Accounting
Tools for Business Decision Making

Seventh Edition

PAUL D. KIMMEL PhD, CPA
University of Wisconsin—Milwaukee
Milwaukee, Wisconsin

JERRY J. WEYGANDT PhD, CPA
University of Wisconsin—Madison
Madison, Wisconsin

DONALD E. KIESO PhD, CPA
Northern Illinois University
DeKalb, Illinois

DEDICATED TO

*Our wives,
Enid, Merlynn, and Donna, for their love,
support, and encouragement.*

DIRECTOR AND VICE PRESIDENT	Michael McDonald
EXECUTIVE EDITOR	Zoe Craig
LEAD PRODUCT DESIGNER	Ed Brislin
PRODUCT DESIGNER	Matthew Origoni
DIRECTOR OF MARKETING	Karolina Zarychta Honsa
EDITORIAL SUPERVISOR	Terry Ann Tatro
EDITORIAL ASSISTANT	Megan Joseph
SENIOR CONTENT MANAGER	Dorothy Sinclair
SENIOR PRODUCTION EDITOR	Valerie Vargas
SENIOR DESIGNER	Wendy Lai
SENIOR PHOTO EDITOR	Mary Ann Price
COVER IMAGE	© carlosalvarez/Getty Images

This book was set in Stix Regular by Aptara®, Inc. and printed and bound by Quad Graphics/Versailles. The cover was printed by Quad Graphics/Versailles.

Founded in 1807, John Wiley & Sons, Inc. has been a valued source of knowledge and understanding for more than 200 years, helping people around the world meet their needs and fulfill their aspirations. Our company is built on a foundation of principles that include responsibility to the communities we serve and where we live and work. In 2008, we launched a Corporate Citizenship Initiative, a global effort to address the environmental, social, economic, and ethical challenges we face in our business. Among the issues we are addressing are carbon impact, paper specifications and procurement, ethical conduct within our business and among our vendors, and community and charitable support. For more information, please visit our website: www.wiley.com/go/citizenship.

Copyright © 2019 John Wiley & Sons, Inc. All rights reserved. No part of this publication may be reproduced, stored in a retrieval system or transmitted in any form or by any means, electronic, mechanical, photocopying, recording, scanning or otherwise, except as permitted under Sections 107 or 108 of the 1976 United States Copyright Act, without either the prior written permission of the Publisher, or authorization through payment of the appropriate per-copy fee to the Copyright Clearance Center, Inc. 222 Rosewood Drive, Danvers, MA 01923, website www.copyright.com. Requests to the Publisher for permission should be addressed to the Permissions Department, John Wiley & Sons, Inc., 111 River Street, Hoboken, NJ 07030-5774, (201)748-6011, fax (201)748-6008, website http://www.wiley.com/go/permissions.

ISBN-13: 978-1-119-49479-9

The inside back cover will contain printing identification and country of origin if omitted from this page. In addition, if the ISBN on the cover differs from the ISBN on this page, the one on the cover is correct.

Printed in America.

SKY10022193_112020

Brief Contents

1. Introduction to Financial Statements 1-1
2. A Further Look at Financial Statements 2-1
3. The Accounting Information System 3-1
4. Accrual Accounting Concepts 4-1
5. Merchandising Operations and the Multiple-Step Income Statement 5-1
6. Reporting and Analyzing Inventory 6-1
7. Fraud, Internal Control, and Cash 7-1
8. Reporting and Analyzing Receivables 8-1
9. Reporting and Analyzing Long-Lived Assets 9-1
10. Reporting and Analyzing Liabilities 10-1
11. Reporting and Analyzing Stockholders' Equity 11-1
12. Statement of Cash Flows 12-1
13. Financial Analysis: The Big Picture 13-1
14. Managerial Accounting 14-1
15. Job Order Costing 15-1
15A. Job Order Costing (non-debit and credit approach)*
16. Process Costing 16-1
16A. Process Costing (non-debit and credit approach)*
17. Activity-Based Costing 17-1
18. Cost-Volume-Profit 18-1
19. Cost-Volume-Profit Analysis: Additional Issues 19-1
20. Incremental Analysis 20-1
21. Pricing 21-1
22. Budgetary Planning 22-1
23. Budgetary Control and Responsibility Accounting 23-1
24. Standard Costs and Balanced Scorecard 24-1
25. Planning for Capital Investments 25-1

APPENDIX A Specimen Financial Statements: Apple Inc. A-1
APPENDIX B Specimen Financial Statements: Columbia Sportswear Company B-1
APPENDIX C Specimen Financial Statements: VF Corporation C-1
APPENDIX D Specimen Financial Statements: Amazon.com, Inc. D-1
APPENDIX E Specimen Financial Statements: Wal-Mart Stores, Inc. E-1
APPENDIX F Specimen Financial Statements: Louis Vuitton F-1
APPENDIX G Time Value of Money G-1
APPENDIX H Reporting and Analyzing Investments H-1
APPENDIX I Payroll Accounting I-1
APPENDIX J Subsidiary Ledgers and Special Journals J-1
APPENDIX K Accounting for Partnerships K-1
APPENDIX L Accounting for Sole Proprietorships L-1

CASES FOR MANAGERIAL DECISION MAKING*

COMPANY INDEX I-1
SUBJECT INDEX I-3

* Available in WileyPLUS and Wiley Custom.

From the Authors

Dear Student,

WHY THIS COURSE? Remember your biology course in high school? Did you have one of those "invisible man" models (or maybe something more high-tech than that) that gave you the opportunity to look "inside" the human body? This accounting course offers something similar. To understand a business, you have to understand the financial insides of a business organization. An accounting course will help you understand the essential financial components of businesses. Whether you are looking at a large multinational company like **Apple** or **Starbucks**, or a single-owner software consulting business or coffee shop, knowing the fundamentals of accounting will help you understand what is happening. As an employee, a manager, an investor, a business owner, or a director of your own personal finances—any of which roles you will have at some point in your life—you will make better decisions for having taken this course.

> "Whether you are looking at a large multinational company like **Apple** or **Starbucks**, or a single-owner software consulting business or coffee shop, knowing the fundamentals of accounting will help you understand what is happening."

WHY THIS TEXT? Your instructor has chosen this text for you because of the authors' trusted reputation. The authors have worked hard to write a text that is engaging, timely, and accurate.

HOW TO SUCCEED? We've asked many students and many instructors whether there is a secret for success in this course. The nearly unanimous answer turns out to be not much of a secret: "Do the homework." This is one course where doing is learning. The more time you spend on the homework assignments—using the various tools that this text provides—the more likely you are to learn the essential concepts, techniques, and methods of accounting. Besides the text itself, WileyPLUS also offers various support resources.

Good luck in this course. We hope you enjoy the experience and that you put to good use throughout a lifetime of success the knowledge you obtain in this course. We are sure you will not be disappointed.

Jerry J. Weygandt
Paul D. Kimmel
Donald E. Kieso

Author Commitment

Jerry Weygandt

JERRY J. WEYGANDT, PhD, CPA, is Arthur Andersen Alumni Emeritus Professor of Accounting at the University of Wisconsin—Madison. He holds a Ph.D. in accounting from the University of Illinois. Articles by Professor Weygandt have appeared in *The Accounting Review, Journal of Accounting Research, Accounting Horizons, Journal of Accountancy,* and other academic and professional journals. These articles have examined such financial reporting issues as accounting for price-level adjustments, pensions, convertible securities, stock option contracts, and interim reports. Professor Weygandt is author of other accounting and financial reporting books and is a member of the American Accounting Association, the American Institute of Certified Public Accountants, and the Wisconsin Society of Certified Public Accountants. He has served on numerous committees of the American Accounting Association and as a member of the editorial board of *The Accounting Review;* he also has served as President and Secretary-Treasurer of the American Accounting Association. In addition, he has been actively involved with the American Institute of Certified Public Accountants and has been a member of the Accounting Standards Executive Committee (AcSEC) of that organization. He has served on the FASB task force that examined the reporting issues related to accounting for income taxes and served as a trustee of the Financial Accounting Foundation. Professor Weygandt has received the Chancellor's Award for Excellence in Teaching and the Beta Gamma Sigma Dean's Teaching Award. He is on the board of directors of M & I Bank of Southern Wisconsin. He is the recipient of the Wisconsin Institute of CPA's Outstanding Educator's Award and the Lifetime Achievement Award. In 2001 he received the American Accounting Association's Outstanding Educator Award.

Paul Kimmel

PAUL D. KIMMEL, PhD, CPA, received his bachelor's degree from the University of Minnesota and his doctorate in accounting from the University of Wisconsin. He teaches at U.W.—Milwaukee and U.W.—Madison. He has public accounting experience with Deloitte & Touche (Minneapolis). He was the recipient of the UWM School of Business Advisory Council Teaching Award, the Reggie Taite Excellence in Teaching Award and a three-time winner of the Outstanding Teaching Assistant Award at the University of Wisconsin. He is also a recipient of the Elijah Watts Sells Award for Honorary Distinction for his results on the CPA exam. He is a member of the American Accounting Association and the Institute of Management Accountants and has published articles in *The Accounting Review, Accounting Horizons, Review of Accounting Studies, Advances in Management Accounting, Managerial Finance, Issues in Accounting Education, Journal of Accounting Education,* as well as other journals. His research interests include accounting for financial instruments and innovation in accounting education. He has published papers and given many presentations regarding accounting instruction, and helped prepare a catalog of critical thinking resources for the Federated Schools of Accountancy.

Don Kieso

DONALD E. KIESO, PhD, CPA, received his bachelor's degree from Aurora University and his doctorate in accounting from the University of Illinois. He has served as chairman of the Department of Accountancy and is currently the KPMG Emeritus Professor of Accountancy at Northern Illinois University. He has public accounting experience with Price Waterhouse & Co. (San Francisco and Chicago) and Arthur Andersen & Co. (Chicago) and research experience with the Research Division of the American Institute of Certified Public Accountants (New York). He has done post doctorate work as a Visiting Scholar at the University of California at Berkeley and is a recipient of NIU's Teaching Excellence Award and four Golden Apple Teaching Awards. Professor Kieso is the author of other accounting and business books and is a member of the American Accounting Association, the American Institute of Certified Public Accountants, and the Illinois CPA Society. He has served as a member of the Board of Directors of the Illinois CPA Society, then AACSB's Accounting Accreditation Committees, the State of Illinois Comptroller's Commission, as Secretary-Treasurer of the Federation of Schools of Accountancy, and as Secretary-Treasurer of the American Accounting Association. Professor Kieso is currently serving on the Board of Trustees and Executive Committee of Aurora University, as a member of the Board of Directors of Kishwaukee Community Hospital, and as Treasurer and Director of Valley West Community Hospital. From 1989 to 1993 he served as a charter member of the national Accounting Education Change Commission. He is the recipient of the Outstanding Accounting Educator Award from the Illinois CPA Society, the FSA's Joseph A. Silvoso Award of Merit, the NIU Foundation's Humanitarian Award for Service to Higher Education, a Distinguished Service Award from the Illinois CPA Society, and in 2003 an honorary doctorate from Aurora University.

Hallmark Features

Accounting, Seventh Edition, provides a simple and practical introduction to financial accounting. It explains the concepts you need to know, while also emphasizing the importance of decision-making, including the use of data analytics.

In this new edition, all content has been carefully reviewed and revised to ensure maximum student understanding. For example, the authors have updated illustrations to show cash flow, balance sheet, and income statement effects of transactions in Chapter 3. At the same time, the time-tested features that have proven to be of most help to students have been retained, such as the following.

DO IT! Exercises

DO IT! Exercises in the body of the text prompt students to stop and review key concepts. They outline the Action Plan necessary to complete the exercise as well as show a detailed solution.

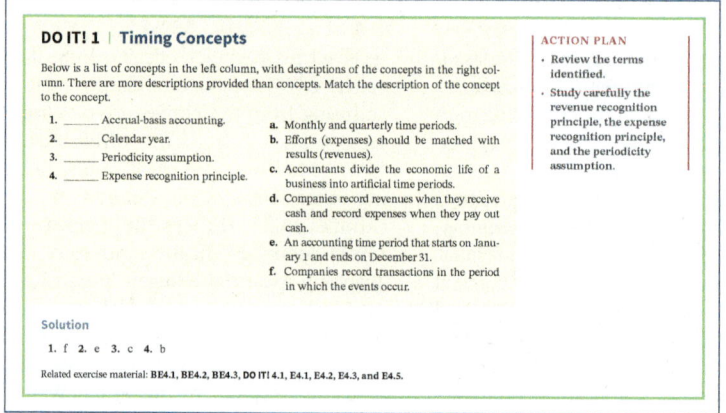

Review and Practice

Each chapter concludes with a Review and Practice section which includes a review of learning objectives, Decision Tools review, key terms glossary, practice multiple-choice questions with annotated solutions, practice brief exercises with solutions, practice exercises with solutions, and a practice problem with a solution.

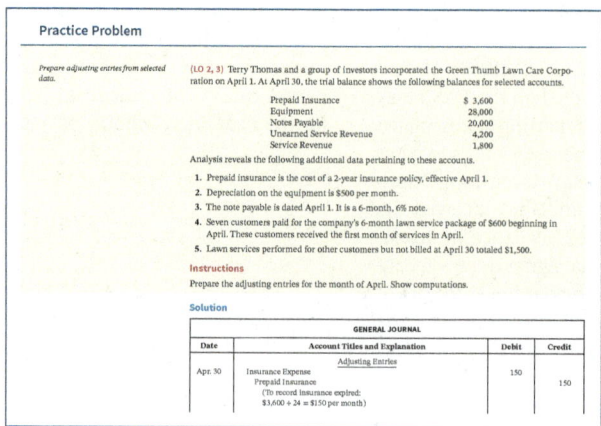

Infographic Learning

Over half of the text is visual, providing students alternative ways of learning about accounting.

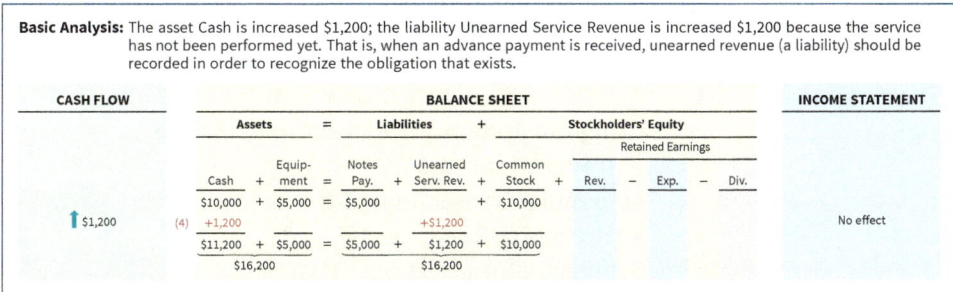

Real-World Decision-Making and Data Analytics

Real-world examples that illustrate interesting situations in companies and how managers make decisions using accounting information are integrated throughout the text, such as in each chapter's opening Feature Story and Insight boxes.

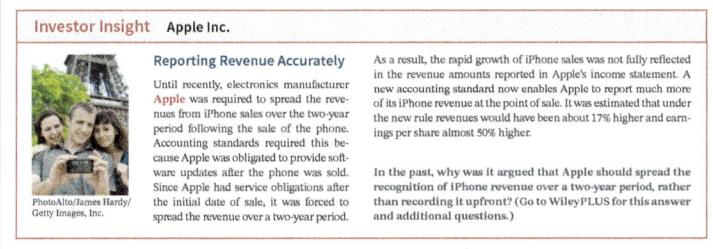

Clearly inventory management is an area that benefits from data analytics. Companies such as **Wal-Mart** collect massive amounts of data about every inventory item and every customer. They analyze customer habits, buying patterns, and sales trends. Using sophisticated models that incorporate economic variables, weather patterns, and many other factors, they strive to optimize inventory levels to maximize sales while minimizing inventory holding costs.

Decision Tools

Accounting concepts that are useful for management decision-making are highlighted throughout the text. A summary of Decision Tools is included in each chapter as well as a practice exercise and solution called Using the Decision Tools.

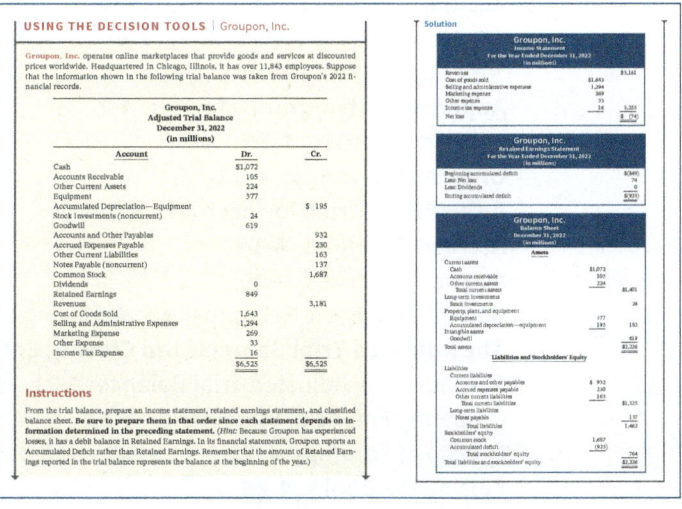

Contents

1 Introduction to Financial Statements 1-1

Knowing the Numbers: **Columbia Sportswear Company** 1-1
Business Organization and Accounting Information Uses 1-2
Forms of Business Organization 1-3
Users and Uses of Financial Information 1-3
Ethics in Financial Reporting 1-5
The Three Types of Business Activity 1-7
Financing Activities 1-7
Investing Activities 1-8
Operating Activities 1-8
The Four Financial Statements 1-9
Income Statement 1-10
Retained Earnings Statement 1-11
Balance Sheet 1-11
Statement of Cash Flows 1-12
Interrelationships of Statements 1-13
Other Elements of an Annual Report 1-16
A Look at IFRS 1-42

2 A Further Look at Financial Statements 2-1

Just Fooling Around?: **The Motley Fool** 2-2
The Classified Balance Sheet 2-3
Current Assets 2-3
Long-Term Investments 2-5
Property, Plant, and Equipment 2-5
Intangible Assets 2-5
Current Liabilities 2-7
Long-Term Liabilities 2-7
Stockholders' Equity 2-7
Analyzing the Financial Statements Using Ratios 2-8
Ratio Analysis 2-8
Using the Income Statement 2-9
Using a Classified Balance Sheet 2-10
Using the Statement of Cash Flows 2-13
Financial Reporting Concepts 2-15
The Standard-Setting Environment 2-16
Qualities of Useful Information 2-16
Assumptions in Financial Reporting 2-17
Principles in Financial Reporting 2-18
Cost Constraint 2-19
A Look at IFRS 2-45

3 The Accounting Information System 3-1

Accidents Happen: **MF Global Holdings Ltd** 3-1
Using the Accounting Equation to Analyze Transactions 3-3
Accounting Transactions 3-3
Analyzing Transactions 3-4
Summary of Transactions 3-10
Accounts, Debits, and Credits 3-11
Debits and Credits 3-11
Debit and Credit Procedures 3-12
Stockholders' Equity Relationships 3-15
Summary of Debit/Credit Rules 3-16
Using a Journal 3-17
The Recording Process 3-17
The Journal 3-18
The Ledger and Posting 3-20
The Ledger 3-20
Chart of Accounts 3-20
Posting 3-21
The Recording Process Illustrated 3-22
Summary Illustration of Journalizing and Posting 3-28
The Trial Balance 3-30
Limitations of a Trial Balance 3-31
A Look at IFRS 3-61

4 Accrual Accounting Concepts 4-1

Keeping Track of Groupons: **Groupon** 4-1
Accrual-Basis Accounting and Adjusting Entries 4-2
The Revenue Recognition Principle 4-3
The Expense Recognition Principle 4-4
Accrual versus Cash Basis of Accounting 4-5
The Need for Adjusting Entries 4-5
Types of Adjusting Entries 4-6
Adjusting Entries for Deferrals 4-7
Prepaid Expenses 4-7
Unearned Revenues 4-11
Adjusting Entries for Accruals 4-14
Accrued Revenues 4-14
Accrued Expenses 4-16
Summary of Basic Relationships 4-19
The Adjusted Trial Balance and Closing Entries 4-21
Preparing the Adjusted Trial Balance 4-21
Preparing Financial Statements 4-22
Quality of Earnings 4-23
Closing the Books 4-26

Summary of the Accounting Cycle 4-28
Appendix 4A: Using a Worksheet 4-33
A Look at IFRS 4-65

5 Merchandising Operations and the Multiple-Step Income Statement 5-1

Buy Now, Vote Later: **REI** 5-1
Merchandising Operations and Inventory Systems 5-3
Operating Cycles 5-3
Flow of Costs 5-4
Recording Purchases Under a Perpetual System 5-6
Freight Costs 5-8
Purchase Returns and Allowances 5-9
Purchase Discounts 5-9
Summary of Purchasing Transactions 5-10
Recording Sales Under a Perpetual System 5-11
Sales Returns and Allowances 5-12
Sales Discounts 5-13
Data Analytics and Credit Sales 5-14
Multiple-Step and Comprehensive Income Statements 5-15
Single-Step Income Statement 5-15
Multiple-Step Income Statement 5-16
Comprehensive Income Statement 5-19
Cost of Goods Sold Under a Periodic System 5-21
Gross Profit Rate and Profit Margin 5-22
Gross Profit Rate 5-22
Profit Margin 5-23
Appendix 5A: Periodic Inventory System 5-26
Recording Merchandise Transactions 5-26
Recording Purchases of Merchandise 5-27
Freight Costs 5-27
Recording Sales of Merchandise 5-27
Comparison of Entries—Perpetual vs. Periodic 5-28
Appendix 5B: Adjusting Entries for Credit Sales with Returns and Allowances 5-29
A Look at IFRS 5-54

6 Reporting and Analyzing Inventory 6-1

"Where Is That Spare Bulldozer Blade?": **Caterpillar** 6-1
Classifying and Determining Inventory 6-2
Classifying Inventory 6-2
Determining Inventory Quantities 6-4
Inventory Methods and Financial Effects 6-6
Specific Identification 6-7
Cost Flow Assumptions 6-7
Financial Statement and Tax Effects of Cost Flow Methods 6-12
Using Inventory Cost Flow Methods Consistently 6-14
Inventory Presentation and Analysis 6-15
Presentation 6-15
Lower-of-Cost-or-Net Realizable Value 6-16
Analysis 6-16
Adjustments for LIFO Reserve 6-18
Appendix 6A: Inventory Cost Flow Methods in Perpetual Inventory Systems 6-21
First-In, First-Out (FIFO) 6-22
Last-In, First-Out (LIFO) 6-22
Average-Cost 6-23
Appendix 6B: Effects of Inventory Errors 6-23
Income Statement Effects 6-24
Balance Sheet Effects 6-25
A Look at IFRS 6-48

7 Fraud, Internal Control, and Cash 7-1

Minding the Money in Madison: **Barriques** 7-1
Fraud and Internal Control 7-3
Fraud 7-3
The Sarbanes-Oxley Act 7-3
Internal Control 7-4
Principles of Internal Control Activities 7-4
Data Analytics and Internal Controls 7-10
Limitations of Internal Control 7-11
Cash Controls 7-12
Cash Receipts Controls 7-12
Cash Disbursements Controls 7-14
Petty Cash Fund 7-16
Control Features of a Bank Account 7-17
Electronic Funds Transfer (EFT) System 7-17
Bank Statements 7-18
Reconciling the Bank Account 7-19
Reporting Cash and Cash Management 7-24
Reporting Cash 7-24
Managing and Monitoring Cash 7-25
Cash Budgeting 7-27
Appendix 7A: Operation of a Petty Cash Fund 7-30
Establishing the Petty Cash Fund 7-30
Making Payments from the Petty Cash Fund 7-31
Replenishing the Petty Cash Fund 7-31
A Look at IFRS 7-56

8 Reporting and Analyzing Receivables 8-1

What's Cooking? **Nike** 8-1
Recognition of Accounts Receivable 8-3
Types of Receivables 8-3
Recognizing Accounts Receivable 8-3

Valuation and Disposition of Accounts Receivable 8-5
Valuing Accounts Receivable 8-5
Disposing of Accounts Receivable 8-12
Notes Receivable 8-14
Determining the Maturity Date 8-15
Computing Interest 8-15
Recognizing Notes Receivable 8-16
Valuing Notes Receivable 8-16
Disposing of Notes Receivable 8-16
Receivables Presentation and Management 8-18
Financial Statement Presentation of Receivables 8-19
Managing Receivables 8-19
Evaluating Liquidity of Receivables 8-21
Accelerating Cash Receipts 8-23
Data Analytics and Receivables Management 8-24
A Look at IFRS 8-47

9 Reporting and Analyzing Long-Lived Assets 9-1

A Tale of Two Airlines: **American Airlines** 9-1
Plant Asset Expenditures 9-3
Determining the Cost of Plant Assets 9-3
Expenditures During Useful Life 9-6
To Buy or Lease? 9-7
Depreciation Methods 9-8
Factors in Computing Depreciation 9-8
Depreciation Methods 9-9
Revising Periodic Depreciation 9-13
Impairments 9-14
Plant Asset Disposals 9-15
Sale of Plant Assets 9-16
Retirement of Plant Assets 9-17
Intangible Assets 9-18
Accounting for Intangible Assets 9-18
Types of Intangible Assets 9-19
Statement Presentation and Analysis 9-21
Presentation 9-21
Analysis 9-23
Appendix 9A: Other Depreciation Methods 9-27
Declining-Balance Method 9-27
Units-of-Activity Method 9-28
A Look at IFRS 9-54

10 Reporting and Analyzing Liabilities 10-1

And Then There Were Two: **Maxwell Car Company** 10-1
Accounting for Current Liabilities 10-3
What Is a Current Liability? 10-3
Notes Payable 10-3
Sales Taxes Payable 10-4
Unearned Revenues 10-5
Current Maturities of Long-Term Debt 10-5
Payroll and Payroll Taxes Payable 10-6
Major Characteristics of Bonds 10-8
Types of Bonds 10-8
Issuing Procedures 10-9
Bond Trading 10-9
Determining the Market Price of a Bond 10-10
Accounting for Bond Transactions 10-12
Issuing Bonds at Face Value 10-13
Discount or Premium on Bonds 10-13
Issuing Bonds at a Discount 10-14
Issuing Bonds at a Premium 10-15
Redeeming Bonds at Maturity 10-17
Redeeming Bonds Before Maturity 10-17
Presentation and Analysis 10-18
Presentation 10-18
Analysis 10-20
Appendix 10A: Straight-Line Amortization 10-24
Amortizing Bond Discount 10-24
Amortizing Bond Premium 10-26
Appendix 10B: Effective-Interest Amortization 10-27
Amortizing Bond Discount 10-27
Amortizing Bond Premium 10-29
Appendix 10C: Accounting for Long-Term Notes Payable 10-30
A Look at IFRS 10-58

11 Reporting and Analyzing Stockholders' Equity 11-1

Oh Well, I Guess I'll Get Rich: **Facebook** 11-1
Corporate Form of Organization 11-3
Characteristics of a Corporation 11-3
Forming a Corporation 11-6
Stockholder Rights 11-6
Stock Issue Considerations 11-7
Corporate Capital 11-9
Accounting for Common, Preferred, and Treasury Stock 11-11
Accounting for Common Stock 11-11
Accounting for Preferred Stock 11-12
Accounting for Treasury Stock 11-13
Cash Dividends, Stock Dividends, and Stock Splits 11-15
Cash Dividends 11-15
Dividend Preferences 11-17
Stock Dividends 11-19
Stock Splits 11-20

Presentation and Analysis   11-22
Retained Earnings   11-22
Retained Earnings Restrictions   11-23
Balance Sheet Presentation of Stockholders' Equity   11-24
Analysis of Stockholders' Equity   11-26
Debt Versus Equity Decision   11-27
Appendix 11A: Entries for Stock Dividends   11-30
A Look at IFRS   11-54

12 Statement of Cash Flows   12-1

Got Cash?: **Microsoft**   12-1
Usefulness and Format of the Statement of Cash Flows   12-3
Usefulness of the Statement of Cash Flows   12-3
Classification of Cash Flows   12-3
Significant Noncash Activities   12-4
Format of the Statement of Cash Flows   12-5
Preparing the Statement of Cash Flows—Indirect Method   12-6
Indirect and Direct Methods   12-7
Indirect Method—Computer Services Company   12-7
Step 1: Operating Activities   12-9
Summary of Conversion to Net Cash Provided by Operating Activities—Indirect Method   12-12
Step 2: Investing and Financing Activities   12-13
Step 3: Net Change in Cash   12-14
Analyzing the Statement of Cash Flows   12-17
The Corporate Life Cycle   12-17
Free Cash Flow   12-19
Appendix 12A: Statement of Cash Flows—Direct Method   12-22
Step 1: Operating Activities   12-23
Step 2: Investing and Financing Activities   12-28
Step 3: Net Change in Cash   12-29
Appendix 12B: Worksheet for the Indirect Method   12-29
Preparing the Worksheet   12-30
Appendix 12C: Statement of Cash Flows—T-Account Approach   12-34
A Look at IFRS   12-61

13 Financial Analysis: The Big Picture   13-1

It Pays to Be Patient: **Warren Buffett**   13-2
Sustainable Income and Quality of Earnings   13-3
Sustainable Income   13-3
Quality of Earnings   13-7
Horizontal Analysis and Vertical Analysis   13-9
Horizontal Analysis   13-10
Vertical Analysis   13-12
Ratio Analysis   13-14
Liquidity Ratios   13-15
Solvency Ratios   13-16
Profitability Ratios   13-16
Financial Analysis and Data Analytics   13-17
Comprehensive Example of Ratio Analysis   13-17
A Look at IFRS   13-54

14 Managerial Accounting   14-1

Just Add Water … and Paddle: **Current Designs**   14-1
Managerial Accounting Basics   14-3
Comparing Managerial and Financial Accounting   14-3
Management Functions   14-3
Organizational Structure   14-4
Managerial Cost Concepts   14-7
Manufacturing Costs   14-7
Product Versus Period Costs   14-8
Illustration of Cost Concepts   14-9
Manufacturing Costs in Financial Statements   14-10
Income Statement   14-11
Cost of Goods Manufactured   14-11
Cost of Goods Manufactured Schedule   14-12
Balance Sheet   14-13
Managerial Accounting Today   14-14
Service Industries   14-14
Focus on the Value Chain   14-15
Balanced Scorecard   14-17
Business Ethics   14-17
Corporate Social Responsibility   14-18

15 Job Order Costing   15-1

Profiting from the Silver Screen: **Disney**   15-1
Cost Accounting Systems   15-3
Process Cost System   15-3
Job Order Cost System   15-3
Job Order Cost Flow   15-4
Accumulating Manufacturing Costs   15-5
Assigning Manufacturing Costs   15-7
Raw Materials Costs   15-8
Factory Labor Costs   15-10
Predetermined Overhead Rates   15-12
Entries for Jobs Completed and Sold   15-15
Assigning Costs to Finished Goods   15-15
Assigning Costs to Cost of Goods Sold   15-16
Summary of Job Order Cost Flows   15-17
Job Order Costing for Service Companies   15-18
Advantages and Disadvantages of Job Order Costing   15-19

xii CONTENTS

Applied Manufacturing Overhead 15-20
Under- or Overapplied Manufacturing Overhead 15-21

16 Process Costing 16-1

The Little Guy Who Could: **Jones Soda** 16-1
Overview of Process Cost Systems 16-3
Uses of Process Cost Systems 16-3
Process Costing for Service Companies 16-4
Similarities and Differences Between Job Order Cost and Process Cost Systems 16-4
Process Cost Flow and Assigning Costs 16-6
Process Cost Flow 16-6
Assigning Manufacturing Costs—Journal Entries 16-6
Equivalent Units 16-9
Weighted-Average Method 16-9
Refinements on the Weighted-Average Method 16-10
The Production Cost Report 16-12
Compute the Physical Unit Flow (Step 1) 16-13
Compute the Equivalent Units of Production (Step 2) 16-13
Compute Unit Production Costs (Step 3) 16-14
Prepare a Cost Reconciliation Schedule (Step 4) 16-15
Preparing the Production Cost Report 16-15
Costing Systems—Final Comments 16-16
Appendix 16A: FIFO Method for Equivalent Units 16-19
Equivalent Units Under FIFO 16-19
Comprehensive Example 16-20
FIFO and Weighted-Average 16-24

17 Activity-Based Costing 17-1

Precor Is on Your Side: **Precor** 17-1
Traditional vs. Activity-Based Costing 17-3
Traditional Costing Systems 17-3
Illustration of a Traditional Costing System 17-3
The Need for a New Approach 17-4
Activity-Based Costing 17-4
ABC and Manufacturers 17-7
Identify and Classify Activities and Allocate Overhead to Cost Pools (Step 1) 17-7
Identify Cost Drivers (Step 2) 17-8
Compute Activity-Based Overhead Rates (Step 3) 17-8
Assign Overhead Costs to Products (Step 4) 17-9
Comparing Unit Costs 17-10
ABC Benefits and Limitations 17-12
The Advantage of Multiple Cost Pools 17-12
The Advantage of Enhanced Cost Control 17-13
The Advantage of Better Management Decisions 17-15
Some Limitations and Knowing When to Use ABC 17-16
ABC and Service Industries 17-17
Traditional Costing Example 17-18
Activity-Based Costing Example 17-18
Appendix 17A: Just-in-Time Processing 17-22
Objective of JIT Processing 17-23
Elements of JIT Processing 17-23
Benefits of JIT Processing 17-23

18 Cost-Volume-Profit 18-1

Don't Worry—Just Get Big: **Amazon.com** 18-1
Cost Behavior Analysis 18-2
Variable Costs 18-3
Fixed Costs 18-4
Relevant Range 18-5
Mixed Costs 18-6
Mixed Costs Analysis 18-7
High-Low Method 18-7
Importance of Identifying Variable and Fixed Costs 18-9
Cost-Volume-Profit Analysis 18-10
Basic Components 18-10
CVP Income Statement 18-11
Break-Even Analysis 18-14
Mathematical Equation 18-15
Contribution Margin Technique 18-15
Graphic Presentation 18-16
Target Net Income and Margin of Safety 18-18
Target Net Income 18-18
Margin of Safety 18-20
Appendix 18A: Regression Analysis 18-22

19 Cost-Volume-Profit Analysis: Additional Issues 19-1

Not Even a Flood Could Stop It: **Whole Foods Market** 19-1
Basic CVP Concepts 19-3
Basic Concepts 19-3
Basic Computations 19-3
CVP and Changes in the Business Environment 19-5
Sales Mix and Break-Even Sales 19-8
Break-Even Sales in Units 19-8
Break-Even Sales in Dollars 19-9
Sales Mix with Limited Resources 19-12
Operating Leverage and Profitability 19-14
Effect on Contribution Margin Ratio 19-15
Effect on Break-Even Point 19-15
Effect on Margin of Safety Ratio 19-16
Operating Leverage 19-16
Appendix 19A: Absorption Costing vs. Variable Costing 19-19
Example Comparing Absorption Costing with Variable Costing 19-19
Net Income Effects 19-21
Decision-Making Concerns 19-25
Potential Advantages of Variable Costing 19-27

CONTENTS xiii

20 Incremental Analysis 20-1

Keeping It Clean: **Method Products** 20-1

Decision-Making and Incremental Analysis 20-3
Incremental Analysis Approach 20-3
How Incremental Analysis Works 20-4
Qualitative Factors 20-5
Relationship of Incremental Analysis and Activity-Based Costing 20-5
Types of Incremental Analysis 20-6
Special Orders 20-6
Make or Buy 20-8
Opportunity Cost 20-9
Sell or Process Further 20-10
Single-Product Case 20-11
Multiple-Product Case 20-11
Repair, Retain, or Replace Equipment 20-14
Eliminate Unprofitable Segment or Product 20-15

21 Pricing 21-1

They've Got Your Size—and Color: **Zappos.com** 21-1

Target Costing 21-3
Establishing a Target Cost 21-4
Cost-Plus and Variable-Cost Pricing 21-5
Cost-Plus Pricing 21-5
Limitations of Cost-Plus Pricing 21-7
Variable-Cost Pricing 21-8
Time-and-Material Pricing 21-10
Transfer Prices 21-13
Negotiated Transfer Prices 21-14
Cost-Based Transfer Prices 21-17
Market-Based Transfer Prices 21-18
Effect of Outsourcing on Transfer Pricing 21-18
Transfers Between Divisions in Different Countries 21-19
Appendix 21A: Absorption-Cost and Variable-Cost Pricing 21-21
Absorption-Cost Pricing 21-21
Variable-Cost Pricing 21-23
Appendix 21B: Transfers Between Divisions in Different Countries 21-24

22 Budgetary Planning 22-1

What's in Your Cupcake?: **BabyCakes NYC** 22-1

Effective Budgeting and the Master Budget 22-3
Budgeting and Accounting 22-3
The Benefits of Budgeting 22-3
Essentials of Effective Budgeting 22-3
The Master Budget 22-6
Sales, Production, and Direct Materials Budgets 22-8
Sales Budget 22-8
Production Budget 22-9
Direct Materials Budget 22-10
Direct Labor, Manufacturing Overhead, and S&A Expense Budgets 22-13
Direct Labor Budget 22-13
Manufacturing Overhead Budget 22-14
Selling and Administrative Expense Budget 22-15
Budgeted Income Statement 22-15
Cash Budget and Budgeted Balance Sheet 22-17
Cash Budget 22-17
Budgeted Balance Sheet 22-20
Budgeting in Nonmanufacturing Companies 22-22
Merchandisers 22-22
Service Companies 22-23
Not-for-Profit Organizations 22-24

23 Budgetary Control and Responsibility Accounting 23-1

Pumpkin Madeleines and a Movie: **Tribeca Grand** 23-1

Budgetary Control and Static Budget Reports 23-3
Budgetary Control 23-3
Static Budget Reports 23-4
Flexible Budget Reports 23-6
Why Flexible Budgets? 23-7
Developing the Flexible Budget 23-9
Flexible Budget—A Case Study 23-9
Flexible Budget Reports 23-11
Responsibility Accounting and Responsibility Centers 23-13
Controllable versus Noncontrollable Revenues and Costs 23-15
Principles of Performance Evaluation 23-15
Responsibility Reporting System 23-17
Types of Responsibility Centers 23-18
Investment Centers 23-22
Return on Investment (ROI) 23-23
Responsibility Report 23-23
Judgmental Factors in ROI 23-24
Improving ROI 23-24
Appendix 23A: ROI vs. Residual Income 23-28
Residual Income Compared to ROI 23-28
Residual Income Weakness 23-29

24 Standard Costs and Balanced Scorecard 24-1

80,000 Different Caffeinated Combinations: **Starbucks** 24-2

Overview of Standard Costs 24-3
Distinguishing Between Standards and Budgets 24-4
Setting Standard Costs 24-4
Direct Materials Variances 24-7
Analyzing and Reporting Variances 24-7
Calculating Direct Materials Variances 24-9

Direct Labor and Manufacturing Overhead Variances 24-11
Direct Labor Variances 24-11
Manufacturing Overhead Variances 24-14
Variance Reports and Balanced Scorecards 24-16
Reporting Variances 24-16
Income Statement Presentation of Variances 24-16
Balanced Scorecard 24-17
Appendix 24A: Standard Cost Accounting System 24-21
Journal Entries 24-21
Ledger Accounts 24-23
Appendix 24B: Overhead Controllable and Volume Variances 24-24
Overhead Controllable Variance 24-24
Overhead Volume Variance 24-25

25 Planning for Capital Investments 25-1

Floating Hotels: **Holland America Line** 25-2
Capital Budgeting and Cash Payback 25-3
Cash Flow Information 25-3
Illustrative Data 25-4
Cash Payback 25-4
Net Present Value Method 25-6
Equal Annual Cash Flows 25-7
Unequal Annual Cash Flows 25-8
Choosing a Discount Rate 25-9
Simplifying Assumptions 25-9
Comprehensive Example 25-10
Capital Budgeting Challenges and Refinements 25-11
Intangible Benefits 25-11
Profitability Index for Mutually Exclusive Projects 25-13
Risk Analysis 25-14
Post-Audit of Investment Projects 25-15
Internal Rate of Return 25-16
Comparing Discounted Cash Flow Methods 25-17
Annual Rate of Return 25-18

APPENDIX A Specimen Financial Statements: Apple Inc. A-1

APPENDIX B Specimen Financial Statements: Columbia Sportswear Company B-1

APPENDIX C Specimen Financial Statements: VF Corporation C-1

APPENDIX D Specimen Financial Statements: Amazon.com, Inc. D-1

APPENDIX E Specimen Financial Statements: Wal-Mart Stores, Inc. E-1

APPENDIX F Specimen Financial Statements: Louis Vuitton F-1

APPENDIX G Time Value of Money G-1
Interest and Future Values G-1
Nature of Interest G-1
Future Value of a Single Amount G-3
Future Value of an Annuity G-5
Present Values G-7
Present Value Variables G-7
Present Value of a Single Amount G-7
Present Value of an Annuity G-9
Time Periods and Discounting G-11
Present Value of a Long-Term Note or Bond G-11
Capital Budgeting Situations G-14
Using Financial Calculators G-15
Present Value of a Single Sum G-16
Present Value of an Annuity G-17
Future Value of a Single Sum G-17
Future Value of an Annuity G-17
Internal Rate of Return G-18
Useful Applications of the Financial Calculator G-18

APPENDIX H Reporting and Analyzing Investments H-1
Accounting for Debt Investments H-1
Why Corporations Invest H-1
Accounting for Debt Investments H-3
Accounting for Stock Investments H-4
Holdings of Less Than 20% H-4
Holdings Between 20% and 50% H-5
Holdings of More Than 50% H-6
Reporting Investments in Financial Statements H-7
Debt Securities H-7
Equity Securities H-10
Balance Sheet Presentation H-11
Presentation of Realized and Unrealized Gain or Loss H-12

*****APPENDIX I** Payroll Accounting I-1
Recording the Payroll I-1
Determining the Payroll I-2
Recording the Payroll I-5
Employer Payroll Taxes I-8
FICA Taxes I-8
Federal Unemployment Taxes I-8
State Unemployment Taxes I-8
Recording Employer Payroll Taxes I-9
Filing and Remitting Payroll Taxes I-9
Internal Control for Payroll I-10

*****APPENDIX J** Subsidiary Ledgers and Special Journals J-1
Subsidiary Ledgers J-1
Subsidiary Ledger Example J-2
Advantages of Subsidiary Ledgers J-3
Special Journals J-4
Sales Journal J-4

* Available online.

Cash Receipts Journal   J-7
Purchases Journal   J-11
Cash Payments Journal   J-13
Effects of Special Journals on the General Journal   J-16
Cybersecurity: A Final Comment   J-17

*APPENDIX K   Accounting for Partnerships   K-1

Forming a Partnership   K-1
Characteristics of Partnerships   K-1
Organizations with Partnerships Characteristics   K-2
Advantages and Disadvantages of Partnerships   K-3
The Partnership Agreement   K-4
Accounting for a Partnership Formation   K-5

Accounting for Partnership Net Income or Net Loss   K-6
Dividing Net Income or Net Loss   K-6
Partnership Financial Statements   K-9

Accounting for Partnership Liquidation   K-10
No Capital Deficiency   K-11
Capital Deficiency   K-12

Admission and Withdrawal of Partners   K-14
Admission of a Partner   K-14
Withdrawal of a Partner   K-18

*APPENDIX L   Accounting for Sole Proprietorships   L-1

Corporation versus Sole Proprietorship Equity Accounts   L-1

Accounts that Change Owner's Equity   L-2
Owner's Equity in a Sole Proprietorship   L-2
Recording Transactions of a Proprietorship   L-3

Retained Earnings Statement versus Owner's Equity Statement   L-3

Closing the Books for a Sole Proprietorship   L-4
Preparing a Post-Closing Trail Balance for a Proprietorship   L-7

Cases for Managerial Decision-Making
(The full text of these cases is available in WileyPLUS.)

Company Index   I-1
Subject Index   I-3

---

* Available online.

Acknowledgments

Accounting has benefitted greatly from the input of focus group participants, manuscript reviewers, those who have sent comments by letter or e-mail, ancillary authors, and proofers. We greatly appreciate the constructive suggestions and innovative ideas of reviewers and the creativity and accuracy of the ancillary authors and checkers.

Dennis Avola
Northeastern University

Ellen Bartley
Farmingdale State College

Thomas Bednarcik
Robert Morris University Illinois

Linda Bell
Park University

Martin Blaine
Columbus State Community College

Bradley Blaylock
Oklahoma State University

Isaac Bonaparte
Towson University

Gary Bower
Community College of Rhode Island

Robert Braun
Southeastern Louisiana University

Lou Bravo
North Lake College

Myra Bruegger
Southeastern Community College

Barry Buchoff
Towson University

Brian Bunce
Bellevue University

Jacqueline Burke
Hofstra University

Matthew Calderisi
Fairleigh Dickinson University

Julia Camp
Providence College

Marian Canada
Ivy Tech Community College at Franklin

James Chiafery
University of Massachusetts—Boston

Bea Chiang
The College of New Jersey

Carolyn Christesen
Westchester Community College

Colleen Chung
Miami Dade College

Shifei Chung
Rowan University

Tony Cioffi
Lorain County Community College

Leslie Cohen
University of Arizona

Jim Coughlin
Robert Morris University

Patricia Crenny
Villanova University

Dori Danko
Grand Valley State University

Mingcherng Deng
Baruch College

Kathy Dunne
Rider University

Barbara Durham
University of Central Florida

Jeanne Eibes
Creighton University

David Emerson
Salisbury University

Caroline Falconetti
Nassau Community College

Nancy Fan
California State Polytechnic University, Pomona

Magdy Farag
California State Polytechnic University, Pomona

Linda Flaming
Monmouth University

Joseph Fournier
University of Rhode Island

Amy Geile
University of Arizona

Alan Glaser
Franklin & Marshall College

J. D. Golub
Northeastern University

Liz Grant
Northern Illinois University

Rita Grant
Grand Valley State University

Steve Groves
Ivy Tech Community College

Konrad Gunderson
Missouri Western State University

Marcye Hampton
University of Central Florida

Deborah Hanks
Cardinal Stritch University

Qian Hao
Wilkes University

Jacory Hickerson
University of Phoenix

Huong Higgins
Worcester Polytechnic Institute

Yongtao Hong
North Dakota State University

Jana Hosmer
Blue Ridge Community College

Robert Hurst
Franklin University

Wayne Ingalls
University of Maine

K. Harold Jackson
Tarrant County College

Jennifer Joe
University of Delaware

James B. Johnson
Community College of Philadelphia

Patricia Johnson
Canisius College

Jordan Kanter
University of Rhode Island

Ann Galligan Kelley
Providence College

Robert Kenny
The College of New Jersey

Emil Koren
Saint Leo University

Leah Kratz
Eastern Mennonite University

Faith Lamprey
Providence College

Gary Laycock
Ivy Tech Community College

Charles Leflar
University of Arkansas

Jennifer LeSure
Ivy Tech Community College

Claudia Lubaski
Lorain County Community College

Susan Lynn
University of Baltimore

Yuanyuan Ma
University of Minnesota

Don McFall
Hiram College

Allison McLeod
University of North Texas

Don Minyard
University of Alabama—Tuscaloosa

Maha Mitrelis
Providence College

Louella Moore
Washburn University

Sia Nassiripour
William Paterson University

Joseph Nesi
Monmouth University

Judith Pagnette
Bellevue College

Glenn Pate
Palm Beach State College

Suzy Pearse
Clemson University

Rachel Pernia
Essex County College

Bob Picard
Idaho State University

George Psaras
Aurora University

Smrity Randhawa
University of Southern California

Patrick Reihing
Nassau Community College

John Ribezzo
Community College of Rhode Island

Barbara Rice
Gateway Community and Technical College

Vernon Richardson
University of Arkansas

Patrick Rogan
Consumnes River College

Juan Roman
Saint Leo University

John Rude
Bloomsburg University

Martin Rudnick
William Paterson University

August Saibeni
Consumnes River College

Barbara Sandler
Queens College

Barbara Scofield
Washburn University

Chris Severson
Franklin University

Suzanne Seymoure
Saint Leo University

Abdus Shahid
The College of New Jersey

Mike Shapeero
Bloomsburg University

Todd Shawver
Bloomsburg University

Eileen Shifflett
James Madison University

Kathy Simmons
Bryant University

Ladd Simms
Mississippi Valley State University

Doug Stives
Monmouth University

Diane Tanner
University of North Florida

Karen Tower
Ivy Tech Community College

Daniel Tschopp
Saint Leo University

Mark Ulrich
St. John's University

Andrea Weickgenannt
Xavier University

Nancy Wilburn
Northern Arizona University

Wayne W. Williams
Community College of Philadelphia

Leon Wlazlo
SUNY Broome Community College

Hannah Wong
William Paterson University

Kenneth Zheng
University at Buffalo

Ancillary Authors, Contributors, Proofers, and Accuracy Checkers

Ellen Bartley
St. Joseph's College

LuAnn Bean
Florida Institute of Technology

Jack Borke
University of Wisconsin—Platteville

Ann K. Brooks
University of New Mexico

Melodi Bunting
Edgewood College

Bea Chiang
The College of New Jersey

Judy Dewitt
Central Michigan University

James Emig
Villanova University

Larry Falcetto
Emporia State University

Heidi Hansel
Kirkwood Community College

Coby Harmon
University of California—Santa Barbara

Lisa Hewes
Northern Arizona University

Derek Jackson
St. Mary's University of Minnesota

Cynthia Lovick
Austin Community College

Kirk Lynch
Sandhills Community College

Jill Misuraca
University of Tampa

Barbara Muller
Arizona State University

Linda Mullins
Georgia State University—Perimeter College

Yvonne Phang
Borough of Manhattan Community College

Laura Prosser
Black Hills State University

Alice Sineath
University of Maryland University College

Teresa Speck
St. Mary's University of Minnesota

Lynn Stallworth
Appalachian State University

Diane Tanner
University of North Florida

Sheila Viel
University of Wisconsin—Milwaukee

Dick Wasson
Southwestern College

Lori Grady Zaher
Bucks County Community College

We appreciate the exemplary support and commitment given to us by editor Zoe Craig, director of marketing Karolina Zarychta Honsa, lead product designer Ed Brislin, product designer Matthew Origoni, editorial supervisor Terry Ann Tatro, designer Wendy Lai, photo editor Mary Ann Price, indexer Steve Ingle, senior production editor Valerie Vargas, and Jackie Henry at Aptara. All of these professionals provided innumerable services that helped the text take shape.

We appreciate suggestions and comments from users—instructors and students alike. You can send your thoughts and ideas about the text to us via email at: *AccountingAuthors@yahoo.com*.

Paul D. Kimmel
Milwaukee, Wisconsin

Jerry J. Weygandt
Madison, Wisconsin

Donald E. Kieso
DeKalb, Illinois

CHAPTER 1

Introduction to Financial Statements

Chapter Preview

How do you start a business? How do you determine whether your business is making or losing money? How should you finance expansion—should you borrow, should you issue stock, should you use your own funds? How do you convince banks to lend you money or investors to buy your stock? Success in business requires making countless decisions, and decisions require financial information.

The purpose of this chapter is to show you what role accounting plays in providing financial information.

*The **Chapter Preview** describes the purpose of the chapter and highlights major topics.*

*The **Feature Story** helps you picture how the chapter topic relates to the real world of accounting and business.*

Feature Story

Knowing the Numbers

Many students who take this course do not plan to be accountants. If you are in that group, you might be thinking, "If I'm not going to be an accountant, why do I need to know accounting?" Well, consider this quote from Harold Geneen, the former chairman of IT&T: "To be good at your business, you have to know the numbers—cold." In business, accounting and financial statements are the means for communicating the numbers. If you don't know how to read financial statements, you can't really know your business.

Knowing the numbers is sometimes even a matter of corporate survival. Consider the story of **Columbia Sportswear Company**, headquartered in Portland, Oregon. Gert Boyle's family fled Nazi Germany when she was 13 years old and then purchased a small hat company in Oregon, Columbia Hat Company. In 1971, Gert's husband, who was then running the company, died suddenly of a heart attack. Gert took over the small, struggling company with help from her son Tim, who was then a senior at the University of Oregon. Somehow, they kept the company afloat. Today, Columbia has more than 4,000 employees and annual sales in excess of $1 billion. Its brands include Columbia, Mountain Hardwear, Sorel, and Montrail.

Columbia doesn't just focus on financial success. Several of its factories continue to participate in a project to increase health awareness of female factory workers in developing countries. Columbia is also a founding member of the Sustainable Apparel Coalition, which strives to reduce the environmental and social impact of the apparel industry. In addition, the company monitors all of the independent factories that produce its products to ensure that they comply with the company's Standards of Manufacturing Practices. These standards address issues including forced labor, child labor, harassment, wages and benefits, health and safety, and the environment.

Employers such as Columbia Sportswear generally assume that managers in all areas of the company are "financially literate." To help prepare you for that, in this text you will learn how to read and prepare financial statements, and how to use key tools to evaluate financial results using basic data analytics.

Chapter Outline

*The **Chapter Outline** presents the chapter's topics and subtopics, as well as practice opportunities.*

LEARNING OBJECTIVES

LO 1 Identify the forms of business organization and the uses of accounting information.	• Forms of business organization • Users and uses of financial information • Ethics in financial reporting	**DO IT! 1** Business Organization Forms
LO 2 Explain the three principal types of business activity.	• Financing activities • Investing activities • Operating activities	**DO IT! 2** Business Activities
LO 3 Describe the four financial statements and how they are prepared.	• Income statement • Retained earnings statement • Balance sheet • Statement of cash flows • Interrelationships of statements • Other annual report elements	**DO IT! 3a** Financial Statements **DO IT! 3b** Components of Annual Reports

Go to the Review and Practice section at the end of the chapter for a targeted summary and practice applications with solutions.
Visit WileyPLUS for additional tutorials and practice opportunities.

Business Organization and Accounting Information Uses

LEARNING OBJECTIVE 1
Identify the forms of business organization and the uses of accounting information.

Suppose you graduate with a business degree and decide you want to start your own business. But what kind of business? You enjoy working with people, especially teaching them new skills. You also spend most of your free time outdoors, kayaking, backpacking, skiing, rock climbing, and mountain biking. You think you might be successful in opening an outdoor guide service where you grew up, in the Sierra Nevada mountains.

Forms of Business Organization

Your next decision is to determine the organizational form of your business. You have three choices—sole proprietorship, partnership, or corporation.

Sole Proprietorship

You might choose the sole proprietorship form for your outdoor guide service. A business owned by one person is a **sole proprietorship**. It is **simple to set up** and **gives you control** over the business. Small owner-operated businesses such as barber shops, law offices, and auto repair shops are often sole proprietorships, as are farms and small retail stores.

Sole Proprietorship
- Simple to establish
- Owner-controlled
- Tax advantages

Partnership

Another possibility is for you to join forces with other individuals to form a partnership. A business owned by two or more persons associated as partners is a **partnership**. Partnerships often are formed because one individual does not have **enough economic resources** to initiate or expand the business. Sometimes **partners bring unique skills or resources** to the partnership. You and your partners should formalize your duties and contributions in a written partnership agreement. Retail and service-type businesses, including professional practices (lawyers, doctors, architects, and certified public accountants), often organize as partnerships.

Partnership
- Simple to establish
- Shared control
- Broader skills and resources
- Tax advantages

Corporation

As a third alternative, you might organize as a corporation. A business organized as a separate legal entity owned by stockholders is a **corporation**. Investors in a corporation receive shares of stock to indicate their ownership claim. Buying stock in a corporation is often more attractive than investing in a partnership because shares of stock are **easy to sell** (transfer ownership). Selling a proprietorship or partnership interest is much more involved. Also, individuals can become **stockholders** by investing relatively small amounts of money (see **Alternative Terminology**). Therefore, it is **easier for corporations to raise funds**. Successful corporations often have thousands of stockholders, and their stock is traded on organized stock exchanges like the **New York Stock Exchange**. Many businesses start as sole proprietorships or partnerships and eventually incorporate.

Corporation
- Easier to transfer ownership
- Easier to raise funds
- No personal liability

ALTERNATIVE TERMINOLOGY

Stockholders are sometimes called *shareholders*.

Alternative Terminology notes present synonymous terms that you may come across in practice.

Other factors to consider in deciding which organizational form to choose are **taxes and legal liability**. If you choose a sole proprietorship or partnership, you generally receive more favorable tax treatment than a corporation. However, proprietors and partners are personally liable for all debts and legal obligations of the business; corporate stockholders are not. In other words, corporate stockholders generally pay higher taxes but have no personal legal liability. We will discuss these issues in more depth in a later chapter.

Finally, while sole proprietorships, partnerships, and corporations represent the main types of business organizations, hybrid forms are now allowed in all states. These hybrid business forms combine the tax advantages of partnerships with the limited liability of corporations. Probably the most common among these hybrids types are limited liability companies (LLCs) and subchapter S corporations. These forms are discussed extensively in business law classes.

The combined number of proprietorships and partnerships in the United States far exceeds the number of corporations. However, the revenue produced by corporations is many times greater. Most of the largest businesses in the United States—for example, **Coca-Cola**, **ExxonMobil**, **General Motors**, **Citigroup**, and **Microsoft**—are corporations. Because the majority of U.S. business is done by corporations, the emphasis in this text is on the corporate form of organization.

Users and Uses of Financial Information

The purpose of financial information is to provide inputs for decision-making. **Accounting** is the information system that identifies, records, and communicates the economic events of an organization to interested users.

Accounting software systems collect vast amounts of data about the economic events experienced by a company and about the parties with whom the company engages, such as suppliers and customers. Business decision-makers take advantage of this wealth of data by using data analytics to make more informed business decisions. Data analytics involves analyzing data, often employing both software and statistics, to draw inferences. As both data access and analytical software improve, the use of data analytics to support decisions is becoming increasingly common at virtually all types of companies (see **Helpful Hint**).

Users of accounting information can be divided broadly into two groups: internal users and external users.

> **HELPFUL HINT**
> Throughout this text, we will highlight examples where accounting information is used to support business decisions using data analytics.
>
> *Helpful Hints* further clarify concepts being discussed.

Internal Users

Internal users of accounting information are managers who plan, organize, and run a business. These include **marketing managers**, **production supervisors**, **finance directors**, **and company officers**. In running a business, managers must answer many important questions, as shown in **Illustration 1.1**.

ILLUSTRATION 1.1 Questions that internal users ask

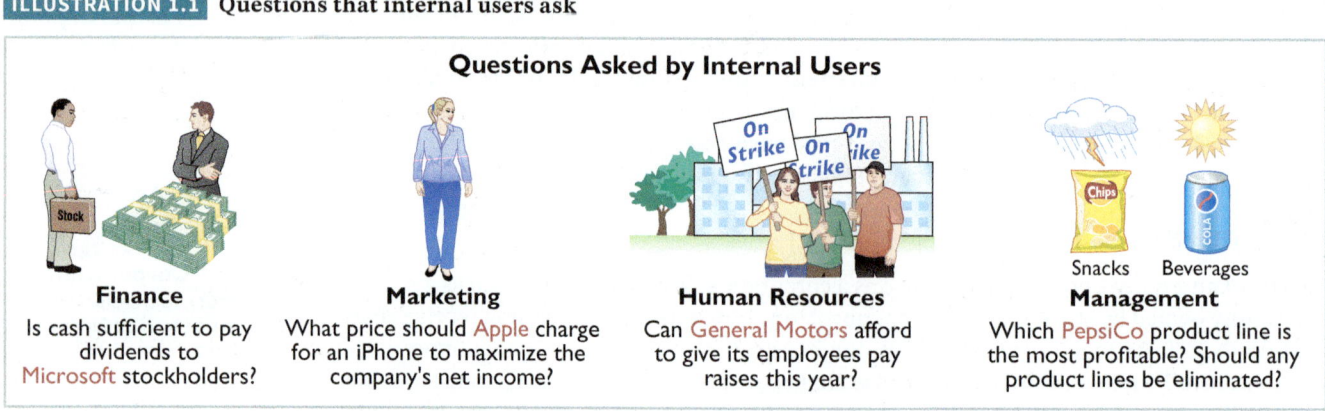

Questions Asked by Internal Users

Finance — Is cash sufficient to pay dividends to Microsoft stockholders?

Marketing — What price should Apple charge for an iPhone to maximize the company's net income?

Human Resources — Can General Motors afford to give its employees pay raises this year?

Management — Which PepsiCo product line is the most profitable? Should any product lines be eliminated?

To answer these and other questions, you need detailed information on a timely basis. For internal users, accounting provides internal reports, such as financial comparisons of operating alternatives, projections of income from new sales campaigns, and forecasts of cash needs for the next year. In addition, companies present summarized financial information in the form of financial statements.

Accounting Across the Organization boxes show applications of accounting information in various business functions.

Accounting Across the Organization — Clif Bar & Company

© Dan Moore/iStockphoto

Owning a Piece of the Bar

The original Clif Bar® energy bar was created in 1990 after six months of experimentation by Gary Erickson and his mother in her kitchen. The company has approximately 1,000 employees and was named one of Landor's Breakaway Brands®. One of **Clif Bar & Company**'s proudest moments was the creation of an employee stock ownership plan (ESOP). This plan gives its employees 20% ownership of the company. The ESOP also resulted in Clif Bar enacting an open-book management program, including the commitment to educate all employee-owners about its finances. Armed with basic accounting knowledge, employees are more aware of the financial impact of their actions, which leads to better decisions.

What are the benefits to the company and to the employees of making the financial statements available to all employees? (Go to WileyPLUS for this answer and additional questions.)

External Users

There are several types of **external users** of accounting information. **Investors** (owners) use accounting information to make decisions to buy, hold, or sell stock. **Creditors** such as suppliers and bankers use accounting information to evaluate the risks of selling on credit or lending money. Some questions that investors and creditors may ask about a company are shown in **Illustration 1.2**.

ILLUSTRATION 1.2 Questions that external users ask

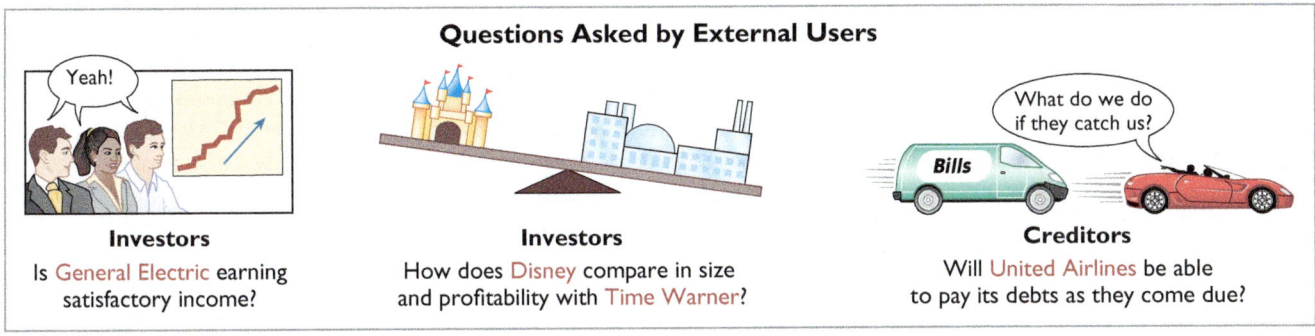

The information needs and questions of other external users vary considerably. **Taxing authorities**, such as the Internal Revenue Service, want to know whether the company complies with the tax laws. **Customers** are interested in whether a company like General Motors will continue to honor product warranties and otherwise support its product lines. **Labor unions**, such as the Major League Baseball Players Association, want to know whether the owners have the ability to pay increased wages and benefits. **Regulatory agencies**, such as the Securities and Exchange Commission or the Federal Trade Commission, want to know whether the company is operating within prescribed rules. For example, Enron, Dynegy, Duke Energy, and other big energy-trading companies reported record profits at the same time as California was paying extremely high prices for energy and suffering from blackouts. This disparity caused regulators to investigate the energy traders to make sure that the profits were earned by legitimate and fair practices.

Accounting Across the Organization

Spinning the Career Wheel

© Josef Volavka/iStockphoto

How will the study of accounting help you? A working knowledge of accounting is desirable for virtually every field of business. Some examples of how accounting is used in business careers include the following.

General management: Managers of Ford Motors, Massachusetts General Hospital, California State University–Fullerton, a McDonald's franchise, and a Trek bike shop all need to understand accounting data in order to make wise business decisions.

Marketing: Marketing specialists at Procter & Gamble must be sensitive to costs and benefits, which accounting helps them quantify and understand. Making a sale is meaningless unless it is a profitable sale.

Finance: Do you want to be a banker for Citicorp, an investment analyst for Goldman Sachs, or a stock broker for Merrill Lynch? These fields rely heavily on accounting knowledge to analyze financial statements. In fact, it is difficult to get a good job in a finance function without two or three courses in accounting.

Real estate: Are you interested in being a real estate broker for Prudential Real Estate? Because a third party—the bank—is almost always involved in financing a real estate transaction, brokers must understand the numbers involved: Can the buyer afford to make the payments to the bank? Does the cash flow from an industrial property justify the purchase price? What are the tax benefits of the purchase?

How might accounting help you? (Go to WileyPLUS for this answer and additional questions.)

Ethics in Financial Reporting

People won't gamble in a casino if they think it is "rigged." Similarly, people won't "play" the stock market if they think stock prices are rigged. At one time, the financial press was full of articles about financial scandals at Enron, WorldCom, HealthSouth, and AIG. As more scandals came to light, a mistrust of financial reporting in general seemed to be developing. One article in the *Wall Street Journal* noted that "repeated disclosures about questionable accounting practices have bruised investors' faith in the reliability of earnings reports, which in turn has sent stock prices tumbling." Imagine trying to carry on a business or invest money if you could not depend on the financial statements to be honestly prepared. Information would have no credibility. There is no doubt that a sound, well-functioning economy depends on accurate and dependable financial reporting.

ETHICS NOTE

Circus-founder P.T. Barnum is alleged to have said, "Trust everyone, but cut the deck." What Sarbanes-Oxley does is to provide measures that (like cutting the deck of playing cards) help ensure that fraud will not occur.

Ethics Notes help sensitize you to some of the ethical issues in accounting.

United States regulators and lawmakers were very concerned that the economy would suffer if investors lost confidence in corporate accounting because of unethical financial reporting. Congress passed the **Sarbanes-Oxley Act (SOX)** to reduce unethical corporate behavior and decrease the likelihood of future corporate scandals (see **Ethics Note**). As a result of SOX, top management must now certify the accuracy of financial information. In addition, penalties for fraudulent financial activity are much more severe. Also, SOX increased both the independence of the outside auditors who review the accuracy of corporate financial statements and the oversight role of boards of directors.

Effective financial reporting depends on sound ethical behavior. To sensitize you to ethical situations and to give you practice at solving ethical dilemmas, we address ethics in a number of ways in this text. (1) A number of the *Feature Stories* and other parts of the text discuss the central importance of ethical behavior to financial reporting. (2) *Ethics Insight boxes* and marginal *Ethics Notes* highlight ethics situations and issues in actual business settings. (3) Many of the *People, Planet, and Profit Insight boxes* focus on ethical issues that companies face in measuring and reporting social and environmental issues. (4) At the end of each chapter, an *Ethics Case* simulates a business situation and asks you to put yourself in the position of a decision-maker in that case.

When analyzing these various ethics cases and your own ethical experiences, you should apply the three steps outlined in **Illustration 1.3**.

ILLUSTRATION 1.3 Steps in analyzing ethics cases

Solving an Ethical Dilemma

1. Recognize an ethical situation and the ethical issues involved.	2. Identify and analyze the principal elements in the situation.	3. Identify the alternatives, and weigh the impact of each alternative on various stakeholders.
Use your personal ethics to identify ethical situations and issues. Some businesses and professional organizations provide written codes of ethics for guidance in some business situations.	Identify the **stakeholders**—persons or groups who may be harmed or benefited. Ask the question: What are the responsibilities and obligations of the parties involved?	Select the most ethical alternative, considering all the consequences. Sometimes there will be one right answer. Other situations involve more than one right solution; these situations require you to evaluate each alternative and select the best one.

*Insight boxes provide examples of business situations from various perspectives—ethics, investor, international, and corporate social responsibility. Guideline answers to the critical thinking questions, as well as additional questions, are available in **WileyPLUS**.*

Ethics Insight   Dewey & LeBoeuf LLP

Alliance/Shutterstock

I Felt the Pressure—Would You?

"I felt the pressure." That's what some of the employees of the now-defunct law firm of **Dewey & LeBoeuf LLP** indicated when they helped to overstate revenue and use accounting tricks to hide losses and cover up cash shortages. These employees worked for the former finance director and former chief financial officer (CFO) of the firm. Here are some of their comments:

- "I was instructed by the CFO to create invoices, knowing they would not be sent to clients. When I created these invoices, I knew that it was inappropriate."

- "I intentionally gave the auditors incorrect information in the course of the audit."

What happened here is that a small group of lower-level employees over a period of years carried out the instructions of their bosses. Their bosses, however, seemed to have no concern as evidenced by various e-mails with one another in which they referred to their financial manipulations as accounting tricks, cooking the books, and fake income.

Sources: Ashby Jones, "Guilty Pleas of Dewey Staff Detail the Alleged Fraud," *Wall Street Journal* (March 28, 2014); and Sara Randazzo, "Dewey CFO Escapes Jail Time in Fraud Case Sentencing," *Wall Street Journal* (October 10, 2017).

Why did these employees lie, and what do you believe should be their penalty for these lies? (Go to WileyPLUS for this answer and additional questions.)

*DO IT! exercises prompt you to stop and review the key points you have just studied. The **Action Plan** offers you tips about how to approach the problem.*

DO IT! 1 | Business Organization Forms

In choosing the organizational form for your outdoor guide service, you should consider the pros and cons of each. Identify each of the following organizational characteristics with the organizational form or forms with which it is associated.

1. Easier to raise funds.
2. Simple to establish.
3. No personal legal liability.
4. Tax advantages.
5. Easier to transfer ownership.

ACTION PLAN
- Know which organizational form best matches the business type, size, and preferences of the owner(s).

Solution

1. Easier to raise funds: Corporation.
2. Simple to establish: Sole proprietorship and partnership.
3. No personal legal liability: Corporation.
4. Tax advantages: Sole proprietorship and partnership.
5. Easier to transfer ownership: Corporation.

Related exercise material: **BE1.1 and DO IT! 1.1.**

The Three Types of Business Activity

LEARNING OBJECTIVE 2
Explain the three principal types of business activity.

All businesses are involved in three types of activity—financing, investing, and operating. For example, Gert Boyle's parents, the founders of **Columbia Sportswear**, obtained cash through financing to start and grow their business. Some of this **financing** came from personal savings, and some likely came from outside sources like banks. The family then **invested** the cash in equipment to run the business, such as sewing equipment and delivery vehicles. Once this equipment was in place, they could begin the **operating** activities of making and selling clothing.

The **accounting information system** keeps track of the results of each of the various business activities—financing, investing, and operating. Let's look at each type of business activity in more detail.

Financing Activities

It takes money to make money. The two primary sources of outside funds for corporations are borrowing money (debt financing) and issuing (selling) shares of stock in exchange for cash (equity financing).

Columbia Sportswear may borrow money in a variety of ways. For example, it can take out a loan at a bank or borrow directly from investors by issuing debt securities called bonds. Persons or entities to whom Columbia owes money are its **creditors**. Amounts owed to creditors—in the form of debt and other obligations—are called **liabilities**. Specific names are given to different types of liabilities, depending on their source. Columbia may have a **note**

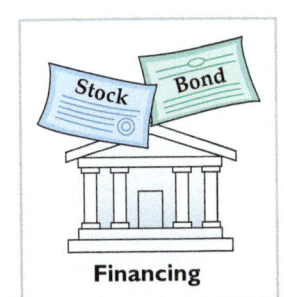

Financing

payable to a bank for the money borrowed to purchase delivery trucks. Debt securities sold to investors that must be repaid at a particular date some years in the future are **bonds payable**.

Corporations also obtain funds by selling shares of stock to investors. **Common stock** is the term used to describe the total amount paid in by stockholders for the shares they purchase.

The claims of creditors differ from those of stockholders. If you loan money to a company, you are one of its creditors. In lending money, you specify a payment schedule (e.g., payment at the end of three months). As a creditor, you have a legal right to be paid at the agreed time. In the event of nonpayment, you may legally force the company to sell property to pay its debts. In the case of financial difficulty, creditor claims must be paid before stockholders' claims.

Stockholders, on the other hand, have no claim to corporate cash until the claims of creditors are satisfied. Suppose you buy a company's stock instead of loaning it money. You have no legal right to expect any payments from your stock ownership until all of the company's creditors are paid amounts currently due. However, many corporations make payments to stockholders on a regular basis as long as there is sufficient cash to cover required payments to creditors. These cash payments to stockholders are called **dividends**.

Investing Activities

Once the company has raised cash through financing activities, it uses that cash in investing activities. Investing activities involve the purchase of the resources a company needs in order to operate. A growing company purchases many resources, such as computers, delivery trucks, furniture, and buildings. Resources owned by a business are called **assets**. Different types of assets are given different names. For example, Columbia Sportswear's sewing equipment is a type of asset referred to as **property, plant, and equipment** (see **Alternative Terminology**).

ALTERNATIVE TERMINOLOGY

Property, plant, and equipment is sometimes called *fixed assets*.

Cash is one of the more important assets owned by Columbia or any other business. If a company has excess cash that it does not need for a while, it might choose to invest in securities (stocks or bonds) of other corporations. **Investments** are another example of an investing activity.

Operating Activities

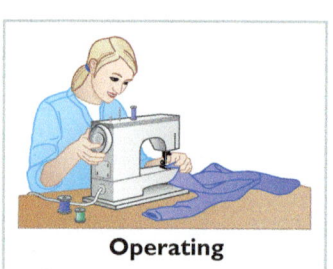

Once a business has the assets it needs to get started, it begins operations. Columbia Sportswear is in the business of selling outdoor clothing and footwear. It sells TurboDown jackets, Millenium snowboard pants, Sorel® snow boots, Bugaboots™, rainwear, and anything else you might need to protect you from the elements. We call amounts earned on the sale of these products **revenues**. **Revenue** is the increase in assets or decrease in liabilities resulting from the sale of goods or the performance of services in the normal course of business. For example, Columbia records revenue when it sells a footwear product.

Revenues arise from different sources and are identified by various names depending on the nature of the business. For instance, Columbia's primary source of revenue is the sale of sportswear. However, it also generates interest revenue on debt securities held as investments. Sources of revenue common to many businesses are **sales revenue**, **service revenue**, and **interest revenue**.

The company purchases its longer-lived assets through investing activities as described earlier. Other assets with shorter lives, however, result from operating activities. For example, **supplies** are assets used in day-to-day operations. Goods available for future sales to customers are assets called **inventory**. Also, if Columbia sells goods to a customer and does not receive cash immediately, then the company has a right to expect payment from that customer in the near future. This right to receive money in the future is called an **account receivable**.

Before Columbia can sell a single Sorel® boot, it must purchase wool, rubber, leather, metal lace loops, laces, and other materials. It then must process, wrap, and ship the finished product. It also incurs costs like salaries, rents, and utilities. All of these costs, referred to as **expenses**, are necessary to produce and sell the product. In accounting language, **expenses** are the cost of assets consumed or services used in the process of generating revenues.

Expenses take many forms and are identified by various names depending on the type of asset consumed or service used. For example, Columbia keeps track of these types of expenses: **cost of goods sold** (such as the cost of materials), **selling expenses** (such as the cost of salespersons' salaries), **marketing expenses** (such as the cost of advertising), **administrative expenses** (such as the salaries of administrative staff, and telephone and heating costs incurred at the corporate office), **interest expense** (amounts of interest paid on various debts), and **income tax expense** (corporate taxes paid to the government).

Columbia may also have liabilities arising from these expenses. For example, it may purchase goods on credit from suppliers. The obligations to pay for these goods are called **accounts payable**. Additionally, Columbia may have **interest payable** on the outstanding amounts owed to the bank. It may also have **wages payable** to its employees and **sales taxes payable**, **property taxes payable**, and **income taxes payable** to the government.

Columbia compares the revenues of a period with the expenses of that period to determine whether it earned a profit. When revenues exceed expenses, *net income* results. When expenses exceed revenues, a *net loss* results.

DO IT! 2 | Business Activities

Classify each item as an asset, liability, common stock, revenue, or expense.

1. Cost of renting property.
2. Truck purchased.
3. Notes payable.
4. Issuance of ownership shares.
5. Amount earned from performing service.
6. Amounts owed to suppliers.

ACTION PLAN
- Classify each item based on its economic characteristics. Proper classification of items is critical if accounting is to provide useful information.

Solution

1. Cost of renting property: Expense.
2. Truck purchased: Asset.
3. Notes payable: Liability.
4. Issuance of ownership shares: Common stock.
5. Amount earned from performing service: Revenue.
6. Amounts owed to suppliers: Liability.

Related exercise material: **BE1.3, DO IT! 1.2, and E1.4.**

International Notes highlight differences between U.S. and international accounting standards.

The Four Financial Statements

LEARNING OBJECTIVE 3
Describe the four financial statements and how they are prepared.

Assets, liabilities, expenses, and revenues are of interest to users of accounting information. This information is arranged in the format of four different **financial statements**, which form the backbone of financial accounting (see *International Note*):

- To show how successfully your business performed during a period of time, you report its revenues and expenses in an **income statement**.
- To indicate how much of previous income was distributed to you and the other owners of your business in the form of dividends, and how much was retained in the business to allow for future growth, you present a **retained earnings statement**.
- To present a picture at a point in time of what your business owns (its assets) and what it owes (its liabilities), you prepare a **balance sheet**.

International Note

The primary types of financial statements required by International Financial Reporting Standards (IFRS) and U.S. generally accepted accounting principles (GAAP) are the same. Neither IFRS nor GAAP is very specific regarding format requirements for the primary financial statements. However, in practice, some format differences do exist in presentations commonly employed by IFRS companies as compared to GAAP companies.

- To show where your business obtained cash during a period of time and how that cash was used, you present a **statement of cash flows**.

To introduce you to these statements, we have prepared the financial statements for your outdoor guide service, Sierra Corporation, after your first month of operations. To summarize, you officially started your business in Truckee, California, on October 1, 2022. Sierra provides guide services in the Lake Tahoe area of the Sierra Nevada mountains. Its promotional materials describe outdoor day trips, such as rafting, snowshoeing, and hiking, as well as multi-day backcountry experiences. To minimize your initial investment, at this point the company has limited outdoor equipment for customer use. Instead, your customers either bring their own equipment or rent equipment through local outfitters. The financial statements for Sierra's first month of business are provided in the following pages.

Income Statement

Decision Tools that are useful for business decision-making are highlighted throughout the text. A summary of the Decision Tools is also provided in each chapter.

> **Decision Tools**
>
> The income statement helps users determine if the company's operations are profitable.

The **income statement** reports a company's revenues and expenses and resulting net income or loss for a period of time (see **Decision Tools**). To indicate that its income statement reports the results of operations for a **specific period of time**, Sierra Corporation dates the income statement "For the Month Ended October 31, 2022." The income statement lists the company's revenues followed by its expenses. Finally, Sierra determines the net income (or net loss) by deducting expenses from revenues. Sierra's income statement is shown in **Illustration 1.4** (see **Helpful Hint**). Congratulations, you are already showing a profit!

ILLUSTRATION 1.4

Sierra Corporation's income statement

> **HELPFUL HINT**
>
> The financial statement heading identifies the company, the type of statement, and the time period covered. Sometimes, another line indicates the unit of measure, e.g., "in thousands" or "in millions."

Sierra Corporation
Income Statement
For the Month Ended October 31, 2022

Revenues		
Service revenue		$10,600
Expenses		
Salaries and wages expense	$5,200	
Rent expense	900	
Supplies expense	1,500	
Depreciation expense	40	
Interest expense	50	
Insurance expense	50	
Total expenses		7,740
Net income		$ 2,860

Why are financial statement users interested in net income? **Investors are interested in a company's past net income because it provides useful information for predicting future net income.** Investors buy and sell stock based on their beliefs about a company's future performance. If investors believe that Sierra will be successful in the future and that this will result in a higher stock price, they will buy its stock.

Creditors also use the income statement to predict future earnings. When a bank loans money to a company, it believes that it will be repaid in the future. If it didn't think it would be repaid, it wouldn't loan the money. Therefore, prior to making the loan the bank loan officer uses the income statement as a source of information to predict whether the company will be profitable enough to repay its loan. Thus, reporting a strong profit will make it easier for Sierra to raise additional cash either by issuing shares of stock or borrowing.

Amounts received from issuing stock are not revenues, and amounts paid out as dividends are not expenses. As a result, they are not reported on the income statement. For example, Sierra Corporation does not treat as revenue the $10,000 of cash received from issuing new stock (see Illustration 1.7), nor does it regard as a business expense the $500 of dividends paid (see Illustration 1.5) (see **Ethics Note**).

> **ETHICS NOTE**
>
> When companies find errors in previously released income statements, they restate those numbers. Perhaps because of the increased scrutiny shortly after Sarbanes-Oxley was implemented, companies filed a record 1,195 restatements.

Retained Earnings Statement

If Sierra Corporation is profitable, at the end of each period it must decide what portion of profits to pay to shareholders in dividends. In theory, it could pay all of its current-period profits, but few companies do this. Why? Because they want to retain part of the profits to allow for further expansion. High-growth companies, such as **Google** and **Facebook**, often pay no dividends. **Retained earnings** is the net income retained in the corporation.

The **retained earnings statement** shows the amounts and causes of changes in retained earnings for a specific time period (see **Decision Tools**). The time period is the same as that covered by the income statement. The beginning retained earnings amount appears on the first line of the statement. Then, the company adds net income and deducts dividends to determine the retained earnings at the end of the period. If a company has a net loss, it deducts (rather than adds) that amount in the retained earnings statement. **Illustration 1.5** presents Sierra's retained earnings statement (see **Helpful Hint**).

> **Decision Tools**
>
> The retained earnings statement helps users determine the company's policy toward dividends and growth.

ILLUSTRATION 1.5

Sierra Corporation's retained earnings statement

> **HELPFUL HINT**
>
> The heading of this statement identifies the company, the type of statement, and the time period covered by the statement.

Sierra Corporation
Retained Earnings Statement
For the Month Ended October 31, 2022

Retained earnings, October 1	$ 0
Add: Net income	2,860
	2,860
Less: Dividends	500
Retained earnings, October 31	$2,360

By monitoring the retained earnings statement, financial statement users can evaluate dividend payment practices. Some investors seek companies, such as **Dow Chemical**, that have a history of paying high dividends. Other investors seek companies, such as **Amazon.com**, that reinvest earnings to increase the company's growth instead of paying dividends. Lenders monitor their corporate customers' dividend payments because any money paid in dividends reduces a company's ability to repay its debts.

Balance Sheet

The **balance sheet** reports assets and claims to assets at a specific **point** in time (see **Decision Tools**). Claims to assets are subdivided into two categories: claims of creditors and claims of owners. As noted earlier, claims of creditors are called **liabilities**. The owners' claim to assets is called **stockholders' equity**.

Illustration 1.6 shows the relationship among the categories on the balance sheet in equation form. This equation is referred to as the **basic accounting equation**.

> **Decision Tools**
>
> The balance sheet helps users determine if the company relies on debt or stockholders' equity to finance its assets.

Assets = Liabilities + Stockholders' Equity

ILLUSTRATION 1.6

Basic accounting equation

This relationship is where the name "balance sheet" comes from. Assets must balance with the claims to assets.

As you can see from looking at Sierra Corporation's balance sheet in **Illustration 1.7**, the balance sheet presents the company's financial position as of a specific date—in this case, October 31, 2022 (see **Helpful Hint**). It lists assets first. Assets are listed in the order of their liquidity, that is, how quickly they could be converted to cash. Assets are followed by liabilities and stockholders' equity (see **Alternative Terminology**). Stockholders' equity is comprised of two parts: (1) common stock and (2) retained earnings. As noted earlier, common stock results when the company sells new shares of stock; retained earnings is the

> **ALTERNATIVE TERMINOLOGY**
>
> Liabilities are also referred to as *debt*.

net income retained in the corporation. Sierra has common stock of $10,000 and retained earnings of $2,360, for total stockholders' equity of $12,360.

ILLUSTRATION 1.7
Sierra Corporation's balance sheet

HELPFUL HINT
The heading of a balance sheet must identify the company, the statement, and the date.

Sierra Corporation
Balance Sheet
October 31, 2022

Assets

Cash		$15,200
Accounts receivable		200
Supplies		1,000
Prepaid insurance		550
Equipment, net		4,960
Total assets		$21,910

Liabilities and Stockholders' Equity

Liabilities		
Notes payable	$ 5,000	
Accounts payable	2,500	
Unearned service revenue	800	
Salaries and wages payable	1,200	
Interest payable	50	
Total liabilities		$ 9,550
Stockholders' equity		
Common stock	10,000	
Retained earnings	2,360	
Total stockholders' equity		12,360
Total liabilities and stockholders' equity		$21,910

Creditors analyze a company's balance sheet to determine the likelihood that they will be repaid. They carefully evaluate the nature of the company's assets and liabilities. In operating Sierra's guide service, the balance sheet will be used to determine whether cash on hand is sufficient for immediate cash needs. The balance sheet will also be used to evaluate the relationship between debt and stockholders' equity to determine whether the company has a satisfactory proportion of debt and common stock financing.

Statement of Cash Flows

Decision Tools
The statement of cash flows helps users determine if the company generates enough cash from operations to fund its investing activities.

The primary purpose of a **statement of cash flows** is to provide financial information about the cash receipts and cash payments of a business for a specific period of time (see **Decision Tools**). To help investors, creditors, and others in their analysis of a company's cash position, the statement of cash flows reports the cash effects of a company's **operating**, **investing**, and **financing** activities. In addition, the statement shows the net increase or decrease in cash during the period, and the amount of cash at the end of the period.

Users are interested in the statement of cash flows because they want to know what is happening to a company's most important resource. The statement of cash flows provides answers to these simple but important questions:

- Where did cash come from during the period?
- How was cash used during the period?
- What was the change in the cash balance during the period?

The statement of cash flows for Sierra Corporation, in **Illustration 1.8**, shows that cash increased $15,200 during the month (see **Helpful Hint**). This increase resulted because operating activities (services to clients) increased cash $5,700, and financing activities increased cash $14,500. Investing activities used $5,000 of cash for the purchase of equipment.

ILLUSTRATION 1.8
Sierra Corporation's statement of cash flows

Sierra Corporation
Statement of Cash Flows
For the Month Ended October 31, 2022

Cash flows from operating activities		
Cash receipts from operating activities	$11,200	
Cash payments for operating activities	(5,500)	
Net cash provided by operating activities		$ 5,700
Cash flows from investing activities		
Purchased office equipment	(5,000)	
Net cash used by investing activities		(5,000)
Cash flows from financing activities		
Issuance of common stock	10,000	
Issuance of note payable	5,000	
Payment of dividend	(500)	
Net cash provided by financing activities		14,500
Net increase in cash		15,200
Cash at beginning of period		0
Cash at end of period		$15,200

HELPFUL HINT
The heading of this statement identifies the company, the type of statement, and the time period covered by the statement. Negative numbers are shown in parentheses.

People, Planet, and Profit Insight

© Marek Uliasz/iStockphoto

Beyond Financial Statements

Should we expand our financial statements beyond the income statement, retained earnings statement, balance sheet, and statement of cash flows? Some believe we should take into account ecological and social performance, in addition to financial results, in evaluating a company. The argument is that a company's responsibility lies with anyone who is influenced by its actions. In other words, a company should be interested in benefiting many different parties, instead of only maximizing stockholders' interests.

A socially responsible business does not exploit or endanger any group of individuals. It follows fair trade practices, provides safe environments for workers, and bears responsibility for environmental damage. Granted, measurement of these factors is difficult. How to report this information is also controversial. But many interesting and useful efforts are underway. Throughout this text, we provide additional insights into how companies are attempting to meet the challenge of measuring and reporting their contributions to society, as well as their financial results, to stockholders.

Why might a company's stockholders be interested in its environmental and social performance? (Go to WileyPLUS for this answer and additional questions.)

Interrelationships of Statements

Illustration 1.9 shows the financial statements of Sierra Corporation (see **Helpful Hints**). Because the results on some financial statements become inputs to other statements, the statements are interrelated. These interrelationships can be seen in Sierra's financial statements, as follows.

1. The retained earnings statement uses the results of the income statement. Sierra reported net income of $2,860 for the period. Net income is added to the beginning amount of retained earnings to determine ending retained earnings.

2. The balance sheet and retained earnings statement are also interrelated. Sierra reports the ending amount of $2,360 on the retained earnings statement as the retained earnings amount on the balance sheet.

3. Finally, the statement of cash flows relates to information on the balance sheet. The statement of cash flows shows how the Cash account changed during the period. It shows the amount of cash at the beginning of the period, the sources and uses of cash during the period, and the $15,200 of cash at the end of the period. The ending amount of cash shown on the statement of cash flows must agree with the amount of cash on the balance sheet.

Study these interrelationships carefully. **To prepare financial statements, you must understand the sequence in which these amounts are determined and how each statement impacts the next.**

ILLUSTRATION 1.9

Sierra Corporation's financial statements

Sierra Corporation
Income Statement
For the Month Ended October 31, 2022

Revenues		
Service revenue		$10,600
Expenses		
Salaries expense	$5,200	
Rent expense	900	
Supplies expense	1,500	
Depreciation expense	40	
Interest expense	50	
Insurance expense	50	
Total expenses		7,740
Net income		$ 2,860

HELPFUL HINT

Note that final sums are double-underlined.

Sierra Corporation
Retained Earnings Statement
For the Month Ended October 31, 2022

Retained earnings, October 1	$ 0
Add: Net income	2,860
	2,860
Less: Dividends	500
Retained earnings, October 31	$2,360

HELPFUL HINT

The arrows in this illustration show interrelationships of the four financial statements.

Sierra Corporation
Balance Sheet
October 31, 2022

Assets

Cash	$15,200
Accounts receivable	200
Advertising supplies	1,000
Prepaid insurance	550
Equipment, net	4,960
Total assets	$21,910

Liabilities and Stockholders' Equity

Liabilities		
Notes payable	$ 5,000	
Accounts payable	2,500	
Unearned service revenue	800	
Salaries and wages payable	1,200	
Interest payable	50	
Total liabilities		$ 9,550
Stockholders' equity		
Common stock	10,000	
Retained earnings	2,360	
Total stockholders' equity		12,360
Total liabilities and stockholders' equity		$21,910

Sierra Corporation
Statement of Cash Flows
For the Month Ended October 31, 2022

Cash flows from operating activities		
Cash receipts from operating activities	$11,200	
Cash payments for operating activities	(5,500)	
Net cash provided by operating activities		$ 5,700
Cash flows from investing activities		
Purchased office equipment	(5,000)	
Net cash used by investing activities		(5,000)
Cash flows from financing activities		
Issuance of common stock	10,000	
Issuance of note payable	5,000	
Payment of dividend	(500)	
Net cash provided by financing activities		14,500
Net increase in cash		15,200
Cash at beginning of period		0
Cash at end of period		$15,200

HELPFUL HINT

Negative amounts are presented in parentheses.

DO IT! 3a | Financial Statements

CSU Corporation began operations on January 1, 2022. The following information is available for CSU on December 31, 2022:

Accounts receivable	1,800	Retained earnings	?	Supplies expense	200
Accounts payable	2,000	Equipment	16,000	Cash	1,400
Rent expense	9,000	Insurance expense	1,000	Dividends	600
Notes payable	5,000	Service revenue	17,000		
Common stock	10,000	Supplies	4,000		

Prepare an income statement, a retained earnings statement, and a balance sheet.

ACTION PLAN
- Report the revenues and expenses for a period of time in an income statement.
- Show the amounts and causes (net income and dividends) of changes in retained earnings during the period in the retained earnings statement.
- Present the assets and claims to those assets (liabilities and equity) at a specific point in time in the balance sheet.

Solution

CSU Corporation
Income Statement
For the Year Ended December 31, 2022

Revenues		
Service revenue		$17,000
Expenses		
Rent expense	$9,000	
Insurance expense	1,000	
Supplies expense	200	
Total expenses		10,200
Net income		$ 6,800

CSU Corporation
Retained Earnings Statement
For the Year Ended December 31, 2022

Retained earnings, January 1	$ 0
Add: Net income	6,800
	6,800
Less: Dividends	600
Retained earnings, December 31	$6,200

CSU Corporation
Balance Sheet
December 31, 2022

Assets

Cash		$ 1,400
Accounts receivable		1,800
Supplies		4,000
Equipment		16,000
Total assets		$23,200

Liabilities and Stockholders' Equity

Liabilities		
Notes payable	$ 5,000	
Accounts payable	2,000	
Total liabilities		$ 7,000
Stockholders' equity		
Common stock	10,000	
Retained earnings	6,200	
Total stockholders' equity		16,200
Total liabilities and stockholders' equity		$23,200

Related exercise material: **BE1.5, BE1.6, BE1.7, BE1.8, BE1.9, BE1.10, DO IT! 1.3a, E1.5, E1.6, E1.7, E1.8, E1.9, E1.10, E1.11, E1.12, E1.13, E1.14, E1.15, and E1.18.**

Other Elements of an Annual Report

Publicly traded U.S. companies must provide shareholders with an **annual report**. The annual report always includes the financial statements introduced in this chapter. The annual report also includes other important information such as a management discussion and analysis section, notes to the financial statements, and an independent auditor's report. No analysis of a company's financial situation and performance is complete without a review of these items.

Management Discussion and Analysis

The **management discussion and analysis (MD&A)** section presents management's views on the company's **ability to pay near-term obligations, its ability to fund operations and expansion, and its results of operations**. Management must highlight favorable or unfavorable trends and identify significant events and uncertainties that affect these three factors. This discussion obviously involves a number of subjective estimates and opinions. A brief excerpt from the MD&A section of **Columbia Sportswear**'s annual report, which addresses its liquidity requirements, is presented in **Illustration 1.10**.

ILLUSTRATION 1.10

Columbia Sportswear's management discussion and analysis

Columbia Sportswear Company
Management's Discussion and Analysis of
Seasonality and Variability of Business

Our operations are affected by seasonal trends typical in the outdoor apparel and footwear industry and have historically resulted in higher sales and profits in the third and fourth calendar quarters. This pattern has resulted primarily from the timing of shipments of fall season products to wholesale customers in the third and fourth quarters and proportionally higher sales in our direct-to-consumer channels in the fourth quarter, combined with an expense base that is spread more consistent throughout the year. We believe that our liquidity requirements for at least the next 12 months will be adequately covered by existing cash, cash provided by operations and existing short-term borrowing arrangements.

Notes to the Financial Statements

Explanatory notes and supporting schedules accompany every set of financial statements and are an integral part of the statements. The **notes to the financial statements** clarify the financial statements and provide additional detail. Information in the notes does not have to be quantifiable (numeric). Examples of notes are descriptions of the significant accounting policies and methods used in preparing the statements, explanations of uncertainties and contingencies, and various statistics and details too voluminous to be included in the statements. The notes are essential to understanding a company's operating performance and financial position.

Illustration 1.11 is an excerpt from the notes to **Columbia Sportswear**'s financial statements. It describes the methods that the company uses to account for revenues.

ILLUSTRATION 1.11

Notes to Columbia Sportswear's financial statements

Columbia Sportswear Company
Notes to Financial Statements
Revenue Recognition

We record wholesale, distributor, e-commerce and licensed product revenues when title passes and the risks and rewards of ownership have passed to the customer. Title generally passes upon shipment to or upon receipt by the customer depending on the terms of sale with the customer. Retail store revenues are recorded at the time of sale.

Auditor's Report

An **auditor's report** is prepared by an independent outside auditor. It states the auditor's opinion as to the fairness of the presentation of the financial position and results of operations and their conformance with generally accepted accounting principles.

An **auditor** is an accounting professional who conducts an independent examination of a company's financial statements. Only accountants who meet certain criteria and thereby attain the designation **certified public accountant (CPA)** may perform audits. If the auditor is satisfied that the financial statements provide a fair representation of the company's financial position and results of operations in accordance with generally accepted accounting principles, then the auditor expresses an **unqualified opinion**. If the auditor expresses anything other than an unqualified opinion, then readers should only use the financial statements with caution. That is, without an unqualified opinion, we cannot have complete confidence that the financial statements give an accurate picture of the company's financial health. For example, **Blockbuster, Inc.**'s auditor at one time stated that its financial situation raised "substantial doubt about the Company's ability to continue as a going concern."

Illustration 1.12 is an excerpt from the auditor's report from Columbia Sportswear's 2016 annual report. Columbia received an unqualified opinion from its auditor, **Deloitte & Touche**.

ILLUSTRATION 1.12

Excerpt from auditor's report on Columbia Sportswear's financial statements

Columbia Sportswear Company
Excerpt from Auditor's Report

Real World

In our opinion, such consolidated financial statements present fairly, in all material respects, the financial position of Columbia Sportswear Company and subsidiaries as of December 31, 2016 and 2015, and the results of their operations and their cash flows for each of the three years in the period ended December 31, 2016, in conformity with accounting principles generally accepted in the United States of America. Also, in our opinion, such financial statement schedules, when considered in relation to the basic consolidated financial statements taken as a whole, presents fairly, in all material respects, the information set forth therein.

DO IT! 3b | Components of Annual Reports

State whether each of the following items is most closely associated with the management discussion and analysis (MD&A), the notes to the financial statements, or the auditor's report.

1. Descriptions of significant accounting policies.
2. Unqualified opinion.
3. Explanations of uncertainties and contingencies.
4. Description of ability to fund operations and expansion.
5. Description of results of operations.
6. Certified public accountant (CPA).

ACTION PLAN
- Realize that financial statements provide information about a company's performance and financial position.
- Be familiar with the other elements of the annual report in order to gain a fuller understanding of a company.

Solution

1. Descriptions of significant accounting policies: Notes.
2. Unqualified opinion: Auditor's report.
3. Explanations of uncertainties and contingencies: Notes.
4. Description of ability to fund operations and expansion: MD&A.
5. Description of results of operations: MD&A.
6. Certified public accountant (CPA): Auditor's report.

Related exercise material: **BE1.11, DO IT! 1.3b, and E1.21.**

Using the Decision Tools comprehensive exercises ask you to apply business information and the decision tools presented in the chapter. Most of these exercises are based on the companies highlighted in the Feature Story.

USING THE DECISION TOOLS | VF Corporation

There is a good chance that you may have never heard of **VF Corporation**. There is also a very good chance that you are wearing one of VF's products right now. VF owns North Face, Lee, Vans, Nautica, Wrangler, Timberland, and numerous other brands. VF is a direct competitor to **Columbia Sportswear**. Suppose that you are considering investing in shares of VF's common stock.

Instructions

Answer these questions related to your decision whether to invest.

a. What financial statements should you evaluate?
b. What should these financial statements tell you?
c. Do you care if the financial statements have been audited? Explain.
d. Appendix B contains financial statements for Columbia, and Appendix C contains those for VF. You can make many comparisons between Columbia and VF in terms of their respective results from operations and financial position. Compare their respective total assets, total revenues, and net cash provided by operating activities for 2016.

Solution

a. Before you invest, you should evaluate the income statement, retained earnings statement, balance sheet, and statement of cash flows.

b. You would probably be most interested in the income statement because it tells about past performance and thus gives an indication of future performance. The retained earnings statement provides a record of the company's dividend history. The balance sheet reveals the relationship between assets and liabilities. The statement of cash flows reveals where the company is getting and spending its cash. This is especially important for a company that wants to grow.

c. You would want audited financial statements. These statements indicate that a CPA (certified public accountant) has examined and expressed an opinion that the statements present fairly the financial position and results of operations of the company. Investors and creditors should not make decisions without studying audited financial statements.

d. Many interesting comparisons can be made between the two companies (all numbers are in thousands). Columbia is smaller, with total assets of $2,013,894 versus $9,739,287 for VF, and it has lower revenue—$2,377,045 versus $12,019,003 for VF. In addition, Columbia's net cash provided by operating activities of $275,167 is less than VF's $1,477,919. However, while useful, these basic measures are not enough to determine whether one company is a better investment than the other. In later chapters, you will learn tools that will allow you to compare the relative profitability and financial health of these and other companies.

The **Review and Practice** section provides opportunities for students to review key concepts and terms as well as complete multiple-choice questions, brief exercises, exercises, and a comprehensive problem. Detailed solutions are also included.

Review and Practice

Learning Objectives Review

1 Identify the forms of business organization and the uses of accounting information.

A sole proprietorship is a business owned by one person. A partnership is a business owned by two or more people associated as partners.

A corporation is a separate legal entity for which evidence of ownership is provided by shares of stock.

Internal users are managers who need accounting information to plan, organize, and run business operations. The primary external users are investors and creditors. Investors (stockholders) use accounting information to decide whether to buy, hold, or sell shares of a company's stock. Creditors (suppliers and bankers) use accounting information to assess the risk of granting credit or loaning money to a business. Other groups who have an indirect interest in a business are taxing authorities, customers, labor unions, and regulatory agencies.

> **2 Explain the three principal types of business activity.**

Financing activities involve collecting the necessary funds to support the business. Investing activities involve acquiring the resources necessary to run the business. Operating activities involve putting the resources of the business into action to generate a profit.

> **3 Describe the four financial statements and how they are prepared.**

An income statement presents the revenues and expenses of a company for a specific period of time. A retained earnings statement summarizes the changes in retained earnings that have occurred for a specific period of time. A balance sheet reports the assets, liabilities, and stockholders' equity of a business at a specific date. A statement of cash flows summarizes information concerning the cash inflows (receipts) and outflows (payments) for a specific period of time.

Assets are resources owned by a business. Liabilities are the debts and obligations of the business. Liabilities represent claims of creditors on the assets of the business. Stockholders' equity represents the claims of owners on the assets of the business. Stockholders' equity is subdivided into two parts: common stock and retained earnings. The basic accounting equation is Assets = Liabilities + Stockholders' Equity.

Within the annual report, the management discussion and analysis provides management's interpretation of the company's results and financial position as well as a discussion of plans for the future. Notes to the financial statements provide additional explanation or detail to make the financial statements more informative. The auditor's report expresses an opinion as to whether the financial statements present fairly the company's results of operations and financial position.

Decision Tools Review

Decision Checkpoints	Info Needed for Decision	Tool to Use for Decision	How to Evaluate Results
Are the company's operations profitable?	Income statement	The income statement reports a company's revenues and expenses and resulting net income or loss for a period of time	If the company's revenues exceed its expenses, it will report net income; otherwise, it will report a net loss.
What is the company's policy toward dividends and growth?	Retained earnings statement	The retained earnings statement reports how much of this year's income the company paid out in dividends to shareholders	A company striving for rapid growth will pay a low (or no) dividend.
Does the company rely primarily on debt or stockholders' equity to finance its assets?	Balance sheet	The balance sheet reports the company's resources and claims to those resources; there are two types of claims: liabilities and stockholders' equity	Compare the amount of debt versus the amount of stockholders' equity to determine whether the company relies more on creditors or owners for its financing.
Does the company generate sufficient cash from operations to fund its investing activities?	Statement of cash flows	The statement of cash flows shows the amount of net cash provided or used by operating activities, investing activities, and financing activities	Compare the amount of net cash provided by operating activities with the amount of net cash used by investing activities. Any deficiency in cash from operating activities must be made up with cash from financing activities.

Glossary Review

Accounting The information system that identifies, records, and communicates the economic events of an organization to interested users. (p. 1-3).

Annual report A report prepared by corporate management that presents financial information including financial statements, a management discussion and analysis section, notes, and an independent auditor's report. (p. 1-16).

Assets Resources owned by a business. (p. 1-8).

Auditor's report A report prepared by an independent outside auditor stating the auditor's opinion as to the fairness of the presentation of the financial position and results of operations and their conformance with generally accepted accounting principles. (p. 1-17).

Balance sheet A financial statement that reports the assets and claims to those assets at a specific point in time. (p. 1-11).

Basic accounting equation Assets = Liabilities + Stockholders' Equity. (p. 1-11).

Certified public accountant (CPA) An individual who has met certain criteria and is thus allowed to perform audits of corporations. (p. 1-17).

Common stock Term used to describe the total amount paid in by stockholders for the shares they purchase. (p. 1-8).

Corporation A business organized as a separate legal entity owned by stockholders. (p. 1-3).

Dividends Payments of cash from a corporation to its stockholders. (p. 1-8).

Expenses The cost of assets consumed or services used in the process of generating revenues. (p. 1-8).

Income statement A financial statement that reports a company's revenues and expenses and resulting net income or net loss for a specific period of time. (p. 1-10).

Liabilities Amounts owed to creditors in the form of debts and other obligations. (p. 1-7).

Management discussion and analysis (MD&A) A section of the annual report that presents management's views on the company's ability to pay near-term obligations, its ability to fund operations and expansion, and its results of operations. (p. 1-16).

Net income The amount by which revenues exceed expenses. (p. 1-9).

Net loss The amount by which expenses exceed revenues. (p. 1-9).

Notes to the financial statements Notes clarify information presented in the financial statements and provide additional detail. (p. 1-16).

Partnership A business owned by two or more persons associated as partners. (p. 1-3).

Retained earnings The amount of net income retained in the corporation. (p. 1-11).

Retained earnings statement A financial statement that summarizes the amounts and causes of changes in retained earnings for a specific time period. (p. 1-11).

Revenue The increase in assets or decrease in liabilities resulting from the sale of goods or the performance of services in the normal course of business. (p. 1-8).

Sarbanes-Oxley Act (SOX) Regulations passed by Congress to reduce unethical corporate behavior. (p. 1-6).

Sole proprietorship A business owned by one person. (p. 1-3).

Statement of cash flows A financial statement that provides financial information about the cash receipts and cash payments of a business for a specific period of time. (p. 1-12).

Stockholders' equity The owners' claim to assets. (p. 1-11).

Practice Multiple-Choice Questions

1. (LO 1) Which is **not** one of the three forms of business organization?
  a. Sole proprietorship.
  b. Creditorship.
  c. Partnership.
  d. Corporation.

2. (LO 1) Which is an advantage of corporations relative to partnerships and sole proprietorships?
  a. Lower taxes.
  b. Harder to transfer ownership.
  c. Reduced legal liability for investors.
  d. Most common form of organization.

3. (LO 1) Which statement about users of accounting information is **incorrect**?
  a. Management is considered an internal user.
  b. Taxing authorities are considered external users.
  c. Present creditors are considered external users.
  d. Regulatory authorities are considered internal users.

4. (LO 1) Which of the following did **not** result from the Sarbanes-Oxley Act?
  a. Top management must now certify the accuracy of financial information.
  b. Penalties for fraudulent activity increased.
  c. Independence of auditors increased.
  d. Tax rates on corporations increased.

5. (LO 2) Which is **not** one of the three primary business activities?
  a. Financing.
  b. Operating.
  c. Advertising.
  d. Investing.

6. (LO 2) Which of the following is an example of a financing activity?
  a. Issuing shares of common stock.
  b. Selling goods on account.
  c. Buying delivery equipment.
  d. Buying inventory.

7. (LO 2) Net income will result during a time period when:
  a. assets exceed liabilities.
  b. assets exceed revenues.
  c. expenses exceed revenues.
  d. revenues exceed expenses.

8. (LO 3) The financial statements for Macias Corporation contained the following information.

Accounts receivable	$ 5,000
Sales revenue	75,000
Cash	15,000
Salaries and wages expense	20,000
Rent expense	10,000

What was Macias Corporation's net income?
  a. $60,000.
  b. $15,000.
  c. $65,000.
  d. $45,000.

9. (LO 3) What section of a statement of cash flows indicates the cash spent on new equipment during the past accounting period?
  a. The investing activities section.
  b. The operating activities section.
  c. The financing activities section.
  d. The statement of cash flows does not give this information.

10. (LO 3) Which statement presents information as of a specific point in time?

   a. Income statement.
   b. Balance sheet.
   c. Statement of cash flows.
   d. Retained earnings statement.

11. (LO 3) Which financial statement reports assets, liabilities, and stockholders' equity?

   a. Income statement.
   b. Retained earnings statement.
   c. Balance sheet.
   d. Statement of cash flows.

12. (LO 3) Stockholders' equity represents:

   a. claims of creditors.
   b. claims of employees.
   c. the difference between revenues and expenses.
   d. claims of owners.

13. (LO 3) As of December 31, 2022, Rockford Corporation has assets of $3,500 and stockholders' equity of $1,500. What are the liabilities for Rockford as of December 31, 2022?

   a. $1,500.   c. $2,500.
   b. $1,000.   d. $2,000.

14. (LO 3) The element of a corporation's annual report that describes the corporation's accounting methods is/are the:

   a. notes to the financial statements.
   b. management discussion and analysis.
   c. auditor's report.
   d. income statement.

15. (LO 3) The element of the annual report that presents an opinion regarding the fairness of the presentation of the financial position and results of operations is/are the:

   a. income statement.
   b. auditor's opinion.
   c. balance sheet.
   d. comparative statements.

Solutions

1. b. Creditorship is not a form of business organization. The other choices are incorrect because (a) sole proprietorship, (c) partnership, and (d) corporation are all forms of business organization.

2. c. An advantage of corporations is that investors are not personally liable for debts of the business. The other choices are incorrect because (a) lower taxes, (b) harder to transfer ownership, and (d) most common form of organization are not true of corporations.

3. d. Regulatory authorities are considered external, not internal, users. The other choices are true statements.

4. d. The Sarbanes-Oxley Act (SOX) was created to reduce unethical corporate behavior and decrease the likelihood of future corporate scandals, not to address tax rates. The other choices are incorrect because (a) top management must now certify the accuracy of financial information, (b) penalties for fraudulent activity increased, and (c) increased independence of auditors all resulted from SOX.

5. c. Advertising is a type of operating activity. The other choices are incorrect because (a) financing, (b) operating, and (d) investing are the three primary business activities.

6. a. Issuing shares of common stock is a financing activity. The other choices are incorrect because (b) selling goods on account is an operating activity, (c) buying delivery equipment is an investing activity, and (d) buying inventory is an operating activity.

7. d. When a company earns more revenues than expenses, it will report net income during a time period. The other choices are incorrect because (a) assets and liabilities are on the balance sheet, not the income statement; (b) assets are on the balance sheet, not the income statement; and (c) net income results when revenues exceed expenses, not when expenses exceed revenues.

8. d. Net income = Sales revenue ($75,000) − Salaries and wages expense ($20,000) − Rent expense ($10,000) = $45,000. The other choices are therefore incorrect.

9. a. The investing activities section of the statement of cash flows provides information about property, plant, and equipment accounts, not (b) the operating activities section or (c) the financing activities section. Choice (d) is incorrect as the statement of cash flows does provide this information.

10. b. The balance sheet presents information as of a specific point in time. The other choices are incorrect because the (a) income statement, (c) statement of cash flows, and (d) retained earnings statement all cover a period of time.

11. c. The balance sheet is a formal presentation of the accounting equation, such that Assets = Liabilities + Stockholders' Equity, not the (a) income statement, (b) retained earnings statement, or (d) statement of cash flows.

12. d. Stockholders' equity represents claims of owners. The other choices are incorrect because (a) claims of creditors and (b) claims of employees are liabilities. Choice (c) is incorrect because the difference between revenues and expenses is net income.

13. d. Using the accounting equation, liabilities can be computed by subtracting stockholders' equity from assets, or $3,500 − $1,500 = $2,000, not (a) $1,500, (b) $1,000, or (c) $2,500.

14. a. The corporation's accounting methods are described in the notes to the financial statements, not in the (b) management discussion and analysis, (c) auditor's report, or (d) income statement.

15. b. The element of the annual report that presents an opinion regarding the fairness of the presentation of the financial position and results of operations is the auditor's opinion, not the (a) income statement, (c) balance sheet, or (d) comparative statements.

Practice Brief Exercises

Use basic accounting equation.

1. (LO 3) At the beginning of the year, Ortiz Company had total assets of $900,000 and total liabilities of $440,000. Answer the following questions.

a. If total assets decreased $100,000 during the year and total liabilities increased $80,000 during the year, what is the amount of stockholders' equity at the end of the year?

b. During the year, total liabilities decreased $100,000 during the year and stockholders' equity increased $200,000. What is the amount of total assets at the end of the year?

c. If total assets increased $50,000 during the year and stockholders' equity increased $60,000 during the year, what is the amount of total liabilities at the end of the year?

Solution

1. a. ($900,000 − $440,000) − $100,000 − $80,000 = $280,000 stockholders' equity
   b. $900,000 − $100,000 + $200,000 = $1,000,000 total assets
   c. $440,000 − $60,000 + $50,000 = $430,000 total liabilities

Determine where items appear on financial statements.

2. (LO 3) Indicate whether the following items would appear on the income statement (IS), balance sheet (BS), or retained earnings statement (RES).

a. _____ Common stock.   d. _____ Service revenue.
b. _____ Cash.   e. _____ Accounts payable.
c. _____ Salaries and wages expense.

Solution

2. a. __BS__ Common stock.
   b. __BS__ Cash.
   c. __IS__ Salaries and wages expense.
   d. __IS__ Service revenue.
   e. __BS__ Accounts payable.

Prepare a balance sheet.

3. (LO 3) Presented below in alphabetical order are balance sheet items for Feagler Company at December 31, 2022. Prepare a balance sheet following the format of Illustration 1.7.

Accounts receivable	$12,500
Cash	38,000
Common stock	5,000
Notes payable	40,000
Retained earnings	5,500

Solution

3.

Feagler Company
Balance Sheet
December 31, 2022

Assets

Cash		$38,000
Accounts receivable		12,500
Total assets		$50,500

Liabilities and Stockholders' Equity

Liabilities		
Notes payable	$40,000	
Total liabilities		$40,000
Stockholders' equity		
Common stock	5,000	
Retained earnings	5,500	
Total stockholders' equity		10,500
Total liabilities and stockholders' equity		$50,500

4. (LO 3) Identify whether the following items would appear on the balance sheet (BS) or income statement (IS) of a corporation.

Determine where items appear on financial statements.

a. _____ Income taxes payable.
b. _____ Cost of goods sold.
c. _____ Supplies.
d. _____ Notes payable.
e. _____ Salaries and wages expense.
f. _____ Service revenue.
g. _____ Depreciation expense.
h. _____ Prepaid insurance.
i. _____ Interest payable.

Solution

4. a. __BS__ Income taxes payable.
   b. __IS__ Cost of goods sold.
   c. __BS__ Supplies.
   d. __BS__ Notes payable.
   e. __IS__ Salaries and wages expense.
   f. __IS__ Service revenue.
   g. __IS__ Depreciation expense.
   h. __BS__ Prepaid insurance.
   i. __BS__ Interest payable.

Practice Exercises

1. (LO 3) The following items and amounts were taken from Ricardo Inc.'s 2022 income statement and balance sheet.

Prepare an income statement.

Cash	$ 84,700	Inventory	$ 64,618
Retained earnings	123,192	Accounts receivable	88,419
Cost of goods sold	483,854	Sales revenue	693,485
Salaries and wages expense	125,000	Income taxes payable	6,499
Prepaid insurance	7,818	Accounts payable	49,384
Interest expense	994	Service revenue	8,998

Instructions

Prepare an income statement for Ricardo Inc. for the year ended December 31, 2022.

Solution

1.

Ricardo Inc.
Income Statement
For the Year Ended December 31, 2022

Revenues		
Sales revenue	$693,485	
Service revenue	8,998	
Total revenues		$702,483
Expenses		
Cost of goods sold	483,854	
Salaries and wages expense	125,000	
Interest expense	994	
Total expenses		609,848
Net income		$ 92,635

Compute net income and prepare a balance sheet.

2. (LO 3) Cozy Bear is a private camping ground near the Mountain Home Recreation Area. It has compiled the following financial information as of December 31, 2022.

Service revenue (from camping fees)	$148,000	Dividends	$ 9,000
Sales revenue (from general store)	35,000	Bonds payable	50,000
Accounts payable	16,000	Expenses during 2022	135,000
Cash	18,500	Supplies	12,500
Equipment	129,000	Common stock	40,000
		Retained earnings (1/1/2022)	15,000

Instructions

a. Determine net income from Cozy Bear for 2022.

b. Prepare a retained earnings statement and a balance sheet for Cozy Bear as of December 31, 2022.

Solution

2. a.

Service revenue	$148,000
Sales revenue	35,000
Total revenue	183,000
Expenses	135,000
Net income	$ 48,000

b.

Cozy Bear
Retained Earnings Statement
For the Year Ended December 31, 2022

Retained earnings, January 1	$15,000
Add: Net income	48,000
	63,000
Less: Dividends	9,000
Retained earnings, December 31	$54,000

Cozy Bear
Balance Sheet
December 31, 2022

Assets

Cash		$ 18,500
Supplies		12,500
Equipment		129,000
Total assets		$160,000

Liabilities and Stockholders' Equity

Liabilities		
Bonds payable	$50,000	
Accounts payable	16,000	
Total liabilities		$ 66,000
Stockholders' equity		
Common stock	40,000	
Retained earnings	54,000	
Total stockholders' equity		94,000
Total liabilities and stockholders' equity		$160,000

Practice Problem

Prepare financial statements.

(LO 3) Jeff Andringa, a former college hockey player, quit his job and started Ice Camp, a hockey camp for kids ages 8 to 18. Eventually, he would like to open hockey camps nationwide. Jeff has asked you to help him prepare financial statements at the end of his first year of operations. He relates the following facts about his business activities.

In order to get the business off the ground, Jeff decided to incorporate. He sold shares of common stock to a few close friends, as well as bought some of the shares himself. He initially raised $25,000 through the sale of these shares. In addition, the company took out a $10,000 loan at a local bank.

Ice Camp purchased, for $12,000 cash, a bus for transporting kids. The company also bought hockey goals and other miscellaneous equipment with $1,500 cash. The company earned camp tuition during the year of $100,000 but had collected only $80,000 of this amount. Thus, at the end of the year, its customers still owed $20,000. The company rents time at a local rink for $50 per hour. Total rink rental costs during the year were $8,000, insurance was $10,000, salary expense was $20,000, and supplies used totaled $9,000, all of which were paid in cash. The company incurred $800 in interest expense on the bank loan, which it still owed at the end of the year.

The company paid dividends during the year of $5,000 cash. The balance in the corporate bank account at December 31, 2022, was $49,500.

Instructions

Using the format of the Sierra Corporation statements in this chapter, prepare an income statement, retained earnings statement, balance sheet, and statement of cash flows. (*Hint:* Prepare the statements in the order stated to take advantage of the flow of information from one statement to the next, as shown in Illustration 1.9.)

Solution

Ice Camp
Income Statement
For the Year Ended December 31, 2022

Revenues		
Service revenue		$100,000
Expenses		
Salaries and wages expense	$20,000	
Insurance expense	10,000	
Supplies expense	9,000	
Rent expense	8,000	
Interest expense	800	
Total expenses		47,800
Net income		$ 52,200

Ice Camp
Retained Earnings Statement
For the Year Ended December 31, 2022

Retained earnings, January 1, 2022	$ 0
Add: Net income	52,200
	52,200
Less: Dividends	5,000
Retained earnings, December 31, 2022	$47,200

Ice Camp
Balance Sheet
December 31, 2022

Assets

Cash		$49,500
Accounts receivable		20,000
Equipment ($12,000 + $1,500)		13,500
Total assets		$83,000

Liabilities and Stockholders' Equity

Liabilities		
Notes payable	$10,000	
Interest payable	800	
Total liabilities		$10,800
Stockholders' equity		
Common stock	25,000	
Retained earnings	47,200	
Total stockholders' equity		72,200
Total liabilities and stockholders' equity		$83,000

Ice Camp
Statement of Cash Flows
For the Year Ended December 31, 2022

Cash flows from operating activities		
Cash receipts from operating activities	$80,000	
Cash payments for operating activities	(47,000)	
Net cash provided by operating activities		$33,000
Cash flows from investing activities		
Purchase of equipment	(13,500)	
Net cash used by investing activities		(13,500)
Cash flows from financing activities		
Issuance of common stock	25,000	
Issuance of notes payable	10,000	
Dividends paid	(5,000)	
Net cash provided by financing activities		30,000
Net increase in cash		49,500
Cash at beginning of period		0
Cash at end of period		$49,500

WileyPLUS

Brief Exercises, DO IT! Exercises, Exercises, Problems, and many additional resources are available for practice in WileyPLUS.

Questions

1. What are the three basic forms of business organizations?
2. What are the advantages to a business of being formed as a corporation? What are the disadvantages?
3. What are the advantages to a business of being formed as a partnership or sole proprietorship? What are the disadvantages?
4. "Accounting is ingrained in our society and is vital to our economic system." Do you agree? Explain.
5. Who are the internal users of accounting data? How does accounting provide relevant data to the internal users?
6. Who are the external users of accounting data? Give examples.

7. What are the three main types of business activity? Give examples of each activity.

8. Listed here are some items found in the financial statements of Finzelberg. Indicate in which financial statement(s) each item would appear.
   a. Service revenue.
   b. Equipment.
   c. Advertising expense.
   d. Accounts receivable.
   e. Common stock.
   f. Interest payable.

9. Why would a bank want to monitor the dividend payment practices of the corporations to which it lends money?

10. "A company's net income appears directly on the income statement and the retained earnings statement, and it is included indirectly in the company's balance sheet." Do you agree? Explain.

11. What is the primary purpose of the statement of cash flows?

12. What are the three main categories of the statement of cash flows? Why do you think these categories were chosen?

13. What is retained earnings? What items increase the balance in retained earnings? What items decrease the balance in retained earnings?

14. What is the basic accounting equation?

15. a. Define the terms assets, liabilities, and stockholders' equity.
    b. What items affect stockholders' equity?

16. Which of these items are liabilities of White Glove Cleaning Service?
    a. Cash.
    b. Accounts payable.
    c. Dividends.
    d. Accounts receivable.
    e. Supplies.
    f. Equipment.
    g. Salaries and wages payable.
    h. Service revenue.
    i. Rent expense.

17. How are each of the following financial statements interrelated? (a) Retained earnings statement and income statement. (b) Retained earnings statement and balance sheet. (c) Balance sheet and statement of cash flows.

18. What is the purpose of the management discussion and analysis section (MD&A)?

19. Why is it important for financial statements to receive an unqualified auditor's opinion?

20. What types of information are presented in the notes to the financial statements?

21. The accounting equation is Assets = Liabilities + Stockholders' Equity. Appendix A reproduces Apple's financial statements. Replacing words in the equation with dollar amounts, what is Apple's accounting equation at September 30, 2017?

Brief Exercises

BE1.1 (LO 1), K Match each of the following forms of business organization with a set of characteristics: sole proprietorship (SP), partnership (P), corporation (C).

Describe forms of business organization.

a. _____ Shared control, tax advantages, increased skills and resources.
b. _____ Simple to set up and maintains control with owner.
c. _____ Easier to transfer ownership and raise funds, no personal liability.

BE1.2 (LO 1), K Match each of the following types of evaluation with one of the listed users of accounting information.

Identify users of accounting information.

1. Trying to determine whether the company complied with tax laws.
2. Trying to determine whether the company can pay its obligations.
3. Trying to determine whether an advertising proposal will be cost-effective.
4. Trying to determine whether the company's net income will result in a stock price increase.
5. Trying to determine whether the company should employ debt or equity financing.

a. _____ Investors in common stock.
b. _____ Marketing managers.
c. _____ Creditors.
d. _____ Chief Financial Officer.
e. _____ Internal Revenue Service.

BE1.3 (LO 2), K Indicate to which business activity, operating activity (O), investing activity (I), or financing activity (F), each item relates.

Classify items by activity.

a. _____ Cash received from customers.
b. _____ Cash paid to stockholders (dividends).
c. _____ Cash received from issuing new common stock.
d. _____ Cash paid to suppliers.
e. _____ Cash paid to purchase a new office building.

BE1.4 (LO 3), C Presented below are a number of transactions. Determine whether each transaction affects common stock (C), dividends (D), revenues (R), expenses (E), or does not affect stockholders' equity (NSE). Provide titles for the revenues and expenses.

Determine effect of transactions on stockholders' equity.

a. Costs incurred for advertising.
b. Cash received for services performed.
c. Costs incurred for insurance.
d. Amounts paid to employees.
e. Cash distributed to stockholders.
f. Cash received in exchange for allowing the use of the company's building.
g. Costs incurred for utilities used.
h. Cash purchase of equipment.
i. Cash received from investors.

Prepare a balance sheet.

BE1.5 (LO 3), AP In alphabetical order below are balance sheet items for Karol Company at December 31, 2022. Prepare a balance sheet following the format of Illustration 1.7.

Accounts payable	$65,000
Accounts receivable	71,000
Cash	22,000
Common stock	18,000
Retained earnings	10,000

Determine where items appear on financial statements.

BE1.6 (LO 3), K Eskimo Pie Corporation markets a broad range of frozen treats, including its famous Eskimo Pie ice cream bars. The following items were taken from a recent income statement and balance sheet. In each case, identify whether the item would appear on the balance sheet (BS) or income statement (IS).

a. _____ Income tax expense.   f. _____ Sales revenue.
b. _____ Inventory.   g. _____ Cost of goods sold.
c. _____ Accounts payable.   h. _____ Common stock.
d. _____ Retained earnings.   i. _____ Accounts receivable.
e. _____ Equipment.   j. _____ Interest expense.

Determine proper financial statement.

BE1.7 (LO 3), K Indicate which statement you would examine to find each of the following items: income statement (IS), balance sheet (BS), retained earnings statement (RES), or statement of cash flows (SCF).

a. Revenue during the period.
b. Supplies on hand at the end of the year.
c. Cash received from issuing new bonds during the period.
d. Total debts outstanding at the end of the period.

Use basic accounting equation.

BE1.8 (LO 3), AP Use the basic accounting equation to answer these questions.

a. The liabilities of Lantz Company are $90,000 and the stockholders' equity is $230,000. What is the amount of Lantz's total assets?

b. The total assets of Salley Company are $170,000 and its stockholders' equity is $80,000. What is the amount of its total liabilities?

c. The total assets of Brandon Co. are $800,000 and its liabilities are equal to one-fourth of its total assets. What is the amount of Brandon's stockholders' equity?

Use basic accounting equation.

BE1.9 (LO 3), AP At the beginning of the year, Morales Company had total assets of $800,000 and total liabilities of $500,000. (Treat each item independently.)

a. If total assets increased $150,000 during the year and total liabilities decreased $80,000, what is the amount of stockholders' equity at the end of the year?

b. During the year, total liabilities increased $100,000 and stockholders' equity decreased $70,000. What is the amount of total assets at the end of the year?

c. If total assets decreased $80,000 and stockholders' equity increased $110,000 during the year, what is the amount of total liabilities at the end of the year?

Identify assets, liabilities, and stockholders' equity.

BE1.10 (LO 3), K Indicate whether each of these items is an asset (A), a liability (L), or part of stockholders' equity (SE).

a. Accounts receivable.   d. Supplies.
b. Salaries and wages payable.   e. Common stock.
c. Equipment.   f. Notes payable.

BE1.11 (LO 3), K Which is **not** a required part of an annual report of a publicly traded company?

Determine required parts of annual report.

a. Statement of cash flows.
b. Notes to the financial statements.
c. Management discussion and analysis.
d. All of these are required.

DO IT! Exercises

DO IT! 1.1 (LO 1), C Identify each of the following organizational characteristics with the business organizational form or forms with which it is associated.

Identify benefits of business organization forms.

a. Easier to transfer ownership.
b. Easier to raise funds.
c. More owner control.
d. Tax advantages.
e. No personal legal liability.

DO IT! 1.2 (LO 2), K Classify each item as an asset, liability, common stock, revenue, or expense.

Classify financial statement elements.

a. Issuance of ownership shares.
b. Land purchased.
c. Amounts owed to suppliers.
d. Bonds payable.
e. Amount earned from selling a product.
f. Cost of advertising.

DO IT! 1.3a (LO 3), AP Gray Corporation began operations on January 1, 2022. The following information is available for Gray on December 31, 2022.

Prepare financial statements.

Accounts payable	$ 5,000	Notes payable	$ 7,000
Accounts receivable	2,000	Rent expense	10,000
Advertising expense	4,000	Retained earnings	?
Cash	3,100	Service revenue	25,000
Common stock	15,000	Supplies	1,900
Dividends	2,500	Supplies expense	1,700
Equipment	26,800		

Prepare an income statement, a retained earnings statement, and a balance sheet for Gray Corporation.

DO IT! 1.3b (LO 3), K Indicate whether each of the following items is most closely associated with the management discussion and analysis (MD&A), the notes to the financial statements, or the auditor's report.

Identify components of annual reports.

a. Description of ability to pay near-term obligations.
b. Unqualified opinion.
c. Details concerning liabilities, too voluminous to be included in the statements.
d. Description of favorable and unfavorable trends.
e. Certified public accountant (CPA).
f. Descriptions of significant accounting policies.

Exercises

E1.1 (LO 1, 2, 3), K Here is a list of words or phrases discussed in this chapter:

Match items with descriptions.

1. Corporation
2. Creditor
3. Accounts receivable
4. Partnership
5. Stockholder
6. Common stock
7. Accounts payable
8. Auditor's opinion

Instructions

Match each word or phrase with the best description of it.

_____ a. An expression about whether financial statements conform with generally accepted accounting principles.

_____ b. A business that raises money by issuing shares of stock.

_____ c. The portion of stockholders' equity that results from receiving cash from investors.

_____ d. Obligations to suppliers of goods.
_____ e. Amounts due from customers.
_____ f. A party to whom a business owes money.
_____ g. A party that invests in common stock.
_____ h. A business that is owned jointly by two or more individuals but does not issue stock.

Match items with descriptions.

E1.2 (LO 1, 2, 3), K The following list of terms or phrases are discussed in this chapter.

1. Certified public accountant (CPA)
2. Management discussion and analysis (MD&A)
3. Revenue
4. Dividends
5. Stockholders' equity
6. Net loss
7. Sole proprietorship
8. Basic accounting equation
9. Expenses
10. Liabilities
11. Sarbanes-Oxley Act (SOX)

Instructions

Match each term or phrase to its description below.

a. _____ Assets = Liabilities + Stockholders' Equity.
b. _____ An individual who has met certain criteria and is thus allowed to perform audits of corporations.
c. _____ Payments of cash from a corporation to its stockholders.
d. _____ The cost of assets consumed or services used in the process of generating revenues.
e. _____ Amounts owed to creditors in the form of debts and other obligations.
f. _____ A section of the annual report that presents management's views on the company's ability to pay near-term obligations, its ability to fund operations and expansion, and its results of operations.
g. _____ The amount by which expenses exceed revenues.
h. _____ The increase in assets or decrease in liabilities resulting from the sale of goods or the performance of services in the normal course of business.
i. _____ Regulations passed by Congress to reduce unethical corporate behavior.
j. _____ A business owned by one person.
k. _____ The owners' claim to assets.

Identify business activities.

E1.3 (LO 2), C All businesses are involved in three types of activities—financing, investing, and operating. Listed below are the names and descriptions of companies in several different industries.

Abitibi Consolidated Inc.—manufacturer and marketer of newsprint
Cal State–Northridge Stdt Union—university student union
Oracle Corporation—computer software developer and retailer
Sportsco Investments—owner of the Vancouver Canucks hockey club
Grant Thornton LLP—professional accounting and business advisory firm
Southwest Airlines—low-cost airline

Instructions

a. For each of the above companies, provide examples of (1) a financing activity, (2) an investing activity, and (3) an operating activity that the company likely engages in.
b. Which of the activities that you identified in (a) are common to most businesses? Which activities are not?

Classify accounts.

E1.4 (LO 2, 3), C The Bonita Vista Golf & Country Club details the following accounts in its financial statements.

Accounts payable _____
Accounts receivable _____
Equipment _____
Sales revenue _____
Service revenue _____
Inventory _____
Mortgage payable _____
Supplies expense _____
Rent expense _____
Salaries and wages expense _____

Instructions

Classify each of the accounts as an asset (A), liability (L), stockholders' equity (SE), revenue (R), or expense (E) item.

E1.5 (LO 3), AP This information relates to Benser Co. for the year 2022.

Prepare income statement and retained earnings statement.

Retained earnings, January 1, 2022	$67,000
Advertising expense	1,800
Dividends	6,000
Rent expense	10,400
Service revenue	58,000
Utilities expense	2,400
Salaries and wages expense	30,000

Instructions

Prepare an income statement and a retained earnings statement for the year ending December 31, 2022.

E1.6 (LO 3), AP Suppose the following information was taken from the 2022 financial statements of pharmaceutical giant **Merck and Co.** (All dollar amounts are in millions.)

Prepare income statement and retained earnings statement.

Retained earnings, January 1, 2022	$43,698.8
Cost of goods sold	9,018.9
Selling and administrative expenses	8,543.2
Dividends	3,597.7
Sales revenue	38,576.0
Research and development expense	5,845.0
Income tax expense	2,267.6

Instructions

a. After analyzing the data, prepare an income statement and a retained earnings statement for the year ending December 31, 2022.

b. Suppose that Merck decided to reduce its research and development expense by 50%. What would be the short-term implications? What would be the long-term implications? How do you think the stock market would react?

E1.7 (LO 3), AP Presented here is information for Zheng Inc. for 2022.

Prepare a retained earnings statement.

Retained earnings, January 1	$130,000
Service revenue	400,000
Total expenses	175,000
Dividends	65,000

Instructions

Prepare the 2022 retained earnings statement for Zheng Inc.

E1.8 (LO 3), AP The following information is available for Randall Inc.

Prepare a balance sheet.

Accounts receivable	$ 2,400	Cash	$ 6,250
Accounts payable	3,700	Supplies	3,760
Interest payable	580	Unearned service revenue	850
Salaries and wages expense	4,500	Service revenue	40,920
Notes payable	31,500	Salaries and wages payable	745
Common stock	50,700	Depreciation expense	670
Inventory	2,840	Equipment (net)	108,200

Instructions

Using the information above, prepare a balance sheet as of December 31, 2022. (*Hint:* Solve for the missing retained earnings amount.)

E1.9 (LO 3), AP Consider each of the following independent situations.

Interpret financial facts.

a. The retained earnings statement of Lee Corporation shows dividends of $68,000, while net income for the year was $75,000.

b. The statement of cash flows for Steele Corporation shows that cash provided by operating activities was $10,000, cash used in investing activities was $110,000, and cash provided by financing activities was $130,000.

Instructions

For each company, provide a brief discussion interpreting these financial facts. For example, you might discuss the company's financial health or its apparent growth philosophy.

Identify financial statement components and prepare income statement.

E1.10 (LO 3), C The following items and amounts were taken from Lonyear Inc.'s 2022 income statement and balance sheet.

_____	Cash	$ 84,700	_____	Accounts receivable	$ 88,419
_____	Retained earnings	123,192	_____	Sales revenue	584,951
_____	Cost of goods sold	438,458	_____	Notes payable	6,499
_____	Salaries and wages expense	115,131	_____	Accounts payable	49,384
_____	Prepaid insurance	7,818	_____	Service revenue	4,806
_____	Inventory	64,618	_____	Interest expense	1,882

Instructions

a. In each, case, identify on the blank line whether the item is an asset (A), liability (L), stockholders' equity (SE), revenue (R), or expense (E) item.

b. Prepare an income statement for Lonyear Inc. for the year ended December 31, 2022.

Identify financial statement components and prepare income statement.

E1.11 (LO 3), AP The following items and amounts were taken from Familia Inc.'s 2022 income statement and balance sheet, the end of its first year of operations.

_____	Interest expense	$ 2,200	_____	Equipment, net	$54,700
_____	Interest payable	700	_____	Depreciation expense	3,200
_____	Notes payable	11,800	_____	Supplies	4,100
_____	Sales revenue	44,300	_____	Common stock	26,800
_____	Cash	2,900	_____	Supplies expense	900
_____	Salaries and wages expense	15,600			

Instructions

a. In each case, identify on the blank line whether the item is an asset (A), liability (L), stockholders' equity (SE), revenue (R), or expense (E) item.

b. Prepare an income statement for Familia Inc. for December 31, 2022.

Calculate missing amounts.

E1.12 (LO 3), AN Here are incomplete financial statements for Donavan, Inc.

Donavan, Inc.
Balance Sheet

Assets		Liabilities and Stockholders' Equity	
Cash	$ 7,000	Liabilities	
Inventory	10,000	Accounts payable	$ 5,000
Buildings (net)	45,000	Stockholders' equity	
Total assets	$62,000	Common stock	(a)
		Retained earnings	(b)
		Total liabilities and stockholders' equity	$62,000

Income Statement

Revenues	$85,000
Cost of goods sold	(c)
Salaries and wages expense	10,000
Net income	$ (d)

Retained Earnings Statement

Beginning retained earnings	$12,000
Add: Net income	(e)
Less: Dividends	5,000
Ending retained earnings	$27,000

Instructions

Calculate the missing amounts.

E1.13 (LO 3), AN Here are incomplete financial statements for Oway Corporation.

Calculate missing amounts.

Oway Corporation.
Balance Sheet

Assets		Liabilities and Stockholders' Equity	
Cash	$ 29,000	Liabilities	
Supplies	(a)	Notes payable	$22,000
Equipment (net)	65,000	Stockholders' equity	
Total assets	$ (b)	Common stock	38,000
		Retained earnings	(c)
		Total liabilities and stockholders' equity	$ (d)

Income Statement

Revenues	$53,000
Depreciation expense	(e)
Salaries and wages expense	10,000
Interest expense	1,000
Net income	$25,000

Retained Earnings Statement

Beginning retained earnings	$ (f)
Add: Net income	(g)
Less: Dividends	6,000
Ending retained earnings	$37,000

Instructions

Calculate the missing amounts.

E1.14 (LO 3), AP Otay Lakes Park is a private camping ground near the Mount Miguel Recreation Area. It has compiled the following financial information as of December 31, 2022.

Compute net income and prepare a balance sheet.

Service revenue (from camping fees)	$132,000	Dividends	$ 9,000
Sales revenue (from general store)	25,000	Notes payable	50,000
Accounts payable	11,000	Expenses during 2022	126,000
Cash	8,500	Supplies	5,500
Equipment	114,000	Common stock	40,000
		Retained earnings (1/1/2022)	5,000

Instructions

a. Determine Otay Lakes Park's net income for 2022.

b. Prepare a retained earnings statement and a balance sheet for Otay Lakes Park as of December 31, 2022.

c. Upon seeing this income statement, Walt Jones, the campground manager, immediately concluded, "The general store is more trouble than it is worth—let's get rid of it." The marketing director isn't so sure this is a good idea. What do you think?

E1.15 (LO 3), AP Kellogg Company is the world's leading producer of ready-to-eat cereal and a leading producer of grain-based convenience foods such as frozen waffles and cereal bars. Suppose the following items were taken from its 2022 income statement and balance sheet. (All dollars are in millions.)

Identify financial statement components and prepare an income statement.

___ Retained earnings	$5,481	___ Bonds payable	$ 4,835
___ Cost of goods sold	7,184	___ Inventory	910
___ Selling and administrative expenses	3,390	___ Sales revenue	12,575
		___ Accounts payable	1,077
___ Cash	334	___ Common stock	105
___ Notes payable	44	___ Income tax expense	498
___ Interest expense	295		

Instructions

a. In each case, identify whether the item is an asset (A), liability (L), stockholders' equity (SE), revenue (R), or expense (E).

b. Prepare an income statement for Kellogg Company for the year ended December 31, 2022.

Prepare a statement of cash flows.

E1.16 (LO 3), AP This information is for Williams Corporation for the year ended December 31, 2022.

Cash received from lenders	$20,000
Cash received from customers	50,000
Cash paid for new equipment	28,000
Cash dividends paid	8,000
Cash paid to suppliers	16,000
Cash balance 1/1/22	12,000

Instructions

a. Prepare the 2022 statement of cash flows for Williams Corporation.

b. Suppose you are one of Williams' creditors. Referring to the statement of cash flows, evaluate Williams' ability to repay its creditors.

Prepare a statement of cash flows.

E1.17 (LO 3), AP Suppose the following data are derived from the 2022 financial statements of **Southwest Airlines**. (All dollars are in millions.) Southwest has a December 31 year-end.

Cash balance, January 1, 2022	$1,390
Cash paid for repayment of debt	122
Cash received from issuance of common stock	144
Cash received from issuance of long-term debt	500
Cash received from customers	9,823
Cash paid for property and equipment	1,529
Cash paid for dividends	14
Cash paid for repurchase of common stock	1,001
Cash paid for goods and services	6,978

Instructions

a. After analyzing the data, prepare a statement of cash flows for Southwest Airlines for the year ended December 31, 2022.

b. Discuss whether the company's net cash provided by operating activities was sufficient to finance its investing activities. If it was not, how did the company finance its investing activities?

Correct an incorrectly prepared balance sheet.

E1.18 (LO 3), AP Wayne Holtz is the bookkeeper for Beeson Company. Wayne has been trying to get the balance sheet of Beeson Company to balance. It finally balanced, but now he's not sure it is correct.

Beeson Company
Balance Sheet
December 31, 2022

Assets		Liabilities and Stockholders' Equity	
Cash	$18,000	Accounts payable	$16,000
Supplies	9,500	Accounts receivable	(12,000)
Equipment	40,000	Common stock	40,000
Dividends	8,000	Retained earnings	31,500
Total assets	$75,500	Total liabilities and stockholders' equity	$75,500

Instructions

Prepare a correct balance sheet.

Classify items as assets, liabilities, and stockholders' equity and prepare accounting equation.

E1.19 (LO 3), AP Suppose the following items were taken from the balance sheet of **Nike, Inc.** (All dollars are in millions.)

1.	Cash	$2,291.1	7.	Inventory	$2,357.0
2.	Accounts receivable	2,883.9	8.	Income taxes payable	86.3
3.	Common stock	2,874.2	9.	Equipment	1,957.7
4.	Notes payable	342.9	10.	Retained earnings	5,818.9
5.	Buildings	3,759.9	11.	Accounts payable	2,815.8
6.	Mortgage payable	1,311.5			

Instructions

Perform each of the following.

a. Classify each of these items as an asset, liability, or stockholders' equity, and determine the total dollar amount for each classification.

b. Determine Nike's accounting equation by calculating the value of total assets, total liabilities, and total stockholders' equity.

c. To what extent does Nike rely on debt versus equity financing?

E1.20 (LO 3), AN The summaries of data from the balance sheet, income statement, and retained earnings statement for two corporations, Walco Corporation and Gunther Enterprises, are presented as follows for 2022.

Use financial statement relationships to determine missing amounts.

	Walco Corporation	Gunther Enterprises
Beginning of year		
Total assets	$110,000	$150,000
Total liabilities	70,000	(d)
Total stockholders' equity	(a)	70,000
End of year		
Total assets	(b)	180,000
Total liabilities	120,000	55,000
Total stockholders' equity	60,000	(e)
Changes during year in retained earnings		
Dividends	(c)	5,000
Total revenues	215,000	(f)
Total expenses	165,000	80,000

Instructions

Determine the missing amounts. Assume all changes in stockholders' equity are due to changes in retained earnings.

E1.21 (LO 3), K The annual report provides financial information in a variety of formats, including the following.

Classify various items in an annual report.

Management discussion and analysis (MD&A)
Financial statements
Notes to the financial statements
Auditor's opinion

Instructions

For each of the following, state in what area of the annual report the item would be presented. If the item would probably not be found in an annual report, state "Not disclosed."

a. The total cumulative amount received from stockholders in exchange for common stock.

b. An independent assessment concerning whether the financial statements present a fair depiction of the company's results and financial position.

c. The interest rate that the company is being charged on all outstanding debts.

d. Total revenue from operating activities.

e. Management's assessment of the company's results.

f. The names and positions of all employees hired in the last year.

Problems: Set A

P1.1A (LO 1), C Writing Presented below are five independent situations.

Determine forms of business organization.

a. Three physics professors at MIT have formed a business to improve the speed of information transfer over the Internet for stock exchange transactions. Each has contributed an equal amount of cash and knowledge to the venture. Although their approach looks promising, they are concerned about the legal liabilities that their business might confront.

b. Bob Colt, a college student looking for summer employment, opened a bait shop in a small shed at a local marina.

c. Alma Ortiz and Jaime Falco each owned separate shoe manufacturing businesses. They have decided to combine their businesses. They expect that within the coming year they will need significant funds to expand their operations.

d. Alice, Donna, and Sam recently graduated with marketing degrees. They have been friends since childhood. They have decided to start a consulting business focused on marketing sporting goods over the Internet.

e. Don Rolls has developed a low-cost GPS device that can be implanted into pets so that they can be easily located when lost. He would like to build a small manufacturing facility to make the devices and then sell them to veterinarians across the country. Don has no savings or personal assets. He wants to maintain control over the business.

Instructions

In each case, explain what form of organization the business is likely to take—sole proprietorship, partnership, or corporation. Give reasons for your choice.

Identify users and uses of financial statements.

P1.2A (LO 3), C Writing Financial decisions often place heavier emphasis on one type of financial statement over the others. Consider each of the following hypothetical situations independently.

a. **The North Face** is considering extending credit to a new customer. The terms of the credit would require the customer to pay within 30 days of receipt of goods.

b. An investor is considering purchasing common stock of **Amazon.com**. The investor plans to hold the investment for at least 5 years.

c. **JPMorgan Chase Bank** is considering extending a loan to a small company. The company would be required to make interest payments at the end of each year for 5 years, and to repay the loan at the end of the fifth year.

d. The president of **Campbell Soup** is trying to determine whether the company is generating enough cash to increase the amount of dividends paid to investors in this and future years, and still have enough cash to buy equipment as it is needed.

Instructions

In each situation, state whether the decision-maker would be most likely to place primary emphasis on information provided by the income statement, balance sheet, or statement of cash flows. In each case provide a brief justification for your choice. Choose only one financial statement in each case.

Prepare an income statement, retained earnings statement, and balance sheet; discuss results.

P1.3A (LO 3), AP On June 1, 2022, Elite Service Co. was started with an initial investment in the company of $22,100 cash. Here are the assets, liabilities, and common stock of the company at June 30, 2022, and the revenues and expenses for the month of June, its first month of operations:

Cash	$ 4,600	Notes payable	$12,000
Accounts receivable	4,000	Accounts payable	500
Service revenue	7,500	Supplies expense	1,000
Supplies	2,400	Maintenance and repairs expense	600
Advertising expense	400	Utilities expense	300
Equipment	26,000	Salaries and wages expense	1,400
Common stock	22,100		

Check figures provide a key number to let you know you are on the right track.

During June, the company issued no additional stock but paid dividends of $1,400.

Instructions

a. Prepare an income statement and a retained earnings statement for the month of June and a balance sheet at June 30, 2022.

b. Briefly discuss whether the company's first month of operations was a success.

c. Discuss the company's decision to distribute a dividend.

a. Net income $ 3,800
    Ret. earnings $ 2,400
    Tot. assets $37,000

Prepare an income statement, retained earnings statement, and balance sheet.

P1.4A (LO 3), AP Reese Inc., a provider of consulting services, was founded on October 1, 2022. At the end of the first month of operations, the company decided to prepare an income statement, retained earnings statement, and balance sheet using the following information.

Accounts payable	$ 3,300	Supplies	$ 2,460
Interest expense	410	Supplies expense	380
Equipment (net)	48,200	Depreciation expense	270
Salaries and wages expense	2,500	Service revenue	20,920
Bonds payable	21,500	Salaries and wages payable	445
Unearned service revenue	4,065	Common stock	9,100
Accounts receivable	1,300	Interest payable	140
Cash	3,950		

Instructions

Using the information, prepare an income statement and retained earnings statement for the month of October 2022 and a balance sheet as of October 31, 2022.

End. retained earnings $17,360

P1.5A (LO 3), AP Presented below is selected financial information for Rojo Corporation for December 31, 2022.

Determine items included in a statement of cash flows, prepare the statement, and comment.

Inventory	$ 25,000	Cash paid to purchase equipment	$ 12,000
Cash paid to suppliers	104,000	Equipment	40,000
Buildings	200,000	Service revenue	100,000
Common stock	50,000	Cash received from customers	132,000
Cash dividends paid	7,000	Cash received from issuing	
Cash at beginning of period	9,000	common stock	22,000

Instructions

a. Prepare the statement of cash flows for Rojo Corporation.

b. Comment on the adequacy of net cash provided by operating activities to fund the company's investing activities and dividend payments.

a. Net cash increase $31,000

P1.6A (LO 3), AN `Writing` Micado Corporation was formed on January 1, 2022. At December 31, 2022, Miko Liu, the president and sole stockholder, decided to prepare a balance sheet, which appeared as follows.

Comment on proper accounting treatment and prepare a corrected balance sheet.

Micado Corporation
Balance Sheet
December 31, 2022

Assets		Liabilities and Stockholders' Equity	
Cash	$20,000	Accounts payable	$30,000
Accounts receivable	50,000	Notes payable	15,000
Inventory	36,000	Boat loan	22,000
Boat	24,000	Stockholders' equity	63,000

Miko willingly admits that she is not an accountant by training. She is concerned that her balance sheet might not be correct. She has provided you with the following additional information.

1. The boat actually belongs to Miko, not to Micado Corporation. However, because she thinks she might take customers out on the boat occasionally, she decided to list it as an asset of the company. To be consistent, she also listed as a liability of the corporation her personal loan that she took out at the bank to buy the boat.

2. The inventory was originally purchased for $25,000, but due to a surge in demand Miko now thinks she could sell it for $36,000. She thought it would be best to record it at $36,000.

3. Included in the accounts receivable balance is $10,000 that Miko loaned to her brother 5 years ago. Miko included this in the receivables of Micado Corporation so she wouldn't forget that her brother owes her money.

Instructions

a. Comment on the proper accounting treatment of the three items above.

b. Provide a corrected balance sheet for Micado Corporation. (*Hint:* To get the balance sheet to balance, adjust stockholders' equity.)

b. Tot. assets $85,000

Continuing Case

*The **Cookie Creations** case starts in Chapter 1 and continues in every chapter. Complete case details and instructions are available in WileyPLUS.*

Cookie Creations

CC1 Natalie Koebel spent much of her childhood learning the art of cookie-making from her grandmother. They spent many happy hours mastering every type of cookie imaginable and later devised new recipes that were both healthy and delicious. Now at the start of her second year in college, Natalie is investigating possibilities for starting her own business as part of the entrepreneurship program in which she is enrolled.

A long-time friend insists that Natalie has to include cookies in her business plan. After a series of brainstorming sessions, Natalie settles on the idea of operating a cookie-making school. She will start on

© leungchopan/ Shutterstock

a part-time basis and offer her services in people's homes. Now that she has started thinking about it, the possibilities seem endless. During the fall, she will concentrate on holiday cookies. She will offer group sessions (which will probably be more entertainment than education) and individual lessons. Natalie also decides to include children in her target market. The first difficult decision is coming up with the perfect name for her business. She settles on "Cookie Creations," and then moves on to more important issues.

Instructions

a. What form of business organization—proprietorship, partnership, or corporation—do you recommend that Natalie use for her business? Discuss the benefits and weaknesses of each form that Natalie might consider.

b. Will Natalie need accounting information? If yes, what information will she need and why? How often will she need this information?

c. Identify specific asset, liability, revenue, and expense accounts that Cookie Creations will likely use to record its business transactions.

d. Should Natalie open a separate bank account for the business? Why or why not?

e. Natalie expects she will have to use her car to drive to people's homes and to pick up supplies, but she also needs to use her car for personal reasons. She recalls from her first-year accounting course something about keeping business and personal assets separate. She wonders what she should do for accounting purposes. What do you recommend?

Expand Your Critical Thinking

Financial Reporting Problem: Apple Inc.

CT1.1 The financial statements of **Apple Inc.** are presented in Appendix A.

Instructions

Refer to Apple's financial statements and answer the following questions.

a. What were Apple's total assets at September 30, 2017? At September 24, 2016?

b. How much cash (and cash equivalents) did Apple have on September 30, 2017?

c. What amount of accounts payable did Apple report on September 30, 2017? On September 24, 2016?

d. What were Apple's net sales in the year ending September 30, 2017? In the year ending September 24, 2016? In the year ending September 26, 2015?

e. What is the amount of the change in Apple's net income from 2016 to 2017?

Comparative Analysis Problem: Columbia Sportswear Company vs. VF Corporation

CT1.2 Columbia Sportswear Company's financial statements are presented in Appendix B. Financial statements of **VF Corporation** are presented in Appendix C.

Instructions

a. Based on the information in these financial statements, determine the following for each company.
   1. Total liabilities at December 31, 2016.
   2. Net property, plant, and equipment at December 31, 2016.
   3. Net cash provided or (used) in investing activities for 2016.
   4. Net income for 2016.

b. What conclusions concerning the two companies can you draw from these data?

Comparative Analysis Problem: Amazon.com, Inc. vs. Wal-Mart Stores, Inc.

CT1.3 Amazon.com, Inc.'s financial statements are presented in Appendix D. Financial statements of **Wal-Mart Stores, Inc.** are presented in Appendix E.

Instructions

a. Based on the information contained in these financial statements, determine the following for each company.
   1. Total assets at December 31, 2016, for Amazon and for Wal-Mart at January 31, 2017.

2. Receivables (net) at December 31, 2016, for Amazon and for Wal-Mart at January 31, 2017.
3. Net sales (product only) for the year ended in 2016 (2017 for Wal-Mart).
4. Net income for year ended in 2016 (2017 for Wal-Mart).

b. What conclusions concerning these two companies can be drawn from these data?

Interpreting Financial Statements

CT1.4 Xerox was not having a particularly pleasant year. The company's stock price had already fallen in the previous year from $60 per share to $30. Just when it seemed things couldn't get worse, Xerox's stock fell to $4 per share. The data below were taken from the statement of cash flows of Xerox. (All dollars are in millions.)

Cash used in operating activities		$ (663)
Cash used in investing activities		(644)
Financing activities		
Dividends paid	$ (587)	
Net cash received from issuing debt	3,498	
Cash provided by financing activities		2,911

Instructions

Analyze the information, and then answer the following questions.

a. If you were a creditor of Xerox, what reaction might you have to the above information?

b. If you were an investor in Xerox, what reaction might you have to the above information?

c. If you were evaluating the company as either a creditor or a stockholder, what other information would you be interested in seeing?

d. Xerox decided to pay a cash dividend. This dividend was approximately equal to the amount paid in the previous year. Discuss the issues that were probably considered in making this decision.

Real-World Focus

CT1.5 You can easily search the Internet to find summary information about companies. This information includes basic descriptions of the company's location, activities, industry, financial health, and financial performance.

Instructions

Go to the **Yahoo! Finance** website, type in a company name, and then use the links (such as Financials) to locate the information necessary to answer the following questions.

a. What is the company's net income? Over what period was this measured?

b. What is the company's total sales? Over what period was this measured?

c. What is the company's industry?

d. What are the names of four companies in this industry?

e. Choose one of the competitors. What is this competitor's name? What is its total sales? What is its net income?

CT1.6 The June 1, 2017, issue of the *Wall Street Journal* includes an article by Michael Rapoport entitled "Coming Soon: What Auditors Really Think About Company Numbers." It provides a discussion about changes to be made to the auditor's report.

Instructions

Read the article and answer the following questions.

a. What does the current auditor's report primarily focus on?

b. What will the new report provide beyond the current report? what are some examples of items that might be discussed?

c. How would the requirements of the new report compare to the requirements of auditor reports in other countries?

d. What criteria must be met in other for an item to be disclosed in the new report?

Decision-Making Across the Organization

CT1.7 Sylvia Ayala recently accepted a job in the production department at **Johnson & Johnson**. Before she starts work, she decides to review the company's annual report to better understand its operations.

The content and organization of corporate annual reports have become fairly standardized. Excluding the public relations part of the report (pictures, products, etc.), the following are the traditional financial portions of the annual report:

- Financial Highlights
- Letter to the Stockholders
- Management's Discussion and Analysis
- Financial Statements
- Notes to the Financial Statements
- Management's Responsibility for Financial Reporting
- Management's Report on Internal Control over Financial Reporting
- Report of Independent Registered Public Accounting Firm
- Selected Financial Data

The official SEC filing of the annual report is called a **Form 10-K**, which often omits the public relations pieces found in most standard annual reports.

Instructions

Use Johnson & Johnson's 10-K report dated January 1, 2017, to answer the following questions.

a. What CPA firm performed the audit of Johnson & Johnson's financial statements?
b. What was the amount of Johnson & Johnson's basic earnings per share in 2016?
c. What are the company's net sales in foreign countries in 2016?
d. What were net sales in 2014?
e. How many shares of common stock have been authorized?
f. How much cash was spent on capital expenditures in 2016?
g. Over what life does the company depreciate its buildings?
h. What was the value of inventory in 2015?

Communication Activity

CT1.8 Marci Ling is the bookkeeper for Samco Company, Inc. Marci has been trying to get the company's balance sheet to balance. She finally got it to balance, but she still isn't sure that it is correct.

Samco Company, Inc.
Balance Sheet
For the Month Ended December 31, 2022

Assets		Liabilities and Stockholders' Equity	
Equipment	$18,000	Common stock	$12,000
Cash	9,000	Accounts receivable	(6,000)
Supplies	1,000	Dividends	(2,000)
Accounts payable	(4,000)	Notes payable	10,000
Total assets	$24,000	Retained earnings	10,000
		Total liabilities and stockholders' equity	$24,000

Instructions

Explain to Marci Ling in a memo (a) the purpose of a balance sheet, and (b) why this balance sheet is incorrect and what she should do to correct it.

Ethics Case

CT1.9 Rules governing the investment practices of individual certified public accountants prohibit them from investing in the stock of a company that their firm audits. The Securities and Exchange Commission (SEC) became concerned that some accountants were violating this rule. In response to an SEC investigation, **PricewaterhouseCoopers** fired 10 people and spent $25 million educating employees about the investment rules and installing an investment tracking system.

Instructions

Answer the following questions.

a. Why do you think rules exist that restrict auditors from investing in companies that are audited by their firms?
b. Some accountants argue that they should be allowed to invest in a company's stock as long as they themselves aren't involved in working on the company's audit or consulting. What do you think of this idea?
c. Today, a very high percentage of publicly traded companies are audited by only four very large public accounting firms. These firms also do a high percentage of the consulting work that is done for publicly traded companies. How does this fact complicate the decision regarding whether CPAs should be allowed to invest in companies audited by their firm?
d. Suppose you were a CPA and you had invested in **IBM** when IBM was not one of your firm's clients. Two years later, after IBM's stock price had fallen considerably, your firm won the IBM audit contract. You will be involved in working with the IBM audit. You know that your firm's rules require that you sell your shares immediately. If you do sell immediately, you will sustain a large loss. Do you think this is fair? What would you do?
e. Why do you think PricewaterhouseCoopers took such extreme steps in response to the SEC investigation?

All About You

CT1.10 Some people are tempted to make their finances look worse to get financial aid. Companies sometimes also manage their financial numbers in order to accomplish certain goals. Earnings management is the planned timing of revenues, expenses, gains, and losses to smooth out bumps in net income. In managing earnings, companies' actions vary from being within the range of ethical activity, to being both unethical and illegal attempts to mislead investors and creditors.

Instructions

Provide responses for each of the following questions.

a. Discuss whether you think each of the following actions (adapted from the **FinAid** website) to increase the chances of receiving financial aid is ethical.
   1. Spend down the student's assets and income first, before spending parents' assets and income.
   2. Accelerate necessary expenses to reduce available cash. For example, if you need a new car, buy it before applying for financial aid.
   3. State that a truly financially dependent child is independent.
   4. Have a parent take an unpaid leave of absence for long enough to get below the "threshold" level of income.
b. What are some reasons why a **company** might want to overstate its earnings?
c. What are some reasons why a **company** might want to understate its earnings?
d. Under what circumstances might an otherwise ethical person decide to illegally overstate or understate earnings?

FASB Codification Activity

CT1.11 The FASB has developed the Financial Accounting Standards Board Accounting Standards Codification (or more simply "the Codification"). The FASB's primary goal in developing the Codification is to provide in one place all the authoritative literature related to a particular topic. To provide easy access to the Codification, the FASB also developed the Financial Accounting Standards Board Codification Research System (CRS). CRS is an online, real-time database that provides easy access to the Codification. The Codification and the related CRS provide a topically organized structure, subdivided into topic, subtopics, sections, and paragraphs, using a numerical index system.

You may find this system useful in your present and future studies, and so we have provided an opportunity to use this online system as part of the *Expand Your Critical Thinking* section.

Instructions

Academic access to the FASB Codification is available through university subscriptions, obtained from the **American Accounting Association**. This subscription covers an unlimited number of students within a single institution. Once this access has been obtained by your school, you should log in and familiarize yourself with the resources that are accessible at the FASB Codification site.

Considering People, Planet, and Profit

CT1.12 Although **Clif Bar & Company** is not a public company, it does share its financial information with its employees as part of its open-book management approach. Further, although it does not publicly share its financial information, it does provide a different form of an annual report to external users. In this report, the company provides information regarding its sustainability efforts.

Instructions

Go to the "Who We Are" page at the Clif Bar website and identify the company's five aspirations.

A Look at IFRS

LEARNING OBJECTIVE 4
Describe the impact of international accounting standards on U.S. financial reporting.

Many people feel that there is a need for one set of international accounting standards. Here is why:

Multinational corporations. Today's companies view the entire world as their market. For example, Coca-Cola, Intel, and McDonald's generate more than 50% of their sales outside the United States. Many foreign companies, such as Toyota, Nestlé, and Sony, find their largest market to be the United States.

Mergers and acquisitions. The mergers between Fiat/Chrysler and Vodafone/Mannesmann suggest that we will see even more such business combinations of companies from different countries in the future.

Information technology. As communication barriers continue to topple through advances in technology, companies and individuals in different countries and markets are becoming more comfortable buying and selling goods and services from one another.

Financial markets. Financial markets are of international significance today. Whether it is currency, equity securities (stocks), bonds, or derivatives, there are active markets throughout the world trading these types of instruments.

Key Points

Following are the key similarities and differences between GAAP and IFRS as related to accounting fundamentals.

Similarities

- The basic techniques for recording business transactions are the same for U.S. and international companies.
- Both international and U.S. accounting standards emphasize transparency in financial reporting. Both sets of standards are primarily driven by meeting the needs of investors and creditors.
- The three most common forms of business organizations, proprietorships, partnerships, and corporations, are also found in countries that use international accounting standards.

Differences

- International standards are referred to as International Financial Reporting Standards (IFRS), developed by the International Accounting Standards Board. Accounting standards in the United States are referred to as generally accepted accounting principles (GAAP) and are developed by the Financial Accounting Standards Board.
- IFRS tends to be simpler in its accounting and disclosure requirements; some people say it is more "principles-based." GAAP is more detailed; some people say it is more "rules-based."
- The internal control standards applicable to Sarbanes-Oxley (SOX) apply only to large public companies listed on U.S. exchanges. There is continuing debate as to whether non-U.S. companies should have to comply with this extra layer of regulation.

IFRS Practice

IFRS Self-Test Questions

1. Which of the following is **not** a reason why a single set of high-quality international accounting standards would be beneficial?
   a. Mergers and acquisition activity.
   b. Financial markets.
   c. Multinational corporations.
   d. GAAP is widely considered to be a superior reporting system.

2. The Sarbanes-Oxley Act determines:
   a. international tax regulations.
   b. internal control standards as enforced by the IASB.
   c. internal control standards of U.S. publicly traded companies.
   d. U.S. tax regulations.

3. IFRS is considered to be more:
   a. principles-based and less rules-based than GAAP.
   b. rules-based and less principles-based than GAAP.
   c. detailed than GAAP.
   d. None of the above.

IFRS Exercises

IFRS1.1 Who are the two key international players in the development of international accounting standards? Explain their role.

IFRS1.2 What is the benefit of a single set of high-quality accounting standards?

International Financial Reporting Problem: Louis Vuitton

IFRS1.3 The financial statements of **Louis Vuitton** are presented in Appendix F. The complete annual report, including the notes to its financial statements, is available at the company's website.

Instructions

Answer the following questions from the company's 2016 annual report.
   a. What accounting firm performed the audit of Louis Vuitton's financial statements?
   b. What is the address of the company's corporate headquarters?
   c. What is the company's reporting currency?

Answers to IFRS Self-Test Questions

1. d   2. c   3. a

CHAPTER 2

A Further Look at Financial Statements

Chapter Preview

If you are thinking of purchasing **Best Buy** stock, or any stock, how can you decide what the shares are worth? If you manage **Columbia Sportswear**'s credit department, how should you determine whether to extend credit to a new customer? If you are a financial executive at **Alphabet Inc.** (**Google**), how do you decide whether your company is generating adequate cash to expand operations without borrowing? Your decision in each of these situations will be influenced by a variety of considerations. One of them should be your careful analysis of a company's financial statements. The reason: Financial statements offer relevant, representationally faithful information that will help you in your decision-making.

In this chapter, we take a closer look at the balance sheet and introduce some useful ways for evaluating the information provided by the financial statements. We also examine the financial reporting concepts underlying the financial statements. We begin by introducing the classified balance sheet.

Feature Story

Just Fooling Around?

Two early pioneers in providing investment information online to the masses were Tom and David Gardner, brothers who created an online investor website called **The Motley Fool**. The name comes from Shakespeare's *As You Like It*. The fool in Shakespeare's play was the only one who could speak unpleasant truths to kings and queens without being killed. Tom and David view themselves as 21st-century "fools," revealing the "truths" of the stock market to the small investor, who they feel has been taken advantage of by Wall Street insiders. The Motley Fool's online bulletin board enables investors to exchange information and insights about companies.

Critics of these bulletin boards contend that they are simply high-tech rumor mills that cause investors to bid up stock prices to unreasonable levels. For example, the stock of **PairGain Technologies** jumped 32% in a single day as a result of a bogus takeover rumor on an investment bulletin board. Some observers are concerned that small investors—ironically, the very people the Gardner brothers are trying to help—will be hurt the most by misinformation and intentional scams.

To show how these bulletin boards work, suppose that you had $10,000 to invest. You were considering **Best Buy Company**, the largest seller of electronics equipment in the United States. You scanned the Internet investment bulletin boards and found messages posted by two different investors. Here are excerpts from actual postings:

TMPVenus: "Where are the prospects for positive movement for this company? Poor margins, poor management, astronomical P/E!"

broachman: "I believe that this is a LONG TERM winner, and presently at a good price."

One says sell, and one says buy. Whom should you believe? If at that time you had taken "broachman's" advice and purchased the stock, the $10,000 you invested would have been worth over $300,000 five years later. Best Buy was one of America's best-performing stocks during that five-year period of time.

Rather than getting swept away by rumors, investors must sort out the good information from the bad. One thing is certain—as information services such as The Motley Fool increase in number, gathering information will become even easier. Evaluating it will be the harder task.

Chapter Outline

LEARNING OBJECTIVES

LO 1 Identify the sections of a classified balance sheet.	• Current assets • Long-term investments • Property, plant, and equipment • Intangible assets • Current liabilities • Long-term liabilities • Stockholders' equity	**DO IT! 1a** Assets Section of Classified Balance Sheet **DO IT! 1b** Balance Sheet Classifications
LO 2 Use ratios to evaluate a company's profitability, liquidity, and solvency.	• Ratio analysis • Using the income statement • Using a classified balance sheet • Using the statement of cash flows	**DO IT! 2** Ratio Analysis
LO 3 Discuss financial reporting concepts.	• The standard-setting environment • Qualities of useful information • Assumptions in financial reporting • Principles in financial reporting • Cost constraint	**DO IT! 3** Financial Accounting Concepts and Principles

Go to the Review and Practice section at the end of the chapter for a targeted summary and practice applications with solutions.
Visit WileyPLUS for additional tutorials and practice opportunities.

The Classified Balance Sheet

> **LEARNING OBJECTIVE 1**
> Identify the sections of a classified balance sheet.

You learned that a balance sheet presents a snapshot of a company's financial position at a point in time. It lists individual asset, liability, and stockholders' equity items. However, to improve users' understanding of a company's financial position, companies often use a **classified** balance sheet instead. A **classified balance sheet** groups together similar assets and similar liabilities, using a number of standard classifications and sections. This is useful because items within a group have similar economic characteristics. A classified balance sheet generally contains the standard classifications listed in **Illustration 2.1**.

Assets	Liabilities and Stockholders' Equity
Current assets	Current liabilities
Long-term investments	Long-term liabilities
Property, plant, and equipment	Stockholders' equity
Intangible assets	

ILLUSTRATION 2.1
Standard balance sheet classifications

These groupings help financial statement readers determine such things as (1) whether the company has enough assets to pay its debts as they come due, and (2) the claims of short- and long-term creditors on the company's total assets. Many of these groupings can be seen in the balance sheet of Franklin Corporation shown in **Illustration 2.2** (see **Helpful Hint**). In the sections that follow, we explain each of these groupings.

Current Assets

Current assets are assets that a company expects to convert to cash or use up within one year or its operating cycle, whichever is longer. In Illustration 2.2, Franklin Corporation had current assets of $22,100. For most businesses, the cutoff for classification as current assets is one year from the balance sheet date. For example, accounts receivable are current assets because the company will collect them and convert them to cash within one year. Supplies is a current asset because the company expects to use the supplies in operations within one year.

Some companies use a period longer than one year to classify assets and liabilities as current because they have an operating cycle longer than one year. The **operating cycle** of a company is the average time required to go from cash to cash in producing revenue—to purchase inventory, sell it on account, and then collect cash from customers. For most businesses, this cycle takes less than a year, so they use a one-year cutoff. But for some businesses, such as vineyards or airplane manufacturers, this period may be longer than a year. **Except where noted, we will assume that companies use one year to determine whether an asset or liability is current or long-term.**

Companies list current assets in order of liquidity, that is, the order in which they expect to convert them into cash (follow this rule when doing your homework). Common types of current assets, listed in order of liquidity, are (1) cash, (2) investments (such as short-term U.S. government securities), (3) receivables (accounts receivable, notes receivable, and interest receivable), (4) inventories, and (5) prepaid expenses (insurance and supplies).

ILLUSTRATION 2.2
Classified balance sheet

Franklin Corporation
Balance Sheet
October 31, 2022

Assets

Current assets			
Cash		$ 6,600	
Debt investments		2,000	
Accounts receivable		7,000	
Notes receivable		1,000	
Inventory		3,000	
Supplies		2,100	
Prepaid insurance		400	
Total current assets			$22,100
Long-term investments			
Stock investments		5,200	
Investment in real estate		2,000	7,200
Property, plant, and equipment			
Land		10,000	
Equipment	$24,000		
Less: Accumulated depreciation—equipment	5,000	19,000	29,000
Intangible assets			
Patents			3,100
Total assets			$61,400

Liabilities and Stockholders' Equity

Current liabilities		
Notes payable	$11,000	
Accounts payable	2,100	
Unearned sales revenue	900	
Salaries and wages payable	1,600	
Interest payable	450	
Total current liabilities		$16,050
Long-term liabilities		
Mortgage payable	10,000	
Notes payable	1,300	
Total long-term liabilities		11,300
Total liabilities		27,350
Stockholders' equity		
Common stock	14,000	
Retained earnings	20,050	
Total stockholders' equity		34,050
Total liabilities and stockholders' equity		$61,400

HELPFUL HINT
Recall that the accounting equation is Assets = Liabilities + Stockholders' Equity.

Illustration 2.3 presents the current assets of **Southwest Airlines Co.** in a recent year.

ILLUSTRATION 2.3
Current assets section

Southwest Airlines Co.
Balance Sheet (partial)
(in millions)

Current assets	
Cash and cash equivalents	$1,680
Short-term investments	1,625
Accounts receivable	546
Inventories	337
Prepaid expenses and other current assets	310
Total current assets	$4,498

As explained later in the chapter, a company's current assets are important in assessing its short-term debt-paying ability.

Long-Term Investments

Long-term investments are generally (1) investments in stocks and bonds of other corporations that are held for more than one year, (2) long-term assets such as land or buildings that a company is not currently using in its operating activities, and (3) long-term notes receivable (see **Alternative Terminology**). In Illustration 2.2, Franklin Corporation reported total long-term investments of $7,200 on its balance sheet.

Alphabet Inc. reported long-term investments on its balance sheet in a recent year as shown in **Illustration 2.4**.

ALTERNATIVE TERMINOLOGY

Long-term investments are often referred to simply as *investments*.

ILLUSTRATION 2.4

Long-term investments section

Alphabet Inc. Balance Sheet (partial) (in millions)	
Long-term investments	
Non-marketable investments	$5,183

Property, Plant, and Equipment

Property, plant, and equipment are assets with relatively long useful lives that are currently used in operating the business (see **Alternative Terminology**). This category includes land, buildings, equipment, delivery vehicles, and furniture. In Illustration 2.2, Franklin Corporation reported property, plant, and equipment of $29,000.

Depreciation is the allocation of the cost of an asset to a number of years. Companies do this by systematically assigning a portion of an asset's cost as an expense each year (rather than expensing the full purchase price in the year of purchase). The assets that the company depreciates are reported on the balance sheet at cost less accumulated depreciation. The **accumulated depreciation** account shows the total amount of depreciation that the company has expensed thus far in the asset's life. In Illustration 2.2, Franklin Corporation reported accumulated depreciation of $5,000.

Illustration 2.5 presents the property, plant, and equipment of **Cooper Tire & Rubber Company** in a recent year. *In your homework, present each accumulated depreciation account immediately below the related plant asset, as shown in Illustration 2.2 for Franklin Corporation.*

ALTERNATIVE TERMINOLOGY

Property, plant, and equipment is sometimes called *fixed assets* or *plant assets*.

ILLUSTRATION 2.5

Property, plant, and equipment section

Cooper Tire & Rubber Company Balance Sheet (partial) (in thousands)		
Property, plant, and equipment		
Land and land improvements	$ 47,767	
Buildings	282,960	
Machinery and equipment	1,742,449	
Molds, cores, and rings	224,662	$2,297,838
Less: Accumulated depreciation		1,433,611
		$ 864,227

Intangible Assets

Many companies have assets that do not have physical substance and yet often are very valuable. We call these assets **intangible assets** (see **Helpful Hint**). One common intangible

HELPFUL HINT

Sometimes intangible assets are reported under a broader heading called "*Other assets.*"

is goodwill. Others include patents, copyrights, and trademarks or trade names that give the company **exclusive right** of use for a specified period of time. In Illustration 2.2, Franklin Corporation reported intangible assets of $3,100.

Illustration 2.6 shows the intangible assets adapted from the balance sheet of media and theme park giant **The Walt Disney Company** in a recent year.

ILLUSTRATION 2.6
Intangible assets section

The Walt Disney Company
Balance Sheet (partial)
(in millions)

Intangible assets and goodwill	
Character/franchise intangibles and copyrights	$ 5,829
Other amortizable intangible assets	893
Accumulated amortization	(1,635)
Net amortizable intangible assets	5,087
FCC licenses	624
Trademarks	1,218
Other indefinite lived intangible assets	20
	6,949
Goodwill	27,810
	$34,759

ACTION PLAN

- Present current assets first. Current assets are cash and other resources that the company expects to convert to cash or use up within one year.
- Present current assets in the order in which the company expects to convert them into cash.
- Subtract accumulated depreciation—equipment from equipment to determine net equipment.

DO IT! 1a | Assets Section of Classified Balance Sheet

Baxter Hoffman recently received the following information related to Hoffman Corporation's December 31, 2022, balance sheet.

Prepaid insurance	$ 2,300	Inventory	$3,400
Cash	800	Accumulated depreciation—	
Equipment	10,700	equipment	2,700
Debt investments (long-term)	2,100	Accounts receivable	1,100
		Trademarks	4,700

Prepare the assets section of Hoffman Corporation's classified balance sheet.

Solution

Hoffman Corporation
Balance Sheet (partial)
December 31, 2022

Assets

Current assets		
Cash		$ 800
Accounts receivable		1,100
Inventory		3,400
Prepaid insurance		2,300
Total current assets		$ 7,600
Long-term investments		
Debt investments		2,100
Property, plant, and equipment		
Equipment	10,700	
Less: Accumulated depreciation—equipment	2,700	8,000
Intangible assets		
Trademarks		4,700
Total assets		$22,400

Related exercise material: **BE2.3, DO IT! 2.1a, E2.3, E2.4, and E2.6.**

Current Liabilities

In the liabilities and stockholders' equity section of the balance sheet, the first grouping is current liabilities. **Current liabilities** are obligations that the company is to pay within the next year or operating cycle, whichever is longer. Common examples are accounts payable, salaries and wages payable, notes payable, interest payable, and income taxes payable. Also included as current liabilities are current maturities of long-term obligations—payments to be made within the next year on long-term obligations. In Illustration 2.2, Franklin Corporation reported five different types of current liabilities, for a total of $16,050.

Illustration 2.7 shows the current liabilities section adapted from the balance sheet of **Alphabet Inc.** in a recent year.

ILLUSTRATION 2.7
Current liabilities section

Alphabet Inc.
Balance Sheet (partial)
(in millions)

Current liabilities	
Accounts payable	$ 1,931
Short-term debt	3,225
Accrued compensation and benefits	3,539
Accrued expenses and other current liabilities	10,313
Income taxes payable, net	302
Total current liabilities	$19,310

Long-Term Liabilities

Long-term liabilities (**long-term debt**) are obligations that a company expects to pay **after** one year. Liabilities in this category include bonds payable, mortgages payable, long-term notes payable, lease liabilities, and pension liabilities. Many companies report long-term debt maturing after one year as a single amount in the balance sheet and show the details of the debt in notes that accompany the financial statements. Others list the various types of long-term liabilities. In Illustration 2.2, Franklin Corporation reported long-term liabilities of $11,300.

Illustration 2.8 shows the long-term liabilities that **Nike, Inc.** reported in its balance sheet in a recent year.

ILLUSTRATION 2.8
Long-term liabilities section

Nike, Inc.
Balance Sheet (partial)
(in millions)

Long-term liabilities	
Bonds payable	$5,474
Deferred income taxes and other	1,907
Total long-term liabilities	$7,381

Stockholders' Equity

Stockholders' equity consists of two parts: common stock and retained earnings. Companies record as **common stock** the investments of assets into the business by the stockholders (see **Alternative Terminology**). They record as **retained earnings** the income retained for use in the business. These two parts, combined, make up **stockholders' equity** on the balance sheet. In Illustration 2.2, Franklin Corporation reported common stock of $14,000 and retained earnings of $20,050.

ALTERNATIVE TERMINOLOGY

Common stock is sometimes called *capital stock*.

ACTION PLAN
- Analyze whether each financial statement item is an asset, liability, or stockholders' equity item.
- Determine if asset and liability items are current or long-term.

DO IT! 1b | Balance Sheet Classifications

The following financial statement items were taken from the financial statements of Callahan Corp.

_____ Salaries and wages payable
_____ Service revenue
_____ Interest payable
_____ Goodwill
_____ Debt investments (short-term)
_____ Mortgage payable (due in 3 years)
_____ Investment in real estate
_____ Equipment
_____ Accumulated depreciation—equipment
_____ Depreciation expense
_____ Retained earnings
_____ Unearned service revenue

Match each of the items to its proper balance sheet classification, shown below. If the item would not appear on a balance sheet, use "NA."

Current assets (CA)
Long-term investments (LTI)
Property, plant, and equipment (PPE)
Intangible assets (IA)
Current liabilities (CL)
Long-term liabilities (LTL)
Stockholders' equity (SE)

Solution

CL	Salaries and wages payable	LTI	Investment in real estate
NA	Service revenue	PPE	Equipment
CL	Interest payable	PPE	Accumulated depreciation—equipment
IA	Goodwill	NA	Depreciation expense
CA	Debt investments (short-term)	SE	Retained earnings
LTL	Mortgage payable (due in 3 years)	CL	Unearned service revenue

Related exercise material: **BE2.1, BE2.2, DO IT! 2.1b, E2.1, E2.2, E2.3, E2.5,** and **E2.7.**

Analyzing the Financial Statements Using Ratios

LEARNING OBJECTIVE 2
Use ratios to evaluate a company's profitability, liquidity, and solvency.

We previously introduced the four financial statements. We discussed how these statements provide information about a company's performance and financial position. Here, we extend this discussion by showing you specific tools that you can use to analyze financial statements in order to make a more meaningful evaluation of a company.

Ratio Analysis

Ratio analysis expresses the relationship among selected items of financial statement data. A **ratio** expresses the mathematical relationship between one quantity and another. For analysis of the primary financial statements, we classify ratios as shown in **Illustration 2.9**.

A single ratio by itself is not very meaningful. Accordingly, in this and the following chapters, we will use various comparisons to shed light on company performance:

1. **Intracompany comparisons** covering two years for the same company.
2. **Industry-average comparisons** based on average ratios for particular industries.
3. **Intercompany comparisons** based on comparisons with a competitor in the same industry.

ILLUSTRATION 2.9
Financial ratio classifications

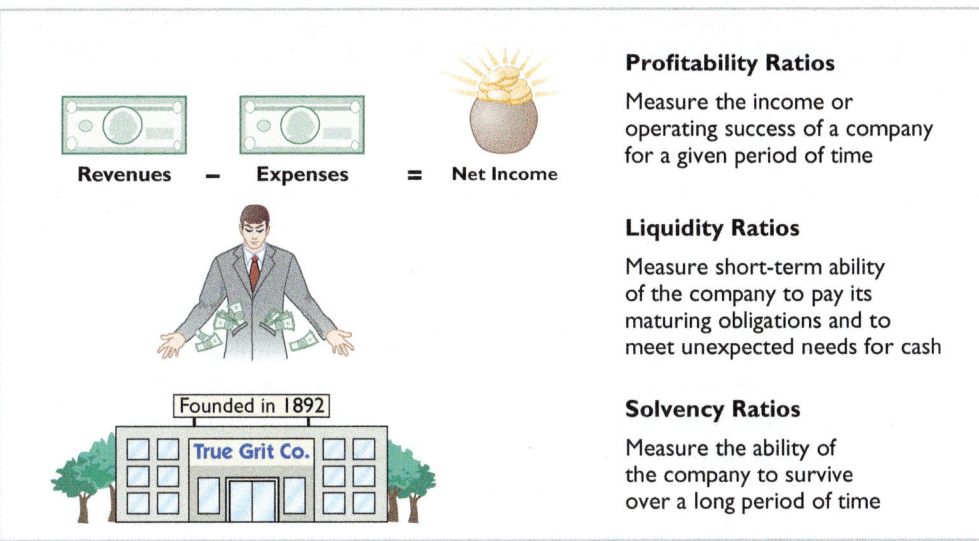

Profitability Ratios
Measure the income or operating success of a company for a given period of time

Liquidity Ratios
Measure short-term ability of the company to pay its maturing obligations and to meet unexpected needs for cash

Solvency Ratios
Measure the ability of the company to survive over a long period of time

Next, we use some ratios and comparisons to analyze the financial statements of **Best Buy**.

Using the Income Statement

Best Buy generates profits for its stockholders by selling electronics. The income statement reveals how successful the company is at generating a profit from its sales. The income statement reports the amount earned during the period (revenues) and the costs incurred during the period (expenses). **Illustration 2.10** shows a simplified income statement for Best Buy.

ILLUSTRATION 2.10
Best Buy's income statement

Best Buy Co., Inc.
Income Statements
For the Year Ended January 28, 2017,
and the Year Ended January 30, 2016 (in millions)

	2017	2016
Revenues		
Net sales and other revenue	$39,403	$39,528
Expenses		
Cost of goods sold	29,963	30,337
Selling, general, and administrative expenses and other	7,603	7,791
Income tax expense	609	503
Total expenses	38,175	38,631
Net income/(loss)	$ 1,228	$ 897

From this income statement, we can see that Best Buy's sales and net income increased during the period. Net income increased from $897 million to $1,228 million. Note that even though the company's revenues declined, net income increased due to a significant decrease in expenses.

A competitor of Best Buy is **hhgregg**. hhgregg is much smaller than Best Buy. At one time, hhgregg operated 228 stores in 20 states. It reported a net loss of $54,879,000 for the year ended March 31, 2016. In early 2017, it filed for bankruptcy. However, just because a company has a net loss does not mean it is about to go bankrupt. We will see if other aspects of its financial position suggested it was in trouble.

To evaluate the profitability of Best Buy, we will use ratio analysis. **Profitability ratios**, such as earnings per share, measure the operating success of a company for a given period of time.

Earnings per Share

Earnings per share (EPS) measures the net income earned on each share of common stock (see **Decision Tools**). Stockholders usually think in terms of the number of shares they own or plan to buy or sell, so stating net income earned as a per share amount provides a useful perspective for determining the investment return. Advanced accounting courses present more refined techniques for calculating earnings per share.

> **Decision Tools**
> Earnings per share helps users compare a company's performance with that of previous years.

For now, a basic approach for calculating earnings per share is to divide earnings available to common stockholders by weighted-average common shares outstanding during the year. What is "earnings available to common stockholders"? It is an earnings amount calculated as net income less dividends paid on another type of stock, called preferred stock (Net income − Preferred dividends).

By comparing earnings per share of **a single company over time**, we can evaluate its relative earnings performance from the perspective of a stockholder—that is, on a per share basis. It is very important to note that comparisons of earnings per share across companies are **not meaningful** because of the wide variations in the numbers of shares of outstanding stock among companies.

Illustration 2.11 shows the earnings per share calculation for **Best Buy** in 2017 and 2016, based on the information presented below. To simplify our calculations, we assumed that any change in the number of shares of common stock for Best Buy occurred in the middle of the year.

(in millions)	2017	2016
Net income	$1,228	$897
Preferred dividends	–0–	–0–
Shares of common stock outstanding at beginning of year	324	352
Shares of common stock outstanding at end of year	311	324

ILLUSTRATION 2.11
Best Buy's earnings per share

$$\text{Earnings per Share} = \frac{\text{Net Income} - \text{Preferred Dividends}}{\text{Weighted-Average Common Shares Outstanding}}$$

($ and shares in millions)	2017	2016
Earnings per share	$\frac{\$1{,}228 - \$0}{(324 + 311)/2} = \$3.87$	$\frac{\$897 - \$0}{(352 + 324)/2} = \$2.65$

Best Buy's earnings per share increased from $2.65 to $3.87. This increase occurred because its net income increased and its outstanding shares decreased.

Using a Classified Balance Sheet

You can learn a lot about a company's financial health by also evaluating the relationship between its various assets and liabilities. **Illustration 2.12** provides a simplified balance sheet for **Best Buy**.

Liquidity

Suppose you are a banker at **Citigroup** considering lending money to Best Buy, or you are a sales manager at **Apple** interested in selling computers and cell phones to Best Buy on credit. You would be concerned about Best Buy's **liquidity**—its ability to pay obligations expected to become due within the next year or operating cycle. You would look closely at the relationship of its current assets to current liabilities.

ILLUSTRATION 2.12
Best Buy's balance sheet

Best Buy Co., Inc.
Balance Sheets
(in millions)

Assets	January 28, 2017	January 30, 2016
Current assets		
Cash and cash equivalents	$ 2,240	$ 1,976
Short-term investments	1,681	1,305
Receivables	1,347	1,162
Merchandise inventories	4,864	5,051
Other current assets	384	392
Total current assets	10,516	9,886
Property and equipment	8,143	8,107
Less: Accumulated depreciation	5,850	5,761
Net property and equipment	2,293	2,346
Other assets	1,047	1,287
Total assets	$13,856	$13,519
Liabilities and Stockholders' Equity		
Current liabilities		
Accounts payable	$ 4,984	$ 4,450
Unredeemed gift card liabilities	427	409
Accrued liabilities	865	802
Accrued income taxes	26	128
Accrued compensation payable	358	384
Other current liabilities	462	752
Total current liabilities	7,122	6,925
Long-term liabilities		
Long-term debt	1,321	1,339
Other long-term liabilities	704	877
Total long-term liabilities	2,025	2,216
Total liabilities	9,147	9,141
Stockholders' equity		
Common stock	31	32
Retained earnings and other	4,678	4,346
Total stockholders' equity	4,709	4,378
Total liabilities and stockholders' equity	$13,856	$13,519

Working Capital One measure of liquidity is **working capital**, which is the difference between the amounts of current assets and current liabilities (see **Illustration 2.13**).

ILLUSTRATION 2.13
Working capital

Working Capital = Current Assets − Current Liabilities

When current assets exceed current liabilities, working capital is positive. When this occurs, there is a greater likelihood that the company will pay its liabilities. When working capital is negative, a company might not be able to pay short-term creditors, and the company might ultimately be forced into bankruptcy. Best Buy had working capital in 2017 of $3,394 million ($10,516 million − $7,122 million).

Current Ratio **Liquidity ratios** measure the short-term ability of the company to pay its maturing obligations and to meet unexpected needs for cash. One liquidity ratio is the **current ratio**, computed as current assets divided by current liabilities (see **Decision Tools**).

> **Decision Tools**
> The current ratio helps users determine if a company can meet its near-term obligations.

The current ratio is a more dependable indicator of liquidity than working capital. Two companies with the same amount of working capital may have significantly different current ratios. **Illustration 2.14** shows the 2017 and 2016 current ratios for **Best Buy** and for **hhgregg**.

ILLUSTRATION 2.14
Current ratio

$$\text{Current Ratio} = \frac{\text{Current Assets}}{\text{Current Liabilities}}$$

Best Buy ($ in millions)		hhgregg
2017	2016	2017
$\frac{\$10,516}{\$7,122} = 1.48:1$	1.43:1	1.51:1

ETHICS NOTE

A company that has more current assets than current liabilities can increase the ratio of current assets to current liabilities by using cash to pay off some current liabilities. This gives the appearance of being more liquid. Do you think this move is ethical?

What does the ratio actually mean? Best Buy's 2017 current ratio of 1.48:1 means that for every dollar of current liabilities, Best Buy has $1.48 of current assets. Best Buy's current ratio increased in 2017. Best Buy's current ratio is very similar to that of hhgregg's.

One potential weakness of the current ratio is that it does not take into account the **composition** of the current assets. For example, a satisfactory current ratio does not disclose whether a portion of the current assets is tied up in slow-moving inventory. The composition of the current assets matters because a dollar of cash is more readily available to pay the bills than is a dollar of inventory. For example, suppose a company's cash balance declined while its merchandise inventory increased substantially. If inventory increased because the company is having difficulty selling its products, then the current ratio might not fully reflect the reduction in the company's liquidity (see **Ethics Note**).

Accounting Across the Organization   REL Consultancy Group

Jorge Salcedo/ iStockphoto

Can a Company Be Too Liquid?

There actually is a point where a company can be too liquid—that is, it can have too much working capital. While it is important to be liquid enough to be able to pay short-term bills as they come due, a company does not want to tie up its cash in extra inventory or receivables that are not earning the company money.

By one estimate from the **REL Consultancy Group**, the thousand largest U.S. companies had cumulative excess working capital of $1.017 trillion in a recent year. This was an 18% increase, which REL said represented a "deterioration in the management of operations." Given that managers throughout a company are interested in improving profitability, it is clear that they should have an eye toward managing working capital. They need to aim for a "Goldilocks solution"—not too much, not too little, but just right.

More recently, a different study found that companies reduced the number of days it took to convert working capital into cash received from customers from 37.1 days down to 35.7 days.

Sources: Maxwell Murphy, "The Big Number," *Wall Street Journal* (November 9, 2011); and Tatyana Shumsky and Nina Trentmann, "Finance Chiefs Look to Free Up Working Capital Ahead of Rate Increases," *Wall Street Journal* (August 21, 2017).

What can various company managers do to ensure that working capital is managed efficiently to maximize net income? (Go to WileyPLUS for this answer and additional questions.)

Solvency

Now suppose that instead of being a short-term creditor, you are interested in either buying Best Buy's stock or extending the company a long-term loan. Long-term creditors and stockholders are interested in a company's **solvency**—its ability to pay interest as it comes due and to repay the balance of a debt due at its maturity. **Solvency ratios** measure the ability of the company to survive over a long period of time.

Debt to Assets Ratio The **debt to assets ratio** is one measure of solvency. It is calculated by dividing total liabilities (both current and long-term) by total assets. It measures the percentage of total financing provided by creditors rather than stockholders (see **Helpful Hint**). Debt financing is more risky than equity financing because debt must be repaid at specific points in time, whether the company is performing well or not. Thus, the higher the percentage of debt financing, the riskier the company.

The higher the percentage of total liabilities (debt) to total assets, the greater the risk that the company may be unable to pay its debts as they come due. **Illustration 2.15** shows the debt to assets ratios for **Best Buy** and **hhgregg**.

HELPFUL HINT
Some users evaluate solvency using a ratio of liabilities divided by stockholders' equity. The higher this "debt to equity" ratio, the lower is a company's solvency.

ILLUSTRATION 2.15
Debt to assets ratio

$$\text{Debt to Assets Ratio} = \frac{\text{Total Liabilities}}{\text{Total Assets}}$$

Best Buy ($ in millions)		hhgregg
2017	2016	2017
$\frac{\$9,147}{\$13,856} = 66\%$	68%	69%

The 2017 ratio of 66% means that every dollar of assets was financed by 66 cents of debt. Best Buy's ratio is similar to hhgregg's ratio of 69%. The higher the ratio, the more reliant the company is on debt financing. This means that a company with a high debt to assets ratio has a lower equity "buffer" available to creditors if the company becomes insolvent. Thus, from the creditors' point of view, a high ratio of debt to assets is undesirable (see **Decision Tools**).

The adequacy of this ratio is often judged in light of the company's earnings. Note that while Best Buy and hhgregg relied on debt financing in a roughly equal fashion, hhgregg went bankrupt. This is largely explained by the fact that hhgregg's income was insufficient to pay its debt obligations as they came due. Generally, companies with relatively stable earnings, such as public utilities, can support higher debt to assets ratios than can cyclical companies with widely fluctuating earnings, such as many high-tech companies. In later chapters, you will learn additional ways to evaluate solvency.

Decision Tools
The debt to assets ratio helps users determine if a company can meet its long-term obligations.

Investor Insight When Debt Is Good

© David Crockett/iStockphoto

Debt financing differs greatly across industries and companies. Here are some debt to assets ratios for selected companies in a recent year:

	Debt to Assets Ratio
Google	23%
Nike	41%
Microsoft	48%
ExxonMobil	48%
General Motors	74%

Discuss the difference in the debt to assets ratio of Microsoft and General Motors. (Go to WileyPLUS for this answer and additional questions.)

Using the Statement of Cash Flows

In the statement of cash flows, net cash provided by operating activities is intended to indicate the cash-generating capability of the company. Analysts have noted, however, that **net cash provided by operating activities fails to take into account that a company must**

> **Decision Tools**
>
> Free cash flow helps users determine the amount of cash a company generated to expand operations, pay off debts, or increase dividends.

invest in new property, plant, and equipment (capital expenditures) just to maintain its current level of operations. Companies also must at least **maintain dividends at current levels** to satisfy investors. A measurement to provide additional insight regarding a company's cash-generating ability is free cash flow. **Free cash flow** describes the net cash provided by operating activities after adjusting for capital expenditures and dividends paid (see **Decision Tools**).

Consider the following example. Suppose that MPC produced and sold 10,000 personal computers this year. It reported $100,000 net cash provided by operating activities. In order to maintain production at 10,000 computers, MPC invested $15,000 in equipment. It chose to pay $5,000 in dividends. Its free cash flow was $80,000 ($100,000 − $15,000 − $5,000). The company could use this $80,000 to purchase new assets to expand the business, pay off debts, or increase its dividend distribution. In practice, analysts often calculate free cash flow with the formula shown in **Illustration 2.16**. (Alternative definitions also exist.)

ILLUSTRATION 2.16
Free cash flow

| Free Cash Flow | = | Net Cash Provided by Operating Activities | − | Capital Expenditures | − | Cash Dividends |

We can calculate Best Buy's 2017 free cash flow as shown in **Illustration 2.17** (dollars in millions).

ILLUSTRATION 2.17
Best Buy's free cash flow

Net cash provided by operating activities	$2,545
Less: Expenditures on property, plant, and equipment	582
Dividends paid	505
Free cash flow	$1,458

Best Buy generated free cash flow of $1,458 million, which is available for the acquisition of new assets, the retirement of stock or debt, or the payment of additional dividends. Long-term creditors consider a high free cash flow amount an indication of solvency. hhgregg's free cash flow for 2016 is negative $34.7 million. Given that hhgregg is considerably smaller than Best Buy, we would expect its free cash flow to be much lower. But clearly the fact that hhgregg had negative free cash flow contributed to its need to file for bankruptcy.

ACTION PLAN
- Use the formula for earnings per share (EPS): (Net income − Preferred dividends) ÷ Weighted-average common shares outstanding.
- Use the formula for the current ratio: Current assets ÷ Current liabilities.
- Use the formula for the debt to assets ratio: Total liabilities ÷ Total assets.

DO IT! 2 | Ratio Analysis

The following information is available for Ozone Inc.

	2022	2021
Current assets	$ 88,000	$ 60,800
Total assets	400,000	341,000
Current liabilities	40,000	38,000
Total liabilities	120,000	150,000
Net income	100,000	50,000
Net cash provided by operating activities	110,000	70,000
Preferred dividends	10,000	10,000
Common dividends	5,000	2,500
Expenditures on property, plant, and equipment	45,000	20,000
Common shares outstanding at beginning of year	60,000	40,000
Common shares outstanding at end of year	120,000	60,000

a. Compute earnings per share for 2022 and 2021 for Ozone, and comment on the change. Ozone's primary competitor, Frost Corporation, had earnings per share of $2 in 2022. Comment on the difference in the ratios of the two companies.

b. Compute the current ratio and debt to assets ratio for each year, and comment on the changes.

c. Compute free cash flow for each year, and comment on the changes.

ACTION PLAN
- Use the formula for free cash flow: Net cash provided by operating activities − Capital expenditures − Cash dividends.

Solution

a. Earnings per share

2022
$$\frac{\$100{,}000 - \$10{,}000}{(120{,}000 + 60{,}000)/2} = \$1.00$$

2021
$$\frac{\$50{,}000 - \$10{,}000}{(60{,}000 + 40{,}000)/2} = \$0.80$$

Ozone's profitability, as measured by the amount of income available to each share of common stock, increased by 25% [($1.00 − $0.80) ÷ $0.80] during 2022. Earnings per share should not be compared across companies because the number of shares issued by companies varies widely. Thus, we cannot conclude that Frost Corporation is more profitable than Ozone based on its higher EPS.

b.

	2022	2021
Current ratio	$\frac{\$88{,}000}{\$40{,}000} = 2.20{:}1$	$\frac{\$60{,}800}{\$38{,}000} = 1.60{:}1$
Debt to assets ratio	$\frac{\$120{,}000}{\$400{,}000} = 30\%$	$\frac{\$150{,}000}{\$341{,}000} = 44\%$

The company's liquidity, as measured by the current ratio, improved from 1.60:1 to 2.20:1. Its solvency also improved, as measured by the debt to assets ratio, which declined from 44% to 30%.

c. Free cash flow

2022: $110,000 − $45,000 − ($10,000 + $5,000) = $50,000
2021: $70,000 − $20,000 − ($10,000 + $2,500) = $37,500

The amount of cash generated by the company above its needs for dividends and capital expenditures increased from $37,500 to $50,000.

Related exercise material: **BE2.4, BE2.5, BE2.6, DO IT! 2.2, E2.8, E2.10, E2.11, and E2.12.**

Financial Reporting Concepts

LEARNING OBJECTIVE 3
Discuss financial reporting concepts.

You have now learned about the four financial statements and some basic ways to interpret those statements. In this section, we will discuss concepts that underlie these financial statements. It would be unwise to make business decisions based on financial statements without understanding the implications of these concepts.

The Standard-Setting Environment

How does **Best Buy** decide on the type of financial information to disclose? What format should it use? How should it measure assets, liabilities, revenues, and expenses? Accounting professionals at Best Buy and all other U.S. companies get guidance from a set of accounting standards that have authoritative support, referred to as **generally accepted accounting principles (GAAP)**. Standard-setting bodies, in consultation with the accounting profession and the business community, determine these accounting standards.

The **Securities and Exchange Commission (SEC)** is the agency of the U.S. government that oversees U.S. financial markets and accounting standard-setting bodies. The **Financial Accounting Standards Board (FASB)** is the primary accounting standard-setting body in the United States. The **International Accounting Standards Board (IASB)** issues standards called **International Financial Reporting Standards (IFRS)**, which have been adopted by many countries outside of the United States (see **International Note**).

Today, the FASB and IASB are working closely together to minimize the differences in their standards. The SEC decided that foreign companies that wish to have their shares traded on U.S stock exchanges no longer have to prepare reports that conform with GAAP, as long as their reports conform with IFRS.

Finally, as a result of the Sarbanes-Oxley Act, the **Public Company Accounting Oversight Board (PCAOB)** was created. Its job is to determine auditing standards and review the performance of auditing firms.

> **International Note**
>
> Over 115 countries use international standards (called IFRS). For example, all companies in the European Union follow IFRS. In this text, we highlight any significant differences using International Notes like this one, as well as a more in-depth discussion in the *A Look at IFRS* section at the end of each chapter.

International Insight

Toru Hanai-Pool/Getty Images

The Korean Discount

If you think that accounting standards don't matter, consider past events in South Korea. For many years, international investors complained that the financial reports of South Korean companies were inadequate and inaccurate. Accounting practices there often resulted in huge differences between stated revenues and actual revenues. Because investors did not have faith in the accuracy of the numbers, they were unwilling to pay as much for the shares of these companies relative to shares of comparable companies in different countries. This difference in share price was often referred to as the "Korean discount."

In response, Korean regulators decided that companies would have to comply with international accounting standards. This change was motivated by a desire to "make the country's businesses more transparent" in order to build investor confidence and spur economic growth. Many other Asian countries, including China, India, Japan, and Hong Kong, have also decided either to adopt international standards or to create standards that are based on the international standards.

Source: Evan Ramstad, "End to 'Korea Discount'?" *Wall Street Journal* (March 16, 2007).

What is meant by the phrase "make the country's businesses more transparent"? Why would increasing transparency spur economic growth? (Go to WileyPLUS for this answer and additional questions.)

Qualities of Useful Information

The FASB and IASB engaged in a joint project in which they developed a conceptual framework to serve as the basis for future accounting standards. The framework begins by stating that the primary objective of financial reporting is to provide financial information that is **useful** to investors and creditors for making decisions about providing capital. According to the FASB, useful information should possess two fundamental qualities, **relevance** and **faithful representation**, as shown in Illustration 2.18.

ILLUSTRATION 2.18
Fundamental qualities of useful information

Relevance Accounting information has relevance if it would make a difference in a business decision. Information is considered relevant if it provides information that has **predictive value**, that is, helps provide accurate expectations about the future, and has **confirmatory value**, that is, confirms or corrects prior expectations. Materiality is a company-specific aspect of relevance. An item is material when its **size** makes it likely to influence the decision of an investor or creditor.

Faithful Representation Faithful representation means that information accurately depicts what really happened. To provide a faithful representation, information must be **complete** (nothing important has been omitted), **neutral** (is not biased toward one position or another), and **free from error**.

Enhancing Qualities

In addition to the two fundamental qualities, the FASB and IASB also describe a number of enhancing qualities of useful information. These include **comparability**, **verifiability**, **timeliness**, and **understandability**. In accounting, comparability results when different companies use the same accounting principles. Another type of comparability is consistency. Consistency means that a company uses the same accounting principles and methods from year to year. Information is verifiable if independent observers, using the same methods, obtain similar results. Recall that certified public accountants (CPAs) perform audits of financial statements to verify their accuracy. For accounting information to have relevance, it must be timely. That is, it must be available to decision-makers before it loses its capacity to influence decisions. The SEC requires that large public companies provide their annual reports to investors within 60 days of their year-end. Information has the quality of understandability if it is presented in a clear and concise fashion, so that reasonably informed users of that information can interpret it and comprehend its meaning.

Accounting Across the Organization

© Skip ODonnell/iStockphoto

What Do These Companies Have in Common?

Another issue related to comparability is the accounting time period. An accounting period that is one-year long is called a **fiscal year**. But a fiscal year need not match the calendar year. For example, a company could end its fiscal year on April 30 rather than on December 31.

Why do companies choose the particular year-ends that they do? For example, why doesn't every company use December 31 as its accounting year-end? Many companies choose to end their accounting year when inventory or operations are at a low point. This is advantageous because compiling accounting information requires much time and effort by managers, so they would rather do it when they aren't as busy operating the business. Also, inventory is easier and less costly to count when its volume is low.

Some companies whose year-ends differ from December 31 are Delta Air Lines, June 30; The Walt Disney Company, September 30; and Dunkin' Donuts, Inc., October 31. In the notes to its financial statements, Best Buy states that its accounting year-end is the Saturday nearest the end of January.

What problems might Best Buy's year-end create for analysts? (Go to WileyPLUS for this answer and additional questions.)

Assumptions in Financial Reporting

To develop accounting standards, the FASB relies on some key assumptions, as shown in **Illustration 2.19** (see **Ethics Note**). These include assumptions about the monetary unit, economic entity, periodicity, and going concern.

ILLUSTRATION 2.19

Key assumptions in financial reporting

ETHICS NOTE

The importance of the economic entity assumption is illustrated by scandals involving Adelphia. In this case, senior company employees entered into transactions that blurred the line between the employees' financial interests and those of the company. For example, Adelphia guaranteed over $2 billion of loans to the founding family.

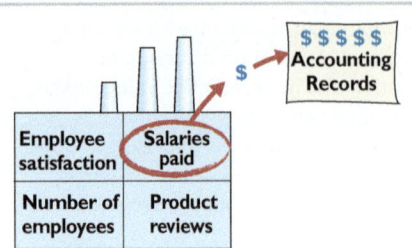

Monetary Unit Assumption The monetary unit assumption requires that only those things that can be expressed in money are included in the accounting records. This means that certain important information needed by investors, creditors, and managers, such as customer satisfaction, is not reported in the financial statements. This assumption relies on the monetary unit remaining relatively stable in value.

Economic Entity Assumption The economic entity assumption states that every economic entity can be separately identified and accounted for. In order to assess a company's performance and financial position accurately, it is important to not blur company transactions with personal transactions (especially those of its managers) or transactions of other companies.

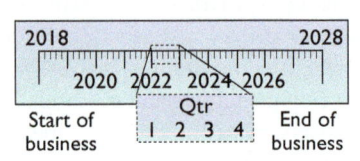

Periodicity Assumption Notice that the income statement, retained earnings statement, and statement of cash flows all cover periods of one year, and the balance sheet is prepared at the end of each year. The periodicity assumption states that the life of a business can be divided into artificial time periods and that useful reports covering those periods can be prepared for the business.

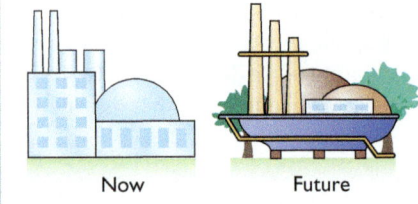

Going Concern Assumption The going concern assumption states that the business will remain in operation for the foreseeable future. Of course, many businesses do fail, but in general it is reasonable to assume that the business will continue operating.

Principles in Financial Reporting

Measurement Principles

GAAP generally uses one of two measurement principles, the historical cost principle or the fair value principle. Selection of which principle to follow generally relates to trade-offs between relevance and faithful representation.

Historical Cost Principle The historical cost principle (or cost principle) dictates that companies record assets at their cost. This is true not only at the time the asset is purchased but also over the time the asset is held. For example, if land that was purchased for $30,000 increases in value to $40,000, it continues to be reported at $30,000.

Fair Value Principle The fair value principle indicates that assets and liabilities should be reported at fair value (the price received to sell an asset or settle a liability). Fair value information may be more useful than historical cost for certain types of assets and liabilities. For example, certain investment securities are reported at fair value because market price information is often readily available for these types of assets. In choosing between cost and fair value, the FASB uses two qualities that make accounting information useful for decision-making—relevance and faithful representation. In determining which measurement principle to use, the FASB weighs the factual nature of cost figures versus the relevance of fair value. In general, the FASB indicates that most assets must follow the historical cost principle because market values may not be representationally faithful. Only in situations where assets are actively traded, such as investment securities, is the fair value principle applied.

Full Disclosure Principle

The **full disclosure principle** requires that companies disclose all circumstances and events that would make a difference to financial statement users. If an important item cannot reasonably be reported directly in one of the four types of financial statements, then it should be discussed in notes that accompany the statements.

Cost Constraint

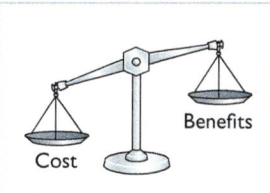

Providing information is costly. In deciding whether companies should be required to provide a certain type of information, accounting standard-setters consider the **cost constraint**. It weighs the cost that companies will incur to provide the information against the benefit that financial statement users will gain from having the information available.

DO IT! 3 | Financial Accounting Concepts and Principles

The following items guide the FASB when it creates accounting standards.

- Relevance
- Faithful representation
- Comparability
- Consistency
- Monetary unit assumption
- Economic entity assumption
- Periodicity assumption
- Going concern assumption
- Historical cost principle
- Full disclosure principle
- Materiality

Match each item above with a description below.

1. _____ Ability to easily evaluate one company's results relative to another's.
2. _____ Belief that a company will continue to operate for the foreseeable future.
3. _____ The judgment concerning whether an item is large enough to matter to decision-makers.
4. _____ The reporting of all information that would make a difference to financial statement users.
5. _____ The practice of preparing financial statements at regular intervals.
6. _____ The quality of information that indicates the information makes a difference in a decision.
7. _____ A belief that items should be reported on the balance sheet at the price that was paid to acquire the item.
8. _____ A company's use of the same accounting principles and methods from year to year.
9. _____ Tracing accounting events to particular companies.
10. _____ The desire to minimize errors and bias in financial statements.
11. _____ Reporting only those things that can be measured in dollars.

ACTION PLAN
- Understand the need for conceptual guidelines in accounting.
- List the characteristics of useful financial information.
- Review the assumptions, principles, and constraint that comprise the guidelines in accounting.

Solution

1. Comparability
2. Going concern assumption
3. Materiality
4. Full disclosure principle
5. Periodicity assumption
6. Relevance
7. Historical cost principle
8. Consistency
9. Economic entity assumption
10. Faithful representation
11. Monetary unit assumption

Related exercise material: **BE2.9, BE2.10, BE2.11, DO IT! 2.3, E2.13, E2.14, and E2.15.**

USING THE DECISION TOOLS | Tweeter Home Entertainment

In this chapter, we evaluated a home electronics giant, **Best Buy**. **Tweeter Home Entertainment** sold consumer electronics products from 154 stores on the East Coast under various names. It specialized in products with high-end features. Tweeter filed for bankruptcy in June 2007 and was acquired by another company in July 2007. Financial data for Tweeter, prior to its bankruptcy, are provided below.

	September 30	
(amounts in millions)	2006	2005
Current assets	$146.4	$158.2
Total assets	258.6	284.0
Current liabilities	107.1	119.0
Total liabilities	190.4	201.1
Total common stockholders' equity	68.2	82.9
Net income (loss)	(16.5)	(74.4)
Net cash provided (used) by operating activities	15.6	(26.7)
Capital expenditures (net)	17.4	22.2
Dividends paid	0	0
Weighted-average shares of common stock (millions)	25.2	24.6

Instructions

Using the data provided, answer the following questions and discuss how these results might have provided an indication of Tweeter's financial troubles.

1. Calculate the current ratio for Tweeter for 2006 and 2005 and discuss its liquidity position.
2. Calculate the debt to assets ratio and free cash flow for Tweeter for 2006 and 2005 and discuss its solvency.
3. Calculate the earnings per share for Tweeter for 2006 and 2005, and discuss its change in profitability.
4. Best Buy's accounting year-end was February 28, 2006; Tweeter's was September 30, 2006. How does this difference affect your ability to compare their profitability?

Solution

1. Current ratio:
   2006: $146.4 ÷ $107.1 = 1.37:1   2005: $158.2 ÷ $119.0 = 1.33:1
   Tweeter's liquidity improved slightly from 2005 to 2006, but in both years it would most likely have been considered inadequate. In 2006, Tweeter had only $1.37 in current assets for every dollar of current liabilities. Sometimes larger companies, such as Best Buy, can function with lower current ratios because they have alternative sources of working capital. But a company of Tweeter's size would normally want a higher ratio.

2. Debt to assets ratio:
   2006: $190.4 ÷ $258.6 = 73.6%   2005: $201.1 ÷ $284.0 = 70.8%
   Tweeter's solvency, as measured by its debt to assets ratio, declined from 2005 to 2006. Its ratio of 73.6% meant that every dollar of assets was financed by 73.6 cents of debt. For a retailer, this is extremely high reliance on debt. This low solvency suggests Tweeter's ability to meet its debt payments was questionable.
   Free cash flow:
   2006: $15.6 − $17.4 − $0 = −$1.8 million
   2005: −$26.7 − $22.2 − $0 = −$48.9 million
   Tweeter's free cash flow was negative in both years. The company did not generate enough net cash provided by operating activities even to cover its capital expenditures, and it was

not paying a dividend. While this is not unusual for new companies in their early years, it is also not sustainable for very long. Part of the reason that its debt to assets ratio, discussed above, was so high was that it had to borrow money to make up for its deficient free cash flow.

3. Loss per share:
   2006: −$16.5 ÷ 25.2 = −$0.65 per share
   2005: −$74.4 ÷ 24.6 = −$3.02 per share
   Tweeter's loss per share declined substantially. However, this was little consolation for its shareholders, who experienced losses in previous years as well. The company's lack of profitability, combined with its poor liquidity and solvency, increased the likelihood that it would eventually file for bankruptcy.

4. Tweeter's income statement covers 7 months not covered by Best Buy's. Suppose that the economy changed dramatically during this 7-month period, either improving or declining. This change in the economy would be reflected in Tweeter's income statement but would not be reflected in Best Buy's income statement until the following March, thus reducing the usefulness of a comparison of the income statements of the two companies.

Review and Practice

Learning Objectives Review

1 Identify the sections of a classified balance sheet.

In a classified balance sheet, companies classify assets as current assets; long-term investments; property, plant, and equipment; and intangibles. They classify liabilities as either current or long-term. A stockholders' equity section shows common stock and retained earnings.

2 Use ratios to evaluate a company's profitability, liquidity, and solvency.

Ratio analysis expresses the relationship among selected items of financial statement data. Profitability ratios, such as earnings per share (EPS), measure aspects of the operating success of a company for a given period of time.

Liquidity ratios, such as the current ratio, measure the short-term ability of a company to pay its maturing obligations and to meet unexpected needs for cash. Solvency ratios, such as the debt to assets ratio, measure the ability of a company to survive over a long period. Free cash flow indicates a company's ability to generate net cash provided by operating activities that is sufficient to pay debts, acquire assets, and distribute dividends.

3 Discuss financial reporting concepts.

Generally accepted accounting principles are a set of rules and practices recognized as a general guide for financial reporting purposes. The basic objective of financial reporting is to provide information that is useful for decision-making.

To be judged useful, information should have the primary characteristics of **relevance** and **faithful representation**. In addition, useful information is comparable, consistent, verifiable, timely, and understandable.

The **monetary unit assumption** requires that companies include in the accounting records only transaction data that can be expressed in terms of money. The **economic entity assumption** states that economic events can be identified with a particular unit of accountability. The **periodicity assumption** states that the economic life of a business can be divided into artificial time periods and that meaningful accounting reports can be prepared for each period. The **going concern assumption** states that the company will continue in operation long enough to carry out its existing objectives and commitments.

The **historical cost principle** states that companies should record assets at their cost. The **fair value principle** indicates that assets and liabilities should be reported at fair value. The **full disclosure principle** requires that companies disclose circumstances and events that matter to financial statement users.

The **cost constraint** weighs the cost that companies incur to provide a type of information against its benefit to financial statement users.

Decision Tools Review

Decision Checkpoints	Info Needed for Decision	Tool to Use for Decision	How to Evaluate Results
How does the company's earnings performance compare with that of previous years?	Net income available to common stockholders and weighted-average common shares outstanding	$$\text{Earnings per share} = \frac{\text{Net income} - \text{Preferred dividends}}{\text{Weighted-average common shares outstanding}}$$	A higher measure suggests improved performance, although the number is subject to manipulation. Values should not be compared across companies.
Can the company meet its near-term obligations?	Current assets and current liabilities	$$\text{Current ratio} = \frac{\text{Current assets}}{\text{Current liabilities}}$$	Higher ratio suggests favorable liquidity.
Can the company meet its long-term obligations?	Total liabilities and total assets	$$\text{Debt to assets ratio} = \frac{\text{Total liabilities}}{\text{Total assets}}$$	Lower value suggests favorable solvency.
How much cash did the company generate to expand operations, pay off debts, or distribute dividends?	Net cash provided by operating activities, cash spent on fixed assets, and cash dividends	$$\text{Free cash flow} = \text{Net cash provided by operating activities} - \text{Capital expenditures} - \text{Cash dividends}$$	Significant free cash flow indicates greater potential to finance new investments and pay additional dividends.

Glossary Review

Classified balance sheet A balance sheet that groups together similar assets and similar liabilities, using a number of standard classifications and sections. (p. 2-3).

Comparability Ability to compare the accounting information of different companies because they use the same accounting principles. (p. 2-17).

Consistency Use of the same accounting principles and methods from year to year within a company. (p. 2-17).

Cost constraint Constraint that weighs the cost that companies will incur to provide the information against the benefit that financial statement users will gain from having the information available. (p. 2-19).

Current assets Assets that companies expect to convert to cash or use up within one year or the operating cycle, whichever is longer. (p. 2-3).

Current liabilities Obligations that a company expects to pay within the next year or operating cycle, whichever is longer. (p. 2-7).

Current ratio A measure of liquidity computed as current assets divided by current liabilities. (p. 2-11).

Debt to assets ratio A measure of solvency calculated as total liabilities divided by total assets. It measures the percentage of total financing provided by creditors. (p. 2-13).

Earnings per share (EPS) A measure of the net income earned on each share of common stock; computed as net income minus preferred dividends divided by the weighted-average number of common shares outstanding during the year. (p. 2-10).

Economic entity assumption An assumption that every economic entity can be separately identified and accounted for. (p. 2-18).

Fair value principle Assets and liabilities should be reported at fair value (the price received to sell an asset or settle a liability). (p. 2-18).

Faithful representation Information that is complete, neutral, and free from error. (p. 2-17).

Financial Accounting Standards Board (FASB) The primary accounting standard-setting body in the United States. (p. 2-16).

Free cash flow Net cash provided by operating activities after adjusting for capital expenditures and cash dividends paid. (p. 2-14).

Full disclosure principle Accounting principle that dictates that companies disclose circumstances and events that make a difference to financial statement users. (p. 2-19).

Generally accepted accounting principles (GAAP) A set of accounting standards that have substantial authoritative support and which guide accounting professionals. (p. 2-16).

Going concern assumption The assumption that the company will continue in operation for the foreseeable future. (p. 2-18).

Historical cost principle An accounting principle that states that companies should record assets at their cost. (p. 2-18).

Intangible assets Assets that do not have physical substance. (p. 2-5).

International Accounting Standards Board (IASB) An accounting standard-setting body that issues standards adopted by many countries outside of the United States. (p. 2-16).

International Financial Reporting Standards (IFRS) Accounting standards, issued by the IASB, that have been adopted by many countries outside of the United States. (p. 2-16).

Liquidity The ability of a company to pay obligations that are expected to become due within the next year or operating cycle. (p. 2-10).

Liquidity ratios Measures of the short-term ability of the company to pay its maturing obligations and to meet unexpected needs for cash. (p. 2-11).

Long-term investments Generally, (1) investments in stocks and bonds of other corporations that companies hold for more than one year; (2) long-term assets, such as land and buildings, not currently being used in the company's operations; and (3) long-term notes receivable. (p. 2-5).

Long-term liabilities (long-term debt) Obligations that a company expects to pay after one year. (p. 2-7).

Materiality Whether an item is large enough to likely influence the decision of an investor or creditor. (p. 2-17).

Monetary unit assumption An assumption that requires that only those things that can be expressed in money are included in the accounting records. (p. 2-18).

Operating cycle The average time required to purchase inventory, sell it on account, and then collect cash from customers—that is, go from cash to cash. (p. 2-3).

Periodicity assumption An assumption that the life of a business can be divided into artificial time periods and that useful reports covering those periods can be prepared for the business. (p. 2-18).

Profitability ratios Measures of the operating success of a company for a given period of time. (p. 2-10).

Property, plant, and equipment Assets with relatively long useful lives that are currently used in operating the business. (p. 2-5).

Public Company Accounting Oversight Board (PCAOB) The group charged with determining auditing standards and reviewing the performance of auditing firms. (p. 2-16).

Ratio An expression of the mathematical relationship between one quantity and another. (p. 2-8).

Ratio analysis A technique that expresses the relationship among selected items of financial statement data. (p. 2-8).

Relevance The quality of information that indicates the information makes a difference in a decision. (p. 2-17).

Securities and Exchange Commission (SEC) The agency of the U.S. government that oversees U.S. financial markets and accounting standard-setting bodies. (p. 2-16).

Solvency The ability of a company to pay interest as it comes due and to repay the balance of debt due at its maturity. (p. 2-12).

Solvency ratios Measures of the ability of the company to survive over a long period of time. (p. 2-12).

Timely Information that is available to decision-makers before it loses its capacity to influence decisions. (p. 2-17).

Understandability Information presented in a clear and concise fashion so that users can interpret it and comprehend its meaning. (p. 2-17).

Verifiable The quality of information that occurs when independent observers, using the same methods, obtain similar results. (p. 2-17).

Working capital The difference between the amounts of current assets and current liabilities. (p. 2-11).

Practice Multiple-Choice Questions

1. **(LO 1)** In a classified balance sheet, assets are usually classified as:
   a. current assets; long-term assets; property, plant, and equipment; and intangible assets.
   b. current assets; long-term investments; property, plant, and equipment; and common stock.
   c. current assets; long-term investments; tangible assets; and intangible assets.
   d. current assets; long-term investments; property, plant, and equipment; and intangible assets.

2. **(LO 1)** Current assets are listed:
   a. by order of expected conversion to cash.
   b. by importance.
   c. by longevity.
   d. alphabetically.

3. **(LO 1)** The correct order of presentation in a classified balance sheet for the following current assets is:
   a. accounts receivable, cash, prepaid insurance, inventory.
   b. cash, inventory, accounts receivable, prepaid insurance.
   c. cash, accounts receivable, inventory, prepaid insurance.
   d. inventory, cash, accounts receivable, prepaid insurance.

4. **(LO 1)** A company has purchased a tract of land. It expects to build a production plant on the land in approximately 5 years. During the 5 years before construction, the land will be idle. The land should be reported as:
   a. property, plant, and equipment.
   b. land expense.
   c. a long-term investment.
   d. an intangible asset.

5. **(LO 1)** The balance in retained earnings is **not** affected by:
   a. net income.
   b. net loss.
   c. issuance of common stock.
   d. dividends.

6. **(LO 2)** Which is an indicator of profitability?
   a. Current ratio.
   b. Earnings per share.
   c. Debt to assets ratio.
   d. Free cash flow.

7. **(LO 2)** For 2022, Spanos Corporation reported net income $26,000, net sales $400,000, and weighted-average common shares outstanding 4,000. There were preferred dividends of $2,000. What was the 2022 earnings per share?
   a. $6.00.
   b. $6.50.
   c. $99.50.
   d. $100.00.

8. **(LO 2)** Which of these measures is an evaluation of a company's ability to pay current liabilities?
   a. Earnings per share.
   b. Current ratio.
   c. Both (a) and (b).
   d. None of the above.

9. **(LO 2)** The following ratios are available for Reilly Inc. and O'Hare Inc.

	Current Ratio	Debt to Assets Ratio	Earnings per Share
Reilly Inc.	2:1	75%	$3.50
O'Hare Inc.	1.5:1	40%	$2.75

Compared to O'Hare Inc., Reilly Inc. has:
a. higher liquidity, higher solvency, and higher profitability.
b. lower liquidity, higher solvency, and higher profitability.
c. higher liquidity, lower solvency, and higher profitability.
d. higher liquidity and lower solvency, but profitability cannot be compared based on information provided.

10. **(LO 2)** Companies can use free cash flow to:
a. pay additional dividends.
b. acquire more property, plant, and equipment.
c. pay off debts.
d. All of the above.

11. **(LO 3)** Generally accepted accounting principles are:
a. a set of standards and rules that are recognized as a general guide for financial reporting.
b. usually established by the Internal Revenue Service.
c. the guidelines used to resolve ethical dilemmas.
d. fundamental truths that can be derived from the laws of nature.

12. **(LO 3)** What organization issues U.S. accounting standards?
a. Financial Accounting Standards Board.
b. International Accounting Standards Committee.
c. International Auditing Standards Committee.
d. None of the above.

13. **(LO 3)** What is the primary criterion by which accounting information can be judged?
a. Consistency.
b. Predictive value.
c. Usefulness for decision-making.
d. Comparability.

14. **(LO 3)** Neutrality is an ingredient of:

	Faithful Representation	Relevance
a.	Yes	Yes
b.	No	No
c.	Yes	No
d.	No	Yes

15. **(LO 3)** The characteristic of information that evaluates whether it is large enough to impact a decision.
a. Comparability.
b. Materiality.
c. Cost.
d. Consistency.

Solutions

1. d. Assets are classified as current assets; long-term investments; property, plant and equipment; and intangible assets. The other choices are incorrect because (a) long-term assets includes long-term investments; property, plant, and equipment; and intangible assets; (b) common stock refers to the equity of the firm and is not an asset; and (c) while tangible assets describes property, plant, and equipment, it is better to use the more common terminology of property, plant, and equipment.

2. a. Current assets should be listed by order of expected conversion to cash (liquidity), not (b) by importance, (c) by longevity, or (d) alphabetically.

3. c. The correct order of presentation for current assets is cash, accounts receivable, inventory, and then prepaid insurance. The other choices are therefore incorrect.

4. c. Land or buildings that are currently not used in operations are considered to be long-term investments. The other choices are incorrect because (a) this classification is for property, plant, and equipment used in operations; (b) land is never expensed; and (d) intangible assets have no physical existence and are used in the production of income.

5. c. Issuance of common stock has no impact on retained earnings. The other choices are incorrect because (a) net income increases retained earnings, (b) net loss decreases retained earnings, and (d) dividends decrease retained earnings.

6. b. Earnings per share is a measure of profitability. The other choices are incorrect because (a) the current ratio is a measure of liquidity, (c) the debt to assets ratio is a measure of solvency, and (d) free cash flow is a measure of solvency.

7. a. Earnings per share = Net income ($26,000) less Preferred dividends ($2,000) divided by Weighted-average common shares outstanding (4,000) = $6.00/share, not (b) $6.50, (c) $99.50, or (d) $100.00.

8. b. The current ratio measures liquidity. Higher current ratios indicate higher liquidity. The other choices are incorrect because (a) earnings per share is a measure of a firm's profitability, not its ability to pay its current liabilities; (c) one of these answers is incorrect; and (d) there is a correct answer.

9. d. Reilly Inc. has higher liquidity as it has a higher current ratio, and lower solvency due to its higher debt to assets ratio. However, profitability cannot be compared across companies using earnings per share because of the wide variations in the number of shares of common stock of different companies. The other choices are therefore incorrect.

10. d. Free cash flow can be used to pay dividends; acquire more property, plant, and equipment; and pay off debts. Although choices (a), (b), and (c) are correct, choice (d) is the better answer.

11. a. All U.S. companies get guidance from a set of rules and practices that have authoritative support, referred to as generally accepted accounting principles (GAAP). Standard-setting bodies, in consultation with the accounting profession and the business community, determine these accounting standards. The other choices are incorrect because GAAP is (b) not established by the Internal Revenue Service, (c) not intended to provide guidance in resolving ethical dilemmas, or (d) created by people and can evolve over time, unlike laws of nature, such as those in physics and chemistry.

12. a. The Financial Accounting Standards Board (FASB) is the organization that issues U.S. accounting standards, not the (b) International Accounting Standards Committee or (c) International Auditing Standards Committee. Choice (d) is wrong as there is a correct answer.

13. c. Usefulness for decision-making is the primary criterion by which accounting information can be judged. The other choices are incorrect because (a) consistency, (b) predictive value, and (d) comparability all help to make accounting information more useful but are not the primary criterion by which accounting information is judged.

14. c. Neutrality is an ingredient of faithful representation but not relevance. The other choices are therefore incorrect.

15. b. Materiality evaluates whether information is large enough to impact a decision, not (a) comparability, (c) cost, or (d) consistency.

Practice Brief Exercises

1. **(LO 1)** A list of financial statement items for Miguel Company includes the following: Accounts Receivable $25,000, Prepaid Insurance $7,000, Cash $8,000, Supplies $11,000, and Stock Investments (short-term) $14,000. Prepare the current assets section of the balance sheet, listing the accounts in proper sequence.

Prepare the current assets section of a balance sheet.

Solution
1.

Miguel Company
Balance Sheet (partial)

Current assets	
Cash	$ 8,000
Stock investments	14,000
Accounts receivable	25,000
Supplies	11,000
Prepaid insurance	7,000
Total current assets	$65,000

2. **(LO 1)** The following are the major balance sheet classifications:

Current assets (CA)   Current liabilities (CL)
Long-term investments (LTI) Long-term liabilities (LTL)
Property, plant, and equipment (PPE) Common stock (CS)
Intangible assets (IA)   Retained earnings (RE)

Match each of the following accounts to its proper balance sheet classification.

Classify accounts on balance sheet.

___ Prepaid insurance   ___ Unearned service revenue
___ Notes payable (short-term)   ___ Debt investments (short-term)
___ Equipment   ___ Accumulated depreciation—equipment
___ Mortgage payable   ___ Stock investments
___ Copyrights   ___ Salaries and wages payable

Solution
2.

CA	Prepaid insurance	CL	Unearned service revenue
CL	Notes payable (short-term)	CA	Debt investments (short-term)
PPE	Equipment	PPE	Accumulated depreciation—equipment
LTL	Mortgage payable	LTI	Stock investments (long-term)
IA	Copyrights	CL	Salaries and wages payable

3. **(LO 2)** Maison Inc. reported the following selected information at December 31.

Calculate liquidity and solvency ratios.

	2022
Total current assets	$ 45,584
Total assets	278,000
Total current liabilities	32,560
Total liabilities	189,040
Net cash provided by operating activities	48,500

Calculate (a) the current ratio, (b) the debt to assets ratio, and (c) free cash flow for December 31, 2022. The company paid dividends of $7,250 and spent $14,400 on capital expenditures.

Solution

3. **a.** Current ratio = $\dfrac{\text{Current assets}}{\text{Current liabilities}} = \dfrac{\$45,584}{\$32,560} = 1.40:1$

b. Debt to assets ratio = $\dfrac{\text{Total liabilities}}{\text{Total assets}} = \dfrac{\$189{,}040}{\$278{,}000} = 68.0\%$

c. Free cash flow = Net cash provided by operating activities − Capital expenditures − Dividends paid = $48,500 − $14,400 − $7,250 = $26,850

Practice Exercises

Prepare assets section of a classified balance sheet.

1. (LO 1) Suppose the following information (in thousands of dollars) is available for **H. J. Heinz Company**—famous for ketchup and other fine food products—for the year ended April 30, 2022.

Prepaid insurance	$ 168,182	Buildings	$4,344,269
Land	56,007	Cash	617,687
Goodwill	4,411,521	Accounts receivable	1,161,481
Trademarks	723,243	Accumulated depreciation—	
Inventory	1,378,216	buildings	2,295,563

Instructions

Prepare the assets section of a classified balance sheet, listing the items in proper sequence and including a statement heading.

Solution

1.

H. J. Heinz Company
Balance Sheet (partial)
April 30, 2022
(in thousands)

Assets

Current assets			
Cash		$ 617,687	
Accounts receivable		1,161,481	
Inventory		1,378,216	
Prepaid insurance		168,182	
Total current assets			$ 3,325,566
Property, plant, and equipment			
Land		56,007	
Buildings	$4,344,269		
Less: Accumulated depr.—buildings	2,295,563	2,048,706	2,104,713
Intangible assets			
Goodwill		4,411,521	
Trademarks		723,243	5,134,764
Total assets			$10,565,043

Compute and interpret various ratios.

2. (LO 2) Suppose the following data were taken from the 2022 and 2021 financial statements of **American Eagle Outfitters**. (All dollars are in thousands.)

	2022	2021
Current assets	$1,020,834	$1,189,108
Total assets	1,867,680	1,979,558
Current liabilities	376,178	464,618
Total liabilities	527,216	562,246
Net income	400,019	387,359
Net cash provided by operating activities	464,270	749,268
Capital expenditures	250,407	225,939
Dividends paid on common stock	80,796	61,521
Weighted-average common shares outstanding	216,119	222,662

Instructions

Perform each of the following.

a. Calculate the current ratio for each year.
b. Calculate earnings per share for each year.
c. Calculate the debt to assets ratio for each year.
d. Calculate the free cash flow for each year.
e. Discuss American Eagle's solvency in 2022 versus 2021.

Solution

2.

	2022	2021
a. Current ratio	$\dfrac{\$1{,}020{,}834}{\$376{,}178} = 2.71\!:\!1$	$\dfrac{\$1{,}189{,}108}{\$464{,}618} = 2.56\!:\!1$
b. Earning per share	$\dfrac{\$400{,}019}{216{,}119} = \$1.85$	$\dfrac{\$387{,}359}{222{,}662} = \$1.74$
c. Debt to assets ratio	$\dfrac{\$527{,}216}{\$1{,}867{,}680} = 28.2\%$	$\dfrac{\$562{,}246}{\$1{,}979{,}558} = 28.4\%$
d. Free cash flow	$\$464{,}270 - \$250{,}407 - \$80{,}796 = \$133{,}067$	$\$749{,}268 - \$225{,}939 - \$61{,}521 = \$461{,}808$

e. Using the debt to assets ratio and free cash flow as measures of solvency produces negative results for American Eagle Outfitters. Its debt to assets ratio decreased slightly from 28.4% for 2021 to 28.2% for 2022, indicating a very small increase in solvency for 2022. Its free cash flow decreased by 71%, indicating a significant decline in solvency.

Practice Problem

(LO 1) Listed here are items taken from the income statement and balance sheet of Bargain Electronics, Inc. for the year ended December 31, 2022. Certain items have been combined for simplification. (Amounts are given in thousands.)

Prepare financial statements.

Notes payable (due in 3 years)	$ 50.5
Cash	141.1
Salaries and wages expense	2,933.6
Common stock	454.9
Accounts payable	922.2
Accounts receivable	723.3
Accumulated depreciation—equipment	110.0
Equipment	1,031.0
Cost of goods sold	9,501.4
Income taxes payable	7.2
Interest expense	1.5
Mortgage payable	451.5
Retained earnings (December 31, 2022)	1,336.3
Inventory	1,636.5
Sales revenue	12,456.9
Debt investments (short-term)	382.6
Income tax expense	30.5
Goodwill	202.7
Notes payable (due in 6 months)	784.6

Instructions

Prepare an income statement and a classified balance sheet using the items listed. Do not use any item more than once.

Solution

Bargain Electronics, Inc.
Income Statement
For the Year Ended December 31, 2022
(in thousands)

Revenues		
Sales revenue		$12,456.9
Expenses		
Cost of goods sold	$9,501.4	
Salaries and wages expense	2,933.6	
Interest expense	1.5	
Income tax expense	30.5	
Total expenses		12,467.0
Net loss		$ (10.1)

Bargain Electronics, Inc.
Balance Sheet
December 31, 2022
(in thousands)

Assets

Current assets		
Cash	$ 141.1	
Debt investments	382.6	
Accounts receivable	723.3	
Inventory	1,636.5	
Total current assets		$2,883.5
Property, plant and equipment		
Equipment	1,031.0	
Less: Accumulated depreciation—equipment	110.0	921.0
Intangible assets		
Goodwill		202.7
Total assets		$4,007.2

Liabilities and Stockholders' Equity

Current liabilities		
Notes payable	$ 784.6	
Accounts payable	922.2	
Income taxes payable	7.2	
Total current liabilities		$1,714.0
Long-term liabilities		
Mortgage payable	451.5	
Notes payable	50.5	502.0
Total liabilities		2,216.0
Stockholders' equity		
Common stock	454.9	
Retained earnings	1,336.3	
Total stockholders' equity		1,791.2
Total liabilities and stockholders' equity		$4,007.2

WileyPLUS

Brief Exercises, DO IT! Exercises, Exercises, Problems, and many additional resources are available for practice in WileyPLUS.

Questions

1. What is meant by the term operating cycle?
2. Define current assets. What basis is used for ordering individual items within the current assets section?
3. Distinguish between long-term investments and property, plant, and equipment.
4. How do current liabilities differ from long-term liabilities?
5. Identify the two parts of stockholders' equity in a corporation and indicate the purpose of each.
6. **a.** Geena Lowe believes that the analysis of financial statements is directed at two characteristics of a company: liquidity and profitability. Is Geena correct? Explain.
   b. Are short-term creditors, long-term creditors, and stockholders primarily interested in the same characteristics of a company? Explain.
7. Name ratios useful in assessing (a) liquidity, (b) solvency, and (c) profitability.
8. Tom Dawes, the founder of Footwear Inc., needs to raise $500,000 to expand his company's operations. He has been told that raising the money through debt will increase the riskiness of his company much more than issuing stock. He doesn't understand why this is true. Explain it to him.
9. What do these classes of ratios measure?
   a. Liquidity ratios.
   b. Profitability ratios.
   c. Solvency ratios.
10. Holding all other factors constant, indicate whether each of the following signals generally good or bad news about a company.
    a. Increase in earnings per share.
    b. Increase in the current ratio.
    c. Increase in the debt to assets ratio.
    d. Decrease in free cash flow.
11. Which ratio or ratios from this chapter do you think should be of greatest interest to:
    a. a pension fund considering investing in a corporation's 20-year bonds?
    b. a bank contemplating a short-term loan?
    c. an investor in common stock?
12. **a.** What are generally accepted accounting principles (GAAP)?
    b. What body provides authoritative support for GAAP?
13. **a.** What is the primary objective of financial reporting?
    b. Identify the characteristics of useful accounting information.
14. Merle Hawkins, the president of Pathway Company, is pleased. Pathway substantially increased its net income in 2022 while keeping its unit inventory relatively the same. Jon Dietz, chief accountant, cautions Merle, however. Dietz says that since Pathway changed its method of inventory valuation, there is a consistency problem and it is difficult to determine whether Pathway is better off. Is Dietz correct? Why or why not?
15. What is the distinction between comparability and consistency?
16. Describe the constraint inherent in the presentation of accounting information.
17. Your roommate believes that accounting standards are uniform throughout the world. Is your roommate correct? Explain.
18. Wanda Roberts is president of Best Texts. She has no accounting background. Wanda cannot understand why fair value is not used as the basis for all accounting measurement and reporting. Discuss.
19. What is the economic entity assumption? Give an example of its violation.
20. What was **Apple**'s largest current asset, largest current liability, and largest item under "Assets" at September 30, 2017?

Brief Exercises

BE2.1 (LO 1), K The following are the major balance sheet classifications:

Classify accounts on balance sheet.

Current assets (CA)
Long-term investments (LTI)
Property, plant, and equipment (PPE)
Intangible assets (IA)
Current liabilities (CL)
Long-term liabilities (LTL)
Common stock (CS)
Retained earnings (RE)

Match each of the following accounts to its proper balance sheet classification.

_____ Accounts payable
_____ Accounts receivable
_____ Accumulated depreciation
_____ Buildings
_____ Cash
_____ Goodwill

CHAPTER 2 A Further Look at Financial Statements

_____ Income taxes payable _____ Inventory
_____ Investment in long-term bonds _____ Patent
_____ Land _____ Supplies

Identify the order of asset classifications.

BE2.2 (LO 1), K Place a number, 1 through 7, in front of each of the following balance sheet categories to designate the order in which they are to be presented in a classified balance sheet.

_____ Long-term investments _____ Current assets
_____ Current liabilities _____ Long-term liabilities
_____ Stockholders' equity _____ Property, plant, and equipment
_____ Intangible assets

Prepare the current assets section of a balance sheet.

BE2.3 (LO 1), AP A list of financial statement items for Chin Company includes the following: accounts receivable $14,000, prepaid insurance $2,600, cash $10,400, supplies $3,800, and debt investments (short-term) $8,200. Prepare the current assets section of the balance sheet listing the items in the proper sequence.

Compute earnings per share.

BE2.4 (LO 2), AP The following information (in millions of dollars) is available for **Limited Brands** for a recent year: sales revenue $9,043, net income $220, preferred dividend $0, and weighted-average common shares outstanding 333 million. Compute the earnings per share for Limited Brands.

Calculate liquidity ratios.

BE2.5 (LO 2), AP These selected condensed data are taken from a recent balance sheet of **Bob Evans Farms** (in millions of dollars).

Cash	$ 29.3
Accounts receivable	20.5
Inventory	28.7
Other current assets	24.0
Total current assets	$102.5
Total current liabilities	$201.2

Compute working capital and the current ratio.

Calculate liquidity and solvency ratios.

BE2.6 (LO 2), AP Ross Music Inc. reported the following selected information at March 31.

	2022
Total current assets	$262,787
Total assets	439,832
Total current liabilities	293,625
Total liabilities	376,002
Net cash provided by operating activities	62,300

Calculate (a) the current ratio, (b) the debt to assets ratio, and (c) free cash flow for March 31, 2022. The company paid dividends of $12,000 and spent $24,787 on capital expenditures.

Recognize generally accepted accounting principles.

BE2.7 (LO 3), K Indicate whether each statement is true or false. If false, indicate how to correct the statement.

a. GAAP is a set of rules and practices established by accounting standard-setting bodies to serve as a general guide for financial reporting purposes.

b. The primary standard-setting body in the United States is the IRS.

Identify characteristics of useful information.

BE2.8 (LO 3), K The accompanying chart shows the qualitative characteristics of useful accounting information. Fill in the blanks.

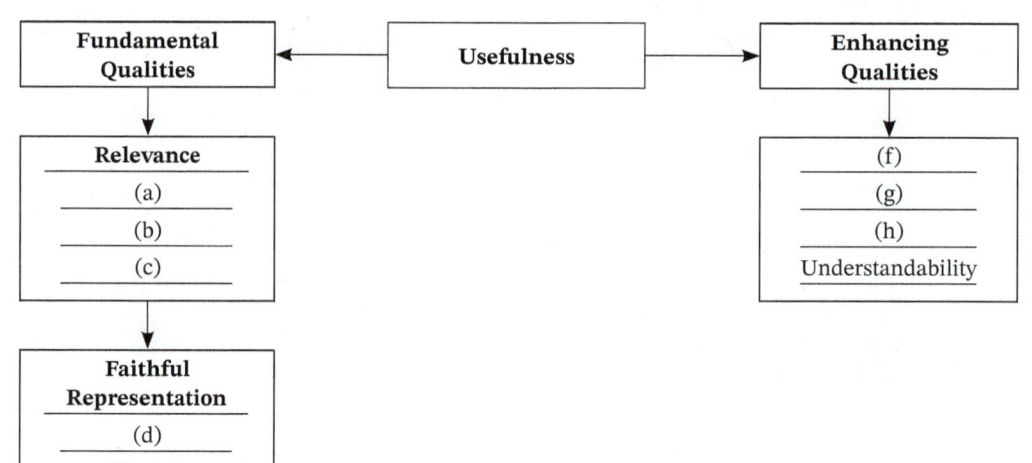

BE2.9 (LO 3), K Given the characteristics of useful accounting information, complete each of the following statements.

Identify characteristics of useful information.

a. For information to be _____, it should have predictive and confirmatory value.

b. _____ means that information accurately depicts what really happened.

c. _____ means using the same accounting principles and methods from year to year within a company.

BE2.10 (LO 3), K Here are some qualitative characteristics of useful accounting information:

Identify characteristics of useful information.

1. Predictive value   3. Verifiable
2. Neutral   4. Timely

Match each qualitative characteristic to one of the following statements.

_____ a. Accounting information should help provide accurate expectations about future events.

_____ b. Accounting information cannot be selected, prepared, or presented to favor one set of interested users over another.

_____ c. The quality of information that occurs when independent observers, using the same methods, obtain similar results.

_____ d. Accounting information must be available to decision-makers before it loses its capacity to influence their decisions.

BE2.11 (LO 3), K The full disclosure principle dictates that:

Define full disclosure principle.

a. financial statements should disclose all assets at their cost.

b. financial statements should disclose only those events that can be measured in dollars.

c. financial statements should disclose all events and circumstances that would matter to users of financial statements.

d. financial statements should not be relied on unless an auditor has expressed an unqualified opinion on them.

DO IT! Exercises

DO IT! 2.1a (LO 1), AP Mylar Corporation has collected the following information related to its December 31, 2022, balance sheet.

Prepare assets section of balance sheet.

Accounts receivable	$22,000	Equipment	$180,000
Accumulated depreciation—equipment	50,000	Inventory	58,000
Cash	13,000	Supplies	7,000
Stock investments (long-term)	1,900	Goodwill	4,100

Prepare the assets section of Mylar Corporation's balance sheet.

DO IT! 2.1b (LO 1), AP The following financial statement items were taken from the financial statements of Gomez Corp.

Classify financial statement items by balance sheet classification.

_____ Trademarks
_____ Notes payable (current)
_____ Interest revenue
_____ Income taxes payable
_____ Debt investments (long-term)
_____ Unearned sales revenue

_____ Inventory
_____ Accumulated depreciation
_____ Land
_____ Common stock
_____ Advertising expense
_____ Mortgage payable (due in 3 years)

Match each of the financial statement items to its proper balance sheet classification. (See E2.1 for a list of the balance sheet classifications.) If the item would not appear on a balance sheet, use "NA."

DO IT! 2.2 (LO 2), AP The following information is available for Nguoi Corporation.

Compute ratios and analyze.

	2022	2021
Current assets	$ 54,000	$ 36,000
Total assets	240,000	205,000
Current liabilities	22,000	30,000
Total liabilities	72,000	100,000
Net income	80,000	40,000
Net cash provided by operating activities	90,000	56,000
Preferred dividends	6,000	6,000
Common dividends	3,000	1,500

	2022	2021
Expenditures on property, plant, and equipment	$ 27,000	$ 12,000
Common shares outstanding at beginning of year	40,000	30,000
Common shares outstanding at end of year	75,000	40,000

a. Compute earnings per share for 2022 and 2021 for Nguoi, and comment on the change. Nguoi's primary competitor, Matisse Corporation, had earnings per share of $1 per share in 2022. Comment on the difference in the ratios of the two companies.

b. Compute the current ratio and debt to assets ratio for each year, and comment on the changes.

c. Compute free cash flow for each year, and comment on the changes.

Identify financial accounting concepts and principles.

DO IT! 2.3 (LO 3), K The following characteristics, assumptions, principles, and constraint guide the FASB when it creates accounting standards.

Relevance
Faithful representation
Comparability
Consistency
Monetary unit assumption
Economic entity assumption

Periodicity assumption
Going concern assumption
Historical cost principle
Full disclosure principle
Materiality
Cost constraint

Match each item above with a description below.

1. _____ Items not easily quantified in dollar terms are not reported in the financial statements.
2. _____ Accounting information must be complete, neutral, and free from error.
3. _____ Personal transactions are not mixed with the company's transactions.
4. _____ The cost to provide information should be weighed against the benefit that users will gain from having the information available.
5. _____ A company's use of the same accounting principles from year to year.
6. _____ Assets are recorded and reported at original purchase price.
7. _____ Accounting information should help users predict future events, and should confirm or correct prior expectations.
8. _____ The life of a business can be divided into artificial segments of time.
9. _____ The reporting of all information that would make a difference to financial statement users.
10. _____ The judgment concerning whether an item's size makes it likely to influence a decision-maker.
11. _____ Assumes a business will remain in operation for the foreseeable future.
12. _____ Different companies use the same accounting principles.

Exercises

Classify accounts on balance sheet.

E2.1 (LO 1), AP The following are the major balance sheet classifications.

Current assets (CA)
Long-term investments (LTI)
Property, plant, and equipment (PPE)
Intangible assets (IA)

Current liabilities (CL)
Long-term liabilities (LTL)
Stockholders' equity (SE)

Instructions

Classify each of the following financial statement items taken from Ming Corporation's balance sheet.

____ Accounts payable
____ Accounts receivable
____ Accumulated depreciation—equipment
____ Buildings
____ Cash
____ Interest payable
____ Goodwill

____ Income taxes payable
____ Inventory
____ Stock investments (to be sold in 7 months)
____ Land (in use)
____ Mortgage payable
____ Supplies
____ Equipment
____ Prepaid rent

E2.2 (LO 1), AP The major balance sheet classifications are listed in E2.1.

Classify financial statement items by balance sheet classification.

Instructions

Classify each of the following financial statement items based upon the major balance sheet classifications listed in E2.1.

___ Prepaid advertising
___ Equipment
___ Trademarks
___ Salaries and wages payable
___ Income taxes payable
___ Retained earnings
___ Accounts receivable
___ Land (held for future use)

___ Patents
___ Bonds payable
___ Common stock
___ Accumulated depreciation—equipment
___ Unearned sales revenue
___ Inventory

E2.3 (LO 1), AP Suppose the following items were taken from the December 31, 2022, assets section of the **Boeing Company** balance sheet. (All dollars are in millions.)

Classify items as current or noncurrent, and prepare assets section of balance sheet.

Inventory	$16,933	Patents	$12,528
Notes receivable—due after December 31, 2023	5,466	Buildings	21,579
		Cash	9,215
Notes receivable—due before December 31, 2023	368	Accounts receivable	5,785
		Debt investments (short-term)	2,008
Accumulated depreciation—buildings	12,795		

Instructions

Prepare the assets section of a classified balance sheet, listing the current assets in order of their liquidity.

E2.4 (LO 1), AP Suppose the following information (in thousands of dollars) is available for **H. J. Heinz Company**—famous for ketchup and other fine food products—at April 30, 2022.

Prepare assets section of a classified balance sheet.

 Excel

Prepaid insurance	$ 125,765	Buildings	$4,033,369
Land	76,193	Cash	373,145
Goodwill	3,982,954	Accounts receivable	1,171,797
Trademarks	757,907	Accumulated depreciation—buildings	2,131,260
Inventory	1,237,613		

Instructions

Prepare the assets section of a classified balance sheet, listing the items in proper sequence and including a statement heading.

E2.5 (LO 1), AP These items are taken from the financial statements of Longhorn Co. at December 31, 2022.

Prepare a classified balance sheet.

Buildings	$105,800
Accounts receivable	12,600
Prepaid insurance	3,200
Cash	11,840
Equipment	82,400
Land	61,200
Insurance expense	780
Depreciation expense	5,300
Interest expense	2,600
Common stock	60,000
Retained earnings (January 1, 2022)	40,000
Accumulated depreciation—buildings	45,600
Accounts payable	9,500
Notes payable	93,600
Accumulated depreciation—equipment	18,720
Interest payable	3,600
Service revenue	14,700

Instructions

Prepare a classified balance sheet. Assume that $13,600 of the note payable will be paid in 2023.

Prepare a classified balance sheet.

E2.6 (LO 1), AP The following items are taken from the financial statements of Carmen Co. at December 31, 2022.

Land	$195,600
Accounts receivable	21,700
Supplies	9,200
Cash	11,840
Equipment	82,400
Buildings	261,200
Land improvements	45,780
Notes receivable (due in 2023)	5,300
Accumulated depreciation—land improvements	12,600
Common stock	75,000
Retained earnings (December 31, 2022)	495,000
Accumulated depreciation—buildings	32,600
Accounts payable	9,500
Mortgage payable	93,600
Accumulated depreciation—equipment	18,720
Interest payable	3,600
Income taxes payable	14,700
Patents	46,700
Investments in stock (long-term)	71,500
Debt investments (short-term)	4,100

Instructions

Prepare a classified balance sheet. Assume that $9,100 of the mortgage payable will be paid in 2023.

Prepare a classified balance sheet.

E2.7 (LO 1), AP Suppose the following items were taken from the 2022 financial statements of Texas Instruments, Inc. (All dollars are in millions.)

Common stock	$2,826	Accumulated depreciation—equipment	$3,547
Prepaid rent	164	Accounts payable	1,459
Equipment	6,705	Patents	2,210
Stock investments (long-term)	637	Notes payable (long-term)	810
Debt investments (short-term)	1,743	Retained earnings	6,896
Income taxes payable	128	Accounts receivable	1,823
Cash	1,182	Inventory	1,202

Instructions

Prepare a classified balance sheet in good form as of December 31, 2022.

Compute and interpret profitability ratio.

E2.8 (LO 2), AP Suppose the following information is available for Callaway Golf Company for the years 2022 and 2021. (Dollars are in thousands, except share information.)

	2022	2021
Net sales	$ 1,117,204	$ 1,124,591
Net income (loss)	66,176	54,587
Total assets	855,338	838,078
Share information		
Common shares outstanding at year-end	64,507,000	66,282,000
Preferred dividends	–0–	–0–

There were 73,139,000 shares of common stock outstanding at the end of 2020.

Instructions

a. What was the company's earnings per share for each year?

b. Based on your findings above, how did the company's profitability change from 2021 to 2022?

c. Suppose the company had paid dividends on preferred stock and on common stock during the year. How would this affect your calculation in part (a)?

Prepare financial statements.

E2.9 (LO 1, 2), AP These financial statement items are for Fairview Corporation at year-end, July 31, 2022.

Salaries and wages payable	$ 2,080
Salaries and wages expense	57,500
Supplies expense	15,600
Equipment	18,500
Accounts payable	4,100
Service revenue	66,100

Rent revenue	$ 8,500
Notes payable (due in 2025)	1,800
Common stock	16,000
Cash	29,200
Accounts receivable	9,780
Accumulated depreciation—equipment	6,000
Dividends	4,000
Depreciation expense	4,000
Retained earnings (beginning of the year)	34,000

Instructions

a. Prepare an income statement and a retained earnings statement for the year. Fairview Corporation did not issue any new stock during the year.

b. Prepare a classified balance sheet at July 31.

c. Compute the current ratio and debt to assets ratio.

d. Suppose that you are the president of Lunar Equipment. Your sales manager has approached you with a proposal to sell $20,000 of equipment to Fairview. He would like to provide a loan to Fairview in the form of a 10%, 5-year note payable. Evaluate how this loan would change Fairview's current ratio and debt to assets ratio, and discuss whether you would make the sale.

E2.10 (LO 2), AP Nordstrom, Inc. operates department stores in numerous states. Selected financial statement data (in millions of dollars) for a recent year follow.

Compute liquidity ratios and compare results.

	End of Year	Beginning of Year
Cash and cash equivalents	$ 72	$ 358
Receivables (net)	1,942	1,788
Merchandise inventory	900	956
Other current assets	303	259
Total current assets	$3,217	$3,361
Total current liabilities	$1,601	$1,635

Instructions

a. Compute working capital and the current ratio at the beginning of the year and at the end of the year.

b. Did Nordstrom's liquidity improve or worsen during the year?

c. Using the data in the chapter, compare Nordstrom's liquidity with **Best Buy**'s.

E2.11 (LO 2), AP The chief financial officer (CFO) of Myeneke Corporation requested that the accounting department prepare a preliminary balance sheet on December 30, 2022, so that the CFO could get an idea of how the company stood. He knows that certain debt agreements with its creditors require the company to maintain a current ratio of at least 2:1. The preliminary balance sheet is as follows.

Compute liquidity measures and discuss findings.

Myeneke Corp.
Balance Sheet
December 30, 2022

Current assets			Current liabilities			
Cash	$25,000		Accounts payable	$ 20,000		
Accounts receivable	30,000		Salaries and wages payable	10,000		$ 30,000
Prepaid insurance	5,000	$ 60,000	Long-term liabilities			
Equipment (net)		200,000	Notes payable			80,000
Total assets		$260,000	Total liabilities			110,000
			Stockholders' equity			
			Common stock		100,000	
			Retained earnings		50,000	150,000
			Total liabilities and stockholders' equity			$260,000

Instructions

a. Calculate the current ratio and working capital based on the preliminary balance sheet.

b. Based on the results in (a), the CFO requested that $20,000 of cash be used to pay off the balance of the Accounts Payable account on December 31, 2022. Calculate the new current ratio and working capital after the company takes these actions.

c. Discuss the pros and cons of the current ratio and working capital as measures of liquidity.

d. Was it unethical for the CFO to take these steps?

Compute and interpret solvency ratios.

E2.12 (LO 2), AP Suppose the following data were taken from the 2022 and 2021 financial statements of **American Eagle Outfitters**. (All numbers, including share data, are in thousands.)

	2022	2021
Current assets	$ 925,359	$1,020,834
Total assets	1,963,676	1,867,680
Current liabilities	401,763	376,178
Total liabilities	554,645	527,216
Net income	179,061	400,019
Net cash provided by operating activities	302,193	464,270
Capital expenditures	265,335	250,407
Dividends paid on common stock	82,394	80,796
Weighted-average common shares outstanding	205,169	216,119

Instructions

Perform each of the following.

a. Calculate the current ratio for each year.

b. Calculate earnings per share for each year.

c. Calculate the debt to assets ratio for each year.

d. Calculate the free cash flow for each year.

e. Discuss American Eagle's solvency in 2022 versus 2021.

f. Discuss American Eagle's ability to finance its investment activities with net cash provided by operating activities, and how any deficiency would be met.

Identify accounting assumptions and principles.

E2.13 (LO 3), K Presented below are the assumptions and principles discussed in this chapter.

1. Full disclosure principle
2. Going concern assumption
3. Monetary unit assumption
4. Periodicity assumption
5. Historical cost principle
6. Economic entity assumption

Instructions

Identify by number the accounting assumption or principle that is described below. Do not use a number more than once.

_____ a. Belief that a company will remain in business for the foreseeable future. (*Note:* Do not use the historical cost principle.)

_____ b. Indicates that personal and business recordkeeping should be separately maintained.

_____ c. Only those things that can be expressed in money are included in the accounting records.

_____ d. Separates financial information into time periods for reporting purposes.

_____ e. Measurement basis used when a reliable estimate of fair value is not available.

_____ f. Dictates that companies should disclose all circumstances and events that make a difference to financial statement users.

Identify accounting terminology.

E2.14 (LO 1, 2, 3), K The following list of terms or phrases are discussed in this chapter.

1. Free cash flow
2. Securities and Exchange Commission (SEC)
3. Solvency
4. Financial Accounting Standards Board (FASB)
5. Materiality
6. Cost constraint
7. Faithful representation
8. Liquidity
9. Working capital
10. Operating cycle
11. Generally accepted accounting principles (GAAP)
12. Current liabilities
13. Relevance
14. Verifiable

Instructions

Match each term or phrase to its description below.

a. _____ Whether an item is large enough to likely influence the decision of an investor or creditor.

b. _____ Constraint that weighs the cost that companies will incur to provide the information against the benefit that financial statement users will gain from having the information available.

c. _____ Obligations that a company expects to pay within the next year or operating cycle, whichever is longer.

d. _____ Information that is complete, neutral, and free from error.

e. _____ The primary accounting standard-setting body in the United States.

f. _____ Net cash provided by operating activities after adjusting for capital expenditures and cash dividends paid.

g. _____ A set of accounting standards that has substantial authoritative support and which guide accounting professionals.

h. _____ The ability of a company to pay obligations that are expected to become due within the next year or operating cycle.

i. _____ The average time required to purchase inventory, sell it on account, and then collect cash from customers—that is, go from cash to cash.

j. _____ The quality of information that indicates the information makes a difference in a decision.

k. _____ The agency of the U.S. government that oversees U.S. financial markets and accounting standard-setting bodies.

l. _____ The quality of information that occurs when independent observers, using the same methods, obtain similar results.

m. _____ The difference between the amounts of current assets and current liabilities.

n. _____ The ability of a company to pay interest as it comes due and to repay the balance of a debt due at its maturity.

E2.15 (LO 3), C Lopez Co. had three major business transactions during 2022.

a. Reported at its fair value of $260,000 merchandise inventory with a cost of $208,000.

b. The president of Lopez Co., Victor Lopez, purchased a truck for personal use and charged it to his expense account.

c. Lopez Co. wanted to make its 2022 income look better, so it added 2 more weeks to its income statement reporting period (a 54-week year). Previous years were 52 weeks.

Identify the assumption or principle that has been violated.

Instructions

In each situation, identify the assumption or principle that has been violated, if any, and discuss what the company should have done.

Problems: Set A

P2.1A (LO 1), AP Suppose the following items are taken from the 2022 balance sheet of **Yahoo! Inc.** (All dollars are in millions.)

Prepare a classified balance sheet.

Goodwill	$3,927
Common stock	6,283
Equipment	1,737
Accounts payable	152
Patents	234
Stock investments (long-term)	3,247
Accounts receivable	1,061
Prepaid rent	233
Debt investments (short-term)	1,160
Retained earnings	6,108
Cash	2,292
Notes payable (long-term)	734
Unearned sales revenue	413
Accumulated depreciation—equipment	201

Tot. current assets	$4,746	
Tot. assets	$13,690	

Instructions

Prepare a classified balance sheet for Yahoo! Inc. as of December 31, 2022.

Prepare financial statements.

P2.2A (LO 1), AP These items are taken from the financial statements of Martin Corporation for 2022.

Retained earnings (beginning of year)	$31,000
Utilities expense	2,000
Equipment	66,000
Accounts payable	18,300
Cash	10,100
Salaries and wages payable	3,000
Common stock	22,800
Dividends	12,000
Supplies	3,100
Debt investment (long-term)	5,700
Trademarks	2,000
Service revenue	68,000
Prepaid insurance	3,500
Maintenance and repairs expense	1,800
Depreciation expense	3,600
Accounts receivable	11,700
Insurance expense	2,200
Salaries and wages expense	37,000
Accumulated depreciation—equipment	17,600

Instructions

Net income	$21,400
Tot. assets	$84,500

Prepare an income statement, a retained earnings statement, and a classified balance sheet as of December 31, 2022.

Prepare financial statements.

P2.3A (LO 1), AP You are provided with the following information for Lazuris Enterprises, effective as of its April 30, 2022, year-end.

Accounts payable	$ 834
Accounts receivable	810
Accumulated depreciation—equipment	670
Cash	1,270
Common stock	16,900
Cost of goods sold	1,060
Depreciation expense	335
Dividends	325
Equipment	2,420
Goodwill	1,800
Income tax expense	165
Income taxes payable	135
Insurance expense	210
Interest expense	400
Inventory	967
Investment in land	14,200
Land	3,100
Mortgage payable (long-term)	3,500
Notes payable (short-term)	61
Prepaid insurance	60
Retained earnings (beginning)	1,600
Salaries and wages expense	700
Salaries and wages payable	222
Sales revenue	5,100
Stock investments (short-term)	1,200

Instructions

a. Net income	$2,230	
b. Tot. current assets	$4,307	
Tot. assets	$25,157	

a. Prepare an income statement and a retained earnings statement for Lazuris Enterprises for the year ended April 30, 2022.

b. Prepare a classified balance sheet for Lazuris Enterprises as of April 30, 2022.

P2.4A (LO 2), AN Writing Comparative financial statement data for Loeb Corporation and Bowsh Corporation, two competitors, appear below. All balance sheet data are as of December 31, 2022.

Compute ratios; comment on relative profitability, liquidity, and solvency.

	Loeb Corporation 2022	Bowsh Corporation 2022
Net sales	$1,800,000	$620,000
Cost of goods sold	1,175,000	340,000
Operating expenses	283,000	98,000
Interest expense	9,000	3,800
Income tax expense	85,000	36,000
Current assets	407,200	190,336
Plant assets (net)	532,000	139,728
Current liabilities	66,325	33,716
Long-term liabilities	108,500	40,684
Net cash common by operating activities	138,000	36,000
Capital expenditures	90,000	20,000
Dividends paid on common stock	36,000	15,000
Weighted-average common shares outstanding	80,000	50,000

Instructions

a. Comment on the relative profitability of the companies by computing the net income and earnings per share for each company for 2022.

b. Comment on the relative liquidity of the companies by computing working capital and the current ratio for each company for 2022.

c. Comment on the relative solvency of the companies by computing the debt to assets ratio and the free cash flow for each company for 2022.

P2.5A (LO 2), AP Writing The following are financial statements of Ohara Company.

Compute and interpret liquidity, solvency, and profitability ratios.

Ohara Company
Income Statement
For the Year Ended December 31, 2022

Net sales	$2,218,500
Cost of goods sold	1,012,400
Selling and administrative expenses	906,000
Interest expense	78,000
Income tax expense	69,000
Net income	$ 153,100

Ohara Company
Balance Sheet
December 31, 2022

Assets

Current assets		
Cash	$ 60,100	
Debt investments	84,000	
Accounts receivable (net)	169,800	
Inventory	145,000	
Total current assets	458,900	
Plant assets (net)	575,300	
Total assets		$1,034,200

Liabilities and Stockholders' Equity

Current liabilities		
Accounts payable	$ 160,000	
Income taxes payable	35,500	
Total current liabilities	195,500	
Bonds payable	200,000	
Total liabilities	395,500	
Stockholders' equity		
Common stock	350,000	
Retained earnings	288,700	
Total stockholders' equity	638,700	
Total liabilities and stockholders' equity	$1,034,200	

Additional information: The net cash provided by operating activities for 2022 was $190,800. The cash used for capital expenditures was $92,000. The cash used for dividends was $31,000. The weighted-average common shares outstanding during the year was 50,000.

Instructions

a. Compute the following values and ratios for 2022. (We provide the results from 2021 for comparative purposes.)

   (i) Working capital. (2021: $160,500)
   (ii) Current ratio. (2021: 1.65:1)
   (iii) Free cash flow. (2021: $48,700)
   (iv) Debt to assets ratio. (2021: 31%)
   (v) Earnings per share. (2021: $3.15)

b. Using your calculations from part (a), discuss changes from 2021 in liquidity, solvency, and profitability.

Compute and interpret liquidity, solvency, and profitability ratios.

P2.6A (LO 2), AP Writing Condensed balance sheet and income statement data for Danke Corporation are presented as follows.

Danke Corporation
Balance Sheets
December 31

	2022	2021
Assets		
Cash	$ 28,000	$ 20,000
Receivables (net)	70,000	62,000
Other current assets	90,000	73,000
Long-term investments	62,000	60,000
Property, plant, and equipment (net)	510,000	470,000
Total assets	$760,000	$685,000
Liabilities and Stockholders' Equity		
Current liabilities	$ 75,000	$ 70,000
Long-term liabilities	80,000	90,000
Common stock	330,000	300,000
Retained earnings	275,000	225,000
Total liabilities and stockholders' equity	$760,000	$685,000

Danke Corporation
Income Statements
For the Years Ended December 31

	2022	2021
Sales revenue	$750,000	$680,000
Cost of goods sold	440,000	400,000
Operating expenses (including income taxes)	240,000	220,000
Net income	$ 70,000	$ 60,000

Additional information:

	2022	2021
Net cash provided by operating activities	$82,000	$56,000
Cash used for capital expenditures	$45,000	$38,000
Dividends paid	$20,000	$15,000
Weighted-average common shares outstanding	33,000	30,000

Instructions

Compute these values and ratios for 2021 and 2022.

a. Earnings per share.
b. Working capital.
c. Current ratio.
d. Debt to assets ratio.
e. Free cash flow.
f. Based on the ratios calculated, discuss briefly the improvement or lack thereof in financial position and operating results from 2021 to 2022 of Danke Corporation.

P2.7A (LO 2), AP Selected financial data of two competitors, **Target** and **Wal-Mart**, are presented here. (All dollars are in millions.) Suppose the data were taken from the 2022 financial statements of each company.

Compute ratios and compare liquidity and solvency for two companies.

	Target (1/31/22)	Wal-Mart (1/31/22)
	Income Statement Data for Year	
Net sales	$64,948	$401,244
Cost of goods sold	44,157	306,158
Selling and administrative expenses	16,389	76,651
Interest expense	894	2,103
Other income	28	4,213
Income taxes	1,322	7,145
Net income	$ 2,214	$ 13,400
	Balance Sheet Data (End of Year)	
Current assets	$17,488	$ 48,949
Noncurrent assets	26,618	114,480
Total assets	$44,106	$163,429
Current liabilities	$10,512	$ 55,390
Long-term liabilities	19,882	42,754
Total stockholders' equity	13,712	65,285
Total liabilities and stockholders' equity	$44,106	$163,429
Net cash provided by operating activities	$4,430	$23,147
Cash paid for capital expenditures	$3,547	$11,499
Dividends declared and paid on common stock	$465	$3,746
Weighted-average common shares outstanding (millions)	774	3,951

Instructions

For each company, compute these values and ratios.

a. Working capital.

b. Current ratio.

c. Debt to assets ratio.

d. Free cash flow.

e. Earnings per share.

f. Compare the liquidity and solvency of the two companies.

P2.8A (LO 3), E Writing A friend of yours, Saira Ortiz, recently completed an undergraduate degree in science and has just started working with a biotechnology company. Saira tells you that the owners of the business are trying to secure new sources of financing which are needed in order for the company to proceed with development of a new healthcare product. Saira said that her boss told her that the company must put together a report to present to potential investors.

Comment on the objectives and qualitative characteristics of financial reporting.

Saira thought that the company should include in this package the detailed scientific findings related to the Phase I clinical trials for this product. She said, "I know that the biotech industry sometimes has only a 10% success rate with new products, but if we report all the scientific findings, everyone will see what a sure success this is going to be! The president was talking about the importance of following some set of accounting principles. Why do we need to look at some accounting rules? What they need to realize is that we have scientific results that are quite encouraging, some of the most talented employees around, and the start of some really great customer relationships. We haven't made any sales yet, but we will. We just need the funds to get through all the clinical testing and get government approval for our product. Then these investors will be quite happy that they bought in to our company early!"

Instructions

a. What is accounting information? Explain to Saira what is meant by generally accepted accounting principles.

b. Comment on how Saira's suggestions for what should be reported to prospective investors conforms to the qualitative characteristics of accounting information. Do you think that the things that Saira wants to include in the information for investors will conform to financial reporting guidelines?

Continuing Case

© leungchopan/ Shutterstock

Cookie Creations

(*Note:* This is a continuation of the Cookie Creations case from Chapter 1.)

CC2 After investigating the different forms of business organization, Natalie Koebel decides to operate her business as a corporation, Cookie Creations Inc. She then begins the process of getting her business running.

Go to WileyPLUS for complete case details and instructions.

Expand Your Critical Thinking

Financial Reporting Problem: Apple Inc.

CT2.1 The financial statements of **Apple Inc.** are presented in Appendix A.

Instructions

Answer the following questions using the financial statements and the notes to the financial statements.

a. What were Apple's total current assets at September 30, 2017, and September 24, 2016?
b. Are the assets included in current assets listed in the proper order? Explain.
c. How are Apple's assets classified?
d. What were Apple's current liabilities at September 30, 2017, and September 24, 2016?

Comparative Analysis Problem: Columbia Sportswear Company vs. VF Corporation

CT2.2 The financial statements of **Columbia Sportswear Company** are presented in Appendix B. Financial statements of **VF Corporation** are presented in Appendix C. Assume Columbia's weighted-average common shares outstanding was 69,683,000, and VF's was 416,103,000.

Instructions

a. For each company, calculate the following values for 2016.
   1. Working capital.
   2. Current ratio.
   3. Debt to assets ratio.
   4. Free cash flow.

   (*Hint:* When calculating free cash flow, **do not** consider business acquisitions to be part of capital expenditures.)

b. Based on your findings above, discuss the relative liquidity and solvency of the two companies.

Comparative Analysis Problem: Amazon.com, Inc. vs. Wal-Mart Stores, Inc.

CT2.3 **Amazon.com, Inc.**'s financial statements are presented in Appendix D. Financial statements of **Wal-Mart Stores, Inc.** are presented in Appendix E.

Instructions

a. For each company, calculate the following values for the most recent year provided.
   1. Working capital.
   2. Current ratio.
   3. Debt to assets ratio.
   4. Free cash flow.

b. Based on your findings above, discuss the relative liquidity and solvency of the two companies.

Interpreting Financial Statements

CT2.4 Suppose the following information was reported by **Gap, Inc.**

	2022	2021	2020	2019	2018
Total assets (millions)	$7,065	$7,985	$7,564	$7,838	$8,544
Working capital	$1,831	$2,533	$1,847	$1,653	$2,757
Current ratio	1.87:1	2.19:1	1.86:1	1.68:1	2.21:1
Debt to assets ratio	.42:1	.39:1	.42:1	.45:1	.39:1
Earnings per share	$1.89	$1.59	$1.35	$1.05	$0.94

a. Determine the overall percentage decrease in Gap's total assets from 2018 to 2022. What was the average decrease per year?

b. Comment on the change in Gap's liquidity. Does working capital or the current ratio appear to provide a better indication of Gap's liquidity? What might explain the change in Gap's liquidity during this period?

c. Comment on the change in Gap's solvency during this period.

d. Comment on the change in Gap's profitability during this period. How might this affect your prediction about Gap's future profitability?

Real-World Focus

CT2.5 You can use the Internet to identify summary liquidity, solvency, and profitability information about companies, and compare this information across companies in the same industry.

Instructions

Select a well-known company and then go to the **Yahoo! Finance** website to locate information to answer the following questions.

a. What is the company's name? What was the company's current ratio and debt to equity ratio (a variation of the debt to assets ratio)?

b. What is the company's industry?

c. What is the name of a competitor? What is the competitor's current ratio and its debt to equity ratio?

d. Based on these measures, which company is more liquid? Which company is more solvent?

CT2.6 The Feature Story described the dramatic effect that investment bulletin boards are having on the investment world. This exercise will allow you to evaluate a bulletin board discussing a company of your choice.

Instructions

Go to the **Yahoo! Finance** website. Type in a company name (or use the index to find it) and then use the Conversations tab to answer the following questions.

a. State the nature of each of these messages (e.g., offering advice, criticizing company, predicting future results, ridiculing other people who have posted messages).

b. For those messages that expressed an opinion about the company, was evidence provided to support the opinion?

c. What effect do you think it would have on bulletin board discussions if the participants provided their actual names? Do you think this would be a good policy?

Decision-Making Across the Organization

CT2.7 As a financial analyst in the planning department for Erin Industries, Inc., you must develop ratios from the comparative financial statements. This information is to be used to convince creditors that, despite a slight decline in sales, Erin Industries, Inc. is liquid, solvent, and profitable, and that it deserves their continued support. Lenders are particularly concerned about the company's ability to continue as a going concern.

Here are the data requested and the computations developed from the financial statements:

	2022	2021
Current ratio	3.1	2.1
Working capital	Up 22%	Down 7%
Free cash flow	Up 25%	Up 18%
Debt to assets ratio	0.60	0.70
Net income	Up 32%	Down 8%
Earnings per share	$2.40	$1.15

Instructions

Erin Industries, Inc. asks you to prepare brief comments stating how each of these items supports the argument that its financial health is improving. The company wishes to use these comments to support presentation of data to its creditors. With the class divided into groups, prepare the comments as requested, giving the implications and the limitations of each item regarding Erin's financial well-being.

Communication Activity

CT2.8 B. P. Palmer is the chief executive officer of Future Products. Palmer is an expert engineer but a novice in accounting.

Instructions

Write a letter to B. P. Palmer that explains (a) the three main types of ratios; (b) examples of each, how they are calculated, and what they measure; and (c) the bases for comparison in analyzing Future Products' financial statements.

Ethics Case

CT2.9 At one time, **Boeing** closed a giant deal to acquire another manufacturer, **McDonnell Douglas**. Boeing paid for the acquisition by issuing shares of its own stock to the stockholders of McDonnell Douglas. In order for the deal not to be revoked, the value of Boeing's stock could not decline below a certain level for a number of months after the deal.

During the first half of the year, Boeing suffered significant cost overruns because of inefficiencies in its production methods. Had these problems been disclosed in the quarterly financial statements during the first and second quarters of the year, the company's stock most likely would have plummeted, and the deal would have been revoked. Company managers spent considerable time debating when the bad news should be disclosed. One public relations manager suggested that the company's problems be revealed on the date of either Princess Diana's or Mother Teresa's funeral, in the hope that it would be lost among those big stories that day. Instead, the company waited until October 22 of that year to announce a $2.6 billion write-off due to cost overruns. Within one week, the company's stock price had fallen 20%, but by this time the McDonnell Douglas deal could not be reversed.

Instructions

Answer the following questions.

a. Who are the stakeholders in this situation?
b. What are the ethical issues?
c. What assumptions or principles of accounting are relevant to this case?
d. Do you think it is ethical to try to "time" the release of a story so as to diminish its effect?
e. What would you have done if you were the chief executive officer of Boeing?
f. Boeing's top management maintains that it did not have an obligation to reveal its problems during the first half of the year. What implications does this have for investors and analysts who follow Boeing's stock?

All About You

CT2.10 Every company needs to plan in order to move forward. Its top management must consider where it wants the company to be in three to five years. Like a company, you need to think about where you want to be three to five years from now, and you need to start taking steps now in order to get there.

Instructions

Provide responses to each of the following items.

a. Where would you like to be working in three to five years? Describe your plan for getting there by identifying between five and 10 specific steps that you need to take in order to get there.
b. In order to get the job you want, you will need a résumé. Your résumé is the equivalent of a company's annual report. It needs to provide relevant information that is a faithful representation about your past accomplishments so that employers can decide whether to "invest" in you. Do a search on the Internet to find a good résumé format. What are the basic elements of a résumé?
c. A company's annual report provides information about a company's accomplishments. In order for investors to use the annual report, the information must provide a faithful representation. How can you assure that the information on your résumé provides a faithful representation about you and your accomplishments?

d. Prepare a résumé assuming that you have accomplished the five to 10 specific steps you identified in part (a). Also, provide evidence that would give assurance that the information is a faithful representation.

FASB Codification Activity

CT2.11 If your school has a subscription to the FASB Codification, log in and prepare responses to the following.

Instructions

a. Access the glossary ("Master Glossary") at the FASB Codification website to answer the following.
   1. What is the definition of current assets?
   2. What is the definition of current liabilities?
b. A company wants to offset its accounts payable against its cash account and show a cash amount net of accounts payable on its balance sheet. Identify the criteria (found in the FASB Codification) under which a company has the right of set off. Does the company have the right to offset accounts payable against the cash account?

Considering People, Planet, and Profit

CT2.12 Auditors provide a type of certification of corporate financial statements. Certification is used in many other aspects of business as well. For example, it plays a critical role in the sustainability movement. The February 7, 2012, issue of the *New York Times* contained an article by S. Amanda Caudill entitled "Better Lives in Better Coffee," which discusses the role of certification in the coffee business.

Instructions

Do an Internet search of "Better Lives in Better Coffee." Read the article and then answer the following questions.

a. The article mentions three different certification types that coffee growers can obtain from three different certification bodies. Using financial reporting as an example, what potential problems might the existence of multiple certification types present to coffee purchasers?
b. According to the author, which certification is most common among coffee growers? What are the possible reasons for this?
c. What social and environmental benefits are coffee certifications trying to achieve? Are there also potential financial benefits to the parties involved?

A Look at IFRS

LEARNING OBJECTIVE 4
Compare the classified balance sheet format under GAAP and IFRS.

The classified balance sheet, although generally required internationally, contains certain variations in format when reporting under IFRS.

Key Points

Following are the key similarities and differences between GAAP and IFRS related to the financial statements.

Similarities

- IFRS generally requires a classified statement of financial position similar to the classified balance sheet under GAAP.
- IFRS follows the same guidelines as this text for distinguishing between current and noncurrent assets and liabilities.

Differences

- IFRS recommends but does not require the use of the title "statement of financial position" rather than balance sheet.

- The format of statement of financial position information is often presented differently under IFRS. Although no specific format is required, many companies that follow IFRS present statement of financial position information in this order:
  - Non-current assets
  - Current assets
  - Equity
  - Non-current liabilities
  - Current liabilities
- Under IFRS, current assets are usually listed in the reverse order of liquidity. For example, under GAAP cash is listed first, but under IFRS it is listed last.
- IFRS has many differences in terminology from what are shown in your text. For example, in the following sample statement of financial position, notice in the investment category that stock is called shares.

Franklin Corporation
Statement of Financial Position
October 31, 2022

Assets

Intangible assets			
Patents			$ 3,100
Property, plant, and equipment			
Land		$10,000	
Equipment	$24,000		
Less: Accumulated depreciation	5,000	19,000	29,000
Long-term investments			
Share investments		5,200	
Investment in real estate		2,000	7,200
Current assets			
Prepaid insurance		400	
Supplies		2,100	
Inventory		3,000	
Notes receivable		1,000	
Accounts receivable		7,000	
Debt investments		2,000	
Cash		6,600	22,100
Total assets			$61,400

Equity and Liabilities

Equity			
Share capital		$20,050	
Retained earnings		14,000	$34,050
Non-current liabilities			
Mortgage payable		10,000	
Notes payable		1,300	11,300
Current liabilities			
Notes payable		11,000	
Accounts payable		2,100	
Salaries and wages payable		1,600	
Unearned service revenue		900	
Interest payable		450	16,050
Total equity and liabilities			$61,400

- Both GAAP and IFRS are increasing the use of fair value to report assets. However, at this point IFRS has adopted it more broadly. As examples, under IFRS companies can apply fair value to property, plant, and equipment, and in some cases intangible assets.

IFRS Practice

IFRS Self-Test Questions

1. A company has purchased a tract of land and expects to build a production plant on the land in approximately 5 years. During the 5 years before construction, the land will be idle. Under IFRS, the land should be reported as:
   a. land expense.
   b. property, plant, and equipment.
   c. an intangible asset.
   d. a long-term investment.

2. Current assets under IFRS are listed generally:
   a. by importance.
   b. in the reverse order of their expected conversion to cash.
   c. by longevity.
   d. alphabetically.

3. Companies that use IFRS:
   a. may report all their assets on the statement of financial position at fair value.
   b. may offset assets against liabilities and show net assets and net liabilities on their statements of financial position, rather than the underlying detailed line items.
   c. may report non-current assets before current assets on the statement of financial position.
   d. do not have any guidelines as to what should be reported on the statement of financial position.

4. Companies that follow IFRS to prepare a statement of financial position generally use the following order of classification:
   a. current assets, current liabilities, non-current assets, non-current liabilities, equity.
   b. non-current assets, non-current liabilities, current assets, current liabilities, equity.
   c. non-current assets, current assets, equity, non-current liabilities, current liabilities.
   d. equity, non-current assets, current assets, non-current liabilities, current liabilities.

IFRS Exercises

IFRS2.1 In what ways does the format of a statement of financial of position under IFRS often differ from a balance sheet presented under GAAP?

IFRS2.2 What term is commonly used under IFRS in reference to the balance sheet?

IFRS2.3 The statement of financial position for Sundell Company includes the following accounts (in British pounds): Accounts Receivable £12,500, Prepaid Insurance £3,600, Cash £15,400, Supplies £5,200, and Debt Investments (short-term) £6,700. Prepare the current assets section of the statement of financial position, listing the accounts in proper sequence.

IFRS2.4 The following information is available for Lessila Bowling Alley at December 31, 2022.

Buildings	$128,800	Share Capital	$100,000
Accounts Receivable	14,520	Retained Earnings (beginning)	15,000
Prepaid Insurance	4,680	Accumulated Depreciation—Buildings	42,600
Cash	18,040	Accounts Payable	12,300
Equipment	62,400	Notes Payable	97,780
Land	64,000	Accumulated Depreciation—Equipment	18,720
Insurance Expense	780	Interest Payable	2,600
Depreciation Expense	7,360	Bowling Revenues	14,180
Interest Expense	2,600		

Prepare a classified statement of financial position. Assume that $13,900 of the notes payable will be paid in 2023.

International Comparative Analysis Problem: Apple vs. Louis Vuitton

IFRS2.5 The financial statements of **Louis Vuitton** are presented in Appendix F. The complete annual report, including the notes to its financial statements, is available at the company's website.

Instructions

Identify five differences in the format of the statement of financial position used by Louis Vuitton compared to a company, such as **Apple**, that follows GAAP. (Apple's financial statements are available in Appendix A.)

Answers to IFRS Self-Test Questions

1. d **2.** b **3.** c **4.** c

CHAPTER 3

The Accounting Information System

Chapter Preview

As indicated in the Feature Story, a reliable information system is a necessity for any company. The purpose of this chapter is to explain and illustrate the features of an accounting information system.

Feature Story

Accidents Happen

How organized are you financially? Take a short quiz. Answer yes or no to each question:

- Does your wallet contain so many cash machine receipts that you've been declared a walking fire hazard?
- Do you wait until your debit card is denied before checking the status of your funds?
- Was Aaron Rodgers (the quarterback for the **Green Bay Packers**) playing high school football the last time you verified the accuracy of your bank account?

If you think it is hard to keep track of the many transactions that make up *your* life, imagine how difficult it is for a big corporation to do so. Not only that, but now consider how important it is for a big company to have good accounting records, especially if it has control of *your* life savings. **MF Global Holdings Ltd** was such a company. As a large investment broker, it held billions of dollars of investments for clients. If you had your life savings invested at MF Global, you might be slightly displeased if you heard this from one of its representatives: "You know, I kind of remember an account for someone with a name like yours—now what did we do with that?"

Unfortunately, that is almost exactly what happened to MF Global's clients shortly before it filed for bankruptcy. During the days immediately following the bankruptcy filing, regulators and auditors struggled to piece things together. In the words of one regulator, "Their books are a disaster . . . we're trying to figure out what numbers are real numbers." One company that considered buying an interest in MF Global walked away from the deal because it "couldn't get a sense of what was on the balance sheet." That company said the information that should have been instantly available instead took days to produce.

It now appears that MF Global did not properly segregate customer accounts from company accounts. And, because of its sloppy recordkeeping, customers were not protected when the company had financial troubles. Total customer losses were approximately $1 billion. As you can see, accounting matters!

Source: S. Patterson and A. Lucchetti, "Inside the Hunt for MF Global Cash," *Wall Street Journal Online* (November 11, 2011).

Chapter Outline

LEARNING OBJECTIVES

LO 1 Analyze the effect of business transactions on the basic accounting equation.	• Accounting transactions • Analyzing transactions • Summary of transactions	**DO IT! 1** Transaction Analysis
LO 2 Explain how accounts, debits, and credits are used to record business transactions.	• Debits and credits • Debit and credit procedures • Stockholders' equity relationships • Summary of debit/credit rules	**DO IT! 2** Debits and Credits for Balance Sheet Accounts
LO 3 Indicate how a journal is used in the recording process.	• The recording process • The journal	**DO IT! 3** Journal Entries
LO 4 Explain how a ledger and posting help in the recording process.	• The ledger • Chart of accounts • Posting • The recording process illustrated • Summary illustration	**DO IT! 4** Posting
LO 5 Prepare a trial balance.	• Limitations of a trial balance	**DO IT! 5** Trial Balance

Go to the Review and Practice section at the end of the chapter for a targeted summary and practice applications with solutions.
Visit WileyPLUS for additional tutorials and practice opportunities.

Using the Accounting Equation to Analyze Transactions

LEARNING OBJECTIVE 1
Analyze the effect of business transactions on the basic accounting equation.

Analyze business transactions → JOURNALIZE → POST → TRIAL BALANCE → ADJUSTING ENTRIES → ADJUSTED TRIAL BALANCE → FINANCIAL STATEMENTS → CLOSING ENTRIES → POST-CLOSING TRIAL BALANCE

The system of collecting and processing transaction data and communicating financial information to decision-makers is known as the **accounting information system**. Factors that shape an accounting information system include the nature of the company's business, the types of transactions, the size of the company, the volume of data, and the information demands of management and others.

This accounting cycle graphic illustrates the steps companies follow each period to record transactions and eventually prepare financial statements.

Most businesses use computerized accounting systems—sometimes referred to as electronic data processing (EDP) systems. These systems handle all the steps involved in the recording process, from initial data entry to preparation of the financial statements. In order to remain competitive, companies continually improve their accounting systems to provide accurate and timely data for decision-making. For example, in its annual report, **Tootsie Roll** at one time stated, "We also invested in additional processing and data storage hardware during the year. We view information technology as a key strategic tool, and are committed to deploying leading edge technology in this area." In addition, many companies upgraded their accounting information systems in response to the requirements of Sarbanes-Oxley.

Accounting information systems rely on a process referred to as **the accounting cycle**. As you can see from the graphic above, the accounting cycle begins with the analysis of business transactions and ends with the preparation of a post-closing trial balance. We explain the first four steps in this chapter.

In this chapter, in order to emphasize the underlying concepts and principles, we focus on a manual accounting system. The accounting concepts and principles do not change whether a system is computerized or manual.

Accounting Transactions

To use an accounting information system, you need to know which economic events to recognize (record). Not all events are recorded and reported in the financial statements. For example, suppose **General Motors** hired a new employee and purchased a new computer. Are these events entered in its accounting records? The first event would not be recorded, but the second event would. We call economic events that require recording in the financial statements **accounting transactions**.

An accounting transaction occurs when assets, liabilities, or stockholders' equity items change as a result of some economic event. The purchase of a computer by **General Motors**, the payment of rent by **Microsoft**, and the sale of a multi-day guided trip by Sierra Corporation are examples of events that change a company's assets, liabilities, or stockholders' equity. **Illustration 3.1** summarizes the decision process companies use to decide whether or not to record economic events.

ILLUSTRATION 3.1 Transaction identification process

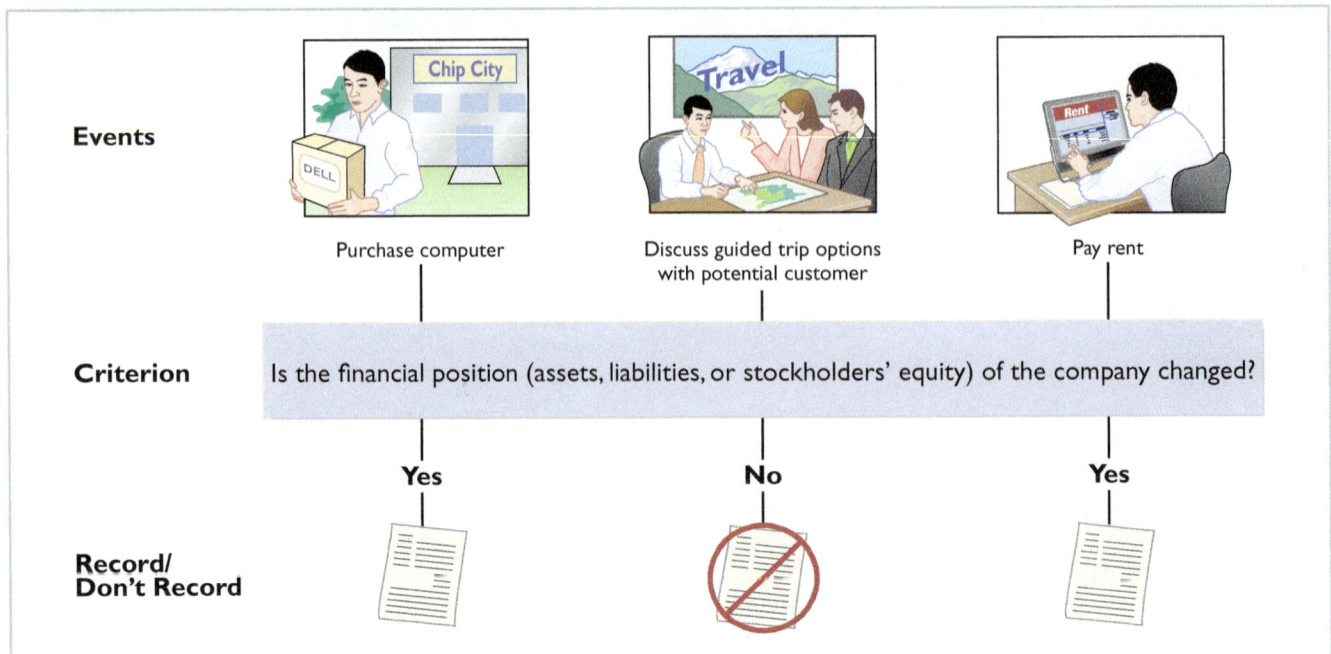

Analyzing Transactions

Recall the basic accounting equation:

> Assets = Liabilities + Stockholders' Equity

Decision Tools

The accounting equation is used to determine if an accounting transaction has occurred.

In this chapter, you will learn how to analyze transactions in terms of their effect on assets, liabilities, and stockholders' equity. **Transaction analysis** is the process of identifying the specific effects of economic events on the accounting equation (see **Decision Tools**).

The accounting equation must always balance. Each transaction has a dual (double-sided) effect on the equation. For example, if an individual asset is increased, there must be a corresponding:

- Decrease in another asset, *or*
- Increase in a specific liability, *or*
- Increase in stockholders' equity.

Two or more items could be affected when an asset is increased. For example, if a company purchases a computer for $10,000 by paying $6,000 in cash and signing a note for $4,000, one asset (equipment) increases $10,000, another asset (cash) decreases $6,000, and a liability (notes payable) increases $4,000. The result is that the accounting equation remains in balance—assets increased by a net $4,000 and liabilities increased by $4,000, as shown below.

Assets		=	Liabilities	+	Stockholders' Equity
Cash	+ Equipment	=	Notes Payable		
−$6,000	+$10,000		+$4,000		

Illustration 1.9 presented the financial statements for Sierra Corporation for its first month. You should review those financial statements at this time. To illustrate how economic events affect the accounting equation, we will examine events affecting Sierra during its first month.

In order to analyze the transactions for Sierra, we will expand the basic accounting equation. This allows us to better illustrate the impact of transactions on stockholders' equity. Recall that stockholders' equity is comprised of two parts: common stock and retained earnings. Common stock is affected when the company issues new shares of stock in exchange for cash. Retained earnings is increased when the company recognizes revenue, and decreased when the company incurs expenses or pays dividends. **Illustration 3.2** shows the expanded equation.

ILLUSTRATION 3.2 Expanded accounting equation

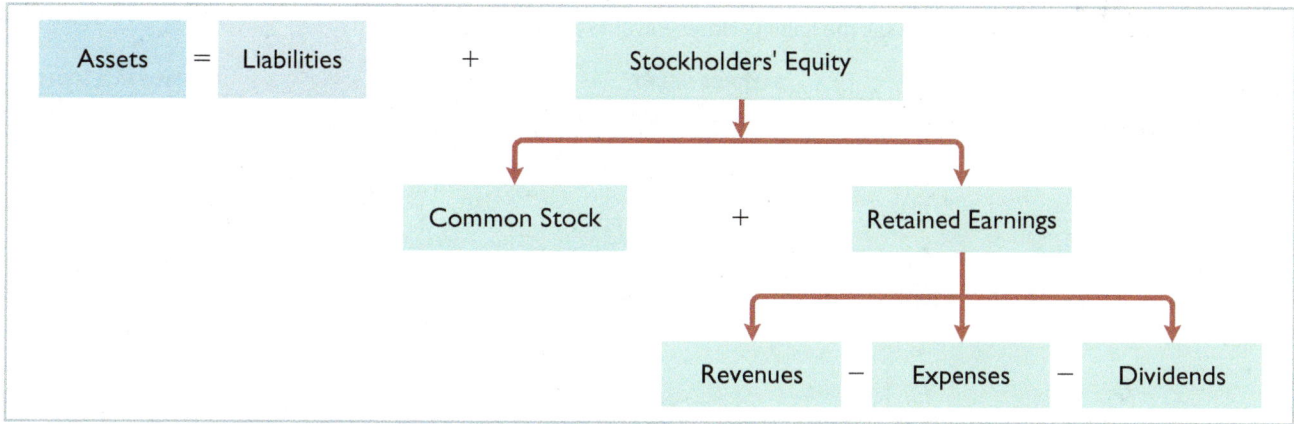

To demonstrate the effect that each transaction has on particular financial statements, we analyze each of Sierra's transactions using the tabular analysis shown in **Illustration 3.3**. Amounts that are reported on the balance sheet are shaded in yellow, income statement items in blue, and dividends (shown on the statement of retained earnings) in gray. Explanations for income statement items are reported in the blue section on the right-hand side. The green section on the left-hand side indicates whether cash flows increased, decreased, or were not affected.

ILLUSTRATION 3.3 Tabular analysis of transactions

CASH FLOW	BALANCE SHEET								INCOME STATEMENT
	Assets	=	Liabilities	+	Stockholders' Equity				
					Common Stock	+	Rev. − Exp.	− Div.	

Event (1). Investment of Cash by Stockholders
On October 1, cash of $10,000 is invested in the business by investors in exchange for $10,000 of common stock. This event is an accounting transaction that results in an increase in both assets and stockholders' equity.

Basic Analysis: The asset Cash is increased $10,000; stockholders' equity (specifically Common Stock) is increased $10,000.

CASH FLOW	BALANCE SHEET								INCOME STATEMENT
	Assets	=	Liabilities	+	Stockholders' Equity				
					Common Stock	+	Rev. − Exp.	− Div.	
↑ $10,000	(1) +$10,000	=			+$10,000				No effect

The equation is in balance after the issuance of common stock. Keeping track of the source of each change in stockholders' equity is essential for later accounting activities. In particular, items recorded in the revenue and expense columns are used for the calculation of net income.

Event (2). Note Issued in Exchange for Cash On October 1, Sierra borrowed $5,000 from Castle Bank by signing a 3-month, 12%, $5,000 note payable. This transaction results in an equal increase in assets and liabilities. The specific effect of this transaction and the cumulative effect of the first two transactions are as follows.

Basic Analysis: The asset Cash is increased $5,000; the liability Notes Payable is increased $5,000.

CASH FLOW		BALANCE SHEET						INCOME STATEMENT
		Assets = Liabilities +		Stockholders' Equity				
					Retained Earnings			
		Cash = Notes Payable +	Common Stock +	Rev. −	Exp. −	Div.		
↑ $5,000	(2)	$10,000 = +5,000 +$5,000	$10,000					No effect
		$15,000 = $5,000 +	$10,000					
			$15,000					

Total assets are now $15,000, and liabilities plus stockholders' equity also total $15,000.

Event (3). Purchase of Equipment for Cash On October 2, Sierra purchased equipment by paying $5,000 cash to Superior Equipment Sales Co. This transaction results in an equal increase and decrease in Sierra's assets.

Basic Analysis: The asset Equipment is increased $5,000; the asset Cash is decreased $5,000.

CASH FLOW		BALANCE SHEET						INCOME STATEMENT
		Assets	= Liabilities +	Stockholders' Equity				
					Retained Earnings			
		Cash + Equip-ment	= Notes Payable +	Common Stock +	Rev. − Exp. − Div.			
↓ $5,000	(3)	$15,000 −5,000 +$5,000	= $5,000 +	$10,000				No effect
		$10,000 + $5,000	= $5,000 +	$10,000				
		$15,000	$15,000					

The balance in total assets did not change; one asset account decreased by the same amount that another increased. The total assets are still $15,000, and liabilities plus stockholders' equity also still total $15,000.

Event (4). Receipt of Cash in Advance from Customer On October 2, Sierra received a $1,200 cash advance from R. Knox, a client. Sierra received cash (an asset) for guide services for multi-day trips that it expects to complete in the future. Although Sierra received cash, **it does not record revenue until it has performed the work**. In some industries, such as the magazine and airline industries, customers are expected to prepay. These companies have a liability to the customer until they deliver the magazines or provide the flight. When the company eventually provides the product or service, it records the revenue.

Since Sierra received cash prior to performance of the service, Sierra has a liability for the work due.

Basic Analysis: The asset Cash is increased $1,200; the liability Unearned Service Revenue is increased $1,200 because the service has not been performed yet. That is, when an advance payment is received, unearned revenue (a liability) should be recorded in order to recognize the obligation that exists.

CASH FLOW			BALANCE SHEET							INCOME STATEMENT
	Assets	=	Liabilities	+	Stockholders' Equity					
							Retained Earnings			
	Cash + Equipment =	Notes Pay. +	Unearned Serv. Rev. +	Common Stock +	Rev. −	Exp. −	Div.			
	$10,000 + $5,000 = $5,000			+ $10,000						
↑ $1,200	(4) +1,200		+$1,200							No effect
	$11,200 + $5,000 = $5,000 +	$1,200 +	$10,000							
	$16,200		$16,200							

Event (5). Services Performed for Cash On October 3, Sierra received $10,000 in cash (an asset) from Copa Company for guide services performed for a corporate event. Guide service is the principal revenue-producing activity of Sierra. **Revenue increases stockholders' equity.** This transaction, then, increases both assets and stockholders' equity.

Basic Analysis: The asset Cash is increased $10,000; the revenue account Service Revenue is increased $10,000.

CASH FLOW			BALANCE SHEET							INCOME STATEMENT
	Assets	=	Liabilities	+	Stockholders' Equity					
							Retained Earnings			
	Cash + Equipment =	Notes Pay. +	Unearned Serv. Rev. +	Common Stock +	Rev. −	Exp. −	Div.			
	$11,200 + $5,000 = $5,000 +	$1,200 +	$10,000							
↑ $10,000	(5) +10,000				+$10,000					Service Revenue
	$21,200 + $5,000 = $5,000 +	$1,200 +	$10,000 +	$10,000						
	$26,200		$26,200							

Often companies perform services "on account." That is, they perform services for which they are paid at a later date. Revenue, however, is recorded when services are performed. Therefore, revenues would increase when services are performed, even though cash has not been received. Instead of receiving cash, the company receives a different type of asset, an **account receivable**. Accounts receivable represent the right to receive payment at a later date. Suppose that Sierra had performed these services on account rather than for cash. This event would be reported using the accounting equation as follows.

Assets	=	Liabilities	+	Stockholders' Equity
Accounts Receivable =				Revenues
+$10,000				+$10,000 Service Revenue

Later, when Sierra collects the $10,000 from the customer, Accounts Receivable decreases by $10,000, and Cash increases by $10,000.

Assets		=	Liabilities	+	Stockholders' Equity
Cash +	Accounts Receivable				
+$10,000	−$10,000				

Note that in this case, revenues are not affected by the collection of cash. Instead Sierra records an exchange of one asset (Accounts Receivable) for a different asset (Cash).

Event (6). Payment of Rent On October 3, Sierra paid its office rent for the month of October in cash, $900 (see **Helpful Hint**). This rent payment is a transaction that results in a decrease in an asset, cash, as well as a decrease in stockholders' equity.

HELPFUL HINT

Note that a minus sign is placed in front of the $900 expense in the following analysis. Since expenses reduce stockholders' equity, we must enter expenses as negatives. This keeps the basic accounting equation in balance.

Rent is a cost incurred by Sierra in its effort to generate revenues. It is treated as an expense because it pertains only to the current month. **Expenses decrease stockholders' equity.** Sierra records the rent payment by decreasing cash and increasing expenses to maintain the balance of the accounting equation.

Basic Analysis: The expense account Rent Expense is increased $900 because the payment pertains only to the current month; the asset Cash is decreased $900.

CASH FLOW		BALANCE SHEET							INCOME STATEMENT
		Assets	=	Liabilities	+	Stockholders' Equity			
							Retained Earnings		
		Cash + Equipment	=	Notes Pay. + Unearned Serv. Rev.	+	Common Stock +	Rev. − Exp. − Div.		
		$21,200 + $5,000	=	$5,000 + $1,200	+	$10,000 +	$10,000		
↓ $900	(6)	−900					−$900		Rent Expense
		$20,300 + $5,000	=	$5,000 + $1,200	+	$10,000 +	$10,000 − $900		
		$25,300					$25,300		

Event (7). Purchase of Insurance Policy for Cash On October 4, Sierra paid $600 for a one-year insurance policy that will expire next year on September 30. Payments of expenses that will benefit more than one accounting period are identified as assets called prepaid expenses or prepayments.

Basic Analysis: The asset Cash is decreased $600; the asset Prepaid Insurance is increased $600.

CASH FLOW		BALANCE SHEET							INCOME STATEMENT
		Assets	=	Liabilities	+	Stockholders' Equity			
							Retained Earnings		
		Cash + Prepaid Insurance + Equipment	=	Notes Pay. + Unearned Serv. Rev.	+	Common Stock +	Rev. − Exp. − Div.		
		$20,300 + $5,000	=	$5,000 + $1,200	+	$10,000 +	$10,000 − $900		
↓ $600	(7)	−600 +$600							No effect
		$19,700 + $600 + $5,000	=	$5,000 + $1,200	+	$10,000 +	$10,000 − $900		
		$25,300					$25,300		

The balance in total assets did not change; one asset account decreased by the same amount that another increased.

Event (8). Purchase of Supplies on Account On October 5, Sierra purchased an estimated three months of supplies on account from Aero Supply for $2,500. In this case, "on account" means that the company receives goods or services that it will pay for at a later date. This transaction increases both an asset (supplies) and a liability (accounts payable).

Basic Analysis: The asset Supplies is increased $2,500; the liability Accounts Payable is increased $2,500.

CASH FLOW		BALANCE SHEET							INCOME STATEMENT
		Assets	=	Liabilities	+	Stockholders' Equity			
							Retained Earnings		
		Cash + Supplies + Prepd. Insur. + Equipment	=	Notes Pay. + Accounts Payable + Unearned Serv. Rev.	+	Common Stock +	Rev. − Exp. − Div.		
		$19,700 + $600 + $5,000	=	$5,000 + $1,200	+	$10,000 +	$10,000 − $900		
No effect	(8)	+$2,500		+$2,500					No effect
		$19,700 + $2,500 + $600 + $5,000	=	$5,000 + $2,500 + $1,200	+	$10,000 +	$10,000 − $900		
		$27,800					$27,800		

Event (9). Hiring of New Employees On October 9, Sierra hired four new employees to begin work on October 15. Each employee will receive a weekly salary of $500 for a five-day work week, payable every two weeks. Employees will receive their first paychecks on October 26.

On the date Sierra hires the employees, there is no effect on the accounting equation because the assets, liabilities, and stockholders' equity of the company have not changed.

Basic Analysis: An accounting transaction has not occurred. There is only an agreement that the employees will begin work on October 15. (See Event (11) for the first payment.)

Event (10). Payment of Dividend
On October 20, Sierra paid a $500 cash dividend (see Helpful Hint). **Dividends are a reduction of stockholders' equity but not an expense.** Dividends are not included in the calculation of net income. Instead, a dividend is a distribution of the company's assets to its stockholders, which is presented in the retained earnings statement.

> **HELPFUL HINT**
> Since dividends reduce stockholders' equity, we place a minus sign in front of the $500 dividend, as shown in the analysis below.

Basic Analysis: The Dividends account is increased $500; the asset Cash is decreased $500.

CASH FLOW		BALANCE SHEET																INCOME STATEMENT
		Assets					=	Liabilities			+	Stockholders' Equity						
														Retained Earnings				
		Cash +	Supplies +	Prepd. Insur. +	Equipment	=	Notes Pay. +	Accts. Pay. +	Unearned Serv. Rev. +		Common Stock +	Rev. −	Exp. −	Div.			
		$19,700 +	$2,500 +	$600 +	$5,000	=	$5,000 +	$2,500 +	$1,200	+	$10,000 +	$10,000 −	$900				
↓ $500	(10)	−500												−$500		No effect
		$19,200 +	$2,500 +	$600 +	$5,000	=	$5,000 +	$2,500 +	$1,200	+	$10,000 +	$10,000 −	$900 −	$500			
				$27,300								$27,300					

Event (11). Payment of Cash for Employee Salaries
Employees have worked two weeks, earning $4,000 in salaries, which were paid on October 26. Salaries and Wages Expense is an expense that reduces stockholders' equity. In this transaction, both assets and stockholders' equity are reduced.

Basic Analysis: The asset Cash is decreased $4,000; the expense account Salaries and Wages Expense is increased $4,000.

CASH FLOW		BALANCE SHEET																INCOME STATEMENT
		Assets					=	Liabilities			+	Stockholders' Equity						
														Retained Earnings				
		Cash +	Supplies +	Prepd. Insur. +	Equipment	=	Notes Pay. +	Accts. Pay. +	Unearned Serv. Rev. +		Common Stock +	Rev. −	Exp. −	Div.			
		$19,200 +	$2,500 +	$600 +	$5,000	=	$5,000 +	$2,500 +	$1,200	+	$10,000 +	$10,000 −	$900 −	$500			
↓ $4,000	(11)	−4,000												−4,000		Sal./Wages Expense
		$15,200 +	$2,500 +	$600 +	$5,000	=	$5,000 +	$2,500 +	$1,200	+	$10,000 +	$10,000 −	$4,900 −	$500			
				$23,300								$23,300					

Investor Insight

© Enviromatic/iStockphoto

Why Accuracy Matters

While most companies record transactions very carefully, the reality is that mistakes still happen. For example, bank regulators fined **Bank One Corporation** (now **JPMorgan Chase**) $1.8 million because they felt that the unreliability of the bank's accounting system caused it to violate regulatory requirements.

Also, in recent years **Fannie Mae**, the government-chartered mortgage association, announced a series of large accounting errors. These announcements caused alarm among investors, regulators, and politicians because they feared that the errors might suggest larger, undetected problems. This was important because the home-mortgage market depends on Fannie Mae to buy hundreds of billions of dollars of mortgages each year from banks, thus enabling the banks to issue new mortgages.

Finally, before a major overhaul of its accounting system, the financial records of **Waste Management Company** were in such disarray that of the company's 57,000 employees, 10,000 were receiving pay slips that were in error.

The Sarbanes-Oxley Act was created to minimize the occurrence of errors like these by increasing every employee's responsibility for accurate financial reporting.

In order for these companies to prepare and issue financial statements, their accounting equations must have been in balance at year-end. How could these errors or misstatements have occurred? (Go to WileyPLUS for this answer and additional questions.)

Summary of Transactions

Illustration 3.4 summarizes the transactions of Sierra Corporation to show their cumulative effect on the basic accounting equation. It includes the transaction number in the first column on the left. The right-most column shows the specific effect of any transaction that affects revenues or expenses. Remember that Event (9) did not result in a transaction, so nothing is recorded for that event. The illustration demonstrates three important points:

1. Each transaction is analyzed in terms of its effect on assets, liabilities, and stockholders' equity.
2. The two sides of the equation must always be equal.
3. The cause of each change in revenues or expenses must be indicated.

ILLUSTRATION 3.4 Summary of transactions

		Assets			=	Liabilities			+	Stockholders' Equity				INCOME STATEMENT
												Retained Earnings		
	Cash	Supplies	Prepd. Insur.	Equipment	=	Notes Pay.	Accts. Pay.	Unearned Serv. Rev.	+	Common Stock	Rev.	Exp.	Div.	
(1)	+$10,000									+$10,000				
(2)	+5,000					+$5,000								
(3)	−5,000			+$5,000										
(4)	+1,200							+$1,200						
(5)	+10,000										+$10,000			Service Revenue
(6)	−900											−$900		Rent Expense
(7)	−600		+$600											
(8)		+$2,500					+$2,500							
(9)														
(10)	−500												−$500	
(11)	−4,000											−4,000		Sal./Wages Expense
	$15,200	+ $2,500	+ $600	+ $5,000	=	$5,000	+ $2,500	+ $1,200	+	$10,000	+ $10,000	− $4,900	− $500	
		$23,300									$23,300			

ACTION PLAN

- Analyze the tabular analysis to determine the nature and effect of each transaction.
- Keep the accounting equation in balance.
- Remember that a change in an asset will require a change in another asset, a liability, or in stockholders' equity.

DO IT! 1 | Transaction Analysis

A tabular analysis of the transactions made by Roberta Mendez & Co., a certified public accounting firm, for the month of August is shown below. Each increase and decrease in stockholders' equity is explained.

	Assets		=	Liabilities	+	Stockholders' Equity			
				Accounts		Common	Retained Earnings		
	Cash	+ Equipment	=	Payable	+	Stock	+ Revenue	− Expenses	
1.	+$25,000					+$25,000			
2.		+$7,000		+$7,000					
3.	+8,000						+$8,000		Service Revenue
4.	−850							−$850	Rent Expense
	$32,150 +	$7,000	=	$7,000	+	$25,000 +	$8,000	− $850	
	$39,150					$39,150			

Describe each transaction that occurred for the month.

Solution

1. The company issued shares of stock to stockholders for $25,000 cash.
2. The company purchased $7,000 of equipment on account.
3. The company received $8,000 of cash in exchange for services performed.
4. The company paid $850 for this month's rent.

Related exercise material: **BE3.1, BE3.2, BE3.3, DO IT! 3.1, E3.1, E3.2, E3.3, and E3.4.**

Accounts, Debits, and Credits

LEARNING OBJECTIVE 2
Explain how accounts, debits, and credits are used to record business transactions.

Rather than using a tabular summary like the one in Illustration 3.4 for Sierra Corporation, an accounting information system uses accounts. An **account** is an individual accounting record of increases and decreases in a specific asset, liability, stockholders' equity, revenue, or expense item. For example, Sierra Corporation has separate accounts for Cash, Accounts Receivable, Accounts Payable, Service Revenue, Salaries and Wages Expense, and so on. (Note that whenever we are referring to a specific account, we capitalize the name.)

In its simplest form, an account consists of three parts: (1) the title of the account, (2) a left or debit side, and (3) a right or credit side. Because the alignment of these parts of an account resembles the letter T, it is referred to as a **T-account**. The basic form of an account is shown in **Illustration 3.5**.

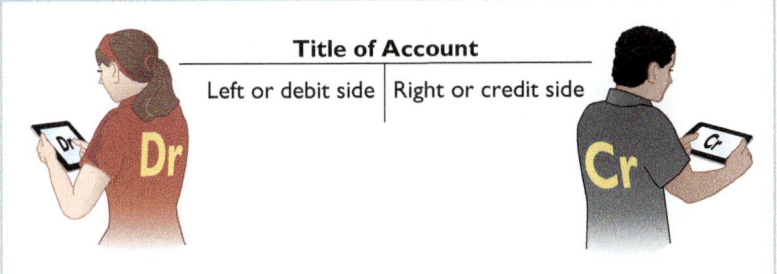

ILLUSTRATION 3.5

Basic form of account

We use this form of account often throughout this text to explain basic accounting relationships.

Debits and Credits

The term **debit** indicates the left side of an account, and **credit** indicates the right side. They are commonly abbreviated as **Dr.** for debit and **Cr.** for credit. They **do not** mean increase or decrease, as is commonly thought. We use the terms debit and credit repeatedly in the recording process to describe **where** entries are made in accounts. For example, the act of entering an amount on the left side of an account is called **debiting** the account. Making an entry on the right side is **crediting** the account.

When comparing the totals of the two sides, an account shows a **debit balance** if the total of the debit amounts exceeds the credits. An account shows a **credit balance** if the credit amounts exceed the debits. Note the position of the debit side and credit side in Illustration 3.5.

The procedure of recording debits and credits in an account is shown in **Illustration 3.6** for the transactions affecting the Cash account of Sierra Corporation. The data are taken from the Cash column of the tabular summary in Illustration 3.4.

ILLUSTRATION 3.6
Tabular summary and account form for Sierra Corporation's Cash account

Tabular Summary	Account Form
Cash	**Cash**
$10,000	(Debits) 10,000 (Credits) 5,000
5,000	5,000 900
−5,000	1,200 600
1,200	10,000 500
10,000	4,000
−900	
−600	Balance 15,200
−500	(Debit)
−4,000	
$15,200	

Every positive item in the tabular summary represents a receipt of cash; every negative amount represents a payment of cash. **Notice that in the account form, we record the increases in cash as debits and the decreases in cash as credits.** For example, the $10,000 receipt of cash (in blue) is debited to Cash, and the −$5,000 payment of cash (in red) is credited to Cash.

Having increases on one side and decreases on the other reduces recording errors and helps in determining the totals of each side of the account as well as the account balance. The balance is determined by netting the two sides (subtracting one amount from the other). The account balance, a debit of $15,200, indicates that Sierra had $15,200 more increases than decreases in cash. That is, since it started with a balance of zero, it has $15,200 in its Cash account.

Debit and Credit Procedures

International Note

Rules for accounting for specific events sometimes differ across countries. For example, European companies rely less on historical cost and more on fair value than U.S. companies. Despite the differences, the double-entry accounting system is the basis of accounting systems worldwide.

Each transaction must affect two or more accounts to keep the basic accounting equation in balance. In other words, **for each transaction, debits must equal credits**. The equality of debits and credits provides the basis for the double-entry accounting system (see **International Note**).

Under the **double-entry system**, the two-sided effect of each transaction is recorded in appropriate accounts. This system provides a logical method for recording transactions. The double-entry system also helps to ensure the accuracy of the recorded amounts and helps to detect errors such as those at **MF Global** as discussed in the Feature Story. If every transaction is recorded with equal debits and credits, then the sum of all the debits to the accounts must equal the sum of all the credits. The double-entry system for determining the equality of the accounting equation is much more efficient than the plus/minus procedure used earlier.

Dr./Cr. Procedures for Assets and Liabilities

In Illustration 3.6 for Sierra Corporation, increases in Cash—an asset—are entered on the left side, and decreases in Cash are entered on the right side. We know that both sides of the basic equation (Assets = Liabilities + Stockholders' Equity) must be equal. It therefore follows that increases and decreases in liabilities have to be recorded **opposite from** increases and decreases in assets. Thus, increases in liabilities are entered on the right or credit side, and decreases in liabilities are entered on the left or debit side. The effects that debits and credits have on assets and liabilities are summarized in **Illustration 3.7**.

Debits	Credits
Increase assets	Decrease assets
Decrease liabilities	Increase liabilities

ILLUSTRATION 3.7

Debit and credit effects–assets and liabilities

Asset accounts normally show debit balances. That is, debits to a specific asset account should exceed credits to that account. Likewise, **liability accounts normally show credit balances**. That is, credits to a liability account should exceed debits to that account. The **normal balances** may be diagrammed as in **Illustration 3.8**.

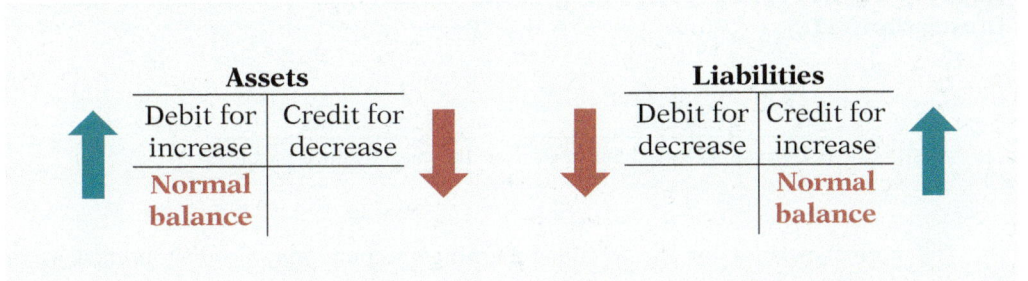

ILLUSTRATION 3.8

Normal balances–assets and liabilities

Knowing which is the normal balance in an account may help when you are trying to identify errors (see **Helpful Hint**). For example, a credit balance in an asset account, such as Land, or a debit balance in a liability account, such as Salaries and Wages Payable, usually indicates errors in recording. Occasionally, however, an abnormal balance may be correct. The Cash account, for example, will have a credit balance when a company has overdrawn its bank balance by spending more than it has in its account. In automated accounting systems, the computer is programmed to flag violations of the normal balance and to print out error or exception reports. In manual systems, careful visual inspection of the accounts is required to detect normal balance problems.

HELPFUL HINT

The normal balance is the side where increases in the account are recorded.

Dr./Cr. Procedures for Stockholders' Equity

Recall that stockholders' equity is comprised of two parts: common stock and retained earnings. In the transaction events earlier in this chapter, you saw that revenues, expenses, and the payment of dividends affect retained earnings. Therefore, the subdivisions of stockholders' equity are common stock, retained earnings, dividends, revenues, and expenses.

Common Stock Common stock is issued to investors in exchange for the stockholders' investment. The Common Stock account is increased by credits and decreased by debits. For example, when cash is invested in the business, Cash is debited and Common Stock is credited. The effects of debits and credits on the Common Stock account are shown in **Illustration 3.9**.

ILLUSTRATION 3.9
Debit and credit effects–common stock

Debits	Credits
Decrease Common Stock	Increase Common Stock

The normal balance in the Common Stock account may be diagrammed as in **Illustration 3.10**.

ILLUSTRATION 3.10
Normal balance–common stock

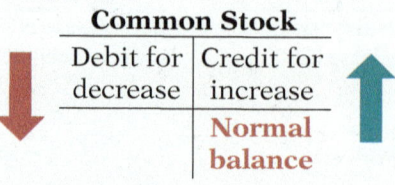

Retained Earnings Retained earnings is net income that is retained in the business. It represents the portion of stockholders' equity that has been accumulated through the profitable operation of the company. Retained Earnings is increased by credits (for example, by net income) and decreased by debits (for example, by a net loss), as shown in **Illustration 3.11**.

ILLUSTRATION 3.11
Debit and credit effects–retained earnings

Debits	Credits
Decrease Retained Earnings	Increase Retained Earnings

The normal balance for the Retained Earnings account may be diagrammed as in **Illustration 3.12**.

ILLUSTRATION 3.12
Normal balance–retained earnings

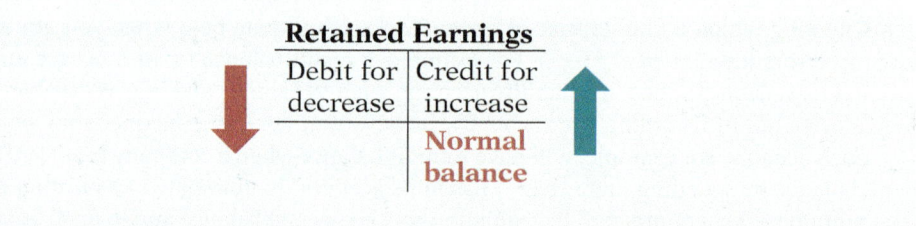

Dividends A dividend is a distribution by a corporation to its stockholders. The most common form of distribution is a cash dividend. Dividends result in a reduction of the stockholders' claims on retained earnings. Because dividends reduce stockholders' equity, increases in the Dividends account are recorded with debits. As shown in **Illustration 3.13**, the Dividends account normally has a debit balance.

ILLUSTRATION 3.13
Normal balance–dividends

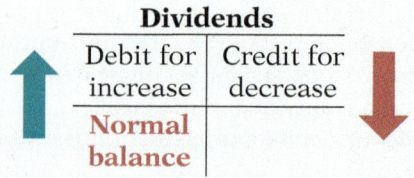

Revenues and Expenses When a company recognizes revenues, stockholders' equity is increased. Revenue accounts are increased by credits and decreased by debits.

Expenses decrease stockholders' equity. Thus, expense accounts are increased by debits and decreased by credits. The effects of debits and credits on revenues and expenses are shown in **Illustration 3.14**.

Debits	Credits
Decrease revenue	Increase revenue
Increase expenses	Decrease expenses

ILLUSTRATION 3.14
Debit and credit effects–revenues and expenses

Credits to revenue accounts should exceed debits; debits to expense accounts should exceed credits. Thus, **revenue accounts normally show credit balances, and expense accounts normally show debit balances**. The normal balances may be diagrammed as in **Illustration 3.15**.

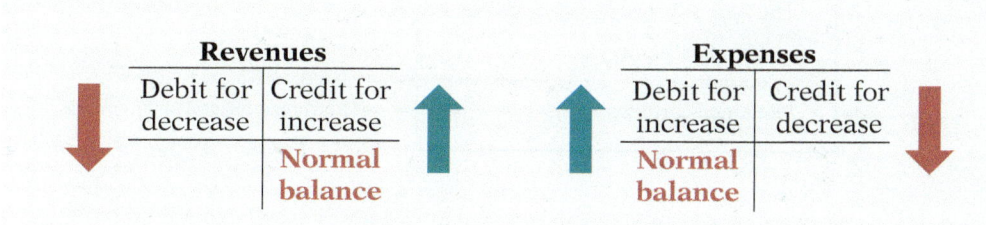

ILLUSTRATION 3.15
Normal balances–revenues and expenses

Investor Insight Chicago Cubs

© Jonathan Daniel/Getty Images, Inc.

Keeping Score

The **Chicago Cubs** baseball team has these major revenue and expense accounts:

Revenues	Expenses
Admissions (ticket sales)	Players' salaries
Concessions	Administrative salaries
Television and radio	Travel
Advertising	Ballpark maintenance

Do you think that the **Chicago Bears** football team would be likely to have the same major revenue and expense accounts as the Cubs? (Go to WileyPLUS for this answer and additional questions.)

Stockholders' Equity Relationships

Companies report the subdivisions of stockholders' equity in various places in the financial statements:

- Common stock and retained earnings: in the stockholders' equity section of the balance sheet.
- Dividends: on the retained earnings statement.
- Revenues and expenses: on the income statement.

Dividends, revenues, and expenses are eventually transferred to retained earnings at the end of the period. As a result, a change in any one of these three items affects stockholders' equity. **Illustration 3.16** shows the relationships of the accounts affecting stockholders' equity.

ILLUSTRATION 3.16
Stockholders' equity relationships

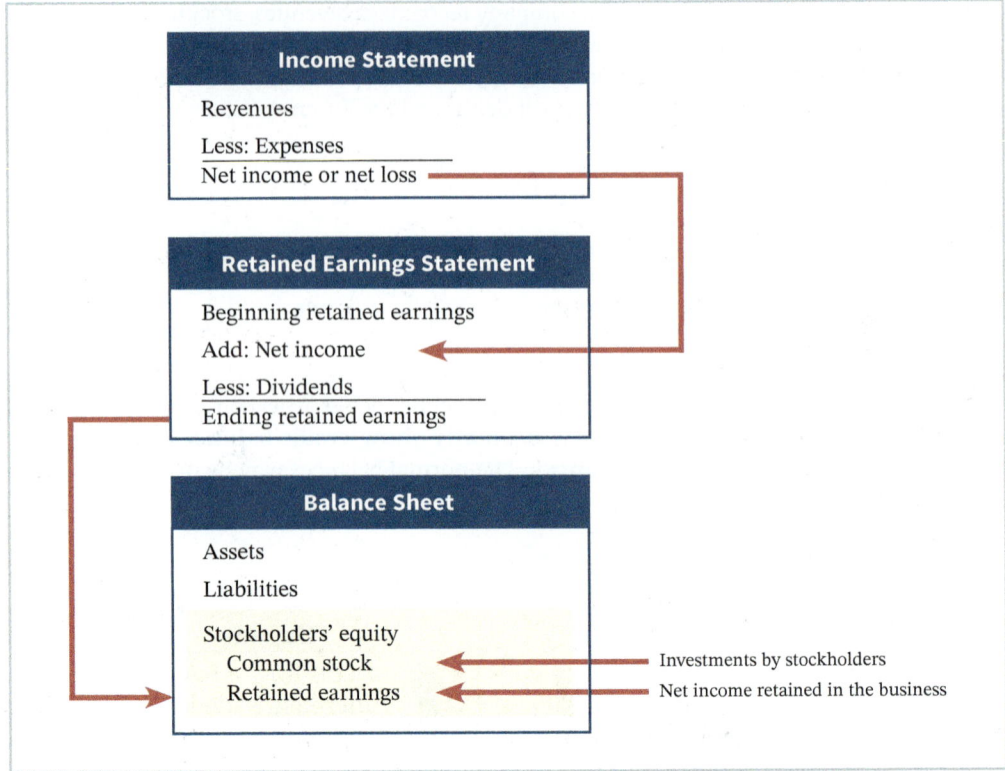

Summary of Debit/Credit Rules

Illustration 3.17 summarizes the debit/credit rules and effects on each type of account. **Study this diagram carefully.** It will help you understand the fundamentals of the double-entry system. No matter what the transaction, total debits must equal total credits in order to keep the accounting equation in balance.

ILLUSTRATION 3.17 Summary of debit/credit rules

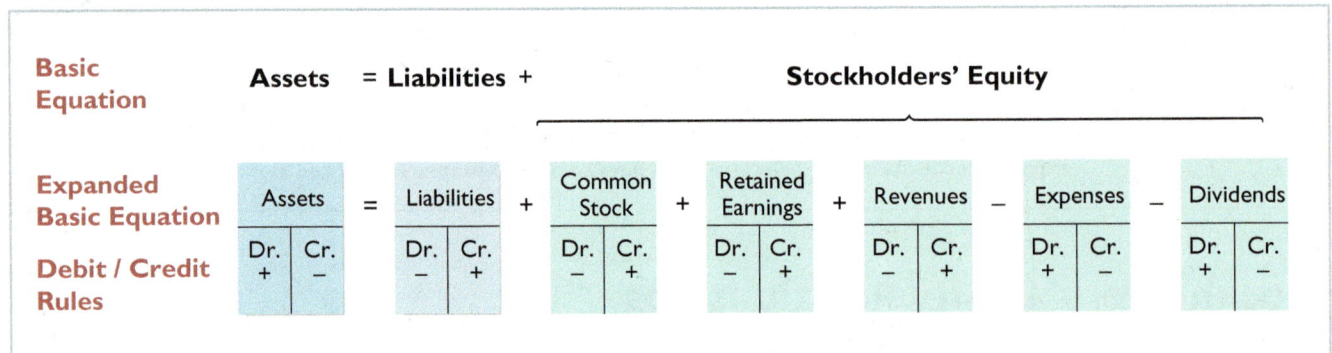

ACTION PLAN
- First identify asset accounts for each different type of asset invested in the business.
- Then identify liability accounts for debts incurred by the business.

DO IT! 2 | Debits and Credits for Balance Sheet Accounts

Kate Browne, president of Hair It Is Inc., has just rented space in a shopping mall for the purpose of opening and operating a beauty salon. Long before opening day and before purchasing equipment, hiring assistants, and remodeling the space, Kate was strongly advised to set up a double-entry set of accounting records in which to record all of her business transactions.

Identify the balance sheet accounts that Hair It Is Inc. will likely need to record the transactions necessary to establish and open for business. Also, indicate whether the normal balance of each account is a debit or a credit.

Solution

Hair It Is Inc. would likely need the following accounts in which to record the transactions necessary to establish and ready the beauty salon for opening day: Cash (debit balance); Equipment (debit balance); Supplies (debit balance); Accounts Payable (credit balance); Notes Payable (credit balance), if the business borrows money; and Common Stock (credit balance).

Related exercise material: **BE3.4, BE3.5, BE3.6, DO IT! 3.2, E3.6, E3.7, and E3.8.**

ACTION PLAN
- Hair It Is Inc. needs only one stockholders' equity account, Common Stock, when it begins the business. The other stockholders' equity account, Retained Earnings, will be needed after the business is operating.

Using a Journal

LEARNING OBJECTIVE 3
Indicate how a journal is used in the recording process.

ANALYZE → **Journalize the transactions** → POST → TRIAL BALANCE → ADJUSTING ENTRIES → ADJUSTED TRIAL BALANCE → FINANCIAL STATEMENTS → CLOSING ENTRIES → POST-CLOSING TRIAL BALANCE

The Recording Process

Although it is possible to enter transaction information directly into the accounts, few businesses do so. Practically every business uses these basic steps in the recording process (an integral part of the accounting cycle):

1. Analyze each transaction in terms of its effect on the accounts.
2. Enter the transaction information in a journal.
3. Transfer the journal information to the appropriate accounts in the ledger.

The actual sequence of events begins with the transaction. Evidence of the transaction comes in the form of a **source document**, such as a sales slip, a check, a bill, or a cash register document (see Ethics Note). This evidence is analyzed to determine the effect of the transaction on specific accounts. The transaction is then entered in the **journal**. Finally, the journal entry is transferred to the designated accounts in the **ledger**. The sequence of events in the recording process is shown in **Illustration 3.18**.

ETHICS NOTE

International Outsourcing Services, LLC was accused of submitting fraudulent documents (store coupons) to companies such as Kraft Foods and PepsiCo for reimbursement of as much as $250 million. Use of proper business documents reduces the likelihood of fraudulent activity.

ILLUSTRATION 3.18 The recording process

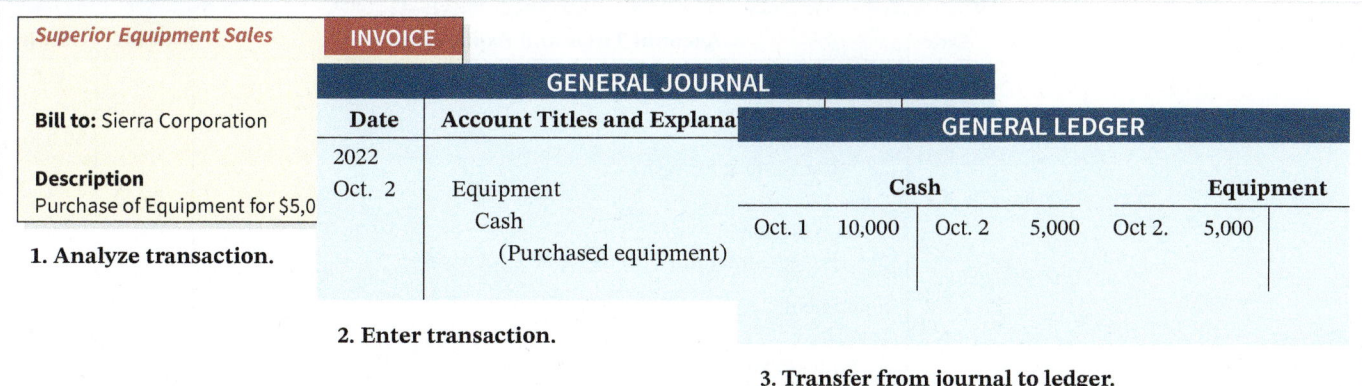

The Journal

Transactions are initially recorded in chronological order in a **journal** before they are transferred to the accounts. For each transaction, the journal shows the debit and credit effects on specific accounts. (In a computerized system, journals are kept as files, and accounts are recorded in computer databases.)

Companies may use various kinds of journals, but every company has at least the most basic form of journal, a **general journal**. **The journal makes three significant contributions to the recording process:**

1. It discloses in one place the **complete effect of a transaction**.
2. It provides a **chronological record** of transactions.
3. It **helps to prevent or locate errors** because the debit and credit amounts for each entry can be readily compared.

Entering transaction data in the journal is known as **journalizing**. To illustrate the technique of journalizing, let's look at the first three transactions of Sierra Corporation in equation form.

On October 1, Sierra issued common stock in exchange for $10,000 cash:

Assets	=	Liabilities	+	Stockholders' Equity	
Cash	=			Common Stock	
+$10,000				+$10,000	Issued stock

On October 1, Sierra borrowed $5,000 by signing a note:

Assets	=	Liabilities	+	Stockholders' Equity
Cash	=	Notes Payable		
+$5,000		+$5,000		

On October 2, Sierra purchased equipment for $5,000:

Assets			=	Liabilities	+	Stockholders' Equity
Cash	+	Equipment				
−$5,000		+$5,000				

Sierra makes separate journal entries for each transaction. A complete entry consists of (1) the date of the transaction, (2) the accounts and amounts to be debited and credited, and (3) a brief explanation of the transaction. These transactions are journalized in **Illustration 3.19**.

ILLUSTRATION 3.19
Recording transactions in journal form

	GENERAL JOURNAL		
Date	Account Titles and Explanation	Debit	Credit
2022			
Oct. 1	Cash	10,000	
	Common Stock		10,000
	(Issued stock for cash)		
1	Cash	5,000	
	Notes Payable		5,000
	(Issued 3-month, 12% note payable for cash)		
2	Equipment	5,000	
	Cash		5,000
	(Purchased equipment for cash)		

Note the following features of the journal entries.

1. The date of the transaction is entered in the Date column.
2. The account to be debited is entered first at the left. The account to be credited is then entered on the next line, indented under the line above. The indentation differentiates debits from credits and decreases the possibility of switching the debit and credit amounts.
3. The amounts for the debits are recorded in the Debit (left) column, and the amounts for the credits are recorded in the Credit (right) column.
4. A brief explanation of the transaction is given.

It is important to use correct and specific account titles in journalizing. Erroneous account titles lead to incorrect financial statements. Some flexibility exists initially in selecting account titles. The main criterion is that each title must appropriately describe the content of the account. For example, a company could use any of these account titles for recording the cost of delivery trucks: Equipment, Delivery Equipment, Delivery Trucks, or Trucks. Once the company chooses the specific title to use, however, it should record under that account title all subsequent transactions involving the account.

Accounting Across the Organization   Hain Celestial Group

It Starts with the Transaction

Keith Homan/ Shutterstock

Recording financial transactions in a company's records should be straightforward. If a company determines that a transaction involves revenue, it records revenue. If it has an expense, then it records an expense. However, sometimes this is difficult to do. For example, for more than a year, **Hain Celestial Group** (an organic food company) did not provide income information to investors and regulators. The reason was that the company discovered revenue irregularities and said it could not release financial results until it determined when and how to record revenue for certain transactions. When Hain missed four deadlines for reporting earnings information, the food company suffered a 34% drop in its stock price. As one analyst noted, it was hard to fathom why a seemingly simple revenue recognition issue took one year to resolve.

In other situations, outright fraud may occur. For example, regulators charged **Obsidian Energy** for fraudulently moving millions of dollars in expenses from operating expenses to capital expenditure accounts. By understating reported operating expenses, Obsidian made it appear that it was efficiently managing its costs as well as increasing its income.

These examples demonstrate that "getting the basic transaction right" is the foundation for relevant and reliable financial statements. Starting with an incorrect or inappropriate transaction leads to distortions in the financial statements.

Sources: Shawn Tully, "The Mystery of Hain Celestial's Accounting," *Fortune.com* (August 20, 2016); and Kelly Cryderman, "U.S. Charges Obsidian, Formerly Penn West, with Accounting Fraud," *The Globe and Mail* (June 28, 2017).

Why is it important for companies to record financial transactions completely and accurately? (Go to WileyPLUS for this answer and additional questions.)

DO IT! 3 | Journal Entries

The following events occurred during the first month of business of Hair It Is Inc., Kate Browne's beauty salon:

1. Issued common stock to shareholders in exchange for $20,000 cash.
2. Purchased $4,800 of equipment on account (to be paid in 30 days).
3. Interviewed three people for the position of stylist.

Prepare the entries to record the transactions.

ACTION PLAN
- Make sure to provide a complete and accurate representation of the transactions' effects on the assets, liabilities, and stockholders' equity of the business.

Solution

The three activities are recorded as follows.

1.	Cash	20,000	
	Common Stock		20,000
	(Issued stock for cash)		
2.	Equipment	4,800	
	Accounts Payable		4,800
	(Purchased equipment on account)		
3.	No entry because no transaction occurred.		

Related exercise material: **BE3.7, BE3.8, BE3.11, DO IT! 3.3, E3.7, E3.9, E3.10, E3.11, and E3.12.**

The Ledger and Posting

LEARNING OBJECTIVE 4
Explain how a ledger and posting help in the recording process.

ANALYZE → JOURNALIZE → **Post to ledger accounts** → TRIAL BALANCE → ADJUSTING ENTRIES → ADJUSTED TRIAL BALANCE → FINANCIAL STATEMENTS → CLOSING ENTRIES → POST-CLOSING TRIAL BALANCE

The Ledger

The record of all accounts maintained by a company and their amounts is referred to collectively as the **ledger**. The ledger provides the balance in each of the accounts as well as keeps track of changes in these balances.

Companies may use various kinds of ledgers, but every company has a general ledger. A **general ledger** contains all the asset, liability, stockholders' equity, revenue, and expense accounts, as shown in **Illustration 3.20**. Whenever we use the term **ledger** in this text without additional specification, it will mean the general ledger.

ILLUSTRATION 3.20
The general ledger

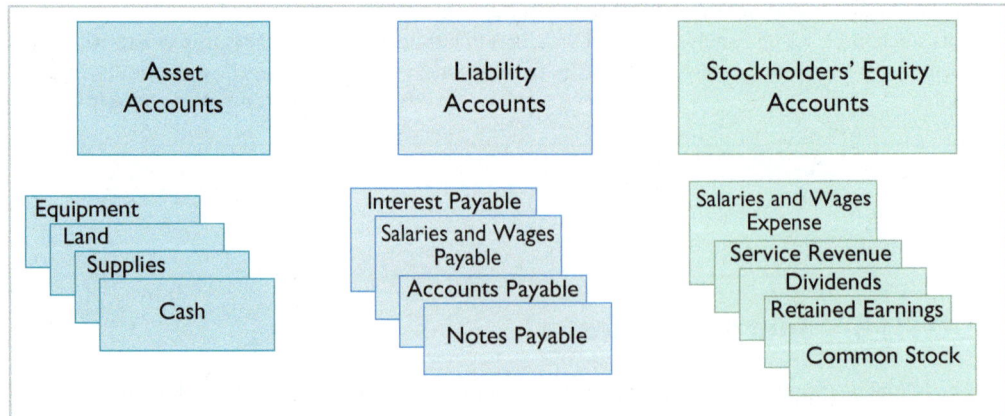

Chart of Accounts

The number and type of accounts used differ for each company, depending on the size, complexity, and type of business. For example, the number of accounts depends on the amount of detail desired by management. The management of one company may want one single account for all types of utility expense. Another may keep separate expense accounts for each type of utility expenditure, such as gas, electricity, and water. A small corporation like Sierra Corporation will not have many accounts compared with a corporate giant like **Ford Motor Company**. Sierra may be able to manage and report its activities in 20 to 30 accounts, whereas Ford requires thousands of accounts to keep track of its worldwide activities.

Most companies list the names of the accounts in a **chart of accounts**. They may create new accounts as needed during the life of the business. **Illustration 3.21** shows the chart of accounts for Sierra in the order that they are typically listed (assets, liabilities, stockholders' equity, revenues, and expenses). **Accounts shown in red are used in this chapter**; accounts shown in black are explained in later chapters.

ILLUSTRATION 3.21 Chart of accounts for Sierra Corporation

Sierra Corporation
Chart of Accounts

Assets	Liabilities	Stockholders' Equity	Revenues	Expenses
Cash	Notes Payable	Common Stock	Service Revenue	Salaries and Wages Expense
Accounts Receivable	Accounts Payable	Retained Earnings		Supplies Expense
Supplies	Interest Payable	Dividends		Rent Expense
Prepaid Insurance	Unearned Service Revenue	Income Summary		Insurance Expense
Equipment	Salaries and Wages Payable			Interest Expense
Accumulated Depreciation—Equipment				Depreciation Expense

Posting

The procedure of transferring journal entry amounts to ledger accounts is called **posting**. **This phase of the recording process accumulates the effects of journalized transactions in the individual accounts.** Posting involves these steps:

1. In the ledger, enter in the appropriate columns of the debited account(s) the date and debit amount shown in the journal.
2. In the ledger, enter in the appropriate columns of the credited account(s) the date and credit amount shown in the journal.

Ethics Insight   Credit Suisse Group

© Nuno Silva/iStockphoto

A Convenient Overstatement

Sometimes a company's investment securities suffer a permanent decline in value below their original cost. When this occurs, the company is supposed to reduce the recorded value of the securities on its balance sheet ("write them down" in common financial lingo) and record a loss. It appears, however, that during the financial crisis of 2008, employees at some financial institutions chose to look the other way as the value of their investments skidded.

A number of Wall Street traders that worked for the investment bank **Credit Suisse Group** were charged with intentionally overstating the value of securities that had suffered declines of approximately $2.85 billion. One reason that they might have been reluctant to record the losses was out of fear that the company's shareholders and clients would panic if they saw the magnitude of the losses. However, personal self-interest might have been equally to blame—the bonuses of the traders were tied to the value of the investment securities.

Source: S. Pulliam, J. Eaglesham, and M. Siconolfi, "U.S. Plans Changes on Bond Fraud," *Wall Street Journal Online* (February 1, 2012).

What incentives might employees have had to overstate the value of these investment securities on the company's financial statements? (Go to WileyPLUS for this answer and additional questions.)

The Recording Process Illustrated

Illustrations 3.22 through 3.32 show the basic steps in the recording process using the October transactions of Sierra Corporation. Sierra's accounting period is a month. A basic analysis and a debit–credit analysis precede the journalizing and posting of each transaction. Study these transaction analyses carefully. **The purpose of transaction analysis is first to identify the type of account involved and then to determine whether a debit or a credit to the account is required.** You should always perform this type of analysis before preparing a journal entry. Doing so will help you understand the journal entries discussed in this chapter as well as more complex journal entries to be described in later chapters.

ILLUSTRATION 3.22

Investment of cash by stockholders

Cash flow analyses show the impact of each transaction on cash.

Cash Flows
+10,000

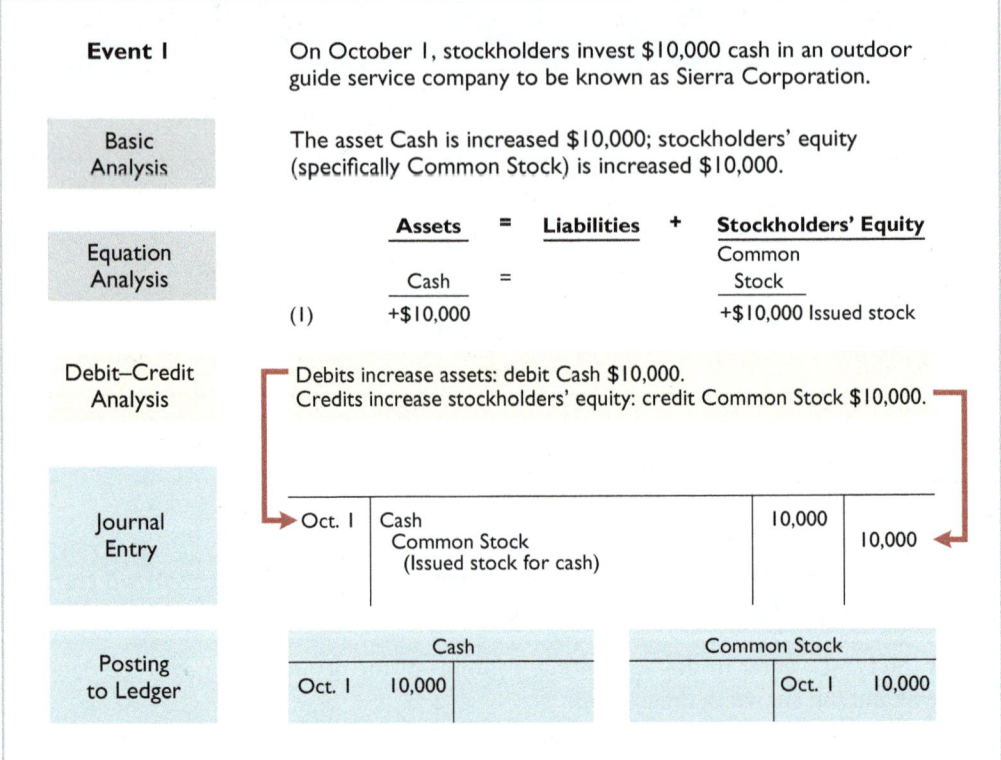

ILLUSTRATION 3.23
Issue of note payable

Event 2 — On October 1, Sierra borrows cash of $5,000 by signing a 3-month, 12%, $5,000 note payable.

Basic Analysis — The asset Cash is increased $5,000; the liability Notes Payable is increased $5,000.

Equation Analysis

	Assets	=	Liabilities	+	Stockholders' Equity
	Cash	=	Notes Payable		
(2)	+$5,000		+$5,000		

Debit–Credit Analysis
Debits increase assets: debit Cash $5,000.
Credits increase liabilities: credit Notes Payable $5,000.

Journal Entry

Oct. 1	Cash	5,000	
	Notes Payable		5,000
	(Issued 3-month, 12% note payable for cash)		

Posting to Ledger

Cash		Notes Payable	
Oct. 1 10,000			Oct. 1 5,000
1 5,000			

Cash Flows +5,000

ILLUSTRATION 3.24
Purchase of equipment

Event 3 — On October 2, Sierra used $5,000 cash to purchase equipment.

Basic Analysis — The asset Equipment is increased $5,000; the asset Cash is decreased $5,000.

Equation Analysis

	Assets			=	Liabilities	+	Stockholders' Equity
	Cash	+	Equipment				
(3)	−$5,000		+$5,000				

Debit–Credit Analysis
Debits increase assets: debit Equipment $5,000.
Credits decrease assets: credit Cash $5,000.

Journal Entry

Oct. 2	Equipment	5,000	
	Cash		5,000
	(Purchased equipment for cash)		

Posting to Ledger

Cash		Equipment	
Oct. 1 10,000	Oct. 2 5,000	Oct. 2 5,000	
1 5,000			

Cash Flows −5,000

ILLUSTRATION 3.25
Receipt of cash in advance from customer

Cash Flows
+1,200

HELPFUL HINT
Many liabilities have the word "payable" in their title. But, note that Unearned Service Revenue is considered a liability even though the word *payable* is not used.

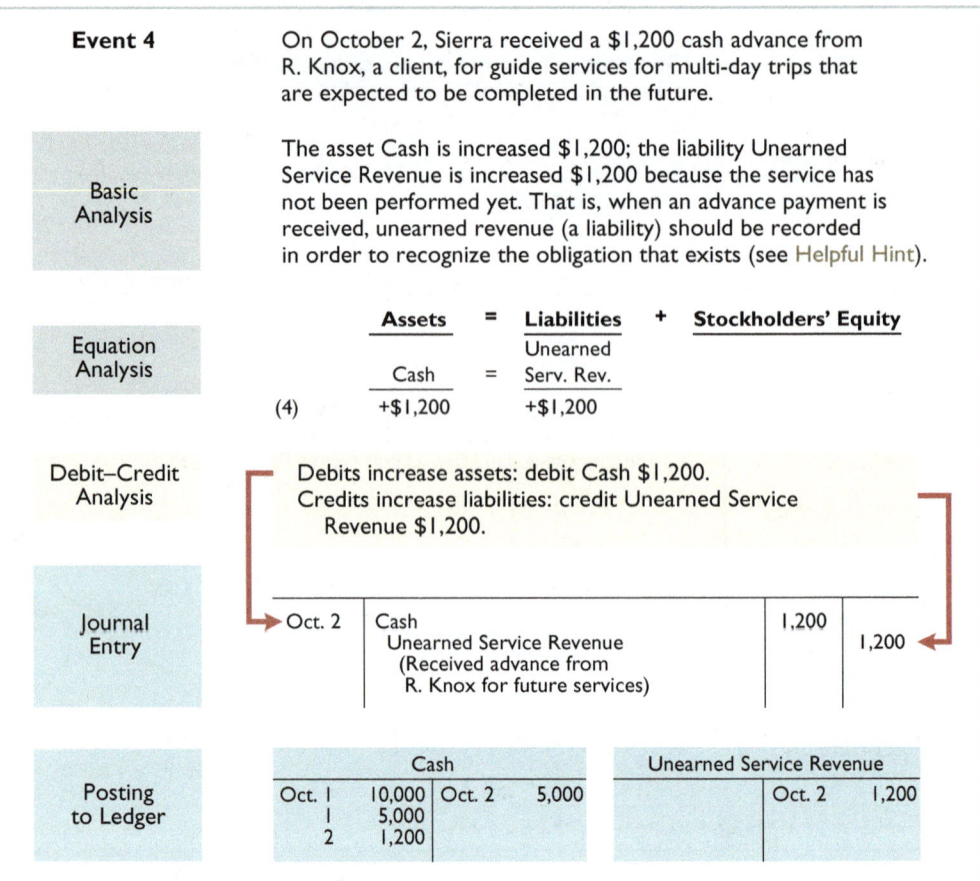

Event 4 — On October 2, Sierra received a $1,200 cash advance from R. Knox, a client, for guide services for multi-day trips that are expected to be completed in the future.

Basic Analysis — The asset Cash is increased $1,200; the liability Unearned Service Revenue is increased $1,200 because the service has not been performed yet. That is, when an advance payment is received, unearned revenue (a liability) should be recorded in order to recognize the obligation that exists (see Helpful Hint).

Equation Analysis

	Assets	=	Liabilities	+	Stockholders' Equity
	Cash	=	Unearned Serv. Rev.		
(4)	+$1,200		+$1,200		

Debit–Credit Analysis — Debits increase assets: debit Cash $1,200. Credits increase liabilities: credit Unearned Service Revenue $1,200.

Journal Entry

Oct. 2	Cash	1,200	
	Unearned Service Revenue		1,200
	(Received advance from R. Knox for future services)		

Posting to Ledger

Cash
Oct. 1	10,000	Oct. 2	5,000
1	5,000		
2	1,200		

Unearned Service Revenue
| | | Oct. 2 | 1,200 |

ILLUSTRATION 3.26
Services performed for cash

Cash Flows
+10,000

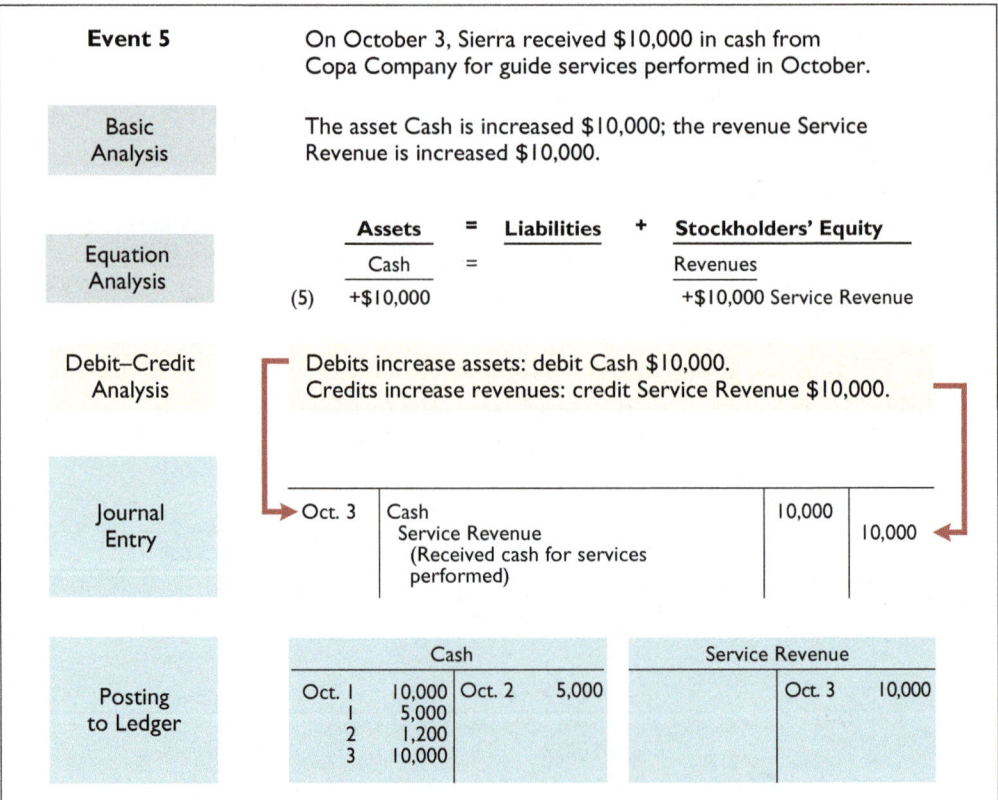

Event 5 — On October 3, Sierra received $10,000 in cash from Copa Company for guide services performed in October.

Basic Analysis — The asset Cash is increased $10,000; the revenue Service Revenue is increased $10,000.

Equation Analysis

	Assets	=	Liabilities	+	Stockholders' Equity
	Cash	=			Revenues
(5)	+$10,000				+$10,000 Service Revenue

Debit–Credit Analysis — Debits increase assets: debit Cash $10,000. Credits increase revenues: credit Service Revenue $10,000.

Journal Entry

Oct. 3	Cash	10,000	
	Service Revenue		10,000
	(Received cash for services performed)		

Posting to Ledger

Cash
Oct. 1	10,000	Oct. 2	5,000
1	5,000		
2	1,200		
3	10,000		

Service Revenue
| | | Oct. 3 | 10,000 |

Event 6	On October 3, Sierra paid office rent for October in cash, $900.	
Basic Analysis	The expense account Rent Expense is increased $900 because the payment pertains only to the current month; the asset Cash is decreased $900.	
Equation Analysis	Assets = Liabilities + Stockholders' Equity Cash = Expenses (6) −$900 −$900 Rent Expense	
Debit–Credit Analysis	Debits increase expenses: debit Rent Expense $900. Credits decrease assets: credit Cash $900.	

Journal Entry	Oct. 3 Rent Expense 900
	           Cash 900
	           (Paid cash for October office rent)	

Posting to Ledger	**Cash**
	Oct. 1 10,000 Oct. 2 5,000
	      1 5,000 3 900
	      2 1,200
	      3 10,000
		Rent Expense
		Oct. 3 900

ILLUSTRATION 3.27
Payment of rent with cash

Cash Flows
−900

Event 7	On October 4, Sierra paid $600 for a 1-year insurance policy that will expire next year on September 30.	
Basic Analysis	The asset Cash is decreased $600. Payments of expenses that will benefit more than one accounting period are identified as prepaid expenses or prepayments. When a payment is made, an asset account is debited in order to show the service or benefit that will be received in the future. Therefore, the asset Prepaid Insurance is increased $600.	
Equation Analysis	Assets = Liabilities + Stockholders' Equity Cash + Prepaid Insurance (7) −$600 +$600	
Debit–Credit Analysis	Debits increase assets: debit Prepaid Insurance $600. Credits decrease assets: credit Cash $600.	

Journal Entry	Oct. 4 Prepaid Insurance 600
	           Cash 600
	           (Paid 1-year policy; effective date October 1)	

Posting to Ledger	**Cash**
	Oct. 1 10,000 Oct. 2 5,000
	      1 5,000 3 900
	      2 1,200 4 600
	      3 10,000
		Prepaid Insurance
		Oct. 4 600

ILLUSTRATION 3.28
Purchase of insurance policy with cash

Cash Flows
−600

ILLUSTRATION 3.29
Purchase of supplies on account

Cash Flows
no effect

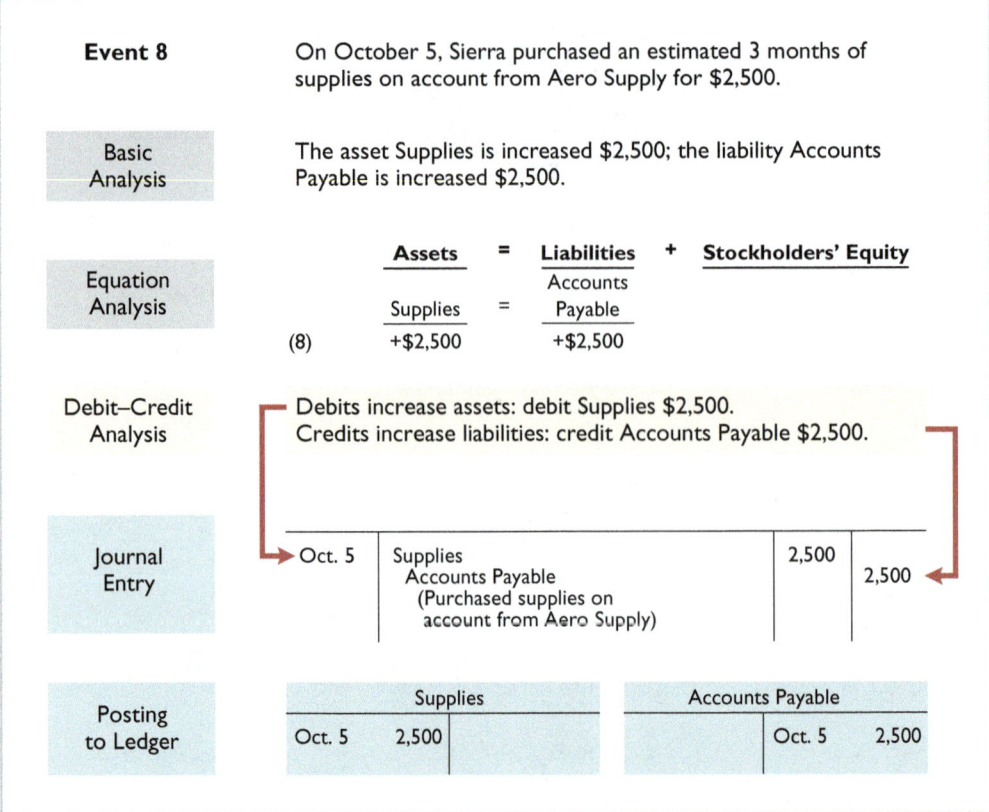

ILLUSTRATION 3.30
Hiring of new employees

Event 9 — On October 9, Sierra hired four employees to begin work on October 15. Each employee will receive a weekly salary of $500 for a 5-day work week, payable every 2 weeks—first payment made on October 26.

Basic Analysis — An accounting transaction has not occurred. There is only an agreement that the employees will begin work on October 15. Thus, a debit–credit analysis is not needed because there is no accounting entry. (See transaction of October 26 (Event 11) for first payment.)

Event 10

On October 20, Sierra paid a $500 cash dividend to stockholders.

Basic Analysis

The Dividends account is increased $500; the asset Cash is decreased $500.

Equation Analysis

Assets	=	Liabilities	+	Stockholders' Equity
Cash	=			Dividends
(10) −$500				−$500

Debit–Credit Analysis

Debits increase dividends: debit Dividends $500.
Credits decrease assets: credit Cash $500.

Journal Entry

Oct. 20	Dividends	500	
	Cash		500
	(Declared and paid a cash dividend)		

Posting to Ledger

Cash				Dividends	
Oct. 1	10,000	Oct. 2	5,000	Oct. 20	500
1	5,000	3	900		
2	1,200	4	600		
3	10,000	20	500		

ILLUSTRATION 3.31
Payment of dividend

Cash Flows
−500

Event 11

On October 26, Sierra paid employee salaries of $4,000 in cash. (See October 9 event.)

Basic Analysis

The expense account Salaries and Wages Expense is increased $4,000; the asset Cash is decreased $4,000.

Equation Analysis

Assets	=	Liabilities	+	Stockholders' Equity
Cash	=			Expenses
(11) −$4,000				−$4,000 Salaries and Wages Expense

Debit–Credit Analysis

Debits increase expenses: debit Salaries and Wages Expense $4,000.
Credits decrease assets: credit Cash $4,000.

Journal Entry

Oct. 26	Salaries and Wages Expense	4,000	
	Cash		4,000
	(Paid salaries to date)		

Posting to Ledger

Cash				Salaries and Wages Expense	
Oct. 1	10,000	Oct. 2	5,000	Oct. 26	4,000
1	5,000	3	900		
2	1,200	4	600		
3	10,000	20	500		
		26	4,000		

ILLUSTRATION 3.32
Payment of cash for employee salaries

Cash Flows
−4,000

Summary Illustration of Journalizing and Posting

The journal for Sierra Corporation for the month of October is summarized in **Illustration 3.33**. The ledger is shown in **Illustration 3.34** with all balances highlighted in red.

ILLUSTRATION 3.33
General journal for Sierra Corporation

		GENERAL JOURNAL		
Date		Account Titles and Explanation	Debit	Credit
2022 Oct. 1		Cash	10,000	
		Common Stock		10,000
		(Issued stock for cash)		
	1	Cash	5,000	
		Notes Payable		5,000
		(Issued 3-month, 12% note payable for cash)		
	2	Equipment	5,000	
		Cash		5,000
		(Purchased equipment for cash)		
	2	Cash	1,200	
		Unearned Service Revenue		1,200
		(Received advance from R. Knox for future service)		
	3	Cash	10,000	
		Service Revenue		10,000
		(Received cash for services performed)		
	3	Rent Expense	900	
		Cash		900
		(Paid cash for October office rent)		
	4	Prepaid Insurance	600	
		Cash		600
		(Paid 1-year policy; effective date October 1)		
	5	Supplies	2,500	
		Accounts Payable		2,500
		(Purchased supplies on account from Aero Supply)		
	20	Dividends	500	
		Cash		500
		(Declared and paid a cash dividend)		
	26	Salaries and Wages Expense	4,000	
		Cash		4,000
		(Paid salaries to date)		

ILLUSTRATION 3.34
General ledger for Sierra Corporation

GENERAL LEDGER

Cash			
Oct. 1	10,000	Oct. 2	5,000
1	5,000	3	900
2	1,200	4	600
3	10,000	20	500
		26	4,000
Bal.	**15,200**		

Supplies			
Oct. 5	2,500		
Bal.	**2,500**		

Prepaid Insurance			
Oct. 4	600		
Bal.	**600**		

Equipment			
Oct. 2	5,000		
Bal.	**5,000**		

Notes Payable			
		Oct. 1	5,000
		Bal.	**5,000**

Accounts Payable			
		Oct. 5	2,500
		Bal.	**2,500**

Unearned Service Revenue			
		Oct. 2	1,200
		Bal.	**1,200**

Common Stock			
		Oct. 1	10,000
		Bal.	**10,000**

Dividends			
Oct. 20	500		
Bal.	**500**		

Service Revenue			
		Oct. 3	10,000
		Bal.	**10,000**

Salaries and Wages Expense			
Oct. 26	4,000		
Bal.	**4,000**		

Rent Expense			
Oct. 3	900		
Bal.	**900**		

DO IT! 4 | Posting

Selected transactions from the journal of Faital Inc. during its first month of operations are presented below. Post these transactions to T-accounts.

Date	Account Titles	Debit	Credit
July 1	Cash	30,000	
	Common Stock		30,000
9	Accounts Receivable	6,000	
	Service Revenue		6,000
24	Cash	4,000	
	Accounts Receivable		4,000

Solution

Cash			
July 1	30,000		
24	4,000		

Accounts Receivable			
July 9	6,000	July 24	4,000

Common Stock			
		July 1	30,000

Service Revenue			
		July 9	6,000

Related exercise material: **BE3.12, DO IT! 3.4, and E3.15.**

ACTION PLAN
- Journalize transactions to keep track of financial activities (receipts, payments, receivables, payables, etc.).
- To make entries useful, classify and summarize them by posting the entries to specific ledger accounts.

The Trial Balance

LEARNING OBJECTIVE 5
Prepare a trial balance.

ANALYZE → JOURNALIZE → POST → **Prepare a trial balance** → ADJUSTING ENTRIES → ADJUSTED TRIAL BALANCE → FINANCIAL STATEMENTS → CLOSING ENTRIES → POST-CLOSING TRIAL BALANCE

> **Decision Tools**
> A trial balance proves that debits equal credits.

A **trial balance** lists accounts and their balances at a given time. A company usually prepares a trial balance at the end of an accounting period. The accounts are listed in the order in which they appear in the ledger. Debit balances are listed in the left column and credit balances in the right column. The totals of the two columns must be equal (see **Decision Tools**).

The trial balance proves the mathematical equality of debits and credits after posting. Under the double-entry system, this equality occurs when the sum of the debit account balances equals the sum of the credit account balances. **A trial balance may also uncover errors in journalizing and posting.** For example, a trial balance may well have detected the error at **MF Global** discussed in the Feature Story. **In addition, a trial balance is useful in the preparation of financial statements.**

These are the procedures for preparing a trial balance:

1. List the account titles and their balances.
2. Total the debit column and total the credit column.
3. Verify the equality of the two columns.

Illustration 3.35 presents the trial balance prepared from the ledger of Sierra Corporation (see **Helpful Hint**). Note that the total debits, $28,700, equal the total credits, $28,700.

ILLUSTRATION 3.35
Sierra Corporation trial balance

> **HELPFUL HINT**
> Note that the order of presentation in the trial balance is:
> Assets
> Liabilities
> Stockholders' equity
> Revenues
> Expenses

Sierra Corporation
Trial Balance
October 31, 2022

	Debit	Credit
Cash	$15,200	
Supplies	2,500	
Prepaid Insurance	600	
Equipment	5,000	
Notes Payable		$ 5,000
Accounts Payable		2,500
Unearned Service Revenue		1,200
Common Stock		10,000
Dividends	500	
Service Revenue		10,000
Salaries and Wages Expense	4,000	
Rent Expense	900	
	$28,700	$28,700

Limitations of a Trial Balance

A trial balance does not prove that all transactions have been recorded or that the ledger is correct. Numerous errors may exist even though the trial balance column totals agree (see **Ethics Note**). For example, the trial balance may balance even when any of the following occurs: (1) a transaction is not journalized, (2) a correct journal entry is not posted, (3) a journal entry is posted twice, (4) incorrect accounts are used in journalizing or posting, or (5) offsetting errors are made in recording the amount of a transaction. In other words, as long as equal debits and credits are posted, even to the wrong account or in the wrong amount, the total debits will equal the total credits. Nevertheless, despite these limitations, the trial balance is a useful screen for finding errors and is frequently used in practice.

> **ETHICS NOTE**
>
> An error is the result of an unintentional mistake. It is neither ethical nor unethical. An irregularity is an intentional misstatement, which is viewed as unethical.

Keeping an Eye on Cash

The Cash account shown below reflects all of the inflows and outflows of cash that occurred during October for Sierra Corporation (see Illustrations 3.22 to 3.32). We have also provided a description of each transaction that affected the Cash account.

1. Oct. 1 Issued stock for $10,000 cash.
2. Oct. 1 Issued note payable for $5,000 cash.
3. Oct. 2 Purchased equipment for $5,000 cash.
4. Oct. 2 Received $1,200 cash in advance from customer.
5. Oct. 3 Received $10,000 cash for services performed.
6. Oct. 3 Paid $900 cash for October rent.
7. Oct. 4 Paid $600 cash for one-year insurance policy.
8. Oct. 20 Paid $500 cash dividend to stockholders.
9. Oct. 26 Paid $4,000 cash salaries.

The Cash account and the related cash transactions indicate why cash changed during October. However, to make this information useful for analysis, it is summarized in a statement of cash flows. The statement of cash flows classifies each transaction as an operating activity, an investing activity, or a financing activity. A user of this statement can then determine the amount of net cash provided by operating activities, the amount of cash used for investing purposes, and the amount of cash provided by financing activities.

Cash

Oct. 1	10,000	Oct. 2	5,000
1	5,000	3	900
2	1,200	4	600
3	10,000	20	500
		26	4,000
Bal.	**15,200**		

Operating activities are the types of activities the company performs to generate profits. Sierra is an outdoor guide business, so its operating activities involve providing guide services. Activities 4, 5, 6, 7, and 9 relate to cash received or spent to directly support its guide services.

Investing activities include the purchase or sale of long-lived assets used in operating the business, or the purchase or sale of investment securities (stocks and bonds of companies other than Sierra). Activity 3, the purchase of equipment, is an investing activity.

The primary types of **financing activities** are borrowing money, issuing shares of stock, and paying dividends. The financing activities of Sierra are Activities 1, 2, and 8.

DO IT! 5 | Trial Balance

The following accounts come from the ledger of SnowGo Corporation at December 31, 2022.

Equipment	$88,000	Common Stock	$20,000
Dividends	8,000	Salaries and Wages Payable	2,000
Accounts Payable	22,000	Notes Payable (due in 3 months)	19,000
Salaries and Wages Expense	42,000	Utilities Expense	3,000
Accounts Receivable	4,000	Prepaid Insurance	6,000
Service Revenue	95,000	Cash	7,000

Prepare a trial balance in good form.

ACTION PLAN
- Determine normal balances and list accounts in the order they appear in the ledger.
- Accounts with debit balances appear in the left column, and those with credit balances in the right column.

ACTION PLAN
- Total the debit and credit columns to prove equality.

Solution

Snowgo Corporation
Trial Balance
December 31, 2022

	Debit	Credit
Cash	$ 7,000	
Accounts Receivable	4,000	
Prepaid Insurance	6,000	
Equipment	88,000	
Notes Payable		$ 19,000
Accounts Payable		22,000
Salaries and Wages Payable		2,000
Common Stock		20,000
Dividends	8,000	
Service Revenue		95,000
Utilities Expense	3,000	
Salaries and Wages Expense	42,000	
	$158,000	$158,000

Related exercise material: **BE3.13, BE3.14, DO IT! 3.5, E3.14, E3.16, E3.17, E3.18, E3.19, E3.20, and E3.21.**

USING THE DECISION TOOLS | Kansas Farmers' Vertically Integrated Cooperative, Inc.

The **Kansas Farmers' Vertically Integrated Cooperative, Inc. (K-VIC)** was formed by over 200 northeast Kansas farmers in the late 1980s. Its purpose is to process raw materials, primarily grain and meat products grown by K-VIC's members, into end-user food products and then to distribute the products nationally. Profits not needed for expansion or investment are returned to the members annually, on a pro rata basis, according to the fair value of the grain and meat products received from each farmer.

Assume that the following trial balance was prepared for K-VIC.

Kansas Farmers' Vertically Integrated Cooperative, Inc.
Trial Balance
December 31, 2022
(in thousands)

	Debit	Credit
Accounts Receivable	$ 712,000	
Accounts Payable		$ 673,000
Buildings	365,000	
Cash	32,000	
Cost of Goods Sold	2,384,000	
Notes Payable (due in 2023)		12,000
Inventory	1,291,000	
Land	110,000	
Mortgage Payable		873,000
Equipment	63,000	
Retained Earnings		822,000
Sales Revenue		3,741,000
Salaries and Wages Payable		62,000
Salaries and Wages Expense	651,000	
Maintenance and Repairs Expense	500,000	
	$6,108,000	$6,183,000

Because the trial balance is not in balance, you have checked with various people responsible for entering accounting data and have discovered the following.

1. The purchase of 35 new trucks, costing $7 million and paid for with cash, was not recorded.
2. A data entry clerk accidentally deleted the account name for an account with a credit balance of $472 million, so the amount was added to the Mortgage Payable account in the trial balance.
3. December cash sales revenue of $75 million was credited to the Sales Revenue account, but the other half of the entry was not made.
4. $50 million of salaries expense were mistakenly charged to Maintenance and Repairs Expense.

Instructions

Answer these questions.

a. Which mistake(s) have caused the trial balance to be out of balance?
b. Should all of the items be corrected? Explain.
c. What is the name of the account the data entry clerk deleted?
d. Make the necessary corrections and prepare a correct trial balance with accounts listed in proper order.
e. On your trial balance, write BAL beside the accounts that go on the balance sheet and INC beside those that go on the income statement.

Solution

a. Only mistake #3 has caused the trial balance to be out of balance.
b. All of the items should be corrected. The misclassification error (mistake #4) on the salaries expense would not affect bottom-line net income, but it does affect the amounts reported in the two expense accounts.
c. There is no Common Stock account, so that must be the account that was deleted by the data entry clerk.
d. and e.

Kansas Farmers' Vertically Integrated Cooperative, Inc.
Trial Balance
December 31, 2022
(in thousands)

	Debit	Credit	
Cash ($32,000 − $7,000 + $75,000)	$ 100,000		BAL
Accounts Receivable	712,000		BAL
Inventory	1,291,000		BAL
Land	110,000		BAL
Buildings	365,000		BAL
Equipment ($63,000 + $7,000)	70,000		BAL
Accounts Payable		$ 673,000	BAL
Salaries and Wages Payable		62,000	BAL
Notes Payable (due in 2023)		12,000	BAL
Mortgage Payable ($873,000 − $472,000)		401,000	BAL
Common Stock		472,000	BAL
Retained Earnings		822,000	BAL
Sales Revenue		3,741,000	INC
Cost of Goods Sold	2,384,000		INC
Salaries and Wages Expense ($651,000 + $50,000)	701,000		INC
Maintenance and Repairs Expense ($500,000 − $50,000)	450,000		INC
	$6,183,000	$6,183,000	

Review and Practice

Learning Objective Review

1 Analyze the effect of business transactions on the basic accounting equation.

Each business transaction must have a dual effect on the accounting equation. For example, if an individual asset is increased, there must be a corresponding (a) decrease in another asset, or (b) increase in a specific liability, or (c) increase in stockholders' equity.

2 Explain how accounts, debits, and credits are used to record business transactions.

An account is an individual accounting record of increases and decreases in specific asset, liability, and stockholders' equity items.

The terms debit and credit are synonymous with left and right. Assets, dividends, and expenses are increased by debits and decreased by credits. Liabilities, common stock, retained earnings, and revenues are increased by credits and decreased by debits.

3 Indicate how a journal is used in the recording process.

The basic steps in the recording process are (a) analyze each transaction in terms of its effect on the accounts, (b) enter the transaction information in a journal, and (c) transfer the journal information to the appropriate accounts in the ledger.

The initial accounting record of a transaction is entered in a journal before the data are entered in the accounts. A journal (a) discloses in one place the complete effect of a transaction, (b) provides a chronological record of transactions, and (c) prevents or locates errors because the debit and credit amounts for each entry can be readily compared.

4 Explain how a ledger and posting help in the recording process.

The entire group of accounts maintained by a company is referred to collectively as a ledger. The ledger provides the balance in each of the accounts as well as keeps track of changes in these balances.

Posting is the procedure of transferring journal entries to the ledger accounts. This phase of the recording process accumulates the effects of journalized transactions in the individual accounts.

5 Prepare a trial balance.

A trial balance is a list of accounts and their balances at a given time. The primary purpose of the trial balance is to prove the mathematical equality of debits and credits after posting. A trial balance also uncovers errors in journalizing and posting and is useful in preparing financial statements.

Decision Tools Review

Decision Checkpoints	Info Needed for Decision	Tool to Use for Decision	How to Evaluate Results
Has an accounting transaction occurred?	Details of the event	Accounting equation	If the event affected assets, liabilities, or stockholders' equity, then record as a transaction.
How do you determine that debits equal credits?	All account balances	Trial balance	List the account titles and their balances; total the debit and credit columns; verify equality.

Glossary Review

Account An individual accounting record of increases and decreases in specific asset, liability, stockholders' equity, revenue, or expense items. (p. 3-11).

Accounting information system The system of collecting and processing transaction data and communicating financial information to decision-makers. (p. 3-3).

Accounting transactions Events that require recording in the financial statements because they affect assets, liabilities, or stockholders' equity. (p. 3-3).

Chart of accounts A list of the names of a company's accounts. (p. 3-21).

Credit The right side of an account. (p. 3-11).

Debit The left side of an account. (p. 3-11).

Double-entry system A system that records the two-sided effect of each transaction in appropriate accounts. (p. 3-12).

General journal The most basic form of journal. (p. 3-18).

General ledger A ledger that contains all asset, liability, stockholders' equity, revenue, and expense accounts. (p. 3-20).

Journal An accounting record in which transactions are initially recorded in chronological order. (p. 3-18).

Journalizing The procedure of entering transaction data in the journal. (p. 3-18).

Ledger A record of all accounts maintained by a company and their amounts. (p.3-20).

Posting The procedure of transferring journal entry amounts to the ledger accounts. (p. 3-21).

T-account The basic form of an account. (p. 3-11).

Trial balance A list of accounts and their balances at a given time. (p. 3-30).

Practice Multiple-Choice Questions

1. **(LO 1)** The effects on the basic accounting equation of performing services for cash are to:
   a. increase assets and decrease stockholders' equity.
   b. increase assets and increase stockholders' equity.
   c. increase assets and increase liabilities.
   d. increase liabilities and increase stockholders' equity.

2. **(LO 1)** Genesis Company buys a $900 machine on credit. This transaction will affect the:
   a. income statement only.
   b. balance sheet only.
   c. income statement and retained earnings statement only.
   d. income statement, retained earnings statement, and balance sheet.

3. **(LO 1)** Which of the following events is **not** recorded in the accounting records?
   a. Equipment is purchased on account.
   b. An employee is terminated.
   c. A cash investment is made into the business.
   d. Company pays dividend to stockholders.

4. **(LO 1)** During 2022, Gibson Company assets decreased $50,000 and its liabilities decreased $90,000. Its stockholders' equity therefore:
   a. increased $40,000.
   b. decreased $140,000.
   c. decreased $40,000.
   d. increased $140,000.

5. **(LO 2)** Which statement about an account is **true**?
   a. An account consists of a title, a debit side, and a ledger side.
   b. An account is an individual accounting record of increases and decreases in specific asset, liability, and stockholders' equity items.
   c. There are separate accounts for specific assets and liabilities but only one account for stockholders' equity items.
   d. The left side of an account is the credit, or decrease, side.

6. **(LO 2)** Debits:
   a. increase both assets and liabilities.
   b. decrease both assets and liabilities.
   c. increase assets and decrease liabilities.
   d. decrease assets and increase liabilities.

7. **(LO 2)** A revenue account:
   a. is increased by debits.
   b. is decreased by credits.
   c. has a normal balance of a debit.
   d. is increased by credits.

8. **(LO 2)** Which accounts normally have debit balances?
   a. Assets, expenses, and revenues.
   b. Assets, expenses, and retained earnings.
   c. Assets, liabilities, and dividends.
   d. Assets, dividends, and expenses.

9. **(LO 2)** Paying an account payable with cash affects the components of the accounting equation in the following way:
   a. Decreases stockholders' equity and decreases liabilities.
   b. Increases assets and decreases liabilities.
   c. Decreases assets and increases stockholders' equity.
   d. Decreases assets and decreases liabilities.

10. **(LO 3)** Which is **not** part of the recording process?
    a. Analyzing transactions.
    b. Preparing an income statement.
    c. Entering transactions in a journal.
    d. Posting journal entries.

11. **(LO 3)** Which of these statements about a journal is **false**?
    a. It contains only revenue and expense accounts.
    b. It provides a chronological record of transactions.
    c. It helps to locate errors because the debit and credit amounts for each entry can be readily compared.
    d. It discloses in one place the complete effect of a transaction.

12. **(LO 4)** A ledger:
    a. contains only asset and liability accounts.
    b. should show accounts in alphabetical order.
    c. is a record of all accounts maintained by a company and their amounts.
    d. provides a chronological record of transactions.

13. **(LO 4)** Posting:
    a. normally occurs before journalizing.
    b. transfers ledger transaction data to the journal.
    c. is an optional step in the recording process.
    d. transfers journal entries to ledger accounts.

14. **(LO 5)** A trial balance:
   a. is a list of accounts with their balances at a given time.
   b. proves that proper account titles were used.
   c. will not balance if a correct journal entry is posted twice.
   d. proves that all transactions have been recorded.

15. **(LO 5)** A trial balance will **not** balance if:
   a. a correct journal entry is posted twice.
   b. the purchase of supplies on account is debited to Supplies and credited to Cash.
   c. a $100 cash dividend is debited to Dividends for $1,000 and credited to Cash for $100.
   d. a $450 payment on account is debited to Accounts Payable for $45 and credited to Cash for $45.

Solutions

1. **b.** When services are performed for cash, assets are increased and stockholders' equity is increased. The other choices are therefore incorrect.

2. **b.** When equipment is purchased on credit, assets are increased and liabilities are increased. These are both balance sheet accounts. The other choices are incorrect because neither the income statement nor the retained earnings statement is affected.

3. **b.** Termination of an employee is not a recordable event in the accounting records. The other choices all represent events that are recorded.

4. **a.** Since assets decreased by $50,000 and liabilities decreased by $90,000, stockholders' equity has to increase by $40,000 to keep the accounting equation balanced. The other choices are therefore incorrect.

5. **b.** An account is an individual accounting record of increases and decreases in specific asset, liability, and stockholders' equity items. The other choices are incorrect because (a) in its simplest form, an account consists of three parts: a title and debit and credit side; (c) there are specific accounts for different types of stockholders' equity, such as Common Stock, Retained Earnings, and Dividends; and (d) the left side of an account is the debit side.

6. **c.** Debits increase assets and decrease liabilities. The other choices are therefore incorrect.

7. **d.** Revenues are increased by credits. Revenues have a normal credit balance. The other choices are therefore incorrect.

8. **d.** Assets, dividends, and expenses have normal debit balances. The other choices are incorrect because (a) revenues have a normal credit balance, (b) retained earnings has a normal credit balance, and (c) liabilities have a normal credit balance.

9. **d.** When paying an account payable with cash, the asset cash decreases. Accounts payable, a liability, decreases as well. The other choices are therefore incorrect.

10. **b.** Preparing an income statement is not part of the recording process. Choices (a) analyzing transactions, (c) entering transactions in a journal, and (d) posting transactions are all steps in the recording process.

11. **a.** A journal contains entries affecting all accounts, not just revenue and expense accounts. The other choices are true statements.

12. **c.** A ledger is a record of all accounts maintained by a company and their amounts. The other choices are incorrect because (a) it contains all types of accounts, not just assets and liabilities; (b) they are not listed in alphabetical order but instead in the order of asset, liability, and stockholders' equity accounts and then revenues and expenses; and (d) the journal provides a chronological record.

13. **d.** Posting transfers journal entries to ledger accounts. The other choices are incorrect because posting (a) occurs after journalizing, (b) transfers the information contained in journal entries to the ledger, and (c) is a required step in the recording process. If posting is not done, the ledger accounts will not reflect changes in the accounts resulting from transactions.

14. **a.** A trial balance is a list of accounts with their balances at a given time. The other choices are incorrect because (b) it does not confirm that proper account titles were used; (c) if a journal entry is posted twice, the trial balance will still balance; and (d) a trial balance does not prove that all transactions have been recorded.

15. **c.** The entry will cause the trial balance to be out of balance. The other choices are incorrect because although these entries are incorrect, they will still allow the trial balance to balance.

Practice Brief Exercises

Identify accounts to be debited and credited.

1. **(LO 2)** Transactions for Warren Potter Inc. for the month of May are presented below. Identify the accounts to be debited and credited for each transaction.

May 1	Stockholders invested $22,000 in the business.
6	Paid office rent of $900.
12	Performed consulting services and billed client $4,400.
18	Purchased equipment on account for $1,200.

Solution

1.

		Account Debited	Account Credited
May	1	Cash	Common Stock
	6	Rent Expense	Cash
	12	Accounts Receivable	Service Revenue
	18	Equipment	Accounts Payable

2. (LO 3) Using the data from **Practice Brief Exercise 1**, journalize the transactions (omit explanations).   *Journalize transactions.*

Solution

2.	May 1	Cash		22,000	
		Common Stock			22,000
	6	Rent Expense		900	
		Cash			900
	12	Accounts Receivable		4,400	
		Service Revenue			4,400
	18	Equipment		1,200	
		Accounts Payable			1,200

3. (LO 4) Selected transactions for Carlos Santana Company are presented in journal form below. Post the transactions to T-accounts. Make one T-account for each and determine each account's ending balance.   *Post journal entries to T-accounts.*

J1

Date	Account Titles and Explanation	Ref.	Debit	Credit
June 6	Cash		22,000	
	Common Stock			22,000
	(Stockholders' investment of cash in business)			
13	Accounts Receivable		8,200	
	Service Revenue			8,200
	(Billed for services performed)			
14	Cash		3,700	
	Accounts Receivable			3,700
	(Received cash in payment of account)			

Solution

3.

Cash

6/6	22,000	
6/14	3,700	
Bal.	25,700	

Accounts Receivable

6/13	8,200	6/14	3,700
Bal. 4,500			

Service Revenue

		6/13	8,200
		Bal.	8,200

Common Stock

		6/6	22,000
		Bal.	22,000

4. (LO 5) From the ledger accounts below, prepare a trial balance for Bundy Corporation at December 31, 2022. List the accounts in the order shown in the text. All account balances are normal.   *Prepare a trial balance.*

Accounts Receivable	$10,000	Salaries and Wages Expense	$ 2,300
Supplies	4,100	Rent Expense	1,200
Accounts Payable	3,500	Common Stock	10,200
Dividends	1,100	Cash	6,000
Service Revenue	11,000		

Solution

4.

Bundy Corporation
Trial Balance
December 31, 2022

	Debit	Credit
Cash	$ 6,000	
Accounts Receivable	10,000	
Supplies	4,100	
Accounts Payable		$ 3,500
Common Stock		10,200
Dividends	1,100	
Service Revenue		11,000
Salaries and Wages Expense	2,300	
Rent Expense	1,200	
	$24,700	$24,700

Practice Exercises

Prepare a tabular presentation.

1. (LO 1) Legal Services Inc. was incorporated on July 1, 2022. During the first month of operations, the following transactions occurred.

1. Stockholders invested $10,000 in cash in exchange for common stock of Legal Services Inc.
2. Paid $800 for July rent on office space.
3. Purchased office equipment on account $3,000.
4. Performed legal services for clients for cash $1,500.
5. Borrowed $700 cash from a bank on a note payable.
6. Performed legal services for client on account $2,000.
7. Paid monthly expenses: salaries $500, utilities $300, and advertising $100.

Instructions

Prepare a tabular summary of the transactions.

Solution

1.

	Assets			=	Liabilities		+	Stockholders' Equity				
Trans-action	Cash +	Accounts Receivable +	Equipment =		Notes Payable +	Accounts Payable +		Common Stock +	Rev. −	Exp. −	Div.	
(1)	+$10,000			=				+$10,000				
(2)	−800									−$800		Rent Expense
(3)			+$3,000	=		+$3,000						
(4)	+1,500								+$1,500			Service Revenue
(5)	+700				+$700							
(6)		+$2,000							+ 2,000			Service Revenue
(7)	−500									−500		Sal./Wages Exp.
	−300									−300		Utilities Expense
	−100									−100		Advertising Expense
	$10,500 +	$2,000 +	$3,000	=	$700 +	$3,000	+	$10,000 +	$3,500 −	$1,700		
		$15,500						$15,500				

2. (LO 3) Presented below is information related to Conan Real Estate Agency.

Journalize transactions.

Oct. 1 Arnold Conan begins business as a real estate agent with a cash investment of $18,000 in exchange for common stock.
2 Hires an administrative assistant.
3 Purchases office equipment for $1,700, on account.
6 Sells a house and lot for B. Clinton; bills B. Clinton $4,200 for realty services performed.
27 Pays $900 on the balance related to the transaction of October 3.
30 Pays the administrative assistant $2,800 in salary for October.

Instructions

Journalize the transactions. (You may omit explanations.)

Solution

2.

GENERAL JOURNAL

Date	Account Titles and Explanation	Debit	Credit
Oct. 1	Cash	18,000	
	Common Stock		18,000
2	No entry required		
3	Equipment	1,700	
	Accounts Payable		1,700
6	Accounts Receivable	4,200	
	Service Revenue		4,200
27	Accounts Payable	900	
	Cash		900
30	Salaries and Wages Expense	2,800	
	Cash		2,800

Practice Problem

(LO 3, 4, 5) Bob Sample and other student-investors opened Campus Carpet Cleaning, Inc. on September 1, 2022. During the first month of operations, the following transactions occurred.

Journalize transactions, post, and prepare a trial balance.

Sept. 1 Stockholders invested $20,000 cash in the business.
2 Paid $1,000 cash for store rent for the month of September.
3 Purchased industrial carpet-cleaning equipment for $25,000, paying $10,000 in cash and signing a $15,000 6-month, 12% note payable.
4 Paid $1,200 for 1-year accident insurance policy.
10 Received bill from the *Daily News* for advertising the opening of the cleaning service, $200.
15 Performed services on account for $6,200.
20 Paid a $700 cash dividend to stockholders.
30 Received $5,000 from customers billed on September 15.

The chart of accounts for the company is the same as for Sierra Corporation except for the following additional account: Advertising Expense.

Instructions

a. Journalize the September transactions.
b. Open ledger accounts and post the September transactions.
c. Prepare a trial balance at September 30, 2022.

Solution

a.

GENERAL JOURNAL

Date		Account Titles and Explanation	Debit	Credit
2022				
Sept.	1	Cash	20,000	
		Common Stock		20,000
		(Issued stock for cash)		
	2	Rent Expense	1,000	
		Cash		1,000
		(Paid September rent)		
	3	Equipment	25,000	
		Cash		10,000
		Notes Payable		15,000
		(Purchased cleaning equipment for cash and 6-month, 12% note payable)		
	4	Prepaid Insurance	1,200	
		Cash		1,200
		(Paid 1-year insurance policy)		
	10	Advertising Expense	200	
		Accounts Payable		200
		(Received bill from *Daily News* for advertising)		
	15	Accounts Receivable	6,200	
		Service Revenue		6,200
		(Services performed on account)		
	20	Dividends	700	
		Cash		700
		(Declared and paid a cash dividend)		
	30	Cash	5,000	
		Accounts Receivable		5,000
		(Collection of accounts receivable)		

b.

GENERAL JOURNAL

Cash						Common Stock			
Sept. 1	20,000	Sept. 2	1,000					Sept. 1	20,000
30	5,000	3	10,000					Bal.	20,000
		4	1,200						
		20	700						
Bal.	12,100								

Accounts Receivable						Dividends			
Sept. 15	6,200	Sept. 30	5,000			Sept. 20	700		
Bal.	1,200					Bal.	700		

Prepaid Insurance						Service Revenue			
Sept. 4	1,200							Sept. 15	6,200
Bal.	1,200							Bal.	6,200

Equipment						Advertising Expense			
Sept. 3	25,000					Sept. 10	200		
Bal.	25,000					Bal.	200		

Notes Payable						Rent Expense			
		Sept. 3	15,000			Sept. 2	1,000		
		Bal.	15,000			Bal.	1,000		

Accounts Payable			
		Sept. 10	200
		Bal.	200

c.

Campus Carpet Cleaning, Inc.
Trial Balance
September 30, 2022

	Debit	Credit
Cash	$12,100	
Accounts Receivable	1,200	
Prepaid Insurance	1,200	
Equipment	25,000	
Notes Payable		$15,000
Accounts Payable		200
Common Stock		20,000
Dividends	700	
Service Revenue		6,200
Advertising Expense	200	
Rent Expense	1,000	
	$41,400	$41,400

WileyPLUS

Brief Exercises, DO IT! Exercises, Exercises, Problems, and many additional resources are available for practice in WileyPLUS.

Questions

1. Describe the accounting information system.

2. Can a business enter into a transaction that affects only the left side of the basic accounting equation? If so, give an example.

3. Are the following events recorded in the accounting records? Explain your answer in each case.
   a. A major stockholder of the company dies.
   b. Supplies are purchased on account.
   c. An employee is fired.
   d. The company pays a cash dividend to its stockholders.

4. Indicate how each business transaction affects the basic accounting equation.
   a. Paid cash for janitorial services.
   b. Purchased equipment for cash.
   c. Issued common stock to investors in exchange for cash.
   d. Paid an account payable in full.

5. Why is an account referred to as a T-account?

6. The terms debit and credit mean "increase" and "decrease," respectively. Do you agree? Explain.

7. Barry Barack, a fellow student, contends that the double-entry system means each transaction must be recorded twice. Is Barry correct? Explain.

8. Misty Reno, a beginning accounting student, believes debit balances are favorable and credit balances are unfavorable. Is Misty correct? Discuss.

9. State the rules of debit and credit as applied to (a) asset accounts, (b) liability accounts, and (c) the Common Stock account.

10. What is the normal balance for each of these accounts?
    a. Accounts Receivable.
    b. Cash.
    c. Dividends.
    d. Accounts Payable.
    e. Service Revenue.
    f. Salaries and Wages Expense.
    g. Common Stock.

11. Indicate whether each account is an asset, a liability, or a stockholders' equity account, and whether it would have a normal debit or credit balance.
    a. Accounts Receivable.
    b. Accounts Payable.
    c. Equipment.
    d. Dividends.
    e. Supplies.

12. For the following transactions, indicate the account debited and the account credited.
    a. Supplies are purchased on account.
    b. Cash is received on signing a note payable.
    c. Employees are paid salaries in cash.

13. For each account listed here, indicate whether it generally will have debit entries only, credit entries only, or both debit and credit entries.
    a. Cash.
    b. Accounts Receivable.
    c. Dividends.
    d. Accounts Payable.
    e. Salaries and Wages Expense.
    f. Service Revenue.

14. What are the normal balances for the following accounts of Apple? (a) Accounts Receivable, (b) Accounts Payable, (c) Sales, and (d) Selling, General, and Administrative Expenses.

15. What are the basic steps in the recording process?

16. a. When entering a transaction in the journal, should the debit or credit be written first?
    b. Which should be indented, the debit or the credit?

17. a. Should accounting transaction debits and credits be recorded directly in the ledger accounts?
    b. What are the advantages of first recording transactions in the journal and then posting to the ledger?

18. Journalize these accounting transactions.
    a. Stockholders invested $12,000 in the business in exchange for common stock.
    b. Insurance of $800 is paid for the year.
    c. Supplies of $1,800 are purchased on account.
    d. Cash of $7,500 is received for services rendered.

19. a. What is a ledger?
    b. Why is a chart of accounts important?

20. What is a trial balance and what are its purposes?

21. Brad Tyler is confused about how accounting information flows through the accounting system. He believes information flows in this order:
    a. Debits and credits are posted to the ledger.
    b. Accounting transaction occurs.
    c. Information is entered in the journal.
    d. Financial statements are prepared.
    e. Trial balance is prepared.

    Indicate to Brad the proper flow of the information.

22. Two students are discussing the use of a trial balance. They wonder whether the following errors, each considered separately, would prevent the trial balance from balancing. What would you tell them?
    a. The bookkeeper debited Cash for $600 and credited Salaries and Wages Expense for $600 for payment of wages.
    b. Cash collected on account was debited to Cash for $800, and Service Revenue was credited for $80.

Brief Exercises

Determine effect of transactions on basic accounting equation.

BE3.1 (LO 1), C Presented below are three economic events. On a sheet of paper, list the letters (a), (b), and (c) with columns for assets, liabilities, and stockholders' equity. In each column, indicate whether the event increased (+), decreased (−), or had no effect (NE) on assets, liabilities, and stockholders' equity.

a. Purchased supplies on account.
b. Received cash for performing a service.
c. Expenses paid in cash.

Determine effect of transactions on basic accounting equation.

BE3.2 (LO 1), AP During 2022, Manion Corp. entered into the following transactions.

1. Borrowed $60,000 by issuing bonds.
2. Paid $9,000 cash dividend to stockholders.
3. Received $13,000 cash from a previously billed customer for services performed.
4. Purchased supplies on account for $3,100.

Using the following tabular analysis, show the effect of each transaction on the accounting equation. Put explanations for changes to revenues or expenses in the right-hand margin. For Retained Earnings, use separate columns for Revenues, Expenses, and Dividends if necessary. Use Illustration 3.4 as a model.

Assets	=	Liabilities	+	Stockholders' Equity	
Cash + Accounts Receivable + Supplies =		Accounts Payable + Bonds Payable +		Common Stock +	Retained Earnings

Determine effect of transactions on basic accounting equation.

BE3.3 (LO 1), AP During 2022, Rostock Company entered into the following transactions.

1. Purchased equipment for $286,176 cash.
2. Issued common stock to investors for $137,590 cash.
3. Purchased inventory of $68,480 on account.

Using the following tabular analysis, show the effect of each transaction on the accounting equation. Put explanations for changes to revenues or expenses in the right-hand margin. For Retained Earnings, use separate columns for Revenues, Expenses, and Dividends if necessary. Use Illustration 3.4 as a model.

Assets	=	Liabilities	+	Stockholders' Equity	
Cash + Inventory + Equipment =		Accounts Payable +		Common Stock +	Retained Earnings

BE3.4 (LO 2), K For each of the following accounts, indicate the effect of a debit or a credit on the account and the normal balance.

a. Accounts Payable.
b. Advertising Expense.
c. Service Revenue.
d. Accounts Receivable.
e. Retained Earnings.
f. Dividends.

Indicate debit and credit effects.

BE3.5 (LO 2), K For each of the following accounts, indicate the effect of a debit or credit on the account and the normal balance.

a. Bonds Payable.
b. Unearned Service Revenue.
c. Depreciation Expense.
d. Common Stock.
e. Buildings.
f. Rent Revenue.

Indicate debit and credit effects.

BE3.6 (LO 2), C Transactions for Jayne Company for the month of June are presented below. Identify the accounts to be debited and credited for each transaction.

June 1 Issues common stock to investors in exchange for $5,000 cash.
    2 Buys equipment on account for $1,100.
    3 Pays $740 to landlord for June rent.
   12 Sends Wil Wheaton a bill for $700 after completing welding work.

Identify accounts to be debited and credited.

BE3.7 (LO 3), AP Use the data in BE3.6 and journalize the transactions. (You may omit explanations.)

Journalize transactions.

BE3.8 (LO 3), AP Journalize the following transactions for Matt's Carpentry, Inc. (You may omit explanations.)

Sept. 1 Purchased supplies for $910 cash.
     5 Paid $300 cash dividend to stockholders.
     7 Received $4,600 down payment from customer for services to be provided in the future.
    16 Received $675 cash from a previously billed customer for payment of services provided in the prior month.
    22 Purchased equipment for $1,900 by paying $600 cash and issued a note payable for the balance.

Journalize transactions.

BE3.9 (LO 3), C Rae Mohlee, a fellow student, is unclear about the basic steps in the recording process. Identify and briefly explain the steps in the order in which they occur.

Identify steps in the recording process.

BE3.10 (LO 3), C Tilton Corporation has the following transactions during August of the current year. Indicate (a) the basic analysis and (b) the debit–credit analysis as shown in Illustrations 3.22 to 3.32.

Aug. 1 Issues shares of common stock to investors in exchange for $10,000.
     4 Pays insurance in advance for 3 months, $1,500.
    16 Receives $900 from clients for services rendered.
    27 Pays the secretary $620 salary.

Indicate basic debit–credit analysis.

BE3.11 (LO 3), AP Use the data in BE3.10 and journalize the transactions. (You may omit explanations.)

Journalize transactions.

BE3.12 (LO 4), AP Selected transactions for Montes Company are presented below in journal form (without explanations). Post the transactions to T-accounts.

Post journal entries to T-accounts.

Date	Account Title	Debit	Credit
May 5	Accounts Receivable	3,800	
	Service Revenue		3,800
12	Cash	1,600	
	Accounts Receivable		1,600
15	Cash	2,000	
	Service Revenue		2,000

BE3.13 (LO 5), AP From the ledger balances below, prepare a trial balance for Peete Company at June 30, 2022. All account balances are normal.

Prepare a trial balance.

Accounts Payable	$ 1,000	Service Revenue	$8,600
Cash	5,400	Accounts Receivable	3,000
Common Stock	18,000	Salaries and Wages Expense	4,000
Dividends	1,200	Rent Expense	1,000
Equipment	13,000		

Prepare a corrected trial balance.

BE3.14 (LO 5), AN An inexperienced bookkeeper prepared the following trial balance that does not balance. Prepare a correct trial balance, assuming all account balances are normal.

Birellie Company
Trial Balance
December 31, 2022

	Debit	Credit
Cash	$20,800	
Prepaid Insurance		$ 3,500
Accounts Payable		2,500
Unearned Service Revenue	1,800	
Common Stock		10,000
Retained Earnings		6,600
Dividends		5,000
Service Revenue		25,600
Salaries and Wages Expense	14,600	
Rent Expense		2,600
	$37,200	$55,800

DO IT! Exercises

Prepare tabular analysis.

DO IT! 3.1 (LO 1), AP Transactions made by Mickelson Co. for the month of March are shown below. Prepare a tabular analysis that shows the effects of these transactions on the expanded accounting equation, similar to that shown in Illustration 3.4.

1. The company performed $20,000 of services for customers on account.
2. The company received $20,000 in cash from customers who had been billed for services [in transaction (1)].
3. The company received a bill for $1,800 of advertising but will not pay it until a later date.
4. Mickelson Co. paid a cash dividend of $3,000.

Identify normal balances.

DO IT! 3.2 (LO 2), C Boyd Docker has just rented space in a strip mall. In this space, he will open a photography studio, to be called SnapShot! A friend has advised Boyd to set up a double-entry set of accounting records in which to record all of his business transactions.

Identify the balance sheet accounts that Boyd will likely need to record the transactions needed to open his business (a corporation). Indicate whether the normal balance of each account is a debit or credit.

Record business activities.

DO IT! 3.3 (LO 3), AP Boyd Docker engaged in the following activities in establishing his photography studio, SnapShot!:

1. Opened a bank account in the name of SnapShot! and deposited $8,000 of his own money into this account in exchange for common stock.
2. Purchased photography supplies at a total cost of $950. The business paid $400 in cash, and the balance is on account.
3. Obtained estimates on the cost of photography equipment from three different manufacturers.

Prepare the journal entries to record the transactions.

Post transactions.

DO IT! 3.4 (LO 4), AP Boyd Docker recorded the following transactions during the month of April.

Apr. 3	Cash	3,400	
	Service Revenue		3,400
16	Rent Expense	500	
	Cash		500
20	Salaries and Wages Expense	300	
	Cash		300

Post these entries to the Cash account of the general ledger to determine the ending balance in cash. The beginning balance in cash on April 1 was $1,900.

DO IT! 3.5 (LO 5), AP The following accounts are taken from the ledger of Chillin' Company at December 31, 2022.

Prepare a trial balance.

Notes Payable	$20,000	Cash	$6,000
Common Stock	25,000	Supplies	5,000
Equipment	76,000	Rent Expense	2,000
Dividends	8,000	Salaries and Wages Payable	3,000
Salaries and Wages Expense	38,000	Accounts Payable	9,000
Service Revenue	86,000	Accounts Receivable	8,000

Prepare a trial balance in good form.

Exercises

E3.1 (LO 1), C Selected transactions for Thyme Advertising Company, Inc. are listed here.

Analyze the effect of transactions.

1. Issued common stock to investors in exchange for cash received from investors.
2. Paid monthly rent.
3. Received cash from customers when service was performed.
4. Billed customers for services performed.
5. Paid dividend to stockholders.
6. Incurred advertising expense on account.
7. Received cash from customers billed in (4).
8. Purchased additional equipment for cash.
9. Purchased equipment on account.

Instructions

Describe the effect of each transaction on assets, liabilities, and stockholders' equity. For example, the first answer is (1) Increase in assets and increase in stockholders' equity.

E3.2 (LO 1), AP Brady Company entered into these transactions during May 2022, its first month of operations.

Analyze the effect of transactions on assets, liabilities, and stockholders' equity.

1. Stockholders invested $40,000 in the business in exchange for common stock of the company.
2. Purchased computers for office use for $30,000 from Ladd on account.
3. Paid $4,000 cash for May rent on storage space.
4. Performed computer services worth $19,000 on account.
5. Performed computer services for Wharton Construction Company for $5,000 cash.
6. Paid Western States Power Co. $8,000 cash for energy usage in May.
7. Paid Ladd for the computers purchased in (2).
8. Incurred advertising expense for May of $1,300 on account.
9. Received $12,000 cash from customers for contracts billed in (4).

Instructions

Using the following tabular analysis, show the effect of each transaction on the accounting equation. Put explanations for changes to revenues or expenses in the right-hand margin. Use Illustration 3.4 as a model.

Assets			=	Liabilities	+	Stockholders' Equity				
	Accounts			Accounts		Common		Retained Earnings		
Cash +	Receivable +	Equipment	=	Payable	+	Stock	+ Revenues	− Expenses	−	Dividends

E3.3 (LO 1), AP During 2022, its first year of operations as a delivery service, Persimmon Corp. entered into the following transactions.

Determine effect of transactions on basic accounting equation.

1. Issued shares of common stock to investors in exchange for $100,000 in cash.
2. Borrowed $45,000 by issuing bonds.
3. Purchased delivery trucks for $60,000 cash.
4. Received $16,000 from customers for services performed.
5. Purchased supplies for $4,700 on account.
6. Paid rent of $5,200.
7. Performed services on account for $10,000.
8. Paid salaries of $28,000.
9. Paid a dividend of $11,000 to shareholders.

Instructions

Using the following tabular analysis, show the effect of each transaction on the accounting equation. Put explanations for changes to Stockholders' Equity in the right-hand margin. Use Illustration 3.4 as a model.

Assets				=	Liabilities	+	Stockholders' Equity				
									Retained Earnings		
Cash	+ Accounts Receivable	+ Supplies	+ Equipment	=	Accounts Payable	+ Bonds Payable	+ Common Stock	+ Revenues	− Expenses	− Dividends	

Analyze transactions and compute net income.

E3.4 (LO 1), AP A tabular analysis of the transactions made during August 2022 by Wolfe Company during its first month of operations is shown as follows. Each increase and decrease in stockholders' equity is explained.

	Assets				=	Liabilities	+	Stockholders' Equity				
						Accounts	Common		Retained Earnings			
	Cash	+ A/R	+ Supp.	+ Equip.	=	Payable	+ Stock	+ Rev.	− Exp.	− Div.	
1.	+$20,000						+$20,000				
2.	−1,000			+$5,000		+$4,000					
3.	−750		+$750								
4.	+4,100	+$5,400						+$9,500			Serv. Rev.
5.	−1,500					−1,500					
6.	−2,000									−$2,000	
7.	−800								−$ 800		Rent Exp.
8.	+450	−450									
9.	−3,000								−3,000		Salar. Exp.
10.						+300			−300		Util. Exp.

Instructions

a. Describe each transaction.
b. Determine how much stockholders' equity increased for the month.
c. Compute the net income for the month.

Prepare an income statement, retained earnings statement, and balance sheet.

E3.5 (LO 2), AP The tabular analysis of transactions for Wolfe Company is presented in E3.4.

Instructions

Prepare an income statement and a retained earnings statement for August and a classified balance sheet at August 31, 2022.

Identify normal account balance and corresponding financial statement.

E3.6 (LO 2), K The following accounts, in alphabetical order, were selected from recent financial statements of **Krispy Kreme Doughnuts, Inc.**

Accounts Payable
Accounts Receivable
Common Stock
Depreciation Expense
Interest Expense

Interest Income
Inventories
Prepaid Expenses
Property and Equipment
Revenues

Instructions

For each account, indicate (a) whether the normal balance is a debit or a credit, and (b) the financial statement—balance sheet or income statement—where the account should be presented.

E3.7 (LO 2, 3), AP Selected transactions for Front Room, an interior decorator corporation, in its first month of business, are as follows.

Identify debits, credits, and normal balances and journalize transactions.

1. Issued stock to investors for $15,000 in cash.
2. Purchased used car for $10,000 cash for use in business.
3. Purchased supplies on account for $300.
4. Billed customers $3,700 for services performed.
5. Paid $200 cash for advertising at the start of the business.
6. Received $1,100 cash from customers billed in transaction (4).
7. Paid creditor $300 cash on account.
8. Paid dividends of $400 cash to stockholders.

Instructions

a. For each transaction indicate (a) the basic type of account debited and credited (asset, liability, stockholders' equity); (b) the specific account debited and credited (Cash, Rent Expense, Service Revenue, etc.); (c) whether the specific account is increased or decreased; and (d) the normal balance of the specific account. Use the following format, in which transaction (1) is given as an example.

	Account Debited				Account Credited			
	(a)	(b)	(c)	(d)	(a)	(b)	(c)	(d)
Trans-action	Basic Type	Specific Account	Effect	Normal Balance	Basic Type	Specific Account	Effect	Normal Balance
1	Asset	Cash	Increase	Debit	Stock-holders' equity	Common Stock	Increase	Credit

b. Journalize the transactions. Do not provide explanations.

E3.8 (LO 2), C This information relates to McCall Real Estate Agency.

Analyze transactions and determine their effect on accounts.

Oct. 1 Stockholders invest $30,000 in exchange for common stock of the corporation.
2 Hires an administrative assistant at an annual salary of $36,000.
3 Buys office furniture for $3,800, on account.
6 Sells a house and lot for E. C. Roads; commissions due from Roads, $10,800 (not paid by Roads at this time).
10 Receives cash of $140 as commission for acting as rental agent renting an apartment.
27 Pays $700 on account for the office furniture purchased on October 3.
30 Pays the administrative assistant $3,000 in salary for October.

Instructions

Prepare the debit–credit analysis for each transaction, as shown in Illustrations 3.22 to 3.32.

E3.9 (LO 3), AP Transaction data for McCall Real Estate Agency are presented in E3.8.

Journalize transactions.

Instructions

Journalize the transactions. Do not provide explanations.

E3.10 (LO 3), AP The May transactions of Chulak Corporation were as follows.

Journalize a series of transactions.

May 4 Paid $700 due for supplies previously purchased on account.
7 Performed advisory services on account for $6,800.
8 Purchased supplies for $850 on account.
9 Purchased equipment for $1,000 in cash.
17 Paid employees $530 in cash.
22 Received bill for equipment repairs of $900.
29 Paid $1,200 for 12 months of insurance policy. Coverage begins June 1.

Instructions

Journalize the transactions. Do not provide explanations.

E3.11 (LO 3), AP Selected transactions for Sophie's Dog Care are as follows during the month of March.

Journalize a series of transactions.

March 1 Paid monthly rent of $1,200.
3 Performed services for $140 on account.
5 Performed services for cash of $75.
8 Purchased equipment for $600. The company paid cash of $80 and the balance was on account.
12 Received cash from customers billed on March 3.
14 Paid wages to employees of $525.
22 Paid utilities of $72.
24 Borrowed $1,500 from Grafton State Bank by signing a note.
27 Paid $220 to repair service for plumbing repairs.
28 Paid balance amount owed from equipment purchase on March 8.
30 Paid $1,800 for six months of insurance.

Instructions

Journalize the transactions. Do not provide explanations.

Record journal entries.

E3.12 (LO 3), AP On April 1, Adventures Travel Agency, Inc. began operations. The following transactions were completed during the month.

1. Issued common stock for $24,000 cash.
2. Obtained a bank loan for $7,000 by issuing a note payable.
3. Paid $11,000 cash to buy equipment.
4. Paid $1,200 cash for April office rent.
5. Paid $1,450 for supplies.
6. Purchased $600 of advertising in the *Daily Herald*, on account.
7. Performed services for $18,000: cash of $2,000 was received from customers, and the balance of $16,000 was billed to customers on account.
8. Paid $400 cash dividend to stockholders.
9. Paid the utility bill for the month, $2,000.
10. Paid *Daily Herald* the amount due in transaction (6).
11. Paid $40 of interest on the bank loan obtained in transaction (2).
12. Paid employees' salaries, $6,400.
13. Received $12,000 cash from customers billed in transaction (7).
14. Paid income tax, $1,500.

Instructions

Journalize the transactions. Do not provide explanations.

Identify key terms.

E3.13 (LO 1, 2, 3, 4, 5), K The following is a list of terms or phrases discussed in the chapter.

1. Credit
2. Journal
3. Ledger
4. Chart of accounts
5. Posting
6. Account
7. Trial balance
8. Accounting transactions
9. Debit

Instructions

Match each term or phrase to its description below.

a. _____ A list of accounts and their balances at a given time.
b. _____ An accounting record in which transactions are initially recorded in chronological order.
c. _____ A record of all accounts maintained by a company and their amounts.
d. _____ An individual accounting record of increases and decreases in specific asset, liability, stockholders' equity, revenue, or expense items.
e. _____ A list of the names of a company's accounts.
f. _____ The right side of an account.
g. _____ The procedure of transferring journal entry amounts to the ledger accounts.
h. _____ The left side of an account.
i. _____ Events that require recording in the financial statements because they affect assets, liabilities, or stockholders' equity.

E3.14 (LO 4, 5), AP Transaction data and journal entries for McCall Real Estate Agency are presented in E3.8 and E3.9.

Post journal entries and prepare a trial balance.

Instructions

a. Post the transactions to T-accounts.

b. Prepare a trial balance at October 31, 2022.

E3.15 (LO 1, 3, 4), AP Selected transactions for Therow Corporation during its first month in business are presented below.

Analyze transactions, prepare journal entries, and post transactions to T-accounts.

Sept.	1	Issued common stock in exchange for $20,000 cash received from investors.
	5	Purchased equipment for $9,000, paying $3,000 in cash and the balance on account.
	8	Performed services on account for $18,000.
	14	Paid salaries of $1,200.
	25	Paid $4,000 cash on balance owed for equipment.
	30	Paid $500 cash dividend.

Therow's chart of accounts shows Cash, Accounts Receivable, Equipment, Accounts Payable, Common Stock, Dividends, Service Revenue, and Salaries and Wages Expense.

Instructions

a. Prepare a tabular analysis of the September transactions. The column headings should be Cash + Accounts Receivable + Equipment = Accounts Payable + Common Stock + Revenues − Expenses − Dividends. For transactions affecting stockholders' equity, provide explanations in the right margin, as shown on Illustration 3.4.

b. Journalize the transactions. Do not provide explanations.

c. Post the transactions to T-accounts.

E3.16 (LO 3, 5), AN The T-accounts below summarize the ledger of Salvador's Gardening Company, Inc. at the end of the first month of operations.

Journalize transactions from T-accounts and prepare a trial balance.

Cash					Unearned Service Revenue		
Apr. 1	15,000	Apr. 15	800			Apr. 30	900
12	700	25	3,500				
29	800						
30	900						

Accounts Receivable					Common Stock		
Apr. 7	3,400	Apr. 29	800			Apr. 1	15,000

Supplies					Service Revenue		
Apr. 4	5,200					Apr. 7	3,400
						12	700

Accounts Payable					Salaries and Wages Expense		
Apr. 25	3,500	Apr. 4	5,200		Apr. 15	800	

Instructions

a. Prepare the journal entries (including explanations) that resulted in the amounts posted to the accounts. Present them in the order they occurred.

b. Prepare a trial balance at April 30, 2022. (*Hint:* Compute ending balances of T-accounts first.)

E3.17 (LO 4, 5), AP Selected transactions from the journal of Baylee Inc. during its first month of operations are presented here.

Post journal entries and prepare a trial balance.

Date		Account Titles	Debit	Credit
Aug. 1		Cash	8,000	
		Common Stock		8,000
	10	Cash	1,700	
		Service Revenue		1,700
	12	Equipment	6,200	
		Cash		1,200
		Notes Payable		5,000
	25	Accounts Receivable	3,400	
		Service Revenue		3,400
	31	Cash	600	
		Accounts Receivable		600

Journalize transactions from T-accounts and prepare a trial balance.

Instructions

a. Post the transactions to T-accounts.
b. Prepare a trial balance at August 31, 2022.

E3.18 (LO 3, 5), AN Here is the ledger for Kriscoe Co.

Cash					Common Stock			
Oct. 1	7,000	Oct. 4	400				Oct. 1	7,000
10	980	12	1,500				25	2,000
10	8,000	15	250					
20	700	30	300					
25	2,000	31	500					

Accounts Receivable					Dividends			
Oct. 6	800	Oct. 20	700		Oct. 30	300		
20	920							

Supplies					Service Revenue			
Oct. 4	400	Oct. 31	180				Oct. 6	800
							10	980
							20	920

Equipment					Salaries and Wages Expense			
Oct. 3	3,000				Oct. 31	500		

Notes Payable					Supplies Expense			
		Oct. 10	8,000		Oct. 31	180		

Accounts Payable					Rent Expense			
Oct. 12	1,500	Oct. 3	3,000		Oct. 15	250		

Instructions

a. Reproduce the journal entries for only the transactions that **occurred on October 1, 10, and 20**, and provide explanations for each.
b. Prepare a trial balance at October 31, 2022. (*Hint:* Compute ending balances of T-accounts first.)

Journalize transactions, post transactions to T-accounts, and prepare trial balance.

E3.19 (LO 3, 4, 5), AP Beyers Corporation provides security services. Selected transactions for Beyers are presented below.

Oct.	1	Issued common stock in exchange for $66,000 cash from investors.
	2	Hired part-time security consultant. Salary will be $2,000 per month. First day of work will be October 15.
	4	Paid 1 month of rent for building for $2,000.
	7	Purchased equipment for $18,000, paying $4,000 cash and the balance on account.
	8	Paid $500 for advertising.
	10	Received bill for equipment repair cost of $390.
	12	Provided security services for event for $3,200 on account.
	16	Purchased supplies for $410 on account.
	21	Paid balance due from October 7 purchase of equipment.
	24	Received and paid utility bill for $148.
	27	Received payment from customer for October 12 services performed.
	31	Paid employee salaries and wages of $5,100.

Instructions

a. Journalize the transactions. Do not provide explanations.
b. Post the transactions to T-accounts.
c. Prepare a trial balance at October 31, 2022. (*Hint:* Compute ending balances of T-accounts first.)

Analyze errors and their effects on trial balance.

E3.20 (LO 5), AN The bookkeeper for Birmingham Corporation made these errors in journalizing and posting.

1. A credit posting of $400 to Accounts Receivable was omitted.
2. A debit posting of $750 for Prepaid Insurance was debited to Insurance Expense.
3. A collection on account of $100 was journalized and posted as a debit to Cash $100 and a credit to Accounts Payable $100.
4. A credit posting of $300 to Income Taxes Payable was made twice.

5. A cash purchase of supplies for $250 was journalized and posted as a debit to Supplies $25 and a credit to Cash $25.
6. A debit of $395 to Advertising Expense was posted as $359.

Instructions

For each error, indicate (a) whether the trial balance will balance; if the trial balance will not balance, indicate (b) the amount of the difference and (c) the trial balance column that will have the larger total. Consider each error separately. Use the following form, in which error 1 is given as an example.

Error	(a) In Balance	(b) Difference	(c) Larger Column
1	No	$400	Debit

E3.21 (LO 5), AP The accounts in the ledger of Rapid Delivery Service contain the following balances on July 31, 2022.

Prepare a trial balance and financial statements.

Accounts Receivable	$13,400	Prepaid Insurance	$ 2,200
Accounts Payable	8,400	Service Revenue	15,500
Cash	?	Dividends	700
Equipment	59,360	Common Stock	40,000
Maintenance and		Salaries and Wages Expense	7,428
Repairs Expense	1,958	Salaries and Wages Payable	820
Insurance Expense	900	Retained Earnings (July 1, 2022)	5,200
Notes Payable (due 2025)	28,450		

Instructions

a. Prepare a trial balance with the accounts arranged as illustrated in the chapter, and fill in the missing amount for Cash.

b. Prepare an income statement, a retained earnings statement, and a classified balance sheet for the month of July 2022.

E3.22 (LO 5), AP Review the transactions listed in E3.1 for Thyme Advertising Company. Classify each transaction as either an operating activity, investing activity, or financing activity, or if no cash is exchanged, as a noncash event.

Classify transactions as cash-flow activities.

E3.23 (LO 5), AP Review the transactions listed in E3.3 for Persimmon Corp. Classify each transaction as either an operating activity, investing activity, or financing activity, or if no cash is exchanged, as a noncash event.

Classify transactions as cash-flow activities.

Problems: Set A

P3.1A (LO 1), AP On April 1, Wonder Travel Agency Inc. was established. These transactions were completed during the month.

Analyze transactions and compute net income.

1. Stockholders invested $30,000 cash in the company in exchange for common stock.
2. Paid $900 cash for April office rent.
3. Purchased office equipment for $3,400 cash.
4. Purchased $200 of advertising in the *Chicago Tribune*, on account.
5. Paid $500 cash for office supplies.
6. Performed services worth $12,000. Cash of $3,000 is received from customers, and the balance of $9,000 is billed to customers on account.
7. Paid $400 cash dividend.
8. Paid *Chicago Tribune* amount due in transaction (4).
9. Paid employees' salaries $1,800.
10. Received $9,000 in cash from customers billed previously in transaction (6).

Instructions

a. Prepare a tabular analysis of the transactions using these column headings: Cash, Accounts Receivable, Supplies, Equipment, Accounts Payable, Common Stock, and Retained Earnings (with separate columns for Revenues, Expenses, and Dividends). Include margin explanations for any changes in Retained Earnings.

b. From an analysis of the Retained Earnings columns, compute the net income or net loss for April.

a. Cash $34,800
Total assets $38,700

3-52 CHAPTER 3 The Accounting Information System

Analyze transactions and prepare financial statements.

P3.2A (LO 1, 2), AP Nona Curry started her own consulting firm, Curry Consulting Inc., on May 1, 2022. The following transactions occurred during the month of May.

May	1	Stockholders invested $15,000 cash in the business in exchange for common stock.
	2	Paid $600 for office rent for the month.
	3	Purchased $500 of supplies on account.
	5	Paid $150 to advertise in the *County News*.
	9	Received $1,400 cash for services performed.
	12	Paid $200 cash dividend.
	15	Performed $4,200 of services on account.
	17	Paid $2,500 for employee salaries.
	20	Paid for the supplies purchased on account on May 3.
	23	Received a cash payment of $1,200 for services performed on account on May 15.
	26	Borrowed $5,000 from the bank on a note payable.
	29	Purchased office equipment for $2,000 paying $200 in cash and the balance on account.
	30	Paid $180 for utilities.

Instructions

a. Cash $18,270
Total assets $23,770

a. Show the effects of the previous transactions on the accounting equation using the following format. Assume the note payable is to be repaid within the year.

	Assets				=	Liabilities		+	Stockholders' Equity			
Date	Cash +	Accounts Receivable +	Supplies +	Equipment	=	Notes Payable +	Accounts Payable	+	Common Stock	+ Revenues	− Expenses	− Dividends

Include margin explanations for any changes in Retained Earnings.

b. Net income $2,170

b. Prepare an income statement for the month of May 2022.

c. Prepare a classified balance sheet at May 31, 2022.

Analyze transactions and prepare an income statement, retained earnings statement, and balance sheet.

P3.3A (LO 1, 2), AP Bindy Crawford created a corporation providing legal services, Bindy Crawford Inc., on July 1, 2022. On July 31 the balance sheet showed Cash $4,000, Accounts Receivable $2,500, Supplies $500, Equipment $5,000, Accounts Payable $4,200, Common Stock $6,200, and Retained Earnings $1,600. During August, the following transactions occurred.

Aug.	1	Collected $1,100 of accounts receivable due from customers.
	4	Paid $2,700 cash for accounts payable due.
	9	Performed services worth $5,400, of which $3,600 is collected in cash and the balance is due in September.
	15	Purchased additional office equipment for $4,000, paying $700 in cash and the balance on account.
	19	Paid salaries $1,400, rent for August $700, and advertising expenses $350.
	23	Paid a cash dividend of $700.
	26	Borrowed $5,000 from American Federal Bank; the money was borrowed on a 4-month note payable.
	31	Incurred utility expenses for the month on account $380.

Instructions

a. Cash $7,150

a. Prepare a tabular analysis of the August transactions beginning with July 31 balances. The column heading should be Cash + Accounts Receivable + Supplies + Equipment = Notes Payable + Accounts Payable + Common Stock + Retained Earnings + Revenues − Expenses − Dividends. Include margin explanations for any changes in Retained Earnings.

b. Net income $2,570
Ret. earnings $3,470

b. Prepare an income statement for August, a retained earnings statement for August, and a classified balance sheet at August 31.

Journalize a series of transactions.

P3.4A (LO 3), AP Bradley's Miniature Golf and Driving Range Inc. was opened on March 1 by Bob Dean. These selected events and transactions occurred during March.

Mar.	1	Stockholders invested $50,000 cash in the business in exchange for common stock of the corporation.
	3	Purchased Snead's Golf Land for $38,000 cash. The price consists of land $23,000, building $9,000, and equipment $6,000. (Record this in a single entry.)
	5	Advertised the opening of the driving range and miniature golf course, paying advertising expenses of $1,200 cash.
	6	Paid cash $2,400 for a 1-year insurance policy.

10 Purchased golf clubs and other equipment for $5,500 from Tahoe Company, payable in 30 days.
18 Received golf fees of $1,600 in cash from customers for golf services performed.
19 Sold 100 coupon books for $25 each in cash. Each book contains 10 coupons that enable the holder to play one round of miniature golf or to hit one bucket of golf balls. (*Hint:* The revenue should not be recognized until the customers use the coupons.)
25 Paid a $500 cash dividend.
30 Paid salaries of $800.
30 Paid Tahoe Company in full for equipment purchased on March 10.
31 Received $900 in cash from customers for golf services performed.

The company uses these accounts: Cash, Prepaid Insurance, Land, Buildings, Equipment, Accounts Payable, Unearned Service Revenue, Common Stock, Retained Earnings, Dividends, Service Revenue, Advertising Expense, and Salaries and Wages Expense.

Instructions

Journalize the March transactions, including explanations. Bradley's records golf fees as service revenue.

P3.5A (LO 3, 4, 5), AP Ayala Architects incorporated as licensed architects on April 1, 2022. During the first month of the operation of the business, these events and transactions occurred:

Journalize transactions, post, and prepare a trial balance.

Apr. 1 Stockholders invested $18,000 cash in exchange for common stock of the corporation.
1 Hired a secretary-receptionist at a salary of $375 per week, payable monthly.
2 Paid office rent for the month $900.
3 Purchased architectural supplies on account from Burmingham Company $1,300.
10 Completed blueprints on a carport and billed client $1,900 for services.
11 Received $700 cash advance from M. Jason to design a new home.
20 Received $2,800 cash for services completed and delivered to S. Melvin.
30 Paid secretary-receptionist for the month $1,500.
30 Paid $300 to Burmingham Company for accounts payable due.

The company uses these accounts: Cash, Accounts Receivable, Supplies, Accounts Payable, Unearned Service Revenue, Common Stock, Service Revenue, Salaries and Wages Expense, and Rent Expense.

Instructions

a. Journalize the transactions, including explanations.
b. Post to the ledger T-accounts.
c. Prepare a trial balance on April 30, 2022.

c. Cash $18,800
Tot. trial balance $24,400

P3.6A (LO 3, 4, 5), AP This is the trial balance of Lacey Company on September 30.

Journalize transactions, post, and prepare a trial balance.

Lacey Company
Trial Balance
September 30, 2022

	Debit	Credit
Cash	$19,200	
Accounts Receivable	2,600	
Supplies	2,100	
Equipment	8,000	
Accounts Payable		$ 4,800
Unearned Service Revenue		1,100
Common Stock		15,000
Retained Earnings		11,000
	$31,900	$31,900

The October transactions were as follows.

Oct. 5 Received $1,300 in cash from customers for accounts receivable due.
10 Billed customers for services performed $5,100.
15 Paid employee salaries $1,200.
17 Performed $600 of services in exchange for cash.
20 Paid $1,900 to creditors for accounts payable due.
29 Paid a $300 cash dividend.
31 Paid utilities $400.

Instructions

a. Prepare a general ledger using T-accounts. Enter the opening balances in the ledger accounts as of October 1. (*Hint:* The October 1 beginning amounts are the September 30 balances in the trial balance above.) Provision should be made for these additional accounts: Dividends, Service Revenue, Salaries and Wages Expense, and Utilities Expense.
b. Journalize the transactions, including explanations.
c. Post to the ledger accounts.
d. Prepare a trial balance on October 31, 2022.

d. Cash $17,300
Tot. trial balance $35,700

Prepare a correct trial balance.

P3.7A (LO 5), AN This trial balance of Washburn Co. does not balance.

Washburn Co.
Trial Balance
June 30, 2022

	Debit	Credit
Cash		$ 3,090
Accounts Receivable	$ 3,190	
Supplies	800	
Equipment	3,000	
Accounts Payable		3,686
Unearned Service Revenue	1,200	
Common Stock		9,000
Dividends	800	
Service Revenue		3,480
Salaries and Wages Expense	3,600	
Utilities Expense	910	
	$13,500	$19,256

Each of the listed accounts has a normal balance per the general ledger. An examination of the ledger and journal reveals the following errors:

1. Cash received from a customer on account was debited for $780, and Accounts Receivable was credited for the same amount. The actual collection was for $870.
2. The purchase of a printer on account for $340 was recorded as a debit to Supplies for $340 and a credit to Accounts Payable for $340.
3. Services were performed on account for a client for $900. Accounts Receivable was debited for $90 and Service Revenue was credited for $900.
4. A debit posting to Salaries and Wages Expense of $700 was omitted.
5. A payment on account for $206 was credited to Cash for $206 and credited to Accounts Payable for $260.
6. Payment of a $600 cash dividend to Washburn's stockholders was debited to Salaries and Wages Expense for $600 and credited to Cash for $600.
7. The amounts for two accounts with normal balances were listed in the wrong column.

Instructions

Tot. trial balance $16,900

Prepare the correct trial balance. (*Hint:* All accounts should have normal balances. Your first step, therefore, should be to move all amounts to the column of their normal balance.)

Journalize transactions, post, and prepare a trial balance.

P3.8A (LO 3, 4, 5), AP The Triquel Theater Inc. was recently formed. It began operations in March 2022. The Triquel is unique in that it will show only triple features of sequential theme movies. On March 1, the ledger of The Triquel showed Cash $16,000, Land $38,000, Buildings (concession stand, projection room, ticket booth, and screen) $22,000, Equipment $16,000, Accounts Payable $12,000, and Common Stock $80,000. During the month of March, the following events and transactions occurred.

Mar. 2 Rented the first three Star Wars movies (*Star Wars®*, *The Empire Strikes Back*, and *The Return of the Jedi*) to be shown for the first three weeks of March. The film rental was $10,000; $2,000 was paid in cash and $8,000 will be paid on March 10.
   3 Ordered the first three *Star Trek* movies to be shown the last 10 days of March. It will cost $500 per night.
   9 Received $9,900 cash from admissions.
   10 Paid balance due on *Star Wars* movies' rental and $2,900 on March 1 accounts payable.
   11 The Triquel Theater contracted with R. Lazlo to operate the concession stand. Lazlo agrees to pay The Triquel 15% of gross receipts, payable monthly, for the rental of the concession stand.

12 Paid advertising expenses $500.
20 Received $8,300 cash from customers for admissions.
20 Received the *Star Trek* movies and paid rental fee of $5,000.
31 Paid salaries of $3,800.
31 Received statement from R. Lazlo showing gross receipts from concessions of $10,000 and the balance due to The Triquel of $1,500 ($10,000 × .15) for March. Lazlo paid half the balance due and will remit the remainder on April 5.
31 Received $20,000 cash from customers for admissions.

In addition to the accounts identified above, the chart of accounts includes Accounts Receivable, Service Revenue, Rent Revenue, Advertising Expense, Rent Expense, and Salaries and Wages Expense.

Instructions

a. Using T-accounts, enter the beginning balances to the ledger.
b. Journalize the March transactions, including explanations. The Triquel records admission revenue as service revenue, concession revenue as sales revenue, and film rental expense as rent expense.
c. Post the March journal entries to the ledger.
d. Prepare a trial balance on March 31, 2022.

d. Cash $32,750
Tot. trial balance $128,800

P3.9A (LO 3, 4, 5), AP On July 31, 2022, the general ledger of Hills Legal Services Inc. showed the following balances: Cash $4,000, Accounts Receivable $1,500, Supplies $500, Equipment $5,000, Accounts Payable $4,100, Common Stock $3,500, and Retained Earnings $3,400. During August, the following transactions occurred.

Journalize transactions, post, and prepare a trial balance.

Aug. 3 Collected $1,200 of accounts receivable due from customers.
5 Received $1,300 cash for issuing common stock to new investors.
6 Paid $2,700 cash on accounts payable.
7 Performed legal services of $6,500, of which $3,000 was collected in cash and the remainder was due on account.
12 Purchased additional equipment for $1,200, paying $400 in cash and the balance on account.
14 Paid salaries $3,500, rent $900, and advertising expenses $275 for the month of August.
18 Collected the balance for the services performed on August 7.
20 Paid cash dividend of $500 to stockholders.
24 Billed a client $1,000 for legal services performed.
26 Received $2,000 from Laurentian Bank; the money was borrowed on a bank note payable that is due in 6 months.
27 Agreed to perform legal services for a client in September for $4,500. The client will pay the amount owing after the services have been performed.
28 Received the utility bill for the month of August in the amount of $275; it is not due until September 15.
31 Paid income tax for the month $500.

Instructions

a. Using T-accounts, enter the beginning balances to the ledger.
b. Journalize the August transactions.
c. Post the August journal entries to the ledger.
d. Prepare a trial balance on August 31, 2022.

d. Cash $6,225
Tot. trial balance $20,175

P3.10A (LO 3, 4, 5), AP Pamper Me Salon Inc.'s general ledger at April 30, 2022, included the following: Cash $5,000, Supplies $500, Equipment $24,000, Accounts Payable $2,100, Notes Payable $10,000, Unearned Service Revenue (from gift certificates) $1,000, Common Stock $5,000, and Retained Earnings $11,400. The following events and transactions occurred during May.

Journalize transactions, post, and prepare trial balance.

May 1 Paid rent for the month of May $1,000.
4 Paid $1,100 of the account payable at April 30.
7 Issued gift certificates for future services for $1,500 cash.
8 Received $1,200 cash from customers for services performed.
14 Paid $1,200 in salaries to employees.
15 Received $800 in cash from customers for services performed.
15 Customers receiving services worth $700 used gift certificates in payment.
21 Paid the remaining accounts payable from April 30.
22 Received $1,000 in cash from customers for services performed.
22 Purchased supplies of $700 on account. All of these were used during the month.
25 Received a bill for advertising for $500. This bill is due on June 13.

25 Received and paid a utilities bill for $400.
29 Received $1,700 in cash from customers for services performed.
29 Customers receiving services worth $600 used gift certificates in payment.
31 Interest of $50 was paid on the note payable.
31 Paid $1,200 in salaries to employees.
31 Paid income tax payment for the month $150.

Instructions

a. Using T-accounts, enter the beginning balances in the general ledger as of April 30, 2022.
b. Journalize the May transactions.
c. Post the May journal entries to the general ledger.
d. Prepare a trial balance on May 31, 2022.

d. Cash $5,100
Tot. trial balance $34,800

Analyze errors and their effects on the trial balance.

P3.11A (LO 5), AN The bookkeeper for Roger's Dance Studio made the following errors in journalizing and posting.

1. A credit to Supplies of $600 was omitted.
2. A debit posting of $300 to Accounts Payable was inadvertently debited to Accounts Receivable.
3. A purchase of supplies on account of $450 was debited to Supplies for $540 and credited to Accounts Payable for $540.
4. A credit posting of $680 to Interest Payable was posted twice.
5. A debit posting to Income Taxes Payable for $250 and a credit posting to Cash for $250 were made twice.
6. A debit posting for $1,200 of Dividends was inadvertently posted to Salaries and Wages Expense instead.
7. A credit to Service Revenue for $450 was inadvertently posted as a debit to Service Revenue.
8. A credit to Accounts Receivable of $250 was credited to Accounts Payable.

Instructions

For each error, indicate (a) whether the trial balance will balance, (b) the amount of the difference if the trial balance will not balance, and (c) the trial balance column that will have the larger total. Consider each error separately. Use the following form, in which error 1 is given as an example.

Error	(a) In Balance	(b) Difference	(c) Larger Column
1	No	$600	Debit

Continuing Case

© leungchopan/Shutterstock

Cookie Creations

(*Note:* This is a continuation of the Cookie Creations case from Chapters 1 and 2.)

CC3 In November 2022, after having incorporated Cookie Creations Inc., Natalie begins operations. She has decided not to pursue the offer to supply cookies to Biscuits. Instead, the company will focus on offering cooking classes.

Go to WileyPLUS for complete case details and instructions.

Expand Your Critical Thinking

Financial Reporting Problem: Apple Inc.

CT3.1 The financial statements of **Apple Inc.** in Appendix A contain the following selected accounts, all in thousands of dollars.

Common Stock	$ 35,867
Accounts Payable	49,049
Accounts Receivable	17,874
Selling, General, and Administrative Expenses	15,261
Inventories	4,855
Net Property, Plant, and Equipment	33,783
Net Sales	229,234

Instructions

a. What is the increase and decrease side for each account? What is the normal balance for each account?

b. Identify the probable other account in the transaction and the effect on that account when:
   1. Accounts Receivable is decreased.
   2. Accounts Payable is decreased.
   3. Inventories is increased.

c. Identify the other account(s) that ordinarily would be involved when:
   1. Interest Expense is increased.
   2. Property, Plant, and Equipment is increased.

Comparative Analysis Problem: Columbia Sportswear Company vs. VF Corporation

CT3.2 The financial statements of **Columbia Sportswear Company** are presented in Appendix B. Financial statements of **VF Corporation** are presented in Appendix C.

Instructions

a. Based on the information contained in these financial statements, determine the normal balance for:

Columbia Sportswear	VF
(1) Accounts Receivable	(1) Inventories
(2) Net Property, Plant, and Equipment	(2) Income Taxes
(3) Accounts Payable	(3) Accrued Liabilities
(4) Retained Earnings	(4) Common Stock
(5) Net Sales	(5) Interest Expense

b. Identify the other account ordinarily involved when:
   1. Accounts Receivable is increased.
   2. Notes Payable is decreased.
   3. Equipment is increased.
   4. Interest Revenue is increased.

Comparative Analysis Problem: Amazon.com, Inc. vs. Wal-Mart Stores, Inc.

CT3.3 Amazon.com, Inc.'s financial statements are presented in Appendix D. Financial statements of **Wal-Mart Stores, Inc.** are presented in Appendix E.

Instructions

a. Based on the information contained in the financial statements, determine the normal balance of the listed accounts for each company.

Amazon	Wal-Mart
1. Interest Expense	1. Product Revenues
2. Cash and Cash Equivalents	2. Inventories
3. Accounts Payable	3. Cost of Sales

b. Identify the other account ordinarily involved when:
   1. Accounts Receivable is increased.
   2. Interest Expense is increased.
   3. Salaries and Wages Payable is decreased.
   4. Service Revenue is increased.

Interpreting Financial Statements

CT3.4 **Chieftain International, Inc.**, is an oil and natural gas exploration and production company. A recent balance sheet reported $208 million in assets with only $4.6 million in liabilities, all of which were short-term accounts payable.

During the year, Chieftain expanded its holdings of oil and gas rights, drilled 37 new wells, and invested in expensive 3-D seismic technology. The company generated $19 million cash from operating activities and paid no dividends. It had a cash balance of $102 million at the end of the year.

Instructions

a. Name at least two advantages to Chieftain from having no long-term debt. Can you think of disadvantages?

b. What are some of the advantages to Chieftain from having this large a cash balance? What is a disadvantage?

c. Why do you suppose Chieftain has the $4.6 million balance in accounts payable, since it appears that it could have made all its purchases for cash?

Real-World Focus

CT3.5 This activity provides information about career opportunities for CPAs.

Instructions

Search the Internet for "start here go places" to access free accounting resources for future CPAs and then answer the following questions.

a. Where do CPAs work?

b. What skills does a CPA need?

c. What is the salary range for a CPA at a large firm during the first three years? What is the salary range for chief financial officers and treasurers at large corporations?

CT3.6 The January 27, 2011, edition of the *New York Times* contains an article by Richard Sandomir entitled "N.F.L. Finances, as Seen Through Packers' Records." The article discusses the fact that the **Green Bay Packers** are the only NFL team that publicly publishes its annual report.

Instructions

Read the article and answer the following questions.

a. Why are the Green Bay Packers the only professional football team to publish and distribute an annual report?

b. Why is the football players' labor union particularly interested in the Packers' annual report?

c. In addition to the players' labor union, what other outside party might be interested in the annual report?

d. Even though the Packers' revenue increased in recent years, the company's operating profit fell significantly. How does the article explain this decline?

Decision-Making Across the Organization

CT3.7 Saira Morrow operates Dressage Riding Academy, Inc. The academy's primary sources of revenue are riding fees and lesson fees, which are provided on a cash basis. Saira also boards horses for owners, who are billed monthly for boarding fees. In a few cases, boarders pay in advance of expected use. For its revenue transactions, the academy maintains these accounts: Cash, Accounts Receivable, Unearned Service Revenue, and Service Revenue.

The academy owns 10 horses, a stable, a riding corral, riding equipment, and office equipment. These assets are accounted for in the following accounts: Horses, Buildings, and Equipment.

The academy employs stable helpers and an office employee, who receive weekly salaries. At the end of each month, the mail usually brings bills for advertising, utilities, and veterinary service. Other expenses include feed for the horses and insurance. For its expenses, the academy maintains the following accounts: Supplies, Prepaid Insurance, Accounts Payable, Salaries and Wages Expense, Advertising Expense, Utilities Expense, Maintenance and Repairs Expense, Supplies Expense, and Insurance Expense.

Saira's sole source of personal income is dividends from the academy. Thus, the corporation declares and pays periodic dividends. To account for stockholders' equity in the business and dividends, two accounts are maintained: Common Stock and Dividends.

During the first month of operations, an inexperienced bookkeeper was employed. Saira asks you to review the following eight entries of the 50 entries made during the month. In each case, the explanation for the entry is correct.

Date		Account	Debit	Credit
May 1		Cash	15,000	
		Unearned Service Revenue		15,000
		(Issued common stock in exchange for $15,000 cash)		
5		Cash	250	
		Service Revenue		250
		(Received $250 cash for lesson fees)		
7		Cash	500	
		Service Revenue		500
		(Received $500 for boarding of horses beginning June 1)		
9		Supplies Expense	1,500	
		Cash		1,500
		(Purchased estimated 5 months' supply of feed and hay for $1,500 on account)		
14		Equipment	80	
		Cash		800
		(Purchased desk and other office equipment for $800 cash)		
15		Salaries and Wages Expense	400	
		Cash		400
		(Issued check to Saira Morrow for personal use)		
20		Cash	145	
		Service Revenue		154
		(Received $154 cash for riding fees)		
31		Maintenance and Repairs Expense	75	
		Accounts Receivable		75
		(Received bill of $75 from carpenter for repair services performed)		

Instructions

With the class divided into groups, answer the following.

a. For each journal entry that is correct, so state. For each journal entry that is incorrect, prepare the entry that should have been made by the bookkeeper.

b. Which of the incorrect entries would prevent the trial balance from balancing?

c. What was the correct net income for May, assuming the bookkeeper originally reported net income of $4,500 after posting all 50 entries?

d. What was the correct cash balance at May 31, assuming the bookkeeper reported a balance of $12,475 after posting all 50 entries?

Communication Activity

CT3.8 Klean Sweep Company offers home cleaning service. Two recurring transactions for the company are billing customers for services performed and paying employee salaries. For example, on March 15 bills totaling $6,000 were sent to customers, and $2,000 was paid in salaries to employees.

Instructions

Write a memorandum to your instructor that explains and illustrates the steps in the recording process for each of the March 15 transactions. Use the format illustrated in the text under the heading "The Recording Process Illustrated."

Ethics Cases

CT3.9 Vanessa Jones is the assistant chief accountant at IBT Company, a manufacturer of computer chips and cell phones. The company presently has total sales of $20 million. It is the end of the first quarter and Vanessa is hurriedly trying to prepare a trial balance so that quarterly financial statements can be prepared and released to management and the regulatory agencies. The total credits on the trial balance exceed the debits by $1,000.

In order to meet the 4 P.M. deadline, Vanessa decides to force the debits and credits into balance by adding the amount of the difference to the Equipment account. She chose Equipment because it is one of the larger account balances; percentage-wise, it will be the least misstated. Vanessa plugs the difference! She believes that the difference is quite small and will not affect anyone's decisions. She wishes that she had another few days to find the error but realizes that the financial statements are already late.

Instructions

a. Who are the stakeholders in this situation?
b. What ethical issues are involved?
c. What are Vanessa's alternatives?

CT3.10 The July 28, 2007, issue of the *Wall Street Journal* includes an article by Kathryn Kranhold entitled "GE's Accounting Draws Fresh Focus on News of Improper Sales Bookings."

Instructions

Read the article and answer the following questions.

a. What improper activity did the employees at GE engage in?
b. Why might the employees have engaged in this activity?
c. What were the implications for the employees who engaged in this activity?
d. What does it mean to "restate" financial results? Why didn't GE restate its results to correct for the improperly reported locomotive sales?

All About You

CT3.11 In their annual reports to stockholders, companies must report or disclose information about all liabilities, including potential liabilities related to environmental clean-up. There are many situations in which you will be asked to provide personal financial information about your assets, liabilities, revenues, and expenses. Sometimes you will face difficult decisions regarding what to disclose and how to disclose it.

Instructions

Suppose that you are putting together a loan application to purchase a home. Based on your income and assets, you qualify for the mortgage loan, but just barely. How would you address each of the following situations in reporting your financial position for the loan application? Provide responses for each of the following questions.

a. You signed a guarantee for a bank loan that a friend took out for $20,000. If your friend doesn't pay, you will have to pay. Your friend has made all of the payments so far, and it appears he will be able to pay in the future.
b. You were involved in an auto accident in which you were at fault. There is the possibility that you may have to pay as much as $50,000 as part of a settlement. The issue will not be resolved before the bank processes your mortgage request.
c. The company at which you work isn't doing very well, and it has recently laid off employees. You are still employed, but it is quite possible that you will lose your job in the next few months.

A Look at IFRS

LEARNING OBJECTIVE 6
Compare the procedures for the recording process under GAAP and IFRS.

International companies use the same set of procedures and records to keep track of transaction data. Thus, the material in this chapter dealing with the account, general rules of debit and credit, and steps in the recording process—the journal, ledger, and chart of accounts—is the same under both GAAP and IFRS.

Key Points

Following are the key similarities and differences between GAAP and IFRS as related to the recording process.

Similarities

- Transaction analysis is the same under IFRS and GAAP.
- Both the IASB and the FASB go beyond the basic definitions provided in the text for the key elements of financial statements, that is assets, liabilities, equity, revenues, and expenses. The implications of the expanded definitions are discussed in more advanced accounting courses.
- As shown in the text, dollar signs are typically used only in the trial balance and the financial statements. The same practice is followed under IFRS, using the currency of the country where the reporting company is headquartered.
- A trial balance under IFRS follows the same format as shown in the text.

Differences

- IFRS relies less on historical cost and more on fair value than do FASB standards.
- Internal controls are a system of checks and balances designed to prevent and detect fraud and errors. While most public U.S. companies have these systems in place, many non-U.S. companies have never completely documented the controls nor had an independent auditor attest to their effectiveness.

IFRS Practice

IFRS Self-Test Questions

1. Which statement is **correct** regarding IFRS?
   a. IFRS reverses the rules of debits and credits, that is, debits are on the right and credits are on the left.
   b. IFRS uses the same process for recording transactions as GAAP.
   c. The chart of accounts under IFRS is different because revenues follow assets.
   d. None of the above statements are correct.

2. The expanded accounting equation under IFRS is as follows:
   a. Assets = Liabilities + Common Stock + Retained Earnings + Revenues − Expenses + Dividends.
   b. Assets + Liabilities = Common Stock + Retained Earnings + Revenues − Expenses − Dividends.
   c. Assets = Liabilities + Common Stock + Retained Earnings + Revenues − Expenses − Dividends.
   d. Assets = Liabilities + Common Stock + Retained Earnings − Revenues − Expenses − Dividends.

3. A trial balance:
   a. is the same under IFRS and GAAP.
   b. proves that transactions are recorded correctly.
   c. proves that all transactions have been recorded.
   d. will not balance if a correct journal entry is posted twice.

4. One difference between IFRS and GAAP is that:
   a. GAAP uses accrual-accounting concepts and IFRS uses primarily the cash basis of accounting.
   b. IFRS uses a different posting process than GAAP.
   c. IFRS uses more fair value measurements than GAAP.
   d. the limitations of a trial balance are different between IFRS and GAAP.

5. The general policy for using proper currency signs (dollar, yen, pound, etc.) is the same for both IFRS and this text. This policy is as follows:
   a. Currency signs only appear in ledgers and journal entries.
   b. Currency signs are only shown in the trial balance.
   c. Currency signs are shown for all compound journal entries.
   d. Currency signs are shown in trial balances and financial statements.

International Financial Reporting Problem: Louis Vuitton

IFRS3.1 The financial statements of Louis Vuitton are presented in Appendix F. The complete annual report, including the notes to its financial statements, is available at the company's website.

Instructions

Describe in which statement each of the following items is reported, and the position in the statement (e.g., current asset).

    a. Other operating income and expense.

    b. Cash and cash equivalents.

    c. Trade accounts payable.

    d. Cost of net financial debt.

Answers to IFRS Self-Test Questions

1. b   **2.** c   **3.** a   **4.** c   **5.** d

CHAPTER 4

Accrual Accounting Concepts

Chapter Preview

As indicated in the Feature Story, making adjustments is necessary to avoid misstatement of revenues and expenses such as those at **Groupon**. In this chapter, we introduce you to the accrual accounting concepts that make such adjustments possible.

Feature Story

Keeping Track of Groupons

Who doesn't like buying things at a discount? That's why it's not surprising that three years after it started as a company, **Groupon, Inc.** was estimated to be worth $16 billion. This translates into an average increase in value of almost $15 million per day.

Now consider that Groupon had previously been estimated to be worth even more than that. What happened? Well, accounting regulators and investors began to question the way that Groupon had accounted for some of its transactions. Groupon sells coupons ("Groupons"), so how hard can it be to account for that? It turns out that accounting for coupons is not as easy as you might think.

First, consider what happens when Groupon makes a sale. Suppose it sells a Groupon for $30 for Highrise Hamburgers. When it receives the $30 from the customer, it must turn over half of that amount ($15) to Highrise Hamburgers. So should Groupon record revenue for the full $30 or just $15? Until recently, Groupon recorded the full $30. But, in response to an SEC ruling on the issue, Groupon now records revenue of $15 instead. This caused Groupon to restate its previous financial statements. This restatement reduced annual revenue by $312.9 million.

A second issue is a matter of timing. When should Groupon record this $15 revenue? Should it record the revenue when it sells the Groupon, or must it wait until the customer uses the Groupon at Highrise Hamburgers? The accounting becomes even more complicated when you consider the company's loyalty programs. Groupon offers free or discounted Groupons to its subscribers for doing things such as referring new customers or participating in promotions. These Groupons are to be used for future purchases, yet the company must record the expense at the time the customer receives the Groupon.

Finally, Groupon, like all other companies, relies on many estimates in its financial reporting. For example, Groupon reports that "estimates are utilized for, but not limited to, stock-based compensation, income taxes, valuation of acquired goodwill and intangible assets, customer refunds, contingent liabilities and the depreciable lives of fixed assets." It notes that "actual results could differ materially from those estimates." So, next time you use a coupon, think about what that means for the company's accountants!

Chapter Outline

LEARNING OBJECTIVES

LO 1 Explain the accrual basis of accounting and the reasons for adjusting entries.	• Revenue recognition principle • Expense recognition principle • Accrual vs. cash basis • Need for adjusting entries • Types of adjusting entries	**DO IT! 1** Timing Concepts
LO 2 Prepare adjusting entries for deferrals.	• Prepaid expenses • Unearned revenues	**DO IT! 2** Adjusting Entries for Deferrals
LO 3 Prepare adjusting entries for accruals.	• Accrued revenues • Accrued expenses • Summary of basic relationships	**DO IT! 3** Adjusting Entries for Accruals
LO 4 Prepare an adjusted trial balance and closing entries.	• Preparing the adjusted trial balance • Preparing financial statements • Quality of earnings • Closing the books • Summary of the accounting cycle	**DO IT! 4a** Trial Balance **DO IT! 4b** Closing Entries

Go to the Review and Practice section at the end of the chapter for a targeted summary and practice applications with solutions.
Visit WileyPLUS for additional tutorials and practice opportunities.

Accrual-Basis Accounting and Adjusting Entries

LEARNING OBJECTIVE 1
Explain the accrual basis of accounting and the reasons for adjusting entries.

Businesses need feedback about how well they are performing during a period of time. For example, management usually wants monthly reports on financial results, most large corporations are required to present quarterly and annual financial statements to stockholders, and the Internal Revenue Service requires all businesses to file annual tax returns. **Accounting** divides the economic life of a business into artificial time periods. Recall that this is the **periodicity assumption**. **Accounting time periods are generally a month, a quarter, or a year** (see **Helpful Hint**). Companies often report using the calendar year (i.e., January 1 to December 31) but sometimes choose a different 12-month period (e.g., August 1 to July 31).

Many business transactions affect more than one of these arbitrary time periods. For example, a new building purchased by **Citigroup** or a new airplane purchased by **Delta Air Lines** will be used for many years. It would not make sense to expense the full cost of the building or the airplane at the time of purchase because each will be used for many subsequent periods. Instead, companies allocate the cost to the periods of use.

Determining the amount of revenues and expenses to report in a given accounting period can be difficult. Proper reporting requires an understanding of the nature of the company's business. Two principles are used as guidelines: the revenue recognition principle and the expense recognition principle.

> **HELPFUL HINT**
> An accounting time period that is one year long is called a fiscal year.

The Revenue Recognition Principle

When a company agrees to perform a service or sell a product to a customer, it has a performance obligation. The **revenue recognition principle** requires that companies **recognize revenue in the accounting period in which the performance obligation is satisfied**. To illustrate, assume Conrad Dry Cleaners performs cleaning services for $100 on June 30, but customers do not claim and pay for their clothes until July 5. Under the revenue recognition principle, Conrad records revenue on June 30 when it satisfies its performance obligation, which is when it performs the service, not in July when it receives the cash. At June 30, Conrad would report a receivable on its balance sheet and revenue in its income statement for the service performed. The journal entries would be as follows.

June 30	Accounts Receivable	100	
	Service Revenue		100
July 5	Cash	100	
	Accounts Receivable		100

> **Revenue Recognition**
>
> Service performed → Cash received
> Customer requests service
>
> Revenue should be recognized in the accounting period in which the service is performed.

Five-Step Revenue Recognition Process—Sierra Corporation Example

Revenue recognition results from a five-step process. This process can best be illustrated with an example. Assume that Sierra Corporation signs a contract with the Lewis family to provide guide services for a one-week backpacking trip for $1,500. **Illustration 4.1** shows the five steps that Sierra follows to recognize revenue.

ILLUSTRATION 4.1 Five steps of revenue recognition

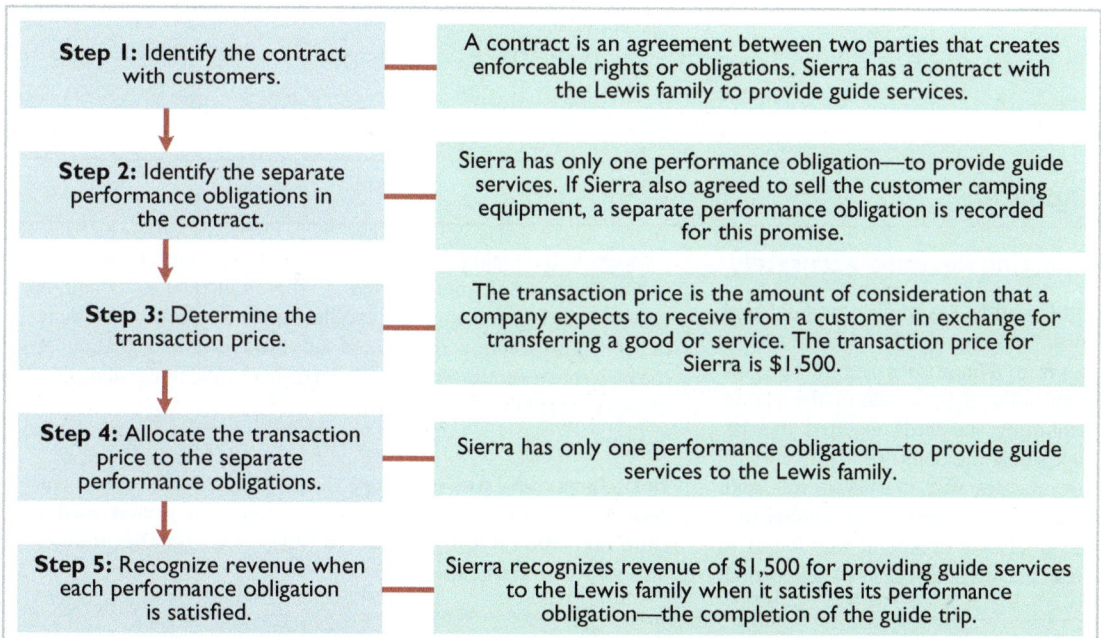

Step 1: Identify the contract with customers. — A contract is an agreement between two parties that creates enforceable rights or obligations. Sierra has a contract with the Lewis family to provide guide services.

Step 2: Identify the separate performance obligations in the contract. — Sierra has only one performance obligation—to provide guide services. If Sierra also agreed to sell the customer camping equipment, a separate performance obligation is recorded for this promise.

Step 3: Determine the transaction price. — The transaction price is the amount of consideration that a company expects to receive from a customer in exchange for transferring a good or service. The transaction price for Sierra is $1,500.

Step 4: Allocate the transaction price to the separate performance obligations. — Sierra has only one performance obligation—to provide guide services to the Lewis family.

Step 5: Recognize revenue when each performance obligation is satisfied. — Sierra recognizes revenue of $1,500 for providing guide services to the Lewis family when it satisfies its performance obligation—the completion of the guide trip.

As indicated, Step 5 is when Sierra recognizes revenue related to providing the guide services to the Lewis family. At this point, Sierra completes the trip and satisfies its performance obligation.

The Expense Recognition Principle

In recognizing expenses, a simple rule is followed: "Let the expenses follow the revenues." Thus, expense recognition is tied to revenue recognition. Applied to the Conrad Dry Cleaners example, this means that the salary expense Conrad incurred in performing the cleaning service on June 30 should be reported in the same period in which it recognizes the service revenue. The critical issue in expense recognition is determining when the expense makes its contribution to revenue. This may or may not be the same period in which the expense is paid. If Conrad does not pay the salary incurred on June 30 until July, it would report salaries and wages payable on its June 30 balance sheet.

The practice of expense recognition is referred to as the **expense recognition principle** (often referred to as the **matching principle**). It dictates that efforts (expenses) be recognized with results (revenues) in the period when the company makes efforts to generate those revenues. Illustration 4.2 shows these relationships (see **Decision Tools**).

ILLUSTRATION 4.2

GAAP relationships in revenue and expense recognition

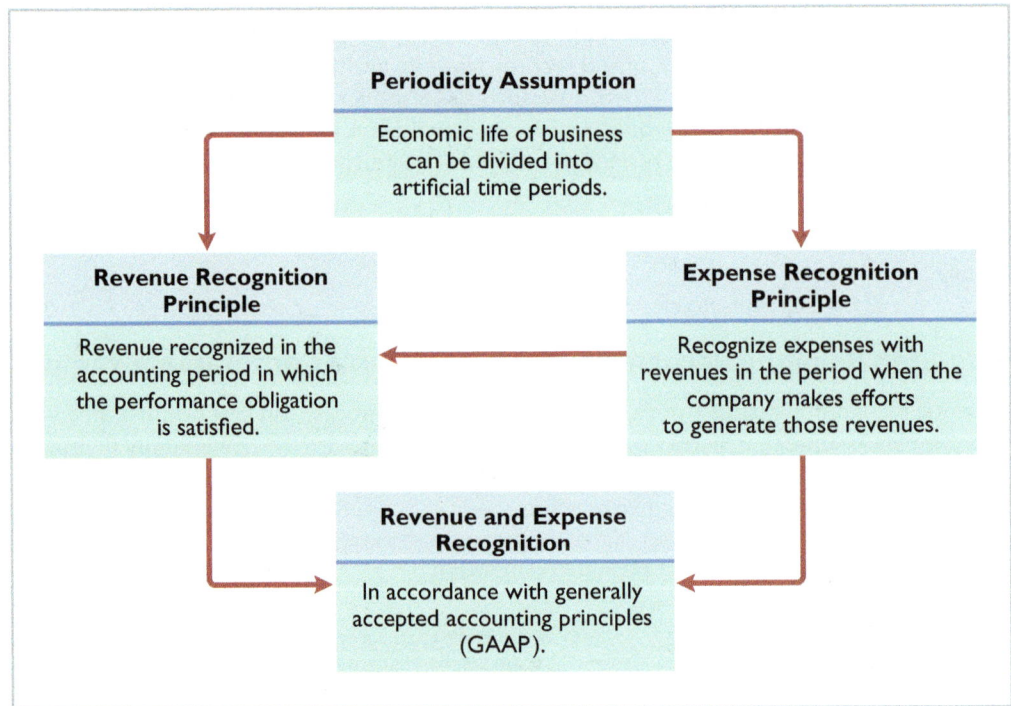

Decision Tools

The revenue recognition principle and the expense recognition principle help to ensure that companies report the correct amount of revenues and expenses in a given period.

Investor Insight   Apple Inc.

PhotoAlto/James Hardy/ Getty Images, Inc.

Reporting Revenue Accurately

Until recently, electronics manufacturer **Apple** was required to spread the revenues from iPhone sales over the two-year period following the sale of the phone. Accounting standards required this because Apple was obligated to provide software updates after the phone was sold. Since Apple had service obligations after the initial date of sale, it was forced to spread the revenue over a two-year period.

As a result, the rapid growth of iPhone sales was not fully reflected in the revenue amounts reported in Apple's income statement. A new accounting standard now enables Apple to report much more of its iPhone revenue at the point of sale. It was estimated that under the new rule revenues would have been about 17% higher and earnings per share almost 50% higher.

In the past, why was it argued that Apple should spread the recognition of iPhone revenue over a two-year period, rather than recording it upfront? (Go to WileyPLUS for this answer and additional questions.)

Accrual versus Cash Basis of Accounting

Accrual-basis accounting means that transactions that change a company's financial statements are recorded **in the periods in which the events occur**, even if cash was not exchanged (see **International Note**). For example, using the accrual basis means that companies recognize revenues when they perform the services (the revenue recognition principle), even if cash was not received. Likewise, under the accrual basis, companies recognize expenses when incurred (the expense recognition principle), even if cash was not paid.

An alternative to the accrual basis is the cash basis. Under **cash-basis accounting**, companies record revenue at the time they receive cash. They record an expense at the time they pay out cash. The cash basis seems appealing due to its simplicity, but it often produces misleading financial statements. For example, it fails to record revenue for a company that has performed services but has not yet received payment. As a result, the cash basis may not reflect revenue in the period that a performance obligation is satisfied. **Cash-basis accounting is not in accordance with generally accepted accounting principles (GAAP).**

Illustration 4.3 compares accrual-based numbers and cash-based numbers. Suppose that Fresh Colors paints a large building in 2021. In 2021, it incurs and pays total expenses (salaries and paint costs) of $50,000. It bills the customer $80,000 but does not receive payment until 2022. On an accrual basis, Fresh Colors reports $80,000 of revenue during 2021 because that is when it performed the service. The company matches expenses of $50,000 to the $80,000 of revenue. Thus, 2021 net income is $30,000 ($80,000 − $50,000). The $30,000 of net income reported for 2021 indicates the profitability of Fresh Colors' efforts during that period.

> **International Note**
>
> Although different accounting standards are often used by companies in other countries, the accrual basis of accounting is central to all of these standards.

ILLUSTRATION 4.3 Accrual-versus cash-basis accounting

	2021	2022
Activity	Purchased paint, painted building, paid employees	Received payment for work done in 2021
Accrual basis	Revenue $80,000 Expense 50,000 Net income $30,000	Revenue $ 0 Expense 0 Net income $ 0
Cash basis	Revenue $ 0 Expense 50,000 Net loss $(50,000)	Revenue $80,000 Expense 0 Net income $80,000

If Fresh Colors instead used cash-basis accounting, it would report $50,000 of expenses in 2021 and $80,000 of revenues during 2022. As shown in Illustration 4.3, it would report a loss of $50,000 in 2021 and net income of $80,000 in 2022. Clearly, the cash-basis measures are misleading because the financial performance of the company would be misstated for both 2021 and 2022.

The Need for Adjusting Entries

In order for revenues to be recorded in the period in which the performance obligations are satisfied and for expenses to be recognized in the period in which they are incurred, companies make adjusting entries. **Adjusting entries ensure that the revenue recognition and expense recognition principles are followed.**

Adjusting entries are necessary because the **trial balance**—the first pulling together of the transaction data—may not contain up-to-date and complete data. This is true for several reasons:

1. Some events are not recorded daily because it is not efficient to do so. Examples are the use of supplies and the earning of wages by employees.
2. Some costs are not recorded during the accounting period because these costs expire with the passage of time rather than as a result of recurring daily transactions. Examples are charges related to the use of buildings and equipment, rent, and insurance.
3. Some items may be unrecorded. An example is a utility service bill that will not be received until the next accounting period.

Adjusting entries are required every time a company prepares financial statements. The company analyzes each account in the trial balance to determine whether it is complete and up-to-date for financial statement purposes. **Every adjusting entry will include one income statement account and one balance sheet account.**

Types of Adjusting Entries

Adjusting entries are classified as either deferrals or accruals. As **Illustration 4.4** shows, each of these classes has two subcategories.

ILLUSTRATION 4.4
Categories of adjusting entries

Deferrals:
1. **Prepaid expenses:** Expenses paid in cash before they are used or consumed.
2. **Unearned revenues:** Cash received before services are performed.

Accruals:
1. **Accrued revenues:** Revenues for services performed but not yet received in cash or recorded.
2. **Accrued expenses:** Expenses incurred but not yet paid in cash or recorded.

Subsequent sections give examples of each type of adjustment. Each example is based on the October 31 trial balance of Sierra Corporation from Illustration 3.35. It is reproduced in **Illustration 4.5**. Note that Retained Earnings has been added to this trial balance with a zero balance. We will explain its use later.

ILLUSTRATION 4.5
Trial balance

Sierra Corporation
Trial Balance
October 31, 2022

	Debit	Credit
Cash	$15,200	
Supplies	2,500	
Prepaid Insurance	600	
Equipment	5,000	
Notes Payable		$ 5,000
Accounts Payable		2,500
Unearned Service Revenue		1,200
Common Stock		10,000
Retained Earnings		0
Dividends	500	
Service Revenue		10,000
Salaries and Wages Expense	4,000	
Rent Expense	900	
	$28,700	$28,700

We assume that Sierra uses an accounting period of one month. Thus, monthly adjusting entries are made. The entries are dated October 31.

> ### DO IT! 1 | Timing Concepts
>
> Below is a list of concepts in the left column, with descriptions of the concepts in the right column. There are more descriptions provided than concepts. Match the description of the concept to the concept.
>
> 1. _____ Accrual-basis accounting.
> 2. _____ Calendar year.
> 3. _____ Periodicity assumption.
> 4. _____ Expense recognition principle.
>
> a. Monthly and quarterly time periods.
> b. Efforts (expenses) should be matched with results (revenues).
> c. Accountants divide the economic life of a business into artificial time periods.
> d. Companies record revenues when they receive cash and record expenses when they pay out cash.
> e. An accounting time period that starts on January 1 and ends on December 31.
> f. Companies record transactions in the period in which the events occur.
>
> **ACTION PLAN**
> - Review the terms identified.
> - Study carefully the revenue recognition principle, the expense recognition principle, and the periodicity assumption.
>
> **Solution**
>
> 1. f 2. e 3. c 4. b
>
> Related exercise material: **BE4.1, BE4.2, BE4.3, DO IT! 4.1, E4.1, E4.2, E4.3, and E4.5.**

Adjusting Entries for Deferrals

LEARNING OBJECTIVE 2
Prepare adjusting entries for deferrals.

ANALYZE → JOURNALIZE → POST → TRIAL BALANCE → **Journalize and post adjusting entries: deferrals/accruals** → ADJUSTED TRIAL BALANCE → FINANCIAL STATEMENTS → CLOSING ENTRIES → POST-CLOSING TRIAL BALANCE

To defer means to postpone or delay. Deferrals are costs or revenues that are recognized at a date later than the point when cash was originally exchanged. Companies make adjusting entries for deferred expenses to record the portion that was incurred during the period. Companies also make adjusting entries for deferred revenues to record services performed during the period. The two types of deferrals are prepaid expenses and unearned revenues.

Prepaid Expenses

Companies record payments of expenses that will benefit more than one accounting period as assets. These **prepaid expenses** or **prepayments** are expenses paid in cash before they are used or consumed. When expenses are prepaid, an asset account is increased (debited) to show the service or benefit that the company will receive in the future. Examples of common prepayments are insurance, supplies, advertising, and rent. In addition, companies make prepayments when they purchase buildings and equipment.

Prepaid expenses are costs that expire either with the passage of time (e.g., rent and insurance) **or through use** (e.g., supplies). The expiration of these costs does not require daily entries, which would be impractical and unnecessary. Accordingly, companies postpone the recognition of such cost expirations until they prepare financial statements. At each statement date, they make adjusting entries to record the expenses applicable to the current accounting period and to show the remaining amounts in the asset accounts.

Prior to adjustment, assets are overstated and expenses are understated. Therefore, as shown in **Illustration 4.6**, **an adjusting entry for prepaid expenses results in an increase (a debit) to an expense account and a decrease (a credit) to an asset account**.

ILLUSTRATION 4.6 Adjusting entries for prepaid expenses

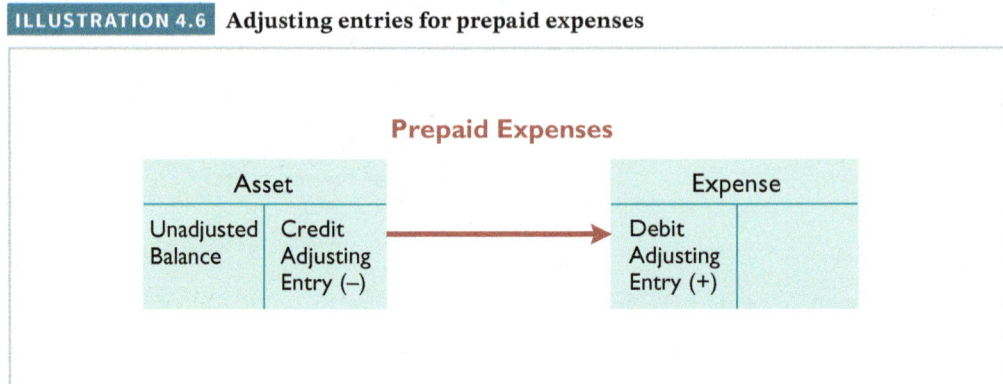

Let's look in more detail at some specific types of prepaid expenses, beginning with supplies.

Supplies

Supplies
Oct. 5
Supplies purchased; record asset

Oct. 31
Supplies used; record supplies expense

The purchase of supplies, such as paper and envelopes, results in an increase (a debit) to an asset account. During the accounting period, the company uses supplies. Rather than record supplies expense as the supplies are used, companies recognize supplies expense at the **end** of the accounting period. At the end of the accounting period, the company counts the remaining supplies. The difference between the unadjusted balance in the Supplies (asset) account and the actual cost of supplies on hand represents the supplies used (an expense) for that period.

Sierra Corporation purchased supplies costing $2,500 on October 5. Sierra recorded the purchase by increasing (debiting) the asset Supplies. This account shows a balance of $2,500 in the October 31 trial balance. A physical count of the inventory at the close of business on October 31 reveals that $1,000 of supplies are still on hand. Thus, the cost of supplies used is $1,500 ($2,500 − $1,000). This use of supplies decreases an asset, Supplies. It also decreases stockholders' equity by increasing an expense account, Supplies Expense. This is shown in **Illustration 4.7** (see **Helpful Hint**).

After adjustment, the asset account Supplies shows a balance of $1,000, which is equal to the cost of supplies on hand at the statement date. In addition, Supplies Expense shows a balance of $1,500, which equals the cost of supplies used in October. **If Sierra does not make the adjusting entry, October expenses will be understated and net income overstated by $1,500. Moreover, both assets and stockholders' equity will be overstated by $1,500 on the October 31 balance sheet.**

Insurance

Companies purchase insurance to protect themselves from losses due to fire, theft, and unforeseen events. Insurance must be paid in advance, often for multiple months. The cost of

ILLUSTRATION 4.7 Adjustment for supplies

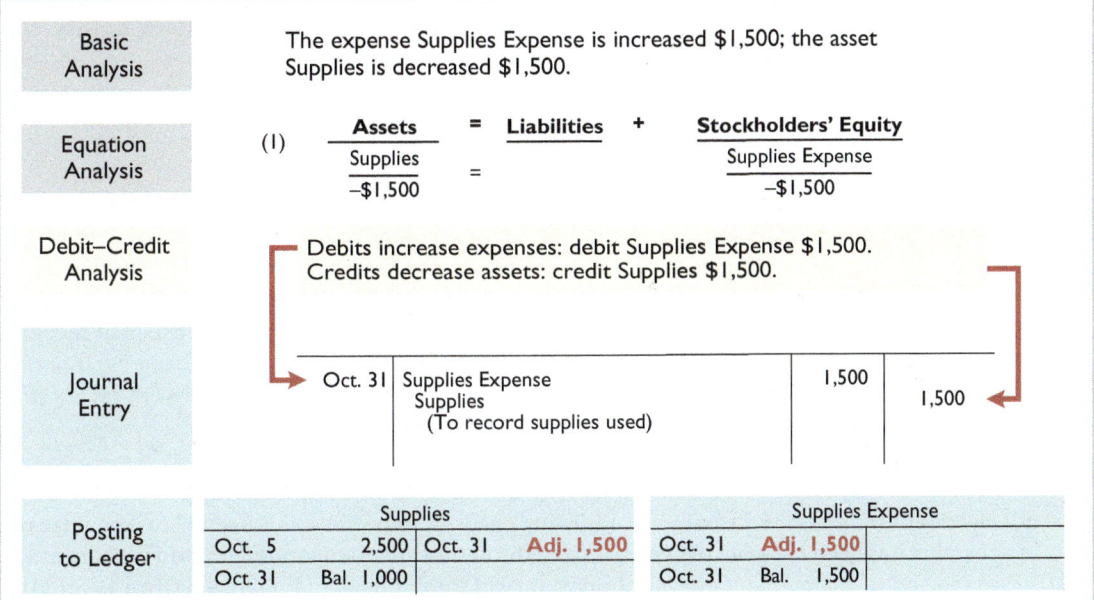

HELPFUL HINT
Due to their nature, adjusting entries have **no effect** on cash flows. As a result, we do not show the cash flow effects in these illustrations.

insurance (premiums) paid in advance is recorded as an increase (debit) in the asset account Prepaid Insurance. At the financial statement date, companies increase (debit) Insurance Expense and decrease (credit) Prepaid Insurance for the cost of insurance that has expired during the period.

On October 4, Sierra Corporation paid $600 for a one-year fire insurance policy. Coverage began on October 1. Sierra recorded the payment by increasing (debiting) Prepaid Insurance. This account shows a balance of $600 in the October 31 trial balance. Insurance of $50 ($600 ÷ 12) expires each month. The expiration of prepaid insurance decreases an asset, Prepaid Insurance. It also decreases stockholders' equity by increasing an expense account, Insurance Expense.

As shown in **Illustration 4.8**, the asset Prepaid Insurance shows a balance of $550, which represents the unexpired cost for the remaining 11 months of coverage. At the same

ILLUSTRATION 4.8 Adjustment for insurance

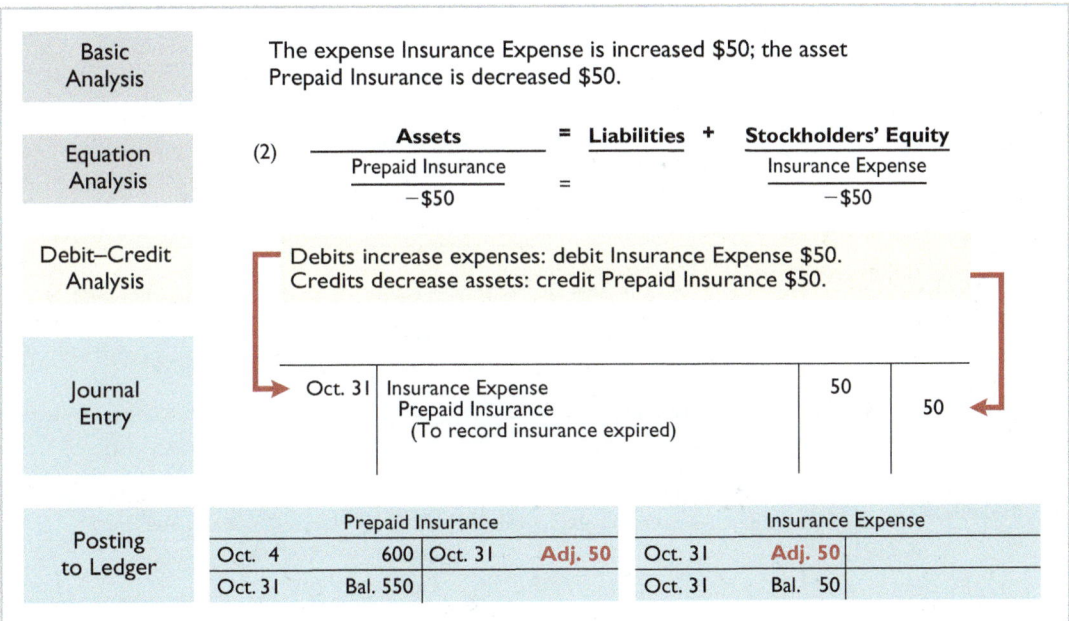

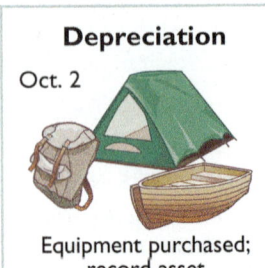

Depreciation

Oct. 2

Equipment purchased; record asset

Equipment			
Oct $40	Nov $40	Dec $40	Jan $40
Feb $40	March $40	April $40	May $40
June $40	July $40	Aug $40	Sept $40
Depreciation = $480/year			

Oct. 31
Depreciation recognized; record depreciation expense

HELPFUL HINT

All contra accounts have increases, decreases, and normal balances opposite to the account to which they relate.

time, the balance in Insurance Expense equals the insurance cost that expired in October. **If Sierra does not make this adjustment, October expenses are understated by $50 and net income is overstated by $50. Moreover, both assets and stockholders' equity will be overstated by $50 on the October 31 balance sheet.**

Depreciation

A company typically owns a variety of assets that have long lives, such as buildings, equipment, and motor vehicles. The period of service is referred to as the **useful life** of the asset. Because a building is expected to be of service for many years, it is recorded as an asset, rather than an expense, on the date it is acquired. Recall that companies record such assets **at cost**, as required by the historical cost principle. To follow the expense recognition principle, companies allocate a portion of this cost as an expense during each period of the asset's useful life. **Depreciation** is the process of allocating the cost of an asset to expense over its useful life.

Need for Adjustment The acquisition of long-lived assets is essentially a long-term prepayment for the use of an asset. An adjusting entry for depreciation is needed to recognize the cost that has been used (an expense) during the period and to report the unused cost (an asset) at the end of the period. One very important point to understand: **Depreciation is an allocation concept, not a valuation concept.** That is, depreciation **allocates an asset's cost to the periods in which it is used. Depreciation does not attempt to report the actual change in the value of the asset.**

For Sierra Corporation, assume that depreciation on the equipment is $480 a year, or $40 per month. As shown in **Illustration 4.9**, rather than decrease (credit) the asset account directly, Sierra instead credits Accumulated Depreciation—Equipment. Accumulated Depreciation is called a **contra asset account**. Such an account is offset against an asset account on the balance sheet (see **Helpful Hint**). Thus, the Accumulated Depreciation—Equipment account offsets the asset Equipment. This account keeps track of the total amount of depreciation expense taken over the life of the asset. To keep the

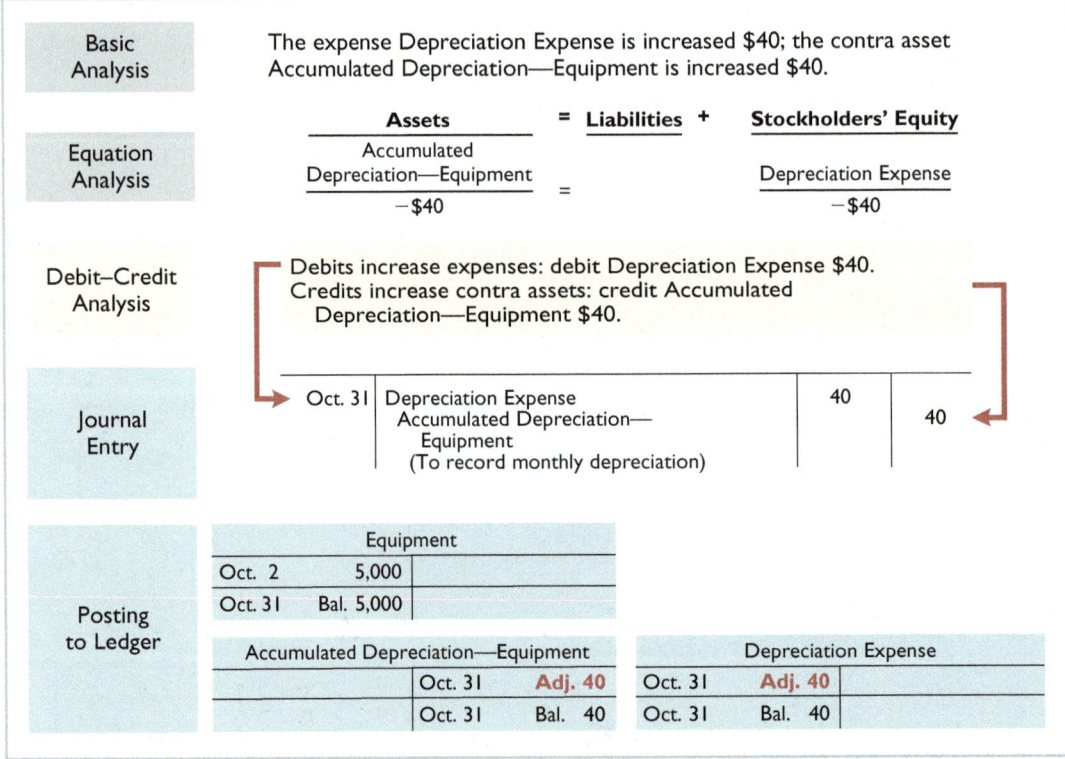

ILLUSTRATION 4.9 Adjustment for depreciation

accounting equation in balance, Sierra decreases stockholders' equity by increasing an expense account, Depreciation Expense.

The balance in the Accumulated Depreciation—Equipment account will increase $40 each month, and the balance in Equipment remains $5,000.

Statement Presentation As noted above, Accumulated Depreciation—Equipment is a contra asset account. It is offset against Equipment on the balance sheet. The normal balance of a contra asset account is a credit. A theoretical alternative to using a contra asset account would be to decrease (credit) the asset account by the amount of depreciation each period. But using the contra account is preferable for a simple reason: It discloses both the original cost of the equipment and the total cost that has expired to date. Thus, in the balance sheet, Sierra deducts Accumulated Depreciation—Equipment from the related asset account, as shown in Illustration 4.10.

Equipment	$5,000
Less: Accumulated depreciation—equipment	40
	$4,960

ILLUSTRATION 4.10
Balance sheet presentation of accumulated depreciation

Book value is the difference between the cost of any depreciable asset and its related accumulated depreciation (see **Alternative Terminology**). In Illustration 4.10, the book value of the equipment at the balance sheet date is $4,960. The book value and the fair value of the asset are generally two different values. As noted earlier, **the purpose of depreciation is not valuation but a means of cost allocation**.

Depreciation expense identifies the portion of an asset's cost that expired during the period (in this case, in October). **Without this adjusting entry, total assets, total stockholders' equity, and net income are overstated by $40 and depreciation expense is understated by $40.**

Illustration 4.11 summarizes the accounting for prepaid expenses.

ALTERNATIVE TERMINOLOGY
Book value is also referred to as *carrying value*.

ACCOUNTING FOR PREPAID EXPENSES

Examples	Reason for Adjustment	Accounts Before Adjustment	Adjusting Entry
Insurance, supplies, advertising, rent, depreciation	Prepaid expenses originally recorded in asset accounts have been used.	Assets overstated. Expenses understated.	Dr. Expenses Cr. Assets or Contra Assets

ILLUSTRATION 4.11
Accounting for prepaid expenses

Unearned Revenues

Companies record cash received before services are performed by increasing (crediting) a liability account called **unearned revenues**. In other words, the **company has a performance obligation** to transfer a service to one of its customers. Items like rent, magazine subscriptions, and customer deposits for future service may result in unearned revenues. Airlines such as **United**, **American**, and **Delta**, for instance, treat receipts from the sale of tickets as unearned revenue until the flight service is provided.

Unearned revenues are the opposite of prepaid expenses. Indeed, unearned revenue on the books of one company is likely to be a prepaid expense on the books of the company that has made the advance payment. For example, if identical accounting periods are assumed, a landlord will have unearned rent revenue when a tenant has prepaid rent.

When a company receives payment for services to be performed in a future accounting period, it increases (credits) an unearned revenue account. Unearned revenue is a liability account used to recognize the obligation that exists. The company subsequently recognizes revenues when it performs the service. During the accounting period, it is not practical to make daily entries as the company performs services. Instead, the company delays recognition of revenue until the adjustment process. The company then makes an adjusting entry to record the revenue for services performed during the period and to show the liability that remains at the end of the accounting period. Prior to adjustment, liabilities are typically overstated and revenues are understated. Therefore, as shown in **Illustration 4.12**, **the adjusting entry for unearned revenues results in a decrease (a debit) to a liability account and an increase (a credit) to a revenue account**.

ILLUSTRATION 4.12 Adjusting entries for unearned revenues

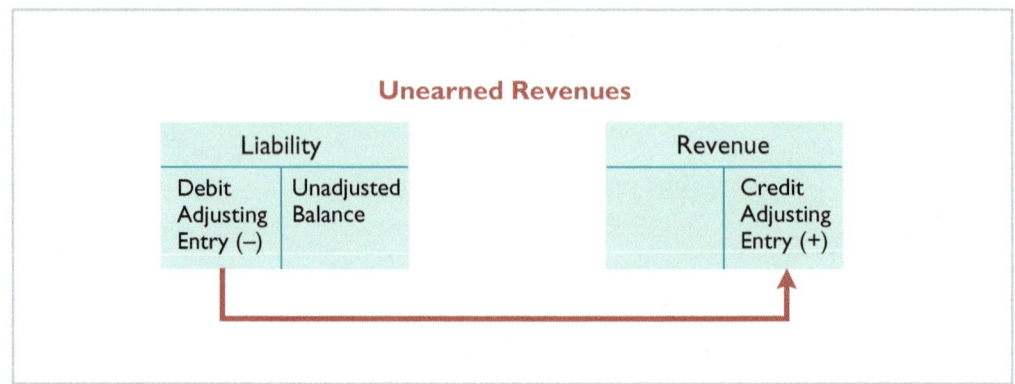

Unearned Revenues

Oct. 2 — Thank you in advance for your work. I will finish by Dec. 31. $1,200

Cash is received in advance; liability is recorded

Oct. 31 — Some service has been performed; some revenue is recorded

Sierra Corporation received $1,200 on October 2 from R. Knox for guide services for multi-day trips expected to be completed by December 31. Sierra credited the payment to Unearned Service Revenue. This liability account shows a balance of $1,200 in the October 31 trial balance. From an evaluation of the service Sierra performed for Knox during October, the company determines that it should recognize $400 of revenue in October. The liability (Unearned Service Revenue) is therefore decreased and stockholders' equity (Service Revenue) is increased.

As shown in **Illustration 4.13**, the liability Unearned Service Revenue now shows a balance of $800. That amount represents the remaining guide services Sierra is obligated

ILLUSTRATION 4.13 Service revenue accounts after adjustment

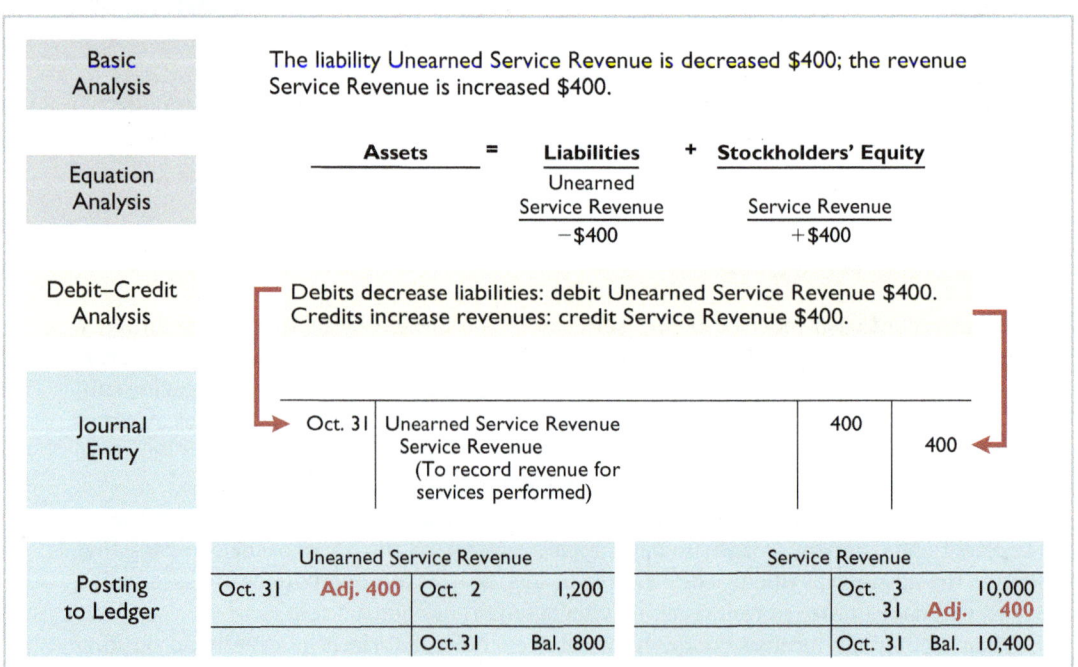

to perform in the future. Service Revenue shows total revenue for October of $10,400. **Without this adjustment, revenues and net income are understated by $400 in the income statement. Moreover, liabilities are overstated and stockholders' equity is understated by $400 on the October 31 balance sheet.**

Illustration 4.14 summarizes the accounting for unearned revenues.

ILLUSTRATION 4.14

Accounting for unearned revenues

ACCOUNTING FOR UNEARNED REVENUES

Examples	Reason for Adjustment	Accounts Before Adjustment	Adjusting Entry
Rent, magazine subscriptions, customer deposits for future service	Unearned revenues recorded in liability accounts are now recognized as revenue for services performed.	Liabilities overstated. Revenues understated.	Dr. Liabilities Cr. Revenues

Accounting Across the Organization Best Buy

© Skip ODonnell/iStockphoto

Turning Gift Cards into Revenue

Those of you who are marketing majors (and even most of you who are not) know that gift cards are among the hottest marketing tools in merchandising today. Customers purchase gift cards and give them to someone for later use. In a recent year, gift-card sales were expected to exceed $124 billion.

Although these programs are popular with marketing executives, they create accounting questions. Should revenue be recorded at the time the gift card is sold, or when it is exercised? How should expired gift cards be accounted for? In a recent balance sheet, **Best Buy** reported unearned revenue related to gift cards of $427 million.

Source: "2014 Gift Card Sales to top $124 Billion, But Growth Slowing," *PRNewswire* (December 10, 2014).

Suppose that Robert Jones purchases a $100 gift card at Best Buy on December 24, 2021, and gives it to his wife, Mary Jones, on December 25, 2021. On January 3, 2022, Mary uses the card to purchase $100 worth of CDs. When do you think Best Buy should recognize revenue and why? (Go to WileyPLUS for this answer and additional questions.)

DO IT! 2 | Adjusting Entries for Deferrals

The ledger of Hammond, Inc. on March 31, 2022, includes these selected accounts before adjusting entries are prepared.

	Debit	Credit
Prepaid Insurance	$ 3,600	
Supplies	2,800	
Equipment	25,000	
Accumulated Depreciation—Equipment		$5,000
Unearned Service Revenue		9,200

An analysis of the accounts shows the following.

1. Insurance expires at the rate of $100 per month.
2. Supplies on hand total $800.
3. The equipment depreciates $200 a month.
4. During March, services were performed for $4,000 of the unearned service revenue.

Prepare the adjusting entries for the month of March.

ACTION PLAN
- Make adjusting entries at the end of the period for revenues recognized and expenses incurred in the period.
- Don't forget to make adjusting entries for deferrals. Failure to adjust for deferrals leads to overstatement of the asset or liability and understatement of the related expense or revenue.

Solution

1.	Insurance Expense	100	
	Prepaid Insurance		100
	(To record insurance expired)		
2.	Supplies Expense ($2,800 − $800)	2,000	
	Supplies		2,000
	(To record supplies used)		
3.	Depreciation Expense	200	
	Accumulated Depreciation—Equipment		200
	(To record monthly depreciation)		
4.	Unearned Service Revenue	4,000	
	Service Revenue		4,000
	(To record revenue for services performed)		

Related exercise material: **BE4.5, BE4.6, BE4.7, BE4.8, BE4.9, DO IT! 4.2, and E4.17.**

Adjusting Entries for Accruals

LEARNING OBJECTIVE 3
Prepare adjusting entries for accruals.

ANALYZE → JOURNALIZE → POST → TRIAL BALANCE → **Journalize and post adjusting entries: deferrals/accruals** → ADJUSTED TRIAL BALANCE → FINANCIAL STATEMENTS → CLOSING ENTRIES → POST-CLOSING TRIAL BALANCE

The second category of adjusting entries is **accruals**. Prior to an accrual adjustment, the revenue account (and the related asset account) or the expense account (and the related liability account) are understated. Thus, the adjusting entry for accruals will **increase both a balance sheet and an income statement account**.

Accrued Revenues

Revenues for services performed but not yet recorded at the statement date are **accrued revenues**. Accrued revenues may accumulate (accrue) with the passing of time, as in the case of interest revenue. These are unrecorded because the earning of interest does not involve daily transactions. Companies do not record interest revenue on a daily basis because it is often impractical to do so. Accrued revenues also may result from services that have been performed but not yet billed nor collected, as in the case of commissions and fees. These may be unrecorded because only a portion of the total service has been performed and the clients won't be billed until the service has been completed.

An adjusting entry records the receivable that exists at the balance sheet date and the revenue for the services performed during the period. Prior to adjustment, both assets and revenues are understated. As shown in **Illustration 4.15**, **an adjusting entry for accrued revenues results in an increase (a debit) to an asset account and an increase (a credit) to a revenue account** (see **Helpful Hint**).

In October, Sierra Corporation performed guide services worth $200 that were not billed to clients on or before October 31. Because these services were not billed, they were not recorded. The accrual of unrecorded service revenue increases an asset account, Accounts

Accrued Revenues

Revenue and receivable are recorded for unbilled services
Nov. 10

Cash is received; receivable is reduced

ILLUSTRATION 4.15
Adjusting entries for accrued revenues

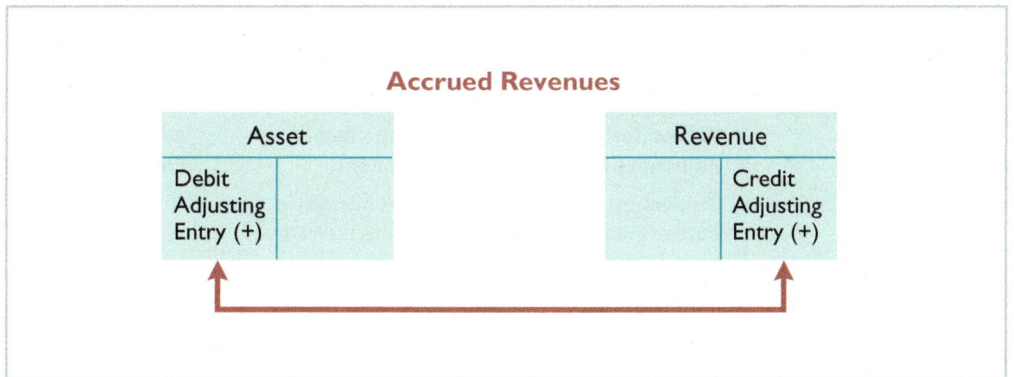

HELPFUL HINT

For accruals, there may have been no prior entry, and the accounts requiring adjustment may both have zero balances prior to adjustment.

Receivable. It also increases stockholders' equity by increasing a revenue account, Service Revenue, as shown in **Illustration 4.16**.

ILLUSTRATION 4.16 Adjustment for accrued revenue

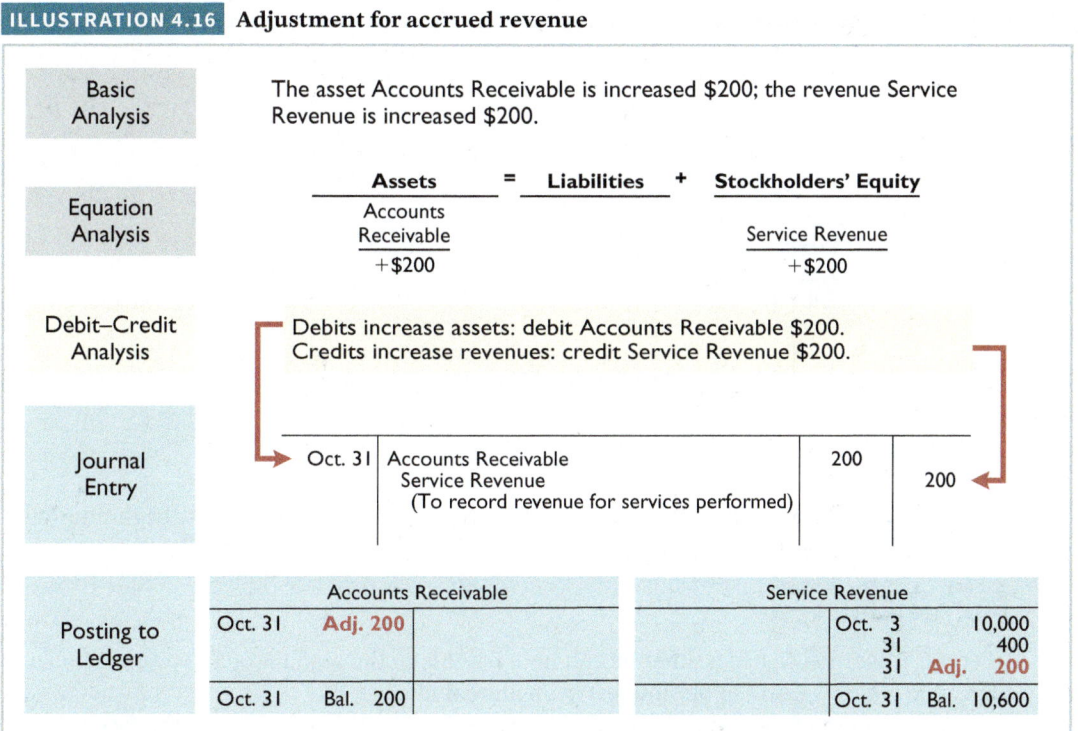

The asset Accounts Receivable shows that clients owe Sierra $200 at the balance sheet date. The balance of $10,600 in Service Revenue represents the total revenue for services Sierra performed during the month ($10,000 + $400 + $200). **Without the adjusting entry, assets and stockholders' equity on the balance sheet and revenues and net income on the income statement are understated.**

On November 10, Sierra receives cash of $200 for the services performed in October and makes the following entry.

Nov. 10	Cash	200	
	Accounts Receivable		200
	(To record cash collected on account)		

The company records the collection of the receivables by a debit (increase) to Cash and a credit (decrease) to Accounts Receivable.

Equation analyses summarize the effects of transactions on the three elements of the accounting equation, as well as the effect on cash flows.

A	=	L	+	SE
+200				
−200				

Cash Flows
+200

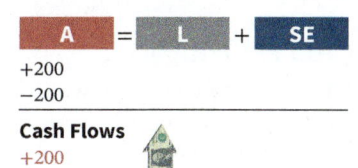

Illustration 4.17 summarizes the accounting for accrued revenues.

ILLUSTRATION 4.17

Accounting for accrued revenues

	ACCOUNTING FOR ACCRUED REVENUES		
Examples	Reason for Adjustment	Accounts Before Adjustment	Adjusting Entry
Interest, rent, services	Services performed but not yet received in cash or recorded.	Assets understated. Revenues understated.	Dr. Assets Cr. Revenues

ETHICS NOTE

A report released by **Fannie Mae**'s board of directors stated that improper adjusting entries at the mortgage-finance company resulted in delayed recognition of expenses caused by interest-rate changes. The motivation for this improper accounting apparently was the desire to meet earnings targets.

Accrued Expenses

Expenses incurred but not yet paid or recorded at the statement date are called **accrued expenses**. Interest, taxes, utilities, and salaries are common examples of accrued expenses.

Companies make adjustments for accrued expenses to record the obligations that exist at the balance sheet date and to recognize the expenses that apply to the current accounting period (see **Ethics Note**). Prior to adjustment, both liabilities and expenses are understated. Therefore, as shown in **Illustration 4.18**, **an adjusting entry for accrued expenses results in an increase (a debit) to an expense account and an increase (a credit) to a liability account**.

ILLUSTRATION 4.18

Adjusting entries for accrued expenses

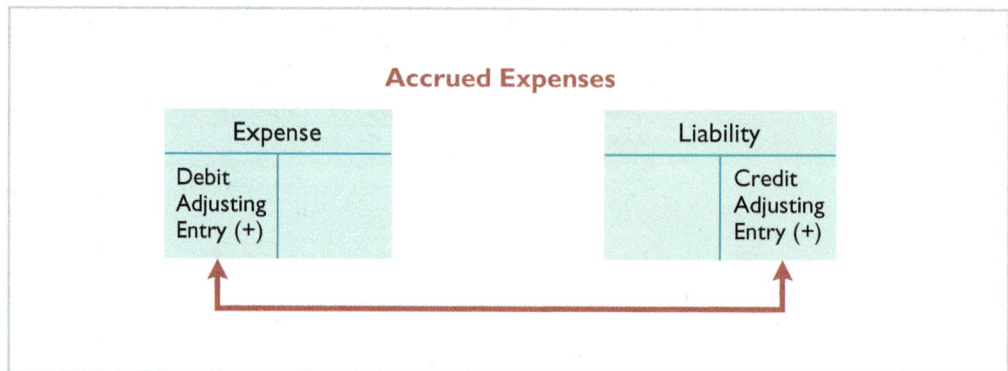

Let's look in more detail at some specific types of accrued expenses, beginning with accrued interest.

Accrued Interest

Sierra Corporation signed a three-month note payable in the amount of $5,000 on October 1. The note requires Sierra to pay interest at an annual rate of 12%.

The amount of the interest recorded is determined by three factors: (1) the face value of the note; (2) the interest rate, which is always expressed as an annual rate; and (3) the length of time the note is outstanding. For Sierra, the total interest due on the $5,000 note at its maturity date three months in the future is $150 ($5,000 × 12% × $\frac{3}{12}$), or $50 for one month. **Illustration 4.19** shows the formula for computing interest and its application to Sierra for the month of October (see **Helpful Hint**).

ILLUSTRATION 4.19

Formula for computing interest

Face Value of Note	×	Annual Interest Rate	×	Time in Terms of One Year	=	Interest
$5,000	×	12%	×	$\frac{1}{12}$	=	$50

HELPFUL HINT

In computing interest, we express the time period as a fraction of a year.

As **Illustration 4.20** shows, the accrual of interest at October 31 increases a liability account, Interest Payable. It also decreases stockholders' equity by increasing an expense account, Interest Expense.

Interest Expense shows the interest charges for the month of October. Interest Payable shows the amount of interest the company owes at the statement date. Sierra will not pay the interest

ILLUSTRATION 4.20 Adjustment for accrued interest

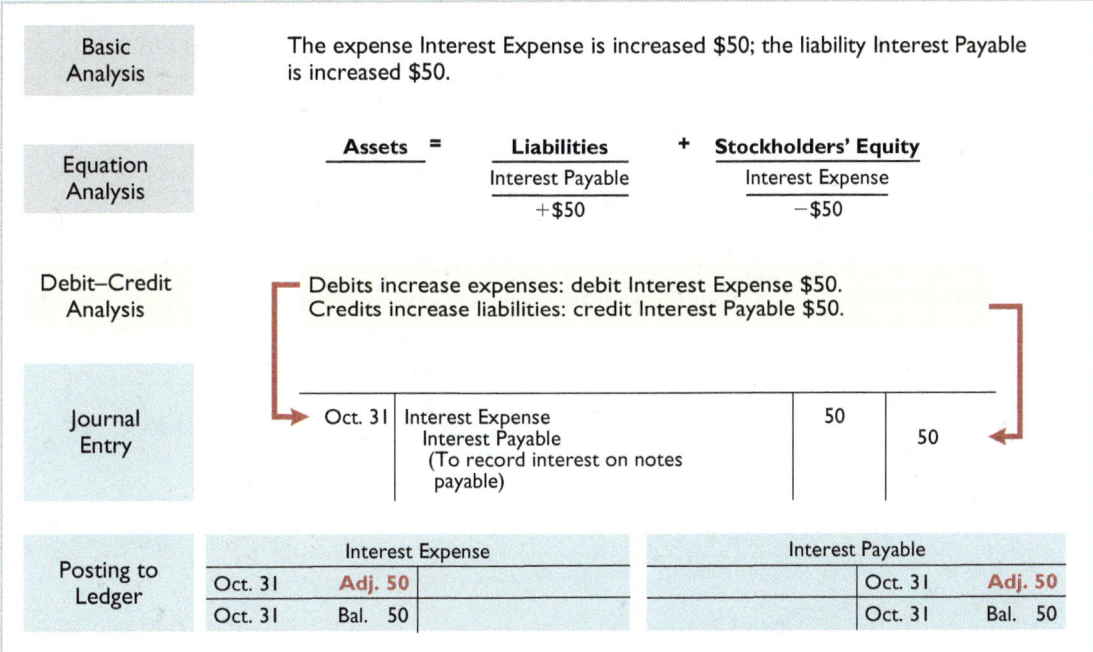

until the note comes due at the end of three months. Companies use the Interest Payable account, instead of crediting Notes Payable, to disclose the two different types of obligations—interest and principal—in the accounts and statements. **Without this adjusting entry, liabilities and interest expense are understated, and net income and stockholders' equity are overstated.**

Accrued Salaries

Companies pay for some types of expenses, such as employee salaries and wages, after the services have been performed. Sierra paid salaries on October 26 for its employees' first two weeks of work; the next payment of salaries will not occur until November 9. As **Illustration 4.21** shows, three working days remain in October (October 29–31).

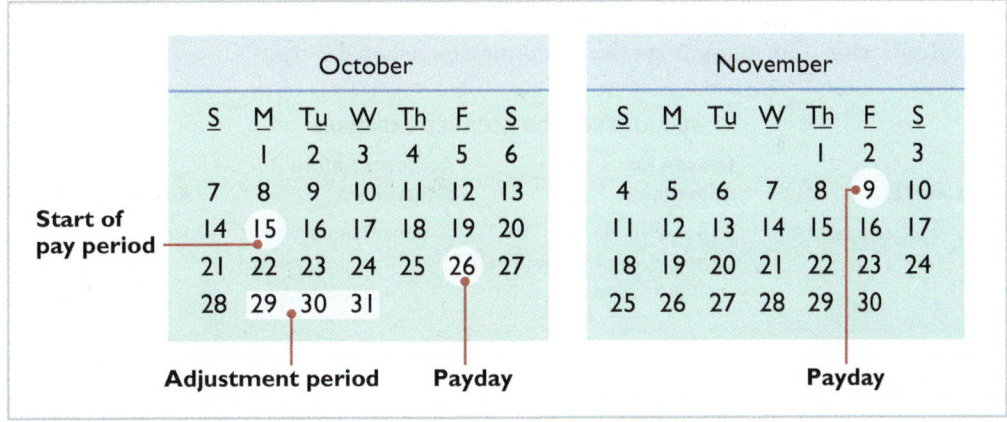

ILLUSTRATION 4.21

Calendar showing Sierra Corporation's pay periods

At October 31, the salaries for these three days represent an accrued expense and a related liability to Sierra. The employees receive total salaries of $2,000 for a five-day work week, or $400 per day. Thus, accrued salaries at October 31 are $1,200 ($400 × 3). This accrual increases a liability, Salaries and Wages Payable. It also decreases stockholders' equity by increasing an expense account, Salaries and Wages Expense, as shown in **Illustration 4.22**.

After this adjustment, the balance in Salaries and Wages Expense of $5,200 (13 days × $400) is the actual salary expense for October. (The employees worked 13 days in October after beginning work on October 15.) The balance in Salaries and Wages Payable of $1,200 is the amount of the liability for salaries Sierra owes as of October 31. **Without the $1,200 adjustment for salaries, Sierra's expenses are understated $1,200 and its liabilities are understated $1,200.**

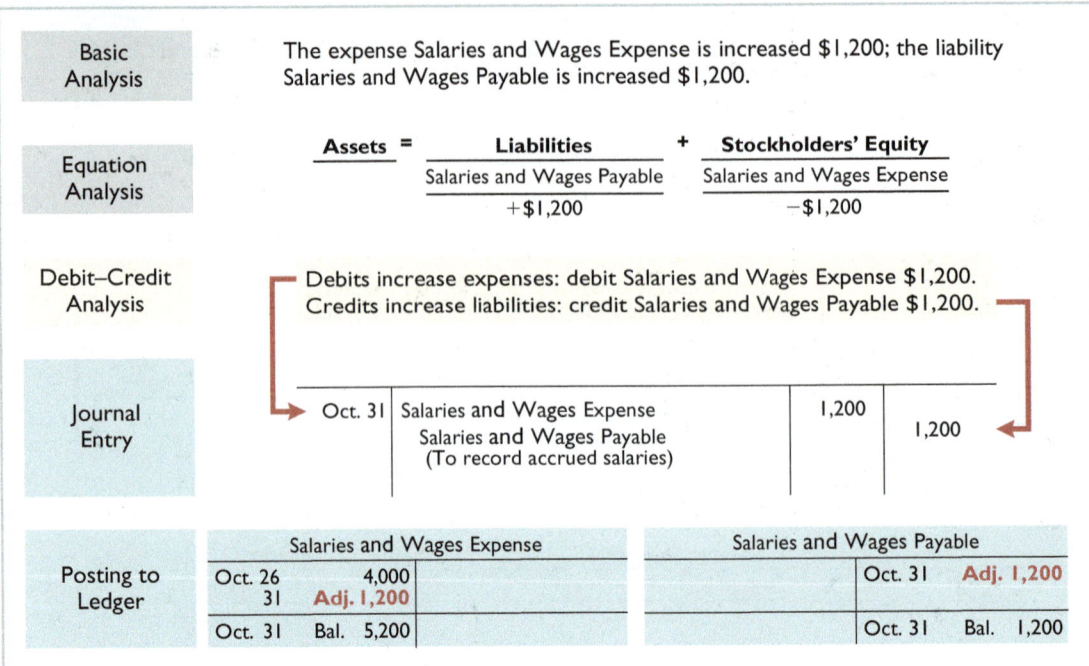

ILLUSTRATION 4.22 Adjustment for accrued salaries

Sierra pays salaries every two weeks. Consequently, the next payday is November 9, when the company will again pay total salaries of $4,000. The payment consists of $1,200 of salaries and wages payable at October 31 plus $2,800 of salaries and wages expense for November (7 working days as shown in the November calendar × $400). Therefore, Sierra makes the following entry on November 9.

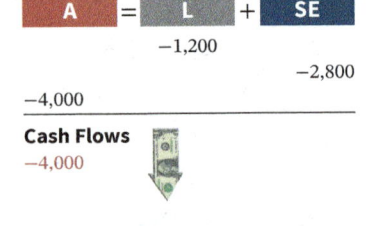

Nov. 9	Salaries and Wages Payable	1,200	
	Salaries and Wages Expense	2,800	
	Cash		4,000
	(To record November 9 payroll)		

This entry eliminates the liability for Salaries and Wages Payable that Sierra recorded in the October 31 adjusting entry, and it records the proper amount of Salaries and Wages Expense for the period between November 1 and November 9.

Illustration 4.23 summarizes the accounting for accrued expenses.

ILLUSTRATION 4.23
Accounting for accrued expenses

		ACCOUNTING FOR ACCRUED EXPENSES		
	Examples	Reason for Adjustment	Accounts Before Adjustment	Adjusting Entry
	Interest, rent, salaries	Expenses have been incurred but not yet paid in cash or recorded.	Expenses understated. Liabilities understated.	Dr. Expenses Cr. Liabilities

People, Planet, and Profit Insight

© Nathan Gleave/ iStockphoto

Got Junk?

Do you have an old computer or two in your garage? How about an old TV that needs replacing? Many people do. Approximately 163,000 computers and televisions become obsolete **each day**. Yet, in a recent year, only 11% of computers were recycled. It is estimated that 75% of all computers ever sold are sitting in storage somewhere, waiting to be disposed of. Each of these old TVs and computers is loaded with lead, cadmium, mercury, and other toxic chemicals. If you have one of these electronic gadgets, you have a responsibility, and a probable cost, for disposing of it. Companies have the same problem, but their discarded materials may include lead paint, asbestos, and other toxic chemicals.

What accounting issue might this cause for companies? (Go to WileyPLUS for this answer and additional questions.)

Summary of Basic Relationships

Illustration 4.24 summarizes the four basic types of adjusting entries. Take some time to study and analyze the adjusting entries. Be sure to note that **each adjusting entry affects one balance sheet account and one income statement account**.

ILLUSTRATION 4.24
Summary of adjusting entries

Type of Adjustment	Accounts Before Adjustment	Adjusting Entry
Prepaid expenses	Assets overstated. Expenses understated.	Dr. Expenses Cr. Assets or Contra Assets
Unearned revenues	Liabilities overstated. Revenues understated.	Dr. Liabilities Cr. Revenues
Accrued revenues	Assets understated. Revenues understated.	Dr. Assets Cr. Revenues
Accrued expenses	Expenses understated. Liabilities understated.	Dr. Expenses Cr. Liabilities

Illustrations **4.25** and **4.26** show the journalizing and posting of adjusting entries for Sierra Corporation on October 31. When reviewing the general ledger in Illustration 4.26, note that for learning purposes we have highlighted the adjustments in red.

ILLUSTRATION 4.25
General journal showing adjusting entries

	GENERAL JOURNAL		
Date	Account Titles and Explanation	Debit	Credit
2022	Adjusting Entries		
Oct. 31	Supplies Expense	1,500	
	Supplies		1,500
	(To record supplies used)		
31	Insurance Expense	50	
	Prepaid Insurance		50
	(To record insurance expired)		
31	Depreciation Expense	40	
	Accumulated Depreciation—Equipment		40
	(To record monthly depreciation)		
31	Unearned Service Revenue	400	
	Service Revenue		400
	(To record revenue for services performed)		
31	Accounts Receivable	200	
	Service Revenue		200
	(To record revenue for services performed)		
31	Interest Expense	50	
	Interest Payable		50
	(To record interest on notes payable)		
31	Salaries and Wages Expense	1,200	
	Salaries and Wages Payable		1,200
	(To record accrued salaries)		

ILLUSTRATION 4.26

General ledger after adjustments

GENERAL LEDGER

Cash

Oct. 1	10,000	Oct. 2	5,000
1	5,000	3	900
2	1,200	4	600
3	10,000	20	500
		26	4,000
Oct. 31	Bal. 15,200		

Accounts Receivable

Oct. 31	200		
Oct. 31	Bal. 200		

Supplies

Oct. 5	2,500	Oct. 31	1,500
Oct. 31	Bal. 1,000		

Prepaid Insurance

Oct. 4	600	Oct. 31	50
Oct. 31	Bal. 550		

Equipment

Oct. 2	5,000		
Oct. 31	Bal. 5,000		

Accumulated Depreciation— Equipment

		Oct. 31	40
		Oct. 31	Bal. 40

Notes Payable

		Oct. 1	5,000
		Oct. 31	Bal. 5,000

Accounts Payable

		Oct. 5	2,500
		Oct. 31	Bal. 2,500

Interest Payable

		Oct. 31	50
		Oct. 31	Bal. 50

Unearned Service Revenue

Oct. 31	400	Oct. 2	1,200
		Oct. 31	Bal. 800

Salaries and Wages Payable

		Oct. 31	1,200
		Oct. 31	Bal. 1,200

Common Stock

		Oct. 1	10,000
		Oct. 31	Bal. 10,000

Retained Earnings

		Oct. 31	Bal. 0

Dividends

Oct. 20	500		
Oct. 31	Bal. 500		

Service Revenue

		Oct. 3	10,000
		31	400
		31	200
		Oct. 31	Bal. 10,600

Salaries and Wages Expense

Oct. 26	4,000		
31	1,200		
Oct. 31	Bal. 5,200		

Supplies Expense

Oct. 31	1,500		
Oct. 31	Bal. 1,500		

Rent Expense

Oct. 3	900		
Oct. 31	Bal. 900		

Insurance Expense

Oct. 31	50		
Oct. 31	Bal. 50		

Interest Expense

Oct. 31	50		
Oct. 31	Bal. 50		

Depreciation Expense

Oct. 31	40		
Oct. 31	Bal. 40		

DO IT! 3 | Adjusting Entries for Accruals

Micro Computer Services Inc. began operations on August 1, 2022. At the end of August 2022, management attempted to prepare monthly financial statements. The following information relates to August.

1. At August 31, the company owed its employees $800 in salaries that will be paid on September 1.
2. On August 1, the company borrowed $30,000 from a local bank on a 15-year mortgage. The annual interest rate is 10%.
3. Revenue for services performed but unrecorded for August totaled $1,100.

Prepare the adjusting entries needed at August 31, 2022.

ACTION PLAN
- Make adjusting entries at the end of the period to recognize revenue for services performed and for expenses incurred.
- Don't forget to make adjusting entries for accruals. Adjusting entries for accruals will increase both a balance sheet and an income statement account.

Solution

1. Salaries and Wages Expense 800
       Salaries and Wages Payable 800
       (To record accrued salaries)

2. Interest Expense 250
       Interest Payable 250
       (To record accrued interest:
       $\$30{,}000 \times 10\% \times \frac{1}{12} = \$250$)

3. Accounts Receivable 1,100
       Service Revenue 1,100
       (To record revenue for services performed)

Related exercise material: **BE4.10**, **BE4.11**, **DO IT! 4.3**, **E4.8**, **E4.9**, **E4.10**, **E4.11**, **E4.12**, **E4.14**, **E4.15**, **E4.16**, **E4.17**, and **E4.18**.

The Adjusted Trial Balance and Closing Entries

LEARNING OBJECTIVE 4
Prepare an adjusted trial balance and closing entries.

ANALYZE → JOURNALIZE → POST → TRIAL BALANCE → ADJUSTING ENTRIES → **Adjusted trial balance** → **Prepare financial statements** → **Journalize and post closing entries** → **Prepare a post-closing trial balance**

After a company has journalized and posted all adjusting entries, it prepares another trial balance from the ledger accounts. This trial balance is called an **adjusted trial balance**. It shows the balances of all accounts, including those adjusted, at the end of the accounting period. The purpose of an adjusted trial balance is to **prove the equality** of the total debit balances and the total credit balances in the ledger after all adjustments. Because the accounts contain all data needed for financial statements, the adjusted trial balance is the **primary basis for the preparation of financial statements**.

Preparing the Adjusted Trial Balance

Illustration 4.27 presents the adjusted trial balance for Sierra Corporation prepared from the ledger accounts in Illustration 4.26. The amounts affected by the adjusting entries are highlighted in red.

ILLUSTRATION 4.27
Adjusted trial balance

Sierra Corporation
Adjusted Trial Balance
October 31, 2022

	Debit	Credit
Cash	$15,200	
Accounts Receivable	200	
Supplies	1,000	
Prepaid Insurance	550	
Equipment	5,000	
Accumulated Depreciation—Equipment		$ 40
Notes Payable		5,000
Accounts Payable		2,500
Interest Payable		50
Unearned Service Revenue		800
Salaries and Wages Payable		1,200
Common Stock		10,000
Retained Earnings		0
Dividends	500	
Service Revenue		10,600
Salaries and Wages Expense	5,200	
Supplies Expense	1,500	
Rent Expense	900	
Insurance Expense	50	
Interest Expense	50	
Depreciation Expense	40	
	$30,190	$30,190

Preparing Financial Statements

Companies can prepare financial statements directly from an adjusted trial balance. Illustrations 4.28 and 4.29 present the relationships between the data in the adjusted trial balance of Sierra Corporation and the corresponding financial statements. As Illustration 4.28 shows, companies prepare the income statement from the revenue and expense accounts. Similarly, they derive the retained earnings statement from the Retained Earnings account, Dividends account, and the net income (or net loss) shown in the income statement. As Illustration 4.29 shows, companies then prepare the balance sheet from the asset, liability, and stockholders' equity accounts. They obtain the amount reported for retained earnings on the balance sheet from the ending balance in the retained earnings statement.

ILLUSTRATION 4.28 Preparation of the income statement and retained earnings statement from the adjusted trial balance

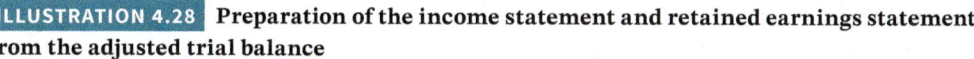

Quality of Earnings

Companies and employees are continually under pressure to "make the numbers"—that is, to have earnings that are in line with expectations. Therefore, it is not surprising that many companies practice earnings management. **Earnings management** is the planned timing of revenues, expenses, gains, and losses to smooth out bumps in net income. The quality of earnings is greatly affected when a company manages earnings up or down to meet some targeted earnings number. A company that has a high **quality of earnings** provides full and transparent information that will not confuse or mislead financial statement users. A company with questionable quality of earnings may mislead investors and creditors, who believe they are relying on relevant information that provides a faithful representation of the company. As a result, investors and creditors lose confidence in financial reporting, and it becomes difficult for our capital markets to work efficiently.

Companies manage earnings in a variety of ways. One way is through the use of **one-time items** to prop up earnings numbers. For example, **ConAgra Foods** recorded a non-recurring

ILLUSTRATION 4.29 Preparation of the balance sheet from the adjusted trial balance

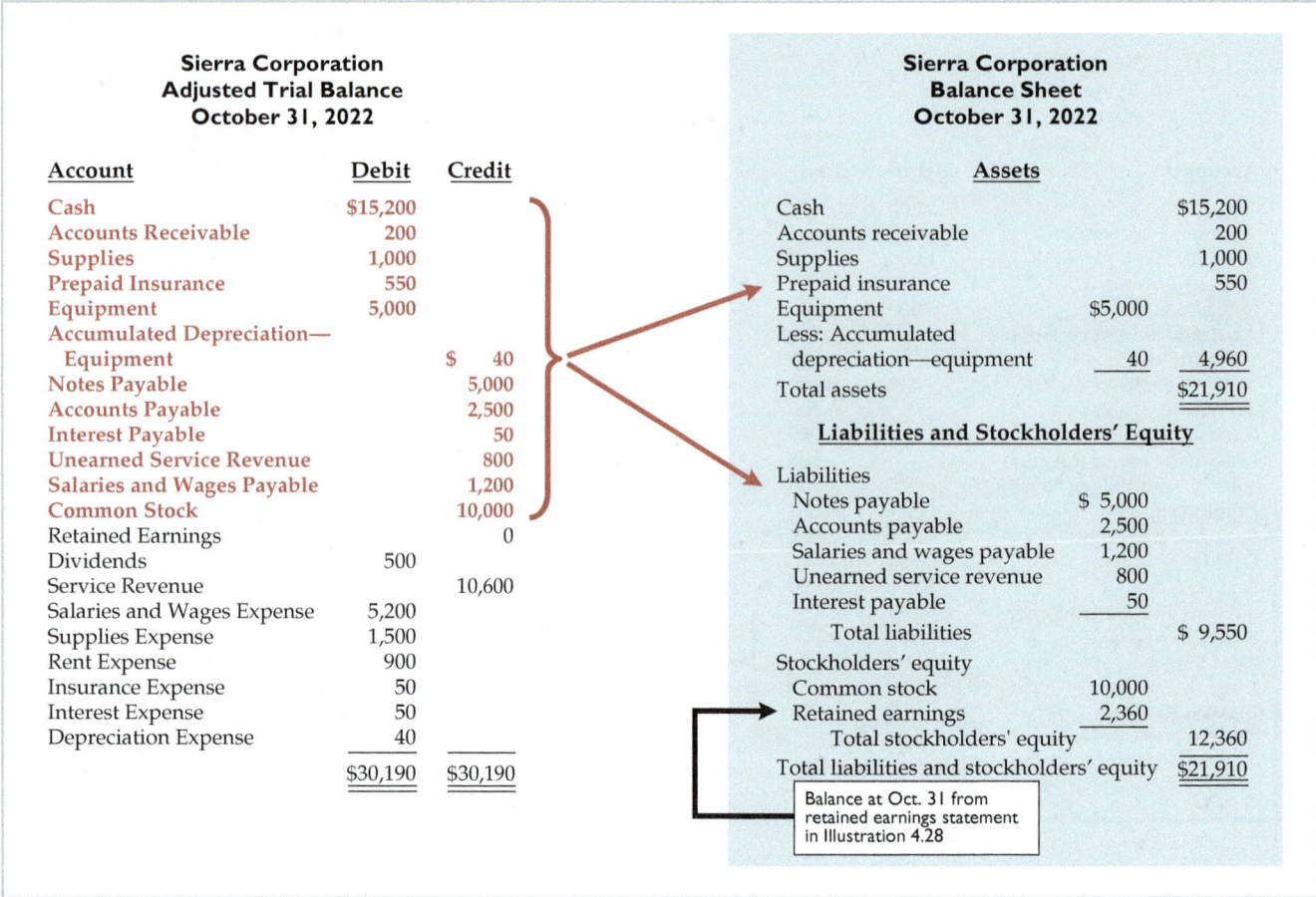

gain from the sale of **Pilgrim's Pride** stock for $186 million to help meet an earnings projection for the quarter.

Another way is to **inflate revenue** numbers in the short-run to the detriment of the long-run. For example, **Bristol-Myers Squibb** provided sales incentives to its wholesalers to encourage them to buy products at the end of the quarter (often referred to as channel-stuffing). This practice allowed Bristol-Myers to meet its sales projections. The problem was that the wholesalers could not sell that amount of merchandise and ended up returning it to Bristol-Myers. The result was that Bristol-Myers had to restate its income numbers.

Companies also manage earnings through **improper adjusting entries**. Regulators investigated **Xerox** for accusations that it was booking too much revenue upfront on multi-year contract sales. Financial executives at **Office Max** resigned amid accusations that the company was recognizing rebates from its vendors too early and therefore overstating revenue. Finally, **WorldCom**'s abuse of adjusting entries to meet its net income targets is unsurpassed. It used adjusting entries to increase net income by reclassifying liabilities as revenue and reclassifying expenses as assets. Investigations of the company's books after it went bankrupt revealed adjusting entries of more than a billion dollars that had no supporting documentation.

DO IT! 4a | Trial Balance

Skolnick Co. was organized on April 1, 2022. The company prepares quarterly financial statements. The adjusted trial balance amounts at June 30 are shown below.

	Debit		Credit
Cash	$ 6,700	Accumulated Depreciation—Equipment	$ 850
Accounts Receivable	600	Notes Payable	5,000
Prepaid Rent	900	Accounts Payable	1,510
Supplies	1,000	Salaries and Wages Payable	400
Equipment	15,000	Interest Payable	50
Dividends	600	Unearned Rent Revenue	500
Salaries and Wages Expense	9,400	Common Stock	14,000
Rent Expense	1,500	Retained Earning	0
Depreciation Expense	850	Service Revenue	14,200
Supplies Expense	200	Rent Revenue	800
Utilities Expense	510		
Interest Expense	50		
	$37,310		$37,310

a. Determine the net income for the quarter April 1 to June 30.
b. Determine the total assets and total liabilities at June 30, 2022, for Skolnick Co.
c. Determine the balance in Retained Earnings at June 30, 2022.

ACTION PLAN
- In an adjusted trial balance, all asset, liability, revenue, and expense accounts are properly stated.
- To determine the ending balance in Retained Earnings, add net income and subtract dividends.

Solution

a. The net income is determined by adding revenues and subtracting expenses. The net income is computed as follows.

Revenues		
Service revenue	$14,200	
Rent revenue	800	
Total revenues		$15,000
Expenses		
Salaries and wages expense	9,400	
Rent expense	1,500	
Depreciation expense	850	
Utilities expense	510	
Supplies expense	200	
Interest expense	50	
Total expenses		12,510
Net income		$ 2,490

b. Total assets and liabilities are computed as follows.

Assets			Liabilities	
Cash		$ 6,700	Notes payable	$5,000
Accounts receivable		600	Accounts payable	1,510
Supplies		1,000	Unearned rent revenue	500
Prepaid rent		900	Salaries and wages payable	400
Equipment	$15,000		Interest payable	50
Less: Accumulated depreciation—equipment	850	14,150		
Total assets		$23,350	Total liabilities	$7,460

c.
Retained earnings, April 1	$ 0
Add: Net income	2,490
Less: Dividends	600
Retained earnings, June 30	$1,890

Related exercise material: **BE4.13, BE4.14, BE4.15, DO IT! 4.4a, and E4.23.**

ALTERNATIVE TERMINOLOGY

Temporary accounts are sometimes called *nominal accounts*, and permanent accounts are sometimes called *real accounts*.

Closing the Books

Previously, you learned that revenue and expense accounts and the Dividends account are subdivisions of retained earnings, which is reported in the stockholders' equity section of the balance sheet. Because revenues, expenses, and dividends relate only to a given accounting period, they are considered **temporary accounts**. In contrast, all balance sheet accounts are considered **permanent accounts** because their balances are carried forward into future accounting periods (see **Alternative Terminology**). **Illustration 4.30** identifies the accounts in each category.

ILLUSTRATION 4.30

Temporary versus permanent accounts

Temporary	Permanent
All revenue accounts All expense accounts Dividends	All asset accounts All liability accounts Stockholders' equity accounts

Preparing Closing Entries

At the end of the accounting period, companies transfer the temporary account balances to the permanent stockholders' equity account—Retained Earnings—through the preparation of closing entries. **Closing entries** transfer net income (or net loss) and dividends to Retained Earnings, so the balance in Retained Earnings agrees with the retained earnings statement. For example, in the adjusted trial balance in Illustration 4.27, Retained Earnings has a balance of zero. Prior to the closing entries, the balance in Retained Earnings is its beginning-of-the-period balance. (For Sierra Corporation, this is zero because it is the company's first month of operations.)

In addition to updating Retained Earnings to its correct ending balance, closing entries produce a **zero balance in each temporary account**. As a result, these accounts are ready to accumulate data about revenues, expenses, and dividends that occur in the next accounting period. **Permanent accounts are not closed.**

When companies prepare closing entries, they could close each income statement account directly to Retained Earnings. However, to do so would result in excessive detail in the Retained Earnings account. Instead, companies close the revenue and expense accounts to another temporary account, **Income Summary**. The balance in Income Summary is the net income or loss for the accounting period. Income Summary is then closed, which transfers the net income or net loss from this account to Retained Earnings. **Illustration 4.31** depicts the closing process. While it still takes the average large company seven days to close, some companies such as **Cisco** employ technology that allows them to do a so-called "virtual close" almost instantaneously any time during the year. Besides dramatically reducing the cost of closing, the virtual close provides companies with accurate data for decision-making whenever they desire it.

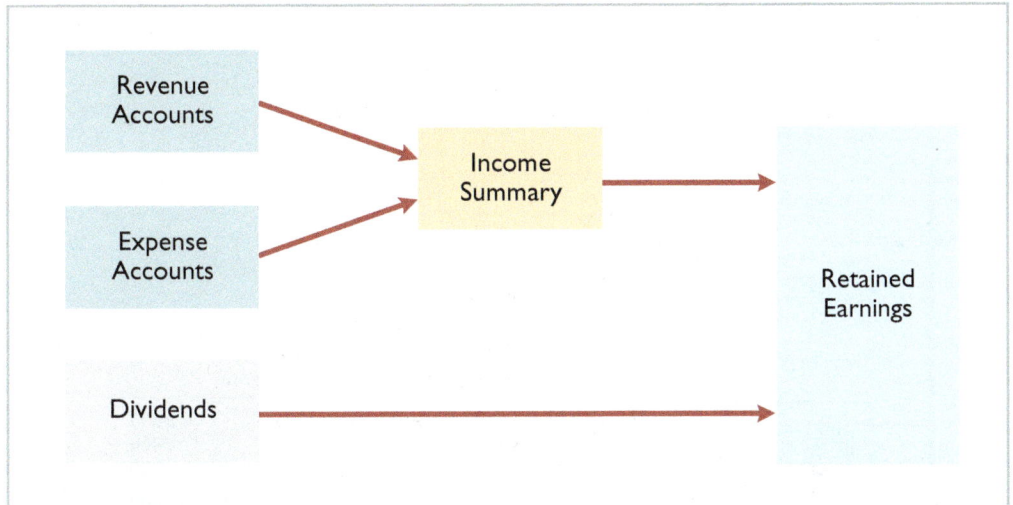

ILLUSTRATION 4.31
The closing process

Illustration 4.32 shows the closing entries for Sierra Corporation (see **Helpful Hint**). Illustration 4.33 diagrams the posting process for Sierra's closing entries.

ILLUSTRATION 4.32
Closing entries journalized

	GENERAL JOURNAL		
Date	Account Titles and Explanation	Debit	Credit
	Closing Entries		
	(1)		
2022 Oct. 31	Service Revenue	10,600	
	Income Summary		10,600
	(To close revenue account)		
	(2)		
31	Income Summary	7,740	
	Salaries and Wages Expense		5,200
	Supplies Expense		1,500
	Rent Expense		900
	Insurance Expense		50
	Interest Expense		50
	Depreciation Expense		40
	(To close expense accounts)		
	(3)		
31	Income Summary	2,860	
	Retained Earnings		2,860
	(To close net income to retained earnings)		
	(4)		
31	Retained Earnings	500	
	Dividends		500
	(To close dividends to retained earnings)		

HELPFUL HINT
Income Summary is a very descriptive title: Companies close total revenues to Income Summary and total expenses to Income Summary. The balance in Income Summary in this case is net income of $2,860.

Preparing a Post-Closing Trial Balance

After a company journalizes and posts all closing entries, it prepares another trial balance, called a **post-closing trial balance**, from the ledger. A post-closing trial balance is a list of all permanent accounts and their balances after closing entries are journalized and posted. **The purpose of this trial balance is to prove the equality of the total debit balances and total credit balances of the permanent account balances that the company carries forward into the next accounting period.** Since all temporary accounts will have zero balances, **the post-closing trial balance will contain only permanent—balance sheet—accounts.**

ILLUSTRATION 4.33 Posting of closing entries

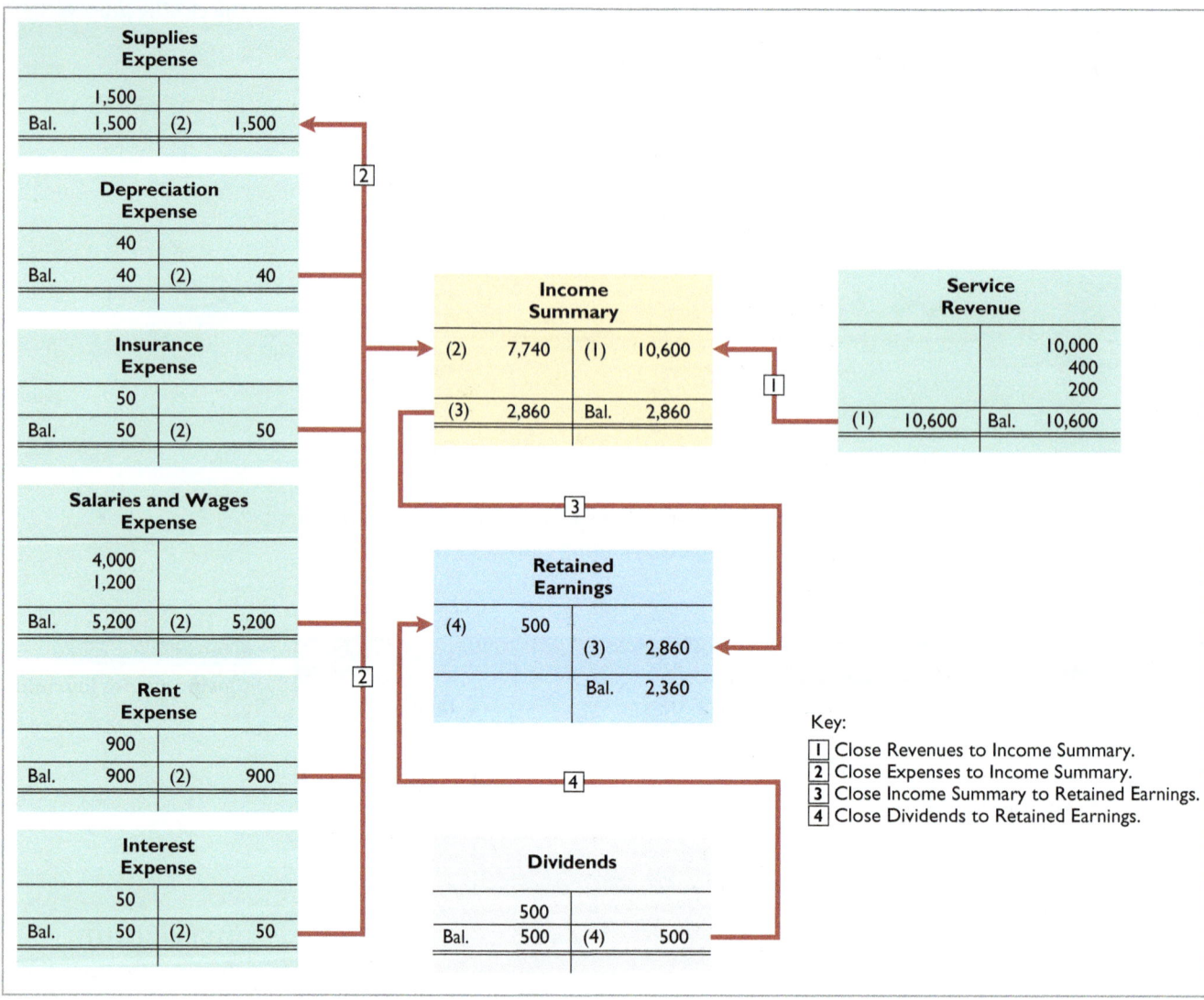

Summary of the Accounting Cycle

HELPFUL HINT

Some companies reverse certain adjusting entries at the beginning of a new accounting period. The company makes a **reversing entry** at the beginning of the next accounting period. This entry is the exact opposite of the adjusting entry made in the previous period.

Illustration 4.34 shows the required steps in the accounting cycle. You can see that the cycle begins with the analysis of business transactions and ends with the preparation of a post-closing trial balance. Companies perform the steps in the cycle in sequence and repeat them in each accounting period.

Steps 1–3 may occur daily during the accounting period. Companies perform Steps 4–7 on a periodic basis, such as monthly, quarterly, or annually (see **Helpful Hint**). Steps 8 and 9, closing entries and a post-closing trial balance, usually take place only at the end of a company's **annual** accounting period.

THE ACCOUNTING CYCLE

ILLUSTRATION 4.34
Required steps in the accounting cycle

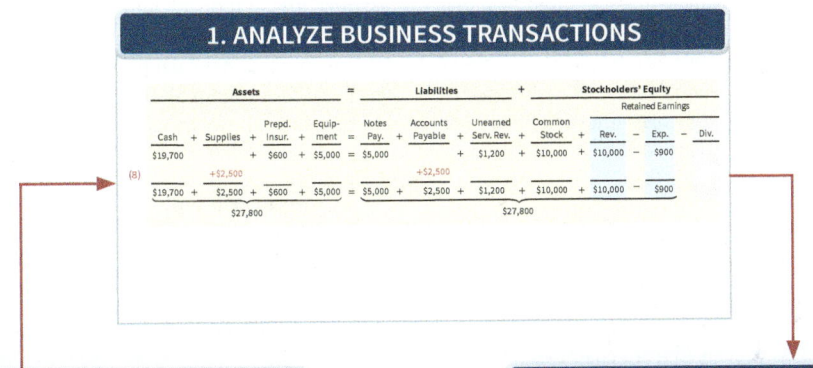

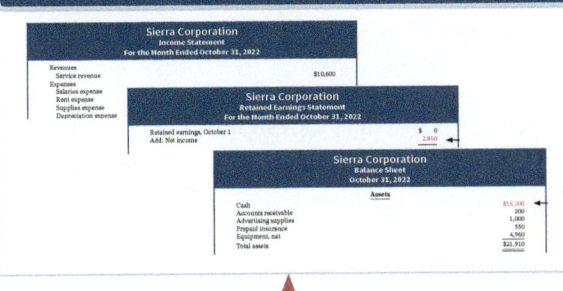

Keeping an Eye on Cash

In this chapter, you learned that adjusting entries are used to adjust numbers that would otherwise be stated on a cash basis. Sierra Corporation's income statement (Illustration 4.28) shows net income of $2,860. The statement of cash flows reports a form of cash-basis income referred to as "Net cash provided by operating activities." For example, Illustration 1.8 which shows a statement of cash flows, reports net cash provided by operating activities of $5,700 for Sierra. Net income and net cash provided by operating activities often differ. The difference for Sierra is $2,840 ($5,700 − $2,860). The following summary shows the causes of this difference of $2,840.

		Computation of Net Cash Provided by Operating Activities	Computation of Net Income
(1)	Cash received in advance from customer	$ 1,200	$ 0
(2)	Cash received from customers for services performed	10,000	10,000
(3)	Services performed for cash received previously in (1)	0	400
(4)	Services performed on account	0	200
(5)	Payment of rent	(900)	(900)
(6)	Purchase of insurance	(600)	0
(7)	Payment of employee salaries	(4,000)	(4,000)
(8)	Use of supplies	0	(1,500)
(9)	Use of insurance	0	(50)
(10)	Depreciation	0	(40)
(11)	Interest cost incurred, but not paid	0	(50)
(12)	Salaries incurred, but not paid	0	(1,200)
		$ 5,700	$ 2,860

For each item included in the computation of net cash provided by operating activities, confirm that cash was either received or paid. For each item in the income statement, confirm that revenue should be recorded because a performance obligation has been satisfied (even when cash was not received) or that an expense was incurred (even when cash was not paid).

ACTION PLAN

- Close revenue and expense accounts to Income Summary.
- Close Income Summary to Retained Earnings.
- Close Dividends to Retained Earnings.

DO IT! 4b | Closing Entries

Hancock Company has the following balances in selected accounts of its adjusted trial balance.

Accounts Payable	$27,000	Dividends	$15,000
Service Revenue	98,000	Retained Earnings	42,000
Rent Expense	22,000	Accounts Receivable	38,000
Salaries and Wages Expense	51,000	Supplies Expense	7,000

Prepare the closing entries at December 31.

Solution

Date	Account	Debit	Credit
Dec. 31	Service Revenue	98,000	
	Income Summary		98,000
	(To close revenue account to Income Summary)		
31	Income Summary	80,000	
	Salaries and Wages Expense		51,000
	Rent Expense		22,000
	Supplies Expense		7,000
	(To close expense accounts to Income Summary)		
31	Income Summary ($98,000 − $80,000)	18,000	
	Retained Earnings		18,000
	(To close net income to retained earnings)		

Dec. 31	Retained Earnings	15,000	
	Dividends		15,000
	(To close dividends to retained earnings)		

Related exercise material: **BE4.16, BE4.17, DO IT! 4.4b, E4.20, E4.21, and E4.24.**

USING THE DECISION TOOLS | Groupon, Inc.

Groupon, Inc. operates online marketplaces that provide goods and services at discounted prices worldwide. Headquartered in Chicago, Illinois, it has over 11,843 employees. Suppose that the information shown in the following trial balance was taken from Groupon's 2022 financial records.

Groupon, Inc.
Adjusted Trial Balance
December 31, 2022
(in millions)

Account	Dr.	Cr.
Cash	$1,072	
Accounts Receivable	105	
Other Current Assets	224	
Equipment	377	
Accumulated Depreciation—Equipment		$ 195
Stock Investments (noncurrent)	24	
Goodwill	619	
Accounts and Other Payables		932
Accrued Expenses Payable		230
Other Current Liabilities		163
Notes Payable (noncurrent)		137
Common Stock		1,687
Dividends	0	
Retained Earnings	849	
Revenues		3,181
Cost of Goods Sold	1,643	
Selling and Administrative Expenses	1,294	
Marketing Expense	269	
Other Expense	33	
Income Tax Expense	16	
	$6,525	$6,525

Instructions

From the trial balance, prepare an income statement, retained earnings statement, and classified balance sheet. **Be sure to prepare them in that order since each statement depends on information determined in the preceding statement.** (*Hint:* Because Groupon has experienced losses, it has a debit balance in Retained Earnings. In its financial statements, Groupon reports an Accumulated Deficit rather than Retained Earnings. Remember that the amount of Retained Earnings reported in the trial balance represents the balance at the beginning of the year.)

Solution

Groupon, Inc.
Income Statement
For the Year Ended December 31, 2022
(in millions)

Revenues		$3,181
Cost of goods sold	$1,643	
Selling and administrative expenses	1,294	
Marketing expense	269	
Other expense	33	
Income tax expense	16	3,255
Net loss		$ (74)

Groupon, Inc.
Retained Earnings Statement
For the Year Ended December 31, 2022
(in millions)

Beginning accumulated deficit	$(849)
Less: Net loss	74
Less: Dividends	0
Ending accumulated deficit	$(923)

Groupon, Inc.
Balance Sheet
December 31, 2022
(in millions)

Assets

Current assets		
Cash	$1,072	
Accounts receivable	105	
Other current assets	224	
Total current assets		$1,401
Long-term investments		
Stock investments		24
Property, plant, and equipment		
Equipment	377	
Accumulated depreciation—equipment	195	182
Intangible assets		
Goodwill		619
Total assets		$2,226

Liabilities and Stockholders' Equity

Liabilities		
Current liabilities		
Accounts and other payables	$ 932	
Accrued expenses payable	230	
Other current liabilities	163	
Total current liabilities		$1,325
Long-term liabilities		
Notes payable		137
Total liabilities		1,462
Stockholders' equity		
Common stock	1,687	
Accumulated deficit	(923)	
Total stockholders' equity		764
Total liabilities and stockholders' equity		$2,226

Appendix 4A Using a Worksheet

LEARNING OBJECTIVE *5
Describe the purpose and the basic form of a worksheet.

We have used T-accounts and trial balances to arrive at the amounts used to prepare financial statements. Accountants, however, frequently use a device known as a worksheet to determine these amounts. A **worksheet** is a multiple-column form that may be used in the adjustment process and in preparing financial statements. Accountants can prepare worksheets manually, but today most use computer spreadsheets.

As its name suggests, the worksheet is a working tool for the accountant. **A worksheet is not a permanent accounting record**; it is neither a journal nor a part of the general ledger. The worksheet is merely a supplemental device used to make it easier to prepare adjusting entries and the financial statements. Small companies with relatively few accounts and adjustments may not need a worksheet. In large companies with numerous accounts and many adjustments, a worksheet is almost indispensable.

Illustration 4A.1 shows the basic form and procedures for preparing a worksheet. Note the headings. The worksheet starts with two columns for the Trial Balance. The next two columns record all Adjustments. Next is the Adjusted Trial Balance. The last two sets of columns correspond to the Income Statement and the Balance Sheet. All items listed in the Adjusted Trial Balance columns are included in either the Income Statement or the Balance Sheet columns.

ILLUSTRATION 4A.1 Form and procedure for a worksheet

Sierra Corporation
Worksheet
For the Month Ended October 31, 2022

Account Titles	Trial Balance Dr.	Trial Balance Cr.	Adjustments Dr.	Adjustments Cr.	Adjusted Trial Balance Dr.	Adjusted Trial Balance Cr.	Income Statement Dr.	Income Statement Cr.	Balance Sheet Dr.	Balance Sheet Cr.
Cash	15,200				15,200				15,200	
Supplies	2,500			(a) 1,500	1,000				1,000	
Prepaid Insurance	600			(b) 50	550				550	
Equipment	5,000				5,000				5,000	
Notes Payable		5,000				5,000				5,000
Accounts Payable		2,500				2,500				2,500
Unearned Service Revenue		1,200	(d) 400			800				800
Common Stock		10,000				10,000				10,000
Retained Earnings		–0–				–0–				–0–
Dividends	500				500				500	
Service Revenue		10,000		(d) 400		10,600		10,600		
				(e) 200						
Salaries and Wages Expense	4,000		(g) 1,200		5,200		5,200			
Rent Expense	900				900		900			
Totals	28,700	28,700								
Supplies Expense			(a) 1,500		1,500		1,500			
Insurance Expense			(b) 50		50		50			
Accum. Depreciation—										
Equipment				(c) 40		40				40
Depreciation Expense			(c) 40		40		40			
Interest Expense			(f) 50		50		50			
Accounts Receivable			(e) 200		200				200	
Interest Payable				(f) 50		50				50
Salaries and Wages Payable				(g) 1,200		1,200				1,200
Totals			3,440	3,440	30,190	30,190	7,740	10,600	22,450	19,590
Net Income							2,860			2,860
Totals							10,600	10,600	22,450	22,450

1 Prepare a trial balance on the worksheet

2 Enter adjustment data

3 Enter adjusted balances

4 Extend adjusted balances to appropriate statement columns

5 Total the statement columns, compute net income (or net loss), and complete worksheet

Review and Practice

Learning Objectives Review

1 Explain the accrual basis of accounting and the reasons for adjusting entries.

The revenue recognition principle dictates that companies recognize revenue when a performance obligation has been satisfied. The expense recognition principle dictates that companies recognize expenses in the period when the company makes efforts to generate those revenues.

Under the cash basis, companies record events only in the periods in which the company receives or pays cash. Accrual-based accounting means that companies record, in the periods in which the events occur, events that change a company's financial statements even if cash has not been exchanged.

Companies make adjusting entries at the end of an accounting period. These entries ensure that companies record revenues in the period in which the performance obligation is satisfied and that companies recognize expenses in the period in which they are incurred. The major types of adjusting entries are prepaid expenses, unearned revenues, accrued revenues, and accrued expenses.

2 Prepare adjusting entries for deferrals.

Deferrals are either prepaid expenses or unearned revenues. Companies make adjusting entries for deferrals at the statement date to record the portion of the deferred item that represents the expense incurred or the revenue for services performed in the current accounting period.

3 Prepare adjusting entries for accruals.

Accruals are either accrued revenues or accrued expenses. Adjusting entries for accruals record revenues for services performed and expenses incurred in the current accounting period that have not been recognized through daily entries.

4 Prepare an adjusted trial balance and closing entries.

An adjusted trial balance is a trial balance that shows the balances of all accounts, including those that have been adjusted, at the end of an accounting period. The purpose of an adjusted trial balance is to show the effects of all financial events that have occurred during the accounting period.

One purpose of closing entries is to transfer net income or net loss for the period to Retained Earnings. A second purpose is to "zero-out" all temporary accounts (revenue accounts, expense accounts, and Dividends) so that they start each new period with a zero balance. To accomplish this, companies "close" all temporary accounts at the end of an accounting period. They make separate entries to close revenues and expenses to Income Summary, Income Summary to Retained Earnings, and Dividends to Retained Earnings. Only temporary accounts are closed.

The required steps in the accounting cycle are (1) analyze business transactions, (2) journalize the transactions, (3) post to ledger accounts, (4) prepare a trial balance, (5) journalize and post adjusting entries, (6) prepare an adjusted trial balance, (7) prepare financial statements, (8) journalize and post closing entries, and (9) prepare a post-closing trial balance.

*5 Describe the purpose and the basic form of a worksheet.

The worksheet is a device to make it easier to prepare adjusting entries and the financial statements. Companies often prepare a worksheet using a computer spreadsheet. The sets of columns of the worksheet are, from left to right, the unadjusted trial balance, adjustments, adjusted trial balance, income statement, and balance sheet.

Decision Tools Review

Decision Checkpoints	Info Needed for Decision	Tool to Use for Decision	How to Evaluate Results
At what point should the company record revenue?	Need to understand the nature of the company's business	Record revenue in the period in which the performance obligation is satisfied.	Recognizing revenue too early overstates current period revenue; recognizing it too late understates current period revenue.
At what point should the company record expenses?	Need to understand the nature of the company's business	Expenses should "follow" revenues—that is, match the effort (expense) with the result (revenue).	Recognizing expenses too early overstates current period expense; recognizing them too late understates current period expense.

Glossary Review

Accrual-basis accounting Accounting basis in which companies record, in the periods in which the events occur, transactions that change a company's financial statements, even if cash was not exchanged. (p. 4-5).

Accrued expenses Expenses incurred but not yet paid in cash or recorded. (p. 4-16).

Accrued revenues Revenues for services performed but not yet received in cash or recorded. (p. 4-14).

Adjusted trial balance A list of accounts and their balances after all adjustments have been made. (p. 4-21).

Adjusting entries Entries made at the end of an accounting period to ensure that the revenue recognition and expense recognition principles are followed. (p. 4-6).

Book value The difference between the cost of a depreciable asset and its related accumulated depreciation. (p. 4-11).

Cash-basis accounting Accounting basis in which a company records revenue only when it receives cash and an expense only when it pays cash. (p. 4-5).

Closing entries Entries at the end of an accounting period to transfer the balances of temporary accounts to a permanent stockholders' equity account, Retained Earnings. (p. 4-26).

Contra asset account An account that is offset against an asset account on the balance sheet. (p. 4-10).

Depreciation The process of allocating the cost of an asset to expense over its useful life. (p. 4-10).

Earnings management The planned timing of revenues, expenses, gains, and losses to smooth out bumps in net income. (p. 4-23).

Expense recognition principle The principle that dictates that efforts (expenses) be recognized with results (revenues) in the period when the company makes efforts to generate those revenues. (p. 4-4).

Fiscal year An accounting period that is one year long. (p. 4-3, in margin).

Income Summary A temporary account used in closing revenue and expense accounts. (p. 4-26).

Periodicity assumption An assumption that the economic life of a business can be divided into artificial time periods. (p. 4-3).

Permanent accounts Balance sheet accounts whose balances are carried forward to the next accounting period. (p. 4-26).

Post-closing trial balance A list of permanent accounts and their balances after a company has journalized and posted closing entries. (p. 4-27).

Prepaid expenses (prepayments) Expenses paid in cash before they are used or consumed. (p. 4-7).

Quality of earnings Indicates the level of full and transparent information that a company provides to users of its financial statements. (p. 4-23).

Revenue recognition principle The principle that companies recognize revenue in the accounting period in which the performance obligation is satisfied. (p. 4-3).

Reversing entry An entry made at the beginning of the next accounting period; the exact opposite of the adjusting entry made in the previous period. (p. 4-28, in margin).

Temporary accounts Revenue, expense, and dividend accounts whose balances a company transfers to Retained Earnings at the end of an accounting period. (p. 4-26).

Unearned revenues Cash received and a liability recorded before services are performed. (p. 4-11).

Useful life The length of service of a productive asset. (p. 4-10).

*Worksheet A multiple-column form that companies may use in the adjustment process and in preparing financial statements. (p. 4-33).

Practice Multiple-Choice Questions

1. **(LO 1)** What is the periodicity assumption?
   a. Companies should recognize revenue in the accounting period in which services are performed.
   b. Companies should match expenses with revenues.
   c. The economic life of a business can be divided into artificial time periods.
   d. The fiscal year should correspond with the calendar year.

2. **(LO 1)** Which principle dictates that efforts (expenses) be recorded with accomplishments (revenues)?
   a. Expense recognition principle.
   b. Historical cost principle.
   c. Periodicity principle.
   d. Revenue recognition principle.

3. **(LO 1)** What are the first step and the final step in the revenue recognition process?
   a. The first step is identify the contract with customers, and the final step is allocate the transaction price to the separate performance obligations.
   b. The first step is identify the separate performance obligations in the contract, and the final step is determine the transaction price.
   c. The first step is identify the contract with customers, and the final step is recognize revenue when each performance obligation is satisfied.
   d. The first step is determine the transaction price, and the final step is identify the separate performance obligations in the contract.

4. **(LO 1)** Which one of these statements about the accrual basis of accounting is **false**?
   a. Companies record events that change their financial statements in the period in which events occur, even if cash was not exchanged.
   b. Companies recognize revenue in the period in which the performance obligation is satisfied.
   c. This basis is in accordance with generally accepted accounting principles.
   d. Companies record revenue only when they receive cash and record expense only when they pay out cash.

5. **(LO 1)** Adjusting entries are made to ensure that:
   a. expenses are recognized in the period in which they are incurred.
   b. revenues are recorded in the period in which the performance obligation is satisfied.

c. balance sheet and income statement accounts have correct balances at the end of an accounting period.

   d. All of the above.

6. **(LO 2, 3)** Each of the following is a major type (or category) of adjusting entry **except**:

   a. prepaid expenses.   c. accrued expenses.
   b. accrued revenues.   d. unearned expenses.

7. **(LO 2)** The trial balance shows Supplies $1,350 and Supplies Expense $0. If $600 of supplies are on hand at the end of the period, the adjusting entry is:

   a. Supplies   600
        Supplies Expense   600
   b. Supplies   750
        Supplies Expense   750
   c. Supplies Expense   750
        Supplies   750
   d. Supplies Expense   600
        Supplies   600

8. **(LO 2)** Adjustments for unearned revenues:

   a. decrease liabilities and increase revenues.
   b. increase liabilities and increase revenues.
   c. increase assets and increase revenues.
   d. decrease revenues and decrease assets.

9. **(LO 2)** Adjustments for prepaid expenses:

   a. decrease assets and increase revenues.
   b. decrease expenses and increase assets.
   c. decrease assets and increase expenses.
   d. decrease revenues and increase assets.

10. **(LO 2)** Queenan Company computes depreciation on delivery equipment at $1,000 for the month of June. The adjusting entry to record this depreciation is as follows:

    a. Depreciation Expense   1,000
         Accumulated Depreciation—
           Queenan Company   1,000
    b. Depreciation Expense   1,000
         Equipment   1,000
    c. Depreciation Expense   1,000
         Accumulated Depreciation—
           Equipment   1,000
    d. Equipment Expense   1,000
         Accumulated Depreciation—
           Equipment   1,000

11. **(LO 3)** Adjustments for accrued revenues:

    a. increase assets and increase liabilities.
    b. increase assets and increase revenues.
    c. decrease assets and decrease revenues.
    d. decrease liabilities and increase revenues.

12. **(LO 3)** Colleen Mooney earned a salary of $400 for the last week of September. She will be paid on October 1. The adjusting entry for Colleen's employer at September 30 is:

    a. No entry is required.
    b. Salaries and Wages Expense   400
         Salaries and Wages Payable   400
    c. Salaries and Wages Expense   400
         Cash   400
    d. Salaries and Wages Payable   400
         Cash   400

13. **(LO 4)** Which statement is **incorrect** concerning the adjusted trial balance?

    a. An adjusted trial balance proves the equality of the total debit balances and the total credit balances in the ledger after all adjustments are made.
    b. The adjusted trial balance provides the primary basis for the preparation of financial statements.
    c. The adjusted trial balance does not list temporary accounts.
    d. The company prepares the adjusted trial balance after it has journalized and posted the adjusting entries.

14. **(LO 4)** Which account will have a zero balance after a company has journalized and posted closing entries?

    a. Service Revenue.
    b. Supplies.
    c. Prepaid Insurance.
    d. Accumulated Depreciation.

15. **(LO 4)** Which types of accounts will appear in the post-closing trial balance?

    a. Permanent accounts.
    b. Temporary accounts.
    c. Expense accounts.
    d. None of the above.

16. **(LO 4)** All of the following are required steps in the accounting cycle **except**:

    a. journalizing and posting closing entries.
    b. preparing an adjusted trial balance.
    c. preparing a post-closing trial balance.
    d. prepare financial statements from the unadjusted trial balance.

Solutions

1. c. The periodicity assumption states that the economic life of a business can be divided into artificial time periods. The other choices are incorrect because (a) this statement describes the revenue recognition principle, (b) this statement describes the expense recognition principle, and (d) the periodicity assumption states that the life of a business can be divided into artificial time periods, not that the fiscal year and calendar year must coincide.

2. a. The expense recognition principle dictates that efforts (expenses) be recorded with accomplishments (revenues). The other choices are incorrect because (b) the historical cost principle states that when assets are purchased, they should be recorded at cost; (c) the periodicity assumption states that the life of a business can be divided into artificial time periods; and (d) the revenue recognition principle states that revenue should be recorded in the period in which the performance obligation is satisfied.

3. c. In the revenue recognition process, the first step is identify the contract with customers, and the final step is recognize revenue when each performance obligation is satisfied. The other choices are incorrect because the five steps in the process in order are (1) Identify the contract with customers, (2) identify the separate performance obligations in the contract, (3) determine the transaction price, (4) allocate the transaction price to the separate performance obligations, and (5) recognize revenue when each performance obligation is satisfied.

4. **d.** If companies record revenue only when they receive cash and record expense only when they pay out cash, they are using the cash basis of accounting. The other choices are true statements about accrual-basis accounting.

5. **d.** Adjusting entries are made to ensure that expenses are recognized in the period in which they are incurred, that revenues are recorded in the period in which the performance obligation is satisfied, and that balance sheet and income statement accounts have correct balances at the end of an accounting period. Although choices (a), (b), and (c) are correct, choice (d) is the better answer.

6. **d.** Unearned expenses are not a major type of adjusting entry. Choices (a) prepaid expenses, (b) accrued revenues, and (c) accrued expenses are all a major type of adjusting entry.

7. **c.** The adjusting entry is to debit Supplies Expense for $750 ($1,350 − $600) and credit Supplies for $750. The other choices are therefore incorrect.

8. **a.** Adjustments for unearned revenues decrease liabilities and increase revenues. The other choices are therefore incorrect.

9. **c.** Adjustments for prepaid expenses decrease assets and increase expenses. The other choices are therefore incorrect.

10. **c.** The adjusting entry is to debit Depreciation Expense and credit Accumulation Depreciation—Equipment. The other choices are incorrect because (a) the contra asset account title includes the asset being depreciated, not the company name; (b) the credit should be to the contra asset account, not the asset; and (d) the debit should be to Depreciation Expense, not Equipment Expense.

11. **b.** When the adjustment is made for accrued revenues, an asset account (usually Accounts Receivable) is increased and a revenue account is increased. The other choices are therefore incorrect.

12. **b.** The adjusting entry should be to debit Salaries and Wages Expense $400 and credit Salaries and Wages Payable for $400. Choice (a) is incorrect because if an adjusting entry is not made, the amount of money owed (liability) that is shown on the balance sheet will be understated and the amount of salaries and wages expense will also be understated. Choices (c) and (d) are incorrect because adjusting entries never affect cash.

13. **c.** The adjusted trial balance does list temporary accounts. The other choices are true statements about the adjusted trial balance.

14. **a.** Service Revenue will have a zero balance after a company has journalized and posted closing entries. The other choices are incorrect because (b) Supplies is an asset, or permanent account, and will not be closed at the end of the year; (c) Prepaid Insurance is an asset, or permanent account, and will not be closed at the end of the year; and (d) Accumulated Depreciation is a contra asset account. Contra asset accounts are permanent accounts and are not closed at the end of the year.

15. **a.** Permanent accounts are the only type of accounts that appear in the post-closing trial balance because they are not closed at the end of the accounting period. Choices (b) and (c) are temporary accounts. Choice (d) is wrong because there is a correct answer.

16. **d.** Financial statements are prepared from the **adjusted** trial balance, not the **un**adjusted trial balance. The other choices are incorrect because (a) journalizing and posting closing entries, (b) preparing an adjusted trial balance, and (c) preparing a post-closing trial balance are all required steps in the accounting cycle.

Practice Brief Exercises

Indicate why adjusting entries are needed.

1. **(LO 1)** The ledger of Dey Company includes the following accounts. Explain why each account may need adjustment.

   a. Supplies.
   b. Unearned Service Revenue.
   c. Salaries and Wages Payable.
   d. Interest Payable.

   Solution

   1. a. Supplies: to recognize supplies used during the period.
      b. Unearned Service Revenue: to record revenue generated for services performed.
      c. Salaries and Wages Payable: to recognize salaries and wages accrued to employees at the end of a reporting period.
      d. Interest Payable: to recognize interest accrued but unpaid on notes payable.

Prepare adjusting entry for depreciation.

2. **(LO 2)** At the end of its first year, the trial balance of Denton Company shows Equipment of $40,000 and zero balances in Accumulated Depreciation—Equipment and Depreciation Expense. Depreciation for the year is estimated to be $8,000. For Denton, (a) prepare the adjusting entry for depreciation at December 31, (b) post the adjustments to T-accounts, and (c) indicate the balance sheet presentation of the equipment at December 31.

   Solution

   2. a. Dec. 31 Depreciation Expense 8,000
                     Accumulated Depreciation—Equipment 8,000

   b.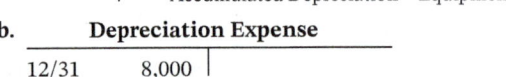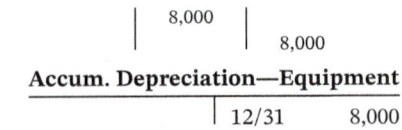

c. Equipment $40,000
   Less: Accumulated Depreciation—Equipment 8,000 $32,000

3. (LO 3) You are asked to prepare the following accrued adjusting entries at December 31. *Prepare adjusting entries for accruals.*

1. Services performed but not recorded are $4,200.
2. Utility expenses incurred but not paid are $660.
3. Salaries and wages earned by employees of $3,000 are unpaid.

Use the following account titles: Accounts Payable, Accounts Receivable, Service Revenue, Salaries and Wages Expense, Salaries and Wages Payable, and Utility Expense.

Solution

3.	Dec. 31	Accounts Receivable	4,200	
		Service Revenue		4,200
	31	Utility Expense	660	
		Accounts Payable		660
	31	Salaries and Wage Expense	3,000	
		Salaries and Wages Payable		3,000

4. (LO 1, 2, 3) The trial balance for Blair Company includes the following balance sheet accounts. Identify the accounts that may require adjustment. For each account that requires adjustment, indicate (a) the type of adjusting entry (prepaid expense, unearned revenue, accrued revenue, or accrued expense) and (b) the related account in the adjusting entry. *Analyze accounts in an unadjusted trial balance.*

Accounts Receivable   Interest Payable
Supplies   Unearned Service Revenue
Prepaid Insurance

Solution

4.

Account	Type of Adjustment	Related Account
Accounts Receivable	Accrued Revenue	Service Revenue
Supplies	Prepaid Expense	Supplies Expense
Prepaid Insurance	Prepaid Expense	Insurance Expense
Interest Payable	Accrued Expense	Interest Expense
Unearned Service Revenue	Unearned Revenue	Service Revenue

5. (LO 4) The adjusted trial balance of Harmony Company includes the following accounts at December 31, 2022: Cash $12,000, Retained Earnings $22,000, Dividends $3,000, Service Revenue $41,000, Rent Expense $900, Salaries and Wages Expense $6,000, Supplies Expense $700, and Depreciation Expense $1,800. Prepare an income statement for the year. *Prepare an income statement from an adjusted trial balance.*

Solution
5.

Harmony Company
Income Statement
For the Year Ended December 31, 2022

Revenues		
Service revenue		$41,000
Expenses		
Salaries and wages expense	$6,000	
Rent expense	900	
Depreciation expense	1,800	
Supplies expense	700	
Total expenses		9,400
Net income		$31,600

Prepare closing entries from ledger balances.

6. (LO 4) The ledger of Quintana Company contains the following balances: Retained Earnings $40,000, Dividends $3,000, Service Revenue $65,000, Salaries and Wages Expense $39,000, and Maintenance and Repairs Expense $9,000. Prepare the closing entries at December 31.

Solution

6.	Dec. 31	Service Revenue	65,000	
		Income Summary		65,000
	31	Income Summary	48,000	
		Salaries and Wages Expense		39,000
		Maintenance and Repairs Expense		9,000
	31	Income Summary	17,000	
		Retained Earnings		17,000
	31	Retained Earnings	3,000	
		Dividends		3,000

Practice Exercises

Prepare correct income statement.

1. (LO 2, 3) The income statement of Bragg Co. for the month of July shows net income of $1,400 based on Service Revenue $5,500, Salaries and Wages Expense $2,300, Supplies Expense $1,200, and Utilities Expense $600. In reviewing the statement, you discover the following.

1. Insurance expired during July of $450 was omitted.
2. Supplies expense includes $300 of supplies that are still on hand at July 31.
3. Depreciation on equipment of $180 was omitted.
4. Accrued but unpaid salaries and wages at July 31 of $400 were not included.
5. Services performed but unrecorded totaled $600.

Instructions

Prepare a correct income statement for July 2022.

Solution

1.

Bragg Co.
Income Statement
For the Month Ended July 31, 2022

Revenues		
Service revenue ($5,500 + $600)		$6,100
Expenses		
Salaries and wages expense ($2,300 + $400)	$2,700	
Supplies expense ($1,200 − $300)	900	
Utilities expense	600	
Insurance expense	450	
Depreciation expense	180	
Total expenses		4,830
Net income		$1,270

Journalize and post closing entries, and prepare a postclosing trial balance.

2. (LO 4) Arapaho Company ended its fiscal year on July 31, 2022. The company's adjusted trial balance as of the end of its fiscal year is as follows.

Arapaho Company
Adjusted Trial Balance
July 31, 2022

Account Titles	Debit	Credit
Cash	$ 15,940	
Accounts Receivable	8,580	
Equipment	16,900	

Account Titles	Debit	Credit
Accumulated Depreciation—Equipment		$ 7,500
Accounts Payable		4,420
Unearned Rent Revenue		1,600
Common Stock		20,500
Retained Earnings		25,000
Dividends	14,000	
Service Revenue		64,000
Rent Revenue		5,500
Depreciation Expense	4,500	
Salaries and Wages Expense	54,700	
Utilities Expense	13,900	
	$128,520	$128,520

Instructions

a. Prepare the closing entries.
b. Post to Retained Earnings and Income Summary T-accounts.
c. Prepare a post-closing trial balance at July 31, 2022.

Solution

2. a.

			Debit	Credit
July 31	Service Revenue		64,000	
	Rent Revenue		5,500	
	Income Summary			69,500
	(To close revenue accounts)			
31	Income Summary		73,100	
	Depreciation Expense			4,500
	Salaries and Wages Expense			54,700
	Utilities Expense			13,900
	(To close expense accounts)			
31	Retained Earnings ($73,100 − $69,500)		3,600	
	Income Summary			3,600
	(To close net loss to retained earnings)			
31	Retained Earnings		14,000	
	Dividends			14,000
	(To close dividends to retained earnings)			

b.

Retained Earnings				Income Summary			
		Bal.	25,000				69,500
	3,600				73,100		
	14,000						3,600
		Bal.	7,400			Bal.	0

c.

Arapaho Company
Post-Closing Trial Balance
July 31, 2022

	Debit	Credit
Cash	$15,940	
Accounts Receivable	8,580	
Equipment	16,900	
Accumulated Depreciation—Equipment		$ 7,500
Accounts Payable		4,420
Unearned Rent Revenue		1,600
Common Stock		20,500
Retained Earnings		7,400
	$41,420	$41,420

Practice Problem

Prepare adjusting entries from selected data.

(LO 2, 3) Terry Thomas and a group of investors incorporated the Green Thumb Lawn Care Corporation on April 1. At April 30, the trial balance shows the following balances for selected accounts.

Prepaid Insurance	$ 3,600
Equipment	28,000
Notes Payable	20,000
Unearned Service Revenue	4,200
Service Revenue	1,800

Analysis reveals the following additional data pertaining to these accounts.

1. Prepaid insurance is the cost of a 2-year insurance policy, effective April 1.
2. Depreciation on the equipment is $500 per month.
3. The note payable is dated April 1. It is a 6-month, 6% note.
4. Seven customers paid for the company's 6-month lawn service package of $600 beginning in April. These customers received the first month of services in April.
5. Lawn services performed for other customers but not billed at April 30 totaled $1,500.

Instructions

Prepare the adjusting entries for the month of April. Show computations.

Solution

GENERAL JOURNAL

Date	Account Titles and Explanation	Debit	Credit
	Adjusting Entries		
Apr. 30	Insurance Expense	150	
	Prepaid Insurance		150
	(To record insurance expired:		
	$3,600 ÷ 24 = $150 per month)		
30	Depreciation Expense	500	
	Accumulated Depreciation—Equipment		500
	(To record monthly depreciation)		
30	Interest Expense	100	
	Interest Payable		100
	(To accrue interest on notes payable:		
	$20,000 × 6% × $\frac{1}{12}$ = $100)		
30	Unearned Service Revenue	700	
	Service Revenue		700
	(To record revenue for services performed:		
	$600 ÷ 6 = $100; $100 per month × 7 = $700)		
30	Accounts Receivable	1,500	
	Service Revenue		1,500
	(To accrue revenue for services performed)		

WileyPLUS

Brief Exercises, DO IT! Exercises, Exercises, Problems, and many additional resources are available for practice in WileyPLUS.

Note: All asterisked Questions, Exercises, and Problems relate to material in the appendix to the chapter.

Questions

1. a. How does the periodicity assumption affect an accountant's analysis of accounting transactions?

b. Explain the term fiscal year.

2. Identify and state two generally accepted accounting principles that relate to adjusting the accounts.

3. What are the five steps of the revenue recognition process?

4. Max Wilson, a lawyer, accepts a legal engagement in March, performs the work in April, and is paid in May. If Wilson's law firm prepares monthly financial statements, when should it recognize revenue from this engagement? Why?

5. In completing the engagement in Question 4, Wilson pays no costs in March, $2,500 in April, and $2,200 in May (incurred in April). How much expense should the firm deduct from revenues in the month when it recognizes the revenue? Why?

6. "The historical cost principle of accounting requires adjusting entries." Do you agree? Explain.

7. Why may the financial information in an unadjusted trial balance not be up-to-date and complete?

8. Distinguish between the two categories of adjusting entries, and identify the types of adjustments applicable to each category.

9. What types of accounts does a company debit and credit in a prepaid expense adjusting entry?

10. "Depreciation is a process of valuation that results in the reporting of the fair value of the asset." Do you agree? Explain.

11. Explain the differences between depreciation expense and accumulated depreciation.

12. Steele Company purchased equipment for $15,000. By the current balance sheet date, the company had depreciated $7,000. Indicate the balance sheet presentation of the data.

13. What types of accounts are debited and credited in an unearned revenue adjusting entry?

14. Abe Technologies provides maintenance service for computers and office equipment for companies throughout the Northeast. The sales manager is elated because she closed a $300,000, 3-year maintenance contract on December 29, 2021, two days before the company's year-end. "Now we will hit this year's net income target for sure," she crowed. The customer is required to pay $100,000 on December 29 (the day the deal was closed). Two more payments of $100,000 each are also required on December 29, 2022 and 2023. Discuss the effect that this event will have on the company's financial statements.

15. BeneMart, a large national retail chain, is nearing its fiscal year-end. It appears that the company is not going to hit its revenue and net income targets. The company's marketing manager, Ed Mellon, suggests running a promotion selling $50 gift cards for $45. He believes that this would be very popular and would enable the company to meet its targets for revenue and net income. What do you think of this idea?

16. Whistler Corp. performed services for a customer but has not received payment, nor has it recorded any entry related to the work. Which of the following types of accounts are involved in the adjusting entry: (a) asset, (b) liability, (c) revenue, or (d) expense? For the accounts selected, indicate whether they would be debited or credited in the entry.

17. A company fails to recognize an expense incurred but not paid. Indicate which of the following types of accounts is debited and which is credited in the adjusting entry: (a) asset, (b) liability, (c) revenue, or (d) expense.

18. A company makes an accrued revenue adjusting entry for $780 and an accrued expense adjusting entry for $510. How much was net income understated or overstated prior to these entries? Explain.

19. On January 9, a company pays $6,200 for salaries, of which $1,100 was reported as Salaries and Wages Payable on December 31. Give the entry to record the payment.

20. For each of the following items before adjustment, indicate the type of adjusting entry—prepaid expense, unearned revenue, accrued revenue, and accrued expense—that is needed to correct the misstatement. If an item could result in more than one type of adjusting entry, indicate each of the types.

   a. Assets are understated.
   b. Liabilities are overstated.
   c. Liabilities are understated.
   d. Expenses are understated.
   e. Assets are overstated.
   f. Revenue is understated.

21. One-half of the adjusting entry is given below. Indicate the account title for the other half of the entry.

   a. Salaries and Wages Expense is debited.
   b. Depreciation Expense is debited.
   c. Interest Payable is credited.
   d. Supplies is credited.
   e. Accounts Receivable is debited.
   f. Unearned Service Revenue is debited.

22. "An adjusting entry may affect more than one balance sheet or income statement account." Do you agree? Why or why not?

23. Which balance sheet account provides evidence that **Apple** records sales on an accrual basis rather than a cash basis? Explain.

24. Why is it possible to prepare financial statements directly from an adjusted trial balance?

25. a. What information do accrual-basis financial statements provide that cash-basis statements do not?
    b. What information do cash-basis financial statements provide that accrual-basis statements do not?

26. What is the relationship, if any, between the amount shown in the adjusted trial balance column for an account and that account's ledger balance?

27. Identify the account(s) debited and credited in each of the four closing entries, assuming the company has net income for the year.

28. Some companies employ technologies that allow them to do a so-called "virtual close." This enables them to close their books nearly instantaneously any time during the year. What advantages does a "virtual close" provide?

29. Describe the nature of the Income Summary account, and identify the types of summary data that may be posted to this account.

30. What items are disclosed on a post-closing trial balance? What is its purpose?

31. Which of these accounts would not appear in the post-closing trial balance? Interest Payable, Equipment, Depreciation Expense, Dividends, Unearned Service Revenue, Accumulated Depreciation—Equipment, and Service Revenue.

32. Indicate, in the sequence in which they are made, the three required steps in the accounting cycle that involve journalizing.

33. Identify, in the sequence in which they are prepared, the three trial balances that are required in the accounting cycle.

CHAPTER 4 Accrual Accounting Concepts

34. Explain the terms earnings management and quality of earnings.
35. Give examples of how companies manage earnings.
*36. What is the purpose of a worksheet?
*37. What is the basic form of a worksheet?

Brief Exercises

Identify the order of the five steps in the revenue recognition process.

BE4.1 (LO 1), K Number the following steps of the revenue recognition process (from 1–5) to place in the correct order.

a. _____ Allocate the transaction price to the separate performance obligations.
b. _____ Identify the contract with customers.
c. _____ Identify the separate performance obligations in the contract.
d. _____ Recognize revenue when each performance obligation is satisfied.
e. _____ Determine the transaction price.

Identify impact of transactions on cash and net income.

BE4.2 (LO 1), C Transactions that affect earnings do not necessarily affect cash. Identify the effect, if any, that each of the following transactions would have upon cash and net income. The first transaction has been completed as an example.

	Cash	Net Income
a. Purchased $100 of supplies for cash.	−$100	$0
b. Recorded an adjusting entry to record use of $20 of the above supplies.		
c. Made sales of $1,300, all on account.		
d. Received $800 from customers in payment of their accounts.		
e. Purchased equipment for cash, $2,500.		
f. Recorded depreciation of building for period used, $600.		

Indicate why adjusting entries are needed.

BE4.3 (LO 1), C The ledger of Melmann Company includes the following accounts. Explain why each account may require adjustment.

a. Prepaid Insurance.
b. Depreciation Expense.
c. Unearned Service Revenue.
d. Interest Payable.

Identify the major types of adjusting entries.

BE4.4 (LO 1), AN Cortina Company accumulates the following adjustment data at December 31. Indicate (1) the type of adjustment (prepaid expense, accrued revenue, and so on) and (2) the status of the accounts before adjustment (for example, "assets understated and revenues understated").

a. Supplies of $400 are on hand. Supplies account shows $1,600 balance.
b. Services performed but unbilled total $700.
c. Interest of $300 has accumulated on a note payable.
d. Rent collected in advance totaling $1,100 has been earned.

Prepare adjusting entry for supplies.

BE4.5 (LO 2), AP Lahey Advertising Company's trial balance at December 31 shows Supplies $8,800 and Supplies Expense $0. On December 31, there are $1,100 of supplies on hand. Prepare the adjusting entry at December 31 and, using T-accounts, enter the balances in the accounts, post the adjusting entry, and indicate the adjusted balance in each account.

Prepare adjusting entry for depreciation.

BE4.6 (LO 2), AP At the end of its first year, the trial balance of Rayburn Company shows Equipment $22,000 and zero balances in Accumulated Depreciation—Equipment and Depreciation Expense. Depreciation for the year is estimated to be $2,750. Prepare the annual adjusting entry for depreciation at December 31, post the adjustments to T-accounts, and indicate the balance sheet presentation of the equipment at December 31.

Prepare adjusting entry for prepaid expense.

BE4.7 (LO 2), AP On July 1, 2022, Ling Co. pays $12,400 to Marsh Insurance Co. for a 2-year insurance contract. Both companies have fiscal years ending December 31. For Ling Co., journalize and post the entry on July 1 and the annual adjusting entry on December 31.

Prepare adjusting entry for unearned revenue.

BE4.8 (LO 2), AP Using the data in BE4.7, journalize and post the entry on July 1 and the adjusting entry on December 31 for Marsh Insurance Co. Marsh uses the accounts Unearned Service Revenue and Service Revenue.

Prepare adjusting entries for deferrals.

BE4.9 (LO 2), AP The unadjusted trial balance of Northern Exposure Inc. had these balances for the following select accounts: Supplies $3,100, Unearned Service Revenue $8,200, and Prepaid Rent

$1,200. At the end of the period, a count showed $500 of supplies on hand. Services of $2,900 had been performed related to the unearned revenue account, and one month's worth of rent, worth $400, had been consumed by Northern Exposure. Record the required adjusting entries related to these events.

BE4.10 (LO 3), AP The bookkeeper for Tran Company asks you to prepare the following accrual adjusting entries at December 31. Use these account titles: Service Revenue, Accounts Receivable, Interest Expense, Interest Payable, Salaries and Wages Expense, and Salaries and Wages Payable.

Prepare adjusting entries for accruals.

a. Interest on notes payable of $300 is accrued.
b. Services performed but unbilled totals $1,700.
c. Salaries of $780 earned by employees have not been recorded.

BE4.11 (LO 3), AP At December 31 of the current year, Cullen Corporation had a number of items that were not reflected in its accounting records. Maintenance and repair costs of $770 were incurred but not paid. Utilities costing $240 were used but not paid, and use of a warehouse space worth $1,900 was provided to a tenant who had not been billed as of the end of the month. Record the required adjusting entries related to these events.

Prepare adjusting entries for accruals.

BE4.12 (LO 2, 3), AN The trial balance of Woods Company includes the following balance sheet accounts. Identify the accounts that might require adjustment. For each account that requires adjustment, indicate (1) the type of adjusting entry (prepaid expense, unearned revenue, accrued revenue, and accrued expense) and (2) the related account in the adjusting entry.

Analyze accounts in a trial balance.

a. Accounts Receivable.
b. Prepaid Insurance.
c. Equipment.
d. Accumulated Depreciation—Equipment.
e. Notes Payable.
f. Interest Payable.
g. Unearned Service Revenue.

BE4.13 (LO 4), AP The adjusted trial balance of Levin Corporation at December 31, 2022, includes the following accounts: Retained Earnings $17,200, Dividends $6,000, Service Revenue $32,000, Salaries and Wages Expense $14,000, Insurance Expense $1,800, Rent Expense $3,900, Supplies Expense $1,500, and Depreciation Expense $1,000. Prepare an income statement for the year.

Prepare an income statement from an adjusted trial balance.

BE4.14 (LO 4), AP Partial adjusted trial balance data for Levin Corporation are presented in BE4.13. The balance in Retained Earnings is the balance as of January 1. Prepare a retained earnings statement for the year assuming net income is $10,400.

Prepare a retained earnings statement from an adjusted trial balance.

BE4.15 (LO 4), K The following selected accounts appear in the adjusted trial balance for Deane Company. Indicate the financial statement on which each account would be reported.

Identify financial statement for selected accounts.

a. Accumulated Depreciation.
b. Depreciation Expense.
c. Retained Earnings (beginning).
d. Dividends.
e. Service Revenue.
f. Supplies.
g. Accounts Payable.

BE4.16 (LO 4), K Using the data in BE4.15, identify the accounts that would be included in a post-closing trial balance.

Identify post-closing trial balance accounts.

BE4.17 (LO 4), AP The income statement for the Bonita Pines Golf Club Inc. for the month ended July 31 shows Service Revenue $16,000, Salaries and Wages Expense $8,400, Maintenance and Repairs Expense $2,500, and Income Tax Expense $1,000. The statement of retained earnings shows an opening balance for Retained Earnings of $20,000 and Dividends $1,300.

Prepare and post closing entries.

a. Prepare closing journal entries.
b. What is the ending balance in Retained Earnings?

BE4.18 (LO4), K The required steps in the accounting cycle are listed in random order below. List the steps in proper sequence.

List required steps in the accounting cycle sequence.

a. Prepare a post-closing trial balance.
b. Prepare an adjusted trial balance.
c. Analyze business transactions.
d. Prepare a trial balance.
e. Journalize the transactions.
f. Journalize and post closing entries.
g. Prepare financial statements.
h. Journalize and post adjusting entries.
i. Post to ledger accounts.

DO IT! Exercises

Identify timing concepts.

DO IT! 4.1 (LO 1), C A list of concepts is provided below in the left column, with descriptions of the concepts in the right column. There are more descriptions provided than concepts. Match the description to the concept.

1. ____ Cash-basis accounting.
2. ____ Fiscal year.
3. ____ Revenue recognition principle.
4. ____ Expense recognition principle.

a. Monthly and quarterly time periods.
b. Accountants divide the economic life of a business into artificial time periods.
c. Efforts (expenses) should be matched with accomplishments (revenues).
d. Companies record revenues when they receive cash and record expenses when they pay out cash.
e. An accounting time period that is one year in length.
f. An accounting time period that starts on January 1 and ends on December 31.
g. Companies record transactions in the period in which the events occur.
h. Recognize revenue in the accounting period in which a performance obligation is satisfied.

Prepare adjusting entries for deferrals.

DO IT! 4.2 (LO 2), AP The ledger of Umatilla, Inc. on March 31, 2022, includes the following selected accounts before adjusting entries.

	Debit	Credit
Supplies	2,500	
Prepaid Insurance	2,400	
Equipment	30,000	
Unearned Service Revenue		10,000

An analysis of the accounts shows the following.

1. Insurance expires at the rate of $300 per month.
2. Supplies on hand total $900.
3. The equipment depreciates $200 per month.
4. During March, services were performed for two-fifths of the unearned service revenue.

Prepare the adjusting entries for the month of March.

Prepare adjusting entries for accruals.

DO IT! 4.3 (LO 3), AP Jean Karns is the new owner of Jean's Computer Services. At the end of July 2022, her first month of ownership, Jean is trying to prepare monthly financial statements. She has the following information for the month.

1. At July 31, Jean owed employees $1,100 in salaries that the company will pay in August.
2. On July 1, Jean borrowed $20,000 from a local bank on a 10-year note. The annual interest rate is 9%.
3. Service revenue unrecorded in July totaled $1,600.

Prepare the adjusting entries needed at July 31, 2022.

Prepare financial statements from adjusted trial balance.

DO IT! 4.4a (LO 4), C Indicate in which financial statement each of the following adjusted trial balance accounts would be presented.

Service Revenue   Accounts Receivable
Notes Payable   Accumulated Depreciation
Common Stock   Utilities Expense

Prepare closing entries.

DO IT! 4.4b (LO 4), AP Paloma Company shows the following balances in selected accounts of its adjusted trial balance.

Supplies	$32,000	Service Revenue	$108,000
Supplies Expense	6,000	Salaries and Wages Expense	40,000
Accounts Receivable	12,000	Utilities Expense	8,000
Dividends	22,000	Rent Expense	18,000
Retained Earnings	70,000		

Prepare the remaining closing entries at December 31.

Exercises

E4.1 (LO 1), C The following independent situations require professional judgment for determining when to recognize revenue from the transactions.

Identify point of revenue recognition.

a. **Southwest Airlines** sells you an advance-purchase airline ticket in September for your flight home in December.

b. **Ultimate Electronics** sells you a home theater on a "no money down and full payment in three months" promotional deal.

c. The **Toronto Blue Jays** sell season tickets online to games in the Skydome. Fans can purchase the tickets at any time, although the season doesn't officially begin until April. The major league baseball season runs from April through October.

d. **RBC Financial Group** loans money on August 1. The loan and the interest are repayable in full in November.

e. In August, a customer orders a sweater from the **Target** website, paying with a Target credit card. The sweater arrives in September. Target sends a bill in October and receives payment in October.

Instructions

Identify when revenue should be recognized in each of the above situations.

E4.2 (LO 1), K These accounting concepts were discussed in this and previous chapters.

Identify accounting assumptions, principles, and constraint.

1. Economic entity assumption.
2. Expense recognition principle.
3. Monetary unit assumption.
4. Periodicity assumption.
5. Historical cost principle.
6. Materiality.
7. Full disclosure principle.
8. Going concern assumption.
9. Revenue recognition principle.
10. Cost constraint.

Instructions

Identify by number the accounting concept that describes each situation below. Do not use a number more than once.

____ a. Is the rationale for why plant assets are not reported at liquidation value. (Do not use the historical cost principle.)

____ b. Indicates that personal and business recordkeeping should be separately maintained.

____ c. Ensures that all relevant financial information is reported.

____ d. Assumes that the dollar is the "measuring stick" used to report on financial performance.

____ e. Requires that accounting standards be followed for all items of **significant** size.

____ f. Separates financial information into time periods for reporting purposes.

____ g. Requires recognition of expenses in the same period as related revenues.

____ h. Indicates that fair value changes subsequent to purchase are not recorded in the accounts.

E4.3 (LO 1), C Here are some accounting reporting situations.

Identify the violated assumption, principle, or constraint.

a. East Lake Company recognizes revenue at the end of the production cycle but before sale. The price of the product, as well as the amount that can be sold, is not certain.

b. Hilo Company is in its fifth year of operation and has yet to issue financial statements. (Do not use the full disclosure principle.)

c. Gomez, Inc. is carrying inventory at its original cost of $100,000. Inventory has a fair value of $110,000.

d. Bly Hospital Supply Corporation reports only current assets and current liabilities on its balance sheet. Equipment and bonds payable are reported as current assets and current liabilities, respectively. Liquidation of the company is unlikely.

e. Chieu Company has inventory on hand that cost $400,000. Chieu reports inventory on its balance sheet at its current fair value of $425,000.

f. Toxy Syles, president of Classic Music Company, bought a computer for her personal use. She paid for the computer by using company funds and debited the "Computers" account.

Instructions

For each situation, list the assumption, principle, or constraint that has been violated, if any. (Some were presented in earlier chapters.) List only one answer for each situation.

Convert earnings from cash to accrual basis.

E4.4 (LO 1, 2, 3), AP Your examination of the records of a company that follows the cash basis of accounting tells you that the company's reported cash-basis earnings in 2022 are $33,640. If this firm had followed accrual-basis accounting practices, it would have reported the following year-end balances.

	2022	2021
Accounts receivable	$3,400	$2,800
Supplies on hand	1,300	1,460
Unpaid wages owed	2,000	2,400
Other unpaid expenses	1,400	1,100

Instructions

Determine the company's net earnings on an accrual basis for 2022. Show all your calculations in an orderly fashion.

Determine cash-basis and accrual-basis earnings.

E4.5 (LO 1), AP In its first year of operations, Gomes Company recognized $28,000 in service revenue, $6,000 of which was on account and still outstanding at year-end. The remaining $22,000 was received in cash from customers.

The company incurred operating expenses of $15,800. Of these expenses, $12,000 were paid in cash; $3,800 was still owed on account at year-end. In addition, Gomes prepaid $2,400 for insurance coverage that would not be used until the second year of operations.

Instructions

a. Calculate the first year's net earnings under the cash basis of accounting, and calculate the first year's net earnings under the accrual basis of accounting.

b. Which basis of accounting (cash or accrual) provides more useful information for decision-makers?

Convert earnings from cash to accrual basis; prepare accrual-based financial statements.

E4.6 (LO1, 2, 3), AP Franken Company, a ski tuning and repair shop, opened on November 1, 2021. The company carefully kept track of all its cash receipts and cash payments. The following information is available at the end of the ski season, April 30, 2022.

	Cash Receipts	Cash Payments
Issuance of common shares	$20,000	
Payment to purchase repair shop equipment		$ 9,200
Rent payments to landlord		1,050
Newspaper advertising payment		375
Utility bill payments		970
Part-time helper's wage payments		2,600
Income tax payment		10,000
Cash receipts from ski and snowboard repair services	32,150	
Subtotals	52,150	24,195
Cash balance		27,955
Totals	$52,150	$52,150

The repair shop equipment was purchased on November 1 and has an estimated useful life of 4 years. Lease payments to the landlord are made at the beginning of each month. The part-time helper is owed

$420 at April 30, 2022, for unpaid wages. At April 30, 2022, customers owe Franken Company $540 for services they have received but have not yet paid for.

Instructions

a. Prepare an accrual-basis income statement for the 6 months ended April 30, 2022.

b. Prepare the April 30, 2022, classified balance sheet.

E4.7 (LO 1, 2, 3), C Writing BizCon, a consulting firm, has just completed its first year of operations. The company's sales growth was explosive. To encourage clients to hire its services, BizCon offered 180-day financing—meaning its largest customers do not pay for nearly 6 months. Because BizCon is a new company, its equipment suppliers insist on being paid cash on delivery. Also, it had to pay up front for 2 years of insurance. At the end of the year, BizCon owed employees for one full month of salaries, but due to a cash shortfall, it promised to pay them the first week of next year.

Identify differences between cash and accrual accounting.

Instructions

a. Explain how cash and accrual accounting would differ for each of the events listed above and describe the proper accrual accounting.

b. Assume that at the end of the year, BizCon reported a favorable net income, yet the company's management is concerned because the company is very short of cash. Explain how BizCon could have positive net income and yet run out of cash.

E4.8 (LO 1, 2, 3), AN Wang Company accumulates the following adjustment data at December 31.

Identify types of adjustments and accounts before adjustment.

a. Services performed but unbilled total $600.

b. Store supplies of $160 are on hand. The supplies account shows a $1,900 balance.

c. Utility expenses of $275 are unpaid.

d. Services performed of $490 collected in advance.

e. Salaries of $620 are unpaid.

f. Prepaid insurance totaling $400 has expired.

Instructions

For each item, indicate (1) the type of adjustment (prepaid expense, unearned revenue, accrued revenue, or accrued expense) and (2) the status of the accounts before adjustment (overstated or understated).

E4.9 (LO 2, 3), AP The ledger of Howard Rental Agency on March 31 of the current year includes the selected accounts below before adjusting entries have been prepared.

Prepare adjusting entries from selected account data.

	Debit	Credit
Supplies	$ 3,000	
Prepaid Insurance	3,600	
Equipment	25,000	
Accumulated Depreciation—Equipment		$ 8,400
Notes Payable		20,000
Unearned Rent Revenue		12,400
Rent Revenue		60,000
Interest Expense	0	
Salaries and Wages Expense	14,000	

An analysis of the accounts shows the following.

1. The equipment depreciates $280 per month.
2. Half of the unearned rent revenue was earned during the quarter.
3. Interest of $400 is accrued on the notes payable.
4. Supplies on hand total $850.
5. Insurance expires at the rate of $400 per month.

Instructions

Prepare the adjusting entries at March 31, assuming that adjusting entries are made quarterly. Additional accounts are Depreciation Expense, Insurance Expense, Interest Payable, and Supplies Expense.

E4.10 (LO 2, 3), AP Al Medina, D.D.S., opened an incorporated dental pfractice on January 1, 2022. During the first month of operations, the following transactions occurred.

Prepare adjusting entries.

1. Performed services for patients who had dental plan insurance. At January 31, $760 of such services was completed but not yet billed to the insurance companies.

2. Utility expenses incurred but not paid prior to January 31 totaled $450.
3. Purchased dental equipment on January 1 for $80,000, paying $20,000 in cash and signing a $60,000, 3-year note payable (interest is paid each December 31). The equipment depreciates $400 per month. Interest is $500 per month.
4. Purchased a 1-year malpractice insurance policy on January 1 for $24,000.
5. Purchased $1,750 of dental supplies (recorded as increase to Supplies). On January 31, determined that $550 of supplies were on hand.

Instructions

Prepare the adjusting entries on January 31. Account titles are Accumulated Depreciation—Equipment, Depreciation Expense, Service Revenue, Accounts Receivable, Insurance Expense, Interest Expense, Interest Payable, Prepaid Insurance, Supplies, Supplies Expense, Utilities Expense, and Accounts Payable.

Prepare adjusting entries.

E4.11 (LO 2, 3), AP The unadjusted trial balance for Sierra Corp. is shown in Illustration 4.5. Instead of the adjusting entries shown in the text at October 31, assume the following adjustment data.

1. Supplies on hand at October 31 total $500.
2. Expired insurance for the month is $100.
3. Depreciation for the month is $75.
4. As of October 31, services worth $800 related to the previously recorded unearned revenue had been performed.
5. Services performed but unbilled (and no receivable has been recorded) at October 31 are $280.
6. Interest expense accrued at October 31 is $70.
7. Accrued salaries at October 31 are $1,400.

Instructions

Prepare the adjusting entries for the items above.

Prepare adjusting entries from selected account data.

E4.12 (LO 2, 3), AP The ledger of Armour Lake Lumber Supply on July 31, 2022, includes the selected accounts below before adjusting entries have been prepared.

	Debit	Credit
Investment in Note Receivable	$ 20,000	
Supplies	24,000	
Prepaid Rent	3,600	
Buildings	250,000	
Accumulated Depreciation—Buildings		$140,000
Unearned Service Revenue		11,500

An analysis of the company's accounts shows the following.

1. The investment in the notes receivable earns interest at a rate of 6% per year.
2. Supplies on hand at the end of the month totaled $18,600.
3. The balance in Prepaid Rent represents 4 months of rent costs.
4. Employees were owed $3,100 related to unpaid salaries and wages.
5. Depreciation on buildings is $6,000 per year.
6. During the month, the company satisfied obligations worth $4,700 related to the Unearned Service Revenue.
7. Unpaid maintenance and repairs costs were $2,300.

Instructions

Prepare the adjusting entries at July 31 assuming that adjusting entries are made monthly. Use additional accounts as needed.

Prepare a correct income statement.

E4.13 (LO 1, 2, 3), AN The income statement of Norski Co. for the month of July shows net income of $2,000 based on Service Revenue $5,500, Salaries and Wages Expense $2,100, Supplies Expense $900, and Utilities Expense $500. In reviewing the statement, you discover the following:

1. Insurance expired during July of $350 was omitted.
2. Supplies expense includes $200 of supplies that are still on hand at July 31.

3. Depreciation on equipment of $150 was omitted.
4. Accrued but unpaid wages at July 31 of $360 were not included.
5. Services performed but unrecorded totaled $700.

Instructions

Prepare a correct income statement for July 2022.

E4.14 (LO 2, 3), AN Selected accounts of Villa Company are shown here.

Journalize basic transactions and adjusting entries.

Supplies Expense				Salaries and Wages Payable			
July 31	750					July 31	1,000

Salaries and Wages Expense				Accounts Receivable			
July 15	1,000			July 31	500		
31	1,000						

Service Revenue				Unearned Service Revenue			
		July 14	3,800	July 31	900	July 1	Bal. 1,500
		31	900			20	600
		31	500				

Supplies			
July 1	Bal. 1,100	July 31	750
10	200		

Instructions

After analyzing the accounts, journalize (a) the July transactions and (b) the adjusting entries that were made on July 31. (*Hint:* July transactions were for cash.)

E4.15 (LO 1, 2, 3), AN This is a partial adjusted trial balance of Ramon Company.

Analyze adjusted data.

Ramon Company
Adjusted Trial Balance
January 31, 2022

	Debit	Credit
Supplies	$ 700	
Prepaid Insurance	1,560	
Salaries and Wages Payable		$1,060
Unearned Service Revenue		750
Supplies Expense	950	
Insurance Expense	520	
Salaries and Wages Expense	1,800	
Service Revenue		4,000

Instructions

Answer these questions, assuming the year begins January 1.

a. If the amount in Supplies Expense is the January 31 adjusting entry and $300 of supplies was purchased in January, what was the balance in Supplies on January 1?

b. If the amount in Insurance Expense is the January 31 adjusting entry and the original insurance premium was for 1 year, what was the total premium and when was the policy purchased?

c. If $2,500 of salaries was paid in January, what was the balance in Salaries and Wages Payable at December 31, 2021?

d. If $1,800 was received in January for services performed in January, what was the balance in Unearned Service Revenue at December 31, 2021?

E4.16 (LO 2, 3), AN On December 31, 2022, Waters Company prepared an income statement and balance sheet, but failed to take into account three adjusting entries. The balance sheet showed total assets $150,000, total liabilities $70,000, and stockholders' equity $80,000. The incorrect income statement showed net income of $70,000.

Determine effect of adjusting entries.

The data for the three adjusting entries were:

1. Salaries and wages amounting to $10,000 for the last 2 days in December were not paid and not recorded. The next payroll will be in January.
2. Rent payments of $8,000 was received for two months in advance on December 1. The entire amount was credited to Unearned Rent Revenue when paid.
3. Depreciation expense for 2022 is $9,000.

Instructions

Complete the following table to correct the financial statement amounts shown (indicate deductions with parentheses).

Item	Net Income	Total Assets	Total Liabilities	Stockholders' Equity
Incorrect balances	$70,000	$150,000	$70,000	$80,000
Effects of:				
Salaries and Wages	_____	_____	_____	_____
Rent Revenue	_____	_____	_____	_____
Depreciation	_____	_____	_____	_____
Correct balances	======	======	======	======

Prepare and post transaction and adjusting entries for prepayments.

E4.17 (LO 2), AP Action Quest Games Inc. adjusts its accounts annually. The following information is available for the year ended December 31, 2022.

1. Purchased a 1-year insurance policy on June 1 for $1,800 cash.
2. Paid $6,500 on August 31 for 5 months' rent in advance.
3. On September 4, received $3,600 cash in advance from a corporation to sponsor a game each month for a total of 9 months for the most improved students at a local school.
4. Signed a contract for cleaning services starting December 1 for $1,000 per month. Paid for the first 2 months on November 30. (*Hint:* Use the account Prepaid Cleaning to record prepayments.)
5. On December 5, received $1,500 in advance from a gaming club. Determined that on December 31, $475 of these games had not yet been played.

Instructions

a. For each of the above transactions, prepare the journal entry to record the initial transaction.
b. For each of the above transactions, prepare the adjusting journal entry that is required on December 31. (*Hint:* Use the account Service Revenue for item 3 and Repairs and Maintenance Expense for item 4.)
c. Post the journal entries in parts (a) and (b) to T-accounts and determine the final balance in each account balance. (*Note:* Posting to the Cash account is not required.)

Prepare adjusting and subsequent entries for accruals.

E4.18 (LO 3), AP Greenock Limited has the following information available for accruals for the year ended December 31, 2022. The company adjusts its accounts annually.

1. The December utility bill for $425 was unrecorded on December 31. Greenock paid the bill on January 11.
2. Greenock is open 7 days a week and employees are paid a total of $3,500 every Monday for a 7-day (Monday–Sunday) workweek. December 31 is a Thursday, so employees will have worked 4 days (Monday, December 28–Thursday, December 31) that they have not been paid for by year-end. Employees will be paid next on January 4.
3. Greenock signed a $45,000, 5% bank loan on November 1, 2021, due in 2 years. Interest is payable on the first day of each following month. (For example, interest incurred during November would be paid on December 1.)
4. Greenock receives a fee from Pizza Shop next door for all pizzas sold to customers using Greenock's facility. The amount owed for December is $300, which Pizza Shop will pay on January 4. (*Hint:* Use the Service Revenue account.)
5. Greenock rented some of its unused warehouse space to a client for $6,000 a month, payable the first day of the following month. It received the rent for the month of December on January 2.

Instructions

a. For each situation, prepare the adjusting entry required at December 31. (Round all calculations to the nearest dollar.)
b. For each situation, prepare the journal entry to record the subsequent cash transaction in 2023.

E4.19 (LO 1, 2, 3, 4), C The following is a list of terms and phrases discussed in the chapter.

Identify accounting terms.

1. Contra asset account
2. Permanent accounts
3. Depreciation
4. Adjusting entries
5. Prepaid expenses (prepayments)
6. Temporary accounts
7. Book value
8. Adjusted trial balance
9. Closing entries
10. Earnings management
11. Income Summary

Instructions

Match each term or phrase with its description below.

a. _____ Expenses paid in cash before they are used or consumed.
b. _____ The difference between the cost of a depreciable asset and its related accumulated depreciation.
c. _____ A list of accounts and their balances after all adjustments have been made.
d. _____ Entries made at the end of an accounting period to ensure that the revenue recognition and expense recognition principles are followed.
e. _____ Entries at the end of an accounting period to transfer the balances of temporary accounts to a permanent stockholders' equity account, Retained Earnings.
f. _____ Revenue, expense, and dividend accounts whose balances a company transfers to Retained Earnings at the end of an accounting period.
g. _____ The planned timing of revenues, expenses, gains, and losses to smooth out bumps in net income.
h. _____ An account that is offset against an asset account on the balance sheet.
i. _____ A temporary account used in closing revenue and expense accounts.
j. _____ Balance sheet accounts whose balances are carried forward to the next accounting period.
k. _____ The process of allocating the cost of an asset to expense over its useful life.

E4.20 (LO 4), AP A partial adjusted trial balance for Ramon Company is given in E4.15.

Prepare closing entries.

Instructions

Prepare the closing entries at January 31, 2022.

E4.21 (LO 4), AP Selected year-end account balances from the adjusted trial balance as of December 31, 2022, for Tippy Corporation is provided below.

Prepare closing entries.

	Debit	Credit
Accounts Receivable	$ 72,600	
Dividends	26,300	
Depreciation Expense	13,200	
Equipment	212,800	
Salaries and Wages Expense	91,100	
Accounts Payable		$ 53,000
Accumulated Depreciation—Equipment		114,800
Unearned Rent Revenue		22,900
Service Revenue		183,800
Rent Revenue		6,200
Rent Expense	3,600	
Retained Earnings		61,800
Supplies Expense	1,400	

Instructions

a. Prepare closing entries
b. Determine the post-closing balance in Retained Earnings.

E4.22 (LO 2, 3, 4), AN The following trial balances are before and after adjustment for Ryan Company at the end of its fiscal year.

Prepare adjusting entries from analysis of trial balance.

Ryan Company
Trial Balance
August 31, 2022

	Before Adjustment		After Adjustment	
	Dr.	Cr.	Dr.	Cr.
Cash	$10,900		$10,900	
Accounts Receivable	8,800		9,400	
Supplies	2,500		500	
Prepaid Insurance	4,000		2,500	
Equipment	16,000		16,000	
Accumulated Depreciation—Equipment		$ 3,600		$ 4,800
Accounts Payable		5,800		5,800
Salaries and Wages Payable		0		1,100
Unearned Rent Revenue		1,800		800
Common Stock		10,000		10,000
Retained Earnings		5,500		5,500
Dividends	2,800		2,800	
Service Revenue		34,000		34,600
Rent Revenue		12,100		13,100
Salaries and Wages Expense	17,000		18,100	
Supplies Expense	0		2,000	
Rent Expense	10,800		10,800	
Insurance Expense	0		1,500	
Depreciation Expense	0		1,200	
	$72,800	$72,800	$75,700	$75,700

Instructions

Prepare the adjusting entries that were made.

Prepare financial statements from adjusted trial balance.

E4.23 (LO 4), AP The adjusted trial balance for Ryan Company is given in E4.22.

Instructions

Prepare the income and retained earnings statements for the year and the classified balance sheet at August 31.

Prepare closing entries.

E4.24 (LO 4), AP The adjusted trial balance for Ryan Company is given in E4.22.

Instructions

Prepare the closing entries for the temporary accounts at August 31.

Problems: Set A

Record transactions on accrual basis; convert revenue to cash receipts.

P4.1A (LO 1, 2, 3), AP The following selected data are taken from the comparative financial statements of Yankee Curling Club. The club prepares its financial statements using the accrual basis of accounting.

September 30	2022	2021
Accounts receivable for member dues	$ 15,000	$ 19,000
Unearned sales revenue	20,000	23,000
Service revenue (from member dues)	151,000	135,000

Dues are billed to members based upon their use of the club's facilities. Unearned sales revenues arise from the sale of tickets to events, such as the Skins Game.

Instructions

(*Hint:* You will find it helpful to use T-accounts to analyze the following data. You must analyze these data sequentially, as missing information must first be deduced before moving on. Post your journal entries as you progress, rather than waiting until the end.)

a. Prepare journal entries for each of the following events that took place during 2022.

1. Dues receivable from members from 2021 were all collected during 2022.
2. During 2022, goods were provided for all of the unearned sales revenue at the end of 2021.

3. Additional tickets were sold for $44,000 cash during 2022; a portion of these were used by the purchasers during the year. The entire balance remaining in Unearned Sales Revenue relates to the upcoming Skins Game in 2022.
4. Dues for the 2021–2022 fiscal year were billed to members.
5. Dues receivable for 2022 (i.e., those billed in item 4 above) were partially collected.

b. Determine the amount of cash received by Yankee from the above transactions during the year ended September 30, 2022.

b. Cash received $199,000

P4.2A (LO 2, 3, 4), AP Len Kumar started his own consulting firm, Kumar Consulting, on June 1, 2022. The trial balance at June 30 is as follows.

Prepare adjusting entries, post to ledger accounts, and prepare adjusted trial balance.

Kumar Consulting
Trial Balance
June 30, 2022

	Debit	Credit
Cash	$ 6,850	
Accounts Receivable	7,000	
Supplies	2,000	
Prepaid Insurance	2,880	
Equipment	15,000	
Accounts Payable		$ 4,230
Unearned Service Revenue		5,200
Common Stock		22,000
Service Revenue		8,300
Salaries and Wages Expense	4,000	
Rent Expense	2,000	
	$39,730	$39,730

In addition to those accounts listed on the trial balance, the chart of accounts for Kumar also contains the following accounts: Accumulated Depreciation—Equipment, Salaries and Wages Payable, Depreciation Expense, Insurance Expense, Utilities Expense, and Supplies Expense.

Other data:

1. Supplies on hand at June 30 total $720.
2. A utility bill for $180 has not been recorded and will not be paid until next month.
3. The insurance policy is for a year.
4. Services were performed for $4,100 of unearned service revenue by the end of the month.
5. Salaries of $1,250 are accrued at June 30.
6. The equipment has a 5-year life with no salvage value and is being depreciated at $250 per month for 60 months.
7. Invoices representing $3,900 of services performed by Kumar during the month have not been recorded as of June 30.

Instructions
a. Prepare the adjusting entries for the month of June.
b. Post the adjusting entries to the ledger accounts. Enter the totals from the trial balance as beginning account balances. (Use T-accounts.)
c. Prepare an adjusted trial balance at June 30, 2022.

b. Service rev. $16,300

c. Tot. trial balance $45,310

P4.3A (LO 2, 3, 4), AP The Moto Hotel opened for business on May 1, 2022. Here is its trial balance before adjustment on May 31.

Prepare adjusting entries, adjusted trial balance, and financial statements.

Moto Hotel
Trial Balance
May 31, 2022

	Debit	Credit
Cash	$ 2,500	
Supplies	2,600	
Prepaid Insurance	1,800	
Land	15,000	
Buildings	70,000	
Equipment	16,800	
Accounts Payable		$ 4,700

	Debit	Credit
Unearned Rent Revenue		$ 3,300
Mortgage Payable		36,000
Common Stock		60,000
Rent Revenue		9,000
Salaries and Wages Expense	$ 3,000	
Utilities Expense	800	
Advertising Expense	500	
	$113,000	$113,000

Other data:

1. Insurance expires at the rate of $450 per month.
2. A count of supplies shows $1,050 of unused supplies on May 31.
3. Annual depreciation is $3,600 on the building and $3,000 on equipment.
4. The mortgage interest rate is 6%. (The mortgage was taken out on May 1.)
5. Unearned rent of $2,500 has been earned.
6. Salaries of $900 are accrued and unpaid at May 31.

Instructions

c. Rent revenue $11,500
Tot. adj. trial balance $114,630
d. Net income $3,570

a. Journalize the adjusting entries on May 31.
b. Prepare a ledger using T-accounts. Enter the trial balance amounts and post the adjusting entries.
c. Prepare an adjusted trial balance on May 31.
d. Prepare (1) an income statement and (2) a retained earnings statement for the month of May and (3) a classified balance sheet at May 31.
e. Identify which accounts should be closed on May 31.

Prepare adjusting entries and financial statements; identify accounts to be closed.

P4.4A (LO 2, 3, 4), AP Salt Creek Golf Inc. was organized on July 1, 2022. Quarterly financial statements are prepared. The trial balance and adjusted trial balance on September 30 are shown as follows.

Salt Creek Golf Inc.
Trial Balance
September 30, 2022

	Unadjusted		Adjusted	
	Dr.	Cr.	Dr.	Cr.
Cash	$ 6,700		$ 6,700	
Accounts Receivable	400		1,000	
Supplies	1,200		180	
Prepaid Rent	1,800		900	
Equipment	15,000		15,000	
Accumulated Depreciation—Equipment				$ 350
Notes Payable		$ 5,000		5,000
Accounts Payable		1,070		1,070
Salaries and Wages Payable				600
Interest Payable				50
Unearned Rent Revenue		1,000		800
Common Stock		14,000		14,000
Retained Earnings		0		0
Dividends	600		600	
Service Revenue		14,100		14,700
Rent Revenue		700		900
Salaries and Wages Expense	8,800		9,400	
Rent Expense	900		1,800	
Depreciation Expense			350	
Supplies Expense			1,020	
Utilities Expense	470		470	
Interest Expense			50	
	$35,870	$35,870	$37,470	$37,470

Instructions

a. Journalize the adjusting entries that were made.

b. Net income $2,510
Tot. assets $23,430

b. Prepare an income statement and a retained earnings statement for the 3 months ending September 30 and a classified balance sheet at September 30.

c. Identify which accounts should be closed on September 30.

d. If the note bears interest at 12%, how many months has it been outstanding?

P4.5A (LO 2, 3), AP A review of the ledger of Lewis Company at December 31, 2022, produces these data pertaining to the preparation of annual adjusting entries.

Prepare adjusting entries.

1. Prepaid Insurance $15,200. The company has separate insurance policies on its buildings and its motor vehicles. Policy B4564 on the building was purchased on July 1, 2021, for $9,600. The policy has a term of 3 years. Policy A2958 on the vehicles was purchased on January 1, 2022, for $7,200. This policy has a term of 18 months.

2. Unearned Rent Revenue $429,000. The company began subleasing office space in its new building on November 1. At December 31, the company had the following rental contracts that are paid in full for the entire term of the lease.

2. Rent revenue $84,000

Date	Term (in months)	Monthly Rent	Number of Leases
Nov. 1	9	$5,000	5
Dec. 1	6	$8,500	4

3. Notes Payable $40,000. This balance consists of a note for 6 months at an annual interest rate of 7%, dated October 1.

4. Salaries and Wages Payable $0. There are eight salaried employees. Salaries are paid every Friday for the current week. Five employees receive a salary of $600 each per week, and three employees earn $700 each per week. Assume December 31 is a Wednesday. Employees do not work weekends. All employees worked the last 3 days of December.

Instructions

Prepare the adjusting entries at December 31, 2022.

P4.6A (LO 2, 3), AN **Writing** Roadside Travel Court was organized on July 1, 2021, by Betty Johnson. Betty is a good manager but a poor accountant. From the trial balance prepared by a part-time bookkeeper, Betty prepared the following income statement for her fourth quarter, which ended June 30, 2022.

Prepare adjusting entries and a corrected income statement.

Roadside Travel Court
Income Statement
For the Quarter Ended June 30, 2022

Revenues		
Rent revenue		$212,000
Operating expenses		
Advertising expense	$ 3,800	
Salaries and wages expense	80,500	
Utilities expense	900	
Depreciation expense	2,700	
Maintenance and repairs expense	4,300	
Total operating expenses		92,200
Net income		$119,800

Betty suspected that something was wrong with the statement because net income had never exceeded $30,000 in any one quarter. Knowing that you are an experienced accountant, she asks you to review the income statement and other data.

You first look at the trial balance. In addition to the account balances reported above in the income statement, the trial balance contains the following additional selected balances at June 30, 2022.

Supplies	$ 8,200
Prepaid Insurance	14,400
Notes Payable	14,000

You then make inquiries and discover the following.

1. Roadside rental revenues include advanced rental payments received for summer occupancy, in the amount of $57,000.

2. There were $1,800 of supplies on hand at June 30.

3. Prepaid insurance resulted from the payment of a 1-year policy on April 1, 2022.

4. The mail in July 2022 brought the following bills: advertising for the week of June 24, $110; repairs made June 18, $4,450; and utilities for the month of June, $215.

5. Wage expense is $300 per day. At June 30, 4 days' wages have been incurred but not paid.

6. The note payable is a 6% note dated May 1, 2022, and due on July 31, 2022.

7. Income tax of $13,400 for the quarter is due in July but has not yet been recorded.

b. Net income $33,285

Journalize transactions and follow through accounting cycle to preparation of financial statements.

f. Cash $3,840
Tot. adj. trial
balance $24,680
g. Net income $970

Instructions

a. Prepare any adjusting journal entries required at June 30, 2022.
b. Prepare a correct income statement for the quarter ended June 30, 2022.
c. Explain the generally accepted accounting principles that Betty did not recognize in preparing her income statement and their effect on her results.

P4.7A (LO 2, 3, 4), AP On November 1, 2022, the following were the account balances of Soho Equipment Repair.

	Debit		Credit
Cash	$ 2,790	Accumulated Depreciation—Equipment	$ 500
Accounts Receivable	2,910	Accounts Payable	2,300
Supplies	1,120	Unearned Service Revenue	400
Equipment	10,000	Salaries and Wages Payable	620
		Common Stock	10,000
		Retained Earnings	3,000
	$16,820		$16,820

During November, the following summary transactions were completed.

Nov. 8 Paid $1,220 for salaries due employees, of which $600 is for November and $620 is for October salaries payable.
10 Received $1,800 cash from customers in payment of account.
12 Received $3,700 cash for services performed in November.
15 Purchased store equipment on account $3,600.
17 Purchased supplies on account $1,300.
20 Paid creditors $2,500 of accounts payable due.
22 Paid November rent $480.
25 Paid salaries $1,000.
27 Performed services on account worth $900 and billed customers.
29 Received $750 from customers for services to be performed in the future.

Adjustment data:

1. Supplies on hand are valued at $1,100.
2. Accrued salaries payable are $480.
3. Depreciation for the month is $250.
4. Services were performed to satisfy $500 of unearned service revenue.

Instructions

a. Enter the November 1 balances in the ledger accounts. (Use T-accounts.)
b. Journalize the November transactions.
c. Post to the ledger accounts. Use Service Revenue, Depreciation Expense, Supplies Expense, Salaries and Wages Expense, and Rent Expense.
d. Prepare a trial balance at November 30.
e. Journalize and post adjusting entries.
f. Prepare an adjusted trial balance.
g. Prepare an income statement and a retained earnings statement for November and a classified balance sheet at November 30.

Continuing Case

© leungchopan/ Shutterstock

Cookie Creations

(*Note:* This is a continuation of the Cookie Creations case from Chapters 1 through 3.)

CC4 It is the end of November and Natalie has been in touch with her grandmother. Her grandmother asked Natalie how well things went in her first month of business. Natalie, too, would like to know if her business has been profitable or not during November. Natalie realizes that in order to determine Cookie Creations' income, she must first make adjustments.

Go to WileyPLUS for complete case details and instructions.

Comprehensive Accounting Cycle Review

ACR4.1 (LO 2, 3, 4), AP Mike Greenberg opened Kleene Window Washing Inc. on July 1, 2022. During July, the following transactions were completed.

Complete all steps in accounting cycle.

July	1	Issued 12,000 shares of common stock for $12,000 cash.
	1	Purchased used truck for $8,000, paying $2,000 cash and the balance on account.
	3	Purchased cleaning supplies for $900 on account.
	5	Paid $1,800 cash on a 1-year insurance policy effective July 1.
	12	Billed customers $3,700 for cleaning services performed.
	18	Paid $1,000 cash on amount owed on truck and $500 on amount owed on cleaning supplies.
	20	Paid $2,000 cash for employee salaries.
	21	Collected $1,600 cash from customers billed on July 12.
	25	Billed customers $2,500 for cleaning services performed.
	31	Paid $290 for maintenance of the truck during month.
	31	Declared and paid $600 cash dividend.

The chart of accounts for Kleene Window Washing contains the following accounts: Cash, Accounts Receivable, Supplies, Prepaid Insurance, Equipment, Accumulated Depreciation—Equipment, Accounts Payable, Salaries and Wages Payable, Common Stock, Retained Earnings, Dividends, Income Summary, Service Revenue, Maintenance and Repairs Expense, Supplies Expense, Depreciation Expense, Insurance Expense, and Salaries and Wages Expense.

Instructions

a. Journalize the July transactions.

b. Post to the ledger accounts. (Use T-accounts.)

c. Prepare a trial balance at July 31.

d. Journalize the following adjustments.

   1. Services performed but unbilled and uncollected at July 31 were $1,700.
   2. Depreciation on equipment for the month was $180.
   3. One-twelfth of the insurance expired.
   4. A count shows $320 of cleaning supplies on hand at July 31.
   5. Accrued but unpaid employee salaries were $400.

e. Post adjusting entries to the T-accounts.

f. Prepare an adjusted trial balance.

g. Prepare the income statement and a retained earnings statement for July and a classified balance sheet at July 31.

h. Journalize and post closing entries and complete the closing process.

i. Prepare a post-closing trial balance at July 31.

f. Cash $5,410
g. Tot. assets $21,500

ACR4.2 (LO 2, 3, 4), AP Lars Linken opened Lars Cleaners on March 1, 2022. During March, the following transactions were completed.

Complete all steps in accounting cycle.

Mar.	1	Issued 10,000 shares of common stock for $15,000 cash.
	1	Borrowed $6,000 cash by signing a 6-month, 6%, $6,000 note payable. Interest will be paid the first day of each subsequent month.
	1	Purchased used truck for $8,000 cash.
	2	Paid $1,500 cash to cover rent from March 1 through May 31.
	3	Paid $2,400 cash on a 6-month insurance policy effective March 1.
	6	Purchased cleaning supplies for $2,000 on account.
	14	Billed customers $3,700 for cleaning services performed.
	18	Paid $500 on amount owed on cleaning supplies.
	20	Paid $1,750 cash for employee salaries.
	21	Collected $1,600 cash from customers billed on March 14.
	28	Billed customers $4,200 for cleaning services performed.
	31	Paid $350 for gas and oil used in truck during month (use Maintenance and Repairs Expense).
	31	Declared and paid a $900 cash dividend.

The chart of accounts for Lars Cleaners contains the following accounts: Cash, Accounts Receivable, Supplies, Prepaid Insurance, Prepaid Rent, Equipment, Accumulated Depreciation—Equipment, Accounts Payable, Salaries and Wages Payable, Notes Payable, Interest Payable, Common Stock, Retained

Earnings, Dividends, Income Summary, Service Revenue, Maintenance and Repairs Expense, Supplies Expense, Depreciation Expense, Insurance Expense, Salaries and Wages Expense, Rent Expense, and Interest Expense.

Instructions

a. Journalize the March transactions.
b. Post to the ledger accounts. (Use T-accounts.)
c. Prepare a trial balance at March 31.
d. Journalize the following adjustments.
   1. Services performed but unbilled and uncollected at March 31 was $200.
   2. Depreciation on equipment for the month was $250.
   3. One-sixth of the insurance expired.
   4. An inventory count shows $280 of cleaning supplies on hand at March 31.
   5. Accrued but unpaid employee salaries were $1,080.
   6. One month of the prepaid rent has expired.
   7. One month of interest expense related to the note payable has accrued and will be paid April 1. (*Hint:* Use the formula from Illustration 4.19 to compute interest.)
e. Post adjusting entries to the T-accounts.

f. Tot. adj. trial balance $31,960

f. Prepare an adjusted trial balance.

g. Tot. assets $24,730

g. Prepare the income statement and a retained earnings statement for March and a classified balance sheet at March 31.

h. Journalize and post closing entries and complete the closing process.
i. Prepare a post-closing trial balance at March 31.

Journalize transactions and follow through accounting cycle to preparation of financial statements.

ACR4.3 (LO 2, 3, 4), AP On August 1, 2022, the following were the account balances of B&B Repair Services.

	Debit		Credit
Cash	$ 6,040	Accumulated Depreciation—Equipment	$ 600
Accounts Receivable	2,910	Accounts Payable	2,300
Notes Receivable	4,000	Unearned Service Revenue	1,260
Supplies	1,030	Salaries and Wages Payable	1,420
Equipment	10,000	Common Stock	12,000
		Retained Earnings	6,400
	$23,980		$23,980

During August, the following summary transactions were completed.

Aug. 1 Paid $400 cash for advertising in local newspapers. Advertising flyers will be included with newspapers delivered during August and September.
3 Paid August rent $380.
5 Received $1,200 cash from customers in payment of account.
10 Paid $3,120 for salaries due employees, of which $1,700 is for August and $1,420 is for July salaries payable.
12 Received $2,800 cash for services performed in August.
15 Purchased store equipment on account $2,000.
20 Paid creditors $2,000 of accounts payable due.
22 Purchased supplies on account $800.
25 Paid $2,900 cash for employees' salaries.
27 Billed customers $3,760 for services performed.
29 Received $780 from customers for services to be performed in the future.

Adjustment data:

1. A count shows supplies on hand of $960.
2. Accrued but unpaid employees' salaries are $1,540.
3. Depreciation on equipment for the month is $320.
4. Services were performed to satisfy $800 of unearned service revenue.
5. One month's worth of advertising services has been received.
6. One month of interest revenue related to the $4,000 note receivable has accrued. The 4-month note has a 6% annual interest rate. (*Hint:* Use the formula from Illustration 4.19 to compute interest.)

Instructions

a. Enter the August 1 balances in the ledger accounts. (Use T-accounts.)
b. Journalize the August transactions.
c. Post to the ledger accounts. B&B's chart of accounts includes Prepaid Advertising, Interest Receivable, Service Revenue, Interest Revenue, Advertising Expense, Depreciation Expense, Supplies Expense, Salaries and Wages Expense, and Rent Expense.
d. Prepare a trial balance at August 31.
e. Journalize and post adjusting entries.
f. Prepare an adjusted trial balance.
g. Prepare an income statement and a retained earnings statement for August and a classified balance sheet at August 31.
h. Journalize and post closing entries and complete the closing process.
i. Prepare a post-closing trial balance at August 31.

f. Cash $2,020
Tot. Adj. trial balance $32,580
g. Net loss $530

ACR4.4 (LO 2, 3, 4), AP At June 30, 2022, the end of its most recent fiscal year, Green River Computer Consultants' post-closing trial balance was as follows:

Record and post transaction, adjusting, and closing journal entries; prepare adjusted trial balance and financial statements.

	Debit	Credit
Cash	$5,230	
Accounts receivable	1,200	
Supplies	690	
Accounts payable		$ 400
Unearned service revenue		1,120
Common stock		3,600
Retained earnings		2,000
	$7,120	$7,120

The company underwent a major expansion in July. New staff was hired and more financing was obtained. Green River conducted the following transactions during July 2022, and adjusts its accounts monthly.

July 1 Purchased equipment, paying $4,000 cash and signing a 2-year note payable for $20,000. The equipment has a 4-year useful life. The note has a 6% interest rate which is payable on the first day of each following month.
2 Issued 20,000 shares of common stock for $50,000 cash.
3 Paid $3,600 cash for a 12-month insurance policy effective July 1.
3 Paid the first 2 (July and August 2022) months' rent for an annual lease of office space for $4,000 per month.
6 Paid $3,800 for supplies.
9 Visited client offices and agreed on the terms of a consulting project. Green River will bill the client, Connor Productions, on the 20th of each month for services performed.
10 Collected $1,200 cash on account from Milani Brothers. This client was billed in June when Green River performed the service.
13 Performed services for Fitzgerald Enterprises. This client paid $1,120 in advance last month. All services relating to this payment are now completed.
14 Paid $400 cash for a utility bill. This related to June utilities that were accrued at the end of June.
16 Met with a new client, Thunder Bay Technologies. Received $12,000 cash in advance for future services to be performed.
18 Paid semi-monthly salaries for $11,000.
20 Performed services worth $28,000 on account and billed customers.
20 Received a bill for $2,200 for advertising services received during July. The amount is not due until August 15.
23 Performed the first phase of the project for Thunder Bay Technologies. Recognized $10,000 of revenue from the cash advance received July 16.
27 Received $15,000 cash from customers billed on July 20.

Adjustment data:

1. Adjustment of prepaid insurance.
2. Adjustment of prepaid rent.
3. Supplies used, $1,250.
4. Equipment depreciation, $500 per month.
5. Accrual of interest on note payable. (*Hint:* Use the formula from Illustration 4.19 to compute interest.)

6. Salaries for the second half of July, $11,000, to be paid on August 1.
7. Estimated utilities expense for July, $800 (invoice will be received in August).
8. Income tax for July, $1,200, will be paid in August.

The chart of accounts for Green River Computer Consultants contains the following accounts: Cash, Accounts Receivable, Supplies, Prepaid Insurance. Prepaid Rent, Equipment, Accumulated Depreciation—Equipment, Accounts Payable, Notes Payable, Interest Payable, Income Taxes Payable, Salaries and Wages Payable, Unearned Service Revenue, Common Stock, Retained Earnings, Dividends, Income Summary, Service Revenue, Supplies Expense, Depreciation Expense, Insurance Expense, Salaries and Wages Expense, Advertising Expense, Income Tax Expense, Interest Expense, Rent Expense, and Utilities Expense.

Instructions

a. Enter the July 1 balances in the ledger accounts. (Use T-accounts.)
b. Journalize the July transactions.
c. Post to the ledger accounts.
d. Prepare a trial balance at July 31.
e. Journalize and post adjusting entries for the month ending July 31.
f. Prepare an adjusted trial balance.
g. Prepare an income statement and a retained earning statement for July and a classified balance sheet at July 31.
h. Journalize and post closing entries and complete the closing process.
i. Prepare a post-closing trial balance at July 31.

g. Net income $6,770
Tot. assets $99,670

Expand Your Critical Thinking

Financial Reporting Problem: Apple Inc.

CT4.1 The financial statements of **Apple Inc.** are presented in Appendix A.

Instructions

a. Using the consolidated income statement and balance sheet, identify items that may result in adjusting entries for deferrals.
b. Using the consolidated income statement, identify two items that may result in adjusting entries for accruals.
c. What was the amount of depreciation and amortization expense for 2017 and 2016? (You will need to examine the notes to the financial statements or the statement of cash flows.) Where was accumulated depreciation and amortization reported?
d. What was the cash paid for income taxes during 2017, reported at the bottom of the consolidated statement of cash flows? What was income tax expense (provision for income taxes) for 2017?

Comparative Analysis Problem: Columbia Sportswear Company vs. VF Corporation

CT4.2 The financial statements of **Columbia Sportswear Company** are presented in Appendix B. Financial statements of **VF Corporation** are presented in Appendix C.

Instructions

a. Identify two accounts on Columbia's balance sheet that provide evidence that Columbia uses accrual accounting. In each case, what income statement account would normally be affected by the adjustment process?
b. Identify two accounts on VF's balance sheet that provide evidence that VF uses accrual accounting (different from the two you listed for Columbia). In each case, what income statement account would normally be affected by the adjustment process?

Comparative Analysis Problem: Amazon.com, Inc. vs. Wal-Mart Stores, Inc.

CT4.3 The financial statements of **Amazon.com, Inc.** are presented in Appendix D. Financial statements of **Wal-Mart Stores, Inc.** are presented in Appendix E.

Instructions

a. Identify two accounts on Amazon's balance sheet that provide evidence that Amazon uses accrual accounting. In each case, what income statement account would normally be affected by the adjustment process?

b. Identify two accounts on Wal-Mart's balance sheet that provide evidence that Wal-Mart uses accrual accounting (different from the two you listed for Amazon). In each case, what income statement account would normally be affected by the adjustment process?

Interpreting Financial Statements

CT4.4 **Laser Recording Systems**, founded in 1981, produces disks for use in the home market. The following is an excerpt from Laser Recording Systems' financial statements (all dollars in thousands).

Laser Recording Systems
Management Discussion

Accrued liabilities increased to $1,642 at January 31, from $138 at the end of the previous fiscal year. Compensation and related accruals increased $195 due primarily to increases in accruals for severance, vacation, commissions, and relocation expenses. Accrued professional services increased by $137 primarily as a result of legal expenses related to several outstanding contractual disputes. Other expenses increased $35, of which $18 was for interest payable.

Instructions

a. Can you tell from the discussion whether Laser Recording Systems has prepaid its legal expenses and is now making an adjustment to the asset account Prepaid Legal Expenses, or whether the company is handling the legal expense via an accrued expense adjustment?

b. Identify each of the adjustments Laser Recording Systems is discussing as one of the four types of possible adjustments discussed in the chapter. How is net income ultimately affected by each of the adjustments?

c. What journal entry did Laser Recording make to record the accrued interest?

Real-World Focus

CT4.5 You can use the Internet to learn about the functions of the **Securities and Exchange Commission (SEC)**.

Instructions

Use the information at the SEC's website to answer the following questions.

a. What event spurred the creation of the SEC? Why was the SEC created?

b. What are the five divisions of the SEC? Briefly describe the purpose of each.

c. What are the responsibilities of the chief accountant?

Decision-Making Across the Organization

CT4.6 Abbey Park was organized on April 1, 2021, by Trudy Crawford. Trudy is a good manager but a poor accountant. From the trial balance prepared by a part-time bookkeeper, Trudy prepared the following income statement for the quarter that ended March 31, 2022.

Abbey Park
Income Statement
For the Quarter Ended March 31, 2022

Revenues		
Rent revenue		$83,000
Operating expenses		
Advertising expense	$ 4,200	
Salaries and wages expense	27,600	
Utilities expense	1,500	
Depreciation expense	800	
Maintenance and repairs expense	2,800	
Total operating expenses		36,900
Net income		$46,100

Trudy knew that something was wrong with the statement because net income had never exceeded $20,000 in any one quarter. Knowing that you are an experienced accountant, she asks you to review the income statement and other data.

You first look at the trial balance. In addition to the account balances reported in the income statement, the ledger contains these selected balances at March 31, 2022.

Supplies	$ 4,500
Prepaid Insurance	7,200
Notes Payable	20,000

You then make inquiries and discover the following.

1. Rent revenue includes advanced rentals for summer-month occupancy, $21,000.
2. There were $600 of supplies on hand at March 31.
3. Prepaid insurance resulted from the payment of a 1-year policy on January 1, 2022.
4. The mail on April 1, 2022, brought the following bills: advertising for week of March 24, $110; repairs made March 10, $1,040; and utilities $240.
5. Wage expense totals $290 per day. At March 31, 3 days' wages have been incurred but not paid.
6. The note payable is a 3-month, 7% note dated January 1, 2022.

Instructions

With the class divided into groups, answer the following.

a. Prepare a correct income statement for the quarter ended March 31, 2022.
b. Explain to Trudy the generally accepted accounting principles that she did not follow in preparing her income statement and their effect on her results.

Communication Activity

CT4.7 On numerous occasions, proposals have surfaced to put the federal government on the accrual basis of accounting. This is no small issue because if this basis were used, it would mean that billions in unrecorded liabilities would have to be booked and the federal deficit would increase substantially.

Instructions

a. What is the difference between accrual-basis accounting and cash-basis accounting?
b. Comment on why politicians prefer a cash-basis accounting system over an accrual-basis system.
c. Write a letter to your senators explaining why you think the federal government should adopt the accrual basis of accounting.

Ethics Case

CT4.8 Wells Company is a pesticide manufacturer. Its sales declined greatly this year due to the passage of legislation outlawing the sale of several of Wells's chemical pesticides. During the coming year, Wells will have environmentally safe and competitive replacement chemicals to replace these discontinued products. Sales in the next year are expected to greatly exceed those of any prior year. Therefore, the decline in this year's sales and profits appears to be a one-year aberration.

Even so, the company president believes that a large dip in the current year's profits could cause a significant drop in the market price of Wells's stock and make it a takeover target. To avoid this possibility, he urges Tim Allen, controller, to accrue every possible revenue and to defer as many expenses as possible in making this period's year-end adjusting entries. The president says to Tim, "We need the revenues this year, and next year we can easily absorb expenses deferred from this year. We can't let our stock price be hammered down!" Tim didn't get around to recording the adjusting entries until January 17, but he dated the entries December 31 as if they were recorded then. Tim also made every effort to comply with the president's request.

Instructions

a. Who are the stakeholders in this situation?
b. What are the ethical considerations of the president's request and Tim's dating the adjusting entries December 31?
c. Can Tim accrue revenues and defer expenses and still be ethical?

All About You

CT4.9 Companies prepare balance sheets in order to know their financial position at a specific point in time. This enables them to make a comparison to their position at previous points in time and gives them a basis for planning for the future. In order to evaluate *your* financial position, you can prepare a personal balance sheet. Assume that you have compiled the following information regarding your finances. (*Hint:* Some of the items might not be used in your personal balance sheet.)

Amount owed on student loan balance (long-term)	$ 5,000
Balance in checking account	1,200
Certificate of deposit (6-month)	3,000
Annual earnings from part-time job	11,300
Automobile	7,000
Balance on automobile loan (current portion)	1,500
Balance on automobile loan (long-term portion)	4,000
Home computer	800
Amount owed to you by younger brother	300
Balance in money market account	1,800
Annual tuition	6,400
Video and stereo equipment	1,250
Balance owed on credit card (current portion)	150
Balance owed on credit card (long-term portion)	1,650

Instructions

Prepare a personal balance sheet using the format you have learned for a classified balance sheet for a company. For the equity account, use M. Y. Own, Capital.

FASB Codification Activity

CT4.10 If your school has a subscription to the FASB Codification, log in and prepare responses to the following.

Instructions

Access the glossary ("Master Glossary") to answer the following.

a. What is the definition of revenue?
b. What is the definition of compensation?

A Look at IFRS

LEARNING OBJECTIVE 6
Compare the procedures for adjusting entries under GAAP and IFRS.

It is often difficult for companies to determine in what time period they should report particular revenues and expenses. Both the IASB and FASB are working on projects to develop conceptual frameworks that will enable companies to better use the same principles to record transactions consistently over time.

Key Points

Following are the key similarities and differences between GAAP and IFRS as related to accrual accounting.

Similarities

- In this chapter, you learned accrual-basis accounting applied under GAAP. Companies applying IFRS also use accrual-basis accounting to ensure that they record transactions that change a company's financial statements in the period in which events occur.
- Similar to GAAP, cash-basis accounting is not in accordance with IFRS.
- IFRS also divides the economic life of companies into artificial time periods. Under both GAAP and IFRS, this is referred to as the **periodicity assumption**.

- The **general** revenue recognition principle required by GAAP that is used in this text is the same as that used under IFRS.
- Revenue recognition fraud is a major issue in U.S. financial reporting. The same situation occurs in other countries, as evidenced by revenue recognition breakdowns at Dutch software company **Baan NV**, Japanese electronics giant **NEC**, and Dutch grocer **Ahold NV**.

Differences

- Under IFRS, revaluation (using fair value) of items such as land and buildings is permitted. IFRS allows depreciation based on revaluation of assets, which is not permitted under GAAP.
- The terminology used for revenues and gains, and expenses and losses, differs somewhat between IFRS and GAAP. For example, income under IFRS includes both revenues, which arise during the normal course of operating activities, and gains, which arise from activities outside of the normal sales of goods and services. The term income is not used this way under GAAP. Instead, under GAAP income refers to the net difference between revenues and expenses.
- Under IFRS, expenses include both those costs incurred in the normal course of operations as well as losses that are not part of normal operations. This is in contrast to GAAP, which defines each separately.

IFRS Practice

IFRS Self-Test Questions

1. IFRS:
   a. uses accrual accounting.
   b. uses cash-basis accounting.
   c. allows revenue to be recognized when a customer makes an order.
   d. requires that revenue not be recognized until cash is received.

2. Which of the following statements is **false**?
   a. IFRS employs the periodicity assumption.
   b. IFRS employs accrual accounting.
   c. IFRS requires that revenues and costs must be capable of being measured reliably.
   d. IFRS uses the cash basis of accounting.

3. As a result of the revenue recognition project by the FASB and IASB:
   a. revenue recognition places more emphasis on when the performance obligation is satisfied.
   b. revenue recognition places more emphasis on when revenue is realized.
   c. revenue recognition places more emphasis on when expenses are incurred.
   d. revenue is no longer recorded unless cash has been received.

4. Which of the following is **false**?
   a. Under IFRS, the term income describes both revenues and gains.
   b. Under IFRS, the term expenses includes losses.
   c. Under IFRS, companies do not engage in the adjusting process.
   d. Under IFRS, revenue recognition fraud is a major issue.

5. Accrual-basis accounting:
   a. is optional under IFRS.
   b. results in companies recording transactions that change a company's financial statements in the period in which events occur.
   c. has been eliminated as a result of the IASB/FASB joint project on revenue recognition.
   d. is not consistent with the IASB conceptual framework.

International Financial Reporting Problem: Louis Vuitton

IFRS4.1 The financial statements of **Louis Vuitton** are presented in Appendix F. The complete annual report, including the notes to its financial statements, is available at the company's website.

Instructions

Visit Louis Vuitton's website and answer the following questions from Louis Vuitton's 2016 annual report.

a. From the notes to the financial statements, how does the company determine the amount of revenue to record at the time of a sale?

b. From the notes to the financial statements, how does the company determine the provision for product returns?

c. Using the consolidated income statement and consolidated statement of financial position, identify items that may result in adjusting entries for deferrals.

d. Using the consolidated income statement, identify two items that may result in adjusting entries for accruals.

Answers to IFRS Self-Test Questions

1. a   2. d   3. a   4. c   5. b

CHAPTER 5

Merchandising Operations and the Multiple-Step Income Statement

Chapter Preview

Merchandising is one of the largest and most influential industries in the United States. It is likely that a number of you will work for a merchandiser. Therefore, understanding the financial statements of merchandising companies is important. In this chapter, you will learn the basics about reporting merchandising transactions. In addition, you will learn how to prepare and analyze a commonly used form of the income statement—the multiple-step income statement.

Feature Story

Buy Now, Vote Later

Have you ever shopped for outdoor gear at an **REI (Recreational Equipment Incorporated)** store? If so, you might have been surprised if a salesclerk asked if you were a member. A member? What do you mean a member? REI is a consumer cooperative, or "co-op" for short. To figure out what that means, consider this quote from the company's annual report:

> As a cooperative, the Company is owned by its members. Each member is entitled to one vote in the election of the Company's

Board of Directors. Since January 1, 2008, the nonrefundable, nontransferable, one-time membership fee has been $20. As of December 31, 2010, there were approximately 10.8 million members.

Voting rights? Now that's something you don't get from shopping at **Wal-Mart**. REI members get other benefits as well, including sharing in the company's profits through a dividend at the end of the year. The more you spend, the bigger your dividend.

Since REI is a co-op, you might wonder whether management's incentives might be a little different. Management is still concerned about making a profit, as it ensures the long-term viability of the company. REI's members also want the company to be run efficiently, so that prices remain low. In order for its members to evaluate just how well management is doing, REI publishes an audited annual report, just like publicly traded companies do.

How well is this business model working for REI? Well, it has consistently been rated as one of the best places to work in the United States by *Fortune* magazine. Also, REI had sustainable business practices long before social responsibility became popular at other companies. The CEO's Stewardship Report states "we reduced the absolute amount of energy we use despite opening four new stores and growing our business; we grew the amount of FSC-certified paper we use to 58.4 percent of our total paper footprint—including our cash register receipt paper; we facilitated 2.2 million volunteer hours and we provided $3.7 million to more than 330 conservation and recreation nonprofits."

So, while REI, like other retailers, closely monitors its financial results, it also strives to succeed in other areas. And, with over 10 million votes at stake, REI's management knows that it has to deliver.

Chapter Outline

LEARNING OBJECTIVES

LO 1 Describe merchandising operations and inventory systems.	• Operating cycles • Flow of costs	**DO IT! 1** Merchandising Operations and Inventory Systems
LO 2 Record purchases under a perpetual inventory system.	• Freight costs • Purchase returns and allowances • Purchase discounts	**DO IT! 2** Purchase Transactions
LO 3 Record sales under a perpetual inventory system.	• Sales returns and allowances • Sales discounts • Data analytics and credit sales	**DO IT! 3** Sales Transactions
LO 4 Prepare a multiple-step income statement and a comprehensive income statement.	• Single-step income statement • Multiple-step income statement • Comprehensive income statement	**DO IT! 4** Multiple-Step Income Statement
LO 5 Determine cost of goods sold under a periodic inventory system.	• Cost of goods purchased • Cost of goods sold	**DO IT! 5** Cost of Goods Sold—Periodic System
LO 6 Compute and analyze gross profit rate and profit margin.	• Gross profit rate • Profit margin	**DO IT! 6** Gross Profit Rate and Profit Margin

Go to the Review and Practice section at the end of the chapter for a targeted summary and practice applications with solutions.
Visit WileyPLUS for additional tutorials and practice opportunities.

Merchandising Operations and Inventory Systems

LEARNING OBJECTIVE 1
Describe merchandising operations and inventory systems.

REI, **Wal-Mart Stores, Inc.**, and **Amazon.com** are called merchandising companies because they buy and sell merchandise rather than perform services as their primary source of revenue. Merchandising companies that purchase and sell directly to consumers are called **retailers**. Merchandising companies that sell to retailers are known as **wholesalers**. For example, retailer **Walgreens** might buy goods from wholesaler **McKesson**. Retailer **Office Depot** might buy office supplies from wholesaler **United Stationers**. The primary source of revenue for merchandising companies is the sale of merchandise, often referred to simply as **sales revenue** or **sales**. A merchandising company has two categories of expenses: cost of goods sold and operating expenses.

Cost of goods sold is the total cost of merchandise sold during the period. This expense is directly related to the revenue recognized from the sale of goods. **Illustration 5.1** shows the income measurement process for a merchandising company. The items in the two blue boxes are unique to a merchandising company; they are not used by a service company.

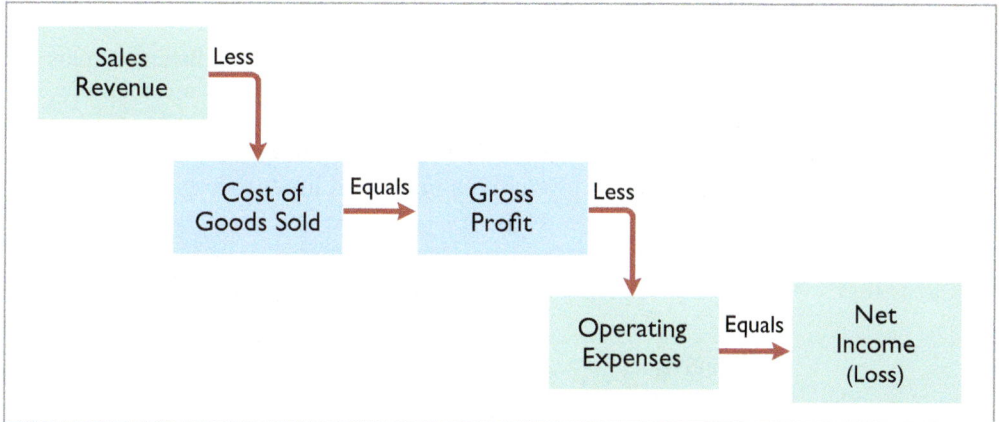

ILLUSTRATION 5.1

Income measurement process for a merchandising company

Operating Cycles

The operating cycle of a merchandising company ordinarily is longer than that of a service company. The purchase of merchandise inventory and its eventual sale lengthen the cycle. **Illustration 5.2** shows the operating cycle of a service company.

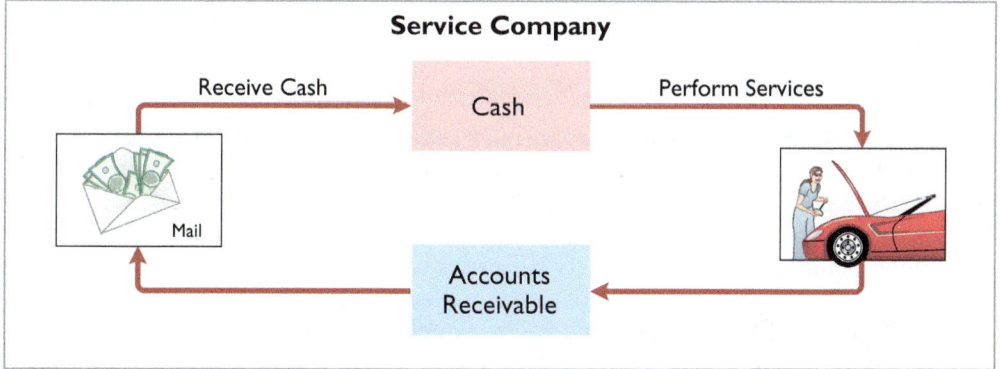

ILLUSTRATION 5.2

Operating cycles for a service company

Illustration 5.3 shows the operating cycle of a merchandising company.

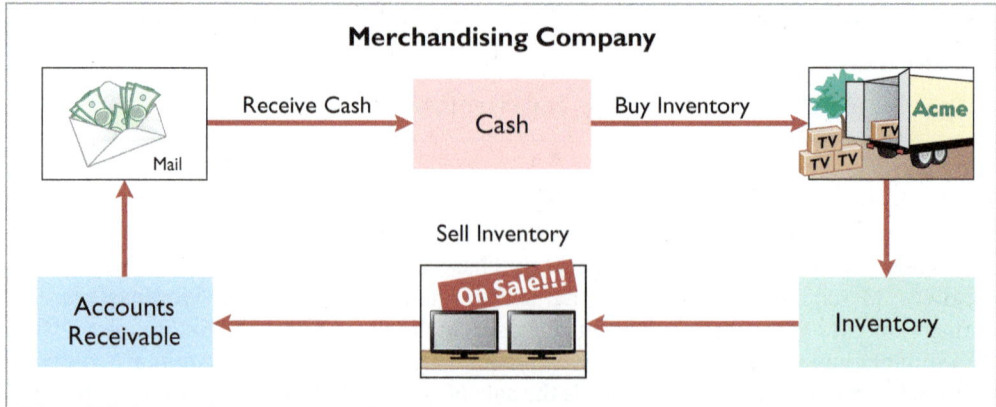

ILLUSTRATION 5.3
Operating cycles for a merchandising company

Note that the added asset account for a merchandising company is the Inventory account. Companies report inventory as a current asset on the balance sheet.

Flow of Costs

The flow of costs for a merchandising company is as follows. Beginning inventory plus the cost of goods purchased is the cost of goods available for sale. As goods are sold, they are assigned to cost of goods sold. Those goods that are not sold by the end of the accounting period represent ending inventory. Illustration 5.4 describes these relationships. Companies use one of two systems to account for inventory: a **perpetual inventory system** or a **periodic inventory system**.

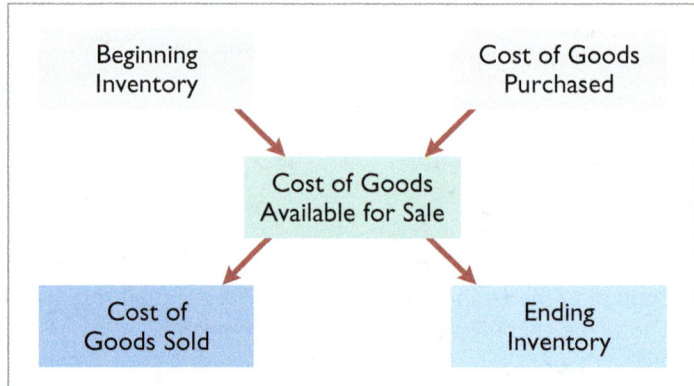

ILLUSTRATION 5.4
Flow of costs

Perpetual System

HELPFUL HINT

Even under perpetual inventory systems, companies take a physical inventory count. This is done as a control procedure to verify inventory levels, in order to detect theft or "shrinkage."

In a **perpetual inventory system**, companies keep detailed records of the cost of each inventory purchase and sale (see **Helpful Hint**). These records continuously—perpetually— show the inventory that should be on hand for every item. For example, a **Ford** dealership has separate inventory records for each automobile, truck, and van on its lot and showroom floor. Similarly, a **Kroger** grocery store uses bar codes and optical scanners to keep a daily running record of every box of cereal and every jar of jelly that it buys and sells. Under a perpetual inventory system, a company determines the cost of goods sold **each time a sale occurs**.

Periodic System

In a **periodic inventory system**, companies do not keep detailed inventory records of the goods on hand throughout the period. Instead, they determine the cost of goods sold **only at the end of the accounting period**—that is, periodically. At that point, the company takes a physical inventory count to determine the cost of goods on hand.

To determine the cost of goods sold under a periodic inventory system, the following steps are necessary:

1. Determine the cost of goods on hand at the beginning of the accounting period.
2. Add to it the cost of goods purchased.
3. Subtract the cost of goods on hand as determined by the physical inventory count at the end of the accounting period.

Illustration 5.5 graphically compares the sequence of activities and the timing of the cost of goods sold computation under the two inventory systems.

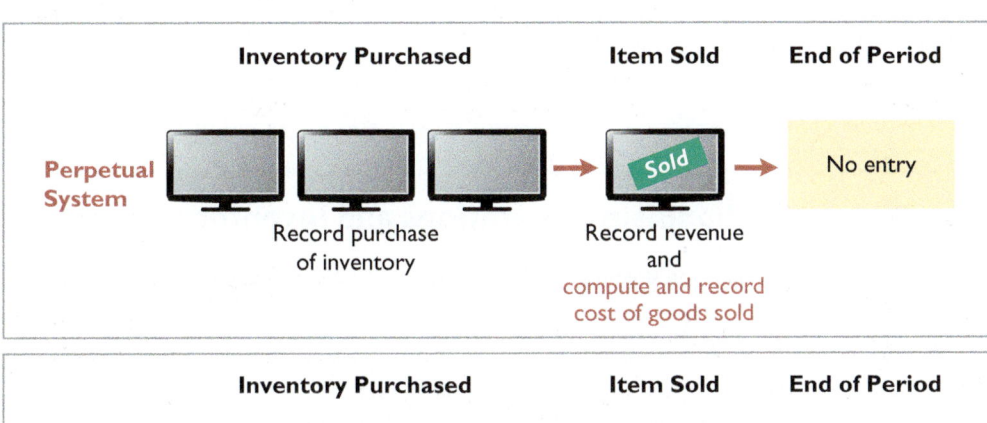
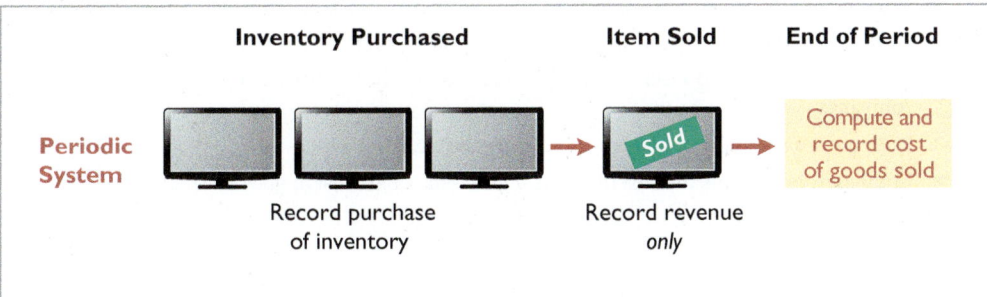

ILLUSTRATION 5.5
Comparing perpetual and periodic inventory systems

Advantages of the Perpetual System

Companies that sell merchandise with high unit values, such as automobiles, furniture, and major home appliances, have traditionally used perpetual systems. The growing use of computers and electronic scanners has enabled many more companies to install perpetual inventory systems. The perpetual inventory system is so named because the accounting records continuously—perpetually—show the quantity and cost of the inventory that should be on hand at any time.

A perpetual inventory system provides better control over inventories than a periodic system. Since the inventory records show the quantities that should be on hand, the company can count the goods at any time to see whether the amount of goods actually on hand agrees with the inventory records. If shortages are uncovered, the company can investigate immediately. Although a perpetual inventory system requires both additional clerical work and expense to maintain the subsidiary records, a computerized system can minimize this cost. Much of **Amazon.com**'s success is attributed to its sophisticated inventory system.

Some businesses find it either unnecessary or uneconomical to invest in a sophisticated, computerized perpetual inventory system such as Amazon's. Many small merchandising businesses now use basic accounting software, which provides some of the essential benefits of a perpetual inventory system. Also, managers of some small businesses still find that they can control their merchandise and manage day-to-day operations using a periodic inventory system.

Because of the widespread use of the perpetual inventory system, we illustrate it in this chapter. We discuss and illustrate the periodic system in Appendix 5A.

Investor Insight   Morrow Snowboards, Inc.

Improving Stock Appeal

© Ben Blankenburg/ iStockphoto

Investors are often eager to invest in a company that has a hot new product. However, when snowboard-maker **Morrow Snowboards, Inc.** issued shares of stock to the public for the first time, some investors expressed reluctance to invest in Morrow because of a number of accounting control problems. To reduce investor concerns, Morrow implemented a perpetual inventory system to improve its control over inventory. In addition, the company stated that it would perform a physical inventory count every quarter until it felt that its perpetual inventory system was reliable.

If a perpetual system keeps track of inventory on a daily basis, why do companies ever need to do a physical count? (Go to WileyPLUS for this answer and additional questions.)

ACTION PLAN
- Review merchandising concepts.
- Understand the flow of costs in a merchandising company.

DO IT! 1 | Merchandising Operations and Inventory Systems

Indicate whether the following statements are true or false. If false, indicate how to correct the statement.

1. The primary source of revenue for a merchandising company results from performing services for customers.
2. The operating cycle of a service company is usually shorter than that of a merchandising company.
3. Sales revenue less cost of goods sold equals gross profit.
4. Ending inventory plus the cost of goods purchased equals cost of goods available for sale.

Solution

1. False. The primary source of revenue for a service company results from performing services for customers. **2.** True. **3.** True. **4.** False. Beginning inventory plus the cost of goods purchased equals cost of goods available for sale.

Related exercise material: **BE5.1, BE5.2, DO IT! 5.1, and E5.1.**

Recording Purchases Under a Perpetual System

LEARNING OBJECTIVE 2
Record purchases under a perpetual inventory system.

Companies purchase inventory using cash or credit (on account). They normally record purchases when they receive the goods from the seller. Every purchase should be supported by business documents that provide written evidence of the transaction. Each cash purchase should be supported by a canceled check or a cash register receipt indicating the items purchased and amounts paid. Companies record cash purchases by an increase in Inventory and a decrease in Cash.

A **purchase invoice** should support each credit purchase. This invoice indicates the total purchase price and other relevant information. However, the purchaser does not prepare a separate purchase invoice. Instead, the purchaser uses as a purchase invoice a copy of the sales invoice sent by the seller. In **Illustration 5.6**, for example, Sauk Stereo (the buyer) uses as a purchase invoice the sales invoice prepared by PW Audio Supply, Inc. (the seller).

ILLUSTRATION 5.6

Sales invoice used as purchase invoice by Sauk Stereo

INVOICE NO. 731

PW AUDIO SUPPLY, INC.
27 CIRCLE DRIVE
HARDING, MICHIGAN 48281

SOLD TO
Firm Name: Sauk Stereo
Attention of: James Hoover, Purchasing Agent
Address: 125 Main Street
City: Chelsea   State: Illinois   Zip: 60915

Date 5/4/22 | Salesperson Malone | Terms 2/10, n/30 | FOB Shipping Point

Catalog No.	Description	Quantity	Price	Amount
X572Y9820	Printed Circuit Board-prototype	1	2,300	$2,300
A2547Z45	Production Model Circuits	5	300	1,500

IMPORTANT: ALL RETURNS MUST BE MADE WITHIN 10 DAYS

TOTAL $3,800

To better understand the contents of this invoice, identify these items:
1. Seller
2. Invoice date
3. Purchaser
4. Salesperson
5. Credit terms
6. Freight terms
7. Goods sold: catalog number, description, quantity, price per unit
8. Total invoice amount

Sauk Stereo makes the following journal entry to record its purchase from PW Audio Supply on account. The entry increases (debits) Inventory and increases (credits) Accounts Payable.

May 4	Inventory	3,800	
	Accounts Payable		3,800
	(To record goods purchased on account from PW Audio Supply)		

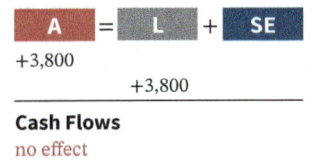

Under the perpetual inventory system, companies record purchases of merchandise for sale in the Inventory account. Thus, **REI** would increase (debit) Inventory for clothing, sporting goods, and anything else purchased for resale to customers.

Not all purchases are debited to Inventory, however. Companies record purchases of assets acquired for use and not for resale, such as supplies, equipment, and similar items, as increases to specific asset accounts rather than to Inventory. For example, to record the purchase of materials used to make shelf signs or for cash register receipt paper, REI would increase (debit) Supplies.

Freight Costs

The sales agreement should indicate who—the seller or the buyer—is to pay for transporting the goods to the buyer's place of business. When a common carrier such as a railroad, trucking company, or airline transports the goods, the carrier prepares a freight bill in accord with the sales agreement.

Freight terms are expressed as either FOB shipping point or FOB destination. The letters FOB mean **free on board**. Thus, **FOB shipping point** means that the seller places the goods free on board the carrier, and the buyer pays the freight costs. Conversely, **FOB destination** means that the seller places the goods free on board to the buyer's place of business, and the seller pays the freight. For example, the sales invoice in Illustration 5.6 indicates FOB shipping point. Thus, the buyer (Sauk Stereo) pays the freight charges. **Illustration 5.7** illustrates these shipping terms.

ILLUSTRATION 5.7 Shipping terms

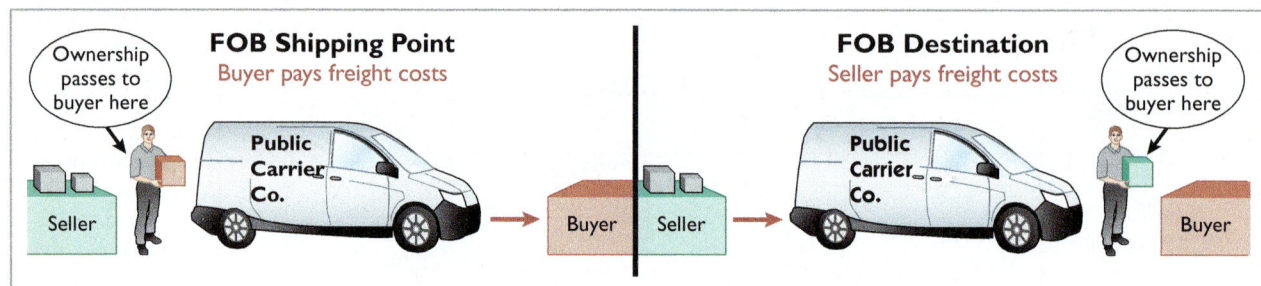

Freight Costs Incurred by the Buyer

When the buyer incurs the transportation costs, these costs are considered part of the cost of purchasing inventory. Therefore, the buyer debits (increases) the Inventory account. For example, if Sauk Stereo (the buyer) pays Public Carrier Co. $150 for freight charges on May 6, the entry on Sauk Stereo's books is:

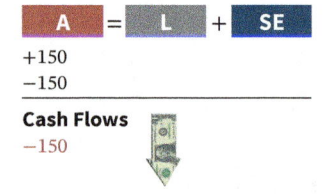
+150
−150

Cash Flows
−150

May 6	Inventory	150	
	Cash		150
	(To record payment of freight on goods purchased)		

Thus, any freight costs incurred by the buyer are part of the cost of merchandise purchased. The reason: Inventory cost should include all costs to acquire the inventory, including freight necessary to deliver the goods to the buyer. Companies recognize these costs as cost of goods sold when inventory is sold.

Freight Costs Incurred by the Seller

In contrast, **freight costs incurred by the seller on outgoing merchandise are an operating expense to the seller**. These costs increase an expense account titled Freight-Out (sometimes called Delivery Expense). For example, if the freight terms on the invoice in Illustration 5.6 had required PW Audio Supply (the seller) to pay the freight charges, the entry by PW Audio Supply would be:

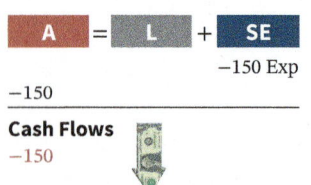
           −150 Exp
−150

Cash Flows
−150

May 4	Freight-Out (or Delivery Expense)	150	
	Cash		150
	(To record payment of freight on goods sold)		

When the seller pays the freight charges, the seller will usually establish a higher invoice price for the goods to cover the shipping expense.

Purchase Returns and Allowances

A purchaser may be dissatisfied with the merchandise received because the goods are damaged or defective, of inferior quality, or do not meet the purchaser's specifications. In such cases, the purchaser may return the goods to the seller for credit if the sale was made on credit, or for a cash refund if the purchase was for cash. This transaction is known as a **purchase return**. Alternatively, the purchaser may choose to keep the merchandise if the seller is willing to grant an allowance (deduction) from the purchase price. This transaction is known as a **purchase allowance**.

Assume that Sauk Stereo returned goods costing $300 to PW Audio Supply on May 8. The following entry by Sauk Stereo for the returned merchandise decreases (debits) Accounts Payable and decreases (credits) Inventory.

May 8	Accounts Payable	300	
	Inventory		300
	(To record return of goods purchased from PW Audio Supply)		

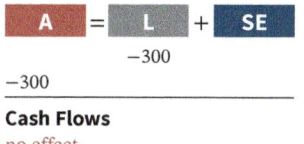

Cash Flows
no effect

Because Sauk Stereo increased Inventory when the goods were received, Inventory is decreased when Sauk Stereo returns the goods.

Suppose instead that Sauk Stereo chose to keep the goods after being granted a $50 allowance (reduction in price). It would reduce (debit) Accounts Payable and reduce (credit) Inventory for $50.

Purchase Discounts

The credit terms of a purchase on account may permit the buyer to claim a cash discount for prompt payment. The buyer calls this cash discount a **purchase discount**. This incentive offers advantages to both parties. The purchaser saves money, and the seller is able to shorten the operating cycle by converting the accounts receivable into cash.

Credit terms specify the amount of the cash discount and time period in which it is offered. They also indicate the time period in which the purchaser is expected to pay the full invoice price. In the sales invoice in Illustration 5.6, credit terms are 2/10, n/30, which is read "two-ten, net thirty" (see **Helpful Hint**). This means that the buyer may take a 2% cash discount on the invoice price, less ("net of") any returns or allowances, if payment is made within 10 days of the invoice date (the **discount period**). Otherwise, the invoice price, less any returns or allowances, is due 30 days from the invoice date.

Alternatively, the discount period may extend to a specified number of days following the month in which the sale occurs. For example, 1/10 EOM (end of month) means that a 1% discount is available if the invoice is paid within the first 10 days of the next month.

When the seller elects not to offer a cash discount for prompt payment, credit terms will specify only the maximum time period for paying the balance due. For example, the invoice may state the time period as n/30, n/60, or n/10 EOM. This means, respectively, that the buyer must pay the net amount in 30 days, 60 days, or within the first 10 days of the next month.

When the buyer pays an invoice within the discount period, the amount of the discount decreases Inventory. Why? Because companies record inventory at cost, and by paying within the discount period, the buyer has reduced its cost. To illustrate, assume Sauk Stereo pays the balance due of $3,500 (gross invoice price of $3,800 less purchase returns and allowances of $300) on May 14, the last day of the discount period. Since the terms are 2/10, n/30, the cash discount is $70 ($3,500 × 2%) and Sauk Stereo pays $3,430 ($3,500 − $70). The entry Sauk Stereo makes to record its May 14 payment decreases (debits) Accounts Payable by the amount of

> **HELPFUL HINT**
> The term *net* in "net 30" means the remaining amount due after subtracting any sales returns and allowances and partial payments.

the gross invoice price, reduces (credits) Inventory by the $70 discount, and reduces (credits) Cash by the net amount owed.

May 14	Accounts Payable		3,500	
	Cash			3,430
	Inventory			70
	(To record payment within discount period)			

If Sauk Stereo failed to take the discount and instead made full payment of $3,500 on June 3, it would debit Accounts Payable and credit Cash for $3,500 each.

June 3	Accounts Payable		3,500	
	Cash			3,500
	(To record payment with no discount taken)			

A merchandising company usually should take all available discounts. Passing up the discount may be viewed as **paying interest** for use of the money. For example, passing up the discount offered by PW Audio Supply would be comparable to Sauk Stereo paying an interest rate of 2% for the use of $3,500 for 20 days. This is the equivalent of an annual interest rate of 36.5% (2% × 365/20). Obviously, it would be better for Sauk Stereo to borrow at prevailing bank interest rates of 6% to 10% than to lose the discount.

Summary of Purchasing Transactions

The following T-account (with transaction descriptions in red) provides a summary of the effect of the previous transactions on Inventory. Sauk Stereo originally purchased $3,800 worth of inventory on account for resale. It then returned $300 of goods. It paid $150 in freight charges, and finally, it received a $70 discount off the balance owed because it paid within the discount period. This results in a balance in Inventory of $3,580.

		Inventory			
Purchase	May 4	3,800	May 8	300	Purchase return
Freight-in	6	150	14	70	Purchase discount
Balance		3,580			

ACTION PLAN
- Purchaser records goods at cost.
- When goods are returned, purchaser reduces Inventory.

DO IT! 2 | Purchase Transactions

On September 5, De La Hoya Company buys merchandise on account from Junot Diaz Company. The purchase price of the goods paid by De La Hoya is $1,500, and the cost to Diaz Company was $800. On September 8, De La Hoya returns defective goods with a selling price of $200. Record the transactions on the books of De La Hoya Company.

Solution

Sept. 5	Inventory		1,500	
	Accounts Payable			1,500
	(To record goods purchased on account)			
8	Accounts Payable		200	
	Inventory			200
	(To record return of defective goods)			

Related exercise material: **BE5.3, BE5.5, DO IT! 5.2, E5.2, E5.3, and E5.5.**

Recording Sales Under a Perpetual System

LEARNING OBJECTIVE 3
Record sales under a perpetual inventory system.

In accordance with the revenue recognition principle, companies record sales revenue when the performance obligation is satisfied. Typically, the performance obligation is satisfied when the goods transfer from the seller to the buyer. At this point, the sales transaction is complete and the sales price established.

Sales may be made on credit or for cash. A **business document** should support every sales transaction, to provide written evidence of the sale. **Cash register documents** provide evidence of cash sales. A **sales invoice**, like the one shown in Illustration 5.6, provides support for a credit sale. The original copy of the invoice goes to the customer, and the seller keeps a copy for use in recording the sale. The invoice shows the date of sale, customer name, total sales price, and other relevant information.

The seller makes two entries for each sale. **The first entry records the sale**: The seller increases (debits) Cash (or Accounts Receivable if a credit sale) and also increases (credits) Sales Revenue. **The second entry records the cost of the merchandise sold**: The seller increases (debits) Cost of Goods Sold and also decreases (credits) Inventory for the cost of those goods. As a result, the Inventory account will show at all times the amount of inventory that should be on hand.

To illustrate a credit sales transaction, PW Audio Supply, Inc. records its May 4 sale of $3,800 to Sauk Stereo (see Illustration 5.6) as follows (assume the merchandise cost PW Audio Supply $2,400).

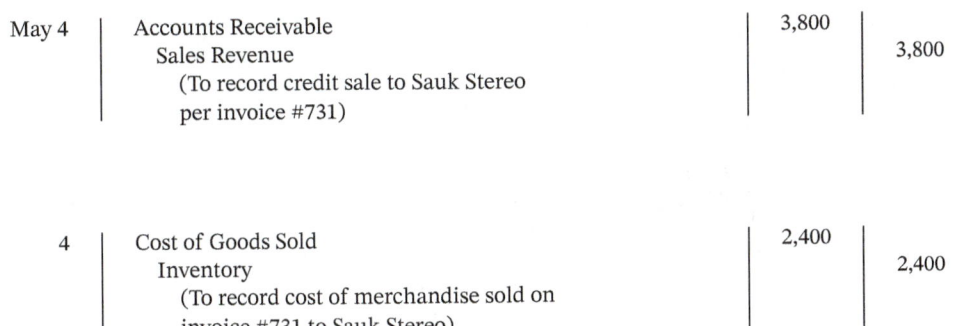

May 4	Accounts Receivable		3,800	
	Sales Revenue			3,800
	(To record credit sale to Sauk Stereo			
	per invoice #731)			
4	Cost of Goods Sold		2,400	
	Inventory			2,400
	(To record cost of merchandise sold on			
	invoice #731 to Sauk Stereo)			

For internal decision-making purposes, merchandising companies may use more than one sales account. For example, PW Audio Supply may decide to keep separate sales accounts for its sales of TVs, Blu-ray players, and headsets. **REI** might use separate accounts for camping gear, children's clothing, and ski equipment—or it might have even more narrowly defined accounts. By using separate sales accounts for major product lines, rather than a single combined sales account, company management can more closely monitor sales trends and respond to changes in sales patterns more strategically. For example, if TV sales are increasing while Blu-ray player sales are decreasing, PW Audio Supply might reevaluate both its advertising and pricing policies on these items to ensure they are optimal.

On its income statement presented to outside investors, a merchandising company normally would provide only a single sales figure—the sum of all of its individual sales accounts. This is done for two reasons. First, providing detail on all of its individual sales accounts would add considerable length to its income statement. Second, companies do not want their competitors to know the details of their operating results. However, **Microsoft** recently expanded its disclosure of revenue from three to five types. The reason: The additional categories enabled financial statement users to better evaluate the growth of the company's consumer and Internet businesses (see **Ethics Note**).

ETHICS NOTE

Many companies are trying to improve the quality of their financial reporting. For example, **General Electric** now provides more detail on its revenues and operating profits.

Anatomy of a Fraud[1]

Holly Harmon was a cashier at a national superstore for only a short time when she began stealing merchandise using three methods. Under the first method, her husband or friends took UPC labels from cheaper items and put them on more expensive items. Holly then scanned the goods at the register. Using the second method, Holly scanned an item at the register but then voided the sale and left the merchandise in the shopping cart. A third approach was to put goods into large plastic containers. She scanned the plastic containers but not the goods within them. After Holly quit, a review of past surveillance tapes enabled the store to observe the thefts and to identify the participants.

Total take: $12,000

The Missing Controls

Human resource controls. A background check would have revealed Holly's previous criminal record. She would not have been hired as a cashier.

Physical controls. Software can flag high numbers of voided transactions or a high number of sales of low-priced goods. Random comparisons of video records with cash register records can ensure that the goods reported as sold on the register are the same goods that are shown being purchased on the video recording. Finally, employees should be aware that they are being monitored.

Source: Adapted from Wells, *Fraud Casebook* (2007), pp. 251–259.

At the end of "Anatomy of a Fraud" stories, which describe some recent real-world frauds, we discuss the missing control activities that would likely have prevented or uncovered the fraud.

Sales Returns and Allowances

We now look at the "flip side" of purchase returns and allowances, which the seller records as **sales returns and allowances**. These are transactions where the seller either accepts goods back from the buyer (a return) or grants a reduction in the purchase price (an allowance) so the buyer will keep the goods. PW Audio Supply's entries to record credit for returned goods involve (1) an increase (debit) in Sales Returns and Allowances (a contra account to Sales Revenue) and a decrease (credit) in Accounts Receivable at the $300 selling price, and (2) an increase (debit) in Inventory (assume a $140 cost) and a decrease (credit) in Cost of Goods Sold, as shown below (assuming that the goods were not defective).

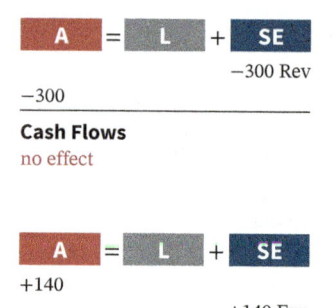

Date	Account	Debit	Credit
May 8	Sales Returns and Allowances	300	
	Accounts Receivable		300
	(To record credit granted to Sauk Stereo for returned goods)		
8	Inventory	140	
	Cost of Goods Sold		140
	(To record cost of goods returned)		

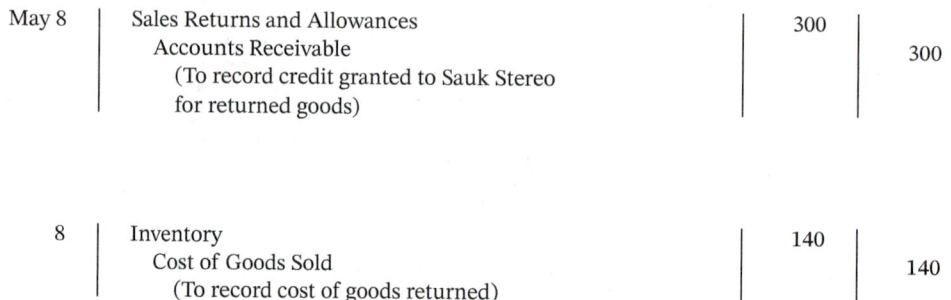

If Sauk Stereo returns goods because they are damaged or defective, then PW Audio Supply's entry to Inventory and Cost of Goods Sold should be for the fair value of the returned goods, rather than their cost. For example, if the returned goods were defective and had a fair value of $50, PW Audio Supply would debit Inventory for $50 and credit Cost of Goods Sold for $50.

What happens if the goods are not returned but the seller grants the buyer an allowance by reducing the purchase price? In this case, the seller debits Sales Returns and Allowances and credits Accounts Receivable for the amount of the allowance. An allowance has no impact on Inventory or Cost of Goods Sold.

---

[1] The "Anatomy of a Fraud" stories in this text are adapted from *Fraud Casebook: Lessons from the Bad Side of Business*, edited by Joseph T. Wells (Hoboken, NJ: John Wiley & Sons, Inc., 2007). Used by permission. The names of some of the people and organizations in the stories are fictitious, but the facts in the stories are true.

Sales Returns and Allowances is a **contra revenue account** to Sales Revenue. This means that it is offset against a revenue account on the income statement. The normal balance of Sales Returns and Allowances is a debit. Companies use a contra account, instead of debiting Sales Revenue, to disclose in the accounts and in the income statement the amount of sales returns and allowances. Disclosure of this information is important to management. Excessive returns and allowances may suggest problems—inferior merchandise, inefficiencies in filling orders, errors in billing customers, or delivery or shipment mistakes. Moreover, a decrease (debit) recorded directly to Sales Revenue would obscure the relative importance of sales returns and allowances as a percentage of sales. It also could distort comparisons between total sales in different accounting periods.

At the end of the accounting period, if the company anticipates that sales returns and allowances will be material, the company should make an adjusting entry to estimate the amount of returns. In some industries, such as those relating to the sale of books and periodicals, returns are often material. The accounting for situations where returns must be estimated is addressed in advanced accounting courses.

Accounting Across the Organization   Costco Wholesale Corp.

© Jacob Wackerhausen/iStockphoto

The Point of No Return?

In most industries, sales returns are relatively minor. But returns of consumer electronics can really take a bite out of profits. At one time, the marketing executives at **Costco Wholesale Corp.** faced a difficult decision. Costco always prided itself on its generous return policy. Most goods had an unlimited grace period for returns. However, a new policy requires that certain electronics must be returned within 90 days of their purchase. The reason? The cost of returned products such as high-definition TVs, computers, and iPods cut an estimated 8¢ per share off Costco's earnings per share, which was $2.30.

Online sales have accentuated the return problem. Many retailers have found that to compete, they must offer free shipping for returned goods.

Sources: Kris Hudson, "Costco Tightens Policy on Returning Electronics," *Wall Street Journal* (February 27, 2007), p. B4; and Loretta Chao, "More Retailers Offering Free Shipping on Returns," *Wall Street Journal* (October 11, 2015).

If a company expects significant returns, what are the implications for revenue recognition? (Go to WileyPLUS for this answer and additional questions.)

Sales Discounts

As mentioned in our discussion of purchase transactions, the seller may offer the customer a cash discount—called by the seller a **sales discount**—for the prompt payment of the balance due. Like a purchase discount, a sales discount is based on the invoice price less returns and allowances, if any. The seller increases (debits) the Sales Discounts account for discounts that are taken. For example, PW Audio Supply makes the following entry to record the cash receipt on May 14 from Sauk Stereo within the discount period.

May 14	Cash	3,430	
	Sales Discounts	70	
	Accounts Receivable		3,500
	(To record collection within 2/10, n/30		
	discount period from Sauk Stereo)		

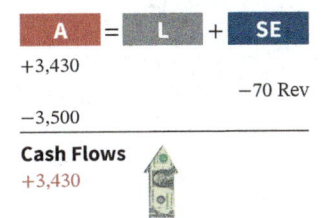

A = L + SE
+3,430
       −70 Rev
−3,500

Cash Flows
+3,430

Like Sales Returns and Allowances, Sales Discounts is a **contra revenue account** to Sales Revenue. Its normal balance is a debit. PW Audio Supply uses this account, instead of debiting Sales Revenue, to disclose the amount of cash discounts taken by customers. If Sauk Stereo does not take the discount, PW Audio Supply increases (debits) Cash for $3,500 and decreases (credits) Accounts Receivable for the same amount at the date of collection.

At the end of the accounting period, if the amount of potential discounts is material, the company should make an adjusting entry to estimate the discounts. This would not usually be the case for sales discounts but might be necessary for other types of discounts such as volume discounts, which are addressed in more advanced accounting courses. The following T-accounts summarize the three sales-related transactions and show their combined effect on net sales.

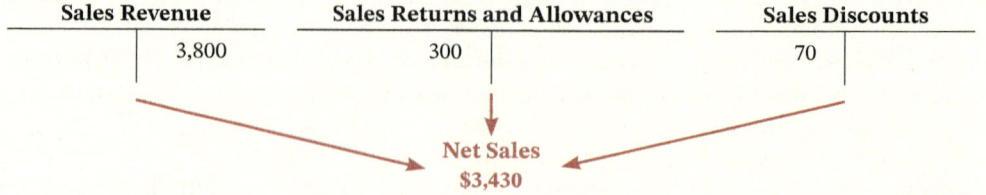

Data Analytics and Credit Sales

Increased access to ever larger amounts of data about customers, suppliers, products, and virtually every other aspect of a business has resulted in a greater reliance by companies on data analytics to support business decisions. Credit sales, sales returns and allowances, and sales discounts all provide rich opportunities for the use of data analytics.

First, the decision to whom to grant credit is very important. Offering credit to customers can substantially increase sales opportunities. However, some credit customers will ultimately not be able to pay the amounts owed. So offering credit to customers has costs. Effectively analyzing data regarding current as well as potential customers can help a company expand its sales base while minimizing the risk of unpaid receivables.

Similarly, companies must develop policies regarding sales return practices. Merchandisers know that generous return policies can enhance customer loyalty. But if returns become common, the company's profitability will suffer. In recent years, companies such as **Best Buy**, **REI**, and **Costco** have all refined their customer return policies, sometimes with unique rules for specific product types, as a result of data analytics applied to their data on product returns.

Finally, sales discounts are offered to customers to encourage early payment of receivables. Offering these discounts is costly. To achieve the optimal cost-benefit balance on sales discounts, companies statistically analyze past discount practices to determine how large the discount should be, how long the payment period should be, and other factors.

People, Planet, and Profit Insight   PepsiCo

Selling Green

Helen Sessions/Alamy

Here is a question an executive of PepsiCo was asked: Should **PepsiCo** market green? The executive indicated that the company should, as he believes it's the No. 1 thing consumers all over the world care about. Here are some of his thoughts on this issue:

"Sun Chips are part of the food business I run. It's a 'healthy snack.' We decided that Sun Chips, if it's a healthy snack, should be made in facilities that have a net-zero footprint. In other words, I want off the electric grid everywhere we make Sun Chips. We did that. Sun Chips should be made in a facility that puts back more water than it uses. It does that. And we partnered with our suppliers and came out with the world's first compostable chip package.

Now, there was an issue with this package: It was louder than the New York subway, louder than jet engines taking off. What would a company that's committed to green do: walk away or stay committed? If your people are passionate, they're going to fix it for you as long as you stay committed. Six months later, the compostable bag has half the noise of our current package.

So the view today is: we should market green, we should be proud to do it . . . it has to be a 360-degree process, both internal and external. And if you do that, you can monetize environmental sustainability for the shareholders."

Source: "Four Problems—and Solutions," *Wall Street Journal* (March 7, 2011), p. R2.

What is meant by "monetize environmental sustainability" for shareholders? (Go to WileyPLUS for this answer and additional questions.)

DO IT! 3 | Sales Transactions

On September 5, De La Hoya Company buys merchandise on account from Junot Diaz Company. The selling price of the goods is $1,500, and the cost to Diaz Company was $800. On September 8, De La Hoya returns defective goods with a selling price of $200 and a fair value of $30. Record the transactions on the books of Junot Diaz Company.

Solution

Sept. 5	Accounts Receivable	1,500	
	Sales Revenue		1,500
	(To record credit sale)		
5	Cost of Goods Sold	800	
	Inventory		800
	(To record cost of goods sold on account)		
8	Sales Returns and Allowances	200	
	Accounts Receivable		200
	(To record credit granted for receipt of returned goods)		
8	Inventory	30	
	Cost of Goods Sold		30
	(To record fair value of goods returned)		

Related exercise material: **BE5.3, BE5.4, DO IT! 5.3, E5.3, E5.4,** and **E5.5.**

ACTION PLAN
- Seller records both the sale and the cost of goods sold at the time of the sale.
- When goods are returned, the seller records the return in a contra account, Sales Returns and Allowances, and reduces Accounts Receivable.
- Any goods returned increase Inventory and reduce Cost of Goods Sold. Defective or damaged inventory is recorded at fair value (scrap value).

Multiple-Step and Comprehensive Income Statements

LEARNING OBJECTIVE 4
Prepare a multiple-step income statement and a comprehensive income statement.

Single-Step Income Statement

Companies widely use two forms of the income statement (see **International Note**). One is the **single-step income statement**. The statement is so named because only one step, subtracting total expenses from total revenues, is required in determining net income (or net loss).

In a single-step statement, all data are classified into two categories: (1) **revenues**, which include both operating revenues and nonoperating revenues and gains (for example, interest revenue and gain on sale of equipment); and (2) **expenses**, which include cost of goods sold, operating expenses, and nonoperating expenses and losses (for example, interest expense, loss on sale of equipment, or income tax expense). The single-step income statement is the form we have used thus far in the text. **Illustration 5.8** shows a single-step statement for **REI**. (Note that REI's 2015 year-end was January 2, 2016.)

There are two primary reasons for using the single-step form. (1) A company does not realize any type of profit or income until total revenues exceed total expenses, so it makes sense to divide the statement into these two categories. (2) The form is simple and easy to read.

International Note

The IASB and FASB are involved in a joint project to evaluate the format of financial statements. The first phase of that project involves a focus on how to best present revenues and expenses. One longer-term result of the project may be an income statement format that better reflects how businesses are run.

ILLUSTRATION 5.8

Single-step income statements

Recreational Equipment, Inc.
Income Statements
(in thousands)

	For the year ended	
	December 31, 2016	January 2, 2016
Revenues		
Net sales	$2,557,543	$2,423,221
Expenses		
Cost of goods sold	1,460,433	1,388,125
Payroll-related expenses	494,820	478,474
Occupancy, general and administrative	420,898	381,147
Patronage refunds and other	121,401	121,853
Income taxes	21,716	18,250
	2,519,268	2,387,849
Net income	$ 38,275	$ 35,372

Multiple-Step Income Statement

A second form of the income statement is the **multiple-step income statement**. The multiple-step income statement is often considered more useful because it highlights the components of net income. The REI income statement in **Illustration 5.9** is an example.

ILLUSTRATION 5.9

Multiple-step income statements

Recreational Equipment, Inc.
Income Statements
(in thousands)

	For the year ended	
	December 31, 2016	January 2, 2016
Net sales	$2,557,543	$2,423,221
Cost of goods sold	1,460,433	1,388,125
Gross profit	1,097,110	1,035,096
Operating expenses		
Payroll-related expenses	494,820	478,474
Occupancy, general and administrative	420,898	381,147
Total operating expenses	915,718	859,621
Income from operations	181,392	175,475
Other revenues and gains		
Other revenues	-0-	-0-
Other expenses and losses		
Patronage refunds and other	121,401	121,853
Income before income taxes	59,991	53,622
Income tax expense	21,716	18,250
Net income	$ 38,275	$ 35,372

The multiple-step income statement has three important line items: gross profit, income from operations, and net income. They are determined as follows.

1. Subtract cost of goods sold from net sales to determine **gross profit**.
2. Deduct operating expenses from gross profit to determine **income from operations**.
3. Add or subtract the results of activities not related to operations to income from operations to determine **net income**.

Note that companies report income tax expense in a separate section of the income statement before net income. The net incomes in Illustrations 5.8 and 5.9 are the same. The two income statements differ in the amount of detail displayed and the order presented. The following discussion provides additional information about the components of a multiple-step income statement.

Sales

The income statement for a merchandising company typically presents gross sales for the period. The company deducts sales returns and allowances and sales discounts (both contra accounts) from sales revenue in the income statement to arrive at **net sales**. **Illustration 5.10** shows the sales section of the income statement for PW Audio Supply.

ILLUSTRATION 5.10

Statement presentation of sales section

PW Audio Supply, Inc.
Income Statement (partial)

Sales			
Sales revenue			$480,000
Less: Sales returns and allowances		$12,000	
Sales discounts		8,000	20,000
Net sales			**$460,000**

Gross Profit

The excess of net sales over cost of goods sold is **gross profit** (see **Alternative Terminology**). It is determined by deducting **cost of goods sold** from net sales. As shown in Illustration 5.9, REI had a gross profit of $1,097 million for the year ended December 31, 2016. This computation uses **net sales**, which takes into account sales returns and allowances and sales discounts.

On the basis of the PW Audio Supply sales data presented in Illustration 5.10 (net sales of $460,000) and the cost of goods sold (assume a balance of $316,000), PW Audio Supply's gross profit is $144,000, computed as follows.

ALTERNATIVE TERMINOLOGY

Gross profit is sometimes referred to as *gross margin*.

Net sales	$460,000
Cost of goods sold	316,000
Gross profit	**$144,000**

It is important to understand what gross profit is—and what it is not. Gross profit represents the **merchandising profit** of a company. Because operating expenses have not been deducted, it is **not a measure of the overall profit** of a company. Nevertheless, management and other interested parties closely watch the amount and trend of gross profit. Comparisons of current gross profit with past amounts and rates and with those in the industry indicate the effectiveness of a company's purchasing and pricing policies.

Operating Expenses

Operating expenses are the next component in measuring net income for a merchandising company. At REI, for example, operating expenses were $916 million for the year ended December 31, 2016.

At PW Audio Supply, operating expenses were $114,000. The firm determines its income from operations by subtracting operating expenses from gross profit. Thus, income from operations is $30,000, as shown below.

Gross profit	$144,000
Operating expenses	**114,000**
Income from operations	$ 30,000

Nonoperating Activities and Income Tax Expense

Nonoperating activities consist of various revenues and expenses and gains and losses that are unrelated to the company's main line of operations. When nonoperating items are included, the label **Income from operations** (or Operating income) precedes them. This label clearly identifies the results of the company's normal operations, an amount determined by subtracting cost of goods sold and operating expenses from net sales. The results of nonoperating activities are shown in the categories **Other revenues and gains** and **Other expenses and losses**. Illustration 5.11 lists examples of each.

ILLUSTRATION 5.11

Examples of nonoperating activities

Other Revenues and Gains

Interest revenue from notes receivable and marketable securities.
Dividend revenue from investments in capital stock.
Rent revenue from subleasing a portion of the store.
Gain from the sale of property, plant, and equipment.

Other Expenses and Losses

Interest expense on notes and loans payable.
Casualty losses from such causes as vandalism and accidents.
Loss from the sale or abandonment of property, plant, and equipment.
Loss from strikes by employees and suppliers.

ETHICS NOTE

Companies manage earnings in various ways. ConAgra Foods recorded a non-recurring gain for $186 million from the sale of Pilgrim's Pride stock to help meet an earnings projection for the quarter.

Nonoperating income is sometimes very significant. For example, in one quarter, Sears Holdings earned more than half of its net income from investments in derivative securities.

The distinction between operating and nonoperating activities is crucial to external users of financial data. These users view operating income as sustainable and many nonoperating activities as non-recurring. When forecasting next year's income, analysts put the most weight on this year's operating income and less weight on this year's nonoperating activities (see Ethics Note).

Ethics Insight IBM

ImageRite/Getty Images, Inc.

Disclosing More Details

After Enron, increased investor criticism and regulator scrutiny forced many companies to improve the clarity of their financial disclosures. For example, IBM began providing more detail regarding its Other gains and losses. It had previously included these items in its selling, general, and administrative expenses, with little disclosure. For example, previously if IBM sold off one of its buildings at a gain, it included this gain in the selling, general, and administrative expense line item, thus reducing that expense. This made it appear that the company had done a better job of controlling operating expenses than it actually had.

As another example, when eBay recently sold the remainder of its investment in Skype to Microsoft, it reported a gain in Other revenues and gains of $1.7 billion. Since eBay's total income from operations was $2.4 billion, it was very important that the gain from the Skype sale not be buried in operating income.

Why have investors and analysts demanded more accuracy in isolating Other gains and losses from operating items? (Go to WileyPLUS for this answer and additional questions.)

Nonoperating activities are reported in the income statement immediately after operating activities. Included among Other revenues and gains in Illustration 5.12 are Interest revenue and Gain on disposal of plant assets. Included in Other expenses and losses are Interest expense and Casualty loss from vandalism.

The net amount resulting from Other revenues and gains and Other expenses and losses is added or subtracted from Income from operations to arrive at Income before income taxes. This amount is then multiplied by the company's corporate income tax rate to arrive at **Income tax expense**. Income tax expense is subtracted from **Income before income taxes** to arrive at net income.

In Illustration 5.12, we have provided the multiple-step income statement of PW Audio Supply. This statement provides more detail than that of REI and thus is useful as a guide for homework. *For homework problems, use the multiple-step form of the income statement unless the requirements state otherwise.*

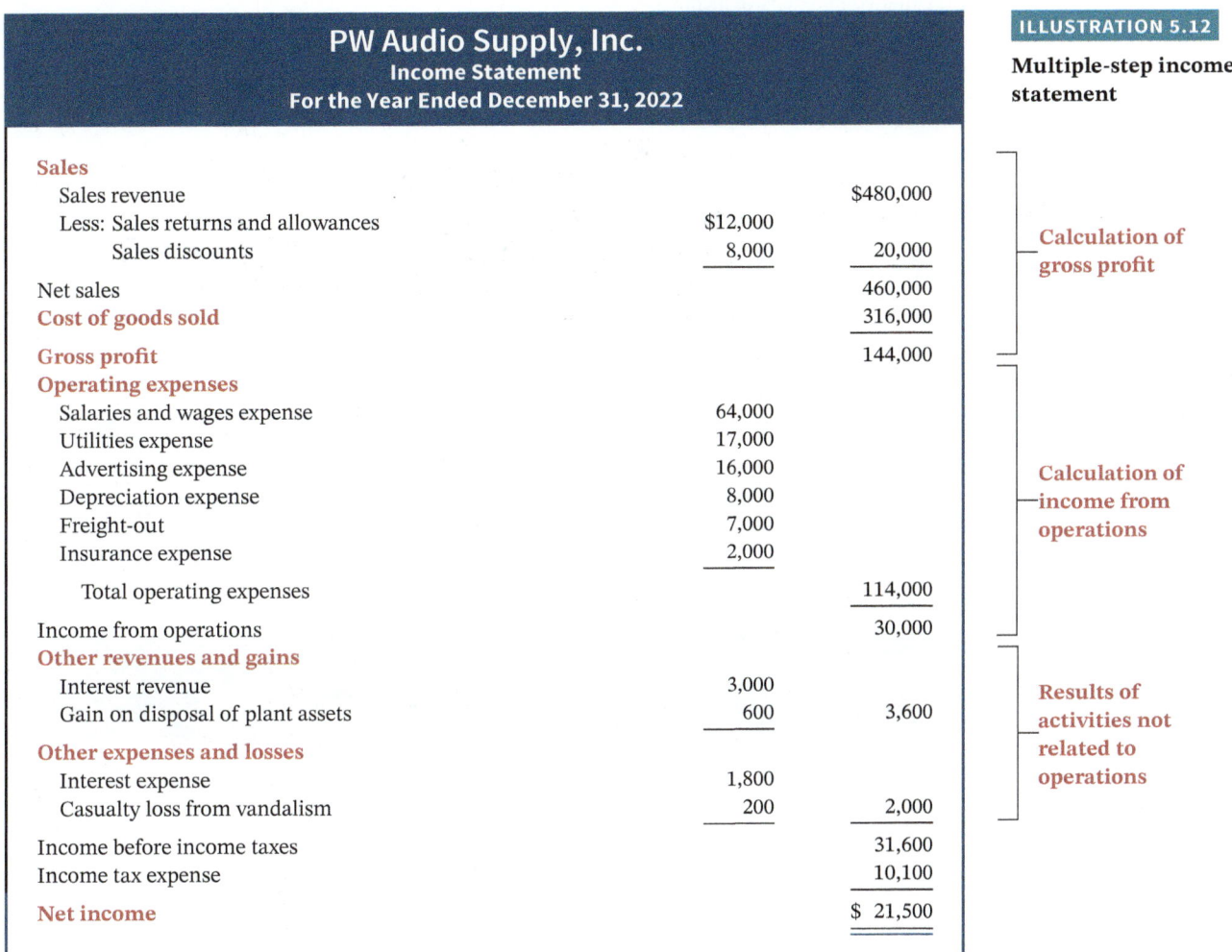

ILLUSTRATION 5.12

Multiple-step income statement

Comprehensive Income Statement

We previously discussed the fair value principle. Recall that accounting standards require companies to mark the recorded values of certain types of assets and liabilities to their fair values at the end of each reporting period. In some instances, the unrealized gains or losses that result from adjusting recorded amounts to fair value are included in net income. However, in other cases, these unrealized gains and losses are not included in net income. Instead, these excluded items are reported as part of a more inclusive earnings measure, called **comprehensive income**. Examples of such items include certain adjustments to pension plan assets, gains and losses on foreign currency translation, and unrealized gains and losses on certain types of investments.

Items that are excluded from net income but included in comprehensive income are either reported in a combined statement of net income and comprehensive income, or in a separate comprehensive income statement. The **comprehensive income statement** presents items that are not included in the determination of net income, referred to as other comprehensive income. **Illustration 5.13** shows how comprehensive income is presented in a separate comprehensive income statement. It assumes that PW Audio Supply had an unrealized gain of $2,700 with $400 of related tax expense. *Use this format when preparing your homework.*

ILLUSTRATION 5.13

Combined statement of net income and comprehensive income

PW Audio Supply, Inc.
Comprehensive Income Statement
For the Year Ended December 31, 2022

Net income	$21,500
Other comprehensive income	
Unrealized holding gain on investment securities (net of $400 tax)	2,300
Comprehensive income	$23,800

DO IT! 4 | Multiple-Step Income Statement

ACTION PLAN
- Subtract cost of goods sold from net sales to determine gross profit.
- Subtract operating expenses from gross profit to determine income from operations.
- Add/subtract nonoperating items to income from operations to determine income before tax.
- Multiply the tax rate by income before tax to determine tax expense.

The following information is available for Art Center Corp. for the year ended December 31, 2022.

Other revenues and gains	$ 8,000	Sales revenue	$462,000
Other expenses and losses	3,000	Operating expenses	187,000
Cost of goods sold	147,000	Sales discounts	20,000
		Other comprehensive income	10,000

Prepare a multiple-step income statement and comprehensive income statement for Art Center Corp. The company has a tax rate of 25%. This rate also applies to other comprehensive income.

Solution

Art Center Corp.
Income Statement
For the Year Ended December 31, 2022

Sales		
Sales revenue		$462,000
Sales discounts		20,000
Net sales		442,000
Cost of goods sold		147,000
Gross profit		295,000
Operating expenses		187,000
Income from operations		108,000
Other revenues and gains	$8,000	
Other expenses and losses	3,000	5,000
Income before income taxes		113,000
Income tax expense		28,250
Net income		$ 84,750

Art Center Corp.
Comprehensive Income Statement
For the Year Ended December 31, 2022

Net income	$84,750
Other comprehensive income (net of $2,500 tax)	7,500
Comprehensive income	$92,250

Related exercise material: **BE5.6, BE5.7, BE5.8, BE5.9, DO IT! 5.4, E5.6, E5.7, E5.8, E5.9, E5.10, E5.11,** and **E5.12**.

Cost of Goods Sold Under a Periodic System

> **LEARNING OBJECTIVE 5**
> Determine cost of goods sold under a periodic inventory system.

Determining cost of goods sold is different when a periodic inventory system is used rather than a perpetual system. As you have seen, a company using a **perpetual system** makes an entry to record cost of goods sold and to reduce inventory **each time a sale is made**. A company using a **periodic system** does not determine cost of goods sold **until the end of the period**. At the end of the period, the company performs a count to determine the ending balance of inventory. It then **calculates cost of goods sold by subtracting ending inventory from the goods available for sale**. Cost of goods available for sale is the sum of beginning inventory plus purchases, as shown in **Illustration 5.14**.

```
  Beginning Inventory
+ Cost of Goods Purchased
  ─────────────────────────
  Cost of Goods Available for Sale
− Ending Inventory
  ─────────────────────────
  Cost of Goods Sold
```

ILLUSTRATION 5.14
Basic formula for cost of goods sold using the periodic system

Another difference between the two approaches is that the perpetual system directly adjusts the Inventory account for any transaction that affects inventory (such as freight costs, purchase returns, and purchase discounts). The periodic system does not do this. Instead, it creates different accounts for purchases, freight costs, purchase returns, and purchase discounts. These various accounts are shown in **Illustration 5.15**, which presents the calculation of cost of goods sold for PW Audio Supply using the periodic approach (see **Helpful Hint**). Note that the basic elements from Illustration 5.14 are highlighted in Illustration 5.15. You will learn in a later chapter about how to determine cost of goods sold using the periodic system.

PW Audio Supply, Inc.
Cost of Goods Sold
For the Year Ended December 31, 2022

Cost of goods sold			
Inventory, January 1			$ 36,000
Purchases		$325,000	
Less: Purchase returns and allowances	$10,400		
Purchase discounts	6,800	17,200	
Net purchases		307,800	
Add: Freight-in		12,200	
Cost of goods purchased			320,000
Cost of goods available for sale			356,000
Inventory, December 31			40,000
Cost of goods sold			**$316,000**

ILLUSTRATION 5.15
Cost of goods sold for a merchandiser using a periodic inventory system

> **HELPFUL HINT**
> The far right column identifies the primary items that make up cost of goods sold of $316,000. The middle column explains cost of goods purchased of $320,000. The left column reports contra purchase items of $17,200.

The use of the periodic inventory system does not affect the form of presentation in the balance sheet. As under the perpetual system, a company reports inventory in the current assets section.

Appendix 5A provides further detail on the use of the periodic system.

ACTION PLAN

- To determine cost of goods purchased, adjust purchases for returns, discounts, and freight-in.
- To determine cost of goods sold, add cost of goods purchased to beginning inventory, and subtract ending inventory.

DO IT! 5 | Cost of Goods Sold—Periodic System

Aerosmith Company's accounting records show the following at the year-end December 31, 2022.

Purchase Discounts	$ 3,400
Freight-In	6,100
Purchases	162,500
Beginning Inventory	18,000
Ending Inventory	20,000
Purchase Returns and Allowances	5,200

Assuming that Aerosmith Company uses the periodic system, compute (a) cost of goods purchased and (b) cost of goods sold.

Solution

a. Cost of goods purchased = $160,000:

$$\text{Purchases} - \text{Purchase returns and allowances} - \text{Purchase discounts} + \text{Freight-in}$$
$$\$162,500 - \$5,200 - \$3,400 + \$6,100 = \$160,000$$

b. Cost of goods sold = $158,000:

$$\text{Beginning inventory} + \text{Cost of goods purchased} - \text{Ending inventory}$$
$$\$18,000 + \$160,000 - \$20,000 = \$158,000$$

Related exercise material: **BE5.10, BE5.11, BE5.12, DO IT! 5.5, E5.13, and E5.14.**

Gross Profit Rate and Profit Margin

LEARNING OBJECTIVE 6
Compute and analyze gross profit rate and profit margin.

Gross Profit Rate

Decision Tools

The gross profit rate helps companies decide if the prices of their goods are in line with changes in the cost of inventory.

A company's gross profit may be expressed as a **percentage** by dividing the amount of gross profit by net sales. This is referred to as the **gross profit rate**. For PW Audio Supply, the gross profit rate is 31.3% ($144,000 ÷ $460,000).

Analysts generally consider the gross profit **rate** to be more informative than the gross profit **amount** because it expresses a more meaningful (qualitative) relationship between gross profit and net sales (see **Decision Tools**). For example, a gross profit amount of $1,000,000 may sound impressive. But if it was the result of sales of $100,000,000, the company's gross profit rate was only 1%. **Illustration 5.16** demonstrates that gross profit rates differ greatly across industries.

ILLUSTRATION 5.16
Gross profit rate by industry

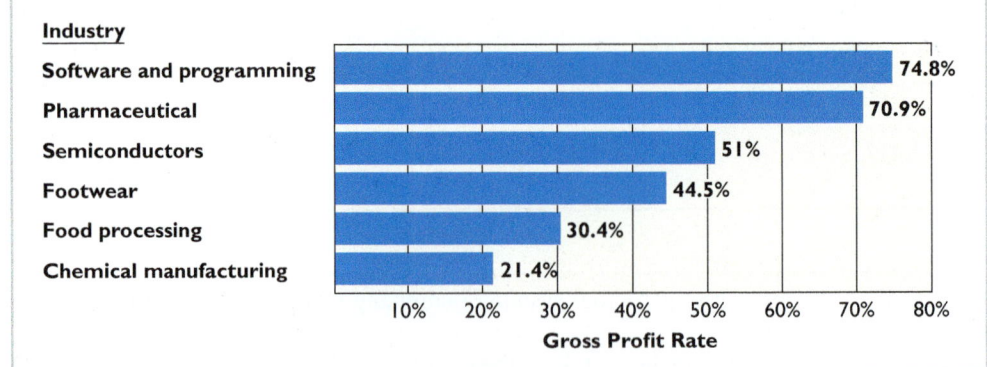

A decline in a company's gross profit rate might have several causes. The company may have begun to sell products with a lower "markup"—for example, budget blue jeans versus designer blue jeans. Increased competition may have resulted in a lower selling price. Or, maybe the company was forced to pay higher prices to its suppliers and was not able to pass these costs on to its customers. The gross profit rates for **REI** and **Dick's Sporting Goods** are presented in **Illustration 5.17**.

ILLUSTRATION 5.17

Gross profit rate

$$\text{Gross Profit Rate} = \frac{\text{Gross Profit}}{\text{Net Sales}}$$

REI ($ in thousands)		Dick's Sporting Goods
2016	2015	2016
$\dfrac{\$1{,}097{,}110}{\$2{,}557{,}543} = 42.9\%$	42.7%	29.9%

REI's gross profit rate increased from 42.7% in 2015 to 42.9% in 2016. What might cause changes in REI's gross profit rate? When the economy changes, retailers also often adjust their selling prices. Changes in national weather patterns can also affect the amount of time people spend outdoors—and therefore impact their purchases of REI merchandise.

Why does REI's gross profit rate differ so much from that of Dick's Sporting Goods? The gross profit rate often differs across retailers because of differences in the nature of their goods. First, REI focuses on outdoor equipment, while Dick's also sells sporting goods and hunting gear. The markup may differ significantly in these different product sectors. Also, although REI and Dick's both sell outdoor equipment, the quality of the equipment they sell might differ. If REI tends to sell more "high-end" goods compared to Dick's, its gross profit rate would tend to be higher. Higher-quality goods often receive a higher markup, but the retailer also sells fewer of them. In general, retailers adopt either a high-volume–low-margin approach (e.g., **Wal-Mart**) or a low-volume–high-margin approach (e.g., **Saks Fifth Avenue**). The strategic choice is often revealed in differences in the companies' gross profit rates.

Profit Margin

The **profit margin** measures the percentage of each dollar of sales that results in net income. We compute this ratio by dividing net income by net sales (revenue) for the period.

How do the gross profit rate and profit margin differ? The gross profit rate measures the margin by which selling price exceeds cost of goods sold. **The profit margin measures the extent by which selling price covers all expenses** (including cost of goods sold) (see **Decision Tools**). A company can improve its profit margin by either increasing its gross profit rate and/or by controlling its operating expenses and other costs. For example, at one time **Radio Shack** reported increased profit margins which it accomplished by closing stores and slashing costs. Eventually, however, it was forced to file for bankruptcy as sales continued to decline.

Profit margins vary across industries. Businesses with high turnovers, such as grocery stores (**Safeway** and **Kroger**) and discount stores (**Target** and **Wal-Mart**), generally experience low profit margins. Low-turnover businesses, such as high-end jewelry stores (**Tiffany and Co.**) or major drug manufacturers (**Merck**), have high profit margins. **Illustration 5.18** shows profit margins from a variety of industries.

Decision Tools

The profit margin helps companies decide if they are maintaining an adequate margin between sales and expenses.

ILLUSTRATION 5.18

Profit margins by industry

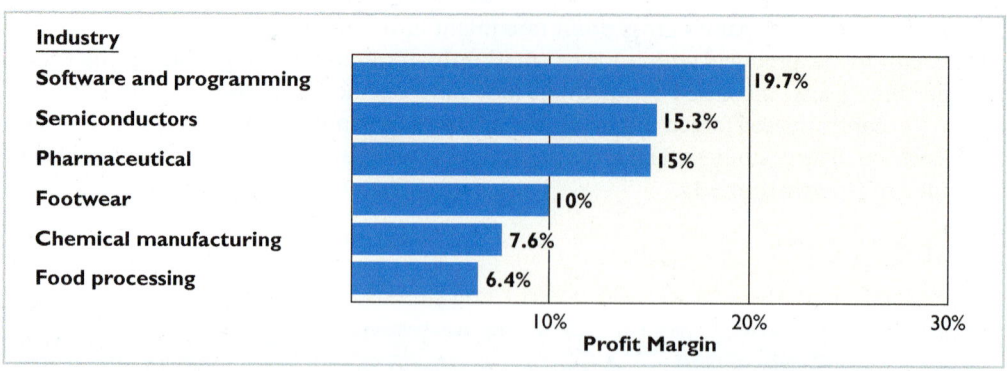

Profit margins for REI and Dick's Sporting Goods are presented in **Illustration 5.19**.

ILLUSTRATION 5.19

Profit margin

$$\text{Profit Margin} = \frac{\text{Net Income}}{\text{Net Sales}}$$

REI ($ in thousands)		Dick's Sporting Goods
2016	2015	2016
$\frac{\$38,275}{\$2,557,543} = 1.5\%$	1.5%	3.6%

REI's profit margin remained at 1.5% between 2015 and 2016. This means that the company generated 1.5¢ of profit on each dollar of sales. This constant profit margin occurred even though the gross profit rate increased.

A change in the profit margin can be caused by a change in the gross profit rate, a change in the amount of operating expenses relative to sales, or a change in the amount of other items (other revenues and gains, or other expenses and losses) relative to sales. From Illustration 5.17, we know that REI's gross profit rate increased slightly. From analyzing the information in Illustration 5.9, we see that operating expenses as a percentage of sales increased from 35.5% ($859,621 ÷ $2,423,221) in 2015 to 35.8% ($915,718 ÷ $2,557,543) in 2016. This increase in operating expenses as a percentage of sales was offset by an increase in the gross profit rate from 42.7% ($1,035,096 ÷ $2,423,221) to 42.9% ($1,097,110 ÷ $2,557,543).

How does REI compare to its competitors? Its profit margin was lower than Dick's in 2016. Thus, its profit margin does not suggest exceptional profitability.

Keeping an Eye on Cash

You learned previously that **earnings have high quality if they provide a full and transparent depiction of how a company performed**. In order to quickly assess earnings quality, analysts sometimes employ the **quality of earnings ratio**. It is calculated as net cash provided by operating activities divided by net income.

$$\text{Quality of Earnings Ratio} = \frac{\text{Net Cash Provided by Operating Activities}}{\text{Net Income}}$$

In general, a measure significantly less than 1 suggests that a company may be using more aggressive accounting techniques in order to accelerate income recognition (record income in earlier periods). A measure significantly greater than 1 suggests that a company is using conservative accounting techniques, which cause it to delay the recognition of income.

Measures that are significantly less than 1 do not provide definitive evidence of low-quality earnings. Low measures do, however, indicate that analysts should investigate the causes of the difference between net income and net cash provided by operating activities. Examples of factors that would cause differences are presented in the "Keeping an Eye on Cash" box in Chapter 4.

The following are recent quality of earnings ratios for a number of well-known companies, all of which have measures in excess of 1.

Company Name ($ in millions)	Net Cash Provided by Operating Activities	÷	Net Income	=	Quality of Earnings Ratio
DuPont	$4,741		$1,769		2.7
Intel	$11,170		$4,369		2.6
Nike	$1,736		$1,487		1.2
Microsoft	$19,037		$14,569		1.3
Wal-Mart	$26,249		$14,335		1.8

DO IT! 6 | Gross Profit Rate and Profit Margin

Rachel Rose, Inc. reported the following in its 2022 and 2021 income statements.

	2022	2021
Net sales	$80,000	$120,000
Cost of goods sold	40,000	60,000
Operating expenses	14,000	28,000
Income tax expense	8,000	12,000
Net income	$18,000	$20,000

Determine the company's gross profit rate and profit margin. Discuss the cause for changes in the ratios.

ACTION PLAN
- To determine gross profit rate, divide gross profit by net sales.
- To find profit margin, divide net income by net sales.

Solution

	2022	2021
Gross profit rate	($80,000 − $40,000) / $80,000 = 50%	($120,000 − $60,000) / $120,000 = 50%
Profit margin	$18,000 ÷ $80,000 = 22.5%	$20,000 ÷ $120,000 = 16.7%

The company's gross profit rate remained constant. However, its profit margin increased significantly due to a sharp decline in its operating costs as a percentage of sales, which declined from 23.3% ($28,000 ÷ $120,000) in 2021 to 17.5% ($14,000 ÷ $80,000) in 2022.

Related exercise material: **BE5.13, BE5.14, BE5.15, DO IT! 5.6, E5.8, E5.9, E5.10, and E5.15**.

USING THE DECISION TOOLS | Mountain Equipment Cooperative

Like **REI**, **Mountain Equipment Cooperative (MEC)** is a retailer of outdoor equipment organized as a cooperative (though MEC *only* sells to its members, who pay a one-time fee of $5). Also like REI, MEC has a significant commitment to sustainability. Many of its stores employ state-of-the-art building techniques to minimize energy use, and it pledges 1% of annual sales revenue to environmental causes. Since MEC is a Canadian company, it follows International Financial Reporting Standards (IFRS) rather than U.S. GAAP. The *A Look at IFRS* section at the end of each chapter of this text discusses some of the main accounting differences that you would need to be aware of to make a thorough comparison of REI and MEC. Here is recent data for MEC.

($ in thousands)	Year ended 2/26/2017	Year ended 12/27/2015
Net income	$ (4,652)	$ 53
Sales revenue	464,876	365,561
Cost of goods sold	318,803	255,757

Instructions

Using the basic facts in the table, evaluate the MEC's profit margin and gross profit rate for the years ended February 26, 2017, and December 27, 2015. (Note that the period ended 2/26/2017 was actually a 14-month period because the company changed its year-end from the last Sunday in December to the last Sunday in February). How do MEC's profit margin and gross profit rate compare to those of REI and Dick's Sporting Goods for 2016?

Solution

	Year ended	
($ in thousands)	2/26/2017	12/27/2015
Profit margin	$\dfrac{\$(4{,}652)}{\$464{,}876} = -1.0\%$	$\dfrac{\$53}{\$365{,}561} = 0.0\%$
Gross profit rate	$\dfrac{\$146{,}073^*}{\$464{,}876} = 31.4\%$	$\dfrac{\$109{,}804^{**}}{\$365{,}561} = 30.0\%$

*$464,876 − $318,803   **$365,561 − $255,757

MEC's profit margin (income per dollar of sales) was 0% in 2015 and then declined to a negative 1% in 2016. This is well below both REI's (1.5%) and Dick's (3.6%). Thus, MEC is not as effective at turning its sales into net income as these two competitors.

MEC's gross profit rate increased from 30.0% to 31.4%. This suggests that its ability to maintain its markup above its cost of goods sold increased during this period. MEC's gross profit rate of 31.4% is lower than REI's (42.9%) but slightly higher than Dick's (29.9%). Dick's gross profit is depressed by the fact that it sells many low-margin products. REI is superior to MEC both in its ability to maintain its markup above its costs of goods sold (its gross profit rate) and in its ability to control operating costs (its profit margin).

Appendix 5A   Periodic Inventory System

LEARNING OBJECTIVE *7
Record purchases and sales of inventory under a periodic inventory system.

As described in this chapter, companies may use one of two basic systems of accounting for inventories: (1) the perpetual inventory system or (2) the periodic inventory system. In the chapter, we focused on the characteristics of the perpetual inventory system. In this appendix, we discuss and illustrate the **periodic inventory system**. One key difference between the two systems is the point at which the company computes cost of goods sold. For a visual reminder of this difference, you may want to refer back to Illustration 5.5.

Recording Merchandise Transactions

In a **periodic inventory system**, companies record revenues from the sale of merchandise when sales are made, just as in a perpetual system. Unlike the perpetual system, however, companies **do not attempt on the date of sale to record the cost of the merchandise sold**. Instead, they take a physical inventory count at the **end of the period** to determine (1) the cost of the merchandise then on hand and (2) the cost of the goods sold during the period. And, **under a periodic system, companies record purchases of merchandise in the Purchases account rather than the Inventory account**. Purchase returns and allowances, purchase discounts, and freight costs on purchases are recorded in separate accounts.

To illustrate the recording of merchandise transactions under a periodic inventory system, we will use purchase/sale transactions between PW Audio Supply, Inc. and Sauk Stereo, as illustrated for the perpetual inventory system in this chapter.

Recording Purchases of Merchandise

On the basis of the sales invoice (Illustration 5.6) and receipt of the merchandise ordered from PW Audio Supply, Sauk Stereo records the $3,800 purchase as follows.

May 4	Purchases	3,800	
	Accounts Payable		3,800
	(To record goods purchased on account from PW Audio Supply)		

Purchases is a temporary account whose normal balance is a debit.

Freight Costs

When the purchaser directly incurs the freight costs, it debits the account Freight-In (or Transportation-In). For example, if Sauk Stereo pays Public Freight Company $150 for freight charges on its purchase from PW Audio Supply on May 6, the entry on Sauk Stereo's books is as follows.

May 6	Freight-In (Transportation-In)	150	
	Cash		150
	(To record payment of freight on goods purchased)		

Like Purchases, Freight-In is a temporary account whose normal balance is a debit. **Freight-In is part of cost of goods purchased.** The reason is that cost of goods purchased should include any freight charges necessary to bring the goods to the purchaser. Freight costs are not subject to a purchase discount. Purchase discounts apply on the invoice cost of the merchandise.

Purchase Returns and Allowances

Sauk Stereo returns goods costing $300 to PW Audio Supply and prepares the following entry to recognize the return.

May 8	Accounts Payable	300	
	Purchase Returns and Allowances		300
	(To record return of goods purchased from PW Audio Supply)		

Purchase Returns and Allowances is a temporary account whose normal balance is a credit.

Purchase Discounts

On May 14, Sauk Stereo pays the balance due on account to PW Audio Supply, taking the 2% cash discount allowed by PW Audio Supply for payment within 10 days. Sauk Stereo records the payment and discount as follows.

May 14	Accounts Payable ($3,800 − $300)	3,500	
	Purchase Discounts ($3,500 × .02)		70
	Cash		3,430
	(To record payment within the discount period)		

Purchase Discounts is a temporary account whose normal balance is a credit.

Recording Sales of Merchandise

The seller, PW Audio Supply, records the sale of $3,800 of merchandise to Sauk Stereo on May 4 (sales invoice No. 731, Illustration 5.6) as follows.

May 4	Accounts Receivable	3,800	
	Sales Revenue		3,800
	(To record credit sale to Sauk Stereo per invoice #731)		

Sales Returns and Allowances

To record the returned goods received from Sauk Stereo on May 8, PW Audio Supply records the $300 sales return as follows.

May 8	Sales Returns and Allowances	300	
	Accounts Receivable		300
	(To record credit granted to Sauk Stereo		
	for returned goods)		

Sales Discounts

On May 14, PW Audio Supply receives payment of $3,430 on account from Sauk Stereo. PW Audio Supply honors the 2% cash discount and records the payment of Sauk Stereo's account receivable in full as follows.

May 14	Cash	3,430	
	Sales Discounts ($3,500 × .02)	70	
	Accounts Receivable ($3,800 − $300)		3,500
	(To record collection within 2/10, n/30		
	discount period from Sauk Stereo)		

Comparison of Entries—Perpetual vs. Periodic

Entries on Sauk Stereo's Books

Transaction		Perpetual Inventory System			Periodic Inventory System		

May 4	Purchase of merchandise on credit.	Inventory
		    Accounts Payable
			3,800	3,800	Purchases
					    Accounts Payable
						3,800	3,800

May 6	Freight costs on purchases.	Inventory
		    Cash
			150	150	Freight-In
					    Cash
						150	150

May 8	Purchase returns and allowances.	Accounts Payable
		    Inventory
			300	300	Accounts Payable
					    Purchase Returns
					    and Allowances
						300	300

May 14	Payment on account with a discount.	Accounts Payable
		    Cash
		    Inventory
			3,500	3,430
				70
					Accounts Payable
					    Cash
					    Purchase Discounts
						3,500	3,430
							70

Entries on PW Audio Supply's Books

Transaction		Perpetual Inventory System			Periodic Inventory System		

May 4	Sale of merchandise on credit.	Accounts Receivable
		    Sales Revenue
			3,800	3,800	Accounts Receivable
					    Sales Revenue
						3,800	3,800

		Cost of Goods Sold Inventory	2,400	2,400	No entry for cost of goods sold		

May 8	Return of merchandise sold.	Sales Returns and Allowances
		    Accounts Receivable
			300	300	Sales Returns and Allowances
					    Accounts Receivable
						300	300

		Inventory Cost of Goods Sold	140	140	No entry		

May 14	Cash received on account with a discount.	Cash
		Sales Discounts
		    Accounts Receivable
			3,430
			70
				3,500	Cash
					Sales Discounts
					    Accounts Receivable
						3,430
						70
							3,500

Appendix 5B | Adjusting Entries for Credit Sales with Returns and Allowances

> **LEARNING OBJECTIVE *8**
> Prepare adjusting entries for credit sales with returns and allowances.

Sales returns are common for many types of businesses. As noted in the chapter, at the end of the accounting period a company must estimate the amount of goods sold during the period that will be returned in subsequent periods and accrue for this amount. To illustrate the accounting for an estimated return situation, assume that Rainbow Company began operations on January 1, 2022. On January 12, 2022, Rainbow sells 100 pairs of shoes for $100 each **on account** to Tanner Inc. Rainbow allows Tanner to return any unused shoes within 45 days of purchase. The cost of each product is $60. Rainbow records the sale as follows.

Accounts Receivable	10,000	
Sales Revenue (100 × $100)		10,000
Cost of Goods Sold	6,000	
Inventory (100 × $60)		6,000
(To record the sale of shoes and related cost of goods sold)		

On January 24, Tanner returns two pairs of shoes because they were the wrong color. Rainbow records the return as follows.

Sales Returns and Allowances	200	
Accounts Receivable (2 × $100)		200
Inventory	120	
Cost of Goods Sold (2 × $60)		120
(To record the return of shoes)		

On January 31, Rainbow prepares monthly financial statements and estimates that it is likely that only one more pair of shoes will be returned. Rainbow records two adjusting entries to account for this estimate. The first entry requires a debit to Sales Returns and Allowances and a credit to Allowance for Sales Returns and Allowances for the selling price of the estimated returns. The second entry requires a debit to Estimated Inventory Returns and a credit to Cost of Goods Sold for the cost of the estimated returns. Rainbow makes the following adjusting entries to account for expected return at January 31, 2022.

Sales Returns and Allowances	100	
Allowance for Sales Returns and Allowances (1 × $100)		100
(To record expected sales return)		
Estimated Inventory Returns	60	
Cost of Goods Sold (1 × $60)		60
(To record the expected return of shoes and related reduction in Cost of Goods Sold)		

The Allowance for Sales Returns and Allowances account is a contra account to Accounts Receivable. The Estimated Inventory Returns account will generally be added to the Inventory account at the end of the reporting period.

On February 18, Tanner returns another pair of shoes to Rainbow. Assuming that Tanner has not already paid Rainbow for the shoes, Rainbow records the entry as follows.

Allowance for Sales Returns and Allowances	100	
Accounts Receivable (1 × $100)		100
Inventory	60	
Estimated Inventory Returns (1 × $60)		60
(To record the return of shoes)		

If Tanner had initially paid for the shoes in cash or paid its balance due on a credit purchase prior to returning the shoes on February 18, Rainbow would credit Accounts Payable rather than Accounts Receivable as shown in the following entry.

Allowance for Sales Returns and Allowances	100	
Accounts Payable (1 × $100)		100
Inventory	60	
Estimated Inventory Returns (1 × $60)		60
(To record the return of shoes)		

Review and Practice

Learning Objectives Review

1 Describe merchandising operations and inventory systems.

Because of the presence of inventory, a merchandising company has sales revenue, cost of goods sold, and gross profit. To account for inventory, a merchandising company must choose between a perpetual inventory system and a periodic inventory system.

2 Record purchases under a perpetual inventory system.

The Inventory account is debited for all purchases of merchandise and for freight costs, and it is credited for purchase discounts and purchase returns and allowances.

3 Record sales under a perpetual inventory system.

When inventory is sold, Accounts Receivable (or Cash) is debited and Sales Revenue is credited for the selling price of the merchandise. At the same time, Cost of Goods Sold is debited and Inventory is credited for the cost of inventory items sold. Separate contra revenue accounts are maintained for Sales Returns and Allowances and Sales Discounts. These accounts are debited as needed to record returns, allowances, or discounts related to the sale.

4 Prepare a multiple-step income statement and a comprehensive income statement.

In a single-step income statement, companies classify all data under two categories, revenues or expenses, and net income is determined in one step. A multiple-step income statement shows numerous steps in determining net income, including results of nonoperating activities. A comprehensive income statement adds or subtracts any items of other comprehensive income to net income to arrive at comprehensive income.

5 Determine cost of goods sold under a periodic inventory system.

The periodic system uses multiple accounts to keep track of transactions that affect inventory. To determine cost of goods sold, first calculate cost of goods purchased by adjusting purchases for returns, allowances, discounts, and freight-in. Then calculate cost of goods sold by adding cost of goods purchased to beginning inventory and subtracting ending inventory.

6 Compute and analyze gross profit rate and profit margin.

Profitability is affected by gross profit, as measured by the gross profit rate, and by management's ability to control costs, as measured by the profit margin.

*7 Record purchases and sales of inventory under a periodic inventory system.

To record purchases, entries are required for (a) cash and credit purchases, (b) purchase returns and allowances, (c) purchase discounts, and (d) freight costs. To record sales, entries are required for (a) cash and credit sales, (b) sales returns and allowances, and (c) sales discounts.

*8 Prepare adjusting entries for credit sales with returns and allowances.

Adjusting credit sales for returns and allowances requires two entries at the end of the period. The first entry requires a debit to Sales Returns and Allowances and a credit to Allowance for Sales Returns and Allowances for the selling price of the estimated returns. The second entry requires a debit to Estimated Inventory Returns and a credit to Cost of Goods Sold for the cost of the estimated returns. The Allowance for Sales Returns and Allowances account is a contra account to Accounts Receivable. The Estimated Inventory Returns will generally be added to the Inventory account at the end of the period.

Decision Tools Review

Decision Checkpoints	Info Needed for Decision	Tool to Use for Decision	How to Evaluate Results
Is the price of goods keeping pace with changes in the cost of inventory?	Gross profit and net sales	Gross profit rate = $\dfrac{\text{Gross profit}}{\text{Net sales}}$	Higher ratio suggests the average margin between selling price and inventory cost is increasing. Too high a margin may result in lost sales.
Is the company maintaining an adequate margin between sales and expenses?	Net income and net sales	Profit margin = $\dfrac{\text{Net income}}{\text{Net sales}}$	Higher value suggests favorable return on each dollar of sales.

Glossary Review

Comprehensive income An income measure that includes gains and losses that are excluded from the determination of net income. (p. 5-19).

Comprehensive income statement A statement that presents items that are not included in the determination of net income, referred to as other comprehensive income. (p. 5-19).

Contra revenue account An account that is offset against a revenue account on the income statement. (p. 5-13).

Cost of goods sold The total cost of merchandise sold during the period. (p. 5-3).

FOB destination Freight terms indicating that ownership of goods remains with the seller until the goods reach the buyer. (p. 5-8).

FOB shipping point Freight terms indicating that ownership of goods passes to the buyer when the public carrier accepts the goods from the seller. (p. 5-8).

Gross profit The excess of net sales over the cost of goods sold. (p. 5-17).

Gross profit rate Gross profit expressed as a percentage by dividing the amount of gross profit by net sales. (p. 5-22).

Income tax expense The product of a company's income before income taxes and its corporate income tax rate. (p. 5-18).

Net sales Sales less sales returns and allowances and sales discounts. (p. 5-17).

Periodic inventory system An inventory system in which a company does not maintain detailed records of goods on hand throughout the period and determines the cost of goods sold only at the end of an accounting period. (p. 5-5).

Perpetual inventory system A detailed inventory system in which a company maintains the cost of each inventory item, and the records continuously show the inventory that should be on hand. (p. 5-4).

Profit margin Measures the percentage of each dollar of sales that results in net income, computed by dividing net income by net sales. (p. 5-23).

Purchase allowance A deduction made to the selling price of merchandise, granted by the seller, so that the buyer will keep the merchandise. (p. 5-9).

Purchase discount A cash discount claimed by a buyer for prompt payment of a balance due. (p. 5-9).

Purchase invoice A document that provides support for each purchase. (p. 5-7).

Purchase return A return of goods from the buyer to the seller for cash or credit. (p. 5-9).

Quality of earnings ratio A measure used to indicate the extent to which a company's earnings provide a full and transparent depiction of its performance; computed as net cash provided by operating activities divided by net income. (p. 5-24).

Sales discount A reduction given by a seller for prompt payment of a credit sale. (p. 5-13).

Sales invoice A document that provides support for each sale. (p. 5-11).

Sales returns and allowances Transactions in which the seller either accepts goods back from the purchaser (a return) or grants a reduction in the purchase price (an allowance) so that the buyer will keep the goods. (p. 5-12).

Sales revenue Primary source of revenue for a merchandising company. (p. 5-3).

Practice Multiple-Choice Questions

1. (LO 1) Which of the following statements about a periodic inventory system is **true**?

   a. Companies determine cost of goods sold only at the end of the accounting period.
   b. Companies continuously maintain detailed records of the cost of each inventory purchase and sale.
   c. The periodic system provides better control over inventories than a perpetual system.
   d. The increased use of computerized systems has increased the use of the periodic system.

2. (LO 2) Under a perpetual inventory system, when goods are purchased for resale by a company:

   a. purchases on account are debited to Inventory.
   b. purchases on account are debited to Purchases.
   c. purchase returns are debited to Purchase Returns and Allowances.
   d. freight costs are debited to Freight-Out.

3. (LO 3) Which sales accounts normally have a debit balance?

   a. Sales Discounts.   c. Both (a) and (b).
   b. Sales Returns and Allowances.   d. Neither (a) nor (b).

4. (LO 3) A company makes a credit sale of $750 on June 13, terms 2/10, n/30, on which it grants a return of $50 on June 16. What amount is received as payment in full on June 23?

a. $700.   c. $685.
b. $686.   d. $650.

5. (LO 3) To record the sale of goods for cash in a perpetual inventory system:

a. only one journal entry is necessary to record cost of goods sold and reduction of inventory.

b. only one journal entry is necessary to record the receipt of cash and the sales revenue.

c. two journal entries are necessary: one to record the receipt of cash and sales revenue, and one to record the cost of goods sold and reduction of inventory.

d. two journal entries are necessary: one to record the receipt of cash and reduction of inventory, and one to record the cost of goods sold and sales revenue.

6. (LO 4) Gross profit will result if:

a. operating expenses are less than net income.
b. net sales are greater than operating expenses.
c. net sales are greater than cost of goods sold.
d. operating expenses are greater than cost of goods sold.

7. (LO 4) If net sales are $400,000, cost of goods sold is $310,000, and operating expenses are $60,000, what is the gross profit?

a. $30,000.   c. $340,000.
b. $90,000.   d. $400,000.

8. (LO 4) The multiple-step income statement for a merchandising company shows each of these features **except**:

a. gross profit.
b. cost of goods sold.
c. a sales section.
d. an investing activities section.

9. (LO 5) If beginning inventory is $60,000, cost of goods purchased is $380,000, and ending inventory is $50,000, what is cost of goods sold under a periodic system?

a. $390,000.   c. $330,000.
b. $370,000.   d. $420,000.

10. (LO 5) Bufford Corporation had reported the following amounts at December 31, 2022: sales revenue $184,000, ending inventory $11,600, beginning inventory $17,200, purchases $60,400, purchase discounts $3,000, purchase returns and allowances $1,100, freight-in $600, and freight-out $900. Calculate the cost of goods available for sale.

a. $69,400.   c. $56,900.
b. $74,100.   d. $197,700.

11. (LO 6) Which of the following would affect the gross profit rate? (Assume sales remains constant.)

a. An increase in advertising expense.
b. A decrease in depreciation expense.
c. An increase in cost of goods sold.
d. A decrease in insurance expense.

12. (LO 6) The gross profit rate is equal to:

a. net income divided by sales.
b. cost of goods sold divided by sales.
c. net sales minus cost of goods sold, divided by net sales.
d. sales minus cost of goods sold, divided by cost of goods sold.

13. (LO 6) During the year ended December 31, 2022, Bjornstad Corporation had the following results: net sales $267,000, cost of goods sold $107,000, net income $92,400, operating expenses $55,400, and net cash provided by operating activities $108,950. What was the company's profit margin?

a. 40%.   c. 20.5%.
b. 60%.   d. 34.6%.

14. (LO 6) A quality of earnings ratio:

a. is computed as net income divided by net cash provided by operating activities.
b. that is less than 1 indicates that a company might be using aggressive accounting tactics.
c. that is greater than 1 indicates that a company might be using aggressive accounting tactics.
d. is computed as net cash provided by operating activities divided by total assets.

*15. (LO 7) When goods are purchased for resale by a company using a periodic inventory system:

a. purchases on account are debited to Inventory.
b. purchases on account are debited to Purchases.
c. purchase returns are debited to Purchase Returns and Allowances.
d. freight costs are debited to Purchases.

Solutions

1. a. Under the periodic inventory system, cost of goods sold is determined only at the end of the accounting period. The other choices are incorrect because (b) detailed records of the cost of each inventory purchase and sale are maintained continuously when a perpetual, not periodic, system is used; (c) the perpetual system provides better control over inventories than a periodic system; and (d) the increased use of computerized systems has increased the use of the perpetual, not periodic, system.

2. a. Under a perpetual inventory system, purchases on account are debited to the Inventory account. Choices (b) and (c) are incorrect because Purchases and Purchase Returns and Allowances are not used in a perpetual inventory system. Choice (d) is incorrect because freight costs incurred for purchased goods are debited to the Inventory account, not the Freight-Out account.

3. c. Both Sales Discounts and Sales Returns and Allowances normally have a debit balance. Choices (a) and (b) are both correct, but (c) is the better answer. Choice (d) is incorrect as both (a) and (b) are correct.

4. b. The full amount of $686 is paid within 10 days of the purchase {($750 − $50) − [($750 − $50) × 2%]}. The other choices are incorrect because (a) does not consider the discount of $14; (c) the amount of the discount is based upon the amount after the return is granted ($700 × 2%), not the amount before the return of merchandise ($750 × 2%); and (d) does not constitute payment in full on June 23.

5. c. Two journal entries are necessary: one to record the receipt of cash and sales revenue, and one to record the cost of goods sold and reduction of inventory. The other choices are incorrect because (a) only considers the recognition of the expense and ignores the revenue, (b) only considers the recognition of revenue and leaves out the expense or cost of merchandise sold, and (d) the receipt of cash and sales revenue, not reduction of inventory, are paired together, and the cost of goods sold and reduction of inventory, not sales revenue, are paired together.

6. c. Gross profit will result if net sales are greater than cost of goods sold. The other choices are incorrect because (a) operating expenses and net income are not used in the computation of gross profit; (b) gross profit results when net sales are greater than cost of goods sold, not operating expenses; and (d) gross profit results when net sales, not operating expenses, are greater than cost of goods sold.

7. b. Gross profit = Net sales ($400,000) − Cost of goods sold ($310,000) = $90,000, not (a) $30,000, (c) $340,000, or (d) $400,000.

8. d. An investing activities section appears on the statement of cash flows, not on a multiple-step income statement. Choices (a) gross profit, (b) cost of goods sold, and (c) a sales section are all features of a multiple-step income statement.

9. a. Beginning inventory ($60,000) + Cost of goods purchased ($380,000) − Ending inventory ($50,000) = Cost of goods sold ($390,000), not (b) $370,000, (c) $330,000, or (d) $420,000.

10. b. Beginning inventory ($17,200) + Purchases ($60,400) − Purchases discounts ($3,000) − Purchase returns and allowances ($1,100) + Freight-in ($600) = Cost of goods available for sale ($74,100). The other choices are therefore incorrect.

11. c. Gross profit rate = Gross profit ÷ Net sales. Therefore, any changes in sale revenue, sales returns and allowances, sales discounts, or cost of goods sold will affect the ratio. Changes in (a) advertising expense, (b) depreciation expense, or (d) insurance expense will not affect the computation of the gross profit rate.

12. c. Gross profit rate = Gross profit (Net sales − Cost of goods sold) ÷ Net sales. The other choices are therefore incorrect.

13. d. Net income ($92,400) ÷ Net sales ($267,000) = Profit margin of 34.6%, not (a) 40%, (b) 60%, or (c) 20.5%.

14. b. A quality of earnings ratio that is less than 1 indicates that a company might be using aggressive accounting tactics. The other choices are incorrect because (a) Quality of earnings = Net cash provided by operating activities ÷ Net income, not vice versa; (c) a ratio that is significantly greater than 1 suggests that a company is using conservative accounting techniques, and (d) Quality of earnings = Net cash provided by operating activities ÷ Net income (not Total assets).

*__15. b.__ Purchases for resale are debited to the Purchases account. The other choices are incorrect because (a) purchases on account are debited to Purchases, not Inventory; (c) Purchase Returns and Allowances are always credited; and (d) freight costs are debited to Freight-In, not Purchases.

Practice Brief Exercises

1. (LO 1, 4) Presented below are the components in determining cost of goods sold for (a) Frazier Company, (b) Todd Company, and (c) Abreu Enterprises. Determine the missing amounts.

Compute the missing amounts in determining cost of goods sold.

	Beginning Inventory	Purchases	Cost of Goods Available for Sale	Ending Inventory	Cost of Goods Sold
a.	$120,000	$150,000	?	?	$160,000
b.	$ 50,000	?	$125,000	$45,000	?
c.	?	$220,000	$330,000	$61,000	?

Solution

1. **a.** Cost of goods available for sale = $120,000 + $150,000 = $270,000
   Ending inventory = $270,000 − $160,000 = $110,000

   b. Purchases = $125,000 − $50,000 = $75,000
   Cost of goods sold = $125,000 − $45,000 = $80,000

   c. Beginning inventory = $330,000 − $220,000 = $110,000
   Cost of goods sold = $330,000 − $61,000 = $269,000

2. (LO 2) Prepare the journal entries to record the following transactions on Robertson Company's books using a perpetual inventory system.

Journalize purchase transactions.

a. On March 2, Melky Company sold $800,000 of merchandise to Robertson Company, terms 2/10, n/30.

b. On March 6, Robertson Company returned $100,000 of the merchandise purchased on March 2.

c. On March 12, Robertson Company paid the balance due to Melky Company.

Solution

2. a.	Inventory	800,000	
	Accounts Payable		800,000
b.	Accounts Payable	100,000	
	Inventory		100,000
c.	Accounts Payable ($800,000 − $100,000)	700,000	
	Inventory ($700,000 × 2%)		14,000
	Cash ($700,000 − $14,000)		686,000

Journalize sales transactions.

3. (LO 3) Prepare the journal entries to record the following transactions on Wendel Company's books using a perpetual inventory system.

a. On March 2, Wendel Company sold $700,000 of merchandise to Krista Company, terms 2/10, n/30. The cost of the merchandise sold was $460,000.

b. On March 6, Krista Company returned $80,000 of the merchandise purchased on March 2. The cost of the merchandise returned was $54,000.

c. On March 12, Wendel Company received the balance due from Krista Company.

Solution

3. a.	March 2		Accounts Receivable	700,000	
			Sales Revenue		700,000
	2		Cost of Goods Sold	460,000	
			Inventory		460,000
b.	6		Sales Returns and Allowances	80,000	
			Accounts Receivable		80,000
	6		Inventory	54,000	
			Cost of Goods Sold		54,000
c.	12		Cash ($620,000 − $12,400)	607,600	
			Sales Discounts ($620,000 × 2%)	12,400	
			Accounts Receivable ($700,000 − $80,000)		620,000

Compute net sales, gross profit, income from operations, and gross profit rate.

4. (LO 4, 6) Assume Yoan Company has the following reported amounts: Sales revenue $400,000, Sales discounts $10,000, Cost of goods sold $234,000, and Operating expenses $60,000. Compute the following: (a) net sales, (b) gross profit, (c) income from operations, and (d) gross profit rate. (Round to one decimal place.)

Solution

4. a. Net sales = $400,000 − $10,000 = $390,000

b. Gross profit = $390,000 − $234,000 = $156,000

c. Income from operations = $156,000 − $60,000 = $96,000

d. Gross profit rate = $156,000 ÷ $390,000 = 40%

Practice Exercises

Prepare purchase and sales entries.

1. (LO 2, 3) On June 10, Vareen Company purchased $8,000 of merchandise from Harrah Company, FOB shipping point, terms 3/10, n/30. Vareen pays the freight costs of $400 on June 11. Damaged goods totaling $300 are returned to Harrah for credit on June 12. The fair value of these goods is $70. On June 19, Vareen pays Harrah Company in full, less the purchase discount. Both companies use a perpetual inventory system.

Instructions

a. Prepare separate entries for each transaction on the books of Vareen Company.

b. Prepare separate entries for each transaction for Harrah Company. The merchandise purchased by Vareen on June 10 had cost Harrah $4,800.

Solution

1. a.

June 10	Inventory		8,000	
	Accounts Payable			8,000
11	Inventory		400	
	Cash			400
12	Accounts Payable		300	
	Inventory			300
19	Accounts Payable ($8,000 – $300)		7,700	
	Inventory ($7,700 × 3%)			231
	Cash ($7,700 – $231)			7,469

b.

June 10	Accounts Receivable		8,000	
	Sales Revenue			8,000
	Cost of Goods Sold		4,800	
	Inventory			4,800
12	Sales Returns and Allowances		300	
	Accounts Receivable			300
	Inventory		70	
	Cost of Goods Sold			70
19	Cash ($7,700 – $231)		7,469	
	Sales Discounts ($7,700 × 3%)		231	
	Accounts Receivable ($8,000 – $300)			7,700

2. (LO 4) In its income statement for the year ended December 31, 2022, Marten Company reported the following condensed data.

Prepare multiple-step and single-step income statements.

Interest expense	$ 70,000	Net sales	$2,200,000
Operating expenses	725,000	Interest revenue	25,000
Cost of goods sold	1,300,000	Loss on disposal of plant assets	17,000
		Income tax expense	10,000

Instructions

a. Prepare a multiple-step income statement.
b. Prepare a single-step income statement.

Solution

2. a.

Marten Company
Income Statement
For the Year Ended December 31, 2022

Net sales		$2,200,000
Cost of goods sold		1,300,000
Gross profit		900,000
Operating expenses		725,000
Income from operations		175,000
Other revenues and gains		
Interest revenue		25,000
Other expenses and losses		
Interest expense	$70,000	
Loss on disposal of plant assets	17,000	(87,000)
Income before income taxes		113,000
Income tax expense		10,000
Net income		$ 103,000

b.

Marten Company
Income Statement
For the Year Ended December 31, 2022

Revenues		
Net sales		$2,200,000
Interest revenue		25,000
Total revenues		2,225,000
Expenses		
Cost of goods sold	$1,300,000	
Operating expenses	725,000	
Interest expense	70,000	
Loss on disposal of plant assets	17,000	
Income tax expense	10,000	
Total expenses		2,122,000
Net income		$ 103,000

Practice Problem

Prepare a multiple-step income statement.

(LO 4) The adjusted trial balance for the year ended December 31, 2022, for Dykstra Company is shown below.

Dykstra Company
Adjusted Trial Balance
For the Year Ended December 31, 2022

	Debit	Credit
Cash	$ 14,500	
Accounts Receivable	11,100	
Inventory	29,000	
Prepaid Insurance	2,500	
Equipment	95,000	
Accumulated Depreciation—Equipment		$ 18,000
Notes Payable		25,000
Accounts Payable		10,600
Common Stock		70,000
Retained Earnings		11,000
Dividends	12,000	
Sales Revenue		536,800
Sales Returns and Allowances	6,700	
Sales Discounts	5,000	
Cost of Goods Sold	363,400	
Freight-Out	7,600	
Advertising Expense	12,000	
Salaries and Wages Expense	56,000	
Utilities Expense	18,000	
Rent Expense	24,000	
Depreciation Expense	9,000	
Insurance Expense	4,500	
Interest Expense	3,600	
Interest Revenue		2,500
	$673,900	$673,900

Instructions

Prepare a multiple-step income statement for Dykstra Company. Assume a tax rate of 30%.

Solution

Dykstra Company
Income Statement
For the Year Ended December 31, 2022

Sales		
Sales revenue		$536,800
Less: Sales returns and allowances	$ 6,700	
Sales discounts	5,000	11,700
Net sales		525,100
Cost of goods sold		363,400
Gross profit		161,700
Operating expenses		
Salaries and wages expense	56,000	
Rent expense	24,000	
Utilities expense	18,000	
Advertising expense	12,000	
Depreciation expense	9,000	
Freight-out	7,600	
Insurance expense	4,500	
Total operating expenses		131,100
Income from operations		30,600
Other revenues and gains		
Interest revenue		2,500
Other expenses and losses		
Interest expense		3,600
Income before income taxes		29,500
Income tax expense		8,850
Net income		$ 20,650

WileyPLUS

Brief Exercises, DO IT! Exercises, Exercises, Problems, and many additional resources are available for practice in WileyPLUS.

Note: All asterisked Questions, Exercises, and Problems relate to material in the appendices to the chapter.

Questions

1. **a.** "The steps in the accounting cycle for a merchandising company differ from the steps in the accounting cycle for a service company." Do you agree or disagree?
   b. Is the measurement of net income in a merchandising company conceptually the same as in a service company? Explain.

2. How do the components of revenues and expenses differ between a merchandising company and a service company?

3. Maria Lopez, CEO of Sales Bin Stores, is considering a recommendation made by both the company's purchasing manager and director of finance that the company should invest in a sophisticated new perpetual inventory system to replace its periodic system. Explain the primary difference between the two systems, and discuss the potential benefits of a perpetual inventory system.

4. **a.** Explain the income measurement process in a merchandising company.
   b. How does income measurement differ between a merchandising company and a service company?

5. Waymon Co. has net sales of $100,000, cost of goods sold of $70,000, and operating expenses of $18,000. What is its gross profit?

6. Masie Ascot believes revenues from credit sales may be recorded before they are collected in cash. Do you agree? Explain.

7. **a.** What is the primary source document for recording (1) cash sales and (2) credit sales?
   b. Using XXs for amounts, give the journal entry for each of the transactions in part (a), assuming perpetual inventory.

8. A credit sale is made on July 10 for $900, terms 1/15, n/30. On July 12, the purchaser returns $100 of goods for credit. Give the journal entry on July 19 to record the receipt of the balance due within the discount period.

9. As the end of Smyle Company's fiscal year approached, it became clear that the company had considerable excess inventory. Marvin Ross, the head of marketing and sales, ordered salespeople to "add 20% more units to each order that you ship. The customers can always ship the extra back next period if they decide they don't want it. We've got to do it to meet this year's sales goal." Discuss the accounting implications of Marvin's action.

10. To encourage bookstores to buy a broader range of book titles and to discourage price discounting, the publishing industry allows bookstores to return unsold books to the publisher. This results in very significant returns each year. To ensure proper recognition of revenues, how should publishing companies account for these returns?

11. Goods costing $1,900 are purchased on account on July 15 with credit terms of 2/10, n/30. On July 18, the purchaser receives a $300 credit from the supplier for damaged goods. Give the journal entry on July 24 to record payment of the balance due within the discount period.

12. Scribe Company reports net sales of $800,000, gross profit of $560,000, and net income of $230,000. What are its operating expenses?

13. Mai Company has always provided its customers with payment terms of 1/10, n/30. Members of its sale force have commented that competitors are offering customers 2/10, n/45. Explain what these terms mean, and discuss the implications to Mai of switching its payment terms to those of its competitors.

14. In its year-end earnings announcement press release, Ransome Corp. announced that its earnings increased by $15 million relative to the previous year. This represented a 20% increase. Inspection of its income statement reveals that the company reported a $20 million gain under "Other revenues and gains" from the sale of one of its factories. Discuss the implications of this gain from the perspective of a potential investor.

15. Identify the distinguishing features of an income statement for a merchandising company.

16. Why is the normal operating cycle for a merchandising company likely to be longer than for a service company?

17. What title does **Apple** use for gross profit? By how much did its total gross profit change, and in what direction, for the year ended September 30, 2017?

18. What merchandising account(s) will appear in the post-closing trial balance?

19. What types of businesses are most likely to use a perpetual inventory system?

20. Identify the accounts that are added to or deducted from purchases to determine the cost of goods purchased under a periodic system. For each account, indicate (a) whether it is added or deducted, and (b) its normal balance.

21. In the following cases, use a periodic inventory system to identify the item(s) designated by the letters X and Y.
   a. Purchases − X − Y = Net purchases.
   b. Cost of goods purchased − Net purchases = X.
   c. Beginning inventory + X = Cost of goods available for sale.
   d. Cost of goods available for sale − Cost of goods sold = X.

22. What two ratios measure factors that affect profitability?

23. What factors affect a company's gross profit rate—that is, what can cause the gross profit rate to increase and what can cause it to decrease?

24. Earl Massey, director of marketing, wants to reduce the selling price of his company's products by 15% to increase market share. He says, "I know this will reduce our gross profit rate, but the increased number of units sold will make up for the lost margin." Before this action is taken, what other factors does the company need to consider?

25. Mark Coney is considering investing in Wiggles Pet Food Company. Wiggles' net income increased considerably during the most recent year even though many other companies in the same industry reported disappointing earnings. Mark wants to know whether the company's earnings provide a reasonable depiction of its results. What initial step can Mark take to help determine whether he needs to investigate further?

*26. On July 15, a company purchases on account goods costing $1,900, with credit terms of 2/10, n/30. On July 18, the company receives a $400 credit memo from the supplier for damaged goods. Give the journal entry on July 24 to record payment of the balance due within the discount period assuming a periodic inventory system.

*27. What are the steps to record an end of period adjustment for credit sales with returns and allowances?

*28. What treatment do Allowance for Sales Returns and Allowances and the Estimated Inventory Returns receive in the financial statements?

Brief Exercises

Compute missing amounts in determining cost of goods sold.

BE5.1 (LO 1), AP Presented below are the components in determining cost of goods sold. Determine the missing amounts.

Beginning Inventory	Purchases	Cost of Goods Available for Sale	Ending Inventory	Cost of Goods Sold
$80,000	$100,000	(a)	(b)	$120,000
$50,000	(c)	$115,000	$35,000	(d)
(e)	$110,000	$160,000	$29,000	(f)

Compute missing amounts in determining net income.

BE5.2 (LO 1, 4), AP Presented here are the components in Salas Company's income statement. Determine the missing amounts.

Sales Revenue	Cost of Goods Sold	Gross Profit	Operating Expenses	Net Income
$ 71,200	(a)	$ 30,000	(b)	$12,100
$108,000	$70,000	(c)	(d)	$29,500
(e)	$71,900	$109,600	$46,200	(f)

BE5.3 (LO 2, 3), AP Rita Company buys merchandise on account from Linus Company. The selling price of the goods is $900 and the cost of the goods sold is $590. Both companies use perpetual inventory systems. Journalize the transactions on the books of both companies.

Journalize perpetual inventory entries.

BE5.4 (LO 3), AP Prepare the journal entries to record the following transactions on Borst Company's books using a perpetual inventory system.

Journalize sales transactions.

a. On March 2, Borst Company sold $800,000 of merchandise to McLeena Company on account, terms 2/10, n/30. The cost of the merchandise sold was $540,000.

b. On March 6, McLeena Company returned $140,000 of the merchandise purchased on March 2. The cost of the merchandise returned was $94,000.

c. On March 12, Borst Company received the balance due from McLeena Company.

BE5.5 (LO 2), AP From the information in BE5.4, prepare the journal entries to record these transactions on McLeena Company's books under a perpetual inventory system.

Journalize purchase transactions.

BE5.6 (LO 4), AP Barto Company provides this information for the month ended October 31, 2022: sales on credit $300,000, cash sales $150,000, sales discounts $5,000, and sales returns and allowances $19,000. Prepare the sales section of the multiple-step income statement based on this information.

Prepare sales section of income statement.

BE 5.7 (LO 4), AP The following information is available for Rancid Corp. for the year ended December 31, 2022.

Prepare multiple-step income statement.

Other revenues and gains	$ 22,600	Sales revenue	$752,000
Other expenses and losses	3,400	Operating expenses	216,000
Cost of goods sold	286,000	Sales returns and allowances	10,000
Sales discounts	3,600		

Prepare a multiple-step income statement for Rancid Corp. The company has a tax rate of 25%.

BE5.8 (LO 4), AP Explain where each of these items would appear on a multiple-step income statement: gain on disposal of plant assets, cost of goods sold, depreciation expense, and sales returns and allowances.

Identify placement of items on a multiple-step income statement.

BE5.9 (LO 4), AP The following information relates to Karen Weigel Inc. for the year 2022.

Prepare a comprehensive income statement.

Retained earnings, January 1, 2022	$48,000	Advertising expense	$ 1,800
Dividends during 2022	5,000	Rent expense	10,400
Service revenue	62,500	Utilities expense	3,100
Salaries and wages expense	28,000	Other comprehensive income (net of tax)	400

After analyzing the data, (a) compute net income and (b) prepare a comprehensive income statement for the year ending December 31, 2022.

BE5.10 (LO 5), AP Silas Company sold goods with a total selling price of $800,000 during the year. It purchased goods for $380,000 and had beginning inventory of $67,000. A count of its ending inventory determined that goods on hand was $50,000. What was its cost of goods sold?

Determine cost of goods sold using basic periodic formula.

BE5.11 (LO 5), AP Assume that Spacey Company uses a periodic inventory system and has these account balances: Purchases $404,000, Purchase Returns and Allowances $13,000, Purchase Discounts $9,000, and Freight-In $16,000. Determine net purchases and cost of goods purchased.

Compute net purchases and cost of goods purchased.

BE5.12 (LO 5), AP Assume the same information as in BE5.11 and also that Spacey Company has beginning inventory of $60,000, ending inventory of $90,000, and net sales of $612,000. Determine the amounts to be reported for cost of goods sold and gross profit.

Compute cost of goods sold and gross profit.

BE5.13 (LO 6), AP Dublin Corporation reported net sales of $250,000, cost of goods sold of $150,000, operating expenses of $50,000, net income of $32,500, beginning total assets of $520,000, and ending total assets of $600,000. Calculate each of the following values and explain what they mean: (a) profit margin and (b) gross profit rate.

Calculate profitability ratios.

Calculate profitability ratios.

BE5.14 (LO 6), AP Garten Corporation reported net sales $800,000, cost of goods sold $520,000, operating expenses $210,000, and net income $68,000. Calculate the following values and explain what they mean: (a) profit margin and (b) gross profit rate.

Evaluate quality of earnings.

BE5.15 (LO 6), C Cabo Corporation reported net income of $346,000, cash of $67,800, and net cash provided by operating activities of $221,200. What does this suggest about the quality of the company's earnings? What further steps should be taken?

Journalize purchase transactions.

*BE5.16 (LO 7), AP Prepare the journal entries to record these transactions on Kimble Company's books using a periodic inventory system.

a. On March 2, Kimble Company purchased $800,000 of merchandise from Poe Company, terms 2/10, n/30.

b. On March 6, Kimble Company returned $95,000 of the merchandise purchased on March 2.

c. On March 12, Kimble Company paid the balance due to Poe Company.

Record entry for estimated sales returns.

*BE5.17 (LO 8), AP At December 31, 2022, Familla Corporation estimates that goods with a selling price of $1,400 and a cost of $650 that were sold on account during the current period will be returned during the next accounting period. Record the entry or entries required to adjust for this information.

DO IT! Exercises

Answer general questions about merchandisers.

DO IT! 5.1 (LO 1), C Indicate whether the following statements are true or false. If false, indicate how to correct the statement.

1. A merchandising company reports gross profit but a service company does not.

2. Under a periodic inventory system, a company determines the cost of goods sold each time a sale occurs.

3. A service company is likely to use accounts receivable but a merchandising company is not likely to do so.

4. Under a periodic inventory system, the cost of goods on hand at the beginning of the accounting period plus the cost of goods purchased less the cost of goods on hand at the end of the accounting period equals cost of goods sold.

Record transactions of purchasing company.

DO IT! 5.2 (LO 2), AP On October 5, Iverson Company buys merchandise on account from Lasse Company. The selling price of the goods is $5,000, and the cost to Lasse Company is $3,000. On October 8, Iverson returns defective goods with a selling price of $640 and a scrap value of $240. Record the transactions of Iverson Company, assuming a perpetual approach.

Record transactions of selling company.

DO IT! 5.3 (LO 3), AP Assume information similar to that in **DO IT!** 5.2. That is: On October 5, Iverson Company buys merchandise on account from Lasse Company. The selling price of the goods is $5,000, and the cost to Lasse Company is $3,000. On October 8, Iverson returns defective goods with a selling price of $640 and a scrap value of $240. Record the transactions on the books of Lasse Company, assuming a perpetual approach.

Prepare multiple-step income statement and comprehensive income statement.

DO IT! 5.4 (LO 4), AP The following information is available for Berlin Corp. for the year ended December 31, 2022:

Other revenues and gains	$ 12,700	Sales revenue	$592,000
Other expenses and losses	13,300	Operating expenses	186,000
Cost of goods sold	156,000	Sales returns and	
Other comprehensive income	5,400	allowances	40,000

Prepare a multiple-step income statement for Berlin Corp. and comprehensive income statement. The company has a tax rate of 30%. This rate also applies to the other comprehensive income.

Determine cost of goods sold using periodic system.

DO IT! 5.5 (LO 5), AP Clean Lake Corporation's accounting records show the following at year-end December 31, 2022:

Purchase Discounts	$ 5,900	Beginning Inventory	$31,720
Freight-In	8,400	Ending Inventory	27,950
Freight-Out	11,100	Purchase Returns and	
Purchases	162,500	Allowances	3,600

Assuming that Clean Lake Corporation uses the periodic system, compute (a) cost of goods purchased and (b) cost of goods sold.

DO IT! 5.6 (LO 6), AN Owen Wise, Inc. reported the following in its 2022 and 2021 income statements.

Compute and analyze profitability ratios.

	2022	2021
Net sales	$150,000	$120,000
Cost of goods sold	90,000	72,000
Operating expenses	32,000	16,000
Income tax expense	18,000	10,000
Net income	$ 10,000	$ 22,000

Determine the company's gross profit rate and profit margin for both years. Discuss the cause for changes in the ratios.

Exercises

E5.1 (LO 1), C Mr. Etemadi has prepared the following list of statements about service companies and merchandisers.

Answer general questions about merchandisers.

1. Measuring net income for a merchandiser is conceptually the same as for a service company.
2. For a merchandiser, sales less operating expenses is called gross profit.
3. For a merchandiser, the primary source of revenues is the sale of inventory.
4. Sales salaries and wages is an example of an operating expense.
5. The operating cycle of a merchandiser is the same as that of a service company.
6. In a perpetual inventory system, no detailed inventory records of goods on hand are maintained.
7. In a periodic inventory system, the cost of goods sold is determined only at the end of the accounting period.
8. A periodic inventory system provides better control over inventories than a perpetual system.

Instructions

Identify each statement as true or false. If false, indicate how to correct the statement.

E5.2 (LO 2), AP This information relates to Rice Co.

Journalize purchase transactions.

1. On April 5, purchased merchandise on account from Jax Company for $28,000, terms 2/10, n/30.
2. On April 6, paid freight costs of $700 on merchandise purchased from Jax.
3. On April 7, purchased equipment on account for $30,000.
4. On April 8, returned $3,600 of April 5 merchandise to Jax Company.
5. On April 15, paid the amount due to Jax Company in full.

Instructions

a. Prepare the journal entries to record the transactions listed above on Rice Co.'s books. Rice Co. uses a perpetual inventory system.

b. Assume that Rice Co. paid the balance due to Jax Company on May 4 instead of April 15. Prepare the journal entry to record this payment.

E5.3 (LO 2, 3), AP Assume that on September 1, **Office Depot** had an inventory that included a variety of calculators. The company uses a perpetual inventory system. During September, these transactions occurred.

Journalize perpetual inventory entries.

Sept. 6   Purchased calculators from Dragoo Co. at a total cost of $1,650, on account, terms n/30.
     9   Paid freight of $50 on calculators purchased from Dragoo Co.
    10   Returned calculators to Dragoo Co. for $66 credit because they did not meet specifications.
    12   Sold calculators costing $520 for $690 to Fryer Book Store, on account, terms n/30.
    14   Granted credit of $45 to Fryer Book Store for the return of one calculator that was not ordered. The calculator cost $34.
    20   Sold calculators costing $570 for $760 to Heasley Card Shop, on account, terms n/30.

Journalize sales transactions.

E5.4 (LO 3), AP The following transactions are for Alonzo Company.

1. On December 3, Alonzo Company sold $500,000 of merchandise to Arte Co., on account, terms 1/10, n/30. The cost of the merchandise sold was $330,000.
2. On December 8, Arte Co. was granted an allowance of $25,000 for merchandise purchased on December 3.
3. On December 13, Alonzo Company received the balance due from Arte Co.

Instructions

a. Prepare the journal entries to record these transactions on the books of Alonzo Company. Alonzo uses a perpetual inventory system.

b. Assume that Alonzo Company received the balance due from Arte Co. on January 2 of the following year instead of December 13. Prepare the journal entry to record the receipt of payment on January 2.

Journalize perpetual inventory entries.

E5.5 (LO 2, 3), AP On June 10, Pais Company purchased $9,000 of merchandise from McGiver Company, on account, terms 3/10, n/30. Pais pays the freight costs of $400 on June 11. Goods totaling $600 are returned to McGiver for credit on June 12. On June 19, Pais Company pays McGiver Company in full, less the purchase discount. Both companies use a perpetual inventory system.

Instructions

a. Prepare separate entries for each transaction on the books of Pais Company.

b. Prepare separate entries for each transaction for McGiver Company. The merchandise purchased by Pais on June 10 cost McGiver $5,000, and the goods returned cost McGiver $310.

Prepare sales section of income statement.

E5.6 (LO 4), AP The adjusted trial balance of Doqe Company shows these data pertaining to sales at the end of its fiscal year, October 31, 2022: Sales Revenue $900,000, Freight-Out $14,000, Sales Returns and Allowances $22,000, and Sales Discounts $13,500.

Instructions

Prepare the sales section of the income statement.

Prepare an income statement, a comprehensive income statement, and calculate profitability ratios.

E5.7 (LO 4, 6), AP Presented below is information for Lieu Co. for the month of January 2022.

Cost of goods sold	$212,000	Rent expense	$ 32,000
Freight-out	7,000	Sales discounts	8,000
Insurance expense	12,000	Sales returns and allowances	20,000
Salaries and wages expense	60,000	Sales revenue	370,000
Income tax expense	5,000	Other comprehensive income (net of $400 tax)	2,000

Instructions

a. Prepare an income statement using the format presented in Illustration 5.12.

b. Prepare a comprehensive income statement.

c. Calculate the profit margin and the gross profit rate.

Compute missing amounts and calculate profitability ratios.

E5.8 (LO 4, 6), AP Financial information is presented here for two companies.

	Yoste Company	Noone Company
Sales revenue	$90,000	(d)
Sales returns and allowances	(a)	$ 5,000
Net sales	84,000	100,000
Cost of goods sold	58,000	(e)
Gross profit	(b)	40,000
Operating expenses	14,380	(f)
Net income	(c)	17,000

Instructions

a. Fill in the missing amounts. Show all computations.

b. Calculate the profit margin and the gross profit rate for each company.

c. Discuss your findings in part (b).

E5.9 (LO 4, 6), AP In its income statement for the year ended December 31, 2022, Darren Company reported the following condensed data.

Prepare multiple-step income statement and calculate profitability ratios.

Salaries and wages expense	$465,000	Loss on disposal of plant assets	$ 83,500
Cost of goods sold	987,000	Sales revenue	2,210,000
Interest expense	71,000	Income tax expense	25,000
Interest revenue	65,000	Sales discounts	160,000
Depreciation expense	310,000	Utilities expense	110,000

Instructions

a. Prepare a multiple-step income statement.

b. Calculate the profit margin and gross profit rate.

c. In 2021, Darren had a profit margin of 5%. Is the decline in 2022 a cause for concern? (Ignore income tax effects.)

E5.10 (LO 4, 6), AP Suppose in its income statement for the year ended June 30, 2022, **The Clorox Company** reported the following condensed data (dollars in millions).

Prepare multiple-step income statement and calculate profitability ratios.

Salaries and wages expense	$ 460	Research and development expense	$ 114
Depreciation expense	90	Income tax expense	276
Sales revenue	5,730	Loss on disposal of plant assets	46
Interest expense	161	Cost of goods sold	3,104
Advertising expense	499	Rent expense	105
Sales returns and allowances	280	Utilities expense	60

Instructions

a. Prepare a multiple-step income statement.

b. Calculate the gross profit rate and the profit margin and explain what each means.

c. Assume the marketing department has presented a plan to increase advertising expenses by $340 million. It expects this plan to result in an increase in both net sales and cost of goods sold of 25%. (*Hint:* Increase both sales revenue and sales returns and allowances by 25%.) Redo parts (a) and (b) and discuss whether this plan has merit. (Assume a tax rate of 34%, and round all amounts to whole dollars.)

E5.11 (LO 4), AP In its income statement for the year ended December 31, 2022, Laine Inc. reported the following condensed data.

Prepare an income statement and comprehensive income statement.

Operating expenses	$ 725,000	Interest revenue	$ 33,000
Cost of goods sold	1,256,000	Loss on disposal of plant assets	17,000
Interest expense	70,000	Net sales	2,200,000
Income tax expense	47,000	Other comprehensive income (net of $1,200 tax)	8,300

Instructions

a. Prepare a multiple-step income statement.

b. Prepare a comprehensive income statement.

E5.12 (LO 4), AP The following selected accounts from the Blue Door Corporation's general ledger are presented below for the year ended December 31, 2022:

Prepare a multiple-step income statement.

Advertising expense	$ 55,000	Interest revenue	$ 30,000
Common stock	250,000	Inventory	67,000
Cost of goods sold	1,085,000	Rent revenue	24,000
Depreciation expense	125,000	Retained earnings	535,000
Dividends	150,000	Salaries and wages expense	675,000
Freight-out	25,000	Sales discounts	8,500
Income tax expense	70,000	Sales returns and allowances	41,000
Insurance expense	15,000	Sales revenue	2,400,000
Interest expense	70,000		

Instructions

Prepare a multiple-step income statement.

Prepare cost of goods sold section using periodic system.

E5.13 (LO 5), AP The trial balance of Mendez Company at the end of its fiscal year, August 31, 2022, includes these accounts: Beginning Inventory $18,700, Purchases $154,000, Sales Revenue $190,000, Freight-In $8,000, Sales Returns and Allowances $3,000, Freight-Out $1,000, and Purchase Returns and Allowances $5,000. The ending inventory is $21,000.

Instructions

Prepare a cost of goods sold section (periodic system) for the year ending August 31, 2022.

Prepare cost of goods sold section using periodic system.

E5.14 (LO 5), AP Below is a series of cost of goods sold sections for companies B, M, O, and S.

	B	M	O	S
Beginning inventory	$ 250	$ 120	$ 700	$ (j)
Purchases	1,500	1,080	(g)	43,590
Purchase returns and allowances	80	(d)	290	(k)
Net purchases	(a)	1,040	7,410	42,290
Freight-in	130	(e)	(h)	2,240
Cost of goods purchased	(b)	1,230	8,050	(l)
Cost of goods available for sale	1,800	1,350	(i)	49,530
Ending inventory	310	(f)	1,150	6,230
Cost of goods sold	(c)	1,230	7,600	43,300

Instructions

Fill in the lettered blanks to complete the cost of goods sold sections.

Evaluate quality of earnings.

E5.15 (LO 6), C Writing Dorsett Corporation reported sales revenue of $257,000, net income of $45,300, cash of $9,300, and net cash provided by operating activities of $23,200. Accounts receivable have increased at three times the rate of sales during the last 3 years.

Instructions

a. Explain what is meant by high quality of earnings.

b. Evaluate the quality of the company's earnings. Discuss your findings.

c. What factors might have contributed to the company's quality of earnings?

Journalize purchase transactions.

*E5.16 (LO 7), AP This information relates to Alfie Co.

1. On April 5, purchased merchandise from Bach Company for $27,000, on account, terms 2/10, n/30.
2. On April 6, paid freight costs of $1,200 on merchandise purchased from Bach Company.
3. On April 7, purchased equipment on account for $30,000.
4. On April 8, returned $3,600 of the April 5 merchandise to Bach Company.
5. On April 15, paid the amount due to Bach Company in full.

Instructions

a. Prepare the journal entries to record these transactions on the books of Alfie Co. using a periodic inventory system.

b. Assume that Alfie Co. paid the balance due to Bach Company on May 4 instead of April 15. Prepare the journal entry to record this payment.

Record entry for estimated sales returns.

*E5.17 (LO 8), AP At December 31, 2022, Highland Corporation estimates that goods with a selling price of $4,700 and a cost of $1,870 that were sold on account during the current period will be returned during the next accounting period. On January 17, 2023, the goods were returned as estimated. The customer had not paid for the goods by the time of the return.

Instructions

Record the entry or entries required to adjust for this information, as well as the subsequent return.

Problems: Set A

Journalize, post, and prepare partial income statement, and calculate ratios.

P5.1A (LO 2, 3, 4, 6), AP Winters Hardware Store completed the following merchandising transactions in the month of May. At the beginning of May, Winters' ledger showed Cash of $8,000 and Common Stock of $8,000.

May 1 Purchased merchandise on account from Black Wholesale Supply for $8,000, terms 1/10, n/30.

2 Sold merchandise on account for $4,400, terms 2/10, n/30. The cost of the merchandise sold was $3,300.

	5	Received credit from Black Wholesale Supply for merchandise returned $200.
	9	Received collections in full, less discounts, from customers billed on May 2.
	10	Paid Black Wholesale Supply in full, less discount.
	11	Purchased supplies for cash $900.
	12	Purchased merchandise for cash $3,100.
	15	Received $230 refund for return of poor-quality merchandise from supplier on cash purchase.
	17	Purchased merchandise on account from Wilhelm Distributors for $2,500, terms 2/10, n/30.
	19	Paid freight on May 17 purchase $250.
	24	Sold merchandise for cash $5,500. The cost of the merchandise sold was $4,100.
	25	Purchased merchandise on account from Clasps Inc. for $800, terms 3/10, n/30.
	27	Paid Wilhelm Distributors in full, less discount.
	29	Made refunds to cash customers for returned merchandise $124. The returned merchandise had cost $90.
	31	Sold merchandise on account for $1,280, terms n/30. The cost of the merchandise sold was $830.

Winters Hardware's chart of accounts includes Cash, Accounts Receivable, Inventory, Supplies, Accounts Payable, Common Stock, Sales Revenue, Sales Returns and Allowances, Sales Discounts, and Cost of Goods Sold.

Instructions

a. Journalize the transactions using a perpetual inventory system.
b. Post the transactions to T-accounts. Be sure to enter the beginning cash and common stock balances.
c. Prepare an income statement through gross profit for the month of May 2022.   **c. Gross profit $2,828**
d. Calculate the profit margin and the gross profit rate. (Assume operating expenses were $1,400.)

P5.2A (LO 2, 3), AP Powell Warehouse distributes hardback books to retail stores and extends credit terms of 2/10, n/30 to all of its customers. During the month of June, the following merchandising transactions occurred.

Journalize purchase and sale transactions under a perpetual system.

June	1	Purchased books on account for $1,040 (including freight) from Catlin Publishers, terms 2/10, n/30.
	3	Sold books on account to Garfunkel Bookstore for $1,200. The cost of the merchandise sold was $720.
	6	Received $40 credit for books returned to Catlin Publishers.
	9	Paid Catlin Publishers in full.
	15	Received payment in full from Garfunkel Bookstore.
	17	Sold books on account to Bell Tower for $1,200. The cost of the merchandise sold was $730.
	20	Purchased books on account for $720 from Priceless Book Publishers, terms 1/15, n/30.
	24	Received payment in full from Bell Tower.
	26	Paid Priceless Book Publishers in full.
	28	Sold books on account to General Bookstore for $1,300. The cost of the merchandise sold was $780.
	30	Granted General Bookstore $130 credit for books returned costing $80.

Instructions

Journalize the transactions for the month of June for Powell Warehouse, using a perpetual inventory system.

P5.3A (LO 2, 3, 4), AP At the beginning of the current season on April 1, the ledger of Granite Hills Pro Shop showed Cash $2,500, Inventory $3,500, and Common Stock $6,000. The following transactions were completed during April 2022.

Journalize, post, and prepare trial balance and partial income statement.

Apr.	5	Purchased golf bags, clubs, and balls on account from Arnie Co. $1,500, terms 3/10, n/60.
	7	Paid freight on Arnie purchase $80.
	9	Received credit from Arnie Co. for merchandise returned $200.
	10	Sold merchandise on account to members $1,340, terms n/30. The merchandise sold had a cost of $820.
	12	Purchased golf shoes, sweaters, and other accessories on account from Woods Sportswear $830, terms 1/10, n/30.
	14	Paid Arnie Co. in full.

17 Received credit from Woods Sportswear for merchandise returned $30.
20 Made sales on account to members $810, terms n/30. The cost of the merchandise sold was $550.
21 Paid Woods Sportswear in full.
27 Granted an allowance to members for clothing that did not fit properly $80.
30 Received payments on account from members $1,220.

The chart of accounts for the pro shop includes Cash, Accounts Receivable, Inventory, Accounts Payable, Common Stock, Sales Revenue, Sales Returns and Allowances, and Cost of Goods Sold.

Instructions

a. Journalize the April transactions using a perpetual inventory system.
b. Using T-accounts, enter the beginning balances in the ledger accounts and post the April transactions.
c. Prepare a trial balance on April 30, 2022.
d. Prepare an income statement through gross profit for the month of April 2022.

c. Tot. trial balance $8,150
d. Gross profit $ 700

Prepare financial statements and calculate profitability ratios.

P5.4A (LO 4, 6), AP Writing Wolford Department Store is located in midtown Metropolis. During the past several years, net income has been declining because suburban shopping centers have been attracting business away from city areas. At the end of the company's fiscal year on November 30, 2022, these accounts appeared in its adjusted trial balance.

Accounts Payable	$ 26,800
Accounts Receivable	17,200
Accumulated Depreciation—Equipment	68,000
Cash	8,000
Common Stock	35,000
Cost of Goods Sold	614,300
Freight-Out	6,200
Equipment	157,000
Depreciation Expense	13,500
Dividends	12,000
Gain on Disposal of Plant Assets	2,000
Income Tax Expense	10,000
Insurance Expense	9,000
Interest Expense	5,000
Inventory	26,200
Notes Payable	43,500
Prepaid Insurance	6,000
Advertising Expense	33,500
Rent Expense	34,000
Retained Earnings	14,200
Salaries and Wages Expense	117,000
Salaries and Wages Payable	6,000
Sales Returns and Allowances	20,000
Sales Revenue	904,000
Utilities Expense	10,600

Additional data: Notes payable are due in 2026.

Instructions

a. Net income $ 32,900
Tot. assets $146,400

a. Prepare a multiple-step income statement, a retained earnings statement, and a classified balance sheet.
b. Calculate the profit margin and the gross profit rate.
c. The vice president of marketing and the director of human resources have developed a proposal whereby the company would compensate the sales force on a strictly commission basis. Given the increased incentive, they expect net sales to increase by 15%. As a result, they estimate that gross profit will increase by $40,443 and expenses by $58,600. Compute the expected new net income. (*Hint:* You do not need to prepare an income statement.) Then, compute the revised profit margin and gross profit rate. Comment on the effect that this plan would have on net income and on the ratios, and evaluate the merit of this proposal. (Ignore income tax effects.)

Prepare a correct multiple-step income statement.

P5.5A (LO 4), AP An inexperienced accountant prepared this condensed income statement for Simon Company, a retail firm that has been in business for a number of years.

Simon Company
Income Statement
For the Year Ended December 31, 2022

Revenues		
Net sales	$850,000	
Other revenues	22,000	
		872,000
Cost of goods sold		555,000
Gross profit		317,000
Operating expenses		
Selling expenses	109,000	
Administrative expenses	103,000	
		212,000
Net earnings		$105,000

As an experienced, knowledgeable accountant, you review the statement and determine that the following steps were taken by the accountant to compute the amounts presented in the income statement.

1. Net sales, as presented, consist of sales $911,000, less freight-out on merchandise sold $33,000, and sales returns and allowances $28,000.

2. Other revenues, as presented, consist of sales discounts $18,000 and rent revenue $4,000.

3. Selling expenses, as presented, consist of salespersons' salaries $80,000, depreciation on equipment $10,000, advertising $13,000, and sales commissions $6,000. The commissions represent commissions paid. At December 31, $3,000 of commissions have been earned by salespersons but have not been paid. All compensation should be recorded as Salaries and Wages Expense.

4. Administrative expenses, as presented, consist of office salaries $47,000, dividends $18,000, utilities $12,000, interest expense $2,000, and rent expense $24,000, which includes prepayments totaling $6,000 for the first quarter of 2023.

Instructions

Evaluate the steps taken by the inexperienced accountant so you can identify corrections that need to be made. Then, prepare a correct detailed multiple-step income statement. (Assume a 25% tax rate.)

Net income $67,500

P5.6A (LO 4), AP The trial balance of People's Choice Wholesale Company contained the following accounts shown at December 31, the end of the company's fiscal year.

Journalize, post, and prepare adjusted trial balance and financial statement.

People's Choice Wholesale Company
Trial Balance
December 31, 2022

	Debit	Credit
Cash	$ 31,400	
Accounts Receivable	37,600	
Inventory	70,000	
Land	92,000	
Buildings	200,000	
Accumulated Depreciation—Buildings		$ 60,000
Equipment	83,500	
Accumulated Depreciation—Equipment		40,500
Notes Payable		54,700
Accounts Payable		17,500
Common Stock		160,000
Retained Earnings		67,200
Dividends	10,000	
Sales Revenue		922,100
Sales Discounts	6,000	
Cost of Goods Sold	709,900	
Salaries and Wages Expense	51,300	
Utilities Expense	11,400	
Maintenance and Repairs Expense	8,900	
Advertising Expense	5,200	
Insurance Expense	4,800	
	$1,322,000	$1,322,000

Adjustment data:

1. Depreciation is $8,000 on buildings and $7,000 on equipment. (Both are operating expenses.)
2. Interest of $4,500 is due and unpaid on notes payable at December 31.
3. Income tax due and unpaid at December 31 is $24,000.

Other data: $15,000 of the notes payable are payable next year.

Instructions

a. Journalize the adjusting entries.
b. Create T-accounts for all accounts used in part (a). Enter the trial balance amounts into the T-accounts and post the adjusting entries.
c. Prepare an adjusted trial balance.
d. Prepare a multiple-step income statement and a retained earnings statement for the year, and a classified balance sheet at December 31, 2022.

c. Tot. trial balance $1,365,500
d. Net income $ 81,100
   Tot. assets $ 399,000

Determine cost of goods sold and gross profit under a periodic system.

P5.7A (LO 4, 5), AP At the end of Oates Department Store's fiscal year on November 30, 2022, these accounts appeared in its adjusted trial balance.

Freight-In	$ 5,060
Inventory (beginning)	41,300
Purchases	613,000
Purchase Discounts	7,000
Purchase Returns and Allowances	6,760
Sales Revenue	902,000
Sales Returns and Allowances	20,000

Additional facts:

1. Inventory on November 30, 2022, is $36,200.
2. Note that Oates Department Store uses a periodic system.

Instructions

Gross profit $272,600

Prepare an income statement through gross profit for the year ended November 30, 2022.

Calculate missing amounts and assess profitability.

P5.8A (LO 4, 5, 6), AN Writing Zhou Inc. operates a retail operation that purchases and sells snowmobiles, among other outdoor products. The company purchases all inventory on credit and uses a periodic inventory system. The Accounts Payable account is used for recording inventory purchases only; all other current liabilities are accrued in separate accounts. You are provided with the following selected information for the fiscal years 2020 through 2023, inclusive.

	2020	2021	2022	2023
Income Statement Data				
Sales revenue		$96,890	$ (e)	$82,220
Cost of goods sold		(a)	28,060	26,490
Gross profit		67,800	59,620	(i)
Operating expenses		63,640	(f)	52,870
Net income		$ (b)	$ 3,510	$ (j)
Balance Sheet Data				
Inventory	$13,000	$ (c)	$14,700	$ (k)
Accounts payable	5,800	6,500	4,600	(l)
Additional Information				
Purchases of inventory on account		$25,890	$ (g)	$24,050
Cash payments to suppliers		(d)	(h)	24,650

Instructions

a. Calculate the missing amounts.
b. The vice presidents of sales, marketing, production, and finance are discussing the company's results with the CEO. They note that sales declined over the 3-year fiscal period, 2021–2023. Does that mean that profitability necessarily also declined? Explain, computing the gross profit rate and the profit margin for each fiscal year to help support your answer.

Journalize, post, and prepare trial balance and partial income statement under a periodic system.

*P5.9A (LO 5, 7), AP At the beginning of the current season on April 1, the ledger of Granite Hills Pro Shop showed Cash $2,500, Inventory $3,500, and Common Stock $6,000. The following transactions occurred during April 2022.

Apr. 5 Purchased golf bags, clubs, and balls on account from Arnie Co. $1,500, terms 3/10, n/60.
7 Paid freight on Arnie Co. purchases $80.
9 Received credit from Arnie Co. for merchandise returned $200.
10 Sold merchandise on account to members $1,340, terms n/30.
12 Purchased golf shoes, sweaters, and other accessories on account from Woods Sportswear $830, terms 1/10, n/30.
14 Paid Arnie Co. in full.
17 Received credit from Woods Sportswear for merchandise returned $30.
20 Made sales on account to members $810, terms n/30.
21 Paid Woods Sportswear in full.
27 Granted credit to members for clothing that did not fit properly $80.
30 Received payments on account from members $1,220.

The chart of accounts for the pro shop includes Cash, Accounts Receivable, Inventory, Accounts Payable, Common Stock, Sales Revenue, Sales Returns and Allowances, Purchases, Purchase Returns and Allowances, Purchase Discounts, and Freight-In.

Instructions

a. Journalize the April transactions using a periodic inventory system.
b. Using T-accounts, enter the beginning balances in the ledger accounts and post the April transactions.
c. Prepare a trial balance on April 30, 2022.
d. Prepare an income statement through gross profit, assuming inventory on hand at April 30 is $4,263.

c. Tot. trial balance $8,427
d. Gross profit $ 700

Continuing Case

Cookie Creations

(*Note:* This is a continuation of the Cookie Creations case from Chapters 1 through 4.)

CC5 Because Natalie has had such a successful first few months, she is considering other opportunities to develop her business. One opportunity is to become the exclusive distributor of a line of fine European mixers. Natalie comes to you for advice on how to account for these mixers.

Go to WileyPLUS for complete case details and instructions.

© leungchopan/Shutterstock

Comprehensive Accounting Cycle Review

ACR5.1 On December 1, 2022, Devine Distributing Company had the following account balances.

	Debit		Credit
Cash	$ 7,200	Accumulated Depreciation—	
Accounts Receivable	4,600	Equipment	$ 2,200
Inventory	12,000	Accounts Payable	4,500
Supplies	1,200	Salaries and Wages Payable	1,000
Equipment	22,000	Common Stock	15,000
	$47,000	Retained Earnings	24,300
			$47,000

During December, the company completed the following summary transactions.

Dec. 6 Paid $1,600 for salaries due employees, of which $600 is for December and $1,000 is for November salaries payable.
8 Received $1,900 cash from customers in payment of account (no discount allowed).
10 Sold merchandise for cash $6,300. The cost of the merchandise sold was $4,100.
13 Purchased merchandise on account from Hecht Co. $9,000, terms 2/10, n/30.
15 Purchased supplies for cash $2,000.
18 Sold merchandise on account $12,000, terms 3/10, n/30. The cost of the merchandise sold was $8,000.
20 Paid salaries $1,800.
23 Paid Hecht Co. in full, less discount.
27 Received collections in full, less discounts, from customers billed on December 18.

Adjustment data:

1. Accrued salaries payable $800.
2. Depreciation $200 per month.
3. Supplies on hand $1,500.
4. Income tax due and unpaid at December 31 is $200.

Instructions

a. Journalize the December transactions using a perpetual inventory system.

b. Enter the December 1 balances in the ledger T-accounts and post the December transactions. Use Cost of Goods Sold, Depreciation Expense, Salaries and Wages Expense, Sales Revenue, Sales Discounts, Supplies Expense, Income Tax Expense, and Income Taxes Payable.

c. Journalize and post adjusting entries.

d. Totals $65,500   d. Prepare an adjusted trial balance.

e. Net income $540   e. Prepare an income statement and a retained earnings statement for December and a classified balance sheet at December 31.

ACR5.2 On November 1, 2022, IKonk, Inc. had the following account balances. The company uses the perpetual inventory method.

	Debit		Credit
Cash	$ 9,000	Accumulated Depreciation—	
Accounts Receivable	2,240	Equipment	$ 1,000
Supplies	860	Accounts Payable	3,400
Equipment	25,000	Unearned Service Revenue	4,000
	$37,100	Salaries and Wages Payable	1,700
		Common Stock	20,000
		Retained Earnings	7,000
			$37,100

During November, the following summary transactions were completed.

Nov. 8 Paid $3,550 for salaries due employees, of which $1,850 is for November and $1,700 is for October.
10 Received $1,900 cash from customers in payment of account.
11 Purchased merchandise on account from Dimas Discount Supply for $8,000, terms 2/10, n/30.
12 Sold merchandise on account for $5,500, terms 2/10, n/30. The cost of the merchandise sold was $4,000.
15 Received credit from Dimas Discount Supply for merchandise returned $300.
19 Received collections in full, less discounts, from customers billed on sales of $5,500 on November 12.
20 Paid Dimas Discount Supply in full, less discount.
22 Received $2,300 cash for services performed in November.
25 Purchased equipment on account $5,000.
27 Purchased supplies on account $1,700.
28 Paid creditors $3,000 of accounts payable due.
29 Paid November rent $375.
29 Paid salaries $1,300.
29 Performed services on account and billed customers $700 for those services.
29 Received $675 from customers for services to be performed in the future.

Adjustment data:

1. Supplies on hand are valued at $1,600.
2. Accrued salaries payable are $500.
3. Depreciation for the month is $250.
4. $650 of services related to the unearned service revenue has not been performed by month-end.

Instructions

a. Enter the November 1 balances in ledger T-accounts.

b. Journalize the November transactions.

c. Post to the ledger accounts. You will need to add some accounts.

d. Journalize and post adjusting entries.

e. Prepare an adjusted trial balance at November 30.

f. Prepare a multiple-step income statement and a retained earnings statement for November and a classified balance sheet at November 30.

g. Journalize and post closing entries.

e. Tot. adj. trial bal. $49,025
f. Tot. assets $38,430

Expand Your Critical Thinking

Financial Reporting Problem: Apple Inc.

CT5.1 The financial statements for **Apple Inc.** are presented in Appendix A.

Instructions

Answer these questions using the Statement of Operations.

a. What was the percentage change in net sales and in net income from the year ended September 24, 2016, to the year ended September 30, 2017?

b. What was the profit margin in each of the 3 years? (Use "Net Sales.") Comment on the trend.

c. What was Apple's gross profit rate in each of the 3 years? (Use "Net Sales" amounts.) Comment on the trend.

Comparative Analysis Problem: Columbia Sportswear Company vs. VF Corporation

CT5.2 The financial statements of **Columbia Sportswear Company** are presented in Appendix B. Financial statements of **VF Corporation** are presented in Appendix C.

Instructions

a. Based on the information contained in these financial statements, determine the following values for each company.
   1. Profit margin for 2016. (For VF, use "Net Sales.")
   2. Gross profit for 2016.
   3. Gross profit rate for 2016.
   4. Operating income for 2016.
   5. Percentage change in operating Income from 2015 to 2016. (For Columbia, use Income from operations.)

b. What conclusions concerning the relative profitability of the two companies can be drawn from these data?

Comparative Analysis Problem: Amazon.com, Inc. vs. Wal-Mart Stores, Inc.

CT5.3 The financial statements of **Amazon.com, Inc.** are presented in Appendix D. Financial statements of **Wal-Mart Stores, Inc.** are presented in Appendix E.

Instructions

a. Based on the information contained in these financial statements, determine the following values for each company.
   1. Profit margin for the most recent year provided. (For Amazon, use "Total net sales.")
   2. Gross profit for the most recent year provided.
   3. Gross profit rate for the most recent year provided.
   4. Operating income for the most recent year provided.
   5. Percentage change in operating income between the most recent year provided and the prior year.

b. What conclusions concerning the relative profitability of the two companies can be drawn from these data?

Interpreting Financial Statements

CT5.4 Recently, it was announced that two giant French retailers, **Carrefour SA** and **Promodes SA**, would merge. A headline in the *Wall Street Journal* blared, "French Retailers Create New Wal-Mart

Rival." While **Wal-Mart**'s total sales would still exceed those of the combined company, Wal-Mart's international sales are far less than those of the combined company. This is a serious concern for Wal-Mart, since its primary opportunity for future growth lies outside of the United States.

Below are basic financial data for the combined corporation (in euros) and Wal-Mart (in U.S. dollars) in a recent year. Even though their results are presented in different currencies, by employing ratios we can make some basic comparisons.

	Carrefour (in millions)	Wal-Mart (in millions)
Sales revenue	€70,486	$256,329
Cost of goods sold	54,630	198,747
Net income	1,738	9,054
Total assets	39,063	104,912
Current assets	14,521	34,421
Current liabilities	13,660	37,418
Total liabilities	29,434	61,289

Instructions

Compare the two companies by answering the following.

a. Calculate the gross profit rate for each of the companies, and discuss their relative abilities to control cost of goods sold.

b. Calculate the profit margin, and discuss the companies' relative profitability.

c. Calculate the current ratio and debt to assets ratio for each of the two companies, and discuss their relative liquidity and solvency.

d. What concerns might you have in relying on this comparison?

Real-World Focus

CT5.5 No financial decision-maker should ever rely solely on the financial information reported in the annual report to make decisions. It is important to keep abreast of financial news. This activity demonstrates how to search for financial news on the Internet.

Instructions

Search the Internet for an article on either **PepsiCo** or **Coca-Cola** that sounds interesting to you and that would be relevant to an investor in these companies, and then answer the following questions.

a. What was the source of the article (e.g., Reuters, Businesswire, Prnewswire)?

b. Assume that you are a personal financial planner and that some of your clients own stock in the company. Write a brief memo to these clients summarizing the article and explaining the implications of the article for their investment.

Decision-Making Across the Organization

CT5.6 Three years ago, Karen Suez and her brother-in-law Reece Jones opened Gigasales Department Store. For the first 2 years, business was good, but the following condensed income statement results for 2022 were disappointing.

Gigasales Department Store
Income Statement
For the Year Ended December 31, 2022

Net sales		$700,000
Cost of goods sold		560,000
Gross profit		140,000
Operating expenses		
Selling expenses	$100,000	
Administrative expenses	20,000	
		120,000
Net income		$ 20,000

Karen believes the problem lies in the relatively low gross profit rate of 20%. Reece believes the problem is that operating expenses are too high.

Karen thinks the gross profit rate can be improved by making two changes. She does not anticipate that these changes will have any effect on operating expenses.

1. Increase average selling prices by 15%; this increase is expected to lower sales volume so that total sales dollars will increase only 4%.
2. Buy merchandise in larger quantities and take all purchase discounts. These changes to selling price and purchasing practices are expected to increase the gross profit rate from its current rate of 20% to a new rate of 25%.

Reece thinks expenses can be cut by making these two changes. He feels that these changes will not have any effect on net sales.

1. Cut 2023 sales salaries of $60,000 in half and give sales personnel a commission of 2% of net sales.
2. Reduce store deliveries to one day per week rather than twice a week. This change will reduce 2023 delivery expenses of $40,000 by 40%.

Karen and Reece come to you for help in deciding the best way to improve net income.

Instructions

With the class divided into groups, answer the following.

a. Prepare a condensed income statement for 2023 assuming (1) Karen's changes are implemented and (2) Reece's ideas are adopted.
b. What is your recommendation to Karen and Reece?
c. Prepare a condensed income statement for 2023 assuming both sets of proposed changes are made.
d. Discuss the impact that other factors might have. For example, would increasing the quantity of inventory increase costs? Would a salary cut affect employee morale? Would decreased morale affect sales? Would decreased store deliveries decrease customer satisfaction? What other suggestions might be considered?

Communication Activity

CT5.7 The following situation is presented in chronological order.

1. Aikan decides to buy a surfboard.
2. He calls Surfing Hawaii Co. to inquire about their surfboards.
3. Two days later, he requests Surfing Hawaii Co. to make him a surfboard.
4. Three days later, Surfing Hawaii Co. sends him a purchase order to fill out.
5. He sends back the purchase order.
6. Surfing Hawaii Co. receives the completed purchase order.
7. Surfing Hawaii Co. completes the surfboard.
8. Aikan picks up the surfboard.
9. Surfing Hawaii Co. bills Aikan.
10. Surfing Hawaii Co. receives payment from Aikan.

Instructions

In a memo to the president of Surfing Hawaii Co., answer the following questions.

a. When should Surfing Hawaii Co. record the sale?
b. Suppose that with his purchase order, Aikan is required to make a down payment. Would that change your answer to part (a)?

Ethics Case

CT5.8 Tabitha Andes was just hired as the assistant treasurer of Southside Stores, a specialty chain store company that has nine retail stores concentrated in one metropolitan area. Among other things, the payment of all invoices is centralized in one of the departments Tabitha will manage. Her primary responsibility is to maintain the company's high credit rating by paying all bills when due and to take advantage of all cash discounts.

Pete Wilson, the former assistant treasurer who has been promoted to treasurer, is training Tabitha in her new duties. He instructs Tabitha that she is to continue the practice of preparing all checks "net of discount" and dating the checks the last day of the discount period. "But," Pete continues, "we always hold the checks at least 4 days beyond the discount period before mailing them. That way we get another 4 days of interest on our money. Most of our creditors need our business and don't complain. And, if they scream about our missing the discount period, we blame it on the mailroom or the post office. We've only lost one discount out of every hundred we take that way. I think everybody does it. By the way, welcome to our team!"

Instructions

a. What are the ethical considerations in this case?
b. What stakeholders are harmed or benefited?
c. Should Tabitha continue the practice started by Pete? Does she have any choice?

All About You

CT5.9 There are many situations in business where it is difficult to determine the proper period in which to record revenue. Suppose that after graduation with a degree in finance, you take a job as a manager at a consumer electronics store called FarWest Electronics. The company has expanded rapidly in order to compete with **Best Buy**.

FarWest has also begun selling gift cards. The cards are available in any dollar amount and allow the holder of the card to purchase an item for up to 2 years from the time the card is purchased. If the card is not used during those 2 years, it expires.

Instructions

At what point should the revenue from the gift cards be recognized? Include the reasoning to support your answer.

FASB Codification Activity

CT5.10 If your school has a subscription to the FASB Codification, log in and prepare responses to the following.

a. Access the glossary ("Master Glossary") to answer the following.
  1. What is the definition provided for inventory?
  2. What is a customer?
b. What guidance does the Codification provide concerning reporting inventories above cost?

A Look at IFRS

LEARNING OBJECTIVE 9
Compare the accounting for merchandising under GAAP and IFRS.

The basic accounting entries for merchandising are the same under both GAAP and IFRS. The income statement is a required statement under both sets of standards. The basic format is similar although some differences do exist.

Key Points

Following are the key similarities and differences between GAAP and IFRS related to inventories.

Similarities

- Under both GAAP and IFRS, a company can choose to use either a perpetual or a periodic inventory system.
- The definition of inventories is basically the same under GAAP and IFRS.
- As indicated above, the basic accounting entries for merchandising are the same under both GAAP and IFRS.
- Both GAAP and IFRS require that income statement information be presented for multiple years. For example, IFRS requires that 2 years of income statement information be presented, whereas GAAP requires 3 years.

Differences

- Under GAAP, companies generally classify income statement items by function. Classification by function leads to descriptions like administration, distribution, and manufacturing. Under IFRS,

companies must classify expenses either by nature or by function. Classification by nature leads to descriptions such as the following: salaries, depreciation expense, and utilities expense. If a company uses the functional-expense method on the income statement, disclosure by nature is required in the notes to the financial statements.
- Presentation of the income statement under GAAP follows either a single-step or multiple-step format. IFRS does not mention a single-step or multiple-step approach.
- Under IFRS, revaluation of land, buildings, and intangible assets is permitted. The initial gains and losses resulting from this revaluation are reported as **other comprehensive income.** The effect of this difference is that the use of IFRS results in more transactions affecting other comprehensive income.

IFRS Practice

IFRS Self-Test Questions

1. Which of the following would **not** be included in the definition of inventory under IFRS?
   a. Photocopy paper held for sale by an office-supply store.
   b. Stereo equipment held for sale by an electronics store.
   c. Used office equipment held for sale by the human relations department of a plastics company.
   d. All of the answer choices would meet the definition.

2. Which of the following would **not** be a line item of a company reporting costs by nature?
   a. Depreciation expense.
   b. Salaries expense.
   c. Interest expense.
   d. Manufacturing expense.

3. Which of the following would **not** be a line item of a company reporting costs by function?
   a. Administration.
   b. Manufacturing.
   c. Utilities expense.
   d. Distribution.

IFRS Exercises

IFRS5.1 Explain the difference between the "nature-of-expense" and "function-of-expense" classifications.

IFRS5.2 For each of the following income statement line items, state whether the item is a "by nature" expense item or a "by function" expense item.
   a. Cost of goods sold.
   b. Depreciation expense.
   c. Salaries and wages expense.
   d. Selling expenses.
   e. Utilities expense.
   f. Delivery expense.
   g. General and administrative expenses.

IFRS5.3 Matilda Company reported the following amounts (in euros) in 2022: Net income, €150,000; Unrealized gain related to revaluation of buildings, €10,000; and Unrealized loss on non-trading securities, €(35,000). Determine Matilda's total comprehensive income for 2022.

International Financial Reporting Problem: Louis Vuitton

IFRS5.4 The financial statements of Louis Vuitton are presented in Appendix F. The complete annual report, including the notes to its financial statements, is available at the company's website.

Instructions

Use Louis Vuitton's annual report to answer the following questions.
   a. Does Louis Vuitton use a multiple-step or a single-step income statement format? Explain how you made your determination.
   b. Instead of "interest expense," what label does Louis Vuitton use for interest costs that it incurs?
   c. Using the notes to the company's financial statements, determine the following:
      1. Composition of the inventory.
      2. Amount of inventory (gross) before impairment.

Answers to IFRS Self-Test Questions

1. c   **2.** d   **3.** c

CHAPTER 6

Reporting and Analyzing Inventory

Chapter Preview

We previously discussed the accounting for merchandise inventory using a perpetual inventory system. In this chapter, we explain the methods used to calculate the cost of inventory on hand at the balance sheet date and the cost of goods sold.

Feature Story

"Where Is That Spare Bulldozer Blade?"

Let's talk inventory—big, bulldozer-size inventory. **Caterpillar Inc.** is the world's largest manufacturer of construction and mining equipment, diesel and natural gas engines, and industrial gas turbines. It sells its products in over 200 countries, making it one of the most successful U.S. exporters. More than 70% of its productive assets are located domestically, and nearly 50% of its sales are foreign.

In the past, Caterpillar's profitability suffered, but today it is very successful. A big part of this turnaround can be attributed to effective management of its inventory. Imagine what it costs Caterpillar to have too many bulldozers sitting around in inventory—a situation the company definitely wants to avoid. Yet Caterpillar must also make sure it has enough inventory to meet demand.

At one time during a 7-year period, Caterpillar's sales increased by 100% while its inventory increased by only 50%. To achieve this dramatic reduction in the amount of resources tied up in inventory while continuing to meet customers' needs, Caterpillar used a two-pronged approach. First, it completed a factory modernization program, which greatly increased its production efficiency. The program reduced by 60% the amount of inventory the company processes at any one time. It also reduced by an incredible 75% the time it takes to manufacture a part.

Second, Caterpillar dramatically improved its parts distribution system. It ships more than 100,000 items daily from its 23 distribution centers strategically located around the world (10 million square feet of warehouse space—remember, we're talking bulldozers). The company can virtually guarantee that it can get any part to anywhere in the world within 24 hours.

These changes led to record exports, profits, and revenues for Caterpillar. It would seem that things couldn't be better. But industry analysts, as well as the company's managers, thought otherwise. In order to maintain Caterpillar's position as the industry leader, management began another major overhaul of inventory production and inventory management processes. The goal: to cut the number of repairs in half, increase productivity by 20%, and increase inventory turnover by 40%.

In short, Caterpillar's ability to manage its inventory has been a key reason for its past success and will very likely play a huge part in its future profitability as well.

Chapter Outline

LEARNING OBJECTIVES

LO 1 Discuss how to classify and determine inventory.	• Classifying inventory • Determine inventory quantities	**DO IT! 1** Rules of Ownership
LO 2 Apply inventory cost flow methods and discuss their financial effects.	• Specific identification • Cost flow assumptions • Financial statement and tax effects • Using inventory cost flow methods consistently	**DO IT! 2** Cost Flow Methods
LO 3 Explain the statement presentation and analysis of inventory.	• Presentation • Lower-of-cost-or-net realizable value • Analysis • Adjustments for LIFO reserve	**DO IT! 3** LCNRV and Inventory Turnover

Go to the Review and Practice section at the end of the chapter for a targeted summary and practice applications with solutions.
Visit WileyPLUS for additional tutorials and practice opportunities.

Classifying and Determining Inventory

LEARNING OBJECTIVE 1
Discuss how to classify and determine inventory.

Two important steps in the reporting of inventory at the end of the accounting period are the classification of inventory based on its degree of completion and the determination of inventory amounts.

Classifying Inventory

How a company classifies its inventory depends on whether the firm is a merchandiser or a manufacturer. Recall that in a **merchandising** company, inventory consists of many different items. For example, in a grocery store, canned goods, dairy products, meats, and produce are just a few of the inventory items on hand. These items have two common characteristics: (1) they are owned by the company, and (2) they are in a form ready for sale to customers in the ordinary course of business. Thus, merchandisers need only one inventory classification, **merchandise inventory**, to describe the many different items that make up the total inventory.

In a **manufacturing** company, some inventory may not yet be ready for sale. As a result, manufacturers usually classify inventory into three categories: finished goods, work in process, and raw materials. **Finished goods inventory** is manufactured items that are completed and ready for sale. **Work in process** is that portion of manufactured inventory that has been placed into the production process but is not yet complete. **Raw materials** are the basic goods that will be used in production but have not yet been placed into production.

For example, **Caterpillar** classifies earth-moving tractors completed and ready for sale as **finished goods**. It classifies the tractors on the assembly line in various stages of production as **work in process**. The steel, glass, tires, and other components that are on hand waiting to be used in the production of tractors are identified as **raw materials** (see **Helpful Hint**). **Illustration 6.1** shows an adapted excerpt from Note 7 of Caterpillar's annual report.

> **HELPFUL HINT**
>
> Regardless of the classification, companies report all inventories under Current Assets on the balance sheet.

ILLUSTRATION 6.1

Composition of Caterpillar's inventory

(millions of dollars)	December 31		
	2015	2014	2013
Raw materials	$2,467	$ 2,986	$ 2,966
Work in process	1,857	2,455	2,589
Finished goods	5,122	6,504	6,785
Other	254	260	285
Total inventories	**$9,700**	**$12,205**	**$12,625**

By observing the levels and changes in the levels of these three inventory types, financial statement users can gain insight into management's production plans. For example, low levels of raw materials and high levels of finished goods suggest that management believes it has enough inventory on hand and production will be slowing down—perhaps in anticipation of a recession. Conversely, high levels of raw materials and low levels of finished goods probably signal that management is planning to step up production.

Many companies have significantly lowered inventory levels and costs using **just-in-time (JIT) inventory** methods. Under a just-in-time method, companies manufacture or purchase goods only when needed. **Dell** is famous for having developed a system for making computers in response to individual customer requests. Even though it makes each computer to meet each customer's particular specifications, Dell is able to assemble the computer and put it on a truck in less than 48 hours. The success of the JIT system depends on reliable suppliers. By integrating its information systems with those of its suppliers, Dell reduced its inventories to nearly zero. This is a huge advantage in an industry where products become obsolete nearly overnight.

The accounting concepts discussed in this chapter apply to the inventory classifications of both merchandising and manufacturing companies. Our focus here is on merchandise inventory. Additional issues specific to manufacturing companies are discussed in managerial accounting courses.

Accounting Across the Organization   Ford

A Big Hiccup

© PeskyMonkey/iStockphoto

JIT can save a company a lot of money, but it isn't without risk. An unexpected disruption in the supply chain can cost a company a lot of money. Japanese automakers experienced just such a disruption when a 6.8-magnitude earthquake caused major damage to the company that produces 50% of their piston rings. The rings themselves cost only $1.50, but you can't make a car without them. As a result, the automakers were forced to shut down production for a few days—a loss of tens of thousands of cars.

Similarly, a major snowstorm halted production at the Canadian plants of **Ford**. A Ford spokesperson said, "Because the plants run with just-in-time inventory, we don't have large stockpiles of parts sitting around. When you have a somewhat significant disruption, you can pretty quickly run out of parts."

Sources: Amy Chozick, "A Key Strategy of Japan's Car Makers Backfires," *Wall Street Journal* (July 20, 2007); and Kate Linebaugh, "Canada Military Evacuates Motorists Stranded by Snow," *Wall Street Journal* (December 15, 2010).

What steps might the companies take to avoid such a serious disruption in the future? (Go to WileyPLUS for this answer and additional questions.)

Determining Inventory Quantities

No matter whether they are using a periodic or perpetual inventory system, all companies need to determine inventory quantities at the end of the accounting period. If using a perpetual system, companies take a physical inventory for the following reasons:

1. To check the accuracy of their perpetual inventory records.
2. To determine the amount of inventory lost due to wasted raw materials, shoplifting, or employee theft.

Companies using a periodic inventory system take a physical inventory for **two different purposes**: to determine the inventory on hand at the balance sheet date, and to determine the cost of goods sold for the period.

Determining inventory quantities involves two steps: (1) taking a physical inventory of goods on hand and (2) determining the ownership of goods.

Taking a Physical Inventory

Companies take a physical inventory at the end of the accounting period. Taking a physical inventory involves actually counting, weighing, or measuring each kind of inventory on hand (see Ethics Note). In many companies, taking an inventory is a formidable task. Retailers such as **Target**, **True Value Hardware**, or **Home Depot** have thousands of different inventory items. An inventory count is generally more accurate when goods are not being sold or received during the counting. Consequently, companies often "take inventory" when the business is closed or when business is slow. Many retailers close early on a chosen day in January—after the holiday sales and returns, when inventories are at their lowest level—to count inventory. **Wal-Mart Stores, Inc.**, for example, has a year-end of January 31.

> **ETHICS NOTE**
>
> In a famous fraud, a salad oil company filled its storage tanks mostly with water. The oil rose to the top, so auditors thought the tanks were full of oil. The company also said it had more tanks than it really did: It repainted numbers on the tanks to confuse auditors.

Determining Ownership of Goods

One challenge in computing inventory quantities is determining what inventory a company owns. To determine ownership of goods, two questions must be answered: Do all of the goods included in the count belong to the company? Does the company own any goods that were not included in the count?

Ethics Insight Leslie Fay

© Greg Brookes/iStockphoto

Falsifying Inventory to Boost Income

Managers at women's apparel maker **Leslie Fay** were convicted of falsifying inventory records to boost net income in an attempt to increase management bonuses. In another case, executives at **Craig Consumer Electronics** were accused of defrauding lenders by manipulating inventory records. The indictment said the company classified "defective goods as new or refurbished" and claimed that it owned certain shipments "from overseas suppliers" when, in fact, Craig either did not own the shipments or the shipments did not exist.

What effect does an overstatement of inventory have on a company's financial statements? (Go to WileyPLUS for this answer and additional questions.)

Goods in Transit A complication in determining ownership is **goods in transit** (on board a truck, train, ship, or plane) at the end of the period. The company may have purchased goods that have not yet been received, or it may have sold goods that have not yet been delivered. To arrive at an accurate count, the company must determine ownership of these goods.

Goods in transit should be included in the inventory of the company that has legal title to the goods. Legal title is determined by the terms of the sale, as shown in **Illustration 6.2** and described below.

ILLUSTRATION 6.2 Terms of sale

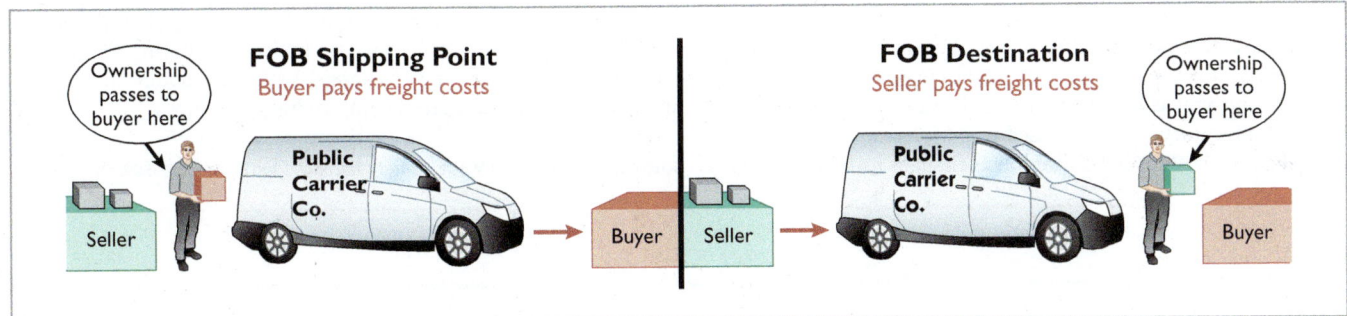

1. When the terms are **FOB (free on board) shipping point**, ownership of the goods passes to the buyer when the public carrier accepts the goods from the seller.
2. When the terms are **FOB destination**, ownership of the goods remains with the seller until the goods reach the buyer.

If goods in transit at the statement date are ignored, inventory quantities may be seriously miscounted. Assume, for example, that Hargrove Company has 20,000 units of inventory on hand on December 31. It also has the following goods in transit:

1. Sales of 1,500 units shipped December 31 FOB destination.
2. Purchases of 2,500 units shipped FOB shipping point by the seller on December 31.

Hargrove has legal title to both the 1,500 units sold and the 2,500 units purchased. If the company ignores the units in transit, it would understate inventory quantities by 4,000 units (1,500 + 2,500).

As we will see later in the chapter, inaccurate inventory counts affect not only the inventory amount shown on the balance sheet but also the cost of goods sold calculation on the income statement.

Consigned Goods In some lines of business, it is common to hold the goods of other parties and try to sell the goods for them for a fee, but without taking ownership of the goods. These are called **consigned goods**.

For example, you might have a used car that you would like to sell. If you take the item to a dealer, the dealer might be willing to put the car on its lot and charge you a commission if it is sold. Under this agreement, the dealer **would not take ownership** of the car, which would still belong to you. Therefore, if an inventory count were taken, the car would not be included in the dealer's inventory because the dealer does not own it.

Many car, boat, and antique dealers sell goods on consignment to keep their inventory costs down and to avoid the risk of purchasing an item that they will not be able to sell. Today, even some manufacturers are making consignment agreements with their suppliers in order to keep their inventory levels low. For example, prior to filing bankruptcy, **Sports Authority Inc.** became embroiled in lawsuits with suppliers over goods that it was holding on consignment. A judge ruled that Sports Authority had to comply with the suppliers' wishes since the consigned goods belonged to the suppliers.

Anatomy of a Fraud

Ted Nickerson, CEO of clock manufacturer Dally Industries, had expensive tastes. To support this habit, Ted took out large loans, which he collateralized with his shares of Dally Industries stock. If the price of Dally's stock fell, he was required to provide the bank with more shares of stock. To achieve target net income figures and thus maintain the stock price, Ted coerced employees in the company to alter inventory figures. Inventory quantities were manipulated by changing the amounts on inventory control tags after the year-end physical inventory count. For example, if a tag said there were 20 units of a particular item, the tag was changed to 220. Similarly, the unit costs that were used to determine the value of ending inventory were increased from, for example, $125 per unit to $1,250. Both of these fraudulent changes had the effect of increasing the amount of reported ending inventory. This reduced cost of goods sold and increased net income.

Total take: $245,000

The Missing Control

Independent internal verification. The company should have spot-checked its inventory records periodically, verifying that the number of units in the records agreed with the amount on hand and that the unit costs agreed with vendor price sheets.

Source: Adapted from Wells, *Fraud Casebook* (2007), pp. 502–509.

ACTION PLAN
- Apply the rules of ownership to goods held on consignment.
- Apply the rules of ownership to goods in transit.

DO IT! 1 | Rules of Ownership

Hasbeen Company completed its inventory count. It arrived at a total inventory value of $200,000. As a new member of Hasbeen's accounting department, you have been given the information listed below. Discuss how this information affects the reported cost of inventory.

1. Hasbeen included in the inventory goods held on consignment for Falls Co., costing $15,000.
2. The company did not include in the count purchased goods of $10,000 which were in transit (terms: FOB shipping point).
3. The company did not include in the count sold inventory with a cost of $12,000 which was in transit (terms: FOB shipping point).

Solution

The goods of $15,000 held on consignment should be deducted from the inventory count. The goods of $10,000 purchased FOB shipping point should be added to the inventory count. Sold goods of $12,000 which were in transit FOB shipping point should not be included in the ending inventory. Thus, inventory should be carried at $195,000 ($200,000 − $15,000 + $10,000).

Related exercise material: **BE6.1, BE6.2, DO IT! 6.1, E6.1, E6.2, and E6.3.**

Inventory Methods and Financial Effects

LEARNING OBJECTIVE 2
Apply inventory cost flow methods and discuss their financial effects.

Inventory is accounted for at cost. Cost includes all expenditures necessary to acquire goods and place them in a condition ready for sale. For example, freight costs incurred to acquire inventory are added to the cost of inventory, but the cost of shipping goods to a customer is a selling expense.

After a company has determined the quantity of units of inventory, it applies unit costs to the quantities to compute the total cost of the inventory and the cost of goods sold. This process can be complicated if a company has purchased inventory items at different times and at different prices.

For example, assume that Crivitz TV Company purchases three identical 50-inch TVs on different dates at costs of $700, $750, and $800. During the year, Crivitz sold two TVs at $1,200 each. These facts are summarized in Illustration 6.3.

ILLUSTRATION 6.3
Data for inventory costing example

Purchases
February 3 1 TV at $700
March 5   1 TV at $750
May 22   1 TV at $800

Sales
June 1   2 TVs for $2,400 ($1,200 × 2)

Cost of goods sold will differ depending on which two TVs the company sold. For example, it might be $1,450 ($700 + $750), or $1,500 ($700 + $800), or $1,550 ($750 + $800). In this section, we discuss alternative costing methods available to Crivitz.

Specific Identification

If Crivitz can positively identify which particular units it sold and which are still in ending inventory, it can use the **specific identification method** of inventory costing. For example, if Crivitz sold the TVs it purchased on February 3 and May 22, then its cost of goods sold is $1,500 ($700 + $800), and its ending inventory is $750 (see Illustration 6.4). Using this method, companies can accurately determine ending inventory and cost of goods sold.

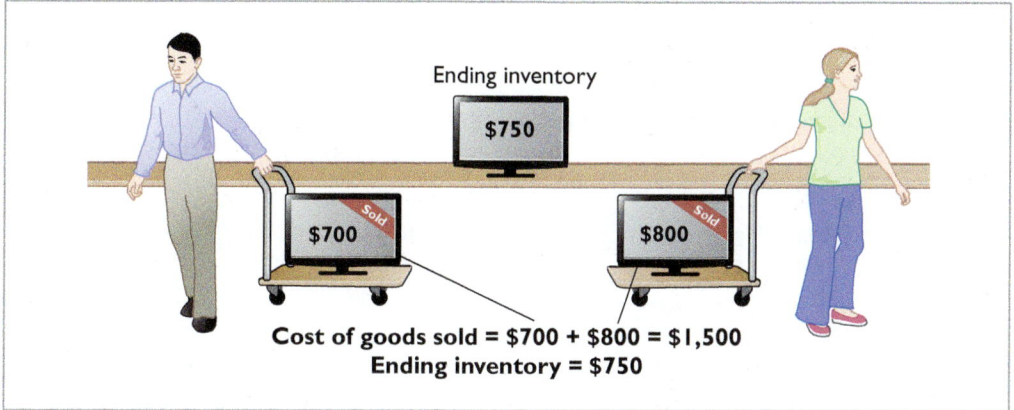

ILLUSTRATION 6.4
Specific identification method

Specific identification requires that companies keep records of the original cost of each individual inventory item. Historically, specific identification was possible only when a company sold a limited variety of high-unit-cost items that could be identified clearly from the time of purchase through the time of sale. Examples of such products are cars, pianos, or expensive antiques (see **Ethics Note**).

Today, bar coding, electronic product codes, and radio frequency identification make it theoretically possible to do specific identification with nearly any type of product. The reality is, however, that this practice is still relatively rare. Instead, rather than keep track of the cost of each particular item sold, most companies make assumptions, called **cost flow assumptions**, about which units were sold.

ETHICS NOTE
A major disadvantage of the specific identification method is that management may be able to manipulate net income. For example, it can boost net income by selling units purchased at a low cost, or reduce net income by selling units purchased at a high cost.

Cost Flow Assumptions

Because specific identification is often impractical, other cost flow methods are permitted. These differ from specific identification in that they **assume** flows of costs that may be unrelated to the physical flow of goods. There are three assumed cost flow methods:

1. First-in, first-out (FIFO).
2. Last-in, first-out (LIFO).
3. Average-cost.

There is no accounting requirement that the cost flow assumption be consistent with the physical movement of the goods. Company management selects the appropriate cost flow method.

To demonstrate the three cost flow methods, we will use a **periodic** inventory system. We assume a periodic system because **very few companies use perpetual LIFO, FIFO, or average-cost** to cost their inventory and related cost of goods sold. Instead, companies that use perpetual systems often use an assumed cost (called a standard cost) to record cost of goods sold at the time of sale. Then, at the end of the period when they count their inventory, they **recalculate cost of goods sold using periodic FIFO, LIFO, or average-cost** as shown in this chapter and adjust cost of goods sold to this recalculated number.[1]

To illustrate the three inventory cost flow methods, we will use the data for Houston Electronics' Astro condensers, shown in **Illustration 6.5**.

ILLUSTRATION 6.5
Data for Houston Electronics

Houston Electronics
Astro Condensers

Date	Explanation	Units	Unit Cost	Total Cost
Jan. 1	Beginning inventory	100	$10	$ 1,000
Apr. 15	Purchase	200	11	2,200
Aug. 24	Purchase	300	12	3,600
Nov. 27	Purchase	400	13	5,200
	Total units available for sale	1,000		$12,000
	Units in ending inventory	(450)		
	Units sold	550		

The cost of goods sold formula in a periodic system is as follows.

$$\text{Beginning Inventory} + \text{Cost of Goods Purchased} - \text{Ending Inventory} = \text{Cost of Goods Sold}$$

Houston Electronics had a total of 1,000 units available to sell during the period (beginning inventory plus purchases). The total cost of these 1,000 units is $12,000, referred to as **cost of goods available for sale**. A physical inventory taken at December 31 determined that there were 450 units in ending inventory. Therefore, Houston sold 550 units (1,000 − 450) during the period. To determine the cost of the 550 units that were sold (the cost of goods sold), we assign a cost to the ending inventory and subtract that value from the cost of goods available for sale. The value assigned to the ending inventory **depends on which cost flow method we use**. No matter which cost flow assumption we use, though, the sum of cost of goods sold plus the cost of the ending inventory must equal the cost of goods available for sale—in this case, $12,000.

First-In, First-Out (FIFO)

The **first-in, first-out (FIFO) method** assumes that the **earliest goods** purchased are the first to be sold. FIFO often parallels the actual physical flow of merchandise. That is, it generally is good business practice to sell the oldest units first. Under the FIFO method, therefore, the **costs of the earliest goods purchased are the first to be recognized in determining cost of goods sold**.

---

[1]Also, some companies use a perpetual system to keep track of units, but they do not make an entry for perpetual cost of goods sold. In addition, firms that employ LIFO tend to use **dollar-value LIFO**, a method discussed in upper-level courses. FIFO periodic and FIFO perpetual give the same result. Therefore, companies should not incur the additional cost to use FIFO perpetual. Few companies use perpetual average-cost because of the added cost of recordkeeping. Finally, for instructional purposes, we believe it is easier to demonstrate the cost flow assumptions under the periodic system, which makes it more pedagogically appropriate.

(This does not necessarily mean that the oldest units **are** sold first, but that the costs of the oldest units are **recognized** first. In a bin of picture hangers at the hardware store, for example, no one really knows, nor would it matter, which hangers are sold first.) **Illustration 6.6** shows the allocation of the cost of goods available for sale at Houston Electronics under FIFO (see **Helpful Hint**).

ILLUSTRATION 6.6
Allocation of costs—FIFO method

Cost of Goods Available for Sale				
Date	Explanation	Units	Unit Cost	Total Cost
Jan. 1	Beginning inventory	100	$10	$ 1,000
Apr. 15	Purchase	200	11	2,200
Aug. 24	Purchase	300	12	3,600
Nov. 27	Purchase	400	13	5,200
	Total	1,000		**$12,000**

Step 1: Ending Inventory

Date	Units	Unit Cost	Total Cost
Nov. 27	400	$13	$5,200
Aug. 24	50	12	600
Total	450		**$5,800**

Step 2: Cost of Goods Sold

Cost of goods available for sale	$12,000
Less: Ending inventory	5,800
Cost of goods sold	**$ 6,200**

HELPFUL HINT

Note the sequencing of the allocation: (1) compute ending inventory, and (2) determine cost of goods sold.

Under FIFO, since it is assumed that the first goods purchased were the first goods sold, ending inventory is based on the prices of the most recent units purchased (see **Helpful Hint**). That is, **under FIFO, companies obtain the cost of the ending inventory by taking the unit cost of the most recent purchase and working backward until all units of inventory have been costed**. In this example, Houston Electronics prices the 450 units of ending inventory using the **most recent** prices. The last purchase was 400 units at $13 on November 27. The remaining 50 units are priced using the unit cost of the second most recent purchase, $12, on August 24. Next, Houston Electronics calculates cost of goods sold by subtracting the cost of the units **not sold** (ending inventory) from the cost of all goods available for sale.

Illustration 6.7 demonstrates that companies also can calculate cost of goods sold by pricing the 550 units sold using the prices of the first 550 units acquired. Note that of the 300 units purchased on August 24, only 250 units are assumed sold. This agrees with our calculation of the cost of ending inventory, where 50 of these units were assumed unsold and thus included in ending inventory.

HELPFUL HINT

Another way of thinking about the calculation of FIFO ending inventory is the LISH assumption—last in still here.

Date	Units	Unit Cost	Total Cost
Jan. 1	100	$10	$1,000
Apr. 15	200	11	2,200
Aug. 24	250	12	3,000
Total	550		**$6,200**

ILLUSTRATION 6.7
Proof of cost of goods sold

Last-In, First-Out (LIFO)

The **last-in, first-out (LIFO) method** assumes that the **latest goods** purchased are the first to be sold. LIFO seldom coincides with the actual physical flow of inventory. (Exceptions include goods stored in piles, such as coal or hay, where goods are removed from the top of the pile as they are sold.) Under the LIFO method, the **costs** of the latest goods purchased are the first to be recognized in determining cost of goods sold. **Illustration 6.8** shows the allocation of the cost of goods available for sale at Houston Electronics under LIFO.

ILLUSTRATION 6.8

Allocation of costs—LIFO method

Cost of Goods Available for Sale

Date	Explanation	Units	Unit Cost	Total Cost
Jan. 1	Beginning inventory	100	$10	$ 1,000
Apr. 15	Purchase	200	11	2,200
Aug. 24	Purchase	300	12	3,600
Nov. 27	Purchase	400	13	5,200
	Total	1,000		$12,000

Step 1: Ending Inventory

Date	Units	Unit Cost	Total Cost
Jan. 1	100	$10	$1,000
Apr. 15	200	11	2,200
Aug. 24	150	12	1,800
Total	450		$5,000

Step 2: Cost of Goods Sold

Cost of goods available for sale	$12,000
Less: Ending inventory	5,000
Cost of goods sold	$ 7,000

HELPFUL HINT

Another way of thinking about the calculation of LIFO ending inventory is the FISH assumption—first in still here.

Under LIFO, since it is assumed that the first goods sold were those that were most recently purchased, ending inventory is based on the prices of the oldest units purchased (see **Helpful Hint**). That is, **under LIFO, companies obtain the cost of the ending inventory by taking the unit cost of the earliest goods available for sale and working forward until all units of inventory have been costed**. In this example, Houston Electronics prices the 450 units of ending inventory using the **earliest** prices. The first purchase was 100 units at $10 in the January 1 beginning inventory. Then, 200 units were purchased at $11. The remaining 150 units needed are priced at $12 per unit (August 24 purchase). Next, Houston Electronics calculates cost of goods sold by subtracting the cost of the units **not sold** (ending inventory) from the cost of all goods available for sale.

Illustration 6.9 demonstrates that companies also can calculate cost of goods sold by pricing the 550 units sold using the prices of the last 550 units acquired. Note that of the 300 units purchased on August 24, only 150 units are assumed sold. This agrees with our calculation of the cost of ending inventory, where 150 of these units were assumed unsold and thus included in ending inventory.

Date	Units	Unit Cost	Total Cost
Nov. 27	400	$13	$5,200
Aug. 24	150	12	1,800
Total	550		**$7,000**

ILLUSTRATION 6.9
Proof of cost of goods sold

Under a periodic inventory system, which we are using here, **all goods purchased during the period are assumed to be available for the first sale, regardless of the date of purchase**.

Average-Cost

The **average-cost method** allocates the cost of goods available for sale on the basis of the **weighted-average unit cost** incurred. **Illustration 6.10** presents the formula and a sample computation of the weighted-average unit cost.

Cost of Goods Available for Sale	÷	Total Units Available for Sale	=	Weighted- Average Unit Cost
$12,000	÷	1,000	=	$12

ILLUSTRATION 6.10
Formula for weighted-average unit cost

The company then applies the weighted-average unit cost to the units on hand to determine the cost of the ending inventory. **Illustration 6.11** shows the allocation of the cost of goods available for sale at Houston Electronics using average-cost.

ILLUSTRATION 6.11
Allocation of costs—average-cost method

Cost of Goods Available for Sale

Date	Explanation	Units	Unit Cost	Total Cost
Jan. 1	Beginning inventory	100	$10	$ 1,000
Apr. 15	Purchase	200	11	2,200
Aug. 24	Purchase	300	12	3,600
Nov. 27	Purchase	400	13	5,200
	Total	1,000		**$12,000**

Step 1: Ending Inventory

$12,000	÷	1,000	=	$12		
		Unit		Total		
Units		Cost		Cost		
450		$12		**$5,400**		

Step 2: Cost of Goods Sold

Cost of goods available for sale	$12,000
Less: Ending inventory	5,400
Cost of goods sold	**$ 6,600**

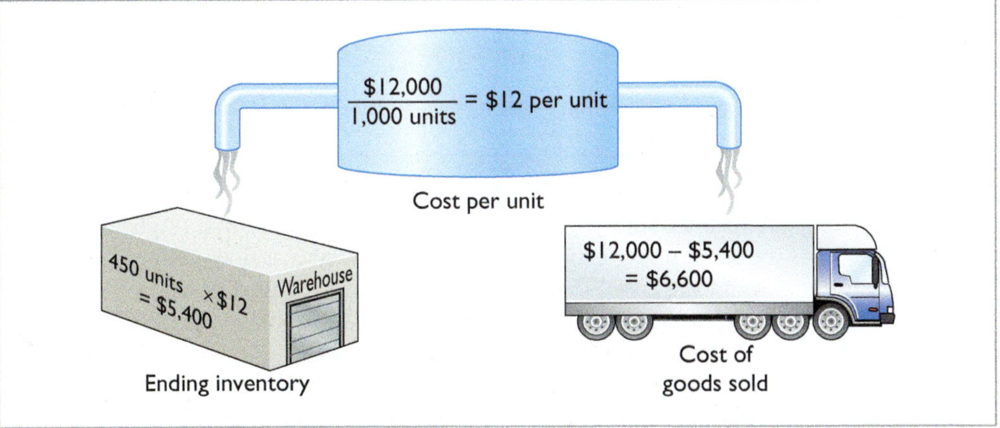

$$\frac{\$12,000}{1,000 \text{ units}} = \$12 \text{ per unit}$$

Cost per unit

450 units × $12 = $5,400
Warehouse
Ending inventory

$12,000 − $5,400 = $6,600
Cost of goods sold

> **Decision Tools**
>
> Analyzing financial statement and tax effects helps users determine which inventory costing method best meets the company's objectives.

We can verify the cost of goods sold under this method by multiplying the units sold times the weighted-average unit cost (550 × $12 = $6,600). Note that this method does **not** use the average of the unit costs. That average is $11.50 ($10 + $11 + $12 + $13 = $46; $46 ÷ 4). The average-cost method instead uses the average **weighted by** the quantities purchased at each unit cost.

Financial Statement and Tax Effects of Cost Flow Methods

Each of the three assumed cost flow methods is acceptable for use. For example, **Reebok International Ltd.** and **Wendy's International** currently use the FIFO method of inventory costing. **Campbell Soup Company**, **Kroger**, and **Walgreen Drugs** use LIFO for part or all of their inventory. **Bristol-Myers Squibb**, **Starbucks**, and **Motorola** use the average-cost method. In fact, a company may also use more than one cost flow method at the same time. **Stanley Black & Decker Manufacturing Company**, for example, uses LIFO for domestic inventories and FIFO for foreign inventories. **Illustration 6.12** shows the use of the three cost flow methods in 500 large U.S. companies.

The reasons companies adopt different inventory cost flow methods are varied, but they usually involve one of three factors: (1) income statement effects, (2) balance sheet effects, or (3) tax effects (see **Decision Tools**).

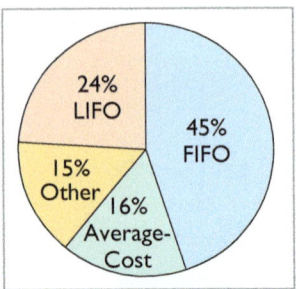

ILLUSTRATION 6.12
Use of cost flow methods in major U.S. companies

Income Statement Effects

To understand why companies might choose a particular cost flow method, let's examine the effects of the different cost flow assumptions on the financial statements of Houston Electronics. The condensed income statements in **Illustration 6.13** assume that Houston sold its 550 units for $18,500, had operating expenses of $9,000, and is subject to an income tax rate of 30%.

ILLUSTRATION 6.13
Comparative effects of cost flow methods

Houston Electronics Condensed Income Statements			
	FIFO	**LIFO**	**Average-Cost**
Sales revenue	$18,500	$18,500	$18,500
Beginning inventory	1,000	1,000	1,000
Purchases	11,000	11,000	11,000
Cost of goods available for sale	12,000	12,000	12,000
Ending inventory	5,800	5,000	5,400
Cost of goods sold	6,200	7,000	6,600
Gross profit	12,300	11,500	11,900
Operating expenses	9,000	9,000	9,000
Income before income taxes*	3,300	2,500	2,900
Income tax expense (30%)	990	750	870
Net income	**$ 2,310**	**$ 1,750**	**$ 2,030**

*We are assuming that Houston Electronics is a corporation, and corporations are required to pay income taxes.

In this example, which assumes equal beginning inventories, the cost of goods available for sale ($12,000) is the same under each of the three inventory cost flow methods. However, the ending inventories and the costs of goods sold are different. This difference is due to the unit costs that the company allocated to cost of goods sold and to ending inventory. Each dollar of difference in ending inventory results in a corresponding dollar difference in income before income taxes. For Houston, an $800 difference exists between FIFO and LIFO cost of goods sold.

In periods of changing prices, the cost flow assumption can have significant impacts both on income and on evaluations of income, such as the following.

1. In a period of inflation, FIFO produces a higher net income because lower unit costs of the first units purchased are matched against revenue.
2. In a period of inflation, LIFO produces a lower net income because higher unit costs of the last goods purchased are matched against revenue.
3. If prices are falling, the results from the use of FIFO and LIFO are reversed. FIFO will report the lowest net income and LIFO the highest.
4. Regardless of whether prices are rising or falling, average-cost produces net income between FIFO and LIFO.

As shown in the Houston example (Illustration 6.13), in a period of rising prices FIFO reports the highest net income ($2,310) and LIFO the lowest ($1,750); average-cost falls between these two amounts ($2,030).

To management, higher net income is an advantage. It causes external users to view the company more favorably. In addition, management bonuses, if based on net income, will be higher. Therefore, when prices are rising (which is usually the case), companies tend to prefer FIFO because it results in higher net income.

Others believe that LIFO presents a more realistic net income number. That is, LIFO matches the more recent costs against current revenues to provide a better measure of net income. During periods of inflation, many challenge the quality of non-LIFO earnings, noting that failing to match current costs against current revenues leads to an understatement of cost of goods sold and an overstatement of net income. As some indicate, net income computed using FIFO creates **"paper or phantom profits"**—that is, earnings that do not really exist.

Balance Sheet Effects

A major advantage of the FIFO method is that in a period of inflation, the costs allocated to ending inventory will approximate their current cost. For example, for Houston Electronics, 400 of the 450 units in the ending inventory are costed under FIFO at the higher November 27 unit cost of $13.

Conversely, a major shortcoming of the LIFO method is that in a period of inflation, the costs allocated to ending inventory may be significantly understated in terms of current cost. The understatement becomes greater over prolonged periods of inflation if the inventory includes goods purchased in one or more prior accounting periods. For example, **Caterpillar** has used LIFO for more than 50 years. Its balance sheet shows ending inventory of $9,700 million. But the inventory's actual current cost if FIFO had been used is $12,189 million.

Tax Effects

We have seen that both inventory on the balance sheet and net income on the income statement are higher when companies use FIFO in a period of inflation. Yet, many companies have selected LIFO. Why? The reason is that LIFO results in the lowest income taxes (because of lower net income) during times of rising prices (see **Helpful Hint**). For example, at Houston Electronics, income taxes are $750 under LIFO, compared to $990 under FIFO. The tax savings of $240 makes more cash available for use in the business.

> **HELPFUL HINT**
> A tax rule, often referred to as the LIFO conformity rule, requires that if companies use LIFO for tax purposes they must also use it for financial reporting purposes. This means that if a company chooses the LIFO method to reduce its tax bills, it will also have to report lower net income in its financial statements.

Keeping an Eye on Cash

You have just seen that when prices are rising the use of LIFO can have a big effect on taxes. The lower taxes paid using LIFO can significantly increase cash flows. To demonstrate the effect of the cost flow assumptions on cash flow, we will calculate net cash provided by operating activities using the data for Houston Electronics from Illustration 6.13. To simplify our example, we assume that Houston's sales and purchases are all cash transactions. We also assume that operating expenses, other than $4,600 of depreciation, are cash transactions.

	FIFO	LIFO	Average-Cost
Cash received from customers	$18,500	$18,500	$18,500
Cash purchases of goods	11,000	11,000	11,000
Cash paid for operating expenses ($9,000 − $4,600)	4,400	4,400	4,400
Cash paid for taxes	990	750	870
Net cash provided by operating activities	$ 2,110	$ 2,350	$ 2,230

LIFO has the highest net cash provided by operating activities because it results in the lowest tax payments. Since cash flow is the lifeblood of any organization, the choice of inventory method is very important.

LIFO also impacts the quality of earnings ratio. Recall that the quality of earnings ratio is net cash provided by operating activities divided by net income. Here, we calculate the quality of earnings ratio under each cost flow assumption.

LIFO has the highest quality of earnings ratio for two reasons. (1) It has the highest net cash provided by operating activities, which increases the ratio's numerator. (2) It reports a conservative measure of net income, which decreases the ratio's denominator. As discussed earlier, LIFO provides a conservative measure of net income because it does not include the phantom profits reported under FIFO.

	FIFO	LIFO	Average-Cost
Net income (from Illustration 6.13)	$2,310	$1,750	$2,030
Quality of earnings ratio	0.91	1.34	1.10

Using Inventory Cost Flow Methods Consistently

Whatever cost flow method a company chooses, it should use that method consistently from one accounting period to another. This approach is often referred to as the **consistency concept**, which means that a company uses the same accounting principles and methods from year to year. Consistent application enhances the comparability of financial statements over successive time periods. In contrast, using the FIFO method one year and the LIFO method the next year would make it difficult to compare the net incomes of the two years.

Although consistent application is preferred, it does not mean that a company may never change its inventory costing method. When a company adopts a different method, it should disclose in the financial statements the change and its effects on net income. **Illustration 6.14** shows a typical disclosure, using information from recent financial statements of **Quaker Oats** (now a unit of **PepsiCo**).

ILLUSTRATION 6.14

Disclosure of change in cost flow method

Quaker Oats
Notes to the Financial Statements

Note 1: Effective July 1, the Company adopted the LIFO cost flow assumption for valuing the majority of U.S. Grocery Products inventories. The Company believes that the use of the LIFO method better matches current costs with current revenues. The effect of this change on the current year was to decrease net income by $16.0 million.

International Insight   ExxonMobil Corporation

Bloomberg/Getty Images

Is LIFO Fair?

ExxonMobil Corporation, like many U.S. companies, uses LIFO to value its inventory for financial reporting and tax purposes. In one recent year, this resulted in a cost of goods sold figure that was $5.6 billion higher than under FIFO. By increasing cost of goods sold, ExxonMobil reduces net income, which reduces taxes. Critics say that LIFO provides an unfair "tax dodge." As Congress looks for more sources of tax revenue, some lawmakers favor the elimination of LIFO. Supporters of LIFO argue that the method is conceptually sound because it matches current costs with current revenues. In addition, they point out that this matching provides protection against inflation.

International accounting standards do not allow the use of LIFO. Because of this, the net income of foreign oil companies such as **BP** and **Royal Dutch Shell** are not directly comparable to U.S. companies, which can make analysis difficult.

Source: David Reilly, "Big Oil's Accounting Methods Fuel Criticism," *Wall Street Journal* (August 8, 2006), p. C1.

What are the arguments for and against the use of LIFO? (Go to WileyPLUS for this answer and additional questions.)

DO IT! 2 | Cost Flow Methods

The accounting records of Shumway Ag Implements show the following data.

Beginning inventory	4,000 units at $ 3
Purchases	6,000 units at $ 4
Sales	7,000 units at $12

Determine the cost of goods sold during the period under a periodic inventory system using (a) the FIFO method, (b) the LIFO method, and (c) the average-cost method.

ACTION PLAN
- Understand the periodic inventory system.
- Allocate costs between goods sold and goods on hand (ending inventory) for each cost flow method.
- Compute cost of goods sold for each method.

Solution

Cost of goods available for sale = (4,000 × $3) + (6,000 × $4) = $36,000
Ending inventory = 10,000 − 7,000 = 3,000 units

a. FIFO: $36,000 − (3,000 × $4) = $24,000
b. LIFO: $36,000 − (3,000 × $3) = $27,000
c. Average cost per unit: [(4,000 @ $3) + (6,000 @ $4)] ÷ 10,000 = $3.60
   Average-cost: $36,000 − (3,000 × $3.60) = $25,200

Related exercise material: **BE6.3, BE6.4, BE6.5, BE6.6, DO IT! 6.2, E6.4, E6.5, and E6.7.**

Inventory Presentation and Analysis

LEARNING OBJECTIVE 3
Explain the statement presentation and analysis of inventory.

Presentation

Recall that inventory is classified in the balance sheet as a current asset immediately below receivables. In a multiple-step income statement, cost of goods sold is subtracted from net sales. There also should be disclosure of (1) the major inventory classifications, (2) the basis of accounting (cost, or lower-of-cost-or-net realizable value), and (3) the cost method (FIFO, LIFO, or average-cost).

Wal-Mart Stores, Inc., for example, in its January 31, 2017, balance sheet reported inventories of $43,046 million under current assets. The accompanying notes to the financial statements, as shown in **Illustration 6.15**, disclosed the following information.

Wal-Mart Stores, Inc.
Notes to the Financial Statements

Note 1. Summary of Significant Accounting Policies

Inventories

The Company values inventories at the lower of cost or market as determined primarily by the retail method of accounting, using the last-in, first-out ("LIFO") method for substantially all of the WalMart U.S. segment's inventories. The inventory at the WalMart International segment is valued primarily by the retail inventory method of accounting, using the first-in, first-out ("FIFO") method. The retail method of accounting results in inventory being valued at the lower of cost or market since permanent markdowns are immediately recorded as a reduction of the retail value of inventory. The inventory at the Sam's Club segment is valued using the LIFO method. At January 31, 2017 and 2016, the Company's inventories valued at LIFO approximate those inventories as if they were valued at FIFO.

ILLUSTRATION 6.15
Inventory disclosures by Wal-Mart

Lower-of-Cost-or-Net Realizable Value

The value of inventory for companies selling high-technology or fashion goods can drop very quickly due to continual changes in technology or fashion. These circumstances sometimes call for inventory valuation methods other than those presented so far. For example, at one time, purchasing managers at **Ford** decided to make a large purchase of palladium, a precious metal used in vehicle emission devices. They made this purchase because they feared a future shortage. The shortage did not materialize, and by the end of the year the price of palladium had plummeted. Ford's inventory was then worth $1 billion less than its original cost. Do you think Ford's inventory should have been stated at cost, in accordance with the historical cost principle, or at its lower net realizable value?

As you probably reasoned, this situation requires a departure from the cost basis of accounting. When the value of inventory is lower than its cost, companies must "write down" the inventory to its net realizable value. This is done by valuing the inventory at the **lower-of-cost-or-net realizable value (LCNRV)** in the period in which the price decline occurs.

LCNRV is an example of the accounting concept of **conservatism**, which means that the best choice among accounting alternatives is the method that is least likely to overstate assets and net income. Critics of accounting conservatism argue that it introduces bias into accounting numbers. This can reduce the representational faithfulness as well as relevance of financial reports.

Under the LCNRV basis, **net realizable value** refers to the net amount that a company expects to realize (receive) from the sale of inventory. Specifically, net realizable value is the estimated selling price in the normal course of business, less estimated costs to complete and sell.

Companies apply LCNRV to the items in inventory after they have used one of the inventory costing methods (specific identification, FIFO, or average-cost) to determine cost. To illustrate the application of LCNRV, assume that Ken Tuckie TV has the following lines of merchandise with costs and net realizable values as indicated. LCNRV produces the results shown in **Illustration 6.16**. Note that the amounts shown in the final column are the lower-of-cost-or-net realizable value amounts for each item.

ILLUSTRATION 6.16
Computation of lower-of-cost-or-net realizable value

	Units	Cost per Unit	Net Realizable Value per Unit	Lower-of-Cost-or-Net Realizable Value	
Flat-screen TVs	100	$600	$550	$ 55,000	($550 × 100)
Satellite radios	500	90	104	45,000	($90 × 500)
DVD recorders	850	50	48	40,800	($48 × 850)
DVDs	3,000	5	6	15,000	($5 × 3,000)
Total inventory				$155,800	

Companies that use the LIFO method or the retail inventory method (such as Wal-Mart in Illustration 6.15) are not required to use lower-of-cost-or-net realizable value for inventory valuation. Instead, they use a lower-of-cost-or-market approach which is a more complex calculation. The computation for the lower-of-cost-or-market method is discussed in more advanced accounting courses.

Analysis

For companies that sell goods, managing inventory levels can be one of the most critical tasks. Having too much inventory on hand costs the company money in storage costs, interest cost (on funds tied up in inventory), and costs associated with the obsolescence of technical goods (e.g., computer chips) or shifts in fashion (e.g., clothes). But having too little inventory on hand results in lost sales.

Clearly inventory management is an area that benefits from data analytics. Companies such as Wal-Mart collect massive amounts of data about every inventory item and every customer. They analyze customer habits, buying patterns, and sales trends. Using sophisticated models that incorporate economic variables, weather patterns, and many other factors, they strive to optimize inventory levels to maximize sales while minimizing inventory holding costs. In this section, we discuss some issues related to evaluating inventory levels.

Inventory Turnover

The **inventory turnover** is calculated as cost of goods sold divided by average inventory. It indicates the liquidity of inventory by measuring the number of times the average inventory "turns over" (is sold) during the year. Inventory turnover can be divided into 365 days to compute **days in inventory**, which indicates the average number of days inventory is held (see **Decision Tools**).

High inventory turnover (low days in inventory) indicates the company has minimal funds tied up in inventory—that it has a minimal amount of inventory on hand at any one time. Although minimizing the funds tied up in inventory is efficient, too high an inventory turnover may indicate that the company is losing sales opportunities because of inventory shortages. For example, investment analysts at one time suggested that **Office Depot** had gone too far in reducing its inventory—they said they were seeing too many empty shelves. Thus, management should closely monitor this ratio to achieve the best balance between too much and too little inventory.

We have previously discussed the increasingly competitive environment of retailers, such as **Wal-Mart** and **Target**. Wal-Mart has implemented **just-in-time inventory procedures** as well as many technological innovations to improve the efficiency of its inventory management. The following data are available for Wal-Mart at January 31, 2017 (labeled 2016), and January 31, 2016 (labeled 2015).

> **Decision Tools**
> Inventory turnover and days in inventory help users determine how long an item is in inventory.

(in millions)	2016	2015
Ending inventory	$ 43,046	$44,469
Cost of goods sold	361,256	

Illustration 6.17 presents the inventory turnovers and days in inventory for Wal-Mart and Target, using data from the financial statements of those corporations for 2016 and 2015.

$$\text{Inventory Turnover} = \frac{\text{Cost of Goods Sold}}{\text{Average Inventory}}$$

$$\text{Days in Inventory} = \frac{365}{\text{Inventory Turnover}}$$

Ratio	Wal-Mart ($ in millions)		Target
	2016	2015	2016
Inventory turnover	$\frac{\$361{,}256}{(\$43{,}046 + \$44{,}469)/2} = 8.3$ times	8.1 times	5.8 times
Days in inventory	$\frac{365 \text{ days}}{8.3} = 44.0$ days	45.1 days	62.9 days

ILLUSTRATION 6.17
Inventory turnovers and days in inventory

The calculations in Illustration 6.17 show that Wal-Mart turns its inventory more frequently than Target (8.3 times for Wal-Mart versus 5.8 times for Target). Consequently, the average time an item spends on a Wal-Mart shelf is shorter (44.0 days for Wal-Mart versus 62.9 days for Target).

This analysis suggests that Wal-Mart is more efficient than Target in its inventory management. Wal-Mart's sophisticated inventory tracking and distribution system allows it to keep minimum amounts of inventory on hand, while still keeping the shelves full of what customers are looking for.

Accounting Across the Organization — Sony

© Dmitry Kutlayev/iStockphoto

Too Many TVs or Too Few?

Financial analysts closely monitor the inventory management practices of companies. For example, some analysts following **Sony** expressed concern because the company built up its inventory of televisions in an attempt to sell 25 million liquid crystal display (LCD) TVs—a 60% increase over the prior year. A year earlier, Sony had cut its inventory levels so that its quarterly days in inventory was down to 38 days, compared to 61 days for the same quarter a year before that. But in the next year, as a result of its inventory build-up, days in inventory rose to 59 days. Management said that it didn't think that Sony's inventory levels were too high. However, analysts were concerned that the company would have to engage in very heavy discounting in order to sell off its inventory. Analysts noted that the losses from discounting can be "punishing."

Source: Daisuke Wakabayashi, "Sony Pledges to Corral Inventory," *Wall Street Journal Online* (November 2, 2010).

For Sony, what are the advantages and disadvantages of having a low days in inventory measure? (Go to WileyPLUS for this answer and additional questions.)

Adjustments for LIFO Reserve

Earlier, we noted that using LIFO rather than FIFO can result in significant differences in the results reported in the balance sheet and the income statement. With increasing prices, FIFO will result in higher income than LIFO. On the balance sheet, FIFO will result in higher reported inventory. The financial statement differences from using LIFO normally increase the longer a company uses LIFO.

Use of different inventory cost flow assumptions complicates analysts' attempts to compare companies' results. Fortunately, companies using LIFO are required to report the difference between inventory reported using LIFO and inventory using FIFO. This amount is referred to as the **LIFO reserve**. Reporting the LIFO reserve enables analysts to make adjustments to compare companies that use different cost flow methods (see **Decision Tools**).

Illustration 6.18 presents an excerpt from the notes to **Caterpillar**'s 2016 financial statements that discloses and discusses Caterpillar's LIFO reserve.

> **Decision Tools**
> Adjusting inventory from LIFO to FIFO helps users analyze the impact of LIFO on the company's reported income.

ILLUSTRATION 6.18
Caterpillar's LIFO reserve

Real World	**Caterpillar Inc.**
	Notes to the Financial Statements

Inventories: Inventories are stated at the lower of cost or market. Cost is principally determined using the last-in, first-out (LIFO) method . . . . If the FIFO (first-in, first-out) method had been in use, inventories would have been $2,139 million and $2,498 million higher than reported at December 31, 2016, and 2015, respectively.

Caterpillar has used LIFO for over 50 years. Thus, the cumulative difference between LIFO and FIFO reflected in the Inventory account is very large. In fact, the 2016 LIFO reserve of $2,498 million is 29% of the 2016 LIFO inventory of $8,614 million. Such a huge difference would clearly distort any comparisons you might try to make with one of Caterpillar's competitors that used FIFO.

To adjust Caterpillar's inventory balance, we add the LIFO reserve to reported inventory, as shown in **Illustration 6.19**. That is, if Caterpillar had used FIFO all along, its inventory would be $11,112 million, rather than $8,614 million.

ILLUSTRATION 6.19
Conversion of inventory from LIFO to FIFO

	(in millions)
2016 inventory using LIFO	$ 8,614
2016 LIFO reserve	2,498
2016 inventory assuming FIFO	**$11,112**

The LIFO reserve can have a significant effect on ratios that analysts commonly use. Using the LIFO reserve adjustment, **Illustration 6.20** calculates the value of the current ratio (current assets ÷ current liabilities) for Caterpillar under both the LIFO and FIFO cost flow assumptions.

ILLUSTRATION 6.20
Impact of LIFO reserve on ratios

($ in millions)	LIFO	FIFO
Current ratio	$\dfrac{\$31{,}967}{\$26{,}132} = 1.22{:}1$	$\dfrac{\$31{,}967 + \$2{,}498}{\$26{,}132} = 1.32{:}1$

As Illustration 6.20 shows, if Caterpillar used FIFO, its current ratio would be 1.32:1 rather than 1.22:1 under LIFO. Thus, Caterpillar's liquidity appears stronger if a FIFO assumption were used in valuing inventories.

CNH Global, a competitor of Caterpillar, uses FIFO to account for its inventory. Comparing Caterpillar to CNH without converting Caterpillar's inventory to FIFO would lead to distortions and potentially erroneous decisions.

DO IT! 3 | LCNRV and Inventory Turnover

ACTION PLAN
- Determine whether cost or net realizable value is lower for each inventory type.
- Sum the lowest value of each inventory type to determine the total value of inventory.

a. Tracy Company sells three different types of home heating stoves (gas, wood, and pellet). The cost and net realizable value of its inventory of stoves are as follows.

	Cost	Net Realizable Value
Gas	$ 84,000	$ 79,000
Wood	250,000	280,000
Pellet	112,000	101,000

Determine the value of the company's inventory under the lower-of-cost-or-net realizable value approach.

Solution
The lowest value for each inventory type is gas $79,000, wood $250,000, and pellet $101,000. The total inventory value is the sum of these amounts, $430,000.

b. Early in 2022, Westmoreland Company switched to a just-in-time inventory system. Its sales revenue, cost of goods sold, and inventory amounts for 2021 and 2022 are shown below.

	2021	2022
Sales revenue	$2,000,000	$1,800,000
Cost of goods sold	1,000,000	910,000
Beginning inventory	290,000	210,000
Ending inventory	210,000	50,000

Determine the inventory turnover and days in inventory for 2021 and 2022. Discuss the changes in the amount of inventory, the inventory turnover and days in inventory, and the amount of sales across the two years.

ACTION PLAN
- To find the inventory turnover, divide cost of goods sold by average inventory.
- To determine days in inventory, divide 365 days by the inventory turnover.

Solution

	2021	2022
Inventory turnover	$\dfrac{\$1{,}000{,}000}{(\$290{,}000 + \$210{,}000)/2} = 4$	$\dfrac{\$910{,}000}{(\$210{,}000 + \$50{,}000)/2} = 7$
Days in inventory	365 ÷ 4 = 91.3 days	365 ÷ 7 = 52.1 days

The company experienced a very significant decline in its ending inventory as a result of the just-in-time inventory. This decline improved its inventory turnover and its days in inventory. However, its sales declined by 10%. It is possible that this decline was caused by the dramatic reduction in the amount of inventory that was on hand, which increased the likelihood of "stock-outs." To determine the optimal inventory level, management must weigh the benefits of reduced inventory against the potential lost sales caused by stock-outs.

Related exercise material: **BE6.9, BE6.10, DO IT! 6.3a, DO IT! 6.3b, E6.9, E6.10, E6.11, and E6.12.**

USING THE DECISION TOOLS | Manitowoc Company

The **Manitowoc Company** is located in Manitowoc, Wisconsin. In recent years, it has made a series of strategic acquisitions to grow and enhance its market-leading positions in each of its three business segments: (1) cranes and related products (crawler cranes, tower cranes, and boom trucks), (2) food service equipment (commercial ice-cube machines, ice-beverage dispensers, and commercial refrigeration equipment), and (3) marine operations (shipbuilding and ship-repair services). The company reported inventory of $644.5 million for 2014 and of $720.8 million for 2013. Here is the inventory note taken from the 2014 financial statements.

The Manitowoc Company
Notes to the Financial Statements

Inventories: The components of inventories at December 31, 2014, and December 31, 2013, are summarized as follows:

(in millions)	2014	2013
Inventories—gross:		
Raw materials	$226.2	$259.0
Work in process	103.7	130.2
Finished goods	414.8	436.8
Total inventories—gross	744.7	826.0
Excess and obsolete inventory reserve	(64.0)	(69.0)
Net inventories at FIFO cost	680.7	757.0
Excess of FIFO costs over LIFO value	(36.2)	(36.2)
Inventories—net (as reported on balance sheet)	$644.5	$720.8

Manitowoc determines inventory cost using the first-in, first-out (FIFO) method for approximately 84% and 87% of total inventory for 2014 and 2013, respectively. The remainder of the inventory is costed using the last-in, first-out (LIFO) method.

Additional facts (amounts in millions):

2014 Current liabilities	$1,011.3
2014 Current assets (as reported)	1,186.1
2014 Cost of goods sold	2,900.4

Instructions

Answer the following questions.

a. Why does the company report its inventory in three components?

b. Why might the company use two methods (LIFO and FIFO) to account for its inventory?

c. Perform each of the following.

   1. Calculate the inventory turnover and days in inventory using the LIFO inventory.
   2. Calculate the 2014 current ratio using LIFO and the current ratio using FIFO. Discuss the difference.

Solution

a. The Manitowoc Company is a manufacturer, so it purchases raw materials and makes them into finished products. At the end of each period, it has some goods that have been started but are not yet complete (work in process).

By reporting all three components of inventory, a company reveals important information about its inventory position. For example, if amounts of raw materials have increased significantly compared to the previous year, we might assume the company is planning to step up production. On the other hand, if levels of finished goods have increased relative to last year and raw materials have declined, we might conclude that sales are slowing down—that the company has too much inventory on hand and is cutting back production.

b. Companies are free to choose different cost flow assumptions for different types of inventory. A company might choose to use FIFO for a product that is expected to decrease in price over time. One common reason for choosing a method other than LIFO is that many foreign countries do not allow LIFO; thus, the company cannot use LIFO for its foreign operations.

c. 1. $\text{Inventory turnover} = \dfrac{\text{Cost of goods sold}}{\text{Average inventory}} = \dfrac{\$2,900.4}{(\$644.5 + \$720.8)/2} = 4.2$

$\dfrac{\text{Days in}}{\text{inventory}} = \dfrac{365}{\text{Inventory turnover}} = \dfrac{365}{4.2} = 86.9 \text{ days}$

2. Current ratio

LIFO	FIFO
$\dfrac{\text{Current assets}}{\text{Current liabilities}} = \dfrac{\$1,186.1}{\$1,011.3} = 1.17{:}1$	$\dfrac{\$1,186.1 + \$36.2}{\$1,011.3} = 1.21{:}1$

This represents a 3.4% increase in the current ratio $[(1.21 - 1.17)/1.17]$.

Appendix 6A Inventory Cost Flow Methods in Perpetual Inventory Systems

LEARNING OBJECTIVE *4
Apply inventory cost flow methods to perpetual inventory records.

What inventory cost flow methods can companies employ if they use a perpetual inventory system? Simple—they can use any of the inventory cost flow methods described in the chapter. To illustrate the application of the three assumed cost flow methods (FIFO, LIFO, and average-cost), we will use the data shown in **Illustration 6A.1** and in this chapter for Houston Electronics' Astro condensers.

ILLUSTRATION 6A.1
Inventoriable units and costs

Houston Electronics
Astro Condensers

Date	Explanation	Units	Unit Cost	Total Cost	Balance in Units
1/1	Beginning inventory	100	$10	$ 1,000	100
4/15	Purchases	200	11	2,200	300
8/24	Purchases	300	12	3,600	600
9/10	Sale	550			50
11/27	Purchases	400	13	5,200	450
				$12,000	

First-In, First-Out (FIFO)

Under perpetual FIFO, the company charges to cost of goods sold the cost of the earliest goods on hand **prior to each sale**. Therefore, the cost of goods sold on September 10 consists of the units on hand January 1 and the units purchased April 15 and August 24. **Illustration 6A.2** shows the inventory under a FIFO method perpetual system.

ILLUSTRATION 6A.2
Perpetual system—FIFO

Date	Purchases		Cost of Goods Sold		Balance (in units and cost)	
January 1					(100 @ $10)	$1,000
April 15	(200 @ $11)	$2,200			(100 @ $10) (200 @ $11)	$3,200
August 24	(300 @ $12)	$3,600			(100 @ $10) (200 @ $11) (300 @ $12)	$6,800
September 10			(100 @ $10) (200 @ $11) (250 @ $12) $6,200		(50 @ $12)	$ 600
November 27	(400 @ $13)	$5,200			(50 @ $12) (400 @ $13)	$5,800

Cost of goods sold → $6,200
Ending inventory → $5,800

The ending inventory in this situation is $5,800, and the cost of goods sold is $6,200 [(100 @ $10) + (200 @ $11) + (250 @ $12)].

Compare Illustrations 6.6 and 6A.2. You can see that the results under FIFO in a perpetual system are the **same as in a periodic system**. In both cases, the ending inventory is $5,800 and cost of goods sold is $6,200. Regardless of the system, the first costs in are the costs assigned to cost of goods sold.

Last-In, First-Out (LIFO)

Under the LIFO method using a perpetual system, the company charges to cost of goods sold the cost of the most recent purchase prior to sale. Therefore, the cost of the goods sold on September 10 consists of all the units from the August 24 and April 15 purchases plus 50 of the units in beginning inventory. **Illustration 6A.3** shows the computation of the ending inventory under the LIFO method.

ILLUSTRATION 6A.3
Perpetual system—LIFO

Date	Purchases		Cost of Goods Sold		Balance (in units and cost)	
January 1					(100 @ $10)	$1,000
April 15	(200 @ $11)	$2,200			(100 @ $10) (200 @ $11)	$3,200
August 24	(300 @ $12)	$3,600			(100 @ $10) (200 @ $11) (300 @ $12)	$6,800
September 10			(300 @ $12) (200 @ $11) (50 @ $10) $6,300		(50 @ $10)	$ 500
November 27	(400 @ $13)	$5,200			(50 @ $10) (400 @ $13)	$5,700

Cost of goods sold → $6,300
Ending inventory → $5,700

The use of LIFO in a perpetual system will usually produce cost allocations that differ from those using LIFO in a periodic system. In a perpetual system, the latest units purchased **prior to each sale** are allocated to cost of goods sold. In contrast, in a periodic system, the latest units purchased **during the period** are allocated to cost of goods sold. Thus, when a purchase is made after the last sale, the LIFO periodic system will apply this purchase to the previous sale. See Illustration 6.9 which shows the proof that the 400 units at $13 purchased on November 27 applied to the sale of 550 units on September 10.

Under the LIFO perpetual system in Illustration 6A.3, the 400 units at $13 purchased on November 27 are all applied to the ending inventory. The ending inventory in this LIFO perpetual illustration is $5,700, and cost of goods sold is $6,300, as compared to the LIFO periodic Illustration 6.8, where the ending inventory is $5,000 and cost of goods sold is $7,000.

Average-Cost

The average-cost method in a perpetual inventory system is called the **moving-average method**. Under this method, the company computes a new average **after each purchase**, by dividing the cost of goods available for sale by the units on hand. The average cost is then applied to (1) the units sold, to determine the cost of goods sold, and (2) the remaining units on hand, to determine the ending inventory amount. **Illustration 6A.4** shows the application of the moving-average cost method by Houston Electronics (computations of the moving-average unit cost are shown after Illustration 6A.4).

Date	Purchases	Cost of Goods Sold	Balance (in units and cost)	
January 1			(100 @ $10)	$1,000
April 15	(200 @ $11) $2,200		(300 @ $10.667)	$3,200
August 24	(300 @ $12) $3,600		(600 @ $11.333)	$6,800
September 10		(550 @ $11.333)	(50 @ $11.333)	$ 567
		$6,233		
November 27	(400 @ $13) $5,200		(450 @ $12.816)	$5,767

ILLUSTRATION 6A.4
Perpetual system—moving-average method

$6,233 — Cost of goods sold
$5,767 — Ending inventory

As indicated, Houston Electronics computes **a new average each time it makes a purchase**.

1. On April 15, after Houston buys 200 units for $2,200, a total of 300 units costing $3,200 ($1,000 + $2,200) are on hand. The average unit cost is $10.667 ($3,200 ÷ 300).

2. On August 24, after Houston buys 300 units for $3,600, a total of 600 units costing $6,800 ($1,000 + $2,200 + $3,600) are on hand. The average cost per unit is $11.333 ($6,800 ÷ 600).

3. On September 10, to compute cost of goods sold, Houston uses this unit cost of $11.333 in costing sales until it makes another purchase, when the company computes a new unit cost. Accordingly, the unit cost of the 550 units sold on September 10 is $11.333, and the total cost of goods sold is $6,233.

4. On November 27, following the purchase of 400 units for $5,200, there are 450 units on hand costing $5,767 ($567 + $5,200) with a new average cost of $12.816 ($5,767 ÷ 450).

Compare this moving-average cost under the perpetual inventory system to Illustration 6.11, which shows the average-cost method under a periodic inventory system.

Appendix 6B Effects of Inventory Errors

LEARNING OBJECTIVE *5
Indicate the effects of inventory errors on the financial statements.

Unfortunately, errors occasionally occur in accounting for inventory. In some cases, errors are caused by failure to count or price the inventory correctly. In other cases, errors occur because companies do not properly recognize the transfer of legal title to goods that are in transit. When errors occur, they affect both the income statement and the balance sheet.

Income Statement Effects

The ending inventory of one period automatically becomes the beginning inventory of the next period. Thus, inventory errors affect the computation of cost of goods sold and net income in two periods.

The effects on cost of goods sold can be computed by first entering incorrect data in the formula in **Illustration 6B.1** and then substituting the correct data.

ILLUSTRATION 6B.1 Formula for cost of goods sold

$$\text{Beginning Inventory} + \text{Cost of Goods Purchased} - \text{Ending Inventory} = \text{Cost of Goods Sold}$$

ETHICS NOTE

Inventory fraud increases during recessions. Such fraud includes pricing inventory at amounts in excess of its actual value, or claiming to have inventory when no inventory exists. Inventory fraud usually overstates ending inventory, thereby understating cost of goods sold and creating higher income.

If **beginning** inventory is understated, cost of goods sold will be understated. If **ending** inventory is understated, cost of goods sold will be overstated. **Illustration 6B.2** shows the effects of inventory errors on the current year's income statement (see **Ethics Note**).

ILLUSTRATION 6B.2 Effects of inventory errors on current year's income statement

When Inventory Error:	Cost of Goods Sold Is:	Net Income Is:
Understates beginning inventory	Understated	Overstated
Overstates beginning inventory	Overstated	Understated
Understates ending inventory	Overstated	Understated
Overstates ending inventory	Understated	Overstated

An error in the ending inventory of the current period will have a **reverse effect on net income of the next accounting period**. Illustration 6B.3 shows this effect. Note that the understatement of ending inventory in 2021 results in an understatement of beginning inventory in 2022 and an overstatement of net income in 2022.

ILLUSTRATION 6B.3 Effects of inventory errors on two years' income statements

Sample Company
Condensed Income Statements

	2021 Incorrect		2021 Correct		2022 Incorrect		2022 Correct	
Sales revenue		$80,000		$80,000		$90,000		$90,000
Beginning inventory	$20,000		$20,000		$12,000		$15,000	
Cost of goods purchased	40,000		40,000		68,000		68,000	
Cost of goods available for sale	60,000		60,000		80,000		83,000	
Ending inventory	12,000		15,000		23,000		23,000	
Cost of goods sold		48,000		45,000		57,000		60,000
Gross profit		32,000		35,000		33,000		30,000
Operating expenses		10,000		10,000		20,000		20,000
Net income		$22,000		$25,000		$13,000		$10,000

$(3,000) Net income understated

$3,000 Net income overstated

The errors cancel. Thus, the combined total income for the 2-year period is correct.

Over the two years, though, total net income is correct because the errors **offset each other**. Notice that total income using incorrect data is $35,000 ($22,000 + $13,000), which is the same as the total income of $35,000 ($25,000 + $10,000) using correct data. Also note in this example that an error in the beginning inventory does not result in a corresponding error in the ending inventory for that period. The correctness of the ending inventory depends entirely on the accuracy of taking and costing the inventory at the balance sheet date under the periodic inventory system.

Balance Sheet Effects

Companies can determine the effect of ending inventory errors on the balance sheet by using the basic accounting equation: Assets = Liabilities + Stockholders' Equity. Errors in the ending inventory have the effects shown in **Illustration 6B.4**.

Ending Inventory Error	Assets	Liabilities	Stockholders' Equity
Overstated	Overstated	No effect	Overstated
Understated	Understated	No effect	Understated

ILLUSTRATION 6B.4
Effects of ending inventory errors on balance sheet

The effect of an error in ending inventory on the subsequent period was shown in Illustration 6B.3. Note that if the error is not corrected, the combined total net income for the two periods would be correct. Thus, total stockholders' equity reported on the balance sheet at the end of 2022 will also be correct.

Review and Practice

Learning Objectives Review

1 Discuss how to classify and determine inventory.

Merchandisers need only one inventory classification, merchandise inventory, to describe the different items that make up total inventory. Manufacturers, on the other hand, usually classify inventory into three categories: finished goods, work in process, and raw materials. To determine inventory quantities, manufacturers (1) take a physical inventory of goods on hand and (2) determine the ownership of goods in transit or on consignment.

2 Apply inventory cost flow methods and discuss their financial effects.

The primary basis of accounting for inventories is cost. Cost includes all expenditures necessary to acquire goods and place them in a condition ready for sale. Cost of goods available for sale includes (a) cost of beginning inventory and (b) cost of goods purchased. The inventory cost flow methods are specific identification and three assumed cost flow methods—FIFO, LIFO, and average-cost.

The cost of goods available for sale may be allocated to cost of goods sold and ending inventory by specific identification or by a method based on an assumed cost flow. When prices are rising, the first-in, first-out (FIFO) method results in lower cost of goods sold and higher net income than the average-cost and the last-in, first-out (LIFO) methods. The reverse is true when prices are falling. In the balance sheet, FIFO results in an ending inventory that is closest to current value, whereas the inventory under LIFO is the farthest from current value. LIFO results in the lowest income taxes (because of lower taxable income).

3 Explain the statement presentation and analysis of inventory.

Companies use the lower-of-cost-or-net realizable value (LCNRV) basis when the net realizable value is less than cost. Under LCNRV, companies recognize the loss in the period in which the price decline occurs.

Inventory turnover is calculated as cost of goods sold divided by average inventory. It can be converted to average days in inventory by dividing 365 days by the inventory turnover. A higher inventory turnover or lower average days in inventory suggests that management is trying to keep inventory levels low relative to its sales level.

The LIFO reserve represents the difference between ending inventory using LIFO and ending inventory if FIFO were employed instead. For some companies this difference can be significant, and ignoring it can lead to inappropriate conclusions when using the current ratio or inventory turnover.

*4 Apply inventory cost flow methods to perpetual inventory records.

Under FIFO, the cost of the earliest goods on hand prior to each sale is charged to cost of goods sold. Under LIFO, the cost of the most recent purchase prior to sale is charged to cost of goods sold. Under the average-cost method, a new average cost is computed after each purchase.

*5 Indicate the effects of inventory errors on the financial statements.

In the income statement of the current year: (1) An error in beginning inventory will have a reverse effect on net income (e.g., overstatement of inventory results in understatement of net income, and vice versa). (2) An error in ending inventory will have a similar effect on net income (e.g., overstatement of inventory results in overstatement of net income). If ending inventory errors are not corrected in the following period, their effect on net income for that period is reversed, and total net income for the two years will be correct.

In the balance sheet: Ending inventory errors will have the same effect on total assets and total stockholders' equity and no effect on liabilities.

Decision Tools Review

Decision Checkpoints	Info Needed for Decision	Tool to Use for Decision	How to Evaluate Results
Which inventory costing method should be used?	Are prices increasing, or are they decreasing?	Income statement, balance sheet, and tax effects	Depends on objective. In a period of rising prices, income and inventory are higher and cash flow is lower under FIFO. LIFO provides opposite results. Average-cost can moderate the impact of changing prices.
How long is an item in inventory?	Cost of goods sold; beginning and ending inventory	$\text{Inventory turnover} = \dfrac{\text{Cost of goods sold}}{\text{Average inventory}}$ $\text{Days in inventory} = \dfrac{365 \text{ days}}{\text{Inventory turnover}}$	A higher inventory turnover or lower average days in inventory suggests that management is reducing the amount of inventory on hand, relative to cost of goods sold.
What is the impact of LIFO on the company's reported inventory?	LIFO reserve, cost of goods sold, ending inventory, current assets, current liabilities	$\text{LIFO inventory} + \text{LIFO reserve} = \text{FIFO inventory}$	If these adjustments are material, they can significantly affect such measures as the current ratio and the inventory turnover.

Glossary Review

Average-cost method An inventory costing method that uses the weighted-average unit cost to allocate the cost of goods available for sale to ending inventory and cost of goods sold. (p. 6-11).

Consigned goods Goods held for sale by one party although ownership of the goods is retained by another party. (p. 6-5).

Consistency concept Companies use the same accounting principles and methods from year to year. (p. 6-14).

Days in inventory Measure of the average number of days inventory is held; calculated as 365 divided by inventory turnover. (p. 6-17).

Finished goods inventory Manufactured items that are completed and ready for sale. (p. 6-3).

First-in, first-out (FIFO) method An inventory costing method that assumes that the earliest goods purchased are the first to be sold. (p. 6-8).

FOB destination Freight terms indicating that ownership of goods remains with the seller until the goods reach the buyer. (p. 6-5).

FOB shipping point Freight terms indicating that ownership of goods passes to the buyer when the public carrier accepts the goods from the seller. (p. 6-5).

Inventory turnover A ratio that indicates the liquidity of inventory by measuring the number of times average inventory is sold during the year; computed by dividing cost of goods sold by the average inventory. (p. 6-17).

Just-in-time (JIT) inventory Inventory system in which companies manufacture or purchase goods only when needed. (p. 6-3).

Last-in, first-out (LIFO) method An inventory costing method that assumes that the latest goods purchased are the first to be sold. (p. 6-10).

LIFO reserve For a company using LIFO, the difference between inventory reported using LIFO and inventory using FIFO. (p. 6-18).

Lower-of-cost-or-net realizable value (LCNRV) A basis whereby inventory is stated at the lower of either its cost or its net realizable value. (p. 6-16).

Moving-average method Perpetual inventory method where the company computes a new average cost after each purchase by dividing the cost of goods available for sale by the units on hand. (p. 6-23).

Net realizable value The estimated selling price in the normal course of business, less estimated costs to complete and sell. (p. 6-16).

Raw materials Basic goods that will be used in production but have not yet been placed in production. (p. 6-3).

Specific identification method An actual physical-flow costing method in which particular items sold and items still in inventory are specifically costed to arrive at cost of goods sold and ending inventory. (p. 6-7).

Weighted-average unit cost Average cost that is weighted by the number of units purchased at each unit cost. (p. 6-11).

Work in process That portion of manufactured inventory that has begun the production process but is not yet complete. (p. 6-3).

Practice Multiple-Choice Questions

1. **(LO 1)** When is a physical inventory usually taken?
   a. When the company has its greatest amount of inventory.
   b. When a limited number of goods are being sold or received.
   c. At the end of the company's fiscal year.
   d. Both (b) and (c).

2. **(LO 1)** Which of the following should **not** be included in the physical inventory of a company?
   a. Goods held on consignment from another company.
   b. Goods shipped on consignment to another company.
   c. Goods in transit from another company shipped FOB shipping point.
   d. All of the above should be included.

3. **(LO 1)** As a result of a thorough physical inventory, Railway Company determined that it had inventory worth $180,000 at December 31, 2022. This count did not take into consideration the following facts. Rogers Consignment Store currently has goods worth $35,000 on its sales floor that belong to Railway but are being sold on consignment by Rogers. The selling price of these goods is $50,000. Railway purchased $13,000 of goods that were shipped on December 27, FOB destination, that will be received by Railway on January 3. Determine the correct amount of inventory that Railway should report.
   a. $230,000.
   b. $215,000.
   c. $228,000.
   d. $193,000.

4. **(LO 2)** Kam Company has the following units and costs.

	Units	Unit Cost
Inventory, Jan. 1	8,000	$11
Purchase, June 19	13,000	12
Purchase, Nov. 8	5,000	13

   If 9,000 units are on hand at December 31, what is the cost of the ending inventory under FIFO?
   a. $99,000.
   b. $108,000.
   c. $113,000.
   d. $117,000.

5. **(LO 2)** From the data in Question 4, what is the cost of the ending inventory under LIFO?
   a. $113,000.
   b. $108,000.
   c. $99,000.
   d. $100,000.

6. **(LO 2)** Davidson Electronics has the following:

	Units	Unit Cost
Inventory, Jan. 1	5,000	$8
Purchase, April 2	15,000	10
Purchase, Aug. 28	20,000	12

   If Davidson has 7,000 units on hand at December 31, the cost of ending inventory under the average-cost method is:
   a. $84,000.
   b. $70,000.
   c. $56,000.
   d. $75,250.

7. **(LO 2)** In periods of rising prices, LIFO will produce:
   a. higher net income than FIFO.
   b. the same net income as FIFO.
   c. lower net income than FIFO.
   d. higher net income than average-cost.

8. **(LO 2)** Cost of goods available for sale consists of two elements: beginning inventory and:
   a. ending inventory.
   b. cost of goods purchased.
   c. cost of goods sold.
   d. All of the answer choices are correct.

9. **(LO 2)** Considerations that affect the selection of an inventory costing method do **not** include:
   a. tax effects.
   b. balance sheet effects.
   c. income statement effects.
   d. perpetual versus periodic inventory system.

10. **(LO 3)** The lower-of-cost-or-net realizable value rule for inventory is an example of the application of:
    a. the conservatism convention.
    b. the historical cost principle.
    c. the materiality concept.
    d. the economic entity assumption.

11. **(LO 3)** Which of these would cause inventory turnover to increase the most?
    a. Increasing the amount of inventory on hand.
    b. Keeping the amount of inventory on hand constant but increasing sales.

c. Keeping the amount of inventory on hand constant but decreasing sales.

d. Decreasing the amount of inventory on hand and increasing sales.

12. (LO 3) Carlos Company had beginning inventory of $80,000, ending inventory of $110,000, cost of goods sold of $285,000, and sales of $475,000. Carlos's days in inventory is:

a. 73 days.   c. 102.5 days.
b. 121.7 days.   d. 84.5 days.

13. (LO 3) Norton Company purchased 1,000 widgets and has 200 widgets in its ending inventory at a cost of $91 each and a net realizable value of $80 each. The ending inventory under lower-of-cost-or-net realizable value is:

a. $91,000.   c. $18,200.
b. $80,000.   d. $16,000.

14. (LO 3) The LIFO reserve is:

a. the difference between the value of the inventory under LIFO and the value under FIFO.

b. an amount used to adjust inventory to the lower-of-cost-or-net realizable value.

c. the difference between the value of the inventory under LIFO and the value under average-cost.

d. an amount used to adjust inventory to historical cost.

*15. (LO 4) In a perpetual inventory system:

a. LIFO cost of goods sold will be the same as in a periodic inventory system.

b. average costs are based entirely on unit-cost simple averages.

c. a new average is computed under the average-cost method after each sale.

d. FIFO cost of goods sold will be the same as in a periodic inventory system.

*16. (LO 5) Fran Company's ending inventory is understated by $4,000. The effects of this error on the current year's cost of goods sold and net income, respectively, are:

a. understated and overstated.
b. overstated and understated.
c. overstated and overstated.
d. understated and understated.

*17. (LO 5) Harold Company overstated its inventory by $15,000 at December 31, 2021. It did not correct the error in 2021 or 2022. As a result, Harold's stockholders' equity was:

a. overstated at December 31, 2021, and understated at December 31, 2022.

b. overstated at December 31, 2021, and properly stated at December 31, 2022.

c. understated at December 31, 2021, and understated at December 31, 2022.

d. overstated at December 31, 2021, and overstated at December 31, 2022.

Solutions

1. d. A physical inventory is usually taken when a limited number of goods are being sold or received, and at the end of the company's fiscal year. Choice (a) is incorrect because a physical inventory count is usually taken when the company has the least, not greatest, amount of inventory. Choices (b) and (c) are correct, but (d) is the better answer.

2. a. Goods held on consignment should not be included because another company has title (ownership) to the goods. The other choices are incorrect because (b) goods shipped on consignment to another company and (c) goods in transit from another company shipped FOB shipping point should be included in a company's ending inventory. Choice (d) is incorrect because (a) is not included in the physical inventory.

3. b. The inventory held on consignment by Rogers should be included in Railway's inventory balance at cost ($35,000). The purchased goods of $13,000 should not be included in inventory until January 3 because the goods are shipped FOB destination. Therefore, the correct amount of inventory is $215,000 ($180,000 + $35,000), not (a) $230,000, (c) $228,000, or (d) $193,000.

4. c. Under FIFO, ending inventory will consist of 5,000 units from the Nov. 8 purchase and 4,000 units from the June 19 purchase. Therefore, ending inventory is (5,000 × $13) + (4,000 × $12) = $113,000, not (a) $99,000, (b) $108,000, or (d) $117,000.

5. d. Under LIFO, ending inventory will consist of 8,000 units from the inventory at Jan. 1 and 1,000 units from the June 19 purchase. Therefore, ending inventory is (8,000 × $11) + (1,000 × $12) = $100,000, not (a) $113,000, (b) $108,000, or (c) $99,000.

6. d. Under the average-cost method, total cost of goods available for sale needs to be calculated in order to determine average cost per unit. The total cost of goods available is $430,000 = (5,000 × $8) + (15,000 × $10) + (20,000 × $12). The average cost per unit = ($430,000/40,000 total units available for sale) = $10.75. Therefore, ending inventory is ($10.75 × 7,000) = $75,250, not (a) $84,000, (b) $70,000, or (c) $56,000.

7. c. In periods of rising prices, LIFO will produce lower net income than FIFO, not (a) higher than FIFO or (b) the same as FIFO. Choice (d) is incorrect because in periods of rising prices, LIFO will produce lower net income than average cost. LIFO therefore charges the highest inventory cost against revenues in a period of rising prices.

8. b. Cost of goods available for sale consists of beginning inventory and cost of goods purchased, not (a) ending inventory or (c) cost of goods sold. Therefore, choice (d) is also incorrect.

9. d. Perpetual vs. periodic inventory system is not one of the factors that affect the selection of an inventory costing method. The other choices are incorrect because (a) tax effects, (b) balance sheet effects, and (c) income statement effects all affect the selection of an inventory costing method.

10. a. Conservatism means that the best choice among accounting alternatives is the method that is least likely to overstate assets and net income. The other choices are incorrect because (b) historical cost means that companies value assets at the original cost, (c) materiality means that an amount is large enough to affect a decision-maker, and (d) economic entity means to keep the company's transactions separate from the transactions of other entities.

11. d. Decreasing the amount of inventory on hand will cause the denominator to decrease, causing inventory turnover to increase. Increasing sales will cause the numerator of the ratio to increase (higher sales means higher COGS), thus causing inventory turnover to increase even more. The other choices are incorrect because (a) increasing the amount of inventory on hand causes the denominator of the ratio to increase while the numerator stays the same, causing inventory turnover to decrease; (b) keeping the amount of inventory on hand constant but increasing sales will cause inventory turnover to increase because the numerator of the ratio will increase (higher sales means higher COGS) while the denominator stays the same, which will result in a lesser inventory increase than decreasing amount of inventory on hand and increasing sales; and (c) keeping the amount of inventory on hand constant but decreasing sales will cause inventory turnover to decrease because the numerator of the ratio will decrease (lower sales means lower COGS) while the denominator stays the same.

12. **b.** Carlos's days in inventory = 365/Inventory turnover = 365/ [$285,000/($80,000 + $110,000)/2)] = 121.7 days, not (a) 73 days, (c) 102.5 days, or (d) 84.5 days.

13. **d.** Under the LCNRV basis, net realizable value is defined as the estimated selling price in the normal course of business, less estimated costs to complete and sell. Therefore, ending inventory would be valued at 200 widgets × $80 each = $16,000, not (a) $91,000, (b) $80,000, or (c) $18,200.

14. **a.** The LIFO reserve is the difference in ending inventory value under LIFO and FIFO. The other choices are therefore incorrect.

*15. **d.** FIFO cost of goods sold is the same under both a periodic and a perpetual inventory system. The other choices are incorrect because (a) LIFO cost of goods sold is not the same under a periodic and a perpetual inventory system; (b) average costs are based on a moving average of unit costs, not an average of unit costs; and (c) a new average is computed under the average-cost method after each purchase, not sale.

*16. **b.** Because ending inventory is too low, cost of goods sold will be too high (overstated) and since cost of goods sold (an expense) is too high, net income will be too low (understated). Therefore, the other choices are incorrect.

*17. **b.** Stockholders' equity is overstated by $15,000 at December 31, 2021, and is properly stated at December 31, 2022. An ending inventory error in one period will have an equal and opposite effect on cost of goods sold and net income in the next period; after two years, the errors have offset each other. The other choices are incorrect because stockholders' equity (a) is properly stated, not understated, at December 31, 2022; (c) is overstated, not understated, by $15,000 at December 31, 2021, and is properly stated, not understated, at December 31, 2022; and (d) is properly stated at December 31, 2022, not overstated.

Practice Brief Exercises

1. (LO 1) Fylus Company took a physical inventory on December 31 and determined that goods costing $180,000 were on hand. Not included in the physical count were $18,000 of goods purchased from Rake Corporation, FOB destination, and $27,000 of goods sold to Shovel Company for $40,000, FOB destination. Both the Rake purchase and the Shovel sale were in transit year-end. What amount should Fylus report as its December 31 inventory?

Determine ending inventory amount.

Solution

1. Physical inventory $180,000
  Add: Goods sold to Shovel   27,000
  Fylus ending inventory $207,000

The $18,000 of goods purchased from Rake are excluded from ending inventory because the terms are FOB destination which means Fylus takes title at the time the goods are received. Goods sold to Shovel FOB destination means that the goods are still Fylus's until delivered.

2. (LO 2) In its first month of operations, Moncada Company made three purchases of merchandise in the following sequence: (1) 200 units at $7, (2) 300 units at $8, and (3) 150 units at $9. Assuming there are 220 units on hand, compute the cost of the ending inventory under the (a) FIFO method and (b) LIFO method. Moncada use a periodic inventory system.

Compute ending inventory using FIFO and LIFO.

Solution

2. **a.** The ending inventory under FIFO consists of (150 units at $9) + (70 units at $8) for a total allocation of $1,910 ($1,350 + $560).

  b. The ending inventory under LIFO consists of (200 units at $7) + (20 units at $8) for a total allocation of $1,560 ($1,400 + $160).

3. (LO 3) At December 31, 2022, the following information was available for Garcia Company: ending inventory $30,000, beginning inventory $42,000, cost of goods sold $240,000, and sales revenue $400,000. Calculate inventory turnover and days in inventory for Garcia Company.

Compute inventory turnover and days in inventory.

Solution

3. Inventory turnover: $\dfrac{\$240,000}{(\$30,000 + \$42,000)/2} = \dfrac{\$240,000}{\$36,000} = 6.67$

Days in inventory: $\dfrac{365}{6.67} = 54.7$ days

Practice Exercises

Determine the correct inventory amount.

1. **(LO 1)** Mika Sorbino, an auditor with Martinez CPAs, is performing a review of Sergei Company's inventory account. Sergei's did not have a good year and top management is under pressure to boost reported income. According to its records, the inventory balance at year-end was $650,000. However, the following information was not considered when determining that amount.

   1. Included in the company's count were goods with a cost of $200,000 that the company is holding on consignment. The goods belong to Bosnia Corporation.
   2. The physical count did not include goods purchased by Sergei with a cost of $40,000 that were shipped FOB shipping point on December 28 and did not arrive at Sergei's warehouse until January 3.
   3. Included in the inventory account was $15,000 of office supplies that were stored in the warehouse and were to be used by the company's supervisors and managers during the coming year.
   4. The company received an order on December 28 that was boxed and was sitting on the loading dock awaiting pick-up on December 31. The shipper picked up the goods on January 1 and delivered them on January 6. The shipping terms were FOB shipping point. The goods had a selling price of $40,000 and a cost of $30,000. The goods were not included in the count because they were sitting on the dock.
   5. On December 29, Sergei shipped goods with a selling price of $80,000 and a cost of $60,000 to Oman Sales Corporation FOB shipping point. The goods arrived on January 3. Oman Sales had only ordered goods with a selling price of $10,000 and a cost of $8,000. However, a Sergei's sales manager had authorized the shipment and said that if Oman wanted to ship the goods back next week, it could.
   6. Included in the count was $30,000 of goods that were parts for a machine that the company no longer made. Given the high-tech nature of Sergei's products, it was unlikely that these obsolete parts had any other use. However, management would prefer to keep them on the books at cost, "since that is what we paid for them, after all."

   Instructions

   Prepare a schedule to determine the correct inventory amount. Provide explanations for each item above, saying why you did or did not make an adjustment for each item.

   Solution

   1. Ending inventory—as reported $650,000
      1. Subtract from inventory: The goods belong to Bosnia Corporation. Sergei is merely holding them for Bosnia. .... (200,000)
      2. Add to inventory: The goods belong to Sergei when they were shipped. 40,000
      3. Subtract from inventory: Office supplies should be carried in a separate account. They are not considered inventory held for resale. .... (15,000)
      4. Add to inventory: The goods belong to Sergei until they are shipped (Jan. 1). 30,000
      5. Add to inventory: Oman Sales ordered goods with a cost of $8,000. Sergei should record the corresponding sales revenue of $10,000. Sergei's decision to ship extra "unordered" goods does not constitute a sale. The manager's statement that Oman could ship the goods back indicates that Sergei knows this overshipment is not a legitimate sale. The manager acted unethically in an attempt to improve Sergei's reported income by overshipping. 52,000

6. Subtract from inventory: GAAP requires that inventory be valued at the lower-of-cost-or-net realizable value. Obsolete parts should be adjusted from cost to zero if they have no other use. (30,000)

Correct inventory $527,000

Determine LCNRV valuation.

2. **(LO 3)** Creve Couer Camera Inc. uses the lower-of-cost-or-net realizable value basis for its inventory. The following data are available at December 31.

	Units	Cost per Unit	Net Realizable Value per Unit
Cameras:			
Minolta	5	$160	$156
Canon	7	145	153
Light Meters:			
Vivitar	12	120	114
Kodak	10	130	142

Instructions

What amount should be reported on Creve Couer Camera's financial statements, assuming the lower-of-cost-or-net realizable value rule is applied?

Solution

2.

	Cost per Unit	Net Realizable Value per Unit	Lower-of-Cost-or-Net Realizable Value	Units	Inventory at Lower-of-Cost-or-Net Realizable Value
Cameras:					
Minolta	$160	$156	$156	5	$ 780
Canon	145	153	145	7	1,015
Light Meters:					
Vivitar	120	114	114	12	1,368
Kodak	130	142	130	10	1,300
Total					$4,463

Practice Problems

Compute inventory and cost of goods sold using three cost flow methods in a periodic inventory system.

1. **(LO 2)** Englehart Company has the following inventory, purchases, and sales data for the month of March.

Inventory: March 1	200 units @ $4.00	$ 800
Purchases:		
March 10	500 units @ $4.50	2,250
March 20	400 units @ $4.75	1,900
March 30	300 units @ $5.00	1,500
Sales:		
March 15	500 units	
March 25	400 units	

The physical inventory count on March 31 shows 500 units on hand.

Instructions

Under a **periodic inventory system**, determine the cost of inventory on hand at March 31 and the cost of goods sold for March under (a) the first-in, first-out (FIFO) method; (b) the last-in, first-out (LIFO) method; and (c) the average-cost method. (For average-cost, carry cost per unit to three decimal places.)

Solution

1. The cost of goods available for sale is $6,450:

Inventory: March 1	200 units @ $4.00	$ 800
Purchases:		
March 10	500 units @ $4.50	2,250
March 20	400 units @ $4.75	1,900
March 30	300 units @ $5.00	1,500
Total cost of goods available for sale		$6,450

a. **FIFO Method**

Ending inventory:

Date	Units	Unit Cost	Total Cost	
Mar. 30	300	$5.00	$1,500	
Mar. 20	200	4.75	950	$2,450

Cost of goods sold: $6,450 − $2,450 = $4,000

b. **LIFO Method**

Ending inventory:

Date	Units	Unit Cost	Total Cost	
Mar. 1	200	$4.00	$ 800	
Mar. 10	300	4.50	1,350	$2,150

Cost of goods sold: $6,450 − $2,150 = $4,300

c. **Average-Cost Method**

Weighted-average unit cost: $6,450 ÷ 1,400 = $4.607
Ending inventory: 500 × $4.607 = $2,303.50
Cost of goods sold: $6,450 − $2,303.50 = $4,146.50

Compute inventory and cost of goods sold using three cost flow methods in a perpetual inventory system.

*2. (LO 4) Practice Problem 1 showed cost of goods sold computations under a periodic inventory system. Now let's assume that Englehart Company uses a perpetual inventory system. The company has the same inventory, purchases, and sales data for the month of March as shown earlier:

Inventory:	March 1	200 units @ $4.00	$ 800
Purchases:			
	March 10	500 units @ $4.50	2,250
	March 20	400 units @ $4.75	1,900
	March 30	300 units @ $5.00	1,500
Sales:			
	March 15	500 units	
	March 25	400 units	

The physical inventory count on March 31 shows 500 units on hand.

Instructions

Under a **perpetual inventory system**, determine the cost of inventory on hand at March 31 and the cost of goods sold for March under (a) FIFO, (b) LIFO, and (c) moving-average cost.

Solution

2. The cost of goods available for sale is $6,450, as follows.

Inventory:		200 units @ $4.00	$ 800
Purchases:	March 10	500 units @ $4.50	2,250
	March 20	400 units @ $4.75	1,900
	March 30	300 units @ $5.00	1,500
Total:		1,400	$6,450

Under a **perpetual inventory system**, the cost of goods sold under each cost flow method is as follows.

a.

FIFO Method

Date	Purchases	Cost of Goods Sold	Balance
March 1			(200 @ $4.00) $800
March 10	(500 @ $4.50) $2,250		(200 @ $4.00) / (500 @ $4.50) $3,050
March 15		(200 @ $4.00) / (300 @ $4.50) = $2,150	(200 @ $4.50) $900
March 20	(400 @ $4.75) $1,900		(200 @ $4.50) / (400 @ $4.75) $2,800
March 25		(200 @ $4.50) / (200 @ $4.75) = $1,850	(200 @ $4.75) $950
March 30	(300 @ $5.00) $1,500		(200 @ $4.75) / (300 @ $5.00) $2,450
	Ending inventory $2,450	Cost of goods sold: $2,150 + $1,850 = $4,000	

b.

LIFO Method

Date	Purchases	Cost of Goods Sold	Balance
March 1			(200 @ $4.00) $800
March 10	(500 @ $4.50) $2,250		(200 @ $4.00) / (500 @ $4.50) $3,050
March 15		(500 @ $4.50) $2,250	(200 @ $4.00) $800
March 20	(400 @ $4.75) $1,900		(200 @ $4.00) / (400 @ $4.75) $2,700
March 25		(400 @ $4.75) $1,900	(200 @ $4.00) $800
March 30	(300 @ $5.00) $1,500		(200 @ $4.00) / (300 @ $5.00) $2,300
	Ending inventory $2,300	Cost of goods sold: $2,250 + $1,900 = $4,150	

c.

Moving-Average Cost Method

Date	Purchases	Cost of Goods Sold	Balance
March 1			(200 @ $4.00) $800
March 10	(500 @ $4.50) $2,250		(700 @ $4.357) $3,050
March 15		(500 @ $4.357) $2,179	(200 @ $4.357) $871
March 20	(400 @ $4.75) $1,900		(600 @ $4.618) $2,771
March 25		(400 @ $4.618) $1,847	(200 @ $4.618) $924
March 30	(300 @ $5.00) $1,500		(500 @ $4.848) $2,424
	Ending inventory $2,424	Cost of goods sold: $2,179 + $1,847 = $4,026	

WileyPLUS

Brief Exercises, DO IT! Exercises, Exercises, Problems, and many additional resources are available for practice in WileyPLUS.

Note: All asterisked Questions, Exercises, and Problems relate to material in the appendices to the chapter.

Questions

1. "The key to successful business operations is effective inventory management." Do you agree? Explain.

2. An item must possess two characteristics to be classified as inventory. What are these two characteristics?

3. What is just-in-time inventory management? What are its potential advantages?

4. Your friend Will Juritz has been hired to help take the physical inventory in Byrd's Hardware Store. Explain to Will what this job will entail.

5. a. Bonita Company ships merchandise to Myan Corporation on December 30. The merchandise reaches the buyer on January 5. Indicate the terms of sale that will result in the goods being included in (1) Bonita's December 31 inventory and (2) Myan's December 31 inventory.

   b. Under what circumstances should Bonita Company include consigned goods in its inventory?

6. Nona Hat Shop received a shipment of hats for which it paid the wholesaler $2,940. The price of the hats was $3,000, but Nona was given a $60 cash discount and required to pay freight charges of $75. What amount should Nona include in inventory? Why?

7. What is the primary basis of accounting for inventories?

8. Ken McCall believes that the allocation of cost of goods available for sale should be based on the actual physical flow of the goods. Explain to Ken why this may be both impractical and inappropriate.

9. What is the major advantage and major disadvantage of the specific identification method of inventory costing?

10. "The selection of an inventory cost flow method is a decision made by accountants." Do you agree? Explain. Once a method has been selected, what accounting requirement applies?

11. Which assumed inventory cost flow method:

    a. usually parallels the actual physical flow of merchandise?

    b. divides cost of goods available for sale by total units available for sale to determine a unit cost?

    c. assumes that the latest units purchased are the first to be sold?

12. In a period of rising prices, the inventory reported in Short Company's balance sheet is close to the current cost of the inventory, whereas King Company's inventory is considerably below its current cost. Identify the inventory cost flow method used by each company. Which company probably has been reporting the higher gross profit?

13. Mamosa Corporation has been using the FIFO cost flow method during a prolonged period of inflation. During the same time period, Mamosa has been paying out all of its net income as dividends. What adverse effects may result from this policy?

14. Oscar Geer, a mid-level product manager for Theresa's Shoes, thinks his company should switch from LIFO to FIFO. He says, "My bonus is based on net income. If we switch it will increase net income and increase my bonus. The company would be better off and so would I." Is he correct? Explain.

15. Discuss the impact the use of LIFO has on taxes paid, cash flows, and the quality of earnings ratio relative to the impact of FIFO when prices are increasing.

16. Hank Artisan is studying for the next accounting midterm examination. What should Hank know about (a) departing from the cost basis of accounting for inventories and (b) the meaning of "net realizable value" in the lower-of-cost-or-net realizable value method?

17. Jackson Music Center has five TVs on hand at the balance sheet date that cost $400 each. The net realizable value is $350 per unit. Under the lower-of-cost-or-net realizable value basis of accounting for inventories, what value should Jackson report for the TVs on the balance sheet? Why?

18. What cost flow assumption may be used under the lower-of-cost-or-net realizable value basis of accounting for inventories?

19. Why is it inappropriate for a company to include freight-out expense in the Cost of Goods Sold account?

20. Tilton Company's balance sheet shows Inventory $162,800. What additional disclosures should be made?

21. Under what circumstances might inventory turnover be too high—that is, what possible negative consequences might occur?

22. What is the LIFO reserve? What are the consequences of ignoring a large LIFO reserve when analyzing a company?

*23. "When perpetual inventory records are kept, the results under the FIFO and LIFO methods are the same as they would be in a periodic inventory system." Do you agree? Explain.

*24. How does the average-cost method of inventory costing differ between a perpetual inventory system and a periodic inventory system?

*25. Albert Company discovers in 2022 that its ending inventory at December 31, 2021, was $5,000 understated. What effect will this error have on (a) 2021 net income, (b) 2022 net income, and (c) the combined net income for the 2 years?

Brief Exercises

Identify items to be included in taking a physical inventory.

BE6.1 (LO 1), C Peete Company identifies the following items for possible inclusion in the physical inventory. Indicate whether each item should be included or excluded from the inventory taking.

  a. 900 units of inventory shipped on consignment by Peete to another company.

  b. 3,000 units of inventory in transit from a supplier shipped FOB destination.

  c. 1,200 units of inventory sold but being held for customer pickup.

  d. 500 units of inventory held on consignment from another company.

Determine ending inventory amount.

BE6.2 (LO 1), AN Stallman Company took a physical inventory on December 31 and determined that goods costing $200,000 were on hand. Not included in the physical count were $25,000 of goods purchased from Pelzer Corporation, FOB shipping point, and $22,000 of goods sold to Alvarez Company for $30,000, FOB destination. Both the Pelzer purchase and the Alvarez sale were in transit at year-end. What amount should Stallman report as its December 31 inventory?

Compute ending inventory using FIFO and LIFO.

BE6.3 (LO 2), AP In its first month of operations, McLanie Company made three purchases of merchandise in the following sequence: (1) 300 units at $6, (2) 400 units at $8, and (3) 500 units at $9. Assuming there are 200 units on hand at the end of the period, compute the cost of the ending inventory under (a) the FIFO method and (b) the LIFO method. McLanie uses a periodic inventory system.

BE6.4 (LO 2), AP Data for McLanie Company are presented in BE6.3. Compute the cost of the ending inventory under the average-cost method. (Round the cost per unit to three decimal places.)

Compute the ending inventory using average-cost.

BE6.5 (LO 2), AP Sunnyside Marine Products began the year with 10 units of marine floats at a cost of $11 each. During the year, it made the following purchases: May 5, 30 unit at $16; July 16, 15 units at $19; and December 7, 20 units at $23. Assuming there are 25 units on hand at the end of the period, determine the cost of goods sold under (a) FIFO, (b) LIFO, and (c) average-cost. Sunnyside uses the periodic approach.

Compute cost of goods sold using FIFO, LIFO, and average-cost.

BE6.6 (LO 2), C The management of Milque Corp. is considering the effects of various inventory-costing methods on its financial statements and its income tax expense. Assuming that the cost the company pays for inventory is increasing, which method will:

Explain the financial statement effect of inventory cost flow assumptions.

a. provide the highest net income?
b. provide the highest ending inventory?
c. result in the lowest income tax expense?
d. result in the most stable earnings over a number of years?

BE6.7 (LO 2), AP In its first month of operation, Hoffman Company purchased 100 units of inventory for $6, then 200 units for $7, and finally 140 units for $8. At the end of the month, 180 units remained. Compute the amount of phantom profit that would result if the company used FIFO rather than LIFO. Explain why this amount is referred to as phantom profit. The company uses the periodic method.

Explain the financial statement effect of inventory cost flow assumptions.

BE6.8 (LO 2), C For each of the following cases, state whether the statement is true for LIFO or for FIFO. Assume that prices are rising.

Identify the impact of LIFO versus FIFO.

a. Results in a higher quality of earnings ratio.
b. Results in higher phantom profits.
c. Results in higher net income.
d. Results in lower taxes.
e. Results in lower net cash provided by operating activities.

BE6.9 (LO 3), AP Wahlowitz Video Center accumulates the following cost and net realizable value data at December 31.

Determine the LCNRV valuation.

Inventory Categories	Cost	Net Realizable Value
Cameras	$12,500	$13,400
Camcorders	9,000	9,500
DVDs	13,000	12,200

Compute the lower-of-cost-or-net realizable value for the company's inventory.

BE6.10 (LO 3), AP Suppose at December 31 of a recent year, the following information (in thousands) was available for sunglasses manufacturer **Oakley, Inc.**: ending inventory $155,377, beginning inventory $119,035, cost of goods sold $349,114, and sales revenue $761,865. Calculate the inventory turnover and days in inventory for Oakley, Inc. (Round inventory turnover to two decimal places.)

Compute inventory turnover and days in inventory.

BE6.11 (LO 3), AP Winnebago Industries, Inc. is a leading manufacturer of motor homes. Suppose Winnebago reported ending inventory at August 29, 2022, of $46,850,000 under the LIFO inventory method. In the notes to its financial statements, assume Winnebago reported a LIFO reserve of $30,346,000 at August 29, 2022. What would Winnebago Industries' ending inventory have been if it had used FIFO?

Determine ending inventory using LIFO reserve.

*BE6.12 (LO 4), AP Loggins Department Store uses a perpetual inventory system. Data for product E2-D2 include the following purchases.

Apply cost flow methods to perpetual inventory records.

Date	Number of Units	Unit Price
May 7	50	$10
July 28	30	15

On June 1, Loggins sold 25 units, and on August 27, 30 more units. Compute the cost of goods sold using (a) FIFO, (b) LIFO, and (c) average-cost. (Round the cost per unit to three decimal places.)

*BE6.13 (LO 5), AN Fennick Company reports net income of $92,000 in 2022. However, ending inventory was understated by $7,000. What is the correct net income for 2022? What effect, if any, will this error have on total assets as reported in the balance sheet at December 31, 2022?

Determine correct financial statement amount.

DO IT! Exercises

Apply rules of ownership to determine inventory cost.

DO IT! 6.1 (LO 1), AN Sheldon Company just took its physical inventory on December 31. The count of inventory items on hand at the company's business locations resulted in a total inventory cost of $300,000. In reviewing the details of the count and related inventory transactions, you have discovered the following items that had not been considered.

1. Sheldon has sent inventory costing $28,000 on consignment to Richfield Company. All of this inventory was at Richfield's showrooms on December 31.
2. The company did not include in the count inventory (cost, $20,000) that was sold on December 28, terms FOB shipping point. The goods were in transit on December 31.
3. The company did not include in the count inventory (cost, $13,000) that was purchased with terms of FOB shipping point. The goods were in transit on December 31.

Compute the correct December 31 inventory.

Compute cost of goods sold under different cost flow methods.

DO IT! 6.2 (LO 2), AP The accounting records of Ohm Electronics show the following data.

Beginning inventory	3,000 units at $5
Purchases	8,000 units at $7
Sales	9,400 units at $10

Determine cost of goods sold during the period under a periodic inventory system using (a) the FIFO method, (b) the LIFO method, and (c) the average-cost method. (Round unit cost to three decimal places.)

Compute inventory value under LCNRV.

DO IT! 6.3a (LO 3), AP Jeri Company sells three different categories of tools (small, medium and large). The cost and net realizable value of its inventory of tools are as follows.

	Cost	Net Realizable Value
Small	$ 64,000	$ 61,000
Medium	290,000	260,000
Large	152,000	167,000

Determine the value of the company's inventory under the lower-of-cost-or-net realizable value approach.

Compute inventory turnover and assess inventory level.

DO IT! 6.3b (LO 3), AN Early in 2022, Fedor Company switched to a just-in-time inventory system. Its sales and inventory amounts for 2021 and 2022 are shown below.

	2021	2022
Sales revenue	$3,120,000	$3,713,000
Cost of goods sold	1,200,000	1,425,000
Beginning inventory	170,000	210,000
Ending inventory	210,000	90,000

Determine the inventory turnover and days in inventory for 2021 and 2022. Discuss the changes in the amount of inventory, the inventory turnover and days in inventory, and the amount of sales across the 2 years.

Exercises

Determine the correct inventory amount.

E6.1 (LO 1), AN Umatilla Bank and Trust is considering giving Pohl Company a loan. Before doing so, it decides that further discussions with Pohl's accountant may be desirable. One area of particular concern is the Inventory account, which has a year-end balance of $275,000. Discussions with the accountant reveal the following.

1. Pohl shipped goods costing $55,000 to Hemlock Company FOB shipping point on December 28. The goods are not expected to reach Hemlock until January 12. The goods were not included in the physical inventory because they were not in the warehouse.
2. The physical count of the inventory did not include goods costing $95,000 that were shipped to Pohl FOB destination on December 27 and were still in transit at year-end.
3. Pohl received goods costing $25,000 on January 2. The goods were shipped FOB shipping point on December 26 by Yanice Co. The goods were not included in the physical count.

4. Pohl shipped goods costing $51,000 to Ehler of Canada FOB destination on December 30. The goods were received in Canada on January 8. They were not included in Pohl's physical inventory.
5. Pohl received goods costing $42,000 on January 2 that were shipped FOB destination on December 29. The shipment was a rush order that was supposed to arrive December 31. This purchase was included in the ending inventory of $275,000.

Instructions

Determine the correct inventory amount on December 31.

E6.2 (LO 1), AN Farley Bains, an auditor with Nolls CPAs, is performing a review of Ryder Company's Inventory account. Ryder did not have a good year, and top management is under pressure to boost reported income. According to its records, the inventory balance at year-end was $740,000. However, the following information was not considered when determining that amount.

Determine the correct inventory amount.

1. Included in the company's count were goods with a cost of $228,000 that the company is holding on consignment. The goods belong to Nader Corporation.
2. The physical count did not include goods purchased by Ryder with a cost of $40,000 that were shipped FOB shipping point on December 28 and did not arrive at Ryder's warehouse until January 3.
3. Included in the Inventory account was $17,000 of office supplies that were stored in the warehouse and were to be used by the company's supervisors and managers during the coming year.
4. The company received an order on December 29 that was boxed and was sitting on the loading dock awaiting pick-up on December 31. The shipper picked up the goods on January 1 and delivered them on January 6. The shipping terms were FOB shipping point. The goods had a selling price of $40,000 and a cost of $29,000. The goods were not included in the count because they were sitting on the dock.
5. Included in the count was $50,000 of goods that were parts for a machine that the company no longer made. Given the high-tech nature of Ryder's products, it was unlikely that these obsolete parts had any other use. However, management would prefer to keep them on the books at cost, "since that is what we paid for them, after all."

Instructions

Prepare a schedule to determine the correct inventory amount. Provide explanations for each item above, stating why you did or did not make an adjustment for each item.

E6.3 (LO 1), K Gato Inc. had the following inventory situations to consider at January 31, its year-end.

Identify items in inventory.

a. Goods held on consignment for Steele Corp. since December 12.
b. Goods shipped on consignment to Logan Holdings Inc. on January 5.
c. Goods shipped to a customer, FOB destination, on January 29 that are still in transit.
d. Goods shipped to a customer, FOB shipping point, on January 29 that are still in transit.
e. Goods purchased FOB destination from a supplier on January 25 that are still in transit.
f. Goods purchased FOB shipping point from a supplier on January 25 that are still in transit.
g. Office supplies on hand at January 31.

Instructions

Identify which of the preceding items should be included in inventory. If the item should not be included in inventory, state in what account, if any, it should have been recorded.

E6.4 (LO 2), AP Mather sells a snowboard, EZslide, that is popular with snowboard enthusiasts. Below is information relating to Mather's purchases of EZslide snowboards during September. During the same month, 102 EZslide snowboards were sold. Mather uses a periodic inventory system.

Compute inventory and cost of goods sold using periodic FIFO, LIFO, and average-cost.

Date	Explanation	Units	Unit Cost	Total Cost
Sept. 1	Inventory	12	$100	$ 1,200
Sept. 12	Purchases	45	103	4,635
Sept. 19	Purchases	50	104	5,200
Sept. 26	Purchases	20	105	2,100
	Totals	127		$13,135

Instructions

Compute the ending inventory at September 30 and the cost of goods sold using the FIFO, LIFO, and average-cost methods. (For average-cost, round the average unit cost to three decimal places.) Prove the amount allocated to cost of goods sold under each method.

Calculate inventory and cost of goods sold using FIFO, average-cost, and LIFO in a periodic inventory system.

E6.5 (LO 2), AP Rusthe Inc. uses a periodic inventory system. Its records show the following for the month of May, in which 74 units were sold.

Date	Explanation	Units	Unit Cost	Total Cost
May 1	Inventory	30	$9	$270
15	Purchase	25	10	250
24	Purchase	38	11	418
	Total	93		$938

Instructions

Calculate the ending inventory at May 31 using the (a) FIFO, (b) LIFO, and (c) average-cost methods. (For average-cost, round the average unit cost to three decimal places.) Prove the amount allocated to cost of goods sold under each method.

Calculate cost of goods sold using specific identification and FIFO periodic.

E6.6 (LO 2), AN On December 1, Premium Electronics has three DVD players left in stock. All are identical, all are priced to sell at $85. One of the three DVD players left in stock, with serial #1012, was purchased on June 1 at a cost of $52. Another, with serial #1045, was purchased on November 1 for $48. The last player, serial #1056, was purchased on November 30 for $40.

Instructions

a. Calculate the cost of goods sold using the FIFO periodic inventory method, assuming that two of the three players were sold by the end of December, Premium Electronics' year-end.

b. If Premium Electronics used the specific identification method instead of the FIFO method, how might it alter its earnings by "selectively choosing" which particular players to sell to the two customers? What would Premium's cost of goods sold be if the company wished to minimize earnings? Maximize earnings?

c. Which inventory method, FIFO or specific identification, do you recommend that Premium use? Explain why.

Compute inventory and cost of goods sold using periodic FIFO, LIFO, and average-cost.

E6.7 (LO 2), AP Jeters Company uses a periodic inventory system and reports the following for the month of June.

Date	Explanation	Units	Unit Cost	Total Cost
June 1	Inventory	120	$5	$600
12	Purchase	370	6	2,220
23	Purchase	200	7	1,400
30	Inventory	230		

Instructions

a. Compute the cost of the ending inventory and the cost of goods sold under (1) FIFO, (2) LIFO, and (3) average-cost. (Round average unit cost to three decimal places.)

b. Which costing method gives the highest ending inventory? The highest cost of goods sold? Why?

c. How do the average-cost values for ending inventory and cost of goods sold relate to ending inventory and cost of goods sold for FIFO and LIFO?

d. Explain why the average cost is not $6.

Evaluate impact of LIFO and FIFO on cash flows and earnings quality.

E6.8 (LO 2), AP The following comparative information is available for Rose Company for 2022.

	LIFO	FIFO
Sales revenue	$86,000	$86,000
Cost of goods sold	38,000	29,000
Operating expenses (including depreciation)	27,000	27,000
Depreciation	10,000	10,000
Cash paid for inventory purchases	32,000	32,000

Instructions

a. Determine net income under each approach. Assume a 30% tax rate.

b. Determine net cash provided by operating activities under each approach. Assume that all sales were on a cash basis and that income taxes and operating expenses, other than depreciation, were on a cash basis.

c. Calculate the quality of earnings ratio under each approach and explain your findings. (Round answer to two decimal places.)

E6.9 (LO 3), AP Digital Camera Shop Inc. uses the lower-of-cost-or-net realizable value basis for its inventory. The following data are available at December 31.

Determine LCNRV valuation.

	Units	Cost per Unit	Net Realizable Value per Unit
Cameras			
Minolta	5	$170	$158
Canon	7	145	152
Light Meters			
Vivitar	12	125	114
Kodak	10	120	135

Instructions

What amount should be reported on Digital Camera Shop's financial statements, assuming the lower-of-cost-or-net realizable value rule is applied?

E6.10 (LO 3), AP Tascon Corporation sells coffee beans, which are sensitive to price fluctuations. The following inventory information is available for this product at December 31, 2022.

Determine LCNRV valuation.

Coffee Bean	Units	Unit Cost	Net Realizable Value
Coffea arabica	13,000 bags	$5.60	$5.55
Coffea robusta	5,000 bags	3.40	3.50

Instructions

Calculate Tascon's inventory by applying the lower-of-cost-or-net realizable value basis.

E6.11 (LO 3), AP Suppose this information is available for **PepsiCo, Inc.** for 2020, 2021, and 2022.

Compute inventory turnover, days in inventory, and gross profit rate.

(in millions)	2020	2021	2022
Beginning inventory	$ 1,926	$ 2,290	$ 2,522
Ending inventory	2,290	2,522	2,618
Cost of goods sold	18,038	20,351	20,099
Sales revenue	39,474	43,251	43,232

Instructions

a. Calculate the inventory turnover for 2020, 2021, and 2022. (Round to one decimal place.)
b. Calculate the days in inventory for 2020, 2021, and 2022.
c. Calculate the gross profit rate for 2020, 2021, and 2022.
d. Comment on any trends observed in your answers to parts (a), (b), and (c).

E6.12 (LO 3), AP The following information is available for Zoe's Activewear Inc. for three recent fiscal years.

Calculate inventory turnover, days in inventory, and gross profit rate.

	2022	2021	2020
Inventory	$ 553,000	$ 568,000	$ 332,000
Net sales	1,948,000	1,725,000	1,311,000
Cost of goods sold	1,552,000	1,288,000	947,000

Instructions

a. Calculate the inventory turnover, days in inventory, and gross profit rate for 2022 and 2021.
b. Based on the ratios calculated in part (a), did Zoe's liquidity and profitability improve or deteriorate in 2022?

E6.13 (LO 3), AP Deere & Company is a global manufacturer and distributor of agricultural, construction, and forestry equipment. Suppose it reported the following information in its 2022 annual report.

Compute inventory turnover and determine the effect of the LIFO reserve on current ratio.

(in millions)	2022	2021
Inventories (LIFO)	$ 2,397	$3,042
Current assets	30,857	
Current liabilities	12,753	
LIFO reserve	1,367	
Cost of goods sold	16,255	

Instructions

a. Compute Deere's inventory turnover and days in inventory for 2022. (Round inventory turnover to 2 decimal places.)

Calculate inventory and cost of goods sold using three cost flow methods in a perpetual inventory system.

b. Compute Deere's current ratio using the 2022 data as presented, and then again after adjusting for the LIFO reserve.

c. Comment on how ignoring the LIFO reserve might affect your evaluation of Deere's liquidity.

*E6.14 (LO 4), AP** Inventory data for Jeters Company are presented in E6.7.

Instructions

a. Calculate the cost of the ending inventory and the cost of goods sold for each cost flow assumption, using a perpetual inventory system. Assume a sale of 410 units occurred on June 15 for a selling price of $8 and a sale of 50 units on June 27 for $9. (*Note:* For the moving-average method, round unit cost to three decimal places.)

b. How do the results differ from E6.7?

c. Why is the average unit cost not $6 [($5 + $6 + $7) ÷ 3 = $6]?

Apply cost flow methods to perpetual records.

*E6.15 (LO 4), AP** Information about Mather is presented in E6.4. Additional data regarding the company's sales of EZslide snowboards are provided below. Assume that Mather uses a perpetual inventory system.

Date		Units
Sept. 5	Sale	8
Sept. 16	Sale	48
Sept. 29	Sale	46
	Totals	102

Instructions

Compute ending inventory at September 30 using FIFO, LIFO, and moving-average. (*Note:* For moving-average, round unit cost to three decimal places.)

Determine effects of inventory errors.

*E6.16 (LO 5), AN** Dowell Hardware reported cost of goods sold as follows.

	2022	2021
Beginning inventory	$ 30,000	$ 20,000
Cost of goods purchased	175,000	164,000
Cost of goods available for sale	205,000	184,000
Less: Ending inventory	37,000	30,000
Cost of goods sold	$168,000	$154,000

Dowell made two errors:

1. 2021 ending inventory was overstated by $2,000.
2. 2022 ending inventory was understated by $5,000.

Instructions

Compute the correct cost of goods sold for each year.

Prepare correct income statements.

*E6.17 (LO 5), AN** Writing Sheen Company reported these income statement data for a 2-year period.

	2022	2021
Sales revenue	$250,000	$210,000
Beginning inventory	40,000	32,000
Cost of goods purchased	202,000	173,000
Cost of goods available for sale	242,000	205,000
Less: Ending inventory	55,000	40,000
Cost of goods sold	187,000	165,000
Gross profit	$ 63,000	$ 45,000

Sheen Company uses a periodic inventory system. The inventories at January 1, 2021, and December 31, 2022, are correct. However, the ending inventory at December 31, 2021, is overstated by $8,000.

Instructions

a. Prepare correct income statement data for the 2 years.

b. What is the cumulative effect of the inventory error on total gross profit for the 2 years?

c. Explain in a letter to the president of Sheen Company what has happened—that is, the nature of the error and its effect on the financial statements.

Problems: Set A

P6.1A (LO 1), AN Pitt Limited is trying to determine the value of its ending inventory as of February 28, 2022, the company's year-end. The accountant counted everything that was in the warehouse as of February 28, which resulted in an ending inventory valuation of $48,000. However, she didn't know how to treat the following transactions so she didn't record them.

Determine items and amounts to be recorded in inventory.

a. On February 26, Pitt shipped to a customer goods costing $800. The goods were shipped FOB shipping point, and the receiving report indicates that the customer received the goods on March 2.

b. On February 26, Martine Inc. shipped goods to Pitt FOB destination. The invoice price was $350 plus $25 for freight. The receiving report indicates that the goods were received by Pitt on March 2.

c. Pitt had $500 of inventory at a customer's warehouse "on approval." The customer was going to let Pitt know whether it wanted the merchandise by the end of the week, March 4.

d. Pitt also had $400 of inventory at a Belle craft shop, on consignment from Pitt.

e. On February 26, Pitt ordered goods costing $750. The goods were shipped FOB shipping point on February 27. Pitt received the goods on March 1.

f. On February 28, Pitt packaged goods and had them ready for shipping to a customer FOB destination. The invoice price was $350 plus $25 for freight; the cost of the items was $280. The receiving report indicates that the goods were received by the customer on March 2.

g. Pitt had damaged goods set aside in the warehouse because they are no longer saleable. These goods originally cost $400 and, originally, Pitt expected to sell these items for $600.

Instructions

For each of the above transactions, specify whether the item in question should be included in ending inventory, and if so, at what amount. For each item that is not included in ending inventory, indicate who owns it and what account, if any, it should have been recorded in.

P6.2A (LO 2), AP Mullins Distribution markets CDs of numerous performing artists. At the beginning of March, Mullins had in beginning inventory 2,500 CDs with a unit cost of $7. During March, Mullins made the following purchases of CDs.

Determine cost of goods sold and ending inventory using FIFO, LIFO, and average-cost with analysis.

March 5	2,000 @ $8	March 21	5,000 @ $10
March 13	3,500 @ $9	March 26	2,000 @ $11

During March 12,000 units were sold. Mullins uses a periodic inventory system.

Instructions

a. Determine the cost of goods available for sale.

b. Determine (1) the ending inventory and (2) the cost of goods sold under each of the assumed cost flow methods (FIFO, LIFO, and average-cost). Prove the accuracy of the cost of goods sold under the FIFO and LIFO methods. (*Note:* For average-cost, round cost per unit to three decimal places.)

b. Cost of goods sold:
FIFO $105,000
LIFO $115,500
Average $109,601

c. Which cost flow method results in (1) the highest inventory amount for the balance sheet and (2) the highest cost of goods sold for the income statement?

P6.3A (LO 2), AP Vista Company Inc. had a beginning inventory of 100 units of Product RST at a cost of $8 per unit. During the year, purchases were:

Determine cost of goods sold and ending inventory using FIFO, LIFO, and average-cost in a periodic inventory system and assess financial statement effects.

Feb. 20	600 units at $ 9	Aug. 12	400 units at $11
May 5	500 units at $10	Dec. 8	100 units at $12

Vista Company uses a periodic inventory system. Sales totaled 1,500 units.

Instructions

a. Determine the cost of goods available for sale.

b. Determine the ending inventory and the cost of goods sold under each of the assumed cost flow methods (FIFO, LIFO, and average-cost). Prove the accuracy of the cost of goods sold under the FIFO and LIFO methods. (Round average unit cost to three decimal places.)

b. Cost of goods sold:
FIFO $14,500
LIFO $15,100
Average $14,824

c. Which cost flow method results in the lowest inventory amount for the balance sheet? The lowest cost of goods sold for the income statement?

Compute ending inventory, prepare income statements, and answer questions using FIFO and LIFO.

P6.4A (LO 2), AN **Writing** The management of National Inc. asks your help in determining the comparative effects of the FIFO and LIFO inventory cost flow methods. For 2022, the accounting records show these data.

Inventory, January 1 (10,000 units)	$ 35,000
Cost of 120,000 units purchased	468,500
Selling price of 98,000 units sold	750,000
Operating expenses	124,000

Units purchased consisted of 35,000 units at $3.70 on May 10, 60,000 units at $3.90 on August 15, and 25,000 units at $4.20 on November 20. Income taxes are 28%.

Instructions

a. Gross profit:
  FIFO $378,800
  LIFO $362,900

a. Prepare comparative condensed income statements for 2022 under FIFO and LIFO. (Show computations of ending inventory.)

b. Answer the following questions for management in the form of a business letter.

  1. Which inventory cost flow method produces the inventory amount that most closely approximates the amount that would have to be paid to replace the inventory? Why?

  2. Which inventory cost flow method produces the net income amount that is a more likely indicator of next period's net income? Why?

  3. Which inventory cost flow method is most likely to approximate the actual physical flow of the goods? Why?

  4. How much more cash will be available under LIFO than under FIFO? Why?

  5. How much of the gross profit under FIFO is illusionary in comparison with the gross profit under LIFO?

Calculate ending inventory, cost of goods sold, gross profit, and gross profit rate under periodic method; compare results.

P6.5A (LO 2), AP You have the following information for Van Gogh Inc. for the month ended October 31, 2022. Van Gogh uses a periodic method for inventory.

Date	Description	Units	Unit Cost or Selling Price
Oct. 1	Beginning inventory	60	$24
Oct. 9	Purchase	120	26
Oct. 11	Sale	100	35
Oct. 17	Purchase	100	27
Oct. 22	Sale	60	40
Oct. 25	Purchase	70	29
Oct. 29	Sale	110	40

Instructions

a. Gross profit:
  LIFO $2,970
  FIFO $3,310
  Average $3,133

a. Calculate (i) ending inventory, (ii) cost of goods sold, (iii) gross profit, and (iv) gross profit rate under each of the following methods.

  1. LIFO.
  2. FIFO.
  3. Average-cost. (Round cost per unit to three decimal places.)

b. Compare results for the three cost flow assumptions.

Compare specific identification, FIFO, and LIFO under periodic method; use cost flow assumption to influence earnings.

P6.6A (LO 2), AP You have the following information for Jewels Gems. Jewels uses the periodic method of accounting for its inventory transactions. Jewels only carries one brand and size of diamonds—all are identical. Each batch of diamonds purchased is carefully coded and marked with its purchase cost.

March 1	Beginning inventory 150 diamonds at a cost of $310 per diamond.
March 3	Purchased 200 diamonds at a cost of $350 each.
March 5	Sold 180 diamonds for $600 each.
March 10	Purchased 330 diamonds at a cost of $375 each.
March 25	Sold 390 diamonds for $650 each.

Instructions

a. Gross profit:
  Maximum $162,500
  Minimum $155,350

a. Assume that Jewels Gems uses the specific identification cost flow method.

  1. Demonstrate how Jewels could maximize its gross profit for the month by specifically selecting which diamonds to sell on March 5 and March 25.

  2. Demonstrate how Jewels could minimize its gross profit for the month by selecting which diamonds to sell on March 5 and March 25.

b. Assume that Jewels uses the FIFO cost flow assumption. Calculate cost of goods sold. How much gross profit would Jewels report under this cost flow assumption?

c. Assume that Jewels uses the LIFO cost flow assumption. Calculate cost of goods sold. How much gross profit would the company report under this cost flow assumption?

d. Which cost flow method should Jewels Gems select? Explain.

P6.7A (LO 3), AP Suppose this information (in millions) is available for the Automotive and Other Operations Divisions of **General Motors Corporation** for a recent year. General Motors uses the LIFO inventory method.

Compute inventory turnover and days in inventory; compute current ratio based on LIFO and after adjusting for LIFO reserve.

Beginning inventory	$ 13,921
Ending inventory	14,939
LIFO reserve	1,423
Current assets	60,135
Current liabilities	70,308
Cost of goods sold	166,259
Sales revenue	178,199

Instructions

a. Calculate the inventory turnover and days in inventory. (Round to one decimal place.)

b. Calculate the current ratio based on inventory as reported using LIFO.

c. Calculate the current ratio after adjusting for the LIFO reserve.

d. Comment on any difference between parts (b) and (c).

*P6.8A (LO 4), AP Bieber Inc. is a retailer operating in Calgary, Alberta. Bieber uses the perpetual inventory method. Assume that there are no credit transactions; all amounts are settled in cash. You are provided with the following information for Bieber for the month of January 2022.

Calculate cost of goods sold, ending inventory, and gross profit for LIFO, FIFO, and moving-average under the perpetual system; compare results.

Date	Description	Quantity	Unit Cost or Selling Price
Dec. 31	Ending inventory	160	$20
Jan. 2	Purchase	100	22
Jan. 6	Sale	180	40
Jan. 9	Purchase	75	24
Jan. 10	Sale	50	45
Jan. 23	Purchase	100	25
Jan. 30	Sale	130	48

Instructions

a. For each of the following cost flow assumptions, calculate (i) cost of goods sold, (ii) ending inventory, and (iii) gross profit.

1. LIFO.
2. FIFO.
3. Moving-average. (Round cost per unit to three decimal places.)

b. Compare results for the three cost flow assumptions.

a. Gross profit:
LIFO	$7,490
FIFO	$7,865
Average	$7,763

*P6.9A (LO 4), AP Lyon Center began operations on July 1. It uses a perpetual inventory system. During July, the company had the following purchases and sales.

Determine ending inventory under a perpetual inventory system.

	Purchases		
Date	Units	Unit Cost	Sales Units
July 1	7	$62	
July 6			5
July 11	3	$66	
July 14			3
July 21	4	$71	
July 27			3

Instructions

a. Determine the ending inventory under a perpetual inventory system using (1) FIFO, (2) moving-average (round unit cost to three decimal places), and (3) LIFO.

b. Which costing method produces the highest ending inventory valuation?

a. FIFO	$213
Average	$207
LIFO	$195

Continuing Case

Cookie Creations

© leungchopan/ Shutterstock

(*Note:* This is a continuation of the Cookie Creations case from Chapters 1 through 5.)

CC6 Natalie is busy establishing both divisions of her business (cookie classes and mixer sales) and completing her business degree. Her goals for the next 11 months are to sell one mixer per month and to give two to three classes per week. Natalie has decided to use a periodic inventory system and now must choose a cost flow assumption for her mixer inventory.

Go to WileyPLUS for complete case details and instructions.

Comprehensive Accounting Cycle Review

ACR6 On December 1, 2022, Waylon Company had the account balances shown below.

	Debit		Credit
Cash	$ 4,800	Accumulated Depreciation—Equipment	$ 1,500
Accounts Receivable	3,900	Accounts Payable	3,000
Inventory	1,800*	Common Stock	10,000
Equipment	21,000	Retained Earnings	17,000
	$31,500		$31,500

*(3,000 × $0.60)

The following transactions occurred during December.

Dec. 3	Purchased 4,000 units of inventory on account at a cost of $0.72 per unit.
5	Sold 4,400 units of inventory on account for $0.90 per unit. (Waylon sold 3,000 of the $0.60 units and 1,400 of the $0.72.)
7	Granted the December 5 customer $180 credit for 200 units of inventory returned costing $144. These units were returned to inventory.
17	Purchased 2,200 units of inventory for cash at $0.80 each.
22	Sold 2,000 units of inventory on account for $0.95 per unit. (Waylon sold 2,000 of the $0.72 units.)

Adjustment data:

1. Accrued salaries and wages payable $400.
2. Depreciation on equipment $200 per month.
3. Income tax expense was $215, to be paid next year.

Instructions

a. Journalize the December transactions and adjusting entries, assuming Waylon uses the perpetual inventory method.
b. Enter the December 1 balances in the ledger T-accounts and post the December transactions. In addition to the accounts mentioned above, use the following additional accounts: Income Taxes Payable, Salaries and Wages Payable, Sales Revenue, Sales Returns and Allowances, Cost of Goods Sold, Depreciation Expense, Salaries and Wages Expense, and Income Tax Expense.
c. Prepare an adjusted trial balance as of December 31, 2022.
d. Prepare an income statement for December 2022 and a classified balance sheet at December 31, 2022.
e. Compute ending inventory and cost of goods sold under FIFO, assuming Waylon Company uses the periodic inventory system.
f. Compute ending inventory and cost of goods sold under LIFO, assuming Waylon Company uses the periodic inventory system.

Expand Your Critical Thinking

Financial Reporting Problem: Apple Inc.

CT6.1 The notes that accompany a company's financial statements provide informative details that would clutter the amounts and descriptions presented in the statements. Refer to the financial statements of **Apple Inc.** in Appendix A. The complete annual report, including the notes to the financial statements, is available at the company's website.

Instructions

Answer the following questions. (Give the amounts in millions of dollars, as shown in Apple's annual report.)

a. What did Apple report for the amount of inventories in its Consolidated Balance Sheet at September 30, 2017? At September 24, 2016?

b. Compute the dollar amount of change and the percentage change in inventories between 2016 and 2017. Compute inventory as a percentage of current assets for 2017.

c. What are the cost of sales reported by Apple for 2017, 2016, and 2015? Compute the ratio of cost of sales to net sales in 2017.

Comparative Analysis Problem: Columbia Sportswear Company vs. VF Corporation

CT6.2 The financial statements of **Columbia Sportswear Company** are presented in Appendix B. Financial statements for **VF Corporation** are presented in Appendix C.

Instructions

a. Based on the information in the financial statements, compute these values for each company for the most recent year.
  1. Inventory turnover. (Use cost of goods sold or cost of sales and inventories.)
  2. Days in inventory.

b. What conclusions concerning the management of the inventory can you draw from these data?

Comparative Analysis Problem: Amazon.com, Inc. vs. Wal-Mart Stores, Inc.

CT6.3 The financial statements of **Amazon.com, Inc.** are presented in Appendix D. Financial statements for **Wal-Mart Stores, Inc.** are presented in Appendix E.

Instructions

a. Based on the information in the financial statements, compute these values for each company for the most recent year.
  1. Inventory turnover. (Use cost of sales and inventories.)
  2. Days in inventory.

b. What conclusions concerning the management of the inventory can you draw from these data?

Interpreting Financial Statements

CT6.4 Suppose the following information is from the 2022 annual report of **American Greetings Corporation** (all dollars in thousands).

	Feb. 28, 2022	Feb. 28, 2021
Inventories		
Finished goods	$232,893	$244,379
Work in process	7,068	10,516
Raw materials and supplies	49,937	43,861
	289,898	298,756
Less: LIFO reserve	86,025	82,085
Total (as reported)	$203,873	$216,671
Cost of goods sold	$809,956	$780,771
Current assets (as reported)	$561,395	$669,340
Current liabilities	$343,405	$432,321

The notes to the company's financial statements also include the following information.

> The last-in, first-out (LIFO) cost method is used for approximately 75% of the domestic inventories in 2022 and approximately 70% in 2021. The foreign subsidiaries principally use the first-in, first-out (FIFO) method. Display material and factory supplies are carried at average-cost.

Instructions

a. Define each of the following: finished goods, work in process, and raw materials.
b. What might be a possible explanation for why the company uses FIFO for its nondomestic inventories?
c. Calculate the company's inventory turnover and days in inventory for 2021 and 2022. (2020 inventory was $182,618.) Discuss the implications of any change in the ratios.
d. What percentage of total inventory does the 2022 LIFO reserve represent? If the company used FIFO in 2022, what would be the value of its inventory? Do you consider this difference a "material" amount from the perspective of an analyst? Which value accurately represents the value of the company's inventory?
e. Calculate the company's 2022 current ratio with the numbers as reported, then recalculate after adjusting for the LIFO reserve.

Real-World Focus

CT6.5 A company's annual report provides various information about inventory.

Instructions

Answer the following questions based on the current year's annual report available at **Cisco**'s website.

a. At Cisco's fiscal year-end, what was the inventory on the balance sheet?
b. How has this changed from the previous fiscal year-end?
c. How much of the inventory was finished goods?

CT6.6 The July 15, 2010, edition of *CFO.com* contains an article by Marie Leone entitled "Sucking the LIFO out of Inventory."

Instructions

Read the article (available online) and then answer the following questions.

a. What type of company benefits most from the use of LIFO?
b. What is the estimated boost in federal tax receipts over 10 years if the use of LIFO for taxes was not allowed?
c. If the United States decides to adopt International Financial Reporting Standards (IFRS), what would be the implications for the use of LIFO?
d. What conceptual justification for LIFO do its proponents provide?
e. What types of companies prefer to use FIFO?

Decision-Making Across the Organization

CT6.7 Solar Electronics has enjoyed tremendous sales growth during the last 10 years. However, even though sales have steadily increased, the company's CEO, Dana Byrnes, is concerned about certain aspects of its performance. She has called a meeting with the corporate controller and the vice presidents of finance, operations, sales, and marketing to discuss the company's performance. Dana begins the meeting by making the following observations:

> We have been forced to take significant write-downs on inventory during each of the last three years because of obsolescence. In addition, inventory storage costs have soared. We rent four additional warehouses to store our increasingly diverse inventory. Five years ago inventory represented only 20% of the value of our total assets. It now exceeds 35%. Yet, even with all of this inventory, "stockouts" (measured by complaints by customers that the desired product is not available) have increased by 40% during the last three years. And worse yet, it seems that we constantly must discount merchandise that we have too much of.

Dana asks the group to review the following data and make suggestions as to how the company's performance might be improved.

(in millions)	2022	2021	2020	2019
Inventory				
Raw materials	$242	$198	$155	$128
Work in process	116	77	49	33
Finished goods	567	482	398	257
Total inventory	$925	$757	$602	$418
Current assets	$1,800	$1,423	$1,183	$841
Total assets	$2,643	$2,523	$2,408	$2,090
Current liabilities	$600	$590	$525	$420
Sales revenue	$9,428	$8,674	$7,536	$6,840
Cost of goods sold	$6,328	$5,474	$4,445	$3,557
Net income	$754	$987	$979	$958

Instructions

Using the information provided, answer the following questions.

a. Compute the current ratio, gross profit rate, profit margin, inventory turnover, and days in inventory for 2020, 2021, and 2022.

b. Discuss the trends and potential causes of the changes in the ratios in part (a).

c. Discuss potential remedies to any problems discussed in part (b).

d. What concerns might be raised by some members of management with regard to your suggestions in part (c)?

Communication Activities

CT6.8 In a discussion of dramatic increases in coffee-bean prices, a *Wall Street Journal* article noted the following fact about **Starbucks**.

> Before this year's bean-price hike, Starbucks added several defenses that analysts say could help it maintain earnings and revenue. The company last year began accounting for its coffee-bean purchases by taking the average price of all beans in inventory.

Prior to this change, the company was using FIFO.

Instructions

Your client, the CEO of Superior Coffee, Inc., read this article and sent you an e-mail message requesting that you explain why Starbucks might have taken this action. Your response should explain what impact this change in accounting method has on earnings, why the company might want to do this, and any possible disadvantages of such a change.

*****CT6.9** You are the controller of Garton Inc. H. K. Logan, the president, recently mentioned to you that she found an error in the 2021 financial statements which she believes has corrected itself. She determined, in discussions with the purchasing department, that 2021 ending inventory was overstated by $1 million. H. K. says that the 2022 ending inventory is correct, and she assumes that 2022 income is correct. H. K. says to you, "What happened has happened—there's no point in worrying about it anymore."

Instructions

You conclude that H. K. is incorrect. Write a brief, tactful memo to her, clarifying the situation.

Ethics Case

CT6.10 Nixon Wholesale Corp. uses the LIFO cost flow method. In the current year, profit at Nixon is running unusually high. The corporate tax rate is also high this year, but it is scheduled to decline significantly next year. In an effort to lower the current year's net income and to take advantage of the changing income tax rate, the president of Nixon Wholesale instructs the plant accountant to recommend to the purchasing department a large purchase of inventory for delivery 3 days before the end of the year. The price of the inventory to be purchased has doubled during the year, and the purchase will represent a major portion of the ending inventory value.

Instructions

a. What is the effect of this transaction on this year's and next year's income statement and income tax expense? Why?

b. If Nixon Wholesale had been using the FIFO method of inventory costing, would the president give the same directive?

c. Should the plant accountant order the inventory purchase to lower income? What are the ethical implications of this order?

All About You

CT6.11 Some of the largest business frauds ever perpetrated have involved the misstatement of inventory. Two classics were at **Leslie Fay** and **McKesson Corporation**.

Instructions

There is considerable information regarding inventory frauds available on the Internet. Search for information about one of the two cases mentioned above, or inventory fraud at any other company, and prepare a short explanation of the nature of the inventory fraud.

FASB Codification Activity

CT6.12 If your school has a subscription to the FASB Codification, log in and prepare responses to the following.

a. The primary basis for accounting for inventories is cost. How is cost defined in the Codification?

b. What does the Codification state regarding the use of consistency in the selection or employment of a basis for inventory?

Considering People, Planet, and Profit

CT6.13 Caterpillar publishes an annual Sustainability Report to explain its position on sustainability, describe its goals, and report on its achievements.

Instructions

Access the most recent report by doing an Internet search of "Caterpillar Sustainability Report" and then answer the following questions.

a. The report describes the company's goals. What are some of these goals?

b. The report describes the company's results with regard to worker safety. Summarize the company's progress in this area.

c. The report describes the company's results regarding energy use. Explain how the company measures its progress, and comment on its results thus far.

A Look at IFRS

LEARNING OBJECTIVE 6
Compare the accounting for inventories under GAAP and IFRS.

The major IFRS requirements related to accounting and reporting for inventories are the same as GAAP. The major differences are that IFRS prohibits the use of the LIFO cost flow assumption and has some differences with regard to lower-of-cost-or-net realizable value.

Key Points

Following are the key similarities and differences between GAAP and IFRS related to inventories.

Similarities

- IFRS and GAAP account for inventory acquisitions at historical cost and value inventory at the lower-of-cost-or-net realizable value subsequent to acquisition.
- Who owns the goods—goods in transit or consigned goods—as well as the costs to include in inventory are essentially accounted for in the same manner under IFRS and GAAP.

Differences

- The requirements for accounting for and reporting inventories are more principles-based under IFRS. That is, GAAP provides more detailed guidelines in inventory accounting.
- A major difference between IFRS and GAAP relates to the LIFO cost flow assumption. GAAP permits the use of LIFO for inventory valuation. IFRS prohibits its use. FIFO and average-cost are the only two acceptable cost flow assumptions permitted under IFRS. Both sets of standards permit specific identification where appropriate.

IFRS Practice

IFRS Self-Test Questions

1. Which of the following should **not** be included in the inventory of a company using IFRS?
   a. Goods held on consignment from another company.
   b. Goods shipped on consignment to another company.
   c. Goods in transit from another company shipped FOB shipping point.
   d. None of the above.

2. Which method of inventory costing is prohibited under IFRS?
   a. Specific identification.
   b. LIFO.
   c. FIFO.
   d. Average-cost.

IFRS Exercises

IFRS6.1 Briefly describe some of the similarities and differences between GAAP and IFRS with respect to the accounting for inventories.

IFRS6.2 LaTour Inc. is based in France and prepares its financial statements (in euros) in accordance with IFRS. In 2022, it reported cost of goods sold of €578 million and average inventory of €154 million. Briefly discuss how analysis of LaTour's inventory turnover (and comparisons to a company using GAAP) might be affected by differences in inventory accounting between IFRS and GAAP.

International Financial Reporting Problem: Louis Vuitton

IFRS6.3 The financial statements of **Louis Vuitton** are presented in Appendix F. The complete annual report, including the notes to its financial statements, is available at the company's website.

Instructions

Using the notes to the company's financial statements, answer the following questions.
a. What cost flow assumption does the company use to value inventory?
b. What amount of goods purchased for retail and finished products did the company report at December 31, 2016?

Answers to IFRS Self-Test Questions

1. a   2. b

CHAPTER 7

Fraud, Internal Control, and Cash

Chapter Preview

As the following Feature Story about recording cash sales at **Barriques** indicates, control of cash is important to ensure that fraud does not occur. Companies also need controls to safeguard other types of assets. For example, Barriques undoubtedly has controls to prevent the theft of food and supplies, and controls to prevent the theft of tableware and dishes from its kitchen.

In this chapter, we explain the essential features of an internal control system and how it prevents fraud. We also describe how those controls apply to a specific asset—cash. The applications include some controls with which you may be already familiar, such as the use of a bank.

Feature Story

Minding the Money in Madison

For many years, **Barriques** in Madison, Wisconsin, has been named the city's favorite coffeehouse. Barriques not only does a booming business in coffee but also has wonderful baked goods, delicious sandwiches, and a fine selection of wines.

"Our customer base ranges from college students to neighborhood residents as well as visitors to our capital city," says bookkeeper Kerry Stoppleworth, who joined the company shortly after it was founded in 1998. "We are unique because we have customers who come in early on their way to work for a cup of coffee and then will stop back after work to pick up a bottle of wine for dinner. We stay very busy throughout all three parts of the day."

Like most businesses where purchases are low-cost and high-volume, cash control has to be simple. "We use a computerized point-of-sale (POS) system to keep track of our inventory and allow us to efficiently ring through an order for a customer," explains Stoppleworth. "You can either scan a barcode for an item or enter in a code for items that don't have a barcode such as cups of coffee or bakery items." The POS system also automatically tracks sales by department and maintains an electronic journal of all the sales transactions that occur during the day.

"There are two POS stations at each store, and throughout the day any of the staff may operate them," says Stoppleworth. At the end of the day, each POS station is reconciled separately. The staff counts the cash in the drawer and enters this amount into the closing totals in the POS system. The POS system then compares the cash and credit amounts, less the cash being carried forward to the next day (the float), to the shift total in the electronic journal. If there are discrepancies, a recount is done and the journal is reviewed transaction by transaction to identify the problem. The staff then creates a deposit ticket for the cash less the float and puts this in a drop safe with the electronic journal summary report for the manager to review and take to the bank the next day. Ultimately, the bookkeeper reviews all of these documents as well as the deposit receipt that the bank produces to make sure they are all in agreement.

As Stoppleworth concludes, "We keep the closing process and accounting simple so that our staff can concentrate on taking care of our customers and making great coffee and food."

Chapter Outline

LEARNING OBJECTIVES

LO 1 Define fraud and the principles of internal control.	• Fraud • The Sarbanes-Oxley Act • Internal control • Principles of internal control activities • Data analytics and internal controls • Limitations of internal control	**DO IT! 1** Control Activities
LO 2 Apply internal control principles to cash.	• Cash receipts controls • Cash disbursements controls • Petty cash fund	**DO IT! 2** Control over Cash Receipts
LO 3 Identify the control features of a bank account.	• EFT system • Bank statements • Reconciling the bank account	**DO IT! 3** Bank Reconciliation
LO 4 Explain the reporting of cash and the basic principles of cash management.	• Reporting cash • Managing and monitoring cash • Cash budgeting	**DO IT! 4a** Reporting Cash **DO IT! 4b** Cash Budget

Go to the Review and Practice section at the end of the chapter for a targeted summary and practice applications with solutions.
Visit WileyPLUS for additional tutorials and practice opportunities.

Fraud and Internal Control

> **LEARNING OBJECTIVE 1**
> Define fraud and the principles of internal control.

The Feature Story describes many of the internal control procedures used by **Barriques**. These procedures are necessary to discourage employees from fraudulent activities.

Fraud

A **fraud** is a dishonest act by an employee that results in personal benefit to the employee at a cost to the employer. Examples of fraud reported in the financial press include the following.

- A bookkeeper in a small company diverted $750,000 of bill payments to a personal bank account over a three-year period.
- A shipping clerk with 28 years of service shipped $125,000 of merchandise to himself.
- A computer operator embezzled $21 million from **Wells Fargo Bank** over a two-year period.
- A church treasurer "borrowed" $150,000 of church funds to finance a friend's business dealings.

Why does fraud occur? The three main factors that contribute to fraudulent activity are depicted by the **fraud triangle** in **Illustration 7.1**.

The most important element of the fraud triangle is **opportunity**. For an employee to commit fraud, the workplace environment must provide opportunities that an employee can take advantage of. Opportunities occur when the workplace lacks sufficient controls to deter and detect fraud. For example, inadequate monitoring of employee actions can create opportunities for theft and can embolden employees because they believe they will not be caught.

A second factor that contributes to fraud is **financial pressure**. Employees sometimes commit fraud because of personal financial problems caused by too much debt. Or, they might commit fraud because they want to lead a lifestyle that they cannot afford on their current salary.

The third factor that contributes to fraud is **rationalization**. In order to justify their fraud, employees rationalize their dishonest actions. For example, employees sometimes justify fraud because they believe they are underpaid while the employer is making lots of money. Employees feel justified in stealing because they believe they deserve to be paid more.

ILLUSTRATION 7.1 Fraud triangle

The Sarbanes-Oxley Act

What can be done to prevent or to detect fraud? After numerous corporate scandals came to light in the early 2000s, Congress addressed this issue by passing the **Sarbanes-Oxley Act (SOX)**. Under SOX, all publicly traded U.S. corporations are required to maintain an adequate system of internal control. Corporate executives and boards of directors must ensure that these controls are reliable and effective. In addition, independent outside auditors must attest to the adequacy of the internal control system. Companies that fail to comply are subject to fines, and company officers can be imprisoned. SOX also created the Public Company Accounting Oversight Board (PCAOB) to establish auditing standards and regulate auditor activity.

One poll found that 60% of investors believe that SOX helps safeguard their stock investments. Many say they would be unlikely to invest in a company that fails to follow SOX requirements. Although some corporate executives have criticized the time and expense involved in following SOX requirements, SOX appears to be working well. For example, the chief accounting officer of **Eli Lily** noted that SOX triggered a comprehensive review of how the company documents its controls. This review uncovered redundancies and pointed out controls that needed to be added. In short, it added up to time and money well spent.

Internal Control

Internal control is a process designed to provide reasonable assurance regarding the achievement of company objectives related to operations, reporting, and compliance. In more detail, the purposes of internal control are to safeguard assets, enhance the reliability of accounting records, increase efficiency of operations, and ensure compliance with laws and regulations. Internal control systems have five primary components as listed below.[1]

- **A control environment.** It is the responsibility of top management to make it clear that the organization values integrity and that unethical activity will not be tolerated. This component is often referred to as the "tone at the top."
- **Risk assessment.** Companies must identify and analyze the various factors that create risk for the business and must determine how to manage these risks.
- **Control activities.** To reduce the occurrence of fraud, management must design policies and procedures to address the specific risks faced by the company.
- **Information and communication.** The internal control system must capture and communicate all pertinent information both down and up the organization, as well as communicate information to appropriate external parties.
- **Monitoring.** Internal control systems must be monitored periodically for their adequacy. Significant deficiencies need to be reported to top management and/or the board of directors.

People, Planet, and Profit Insight

© Karl Dolenc/iStockphoto

And the Controls Are . . .

Internal controls are important for an effective financial reporting system. The same is true for sustainability reporting. An effective system of internal controls for sustainability reporting will help in the following ways: (1) prevent the unauthorized use of data; (2) provide reasonable assurance that the information is accurate, valid, and complete; and (3) report information that is consistent with overall sustainability accounting policies. With these types of controls, users will have the confidence that they can use the sustainability information effectively.

Some regulators are calling for even more assurance through audits of this information. Companies that potentially can cause environmental damage through greenhouse gases, as well as companies in the mining and extractive industries, are subject to reporting requirements. And, as demand for more information in the sustainability area expands, the need for audits of this information will grow.

Why is sustainability information important to investors? (Go to WileyPLUS for this answer and additional questions.)

Principles of Internal Control Activities

Each of the five components of an internal control system is important. Here, we will focus on one component, the control activities. The reason? These activities are the backbone of the company's efforts to address the risks it faces, such as fraud. The specific control activities

---

[1] The Committee of Sponsoring Organizations of the Treadway Commission, "Internal Control—Integrated Framework," www.coso.org/documents/990025P_Executive_Summary_final_may20_e.pdf; and Stephen J. McNally, "The 2013 COSO Framework and SOX Compliance," *Strategic Finance* (June 2013).

used by a company will vary, depending on management's assessment of the risks faced. This assessment is heavily influenced by the size and nature of the company.

The six principles of control activities are as follows (see **Decision Tools**).

- Establishment of responsibility
- Segregation of duties
- Documentation procedures
- Physical controls
- Independent internal verification
- Human resource controls

> **Decision Tools**
>
> The six principles of internal control activities help to ensure that a company's financial statements are adequately supported by internal controls.

We explain these principles in the following sections. You should recognize that they apply to most companies and are relevant to both manual and computerized accounting systems.

Establishment of Responsibility

An essential principle of internal control is to assign responsibility to specific employees. **Control is most effective when only one person is responsible for a given task.**

To illustrate, assume that the cash on hand at the end of the day in a **Safeway** supermarket is $10 short of the cash entered in the cash register. If only one person has operated the register, the shift manager can quickly determine responsibility for the shortage. If two or more individuals have worked the register, it may be impossible to determine who is responsible for the error.

Many retailers solve this problem by having registers with multiple drawers. This makes it possible for more than one person to operate a register but still allows identification of a particular employee with a specific drawer. Only the signed-in cashier has access to his or her drawer.

Establishing responsibility often requires limiting access only to authorized personnel, and then identifying those personnel. For example, the automated systems used by many companies have mechanisms such as identifying passcodes that keep track of who made a journal entry, who entered a sale, or who went into an inventory storeroom at a particular time. Use of identifying passcodes enables the company to establish responsibility by identifying the particular employee who carried out the activity.

Transfer of cash drawers

Anatomy of a Fraud

Maureen Frugali was a training supervisor for claims processing at Colossal Healthcare. As a standard part of the claims-processing training program, Maureen created fictitious claims for use by trainees. These fictitious claims were then sent to the accounts payable department. After the training claims had been processed, she was to notify Accounts Payable of all fictitious claims, so that they would not be paid. However, she did not inform Accounts Payable about every fictitious claim. She created some fictitious claims for entities that she controlled (that is, she would receive the payment), and she let Accounts Payable pay her.

Total take: $11 million

The Missing Control

Establishment of responsibility. The healthcare company did not adequately restrict the responsibility for authorizing and approving claims transactions. The training supervisor should not have been authorized to create claims in the company's "live" system.

Source: Adapted from Wells, *Fraud Casebook* (2007), pp. 61–70.

Segregation of Duties

Segregation of duties is indispensable in an internal control system. There are two common applications of this principle:

1. Different individuals should be responsible for related activities.
2. The responsibility for recordkeeping for an asset should be separate from the physical custody of that asset.

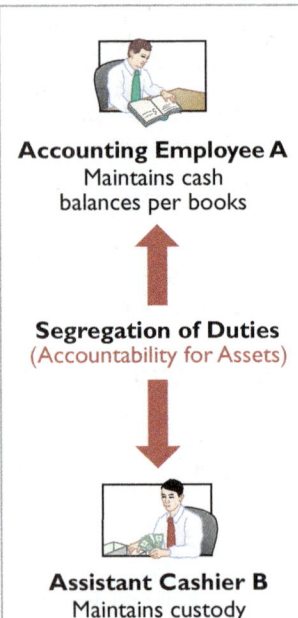

The rationale for segregation of duties is this: **The work of one employee should, without a duplication of effort, provide a reliable basis for evaluating the work of another employee.** For example, the personnel that design and program computerized systems should not be assigned duties related to day-to-day use of the system. Otherwise, they could design the system to benefit them personally and conceal the fraud through day-to-day use.

Segregation of Related Activities   Making one individual responsible for related activities increases the potential for errors and irregularities.

Purchasing Activities   Companies should, for example, assign related **purchasing activities** to different individuals. Related purchasing activities include ordering merchandise, approving orders, receiving goods, authorizing payment, and paying for goods or services. Various frauds are possible when one person handles related purchasing activities:

- If a purchasing agent is allowed to order goods without obtaining supervisory approval, the likelihood of the purchasing agent receiving kickbacks from suppliers increases.
- If an employee who orders goods also handles the invoice and receipt of the goods, as well as payment authorization, he or she might authorize payment for a fictitious invoice.

These abuses are less likely to occur when companies divide the purchasing tasks.

Sales Activities   Similarly, companies should assign related **sales activities** to different individuals. Related selling activities include making a sale, shipping (or delivering) the goods to the customer, billing the customer, and receiving payment. Various frauds are possible when one person handles related sales activities:

- If a salesperson can make a sale without obtaining supervisory approval, he or she might make sales at unauthorized prices to increase sales commissions.
- A shipping clerk who also has access to accounting records could ship goods to himself.
- A billing clerk who handles billing and receipt could understate the amount billed for sales made to friends and relatives.

These abuses are less likely to occur when companies divide the sales tasks. The salespeople make the sale, the shipping department ships the goods on the basis of the sales order, and the billing department prepares the sales invoice after comparing the sales order with the report of goods shipped.

Anatomy of a Fraud

Lawrence Fairbanks, the assistant vice-chancellor of communications at Aesop University, was allowed to make purchases of under $2,500 for his department without external approval. Unfortunately, he also sometimes bought items for himself, such as expensive antiques and other collectibles. How did he do it? He replaced the vendor invoices he received with fake vendor invoices that he created. The fake invoices had descriptions that were more consistent with the communications department's purchases. He submitted these fake invoices to the accounting department as the basis for their journal entries and to the accounts payable department as the basis for payment.

Total take: $475,000

The Missing Control

Segregation of duties. The university had not properly segregated related purchasing activities. Lawrence was ordering items, receiving the items, and receiving the invoice. By receiving the invoice, he had control over the documents that were used to account for the purchase and thus was able to substitute a fake invoice.

Source: Adapted from Wells, *Fraud Casebook* (2007), pp. 3–15.

Segregation of Recordkeeping from Physical Custody   The accountant should have neither physical custody of the asset nor access to it. Likewise, the custodian of the asset should not maintain or have access to the accounting records. **The custodian of the asset is not likely to convert the asset to personal use when one employee maintains the record of the asset, and a different employee has physical custody of the asset.** The separation of accounting responsibility from the custody of assets is especially important for cash and inventories because these assets are very vulnerable to fraud.

Anatomy of a Fraud

Angela Bauer was an accounts payable clerk for Aggasiz Construction Company. Angela prepared and issued checks to vendors and reconciled bank statements. She perpetrated a fraud in this way: She wrote checks for costs that the company had not actually incurred (e.g., fake taxes). A supervisor then approved and signed the checks. Before issuing the check, though, Angela would "white-out" the payee line on the check and change it to personal accounts that she controlled. She was able to conceal the theft because she also reconciled the bank account. That is, nobody else ever saw that the checks had been altered.

Total take: $570,000

The Missing Control

Segregation of duties. Aggasiz Construction Company did not properly segregate recordkeeping from physical custody. Angela had physical custody of the checks, which essentially was control of the cash. She also had recordkeeping responsibility because she prepared the bank reconciliation.

Source: Adapted from Wells, *Fraud Casebook* (2007), pp. 100–107.

Documentation Procedures

Documents provide evidence that transactions and events have occurred. For example, point-of-sale terminals are networked with a company's computing and accounting records, which results in direct documentation.

Similarly, a shipping document indicates that the goods have been shipped, and a sales invoice indicates that the company has billed the customer for the goods. By requiring signatures (or initials) on the documents, the company can identify the individual(s) responsible for the transaction or event. Companies should document transactions when they occur.

Companies should establish procedures for documents. First, whenever possible, companies should use **prenumbered documents, and all documents should be accounted for**. Prenumbering helps to prevent a transaction from being recorded more than once, or conversely, from not being recorded at all. Second, the control system should require that employees **promptly forward source documents for accounting entries to the accounting department. This control measure helps to ensure timely recording of the transaction** and contributes directly to the accuracy and reliability of the accounting records.

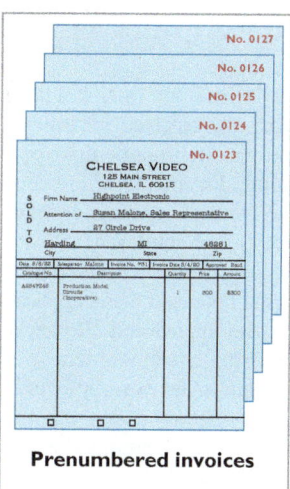

Prenumbered invoices

Anatomy of a Fraud

To support their reimbursement requests for travel costs incurred, employees at Mod Fashions Corporation's design center were required to submit receipts. The receipts could include the detailed bill provided for a meal, the credit card receipt provided when the credit card payment is made, or a copy of the employee's monthly credit card bill that listed the item. A number of the designers who frequently traveled together came up with a fraud scheme: They submitted claims for the same expenses. For example, if they had a meal together that cost $200, one person submitted the detailed meal bill, another submitted the credit card receipt, and a third submitted a monthly credit card bill showing the meal as a line item. Thus, all three received a $200 reimbursement.

Total take: $75,000

The Missing Control

Documentation procedures. Mod Fashions should require the original, detailed receipt. It should not accept photocopies, and it should not accept credit card statements. In addition, documentation procedures could be further improved by requiring the use of a corporate credit card (rather than a personal credit card) for all business expenses.

Source: Adapted from Wells, *Fraud Casebook* (2007), pp. 79–90.

Physical Controls

Use of physical controls is essential. **Physical controls** relate to the safeguarding of assets and enhance the accuracy and reliability of the accounting records. **Illustration 7.2** shows examples of these controls.

> **ILLUSTRATION 7.2** Physical controls

Physical Controls

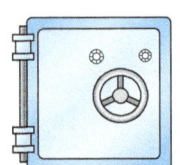
Safes, vaults, and safety deposit boxes for cash and business papers

Locked warehouses and storage cabinets for inventories and records

Computer facilities with passkey access or fingerprint or eyeball scans

Alarms to prevent break-ins

Television monitors and garment sensors to deter theft

Time clocks for recording time worked

Anatomy of a Fraud

At Centerstone Health, a large insurance company, the mailroom each day received insurance applications from prospective customers. Mailroom employees scanned the applications into electronic documents before the applications were processed. Once the applications were scanned, they could be accessed online by authorized employees.

Insurance agents at Centerstone Health earn commissions based upon successful applications. The sales agent's name is listed on the application. However, roughly 15% of the applications are from customers who did not work with a sales agent. Two friends—Alex, an employee in recordkeeping, and Parviz, a sales agent—thought up a way to perpetrate a fraud. Alex identified scanned applications that did not list a sales agent. After business hours, he entered the mailroom and found the hard-copy applications that did not show a sales agent. He wrote in Parviz's name as the sales agent and then rescanned the application for processing. Parviz received the commission, which the friends then split.

Total take: $240,000

The Missing Control

Physical controls. Centerstone Health lacked two basic physical controls that could have prevented this fraud. First, the mailroom should have been locked during nonbusiness hours, and access during business hours should have been tightly controlled. Second, the scanned applications supposedly could be accessed only by authorized employees using their passwords. However, the password for each employee was the same as the employee's user ID. Since employee user-ID numbers were available to all other employees, all employees knew each other's passwords. Thus, Alex could enter the system using another employee's password and access the scanned applications.

Source: Adapted from Wells, *Fraud Casebook* (2007), pp. 316–326.

Independent Internal Verification

Most internal control systems provide for **independent internal verification**. This principle involves the review of data prepared by employees. To obtain maximum benefit from independent internal verification:

1. Companies should verify records periodically or on a surprise basis.
2. An employee who is independent of the personnel responsible for the information should make the verification.
3. Discrepancies and exceptions should be reported to a management level that can take appropriate corrective action.

Independent internal verification is especially useful in comparing recorded accountability with existing assets. The reconciliation of the electronic journal with the cash in the point-of-sale terminal at **Barriques** is an example of this internal control principle. Other common examples are the reconciliation of a company's cash balance per books with the cash balance per bank, and the verification of the perpetual inventory records through a count of physical inventory. Illustration 7.3 shows the relationship between this principle and the segregation of duties principle.

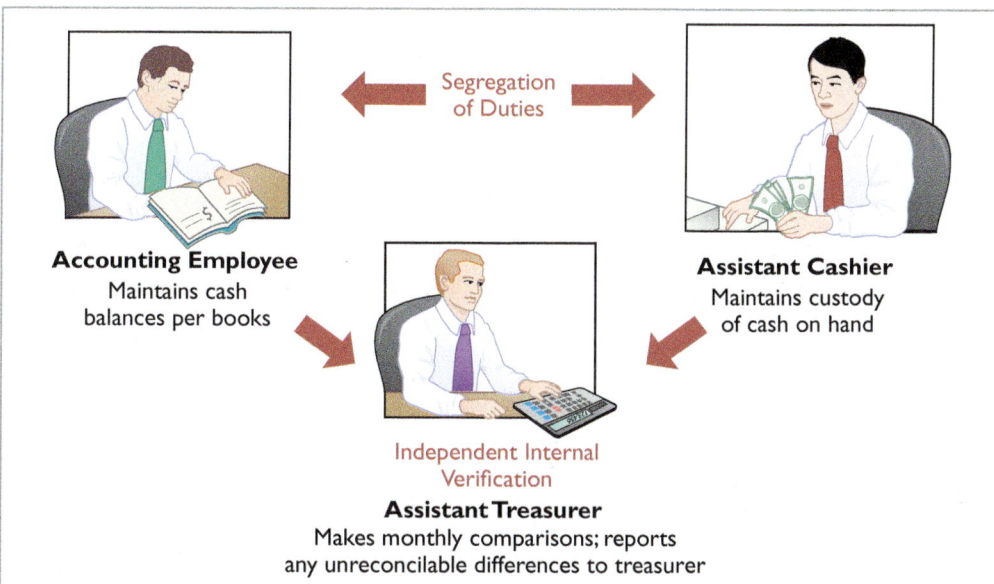

ILLUSTRATION 7.3

Comparison of segregation of duties principle with independent internal verification principle

Anatomy of a Fraud

Bobbi Jean Donnelly, the office manager for Mod Fashions Corporation's design center, was responsible for preparing the design center budget and reviewing expense reports submitted by design center employees. Her desire to upgrade her wardrobe got the better of her, and she enacted a fraud that involved filing expense-reimbursement requests for her own personal clothing purchases. Bobbi Jean was able to conceal the fraud because she was responsible for reviewing all expense reports, including her own. In addition, she sometimes was given ultimate responsibility for signing off on the expense reports when her boss was "too busy." Also, because she controlled the budget, when she submitted her expenses, she coded them to budget items that she knew were running under budget, so that they would not catch anyone's attention.

Total take: $275,000

The Missing Control

Independent internal verification. Bobbi Jean's boss should have verified her expense reports. When asked what he thought her expenses for a year were, the boss said about $10,000. At $115,000 per year, her actual expenses were more than 10 times what would have been expected. However, because he was "too busy" to verify her expense reports or to review the budget, he never noticed.

Source: Adapted from Wells, *Fraud Casebook* (2007), pp. 79–90.

Large companies often assign independent internal verification to internal auditors. **Internal auditors** are company employees who continuously evaluate the effectiveness of the company's internal control systems. They review the activities of departments and individuals to determine whether prescribed internal controls are being followed. They also recommend improvements when needed. For example, **WorldCom** was at one time the second largest U.S. telecommunications company. The fraud that caused its bankruptcy (the largest ever when it occurred) involved billions of dollars. It was uncovered by an internal auditor.

Human Resource Controls

Human resource control activities include the following.

1. **Bond employees who handle cash. Bonding** involves obtaining insurance protection against theft by employees. It contributes to the safeguarding of cash in two ways. First, the insurance company carefully screens all individuals before adding them to the policy and may reject risky applicants. Second, bonded employees know that the insurance company will vigorously prosecute all offenders.

2. **Rotate employees' duties and require employees to take vacations.** These measures deter employees from attempting thefts since they will not be able to permanently conceal their improper actions. Many banks, for example, have discovered employee thefts when the employee was on vacation or assigned to a new position.

3. **Conduct thorough background checks.** Many believe that the most important and inexpensive measure any business can take to reduce employee theft and fraud is for the human resource department to conduct thorough background checks. Two tips: (1) Check to see whether job applicants actually graduated from the schools they list. (2) Never use telephone numbers for previous employers provided by the applicant. Always look them up yourself.

Anatomy of a Fraud

Ellen Lowry was the desk manager and Josephine Rodriguez was the head of housekeeping at the Excelsior Inn, a luxury hotel. The two best friends were so dedicated to their jobs that they never took vacations, and they frequently filled in for other employees. In fact, Ms. Rodriguez, whose job as head of housekeeping did not include cleaning rooms, often cleaned rooms herself, "just to help the staff keep up." These two "dedicated" employees, working as a team, found a way to earn a little more cash. Ellen, the desk manager, provided significant discounts to guests who paid with cash. She kept the cash and did not register the guests in the hotel's computerized system. Instead, she took the room out of circulation "due to routine maintenance." Because the room did not show up as being used, it did not receive a normal housekeeping assignment. Instead, Josephine, the head of housekeeping, cleaned the rooms during the guests' stay.

Total take: $95,000

The Missing Control

Human resource controls. Ellen, the desk manager, had been fired by a previous employer after being accused of fraud. If the Excelsior Inn had conducted a thorough background check, it would not have hired her. The hotel fraud was detected when Ellen missed work for a few days due to illness. A system of mandatory vacations and rotating days off would have increased the chances of detecting the fraud before it became so large.

Source: Adapted from Wells, *Fraud Casebook* (2007), pp. 145–155.

Accounting Across the Organization

Stockbyte/Getty Images, Inc.

SOX Boosts the Role of Human Resources

Under SOX, a company needs to keep track of employees' degrees and certifications to ensure that employees continue to meet the specified requirements of a job. Also, to ensure proper employee supervision and proper separation of duties, companies must develop and monitor an organizational chart. When one corporation went through this exercise, it found that out of 17,000 employees, there were 400 people who did not report to anyone. The corporation also had 35 people who reported to each other. In addition, if an employee complains of an unfair firing and mentions financial issues at the company, the human resource department must refer the case to the company audit committee and possibly to its legal counsel.

Why would unsupervised employees or employees who report to each other represent potential internal control threats? (Go to WileyPLUS for this answer and additional questions.)

Data Analytics and Internal Controls

Data analytics has dramatically changed many aspects of internal control practices. In the past, internal and external auditors tended to rely heavily on investigations of period-end samples of transactions to identify potential violations. Now, rather than wait for a period-end sample, many companies employ continuous monitoring of virtually every transaction. As a result, spikes in certain types of activity or developing trends are more quickly identified and investigated.

Many different aspects of journal entries can be monitored continuously. For example, systems can automatically identify who recorded a particular journal entry. This is important to ensure that segregation of duties is not violated, that is, that the entry is only made by a current (as opposed to recently terminated) employee and that the employee is authorized to make that type of entry.

Large dollar amounts in risky areas can also be flagged and investigated quickly. Recipients of payments can be easily screened to ensure, for example, that bonus amounts are correctly determined based on results and bonus formulas, and that bonuses are only paid to employees who are designated for bonus payments. Similarly, vendor payments can be easily screened to ensure that payments only go to authorized vendors and that amounts are within an anticipated range. Sophisticated models can be used to continually estimate critical measures, and those estimates are then compared to actual results to identify outliers.

Limitations of Internal Control

Companies generally design their systems of internal control to provide **reasonable assurance** of proper safeguarding of assets and reliability of the accounting records. The concept of reasonable assurance rests on the premise that the costs of establishing control procedures should not exceed their expected benefit (see **Helpful Hint**).

To illustrate, consider shoplifting losses in retail stores. Stores could eliminate such losses by having a security guard stop and search customers as they leave the store. But store managers have concluded that the negative effects of such a procedure cannot be justified. Instead, they have attempted to control shoplifting losses by less costly procedures. They post signs saying, "We reserve the right to inspect all packages" and "All shoplifters will be prosecuted." They use hidden cameras and store detectives to monitor customer activity, and they install sensor equipment at exits.

The **human element** is an important factor in every system of internal control. A good system can become ineffective as a result of employee fatigue, carelessness, or indifference. For example, a receiving clerk may not bother to count goods received and may just "fudge" the counts. Occasionally, two or more individuals may work together to get around prescribed controls. Such **collusion** can significantly reduce the effectiveness of a system, eliminating the protection offered by segregation of duties. No system of internal control is perfect.

The **size of the business** also may impose limitations on internal control. Small companies often find it difficult to segregate duties or to provide for independent internal verification. A study by the Association of Certified Fraud Examiners indicates that businesses with fewer than 100 employees are most at risk for employee theft. In fact, 29% of frauds occurred at companies with fewer than 100 employees. The median loss at small companies was $154,000, which was nearly as high as the median fraud at companies with more than 10,000 employees ($160,000). A $154,000 loss can threaten the very existence of a small company.

> **HELPFUL HINT**
> Controls may vary with the risk level of the activity. For example, management may consider cash to be high risk and maintaining inventories in the stockroom as low risk. Thus, management would have stricter controls for cash.

DO IT! 1 | Control Activities

Identify which control activity is violated in each of the following situations, and explain how the situation creates an opportunity for a fraud.

1. The person with primary responsibility for reconciling the bank account and making all bank deposits is also the company's accountant.
2. Wellstone Company's treasurer received an award for distinguished service because he had not taken a vacation in 30 years.
3. In order to save money spent on order slips and to reduce time spent keeping track of order slips, a local bar/restaurant does not buy prenumbered order slips.

Solution

1. Violates the control activity of segregation of duties. Recordkeeping should be separate from physical custody. As a consequence, the employee could embezzle cash and make journal entries to hide the theft.
2. Violates the control activity of human resource controls. Key employees must take vacations. Otherwise, the treasurer, who manages the company's cash, might embezzle cash and use his position to conceal the theft.

ACTION PLAN
- Familiarize yourself with each of the control activities discussed.
- Understand the nature of the frauds that each control activity is intended to address.

> 3. Violates the control activity of documentation procedures. If prenumbered documents are not used, then it is virtually impossible to account for the documents. As a consequence, an employee could write up a dinner sale, receive the cash from the customer, and then throw away the order slip and keep the cash.
>
> Related exercise material: **BE7.1, BE7.2, BE7.3, BE7.4, DO IT! 7.1, E7.1,** and **E7.2.**

Cash Controls

LEARNING OBJECTIVE 2
Apply internal control principles to cash.

Cash is the one asset that is readily convertible into any other type of asset. It also is easily concealed and transported, and is highly desired. Because of these characteristics, **cash is the asset most susceptible to fraudulent activities**. In addition, because of the large volume of cash transactions, numerous errors may occur in executing and recording them. To safeguard cash and to ensure the accuracy of the accounting records for cash, effective internal control over cash is critical.

Cash Receipts Controls

Illustration 7.4 shows how the internal control principles explained earlier apply to cash receipts transactions. As you might expect, companies vary considerably in how they apply

ILLUSTRATION 7.4 Application of internal control principles to cash receipts

Cash Receipts Controls

Establishment of Responsibility
Only designated personnel are authorized to handle cash receipts (cashiers)

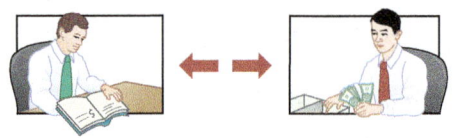

Segregation of Duties
Different individuals receive cash, record cash receipts, and hold the cash

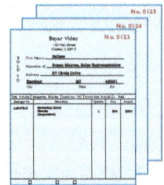

Documentation Procedures
Use remittance advice (mail receipts), cash register tapes or computer records, and deposit slips

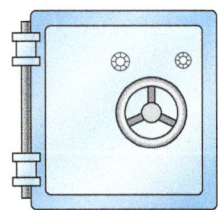

Physical Controls
Store cash in safes and bank vaults; limit access to storage areas; use cash registers or point-of-sale terminals

Independent Internal Verification
Supervisors count cash receipts daily; assistant treasurer compares total receipts to bank deposits daily

Human Resource Controls
Bond personnel who handle cash; require employees to take vacations; conduct background checks

these principles. To illustrate internal control over cash receipts, we will examine control activities for a retail store with both over-the-counter and mail receipts.

Over-the-Counter Receipts

In retail businesses, control of over-the-counter receipts centers on cash registers that are visible to customers. A cash sale is entered in a cash register (or point-of-sale terminal), with the amount clearly visible to the customer. This activity prevents the sales clerk from entering a lower amount and pocketing the difference. The customer receives an itemized cash register receipt and is expected to count the change received. (One weakness at **Barriques** in the Feature Story is that customers are only given a receipt if requested.) The cash register's tape is locked in the register until a supervisor removes it. This tape accumulates the daily transactions and totals.

At the end of the clerk's shift, the clerk counts the cash and sends the cash and the count to the cashier. The cashier (or manager) counts the cash, prepares a deposit slip, and deposits the cash at the bank. The cashier also sends a duplicate of the deposit slip to the accounting department to indicate cash received. The supervisor removes the cash register tape and sends it to the accounting department as the basis for a journal entry to record the cash received. (For point-of-sale systems, the accounting department receives information on daily transactions and totals through the computer network.) **Illustration 7.5** summarizes this process (see **Helpful Hint**).

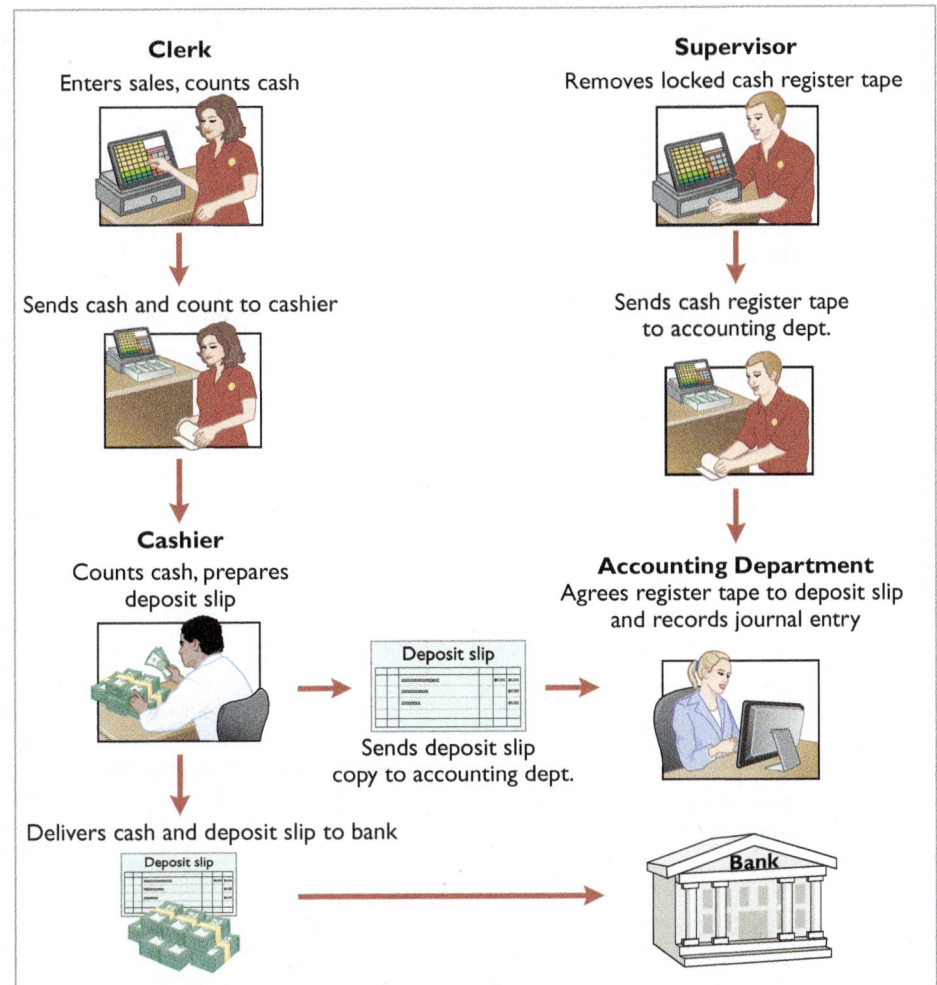

ILLUSTRATION 7.5

Control of over-the-counter receipts

HELPFUL HINT

Flowcharts such as this one enhance the understanding of the flow of documents, the processing steps, and the internal control procedures.

This system for handling cash receipts uses an important internal control principle—segregation of recordkeeping from physical custody. The supervisor has access to the cash register tape but **not** to the cash. The clerk and the cashier have access to the cash but **not** to the register tape. In addition, the cash register tape provides documentation and enables independent internal verification. Use of these three principles of internal control (segregation of recordkeeping from physical custody, documentation, and independent internal verification) provides an effective system of internal control. Any attempt at fraudulent activity should be detected unless there is collusion among the employees.

In some instances, the amount deposited at the bank will not agree with the cash recorded in the accounting records based on the cash register tape. These differences often result because the clerk hands incorrect change back to the retail customer. In this case, the difference between the actual cash and the amount reported on the cash register tape is reported in a Cash Over and Short account. For example, suppose that the cash register tape indicated sales of $6,956.20 but the amount of cash was only $6,946.10. A cash shortfall of $10.10 exists. To account for this cash shortfall and related cash, the company makes the following entry.

Cash	6,946.10	
Cash Over and Short	10.10	
Sales Revenue		6,956.20
(To record cash shortfall)		

Cash Over and Short is an income statement item. It is reported as miscellaneous expense when there is a cash shortfall, and as miscellaneous revenue when there is an overage. Clearly, the amount should be small. Any material amounts in this account should be investigated.

Mail Receipts

All mail receipts should be opened in the presence of at least two mail clerks. These receipts are generally in the form of checks. A mail clerk should endorse each check "For Deposit Only." This restrictive endorsement reduces the likelihood that someone could divert the check to personal use. Banks will not give an individual cash when presented with a check that has this type of endorsement.

The mail clerks prepare, in triplicate, a list of the checks received each day. This list shows the name of the check issuer, the purpose of the payment, and the amount of the check. Each mail clerk signs the list to establish responsibility for the data. The original copy of the list, along with the checks, is then sent to the cashier's department. A copy of the list is sent to the accounting department for recording in the accounting records. The clerks also keep a copy.

This process provides excellent internal control for the company. By employing at least two clerks, the chance of fraud is reduced. Each clerk knows he or she is being observed by the other clerk(s). To engage in fraud, they would have to collude. The customers who submit payments also provide control because they will contact the company with a complaint if they are not properly credited for payment. Because the cashier has access to the cash but not the records, and the accounting department has access to the records but not the cash, neither can engage in undetected fraud.

Cash Disbursements Controls

Companies disburse cash for a variety of reasons, such as to pay expenses and liabilities or to purchase assets. **Generally, internal control over cash disbursements is more effective when companies pay by check or electronic funds transfer (EFT) rather than by cash.** One exception is **payments for incidental amounts that are paid out of petty cash.**[2]

Companies generally issue checks only after following specified control procedures. **Illustration 7.6** shows how principles of internal control apply to cash disbursements.

Voucher System Controls

Most medium and large companies use vouchers as part of their internal control over cash disbursements. A **voucher system** is a network of approvals by authorized individuals, acting independently, to ensure that all disbursements by check are proper.

---

[2]We explain the operation of a petty cash fund in Appendix 7A.

ILLUSTRATION 7.6 Application of internal control principles to cash disbursements

Cash Disbursements Controls

Establishment of Responsibility
Only designated personnel are authorized to sign checks (treasurer) and approve vendors

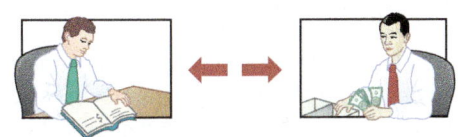

Segregation of Duties
Different individuals approve and make payments; check-signers do not record disbursements

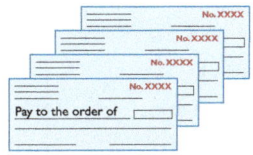

Documentation Procedures
Use prenumbered checks and account for them in sequence; each check must have an approved invoice; require employees to use corporate credit cards for reimbursable expenses; stamp invoices "paid"

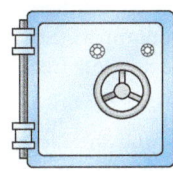

Physical Controls
Store blank checks in safes, with limited access; print check amounts by machine in indelible ink

Independent Internal Verification
Compare checks to invoices; reconcile bank statement monthly

Human Resource Controls
Bond personnel who handle cash; require employees to take vacations; conduct background checks

The system begins with the authorization to incur a cost or expense. It ends with the issuance of a check for the liability incurred. A **voucher** is an authorization form prepared for each expenditure. Companies require vouchers for all types of cash disbursements except those from petty cash.

The starting point in preparing a voucher is to fill in the appropriate information about the liability on the face of the voucher. The vendor's invoice provides most of the needed information. Then, an employee in the accounts payable department records the voucher (in a journal called a **voucher register**) and files it according to the date on which it is to be paid. The company issues and sends a check on that date, and stamps the voucher "paid." The paid voucher is sent to the accounting department for recording (in a journal called the **check register**). A voucher system involves two journal entries, one to record the liability when the voucher is issued and a second to pay the liability that relates to the voucher.

The use of a voucher system, whether done manually or electronically, improves internal control over cash disbursements. First, the authorization process inherent in a voucher system establishes responsibility. Each individual has responsibility to review the underlying documentation to ensure that it is correct. In addition, the voucher system keeps track of the documents that back up each transaction. By keeping these documents in one place, a supervisor can independently verify the authenticity of each transaction. Consider, for example, the case of Aesop University presented earlier in the Anatomy of a Fraud box. Aesop did not use a voucher system for transactions under $2,500. As a consequence, there was no independent verification of the documents, which enabled the employee to submit fake invoices to hide his unauthorized purchases.

Petty Cash Fund

ETHICS NOTE
Petty cash funds are authorized and legitimate. In contrast, "slush" funds are unauthorized and hidden (under the table).

As you just learned, better internal control over cash disbursements is possible when companies make payments by check. However, using checks to pay small amounts is both impractical and a nuisance. For instance, a company would not want to write checks to pay for postage due, working lunches, or taxi fares. A common way of handling such payments, while maintaining satisfactory control, is to use a **petty cash fund** to pay relatively small amounts (see Ethics Note). The operation of a petty cash fund, often called an **imprest system**, involves (1) establishing the fund, (2) making payments from the fund, and (3) replenishing the fund.[3] We explain the operation of a petty cash fund in Appendix 7A.

Ethics Insight

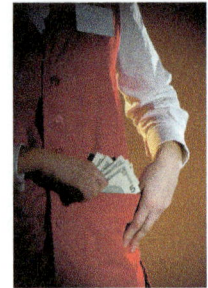
© Chris Fernig/iStockphoto

How Employees Steal

Occupational fraud is using your own occupation for personal gain through the misuse or misapplication of the company's resources or assets. This type of fraud is one of three types:

1. **Asset misappropriation**, such as theft of cash on hand, fraudulent disbursements, false refunds, ghost employees, personal purchases, and fictitious employees. This fraud is the most common but the least costly.

2. **Corruption**, such as bribery, illegal gratuities, and economic extortion. This fraud generally falls in the middle between asset misappropriation and financial statement fraud as regards frequency and cost.

3. **Financial statement fraud**, such as fictitious revenues, concealed liabilities and expenses, improper disclosures, and improper asset values. This fraud occurs less frequently than other types of fraud but it is the most costly.

The graph below shows the frequency and the median loss for each type of occupational fraud. (Note that the sum of percentages exceeds 100% because some cases of fraud involved more than one type.)

Source: *2016 Report to the Nations on Occupational Fraud and Abuse,* Association of Certified Fraud Examiners, p. 12.

How can companies reduce the likelihood of occupational fraud? (Go to WileyPLUS for this answer and additional questions.)

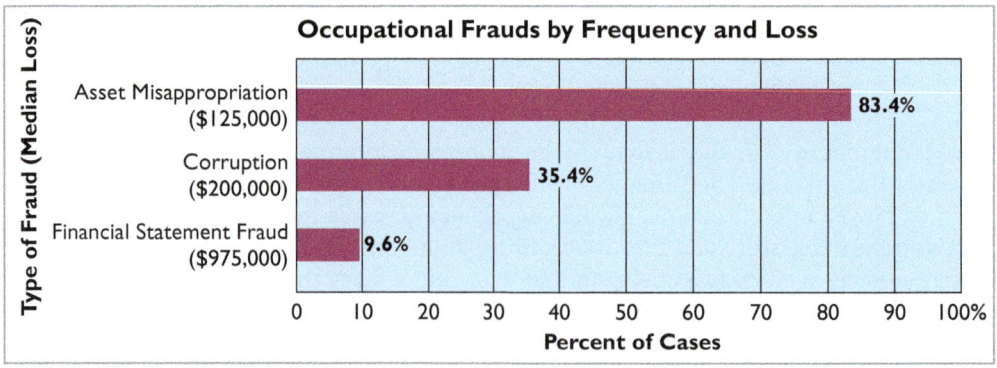

---

[3] The term "imprest" means an advance of money for a designated purpose.

DO IT! 2 | Control over Cash Receipts

L. R. Cortez is concerned about the control over cash receipts in his fast-food restaurant, Big Cheese. The restaurant has two cash registers. At no time do more than two employees take customer orders and enter sales. Work shifts for employees range from 4 to 8 hours. Cortez asks your help in installing a good system of internal control over cash receipts.

Solution

Cortez should assign a separate cash register drawer to each employee at the start of each work shift, with register totals set at zero. Each employee should have access to only the assigned register drawer to enter all sales. Each customer should be given a receipt. At the end of the shift, the employee should do a cash count. A separate employee should compare the cash count with the register tape (or point-of-sale records) to be sure they agree. In addition, Cortez should install an automated point-of-sale system that would enable the company to compare orders entered in the register to orders processed by the kitchen.

Related exercise material: **BE7.5, BE7.6, BE7.7, BE7.8, DO IT! 7.2, E7.3, E7.4, E7.5, E7.6, and E7.7.**

ACTION PLAN
- Differentiate among the internal control principles of (1) establishing responsibility, (2) physical controls, and (3) independent internal verification.
- Design an effective system of internal control over cash receipts.

Control Features of a Bank Account

LEARNING OBJECTIVE 3
Identify the control features of a bank account.

The use of a bank contributes significantly to good internal control over cash. A company safeguards its cash by using a bank as a depository and clearinghouse for checks received and checks written. The use of a bank checking account minimizes the amount of currency that must be kept on hand. It also facilitates control of cash because a double record is maintained of all bank transactions—one by the business and the other by the bank. The asset account Cash maintained by the company is the "flipside" of the bank's liability account for that company. A **bank reconciliation** is the process of comparing the bank's balance with the company's balance, and explaining the differences to make them agree.

Many companies have more than one bank account. For efficiency of operations and better control, national retailers like **Wal-Mart** and **Target** often have regional bank accounts. Similarly, a company such as **ExxonMobil** with more than 100,000 employees may have a payroll bank account as well as one or more general bank accounts. In addition, a company may maintain several bank accounts in order to have more than one source for short-term loans.

Electronic Funds Transfer (EFT) System

It is not surprising that companies and banks have developed approaches to transfer funds among parties without the use of paper (deposit tickets, checks, etc.). Such procedures, called **electronic funds transfers (EFTs)**, are disbursement systems that use wire, telephone, or computers to transfer cash from one location to another. Use of EFT is quite common. For example, many employees receive no formal payroll checks from their employers. Instead, employers send electronic payroll data to the appropriate banks. Also, companies now frequently make regular payments such as those for utilities, rent, and insurance by EFT.

EFT transactions normally result in better internal control since no cash or checks are handled by company employees. This does not mean that opportunities for fraud are eliminated. In fact, the same basic principles related to internal control apply to EFT transactions.

For example, without proper segregation of duties and authorizations, an employee might be able to redirect electronic payments into a personal bank account and conceal the theft with fraudulent accounting entries.

Bank Statements

Each month, the company receives from the bank a **bank statement** showing its bank transactions and balances.[4] For example, the statement for Laird Company in **Illustration 7.7** shows the following: (1) checks paid and other debits (such as debit card transactions or electronic funds transfers for bill payments) that reduce the balance in the depositor's account, (2) deposits (by direct deposit, automated teller machine, or electronic funds transfer) and other credits that increase the balance in the depositor's account, and (3) the account balance after each day's transactions (see **Helpful Hint**).

ILLUSTRATION 7.7

Bank statement

HELPFUL HINT

Essentially, the bank statement is a copy of the bank's records sent to the customer or made available online for review.

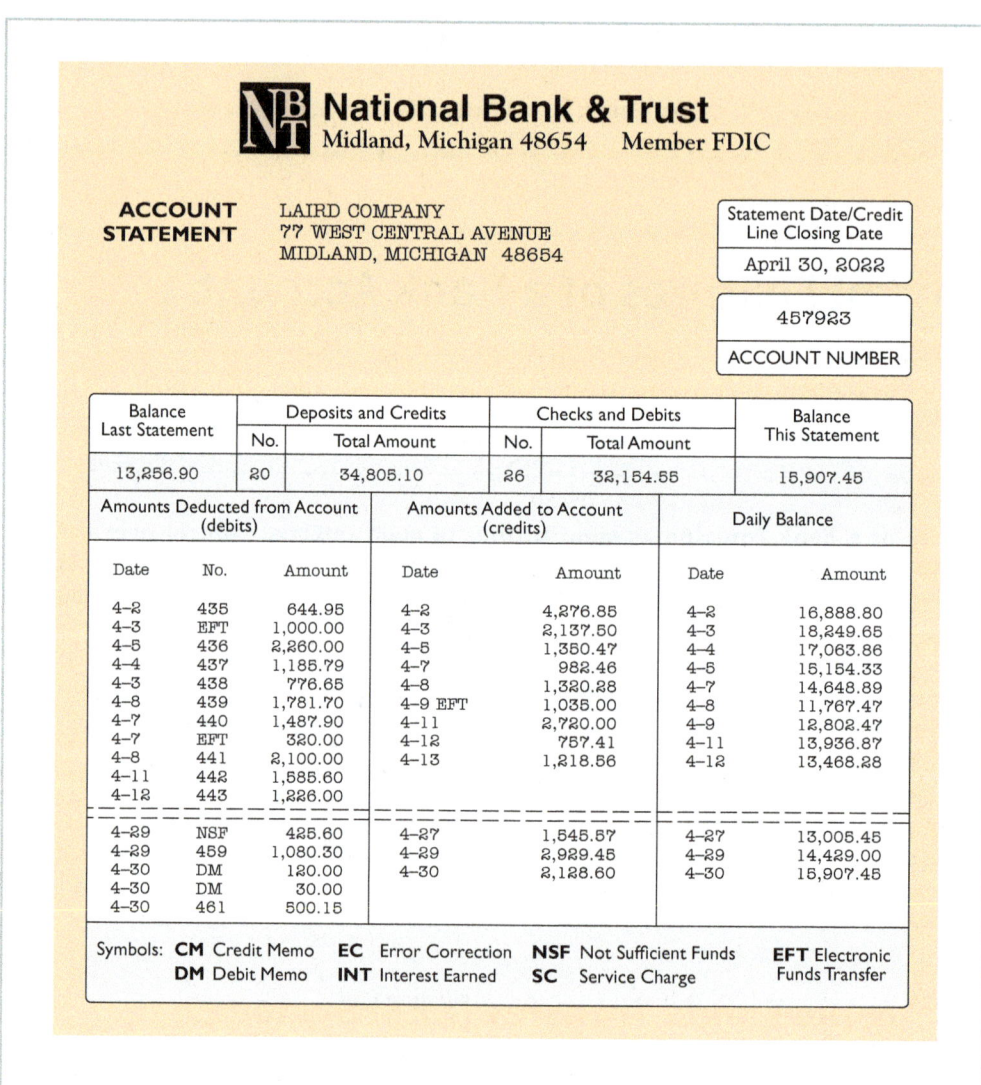

Remember that **bank statements are prepared from the *bank's* perspective**. For example, **every deposit the bank receives is an increase in the bank's liabilities (an account payable to the depositor)**. Therefore, in Illustration 7.7, National Bank and Trust **credits** to Laird Company every deposit it received from Laird. The reverse occurs

---

[4]Our presentation assumes that a company makes all adjustments at the end of the month. In practice, a company may also make journal entries during the month as it reviews information from the bank regarding its account.

when the bank "pays" a check issued by Laird Company on its checking account balance: Payment reduces the bank's liability and is therefore **debited** to Laird's account with the bank.

The bank statement lists in numerical sequence all paid checks along with the date the check was paid and its amount. Upon paying a check, the bank stamps the check "paid"; a paid check is sometimes referred to as a **canceled** check. In addition, the bank includes with the bank statement memoranda explaining other debits and credits it made to the depositor's account.

A check that is not paid by a bank because of insufficient funds in a bank account is called an **NSF check** (not sufficient funds). The bank uses a debit memorandum when a previously deposited customer's check "bounces" because of insufficient funds. In such a case, the customer's bank marks the check NSF (not sufficient funds) and returns it to the depositor's bank. The bank then debits (decreases) the depositor's account, as shown by the symbol NSF in Illustration 7.7, and sends the NSF check and debit memorandum to the depositor as notification of the charge. The NSF check creates an account receivable for the depositor and reduces cash in the bank account.

Reconciling the Bank Account

Because the bank and the company maintain independent records of the company's checking account, you might assume that the respective balances will always agree. In fact, the two balances are seldom the same at any given time, and both balances differ from the "correct or true" balance. Therefore, it is necessary to make the balance per books and the balance per bank agree with the correct or true amount—a process called **reconciling the bank account**. The need for reconciliation has two causes:

1. **Time lags** that prevent one of the parties from recording the transaction in the same period.
2. **Errors** by either party in recording transactions.

Time lags occur frequently. For example, several days may elapse between the time a company pays by check and the date the bank pays the check. Similarly, when a company uses the bank's night depository to make its deposits, there will be a difference of one day between the time the company records the receipts and the time the bank does so. A time lag also occurs whenever the bank mails a debit or credit memorandum to the company.

You might think that if a company never writes checks (for example, if a small company uses only a debit card or electronic bill funds transfers), it does not need to reconcile its account. However, **the possibility of errors or fraud still necessitates periodic reconciliation**. The incidence of errors or fraud depends on the effectiveness of the internal controls maintained by the company and the bank. Bank errors are infrequent. However, either party could accidentally record a $450 check as $45 or $540. In addition, the bank might mistakenly charge a check drawn by C. D. Berg to the account of C. D. Burg.

Reconciliation Procedure

In reconciling the bank account, it is customary to reconcile the balance per books and balance per bank to their adjusted (correct or true) cash balances. **To obtain maximum benefit from a bank reconciliation, an employee who has no other responsibilities related to cash should prepare the reconciliation.** When companies do not follow the internal control principle of independent internal verification in preparing the reconciliation, cash embezzlements may escape unnoticed. For example, in the Anatomy of a Fraud box presented earlier, a bank reconciliation by someone other than Angela Bauer might have exposed her embezzlement.

Illustration 7.8 shows the reconciliation process (see **Helpful Hint**). The starting point in preparing the reconciliation is to enter the balance per bank statement and balance per books on a schedule. The following steps should reveal all the reconciling items that cause the difference between the two balances.

ILLUSTRATION 7.8
Bank reconciliation adjustments

HELPFUL HINT
Deposits in transit and outstanding checks are reconciling items because of time lags.

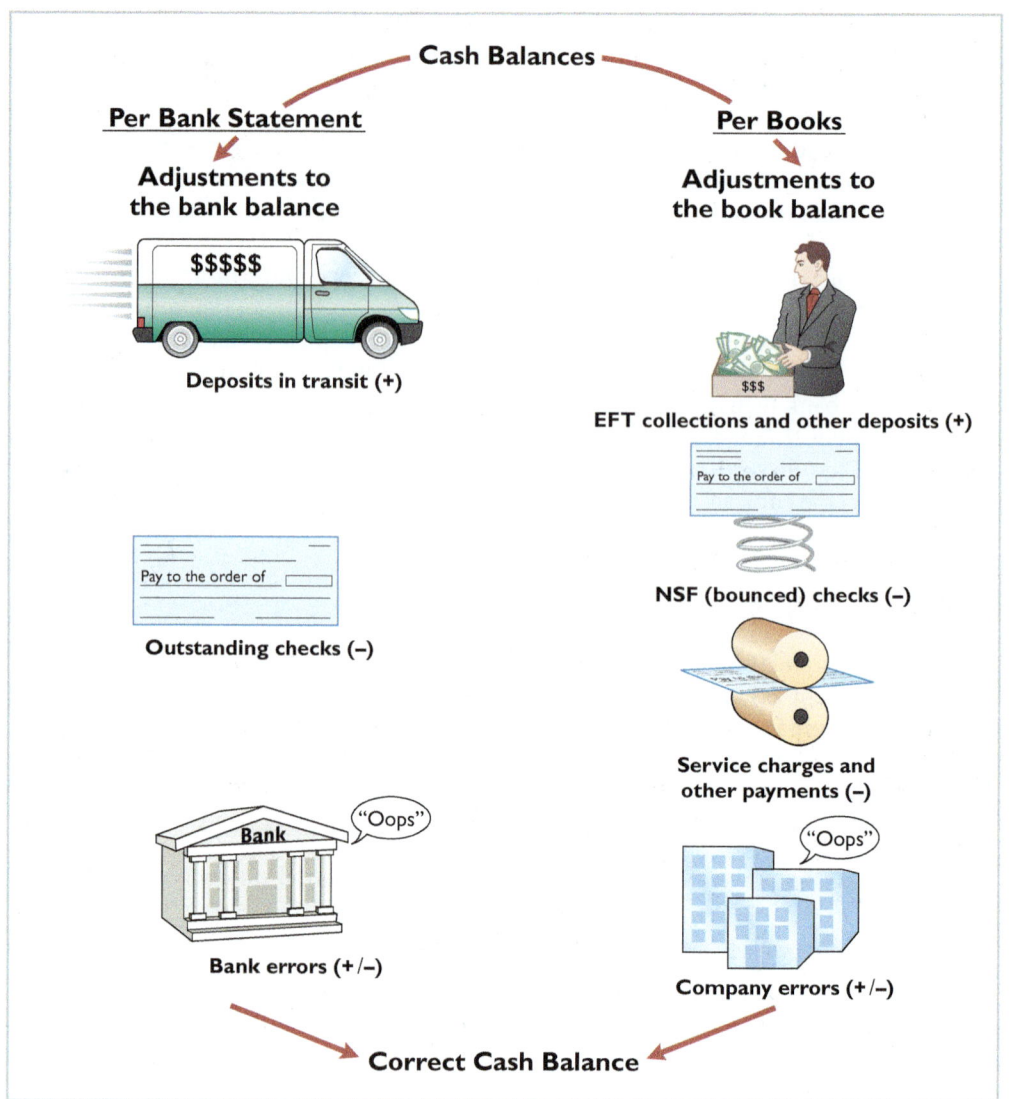

Reconciling Items per Bank On the bank side of the reconciliation, the items to reconcile are deposits in transit (amounts added), outstanding checks (amounts deducted), and bank errors (if any). By adjusting the bank balance for these items, a company brings that balance up to date.

Step 1 **Deposits in transit (+).** Compare the individual deposits on the bank statement with the deposits in transit from the preceding bank reconciliation and with the deposits per company records or copies of duplicate deposit slips. Deposits recorded by the depositor that have not been recorded by the bank represent **deposits in transit**. Add these deposits to the balance per bank.

Step 2 **Outstanding checks (−).** Compare the paid checks shown on the bank statement or the paid checks returned with the bank statement with (a) checks outstanding from the preceding bank reconciliation, and (b) checks issued by the company as recorded in the cash payments journal. Issued checks recorded by the company that have not been paid by the bank represent **outstanding checks**. Deduct outstanding checks from the balance per bank.

Step 3 **Bank errors (+/−).** Note any errors made by the bank that were discovered in the previous steps. For example, if the bank processed a deposit of $1,693 as $1,639 in error, the difference of $54 ($1,693 − $1,639) is added to the balance per bank on the bank reconciliation. All errors made by the bank are reconciling items in determining the adjusted cash balance per the bank.

Reconciling Items per Books Reconciling items on the book side relate to amounts not yet recorded on the company's books and include adjustments from deposits and other amounts added, payments and other amounts deducted, and company errors (if any).

Step 1 **Other deposits (+).** Compare the other deposits on the bank statement with the company records. Any unrecorded amounts should be added to the balance per books. For example, if the bank statement shows electronic funds transfers from customers paying their accounts online, these amounts should be added to the balance per books on the bank reconciliation to update the company's records unless they had previously been recorded by the company.

Step 2 **Other payments (−).** Similarly, any unrecorded other payments should be deducted from the balance per books. For example, if the bank statement shows service charges (such as debit and credit card fees and other bank service charges), this amount is deducted from the balance per books on the bank reconciliation to make the company's records agree with the bank's records. **Normally, the company will already have recorded electronic payments.** However, if this has not been the case then these payments must be deducted from the balance per books on the bank reconciliation to make the company's records agree with the bank's records.

Step 3 **Book errors (+/−).** Note any errors made by the depositor that have been discovered in the previous steps. For example, say a company wrote check No. 443 to a supplier in the amount of $1,226 on April 12, but the accounting clerk recorded the check amount as $1,262. The error of $36 ($1,262 − $1,226) is added to the balance per books because the company reduced the balance per books by $36 too much when it recorded the check as $1,262 instead of $1,226. Only errors made by the company, not the bank, are included as reconciling items in determining the adjusted cash balance per books.

Bank Reconciliation Illustrated

Illustration 7.7 presented the bank statement for Laird Company which the company accessed online (see **Helpful Hint**). It shows a balance per bank of $15,907.45 on April 30, 2022. On this date the balance of cash per books is $11,709.45.

From the foregoing steps, Laird determines the following reconciling items for the bank.

Step 1 **Deposits in transit (+):** April 30 deposit (received by bank on May 1). $2,201.40

Step 2 **Outstanding checks (−):** No. 453, $3,000.00; No. 457, $1,401.30; No. 460, $1,502.70. 5,904.00

Step 3 **Bank errors (+/−):** None.

Reconciling items per books are as follows.

Step 1 **Other deposits (+):** Unrecorded electronic receipt from customer on account on April 9 determined from the bank statement. $1,035.00

Step 2 **Other payments (−):** The electronic payments on April 3 and 7 were previously recorded by the company when they were initiated. Unrecorded charges determined from the bank statement are as follows:

Returned NSF check on April 29	425.60
Debit and credit card fees on April 30	120.00
Bank service charges on April 30	30.00

Step 3 **Company errors (+):** Check No. 443 was correctly written by Laird for $1,226 and was correctly paid by the bank on April 12. However, it was recorded as $1,262 on Laird's books. 36.00

Illustration 7.9 shows Laird's bank reconciliation (see **Alternative Terminology**).

> **HELPFUL HINT**
> Note in the bank statement in Illustration 7.7 that the bank has paid checks No. 459 and 461, but check No. 460 is not listed. Thus, this check is outstanding. If a complete bank statement were provided, checks No. 453 and 457 also would not be listed. Laird obtains the amounts for these three checks from its cash payments records.

ILLUSTRATION 7.9
Bank reconciliation

Laird Company
Bank Reconciliation
April 30, 2022

Cash balance per bank statement		$15,907.45
Add: Deposits in transit		2,201.40
		18,108.85
Less: Outstanding checks		
No. 453	$3,000.00	
No. 457	1,401.30	
No. 460	1,502.70	5,904.00
Adjusted cash balance per bank		**$12,204.85**
Cash balance per books		$11,709.45
Add: Electronic funds transfer received	$1,035.00	
Error in recording check No. 443	36.00	1,071.00
		12,780.45
Less: NSF check	425.60	
Debit and credit card fees	120.00	
Bank service charge	30.00	575.60
Adjusted cash balance per books		**$12,204.85**

ALTERNATIVE TERMINOLOGY
The terms *adjusted cash balance*, *true cash balance*, and *correct cash balance* are used interchangeably.

HELPFUL HINT
These entries are adjusting entries. In prior chapters, we considered Cash an account that did not require adjustment because we had not yet explained a bank reconciliation.

Entries from Bank Reconciliation

The depositor (that is, the company) next must record each reconciling item used to determine the **adjusted cash balance per books**. If the company does not journalize and post these items, the Cash account will not show the correct balance. The adjusting entries for the Laird Company bank reconciliation on April 30 are as follows (see **Helpful Hint**).

Collection of Electronic Funds Transfer   A payment of an account by a customer is recorded in the same way, whether the cash is received through the mail or electronically. The entry by Laird to record the EFT collection (which it learned of from the bank statement) is as follows.

Apr. 30	Cash	1,035	
	Accounts Receivable		1,035
	(To record receipt of electronic funds transfer)		

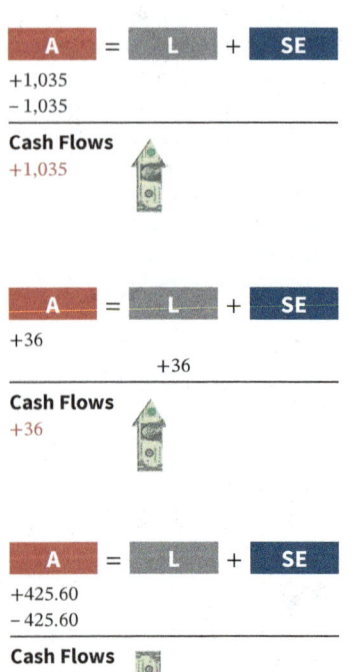

A = L + SE
+1,035
−1,035

Cash Flows
+1,035

Book Error   An examination of the cash disbursements journal shows that check No. 443 was a payment on account to Andrea Company, a supplier. The correcting entry is as follows.

Apr. 30	Cash	36	
	Accounts Payable—Andrea Company		36
	(To correct error in recording check No. 443)		

A = L + SE
+36   +36

Cash Flows
+36

NSF Check   As indicated earlier, an NSF check becomes an accounts receivable to the depositor. The entry is as follows.

Apr. 30	Accounts Receivable—J. R. Baron	425.60	
	Cash		425.60
	(To record NSF check)		

A = L + SE
+425.60
−425.60

Cash Flows
−425.60

Bank Charges Expense   Fees for processing debit and credit card transactions are normally debited to the Bank Charges Expense account, as are bank service charges. We have chosen to combine and record these in one journal entry, as the following shows, although they also could be journalized separately.

Apr. 30	Bank Charges Expense	150	
	Cash		150
	(To record charges for debit and credit card fees of $120 and bank service charges of $30)		

A	=	L	+	SE
				−150 Exp
−150				

Cash Flows
−150

After Laird posts the entries, the Cash account will appear as in **Illustration 7.10**. The adjusted cash balance in the ledger should agree with the adjusted cash balance per books in the bank reconciliation in Illustration 7.9.

		Cash		
Apr. 30	Bal.	11,709.45	Apr. 30	425.60
30		1,035.00	30	150.00
30		36.00		
Apr. 30	Bal.	**12,204.85**		

ILLUSTRATION 7.10

Adjusted balance in Cash account

What entries does the bank make? If the company discovers any bank errors in preparing the reconciliation, it should notify the bank so the bank can make the necessary corrections on its records. The bank does not make any entries for deposits in transit or outstanding checks. Only when these items reach the bank will the bank record these items.

Investor Insight

Madoff's Ponzi Scheme

Mary Altaffer/©AP/ Wide World Photos

No recent fraud has generated more interest and rage than the one perpetrated by Bernard Madoff. Madoff was an elite New York investment fund manager who was highly regarded by securities regulators. Investors flocked to him because he delivered steady returns of between 10% and 15%, no matter whether the market was going up or going down. However, for many years, Madoff did not actually invest the cash that people gave to him. Instead, he was running a Ponzi scheme: He paid returns to existing investors using cash received from new investors. As long as the size of his investment fund continued to grow from new investments at a rate that exceeded the amounts that he needed to pay out in returns, Madoff was able to operate his fraud smoothly.

To conceal his misdeeds, Madoff fabricated false investment statements that were provided to investors. In addition, Madoff hired an auditor that never verified the accuracy of the investment records but automatically issued unqualified opinions each year. A competing fund manager warned the SEC a number of times over a nearly 10-year period that he thought Madoff was engaged in fraud. The SEC never aggressively investigated the allegations. Investors, many of which were charitable organizations, lost more than $18 billion. Madoff was sentenced to a jail term of 150 years.

How was Madoff able to conceal such a giant fraud? (Go to WileyPLUS for this answer and additional questions.)

DO IT! 3 | Bank Reconciliation

Sally Kist owns Linen Kist Fabrics. Sally asks you to explain how she should treat the following reconciling items when reconciling the company's bank account: (1) a debit memorandum for an NSF check, (2) a credit memorandum for an electronic funds transfer from one of the company's customers received by the bank, (3) outstanding checks, and (4) a deposit in transit.

ACTION PLAN

- **Understand the purpose of a bank reconciliation.**
- **Identify time lags and explain how they cause reconciling items.**

Solution

Sally should treat the reconciling items as follows.

1. NSF check: Deduct from balance per books.
2. Electronic funds transfer received by bank: Add to balance per books.
3. Outstanding checks: Deduct from balance per bank.
4. Deposit in transit: Add to balance per bank.

Related exercise material: **BE7.10, BE7.11, BE7.12, BE7.13, DO IT! 7.3, E7.8, E7.9, E7.11, E7.12, E7.13, and E7.14.**

Reporting Cash and Cash Management

LEARNING OBJECTIVE 4
Explain the reporting of cash and the basic principles of cash management.

Reporting Cash

Cash consists of coins, currency (paper money), checks, money orders, and money on hand or on deposit in a bank or similar depository. Checks that are dated later than the current date (post-dated checks) are not included in cash. Companies report cash in two different statements: the balance sheet and the statement of cash flows. The balance sheet reports the amount of cash available at a given point in time. The statement of cash flows shows the sources and uses of cash during a period of time. The statement of cash flows was introduced in Chapters 1 and 2, and will be discussed in much detail in Chapter 12. In this section, we discuss some important points regarding the presentation of cash in the balance sheet.

When presented in a balance sheet, cash on hand, cash in banks, and petty cash are often combined and reported simply as **Cash**. Because it is the most liquid asset owned by the company, cash is listed first in the current assets section of the balance sheet.

Cash Equivalents

Many companies use the designation "Cash and cash equivalents" in reporting cash. (See Illustration 7.11 for an example.) **Cash equivalents** are short-term, highly liquid investments that are both:

1. Readily convertible to known amounts of cash.
2. So near their maturity that their market value is relatively insensitive to changes in interest rates. (Generally, only investments with maturities of three months or less qualify under this definition.)

ILLUSTRATION 7.11
Balance sheet presentation of cash

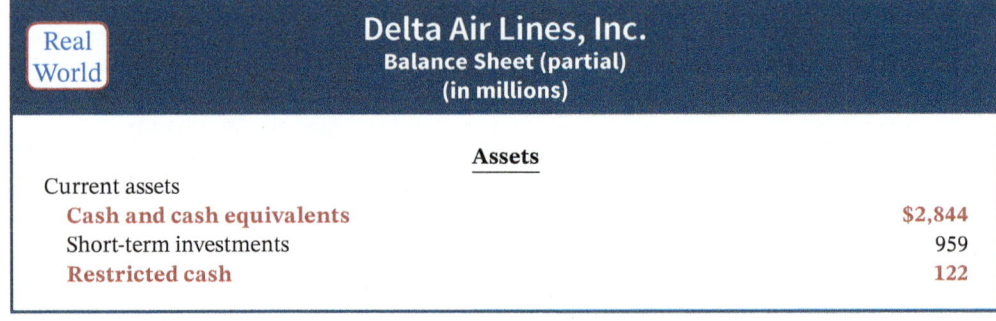

ETHICS NOTE
Recently, some companies were forced to restate their financial statements because they had too broadly interpreted which types of investments could be treated as cash equivalents. By reporting these items as cash equivalents, the companies made themselves look more liquid.

Examples of cash equivalents are Treasury bills, commercial paper (short-term corporate notes), and money market funds (see **Ethics Note**). All typically are purchased with cash that is in excess of immediate needs.

Occasionally a company will have a net negative balance in its bank account. In this case, the company should report the negative balance among current liabilities. For example, farm equipment manufacturer **Ag-Chem** at one time reported "Checks outstanding in excess of cash balances" of $2,145,000 among its current liabilities.

Restricted Cash

A company may have **restricted cash**, cash that is not available for general use but rather is restricted for a special purpose (see **Decision Tools**). For example, landfill companies are often required to maintain a fund of restricted cash to ensure they will have adequate resources to cover closing and clean-up costs at the end of a landfill site's useful life. **McKesson Corp.** recently reported restricted cash of $962 million to be paid out as the result of investor lawsuits.

Cash restricted in use should be reported separately on the balance sheet as restricted cash. If the company expects to use the restricted cash within the next year, it reports the amount as a current asset. When this is not the case, it reports the restricted funds as a noncurrent asset. The FASB now requires that restricted cash be included with cash and cash equivalents when reconciling the beginning and ending amounts on a statement of cash flows.

Illustration 7.11 shows restricted cash reported in the financial statements of **Delta Air Lines** during a recent year. The company was required to maintain restricted cash as collateral to support insurance obligations related to workers' compensation claims. Delta did not have access to these funds for general use, and so it had to report them separately, rather than as part of cash and cash equivalents.

> **Decision Tools**
> Reporting restricted cash separately helps users determine the amount of cash available for a company's general use.

DO IT! 4a | Reporting Cash

Indicate whether each of the following statements is true or false. If false, indicate how to correct the statement.

1. Cash and cash equivalents are comprised of coins, currency (paper money), money orders, and NSF checks.
2. Restricted cash is classified as either a current asset or noncurrent asset, depending on the circumstances.
3. A company may have a negative balance in its bank account. In this case, it should offset this negative balance against cash and cash equivalents on the balance sheet.
4. Because cash and cash equivalents often includes short-term investments, accounts receivable should be reported as the first item on the balance sheet.

ACTION PLAN
- Understand how companies present cash and restricted cash on the balance sheet.
- Review the designations of cash equivalents and restricted cash, and how companies typically handle them.

Solution

1. False. NSF checks should be reported as receivables, not cash and cash equivalents. **2.** True. **3.** False. Companies that have a negative balance in their bank accounts should report the negative balance as a current liability. **4.** False. Cash equivalents are readily convertible to known amounts of cash, and so near maturity (less than 3 months) that they are considered more liquid than accounts receivable and therefore are reported before accounts receivable on the balance sheet.

Related exercise material: **BE7.15, DO IT! 7.4a, and E7.15.**

Managing and Monitoring Cash

Many companies struggle, not because they fail to generate sales, but because they cannot manage their cash. A real-life example of this is a clothing manufacturing company owned by Sharon McCollick. McCollick gave up a stable, high-paying marketing job with **Intel Corporation** to start her own company. Soon she had more orders from stores such as **JC Penney** and **Dayton Hudson** (now **Target**) than she could fill. Yet she found herself on the brink of financial disaster, owing three mortgage payments on her house and $2,000 to the IRS. Her company could generate sales, but it was not collecting cash fast enough to support its operations. The bottom line is that a business must have cash.[5]

A merchandising company's operating cycle is generally shorter than that of a manufacturing company. **Illustration 7.12** shows the cash to cash operating cycle of a merchandising operation.

---

[5]Adapted from T. Petzinger, Jr., "The Front Lines—Sharon McCollick Got Mad and Tore Down a Bank's Barriers," *Wall Street Journal* (May 19, 1995), p. B1.

> **ILLUSTRATION 7.12**
> Operating cycle of a merchandising company

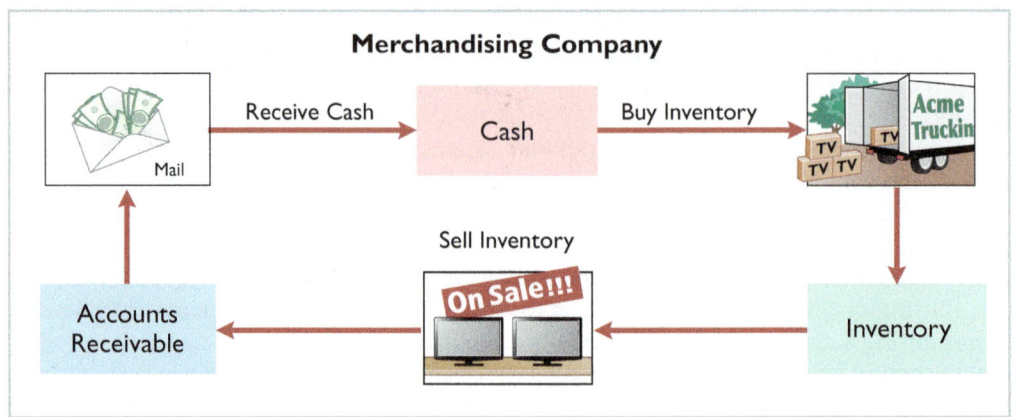

To understand cash management, consider the operating cycle of Sharon McCollick's clothing manufacturing company. First, it purchases cloth. Let's assume that it purchases the cloth on credit provided by the supplier, so the company owes its supplier money. Second, employees convert the cloth to clothing. Now the company also owes its employees money. Third, it sells the clothing to retailers, on credit. McCollick's company will have no money to repay suppliers or employees until it receives payments from customers. In a manufacturing operation, there may be a significant lag between the original purchase of raw materials and the ultimate receipt of cash from customers.

Managing the often-precarious balance created by the ebb and flow of cash during the operating cycle is one of a company's greatest challenges. The objective is to ensure that a company has sufficient cash to meet payments as they come due, yet minimize the amount of non-revenue-generating cash on hand.

Basic Principles of Cash Management

Management of cash is the responsibility of the company **treasurer**. Any company can improve its chances of having adequate cash by following five basic principles of cash management.

1. **Increase the speed of receivables collection.** Money owed Sharon McCollick by her customers is money that she cannot use. The more quickly customers pay her, the more quickly she can use those funds. Thus, rather than have an average collection period of 30 days, she may want an average collection period of 15 days. However, she must carefully weigh any attempt to force her customers to pay earlier against the possibility that she may anger or alienate them. Perhaps her competitors are willing to provide a 30-day grace period. As noted in Chapter 5, one common way to encourage customers to pay more quickly is to offer cash discounts for early payment under such terms as 2/10, n/30.

2. **Keep inventory levels low.** Maintaining a large inventory of cloth and finished clothing is costly. It ties up large amounts of cash, as well as warehouse space. Increasingly, companies are using techniques to reduce the inventory on hand, thus conserving their cash. Of course, if Sharon McCollick has inadequate inventory, she will lose sales. The proper level of inventory is an important decision.

3. **Monitor payment of liabilities.** Sharon McCollick should monitor when her bills are due, so she avoids paying them too early. Let's say her supplier allows 30 days for payment. If she pays in 10 days, she has lost the use of that cash for 20 days. Therefore, she should use the full payment period. But, she should not pay late. This could damage her credit rating (and future borrowing ability). Also, late payments to suppliers can damage important supplier relationships and may even threaten a supplier's viability. McCollick's company also should conserve cash by taking cash discounts offered by suppliers, when possible (see **International Note**).

4. **Plan the timing of major expenditures.** To maintain operations or to grow, all companies must make major expenditures. These often require some form of outside financing. To increase the likelihood of obtaining outside financing, Sharon McCollick should carefully consider the timing of major expenditures in light of her company's operating cycle. If

> **International Note**
> International sales complicate cash management. For example, if **Nike** must repay a Japanese supplier 30 days from today in Japanese yen, Nike will be concerned about how the exchange rate of U.S. dollars for yen might change during those 30 days. Often, corporate treasurers make investments known as *hedges* to lock in an exchange rate to reduce the company's exposure to exchange-rate fluctuation.

at all possible, she should make any major expenditure when the company normally has excess cash—usually during the off-season.

5. **Invest idle cash.** Cash on hand earns nothing. An important part of the treasurer's job is to ensure that the company invests any excess cash, even if it is only overnight. Many businesses, such as Sharon McCollick's clothing company, are seasonal. During her slow season, when she has excess cash, she should invest it.

To avoid a cash crisis, it is very important that investments of idle cash be highly liquid and risk-free. A **liquid investment** is one with a market in which someone is always willing to buy or sell the investment. A **risk-free investment** means there is no concern that the party will default on its promise to pay its principal and interest. For example, using excess cash to purchase stock in a small company because you heard that it was probably going to increase in value in the near term is totally inappropriate. First, the stock of small companies is often illiquid. Second, if the stock suddenly decreases in value, you might be forced to sell the stock at a loss in order to pay your bills as they come due. The most common form of liquid investments is interest-paying U.S. government securities.

Illustration 7.13 summarizes these five principles of cash management.

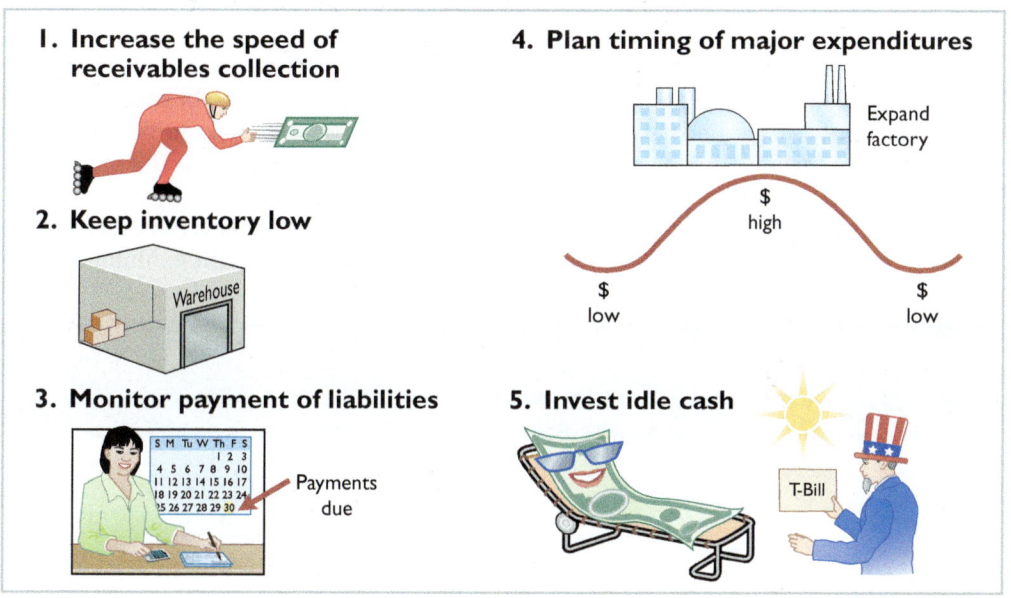

ILLUSTRATION 7.13

Five principles of sound cash management

Cash Budgeting

Because cash is so vital to a company, **planning the company's cash needs** is a key business activity. It enables the company to plan ahead to cover possible cash shortfalls and to make investments of idle funds. The **cash budget** shows anticipated cash flows, usually over a one- to two-year period (see **Decision Tools**). In this section, we introduce the basics of cash budgeting. More advanced discussion of cash budgets and budgets in general is provided in managerial accounting texts.

As shown in Illustration 7.14, the cash budget contains three sections—cash receipts, cash disbursements, and financing—and the beginning and ending cash balances.

The **Cash receipts** section includes expected receipts from the company's principal source(s) of cash, such as cash sales and collections from customers on credit sales. This section also shows anticipated receipts of interest and dividends, and proceeds from planned sales of investments, plant assets, and the company's capital stock.

The **Cash disbursements** section shows expected payments for inventory, labor, overhead, and selling and administrative expenses. It also includes projected payments for income taxes, dividends, investments, and plant assets. Note that it does not include depreciation since depreciation expense does not use cash.

Decision Tools

The cash budget helps users determine if the company will be able to meet its projected cash needs.

ILLUSTRATION 7.14
Basic form of cash budget

Any Company
Cash Budget

Beginning cash balance	$X,XXX
Add: **Cash receipts** (itemized)	X,XXX
Total available cash	X,XXX
Less: **Cash disbursements** (itemized)	X,XXX
Excess (deficiency) of available cash over cash disbursements	X,XXX
Financing	
Add: Borrowings	X,XXX
Less: Repayments	X,XXX
Ending cash balance	$X,XXX

The **Financing** section shows expected borrowings and repayments of borrowed funds plus interest. Financing is needed when there is a cash deficiency or when the cash balance is less than management's minimum required balance.

Companies must prepare multi-period cash budgets in sequence because the ending cash balance of one period becomes the beginning cash balance for the next period. In practice, companies often prepare cash budgets for the next 12 months on a monthly basis.

To minimize detail, we will assume that Hayes Company prepares an annual cash budget by quarters. Preparing a cash budget requires making some assumptions. For example, Hayes makes assumptions regarding collection of accounts receivable, sales of securities, payments for materials and salaries, and purchases of property, plant, and equipment. The accuracy of the cash budget is very dependent on the accuracy of these assumptions.

In **Illustration 7.15**, we present the cash budget for Hayes. The budget indicates that the company will need $3,000 of financing in the second quarter to maintain a minimum cash

ILLUSTRATION 7.15
Sample cash budget

Hayes Company
Cash Budget
For the Year Ending December 31, 2022

	Quarter			
	1	2	3	4
Beginning cash balance	$ 38,000	$ 25,500	$ 15,000	$ 19,400
Add: **Cash receipts**				
Collections from customers	168,000	198,000	228,000	258,000
Sale of securities	2,000	0	0	0
Total receipts	170,000	198,000	228,000	258,000
Total available cash	208,000	223,500	243,000	277,400
Less: **Cash disbursements**				
Inventory	23,200	27,200	31,200	35,200
Salaries	62,000	72,000	82,000	92,000
Selling and administrative expenses (excluding depreciation)	94,300	99,300	104,300	109,300
Purchase of truck	0	10,000	0	0
Income tax expense	3,000	3,000	3,000	3,000
Total disbursements	182,500	211,500	220,500	239,500
Excess (deficiency) of available cash over disbursements	25,500	12,000	22,500	37,900
Financing				
Add: Borrowings	0	3,000	0	0
Less: Repayments—plus $100 interest	0	0	3,100	0
Ending cash balance	$ 25,500	$ 15,000	$ 19,400	$ 37,900

balance of $15,000. Since there is an excess of available cash over disbursements of $22,500 at the end of the third quarter, Hayes will repay the borrowing, plus $100 interest, in that quarter.

A cash budget contributes to more effective cash management. For example, it can show when a company will need additional financing well before the actual need arises. Conversely, it can indicate when the company will have excess cash available for investments or other purposes.

DO IT! 4b | Cash Budget

Martian Company's management wants to maintain a minimum monthly cash balance of $15,000. At the beginning of March, the cash balance is $16,500, expected cash receipts for March are $210,000, and cash disbursements are expected to be $220,000. How much cash, if any, must Martian borrow to maintain the desired minimum monthly balance?

Solution

Beginning cash balance	$ 16,500
Add: Cash receipts for March	210,000
Total available cash	226,500
Less: Cash disbursements for March	220,000
Excess of available cash over cash disbursements	6,500
Financing	
Add: **Borrowings**	8,500
Ending cash balance	$ 15,000

To maintain the desired minimum cash balance of $15,000, Martian Company must borrow $8,500 of cash.

Related exercise material: **BE7.16, DO IT! 7.4b, and E7.17.**

ACTION PLAN
- Add the beginning cash balance to receipts to determine total available cash.
- Subtract disbursements to determine excess or deficiency.
- Compare excess or deficiency with desired minimum cash to determine borrowing needs.

USING THE DECISION TOOLS | Mattel Corporation

Presented below is hypothetical financial information for **Mattel Corporation** from the year ended December 31, 2021. Mattel is a toy manufacturing company, at one time named by *Fortune* magazine as one of the top 100 companies for which to work.

Selected Financial Information
Year Ended December 31, 2021
(in millions)

Net cash provided by operating activities	$325
Capital expenditures	162
Dividends paid	80
Total expenses	680
Depreciation expense	40
Cash balance	206

Also provided below are estimates of the company's sources and uses of cash during the year ended December 31, 2022. This information should be used to prepare a cash budget for 2022.

Projected Sources and Uses of Cash
(in millions)

Beginning cash balance	$206
Cash receipts from sales of product	355
Cash receipts from sale of short-term investments	20
Cash payments for inventory	357
Cash payments for selling and administrative costs	201
Cash payments for property, plant, and equipment	45
Cash payments for taxes	17

Mattel's management believes it should maintain a balance of $200 million cash.

Instructions

a. Using the hypothetical projected sources and uses of cash information presented above, prepare a cash budget for 2022 for Mattel Corporation.
b. Comment on the company's cash adequacy, and discuss steps that might be taken to improve its cash position.

Solution

a.

Mattel Corporation
Cash Budget
For the Year Ending December 31, 2022
(in millions)

Beginning cash balance		$206
Add: Cash receipts		
From sales of product	$355	
From sale of short-term investments	20	375
Total available cash		581
Less: Cash disbursements		
Payments for inventory	357	
Payments for selling and administrative costs	201	
Payments for property, plant, and equipment	45	
Payments for taxes	17	
Total disbursements		620
Excess (deficiency) of available cash over disbursements		(39)
Financing		
Add: **Borrowings**		**239**
Ending cash balance		$200

b. Using these hypothetical data, Mattel's cash position appears adequate. For 2022, Mattel is projecting a cash shortfall. This is not necessarily of concern, but it should be investigated. Its primary line of business is toys. Most toys are sold during December. We would expect Mattel's cash position to vary significantly during the course of the year. After the holiday season, once its customers have paid Mattel, it probably has a lot of excess cash. However, when it is making and selling its product but has not yet been paid, it may need to borrow to meet any temporary cash shortfalls.

    If Mattel's management is concerned with its cash position, it could take the following steps. (1) Offer its customers cash discounts for early payment, such as 2/10, n/30. (2) Implement inventory management techniques to reduce the need for large inventories of such things as the plastics used to make its toys. (3) Carefully time payments to suppliers by keeping track of when payments are due, so as not to pay too early. (4) If it has plans for major expenditures, time those expenditures to coincide with its seasonal period of excess cash.

Appendix 7A | Operation of a Petty Cash Fund

LEARNING OBJECTIVE *5
Explain the operation of a petty cash fund.

The operation of a petty cash fund involves (1) establishing the fund, (2) making payments from the fund, and (3) replenishing the fund.

Establishing the Petty Cash Fund

Two essential steps in establishing a petty cash fund are (1) appointing a petty cash custodian who will be responsible for the fund, and (2) determining the size of the fund. Ordinarily, a company expects the amount in the fund to cover anticipated disbursements for a three- to four-week period.

To establish the fund, a company issues a check payable to the petty cash custodian for the stipulated amount. For example, if Laird Company decides to establish a $100 fund on March 1, the general journal entry is as follows.

Mar. 1	Petty Cash	100	
	Cash		100
	(To establish a petty cash fund)		

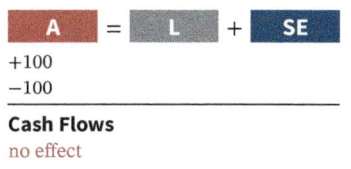

Cash Flows
no effect

The fund custodian cashes the check and places the proceeds in a locked petty cash box or drawer. Most petty cash funds are established on a fixed-amount basis. The company will make no additional entries to the Petty Cash account unless management changes the stipulated amount of the fund. For example, if Laird decides on July 1 to increase the size of the fund to $250, it would debit Petty Cash $150 and credit Cash $150.

Making Payments from the Petty Cash Fund

The petty cash custodian has the authority to make payments from the fund that conform to prescribed management policies. Usually, management limits the size of expenditures that come from petty cash. Likewise, it may not permit use of the fund for certain types of transactions (such as making short-term loans to employees).

Each payment from the fund must be documented on a prenumbered petty cash receipt (or petty cash voucher), as shown in **Illustration 7A.1**. The signatures of both the fund custodian and the person receiving payment are required on the receipt. If other supporting documents such as a freight bill or invoice are available, they should be attached to the petty cash receipt (see **Helpful Hint**).

HELPFUL HINT
The petty cash receipt satisfies two internal control principles: (1) establishment of responsibility (signature of custodian), and (2) documentation procedures.

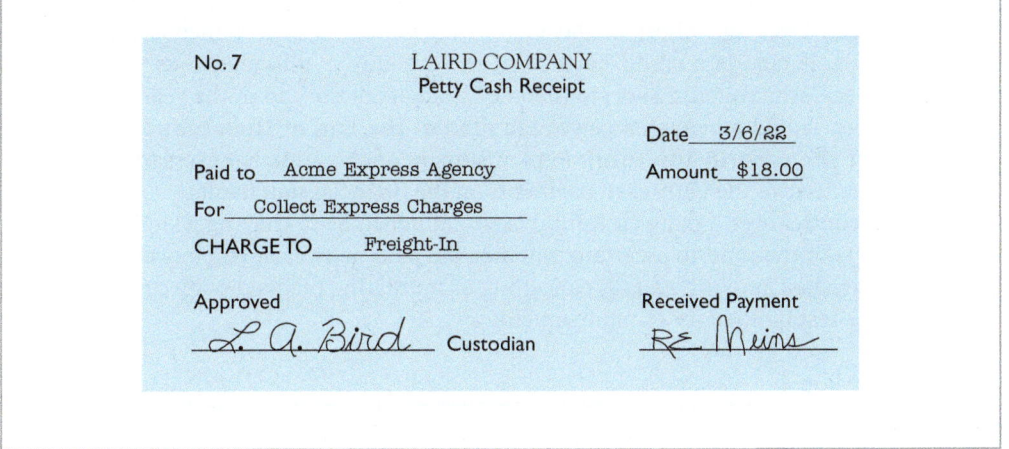

ILLUSTRATION 7A.1
Petty cash receipt

The petty cash custodian keeps the receipts in the petty cash box until the fund is replenished. The sum of the petty cash receipts and the money in the fund should equal the established total at all times. Management can (and should) make surprise counts at any time by an independent person, such as an internal auditor, to determine the correctness of the fund.

The company does not make an accounting entry to record a payment when it is made from petty cash. It is considered both inexpedient and unnecessary to do so. Instead, the company recognizes the accounting effects of each payment when it replenishes the fund.

Replenishing the Petty Cash Fund

When the money in the petty cash fund reaches a minimum level, the company replenishes the fund (see **Helpful Hint**). The petty cash custodian initiates a request for reimbursement. The individual prepares a schedule (or summary) of the payments that have been made and sends the schedule, supported by petty cash receipts and other documentation, to the treasurer's office. The treasurer's office examines the receipts and supporting documents to verify that proper payments from the fund were made. The treasurer then approves the request and

HELPFUL HINT
Replenishing the petty cash fund involves three internal control procedures: (1) segregation of duties, (2) documentation procedures, and (3) independent internal verification.

issues a check to restore the fund to its established amount. At the same time, all supporting documentation is stamped "paid" so that it cannot be submitted again for payment.

To illustrate, assume that on March 15 Laird's petty cash custodian requests a check for $87. The fund contains $13 cash and petty cash receipts for postage $44, freight-out $38, and miscellaneous expenses $5. The general journal entry to record the check is as follows.

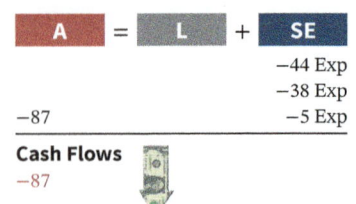

Mar. 15	Postage Expense	44	
	Freight-Out	38	
	Miscellaneous Expense	5	
	Cash		87
	(To replenish petty cash fund)		

Note that the reimbursement entry does not affect the Petty Cash account. Replenishment changes the composition of the fund by replacing the petty cash receipts with cash. It does not change the balance in the fund.

Occasionally, in replenishing a petty cash fund, the company may need to recognize a cash shortage or overage. This results when the total of the cash plus receipts in the petty cash box does not equal the established amount of the petty cash fund. To illustrate, assume that Laird's petty cash custodian has only $12 in cash in the fund plus the receipts as listed. The request for reimbursement would therefore be for $88, and Laird would make the following entry.

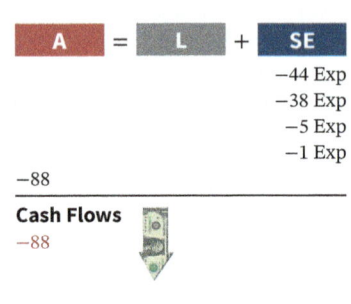

Mar. 15	Postage Expense	44	
	Freight-Out	38	
	Miscellaneous Expense	5	
	Cash Over and Short	1	
	Cash		88
	(To replenish petty cash fund)		

Conversely, if the custodian has $14 in cash, the reimbursement request would be for $86. The company would credit Cash Over and Short for $1 (overage). A company reports a debit balance in Cash Over and Short in the income statement as miscellaneous expense (see **Helpful Hint**). It reports a credit balance in the account as miscellaneous revenue. The company closes Cash Over and Short to Income Summary at the end of the year.

Companies should replenish a petty cash fund **at the end of the accounting period, regardless of the cash in the fund**. Replenishment at this time is necessary in order to recognize the effects of the petty cash payments on the financial statements.

Internal control over a petty cash fund is strengthened by (1) having a supervisor make surprise counts of the fund to ascertain whether the paid petty cash receipts and fund cash equal the designated amount, and (2) cancelling or mutilating the paid petty cash receipts so they cannot be resubmitted for reimbursement.

HELPFUL HINT

Cash over and short situations result from mathematical errors or from failure to keep accurate records.

Review and Practice

Learning Objectives Review

1 Define fraud and the principles of internal control.

A fraud is a dishonest act by an employee that results in personal benefit to the employee at a cost to the employer. The fraud triangle refers to the three factors that contribute to fraudulent activity by employees: opportunity, financial pressure, and rationalization. Internal control consists of all the related methods and measures adopted within an organization to safeguard assets, enhance the reliability of accounting records, increase efficiency of operations, and ensure compliance with laws and regulations.

The principles of internal control are establishment of responsibility, segregation of duties, documentation procedures, physical controls, independent internal verification, and human resource controls.

2 Apply internal control principles to cash.

Internal controls over cash receipts include (a) designating only personnel such as cashiers to handle cash; (b) assigning the duties of receiving cash, recording cash, and having custody of cash to different individuals; (c) obtaining remittance advices for mail receipts, cash register tapes or computer records for over-the-counter receipts, and deposit slips for bank deposits; (d) using company safes and bank vaults to store cash with access limited to authorized personnel, and using cash registers or point-of-sale terminals in executing over-the-counter receipts; (e) making independent daily counts of register receipts and daily comparisons of total receipts with total deposits; and (f) conducting background checks and bonding personnel who handle cash, as well as requiring them to take vacations.

Internal controls over cash disbursements include (a) having only specified individuals such as the treasurer authorized to sign checks and approve vendors; (b) assigning the duties of approving items for payment, paying the items, and recording the payment to different individuals; (c) using prenumbered checks and accounting for all checks, with each check supported by an approved invoice; after payment, stamping each approved invoice "paid"; (d) storing blank checks in a safe or vault with access restricted to authorized personnel, and using a machine with indelible ink to imprint amounts on checks; (e) comparing each check with the approved invoice before issuing the check, and making monthly reconciliations of bank and book balances; and (f) bonding personnel who handle cash, requiring employees to take vacations, and conducting background checks.

3 Identify the control features of a bank account.

In reconciling the bank account, it is customary to reconcile the balance per books and the balance per bank to their adjusted balance. The steps reconciling the Cash account are to determine deposits in transit and electronic funds transfers received by bank, outstanding checks and electronic payments, errors by the depositor or the bank, and unrecorded bank memoranda.

4 Explain the reporting of cash and the basic principles of cash management.

Cash is listed first in the current assets section of the balance sheet. Companies often report cash together with cash equivalents. Cash restricted for a special purpose is reported separately as a current asset or as a noncurrent asset, depending on when the company expects to use the cash.

The basic principles of cash management include (a) increase the speed of receivables collection, (b) keep inventory levels low, (c) monitor the timing of payment of liabilities, (d) plan timing of major expenditures, and (e) invest idle cash.

The three main elements of a cash budget are the cash receipts section, cash disbursements section, and financing section.

*5 Explain the operation of a petty cash fund.

In operating a petty cash fund, a company establishes the fund by appointing a custodian and determining the size of the fund. The custodian makes payments from the fund for documented expenditures. The company replenishes the fund as needed, and at the end of each accounting period. Accounting entries to record payments are made each time the fund is replenished.

Decision Tools Review

Decision Checkpoints	Info Needed for Decision	Tool to Use for Decision	How to Evaluate Results
Are the company's financial statements supported by adequate internal controls?	Auditor's report, management discussion and analysis, articles in financial press	The principles of internal control activities are (1) establishment of responsibility, (2) segregation of duties, (3) documentation procedures, (4) physical controls, (5) independent internal verification, and (6) human resource controls.	If any indication is given that these or other controls are lacking, use the financial statements with caution.
Is all of the company's cash available for general use?	Balance sheet and notes to financial statements	The company reports restricted cash in assets section of balance sheet.	A restriction on the use of cash limits management's ability to use those resources for general obligations. This might be considered when assessing liquidity.
Will the company be able to meet its projected cash needs?	Cash budget (typically available only to management)	The cash budget shows projected sources and uses of cash. If cash uses exceed internal cash sources, then the company must look for outside sources.	Two issues: (1) Are management's projections reasonable? (2) If outside sources are needed, are they available?

Glossary Review

Bank reconciliation The process of comparing the bank's account balance with the company's balance, and explaining the differences to make them agree. (p. 7-17).

Bank statement A statement received monthly from the bank that shows the depositor's bank transactions and balances. (p. 7-18).

Bonding Obtaining insurance protection against theft by employees. (p. 7-9).

Cash Resources that consist of coins, currency, checks, money orders, and money on hand or on deposit in a bank or similar depository. (p. 7-24).

Cash budget A projection of anticipated cash flows, usually over a one- to two-year period. (p. 7-27).

Cash equivalents Short-term, highly liquid investments that can be readily converted to a specific amount of cash and which are relatively insensitive to interest rate changes. (p. 7-24).

Deposits in transit Deposits recorded by the depositor that have not been recorded by the bank. (p. 7-20).

Electronic funds transfer (EFT) A disbursement system that uses wire, telephone, or computer to transfer cash from one location to another. (p. 7-17).

Fraud A dishonest act by an employee that results in personal benefit to the employee at a cost to the employer. (p. 7-3).

Fraud triangle The three factors that contribute to fraudulent activity by employees: opportunity, financial pressure, and rationalization. (p. 7-3).

Internal auditors Company employees who continuously evaluate the effectiveness of the company's internal control systems. (p. 7-9).

Internal control A process designed to provide reasonable assurance regarding the achievement of company objectives related to operations, reporting, and compliance. (p. 7-4).

NSF check A check that is not paid by a bank because of insufficient funds in a bank account. (p. 7-19).

Outstanding checks Checks issued and recorded by a company that have not been paid by the bank. (p. 7-20).

Petty cash fund A cash fund used to pay relatively small amounts. (p. 7-16).

Restricted cash Cash that is not available for general use but instead is restricted for a particular purpose. (p. 7-24).

Sarbanes-Oxley Act (SOX) Law that requires publicly traded companies to maintain adequate systems of internal control. (p. 7-3).

Treasurer Employee responsible for the management of a company's cash. (p. 7-26).

Voucher An authorization form prepared for each expenditure in a voucher system. (p. 7-15).

Voucher system A network of approvals by authorized individuals, acting independently, to ensure that all disbursements by check are proper. (p. 7-14).

Practice Multiple-Choice Questions

1. **(LO 1)** Which of the following is **not** an element of the fraud triangle?
    a. Rationalization.
    b. Financial pressure.
    c. Segregation of duties.
    d. Opportunity.

2. **(LO 1)** Internal control is used in a business to:
    a. safeguard its assets.
    b. enhance the accuracy and reliability of its accounting records.
    c. ensure compliance with laws and regulations.
    d. All of these answer choices are correct.

3. **(LO 1)** The principles of internal control do **not** include:
    a. establishment of responsibility.
    b. documentation procedures.
    c. management responsibility.
    d. independent internal verification.

4. **(LO 1)** Physical controls do **not** include:
    a. safes and vaults to store cash.
    b. independent bank reconciliations.
    c. locked warehouses for inventories.
    d. bank safety deposit boxes for important papers.

5. **(LO 1)** Which of the following was **not** a result of the Sarbanes-Oxley Act?
    a. Companies must file financial statements with the Internal Revenue Service.
    b. All publicly traded companies must maintain adequate internal controls.
    c. The Public Company Accounting Oversight Board was created to establish auditing standards and regulate auditor activity.
    d. Corporate executives and boards of directors must ensure that controls are reliable and effective, and they can be fined or imprisoned for failure to do so.

6. **(LO 1)** Which of the following control activities is **not** relevant when a company uses a computerized (rather than manual) accounting system?
    a. Establishment of responsibility.
    b. Segregation of duties.
    c. Independent internal verification.
    d. All of these control activities are relevant to a computerized system.

7. **(LO 2)** Permitting only designated personnel such as cashiers to handle cash receipts is an application of the principle of:
    a. segregation of duties.
    b. establishment of responsibility.
    c. independent internal verification.
    d. human resource controls.

8. **(LO 2)** The use of prenumbered checks in disbursing cash is an application of the principle of:

 a. establishment of responsibility.
 b. segregation of duties.
 c. physical controls.
 d. documentation procedures.

9. **(LO 3)** The control features of a bank account do **not** include:

 a. having bank auditors verify the correctness of the bank balance per books.
 b. minimizing the amount of cash that must be kept on hand.
 c. providing a double record of all bank transactions.
 d. safeguarding cash by using a bank as a depository.

10. **(LO 3)** In a bank reconciliation, deposits in transit are:

 a. deducted from the book balance.
 b. added to the book balance.
 c. added to the bank balance.
 d. deducted from the bank balance.

11. **(LO 3)** The reconciling item in a bank reconciliation that will result in an adjusting entry by the depositor is:

 a. outstanding checks.   c. a bank error.
 b. deposit in transit.   d. bank service charges.

12. **(LO 4)** Which of the following items in a cash drawer at November 30 is **not** cash?

 a. Money orders.
 b. Coins and currency.
 c. An NSF check.
 d. A customer check dated November 28.

13. **(LO 4)** Which statement correctly describes the reporting of cash?

 a. Cash cannot be combined with cash equivalents.
 b. Restricted cash funds may be combined with cash.
 c. Cash is listed first in the current assets section.
 d. Restricted cash funds cannot be reported as a current asset.

14. **(LO 4)** Which of the following would **not** be an example of good cash management?

 a. Provide discounts to customers to encourage early payment.
 b. Invest temporary excess cash in stock of a small company.
 c. Carefully monitor payments so that payments are not made early.
 d. Employ just-in-time inventory methods to keep inventory low.

15. **(LO 4)** Which of the following is **not** one of the sections of a cash budget?

 a. Cash receipts section.
 b. Cash disbursements section.
 c. Financing section.
 d. Cash from operations section.

*16. **(LO 5)** A check is written to replenish a $100 petty cash fund when the fund contains receipts of $94 and $4 in cash. In recording the check:

 a. debit Cash Over and Short for $2.
 b. debit Petty Cash for $94.
 c. credit Cash for $94.
 d. credit Petty Cash for $2.

Solutions

1. c. Segregation of duties is not an element of the fraud triangle. The other choices are fraud triangle elements.

2. d. Safeguarding a company's assets, enhancing the accuracy and reliability of its accounting records, and ensuring compliance with laws and regulations are all aspects of internal control.

3. c. Management responsibility is not one of the principles of internal control. The other choices are true statements.

4. b. Independent bank reconciliations are not a physical control. The other choices are true statements.

5. a. Filing financial statements with the IRS is not a result of the Sarbanes-Oxley Act (SOX); SOX focuses on the prevention or detection of fraud. The other choices are results of SOX.

6. d. Establishment of responsibility, segregation of duties, and independent internal verification are all relevant to a computerized system. Although choices (a), (b), and (c) are correct, choice (d) is the better answer.

7. b. Permitting only designated personnel to handle cash receipts is an application of the principle of establishment of responsibility, not (a) segregation of duties, (c) independent internal verification, or (d) human resource controls.

8. d. The use of prenumbered checks in disbursing cash is an application of the principle of documentation procedures, not (a) establishment of responsibility, (b) segregation of duties, or (c) physical controls.

9. a. Having bank auditors verify the correctness of the bank balance per books is not one of the control features of a bank account. The other choices are true statements.

10. c. Deposits in transit are added to the bank balance on a bank reconciliation, not (a) deducted from the book balance, (b) added to the book balance, or (d) deducted from the bank balance.

11. d. Because the depositor does not know the amount of the bank service charges until the bank statement is received, an adjusting entry must be made when the statement is received. The other choices are incorrect because (a) outstanding checks do not require an adjusting entry by the depositor because the checks have already been recorded in the depositor's books, (b) deposits in transit do not require an adjusting entry by the depositor because the deposits have already been recorded in the depositor's books, and (c) bank errors do not require an adjusting entry by the depositor, but the depositor does need to inform the bank of the error so it can be corrected.

12. c. An NSF check should not be considered cash. The other choices are true statements.

13. c. Cash is listed first in the current assets section. The other choices are incorrect because (a) cash and cash equivalents can be appropriately combined when reporting cash on the balance sheet, (b) restricted cash is not to be combined with cash when reporting cash on the balance sheet, and (d) restricted funds can be reported as current assets if they will be used within one year.

14. **b.** Investing excess cash to purchase stock in a small company is inappropriate because the stock of small companies is often not easily converted to cash. Choices (a) providing discounts to customers to encourage early payment, (c) carefully monitoring payments so that cash is held until just before the payment date of liabilities, and (d) keeping inventory levels low are all good cash management practices.

15. **d.** Cash from operations is not a section of a cash budget. Choices (a) cash receipts section, (b) cash disbursements section, and (c) financing section are all elements of a cash budget.

*16. **a.** When this check is recorded, the company should debit Cash Over and Short for the shortage of $2 (total of the receipts plus cash in the drawer ($98) versus $100), not (b) debit Petty Cash for $94, (c) credit Cash for $94, or (d) credit Petty Cash for $2.

Practice Brief Exercises

Prepare partial bank reconciliation.

1. (LO 3) At August 31, Saladino Company has the following bank information: cash balance per bank $5,200, outstanding checks $1,462, deposits in transit $1,211, and a bank debit memo $110. Determine the adjusted cash balance per bank at July 31.

Solution

1.

	Cash balance per bank	$5,200
	Add: Deposits in transit	1,211
		6,411
	Less: Outstanding checks	1,462
	Adjusted cash balance per bank	$4,949

Explain the statement presentation of cash balances.

2. (LO 4) Zian Company has the following cash balances: Cash in Bank $18,762, Payroll Bank Account $8,000, Petty Cash $150, and Plant Expansion Fund Cash $30,000 to be used 2 years from now. Explain how each balance should be reported on the balance sheet.

Solution

2. Zian Company should report Cash in Bank, Payroll Bank Account, and Petty Cash as current assets (usually combined as one Cash amount). Plant Expansion Fund Cash should be reported as a noncurrent asset, assuming the fund is not expected to be used during the next year.

Prepare a cash budget.

3. (LO 4) The following information is available for Bohemia Company for the month of June: expected cash receipts $73,000, expected cash disbursements $81,000, and cash balance on June 1, $10,000. Management wishes to maintain a minimum cash balance of $11,000. Prepare a basic cash budget for the month of June.

Solution

3.

Bohemia Company
Cash Budget
For the Month of June

Beginning cash balance	$10,000
Add: Cash receipts	73,000
Total available cash	83,000
Less: Cash disbursements	81,000
Excess of available cash over cash disbursements	2,000
Add: Borrowings	9,000
Ending cash balance	$11,000

Prepare entry to replenish a petty cash fund.

*****4. (LO 5)** On May 31, Tyler's petty cash fund of $200 is replenished when the fund contains $7 in cash and receipts for postage $105, freight-out $49, and miscellaneous expense $40. Prepare the journal entry to record the replenishment of the petty cash fund.

Solution

*4. May 31	Postage Expense	105	
	Freight-Out	49	
	Miscellaneous Expense	40	
	Cash		193
	Cash Over and Short		1

Practice Exercises

1. **(LO 1, 2)** Listed below are five procedures followed by Shepherd Company.

   Indicate whether procedure is good or weak internal control.

   1. Total cash receipts are compared to bank deposits daily by someone who has no other cash responsibilities.
   2. Time clocks are used for recording time worked by employees.
   3. Employees are required to take vacations.
   4. Any member of the sales department can approve credit sales.
   5. Sam Hill ships goods to customers, bills customers, and receives payment from customers.

   Instructions

   Indicate whether each procedure is an example of good internal control or of weak internal control. If it is an example of good internal control, indicate which internal control principle is being followed. If it is an example of weak internal control, indicate which internal control principle is violated. Use the table below.

Procedure	IC Good or Weak?	Related Internal Control Principle
1.		
2.		
3.		
4.		
5.		

   Solution

1. Procedure	IC Good or Weak?	Related Internal Control Principle
1.	Good	Independent internal verification
2.	Good	Physical controls
3.	Good	Human resource controls
4.	Weak	Establishment of responsibility
5.	Weak	Segregation of duties

2. **(LO 3)** The information below relates to the Cash account in the ledger of Ansel Company.

   Prepare bank reconciliation and adjusting entries.

   Balance June 1—$17,450; Cash deposited—$64,000.
   Balance June 30—$17,704; Checks written—$63,746.

   The June bank statement shows a balance of $16,422 on June 30 and the following memoranda.

Credits		Debits	
Collection of $1,530 from customers through electronic funds transfer	$1,530	NSF check: Anne Adams	$425
Interest earned on checking account	$35	Safety deposit box rent	$55

   At June 30, deposits in transit were $4,750, and outstanding checks totaled $2,383.

   Instructions

   a. Prepare the bank reconciliation at June 30.
   b. Prepare the adjusting entries at June 30, assuming (1) the NSF check was from a customer on account, and (2) no interest had been accrued on the checking account.

Solution

2. a.

Ansel Company
Bank Reconciliation
June 30

Cash balance per bank statement			$16,422
Add: Deposits in transit			4,750
			21,172
Less: Outstanding checks			2,383
Adjusted cash balance per bank			$18,789
Cash balance per books			$17,704
Add: Electronic funds transfer received		$1,530	
Interest earned		35	1,565
			19,269
Less: NSF check		425	
Safety deposit box rent		55	480
Adjusted cash balance per books			$18,789

b.

Date	Account	Debit	Credit
June 30	Cash	1,530	
	Accounts Receivable		1,530
30	Cash	35	
	Interest Revenue		35
30	Accounts Receivable (Anne Adams)	425	
	Cash		425
30	Bank Charges Expense	55	
	Cash		55

Practice Problem

Prepare bank reconciliation and journalize entries.

(LO 3) Trillo Company's bank statement for May 2022 shows these data.

Balance May 1	$12,650	Balance May 31	$14,280
Debit memorandum:		Credit memorandum:	
NSF check	175	Collection from customer of electronic funds transfer	505

The cash balance per books at May 31 is $13,319. Your review of the data reveals the following.

1. The NSF check was from Hup Co., a customer.
2. Outstanding checks at May 31 total $2,410.
3. Deposits in transit at May 31 total $1,752.
4. A Trillo Company check for $352 dated May 10 cleared the bank on May 25. This check, which was a payment on account, was journalized for $325.

Instructions

a. Prepare a bank reconciliation at May 31.
b. Journalize the entries required by the reconciliation.

Solution

a.

Cash balance per bank statement	$14,280
Add: Deposits in transit	1,752
	16,032
Less: Outstanding checks	2,410
Adjusted cash balance per bank	$13,622

Cash balance per books			$13,319
Add: Electronic funds transfer received			505
			13,824
Less: NSF check		$175	
Error in recording check ($352 − $325)		27	202
Adjusted cash balance per books			$13,622

b.
May 31	Cash		505	
	Accounts Receivable			505
	(To record receipt of electronic funds transfer)			
31	Accounts Receivable (Hup Co.)		175	
	Cash			175
	(To record NSF check from Hup Co.)			
31	Accounts Payable		27	
	Cash			27
	(To correct error in recording check)			

WileyPLUS

Brief Exercises, DO IT! Exercises, Exercises, Problems, and many additional resources are available for practice in WileyPLUS.

Note: All asterisked Questions, Exercises, and Problems relate to material in the appendix to the chapter.

Questions

1. A local bank reported that it lost $150,000 as the result of employee fraud. Ray Fairburn is not clear on what is meant by "employee fraud." Explain the meaning of fraud to Ray and give an example of fraud that might occur at a bank.

2. Fraud experts often say that there are three primary factors that contribute to employee fraud. Identify the three factors and explain what is meant by each.

3. Identify the five components of a good internal control system.

4. "Internal control is concerned only with enhancing the accuracy of the accounting records." Do you agree? Explain.

5. Discuss how the Sarbanes-Oxley Act has increased the importance of internal control to top managers of a company.

6. What principles of internal control apply to most businesses?

7. In the corner grocery store, all sales clerks make change out of one cash register drawer. Is this a violation of internal control? Why?

8. Branden Doyle is reviewing the principle of segregation of duties. What are the two common applications of this principle?

9. How do documentation procedures contribute to good internal control?

10. What internal control objectives are met by physical controls?

11. **a.** Explain the control principle of independent internal verification.
    b. What practices are important in applying this principle?

12. As the company accountant, explain the following ideas to the management of Ortiz Company.
    a. The concept of reasonable assurance in internal control.
    b. The importance of the human factor in internal control.

13. Discuss the human resources department's involvement in internal controls.

14. Robbins Inc. owns the following assets at the balance sheet date.

Cash in bank—savings account	$ 8,000
Cash on hand	1,100
Cash refund due from the IRS	1,000
Checking account balance	12,000
Postdated checks	500

What amount should be reported as Cash in the balance sheet?

15. What principle(s) of internal control is (are) involved in making daily cash counts of over-the-counter receipts?

16. Assume that **Kohl's Department Stores** installed new cash registers in its stores. How do cash registers improve internal control over cash receipts?

17. At Lazlo Wholesale Company, two mail clerks open all mail receipts. How does this strengthen internal control?

18. "To have maximum effective internal control over cash disbursements, all payments should be made by check or electronic funds transfer." Is this true? Explain.

19. Pauli Company's internal controls over cash disbursements provide for the treasurer to sign checks imprinted by a checkwriter after comparing the check with the approved invoice. Identify the internal control principles that are present in these controls.

20. How do these principles apply to cash disbursements?
    a. Physical controls.
    b. Human resource controls.

CHAPTER 7 Fraud, Internal Control, and Cash

21. What is the essential feature of an electronic funds transfer (EFT) procedure?

22. "The use of a bank contributes significantly to good internal control over cash." Is this true? Why?

23. Hank Cook is confused about the lack of agreement between the cash balance per books and the balance per bank. Explain the causes for the lack of agreement to Hank and give an example of each cause.

24. Identify the basic principles of cash management.

25. Trisha Massey asks for your help concerning an NSF check. Explain to Trisha (a) what an NSF check is, (b) how it is treated in a bank reconciliation, and (c) whether it will require an adjusting entry on the company's books.

26. a. Describe cash equivalents and explain how they are reported.
    b. How should restricted cash funds be reported on the balance sheet?

27. What was **Apple**'s balance in cash and cash equivalents at September 30, 2017? Did it report any restricted cash? How did Apple define cash equivalents?

*28. a. Identify the three activities that pertain to a petty cash fund, and indicate an internal control principle that is applicable to each activity.
    b. When are journal entries required in the operation of a petty cash fund?

Brief Exercises

Identify fraud triangle concepts.

BE7.1 (LO 1), K Match each situation with the fraud triangle factor (opportunity, financial pressure, or rationalization) that best describes it.
  a. An employee's monthly credit card payments are nearly 75% of their monthly earnings.
  b. An employee earns minimum wage at a firm that has reported record earnings for each of the last five years.
  c. An employee has an expensive gambling habit.
  d. An employee has check-writing and -signing responsibilities for a small company, and is also responsible for reconciling the bank account.

Indicate internal control concepts.

BE7.2 (LO 1), C Shelly Eckert has prepared the following list of statements about internal control.
  a. One of the objectives of internal control is to safeguard assets from employee theft, robbery, and unauthorized use.
  b. One of the objectives of internal control is to enhance the accuracy and reliability of the accounting records.
  c. No laws require U.S. corporations to maintain an adequate system of internal control.
Identify each statement as true or false. If false, indicate how to correct the statement.

Explain the importance of internal control.

BE7.3 (LO 1), C Pat Buhn is the new owner of Young Co. She has heard about internal control but is not clear about its importance for her business. Explain to Pat the four purposes of internal control, and give her one application of each purpose for Young Co.

Identify internal control principles.

BE7.4 (LO 1), C The internal control procedures in Dayton Company result in the following provisions. Identify the principles of internal control that are being followed in each case.
  a. Employees who have physical custody of assets do not have access to the accounting records.
  b. Each month, the assets on hand are compared to the accounting records by an internal auditor.
  c. A prenumbered shipping document is prepared for each shipment of goods to customers.

Identify the internal control principles applicable to cash receipts.

BE7.5 (LO 2), C Jolson Company has the following internal control procedures over cash receipts. Identify the internal control principle that is applicable to each procedure.
  a. All over-the-counter receipts are entered in cash registers.
  b. All cashiers are bonded.
  c. Daily cash counts are made by cashier department supervisors.
  d. The duties of receiving cash, recording cash, and having custody of cash are assigned to different individuals.
  e. Only cashiers may operate cash registers.

Make journal entries for cash overage and shortfall.

BE7.6 (LO 2), AP The cash register tape for Bluestem Industries reported sales of $6,871.50. Record the journal entry that would be necessary for each of the following situations. (a) Sales per cash register tape exceeds cash on hand by $50.75. (b) Cash on hand exceeds cash reported by cash register tape by $28.32.

BE7.7 (LO 2), AP While examining cash receipts information, the accounting department determined the following information: opening cash balance $150, cash on hand $1,125.74, and cash sales per register tape $988.62. Prepare the required journal entry based upon the cash count sheet.

Make journal entry using cash count sheet.

BE7.8 (LO 2), C Tott Company has the following internal control procedures over cash disbursements. Identify the internal control principle that is applicable to each procedure.

Identify the internal control principles applicable to cash disbursements.

a. Company checks are prenumbered.

b. The bank statement is reconciled monthly by an internal auditor.

c. Blank checks are stored in a safe in the treasurer's office.

d. Only the treasurer or assistant treasurer may sign checks.

e. Check-signers are not allowed to record cash disbursement transactions.

BE7.9 (LO 3), C Luke Roye is uncertain about the control features of a bank account. Explain the control benefits of (a) a checking account and (b) a bank statement.

Identify the control features of a bank account.

BE7.10 (LO 3), C The following reconciling items are applicable to the bank reconciliation for Forde Co. Indicate how each item should be shown on a bank reconciliation.

Indicate location of reconciling items in a bank reconciliation.

a. Outstanding checks.

b. Bank debit memorandum for service charge.

c. Bank credit memorandum for collecting from customer an electronic funds transfer.

d. Deposit in transit.

BE7.11 (LO 3), C Using the data in BE7.10, indicate (a) the items that will result in an adjustment to the depositor's records and (b) why the other items do not require adjustment.

Identify reconciling items that require adjusting entries.

BE7.12 (LO 3), AP At July 31, Planter Company has this bank information: cash balance per bank $7,291, outstanding checks $762, deposits in transit $1,350, and a bank service charge $40. Determine the adjusted cash balance per bank at July 31.

Prepare partial bank reconciliation.

BE7.13 (LO 3), AP In the month of November, Fiesta Company Inc. wrote checks in the amount of $9,750. In December, checks in the amount of $11,762 were written. In November, $8,800 of these checks were presented to the bank for payment, and $10,889 in December. There were no outstanding checks at the beginning of November. What is the amount of outstanding checks at the end of November? At the end of December?

Analyze outstanding checks.

BE7.14 (LO 3), AP At August 31, Pratt Company has a cash balance per books of $9,500 and the following additional data from the bank statement: charge for printing Pratt Company checks $35 and interest earned on checking account balance $40. In addition, Pratt Company has outstanding checks of $800. Determine the adjusted cash balance per books at August 31.

Prepare partial bank reconciliation.

BE7.15 (LO 4), C Spahn Company has these cash balances: cash in bank $12,742, payroll bank account $6,000, and plant expansion fund cash $25,000. Explain how each balance should be reported on the balance sheet.

Explain the statement presentation of cash balances.

BE7.16 (LO 4), AP The following information is available for Bonkers Company for the month of January: expected cash receipts $59,000, expected cash disbursements $67,000, and cash balance on January 1, $12,000. Management wishes to maintain a minimum cash balance of $9,000. Prepare a basic cash budget for the month of January.

Prepare a cash budget.

*BE7.17 (LO 5), AP On March 20, Harbor's petty cash fund of $100 is replenished when the fund contains $19 in cash and receipts for postage $40, supplies $26, and travel expense $15. Prepare the journal entry to record the replenishment of the petty cash fund.

Prepare entry to replenish a petty cash fund.

DO IT! Exercises

DO IT! 7.1 (LO 1), C Identify which control activity is violated in each of the following situations, and explain how the situation creates an opportunity for fraud or inappropriate accounting practices.

Identify violations of control activities.

1. Once a month, the sales department sends sales invoices to the accounting department to be recorded.

2. Steve Nicoles orders merchandise for Binn Company; he also receives merchandise and authorizes payment for merchandise.

3. Several clerks at Draper's Groceries use the same cash register drawer.

Design system of internal control over cash receipts.

DO IT! 7.2 (LO 2), C Wes Unsel is concerned with control over mail receipts at Wooden Sporting Goods. All mail receipts are opened by Mel Blount. Mel sends the checks to the accounting department, where they are stamped "For Deposit Only." The accounting department records and deposits the mail receipts weekly. Wes asks your help in installing a good system of internal control over mail receipts.

Explain treatment of items in bank reconciliation.

DO IT! 7.3 (LO 3), C Ned Douglas owns Ned's Blankets. Ned asks you to explain how he should treat the following reconciling items when reconciling the company's bank account.

1. Outstanding checks.
2. A deposit in transit.
3. The bank charged to our account a check written by another company.
4. A debit memorandum for a bank service charge.

Analyze statements about the reporting of cash.

DO IT! 7.4a (LO 4), AP Indicate whether each of the following statements is true or false. If false, indicate how to correct the statement.

1. A company has the following assets at the end of the year: cash on hand $40,000, cash refund due from customer $30,000, and checking account balance $22,000. Cash and cash equivalents is therefore $62,000.
2. A company that has received NSF checks should report these checks as a current liability on the balance sheet.
3. Restricted cash that is a current asset is reported as part of cash and cash equivalents.
4. A company has cash in the bank of $50,000, petty cash of $400, and stock investments of $100,000. Total cash and cash equivalents is therefore $50,400.

Prepare a cash budget.

DO IT! 7.4b (LO 4), AP Stern Corporation's management wants to maintain a minimum monthly cash balance of $8,000. At the beginning of September, the cash balance is $12,270, expected cash receipts for September are $97,200, and cash disbursements are expected to be $115,000. How much cash, if any, must Stern borrow to maintain the desired minimum monthly balance? Determine your answer by using the basic form of the cash budget.

Exercises

Identify the principles of internal control.

E7.1 (LO 1), C Bank employees use a system known as the "maker-checker" system. An employee will record an entry in the appropriate journal, and then a supervisor will verify and approve the entry. These days, as all of a bank's accounts are computerized, the employee first enters a batch of entries into the computer, and then the entries are posted automatically to the general ledger account after the supervisor approves them on the system.

Access to the computer system is password-protected and task-specific, which means that the computer system will not allow the employee to approve a transaction or the supervisor to record a transaction.

Instructions

Identify the principles of internal control inherent in the "maker-checker" procedure used by banks.

Identify the principles of internal control.

E7.2 (LO 1), C Ricci's Pizza operates strictly on a carryout basis. Customers pick up their orders at a counter where a clerk exchanges the pizza for cash. While at the counter, the customer can see other employees making the pizzas and the large ovens in which the pizzas are baked.

Instructions

Identify the six principles of internal control and give an example of each principle that you might observe when picking up your pizza. (*Note:* It may not be possible to observe all the principles.)

Indicate whether procedure is good or weak internal control.

E7.3 (LO 1, 2), C Listed below are five procedures followed by Eikenberry Company.

1. Several individuals operate the cash register using the same register drawer.
2. A monthly bank reconciliation is prepared by someone who has no other cash responsibilities.
3. Joe Cockrell writes checks and also records cash payment entries.
4. One individual orders inventory, while a different individual authorizes payments.
5. Unnumbered sales invoices from credit sales are forwarded to the accounting department every four weeks for recording.

Instructions

Indicate whether each procedure is an example of good internal control or of weak internal control. If it is an example of good internal control, indicate which internal control principle is being followed. If it is an example of weak internal control, indicate which internal control principle is violated. Use the table below.

Procedure	IC Good or Weak?	Related Internal Control Principle
1.		
2.		
3.		
4.		
5.		

E7.4 (LO 1, 2), C Listed below are five procedures followed by Gilmore Company.

1. Employees are required to take vacations.
2. Any member of the sales department can approve credit sales.
3. Paul Jaggard ships goods to customers, bills customers, and receives payment from customers.
4. Total cash receipts are compared to bank deposits daily by someone who has no other cash responsibilities.
5. Time clocks are used for recording time worked by employees.

Indicate whether procedure is good or weak internal control.

Instructions

Indicate whether each procedure is an example of good internal control or of weak internal control. If it is an example of good internal control, indicate which internal control principle is being followed. If it is an example of weak internal control, indicate which internal control principle is violated. Use the table below.

Procedure	IC Good or Weak?	Related Internal Control Principle
1.		
2.		
3.		
4.		
5.		

E7.5 (LO 2), E The following control procedures are used in Keaton Company for over-the-counter cash receipts.

1. Each store manager is responsible for interviewing applicants for cashier jobs. They are hired if they seem honest and trustworthy.
2. All over-the-counter receipts are registered by three clerks who share a cash register with a single cash drawer.
3. To minimize the risk of robbery, cash in excess of $100 is stored in an unlocked briefcase in the stock room until it is deposited in the bank.
4. At the end of each day, the total receipts are counted by the cashier on duty and reconciled to the cash register total.
5. The company accountant makes the bank deposit and then records the day's receipts.

List internal control weaknesses over cash receipts and suggest improvements.

Instructions

a. For each procedure, explain the weakness in internal control and identify the control principle that is violated.
b. For each weakness, suggest a change in the procedure that will result in good internal control.

E7.6 (LO 2), E The following control procedures are used in Bunny's Boutique Shoppe for cash disbursements.

1. Each week, 100 company checks are left in an unmarked envelope on a shelf behind the cash register.
2. The store manager personally approves all payments before she signs and issues checks.
3. The store purchases used goods for resale from people that bring items to the store. Since that can occur anytime that the store is open, all employees are authorized to purchase goods for resale by disbursing cash from the register. The purchase is documented by having the store employee write on a piece of paper a description of the item that was purchased and the amount that was paid. The employee then signs the paper and puts it in the register.

List internal control weaknesses for cash disbursements and suggest improvements.

4. After payment, bills are "filed" in a paid invoice folder.

5. The company accountant prepares the bank reconciliation and reports any discrepancies to the owner.

Instructions

a. For each procedure, explain the weakness in internal control and identify the internal control principle that is violated.

b. For each weakness, suggest a change in the procedure that will result in good internal control.

Identify internal control weaknesses for cash disbursements and suggest improvements.

E7.7 (LO 2), E At Martinez Company, checks are not prenumbered because both the purchasing agent and the treasurer are authorized to issue checks. Each signer has access to unissued checks kept in an unlocked file cabinet. The purchasing agent pays all bills pertaining to goods purchased for resale. Prior to payment, the purchasing agent determines that the goods have been received and verifies the mathematical accuracy of the vendor's invoice. After payment, the invoice is filed by vendor name and the purchasing agent records the payment in the cash disbursements journal. The treasurer pays all other bills following approval by authorized employees. After payment, the treasurer stamps all bills "paid," files them by payment date, and records the checks in the cash disbursements journal. Martinez Company maintains one checking account that is reconciled by the treasurer.

Instructions

a. List the weaknesses in internal control over cash disbursements.

b. Identify improvements for correcting these weaknesses.

Prepare bank reconciliation and adjusting entries.

E7.8 (LO 3), AP The following information pertains to Ranchero Company.

1. Cash balance per books, August 31, $7,364.
2. Cash balance per bank, August 31, $7,328.
3. Outstanding checks, August 31, $686.
4. August bank service charge not recorded by the depositor $38.
5. Deposits in transit, August 31, $2,700.

In addition, $2,016 was collected for Ranchero Company in August by the bank through electronic funds transfer. The collection has not been recorded by Ranchero Company.

Instructions

a. Prepare a bank reconciliation at August 31, 2022.

b. Journalize the adjusting entries at August 31 on the books of Ranchero Company.

Prepare bank reconciliation and adjusting entries.

E7.9 (LO 3), AP Rachel Sells is unable to reconcile the bank balance at January 31. Rachel's reconciliation is shown here.

Cash balance per bank	$3,677.20
Add: NSF check	450.00
Less: Bank service charge	28.00
Adjusted balance per bank	$4,099.20
Cash balance per books	$3,975.20
Less: Deposits in transit	590.00
Add: Outstanding checks	770.00
Adjusted balance per books	$4,155.20

Instructions

a. What is the proper adjusted cash balance per bank?

b. What is the proper adjusted cash balance per books?

c. Prepare the adjusting journal entries necessary to determine the adjusted cash balance per books.

Determine outstanding checks.

E7.10 (LO 3), AP At April 30, the bank reconciliation of Back 40 Company shows three outstanding checks: No. 254 $650, No. 255 $700, and No. 257 $410. The May bank statement and the May cash payments journal are given here.

Bank Statement Checks Paid			Cash Payments Journal Checks Issued		
Date	Check No.	Amount	Date	Check No.	Amount
5-4	254	$650	5-2	258	$159
5-2	257	410	5-5	259	275
5-17	258	159	5-10	260	925
5-12	259	275	5-15	261	500
5-20	260	925	5-22	262	750
5-29	263	480	5-24	263	480
5-30	262	750	5-29	264	360

Instructions

Using step 2 in the reconciliation procedure, list the outstanding checks at May 31.

E7.11 (LO 3), AP The following information pertains to Lance Company.

Prepare bank reconciliation and adjusting entries.

1. Cash balance per bank, July 31, $8,732.
2. July bank service charge not recorded by the depositor $45.
3. Cash balance per books, July 31, $8,768.
4. Deposits in transit, July 31, $3,500.
5. $2,023 collected from a customer for Lance Company in July by the bank through electronic funds transfer. The collection has not been recorded by Lance Company.
6. Outstanding checks, July 31, $1,486.

Instructions

a. Prepare a bank reconciliation at July 31, 2022.
b. Journalize the adjusting entries at July 31 on the books of Lance Company.

E7.12 (LO 3), AP This information relates to the Cash account in the ledger of Howard Company.

Prepare bank reconciliation and adjusting entries.

Balance September 1—$16,400; Cash deposited—$64,000
Balance September 30—$17,600; Checks written—$62,800

The September bank statement shows a balance of $16,500 at September 30 and the following memoranda.

Credits		Debits	
Collection from customer of electronic funds transfer	$1,830	NSF check: H. Kane	$560
Interest earned on checking account	45	Safety deposit box rent	60

At September 30, deposits in transit were $4,738 and outstanding checks totaled $2,383.

Instructions

a. Prepare the bank reconciliation at September 30, 2022.
b. Prepare the adjusting entries at September 30, assuming the NSF check was from a customer on account.

E7.13 (LO 3), AP The cash records of Upton Company show the following.

Compute deposits in transit and outstanding checks for two bank reconciliations.

For July:

1. The June 30 bank reconciliation indicated that deposits in transit total $580. During July, the general ledger account Cash shows deposits of $16,900, but the bank statement indicates that only $15,600 in deposits were received during the month.
2. The June 30 bank reconciliation also reported outstanding checks of $940. During the month of July, Upton Company books show that $17,500 of checks were issued, yet the bank statement showed that $16,400 of checks cleared the bank in July.

For September:

3. In September, deposits per bank statement totaled $25,900, deposits per books were $26,400, and deposits in transit at September 30 were $2,200.
4. In September, cash disbursements per books were $23,500, checks clearing the bank were $24,000, and outstanding checks at September 30 were $2,100.

There were no bank debit or credit memoranda, and no errors were made by either the bank or Upton Company.

Instructions

Answer the following questions.

a. In situation 1, what were the deposits in transit at July 31?

b. In situation 2, what were the outstanding checks at July 31?

c. In situation 3, what were the deposits in transit at August 31?

d. In situation 4, what were the outstanding checks at August 31?

Prepare bank reconciliation and adjusting entries.

E7.14 (LO 3), AP Perth Inc.'s bank statement from Main Street Bank at August 31, 2022, gives the following information.

Balance, August 1	$18,400	Bank debit memorandum:		
August deposits	71,000	Safety deposit box fee	$	25
Checks cleared in August	68,678	Service charge		50
Bank credit memorandum:		Balance, August 31		20,692
Interest earned	45			

A summary of the Cash account in the ledger for August shows the following: balance, August 1, $18,700; receipts $74,000; disbursements $73,570; and balance, August 31, $19,130. Analysis reveals that the only reconciling items on the July 31 bank reconciliation were a deposit in transit for $4,800 and outstanding checks of $4,500. In addition, you determine that there was an error involving a company check drawn in August: A check for $400 to a creditor on account that cleared the bank in August was journalized and posted for $40.

Instructions

a. Determine deposits in transit.

b. Determine outstanding checks. (*Hint:* You need to correct disbursements for the check error.)

c. Prepare a bank reconciliation at August 31.

d. Journalize the adjusting entry(ies) to be made by Perth Inc. at August 31.

Identify reporting of cash.

E7.15 (LO 4), AP A new accountant at Wyne Inc. is trying to identify which of the amounts shown below should be reported as the current asset "Cash and cash equivalents" in the year-end balance sheet, as of April 30, 2022.

1. $60 of currency and coin in a locked box used for incidental cash transactions.
2. A $10,000 U.S. Treasury bill, due May 31, 2022.
3. $260 of April-dated checks that Wyne has received from customers but not yet deposited.
4. An $85 check received from a customer in payment of its April account, but postdated to May 1.
5. $2,500 in the company's checking account.
6. $4,800 in its savings account.
7. $75 of prepaid postage in its postage meter.
8. A $25 IOU from the company receptionist.

Instructions

a. What balance should Wyne report as its "Cash and cash equivalents" balance at April 30, 2022?

b. In what account(s) and in what financial statement(s) should the items not included in "Cash and cash equivalents" be reported?

Review cash management practices.

E7.16 (LO 4), C Lance, Art, and Wayne have joined together to open a law practice but are struggling to manage their cash flow. They haven't yet built up sufficient clientele and revenues to support their legal practice's ongoing costs. Initial costs, such as advertising, renovations to their premises, and the like, all result in outgoing cash flow at a time when little is coming in. Lance, Art, and Wayne haven't had time to establish a billing system since most of their clients' cases haven't yet reached the courts, and the lawyers didn't think it would be right to bill them until "results were achieved."

Unfortunately, Lance, Art, and Wayne's suppliers don't feel the same way. Their suppliers expect them to pay their accounts payable within a few days of receiving their bills. So far, there hasn't even been enough money to pay the three lawyers, and they are not sure how long they can keep practicing law without getting some money into their pockets.

Instructions

Can you provide any suggestions for Lance, Art, and Wayne to improve their cash management practices?

E7.17 (LO 4), AP Rigley Company expects to have a cash balance of $46,000 on January 1, 2022. These are the relevant monthly budget data for the first two months of 2022.

Prepare a cash budget for two months.

➡ **Excel**

1. Collections from customers: January $71,000 and February $146,000.
2. Payments to suppliers: January $40,000 and February $75,000.
3. Wages: January $30,000 and February $40,000. Wages are paid in the month they are incurred.
4. Administrative expenses: January $21,000 and February $24,000. These costs include depreciation of $1,000 per month. All other costs are paid as incurred.
5. Selling expenses: January $15,000 and February $20,000. These costs are exclusive of depreciation. They are paid as incurred.
6. Sales of short-term investments in January are expected to realize $12,000 in cash. Rigley has a line of credit at a local bank that enables it to borrow up to $25,000. The company wants to maintain a minimum monthly cash balance of $20,000.

Instructions

Prepare a cash budget for January and February.

*E7.18 (LO 5), AP During October, Bismark Light Company experiences the following transactions in establishing a petty cash fund.

Prepare journal entries for a petty cash fund.

Oct. 1   A petty cash fund is established with a check for $150 issued to the petty cash custodian.

     31   A check was written to reimburse the fund and increase the fund to $200. A count of the petty cash fund disclosed the following items:

Currency	$59.00
Coins	0.70
Expenditure receipts (vouchers):	
Supplies	$26.10
Telephone, Internet, and fax	16.40
Postage	39.70
Freight-out	6.80

Instructions

Journalize the entries in October that pertain to the petty cash fund.

*E7.19 (LO 5), AP Kael Company maintains a petty cash fund for small expenditures. These transactions occurred during the month of August.

Journalize and post petty cash fund transactions.

Aug. 1   Established the petty cash fund by writing a check payable to the petty cash custodian for $200.

     15   Replenished the petty cash fund by writing a check for $175. On this date, the fund consisted of $25 in cash and these petty cash receipts: freight-out $74.40, entertainment expense $36, postage expense $33.70, and miscellaneous expense $27.50.

     16   Increased the amount of the petty cash fund to $400 by writing a check for $200.

     31   Replenished the petty cash fund by writing a check for $283. On this date, the fund consisted of $117 in cash and these petty cash receipts: postage expense $145, entertainment expense $90.60, and freight-out $46.40.

Instructions

a. Journalize the petty cash transactions.
b. Post to the Petty Cash account.
c. What internal control features exist in a petty cash fund?

Problems: Set A

P7.1A (LO 2), C Gary Theater is in the Hoosier Mall. A cashier's booth is located near the entrance to the theater. Two cashiers are employed. One works from 1:00 to 5:00 P.M., the other from 5:00 to 9:00 P.M. Each cashier is bonded. The cashiers receive cash from customers and operate a machine that ejects serially numbered tickets. The rolls of tickets are inserted and locked into the machine by the theater manager at the beginning of each cashier's shift.

Identify internal control weaknesses for cash receipts.

After purchasing a ticket, the customer takes the ticket to a doorperson stationed at the entrance of the theater lobby some 60 feet from the cashier's booth. The doorperson tears the ticket in half, admits the customer, and returns the ticket stub to the customer. The other half of the ticket is dropped into a locked box by the doorperson.

At the end of each cashier's shift, the theater manager removes the ticket rolls from the machine and makes a cash count. The cash count sheet is initialed by the cashier. At the end of the day, the manager deposits the receipts in total in a bank night deposit vault located in the mall. In addition, the manager sends copies of the deposit slip and the initialed cash count sheets to the theater company treasurer for verification and to the company's accounting department. Receipts from the first shift are stored in a safe located in the manager's office.

Instructions

a. Identify the internal control principles and their application to the cash receipts transactions of Gary Theater.

b. If the doorperson and cashier decided to collaborate to misappropriate cash, what actions might they take?

Identify internal control weaknesses in cash receipts and cash disbursements.

P7.2A (LO 2), C Blue Bayou Middle School wants to raise money for a new sound system for its auditorium. The primary fund-raising event is a dance at which the famous disc jockey Kray Zee will play classic and not-so-classic dance tunes. Grant Hill, the music and theater instructor, has been given the responsibility for coordinating the fund-raising efforts. This is Grant's first experience with fund-raising. He decides to put the eighth-grade choir in charge of the event; he will be a relatively passive observer.

Grant had 500 unnumbered tickets printed for the dance. He left the tickets in a box on his desk and told the choir students to take as many tickets as they thought they could sell for $5 each. In order to ensure that no extra tickets would be floating around, he told them to dispose of any unsold tickets. When the students received payment for the tickets, they were to bring the cash back to Grant, and he would put it in a locked box in his desk drawer.

Some of the students were responsible for decorating the gymnasium for the dance. Grant gave each of them a key to the money box and told them that if they took money out to purchase materials, they should put a note in the box saying how much they took and what it was used for. After 2 weeks, the money box appeared to be getting full, so Grant asked Lynn Dandi to count the money, prepare a deposit slip, and deposit the money in a bank account that Grant had opened.

The day of the dance, Grant wrote a check from the account to pay Kray Zee. The DJ said, however, that he accepted only cash and did not give receipts. So Grant took $200 out of the cash box and gave it to Kray. At the dance, Grant had Dana Uhler working at the entrance to the gymnasium, collecting tickets from students and selling tickets to those who had not pre-purchased them. Grant estimated that 400 students attended the dance.

The following day, Grant closed out the bank account, which had $250 in it, and gave that amount plus the $180 in the cash box to Principal Sanchez. Principal Sanchez seemed surprised that, after generating roughly $2,000 in sales, the dance netted only $430 in cash. Grant did not know how to respond.

Instructions

Identify as many internal control weaknesses as you can in this scenario, and suggest how each could be addressed.

Prepare a bank reconciliation and adjusting entries.

P7.3A (LO 3), AP On July 31, 2022, Keeds Company had a cash balance per books of $6,140. The statement from Dakota State Bank on that date showed a balance of $7,690.80. A comparison of the bank statement with the Cash account revealed the following facts.

1. The bank service charge for July was $25.
2. The bank collected $1,520 from a customer for Keeds Company through electronic funds transfer.
3. The July 31 receipts of $1,193.30 were not included in the bank deposits for July. These receipts were deposited by the company in a night deposit vault on July 31.
4. Company check No. 2480 issued to L. Taylor, a creditor, for $384 that cleared the bank in July was incorrectly entered in the cash payments journal on July 10 for $348.
5. Checks outstanding on July 31 totaled $1,860.10.
6. On July 31, the bank statement showed an NSF charge of $575 for a check received by the company from W. Krueger, a customer, on account.

Instructions

a. Prepare the bank reconciliation as of July 31.

b. Prepare the necessary adjusting entries at July 31.

a. Adjusted cash bal. $7,024.00

P7.4A (LO 3), AP The bank portion of the bank reconciliation for Bogalusa Company at October 31, 2022, is shown below.

Prepare a bank reconciliation and adjusting entries from detailed data.

Bogalusa Company
Bank Reconciliation
October 31, 2022

Cash balance per bank			$12,367.90
Add: Deposits in transit			1,530.20
			13,898.10
Less: Outstanding checks			
Check Number		Check Amount	
2451		$1,260.40	
2470		684.20	
2471		844.50	
2472		426.80	
2474		1,050.00	4,265.90
Adjusted cash balance per bank			$9,632.20

The adjusted cash balance per bank agreed with the cash balance per books at October 31. The November bank statement showed the following checks and deposits.

Bank Statement

Checks and Debits			Deposits and Credits	
Date	Number	Amount	Date	Amount
11-1	2470	$ 684.20	11-1	$ 1,530.20
11-2	2471	844.50	11-4	1,211.60
11-5	2474	1,050.00	11-8	990.10
11-4	2475	1,640.70	11-13	2,575.00
11-8	2476	2,830.00	11-18	1,472.70
11-10	2477	600.00	11-19 EFT	2,242.00
11-15	2479	1,750.00	11-21	2,945.00
11-18	2480	1,330.00	11-25	2,567.30
11-27	2481	695.40	11-28	1,650.00
11-28	SC	85.00	11-30	1,186.00
11-30	2483	575.50	Total	$18,369.90
11-29	2486	940.00		
	Total	$13,025.30		

The cash records per books for November showed the following.

Cash Payments Journal							Cash Receipts Journal	
Date	Number	Amount	Date	Number	Amount		Date	Amount
11-1	2475	$1,640.70	11-20	2483	$ 575.50		11-3	$ 1,211.60
11-2	2476	2,830.00	11-22	2484	829.50		11-7	990.10
11-2	2477	600.00	11-23	2485	974.80		11-12	2,575.00
11-4	2478	538.20	11-24	2486	940.00		11-17	1,472.70
11-8	2479	1,705.00	11-29	2487	398.00		11-20	2,954.00
11-10	2480	1,330.00	11-30	2488	800.00		11-24	2,567.30
11-15	2481	695.40	Total		$14,469.10		11-27	1,650.00
11-18	2482	612.00					11-29	1,186.00
							11-30	1,304.00
							Total	$15,910.70

The bank statement contained two bank memoranda:

1. A credit of $2,242 for the collection from a customer for Bogalusa Company of an electronic funds transfer.
2. A debit for the printing of additional company checks $85.

At November 30, the cash balance per books was $11,073.80 and the cash balance per bank statement was $17,712.50. The bank did not make any errors, but **Bogalusa Company made two errors.**

Instructions

a. Adjusted cash bal. $13,176.80

a. Using the steps in the reconciliation procedure described in the chapter, prepare a bank reconciliation at November 30, 2022.

b. Prepare the adjusting entries based on the reconciliation. (*Note:* The correction of any errors pertaining to recording checks should be made to Accounts Payable. The correction of any errors relating to recording cash receipts should be made to Accounts Receivable.)

Prepare a bank reconciliation and adjusting entries.

P7.5A (LO 3), AP Timmins Company of Emporia, Kansas, spreads herbicides and applies liquid fertilizer for local farmers. On May 31, 2022, the company's Cash account per its general ledger showed a balance of $6,738.90.

The bank statement from Emporia State Bank on that date showed the following balance.

Emporia State Bank		
Checks and Debits	Deposits and Credits	Daily Balance
XXX	XXX	5-31 6,968.00

A comparison of the details on the bank statement with the details in the Cash account revealed the following facts.

1. The statement included a debit memo of $40 for the printing of additional company checks.
2. Cash sales of $883.15 on May 12 were deposited in the bank. The cash receipts journal entry and the deposit slip were incorrectly made for $933.15. The bank credited Timmins Company for the correct amount.
3. Outstanding checks at May 31 totaled $276.25, and deposits in transit were $1,880.15.
4. On May 18, the company issued check No. 1181 for $685 to H. Moses, on account. The check, which cleared the bank in May, was incorrectly journalized and posted by Timmins Company for $658.
5. $2,690 was collected from a customer's note receivable by the bank for Timmins Company on May 31 through electronic funds transfer.
6. Included with the canceled checks was a check issued by Tomins Company to C. Pernod for $360 that was incorrectly charged to Timmins Company by the bank.
7. On May 31, the bank statement showed an NSF charge of $380 for a check issued by Sara Ballard, a customer, to Timmins Company on account.

Instructions

a. Adjusted cash bal. $8,931.90

a. Prepare the bank reconciliation at May 31, 2022.

b. Prepare the necessary adjusting entries for Timmins Company at May 31, 2022.

Prepare a comprehensive bank reconciliation with theft and internal control deficiencies.

P7.6A (LO 1, 2, 3), E Daisey Company is a very profitable small business. It has not, however, given much consideration to internal control. For example, in an attempt to keep clerical and office expenses to a minimum, the company has combined the jobs of cashier and bookkeeper. As a result, Bret Turrin handles all cash receipts, keeps the accounting records, and prepares the monthly bank reconciliations.

The balance per the bank statement on October 31, 2022, was $18,380. Outstanding checks were No. 62 for $140.75, No. 183 for $180, No. 284 for $253.25, No. 862 for $190.71, No. 863 for $226.80, and No. 864 for $165.28. Included with the statement was a credit memorandum of $185 indicating the collection of a note receivable for Daisey Company by the bank on October 25. This memorandum has not been recorded by Daisey.

The company's ledger showed one Cash account with a balance of $21,877.72. The balance included undeposited cash on hand. Because of the lack of internal controls, Bret took for personal use all of the undeposited receipts in excess of $3,795.51. He then prepared the following bank reconciliation in an effort to conceal his theft of cash.

Cash balance per books, October 31		$21,877.72
Add: Outstanding checks		
No. 862	$190.71	
No. 863	226.80	
No. 864	165.28	482.79
		22,360.51
Less: Undeposited receipts		3,795.51
Unadjusted balance per bank, October 31		18,565.00
Less: Bank credit memorandum		185.00
Cash balance per bank statement, October 31		$18,380.00

Instructions

a. Prepare a correct bank reconciliation. (*Hint:* Deduct the amount of the theft from the adjusted balance per books.)

a. Adjusted cash bal. $21,018.72

b. Indicate the three ways that Bret attempted to conceal the theft and the dollar amount involved in each method.

c. What principles of internal control were violated in this case?

P7.7A (LO 4), AP You are provided with the following information taken from Moynahan Inc.'s March 31, 2022, balance sheet.

Prepare a cash budget.

Cash	$ 11,000
Accounts receivable	20,000
Inventory	36,000
Property, plant, and equipment, net of depreciation	120,000
Accounts payable	22,400
Common stock	150,000
Retained earnings	11,600

Additional information concerning Moynahan Inc. is as follows.

1. Gross profit is 25% of sales.
2. Actual and budgeted sales data:

March (actual)	$46,000
April (budgeted)	70,000

3. Sales are both cash and credit. Cash collections expected in April are:

March	$18,400	(40% of $46,000)
April	42,000	(60% of $70,000)
	$60,400	

4. Half of a month's purchases are paid for in the month of purchase and half in the following month. Cash disbursements expected in April are:

Purchases March	$22,400
Purchases April	28,100
	$50,500

5. Cash operating costs are anticipated to be $11,200 for the month of April.
6. Equipment costing $2,500 will be purchased for cash in April.
7. The company wishes to maintain a minimum cash balance of $9,000. An open line of credit is available at the bank. All borrowing is done at the beginning of the month, and all repayments are made at the end of the month. The interest rate is 12% per year, and interest expense is accrued at the end of the month and paid in the following month.

Instructions

Prepare a cash budget for the month of April. Determine how much cash Moynahan Inc. must borrow, or can repay, in April.

Apr. borrowings $1,800

P7.8A (LO 4), AP Bastille Corporation prepares monthly cash budgets. Here are relevant data from operating budgets for 2022.

Prepare a cash budget.

	January	February
Sales	$360,000	$400,000
Purchases	120,000	130,000
Salaries	84,000	81,000
Administrative expenses	72,000	75,000
Selling expenses	79,000	88,000

All sales and purchases are on account. Budgeted collections and disbursement data are given below. All other expenses are paid in the month incurred. Administrative expenses include $1,000 of depreciation per month.

Other data.

1. Collections from customers: January $326,000; February $378,000.
2. Payments for purchases: January $110,000; February $135,000.
3. Other receipts: January: collection of December 31, 2021, notes receivable $15,000; February: proceeds from sale of securities $4,000.
4. Other disbursements: February $10,000 cash dividend.

The company's cash balance on January 1, 2022, is expected to be $46,000. The company wants to maintain a minimum cash balance of $40,000.

Instructions

Jan. 31 cash bal. $43,000   Prepare a cash budget for January and February.

Continuing Case

© leungchopan/
Shutterstock

Cookie Creations

(*Note:* This is a continuation of the Cookie Creations case from Chapters 1 through 6.)

CC7 Part 1 Natalie is struggling to keep up with the recording of her accounting transactions. She is spending a lot of time marketing and selling mixers and giving her cookie classes. Her friend John is an accounting student who runs his own accounting service. He has asked Natalie if she would like to have him do her accounting. John and Natalie meet and discuss her business.

Part 2 Natalie decides that she cannot afford to hire John to do her accounting. One way that she can ensure that her Cash account does not have any errors and is accurate and up-to-date is to prepare a bank reconciliation at the end of each month. Natalie would like you to help her.

Go to WileyPLUS for complete case details and instructions.

Comprehensive Accounting Cycle Review

ACR7 On December 1, 2022, Ravenwood Company had the following account balances.

	Debit		Credit
Cash	$18,200	Accumulated Depreciation—	
Notes Receivable	2,000	Equipment	$ 3,000
Accounts Receivable	7,500	Accounts Payable	6,100
Inventory	16,000	Common Stock	50,000
Prepaid Insurance	1,600	Retained Earnings	14,200
Equipment	28,000		$73,300
	$73,300		

During December, the company completed the following transactions.

Dec. 7 Received $3,600 cash from customers in payment of account (no discount allowed).
12 Purchased merchandise on account from Greene Co. $12,000, terms 1/10, n/30.
17 Sold merchandise on account $16,000, terms 2/10, n/30. The cost of the merchandise sold was $10,000.
19 Paid salaries $2,200.
22 Paid Greene Co. in full, less discount.
26 Received collections in full, less discounts, from customers billed on December 17.
31 Received $2,700 cash from customers in payment of account (no discount allowed).

Adjustment data:

1. Depreciation $200 per month.
2. Insurance expired $400.
3. Income tax expense was $425. It was unpaid at December 31.

Instructions

a. Journalize the December transactions. (Assume a perpetual inventory system.)

b. Enter the December 1 balances in the ledger T-accounts and post the December transactions. Use Cost of Goods Sold, Depreciation Expense, Insurance Expense, Salaries and Wages Expense, Sales Revenue, Sales Discounts, Income Taxes Payable, and Income Tax Expense.

c. The statement from Lyon County Bank on December 31 showed a balance of $25,930. A comparison of the bank statement with the Cash account revealed the following facts.

   1. The bank collected the $2,000 note receivable for Ravenwood Company on December 15 through electronic funds transfer.
   2. The December 31 receipts were deposited in a night deposit vault on December 31. These deposits were recorded by the bank in January.
   3. Checks outstanding on December 31 totaled $1,210.
   4. On December 31, the bank statement showed a NSF charge of $680 for a check received by the company from M. Lawrence, a customer, on account.

   Prepare a bank reconciliation as of December 31 based on the available information. (*Hint:* The cash balance per books is $26,100. This can be proven by finding the balance in the Cash account from parts (a) and (b).)

d. Journalize the adjusting entries resulting from the bank reconciliation and adjustment data.

e. Post the adjusting entries to the ledger T-accounts.

f. Prepare an adjusted trial balance.

g. Prepare an income statement for December and a classified balance sheet at December 31.

f. Totals	$89,925
g. Net income	$ 2,455
Total assets	$73,180

Expand Your Critical Thinking

Financial Reporting Problem: Apple Inc.

CT7.1 The financial statements of **Apple Inc.** are presented in Appendix A. The complete annual report, including the notes to its financial statements, is available at the company's website.

Instructions

Using the financial statements and reports, answer these questions about Apple's internal controls and cash.

a. What comments, if any, are made about cash in the "Report of Independent Registered Public Accounting Firm"?

b. What data about cash and cash equivalents are shown in the consolidated balance sheet (statement of financial position)?

c. What activities are identified in the consolidated statement of cash flows as being responsible for the changes in cash during 2017?

d. How are cash equivalents defined in the Notes to Consolidated Financial Statements?

e. Read the section of the report titled "Management's Report on Internal Control Over Financial Reporting." Summarize the statements made in that section of the report.

Comparative Analysis Problem: Columbia Sportswear Company vs. VF Corporation

CT7.2 The financial statements of **Columbia Sportswear Company** are presented in Appendix B. Financial statements of **VF Corporation** are presented in Appendix C.

Instructions

Answer the following questions for each company.

a. What is the balance in cash and cash equivalents at December 31, 2016?

b. What percentage of total assets does cash represent for each company over the last 2 years? Has it changed significantly for either company?

c. How much cash was provided by operating activities during 2016?

d. Comment on your findings in parts (a) through (c).

Comparative Analysis Problem: Amazon.com, Inc. vs. Wal-Mart Stores, Inc.

CT7.3 The financial statements of **Amazon.com, Inc.** are presented in Appendix D. Financial statements of **Wal-Mart Stores, Inc.** are presented in Appendix E.

Instructions

Answer the following questions for each company.

a. What is the balance in cash and cash equivalents at December 31, 2016, for Amazon and at January 31, 2017, for Wal-Mart?

b. What percentage of total assets does cash represent for each company over the last two years provided? Has it changed significantly for either company?

c. How much cash was provided by operating activities during the year ended December 31, 2016, for Amazon and January 31, 2017, for Wal-Mart?

d. Comment on your findings in parts (a) through (c).

Interpreting Financial Statements

CT7.4 The international accounting firm **Ernst & Young** performed a global survey on fraud. The results of that survey are summarized in a report titled *Global Fraud Survey 2016*. You can find this report by doing an Internet search on the title.

Instructions

Read the Overview section and then answer the following questions.

a. What steps should businesses take to minimize risk?

b. What percentage of survey respondents consider bribery and fraud to happen widely in their country?

c. What percentage of finance team members said they would engage in unethical behavior to meet targets or protect corporate survival?

Real-World Focus

CT7.5 The **Financial Accounting Standards Board (FASB)** is a private organization established to improve accounting standards and financial reporting. The FASB conducts extensive research before issuing a "Statement of Financial Accounting Standards," which represents an authoritative expression of generally accepted accounting principles.

Instructions

Go to the FASB website to answer the following questions.

a. What are the 10 steps of the standard-setting process?

b. What are the advisory groups that provide service to the FASB?

c. What characteristics make the FASB's procedures an "open" decision-making process?

CT7.6 The **Public Company Accounting Oversight Board (PCAOB)** was created as a result of the Sarbanes-Oxley Act. It has oversight and enforcement responsibilities over accounting firms in the United States.

Instructions

Go to the PCAOB website to answer the following questions.

a. What is the mission of the PCAOB?

b. Briefly summarize its responsibilities related to inspections.

c. Briefly summarize its responsibilities related to enforcement.

Decision-Making Across the Organization

CT7.7 Alternative Distributor Corp., a distributor of groceries and related products, is headquartered in Medford, Massachusetts.

During a recent audit, Alternative Distributor Corp. was advised that existing internal controls necessary for the company to develop reliable financial statements were inadequate. The audit report stated that the current system of accounting for sales, receivables, and cash receipts constituted a material weakness. Among other items, the report focused on nontimely deposit of cash receipts, exposing Alternative Distributor to potential loss or misappropriation, excessive past due accounts receivable due to lack of collection efforts, disregard of advantages offered by vendors for prompt payment of invoices, absence of appropriate segregation of duties by personnel consistent with appropriate control objectives, inadequate procedures for applying accounting principles, lack of qualified management personnel, lack of supervision by an outside board of directors, and overall poor recordkeeping.

Instructions

a. Identify the principles of internal control violated by Alternative Distributor Corp.

b. Explain why managers of various functional areas in the company should be concerned about internal controls.

Communication Activity

CT7.8 As a new auditor for the CPA firm of Blacke and Whyte, you have been assigned to review the internal controls over mail cash receipts of Simon Company. Your review reveals that checks are promptly endorsed "For Deposit Only," but no list of the checks is prepared by the person opening the mail. The mail is opened either by the cashier or by the employee who maintains the accounts receivable records. Mail receipts are deposited in the bank weekly by the cashier.

Instructions

Write a letter to Frank Simon, owner of Simon Company, explaining the weaknesses in internal control and your recommendations for improving the system.

Ethics Cases

CT7.9 Banks charge fees for "bounced" checks—that is, checks that exceed the balance in the account. It has been estimated that processing bounced checks costs a bank roughly $1.50 per check. Thus, the profit margin on bounced checks is very high. Recognizing this, some banks have started to process checks from largest to smallest. By doing this, they maximize the number of checks that bounce if a customer overdraws an account. For example, **NationsBank** (now **Bank of America**) projected a $14 million increase in fee revenue as a result of processing largest checks first. In response to criticism, banks have responded that their customers prefer to have large checks processed first, because those tend to be the most important. At the other extreme, some banks will cover their customers' bounced checks, effectively extending them an interest-free loan while their account is overdrawn.

Instructions

Answer each of the following questions.

a. Carl Roen had a balance of $1,500 in his checking account at First National Bank on a day when the bank received the following five checks for processing against his account.

Check Number	Amount	Check Number	Amount
3150	$ 35	3165	$ 550
3162	400	3166	1,510
		3169	180

Assuming a $30 fee assessed by the bank for each bounced check, how much fee revenue would the bank generate if it processed checks (1) from largest to smallest, (2) from smallest to largest, and (3) in order of check number?

b. Do you think that processing checks from largest to smallest is an ethical business practice?

c. In addition to ethical issues, what other issues must a bank consider in deciding whether to process checks from largest to smallest?

d. If you were managing a bank, what policy would you adopt on bounced checks?

CT7.10 The **National Fraud Information Center (NFIC)** was originally established in 1992 by the National Consumers League, the oldest nonprofit consumer organization in the United States, to fight the growing menace of telemarketing fraud by improving prevention and enforcement. It maintains a website that provides many useful fraud-related resources.

Instructions

Go to the NFIC website and find an item of interest to you. Write a short summary of your findings.

All About You

CT7.11 The print and electronic media are full of stories about potential security risks that can arise from your personal computer. It is important to keep in mind, however, that there are also many ways that your identity can be stolen other than from your computer. The federal government provides many resources to help protect you from identity thieves.

Instructions

Search the Internet for "ID Theft Faceoff Game" and then complete the quiz provided.

FASB Codification Activity

CT7.12 If your school has a subscription to the FASB Codification, log in and prepare responses to the following.

   a. How is cash defined in the Codification?
   b. How are cash equivalents defined in the Codification?
   c. What are the disclosure requirements related to cash and cash equivalents?

A Look at IFRS

> **LEARNING OBJECTIVE 6**
> Compare the accounting procedures for fraud, internal control, and cash under GAAP and IFRS.

Fraud can occur anywhere. And because the three main factors that contribute to fraud are universal in nature, the principles of internal control activities are used globally by companies. While Sarbanes-Oxley (SOX) does not apply to international companies, most large international companies have internal controls similar to those indicated in the chapter. IFRS and GAAP are also very similar in accounting for cash. *IAS No. 1 (revised),* "Presentation of Financial Statements," is the only standard that discusses issues specifically related to cash.

Key Points

Following are the key similarities and differences between GAAP and IFRS related to fraud, internal control, and cash.

Similarities

- The fraud triangle discussed in this chapter is applicable to all international companies. Some of the major frauds on an international basis are **Parmalat** (Italy), **Royal Ahold** (the Netherlands), and **Satyam Computer Services** (India).
- Rising economic crime poses a growing threat to companies, with 34% of all organizations worldwide being victims of fraud in a recent 12-month period.
- Accounting scandals both in the United States and internationally have re-ignited the debate over the relative merits of GAAP, which takes a "rules-based" approach to accounting, versus IFRS, which takes a "principles-based" approach. The FASB has introduced more principles-based standards.
- On a lighter note, at one time the Ig Nobel Prize in Economics went to the CEOs of those companies involved in the corporate accounting scandals of that year for "adapting the mathematical concept of imaginary numbers for use in the business world." A parody of the Nobel Prizes, the Ig Nobel Prizes (read Ignoble, as not noble) are given each year in early October for 10 achievements that "first make people laugh, and then make them think." Organized by the scientific humor magazine *Annals of Improbable Research* (*AIR*), they are presented by a group that includes genuine Nobel laureates at a ceremony at Harvard University's Sanders Theater.
- Internal controls are a system of checks and balances designed to prevent and detect fraud and errors. While most companies have these systems in place, many have never completely documented them, nor had an independent auditor attest to their effectiveness. Both of these actions are required under SOX.
- Companies find that internal control review is a costly process but badly needed. One study estimates the cost of SOX compliance for U.S. companies at over $35 billion, with audit fees doubling in the first year of compliance. At the same time, examination of internal controls indicates lingering problems in the way companies operate. One study of first compliance with the internal-control testing provisions documented material weaknesses for about 13% of companies reporting in a two-year period (*PricewaterhouseCoopers' Global Economic Crime Survey,* 2005).

- The accounting and internal control procedures related to cash are essentially the same under both IFRS and this text. In addition, the definition used for cash equivalents is the same.
- Most companies report cash and cash equivalents together under IFRS, as shown in this text. In addition, IFRS follows the same accounting policies related to the reporting of restricted cash.

Differences

- The SOX internal control standards apply only to companies listed on U.S. exchanges. There is continuing debate over whether foreign issuers should have to comply with this extra layer of regulation.

IFRS Practice

IFRS Self-Test Questions

1. Non-U.S companies that follow IFRS:
   a. do not normally use the principles of internal control activities described in this text.
   b. often offset cash with accounts payable on the balance sheet.
   c. are not required to follow SOX.
   d. None of the above.
2. The Sarbanes-Oxley Act applies to:
   a. all U.S. companies listed on U.S. exchanges.
   b. all companies that list stock on any stock exchange in any country.
   c. all European companies listed on European exchanges.
   d. Both (a) and (c).
3. High-quality international accounting requires both high-quality accounting standards and:
   a. a reconsideration of SOX to make it less onerous.
   b. high-quality auditing standards.
   c. government intervention to ensure that the public interest is protected.
   d. the development of new principles of internal control activities.

IFRS Exercises

IFRS7.1 Some people argue that the internal control requirements of the Sarbanes-Oxley Act (SOX) put U.S. companies at a competitive disadvantage to companies outside the United States. Discuss the competitive implications (both pros and cons) of SOX.

International Financial Reporting Problem: Louis Vuitton

IFRS7.2 The financial statements of **Louis Vuitton** are presented in Appendix F. The complete annual report, including the notes to its financial statements, is available at the company's website.

Instructions

Using the notes to the company's financial statements, what are Louis Vuitton's accounting policies related to cash and cash equivalents?

Answers to IFRS Self-Test Questions

1. c **2.** a **3.** b

CHAPTER 8

Reporting and Analyzing Receivables

Chapter Preview

In this chapter, we discuss some of the decisions related to reporting and analyzing receivables. As indicated in the Feature Story, receivables are a significant asset on the books of **Nike**. Receivables are important to companies in other industries as well because a large portion of sales in the United States are credit sales. As a consequence, companies must pay close attention to their receivables balances and manage them carefully. In this chapter, we will look at the accounting and management of receivables at Nike and one of its competitors, **Skechers USA**.

Feature Story

What's Cooking?

What major U.S corporation got its start 38 years ago with a waffle iron? *Hint:* It doesn't sell food. *Another hint:* Swoosh. *Another hint:* "Just do it." That's right, **Nike**. In 1971, Nike co-founder Bill Bowerman put a piece of rubber into a kitchen waffle iron, and the trademark waffle sole was born. It seems fair to say that at Nike, "They don't make 'em like they used to."

Nike was co-founded by Bowerman and Phil Knight, a member of Bowerman's University of Oregon track team. Each began in the shoe business independently during the early 1960s. Bowerman got his start by making hand-crafted running shoes for his University of Oregon track team. Knight, after completing graduate school, started a small business importing low-cost, high-quality shoes from Japan. In 1964, the two joined forces, each contributing $500, and formed Blue Ribbon Sports, a partnership that marketed Japanese shoes.

It wasn't until 1971 that the company began manufacturing its own line of shoes. With the new shoes came a new corporate name—Nike—the Greek goddess of victory. It is hard to imagine that the company that now boasts a stable full of world-class athletes as promoters at one time had part-time employees selling shoes out of car trunks at track meets on a cash-and-carry basis.

As the business grew, Nike sold its shoes to sporting good shops and department stores on a credit basis. This necessitated receivables management. Today, with sales of $20.8 billion and accounts receivable of $3.1 billion, managing accounts receivable is vitally important to Nike's success. If it makes a major mistake with its receivables, it will definitely affect the bottom line.

In recent years, Nike has expanded its product line to a diverse range of products, including performance equipment such as soccer balls and golf clubs. While this has increased sales revenue, it has also complicated Nike's receivables management efforts. Now, instead of selling shoes at a limited number of retail outlets, it sells its vast number of products to a diverse array of stores, large and small. For example, Nike golf clubs are sold at local country clubs and golf shops across the country, while soccer equipment can be sold directly to customers through Internet sales. This diversification of its customer list complicates matters because Nike has to approve each new store or customer for credit sales, monitor cash collections, and pursue slow-paying accounts. That's a lot of work. Maybe cash-and-carry wasn't so bad after all.

Chapter Outline

LEARNING OBJECTIVES

LO 1 Explain how companies recognize accounts receivable.	• Types of receivables • Recognizing accounts receivable	**DO IT! 1** Recognizing Accounts Receivable
LO 2 Describe how companies value accounts receivable and record their disposition.	• Valuing accounts receivable • Disposing of accounts receivable	**DO IT! 2a** Bad Debt Expense **DO IT! 2b** Factoring
LO 3 Explain how companies recognize, value, and dispose of notes receivable.	• Determining the maturity date • Computing interest • Recognizing notes receivable • Valuing notes receivable • Disposing of notes receivable	**DO IT! 3** Recognizing Notes Receivable
LO 4 Describe the statement presentation of receivables and the principles of receivables management.	• Financial statement presentation of receivables • Managing receivables • Evaluating liquidity • Accelerating cash receipts • Data analytics and receivables management	**DO IT! 4** Analysis of Receivables

Go to the Review and Practice section at the end of the chapter for a targeted summary and practice applications with solutions.
Visit WileyPLUS for additional tutorials and practice opportunities.

Recognition of Accounts Receivable

LEARNING OBJECTIVE 1
Explain how companies recognize accounts receivable.

The term **receivables** refers to amounts due from individuals and companies. Receivables are claims that are expected to be collected in cash. The management of receivables is a very important activity for any company that sells goods or services on credit.

Receivables are important because they represent one of a company's most liquid assets. For many companies, receivables are also one of the largest assets. For example, receivables represent 13.7% of the current assets of pharmaceutical giant **Rite Aid**. Illustration 8.1 lists receivables as a percentage of total assets for five other well-known companies in a recent year.

Company	Receivables as a Percentage of Total Assets
Ford Motor Company	43.2%
General Electric	41.5
Minnesota Mining and Manufacturing Company (3M)	12.7
DuPont Co.	11.7
Intel Corporation	3.9

ILLUSTRATION 8.1
Receivables as a percentage of assets

Types of Receivables

The relative significance of a company's receivables as a percentage of its assets depends on various factors: its industry, the time of year, whether it extends long-term financing, and its credit policies. To reflect important differences among receivables, they are frequently classified as (1) accounts receivable, (2) notes receivable, and (3) other receivables.

Accounts receivable are amounts customers owe on account. They result from the sale of goods and services. Companies generally expect to collect accounts receivable within 30 to 60 days. They are usually the most significant type of claim held by a company.

Notes receivable are a written promise (as evidenced by a formal instrument) for amounts to be received. The note normally requires the collection of interest and extends for time periods of 60–90 days or longer. Notes and accounts receivable that result from sales transactions are often called **trade receivables**.

Other receivables include nontrade receivables such as interest receivable, loans to company officers, advances to employees, and income taxes refundable. These do not generally result from the operations of the business. Therefore, they are generally classified and reported as separate items in the balance sheet (see **Ethics Note**).

ETHICS NOTE
Companies report receivables from employees separately in the financial statements. The reason: Sometimes these receivables are not the result of an "arm's-length" transaction.

Recognizing Accounts Receivable

Recognizing accounts receivable is relatively straightforward. A service organization records a receivable when it performs a service on account. A merchandiser records accounts receivable at the point of sale of merchandise on account. When a merchandiser sells goods, it increases (debits) Accounts Receivable and increases (credits) Sales Revenue.

As discussed in Chapter 5, sometimes sellers offer sales discounts to encourage early payment by the buyer. If the buyer pays during the discount period, the receivable balance will be satisfied with a smaller cash payment. Also, the buyer might find some of the goods unacceptable and choose to return the unwanted goods. When a buyer returns goods, the receivable balance is reduced.

To review, assume that Jordache Co. on July 1, 2022, sells merchandise on account to Polo Company for $1,000, terms 2/10, n/30. On July 5, Polo returns merchandise with a sales price of $100 to Jordache Co. On July 11, Jordache receives payment from Polo Company for the balance due. The journal entries to record these transactions on the books of Jordache Co. are as follows (see **Helpful Hint**). **(Cost of goods sold entries are omitted.)**

HELPFUL HINT
These entries are the same as those described in Chapter 5. For simplicity, we have omitted inventory and cost of goods sold from this set of journal entries and from end-of-chapter material.

Date	Account	Debit	Credit
July 1	Accounts Receivable	1,000	
	Sales Revenue		1,000
	(To record sales on account)		
July 5	Sales Returns and Allowances	100	
	Accounts Receivable		100
	(To record merchandise returned)		
July 11	Cash ($900 − $18)	882	
	Sales Discounts ($900 × .02)	18	
	Accounts Receivable		900
	(To record collection of accounts receivable)		

Some retailers issue their own credit cards. When you use a retailer's credit card (**JCPenney**, for example), the retailer charges interest on the balance due if not paid within a specified period (usually 25–30 days).

To illustrate, assume that you use your JCPenney Company credit card to purchase clothing with a sales price of $300 on June 15, 2022. JCPenney will increase (debit) Accounts Receivable for $300 and increase (credit) Sales Revenue for $300 (cost of goods sold entry omitted) as follows.

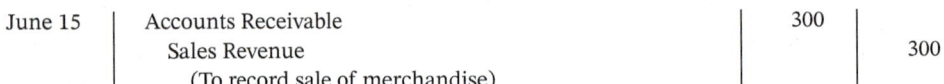

June 15	Accounts Receivable	300	
	Sales Revenue		300
	(To record sale of merchandise)		

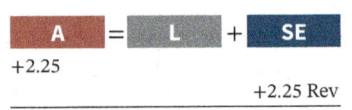

A = L + SE
+300
          +300 Rev

Cash Flows
no effect

If you still owe the $300 from the June 15 transaction at the end of the month, JCPenney charges interest of 1.5% per month on the balance due. JCPenney makes an adjusting entry to record interest revenue of $2.25 ($300 × 1.5% × ½) on June 30 as follows.

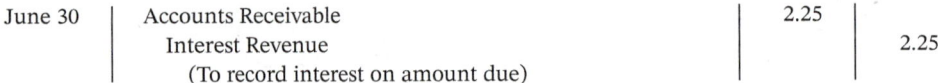

A = L + SE
+2.25
          +2.25 Rev

Cash Flows
no effect

June 30	Accounts Receivable	2.25	
	Interest Revenue		2.25
	(To record interest on amount due)		

Interest revenue is often substantial for many retailers.

Anatomy of a Fraud

Tasanee was the accounts receivable clerk for a large nonprofit foundation that provided performance and exhibition space for the performing and visual arts. Her responsibilities included activities normally assigned to an accounts receivable clerk, such as recording revenues from various sources (donations, facility rental fees, ticket revenue, and bar receipts). However, she was also responsible for handling all cash and checks from the time they were received until the time she deposited them, as well as preparing the bank reconciliation. Tasanee took advantage of her situation by falsifying bank deposits and bank reconciliations so that she could steal cash from the bar receipts. Since nobody else logged the donations or matched the donation receipts to pledges prior to Tasanee receiving them, she was able to offset the cash that was stolen against donations that she received but didn't record. Her crime was made easier by the fact that her boss, the company's controller, only did a very superficial review of the bank reconciliation and thus didn't notice that some numbers had been cut out from other documents and taped onto the bank reconciliation.

Total take: $1.5 million

The Missing Controls

Segregation of duties. The foundation should not have allowed an accounts receivable clerk, whose job was to record receivables, to also handle cash, record cash, make deposits, and especially prepare the bank reconciliation.

Independent internal verification. The controller was supposed to perform a thorough review of the bank reconciliation. Because he did not, he was terminated from his position.

Source: Adapted from Wells, *Fraud Casebook* (2007), pp. 183–194.

> **DO IT! 1** | **Recognizing Accounts Receivable**
>
> On May 1, Wilton sold merchandise on account to Bates for $50,000 terms 3/15, net 45. On May 4, Bates returns merchandise with a sales price of $2,000. On May 16, Wilton receives payment from Bates for the balance due. Prepare journal entries to record the May transactions on Wilton's books. (You may ignore cost of goods sold entries and explanations.)
>
> **ACTION PLAN**
> - Prepare entry to record the receivable and related return.
> - Compute the sales discount and related entry.
>
> **Solution**
>
> | May 1 | Accounts Receivable | 50,000 | |
> |---|---|---|---|
> | | Sales Revenue | | 50,000 |
> | 4 | Sales Returns and Allowances | 2,000 | |
> | | Accounts Receivable | | 2,000 |
> | 16 | Cash ($48,000 − $1,440) | 46,560 | |
> | | Sales Discounts ($48,000 × .03) | 1,440 | |
> | | Accounts Receivable | | 48,000 |
>
> Related exercise material: **BE8.1, BE8.2, DO IT! 8.1, E8.1, and E8.2.**

Valuation and Disposition of Accounts Receivable

LEARNING OBJECTIVE 2
Describe how companies value accounts receivable and record their disposition.

Valuing Accounts Receivable

Once companies record receivables in the accounts, the next question is: How should they report receivables in the financial statements? Companies report accounts receivable on the balance sheet as an asset. But determining the **amount** to report is sometimes difficult because some receivables will become uncollectible.

Each customer must satisfy the credit requirements of the seller before the credit sale is approved. Inevitably, though, some accounts receivable become uncollectible. For example, a customer may not be able to pay because of a decline in its sales revenue due to a downturn in the economy. Similarly, individuals may be laid off from their jobs or faced with unexpected hospital bills. Companies record credit losses as **Bad Debt Expense** (or Uncollectible Accounts Expense). Such losses are a normal and necessary risk of doing business on a credit basis.

When U.S. home prices fell, home foreclosures rose, and the economy in general slowed as a result of the financial crisis of 2008, lenders experienced huge increases in their bad debt expense. For example, during one quarter **Wachovia** (a large U.S. bank now owned by **Wells Fargo**) increased bad debt expense from $108 million to $408 million. Similarly, **American Express** increased its bad debt expense by 70%.

Two methods are used in accounting for uncollectible accounts: (1) the direct write-off method and (2) the allowance method. The following sections explain these methods.

Direct Write-Off Method for Uncollectible Accounts

Under the **direct write-off method**, when a company determines a particular account to be uncollectible, it charges the loss to Bad Debt Expense. Assume, for example, that Warden

Co. writes off as uncollectible M. E. Doran's $200 balance on December 12. Warden's entry is as follows.

Dec. 12	Bad Debt Expense	200	
	Accounts Receivable		200
	(To record write-off of M. E. Doran account)		

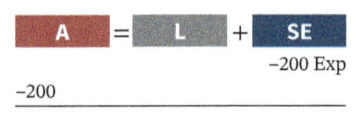

Cash Flows
no effect

Under this method, Bad Debt Expense will show only **actual losses** from uncollectibles. The company will report accounts receivable at its gross amount.

Use of the direct write-off method can reduce the relevance of both the income statement and the balance sheet. Consider the following example. In 2022, Quick Buck Computer Company decided it could increase its revenues by offering computers to college students without requiring any money down and with no credit-approval process. On campuses across the country, it sold one million computers with a selling price of $800 each. This increased Quick Buck's revenues and receivables by $800 million. The promotion was a huge success! The 2022 balance sheet and income statement looked great. Unfortunately, during 2023, nearly 40% of the customers defaulted on their loans. This made the 2023 income statement and balance sheet look terrible. **Illustration 8.2** shows the effect of these events on the financial statements if the direct write-off method is used.

ILLUSTRATION 8.2

Effects of direct write-off method

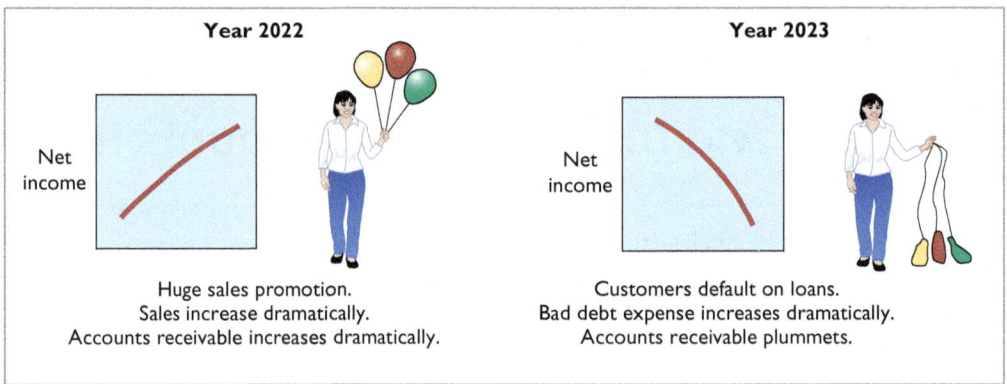

Under the direct write-off method, companies often record bad debt expense in a period different from the period in which they record the revenue. The method does not attempt to match bad debt expense to sales revenue in the income statement. Nor does the direct write-off method show accounts receivable in the balance sheet at the amount the company actually expects to receive. **Consequently, unless bad debt losses are insignificant, the direct write-off method is not acceptable for financial reporting purposes.**

Allowance Method for Uncollectible Accounts

The **allowance method** of accounting for bad debts involves estimating uncollectible accounts at the end of each period. This provides better matching of expenses with revenues on the income statement. It also ensures that companies state receivables on the balance sheet at their cash (net) realizable value. **Cash (net) realizable value** is the net amount the company expects to receive in cash. It excludes amounts that the company estimates it will not collect. Thus, this method reduces receivables in the balance sheet by the amount of estimated uncollectible receivables.

Companies must use the allowance method for financial reporting purposes when bad debts are material in amount (see **Helpful Hint**). This method has three essential features:

HELPFUL HINT

In this context, *material* means significant or important to financial statement users.

1. Companies **estimate** uncollectible accounts receivable. They match this estimated expense **against revenues** in the same accounting period in which they record the revenues.

2. Companies debit estimated uncollectibles to Bad Debt Expense and credit them to Allowance for Doubtful Accounts through an adjusting entry at the end of each period. Allowance for Doubtful Accounts is a contra account to Accounts Receivable.

3. When companies write off a specific account, they debit actual uncollectibles to Allowance for Doubtful Accounts and credit that amount to Accounts Receivable.

Recording Estimated Uncollectibles To illustrate the allowance method, assume that in its first year of operations, Hampson Furniture has credit sales of $1,200,000 in 2022. Of this amount, $200,000 of receivables remains uncollected at December 31. The credit manager estimates that $12,000 of these receivables will be uncollectible. The adjusting entry to record the estimated uncollectibles increases (debits) Bad Debt Expense and increases (credits) Allowance for Doubtful Accounts, as follows.

Dec. 31	Bad Debt Expense	12,000	
	Allowance for Doubtful Accounts		12,000
	(To record estimate of uncollectible accounts)		

A	=	L	+	SE
				−12,000 Exp
−12,000				

Cash Flows
no effect

Hampson reports Bad Debt Expense in the income statement as an operating expense. Thus, the estimated uncollectibles are matched with sales in 2022. Hampson records the expense in the same year it made the sales.

Allowance for Doubtful Accounts shows the estimated amount of claims on customers that the company expects will become uncollectible in the future. Companies use a contra account instead of a direct credit to Accounts Receivable because they do not know which customers will not pay. The credit balance in the allowance account will absorb the specific write-offs when they occur. As **Illustration 8.3** shows, the company deducts the allowance account from accounts receivable in the current assets section of the balance sheet.

Hampson Furniture
Balance Sheet (partial)

Current assets		
Cash		$ 14,800
Accounts receivable	**$200,000**	
Less: Allowance for doubtful accounts	**12,000**	188,000
Inventory		310,000
Supplies		25,000
Total current assets		$537,800

ILLUSTRATION 8.3
Presentation of allowance for doubtful accounts

The amount of $188,000 in Illustration 8.3 represents the expected **cash realizable value** of the accounts receivable at the statement date (see **Helpful Hint**). **Companies do not close Allowance for Doubtful Accounts at the end of the fiscal year.**

HELPFUL HINT
Cash realizable value is sometimes referred to as *accounts receivable (net)*.

Recording the Write-Off of an Uncollectible Account As described in the Feature Story, companies use various methods of collecting past-due accounts, such as letters, calls, and legal action. When they have exhausted all means of collecting a past-due account and collection appears impossible, the company writes off the account. In the credit card industry, for example, it is standard practice to write off accounts that are 210 days past due. To prevent premature or unauthorized write-offs, authorized management personnel should formally approve each write-off. **To maintain segregation of duties, the employee authorized to write off accounts should not have daily responsibilities related to cash or receivables.**

To illustrate a receivables write-off, assume that the financial vice president of Hampson Furniture authorizes a write-off of the $500 balance owed by R. A. Ware on March 1, 2023. The entry to record the write-off is as follows.

Mar. 1	Allowance for Doubtful Accounts	500	
	Accounts Receivable		500
	(Write-off of R. A. Ware account)		

A	=	L	+	SE
+500				
−500				

Cash Flows
no effect

The company does not increase bad debt expense when the write-off occurs. **Under the allowance method, companies debit every bad debt write-off to the allowance account rather than to Bad Debt Expense.** A debit to Bad Debt Expense would be incorrect because the company has already recognized the expense when it made the adjusting entry for estimated bad debts. Instead, the entry to record the write-off of an uncollectible account reduces both Accounts Receivable and Allowance for Doubtful Accounts. After posting, the general ledger accounts appear as shown in **Illustration 8.4**.

ILLUSTRATION 8.4
General ledger balances after write-off

Accounts Receivable				Allowance for Doubtful Accounts			
Jan. 1 Bal.	200,000	Mar. 1	500	Mar. 1	500	Jan. 1 Bal.	12,000
Mar. 1 Bal.	199,500					Mar. 1 Bal.	11,500

A write-off affects **only balance sheet accounts**—not income statement accounts. The write-off of the account reduces both Accounts Receivable and Allowance for Doubtful Accounts. Cash realizable value in the balance sheet, therefore, remains the same, as **Illustration 8.5** shows.

ILLUSTRATION 8.5
Cash realizable value comparison

	Before Write-Off	After Write-Off
Accounts receivable	$200,000	$199,500
Allowance for doubtful accounts	12,000	11,500
Cash realizable value	**$188,000**	**$188,000**

Recovery of an Uncollectible Account Occasionally, a company collects from a customer after it has written off the account as uncollectible. The company makes two entries to record the recovery of a bad debt. (1) It reverses the entry made in writing off the account. This reinstates the customer's account. (2) It journalizes the collection in the usual manner.

To illustrate, assume that on July 1, R. A. Ware pays the $500 amount that Hampson had written off on March 1. Hampson makes the following entries.

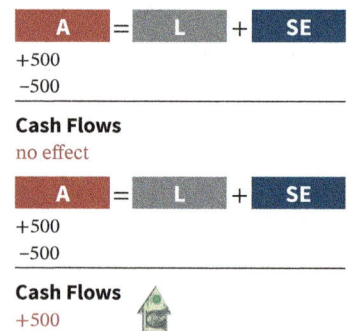

(1)
July 1 | Accounts Receivable | 500 |
 | Allowance for Doubtful Accounts | | 500
 | (To reverse write-off of R. A. Ware account) | |

(2)
July 1 | Cash | 500 |
 | Accounts Receivable | | 500
 | (To record collection from R. A. Ware) | |

Note that the recovery of a bad debt, like the write-off of a bad debt, affects **only balance sheet accounts**. The net effect of the two entries above is a debit to Cash and a credit to Allowance for Doubtful Accounts for $500. Accounts Receivable and Allowance for Doubtful Accounts both increase in entry (1) for two reasons. First, the company made an error in judgment when it wrote off the account receivable. Second, after R. A. Ware did pay, Accounts Receivable in the general ledger and Ware's account in the subsidiary ledger should show the collection for possible future credit purposes.

Estimating the Allowance For Hampson Furniture in Illustration 8.3, the amount of the expected uncollectibles was given. However, in "real life," companies must estimate the amount of expected uncollectible accounts if they use the allowance method. **Illustration 8.6** shows an excerpt from the notes to **Nike**'s financial statements discussing its use of the allowance method.

ILLUSTRATION 8.6
Nike's allowance method disclosure

Nike, Inc.
Notes to the Financial Statements

Allowance for Uncollectible Accounts Receivable

Accounts receivable, net consist primarily of amounts receivable from customers. The Company makes ongoing estimates relating to the collectability of its accounts receivable and maintains an allowance for estimated losses resulting from the inability of its customers to make required payments. In determining the amount of the allowance, the Company considers historical levels of credit losses and makes judgments about the creditworthiness of significant customers based on ongoing credit on evaluations. Accounts receivable with anticipated collection dates greater than 12 months from the balance sheet date and related allowances are considered non-current and recorded in *Deferred income taxes and other assets*. The allowance for uncollectible accounts receivable was $19 million and $43 million at May 31, 2017 and 2016, respectively.

Frequently, companies estimate the allowance as a percentage of the outstanding receivables. Under the **percentage-of-receivables basis**, management establishes a percentage relationship between the amount of receivables and expected losses from uncollectible accounts (see **Helpful Hint**). For example, suppose Steffen Company has an ending balance in Accounts Receivable of $200,000 and an unadjusted credit balance in Allowance for Doubtful Accounts of $1,500. It estimates that 5% of its accounts receivable will eventually be uncollectible. It should report a balance in Allowance for Doubtful Accounts of $10,000 (.05 × $200,000). To increase the balance in Allowance for Doubtful Accounts from $1,500 to $10,000, the company debits (increases) Bad Debt Expense and credits (increases) Allowance for Doubtful Accounts by $8,500 ($10,000 − $1,500).

To more accurately estimate the ending balance in the allowance account, a company often prepares a schedule, called **aging the accounts receivable**. This schedule classifies customer balances by the length of time they have been unpaid.

After the company arranges the accounts by age, it determines the expected bad debt losses by applying percentages, based on past experience and other factors, to the totals of each category. The longer a receivable is past due, the less likely it is to be collected. As a result, the estimated percentage of uncollectible debts increases as the number of days past due increases (see **Helpful Hint**). Illustration 8.7 shows an aging schedule for Dart Company (see **Decision Tools**). Note the increasing uncollectible percentages from 2% to 40%.

> **HELPFUL HINT**
> Where appropriate, the percentage-of-receivables basis may use only a single percentage rate.

Allowance for Doubtful Accounts

Dec. 31 Unadj. Bal.	1,500
Dec. 31 Adj.	**8,500**
Dec. 31 Bal.	10,000

> **Decision Tools**
> An aging schedule helps users determine if the amount of past due accounts is increasing and which accounts require management's attention.

ILLUSTRATION 8.7
Aging schedule

Customer	Total	Not Yet Due	1–30	31–60	61–90	Over 90
			\multicolumn{4}{c}{Number of Days Past Due}			
T. E. Adert	$ 600		$ 300		$ 200	$ 100
R. C. Bortz	300	$ 300				
B. A. Carl	450		200	$ 250		
O. L. Diker	700	500			200	
T. O. Ebbet	600			300		300
Others	36,950	26,200	5,200	2,450	1,600	1,500
	$39,600	$27,000	$5,700	$3,000	$2,000	$1,900
Estimated percentage uncollectible		2%	4%	10%	20%	40%
Total estimated uncollectible accounts	$ 2,228	$ 540	$ 228	$ 300	$ 400	$ 760

> **HELPFUL HINT**
> The older categories have higher percentages because the longer an account is past due, the less likely it is to be collected.

Total estimated uncollectible accounts for Dart Company ($2,228) represent the existing customer claims expected to become uncollectible in the future. Thus, this amount represents the **required balance** in Allowance for Doubtful Accounts at the balance sheet date. Accordingly, **the amount of bad debt expense that should be recorded in the adjusting entry is the difference between the required balance and the existing balance in the allowance account**. The existing, unadjusted balance in Allowance for Doubtful Accounts is the net result of the beginning balance (a normal credit balance) less the write-offs of specific accounts during the year (debits to the allowance account).

For example, if the unadjusted trial balance shows Allowance for Doubtful Accounts with a credit balance of $528, then an adjusting entry for $1,700 ($2,228 − $528) is necessary:

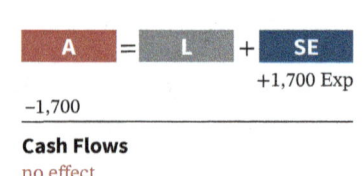

Cash Flows
no effect

Dec. 31	Bad Debt Expense	1,700	
	Allowance for Doubtful Accounts		1,700
	(To adjust allowance account to total estimated uncollectibles)		

After Dart posts the adjusting entry, its accounts appear as shown in **Illustration 8.8**.

ILLUSTRATION 8.8
Bad debt accounts after posting

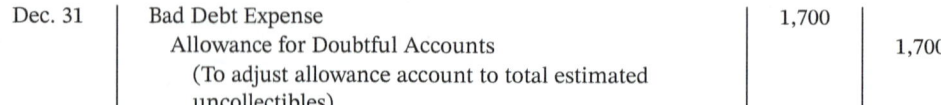

Bad Debt Expense		Allowance for Doubtful Accounts	
Dec. 31 Adj. 1,700			Dec. 31 Unadj. Bal. 528
			Dec. 31 Adj. 1,700
			Dec. 31 Bal. 2,228

An important aspect of accounts receivable management is simply maintaining a close watch on the accounts. Studies have shown that accounts more than 60 days past due lose approximately 50% of their value if no payment activity occurs within the next 30 days. For each additional 30 days that pass, the collectible value halves once again.

Occasionally, the allowance account will have a **debit balance** prior to adjustment. This occurs because the debits to the allowance account from write-offs during the year **exceeded** the beginning balance in the account which was based on previous estimates for bad debts. In such a case, the company **adds the debit balance to the required balance** when it makes the adjusting entry. Thus, if there was a $500 **debit** balance in the allowance account before adjustment, the adjusting entry would be for $2,728 ($2,228 + $500) to arrive at a credit balance of $2,228 as shown below.

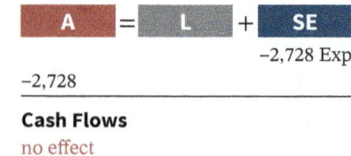

Cash Flows
no effect

Dec. 31	Bad Debt Expense	2,728	
	Allowance for Doubtful Accounts		2,728
	(To adjust allowance account to total estimated uncollectibles)		

After Dart posts the adjusting entry, its accounts appear as shown in **Illustration 8.9**.

ILLUSTRATION 8.9
Bad debt accounts after posting

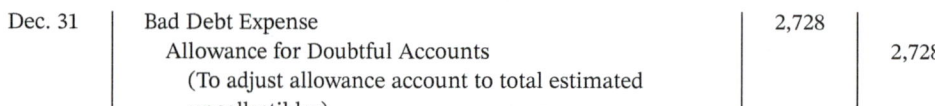

Bad Debt Expense		Allowance for Doubtful Accounts	
Dec. 31 Adj. 2,728		Dec. 31 Unadj. Bal. 500	Dec. 31 Adj. 2,728
			Dec. 31 Bal. 2,228

The percentage-of-receivables basis provides an estimate of the cash realizable value of the receivables. It also provides a reasonable matching of expenses to revenue. The FASB now employs an expected credit loss model which requires that companies must measure expected uncollectible accounts and record bad debt expense on all receivables, even those with a low risk of loss. Companies use sophisticated models employing data analytics to arrive at accurate estimates on a timely basis.

The note in **Illustration 8.10** regarding accounts receivable comes from the annual report of the shoe company **Skechers USA**.

ILLUSTRATION 8.10
Skechers USA's disclosure of accounts receivable

Skechers USA
Notes to the Financial Statements

The likelihood of a material loss on an uncollectible account would be mainly dependent on deterioration in the overall economic conditions in a particular country or region. Reserves are fully provided for all probable losses of this nature. For receivables that are not specifically identified as high risk, we provide a reserve based upon our historical loss rate as a percentage of sales. Gross trade accounts receivable were $368.5 million and $368.2 million, and the allowance for bad debts, returns, sales allowances and customer chargebacks were $41.6 million and $24.3 million, at December 31, 2016 and 2015, respectively. Our credit losses charged to expense for the years ended December 31, 2016, 2015 and 2014 were $12.7 million, $5.3 million, and $11.8 million, respectively. In addition, we recorded sales return and allowance expense for the years ended December 31, 2016, 2015 and 2014 of $18.1 million, $2.3 million, and $2.3 million, respectively.

Ethics Insight

Cookie Jar Allowances

© Christy Thompson/Shutterstock

There are many pressures on companies to achieve earnings targets. For managers, poor earnings can lead to dismissal or lack of promotion. It is not surprising then that management may be tempted to look for ways to boost their earnings number.

One way a company can achieve greater earnings is to lower its estimate of what is needed in its Allowance for Doubtful Accounts (sometimes referred to as "tapping the cookie jar"). For example, suppose a company has an Allowance for Doubtful Accounts of $10 million and decides to reduce this balance to $9 million. As a result of this change, Bad Debt Expense decreases by $1 million and earnings increase by $1 million.

Large banks such as **JP Morgan Chase**, **Wells Fargo**, and **Bank of America** recently decreased their Allowance for Doubtful Accounts by over $4 billion. These reductions came at a time when these big banks were still suffering from lower mortgage lending and trading activity, both of which lead to lower earnings. They justified these reductions in the allowance balances by noting that credit quality and economic conditions had improved. This may be so, but it sure is great to have a cookie jar that might be tapped when a boost in earnings is needed.

How might investors determine that a company is managing its earnings? (Go to WileyPLUS for this answer and additional questions.)

DO IT! 2a | Bad Debt Expense

Brule Corporation has been in business for 5 years. The unadjusted trial balance at the end of the current year shows Accounts Receivable $30,000, Sales Revenue $180,000, and Allowance for Doubtful Accounts with a debit balance of $2,000. Brule estimates bad debts to be 10% of accounts receivable. Prepare the entry necessary to adjust Allowance for Doubtful Accounts.

Solution

Brule should make the following entry to bring the debit balance in Allowance for Doubtful Accounts up to a normal, credit balance of $3,000 (10% × $30,000):

Bad Debt Expense [(10% × $30,000) + $2,000]	5,000	
Allowance for Doubtful Accounts		5,000
(To record estimate of uncollectible accounts)		

Related exercise material: **BE8.3, BE8.4, BE8.5, BE8.6, DO IT! 8.2a, E8.3, E8.4, E8.5, E8.6, and E8.7.**

ACTION PLAN
- Estimate the amount the company does not expect to collect.
- Consider the existing balance in the allowance account when using the percentage-of-receivables basis.
- Report receivables at their cash (net) realizable value—that is, the amount the company expects to collect in cash.

Disposing of Accounts Receivable

In the normal course of events, companies collect accounts receivable in cash and remove the receivables from the books. However, as credit sales and receivables have grown in significance, the "normal course of events" has changed. Companies now frequently sell their receivables to another company for cash, thereby shortening the cash-to-cash operating cycle.

Companies sell receivables for two major reasons. First, **they may be the only reasonable source of cash**. When money is tight, companies may not be able to borrow money in the usual credit markets. Or if money is available, the cost of borrowing may be prohibitive.

A second reason for selling receivables is that **billing and collection are often time-consuming and costly**. It is often easier for a retailer to sell the receivables to another party with expertise in billing and collection matters. Credit card companies such as MasterCard, Visa, and Discover specialize in billing and collecting accounts receivable.

Sale of Receivables to a Factor

A common sale of receivables is a sale to a factor. A **factor** is a finance company or bank that buys receivables from businesses and then collects the payments directly from the customers. Factoring is a multibillion dollar business.

Factoring arrangements vary widely. Typically, the factor charges a commission to the company that is selling the receivables. This fee often ranges from 1–3% of the amount of receivables purchased. To illustrate, assume that Hendredon Furniture factors $600,000 of receivables to Federal Factors. Federal Factors assesses a service charge of 2% of the amount of receivables sold. The journal entry to record the sale by Hendredon Furniture on April 2, 2022, is as follows.

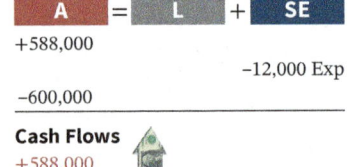

A = L + SE
+588,000
               −12,000 Exp
−600,000

Cash Flows
+588,000

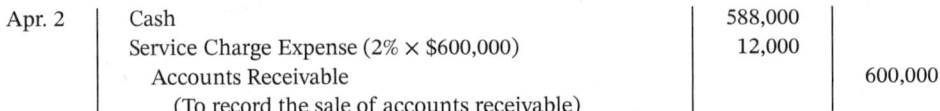

Apr. 2	Cash		588,000	
	Service Charge Expense (2% × $600,000)		12,000	
	Accounts Receivable			600,000
	(To record the sale of accounts receivable)			

If Hendredon often sells its receivables, it records the service charge expense as an operating expense. If the company infrequently sells receivables, it may report this amount in the Other expenses and losses section of the income statement.

National Credit Card Sales

Over one billion credit cards are in use in the United States—more than three credit cards for every man, woman, and child in this country. Visa, MasterCard, and American Express are the national credit cards that most individuals use. Three parties are involved when national credit cards are used in retail sales: (1) the credit card issuer, who is independent of the retailer; (2) the retailer; and (3) the customer. **A retailer's acceptance of a national credit card is another form of selling (factoring) the receivable.**

Illustration 8.11 shows the major advantages of national credit cards to the retailer. In exchange for these advantages, the retailer pays the credit card issuer a fee of 2–4% of the invoice price for its services (see Ethics Note).

> **ETHICS NOTE**
>
> In exchange for lower interest rates, some companies have eliminated the 25-day grace period before finance charges kick in. Be sure you read the fine print in any credit agreement you sign.

Accounting for Credit Card Sales The retailer generally considers sales from the use of national credit card sales as **cash sales**. The retailer must pay to the bank that issues the card a fee for processing the transactions. The retailer records the credit card slips in a similar manner as checks deposited from a cash sale.

To illustrate, Anita Ferreri purchases $1,000 of sound equipment for her restaurant from Karen Kerr Music Co., using her Visa First Bank Card. First Bank charges a service

ILLUSTRATION 8.11
Advantages of credit cards to the retailer

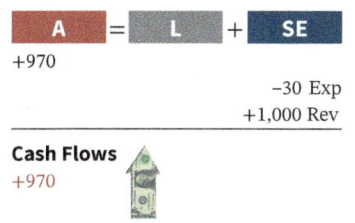

fee of 3%. The entry to record this transaction by Karen Kerr Music on March 22, 2022, is as follows.

Mar. 22	Cash	970	
	Service Charge Expense	30	
	Sales Revenue		1,000
	(To record Visa credit card sales)		

A = L + SE
+970
                  −30 Exp
                +1,000 Rev

Cash Flows
+970

Accounting Across the Organization   Nordstrom

© Zibedik/iStockphoto

How Does a Credit Card Work?

Most of you know how to use a credit card, but do you know what happens in the transaction and how the transaction is processed? Suppose that you use a **Visa** card to purchase some new ties at **Nordstrom**. You swipe your credit card (or insert it if it is a chip card), which allows the information to be read. The salesperson enters the amount of the purchase. The machine contacts the Visa computer, which routes the call back to the bank that issued your Visa card. The issuing bank verifies that the account exists, that the card is not stolen, and that you have not exceeded your credit limit. At this point, you sign to authorize the transaction.

Visa acts as the clearing agent for the transaction. It transfers funds from the issuing bank to Nordstrom's bank account. Generally this transfer of funds, from sale to the receipt of funds in the merchant's account, takes two to three days.

In the meantime, Visa puts a pending charge on your account for the amount of the tie purchase; that amount counts immediately against your available credit limit. At the end of the billing period, Visa sends you an invoice (your credit card bill) which shows the various charges you made, and the amounts that Visa expended on your behalf, for the month. You then must "pay the piper" for your stylish new ties.

Assume that Nordstrom prepares a bank reconciliation at the end of each month. If some credit card sales have not been processed by the bank, how should Nordstrom treat these transactions on its bank reconciliation? (Go to WileyPLUS for this answer and additional questions.)

ACTION PLAN
- Consider sale of receivables to a factor.
- Weigh cost of factoring against benefit of having cash in hand.

DO IT! 2b | Factoring

Peter M. Kell Wholesalers Co. needs to raise $120,000 in cash to safely cover next Friday's employee payroll. Kell has reached its debt ceiling. Kell's present balance of outstanding receivables totals $750,000. Kell decides to factor $125,000 of its receivables on September 7, 2022, to alleviate this cash crunch. Record the entry that Kell would make when it raises the needed cash. (Assume a 1% service charge.)

Solution

Assuming that Kell Co. factors $125,000 of its accounts receivable at a 1% service charge, it would make this entry:

Sept. 7	Cash	123,750	
	Service Charge Expense (1% × $125,000)	1,250	
	Accounts Receivable		125,000
	(To record sale of receivables to factor)		

Related exercise material: **BE 8.7, DO IT! 8.2b,** and **E8.8.**

Notes Receivable

LEARNING OBJECTIVE 3
Explain how companies recognize, value, and dispose of notes receivable.

Companies may also grant credit in exchange for a formal credit instrument known as a promissory note. A **promissory note** is a written promise to pay a specified amount of money on demand or at a definite time. Promissory notes may be used (1) when individuals and companies lend or borrow money, (2) when the amount of the transaction and the credit period exceed normal limits, or (3) in settlement of accounts receivable.

In a promissory note, the party making the promise to pay is called the **maker**. The party to whom payment is to be made is called the **payee**. The note may specifically identify the payee by name or may designate the payee simply as the bearer of the note.

In the note shown in **Illustration 8.12**, Calhoun Company is the maker and Wilma Company is the payee. To Wilma Company, the promissory note is a note receivable. To Calhoun Company, it is a note payable (see **Helpful Hint**).

ILLUSTRATION 8.12

Promissory note

HELPFUL HINT

For this note, the maker, Calhoun Company, debits Cash and credits Notes Payable. The payee, Wilma Company, debits Notes Receivable and credits Cash.

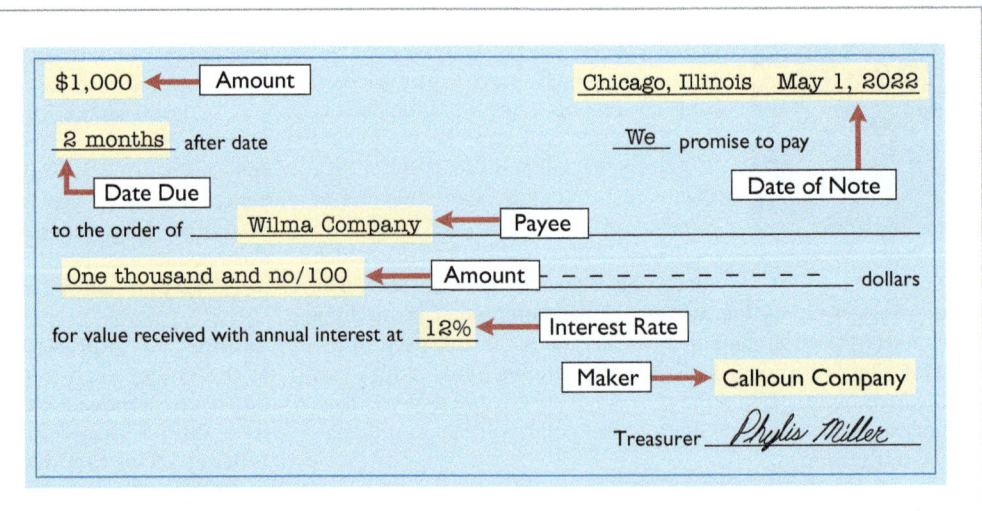

Notes receivable give the holder a stronger legal claim to assets than do accounts receivable. Like accounts receivable, notes receivable can be readily sold to another party. Promissory notes are negotiable instruments (as are checks), which means that they can be transferred to another party by endorsement.

Companies frequently accept notes receivable from customers who need to extend the payment of an outstanding account receivable. They often require such notes from high-risk customers. In some industries (such as the pleasure and sport boat industry), all credit sales are supported by notes. The majority of notes, however, originate from lending transactions.

The basic issues in accounting for notes receivable are the same as those for accounts receivable. On the following pages, we look at these issues. Before we do, however, we need to consider two issues that do not apply to accounts receivable: determining the maturity date and computing interest.

Determining the Maturity Date

Illustration 8.13 shows three ways of stating the maturity date of a promissory note.

ILLUSTRATION 8.13

Maturity date of different notes

When the life of a note is expressed in terms of months, you find the date when it matures by counting the months from the date of issue. For example, the maturity date of a three-month note dated May 1 is August 1. A note drawn on the last day of a month matures on the last day of a subsequent month. That is, a July 31 note due in two months matures on September 30.

When the due date is stated in terms of days, you need to count the exact number of days to determine the maturity date. In counting, **omit the date the note is issued but include the due date**. For example, the maturity date of a 60-day note dated July 17 is September 15, computed as shown in Illustration 8.14.

Term of note		60 days
July (31–17)	14	
August	31	45
Maturity date: September		15

ILLUSTRATION 8.14

Computation of maturity date

Computing Interest

Illustration 8.15 gives the basic formula for computing interest on an interest-bearing note.

ILLUSTRATION 8.15
Formula for computing interest

| Face Value of Note | × | Annual Interest Rate | × | Time in Terms of One Year | = | Interest |

HELPFUL HINT
The interest rate specified is the *annual* rate.

The interest rate specified in a note is an **annual** rate of interest (see **Helpful Hint**). The time factor in the formula in Illustration 8.15 expresses the fraction of a year that the note is outstanding. When the maturity date is stated in days, the time factor is often the number of days divided by 360. Remember that when counting days, omit the date that the note is issued but include the due date. When the due date is stated in months, the time factor is the number of months divided by 12. **Illustration 8.16** shows computation of interest for various time periods.

ILLUSTRATION 8.16
Computation of interest

Terms of Note	Interest Computation
	Face × Rate × Time = Interest
$ 730, 12%, 120 days	$ 730 × 12% × 120/360 = $ 29.20
$1,000, 9%, 6 months	$1,000 × 9% × 6/12 = $ 45.00
$2,000, 6%, 1 year	$2,000 × 6% × 1/1 = $120.00

There are different ways to calculate interest. For example, the computation in Illustration 8.15 assumes 360 days for the length of the year. Most financial institutions use 365 days to compute interest. *For homework problems, assume 360 days to simplify computations.*

Recognizing Notes Receivable

To illustrate the basic entry for notes receivable, we will use Calhoun Company's $1,000, two-month, 12% promissory note dated May 1. Assuming that Calhoun Company wrote the note to settle an open account, Wilma Company makes the following entry for the receipt of the note.

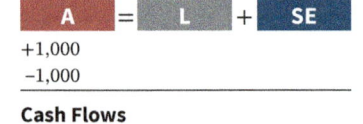
+1,000
−1,000

Cash Flows
no effect

May 1	Notes Receivable	1,000	
	Accounts Receivable		1,000
	(To record acceptance of Calhoun Company note)		

The company records the note receivable at its **face value**, the value shown on the face of the note. No interest revenue is reported when the note is accepted because the revenue recognition principle does not recognize revenue until the performance obligation is satisfied. Interest is earned (accrued) as time passes.

If a company issues cash in exchange for a note, the entry is a debit to Notes Receivable and a credit to Cash in the amount of the loan.

Valuing Notes Receivable

Valuing short-term notes receivable is the same as valuing accounts receivable. Like accounts receivable, companies report short-term notes receivable at their **cash (net) realizable value**. The notes receivable allowance account is Allowance for Doubtful Accounts. The estimations involved in determining cash realizable value and in recording bad debt expense and the related allowance are done similarly to accounts receivable.

Disposing of Notes Receivable

Notes may be held to their maturity date, at which time the face value plus accrued interest is due. In some situations, the maker of the note defaults, and the payee must make an appropriate adjustment. In other situations, similar to accounts receivable, the holder of the note speeds up the conversion to cash by selling the receivables (as described earlier in this chapter).

Honor of Notes Receivable

A note is **honored** when its maker pays in full at its maturity date. For each interest-bearing note, the **amount due at maturity** is the face value of the note plus interest for the length of time specified on the note.

To illustrate, assume that Wolder Co. lends Higley Co. $10,000 on June 1, accepting a five-month, 9% interest note. In this situation, interest is $375 ($10,000 × 9% × $\frac{5}{12}$). The amount due, **the maturity value**, is $10,375 ($10,000 + $375). To obtain payment, Wolder (the payee) must present the note either to Higley Co. (the maker) or to the maker's agent, such as a bank. If Wolder presents the note to Higley Co. on November 1, the maturity date, Wolder's entry to record the collection is as follows.

Nov. 1	Cash	10,375	
	Notes Receivable		10,000
	Interest Revenue ($10,000 × 9% × $\frac{5}{12}$)		375
	(To record collection of Higley note and interest)		

A	=	L	+	SE
+10,375				
−10,000				
				+375 Rev

Cash Flows
+10,375

Accrual of Interest Receivable

Suppose instead that Wolder Co. prepares financial statements as of September 30. The timeline in **Illustration 8.17** presents this situation.

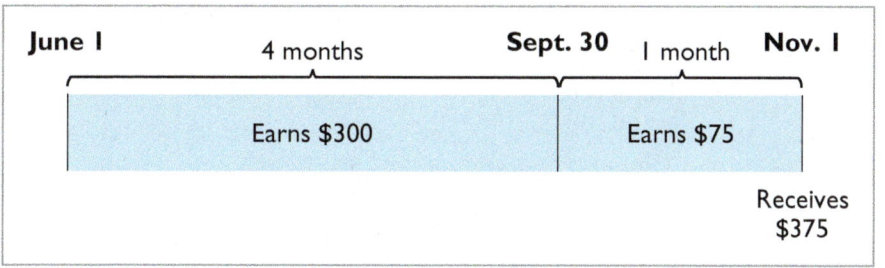

ILLUSTRATION 8.17
Timeline of interest earned

To reflect interest earned but not yet received, Wolder must accrue interest on September 30. In this case, the adjusting entry by Wolder is for four months of interest, or $300, as shown below.

Sept. 30	Interest Receivable ($10,000 × 9% × $\frac{4}{12}$)	300	
	Interest Revenue		300
	(To accrue 4 months' interest on Higley note)		

A	=	L	+	SE
+300				
				+300 Rev

Cash Flows
no effect

At the note's maturity on November 1, Wolder receives $10,375. This amount represents repayment of the $10,000 note as well as five months of interest, or $375, as shown below. The $375 is comprised of the $300 Interest Receivable accrued on September 30 plus $75 earned during October. Wolder's entry to record the honoring of the Higley note on November 1 is as follows.

Nov. 1	Cash [$10,000 + ($10,000 × 9% × $\frac{5}{12}$)]	10,375	
	Notes Receivable		10,000
	Interest Receivable		300
	Interest Revenue ($10,000 × 9% × $\frac{1}{12}$)		75
	(To record collection of Higley note and interest)		

A	=	L	+	SE
+10,375				
−10,000				
−300				
				+75 Rev

Cash Flows
+10,375

In this case, Wolder credits Interest Receivable because the receivable was established in the adjusting entry on September 30.

Dishonor of Notes Receivable

A **dishonored (defaulted) note** is a note that is not paid in full at maturity. A dishonored note receivable is no longer negotiable. However, the payee still has a claim against the maker of the note for both the note and the interest. Therefore, the note holder usually transfers the Notes Receivable account to an Accounts Receivable account.

To illustrate, assume that Higley Co. on November 1 indicates that it cannot pay at the present time. The entry to record the dishonor of the note depends on whether Wolder Co. expects eventual collection. If it does expect eventual collection, Wolder Co. debits the amount due (face value and interest) on the note to Accounts Receivable. It would make the following entry at the time the note is dishonored (assuming no previous accrual of interest).

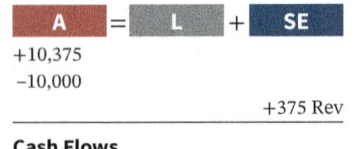
+10,375
−10,000
+375 Rev

Cash Flows
no effect

Nov. 1	Accounts Receivable	10,375	
	Notes Receivable		10,000
	Interest Revenue		375
	(To record the dishonor of Higley note)		

If instead on November 1 there is no hope of collection, the note holder would write off the face value of the note by debiting Allowance for Doubtful Accounts. No interest revenue would be recorded because collection will not occur.

ACTION PLAN

- Count the exact number of days to determine the maturity date. Omit the date the note is issued, but include the due date.
- Compute the accrued interest.
- Prepare the entry for payment of the note and the interest.

DO IT! 3 | Recognizing Notes Receivable

Gambit Stores accepts from Leonard Co. a $3,400, 90-day, 6% note dated May 10 in settlement of Leonard's overdue account. (a) What is the maturity date of the note? (b) What is the interest payable at the maturity date? (c) What entry does Gambit make at the maturity date, assuming Leonard pays the note and interest in full at that time?

Solution

a. The maturity date is August 8, computed as follows.

Term of note:		90 days
May (31–10)	21	
June	30	
July	31	82
Maturity date: August		8

b. The interest payable at the maturity date is $51, computed as follows.

Face	×	Rate	×	Time	=	Interest
$3,400	×	6%	×	90/360	=	$51

c. Gambit Stores records this entry at the maturity date:

Cash	3,451	
Interest Revenue		51
Notes Receivable		3,400
(To record collection of Leonard note and interest)		

Related exercise material: **BE8.8, BE8.9, DO IT! 8.3, E8.11, E8.12, and E8.13.**

Receivables Presentation and Management

LEARNING OBJECTIVE 4

Describe the statement presentation of receivables and the principles of receivables management.

If a company has significant receivables, analysts carefully review the company's financial statement disclosures to evaluate how well the company is managing its receivables.

Financial Statement Presentation of Receivables

Companies should identify in the balance sheet or in the notes to the financial statements each of the major types of receivables. Short-term receivables are reported in the current assets section of the balance sheet, below short-term investments. Short-term investments appear before short-term receivables because these investments are nearer to cash. Companies report both the gross amount of receivables and the allowance for doubtful accounts.

Receivables represent 60% of the total assets of heavy equipment manufacturer **Deere & Company**. **Illustration 8.18** shows a presentation of receivables for Deere & Company from its balance sheet and notes in a recent year.

ILLUSTRATION 8.18

Balance sheet presentation of receivables

Deere & Company Balance Sheet (partial) (in millions)	
Receivables	
Receivables from unconsolidated subsidiaries	$ 30
Trade accounts and notes receivable	3,278
Financing receivables	27,583
Restricted financing receivables	4,616
Other receivables	1,500
Total receivables	37,007
Less: Allowance for doubtful trade receivables	175
Net receivables	$36,832

In the income statement, companies report bad debt expense under Selling expenses in the operating expenses section. They show interest revenue under Other revenues and gains in the nonoperating section of the income statement.

If a company has significant risk of uncollectible accounts or other problems with its receivables, it is required to discuss this possibility in the notes to the financial statements.

Managing Receivables

Managing accounts receivable involves five steps:

1. Determine to whom to extend credit.
2. Establish a payment period.
3. Monitor collections.
4. Evaluate the liquidity of receivables.
5. Accelerate cash receipts from receivables when necessary.

Extending Credit

Every entrepreneur struggles with financing issues. For example, the very first order that **Apple**'s founders received was 50 circuit boards for a computer hobby shop. To produce the $25,000 order, Steve Jobs and Steve Wozniak needed $15,000 of parts. To purchase the parts, they borrowed $5,000 from friends but then were turned down when they applied for a bank loan for the $10,000 balance. They approached two parts suppliers in an effort to negotiate a purchase on credit, but both suppliers said no. Finally, a third supplier agreed to sell them the parts on 30-day credit after he called the computer hobby shop to confirm that it had, in fact, placed a $25,000 order to purchase goods.

A critical part of managing receivables is determining who should be extended credit and who should not. Many companies increase sales by being generous with their credit policy. However, they sometimes extend credit to risky customers who do not pay. But if your credit policy is too tight, you will lose sales. If it is too loose, you may sell to "deadbeats" who will pay either very late or not at all. One CEO noted that prior to getting his credit and collection department in order, his salespeople had 300 square feet of office space **per person**, while the people in credit and collections had six people crammed into a single 300-square-foot space. Although this focus on sales boosted sales revenue, it had very expensive consequences in bad debt expense.

Companies can take certain steps to help minimize losses due to bad debts when they decide to relax credit standards for new customers. They might require risky customers to provide letters of credit or bank guarantees. Then, if the customer does not pay, the bank that provided the guarantee will do so. Particularly risky customers might be required to pay cash on delivery. For example, at one time retailer **Linens'n Things, Inc.** reported that its largest suppliers were requiring cash payment before delivery. The suppliers had cut off shipments because the company had been slow in paying. **Kmart**'s suppliers also required it to pay cash in advance when it was financially troubled.

In addition, companies should ask potential customers for references from banks and suppliers, to determine their payment history. It is important to check references of potential new customers as well as periodically to check the financial health of continuing customers. Many resources are available for investigating customers. For example, *The Dun & Bradstreet Reference Book of American Business* lists millions of companies and provides credit ratings for many of them.

Accounting Across the Organization   Countrywide Financial Corporation

Bad Information Can Lead to Bad Loans

© Andy Dean/iStockphoto

Many factors contributed to the recent credit crisis. One significant factor that resulted in many bad loans was a failure by lenders to investigate loan customers sufficiently. For example, **Countrywide Financial Corporation** wrote many loans under its "Fast and Easy" loan program. That program allowed borrowers to provide little or no documentation for their income or their assets. Other lenders had similar programs, which earned the nickname "liars' loans." One study found that in these situations, 60% of applicants overstated their incomes by more than 50% in order to qualify for a loan. Critics of the banking industry say that because loan officers were compensated for loan volume, and because banks were selling the loans to investors rather than holding them, the lenders had little incentive to investigate the borrowers' creditworthiness.

Sources: Glenn R. Simpson and James R. Hagerty, "Countrywide Loss Focuses Attention on Underwriting," *Wall Street Journal* (April 30, 2008), p. B1; and Michael Corkery, "Fraud Seen as Driver in Wave of Foreclosures," *Wall Street Journal* (December 21, 2007), p. A1.

What steps should the banks have taken to ensure the accuracy of financial information provided on loan applications? (Go to WileyPLUS for this answer and additional questions.)

Establishing a Payment Period

Companies that extend credit should determine a required payment period and communicate that policy to their customers. It is important that the payment period is consistent with that of competitors. For example, if you require payment within 15 days but your competitors allow payment within 45 days, you may lose sales to your competitors. To match your competitors' generous terms yet still encourage prompt payment of accounts, you might allow up to 45 days to pay but offer a sales discount for people paying within 15 days.

Monitoring Collections

We discussed preparation of the accounts receivable aging schedule earlier in the chapter. Companies should prepare an accounts receivable aging schedule at least monthly (see **Decision Tools**). In addition to estimating the allowance for doubtful accounts, the aging schedule has other uses. It helps managers estimate the timing of future cash inflows, which is very important to the treasurer's efforts to prepare a cash budget. It provides information about the overall collection experience of the company and identifies problem accounts. For example, management would compute and compare the percentage of receivables that are over 90 days past due. **Illustration 8.19** contains an excerpt from the notes to **Skechers**' financial statements discussing how it monitors receivables.

> **Decision Tools**
>
> Monitoring the accounts receivable aging schedule helps users determine if the company's credit risk is increasing.

> **Skechers USA**
> **Notes to the Financial Statements**
>
> To minimize the likelihood of uncollectibility, customers' credit-worthiness is reviewed and adjusted periodically in accordance with external credit reporting services, financial statements issued by the customer and our experience with the account. When a customer's account becomes significantly past due, we generally place a hold on the account and discontinue further shipments to that customer, minimizing further risk of loss.

ILLUSTRATION 8.19
Note on monitoring Skechers' receivables

The aging schedule identifies problem accounts that the company needs to pursue with phone calls, letters, and occasionally legal action. Sometimes, special arrangements must be made with problem accounts. For example, it was reported that **Intel Corporation** (a major manufacturer of computer chips) required that **Packard Bell** (at one time one of the largest U.S. sellers of personal computers) exchange its past-due account receivable for an interest-bearing note receivable. This caused concern within the investment community. The move suggested that Packard Bell was in trouble, which worried Intel investors concerned about Intel's accounts receivable.

If a company has significant concentrations of credit risk, it must discuss this risk in the notes to its financial statements (see **Decision Tools**). A **concentration of credit risk** is a threat of nonpayment from a single large customer or class of customers that could adversely affect the financial health of the company. **Illustration 8.20** shows an excerpt from the credit risk note from a recent annual report of **Skechers**. Skechers reports that its five largest customers account for 11.3% of its net sales.

Decision Tools
Identifying risky credit customers helps users determine if the company has significant concentrations of credit risk.

> **Skechers USA**
> **Notes to the Financial Statements**
>
> **We Depend Upon a Relatively Small Group of Customers for a Large Portion of Our Sales.**
>
> During 2016, 2015 and 2014, our net sales to our five largest customers accounted for approximately 11.3%, 14.6% and 15.7% of total net sales, respectively. No customer accounted for more than 10.0% of our net sales during 2016, 2015 and 2014. No customer accounted for more than 10.0% of trade receivables at December 31, 2016 and 2014. As of December 31, 2015, one customer accounted for 10.6% of trade receivables. Although we have long-term relationships with many of our customers, our customers do not have a contractual obligation to purchase our products and we cannot be certain that we will be able to retain our existing major customers. Furthermore, the retail industry regularly experiences consolidation, contractions and closings which may result in our loss of customers or our inability to collect accounts receivable of major customers. If we lose a major customer, experience a significant decrease in sales to a major customer or are unable to collect the accounts receivable of a major customer, our business could be harmed.

ILLUSTRATION 8.20
Excerpt from Skechers' note on concentration of credit risk

This note to Skechers' financial statements indicates it has a relatively high concentration of credit risk. A default by any of these large customers could have a significant negative impact on its financial performance.

Evaluating Liquidity of Receivables

Investors and managers keep a watchful eye on the relationship among sales, accounts receivable, and cash collections. If sales increase, then accounts receivable are also expected to increase. But a disproportionate increase in accounts receivable might signal trouble. Perhaps the company increased its sales by loosening its credit policy, and these receivables may be difficult or impossible to collect. Such receivables are considered less liquid. Recall that liquidity is measured by how quickly certain assets can be converted to cash.

> **Decision Tools**
>
> The accounts receivable turnover and the average collection period help users determine if a company's collections are being made in a timely fashion.

The ratio that analysts use to assess the liquidity of receivables is the **accounts receivable turnover**, computed by dividing net credit sales (net sales less cash sales) by the average net accounts receivable during the year (see **Decision Tools**). This ratio measures the number of times, on average, a company collects receivables during the period. Unless seasonal factors are significant, **average** accounts receivable outstanding can be computed from the beginning and ending balances of the net receivables.[1]

A popular variant of the accounts receivable turnover is the **average collection period**, which measures the average amount of time that a receivable is outstanding. This is done by dividing the accounts receivable turnover into 365 days. Companies use the average collection period to assess the effectiveness of a company's credit and collection policies. The average collection period should not greatly exceed the credit term period (i.e., the time allowed for payment).

The following data (in millions) are available for **Nike**.

	For the Year Ended May 31,	
	2017	2016
Sales	$34,350	$32,376
Accounts receivable (net)	3,677	3,241

Illustration 8.21 shows the accounts receivable turnover and average collection period for Nike and **Skechers**. These calculations assume that all sales were credit sales.

ILLUSTRATION 8.21 Accounts receivable turnover and average collection period

$$\text{Accounts Receivable Turnover} = \frac{\text{Net Credit Sales}}{\text{Average Net Accounts Receivable}}$$

$$\text{Average Collection Period} = \frac{365}{\text{Accounts Receivable Turnover}}$$

Ratio	Nike ($ in millions)		Skechers USA
	2017	2016	2016
Accounts receivable turnover	$\frac{\$34{,}350}{(\$3{,}677 + \$3{,}241)/2} = 9.9$ times	9.8 times	10.6 times
Average collection period	$\frac{365 \text{ days}}{9.9} = 36.9$ days	37.2 days	34.4 days

Nike's accounts receivable turnover was 9.9 times in 2017, with a corresponding average collection period of 36.9 days. This was slightly faster than its 2016 collection period. It was slower than **Skechers**, which was 34.4 days. What this means is that Nike turned its receivables into cash more slowly than Skechers. Therefore, it might be less likely to pay its current obligations than a company with a quicker accounts receivable turnover (all else equal) and is more likely to need outside financing to meet cash shortfalls.

In some cases, accounts receivable turnover may be misleading. Some large retail chains that issue their own credit cards encourage customers to use these cards for purchases. If customers pay slowly, the stores earn a healthy return on the outstanding receivables in the form of interest at rates of 18% to 22%. On the other hand, companies that sell (factor) their receivables on a consistent basis will have a faster turnover than those that do not. Thus, to interpret accounts receivable turnover, you must know how a company manages its receivables. In general, the faster the turnover, the greater the reliability of the current ratio for assessing liquidity.

---

[1]If seasonal factors are significant, determine the average accounts receivable balance by using monthly or quarterly amounts.

Accelerating Cash Receipts

In the normal course of events, companies collect accounts receivable in cash and remove them from the books. However, as credit sales and receivables have grown in size and significance, the "normal course of events" has changed. Two common expressions apply to the collection of receivables: (1) "Time is money"—that is, waiting for the normal collection process costs money. (2) "A bird in the hand is worth two in the bush"—that is, getting the cash now is better than getting it later or not at all. Therefore, in order to accelerate the receipt of cash from receivables, companies frequently sell their receivables to another company for cash, thereby shortening the cash-to-cash operating cycle.

There are three reasons for the sale of receivables. The first is their **size**. In recent years, for competitive reasons, sellers (retailers, wholesalers, and manufacturers) often have provided financing to purchasers of their goods. For example, many major companies in the automobile, truck, industrial and farm equipment, computer, and appliance industries have created companies that accept responsibility for accounts receivable financing. **Caterpillar** has **Caterpillar Financial Services**, **General Electric** has **GE Capital**, and **Ford** has **Ford Motor Credit Corp. (FMCC)**. These companies are referred to as **captive finance companies** because they are owned by the company selling the product. The purpose of captive finance companies is to encourage the sale of the company's products by assuring financing to buyers. However, the parent companies involved do not necessarily want to hold large amounts of receivables, so they may sell them.

Second, **companies may sell receivables because they may be the only reasonable source of cash**. When credit is tight, companies may not be able to borrow money in the usual credit markets. Even if credit is available, the cost of borrowing may be prohibitive.

A final reason for selling receivables is that **billing and collection are often time-consuming and costly**. As a result, it is often easier for a retailer to sell the receivables to another party that has expertise in billing and collection matters. Credit card companies such as **MasterCard**, **Visa**, **American Express**, and **Discover** specialize in billing and collecting accounts receivable.

Illustration 8.22 summarizes the basic principles of managing accounts receivable.

ILLUSTRATION 8.22 Managing receivables

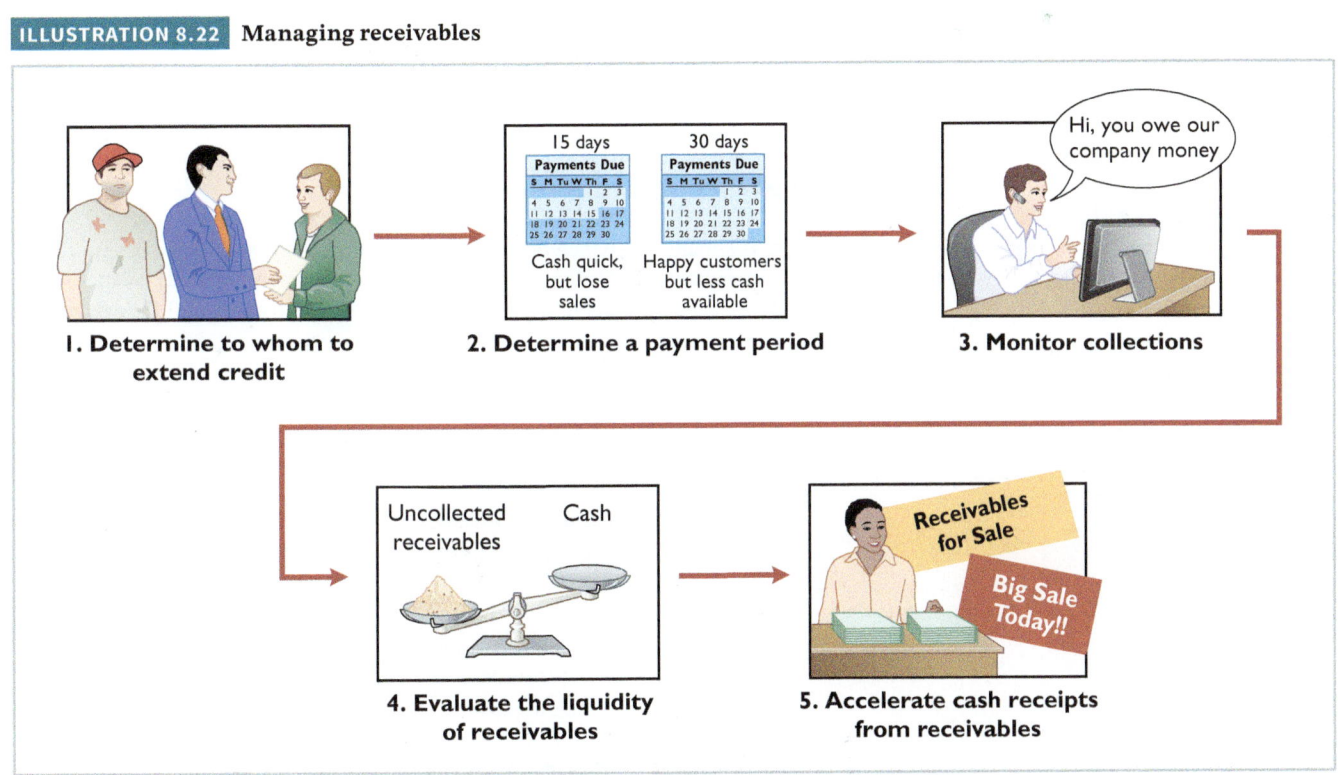

Data Analytics and Receivables Management

Opportunities abound to improve receivables management through data analytics. Software packages promise increases in working capital, improved revenues, and enhanced customer relations. So-called visualization software, which presents data in sophisticated graph format, enables managers to more quickly identify issues and obtain a deeper understanding of the factors that influence successful receivables management. Use of such software helps identify which currencies, sales representatives, customers, product lines, or geographic regions need closer attention. This sometimes enables management to do a more granular investigation of the cash-to-cash cycle time (discussed in Chapter 5) to evaluate which product lines are meeting company goals.

Data analytics of receivables is particularly valuable for predictive analysis which allows improved evaluation of customers' risk profiles. In many instances, the company can identify risky customers and take corrective action before problems arise. Software provided by companies such as **Workday** use artificial intelligence to forecast which customers are likely to pay late.

Keeping an Eye on Cash

A lot of companies report strong sales growth but have cash flow problems. How can this be? The reason for the difference is timing: Sales revenue is recorded when goods are delivered even if cash is not received until later. For example, **Nike** had sales of $34,350 million during 2017. Does that mean it received cash of $34,350 million from its customers? Most likely not. So how do we determine the amount of cash related to sales revenue that is actually received from customers? We analyze the changes that take place in Accounts Receivable.

To illustrate, suppose Bestor Corporation started the year with $10,000 in accounts receivable. During the year, it had credit sales of $100,000. At the end of the year, the balance in accounts receivable was $25,000. As a result, accounts receivable increased $15,000 during the year. How much cash did Bestor collect from customers during the year? Using the following T-account, we can determine that collections were $85,000.

Accounts Receivable

Beginning balance	10,000	85,000	Collections
Sales	100,000		
Ending balance	25,000		

As shown, the difference between sales and cash collections is explained by the change in Accounts Receivable. Accounts Receivable increased by $15,000. Therefore, since credit sales were $100,000, cash collections were only $85,000.

To illustrate another situation, let's use Nike. Recall that it had net credit sales of $34,350 million. Its ending receivables balance was $3,677 million, and its beginning receivables balance was $3,241 million—an increase of $436 million. Given this change, we can determine that the cash collected from customers during the year was $33,914 million ($34,350 − $436). This is shown in the following T-account.

Accounts Receivable

Beginning balance	3,241	33,914	Collections
Sales	34,350		
Ending balance	3,677		

DO IT! 4 | Analysis of Receivables

In 2022, Lebron James Company had net credit sales of $923,795 for the year. It had a beginning accounts receivable (net) balance of $38,275 and an ending accounts receivable (net) balance of $35,988. Compute Lebron James Company's (a) accounts receivable turnover and (b) average collection period in days.

ACTION PLAN

- Review the formula to compute the accounts receivable turnover.
- Make sure that both the beginning and ending accounts receivable are considered in the computation.
- Review the formula to compute the average collection period in days.

Solution

a.

$$\text{Net credit sales} \div \text{Average net accounts receivable} = \text{Accounts receivable turnover}$$

$$\$923{,}795 \div \frac{\$38{,}275 + \$35{,}988}{2} = 24.9 \text{ times}$$

b.

$$\text{Days in year} \div \text{Accounts receivable turnover} = \text{Average collection period in days}$$

$$365 \div 24.9 \text{ times} = 14.7 \text{ days}$$

Related exercise material: **BE8.11, BE8.12, DO IT! 8.4, E8.16,** and **E8.17.**

USING THE DECISION TOOLS | adidas

Suppose the following information was taken from the 2017 financial statements of **adidas**. Similar to **Nike** and **Skechers**, adidas sells shoes as well as other products.

adidas AG
Selected Financial Information
(in millions)

	2017	2016
Sales	€14,534	€14,203
Accounts receivable (net)	€ 1,946	€ 1,809
Total current assets	€ 7,347	€ 6,857
Total current liabilities	€ 4,378	€ 4,732

Instructions

Comment on adidas' accounts receivable management and liquidity relative to that of Nike, using (a) the current ratio and (b) the accounts receivable turnover and average collection period. Nike's current ratio was 2.80:1. The other ratio values for Nike were calculated earlier in the chapter.

Solution

a. Here is the 2017 current ratio (Current assets ÷ Current liabilities) for each company.

Nike	adidas
2.80:1	$\dfrac{\$7{,}347}{\$4{,}378} = 1.68{:}1$

Based on the assumed information for adidas, Nike's current ratio far exceeds that of adidas. In fact, Nike's might be excessive. A company of its size would not normally want to have so much capital tied up in current assets.

b. The accounts receivable turnover and average collection period for each company are:

	Nike	adidas
Accounts receivable turnover	9.9 times	$\dfrac{\$14{,}534}{(\$1{,}946 + \$1{,}809)/2} = 7.7$ times
Average collection period	36.9 days	$\dfrac{365}{7.7} = 47.4$ days

Based on the assumed information for adidas, its accounts receivable turnover of 7.7 compared to Nike's 9.9, and its average collection period of 47.4 days versus Nike's 36.9 days, suggest that adidas is able to collect from its customers slightly less quickly. It is important to note, however, that adidas is a German company. It reports under IFRS. A thorough comparison of adidas and Nike would require consideration of differences in the treatment of accounts receivable under IFRS and GAAP.

Review and Practice

Learning Objectives Review

1 Explain how companies recognize accounts receivable.

Receivables are frequently classified as accounts, notes, and other. Accounts receivable are amounts customers owe on account. Notes receivable represent claims that are evidenced by formal instruments of credit. Other receivables include nontrade receivables such as interest receivable, loans to company officers, advances to employees, and income taxes refundable.

Companies record accounts receivable when they perform a service on account or at the point-of-sale of merchandise on account. Sales returns and allowances and cash discounts reduce the amount received on accounts receivable.

2 Describe how companies value accounts receivable and record their disposition.

The two methods of accounting for uncollectible accounts are the allowance method and the direct write-off method. Under the allowance method, companies estimate uncollectible accounts as a percentage of receivables. It emphasizes the cash realizable value of the accounts receivable. An aging schedule is frequently used with this approach.

3 Explain how companies recognize, value, and dispose of notes receivable.

The formula for computing interest is Face value of note × Annual interest rate × Time in terms of one year. Notes can be held to maturity, at which time the borrower (maker) pays the face value plus accrued interest and the payee removes the note from the accounts. In many cases, however, similar to accounts receivable, the holder of the note speeds up the conversion by selling the receivable to another party. In some situations, the maker of the note dishonors the note (defaults), and the note is written off.

4 Describe the statement presentation of receivables and the principles of receivables management.

Companies should identify each major type of receivable in the balance sheet or in the notes to the financial statements. Short-term receivables are considered current assets. Companies report the gross amount of receivables and the allowance for doubtful accounts. They report bad debt and service charge expenses in the income statement as operating (selling) expenses, and interest revenue as other revenues and gains in the nonoperating section of the statement.

To properly manage receivables, management must (a) determine to whom to extend credit, (b) establish a payment period, (c) monitor collections, (d) evaluate the liquidity of receivables, and (e) accelerate cash receipts from receivables when necessary. The accounts receivable turnover and the average collection period both are useful in analyzing management's effectiveness in managing receivables. The accounts receivable aging schedule also provides useful information. If the company needs additional cash, management can accelerate the collection of cash from receivables by selling (factoring) its receivables or by allowing customers to pay with bank credit cards.

Decision Tools Review

Decision Checkpoints	Info Needed for Decision	Tool to Use for Decision	How to Evaluate Results
Is the amount of past due accounts increasing? Which accounts require management's attention?	List of outstanding receivables and their due dates	Prepare an aging schedule showing the receivables in various stages: outstanding 0–30 days, 31–60 days, 61–90 days, and over 90 days.	Accounts in the older categories require follow-up: letters, phone calls, and possible renegotiation of terms.
Is the company's credit risk increasing?	Customer account balances and due dates	Accounts receivable aging schedule	Compute and compare the percentage of receivables over 90 days old.
Does the company have significant concentrations of credit risk?	Note to the financial statements on concentrations of credit risk	If risky credit customers are identified, the financial health of those customers should be evaluated to gain an independent assessment of the potential for a material credit loss.	If a material loss appears likely, the potential negative impact of that loss on the company should be carefully evaluated, along with the adequacy of the allowance for doubtful accounts.
Are collections being made in a timely fashion?	Net credit sales and average net accounts receivable balance	$$\text{Accounts receivable turnover} = \frac{\text{Net credit sales}}{\text{Average net accounts receivable}}$$ $$\text{Average collection period} = \frac{365 \text{ days}}{\text{Accounts receivable turnover}}$$	Average collection period should be consistent with corporate credit policy. An increase may suggest a decline in financial health of customers.

Glossary Review

Accounts receivable Amounts customers owe on account. (p. 8-3).

Accounts receivable turnover A measure of the liquidity of accounts receivable, computed by dividing net credit sales by average net accounts receivable. (p. 8-22).

Aging the accounts receivable A schedule of customer balances classified by the length of time they have been unpaid. (p. 8-9).

Allowance method A method of accounting for bad debts that involves estimating uncollectible accounts at the end of each period. (p. 8-6).

Average collection period The average amount of time that a receivable is outstanding, calculated by dividing 365 days by the accounts receivable turnover. (p. 8-22).

Bad Debt Expense An expense account to record losses from extending credit. (p. 8-5).

Cash (net) realizable value The net amount a company expects to receive in cash from receivables. (p. 8-6).

Concentration of credit risk The threat of nonpayment from a single large customer or class of customers that could adversely affect the financial health of the company. (p. 8-21).

Direct write-off method A method of accounting for bad debts that involves charging receivable balances to Bad Debt Expense at the time receivables from a particular company are determined to be uncollectible. (p. 8-5).

Dishonored (defaulted) note A note that is not paid in full at maturity. (p. 8-17).

Factor A finance company or bank that buys receivables from businesses for a fee and then collects the payments directly from the customers. (p. 8-12).

Maker The party in a promissory note who is making the promise to pay. (p. 8-14).

Notes receivable Written promise (as evidenced by a formal instrument) for amounts to be received. (p. 8-3).

Other receivables Nontrade receivables that generally do not result from the operations of the business such as interest receivable and income taxes refundable. (p. 8-3)

Payee The party to whom payment of a promissory note is to be made. (p. 8-14).

Percentage-of-receivables basis A method of estimating the amount of bad debt expense whereby management establishes a percentage relationship between the amount of receivables and the expected losses from uncollectible accounts. (p. 8-9).

Promissory note A written promise to pay a specified amount of money on demand or at a definite time. (p. 8-14).

Receivables Amounts due from individuals and companies that are expected to be collected in cash. (p. 8-3).

Trade receivables Notes and accounts receivable that result from sales transactions. (p. 8-3).

Practice Multiple-Choice Questions

1. (**LO 1**) A receivable that is evidenced by a formal instrument and that normally requires the payment of interest is:

   a. an account receivable.
   b. a trade receivable.
   c. a note receivable.
   d. a classified receivable.

2. (**LO 1**) Receivables are frequently classified as:

   a. accounts receivable, company receivables, and other receivables.
   b. accounts receivable, notes receivable, and employee receivables.
   c. accounts receivable and general receivables.
   d. accounts receivable, notes receivable, and other receivables.

3. (**LO 1**) Kersee Company on June 15 sells merchandise on account to Eng Co. for $1,000, terms 2/10, n/30. On June 20, Eng Co. returns merchandise worth $300 to Kersee Company. On June 24, payment is received from Eng Co. for the balance due. What is the amount of cash received?

   a. $700.   c. $686.
   b. $680.   d. None of the above.

4. (**LO 2, 4**) Accounts and notes receivable are reported in the current assets section of the balance sheet at:

   a. cash (net) realizable value
   b. net book value.
   c. lower-of-cost-or-market value.
   d. invoice cost.

5. (**LO 2**) Net credit sales for the month are $800,000. The accounts receivable balance is $160,000. The allowance is calculated as 7.5% of the receivables balance using the percentage-of-receivables basis. If Allowance for Doubtful Accounts has a credit balance of $5,000 before adjustment, what is the balance after adjustment?

   a. $12,000.   c. $17,000.
   b. $7,000.   d. $31,000.

6. (**LO 2**) In 2022, Patterson Wholesale Company had net credit sales of $750,000. On January 1, 2022, Allowance for Doubtful Accounts had a credit balance of $18,000. During 2022, $30,000 of uncollectible accounts receivable were written off. Past experience indicates that the allowance should be 10% of the balance in receivables (percentage-of-receivables basis). If the accounts receivable balance at December 31 was $200,000, what is the required adjustment to Allowance for Doubtful Accounts at December 31, 2022?

   a. $20,000.   c. $32,000.
   b. $75,000.   d. $30,000.

7. (**LO 2**) An analysis and aging of the accounts receivable of Raja Company at December 31 reveal these data:

Accounts receivable	$800,000
Allowance for doubtful accounts per books before adjustment (credit)	50,000
Amounts expected to become uncollectible	65,000

What is the cash realizable value of the accounts receivable at December 31, after adjustment?

   a. $685,000.   c. $800,000.
   b. $750,000.   d. $735,000.

8. (**LO 2**) Which of these statements about **Visa** credit card sales is **incorrect**?

   a. The credit card issuer conducts the credit investigation of the customer.
   b. The retailer is not involved in the collection process.

c. The retailer must wait to receive payment from the issuer.

d. The retailer receives cash more quickly than it would from individual customers.

9. **(LO 2)** Good Stuff Retailers accepted $50,000 of **Citibank Visa** credit card charges for merchandise sold on July 1. Citibank charges 4% for its credit card use. The entry to record this transaction by Good Stuff Retailers will include a credit to Sales Revenue of $50,000 and a debit(s) to:

   a. Cash $48,000 and Service Charge Expense $2,000.
   b. Accounts Receivable $48,000 and Service Charge Expense $2,000.
   c. Cash $50,000.
   d. Accounts Receivable $50,000.

10. **(LO 2)** A company can accelerate its cash receipts by all of the following **except**:

    a. offering discounts for early payment.
    b. accepting national credit cards for customer purchases.
    c. selling receivables to a factor.
    d. writing off receivables.

11. **(LO 2)** Hughes Company has a credit balance of $5,000 in its Allowance for Doubtful Accounts before any adjustments are made at the end of the year. Based on review and aging of its accounts receivable at the end of the year, Hughes estimates that $60,000 of its receivables are uncollectible. The amount of bad debt expense which should be reported for the year is:

    a. $5,000.   c. $60,000.
    b. $55,000.   d. $65,000.

12. **(LO 2)** Use the same information as in Question 11, except that Hughes has a debit balance of $5,000 in its Allowance for Doubtful Accounts before any adjustments are made at the end of the year. In this situation, the amount of bad debt expense that should be reported for the year is:

    a. $5,000.   c. $60,000.
    b. $55,000.   d. $65,000.

13. **(LO 3)** Which of these statements about promissory notes is **incorrect**?

    a. The party making the promise to pay is called the maker.
    b. The party to whom payment is to be made is called the payee.
    c. A promissory note is not a negotiable instrument.
    d. A promissory note is more liquid than an account receivable.

14. **(LO 3)** Michael Co. accepts a $1,000, 3-month, 12% promissory note in settlement of an account with Tani Co. The entry to record this transaction is:

    a. Notes Receivable   1,030
         Accounts Receivable   1,030
    b. Notes Receivable   1,000
         Accounts Receivable   1,000
    c. Notes Receivable   1,000
         Sales Revenue   1,000
    d. Notes Receivable   1,020
         Accounts Receivable   1,020

15. **(LO 3)** Schleis Co. holds Murphy Inc.'s $10,000, 120-day, 9% note. The entry made by Schleis Co. when the note is collected, assuming no interest has previously been accrued, is:

    a. Cash   10,300
         Notes Receivable   10,300
    b. Cash   10,000
         Notes Receivable   10,000
    c. Accounts Receivable   10,300
         Notes Receivable   10,000
         Interest Revenue   300
    d. Cash   10,300
         Notes Receivable   10,000
         Interest Revenue   300

16. **(LO 4)** If a company is concerned about extending credit to a risky customer, it could do any of the following **except**:

    a. require the customer to pay cash in advance.
    b. require the customer to provide a letter of credit or a bank guarantee.
    c. contact references provided by the customer, such as banks and other suppliers.
    d. provide the customer a lengthy payment period to increase the chance of paying.

17. **(LO 4)** Eddy Corporation had net credit sales during the year of $800,000 and cost of goods sold of $500,000. The balance in receivables at the beginning of the year was $100,000 and at the end of the year was $150,000. What was the accounts receivable turnover and average collection period in days?

    a. 4.0 and 91.3 days.   c. 6.4 and 57 days.
    b. 5.3 and 68.9 days.   d. 8.0 and 45.6 days.

18. **(LO 4)** Prall Corporation sells its goods on terms of 2/10, n/30. It has an accounts receivable turnover of 7. What is its average collection period (days)?

    a. 2,555   c. 52
    b. 30   d. 210

Solutions

1. **c.** A note receivable represent claims for which formal instruments of credit are issued as evidence of the debt. The note normally requires the payment of the principal and interest on a specific date. Choices (a) account receivable, (b) trade receivable, and (d) classified receivable rarely require the payment of interest if paid within a 30-day period.

2. **d.** Receivables are frequently classified as accounts receivable, notes receivable, and other receivables. The other choices are incorrect because receivables are not frequently classified as (a) company receivables, (b) employee receivables, or (c) general receivables.

3. **c.** Because payment is made within the discount period of 10 days, the amount received is $700 ($1,000 − $300 return) minus the discount of $14 ($700 × 2%), for a cash amount of $686, not (a) $700 or (b) $680. Choice (d) is wrong as there is a correct answer.

4. **a.** Accounts and notes receivable are reported in the current assets section of the balance sheet at cash (net) realizable value, not (b) net book value, (c) lower-of-cost-or-market value, or (d) invoice cost.

5. a. The ending balance required in the allowance account is 7.5% × $160,000, or $12,000. Since there is already a balance of $5,000 in Allowance for Doubtful Accounts, the difference of $7,000 should be added, resulting in a balance of $12,000, not (b) $7,000, (c) $17,000, or (d) $31,000.

6. c. After the write-offs are recorded, Allowance for Doubtful Accounts will have a debit balance of $12,000 ($18,000 credit beginning balance combined with a $30,000 debit for the write-offs). The desired balance, using the percentage-of-receivables basis, is a credit balance of $20,000 ($200,000 × 10%). In order to have an ending balance of $20,000, the required adjustment to Allowance for Doubtful Accounts is $32,000, not (a) $20,000, (b) $75,000, or (d) $30,000.

7. d. The cash realizable value of the accounts receivable is Accounts Receivable ($800,000) less the expected ending balance in Allowance for Doubtful Accounts after adjustments ($65,000) = $735,000, not (a) $685,000, (b) $750,000, or (c) $800,000.

8. c. There is no wait for payment. The retailer receives payment at the time the credit card is accepted from the customer. The other choices are true statements.

9. a. The entry includes a credit to Sales Revenue for $50,000, a $48,000 debit to Cash, and a debit to Service Charge Expense for $2,000. The other choices are therefore incorrect.

10. d. Writing off receivables will result in a company failing to collect any money. Instead, choices (a) offering discounts for early payment, (b) accepting national credit cards for customer purchases, and (c) selling receivables to a factor will all allow a company to accelerate its cash receipts.

11. b. By crediting Allowance for Doubtful Accounts for $55,000, the new balance will be the required balance of $60,000. This adjusting entry debits Bad Debt Expense for $55,000 and credits Allowance for Doubtful Accounts for $55,000, not (a) $5,000, (c) $60,000, or (d) $65,000.

12. d. By crediting Allowance for Doubtful Accounts for $65,000, the new balance will be the required balance of $60,000. This adjusting entry debits Bad Debt Expense for $65,000 and credits Allowance for Doubtful Accounts for $65,000, not (a) $5,000, (b) $55,000, or (c) $60,000.

13. c. Promissory notes are negotiable instruments, meaning if sold, the seller can transfer to another party by endorsement. The other choices are true statements.

14. b. On the date Michael accepts the note, Notes Receivable is debited for $1,000 and Accounts Receivable is credited for $1,000. Interest is accrued only with the passage of time. The other choices are therefore incorrect.

15. d. When Schleis receives payment, it will increase cash, reduce the notes receivable account, and recognize interest earned for the term of the note. Interest = $10,000 × 9% × 120/360 = $300. Total cash received = $10,000 + $300 = $10,300. The other choices are therefore incorrect.

16. d. A longer payment period will increase the chances the customer will not pay. The other choices are incorrect as companies might require risky customers to (a) pay cash in advance, (b) provide letters of credit or bank guarantees, or (c) ask for references from banks and suppliers to determine their payment history.

17. c. Accounts receivable turnover = Net credit sales ($800,000) ÷ Average net accounts receivable [($100,000 + $150,000)/2] = 6.4. The average collection period in days = (365 ÷ 6.4) = 57 days. The other choices are therefore incorrect.

18. c. Average collection period = Number of days in the year (365) ÷ Accounts receivable turnover (7) = 52 days, not (a) 2.555, (b) 30, or (d) 210.

Practice Brief Exercises

1. (LO 1) Record the following transactions on the books of Gonzalez Co.

Record basic accounts receivable transactions.

a. On August 1, Gonzalez Co. sold merchandise on account to Miguel Inc. for $15,500, terms 1/10, n/30.

b. On August 8, Miguel Inc. returned merchandise worth $3,100 to Gonzalez Co.

c. On August 11, Miguel Inc. paid for the merchandise.

Solution

1. a.	Accounts Receivable	15,500	
	Sales Revenue		15,500
b.	Sales Returns and Allowances	3,100	
	Accounts Receivable		3,100
c.	Cash ($12,400 − $124)	12,276	
	Sales Discounts ($12,400 × 1%)	124	
	Accounts Receivable ($15,500 − $3,100)		12,400

2. (LO 2) Sanchez Co. uses the percentage-of-receivables basis in 2022 to record bad debt expense. It estimates that 3% of accounts receivable will become uncollectible. Sales revenues are $900,000 for 2022, and sales returns and allowances are $50,000 at December 31, 2022. Accounts receivable has a balance of $139,000, and the allowance for doubtful accounts has a credit balance of $3,000. Prepare the adjusting entry to record bad debt expense in 2022.

Prepare entry using percentage-of-receivables method.

Prepare entry for notes receivable exchanged for account receivable.

Solution

2. Bad Debt Expense [($139,000 × 3%) − $3,000]   1,170
    Allowance for Doubtful Accounts   1,170

3. **(LO 3)** On January 20, 2022, Carlos Co. sold merchandise on account to Carson Co. for $20,000, n/30. On February 19, Carson Co. gave Carlos Co. an 8% promissory note in settlement of this account. Prepare the journal entry to record the sale and the settlement of the account receivable.

Solution

Jan. 20	Accounts Receivable		20,000	
	Sales Revenue			20,000
Feb. 19	Notes Receivable		20,000	
	Accounts Receivable			20,000

Practice Exercises

Journalize entries to record allowance for doubtful accounts using two different bases.

1. **(LO 2)** The ledger of J.C. Cobb Company at the end of the current year shows Accounts Receivable $150,000, Sales Revenue $850,000, and Sales Returns and Allowances $30,000.

   Instructions

   a. If J.C. Cobb uses the direct write-off method to account for uncollectible accounts, journalize the adjusting entry at December 31, assuming J.C. Cobb determines that M. Jack's $1,500 balance is uncollectible.

   b. If Allowance for Doubtful Accounts has a credit balance of $2,400 in the trial balance, journalize the adjusting entry at December 31, assuming bad debts are expected to be 10% of accounts receivable.

   c. If Allowance for Doubtful Accounts has a debit balance of $200 in the trial balance, journalize the adjusting entry at December 31, assuming bad debts are expected to be 6% of accounts receivable.

Solution

1. a. Dec. 31	Bad Debt Expense		1,500	
	Accounts Receivable			1,500
b. Dec. 31	Bad Debt Expense		12,600	
	Allowance for Doubtful Accounts			
	[($150,000 × 10%) − $2,400]			12,600
c. Dec. 31	Bad Debt Expense		9,200	
	Allowance for Doubtful Accounts			
	[($150,000 × 6%) + $200]			9,200

Journalize entries for notes receivable transactions.

2. **(LO 3)** Troope Supply Co. has the following transactions related to notes receivable during the last 3 months of 2022.

   Oct. 1   Loaned $16,000 cash to Juan Vasquez on a 1-year, 10% note.
   Dec. 11 Sold goods to A. Palmer, Inc., receiving a $6,750, 90-day, 8% note.
        16 Received a $6,400, 6-month, 9% note in exchange for J. Nicholas's outstanding accounts receivable.
        31 Accrued interest revenue on all notes receivable.

   Instructions

   a. Journalize the transactions for Troope Supply Co.

   b. Record the collection of the Vasquez note at its maturity in 2023.

Solution

2. a.

			2022		
Oct. 1		Notes Receivable		16,000	
		Cash			16,000
Dec. 11		Notes Receivable		6,750	
		Sales Revenue			6,750
Dec. 16		Notes Receivable		6,400	
		Accounts Receivable			6,400
31		Interest Receivable		454	
		Interest Revenue*			454

*Calculation of interest revenue:

Vasquez's note:	$16,000 × 10% × 3/12 =	$400
Palmer's note:	6,750 × 8% × 20/360 =	30
Nicholas's note:	6,400 × 9% × 15/360 =	24
Total accrued interest		$454

b.

			2023		
Oct. 1		Cash		17,600	
		Interest Receivable			400
		Interest Revenue**			1,200
		Notes Receivable			16,000

**($16,000 × 10% × 9/12)

Practice Problem

(LO 1, 2, 3) Presented here are selected transactions related to B. Dylan Corp.

Prepare entries for various receivables transactions.

Mar. 1   Sold $20,000 of merchandise to Potter Company, terms 2/10, n/30.
       11   Received payment in full from Potter Company for balance due on existing accounts receivable.
       12   Accepted Juno Company's $20,000, 6-month, 12% note for balance due on outstanding account receivable.
       13   Made B. Dylan Corp. credit card sales for $13,200.
       15   Made Visa credit sales totaling $6,700. A 5% service fee is charged by Visa.
Apr. 11   Sold accounts receivable of $8,000 to Harcot Factor. Harcot Factor assesses a service charge of 2% of the amount of receivables sold.
       13   Received collections of $8,200 on B. Dylan Corp. credit card sales.
May 10   Wrote off as uncollectible $16,000 of accounts receivable. (B. Dylan Corp. uses the percentage-of-receivables basis to estimate bad debts.)
June 30   The balance in accounts receivable at the end of the first 6 months is $200,000. The company estimates that 10% of accounts receivable will become uncollectible. At June 30, the credit balance in the allowance account prior to adjustment is $3,500. Recorded bad debt expense.
July 16   One of the accounts receivable written off in May pays the amount due, $4,000, in full.

Instructions

Prepare the journal entries for the transactions. (Omit cost of goods sold entries.)

Solution*

Mar. 1		Accounts Receivable		20,000	
		Sales Revenue			20,000
		(To record sales on account)			
11		Cash		19,600	
		Sales Discounts (2% × $20,000)		400	
		Accounts Receivable			20,000
		(To record collection of accounts receivable)			

	12	Notes Receivable		20,000	
		Accounts Receivable			20,000
		(To record acceptance of Juno Company note)			
	13	Accounts Receivable		13,200	
		Sales Revenue			13,200
		(To record company credit card sales)			
	15	Cash		6,365	
		Service Charge Expense (5% × $6,700)		335	
		Sales Revenue			6,700
		(To record credit card sales)			
Apr.	11	Cash		7,840	
		Service Charge Expense (2% × $8,000)		160	
		Accounts Receivable			8,000
		(To record sale of receivables to factor)			
	13	Cash		8,200	
		Accounts Receivable			8,200
		(To record collection of accounts receivable)			
May	10	Allowance for Doubtful Accounts		16,000	
		Accounts Receivable			16,000
		(To record write-off of accounts receivable)			
June	30	Bad Debt Expense		16,500	
		Allowance for Doubtful Accounts			16,500
		[($200,000 × 10%) − $3,500]			
		(To record estimate of uncollectible accounts)			
July	16	Accounts Receivable		4,000	
		Allowance for Doubtful Accounts			4,000
		(To reverse write-off of accounts receivable)			
		Cash		4,000	
		Accounts Receivable			4,000
		(To record collection of accounts receivable)			

*Cost of goods sold entries are omitted here as well as in homework material.

WileyPLUS

Brief Exercises, DO IT! Exercises, Exercises, Problems, and many additional resources are available for practice in WileyPLUS.

Questions

1. What is the difference between an account receivable and a note receivable?

2. What are some common types of receivables other than accounts receivable or notes receivable?

3. What are the essential features of the allowance method of accounting for bad debts?

4. Lance Morrow cannot understand why the cash realizable value does not decrease when an uncollectible account is written off under the allowance method. Clarify this point for Lance.

5. Sarasota Company has a credit balance of $2,200 in Allowance for Doubtful Accounts before adjustment. The estimated uncollectibles under the percentage-of-receivables basis is $5,100. Prepare the adjusting entry.

6. What types of receivables does **Apple** report on its balance sheet? Does it use the allowance method or the direct write-off method to account for uncollectibles?

7. How are bad debts accounted for under the direct write-off method? What are the disadvantages of this method?

8. Tawnya Dobbs, the vice president of sales for Tropical Pools and Spas, wants the company's credit department to be less restrictive in granting credit. "How can we sell anything when you guys won't approve anybody?" she asks. Discuss the pros and cons of "easy credit." What are the accounting implications?

9. **JCPenney Company** accepts both its own credit cards and national credit cards. What are the advantages of accepting both types of cards?

10. An article in the *Wall Street Journal* indicated that companies are selling their receivables at a record rate. Why do companies sell their receivables?

11. **Calico Corners** decides to sell $400,000 of its accounts receivable to Fast Cash Factors Inc. Fast Cash Factors assesses a service charge of 3% of the amount of receivables sold. Prepare the journal entry that Calico Corners makes to record this sale.

12. Your roommate is uncertain about the advantages of a promissory note. Compare the advantages of a note receivable with those of an account receivable.

13. How may the maturity date of a promissory note be stated?

14. Compute the missing amounts for each of the following notes.

Principal	Annual Interest Rate	Time	Total Interest
(a)	6%	60 days	$ 270
$60,000	(b)	5 months	$2,500
$50,000	11%	(c)	$2,750
$30,000	8%	3 years	(d)

15. Mendosa Company dishonors a note at maturity. What are the options available to the lender?

16. **General Motors Company** has accounts receivable and notes receivable. How should the receivables be reported on the balance sheet?

17. What are the steps to good receivables management?

18. How might a company monitor the risk related to its accounts receivable?

19. What is meant by a concentration of credit risk?

20. The president of Ericson Inc. proudly announces her company's improved liquidity since its current ratio has increased substantially from one year to the next. Does an increase in the current ratio always indicate improved liquidity? What other ratio or ratios might you review to determine whether or not the increase in the current ratio is an improvement in financial health?

21. Since hiring a new sales director, Tilton Inc. has enjoyed a 50% increase in sales. The CEO has also noticed, however, that the company's average collection period has increased from 17 days to 38 days. What might be the cause of this increase? What are the implications to management of this increase?

22. Assume **The Coca-Cola Company**'s accounts receivable turnover was 9.05, and its average amount of net receivables during the period was $3,424 million. What is the amount of its net credit sales for the period? What is the average collection period in days?

23. Douglas Corp. has experienced tremendous sales growth this year, but it is always short of cash. What is one explanation for this occurrence?

24. How can the amount of collections from customers be determined?

Brief Exercises

BE8.1 (LO 1), C Presented below are three receivables transactions. Indicate whether these receivables are reported as accounts receivable, notes receivable, or other receivables on a balance sheet.

Identify different types of receivables.

a. Advanced $10,000 to an employee.
b. Received a promissory note of $34,000 for services performed.
c. Sold merchandise on account for $60,000 to a customer.

BE8.2 (LO 1), AP Record the following transactions on the books of Jarvis Co. (Omit cost of goods sold entries.)

Record basic accounts receivable transactions.

a. On July 1, Jarvis Co. sold merchandise on account to Stacey Inc. for $23,000, terms 2/10, n/30.
b. On July 8, Stacey Inc. returned merchandise worth $2,400 to Jarvis Co.
c. On July 11, Stacey Inc. paid for the merchandise.

BE8.3 (LO 2), AP At the end of 2021, Safer Co. has accounts receivable of $700,000 and an allowance for doubtful accounts of $25,000. On January 24, 2022, it is learned that the company's receivable from Madonna Inc. is not collectible and therefore management authorizes a write-off of $4,300.

Prepare entry for write-off, and determine cash realizable value.

a. Prepare the journal entry to record the write-off.
b. What is the cash realizable value of the accounts receivable (1) before the write-off and (2) after the write-off?

BE8.4 (LO 2), AP Assume the same information as BE8.3 and that on March 4, 2022, Safer Co. receives payment of $4,300 in full from Madonna Inc. Prepare the journal entries to record this transaction.

Prepare entries for collection of bad debt write-off.

BE8.5 (LO 2), AP Byrd Co. uses the percentage-of-receivables basis to record bad debt expense and concludes that 2% of accounts receivable will become uncollectible. Accounts receivable are $400,000 at the end of the year, and the allowance for doubtful accounts has a credit balance of $2,800.

Prepare entry using percentage-of-receivables method.

a. Prepare the adjusting journal entry to record bad debt expense for the year.
b. If the allowance for doubtful accounts had a debit balance of $900 instead of a credit balance of $2,800, prepare the adjusting journal entry for bad debt expense.

Prepare entry using the percentage-of-receivables method.

BE8.6 (LO 2), AP Bayfiew Corp uses the percentage-of-receivables basis to record bad debt expense.

Accounts receivable (ending balance)	$550,000 (debit)
Allowance for doubtful accounts (unadjusted)	4,200 (debit)

The company estimates that 3% of accounts receivable will become uncollectible.

a. Prepare the adjusting journal entry to record bad debt expense for the year.
b. What is the ending (adjusted) balance in Allowance for Doubtful Accounts?
c. What is the cash (net) realizable value?

Prepare entries for credit card sale and sale of accounts receivable.

BE8.7 (LO 2), AP Consider these transactions:

a. Tastee Restaurant accepted a Visa card in payment of a $200 lunch bill. The bank charges a 3% fee. What entry should Tastee make?
b. Martin Company sold its accounts receivable of $65,000. What entry should Martin make, given a service charge of 3% on the amount of receivables sold?

Compute interest and determine maturity dates on notes.

BE8.8 (LO 3), AP Compute interest and find the maturity date for the following notes.

	Date of Note	Principal	Interest Rate (%)	Terms
a.	June 10	$80,000	6%	60 days
b.	July 14	$50,000	7%	90 days
c.	April 27	$12,000	8%	75 days

Determine maturity dates and compute interest and rates on notes.

BE8.9 (LO 3), AN Presented below are data on three promissory notes. Determine the missing amounts.

	Date of Note	Terms	Maturity Date	Principal	Annual Interest Rate	Total Interest
a.	April 1	60 days	?	$600,000	9%	?
b.	July 2	30 days	?	90,000	?	$600
c.	March 7	6 months	?	120,000	10%	?

Prepare entry for note receivable exchanged for accounts receivable.

BE8.10 (LO 3), AP On January 10, 2022, Masterson Co. sold merchandise on account to Tompkins for $8,000, terms n/30. On February 9, Tompkins gave Masterson Co. a 7% promissory note in settlement of this account. Prepare the journal entry to record the sale and the settlement of the accounts receivable. (Omit cost of goods sold entries.)

Prepare entry for estimated uncollectibles and classifications, and compute ratios.

BE8.11 (LO 2, 4), AP During its first year of operations, Fertig Company had credit sales of $3,000,000, of which $400,000 remained uncollected at year-end. The credit manager estimates that $18,000 of these receivables will become uncollectible.

a. Prepare the journal entry to record the estimated uncollectibles. (Assume an unadjusted balance of zero in Allowance for Doubtful Accounts.)
b. Prepare the current assets section of the balance sheet for Fertig Company, assuming that in addition to the receivables it has cash of $90,000, merchandise inventory of $180,000, and supplies of $13,000.
c. Calculate the accounts receivable turnover and average collection period. Assume that average net accounts receivable were $300,000. Explain what these measures tell us.

Analyze accounts receivable.

BE8.12 (LO 4), AP Suppose the 2022 financial statements of **3M Company** report net sales of $23.1 billion. Accounts receivable (net) are $3.2 billion at the beginning of the year and $3.25 billion at the end of the year. Compute 3M's accounts receivable turnover. Compute 3M's average collection period for accounts receivable in days.

Determine cash collections.

BE8.13 (LO 4), AP Kennewick Corp. had a beginning balance in accounts receivable of $70,000 and an ending balance of $91,000. Credit sales during the period were $598,000. Determine cash collections.

DO IT! Exercises

Prepare entries to recognize accounts receivable.

DO IT! 8.1 (LO 1), AP On March 1, Lincoln sold merchandise on account to Amelia Company for $28,000, terms 1/10, net 45. On March 6, Amelia returns merchandise with a sales price of $1,000. On March 11, Lincoln receives payment from Amelia for the balance due. Prepare journal entries to record the March transactions on Lincoln's books. (Ignore cost of goods sold entries and explanations.)

DO IT! 8.2a (LO 2), AP Mantle Company has been in business several years. At the end of the current year, the unadjusted trial balance shows:

Accounts Receivable	$ 310,000 Dr.
Sales Revenue	2,200,000 Cr.
Allowance for Doubtful Accounts	5,700 Cr.

Bad debts are estimated to be 7% of receivables. Prepare the entry to adjust Allowance for Doubtful Accounts.

Prepare entry for uncollectible accounts.

DO IT! 8.2b (LO 2), AP Neumann Distributors is a growing company whose ability to raise capital has not been growing as quickly as its expanding assets and sales. Neumann's local banker has indicated that the company cannot increase its borrowing for the foreseeable future. Neumann's suppliers are demanding payment for goods acquired within 30 days of the invoice date, but Neumann's customers are slow in paying for their purchases (60–90 days). As a result, Neumann has a cash flow problem.

Neumann needs $160,000 to cover next Friday's payroll. Its balance of outstanding accounts receivable totals $800,000. To alleviate this cash crunch, the company sells $170,000 of its receivables. Record the entry that Neumann would make. (Assume a 2% service charge.)

Prepare entry for factored accounts.

DO IT! 8.3 (LO 3), AP Buffet Wholesalers accepts from Gates Stores a $6,200, 4-month, 9% note dated May 31 in settlement of Gates' overdue account. The maturity date of the note is September 30. What entry does Buffet make at the maturity date, assuming Gates pays the note and interest in full at that time?

Prepare entries for notes receivable.

DO IT! 8.4 (LO 4), AP In 2022, Bismark Company has net credit sales of $1,600,000 for the year. It had a beginning accounts receivable (net) balance of $108,000 and an ending accounts receivable (net) balance of $120,000. Compute Bismark Company's (a) accounts receivable turnover and (b) average collection period in days.

Compute ratios for receivables.

Exercises

E8.1 (LO 1), AP On January 6, Jacob Co. sells merchandise on account to Harley Inc. for $9,200, terms 1/10, n/30. On January 16, Harley pays the amount due.

Prepare entries for recognizing accounts receivable.

Instructions

Prepare the entries on Jacob Co.'s books to record the sale and related collection. (Omit cost of goods sold entries.)

E8.2 (LO 1), AP On January 10, Molly Amise uses her Lawton Co. credit card to purchase merchandise from Lawton Co. for $1,700. On February 10, Molly is billed for the amount due of $1,700. On February 12, Molly pays $1,100 on the balance due. On March 10, Molly is billed for the amount due, including interest at 1% per month on the unpaid balance as of February 12.

Prepare entries for recognizing accounts receivable.

Instructions

Prepare the entries on Lawton Co.'s books related to the transactions that occurred on January 10, February 12, and March 10. (Omit cost of goods sold entries.)

E8.3 (LO 1, 2), AP At the beginning of the current period, Rose Corp. had balances in Accounts Receivable of $200,000 and in Allowance for Doubtful Accounts of $9,000 (credit). During the period, it had net credit sales of $800,000 and collections of $763,000. It wrote off as uncollectible accounts receivable of $7,300. However, a $3,100 account previously written off as uncollectible was recovered before the end of the current period. Uncollectible accounts are estimated to total $25,000 at the end of the period. (Omit cost of goods sold entries.)

Journalize receivables transactions.

Instructions

a. Prepare the entries to record sales and collections during the period.
b. Prepare the entry to record the write-off of uncollectible accounts during the period.
c. Prepare the entries to record the recovery of the uncollectible account during the period.
d. Prepare the entry to record bad debt expense for the period.
e. Determine the ending balances in Accounts Receivable and Allowance for Doubtful Accounts.
f. What is the net realizable value of the receivables at the end of the period?

Journalize receivables transactions.

E8.4 (LO 1, 2), AP Assume the following information for Larry Corp.

Accounts receivable (beginning balance)	$142,000
Allowance for doubtful accounts (beginning balance)	11,360
Net credit sales	945,000
Collections	910,000
Write-offs of accounts receivable	5,200
Collections of accounts previously written off	1,900

Uncollectible accounts are expected to be 8% of the ending balance in accounts receivable.

Instructions

a. Prepare the entries to record sales and collections during the period.

b. Prepare the entry to record the write-off of uncollectible accounts during the period.

c. Prepare the entries to record the recovery of the uncollectible account during the period.

d. Determine the ending balance in Accounts Receivable and the unadjusted balance in Allowance for Doubtful Accounts.

e. Prepare the entry to record bad debt expense for the period.

f. Determine the ending (adjusted) balance in Allowance for Doubtful Accounts.

Prepare entries to record allowance for doubtful accounts.

E8.5 (LO 2), AP The ledger of Macarty Company at the end of the current year shows Accounts Receivable $78,000, Credit Sales $810,000, and Sales Returns and Allowances $40,000.

Instructions

a. If Macarty uses the direct write-off method to account for uncollectible accounts, journalize the adjusting entry at December 31, assuming Macarty determines that Matisse's $900 balance is uncollectible.

b. If Allowance for Doubtful Accounts has a credit balance of $1,100 in the trial balance, journalize the adjusting entry at December 31, assuming bad debts are expected to be 10% of accounts receivable.

c. If Allowance for Doubtful Accounts has a debit balance of $500 in the trial balance, journalize the adjusting entry at December 31, assuming bad debts are expected to be 8% of accounts receivable.

Determine bad debt expense, and prepare the adjusting entry.

E8.6 (LO 2), AP Godfreid Company has accounts receivable of $95,400 at March 31, 2022. Credit terms are 2/10, n/30. At March 31, 2022, there is a $2,100 credit balance in Allowance for Doubtful Accounts prior to adjustment. The company uses the percentage-of-receivables basis for estimating uncollectible accounts. The company's estimates of bad debts are as shown below.

	Balance, March 31		Estimated Percentage
Age of Accounts	2022	2021	Uncollectible
Current	$65,000	$75,000	2%
1–30 days past due	12,900	8,000	5
31–90 days past due	10,100	2,400	30
Over 90 days past due	7,400	1,100	50
	$95,400	$86,500	

Instructions

a. Determine the total estimated uncollectibles at March 31, 2022.

b. Prepare the adjusting entry at March 31, 2022, to record bad debt expense.

c. Discuss the implications of the changes in the aging schedule from 2021 to 2022.

Prepare entry for estimated uncollectibles, write-off, and recovery.

E8.7 (LO 2), AP On December 31, 2021, when its Allowance for Doubtful Accounts had a debit balance of $1,400, Dallas Co. estimates that 9% of its accounts receivable balance of $90,000 will become uncollectible and records the necessary adjustment to Allowance for Doubtful Accounts. On May 11, 2022, Dallas Co. determined that B. Jared's account was uncollectible and wrote off $1,200. On June 12, 2022, Jared paid the amount previously written off.

Instructions

Prepare the journal entries on December 31, 2021, May 11, 2022, and June 12, 2022.

E8.8 (LO 2), AP On March 3, Plume Appliances sells $710,000 of its receivables to Western Factors Inc. Western Factors Inc. assesses a service charge of 4% of the amount of receivables sold.

Prepare entry for sale of accounts receivable.

Instructions

Prepare the entry on Plume Appliances' books to record the sale of the receivables.

E8.9 (LO 2), AP On May 10, Keene Company sold merchandise for $4,000 and accepted the customer's Best Business Bank MasterCard. At the end of the day, the Best Business Bank MasterCard receipts were deposited in the company's bank account. Best Business Bank charges a 3.8% service charge for credit card sales.

Prepare entry for credit card sale.

Instructions

Prepare the entry on Keene Company's books to record the sale of merchandise.

E8.10 (LO 2), AP On July 4, Mazie's Restaurant accepts a Visa card for a $250 dinner bill. Visa charges a 4% service fee.

Prepare entry for credit card sale.

Instructions

Prepare the entry on Mazie's books related to the transaction.

E8.11 (LO 3), AP Moses Supply Co. has the following transactions related to notes receivable during the last 2 months of the year. The company does not make entries to accrue interest except at December 31.

Prepare entries for notes receivable transactions.

Nov.	1	Loaned $60,000 cash to C. Bohr on a 12-month, 7% note.
Dec.	11	Sold goods to K. R. Pine, Inc., receiving a $3,600, 90-day, 8% note.
	16	Received a $12,000, 180-day, 9% note to settle an open account from A. Murdock.
	31	Accrued interest revenue on all notes receivable.

Instructions

Journalize the transactions for Moses Supply Co. (Omit cost of goods sold entries.)

E8.12 (LO 3), AP These transactions took place for Bramson Co.

Journalize notes receivable transactions.

2021

| May | 1 | Received a $5,000, 12-month, 6% note in exchange for an outstanding account receivable from R. Stoney. |
| Dec. | 31 | Accrued interest revenue on the R. Stoney note. |

2022

| May | 1 | Received principal plus interest on the R. Stoney note. (No interest has been accrued since December 31, 2021.) |

Instructions

Record the transactions in the general journal. The company does not make entries to accrue interest except at December 31.

E8.13 (LO 3), AP Vandiver Company had the following select transactions.

Prepare entries for notes receivable transactions.

Apr. 1, 2022	Accepted Goodwin Company's 12-month, 6% note in settlement of a $30,000 account receivable.
July 1, 2022	Loaned $25,000 cash to Thomas Slocombe on a 9-month, 10% note.
Dec. 31, 2022	Accrued interest on all notes receivable.
Apr. 1, 2023	Received principal plus interest on the Goodwin note.
Apr. 1, 2023	Thomas Slocombe dishonored its note; Vandiver expects it will eventually collect.

Instructions

Prepare journal entries to record the transactions. Vandiver prepares adjusting entries once a year on December 31.

E8.14 (LO 4), AP Eileen Corp. had the following balances in receivable accounts at October 31, 2022 (in thousands): Allowance for Doubtful Accounts $52, Accounts Receivable $2,910, Other Receivables $189, and Notes Receivable $1,353.

Prepare a balance sheet presentation of receivables.

Instructions

Prepare the balance sheet presentation of Eileen Corp.'s receivables in good form.

Identify the principles of receivables management.

E8.15 (LO 4), K The following is a list of activities that companies perform in relation to their receivables.

1. Selling receivables to a factor.
2. Reviewing company ratings in *The Dun and Bradstreet Reference Book of American Business*.
3. Collecting information on competitors' payment period policies.
4. Preparing monthly accounts receivable aging schedule and investigating problem accounts.
5. Calculating the accounts receivable turnover and average collection period.

Instructions

Match each of the activities listed above with a purpose of the activity listed below.

a. Determine to whom to extend credit.
b. Establish a payment period.
c. Monitor collections.
d. Evaluate the liquidity of receivables.
e. Accelerate cash receipts from receivable when necessary.

Compute ratios to evaluate a company's receivables balance.

E8.16 (LO 4), AN Suppose the following information was taken from the 2022 financial statements of **FedEx Corporation**, a major global transportation/delivery company.

(in millions)	2022	2021
Accounts receivable (gross)	$ 3,587	$ 4,517
Accounts receivable (net)	3,391	4,359
Allowance for doubtful accounts	196	158
Sales revenue	35,497	37,953
Total current assets	7,116	7,244

Instructions

Answer each of the following questions.

a. Calculate the accounts receivable turnover and the average collection period for 2022 for FedEx.
b. Is accounts receivable a material component of the company's total current assets?
c. Evaluate the balance in FedEx's allowance for doubtful accounts.

Evaluate liquidity.

E8.17 (LO 4), AN The following ratios are available for Ming Inc.

	2022	2021
Current ratio	1.3:1	1.5:1
Accounts receivable turnover	12 times	10 times
Inventory turnover	11 times	9 times

Instructions

a. Is Ming's short-term liquidity improving or deteriorating in 2022? Be specific in your answer, referring to relevant ratios.
b. Do changes in turnover ratios affect profitability? Explain.
c. Identify any steps Ming might have taken, or might wish to take, to improve its management of its accounts receivable and inventory turnovers.

Identify reason for sale of receivables.

E8.18 (LO 4), C In a recent annual report, **Office Depot, Inc.** notes that the company entered into an agreement to sell all of its credit card program receivables to financial service companies.

Instructions

Explain why Office Depot, a financially stable company with positive cash flow, would choose to sell its receivables.

Determine cash flows and evaluate quality of earnings.

E8.19 (LO 4), AN Bailey Corp. significantly reduced its requirements for credit sales. As a result, sales during the current year increased dramatically. It had receivables at the beginning of the year of $38,000 and ending receivables of $191,000. Credit sales were $380,000.

Instructions

a. Determine cash collections during the period.
b. Discuss how your findings in part (a) would affect Bailey Corp.'s quality of earnings ratio. (Do not compute.)
c. What concerns might you have regarding Bailey's accounting?

E8.20 (LO 1, 2, 3, 4), K The following words and phrases were discussed in this chapter.

Identify key terms.

1. Notes receivable.
2. Cash (net) realizable value.
3. Accounts receivable turnover.
4. Aging the accounts receivable.
5. Percentage-of-receivables basis.
6. Dishonored (defaulted) note.
7. Concentration of credit risk.
8. Allowance method.
9. Direct write-off method.
10. Factor.

Instructions

Match each word or phrase with its description below.

a. _____ Written promise (as evidenced by a formal instrument) for amounts to be received.
b. _____ A method of accounting for bad debts that involves estimating uncollectible accounts at the end of each period.
c. _____ A measure of the liquidity of accounts receivable, computed by dividing net credit sales by average net accounts receivable.
d. _____ A method of accounting for bad debts that involves charging receivable balances to Bad Debt Expense at the time receivables from a particular company are determined to be uncollectible.
e. _____ A finance company or bank that buys receivables from businesses for a fee and then collects the payments directly from the customers.
f. _____ The net amount a company expects to receive in cash from receivables.
g. _____ The threat of nonpayment from a single large customer or class of customers that could adversely affect the financial health of the company.
h. _____ A note that is not paid in full at maturity.
i. _____ A method of estimating the amount of bad debt expense whereby management establishes a percentage relationship between the amount of receivables and the expected losses from uncollectible accounts.
j. _____ A schedule of customer balances classified by the length of time they have been unpaid.

Problems: Set A

P8.1A (LO 2), AP Rianna.com uses the allowance method of accounting for bad debts. The company produced the following aging of the accounts receivable at year-end.

Journalize transactions related to bad debts.

	Total	Number of Days Outstanding				
		0–30	31–60	61–90	91–120	Over 120
Accounts receivable	$377,000	$222,000	$90,000	$38,000	$15,000	$12,000
% uncollectible		1%	4%	5%	8%	10%
Estimated bad debts						

Instructions

a. Calculate the total estimated bad debts based on the above information.
b. Prepare the year-end adjusting journal entry to record the bad debts using the aged uncollectible accounts receivable determined in (a). Assume the unadjusted balance in Allowance for Doubtful Accounts is a $4,000 debit.
c. Of the above accounts, $5,000 is determined to be specifically uncollectible. Prepare the journal entry to write off the uncollectible account.
d. The company collects $5,000 subsequently on a specific account that had previously been determined to be uncollectible in (c). Prepare the journal entry(ies) necessary to restore the account and record the cash collection.
e. Comment on how your answers to (a)–(d) would change if Rianna.com used 3% of total accounts receivable, rather than aging the accounts receivable. What are the advantages to the company of aging the accounts receivable rather than applying a percentage to total accounts receivable?

a. Tot. est. bad debts $10,120

CHAPTER 8 Reporting and Analyzing Receivables

Prepare journal entries related to bad debt expense, and compute ratios.

P8.2A (LO 2, 4), AP At December 31, 2021, Suisse Imports reported this information on its balance sheet.

Accounts receivable	$600,000
Less: Allowance for doubtful accounts	37,000

During 2022, the company had the following transactions related to receivables.

1. Sales on account	$2,500,000
2. Sales returns and allowances	50,000
3. Collections of accounts receivable	2,200,000
4. Write-offs of accounts receivable deemed uncollectible	41,000
5. Recovery of bad debts previously written off as uncollectible	15,000

Instructions

a. Prepare the journal entries to record each of these five transactions. Assume that no cash discounts were taken on the collections of accounts receivable. (Omit cost of goods sold entries.)

b. A/R bal. $809,000

b. Enter the January 1, 2022, balances in Accounts Receivable and Allowance for Doubtful Accounts, post the entries to the two accounts (use T-accounts), and determine the balances.

c. Prepare the journal entry to record bad debt expense for 2022, assuming that aging the accounts receivable indicates that estimated bad debts are $46,000.

d. Compute the accounts receivable turnover and average collection period.

Journalize transactions related to bad debts.

P8.3A (LO 2), AP Presented below is an aging schedule for Bryan Company at December 31, 2021.

			Number of Days Past Due			
Customer	Total	Not Yet Due	1–30	31–60	61–90	Over 90
Aneesh	$ 24,000		$ 9,000	$15,000		
Bird	30,000	$ 30,000				
Cope	50,000	5,000	5,000		$40,000	
DeSpears	38,000					$38,000
Others	120,000	72,000	35,000	13,000		
	$262,000	$107,000	$49,000	$28,000	$40,000	$38,000
Estimated percentage uncollectible			3%	7%	12%	24%	60%
Total estimated bad debts	$ 42,400	$ 3,210	$ 3,430	$ 3,360	$ 9,600	$22,800

At December 31, 2021, the unadjusted balance in Allowance for Doubtful Accounts is a credit of $8,000.

Instructions

a. Bad Debt Exp. $34,400

a. Journalize and post the adjusting entry for bad debts at December 31, 2021. (Use T-accounts.)

b. Journalize and post to the allowance account these 2022 events and transactions:

1. March 1, a $600 customer balance originating in 2021 is judged uncollectible.

2. May 1, a check for $600 is received from the customer whose account was written off as uncollectible on March 1.

c. Journalize the adjusting entry for bad debts at December 31, 2022, assuming that the unadjusted balance in Allowance for Doubtful Accounts is a debit of $1,400 and the aging schedule indicates that total estimated bad debts will be $36,700.

Compute bad debt amounts.

P8.4A (LO 2), AP Writing Here is information related to Morgane Company for 2022.

Total credit sales	$1,500,000
Accounts receivable at December 31	840,000
Bad debts written off	37,000

Instructions

a. What amount of bad debt expense will Morgane Company report if it uses the direct write-off method of accounting for bad debts?

b. Bad Debt Exp. $30,600

b. Assume that Morgane Company uses the percentage-of-receivables basis to record bad debt expense and concludes that 4% of accounts receivable will become uncollectible. What amount of bad debt expense will the company record if Allowance for Doubtful Accounts has a credit balance of $3,000?

c. Assume the same facts as in part (b), except that there is a $1,000 debit balance in Allowance for Doubtful Accounts. What amount of bad debt expense will Morgane record?

d. What is a weakness of the direct write-off method of reporting bad debt expense?

P8.5A (LO 2), AP Writing At December 31, 2022, the trial balance of Malone Company contained the following amounts before adjustment.

Journalize entries to record transactions related to bad debts.

	Debit	Credit
Accounts Receivable	$180,000	
Allowance for Doubtful Accounts		$ 1,500
Sales Revenue		875,000

Instructions

a. Prepare the adjusting entry at December 31, 2022, to record bad debt expense, assuming that the aging schedule indicates that $10,200 of accounts receivable will be uncollectible.

b. Repeat part (a), assuming that instead of a credit balance there is a $1,500 debit balance in Allowance for Doubtful Accounts.

b. Bad Debt Exp. $11,700

c. During the next month, January 2023, a $2,100 account receivable is written off as uncollectible. Prepare the journal entry to record the write-off.

d. Repeat part (c), assuming that Malone Company uses the direct write-off method instead of the allowance method in accounting for uncollectible accounts receivable.

e. What are the advantages of using the allowance method in accounting for uncollectible accounts as compared to the direct write-off method?

P8.6A (LO 1, 3), AP On January 1, 2022, Harvee Company had Accounts Receivable of $54,200 and Allowance for Doubtful Accounts of $3,700. Harvee Company prepares financial statements annually. During the year, the following selected transactions occurred.

Journalize various receivables transactions.

Jan.	5	Sold $4,000 of merchandise to Rian Company, terms n/30.
Feb.	2	Accepted a $4,000, 4-month, 9% promissory note from Rian Company for balance due.
	12	Sold $12,000 of merchandise to Cato Company and accepted Cato's $12,000, 2-month, 10% note for the balance due.
	26	Sold $5,200 of merchandise to Malcolm Co., terms n/10.
Apr.	5	Accepted a $5,200, 3-month, 8% note from Malcolm Co. for balance due.
	12	Collected Cato Company note in full.
June	2	Collected Rian Company note in full.
	15	Sold $2,000 of merchandise to Gerri Inc. and accepted a $2,000, 6-month, 12% note for the amount due.

Instructions

Journalize the transactions. (Omit cost of goods sold entries.)

P8.7A (LO 4), C The president of Mossy Enterprises asks if you could indicate the impact certain transactions have on the following ratios.

Explain the impact of transactions on ratios.

Transaction	Current Ratio (2:1)	Accounts Receivable Turnover (10×)	Average Collection Period (36.5 days)
1. Received $5,000 on cash sale. The cost of the goods sold was $2,600.			
2. Recorded bad debt expense of $500 using allowance method.			
3. Wrote off a $100 account receivable as uncollectible (Uses allowance method.)			
4. Recorded $2,500 sales on account. The cost of the goods sold was $1,500.			

Instructions

Complete the table, indicating whether each transaction will increase (I), decrease (D), or have no effect (NE) on the specific ratios provided for Mossy Enterprises.

Prepare entries for various credit card and notes receivable transactions.

P8.8A (LO 1, 2, 3, 4), AP Milton Company closes its books on its July 31 year-end. The company does not make entries to accrue for interest except at its year-end. On June 30, the Notes Receivable account balance is $23,800. Notes Receivable include the following.

Date	Maker	Face Value	Term	Maturity Date	Interest Rate
April 21	Coote Inc.	$ 6,000	90 days	July 20	8%
May 25	Brady Co.	7,800	60 days	July 24	10%
June 30	BMG Corp.	10,000	6 months	December 31	6%

During July, the following transactions were completed.

July 5   Made sales of $4,500 on Milton credit cards.
     14   Made sales of $600 on Visa credit cards. The credit card service charge is 3%.
     20   Received payment in full from Coote Inc. on the amount due.
     24   Received payment in full from Brady Co. on the amount due.

Instructions

a. Journalize the July transactions and the July 31 adjusting entry for accrued interest receivable. (Interest is computed using 360 days; omit cost of goods sold entries.)

b. A/R bal. $ 4,500

b. Enter the balances at July 1 in the receivable accounts and post the entries to all of the receivable accounts. (Use T-accounts.)

c. Tot. receivables $14,550

c. Show the balance sheet presentation of the receivable accounts at July 31.

Calculate and interpret various ratios.

P8.9A (LO 4), AN Suppose the amounts presented here are basic financial information (in millions) from the 2022 annual reports of **Nike** and **adidas**.

	Nike	adidas
Sales revenue	$19,176.1	$10,381
Allowance for doubtful accounts, beginning	78.4	119
Allowance for doubtful accounts, ending	110.8	124
Accounts receivable balance (gross), beginning	2,873.7	1,743
Accounts receivable balance (gross), ending	2,994.7	1,553

Instructions

Calculate the accounts receivable turnover and average collection period for both companies. Comment on the difference in their collection experiences.

Continuing Case

© leungchopan/ Shutterstock

Cookie Creations

(*Note:* This is a continuation of the Cookie Creations case from Chapters 1 through 7.)

CC8 One of Natalie's friends, Curtis Lesperance, runs a coffee shop where he sells specialty coffees and prepares and sells muffins and cookies. He is eager to buy one of Natalie's fine European mixers, which would enable him to make larger batches of muffins and cookies. However, Curtis cannot afford to pay for the mixer for at least 30 days. He asks Natalie if she would be willing to sell him the mixer on credit. Natalie comes to you for advice.

Go to WileyPLUS for complete case details and instructions.

Comprehensive Accounting Cycle Review

ACR8 Hudson Corporation's balance sheet at December 31, 2021, is presented below.

Hudson Corporation
Balance Sheet
December 31, 2021

Cash	$13,100	Accounts payable	$ 8,750
Accounts receivable	19,780	Common stock	20,000
Allowance for doubtful accounts	(800)	Retained earnings	12,730
Inventory	9,400		
	$41,480		$41,480

During January 2022, the following transactions occurred. Hudson uses the perpetual inventory method.

Jan. 1 Hudson accepted a 4-month, 8% note from Betheny Company in payment of Betheny's $1,200 account.
3 Hudson wrote off as uncollectible the accounts of Walter Corporation ($450) and Drake Company ($280).
8 Hudson purchased $17,200 of inventory on account.
11 Hudson sold for $25,000 on account inventory that cost $17,500.
15 Hudson sold inventory that cost $700 to Jack Rice for $1,000. Rice charged this amount on his Visa First Bank card. The service fee charged Hudson by First Bank is 3%.
17 Hudson collected $22,900 from customers on account.
21 Hudson paid $16,300 on accounts payable.
24 Hudson received payment in full ($280) from Drake Company on the account written off on January 3.
27 Hudson purchased advertising supplies for $1,400 cash.
31 Hudson paid other operating expenses, $3,218.

Adjustment data:

1. Interest is recorded for the month on the note from January 1.
2. Bad debts are expected to be 6% of the January 31, 2022, accounts receivable.
3. A count of advertising supplies on January 31, 2022, reveals that $560 remains unused.
4. The income tax rate is 30%. (*Hint:* Prepare the income statement up to Income before taxes and multiply by 30% to compute the amount; round to whole dollars.)

Instructions

(You may want to set up T-accounts to determine ending balances.)

a. Prepare journal entries for the transactions listed above and adjusting entries. (Include entries for cost of goods sold using the perpetual inventory system.)
b. Prepare an adjusted trial balance at January 31, 2022.
c. Prepare an income statement and a retained earnings statement for the month ending January 31, 2022, and a classified balance sheet as of January 31, 2022.

Expand Your Critical Thinking

Financial Reporting Problem: Apple Inc.

CT8.1 Refer to the financial statements of Apple Inc. in Appendix A.

Instructions

a. Calculate the accounts receivable turnover and average collection period for 2017. (Assume all sales were credit sales.)
b. Did Apple have any potentially significant credit risks in 2017?
c. What conclusions can you draw from the information in parts (a) and (b)?

Comparative Analysis Problem: Columbia Sportswear Company vs. VF Corporation

CT8.2 The financial statements of Columbia Sportswear Company are presented in Appendix B. Financial statements of VF Corporation are presented in Appendix C.

Instructions

a. Based on the information contained in these financial statements, compute the following 2016 values for each company.
   1. Accounts receivable turnover. (For VF, use "Net sales." Assume all sales were credit sales.)
   2. Average collection period for accounts receivable.
b. What conclusions concerning the management of accounts receivable can be drawn from these data?

Comparative Analysis Problem: Amazon.com, Inc. vs. Wal-Mart Stores, Inc.

CT8.3 The financial statements of Amazon.com, Inc. are presented in Appendix D. Financial statements of Wal-Mart Stores, Inc. are presented in Appendix E.

Instructions

a. Based on the information contained in these financial statements, compute the following values for each company for the most recent fiscal year provided.

1. Accounts receivable turnover. (For Amazon.com, use "Net product sales." Assume all sales were credit sales.)
2. Average collection period for accounts receivable.

b. What conclusions concerning the management of accounts receivable can be drawn from these data?

Interpreting Financial Statements

CT8.4 Suppose the information below is from the 2022 financial statements and accompanying notes of The Scotts Company, a major manufacturer of lawn-care products.

(in millions)	2022	2021
Accounts receivable	$ 270.4	$ 259.7
Allowance for uncollectible accounts	10.6	11.4
Sales revenue	2,981.8	2,871.8
Total current assets	1,044.9	999.3

The Scotts Company
Notes to the Financial Statements

Note 19. Concentrations of Credit Risk

Financial instruments which potentially subject the Company to concentration of credit risk consist principally of trade accounts receivable. The Company sells its consumer products to a wide variety of retailers, including mass merchandisers, home centers, independent hardware stores, nurseries, garden outlets, warehouse clubs, food and drug stores and local and regional chains. Professional products are sold to commercial nurseries, greenhouses, landscape services and growers of specialty agriculture crops. Concentrations of accounts receivable at September 30, net of accounts receivable pledged under the terms of the New MARP Agreement whereby the purchaser has assumed the risk associated with the debtor's financial inability to pay ($146.6 million and $149.5 million for 2022 and 2021, respectively), were as follows.

	2022	2021
Due from customers geographically located in North America	53%	52%
Applicable to the consumer business	61%	54%
Applicable to Scotts LawnService®, the professional businesses (primarily distributors), Smith & Hawken® and Morning Song®	39%	46%
Top 3 customers within consumer business as a percent of total consumer accounts receivable	0%	0%

The remainder of the Company's accounts receivable at September 30, 2022 and 2021, were generated from customers located outside of North America, primary retailers, distributors, nurseries and growers in Europe. No concentrations of customers or individual customers within this group account for more than 10% of the Company's accounts receivable at either balance sheet date.

The Company's three largest customers are reported within the Global Consumer segment, and are the only customers that individually represent more than 10% of reported consolidated net sales for each of the last three fiscal years. These three customers accounted for the following percentages of consolidated net sales for the fiscal years ended September 30:

	Largest Customer	2nd Largest Customer	3rd Largest Customer
2022	21.0%	13.5%	13.4%
2021	20.2%	10.9%	10.2%
2020	21.5%	11.2%	10.5%

Instructions

Answer each of the following questions.

   a. Calculate the accounts receivable turnover and average collection period for 2022 for the company.
   b. Is accounts receivable a material component of the company's total 2022 current assets?
   c. Scotts sells seasonal products. How might this affect the accuracy of your answer to part (a)?
   d. Evaluate the credit risk of Scotts' 2022 concentrated receivables.
   e. Comment on the informational value of Scotts' Note 19 on concentrations of credit risk.

Real-World Focus

CT8.5 Purpose: To learn more about factoring.

Instructions

Go to the **Commercial Capital LLC** website, click on **Invoice Factoring**, and then answer the following questions.

   a. What are some of the benefits of factoring?
   b. What is the range of the percentages of the typical discount rate?
   c. If a company factors its receivables, what percentage of the value of the receivables can it expect to receive from the factor in the form of cash, and how quickly will it receive the cash?

CT8.6 The October 31, 2017, issue of the *Wall Street Journal* includes an article by Suzanne Kapner entitled "Inside the Decline of Sears, the Amazon of the 20th Century."

Instructions

Read the article and then answer the following questions.

   a. Describe some of the steps that suppliers took in response to the decline of **Sears'** credit quality.
   b. As its suppliers took the steps described in part (a), what were the implications for Sears' ability to compete as a retailer?
   c. How did companies that provide factoring services respond to Sears' troubles?

Decision-Making Across the Organization

CT8.7 Emilio and René Santos own Club Fandango. From its inception, Club Fandango has sold merchandise on either a cash or credit basis, but no credit cards have been accepted. During the past several months, the Santos have begun to question their credit-sales policies. First, they have lost some sales because of their refusal to accept credit cards. Second, representatives of two metropolitan banks have convinced them to accept their national credit cards. One bank, Business National Bank, has stated that (1) its credit card fee is 4% and (2) it pays the retailer 96 cents on each $1 of sales within 3 days of receiving the credit card billings.

The Santos decide that they should determine the cost of carrying their own credit sales. From the accounting records of the past 3 years, they accumulate these data:

	2022	2021	2020
Net credit sales	$500,000	$600,000	$400,000
Collection agency fees for slow-paying customers	2,900	2,600	1,600
Salary of part-time accounts receivable clerk	4,400	4,400	4,400

Credit and collection expenses as a percentage of net credit sales are as follows: uncollectible accounts 1.6%, billing and mailing costs .5%, and credit investigation fee on new customers .2%.

Emilio and René also determine that the average accounts receivable balance outstanding during the year is 5% of net credit sales. The Santos estimate that they could earn an average of 10% annually on cash invested in other business opportunities.

Instructions

With the class divided into groups, answer the following.

   a. Prepare a tabulation for each year showing total credit and collection expenses in dollars and as a percentage of net credit sales.

b. Determine the net credit and collection expenses in dollars and as a percentage of sales after considering the revenue not earned from other investment opportunities. (*Note:* The income lost on the cash held by the bank for 3 days is considered to be immaterial.)

c. Discuss both the financial and nonfinancial factors that are relevant to the decision.

Communication Activity

CT8.8 Chien Corporation is a recently formed business selling the "World's Best Doormat." The corporation is selling doormats faster than Chien can make them. It has been selling the product on a credit basis, telling customers to "pay when they can." Oddly, even though sales are tremendous, the company is having trouble paying its bills.

Instructions

Write a memo to the president of Chien Corporation discussing these questions:

a. What steps should be taken to improve the company's ability to pay its bills?

b. What accounting steps should be taken to measure its success in improving collections and in recording its collection success?

c. If the corporation is still unable to pay its bills, what additional steps can be taken with its receivables to ease its liquidity problems?

Ethics Case

CT8.9 As its year-end approaches, it appears that Mendez Corporation's net income will increase 10% this year. The president of Mendez Corporation, nervous that the stockholders might expect the company to sustain this 10% growth rate in net income in future years, suggests that the controller increase the allowance for doubtful accounts to 4% of receivables in order to lower this year's net income. The president thinks that the lower net income, which reflects a 6% growth rate, will be a more sustainable rate of growth for Mendez Corporation in future years. The controller of Mendez Corporation believes that the company's yearly allowance for doubtful accounts should be 2% of receivables.

Instructions

a. Who are the stakeholders in this case?

b. Does the president's request pose an ethical dilemma for the controller?

c. Should the controller be concerned with Mendez Corporation's growth rate in estimating the allowance? Explain your answer.

All About You

CT8.10 Credit card usage in the United States is substantial. Many startup companies use credit cards as a way to help meet short-term financial needs. The most common forms of debt for startups are use of credit cards and loans from relatives.

Suppose that you start up Fantastic Sandwich Shop. You invested your savings of $20,000 and borrowed $70,000 from your relatives. Although sales in the first few months are good, you see that you may not have sufficient cash to pay expenses and maintain your inventory at acceptable levels, at least in the short term. You decide you may need to use one or more credit cards to fund the possible cash shortfall.

Instructions

a. Go to the Internet and find two sources that provide insight into how to compare credit card terms.

b. Develop a list, in descending order of importance, as to what features are most important to you in selecting a credit card for your business.

c. Examine the features of your present credit card. (If you do not have a credit card, select a likely one online for this exercise.) Given your analysis above, what are the three major disadvantages of your present credit card?

FASB Codification Activity

CT8.11 If your school has a subscription to the FASB Codification, log in and prepare responses to the following.

a. How are receivables defined in the Codification?

b. What are the conditions under which losses from uncollectible receivables (Bad Debt Expense) should be reported?

A Look at IFRS

LEARNING OBJECTIVE 5
Compare the accounting for receivables under GAAP and IFRS.

The basic accounting and reporting issues related to the recognition, measurement, and disposition of receivables are very similar between IFRS and GAAP.

Key Points

Following are the key similarities and differences between GAAP and IFRS related to the accounting for receivables.

Similarities

- The recording of receivables, recognition of sales returns and allowances and sales discounts, and the allowance method to record bad debts are the same between GAAP and IFRS.
- Both IFRS and GAAP often use the term impairment to indicate that a receivable or a percentage of receivables may not be collected.
- The FASB and IASB have worked to implement fair value measurement (the amount they currently could be sold for) for financial instruments, such as receivables. Both Boards have faced bitter opposition from various factions.

Differences

- Although IFRS implies that receivables with different characteristics should be reported separately, there is no standard that mandates this segregation.
- IFRS has a different approach for estimating uncollectible accounts for receivables with a significant financing component (e.g., notes receivable). It differentiates based on whether the receivables have experienced a deterioration in credit quality.
- IFRS and GAAP differ in the criteria used to determine how to record a factoring transaction. IFRS uses a combination approach focused on risks and rewards and loss of control. GAAP uses loss of control as the primary criterion. In addition, IFRS permits partial derecognition of receivables; GAAP does not.

IFRS Practice

IFRS Self-Test Questions

1. Which of the following statements is **false**?
   a. Receivables include equity securities purchased by the company.
   b. Receivables include credit card receivables.
   c. Receivables include amounts owed by employees as a result of company loans to employees.
   d. Receivables include amounts resulting from transactions with customers.

2. In recording a factoring transaction:
   a. IFRS focuses on loss of control.
   b. GAAP focuses on loss of control and risks and rewards.
   c. IFRS and GAAP allow partial derecognition.
   d. IFRS allows partial derecognition.

3. Under IFRS:
   a. the entry to record estimated uncollected accounts is the same as GAAP.
   b. it is always acceptable to use the direct write-off method.
   c. all financial instruments are recorded at fair value.
   d. None of the above.

International Financial Reporting Problem: Louis Vuitton

IFRS8.1 The financial statements of **Louis Vuitton** are presented in Appendix F. The complete annual report, including the notes to its financial statements, is available at the company's website.

Instructions

Use the company's annual report to answer the following questions.

a. What is the accounting policy related to accounting for trade accounts receivable?

b. According to the notes to the financial statements, what accounted for the difference between gross trade accounts receivable and net accounts receivable?

c. According to the notes to the financial statements, what was the major reason why the balance in receivables increased relative to the previous year?

d. Using information in the notes to the financial statements, determine what percentage the provision for impairment of receivables was as a percentage of total trade receivables for 2016 and 2015. How did the ratio change from 2015 to 2016, and what does this suggest about the company's receivables?

Answers to IFRS Self-Test Questions

1. a **2.** d **3.** a

CHAPTER 9

Reporting and Analyzing Long-Lived Assets

Chapter Preview

For airlines and many other companies, making the right decisions regarding long-lived assets is critical because these assets represent huge investments. The discussion in this chapter is in two parts: plant assets and intangible assets. **Plant assets** are the property, plant, and equipment (physical assets) that commonly come to mind when we think of what a company owns. **Intangible assets**, such as copyrights and patents, lack physical substance but can be extremely valuable and vital to a company's success.

Feature Story

A Tale of Two Airlines

So, you're interested in starting a new business. Have you thought about the airline industry? Today, the most profitable airlines in the industry are not well-known majors like **American Airlines** and **United**. In fact, most giant, older airlines seem to be either bankrupt or on the verge of bankruptcy. In a recent year, five major airlines representing 24% of total U.S. capacity were operating under bankruptcy protection.

Not all airlines are hurting. The growth and profitability in the airline industry today is found at relative newcomers like **Southwest Airlines** and **JetBlue Airways**. These and other new airlines compete primarily on ticket prices. During a recent five-year period, the low-fare airline market share increased by 47%, reaching 22% of U.S. airline capacity.

Southwest was the first upstart to make it big. It did so by taking a different approach. It bought small, new, fuel-efficient planes. Also, instead of the "hub-and-spoke" approach used by the majors, it opted for direct, short hop, no frills flights. It was all about controlling costs—getting the most out of its efficient new planes.

JetBlue, founded by former employees of Southwest, was recently ranked as the number 1 airline in the United States by the airline rating company **SkyTrax**. Management initially attempted to differentiate JetBlue by offering amenities not found on other airlines, such as seatback entertainment systems, while adopting Southwest's low-fare model. This approach was successful during JetBlue's early years, as it enjoyed both profitability and rapid growth. However, more recently the company has had to take aggressive steps to rein in costs in order to return to profitability.

In the past, upstarts such as **ValuJet** chose a different approach. The company bought planes that were 20 to 30 years old (known in the industry as *zombies*), which allowed it to quickly add planes to its fleet. Valujet started with a $3.4 million investment and grew to be worth $630 million in its first three years.

But with high fuel costs, airlines are no longer in the market for old planes which generally can't be operated efficiently. Today, success in the airline business comes from owning the newest and most efficient equipment, and knowing how to get the most out of it.

Chapter Outline

LEARNING OBJECTIVES

LO 1 Explain the accounting for plant asset expenditures.	• Determining the cost of plant assets • Expenditures during useful life • To buy or lease?	**DO IT! 1** Cost of Plant Assets
LO 2 Apply depreciation methods to plant assets.	• Factors in computing depreciation • Depreciation methods • Revising depreciation • Impairments	**DO IT! 2a** Straight-Line Depreciation **DO IT! 2b** Revised Depreciation
LO 3 Explain how to account for the disposal of plant assets.	• Sale of plant assets • Retirement of plant assets	**DO IT! 3** Plant Asset Disposals
LO 4 Identify the basic issues related to reporting intangible assets.	• Accounting for intangible assets • Types of intangible assets	**DO IT! 4** Classification Concepts
LO 5 Discuss how long-lived assets are reported and analyzed.	• Presentation • Analysis	**DO IT! 5** Asset Turnover

Go to the Review and Practice section at the end of the chapter for a targeted summary and practice applications with solutions.
Visit WileyPLUS for additional tutorials and practice opportunities.

Plant Asset Expenditures

LEARNING OBJECTIVE 1
Explain the accounting for plant asset expenditures.

Plant assets are resources that have physical substance (a definite size and shape), are used in the operations of a business, and are not intended for sale to customers. They are called various names—property, plant, and equipment; plant and equipment; and fixed assets. By whatever name, these assets are expected to be of service to the company for a number of years. Except for land, plant assets decline in service potential (ability to produce revenue) over their useful lives.

Plant assets are critical to a company's success because they determine the company's capacity and therefore its ability to satisfy customers. With too few planes, for example, **JetBlue Airways** and **Southwest Airlines** would lose customers to their competitors. But with too many planes, they would be flying with empty seats. Management must constantly monitor its needs and acquire assets accordingly. Failure to do so results in lost business opportunities or inefficient use of existing assets and, eventually, poor financial results.

It is important for a company to (1) keep assets in good operating condition, (2) replace worn-out or outdated assets, and (3) expand its productive assets as needed. The decline of rail travel in the United States can be traced in part to the failure of railroad companies to maintain and update their assets. Conversely, the growth of air travel in this country can be attributed in part to the general willingness of airline companies to follow these essential guidelines.

For many companies, investments in plant assets are substantial. **Illustration 9.1** shows the percentages of plant assets in relation to total assets in various companies in a recent year.

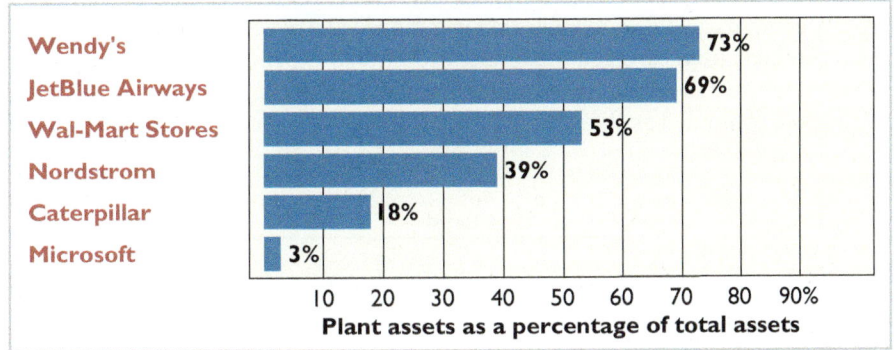

ILLUSTRATION 9.1
Percentages of plant assets in relation to total assets

Determining the Cost of Plant Assets

The **historical cost principle** requires that companies record plant assets at cost. Thus, JetBlue Airways and Southwest Airlines record their planes at cost. **Cost consists of all expenditures necessary to acquire an asset and make it ready for its intended use.** For example, when **Boeing** buys equipment, the purchase price, freight costs paid by Boeing, and installation costs are all part of the cost of the equipment.

Determining which costs to include in a plant asset account and which costs not to include is very important. If a cost is not included in a plant asset account, then it must be expensed immediately. Such costs are referred to as **revenue expenditures**. On the other hand, costs that are not expensed immediately but are instead included in a plant asset account are referred to as **capital expenditures**. JetBlue reported capital expenditures of $1,074 million during 2017.

This distinction is important; it has immediate, and often material, implications for the income statement. Some companies, in order to boost current income, have **improperly** capitalized expenditures that they should have expensed. For example, suppose that a company improperly capitalizes to a building account $1,000 of maintenance costs incurred at the end of the year. (That is, the costs are included in the asset account Buildings rather than being expensed immediately as Maintenance and Repairs Expense.) If the company is allocating the cost of the building as an expense (depreciating it) over a 40-year life, then the maintenance cost of $1,000 will be incorrectly spread across 40 years instead of being expensed in the current year. As a result, the company will understate current-year expenses by approximately $1,000 and will overstate current-year income by approximately $1,000. Thus, determining which costs to capitalize and which to expense is very important.

Cost is measured by the cash paid in a cash transaction or by the **cash equivalent price** paid when companies use noncash assets in payment. **The cash equivalent price is equal to the fair value of the asset given up or the fair value of the asset received, whichever is more clearly determinable** (see **International Note**). Once cost is established, it becomes the basis of accounting for the plant asset over its useful life. Current fair value is not used to increase the recorded cost after acquisition. We explain the application of the historical cost principle to each of the major classes of plant assets in the following sections.

> **International Note**
>
> IFRS is more flexible regarding asset valuation. Companies revalue to fair value when they believe this information is more relevant.

Land

Companies often use land as a building site for a manufacturing plant or office site. The cost of land includes (1) the cash purchase price, (2) closing costs such as title and attorney's fees, (3) real estate brokers' commissions, and (4) accrued property taxes and other liens on the land assumed by the purchaser. For example, if the cash price is $50,000 and the purchaser agrees to pay accrued property taxes of $5,000, the cost of the land is $55,000.

All necessary costs incurred in making land **ready for its intended use** increase (debit) the Land account. When a company acquires vacant land, its cost includes expenditures for clearing, draining, filling, and grading. If the land has a building on it that must be removed to make the site suitable for construction of a new building, the company includes all demolition and removal costs, less any proceeds from salvaged materials, in the Land account.

To illustrate, assume that Hayes Company acquires real estate at a cash cost of $100,000. The property contains an old warehouse that is removed at a net cost of $6,000 ($7,500 in costs less $1,500 proceeds from salvaged materials). Additional expenditures are for the attorney's fee $1,000 and the real estate broker's commission $8,000. Given these factors, the cost of the land is $115,000, computed as shown in **Illustration 9.2**.

ILLUSTRATION 9.2
Computation of cost of land

Land	
Cash price of property	$100,000
Net removal cost of warehouse	6,000
Attorney's fee	1,000
Real estate broker's commission	8,000
Cost of land	**$115,000**

When Hayes records the acquisition, it debits Land and credits Cash for $115,000.

Land Improvements

Land improvements are structural additions with limited lives that are made to land, such as driveways, parking lots, fences, landscaping, and underground sprinklers. The cost of land improvements includes all expenditures necessary to make the improvements ready for their intended use. For example, the cost of a new company parking lot includes the amount paid for paving, fencing, and lighting. Thus, the company would debit the total of all of these costs to Land Improvements.

Land improvements have limited useful lives. Even when well-maintained, they will eventually need to be replaced. As a result, companies expense (depreciate) the cost of land improvements over their useful lives.

Buildings

Buildings are facilities used in operations, such as stores, offices, factories, warehouses, and airplane hangars. Companies charge to the Buildings account all necessary expenditures relating to the purchase or construction of a building. When a building is **purchased**, such costs include the purchase price, closing costs (attorney's fees, title insurance, etc.), and real estate broker's commission. Costs to make the building ready for its intended use consist of expenditures for remodeling rooms and offices and replacing or repairing the roof, floors, electrical wiring, and plumbing. When a new building is **constructed**, its cost consists of the contract price plus payments made by the owner for architects' fees, building permits, and excavation costs.

In addition, companies add certain interest costs to the cost of a building. Interest costs incurred to finance a construction project are included in the cost of the asset when a significant period of time is required to get the asset ready for use. In these circumstances, interest costs are considered as necessary as materials and labor. However, the inclusion of interest costs in the cost of a constructed building is **limited to interest costs incurred during the construction period**. When construction has been completed, subsequent interest payments on funds borrowed to finance the construction are recorded as increases (debits) to Interest Expense.

Equipment

Equipment includes assets used in operations, such as store check-out counters, office furniture, factory machinery, and delivery trucks. **JetBlue Airways**' equipment includes aircraft, in-flight entertainment systems, and trucks for ground operations. The cost of equipment consists of the cash purchase price, sales taxes, freight charges, and insurance during transit paid by the purchaser. It also includes expenditures required in assembling, installing, and testing the unit. However, companies treat as expenses the costs of motor vehicle licenses and accident insurance on company trucks and cars. Such items are **annual recurring expenditures and do not benefit future periods**. Two criteria apply in determining the cost of equipment: (1) the frequency of the cost—one time or recurring, and (2) the benefit period—the life of the asset or one year.

To illustrate, assume that Lenard Company purchases a delivery truck on January 1 at a cash price of $22,000. Related expenditures are sales taxes $1,320, painting and lettering $500, motor vehicle license $80, and a three-year accident insurance policy $1,600. The cost of the delivery truck is $23,820, computed as shown in **Illustration 9.3**.

Delivery Truck	
Cash price	$22,000
Sales taxes	1,320
Painting and lettering	500
Cost of delivery truck	**$23,820**

ILLUSTRATION 9.3
Computation of cost of delivery truck

Lenard treats the cost of a motor vehicle license as an expense and the cost of an insurance policy as a prepaid asset. Thus, the company records the purchase of the truck and related expenditures as follows.

Equipment	23,820	
License Expense	80	
Prepaid Insurance	1,600	
Cash		25,500
(To record purchase of delivery truck and related expenditures)		

A = L + SE
+23,820
               −80 Exp
+1,600
−25,500

Cash Flows
−25,500

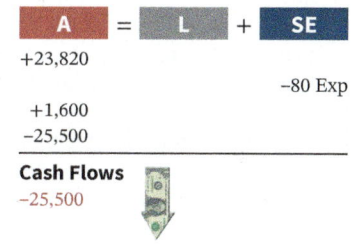

For another example, assume Merten Company purchases factory machinery at a cash price of $50,000. Related expenditures are sales taxes $3,000, insurance during shipping $500, and installation and testing $1,000. The cost of the factory machinery is $54,500, computed as shown in **Illustration 9.4**.

ILLUSTRATION 9.4
Computation of cost of factory machinery

Factory Machinery	
Cash price	$50,000
Sales taxes	3,000
Insurance during shipping	500
Installation and testing	1,000
Cost of factory machinery	**$54,500**

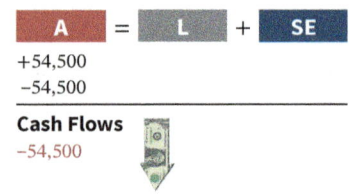

Thus, Merten records the purchase and related expenditures as follows.

Equipment	54,500	
Cash		54,500
(To record purchase of factory machinery and related expenditures)		

Expenditures During Useful Life

During the useful life of a plant asset, a company may incur costs for ordinary repairs, additions, and improvements. **Ordinary repairs** are expenditures to maintain the operating efficiency and expected productive life of the unit. They usually are fairly small amounts that occur frequently throughout the service life. Examples are motor tune-ups and oil changes, the painting of buildings, and the replacing of worn-out gears on factory machinery. Ordinary repairs are debited to Maintenance and Repairs Expense as incurred.

In contrast, **additions and improvements** are costs incurred to **increase** the operating efficiency, productive capacity, or expected useful life of the plant asset. These expenditures are usually material in amount and occur infrequently during the period of ownership. Expenditures for additions and improvements increase the company's investment in productive facilities and are generally debited to the plant asset affected. Thus, they are **capital expenditures**. The accounting for capital expenditures varies depending on the nature of the expenditure.

Northwest Airlines at one time spent $120 million to spruce up 40 jets. The improvements were designed to extend the lives of the planes, meet stricter government noise limits, and save money. The capital expenditure was expected to extend the life of the jets by 10 to 15 years and save about $560 million compared to the cost of buying new planes. The jets were, on average, 24 years old.

Anatomy of a Fraud

Bernie Ebbers was the founder and CEO of the phone company **WorldCom**. The company engaged in a series of increasingly large, debt-financed acquisitions of other companies. These acquisitions made the company grow quickly, which made the stock price increase dramatically. However, because the acquired companies all had different accounting systems, WorldCom's financial records were a mess. When WorldCom's performance started to flatten out, Bernie coerced WorldCom's accountants to engage in a number of fraudulent activities to make net income look better than it really was and thus prop up the stock price. One of these frauds involved treating $7 billion of line costs as capital expenditures. The line costs, which were rental fees paid to other phone companies to use their phone lines, had always been properly expensed in previous years. Capitalization delayed expense recognition to future periods and thus boosted current-period profits.

Total take: $7 billion

The Missing Controls

Documentation procedures. The company's accounting system was a disorganized collection of non-integrated systems, which resulted from a series of corporate acquisitions. Top management took advantage of this disorganization to conceal its fraudulent activities.

Independent internal verification. A fraud of this size should have been detected by a routine comparison of the actual physical assets with the list of physical assets shown in the accounting records.

To Buy or Lease?

In this chapter, we focus on purchased assets, but we want to expose you briefly to an alternative—leasing. A **lease** is a contractual agreement in which the owner of an asset (the **lessor**) allows another party (the **lessee**) to use the asset for a period of time at an agreed price. In many industries, leasing is quite common. For example, one-third of heavy-duty commercial trucks are leased.

Some advantages of leasing an asset versus purchasing it are as follows.

1. **Reduced risk of obsolescence.** Frequently, lease terms allow the party using the asset (the lessee) to exchange the asset for a more modern one if it becomes outdated. This is much easier than trying to sell an obsolete asset.
2. **Little or no down payment.** To purchase an asset, most companies must borrow money, which usually requires a down payment of at least 20%. Leasing an asset requires little or no down payment.
3. **Shared tax advantages.** Startup companies typically earn little or no profit in their early years, and so they have little need for the tax deductions available from owning an asset. In a lease, the lessor gets the tax advantage because it owns the asset. It often will pass these tax savings on to the lessee in the form of lower lease payments.

Airlines often choose to lease many of their airplanes in long-term lease agreements. In recent financial statements, **JetBlue Airways** stated that it leased 50 of its 243 planes.

Accounting Across the Organization

Many U.S. Firms Use Leases

© Brian Raisbeck/iStockphoto

Leasing is big business for U.S. companies. For example, in a recent year leasing accounted for about 33% of all business investment ($264 billion).

Who does the most leasing? Interestingly, major banks such as **Continental Bank**, **J.P. Morgan Leasing**, and **US Bancorp Equipment Finance** are the major lessors. Also, many companies have established separate leasing companies, such as **Boeing Capital Corporation**, **Dell Financial Services**, and **John Deere Capital Corporation**. As an example of the magnitude of leasing, leased planes account for nearly 40% of the U.S. fleet of commercial airlines. **Lease Finance Corporation** in Los Angeles owns more planes than any airline in the world.

Leasing is also becoming increasingly common in the hotel industry. **Marriott**, **Hilton**, and **InterContinental** are increasingly choosing to lease hotels that are owned by someone else.

Why might airline managers choose to lease rather than purchase their planes? (Go to WileyPLUS for this answer and additional questions.)

DO IT! 1 | Cost of Plant Assets

Assume that Drummond Corp. purchases a delivery truck for $15,000 cash plus sales taxes of $900 and delivery costs of $500. The buyer also pays $200 for painting and lettering, $600 for an annual insurance policy, and $80 for a motor vehicle license. Explain how the company should account for each of these costs.

ACTION PLAN
- Identify expenditures made in order to get delivery equipment ready for its intended use.
- Expense operating costs incurred during the useful life of the equipment.

Solution

The first four payments ($15,000 purchase price, $900 sales taxes, $500 delivery, and $200 painting and lettering) are expenditures necessary to make the truck ready for its intended use. Thus, the cost of the truck is $16,600. The payments for insurance and the license are operating expenses incurred annually during the useful life of the asset.

Related exercise material: **BE9.1, BE9.2, BE9.3, DO IT! 9.1, E9.1, E9.2,** and **E9.3.**

Depreciation Methods

LEARNING OBJECTIVE 2
Apply depreciation methods to plant assets.

As explained in Chapter 4, **depreciation is the process of allocating to expense the cost of a plant asset over its useful (service) life in a rational and systematic manner.** Such cost allocation is designed to properly record expenses (efforts) with associated revenues (results) (see **Illustration 9.5**).

ILLUSTRATION 9.5
Depreciation as a cost allocation concept

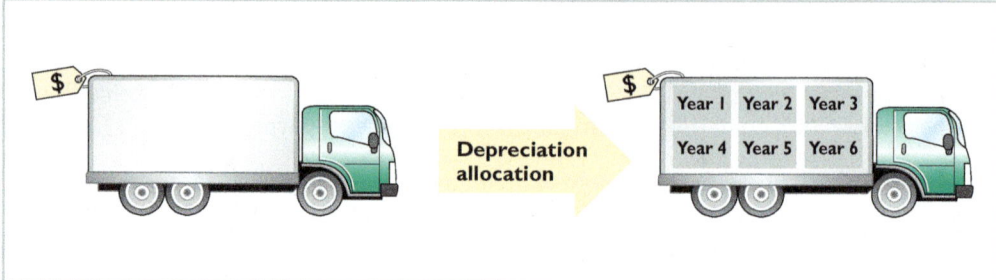

Depreciation affects the balance sheet through accumulated depreciation, which companies report as a deduction from plant assets. It affects the income statement through depreciation expense.

It is important to understand that **depreciation is a cost allocation process**, not an **asset valuation process**. No attempt is made to measure the change in an asset's fair value during ownership. Thus, the **book value**—cost less accumulated depreciation—of a plant asset may differ significantly from its **fair value**. In fact, if an asset is fully depreciated, it can have zero book value but still have a significant fair value.

Depreciation applies to **three classes of plant assets**: land improvements, buildings, and equipment (see **Ethics Note**). Each of these classes is considered to be a **depreciable asset** because the usefulness to the company and the revenue-producing ability of each class decline over the asset's useful life. Depreciation **does not apply to land** because its usefulness and revenue-producing ability generally remain intact as long as the land is owned. In fact, in many cases, the usefulness of land increases over time because of the scarcity of good sites. Thus, **land is not a depreciable asset**.

During a depreciable asset's useful life, its revenue-producing ability declines because of wear and tear. A delivery truck that has been driven 100,000 miles will be less useful to a company than one driven only 800 miles.

A decline in revenue-producing ability may also occur because of obsolescence. **Obsolescence** is the process by which an asset becomes out of date before it physically wears out. The rerouting of major airlines from Chicago's Midway Airport to Chicago-O'Hare International Airport because Midway's runways were too short for giant jets is an example. Similarly, many companies replace their computers long before they originally planned to do so because technological improvements make their old hardware obsolete.

Recognizing depreciation for an asset does not result in the accumulation of cash for replacement of the asset. The balance in Accumulated Depreciation represents the total amount of the asset's cost that the company has charged to expense to date; **it is not a cash fund**.

ETHICS NOTE
When a business is acquired, proper allocation of the purchase price to various asset classes is important since different depreciation treatment can materially affect income. For example, buildings are depreciated, but land is not.

Factors in Computing Depreciation

Three factors affect the computation of depreciation, as shown in **Illustration 9.6** (see **Helpful Hint**).

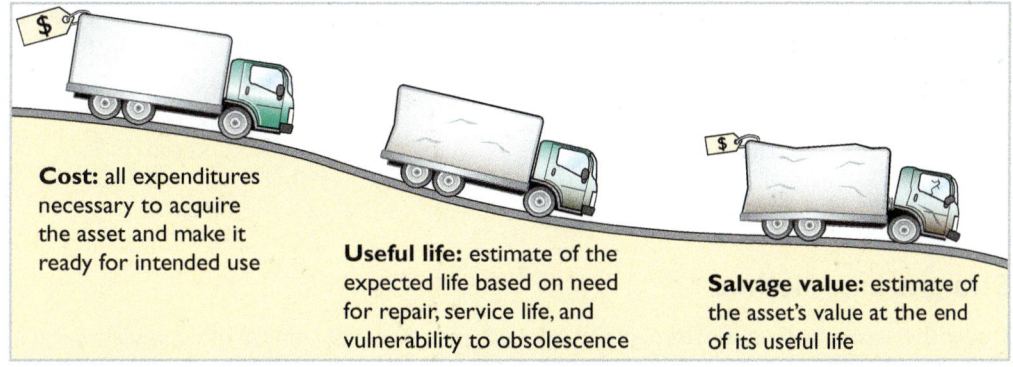

ILLUSTRATION 9.6
Three factors in computing depreciation

HELPFUL HINT
Depreciation expense is reported on the income statement. Accumulated depreciation is reported on the balance sheet as a deduction from plant assets.

1. **Cost.** Earlier in the chapter, we explained the considerations that affect the cost of a depreciable asset. Remember that companies record plant assets at cost, in accordance with the historical cost principle.

2. **Useful life.** Useful life is an estimate of the expected productive life, also called service life, of the asset for its owner. Useful life may be expressed in terms of time, units of activity (such as machine hours), or units of output. Useful life is an estimate. In making the estimate, management considers such factors as the intended use of the asset, repair and maintenance policies, and vulnerability of the asset to obsolescence. The company's past experience with similar assets is often helpful in deciding on expected useful life.

3. **Salvage value.** Salvage value is an estimate of the asset's value at the end of its useful life for its owner. Companies may base the value on the asset's worth as scrap or on its expected trade-in value. Like useful life, salvage value is an estimate. In making the estimate, management considers how it plans to dispose of the asset and its experience with similar assets.

Depreciation Methods

Although a number of methods exist, depreciation is generally computed using one of three methods:

1. Straight-line
2. Declining-balance
3. Units-of-activity

Like the alternative inventory methods discussed in Chapter 6, each of these depreciation methods is acceptable under generally accepted accounting principles. Management selects the method it believes best measures an asset's contribution to revenue over its useful life. Once a company chooses a method, it should apply that method consistently over the useful life of the asset. Consistency enhances the ability to analyze financial statements over multiple years.

Illustration 9.7 shows the distribution of the primary depreciation methods in a sample of the largest U.S. companies. Clearly, straight-line depreciation is the most widely used approach. In fact, because some companies use more than one method, **straight-line depreciation is used for some or all of the depreciation taken by more than 95% of U.S. companies**. For this reason, we illustrate procedures for straight-line depreciation and discuss the alternative depreciation approaches only at a conceptual level. This coverage introduces you to the basic idea of depreciation as an allocation concept without entangling you in too much procedural detail. (Also, note that many calculators are preprogrammed to perform the basic depreciation methods.) Details on the alternative approaches are presented in Appendix 9A.

No matter what method is used, the total amount depreciated over the useful life of the asset is its depreciable cost. **Depreciable cost** is equal to the cost of the asset less its salvage value.

ILLUSTRATION 9.7
Use of depreciation methods in major U.S. companies

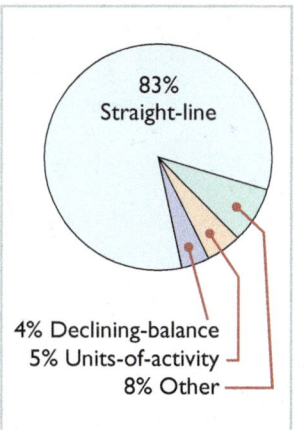

83% Straight-line
4% Declining-balance
5% Units-of-activity
8% Other

Our illustration of depreciation methods, both here and in the chapter appendix, is based on the following data relating to a small delivery truck purchased by Bill's Pizzas on January 1, 2022.

Cost	$13,000
Expected salvage value	$1,000
Estimated useful life (in years)	5
Estimated useful life (in miles)	100,000

Straight-Line Method

Under the **straight-line method**, companies expense an equal amount of depreciation each year of the asset's useful life. Management must choose the useful life of an asset based on its own expectations and experience.

To compute the annual depreciation expense, we divide depreciable cost by the estimated useful life. As indicated above, depreciable cost represents the total amount subject to depreciation; it is calculated as the cost of the plant asset less its salvage value. **Illustration 9.8** shows the computation of depreciation expense in the first year for Bill's Pizzas' delivery truck.

ILLUSTRATION 9.8
Formula for straight-line method

Cost	−	Salvage Value	=	Depreciable Cost
$13,000	−	$1,000	=	$12,000

Depreciable Cost	÷	Useful Life (in years)	=	Depreciation Expense
$12,000	÷	5	=	$2,400

Alternatively, we can compute an annual **rate** at which the company depreciates the delivery truck. In this case, the rate is 20% (100% ÷ 5 years). When an annual rate is used under the straight-line method, the company applies the percentage rate to the depreciable cost of the asset, as shown in the **depreciation schedule** in **Illustration 9.9**.

ILLUSTRATION 9.9
Straight-line depreciation schedule

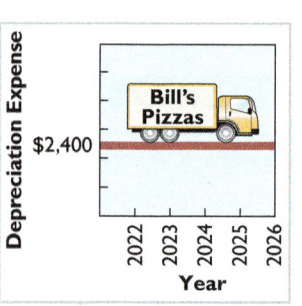

Bill's Pizzas

	Computation			Annual	End of Year	
Year	Depreciable Cost	× Depreciation Rate	=	Depreciation Expense	Accumulated Depreciation	Book Value
2022	$12,000	20%		$ 2,400	$ 2,400	$10,600*
2023	12,000	20		2,400	4,800	8,200
2024	12,000	20		2,400	7,200	5,800
2025	12,000	20		2,400	9,600	3,400
2026	12,000	20		2,400	12,000	1,000
			Total	$12,000		

*$13,000 − $2,400

Note that the depreciation expense of $2,400 is the same each year. The book value at the end of the useful life is equal to the estimated $1,000 salvage value.

What happens when an asset is purchased **during** the year, rather than on January 1 as in our example? In that case, it is necessary to **prorate the annual depreciation** for the portion of a year used. If Bill's Pizzas had purchased the delivery truck on April 1, 2022, the company would use the truck for 9 months in 2022. The depreciation for 2022 would be $1,800 ($12,000 × 20% × $\frac{9}{12}$ of a year).

As indicated earlier, the straight-line method predominates in practice. For example, such large companies as **Campbell Soup**, **Marriott**, and **General Mills** use the straight-line method. It is simple to apply, and it records expenses with associated revenues appropriately when the use of the asset is reasonably uniform throughout the service life. Generally, the types of assets that give equal benefits over their useful lives are those for which daily use does not affect productivity. Examples are office furniture and fixtures, buildings, warehouses, and garages for motor vehicles.

DO IT! 2a | Straight-Line Depreciation

On January 1, 2022, Iron Mountain Ski Corporation purchased a new snow-grooming machine for $50,000. The machine is estimated to have a 10-year life with a $2,000 salvage value. What journal entry would Iron Mountain Ski Corporation make at December 31, 2022, if it uses the straight-line method of depreciation?

ACTION PLAN
- Calculate depreciable cost (Cost − Salvage value).
- Divide the depreciable cost by the asset's estimated useful life.

Solution

$$\text{Depreciation expense} = \frac{\text{Cost} - \text{Salvage value}}{\text{Useful life}} = \frac{\$50{,}000 - \$2{,}000}{10} = \$4{,}800$$

Iron Mountain would record the first year's depreciation as follows.

Dec. 31	Depreciation Expense	4,800	
	Accumulated Depreciation—Equipment		4,800
	(To record annual depreciation on snow-grooming machine)		

Related exercise material: **BE9.4, DO IT! 9.2a, E9.4, E9.5, and E9.6**.

Declining-Balance Method

The **declining-balance method** computes depreciation expense using a constant rate applied to a declining book value. This method is called an **accelerated-depreciation method** because it results in higher depreciation in the early years of an asset's life than does the straight-line approach. However, because the total amount of depreciation (the depreciable cost) taken over an asset's life is the same **no matter what approach** is used, the declining-balance method produces a decreasing annual depreciation expense over the asset's useful life. In early years, declining-balance depreciation expense will exceed straight-line. In later years, it will be less than straight-line. Managers might choose an accelerated approach if they think that an asset's utility will decline quickly.

Companies can apply the declining-balance approach at different rates, which result in varying speeds of depreciation. A common declining-balance rate is double the straight-line rate. Using that rate, the method is referred to as the **double-declining-balance method**.

If we apply the double-declining-balance method to Bill's Pizzas' delivery truck, assuming a five-year life, we get the pattern of depreciation shown in **Illustration 9.10**. **Illustration 9A.2 presents the computations behind these numbers.** Again, note that total depreciation over the life of the truck is $12,000, the depreciable cost.

Bill's Pizzas

Year	Annual Depreciation Expense	Accumulated Depreciation	Book Value
2022	$ 5,200	$ 5,200	$7,800
2023	3,120	8,320	4,680
2024	1,872	10,192	2,808
2025	1,123	11,315	1,685
2026	685	12,000	1,000
Total	$12,000		

ILLUSTRATION 9.10
Declining-balance depreciation schedule

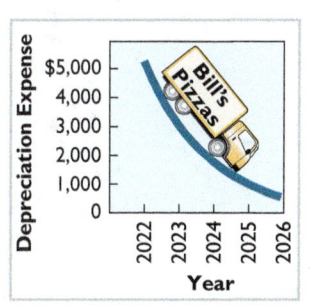

Units-of-Activity Method

As indicated earlier, useful life can be expressed in ways other than a time period. Under the **units-of-activity method**, useful life is expressed in terms of the total units of production or the use expected from the asset. The units-of-activity method is ideally suited to factory machinery: Companies can measure production in terms of units of output or in terms of machine hours used in operating the machinery. It is also possible to use the method for such items as delivery equipment (miles driven) and airplanes (hours in use). The units-of-activity method is generally not suitable for such assets as buildings or furniture because activity levels are difficult to measure for these assets.

Applying the units-of-activity method to the delivery truck owned by Bill's Pizzas, we first must know some basic information. Bill's expects to be able to drive the truck a total of 100,000 miles. **Illustration 9.11** shows depreciation over the five-year life based on an assumed mileage pattern. **Illustration 9A.4 presents the computations used to arrive at these results.**

ILLUSTRATION 9.11

Units-of-activity depreciation schedule

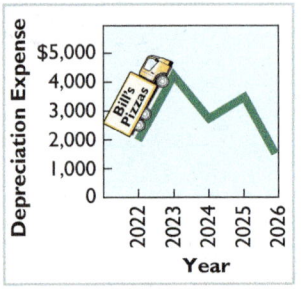

Bill's Pizzas

Year	Units of Activity (miles)	Annual Depreciation Expense	End of Year Accumulated Depreciation	End of Year Book Value
2022	15,000	$ 1,800	$ 1,800	$11,200
2023	30,000	3,600	5,400	7,600
2024	20,000	2,400	7,800	5,200
2025	25,000	3,000	10,800	2,200
2026	10,000	1,200	12,000	1,000
Total	$100,000	$12,000		

As the name implies, under units-of-activity depreciation, the amount of depreciation is proportional to the activity that took place during that period. For example, the delivery truck was driven twice as many miles in 2023 as in 2022, and depreciation was exactly twice as much in 2023 as it was in 2022.

Management's Choice: Comparison of Methods

Illustration 9.12 compares annual and total depreciation expense for Bill's Pizzas under the three methods.

ILLUSTRATION 9.12

Comparison of depreciation methods

Year	Straight-Line	Declining-Balance	Units-of-Activity
2022	$ 2,400	$ 5,200	$ 1,800
2023	2,400	3,120	3,600
2024	2,400	1,872	2,400
2025	2,400	1,123	3,000
2026	2,400	685	1,200
	$12,000	$12,000	$12,000

Annual depreciation expense varies considerably among the methods, but **total depreciation expense is the same ($12,000) for the five-year period**. Each method is acceptable in accounting because each recognizes the decline in service potential of the asset in a rational and systematic manner. **Illustration 9.13** graphs the depreciation expense pattern under each method.

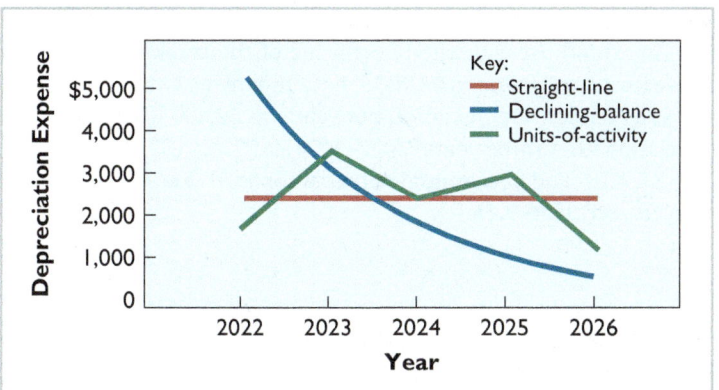

ILLUSTRATION 9.13
Patterns of depreciation

Depreciation and Income Taxes

The Internal Revenue Service (IRS) allows corporate taxpayers to deduct depreciation expense when computing taxable income. However, the tax regulations of the IRS do not require the taxpayer to use the same depreciation method on the tax return that it uses in preparing financial statements (see **Helpful Hint**).

Consequently, many large corporations use straight-line depreciation in their financial statements in order to maximize net income; at the same time, they use a special accelerated-depreciation method on their tax returns in order to minimize their income taxes. For tax purposes, taxpayers must use on their tax returns either the straight-line method or a special accelerated-depreciation method called the **Modified Accelerated Cost Recovery System** (MACRS).

HELPFUL HINT
Depreciation per financial statements is usually different from depreciation per tax returns.

Depreciation Disclosure in the Notes

Companies must disclose the choice of depreciation method in their financial statements or in related notes that accompany the statements. **Illustration 9.14** shows excerpts from the "Property and equipment" notes from the financial statements of **Southwest Airlines**.

Real World	**Southwest Airlines**
	Notes to the Financial Statements

Property and equipment Depreciation is provided by the straight-line method to estimated residual values over periods generally ranging from 23 to 25 years for flight equipment.

ILLUSTRATION 9.14
Disclosure of depreciation policies

From this note, we learn that Southwest Airlines uses the straight-line method to depreciate its planes over periods of 23 to 25 years.

Revising Periodic Depreciation

Management should periodically review annual depreciation expense. If wear and tear or obsolescence indicates that annual depreciation is either inadequate or excessive, the company should change the depreciation expense amount.

When a change in an estimate is required, the company makes the change in **current and future years but not to prior periods**. Thus, when making the change, the company (1) does not change previously recorded depreciation expense, but (2) revises depreciation expense for current and future years. The rationale for this treatment is that continual restatement of prior periods would adversely affect users' confidence in financial statements.

To determine the new annual depreciation expense, the company first computes the asset's depreciable cost at the time of the revision. It then allocates the revised depreciable cost to the remaining useful life (see **Helpful Hint**).

HELPFUL HINT
Use a step-by-step approach: (1) determine new depreciable cost; (2) divide by remaining useful life.

To illustrate, assume that Bill's Pizzas decides at the end of 2025 (prior to the year-end adjusting entries) to extend the estimated useful life of the truck one year (a total life of six years) and increase its salvage value to $2,200. The company has used the straight-line method to depreciate the asset to date. Depreciation per year was $2,400 [($13,000 − $1,000) ÷ 5]. Accumulated depreciation after three years (2022–2024) is $7,200 ($2,400 × 3), and book value is $5,800 ($13,000 − $7,200). The new annual depreciation is $1,200, computed on December 31, 2025, as shown in **Illustration 9.15**.

ILLUSTRATION 9.15
Revised depreciation computation

Book value, 1/1/25	$ 5,800
Less: New salvage value	2,200
Depreciable cost	$ 3,600
Remaining useful life	3 years (2025–2027)
Revised annual depreciation ($3,600 ÷ 3)	**$ 1,200**

Bill's Pizzas does not make a special entry for the change in estimate. On December 31, 2025, during the preparation of adjusting entries, it records depreciation expense of $1,200 instead of the amount recorded in previous years.

Companies must disclose in the financial statements significant changes in estimates. Although a company may have a legitimate reason for changing an estimated life, financial statement users should be aware that some companies might change an estimate simply to achieve financial statement goals. For example, extending an asset's estimated life reduces depreciation expense and increases current period income.

At one time, **AirTran Airways** (now owned by **Southwest Airlines**) increased the estimated useful lives of some of its planes from 25 to 30 years and increased the estimated lives of related aircraft parts from 5 years to 30 years. It disclosed that the change in estimate decreased its net loss for the year by approximately $0.6 million, or about $0.01 per share. Whether these changes were appropriate depends on how reasonable it is to assume that planes will continue to be used for a long time. Our Feature Story suggests that although in the past many planes lasted a long time, it is also clear that because of high fuel costs, airlines are now scrapping many of their old, inefficient planes.

Impairments

As noted earlier, the book value of plant assets is rarely the same as the fair value. In instances where the value of a plant asset declines substantially, its fair value might fall materially below book value. This may happen because a machine has become obsolete, or the market for the product made by the machine has dried up or has become very competitive. A **permanent decline** in the fair value of an asset is referred to as an **impairment**. So as not to overstate the asset on the books, the company records a write-down, whereby the asset's cost is reduced to its new fair value during the year in which the decline in value occurs. For example, **Disney** recorded a $200 million write-down on its action movie *John Carter*. Disney spent more than $300 million producing the film.

In the past, some companies **improperly** delayed recording losses on impairments until a year when it was "convenient" to do so—when the impact on the company's reported results was minimized. For example, in a year when a company has record profits, it can afford to write down some of its bad assets without hurting its reported results too much. As discussed in Chapter 4, the practice of timing the recognition of gains and losses to achieve certain income results is known as **earnings management**. Earnings management reduces earnings quality. To minimize earnings management, accounting standards now require immediate loss recognition on impaired assets.

Write-downs can create problems for users of financial statements. Critics of write-downs note that after a company writes down assets, its depreciation expense will be lower in all subsequent periods. Some companies improperly inflate asset write-downs in bad years, when they are going to report poor results anyway. (This practice is referred to as "taking a big bath.") Then in subsequent years, when the company recovers, its results will look even better because of lower depreciation expense.

DO IT! 2b | Revised Depreciation

Chambers Corporation purchased a piece of equipment for $36,000. It estimated a 6-year life and $6,000 salvage value. Thus, straight-line depreciation was $5,000 per year [($36,000 − $6,000) ÷ 6]. At the end of year three (before the depreciation adjustment), it estimated the new total life to be 10 years and the new salvage value to be $2,000. Compute the revised depreciation.

ACTION PLAN
- Calculate depreciable cost.
- Divide depreciable cost by new remaining life.

Solution

Original depreciation expense = [($36,000 − $6,000) ÷ 6] = $5,000
Accumulated depreciation after 2 years = 2 × $5,000 = $10,000
Book value = $36,000 − $10,000 = $26,000

Book value after 2 years of depreciation	$26,000
Less: New salvage value	2,000
Depreciable cost	$24,000
Remaining useful life	8 years
Revised annual depreciation ($24,000 ÷ 8)	$ 3,000

Related exercise material: **BE9.6, DO IT! 9.2b, E9.7, and E9.8.**

Plant Asset Disposals

LEARNING OBJECTIVE 3
Explain how to account for the disposal of plant assets.

Companies dispose of plant assets that are no longer useful to them. **Illustration 9.16** shows the three ways in which companies make plant asset disposals.

ILLUSTRATION 9.16

Methods of plant asset disposal

Sale — Equipment is sold to another party.
Retirement — Equipment is scrapped or discarded.
Exchange — Existing equipment is traded for new equipment.

Whatever the disposal method, the company must determine the book value of the plant asset at the time of disposal in order to determine the gain or loss. Recall that the book value is the difference between the cost of the plant asset and the accumulated depreciation to date. If the disposal does not occur on the first day of the year, the company must record depreciation for the fraction of the year to the date of disposal. The company then eliminates the book value by reducing (debiting) Accumulated Depreciation for the total depreciation associated with that asset to the date of disposal and reducing (crediting) the

Sale of Plant Assets

In a disposal by sale, the company compares the book value of the asset with the proceeds received from the sale. If the proceeds from the sale **exceed** the book value of the plant asset, a **gain on disposal** occurs. If the proceeds from the sale **are less than** the book value of the plant asset sold, a **loss on disposal** occurs.

Only by coincidence will the book value and the fair value of the asset be the same at the time the asset is sold. Gains and losses on sales of plant assets are therefore quite common. As an example, **Delta Air Lines** at one time reported a $94 million gain on the sale of five **Boeing** B-727-200 aircraft and five **Lockheed** L-1011-1 aircraft.

Gain on Sale

To illustrate a gain on sale of plant assets, assume that on July 1, 2022, Wright Company sells office furniture for $16,000 cash. The office furniture originally cost $60,000 and as of January 1, 2022, had accumulated depreciation of $41,000. Depreciation for the first six months of 2022 is $8,000. Wright records depreciation expense and updates accumulated depreciation to July 1 as follows.

July 1	Depreciation Expense	8,000	
	Accumulated Depreciation—Equipment		8,000
	(To record depreciation expense for the first 6 months of 2022)		

After the accumulated depreciation balance is updated, the company computes the gain or loss as the difference between the proceeds from sale and the book value at the date of disposal. Wright Company has a gain on disposal of $5,000, as computed in **Illustration 9.17**.

ILLUSTRATION 9.17
Computation of gain on disposal

Cost of office furniture	$60,000
Less: Accumulated depreciation ($41,000 + $8,000)	49,000
Book value at date of disposal	11,000
Proceeds from sale	16,000
Gain on disposal of plant asset	$ 5,000

Wright records the sale and the gain on sale of the plant asset as follows.

July 1	Cash	16,000	
	Accumulated Depreciation—Equipment	49,000	
	Equipment		60,000
	Gain on Disposal of Plant Assets		5,000
	(To record sale of office furniture at a gain)		

Companies report a gain on disposal of plant assets in the "Other revenues and gains" section of the income statement.

Loss on Sale

Assume that instead of selling the office furniture for $16,000, Wright sells it for $9,000. In this case, Wright experiences a loss of $2,000, as computed in **Illustration 9.18**.

Cost of office furniture	$60,000	
Less: Accumulated depreciation	49,000	
Book value at date of disposal	11,000	
Proceeds from sale	9,000	
Loss on disposal of plant asset	**$ 2,000**	

ILLUSTRATION 9.18
Computation of loss on disposal

Wright records the sale and the loss on sale of the plant asset as follows.

July 1	Cash	9,000	
	Accumulated Depreciation—Equipment	49,000	
	Loss on Disposal of Plant Assets	2,000	
	Equipment		60,000
	(To record sale of office furniture at a loss)		

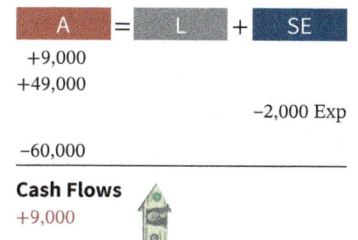

Companies report a loss on disposal of the plant asset in the "Other expenses and losses" section of the income statement.

Retirement of Plant Assets

Companies simply retire, rather than sell, some assets at the end of their useful lives. For example, some productive assets used in manufacturing may have very specific uses, and they consequently have no ready market when the company no longer needs them. In such a case, the asset is simply retired.

Companies record retirement of an asset as a special case of a disposal where no cash is received. They decrease (debit) Accumulated Depreciation for the full amount of depreciation taken over the life of the asset and decrease (credit) the asset account for the original cost of the asset. The loss (a gain is not possible on a retirement) is equal to the asset's book value on the date of retirement.[1]

DO IT! 3 | Plant Asset Disposals

Overland Trucking has an old truck that cost $30,000 and has accumulated depreciation of $16,000. Assume two different situations:

1. The company sells the old truck for $17,000 cash.
2. The truck is worthless, so the company simply retires it.

What entry should Overland use to record each scenario?

Solution

1. Sale of truck for cash:

	Cash	17,000	
	Accumulated Depreciation—Equipment	16,000	
	Equipment		30,000
	Gain on Disposal of Plant Assets		3,000
	[$17,000 − ($30,000 − $16,000)]		
	(To record sale of truck at a gain)		

2. Retirement of truck:

	Accumulated Depreciation—Equipment	16,000	
	Loss on Disposal of Plant Assets	14,000	
	Equipment		30,000
	(To record retirement of truck at a loss)		

ACTION PLAN
- Compare the asset's book value and its fair value to determine whether a gain or loss has occurred.
- Make sure that both the Equipment account and Accumulated Depreciation—Equipment are reduced upon disposal.

Related exercise material: **BE9.7, BE9.8, DO IT! 9.3, E9.9, E9.10, E9.11, and E9.12.**

---

[1]More advanced courses discuss the accounting for exchanges, the third method of plant asset disposal.

Intangible Assets

LEARNING OBJECTIVE 4
Identify the basic issues related to reporting intangible assets.

Intangible assets are rights, privileges, and competitive advantages that result from ownership of long-lived assets that do not possess physical substance. Many companies' most valuable assets are intangible. Some widely known intangibles are **Microsoft**'s patents, **McDonald's** franchises, the trade name iPod, and **Nike**'s trademark "swoosh."

As you will learn in this section, financial statements report numerous intangibles. Yet, many other financially significant intangibles are not reported. To give an example, according to its financial statements in a recent year, **Google** had total stockholders' equity of $22.7 billion. But its market value—the total market price of all its shares on that same date—was roughly $178.5 billion. Thus, its actual market value was about $155.8 billion greater than the amount reported for stockholders' equity on the balance sheet. It is not uncommon for a company's reported book value to differ from its market value because balance sheets are reported at historical cost. But such an extreme difference seriously diminishes the usefulness of the balance sheet to decision-makers. In the case of Google, the difference is due to unrecorded intangibles. For many high-tech or so-called intellectual-property companies, most of their value is from intangibles, many of which are not reported under current accounting rules.

Intangibles may be evidenced by contracts, licenses, and other documents. Intangibles may arise from the following sources:

1. Government grants, such as patents, copyrights, licenses, trademarks, and trade names.
2. Acquisition of another business in which the purchase price includes a payment for goodwill.
3. Private monopolistic arrangements arising from contractual agreements, such as franchises and leases.

Accounting for Intangible Assets

Companies record intangible assets at cost. Cost is comprised of all expenditures necessary for the company to acquire the right, privilege, or competitive advantage. Intangibles are categorized as having either a limited life or an indefinite life. If an intangible has a **limited life**, the company allocates its cost over the asset's useful life using a process similar to depreciation. The process of allocating to expense the cost of intangibles is referred to as **amortization**. The cost of intangible assets with **indefinite lives should not be amortized**.

To record amortization of an intangible asset, a company increases (debits) Amortization Expense and decreases (credits) the specific intangible asset. (Alternatively, some companies choose to credit a contra account, such as Accumulated Amortization. *For homework, you should directly credit the specific intangible asset.*)

Intangible assets are typically amortized on a straight-line basis. For example, the legal life of a patent is 20 years. Companies **amortize the cost of a patent over its 20-year life or its useful life, whichever is shorter**. To illustrate the computation of patent amortization, assume that National Labs purchases a patent at a cost of $60,000 on June 30. If National estimates the useful life of the patent to be eight years, the annual amortization expense is $7,500 ($60,000 ÷ 8) per year. National records $3,750 ($7,500 × $\frac{6}{12}$) of amortization for the six-month period ended December 31 as follows.

A = L + SE
−3,750 Exp
−3,750

Cash Flows
no effect

Dec. 31	Amortization Expense	3,750	
	Patents		3,750
	(To record patent amortization)		

When a company has significant intangibles, analysts should evaluate the reasonableness of the useful life estimates that the company discloses in the notes to its financial statements. In determining useful life, the company should consider obsolescence, inadequacy, and other factors. These may cause a patent or other intangible to become economically ineffective before the end of its legal life (see **Decision Tools**).

For example, suppose **Intel** obtained a patent on a new computer chip it had developed. The legal life of the patent is 20 years. From experience, however, we know that the useful life of a computer chip patent is rarely more than five years. Because new superior chips are developed so rapidly, existing chips become obsolete. Consequently, we would question the amortization expense of Intel if it amortized its patent on a computer chip for a life significantly longer than a five-year period. Amortizing an intangible over a period that is too long will understate amortization expense, overstate Intel's net income, and overstate its assets.

> **Decision Tools**
> Evaluating a company's amortization of intangibles helps users determine if net income is overstated.

Types of Intangible Assets

Patents

A **patent** is an exclusive right issued by the U.S. Patent Office that enables the recipient to manufacture, sell, or otherwise control an invention for a period of 20 years from the date of the grant. **The initial cost of a patent is the cash or cash equivalent price paid to acquire the patent.**

The saying "A patent is only as good as the money you're prepared to spend defending it" is very true. Most patents are subject to some type of litigation by competitors. A well-known example is the patent infringement suit brought by **Amazon.com** against **Barnes & Noble.com** regarding its online shopping software. If the owner incurs legal costs in successfully defending the patent in an infringement suit, such costs are considered necessary to establish the validity of the patent. Thus, **the owner adds those costs to the Patents account and amortizes them over the remaining life of the patent**.

Research and Development Costs

Research and development costs are expenditures that may lead to patents, copyrights, new processes, and new products (see **Helpful Hint**). Many companies spend considerable sums of money on research and development (R&D) in an ongoing effort to develop new products or processes. For example, in a recent year **Google** spent over $9.8 billion on research and development. There are uncertainties in identifying the extent and timing of the future benefits of these expenditures. As a result, companies usually record research and development costs **as an expense when incurred**, whether the R&D is successful or not.

To illustrate, assume that Laser Scanner Company spent $3 million on research and development that resulted in two highly successful patents. It spent $20,000 on legal fees for the patents. It can include the legal fees in the cost of the patents but cannot include the R&D costs in the cost of the patents. Instead, Laser Scanner records the R&D costs as an expense when incurred.

Many disagree with this accounting approach (see **International Note**). They argue that to expense these costs leads to understated assets and net income. Others argue that capitalizing these costs would lead to highly speculative assets on the balance sheet. Who is right is difficult to determine.

> **HELPFUL HINT**
> Research and development costs are not intangible costs, but because these expenditures may lead to patents and copyrights, we discuss them in this section.

> **International Note**
> IFRS allows capitalization of some development costs. This may contribute to differences in R&D expenditures across nations.

Copyrights

The federal government grants **copyrights**, which give the owner the exclusive right to reproduce and sell an artistic or published work. Copyrights last for the life of the creator plus 70 years. The cost of the copyright consists of the **cost of acquiring and defending it**. The cost may be only the small fee paid to the U.S. Copyright Office, or it may amount to a great deal more if a copyright is acquired from another party. The useful life of a copyright generally is significantly shorter than its legal life.

Trademarks and Trade Names

A **trademark** or **trade name** is a word, phrase, jingle, or symbol that distinguishes or identifies a particular enterprise or product. Trade names like Wheaties, Monopoly, Sunkist, Kleenex, Coca-Cola, Big Mac, and Jeep create immediate product identification and generally enhance the sale of the product. The creator or original user may obtain the exclusive legal right to the trademark or trade name by registering it with the U.S. Patent Office. Such registration provides 20 years' protection and may be renewed indefinitely as long as the trademark or trade name is in use.

If a company purchases the trademark or trade name, the cost is the purchase price. If the company develops the trademark or trade name itself, the cost includes attorney's fees, registration fees, design costs, successful legal defense costs, and other expenditures directly related to securing it. Because trademarks and trade names have indefinite lives, they are not amortized.

Accounting Across the Organization Google

We Want to Own Glass

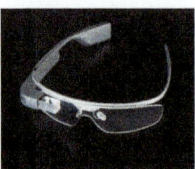
© Hattanas Kumchai/ Shutterstock

Google, which has trademarked the term "Google Glass," now wants to trademark the term "Glass." Why? Because the simple word Glass has marketing advantages over the term Google Glass. It is easy to remember and is more universal. Regulators, however, are balking at Google's request. They say that the possible trademark is too similar to other existing or pending software trademarks that contain the word "glass." Also, regulators suggest that the term Glass is merely descriptive and therefore lacks trademark protection. For example, regulators note that a company that makes salsa could not trademark the term "Spicy Salsa."

BorderStylo LLC, which developed a Web-browser extension called Write on Glass, has filed a notice of opposition to Google's request. Google is fighting back and has sent the trademark examiner a 1,928-page application defense.

Source: Jacob Gershman, "Google Wants to Own 'Glass'," *Wall Street Journal* (April 4, 2014), p. B5.

If Google is successful in registering the term Glass, where will this trademark be reported on its financial statements? (Go to WileyPLUS for this answer and additional questions.)

Franchises

When you purchase a RAV4 from a **Toyota** dealer, fill up your tank at the corner **Shell** station, eat lunch at **Subway**, or make reservations at a **Marriott** hotel, you are dealing with franchises. A **franchise** is a contractual arrangement under which the franchisor grants the franchisee the right to sell certain products, to perform specific services, or to use certain trademarks or trade names, usually within a designated geographic area.

Another type of franchise is a license. Licenses granted by a governmental body permit a business to use public property in performing its services. Examples are the use of city streets for a bus line or taxi service; the use of public land for telephone, electric, and cable television lines; and the use of airwaves for radio or TV broadcasting. In a recent license agreement, **Fox**, **CBS**, and **NBC** agreed to pay $27.9 billion for the right to broadcast **NFL** football games over an eight-year period.

Franchises and licenses may be granted for a definite period of time, or the time period may be indefinite or perpetual. **When a company incurs costs in connection with the acquisition of the franchise or license, it should recognize an intangible asset.** Companies record as **operating expenses** annual payments made under a franchise agreement in the period in which they are incurred. In the case of a limited life, a company amortizes the cost of a franchise (or license) as operating expense over the useful life. If the life is indefinite or perpetual, the cost is not amortized.

Goodwill

Usually, the largest intangible asset that appears on a company's balance sheet is goodwill. **Goodwill** represents the value of all favorable attributes that relate to a company that are not attributable to any other specific asset. These include exceptional management, desirable location, good customer relations, skilled employees, high-quality products, fair pricing policies, and harmonious relations with labor unions. Goodwill is unique because unlike other assets such as investments, plant assets, and even other intangibles, which can be sold **individually** in the marketplace, goodwill can be identified only with the business **as a whole**.

If goodwill can be identified only with the business as a whole, how can it be determined? Certainly, many business enterprises have many of the factors cited above (exceptional management, desirable location, and so on). However, to determine the amount of goodwill in these situations would be difficult and very subjective. In other words, to recognize goodwill without an exchange transaction that puts a value on the goodwill would lead to subjective valuations that do not contribute to the reliability of financial statements. **Therefore, companies record goodwill only when there is an exchange transaction that involves the purchase of an entire business. When an entire business is purchased, goodwill is the excess of cost over the fair value of the net assets (assets less liabilities) acquired.**

In recording the purchase of a business, a company debits the identifiable acquired assets and credits liabilities at their fair values, credits cash for the purchase price, and records the difference as the cost of goodwill. Goodwill is not amortized because it is considered to have an indefinite life. However, it must be written down if a company determines the value of goodwill has been permanently impaired.

DO IT! 4 | Classification Concepts

Match the following terms or phrases with the statement most directly associated with it.

1. Copyright.
2. Intangible assets.
3. Research and development costs.
4. Amortization.
5. Franchise.

a. _____ The allocation to expense of the cost of an intangible asset over the asset's useful life.

b. _____ Rights, privileges, and competitive advantages that result from the ownership of long-lived assets that do not possess physical substance.

c. _____ An exclusive right granted by the federal government to reproduce and sell an artistic or published work.

d. _____ A right to sell certain products or services or to use certain trademarks or trade names within a designated geographic area.

e. _____ Costs incurred by a company that often lead to patents or new products. These costs must be expensed as incurred.

ACTION PLAN
- Know that the accounting for intangibles often depends on whether the item has a finite or indefinite life.
- Recognize the many similarities and differences between the accounting for plant assets and intangible assets.

Solution

a. 4.   d. 5.
b. 2.   e. 3.
c. 1.

Related exercise material: **BE9.9, DO IT! 9.4, E9.14, E9.15, and E9.16.**

Statement Presentation and Analysis

LEARNING OBJECTIVE 5
Discuss how long-lived assets are reported and analyzed.

Presentation

Usually, companies show plant assets in the financial statements under "Property, plant, and equipment," and they show intangibles separately under "Intangible assets." **Illustration 9.19** shows a typical balance sheet presentation of long-lived assets.

> **ILLUSTRATION 9.19**
>
> Presentation of property, plant, and equipment, and intangible assets

Artex Company
Balance Sheet (partial)
(in thousands)

Current assets		
Cash		$ 430
Accounts receivable		100
Inventory		910
Total current assets		$ 1,440
Property, plant, and equipment		
Land		920
Buildings	$7,600	
Less: Accumulated depreciation—buildings	500	7,100
Equipment	3,870	
Less: Accumulated depreciation—equipment	620	3,250
Total property, plant, and equipment		11,270
Intangible assets		
Patents		440
Trademarks		180
Goodwill		900
		1,520
Total assets		$14,230

When a plant asset is fully depreciated, the plant asset and related accumulated depreciation should continue to be reported on the balance sheet without further depreciation or adjustment until the asset is retired. Intangibles do not usually use a contra asset account like the contra asset account Accumulated Depreciation used for plant assets. Instead, companies record amortization of intangibles as a direct decrease (credit) to the asset account.

Either within the balance sheet or in the notes, companies should disclose the balances of the major classes of assets, such as land, buildings, and equipment, and of accumulated depreciation by major classes or in total. In addition, they should describe the depreciation and amortization methods used and disclose the amount of depreciation and amortization expense for the period.

People, Planet, and Profit Insight   BHP Billiton

© Christian Uhrig/ iStockphoto

Sustainability Report Please

Sustainability reports identify how the company is meeting its corporate social responsibilities. Many companies, both large and small, are now issuing these reports. For example, companies such as **Disney**, **Best Buy**, **Microsoft**, **Ford**, and **ConocoPhillips** issue these reports. Presented below is an adapted section of a recent **BHP Billiton** (a global mining, oil, and gas company) sustainability report on its environmental policies. These policies are to (1) take action to address the challenges of climate change, (2) set and achieve targets that reduce pollution, and (3) enhance biodiversity by assessing and considering ecological values and land-use aspects. Here is how BHP Billiton measures the success or failure of some of these policies:

	Target	Target date
Safety	• Zero work-related fatalities. • Year-on-year improvement of our total recordable injury frequency (TRIF).	Annual Annual
Health	For our most material exposures of respirable silica, diesel particulate and coal mine dust, we will achieve a 50 per cent reduction in the number of workers potentially exposed as compared with the FY2017 baseline.	30 June 2022

Community	Zero significant community events.	Annual
	Our social investment will contribute to improved quality of life in host communities and support achievement of the UN Sustainable Development Goals. We will invest not less than one per cent of pre-tax profit (three-year rolling average) in meeting these objectives.	30 June 2022
	Regional Indigenous Peoples Plans will be developed, which support implementation of BHP's Indigenous Peoples Strategy. Plans will include all geographically relevant assets.	30 June 2022
Climate change	Maintain FY2022 greenhouse gas (GHG) emissions at or below FY2017 levels while we continue to grow our business.	30 June 2022
	Longer-term goal: In line with international commitments, BHP aims to achieve net-zero operational GHG emissions in the second half of this century.	The second half of this century.

In addition to the environment, BHP Billiton has sections in its sustainability report that discuss people, safety, health, and community.

Why do you believe companies issue sustainability reports? (Go to WileyPLUS for this answer and additional questions.)

Analysis

The presentation of financial statement information about plant assets enables decision makers to analyze the company's use of its plant assets. We will use two measures to analyze plant assets: return on assets and asset turnover. We also show how profit margin relates to both.

Return on Assets

An overall measure of profitability is the **return on assets** (see **Decision Tools**). This ratio is computed by dividing net income by average total assets. (Average assets are commonly calculated by adding the beginning and ending values of assets and dividing by 2.) Return on assets indicates the amount of net income generated by each dollar of assets. Thus, the higher the return on assets, the more profitable the company.

Information is provided below related to **JetBlue Airways**.

	JetBlue (in millions)
Net income, 2017	$1,147
Total assets, 12/31/17	9,781
Total assets, 12/31/16	9,323
Net sales, 2017	7,015

Decision Tools

Return on assets helps users determine if a company is using its assets effectively.

Illustration 9.20 presents the 2017 and 2016 return on assets of JetBlue Airways and Southwest Airlines.

ILLUSTRATION 9.20

Return on assets for JetBlue and Southwest

$$\text{Return on Assets} = \frac{\text{Net Income}}{\text{Average Total Assets}}$$

JetBlue Airways ($ in millions)		Southwest Airlines
2017	2016	2017
$\dfrac{\$1{,}147}{(\$9{,}781 + \$9{,}323)/2} = 12.0\%$	8.4%	14.4%

JetBlue's return on assets was less than that of Southwest's. At one time, the airline industry experienced financial difficulties as it attempted to cover high labor, fuel, and security costs while offering fares low enough to attract customers. Such difficulties were reflected in a low industry average for return on assets. In response, Southwest announced that it would not add additional planes beyond the 700 it already had until it met its investment-return targets. Instead, the company added seats to existing planes and replaced some smaller planes with larger ones.

Accounting Across the Organization

Marketing ROI as Profit Indicator

© Walter G Arce/Cal Sport Media/NewsCom

Marketing executives use the basic finance concept underlying return on assets to determine "marketing return on investment (ROI)." They calculate *marketing ROI* as the profit generated by a marketing initiative divided by the investment in that initiative.

It can be tricky to determine what to include in the "investment" amount and how to attribute profit to a particular marketing initiative. However, many firms feel that measuring marketing ROI is worth the effort because it allows managers to evaluate the relative effectiveness of various programs. In addition, it helps quantify the benefits that marketing provides to the organization. In periods of tight budgets, the marketing ROI number can provide particularly valuable evidence to help a marketing manager avoid budget cuts.

Source: James O. Mitchel, "Marketing ROI," *LIMRA's MarketFacts Quarterly* (Summer 2004), p. 15.

How does measuring marketing ROI support the overall efforts of the organization? (Go to WileyPLUS for this answer and additional questions.)

Decision Tools

The asset turnover helps users determine how effectively a company is generating sales from its assets.

Asset Turnover

Asset turnover indicates how efficiently a company uses its assets to generate sales—that is, how many dollars of sales a company generates for each dollar invested in assets (see **Decision Tools**). It is calculated by dividing net sales by average total assets. When we compare two companies in the same industry, the one with the higher asset turnover is operating more efficiently. It is generating more sales per dollar invested in assets. **Illustration 9.21** presents the asset turnovers for JetBlue Airways and Southwest Airlines.

ILLUSTRATION 9.21

Asset turnovers for JetBlue and Southwest

$$\text{Asset Turnover} = \frac{\text{Net Sales}}{\text{Average Total Assets}}$$

JetBlue Airways ($ in millions)		Southwest Airlines
2017	2016	2017
$\dfrac{\$7{,}015}{(\$9{,}781 + \$9{,}323)/2} = 0.73$ times	0.74 times	0.92 times

These asset turnover values tell us that for each dollar of assets, JetBlue generates sales of $0.73 and Southwest $0.92. Southwest is more successful in generating sales per dollar invested in assets. In recent years, airlines have reduced both the number of planes used and routes flown to try to pack more customers on a plane. This would increase the asset turnover.

Asset turnovers vary considerably across industries. During a recent year, the average asset turnover for electric utility companies was 0.34. The grocery industry had an average asset turnover of 2.89. Asset turnover values, therefore, are only comparable within—not between—industries.

Profit Margin Revisited

In Chapter 5, you learned about **profit margin**. That ratio is calculated by dividing net income by net sales. It tells how effective a company is in turning its sales into income—that is, how much income each dollar of sales provides. **Illustration 9.22** shows that return on assets can be computed as the product of profit margin and asset turnover.

ILLUSTRATION 9.22

Composition of return on assets

Profit Margin	×	Asset Turnover	=	Return on Assets
$\dfrac{\text{Net Income}}{\text{Net Sales}}$	×	$\dfrac{\text{Net Sales}}{\text{Average Total Assets}}$	=	$\dfrac{\text{Net Income}}{\text{Average Total Assets}}$

This relationship has very important strategic implications for management. From Illustration 9.22, we can see that if a company wants to increase its return on assets, it can do so in two ways: (1) by increasing the margin it generates from each dollar of goods that it sells (the profit margin), or (2) by increasing the volume of goods that it sells (the asset turnover). For example, most grocery stores have very low profit margins, often in the range of 1 or 2 cents for every dollar of goods sold. Grocery stores, therefore, focus on asset turnover: They rely on high turnover to increase their return on assets. Alternatively, a store selling luxury goods, such as expensive jewelry, does not generally have a high turnover. Consequently, a seller of luxury goods focuses on having a high profit margin. Recently, **Apple** decided to offer a more expensive version of its popular iPhone. This new product would provide a higher margin but lower volume than Apple's less expensive version.

Let's evaluate the return on assets of JetBlue and Southwest for 2017 by evaluating its components—profit margin and asset turnover. See **Illustration 9.23**.

	Profit Margin	×	Asset Turnover	=	Return on Assets
JetBlue Airways	16.4%	×	0.73	=	12.0%
Southwest Airlines	15.7%	×	0.92	=	14.4%

ILLUSTRATION 9.23
Components of rate of return for JetBlue and Southwest

JetBlue's return on asset of 12% versus Southwest's 14.4% means that JetBlue generates 12.0 cents per each dollar invested in assets, while Southwest generates 14.4 cents. Illustration 9.23 reveals that although these two airlines have similar return on asset values, they achieve this return in a slightly different fashion. First, JetBlue's profit margin of 16.4% versus Southwest's 15.7% means that for every dollar of sales, JetBlue generates approximately 16.4 cents of net income, while Southwest generates approximately 15.7 cents. Second, JetBlue's asset turnover of 0.73 means that it generates 73 cents of sales per each dollar invested in assets, while Southwest generates 92 cents. Therefore, in 2017, Southwest was more effective at generating sales from its assets, while JetBlue was better at deriving profit from its sales.

Keeping an Eye on Cash

Depreciation and amortization expense are among the biggest causes of differences between accrual-accounting net income and net cash provided by operating activities. Depreciation and amortization reduce net income, but they do not use up any cash. Therefore, to determine net cash provided by operating activities under a common approach referred to as the indirect method, companies add depreciation and amortization back to net income. For example, if a company reported net income of $175,000 during the year and had depreciation expense of $40,000, net cash provided by operating activities would be $215,000 (assuming no other accrual-accounting differences). The operating activities section of a recent statement of cash flows for **The Coca-Cola Company** reports the following adjustment for depreciation and amortization.

The adjustment for depreciation and amortization was more than twice as big as any other adjustment required to convert net income to net cash provided by operating activities.

It is also interesting to examine the statement of cash flows to determine the amount of property, plant, and equipment a company purchased and the cash it received from property, plant, and equipment sold in a given year. For example, the investing activities section of Coca-Cola reports the following.

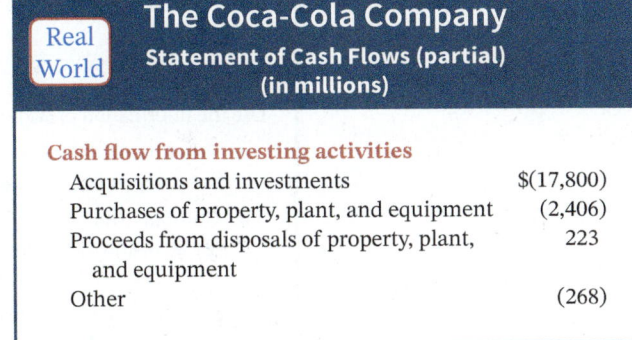

The Coca-Cola Company
Statement of Cash Flows (partial)
(in millions)

Cash flow from investing activities
Acquisitions and investments $(17,800)
Purchases of property, plant, and equipment (2,406)
Proceeds from disposals of property, plant, and equipment 223
Other (268)

As indicated, Coca-Cola made significant purchases and sales of property, plant, and equipment. The level of purchases suggests that Coca-Cola believes that it can earn a reasonable rate of return on these assets.

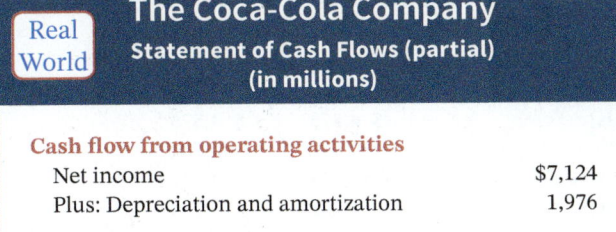

The Coca-Cola Company
Statement of Cash Flows (partial)
(in millions)

Cash flow from operating activities
Net income $7,124
Plus: Depreciation and amortization 1,976

ACTION PLAN	DO IT! 5	Asset Turnover

ACTION PLAN
- Recognize that the asset turnover analyzes the productivity of a company's assets.
- Know the formula Net sales ÷ Average total assets equals Asset turnover.

DO IT! 5 | Asset Turnover

Paramour Company reported net income of $180,000, net sales of $420,000, and had total assets of $460,000 on January 1, 2022, and total assets on December 31, 2022, of $540,000. Determine Paramour's asset turnover for 2022.

Solution

The asset turnover for Paramour Company is computed as follows.

Net Sales	÷	Average Total Assets	=	Asset Turnover
$420,000	÷	$\dfrac{\$460,000 + \$540,000}{2}$	=	.84 times

Related exercise material: **BE9.10, DO IT! 9.5, E9.18, E9.19, and E9.20.**

USING THE DECISION TOOLS | Delta Air Lines

Delta Air Lines, Inc., headquartered in Atlanta, Georgia, is one of the largest airlines in the world. It serves 342 destinations in 61 countries. Delta provided the following information in its 2016 annual report.

Delta Air Lines, Inc.
Notes to the Financial Statements (Partial)

Long-Lived Assets
The following table summarizes our property and equipment:

(in millions, except for estimated useful life)	Estimated Useful Life	December 31, 2016	2015
Flight equipment	20–32 years	$28,135	$26,057
Ground property and equipment	3–40 years	6,581	5,862
Flight and ground equipment under capital leases	Shorter of lease term or estimated useful life	1,056	1,112
Advance payments for equipment		1,059	879
Less: accumulated depreciation and amortization[1]		(12,456)	(10,871)
Total property and equipment, net		$24,375	$23,039

[1]Includes accumulated amortization for flight and ground equipment under capital leases in the amount of $757 million and $782 million at December 31, 2016 and 2015, respectively.

We record property and equipment at cost and depreciate or amortize these assets on a straight-line basis to their estimated residual values over their estimated useful lives.

Instructions

Use the information provided to answer the following questions.

a. What method does the company use to depreciate its aircraft? Over what period is the company depreciating these aircraft?

b. Compute the company's return on assets ratio, asset turnover ratio, and profit margin ratio for 2016 and 2015. Comment on your results.

(in millions)	2016	2015
Net income (loss)	$ 4,373	$ 4,526
Net sales	39,639	40,704
Beginning total assets	53,134	54,121
Ending total assets	51,261	53,134

Solution

a. The company depreciates property and equipment using the straight-line approach. It depreciates aircraft over a 20–32-year life.

b.

	2016	2015
Return on assets	$\dfrac{\$4{,}373}{(\$53{,}134 + \$51{,}261)/2} = 8.4\%$	$\dfrac{\$4{,}526}{(\$54{,}121 + \$53{,}134)/2} = 8.4\%$
Asset turnover	$\dfrac{\$39{,}639}{(\$53{,}134 + \$51{,}261)/2} = 0.76 \text{ times}$	$\dfrac{\$40{,}704}{(\$54{,}121 + \$53{,}134)/2} = 0.76 \text{ times}$
Profit margin	$\dfrac{\$4{,}373}{\$39{,}639} = 11.0\%$	$\dfrac{\$4{,}526}{\$40{,}704} = 11.1\%$

Delta's return on assets, asset turnover, and profit margin ratios were virtually unchanged from 2015 to 2016.

Appendix 9A Other Depreciation Methods

LEARNING OBJECTIVE *6
Compute periodic depreciation using the declining-balance method and the units-of-activity method.

In this appendix, we show the calculations of the depreciation expense amounts that we used in the chapter for the declining-balance and units-of-activity methods.

Declining-Balance Method

The **declining-balance method** produces a decreasing annual depreciation expense over the useful life of the asset. The method is so named because the computation of periodic depreciation is based on a **declining book value** (cost less accumulated depreciation) of the asset. Annual depreciation expense is computed by multiplying the book value at the beginning of the year by the declining-balance depreciation rate. **The depreciation rate remains constant from year to year, but the book value to which the rate is applied declines each year.**

Book value for the first year is the cost of the asset because the balance in accumulated depreciation at the beginning of the asset's useful life is zero. In subsequent years, book value is the difference between cost and accumulated depreciation at the beginning of the year. **Unlike other depreciation methods, the declining-balance method ignores salvage value in determining the amount to which the declining-balance rate is applied.** Salvage value, however, does limit the total depreciation that can be taken. Depreciation stops when the asset's book value equals its expected salvage value.

Depreciation must be completed by the end of the asset's useful life. Therefore, in the last year of the asset's useful life, it is sometimes necessary to adjust the amount of depreciation expense so that the book value equals the expected salvage value. For example, note the adjustment to the final year in Illustration 9A.2.

As noted in the chapter, a common declining-balance rate is double the straight-line rate—the **double-declining-balance method** (see **Helpful Hint**). If Bill's Pizzas uses the double-declining-balance method, the depreciation rate is 40% (2 × the straight-line rate of 20%). **Illustration 9A.1** presents the formula and computation of depreciation for the first year on the delivery truck.

HELPFUL HINT
The straight-line rate is approximated as 1 ÷ Estimated life. In this case, it is 1 ÷ 5 = 20%.

ILLUSTRATION 9A.1
Formula for declining-balance method

Book Value at Beginning of Year	×	Declining-Balance Rate	=	Depreciation Expense
$13,000	×	40%	=	$5,200

Illustration 9A.2 presents the depreciation schedule under this method (see **Helpful Hint**).

ILLUSTRATION 9A.2
Double-declining-balance depreciation schedule

HELPFUL HINT
Depreciation stops when the asset's book value equals its expected salvage value.

Bill's Pizzas

	Computation			Annual	End of Year	
Year	Book Value Beginning of Year	×	Depreciation Rate =	Depreciation Expense	Accumulated Depreciation	Book Value
2022	$13,000		40%	$5,200	$ 5,200	$7,800*
2023	7,800		40	3,120	8,320	4,680
2024	4,680		40	1,872	10,192	2,808
2025	2,808		40	1,123	11,315	1,685
2026	1,685		40	685**	12,000	1,000

*$13,000 − $5,200
**Computation of $674 ($1,685 × 40%) is adjusted to $685 in order for book value to equal salvage value.

The delivery equipment is 69% depreciated ($8,320 ÷ $12,000) at the end of the second year. Under the straight-line method, it would be depreciated 40% ($4,800 ÷ $12,000) at that time. Because the declining-balance method produces higher depreciation expense in the early years than in the later years, it is considered an **accelerated-depreciation method**.

The declining-balance method is compatible with the expense recognition principle. It recognizes the higher depreciation expense in early years with the associated higher benefits received in these years. Conversely, it recognizes lower depreciation expense in later years when the asset's contribution to revenue is likely to be lower. Also, some assets lose their usefulness rapidly because of obsolescence. In these cases, the declining-balance method provides a more appropriate depreciation amount.

When an asset is purchased during the year, it is necessary to prorate the declining-balance depreciation in the first year on a time basis. For example, if Bill's Pizzas had purchased the delivery equipment on April 1, 2022, depreciation for 2022 would be $3,900 ($13,000 × 40% × $\frac{9}{12}$). The book value for computing depreciation in 2023 then becomes $9,100 ($13,000 − $3,900), and the 2023 depreciation is $3,640 ($9,100 × 40%).

Units-of-Activity Method

ALTERNATIVE TERMINOLOGY
Another term often used is the *units-of-production method*.

Under the **units-of-activity method**, useful life is expressed in terms of the total units of production or use expected from the asset (see **Alternative Terminology**). The units-of-activity method is ideally suited to equipment whose activity can be measured in units of output, miles driven, or hours in use. The units-of-activity method is generally not suitable for assets for which depreciation is a function more of time than of use.

To use this method, a company estimates the total units of activity for the entire useful life and divides that amount into the depreciable cost to determine the depreciation cost per unit. It then multiplies the depreciation cost per unit by the units of activity during the year to find the annual depreciation for that year.

To illustrate, assume that Bill's Pizzas estimates it will drive its new delivery truck 15,000 miles in the first year. **Illustration 9A.3** presents the formula and computation of depreciation expense in the first year.

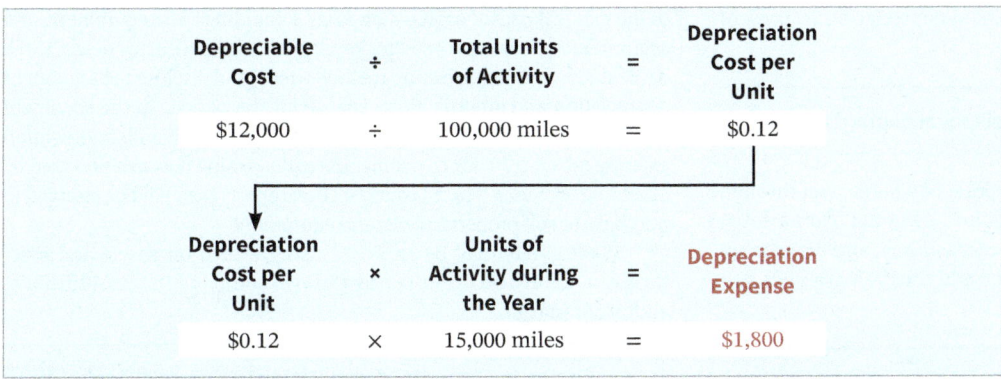

ILLUSTRATION 9A.3
Formula for units-of-activity method

Illustration 9A.4 shows the depreciation schedule, using assumed mileage data (see Helpful Hint).

Bill's Pizzas

Year	Units of Activity	×	Depreciation Cost/Unit	=	Annual Depreciation Expense	Accumulated Depreciation	Book Value
2022	15,000		$0.12		**$1,800**	$ 1,800	$11,200*
2023	30,000		0.12		**3,600**	5,400	7,600
2024	20,000		0.12		**2,400**	7,800	5,200
2025	25,000		0.12		**3,000**	10,800	2,200
2026	10,000		0.12		**1,200**	12,000	**1,000**

*$13,000 − $1,800

ILLUSTRATION 9A.4
Units-of-activity depreciation schedule

HELPFUL HINT
Depreciation stops when the asset's book value equals its expected salvage value.

The units-of-activity method is not nearly as popular as the straight-line method, primarily because it is often difficult to make a reasonable estimate of total activity. However, this method is used by some very large companies, such as **Standard Oil Company of California** and **Boise Cascade Corporation**. When the productivity of the asset varies significantly from one period to another, the units-of-activity method results in the best association of expenses (efforts) with related revenues (results).

This method is easy to apply when assets are purchased during the year. In such a case, companies use the productivity of the asset for the partial year in computing the depreciation.

Review and Practice

Learning Objectives Review

1 Explain the accounting for plant asset expenditures.

The cost of plant assets includes all expenditures necessary to acquire the asset and make it ready for its intended use. Once cost is established, a company uses that amount as the basis of accounting for the plant asset over its useful life.

2 Apply depreciation methods to plant assets.

Depreciation is the process of allocating to expense the cost of a plant asset over its useful (service) life in a rational and systematic manner. Depreciation is not a process of valuation, and it is not a process that results in an accumulation of cash. Depreciation reflects an asset's decreasing usefulness and revenue-producing ability, resulting from wear and tear and from obsolescence.

The formula for straight-line depreciation is:

$$\frac{\text{Cost} - \text{Salvage value}}{\text{Useful life (in years)}}$$

The expense patterns of the three depreciation methods are as follows.

Method	Annual Depreciation Pattern
Straight-line	Constant amount
Declining-balance	Decreasing amount
Units-of-activity	Varying amount

Companies make revisions of periodic depreciation in present and future periods, not retroactively.

3 Explain how to account for the disposal of plant assets.

The procedure for accounting for the disposal of a plant asset through sale or retirement is (a) eliminate the book value of the plant asset at the date of disposal; (b) record cash proceeds, if any; and (c) account for the difference between the book value and the cash proceeds as a gain or a loss on disposal.

4 Identify the basic issues related to reporting intangible assets.

Companies report intangible assets at their cost less any amounts amortized. If an intangible asset has a limited life, its cost should be allocated (amortized) over its useful life. Intangible assets with indefinite lives should not be amortized.

5 Discuss how long-lived assets are reported and analyzed.

Companies usually show plant assets under "Property, plant, and equipment"; they show intangibles separately under "Intangible assets." Either within the balance sheet or in the notes, companies disclose the balances of the major classes of assets, such as land, buildings, and equipment, and accumulated depreciation by major classes or in total. They describe the depreciation and amortization methods used, and disclose the amount of depreciation and amortization expense for the period. In the statement of cash flows, under the indirect method, depreciation and amortization expense are added back to net income to determine net cash provided by operating activities. The investing section reports cash paid or received to purchase or sell property, plant, and equipment.

Plant assets may be analyzed using return on assets and asset turnover. Return on assets consists of two components: asset turnover and profit margin.

*6 Compute periodic depreciation using the declining-balance method and the units-of-activity method.

The depreciation expense calculation for each of these methods is:

Declining-balance:

$$\text{Book value at beginning of year} \times \text{Declining-balance rate} = \text{Depreciation expense}$$

Units-of-activity:

$$\text{Depreciable cost} \div \text{Total units of activity} = \text{Depreciation cost per unit}$$

$$\text{Depreciation cost per unit} \times \text{Units of activity during year} = \text{Depreciation expense}$$

Decision Tools Review

Decision Checkpoints	Info Needed for Decision	Tool to Use for Decision	How to Evaluate Results
Is the company's amortization of intangibles reasonable?	Estimated useful life of intangibles from notes to financial statements of this company and its competitors	If the company's estimated useful life significantly exceeds that of competitors or does not seem reasonable in light of the circumstances, the reason for the difference should be investigated.	Too high an estimated useful life will result in understating amortization expense and overstating net income.
Is the company using its assets effectively?	Net income and average total assets	$\text{Return on assets} = \dfrac{\text{Net income}}{\text{Average total assets}}$	Higher value suggests favorable efficiency (use of assets).
How effective is the company at generating sales from its assets?	Net sales and average total assets	$\text{Asset turnover} = \dfrac{\text{Net sales}}{\text{Average total assets}}$	Indicates the sales dollars generated per dollar of assets. A high value suggests the company is effective in using its resources to generate sales.

Glossary Review

Accelerated-depreciation method A depreciation method that produces higher depreciation expense in the early years than the straight-line approach. (p. 9-11).

Additions and improvements Costs incurred to increase the operating efficiency, productive capacity, or expected useful life of a plant asset. (p. 9-6).

Amortization The process of allocating to expense the cost of an intangible asset. (p. 9-18).

Asset turnover Indicates how efficiently a company uses its assets to generate sales; calculated as net sales divided by average total assets. (p. 9-24).

Capital expenditures Expenditures that increase the company's investment in plant assets. (p. 9-3).

Cash equivalent price An amount equal to the fair value of the asset given up or the fair value of the asset received, whichever is more clearly determinable. (p. 9-4).

Copyright An exclusive right granted by the federal government allowing the owner to reproduce and sell an artistic or published work. (p. 9-19).

Declining-balance method A depreciation method that applies a constant rate to the declining book value of the asset and produces a decreasing annual depreciation expense over the asset's useful life. (pp. 9-11, 9-27).

Depreciable cost The cost of a plant asset less its salvage value. (p. 9-9).

Depreciation The process of allocating to expense the cost of a plant asset over its useful life in a rational and systematic manner. (p. 9-8).

Franchise A contractual arrangement under which the franchisor grants the franchisee the right to sell certain products, to perform specific services, or to use certain trademarks or trade names, usually within a designated geographic area. (p. 9-20).

Goodwill The value of all favorable attributes that relate to a company that are not attributable to any other specific asset. (p. 9-20).

Impairment A permanent decline in the fair value of an asset. (p. 9-14).

Intangible assets Rights, privileges, and competitive advantages that result from the ownership of long-lived assets that do not possess physical substance. (p. 9-18).

Lease A contractual agreement allowing one party (the lessee) to use the asset of another party (the lessor) for a period of time at an agreed price. (p. 9-7).

Lessee A party that has made contractual arrangements to use another party's asset for a period at an agreed price. (p. 9-7).

Lessor A party that has agreed contractually to let another party use its asset for a period at an agreed price. (p. 9-7).

Ordinary repairs Expenditures to maintain the operating efficiency and expected productive life of the asset. (p. 9-6).

Patent An exclusive right issued by the U.S. Patent Office that enables the recipient to manufacture, sell, or otherwise control an invention for a period of 20 years from the date of the grant. (p. 9-19).

Plant assets Resources that have physical substance, are used in the operations of a business, and are not intended for sale to customers. (p. 9-3).

Research and development costs Expenditures that may lead to patents, copyrights, new processes, and new products; must be expensed as incurred. (p. 9-19).

Return on assets A profitability measure that indicates the amount of net income generated by each dollar of assets; computed as net income divided by average total assets. (p. 9-23).

Revenue expenditures Expenditures that are immediately charged against revenues as an expense. (p. 9-3).

Straight-line method A depreciation method in which companies expense an equal amount of depreciation for each year of the asset's useful life. (p. 9-10).

Trademark (trade name) A word, phrase, jingle, or symbol that distinguishes or identifies a particular enterprise or product. (p. 9-20).

Units-of-activity method A depreciation method in which useful life is expressed in terms of the total units of production or use expected from the asset. (pp. 9-12, 9-28).

Practice Multiple-Choice Questions

1. **(LO 1, 6)** Corrieten Company purchased equipment and incurred these costs:

Cash price	$24,000
Sales taxes	1,200
Insurance during transit	200
Installation and testing	400
Total costs	$25,800

   What amount should be recorded as the cost of the equipment?
   a. $24,000.
   b. $25,200.
   c. $25,400.
   d. $25,800.

2. **(LO 1)** The benefits to leasing include each of the following **except**:
   a. higher resale value.
   b. reduced risk of obsolescence.
   c. little or no down payment.
   d. shared tax advantages.

3. **(LO 1)** Additions to plant assets are:
   a. revenue expenditures.
   b. debited to the Maintenance and Repairs Expense account.
   c. debited to the Purchases account.
   d. capital expenditures.

4. **(LO 2)** Depreciation is a process of:
   a. valuation.
   b. cost allocation.
   c. cash accumulation.
   d. appraisal.

5. **(LO 2)** Cuso Company purchased equipment on January 1, 2021, at a total invoice cost of $400,000. The equipment has an estimated salvage value of $10,000 and an estimated useful life of 5 years. What is the amount of accumulated depreciation at December 31, 2022, if the straight-line method of depreciation is used?
   a. $80,000.
   b. $160,000.
   c. $78,000.
   d. $156,000.

6. **(LO 2)** A company would minimize its depreciation expense in the first year of owning an asset if it used:
   a. a high estimated life, a high salvage value, and declining-balance depreciation.
   b. a low estimated life, a high salvage value, and straight-line depreciation.
   c. a high estimated life, a high salvage value, and straight-line depreciation.
   d. a low estimated life, a low salvage value, and declining-balance depreciation.

7. **(LO 2)** When there is a change in estimated depreciation:
   a. previous depreciation should be corrected.

b. current and future years' depreciation should be revised.

c. only future years' depreciation should be revised.

d. None of the above.

8. **(LO 2)** Able Towing Company purchased a tow truck for $60,000 on January 1, 2022. It was originally depreciated on a straight-line basis over 10 years with an assumed salvage value of $12,000. On December 31, 2024, before adjusting entries had been made, the company decided to change the remaining estimated life to 4 years (including 2024) and the salvage value to $2,000. What was the depreciation expense for 2024?

a. $6,000.   c. $15,000.

b. $4,800.   d. $12,100.

9. **(LO 3)** Bennie Razor Company has decided to sell one of its old manufacturing machines on June 30, 2022. The machine was purchased for $80,000 on January 1, 2018, and was depreciated on a straight-line basis for 10 years assuming no salvage value. If the machine was sold for $26,000, what was the amount of the gain or loss recorded at the time of the sale?

a. $18,000 loss.   c. $22,000 gain.

b. $54,000 loss.   d. $46,000 gain.

10. **(LO 4)** Pierce Company incurred $150,000 of research and development costs in its laboratory to develop a new product. It spent $20,000 in legal fees for a patent granted on January 2, 2022. On July 31, 2022, Pierce paid $15,000 for legal fees in a successful defense of the patent. What is the total amount that should be debited to Patents through July 31, 2022?

a. $150,000.   c. $185,000.

b. $35,000.   d. $170,000.

11. **(LO 4)** Indicate which one of these statements is **true**.

a. Since intangible assets lack physical substance, they need to be disclosed only in the notes to the financial statements.

b. Goodwill should be reported as a contra account in the stockholders' equity section.

c. Totals of major classes of assets can be shown in the balance sheet, with asset details disclosed in the notes to the financial statements.

d. Intangible assets are typically combined with plant assets and inventory and then shown in the property, plant, and equipment section.

12. **(LO 4)** If a company reports goodwill as an intangible asset on its books, what is the one thing you know with certainty?

a. The company is a valuable company worth investing in.

b. The company has a well-established brand name.

c. The company purchased another company.

d. The goodwill will generate a lot of positive business for the company for many years to come.

13. **(LO 4)** Which of the following statements is **false**?

a. If an intangible asset has a finite life, it should be amortized.

b. The amortization period of an intangible asset can exceed 20 years.

c. Goodwill is recorded only when a business is purchased.

d. Research and development costs are expensed when incurred, except when the research and development expenditures result in a successful patent.

14. **(LO 5)** Which of the following measures provides an indication of how efficient a company is in employing its assets?

a. Current ratio.   c. Debt to assets ratio.

b. Profit margin.   d. Asset turnover.

15. **(LO 5)** Lake Coffee Company reported net sales of $180,000, net income of $54,000, beginning total assets of $200,000, and ending total assets of $300,000. What was the company's asset turnover?

a. 0.90   c. 0.72

b. 0.20   d. 1.39

*16. **(LO 6)** Kant Enterprises purchased a truck for $11,000 on January 1, 2021. The truck will have an estimated salvage value of $1,000 at the end of 5 years. If you use the units-of-activity method, the balance in accumulated depreciation at December 31, 2022, can be computed by the following formula:

a. ($11,000 ÷ Total estimated activity) × Units of activity for 2022.

b. ($10,000 ÷ Total estimated activity) × Units of activity for 2022.

c. ($11,000 ÷ Total estimated activity) × Units of activity for 2021 and 2022.

d. ($10,000 ÷ Total estimated activity) × Units of activity for 2021 and 2022.

*17. **(LO 6)** Jefferson Company purchased a piece of equipment on January 1, 2022. The equipment cost $60,000 and has an estimated life of 8 years and a salvage value of $8,000. What was the depreciation expense for the asset for 2023 under the double-declining-balance method?

a. $6,500.   c. $15,000.

b. $11,250.   d. $6,562.

Solutions

1. d. All of the costs ($1,200 + $200 + $400) in addition to the cash price ($24,000) should be included in the cost of the equipment because they were necessary expenditures to acquire the asset and make it ready for its intended use. The other choices are therefore incorrect.

2. a. Higher resale value is not a benefit of leasing. The benefits of leasing include (b) reduced risk of obsolescence, (c) little or no down payment, and (d) shared tax advantages.

3. d. When an addition is made to plant assets, it is intended to increase productive capacity, increase the assets' useful life, or increase the efficiency of the assets. This is called a capital expenditure. The other choices are incorrect because (a) additions to plant assets are not revenue expenditures because the additions will have a long-term useful life whereas revenue expenditures are minor repairs and maintenance that do not prolong the life of the assets; (b) additions to plant assets are debited to Plant Assets, not Maintenance and Repairs Expense, because the Maintenance and Repairs Expense account is used to record expenditures not intended to increase the life of the assets; and (c) additions to plant assets are debited to Plant Assets, not Purchases, because the Purchases account is used to record assets intended for resale (inventory).

4. b. Depreciation is a process of allocating the cost of an asset over its useful life, not a process of (a) valuation, (c) cash accumulation, or (d) appraisal.

5. d. Accumulated depreciation will be the sum of 2 years of depreciation expense. Annual depreciation for this asset is ($400,000 − $10,000)/5 = $78,000. The sum of 2 years' depreciation is therefore $156,000 ($78,000 + $78,000), not (a) $80,000, (b) $160,000, or (c) $78,000.

6. c. A high estimated life spreads the cost over a longer period of time, resulting in a smaller expense each year. The high salvage value limits the cost to be allocated. Straight-line depreciation yields a smaller depreciation charge in the first year than the declining-balance method. The other choices are therefore incorrect.

7. b. When there is a change in estimated depreciation, the current and future years' depreciation computation should reflect the new estimates. The other choices are incorrect because (a) previous years' depreciation should not be adjusted when new estimates are made for depreciation, and (c) when there is a change in estimated depreciation, the current and future years' depreciation computation should reflect the new estimates. Choice (d) is wrong because there is a correct answer.

8. d. First, calculate accumulated depreciation from January 1, 2022, through December 31, 2023, which is $9,600 {[($60,000 − $12,000)/10 years] × 2 years}. Next, calculate the revised depreciable cost, which is $48,400 ($60,000 − $9,600 − $2,000). Thus, the depreciation expense for 2024 is $12,100 ($48,400/4), not (a) $6,000, (b) $4,800, or (c) $15,000.

9. a. First, the book value needs to be determined. The accumulated depreciation as of June 30, 2022, is $36,000 [($80,000/10) × 4.5 years]. Thus, the cost of the machine less accumulated depreciation equals $44,000 ($80,000 − $36,000). The loss recorded at the time of sale is $18,000 ($26,000 − $44,000), not (b) $54,000, (c) $22,000, or (d) $46,000.

10. b. Because the $150,000 was spent developing the patent rather than buying it from another firm, it is debited to Research and Development Expense. Only the $35,000 spent on legal fees ($20,000 for granting patent and $15,000 for defense) can be debited to Patents, not (a) $150,000, (c) $185,000, or (d) $170,000.

11. c. Reporting only totals of major classes of assets in the balance sheet is appropriate. Additional details can be shown in the notes to the financial statements. The other choices are false statements.

12. c. In order to report goodwill, a company must have entered into an exchange transaction that involves the purchase of another business. Choices (a) the company is a valuable company worth investing in, (b) the company has a well-established brand name, and (d) the goodwill will generate a lot of positive business for the company for many years to come are not necessarily valid assumptions.

13. d. Research and development (R&D) costs are expensed when incurred, regardless of whether the research and development expenditures result in a successful patent or not. The other choices are true statements.

14. d. The asset turnover indicates how efficiently a company is employing its assets. The other choices are incorrect because (a) the current ratio is an indicator of liquidity and the company's ability to pay its obligations when they come due, (b) the profit margin is an indicator of how profitable a company is, and (c) the debt to assets ratio indicates the proportion of assets that are financed by debt rather than by equity.

15. c. Asset turnover = Net sales ($180,000)/Average total assets [($200,000 + $300,000)/2] = 0.72 times, not (a) 0.90, (b) 0.20, or (d) 1.39 times.

*****16. d.** The units-of-activity method takes salvage value into consideration; therefore, the depreciable cost is $10,000. This amount is divided by total estimated activity. The resulting number is multiplied by the units of activity used in 2021 and 2022 to compute the accumulated depreciation at the end of 2022, the second year of the asset's use. The other choices are therefore incorrect.

*****17. b.** For the double-declining method, the depreciation rate would be 25% or (1/8 × 2). For 2022, annual depreciation expense is $15,000 ($60,000 book value × 25%); for 2023, annual depreciation expense is $11,250 [($60,000 − $15,000) × 25%], not (a) $6,500, (c) $15,000, or (d) $6,562.

Practice Brief Exercises

1. (LO 2, 6) Fulmer Company acquires a delivery truck at a cost of $50,000. The truck is expected to have a salvage value of $5,000 at the end of its 5-year useful life.

Compute straight-line and declining-balance depreciation.

a. Compute annual depreciation expense for the first and second years using the straight-line method.

*****b.** Compute annual depreciation expense for the first and second years using double-declining balance.

Solution

1. a. Depreciable cost of $45,000, ($50,000 − $5,000). With a 5-year useful life, annual depreciation is $9,000, ($45,000 ÷ 5). Under the straight-line method, depreciation is the same each year. Thus, depreciation is $9,000 for both the first and second years.

*****b.** The declining-balance rate is 40% (20% × 2), which is applied to book value at the beginning of the year. The computations are:

	Book Value	×	Rate	=	Depreciation
Year 1	$50,000		40%		$20,000
Year 2	($50,000 − $20,000)		40%		$12,000

Prepare entries for disposal by sale.

2. (LO 3) Giolito Company sells equipment on August 31, 2022, for $20,000 cash. The equipment originally cost $60,000 and as of January 1, 2022, had accumulated depreciation of $38,000. Depreciation for the first 8 months of 2022 is $6,000. Prepare the journal entries to (a) update depreciation to August 31, 2022, and (b) record the sale of the equipment.

Solution

2. **a.** Depreciation Expense   6,000
              Accumulated Depreciation—Equipment   6,000

   b. Cash   20,000
              Accumulated Depreciation—Equipment   44,000
                  Equipment   60,000
                  Gain on Disposal of Plant Assets   4,000

Cost of equipment	$60,000
Less: Accumulated depreciation	44,000*
Book value at date of disposal	16,000
Proceeds from sale	20,000
Gain on disposal	$ 4,000

*$38,000 + $6,000

Prepare amortization expense entry and balance sheet presentation for intangibles.

3. (LO 4) Lucas Company acquires a limited-life franchise for $200,000 on January 2, 2022. Its estimated useful life is 10 years. (a) Prepare the journal entry to record amortization expense for the first year. (b) Show how this franchise is reported on the balance sheet at the end of the first year.

Solution

3. **a.** Amortization Expense ($200,000 ÷ 10)   20,000
              Franchises   20,000

   b. Intangible assets
              Franchises $180,000

Practice Exercises

Compute revised annual depreciation.

1. (LO 2) Will Smith, the new controller of Alexandria Company, has reviewed the expected useful lives and salvage values of selected depreciable assets at the beginning of 2022. Here are his findings:

Type of Asset	Date Acquired	Cost	Accumulated Depreciation, Jan. 1, 2022	Useful Life (in Years) Old	Useful Life (in Years) Proposed	Salvage Value Old	Salvage Value Proposed
Building	Jan. 1, 2014	$900,000	$172,000	40	50	$40,000	$47,600
Warehouse	Jan. 1, 2016	120,000	27,600	25	20	5,000	3,600

All assets are depreciated by the straight-line method. Alexandria Company uses a calendar year in preparing annual financial statements. After discussion, management has agreed to accept Will's proposed changes. (The "Proposed" useful life is total life, not remaining life.)

Instructions

a. Compute the revised annual depreciation on each asset in 2022. (Show computations.)

b. Prepare the entry (or entries) to record depreciation on the building in 2022.

Solution

1. a.

	Type of Asset	
	Building	**Warehouse**
Book value, 1/1/22	$728,000	$92,400
Less: Salvage value	47,600	3,600
Depreciable cost (1)	$680,400	$88,800
Revised remaining useful life in years (2)	42*	14**
Revised annual depreciation (1) ÷ (2)	$16,200	$6,343

*(50 − 8); **(20 − 6)

b. Dec. 31 Depreciation Expense 16,200
 Accumulated Depreciation—
  Buildings   16,200

2. (LO 4) Lake Company, organized in 2022, has the following transactions related to intangible assets.

1/2/22	Purchased patent (8-year life)	$560,000
4/1/22	Goodwill purchased (indefinite life)	360,000
7/1/22	10-year franchise; expiration date 7/1/2032	440,000
9/1/22	Research and development costs	185,000

Prepare entries to set up appropriate accounts for different intangibles; amortize intangible assets.

Instructions

Prepare the necessary entries to record these intangibles. All costs incurred were for cash. Make the adjusting entries as of December 31, 2022, recording any necessary amortization and reflecting all balances accurately as of that date.

Solution

2.
1/2/22	Patents	560,000	
	Cash		560,000
4/1/22	Goodwill	360,000	
	Cash		360,000
	(Part of the entry to record purchase of another company)		
7/1/22	Franchises	440,000	
	Cash		440,000
9/1/22	Research and Development Expense	185,000	
	Cash		185,000
12/31/22	Amortization Expense	92,000	
	($560,000 ÷ 8) + [($440,000 ÷ 10) × 1/2]		
	Patents		70,000
	Franchises		22,000

Ending balances, 12/31/22:
Patents = $490,000 ($560,000 − $70,000)
Goodwill = $360,000
Franchises = $418,000 ($440,000 − $22,000)
R&D expense = $185,000

Practice Problems

1. (LO 2, 6) DuPage Company purchases a factory machine at a cost of $18,000 on January 1, 2022. DuPage expects the machine to have a salvage value of $2,000 at the end of its 4-year useful life.

During its useful life, the machine is expected to be used 160,000 hours. Actual annual hourly use was 2022, 40,000; 2023, 60,000; 2024, 35,000; and 2025, 25,000.

Compute depreciation under different methods.

Instructions

a. Prepare a depreciation schedule for the straight-line method.

*b. Prepare a depreciation schedule for the units-of-activity method.

*c. Prepare a depreciation schedule for the declining-balance method using double the straight-line rate.

Solution

1. a.

Straight-Line Method

	Computation			Annual	End of Year	
Year	Depreciable Cost*	×	Depreciation Rate =	Depreciation Expense	Accumulated Depreciation	Book Value
2022	$16,000		25%	$4,000	$ 4,000	$14,000**
2023	16,000		25%	4,000	8,000	10,000
2024	16,000		25%	4,000	12,000	6,000
2025	16,000		25%	4,000	16,000	2,000

*$18,000 − $2,000.
**$18,000 − $4,000.

*b.

Units-of-Activity Method

	Computation			Annual	End of Year	
Year	Units of Activity	×	Depreciable Cost/Unit =	Depreciation Expense	Accumulated Depreciation	Book Value
2022	40,000		$0.10*	$4,000	$ 4,000	$14,000
2023	60,000		0.10	6,000	10,000	8,000
2024	35,000		0.10	3,500	13,500	4,500
2025	25,000		0.10	2,500	16,000	2,000

*($18,000 − $2,000) ÷ 160,000.

*c.

Declining-Balance Method

	Computation			Annual	End of Year	
Year	Book Value Beginning of Year	×	Depreciation Rate* =	Depreciation Expense	Accumulated Depreciation	Book Value
2022	$18,000		50%	$9,000	$ 9,000	$9,000
2023	9,000		50%	4,500	13,500	4,500
2024	4,500		50%	2,250	15,750	2,250
2025	2,250		50%	250**	16,000	2,000

*¼ × 2.
**Adjusted to $250 because ending book value should not be less than expected salvage value.

Record disposal of plant asset.

2. (LO 3) On January 1, 2019, Skyline Limousine Co. purchased a limousine at an acquisition cost of $28,000. Skyline depreciated the vehicle by the straight-line method using a 4-year service life and a $4,000 salvage value. The company's fiscal year ends on December 31.

Instructions

Prepare the journal entry or entries to record the disposal of the limousine, assuming that it was:

a. Retired and scrapped with no salvage value on January 1, 2023.

b. Sold for $5,000 on July 1, 2022.

Solution

2. a.

Jan. 1, 2023	Accumulated Depreciation—Equipment		24,000*	
	Loss on Disposal of Plant Assets		4,000	
	Equipment			28,000
	(To record retirement of limousine)			

*[($28,000 − $4,000) ÷ 4] × 4

b.

July 1, 2022	Depreciation Expense		3,000*	
	Accumulated Depreciation—Equipment			3,000
	(To record depreciation to date of disposal)			

*[($28,000 − $4,000) ÷ 4] × $\frac{1}{2}$

Cash	5,000	
Accumulated Depreciation—Equipment	21,000*	
Loss on Disposal of Plant Assets	2,000	
Equipment		28,000
(To record sale of limousine)		

*[($28,000 − $4,000) ÷ 4] × 3.5

WileyPLUS

Brief Exercises, DO IT! Exercises, Exercises, Problems, and many additional resources are available for practice in WileyPLUS.

Note: All asterisked Questions, Exercises, and Problems relate to material in the appendix to the chapter.

Questions

1. Mrs. Harcross is uncertain about how the historical cost principle applies to plant assets. Explain the principle to Mrs. Harcross.

2. How is the cost for a plant asset measured in a cash transaction? In a noncash transaction?

3. Barrister Company acquires the land and building owned by Ansel Company. What types of costs may be incurred to make the asset ready for its intended use if Barrister Company wants to use only the land? If it wants to use both the land and the building?

4. Distinguish between ordinary repairs and capital expenditures during an asset's useful life.

5. Breton Inc. needs to upgrade its diagnostic equipment. At the time of purchase, Breton had expected the equipment to last 8 years. Unfortunately, it was obsolete after only 4 years. Nolan Rush, CFO of Breton Inc., is considering leasing new equipment rather than buying it. What are the potential benefits of leasing?

6. In a recent newspaper release, the president of Magnusson Company asserted that something has to be done about depreciation. The president said, "Depreciation does not come close to accumulating the cash needed to replace the asset at the end of its useful life." What is your response to the president?

7. Melanie is studying for the next accounting examination. She asks your help on two questions: (a) What is salvage value? (b) How is salvage value used in determining depreciable cost under the straight-line method? Answer Melanie's questions.

8. Contrast the straight-line method and the units-of-activity method in relation to (a) useful life and (b) the pattern of periodic depreciation over useful life.

9. Contrast the effects of the three depreciation methods on annual depreciation expense.

10. In the fourth year of an asset's 5-year useful life, the company decides that the asset will have a 6-year service life. How should the revision of depreciation be recorded? Why?

11. How is a gain or a loss on the sale of a plant asset computed?

12. Marsh Corporation owns a machine that is fully depreciated but is still being used. How should Marsh account for this asset and report it in the financial statements?

13. What does **Apple** use as the estimated useful life on its buildings? On its machinery and equipment? (*Hint:* You will need to use the notes to Apple's financial statements, available at the company's website.)

14. What are the similarities and differences between depreciation and amortization?

15. During a recent management meeting, Bruce Dunn, director of marketing, proposed that the company begin capitalizing its marketing expenditures as goodwill. In his words, "Marketing expenditures create goodwill for the company which benefits the company for multiple periods. Therefore it doesn't make good sense to have to expense it as it is incurred. Besides, if we capitalize it as goodwill, we won't have to amortize it, and this will boost reported income." Discuss the merits of Bruce's proposal.

16. Warwick Company hires an accounting intern who says that intangible assets should always be amortized over their legal lives. Is the intern correct? Explain.

17. Goodwill has been defined as the value of all favorable attributes that relate to a business enterprise. What types of attributes could result in goodwill?

18. Kathy Malone, a business major, is working on a case problem for one of her classes. In this case problem, the company needs to raise cash to market a new product it developed. Doug Price, an engineering major, takes one look at the company's balance sheet and says, "This company has an awful lot of goodwill. Why don't you recommend that they sell some of it to raise cash?" How should Kathy respond to Doug?

19. Under what conditions is goodwill recorded? What is the proper accounting treatment for amortizing goodwill?

20. Often research and development costs provide companies with benefits that last a number of years. (For example, these costs can lead to the development of a patent that will increase the company's income for many years.) However, generally accepted accounting principles require that such costs be recorded as an expense when incurred. Why?

21. Suppose in 2022 that **Campbell Soup Company** reported average total assets of $6,265 million, net sales of $7,586 million, and net income of $736 million. What was Campbell Soup's return on assets?

22. Cassy Dominic, a marketing executive for Fresh Views Inc., has proposed expanding its product line of framed graphic art by producing a line of lower-quality products. These would require less processing by the company and would provide a lower profit margin. Mel Joss, the company's CFO, is concerned that this new product line would reduce the company's return on assets. Discuss the potential effect on return on assets that this product might have.

23. Give an example of an industry that would be characterized by (a) a high asset turnover and a low profit margin, and (b) a low asset turnover and a high profit margin.

24. Peyton Corporation and Rogers Corporation operate in the same industry. Peyton uses the straight-line method to account for depreciation, whereas Rogers uses an accelerated method. Explain what complications might arise in trying to compare the results of these two companies.

25. Mesa Corporation uses straight-line depreciation for financial reporting purposes but an accelerated method for tax purposes. Is it acceptable to use different methods for the two purposes? What is Mesa Corporation's motivation for doing this?

26. You are comparing two companies in the same industry. You have determined that Gore Corp. depreciates its plant assets over a 40-year life, whereas Ross Corp. depreciates its plant assets over a 20-year life. Discuss the implications this has for comparing the results of the two companies.

27. Explain how transactions related to plant assets and intangibles are reported in the statement of cash flows under the indirect method.

Brief Exercises

Determine the cost of land.

BE9.1 (LO 1), AP These expenditures were incurred by Dobbin Company in purchasing land: cash price $60,000, assumed accrued taxes $5,000, attorney's fees $2,100, real estate broker's commission $3,300, and clearing and grading $3,500. What is the cost of the land?

Determine the cost of a truck.

BE9.2 (LO 1), AP Thoms Company incurs these expenditures in purchasing a truck: cash price $24,000, accident insurance (during use) $2,000, sales taxes $1,080, motor vehicle license $300, and painting and lettering $1,700. What is the cost of the truck?

Prepare entries for delivery truck costs.

BE9.3 (LO 1), AP Krieg Company had the following two transactions related to its delivery truck.

1. Paid $38 for an oil change.
2. Paid $400 to install special shelving units, which increase the operating efficiency of the truck.

Prepare Krieg's journal entries to record these two transactions.

Compute straight-line depreciation.

BE9.4 (LO 2), AP Gordon Chemicals Company acquires a delivery truck at a cost of $31,000 on January 1, 2022. The truck is expected to have a salvage value of $4,000 at the end of its 4-year useful life. Compute annual depreciation for the first and second years using the straight-line method.

Compute depreciation and evaluate treatment.

BE9.5 (LO 2), AN Ivy Company purchased land and a building on January 1, 2022. Management's best estimate of the value of the land was $100,000 and of the building $250,000. However, management told the accounting department to record the land at $230,000 and the building at $120,000. The building is being depreciated on a straight-line basis over 20 years with no salvage value. Why do you suppose management requested this accounting treatment? Is it ethical?

Compute revised depreciation.

BE9.6 (LO 2), AP On January 1, 2022, the Hermann Company general ledger shows Equipment $36,000 and Accumulated Depreciation $13,600. The depreciation resulted from using the straight-line method with a useful life of 10 years and a salvage value of $2,000. On this date, the company concludes that the equipment has a remaining useful life of only 2 years with the same salvage value. Compute the revised annual depreciation.

Journalize entries for disposal of plant assets.

BE9.7 (LO 3), AP Prepare journal entries to record these transactions. (a) Echo Company retires its delivery equipment, which cost $41,000. Accumulated depreciation is also $41,000 on this delivery equipment. No salvage value is received. (b) Assume the same information as in part (a), except that accumulated depreciation for the equipment is $37,200 instead of $41,000.

Journalize entries for sale of plant assets.

BE9.8 (LO 3), AP Antone Company sells office equipment on July 31, 2022, for $21,000 cash. The office equipment originally cost $72,000 and as of January 1, 2022, had accumulated depreciation of $42,000. Depreciation for the first 7 months of 2022 is $4,600. Prepare the journal entries to (a) update depreciation to July 31, 2022, and (b) record the sale of the equipment.

Account for intangibles—patents.

BE9.9 (LO 4), AP Abner Company purchases a patent for $156,000 on January 2, 2022. Its estimated useful life is 6 years.

a. Prepare the journal entry to record amortization expense for the first year.
b. Show how this patent is reported on the balance sheet at the end of the first year.

Compute return on assets and asset turnover.

BE9.10 (LO 5), AP Suppose in its 2022 annual report that **McDonald's Corporation** reports beginning total assets of $28.46 billion, ending total assets of $30.22 billion, net sales of $22.74 billion, and net income of $4.55 billion.

a. Compute McDonald's return on assets.
b. Compute McDonald's asset turnover.

Classification of long-lived assets on balance sheet.

BE9.11 (LO 5), AP Suppose **Nike, Inc.** reported the following plant assets and intangible assets for the year ended May 31, 2022 (in millions): other plant assets $965.8, land $221.6, patents and trademarks (at cost)

$515.1, machinery and equipment $2,094.3, buildings $974.0, goodwill (at cost) $193.5, accumulated amortization $47.7, and accumulated depreciation $2,298.0. Prepare a partial balance sheet for Nike for these items.

BE9.12 (LO 5), AP Hunt Company reported net income of $157,000. It reported depreciation expense of $12,000 and accumulated depreciation of $47,000. Amortization expense was $8,000. Hunt purchased new equipment during the year for $50,000. Show how this information would be used to determine net cash provided by operating activities under the indirect method.

Determine net cash provided by operating activities.

*BE9.13 (LO 6), AP Depreciation information for Gordon Chemicals Company is given in BE9.4. Assuming the declining-balance depreciation rate is double the straight-line rate, compute annual depreciation for the first and second years under the declining-balance method.

Compute declining-balance depreciation.

*BE9.14 (LO 6), AP Kwik Taxi Service uses the units-of-activity method in computing depreciation on its taxicabs. Each cab is expected to be driven 150,000 miles. Taxi 10 cost $27,500 and is expected to have a salvage value of $500. Taxi 10 was driven 32,000 miles in 2021 and 33,000 miles in 2022. Compute the depreciation for each year.

Compute depreciation using units-of-activity method.

DO IT! Exercises

DO IT! 9.1 (LO 1), C Hummer Company purchased a delivery truck. The total cash payment was $30,020, including the following items.

Explain accounting for cost of plant assets.

Negotiated purchase price	$24,000
Installation of special shelving	1,100
Painting and lettering	900
Motor vehicle license	180
Two-year insurance policy	2,400
Sales tax	1,440
Total paid	$30,020

Explain how each of these costs would be accounted for.

DO IT! 9.2a (LO 2), AP On January 1, 2022, Salt Creek Country Club purchased a new riding mower for $15,000. The mower is expected to have a 10-year life with a $1,000 salvage value. What journal entry would Salt Creek make on December 31, 2022, if it uses straight-line depreciation?

Calculate depreciation expense and make journal entry.

DO IT! 9.2b (LO 2), AP Fordon Corporation purchased a piece of equipment for $50,000. It estimated an 8-year life and $2,000 salvage value. At the end of year four (before the depreciation adjustment), it estimated the new total life to be 10 years and the new salvage value to be $4,000. Compute the revised depreciation.

Calculated revised depreciation

DO IT! 9.3 (LO 3), AP Bylie Company has an old factory machine that cost $50,000. The machine has accumulated depreciation of $28,000. Bylie has decided to sell the machine.

Make journal entries to record plant asset disposal.

a. What entry would Bylie make to record the sale of the machine for $25,000 cash?
b. What entry would Bylie make to record the sale of the machine for $15,000 cash?

DO IT! 9.4 (LO 4), C Match the statement with the term most directly associated with it.

Match intangible assets with concepts.

    Goodwill   Amortization
    Intangible assets   Franchise
    Research and development costs

1. _____ Rights, privileges, and competitive advantages that result from the ownership of long-lived assets that do not possess physical substance.
2. _____ The allocation of the cost of an intangible asset to expense in a rational and systematic manner.
3. _____ A right to sell certain products or services, or use certain trademarks or trade names within a designated geographic area.
4. _____ Costs incurred by a company that often lead to patents or new products. These costs must be expensed as incurred.
5. _____ The excess of the cost of a company over the fair value of the net assets required.

DO IT! 9.5 (LO 5), AP For 2022, Sale Company reported beginning total assets of $300,000 and ending total assets of $340,000. Its net income for this period was $50,000, and its net sales were $400,000. Compute the company's asset turnover for 2022.

Calculate asset turnover.

Exercises

Determine cost of plant acquisitions.

E9.1 (LO 1), C **Writing** The following expenditures relating to plant assets were made by Glenn Company during the first 2 months of 2022.

1. Paid $7,000 of accrued taxes at the time the plant site was acquired.
2. Paid $200 insurance to cover a possible accident loss on new factory machinery while the machinery was in transit.
3. Paid $850 sales taxes on a new delivery truck.
4. Paid $21,000 for parking lots and driveways on the new plant site.
5. Paid $250 to have the company name and slogan painted on the new delivery truck.
6. Paid $8,000 for installation of new factory machinery.
7. Paid $900 for a 2-year accident insurance policy on the new delivery truck.
8. Paid $75 motor vehicle license fee on the new truck.

Instructions

a. Explain the application of the historical cost principle in determining the acquisition cost of plant assets.
b. List the numbers of the transactions, and opposite each indicate the account title to which each expenditure should be debited.

Determine property, plant, and equipment costs.

E9.2 (LO 1), C Adama Company incurred the following costs.

1. Sales tax on factory machinery purchased	$ 5,000
2. Painting of and lettering on truck immediately upon purchase	700
3. Installation and testing of factory machinery	2,000
4. Real estate broker's commission on land purchased	3,500
5. Insurance premium paid for first year's insurance on new truck	880
6. Cost of landscaping on property purchased	7,200
7. Cost of paving parking lot for new building constructed	17,900
8. Cost of clearing, draining, and filling land	13,300
9. Architect's fees on self-constructed building	10,000

Instructions

Indicate to which account Adama would debit each of the costs.

Determine acquisition costs of land.

E9.3 (LO 1), AP On March 1, 2022, Boyd Company acquired real estate, on which it planned to construct a small office building, by paying $80,000 in cash. An old warehouse on the property was demolished at a cost of $8,200; the salvaged materials were sold for $1,700. Additional expenditures before construction began included $1,900 attorney's fee for work concerning the land purchase, $5,200 real estate broker's fee, $9,100 architect's fee, and $14,000 to put in driveways and a parking lot.

Instructions

a. Determine the amount to be reported as the cost of the land.
b. For each cost not used in part (a), indicate the account to be debited.

Understand depreciation concepts.

E9.4 (LO 2), C Alysha Monet has prepared the following list of statements about depreciation.

1. Depreciation is a process of asset valuation, not cost allocation.
2. Depreciation provides for the proper recording of expenses (efforts) with revenues (results).
3. The book value of a plant asset should approximate its fair value.
4. Depreciation applies to three classes of plant assets: land, buildings, and equipment.
5. Depreciation does not apply to a building because its usefulness and revenue-producing ability generally remain intact over time.
6. The revenue-producing ability of a depreciable asset will decline due to wear and tear and to obsolescence.
7. Recognizing depreciation on an asset results in an accumulation of cash for replacement of the asset.

8. The balance in accumulated depreciation represents the total cost that has been charged to expense since placing the asset in service.
9. Depreciation expense and accumulated depreciation are reported on the income statement.
10. Three factors affect the computation of depreciation: cost, useful life, and salvage value.

Instructions

Identify each statement as true or false. If false, indicate how to correct the statement.

E9.5 (LO 2), AP Gotham Company purchased a new machine on October 1, 2022, at a cost of $90,000. The company estimated that the machine has a salvage value of $8,100. The machine is expected to be used for 70,000 working hours during its 10-year life.

Determine straight-line depreciation for partial period.

Instructions

Compute the depreciation expense under the straight-line method for 2022 and 2023, assuming a December 31 year-end.

E9.6 (LO 2), AP Linton Company purchased a delivery truck for $34,000 on July 1, 2022. The truck has an expected salvage value of $2,000, and is expected to be driven 100,000 miles over its estimated useful life of 8 years. Actual miles driven were 15,000 in 2022 and 12,000 in 2023. Linton uses the straight-line method of depreciation.

Compute depreciation using the straight-line method.

Instructions

a. Compute depreciation expense for 2022 and 2023.
b. Prepare the journal entry to record 2022 depreciation.
c. Prepare the journal entry to record 2023 depreciation.
d. Show how the truck would be reported in the December 31, 2023, balance sheet.

E9.7 (LO 2), AN Victor Mineli, the new controller of Santorini Company, has reviewed the expected useful lives and salvage values of selected depreciable assets at the beginning of 2022. Here are his findings:

Compute revised annual depreciation.

Type of Asset	Date Acquired	Cost	Accumulated Depreciation, Jan. 1, 2022	Useful Life (in years)		Salvage Value	
				Old	Proposed	Old	Proposed
Building	Jan. 1, 2014	$700,000	$130,000	40	58	$50,000	$35,000
Warehouse	Jan. 1, 2017	120,000	23,000	25	20	5,000	3,600

All assets are depreciated by the straight-line method. Santorini Company uses a calendar year in preparing annual financial statements. After discussion, management has agreed to accept Victor's proposed changes. (The "Proposed" useful life is total life, not remaining life.)

Instructions

a. Compute the revised annual depreciation on each asset in 2022. (Show computations.)
b. Prepare the entry (or entries) to record depreciation on the building in 2022.

E9.8 (LO 2), AP On July 1, 2019, April Company purchased new equipment for $80,000. Its estimated useful life was 7 years with a $10,000 salvage value. On December 31, 2022, the company estimated that the equipment's remaining useful life was 10 years, with a revised salvage value of $5,000.

Compute revised depreciation and record entries.

Instructions

a. Prepare the journal entry to record depreciation on December 31, 2019.
b. Prepare the journal entry to record depreciation on December 31, 2020.
c. Compute the revised annual depreciation on December 31, 2022.
d. Prepare the journal entry to record depreciation on December 31, 2022.
e. Compute the balance in Accumulated Depreciation—Equipment for this equipment after depreciation expense has been recorded on December 31, 2022.

E9.9 (LO 3), AP Thieu Co. has delivery equipment that cost $50,000 and has been depreciated $24,000.

Journalize transactions related to disposals of plant assets.

Instructions

Record entries for the disposal under the following assumptions.

a. It was scrapped as having no value.
b. It was sold for $37,000.
c. It was sold for $20,000.

Record disposal of equipment.

E9.10 (LO 3), AP Here are selected 2022 transactions of Akron Corporation.

Jan. 1 Retired a piece of machinery that was purchased on January 1, 2012. The machine cost $62,000 and had a useful life of 10 years with no salvage value.

June 30 Sold a computer that was purchased on January 1, 2020. The computer cost $36,000 and had a useful life of 3 years with no salvage value. The computer was sold for $5,000 cash.

Dec. 31 Sold a delivery truck for $9,000 cash. The truck cost $25,000 when it was purchased on January 1, 2019, and was depreciated based on a 5-year useful life with a $4,000 salvage value.

Instructions

Journalize all entries required on the above dates, including entries to update depreciation on assets disposed of, where applicable. Akron Corporation uses straight-line depreciation.

Journalize entries for disposal of equipment.

E9.11 (LO 3), AP Pryce Company owns equipment that cost $65,000 when purchased on January 1, 2019. It has been depreciated using the straight-line method based on an estimated salvage value of $5,000 and an estimated useful life of 5 years.

Instructions

Prepare Pryce Company's journal entries to record the sale of the equipment in these four independent situations.

a. Sold for $31,000 on January 1, 2022.
b. Sold for $31,000 on May 1, 2022.
c. Sold for $11,000 on January 1, 2022.
d. Sold for $11,000 on October 1, 2022.

Record equipment transactions and determine missing amounts.

E9.12 (LO 1, 2, 3), AN Shown below are the T-accounts relating to equipment that was purchased for cash by a company on the first day of the current year. The equipment was depreciated on a straight-line basis with an estimated useful life of 10 years and a salvage value of $100. Part of the equipment was sold on the last day of the current year for cash proceeds.

Cash		Equipment		Accumulated Depreciation—Equipment	
	Jan. 1 (a)	Jan. 1 1,100			Dec. 31 100
Dec. 31 450			Dec. 31 440	Dec. 31 40	

Depreciation Expense	Gain on Disposal of Plant Assets
Dec. 31 (b)	Dec. 31 (c)

Instructions

Prepare the journal entries to record the following and derive the missing amounts:

a. Purchase of equipment on January 1. What was the cash paid?
b. Depreciation recorded on December 31. What was the depreciation expense?
c. Sale of part of the equipment on December 31. What was the gain on disposal?

Apply accounting concepts.

E9.13 (LO 1, 2, 3, 4), C Writing The following situations are independent of one another.

1. An accounting student recently employed by a small company doesn't understand why the company is only depreciating its buildings and equipment, but not its land. The student prepared journal entries to depreciate all the company's property, plant, and equipment for the current year-end.

2. The same student also thinks the company's amortization policy on its intangible assets is wrong. The company is currently amortizing its patents but not its goodwill. As a result, the student added goodwill to her adjusting entry for amortization at the end of the current year. She told a fellow employee that she felt she had improved the consistency of the company's accounting policies by making these changes.

3. The same company has a building still in use that has a zero book value but a substantial fair value. The student felt that this practice didn't benefit the company's users—especially the bank—and wrote the building up to its fair value. After all, she reasoned, you can write down assets if fair values are lower. Writing them up if fair value is higher is yet another example of the improved consistency that she has brought to the company's accounting practices.

Instructions

Explain whether or not the accounting treatment in each of the above situations is in accordance with generally accepted accounting principles. Explain what accounting principle or assumption, if any, has been violated and what the appropriate accounting treatment should be.

E9.14 (LO 4), AN These are selected 2022 transactions for Wyle Corporation:

Jan. 1   Purchased a copyright for $120,000. The copyright has a useful life of 6 years and a remaining legal life of 30 years.

Mar. 1   Purchased a patent with an estimated useful life of 4 years and a legal life of 20 years for $54,000.

Sept. 1   Purchased a small company and recorded goodwill of $150,000. Its useful life is indefinite.

Prepare adjusting entries for amortization.

Instructions

Prepare all adjusting entries at December 31 to record amortization required by the events.

E9.15 (LO 4), AN On January 1, 2022, Haley Company had a balance of $360,000 of goodwill on its balance sheet that resulted from the purchase of a small business in a prior year. The goodwill had an indefinite life. During 2022, the company had the following additional transactions.

Prepare entries to set up appropriate accounts for different intangibles; calculate amortization.

Jan. 2   Purchased a patent (5-year life) $280,000.

July 1   Acquired a 9-year franchise; expiration date July 1, 2031, $540,000.

Sept. 1   Research and development costs $185,000.

Instructions

a. Prepare the necessary entries to record the transactions related to intangibles. All costs incurred were for cash.

b. Make the entries as of December 31, 2022, recording any necessary amortization.

c. Indicate what the intangible asset account balances should be on December 31, 2022.

E9.16 (LO 4), C Writing Alliance Atlantis Communications Inc. changed its accounting policy to amortize broadcast rights over the contracted exhibition period, which is based on the estimated useful life of the program. Previously, the company amortized broadcast rights over the lesser of 2 years or the contracted exhibition period.

Discuss implications of amortization period.

Instructions

Write a short memo to your client explaining the implications this has for the analysis of Alliance Atlantis's results.

E9.17 (LO 2, 4), C The questions listed below are independent of one another.

Answer questions on depreciation and intangibles.

Instructions

Provide a brief answer to each question.

a. Why should a company depreciate its buildings?

b. How can a company have a building that has a zero reported book value but substantial fair value?

c. What are some examples of intangibles that you might find on your college campus?

d. Give some examples of company or product trademarks or trade names. Are trade names and trademarks reported on a company's balance sheet?

E9.18 (LO 5), AP Suppose during 2022 that **Federal Express** reported the following information (in millions): net sales of $35,497 and net income of $98. Its balance sheet also showed total assets at the beginning of the year of $25,633 and total assets at the end of the year of $24,244.

Calculate asset turnover and return on assets.

Instructions

Calculate the (a) asset turnover and (b) return on assets.

E9.19 (LO 5), AP Lymen International is considering a significant expansion to its product line. The sales force is excited about the opportunities that the new products will bring. The new products are a significant step up in quality above the company's current offerings, but offer a complementary fit to its existing product line. Fred Ridtdick, senior production department manager, is very excited about the high-tech new equipment that will have to be acquired to produce the new products. Barbara Dyson, the company's CFO, has provided the following projections based on results with and without the new products.

Calculate and interpret ratios.

	Without New Products	With New Products
Sales revenue	$10,000,000	$16,000,000
Net income	$500,000	$960,000
Average total assets	$5,000,000	$12,000,000

Instructions

a. Compute the company's return on assets, profit margin, and asset turnover, both with and without the new product line.

b. Discuss the implications that your findings in part (a) have for the company's decision.

Calculate and interpret ratios.

E9.20 (LO 5), AP Linley Company reports the following information (in millions) during a recent year: net sales, $11,408.5; net earnings, $264.8; total assets, ending, $4,312.6; and total assets, beginning, $4,254.3.

Instructions

a. Calculate the (1) return on assets, (2) asset turnover, and (3) profit margin.

b. Prove mathematically how the profit margin and asset turnover work together to explain return on assets, by showing the appropriate calculation.

c. Linley Company owns Northgate (grocery), Linley Theaters, Oz Drugstores, and Ransome (heavy equipment), and manages commercial real estate, among other activities. Does this diversity of activities affect your ability to interpret the ratios you calculated in (a)? Explain.

Determine net cash provided by operating activities.

E9.21 (LO 5), AN Mendez Corporation reported net income of $58,000. Depreciation expense for the year was $132,000. The company calculates depreciation expense using the straight-line method, with a useful life of 10 years. Top management would like to switch to a 15-year useful life because depreciation expense would be reduced to $88,000. The CEO says, "Increasing the useful life would increase net income and net cash provided by operating activities."

Instructions

Provide a comparative analysis showing net income and net cash provided by operating activities (ignoring other accrual adjustments) under the indirect method using a 10-year and a 15-year useful life. (Ignore income taxes.) Evaluate the CEO's suggestion.

Identify key terms.

E9.22 (LO 1, 2, 3, 4), K The following is a list of words or phrases introduced in the chapter.

1. Capital expenditures.
2. Goodwill.
3. Plant assets.
4. Lessor.
5. Patent.
6. Copyright.
7. Impairment.
8. Accelerated-depreciation method.
9. Intangible assets.
10. Declining-balance method.
11. Amortization.
12. Lessee.
13. Trademark (trade name).
14. Ordinary repairs.
15. Units-of-activity method.

Instructions

Match the word or phrase above with its description below.

a. _____ Any depreciation method that produces higher depreciation expense in the early years than the straight-line approach.

b. _____ The process of allocating to expense the cost of an intangible asset.

c. _____ Expenditures that increase the company's investment in plant assets.

d. _____ A depreciation method that applies a constant rate to the declining book value of the asset and produces a decreasing annual depreciation expense over the asset's useful life.

e. _____ A permanent decline in the fair value of an asset.

f. _____ Rights, privileges, and competitive advantages that result from the ownership of long-lived assets that do not possess physical substance.

g. _____ A party that has made contractual arrangements to use another party's asset for a period at an agreed price.

h. _____ A party that has agreed contractually to let another party use its asset for a period at an agreed price.

i. _____ Expenditures to maintain the operating efficiency and expected productive life of the asset.

j. _____ Resources that have physical substance, are used in the operations of a business, and are not intended for sale to customers.

k. _____ A depreciation method in which useful life is expressed in terms of the total units of production or use expected from the asset.

l. _____ An exclusive right granted by the federal government allowing the owner to reproduce and sell an artistic or published work.

m. _____ A word, phrase, jingle, or symbol that distinguishes or identifies a particular enterprise or product.

n. _____ An exclusive right issued by the U.S. Patent Office that enables the recipient to manufacture, sell, or otherwise control an invention for a period of 20 years from the date of the grant.

o. _____ The value of all favorable attributes that relate to a company that are not attributable to any other specific asset.

*E9.23 (LO 6), AP Whippet Bus Lines uses the units-of-activity method in depreciating its buses. One bus was purchased on January 1, 2022, at a cost of $100,000. Over its 4-year useful life, the bus is expected to be driven 160,000 miles. Salvage value is expected to be $8,000.

Compute depreciation under units-of-activity method.

Instructions

a. Compute the depreciation cost per unit.

b. Prepare a depreciation schedule assuming actual mileage was 2022, 40,000; 2023, 52,000; 2024, 41,000; and 2025, 27,000.

*E9.24 (LO 6), AP Basic information relating to a new machine purchased by Gotham Company is presented in E9.5.

Compute declining-balance and units-of-activity depreciation.

Instructions

Using the facts presented in E9.5, compute depreciation using the following methods in the year indicated.

a. Declining-balance using double the straight-line rate for 2022 and 2023.

b. Units-of-activity for 2022, assuming machine usage was 500 hours. (Round depreciation per unit to the nearest cent.)

Problems: Set A

P9.1A (LO 1), C Peete Company was organized on January 1. During the first year of operations, the following plant asset expenditures and receipts were recorded in random order.

Determine acquisition costs of land and building.

Debit

1. Excavation costs for new building	$ 23,000
2. Architect's fees on building plans	33,000
3. Full payment to building contractor	640,000
4. Cost of real estate purchased as a plant site (land $255,000 and building $25,000)	280,000
5. Cost of parking lots and driveways	29,000
6. Accrued real estate taxes paid at time of purchase of land	3,170
7. Installation cost of fences around property	6,800
8. Cost of demolishing building to make land suitable for construction of new building	31,000
9. Real estate taxes paid for the current year on land	6,400
	$1,052,370

Credit

10. Proceeds from salvage of demolished building	$ 12,000

Instructions

Analyze the transactions using the following table column headings. Enter the number of each transaction in the Item column, and enter the amounts in the appropriate columns. For amounts in the Other Accounts column, also indicate the account title.

Item	Land	Buildings	Other Accounts

Land $302,170

Journalize equipment transactions related to purchase, sale, retirement, and depreciation.

P9.2A (LO 2, 3, 5), AP At December 31, 2022, Arnold Corporation reported the following plant assets.

Land		$ 3,000,000
Buildings	$26,500,000	
Less: Accumulated depreciation—buildings	11,925,000	14,575,000
Equipment	40,000,000	
Less: Accumulated depreciation—equipment	5,000,000	35,000,000
Total plant assets		$52,575,000

During 2023, the following selected cash transactions occurred.

Apr. 1 Purchased land for $2,200,000.
May 1 Sold equipment that cost $600,000 when purchased on January 1, 2016. The equipment was sold for $170,000.
June 1 Sold land for $1,600,000. The land cost $1,000,000.
July 1 Purchased equipment for $1,100,000.
Dec. 31 Retired equipment that cost $700,000 when purchased on December 31, 2013. No salvage value was received.

Instructions

a. Journalize the transactions. (*Hint:* You may wish to set up T-accounts, post beginning balances, and then post 2023 transactions.) Arnold uses straight-line depreciation for buildings and equipment. The buildings are estimated to have a 40-year useful life and no salvage value; the equipment is estimated to have a 10-year useful life and no salvage value. Update depreciation on assets disposed of at the time of sale or retirement.

b. Record adjusting entries for depreciation for 2023.

c. Prepare the plant assets section of Arnold's balance sheet at December 31, 2023.

c. Tot. plant assets $50,037,500

Journalize entries for disposal of plant assets.

P9.3A (LO 3), AP Pine Company had the following assets on January 1, 2022.

Item	Cost	Purchase Date	Useful life (in years)	Salvage Value
Machinery	$71,000	Jan. 1, 2012	10	$ -0-
Forklift	30,000	Jan. 1, 2019	5	-0-
Truck	33,400	Jan. 1, 2017	8	3,000

During 2022, each of the assets was removed from service. The machinery was retired on January 1. The forklift was sold on June 30 for $12,000. The truck was discarded on December 31.

Instructions

Journalize all entries required on the above dates, including entries to update depreciation, where applicable, on disposed assets. The company uses straight-line depreciation. All depreciation was up to date as of December 31, 2021.

Loss on truck disposal $10,600

Record property, plant, and equipment transactions; prepare partial balance sheet.

P9.4A (LO 1, 2, 3, 5), AP At January 1, 2022, Youngstown Company reported the following property, plant, and equipment accounts:

Accumulated depreciation—buildings	$ 62,200,000
Accumulated depreciation—equipment	54,000,000
Buildings	97,400,000
Equipment	150,000,000
Land	20,000,000

The company uses straight-line depreciation for buildings and equipment, its year-end is December 31, and it makes adjusting entries annually. The buildings are estimated to have a 40-year useful life and no salvage value; the equipment is estimated to have a 10-year useful life and no salvage value.

During 2022, the following selected transactions occurred:

Apr. 1 Purchased land for $4.4 million. Paid $1.1 million cash and issued a 3-year, 6% note payable for the balance. Interest on the note is payable annually each April 1.
May 1 Sold equipment for $300,000 cash. The equipment cost $2.8 million when originally purchased on January 1, 2014.
June 1 Sold land for $3.6 million. Received $900,000 cash and accepted a 3-year, 5% note for the balance. The land cost $1.4 million when purchased on June 1, 2016. Interest on the note is due annually each June 1.
July 1 Purchased equipment for $2.2 million cash.
Dec. 31 Retired equipment that cost $1 million when purchased on December 31, 2012. No proceeds were received.

Instructions

a. Journalize the above transactions. (*Hint:* You may wish to set up T-accounts, post beginning balances, and then post 2022 transactions.)

b. Record any adjusting entries for depreciation required at December 31.

c. Prepare the property, plant, and equipment section of the company's statement of financial position at December 31.

Total PP&E $138,575,000

P9.5A (LO 4, 5), AP The intangible assets section of Amato Corporation's balance sheet at December 31, 2022, is presented here.

Prepare entries to record transactions related to acquisition and amortization of intangibles; prepare the intangible assets section and note.

Patents ($60,000 cost less $6,000 amortization)	$54,000
Copyrights ($36,000 cost less $25,200 amortization)	10,800
Total	$64,800

The patent was acquired in January 2022 and has a useful life of 10 years. The copyright was acquired in January 2016 and also has a useful life of 10 years. The following cash transactions may have affected intangible assets during 2023.

Jan.	2	Paid $46,800 legal costs to successfully defend the patent against infringement by another company.
Jan.–June		Developed a new product, incurring $230,000 in research and development costs. A patent was granted for the product on July 1, and its useful life is equal to its legal life. Legal and other costs for the patent were $20,000.
Sept.	1	Paid $40,000 to a quarterback to appear in commercials advertising the company's products. The commercials will air in September and October.
Oct.	1	Acquired a copyright for $200,000. The copyright has a useful life and legal life of 50 years.

Instructions

a. Prepare journal entries to record the transactions.

b. Prepare journal entries to record the 2023 amortization expense for intangible assets.

c. Prepare the intangible assets section of the balance sheet at December 31, 2023.

c. Tot. intangibles $315,300

d. Prepare the note to the financial statements on Amato Corporation's intangible assets as of December 31, 2023.

P9.6A (LO 4), AP Due to rapid employee turnover in the accounting department, the following transactions involving intangible assets were improperly recorded by Inland Corporation.

Prepare entries to correct errors in recording and amortizing intangible assets.

1. Inland developed a new manufacturing process, incurring research and development costs of $160,000. The company also purchased a patent for $40,000. In early January, Inland capitalized $200,000 as the cost of the patents. Patent amortization expense of $10,000 was recorded based on a 20-year useful life.

2. On July 1, 2022, Inland purchased a small company and as a result recorded goodwill of $80,000. Inland recorded a half-year's amortization in 2022, based on a 20-year life ($2,000 amortization). The goodwill has an indefinite life.

Instructions

Prepare all journal entries necessary to correct any errors made during 2022. Assume the books have not yet been closed for 2022.

P9.7A (LO 5), AN Blythe Corporation and Jacke Corporation, two companies of roughly the same size, are both involved in the manufacture of shoe-tracing devices. Each company depreciates its plant assets using the straight-line approach. An investigation of their financial statements reveals the information shown below.

Calculate and comment on return on assets, profit margin, and asset turnover.

	Blythe Corp.	Jacke Corp.
Net income	$ 240,000	$ 300,000
Sales revenue	1,150,000	1,200,000
Total assets (average)	3,200,000	3,000,000
Plant assets (average)	2,400,000	1,800,000
Intangible assets (goodwill)	300,000	0

Instructions

a. For each company, calculate these values:

1. Return on assets.
2. Profit margin.
3. Asset turnover.

b. Based on your calculations in part (a), comment on the relative effectiveness of the two companies in using their assets to generate sales. What factors complicate your ability to compare the two companies?

Compute depreciation under different methods.

*P9.8A (LO 2, 6), AP In recent years, Jayme Company has purchased three machines. Because of frequent employee turnover in the accounting department, a different accountant was in charge of selecting the depreciation method for each machine, and various methods have been used. Information concerning the machines is summarized in the table below.

Machine	Acquired	Cost	Salvage Value	Useful Life (in years)	Depreciation Method
1	Jan. 1, 2020	$96,000	$12,000	8	Straight-line
2	July 1, 2021	85,000	10,000	5	Declining-balance
3	Nov. 1, 2021	66,000	6,000	6	Units-of-activity

For the declining-balance method, Jayme Company uses the double-declining rate. For the units-of-activity method, total machine hours are expected to be 30,000. Actual hours of use in the first 3 years were 2021, 800; 2022, 4,500; and 2023, 6,000.

Instructions

a. Machine 2 $60,520

a. Compute the amount of accumulated depreciation on each machine at December 31, 2023.

b. If machine 2 was purchased on April 1 instead of July 1, what would be the depreciation expense for this machine in 2021? In 2022?

Compute depreciation under different methods.

*P9.9A (LO 2, 6), AP Megan Corporation purchased machinery on January 1, 2022, at a cost of $250,000. The estimated useful life of the machinery is 4 years, with an estimated salvage value at the end of that period of $30,000. The company is considering different depreciation methods that could be used for financial reporting purposes.

Instructions

a. Double-declining-balance expense 2024 $31,250

a. Prepare separate depreciation schedules for the machinery using the straight-line method, and the declining-balance method using double the straight-line rate. (Round to the nearest dollar.)

b. Which method would result in the higher reported 2022 income? In the highest total reported income over the 4-year period?

c. Which method would result in the lower reported 2022 income? In the lowest total reported income over the 4-year period?

Continuing Case

© leungchopan/ Shutterstock

Cookie Creations

(*Note:* This is a continuation of the Cookie Creations case from Chapters 1 through 8.)

CC9 Part 1 Now that she is selling mixers and her customers can use credit cards to pay for them, Natalie is thinking of upgrading her website so that she can sell mixers online, to broaden her range of customers. She will need to know how to account for the costs of upgrading the site.

Part 2 Natalie is also thinking of buying a van that will be used only for business. Natalie is concerned about the impact of the van's cost on her income statement and balance sheet. She has come to you for advice on calculating the van's depreciation.

Go to WileyPLUS for complete case details and instructions.

Comprehensive Accounting Cycle Review

ACR9.1 Milo Corporation's unadjusted trial balance at December 1, 2022, is presented below.

	Debit	Credit
Cash	$ 22,000	
Accounts Receivable	36,800	
Notes Receivable	10,000	
Interest Receivable	–0–	
Inventory	36,200	
Prepaid Insurance	3,600	

	Debit	Credit
Land	$ 20,000	
Buildings	150,000	
Equipment	60,000	
Patent	9,000	
Allowance for Doubtful Accounts		$ 500
Accumulated Depreciation—Buildings		50,000
Accumulated Depreciation—Equipment		24,000
Accounts Payable		27,300
Salaries and Wages Payable		-0-
Notes Payable (due April 30, 2023)		11,000
Income Taxes Payable		-0-
Interest Payable		-0-
Notes Payable (due in 2028)		35,000
Common Stock		50,000
Retained Earnings		63,600
Dividends	12,000	
Sales Revenue		900,000
Interest Revenue		-0-
Gain on Disposal of Plant Assets		-0-
Bad Debt Expense	-0-	
Cost of Goods Sold	630,000	
Depreciation Expense	-0-	
Income Tax Expense	-0-	
Insurance Expense	-0-	
Interest Expense	-0-	
Other Operating Expenses	61,800	
Amortization Expense	-0-	
Salaries and Wages Expense	110,000	
	$1,161,400	$1,161,400

The following transactions occurred during December.

Dec. 2 Purchased equipment for $16,000, plus sales taxes of $800 (paid in cash).
2 Milo sold for $3,500 equipment which originally cost $5,000. Accumulated depreciation on this equipment at January 1, 2022, was $1,800; 2022 depreciation prior to the sale of equipment was $825.
15 Milo sold for $5,000 on account inventory that cost $3,500.
23 Salaries and wages of $6,600 were paid.

Adjustment data:

1. Milo estimates that uncollectible accounts receivable at year-end are $4,000.
2. The note receivable is a 1-year, 8% note dated April 1, 2022. No interest has been recorded.
3. The balance in prepaid insurance represents payment of a $3,600, 6-month premium on September 1, 2022.
4. The building is being depreciated using the straight-line method over 30 years. The salvage value is $30,000.
5. The equipment owned prior to this year is being depreciated using the straight-line method over 5 years. The salvage value is 10% of cost.
6. The equipment purchased on December 2, 2022, is being depreciated using the straight-line method over 5 years, with a salvage value of $1,800.
7. The patent was acquired on January 1, 2022, and has a useful life of 9 years from that date.
8. Unpaid salaries at December 31, 2022, total $2,200.
9. Both the short-term and long-term notes payable are dated January 1, 2022, and carry a 10% interest rate. All interest is payable in the next 12 months.
10. Income tax expense was $15,000. It was unpaid at December 31.

Instructions

a. Prepare journal entries for the transactions listed above and adjusting entries.
b. Prepare an adjusted trial balance at December 31, 2022.
c. Prepare a 2022 income statement and a 2022 retained earnings statement.
d. Prepare a December 31, 2022, balance sheet.

b. Totals $1,205,775
c. Net income $51,150
d. Total assets $247,850

ACR9.2 Aberkonkie Corporation prepares quarterly financial statements. The post-closing trial balance at December 31, 2021, is presented below.

Aberkonkie Corporation
Post-Closing Trial Balance
December 31, 2021

	Debit	Credit
Cash	$ 24,300	
Accounts Receivable	22,400	
Allowance for Doubtful Accounts		$ 1,200
Equipment	20,000	
Accumulated Depreciation—Equipment		15,000
Buildings	100,000	
Accumulated Depreciation—Buildings		15,000
Land	20,000	
Accounts Payable		12,370
Common Stock		90,000
Retained Earnings		53,130
	$186,700	$186,700

During the first quarter of 2022, the following transaction occurred:

1. On February 1, Aberkonkie collected fees of $12,000 in advance. The company will perform $1,000 of services each month from February 1, 2022, to January 31, 2023.
2. On February 1, Aberkonkie purchased computer equipment for $9,000 plus sales taxes of $600. $3,000 cash was paid with the rest on account. Check #455 was used.
3. On March 1, Aberkonkie acquired a patent with a 10-year life for $9,600 cash. Check #456 was used.
4. On March 28, Aberkonkie recorded the quarter's sales in a single entry. During this period, Aberkonkie had total sales of $140,000 (not including the sales referred to in item 1 above). All of the sales were on account.
5. On March 29, Aberkonkie collected $133,000 from customers on account.
6. On March 29, Aberkonkie paid $16,370 on accounts payable. Check #457 was used.
7. On March 29, Aberkonkie paid other operating expenses of $97,525. Check #458 was used.
8. On March 31, Aberkonkie wrote off a receivable of $200 for a customer who declared bankruptcy.
9. On March 31, Aberkonkie sold for $1,620 equipment that originally cost $11,000. It had an estimated life of 5 years and salvage of $1,000. Accumulated depreciation as of December 31, 2021, was $8,000 using the straight line method. (*Hint:* Record depreciation on the equipment sold, then record the sale.)

Bank reconciliation data and adjustment data:

1. The company reconciles its bank statement every quarter. Information from the December 31, 2021, bank reconciliation is:

Deposit in transit:	12/30/2021	$5,000
Outstanding checks	#440	3,444
	#452	333
	#453	865
	#454	5,845

The bank statement received for the quarter ended March 31, 2022, is as follows:

Beginning balance per bank		$ 29,787
Deposits: 1/2/2022, $5,000; 2/2/2022, $12,000; 3/30/2022, $133,000		150,000
Checks: #452, $333; #453, $865; #457, $16,370; #458, $97,525		(115,093)
Debit memo: Bank service charge (record as operating expense)		(100)
Ending bank balance		$ 64,594

2. Record revenue earned from item 1 above.
3. $26,000 of accounts receivable at March 31, 2022, are not past due yet. The bad debt percentage for these is 4%. The remaining balance of accounts receivable is past due. The bad debt percentage for these is 23.75%. Record bad debt expense. (*Hint:* You will need to compute the balance in accounts receivable before calculating this.)
4. Depreciation is recorded on the equipment still owned at March 31, 2022. The new equipment purchased in February is being depreciated on a straight-line basis over 5 years and salvage value was estimated at $1,200. The old equipment still owned is being depreciated over a 10-year life using straight-line with no salvage value.

5. Depreciation is recorded on the building on a straight-line basis based on a 30-year life and a salvage value of $10,000.

6. Amortization is recorded on the patent.

7. The income tax rate is 30%. This amount will be paid when the tax return is due in April. (*Hint:* Prepare the income statement up to income before taxes and multiply by 30% to compute the amount.)

Instructions

a. Record journal entries for transactions 1–9.

b. Enter the December 31, 2021, balances in ledger accounts using T-accounts.

c. Post the journal entries to the ledger accounts for items 1–9.

d. Prepare an unadjusted trial balance at March 31.

e. Prepare a bank reconciliation in good form.

f. Journalize and post entries related to bank reconciliation and all adjusting entries.

g. Prepare an adjusted trial balance.

h. Prepare an income statement and a retained earnings statement for the quarter ended March 31, 2022, and a classified balance sheet at March 31, 2022.

d. Trial balance total $320,730
e. Adjusted balance
    per bank $44,325
f. Total assets $196,590

Expand Your Critical Thinking

Financial Reporting Problem: Apple Inc.

CT9.1 The financial statements of **Apple Inc.** are presented in Appendix A. The complete annual report, including the notes to the financial statements, is available at the company's website.

Instructions

Answer the following questions.

a. What were the total cost and book value of property, plant, and equipment at September 30, 2017?

b. Using the notes to the financial statements, what method or methods of depreciation are used by Apple for financial reporting purposes?

c. What was the amount of depreciation and amortization expense for each of the 3 years 2015–2017? (*Hint:* Use the statement of cash flows.)

d. Using the statement of cash flows, what are the amounts of property, plant, and equipment purchased in 2017 and 2016?

e. Using the notes to the financial statements, explain how Apple accounted for its intangible assets in 2017.

Comparative Analysis Problem: Columbia Sportswear Company vs. VF Corporation

CT9.2 The financial statements of **Columbia Sportswear Company** are presented in Appendix B. Financial statements of **VF Corporation** are presented in Appendix C. The complete annual reports, including the notes to the financial statements, are available at each company's respective website.

Instructions

a. Based on the information in these financial statements and the accompanying notes and schedules, compute the following values for each company in 2016.

   1. Return on assets.
   2. Profit margin (use "Total Revenue").
   3. Asset turnover.

b. What conclusions concerning the management of plant assets can be drawn from these data?

Comparative Analysis Problem: Amazon.com, Inc. vs. Wal-Mart Stores, Inc.

CT9.3 The financial statements of **Amazon.com, Inc.** are presented in Appendix D. Financial statements of **Wal-Mart Stores, Inc.** are presented in Appendix E. The complete annual reports, including the notes to the financial statements, are available at each company's respective website.

Instructions

a. Based on the information in these financial statements and the accompanying notes and schedules, compute the following values for each company for the most recent fiscal year provided.

1. Return on assets.
2. Profit margin (use "Total Revenue").
3. Asset turnover.

b. What conclusions concerning the management of plant assets can be drawn from these data?

Interpreting Financial Statements

CT9.4 The March 29, 2012, edition of the *Wall Street Journal Online* contains an article by Miguel Bustillo entitled, "Best Buy Forced to Rethink Big Box." The article explains how the 1,100 giant stores, which enabled **Best Buy** to obtain its position as the largest retailer of electronics, are now reducing the company's profitability and even threatening its survival. The problem is that many customers go to Best Buy stores to see items but then buy them for less from online retailers. As a result, Best Buy recently announced that it would close 50 stores and switch to smaller stores. However, some analysts think that these changes are not big enough.

Suppose the following data were extracted from the 2022 and 2017 annual reports of Best Buy. (All amounts are in millions.)

	2022	2021	2017	2016
Total assets at year-end	$17,849	$18,302	$11,864	$10,294
Net sales	50,272		30,848	
Net income	1,277		1,140	

Instructions

Using the data above, answer the following questions.

a. How might the return on assets and asset turnover of Best Buy differ from an online retailer?
b. Compute the profit margin, asset turnover, and return on assets for 2022 and 2017.
c. Present the ratios calculated in part (b) in the equation format shown in Illustration 9.22.
d. Discuss the implications of the ratios calculated in parts (b) and (c).

Real-World Focus

CT9.5 A company's annual report identifies the amount of its plant assets and the depreciation method used.

Instructions

Select a particular company, search the Internet for the company's website address, and then answer the following questions.

a. What is the name of the company?
b. What is the Internet address of the annual report?
c. At fiscal year-end, what is the net amount of its plant assets?
d. What is the accumulated depreciation?
e. Which method of depreciation does the company use?

CT9.6 The November 16, 2011, edition of the *Wall Street Journal Online* contains an article by Maxwell Murphy entitled "The Big Number: 51."

Instructions

Read the article and then answer the following questions.

a. What do the 51 companies referred to in the title have in common? What implications does this have regarding the fair value of a company's assets?
b. What significance does the common trait referred to in part (a) have for a company's goodwill?
c. How does a company get to record goodwill on its books—that is, what must have occurred for goodwill to show up on a company's books?
d. If these companies write down their goodwill, will this reduce their cash?

Decision-Making Across the Organization

CT9.7 Brady Furniture Corp. is nationally recognized for making high-quality products. Management is concerned that it is not fully exploiting its brand power. Brady's production managers are also concerned because their plants are not operating at anywhere near full capacity. Management is currently considering a proposal to offer a new line of affordable furniture.

Those in favor of the proposal (including the vice president of production) believe that, by offering these new products, the company could attract a clientele that it is not currently servicing. Also, it could operate its plants at full capacity, thus taking better advantage of its assets.

The vice president of marketing, however, believes that the lower-priced (and lower-margin) product would have a negative impact on the sales of existing products. The vice president believes that $10,000,000 of the sales of the new product will be from customers that would have purchased the more expensive product but switched to the lower-margin product because it was available. (This is often referred to as cannibalization of existing sales.) Top management feels, however, that even with cannibalization, the company's sales will increase and the company will be better off.

The following data are available.

(in thousands)	Current Results	Proposed Results without Cannibalization	Proposed Results with Cannibalization
Sales revenue	$45,000	$60,000	$50,000
Net income	$12,000	$13,500	$12,000
Average total assets	$100,000	$100,000	$100,000

Instructions

a. Compute Brady's return on assets, profit margin, and asset turnover, both with and without the new product line.

b. Discuss the implications that your findings in part (a) have for Brady's decision.

c. Are there any other options that Brady should consider? What impact would each of these have on the above ratios?

Communication Activity

CT9.8 The chapter presented some concerns regarding the current accounting standards for research and development expenditures.

Instructions

Assume that you are either (a) the president of a company that is very dependent on ongoing research and development, writing a memo to the FASB complaining about the current accounting standards regarding research and development, or (b) the FASB member defending the current standards regarding research and development. Your memo should address the following questions.

1. By requiring expensing of R&D, do you think companies will spend less on R&D? Why or why not? What are the possible implications for the competitiveness of U.S. companies?

2. If a company makes a commitment to spend money for R&D, it must believe it has future benefits. Shouldn't these costs therefore be capitalized just like the purchase of any long-lived asset that you believe will have future benefits?

Ethics Case

CT9.9 Clean Aire Anti-Pollution Company is suffering declining sales of its principal product, non-biodegradable plastic cartons. The president, Wade Truman, instructs his controller, Kate Rollins, to lengthen asset lives to reduce depreciation expense. A processing line of automated plastic extruding equipment, purchased for $3.5 million in January 2022, was originally estimated to have a useful life of 8 years and a salvage value of $400,000. Depreciation has been recorded for 2 years on that basis. Wade wants the estimated life changed to 12 years total and the straight-line method continued with no change in the salvage value. Kate is hesitant to make the change, believing it is unethical to increase net income in this manner. Wade says, "Hey, the life is only an estimate, and I've heard that our competition uses a 12-year life on their production equipment."

Instructions

a. Who are the stakeholders in this situation?

b. Is the proposed change in asset life unethical, or is it simply a good business practice by an astute president?

c. What is the effect of Wade's proposed change on income before taxes in the year of change?

All About You

CT9.10 A company's tradename is a very important asset to the company, as it creates immediate product identification. Companies invest substantial sums to ensure that their product is well-known to the consumer. Test your knowledge of who owns some famous brands and their impact on the financial statements.

Instructions

a. Provide an answer to the four multiple-choice questions below.

1. Which company owns both Taco Bell and Pizza Hut?
   a. McDonald's.   b. CKE.   c. Yum Brands.   d. Wendy's.
2. Dairy Queen belongs to:
   a. Breyer.   b. Berkshire Hathaway.   c. GE.   d. The Coca-Cola Company.
3. Phillip Morris, the cigarette maker, is owned by:
   a. Altria.   b. GE.   c. Boeing.   d. ExxonMobil.
4. AOL, a major Internet provider, belongs to:
   a. Microsoft.   b. Cisco.   c. NBC.   d. Time Warner.

b. How do you think the value of these brands is reported on the appropriate company's balance sheet?

FASB Codification Activity

CT9.11 If your school has a subscription to the FASB Codification, log in and prepare responses to the following.

a. What does it mean to capitalize an item?
b. What is the definition provided for an intangible asset?
c. Your great-uncle, who is a CPA, is impressed that you are taking an accounting class. Based on his experience, he believes that depreciation is something that companies do based on past practice, not on the basis of authoritative guidance. Provide the authoritative literature to support the practice of fixed-asset depreciation.

Considering People, Planet, and Profit

CT9.12 The March 6, 2012, edition of the *Wall Street Journal Online* contains an article by David Kesmodel entitled "Air War: 'Winglet' Versus 'Sharklet'." This article demonstrates how a company focused on green technology has also been profitable.

Instructions

Read the article and then answer the following questions.

a. Why did **Airbus** file a lawsuit against **Aviation Partners**?
b. What are the percentage fuel savings provided by Aviation Partners' Winglets on **Boeing** jetliners? How much total jet fuel did Aviation Partners say that its Winglets have provided at the time the article was written?
c. Describe the history of the relationship between Aviation Partners and Airbus, and the development of the Airbus Sharklet.
d. What would be the likely accounting implications if Aviation Partners were to lose the lawsuit?

A Look at IFRS

LEARNING OBJECTIVE 7
Compare the accounting for long-lived assets under GAAP and IFRS.

IFRS follows most of the same principles as GAAP in the accounting for property, plant, and equipment. There are, however, some significant differences in the implementation. IFRS allows the use of revaluation of property, plant, and equipment, and it also requires the use of component depreciation.

In addition, there are some significant differences in the accounting for both intangible assets and impairments.

Key Points

The following are the key similarities and differences between GAAP and IFRS as related to the recording process for long-lived assets.

Similarities

- The definition for plant assets for both IFRS and GAAP is essentially the same.
- Both IFRS and GAAP follow the historical cost principle when accounting for property, plant, and equipment at date of acquisition. Cost consists of all expenditures necessary to acquire the asset and make it ready for its intended use.
- Under both IFRS and GAAP, interest costs incurred during construction are capitalized. Recently, IFRS converged to GAAP requirements in this area.
- The accounting for subsequent expenditures (such as ordinary repairs and additions) is essentially the same under IFRS and GAAP.
- IFRS also views depreciation as an allocation of cost over an asset's useful life. IFRS permits the same depreciation methods (e.g., straight-line, accelerated, and units-of-activity) as GAAP.
- Under both GAAP and IFRS, changes in the depreciation method used and changes in useful life are handled in current and future periods. Prior periods are not affected. GAAP recently conformed to international standards in the accounting for changes in depreciation methods.
- The accounting for plant asset disposals is essentially the same under IFRS and GAAP.
- The definition of intangible assets is essentially the same under IFRS and GAAP.
- The accounting for exchanges of nonmonetary assets has recently converged between IFRS and GAAP. GAAP now requires that gains on exchanges of nonmonetary assets be recognized if the exchange has commercial substance. This is the same framework used in IFRS.

Differences

- IFRS uses the term **residual value** rather than salvage value to refer to an owner's estimate of an asset's value at the end of its useful life for that owner.
- IFRS allows companies to revalue plant assets to fair value at the reporting date. Companies that choose to use the revaluation framework must follow revaluation procedures. If revaluation is used, it must be applied to all assets in a class of assets. Assets that are experiencing rapid price changes must be revalued on an annual basis, otherwise less frequent revaluation is acceptable.
- IFRS requires component depreciation. **Component depreciation** specifies that any significant parts of a depreciable asset that have different estimated useful lives should be separately depreciated. Component depreciation is allowed under GAAP but is seldom used.
- As in GAAP, under IFRS the costs associated with research and development are segregated into the two components. Costs in the research phase are always expensed under both IFRS and GAAP. Under IFRS, however, costs in the development phase are capitalized as Development Costs once technological feasibility is achieved.
- IFRS permits revaluation of intangible assets (except for goodwill). GAAP prohibits revaluation of intangible assets.

IFRS Practice

IFRS Self-Test Questions

1. Which of the following statements is **correct**?
    a. Both IFRS and GAAP permit revaluation of property, plant, and equipment and intangible assets (except for goodwill).
    b. IFRS permits revaluation of property, plant, and equipment and intangible assets (except for goodwill).
    c. Both IFRS and GAAP permit revaluation of property, plant, and equipment but not intangible assets.
    d. GAAP permits revaluation of property, plant, and equipment but not intangible assets.

2. All research and development costs are:
    a. expensed under GAAP.
    b. expensed under IFRS.
    c. expensed under both GAAP and IFRS.
    d. None of the above.

IFRS Exercises

IFRS9.1 What is component depreciation, and when must it be used?

IFRS9.2 What is revaluation of plant assets? When should revaluation be applied?

IFRS9.3 Some product development expenditures are recorded as development expenses and others as development costs. Explain the difference between these accounts and how a company decides which classification is appropriate.

International Financial Statement Analysis: Louis Vuitton

IFRS9.4 The financial statements of **Louis Vuitton** are presented in Appendix F. The complete annual report, including the notes to its financial statements, is available at the company's website.

Instructions

Use the company's annual report to answer the following questions.

a. According to the notes to the financial statements, what method or methods does the company use to depreciate "property, plant, and equipment?" What useful lives does it use to depreciate property, plant, and equipment?

b. Using the notes to the financial statements, explain how the company accounted for its intangible assets with indefinite lives.

c. Using the notes to the financial statements, determine (1) the balance in Accumulated Amortization and Impairment for intangible assets (other than goodwill), and (2) the balance in Depreciation (and impairment) for property, plant, and equipment.

Answers to IFRS Self-Test Questions

1. b **2.** a

CHAPTER 10

Reporting and Analyzing Liabilities

Chapter Preview

The following Feature Story suggests that **General Motors (GM)** and **Ford** accumulated tremendous amounts of debt in their pursuit of auto industry dominance. It is unlikely that they could have grown so large without this debt, but at times the debt threatened their very existence. Given this risk, why do companies borrow money? Why do they sometimes borrow short-term and other times long-term? Besides bank borrowings, what other kinds of debts do companies incur? In this chapter, we address these issues.

Feature Story

And Then There Were Two

Debt can help a company acquire the things it needs to grow. But, it is often the very thing that can also kill a company. A brief history of **Maxwell Car Company** illustrates the role of debt in the U.S. auto industry. In 1920, Maxwell Car Company was on the brink of financial ruin. Because it was unable to pay its bills, its creditors stepped in and took over. They hired a former **General Motors (GM)** executive named Walter Chrysler to reorganize the company. By 1925, he had taken over the company and renamed it Chrysler. By 1933, **Chrysler** was booming, with sales surpassing even those of **Ford**.

But the next few decades saw Chrysler make a series of blunders. By 1980, with its creditors pounding at the gates, Chrysler was again on the brink of financial ruin.

At that point, Chrysler brought in a former Ford executive named Lee Iacocca to save the company. Iacocca argued that the United States could not afford to let Chrysler fail because of the loss of jobs. He convinced the federal government to grant loan guarantees—promises that if Chrysler failed to pay its creditors, the government would pay them. Iacocca then streamlined operations and brought out some profitable products. Chrysler repaid all of its government-guaranteed loans by 1983, seven years ahead of the scheduled final payment.

To compete in today's global vehicle market, you must be big—really big. So in 1998, Chrysler merged with German automaker **Daimler-Benz** to form **DaimlerChrysler**. For a time, this left just two U.S.-based auto manufacturers—GM and Ford. But in 2007, DaimlerChrysler sold 81% of Chrysler to **Cerberus**, an investment group, to provide much-needed cash infusions to the automaker. In 2009, Daimler turned over its remaining stake to Cerberus. Three days later, Chrysler filed for bankruptcy. But by 2010, it was beginning to show signs of a turnaround.

The car companies are giants. GM and Ford typically rank among the top five U.S. firms in total assets. But GM and Ford accumulated truckloads of debt on their way to getting big. Although debt made it possible to get so big, the Chrysler story, and GM's recent bankruptcy, make it clear that debt can also threaten a company's survival.

Chapter Outline

LEARNING OBJECTIVES

LO 1 Explain how to account for current liabilities.	• What is a current liability? • Notes payable • Sales taxes payable • Unearned revenues • Current maturities of long-term debt • Payroll and payroll taxes payable	**DO IT! 1a** Current Liabilities **DO IT! 1b** Wages and Payroll Taxes
LO 2 Describe the major characteristics of bonds.	• Types of bonds • Issuing procedures • Bond trading • Determining the market price of a bond	**DO IT! 2** Bond Terminology
LO 3 Explain how to account for bond transactions.	• Issuing bonds at face value • Discount or premium on bonds • Issuing bonds at a discount • Issuing bonds at a premium • Redeeming bonds at maturity • Redeeming bonds before maturity	**DO IT! 3a** Bond Issuance **DO IT! 3b** Bond Redemption
LO 4 Discuss how liabilities are reported and analyzed.	• Presentation • Analysis	**DO IT! 4** Analyzing Liabilities

Go to the Review and Practice section at the end of the chapter for a targeted summary and practice applications with solutions.
Visit WileyPLUS for additional tutorials and practice opportunities.

Accounting for Current Liabilities

LEARNING OBJECTIVE 1
Explain how to account for current liabilities.

What Is a Current Liability?

You have learned that liabilities are defined as "creditors' claims on total assets" and as "existing debts and obligations." Companies must settle or pay these claims, debts, and obligations at some time in the future by transferring assets or services. The future date on which they are due or payable (the maturity date) is a significant feature of liabilities.

As explained in Chapter 4, a **current liability** is a debt that a company expects to pay (1) from existing current assets or through the creation of other current liabilities, and (2) within one year or the operating cycle, whichever is longer. Debts that do not meet this criterion are **long-term liabilities**.

Financial statement users want to know whether a company's obligations are current or long-term. A company that has more current liabilities than current assets often lacks liquidity, or short-term debt-paying ability. In addition, users want to know the types of liabilities a company has. If a company declares bankruptcy, a specific, predetermined order of payment to creditors exists. Thus, the amount and type of liabilities are of critical importance.

The different types of current liabilities include notes payable, accounts payable, unearned revenues, and accrued liabilities such as taxes, salaries and wages, and interest payable. In the sections that follow, we discuss common types of current liabilities (see **Helpful Hint**).

HELPFUL HINT
In previous chapters, we explained the entries for accounts payable and the adjusting entries for some current liabilities.

Notes Payable

Companies record obligations in the form of written notes as **notes payable**. Notes payable are often used instead of accounts payable because they give the lender formal proof of the obligation in case legal remedies are needed to collect the debt. Companies frequently issue notes payable to meet short-term financing needs. Notes payable usually require the borrower to pay interest.

Notes are issued for varying periods of time. **Those due for payment within one year of the balance sheet date are usually classified as current liabilities.**

To illustrate the accounting for notes payable, assume that First National Bank agrees to lend $100,000 on September 1, 2022, if Cole Williams Co. signs a $100,000, 12%, four-month note maturing on January 1. When a company issues an interest-bearing note, the amount of assets it receives upon issuance of the note generally equals the note's face value. Cole Williams therefore will receive $100,000 cash and will make the following journal entry.

Sept. 1	Cash	100,000	
	Notes Payable		100,000
	(To record issuance of 12%, 4-month note to First National Bank)		

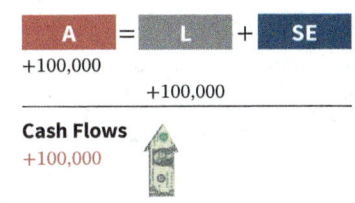

Interest accrues over the life of the note, and the company must periodically record that accrual. If Cole Williams prepares financial statements annually, it makes an adjusting entry at December 31 to recognize interest expense and interest payable of $4,000 ($100,000 × 12% × 4/12). **Illustration 10.1** shows the formula for computing interest and its application to Cole Williams' note.

Face Value of Note	×	Annual Interest Rate	×	Time in Terms of One Year	=	Interest
$100,000	×	12%	×	4/12	=	$4,000

ILLUSTRATION 10.1
Formula for computing interest

Cole Williams makes an adjusting entry as follows.

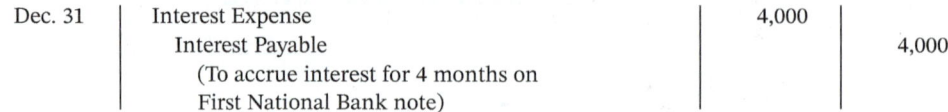

Dec. 31	Interest Expense	4,000	
	Interest Payable		4,000
	(To accrue interest for 4 months on First National Bank note)		

In the December 31 financial statements, the current liabilities section of the balance sheet will show notes payable $100,000 and interest payable $4,000. In addition, the company will report interest expense of $4,000 under "Other expenses and losses" in the income statement. If Cole Williams prepared financial statements monthly, the adjusting entry at the end of each month would be $1,000 ($100,000 × 12% × 1/12).

At maturity (January 1, 2023), Cole Williams must pay the face value of the note ($100,000) plus $4,000 interest ($100,000 × 12% × 4/12). It records payment of the note and accrued interest as follows.

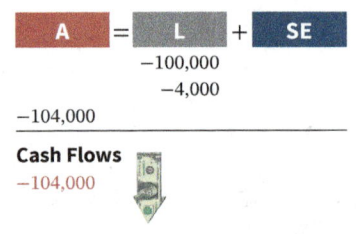

Jan. 1	Notes Payable	100,000	
	Interest Payable	4,000	
	Cash		104,000
	(To record payment of First National Bank interest-bearing note and accrued interest at maturity)		

Sales Taxes Payable

Many of the products we purchase at retail stores are subject to sales taxes. Many states also are now collecting sales taxes on purchases made on the Internet as well. Sales taxes are expressed as a percentage of the sales price. The selling company collects the tax from the customer when the sale occurs. Periodically (usually monthly), the retailer remits the collections to the state's department of revenue. Collecting sales taxes is important. For example, the State of New York recently sued **Sprint Corporation** for $300 million for its alleged failure to collect sales taxes on phone calls.

Under most state sales tax laws, the selling company must enter separately in the cash register the amount of the sale and the amount of the sales tax collected (see **Helpful Hint**). (Gasoline sales are a major exception.) The company then uses the cash register readings to credit Sales Revenue and Sales Taxes Payable. For example, if the March 25 cash register reading for Cooley Grocery shows sales of $10,000 and sales taxes of $600 (sales tax rate of 6%), the journal entry is as follows.

HELPFUL HINT

For point-of-sale systems, the company receives sales information through the computer network.

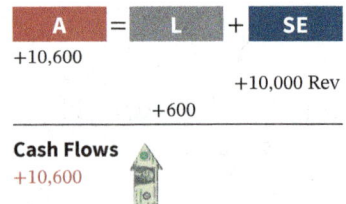

Mar. 25	Cash	10,600	
	Sales Revenue		10,000
	Sales Taxes Payable		600
	(To record daily sales and sales taxes)		

When the company remits the taxes to the taxing agency, it debits Sales Taxes Payable and credits Cash. The company does not report sales taxes as an expense. It simply forwards to the government the amount paid by the customers. Thus, Cooley Grocery serves only as a **collection agent** for the taxing authority.

Sometimes companies do not enter sales taxes separately in the cash register. To determine the amount of sales in such cases, divide total receipts by 100% plus the sales tax percentage. For example, assume that Cooley Grocery enters total receipts of $10,600. The receipts from the sales are equal to the sales price (100%) plus the tax percentage (6% of sales), or 1.06 times the sales total. We can compute the sales amount as follows.

$$\$10,600 \div 1.06 = \$10,000$$

Thus, we can find the sales tax amount of $600 by either (1) subtracting sales from total receipts ($10,600 − $10,000) or (2) multiply sales by the sales tax rate ($10,000 × .06).

Unearned Revenues

A magazine publisher, such as **Sports Illustrated**, receives customers' checks when they order magazines. An airline company, such as **Southwest Airlines**, often receives cash when it sells tickets for future flights. Season tickets for concerts, sporting events, and theater programs are also paid for in advance. How do companies account for unearned revenues that are received before goods are delivered or services are performed?

1. When a company receives the advance payment, it debits Cash and credits a current liability account identifying the source of the unearned revenue.
2. When the company recognizes revenue, it debits an unearned revenue account and credits a revenue account.

To illustrate, assume that Superior University sells 10,000 season football tickets at $50 each for its five-game home schedule. The university makes the following entry for the sale of season tickets.

Aug. 6	Cash (10,000 × $50)	500,000	
	Unearned Ticket Revenue		500,000
	(To record sale of 10,000 season tickets)		

As each game is completed, Superior records the recognition of revenue with the following entry.

Sept. 7	Unearned Ticket Revenue ($500,000 ÷ 5)	100,000	
	Ticket Revenue		100,000
	(To record football ticket revenue)		

The account Unearned Ticket Revenue represents unearned revenue, and Superior reports it as a current liability. As the school recognizes revenue, it reclassifies the amount from unearned revenue to Ticket Revenue. Unearned revenue is substantial for some companies. In the airline industry, for example, tickets sold for future flights represent almost 50% of total current liabilities. At **United Air Lines**, unearned ticket revenue is its largest current liability, recently amounting to over $1 billion.

Illustration 10.2 shows specific unearned revenue and revenue accounts used in selected types of businesses.

Type of Business	Account Title	
	Unearned Revenue	Revenue
Airline	Unearned Ticket Revenue	Ticket Revenue
Magazine publisher	Unearned Subscription Revenue	Subscription Revenue
Hotel	Unearned Rent Revenue	Rent Revenue

ILLUSTRATION 10.2
Unearned revenue and revenue accounts

Current Maturities of Long-Term Debt

Companies often have a portion of long-term debt that comes due in the current year. That amount is considered a current liability. As an example, assume that Wendy Construction issues a five-year, interest-bearing $25,000 note on January 1, 2022. This note specifies that each January 1, starting January 1, 2023, Wendy should pay $5,000 of the note. When the company prepares financial statements on December 31, 2022, it should report $5,000 as a current liability and $20,000 as a long-term liability. (The $5,000 amount is the portion of the note that is due to be paid within the next 12 months.) Companies often identify current maturities of long-term debt on the balance sheet as **long-term debt due within one year**. In a recent year, **General Motors** had $724 million of such debt.

It is not necessary to prepare an adjusting entry to recognize the current maturity of long-term debt. At the balance sheet date, all obligations due within one year are classified as current, and all other obligations as long-term.

ACTION PLAN

- Use the interest formula: Face value of note × Annual interest rate × Time in terms of one year.
- Divide total receipts by 100% plus the tax rate to determine sales revenue; then subtract sales revenue from the total receipts.
- Determine what fraction of the total unearned rent should be recognized this year.

DO IT! 1a | Current Liabilities

You and several classmates are studying for the next accounting examination. They ask you to answer the following questions.

1. If cash is borrowed on a $50,000, 6-month, 12% note on September 1, how much interest expense would be incurred by December 31?
2. How is the sales tax amount determined when the cash register total includes sales taxes?
3. If $15,000 is collected in advance on November 1 for 3 months' rent, what amount of rent revenue should be recognized by December 31?

Solution

1. $50,000 × 12% × 4/12 = $2,000
2. First, divide the total cash register receipts by 100% plus the sales tax percentage to find the sales revenue amount. Second, subtract the sales revenue amount from the total cash register receipts to determine the sales taxes.
3. $15,000 × 2/3 = $10,000

Related exercise material: **BE10.1, BE10.2, BE10.3, BE10.4, BE10.5, DO IT! 10.1a, E10.1, E10.2, E10.3, E10.4, and E10.5.**

Payroll and Payroll Taxes Payable

Assume that Susan Alena works 40 hours this week for Pepitone Inc., earning a wage of $10 per hour. Will Susan receive a $400 check at the end of the week? Not likely. The reason: Pepitone is required to withhold amounts from her wages to pay various governmental authorities. For example, Pepitone will withhold amounts for FICA taxes (Social Security and Medicare)[1] and for federal and state income taxes. If these withholdings total $100, Susan will receive a check for only $300. **Illustration 10.3** summarizes the types of payroll deductions that normally occur for most companies.

ILLUSTRATION 10.3
Payroll deductions

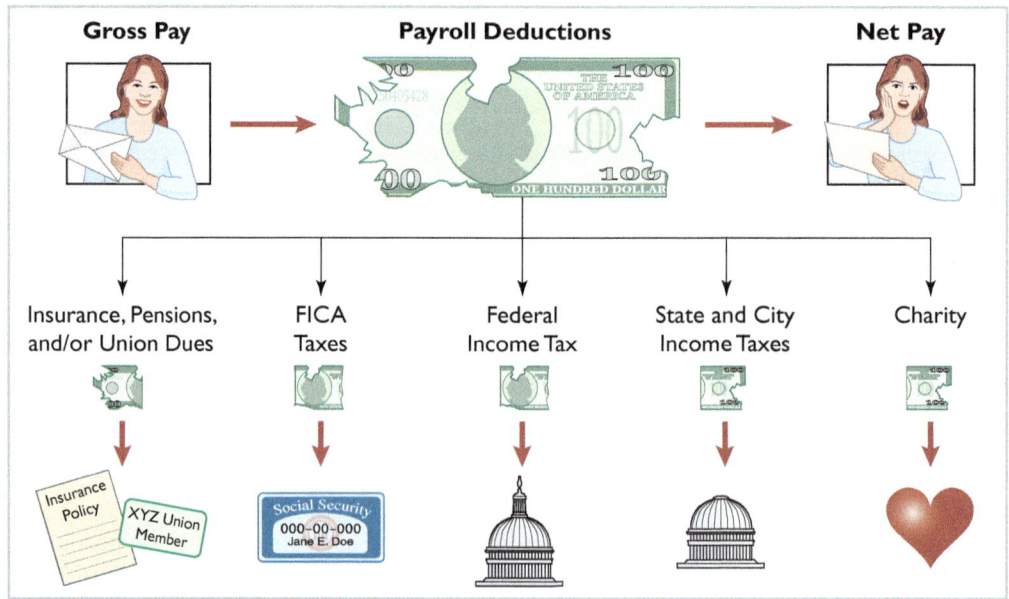

[1]Social Security and Medicare taxes are commonly called FICA taxes. In 1937, Congress enacted the Federal Insurance Contributions Act (FICA) whereby both the employee and employer must make equal contributions. The recent combined Social Security and Medicare rate was 7.65%. *Our examples and homework use 7.65% as the FICA rate.*

As a result of these deductions, companies withhold from employee paychecks amounts that must be paid to other parties. Pepitone therefore has incurred liabilities to pay these third parties and must report these liabilities on its balance sheet.

As a second illustration, assume that Cargo Corporation records its payroll for the week of March 7 with the following journal entry.

Mar. 7	Salaries and Wages Expense	100,000	
	FICA Taxes Payable		7,650
	Federal Income Taxes Payable		21,864
	State Income Taxes Payable		2,922
	Salaries and Wages Payable		67,564
	(To record payroll and withholding taxes for the week ending March 7)		

Cargo then records payment of this payroll on March 7 as follows.

Mar. 7	Salaries and Wages Payable	67,564	
	Cash		67,564
	(To record payment of the March 7 payroll)		

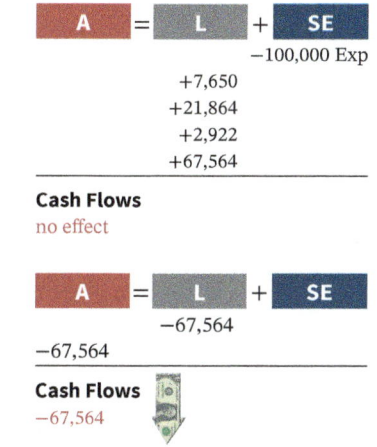

In this case, Cargo reports $100,000 in salaries and wages expense. In addition, it reports liabilities for the salaries and wages payable as well as liabilities to governmental agencies. Rather than pay the employees $100,000, Cargo instead must withhold the taxes and make the tax payments directly to the government entities. In summary, Cargo is essentially serving as a tax collector.

In addition to the liabilities incurred as a result of withholdings, employers also incur a second type of payroll-related liability. With every payroll, the employer incurs liabilities to pay various **payroll taxes** levied upon the employer. These payroll taxes include the **employer's share** of FICA (Social Security and Medicare) taxes and state and federal unemployment taxes. Based on Cargo's $100,000 payroll, the company would record the employer's expense and liability for these payroll taxes as follows.

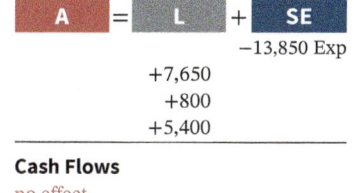

Mar. 7	Payroll Tax Expense	13,850	
	FICA Taxes Payable		7,650
	Federal Unemployment Taxes Payable		800
	State Unemployment Taxes Payable		5,400
	(To record employer's payroll taxes on March 7 payroll)		

Companies classify the payroll and payroll tax liability accounts as current liabilities because they must be paid to employees or remitted to taxing authorities periodically and in the near term. Taxing authorities impose substantial fines and penalties on employers if the withholding and payroll taxes are not computed correctly and paid on time.

Anatomy of a Fraud

Art was a custodial supervisor for a large school district. The district was supposed to employ between 35 and 40 regular custodians, as well as 3 or 4 substitute custodians to fill in when regular custodians were absent. Instead, in addition to the regular custodians, Art "hired" 77 substitutes. In fact, almost none of these people worked for the district. Instead, Art submitted time cards for these people, collected their checks at the district office, and personally distributed the checks to the "employees." If a substitute's check was for $1,200, that person would cash the check, keep $200, and pay Art $1,000.

Total take: $150,000

The Missing Controls

Human resource controls. Thorough background checks should be performed. No employees should begin work until they have been approved by the Board of Education and entered into the payroll system. No employees should be entered into the payroll system until they have been approved by a supervisor. All paychecks should be distributed directly to employees at the official school locations by designated employees or direct-deposited into approved employee bank accounts.

Independent internal verification. Budgets should be reviewed monthly to identify situations where actual costs significantly exceed budgeted amounts.

Source: Adapted from Wells, *Fraud Casebook* (2007), pp. 164–171.

> **ACTION PLAN**
> - Remember that wages earned are an expense to the company, but withholdings reduce the amount due to be paid to the employee.
> - Payroll taxes are taxes the company incurs related to its employees.

DO IT! 1b | Wages and Payroll Taxes

During the month of September, Lake Corporation's employees earned wages of $60,000. Withholdings related to these wages were $4,590 for FICA, $6,500 for federal income tax, and $2,000 for state income tax. Costs incurred for unemployment taxes were $90 for federal and $150 for state.

Prepare the September 30 journal entries for (a) salaries and wages expense and salaries and wages payable, assuming that all September wages will be paid in October, and (b) the company's payroll tax expense.

Solution

a. To determine wages payable, reduce wages expense by the withholdings for FICA, federal income tax, and state income tax.

Sept. 30	Salaries and Wages Expense	60,000	
	FICA Taxes Payable		4,590
	Federal Income Taxes Payable		6,500
	State Income Taxes Payable		2,000
	Salaries and Wages Payable		46,910

b. Payroll taxes would be for the company's share of FICA, as well as for federal and state unemployment tax.

Sept. 30	Payroll Tax Expense	4,830	
	FICA Taxes Payable		4,590
	Federal Unemployment Taxes Payable		90
	State Unemployment Taxes Payable		150

Related exercise material: **BE10.5, BE10.6, BE10.7, DO IT! 10.1b, E10.6, E10.7, and E10.8.**

Major Characteristics of Bonds

> **LEARNING OBJECTIVE 2**
> Describe the major characteristics of bonds.

Long-term liabilities are obligations that a company expects to pay more than one year in the future. In this section, we explain the accounting for the principal types of obligations reported in the long-term liabilities section of the balance sheet. These obligations often are in the form of bonds or long-term notes.

Bonds are a form of interest-bearing notes payable issued by corporations, universities, and governmental agencies. Bonds, like common stock, are sold in small denominations (usually $1,000 or multiples of $1,000). As a result, bonds attract many investors. When a corporation issues bonds, it is borrowing money. The person who buys the bonds (the bondholder) is lending money.

Types of Bonds

Bonds may have many different features. In the following sections, we describe the types of bonds commonly issued.

Secured and Unsecured Bonds

Secured bonds have specific assets of the issuer pledged as collateral for the bonds. A bond secured by real estate, for example, is called a **mortgage bond**. A bond secured by specific assets set aside to redeem (retire) the bonds is called a **sinking fund bond**.

Unsecured bonds, also called **debenture bonds**, are issued against the general credit of the borrower. Companies with good credit ratings use these bonds extensively. For example, at one time, **DuPont** reported over $2 billion of debenture bonds outstanding.

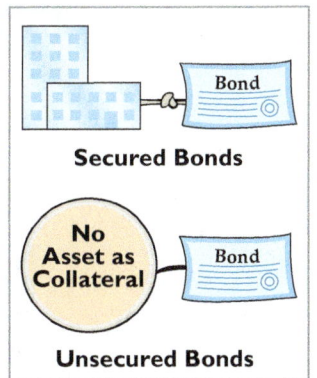

Convertible and Callable Bonds

Bonds that can be converted into common stock at the bondholder's option are **convertible bonds**. Bonds that the issuing company can redeem (buy back) at a stated dollar amount prior to maturity are **callable bonds**. Convertible bonds have features that are attractive both to bondholders and to the issuer. The conversion feature often gives bondholders an opportunity to benefit if the market price of the common stock increases substantially. Furthermore, until conversion, the bondholder receives interest on the bond. For the issuer, the bonds sell at a higher price and pay a lower rate of interest than comparable debt securities that do not have a conversion option. Many corporations, such as **USAir**, **United States Steel Corp.**, and **General Motors Corporation**, have issued convertible bonds.

Issuing Procedures

State laws grant corporations the power to issue bonds. Both the board of directors and stockholders usually must approve bond issues. **In authorizing the bond issue, the board of directors must stipulate the number of bonds to be authorized, total face value, and contractual interest rate.** The total bond authorization often exceeds the number of bonds the company originally issues. This gives the corporation the flexibility to issue more bonds, if needed, to meet future cash requirements.

The **face value** is the amount of principal due at the maturity date. The **maturity date** is the date that the final payment is due to the investor from the issuing company. The **contractual interest rate**, often referred to as the **stated rate**, is the rate used to determine the amount of cash interest the issuing company pays and the investor receives. Usually, the contractual rate is stated as an annual rate.

The terms of the bond issue are set forth in a legal document called a **bond indenture**. The indenture shows the terms and summarizes the rights of the bondholders and their trustees, and the obligations of the issuing company. The **trustee** (usually a financial institution) keeps records of each bondholder, maintains custody of unissued bonds, and holds conditional title to pledged property.

In addition, the issuing company arranges for the printing of **bond certificates**. The indenture and the certificate are separate documents. As shown in **Illustration 10.4**, a bond certificate, which is sometimes an electronic record, provides the following information: name of the issuer, face value, contractual interest rate, and maturity date. An investment company that specializes in selling securities generally sells the bonds for the issuing company.

Bond Trading

Bondholders have the opportunity to convert their holdings into cash at any time by selling the bonds at the current market price on national securities exchanges. **Bond prices are quoted as a percentage of the face value of the bond, which is usually $1,000.** A $1,000 bond with a quoted price of 97 means that the selling price of the bond is 97% of face value, or $970. Newspapers and the financial press publish bond prices and trading activity daily, as shown in **Illustration 10.5**.

ILLUSTRATION 10.4 Bond certificate

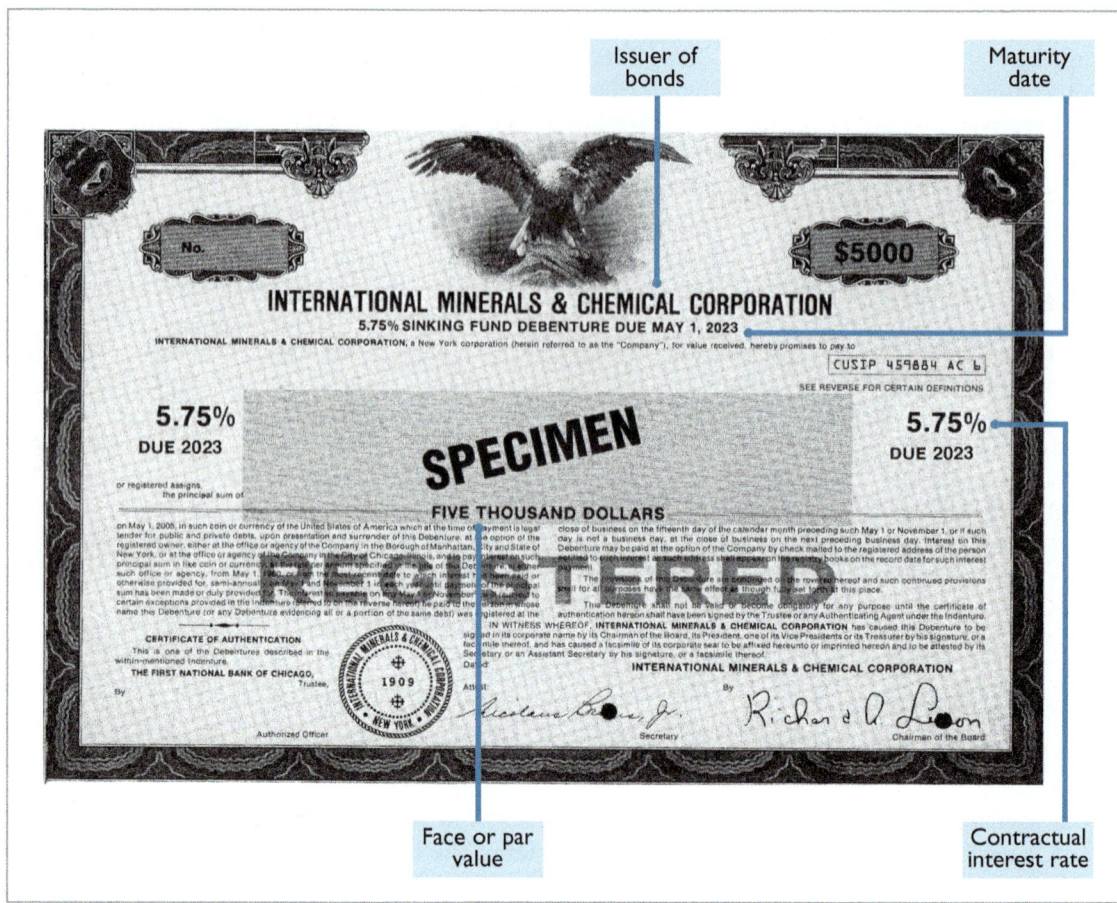

ILLUSTRATION 10.5
Market information for bonds

Issuer	Bonds	Maturity	Close	Yield
Time Warner Cable	6.75	June 15, 2039	116.4	5.49

HELPFUL HINT

The price of a $1,000 bond trading at 95¼ is $952.50.

This bond listing indicates that **Time Warner Cable** has outstanding 6.75%, $1,000 bonds that mature in 2039 (see **Helpful Hint**). They currently yield a 5.49% return. At the close of trading, the price was 116.4% of face value, or $1,164.

A corporation makes journal entries **only when it issues or buys back bonds**, or when bondholders convert bonds into common stock. For example, **DuPont does not journalize** transactions between its bondholders and other investors. If Tom Smith sells his DuPont bonds to Faith Jones, DuPont does not journalize the transaction.

Determining the Market Price of a Bond

If your company needed financing and wanted to attract investors to purchase your bonds, how would the market set the price for these bonds? To be more specific, assume that Coronet, Inc. issues a **zero-interest bond** (pays no interest) with a face value of $1,000,000 due in 20 years. For this bond, the only cash Coronet pays to bond investors is a million dollars at the end of 20 years. Would investors pay a million dollars for this bond? We hope not because a million dollars received 20 years from now is not the same as a million dollars received today.

The term **time value of money** is used to indicate the relationship between time and money—that a dollar received today is worth more than a dollar promised at some time in the future. If you had $1 million today, you would invest it. From that investment, you would earn interest such that at the end of 20 years, you would have much more than $1 million. Thus, if

Same dollars at different times are not equal.

someone is going to pay you $1 million 20 years from now, you would want to find its equivalent today, or its **present value**. In other words, you would want to determine the value today of the amount to be received in the future after taking into account current interest rates.

The current market price (present value) of a bond is the value at which it should sell in the marketplace. Market price therefore is a function of the three factors that determine present value: (1) the dollar amounts to be received, (2) the length of time until the amounts are received, and (3) the market rate of interest. The **market interest rate** is the rate investors demand for loaning funds.

To illustrate, assume that Acropolis Company on January 1, 2022, issues $100,000 of 9% bonds, due in five years, with interest payable annually at year-end. The purchaser of the bonds would receive the following two types of cash payments: (1) **principal** of $100,000 to be paid at maturity, and (2) five $9,000 **interest payments** ($100,000 × 9%) over the term of the bonds. **Illustration 10.6** shows a time diagram depicting both cash flows.

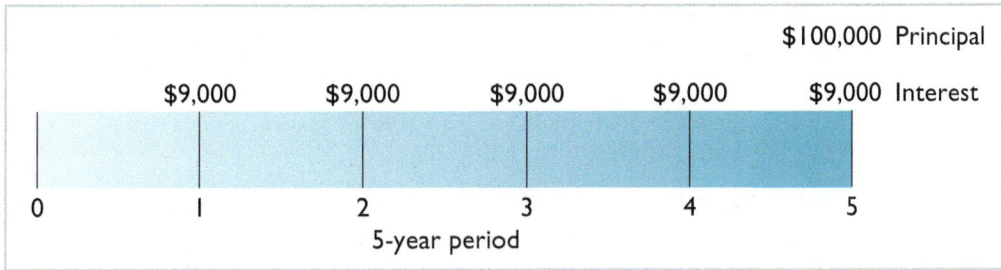

ILLUSTRATION 10.6
Time diagram depicting cash flows

The current market price of a bond is equal to the present value of all the future cash payments promised by the bond. **Illustration 10.7** lists and totals the present values of these amounts, assuming the market rate of interest is 9%.

Present value of $100,000 received in 5 years	$ 64,993
Present value of $9,000 received annually for 5 years	35,007
Market price of bonds	**$100,000**

ILLUSTRATION 10.7
Computing the market price of bonds

Tables are available to provide the present value numbers to be used, or these values can be determined mathematically or with financial calculators.[2] Appendix G provides further discussion of the concepts and the mechanics of the time value of money computations.

Investor Insight

Running Hot!

© alphaspirit/Shutterstock

Recently, the market for bonds was running hot. For example, consider these two large deals: **Apple Inc.** sold $17 billion of debt, which at the time was the largest corporate bond ever sold. But shortly thereafter, it was beat by **Verizon Communications Inc.**, which sold $49 billion of debt. The chart highlights the increased issuance of bonds.

As one expert noted about these increases, "Companies are taking advantage of this lower-rate environment in the limited period of time it is going to be around." An interesting aspect of these bond issuances is that companies, like

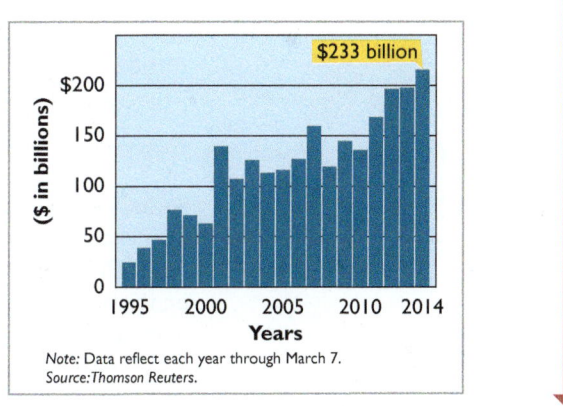

---

[2]For those knowledgeable in the use of present value tables, the computations in the example shown in Illustration 10.7 are $100,000 × .64993 = $64,993, and $9,000 × 3.88965 = $35,007 (rounded).

Philip Morris International, Medtronic, Inc., and **Simon Properties,** are even selling 30-year bonds. These bond issuers are benefiting from "a massive sentiment shift," says one bond expert. The belief that the economy will recover is making investors more comfortable holding longer-term bonds, as they search for investments that offer better returns than U.S. Treasury bonds.

Sources: Vipal Monga, "The Big Number," *Wall Street Journal* (March 20, 2012), p. B5; and Mike Cherney, "Renewed Embrace of Bonds Sparks Boom," *Wall Street Journal* (March 8–9, 2014), p. B5.

What are the advantages for companies of issuing 30-year bonds instead of 5-year bonds? (Go to WileyPLUS for this answer and additional questions.)

ACTION PLAN
- Review the types of bonds and the basic terms associated with bonds.

DO IT! 2 | Bond Terminology

State whether each of the following statements is true or false. If false, indicate how to correct the statement.

_____ 1. Mortgage bonds and sinking fund bonds are both examples of secured bonds.
_____ 2. Unsecured bonds are also known as debenture bonds.
_____ 3. The contractual interest rate is the rate investors demand for loaning funds.
_____ 4. The face value is the amount of principal the issuing company must pay at the maturity date.
_____ 5. The market price of a bond is equal to its maturity value.

Solution

1. True. 2. True. 3. False. The contractual interest rate is used to determine the amount of cash interest the borrower pays. 4. True. 5. False. The market price of a bond is the value at which it should sell in the marketplace. As a result, the market price of the bond and its maturity value are often different.

Related exercise material: **DO IT! 10.2 and E10.11.**

Accounting for Bond Transactions

LEARNING OBJECTIVE 3
Explain how to account for bond transactions.

As indicated earlier, a corporation records bond transactions when it issues (sells) or redeems (buys back) bonds and when bondholders convert bonds into common stock. If bondholders sell their bond investments to other investors, the issuing company receives no further money on the transaction, **nor does the issuing company journalize the transaction** (although it does keep records of the names of bondholders in some cases).

Bonds may be issued at face value, below face value (discount), or above face value (premium). Recall that bond prices for both new issues and existing bonds are quoted as **a percentage of the face value of the bond, and that face value is usually $1,000.** Thus, a $1,000 bond with a quoted price of 97 means that the selling price of the bond is 97% of face value, or $970.

Issuing Bonds at Face Value

To illustrate the accounting for bonds issued at face value, assume that on January 1, 2022, Candlestick Inc. issues $100,000, five-year, 10% bonds at 100 (100% of face value). The entry to record the sale is as follows.

Jan. 1	Cash	100,000	
	Bonds Payable		100,000
	(To record sale of bonds at face value)		

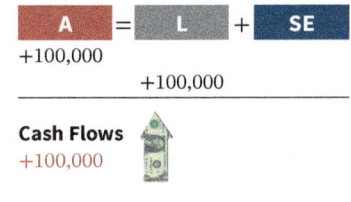

Candlestick reports bonds payable in the long-term liabilities section of the balance sheet because the maturity date is January 1, 2027 (more than one year away).

Over the term (life) of the bonds, companies make entries to record bond interest. Interest on bonds payable is computed in the same manner as interest on notes payable. Assume that interest is payable annually on January 1 on the Candlestick bonds. In that case, Candlestick accrues interest of $10,000 ($100,000 × 10%) on December 31. At December 31, Candlestick recognizes the $10,000 of interest expense incurred with the following entry.

Dec. 31	Interest Expense	10,000	
	Interest Payable		10,000
	(To accrue bond interest)		

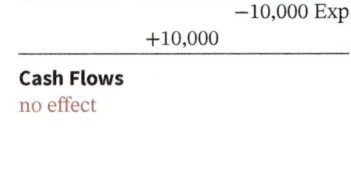

The company classifies interest payable as a current liability because it is scheduled for payment within the next year. When Candlestick pays the interest on January 1, 2023, it debits (decreases) Interest Payable and credits (decreases) Cash for $10,000.

Candlestick records the payment on January 1 as follows.

Jan. 1	Interest Payable	10,000	
	Cash		10,000
	(To record payment of bond interest)		

Discount or Premium on Bonds

The previous example assumed that the contractual (stated) interest rate and the market (effective) interest rate paid on the bonds were the same. Recall that the **contractual interest rate** is the rate applied to the face (par) value to arrive at the interest paid in a year. The **market interest rate** is the rate investors demand for loaning funds to the corporation. When the contractual interest rate and the market interest rate are the same, bonds sell **at face value (par value)**.

However, market interest rates change daily. The type of bond issued, the state of the economy, current industry conditions, and the company's performance all affect market interest rates. As a result, contractual and market interest rates often differ. To make bonds salable when the two rates differ, bonds sell below or above face value.

To illustrate, suppose that a company issues 10% bonds at a time when other bonds of similar risk are paying 12%. Investors will not be interested in buying the 10% bonds, so their value will fall below their face value. When a bond is sold for less than its face value, the difference between the face value of a bond and its selling price is called a **discount**. As a result of the decline in the bonds' selling price, the actual interest rate incurred by the company increases to the level of the current market interest rate.

Conversely, if the market rate of interest is **lower than** the contractual interest rate, investors will have to pay more than face value for the bonds. That is, if the market rate of interest is 8% but the contractual interest rate on the bonds is 10%, the price of the bonds will be bid up. When a bond is sold for more than its face value, the difference between its selling price and the face value is called a **premium**. **Illustration 10.8** shows these relationships.

ILLUSTRATION 10.8
Interest rates and bond prices

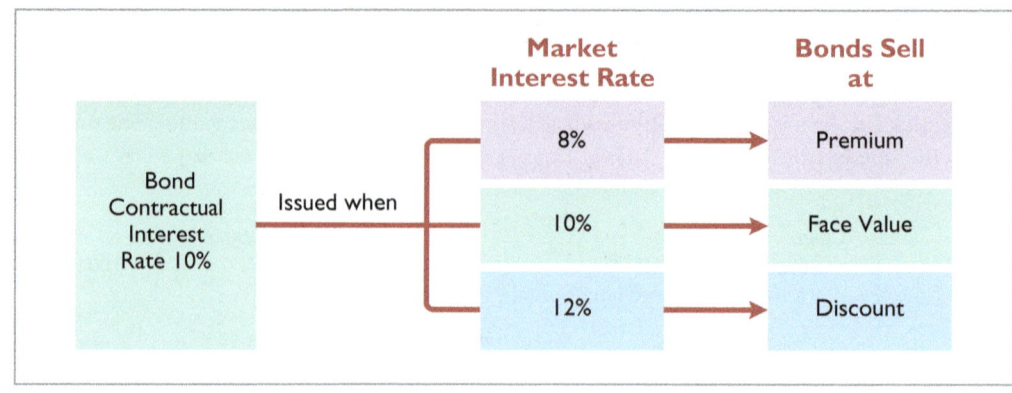

Issuance of bonds at an amount different from face value is quite common. By the time a company completes the necessary paperwork and markets the bonds, it will be a coincidence if the market rate and the contractual rate are the same. Thus, the issuance of bonds at a discount does not mean that the issuer's financial strength is suspect. Conversely, the sale of bonds at a premium does not indicate that the financial strength of the issuer is exceptional.

HELPFUL HINT

Discount on Bonds Payable	
Increase Debit	Decrease Credit
Normal Balance	

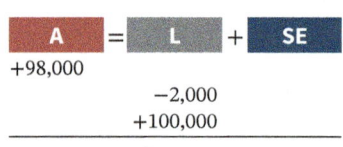

Cash Flows
+98,000

Issuing Bonds at a Discount

To illustrate issuance of bonds at a discount, assume that on January 1, 2022, Candlestick Inc. sells $100,000, five-year, 10% bonds for $98,000 (98% of face value). Interest is payable annually on January 1. The entry to record the issuance is as follows (see **Helpful Hint**).

Jan. 1	Cash	98,000	
	Discount on Bonds Payable	2,000	
	Bonds Payable		100,000
	(To record sale of bonds at a discount)		

Although Discount on Bonds Payable has a debit balance, **it is not an asset**. Rather, it is a **contra account**. This account is **deducted from bonds payable** on the balance sheet, as shown in **Illustration 10.9**.

ILLUSTRATION 10.9
Statement presentation of discount on bonds payable

Candlestick Inc.
Balance Sheet (partial)

Long-term liabilities		
Bonds payable	$100,000	
Less: Discount on bonds payable	2,000	$98,000

HELPFUL HINT

Carrying value (book value) of bonds issued at a discount is determined by subtracting the balance of the discount account from the balance of the Bonds Payable account.

The $98,000 represents the **carrying (or book) value** of the bonds (see **Helpful Hint**). On the date of issue, this amount equals the market price of the bonds.

The issuance of bonds below face value—at a discount—causes the total cost of borrowing to differ from the bond interest paid. That is, the issuing corporation must pay not only the contractual interest rate over the term of the bonds but also the face value (rather than the issuance price) at maturity. Therefore, the difference between the issuance price and face value of the bonds—the discount—is an **additional cost of borrowing**. The company records this additional cost as **interest expense** over the life of the bonds. The total cost of borrowing $98,000 for Candlestick is therefore $52,000, computed as shown in **Illustration 10.10**.

ILLUSTRATION 10.10
Total cost of borrowing—bonds issued at a discount

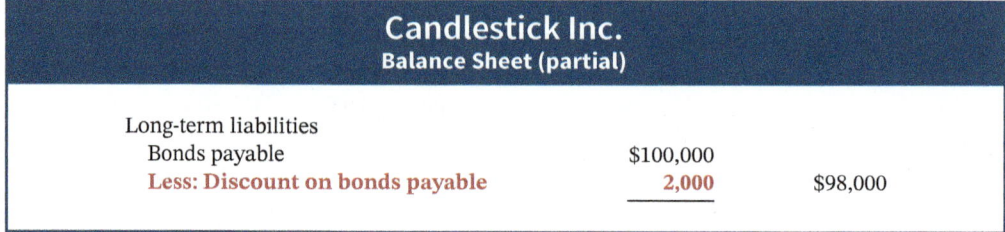

Alternatively, we can compute the total cost of borrowing as shown in **Illustration 10.11**.

Bonds Issued at a Discount	
Principal at maturity	$100,000
Annual interest payments ($10,000 × 5)	50,000
Cash to be paid to bondholders	150,000
Less: Cash received from bondholders	98,000
Total cost of borrowing	**$ 52,000**

ILLUSTRATION 10.11
Alternative computation of total cost of borrowing—bonds issued at a discount

To follow the expense recognition principle, companies allocate bond discount to expense in each period in which the bonds are outstanding. This is referred to as **amortizing the discount**. Amortization of the discount **increases** the amount of interest expense reported each period. That is, after the company amortizes the discount, the amount of interest expense it reports in a period will exceed the contractual amount. As shown in Illustration 10.10, for the bonds issued by Candlestick, total interest expense will exceed the contractual interest by $2,000 over the life of the bonds.

As the discount is amortized, its balance declines. As a consequence, the carrying value of the bonds will increase, until at maturity the carrying value of the bonds equals their face amount. This is shown in **Illustration 10.12**. Appendices 10A and 10B at the end of this chapter discuss procedures for amortizing bond discount.

ILLUSTRATION 10.12
Amortization of bond discount

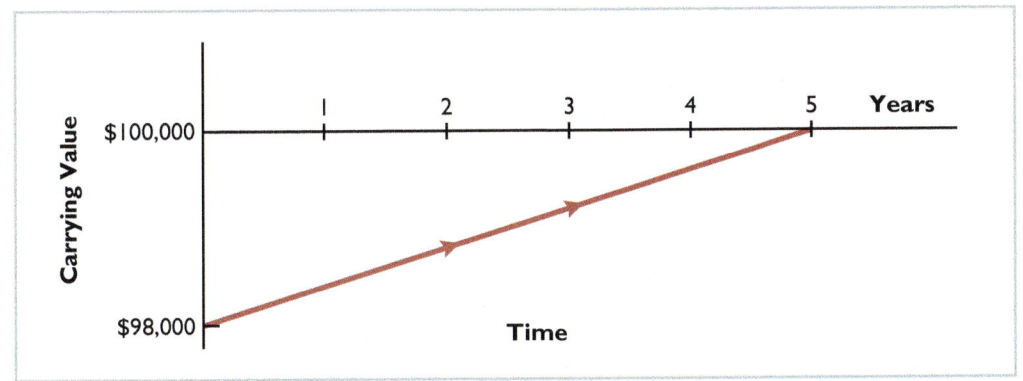

Issuing Bonds at a Premium

To illustrate the issuance of bonds at a premium, we now assume the Candlestick Inc. bonds described above sell for $102,000 (102% of face value) rather than for $98,000. The entry to record the sale is as follows.

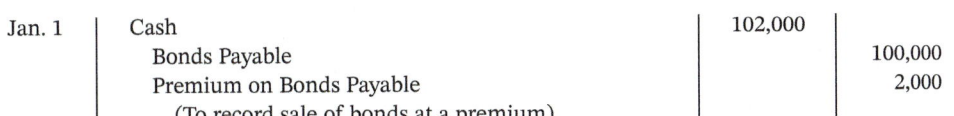

Jan. 1	Cash	102,000	
	Bonds Payable		100,000
	Premium on Bonds Payable		2,000
	(To record sale of bonds at a premium)		

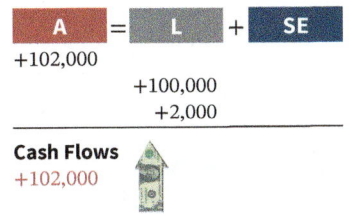

A	=	L	+	SE
+102,000		+100,000		
		+2,000		

Cash Flows
+102,000

Candlestick adds the premium on bonds payable **to the bonds payable amount** on the balance sheet, as shown in **Illustration 10.13**.

ILLUSTRATION 10.13
Statement presentation of bond premium

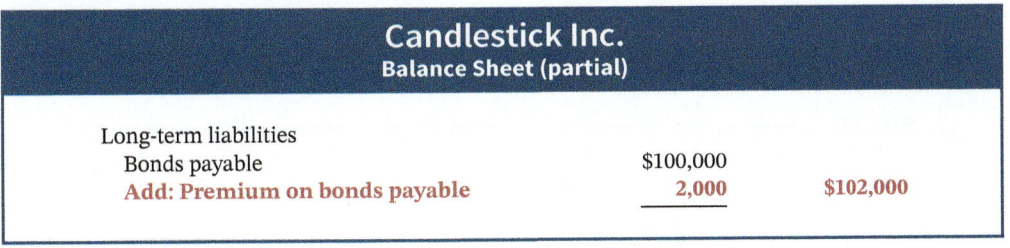

Candlestick Inc.
Balance Sheet (partial)

Long-term liabilities		
Bonds payable	$100,000	
Add: Premium on bonds payable	2,000	$102,000

> **HELPFUL HINT**
>
> **Premium on Bonds Payable**
>
> | Decrease Debit | Increase Credit |
> |---|---|
> | | ↓ |
> | | Normal Balance |

The sale of bonds above face value causes the total cost of borrowing to be **less than the bond interest paid**. The reason: The borrower is not required to pay the bond premium at the maturity date of the bonds. Thus, the bond premium is considered to be **a reduction in the cost of borrowing** that reduces bond interest over the life of the bonds. The total cost of borrowing $102,000 for Candlestick is shown in **Illustration 10.14** (see **Helpful Hint**).

ILLUSTRATION 10.14
Total cost of borrowing—bonds issued at a premium

Bonds Issued at a Premium	
Annual interest payments	
($100,000 × 10% = $10,000; $10,000 × 5)	$50,000
Less: Bond premium ($102,000 − $100,000)	2,000
Total cost of borrowing	**$48,000**

Alternatively, we can compute the cost of borrowing as shown in **Illustration 10.15**.

ILLUSTRATION 10.15
Alternative computation of total cost of borrowing—bonds issued at a premium

Bonds Issued at a Premium	
Principal at maturity	$100,000
Annual interest payments ($10,000 × 5)	50,000
Cash to be paid to bondholders	150,000
Less: Cash received from bondholders	102,000
Total cost of borrowing	**$ 48,000**

> **HELPFUL HINT**
>
> Both a discount and a premium account are valuation accounts. A *valuation account* is one that is needed to value properly the item to which it relates.

Similar to bond discount, companies allocate bond premium to expense in each period in which the bonds are outstanding (see **Helpful Hint**). This is referred to as **amortizing the premium**. Amortization of the premium **decreases** the amount of interest expense reported each period. That is, after the company amortizes the premium, the amount of interest expense it reports in a period will be less than the contractual amount. As shown in Illustration 10.14, for the bonds issued by Candlestick, contractual interest will exceed the interest expense by $2,000 over the life of the bonds.

As the premium is amortized, its balance declines. As a consequence, the carrying value of the bonds will decrease, until at maturity the carrying value of the bonds equals their face amount. This is shown in **Illustration 10.16**. Appendices 10A and 10B at the end of this chapter discuss procedures for amortizing bond premium.

ILLUSTRATION 10.16
Amortization of bond premium

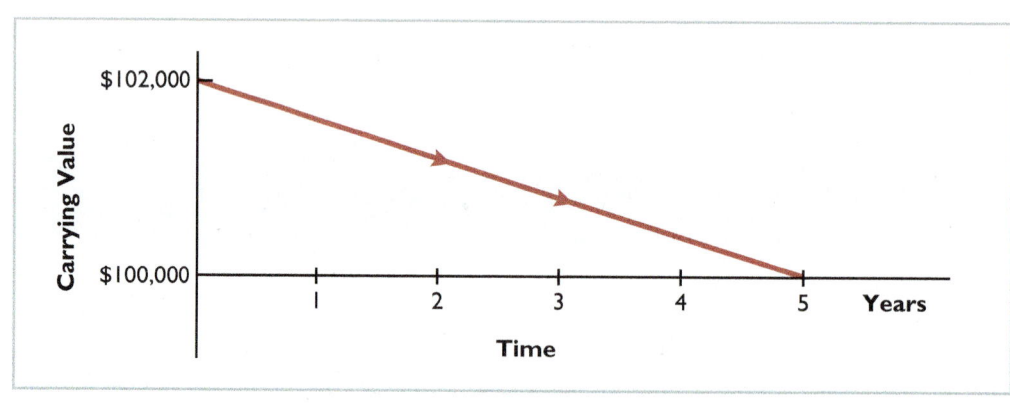

DO IT! 3a | Bond Issuance

Giant Corporation issues $200,000 of bonds for $189,000. (a) Prepare the journal entry to record the issuance of the bonds, and (b) show how the bonds would be reported on the balance sheet at the date of issuance.

Solution

a.
Cash	189,000	
Discount on Bonds Payable	11,000	
Bonds Payable		200,000
(To record sale of bonds at a discount)		

b. Long-term liabilities
    Bonds payable $200,000
    Less: Discount on bonds payable   11,000 $189,000

Related exercise material: BE10.8, BE10.9, BE10.10, BE10.12, DO IT! 10.3a, E10.12, E10.13, E10.14, E10.15, and E10.16.

ACTION PLAN
- Record cash received, bonds payable at face value, and the difference as a discount or premium.
- Report discount as a deduction from bonds payable and premium as an addition to bonds payable.

Redeeming Bonds at Maturity

Regardless of the issue price of bonds, the book value of the bonds at maturity will equal their face value. Assuming that the company pays and records separately the interest for the last interest period, Candlestick Inc. records the redemption of its bonds at maturity as follows.

Jan. 1	Bonds Payable	100,000	
	Cash		100,000
	(To record redemption of bonds at maturity)		

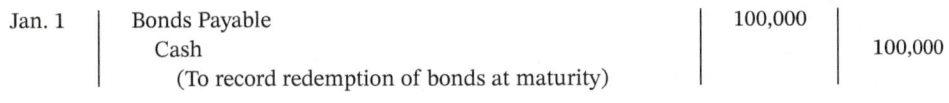
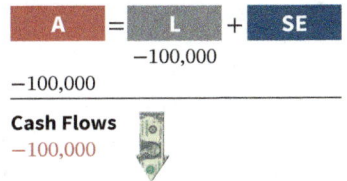

Redeeming Bonds Before Maturity

Bonds may be redeemed before maturity. A company may decide to redeem bonds before maturity to reduce interest cost and to remove debt from its balance sheet. A company should redeem debt early only if it has sufficient cash resources.

When a company redeems bonds before maturity, it is necessary to (1) eliminate the carrying value of the bonds at the redemption date, (2) record the cash paid, and (3) recognize the gain or loss on redemption. The **carrying value** of the bonds is the face value of the bonds less any remaining bond discount or plus any remaining bond premium at the redemption date (see **Helpful Hint**).

To illustrate, assume that Candlestick Inc. has sold its bonds at a premium. At the end of the fourth period, Candlestick redeems these bonds at 103 after paying the annual interest. Assume that the carrying value of the bonds at the redemption date is $100,400 (principal $100,000 and premium $400). Candlestick records the redemption at the end of the fourth interest period (January 1, 2026) as follows.

HELPFUL HINT

If a bond is redeemed prior to its maturity date and its carrying value exceeds its redemption price, this results in a gain.

Jan. 1	Bonds Payable	100,000	
	Premium on Bonds Payable	400	
	Loss on Bond Redemption	2,600	
	Cash		103,000
	(To record redemption of bonds at 103)		

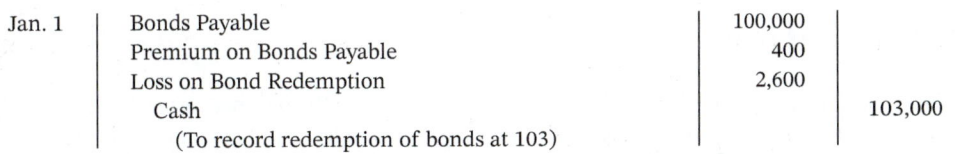
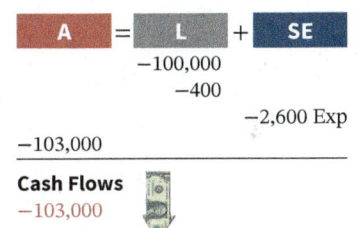

Note that the loss of $2,600 is the difference between the cash paid of $103,000 and the carrying value of the bonds of $100,400.

People, Planet, and Profit Insight

© CarpathianPrince/ Shutterstock

How About Some Green Bonds?

Green bonds are debt used to fund activities such as renewable-energy projects. For example, a company may use the proceeds from the sale of green bonds to clean up its manufacturing operations and cut waste (such as related to energy consumption).

The use of green bonds has taken off as companies now have guidelines as to how to disclose and report on these green-bond proceeds. These standardized disclosures provide transparency as to how these bonds are used and their effect on overall profitability.

Investors are taking a strong interest in these bonds. Investing companies are installing socially responsible investing teams and have started to integrate sustainability into their investment processes. The disclosures of how companies are using the bond proceeds help investors to make better financial decisions.

Source: Ben Edwards, "Green Bonds Catch On." *Wall Street Journal* (April 3, 2014), p. C5.

Why might standardized disclosure help investors to better understand how proceeds from the sale or issuance of bonds are used? (Go to WileyPLUS for this answer and additional questions.)

ACTION PLAN
- Determine and eliminate the carrying value of the bonds.
- Record the cash paid.
- Compute and record the gain or loss (the difference between the first two items).

DO IT! 3b | Bond Redemption

R & B Inc. issued $500,000, 10-year bonds at a discount. Prior to maturity, when the carrying value of the bonds is $496,000, the company redeems the bonds at 98. Prepare the entry to record the redemption of the bonds.

Solution

There is a gain on redemption. The cash paid, $490,000 ($500,000 × 98%), is less than the carrying value of $496,000. The entry is:

Bonds Payable	500,000	
Discount on Bonds Payable		4,000
Gain on Bond Redemption		6,000
Cash		490,000
(To record redemption of bonds at 98)		

Related exercise material: **BE10.11, DO IT! 10.3b, E10.17, and E10.18.**

Presentation and Analysis

LEARNING OBJECTIVE 4
Discuss how liabilities are reported and analyzed.

Presentation

Current liabilities are the first category under "Liabilities" on the balance sheet. Companies list each of the principal types of current liabilities separately within the category. Within the current liabilities section, companies often list notes payable first, followed by accounts payable.

Companies report long-term liabilities in a separate section of the balance sheet immediately following "Current liabilities." **Illustration 10.17** shows an example.

ILLUSTRATION 10.17
Balance sheet presentation of liabilities

Marais Company
Balance Sheet (partial)

Liabilities

Current liabilities
Notes payable	$ 250,000	
Accounts payable	125,000	
Current maturities of long-term debt	300,000	
Accrued liabilities	75,000	
Total current liabilities		$ 750,000

Long-term liabilities
Bonds payable	1,000,000	
Less: Discount on bonds payable	80,000	920,000
Notes payable, secured by plant assets		540,000
Lease liability		500,000
Total long-term liabilities		1,960,000
Total liabilities		$2,710,000

Disclosure of debt is very important. Failures at **Enron**, **WorldCom**, and **Global Crossing** have made investors very concerned about companies' debt obligations (see **Ethics Note**). Summary data regarding debts may be presented in the balance sheet with detailed data (such as interest rates, maturity dates, conversion privileges, and assets pledged as collateral) shown in a supporting schedule in the notes. Companies should report current maturities of long-term debt as a current liability.

ETHICS NOTE

Some companies try to minimize the amount of debt reported on their balance sheets by not reporting certain types of commitments as liabilities. This subject is of intense interest in the financial community.

Keeping an Eye on Cash

The balance sheet presents the balances of a company's debts at a point in time. The statement of cash flows also presents information about a company's debts. Information regarding cash inflows and outflows during the year that resulted from the principal portion of debt transactions appears in the "Financing activities" section of the statement of cash flows. Interest expense is reported in the "Operating activities" section even though it resulted from debt transactions.

The following statement of cash flows presents the cash flows from financing activities for **General Motors Company** from a recent year. From this we learn that the company issued new debt of $31,373 million and repaid debt of $19,524 million.

General Motors Company
Statement of Cash Flows (partial)
(in millions)

Cash flows from financing activities
Payments to repurchase stock	$ (3,277)
Proceeds from issuance of debt	31,373
Payments of debt	(19,524)
Increase in short-term debt	391
Dividends paid	(3,165)
Other	(123)
Net cash provided by (used in) financing activities	$ 5,675

Analysis

Careful examination of debt obligations helps you assess a company's ability to pay its current and long-term obligations. It also helps you determine whether a company can obtain debt financing in order to grow. We will use the information from the financial statements of **General Motors** (see **Illustration 10.18**) to illustrate the analysis of a company's liquidity and solvency.

ILLUSTRATION 10.18
Simplified balance sheets for General Motors

General Motors Company
Balance Sheets
December 31, 2017 and 2016
(in millions)

Assets	2017	2016
Total current assets	$ 68,744	$ 76,203
Noncurrent assets	143,738	145,487
Total assets	$212,482	$221,690
Liabilities and Stockholders' Equity		
Total current liabilities	$ 76,890	$ 85,181
Noncurrent liabilities	99,392	92,434
Total liabilities	176,282	177,615
Total stockholders' equity	36,200	44,075
Total liabilities and stockholders' equity	$212,482	$221,690

Liquidity

Liquidity ratios measure the short-term ability of a company to pay its maturing obligations and to meet unexpected needs for cash. A commonly used measure of liquidity is the current ratio (presented in Chapter 2). The current ratio is calculated as current assets divided by current liabilities. **Illustration 10.19** presents the current ratio for General Motors.

ILLUSTRATION 10.19
Current ratio

General Motors
($ in millions)

Ratio	2017	2016
Current Ratio	$\dfrac{\$68,744}{\$76,890} = .89\!:\!1$	$\dfrac{\$76,203}{\$85,181} = .89\!:\!1$

> **Decision Tools**
> Comparing available lines of credit to current liabilities as well as evaluating liquidity ratios helps users determine if a company can obtain short-term financing when necessary.

General Motors' current ratio remained constant at .89:1 from 2016 to 2017. This ratio is quite low. Many companies today minimize their liquid assets (such as accounts receivable and inventory) in order to improve profitability measures, such as return on assets. This is particularly true of large companies such as **Ford**, General Motors, and **Toyota**. Companies that keep fewer liquid assets on hand must rely on other sources of liquidity. One such source is a **bank line of credit**. A line of credit is a prearranged agreement between a company and a lender that permits the company, should it be necessary, to borrow up to an agreed-upon amount. For example, a recent disclosure regarding debt in General Motors' annual report stated that it had $12 billion of unused lines of credit (see **Decision Tools**).

Solvency

Solvency ratios measure the ability of a company to survive over a long period of time. The Feature Story in this chapter mentioned that, although there once were many U.S. automobile manufacturers, only three U.S.-based companies remain today. Many of the others went bankrupt. This highlights the fact that when making a long-term loan or purchasing a company's stock, you must give consideration to a company's solvency.

To reduce the risks associated with having a large amount of debt during an economic downturn, some U.S. automobile manufacturers took two precautionary steps while they enjoyed strong profits. First, they built up large balances of cash and cash equivalents to avoid a cash crisis. Second, they were reluctant to build new plants or hire new workers to meet their production needs. Instead, they asked workers to put in overtime, or they "outsourced" work to other companies. In this way, when the economic downturn occurred, they hoped to avoid having to make debt payments on idle production plants and to minimize layoffs. As a result, when the crisis first hit, Ford had cash of $29 billion, about double the amount of cash it would expect to use over a two-year period.

In Chapter 2, you learned that one measure of a company's solvency is the debt to assets ratio. This is calculated as total liabilities (debt) divided by total assets. This ratio indicates the extent to which a company's assets are financed with debt.

Another useful solvency measure is the **times interest earned** (see **Decision Tools**). It provides an indication of a company's ability to meet interest payments as they come due. It is computed by dividing the sum of net income, interest expense, and income tax expense by interest expense. It uses income before interest expense and taxes because this number best represents the amount available to pay interest.

> **Decision Tools**
> Times interest earned helps users determine if a company can meet its obligations in the long term.

We can use the balance sheet information presented in Illustration 10.18 and the additional information below to calculate solvency ratios for General Motors.

($ in millions)	2017	2016
Net income	$ (3,882)	$9,268
Interest expense	575	563
Income tax expense	11,533	2,739

The debt to assets ratios and times interest earned for General Motors are shown in **Illustration 10.20**.

ILLUSTRATION 10.20
Solvency ratios

$$\text{Debt to Assets Ratio} = \frac{\text{Total Liabilities}}{\text{Total Assets}}$$

$$\text{Times Interest Earned} = \frac{\text{Net Income} + \text{Interest Expense} + \text{Income Tax Expense}}{\text{Interest Expense}}$$

General Motors
($ in millions)

Ratio	2017	2016
Debt to Assets Ratio	$\frac{\$176,282}{\$212,482} = 83\%$	80%
Times Interest Earned	$\frac{\$(3,882) + \$575 + \$11,533}{\$575} = 14.3 \text{ times}$	22.3 times

General Motors' debt to assets ratio was 83% in 2017. Thus, General Motors is quite reliant on debt financing. In part, General Motors' heavy reliance on debt is due to its substantial finance division.

General Motors' times interest earned decreased from 22.3 times in 2016 to 14.3 in 2017. This means that in 2017 General Motors had earnings before interest and taxes that were more than 14.3 times the amount needed to pay interest. The higher the multiple, the lower the likelihood that the company will default on interest payments. This suggests that General Motors' ability to meet interest payments was high.

Investor Insight

© Yenwen Lu/iStockphoto

Debt Masking

In the wake of the financial crisis, many financial institutions are wary of reporting too much debt on their financial statements, for fear that investors will consider them too risky. The Securities and Exchange Commission (SEC) is concerned that some companies engage in "debt masking" to make it appear that they use less debt than they actually do. These companies enter into transactions at the end of the accounting period that essentially remove debt from their books. Shortly after the end of the period, they reverse the transaction and the debt goes back on their books. The *Wall Street Journal* reported that 18 large banks "had consistently lowered one type of debt at the end of each of the past five quarters, reducing it on average by 42% from quarterly peaks."

Source: Tom McGinty, Kate Kelly, and Kara Scannell, "Debt 'Masking' Under Fire," *Wall Street Journal Online* (April 21, 2010).

What implications does debt masking have for an investor that is using the debt to assets ratio to evaluate a company's solvency? (Go to WileyPLUS for this answer and additional questions.)

Contingencies

> **Decision Tools**
>
> Understanding a company's contingencies and significant off-balance-sheet financing helps users determine the potential impact on a company's financial position.

One reason a company's balance sheet might not fully reflect its potential obligations is due to contingencies. **Contingencies** are events with uncertain outcomes that may represent potential liabilities (see **Decision Tools**). A common type of contingency is lawsuits. Suppose, for example, that you were analyzing the financial statements of a cigarette manufacturer and did not consider the possible negative implications of existing unsettled lawsuits. Your analysis of the company's financial position would certainly be misleading. Other common types of contingencies are product warranties and environmental cleanup obligations. For example, in a recent year, **Novartis AG** began offering a money-back guarantee on its blood-pressure medications. This guarantee would necessitate an accrual for the estimated claims that will result from returns.

Accounting rules require that companies disclose contingencies in the notes. In some cases, they must accrue them as liabilities. For example, suppose that Waterbury Inc. is sued by a customer for $1 million due to an injury sustained by a defective product. If at the company's year-end the lawsuit had not yet been resolved, how should Waterbury account for this event? If the company can determine **a reasonable estimate** of the expected loss and if it is **probable** it will lose the suit, then the company should accrue for the loss. It records the loss by increasing (debiting) a loss account and increasing (crediting) a liability such as Lawsuit Liability. If **both** of these conditions are not met, then the company does not make a journal entry and instead discloses the basic facts regarding this suit in the notes to its financial statements.

Off-Balance-Sheet Financing

A concern for analysts when they evaluate a company's liquidity and solvency is whether that company has properly recorded all of its obligations. The bankruptcy of **Enron Corporation**, one of the largest bankruptcies in U.S. history, demonstrated how much damage can result when a company does not properly record or disclose all of its debts. Many would say Enron was practicing off-balance-sheet financing. **Off-balance-sheet financing** is an intentional effort by a company to structure its financing arrangements so as to avoid showing liabilities on its balance sheet.

Investor Insight

Paul Fleet/Alamy

"Covenant-Lite" Debt

In many corporate loans and bond issuances, the lending agreement specifies **debt covenants**. These covenants typically are specific financial measures, such as minimum levels of retained earnings, cash flows, times interest earned, or other measures that a company must maintain during the life of the loan. If the company violates a covenant, it is considered to have violated the loan agreement. The creditors can then demand immediate repayment, or they can renegotiate the loan's terms. Covenants protect lenders because they enable lenders to step in and try to get their money back before the borrower gets too deep into trouble.

During the 1990s, most traditional loans specified between three to six covenants or "triggers." In subsequent years, however, when there was lots of cash available, lenders began reducing or completely eliminating covenants from loan agreements in order to be more competitive with other lenders. Then, when the economy declined, these lenders lost big money when companies defaulted.

Sources: Cynthia Koons, "Risky Business: Growth of 'Covenant-Lite' Debt," *Wall Street Journal* (June 18, 2007), p. C2; and Katy Burne, "More Loans Come with Few Strings Attached," *Wall Street Journal* (June 12, 2014).

How can financial ratios such as those covered in this chapter provide protection for creditors? (Go to WileyPLUS for this answer and additional questions.)

DO IT! 4 | Analyzing Liabilities

Trout Company provides you with the following balance sheet information as of December 31, 2022.

Current assets	$10,500	Current liabilities	$ 8,000
Long-term assets	24,200	Long-term liabilities	16,000
Total assets	$34,700	Stockholders' equity	10,700
		Total liabilities and stockholders' equity	$34,700

In addition, Trout reported net income for 2022 of $14,000, income tax expense of $2,800, and interest expense of $900.

Instructions

a. Compute the current ratio and working capital for Trout for 2022.

b. Assume that at the end of 2022, Trout used $2,000 cash to pay off $2,000 of accounts payable. How would the current ratio and working capital have changed?

c. Compute the debt to assets ratio and the times interest earned for Trout for 2022.

Solution

a. Current ratio is 1.31:1 ($10,500/$8,000). Working capital is $2,500 ($10,500 − $8,000).

b. Current ratio is 1.42:1 ($8,500/$6,000). Working capital is $2,500 ($8,500 − $6,000).

c. Debt to assets ratio is 69.2% ($24,000/$34,700). Times interest earned is 19.67 times [($14,000 + $2,800 + $900)/$900].

Related exercise material: **BE10.14, DO IT! 10.4, E10.20, E10.21, and E10.22.**

ACTION PLAN
- Use the formula for the current ratio: Current assets ÷ Current liabilities.
- Use the formula for working capital: Current assets − Current liabilities.
- Use the formula for the debt to assets ratio: Total liabilities ÷ Total assets.

USING THE DECISION TOOLS | Ford Motor Company

Ford Motor Company has enjoyed some tremendous successes, including its popular F-10 pickup truck. Development of a new vehicle costs billions. A flop is financially devastating, and the financial effect is magnified if the company has large amounts of outstanding debt.

The following balance sheets provide financial information for Ford Motor Company as of December 31, 2017 and 2016.

Ford Motor Company
Balance Sheets
December 31, 2017 and 2016
(in millions)

Assets	2017	2016
Current assets	$115,902	$108,461
Noncurrent assets	141,906	129,490
Total assets	$257,808	$237,951

Liabilities and Shareholders' Equity		
Current liabilities	$ 94,600	$ 90,281
Noncurrent liabilities	128,192	118,387
Total liabilities	222,792	208,668
Total shareholders' equity (deficit)	35,016	29,283
Total liabilities and shareholders' equity	$257,808	$237,951
Other Information		
Net income	$ 7,628	$ 4,607
Income tax expense (benefit)	520	2,189
Interest expense	1,133	894
Available lines of credit (Automotive Division)	12,100	

Instructions

1. Evaluate Ford's liquidity using appropriate ratios and compare to those of **General Motors** presented in Illustration 10.19.
2. Evaluate Ford's solvency using appropriate ratios and compare to those of General Motors presented in Illustration 10.20.
3. Comment on Ford's available lines of credit.

Solution

1. Ford's liquidity can be measured using the current ratio:

	2017	2016
Current ratio	$\frac{\$115,902}{\$94,600} = 1.23{:}1$	$\frac{\$108,461}{\$90,281} = 1.20{:}1$

Ford's current ratio increased slightly from 2016 to 2017. Ford's 2017 current ratio exceeds General Motors' ratio by a fairly large amount, suggesting Ford is more liquid.

2. Ford's solvency can be measured with the debt to assets ratio and the times interest earned:

	2017	2016
Debt to assets ratio	$\frac{\$222,792}{\$257,808} = 86\%$	$\frac{\$208,668}{\$237,951} = 88\%$
Times interest earned	$\frac{\$7,628 + \$1,133 + \$520}{\$1,133} = 8.2 \text{ times}$	$\frac{\$4,607 + \$894 + \$2,189}{\$894} = 8.6 \text{ times}$

The debt to assets ratio suggests that Ford relies very heavily on debt financing. The ratio decreased slightly from 2016 to 2017, indicating that the company's solvency improved slightly. Ford's reliance on debt, as measured by the debt to assets ratio, slightly exceeds that of General Motors.

The times interest earned is 8.2 times in 2017 and 8.6 times in 2016. While not as high as that of General Motors, it is very strong.

3. Ford has available lines of credit of $12.1 billion. These financing sources significantly improve its liquidity and help reduce the concerns of its short-term creditors.

Appendix 10A Straight-Line Amortization

LEARNING OBJECTIVE *5
Apply the straight-line method of amortizing bond discount and bond premium.

Amortizing Bond Discount

To follow the expense recognition principle, companies allocate bond discount to expense in each period in which the bonds are outstanding. The **straight-line method of amortization** allocates the same amount to interest expense in each interest period. The calculation is presented in **Illustration 10A.1**.

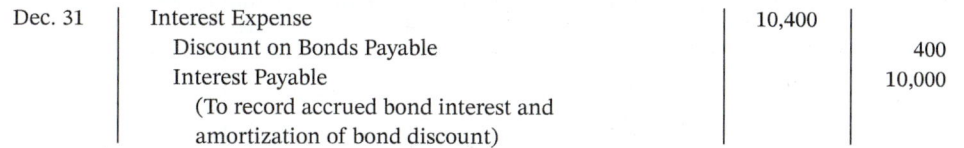

ILLUSTRATION 10A.1
Formula for straight-line method of bond discount amortization

In the Candlestick Inc. example, the company sold $100,000, five-year, 10% bonds on January 1, 2022, for $98,000. This resulted in a $2,000 bond discount ($100,000 − $98,000). The bond discount amortization is $400 ($2,000 ÷ 5) for each of the five amortization periods. Candlestick records the first accrual of bond interest and the amortization of bond discount on December 31 as follows.

Dec. 31	Interest Expense	10,400	
	Discount on Bonds Payable		400
	Interest Payable		10,000
	(To record accrued bond interest and amortization of bond discount)		

A	=	L	+	SE
				−10,400 Exp
		+400		
		+10,000		

Cash Flows
no effect

Over the term of the bonds, the balance in Discount on Bonds Payable will decrease annually by the same amount until it has a zero balance at the maturity date of the bonds (see **Alternative Terminology**). Thus, the carrying value of the bonds at maturity will be equal to the face value of the bonds.

Preparing a bond discount amortization schedule, as shown in **Illustration 10A.2**, is useful to determine interest expense, discount amortization, and the carrying value of the bond. As indicated, the interest expense recorded each period is $10,400. Also note that the carrying value of the bond increases $400 each period until it reaches its face value of $100,000 at the end of period 5.

ALTERNATIVE TERMINOLOGY

The amount in the Discount on Bonds Payable account is often referred to as *Unamortized Discount on Bonds Payable*.

ILLUSTRATION 10A.2
Bond discount amortization schedule

Candlestick Inc.
Bond Discount Amortization Schedule
Straight-Line Method—Annual Interest Payments
$100,000 of 10%, 5-Year Bonds

Interest Periods	(A) Interest to Be Paid (10% × $100,000)	(B) Interest Expense to Be Recorded (A) + (C)	(C) Discount Amortization ($2,000 ÷ 5)	(D) Unamortized Discount (D) − (C)	(E) Bond Carrying Value ($100,000 − D)
Issue date				$2,000	$ 98,000
1	$10,000	$10,400	$ 400	1,600	98,400
2	10,000	10,400	400	1,200	98,800
3	10,000	10,400	400	800	99,200
4	10,000	10,400	400	400	99,600
5	10,000	10,400	400	0	100,000
	$50,000	$52,000	$2,000		

Column **(A)** remains constant because the face value of the bonds ($100,000) is multiplied by the annual contractual interest rate (10%) each period.

Column **(B)** is computed as the interest paid (Column A) plus the discount amortization (Column C).

Column **(C)** indicates the discount amortization each period.

Column **(D)** decreases each period by the same amount until it reaches zero at maturity.

Column **(E)** increases each period by the amount of discount amortization until it equals the face value at maturity.

Amortizing Bond Premium

The amortization of bond premium parallels that of bond discount. **Illustration 10A.3** presents the formula for determining bond premium amortization under the straight-line method.

ILLUSTRATION 10A.3
Formula for straight-line method of bond premium amortization

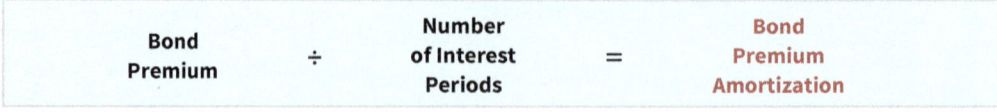

Continuing our example, assume Candlestick Inc., sells the bonds described above for $102,000, rather than $98,000. This results in a bond premium of $2,000 ($102,000 − $100,000). The premium amortization for each interest period is $400 ($2,000 ÷ 5). Candlestick records the first accrual of interest on December 31 as follows.

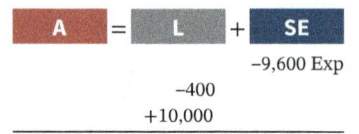

-9,600 Exp
-400
+10,000

Cash Flows
no effect

Dec. 31	Interest Expense	9,600	
	Premium on Bonds Payable	400	
	Interest Payable		10,000
	(To record accrued bond interest and		
	amortization of bond premium)		

Over the term of the bonds, the balance in Premium on Bonds Payable will decrease annually by the same amount until it has a zero balance at maturity.

A bond premium amortization schedule, as shown in **Illustration 10A.4**, is useful to determine interest expense, premium amortization, and the carrying value of the bond. As indicated, the interest expense Candlestick records each period is $9,600. Note that the carrying value of the bond decreases $400 each period until it reaches its face value of $100,000 at the end of period 5.

ILLUSTRATION 10A.4
Bond premium amortization schedule

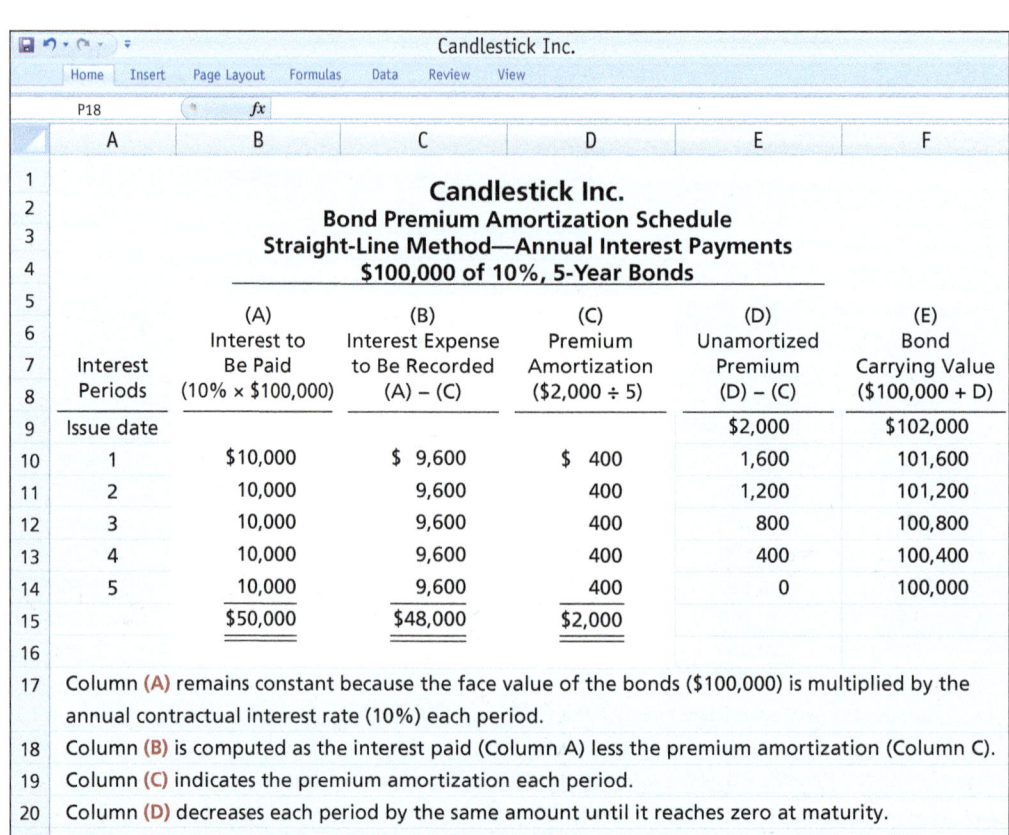

Appendix 10B Effective-Interest Amortization

LEARNING OBJECTIVE *6
Apply the effective-interest method of amortizing bond discount and bond premium.

To follow the expense recognition principle, companies allocate bond discount to expense in each period in which the bonds are outstanding. However, to completely comply with the expense recognition principle, interest expense as a percentage of carrying value should not change over the life of the bonds.

This percentage, referred to as the **effective-interest rate**, is established when the bonds are issued and remains constant in each interest period. Unlike the straight-line method, the effective-interest method of amortization accomplishes this result.

Under the **effective-interest method of amortization**, the amortization of bond discount or bond premium results in periodic interest expense equal to a constant percentage of the carrying value of the bonds. The effective-interest method results in **varying amounts** of amortization and interest expense per period but a **constant percentage rate**. In contrast, the straight-line method results in constant amounts of amortization and interest expense per period but a varying percentage rate.

Companies follow three steps under the effective-interest method:

1. Compute the **bond interest expense** by multiplying the carrying value of the bonds at the beginning of the interest period by the effective-interest rate.
2. Compute the **bond interest paid** (or accrued) by multiplying the face value of the bonds by the contractual interest rate.
3. Compute the **amortization amount** by determining the difference between the amounts computed in steps (1) and (2).

Illustration 10B.1 depicts these steps.

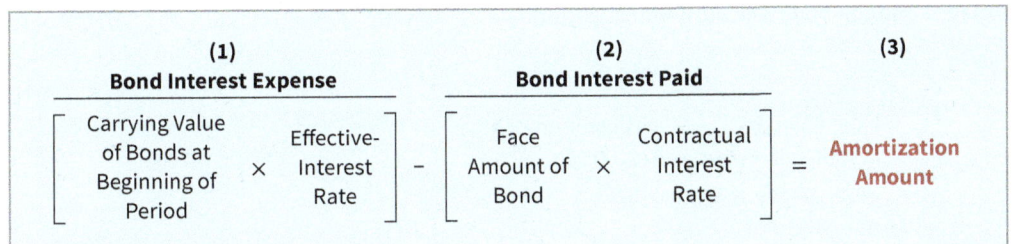

ILLUSTRATION 10B.1
Computation of amortization using effective-interest method

Both the straight-line and effective-interest methods of amortization result in the same total amount of interest expense over the term of the bonds. Furthermore, interest expense each interest period is generally comparable in amount. However, **when the amounts are materially different, generally accepted accounting principles (GAAP) require use of the effective-interest method.**

Amortizing Bond Discount

In the Candlestick Inc. example, the company sold $100,000, five-year, 10% bonds on January 1, 2022, for $98,000. This resulted in a $2,000 bond discount ($100,000 − $98,000). This discount results in an effective-interest rate of approximately 10.5348%. (The effective-interest rate can be computed using the techniques shown in Appendix G.)

Preparing a bond discount amortization schedule as shown in **Illustration 10B.2** facilitates the recording of interest expense and the discount amortization. Note that interest expense as a percentage of carrying value remains constant at 10.5348% (see **Helpful Hint**).

HELPFUL HINT
Note that the amount of periodic interest expense increases over the life of the bonds when the effective-interest method is used for bonds issued at a discount. The reason is that a constant percentage is applied to an increasing bond carrying value to compute interest expense. The carrying value is increasing because of the amortization of the discount.

ILLUSTRATION 10B.2 Bond discount amortization schedule

Candlestick Inc.
Bond Discount Amortization Schedule
Effective-Interest Method—Annual Interest Payments
10% Bonds Issued at 10.5348%

Interest Periods	(A) Interest to Be Paid (10% × $100,000)	(B) Interest Expense to Be Recorded (10.5348% × Preceding Bond Carrying Value)	(C) Discount Amortization (B) − (A)	(D) Unamortized Discount (D) − (C)	(E) Bond Carrying Value ($100,000 − D)
Issue date				$2,000	$ 98,000
1	$10,000	$10,324 (10.5348% × $98,000)	$ 324	1,676	98,324
2	10,000	10,358 (10.5348% × $98,324)	358	1,318	98,682
3	10,000	10,396 (10.5348% × $98,682)	396	922	99,078
4	10,000	10,438 (10.5348% × $99,078)	438	484	99,516
5	10,000	10,484 (10.5348% × $99,516)	484	–0–	100,000
	$50,000	$52,000	$2,000		

Column **(A)** remains constant because the face value of the bonds ($100,000) is multiplied by the annual contractual interest rate (10%) each period.

Column **(B)** is computed as the preceding bond carrying value times the annual effective-interest rate (10.5348%).

Column **(C)** indicates the discount amortization each period.

Column **(D)** decreases each period until it reaches zero at maturity.

Column **(E)** increases each period until it equals face value at maturity.

For the first interest period, **Illustration 10B.3** shows the computations of bond interest expense and the bond discount amortization.

ILLUSTRATION 10B.3
Computation of bond discount amortization

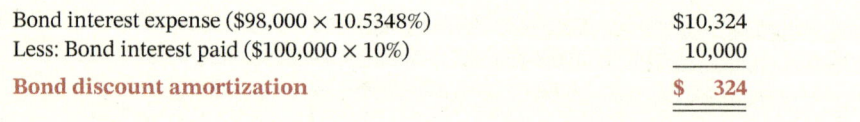

Bond interest expense ($98,000 × 10.5348%)	$10,324
Less: Bond interest paid ($100,000 × 10%)	10,000
Bond discount amortization	$ 324

As a result, Candlestick records the accrual of interest and amortization of bond discount on December 31 as follows.

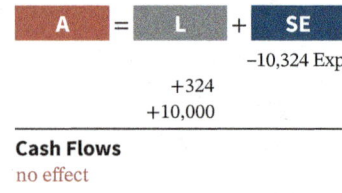

Cash Flows
no effect

Dec. 31	Interest Expense	10,324	
	Discount on Bonds Payable		324
	Interest Payable		10,000
	(To record accrued interest and amortization of bond discount)		

For the second interest period, bond interest expense will be $10,358 ($98,324 × 10.5348%), and the discount amortization will be $358. At December 31, Candlestick makes the following adjusting entry.

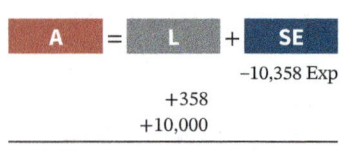

Cash Flows
no effect

Dec. 31	Interest Expense	10,358	
	Discount on Bonds Payable		358
	Interest Payable		10,000
	(To record accrued interest and amortization of bond discount)		

Amortizing Bond Premium

Continuing our example, assume Candlestick Inc. sells the bonds described above for $102,000 rather than $98,000. This would result in a bond premium of $2,000 ($102,000 − $100,000). This premium results in an effective-interest rate of approximately 9.4794%. (The effective-interest rate can be solved for using the techniques shown in Appendix G.) **Illustration 10B.4** shows the bond premium amortization schedule.

ILLUSTRATION 10B.4 Bond premium amortization schedule

Candlestick Inc.
Bond Premium Amortization Schedule
Effective-Interest Method—Annual Interest Payments
10% Bonds Issued at 9.4794%

Interest Periods	(A) Interest to Be Paid (10% × $100,000)	(B) Interest Expense to Be Recorded (9.4794% × Preceding Bond Carrying Value)	(C) Premium Amortization (A) − (B)	(D) Unamortized Premium (D) − (C)	(E) Bond Carrying Value ($100,000 + D)
Issue date				$2,000	$102,000
1	$10,000	$ 9,669 (9.4794% × $102,000)	$ 331	1,669	101,669
2	10,000	9,638 (9.4794% × $101,669)	362	1,307	101,307
3	10,000	9,603 (9.4794% × $101,307)	397	910	100,910
4	10,000	9,566 (9.4794% × $100,910)	434	476	100,476
5	10,000	9,524 * (9.4794% × $100,476)	476*	–0–	100,000
	$50,000	$48,000	$2,000		

Column **(A)** remains constant because the face value of the bonds ($100,000) is multiplied by the contractual interest rate (10%) each period.
Column **(B)** is computed as the carrying value of the bonds times the annual effective-interest rate (9.4794%).
Column **(C)** indicates the premium amortization each period.
Column **(D)** decreases each period until it reaches zero at maturity.
Column **(E)** decreases each period until it equals face value at maturity.

*Rounded to eliminate remaining premium resulting from rounding the effective rate.

For the first interest period, **Illustration 10B.5** shows the computations of bond interest expense and the bond premium amortization.

ILLUSTRATION 10B.5 Computation of bond premium amortization

Bond interest paid ($100,000 × 10%)	$10,000
Less: Bond interest expense ($102,000 × 9.4794%)	9,669
Bond premium amortization	**$ 331**

The entry Candlestick makes on December 31 is as follows.

Dec. 31	Interest Expense	9,669	
	Premium on Bonds Payable	331	
	Interest Payable		10,000
	(To record accrued interest and amortization of bond premium)		

A = L + SE
−9,669 Exp
−331
+10,000

Cash Flows
no effect

For the second interest period, interest expense will be $9,638, and the premium amortization will be $362. Note that the amount of periodic interest expense decreases over the life of the bond when companies apply the effective-interest method to bonds issued at a premium. The reason is that a constant percentage is applied to a decreasing bond carrying value to compute interest expense. The carrying value is decreasing because of the amortization of the premium.

Appendix 10C Accounting for Long-Term Notes Payable

LEARNING OBJECTIVE *7
Explain how to account for long-term notes payable.

The use of notes payable in long-term debt financing is quite common. **Long-term notes payable** are similar to short-term interest-bearing notes payable except that the term of the notes exceeds one year. In periods of unstable interest rates, lenders may tie the interest rate on long-term notes to changes in the market rate for comparable loans.

A long-term note may be secured by a **mortgage** that pledges title to specific assets as security for a loan. Individuals widely use **mortgage notes payable** to purchase homes, and many small and some large companies use them to acquire plant assets. At one time, approximately 18% of **McDonald's** long-term debt related to mortgage notes on land, buildings, and improvements.

Like other long-term notes payable, the mortgage loan terms may stipulate either a **fixed** or an **adjustable** interest rate. The interest rate on a fixed-rate mortgage remains the same over the life of the mortgage. The interest rate on an adjustable-rate mortgage is adjusted periodically to reflect changes in the market rate of interest. Typically, the terms require the borrower to make equal installment payments over the term of the loan. Each payment consists of (1) interest on the unpaid balance of the loan and (2) a reduction of loan principal. While the total amount of the payment remains constant, the interest decreases each period, and the portion applied to the loan principal increases.

Companies initially record mortgage notes payable at face value. They subsequently make entries for each installment payment. To illustrate, assume that Porter Technology Inc. issues a $500,000, 8%, 20-year mortgage note on December 31, 2022, to obtain needed financing for a new research laboratory. The terms provide for annual installment payments of $50,926 (not including real estate taxes and insurance). **Illustration 10C.1** shows the installment payment schedule for the first four years.

ILLUSTRATION 10C.1

Mortgage installment payment schedule

Interest Period	(A) Cash Payment	(B) Interest Expense (D) × 8%	(C) Reduction of Principal (A) – (B)	(D) Principal Balance (D) – (C)
Issue date				$500,000
1	$50,926	$40,000	$10,926	489,074
2	50,926	39,126	11,800	477,274
3	50,926	38,182	12,744	464,530
4	50,926	37,162	13,764	450,766

A	=	L	+	SE
+500,000		+500,000		

Cash Flows
+500,000

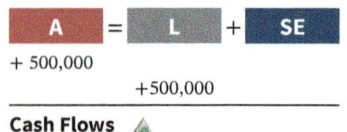

Porter records the mortgage loan on December 31, 2022, as follows.

Dec. 31	Cash	500,000	
	Mortgage Payable		500,000
	(To record mortgage loan)		

On December 31, 2023, Porter records the first installment payment as follows.

Dec. 31	Interest Expense		40,000	
	Mortgage Payable		10,926	
	Cash			50,926
	(To record annual payment on mortgage)			

A = L + SE
−50,926 = −10,926 + −40,000 Exp

Cash Flows
−50,926

In the balance sheet, the company reports the reduction in principal for the next year as a current liability, and it classifies the remaining unpaid principal balance as a long-term liability. At December 31, 2023, the total liability is $489,074. Of that amount, $11,800 is current and $477,274 ($489,074 − $11,800) is long-term.

Review and Practice

Learning Objectives Review

1 Explain how to account for current liabilities.

A current liability is a debt that a company can reasonably expect to pay (a) from existing current assets or through the creation of other current liabilities and (b) within one year or the operating cycle, whichever is longer. The major types of current liabilities are notes payable, accounts payable, sales taxes payable, unearned revenues, and accrued liabilities such as taxes, salaries and wages, and interest payable.

When a note payable is interest-bearing, the amount of assets received upon the issuance of the note is generally equal to the face value of the note, and interest expense is accrued over the life of the note. At maturity, the amount paid is equal to the face value of the note plus accrued interest.

Companies record sales taxes payable at the time the related sales occur. The company serves as a collection agent for the taxing authority. Sales taxes are not an expense to the company. Companies hold employee withholding taxes and credit them to appropriate liability accounts, until they remit these taxes to the governmental taxing authorities. Unearned revenues are initially recorded in an unearned revenue account. As a company recognizes revenue, a transfer from unearned revenue to revenue occurs. Companies report the current maturities of long-term debt as a current liability in the balance sheet.

2 Describe the major characteristics of bonds.

The following different types of bonds may be issued: secured and unsecured bonds, and convertible and callable bonds.

3 Explain how to account for bond transactions.

When companies issue bonds, they debit Cash for the cash proceeds and credit Bonds Payable for the face value of the bonds. In addition, they use the accounts Premium on Bonds Payable and Discount on Bonds Payable to show the bond premium and bond discount, respectively. Bond discount and bond premium are amortized over the life of the bond, which increases or decreases interest expense, respectively.

When companies redeem bonds at maturity, they credit Cash and debit Bonds Payable for the face value of the bonds. When companies redeem bonds before maturity, they (a) eliminate the carrying value of the bonds at the redemption date, (b) record the cash paid, and (c) recognize the gain or loss on redemption.

4 Discuss how liabilities are reported and analyzed.

Current liabilities appear first on the balance sheet, followed by long-term liabilities. Companies should report the nature and amount of each liability in the balance sheet or in schedules in the notes accompanying the statements. They report inflows and outflows of cash related to the principal portion of long-term debt in the financing section of the statement of cash flows.

The liquidity of a company may be analyzed by computing the current ratio. The long-run solvency of a company may be analyzed by computing the debt to assets ratio and the times interest earned. Other factors to consider are contingencies and off-balance-sheet financing.

*5 Apply the straight-line method of amortizing bond discount and bond premium.

The straight-line method of amortization results in a constant amount of amortization and interest expense per period.

*6 Apply the effective-interest method of amortizing bond discount and bond premium.

The effective-interest method results in varying amounts of amortization and interest expense per period but a constant percentage rate of interest. When the difference between the straight-line and effective-interest methods is material, GAAP requires use of the effective-interest method.

*7 Explain how to account for long-term notes payable.

Each payment consists of (1) interest on the unpaid balance of the loan, and (2) a reduction of loan principal. The interest decreases each period, while the portion applied to the loan principal increases each period.

Decision Tools Review

Decision Checkpoints	Info Needed for Decision	Tool to Use for Decision	How to Evaluate Results
Can the company obtain short-term financing when necessary?	Available lines of credit, from notes to the financial statements.	Compare available lines of credit to current liabilities. Also, evaluate liquidity ratios.	If liquidity ratios are low, then lines of credit should be high to compensate.
Can the company meet its obligations in the long term?	Interest expense and net income before interest and taxes	Times interest earned = $\dfrac{\text{Net income} + \text{Interest expense} + \text{Income tax expense}}{\text{Interest expense}}$	High ratio indicates ability to meet interest payments as scheduled.
Does the company have any contingencies?	Knowledge of events with uncertain negative outcomes	Notes to financial statements and financial statements	If negative outcomes are possible, determine the probability, the amount of loss, and the potential impact on financial statements.

Glossary Review

Bond certificate A legal document that indicates the name of the issuer, the face value of the bonds, and other data such as the contractual interest rate and the maturity date of the bonds. (p. 10-9).

Bond indenture A legal document that sets forth the terms of the bond issue. (p. 10-9).

Bonds A form of interest-bearing notes payable issued by corporations, universities, and governmental agencies. (p. 10-8).

Callable bonds Bonds that the issuing company can redeem (buy back) at a stated dollar amount prior to maturity. (p. 10-9).

Contingencies Events with uncertain outcomes that may represent potential liabilities. (p. 10-22).

Contractual (stated) interest rate Rate used to determine the amount of interest the issuer pays and the investor receives. (p. 10-9).

Convertible bonds Bonds that can be converted into common stock at the bondholder's option. (p. 10-9).

Current liability A debt that a company reasonably expects to pay (1) from existing current assets or through the creation of other current liabilities, and (2) within one year or the operating cycle, whichever is longer. (p. 10-3).

Debenture bonds Bonds issued against the general credit of the borrower. Also called unsecured bonds. (p. 10-9).

Discount (on a bond) The difference between the face value of a bond and its selling price when a bond is sold for less than its face value. (p. 10-13).

*__Effective-interest method of amortization__ A method of amortizing bond discount or bond premium that results in periodic interest expense equal to a constant percentage of the carrying value of the bonds. (p. 10-27).

*__Effective-interest rate__ Rate established when bonds are issued that maintains a constant value for interest expense as a percentage of bond carrying value in each interest period. (p. 10-27).

Face value Amount of principal due at the maturity date of the bond. (p. 10-9).

Long-term liabilities Obligations that a company expects to pay more than one year in the future. (p. 10-8).

Market interest rate The rate investors demand for loaning funds to the corporation. (p. 10-11).

Maturity date The date on which the final payment on a bond is due from the bond issuer to the investor. (p. 10-9).

Mortgage bond A bond secured by real estate. (p. 10-9).

*__Mortgage note payable__ A long-term note secured by a mortgage that pledges title to specific assets as security for the loan. (p. 10-30).

Notes payable An obligation in the form of a written note. (p. 10-3).

Off-balance-sheet financing The intentional effort by a company to structure its financing arrangements so as to avoid showing liabilities on its balance sheet. (p. 10-22).

Premium (on a bond) The difference between the selling price and the face value of a bond when a bond is sold for more than its face value. (p. 10-13).

Present value The value today of an amount to be received at some date in the future after taking into account current interest rates. (p. 10-11).

Secured bonds Bonds that have specific assets of the issuer pledged as collateral. (p. 10-9).

Sinking fund bonds Bonds secured by specific assets set aside to redeem them. (p. 10-9).

*__Straight-line method of amortization__ A method of amortizing bond discount or bond premium that allocates the same amount to interest expense in each interest period. (p. 10-24).

Times interest earned A measure of a company's solvency, calculated by dividing the sum of net income, interest expense, and income tax expense by interest expense. (p. 10-21).

Time value of money The relationship between time and money. A dollar received today is worth more than a dollar promised at some time in the future. (p. 10-10).

Unsecured bonds Bonds issued against the general credit of the borrower. (p. 10-9).

Practice Multiple-Choice Questions

1. **(LO 1)** The time period for classifying a liability as current is one year or the operating cycle, whichever is:
   a. longer.
   b. shorter.
   c. probable.
   d. possible.

2. **(LO 1)** To be classified as a current liability, a debt must be expected to be paid within:
   a. 1 year.
   b. the operating cycle.
   c. 2 years.
   d. (a) or (b), whichever is longer.

3. **(LO 1)** Ottman Company borrows $88,500 on September 1, 2022, from Farley State Bank by signing an $88,500, 12%, 1-year note. What is the accrued interest at December 31, 2022?
   a. $2,655.
   b. $3,540.
   c. $4,425.
   d. $10,620.

4. **(LO 1)** JD Company borrowed $70,000 on December 1 on a 6-month, 12% note. At December 31:
   a. neither the note payable nor the interest payable is a current liability.
   b. the note payable is a current liability but the interest payable is not.
   c. the interest payable is a current liability but the note payable is not.
   d. both the note payable and the interest payable are current liabilities.

5. **(LO 1)** Alexis Company has total proceeds from sales of $4,515. If the proceeds include sales taxes of 5%, what is the amount to be credited to Sales Revenue?
   a. $4,000.
   b. $4,300.
   c. $4,289.25.
   d. The correct answer is not given.

6. **(LO 1)** When recording payroll:
   a. gross earnings are recorded as salaries and wages payable.
   b. net pay is recorded as salaries and wages expense.
   c. payroll deductions are recorded as liabilities.
   d. More than one of the above.

7. **(LO 1)** No Fault Insurance Company collected a premium of $18,000 for a 1-year insurance policy on April 1. What amount should No Fault report as a current liability for Unearned Insurance Premiums at December 31?
   a. $0.
   b. $4,500.
   c. $13,500.
   d. $18,000.

8. **(LO 1)** Employer payroll taxes do **not** include:
   a. federal unemployment taxes.
   b. state unemployment taxes.
   c. federal income taxes.
   d. FICA taxes.

9. **(LO 2)** What term is used for bonds that have specific assets pledged as collateral?
   a. Callable bonds.
   b. Convertible bonds.
   c. Secured bonds.
   d. Discount bonds.

10. **(LO 2)** The market interest rate:
    a. is the contractual interest rate used to determine the amount of cash interest paid by the borrower.
    b. is listed in the bond indenture.
    c. is the rate investors demand for loaning funds.
    d. More than one of the above is true.

11. **(LO 3)** Laurel Inc. issues 10-year bonds with a maturity value of $200,000. If the bonds are issued at a premium, this indicates that:
    a. the contractual interest rate exceeds the market interest rate.
    b. the market interest rate exceeds the contractual interest rate.
    c. the contractual interest rate and the market interest rate are the same.
    d. no relationship exists between the two rates.

12. **(LO 3)** On January 1, 2022, Kelly Corp. issues $200,000, 5-year, 7% bonds at face value. The entry to record the issuance of the bonds would include a:
    a. debit to Cash for $14,000.
    b. debit to Bonds Payable for $200,000.
    c. credit to Bonds Payable for $200,000.
    d. credit to Interest Expense of $14,000.

13. **(LO 3)** Prescher Corporation issued bonds that pay interest every January 1. The entry to accrue bond interest at December 31 includes a:
    a. debit to Interest Payable.
    b. credit to Cash.
    c. credit to Interest Expense.
    d. credit to Interest Payable.

14. **(LO 3)** Goethe Corporation redeems its $100,000 face value bonds at 105 on January 1, following the payment of interest. The carrying value of the bonds at the redemption date is $103,745. The entry to record the redemption will include a:
    a. credit of $3,745 to Loss on Bond Redemption.
    b. debit of $3,745 to Premium on Bonds Payable.
    c. credit of $1,255 to Gain on Bond Redemption.
    d. debit of $5,000 to Premium on Bonds Payable.

15. **(LO 4)** In a recent year, Derek Corporation had net income of $150,000, interest expense of $30,000, and income tax expense of $20,000. What was Derek Corporation's times interest earned for the year?
    a. 5.00.
    b. 4.00.
    c. 6.67.
    d. 7.50.

16. (LO 4) Which of the following is a measure of liquidity?

   a. Debt to assets ratio.
   b. Working capital.
   c. Current ratio.
   d. Both working capital and current ratio.

*17. (LO 5) On January 1, Xiang Corporation issues $500,000, 5-year, 12% bonds at 96 with interest payable on January 1. The entry on December 31 to record accrued bond interest and the amortization of bond discount using the straight-line method will include a:

   a. debit to Interest Expense $57,600.
   b. debit to Interest Expense $60,000.
   c. credit to Discount on Bonds Payable $4,000.
   d. credit to Discount on Bonds Payable $2,000.

*18. (LO 5) For the bonds issued in Question 17, what is the carrying value of the bonds at the end of the third interest period?

   a. $492,000.
   b. $488,000.
   c. $472,000.
   d. $464,000.

*19. (LO 6) On January 1, Holly Ester Inc. issued $1,000,000, 10-year, 9% bonds for $938,554. The market rate of interest for these bonds is 10%. Interest is payable annually on December 31. Holly Ester uses the effective-interest method of amortizing bond discount. At the end of the first year, Holly Ester should report unamortized bond discount of:

   a. $54,900.
   b. $57,591.
   c. $51,610.
   d. $51,000.

*20. (LO 6) On January 1, Nicholas Corporation issued $1,000,000, 14%, 5-year bonds with interest payable on December 31. The bonds sold for $1,072,096. The market rate of interest for these bonds was 12%. On the first interest date, using the effective-interest method, the debit entry to Interest Expense is for:

   a. $120,000.
   b. $125,581.
   c. $128,652.
   d. $140,000.

*21. (LO 7) Sampson Corp. purchased a piece of equipment by issuing a $20,000, 6% installment note payable. Quarterly payments on the note are $1,165. What will be the reduction in the principal portion of the note payable that results from the first payment?

   a. $1,165.
   b. $300.
   c. $865.
   d. $1,200.

*22. (LO 7) Andrews Inc. issues a $497,000, 10% 3-year mortgage note on January 1. The note will be paid in three annual installments of $200,000, each payable at the end of the year. What is the amount of interest expense that should be recognized by Andrews Inc. in the second year?

   a. $16,567.
   b. $49,700.
   c. $34,670.
   d. $346,700.

*23. (LO 7) Howard Corporation issued a 20-year mortgage note payable on January 1, 2022. At December 31, 2022, the unpaid principal balance will be reported as:

   a. a current liability.
   b. a long-term liability.
   c. part current and part long-term liability.
   d. interest payable.

Solutions

1. a. The time period for classifying a liability as current is one year or the operating cycle, whichever is longer, not (b) shorter, (c) probable, or (d) possible.

2. d. To be classified as a current liability, a debt must be expected to be paid within 1 year or the operating cycle, whichever is longer. Choices (a) and (b) are both correct, but (d) is the better answer. Choice (c) is incorrect.

3. b. Accrued interest at 12/31/22 is computed as the face value ($88,500) times the interest rate (12%) times the portion of the year the debt was outstanding (4 months out of 12), or $3,540 ($88,500 × 12% × $\frac{4}{12}$), not (a) $2,655, (c) $4,425, or (d) $10,620.

4. d. A current liability is a debt the company reasonably expects to pay (1) from existing current assets or through the creation of other current liabilities, and (2) within the next year or the operating cycle, whichever is longer. Since both the interest payable and the note payable are expected to be paid within one year, they both will be considered current liabilities. The other choices are therefore incorrect.

5. b. Dividing the total proceeds ($4,515) by one plus the sales tax rate (1.05) will result in the amount of sales to be credited to the Sales Revenue account of $4,300 ($4,515 ÷ 1.05). The other choices are therefore incorrect.

6. c. Payroll deductions are recorded as liabilities. The other choices are incorrect because (a) gross earnings are recorded as salaries and wages expense, and (b) net pay is recorded as salaries and wages payable. Choice (d) is wrong as there is only one correct answer.

7. b. The monthly premium is $1,500 or $18,000 divided by 12. Because No Fault has recognized 9 months of insurance revenue (April 1–December 31), 3 months' insurance premium is still unearned. The amount that No Fault should report as Unearned Service Revenue is therefore $4,500 (3 months × $1,500), not (a) $0, (c) $13,500, or (d) $18,000.

8. c. Federal income taxes are a payroll deduction, not an employer payroll tax. The employer is merely a collection agent. The other choices are all included in employer payroll taxes.

9. c. Secured bonds are those that have specific assets of the issuer pledged as collateral. The other choices are incorrect because (a) callable bonds can be redeemed (bought back) by the issuer at a stated dollar amount prior to the maturity date, (b) convertible bonds can be converted into common stock at the option of the bondholder, and (d) discount bonds is not a term that is generally used when describing bonds.

10. c. The market interest rate is the rate investors demand for loaning funds to the corporation. The other choices are incorrect because (a) the rate on the bond certificate is used to determine the interest payments, (b) the contract interest rate is listed in the bond indenture, and (d) there is only one correct answer.

11. a. When bonds are issued at a premium, this indicates that the contractual interest rate is higher than the market interest rate. The other choices are incorrect because (b) when the market interest rate exceeds the contractual interest rate, bonds are sold at a discount; (c) when the contractual interest rate and the market interest rate are the same, bonds will be issued at par; and (d) the relationship between the market rate of interest and the contractual rate of interest determines whether bonds are issued at par, a discount, or a premium.

12. c. The issuance entry for the bonds includes a debit to Cash for $200,000 and a credit to Bonds Payable for $200,000. The other choices are therefore incorrect.

13. d. Since the interest has been accrued but not yet paid, it has to be recognized as an increase in expenses and liabilities. The entry would be a debit to Interest Expense and a credit to Interest Payable. The other choices are incorrect because (a) an interest accrual will increase, not decrease, Interest Payable; (b) interest accruals do not affect Cash; and (c) an interest accrual will increase, not decrease, Interest Expense.

14. b. The entry to record the redemption of bonds will include a debit to Bonds Payable of $100,000, a debit to Premium on Bonds Payable of $3,745 ($103,745 − $100,000), a credit to Cash of $105,000 ($100,000 × 1.05) and a debit to Loss on Bond Redemption of $1,255 ($105,000 − $103,745). The other choices are therefore incorrect.

15. c. Times interest earned = (Net income + Interest expense + Income tax expense) ÷ Interest expense = ($150,000 + $30,000 + $20,000) ÷ $30,000 = 6.67, not (a) 5.00, (b) 4.00, or (d) 7.50.

16. d. Working capital and current ratio are measures of liquidity. Choice (a) is incorrect because the debt to assets ratio measures solvency, which is the ability of a company to survive over a long period of time.

*17. c. [$500,000 − (96% × $500,000)] = $20,000; $20,000 ÷ 5 = $4,000 of discount to amortize annually. As a result, the entry would involve a credit to Discount on Bonds Payable $4,000. The other choices are therefore incorrect.

*18. a. The carrying value of bonds increases by the amount of the periodic discount amortization. Discount amortization using the straight-line method is $4,000 each period. Total discount amortization for three periods is $12,000 ($4,000 × 3 periods) which is added to the initial carrying value ($480,000) to arrive at $492,000, the carrying value at the end of the third interest period, not (b) $488,000, (c) $472,000, or (d) $464,000.

*19. b. The beginning balance of unamortized discount is $61,446 ($1,000,000 − $938,554). The discount amortization is $3,855, the difference between the cash interest payment of $90,000 ($1,000,000 × 9%) and the interest expense recorded of $93,855 ($938,554 × 10%). This discount amortization ($3,855) is then subtracted from the beginning balance of unamortized discount ($61,446), to arrive at a balance of $57,591 at the end of the first year, not (a) $54,900, (c) $51,610, or (d) $51,000.

*20. c. The debit to Interest Expense = $1,072,096 (initial carrying value of bond) × 12% (market rate) = $128,652, not (a) $120,000, (b) $125,581, or (d) $140,000.

*21. c. The reduction in the principal portion of the note payable that results from the first payment = $1,165 − ($20,000 × 0.06 × 1/4) = $865, not (a) $1,165, (b) $300, or (d) $1,200.

*22. c. In the first year, Andrews will recognize $49,700 of interest expense ($497,000 × 10%). After the first payment is made, the amount remaining on the note will be $346,700 [$497,000 principal − ($200,000 payment − $49,700 interest)]. The remaining balance ($346,700) is multiplied by the interest rate (10%) to compute the interest expense to be recognized for the second year, $34,670 ($346,700 × 10%), not (a) $16,567, (b) $49,700, or (d) $346,700.

*23. c. Howard Corporation reports the reduction in principal for the next year as a current liability, and it classifies the remaining unpaid principal balance as a long-term liability. The other choices are therefore incorrect.

Practice Brief Exercises

1. (LO 1) Amy Pond Discounts does not segregate sales and sales taxes at the time of sale. The register total for March 17 is $19,928. All sales are subject to a 6% sales tax. Compute sales taxes payable and make the entry to record sales taxes payable and sales revenue.

Compute and record sales taxes payable.

Solution

1. Sales tax payable:

   Sales = $18,800 ($19,928 ÷ 1.06)

   Sales taxes payable = $1,128 ($18,800 × 6%)

Mar. 17	Cash	19,928	
	Sales Revenue		18,800
	Sales Taxes Payable		1,128

2. (LO 2) Ben Borke's regular hourly wage rate is $20, and he receives an hourly rate of $30 for work in excess of 40 hours. During a January pay period, Ben works 46 hours. Ben's federal income tax withholding is $123, he has no voluntary deductions, and the FICA tax rate is 7.65%. There are no state income taxes. Compute Ben's gross earnings and net pay for the pay period.

Compute gross earnings and net pay.

Solution

2. Gross earnings:

Regular pay (40 × $20)		$800.00
Overtime pay (6 × $30)		180.00
Gross earnings		$980.00
Less: FICA taxes payable ($980 × 7.65%)	$ 74.97	
Federal income taxes payable	123.00	197.97
Net pay		$782.03

Prepare entries for bonds issued at face value.

3. (LO 3) Kahnle Corporation issued 3,000, 7%, 5-year, $1,000 bonds dated January 1, 2022, at 100. Interest is paid each January 1. (a) Prepare the journal entry to record the sale of these bonds on January 1, 2022. (b) Prepare the adjusting journal entry on December 31, 2022, to record interest expense. (c) Prepare the journal entry on January 1, 2023, to record interest paid.

Solution

3. **a.** Jan. 1   Cash   3,000,000
               Bonds Payable (3,000 × $1,000)   3,000,000

    b. Dec. 31   Interest Expense   210,000
                Interest Payable ($3,000,000 × 7%)   210,000

    c. Jan. 1   Interest Payable   210,000
                Cash ($3,000,000 × 7%)   210,000

Prepare statement presentation of long-term liabilities.

4. (LO 4) Presented below are liability items for Rymer Company at December 31, 2022. Prepare the long-term liabilities section of the balance sheet for Rymer Company.

Bonds payable, due 2024	$700,000
Accounts Payable	100,000
Lease liability	120,000
Notes payable, due 2027	110,000
Premium on bonds payable	40,000

Solution

4. Long-term liabilities*

Bonds payable, due 2024	$700,000	
Plus: Premium on bonds payable	40,000	$740,000
Notes payable, due 2027		110,000
Lease liability		120,000
Total long-term liabilities		$970,000

*Accounts Payable is a current liability.

Prepare entries for long-term notes payable.

*5. (LO 7) Tyler-Danish Inc. issues a $600,000, 10%, 10-year mortgage note on December 31, 2022, to obtain financing for a new building. The terms provide for annual installment payments of $97,647, Prepare the entry to record the mortgage loan on December 31, 2022, and the first installment payment on December 31, 2023.

Solution

*5.

Annual Interest Period	(A) Cash Payment	(B) Interest Expense (D) × 10%	(C) Reduction of Principal (A) − (B)	(D) Principal Balance (D) − (C)
Issue Date				$600,000
1	$97,647	$60,000	$37,647	562,353

2022
Dec. 31   Cash   600,000
          Mortgage Payable   600,000

2023
Dec. 31   Interest Expense   60,000
         Mortgage Payable   37,647
            Cash   97,647

Practice Exercises

Prepare entries for interest-bearing notes.

1. (LO 1) On June 1, JetSet Company borrows $150,000 from First Bank on a 6-month, $150,000, 8% note.

Instructions

a. Prepare the entry on June 1.

b. Prepare the adjusting entry on June 30.

c. Prepare the entry at maturity (December 1), assuming monthly adjusting entries have been made through November 30.

d. What was the total financing cost (interest expense)?

Solution

1. a. June 1 | Cash | 150,000 | |
    |---|---|---|
    | Notes Payable | | 150,000 |

    b. June 30 | Interest Expense | 1,000 | |
    |---|---|---|
    | Interest Payable | | 1,000 |
    | ($150,000 × 8% × 1/12) | | |

    c. Dec. 1 | Notes Payable | 150,000 | |
    |---|---|---|
    | Interest Payable | 6,000 | |
    | ($150,000 × 8% × 6/12) | | |
    | Cash | | 156,000 |

    d. $6,000

---

2. **(LO 3)** Global Airlines Company issued $900,000 of 8%, 10-year bonds on January 1, 2022, at face value. Interest is payable annually on January 1.

Prepare entries for bonds issued at face value.

Instructions

Prepare the journal entries to record the following events.

a. The issuance of the bonds.

b. The accrual of interest on December 31.

c. The payment of interest on January 1, 2023.

d. The redemption of bonds at maturity, assuming interest for the last interest period has been paid and recorded.

Solution

2.

January 1, 2022

a. Cash	900,000	
Bonds Payable		900,000

December 31, 2022

b. Interest Expense	72,000	
Interest Payable ($900,000 × 8%)		72,000

January 1, 2023

c. Interest Payable	72,000	
Cash		72,000

January 1, 2032

d. Bonds Payable	900,000	
Cash		900,000

---

*3. **(LO 7)** Trawler Company borrowed $500,000 on December 31, 2022, by issuing a $500,000, 7% mortgage note payable. The terms call for annual installment payments of $80,000 on December 31.

Prepare entries to record mortgage note and installment payments.

Instructions

a. Prepare the journal entries to record the mortgage loan and the first two installment payments.

b. Indicate the amount of mortgage note payable to be reported as a current liability and as a long-term liability at December 31, 2023.

Solution

3.

December 31, 2022

a. Cash	500,000	
Mortgage Payable		500,000

December 31, 2023

Interest Expense ($500,000 × 7%)	35,000	
Mortgage Payable	45,000	
Cash		80,000

December 31, 2024

Interest Expense [($500,000 − $45,000) × 7%]	31,850	
Mortgage Payable	48,150	
Cash		80,000

b. Current: $48,150
Long-term: $406,850 ($500,000 − $45,000 − $48,150)

Practice Problem

Prepare entries to record issuance of bonds, interest accrual, and bond redemption.

(LO 3, 5) Snyder Software Inc. successfully developed a new spreadsheet program. However, to produce and market the program, the company needed additional financing. On January 1, 2021, Snyder borrowed money as follows.

1. Snyder issued $500,000, 11%, 10-year bonds. The bonds sold at face value and pay interest on January 1.

2. Snyder issued $1.0 million, 10%, 10-year bonds for $886,996. Interest is payable on January 1. Snyder uses the straight-line method of amortization.

Instructions

a. For the 11% bonds, prepare journal entries for the following items.
   1. The issuance of the bonds on January 1, 2021.
   2. Accrue interest expense on December 31, 2021.
   3. The payment of interest on January 1, 2022.

*b. For the 10-year, 10% bonds:
   1. Journalize the issuance of the bonds on January 1, 2021.
   2. Prepare the entry for the redemption of the bonds at 101 on January 1, 2024, after paying the interest due on this date. The carrying value of the bonds at the redemption date was $920,897.

Solution

a. 1. 2021

Jan. 1	Cash	500,000	
	Bonds Payable		500,000
	(To record issue of 11%, 10-year bonds at face value)		

2. 2021

Dec. 31	Interest Expense	55,000	
	Interest Payable		55,000
	(To record accrual of bond interest)		

3. 2022

Jan. 1	Interest Payable	55,000	
	Cash		55,000
	(To record payment of accrued interest)		

***b. 1. 2021**

Jan. 1	Cash	886,996	
	Discount on Bonds Payable	113,004	
	Bonds Payable		1,000,000
	(To record issuance of bonds at a discount)		

2. 2024

Jan. 1	Bonds Payable	1,000,000	
	Loss on Bond Redemption	89,103*	
	Discount on Bonds Payable		79,103
	Cash		1,010,000
	(To record redemption of bonds at 101)		

*($1,010,000 − $920,897)

WileyPLUS

Brief Exercises, DO IT! Exercises, Exercises, Problems, and many additional resources are available for practice in WileyPLUS.

Note: All asterisked Questions, Exercises, and Problems relate to material in the appendices to the chapter.

Questions

1. Jenny Perez believes a current liability is a debt that can be expected to be paid in one year. Is Jenny correct? Explain.

2. Rayborn Company obtains $20,000 in cash by signing a 9%, 6-month, $20,000 note payable to First Bank on July 1. Rayborn's fiscal year ends on September 30. What information should be reported for the note payable in the annual financial statements?

3. a. Your roommate says, "Sales taxes are reported as an expense in the income statement." Do you agree? Explain.

   b. Leiana's Cafe has cash proceeds from sales of $8,550. This amount includes $550 of sales taxes. Give the entry to record the proceeds.

4. Carolina University sold 9,000 season football tickets at $100 each for its five-game home schedule. What entries should be made (a) when the tickets are sold and (b) after each game?

5. Identify three taxes commonly withheld by the employer from an employee's gross pay.

6. a. Identify three taxes commonly paid by employers on employees' salaries and wages.

   b. Where in the financial statements does the employer report taxes withheld from employees' pay?

7. Identify the liabilities classified by **Apple** as current.

8. a. What are long-term liabilities? Give two examples.

   b. What is a bond?

9. Contrast these types of bonds:

   a. Secured and unsecured.

   b. Convertible and callable.

10. Explain each of these important terms in issuing bonds:

    a. Face value.

    b. Contractual interest rate.

    c. Bond certificate.

11. a. What is a convertible bond?

    b. Discuss the advantages of a convertible bond from the standpoint of the bondholders and of the issuing corporation.

12. Describe the two major obligations incurred by a company when bonds are issued.

13. Assume that Acorn Inc. sold bonds with a face value of $100,000 for $104,000. Was the market interest rate equal to, less than, or greater than the bonds' contractual interest rate? Explain.

14. Lee and Jay are discussing how the market price of a bond is determined. Lee believes that the market price of a bond is solely a function of the amount of the principal payment at the end of the term of a bond. Is he right? Discuss.

15. If a 6%, 10-year, $800,000 bond is issued at face value and interest is paid annually, what is the amount of the interest payment at the end of the first period?

16. If the Bonds Payable account has a balance of $700,000 and the Discount on Bonds Payable account has a balance of $36,000, what is the carrying value of the bonds?

17. Which accounts are debited and which are credited if a bond issue originally sold at a premium is redeemed before maturity at 97 immediately following the payment of interest?

18. Penny Lennon, the chief financial officer of Johnson Inc., is considering the options available to her for financing the company's new plant. Short-term interest rates right now are 6%, and long-term rates are 8%. The company's current ratio is 2.2:1. If she finances the new plant with short-term debt, the current ratio will fall to 1.5:1. Briefly discuss the issues that Penny should consider.

19. a. In general, what are the requirements for the financial statement presentation of long-term liabilities?

    b. What ratios may be computed to evaluate a company's liquidity and solvency?

20. Ernie Sams says that liquidity and solvency are the same thing. Is he correct? If not, how do they differ?

21. Anglo Corporation has a current ratio of 1.1:1. Jon has always been told that a corporation's current ratio should exceed 2.0:1. The company maintains that its ratio is low because it has a minimal amount of inventory on hand so as to reduce operating costs. Anglo also has significant available lines of credit. Is Jon still correct? What do some companies do to compensate for having fewer liquid assets?

22. What criteria must be met before a contingency must be recorded as a liability? How should the contingency be disclosed if the criteria are not met?

*23. Explain the straight-line method of amortizing discount and premium on bonds payable.

*24. Robbins Corporation issues $200,000 of 6%, 5-year bonds on January 1, 2022, at 103. Assuming that the straight-line method is used to amortize the premium, what is the total amount of interest expense for 2022?

*25. Honore Draper is discussing the advantages of the effective-interest method of bond amortization with her accounting staff. What do you think Honore is saying?

*26. Dotsin Corporation issues $400,000 of 9%, 5-year bonds on January 1, 2022, at 104. If Dotsin uses the effective-interest method in amortizing the premium, will the annual interest expense increase or decrease over the life of the bonds? Explain.

*27. Your friend just received a car loan. It is a 7-year installment note. He does not understand the mechanics of how the loan works. Explain the important aspects of the installment note.

*28. Tim Rian, a friend of yours, has recently purchased a home for $125,000, paying $25,000 down and the remainder financed by a 6.5%, 20-year mortgage, payable at $745.57 per month. At the end of the first month, Tim receives a statement from the bank indicating that only $203.90 of principal was paid during the month. At this rate, he calculates that it will take over 40 years to pay off the mortgage. Is he right? Discuss.

Brief Exercises

Identify whether obligations are current liabilities.

BE10.1 (LO 1), C Busch Company has these obligations at December 31: (a) a note payable for $100,000 due in 2 years, (b) a 10-year mortgage payable of $200,000 payable in ten $20,000 annual payments and (c) interest payable of $15,000 on the mortgage, and (d) accounts payable of $60,000. For each obligation, indicate whether it should be classified as a current liability, long-term liability, or both.

Prepare entries for an interest-bearing note payable.

BE10.2 (LO 1), AP Hive Company borrows $90,000 on July 1 from the bank by signing a $90,000, 7%, 1-year note payable. Prepare the journal entries to record (a) the proceeds of the note and (b) accrued interest at December 31, assuming adjusting entries are made only at the end of the year.

Compute and record sales taxes payable.

BE10.3 (LO 1), AP Greenspan Supply does not segregate sales and sales taxes at the time of sale. The register total for March 16 is $10,388. All sales are subject to a 6% sales tax. Compute sales taxes payable and make the entry to record sales taxes payable and sales.

Prepare entries for unearned revenues.

BE10.4 (LO 1), AP Bramble University sells 3,500 season basketball tickets at $80 each for its 10-game home schedule. Give the entry to record (a) the sale of the season tickets and (b) the revenue recognized after playing the first home game.

Compute gross earnings and net pay.

BE10.5 (LO 1), AP Betsy Strand's regular hourly wage rate is $16, and she receives an hourly rate of $24 for work in excess of 40 hours. During a January pay period, Betsy works 47 hours. Betsy's federal income tax withholding is $95, and she has no voluntary deductions. Compute Betsy Strand's gross earnings and net pay for the pay period. Assume that the FICA tax rate is 7.65%.

Record a payroll and the payment of wages.

BE10.6 (LO 1), AP Data for Betsy Strand are presented in BE10.5. Prepare the employer's journal entries to record (a) Betsy's pay for the period and (b) the payment of Betsy's wages. Use January 15 for the end of the pay period and the payment date.

Prepare entries for payroll taxes.

BE10.7 (LO 1), AP Data for Betsy Strand are presented in BE10.5. Prepare the employer's journal entry to record payroll taxes for the period. Ignore unemployment taxes.

Prepare entries for issuance of bonds.

BE10.8 (LO 3), AP Bridle Inc. issues $300,000, 10-year, 8% bonds at 98. Prepare the journal entry to record the sale of these bonds on March 1, 2022.

Prepare entries for issuance of bonds.

BE10.9 (LO 3), AP Ravine Company issues $400,000, 20-year, 7% bonds at 101. Prepare the journal entry to record the sale of these bonds on June 1, 2022.

Prepare journal entries for bonds issued at face value.

BE10.10 (LO 3), AP Clooney Corporation issued 3,000 7%, 5-year, $1,000 bonds dated January 1, 2022, at face value. Interest is paid each January 1.

a. Prepare the journal entry to record the sale of these bonds on January 1, 2022.

b. Prepare the adjusting journal entry on December 31, 2022, to record interest expense.

c. Prepare the journal entry on January 1, 2023, to record interest paid.

Prepare journal entry for redemption of bonds.

BE10.11 (LO 3), AP The balance sheet for Gelher Company reports the following information on July 1, 2022.

Gelher Company
Balance Sheet (partial)

Long-term liabilities		
Bonds payable	$2,000,000	
Less: Discount on bonds payable	45,000	$1,955,000

Gelher decides to redeem these bonds at 102 after paying annual interest. Prepare the journal entry to record the redemption on July 1, 2022.

BE10.12 (LO 4), AP Presented here are long-term liability items for Stevens Inc. at December 31, 2022. Prepare the long-term liabilities section of the balance sheet for Stevens Inc.

Prepare statement presentation of long-term liabilities.

Bonds payable (due 2026)	$700,000
Notes payable (due 2024)	80,000
Discount on bonds payable	28,000

BE10.13 (LO 4), AP Presented here are liability items for O'Brian Inc. at December 31, 2022. Prepare the liabilities section of O'Brian's balance sheet.

Prepare liabilities section of balance sheet.

Accounts payable	$157,000	FICA taxes payable	$ 7,800
Notes payable	20,000	Interest payable	40,000
(due May 1, 2023)		Notes payable (due 2024)	80,000
Bonds payable (due 2026)	900,000	Income taxes payable	3,500
Unearned rent revenue	240,000	Sales taxes payable	1,700
Discount on bonds payable	41,000		

BE10.14 (LO 4), AP Suppose the 2022 adidas financial statements contain the following selected data (in millions).

Analyze solvency.

Current assets	$4,485	Interest expense	$169
Total assets	8,875	Income taxes	113
Current liabilities	2,836	Net income	245
Total liabilities	5,099		
Cash	775		

Compute the following values and provide a brief interpretation of each.

a. Working capital.   c. Debt to assets ratio.
b. Current ratio.   d. Times interest earned.

*****BE10.15 (LO 5), AP** Alpine Company issues $2 million, 10-year, 7% bonds at 99, with interest payable on December 31. The straight-line method is used to amortize bond discount.

Prepare journal entries for bonds issued at a discount.

a. Prepare the journal entry to record the sale of these bonds on January 1, 2022.

b. Prepare the journal entry to record interest expense and bond discount amortization on December 31, 2022, assuming no previous accrual of interest.

*****BE10.16 (LO 5), AP** Harvard Inc. issues $4 million, 5-year, 8% bonds at 102, with interest payable on January 1. The straight-line method is used to amortize bond premium.

Prepare journal entries for bonds issued at a premium.

a. Prepare the journal entry to record the sale of these bonds on January 1, 2022.

b. Prepare the journal entry to record interest expense and bond premium amortization on December 31, 2022, assuming no previous accrual of interest.

*****BE10.17 (LO 6), AP** **Writing** Presented below is the partial bond discount amortization schedule for Rohr Corp., which uses the effective-interest method of amortization.

Use effective-interest method of bond amortization.

Interest Periods	Interest to Be Paid	Interest Expense to Be Recorded	Discount Amortization	Unamortized Discount	Bond Carrying Value
Issue date				$38,609	$961,391
1	$45,000	$48,070	$3,070	35,539	964,461
2	45,000	48,223	3,223	32,316	967,684

Instructions

a. Prepare the journal entry to record the payment of interest and the discount amortization at the end of period 1.

b. Explain why interest expense is greater than interest paid.

c. Explain why interest expense will increase each period.

*****BE10.18 (LO 7), AP** Jenseng Inc. issues a $800,000, 10%, 10-year mortgage note on December 31, 2022, to obtain financing for a new building. The terms provide for annual installment payments of $130,196. Prepare the entry to record the mortgage loan on December 31, 2022, and the first installment payment on December 31, 2023.

Prepare entries for long-term notes payable.

DO IT! Exercises

Answer questions about current liabilities.

DO IT! 10.1a (LO 1), AP You and several classmates are studying for the next accounting examination. They ask you to answer the following questions.

1. If cash is borrowed on a $60,000, 9-month, 10% note on August 1, how much interest expense would be incurred by December 31?
2. The cash register total including sales taxes is $42,000, and the sales tax rate is 5%. What is the sales taxes payable?
3. If $42,000 is collected in advance on November 1 for 6-month magazine subscriptions, what amount of subscription revenue should be recognized on December 31?

Prepare entries for payroll and payroll taxes.

DO IT! 10.1b (LO 1), AP During the month of February, Hennesey Corporation's employees earned wages of $74,000. Withholdings related to these wages were $5,661 for FICA, $7,100 for federal income tax, and $1,900 for state income tax. Costs incurred for unemployment taxes were $110 for federal and $160 for state.

Prepare the February 28 journal entries for (a) salaries and wages expense and salaries and wages payable assuming that all February wages will be paid in March and (b) the company's payroll tax expense.

Evaluate statements about bonds.

DO IT! 10.2 (LO 2), C State whether each of the following statements is true or false. If false, indicate how to correct the statement.

1. Convertible bonds are also known as callable bonds.
2. The market rate is the rate investors demand for loaning funds.
3. Annual interest payments on bonds are equal to the face value times the stated rate.
4. The present value of a bond is the value at which it should sell in the market.

Prepare journal entry for bond issuance and show balance sheet presentation.

DO IT! 10.3a (LO 3), AP Smiley Corporation issues $300,000 of bonds for $315,000. (a) Prepare the journal entry to record the issuance of the bonds, and (b) show how the bonds would be reported on the balance sheet at the date of issuance.

Prepare entry for bond redemption.

DO IT! 10.3b (LO 3), AP Farmland Corporation issued $400,000 of 10-year bonds at a discount. Prior to maturity, when the carrying value of the bonds was $388,000, the company redeemed the bonds at 99. Prepare the entry to record the redemption of the bonds.

Analyze liabilities.

DO IT! 10.4 (LO 4), AN Grouper Company provides you with the following balance sheet information as of December 31, 2022.

Current assets	$11,500	Current liabilities	$12,000
Long-term assets	26,500	Long-term liabilities	14,000
Total assets	$38,000	Stockholders' equity	12,000
		Total liabilities and stockholders' equity	$38,000

In addition, Grouper reported net income for 2022 of $16,000, income tax expense of $3,200, and interest expense of $1,300.

a. Compute the current ratio and working capital for Grouper for 2022.
b. Assume that at the end of 2022, Grouper used $3,000 cash to pay off $3,000 of accounts payable. How would the current ratio and working capital have changed?
c. Compute the debt to assets ratio and the times interest earned for Grouper for 2022.

Exercises

Prepare entries for interest-bearing notes.

E10.1 (LO 1), AP Kelly Jones and Tami Crawford borrowed $15,000 on a 7-month, 8% note from Gem State Bank to open their business, JC's Coffee House. The money was borrowed on June 1, 2022, and the note matures January 1, 2023.

Instructions

a. Prepare the entry to record the receipt of the funds from the loan.
b. Prepare the entry to accrue the interest on June 30.

c. Assuming adjusting entries are made at the end of each month, determine the balance in the Interest Payable account at December 31, 2022.

d. Prepare the entry required on January 1, 2023, when the loan is paid back.

E10.2 (LO 1), AP On May 15, Wild Quest Clothiers borrowed some money on a 4-month note to provide cash during the slow season of the year. The interest rate on the note was 8%. At the time the note was due, the amount of interest owed was $480.

Prepare entries for interest-bearing notes.

Instructions

a. Determine the amount borrowed by Wild Quest.

b. Independent of your answer in part (a), assume the amount borrowed was $18,500. What was the interest rate if the amount of interest owed was $555?

c. Prepare the entry for the initial borrowing and the repayment for the facts in part (a).

E10.3 (LO 1), AP On June 1, Marchon Company Ltd. borrows $60,000 from Acme Bank on a 6-month, $60,000, 8% note. The note matures on December 1.

Prepare entries for interest-bearing notes.

Instructions

a. Prepare the entry on June 1.

b. Prepare the adjusting entry on June 30.

c. Prepare the entry at maturity (December 1), assuming monthly adjusting entries have been made through November 30.

d. What was the total financing cost (interest expense)?

E10.4 (LO 1), AP C.S. Lewis Company had the following transactions involving notes payable.

Prepare entries for interest-bearing notes.

July 1, 2022	Borrows $50,000 from First National Bank by signing a 9-month, 8% note.
Nov. 1, 2022	Borrows $60,000 from Lyon County State Bank by signing a 3-month, 6% note.
Dec. 31, 2022	Prepares adjusting entries.
Feb. 1, 2023	Pays principal and interest to Lyon County State Bank.
Apr. 1, 2023	Pays principal and interest to First National Bank.

Instructions

Prepare journal entries for each of the transactions.

E10.5 (LO 1), AP In performing accounting services for small businesses, you encounter the following situations pertaining to cash sales.

Journalize sales and related taxes.

1. Cerviq Company enters sales and sales taxes separately on its cash register. On April 10, the register totals are sales $22,000 and sales taxes $1,100.

2. Quartz Company does not segregate sales and sales taxes. Its register total for April 15 is $13,780, which includes a 6% sales tax.

Instructions

Prepare the entries to record the sales transactions and related taxes for (a) Cerviq Company and (b) Quartz Company.

E10.6 (LO 1), AP During the month of March, Munster Company's employees earned wages of $64,000. Withholdings related to these wages were $4,896 for FICA, $7,500 for federal income tax, $3,100 for state income tax, and $400 for union dues. The company incurred no cost related to these earnings for federal unemployment tax but incurred $700 for state unemployment tax.

Journalize payroll entries.

Instructions

a. Prepare the necessary March 31 journal entry to record salaries and wages expense and salaries and wages payable. Assume that wages earned during March will be paid during April.

b. Prepare the entry to record the company's payroll tax expense.

E10.7 (LO 1), AP Dan Noll's gross earnings for the week were $1,780, his federal income tax withholding was $303, and his FICA total was $136. There were no state income taxes.

Calculate and record net pay.

Instructions

a. What was Noll's net pay for the week?

b. Journalize the entry for the recording of his pay in the general journal. (*Note:* Use Salaries and Wages Payable, not Cash.)

c. Record the issuing of the check for Noll's pay in the general journal.

Record accrual of payroll taxes.

E10.8 (LO 1), AP According to the accountant of Ulster Inc., its payroll taxes for the week were as follows: $137.68 for FICA taxes, $13.77 for federal unemployment taxes, and $92.93 for state unemployment taxes.

Instructions

Journalize the entry to record the accrual of the payroll taxes.

Journalize unearned revenue transactions.

E10.9 (LO 1), AP Season tickets for the Dingos are priced at $320 and include 16 home games. An equal amount of revenue is recognized after each game is played. When the season began, the amount credited to Unearned Ticket Revenue was $1,728,000. By the end of October, $1,188,000 of the Unearned Ticket Revenue had been recognized as revenue.

Instructions

a. How many season tickets did the Dingos sell?

b. How many home games had the Dingos played by the end of October?

c. Prepare the entry for the initial recording of the Unearned Ticket Revenue.

d. Prepare the entry to recognize the revenue after the first home game had been played.

Journalize unearned subscription revenue.

E10.10 (LO 1), AP Cassini Company Ltd. publishes a monthly sports magazine, *Fishing Preview*. Subscriptions to the magazine cost $28 per year. During November 2022, Cassini sells 6,300 subscriptions for cash, beginning with the December issue. Cassini prepares financial statements quarterly and recognizes subscription revenue at the end of the quarter. The company uses the accounts Unearned Subscription Revenue and Subscription Revenue. The company has a December 31 year-end.

Instructions

a. Prepare the entry in November for the receipt of the subscriptions.

b. Prepare the adjusting entry at December 31, 2022, to record subscription revenue in December 2022.

c. Prepare the adjusting entry at March 31, 2023, to record subscription revenue in the first quarter of 2023.

Evaluate statements about bonds.

E10.11 (LO 2), AN Nick Bosch has prepared the following list of statements about bonds.

1. Bonds are a form of interest-bearing notes payable.
2. Secured bonds have specific assets of the issuer pledged as collateral for the bonds.
3. Secured bonds are also known as debenture bonds.
4. A conversion feature may be added to bonds to make them more attractive to bond buyers.
5. The rate used to determine the amount of cash interest the borrower pays is called the stated rate.
6. Bond prices are usually quoted as a percentage of the face value of the bond.
7. The present value of a bond is the value at which it should sell in the marketplace.

Instructions

Identify each statement as true or false. If false, indicate how to correct the statement.

Prepare journal entries for issuance of bonds and payment and accrual of interest.

E10.12 (LO 3), AP On August 1, 2022, Gonzaga Corporation issued $600,000, 7%, 10-year bonds at face value. Interest is payable annually on August 1. Gonzaga's year-end is December 31.

Instructions

Prepare journal entries to record the following events.

a. The issuance of the bonds.

b. The accrual of interest on December 31, 2022.

c. The payment of interest on August 1, 2023.

Prepare journal entries for issuance of bonds and payment and accrual of interest.

E10.13 (LO 3), AP On January 1, Kirkland Company issued $300,000, 8%, 10-year bonds at face value. Interest is payable annually on January 1.

Instructions

Prepare journal entries to record the following events.

a. The issuance of the bonds.

b. The accrual of interest on December 31.

c. The payment of interest on January 1.

E10.14 (LO 3), AP Arroyo Company issued $600,000, 10-year, 6% bonds at 103.

Prepare entries for issuance of bonds, balance sheet presentation, and cause of deviations from face value.

Instructions

a. Prepare the journal entry to record the sale of these bonds on January 1, 2022.

b. Suppose the remaining Premium on Bonds Payable was $10,800 on December 31, 2025. Show the balance sheet presentation on this date.

c. Explain why the bonds sold at a price above the face amount.

E10.15 (LO 3), AP Mobbe Company issued $500,000, 15-year, 7% bonds at 96.

Prepare entries for issuance of bonds, balance sheet presentation, and cause of deviations from face value.

Instructions

a. Prepare the journal entry to record the sale of these bonds on January 1, 2022.

b. Suppose the remaining Discount on Bonds Payable was $12,000 on December 31, 2027. Show the balance sheet presentation on this date.

c. Explain why the bonds sold at a price below the face amount.

E10.16 (LO 3), AN Assume that the following are independent situations recently reported in the *Wall Street Journal*.

Prepare entries for issue of bonds.

1. **General Electric (GE)** 7% bonds, maturing January 28, 2023, were issued at 111.12.
2. **Boeing** 7% bonds, maturing September 24, 2037, were issued at 99.08.

Instructions

a. Were GE and Boeing bonds issued at a premium or a discount?

b. Explain how bonds, both paying the same contractual interest rate, could be issued at different prices.

c. Prepare the journal entry to record the issue of each of these two bonds, assuming each company issued $800,000 of bonds in total.

E10.17 (LO 3), AP Kale Company issued $350,000 of 8%, 20-year bonds on January 1, 2022, at face value. Interest is payable annually on January 1.

Prepare journal entries to record issuance of bonds, payment of interest, and redemption at maturity.

Instructions

Prepare the journal entries to record the following events.

a. The issuance of the bonds.

b. The accrual of interest on December 31, 2022.

c. The payment of interest on January 1, 2023.

d. The redemption of the bonds at maturity, assuming interest for the last interest period has been paid and recorded.

E10.18 (LO 3), AP The following situations are independent of each other.

Prepare journal entries for redemption of bonds.

Instructions

For each situation, prepare the appropriate journal entry for the redemption of the bonds.

a. Mikhail Corporation redeemed $140,000 face value, 9% bonds on April 30, 2022, at 101. The carrying value of the bonds at the redemption date was $126,500. The bonds pay annual interest, and the interest payment due on April 30, 2022, has been made and recorded.

b. Oldman, Inc., redeemed $170,000 face value, 12.5% bonds on June 30, 2022, at 98. The carrying value of the bonds at the redemption date was $184,000. The bonds pay annual interest, and the interest payment due on June 30, 2022, has been made and recorded.

E10.19 (LO 4), AP Sanchez, Inc. reports the following liabilities (in thousands) on its December 31, 2022, balance sheet and notes to the financial statements.

Prepare liabilities section of balance sheet.

Accounts payable	$4,263.9	Mortgage payable	$6,746.7
Unearned rent revenue	1,058.1	Notes payable (due in 2025)	335.6
Bonds payable	1,961.2	Salaries and wages payable	858.1
Current portion of mortgage payable	1,992.2	Notes payable (due in 2023)	2,563.6
Income taxes payable	265.2	Warranty liability—current	1,417.3

Instructions

a. Identify which of the above liabilities are likely current and which are likely long-term. List any items that do not fit in either category. Explain the reasoning for your selection.

b. Prepare the liabilities section of Sanchez's balance sheet as at December 31, 2022.

Calculate liquidity and solvency measures.

E10.20 (LO 4), AP Suppose **McDonald's** 2022 financial statements contain the following selected data (in millions).

Current assets	$ 3,416.3	Interest expense	$ 473.2
Total assets	30,224.9	Income taxes	1,936.0
Current liabilities	2,988.7	Net income	4,551.0
Total liabilities	16,191.0		

Instructions

Compute the following values and provide a brief interpretation of each.

a. Working capital.
b. Current ratio.
c. Debt to assets ratio.
d. Times interest earned.

Calculate current ratio before and after paying accounts payable.

E10.21 (LO 4), AN Suppose **3M Company** reported the following financial data for 2022 and 2021 (in millions).

3M Company
Balance Sheet (partial)

	2022	2021
Current assets		
Cash and cash equivalents	$ 3,040	$1,849
Accounts receivable, net	3,250	3,195
Inventories	2,639	3,013
Other current assets	1,866	1,541
Total current assets	$10,795	$9,598
Current liabilities	$ 4,897	$5,839

Instructions

a. Calculate the current ratio for 3M for 2022 and 2021.

b. Suppose that at the end of 2022, 3M management used $300 million cash to pay off $300 million of accounts payable. How would its current ratio change?

Calculate current ratio before and after paying accounts payable.

E10.22 (LO 4), AN Underwood Boutique reported the following financial data for 2022 and 2021.

Underwood Boutique
Balance Sheet (partial)
September 30 (in thousands)

	2022	2021
Current assets		
Cash and short-term deposits	$2,574	$1,021
Accounts receivable	2,147	1,575
Inventories	1,201	1,010
Other current assets	322	192
Total current assets	$6,244	$3,798
Current liabilities	$4,503	$2,619

Instructions

a. Calculate the current ratio for Underwood Boutique for 2022 and 2021.

b. Suppose that at the end of 2022, Underwood Boutique used $1.5 million cash to pay off $1.5 million of accounts payable. How would its current ratio change?

c. At September 30, Underwood Boutique has an undrawn operating line of credit of $12.5 million. Would this affect any assessment that you might make of Underwood Boutique's short-term liquidity? Explain.

E10.23 (LO 4), C A large retailer was sued nearly 5,000 times in a recent year—about once every 2 hours every day of the year. It has been sued for everything imaginable—ranging from falls on icy parking lots to injuries sustained in shoppers' stampedes to a murder with a rifle purchased at one of its stores. The company reported the following in the notes to its financial statements.

Discuss contingencies.

> The Company and its subsidiaries are involved from time to time in claims, proceedings, and litigation arising from the operation of its business. The Company does not believe that any such claim, proceeding, or litigation, either alone or in the aggregate, will have a material adverse effect on the Company's financial position or results of its operations.

Instructions
a. Explain why the company does not have to record these contingencies.
b. Comment on any implications for analysis of the financial statements.

E10.24 (LO 1, 2, 3, 4), K The following are terms or phrases that were introduced in the chapter.

Identify key terms.

1. Bond certificate.
2. Premium (on a bond).
3. Discount (on a bond).
4. Times interest earned.
5. Present value.
6. Maturity date.
7. Callable bonds.
8. Market interest rate.
9. Contingencies.
10. Secured bonds.
11. Contractual (stated) interest rate.
12. Unsecured bonds.
13. Off-balance-sheet financing.
14. Face value.
15. Convertible bonds

Instructions
Match the term or phrase with the appropriate description below.

a. _____ The value today of an amount to be received at some date in the future after taking into account current interest rates.
b. _____ Bonds that have specific assets of the issuer pledged as collateral.
c. _____ Events with uncertain outcomes that may represent potential liabilities.
d. _____ Bonds that can be converted into common stock at the bondholder's option.
e. _____ A legal document that indicates the name of the issuer, the face value of the bonds, and other data such as the contractual interest rate and the maturity date of the bonds.
f. _____ Bonds that the issuing company can redeem (buy back) at a stated dollar amount prior to maturity.
g. _____ The date on which the final payment on a bond is due from the bond issuer to the investor.
h. _____ Rate used to determine the amount of interest the issuer pays and the investor receives.
i. _____ The difference between the face value of a bond and its selling price when a bond is sold for less than its face value.
j. _____ A measure of a company's solvency, calculated by dividing the sum of net income, interest expense, and income tax expense by interest expense.
k. _____ The rate investors demand for loaning funds to the corporation.
l. _____ Amount of principal due at the maturity date of the bond.
m. _____ Bonds issued against the general credit of the borrower.
n. _____ The intentional effort by a company to structure its financing arrangements so as to avoid showing liabilities on its balance sheet
o. _____ The difference between the selling price and the face value of a bond when a bond is sold for more than its face value.

*E10.25 (LO 3, 5), AP Sehr Company issued $500,000, 6%, 30-year bonds on January 1, 2022, at 103. Interest is payable annually on January 1. Sehr uses straight-line amortization for bond premium or discount.

Prepare journal entries to record issuance of bonds, payment of interest, amortization of premium using straight-line, and redemption at maturity.

Instructions

Prepare the journal entries to record the following events.

a. The issuance of the bonds.

b. The accrual of interest and the premium amortization on December 31, 2022.

c. The payment of interest on January 1, 2023.

d. The redemption of the bonds at maturity, assuming interest for the last interest period has been paid and recorded.

Prepare journal entries to record issuance of bonds, payment of interest, amortization of discount using straight-line, and redemption at maturity.

*E10.26 (LO 3, 5), AP** Motley Company issued $300,000, 8%, 15-year bonds on December 31, 2021, for $288,000. Interest is payable annually on December 31. Motley uses the straight-line method to amortize bond premium or discount.

Instructions

Prepare the journal entries to record the following events.

a. The issuance of the bonds.

b. The payment of interest and the discount amortization on December 31, 2022.

c. The redemption of the bonds at maturity, assuming interest for the last interest period has been paid and recorded.

Prepare journal entries for issuance of bonds, payment of interest, and amortization of discount using effective-interest method.

*E10.27 (LO 3, 6), AP** Woode Corporation issued $400,000, 7%, 20-year bonds on January 1, 2022, for $360,727. This price resulted in an effective-interest rate of 8% on the bonds. Interest is payable annually on January 1. Woode uses the effective-interest method to amortize bond premium or discount.

Instructions

Prepare the journal entries to record (round to the nearest dollar):

a. The issuance of the bonds.

b. The accrual of interest and the discount amortization on December 31, 2022.

c. The payment of interest on January 1, 2023.

Prepare journal entries for issuance of bonds, payment of interest, and amortization of premium using effective-interest method.

*E10.28 (LO 3, 6), AP** Hernandez Company issued $380,000, 7%, 10-year bonds on January 1, 2022, for $407,968. This price resulted in an effective-interest rate of 6% on the bonds. Interest is payable annually on January 1. Hernandez uses the effective-interest method to amortize bond premium or discount.

Instructions

Prepare the journal entries (rounded to the nearest dollar) to record:

a. The issuance of the bonds.

b. The accrual of interest and the premium amortization on December 31, 2022.

c. The payment of interest on January 1, 2023.

Prepare journal entries to record mortgage note and installment payments.

*E10.29 (LO 7), AP** Yancey Co. receives $300,000 when it issues a $300,000, 10%, mortgage note payable to finance the construction of a building at December 31, 2022. The terms provide for annual installment payments of $50,000 on December 31.

Instructions

Prepare the journal entries to record the mortgage loan and the first two installment payments.

Determine balance sheet presentation of installment note payable.

*E10.30 (LO 7), AP** Waite Corporation issued a $50,000, 10%, 10-year installment note payable on January 1, 2022. Payments of $8,137 are made each January 1, beginning January 1, 2023.

Instructions

a. What amounts should be reported under current liabilities related to the note on December 31, 2022?

b. What should be reported under long-term liabilities?

Problems: Set A

P10.1A (LO 1, 4), AP On January 1, 2022, the ledger of Romada Company contained these liability accounts.

Accounts Payable	$42,500
Sales Taxes Payable	6,600
Unearned Service Revenue	19,000

Prepare current liability entries, adjusting entries, and current liabilities section.

During January, the following selected transactions occurred.

Jan.	1	Borrowed $18,000 in cash from Apex Bank on a 4-month, 5%, $18,000 note.
	5	Sold merchandise for cash totaling $6,254, which includes 6% sales taxes.
	12	Performed services for customers who had made advance payments of $10,000. (Credit Service Revenue.)
	14	Paid state treasurer's department for sales taxes collected in December 2021, $6,600.
	20	Sold 500 units of a new product on credit at $48 per unit, plus 6% sales tax.

During January, the company's employees earned wages of $70,000. Withholdings related to these wages were $5,355 for FICA, $5,000 for federal income tax, and $1,500 for state income tax. The company owed no money related to these earnings for federal or state unemployment tax. Assume that wages earned during January will be paid during February. No entry had been recorded for wages or payroll tax expense as of January 31.

Instructions

a. Journalize the January transactions.

b. Journalize the adjusting entries at January 31 for the outstanding note payable and for salaries and wages expense and payroll tax expense.

c. Prepare the current liabilities section of the balance sheet at January 31, 2022. Assume no change in Accounts Payable.

c. Tot. current liabilities $146,724

P10.2A (LO 1, 4), AP Ehler Corporation sells rock-climbing products and also operates an indoor climbing facility for climbing enthusiasts. During the last part of 2022, Ehler had the following transactions related to notes payable.

Journalize and post note transactions; show balance sheet presentation.

Sept.	1	Issued a $12,000 note to Pippen to purchase inventory. The 3-month note payable bears interest of 6% and is due December 1. (Ehler uses a perpetual inventory system.)
Sept.	30	Recorded accrued interest for the Pippen note.
Oct.	1	Issued a $16,500, 8%, 4-month note to Prime Bank to finance the purchase of a new climbing wall for advanced climbers. The note is due February 1.
Oct.	31	Recorded accrued interest for the Pippen note and the Prime Bank note.
Nov.	1	Issued a $26,000 note and paid $8,000 cash to purchase a vehicle to transport clients to nearby climbing sites as part of a new series of climbing classes. This note bears interest of 6% and matures in 12 months.
Nov.	30	Recorded accrued interest for the Pippen note, the Prime Bank note, and the vehicle note.
Dec.	1	Paid principal and interest on the Pippen note.
Dec.	31	Recorded accrued interest for the Prime Bank note and the vehicle note.

Instructions

a. Prepare journal entries for the transactions noted above.

b. Post the above entries to the Notes Payable, Interest Payable, and Interest Expense accounts. (Use T-accounts.)

c. Show the balance sheet presentation of notes payable and interest payable at December 31.

d. How much interest expense relating to notes payable did Ehler incur during the year?

b. Interest Payable $590

P10.3A (LO 3), AP The following section is taken from Hardesty's balance sheet at December 31, 2021.

Prepare journal entries to record interest payments and redemption of bonds.

Current liabilities	
Interest payable	$ 40,000
Long-term liabilities	
Bonds payable (8%, due January 1, 2025)	500,000

Interest is payable annually on January 1. The bonds are callable on any annual interest date.

b. Loss $6,000

Instructions

a. Journalize the payment of the bond interest on January 1, 2022.
b. Assume that on January 1, 2022, after paying interest, Hardesty calls bonds having a face value of $200,000. The call price is 103. Record the redemption of the bonds.
c. Prepare the adjusting entry on December 31, 2022, to accrue the interest on the remaining bonds.

Prepare journal entries to record issuance of bonds, interest, balance sheet presentation, and bond redemption.

P10.4A (LO 3, 4), AP On October 1, 2021, Kristal Corp. issued $700,000, 5%, 10-year bonds at face value. The bonds were dated October 1, 2021, and pay interest annually on October 1. Financial statements are prepared annually on December 31.

Instructions

a. Prepare the journal entry to record the issuance of the bonds.
b. Prepare the adjusting entry to record the accrual of interest on December 31, 2021.
c. Show the balance sheet presentation of bonds payable and bond interest payable on December 31, 2021.
d. Prepare the journal entry to record the payment of interest on October 1, 2022.
e. Prepare the adjusting entry to record the accrual of interest on December 31, 2022.

f. Loss $28,000

f. Assume that on January 1, 2023, Kristal pays the accrued bond interest and calls the bonds. The call price is 104. Record the payment of interest and redemption of the bonds.

Prepare journal entries to record issuance of bonds, show balance sheet presentation, and record bond redemption.

P10.5A (LO 3, 4), AP Malcolm Company sold $6,000,000, 7%, 15-year bonds on January 1, 2022. The bonds were dated January 1, 2022, and pay interest on December 31. The bonds were sold at 98.

Instructions

a. Prepare the journal entry to record the issuance of the bonds on January 1, 2022.
b. At December 31, 2022, $8,000 of the bond discount had been amortized. Show the long-term liability balance sheet presentation of the bond liability at December 31, 2022.

c. Loss $224,000

c. At January 1, 2024, when the carrying value of the bonds was $5,896,000, the company redeemed the bonds at 102. Record the redemption of the bonds assuming that interest for the year had already been paid.

Calculate and comment on ratios.

P10.6A (LO 4), AN Suppose you have been presented with selected information taken from the financial statements of **Southwest Airlines Co.**

Southwest Airlines Co.
Balance Sheet (partial)
December 31
(in millions)

	2022	2021
Total current assets	$ 2,893	$ 4,443
Noncurrent assets	11,415	12,329
Total assets	$14,308	$16,772
Current liabilities	$ 2,806	$ 4,836
Long-term liabilities	6,549	4,995
Total liabilities	9,355	9,831
Shareholders' equity	4,953	6,941
Total liabilities and shareholders' equity	$14,308	$16,772

Other information:

	2022	2021
Net income (loss)	$ 178	$ 645
Income tax expense	100	413
Interest expense	130	119
Cash provided by operations	(1,521)	2,845
Capital expenditures	923	1,331
Cash dividends	13	14

Instructions

a. Calculate each of the following ratios for 2022 and 2021.

1. Current ratio.
2. Free cash flow.
3. Debt to assets ratio.
4. Times interest earned.

b. Comment on the trend in ratios.

P10.7A (LO 3, 5), AP The following information is taken from Lassen Corp.'s balance sheet at December 31, 2021.

Prepare journal entries to record interest payments, straight-line discount amortization, and redemption of bonds.

Current liabilities		
Interest payable		$ 96,000
Long-term liabilities		
Bonds payable (4%, due January 1, 2032)	$2,400,000	
Less: Discount on bonds payable	24,000	2,376,000

Interest is payable annually on January 1. The bonds are callable on any annual interest date. Lassen uses straight-line amortization for any bond premium or discount. From December 31, 2021, the bonds will be outstanding for an additional 10 years (120 months).

Instructions

(Round all computations to the nearest dollar.)

a. Journalize the payment of bond interest on January 1, 2022.

b. Prepare the entry to amortize bond discount and to accrue the interest on December 31, 2022.

c. Assume on January 1, 2023, after paying interest, that Lassen Corp. calls bonds having a face value of $400,000. The call price is 102. Record the redemption of the bonds.

c. Loss $11,600

d. Prepare the adjusting entry at December 31, 2023, to amortize bond discount and to accrue interest on the remaining bonds.

P10.8A (LO 3, 4, 5), AP Fong Corporation sold $2,000,000, 7%, 5-year bonds on January 1, 2022. The bonds were dated January 1, 2022, and pay interest on January 1. Fong Corporation uses the straight-line method to amortize bond premium or discount.

Prepare journal entries to record issuance of bonds, interest, and straight-line amortization, and balance sheet presentation.

Instructions

a. Prepare all the necessary journal entries to record the issuance of the bonds and bond interest expense for 2022, assuming that the bonds sold at 102.

b. Prepare journal entries as in part (a) assuming that the bonds sold at 97.

c. Show the balance sheet presentation for the bond issue at December 31, 2022, using (1) the 102 selling price, and then (2) the 97 selling price.

P10.9A (LO 3, 4, 5), AP Saylor Co. sold $3,000,000, 8%, 10-year bonds on January 1, 2022. The bonds were dated January 1, 2022, and pay interest on January 1. The company uses straight-line amortization on bond premiums and discounts. Financial statements are prepared annually.

Prepare journal entries to record issuance of bonds, interest, and straight-line amortization, and balance sheet presentation.

Instructions

a. Prepare the journal entries to record the issuance of the bonds assuming they sold at:

1. 103.
2. 98.

b. Prepare amortization tables for both assumed sales for the first three interest payments.

c. Prepare the journal entries to record interest expense for 2022 under both of the bond issuances assumed in part (a).

c. (2) 12/31/22
*   Interest Expense $246,000*

d. Show the long-term liabilities balance sheet presentation for both of the bond issuances assumed in part (a) at December 31, 2022.

P10.10A (LO 3, 6), AP On January 1, 2022, Lachte Corporation issued $1,800,000 face value, 5%, 10-year bonds at $1,667,518. This price resulted in an effective-interest rate of 6% on the bonds. Lachte uses the effective-interest method to amortize bond premium or discount. The bonds pay annual interest January 1.

Prepare journal entries to record issuance of bonds, payment of interest, and amortization of bond discount using effective-interest method.

Instructions

(Round all computations to the nearest dollar.)

a. Prepare the journal entry to record the issuance of the bonds on January 1, 2022.

b. Prepare an amortization table through December 31, 2024 (three interest periods), for this bond issue.

*c. Interest
   Expense $100,051*

c. Prepare the journal entry to record the accrual of interest and the amortization of the discount on December 31, 2022.

d. Prepare the journal entry to record the payment of interest on January 1, 2023.

e. Prepare the journal entry to record the accrual of interest and the amortization of the discount on December 31, 2023.

Prepare journal entries to record issuance of bonds, payment of interest, and effective-interest amortization, and balance sheet presentation.

*P10.11A (LO 3, 4, 6), AP On January 1, 2022, Opal Company issued $2,000,000 face value, 7%, 10-year bonds at $2,147,202. This price resulted in a 6% effective-interest rate on the bonds. Opal uses the effective-interest method to amortize bond premium or discount. The bonds pay annual interest on each January 1.

Instructions

*a. (4) Interest
   Expense $128,162*

a. Prepare the journal entries to record the following transactions.
   1. The issuance of the bonds on January 1, 2022.
   2. Accrual of interest and amortization of the premium on December 31, 2022.
   3. The payment of interest on January 1, 2023.
   4. Accrual of interest and amortization of the premium on December 31, 2023.

b. Show the proper long-term liabilities balance sheet presentation for the liability for bonds payable at December 31, 2023.

c. Provide the answers to the following questions in narrative form.
   1. What amount of interest expense is reported for 2023?
   2. Would the bond interest expense reported in 2023 be the same as, greater than, or less than the amount that would be reported if the straight-line method of amortization were used?

Prepare installment payments schedule, journal entries, and balance sheet presentation for a mortgage note payable.

*P10.12A (LO 4, 7), AP Laverne purchased a new piece of equipment to be used in its new facility. The $370,000 piece of equipment was purchased with a $50,000 down payment and with cash received through the issuance of a $320,000, 8%, 5-year mortgage payable issued on January 1, 2022. The terms provide for annual installment payments of $80,146 on December 31.

Instructions

(Round all computations to the nearest dollar.)

a. Prepare an installment payments schedule for the first three payments of the notes payable.

b. Prepare the journal entry related to the notes payable for December 31, 2022.

c. Current portion $58,910

c. Show the balance sheet presentation for this obligation for December 31, 2022. (*Hint:* Be sure to distinguish between the current and long-term portions of the note.)

Prepare journal entries to record payments for long-term note payable, and balance sheet presentation.

*P10.13A (LO 4, 7), AP Hetty Grey has just approached a venture capitalist for financing for her new business venture, the development of a local ski hill. On July 1, 2021, Hetty was loaned $150,000 at an annual interest rate of 7%. The loan is repayable over 5 years in annual installments of $36,584, principal and interest, due each June 30. The first payment is due June 30, 2022. Hetty uses the effective-interest method for amortizing debt. Her ski hill company's year-end will be June 30.

Instructions

a. Prepare an amortization schedule for the 5 years, 2021–2026. (Round all calculations to the nearest dollar.)

*b. 6/30/22 Interest
   Expense $10,500*

b. Prepare all journal entries for Hetty Grey for the first 2 fiscal years ended June 30, 2022, and June 30, 2023. (Round all calculations to the nearest dollar.)

c. Show the balance sheet presentation of the note payable as of June 30, 2023. (*Hint:* Be sure to distinguish between the current and long-term portions of the note.)

Continuing Case

Cookie Creations

(*Note:* This is a continuation of the Cookie Creations case from Chapters 1 through 9.)

CC10 Recall that Cookie Creations borrowed $2,000 from Natalie's grandmother. Natalie now is thinking of repaying all amounts outstanding on that loan. She needs to know the amounts of interest payable and interest expense to make the correct journal entries for repayment of the loan.

Go to WileyPLUS for complete case details and instructions.

Comprehensive Accounting Cycle Review

ACR10 Aimes Corporation's balance sheet at December 31, 2021, is presented below.

Aimes Corporation
Balance Sheet
December 31, 2021

Cash	$ 30,000	Accounts payable	$ 13,750
Inventory	30,750	Interest payable	2,500
Prepaid insurance	5,600	Bonds payable	50,000
Equipment	38,000	Common stock	25,000
	$104,350	Retained earnings	13,100
			$104,350

During 2022, the following transactions occurred. Aimes uses a perpetual inventory system.

1. Aimes paid $2,500 interest on the bonds on January 1, 2022.
2. Aimes purchased $241,100 of inventory on account.
3. Aimes sold for $480,000 cash inventory which cost $265,000. Aimes also collected $28,800 sales taxes.
4. Aimes paid $230,000 on accounts payable.
5. Aimes paid $2,500 interest on the bonds on July 1, 2022.
6. The prepaid insurance ($5,600) expired on July 31.
7. On August 1, Aimes paid $10,200 for insurance coverage from August 1, 2022, through July 31, 2023.
8. Aimes paid $17,000 sales taxes to the state.
9. Paid other operating expenses, $91,000.
10. Redeemed the bonds on December 31, 2022, by paying $48,000 plus $2,500 interest.
11. Issued $90,000 of 8% bonds on December 31, 2022, at 103. The bonds pay interest every June 30 and December 31.

Adjustment data:

1. Recorded the insurance expired from item 7.
2. The equipment was acquired on December 31, 2021, and will be depreciated on a straight-line basis over 5 years with a $3,000 salvage value.
3. The income tax rate is 30%. (*Hint:* Prepare the income statement up to income before taxes and multiply by 30% to compute the amount.)

Instructions

(You may want to set up T-accounts to determine ending balances.)

a. Prepare journal entries for the transactions listed above and adjusting entries.
b. Prepare an adjusted trial balance at December 31, 2022.   b. Totals $687,695
c. Prepare an income statement and a retained earnings statement for the year ending December 31, 2022, and a classified balance sheet as of December 31, 2022.   c. N.I. $72,905

Expand Your Critical Thinking

Financial Reporting Problem: Apple Inc.

CT10.1 Refer to the financial statements of **Apple Inc.** in Appendix A.

Instructions

Answer the following questions.

a. What were Apple's total current liabilities at September 30, 2017? What was the increase/decrease in Apple's total current liabilities from the prior year?
b. How much were the accounts payable at September 30, 2017?
c. What were the components of total current liabilities on September 30, 2017 (other than accounts payable already discussed above)?

Comparative Analysis Problem: Columbia Sportswear Company vs. VF Corporation

CT10.2 The financial statements of **Columbia Sportswear Company** are presented in Appendix B. Financial statements of **VF Corporation** are presented in Appendix C.

Instructions

a. Based on the information contained in these financial statements, compute the current ratio for 2016 for each company. What conclusions concerning the companies' liquidity can be drawn from these ratios?

b. Based on the information contained in these financial statements, compute the following 2016 ratios for each company.

1. Debt to assets ratio.
2. Times interest earned.

What conclusions about the companies' long-run solvency can be drawn from the ratios?

Comparative Analysis Problem: Amazon.com, Inc. vs. Wal-Mart Stores, Inc.

CT10.3 The financial statements of **Amazon.com, Inc.** are presented in Appendix D. Financial statements of **Wal-Mart Stores, Inc.** are presented in Appendix E.

Instructions

a. Based on the information contained in these financial statements, compute the current ratio for the most recent fiscal year provided for each company. What conclusions concerning the companies' liquidity can be drawn from these ratios?

b. Based on the information contained in these financial statements, compute the following ratios for each company's most recent fiscal year.

1. Debt to assets ratio.
2. Times interest earned.

What conclusions about the companies' long-run solvency can be drawn from the ratios?

Interpreting Financial Statements

CT10.4 **Hechinger Co.** and **Home Depot** are two home improvement retailers. Compared to Hechinger, founded in the early 1900s, Home Depot is a relative newcomer. But in recent years, while Home Depot was reporting large increases in net income, Hechinger was reporting increasingly large net losses. Finally, largely due to competition from Home Depot, Hechinger was forced to file for bankruptcy. Here are financial data for both companies (in millions).

	Hechinger	Home Depot
Cash	$ 21	$ 62
Receivables	0	469
Total current assets	1,153	4,933
Beginning total assets	1,668	11,229
Ending total assets	1,577	13,465
Beginning current liabilities	935	2,456
Ending current liabilities	938	2,857
Beginning total liabilities	1,392	4,015
Ending total liabilities	1,339	4,716
Interest expense	67	37
Income tax expense	3	1,040
Cash provided (used) by operations	(257)	1,917
Net income	(93)	1,614
Net sales	3,444	30,219

Instructions

Using the data provided, perform the following analysis.

a. Calculate working capital and the current ratio for each company. Discuss their relative liquidity.

b. Calculate the debt to assets ratio and times interest earned for each company. Discuss their relative solvency.

c. Calculate the return on assets and profit margin for each company. Comment on their relative profitability.

CT10.5 For many years, **Borders Group** and **Barnes and Noble** were the dominant booksellers in the United States. They experienced rapid growth, and in the process they forced many small, independent bookstores out of business. Recently, Borders filed for bankruptcy. It was the victim of its inability to change with the times. It did not develop a viable business plan for dealing with digital books and online sales. Below is financial information (in millions) for the two companies, taken from the annual reports of each company one year before Borders filed for bankruptcy.

	Borders	Barnes and Noble
Current assets	$ 978.7	$1,719.5
Total assets	1,415.6	3,705.7
Current liabilities	918.1	1,724.4
Total liabilities	1,257.3	2,802.3
Net income/(loss)	(109.4)	36.7
Interest expense	24.1	28.2
Tax expense/(income tax benefit)	(31.3)	8.4

Instructions

a. Compute the current ratio for each company.

b. Compute the debt to assets ratio and times interest earned for each company. (*Hint:* A tax benefit means that rather than pay taxes, the company was due a refund because of its losses. For ratio purposes, a tax benefit is treated the opposite of tax expense.)

c. Discuss the relative liquidity and solvency of each company. Did the bankruptcy of Borders seem likely?

Real-World Focus

CT10.6 Bond or debt securities pay a stated rate of interest. This rate of interest is dependent on the risk associated with the investment. Also, bond prices change when the risks associated with those bonds change. **Standard & Poor's** provides ratings for companies that issue debt securities.

Instructions

Go to the Standard & Poor's website and then answer the following questions.

a. Explain the meaning of an "A" rating. Explain the meaning of a "C" rating.

b. What types of things can cause a change in a company's credit rating?

c. Explain the relationship between a company's credit rating and the merit of an investment in that company's bonds.

CT10.7 The September 1, 2009, edition of *CFO.com* contains an article by Marie Leone and Tim Reason entitled "Dirty Secrets." You can access this article by doing an Internet search on "CFO.com Dirty Secrets."

Instructions

Read the article and then answer the following questions.

a. Summarize the accounting for contingent items that is provided in this text.

b. The authors of the article suggest that many companies are basically accounting for contingencies on a cash basis. Is this consistent with the approach you described in part (a)?

c. The article suggests that many companies report one set of liability estimates to insurers and a different (lower) set of numbers in their financial statements. How is this possible, and what are the implications for investors?

d. How do international accounting standards differ in terms of the amounts reported in these types of situations?

Decision-Making Across the Organization

CT10.8 On January 1, 2020, Picard Corporation issued $3,000,000, 5-year, 8% bonds at 97. The bonds pay interest annually on January 1. By January 1, 2022, the market rate of interest for bonds of risk similar to those of Picard Corporation had risen. As a result, the market price of these bonds was $2,500,000 on January 1, 2022—below their carrying value of $2,946,000.

Geoff Marquis, president of the company, suggests repurchasing all of these bonds in the open market at the $2,500,000 price. But to do so the company will have to issue $2,500,000 (face value) of new 10-year, 12% bonds at par. The president asks you, as controller, "What is the feasibility of my proposed repurchase plan?"

Instructions

With the class divided into groups, answer the following.

a. Prepare the journal entry to redeem the 5-year bonds on January 1, 2022. Prepare the journal entry to issue the new 10-year bonds.

b. Prepare a short memo to the president in response to his request for advice. List the economic factors that you believe should be considered for his repurchase proposal.

Communication Activity

CT10.9 Jerry Hogan, president of Norwest, Inc., is considering the issuance of bonds to finance an expansion of his business. He has asked you to do the following: (1) discuss the advantages of bonds over common stock financing, (2) indicate the types of bonds he might issue, and (3) explain the issuing procedures used in bond transactions.

Instructions

Write a memorandum to the president, answering his request.

Ethics Cases

CT10.10 The July 1998 issue of *Inc.* magazine included an article by Jeffrey L. Seglin entitled "Would You Lie to Save Your Company?" It recounts the following true situation:

"A Chief Executive Officer (CEO) of a $20-million company that repairs aircraft engines received notice from a number of its customers that engines that it had recently repaired had failed, and that the company's parts were to blame. The CEO had not yet determined whether his company's parts were, in fact, the cause of the problem. The Federal Aviation Administration (FAA) had been notified and was investigating the matter.

What complicated the situation was that the company was in the midst of its year-end audit. As part of the audit, the CEO was required to sign a letter saying that he was not aware of any significant outstanding circumstances that could negatively impact the company—in accounting terms, of any contingencies. The auditor was not aware of the customer complaints or the FAA investigation.

The company relied heavily on short-term loans from eight banks. The CEO feared that if these lenders learned of the situation, they would pull their loans. The loss of these loans would force the company into bankruptcy, leaving hundreds of people without jobs. Prior to this problem, the company had a stellar performance record."

Instructions

Answer the following questions.

a. Who are the stakeholders in this situation?

b. What are the CEO's possible courses of action? What are the potential results of each course of action? (Take into account the two alternative outcomes: the FAA determines the company (1) was not at fault, and (2) was at fault.)

c. What would you do, and why?

d. Suppose the CEO decides to conceal the situation, and that during the next year the company is found to be at fault and is forced into bankruptcy. What losses are incurred by the stakeholders in this situation? Do you think the CEO should suffer legal consequences if he decides to conceal the situation?

CT10.11 During the summer of 2002, the financial press reported that **Citigroup** was being investigated for allegations that it had arranged transactions for **Enron** so as to intentionally misrepresent the nature of the transactions and consequently achieve favorable balance sheet treatment. Essentially, the deals were structured to make it appear that money was coming into Enron from trading activities, rather than from loans.

A July 23, 2002, *The New York Times* article by Richard Oppel and Kurt Eichenwald entitled "Citigroup Said to Mold Deal to Help Enron Skirt Rules" suggested that Citigroup intentionally kept certain parts of a secret oral agreement out of the written record for fear that it would change the accounting treatment. Critics contend that this had the effect of significantly understating Enron's liabilities, thus misleading investors and creditors. Citigroup maintains that, as a lender, it has no obligation to ensure that its clients account for transactions properly. The proper accounting, Citigroup insists, is the responsibility of the client and its auditor.

Instructions

Answer the following questions.

a. Who are the stakeholders in this situation?

b. Do you think that a lender, in general, in arranging so-called "structured financing" has a responsibility to ensure that its clients account for the financing in an appropriate fashion, or is this the responsibility of the client and its auditor?

c. What effect did the fact that the written record did not disclose all characteristics of the transaction probably have on the auditor's ability to evaluate the accounting treatment of this transaction?

d. *The New York Times* article noted that in one presentation made to sell this kind of deal to Enron and other energy companies, Citigroup stated that using such an arrangement "eliminates the need for capital markets disclosure, keeping structure mechanics private." Why might a company wish to conceal the terms of a financing arrangement from the capital markets (investors and creditors)? Is this appropriate? Do you think it is ethical for a lender to market deals in this way?

e. Why was this deal more potentially harmful to shareholders than other off-balance-sheet transactions (for example, lease financing)?

All About You

CT10.12 For most U.S. families, medical costs are substantial and rising. But will medical costs be your most substantial expense over your lifetime? Not likely. Will it be housing or food? Again, not likely. The answer: Taxes are likely to be your biggest expense. On average, Americans work 74 days each year to afford their federal taxes. Companies, too, have large tax burdens. They look very hard at tax issues in deciding where to build their plants and where to locate their administrative headquarters.

Instructions

a. Determine what your state income taxes are if your taxable income is $60,000 and you file as a single taxpayer in the state in which you live.

b. Assume that you own a home worth $200,000 in your community and the tax rate is 2.1%. Compute the property taxes you would pay.

c. Assume that the total gasoline bill for your automobile is $1,200 a year (300 gallons at $4 per gallon). What are the amounts of state and federal taxes that you pay on the $1,200?

d. Assume that your purchases for the year total $9,000. Of this amount, $5,000 was for food and prescription drugs. What is the amount of sales tax you would pay on these purchases? (*Note:* Many states do not have a sales tax for food or prescription drug purchases. Does yours?)

e. Determine what your FICA taxes are if your income is $60,000.

f. Determine what your federal income taxes are if your taxable income is $60,000 and you file as a single taxpayer.

g. Determine your total taxes paid based on the above calculations, and determine the percentage of income that you would pay in taxes based on the following formula: Total taxes paid ÷ Total income.

FASB Codification Activity

CT10.13 If your school has a subscription to the FASB Codification, log in and prepare responses to the following.

a. What is the definition of current liabilities?

b. What is the definition of long-term obligations?

c. What guidance does the Codification provide for the disclosure of long-term obligations?

Considering People, Planet, and Profit

CT10.14 The December 10, 2011, edition of *The Economist* contains an article entitled "Helping the Poor to Save: Small Wonder." This article discusses how many of the world's poorest people benefit from borrowing small amounts of money.

Instructions

Read the article and answer the following questions. (The article can be accessed by doing an Internet search that includes the title of the article and magazine.)

a. What monthly rate of interest do people pay on the loans they borrow from the microfinance organizations described in the article? What would these rates be on an annualized basis?

b. The rates described in your answer to part (a) are very high. Explain how somebody can pay such high rates and yet still benefit from borrowing.

c. Describe the structure of the typical village savings and loan organization.

A Look at IFRS

LEARNING OBJECTIVE 8
Compare the accounting for liabilities under GAAP and IFRS.

IFRS and GAAP have similar definitions of liabilities but have a different approach for recording certain liabilities.

Key Points

Following are the key similarities and differences between GAAP and IFRS as related to accounting for liabilities.

Similarities

- The basic definition of a liability under GAAP and IFRS is very similar. In a more technical way, liabilities are defined by the IASB as a present obligation of the entity arising from past events, the settlement of which is expected to result in an outflow from the entity of resources embodying economic benefits.
- The accounting for current liabilities such as notes payable, unearned revenue, and payroll taxes payable are similar between GAAP and IFRS.
- IFRS requires that companies classify liabilities as current or noncurrent on the face of the statement of financial position (balance sheet), except in industries where a **presentation** based on liquidity would be considered to provide more useful information (such as financial institutions). When current liabilities (also called short-term liabilities) are presented, they are generally presented in order of liquidity.
- Under IFRS, liabilities are classified as current if they are expected to be paid within 12 months.
- Similar to GAAP, items are normally reported in order of liquidity. Companies sometimes show liabilities before assets. Also, they will sometimes show long-term liabilities before current liabilities.
- The basic calculation for bond valuation is the same under GAAP and IFRS. In addition, the accounting for bond liability transactions is essentially the same between GAAP and IFRS.
- IFRS requires use of the effective-interest method for amortization of bond discounts and premiums. GAAP also requires the effective-interest method, except that it allows use of the straight-line method where the difference is not material. Under IFRS, companies do not use a premium or discount account but instead show the bond at its net amount. For example, if a $100,000 bond was issued at 97, under IFRS a company would record:

Cash	97,000	
Bonds Payable		97,000

Differences

- The accounting for convertible bonds differs between IFRS and GAAP. Unlike GAAP, IFRS splits the proceeds from the convertible bond between an equity component and a debt component. The equity conversion rights are reported in equity.

    To illustrate, assume that Harris Corp. issues convertible 7% bonds with a face value of $1,000,000 and receives $1,000,000. Comparable bonds without a conversion feature would have required a 9% rate of interest. To determine how much of the proceeds would be allocated to debt and how much to equity, the promised payments of the bond obligation would be discounted at the market rate of 9%. Suppose that this results in a present value of $850,000. The entry to record the issuance would be:

Cash	1,000,000	
Bonds Payable		850,000
Share Premium—Conversion Equity		150,000

- Under IFRS, companies sometimes will net current liabilities against current assets to show working capital on the face of the statement of financial position.

IFRS Practice

IFRS Self-Test Questions

1. Which of the following is **false**?
   a. Under IFRS, current liabilities must always be presented before noncurrent liabilities.
   b. Under IFRS, an item is a current liability if it will be paid within the next 12 months.
   c. Under IFRS, current liabilities are sometimes netted against current assets on the statement of financial position.
   d. Under IFRS, a liability is only recognized if it is a present obligation.

2. The accounting for bonds payable is:
   a. essentially the same under IFRS and GAAP.
   b. differs in that GAAP requires use of the straight-line method for amortization of bond premium and discount.
   c. the same except that market prices may be different because the present value calculations are different between IFRS and GAAP.
   d. not covered by IFRS.

3. Stevens Corporation issued 5% convertible bonds with a total face value of $3,000,000 for $3,000,000. If the bonds had not had a conversion feature, they would have sold for $2,600,000. Under IFRS, the entry to record the transaction would require a credit to:
   a. Bonds Payable for $3,000,000.
   b. Bonds Payable for $400,000.
   c. Share Premium—Conversion Equity for $400,000.
   d. Discount on Bonds Payable for $400,000.

4. Which of the following is **true** regarding accounting for amortization of bond discount and premium?
   a. Both IFRS and GAAP must use the effective-interest method.
   b. GAAP must use the effective-interest method, but IFRS may use either the effective-interest method or the straight-line method.
   c. IFRS is required to use the effective-interest method.
   d. GAAP is required to use the straight-line method.

IFRS Exercises

IFRS10.1 Briefly describe some of the similarities and differences between GAAP and IFRS with respect to the accounting for liabilities.

IFRS10.2 Ratzlaff Company issues (in euros) €2 million, 10-year, 8% bonds at 97, with interest payable annually on January 1.

Instructions

a. Prepare the journal entry to record the sale of these bonds on January 1, 2022.
b. Assuming instead that the above bonds sold for 104, prepare the journal entry to record the sale of these bonds on January 1, 2022.

IFRS10.3 Archer Company issued (in pounds) £4,000,000 par value, 7% convertible bonds at 99 for cash. The net present value of the debt without the conversion feature is £3,800,000. Prepare the journal entry to record the issuance of the convertible bonds.

International Financial Statement Analysis: Louis Vuitton

IFRS10.4 The financial statements of **Louis Vuitton** are presented in Appendix F. The complete annual report, including the notes to its financial statements, is available at the company's website.

Instructions

Use the company's annual report to answer the following questions.
a. What were the total current liabilities for the company as of December 31, 2016? What portion of these current liabilities related to provisions?
b. According to the notes to the financial statements, what is the composition of long-term gross borrowings?
c. According to the accounting policy note to the financial statements, how are borrowings measured?
d. Determine the amount of fixed-rate and adjustable-rate (floating) borrowings (gross) that the company reports.

Answers to IFRS Self-Test Questions

1. a 2. a 3. c 4. c

CHAPTER 11

Reporting and Analyzing Stockholders' Equity

Chapter Preview

Corporations like **Facebook** and **Google** have substantial resources at their disposal. In fact, the corporation is the dominant form of business organization in the United States in terms of sales, earnings, and number of employees. All of the 500 largest U.S. companies are corporations. In this chapter, we look at the essential features of a corporation and explain the accounting for a corporation's capital stock transactions.

Feature Story

Oh Well, I Guess I'll Get Rich

Suppose you started one of the fastest-growing companies in the history of business. Now suppose that by "going public"— issuing stock of your company to outside investors who are foaming at the mouth for the chance to buy its shares—you would instantly become one of the richest people in the world. Would you hesitate?

That is exactly what Mark Zuckerberg, the founder of **Facebook**, did. Many people who start high-tech companies go public as soon as possible to cash in on their riches. But Zuckerberg was reluctant to do so. To understand why, you need to understand the advantages and disadvantages of being a public company.

The main motivation for issuing shares to the public is to raise money so you can grow your business. However, unlike a manufacturer or even an online retailer, Facebook doesn't need major physical resources, it doesn't have inventory, and it doesn't really need much money for marketing. But why not go public anyway, so the company would have some extra cash on hand—and so you personally get rich? As head of a closely held, nonpublic company, Zuckerberg was subject to far fewer regulations than a public company. Prior to going public, Zuckerberg could basically run the company however he wanted to.

For example, early in 2012, Facebook shocked the investment community by purchasing the photo-sharing service Instagram. The purchase was startling both for its speed (over a weekend) and price ($1 billion). Zuckerberg basically didn't seek anyone's approval. He thought it was a good idea, so he just did it. The structured decision-making process of a public company would make it very difficult for a public company to move that fast.

Speed is useful, but it is likely that Facebook will make even bigger acquisitions in the future. To survive among the likes of **Microsoft**, **Google**, and **Apple**, it needs lots of cash. To raise that amount of money, the company really needed to go public. So in 2012, Mark Zuckerberg reluctantly made Facebook a public company, thus becoming one of the richest people in the world.

Chapter Outline

LEARNING OBJECTIVES

LO 1 Discuss the major characteristics of a corporation.	• Characteristics of a corporation • Forming a corporation • Stockholder rights • Stock issue considerations • Corporate capital	**DO IT! 1a** Corporate Organization **DO IT! 1b** Corporate Capital
LO 2 Explain how to account for the issuance of common, preferred, and treasury stock.	• Accounting for common stock • Accounting for preferred stock • Accounting for treasury stock	**DO IT! 2a** Issuance of Stock **DO IT! 2b** Treasury Stock
LO 3 Explain how to account for cash dividends, stock dividends, and stock splits.	• Cash dividends • Dividend preferences • Stock dividends • Stock splits	**DO IT! 3a** Preferred Stock Dividends **DO IT! 3b** Stock Dividends and Stock Splits
LO 4 Discuss how stockholders' equity is reported and analyzed.	• Retained earnings • Retained earnings restrictions • Balance sheet presentation of stockholders' equity • Analysis of stockholders' equity • Debt versus equity decision	**DO IT! 4a** Stockholders' Equity Section **DO IT! 4b** Analyzing Stockholders' Equity

Go to the Review and Practice section at the end of the chapter for a targeted summary and practice applications with solutions.
Visit WileyPLUS for additional tutorials and practice opportunities.

Corporate Form of Organization

LEARNING OBJECTIVE 1
Discuss the major characteristics of a corporation.

In 1819, Chief Justice John Marshall defined a corporation as "an artificial being, invisible, intangible, and existing only in contemplation of law." This definition is the foundation for the prevailing legal interpretation that a **corporation** is an **entity separate and distinct from its owners** (see **Decision Tools**).

A corporation is created by law, and its continued existence depends upon the statutes of the state in which it is incorporated. As a legal entity, a corporation has most of the rights and privileges of a person. The major exceptions relate to privileges that only a living person can exercise, such as the right to vote or to hold public office. A corporation is subject to the same duties and responsibilities as a person. For example, it must abide by the laws, and it must pay taxes.

Two common ways to classify corporations are by **purpose** and by **ownership**. A corporation may be organized for the purpose of making a profit, or it may be not-for-profit. For-profit corporations include such well-known companies as **McDonald's**, **Nike**, **PepsiCo**, and **Facebook**. Not-for-profit corporations are organized for charitable, medical, or educational purposes. Examples are the **Salvation Army** and the **American Cancer Society**.

Classification by ownership differentiates publicly held and privately held corporations. A **publicly held corporation** may have thousands of stockholders. Its stock is regularly traded on a national securities exchange such as the New York Stock Exchange or NASDAQ. Examples are **IBM**, **Caterpillar**, and **Apple**.

In contrast, a **privately held corporation** usually has only a few stockholders, and does not offer its stock for sale to the general public (see **Alternative Terminology**). Privately held companies are generally much smaller than publicly held companies, although some notable exceptions exist. Before going public, Facebook was one example; **Cargill Inc.**, a private corporation that trades in grain and other commodities, is one of the largest companies in the United States.

> **Decision Tools**
> Understanding the costs and benefits of different types of business organizations helps managers determine if incorporating is in the best interest of the company.

> **ALTERNATIVE TERMINOLOGY**
> Privately held corporations are also referred to as *closely held corporations.*

Characteristics of a Corporation

In 1964, when **Nike**'s founders Phil Knight and Bill Bowerman were just getting started in the running shoe business, they formed their original organization as a partnership. In 1968, they reorganized the company as a corporation. A number of characteristics distinguish corporations from proprietorships and partnerships. We explain the most important of these characteristics below.

Separate Legal Existence

As an entity separate and distinct from its owners, the corporation acts under its own name rather than in the name of its stockholders. **Facebook** may buy, own, and sell property. It may borrow money, and it may enter into legally binding contracts in its own name. It may also sue or be sued, and it pays its own taxes.

In a partnership, the acts of the owners (partners) bind the partnership. In contrast, the acts of its owners (stockholders) do not bind the corporation unless such owners are **agents** of the corporation. For example, if you owned shares of Facebook stock, you would not have the right to purchase inventory for the company unless you were designated as an agent of the corporation.

Stockholders
Legal existence separate from owners

Limited Liability of Stockholders

Since a corporation is a separate legal entity, creditors have recourse only to corporate assets to satisfy their claims. The liability of stockholders is normally limited to their investment in the corporation. Creditors have no legal claim on the personal assets of the owners unless fraud has occurred. Even in the event of bankruptcy, stockholders' losses are generally limited to their capital investment in the corporation.

Stockholders
Limited liability of stockholders

Transferable Ownership Rights

Transferable ownership rights

Shares of capital stock give ownership in a corporation. These shares are transferable units. Stockholders may dispose of part or all of their interest in a corporation simply by selling their stock. The transfer of an ownership interest in a partnership requires the consent of each owner. In contrast, the transfer of stock is entirely at the discretion of the stockholder. It does not require the approval of either the corporation or other stockholders.

The transfer of ownership rights between stockholders normally has no effect on the daily operating activities of the corporation. Nor does it affect the corporation's assets, liabilities, and total ownership equity. The transfer of these ownership rights is a transaction between individual owners. The company does not participate in the transfer of these ownership rights after the original sale of the capital stock.

Ability to Acquire Capital

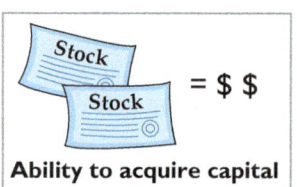
Ability to acquire capital

It is relatively easy for a corporation to obtain capital through the issuance of stock. Buying stock in a corporation is often attractive to an investor because a stockholder has limited liability and shares of stock are readily transferable. Also, numerous individuals can become stockholders by investing relatively small amounts of money.

Continuous Life

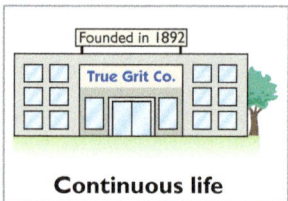
Continuous life

The life of a corporation is stated in its charter. The life may be perpetual, or it may be limited to a specific number of years. If it is limited, the company can extend the life through renewal of the charter. Since a corporation is a separate legal entity, its continuance as a going concern is not affected by the withdrawal, death, or incapacity of a stockholder, employee, or officer. As a result, a successful company can have a continuous and perpetual life.

Corporation Management

Stockholders legally own the corporation. However, they manage the corporation indirectly through a board of directors they elect. Mark Zuckerberg is the chairman of Facebook's board of directors. The board, in turn, formulates the operating policies for the company. The board also selects officers, such as a president and one or more vice presidents, to execute policy and to perform daily management functions. As a result of the Sarbanes-Oxley Act, the board is now required to monitor management's actions more closely. Many feel that the failures of **Enron**, **WorldCom**, and more recently **MF Global** could have been avoided by more diligent boards.

Illustration 11.1 presents a typical organization chart showing the delegation of responsibility. The chief executive officer (CEO) has overall responsibility for managing the business. As the organization chart shows, the CEO delegates responsibility to other officers. The chief accounting officer is the **controller**. The controller's responsibilities include (1) maintaining the accounting records, (2) ensuring an adequate system of internal control, and (3) preparing financial statements, tax returns, and internal reports. The **treasurer** has custody of the corporation's funds and is responsible for maintaining the company's cash position.

The organizational structure of a corporation enables a company to hire professional managers to run the business (see **Ethics Note**). On the other hand, the separation of ownership and management often reduces an owner's ability to actively manage the company.

ETHICS NOTE

Managers who are not owners are often compensated based on the performance of the firm. They thus may be tempted to exaggerate firm performance by inflating income figures.

Government Regulations

Government regulations

A corporation is subject to numerous state and federal regulations. For example, state laws usually prescribe the requirements for issuing stock, the distributions of earnings permitted to stockholders, and the acceptable methods for buying back and retiring stock. Federal securities laws govern the sale of capital stock to the general public. Also, most publicly held corporations are required to make extensive disclosure of their financial affairs to the Securities and Exchange Commission (SEC) through quarterly and annual reports (Forms 10Q and 10K). In addition, when a corporation lists its stock on organized securities exchanges, it must comply with the reporting requirements of these exchanges. Government regulations are designed to protect the owners of the corporation.

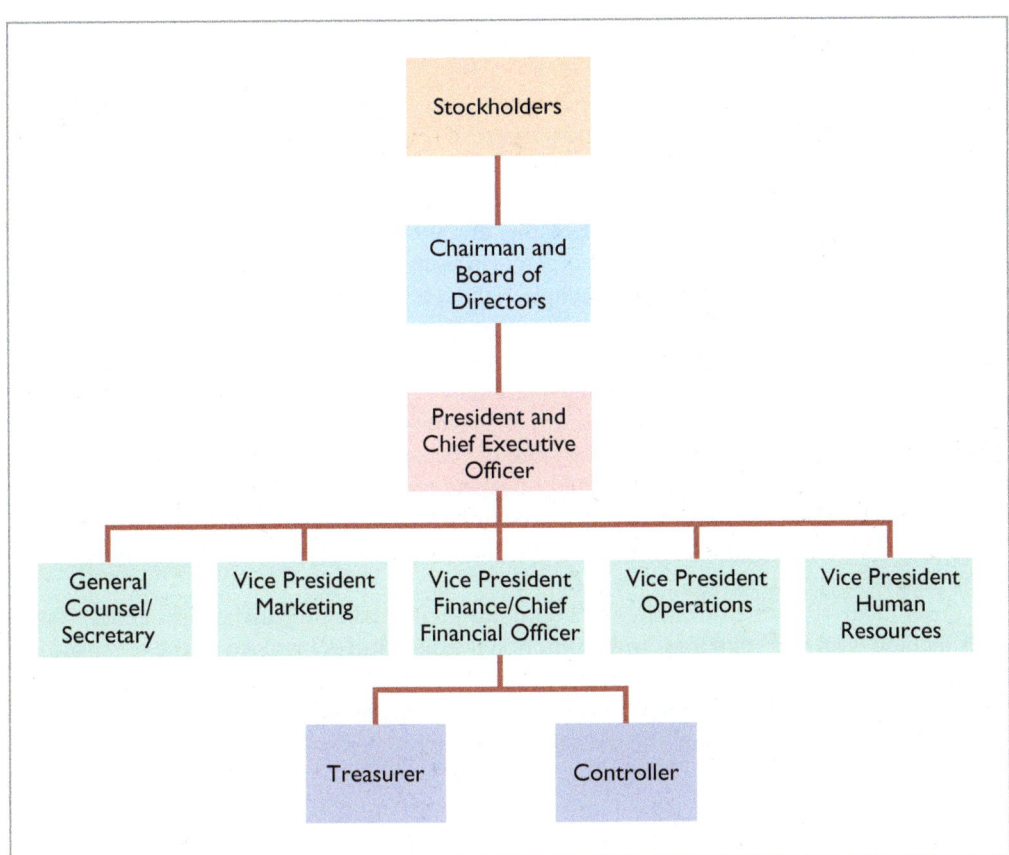

ILLUSTRATION 11.1

Corporation organization chart

Additional Taxes

Owners of proprietorships and partnerships report their share of earnings on their personal income tax returns. The individual owner then pays taxes on this amount. Corporations, on the other hand, must pay federal and state income taxes **as a separate legal entity**. These taxes can be substantial. They can amount to as much as 40% of taxable income.

In addition, stockholders must pay taxes on cash dividends (pro rata distributions of net income). Thus, many argue that the government taxes corporate income **twice (double taxation)**—once at the corporate level and again at the individual level.

In summary, Illustration 11.2 shows the advantages and disadvantages of a corporation compared to a proprietorship and a partnership.

Additional taxes

Advantages	Disadvantages
Separate legal existence	Corporation management—separation of ownership and management
Limited liability of stockholders	Government regulations
Transferable ownership rights	Additional taxes
Ability to acquire capital	
Continuous life	
Corporation management—professional managers	

ILLUSTRATION 11.2

Advantages and disadvantages of a corporation

Other Forms of Business Organization

A variety of "hybrid" organizational forms—forms that combine different attributes of partnerships and corporations—now exist. For example, one type of corporate form, called an **S corporation**, allows for legal treatment as a corporation but tax treatment as a partnership—that is, no double taxation. Because of changes to the S corporation's rules, more small- and medium-sized businesses now may choose S corporation treatment. One of the primary criteria is that the company cannot have more than 100 shareholders. Other forms of organization include limited partnerships, limited liability partnerships (LLPs), and limited liability companies (LLCs).

Forming a Corporation

ALTERNATIVE TERMINOLOGY
The charter is often referred to as the *articles of incorporation.*

A corporation is formed by grant of a state **charter** (see **Alternative Terminology**). The charter is a document that describes the name and purpose of the corporation, the types and number of shares of stock that are authorized to be issued, the names of the individuals that formed the company, and the number of shares that these individuals agreed to purchase. Regardless of the number of states in which a corporation has operating divisions, it is incorporated in only one state.

It is to the company's advantage to incorporate in a state whose laws are favorable to the corporate form of business organization. For example, although **Facebook** has its headquarters in California, it is incorporated in Delaware. In fact, more and more corporations have been incorporating in states with rules that favor existing management. For example, **Gulf Oil** changed its state of incorporation to Delaware to thwart possible unfriendly takeovers. There, certain defensive tactics against takeovers can be approved by the board of directors alone, without a vote by shareholders.

Upon receipt of its charter from the state of incorporation, the corporation establishes **by-laws**. The by-laws establish the internal rules and procedures for conducting the affairs of the corporation. Corporations engaged in interstate commerce must also obtain a **license** from each state in which they do business. The license subjects the corporation's operating activities to the general corporation laws of the state.

Costs incurred in the formation of a corporation are called **organization costs**. These costs include legal and state fees, and promotional expenditures involved in the organization of the business. **Corporations expense organization costs as incurred.** Determining the amount and timing of future benefits is so difficult that it is standard procedure to take a conservative approach of expensing these costs immediately.

Stockholder Rights

When chartered, the corporation may begin selling shares of stock. When a corporation has only one class of stock, it is **common stock**. Each share of common stock gives the stockholder the ownership rights pictured in **Illustration 11.3**. The articles of incorporation or the by-laws state the ownership rights of a share of stock.

ILLUSTRATION 11.3
Ownership rights of stockholders

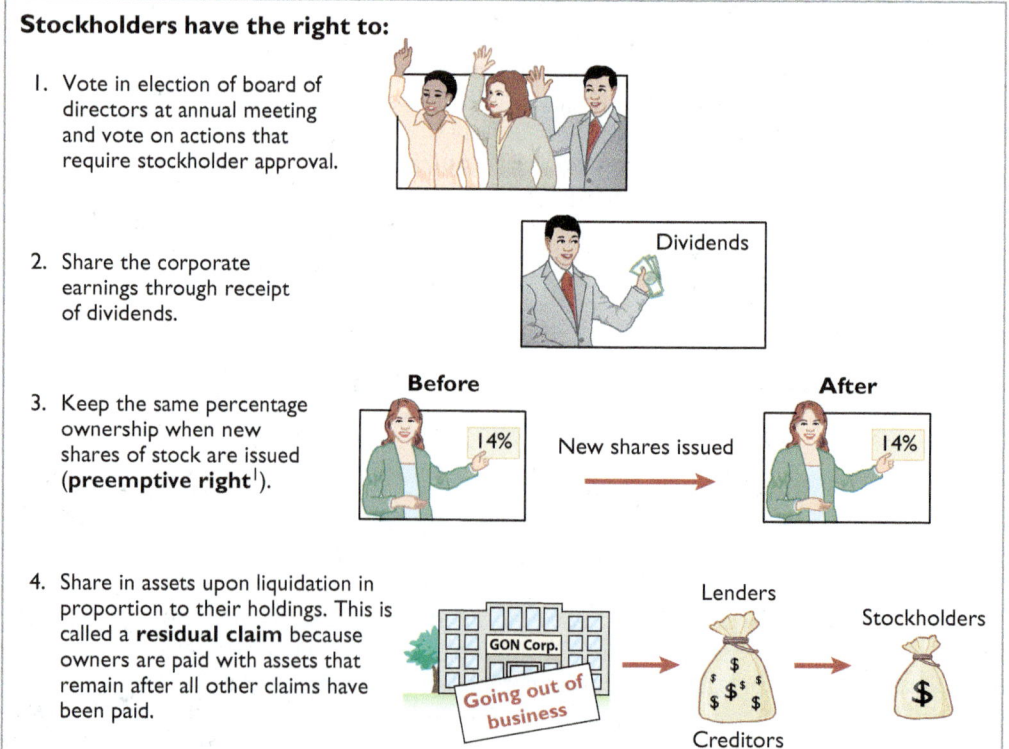

[1] A number of companies have eliminated the preemptive right because they believe it makes an unnecessary and cumbersome demand on management. For example, by stockholder approval, **IBM** has dropped its preemptive right for stockholders.

Proof of stock ownership is evidenced by a form known as a **stock certificate**. As **Illustration 11.4** shows, the face of the certificate shows the name of the corporation, the stockholder's name, the class and special features of the stock, the number of shares owned, and the signatures of authorized corporate officials. Prenumbered certificates facilitate accountability. They may be issued for any quantity of shares.

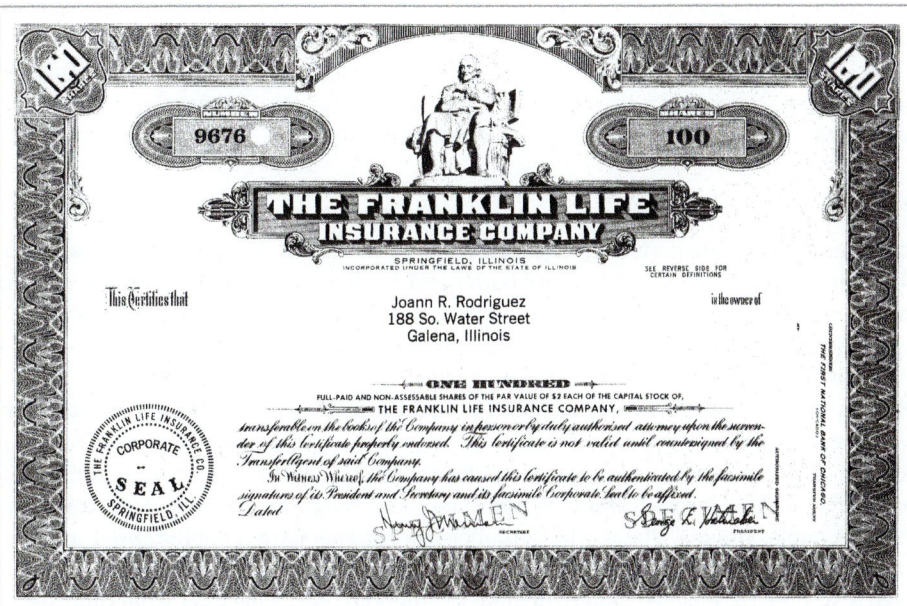

ILLUSTRATION 11.4

A stock certificate

People, Planet, and Profit Insight

© Robert Churchill/iStockphoto

The Impact of Corporate Social Responsibility

A survey conducted by **Institutional Shareholder Services**, a proxy advisory firm, shows that 83% of investors now believe environmental and social factors can significantly impact shareholder value over the long term. This belief is clearly visible in the rising level of support for shareholder proposals requesting action related to social and environmental issues.

The following table shows that the number of corporate social responsibility (CSR) related shareholder proposals rose from 150 in 2000 to 191 in 2010. Moreover, those proposals received average voting support of 18.4% of votes cast versus just 7.5% a decade earlier.

Trends in Shareholder Proposals on Corporate Responsibility			
	2000	2005	2010
Number of proposals voted	150	155	191
Average voting support	7.5%	9.9%	18.4%
Percent proposals receiving >10% support	16.7%	31.2%	52.1%

Source: Investor Responsibility Research Center, Ernst & Young, *Seven Questions CEOs and Boards Should Ask About: "Triple Bottom Line" Reporting.*

Why are CSR-related shareholder proposals increasing? (Go to WileyPLUS for this answer and additional questions.)

Stock Issue Considerations

Although **Facebook** incorporated in 2004, it did not sell stock to the public until 2012. At that time, Facebook evidently decided it would benefit from the infusion of cash that a public sale would bring. When a corporation decides to issue stock, it must resolve a number of basic questions: How many shares should it authorize for sale? How should it issue the stock? What value should the corporation assign to the stock? We address these questions in the following sections.

Authorized Stock

The charter indicates the amount of stock that a corporation is **authorized** to sell. The total amount of **authorized stock** at the time of incorporation normally anticipates both initial

Indirect issuance

and subsequent capital needs. As a result, the number of shares authorized generally exceeds the number initially sold. If it sells all authorized stock, a corporation must obtain consent of the state to amend its charter before it can issue additional shares.

The authorization of capital stock does not result in a formal accounting entry. The reason is that the event has no immediate effect on either corporate assets or stockholders' equity. However, the number of authorized shares is often reported in the stockholders' equity section. For example, Facebook has approximately 9 billion authorized shares. It is then simple to determine the number of unissued shares that the corporation can issue without amending the charter: subtract the total shares issued from the total authorized. For example, if Advanced Micro was authorized to sell 100,000 shares of common stock and issued 80,000 shares, 20,000 shares would remain unissued.

Issuance of Stock

A corporation can issue common stock **directly** to investors. Alternatively, it can issue the stock **indirectly** through an investment banking firm that specializes in bringing securities to the attention of prospective investors. Direct issue is typical in closely held companies. Indirect issue is customary for a publicly held corporation.

In an indirect issue, the investment banking firm may agree to **underwrite** the entire stock issue. In this arrangement, the investment banker buys the stock from the corporation at a stipulated price and resells the shares to investors. The corporation thus avoids any risk of being unable to sell the shares. Also, it obtains immediate use of the cash received from the underwriter. The investment banking firm, in turn, assumes the risk of reselling the shares, in return for an underwriting fee.[2] For example, Google (the world's number-one Internet search engine) used underwriters when it issued a highly successful initial public offering, raising $1.67 billion. The underwriters charged a 3% underwriting fee (approximately $50 million) on Google's stock offering.

How does a corporation set the price for a new issue of stock? Among the factors to be considered are (1) the company's anticipated future earnings, (2) its expected dividend rate per share, (3) its current financial position, (4) the current state of the economy, and (5) the current state of the securities market. The calculation can be complex and is properly the subject of a finance course.

Anatomy of a Fraud

The president, chief operating officer, and chief financial officer of SafeNet, a software encryption company, were each awarded employee stock options by the company's board of directors as part of their compensation package. Stock options enable an employee to buy a company's stock sometime in the future at the price that existed when the stock option was awarded. For example, suppose that you received stock options today, when the stock price of your company was $30. Three years later, if the stock price rose to $100, you could "exercise" your options and buy the stock for $30 per share, thereby making $70 per share. After being awarded their stock options, the three employees changed the award dates in the company's records to dates in the past, when the company's stock was trading at historical lows. For instance, using the previous example, they would choose a past date when the stock was selling for $10 per share, rather than the $30 price on the actual award date. This would increase the profit from exercising the options to $90 per share.

Total take: $1.7 million

The Missing Control

Independent internal verification. The company's board of directors should have ensured that the awards were properly administered. For example, the date on the minutes from the board meeting could be compared to the dates that were recorded for the awards. In addition, the dates should again be confirmed upon exercise.

Par and No-Par Value Stocks

Par value stock is capital stock to which the charter has assigned a value per share. Years ago, par value determined the **legal capital** per share that a company must retain in the business for

---

[2]Alternatively, the investment banking firm may agree only to enter into a **best-efforts contract** with the corporation. In such cases, the banker agrees to sell as many shares as possible at a specified price. The corporation bears the risk of unsold stock. Under a best-efforts arrangement, the banking firm is paid a fee or commission for its services.

the protection of corporate creditors. That amount was not available for withdrawal by stockholders. Thus, in the past, most states required the corporation to sell its shares at par or above.

However, par value was often immaterial relative to the value of the company's stock—even at the time of issue. Thus, its usefulness as a protective device to creditors was questionable. For example, **Facebook**'s par value is $0.000006 per share, yet its market price recently was $84. Thus, par has no relationship with market price. In the vast majority of cases, it is an immaterial amount. As a consequence, today many states do not require a par value. Instead, they use other means to protect creditors.

No-par value stock is capital stock to which the charter has not assigned a value. No-par value stock is fairly common today. For example, **Nike** and **Procter & Gamble** both have no-par stock. In many states, the board of directors assigns a **stated value** to no-par shares.

DO IT! 1a | Corporate Organization

Indicate whether each of the following statements is true or false. If false, indicate how to correct the statement.

_____ 1. Similar to partners in a partnership, stockholders of a corporation have unlimited liability.

_____ 2. It is relatively easy for a corporation to obtain capital through the issuance of stock.

_____ 3. The separation of ownership and management is an advantage of the corporate form of business.

_____ 4. The journal entry to record the authorization of capital stock includes a credit to the appropriate capital stock account.

_____ 5. All states require a par value per share for capital stock.

ACTION PLAN
- Review the characteristics of a corporation and understand which are advantages and which are disadvantages.
- Understand that corporations raise capital through the issuance of stock, which can be par or no-par.

Solution

1. False. The liability of stockholders is normally limited to their investment in the corporation.
2. True. **3.** False. The separation of ownership and management is a disadvantage of the corporate form of business. **4.** False. The authorization of capital stock does not result in a formal accounting entry. **5.** False. Many states do not require a par value.

Related exercise material: **BE11.1, DO IT! 11.1a, E11.1, and E11.2.**

Corporate Capital

Owners' equity is identified by various names: **stockholders' equity, shareholders' equity,** or **corporate capital**. The stockholders' equity section of a corporation's balance sheet consists of two parts: (1) paid-in (contributed) capital and (2) retained earnings (earned capital).

The distinction between **paid-in capital** and **retained earnings** is important from both a legal and a financial point of view. Legally, corporations can make distributions of earnings (declare dividends) out of retained earnings in all states. However, in many states they cannot declare dividends out of paid-in capital. Management, stockholders, and others often look to retained earnings for the continued existence and growth of the corporation.

Paid-In Capital

Paid-in capital is the total amount of cash and other assets paid in to the corporation by stockholders in exchange for capital stock. As noted earlier, when a corporation has only one class of stock, it is **common stock**.

Retained Earnings

Retained earnings is net income that a corporation retains for future use. Net income is recorded in Retained Earnings by a closing entry that debits Income Summary and credits

Retained Earnings. For example, assuming that net income for Delta Robotics in its first year of operations is $130,000, the closing entry is:

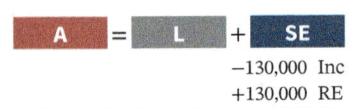

Cash Flows
no effect

Income Summary	130,000	
Retained Earnings		130,000
(To close Income Summary and transfer net income		
to Retained Earnings)		

If Delta Robotics has a balance of $800,000 in common stock at the end of its first year, its stockholders' equity section is as shown in **Illustration 11.5**.

ILLUSTRATION 11.5
Stockholders' equity section

Delta Robotics
Balance Sheet (partial)

Stockholders' equity		
Paid-in capital		
Common stock	$800,000	
Retained earnings	130,000	
Total stockholders' equity		$930,000

Illustration 11.6 compares the owners' equity (stockholders' equity) accounts reported on a balance sheet for a proprietorship and a corporation.

ILLUSTRATION 11.6
Comparison of owners' equity accounts

Proprietorship

Owner's Capital
| | Normal bal. |

Corporation

Common Stock
| | Normal bal. |

Retained Earnings
| | Normal bal. |

ACTION PLAN
- Record net income in Retained Earnings by a closing entry in which Income Summary is debited and Retained Earnings is credited.
- In the stockholders' equity section, show (1) paid-in capital and (2) retained earnings.

DO IT! 1b | Corporate Capital

At the end of its first year of operation, Doral Corporation has $750,000 of common stock and net income of $122,000. Prepare (a) the closing entry for net income and (b) the stockholders' equity section at year-end.

Solution

a.
Income Summary	122,000	
Retained Earnings		122,000
(To close Income Summary and transfer net		
income to Retained Earnings)		

b.
Stockholders' equity		
Paid-in capital		
Common stock	$750,000	
Retained earnings	122,000	
Total stockholders' equity		$872,000

Related exercise material: **DO IT! 11.1b**.

Accounting for Common, Preferred, and Treasury Stock

LEARNING OBJECTIVE 2
Explain how to account for the issuance of common, preferred, and treasury stock.

Accounting for Common Stock

Let's now look at how to account for new issues of common stock (see **Helpful Hint**). The primary objectives in accounting for the issuance of common stock are (1) to identify the specific sources of paid-in capital and (2) to maintain the distinction between paid-in capital and retained earnings. As shown below, **the issuance of common stock affects only paid-in capital accounts**.

HELPFUL HINT
Stock is sometimes issued in exchange for services (payment to attorneys or consultants, for example) or for noncash assets (land or buildings). The value recorded for the shares issued is determined by either the market price of the shares or the value of the good or service received, depending upon which amount the company can more readily determine.

Issuing Par Value Common Stock for Cash

As discussed earlier, par value does not indicate a stock's market price. The cash proceeds from issuing par value stock may be equal to, greater than, or less than par value. When a company records the issuance of common stock for cash, it credits the par value of the shares to Common Stock and records in a separate paid-in capital account the portion of the proceeds that is above or below par value.

To illustrate, assume that Hydro-Slide, Inc. issues 1,000 shares of $1 par value common stock at par for cash. The entry to record this transaction is as follows.

Cash	1,000	
Common Stock		1,000
(To record issuance of 1,000 shares of $1 par common stock at par)		

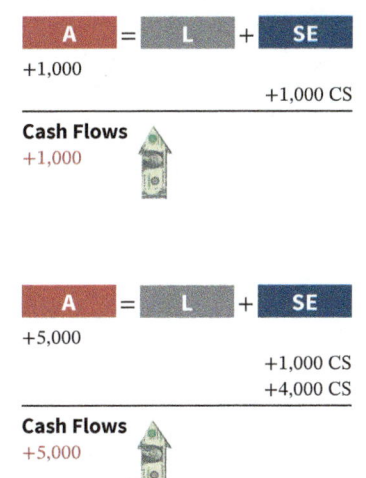

Now assume Hydro-Slide, Inc. issues an additional 1,000 shares of the $1 par value common stock for cash at $5 per share. The amount received above the par value, in this case $4 ($5 − $1), would be credited to Paid-in Capital in Excess of Par Value. The entry is as follows.

Cash	5,000	
Common Stock (1,000 × $1)		1,000
Paid-in Capital in Excess of Par Value		4,000
(To record issuance of 1,000 shares of common stock in excess of par)		

The total paid-in capital from these two transactions is $6,000. If Hydro-Slide, Inc. has retained earnings of $27,000, the stockholders' equity section of the balance sheet is as shown in **Illustration 11.7**.

Hydro-Slide, Inc.
Balance Sheet (partial)

Stockholders' equity	
Paid-in capital	
Common stock	$ 2,000
Paid-in capital in excess of par value	**4,000**
Total paid-in capital	6,000
Retained earnings	27,000
Total stockholders' equity	$33,000

ILLUSTRATION 11.7
Stockholders' equity—paid-in capital in excess of par value

Some companies issue no-par stock with a stated value. For accounting purposes, companies treat the stated value in the same way as the par value. For example, if in our Hydro-Slide example the stock was no-par stock with a stated value of $1, the entries would be the same as those presented for the par stock except the term "Par Value" would be replaced with "Stated Value." If a company issues no-par stock that does not have a stated value, then it credits to the Common Stock account the full amount received. In such a case, there is no need for the Paid-in Capital in Excess of Stated Value account.

Accounting for Preferred Stock

To appeal to a larger segment of potential investors, a corporation may issue an additional class of stock, called preferred stock. **Preferred stock** has contractual provisions that give it preference or priority over common stock in certain areas. Typically, preferred stockholders have a priority in relation to (1) dividends and (2) assets in the event of liquidation. However, they sometimes do not have voting rights. **Facebook** had 543 million preferred shares held by investors at the end of 2011, prior to going public. Approximately 6% of U.S. companies have one or more classes of preferred stock.

Like common stock, companies issue preferred stock for cash or for noncash consideration. The entries for these transactions are similar to the entries for common stock. When a corporation has more than one class of stock, each paid-in capital account title should identify the stock to which it relates (e.g., Preferred Stock, Common Stock, Paid-in Capital in Excess of Par Value—Preferred Stock, and Paid-in Capital in Excess of Par Value—Common Stock).

Assume that Stine Corporation issues 10,000 shares of $10 par value preferred stock for $12 cash per share. The entry to record the issuance is as follows.

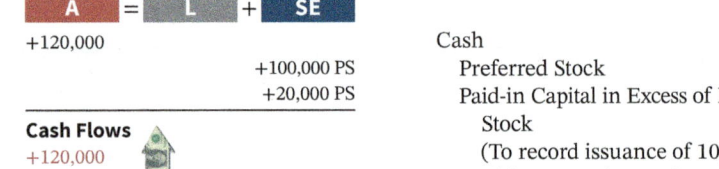

Cash	120,000	
Preferred Stock		100,000
Paid-in Capital in Excess of Par Value—Preferred		
Stock		20,000
(To record issuance of 10,000 shares		
of $10 par value preferred stock)		

Preferred stock has either a par value or no-par value. In the stockholders' equity section of the balance sheet, companies show preferred stock first because of its dividend and liquidation preferences over common stock.

Investor Insight   Facebook

How to Read Stock Quotes

Emmanuel Dunand/ AFP/Getty Images

Organized exchanges trade the stock of publicly held companies at dollar prices per share established by the interaction between buyers and sellers. For each listed security, the financial press reports the high and low prices of the stock during the year, the total volume of stock traded on a given day, the high and low prices for the day, and the closing market price, with the net change for the day. **Facebook** is listed on the Nasdaq exchange. Here is a recent listing for Facebook:

	52 Weeks						Net
Stock	High	Low	Volume	High	Low	Close	Change
Facebook	86.07	54.66	54,156,600	85.59	83.11	84.63	.629

These numbers indicate the following. The high and low market prices for the last 52 weeks have been $86.07 and $54.66. The trading volume for the day was 54,156,600 shares. The high, low, and closing prices for that date were $85.59, $83.11, and $84.63, respectively. The net change for the day was a decrease of $0.629 per share.

For stocks traded on organized exchanges, how are the dollar prices per share established? What factors might influence the price of shares in the marketplace? (Go to WileyPLUS for this answer and additional questions.)

> ### DO IT! 2a | Issuance of Stock
>
> Cayman Corporation begins operations on March 1 by issuing 100,000 shares of $1 par value common stock for cash at $12 per share. On March 28, Cayman issues 1,500 shares of $10 par value preferred stock for cash at $30 per share. Journalize the issuance of the common and preferred shares.
>
> **Solution**
>
> | Date | Account | Debit | Credit |
> |---|---|---|---|
> | Mar. 1 | Cash | 1,200,000 | |
> | | Common Stock (100,000 × $1) | | 100,000 |
> | | Paid-in Capital in Excess of Par Value— | | |
> | | Common Stock | | 1,100,000 |
> | | (To record issuance of 100,000 shares at $12 per share) | | |
> | Mar. 28 | Cash | 45,000 | |
> | | Preferred Stock (1,500 × $10) | | 15,000 |
> | | Paid-in Capital in Excess of Par Value— | | |
> | | Preferred Stock | | 30,000 |
> | | (To record issuance of 1,500 shares at $30 per share) | | |
>
> Related exercise material: **BE11.2, BE11.3, BE11.4, DO IT! 11.2a, and E11.3.**
>
> **ACTION PLAN**
> - In issuing shares for cash, credit Common Stock for par value per share.
> - Credit any additional proceeds in excess of par to a separate paid-in capital account.
> - For the cash equivalent price, use either the fair value of what is given up or the fair value of what is received, whichever is more clearly determinable.

Accounting for Treasury Stock

Treasury stock is a corporation's own stock that has been reacquired by the corporation and is being held for future use. A corporation may acquire treasury stock for various reasons:

1. To reissue the shares to officers and employees under bonus and stock compensation plans.
2. To increase trading of the company's stock in the securities market. Companies expect that buying their own stock will signal that management believes the stock is underpriced, which they hope will enhance its market price.
3. To have additional shares available for use in acquiring other companies.
4. To reduce the number of shares outstanding and thereby increase earnings per share.

A less frequent reason for purchasing treasury shares is to eliminate hostile shareholders by buying them out.

Many corporations have treasury stock. For example, in the United States approximately 65% of companies have treasury stock. During one quarter, companies in the **Standard & Poor's** 500-stock index spent a record of about $118 billion to buy treasury stock. In a recent year, **Nike** purchased more than 6 million treasury shares. At one point, stock repurchases were so substantial that a study by two Federal Reserve economists suggested that a sharp reduction in corporate purchases of treasury shares might result in a sharp drop in the value of the U.S. stock market.

Purchase of Treasury Stock

The purchase of treasury stock is generally accounted for by the **cost method**. This method derives its name from the fact that the Treasury Stock account is maintained at the cost of shares purchased. Under the cost method, **companies increase (debit) Treasury Stock by the price paid to reacquire the shares. Treasury Stock decreases by the same amount when the company later sells the shares.**

To illustrate, assume that on January 1, 2022, the stockholders' equity section for Mead, Inc. has 100,000 shares of $5 par value common stock issued and outstanding (currently held by stockholders). All of the shares were issued at par value. Retained earnings is $200,000. **Illustration 11.8** shows the stockholders' equity section of the balance sheet before purchase of treasury stock.

ILLUSTRATION 11.8
Stockholders' equity with no treasury stock

Mead, Inc.
Balance Sheet (partial)

Stockholders' equity	
Paid-in capital	
Common stock, $5 par value, 400,000 shares authorized,	
100,000 shares issued and outstanding	$500,000
Retained earnings	200,000
Total stockholders' equity	$700,000

On February 1, 2022, Mead acquires 4,000 shares of its stock at $8 per share. The entry is as follows.

Feb. 1	Treasury Stock		32,000	
	Cash			32,000
	(To record purchase of 4,000 shares of treasury stock at $8 per share)			

HELPFUL HINT
Treasury Stock is a contra stockholders' equity account.

The Treasury Stock account would increase by the cost of the shares purchased ($32,000), (see **Helpful Hint**). The original paid-in capital account, Common Stock, would not be affected because **the number of issued shares does not change**. That is, once a share has been issued, a subsequent repurchase of that share as treasury stock does not affect its status as "issued."

Companies show treasury stock as a deduction from total paid-in capital and retained earnings in the stockholders' equity section of the balance sheet. **Illustration 11.9** shows this presentation for Mead, Inc. Thus, the acquisition of treasury stock reduces stockholders' equity.

ILLUSTRATION 11.9
Stockholders' equity with treasury stock

Mead, Inc.
Balance Sheet (partial)

Stockholders' equity	
Paid-in capital	
Common stock, $5 par value, 400,000 shares authorized,	
100,000 shares issued and 96,000 shares outstanding	$500,000
Retained earnings	200,000
Total paid-in capital and retained earnings	700,000
Less: Treasury stock (4,000 shares)	**32,000**
Total stockholders' equity	$668,000

ETHICS NOTE
The purchase of treasury stock reduces the cushion for creditors. To protect creditors, many states require that a portion of retained earnings equal to the cost of the treasury stock purchased be restricted from being paid as dividends.

Company balance sheets disclose both the number of shares issued (100,000) and the number in the treasury (4,000). The difference is the number of shares of stock outstanding (96,000). The term **outstanding stock** means the number of shares of issued stock that are currently being held by stockholders.

In a bold (and some would say risky) move, **Reebok** at one time bought back nearly a third of its shares. This repurchase of shares dramatically reduced Reebok's available cash (see **Ethics Note**). In fact, the company borrowed significant funds to accomplish the repurchase. In a press release, management stated that it was repurchasing the shares because it believed that the stock was severely underpriced. The repurchase of so many shares was meant to signal management's belief in good future earnings.

Skeptics, however, suggested that Reebok's management repurchased the shares to make it less likely that the company would be acquired by another company (in which case Reebok's top managers would likely lose their jobs). Acquiring companies like to purchase companies with large cash reserves so they can pay off debt used in the acquisition. By depleting its cash through the purchase of treasury shares, Reebok became a less likely acquisition target.

DO IT! 2b | Treasury Stock

Santa Anita Inc. purchases 3,000 shares of its $50 par value common stock for $180,000 cash on July 1. It expects to hold the shares in the treasury until resold. Journalize the treasury stock transaction.

Solution

July 1	Treasury Stock	180,000	
	Cash		180,000
	(To record the purchase of 3,000 shares at $60 per share)		

Related exercise material: **BE11.5, DO IT! 11.2b, E11.4, E11.5, and E11.8.**

ACTION PLAN
- Record the purchase of treasury stock at cost.
- Report treasury stock as a deduction from stockholders' equity (contra account) at the bottom of the stockholders' equity section.

Cash Dividends, Stock Dividends, and Stock Splits

LEARNING OBJECTIVE 3
Explain how to account for cash dividends, stock dividends, and stock splits.

As noted earlier, a **dividend is a distribution by a corporation to its stockholders on a pro rata** (proportional to ownership) **basis**. Pro rata means that if you own, say, 10% of the common shares, you will receive 10% of the dividend. Dividends can take four forms: cash, property, scrip (promissory note to pay cash), or stock. Cash dividends predominate in practice, although companies also declare stock dividends with some frequency.

Investors are very interested in a company's dividend practices. In the financial press, **dividends are generally reported quarterly as a dollar amount per share**. (Sometimes they are reported on an annual basis.) For example, the recent **quarterly** dividend rate was 24 cents per share for **Nike**, 22 cents per share for **GE**, and 25 cents per share for **ConAgra Foods**. **Facebook** does not pay dividends.

Cash Dividends

A **cash dividend** is a pro rata (proportional to ownership) distribution of cash to stockholders. Cash dividends are not paid on treasury shares. For a corporation to pay a cash dividend, it must have the following.

1. **Retained earnings.** Payment of dividends from retained earnings is legal in all states. In addition, loan agreements frequently constrain companies to pay dividends only from retained earnings. Many states prohibit payment of dividends from legal capital. However, payment of dividends from paid-in capital in excess of par value is legal in some states.

2. **Adequate cash.** Recently, Facebook had a balance in retained earnings of $6,099 million but a cash balance of only $4,315 million. If it had wanted to pay a dividend equal to

its retained earnings, Facebook would have had to raise $1,784 million more in cash. It would have been unlikely to do this because it would not be able to pay this much in dividends in future years. In addition, such a dividend would completely deplete Facebook's balance in retained earnings, so it would not be able to pay a dividend in the next year unless it had positive net income.

3. **Declared dividends.** The board of directors has full authority to determine the amount of income to distribute in the form of dividends. Dividends are not a liability until they are declared.

The amount and timing of a dividend are important issues for management to consider. The payment of a large cash dividend could lead to liquidity problems for the company. Conversely, a small dividend or a missed dividend may cause unhappiness among stockholders who expect to receive a reasonable cash payment from the company on a periodic basis. Many companies declare and pay cash dividends quarterly. On the other hand, a number of high-growth companies pay no dividends, preferring to conserve cash to finance future capital expenditures.

Investors monitor a company's dividend practices. For example, regular dividend boosts in the face of irregular earnings can be a warning signal. Companies with high dividends and rising debt may be borrowing money to pay shareholders. On the other hand, low dividends may not be a negative sign because it may mean the company is reinvesting in itself, which may result in high returns through increases in the stock price. Presumably, investors seeking regular dividends buy stock in companies that pay periodic dividends, and those seeking growth in the stock price (capital gains) buy stock in companies that retain their earnings rather than pay dividends.

Entries for Cash Dividends

Three dates are important in connection with dividends: (1) the declaration date, (2) the record date, and (3) the payment date. Companies make accounting entries on the declaration date and the payment date.

On the **declaration date**, the board of directors formally authorizes the cash dividend and announces it to stockholders. The declaration of a cash dividend **commits the corporation to a binding legal obligation**. Thus, the company must make an entry to recognize the increase in Cash Dividends and the increase in the liability Dividends Payable.

To illustrate, assume that on December 1, 2022, the directors of Media General declare a $0.50 per share cash dividend on 100,000 shares of $10 par value common stock. The dividend is $50,000 (100,000 × $0.50). The entry to record the declaration is as follows.

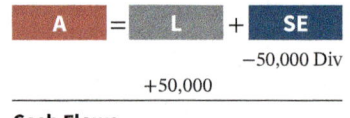

Cash Flows
no effect

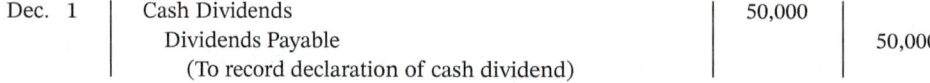

Declaration Date

Dec. 1	Cash Dividends	50,000	
	Dividends Payable		50,000
	(To record declaration of cash dividend)		

In Chapter 3, we used an account called Dividends to record a cash dividend. Here, we use the more specific title Cash Dividends to differentiate from other types of dividends, such as stock dividends. (*For homework problems, you should use the Cash Dividends account for recording dividend declarations*). Dividends Payable is a current liability. It will normally be paid within the next several months.

At the **record date**, the company determines ownership of the outstanding shares for dividend purposes (see **Helpful Hint**). The stockholders' records maintained by the corporation supply this information.

For Media General, the record date is December 22. No entry is required on the record date.

HELPFUL HINT

The record date is important in determining the dividend to be paid to each stockholder.

Record Date

Dec. 22 | No entry necessary

On the **payment date**, the company makes cash dividend payments to the stockholders on record as of December 22. It also records the payment of the dividend. If January 20 is the payment date for Media General, the entry on that date is as follows.

Cash Dividends, Stock Dividends, and Stock Splits 11-17

Payment Date

Jan. 20	Dividends Payable	50,000	
	Cash		50,000
	(To record payment of cash dividend)		

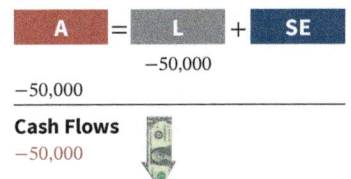

Note that payment of the dividend on the payment date reduces both current assets and current liabilities, but it has no effect on stockholders' equity. Cash Dividends is closed to Retained Earnings at the end of the accounting period. Thus, the cumulative effect of the **declaration and payment** of a cash dividend on a company's financial statements is to **decrease both stockholders' equity and total assets**.

Accounting Across the Organization

Palto/iStockphoto

Up, Down, and ??

The decision whether to pay a dividend, and how much to pay, is a very important management decision. As the chart below shows, from 2002 to 2007, many companies substantially increased their dividends, and total dividends paid by U.S. companies hit record levels. One reason for the increase is that Congress lowered, from 39% to 15%, the tax rate paid by investors on dividends received, making dividends more attractive to investors.

Then the financial crisis of 2008 occurred. As a result, in 2009, 804 companies cut their dividends (see the chart), the highest level since **Standard & Poor's** started collecting data in 1995. In 2010, some companies started to increase their dividends. In 2018, many companies increased dividend payouts in response to higher rates being paid on bonds.

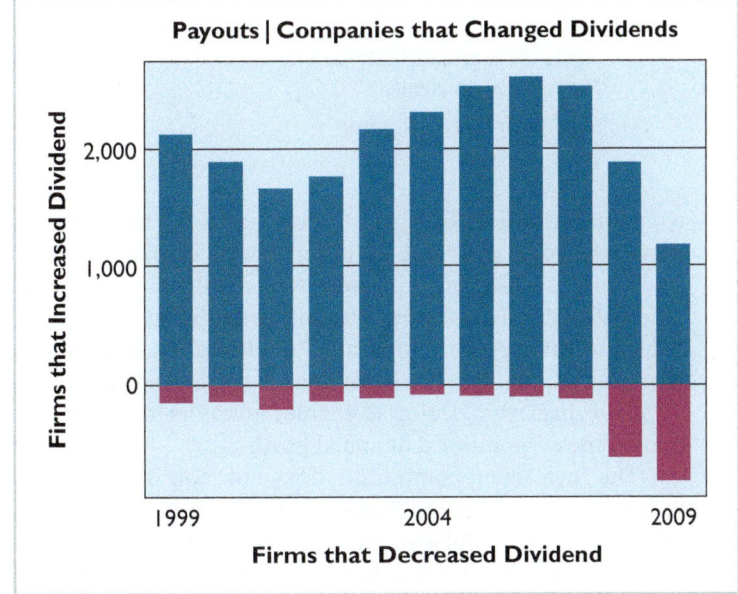

Sources: Matt Phillips and Jay Miller, "Last Year's Dividend Slash Was $58 Billion," *Wall Street Journal* (January 8, 2010), p. C5; and Michael Wursthorn, "Dividends Climb Amid Rising Competition from Bonds," *Wall Street Journal* (February 27, 2018).

What factors must management consider in deciding how large a dividend to pay? (Go to WileyPLUS for this answer and additional questions.)

Dividend Preferences

Preferred stockholders have the right to share in the distribution of corporate income before common stockholders. For example, if the dividend rate on preferred stock is $5 per share, common shareholders cannot receive any dividends in the current year until preferred stockholders have received $5 per share. The first claim to dividends does not, however, **guarantee** dividends. Dividends depend on many factors, such as adequate retained earnings and availability of cash.

For preferred stock, companies state the per share dividend amount as a percentage of the par value of the stock or as a specified amount. For example, **EarthLink** (before it merged with **Windstream Holdings**) specified a 3% dividend.

Most preferred stocks have a preference on corporate assets if the corporation fails. This feature provides security for the preferred stockholder. The preference to assets may be for the par value of the shares or for a specified liquidating value. For example, **Commonwealth Edison** issued preferred stock that entitled the holders to receive $31.80 per share, plus accrued and unpaid dividends, in the event of involuntary liquidation. The liquidation preference is used in litigation pertaining to bankruptcy lawsuits involving the respective claims of creditors and preferred stockholders.

Cumulative Dividend

Preferred stock contracts often contain a **cumulative dividend** feature. This feature stipulates that preferred stockholders must be paid both current-year dividends and any unpaid prior-year dividends before common stockholders are paid dividends. When preferred stock is cumulative, preferred dividends not declared that were supposed to be declared in a given period are called **dividends in arrears**.

To illustrate, assume that Scientific Leasing has 5,000 shares of 7%, $100 par value cumulative preferred stock outstanding. Each $100 share pays a $7 dividend (.07 × $100). The annual dividend is $35,000 (5,000 × $7 per share). If dividends are two years in arrears, preferred stockholders are entitled to receive in the current year the dividends as shown in **Illustration 11.10**.

ILLUSTRATION 11.10
Computation of total dividends to preferred stock

Dividends in arrears ($35,000 × 2)	$ 70,000
Current-year dividends	35,000
Total preferred dividends	**$105,000**

No distribution can be made to common stockholders until Scientific Leasing pays this entire preferred dividend. In other words, companies cannot pay dividends to common stockholders while any preferred stock dividend is in arrears.

Dividends in arrears are not considered a liability. No obligation exists until the board of directors formally "declares" that the corporation will pay a dividend. However, companies should disclose in the notes to the financial statements the amount of dividends in arrears. Doing so enables investors to assess the impact of this potential obligation on the corporation's financial position.

The investment community does not look favorably upon companies that are unable to meet their dividend obligations. As a financial officer noted in discussing one company's failure to pay its cumulative preferred dividend for a period of time, "Not meeting your obligations on something like that is a major black mark on your record."

ACTION PLAN
- Determine dividends on preferred shares by multiplying the dividend rate times the par value of the stock times the number of preferred shares.

DO IT! 3a | Preferred Stock Dividends

MasterMind Corporation has 2,000 shares of 6%, $100 par value preferred stock outstanding at December 31, 2022. At December 31, 2022, the company declared a $60,000 cash dividend. Determine the dividend paid to preferred stockholders and common stockholders under each of the following scenarios.

1. The preferred stock is noncumulative, and the company has not missed any dividends in previous years.
2. The preferred stock is noncumulative, and the company did not pay a dividend in each of the two previous years.
3. The preferred stock is cumulative, and the company did not pay a dividend in each of the two previous years.

Solution

1. The company has not missed past dividends and the preferred stock is noncumulative. Thus, the preferred stockholders are paid only this year's dividends. The dividend paid to preferred stockholders would be $12,000 (2,000 × .06 × $100). The dividend paid to common stockholders would be $48,000 ($60,000 − $12,000).

2. The preferred stock is noncumulative. Thus, past unpaid dividends do not have to be paid. The dividend paid to preferred stockholders would be $12,000 (2,000 × .06 × $100). The dividend paid to common stockholders would be $48,000 ($60,000 − $12,000).

3. The preferred stock is cumulative. Thus, dividends that have been missed (dividends in arrears) must be paid. The dividend paid to preferred stockholders would be $36,000 (3 × 2,000 × .06 × $100). Of the $36,000, $24,000 relates to dividends in arrears and $12,000 relates to the current dividend on preferred stock. The dividend paid to common stockholders would be $24,000 ($60,000 − $36,000).

Related exercise material: **BE 11.7, DO IT! 11.3a, and E11.10.**

ACTION PLAN
- Understand the cumulative feature: If preferred stock is cumulative, then any missed dividends (dividends in arrears) and the current year's dividend must be paid to preferred stockholders before dividends are paid to common stockholders.

Stock Dividends

A **stock dividend** is a pro rata (proportional to ownership) distribution of the corporation's own stock to stockholders. Whereas a cash dividend is paid in cash, a stock dividend is paid in stock. **A stock dividend results in a decrease in retained earnings and an increase in paid-in capital.** Unlike a cash dividend, a stock dividend does not decrease total stockholders' equity or total assets.

Because a stock dividend does not result in a distribution of assets, some view it as nothing more than a publicity gesture. Stock dividends are often issued by companies that do not have adequate cash to issue a cash dividend. Such companies may not want to announce that they are not going to issue a cash dividend at their expected time. By issuing a stock dividend, they "save face" by giving the appearance of distributing a dividend. Note that since a stock dividend neither increases nor decreases the assets in the company, investors are not receiving anything they didn't already own. In a sense, it is like asking for two pieces of pie and having your host take one piece of pie and cut it into two smaller pieces. You are not better off, but you got your two pieces of pie.

To illustrate a stock dividend, assume that you have a 2% ownership interest in Cetus Inc.; you own 20 of its 1,000 shares of common stock. If Cetus declares a 10% stock dividend, it issues 100 shares (1,000 × 10%) of stock. You receive two shares (2% × 100), but your ownership interest remains at 2% (22 ÷ 1,100). **You now own more shares of stock, but your ownership interest has not changed.** Moreover, the company disburses no cash and assumes no liabilities.

What, then, are the purposes and benefits of a stock dividend? Corporations generally issue stock dividends for one of the following reasons:

1. To satisfy stockholders' dividend expectations without spending cash.
2. To increase the marketability of the stock by increasing the number of shares outstanding and thereby decreasing the market price per share. Decreasing the market price of the stock makes it easier for smaller investors to purchase the shares.
3. To emphasize that the company has permanently reinvested in the business a portion of stockholders' equity, which therefore is unavailable for cash dividends.

When the dividend is declared, the board of directors determines the size of the stock dividend and the value per share to use to record the transaction. In order to meet legal requirements, the per share amount must be at least equal to the par or stated value.

The accounting profession distinguishes between a **small stock dividend** (less than 20%–25% of the corporation's issued stock) and a **large stock dividend** (greater than 20%–25%). It recommends that the company use the **fair value per share** to record small stock dividends. The recommendation is based on the assumption that a small stock dividend will have little effect on the market price of the shares previously outstanding. Thus, many stockholders consider small stock dividends to be distributions of earnings equal to the fair value of the shares distributed. The accounting profession does not specify the value to use to record a large stock dividend. However, companies normally use **par or stated value per share**. Small stock dividends predominate in practice. In Appendix 11A at the end of the chapter, we illustrate the journal entries for small stock dividends.

Effects of Stock Dividends

How do stock dividends affect stockholders' equity? They **change the composition of stockholders' equity** because they result in a transfer of a portion of retained earnings to paid-in capital (see **Helpful Hint**). However, **total stockholders' equity remains the same**. Stock dividends also have no effect on the par or stated value per share, but the number of shares outstanding increases.

Illustration 11.11 shows the effects that result when Medland Corp. declares a 10% stock dividend on its $10 par common stock when 50,000 shares were outstanding. The market price was $15 per share.

HELPFUL HINT

Because of its effects, a stock dividend is also referred to as *capitalizing retained earnings*.

ILLUSTRATION 11.11
Stock dividend effects

	Before Dividend	Change	After Dividend
Stockholders' equity			
Paid-in capital			
Common stock, $10 par	$ 500,000	$ 50,000	$ 550,000
Paid-in capital in excess of par value	—	25,000	25,000
Total paid-in capital	500,000	+75,000	575,000
Retained earnings	300,000	−75,000	225,000
Total stockholders' equity	$800,000	$ 0	$800,000
Outstanding shares	50,000	+ 5,000	55,000
Par value per share	$ 10.00	$ 0	$ 10.00

In this example, total paid-in capital increased by $75,000 (50,000 shares × 10% × $15), and retained earnings decreased by the same amount. Note also that total stockholders' equity remains unchanged at $800,000. The number of shares increases by 5,000 (50,000 × 10%).

Stock Splits

A **stock split**, like a stock dividend, involves the issuance of additional shares of stock to stockholders according to their percentage ownership. However, **a stock split results in a reduction in the par or stated value per share** (see **Helpful Hint**). The purpose of a stock split is to increase the marketability of the stock by lowering its market price per share. This, in turn, makes it easier for the corporation to issue additional stock. After hitting a peak of 114 stock splits in 1986, the number of splits in the United States has fallen to about 30 per year. **Google** announced a 2-for-1 split recently when its stock was selling for $650 per share.

HELPFUL HINT

A stock split changes the par value per share but does not affect any balances in stockholders' equity.

Like a stock dividend, a stock split increases the number of shares owned by a shareholder, but it does not change the percentage of the total company that the shareholder owns. The effects of a 4-for-1 split are shown in **Illustration 11.12**.

The effect of a split on market price is generally **inversely proportional** to the size of the split. For example, after a recent 2-for-1 stock split, the market price of **Nike**'s stock fell from $111 to approximately $55.

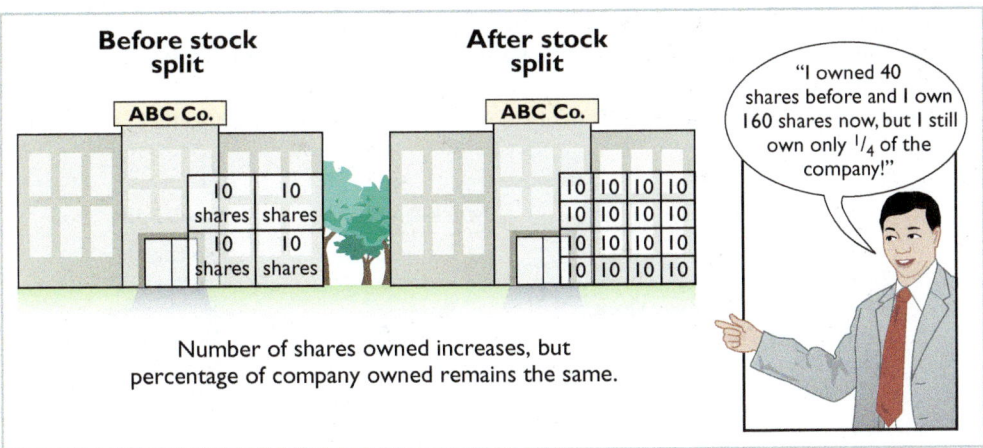

ILLUSTRATION 11.12

Effect of stock split for stockholders

Investor Insight — Berkshire Hathaway

Dietmar Klement/ iStockphoto

A No-Split Philosophy

Warren Buffett's company, **Berkshire Hathaway**, has two classes of shares. Until recently, the company had never split either class of stock. As a result, the class A stock recently had a market price of $300,000 and the class B at one time sold for about $3,200 per share. Because the price per share is so high, the stock does not trade as frequently as the stock of other companies. Buffett has always opposed stock splits because he feels that a lower stock price attracts short-term investors. He appears to be correct. For example, while more than 6 million shares of IBM are exchanged on the average day, only about 1,000 class A shares of Berkshire are traded. Despite Buffett's aversion to splits, in order to accomplish an acquisition, Berkshire split its class B shares 50 to 1.

Source: Scott Patterson, "Berkshire Nears Smaller Baby B's," *Wall Street Journal Online* (January 19, 2010).

Why does Warren Buffett usually oppose stock splits? (Go to WileyPLUS for this answer and additional questions.)

In a stock split, the company increases the number of shares in the same proportion that it decreases the par or stated value per share. For example, in a 2-for-1 split, the company exchanges one share of $10 par value stock for two shares of $5 par value stock. **A stock split does not have any effect on paid-in capital, retained earnings, and total stockholders' equity.** However, the number of shares outstanding increases. The effects of a 2-for-1 stock split of Medland Corporation's common stock are shown in Illustration 11.13.

	Before Stock Split	Change	After Stock Split
Stockholders' equity			
Paid-in capital			
Common stock			
(before: 50,000 $10 par shares; after: 100,000 $5 par shares)	$ 500,000		$ 500,000
Paid-in capital in excess of par value	0		0
Total paid-in capital	500,000	$ 0	500,000
Retained earnings	300,000	0	300,000
Total stockholders' equity	**$800,000**	$ 0	**$800,000**
Outstanding shares	50,000	+ 50,000	100,000
Par value per share	$ 10.00	–$ 5.00	$ 5.00

ILLUSTRATION 11.13

Stock split effects

Because a stock split does not affect the balances in any stockholders' equity accounts, a company **does not need to journalize a stock split**. However, a memorandum entry explaining the effect of the split is typically made.

Illustration 11.14 compares the effects of stock dividends and stock splits.

ILLUSTRATION 11.14
Effects of stock splits and stock dividends differentiated

Item	Stock Dividend	Stock Split
Total paid-in capital	Increase	No change
Total retained earnings	Decrease	No change
Total par value (common stock)	Increase	No change
Par value per share	No change	Decrease
Shares outstanding	Increase	Increase
Total stockholders' equity	No change	No change

ACTION PLAN
- Calculate the stock dividend's effect on retained earnings by multiplying the number of new shares times the market price of the stock (or par value for a large stock dividend).
- Recall that a stock dividend increases the number of shares without affecting total equity.
- Recall that a stock split only increases the number of shares outstanding and decreases the par value per share without affecting total equity.

DO IT! 3b | Stock Dividends and Stock Splits

Due to five years of record earnings at Sing CD Corporation, the market price of its 500,000 shares of $2 par value common stock tripled from $15 per share to $45. During this period, paid-in capital remained the same at $2,000,000. Retained earnings increased from $1,500,000 to $10,000,000. President Joan Elbert is considering either a 10% stock dividend or a 2-for-1 stock split. She asks you to show the before-and-after effects of each option on (a) retained earnings, (b) total stockholders' equity, and (c) par value per share.

Solution

The stock dividend amount is $2,250,000 [(500,000 × 10%) × $45]. The new balance in retained earnings is $7,750,000 ($10,000,000 − $2,250,000). The retained earnings balance after the stock split is the same as it was before the split: $10,000,000. The effects on the stockholders' equity accounts are as follows.

	Original Balances	After Dividend	After Split
Paid-in capital	$ 2,000,000	$ 4,250,000	$ 2,000,000
Retained earnings	10,000,000	7,750,000	10,000,000
Total stockholders' equity	$12,000,000	$12,000,000	$12,000,000
Shares outstanding	500,000	550,000	1,000,000
Par value per share	$ 2.00	$ 2.00	$ 1.00

Related exercise material: **BE11.8, DO IT! 11.3b,** and **E11.11.**

Presentation and Analysis

LEARNING OBJECTIVE 4
Discuss how stockholders' equity is reported and analyzed.

Retained Earnings

Retained earnings is net income that a company retains in the business. The balance in retained earnings is part of the stockholders' claim on the total assets of the corporation. It does not, however, represent a claim on any specific asset. Nor can the amount of retained earnings be associated with the balance of any asset account. For example, a $100,000 balance in retained earnings does not mean that there should be $100,000 in cash. The reason is that the company may have used the cash resulting from the excess of revenues over expenses to purchase buildings, equipment, and other assets. **Illustration 11.15** shows recent amounts of retained earnings and cash in selected companies.

ILLUSTRATION 11.15

Retained earnings and cash balances

Company	Retained Earnings	Cash
Facebook	$ 3,159	$3,323
Google	61,262	8,989
Nike	5,695	3,337
Starbucks	4,130	2,576

(in millions)

When expenses exceed revenues, a **net loss** results. In contrast to net income, a net loss decreases retained earnings. In closing entries, a company debits a net loss to the Retained Earnings account. **It does not debit net losses to paid-in capital accounts.** To do so would destroy the distinction between paid-in and earned capital. If cumulative losses and dividends exceed cumulative income over a company's life, a debit balance in Retained Earnings results. A debit balance in Retained Earnings, such as that of **Groupon, Inc.** in a recent year, is a **deficit**. A company reports a deficit as a deduction in the stockholders' equity section of the balance sheet, as shown in **Illustration 11.16**.

ILLUSTRATION 11.16

Stockholders' equity with deficit

Groupon, Inc.
Balance Sheet (partial)
(in thousands)

Stockholders' equity
  Paid-in capital
    Common stock $ 70
    Paid-in capital in excess of par value   1,885,301
    Total paid-in capital   1,885,371
  Accumulated deficit   (921,960)
    Total paid-in capital and retained earnings   963,411
  Less: Treasury stock   198,467
Total stockholders' equity $ 764,944

Retained Earnings Restrictions

The balance in retained earnings is generally available for dividend declarations. Some companies state this fact. In some circumstances, however, there may be **retained earnings restrictions**. These make a portion of the balance currently unavailable for dividends. Restrictions result from one or more of these causes: legal, contractual, or voluntary.

Companies generally disclose retained earnings restrictions in the notes to the financial statements. For example, as shown in **Illustration 11.17**, **Tektronix Inc.**, a manufacturer of electronic measurement devices, recently had total retained earnings of $774 million, but the unrestricted portion was only $223.8 million.

ILLUSTRATION 11.17

Disclosure of unrestricted retained earnings

Tektronix Inc.
Notes to the Financial Statements

Certain of the Company's debt agreements require compliance with debt covenants. The Company had unrestricted retained earnings of $223.8 million after meeting those requirements.

Balance Sheet Presentation of Stockholders' Equity

In the stockholders' equity section of the balance sheet, companies report paid-in capital, retained earnings, accumulated other comprehensive income, and treasury stock. Within paid-in capital, two classifications are recognized:

1. **Capital stock**, which consists of preferred and common stock. Companies show preferred stock before common stock because of its preferential rights. They report information about the par value, shares authorized, shares issued, and shares outstanding for each class of stock.
2. **Additional paid-in capital**, which includes the excess of amounts paid in over par or stated value.

As discussed in Chapter 5, in some instances unrealized gains and losses are not included in net income. Instead, these excluded items, referred to as other comprehensive income items, are reported as part of a more inclusive earnings measure called comprehensive income. Examples of other comprehensive income items include certain adjustments to pension plan assets, types of foreign currency gains and losses, and some gains and losses on investments. The items reported as other comprehensive income are closed each year to the **Accumulated Other Comprehensive Income** account. Thus, this account includes the cumulative amount of all previous items reported as other comprehensive income. This account can have either a debit or credit balance depending on whether or not accumulated gains exceed accumulated losses over the years. If accumulated losses exceed gains, then the company reports accumulated other comprehensive loss.

Illustration 11.18 presents the stockholders' equity section of the balance sheet of Graber Inc. (see **International Note**). The company discloses a retained earnings restriction in the notes. The stockholders' equity section for Graber Inc. includes most of the accounts discussed in this chapter. The disclosures pertaining to Graber's common stock indicate that 400,000 shares are issued, 100,000 shares are unissued (500,000 authorized less 400,000 issued), and 390,000 shares are outstanding (400,000 issued less 10,000 shares in treasury).

ILLUSTRATION 11.18
Stockholders' equity section of balance sheet

International Note

Like GAAP, under IFRS companies typically disclose separate categories of capital on the balance sheet. However, because of varying accounting treatments of certain transactions (such as treasury stock or asset revaluations), some categories used under IFRS vary from those under GAAP.

Graber Inc.
Balance Sheet (partial)

Stockholders' equity		
Paid-in capital		
Capital stock		
9% preferred stock, $100 par value, cumulative, 10,000 shares authorized, 6,000 shares issued and outstanding		$ 600,000
Common stock, no par, $5 stated value, 500,000 shares authorized, 400,000 shares issued, and 390,000 outstanding		2,000,000
Total capital stock		2,600,000
Additional paid-in capital		
Paid-in capital in excess of par value—preferred stock	$ 30,000	
Paid-in capital in excess of stated value—common stock	1,050,000	
Total additional paid-in capital		1,080,000
Total paid-in capital		3,680,000
Retained earnings **(see Note R)**		1,050,000
Total paid-in capital and retained earnings		4,730,000
Accumulated other comprehensive income		110,000
Less: Treasury stock (10,000 common shares)		80,000
Total stockholders' equity		$4,760,000

Note R: Retained earnings is restricted for the cost of treasury stock, $80,000.

Keeping an Eye on Cash

The balance sheet presents the balances of a company's stockholders' equity accounts at a point in time. Companies report in the financing activities section of the statement of cash flows information regarding cash inflows and outflows during the year that resulted from equity transactions. The excerpt shown presents the cash flows from financing activities from the statement of cash flows of **Tootsie Roll Industries, Inc.** in a recent year. From this information, we learn that the company's purchased treasury stock during the period, and its financing activities resulted in a net reduction in its cash balance.

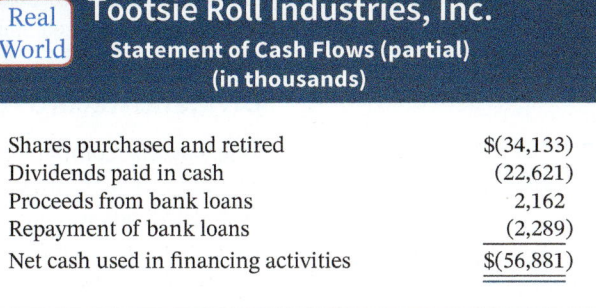

Tootsie Roll Industries, Inc.
Statement of Cash Flows (partial)
(in thousands)

Shares purchased and retired	$(34,133)
Dividends paid in cash	(22,621)
Proceeds from bank loans	2,162
Repayment of bank loans	(2,289)
Net cash used in financing activities	$(56,881)

DO IT! 4a | Stockholders' Equity Section

Jennifer Corporation has issued 300,000 shares of $3 par value common stock. It is authorized to issue 600,000 shares. The paid-in capital in excess of par value on the common stock is $380,000. The corporation has reacquired 15,000 shares at a cost of $50,000 and is currently holding those shares. It also had a cumulative other comprehensive loss of $82,000.

The corporation also has 4,000 shares issued and outstanding of 8%, $100 par value preferred stock. It is authorized to issue 10,000 shares. The paid-in capital in excess of par value on the preferred stock is $97,000. Retained earnings is $610,000.

Prepare the stockholders' equity section of the balance sheet.

ACTION PLAN
- Present capital stock first; list preferred stock before common stock.
- Present additional paid-in capital after capital stock.
- Report retained earnings after capital stock and additional paid-in capital.
- Deduct treasury stock from total paid-in capital and retained earnings.

Solution

Jennifer Corporation
Balance Sheet (partial)

Stockholders' equity		
Paid-in capital		
Capital stock		
8% preferred stock, $100 par value, 10,000 shares authorized, 4,000 shares issued and outstanding	$400,000	
Common stock, $3 par value, 600,000 shares authorized, 300,000 shares issued, and 285,000 shares outstanding	900,000	
Total capital stock		$1,300,000
Additional paid-in capital		
Paid-in capital in excess of par value—preferred stock	97,000	
Paid-in capital in excess of par value—common stock	380,000	
Total additional paid-in capital		477,000
Total paid-in capital		1,777,000
Retained earnings		610,000
Total paid-in capital and retained earnings		2,387,000
Accumulated other comprehensive loss		82,000
Less: Treasury stock (15,000 common shares) (at cost)		50,000
Total stockholders' equity		$2,255,000

Related exercise material: **BE11.10, DO IT! 11.4a, E11.13, E11.14, and E11.15.**

Analysis of Stockholders' Equity

Investors are interested in both a company's dividend record and its earnings performance. Although those two measures are often parallel, that is not always the case. Thus, investors should investigate each one separately.

Dividend Record

Decision Tools
The payout ratio helps users determine the portion of a company's earnings that its pays out in dividends.

One way that companies reward stock investors for their investment is to pay them dividends. The **payout ratio** measures the percentage of earnings a company distributes in the form of cash dividends to common stockholders (see **Decision Tools**). It is computed by **dividing total cash dividends declared to common shareholders by net income**. Using the information shown below, the payout ratio for **Nike** in 2016 and 2015 (years ended May 31, 2017 and 2016, respectively) is calculated in **Illustration 11.19**.

	2016	2015
Dividends (in millions)	$1,133	$1,022
Net income (in millions)	4,240	3,760

ILLUSTRATION 11.19
Nike's payout ratio

$$\text{Payout Ratio} = \frac{\text{Cash Dividends Declared on Common Stock}}{\text{Net Income}}$$

($ in millions)	2016	2015
Payout Ratio	$\frac{\$1,133}{\$4,240} = 26.7\%$	$\frac{\$1,022}{\$3,760} = 27.2\%$

Nike's payout ratio was relatively constant at approximately 27%. Companies attempt to set their dividend rate at a level that will be sustainable.

Companies that have high growth rates are characterized by low payout ratios because they reinvest most of their net income in the business. Thus, a low payout ratio is not necessarily bad news. Companies that believe they have many good opportunities for growth, such as **Facebook**, will reinvest those funds in the company rather than pay dividends. However, low dividend payments, or a cut in dividend payments, might signal that a company has liquidity or solvency problems and is trying to conserve cash by not paying dividends. Thus, investors and analysts should investigate the reason for low dividend payments.

Illustration 11.20 lists recent payout ratios of four well-known companies.

ILLUSTRATION 11.20
Payout ratios of companies

Company	Payout Ratio
Microsoft	24.5%
Kellogg	43.3%
Facebook	0%
Wal-Mart	49.0%

Earnings Performance

Decision Tools
Return on common stockholders' equity helps users determine a company's return on its common stockholders' investment.

Another way to measure corporate performance is through profitability. A widely used ratio that measures profitability from the common stockholders' viewpoint is **return on common stockholders' equity (ROE)** (see **Decision Tools**). This ratio shows how many dollars of net income a company earned for each dollar of common stockholders' equity. It is computed by dividing net income available to common stockholders (Net income − Preferred dividends) by average common stockholders' equity. Common stockholders' equity is equal to total stockholders' equity minus any equity from preferred stock.

Using the information on the previous page and the additional information presented below, **Illustration 11.21** shows **Nike**'s return on common stockholders' equity.

(in millions)	2016	2015	2014
Preferred dividends	$ –0–	$ –0–	$ –0–
Common stockholders' equity	12,407	12,258	12,707

ILLUSTRATION 11.21
Nike's return on common stockholders' equity

$$\text{Return on Common Stockholders' Equity} = \frac{\text{Net Income} - \text{Preferred Dividends}}{\text{Average Common Stockholders' Equity}}$$

($ in millions)	2016	2015
Return on Common Stockholders' Equity	$\frac{\$4{,}240 - \$0}{(\$12{,}407 + \$12{,}258)/2} = 34.4\%$	$\frac{\$3{,}760 - \$0}{(\$12{,}258 + \$12{,}707)/2} = 30.1\%$

From 2015 to 2016, Nike's return on common shareholders' equity increased. As a company grows larger, it becomes increasingly hard to sustain a high return. In Nike's case, since many believe the U.S. market for expensive sports shoes is saturated, it will need to grow either along new product lines, such as hiking shoes and golf equipment, or in new markets, such as Europe and Asia.

Debt Versus Equity Decision

When obtaining long-term capital, corporate managers must decide whether to issue bonds or to sell common stock. Bonds have three primary advantages relative to common stock, as shown in **Illustration 11.22**.

Bond Financing	Advantages
	1. **Stockholder control is not affected.** Bondholders do not have voting rights, so current owners (stockholders) retain full control of the company.
	2. **Tax savings result.** Bond interest is deductible for tax purposes; dividends on stock are not.
	3. **Return on common stockholders' equity may be higher.** Although bond interest expense reduces net income, return on common stockholders' equity often is higher under bond financing because no additional shares of common stock are issued.

ILLUSTRATION 11.22
Advantages of bond financing over common stock

How does the debt versus equity decision affect the return on common stockholders' equity? **Illustration 11.23** shows that the return on common stockholders' equity is affected by the return on assets and the amount of leverage a company uses—that is, by the company's reliance on debt (often measured by the debt to assets ratio). **If a company wants to increase its return on common stockholders' equity, it can either increase its return on assets or increase its reliance on debt financing.**

To illustrate the potential effect of debt financing on the return on common stockholders' equity, assume that Microsystems Inc. currently has 100,000 shares of common stock outstanding issued at $25 per share and no debt. It is considering two alternatives for raising an additional $5 million. Plan A involves issuing 200,000 shares of common stock at the current market price of $25 per share. Plan B involves issuing $5 million of 12% bonds at

ILLUSTRATION 11.23
Components of the return on common stockholders' equity

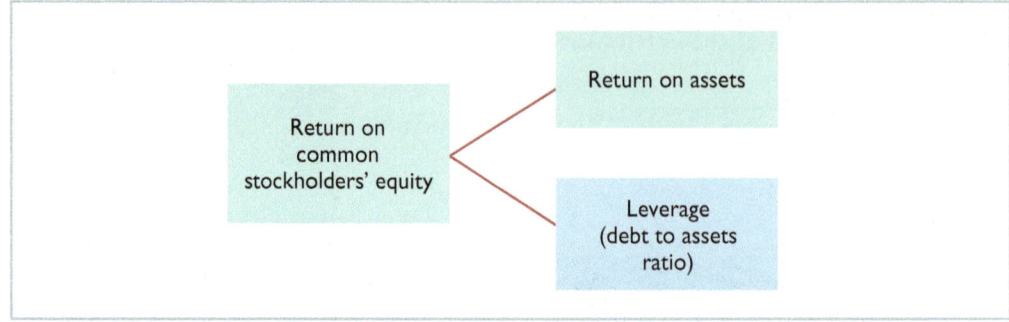

face value. Income before interest and taxes will be $1.5 million; income taxes are expected to be 30%. The alternative effects on the return on common stockholders' equity are shown in **Illustration 11.24**.

ILLUSTRATION 11.24
Effects on return on common stockholders' equity of issuing debt

	Plan A: Issue Stock	Plan B: Issue Bonds
Income before interest and taxes	$1,500,000	$1,500,000
Interest (12% × $5,000,000)	—	600,000
Income before income taxes	1,500,000	900,000
Income tax expense (30%)	450,000	270,000
Net income	$1,050,000	$ 630,000
Common stockholders' equity	$7,500,000	$2,500,000
Return on common stockholders' equity	14%	25.2%

Note that with long-term debt financing (bonds), net income is $420,000 ($1,050,000 − $630,000) less. However, the return on common stockholders' equity increases from 14% to 25.2% with the use of debt financing because net income is spread over a smaller amount of common stockholders' equity. **In general, as long as the return on assets rate exceeds the rate paid on debt, a company will increase the return on common stockholders' equity by the use of debt.**

After seeing this illustration, you might ask, why don't companies rely almost exclusively on debt financing rather than equity? Debt has one major disadvantage: **Debt reduces solvency. The company locks in fixed payments that it must make in good times and bad. The company must pay interest on a periodic basis and must pay the principal (face value) of the bonds at maturity.** A company with fluctuating earnings and a relatively weak cash position may experience great difficulty in meeting interest requirements in periods of low earnings. In the extreme, this can result in bankruptcy. With common stock financing, on the other hand, the company can decide to pay low (or no) dividends if earnings are low.

ACTION PLAN
- Determine return on common stockholders' equity by dividing net income available to common stockholders by average common stockholders' equity.

DO IT! 4b | Analyzing Stockholders' Equity

On January 1, 2022, Siena Corporation purchased 2,000 shares of treasury stock. Other information regarding Siena Corporation is provided below.

	2022	2021
Net income	$110,000	$110,000
Dividends on preferred stock	$10,000	$10,000
Dividends on common stock	$1,600	$2,000
Common stockholders' equity, beginning of year	$400,000*	$500,000
Common stockholders' equity, end of year	$400,000	$500,000

*Adjusted for purchase of treasury stock.

Compute (a) return on common stockholders' equity for each year, and (b) discuss its change from 2021 to 2022.

Solution

a.

	2022	2021
Return on common stockholders' equity	$\dfrac{\$110{,}000 - \$10{,}000}{(\$400{,}000 + \$400{,}000)/2} = 25\%$	$\dfrac{\$110{,}000 - \$10{,}000}{(\$500{,}000 + \$500{,}000)/2} = 20\%$

b. Between 2021 and 2022, return on common stockholders' equity improved from 20% to 25%. While this would appear to be good news for the company's common stockholders, this increase should be carefully evaluated. It is important to note that net income did not change during this period. The increase in the ratio was due to the purchase of treasury shares, which reduced the denominator of the ratio. As the company repurchases its own shares, it becomes more reliant on debt and thus increases its risk.

Related exercise material: **BE11.12, DO IT! 11.4b, E11.16, E11.17, and E11.18.**

USING THE DECISION TOOLS | adidas

adidas is one of **Nike**'s competitors. In such a competitive and rapidly changing environment, one wrong step can spell financial disaster.

Instructions

The following facts are available from adidas's annual report. As a German company, adidas reports under International Financial Reporting Standards (IFRS). Using this information, evaluate its (a) payout ratio and (b) earnings per share and return on common stockholders' equity (ROE). (c) Compare the payout ratio and ROE with those for Nike for 2016 and 2015.

(in millions)	2016	2015	2014
Dividends declared	€320	€303	
Net income	€1,017	€634	
Preferred dividends	0	0	
Shares outstanding at end of year	201	200	204
Common stockholders' equity	€6,472	€5,666	€5,625

Solution

a. A measure to evaluate a company's dividend record is the payout ratio. For adidas, this measure in 2016 and 2015 is calculated as follows.

	2016	2015
Payout ratio	$\dfrac{€320}{€1{,}017} = 31.5\%$	$\dfrac{€303}{€634} = 47.8\%$

b. There are many measures of earnings performance. Some of those presented thus far in the text were earnings per share and the return on common stockholders' equity. These measures for adidas in 2016 and 2015 are calculated as follows.

	2016	2015
Earnings per share	$\dfrac{€1{,}017 - 0}{(201 + 200)/2} = €5.07$	$\dfrac{€634 - 0}{(200 + 204)/2} = €3.14$
Return on common stockholders' equity	$\dfrac{€1{,}017 - 0}{(€6{,}472 + €5{,}666)/2} = 16.8\%$	$\dfrac{€634 - 0}{(€5{,}666 + €5{,}625)/2} = 11.2\%$

c. Nike's payout ratio was 26.7%. adidas's payout ratio decreased from 2015 to 2016 but was still higher than Nike's ratio in 2016. This means that adidas paid a higher percentage of its earnings as dividends. Nike had a higher return on shareholders' equity (30.1% and 34.4%) during this 2-year period than adidas.

Appendix 11A: Entries for Stock Dividends

LEARNING OBJECTIVE *5
Prepare entries for stock dividends.

To illustrate the accounting for stock dividends, assume that Medland Corporation has a balance of $300,000 in retained earnings and declares a 10% stock dividend on its 50,000 shares of $10 par value common stock. The current fair value of its stock is $15 per share. The number of shares to be issued is 5,000 (10% × 50,000), and the total amount to be debited to Stock Dividends is $75,000 (5,000 × $15). The entry to record this transaction at the declaration date is as follows.

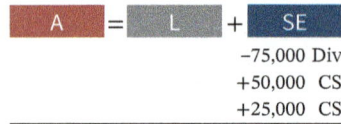

Stock Dividends	75,000	
Common Stock Dividends Distributable		50,000
Paid-in Capital in Excess of Par Value		25,000
(To record declaration of 10% stock dividend)		

A = L + SE
−75,000 Div
+50,000 CS
+25,000 CS

Cash Flows
no effect

At the declaration date, Medland increases (debits) Stock Dividends for the fair value of the stock issued, increases (credits) Common Stock Dividends Distributable for the par value of the dividend shares (5,000 × $10), and increases (credits) the excess over par (5,000 × $5) to an additional paid-in capital account.

Stock Dividends is closed to Retained Earnings at the end of the accounting period. Common Stock Dividends Distributable is a stockholders' equity account (see **Helpful Hint**). It is not a liability because assets will not be used to pay the dividend. If Medland prepares a balance sheet before it issues the dividend shares, it reports the distributable account in paid-in capital as an addition to common stock issued, as shown in **Illustration 11A.1**.

HELPFUL HINT
Note that the dividend account title is *distributable*, not *payable*.

ILLUSTRATION 11A.1
Statement presentation of common stock dividends distributable

Medland Corporation
Balance Sheet (partial)

Paid-in capital	
Common stock	$500,000
Common stock dividends distributable	**50,000**
Paid-in capital in excess of par—common stock	25,000
Total paid-in capital	$575,000

When Medland issues the dividend shares, it decreases Common Stock Dividends Distributable and increases Common Stock as follows.

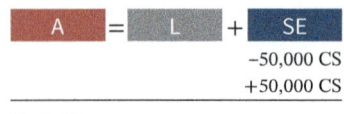

A = L + SE
−50,000 CS
+50,000 CS

Cash Flows
no effect

Common Stock Dividends Distributable	50,000	
Common Stock		50,000
(To record issuance of 5,000 shares in a stock dividend)		

Review and Practice

Learning Objectives Review

1 Discuss the major characteristics of a corporation.

The major characteristics of a corporation are separate legal existence, limited liability of stockholders, transferable ownership rights, ability to acquire capital, continuous life, corporation management, government regulations, and additional taxes.

2 Explain how to account for the issuance of common, preferred, and treasury stock.

When a company records issuance of common stock for cash, it credits the par value of the shares to Common Stock. It records in a separate paid-in capital account the portion of the proceeds that is above par value. When no-par common stock has a stated value, the entries are similar to those for par value stock. When no-par common stock does not have a stated value, the entire proceeds from the issue are credited to Common Stock.

Companies generally use the cost method in accounting for treasury stock. Under this approach, a company debits Treasury Stock at the price paid to reacquire the shares.

3 Explain how to account for cash dividends, stock dividends, and stock splits.

Companies make entries for dividends at the declaration date and the payment date. At the declaration date, the entries for a cash dividend are debit Cash Dividends and credit Dividends Payable.

Preferred stock has contractual provisions that give it priority over common stock in certain areas. Typically, preferred stockholders have a preference as to (1) dividends and (2) assets in the event of liquidation. However, they sometimes do not have voting rights.

The effects of stock dividends and splits are as follows. Small stock dividends transfer an amount equal to the fair value of the shares issued from retained earnings to the paid-in capital accounts. Stock splits reduce the par value per share of the common stock while increasing the number of shares so that the balance in the Common Stock account remains the same.

4 Discuss how stockholders' equity is reported and analyzed.

Additions to retained earnings consist of net income. Deductions consist of net loss and cash and stock dividends. In some instances, portions of retained earnings are restricted, making that portion unavailable for the payment of dividends.

In the stockholders' equity section of the balance sheet, companies report paid-in capital and retained earnings and identify specific sources of paid-in capital. Within paid-in capital, companies show two classifications: capital stock and additional paid-in capital. If a corporation has treasury stock, it deducts the cost of treasury stock from total paid-in capital and retained earnings to determine total stockholders' equity.

A company's dividend record can be evaluated by looking at what percentage of net income it chooses to pay out in dividends, as measured by the payout ratio (dividends divided by net income). Earnings performance is measured with the return on common stockholders' equity (income available to common stockholders divided by average common stockholders' equity).

*5 Prepare entries for stock dividends.

To record the declaration of a small stock dividend (less than 20%), debit Stock Dividends for an amount equal to the fair value of the shares issued. Record a credit to a temporary stockholders' equity account—Common Stock Dividends Distributable—for the par value of the shares, and credit the balance to Paid-in Capital in Excess of Par Value. When the shares are issued, debit Common Stock Dividends Distributable and credit Common Stock.

Decision Tools Review

Decision Checkpoints	Info Needed for Decision	Tool to Use for Decision	How to Evaluate Results
Should the company incorporate?	Capital needs, growth expectations, type of business, tax status	Corporations have limited liability, better capital-raising ability, and professional managers. But they suffer from additional taxes, government regulations, and separation of ownership from management.	Must carefully weigh the costs and benefits in light of the particular circumstances.

(continues)

(continued)

Decision Checkpoints	Info Needed for Decision	Tool to Use for Decision	How to Evaluate Results
What portion of its earnings does the company pay out in dividends?	Net income and total cash dividends on common stock	Payout ratio = Cash dividends declared on common stock / Net income	A low ratio may suggest that the company is retaining its earnings for investment in future growth.
What is the company's return on common stockholders' investment?	Earnings available to common stockholders and average common stockholders' equity	Return on common stockholders' equity = (Net income − Preferred dividends) / Average common stockholders' equity	A high measure suggests strong earnings performance from common stockholders' perspective.

Glossary Review

Accumulated Other Comprehensive Income This account includes the cumulative amount of all previous items reported as other comprehensive income. (p. 11-24).

Authorized stock The amount of stock that a corporation is authorized to sell as indicated in its charter. (p. 11-7).

Cash dividend A pro rata (proportional to ownership) distribution of cash to stockholders. (p. 11-15).

Charter A document that describes a corporation's name and purpose, types of stock and number of shares authorized, names of individuals involved in the formation, and number of shares each individual has agreed to purchase. (p. 11-6).

Corporation A company organized as a separate legal entity, with most of the rights and privileges of a person. (p. 11-3).

Cumulative dividend A feature of preferred stock entitling the stockholder to receive current and unpaid prior-year dividends before common stockholders receive any dividends. (p. 11-18).

Declaration date The date the board of directors formally authorizes the dividend and announces it to stockholders. (p. 11-16).

Deficit A debit balance in Retained Earnings. (p. 11-23).

Dividend A distribution by a corporation to its stockholders on a pro rata (proportional to ownership) basis. (p. 11-15).

Dividends in arrears Preferred dividends that were supposed to be declared but were not declared during a given period. (p. 11-18).

No-par value stock Capital stock that has not been assigned a value in the corporate charter. (p. 11-9).

Organization costs Costs incurred in the formation of a corporation, including legal and state fees and promotional expenditures. (p. 11-6).

Outstanding stock Capital stock that has been issued and is being held by stockholders. (p. 11-14).

Paid-in capital The amount stockholders paid in to the corporation in exchange for shares of ownership. (p. 11-9).

Par value stock Capital stock that has been assigned a value per share in the corporate charter. (p. 11-8).

Payment date The date cash dividend payments are made to stockholders. (p. 11-16).

Payout ratio A measure of the percentage of earnings a company distributes in the form of cash dividends to common stockholders. (p. 11-26).

Preferred stock Capital stock that has contractual preferences over common stock in certain areas. (p. 11-12).

Privately held corporation A corporation that has only a few stockholders and whose stock is not available for sale to the general public. (p. 11-3).

Publicly held corporation A corporation that may have thousands of stockholders and whose stock is traded on a national securities market. (p. 11-3).

Record date The date when the company determines ownership of outstanding shares for dividend purposes. (p. 11-16).

Retained earnings Net income that a company retains in the business. (p. 11-9).

Retained earnings restrictions Circumstances that make a portion of retained earnings currently unavailable for dividends. (p. 11-23).

Return on common stockholders' equity (ROE) A measure of profitability from the stockholders' point of view; computed by dividing net income minus preferred dividends by average common stockholders' equity. (p. 11-26).

Stated value The amount per share assigned by the board of directors to no-par stock. (p. 11-9).

Stock dividend A pro rata (proportional to ownership) distribution of the corporation's own stock to stockholders. (p. 11-19).

Stock split The issuance of additional shares of stock to stockholders accompanied by a reduction in the par or stated value per share. (p. 11-20).

Treasury stock A corporation's own stock that has been reacquired by the corporation and is being held for future use. (p. 11-13).

Practice Multiple-Choice Questions

1. **(LO 1)** Which of these is **not** a major advantage of a corporation?
   a. Separate legal existence.
   b. Continuous life.
   c. Government regulations.
   d. Transferable ownership rights.

2. **(LO 1)** A major **disadvantage** of a corporation is:
   a. limited liability of stockholders.
   b. additional taxes.
   c. transferable ownership rights.
   d. None of the above.

3. **(LO 1)** Which of these statements is **false**?
   a. Ownership of common stock gives the owner a voting right.
   b. The stockholders' equity section begins with paid-in capital.
   c. The authorization of capital stock does not result in a formal accounting entry.
   d. Legal capital is intended to protect stockholders.

4. **(LO 2)** ABC Corp. issues 1,000 shares of $10 par value common stock at $12 per share. When the transaction is recorded, credits are made to:
   a. Common Stock $10,000 and Paid-in Capital in Excess of Stated Value $2,000.
   b. Common Stock $12,000.
   c. Common Stock $10,000 and Paid-in Capital in Excess of Par Value $2,000.
   d. Common Stock $10,000 and Retained Earnings $2,000.

5. **(LO 2)** Treasury stock may be repurchased:
   a. to reissue the shares to officers and employees under bonus and stock compensation plans.
   b. to signal to the stock market that management believes the stock is underpriced.
   c. to have additional shares available for use in the acquisition of other companies.
   d. More than one of the above.

6. **(LO 3)** Preferred stock may have priority over common stock **except** in:
   a. dividend preference.
   b. preference to assets in the event of liquidation.
   c. cumulative dividends.
   d. voting.

7. **(LO 3)** U-Bet Corporation has 10,000 shares of 8%, $100 par value, cumulative preferred stock outstanding at December 31, 2022. No dividends were declared in 2020 or 2021. If U-Bet wants to pay $375,000 of dividends in 2022, common stockholders will receive:
   a. $0.
   b. $295,000.
   c. $215,000.
   d. $135,000.

8. **(LO 3)** Entries for cash dividends are required on the:
   a. declaration date and the record date.
   b. record date and the payment date.
   c. declaration date, record date, and payment date.
   d. declaration date and the payment date.

9. **(LO 3)** Which of these statements about stock dividends is **true**?
   a. Stock dividends reduce a company's cash balance.
   b. A stock dividend has no effect on total stockholders' equity.
   c. A stock dividend decreases total stockholders' equity.
   d. A stock dividend ordinarily will increase total stockholders' equity.

10. **(LO 3)** Zealot Inc. has retained earnings of $500,000 and total stockholders' equity of $2,000,000. It has 100,000 shares of $8 par value common stock outstanding, which is currently selling for $30 per share. If Zealot declares a 10% stock dividend on its common stock:
    a. net income will decrease by $80,000.
    b. retained earnings will decrease by $80,000 and total stockholders' equity will increase by $80,000.
    c. retained earnings will decrease by $300,000 and total stockholders' equity will increase by $300,000.
    d. retained earnings will decrease by $300,000 and total paid-in capital will increase by $300,000.

11. **(LO 4)** In the stockholders' equity section of the balance sheet, common stock:
    a. is listed before preferred stock.
    b. is added to total capital stock.
    c. is part of paid-in capital.
    d. is part of additional paid-in capital.

12. **(LO 4)** In the stockholders' equity section, the cost of treasury stock is deducted from:
    a. total paid-in capital and retained earnings.
    b. retained earnings.
    c. total stockholders' equity.
    d. common stock in paid-in capital.

13. **(LO 4)** The return on common stockholders' equity is usually increased by all of the following, **except**:
    a. an increase in the return on assets ratio.
    b. an increase in the use of debt financing.
    c. an increase in the company's stock price.
    d. an increase in the company's net income.

14. **(LO 4)** Thomas is nearing retirement and would like to invest in a stock that will provide a good steady income. Thomas should choose a stock with a:
    a. high current ratio.
    b. high dividend payout.
    c. high earnings per share.
    d. high price-earnings ratio.

15. **(LO 4)** Jackson Inc. reported net income of $186,000 during 2022 and paid dividends of $26,000 on common stock. It also paid dividends on its 10,000 shares of 6%, $100 par value, non-cumulative preferred stock. Common stockholders' equity was $1,200,000 on January 1, 2022, and $1,600,000 on December 31, 2022. The company's return on common stockholders' equity for 2022 is:
    a. 10.0%.
    b. 9.0%.
    c. 7.1%.
    d. 13.3%.

16. **(LO 4)** If everything else is held constant, earnings per share is increased by:
    a. the payment of a cash dividend to common shareholders.
    b. the payment of a cash dividend to preferred shareholders.
    c. the issuance of new shares of common stock.
    d. the purchase of treasury stock.

Solutions

1. c. Government regulations are a disadvantage of a corporation. The other choices are advantages of a corporation.

2. b. Additional taxes are a disadvantage of a corporation. The other choices are advantages of a corporation.

3. d. Legal capital is intended to protect creditors, not stockholders. The other choices are true statements.

4. c. Common Stock should be credited for $10,000 and Paid-in Capital in Excess of Par Value should be credited for $2,000. The stock is par value stock, not stated value stock, and this excess is contributed, not earned, capital. The other choices are therefore incorrect.

5. d. Treasury stock may be repurchased to reissue the shares as part of bonus and stock compensation plans, to signal to the stock market that the stock is underpriced, and to have additional shares available for use in the acquisition of other companies. Choice (a), (b), (c) are all correct, but (d) is the best answer.

6. d. Preferred stock usually does not have voting rights and therefore does not have priority over common stock on this issue. The other choices are true statements.

7. d. The preferred stockholders will receive a total of $240,000 of dividends [dividends in arrears ($80,000 × 2 years) + current-year dividends ($80,000)]. If U-Bet wants to pay a total of $375,000 in 2022, then common stockholders will receive $135,000 ($375,000 − $240,000), not (a) $0, (b) $295,000, or (c) $215,000.

8. d. Entries are required for dividends on the declaration date and the payment date, but not the record date. The other choices are therefore incorrect.

9. b. A stock dividend moves amounts from retained earnings to paid-in capital and has no effect on stockholders' equity or cash. The other choices are therefore incorrect.

10. d. A 10% stock dividend on the company's common stock will increase the number of shares issued by 10,000 (100,000 × 10%). At a market price of $30 per share, total paid-in capital will increase by $300,000 (10,000 shares × $30/share) and retained earnings will decrease by that same amount. The other choices are therefore incorrect.

11. c. Common stock is part of paid-in capital. The other choices are incorrect because common stock (a) is listed after preferred stock, (b) is not added to total capital stock but is part of capital stock, and (d) is part of capital stock, not additional paid-in capital.

12. a. The cost of treasury stock is deducted from total paid-in capital and retained earnings. The other choices are therefore incorrect.

13. c. An increase in the company's stock price has no effect on the return on common stockholders' equity. The other choices are incorrect because (a) an increase in a firm's return on assets, (b) an increase in a firm's use of debt financing, and (c) an increase in a firm's net income will all increase the return on common stockholders' equity.

14. b. Thomas should focus on a high dividend payout. The other choices are incorrect because a stock with a (a) high current ratio, (c) high earnings per share, or (d) high price-earnings ratio may or may not pay dividends on a consistent basis.

15. b. Return on common stockholders' equity is net income available to common stockholders divided by average common stockholders' equity. Net income available to common stockholders is net income less preferred dividends = $126,000 [$186,000 − (10,000 × .06 × $100)]. The company's return on common stockholders' equity for the year is therefore 9.0% [$126,000/($1,200,000 + $1,600,000)/2)], not (a) 10.0%, (c) 7.1%, or (d) 13.3%.

16. d. The purchase of treasury stock reduces the number of shares outstanding, which is the denominator of earnings per share (EPS). With a smaller denominator, EPS is larger. The other choices are incorrect because (a) the payment of a cash dividend to common stockholders does not affect the earnings or the number of outstanding shares, so EPS will stay the same; (b) the payment of a cash dividend to preferred stockholders will reduce the amount of earnings available to the common stockholders, thus reducing EPS; and (c) the issuance of new shares of common stock would not affect earnings but will increase the number of outstanding shares, thereby reducing EPS.

Practice Brief Exercises

Prepare entries for issuance of par value common stock.

1. (LO 2) On April 10, Leury Corporation issues 3,000 shares of $5 par value common stock for cash at $14 per share. Journalize the issuance of the stock.

Solution

1. April 10	Cash (3,000 × $14)	42,000	
	Common Stock (3,000 × $5)		15,000
	Paid-in Capital in Excess of Par—Common Stock (3,000 × $9)		27,000

Prepare entries for treasury stock transactions.

2. (LO 2) On June 1, Omar Corporation purchases 600 shares of its $5 par value common stock for the treasury at a cash price of $10 per share. Journalize the treasury stock transaction.

Solution

2. June 1	Treasury Stock (600 × $10)	6,000	
	Cash		6,000

Prepare entries for a cash dividend.

3. (LO 3) Giovanni Corporation has 70,000 shares of common stock outstanding. It declares a $2 per share cash dividend on November 15 to stockholders of record on December 15. The dividend is paid on December 31. Prepare the entries on the appropriate dates to record the declaration and payment of the cash dividend.

Solution

3.

Nov. 15	Cash Dividends (70,000 × $2/share)		140,000	
	Dividends Payable			140,000
Dec. 31	Dividends Payable		140,000	
	Cash			140,000

4. (LO 3) The stockholders' equity section of Ynoa Corporation consists of common stock ($5 par) $3,000,000 and retained earnings $1,000,000. A 15% stock dividend (90,000 shares) is declared when the market price per share is $11. Show the before-and-after effects of the dividend on (a) the components of stockholders' equity, (b) shares outstanding, and (c) par value per share.

Show before-and-after effects of a stock dividend.

Solution

	Before Dividend	After Dividend
4. a. Stockholders' equity		
Paid-in capital		
Common stock, $5 par	$3,000,000	$3,450,000
In excess of par	—	540,000
Total paid-in capital	3,000,000	3,990,000
Retained earnings	1,000,000	10,000
Total stockholders' equity	$4,000,000	$4,000,000
b. Outstanding shares	600,000	690,000
c. Par value per share	$5.00	$5.00

5. (LO 4) Navarez Corporation has the following accounts at December 31: Common Stock, $2 par, 50,000 shares issued, $100,000; Paid-in Capital in Excess of Par—Common Stock $40,000; Retained Earnings $65,000; and Treasury Stock, 2,000 shares, $17,000. Prepare the stockholders' equity section of the balance sheet.

Prepare stockholders' equity section.

Solution

5. Stockholders' equity
  Paid-in capital

Common stock, $2 par value, 50,000 shares issued, and 48,000 shares outstanding	$100,000
In excess of par—common stock	40,000
Total paid-in capital	140,000
Retained earnings	65,000
Total paid-in capital and retained earnings	205,000
Less: Treasury stock (2,000 common shares)	17,000
Total stockholders' equity	$188,000

Practice Exercises

1. (LO 2) Maci Co. had the following transactions during the current period.

June 12   Issued 60,000 shares of $5 par value common stock for cash of $370,000.
July 11   Issued 1,000 shares of $100 par value preferred stock for cash at $112 per share.
Nov. 28   Purchased 2,000 shares of treasury stock for $70,000.

Journalize issuance of common and preferred stock and purchase of treasury stock.

Instructions
Journalize the transactions.

Solution

1.

June 12	Cash		370,000	
	Common Stock (60,000 × $5)			300,000
	Paid-in Capital in Excess of Par Value—			
	Common Stock			70,000
July 11	Cash (1,000 × $112)		112,000	
	Preferred Stock (1,000 × $100)			100,000
	Paid-in Capital in Excess of Par Value—			
	Preferred Stock (1,000 × $12)			12,000
Nov. 28	Treasury Stock		70,000	
	Cash			70,000

Journalize cash dividends; indicate statement presentation.

2. (LO 3, 4) On January 1, Chong Corporation had 95,000 shares of no-par common stock issued and outstanding. The stock has a stated value of $5 per share. During the year, the following occurred.

- Apr. 1   Issued 25,000 additional shares of common stock for $17 per share.
- June 15   Declared a cash dividend of $1 per share to stockholders of record on June 30.
- July 10   Paid the $1 cash dividend.
- Dec. 1   Issued 2,000 additional shares of common stock for $19 per share.
-      15   Declared a cash dividend on outstanding shares of $1.20 per share to stockholders of record on December 31.

Instructions

a. Prepare the entries, if any, on each of the three dividend dates.

b. How are dividends and dividends payable reported in the financial statements prepared at December 31?

Solution

2. a.

June 15	Cash Dividends (120,000 × $1)		120,000	
	Dividends Payable			120,000
July 10	Dividends Payable		120,000	
	Cash			120,000
Dec. 15	Cash Dividends (122,000 × $1.20)		146,400	
	Dividends Payable			146,400

b. In the retained earnings statement, dividends of $266,400 will be deducted. In the balance sheet, Dividends Payable of $146,400 will be reported as a current liability.

Practice Problem

Journalize transactions and prepare stockholders' equity section.

Rolman Corporation is authorized to issue 1,000,000 shares of $5 par value common stock. In its first year, the company has the following stock transactions.

- Jan. 10   Issued 400,000 shares of stock at $8 per share.
- Sept. 21   Purchased 10,000 shares of common stock for the treasury at $9 per share.
- Dec. 24   Declared a cash dividend of 10 cents per share on common stock outstanding.

Instructions

a. Journalize the transactions.

b. Prepare the stockholders' equity section of the balance sheet, assuming the company had retained earnings of $150,600 at December 31 and an accumulated other comprehensive loss of $105,000.

Solution

a.

Jan. 10	Cash		3,200,000	
	Common Stock			2,000,000
	Paid-in Capital in Excess of Par Value			1,200,000
	(To record issuance of 400,000 shares			
	of $5 par value stock)			
Sept. 21	Treasury Stock		90,000	
	Cash			90,000
	(To record purchase of 10,000 shares			
	of treasury stock at cost)			

Dec. 24	Cash Dividends	39,000	
	Dividends Payable		39,000
	(To record declaration of 10 cents per share cash dividend)		

b.

Rolman Corporation
Balance Sheet (partial)

Stockholders' equity	
Paid-in capital	
Capital stock	
Common stock, $5 par value, 1,000,000 shares authorized, 400,000 shares issued, 390,000 outstanding	$2,000,000
Additional paid-in capital	
Paid-in capital in excess of par value—common stock	1,200,000
Total paid-in capital	3,200,000
Retained earnings	150,600
Total paid-in capital and retained earnings	3,350,600
Accumulated other comprehensive loss	105,000
Less: Treasury stock (10,000 shares)	90,000
Total stockholders' equity	$3,155,600

WileyPLUS

Brief Exercises, DO IT! Exercises, Exercises, Problems, and many additional resources are available for practice in WileyPLUS.

Note: All asterisked Questions, Exercises, and Problems relate to material in the appendix to the chapter.

Questions

1. Joe, a student, asks your help in understanding some characteristics of a corporation. Explain each of these to Joe.
   a. Separate legal existence.
   b. Limited liability of stockholders.
   c. Transferable ownership rights.

2. a. Your friend G. C. Jones cannot understand how the characteristic of corporate management is both an advantage and a disadvantage. Clarify this problem for G. C.
   b. Identify and explain two other disadvantages of a corporation.

3. Nona Jaymes believes a corporation must be incorporated in the state in which its headquarters office is located. Is Nona correct? Explain.

4. What are the basic ownership rights of common stockholders in the absence of restrictive provisions?

5. A corporation has been defined as an entity separate and distinct from its owners. In what ways is a corporation a separate legal entity?

6. What are the two principal components of stockholders' equity?

7. The corporate charter of Gage Corporation allows the issuance of a maximum of 100,000 shares of common stock. During its first 2 years of operation, Gage sold 70,000 shares to shareholders and reacquired 4,000 of these shares. After these transactions, how many shares are authorized, issued, and outstanding?

8. Which is the better investment—common stock with a par value of $5 per share or common stock with a par value of $20 per share?

9. For what reasons might a company like **IBM** repurchase some of its stock (treasury stock)?

10. Monet, Inc. purchases 1,000 shares of its own previously issued $5 par common stock for $11,000. Assuming the shares are held in the treasury, what effect does this transaction have on (a) net income, (b) total assets, (c) total paid-in capital, and (d) total stockholders' equity?

11. a. What are the principal differences between common stock and preferred stock?
    b. Preferred stock may be cumulative. Discuss this feature.
    c. How are dividends in arrears presented in the financial statements?

12. Identify the events that result in credits and debits to retained earnings.

13. Indicate how each of these accounts should be classified in the stockholders' equity section of the balance sheet.

a. Common Stock.
b. Paid-in Capital in Excess of Par Value.
c. Retained Earnings.
d. Treasury Stock.
e. Paid-in Capital in Excess of Stated Value.
f. Preferred Stock.

14. What three conditions must be met before a cash dividend is paid?

15. Three dates associated with Petrie Company's cash dividend are May 1, May 15, and May 31. Discuss the significance of each date and give the entry at each date.

16. Contrast the effects of a cash dividend and a stock dividend on a corporation's balance sheet.

17. Doris Angel asks, "Since stock dividends don't change anything, why declare them?" What is your answer to Doris?

18. Jayne Corporation has 10,000 shares of $15 par value common stock outstanding when it announces a 3-for-1 split. Before the split, the stock had a market price of $120 per share. After the split, how many shares of stock will be outstanding, and what will be the approximate market price per share?

19. The board of directors is considering a stock split or a stock dividend. They understand that total stockholders' equity will remain the same under either action. However, they are not sure of the different effects of the two actions on other aspects of stockholders' equity. Explain the differences to the directors.

20. What was the cost of **Apple**'s treasury stock acquired in fiscal year 2017? (*Hint:* Refer to Apple's statement of cash flows.)

21. a. What is the purpose of a retained earnings restriction?
   b. Identify the possible causes of retained earnings restrictions.

22. Thom Inc.'s common stock has a par value of $1 and a current market price of $15. Explain why these amounts are different.

23. What is the formula for the payout ratio? What does it indicate?

24. Explain the circumstances under which debt financing will increase the return on common stockholders' equity.

25. Under what circumstances will the return on assets and the return on common stockholders' equity be equal?

26. Sauer Corp. has a return on assets of 12%. It plans to issue bonds at 8% and use the cash to repurchase stock. What effect will this have on its debt to assets ratio and on its return on common stockholders' equity?

Brief Exercises

List advantages and disadvantages of a corporation.

BE11.1 (LO 1), K Hana Ascot is planning to start a business. Identify for Hana the advantages and disadvantages of the corporate form of business organization.

Journalize issuance of par value common stock.

BE11.2 (LO 2), AP On May 10, Pilar Corporation issues 2,500 shares of $5 par value common stock for cash at $13 per share. Journalize the issuance of the stock.

Journalize issuance of no-par common stock.

BE11.3 (LO 2), AP On June 1, Forrest Inc. issues 3,000 shares of no-par common stock at a cash price of $7 per share. Journalize the issuance of the shares.

Journalize issuance of preferred stock.

BE11.4 (LO 2), AP Layes Inc. issues 8,000 shares of $100 par value preferred stock for cash at $106 per share. Journalize the issuance of the preferred stock.

Prepare entries for treasury stock transactions.

BE11.5 (LO 2), AP On July 1, Raney Corporation purchases 500 shares of its $5 par value common stock for the treasury at a cash price of $9 per share. Journalize the treasury stock transaction.

Prepare entries for a cash dividend.

BE11.6 (LO 3), AP Basse Corporation has 7,000 shares of common stock outstanding. It declares a $1 per share cash dividend on November 1 to stockholders of record on December 1. The dividend is paid on December 31. Prepare the entries on the appropriate dates to record the declaration and payment of the cash dividend.

Determine dividends paid to common stockholders.

BE11.7 (LO 3), AP M. Bot Corporation has 10,000 shares of 8%, $100 par value, cumulative preferred stock outstanding at December 31, 2022. No dividends were declared in 2020 or 2021. If M. Bot wants to pay $375,000 of dividends in 2022, what amount of dividends will common stockholders receive?

Show before-and-after effects of a stock dividend.

BE11.8 (LO 3), AP The stockholders' equity section of Mabry Corporation's balance sheet consists of common stock ($8 par) $1,000,000 and retained earnings $300,000. A 10% stock dividend (12,500 shares) is declared when the market price per share is $19. Show the before-and-after effects of the dividend on (a) the components of stockholders' equity and (b) the shares outstanding.

Compare impact of cash dividend, stock dividend, and stock split.

BE11.9 (LO 3), K Indicate whether each of the following transactions would increase (+), decrease (−), or not affect (N/A) total assets, total liabilities, and total stockholders' equity.

Transaction	Assets	Liabilities	Stockholders' Equity
a. Declared cash dividend.			
b. Paid cash dividend declared in (a).			
c. Declared stock dividend.			
d. Distributed stock dividend declared in (c).			
e. Split stock 3-for-1.			

BE11.10 (LO 4), AP Sudz Corporation has these accounts at December 31: Common Stock, $10 par, 5,000 shares issued, $50,000; Paid-in Capital in Excess of Par Value $22,000; Retained Earnings $42,000; and Treasury Stock, 500 shares, $11,000. Prepare the stockholders' equity section of the balance sheet.

Prepare a stockholders' equity section.

BE11.11 (LO 4), C Hans Miken, president of Miken Corporation, believes that it is a good practice for a company to maintain a constant payout of dividends relative to its earnings. Last year, net income was $600,000, and the corporation paid $120,000 in dividends. This year, due to some unusual circumstances, the corporation had income of $1,600,000. Hans expects next year's net income to be about $700,000. What was Miken Corporation's payout ratio last year? If it is to maintain the same payout ratio, what amount of dividends would it pay this year? Is this necessarily a good idea—that is, what are the pros and cons of maintaining a constant payout ratio in this scenario?

Evaluate a company's dividend record.

BE11.12 (LO 4), AP SUPERVALU, one of the largest grocery retailers in the United States, is headquartered in Minneapolis. Suppose the following financial information (in millions) was taken from the company's 2022 annual report: net sales $44,597, net income $393, beginning stockholders' equity $2,581, and ending stockholders' equity $2,887. There were no dividends paid on preferred stock. Compute the return on common stockholders' equity. Provide a brief interpretation of your findings.

Calculate the return on stockholders' equity.

BE11.13 (LO 4), AP Emron Inc. is considering these two alternatives to finance its construction of a new $2 million plant:

Compare bond financing to stock financing.

1. Issuance of 200,000 shares of common stock at the market price of $10 per share.
2. Issuance of $2 million, 6% bonds at face value.

Complete the table and indicate which alternative is preferable.

	Issue Stock	Issue Bonds
Income before interest and taxes	$1,500,000	$1,500,000
Interest expense from bonds		
Income before income taxes		
Income tax expense (30%)		
Net income	$	$
Outstanding shares		700,000
Earnings per share	$	$

*****BE11.14 (LO 5), AP** Stossel Corporation has 200,000 shares of $10 par value common stock outstanding. It declares a 12% stock dividend on December 1 when the market price per share is $17. The dividend shares are issued on December 31. Prepare the entries for the declaration and distribution of the stock dividend.

Prepare entries for a stock dividend.

DO IT! Exercises

DO IT! 11.1a (LO 1), C Indicate whether each of the following statements is true or false. If false, indicate how to correct the statement.

Analyze statements about corporate organization.

_____ 1. The corporation is an entity separate and distinct from its owners.

_____ 2. The liability of stockholders is normally limited to their investment in the corporation.

_____ 3. The relatively low amount of government regulation of corporations is an advantage of the corporate form of business.

_____ 4. There is no journal entry to record the authorization of capital stock.

_____ 5. No-par value stock is quite rare today.

DO IT! 11.1b (LO 1), AP At the end of its first year of operation, Goss Corporation has $1,000,000 of common stock and net income of $236,000. Prepare (a) the closing entry for net income and (b) the stockholders' equity section at year-end.

Close net income and prepare stockholders' equity section.

DO IT! 11.2a (LO 2), AP Beauty Island Corporation began operations on April 1 by issuing 55,000 shares of $5 par value common stock for cash at $13 per share. In addition, Beauty Island issued 1,000 shares of $1 par value preferred stock for $6 per share. Journalize the issuance of the common and preferred shares.

Journalize issuance of stock.

DO IT! 11.2b (LO 2), AP Dinosso Corporation purchased 2,000 shares of its $10 par value common stock for $76,000 on August 1. It will hold these in the treasury until resold. Journalize the treasury stock transaction.

Journalize treasury stock transaction.

Determine dividends paid to preferred and common stockholders.

DO IT! 11.3a (LO 3), AP Sparks Corporation has 3,000 shares of 8%, $100 par value preferred stock outstanding at December 31, 2022. At December 31, 2022, the company declared a $105,000 cash dividend. Determine the dividend paid to preferred stockholders and common stockholders under each of the following scenarios.

1. The preferred stock is noncumulative, and the company has not missed any dividends in previous years.
2. The preferred stock is noncumulative, and the company did not pay a dividend in each of the two previous years.
3. The preferred stock is cumulative, and the company did not pay a dividend in each of the two previous years.

Determine effects of stock dividend and stock split.

DO IT! 11.3b (LO 3), AP Spears Company has had 4 years of record earnings. Due to this success, the market price of its 400,000 shares of $2 par value common stock has increased from $6 per share to $50. During this period, paid-in capital remained the same at $2,400,000. Retained earnings increased from $1,800,000 to $12,000,000. CEO Don Ames is considering either (1) a 15% stock dividend or (2) a 2-for-1 stock split. He asks you to show the before-and-after effects of each option on (a) retained earnings, (b) total stockholders' equity, and (c) par value per share.

Prepare stockholders' equity section.

DO IT! 11.4a (LO 4), AP Hoyle Corporation has issued 100,000 shares of $5 par value common stock. It was authorized 500,000 shares. The paid-in capital in excess of par value on the common stock is $263,000. The corporation has reacquired 7,000 shares at a cost of $46,000 and is currently holding those shares. It also had accumulated other comprehensive income of $67,000.

The corporation also has 2,000 shares issued and outstanding of 9%, $100 par value preferred stock. It was authorized 10,000 shares. The paid-in capital in excess of par value on the preferred stock is $23,000. Retained earnings is $372,000. Prepare the stockholders' equity section of the balance sheet.

Compute return on stock-holders' equity and discuss changes.

DO IT! 11.4b (LO 4), AP On January 1, 2022, Vahsholtz Corporation purchased 5,000 shares of treasury stock. Other information regarding Vahsholtz Corporation is provided as follows.

	2022	2021
Net income	$110,000	$100,000
Dividends on preferred stock	$ 30,000	$ 30,000
Dividends on common stock	$ 25,000	$ 20,000
Weighted-average number of common shares outstanding	45,000	50,000
Common stockholders' equity beginning of year	$750,000	$600,000
Common stockholders' equity end of year	$830,000	$750,000

Compute (a) return on common stockholders' equity for each year, and (b) discuss the changes in each.

Exercises

Identify characteristics of a corporation.

E11.1 (LO 1), C Andrea has prepared the following list of statements about corporations.

1. A corporation is an entity separate and distinct from its owners.
2. As a legal entity, a corporation has most of the rights and privileges of a person.
3. Most of the largest U.S. corporations are privately held corporations.
4. Corporations may buy, own, and sell property; borrow money; enter into legally binding contracts; and sue and be sued.
5. The net income of a corporation is not taxed as a separate entity.
6. Creditors have a legal claim on the personal assets of the owners of a corporation if the corporation does not pay its debts.
7. The transfer of stock from one owner to another requires the approval of either the corporation or other stockholders.
8. The board of directors of a corporation legally owns the corporation.
9. The chief accounting officer of a corporation is the controller.
10. Corporations are subject to fewer state and federal regulations than partnerships or proprietorships.

Instructions

Identify each statement as true or false. If false, indicate how to correct the statement.

E11.2 (LO 1), C Andrea (see E11.1) has studied the information you gave her in that exercise and has come to you with more statements about corporations.

Identify characteristics of a corporation.

1. Corporation management is both an advantage and a disadvantage of a corporation compared to a proprietorship or a partnership.
2. Limited liability of stockholders, government regulations, and additional taxes are the major disadvantages of a corporation.
3. When a corporation is formed, organization costs are recorded as an asset.
4. Each share of common stock gives the stockholder the ownership rights to vote at stockholder meetings, share in corporate earnings, keep the same percentage ownership when new shares of stock are issued, and share in assets upon liquidation.
5. The number of issued shares is always greater than or equal to the number of authorized shares.
6. A journal entry is required for the authorization of capital stock.
7. Publicly held corporations usually issue stock directly to investors.
8. The trading of capital stock on a securities exchange involves the transfer of already issued shares from an existing stockholder to another investor.
9. The market price of common stock is usually the same as its par value.
10. Retained earnings is the total amount of cash and other assets paid in to the corporation by stockholders in exchange for capital stock.

Instructions

Identify each statement as true or false. If false, indicate how to correct the statement.

E11.3 (LO 2), AP During its first year of operations, Mona Corporation had these transactions pertaining to its common stock.

Journalize issuance of common stock.

| Jan. 10 | Issued 30,000 shares for cash at $5 per share. |
| July 1 | Issued 60,000 shares for cash at $7 per share. |

Instructions

a. Journalize the transactions, assuming that the common stock has a par value of $5 per share.
b. Journalize the transactions, assuming that the common stock is no-par with a stated value of $1 per share.

E11.4 (LO 2), AP Sagan Co. had these transactions during the current period.

Journalize issuance of common stock and preferred stock and purchase of treasury stock.

June 12	Issued 80,000 shares of $1 par value common stock for cash of $300,000.
July 11	Issued 3,000 shares of $100 par value preferred stock for cash at $106 per share.
Nov. 28	Purchased 2,000 shares of treasury stock for $9,000.

Instructions

Prepare the journal entries for the Sagan Co. transactions.

E11.5 (LO 2), AP Quay Co. had the following transactions during the current period.

Journalize issuance of common and preferred stock and purchase of treasury stock.

Mar. 2	Issued 5,000 shares of $5 par value common stock to attorneys in payment of a bill for $30,000 for services performed in helping the company to incorporate.
June 12	Issued 60,000 shares of $5 par value common stock for cash of $375,000.
July 11	Issued 1,000 shares of $100 par value preferred stock for cash at $110 per share.
Nov. 28	Purchased 2,000 shares of treasury stock for $80,000.

Instructions

Journalize the transactions.

E11.6 (LO 2, 4), AP Penland Corporation is authorized to issue both preferred and common stock. The par value of the preferred is $50. During the first year of operations, the company had the following events and transactions pertaining to its preferred stock.

Journalize preferred stock transactions and indicate statement presentation.

| Feb. 1 | Issued 40,000 shares for cash at $51 per share. |
| July 1 | Issued 60,000 shares for cash at $56 per share. |

Instructions

a. Journalize the transactions.
b. Post to the stockholders' equity accounts. (Use T-accounts.)
c. Discuss the statement presentation of the accounts.

Answer questions about stockholders' equity section.

E11.7 (LO 2, 4), C The stockholders' equity section of Lachlin Corporation's balance sheet at December 31 is presented here.

Lachlin Corporation
Balance Sheet (partial)

Stockholders' equity	
Paid-in capital	
Preferred stock, cumulative, 10,000 shares authorized, 6,000 shares issued and outstanding	$ 600,000
Common stock, no par, 750,000 shares authorized, 580,000 shares issued	2,900,000
Total paid-in capital	3,500,000
Retained earnings	1,158,000
Total paid-in capital and retained earnings	4,658,000
Less: Treasury stock (6,000 common shares)	32,000
Total stockholders' equity	$4,626,000

Instructions

From a review of the stockholders' equity section, answer the following questions.

a. How many shares of common stock are outstanding?
b. Assuming there is a stated value, what is the stated value of the common stock?
c. What is the par value of the preferred stock?
d. If the annual dividend on preferred stock is $36,000, what is the dividend rate on preferred stock?
e. If dividends of $72,000 were in arrears on preferred stock, what would be the balance reported for retained earnings?

Prepare correct entries for capital stock transactions.

E11.8 (LO 2), AN Mesa Corporation recently hired a new accountant with extensive experience in accounting for partnerships. Because of the pressure of the new job, the accountant was unable to review what he had learned earlier about corporation accounting. During the first month, he made the following entries for the corporation's capital stock.

May 2	Cash	104,000	
	Capital Stock		104,000
	(Issued 8,000 shares of $10 par value common stock at $13 per share)		
10	Cash	530,000	
	Capital Stock		530,000
	(Issued 10,000 shares of $20 par value preferred stock at $53 per share)		
15	Capital Stock	7,200	
	Cash		7,200
	(Purchased 600 shares of common stock for the treasury at $12 per share)		

Instructions

On the basis of the explanation for each entry, prepare the entries that should have been made for the capital stock transactions.

Journalize cash dividends and indicate statement presentation.

E11.9 (LO 3), AP On January 1, Graves Corporation had 60,000 shares of no-par common stock issued and outstanding. The stock has a stated value of $4 per share. During the year, the following transactions occurred.

Apr. 1	Issued 9,000 additional shares of common stock for $11 per share.	
June 15	Declared a cash dividend of $1.50 per share to stockholders of record on June 30.	
July 10	Paid the $1.50 cash dividend.	
Dec. 1	Issued 4,000 additional shares of common stock for $12 per share.	
15	Declared a cash dividend on outstanding shares of $1.60 per share to stockholders of record on December 31.	

Instructions

a. Prepare the entries, if any, on each of the three dates that involved dividends.

b. How are dividends and dividends payable reported in the financial statements prepared at December 31?

E11.10 (LO 3), AP Knudsen Corporation was organized on January 1, 2021. During its first year, the corporation issued 2,000 shares of $50 par value preferred stock and 100,000 shares of $10 par value common stock. At December 31, the company declared the following cash dividends: 2021, $5,000; 2022, $12,000; and 2023, $28,000.

Allocate cash dividends to preferred and common stock.

Instructions

a. Show the allocation of dividends to each class of stock, assuming the preferred stock dividend is 6% and noncumulative.

b. Show the allocation of dividends to each class of stock, assuming the preferred stock dividend is 7% and cumulative.

c. Journalize the declaration of the cash dividend at December 31, 2023, under part (b).

E11.11 (LO 3), AP On October 31, the stockholders' equity section of Manolo Company's balance sheet consists of common stock $648,000 and retained earnings $400,000. Manolo is considering the following two courses of action: (1) declaring a 5% stock dividend on the 81,000 $8 par value shares outstanding or (2) effecting a 2-for-1 stock split that will reduce par value to $4 per share. The current market price is $17 per share.

Compare effects of a stock dividend and a stock split.

Instructions

Prepare a tabular summary of the effects of the alternative actions on the company's stockholders' equity and outstanding shares. Use these column headings: **Before Action**, **After Stock Dividend**, and **After Stock Split**.

E11.12 (LO 2, 3), AP The stockholders' equity accounts of Ripley Corporation on January 1, 2022, were as follows.

Journalize transactions for stock issuance, treasury stock purchase, cash dividend, and closing entries.

Preferred Stock (8%, $100 par noncumulative, 5,000 shares authorized)	$ 400,000
Common Stock ($10 stated value, 800,000 shares authorized)	1,500,000
Paid-in Capital in Excess of Par Value—Preferred Stock	55,000
Paid-in Capital in Excess of Stated Value—Common Stock	880,000
Retained Earnings	760,000
Treasury Stock (8,000 common shares)	64,000

During 2022, the corporation had the following transactions and events pertaining to its stockholders' equity.

Mar 1	Issued 6,000 shares of common stock for $85 per share.
June 22	Purchased 1,000 additional shares of common treasury stock at $11 per share.
Sept. 1	Declared a 8% cash dividend on preferred stock, payable October 1.
Oct. 1	Paid the dividend declared on September 1.
Dec. 1	Declared a $0.70 per share cash dividend to common stockholders of record on December 15, payable December 31, 2022.
31	Determined that net income for the year was $110,000. Paid the dividend declared on December 1.

Instructions

Journalize the transactions for the dates shown. Include entries to close net income and dividends to Retained Earnings.

Prepare a stockholders' equity section.

E11.13 (LO 4), AP Wells Fargo & Company, headquartered in San Francisco, is one of the nation's largest financial institutions. Suppose it reported the following selected accounts (in millions) as of December 31, 2022.

Retained Earnings	$41,563
Preferred Stock	8,485
Common Stock—$1⅔ par value, authorized 6,000,000,000 shares; issued 5,245,971,422 shares	8,743
Treasury Stock—67,346,829 common shares	(2,450)
Paid-in Capital in Excess of Par Value—Common Stock	52,878
Accumulated Other Comprehensive Income	8,327

Instructions

Prepare the stockholders' equity section of the balance sheet for Wells Fargo as of December 31, 2022.

Prepare a stockholders' equity section.

E11.14 (LO 4), AP The following stockholders' equity accounts, arranged alphabetically, are in the ledger of Ryder Corporation at December 31, 2022.

Common Stock ($2 stated value)	$1,600,000
Paid-in Capital in Excess of Par Value—Preferred Stock	45,000
Paid-in Capital in Excess of Stated Value—Common Stock	1,050,000
Preferred Stock (8%, $100 par, noncumulative)	600,000
Retained Earnings	1,334,000
Treasury Stock (12,000 common shares)	72,000

Instructions

Prepare the stockholders' equity section of the balance sheet at December 31, 2022.

Prepare a stockholders' equity section.

E11.15 (LO 4), AP The following accounts appear in the ledger of Paisan Inc. after the books are closed at December 31, 2022.

Common Stock (no-par, $1 stated value, 400,000 shares authorized, 250,000 shares issued)	$ 250,000
Paid-in Capital in Excess of Stated Value—Common Stock	1,200,000
Preferred Stock ($50 par value, 8%, 40,000 shares authorized, 14,000 shares issued)	700,000
Retained Earnings	920,000
Treasury Stock (9,000 common shares)	64,000
Paid-in Capital in Excess of Par Value—Preferred Stock	24,000
Accumulated Other Comprehensive Loss	31,000

Instructions

Prepare the stockholders' equity section at December 31, assuming $100,000 of retained earnings is restricted for plant expansion. (Use Note R.)

Calculate ratios to evaluate dividend and earnings performance.

E11.16 (LO 4), AP The following financial information is available for Flintlock Corporation.

(in millions)	2022	2021
Average common stockholders' equity	$2,532	$2,591
Dividends declared for common stockholders	298	611
Dividends declared for preferred stockholders	40	40
Net income	504	555

Instructions

Calculate the payout ratio and return on common stockholders' equity for 2022 and 2021. Comment on your findings.

Calculate ratios to evaluate dividend and earnings performance.

E11.17 (LO 4), AP Suppose the following financial information is available for **Walgreen Company**.

(in millions)	2022	2021
Average common stockholders' equity	$13,622.5	$11,986.5
Dividends declared for common stockholders	471	394
Dividends declared for preferred stockholders	0	0
Net income	2,006	2,157

Instructions

Calculate the payout ratio and return on common stockholders' equity for 2022 and 2021. Comment on your findings.

E11.18 (LO 4), AN Kojak Corporation decided to issue common stock and used the $300,000 proceeds to redeem all of its outstanding bonds on January 1, 2022. The following information is available for the company for 2022 and 2021.

Calculate ratios to evaluate profitability and solvency.

	2022	2021
Net income	$ 182,000	$ 150,000
Dividends declared for preferred stockholders	8,000	8,000
Average common stockholders' equity	1,000,000	700,000
Total assets	1,200,000	1,200,000
Current liabilities	100,000	100,000
Total liabilities	200,000	500,000

Instructions

a. Compute the return on common stockholders' equity for both years.

b. Explain how it is possible that net income increased but the return on common stockholders' equity decreased.

c. Compute the debt to assets ratio for both years, and comment on the implications of this change in the company's solvency.

E11.19 (LO 4), AN Baja Airlines is considering these two alternatives for financing the purchase of a fleet of airplanes:

Compare issuance of stock financing to issuance of bond financing.

1. Issue 50,000 shares of common stock at $40 per share. (Cash dividends have not been paid nor is the payment of any contemplated.)
2. Issue 12%, 10-year bonds at face value for $2,000,000.

It is estimated that the company will earn $800,000 before interest and taxes as a result of this purchase. The company has an estimated tax rate of 30% and has 90,000 shares of common stock outstanding prior to the new financing.

Instructions

Determine the effect on net income and earnings per share for (a) issuing stock and (b) issuing bonds. Assume the new shares or new bonds will be outstanding for the entire year.

E11.20 (LO 4), AN Cabo Company has $1,000,000 in assets and $1,000,000 in stockholders' equity, with 40,000 shares outstanding the entire year. It has a return on assets of 10%. During 2021, it had net income of $100,000. On January 1, 2022, it issued $400,000 in debt at 4% and immediately repurchased 20,000 shares for $400,000. Management expected that, had it not issued the debt, it would have had net income of $100,000 in 2022.

Compute ratios and interpret.

Instructions

a. Determine the company's net income and earnings per share for 2021 and 2022. (Ignore taxes in your computations.)

b. Compute the company's return on common stockholders' equity for 2021 and 2022.

c. Compute the company's debt to assets ratio for 2021 and 2022.

d. Discuss the impact that the borrowing had on the company's profitability and solvency. Was it a good idea to borrow the money to buy the treasury stock?

*E11.21 (LO 5), AP On January 1, 2022, Lenne Corporation had $1,200,000 of common stock outstanding that was issued at par and retained earnings of $750,000. The company issued 30,000 shares of common stock at par on July 1 and earned net income of $400,000 for the year.

Journalize stock dividends.

Instructions

Journalize the declaration of a 15% stock dividend on December 10, 2022, for the following two independent assumptions.

a. Par value is $10 and market price is $15.

b. Par value is $5 and market price is $8.

Problems: Set A

Journalize stock transactions, post, and prepare paid-in capital section.

P11.1A (LO 2, 4), AP Tidal Corporation was organized on January 1, 2022. It is authorized to issue 20,000 shares of 6%, $50 par value preferred stock and 500,000 shares of no-par common stock with a stated value of $1 per share. The following stock transactions were completed during the first year.

Jan. 10	Issued 70,000 shares of common stock for cash at $4 per share.
Mar. 1	Issued 12,000 shares of preferred stock for cash at $53 per share.
May 1	Issued 120,000 shares of common stock for cash at $6 per share.
Sept. 1	Issued 5,000 shares of common stock for cash at $5 per share.
Nov. 1	Issued 3,000 shares of preferred stock for cash at $56 per share.

Instructions

a. Journalize the transactions.
b. Post to the stockholders' equity accounts. (Use T-accounts.)
c. Prepare the paid-in capital portion of the stockholders' equity section at December 31, 2022.

c. Tot. paid-in capital $1,829,000

Journalize transactions, post, and prepare a stockholders' equity section; calculate ratios.

P11.2A (LO 2, 3, 4), AP The stockholders' equity accounts of Cyrus Corporation on January 1, 2022, were as follows.

Preferred Stock (7%, $100 par noncumulative, 5,000 shares authorized)	$ 300,000
Common Stock ($4 stated value, 300,000 shares authorized)	1,000,000
Paid-in Capital in Excess of Par Value—Preferred Stock	15,000
Paid-in Capital in Excess of Stated Value—Common Stock	480,000
Retained Earnings	688,000
Treasury Stock (5,000 common shares)	40,000

During 2022, the corporation had the following transactions and events pertaining to its stockholders' equity.

Feb. 1	Issued 5,000 shares of common stock for $30,000.
Mar. 20	Purchased 1,000 additional shares of common treasury stock at $7 per share.
Oct. 1	Declared a 7% cash dividend on preferred stock, payable November 1.
Nov. 1	Paid the dividend declared on October 1.
Dec. 1	Declared a $0.50 per share cash dividend to common stockholders of record on December 15, payable December 31, 2022.
31	Determined that net income for the year was $280,000. Paid the dividend declared on December 1.

Instructions

a. Journalize the transactions. (Include entries to close net income and dividends to Retained Earnings.)
b. Enter the beginning balances in the accounts and post the journal entries to the stockholders' equity accounts. (Use T-accounts.)
c. Prepare the stockholders' equity section of the balance sheet at December 31, 2022.
d. Calculate the payout ratio, earnings per share, and return on common stockholders' equity. (*Note:* Use the common shares outstanding on January 1 and December 31 to determine the average shares outstanding.)

c. Tot. paid-in capital $1,825,000

Prepare a stockholders' equity section.

P11.3A (LO 2, 3, 4), AP On December 31, 2021, Jons Company had 1,300,000 shares of $5 par common stock issued and outstanding. At December 31, 2021, stockholders' equity had the amounts listed here.

Common Stock	$6,500,000
Additional Paid-in Capital	1,800,000
Retained Earnings	1,200,000

Transactions during 2022 and other information related to stockholders' equity accounts were as follows.

1. On January 10, issued at $107 per share 120,000 shares of $100 par value, 9% cumulative preferred stock.
2. On February 8, reacquired 15,000 shares of its common stock for $11 per share.
3. On May 9, declared the yearly cash dividend on preferred stock, payable June 10, to stockholders of record on May 31.

4. On June 8, declared a cash dividend of $1.20 per share on the common stock outstanding, payable on July 10 to stockholders of record on July 1.

5. Net income for 2022 was $3,600,000.

Instructions

a. Record the journal entries that are required for items 1–5 above.

b. Prepare the stockholders' equity section of Jons' balance sheet at December 31, 2022.

Tot. stockholders' equity $23,153,000

P11.4A (LO 3, 4), AP The ledger of Waite Corporation at December 31, 2022, after the books have been closed, contains the following stockholders' equity accounts.

Preferred Stock (10,000 shares issued)	$1,000,000
Common Stock (300,000 shares issued)	1,500,000
Paid-in Capital in Excess of Par Value—Preferred Stock	200,000
Paid-in Capital in Excess of Stated Value—Common Stock	1,600,000
Retained Earnings	2,860,000

Reproduce Retained Earnings account, and prepare a stockholders' equity section.

A review of the accounting records reveals this information:

1. Preferred stock is 8%, $100 par value, noncumulative. Since January 1, 2021, 10,000 shares have been outstanding; 20,000 shares are authorized.

2. Common stock is no-par with a stated value of $5 per share; 600,000 shares are authorized.

3. The January 1, 2022, balance in Retained Earnings was $2,380,000.

4. On October 1, 60,000 shares of common stock were sold for cash at $9 per share.

5. A cash dividend of $400,000 was declared and properly allocated to preferred and common stock on November 1. No dividends were paid to preferred stockholders in 2021.

6. Net income for the year was $880,000.

7. On December 31, 2022, the directors authorized disclosure of a $160,000 restriction of retained earnings for plant expansion. (Use Note A.)

Instructions

a. Reproduce the Retained Earnings account (T-account) for the year.

b. Prepare the stockholders' equity section of the balance sheet at December 31.

b. Tot. paid-in capital $4,300,000

P11.5A (LO 2, 4), AP Layes Corporation has been authorized to issue 20,000 shares of $100 par value, 7%, noncumulative preferred stock and 1,000,000 shares of no-par common stock. The corporation assigned a $5 stated value to the common stock. At December 31, 2022, the ledger contained the following balances pertaining to stockholders' equity.

Prepare entries for stock transactions, and prepare a stockholders' equity section.

Preferred Stock	$ 150,000
Paid-in Capital in Excess of Par Value—Preferred Stock	20,000
Common Stock	2,000,000
Paid-in Capital in Excess of Stated Value—Common Stock	1,520,000
Treasury Stock (4,000 common shares)	36,000
Retained Earnings	82,000
Accumulated Other Comprehensive Income	51,000

The preferred stock was issued for $170,000 cash. All common stock issued was for cash. In November 4,000 shares of common stock were purchased for the treasury at a per share cost of $9. No dividends were declared in 2022.

Instructions

a. Prepare the journal entries for the following.

1. Issuance of preferred stock for cash.
2. Issuance of common stock for cash.
3. Purchase of common treasury stock for cash.

b. Prepare the stockholders' equity section of the balance sheet at December 31, 2022.

b. Tot. stockholders' equity $3,787,000

P11.6A (LO 2, 3, 4), AP On January 1, 2022, Kimbel Inc. had these stockholders' equity balances.

Prepare a stockholders' equity section.

Common Stock, $1 par (2,000,000 shares authorized, 600,000 shares issued and outstanding)	$ 600,000
Paid-in Capital in Excess of Par Value	1,500,000
Retained Earnings	700,000
Accumulated Other Comprehensive Income	60,000

During 2022, the following transactions and events occurred.

1. Issued 50,000 shares of $1 par value common stock for $3 per share.
2. Issued 60,000 shares of common stock for cash at $4 per share.
3. Purchased 20,000 shares of common stock for the treasury at $3.80 per share.
4. Declared and paid a cash dividend of $207,000.
5. Earned net income of $410,000.
6. Had other comprehensive income of $17,000.

Tot. stockholders' equity $3,394,000

Instructions

Prepare the stockholders' equity section of the balance sheet at December 31, 2022.

Evaluate a company's profitability and solvency.

P11.7A (LO 4), AP Writing Spahn Company manufactures backpacks. During 2022, Spahn issued bonds at 10% interest and used the cash proceeds to purchase treasury stock. The following financial information is available for Spahn Company for the years 2022 and 2021.

	2022	2021
Sales revenue	$ 9,000,000	$ 9,000,000
Net income	2,240,000	2,500,000
Interest expense	500,000	140,000
Tax expense	670,000	750,000
Dividends paid on common stock	890,000	1,026,000
Dividends paid on preferred stock	300,000	300,000
Total assets (year-end)	14,500,000	16,875,000
Average total assets	15,687,500	17,763,000
Total liabilities (year-end)	6,000,000	3,000,000
Avg. total common stockholders' equity	9,400,000	14,100,000

Instructions

a. Use the information above to calculate the following ratios for both years: (1) return on assets, (2) return on common stockholders' equity, (3) payout ratio, (4) debt to assets ratio, and (5) times interest earned.

b. Referring to your findings in part (a), discuss the changes in the company's profitability from 2021 to 2022.

c. Referring to your findings in part (a), discuss the changes in the company's solvency from 2021 to 2022.

d. Based on your findings in (b), was the decision to issue debt to purchase common stock a wise one?

Prepare dividend entries, prepare a stockholders' equity section, and calculate ratios.

*P11.8A (LO 3, 4, 5), AP On January 1, 2022, Tacoma Corporation had these stockholders' equity accounts.

Common Stock ($10 par value, 70,000 shares issued and outstanding)	$700,000
Paid-in Capital in Excess of Par Value	500,000
Retained Earnings	620,000

During the year, the following transactions occurred.

Jan. 15	Declared a $0.50 cash dividend per share to stockholders of record on January 31, payable February 15.
Feb. 15	Paid the dividend declared in January.
Apr. 15	Declared a 10% stock dividend to stockholders of record on April 30, distributable May 15. On April 15, the market price of the stock was $14 per share.
May 15	Issued the shares for the stock dividend.
Dec. 1	Declared a $0.60 per share cash dividend to stockholders of record on December 15, payable January 10, 2023.
31	Determined that net income for the year was $400,000.

Instructions

a. Journalize the transactions. (Include entries to close net income and dividends to Retained Earnings.)

b. Enter the beginning balances and post the entries to the stockholders' equity T-accounts. (*Note:* Open additional stockholders' equity accounts as needed.)

c. Prepare the stockholders' equity section of the balance sheet at December 31.

d. Calculate the payout ratio and return on common stockholders' equity.

c. Tot. stockholders' equity $2,138,800

Continuing Case

Cookie Creations

(*Note:* This is a continuation of the Cookie Creations case from Chapters 1 through 10.)

CC11 Part 1 Because Natalie has been so successful with Cookie Creations and her friend Curtis Lesperance has been just as successful with his coffee shop, they conclude that they could benefit from each other's business expertise. Curtis and Natalie next evaluate the different types of business organization. Because of the advantage of limited personal liability, they decide to form a corporation.

Natalie and Curtis are very excited about this new business venture. They come to you with information they have gathered about their companies and with a number of questions.

© leungchopan/ Shutterstock

Part 2 After establishing their company's fiscal year to be October 31, Natalie and Curtis began operating Cookie & Coffee Creations Inc. on November 1, 2022. On that date, they issued both preferred and common stock. Natalie and Curtis now want to prepare financial information for the first year of operations.

Go to WileyPLUS for complete case details and instructions.

Comprehensive Accounting Cycle Review

ACR11.1 (LO 2, 3, 4), AP Hawkeye Corporation's balance sheet at December 31, 2021, is presented as follow.

Journalize transactions and prepare financial statements.

Hawkeye Corporation
Balance Sheet
December 31, 2021

Cash	$ 24,600	Accounts payable	$ 25,600
Accounts receivable	45,500	Common stock ($10 par)	80,000
Allowance for doubtful		Retained earnings	127,400
accounts	(1,500)		$233,000
Supplies	4,400		
Land	40,000		
Buildings	142,000		
Accumulated depreciation—			
buildings	(22,000)		
	$233,000		

During 2022, the following transactions occurred.

1. On January 1, Hawkeye issued 1,200 shares of $40 par, 7% preferred stock for $49,200.
2. On January 1, Hawkeye also issued 900 shares of the $10 par value common stock for $21,000.
3. Hawkeye performed services for $320,000 on account.
4. On April 1, 2022, Hawkeye collected fees of $36,000 in advance for services to be performed from April 1, 2022, to March 31, 2023.
5. Hawkeye collected $276,000 from customers on account.
6. Hawkeye bought $35,100 of supplies on account.
7. Hawkeye paid $32,200 on accounts payable.
8. Hawkeye reacquired 400 shares of its common stock on June 1 for $28 per share.
9. Paid other operating expenses of $188,200.
10. On December 31, 2022, Hawkeye declared the annual cash dividend on preferred stock and a $1.20 per share dividend on the outstanding common stock, all payable on January 15, 2023.
11. An account receivable of $1,700 which originated in 2021 is written off as uncollectible.

Adjustment data:

1. A count of supplies indicates that $5,900 of supplies remain unused at year-end.
2. Recorded revenue from item 4 above.

3. The allowance for doubtful accounts should have a balance of $3,500 at year end.
4. Depreciation is recorded on the building on a straight-line basis based on a 30-year life and a salvage value of $10,000.
5. The income tax rate is 30%. (*Hint:* Prepare the income statement up to income before taxes and multiply by 30% to compute the amount.)

Instructions

(You may want to set up T-accounts to determine ending balances.)

a. Prepare journal entries for the transactions listed above and adjusting entries.
b. Prepare an adjusted trial balance at December 31, 2022.
c. Prepare an income statement and a retained earnings statement for the year ending December 31, 2022, and a classified balance sheet as of December 31, 2022.

b. Totals $740,690
c. Net income $81,970
   Tot. assets $421,000

Journalize transactions and prepare financial statements.

ACR11.2 (LO 2, 3, 4), AP Karen Noonan opened Clean Sweep Inc. on February 1, 2022. During February, the following transactions were completed.

Feb.	1	Issued 5,000 shares of Clean Sweep common stock for $13,000. Each share has a $1.50 par.
	1	Borrowed $8,000 on a 2-year, 6% note payable.
	1	Paid $9,020 to purchase used floor and window cleaning equipment from a company going out of business ($4,820 was for the floor equipment and $4,200 for the window equipment).
	1	Paid $220 for February Internet and phone services.
	3	Purchased cleaning supplies for $980 on account.
	4	Hired 4 employees. Each will be paid $480 per 5-day work week (Monday–Friday). Employees will begin working Monday, February 9.
	5	Obtained insurance coverage for $9,840 per year. Coverage runs from February 1, 2022, through January 31, 2023. Karen paid $2,460 cash for the first quarter of coverage.
	5	Discussions with the insurance agent indicated that providing outside window cleaning services would cost too much to insure. Karen sold the window cleaning equipment for $3,950 cash.
	16	Billed customers $3,900 for cleaning services performed through February 13, 2022.
	17	Received $540 from a customer for 4 weeks of cleaning services to begin February 21, 2022. (By paying in advance, this customer received 10% off the normal weekly fee of $150.)
	18	Paid $300 on amount owed on cleaning supplies.
	20	Paid $3 per share to buy 300 shares of Clean Sweep common stock from a shareholder who disagreed with management goals. The shares will be held as treasury shares.
	23	Billed customers $4,300 for cleaning services performed through February 20.
	24	Paid cash for employees' wages for 2 weeks (February 9–13 and 16–20).
	25	Collected $2,500 cash from customers billed on February 16.
	27	Paid $220 for Internet and phone services for March.
	28	Declared and paid a cash dividend of $0.20 per share.

Instructions

a. Journalize the February transactions. (You do not need to include an explanation for each journal entry.)
b. Post to the ledger accounts (Use T-accounts.)
c. Prepare a trial balance at February 28, 2022.
d. Journalize the following adjustments. (Round all amounts to whole dollars.)

c. Trial bal. totals $30,420

1. Services performed for customers through February 27, 2022, but unbilled and uncollected were $3,800.
2. Received notice that a customer who was billed $200 for services performed February 10 has filed for bankruptcy. Clean Sweep does not expect to collect any portion of this outstanding receivable.
3. Clean Sweep uses the allowance method to estimate bad debts. Clean Sweep estimates that 3% of its month-end receivables will not be collected.
4. Record 1 month of depreciation for the floor equipment. Use the straight-line method, an estimated life of 4 years, and $500 salvage value.
5. Record 1 month of insurance expense.
6. An inventory count shows $400 of supplies on hand at February 28.

7. One week of services were performed for the customer who paid in advance on February 17.
8. Accrue for wages owed through February 28, 2022.
9. Accrue for interest expense for 1 month.
10. Karen estimates a 20% income tax rate. (*Hint:* Prepare an income statement up to "income before taxes" to help with the income tax calculation.)

e. Post adjusting entries to the T-accounts.
f. Prepare an adjusted trial balance.
g. Prepare a multiple-step income statement, a retained earnings statement, and a properly classified balance sheet as of February 28, 2022.
h. Journalize closing entries.

g. Net income $3,117
Tot. assets $26,101

Expand Your Critical Thinking

Financial Reporting Problem: Apple Inc.

CT11.1 The stockholders' equity section of **Apple Inc.**'s balance sheet is shown in the Consolidated Statement of Financial Position in Appendix A. The complete annual report, including the notes to its financial statements, is available at the company's website.

Instructions

Answer the following questions.

a. What is the par or stated value per share of Apple's common stock?
b. What percentage of Apple's authorized common stock was issued at September 30, 2017? (Round to the nearest full percent.)
c. How many shares of common stock were outstanding at September 24, 2016, and at September 30, 2017?
d. Calculate the payout ratio, earnings per share, and return on common stockholders' equity for 2017.

Comparative Analysis Problem: Columbia Sportswear Company vs. VF Corporation

CT11.2 The financial statements of **Columbia Sportswear Company** are presented in Appendix B. Financial statements of **VF Corporation** are presented in Appendix C.

Instructions

a. Based on the information in these financial statements, compute the 2016 return on common stockholders' equity, debt to assets ratio, and return on assets for each company.
b. What conclusions concerning the companies' profitability can be drawn from these ratios? Which company relies more on debt to boost its return to common shareholders?
c. Compute the payout ratio for each company. Which pays out a higher percentage of its earnings?

Comparative Analysis Problem: Amazon.com, Inc. vs. Wal-Mart Stores, Inc.

CT11.3 The financial statements of **Amazon.com, Inc.** are presented in Appendix D. Financial statements of **Wal-Mart Stores, Inc.** are presented in Appendix E.

Instructions

a. Based on the information in these financial statements, compute the return on common stockholders' equity, debt to assets ratio, and return on assets for each company for the most recent year provided.
b. What conclusions concerning the companies' profitability can be drawn from these ratios? Which company relies more on debt to boost its return to common shareholders?
c. Compute the payout ratio for each company. Which pays out a higher percentage of its earnings?

Interpreting Financial Statements

CT11.4 Marriott Corporation split into two companies: **Host Marriott Corporation** and **Marriott International**. Host Marriott retained ownership of the corporation's vast hotel and other properties, while Marriott International, rather than owning hotels, managed them. The purpose of this split was to free Marriott International from the "baggage" associated with Host Marriott, thus allowing it to be more aggressive in its pursuit of growth. The following information (in millions) is provided for each corporation for their first full year operating as independent companies.

	Host Marriott	Marriott International
Sales revenue	$1,501	$8,415
Net income	(25)	200
Total assets	3,822	3,207
Total liabilities	3,112	2,440
Common stockholders' equity	710	767

Instructions

a. The two companies were split by the issuance of shares of Marriott International to all shareholders of the previous combined company. Discuss the nature of this transaction.

b. Calculate the debt to assets ratio for each company.

c. Calculate the return on assets and return on common stockholders' equity for each company.

d. The company's debtholders were fiercely opposed to the original plan to split the two companies because the original plan had Host Marriott absorbing the majority of the company's debt. They relented only when Marriott International agreed to absorb a larger share of the debt. Discuss the possible reasons the debtholders were opposed to the plan to split the company.

Real-World Focus

CT11.5 You should become familiar with reviewing the stockholders' equity section of an annual report to identify its major components.

Instructions

Select a well-known company, search the Internet for its most recent annual report, and then answer the following questions.

a. What is the company's name?

b. What classes of capital stock has the company issued?

c. For each class of stock:

   1. How many shares are authorized, issued, and/or outstanding?
   2. What is the par value?

d. What are the company's retained earnings?

e. Has the company acquired treasury stock? How many shares?

Decision-Making Across the Organization

CT11.6 During a recent period, the fast-food chain **Wendy's International** purchased many treasury shares. This caused the number of shares outstanding to fall from 124 million to 105 million. The following information was drawn from the company's financial statements (in millions).

	Information for the Year after Purchase of Treasury Stock	Information for the Year before Purchase of Treasury Stock
Net income	$ 193.6	$ 123.4
Total assets	2,076.0	1,837.9
Average total assets	2,016.9	1,889.8
Total common stockholders' equity	1,029.8	1,068.1
Average common stockholders' equity	1,078.0	1,126.2
Total liabilities	1,046.3	769.9
Average total liabilities	939.0	763.7
Interest expense	30.2	19.8
Income taxes	113.7	84.3
Cash provided by operations	305.2	233.8
Cash dividends paid on common stock	26.8	31.0
Preferred stock dividends	0	0
Average number of common shares outstanding	109.7	119.9

Instructions

Use the information provided to answer the following questions.

a. Compute earnings per share, return on common stockholders' equity, and return on assets for both years. Discuss the change in the company's profitability over this period.

b. Compute the dividend payout ratio. Also compute the average cash dividend paid per share of common stock (dividends paid divided by the average number of common shares outstanding). Discuss any change in these ratios during this period and the implications for the company's dividend policy.

c. Compute the debt to assets ratio and times interest earned. Discuss the change in the company's solvency.

d. Based on your findings in (a) and (c), discuss to what extent any change in the return on common stockholders' equity was the result of increased reliance on debt.

e. Does it appear that the purchase of treasury stock and the shift toward more reliance on debt were wise strategic moves?

Communication Activity

CT11.7 Earl Kent, your uncle, is an inventor who has decided to incorporate. Uncle Earl knows that you are an accounting major at U.N.O. In a recent letter to you, he ends with the question, "I'm filling out a state incorporation application. Can you tell me the difference among the following terms: (1) authorized stock, (2) issued stock, (3) outstanding stock, and (4) preferred stock?"

Instructions

In a brief note, differentiate for Uncle Earl the four different stock terms. Write the letter to be friendly, yet professional.

Ethics Cases

CT11.8 The R&D division of Pele Corp. has just developed a chemical for sterilizing the vicious Brazilian "killer bees" which are invading Mexico and the southern United States. The president of Pele is anxious to get the chemical on the market because Pele profits need a boost—and his job is in jeopardy because of decreasing sales and profits. Pele has an opportunity to sell this chemical in Central American countries, where the laws are much more relaxed than in the United States.

The director of Pele's R&D division strongly recommends further research in the laboratory to test the side effects of this chemical on other insects, birds, animals, plants, and even humans. He cautions the president, "We could be sued from all sides if the chemical has tragic side effects that we didn't even test for in the lab." The president answers, "We can't wait an additional year for your lab tests. We can avoid losses from such lawsuits by establishing a separate wholly owned corporation to shield Pele Corp. from such lawsuits. We can't lose any more than our investment in the new corporation, and we'll invest just the patent covering this chemical. We'll reap the benefits if the chemical works and is safe, and avoid the losses from lawsuits if it's a disaster." The following week, Pele creates a new wholly owned corporation called Cabo Inc., sells the chemical patent to it for $10, and watches the spraying begin.

Instructions

a. Who are the stakeholders in this situation?

b. Are the president's motives and actions ethical?

c. Can Pele shield itself against losses of Cabo Inc.?

CT11.9 Cooper Corporation has paid 60 consecutive quarterly cash dividends (15 years). The last 6 months have been a real cash drain on the company, however, as profit margins have been greatly narrowed by increasing competition. With a cash balance sufficient to meet only day-to-day operating needs, the president, Sonny Boyd, has decided that a stock dividend instead of a cash dividend should be declared. He tells Cooper's financial vice president, Dana Marks, to issue a press release stating that the company is extending its consecutive dividend record with the issuance of a 5% stock dividend. "Write the press release convincing the stockholders that the stock dividend is just as good as a cash dividend," he orders. "Just watch our stock rise when we announce the stock dividend; it must be a good thing if that happens."

Instructions

a. Who are the stakeholders in this situation?

b. Is there anything unethical about president Boyd's intentions or actions?

c. What is the effect of a stock dividend on a corporation's stockholders' equity accounts? Which would you rather receive as a stockholder—a cash dividend or a stock dividend? Why?

All About You

CT11.10 In response to the Sarbanes-Oxley Act, many companies have implemented formal ethics codes. Many other organizations also have ethics codes.

Instructions

Obtain the ethics code from an organization that you belong to (e.g., student organization, business school, employer, or a volunteer organization). Evaluate the ethics code based on how clearly it identifies proper and improper behavior. Discuss its strengths, and how it might be improved.

FASB Codification Activity

CT11.11 If your school has a subscription to the FASB Codification, log in and prepare responses to the following.

a. What is the stock dividend?

b. What is a stock split?

c. At what percentage point does the issuance of additional shares qualify as a stock dividend, as opposed to a stock split?

Considering People, Planet, and Profit

CT11.12 The January 19, 2012, edition of the *Wall Street Journal* contains an article by Angus Loten entitled "With New Law, Profits Take a Back Seat."

Instructions

Read the article online and then answer the following questions.

a. Summarize the nature of the new law that is discussed in the article.

b. What do some proponents of the law say is the "biggest value" of the law? How does the article say that this would have impacted **Ben & Jerry's**?

c. What are some criticisms of the law?

d. How does incorporation as a benefit corporation differ from B Corp certification?

e. What are some of the companies that the article cites as either having adopted benefit corporation standing or are considering it?

A Look at IFRS

LEARNING OBJECTIVE 6
Compare the accounting for stockholders' equity under GAAP and IFRS.

The accounting for transactions related to stockholders' equity, such as issuance of shares and purchase of treasury stock, are similar under both IFRS and GAAP. Major differences relate to terminology used, introduction of items such as revaluation surplus, and presentation of stockholders' equity information.

Key Points

Following are the key similarities and differences between GAAP and IFRS as related to stockholders' equity, dividends, retained earnings, and income reporting.

Similarities

- Aside from the terminology used, the accounting transactions for the issuance of shares and the purchase of treasury stock are similar.
- Like GAAP, IFRS does not allow a company to record gains or losses on purchases of its own shares.
- The accounting related to prior period adjustment is essentially the same under IFRS and GAAP.
- The income statement using IFRS is called the **statement of comprehensive income**. A statement of comprehensive income is presented in a one- or two-statement format. The single-statement approach includes all items of income and expense, as well as each component of other

comprehensive income or loss by its individual characteristic. In the two-statement approach, a traditional income statement is prepared. It is then followed by a statement of comprehensive income, which starts with net income or loss and then adds other comprehensive income or loss items. Regardless of which approach is reported, income tax expense is required to be reported.

- The computations related to earnings per share are essentially the same under IFRS and GAAP.

Differences

- Under IFRS, the term **reserves** is used to describe all equity accounts other than those arising from contributed (paid-in) capital. This would include, for example, reserves related to retained earnings, asset revaluations, and fair value differences.
- Many countries have a different mix of investor groups than in the United States. For example, in Germany, financial institutions like banks are not only major creditors of corporations but often are the largest corporate stockholders as well. In the United States, Asia, and the United Kingdom, many companies rely on substantial investment from private investors.
- There are often terminology differences for equity accounts. The following summarizes some of the common differences in terminology.

GAAP	IFRS
Common stock	Share capital—ordinary
Stockholders	Shareholders
Par value	Nominal or face value
Authorized stock	Authorized share capital
Preferred stock	Share capital—preference
Paid-in capital	Issued/allocated share capital
Paid-in capital in excess of par—common stock	Share premium—ordinary
Paid-in capital in excess of par—preferred stock	Share premium—preference
Retained earnings	Retained earnings or Retained profits
Retained earnings deficit	Accumulated losses
Accumulated other comprehensive income	General reserve and other reserve accounts

As an example of how similar transactions use different terminology under IFRS, consider the accounting for the issuance of 1,000 shares of $1 par value common stock for $5 per share. Under IFRS, the entry is as follows.

Cash	5,000	
Share Capital—Ordinary		1,000
Share Premium—Ordinary		4,000

- A major difference between IFRS and GAAP relates to the account Revaluation Surplus. Revaluation surplus arises under IFRS because companies are permitted to revalue their property, plant, and equipment to fair value under certain circumstances. This account is part of general reserves under IFRS and is not considered contributed capital.
- IFRS often uses terms such as **retained profits** or **accumulated profit or loss** to describe retained earnings. The term retained earnings is also often used.
- Equity is given various descriptions under IFRS, such as shareholders' equity, owners' equity, capital and reserves, and shareholders' funds.

IFRS Practice

IFRS Self-Test Questions

1. Which of the following is **true**?
   a. In the United States, the primary corporate stockholders are financial institutions.
   b. Share capital means total assets under IFRS.
   c. The IASB and FASB are presently studying how financial statement information should be presented.
   d. The accounting for treasury stock differs extensively between GAAP and IFRS.

2. Under IFRS, the amount of capital received in excess of par value would be credited to:
   a. Retained Earnings.
   b. Contributed Capital.
   c. Share Premium.
   d. Par value is not used under IFRS.

3. Which of the following is **false**?
   a. Under GAAP, companies cannot record gains on transactions involving their own shares.
   b. Under IFRS, companies cannot record gains on transactions involving their own shares.

c. Under IFRS, the statement of stockholders' equity is a required statement.

d. Under IFRS, a company records a revaluation surplus when it experiences an increase in the price of its common stock.

4. Which of the following does **not** represent a pair of GAAP/IFRS-comparable terms?

   a. Additional paid-in capital/Share premium.
   b. Treasury stock/Repurchase reserve.
   c. Common stock/Share capital.
   d. Preferred stock/Preference shares.

5. The basic accounting for cash dividends and stock dividends:

   a. is different under IFRS versus GAAP.
   b. is the same under IFRS and GAAP.
   c. differs only for the accounting for cash dividends between GAAP and IFRS.
   d. differs only for the accounting for stock dividends between GAAP and IFRS.

6. Which item in **not** considered part of reserves?

   a. Unrealized loss on available-for-sale investments.
   b. Revaluation surplus.
   c. Retained earnings.
   d. Issued shares.

7. Under IFRS, a statement of comprehensive income must include:

   a. accounts payable.   c. income tax expense.
   b. retained earnings.   d. preference stock.

8. Which set of terms can be used to describe total stockholders' equity under IFRS?

   a. Shareholders' equity, capital and reserves, other comprehensive income.
   b. Capital and reserves, shareholders' equity, shareholders' funds.
   c. Capital and reserves, retained earnings, shareholders' equity.
   d. All of the answer choices are correct.

9. Earnings per share computations related to IFRS and GAAP:

   a. are essentially similar.
   b. result in an amount referred to as earnings per share.
   c. must deduct preferred (preference) dividends when computing earnings per share.
   d. All of the answer choices are correct.

IFRS Exercises

IFRS11.1 On May 10, Jaurez Corporation issues 1,000 shares of $10 par value ordinary shares for cash at $18 per share. Journalize the issuance of the shares.

IFRS11.2 Meenen Corporation has the following accounts at December 31, 2022 (in euros): Share Capital—Ordinary, €10 par, 5,000 shares issued, €50,000; Share Premium—Ordinary €10,000; Retained Earnings €45,000; and Treasury Shares—Ordinary, 500 shares, €11,000. Prepare the equity section of the statement of financial position (balance sheet).

IFRS11.3 Overton Co. had the following transactions during the current period.

Mar. 2	Issued 5,000 shares of $1 par value ordinary shares to attorneys in payment of a bill for $30,000 for services performed in helping the company to incorporate.
June 12	Issued 60,000 shares of $1 par value ordinary shares for cash of $375,000.
July 11	Issued 1,000 shares of $100 par value preference shares for cash at $110 per share.
Nov. 28	Purchased 2,000 treasury shares for $80,000.

Instructions

Journalize the above transactions.

International Financial Reporting Problem: Louis Vuitton

IFRS11.4 The financial statements of **Louis Vuitton** are presented in Appendix F. The complete annual report, including the notes to its financial statements, is available at the company's website.

Instructions

Use the company's annual report to answer the following questions.

   a. Determine the following amounts at December 31, 2016: (1) total equity, (2) total revaluation reserve, and (3) number of treasury shares.
   b. Examine the equity section of the company's balance sheet. For each of the following, provide the comparable label that would be used under GAAP: (1) share capital, (2) share premium, and (3) net profit, group share.
   c. Did the company declare and pay any dividends for the year ended December 31, 2016?
   d. Compute the company's return on ordinary shareholders' equity for the year ended December 31, 2016.
   e. What was Louis Vuitton's earnings per share for the year ended December 31, 2016?

Answers to IFRS Self-Test Questions

1. c 2. c 3. d 4. b 5. b 6. d 7. c 8. b 9. d

CHAPTER 12

Statement of Cash Flows

Chapter Preview

The balance sheet, income statement, and retained earnings statement do not always show the whole picture of the financial condition of a company or institution. In fact, looking at the financial statements of some well-known companies, a thoughtful investor might ask questions like these: How did **Eastman Kodak** finance cash dividends of $649 million in a year in which it earned only $17 million? How could **United Air Lines** purchase new planes that cost $1.9 billion in a year in which it reported a net loss of over $2 billion? How did the companies that spent a combined fantastic $3.4 trillion on mergers and acquisitions in a recent year finance those deals? Answers to these and similar questions can be found in this chapter, which presents the statement of cash flows.

Feature Story

Got Cash?

Companies must be ready to respond to changes quickly in order to survive and thrive. This requires careful management of cash. One company that managed cash successfully in its early years was **Microsoft**. During those years, the company paid much of its payroll with stock options (rights to purchase company stock in the future at a given price) instead of cash. This conserved cash and turned more than a thousand of its employees into millionaires.

In recent years, Microsoft has had a different kind of cash problem. Now that it has reached a more "mature" stage in life, it generates so much cash—roughly $1 billion per month—that it cannot always figure out what to do with it. At one time, Microsoft had accumulated $60 billion.

The company said it was accumulating cash to invest in new opportunities, buy other companies, and pay off pending lawsuits. Microsoft's stockholders complained that holding all this cash was putting a drag on the company's profitability. Why? Because Microsoft had the cash invested in very low-yielding government securities. Stockholders felt that the company either should find new investment projects that would bring higher returns, or return some of the cash to stockholders.

Finally, Microsoft announced a plan to return cash to stockholders by paying a special one-time $32 billion dividend. This special dividend was so large that, according to the U.S. Commerce Department, it caused total personal income in the United States to rise by 3.7% in one month—the largest increase ever recorded by the agency. (It also made the holiday season brighter, especially for retailers in the Seattle area.) Microsoft also doubled its regular annual dividend to $3.50 per share. Further, it announced that it would spend another $30 billion buying treasury stock.

Apple also has encountered this cash "problem." Recently, Apple had nearly $100 billion in liquid assets (cash, cash equivalents, and investment securities). The company was generating $37 billion of cash per year from its operating activities but spending only about $7 billion on plant assets and purchases of patents. In response to shareholder pressure, Apple announced that it would begin to pay a quarterly dividend of $2.65 per share and buy back up to $10 billion of its stock. Analysts noted that the dividend consumes only $10 billion of cash per year. This leaves Apple wallowing in cash. The rest of us should have such problems.

Source: "Business: An End to Growth? Microsoft's Cash Bonanza," *The Economist* (July 23, 2005), p. 61.

Chapter Outline

LEARNING OBJECTIVES

LO 1 Discuss the usefulness and format of the statement of cash flows.	• Usefulness of the statement of cash flows • Classification of cash flows • Significant noncash activities • Format of the statement of cash flows	**DO IT! 1** Classification of Cash Flows
LO 2 Prepare a statement of cash flows using the indirect method.	• Indirect and direct methods • Indirect method—Computer Services Company • Step 1: Operating activities • Summary of conversion to net cash provided by operating activities • Step 2: Investing and financing activities • Step 3: Net change in cash	**DO IT! 2a** Cash from Operating Activities **DO IT! 2b** Indirect Method
LO 3 Use the statement of cash flows to evaluate a company.	• The corporate life cycle • Free cash flow	**DO IT! 3** Free Cash Flow

Go to the Review and Practice section at the end of the chapter for a targeted summary and practice applications with solutions.
Visit WileyPLUS for additional tutorials and practice opportunities.

Usefulness and Format of the Statement of Cash Flows

> **LEARNING OBJECTIVE 1**
> Discuss the usefulness and format of the statement of cash flows.

The balance sheet, income statement, and retained earnings statement provide only limited information about a company's cash flows (cash receipts and cash payments). For example, comparative balance sheets show the net increase in property, plant, and equipment during the year. But, they do not show how the additions were financed or paid for. The income statement shows net income based on the accrual basis of accounting. But, it does not indicate the amount of cash generated by operating activities. The retained earnings statement shows cash dividends declared but not the cash dividends paid during the year. None of these statements presents a detailed summary of where cash came from and how it was used.

Usefulness of the Statement of Cash Flows

The **statement of cash flows** reports the cash receipts, cash payments, and net change in cash resulting from operating, investing, and financing activities during a period. The information in a statement of cash flows helps investors, creditors, and others assess the following.

1. **The entity's ability to generate future cash flows.** By examining relationships between items in the statement of cash flows, investors can better predict the amounts, timing, and uncertainty of future cash flows than they can from accrual-basis data.
2. **The entity's ability to pay dividends and meet obligations.** If a company does not have adequate cash, it cannot pay employees, settle debts, or pay dividends. Employees, creditors, and stockholders should be particularly interested in this statement because it alone shows the flows of cash in a business.
3. **The reasons for the difference between net income and net cash provided (used) by operating activities.** Net income provides information on the success or failure of a business. However, some financial statement users are critical of accrual-basis net income because it requires many estimates (see **Ethics Note**). As a result, users often challenge the reliability of the number. Such is not the case with cash. Many readers of the statement of cash flows want to know the reasons for the difference between net income and net cash provided by operating activities. Then, they can assess for themselves the reliability of the income number.
4. **The cash investing and financing transactions during the period.** By examining a company's investing and financing transactions, a financial statement reader can better understand why assets and liabilities changed during the period.

> **ETHICS NOTE**
> Though we discourage reliance on cash flows to the exclusion of accrual accounting, comparing net cash provided by operating activities to net income can reveal important information about the "quality" of reported net income. Such a comparison can reveal the extent to which net income provides a good measure of actual performance.

Classification of Cash Flows

The statement of cash flows classifies cash receipts and cash payments as operating, investing, and financing activities. Transactions and other events characteristic of each kind of activity are as follows.

1. **Operating activities** include the cash effects of transactions that create revenues and expenses. They thus enter into the determination of net income.
2. **Investing activities** include (a) acquiring and disposing of investments and property, plant, and equipment, and (b) lending money and collecting the loans.
3. **Financing activities** include (a) obtaining cash from issuing debt and repaying the amounts borrowed, and (b) obtaining cash from stockholders, repurchasing shares, and paying dividends.

The operating activities category is the most important. It shows the cash provided by company operations. This source of cash is generally considered to be the best measure of a company's ability to generate sufficient cash to continue as a going concern.

Illustration 12.1 lists typical cash receipts and cash payments within each of the three classifications. **Study the list carefully.** It will prove very useful in solving homework exercises and problems.

ILLUSTRATION 12.1
Typical receipt and payment classifications

Operating activities

Investing activities

Financing activities

TYPES OF CASH INFLOWS AND OUTFLOWS

Operating activities—Income statement items
Cash inflows:
   From sale of goods or services.
   From interest received and dividends received.
Cash outflows:
   To suppliers for inventory.
   To employees for wages.
   To government for taxes.
   To lenders for interest.
   To others for expenses.

Investing activities—Changes in investments and long-term assets
Cash inflows:
   From sale of property, plant, and equipment.
   From sale of investments in debt or equity securities of other entities.
   From collection of principal on loans to other entities.
Cash outflows:
   To purchase property, plant, and equipment.
   To purchase investments in debt or equity securities of other entities.
   To make loans to other entities.

Financing activities—Changes in long-term liabilities and stockholders' equity
Cash inflows:
   From sale of common stock.
   From issuance of debt (bonds and notes).
Cash outflows:
   To stockholders as dividends.
   To redeem long-term debt or reacquire capital stock (treasury stock).

Note the following general guidelines:

1. Operating activities involve income statement items.
2. Investing activities involve cash flows resulting from changes in investments and long-term asset items.
3. Financing activities involve cash flows resulting from changes in long-term liability and stockholders' equity items.

Companies classify as operating activities some cash flows related to investing or financing activities. For example, receipts of investment revenue (interest and dividends) are classified as operating activities. So are payments of interest to lenders. Why are these considered operating activities? **Because companies report these items in the income statement, where results of operations are shown.**

Significant Noncash Activities

Not all of a company's significant activities involve cash. Examples of significant noncash activities are as follows.

1. Direct issuance of common stock to purchase assets.
2. Conversion of bonds into common stock.

3. Direct issuance of debt to purchase assets.
4. Exchanges of plant assets.

Companies do not report in the body of the statement of cash flows significant financing and investing activities that do not affect cash. Instead, they report these activities in either a **separate schedule** at the bottom of the statement of cash flows or in a **separate note or supplementary schedule** to the financial statements (see **Helpful Hint**). The reporting of these noncash activities in a separate schedule satisfies the **full disclosure principle**.

In solving homework assignments, you should present significant noncash investing and financing activities in a separate schedule at the bottom of the statement of cash flows (see the last item in Illustration 12.2 below).

> **HELPFUL HINT**
> Do not include noncash investing and financing activities in the body of the statement of cash flows. Report this information in a separate schedule.

Accounting Across the Organization   Target Corporation

Darren McCollester/
Getty Images, Inc.

Net What?

Net income is not the same as net cash provided by operating activities. The table shows some results from recent annual reports (dollars in millions), including **Target Corporation**. Note how the numbers differ greatly across the list even though all these companies engage in retail merchandising.

Company	Net Income	Net Cash Provided by Operating Activities
Kohl's Corporation	$ 889	$ 1,884
Wal-Mart Stores, Inc.	16,669	25,591
J. C. Penney Company, Inc.	(1,388)	(1,814)
Costco Wholesale Corp.	20,391	3,437
Target Corporation	1,971	6,520

In general, why do differences exist between net income and net cash provided by operating activities? (Go to WileyPLUS for this answer and additional questions.)

Format of the Statement of Cash Flows

The general format of the statement of cash flows presents the results of the three activities discussed previously—operating, investing, and financing—plus the significant noncash investing and financing activities. **Illustration 12.2** shows a widely used form of the statement of cash flows.

ILLUSTRATION 12.2
Format of statement of cash flows

Company Name
Statement of Cash Flows
For the Period Covered

Cash flows from operating activities		
(List of individual items)	XX	
Net cash provided (used) by operating activities		XXX
Cash flows from investing activities		
(List of individual inflows and outflows)	XX	
Net cash provided (used) by investing activities		XXX
Cash flows from financing activities		
(List of individual inflows and outflows)	XX	
Net cash provided (used) by financing activities		XXX
Net increase (decrease) in cash		XXX
Cash at beginning of period		XXX
Cash at end of period		XXX
Noncash investing and financing activities		
(List of individual noncash transactions)		XXX

The cash flows from operating activities section always appears first, followed by the investing activities section and then the financing activities section. The sum of the operating, investing, and financing sections equals the net increase or decrease in cash for the period. This amount is added to the beginning cash balance to arrive at the ending cash balance—the same amount reported on the balance sheet. The FASB now requires that restricted cash be included with cash and cash equivalents when reconciling the beginning and ending amounts on the statement of cash flows.

ACTION PLAN
- Identify the three types of activities used to report all cash inflows and outflows.
- Report as operating activities the cash effects of transactions that create revenues and expenses and enter into the determination of net income.
- Report as investing activities transactions that (a) acquire and dispose of investments and long-term assets and (b) lend money and collect loans.
- Report as financing activities transactions that (a) obtain cash from issuing debt and repay the amounts borrowed and (b) obtain cash from stockholders and pay them dividends.

DO IT! 1 | Classification of Cash Flows

During its first week, Duffy & Stevenson Company had these transactions.

1. Issued 100,000 shares of $5 par value common stock for $800,000 cash.
2. Borrowed $200,000 from Castle Bank, signing a 5-year note bearing 8% interest.
3. Purchased two semi-trailer trucks for $170,000 cash.
4. Paid employees $12,000 for salaries and wages.
5. Collected $20,000 cash for services performed.

Classify each of these transactions by type of cash flow activity. (*Hint:* Refer to Illustration 12.1.)

Solution

1. Financing activity.
2. Financing activity.
3. Investing activity.
4. Operating activity.
5. Operating activity.

Related exercise material: **BE12.1, BE12.2, BE12.3, DO IT! 12.1, E12.1, E12.2, and E12.3.**

Preparing the Statement of Cash Flows—Indirect Method

LEARNING OBJECTIVE 2
Prepare a statement of cash flows using the indirect method.

Companies prepare the statement of cash flows differently from the three other basic financial statements. First, it is not prepared from an adjusted trial balance. It requires detailed information concerning the changes in account balances that occurred between two points in time. An adjusted trial balance will not provide the necessary data. Second, the statement of cash flows deals with cash receipts and payments. As a result, the company **adjusts** the effects of the use of accrual accounting **to determine cash flows**.

The information to prepare this statement usually comes from three sources:

- **Comparative balance sheets.** Information in the comparative balance sheets indicates the amount of the changes in assets, liabilities, and stockholders' equity from the beginning to the end of the period.

- **Current income statement.** Information in this statement helps determine the amount of net cash provided or used by operating activities during the period.
- **Additional information.** Such information includes transaction data that are needed to determine how cash was provided or used during the period.

Preparing the statement of cash flows from these data sources involves three major steps, explained in **Illustration 12.3**.

Step 1: Determine net cash provided/used by operating activities by converting net income from an accrual basis to a cash basis.

This step involves analyzing not only the current year's income statement but also comparative balance sheets and selected additional data.

Step 2: Analyze changes in noncurrent asset and liability accounts and stockholders' equity accounts and record as investing and financing activities, or disclose as noncash transactions.

This step involves analyzing comparative balance sheet data and selected additional information for their effects on cash.

Step 3: Compare the net change in cash on the statement of cash flows with the change in the Cash account reported on the balance sheet to make sure the amounts agree.

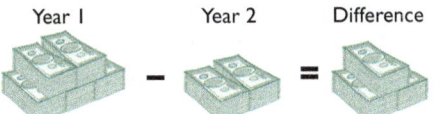

The difference between the beginning and ending cash balances can be easily computed from comparative balance sheets.

ILLUSTRATION 12.3

Three major steps in preparing the statement of cash flows

Indirect and Direct Methods

In order to perform Step 1, a company **must convert net income from an accrual basis to a cash basis.** This conversion may be done by either of two methods: (1) the indirect method or (2) the direct method. **Both methods arrive at the same amount** for "Net cash provided by operating activities." They differ in **how** they arrive at the amount.

The **indirect method** adjusts net income for items that do not affect cash. A great majority of companies (98%) use this method. Companies favor the indirect method for two reasons: (1) it is easier and less costly to prepare, and (2) it focuses on the differences between net income and net cash flow from operating activities.

The **direct method** shows operating cash receipts and payments. It is prepared by adjusting each item in the income statement from the accrual basis to the cash basis. The FASB has expressed a preference for the direct method but allows the use of either method.

The next section illustrates the more popular indirect method. Appendix 12A illustrates the direct method.

Indirect Method—Computer Services Company

To explain how to prepare a statement of cash flows using the indirect method, we use financial information from Computer Services Company. **Illustration 12.4** presents Computer Services' current- and previous-year balance sheets, its current-year income statement, and related financial information for the current year.

ILLUSTRATION 12.4
Comparative balance sheets, income statement, and additional information for Computer Services Company

Computer Services Company
Comparative Balance Sheets
December 31

Assets	2022	2021	Change in Account Balance Increase/Decrease
Current assets			
Cash	$ 55,000	$ 33,000	$ 22,000 Increase
Accounts receivable	20,000	30,000	10,000 Decrease
Inventory	15,000	10,000	5,000 Increase
Prepaid expenses	5,000	1,000	4,000 Increase
Property, plant, and equipment			
Land	130,000	20,000	110,000 Increase
Buildings	160,000	40,000	120,000 Increase
Accumulated depreciation—buildings	(11,000)	(5,000)	6,000 Increase
Equipment	27,000	10,000	17,000 Increase
Accumulated depreciation—equipment	(3,000)	(1,000)	2,000 Increase
Total assets	$398,000	$138,000	
Liabilities and Stockholders' Equity			
Current liabilities			
Accounts payable	$ 28,000	$ 12,000	$ 16,000 Increase
Income taxes payable	6,000	8,000	2,000 Decrease
Long-term liabilities			
Bonds payable	130,000	20,000	110,000 Increase
Stockholders' equity			
Common stock	70,000	50,000	20,000 Increase
Retained earnings	164,000	48,000	116,000 Increase
Total liabilities and stockholders' equity	$398,000	$138,000	

Computer Services Company
Income Statement
For the Year Ended December 31, 2022

Sales revenue		$507,000
Cost of goods sold	$150,000	
Operating expenses (excluding depreciation)	111,000	
Depreciation expense	9,000	
Loss on disposal of plant assets	3,000	
Interest expense	42,000	315,000
Income before income tax		192,000
Income tax expense		47,000
Net income		$145,000

Additional information for 2022:

1. Depreciation expense was comprised of $6,000 for building and $3,000 for equipment.
2. The company sold equipment with a book value of $7,000 (cost $8,000, less accumulated depreciation $1,000) for $4,000 cash.
3. Issued $110,000 of long-term bonds in direct exchange for land.
4. A building costing $120,000 was purchased for cash. Equipment costing $25,000 was also purchased for cash.
5. Issued common stock for $20,000 cash.
6. The company declared and paid a $29,000 cash dividend.

We now apply the three steps for preparing a statement of cash flows to the information provided for Computer Services Company.

Step 1: Operating Activities

Determine Net Cash Provided/Used by Operating Activities by Converting Net Income from an Accrual Basis to a Cash Basis

To determine net cash provided by operating activities under the indirect method, companies **adjust net income in numerous ways**. A useful starting point is to understand **why** net income must be converted to net cash provided by operating activities.

Under generally accepted accounting principles, most companies use the accrual basis of accounting. This basis requires that companies record revenue when a performance obligation is satisfied and record expenses when incurred. Revenues include credit sales for which the company has not yet collected cash. Expenses incurred include some items that have not yet been paid in cash. Thus, under the accrual basis, net income is not the same as net cash provided by operating activities.

Therefore, under the **indirect method**, companies must adjust net income to convert certain items to the cash basis. The indirect method (or reconciliation method) starts with net income and converts it to net cash provided by operating activities. **Illustration 12.5** lists the three types of adjustments.

Net Income   +/−   **Adjustments**   =   Net Cash Provided/Used by Operating Activities

- **Add back noncash expenses**, such as depreciation expense and amortization expense.
- **Deduct gains and add losses** that resulted from investing and financing activities.
- **Analyze changes** to noncash current asset and current liability accounts.

ILLUSTRATION 12.5
Three types of adjustments to convert net income to net cash provided by operating activities

We explain the three types of adjustments in the next three sections.

Depreciation Expense

Computer Services' income statement reports depreciation expense of $9,000. Although depreciation expense reduces net income, it does not reduce cash. In other words, depreciation expense is a noncash charge. The company must add it back to net income to negate the effect of the expense to arrive at net cash provided by operating activities (see **Helpful Hint**). Computer Services reports depreciation expense in the statement of cash flows as in **Illustration 12.6**.

HELPFUL HINT
Depreciation is similar to any other expense in that it reduces net income. It differs in that it does not involve a current cash outflow. That is why it must be *added back* to net income to arrive at net cash provided by operating activities.

Cash flows from operating activities		
Net income		$145,000
Adjustments to reconcile net income to net cash provided by operating activities:		
Depreciation expense		9,000
Net cash provided by operating activities		$154,000

ILLUSTRATION 12.6
Adjustment for depreciation

As the first adjustment to net income in the statement of cash flows, companies frequently list depreciation and similar noncash charges such as amortization of intangible assets and bad debt expense.

Loss on Disposal of Plant Assets

Illustration 12.1 states that cash received from the sale (disposal) of plant assets is reported in the investing activities section. Because of this, **companies eliminate from net income all gains and losses related to the disposal of plant assets, to arrive at net cash provided by operating activities.**

In our example, Computer Services' income statement reports a $3,000 loss on the disposal of plant assets (book value $7,000, less $4,000 cash received from disposal of plant assets). The journal entry to record this transaction would have been as follows.

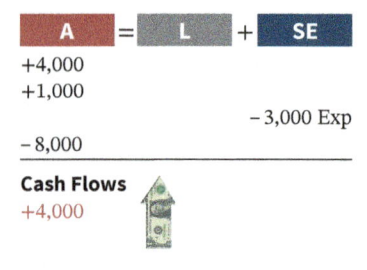

Cash	4,000	
Accumulated Depreciation—Equipment	1,000	
Loss on Disposal of Plant Assets	3,000	
Equipment		8,000

The company's loss of $3,000 should be added to net income in order to determine net cash provided by operating activities. The loss reduced net income but did not reduce cash. **Illustration 12.7** shows that the $3,000 loss is eliminated by adding $3,000 back to net income to arrive at net cash provided by operating activities. (The cash received of $4,000 will be reported in the investing activities section, as discussed later.)

ILLUSTRATION 12.7
Adjustment for loss on disposal of plant assets

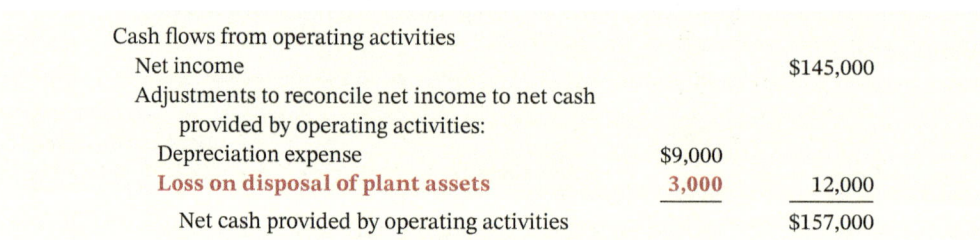

If a gain on disposal occurs, the company deducts the gain from net income in order to determine net cash provided by operating activities. **In the case of either a gain or a loss, companies report as a source of cash in the investing activities section of the statement of cash flows the actual amount of cash received from the sale.**

Changes to Noncash Current Asset and Current Liability Accounts

A final adjustment in reconciling net income to net cash provided by operating activities involves examining all changes in noncash current asset and current liability accounts. The accrual-accounting process records revenues in the period in which the performance obligation is satisfied and expenses as incurred. For example, Accounts Receivable reflects amounts owed to the company for sales that have been made but for which cash collections have not yet been received. Prepaid Insurance reflects insurance that has been paid for but which has not yet expired (therefore has not been expensed). Similarly, Salaries and Wages Payable reflects salaries and wages expense that has been incurred but has not been paid.

As a result, companies need to adjust net income for these accruals and prepayments to determine net cash provided by operating activities. Thus, they must analyze the change in each noncash current asset and current liability account to determine its impact on net income and cash.

Changes in Noncash Current Assets The adjustments required for changes in noncash current asset accounts are as follows. **Deduct from net income increases in current asset accounts, and add to net income decreases in current asset accounts, to arrive at net cash provided by operating activities.** We observe these relationships by analyzing the accounts of Computer Services.

Decrease in Accounts Receivable Computer Services' accounts receivable decreased by $10,000 (from $30,000 to $20,000) during the period. For Computer Services, this means that cash receipts were $10,000 higher than sales revenue. The Accounts Receivable account in **Illustration 12.8** shows that Computer Services had $507,000 in sales revenue (as reported on the income statement). Since the beginning balance was $30,000 and accounts receivable increased by $507,000 because of sales, then receipts during the period must have been $517,000, to arrive at an ending balance of $20,000. Thus, receipts exceeded sales by $10,000, the amount of the decline in accounts receivable.

Accounts Receivable

1/1/22	Balance	30,000	Receipts from customers	517,000
	Sales revenue	507,000		
12/31/22	Balance	20,000		

ILLUSTRATION 12.8
Analysis of accounts receivable

As shown in Illustration 12.9, to adjust net income to net cash provided by operating activities, the company adds to net income the decrease of $10,000 in accounts receivable. When the Accounts Receivable balance increases, cash receipts are lower than sales revenue earned under the accrual basis. Therefore, the company deducts from net income the amount of the increase in accounts receivable, to arrive at net cash provided by operating activities.

Increase in Inventory Computer Services' inventory increased $5,000 (from $10,000 to $15,000) during the period. The change in the Inventory account reflects the difference between the amount of inventory purchased and the amount sold. For Computer Services, this means that the cost of merchandise purchased exceeded the cost of goods sold by $5,000. As a result, cost of goods sold does not reflect $5,000 of cash payments made for merchandise. The company deducts from net income this inventory increase of $5,000 during the period, to arrive at net cash provided by operating activities (see Illustration 12.9). If inventory decreases, the company adds to net income the amount of the change, to arrive at net cash provided by operating activities.

Increase in Prepaid Expenses Computer Services' prepaid expenses increased during the period by $4,000. This means that cash paid for expenses is higher than expenses reported on an accrual basis. In other words, the company has made cash payments in the current period that will not be charged to expenses until future periods. To adjust net income to net cash provided by operating activities, the company deducts from net income the $4,000 increase in prepaid expenses (see **Illustration 12.9**).

Cash flows from operating activities			
Net income			$145,000
Adjustments to reconcile net income to net cash provided by operating activities:			
Depreciation expense		$ 9,000	
Loss on disposal of plant assets		3,000	
Decrease in accounts receivable		10,000	
Increase in inventory		(5,000)	
Increase in prepaid expenses		(4,000)	13,000
Net cash provided by operating activities			$158,000

ILLUSTRATION 12.9
Adjustments for changes in current asset accounts

If prepaid expenses decrease, reported expenses are higher than the expenses paid. Therefore, the company adds to net income the decrease in prepaid expenses, to arrive at net cash provided by operating activities.

Changes in Current Liabilities The adjustments required for changes in current liability accounts are as follows. **Add to net income increases in current liability accounts and deduct from net income decreases in current liability accounts, to arrive at net cash provided by operating activities.**

Increase in Accounts Payable For Computer Services, Accounts Payable increased by $16,000 (from $12,000 to $28,000) during the period. That means the company received $16,000 more in goods than it actually paid for. As shown in Illustration 12.10, to adjust net income to determine net cash provided by operating activities, the company adds to net income the $16,000 increase in Accounts Payable.

Decrease in Income Taxes Payable When a company incurs income tax expense but has not yet paid its taxes, it records income taxes payable. A change in the Income Taxes Payable account reflects the difference between income tax expense incurred and income tax actually paid. Computer Services' Income Taxes Payable account decreased by $2,000. That means the $47,000 of income tax expense reported on the income statement was $2,000 less than the amount of taxes paid during the period of $49,000. As shown in **Illustration 12.10**, to adjust net income to a cash basis, the company must reduce net income by $2,000.

ILLUSTRATION 12.10
Adjustments for changes in current liability accounts

Cash flows from operating activities		
Net income		$145,000
Adjustments to reconcile net income to net cash provided by operating activities:		
Depreciation expense	$ 9,000	
Loss on disposal of plant assets	3,000	
Decrease in accounts receivable	10,000	
Increase in inventory	(5,000)	
Increase in prepaid expenses	(4,000)	
Increase in accounts payable	**16,000**	
Decrease in income taxes payable	**(2,000)**	27,000
Net cash provided by operating activities		$172,000

Illustration 12.10 shows that after starting with net income of $145,000, the sum of all of the adjustments to net income was $27,000. This resulted in net cash provided by operating activities of $172,000.

Summary of Conversion to Net Cash Provided by Operating Activities—Indirect Method

As shown in the previous illustrations, the statement of cash flows prepared by the indirect method starts with net income. It then adds or deducts items to arrive at net cash provided by operating activities. The required adjustments are of three types:

1. Noncash charges such as depreciation and amortization.
2. Gains and losses on the disposal of plant assets.
3. Changes in noncash current asset and current liability accounts.

Illustration 12.11 provides a summary of these changes and required adjustments.

ILLUSTRATION 12.11
Adjustments required to convert net income to net cash provided by operating activities

		Adjustments Required to Convert Net Income to Net Cash Provided by Operating Activities
Noncash Charges	Depreciation expense	Add
	Amortization expense	Add
Gains and Losses	Loss on disposal of plant assets	Add
	Gain on disposal of plant assets	Deduct
Changes in Current Assets and Current Liabilities	Increase in current asset account	Deduct
	Decrease in current asset account	Add
	Increase in current liability account	Add
	Decrease in current liability account	Deduct

Anatomy of a Fraud

For more than a decade, the top executives at the Italian dairy products company **Parmalat** engaged in multiple frauds that overstated cash and other assets by more than $1 billion while understating liabilities by between $8 and $12 billion. Much of the fraud involved creating fictitious sources and uses of cash. Some of these activities incorporated sophisticated financial transactions with subsidiaries created with the help of large international financial institutions. However, much of the fraud employed very basic, even sloppy, forgery of documents. For example, when outside auditors requested confirmation of bank accounts (such as a fake $4.8 billion account in the Cayman Islands), documents were created on scanners, with signatures that were cut and pasted from other documents. These were then passed through a fax machine numerous times to make them look real (if difficult to read). Similarly, fictitious bills were created in order to divert funds to other businesses owned by the Tanzi family (who controlled Parmalat).

Total take: Billions of dollars

The Missing Control

Independent internal verification. Internal auditors at the company should have independently verified bank accounts and major transfers of cash to outside companies that were controlled by the Tanzi family.

DO IT! 2a | Cash from Operating Activities

Josh's PhotoPlus reported net income of $73,000 for 2022. Included in the income statement were depreciation expense of $7,000 and a gain on disposal of plant assets of $2,500. Josh's comparative balance sheets show the following balances.

	12/31/21	12/31/22
Accounts receivable	$17,000	$21,000
Accounts payable	6,000	2,200

Calculate net cash provided by operating activities for Josh's PhotoPlus.

Solution

Cash flows from operating activities		
Net income		$73,000
Adjustments to reconcile net income to net cash provided by operating activities:		
Depreciation expense	$ 7,000	
Gain on disposal of plant assets	(2,500)	
Increase in accounts receivable	(4,000)	
Decrease in accounts payable	(3,800)	(3,300)
Net cash provided by operating activities		$69,700

Related exercise material: **BE12.4, BE12.5, BE12.6, DO IT! 12.2a, E12.4, E12.5, E12.6, E12.7,** and **E12.8.**

ACTION PLAN
- Add noncash charges such as depreciation back to net income to compute net cash provided by operating activities.
- Deduct from net income gains on the disposal of plant assets, or add losses back to net income, to compute net cash provided by operating activities.
- Use changes in noncash current asset and current liability accounts to compute net cash provided by operating activities.

Step 2: Investing and Financing Activities

Analyze Changes in Noncurrent Asset and Liability Accounts and Stockholders' Equity Accounts and Record as Investing and Financing Activities, or as Noncash Investing and Financing Activities

Increase in Land As indicated from the change in the Land account and the additional information, Computer Services purchased land of $110,000 by directly exchanging bonds for land. The issuance of bonds payable for land has no effect on cash. But, it is a significant noncash investing and financing activity that merits disclosure in a separate schedule (see Illustration 12.14).

Increase in Buildings As the additional data indicate, Computer Services acquired an office building for $120,000 cash. This is a cash outflow reported in the investing activities section (see Illustration 12.14).

HELPFUL HINT

The investing and financing activities are measured and reported the same way under both the direct and indirect methods.

Increase in Equipment The Equipment account increased $17,000. The additional information explains that this net increase resulted from two transactions: (1) a purchase of equipment of $25,000, and (2) the sale for $4,000 of equipment costing $8,000. These transactions are investing activities (see **Helpful Hint**). The company should report each transaction separately. Thus, it reports the purchase of equipment as an outflow of cash for $25,000. It reports the sale as an inflow of cash for $4,000. The T-account in **Illustration 12.12** shows the reasons for the change in this account during the year.

ILLUSTRATION 12.12
Analysis of equipment

Equipment			
1/1/22 Balance	10,000	Cost of equipment sold	8,000
Purchase of equipment	25,000		
12/31/22 Balance	27,000		

The following entry shows the details of the equipment sale transaction.

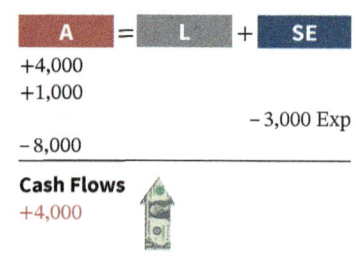

Cash	4,000	
Accumulated Depreciation—Equipment	1,000	
Loss on Disposal of Plant Assets	3,000	
Equipment		8,000

Increase in Bonds Payable The Bonds Payable account increased $110,000. As indicated in the additional information, the company acquired land from the issuance of these bonds. It reports this noncash transaction in a separate schedule at the bottom of the statement.

Increase in Common Stock The balance sheet reports an increase in Common Stock of $20,000. The additional information section notes that this increase resulted from the issuance of new shares of stock. This is a cash inflow reported in the financing activities section (see **Helpful Hint**).

HELPFUL HINT

When companies issue stocks or bonds for cash, the actual proceeds will appear in the statement of cash flows as a financing inflow (rather than the par value of the stocks or face value of bonds).

Increase in Retained Earnings Retained earnings increased $116,000 during the year. This increase can be explained by two factors: (1) net income of $145,000 increased retained earnings, and (2) dividends of $29,000 decreased retained earnings. The company adjusts net income to net cash provided by operating activities in the operating activities section. Payment of the dividends (not the declaration) is a **cash outflow that the company reports as a financing activity**. The T-account shown in **Illustration 12.13** shows the reasons for the change in this account during the year.

ILLUSTRATION 12.13
Analysis of retained earnings

Retained Earnings				
Dividends declared	29,000	1/1/22	Balance	48,000
			Net income	145,000
		12/31/22	Balance	164,000

Statement of Cash Flows—2022

Using the previous information, we can now prepare a statement of cash flows for 2022 for Computer Services Company as shown in **Illustration 12.14** (see **Helpful Hint**).

Step 3: Net Change in Cash

Compare the Net Change in Cash on the Statement of Cash Flows with the Change in the Cash Account Reported on the Balance Sheet to Make Sure the Amounts Agree

Illustration 12.14 indicates that the net change in cash during the period was an increase of $22,000. This agrees with the change in Cash account reported on the balance sheet in Illustration 12.4.

ILLUSTRATION 12.14
Statement of cash flows, 2022—indirect method

Computer Services Company
Statement of Cash Flows—Indirect Method
For the Year Ended December 31, 2022

Cash flows from operating activities		
Net income		$145,000
Adjustments to reconcile net income to net cash provided by operating activities:		
Depreciation expense	$ 9,000	
Loss on disposal of plant assets	3,000	
Decrease in accounts receivable	10,000	
Increase in inventory	(5,000)	
Increase in prepaid expenses	(4,000)	
Increase in accounts payable	16,000	
Decrease in income taxes payable	(2,000)	27,000
Net cash provided by operating activities		172,000
Cash flows from investing activities		
Purchase of building	(120,000)	
Purchase of equipment	(25,000)	
Sale of equipment	4,000	
Net cash used by investing activities		(141,000)
Cash flows from financing activities		
Issuance of common stock	20,000	
Payment of cash dividends	(29,000)	
Net cash used by financing activities		(9,000)
Net increase in cash		22,000
Cash at beginning of period		33,000
Cash at end of period		$ 55,000
Noncash investing and financing activities		
Issuance of bonds payable to purchase land		$110,000

> **HELPFUL HINT**
> Note that in the investing and financing activities sections, positive numbers indicate cash inflows (receipts), and negative numbers indicate cash outflows (payments).

Accounting Across the Organization

Burning Through Our Cash

© Soubrette/iStockphoto

Box (cloud storage), **Cyan** (game creator), **FireEye** (cyber security), and **MobileIron** (mobile security of data) are a few of the tech companies that recently have issued or are about to issue stock to the public. Investors now have to determine whether these tech companies have viable products and high chances for success.

An important consideration in evaluating a tech company is determining its financial flexibility—its ability to withstand adversity if an economic setback occurs. One way to measure financial flexibility is to assess a company's cash burn rate, which determines how long its cash will hold out if the company is expending more cash than it is receiving.

FireEye, for example, used cash in excess of $50 million in 2013. But the company also had over $150 million as a cash cushion, so it would take over three years before it runs out of cash. And even though Box has a much lower cash burn rate than FireEye, it still has over a year's cushion. Compare that to the tech companies in 2000, when over one-quarter of them were on track to run out of cash within a year. And many did. Fortunately, the tech companies of today seem to be better equipped to withstand an economic setback.

Source: Shira Ovide, "Tech Firms' Cash Hoards Cool Fears of a Meltdown," *Wall Street Journal* (May 14, 2014).

What implications does a company's cash burn rate have for its survival? (See WileyPLUS for this answer and additional questions.)

DO IT! 2b | Indirect Method

ACTION PLAN
- Determine net cash provided/used by operating activities by adjusting net income for items that did not affect cash.
- Determine net cash provided/used by investing activities and financing activities.
- Determine the net increase/decrease in cash.

Use the following information to prepare a statement of cash flows using the indirect method.

Reynolds Company
Comparative Balance Sheets
December 31

Assets	2022	2021	Change Increase/Decrease
Cash	$ 54,000	$ 37,000	$ 17,000 Increase
Accounts receivable	68,000	26,000	42,000 Increase
Inventory	54,000	-0-	54,000 Increase
Prepaid expenses	4,000	6,000	2,000 Decrease
Land	45,000	70,000	25,000 Decrease
Buildings	200,000	200,000	-0-
Accumulated depreciation—buildings	(21,000)	(11,000)	10,000 Increase
Equipment	193,000	68,000	125,000 Increase
Accumulated depreciation—equipment	(28,000)	(10,000)	18,000 Increase
Totals	$569,000	$386,000	

Liabilities and Stockholders' Equity	2022	2021	Change Increase/Decrease
Accounts payable	$ 23,000	$ 40,000	$ 17,000 Decrease
Accrued expenses payable	10,000	-0-	10,000 Increase
Bonds payable	110,000	150,000	40,000 Decrease
Common stock ($1 par)	220,000	60,000	160,000 Increase
Retained earnings	206,000	136,000	70,000 Increase
Totals	$569,000	$386,000	

Reynolds Company
Income Statement
For the Year Ended December 31, 2022

Sales revenue		$890,000
Cost of goods sold	$465,000	
Operating expenses	221,000	
Interest expense	12,000	
Loss on disposal of plant assets	2,000	700,000
Income before income taxes		190,000
Income tax expense		65,000
Net income		$125,000

Additional information:

1. Operating expenses include depreciation expense of $33,000 ($10,000 of depreciation expense for buildings and $23,000 for equipment).
2. Land was sold at its book value for cash.
3. Cash dividends of $55,000 were declared and paid in 2022.
4. Equipment with a cost of $166,000 was purchased for cash. Equipment with a cost of $41,000 and a book value of $36,000 was sold for $34,000 cash.
5. Bonds of $40,000 were redeemed at their face value for cash.
6. Common stock ($1 par) of $160,000 was issued for cash.

Solution

Reynolds Company
Statement of Cash Flows—Indirect Method
For the Year Ended December 31, 2022

Cash flows from operating activities		
Net income		$ 125,000
Adjustments to reconcile net income to net cash provided by operating activities:		
Depreciation expense	$ 33,000	
Loss on disposal of plant assets*	2,000	
Increase in accounts receivable	(42,000)	
Increase in inventory	(54,000)	
Decrease in prepaid expenses	2,000	
Decrease in accounts payable	(17,000)	
Increase in accrued expenses payable	10,000	(66,000)
Net cash provided by operating activities		59,000
Cash flows from investing activities		
Sale of land	25,000	
Sale of equipment	34,000	
Purchase of equipment	(166,000)	
Net cash used by investing activities		(107,000)
Cash flows from financing activities		
Redemption of bonds	(40,000)	
Sale of common stock	160,000	
Payment of dividends	(55,000)	
Net cash provided by financing activities		65,000
Net increase in cash		17,000
Cash at beginning of period		37,000
Cash at end of period		$ 54,000

*Cash		34,000
Accumulated Depreciation—Equipment ($41,000 − $36,000)		5,000
Loss on Disposal of Plant Assets		2,000
Equipment		41,000

Related exercise material: **BE12.4, BE12.5, BE12.6, BE12.7, DO IT! 12.2b, E12.4, E12.5, E12.6, E12.7, E12.8, E12.9, and E12.10.**

Analyzing the Statement of Cash Flows

LEARNING OBJECTIVE 3
Use the statement of cash flows to evaluate a company.

Traditionally, investors and creditors used ratios based on accrual accounting. These days, cash-based ratios are gaining increased acceptance among analysts. In this section, we review the corporate life cycle and free cash flow.

The Corporate Life Cycle

All products go through a series of phases called the **product life cycle**. The phases (in order of their occurrence) are **introductory phase**, **growth phase**, **maturity phase**, and **decline**

phase. The introductory phase occurs at the beginning of a company's life, when it purchases fixed assets and begins to produce and sell products. During the growth phase, the company strives to expand its production and sales. In the maturity phase, sales and production level off. During the decline phase, sales of the product decrease due to a weakening in consumer demand.

In the same way that products have life cycles, companies have life cycles as well. Companies generally have more than one product, and not all of a company's products are in the same phase of the product life cycle at the same time. This sometimes makes it difficult to classify a company's phase. Still, we can characterize a company as being in one of the four phases because the majority of its products are in a particular phase.

Illustration 12.15 shows that the phase a company is in affects its cash flows. In the **introductory phase**, we expect that the company will not generate positive cash from operations. That is, cash used in operations will exceed cash generated by operations in the introductory phase. Also, the company spends considerable amounts to purchase productive assets such as buildings and equipment. To support its asset purchases, the company issues stock or debt. Thus, during the introductory phase, we expect negative cash from operations, negative cash from investing, and positive cash from financing.

ILLUSTRATION 12.15
Impact of product life cycle on cash flows

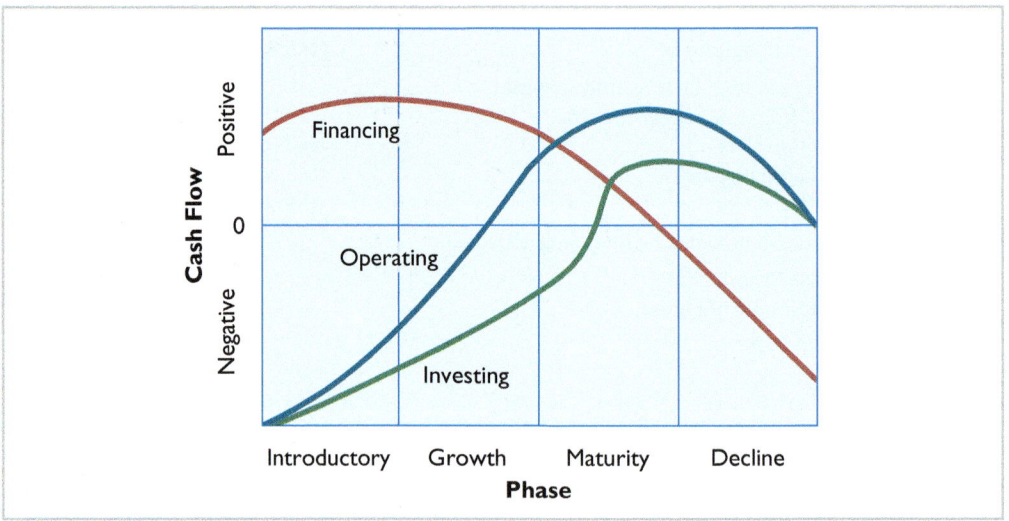

During the **growth phase**, we expect to see the company start to generate small amounts of cash from operations. During this phase, net cash provided by operating activities on the statement of cash flows is less than net income. One reason net income exceeds cash flow from operations during this period is explained by the difference between the cash paid for inventory and the amount expensed as cost of goods sold. Since the company projects increasing sales, the size of inventory purchases increases. Thus, in the growth phase, the company expenses less inventory on an accrual basis than it purchases on a cash basis. Also, collections on accounts receivable lag behind sales, and accrual sales during a period exceed cash collections during that period. Cash needed for asset acquisitions will continue to exceed net cash provided by operating activities. The company makes up the deficiency by issuing new stock or debt. Thus, in the growth phase, the company continues to show negative cash from investing activities and positive cash from financing activities.

During the **maturity phase**, net cash provided by operating activities and net income are approximately the same. Cash generated from operations exceeds investing needs. Thus, in the maturity phase, the company starts to pay dividends, retire debt, or buy back stock.

Finally, during the **decline phase**, net cash provided by operating activities decreases. Cash from investing activities might actually become positive as the company sells off excess assets. Cash from financing activities may be negative as the company buys back stock and redeems debt.

Consider **Microsoft**. During its early years, it had significant product development costs and little revenue. Microsoft was lucky in that its agreement with **IBM** to provide the operating system for IBM PCs gave it an early steady source of cash to support growth. As noted in the Feature Story, Microsoft conserved cash by paying employees with stock options rather than cash. Today, Microsoft could be characterized as being in the maturity phase. It continues to spend considerable amounts on research and development and investment in new assets. In recent years, though, its net cash provided by operating activities has exceeded its net income. Also, cash from operations over this period exceeded cash used for investing, and common stock repurchased exceeded common stock issued. For Microsoft, as for any large company, the challenge is to maintain its growth. In the software industry, where products become obsolete very quickly, the challenge is particularly great.

Investor Insight

Alfonso Ianniello/Shutterstock

Operating with Negative Cash

Listed here are amounts (in millions) of net income and net cash provided (used) by operating, investing, and financing activities for a variety of companies at one time. The final column suggests each company's likely phase in the life cycle based on these figures.

Company	Net Income	Net Cash Provided (Used) by Operating Activities	Net Cash Provided (Used) by Investing Activities	Net Cash Provided (Used) by Financing Activities	Likely Phase in Life Cycle
Amazon.com	$ 476	$1,405	$ (42)	$ (50)	Early maturity
LDK Solar	(144)	(81)	(329)	462	Introductory/ early growth
United States Steel	879	1,745	(4,675)	(1,891)	Maturity
Kellogg	1,103	1,503	(601)	(788)	Early decline
Southwest Airlines	645	2,845	(1,529)	493	Maturity
Starbucks	673	1,331	(1,202)	(172)	Maturity

Why do companies have negative net cash provided by operating activities during the introductory phase? (Go to WileyPLUS for this answer and additional questions.)

Free Cash Flow

In the statement of cash flows, net cash provided by operating activities is intended to indicate the cash-generating capability of the company. Analysts have noted, however, that **cash provided by operating activities fails to take into account that a company must invest in new fixed assets** just to maintain its current level of operations. Companies also must at least **maintain dividends at current levels** to satisfy investors. As we discussed in Chapter 2, the measurement of free cash flow provides additional insight regarding a company's cash-generating ability. **Free cash flow** describes the net cash provided by operating activities after adjustment for capital expenditures and dividends (see **Decision Tools**).

Consider the following example. Suppose that MPC produced and sold 10,000 personal computers this year. It reported $100,000 cash provided by operating activities. In order to maintain production at 10,000 computers, MPC invested $15,000 in equipment. It chose to pay $5,000 in dividends. Its free cash flow was $80,000 ($100,000 − $15,000 − $5,000). The company could use this $80,000 either to purchase new assets, pay off debt, or pay an $80,000 dividend. In practice, free cash flow is often calculated with the formula in **Illustration 12.16**. Alternative definitions also exist.

> **Decision Tools**
> Free cash flows helps users determine the amount of cash the company generated to expand operations or pay dividends.

ILLUSTRATION 12.16
Free cash flow

$$\text{Free Cash Flow} = \text{Net Cash Provided by Operating Activities} - \text{Capital Expenditures} - \text{Cash Dividends}$$

Illustration 12.17 provides basic information excerpted from the 2017 statement of cash flows of **Apple**.

ILLUSTRATION 12.17
Apple's cash flow information ($ in millions)

Apple Inc.
Statement of Cash Flows Information (partial)
2017

Net cash provided by operating activities		$ 63,598
Cash flows from investing activities		
Additions to property and equipment and intangibles	$ (12,451)	
Purchases of investments	(159,486)	
Sales of investments	94,564	
Acquisitions of companies	(329)	
Maturities of investments	31,775	
Other	(519)	
Net cash used by investing activities		(46,446)
Cash paid for dividends		(12,769)

Apple's free cash flow is calculated as shown in **Illustration 12.18** (in millions). Apple generated approximately $38 billion of free cash flow. This is a tremendous amount of cash generated in a single year. It is available for the acquisition of new assets, the buyback and retirement of stock or debt, or the payment of dividends.

ILLUSTRATION 12.18
Calculation of Apple's free cash flow ($ in millions)

Net cash provided by operating activities	$63,598
Less: Expenditures on property, plant, and equipment	12,451
Dividends paid	12,769
Free cash flow	$38,378

Apple's cash from operations of $63.6 billion exceeds its 2017 net income of $48.4 billion by $15.2 billion. This lends additional credibility to Apple's income number as an indicator of potential future performance. If anything, Apple's net income might understate its actual performance.

Keeping an Eye on Cash

Cash flow is closely monitored by analysts and investors for many reasons and in a variety of ways. One measure that is gaining increased attention is "price to cash flow." This is a variant of the price to earnings (P-E) ratio, which has been a staple of analysts for a long time. The difference is that rather than divide the company's stock price by its earnings per share (an accrual-accounting–based number), the price to cash flow ratio divides the company's stock price by its cash flow per share. A high measure suggests that the stock price is high relative to the company's ability to generate cash. A low measure indicates that the company's stock might be a bargain.

The following table provides values for some well-known companies in a recent year. While you should not use this measure as the sole factor in choosing a stock, it can serve as a useful screen by which to identify companies that merit further investigation.

Company	Price/Cash Flow	Price/EPS
Microsoft	55.6	62.5
Apple	11.1	12.5
Nike	19.1	24.8
Wal-Mart	9.0	15.7
Jet Blue	7.9	11.1

DO IT! 3 | Free Cash Flow

Chicago Corporation issued the following statement of cash flows for 2022.

ACTION PLAN
- Compute free cash flow as Net cash provided by operating activities − Capital expenditures − Cash dividends.

Chicago Corporation
Statement of Cash Flows—Indirect Method
For the Year Ended December 31, 2022

Cash flows from operating activities		
Net income		$ 19,000
Adjustments to reconcile net income to net cash provided by operating activities:		
Depreciation expense	$ 8,100	
Loss on disposal of plant assets	1,300	
Decrease in accounts receivable	6,900	
Increase in inventory	(4,000)	
Decrease in accounts payable	(2,000)	10,300
Net cash provided by operating activities		29,300
Cash flows from investing activities		
Sale of investments	1,100	
Purchase of equipment	(19,000)	
Net cash used by investing activities		(17,900)
Cash flows from financing activities		
Issuance of stock	10,000	
Payment on long-term note payable	(5,000)	
Payment for dividends	(9,000)	
Net cash used by financing activities		(4,000)
Net increase in cash		7,400
Cash at beginning of year		10,000
Cash at end of year		$ 17,400

a. Compute free cash flow for Chicago Corporation.

b. Explain why free cash flow often provides better information than "Net cash provided by operating activities."

Solution

a. Free cash flow = $29,300 − $19,000 − $9,000 = $1,300

b. Net cash provided by operating activities fails to take into account that a company must invest in new plant assets just to maintain the current level of operation. Companies must also maintain dividends at current levels to satisfy investors. The measurement of free cash flow provides additional insight regarding a company's cash-generating ability.

Related exercise material: **BE12.9, BE12.10, BE12.11, BE12.12, DO IT! 12.3, E12.12, and E12.13.**

USING THE DECISION TOOLS | Intel Corporation

Intel Corporation is the leading producer of computer chips for personal computers. A primary competitor is **Qualcomm**. Financial statement data for Intel are as follows.

Intel Corporation
Statement of Cash Flows
For the Year Ended December 31, 2017
(in millions)

	2017
Net cash provided by operating activities	$ 22,110
Net cash used for investing activities	(15,762)
Net cash used for financing activities	(8,475)
Net increase (decrease) in cash and cash equivalents	$ (2,127)

Note. Cash spent on property, plant, and equipment in 2017 was $11,778. Cash paid for dividends was $5,072.

Instructions

Calculate free cash flow for Intel and then compare it to Qualcomm's free cash flow of $1,381 million.

Solution

Intel's free cash flow is $5,260 million ($22,110 − $11,778 − $5,072). Qualcomm's is $1,381 million. This nearly $4 billion difference gives Intel an advantage in the ability to move quickly to invest in new projects.

Appendix 12A | Statement of Cash Flows—Direct Method

LEARNING OBJECTIVE *4
Prepare a statement of cash flows using the direct method.

To explain and illustrate the direct method for preparing a statement of cash flows, we use the transactions of Computer Services Company for 2022. **Illustration 12A.1** presents information related to 2022 for the company.

ILLUSTRATION 12A.1
Comparative balance sheets, income statement, and additional information for Computer Services Company

Computer Services Company
Comparative Balance Sheets
December 31

Assets	2022	2021	Change in Account Balance Increase/Decrease
Current assets			
Cash	$ 55,000	$ 33,000	$ 22,000 Increase
Accounts receivable	20,000	30,000	10,000 Decrease
Inventory	15,000	10,000	5,000 Increase
Prepaid expenses	5,000	1,000	4,000 Increase
Property, plant, and equipment			
Land	130,000	20,000	110,000 Increase
Buildings	160,000	40,000	120,000 Increase
Accumulated depreciation—buildings	(11,000)	(5,000)	6,000 Increase
Equipment	27,000	10,000	17,000 Increase
Accumulated depreciation—equipment	(3,000)	(1,000)	2,000 Increase
Total assets	$398,000	$138,000	

Liabilities and Stockholders' Equity			
Current liabilities			
Accounts payable	$ 28,000	$ 12,000	$ 16,000 Increase
Income taxes payable	6,000	8,000	2,000 Decrease
Long-term liabilities			
Bonds payable	130,000	20,000	110,000 Increase
Stockholders' equity			
Common stock	70,000	50,000	20,000 Increase
Retained earnings	164,000	48,000	116,000 Increase
Total liabilities and stockholders' equity	$398,000	$138,000	

Computer Services Company
Income Statement
For the Year Ended December 31, 2022

Sales revenue		$507,000
Cost of goods sold	$150,000	
Operating expenses (excluding depreciation)	111,000	
Depreciation expense	9,000	
Loss on disposal of plant assets	3,000	
Interest expense	42,000	315,000
Income before income tax		192,000
Income tax expense		47,000
Net income		$145,000

Additional information for 2022:

1. Depreciation expense was comprised of $6,000 for building and $3,000 for equipment.
2. The company sold equipment with a book value of $7,000 (cost $8,000, less accumulated depreciation $1,000) for $4,000 cash.
3. Issued $110,000 of long-term bonds in direct exchange for land.
4. A building costing $120,000 was purchased for cash. Equipment costing $25,000 was also purchased for cash.
5. Issued common stock for $20,000 cash.
6. The company declared and paid a $29,000 cash dividend.

To prepare a statement of cash flows under the direct approach, we apply the three steps outlined in Illustration 12.3.

Step 1: Operating Activities

Determine Net Cash Provided/Used by Operating Activities by Converting Net Income Components from an Accrual Basis to a Cash Basis

Under the **direct method**, companies compute net cash provided by operating activities by **adjusting each item in the income statement** from the accrual basis to the cash basis. To simplify and condense the operating activities section, companies **report only major classes of operating cash receipts and cash payments**. For these major classes, the difference between cash receipts and cash payments is the net cash provided by operating activities. These relationships are as shown in **Illustration 12A.2**.

> **ILLUSTRATION 12A.2** Major classes of cash receipts and payments

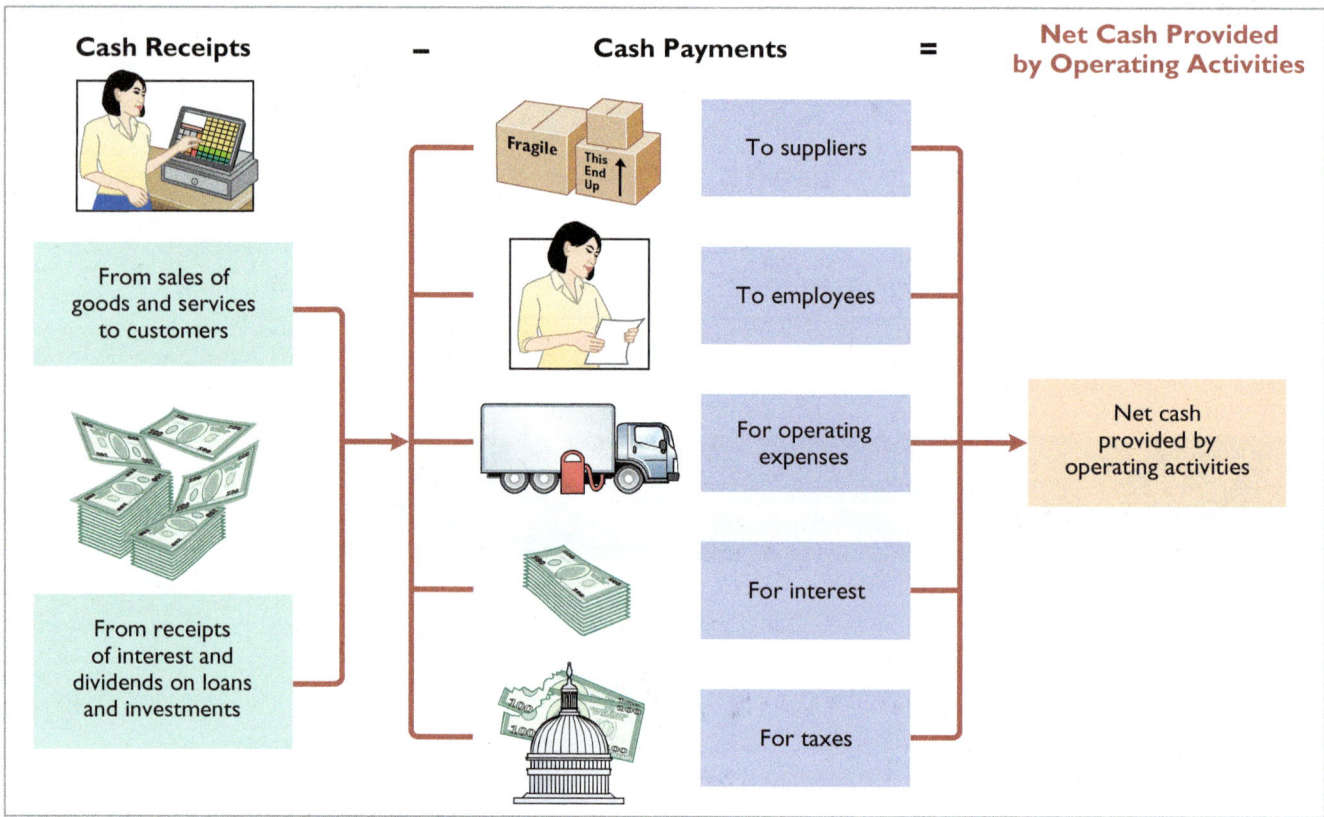

An efficient way to apply the direct method is to analyze the items reported in the income statement in the order in which they are listed. We then determine cash receipts and cash payments related to these revenues and expenses. The following presents the adjustments required to prepare a statement of cash flows for Computer Services Company using the direct approach.

Cash Receipts from Customers The income statement for Computer Services reported sales revenue from customers of $507,000. How much of that was cash receipts? To answer that, a company considers the change in accounts receivable during the year. When accounts receivable increase during the year, revenues on an accrual basis are higher than cash receipts from customers. Operations led to revenues, but not all of those revenues resulted in cash receipts.

To determine the amount of cash receipts, a company deducts from sales revenue the increase in accounts receivable. On the other hand, there may be a decrease in accounts receivable. That would occur if cash receipts from customers exceeded sales revenue. In that case, a company adds to sales revenue the decrease in accounts receivable. For Computer Services, accounts receivable decreased $10,000. Thus, cash receipts from customers were $517,000, computed as shown in **Illustration 12A.3**.

> **ILLUSTRATION 12A.3**
> Computation of cash receipts from customers

Sales revenue	$507,000
Add: Decrease in accounts receivable	10,000
Cash receipts from customers	**$517,000**

Computer Services can also determine cash receipts from customers from an analysis of the Accounts Receivable account, as shown in **Illustration 12A.4**.

Accounts Receivable

1/1/22	Balance	30,000	Receipts from customers	517,000
	Sales revenue	507,000		
12/31/22	Balance	20,000		

ILLUSTRATION 12A.4
Analysis of accounts receivable

HELPFUL HINT
The T-account shows that sales revenue plus decrease in accounts receivable equals cash receipts.

Illustration 12A.5 shows the relationships among cash receipts from customers, sales revenue, and changes in accounts receivable (see **Helpful Hint**).

$$\text{Cash Receipts from Customers} = \text{Sales Revenue} \begin{cases} + \text{Decrease in Accounts Receivable} \\ \text{or} \\ - \text{Increase in Accounts Receivable} \end{cases}$$

ILLUSTRATION 12A.5
Formula to compute cash receipts from customers—direct method

Cash Payments to Suppliers Computer Services reported cost of goods sold of $150,000 on its income statement. How much of that was cash payments to suppliers? To answer that, it is first necessary to find purchases for the year. To find purchases, a company adjusts cost of goods sold for the change in inventory. When inventory increases during the year, purchases for the year have exceeded cost of goods sold. As a result, to determine the amount of purchases, a company adds to cost of goods sold the increase in inventory.

In 2022, Computer Services' inventory increased $5,000. It computes purchases as shown in **Illustration 12A.6**.

Cost of goods sold	$150,000
Add: Increase in inventory	5,000
Purchases	$155,000

ILLUSTRATION 12A.6
Computation of purchases

Computer Services can also determine purchases from an analysis of the Inventory account, as shown in **Illustration 12A.7**.

Inventory

1/1/22	Balance	10,000	Cost of goods sold	150,000
	Purchases	155,000		
12/31/22	Balance	15,000		

ILLUSTRATION 12A.7
Analysis of inventory

After computing purchases, a company can determine cash payments to suppliers. This is done by adjusting purchases for the change in accounts payable. When accounts payable increase during the year, purchases on an accrual basis are higher than they are on a cash basis. As a result, to determine cash payments to suppliers, a company deducts from purchases the increase in accounts payable. On the other hand, if cash payments to suppliers exceed purchases, there will be a decrease in accounts payable. In that case, a company adds to purchases the decrease in accounts payable. For Computer Services, cash payments to suppliers were $139,000, computed as shown in **Illustration 12A.8**.

Purchases	$155,000
Deduct: Increase in accounts payable	16,000
Cash payments to suppliers	$139,000

ILLUSTRATION 12A.8
Computation of cash payments to suppliers

Computer Services also can determine cash payments to suppliers from an analysis of the Accounts Payable account, as shown in Illustration 12A.9.

ILLUSTRATION 12A.9
Analysis of accounts payable

Accounts Payable				
Payments to suppliers	139,000	1/1/22	Balance	12,000
			Purchases	155,000
		12/31/22	Balance	28,000

HELPFUL HINT
The T-account shows that purchases less increase in accounts payable equals payments to suppliers.

Illustration 12A.10 shows the relationships among cash payments to suppliers, cost of goods sold, changes in inventory, and changes in accounts payable (see **Helpful Hint**).

ILLUSTRATION 12A.10
Formula to compute cash payments to suppliers—direct method

$$\text{Cash Payments to Suppliers} = \text{Cost of Goods Sold} + \begin{cases} +\text{ Increase in Inventory} \\ \text{or} \\ -\text{ Decrease in Inventory} \end{cases} + \begin{cases} +\text{ Decrease in Accounts Payable} \\ \text{or} \\ -\text{ Increase in Accounts Payable} \end{cases}$$

Cash Payments for Operating Expenses Computer Services reported on its income statement operating expenses of $111,000. How much of that amount was cash paid for operating expenses? To answer that, we need to adjust this amount for any changes in prepaid expenses and accrued expenses payable. For example, if prepaid expenses increased during the year, cash paid for operating expenses is higher than operating expenses reported on the income statement. To convert operating expenses to cash payments for operating expenses, a company adds the increase in prepaid expenses to operating expenses. On the other hand, if prepaid expenses decrease during the year, it deducts the decrease from operating expenses.

Companies must also adjust operating expenses for changes in accrued expenses payable. When accrued expenses payable increase during the year, operating expenses on an accrual basis are higher than they are in a cash basis. As a result, to determine cash payments for operating expenses, a company deducts from operating expenses an increase in accrued expenses payable. On the other hand, a company adds to operating expenses a decrease in accrued expenses payable because cash payments exceed operating expenses.

Computer Services' cash payments for operating expenses were $115,000, computed as shown in Illustration 12A.11.

ILLUSTRATION 12A.11
Computation of cash payments for operating expenses

Operating expenses	$111,000
Add: Increase in prepaid expenses	4,000
Cash payments for operating expenses	**$115,000**

Illustration 12A.12 shows the relationships among cash payments for operating expenses, changes in prepaid expenses, and changes in accrued expenses payable.

ILLUSTRATION 12A.12
Formula to compute cash payments for operating expenses—direct method

$$\text{Cash Payments for Operating Expenses} = \text{Operating Expenses} + \begin{cases} +\text{ Increase in Prepaid Expenses} \\ \text{or} \\ -\text{ Decrease in Prepaid Expenses} \end{cases} + \begin{cases} +\text{ Decrease in Accrued Expenses Payable} \\ \text{or} \\ -\text{ Increase in Accrued Expenses Payable} \end{cases}$$

Depreciation Expense and Loss on Disposal of Plant Assets Computer Services' depreciation expense in 2022 was $9,000. Depreciation expense is not shown on a statement of cash flows under the direct method because it is a noncash charge. If the amount for operating expenses includes depreciation expense, operating expenses must be reduced by the amount of depreciation to determine cash payments for operating expenses.

The loss on disposal of plant assets of $3,000 is also a noncash charge. The loss on disposal of plant assets reduces net income, but it does not reduce cash. Thus, the loss on disposal of plant assets is not shown on the statement of cash flows under the direct method.

Other charges to expense that do not require the use of cash, such as the amortization of intangible assets and bad debt expense, are treated in the same manner as depreciation.

Cash Payments for Interest Computer Services reported on the income statement interest expense of $42,000. Since the balance sheet did not include an accrual for interest payable for 2021 or 2022, the amount reported as expense is the same as the amount of interest paid.

Cash Payments for Income Taxes Computer Services reported income tax expense of $47,000 on the income statement. Income taxes payable, however, decreased $2,000. This decrease means that income taxes paid were more than income taxes reported in the income statement. Cash payments for income taxes were therefore $49,000 as shown in **Illustration 12A.13**.

Income tax expense	$47,000
Add: Decrease in income taxes payable	2,000
Cash payments for income taxes	**$49,000**

ILLUSTRATION 12A.13
Computation of cash payments for income taxes

Computer Services can also determine cash payments for income taxes from an analysis of the Income Taxes Payable account, as shown in **Illustration 12A.14**.

Income Taxes Payable

Cash payments for income taxes	49,000	1/1/22 Balance	8,000
		Income tax expense	47,000
		12/31/22 Balance	6,000

ILLUSTRATION 12A.14
Analysis of income taxes payable

Illustration 12A.15 shows the relationships among cash payments for income taxes, income tax expense, and changes in income taxes payable.

Cash Payments for Income Taxes = Income Tax Expense + Decrease in Income Taxes Payable **or** − Increase in Income Taxes Payable

ILLUSTRATION 12A.15
Formula to compute cash payments for income taxes—direct method

The operating activities section of the statement of cash flows of Computer Services is shown in **Illustration 12A.16**.

Cash flows from operating activities		
Cash receipts from customers		$517,000
Less: Cash payments:		
To suppliers	$139,000	
For operating expenses	115,000	
For interest expense	42,000	
For income taxes	49,000	345,000
Net cash provided by operating activities		$172,000

ILLUSTRATION 12A.16
Operating activities section of the statement of cash flows

When a company uses the direct method, it must also provide in a **separate schedule** (not shown here) the net cash flows from operating activities as computed under the indirect method. Note that whether a company uses the indirect or direct method, the net cash provided by operating activities is the same for both methods.

Step 2: Investing and Financing Activities

Analyze Changes in Noncurrent Asset and Liability Accounts and Stockholders' Equity Accounts and Record as Investing and Financing Activities, or Disclose as Noncash Transactions

Increase in Land As indicated from the change in the Land account and the additional information, Computer Services purchased land of $110,000 by directly exchanging bonds for land. The exchange of bonds payable for land has no effect on cash. But, it is a significant noncash investing and financing activity that merits disclosure in a separate schedule (see Illustration 12A.18).

Increase in Buildings As the additional data indicate, Computer Services acquired an office building for $120,000 cash. This is a cash outflow reported in the investing activities section (see Illustration 12A.18).

> **HELPFUL HINT**
> The investing and financing activities are measured and reported the same under both the direct and indirect methods.

Increase in Equipment The Equipment account increased $17,000. The additional information explains that this was a net increase that resulted from two transactions: (1) a purchase of equipment of $25,000, and (2) the sale for $4,000 of equipment costing $8,000. These transactions are investing activities (see **Helpful Hint**). The company should report each transaction separately. The statement in Illustration 12A.18 reports the purchase of equipment as an outflow of cash for $25,000. It reports the sale as an inflow of cash for $4,000. The T-account in **Illustration 12A.17** shows the reasons for the change in this account during the year.

ILLUSTRATION 12A.17
Analysis of equipment

	Equipment		
1/1/22 Balance	10,000	Cost of equipment sold	8,000
Purchase of equipment	25,000		
12/31/22 Balance	27,000		

The following entry shows the details of the equipment sale transaction.

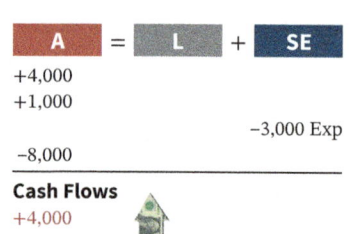

Cash	4,000	
Accumulated Depreciation—Equipment	1,000	
Loss on Disposal of Plant Assets	3,000	
Equipment		8,000

Increase in Bonds Payable The Bonds Payable account increased $110,000. As indicated in the additional information, the company acquired land by directly exchanging bonds for land. Illustration 12A.18 reports this noncash transaction in a separate schedule at the bottom of the statement.

> **HELPFUL HINT**
> When companies issue stocks or bonds for cash, the actual proceeds will appear in the statement of cash flows as a financing inflow (rather than the par value of the stocks or face value of bonds).

Increase in Common Stock The balance sheet reports an increase in Common Stock of $20,000. The additional information section notes that this increase resulted from the issuance of new shares of stock. This is a cash inflow reported in the financing activities section in Illustration 12A.18 (see **Helpful Hint**).

Increase in Retained Earnings Retained earnings increased $116,000 during the year. This increase can be explained by two factors: (1) net income of $145,000 increased retained earnings, and (2) dividends of $29,000 decreased retained earnings. **Payment** of the dividends (not the declaration) is a **cash outflow that the company reports as a financing activity in Illustration 12A.18.**

Statement of Cash Flows—2022

Illustration 12A.18 shows the statement of cash flows for Computer Services Company.

ILLUSTRATION 12A.18
Statement of cash flows, 2022—direct method

Computer Services Company
Statement of Cash Flows—Direct Method
For the Year Ended December 31, 2022

Cash flows from operating activities		
Cash receipts from customers		$ 517,000
Less: Cash payments:		
To suppliers	$ 139,000	
For operating expenses	115,000	
For income taxes	49,000	
For interest expense	42,000	345,000
Net cash provided by operating activities		172,000
Cash flows from investing activities		
Sale of equipment	4,000	
Purchase of building	(120,000)	
Purchase of equipment	(25,000)	
Net cash used by investing activities		(141,000)
Cash flows from financing activities		
Issuance of common stock	20,000	
Payment of cash dividends	(29,000)	
Net cash used by financing activities		(9,000)
Net increase in cash		22,000
Cash at beginning of period		33,000
Cash at end of period		$ 55,000
Noncash investing and financing activities		
Issuance of bonds payable to purchase land		$ 110,000

Step 3: Net Change in Cash

Compare the Net Change in Cash on the Statement of Cash Flows with the Change in the Cash Account Reported on the Balance Sheet to Make Sure the Amounts Agree

Illustration 12A.18 indicates that the net change in cash during the period was an increase of $22,000. This agrees with the change in balances in the Cash account reported on the balance sheets in Illustration 12A.1.

Appendix 12B: Worksheet for the Indirect Method

LEARNING OBJECTIVE *5
Use a worksheet to prepare the statement of cash flows using the indirect method.

When preparing a statement of cash flows, companies may need to make numerous adjustments of net income. In such cases, they often use **a worksheet to assemble and classify the data that will appear on the statement**. The worksheet is merely an aid in preparing the statement. Its use is optional. **Illustration 12B.1** shows the skeleton format of the worksheet for preparation of the statement of cash flows.

The following guidelines are important in preparing a worksheet.

1. In the balance sheet accounts section, **list accounts with debit balances separately from those with credit balances**. This means, for example, that Accumulated Depreciation appears under credit balances and not as a contra account under debit balances.

ILLUSTRATION 12B.1
Format of worksheet

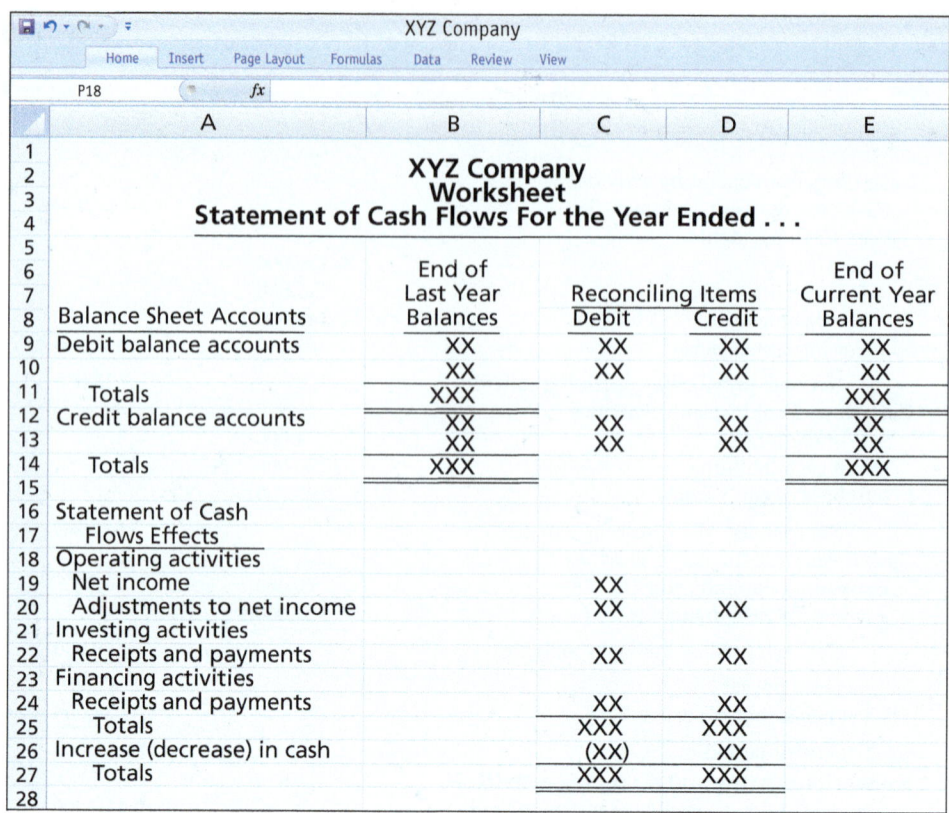

Enter the beginning and ending balances of each account in the appropriate columns. Enter as reconciling items in the two middle columns the transactions that caused the change in the account balance during the year.

After all reconciling items have been entered, each line pertaining to a balance sheet account should "foot across." That is, the beginning balance plus or minus the reconciling item(s) must equal the ending balance. When this agreement exists for all balance sheet accounts, all changes in account balances have been reconciled.

2. The bottom portion of the worksheet consists of the operating, investing, and financing activities sections. It provides the information necessary to prepare the formal statement of cash flows. **Enter inflows of cash as debits in the reconciling columns. Enter outflows of cash as credits in the reconciling columns.** Thus, in this section, the sale of equipment for cash at book value appears as a debit under investing activities. Similarly, the purchase of land for cash appears as a credit under investing activities.

3. **The reconciling items shown in the worksheet are not entered in any journal or posted to any account.** They do not represent either adjustments or corrections of the balance sheet accounts. They are used only to facilitate the preparation of the statement of cash flows.

Preparing the Worksheet

Preparing a worksheet involves a series of prescribed steps. The steps in this case are:

1. Enter in the balance sheet accounts section the balance sheet accounts and their beginning and ending balances.

2. Enter in the reconciling columns of the worksheet the data that explain the changes in the balance sheet accounts other than cash and their effects on the statement of cash flows.

3. Enter on the cash line and at the bottom of the worksheet the increase or decrease in cash. This entry should enable the totals of the reconciling columns to be in agreement.

To illustrate the preparation of a worksheet, we will use the 2022 data for Computer Services Company. Your familiarity with these data (from the chapter) should help you understand the use of a worksheet. For ease of reference, the comparative balance sheets, income statement, and selected data for 2022 are presented in **Illustration 12B.2**.

ILLUSTRATION 12B.2
Comparative balance sheets, income statement, and additional information for Computer Services Company

Computer Services Company
Comparative Balance Sheets
December 31

	2022	2021	Change in Account Balance Increase/Decrease
Assets			
Current assets			
Cash	$ 55,000	$ 33,000	$ 22,000 Increase
Accounts receivable	20,000	30,000	10,000 Decrease
Inventory	15,000	10,000	5,000 Increase
Prepaid expenses	5,000	1,000	4,000 Increase
Property, plant, and equipment			
Land	130,000	20,000	110,000 Increase
Buildings	160,000	40,000	120,000 Increase
Accumulated depreciation—buildings	(11,000)	(5,000)	6,000 Increase
Equipment	27,000	10,000	17,000 Increase
Accumulated depreciation—equipment	(3,000)	(1,000)	2,000 Increase
Total assets	$398,000	$138,000	
Liabilities and Stockholders' Equity			
Current liabilities			
Accounts payable	$ 28,000	$ 12,000	$ 16,000 Increase
Income taxes payable	6,000	8,000	2,000 Decrease
Long-term liabilities			
Bonds payable	130,000	20,000	110,000 Increase
Stockholders' equity			
Common stock	70,000	50,000	20,000 Increase
Retained earnings	164,000	48,000	116,000 Increase
Total liabilities and stockholders' equity	$398,000	$138,000	

Computer Services Company
Income Statement
For the Year Ended December 31, 2022

Sales revenue		$507,000
Cost of goods sold	$150,000	
Operating expenses (excluding depreciation)	111,000	
Depreciation expense	9,000	
Loss on disposal of plant assets	3,000	
Interest expense	42,000	315,000
Income before income taxes		192,000
Income tax expense		47,000
Net income		$145,000

Additional information for 2022:
1. Depreciation expense was comprised of $6,000 for building and $3,000 for equipment.
2. The company sold equipment with a book value of $7,000 (cost $8,000, less accumulated depreciation $1,000) for $4,000 cash.
3. Issued $110,000 of long-term bonds in direct exchange for land.
4. A building costing $120,000 was purchased for cash. Equipment costing $25,000 was also purchased for cash.
5. Issued common stock for $20,000 cash.
6. The company declared and paid a $29,000 cash dividend.

Determining the Reconciling Items

Companies can use one of several approaches to determine the reconciling items. For example, they can first complete the changes affecting net cash provided by operating activities, and then can determine the effects of financing and investing transactions. Or, they can analyze the balance sheet accounts in the order in which they are listed on the worksheet. We will follow this latter approach for Computer Services, except for cash. As indicated in Step 3, **cash is handled last**.

Accounts Receivable The decrease of $10,000 in accounts receivable means that cash collections from sales revenue are higher than the sales revenue reported in the income statement. To convert net income to net cash provided by operating activities, we add the decrease of $10,000 to net income. The entry in the reconciling columns of the worksheet is:

a. Operating—Decrease in Accounts Receivable	10,000	
Accounts Receivable		10,000

Inventory Computer Services' inventory balance increases $5,000 during the period. The Inventory account reflects the difference between the amount of inventory that the company purchased and the amount that it sold. For Computer Services, this means that the cost of merchandise purchased exceeds the cost of goods sold by $5,000. As a result, cost of goods sold does not reflect $5,000 of cash payments made for merchandise. We deduct this inventory increase of $5,000 during the period from net income to arrive at net cash provided by operating activities. The worksheet entry is:

b. Inventory	5,000	
Operating—Increase in Inventory		5,000

Prepaid Expenses An increase of $4,000 in prepaid expenses means that expenses deducted in determining net income are less than expenses that were paid in cash. We deduct the increase of $4,000 from net income in determining net cash provided by operating activities. The worksheet entry is:

c. Prepaid Expenses	4,000	
Operating—Increase in Prepaid Expenses		4,000

> **HELPFUL HINT**
> These amounts are asterisked in the worksheet to indicate that they result from a significant noncash transaction.

Land The increase in land of $110,000 resulted from a purchase through the issuance of long-term bonds. The company should report this transaction as a significant noncash investing and financing activity (see **Helpful Hint**). The worksheet entry is:

d. Land	110,000	
Bonds Payable		110,000

Buildings The cash purchase of a building for $120,000 is an investing activity cash outflow. The entry in the reconciling columns of the worksheet is:

e. Buildings	120,000	
Investing—Purchase of Building		120,000

Equipment The increase in equipment of $17,000 resulted from a cash purchase of $25,000 and the disposal of plant assets (equipment) costing $8,000. The book value of the equipment was $7,000, the cash proceeds were $4,000, and a loss of $3,000 was recorded. The worksheet entries are:

f. Equipment	25,000	
Investing—Purchase of Equipment		25,000
g. Investing—Sale of Equipment	4,000	
Operating—Loss on Disposal of Plant Assets	3,000	
Accumulated Depreciation—Equipment	1,000	
Equipment		8,000

Accounts Payable We must add the increase of $16,000 in accounts payable to net income to determine net cash provided by operating activities. The worksheet entry is:

h. Operating—Increase in Accounts Payable		16,000	
Accounts Payable			16,000

Income Taxes Payable When a company incurs income tax expense but has not yet paid its taxes, it records income taxes payable. A change in the Income Taxes Payable account reflects the difference between income tax expense incurred and income tax actually paid. Computer Services' Income Taxes Payable account decreases by $2,000. That means the $47,000 of income tax expense reported on the income statement was $2,000 less than the amount of taxes paid during the period of $49,000. To adjust net income to a cash basis, we must reduce net income by $2,000. The worksheet entry is:

i. Income Taxes Payable		2,000	
Operating—Decrease in Income Taxes Payable			2,000

Bonds Payable The increase of $110,000 in this account resulted from the issuance of bonds for land. This is a significant noncash investing and financing activity. Worksheet entry (d) above is the only entry necessary.

Common Stock The balance sheet reports an increase in Common Stock of $20,000. The additional information section notes that this increase resulted from the issuance of new shares of stock. This is a cash inflow reported in the financing section. The worksheet entry is:

j. Financing—Issuance of Common Stock		20,000	
Common Stock			20,000

Accumulated Depreciation—Buildings, and Accumulated Depreciation—Equipment Increases in these accounts of $6,000 and $3,000, respectively, resulted from depreciation expense. Depreciation expense is a **noncash charge that we must add to net income** to determine net cash provided by operating activities. The worksheet entries are:

k. Operating—Depreciation Expense		6,000	
Accumulated Depreciation—Buildings			6,000
l. Operating—Depreciation Expense		3,000	
Accumulated Depreciation—Equipment			3,000

Retained Earnings The $116,000 increase in retained earnings resulted from net income of $145,000 and the declaration and payment of a $29,000 cash dividend. Net income is included in net cash provided by operating activities, and the dividends are a financing activity cash outflow. The entries in the reconciling columns of the worksheet are:

m. Operating—Net Income		145,000	
Retained Earnings			145,000
n. Retained Earnings		29,000	
Financing—Payment of Dividends			29,000

Disposition of Change in Cash The firm's cash increased $22,000 in 2022. The final entry on the worksheet, therefore, is:

o. Cash		22,000	
Increase in Cash			22,000

As shown in the worksheet, we enter the increase in cash in the reconciling credit column as a **balancing** amount. This entry should complete the reconciliation of the changes in the balance sheet accounts. Also, it should permit the totals of the reconciling columns to be in agreement. When all changes have been explained and the reconciling columns are in agreement, the reconciling columns are ruled to complete the worksheet. The completed worksheet for Computer Services Company is shown in **Illustration 12B.3**.

ILLUSTRATION 12B.3
Completed worksheet—indirect method

Computer Services Company
Worksheet
Statement of Cash Flows For the Year Ended December 31, 2022

Balance Sheet Accounts	Balance 12/31/21	Reconciling Items Debit	Reconciling Items Credit	Balance 12/31/22
Debits				
Cash	33,000	(o) 22,000		55,000
Accounts Receivable	30,000		(a) 10,000	20,000
Inventory	10,000	(b) 5,000		15,000
Prepaid Expenses	1,000	(c) 4,000		5,000
Land	20,000	(d) 110,000*		130,000
Buildings	40,000	(e) 120,000		160,000
Equipment	10,000	(f) 25,000	(g) 8,000	27,000
Total	144,000			412,000
Credits				
Accounts Payable	12,000		(h) 16,000	28,000
Income Taxes Payable	8,000	(i) 2,000		6,000
Bonds Payable	20,000		(d) 110,000*	130,000
Accumulated Depreciation—Buildings	5,000		(k) 6,000	11,000
Accumulated Depreciation—Equipment	1,000	(g) 1,000	(l) 3,000	3,000
Common Stock	50,000		(j) 20,000	70,000
Retained Earnings	48,000	(n) 29,000	(m) 145,000	164,000
Total	144,000			412,000
Statement of Cash Flows Effects				
Operating activities				
Net income		(m) 145,000		
Decrease in accounts receivable		(a) 10,000		
Increase in inventory			(b) 5,000	
Increase in prepaid expenses			(c) 4,000	
Increase in accounts payable		(h) 16,000		
Decrease in income taxes payable			(i) 2,000	
Depreciation expense		(k) 6,000		
		(l) 3,000		
Loss on disposal of plant assets		(g) 3,000		
Investing activities				
Purchase of building			(e) 120,000	
Purchase of equipment			(f) 25,000	
Sale of equipment		(g) 4,000		
Financing activities				
Issuance of common stock		(j) 20,000		
Payment of dividends			(n) 29,000	
Totals		525,000	503,000	
Increase in cash			(o) 22,000	
Totals		525,000	525,000	

*Significant noncash investing and financing activity.

Appendix 12C Statement of Cash Flows—T-Account Approach

LEARNING OBJECTIVE *6
Use the T-account approach to prepare a statement of cash flows.

Many people like to use T-accounts to provide structure to the preparation of a statement of cash flows. The use of T-accounts is based on the accounting equation:

Assets = Liabilities + Equity

Now, let's rewrite the left-hand side as:

> **Cash + Noncash Assets = Liabilities + Equity**

Next, rewrite the equation by subtracting Noncash Assets from each side to isolate Cash on the left-hand side:

> **Cash = Liabilities + Equity − Noncash Assets**

Finally, if we insert the Δ symbol (which means "change in"), we have:

> **Δ Cash = Δ Liabilities + Δ Equity − Δ Noncash Assets**

What this means is that the change in cash is equal to the change in all of the other balance sheet accounts. Another way to think about this is that if we analyze the changes in all of the noncash balance sheet accounts, we will explain the change in the Cash account. This, of course, is exactly what we are trying to do with the statement of cash flows.

To implement this approach, first prepare a large Cash T-account with sections for operating, investing, and financing activities. Then, prepare smaller T-accounts for all of the other noncash balance sheet accounts. Insert the beginning and ending balances for each of these accounts. Once you have done this, then walk through the steps outlined in Illustration 12.3. As you walk through the steps, enter debit and credit amounts into the affected accounts. When all of the changes in the T-accounts have been explained, you are done. To demonstrate, we apply this approach to the example of Computer Services Company that is presented in the chapter. Each of the adjustments in **Illustration 12C.1** is numbered so you can follow them through the T-accounts.

1. Post net income as a debit to the operating section of the Cash T-account and a credit to Retained Earnings. Make sure to label all adjustments to the Cash T-account. It also helps to number each adjustment so you can trace all of them if you make an error.

2. Post depreciation expense as a debit to the operating section of Cash and a credit to each of the appropriate accumulated depreciation accounts.

3. Post any gains or losses on the sale of property, plant, and equipment. To do this, it is best to first prepare the journal entry that was recorded at the time of the sale and then post each element of the journal entry. For example, for Computer Services the entry was as follows.

Cash	4,000	
Accumulated Depreciation—Equipment	1,000	
Loss on Disposal of Plant Assets	3,000	
Equipment		8,000

The $4,000 cash entry is a source of cash in the investing section of the Cash account. Accumulated Depreciation—Equipment is debited for $1,000. The Loss on Disposal of Plant Assets (equipment) is a debit to the operating section of the Cash T-account. Finally, Equipment is credited for $8,000.

4–8. Next, post each of the changes to the noncash current asset and current liability accounts. For example, to explain the $10,000 decline in Computer Services' accounts receivable, credit Accounts Receivable for $10,000 and debit the operating section of the Cash T-account for $10,000.

ILLUSTRATION 12C.1 T-account approach

Cash

Operating			
(1) Net income	145,000	5,000	Inventory (5)
(2) Depreciation expense	9,000	4,000	Prepaid expenses (6)
(3) Loss on equipment	3,000	2,000	Income taxes payable (8)
(4) Accounts receivable	10,000		
(7) Accounts payable	16,000		
Net cash provided by operating activities	172,000		
Investing			
(3) Sold equipment	4,000	120,000	Purchased building (10)
		25,000	Purchased equipment (11)
		141,000	Net cash used by investing activities
Financing			
(12) Issued common stock	20,000	29,000	Dividend paid (13)
		9,000	Net cash used by financing activities
Net increase in cash		22,000	

Accounts Receivable		Inventory		Prepaid Expenses		Land	
30,000		10,000		1,000		20,000	
	10,000 (4)	(5) 5,000		(6) 4,000		(9) 110,000	
20,000		15,000		5,000		130,000	

Buildings		Accumulated Depreciation—Buildings		Equipment		Accumulated Depreciation—Equipment	
40,000			5,000	10,000			1,000
(10) 120,000			6,000 (2)	(11) 25,000	8,000 (3)	(3) 1,000	3,000 (2)
160,000			11,000	27,000			3,000

Accounts Payable		Income Taxes Payable		Bonds Payable		Common Stock		Retained Earnings	
	12,000		8,000		20,000		50,000		48,000
	16,000 (7)	(8) 2,000			110,000 (9)		20,000 (12)		145,000 (1)
	28,000		6,000		130,000		70,000	(13) 29,000	
									164,000

9. Analyze the changes in the noncurrent accounts. Land was purchased by issuing bonds payable. This requires a debit to Land for $110,000 and a credit to Bonds Payable for $110,000. Note that this is a significant noncash event that requires disclosure at the bottom of the statement of cash flows.

10. Buildings is debited for $120,000, and the investing section of the Cash T-account is credited for $120,000 as a use of cash from investing.

11. Equipment is debited for $25,000 and the investing section of the Cash T-account is credited for $25,000 as a use of cash from investing.

12. Common Stock is credited for $20,000 for the issuance of shares of stock, and the financing section of the Cash T-account is debited for $20,000.

13. Retained Earnings is debited to reflect the payment of the $29,000 dividend, and the financing section of the Cash T-account is credited to reflect the use of Cash.

At this point, all of the changes in the noncash accounts have been explained. All that remains is to subtotal each section of the Cash T-account and compare the total change in cash with the change shown on the balance sheet. Once this is done, the information in the Cash T-account can be used to prepare a statement of cash flows.

Review and Practice

Learning Objectives Review

1. Discuss the usefulness and format of the statement of cash flows.

The statement of cash flows provides information about the cash receipts, cash payments, and net change in cash resulting from the operating, investing, and financing activities of a company during the period.

Operating activities include the cash effects of transactions that enter into the determination of net income. Investing activities involve cash flows resulting from changes in investments and long-term asset items. Financing activities involve cash flows resulting from changes in long-term liability and stockholders' equity items.

2. Prepare a statement of cash flows using the indirect method.

The preparation of a statement of cash flows involves three major steps. (1) Determine net cash provided/used by operating activities by converting net income from an accrual basis to a cash basis. (2) Analyze changes in noncurrent asset and liability accounts and record as investing and financing activities, or disclose as noncash transactions. (3) Compare the net change in cash on the statement of cash flows with the change in the Cash account reported on the balance sheet to make sure the amounts agree.

3. Use the statement of cash flows to evaluate a company.

During the introductory stage, net cash provided by operating activities and net cash provided by investing activities are negative, and net cash provided by financing activities is positive. During the growth stage, net cash provided by operating activities becomes positive but is still not sufficient to meet investing needs. During the maturity stage, net cash provided by operating activities exceeds investing needs, so the company begins to retire debt. During the decline stage, net cash provided by operating activities is reduced, net cash provided by investing activities becomes positive (from selling off assets), and net cash provided by financing activities becomes more negative.

Free cash flow indicates the amount of cash a company generated during the current year that is available for the payment of dividends or for expansion.

*4. Prepare a statement of cash flows using the direct method.

The preparation of the statement of cash flows involves three major steps. (1) Determine net cash provided/used by operating activities by converting net income from an accrual basis to a cash basis. (2) Analyze changes in noncurrent asset and liability accounts and record as investing and financing activities, or disclose as noncash transactions. (3) Compare the net change in cash on the statement of cash flows with the change in the Cash account reported on the balance sheet to make sure the amounts agree. The direct method reports cash receipts less cash payments to arrive at net cash provided by operating activities.

*5. Use a worksheet to prepare the statement of cash flows using the indirect method.

When there are numerous adjustments, a worksheet can be a helpful tool in preparing the statement of cash flows. Key guidelines for using a worksheet are as follows. (1) List accounts with debit balances separately from those with credit balances. (2) In the reconciling columns in the bottom portion of the worksheet, show cash inflows as debits and cash outflows as credits. (3) Do not enter reconciling items in any journal or account, but use them only to help prepare the statement of cash flows.

The steps in preparing the worksheet are as follows. (1) Enter beginning and ending balances of balance sheet accounts. (2) Enter debits and credits in reconciling columns. (3) Enter the increase or decrease in cash in two places as a balancing amount.

*6. Use the T-account approach to prepare a statement of cash flows.

To use T-accounts to prepare the statement of cash flows: (1) prepare a large Cash T-account with sections for operating, investing, and financing activities; (2) prepare smaller T-accounts for all other noncash accounts; (3) insert beginning and ending balances for all accounts; and (4) follows the steps in Illustration 12C.1, entering debit and credit amounts as needed.

Decision Tools Review

Decision Checkpoints	Info Needed for Decision	Tool to Use for Decision	How to Evaluate Results
How much cash did the company generate to either expand operations or pay dividends?	Net cash provided by operating activities, cash spent on fixed assets, and cash dividends	Free cash flow = Net cash provided by operating activities − Capital expenditures − Cash dividends	Significant free cash flow indicates greater potential to finance new investment and pay additional dividends.

Glossary Review

*Direct method A method of determining net cash provided by operating activities by adjusting each item in the income statement from the accrual basis to the cash basis. The direct method shows operating cash receipts and payments. (pp. 12-7, 12-23).

Financing activities Cash flow activities that include (a) obtaining cash from issuing debt and repaying the amounts borrowed and (b) obtaining cash from stockholders, repurchasing shares, and paying dividends. (p. 12-3).

Free cash flow Net cash provided by operating activities after adjusting for capital expenditures and cash dividends paid. (p. 12-19).

Indirect method A method of preparing a statement of cash flows in which net income is adjusted for items that do not affect cash, to determine net cash provided by operating activities. (pp. 12-7, 12-9).

Investing activities Cash flow activities that include (a) transactions that involve the purchase or disposal of investments and property, plant, and equipment using cash, and (b) lending money and collecting the loans. (p. 12-3).

Operating activities Cash flow activities that include the cash effects of transactions that create revenues and expenses and thus enter into the determination of net income. (p. 12-3).

Product life cycle A series of phases in a product's sales and cash flows over time. These phases, in order of occurrence, are introductory, growth, maturity, and decline. (p. 12-17).

Statement of cash flows A basic financial statement that provides information about the cash receipts and cash payments of an entity during a period, classified as operating, investing, and financing activities, in a format that reconciles the beginning and ending cash balances. (p. 12-3).

Practice Multiple-Choice Questions

1. **(LO 1)** Which of the following is **incorrect** about the statement of cash flows?
   a. It is a fourth basic financial statement.
   b. It provides information about cash receipts and cash payments of an entity during a period.
   c. It reconciles the ending cash account balance to the balance per the bank statement.
   d. It provides information about the operating, investing, and financing activities of the business.

2. **(LO 1)** Which of the following will **not** be reported in the statement of cash flows?
   a. The net change in stockholders' equity during the year.
   b. Cash payments for plant assets during the year.
   c. Cash receipts from sales of plant assets during the year.
   d. Sources of financing during the period.

3. **(LO 1)** The statement of cash flows classifies cash receipts and cash payments by these activities:
   a. operating and nonoperating.
   b. operating, investing, and financing.
   c. financing, operating, and nonoperating.
   d. investing, financing, and nonoperating.

4. **(LO 1)** Which is an example of a cash flow from an operating activity?
   a. Payment of cash to lenders for interest.
   b. Receipt of cash from the sale of common stock.
   c. Payment of cash dividends to the company's stockholders.
   d. None of the above.

5. **(LO 1)** Which is an example of a cash flow from an investing activity?
   a. Receipt of cash from the issuance of bonds payable.
   b. Payment of cash to repurchase outstanding common stock.
   c. Receipt of cash from the sale of equipment.
   d. Payment of cash to suppliers for inventory.

6. **(LO 1)** Cash dividends paid to stockholders are classified on the statement of cash flows as:
   a. operating activities.
   b. investing activities.
   c. a combination of (a) and (b).
   d. financing activities.

7. **(LO 1)** Which is an example of a cash flow from a financing activity?
   a. Receipt of cash from sale of land.
   b. Issuance of debt for cash.
   c. Purchase of equipment for cash.
   d. None of the above

8. **(LO 1)** Which of the following is **incorrect** about the statement of cash flows?
   a. The direct method may be used to report net cash provided by operating activities.
   b. The statement shows the net cash provided (used) for three categories of activity.
   c. The operating activities section is the last section of the statement.
   d. The indirect method may be used to report net cash provided by operating activities.

Use the indirect method to solve Questions 9 through 11.

9. **(LO 2)** Net income is $132,000, accounts payable increased $10,000 during the year, inventory decreased $6,000 during the year, and accounts receivable increased $12,000 during the year. Under the indirect method, what is net cash provided by operating activities?
   a. $102,000.
   b. $112,000.
   c. $124,000.
   d. $136,000.

10. (LO 2) Items that are added back to net income in determining net cash provided by operating activities under the indirect method do **not** include:

  a. depreciation expense.
  b. an increase in inventory.
  c. amortization expense.
  d. loss on disposal of equipment.

11. (LO 2) The following data are available for Bill Mack Corporation.

Net income	$200,000
Depreciation expense	40,000
Dividends paid	60,000
Gain on sale of land	10,000
Decrease in accounts receivable	20,000
Decrease in accounts payable	30,000

Net cash provided by operating activities is:

  a. $160,000.   c. $240,000.
  b. $220,000.   d. $280,000.

12. (LO 2) The following are data concerning cash received or paid from various transactions for Orange Peels Corporation.

Sale of land	$100,000
Sale of equipment	50,000
Issuance of common stock	70,000
Purchase of equipment	30,000
Payment of cash dividends	60,000

Net cash provided by investing activities is:

  a. $120,000.   c. $150,000.
  b. $130,000.   d. $190,000.

13. (LO 2) The following data are available for Retique!

Increase in accounts payable	$ 40,000
Increase in bonds payable	100,000
Sale of investment	50,000
Issuance of common stock	60,000
Payment of cash dividends	30,000

Net cash provided by financing activities is:

  a. $90,000.   c. $160,000.
  b. $130,000.   d. $170,000.

14. (LO 3) Free cash flow provides an indication of a company's ability to:

  a. manage inventory.
  b. generate cash to pay dividends.
  c. generate cash to invest in new capital expenditures.
  d. Both (b) and (c).

15. (LO 3) During the introductory phase of a company's life cycle, one would normally expect to see:

  a. negative cash from operations, negative cash from investing, and positive cash from financing.
  b. negative cash from operations, positive cash from investing, and positive cash from financing.
  c. positive cash from operations, negative cash from investing, and negative cash from financing.
  d. positive cash from operations, negative cash from investing, and positive cash from financing.

Use the direct method to solve Questions 16 and 17.

*16. (LO 4) The beginning balance in accounts receivable is $44,000, the ending balance is $42,000, and sales during the period are $129,000. What are cash receipts from customers?

  a. $127,000.   c. $131,000.
  b. $129,000.   d. $141,000.

*17. (LO 4) Which of the following items is reported on a statement of cash flows prepared by the direct method?

  a. Loss on disposal of building.
  b. Increase in accounts receivable.
  c. Depreciation expense.
  d. Cash payments to suppliers.

Solutions

1. c. The statement of cash flows does not reconcile the ending cash balance to the balance per the bank statement. The other choices are true statements.

2. a. The net change in stockholders' equity during the year is not reported in the statement of cash flows. The other choices are true statements.

3. b. Operating, investing, and financing activities are the three classifications of cash receipts and cash payments used in the statement of cash flows. The other choices are therefore incorrect.

4. a. Payment of cash to lenders for interest is an operating activity. The other choices are incorrect because (b) receipt of cash from the sale of common stock is a financing activity, (c) payment of cash dividends to the company's stockholders is a financing activity, and (d) there is a correct answer.

5. c. Receipt of cash from the sale of equipment is an investing activity. The other choices are incorrect because (a) the receipt of cash from the issuance of bonds payable is a financing activity, (b) payment of cash to repurchase outstanding common stock is a financing activity, and (d) payment of cash to suppliers for inventory is an operating activity.

6. d. Cash dividends paid to stockholders are classified as a financing activity, not (a) an operating activity, (b) an investing activity, or (c) a combination of (a) and (b).

7. b. Issuance of debt for cash is a financing activity. The other choices are incorrect because (a) the receipt of cash for the sale of land is an investing activity, (c) the purchase of equipment for cash is an investing activity, and (d) there is a correct answer.

8. c. The operating section of the statement of cash flows is the first, not the last, section of the statement. The other choices are true statements.

9. d. Net cash provided by operating activities is computed by adjusting net income for the changes in the three current asset/current liability accounts listed. An increase in accounts payable ($10,000) and a decrease in inventory ($6,000) are added to net income ($132,000), while an increase in accounts receivable ($12,000) is subtracted from net income, or $132,000 + $10,000 + $6,000 − $12,000 = $136,000, not (a) $102,000, (b) $112,000, or (c) $124,000.

10. b. An increase in inventory is subtracted, not added, to net income in determining net cash provided by operating activities. The other choices are incorrect because (a) depreciation expense, (c) amortization expense, and (d) loss on disposal of equipment are all added back to net income in determining net cash provided by operating activities.

11. b. Net cash provided by operating activities is $220,000 (Net income $200,000 + Depreciation expense $40,000 − Gain on disposal of land $10,000 + Decrease in accounts receivable $20,000 − Decrease in accounts payable $30,000), not (a) $160,000, (c) $240,000, or (d) $280,000.

12. a. Net cash provided by investing activities is $120,000 (Sale of land $100,000 + Sale of equipment $50,000 − Purchase of equipment $30,000), not (b) $130,000, (c) $150,000, or (d) $190,000. Issuance of common stock and payment of cash dividends are financing activities.

13. b. Net cash provided by financing activities is $130,000 (Increase in bonds payable $100,000 + Issuance of common stock $60,000 − Payment of cash dividends $30,000), not (a) $90,000, (c) $160,000, or (d) $170,000. Increase in accounts payable is an operating activity, and sale of investment is an investing activity.

14. d. Free cash flow provides an indication of a company's ability to generate cash to pay dividends and to invest in new capital expenditures. Choice (a) is incorrect because other measures besides free cash flow provide the best measure of a company's ability to manage inventory. Choices (b) and (c) are true statements, but (d) is the better answer.

15. a. During the introductory phase of a company's life cycle, the company will most likely finance its operations and investing activities through borrowing or the issuance of stock. This means negative cash from operations and investing, and positive cash from financing. The other choices are incorrect because during the introductory phase of a company's life cycle, the company will most likely (b) purchase long-term assets which requires a cash outflow, (c) finance its operations and investing activities through borrowing or the issuance of stock which generates cash inflows from financing, and (d) use cash to fund operations until it establishes a customer base.

*__16. c.__ Cash receipts from customers amount to $131,000 ($129,000 + $2,000). The other choices are therefore incorrect.

*__17. d.__ Cash payments to suppliers are reported on a statement of cash flows prepared by the direct method. The other choices are incorrect because (a) loss on disposal of building, (b) increase in accounts receivable, and (c) depreciation expense are reported in the operating activities section of the statement of cash flows when the indirect, not direct, method is used.

Practice Brief Exercises

Identify investing activity transactions.

1. (LO 1) The following is a summary of the Cash account of Covey Company:

Cash (Summary Form)

Balance, Jan. 1	8,000		
Receipts from customers	364,000	Payments for goods	200,000
Dividends on stock investments	6,000	Payments for operating expenses	140,000
Proceeds from sale of land	96,000	Purchase of equipment	70,000
Proceeds from issuance of bonds payable	300,000	Taxes paid	8,000
		Dividends paid	50,000
Balance, Dec. 31	306,000		

What amount of net cash provided (used) by investing activities should be reported in the statement of cash flows?

Solution

1. Cash flows from investing activities
   Proceeds from sale of land $96,000
   Purchase of equipment .... (70,000)
   Net cash provided by financing activities $26,000

Compute net cash provided by operating activities—indirect method.

2. (LO 2) Engel, Inc. reported net income of $1.6 million in 2022. Depreciation for the year was $140,000, accounts receivable increased $250,000, and accounts payable increased $210,000. The company also had a gain on disposal of plant assets of $19,000. Compute net cash provided by operating activities using the indirect method.

Solution

2. Net income $1,600,000
   Adjustments to reconcile net income to net cash
     provided by operating activities
     Depreciation expense .... $ 140,000
     Gain on disposal of plant assets .... (19,000)
     Accounts receivable increase .... (250,000)
     Accounts payable increase 210,000   81,000
   Net cash provided by operating activities $1,681,000

3. **(LO 3)** Goldberg Corporation reported net cash provided by operating activities of $410,000, net cash used by investing activities of $200,000 (including cash spent for equipment of $160,000), and net cash provided by financing activities of $60,000. Dividends of $110,000 were paid. Calculate free cash flow.

Calculate free cash flow.

Solution

3. Free cash flow = $410,000 − $160,000 − $110,000 = $140,000

Practice Exercises

1. **(LO 2)** Furst Corporation had the following transactions.
   1. Paid salaries of $14,000.
   2. Issued 1,000 shares of $1 par value common stock for equipment worth $16,000.
   3. Sold equipment (cost $10,000, accumulated depreciation $6,000) for $3,000.
   4. Sold land (cost $12,000) for $16,000.
   5. Issued another 1,000 shares of $1 par value common stock for $18,000.
   6. Recorded depreciation of $20,000.

   Prepare journal entries to determine effect on statement of cash flows.

   ### Instructions
   For each transaction above, (a) prepare the journal entry and (b) indicate how it would affect the statement of cash flows. Assume the indirect method.

   ### Solution

   1. 1. a. Salaries and Wages Expense | 14,000 |
              Cash | | 14,000
         b. Salaries and wages expense is not reported separately on the statement of cash flows. It is part of the computation of net income in the income statement and is included in the net income amount on the statement of cash flows.
      2. a. Equipment | 16,000 |
              Common Stock | | 1,000
              Paid-in Capital in Excess of Par—Common Stock | | 15,000
         b. The issuance of common stock for equipment ($16,000) is reported as a noncash financing and investing activity at the bottom of the statement of cash flows.
      3. a. Cash | 3,000 |
              Loss on Disposal of Plant Assets | 1,000 |
              Accumulated Depreciation—Equipment | 6,000 |
              Equipment | | 10,000
         b. The cash receipt ($3,000) is reported in the investing section. The loss ($1,000) is added to net income in the operating section.
      4. a. Cash | 16,000 |
              Land | | 12,000
              Gain on Disposal of Plant Assets | | 4,000
         b. The cash receipt ($16,000) is reported in the investing section. The gain ($4,000) is deducted from net income in the operating section.
      5. a. Cash | 18,000 |
              Common Stock | | 1,000
              Paid-in Capital in Excess of Par—Common Stock | | 17,000
         b. The cash receipt ($18,000) is reported in the financing section.
      6. a. Depreciation Expense | 20,000 |
              Accumulated Depreciation—Equipment | | 20,000
         b. Depreciation expense ($20,000) is added to net income in the operating section.

2. **(LO 2, 3)** Strong Corporation's comparative balance sheets are presented as follows.

   Prepare statement of cash flows and compute free cash flow.

Strong Corporation
Comparative Balance Sheets
December 31

	2022	2021
Cash	$ 28,200	$ 17,700
Accounts receivable	24,200	22,300
Investments	23,000	16,000
Equipment	60,000	70,000
Accumulated depreciation—equipment	(14,000)	(10,000)
Total	$121,400	$116,000
Accounts payable	$ 19,600	$ 11,100
Bonds payable	10,000	30,000
Common stock	60,000	45,000
Retained earnings	31,800	29,900
Total	$121,400	$116,000

Additional information:

1. Net income was $28,300. Depreciation expense was $5,200. Dividends declared and paid were $26,400.
2. Equipment which cost $10,000 and had accumulated depreciation of $1,200 was sold for $4,300.
3. All other changes in noncurrent account balances had a direct effect on cash flows, except the change in accumulated depreciation.

Instructions

a. Prepare a statement of cash flows for 2022 using the indirect method.
b. Compute free cash flow.

Solution

2. a.

Strong Corporation
Statement of Cash Flows
For the Year Ended December 31, 2022

Cash flows from operating activities			
Net income			$ 28,300
Adjustments to reconcile net income to net cash provided by operating activities:			
Depreciation expense		$ 5,200	
Loss on disposal of plants assets		4,500*	
Increase in accounts payable		8,500	
Increase in accounts receivable		(1,900)	16,300
Net cash provided by operating activities			44,600
Cash flows from investing activities			
Sale of equipment		4,300	
Purchase of investments		(7,000)	
Net cash used by investing activities			(2,700)
Cash flows from financing activities			
Issuance of common stock		15,000	
Retirement of bonds		(20,000)	
Payment of dividends		(26,400)	
Net cash used by financing activities			(31,400)
Net increase in cash			10,500
Cash at beginning of period			17,700
Cash at end of period			$ 28,200

*[$4,300 − ($10,000 − $1,200)]

b. $44,600 − $0 − $26,400 = $18,200

Practice Problem

The income statement for Kosinski Manufacturing contains the following condensed information.

Prepare statement of cash flows using indirect and direct methods.

Kosinski Manufacturing
Income Statement
For the Year Ended December 31, 2022

Sales revenue		$6,583,000
Cost of goods sold	$2,810,000	
Operating expenses (excluding depreciation)	2,086,000	
Depreciation expense	880,000	
Loss on disposal of plant assets	24,000	5,800,000
Income before income taxes		783,000
Income tax expense		353,000
Net income		$ 430,000

The $24,000 loss resulting from the sale of machinery resulted from selling equipment for $270,000 cash. Machinery was purchased at a cost of $750,000. The following balances are reported on Kosinski's comparative balance sheets at December 31.

	2022	2021
Cash	$672,000	$130,000
Accounts receivable	775,000	610,000
Inventory	834,000	867,000
Accounts payable	521,000	501,000

Income tax expense of $353,000 represents the amount paid in 2022. Dividends declared and paid in 2022 totaled $200,000.

Instructions

a. Prepare the statement of cash flows using the indirect method.

*b. Prepare the statement of cash flows using the direct method.

Solution

a.

Kosinski Manufacturing
Statement of Cash Flows—Indirect Method
For the Year Ended December 31, 2022

Cash flows from operating activities		
Net income		$ 430,000
Adjustments to reconcile net income to net cash provided by operating activities:		
Depreciation expense	$ 880,000	
Loss on disposal of plant assets	24,000	
Increase in accounts receivable	(165,000)	
Decrease in inventory	33,000	
Increase in accounts payable	20,000	792,000
Net cash provided by operating activities		1,222,000
Cash flows from investing activities		
Sale of equipment	270,000	
Purchase of equipment	(750,000)	
Net cash used by investing activities		(480,000)
Cash flows from financing activities		
Payment of cash dividends	(200,000)	
Net cash used by financing activities		(200,000)
Net increase in cash		542,000
Cash at beginning of period		130,000
Cash at end of period		$ 672,000

*b.

Kosinski Manufacturing
Statement of Cash Flows—Direct Method
For the Year Ended December 31, 2022

Cash flows from operating activities		
Cash collections from customers		$6,418,000*
Cash payments:		
To suppliers	$2,757,000**	
For operating expenses	2,086,000	
For income taxes	353,000	5,196,000
Net cash provided by operating activities		1,222,000
Cash flows from investing activities		
Sale of machinery	270,000	
Purchase of machinery	(750,000)	
Net cash used by investing activities		(480,000)
Cash flows from financing activities		
Payment of cash dividends	(200,000)	
Net cash used by financing activities		(200,000)
Net increase in cash		542,000
Cash at beginning of period		130,000
Cash at end of period		$ 672,000

Direct-Method Computations:

*Computation of cash collections from customers:	
Sales revenue per the income statement	$ 6,583,000
Deduct: Increase in accounts receivable	(165,000)
Cash collections from customers	$ 6,418,000
**Computation of cash payments to suppliers	
Cost of goods sold per income statement	$ 2,810,000
Deduct: Decrease in inventories	(33,000)
Deduct: Increase in accounts payable	(20,000)
	$ 2,757,000

WileyPLUS

Brief Exercises, DO IT! Exercises, Exercises, Problems, and many additional resources are available for practice in WileyPLUS.

Note: All asterisked Questions, Exercises, and Problems relate to material in the appendices to the chapter.

Questions

1. a. What is a statement of cash flows?
   b. Pat Marx maintains that the statement of cash flows is an optional financial statement. Do you agree? Explain.

2. What questions about cash are answered by the statement of cash flows?

3. Distinguish among the three activities reported in the statement of cash flows.

4. a. What are the sources (inflows) of cash in a statement of cash flows?
   b. What are the uses (outflows) of cash?

5. Why is it important to disclose certain noncash transactions? How should they be disclosed?

6. Helen Powell and Paul Tang were discussing the format of the statement of cash flows of Baumgarten Co. At the bottom of

Baumgarten's statement of cash flows was a separate section entitled "Noncash investing and financing activities." Give three examples of significant noncash transactions that would be reported in this section.

7. Why is it necessary to use comparative balance sheets, a current income statement, and certain transaction data in preparing a statement of cash flows?

8. Contrast the advantages and disadvantages of the direct and indirect methods of preparing the statement of cash flows. Are both methods acceptable? Which method is preferred by the FASB? Which method is more popular?

9. When the total cash inflows exceed the total cash outflows in the statement of cash flows, how and where is this excess identified?

10. Describe the indirect method for determining net cash provided (used) by operating activities.

11. Why is it necessary to convert accrual-basis net income to cash-basis net income when preparing a statement of cash flows?

12. The president of Murquery Company is puzzled. During the last year, the company experienced a net loss of $800,000, yet its cash increased $300,000 during the same period of time. Explain to the president how this could occur.

13. Identify five items that are adjustments to convert net income to net cash provided by operating activities under the indirect method.

14. Why and how is depreciation expense reported in a statement of cash flows prepared using the indirect method?

15. Why is the statement of cash flows useful?

16. During 2022, Slivowitz Company exchanged $1,700,000 of its common stock for land. Indicate how the transaction would be reported on a statement of cash flows, if at all.

17. a. What are the phases of the corporate life cycle?
    b. What effect does each phase have on the amounts reported in a statement of cash flows?

18. Based on its statement of cash flows, in what stage of the product life cycle is **Apple**?

*19. Describe the direct method for determining net cash provided by operating activities.

*20. Give the formulas under the direct method for computing (a) cash receipts from customers and (b) cash payments to suppliers.

*21. Harbinger Inc. reported sales of $2 million for 2022. Accounts receivable decreased $150,000 and accounts payable increased $300,000. Compute cash receipts from customers, assuming that the receivable and payable transactions are related to operations.

*22. In the direct method, why is depreciation expense not reported in the cash flows from operating activities section?

Brief Exercises

BE12.1 (LO 1), K Each of these items must be considered in preparing a statement of cash flows for Irvin Co. for the year ended December 31, 2022. For each item, state how it should be shown in the statement of cash flows for 2022.

Indicate statement presentation of selected transactions.

a. Issued bonds for $200,000 cash.
b. Purchased equipment for $180,000 cash.
c. Sold land costing $20,000 for $20,000 cash.
d. Declared and paid a $50,000 cash dividend.

BE12.2 (LO 1), C Classify each item as an operating, investing, or financing activity. Assume all items involve cash unless there is information to the contrary.

Classify items by activities.

a. Purchase of equipment.
b. Sale of building.
c. Redemption of bonds.
d. Cash received from sale of goods.
e. Payment of dividends.
f. Issuance of capital stock.

BE12.3 (LO 1), AP The following T-account is a summary of the Cash account of Alixon Company.

Identify financing activity transactions.

Cash (Summary Form)

Balance, Jan. 1	8,000		
Receipts from customers	364,000	Payments for goods	200,000
Dividends on stock investments	6,000	Payments for operating expenses	140,000
Proceeds from sale of equipment	36,000	Interest paid	10,000
Proceeds from issuance of		Taxes paid	8,000
bonds payable	300,000	Dividends paid	40,000
Balance, Dec. 31	316,000		

What amount of net cash provided (used) by financing activities should be reported in the statement of cash flows?

BE12.4 (LO 2), AP Miguel, Inc. reported net income of $2.5 million in 2022. Depreciation for the year was $160,000, accounts receivable decreased $350,000, and accounts payable decreased $280,000. Compute net cash provided by operating activities using the indirect approach.

Compute net cash provided by operating activities—indirect method.

Compute net cash provided by operating activities—indirect method.

BE12.5 (LO 2), AP The net income for Mongan Co. for 2022 was $280,000. For 2022, depreciation on plant assets was $70,000, and the company incurred a loss on disposal of plant assets of $28,000. Compute net cash provided by operating activities under the indirect method, assuming there were no other changes in the company's accounts.

Compute net cash provided by operating activities—indirect method.

BE12.6 (LO 2), AP The comparative balance sheets for Gale Company show these changes in noncash current asset accounts: accounts receivable decreased $80,000, prepaid expenses increased $28,000, and inventories increased $40,000. Compute net cash provided by operating activities using the indirect method, assuming that net income is $186,000.

Determine cash received from sale of equipment.

BE12.7 (LO 2), AN The T-accounts for Equipment and the related Accumulated Depreciation—Equipment for Goldstone Company at the end of 2022 are shown here.

Equipment					Accum. Depr.—Equipment			
Beg. bal.	80,000	Disposals	22,000		Disposals	5,100	Beg. bal.	44,500
Acquisitions	41,600						Depr. exp.	12,000
End. bal.	99,600						End. bal.	51,400

In addition, Goldstone's income statement reported a loss on the disposal of plant assets of $3,500. What amount was reported on the statement of cash flows as "cash flow from sale of equipment"?

Answer questions related to the phases of product life cycle.

BE12.8 (LO 3), C Answer the following questions.

a. Why is net cash provided by operating activities likely to be lower than reported net income during the growth phase?

b. Why is net cash from investing activities often positive during the late maturity phase and during the decline phase?

Calculate free cash flow.

BE12.9 (LO 3), AP Suppose during 2022 that **Cypress Semiconductor Corporation** reported net cash provided by operating activities of $89,303,000, cash used in investing of $43,126,000, and cash used in financing of $7,368,000. In addition, cash spent for fixed assets during the period was $25,823,000. No dividends were paid. Calculate free cash flow.

Calculate free cash flow.

BE12.10 (LO 3), AP Sprouts Corporation reported net cash provided by operating activities of $412,000, net cash used by investing activities of $250,000, and net cash provided by financing activities of $70,000. In addition, cash spent for capital assets during the period was $200,000. No dividends were paid. Calculate free cash flow.

Calculate free cash flow.

BE12.11 (LO 3), AP Suppose **Canwest Global Communications Corp.** reported net cash used by operating activities of $104,539,000 and sales revenue of $2,867,459,000 during 2022. Cash spent on plant asset additions during the year was $79,330,000. Calculate free cash flow.

Calculate and analyze free cash flow.

BE12.12 (LO 3), AN The management of Uhuru Inc. is trying to decide whether it can increase its dividend. During the current year, it reported net income of $875,000. It had net cash provided by operating activities of $734,000, paid cash dividends of $92,000, and had capital expenditures of $310,000. Compute the company's free cash flow, and discuss whether an increase in the dividend appears warranted. What other factors should be considered?

Compute receipts from customers—direct method.

*****BE12.13** (LO 4), AP Suppose **Columbia Sportswear Company** had accounts receivable of $299,585,000 at January 1, 2022, and $226,548,000 at December 31, 2022. Assume sales revenue was $1,244,023,000 for the year 2022. What is the amount of cash receipts from customers in 2022?

Compute cash payments for income taxes—direct method.

*****BE12.14** (LO 4), AP Hoffman Corporation reported income taxes of $370,000,000 on its 2022 income statement and income taxes payable of $277,000,000 at December 31, 2021, and $528,000,000 at December 31, 2022. What amount of cash payments were made for income taxes during 2022?

Compute cash payments for operating expenses—direct method.

*****BE12.15** (LO 4), AP Pietr Corporation reports operating expenses of $90,000, excluding depreciation expense of $15,000, for 2022. During the year, prepaid expenses decreased $7,200 and accrued expenses payable increased $4,400. Compute the cash payments for operating expenses in 2022.

DO IT! Exercises

Classify transactions by type of cash flow activity.

DO IT! 12.1 (LO 1), C Moss Corporation had the following transactions.

1. Issued $160,000 of bonds payable.
2. Paid utilities expense.
3. Issued 500 shares of preferred stock for $45,000.

4. Sold land and a building for $250,000.

5. Loaned $30,000 to Dead End Corporation, receiving Dead End's 1-year, 12% note.

Classify each of these transactions by type of cash flow activity (operating, investing, or financing). (*Hint:* Refer to Illustration 12.1.)

DO IT! 12.2a (LO 2), AP PK Photography reported net income of $100,000 for 2022. Included in the income statement were depreciation expense of $6,300, patent amortization expense of $4,000, and a gain on disposal of plant assets of $3,600. PK's comparative balance sheets show the following balances.

Calculate net cash from operating activities.

	12/31/22	12/31/21
Accounts receivable	$21,000	$27,000
Accounts payable	9,200	6,000

Calculate net cash provided by operating activities for PK Photography.

DO IT! 12.2b (LO 2), AP Alex Company reported the following information for 2022.

Prepare statement of cash flows—indirect method.

Alex Company
Comparative Balance Sheets
December 31

Assets	2022	2021	Change Increase/Decrease
Cash	$ 59,000	$ 36,000	$ 23,000 Increase
Accounts receivable	62,000	22,000	40,000 Increase
Inventory	44,000	-0-	44,000 Increase
Prepaid expenses	6,000	4,000	2,000 Increase
Land	55,000	70,000	15,000 Decrease
Buildings	200,000	200,000	-0-
Accumulated depreciation—buildings	(21,000)	(14,000)	7,000 Increase
Equipment	183,000	68,000	115,000 Increase
Accumulated depreciation—equipment	(28,000)	(10,000)	18,000 Increase
Totals	$560,000	$376,000	
Liabilities and Stockholders' Equity			
Accounts payable	$ 43,000	$ 40,000	$ 3,000 Increase
Accrued expenses payable	-0-	10,000	10,000 Decrease
Bonds payable	100,000	150,000	50,000 Decrease
Common stock ($1 par)	230,000	60,000	170,000 Increase
Retained earnings	187,000	116,000	71,000 Increase
Totals	$560,000	$376,000	

Alex Company
Income Statement
For the Year Ended December 31, 2022

Sales revenue		$941,000
Cost of goods sold	$475,000	
Operating expenses	231,000	
Interest expense	12,000	
Loss on disposal of equipment	2,000	720,000
Income before income taxes		221,000
Income tax expense		65,000
Net income		$156,000

Additional information:

1. Operating expenses include depreciation expense of $40,000.
2. Land was sold at its book value for cash.
3. Cash dividends of $85,000 were declared and paid in 2022.
4. Equipment with a cost of $166,000 was purchased for cash. Equipment with a cost of $51,000 and a book value of $36,000 was sold for $34,000 cash.
5. Bonds of $50,000 were redeemed at their face value for cash.
6. Common stock ($1 par) of $170,000 was issued for cash.

Use this information to prepare a statement of cash flows using the indirect method.

Compute and discuss free cash flow.

DO IT! 12.3 (LO 3), AP Moskow Corporation issued the following statement of cash flows for 2022.

Moskow Corporation
Statement of Cash Flows—Indirect Method
For the Year Ended December 31, 2022

Cash flows from operating activities		
Net income		$ 59,000
Adjustments to reconcile net income to net cash provided by operating activities:		
Depreciation expense	$ 9,100	
Decrease in accounts receivable	9,500	
Increase in inventory	(5,000)	
Decrease in accounts payable	(2,200)	
Loss on disposal of plant assets	3,300	14,700
Net cash provided by operating activities		73,700
Cash flows from investing activities		
Sale of investments	3,100	
Purchase of equipment	(24,200)	
Net cash used by investing activities		(21,100)
Cash flows from financing activities		
Issuance of stock	20,000	
Payment on long-term note payable	(10,000)	
Payment for dividends	(13,000)	
Net cash used by financing activities		(3,000)
Net increase in cash		49,600
Cash at beginning of year		13,000
Cash at end of year		$ 62,600

a. Compute free cash flow for Moskow Corporation.

b. Explain why free cash flow often provides better information than "Net cash provided by operating activities."

Exercises

Classify transactions by type of activity.

E12.1 (LO 1), C Kiley Corporation had these transactions during 2022.

a. Purchased a machine for $30,000, giving a long-term note in exchange.
b. Issued $50,000 par value common stock for cash.
c. Issued $200,000 par value common stock upon conversion of bonds having a face value of $200,000.
d. Declared and paid a cash dividend of $13,000.
e. Sold a long-term investment with a cost of $15,000 for $15,000 cash.

f. Collected $16,000 from sale of goods.

g. Paid $18,000 to suppliers.

Instructions

Analyze the transactions and indicate whether each transaction is an operating activity, investing activity, financing activity, or noncash investing and financing activity.

E12.2 (LO 1), C An analysis of comparative balance sheets, the current year's income statement, and the general ledger accounts of Hailey Corp. uncovered the following items. Assume all items involve cash unless there is information to the contrary.

Classify transactions by type of activity.

a. Exchange of land for patent.
b. Sale of building at book value.
c. Payment of dividends.
d. Depreciation.
e. Conversion of bonds into common stock.
f. Issuance of capital stock.
g. Amortization of patent.
h. Issuance of bonds for land.
i. Purchase of land.
j. Loss on disposal of plant assets.
k. Retirement of bonds.

Instructions

Indicate where each item should be presented in the statement of cash flows (indirect method) using these four major classifications: operating activity (that is, the item would be listed among the adjustments to net income to determine net cash provided by operating activities under the indirect method), investing activity, financing activity, or significant noncash investing and financing activity.

E12.3 (LO 1), AP Cushenberry Corporation had the following transactions.

Prepare journal entry and determine effect on cash flows.

1. Sold land (cost $12,000) for $15,000.
2. Issued common stock at par for $20,000.
3. Recorded depreciation on buildings for $17,000.
4. Paid salaries of $9,000.
5. Issued 1,000 shares of $1 par value common stock for equipment worth $8,000.
6. Sold equipment (cost $10,000, accumulated depreciation $7,000) for $1,200.

Instructions

For each transaction above, (a) prepare the journal entry, and (b) indicate how it would affect the statement of cash flows using the indirect method.

E12.4 (LO 2), AP Sosa Company reported net income of $190,000 for 2022. Sosa also reported depreciation expense of $35,000 and a loss of $5,000 on the disposal of plant assets. The comparative balance sheets show an increase in accounts receivable of $15,000 for the year, a $17,000 increase in accounts payable, and a $4,000 increase in prepaid expenses.

Prepare the operating activities section—indirect method.

Instructions

Prepare the operating activities section of the statement of cash flows for 2022. Use the indirect method.

E12.5 (LO 2), AP The current sections of Sunn Inc.'s balance sheets at December 31, 2021 and 2022, are presented here. Sunn's net income for 2022 was $153,000. Depreciation expense was $27,000.

Prepare the operating activities section—indirect method.

	2022	2021
Current assets		
Cash	$105,000	$ 99,000
Accounts receivable	80,000	89,000
Inventory	168,000	172,000
Prepaid expenses	27,000	22,000
Total current assets	$380,000	$382,000
Current liabilities		
Accrued expenses payable	$ 15,000	$ 5,000
Accounts payable	85,000	92,000
Total current liabilities	$100,000	$ 97,000

Instructions

Prepare the net cash provided by operating activities section of the company's statement of cash flows for the year ended December 31, 2022, using the indirect method.

Prepare the operating activities section—indirect method.

E12.6 (LO 2), AP The current sections of Ray Inc.'s balance sheets at December 31, 2021 and 2022, are presented here. Ray's net income for 2022 was $254,000. Depreciation expense was $42,000.

	2022	2021
Current assets		
Cash	$ 62,000	$ 89,000
Accounts receivable	85,000	69,000
Inventory	78,000	62,000
Prepaid expenses	17,000	19,000
Total current assets	$242,000	$239,000
Current liabilities		
Accrued expenses payable	$ 6,000	$ 16,000
Accounts payable	88,000	72,000
Total current liabilities	$ 94,000	$ 88,000

Instructions

Prepare the net cash provided by operating activities section of the company's statement of cash flows for the year ended December 31, 2022, using the indirect method.

Prepare statement of cash flows—indirect method.

E12.7 (LO 2), AP The following information is available for Stamos Corporation for the year ended December 31, 2022.

Beginning cash balance	$ 45,000
Accounts payable decrease	3,700
Depreciation expense	162,000
Accounts receivable increase	8,200
Inventory increase	11,000
Net income	284,100
Cash received for sale of land at book value	35,000
Cash dividends paid	12,000
Income taxes payable increase	4,700
Cash used to purchase building	289,000
Cash used to purchase treasury stock	26,000
Cash received from issuing bonds	200,000

Instructions

Prepare a statement of cash flows using the indirect method.

Prepare statement of cash flows—indirect method.

E12.8 (LO 2), AP The following information is available for Moab Corporation for the year ended December 31, 2022.

Beginning cash balance	$ 24,000
Accounts payable increase	5,700
Depreciation expense	41,000
Accounts receivable decrease	4,800
Inventory decrease	3,100
Net income	57,200
Cash received for sale of land at book value	104,000
Cash dividends paid	38,000
Income taxes payable decrease	3,900
Cash used to purchase land	81,000
Cash used to redeem bonds	66,000
Cash received from issuing stock	160,000

Instructions

Prepare a statement of cash flows using the indirect method.

Prepare partial statement of cash flows—indirect method.

E12.9 (LO 2), AN The following three accounts appear in the general ledger of Beiber Corp. during 2022.

Equipment

Date		Debit	Credit	Balance
Jan. 1	Balance			160,000
July 31	Purchase of equipment	70,000		230,000
Sept. 2	Cost of equipment constructed	53,000		283,000
Nov. 10	Cost of equipment sold		49,000	234,000

Accumulated Depreciation—Equipment

Date		Debit	Credit	Balance
Jan. 1	Balance			71,000
Nov. 10	Accumulated depreciation on equipment sold	16,000		55,000
Dec. 31	Depreciation for year		28,000	83,000

Retained Earnings

Date		Debit	Credit	Balance
Jan. 1	Balance			105,000
Aug. 23	Dividends (cash)	14,000		91,000
Dec. 31	Net income		72,000	163,000

Instructions

From the postings in the accounts, indicate how the information is reported on a statement of cash flows using the indirect method. The loss on disposal of plant assets was $8,000. (*Hint:* Cost of equipment constructed is reported in the investing activities section as a decrease in cash of $53,000.)

E12.10 (LO 2), AP The following are comparative balance sheets for Mitch Company.

Prepare a statement of cash flows—indirect method.

Mitch Company
Comparative Balance Sheets
December 31

Assets	2022	2021
Cash	$ 68,000	$ 22,000
Accounts receivable	88,000	76,000
Inventory	167,000	189,000
Land	80,000	100,000
Equipment	260,000	200,000
Accumulated depreciation—equipment	(66,000)	(32,000)
Total	$597,000	$555,000

Liabilities and Stockholders' Equity		
Accounts payable	$ 39,000	$ 43,000
Bonds payable	150,000	200,000
Common stock ($1 par)	216,000	174,000
Retained earnings	192,000	138,000
Total	$597,000	$555,000

Additional information:

1. Net income for 2022 was $93,000.
2. Depreciation expense was $34,000.
3. Cash dividends of $39,000 were declared and paid.
4. Bonds payable amounting to $50,000 were redeemed for cash $50,000.
5. Common stock was issued for $42,000 cash.
6. No equipment was sold during 2022.
7. Land was sold for its book value.

Instructions

Prepare a statement of cash flows for 2022 using the indirect method.

E12.11 (LO 3), C The information in the table is from the statement of cash flows for a company at four different points in time (M, N, O, and P). Negative values are presented in parentheses.

Identify phases of product life cycle.

	Point in Time			
	M	N	O	P
Net cash provided by operating activities	$ (60,000)	$ 30,000	$120,000	$(10,000)
Cash provided by investing activities	(100,000)	25,000	30,000	(40,000)
Cash provided by financing activities	70,000	(90,000)	(50,000)	120,000
Net income	(38,000)	10,000	100,000	(5,000)

Instructions

For each point in time, state whether the company is most likely in the introductory phase, growth phase, maturity phase, or decline phase. In each case, explain your choice.

Compare free cash flow of two companies.

E12.12 (LO 3), AN Suppose the following is 2022 information for **PepsiCo, Inc.** and **The Coca-Cola Company**.

($ in millions)	PepsiCo	Coca-Cola
Net cash provided by operating activities	$ 6,796	$ 8,186
Average current liabilities	8,772	13,355
Net income	5,979	6,906
Sales revenue	43,232	30,990
Capital expenditures	2,128	1,993
Dividends paid	2,732	3,800

Instructions

Compute free cash flow for both companies and compare.

Compare free cash flow of two companies.

E12.13 (LO 3), AN Information for two companies in the same industry, Merrill Corporation and Wingate Corporation, is presented here.

	Merrill Corporation	Wingate Corporation
Net cash provided by operating activities	$ 80,000	$100,000
Average current liabilities	50,000	100,000
Net income	200,000	200,000
Capital expenditures	40,000	70,000
Dividends paid	5,000	10,000

Instructions

Compute free cash flow for both companies and compare.

Compute cash provided by operating activities—direct method.

*E12.14 (LO 4), AP Zimmer Company completed its first year of operations on December 31, 2022. Its initial income statement showed that Zimmer had sales revenue of $198,000 and operating expenses of $83,000. Accounts receivable and accounts payable at year-end were $60,000 and $23,000, respectively. Assume that accounts payable related to operating expenses. Ignore income taxes.

Instructions

Compute net cash provided by operating activity using the direct method.

Compute cash payments—direct method.

*E12.15 (LO 4), AP Suppose the 2022 income statement for **McDonald's Corporation** shows cost of goods sold $5,178.0 million and operating expenses (including depreciation expense of $1,216.2 million) $10,725.7 million. The comparative balance sheets for the year show that inventory decreased $5.3 million, prepaid expenses increased $42.2 million, accounts payable (merchandise suppliers) increased $15.6 million, and accrued expenses payable increased $199.8 million.

Instructions

Using the direct method, compute (a) cash payments to suppliers and (b) cash payments for operating expenses.

Compute cash flow from operating activities—direct method.

*E12.16 (LO 4), AP The 2022 accounting records of Megan Transport reveal these transactions and events.

Payment of interest	$ 10,000	Payment of salaries and wages	$ 53,000
Cash sales	48,000	Depreciation expense	16,000
Receipt of dividend revenue	18,000	Proceeds from sale of vehicles	812,000
Payment of income taxes	12,000	Purchase of equipment for cash	22,000
Net income	38,000	Loss on sale of vehicles	3,000
Payment for merchandise	97,000	Payment of dividends	14,000
Payment for land	74,000	Payment of operating expenses	28,000
Collection of accounts receivable	195,000		

Instructions

Prepare the cash flows from operating activities section using the direct method.

*E12.17 (LO 4), AP The following information is available for Balboa Corp. for 2022.

Prepare statement of cash flows—direct method.

Cash used to purchase treasury stock	$ 48,100
Cash dividends paid	21,800
Cash paid for interest	22,400
Net income	464,300
Sales revenue	802,000
Cash paid for taxes	99,000
Cash received from customers	566,100
Cash received from sale of building (at book value)	197,600
Cash paid for operating expenses	77,000
Beginning cash balance	11,000
Cash paid for goods and services	279,100
Cash received from issuing common stock	355,000
Cash paid to redeem bonds at maturity	200,000
Cash paid to purchase equipment	113,200

Instructions

Prepare a statement of cash flows using the direct method.

*E12.18 (LO 4), AN The following information is taken from the 2022 general ledger of Preminger Company.

Calculate cash flows—direct method.

Rent		Rent expense	$ 30,000
		Prepaid rent, January 1	5,900
		Prepaid rent, December 31	7,400
Salaries		Salaries and wages expense	$ 54,000
		Salaries and wages payable, January 1	2,000
		Salaries and wages payable, December 31	8,000
Sales		Sales revenue	$160,000
		Accounts receivable, January 1	16,000
		Accounts receivable, December 31	7,000

Instructions

In each case, compute the amount that should be reported in the operating activities section of the statement of cash flows under the direct method.

Problems: Set A

P12.1A (LO 1, 2), AP You are provided with the following information regarding events that occurred at Moore Corporation during 2022 or changes in account balances as of December 31, 2022.

Distinguish among operating, investing, and financing activities.

	(1) Statement of Cash Flow Section Affected	(2) If Operating, Did It Increase or Decrease Reported Cash from Operating Activities?
a. Depreciation expense was $80,000.		
b. Interest Payable account increased $5,000.		
c. Received $26,000 from sale of plant assets.		
d. Acquired land by issuing common stock to seller.		
e. Paid $17,000 cash dividend to preferred stockholders.		
f. Paid $4,000 cash dividend to common stockholders.		
g. Accounts Receivable account decreased $10,000.		
h. Inventory increased $2,000.		
i. Received $100,000 from issuing bonds payable.		
j. Acquired equipment for $16,000 cash.		

Instructions

Moore prepares its statement of cash flows using the indirect approach. Complete the first column of the table, indicating whether each item affects the operating activities section (O) (that is, the item would be listed among the adjustments to net income to determine net cash provided by operating activities under the indirect approach), investing activities section (I), financing activities section (F), or is a noncash (NC) transaction reported in a separate schedule. For those items classified as operating activities (O), indicate whether the item is added (A) or subtracted (S) from net income to determine net cash provided by operating activities.

Determine cash flow effects of changes in equity accounts.

P12.2A (LO 2), AN The following account balances relate to the stockholders' equity accounts of Molder Corp. at year-end.

	2022	2021
Common stock, 10,500 and 10,000 shares, respectively, for 2022 and 2021	$160,800	$140,000
Preferred stock, 5,000 shares	125,000	125,000
Retained earnings	300,000	270,000

A small stock dividend was declared and issued in 2022. The market price of the shares was $8,800. Cash dividends were $20,000 in both 2022 and 2021. The common stock has no par or stated value.

Instructions

a. Net income $58,800

a. What was the amount of net income reported by Molder Corp. in 2022?

b. Determine the amounts of any cash inflows or outflows related to the common stock and dividend accounts in 2022.

c. Indicate where each of the cash inflows or outflows identified in (b) would be classified on the statement of cash flows.

Prepare the operating activities section—indirect method.

P12.3A (LO 2), AP The income statement of Munsun Company is presented here.

Munsun Company
Income Statement
For the Year Ended November 30, 2022

Sales revenue		$7,600,000
Cost of goods sold		
Beginning inventory	$1,900,000	
Purchases	4,400,000	
Goods available for sale	6,300,000	
Ending inventory	1,600,000	
Total cost of goods sold		4,700,000
Gross profit		2,900,000
Operating expenses		
Selling expenses	450,000	
Administrative expenses	700,000	1,150,000
Net income		$1,750,000

Additional information:

1. Accounts receivable decreased $380,000 during the year, and inventory decreased $300,000.
2. Prepaid expenses increased $150,000 during the year.
3. Accounts payable to suppliers of merchandise decreased $350,000 during the year.
4. Accrued expenses payable decreased $100,000 during the year.
5. Administrative expenses include depreciation expense of $110,000.

Instructions

Net cash provided $1,940,000

Prepare the operating activities section of the statement of cash flows for the year ended November 30, 2022, for Munsun Company, using the indirect method.

Prepare the operating activities section—direct method.

Net cash provided—
oper. act. $1,940,000

*P12.4A (LO 4), AP Data for Munsun Company are presented in P12.3A.

Instructions

Prepare the operating activities section of the statement of cash flows using the direct method.

P12.5A (LO 2), AP Rewe Company's income statement contained the condensed information below.

Prepare the operating activities section—indirect method.

Rewe Company
Income Statement
For the Year Ended December 31, 2022

Service revenue		$970,000
Operating expenses, excluding depreciation	$614,000	
Depreciation expense	55,000	
Loss on disposal of plant assets	16,000	685,000
Income before income taxes		285,000
Income tax expense		56,000
Net income		$229,000

Rewe's balance sheets contained the following comparative data at December 31.

	2022	2021
Accounts receivable	$70,000	$60,000
Accounts payable	41,000	32,000
Income taxes payable	13,000	7,000

Accounts payable pertain to operating expenses.

Instructions

Prepare the operating activities section of the statement of cash flows using the indirect method.

Net cash provided $305,000

*P12.6A (LO 4), AP Data for Rewe Company are presented in P12.5A.

Prepare the operating activities section—direct method.

Instructions

Prepare the operating activities section of the statement of cash flows using the direct method.

Net cash provided $305,000

P12.7A (LO 2, 3), AP Presented below are the financial statements of Warner Company.

Prepare a statement of cash flows—indirect method, and compute free cash flow.

Warner Company
Comparative Balance Sheets
December 31

Assets	2022	2021
Cash	$ 35,000	$ 20,000
Accounts receivable	20,000	14,000
Inventory	28,000	20,000
Property, plant, and equipment	60,000	78,000
Accumulated depreciation	(32,000)	(24,000)
Total	$111,000	$108,000
Liabilities and Stockholders' Equity		
Accounts payable	$ 19,000	$ 15,000
Income taxes payable	7,000	8,000
Bonds payable	17,000	33,000
Common stock	18,000	14,000
Retained earnings	50,000	38,000
Total	$111,000	$108,000

Warner Company
Income Statement
For the Year Ended December 31, 2022

Sales revenue		$242,000
Cost of goods sold		175,000
Gross profit		67,000
Selling expenses	$18,000	
Administrative expenses	6,000	24,000
Income from operations		43,000
Interest expense		3,000
Income before income taxes		40,000
Income tax expense		8,000
Net income		$ 32,000

Additional data:

1. Depreciation expense was $17,500.
2. Dividends declared and paid were $20,000.
3. During the year equipment was sold for $8,500 cash. This equipment cost $18,000 originally and had accumulated depreciation of $9,500 at the time of sale.

Instructions

a. Prepare a statement of cash flows using the indirect method.
b. Compute free cash flow.

a. Net cash provided— oper. act. $38,500

Prepare a statement of cash flows— direct method, and compute free cash flow.

*P12.8A (LO 3, 4), AP Data for Warner Company are presented in P12.7A. Further analysis reveals the following.

1. Accounts payable pertain to merchandise suppliers.
2. All operating expenses except for depreciation were paid in cash.
3. All depreciation expense is in the selling expense category.
4. All sales and purchases are on account.

Instructions

a. Prepare a statement of cash flows for Warner Company using the direct method.
b. Compute free cash flow.

a. Net cash provided— oper. act. $38,500

Prepare a statement of cash flows— indirect method.

P12.9A (LO 2), AP Condensed financial data of Granger Inc. follow.

Granger Inc.
Comparative Balance Sheets
December 31

Assets	2022	2021
Cash	$ 80,800	$ 48,400
Accounts receivable	87,800	38,000
Inventory	112,500	102,850
Prepaid expenses	28,400	26,000
Long-term investments	138,000	109,000
Plant assets	285,000	242,500
Accumulated depreciation	(50,000)	(52,000)
Total	$682,500	$514,750
Liabilities and Stockholders' Equity		
Accounts payable	$102,000	$ 67,300
Accrued expenses payable	16,500	21,000
Bonds payable	110,000	146,000
Common stock	220,000	175,000
Retained earnings	234,000	105,450
Total	$682,500	$514,750

Granger Inc.
Income Statement Data
For the Year Ended December 31, 2022

Sales revenue		$388,460
Less:		
Cost of goods sold	$135,460	
Operating expenses, excluding depreciation	12,410	
Depreciation expense	46,500	
Income tax expense	27,280	
Interest expense	4,730	
Loss on disposal of plant assets	7,500	233,880
Net income		$154,580

Additional information:

1. New plant assets costing $100,000 were purchased for cash during the year.
2. Old plant assets having an original cost of $57,500 and accumulated depreciation of $48,500 were sold for $1,500 cash.
3. Bonds payable matured and were paid off at face value for cash.
4. A cash dividend of $26,030 was declared and paid during the year.

Instructions

Prepare a statement of cash flows using the indirect method.

Net cash provided—
oper. act. $176,930

*P12.10A (LO 4), AP Data for Granger Inc. are presented in P12.9A. Further analysis reveals that accounts payable pertain to merchandise creditors.

Prepare a statement of cash flows—direct method.

Instructions

Prepare a statement of cash flows for Granger Inc. using the direct method.

Net cash provided—
oper. act. $176,930

P12.11A (LO 2), AP The comparative balance sheets for Spicer Company as of December 31 are presented below.

Prepare a statement of cash flows—indirect method.

Spicer Company
Comparative Balance Sheets
December 31

Assets	2022	2021
Cash	$ 68,000	$ 45,000
Accounts receivable	50,000	58,000
Inventory	151,450	142,000
Prepaid expenses	15,280	21,000
Land	145,000	130,000
Buildings	200,000	200,000
Accumulated depreciation—buildings	(60,000)	(40,000)
Equipment	225,000	155,000
Accumulated depreciation—equipment	(45,000)	(35,000)
Total	$749,730	$676,000
Liabilities and Stockholders' Equity		
Accounts payable	$ 44,730	$ 36,000
Bonds payable	300,000	300,000
Common stock, $1 par	200,000	160,000
Retained earnings	205,000	180,000
Total	$749,730	$676,000

Additional information:

1. Operating expenses include depreciation expense of $42,000 ($20,000 of depreciation expense for buildings and $22,000 for equipment).
2. Land was sold for cash at book value.
3. Cash dividends of $12,000 were paid.
4. Net income for 2022 was $37,000.
5. Equipment was purchased for $92,000 cash. In addition, equipment costing $22,000 with a book value of $10,000 was sold for $8,000 cash.
6. 40,000 shares of $1 par value common stock were issued in exchange for land with a fair value of $40,000.

Instructions

Prepare a statement of cash flows for the year ended December 31, 2022, using the indirect method.

Net cash provided—
oper. act. $94,000

P12.12A (LO 3), C You are provided with the following transactions that took place during the year.

Identify the impact of transactions on free cash flow.

Transactions	Free Cash Flow ($125,000)
a. Recorded credit sales $2,500.	
b. Collected $1,900 owed by customers.	

Transactions	Free Cash Flow ($125,000)
c. Paid amount owed to suppliers $2,750.	
d. Recorded sales returns of $500 and credited the customer's account.	
e. Purchased new equipment $5,000.	
f. Purchased a patent and paid $65,000 cash for the asset.	

Instructions

For each transaction listed, indicate whether it will increase (I), decrease (D), or have no effect (NE) on free cash flow.

Continuing Case

© leungchopan/ Shutterstock

Cookie Creations

(*Note:* This is a continuation of the Cookie Creations case from Chapters 1 through 11.)

CC12 Natalie has prepared the balance sheet and income statement of Cookie & Coffee Creations Inc. and would like you to prepare the statement of cash flows.

Go to WileyPLUS for complete case details and instructions.

Expand Your Critical Thinking

Financial Reporting Problem: Apple Inc.

CT12.1 The financial statements of **Apple Inc.** are presented in Appendix A.

Instructions

Answer the following questions.

a. What was the amount of net cash provided by operating activities for the year ended September 30, 2017? For the year ended September 24, 2016?

b. What was the amount of increase or decrease in cash and cash equivalents for the year ended September 30, 2017?

c. Which method of computing net cash provided by operating activities does Apple use?

d. From your analysis of the September 30, 2017, statement of cash flows, was the change in accounts receivable a decrease or an increase? Was the change in inventories a decrease or an increase? Was the change in accounts payable a decrease or an increase?

e. What was the net cash used by investing activities for the year ended September 30, 2017?

f. What was the amount of interest paid in the year ended September 30, 2017? What was the amount of income taxes paid for the same period?

Comparative Analysis Problem: Columbia Sportswear Company vs. VF Corporation

CT12.2 **Columbia Sportswear Company**'s financial statements are presented in Appendix B. Financial statements of **VF Corporation** are presented in Appendix C.

Instructions

a. Based on the information contained in these financial statements, compute free cash flow for each company.

b. What conclusions concerning the management of cash can be drawn from these data?

Comparative Analysis Problem: Amazon.com, Inc. vs. Wal-Mart Stores, Inc.

CT12.3 **Amazon.com, Inc.**'s financial statements are presented in Appendix D. Financial statements of **Wal-Mart Stores, Inc.** are presented in Appendix E.

Instructions

a. Based on the information contained in these financial statements, compute free cash flow for each company for the most recent year provided.

b. What conclusions concerning the management of cash can be drawn from these data?

Real-World Focus

CT12.4 You can use the Internet to view **SEC** filings.

Instructions

Choose a company, go to the **Yahoo! Finance** website, and then answer the following questions.

a. What company did you select?

b. What is its stock symbol? What is its selling price?

c. What recent SEC filings are available for your viewing? (*Hint:* Use the Profile link.)

d. Which filing is the most recent? What is the date?

CT12.5 The April 30, 2017, edition of the *Wall Street Journal* contains an article by Tripp Mickle entitled "Apple's Cash Hoard Set to Top $250 Billion."

Instructions

Read the article and then answer the following questions.

a. In comparison to other large values, how big is **Apple**'s cash amount of $250 billion?

b. In what form does Apple hold its cash and cash equivalents?

c. At the time of the article, how much money had Apple returned to shareholders in the form of dividends and stock buybacks since starting those programs in 2012?

d. What is the largest acquisition of another company? What acquisitions have some investors proposed to Apple, and what was the market value of those companies at the time of the article?

CT12.6 The November 23, 2011, edition of the *Wall Street Journal Online* contains an article by John Jannarone entitled "Backlash from Netflix Buybacks."

Instructions

Read the article and then answer the following questions.

a. What was the stock price for the shares of common stock issued by **Netflix** in the article? What was the price of the stock a few months previously?

b. Why did Netflix issue new shares at a time when its stock price was so depressed relative to previous valuations for its stock?

c. What previous actions had Netflix taken to reduce its cash balance?

d. What does the article say is the lesson that growth companies should learn from the Netflix example?

Decision-Making Across the Organization

CT12.7 Pete Kent and Maria Robles are examining the following statement of cash flows for Sullivan Company for the year ended January 31, 2022.

Sullivan Company
Statement of Cash Flows
For the Year Ended January 31, 2022

Sources of cash	
From sales of merchandise	$385,000
From sale of capital stock	405,000
From sale of investment (purchased below)	80,000
From depreciation	55,000
From issuance of note for truck	20,000
From interest on investments	6,000
Total sources of cash	951,000

Uses of cash	
For purchase of fixtures and equipment	$320,000
For merchandise purchased for resale	258,000
For operating expenses (including depreciation)	170,000
For purchase of investment	75,000
For purchase of truck by issuance of note	20,000
For purchase of treasury stock	10,000
For interest on note payable	3,000
Total uses of cash	856,000
Net increase in cash	$ 95,000

Pete claims that Sullivan's statement of cash flows is an excellent portrayal of a superb first year with cash increasing $95,000. Maria replies that it was not a superb first year. Rather, she says, the year was an operating failure, that the statement is presented incorrectly, and that $95,000 is not the actual increase in cash. The cash balance at the beginning of the year was $140,000.

Instructions

With the class divided into groups, answer the following.

a. Using the data provided, prepare a statement of cash flows in proper form using the indirect method. The only noncash items in the income statement are depreciation and the gain from the sale of the investment.

b. With whom do you agree, Pete or Maria? Explain your position.

Communication Activity

CT12.8 Walt Jax, the owner-president of Computer Services Company, is unfamiliar with the statement of cash flows that you, as his accountant, prepared. He asks for further explanation.

Instructions

Write him a brief memo explaining the form and content of the statement of cash flows as shown in Illustration 12.14.

Ethics Case

CT12.9 Pendleton Automotive Corp. is a medium-sized wholesaler of automotive parts. It has 10 stockholders who have been paid a total of $1 million in cash dividends for 8 consecutive years. The board's policy requires that, for this dividend to be declared, net cash provided by operating activities as reported in Pendleton Automotive's current year's statement of cash flows must exceed $1 million. President and CEO Hans Pfizer's job is secure so long as he produces annual operating cash flows to support the usual dividend.

At the end of the current year, controller Kurt Nolte presents president Hans Pfizer with some disappointing news. The net cash provided by operating activities is calculated by the indirect method to be only $970,000. The president says to Kurt, "We must get that amount above $1 million. Isn't there some way to increase operating cash flow by another $30,000?" Kurt answers, "These figures were prepared by my assistant. I'll go back to my office and see what I can do." The president replies, "I know you won't let me down, Kurt."

Upon close scrutiny of the statement of cash flows, Kurt concludes that he can get the operating cash flows above $1 million by reclassifying a $60,000, 2-year note payable listed in the financing activities section as "Proceeds from bank loan—$60,000." He will report the note instead as "Increase in payables—$60,000" and treat it as an adjustment of net income in the operating activities section. He returns to the president, saying, "You can tell the board to declare their usual dividend. Our net cash flow provided by operating activities is $1,030,000." "Good man, Kurt! I knew I could count on you," exults the president.

Instructions

a. Who are the stakeholders in this situation?

b. Was there anything unethical about the president's actions? Was there anything unethical about the controller's actions?

c. Are the board members or anyone else likely to discover the misclassification?

All About You

CT12.10 In this chapter, you learned that companies prepare a statement of cash flows in order to keep track of their sources and uses of cash and to help them plan for their future cash needs. Planning for your own short- and long-term cash needs is every bit as important as it is for a company.

Instructions

Read the article "Financial 'Uh-Oh'? No Problem" (available online) and then answer the following questions.

a. Describe the three factors that determine how much money you should set aside for short-term needs.

b. How many months of living expenses does the article suggest to set aside?

c. Estimate how much you should set aside based upon your current situation. Are you closer to Cliff's scenario or to Prudence's?

FASB Codification Activity

CT12.11 If your school has a subscription to the FASB Codification, log in and prepare responses to the following. Use the Master Glossary to determine the proper definitions.

a. What are cash equivalents?

b. What are financing activities?

c. What are investing activities?

d. What are operating activities?

e. What is the primary objective for the statement of cash flow? Is working capital the basis for meeting this objective?

f. Do companies need to disclose information about investing and financing activities that do not affect cash receipts or cash payments? If so, how should such information be disclosed?

A Look at IFRS

LEARNING OBJECTIVE 7
Compare the procedures for the statement of cash flows under GAAP and IFRS.

As in GAAP, the statement of cash flows is a required statement for IFRS. In addition, the content and presentation of an IFRS statement of cash flows is similar to the one used for GAAP. However, the disclosure requirements related to the statement of cash flows are more extensive under GAAP. *IAS 7* ("Cash Flow Statements") provides the overall IFRS requirements for cash flow information.

Key Points

Following are the key similarities and differences between GAAP and IFRS as related to the statement of cash flows.

Similarities

- Companies preparing financial statements under IFRS must also prepare a statement of cash flows as an integral part of the financial statements.
- Both IFRS and GAAP require that the statement of cash flows should have three major sections—operating, investing, and financing activities—along with changes in cash and cash equivalents.
- Similar to GAAP, the statement of cash flows can be prepared using either the indirect or direct method under IFRS. In both U.S. and international settings, companies choose for the most part to use the indirect method for reporting net cash flows from operating activities.
- The definition of cash equivalents used in IFRS is similar to that used in GAAP. A major difference is that in certain situations, bank overdrafts are considered part of cash and cash equivalents under IFRS (which is not the case in GAAP). Under GAAP, bank overdrafts are classified as financing activities in the statement of cash flows and are reported as liabilities on the balance sheet.

Differences

- IFRS requires that noncash investing and financing activities be excluded from the statement of cash flows. Instead, these noncash activities should be reported elsewhere. This requirement is interpreted to mean that noncash investing and financing activities should be disclosed in the notes to the financial statements instead of in the financial statements. Under GAAP, companies may present this information on the face of the statement of cash flows.

- One area where there can be substantial differences between IFRS and GAAP relates to the classification of interest, dividends, and taxes. The following table indicates the differences between the two approaches.

Item	IFRS	GAAP
Interest paid	Operating or financing	Operating
Interest received	Operating or investing	Operating
Dividends paid	Operating or financing	Financing
Dividends received	Operating or investing	Operating
Taxes paid	Operating—unless specific identification with financing or investing activity	Operating

- Under IFRS, some companies present the operating section in a single line item, with a full reconciliation provided in the notes to the financial statements. This presentation is not seen under GAAP.

IFRS Practice

IFRS Self-Test Questions

1. Under IFRS, interest paid can be reported as:
   a. only a financing activity.
   b. a financing activity or an investing activity.
   c. a financing activity or an operating activity.
   d. only an operating activity.

2. IFRS requires that noncash items:
   a. be reported in the section to which they relate, that is, a noncash investing activity would be reported in the investing section.
   b. be disclosed in the notes to the financial statements.
   c. do not need to be reported.
   d. be treated in a fashion similar to cash equivalents.

3. Under IFRS:
   a. taxes are always treated as an operating activity.
   b. the income statement uses the headings operating, investing, and financing activities.
   c. dividends received can be either an operating or investing activity.
   d. dividends paid can be either an operating or investing activity.

4. Which of the following is **correct**?
   a. Under IFRS, the statement of cash flows is optional.
   b. IFRS requires use of the direct approach in preparing the statement of cash flows.
   c. The majority of companies following GAAP and the majority following IFRS employ the indirect approach to the statement of cash flows.
   d. Under IFRS, companies offset financing activities against investing activities.

IFRS Exercises

IFRS12.1 Discuss the differences that exist in the treatment of bank overdrafts under GAAP and IFRS.

IFRS12.2 Describe the treatment of each of the following items under IFRS versus GAAP.
a. Interest paid.
b. Interest received.
c. Dividends paid.
d. Dividends received.

International Financial Reporting Problem: Louis Vuitton

IFRS12.3 The financial statements of **Louis Vuitton** are presented in Appendix F. The complete annual report, including the notes to its financial statements, is available at the company's website.

Instructions

Use the company's annual report to answer the following questions.

a. In which section (operating, investing, or financing) does Louis Vuitton report interest paid (finance costs)?
b. In which section (operating, investing, or financing) does Louis Vuitton report dividends received?
c. If Louis Vuitton reported under GAAP rather than IFRS, how would its treatment of bank overdrafts differ?

Answers to IFRS Self-Test Questions

1. c 2. b 3. c 4. c

CHAPTER 13

Financial Analysis: The Big Picture

Chapter Preview

We can all learn an important lesson from Warren Buffett: Study companies carefully if you wish to invest. Do not get caught up in fads but instead find companies that are financially healthy. Using some of the basic decision tools presented in this text, you can perform a rudimentary analysis on any company and draw basic conclusions about its financial health. Although it would not be wise for you to bet your life savings on a company's stock relying solely on your current level of knowledge, we strongly encourage you to practice your new skills wherever possible. Only with practice will you improve your ability to interpret financial numbers.

Before we unleash you on the world of high finance, we present a few more important concepts and techniques as well as one more comprehensive review of corporate financial statements. We use all of the decision tools presented in this text to analyze a single company, with comparisons to a competitor and industry averages.

Feature Story

It Pays to Be Patient

A recent issue of *Forbes* magazine listed Warren Buffett as the second richest person in the world. His estimated wealth was $69 billion, give or take a few million. How much is $69 billion? If you invested $69 billion in an investment earning just 4%, you could spend $7.6 million per day—every day—forever.

So, how does Buffett spend his money? Basically, he doesn't! He still lives in the same house that he purchased in Omaha, Nebraska, in 1958 for $31,500. He still drives his own car (a Cadillac DTS). And, in case you were thinking that his kids are riding the road to Easy Street, think again. Buffett has committed to donate virtually all of his money to charity before he dies.

How did Buffett amass this wealth? Through careful investing. Buffett epitomizes a "value investor." He applies the basic techniques he learned in the 1950s from the great value investor Benjamin Graham. He looks for companies that have good long-term potential but are currently underpriced. He invests in companies that have low exposure to debt and that reinvest their earnings for future growth. He does not get caught up in fads or the latest trends.

For example, Buffett sat out on the dot-com mania in the 1990s. When other investors put lots of money into fledgling high-tech firms, Buffett didn't bite because he did not find dot-com companies that met his criteria. He didn't get to enjoy the stock price boom on the way up, but on the other hand, he didn't have to ride the price back down to Earth. When the dot-com bubble burst, everyone else was suffering from investment shock. Buffett swooped in and scooped up deals on companies that he had been following for years.

In 2012, the stock market had again reached near record highs. Buffett's returns had been significantly lagging the market. Only 26% of his investments at that time were in stock, and he was sitting on $38 billion in cash. One commentator noted that "if the past is any guide, just when Buffett seems to look most like a loser, the party is about to end."

If you think you want to follow Buffett's example and transform your humble nest egg into a mountain of cash, be warned. His techniques have been widely circulated and emulated, but never practiced with the same degree of success. You should probably start by honing your financial analysis skills. A good way for you to begin your career as a successful investor is to master the fundamentals of financial analysis discussed in this chapter.

Source: Jason Zweig, "Buffett Is Out of Step," *Wall Street Journal* (May 7, 2012).

Chapter Outline

LEARNING OBJECTIVES

LO 1 Apply the concepts of sustainable income and quality of earnings.	• Sustainable income • Quality of earnings	**DO IT! 1** Unusual Items
LO 2 Apply horizontal analysis and vertical analysis.	• Horizontal analysis • Vertical analysis	**DO IT! 2** Horizontal Analysis
LO 3 Analyze a company's performance using ratio analysis.	• Liquidity ratios • Solvency ratios • Profitability ratios • Financial analysis and data analytics • Comprehensive example	**DO IT! 3** Ratio Analysis

Go to the Review and Practice section at the end of the chapter for a targeted summary and practice applications with solutions.
Visit WileyPLUS for additional tutorials and practice opportunities.

Sustainable Income and Quality of Earnings

LEARNING OBJECTIVE 1
Apply the concepts of sustainable income and quality of earnings.

Sustainable Income

The value of a company like **Google** is a function of the amount, timing, and uncertainty of its future cash flows. Google's current and past income statements are particularly useful in helping analysts predict these future cash flows. In using this approach, analysts must make sure that Google's past income numbers reflect its **sustainable income**, that is, do not include unusual (out-of-the-ordinary) revenues, expenses, gains, and losses. **Sustainable income** is, therefore, the most likely level of income to be obtained by a company in the future. Sustainable income differs from actual net income by the amount of unusual revenues, expenses, gains, and losses included in the current year's income. Analysts are interested in sustainable income because it helps them derive an estimate of future earnings without the "noise" of unusual items.

Fortunately, an income statement provides information on sustainable income by separating operating transactions from nonoperating transactions. This statement also highlights intermediate components of income such as income from operations, income before income taxes, and income from continuing operations. In addition, information on unusual items such as gains or losses on discontinued items and components of other comprehensive income are disclosed.

Illustration 13.1 presents a statement of comprehensive income for Cruz Company for the year 2022. A statement of comprehensive income includes not only net income but a broader measure of income called comprehensive income. The two major unusual items in this statement are discontinued operations and other comprehensive income (highlighted in red). When estimating future cash flows, analysts must consider the implications of each of these components.

ILLUSTRATION 13.1
Statement of comprehensive income

Cruz Company
Statement of Comprehensive Income
For the Year Ended 2022

Sales revenue	$900,000
Cost of goods sold	650,000
Gross profit	250,000
Operating expenses	100,000
Income from operations	150,000
Other revenues (expenses) and gains (losses)	20,000
Income before income taxes	170,000
Income tax expense	24,000
Income from continuing operations	146,000
Discontinued operations (net of tax)	**30,000**
Net income	176,000
Other comprehensive income items (net of tax)	**10,000**
Comprehensive income	$186,000

In looking at Illustration 13.1, note that Cruz Company's two major types of unusual items, discontinued operations and other comprehensive income, are reported net of tax. That is, Cruz first calculates income tax expense before income from continuing operations. Then, it calculates income tax expense related to the discontinued operations and other comprehensive income, and displays each item separately, net of tax. The general concept is, "Let the

Discontinued Operations

Decision Tools

The discontinued operations section alerts users to the sale of any of a company's major components of its business.

Discontinued operations refers to the disposal of a **significant component** of a business, such as the elimination of a major class of customers or an entire activity (see **Decision Tools**). For example, to downsize its operations, **General Dynamics Corp.** sold its missile business to **Hughes Aircraft Co.** for $450 million. In the net income section of its statement of comprehensive income, General Dynamics reported the sale in a separate section entitled "Discontinued operations."

Following the disposal of a significant component, the company should report on its statement both income from continuing operations and income (or loss) from discontinued operations. **The income (loss) from discontinued operations consists of two parts: the income (loss) from operations** and **the gain (loss) on disposal of the component.**

To illustrate, assume that during 2022 Acro Energy Inc. has income before income taxes of $800,000. During 2022, Acro discontinued and sold its unprofitable chemical division. The loss in 2022 from chemical operations (net of $60,000 taxes) was $140,000. The loss on disposal of the chemical division (net of $30,000 taxes) was $70,000. Assuming a 30% tax rate on income, **Illustration 13.2** shows Acro's statement of comprehensive income presentation (see **Helpful Hint**).

ILLUSTRATION 13.2

Statement presentation of discontinued operations

HELPFUL HINT

Observe the dual disclosures: (1) the results of operation of the discontinued division must be separated from the results of continuing operations, and (2) the company must also report the gain or loss on disposal of the division.

Acro Energy Inc.
Statement of Comprehensive Income (partial)
For the Year Ended December 31, 2022

Income before income taxes		$800,000
Income tax expense		240,000
Income from continuing operations		560,000
Discontinued operations		
Loss from operation of chemical division, net of $60,000 income tax savings	$140,000	
Loss from disposal of chemical division, net of $30,000 income tax savings	70,000	210,000
Net income		$350,000

Note that the statement uses the caption "Income from continuing operations" and adds a new section "Discontinued operations." **The new section reports both the operating loss and the loss on disposal net of applicable income taxes.** This presentation clearly indicates the separate effects of continuing operations and discontinued operations on net income.

Investor Insight

What Does "Non-Recurring" Really Mean?

© Andrey Armyagov/iStockphoto

Many companies incur restructuring charges as they attempt to reduce costs. They often label these items in the income statement as "non-recurring" charges, to suggest that they are isolated events, unlikely to occur in future periods. The question for analysts is, are these costs really one-time, "non-recurring events" or do they reflect problems that the company will be facing for many periods in the future? If they are one-time events, then they can be largely ignored when trying to predict future earnings.

But, some companies report "one-time" restructuring charges over and over again. For example, **Procter & Gamble** reported a restructuring charge in 12 consecutive quarters, and **Motorola** had "special" charges in 14 consecutive quarters. On the other hand, other companies have a restructuring charge only once in a 5- or 10-year period. There appears to be no substitute for careful analysis of the numbers that comprise net income.

If a company takes a large restructuring charge, what is the effect on the company's current income statement versus future ones? (Go to WileyPLUS for this answer and additional questions.)

Comprehensive Income

Most revenues, expenses, gains, and losses are included in net income. However, as discussed in earlier chapters, certain gains and losses that bypass net income are reported as part of a more inclusive earnings measure called comprehensive income. **Comprehensive income** is the sum of net income and other comprehensive income items.[1]

Illustration of Comprehensive Income

Accounting standards require that companies adjust most investments in stocks and bonds up or down to their market price at the end of each accounting period. For example, assume that during 2022, its first year of operations, Stassi Corporation purchased **IBM** bonds for $10,500 as an investment, which it intends to sell sometime in the future. At the end of 2022, Stassi was still holding the investment, but the bonds' market price was now $8,000. In this case, Stassi is required to reduce the recorded value of its IBM investment by $2,500. The $2,500 difference is an "unrealized" loss. A gain or loss is referred to as unrealized when as asset has experienced a change in value but the owner has not sold the asset. The sale of the asset results in "realization" of the gain or loss.

Should Stassi include this $2,500 unrealized loss in net income? It depends on whether Stassi classifies the IBM bonds as a trading security or an available-for-sale security. A **trading security** is bought and held primarily for sale in the near term to generate income on short-term price differences. Companies report unrealized losses on trading securities in the "Other expenses and losses" section of the income statement. The rationale: It is likely that the company will realize the unrealized loss (or an unrealized gain), so the company should report the loss (gain) as part of net income.

If Stassi did not purchase the investment for trading purposes, it is classified as available-for-sale. **Available-for-sale securities** are held with the intent of selling them sometime in the future. Companies do not include unrealized gains or losses on available-for-sale securities in net income. Instead, they report them as part of "Other comprehensive income." Other comprehensive income is not included in net income.

Format

One format for reporting other comprehensive income is to report a separate comprehensive income statement. For example, assuming that Stassi Corporation has a net income of $300,000 and a 20% tax rate, the unrealized loss would be reported below net income, net of tax, as shown in **Illustration 13.3**.

Stassi Corporation
Comprehensive Income Statement
For the Year Ended December 31, 2022

Net income	$300,000
Other comprehensive income	
Unrealized loss on available-for-sale securities, net of $500 income tax savings	2,000
Comprehensive income	$298,000

ILLUSTRATION 13.3
Lower portion of combined statement of income and comprehensive income

Companies report the cumulative amount of other comprehensive income from all years as a separate component of stockholders' equity. To illustrate, assume Stassi has common stock of $3,000,000, retained earnings of $300,000, and accumulated other comprehensive loss of $2,000. (To simplify, we are assuming that this is Stassi's first year of operations. Since it has only operated for one year, the cumulative amount of other comprehensive income is this year's loss of $2,000.) **Illustration 13.4** shows the balance sheet presentation of the accumulated other comprehensive loss.

---

[1] The FASB's Conceptual Framework describes comprehensive income as including all changes in stockholders' equity during a period except those changes resulting from investments by stockholders and distributions to stockholders.

ILLUSTRATION 13.4
Unrealized loss in stockholders' equity section

Stassi Corporation
Balance Sheet (partial)

Stockholders' equity		
Common stock		$3,000,000
Retained earnings		300,000
Total paid-in capital and retained earnings		3,300,000
Accumulated other comprehensive loss		(2,000)
Total stockholders' equity		$3,298,000

Note that the presentation of the accumulated other comprehensive loss is similar to the presentation of the cost of treasury stock in the stockholders' equity section. (An unrealized gain would be added in this section of the balance sheet.)

Complete Statement of Comprehensive Income As seen in Illustration 13.1, as an alternative to preparing a separate comprehensive income statement, many companies report net income and other comprehensive income in a combined statement of comprehensive income. (*For your homework in this chapter, use this combined format.*) The statement of comprehensive income for Pace Corporation in **Illustration 13.5** presents the types of items found on this statement, such as net sales, cost of goods sold, operating expenses, and income taxes. In addition, it shows how companies report discontinued operations and other comprehensive income (highlighted in red).

ILLUSTRATION 13.5
Complete statement of comprehensive income

Pace Corporation
Statement of Comprehensive Income
For the Year Ended December 31, 2022

Net sales		$440,000
Cost of goods sold		260,000
Gross profit		180,000
Operating expenses		110,000
Income from operations		70,000
Other revenues and gains		5,600
Other expenses and losses		9,600
Income before income taxes		66,000
Income tax expense ($66,000 × 30%)		19,800
Income from continuing operations		46,200
Discontinued operations		
Loss from operation of plastics division, net of		
income tax savings $18,000 ($60,000 × 30%)	$42,000	
Gain on disposal of plastics division, net of		
$15,000 income taxes ($50,000 × 30%)	35,000	7,000
Net income		39,200
Other comprehensive income		
Unrealized gain on available-for-sale securities,		
net of income taxes ($15,000 × 30%)		10,500
Comprehensive income		$ 49,700

Changes in Accounting Principle

For ease of comparison, users of financial statements expect companies to prepare their statements on a basis **consistent** with the preceding period. A **change in accounting principle** occurs when the principle used in the current year is different from the one used in the preceding year (see **Decision Tools**). An example is a change in inventory costing methods (such as FIFO to average-cost). Accounting rules permit a change when management can show that the new principle is preferable to the old principle.

Companies report most changes in accounting principle retroactively.[2] That is, they report both the current period and previous periods using the new principle. As a result, the same principle applies in all periods. This treatment improves the ability to compare results across years.

> **Decision Tools**
>
> Informing users of a change in accounting principle helps them determine the effect of this change on current and prior periods.

Investor Insight   United Parcel Service (UPS)

More Frequent Ups and Downs

Larry MacDougal/AP/Wide World Photos

In the past, U.S. companies used a method to account for their pension plans that smoothed out the gains and losses on their pension portfolios by spreading gains and losses over multiple years. Many felt that this approach was beneficial because it reduced the volatility of reported net income. However, recently some companies have opted to adopt a method that comes closer to recognizing gains and losses in the period in which they occur. Some of the companies that have adopted this approach are **United Parcel Service (UPS)**, **Honeywell International**, **IBM**, **AT&T**, and **Verizon Communications**. The CFO at UPS said he favored the new approach because "events that occurred in prior years will no longer distort current-year results. It will result in better transparency by eliminating the noise of past plan performance." When UPS switched, it resulted in a charge of $827 million from the change in accounting principle.

Source: Bob Sechler and Doug Cameron, "UPS Alters Pension-Plan Accounting," *Wall Street Journal* (January 30, 2012).

When predicting future earnings, how should analysts treat the one-time charge that results from a switch to the different approach for accounting for pension plans? (Go to WileyPLUS for this answer and additional questions.)

Quality of Earnings

The quality of a company's earnings is of extreme importance to analysts. A company that has a high **quality of earnings** provides full and transparent information that will not confuse or mislead users of the financial statements.

Recent accounting scandals suggest that some companies are spending too much time managing their income and not enough time managing their business. Here are some of the factors affecting quality of earnings.

Alternative Accounting Methods

Variations among companies in the application of generally accepted accounting principles may hamper comparability and reduce quality of earnings. For example, suppose one company uses the FIFO method of inventory costing, while another company in the same industry uses LIFO. If inventory is a significant asset to both companies, it is unlikely that their current ratios are comparable. For example, if **General Motors Corporation** used FIFO instead of LIFO for inventory valuation, its inventories in a recent year would have been 26% higher, which significantly affects the current ratio (and other ratios as well).

In addition to differences in inventory costing methods, differences also exist in reporting such items as depreciation and amortization. Although these differences in accounting methods might be detectable from reading the notes to the financial statements, adjusting the financial data to compensate for the different methods is often difficult, if not impossible.

---

[2] An exception to the general rule is a change in depreciation methods. The effects of this change are reported in current and future periods. Discussion of this approach is left for more advanced courses.

Pro Forma Income

Companies whose stock is publicly traded are required to present their income statement following generally accepted accounting principles (GAAP). In recent years, many companies have been also reporting a second measure of income, called pro forma income. **Pro forma income** usually excludes items that the company thinks are unusual or non-recurring. For example, in a recent year, **Cisco Systems** (a high-tech company) reported a quarterly net loss under GAAP of $2.7 billion. Cisco reported pro forma income for the same quarter as a profit of $230 million. This large difference in profits between GAAP income numbers and pro forma income is not unusual. For example, during one nine-month period, the 100 largest companies on the Nasdaq stock exchange reported a total pro forma income of $19.1 billion but a total loss as measured by GAAP of $82.3 billion—a difference of about $100 billion!

To compute pro forma income, companies generally exclude any items they deem inappropriate for measuring their performance. Many analysts and investors are critical of the practice of using pro forma income because these numbers often make companies look better than they really are. As the financial press noted, pro forma numbers might be called "earnings before bad stuff." Companies, on the other hand, argue that pro forma numbers more clearly indicate sustainable income because they exclude unusual and non-recurring expenses. "Cisco's technique gives readers of financial statements a clear picture of Cisco's normal business activities," the company said in a statement issued in response to questions about its pro forma income accounting.

Recently, the SEC provided some guidance on how companies should present pro forma information. Stay tuned: Everyone seems to agree that pro forma numbers can be useful if they provide insights into determining a company's sustainable income. However, many companies have abused the flexibility that pro forma numbers allow and have used the measure as a way to put their companies in a more favorable light.

Improper Recognition

Because some managers feel pressure from Wall Street to continually increase earnings, they manipulate earnings numbers to meet these expectations. The most common abuse is the improper recognition of revenue. One practice that some companies use is called **channel stuffing**. Offering deep discounts, companies encourage customers to buy early (stuff the channel) rather than later. This boosts the seller's earnings in the current period, but it often leads to a disaster in subsequent periods because customers have no need for additional goods. To illustrate, **Bristol-Myers Squibb** at one time indicated that it used sales incentives to encourage wholesalers to buy more drugs than they needed. As a result, the company had to issue revised financial statements showing corrected revenues and income.

Another practice is the improper capitalization of operating expenses. **WorldCom** capitalized over $7 billion of operating expenses in order to report positive net income. In other situations, companies fail to report all their liabilities. **Enron** promised to make payments on certain contracts if financial difficulty developed, but these guarantees were not reported as liabilities. In addition, disclosure was so lacking in transparency that it was impossible to understand what was happening at the company.

ACTION PLAN
- Show discontinued operations and other comprehensive income net of tax.

DO IT! 1 | Unusual Items

In its proposed 2022 income statement, AIR Corporation reports income before income taxes $400,000, unrealized gain on available-for-sale securities $100,000, income taxes $120,000 (not including unusual items), loss from operation of discontinued flower division $50,000, and loss on disposal of discontinued flower division $90,000. The income tax rate is 30%. Prepare a correct statement of comprehensive income, beginning with "Income before income taxes."

Solution

AIR Corporation
Statement of Comprehensive Income (partial)
For the Year Ended December 31, 2022

Income before income taxes		$400,000
Income tax expense		120,000
Income from continuing operations		280,000
Discontinued operations		
Loss from operation of flower division,		
net of $15,000 income tax savings	$35,000	
Loss on disposal of flower division,		
net of $27,000 income tax savings	63,000	98,000
Net income		182,000
Other comprehensive income		
Unrealized gain on available-for-sale		
securities, net of $30,000 income taxes		70,000
Comprehensive income		$252,000

Related exercise material: **BE13.1, BE13.2, DO IT! 13.1, E13.1, and E13.2.**

Horizontal Analysis and Vertical Analysis

LEARNING OBJECTIVE 2
Apply horizontal analysis and vertical analysis.

As indicated, in assessing the financial performance of a company, investors are interested in the core or sustainable earnings of a company. In addition, investors are interested in making comparisons from period to period. Throughout this text, we have relied on three types of comparisons to improve the decision-usefulness of financial information:

1. **Intracompany basis.** Comparisons within a company are often useful to detect changes in financial relationships and significant trends. For example, a comparison of **Kellogg**'s current year's cash amount with the prior year's cash amount shows either an increase or a decrease. Likewise, a comparison of Kellogg's year-end cash amount with the amount of its total assets at year-end shows the proportion of total assets in the form of cash.

2. **Intercompany basis.** Comparisons with other companies provide insight into a company's competitive position. For example, investors can compare Kellogg's total sales for the year with the total sales of its competitors in the breakfast cereal area, such as **General Mills**.

3. **Industry averages.** Comparisons with industry averages provide information about a company's relative position within the industry. For example, financial statement readers can compare Kellogg's financial data with the averages for its industry compiled by financial rating organizations such as **Dun & Bradstreet**, **Moody's**, and **Standard & Poor's**, or with information provided on the Internet by organizations such as **Yahoo!** on its financial site.

We use three basic tools in financial statement analysis to highlight the significance of financial statement data:

1. Horizontal analysis.
2. Vertical analysis.
3. Ratio analysis.

In previous chapters, we relied primarily on ratio analysis, supplemented with some basic horizontal and vertical analysis. In the remainder of this section, we introduce more formal forms of horizontal and vertical analysis. In the next section, we review ratio analysis in some detail.

Horizontal Analysis

Decision Tools

Horizontal analysis helps users compare a company's financial position and operating results with those of the previous period.

Horizontal analysis, also known as trend analysis, is a technique for evaluating a series of financial statement data over a period of time (see **Decision Tools**). Its purpose is to determine the increase or decrease that has taken place, expressed as either an amount or a percentage. For example, here are recent net sales figures (in thousands) of Chicago Cereal Company:

2022	2021	2020	2019	2018
$11,776	$10,907	$10,177	$9,614	$8,812

If we assume that 2018 is the base year, we can measure all percentage increases or decreases relative to this base-period amount with the formula shown in **Illustration 13.6**.

ILLUSTRATION 13.6
Horizontal analysis—computation of changes since base period

$$\text{Change Since Base Period} = \frac{\text{Current-Year Amount} - \text{Base-Year Amount}}{\text{Base-Year Amount}}$$

For example, we can determine that net sales for Chicago Cereal increased approximately 9.1% [($9,614 − $8,812) ÷ $8,812] from 2018 to 2019. Similarly, we can also determine that net sales increased by 33.6% [($11,776 − $8,812) ÷ $8,812] from 2018 to 2022.

Alternatively, we can express current-year sales as a percentage of the base period. To do so, we would divide the current-year amount by the base-year amount, as shown in **Illustration 13.7**.

ILLUSTRATION 13.7
Horizontal analysis—computation of current year in relation to base year

$$\text{Current Results in Relation to Base Period} = \frac{\text{Current-Year Amount}}{\text{Base-Year Amount}}$$

Current-period sales expressed as a percentage of the base period for each of the five years, using 2018 as the base period, are shown in **Illustration 13.8**.

ILLUSTRATION 13.8
Horizontal analysis of net sales

Chicago Cereal Company
Net Sales (in thousands)
Base Period 2018

2022	2021	2020	2019	2018
$11,776	$10,907	$10,177	$9,614	$8,812
133.6%	123.8%	115.5%	109.1%	100%

The large increase in net sales during 2019 would raise questions regarding possible reasons for such a significant change. Chicago Cereal's 2019 notes to the financial statements explain that the company completed an acquisition of Elf Foods Company during 2019. This major acquisition would help explain the increase in sales highlighted by horizontal analysis.

To further illustrate horizontal analysis, we use the financial statements of Chicago Cereal Company. Its two-year condensed balance sheets for 2022 and 2021, showing dollar and percentage changes, are presented in Illustration 13.9 (see **Helpful Hint**).

ILLUSTRATION 13.9
Horizontal analysis of balance sheets

Chicago Cereal Company
Condensed Balance Sheets
December 31 (in thousands)

			Increase (Decrease) during 2022	
Assets	2022	2021	Amount	Percent
Current assets	$ 2,717	$ 2,427	$ 290	11.9
Property assets (net)	2,990	2,816	174	6.2
Other assets	5,690	5,471	219	4.0
Total assets	$11,397	$10,714	$ 683	6.4
Liabilities and Stockholders' Equity				
Current liabilities	$ 4,044	$ 4,020	$ 24	0.6
Long-term liabilities	4,827	4,625	202	4.4
Total liabilities	8,871	8,645	226	2.6
Stockholders' equity				
Common stock	493	397	96	24.2
Retained earnings	3,390	2,584	806	31.2
Treasury stock (cost)	(1,357)	(912)	445	48.8
Total stockholders' equity	2,526	2,069	457	22.1
Total liabilities and stockholders' equity	$11,397	$10,714	$ 683	6.4

HELPFUL HINT
When using horizontal analysis, be sure to examine both dollar amount changes and percentage changes. It is not necessarily bad if a company's earnings are growing at a declining rate. The amount of increase may be the same as or more than the base year, but the percentage change may be less because the base is greater each year.

The comparative balance sheets show that a number of changes occurred in Chicago Cereal's financial position from 2021 to 2022. In the assets section, current assets increased $290,000, or 11.9% ($290 ÷ $2,427), and property assets (net) increased $174,000, or 6.2%. Other assets increased $219,000, or 4.0%. In the liabilities section, current liabilities increased $24,000, or 0.6%, while long-term liabilities increased $202,000, or 4.4%. In the stockholders' equity section, we find that retained earnings increased $806,000, or 31.2%.

Illustration 13.10 presents two-year comparative income statements of Chicago Cereal Company for 2022 and 2021, showing dollar and percentage changes (see **Helpful Hint**).

ILLUSTRATION 13.10
Horizontal analysis of income statements

Chicago Cereal Company
Condensed Income Statements
For the Years Ended December 31 (in thousands)

			Increase (Decrease) during 2022	
	2022	2021	Amount	Percent
Net sales	$11,776	$10,907	$869	8.0
Cost of goods sold	6,597	6,082	515	8.5
Gross profit	5,179	4,825	354	7.3
Selling and administrative expenses	3,311	3,059	252	8.2
Income from operations	1,868	1,766	102	5.8
Interest expense	321	294	27	9.2
Income before income taxes	1,547	1,472	75	5.1
Income tax expense	444	468	(24)	(5.1)
Net income	$ 1,103	$ 1,004	$ 99	9.9

HELPFUL HINT
The increase in the Amount column of $99 results by adding and subtracting the amounts shown. In the Percent column, the 9.9% cannot be determined by adding and subtracting the percentages shown.

Horizontal analysis of the income statements shows the following changes. Net sales increased $869,000, or 8.0% ($869 ÷ $10,907). Cost of goods sold increased $515,000, or 8.5% ($515 ÷ $6,082). Selling and administrative expenses increased $252,000, or 8.2% ($252 ÷ $3,059). Overall, gross profit increased 7.3% and net income increased 9.9%. The increase in net income can be attributed to the increase in net sales and a decrease in income tax expense.

The measurement of changes from period to period in percentages is relatively straightforward and quite useful. However, complications can result in making the computations. If an item has no value in a base year or preceding year and a value in the next year, no percentage change can be computed.

Vertical Analysis

> **Decision Tools**
> Vertical analysis helps users compare relationships between financial statement items with those of last year or of competitors.

Vertical analysis, also called common-size analysis, is a technique for evaluating financial statement data that expresses each item in a financial statement as a **percentage of a base amount** (see **Decision Tools**). For example, on a balance sheet we might express current assets as 22% of total assets (total assets being the base amount). Or, on an income statement we might express selling expenses as 16% of net sales (net sales being the base amount).

Presented in **Illustration 13.11** are the comparative balance sheets of Chicago Cereal for 2022 and 2021, analyzed vertically. The base for the asset items is **total assets**, and the base for the liability and stockholders' equity items is **total liabilities and stockholders' equity**.

ILLUSTRATION 13.11
Vertical analysis of balance sheets

Chicago Cereal Company
Condensed Balance Sheets
December 31 (in thousands)

	2022 Amount	2022 Percent*	2021 Amount	2021 Percent*
Assets				
Current assets	$ 2,717	23.8	$ 2,427	22.6
Property assets (net)	2,990	26.2	2,816	26.3
Other assets	5,690	50.0	5,471	51.1
Total assets	$11,397	100.0	$10,714	100.0
Liabilities and Stockholders' Equity				
Current liabilities	$ 4,044	35.5	$ 4,020	37.5
Long-term liabilities	4,827	42.4	4,625	43.2
Total liabilities	8,871	77.9	8,645	80.7
Stockholders' equity				
Common stock	493	4.3	397	3.7
Retained earnings	3,390	29.7	2,584	24.1
Treasury stock (cost)	(1,357)	(11.9)	(912)	(8.5)
Total stockholders' equity	2,526	22.1	2,069	19.3
Total liabilities and stockholders' equity	$11,397	100.0	$10,714	100.0

*Numbers have been rounded to total 100%.

In addition to showing the relative size of each category on the balance sheets, vertical analysis can show the percentage change in the individual asset, liability, and stockholders' equity items. In this case, current assets increased $290,000 from 2021 to 2022, and they increased from 22.6% to 23.8% of total assets. Property assets (net) decreased from 26.3% to 26.2% of total assets. Other assets decreased from 51.1% to 50.0% of total assets. Also, retained earnings increased by $806,000 from 2021 to 2022, and total stockholders' equity increased from 19.3% to 22.1% of total liabilities and stockholders' equity. This switch to a higher percentage of equity financing has two causes. First, while total liabilities increased by $226,000, the percentage of liabilities declined from 80.7% to 77.9% of total liabilities and stockholders' equity. Second, retained earnings increased by $806,000, from 24.1% to 29.7% of total liabilities and stockholders' equity. Thus, the company shifted toward equity financing by relying less on debt and by increasing the amount of retained earnings.

Vertical analysis of the comparative income statements of Chicago Cereal, shown in **Illustration 13.12**, reveals that cost of goods sold **as a percentage of net sales** increased from 55.8% to 56.0%, and selling and administrative expenses increased from 28.0% to 28.1%. Net income as a percentage of net sales increased from 9.2% to 9.4%. Chicago Cereal's increase in net income as a percentage of sales is due primarily to the decrease in income tax expense as a percentage of sales.

ILLUSTRATION 13.12
Vertical analysis of income statements

Chicago Cereal Company
Condensed Income Statements
For the Years Ended December 31 (in thousands)

	2022		2021	
	Amount	Percent*	Amount	Percent*
Net sales	$11,776	100.0	$10,907	100.0
Cost of goods sold	6,597	56.0	6,082	55.8
Gross profit	5,179	44.0	4,825	44.2
Selling and administrative expenses	3,311	28.1	3,059	28.0
Income from operations	1,868	15.9	1,766	16.2
Interest expense	321	2.7	294	2.7
Income before income taxes	1,547	13.2	1,472	13.5
Income tax expense	444	3.8	468	4.3
Net income	$ 1,103	9.4	$ 1,004	9.2

*Numbers have been rounded to total 100%.

Vertical analysis also enables you to compare companies of different sizes. For example, one of Chicago Cereal's competitors is Giant Mills. Giant Mills' sales are 1,000 times larger than those of Chicago Cereal. Vertical analysis enables us to meaningfully compare the condensed income statements of Chicago Cereal and Giant Mills, as shown in **Illustration 13.13**.

ILLUSTRATION 13.13
Intercompany comparison by vertical analysis

Condensed Income Statements
For the Year Ended December 31, 2022

	Chicago Cereal (in thousands)		Giant Mills, Inc. (in millions)	
	Amount	Percent*	Amount	Percent*
Net sales	$11,776	100.0	$17,910	100.0
Cost of goods sold	6,597	56.0	11,540	64.4
Gross profit	5,179	44.0	6,370	35.6
Selling and administrative expenses	3,311	28.1	3,474	19.4
Non-recurring charges and (gains)	0	—	(62)	(0.3)
Income from operations	1,868	15.9	2,958	16.5
Other expenses and revenues (including income taxes)	765	6.5	1,134	6.3
Net income	$ 1,103	9.4	$ 1,824	10.2

*Numbers have been rounded to total 100%.

Although Chicago Cereal's net sales are much less than those of Giant Mills, vertical analysis eliminates the impact of this size difference for our analysis. Chicago Cereal has a higher gross profit percentage 44.0%, compared to 35.6% for Giant Mills. But, Chicago Cereal's selling and administrative expenses are 28.1% of net sales, while those of Giant Mills are 19.4% of net sales. Looking at net income, we see that Giant Mills' percentage is higher. Chicago Cereal's net income as a percentage of net sales is 9.4%, compared to 10.2% for Giant Mills.

Anatomy of a Fraud

Sometimes relationships between numbers can be used to detect fraud. Financial ratios that appear abnormal or statistical abnormalities in the numbers themselves can reveal fraud. For example, the fact that **WorldCom**'s line costs, as a percentage of either total expenses or revenues, differed very significantly from its competitors should have alerted people to the possibility of fraud. Or, consider the case of a bank manager, who cooperated with a group of his friends to defraud the bank's credit card department. The manager's friends would apply for credit cards and then run up balances of slightly less than $5,000. The bank had a policy of allowing bank personnel to write-off balances of less than $5,000 without seeking supervisor approval. The fraud was detected by applying statistical analysis based on Benford's Law. Benford's Law states that in a random collection of numbers, the frequency of lower digits (e.g., 1, 2, or 3) should be much higher than higher digits (e.g., 7, 8, or 9). In this case, bank auditors analyzed the first two digits of amounts written off. There was a spike at 48 and 49, which was not consistent with what would be expected if the numbers were random.

Total take: Thousands of dollars

The Missing Control

Independent internal verification. While it might be efficient to allow employees to write off accounts below a certain level, it is important that these write-offs be reviewed and verified periodically. Such a review would likely call attention to an employee with large amounts of write-offs, or in this case, write-offs that were frequently very close to the approval threshold.

Source: Mark J. Nigrini, "I've Got Your Number," *Journal of Accountancy Online* (May 1999).

ACTION PLAN
- Find the percentage change by dividing the amount of the increase by the 2021 amount (base year).

DO IT! 2 | Horizontal Analysis

Summary financial information for Rosepatch Company is as follows.

	December 31, 2022	December 31, 2021
Current assets	$234,000	$180,000
Plant assets (net)	756,000	420,000
Total assets	$990,000	$600,000

Compute the amount and percentage changes in 2022 using horizontal analysis, assuming 2021 is the base year.

Solution

	Increase in 2022	
	Amount	Percent
Current assets	$ 54,000	30% [($234,000 − $180,000) ÷ $180,000]
Plant assets (net)	336,000	80% [($756,000 − $420,000) ÷ $420,000]
Total assets	$390,000	65% [($990,000 − $600,000) ÷ $600,000]

Related exercise material: **BE13.4, BE13.6, BE13.7, BE13.9, DO IT! 13.2, E13.3, E13.5, and E13.6.**

Ratio Analysis

Decision Tools
Ratio analysis helps users evaluate mathematical relationships between financial statement items and compare across years, competitors, and industry.

LEARNING OBJECTIVE 3
Analyze a company's performance using ratio analysis.

Ratio analysis expresses the relationship among selected items of financial statement data (see **Decision Tools**). A **ratio** expresses the mathematical relationship between one quantity and another. The relationship is expressed in terms of either a percentage, a rate, or a simple proportion. To illustrate, in a recent year, **Nike, Inc.** had current assets of $13,626 million and current liabilities of $3,926 million. We can find the relationship between these two measures by dividing current assets by current liabilities. The alternative means of expression are as follows.

Percentage: Current assets are 347% of current liabilities.
Rate: Current assets are 3.47 times current liabilities.
Proportion: The relationship of current assets to liabilities is 3.47:1.

To analyze the primary financial statements, we can use ratios to evaluate liquidity, profitability, and solvency. **Illustration 13.14** describes these classifications.

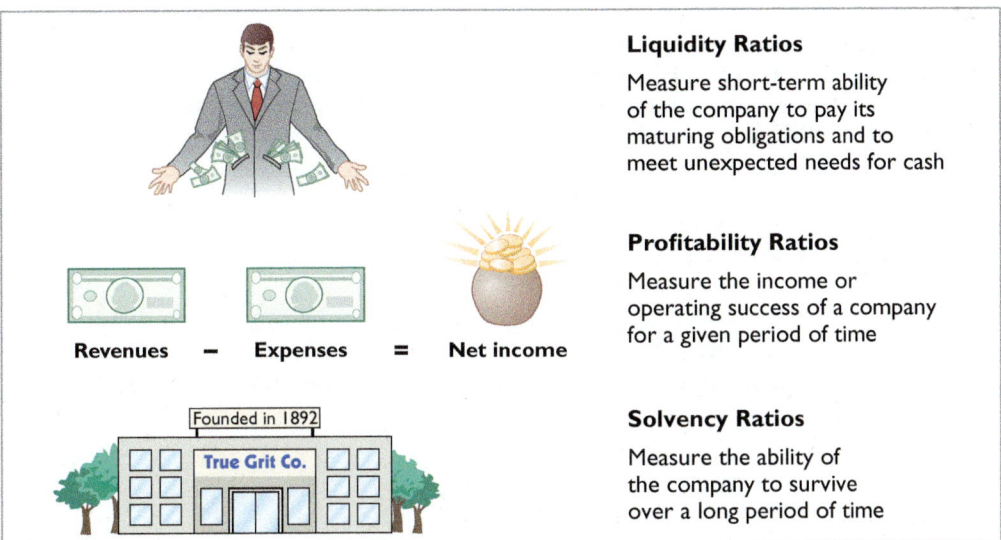

ILLUSTRATION 13.14
Financial ratio classifications

Ratios can provide clues to underlying conditions that may not be apparent from individual financial statement components. However, a single ratio by itself is not very meaningful. Thus, in the discussion of ratios we will use the following types of comparisons.

1. **Intracompany comparisons** for two years for Chicago Cereal.
2. **Industry average comparisons** based on median ratios for the industry.
3. **Intercompany comparisons** based on Giant Mills as Chicago Cereal's principal competitor.

Liquidity Ratios

Liquidity ratios (**Illustration 13.15**) measure the short-term ability of the company to pay its maturing obligations and to meet unexpected needs for cash. Short-term creditors such as bankers and suppliers are particularly interested in assessing liquidity.

ILLUSTRATION 13.15
Summary of liquidity ratios

Liquidity Ratios	
Working capital	Current assets − Current liabilities
Current ratio	$\dfrac{\text{Current assets}}{\text{Current liabilities}}$
Inventory turnover	$\dfrac{\text{Cost of goods sold}}{\text{Average inventory}}$
Days in inventory	$\dfrac{365 \text{ days}}{\text{Inventory turnover}}$
Accounts receivable turnover	$\dfrac{\text{Net credit sales}}{\text{Average net accounts receivable}}$
Average collection period	$\dfrac{365 \text{ days}}{\text{Accounts receivable turnover}}$

> **Investor Insight**
>
>
> Nova Stock/SuperStock
>
> **How to Manage the Current Ratio**
>
> The apparent simplicity of the current ratio can have real-world limitations because adding equal amounts to both the numerator and the denominator causes the ratio to decrease.
>
> Assume, for example, that a company has $2,000,000 of current assets and $1,000,000 of current liabilities. Its current ratio is 2:1. If it purchases $1,000,000 of inventory on account, it will have $3,000,000 of current assets and $2,000,000 of current liabilities. Its current ratio decreases to 1.5:1. If, instead, the company pays off $500,000 of its current liabilities, it will have $1,500,000 of current assets and $500,000 of current liabilities. Its current ratio increases to 3:1. Thus, any trend analysis should be done with care because the ratio is susceptible to quick changes and is easily influenced by management.
>
> **How might management influence a company's current ratio? (Go to WileyPLUS for this answer and additional questions.)**

Solvency Ratios

Solvency ratios (**Illustration 13.16**) measure the ability of the company to survive over a long period of time. Long-term creditors and stockholders are interested in a company's long-run solvency, particularly its ability to pay interest as it comes due and to repay the balance of debt at its maturity.

ILLUSTRATION 13.16
Summary of solvency ratios

Solvency Ratios

Debt to assets ratio	$\dfrac{\text{Total liabilities}}{\text{Total assets}}$
Times interest earned	$\dfrac{\text{Net income} + \text{Interest expense} + \text{Income tax expense}}{\text{Interest expense}}$
Free cash flow	Net cash provided by operating activities $-$ Capital expenditures $-$ Cash dividends

Profitability Ratios

Profitability ratios (**Illustration 13.17**) measure the income or operating success of a company for a given period of time. A company's income, or lack of it, affects its ability to obtain debt and equity financing, its liquidity position, and its ability to grow. As a consequence,

ILLUSTRATION 13.17
Summary of profitability ratios

Profitability Ratios

Earnings per share	$\dfrac{\text{Net income} - \text{Preferred dividends}}{\text{Weighted-average common shares outstanding}}$
Price-earnings ratio	$\dfrac{\text{Market price per share}}{\text{Earnings per share}}$
Gross profit rate	$\dfrac{\text{Gross profit}}{\text{Net sales}}$
Profit margin	$\dfrac{\text{Net income}}{\text{Net sales}}$
Return on assets	$\dfrac{\text{Net income}}{\text{Average total assets}}$
Asset turnover	$\dfrac{\text{Net sales}}{\text{Average total assets}}$
Payout ratio	$\dfrac{\text{Cash dividends declared on common stock}}{\text{Net income}}$
Return on common stockholders' equity	$\dfrac{\text{Net income} - \text{Preferred dividends}}{\text{Average common stockholders' equity}}$

creditors and investors alike are interested in evaluating profitability. Profitability is frequently used as the ultimate test of management's operating effectiveness.

> **Investor Insight**
>
>
>
> © Ferran Traite Soler/ iStockphoto
>
> **High Ratings Can Bring Low Returns**
>
> **Moody's**, **Standard & Poor's**, and **Fitch** are three big firms that perform financial analysis on publicly traded companies and then publish ratings of the companies' creditworthiness. Investors and lenders rely heavily on these ratings in making investment and lending decisions. Some people feel that the collapse of the financial markets was worsened by inadequate research reports and ratings provided by the financial rating agencies. Critics contend that the rating agencies were reluctant to give large companies low ratings because they feared that by offending them they would lose out on business opportunities. For example, the rating agencies gave many so-called mortgage-backed securities ratings that suggested that they were low risk. Later, many of these very securities became completely worthless. Steps have been taken to reduce the conflicts of interest that lead to these faulty ratings.
>
> **Sources:** Aaron Lucchetti and Judith Burns, "Moody's CEO Warned Profit Push Posed a Risk to Quality of Ratings," *Wall Street Journal Online* (October 23, 2008); and Alan S. Binder, "A Better Way to Run Rating Agencies," *Wall Street Journal* (April 17, 2014).
>
> **Why are credit rating agencies important to the financial markets? (Go to WileyPLUS for this answer and additional questions.)**

Financial Analysis and Data Analytics

In the age of "Big Data," opportunities for investors to apply data analytics to financial data are boundless. Immense quantities and types of data are available to investors. Free financial data about corporations, for example, can be obtained from the SEC's Edgar database and other sources. Alternatively, database services such as Compustat and WorldScope sell financial and other information regarding a wide range of company and industry characteristics. In addition, each day massive amounts of trading data are collected from financial exchanges.

Professional analysts employ sophisticated computerized valuation models which use financial, nonfinancial, and trading data to identify investment opportunities. Since these valuation models frequently rely heavily on accounting data, it is important to have a sound understanding of the financial accounting standards on which the numbers used in the models are based. If you desire to someday use data analytics to evaluate companies, the accounting skills and financial analysis tools acquired in this course are a good start.

Comprehensive Example of Ratio Analysis

In this section, we provide a comprehensive review of ratios used for evaluating the financial health and performance of a company. We use the financial information in Illustrations 13.18 through 13.21 to calculate Chicago Cereal Company's 2022 ratios. You can use these data to review the computations.

ILLUSTRATION 13.18

Chicago Cereal Company's balance sheets

Chicago Cereal Company
Balance Sheets
December 31 (in thousands)

Assets	2022	2021
Current assets		
Cash	$ 524	$ 411
Accounts receivable	1,026	945
Inventory	924	824
Prepaid expenses and other current assets	243	247
Total current assets	2,717	2,427
Property assets (net)	2,990	2,816
Intangibles and other assets	5,690	5,471
Total assets	$11,397	$10,714

Liabilities and Stockholders' Equity		
Current liabilities	$ 4,044	$ 4,020
Long-term liabilities	4,827	4,625
Stockholders' equity—common	2,526	2,069
Total liabilities and stockholders' equity	$11,397	$10,714

ILLUSTRATION 13.19
Chicago Cereal Company's income statements

Chicago Cereal Company
Condensed Income Statements
For the Years Ended December 31 (in thousands)

	2022	2021
Net sales	$11,776	$10,907
Cost of goods sold	6,597	6,082
Gross profit	5,179	4,825
Selling and administrative expenses	3,311	3,059
Income from operations	1,868	1,766
Interest expense	321	294
Income before income taxes	1,547	1,472
Income tax expense	444	468
Net income	$ 1,103	$ 1,004

ILLUSTRATION 13.20
Chicago Cereal Company's statements of cash flows

Chicago Cereal Company
Condensed Statements of Cash Flows
For the Years Ended December 31 (in thousands)

	2022	2021
Cash flows from operating activities		
Cash receipts from operating activities	$11,695	$10,841
Cash payments for operating activities	10,192	9,431
Net cash provided by operating activities	1,503	1,410
Cash flows from investing activities		
Purchases of property, plant, and equipment	(472)	(453)
Other investing activities	(129)	8
Net cash used in investing activities	(601)	(445)
Cash flows from financing activities		
Issuance of common stock	163	218
Issuance of debt	2,179	721
Reductions of debt	(2,011)	(650)
Payment of dividends	(475)	(450)
Repurchase of common stock and other items	(645)	(612)
Net cash provided (used) by financing activities	(789)	(773)
Increase (decrease) in cash and cash equivalents	113	192
Cash and cash equivalents at beginning of year	411	219
Cash and cash equivalents at end of year	$ 524	$ 411

ILLUSTRATION 13.21
Additional information for Chicago Cereal Company

Additional information:

	2022	2021
Weighted-average number of shares (thousands)	418.7	418.5
Stock price at year-end	$52.92	$50.06

As indicated in the chapter, we can classify ratios into three types for analysis of the primary financial statements:

1. **Liquidity ratios.** Measures of the short-term ability of the company to pay its maturing obligations and to meet unexpected needs for cash.
2. **Solvency ratios.** Measures of the ability of the company to survive over a long period of time.
3. **Profitability ratios.** Measures of the income or operating success of a company for a given period of time.

As a tool of analysis, ratios can provide clues to underlying conditions that may not be apparent from an inspection of the individual components of a particular ratio. But, a single ratio by itself is not very meaningful. Accordingly, in this discussion we use the following three comparisons.

1. **Intracompany comparisons** covering two years for Chicago Cereal (using comparative financial information from Illustrations 13.18 through 13.21).
2. **Intercompany comparisons** using Giant Mills as one of Chicago Cereal's competitors.
3. **Industry average comparisons** based on **MSN.com** median ratios for manufacturers of flour and other grain mill products and comparisons with other sources. For some of the ratios that we use, industry comparisons are not available (denoted "na").

Liquidity Ratios

Liquidity ratios measure the short-term ability of the company to pay its maturing obligations and to meet unexpected needs for cash. Short-term creditors such as bankers and suppliers are particularly interested in assessing liquidity. The measures used to determine the company's short-term debt-paying ability are the current ratio, the accounts receivable turnover, the average collection period, the inventory turnover, and days in inventory.

1. **Current ratio.** The **current ratio** expresses the relationship of current assets to current liabilities, computed by dividing current assets by current liabilities. It is widely used for evaluating a company's liquidity and short-term debt-paying ability. The 2022 and 2021 current ratios for Chicago Cereal and comparative data are shown in **Illustration 13.22**.

ILLUSTRATION 13.22 Current ratio

Ratio	Formula	Chicago Cereal			Giant Mills 2022	Industry Average
			2022	2021		
Current ratio	Current assets / Current liabilities	$\frac{\$2,717}{\$4,044} =$	.67	.60	.67	1.06

What do the measures tell us? Chicago Cereal's 2022 current ratio of .67 means that for every dollar of current liabilities, it has $0.67 of current assets. We sometimes state such ratios as .67:1 to reinforce this interpretation. Its current ratio—and therefore its liquidity—increased significantly in 2022. It is well below the industry average but the same as that of Giant Mills.

2. **Accounts receivable turnover.** Analysts can measure liquidity by how quickly a company converts certain assets to cash. A low value for the current ratio can sometimes be compensated for if some of the company's current assets are highly liquid.

   How liquid, for example, are the receivables? The ratio used to assess the liquidity of the receivables is the **accounts receivable turnover**, which measures the number of times, on average, a company collects receivables during the period. The accounts receivable turnover is computed by dividing net credit sales (net sales less cash sales) by average net accounts receivable during the year. The accounts receivable turnover for Chicago Cereal is shown in **Illustration 13.23**.

ILLUSTRATION 13.23 Accounts receivable turnover

Ratio	Formula	Chicago Cereal 2022		Chicago Cereal 2021	Giant Mills 2022	Industry Average
Accounts receivable turnover	Net credit sales / Average net accounts receivable	$\dfrac{\$11{,}776}{(\$1{,}026 + \$945) \div 2}$	= 11.9	12.0	12.2	11.2

In computing the rate, we assumed that all Chicago Cereal's sales are credit sales. Its accounts receivable turnover declined slightly in 2022. The turnover of 11.9 times is higher than the industry average of 11.2 times, and slightly lower than Giant Mills' turnover of 12.2 times. A higher value suggests better liquidity because the receivables are being collected more quickly.

3. **Average collection period.** A popular variant of the accounts receivable turnover converts it into an **average collection period** in days. This is done by dividing the accounts receivable turnover into 365 days. The average collection period for Chicago Cereal is shown in **Illustration 13.24**.

ILLUSTRATION 13.24 Average collection period

Ratio	Formula	Chicago Cereal 2022		Chicago Cereal 2021	Giant Mills 2022	Industry Average
Average collection period	365 days / Accounts receivable turnover	$\dfrac{365}{11.9}$	= 30.7	30.4	29.9	32.6

Chicago Cereal's 2022 accounts receivable turnover of 11.9 times is divided into 365 days to obtain approximately 31 days. This means that the average collection period for receivables is about 31 days. Its average collection period is slightly longer than that of Giant Mills and shorter than that of the industry. A shorter collection period means receivables are being collected more quickly and thus are more liquid.

Analysts frequently use the average collection period to assess the effectiveness of a company's credit and collection policies. The general rule is that the collection period should not greatly exceed the credit term period (i.e., the time allowed for payment, which is 30 days for many companies).

4. **Inventory turnover.** The **inventory turnover** measures the number of times average inventory was sold during the period. Its purpose is to measure the liquidity of the inventory. A high measure indicates that inventory is being sold and replenished frequently. The inventory turnover is computed by dividing the cost of goods sold by the average inventory during the period. Unless seasonal factors are significant, average inventory can be computed from the beginning and ending inventory balances. Chicago Cereal's inventory turnover is shown in **Illustration 13.25**.

ILLUSTRATION 13.25 Inventory turnover

Ratio	Formula	Chicago Cereal 2022		Chicago Cereal 2021	Giant Mills 2022	Industry Average
Inventory turnover	Cost of goods sold / Average inventory	$\dfrac{\$6{,}597}{(\$924 + \$824) \div 2}$	= 7.5	7.9	7.4	6.7

Chicago Cereal's inventory turnover decreased slightly in 2022. The turnover of 7.5 times is higher than the industry average of 6.7 times and similar to that of Giant Mills. Generally, the faster the inventory turnover, the less cash is tied up in inventory and the less the chance of inventory becoming obsolete. Of course, a downside of high inventory turnover is that it sometimes results in lost sales because if a company keeps less inventory on hand, it is more likely to run out of inventory when it is needed.

5. **Days in inventory.** A variant of the inventory turnover is the **days in inventory**, which measures the average number of days inventory is held. The days in inventory for Chicago Cereal is shown in **Illustration 13.26**.

ILLUSTRATION 13.26
Days in inventory

Ratio	Formula	Chicago Cereal 2022	Chicago Cereal 2021	Giant Mills 2022	Industry Average
Days in inventory	365 days / Inventory turnover	$\frac{365}{7.5} =$ 48.7	46.2	49.3	54.5

Chicago Cereal's 2022 inventory turnover of 7.5 divided into 365 is approximately 49 days. An average selling time of 49 days is faster than the industry average and similar to that of Giant Mills.

Inventory turnovers vary considerably among industries. For example, grocery store chains have a turnover of 10 times and an average selling period of 37 days. In contrast, jewelry stores have an average turnover of 1.3 times and an average selling period of 281 days. Within a company, there may even be significant differences in inventory turnover among different types of products. Thus, in a grocery store the turnover of perishable items such as produce, meats, and dairy products is faster than the turnover of soaps and detergents.

To conclude, nearly all of these liquidity measures suggest that Chicago Cereal's liquidity changed little during 2022. Its liquidity appears acceptable when compared to the industry as a whole and when compared to Giant Mills.

Solvency Ratios

Solvency ratios measure the ability of the company to survive over a long period of time. Long-term creditors and stockholders are interested in a company's long-run solvency, particularly its ability to pay interest as it comes due and to repay the face value of debt at maturity. The debt to assets ratio and times interest earned provide information about debt-paying ability. In addition, free cash flow provides information about the company's solvency and its ability to pay additional dividends or invest in new projects.

6. **Debt to assets ratio.** The **debt to assets ratio** measures the percentage of total financing provided by creditors. It is computed by dividing total liabilities (both current and long-term debt) by total assets. This ratio indicates the degree of financial leveraging. It also provides some indication of the company's ability to withstand losses without impairing the interests of its creditors. The higher the percentage of debt to assets, the greater the risk that the company may be unable to meet its maturing obligations. Thus, from the creditors' point of view, a low ratio of debt to assets is desirable. Chicago Cereal's debt to assets ratio is shown in **Illustration 13.27**.

ILLUSTRATION 13.27
Debt to assets ratio

Ratio	Formula	Chicago Cereal 2022	Chicago Cereal 2021	Giant Mills 2022	Industry Average
Debt to assets ratio	Total liabilities / Total assets	$\frac{\$8,871}{\$11,397} =$ 78%	81%	55%	55%

Chicago Cereal's 2022 ratio of 78% means that creditors have provided financing sufficient to cover 78% of the company's total assets. Alternatively, it says that it would have to liquidate 78% of its assets at their book value in order to pay off all of its debts. Its ratio is above the industry average of 55%, as well as that of Giant Mills. This suggests that it is less solvent than the industry average and Giant Mills. Chicago Cereal's solvency improved slightly during the year.

The adequacy of this ratio is often judged in light of the company's earnings. Generally, companies with relatively stable earnings, such as public utilities, have higher debt to assets ratios than cyclical companies with widely fluctuating earnings, such as many high-tech companies.

Another ratio with a similar meaning is the **debt to equity ratio**. It shows the relative use of borrowed funds (total liabilities) compared with resources invested by the owners. Because this ratio can be computed in several ways, be careful when making comparisons with it. Debt may be defined to include only the noncurrent portion of liabilities, and intangible assets may be excluded from stockholders' equity (which would equal tangible net worth). If debt and assets are defined as above (all liabilities and all assets), then when the debt to assets ratio equals 50%, the debt to equity ratio is 1:1.

7. **Times interest earned.** The **times interest earned** (also called interest coverage) indicates the company's ability to meet interest payments as they come due. It is computed by dividing the sum of net income, interest expense, and income tax expense by interest expense. Note that this ratio uses income before interest expense and income taxes because this amount represents what is available to cover interest. Chicago Cereal's times interest earned is shown in **Illustration 13.28**.

ILLUSTRATION 13.28 Times interest earned

Ratio	Formula		Chicago Cereal		Giant Mills	Industry Average
			2022	2021	2022	
Times interest earned	$\dfrac{\text{Net Income} + \text{Interest expense} + \text{Income tax expense}}{\text{Interest expense}}$	$\dfrac{\$1{,}103 + \$321 + \$444}{\$321} =$	5.8	6.0	9.9	5.5

For Chicago Cereal, the 2022 interest coverage was 5.8 times, which indicates that income before interest and taxes was 5.8 times the amount needed for interest expense. This is less than the rate for Giant Mills, but it slightly exceeds the rate for the industry. The debt to assets ratio decreased for Chicago Cereal during 2022, and its times interest earned held relatively constant. A low debt to assets ratio and high times interest earned suggest better solvency.

8. **Free cash flow.** One indication of a company's solvency, as well as of its ability to pay dividends or expand operations, is the amount of excess cash it generated after investing in capital expenditures and paying dividends. This amount is referred to as **free cash flow**. For example, if you generate $100,000 of net cash provided by operating activities but you spend $30,000 on capital expenditures and pay $10,000 in dividends, you have $60,000 ($100,000 − $30,000 − $10,000) to use either to expand operations, pay additional dividends, or pay down debt. Chicago Cereal's free cash flow is shown in **Illustration 13.29**.

ILLUSTRATION 13.29 Free cash flow

Ratio	Formula		Chicago Cereal		Giant Mills	Industry Average
			2022	2021	2022	
Free cash flow	Net cash provided by operating activities − Capital expenditures − Cash dividends	$1,503 − $472 − $475 =	$556 (in thousands)	$507	$895 (in millions)	na

Chicago Cereal's free cash flow increased slightly from 2021 to 2022. During both years, the net cash provided by operating activities was more than enough to allow it to acquire additional productive assets and maintain dividend payments. It could have used the remaining cash to reduce debt if necessary. Given that Chicago Cereal is much smaller than Giant Mills, we would expect its free cash flow to be substantially smaller, which it is.

Profitability Ratios

Profitability ratios measure the income or operating success of a company for a given period of time. A company's income, or the lack of it, affects its ability to obtain debt and equity financing, its liquidity position, and its ability to grow. As a consequence, creditors and investors alike are interested in evaluating profitability. Analysts frequently use profitability as the ultimate test of management's operating effectiveness.

The relationships among measures of profitability are very important. Understanding them can help management determine where to focus its efforts to improve profitability. **Illustration 13.30** diagrams these relationships. Our discussion of Chicago Cereal's profitability is structured around this diagram.

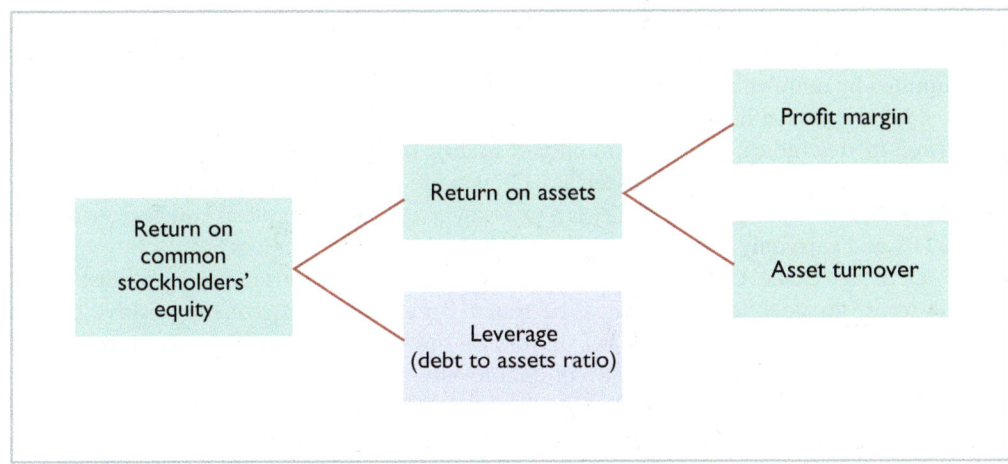

ILLUSTRATION 13.30

Relationships among profitability measures

9. **Return on common stockholders' equity (ROE).** A widely used measure of profitability from the common stockholder's viewpoint is the **return on common stockholders' equity (ROE)**. This ratio shows how many dollars of net income the company earned for each dollar invested by the owners. It is computed by dividing net income minus any preferred dividends—that is, income available to common stockholders—by average common stockholders' equity. The return on common stockholders' equity for Chicago Cereal is shown in **Illustration 13.31**.

ILLUSTRATION 13.31 Return on common stockholders' equity

Ratio	Formula	Chicago Cereal		2022	2021	Giant Mills 2022	Industry Average
Return on common stockholders' equity	$\dfrac{\text{Net Income} - \text{Preferred dividends}}{\text{Average common stockholders' equity}}$	$\dfrac{\$1{,}103 - \$0}{(\$2{,}526 + \$2{,}069) \div 2}$	=	48%	46%	25%	19%

Chicago Cereal's 2022 return on common stockholders' equity is unusually high at 48%. The industry average is 19% and Giant Mills' return is 25%. In the subsequent sections, we investigate the causes of this high return.

10. **Return on assets.** The return on common stockholders' equity is affected by two factors: the **return on assets** and the degree of leverage. The return on assets measures the overall profitability of assets in terms of the income earned on each dollar invested in assets. It is computed by dividing net income by average total assets. Chicago Cereal's return on assets is shown in **Illustration 13.32**.

ILLUSTRATION 13.32 Return on assets

Ratio	Formula	Chicago Cereal			Giant Mills 2022	Industry Average
			2022	2021		
Return on assets	$\dfrac{\text{Net income}}{\text{Average total assets}}$	$\dfrac{\$1{,}103}{(\$11{,}397 + \$10{,}714) \div 2} =$	10.0%	9.4%	6.2%	5.3%

Chicago Cereal had a 10.0% return on assets in 2022. This rate is significantly higher than that of Giant Mills and the industry average.

Note that its rate of return on common stockholders' equity (48%) is substantially higher than its rate of return on assets (10%). The reason is that it has made effective use of **leverage**. **Leveraging** or **trading on the equity** at a gain means that the company has borrowed money at a lower rate of interest than the rate of return it earns on the assets it purchased with the borrowed funds. Leverage enables management to use money supplied by nonowners to increase the return to owners.

A comparison of the rate of return on assets with the rate of interest paid for borrowed money indicates the profitability of trading on the equity. If you borrow money at 8% and your rate of return on assets is 11%, you are trading on the equity at a gain. Note, however, that trading on the equity is a two-way street. For example, if you borrow money at 11% and earn only 8% on it, you are trading on the equity at a loss.

Chicago Cereal earns more on its borrowed funds than it has to pay in interest. Thus, the return to stockholders exceeds the return on assets because of the positive benefit of leverage. Recall from our earlier discussion that Chicago Cereal's percentage of debt financing, as measured by the ratio of debt to assets (or debt to equity), was higher than Giant Mills' and the industry average. It appears that Chicago Cereal's high return on common stockholders' equity is due in part to its use of leverage.

11. **Profit margin.** The return on assets is affected by two factors, the first of which is the profit margin. The **profit margin**, or rate of return on sales, is a measure of the percentage of each dollar of sales that results in net income. It is computed by dividing net income by net sales for the period. Chicago Cereal's profit margin is shown in **Illustration 13.33**.

ILLUSTRATION 13.33 Profit margin

Ratio	Formula	Chicago Cereal			Giant Mills 2022	Industry Average
			2022	2021		
Profit margin	$\dfrac{\text{Net income}}{\text{Net sales}}$	$\dfrac{\$1{,}103}{\$11{,}776} =$	9.4%	9.2%	8.2%	6.1%

Chicago Cereal experienced a slight increase in its profit margin from 2021 to 2022 of 9.2% to 9.4%. Its profit margin was higher, indicating the company earned more profit out of each dollar of sales, than the industry average and that of Giant Mills.

High-volume (high inventory turnover) businesses such as grocery stores and pharmacy chains generally have low profit margins. Low-volume businesses such as jewelry stores and airplane manufacturers have high profit margins.

12. **Asset turnover.** The other factor that affects the return on assets is the asset turnover. The **asset turnover** measures how efficiently a company uses its assets to generate sales. It is determined by dividing net sales by average total assets for the period. The resulting number shows the dollars of sales produced by each dollar invested in assets. **Illustration 13.34** shows the asset turnover for Chicago Cereal.

ILLUSTRATION 13.34
Asset turnover

Ratio	Formula	Chicago Cereal		Giant Mills 2022	Industry Average
		2022	2021		
Asset turnover	Net sales / Average total assets	$\frac{\$11{,}776}{(\$11{,}397 + \$10{,}714) \div 2} =$ 1.07	1.02	.76	.87

The asset turnover shows that in 2022, Chicago Cereal generated sales of $1.07 for each dollar it had invested in assets. The ratio rose from 2021 to 2022. Its asset turnover is above the industry average and that of Giant Mills.

Asset turnovers vary considerably among industries. The average asset turnover for utility companies is .45, for example, while the grocery store industry has an average asset turnover of 3.49.

In summary, Chicago Cereal's return on assets increased from 9.4% in 2021 to 10.0% in 2022. Underlying this increase was an increased profitability on each dollar of sales (as measured by the profit margin) and a rise in the sales-generating efficiency of its assets (as measured by the asset turnover). We can analyze the combined effects of profit margin and asset turnover on return on assets for Chicago Cereal as shown in **Illustration 13.35**.

ILLUSTRATION 13.35 Composition of return on assets

Ratios:	Profit Margin	×	Asset Turnover	=	Return on Assets
	Net Income / Net Sales	×	Net Sales / Average Total Assets	=	Net Income / Average Total Assets
Chicago Cereal					
2022	9.4%	×	1.07 times	=	10.1%*
2021	9.2%	×	1.02 times	=	9.4%

*Difference from value in Illustration 13.32 due to rounding.

13. **Gross profit rate.** One factor that strongly influences the profit margin is the gross profit rate. The **gross profit rate** is determined by dividing gross profit (net sales less cost of goods sold) by net sales. This rate indicates a company's ability to maintain an adequate selling price above its cost of goods sold.

As an industry becomes more competitive, this ratio declines. For example, in the early years of the personal computer industry, gross profit rates were quite high. Today, because of increased competition and a belief that most brands of personal computers are similar in quality, gross profit rates have become thin. Analysts should closely monitor gross profit rates over time. **Illustration 13.36** shows Chicago Cereal's gross profit rate.

ILLUSTRATION 13.36
Gross profit rate

Ratio	Formula	Chicago Cereal		Giant Mills 2022	Industry Average
		2022	2021		
Gross profit rate	Gross profit / Net sales	$\frac{\$5{,}179}{\$11{,}776} =$ 44%	44%	34%	30%

Chicago Cereal's gross profit rate remained constant from 2021 to 2022.

14. **Earnings per share (EPS).** Stockholders usually think in terms of the number of shares they own or plan to buy or sell. Expressing net income earned on a per share basis provides a useful perspective for determining profitability. **Earnings per share** is a measure of the net income earned on each share of common stock. It is computed by dividing net income by the average number of common shares outstanding during the year.

The terms "net income per share" or "earnings per share" refer to the amount of net income applicable to each share of **common stock**. Therefore, when we compute earnings per share, if there are preferred dividends declared for the period, we must deduct them from net income to arrive at income available to the common stockholders. Chicago Cereal's earnings per share is shown in **Illustration 13.37**.

ILLUSTRATION 13.37
Earnings per share

Ratio	Formula	Chicago Cereal		Giant Mills	Industry Average
		2022	2021	2022	
Earnings per share (EPS)	$\dfrac{\text{Net income} - \text{Preferred dividends}}{\text{Weighted-average common shares outstanding}}$	$\dfrac{\$1{,}103 - \$0}{418.7} = \$2.63$	$2.40	$2.90	na

Note that no industry average is presented in Illustration 13.37. Industry data for earnings per share are not reported, and in fact the Chicago Cereal and Giant Mills ratios should not be compared. Such comparisons are not meaningful because of the wide variations in the number of shares of outstanding stock among companies. Chicago Cereal's earnings per share increased 23 cents per share in 2022. This represents a 9.6% increase from the 2021 EPS of $2.40.

15. **Price-earnings ratio.** The **price-earnings ratio** is an oft-quoted statistic that measures the ratio of the market price of each share of common stock to the earnings per share. The price-earnings (P-E) ratio reflects investors' assessments of a company's future earnings. It is computed by dividing the market price per share of the stock by earnings per share. Chicago Cereal's price-earnings ratio is shown in **Illustration 13.38**.

ILLUSTRATION 13.38
Price-earnings ratio

Ratio	Formula	Chicago Cereal		Giant Mills	Industry Average
		2022	2021	2022	
Price-earnings ratio	$\dfrac{\text{Market price per share}}{\text{Earnings per share}}$	$\dfrac{\$52.92}{\$2.63} = 20.1$	20.9	24.3	35.8

At the end of 2022 and 2021, the market price of Chicago Cereal's stock was $52.92 and $50.06, respectively.

In 2022, each share of Chicago Cereal's stock sold for 20.1 times the amount that was earned on each share. Chicago Cereal's price-earnings ratio is lower than Giant Mills' ratio of 24.3 and lower than the industry average of 35.8 times. Its lower P-E ratio suggests that the market is less optimistic about Chicago Cereal than about Giant Mills. However, it might also signal that Chicago Cereal's stock is underpriced.

16. **Payout ratio.** The **payout ratio** measures the percentage of earnings distributed in the form of cash dividends. It is computed by dividing cash dividends declared on common stock by net income. Companies that have high growth rates are characterized by low payout ratios because they reinvest most of their net income in the business. The payout ratio for Chicago Cereal is shown in **Illustration 13.39**.

ILLUSTRATION 13.39
Payout ratio

Ratio	Formula	Chicago Cereal		Giant Mills	Industry Average
		2022	2021	2022	
Payout ratio	$\dfrac{\text{Cash dividends declared on common stock}}{\text{Net income}}$	$\dfrac{\$475}{\$1{,}103} = 43\%$	45%	54%	37%

The 2022 and 2021 payout ratios for Chicago Cereal are slightly lower than that of Giant Mills (54%) but higher than the industry average (37%). A lower payout ratio means a company has chosen to pay out a lower percentage of its net income as dividends.

Management has some control over the amount of dividends paid each year, and companies are generally reluctant to reduce a dividend below the amount paid in a previous year. Therefore, the payout ratio will actually increase if a company's net income declines but the company keeps its total dividend payment the same. Of course, unless the company returns to its previous level of profitability, maintaining this higher dividend payout ratio is probably not possible over the long run.

Before drawing any conclusions regarding Chicago Cereal's dividend payout ratio, we should calculate this ratio over a longer period of time to evaluate any trends and also try to find out whether management's philosophy regarding dividends has changed recently. The "Selected Financial Data" section of Chicago Cereal's Management Discussion and Analysis shows that over a 5-year period, earnings per share rose 45%, while dividends per share grew only 19%.

In terms of the types of financial information available and the ratios used by various industries, what can be practically covered in this text gives you only the "Titanic approach." That is, you are seeing only the tip of the iceberg compared to the vast databases and types of ratio analysis that are available on computers. The availability of information is not a problem. The real trick is to be discriminating enough to perform relevant analysis and select pertinent comparative data.

DO IT! 3 | Ratio Analysis

The condensed financial statements of John Cully Company, for the years ended June 30, 2022 and 2021, are presented as follows.

John Cully Company
Balance Sheets
June 30

		(in thousands)
Assets	2022	2021
Current assets		
Cash and cash equivalents	$ 553.3	$ 611.6
Accounts receivable (net)	776.6	664.9
Inventory	768.3	653.5
Prepaid expenses and other current assets	204.4	269.2
Total current assets	2,302.6	2,199.2
Investments	12.3	12.6
Property, plant, and equipment (net)	694.2	647.0
Intangibles and other assets	876.7	849.3
Total assets	$3,885.8	$3,708.1
Liabilities and Stockholders' Equity		
Current liabilities	$1,497.7	$1,322.0
Long-term liabilities	679.5	637.1
Stockholders' equity—common	1,708.6	1,749.0
Total liabilities and stockholders' equity	$3,885.8	$3,708.1

ACTION PLAN
- Remember that the current ratio includes all current assets.
- Use average balances for turnover ratios like inventory, accounts receivable, and return on assets.

John Cully Company
Income Statements
For the Years Ended June 30

	(in thousands)	
	2022	2021
Sales revenue	$6,336.3	$5,790.4
Costs and expenses		
Cost of goods sold	1,617.4	1,476.3
Selling and administrative expenses	4,007.6	3,679.0
Interest expense	13.9	27.1
Total costs and expenses	5,638.9	5,182.4
Income before income taxes	697.4	608.0
Income tax expense	291.3	232.6
Net income	$ 406.1	$ 375.4

Compute the following ratios for 2022 and 2021.

  a. Current ratio.

  b. Inventory turnover. (Inventory on 6/30/20 was $599.0.)

  c. Profit margin.

  d. Return on assets. (Assets on 6/30/20 were $3,349.9.)

  e. Return on common stockholders' equity. (Stockholders' equity on 6/30/20 was $1,795.9.)

  f. Debt to assets ratio.

  g. Times interest earned.

Solution

	2022	2021
a. Current ratio:		
$2,302.6 ÷ $1,497.7 =	1.5:1	
$2,199.2 ÷ $1,322.0 =		1.7:1
b. Inventory turnover:		
$1,617.4 ÷ [($768.3 + $653.5) ÷ 2] =	2.3 times	
$1,476.3 ÷ [($653.5 + $599.0) ÷ 2] =		2.4 times
c. Profit margin:		
$406.1 ÷ $6,336.3 =	6.4%	
$375.4 ÷ $5,790.4 =		6.5%
d. Return on assets:		
$406.1 ÷ [($3,885.8 + $3,708.1) ÷ 2] =	10.7%	
$375.4 ÷ [($3,708.1 + $3,349.9) ÷ 2] =		10.6%
e. Return on common stockholders' equity:		
($406.1 − $0) ÷ [($1,708.6 + $1,749.0) ÷ 2] =	23.5%	
($375.4 − $0) ÷ [($1,749.0 + $1,795.9) ÷ 2] =		21.2%
f. Debt to assets ratio:		
($1,497.7 + $679.5) ÷ $3,885.8 =	56.0%	
($1,322.0 + $637.1) ÷ $3,708.1 =		52.8%
g. Times interest earned:		
($406.1 + $13.9 + $291.3) ÷ $13.9 =	51.2 times	
($375.4 + $27.1 + $232.6) ÷ $27.1 =		23.4 times

Related exercise material: **BE13.10, BE13.11, BE13.12, BE13.13, BE13.14, BE13.15, DO IT! 13.3, E13.7, E13.8, E13.9, E13.10, E13.11, E13.12,** and **E13.13.**

USING THE DECISION TOOLS | Kellogg Company

In analyzing a company, you should always investigate an extended period of time in order to determine whether the condition and performance of the company are changing. The condensed financial statements of **Kellogg Company** for 2017 and 2016 are presented here.

Kellogg Company, Inc.
Balance Sheets
December 30, 2017, and December 31, 2016
(in millions)

Assets	2017	2016
Current assets		
Cash	$ 281	$ 280
Accounts receivable (net)	1,389	1,231
Inventories	1,217	1,238
Other current assets	149	191
Total current assets	3,036	2,940
Property (net)	3,716	5,166
Other assets	9,598	7,005
Total assets	$16,350	$15,111
Liabilities and Stockholders' Equity		
Current liabilities	$ 4,479	$ 4,474
Long-term liabilities	9,643	8,711
Stockholders' equity—common	2,228	1,926
Total liabilities and stockholders' equity	$16,350	$15,111

Kellogg Company, Inc.
Condensed Income Statements
For the Years Ended December 30, 2017, and December 31, 2016
(in millions)

	2017	2016
Net sales	$12,923	$13,014
Cost of goods sold	7,901	8,259
Gross profit	5,022	4,755
Selling and administrative expenses	3,076	3,360
Income from operations	1,946	1,395
Interest expense	256	406
Other income (expense), net	(16)	(62)
Income before income taxes	1,674	927
Income tax expense	412	233
Other earnings (loss)	7	0
Net income	$ 1,269	$ 694

Instructions

Compute the following ratios for Kellogg for 2017 and discuss your findings (2016 values are provided for comparison).

1. Liquidity:
   a. Current ratio (2016: .66:1).
   b. Inventory turnover (2016: 6.6 times).
2. Solvency:
   a. Debt to assets ratio (2016: 87%).
   b. Times interest earned (2016: 3.3 times).

3. Profitability:
   a. Return on assets (2016: 4.6%).
   b. Profit margin (2016: 5.3%).
   c. Return on common stockholders' equity (2016: 33%).

Solution

1. Liquidity

   a. Current ratio:

   2017: $\dfrac{\$3,036}{\$4,479} = .68:1$ 2016: .66:1

   b. Inventory turnover:

   2017: $\dfrac{\$7,901}{(\$1,217 + \$1,238)/2} = 6.4 \text{ times}$ 2016: 6.6 times

   We see that between 2016 and 2017, the current ratio increased, which suggests an increase in liquidity. The inventory turnover decreased, which suggests a decline in liquidity.

2. Solvency

   a. Debt to assets ratio:

   2017: $\dfrac{\$4,479 + \$9,643}{\$16,350} = 86\%$ 2016: 87%

   b. Times interest earned:

   2017: $\dfrac{\$1,269 + \$256 + \$412}{\$256} = 7.6 \text{ times}$ 2016: 3.3 times

   Kellogg's debt to assets ratio decreased in 2017, and its times interest earned increased. Both changes suggest improved solvency.

3. Profitability

   a. Return on assets:

   2017: $\dfrac{\$1,269}{(\$16,350 + \$15,111)/2} = 8.0\%$ 2016: 4.6%

   b. Profit margin:

   2017: $\dfrac{\$1,269}{\$12,923} = 9.8\%$ 2016: 5.3%

   c. Return on common stockholders' equity:

   2017: $\dfrac{\$1,269}{(\$2,228 + \$1,926)/2} = 61\%$ 2016: 33%

   Kellogg's return on assets, profit margin, and return on stockholders' equity increased. The company experienced a sharp increase in net income, while its total assets, sales, and equity were relatively constant.

Review and Practice

Learning Objectives Review

1 Apply the concepts of sustainable income and quality of earnings.

Sustainable income analysis is useful in evaluating a company's performance. Sustainable income is the most likely level of income to be obtained by the company in the future and omits unusual items. Discontinued operations and other comprehensive income are presented on the statement of comprehensive income to highlight their unusual nature. Items below income from continuing operations must be presented net of tax.

A high quality of earnings provides full and transparent information that will not confuse or mislead users of the financial statements. Issues related to quality of earnings are (1) alternative accounting methods, (2) pro forma income, and (3) improper recognition.

2 Apply horizontal analysis and vertical analysis.

Horizontal analysis is a technique for evaluating a series of data over a period of time to determine the increase or decrease that has taken place, expressed as either a dollar amount or a percentage.

Vertical analysis is a technique that expresses each item in a financial statement as a percentage of a relevant total or a base amount.

3 Analyze a company's performance using ratio analysis.

Financial ratios are provided in Illustration 13.15 (liquidity), Illustration 13.16 (solvency), and Illustration 13.17 (profitability). Analysis is enhanced by intracompany, intercompany, and industry comparisons of these three classes of ratios.

Decision Tools Review

Decision Checkpoints	Info Needed for Decision	Tool to Use for Decision	How to Evaluate Results
Has the company sold any major components of its business?	Discontinued operations section of income statement	Anything reported in this section indicates that the company has discontinued a major component of its business.	If a major component has been discontinued, its results during the current period should not be included in estimates of future net income.
Has the company changed any of its accounting principles?	Effect of change in accounting principle on current and prior periods	Management indicates that the new principle is preferable to the old principle.	Examine current and prior years' reported income, using new-principle basis to assess trends for estimating future income.
How do the company's financial position and operating results compare with those of the previous period?	Income statement and balance sheet	Comparative financial statements should be prepared over at least two years, with the first year reported being the base year. Changes in each line item relative to the base year should be presented both by amount and by percentage. This is called **horizontal analysis**.	Significant changes should be investigated to determine the reason for the change.
How do the relationships between items in this year's financial statements compare with those of last year or those of competitors?	Income statement and balance sheet	Each line item on the income statement should be presented as a percentage of net sales, and each line item on the balance sheet should be presented as a percentage of total assets or total liabilities and stockholders' equity. These percentages should be investigated for differences either across years in the same company or in the same year across different companies. This is called **vertical analysis**.	Any significant differences either across years or between companies should be investigated to determine the cause.
How do mathematical relationships between financial statement items compare to prior years, competitors, and industry?	Financial statements	Various ratios that measure liquidity, solvency, and profitability.	Significant differences from prior-year values, or from competitor or industry values, should be investigated to determine the cause.

Glossary Review

Accounts receivable turnover A measure of the liquidity of receivables; computed as net credit sales divided by average net accounts receivable. (p. 13-19).

Asset turnover A measure of how efficiently a company uses its assets to generate sales; computed as net sales divided by average total assets. (p. 13-24).

Available-for-sale securities Securities that are held with the intent of selling them sometime in the future. (p. 13-5).

Average collection period The average number of days that receivables are outstanding; calculated as accounts receivable turnover divided into 365 days. (p. 13-20).

Change in accounting principle Use of an accounting principle in the current year different from the one used in the preceding year. (p. 13-6).

Comprehensive income The sum of net income and other comprehensive income items. (p. 13-5).

Current ratio A measure used to evaluate a company's liquidity and short-term debt-paying ability; calculated as current assets divided by current liabilities. (p. 13-19).

Days in inventory A measure of the average number of days inventory is held; computed as inventory turnover divided into 365 days. (p. 13-21).

Debt to assets ratio A measure of the percentage of total financing provided by creditors; computed as total liabilities divided by total assets. (p. 13-21).

Discontinued operations The disposal of a significant component of a business. (p. 13-4).

Earnings per share The net income earned by each share of outstanding common stock; computed as net income less preferred dividends divided by the weighted-average common shares outstanding. (p. 13-25).

Free cash flow A measure of solvency. Cash remaining from operating activities after adjusting for capital expenditures and dividends paid. (p. 13-22).

Gross profit rate Gross profit expressed as a percentage of sales; computed as gross profit divided by net sales. (p. 13-25).

Horizontal analysis A technique for evaluating a series of financial statement data over a period of time to determine the increase (decrease) that has taken place, expressed as either a dollar amount or a percentage. (p. 13-10).

Inventory turnover A measure of the liquidity of inventory. Measures the number of times average inventory was sold during the period; computed as cost of goods sold divided by average inventory. (p. 13-20).

Leveraging Borrowing money at a lower rate of interest than can be earned by using the borrowed money; also referred to as *trading on the equity*. (p. 13-24).

Liquidity ratios Measures of the short-term ability of the company to pay its maturing obligations and to meet unexpected needs for cash. (p. 13-15).

Payout ratio A measure of the percentage of earnings distributed in the form of cash dividends; calculated as cash dividends declared on common stock divided by net income. (p. 13-26).

Price-earnings (P-E) ratio A comparison of the market price of each share of common stock to the earnings per share; computed as the market price of the stock divided by earnings per share. (p. 13-26).

Profitability ratios Measures of the income or operating success of a company for a given period of time. (p. 13-16).

Profit margin A measure of the net income generated by each dollar of sales; computed as net income divided by net sales. (p. 13-24).

Pro forma income A measure of income that usually excludes items that a company thinks are unusual or non-recurring. (p. 13-8).

Quality of earnings Indicates the level of full and transparent information that is provided to users of the financial statements. (p. 13-7).

Ratio The mathematical relationship between one quantity and another. The relationship may be expressed either as a percentage, a rate, or a simple proportion. (p. 13-14).

Ratio analysis A technique for evaluating financial statements that expresses the relationship between selected financial statement data. (p. 13-14).

Return on assets A profitability measure that indicates the amount of net income generated by each dollar of assets; calculated as net income divided by average total assets. (p. 13-24).

Return on common stockholders' equity (ROE) A measure of the dollars of net income earned for each dollar invested by the owners; computed as income available to common stockholders divided by average common stockholders' equity. (p. 13-23).

Solvency ratios Measures of the ability of a company to survive over a long period of time, particularly to pay interest as it comes due and to repay the balance of debt at its maturity. (p. 13-16).

Sustainable income The most likely level of income to be obtained by a company in the future. (p. 13-3).

Times interest earned A measure of a company's solvency and ability to meet interest payments as they come due; calculated as the sum of net income, interest expense, and income tax expense divided by interest expense. (p. 13-22).

Trading on the equity See *leveraging*. (p. 13-24).

Trading securities Securities bought and held primarily for sale in the near term to generate income on short-term price differences. (p. 13-5).

Vertical analysis A technique for evaluating financial statement data that expresses each item in a financial statement as a percentage of a base amount. (p. 13-12).

Practice Multiple-Choice Questions

1. **(LO 1)** In reporting discontinued operations, the income statement should show in a special section:

    a. gains on the disposal of the discontinued component.

    b. losses on the disposal of the discontinued component.

    c. Neither (a) nor (b).

    d. Both (a) and (b).

2. **(LO 1)** Cool Stools Corporation has income before taxes of $400,000 and a loss on discontinued operations of $100,000. If the

income tax rate is 25% on all items, the statement of comprehensive income should show income from continuing operations and discontinued operations, respectively, of

a. $325,000 and $100,000.
b. $325,000 and $75,000.
c. $300,000 and $100,000.
d. $300,000 and $75,000.

3. **(LO 1)** Which of the following would be considered an "Other comprehensive income" item?

a. Gain on disposal of discontinued operations.
b. Unrealized loss on available-for-sale securities.
c. Loss related to flood.
d. Net income.

4. **(LO 1)** Which situation below might indicate a company has a low quality of earnings?

a. The same accounting principles are used each year.
b. Revenue is recognized when the performance obligation is satisfied.
c. Maintenance costs are capitalized and then depreciated.
d. The company's P-E ratio is high relative to competitors.

5. **(LO 2)** In horizontal analysis, each item is expressed as a percentage of the:

a. net income amount.
b. stockholders' equity amount.
c. total assets amount.
d. base-year amount.

6. **(LO 2)** Adams Corporation reported net sales of $300,000, $330,000, and $360,000 in the years 2020, 2021, and 2022, respectively. If 2020 is the base year, what percentage do 2022 sales represent of the base?

a. 77%.
b. 108%.
c. 120%.
d. 130%.

7. **(LO 2)** The following schedule is a display of what type of analysis?

	Amount	Percent
Current assets	$200,000	25%
Property, plant, and equipment	600,000	75%
Total assets	$800,000	

a. Horizontal analysis.
b. Differential analysis.
c. Vertical analysis.
d. Ratio analysis.

8. **(LO 2)** In vertical analysis, the base amount for depreciation expense is generally:

a. net sales.
b. depreciation expense in a previous year.
c. gross profit.
d. fixed assets.

9. **(LO 3)** Which measure is an evaluation of a company's ability to pay current liabilities?

a. Accounts receivable turnover.
b. Current ratio.

c. Both (a) and (b).
d. None of the above.

10. **(LO 3)** Which measure is useful in evaluating the efficiency in managing inventories?

a. Inventory turnover.
b. Days in inventory.
c. Both (a) and (b).
d. None of the above.

11. **(LO 3)** Which of these is **not** a liquidity ratio?

a. Current ratio.
b. Asset turnover.
c. Inventory turnover.
d. Accounts receivable turnover.

12. **(LO 3)** Plano Corporation reported net income $24,000, net sales $400,000, and average assets $600,000 for 2022. What is the 2022 profit margin?

a. 6%.
b. 12%.
c. 40%.
d. 200%.

Use the following financial statement information as of the end of each year to answer Questions 13–17.

	2022	2021
Inventory	$ 54,000	$ 48,000
Current assets	81,000	106,000
Total assets	382,000	326,000
Current liabilities	27,000	36,000
Total liabilities	102,000	88,000
Common stockholders' equity	240,000	198,000
Net sales	784,000	697,000
Cost of goods sold	306,000	277,000
Net income	134,000	90,000
Income tax expense	22,000	18,000
Interest expense	12,000	12,000
Dividends paid to preferred stockholders	4,000	4,000
Dividends paid to common stockholders	15,000	10,000

13. **(LO 3)** Compute the days in inventory for 2022.

a. 64.4 days.
b. 60.8 days.
c. 6 days.
d. 24 days.

14. **(LO 3)** Compute the current ratio for 2022.

a. 1.26:1.
b. 3.0:1.
c. 0.80:1.
d. 3.75:1.

15. **(LO 3)** Compute the profit margin for 2022.

a. 17.1%.
b. 18.1%.
c. 37.9%.
d. 5.9%.

16. **(LO 3)** Compute the return on common stockholders' equity for 2022.

a. 54.2%.
b. 52.5%.
c. 61.2%.
d. 59.4%.

17. **(LO 3)** Compute the times interest earned for 2022.

a. 11.2 times.
b. 65.3 times.
c. 14.0 times.
d. 13.0 times.

Solutions

1. d. Gains and losses from the operations of a discontinued segment and gains and losses on the disposal of the discontinued segment are shown in a separate section immediately after continuing operations in the income statement. Choices (a) and (b) are correct, but (d) is the better answer. Choice (c) is wrong as there is a correct answer.

2. d. Income tax expense = 25% × $400,000 = $100,000; therefore, income from continuing operations = $400,000 − $100,000 = $300,000. The loss on discontinued operations is shown net of tax, $100,000 × 75% = $75,000. The other choices are therefore incorrect.

3. b. Unrealized gains and losses on available-for-sale securities are part of other comprehensive income. The other choices are incorrect because (a) a gain on the disposal of discontinued operations is reported as an unusual item, (c) loss related to a flood is reported among other expenses and losses, and (d) net income is a separate line item.

4. c. Capitalizing and then depreciating maintenance costs suggests that a company is trying to avoid expensing certain costs by deferring them to future accounting periods to increase current-period income. The other choices are incorrect because (a) using the same accounting principles each year and (b) recognizing revenue when the performance obligation is satisfied is in accordance with GAAP. Choice (d) is incorrect because a high P-E ratio does not suggest that a firm has low quality of earnings.

5. d. Horizontal analysis converts each succeeding year's balance to a percentage of the base year amount, not (a) net income amount, (b) stockholders' equity amount, or (c) total assets amount.

6. c. The trend percentage for 2022 is 120% ($360,000/$300,000), not (a) 77%, (b) 108%, or (d) 130%.

7. c. The data in the schedule is a display of vertical analysis because the individual asset items are expressed as a percentage of total assets. The other choices are therefore incorrect. Horizontal analysis is a technique for evaluating a series of data over a period of time.

8. a. In vertical analysis, net sales is used as the base amount for income statement items, not (b) depreciation expense in a previous year, (c) gross profit, or (d) fixed assets.

9. c. Both the accounts receivable turnover and the current ratio measure a firm's ability to pay current liabilities. Choices (a) and (b) are correct but (c) is the better choice. Choice (d) is incorrect because there is a correct answer.

10. c. Both inventory turnover and days in inventory measure a firm's efficiency in managing inventories. Choices (a) and (b) are correct but (c) is the better answer. Choice (d) is incorrect because there is a correct answer.

11. b. Asset turnover is a measure of profitability. The other choices are incorrect because the (a) current ratio, (c) inventory turnover, and (d) accounts receivable turnover are all measures of a firm's liquidity.

12. a. Profit margin = Net income ($24,000) ÷ Net sales ($400,000) = 6%, not (b) 12%, (c) 40%, or (d) 200%.

13. b. Inventory turnover = Cost of goods sold/Average inventory {$306,000/[($54,000 + $48,000)/2]} = 6 times. Thus, days in inventory = 60.8 (365/6), not (a) 64.4, (c) 6, or (d) 24 days.

14. b. Current ratio = Current assets/Current liabilities ($81,000/$27,000) = 3.0:1, not (a) 1.26:1, (c) 0.80:1, or (d) 3.75:1.

15. a. Profit margin = Net income/Net sales ($134,000/$784,000) = 17.1%, not (b) 18.1%, (c) 37.9%, or (d) 5.9%.

16. d. Return on common stockholders' equity = Net income ($134,000) − Dividends to preferred stockholders ($4,000)/Average common stockholders' equity [($240,000 + $198,000)/2] = 59.4%, not (a) 54.2%, (b) 52.5%, or (c) 61.2%.

17. c. Times interest earned = (Net income + Interest expense + Income tax expense) ÷ Interest expense [($134,000 + $12,000 + $22,000)/$12,000] = 14.0 times, not (a) 11.2, (b) 65.3, or (d) 13.0 times.

Practice Brief Exercises

Prepare a discontinued operations section.

1. (LO 1) On September 30, Reynaldo Corporation discontinued its operations in Africa. During the year, the operating gain was $100,000 before taxes. On September 1, Reynaldo disposed of its African facilities at a pretax loss of $350.000. The applicable tax rate is 30%. Show the discontinued operations section of the statement of comprehensive income.

Solution

1.

Reynaldo Corporation
Partial Income Statement

Gain from operations of discontinued division, net of $30,000 income taxes ($100,000 × 30%)	$ 70,000	
Loss from disposal of discontinued division, net of $105,000 income tax savings ($350,000 × 30%)	(245,000)	$(175,000)

Prepare horizontal analysis.

2. (LO 2) Using the following data from the comparative balance sheet of Alfredo Company, perform horizontal analysis.

	December 31, 2022	December 31, 2021
Accounts payable	$ 300,000	$ 200,000
Common stock	700,000	600,000
Total liabilities and equity	2,000,000	1,800,000

Solution

2.

	December 31, 2022	December 31, 2021	Increase or (Decrease) Amount	Percent*
Accounts payable	$ 300,000	$ 200,000	$100,000	50%
Common stock	700,000	600,000	100,000	17
Total liabilities and stockholders' equity	2,000,000	1,800,000	200,000	11

*100/200 = 50%; 100/600 = 16.7%; 200/1,800 = 11.1%

3. (LO 3) Gonzalez Company has beginning inventory of $400,000, cost of goods sold of $2,200,000, and days in inventory of 73. What is Gonzalez' inventory turnover and ending inventory?

Calculate ratios.

Solution

3. Days in inventory = 365/Inventory turnover
    73 = 365/Inventory turnover.
    Inventory turnover = 5 (365/73)

    Inventory turnover = Cost of goods sold/Average inventory
    5 = $2,200,000/Average inventory
    Average inventory = $2,200,000/5 = $440,000.

    Since beginning inventory is $400,000, ending inventory must be $480,000: ($400,000 + $480,000)/2 = $440,000.

Practice Exercises

1. (LO 2) The comparative condensed balance sheets of Roadway Corporation are presented below.

Prepare horizontal and vertical analysis.

Roadway Corporation
Condensed Balance Sheets
December 31

	2022	2021
Assets		
Current assets	$ 76,000	$ 80,000
Property, plant, and equipment (net)	99,000	90,000
Intangibles	25,000	40,000
Total assets	$200,000	$210,000
Liabilities and Stockholders' Equity		
Current liabilities	$ 40,800	$ 48,000
Long-term liabilities	143,000	150,000
Stockholders' equity	16,200	12,000
Total liabilities and stockholders' equity	$200,000	$210,000

Instructions

a. Prepare a horizontal analysis of the balance sheet data for Roadway Corporation using 2021 as a base.

b. Prepare a vertical analysis of the balance sheet data for Roadway Corporation in columnar form for 2022.

Solution

1. a.

Roadway Corporation
Condensed Balance Sheets
December 31

	2022	2021	Increase (Decrease)	Percent Change from 2021
Assets				
Current assets	$ 76,000	$ 80,000	$ (4,000)	(5.0%)
Property, plant, and equipment (net)	99,000	90,000	9,000	10.0%
Intangibles	25,000	40,000	(15,000)	(37.5%)
Total assets	$200,000	$210,000	$(10,000)	(4.8%)
Liabilities and Stockholders' Equity				
Current liabilities	$ 40,800	$ 48,000	$ (7,200)	(15.0%)
Long-term liabilities	143,000	150,000	(7,000)	(4.7%)
Stockholders' equity	16,200	12,000	4,200	35.0%
Total liabilities and stockholders' equity	$200,000	$210,000	$(10,000)	(4.8%)

b.

Roadway Corporation
Condensed Balance Sheet
December 31, 2022

	Amount	Percent
Assets		
Current assets	$ 76,000	38.0%
Property, plant, and equipment (net)	99,000	49.5%
Intangibles	25,000	12.5%
Total assets	$200,000	100.0%
Liabilities and Stockholders' Equity		
Current liabilities	$ 40,800	20.4%
Long-term liabilities	143,000	71.5%
Stockholders' equity	16,200	8.1%
Total liabilities and stockholders' equity	$200,000	100.0%

Compute ratios.

2. (LO 3) Rondo Corporation's comparative balance sheets are presented below.

Rondo Corporation
Balance Sheets
December 31

	2022	2021
Cash	$ 5,300	$ 3,700
Accounts receivable	21,200	23,400
Inventory	9,000	7,000
Land	20,000	26,000
Buildings	70,000	70,000
Accumulated depreciation—buildings	(15,000)	(10,000)
Total	$110,500	$120,100
Accounts payable	$ 10,370	$ 31,100
Common stock	75,000	69,000
Retained earnings	25,130	20,000
Total	$110,500	$120,100

Rondo's 2022 income statement included net sales of $120,000, cost of goods sold of $70,000, and net income of $14,000.

Instructions

Compute the following ratios for 2022.

a. Current ratio.
b. Accounts receivable turnover.
c. Inventory turnover.
d. Profit margin.
e. Asset turnover.
f. Return on assets.
g. Return on common stockholders' equity.
h. Debt to assets ratio.

Solution

2. a. ($5,300 + $21,200 + $9,000)/$10,370 = 3.42:1
   b. $120,000/[($21,200 + $23,400)/2] = 5.38 times
   c. $70,000/[($9,000 + $7,000)/2] = 8.8 times
   d. $14,000/$120,000 = 11.7%
   e. $120,000/[($110,500 + $120,100)/2] = 1.04 times
   f. $14,000/[($110,500 + $120,100)/2] = 12.1%
   g. $14,000/[($100,130 + $89,000)/2] = 14.8%
   h. $10,370/$110,500 = 9.4%

Practice Problem

(LO 1) The events and transactions of Dever Corporation for the year ending December 31, 2022, resulted in the following data.

Cost of goods sold	$2,600,000
Net sales	4,400,000
Other expenses and losses	9,600
Other revenues and gains	5,600
Selling and administrative expenses	1,100,000
Income from operations of plastics division	70,000
Gain from disposal of plastics division	500,000
Unrealized loss on available-for-sale securities	60,000

Prepare a statement of comprehensive income.

Analysis reveals the following:

1. All items are before the applicable income tax rate of 30%.
2. The plastics division was sold on July 1.
3. All operating data for the plastics division have been segregated.

Instructions

Prepare a statement of comprehensive income for the year.

Solution

Dever Corporation
Statement of Comprehensive Income
For the Year Ended December 31, 2022

Net sales	$4,400,000
Cost of goods sold	2,600,000
Gross profit	1,800,000
Selling and administrative expenses	1,100,000
Income from operations	700,000
Other revenues and gains	5,600
Other expenses and losses	9,600
Income before income taxes	696,000
Income tax expense ($696,000 × 30%)	208,800

Income from continuing operations		487,200
Discontinued operations		
Income from operation of plastics division, net of $21,000		
income taxes ($70,000 × 30%)	49,000	
Gain from disposal of plastics division, net of $150,000		
income taxes ($500,000 × 30%)	350,000	399,000
Net income		886,200
Unrealized loss on available-for-sale securities, net of $18,000		
income tax savings ($60,000 × 30%)		42,000
Comprehensive income		$ 844,200

WileyPLUS

Brief Exercises, DO IT! Exercises, Exercises, Problems, and many additional resources are available for practice in WileyPLUS.

Questions

1. Explain sustainable income. What relationship does this concept have to the treatment of discontinued operations on the income statement?

2. Hogan Inc. reported 2021 earnings per share of $3.26 and had no discontinued operations. In 2022, earnings per share on income from continuing operations was $2.99, and earnings per share on net income was $3.49. Do you consider this trend to be favorable? Why or why not?

3. Moosier Inc. has been in operation for 3 years and uses the FIFO method of pricing inventory. During the fourth year, Moosier changes to the average-cost method for all its inventory. How will Moosier report this change?

4. What amount did **Apple** report as "Other comprehensive earnings" in its consolidated statement of comprehensive income ending September 30, 2017? By what percentage did Apple's "Comprehensive income" differ from its "Net income"?

5. Identify and explain factors that affect quality of earnings.

6. Explain how the choice of one of the following accounting methods over the other raises or lowers a company's net income during a period of continuing inflation.

   a. Use of FIFO instead of LIFO for inventory costing.

   b. Use of a 6-year life for machinery instead of a 9-year life.

   c. Use of straight-line depreciation instead of declining-balance depreciation.

7. Two popular methods of financial statement analysis are horizontal analysis and vertical analysis. Explain the difference between these two methods.

8. a. If Erin Company had net income of $300,000 in 2021 and it experienced a 24.5% increase in net income for 2022, what is its net income for 2022?

   b. If 6 cents of every dollar of Erin's revenue is net income in 2021, what is the dollar amount of 2021 revenue?

9. a. Gina Jaimes believes that the analysis of financial statements is directed at two characteristics of a company: liquidity and profitability. Is Gina correct? Explain.

   b. Are short-term creditors, long-term creditors, and stockholders interested in primarily the same characteristics of a company? Explain.

10. a. Distinguish among the following bases of comparison: intracompany, intercompany, and industry averages.

   b. Give the principal value of using each of the three bases of comparison.

11. Name the major ratios useful in assessing (a) liquidity and (b) solvency.

12. Vern Thoms is puzzled. His company had a profit margin of 10% in 2022. He feels that this is an indication that the company is doing well. Tina Amos, his accountant, says that more information is needed to determine the company's financial well-being. Who is correct? Why?

13. What does each type of ratio measure?

   a. Liquidity ratios.

   b. Solvency ratios.

   c. Profitability ratios.

14. What is the difference between the current ratio and working capital?

15. Handi Mart, a retail store, has an accounts receivable turnover of 4.5 times. The industry average is 12.5 times. Does Handi Mart have a collection problem with its receivables?

16. Which ratios should be used to help answer each of these questions?

   a. How efficient is a company in using its assets to produce sales?

   b. How near to sale is the inventory on hand?

   c. How many dollars of net income were earned for each dollar invested by the owners?

   d. How able is a company to meet interest charges as they fall due?

17. At year-end, the price-earnings ratio of General Motors was 11.3, and the price-earnings ratio of Microsoft was 28.14. Which company did the stock market favor? Explain.

18. What is the formula for computing the payout ratio? Do you expect this ratio to be high or low for a growth company?

19. Holding all other factors constant, indicate whether each of the following changes generally signals good or bad news about a company.
   a. Increase in profit margin.
   b. Decrease in inventory turnover.
   c. Increase in current ratio.
   d. Decrease in earnings per share.
   e. Increase in price-earnings ratio.
   f. Increase in debt to assets ratio.
   g. Decrease in times interest earned.

20. The return on assets for Ayala Corporation is 7.6%. During the same year, Ayala's return on common stockholders' equity is 12.8%. What is the explanation for the difference in the two rates?

21. Which two ratios do you think should be of greatest interest in each of the following cases?
   a. A pension fund considering the purchase of 20-year bonds.
   b. A bank contemplating a short-term loan.
   c. A common stockholder.

22. Keanu Inc. has net income of $200,000, average shares of common stock outstanding of 40,000, and preferred dividends for the period of $20,000. What is Keanu's earnings per share of common stock? Fred Tyme, the president of Keanu, believes that the computed EPS of the company is high. Comment.

Brief Exercises

BE13.1 (LO 1), AP On June 30, Flores Corporation discontinued its operations in Mexico. On September 1, Flores disposed of the Mexico facility at a pretax loss of $640,000. The applicable tax rate is 25%. Show the discontinued operations section of Flores's statement of comprehensive income.

Prepare a discontinued operations section of an income statement.

BE13.2 (LO 1), AP An inexperienced accountant for Silva Corporation showed the following in the income statement: income before income taxes $450,000 and unrealized gain on available-for-sale securities (before taxes) $70,000. The unrealized gain on available-for-sale securities and income before income taxes are both subject to a 25% tax rate. Prepare a correct statement of comprehensive income.

Prepare statement of comprehensive income including unusual items.

BE13.3 (LO 1), C On January 1, 2022, Bryce Inc. changed from the LIFO method of inventory pricing to the FIFO method. Explain how this change in accounting principle should be treated in the company's financial statements.

Indicate how a change in accounting principle is reported.

BE13.4 (LO 2), AP Using these data from the comparative balance sheet of Rollaird Company, perform horizontal analysis.

Prepare horizontal analysis.

	December 31, 2022	December 31, 2021
Accounts receivable	$ 460,000	$ 400,000
Inventory	780,000	650,000
Total assets	3,164,000	2,800,000

BE13.5 (LO 2), AP Using the data presented in BE13.4 for Rollaird Company, perform vertical analysis.

Prepare vertical analysis.

BE13.6 (LO 2), AP Net income was $500,000 in 2020, $485,000 in 2021, and $518,400 in 2022. What is the percentage of change from (a) 2020 to 2021, and (b) from 2021 to 2022? Is the change an increase or a decrease?

Calculate percentage of change.

BE13.7 (LO 2), AP If Coho Company had net income of $382,800 in 2022 and it experienced a 16% increase in net income over 2021, what was its 2021 net income?

Calculate net income.

BE13.8 (LO 2), AP Vertical analysis (common-size) percentages for Palau Company's sales revenue, cost of goods sold, and expenses are listed here.

Analyze change in net income.

Vertical Analysis	2022	2021	2020
Sales revenue	100.0%	100.0%	100.0%
Cost of goods sold	60.5	62.9	64.8
Expenses	26.0	26.6	27.5

Did Palau's net income as a percent of sales increase, decrease, or remain unchanged over the 3-year period? Provide numerical support for your answer.

BE13.9 (LO 2), AP Writing Horizontal analysis (trend analysis) percentages for Phoenix Company's sales revenue, cost of goods sold, and expenses are listed here.

Analyze change in net income.

Horizontal Analysis	2022	2021	2020
Sales revenue	96.2%	104.8%	100.0%
Cost of goods sold	101.0	98.0	100.0
Expenses	105.6	95.4	100.0

Explain whether Phoenix's net income increased, decreased, or remained unchanged over the 3-year period.

Calculate current ratio.

BE13.10 (LO 3), AP Suppose these selected condensed data are taken from recent balance sheets of **Bob Evans Farms** (in thousands).

	2022	2021
Cash	$ 13,606	$ 7,669
Accounts receivable	23,045	19,951
Inventory	31,087	31,345
Other current assets	12,522	11,909
Total current assets	$ 80,260	$ 70,874
Total current liabilities	$245,805	$326,203

Compute the current ratio for each year and comment on your results.

Evaluate collection of accounts receivable.

BE13.11 (LO 3), AN Writing The following data are taken from the financial statements of Colby Company.

	2022	2021
Accounts receivable (net), end of year	$ 550,000	$ 540,000
Net sales on account	4,300,000	4,000,000
Terms for all sales are 1/10, n/45		

Compute for each year (a) the accounts receivable turnover and (b) the average collection period. What conclusions about the management of accounts receivable can be drawn from these data? At the end of 2020, accounts receivable was $520,000.

Evaluate management of inventory.

BE13.12 (LO 3), AN Writing The following data were taken from the income statements of Mydorf Company.

	2022	2021
Sales revenue	$6,420,000	$6,240,000
Beginning inventory	960,000	840,000
Purchases	4,840,000	4,661,000
Ending inventory	1,020,000	960,000

Compute for each year (a) the inventory turnover and (b) days in inventory. What conclusions concerning the management of the inventory can be drawn from these data?

Calculate profitability ratios.

BE13.13 (LO 3), AN Staples, Inc. is one of the largest suppliers of office products in the United States. Suppose it had net income of $738.7 million and sales of $24,275.5 million in 2022. Its total assets were $13,073.1 million at the beginning of the year and $13,717.3 million at the end of the year. What is Staples, Inc.'s (a) asset turnover and (b) profit margin? (Round to two decimals.) Provide a brief interpretation of your results.

Calculate profitability ratios.

BE13.14 (LO 3), AN Hollie Company has stockholders' equity of $400,000 and net income of $72,000. It has a payout ratio of 18% and a return on assets of 20%. How much did Hollie pay in cash dividends, and what were its average total assets?

Calculate and analyze free cash flow.

BE13.15 (LO 3), AN Selected data taken from a recent year's financial statements of trading card company **Topps Company, Inc.** are as follows (in millions).

Net sales	$326.7
Current liabilities, beginning of year	41.1
Current liabilities, end of year	62.4
Net cash provided by operating activities	10.4
Total liabilities, beginning of year	65.2
Total liabilities, end of year	73.2
Capital expenditures	3.7
Cash dividends	6.2

Compute the free cash flow. Provide a brief interpretation of your results.

DO IT! Exercises

Prepare statement of comprehensive income including unusual items.

DO IT! 13.1 (LO 1), AP In its proposed 2022 income statement, Hrabik Corporation reports income before income taxes $500,000, income taxes $100,000 (not including unusual items), loss on operation of discontinued music division $60,000, gain on disposal of discontinued music division $40,000, and unrealized loss on available-for-sale securities $150,000. The income tax rate is 20%. Prepare a correct statement of comprehensive income, beginning with income before income taxes.

DO IT! 13.2 (LO 2), AP Summary financial information for Gandaulf Company is as follows.

Prepare horizontal analysis.

	Dec. 31, 2022	Dec. 31, 2021
Current assets	$ 200,000	$ 220,000
Plant assets	1,040,000	780,000
Total assets	$1,240,000	$1,000,000

Compute the amount and percentage changes in 2022 using horizontal analysis, assuming 2021 is the base year.

DO IT! 13.3 (LO 3), AP The condensed financial statements of Murawski Company for the years 2021 and 2022 are presented as follows. (Amounts in thousands.)

Compute ratios.

Murawski Company
Balance Sheets
December 31

	2022	2021
Current assets		
Cash and cash equivalents	$ 330	$ 360
Accounts receivable (net)	470	400
Inventory	460	390
Prepaid expenses	120	160
Total current assets	1,380	1,310
Investments	10	10
Property, plant, and equipment	420	380
Intangibles and other assets	530	510
Total assets	$2,340	$2,210
Current liabilities	$ 900	$ 790
Long-term liabilities	410	380
Stockholders' equity—common	1,030	1,040
Total liabilities and stockholders' equity	$2,340	$2,210

Murawski Company
Income Statements
For the Years Ended December 31

	2022	2021
Sales revenue	$3,800	$3,460
Costs and expenses		
Cost of goods sold	955	890
Selling & administrative expenses	2,400	2,330
Interest expense	25	20
Total costs and expenses	3,380	3,240
Income before income taxes	420	220
Income tax expense	126	66
Net income	$ 294	$ 154

Compute the following ratios for 2022 and 2021.

a. Current ratio.

b. Inventory turnover. (Inventory on 12/31/20 was $340.)

c. Profit margin.

d. Return on assets. (Assets on 12/31/20 were $1,900.)

e. Return on common stockholders' equity. (Stockholders' equity on 12/31/20 was $900.)

f. Debt to assets ratio.

g. Times interest earned.

Exercises

Prepare a correct statement of comprehensive income.

E13.1 (LO 1), AP **Writing** For its fiscal year ending October 31, 2022, Haas Corporation reports the following partial data shown below.

Income before income taxes	$540,000
Income tax expense (20% × $420,000)	84,000
Income from continuing operations	456,000
Loss on discontinued operations	120,000
Net income	$336,000

The loss on discontinued operations was comprised of a $50,000 loss from operations and a $70,000 loss from disposal. The income tax rate is 20% on all items.

Instructions

a. Prepare a correct statement of comprehensive income beginning with income before income taxes.

b. Explain in memo form why the income statement data are misleading.

Prepare statement of comprehensive income.

E13.2 (LO 1), AP Trayer Corporation has income from continuing operations of $290,000 for the year ended December 31, 2022. It also has the following items (before considering income taxes).

1. An unrealized loss of $80,000 on available-for-sale securities.
2. A gain of $30,000 on the discontinuance of a division (comprised of a $10,000 loss from operations and a $40,000 gain on disposal).

Assume all items are subject to income taxes at a 20% tax rate.

Instructions

Prepare a statement of comprehensive income, beginning with income from continuing operations.

Prepare horizontal analysis.

E13.3 (LO 2), AP Here is financial information for Glitter Inc.

	December 31, 2022	December 31, 2021
Current assets	$106,000	$ 90,000
Plant assets (net)	400,000	350,000
Current liabilities	99,000	65,000
Long-term liabilities	122,000	90,000
Common stock, $1 par	130,000	115,000
Retained earnings	155,000	170,000

Instructions

Prepare a schedule showing a horizontal analysis for 2022, using 2021 as the base year.

Prepare vertical analysis.

E13.4 (LO 2), AP Operating data for Joshua Corporation are presented below.

	2022	2021
Sales revenue	$800,000	$600,000
Cost of goods sold	520,000	408,000
Selling expenses	120,000	72,000
Administrative expenses	60,000	48,000
Income tax expense	30,000	24,000
Net income	70,000	48,000

Instructions

Prepare a schedule showing a vertical analysis for 2022 and 2021.

Prepare horizontal and vertical analyses.

E13.5 (LO 2), AP Hypothetical balance sheets of **Nike, Inc.** are presented here.

Nike, Inc.
Comparative Balance Sheets
May 31
($ in millions)

Assets	2022	2021
Current assets	$ 9,734	$ 8,839
Property, plant, and equipment (net)	1,958	1,891
Other assets	1,558	1,713
Total assets	$13,250	$12,443
Liabilities and Stockholders' Equity		
Current liabilities	$ 3,277	$ 3,322
Long-term liabilities	1,280	1,296
Stockholders' equity	8,693	7,825
Total liabilities and stockholders' equity	$13,250	$12,443

Instructions

a. Prepare a horizontal analysis of the balance sheet data for Nike, using 2021 as a base. (Show the amount of increase or decrease as well.)

b. Prepare a vertical analysis of the balance sheet data for Nike for 2022.

E13.6 (LO 2), AP Here are the comparative income statements of Delaney Corporation.

Prepare horizontal and vertical analyses.

Delaney Corporation
Comparative Income Statements
For the Years Ended December 31

	2022	2021
Net sales	$598,000	$500,000
Cost of goods sold	477,000	420,000
Gross profit	121,000	80,000
Operating expenses	80,000	44,000
Net income	$ 41,000	$ 36,000

Instructions

a. Prepare a horizontal analysis of the income statement data for Delaney Corporation, using 2021 as a base. (Show the amounts of increase or decrease.)

b. Prepare a vertical analysis of the income statement data for Delaney Corporation for both years.

E13.7 (LO 3), AP Nordstrom, Inc. operates department stores in numerous states. Selected hypothetical financial statement data (in millions) for 2022 are presented below.

Compute liquidity ratios.

	End of Year	Beginning of Year
Cash and cash equivalents	$ 795	$ 72
Accounts receivable (net)	2,035	1,942
Inventory	898	900
Other current assets	326	303
Total current assets	$4,054	$3,217
Total current liabilities	$2,014	$1,601

For the year, net credit sales were $8,258 million, cost of goods sold was $5,328 million, and net cash provided by operating activities was $1,251 million.

Instructions

Compute the current ratio, accounts receivable turnover, average collection period, inventory turnover, and days in inventory at the end of the current year.

E13.8 (LO 3), AP Gwynn Incorporated had the following transactions involving current assets and current liabilities during February 2022.

Perform current ratio analysis.

Feb. 3 Collected accounts receivable of $15,000.
7 Purchased equipment for $23,000 cash.
11 Paid $3,000 for a 1-year insurance policy.
14 Paid accounts payable of $12,000.
18 Declared cash dividends, $4,000.

Additional information:
As of February 1, 2022, current assets were $120,000 and current liabilities were $40,000.

Instructions

Compute the current ratio as of the beginning of the month and after each transaction.

E13.9 (LO 3), AP Lendell Company has these comparative balance sheet data:

Lendell Company
Balance Sheets
December 31

	2022	2021
Cash	$ 15,000	$ 30,000
Accounts receivable (net)	70,000	60,000
Inventory	60,000	50,000
Plant assets (net)	200,000	180,000
	$345,000	$320,000
Accounts payable	$ 50,000	$ 60,000
Mortgage payable (15%)	100,000	100,000
Common stock, $10 par	140,000	120,000
Retained earnings	55,000	40,000
	$345,000	$320,000

Additional information for 2022:

1. Net income was $25,000.
2. Sales on account were $375,000. Sales returns and allowances amounted to $25,000.
3. Cost of goods sold was $198,000.
4. Net cash provided by operating activities was $48,000.
5. Capital expenditures were $25,000, and cash dividends were $10,000.

Instructions

Compute the following ratios at December 31, 2022.

a. Current ratio.
b. Accounts receivable turnover.
c. Average collection period.
d. Inventory turnover.
e. Days in inventory.
f. Free cash flow.

E13.10 (LO 3), AP Selected hypothetical comparative statement data for the giant bookseller **Barnes & Noble** are presented here. All balance sheet data are as of the end of the fiscal year (in millions).

	2022	2021
Net sales	$5,121.8	$5,286.7
Cost of goods sold	3,540.6	3,679.8
Net income	75.9	135.8
Accounts receivable	81.0	107.1
Inventory	1,203.5	1,358.2
Total assets	2,993.9	3,249.8
Total common stockholders' equity	921.6	1,074.7

Instructions

Compute the following ratios for 2022.

a. Profit margin.
b. Asset turnover.
c. Return on assets.
d. Return on common stockholders' equity.
e. Gross profit rate.

E13.11 (LO 3), AP Here is the income statement for Myers, Inc.

Myers, Inc.
Income Statement
For the Year Ended December 31, 2022

Sales revenue	$400,000
Cost of goods sold	230,000
Gross profit	170,000
Expenses (including $16,000 interest and $24,000 income taxes)	98,000
Net income	$ 72,000

Additional information:

1. Common stock outstanding January 1, 2022, was 32,000 shares, and 40,000 shares were outstanding at December 31, 2022.
2. The market price of Myers stock was $14 in 2022.
3. Cash dividends of $21,000 were paid, $5,000 of which were to preferred stockholders.

Instructions

Compute the following measures for 2022.

a. Earnings per share.
b. Price-earnings ratio.
c. Payout ratio.
d. Times interest earned.

E13.12 (LO 3), AP Panza Corporation experienced a fire on December 31, 2022, in which its financial records were partially destroyed. It has been able to salvage some of the records and has ascertained the following balances.

Compute amounts from ratios.

	December 31, 2022	December 31, 2021
Cash	$ 30,000	$ 10,000
Accounts receivable (net)	72,500	126,000
Inventory	200,000	180,000
Accounts payable	50,000	90,000
Notes payable	30,000	60,000
Common stock, $100 par	400,000	400,000
Retained earnings	113,500	101,000

Additional information:

1. The inventory turnover is 3.8 times.
2. The return on common stockholders' equity is 22%. The company had no additional paid-in capital.
3. The accounts receivable turnover is 11.2 times.
4. The return on assets is 18%.
5. Total assets at December 31, 2021, were $605,000.

Instructions

Compute the following for Panza Corporation.

a. Cost of goods sold for 2022.
b. Net credit sales for 2022.
c. Net income for 2022.
d. Total assets at December 31, 2022.

E13.13 (LO 3), AP The condensed financial statements of Ness Company for the years 2021 and 2022 are presented below.

Compute ratios.

Ness Company
Balance Sheets
December 31 (in thousands)

	2022	2021
Current assets		
Cash and cash equivalents	$ 330	$ 360
Accounts receivable (net)	470	400
Inventory	460	390
Prepaid expenses	130	160
Total current assets	1,390	1,310

	2022	2021
Property, plant, and equipment (net)	$ 410	$ 380
Investments	10	10
Intangibles and other assets	530	510
Total assets	$2,340	$2,210
Current liabilities	$ 820	$ 790
Long-term liabilities	480	380
Stockholders' equity—common	1,040	1,040
Total liabilities and stockholders' equity	$2,340	$2,210

Ness Company
Income Statements
For the Year Ended December 31 (in thousands)

	2022	2021
Sales revenue	$3,800	$3,460
Costs and expenses		
Cost of goods sold	970	890
Selling & administrative expenses	2,400	2,330
Interest expense	10	20
Total costs and expenses	3,380	3,240
Income before income taxes	420	220
Income tax expense	168	88
Net income	$ 252	$ 132

Compute the following ratios for 2022 and 2021.

a. Current ratio.

b. Inventory turnover. (Inventory on December 31, 2020, was $340.)

c. Profit margin.

d. Return on assets. (Assets on December 31, 2020, were $1,900.)

e. Return on common stockholders' equity. (Equity on December 31, 2020, was $900.)

f. Debt to assets ratio.

g. Times interest earned.

Problems: Set A

Prepare vertical analysis and comment on profitability.

P13.1A (LO 2, 3), AN Writing Here are comparative statement data for Duke Company and Lord Company, two competitors. All balance sheet data are as of December 31, 2022, and December 31, 2021.

	Duke Company		Lord Company	
	2022	2021	2022	2021
Net sales	$1,849,000		$546,000	
Cost of goods sold	1,063,200		289,000	
Operating expenses	240,000		82,000	
Interest expense	6,800		3,600	
Income tax expense	62,000		28,000	
Current assets	325,975	$312,410	83,336	$ 79,467
Plant assets (net)	526,800	500,000	139,728	125,812
Current liabilities	66,325	75,815	35,348	30,281
Long-term liabilities	113,990	90,000	29,620	25,000
Common stock, $10 par	500,000	500,000	120,000	120,000
Retained earnings	172,460	146,595	38,096	29,998

Instructions

a. Prepare a vertical analysis of the 2022 income statement data for Duke Company and Lord Company.

b. Comment on the relative profitability of the companies by computing the 2022 return on assets and the return on common stockholders' equity for both companies.

P13.2A (LO 3), AP The comparative statements of Wahlberg Company are presented here.

Compute ratios from balance sheets and income statements.

Wahlberg Company
Income Statements
For the Years Ended December 31

	2022	2021
Net sales	$1,890,540	$1,750,500
Cost of goods sold	1,058,540	1,006,000
Gross profit	832,000	744,500
Selling and administrative expenses	500,000	479,000
Income from operations	332,000	265,500
Other expenses and losses		
Interest expense	22,000	20,000
Income before income taxes	310,000	245,500
Income tax expense	92,000	73,000
Net income	$ 218,000	$ 172,500

Wahlberg Company
Balance Sheets
December 31

Assets	2022	2021
Current assets		
Cash	$ 60,100	$ 64,200
Debt investments (short-term)	74,000	50,000
Accounts receivable	117,800	102,800
Inventory	126,000	115,500
Total current assets	377,900	332,500
Plant assets (net)	649,000	520,300
Total assets	$1,026,900	$852,800
Liabilities and Stockholders' Equity		
Current liabilities		
Accounts payable	$ 160,000	$145,400
Income taxes payable	43,500	42,000
Total current liabilities	203,500	187,400
Bonds payable	220,000	200,000
Total liabilities	423,500	387,400
Stockholders' equity		
Common stock ($5 par)	290,000	300,000
Retained earnings	313,400	165,400
Total stockholders' equity	603,400	465,400
Total liabilities and stockholders' equity	$1,026,900	$852,800

All sales were on account. Net cash provided by operating activities for 2022 was $220,000. Capital expenditures were $136,000, and cash dividends were $70,000.

Instructions

Compute the following ratios for 2022.

a. Earnings per share.
b. Return on common stockholders' equity.
c. Return on assets.
d. Current ratio.

e. Accounts receivable turnover.
f. Average collection period.
g. Inventory turnover.
h. Days in inventory.
i. Times interest earned.
j. Asset turnover.
k. Debt to assets ratio.
l. Free cash flow.

Perform ratio analysis, and discuss changes in financial position and operating results.

P13.3A (LO 3), AN Writing Condensed balance sheet and income statement data for Jergan Corporation are presented here.

Jergan Corporation
Balance Sheets
December 31

	2022	2021	2020
Cash	$ 30,000	$ 20,000	$ 18,000
Accounts receivable (net)	50,000	45,000	48,000
Other current assets	90,000	95,000	64,000
Investments	55,000	70,000	45,000
Plant and equipment (net)	500,000	370,000	358,000
	$725,000	$600,000	$533,000
Current liabilities	$ 85,000	$ 80,000	$ 70,000
Long-term debt	145,000	85,000	50,000
Common stock, $10 par	320,000	310,000	300,000
Retained earnings	175,000	125,000	113,000
	$725,000	$600,000	$533,000

Jergan Corporation
Income Statements
For the Years Ended December 31

	2022	2021
Sales revenue	$740,000	$600,000
Less: Sales returns and allowances	40,000	30,000
Net sales	700,000	570,000
Cost of goods sold	425,000	350,000
Gross profit	275,000	220,000
Operating expenses (including income taxes)	180,000	150,000
Net income	$ 95,000	$ 70,000

Additional information:

1. The market price of Jergan's common stock was $7.00, $7.50, and $8.50 for 2020, 2021, and 2022, respectively.
2. You must compute dividends paid. All dividends were paid in cash.

Instructions

a. Compute the following ratios for 2021 and 2022.
   1. Profit margin.
   2. Gross profit rate.
   3. Asset turnover.
   4. Earnings per share.
   5. Price-earnings ratio.
   6. Payout ratio.
   7. Debt to assets ratio.

b. Based on the ratios calculated, discuss briefly the improvement or lack thereof in the financial position and operating results from 2021 to 2022 of Jergan Corporation.

Compute ratios; comment on overall liquidity and profitability.

P13.4A (LO 3), AN The following financial information is for Priscoll Company.

Priscoll Company
Balance Sheets
December 31

Assets	2022	2021
Cash	$ 70,000	$ 65,000
Debt investments (short-term)	55,000	40,000
Accounts receivable	104,000	90,000
Inventory	230,000	165,000
Prepaid expenses	25,000	23,000
Land	130,000	130,000
Building and equipment (net)	260,000	185,000
Total assets	$874,000	$698,000

Liabilities and Stockholders' Equity		
Notes payable	$170,000	$120,000
Accounts payable	65,000	52,000
Accrued liabilities	40,000	40,000
Bonds payable, due 2025	250,000	170,000
Common stock, $10 par	200,000	200,000
Retained earnings	149,000	116,000
Total liabilities and stockholders' equity	$874,000	$698,000

Priscoll Company
Income Statements
For the Years Ended December 31

	2022	2021
Sales revenue	$882,000	$790,000
Cost of goods sold	640,000	575,000
Gross profit	242,000	215,000
Operating expenses	190,000	167,000
Net income	$ 52,000	$ 48,000

Additional information:

1. Inventory at the beginning of 2021 was $115,000.
2. Accounts receivable (net) at the beginning of 2021 were $86,000.
3. Total assets at the beginning of 2021 were $660,000.
4. No common stock transactions occurred during 2021 or 2022.
5. All sales were on account.

Instructions

a. Indicate, by using ratios, the change in liquidity and profitability of Priscoll Company from 2021 to 2022. (*Note:* Not all profitability ratios can be computed nor can cash-basis ratios be computed.)

b. The following are three independent situations and a ratio that may be affected. For each situation, compute the affected ratio (1) as of December 31, 2022, and (2) as of December 31, 2023, after giving effect to the situation.

Situation	Ratio
1. 18,000 shares of common stock were sold at par on July 1, 2023. Net income for 2023 was $54,000.	Return on common stockholders' equity
2. All of the notes payable were paid in 2023. All other liabilities remained at their December 31, 2022, levels. Total assets on December 31, 2023, were $900,000.	Debt to assets ratio
3. The market price of common stock was $9 and $12 on December 31, 2022 and 2023, respectively. Net income for 2023 was $54,000.	Price-earnings ratio

CHAPTER 13 Financial Analysis: The Big Picture

Compute selected ratios, and compare liquidity, profitability, and solvency for two companies.

P13.5A (LO 3), AN Selected hypothetical financial data of **Target** and **Wal-Mart** for 2022 are presented here (in millions).

	Target Corporation	Wal-Mart Stores, Inc.
Income Statement Data for Year		
Net sales	$65,357	$408,214
Cost of goods sold	45,583	304,657
Selling and administrative expenses	15,101	79,607
Interest expense	707	2,065
Other income (expense)	(94)	(411)
Income tax expense	1,384	7,139
Net income	$ 2,488	$ 14,335
Balance Sheet Data (End of Year)		
Current assets	$18,424	$ 48,331
Noncurrent assets	26,109	122,375
Total assets	$44,533	$170,706
Current liabilities	$11,327	$ 55,561
Long-term debt	17,859	44,089
Total stockholders' equity	15,347	71,056
Total liabilities and stockholders' equity	$44,533	$170,706
Beginning-of-Year Balances		
Total assets	$44,106	$163,429
Total stockholders' equity	13,712	65,682
Current liabilities	10,512	55,390
Total liabilities	30,394	97,747
Other Data		
Average net accounts receivable	$ 7,525	$ 4,025
Average inventory	6,942	33,836
Net cash provided by operating activities	5,881	26,249
Capital expenditures	1,729	12,184
Dividends	496	4,217

Instructions

a. For each company, compute the following ratios.

1. Current ratio.
2. Accounts receivable turnover.
3. Average collection period.
4. Inventory turnover.
5. Days in inventory.
6. Profit margin.
7. Asset turnover.
8. Return on assets.
9. Return on common stockholders' equity.
10. Debt to assets ratio.
11. Times interest earned.
12. Free cash flow.

b. Compare the liquidity, solvency, and profitability of the two companies.

Continuing Case

© leungchopan/ Shutterstock

Cookie Creations

(*Note:* This is a continuation of the Cookie Creations case from Chapters 1 through 12.)

CC13 Natalie and Curtis have comparative balance sheets and income statements for Cookie & Coffee Creations Inc. They have been told that they can use these financial statements to prepare horizontal and vertical analyses, to calculate financial ratios, to analyze how their business is doing, and to make some decisions they have been considering.

Go to WileyPLUS for complete case details and instructions.

Expand Your Critical Thinking

Financial Reporting Problem: Apple Inc.

CT13.1 Your parents are considering investing in **Apple Inc.** common stock. They ask you, as an accounting expert, to make an analysis of the company for them. Financial statements of Apple are presented in Appendix A. The complete annual report, including the notes to its financial statements, is available at the company's website.

Instructions

a. Make a 5-year trend analysis, using 2013 as the base year, of (1) net sales and (2) net income. Comment on the significance of the trend results.

b. Compute for 2017 and 2016 the (1) debt to assets ratio and (2) times interest earned. (See Note 3 for interest expense.) How would you evaluate Apple's long-term solvency?

c. Compute for 2017 and 2016 the (1) profit margin, (2) asset turnover, (3) return on assets, and (4) return on common stockholders' equity. How would you evaluate Apple's profitability? Total assets at September 26, 2015, were $290,479 million and total stockholders' equity at September 26, 2015, was $119,355 million.

d. What information outside the annual report may also be useful to your parents in making a decision about Apple?

Comparative Analysis Problem: Columbia Sportswear Company vs. VF Corporation

CT13.2 The financial statements of **Columbia Sportswear Company** are presented in Appendix B. Financial statements of **VF Corporation** are presented in Appendix C.

Instructions

a. Based on the information in the financial statements, determine each of the following for each company:
   1. The percentage increase (i) in net sales and (ii) in net income from 2015 to 2016.
   2. The percentage increase (i) in total assets and (ii) in total stockholders' equity from 2015 to 2016.
   3. The basic earnings per share for 2016.

b. What conclusions concerning the two companies can be drawn from these data?

Comparative Analysis Problem: Amazon.com, Inc. vs. Wal-Mart Stores, Inc.

CT13.3 The financial statements of **Amazon.com, Inc.** are presented in Appendix D. Financial statements of **Wal-Mart Stores, Inc.** are presented in Appendix E.

Instructions

a. Based on the information in the financial statements, determine each of the following for each company:
   1. The percentage increase (i) in net sales and (ii) in net income between the two most recent years provided.
   2. The percentage increase (i) in total assets and (ii) in total stockholders' equity between the two most recent years provided.
   3. The basic earnings per share for the most recent year provided.

b. What conclusions concerning the two companies can be drawn from these data?

Interpreting Financial Statements

CT13.4 **The Coca-Cola Company** and **PepsiCo, Inc.** provide refreshments to every corner of the world. Selected data from hypothetical consolidated financial statements for The Coca-Cola Company and for PepsiCo, Inc. are presented here (in millions).

	Coca-Cola	PepsiCo
Total current assets	$17,551	$12,571
Total current liabilities	13,721	8,756
Net sales	30,990	43,232
Cost of goods sold	11,088	20,099
Net income	6,824	5,946
Average (net) accounts receivable for the year	3,424	4,654

	Coca-Cola	PepsiCo
Average inventories for the year	$ 2,271	$ 2,570
Average total assets	44,595	37,921
Average common stockholders' equity	22,636	14,556
Average current liabilities	13,355	8,772
Average total liabilities	21,960	23,466
Total assets	48,671	39,848
Total liabilities	23,872	23,044
Income taxes	2,040	2,100
Interest expense	355	397
Net cash provided by operating activities	8,186	6,796
Capital expenditures	1,993	2,128
Cash dividends	3,800	2,732

Instructions

a. Compute the following liquidity ratios for Coca-Cola and for PepsiCo and comment on the relative liquidity of the two competitors.

1. Current ratio.
2. Accounts receivable turnover.
3. Average collection period.
4. Inventory turnover.
5. Days in inventory.

b. Compute the following solvency ratios for the two companies and comment on the relative solvency of the two competitors.

1. Debt to assets ratio.
2. Times interest earned.
3. Free cash flow.

c. Compute the following profitability ratios for the two companies and comment on the relative profitability of the two competitors.

1. Profit margin.
2. Asset turnover.
3. Return on assets.
4. Return on common stockholders' equity.

Real-World Focus

CT13.5 You can use the Internet to employ comparative data and industry data to evaluate a company's performance and financial position.

Instructions

Identify two competing companies and then go to the **MarketWatch** website. Type in the company name, for example, **Best Buy**, in the search box and then use the information from the Profile tab to answer the following questions.

a. Evaluate the company's liquidity relative to the industry averages and to the competitor that you chose.

b. Evaluate the company's solvency relative to the industry averages and to the competitor that you chose.

c. Evaluate the company's profitability relative to the industry averages and to the competitor that you chose.

CT13.6 The April 25, 2012, edition of the *Wall Street Journal* contains an article by Spencer Jakab entitled "Amazon's Valuation Is Hard to Justify."

Instructions

Read the article and answer the following questions.

a. Explain what is meant by the statement that "On a split-adjusted basis, today's share price is the equivalent of $1,166."

b. The article says that **Amazon.com** nearly doubled its capital spending on items such as fulfillment centers (sophisticated warehouses where it finds, packages, and ships goods to customers). Discuss the implications that this spending would have on the company's return on assets in the short-term and in the long-term.

c. How does Amazon's P-E ratio compare to that of **Apple**, **Netflix**, and **Wal-Mart**? What does this suggest about investors' expectations about Amazon's future earnings?

d. What factor does the article cite as a possible hurdle that might reduce Amazon's ability to raise its operating margin back to previous levels?

Decision-Making Across the Organization

CT13.7 You are a loan officer for White Sands Bank of Taos. Paul Jason, president of P. Jason Corporation, has just left your office. He is interested in an 8-year loan to expand the company's operations. The borrowed funds would be used to purchase new equipment. As evidence of the company's debtworthiness, Jason provided you with the following facts.

	2022	2021
Current ratio	3.1	2.1
Asset turnover	2.8	2.2
Net income	Up 32%	Down 8%
Earnings per share	$3.30	$2.50

Jason is a very insistent (some would say pushy) man. When you told him that you would need additional information before making your decision, he acted offended and said, "What more could you possibly want to know?" You responded that, at a minimum, you would need complete, audited financial statements.

Instructions

With the class divided into groups, answer the following.

a. Explain why you would want the financial statements to be audited.

b. Discuss the implications of the ratios provided for the lending decision you are to make. That is, does the information paint a favorable picture? Are these ratios relevant to the decision?

c. List three other ratios that you would want to calculate for this company, and explain why you would use each.

Communication Activity

CT13.8 Larry Dundee is the chief executive officer of Palmer Electronics. Dundee is an expert engineer but a novice in accounting. Dundee asks you, as an accounting student, to explain (a) the bases for comparison in analyzing Palmer's financial statements and (b) the limitations, if any, in financial statement analysis.

Instructions

Write a memo to Larry Dundee that explains the basis for comparison and the factors affecting quality of earnings.

Ethics Case

CT13.9 René Kelly, president of RL Industries, wishes to issue a press release to bolster her company's image and maybe even its stock price, which has been gradually falling. As controller, you have been asked to provide a list of 20 financial ratios and other operating statistics for RL Industries' first-quarter financials and operations.

Two days after you provide the data requested, Erin Lourdes, the public relations director of RL, asks you to prove the accuracy of the financial and operating data contained in the press release written by the president and edited by Erin. In the news release, the president highlights the sales increase of 25% over last year's first quarter and the positive change in the current ratio from 1.5:1 last year to 3:1 this year. She also emphasizes that production was up 50% over the prior year's first quarter.

You note that the release contains only positive or improved ratios and none of the negative or deteriorated ratios. For instance, no mention is made that the debt to assets ratio has increased from 35% to 55%, that inventories are up 89%, and that although the current ratio improved, the accounts receivable turnover fell from 12 to 9. Nor is there any mention that the reported profit for the quarter would have been a loss had not the estimated lives of RL plant and machinery been increased by 30%. Erin emphasized, "The Pres wants this release by early this afternoon."

Instructions

a. Who are the stakeholders in this situation?

b. Is there anything unethical in the president's actions?

c. Should you as controller remain silent? Does Erin have any responsibility?

All About You

CT13.10 In this chapter, you learned how to use many tools for performing a financial analysis of a company. When making personal investments, however, it is most likely that you won't be buying stocks and bonds in individual companies. Instead, when most people want to invest in stock, they buy mutual funds. By investing in a mutual fund, you reduce your risk because the fund diversifies by buying the stock of a variety of different companies, bonds, and other investments, depending on the stated goals of the fund.

Before you invest in a fund, you will need to decide what type of fund you want. For example, do you want a fund that has the potential of high growth (but also high risk), or are you looking for lower risk and a steady stream of income? Do you want a fund that invests only in U.S. companies, or do you want one that invests globally? Many resources are available to help you with these types of decisions.

Instructions

Do an Internet search on "Motley Fool Here's How to Determine Your Ideal Asset Allocation Strategy" and then complete the investment allocation questionnaire. Add up your total points to determine the type of investment fund that would be appropriate for you.

FASB Codification Activity

CT13.11 If your school has a subscription to the FASB Codification, log in and prepare responses to the following. Use the Master Glossary for determining the proper definitions.

   a. Discontinued operations.
   b. Comprehensive income.

A Look at IFRS

LEARNING OBJECTIVE 4
Compare financial statement analysis and income statement presentation under GAAP and IFRS.

The tools of financial statement analysis are the same throughout the world. Techniques such as vertical and horizontal analysis, for example, are tools used by analysts regardless of whether GAAP- or IFRS-related financial statements are being evaluated. In addition, the ratios provided in the text are the same ones that are used internationally.

As in GAAP, the income statement is a required statement under IFRS. In addition, the content and presentation of an IFRS income statement is similar to the one used for GAAP. *IAS 1* (revised), "Presentation of Financial Statements," provides general guidelines for the reporting of income statement information. In general, the differences in the presentation of financial statement information are relatively minor.

Key Points

Following are the key similarities between GAAP and IFRS as related to financial statement analysis and income statement presentation. There are no significant differences between the two standards.

- The tools of financial statement analysis covered in this chapter are universal and therefore no significant differences exist in the analysis methods used.
- The basic objectives of the income statement are the same under both GAAP and IFRS. As indicated in the text, a very important objective is to ensure that users of the income statement can evaluate the sustainable income of the company. Thus, both the IASB and the FASB are interested in distinguishing normal levels of income from unusual items in order to better predict a company's future profitability.
- The basic accounting for discontinued operations is the same under IFRS and GAAP.
- The accounting for changes in accounting principles and changes in accounting estimates are the same for both GAAP and IFRS.
- Both GAAP and IFRS follow the same approach in reporting comprehensive income.

IFRS Practice

IFRS Self-Test Questions

1. The basic tools of financial analysis are the same under both GAAP and IFRS **except** that:
   a. horizontal analysis cannot be done because the format of the statements is sometimes different.
   b. analysis is different because vertical analysis cannot be done under IFRS.
   c. the current ratio cannot be computed because current liabilities are often reported before current assets in IFRS statements of position.
   d. None of the above.

2. Presentation of comprehensive income must be reported under IFRS in:
   a. the statement of stockholders' equity.
   b. the income statement ending with net income.
   c. the notes to the financial statements.
   d. a statement of comprehensive income.

3. In preparing its income statement for 2022, Parmalane assembles the following information.

Sales revenue	$500,000
Cost of goods sold	300,000
Operating expenses	40,000
Loss on discontinued operations	20,000

   Ignoring income taxes, what is Parmalane's income from continuing operations for 2022 under IFRS?
   a. $260,000.
   b. $250,000.
   c. $240,000.
   d. $160,000.

International Financial Reporting Problem: Louis Vuitton

IFRS13.1 The financial statements of **Louis Vuitton** are presented in Appendix F. The complete annual report, including the notes to its financial statements, is available at the company's website.

Instructions

Use the company's **2016 annual report** to answer the following questions.

a. What was the company's profit margin for 2016? Has it increased or decreased from 2015?
b. What was the company's operating profit for 2016?
c. The company reported comprehensive income of €4,543 billion in 2016. What are the other comprehensive gains and losses recorded in 2016?

Answers to IFRS Self-Test Questions

1. d **2.** d **3.** d

CHAPTER 14

Managerial Accounting

Chapter Preview

This chapter focuses on issues illustrated in the following Feature Story about **Current Designs** and its parent company **Wenonah Canoe**. To succeed, the company needs to determine and control the costs of material, labor, and overhead, and understand the relationship between costs and profits. Managers often make decisions that determine their company's fate—and their own. Managers are evaluated on the results of their decisions. Managerial accounting provides tools to assist management in making decisions and to evaluate the effectiveness of those decisions.

Feature Story

Just Add Water ... and Paddle

Mike Cichanowski grew up on the Mississippi River in Winona, Minnesota. At a young age, he learned to paddle a canoe so he could explore the river. Before long, Mike began crafting his own canoes from bent wood and fiberglass in his dad's garage. Then, when his canoe-making shop outgrew the garage, he moved it into an old warehouse. When that was going to be torn down, Mike came to a critical juncture in his life. He took out a bank loan and built his own small shop, giving birth to the company **Wenonah Canoe**.

Wenonah Canoe soon became known as a pioneer in developing techniques to get the most out of new materials such as plastics, composites, and carbon fibers—maximizing strength while minimizing weight.

In the 1990s, as kayaking became popular, Mike made another critical decision when he acquired **Current Designs**, a premier Canadian kayak manufacturer. This venture allowed

Wenonah to branch out with new product lines while providing Current Designs with much-needed capacity expansion and manufacturing expertise. Mike moved Current Designs' headquarters to Minnesota and made a big (and potentially risky) investment in a new production facility. Today, the company's 90 employees produce about 12,000 canoes and kayaks per year. These are sold across the country and around the world.

Mike will tell you that business success is "a three-legged stool." The first leg is the knowledge and commitment to make a great product. Wenonah's canoes and Current Designs' kayaks are widely regarded as among the very best. The second leg is the ability to sell your product. Mike's company started off making great canoes, but it took a little longer to figure out how to sell them. The third leg is not something that most of you would immediately associate with entrepreneurial success. It is what goes on behind the scenes—accounting. Good accounting information is absolutely critical to the countless decisions, big and small, that ensure the survival and growth of the company.

Bottom line: No matter how good your product is, and no matter how many units you sell, if you don't have a firm grip on your numbers, you are up a creek without a paddle.

Source: www.wenonah.com.

 Watch the *What Is Managerial Accounting?* video in WileyPLUS for an introduction to managerial accounting and the topics presented in the remaining chapters.

Chapter Outline

LEARNING OBJECTIVES

LO 1 Identify the features of managerial accounting and the functions of management.	• Comparing managerial and financial accounting • Management functions • Organizational structure	**DO IT! 1** Managerial Accounting Overview
LO 2 Describe the classes of manufacturing costs and the differences between product and period costs.	• Manufacturing costs • Product vs. period costs • Illustration of cost concepts	**DO IT! 2** Managerial Cost Concepts
LO 3 Demonstrate how to compute cost of goods manufactured and prepare financial statements for a manufacturer.	• Income statement • Cost of goods manufactured • Cost of goods manufactured schedule • Balance sheet	**DO IT! 3** Cost of Goods Manufactured
LO 4 Discuss trends in managerial accounting.	• Service industries • Value chain • Balanced scorecard • Business ethics • Corporate social responsibility	**DO IT! 4** Trends in Managerial Accounting

Go to the Review and Practice section at the end of the chapter for a targeted summary and practice applications with solutions.
Visit WileyPLUS for additional tutorials and practice opportunities.

Managerial Accounting Basics

> **LEARNING OBJECTIVE 1**
> Identify the features of managerial accounting and the functions of management.

Managerial accounting provides economic and financial information for managers and other internal users. The skills that you learn in this course will be vital to your future success in business. You don't believe us? Let's look at some examples of some of the crucial activities of employees at **Current Designs** and where those activities are addressed in this text.

In order to know whether it is making a profit, Current Designs needs accurate information about the cost of each kayak (Chapters 15, 16, and 17). To be profitable, Current Designs adjusts the number of kayaks it produces in response to changes in economic conditions and consumer tastes. It needs to understand how changes in the number of kayaks it produces impact its production costs and profitability (Chapters 18 and 19). Further, Current Designs' managers often consider alternative courses of action. For example, should the company accept a special order from a customer, produce a particular kayak component internally or outsource it, or continue or discontinue a particular product line (Chapter 20)? Finally, one of the most important and most difficult decisions is what price to charge for the kayaks (Chapter 21).

In order to plan for the future, Current Designs prepares budgets (Chapter 22), and it then compares its budgeted numbers with its actual results to evaluate performance and identify areas that need to change (Chapters 23 and 24). Finally, it sometimes needs to make substantial investment decisions, such as the building of a new plant or the purchase of new equipment (Chapter 25).

Someday, you are going to face decisions just like these. You may end up in sales, marketing, management, production, or finance. You may work for a company that provides medical care, produces software, or serves up mouth-watering meals. No matter what your position is and no matter what your product, the skills you acquire in this class will increase your chances of business success. Put another way, in business you can either guess or you can make an informed decision. As a CEO of **Microsoft** once noted: "If you're supposed to be making money in business and supposed to be satisfying customers and building market share, there are numbers that characterize those things. And if somebody can't speak to me quantitatively about it, then I'm nervous." This course gives you the skills you need to quantify information so you can make informed business decisions.

Comparing Managerial and Financial Accounting

There are both similarities and differences between managerial and financial accounting. First, each field of accounting deals with the economic events of a business. For example, *determining* the unit cost of manufacturing a product is part of managerial accounting. *Reporting* the total cost of goods manufactured and sold is part of financial accounting. In addition, both managerial and financial accounting require that a company's economic events be quantified and communicated to interested parties. **Illustration 14.1** summarizes the principal differences between financial accounting and managerial accounting.

Management Functions

Managers' activities and responsibilities can be classified into three broad functions:

1. Planning.
2. Directing.
3. Controlling.

In performing these functions, managers make decisions that have a significant impact on the organization.

ILLUSTRATION 14.1 Differences between financial and managerial accounting

Feature	Financial Accounting	Managerial Accounting
Primary Users of Reports	External users: stockholders, creditors, and regulators.	Internal users: officers and managers.
Types and Frequency of Reports	Financial statements. Quarterly and annually.	Internal reports. As frequently as needed.
Purpose of Reports	General-purpose.	Special-purpose for specific decisions.
Content of Reports	Pertains to business as a whole. Highly aggregated (condensed). Limited to double-entry accounting and cost data. Generally accepted accounting principles.	Pertains to subunits of the business. Very detailed. Extends beyond double-entry accounting to any relevant data. Evaluated based on relevance to decisions.
Verification Process	Audited by CPA.	No independent audits.

Planning requires managers to look ahead and to establish objectives. These objectives are often diverse: maximizing short-term profits and market share, maintaining a commitment to environmental protection, and contributing to social programs. For example, **Hewlett-Packard**, in an attempt to gain a stronger foothold in the computer industry, greatly reduced its prices to compete with **Dell**. A key objective of management is to **add value** to the business under its control. Value is usually measured by the price of the company's stock and by the potential selling price of the company.

Directing involves coordinating a company's diverse activities and human resources to produce a smooth-running operation. This function relates to implementing planned objectives and providing necessary incentives to motivate employees. For example, manufacturers such as **Campbell Soup Company**, **General Motors**, and **Dell** need to coordinate purchasing, manufacturing, warehousing, and selling. Service corporations such as **American Airlines**, **Federal Express**, and **AT&T** coordinate scheduling, sales, service, and acquisitions of equipment and supplies. Directing also involves selecting executives, appointing managers and supervisors, and hiring and training employees.

The third management function, **controlling**, is the process of keeping the company's activities on track. In controlling operations, managers determine whether planned goals are met. When there are deviations from targeted objectives, managers decide what changes are needed to get back on track. Scandals at companies like **Enron**, **Lucent**, and **Xerox** attest to the fact that companies need adequate controls to ensure that the company develops and distributes accurate information.

How do managers achieve control? A smart manager in a very small operation can make personal observations, ask good questions, and know how to evaluate the answers. But using this approach in a larger organization would result in chaos. Imagine the president of **Current Designs** attempting to determine whether the company is meeting its planned objectives without some record of what has happened and what is expected to occur. Thus, large businesses typically use a formal system of evaluation. These systems include such features as budgets, responsibility centers, and performance evaluation reports—all of which are features of managerial accounting.

Decision-making is not a separate management function. Rather, it is the outcome of the exercise of good judgment in planning, directing, and controlling.

Organizational Structure

Most companies prepare **organization charts** to show the interrelationships of activities and the delegation of authority and responsibility within the company. **Illustration 14.2** shows a typical organization chart.

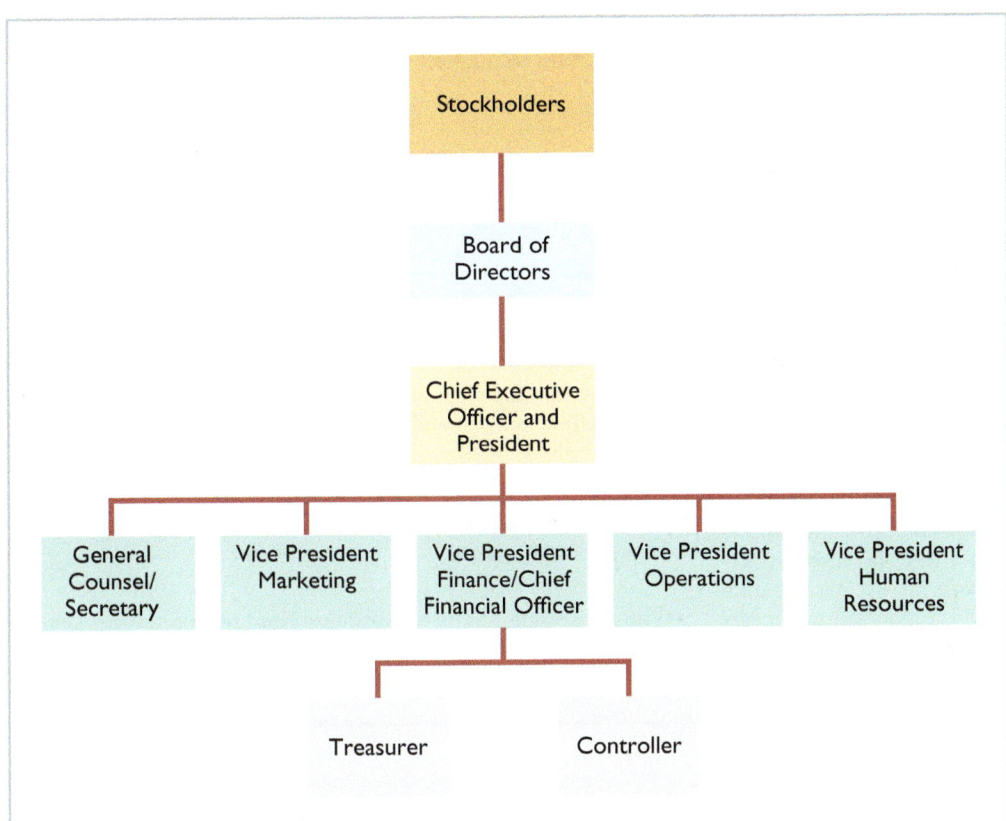

ILLUSTRATION 14.2

A typical corporate organization chart

Stockholders own the corporation, but they manage it indirectly through a **board of directors** they elect. The board formulates the operating policies for the company or organization. The board also selects officers, such as a president and one or more vice presidents, to execute policy and to perform daily management functions.

The **chief executive officer (CEO)** has overall responsibility for managing the business. As the organization chart shows, the CEO delegates responsibilities to other officers.

Responsibilities within the company are frequently classified as either line or staff positions. Employees with **line positions** are directly involved in the company's primary revenue-generating operating activities. Examples of line positions include the vice president of operations, vice president of marketing, plant managers, supervisors, and production personnel. Employees with **staff positions** are involved in activities that support the efforts of the line employees. In a company like **General Electric** or **Facebook**, employees in finance, legal, and human resources have staff positions. While activities of staff employees are vital to the company, these employees are nonetheless there to serve the line employees who engage in the company's primary operations.

The **chief financial officer (CFO)** is responsible for all of the accounting and finance issues the company faces. The CFO is supported by the **controller** and the **treasurer**. The controller's responsibilities include (1) maintaining the accounting records, (2) ensuring an adequate system of internal control, and (3) preparing financial statements, tax returns, and internal reports. The treasurer has custody of the corporation's funds and is responsible for maintaining the company's cash position.

Also serving the CFO is the internal audit staff. The staff's responsibilities include reviewing the reliability and integrity of financial information provided by the controller and treasurer. Staff members also ensure that internal control systems are functioning properly to safeguard corporate assets. In addition, they investigate compliance with policies and regulations. In many companies, these staff members also determine whether resources are used in the most economical and efficient fashion.

The vice president of operations oversees employees with line positions. For example, the company might have multiple plant managers, each of whom reports to the vice president of operations. Each plant also has department managers, such as fabricating, painting, and shipping, each of whom reports to the plant manager.

Management Insight   DPR Construction

Sam Edwards/ Caiaimage/Getty Images

Does a Company Need a CEO?

Can a company function without a person at the top? Nearly all companies have a CEO although some, such as **Oracle**, **Chipotle**, and **Whole Foods**, have operated with two people in the CEO position. **Samsung** even had three CEOs at the same time. On the other hand, **Abercrombie and Fitch** operated for more than two years without a CEO because its CEO unexpectedly quit and a suitable replacement was hard to find. In fact, some companies replace the CEO position with a management committee. These companies feel this structure improves decision-making and increases collaboration. For example, the 4,000 employees of **DPR Construction** are overseen by an eight-person committee. Committee members are rotated off gradually but then continue to advise current members. The company notes that this approach provides more continuity over time than the sometimes sudden and harsh changes that occur when CEOs are replaced.

Source: Rachel Feintzeig, "Companies Manage with No CEO," *Wall Street Journal* (December 13, 2016).

What are some of the advantages cited by companies that choose a structure that lacks a CEO? (Go to WileyPLUS for this answer and additional questions).

ACTION PLAN

- Understand that managerial accounting is a field of accounting that provides economic and financial information for managers and other internal users.
- Understand that financial accounting provides information for external users.
- Analyze which users require which different types of information.

DO IT! 1 | Managerial Accounting Overview

Indicate whether the following statements are true or false. If false, explain why.

1. Managerial accountants have a single role within an organization: collecting and reporting costs to management.
2. Financial accounting reports are general-purpose and intended for external users.
3. Managerial accounting reports are special-purpose and issued as frequently as needed.
4. Managers' activities and responsibilities can be classified into three broad functions: cost accounting, budgeting, and internal control.
5. Managerial accounting reports must now comply with generally accepted accounting principles (GAAP).

Solution

1. False. Managerial accountants do determine product costs, but they are also responsible for evaluating how well the company employs its resources. As a result, when the company makes critical strategic decisions, managerial accountants serve as team members alongside personnel from production, marketing, and engineering.
2. True.
3. True.
4. False. Managers' activities are classified into three broad functions: planning, directing, and controlling. Planning requires managers to look ahead to establish objectives. Directing involves coordinating a company's diverse activities and human resources to produce a smooth-running operation. Controlling keeps the company's activities on track.
5. False. Managerial accounting reports are for internal use and thus do not have to comply with GAAP.

Related exercise material: **BE14.1, BE14.2, DO IT! 14.1, and E14.1.**

Managerial Cost Concepts

> **LEARNING OBJECTIVE 2**
> Describe the classes of manufacturing costs and the differences between product and period costs.

In order for managers at **Current Designs** to plan, direct, and control operations effectively, they need good information. One very important type of information relates to costs. Managers should ask questions such as the following.

1. What costs are involved in making a product or performing a service?
2. If we decrease production volume, will costs change?
3. What impact will automation have on total costs?
4. How can we best control costs?

To answer these questions, managers obtain and analyze reliable and relevant cost information. The first step is to understand the various cost categories that companies use.

Manufacturing Costs

Manufacturing consists of activities and processes that convert raw materials into finished goods. Contrast this type of operation with merchandising, which sells products in the form in which they are purchased. Manufacturing costs incurred to produce a product are classified as direct materials, direct labor, and manufacturing overhead.

Direct Materials

To obtain the materials that will be converted into the finished product, the manufacturer purchases raw materials. **Raw materials** are the basic materials and parts used in the manufacturing process.

Raw materials that can be physically and directly associated with the finished product during the manufacturing process are **direct materials**. Examples include flour in the baking of bread, syrup in the bottling of soft drinks, and steel in the making of automobiles. A primary direct material of many Current Designs' kayaks is polyethylene powder. Some of its high-performance kayaks use Kevlar®.

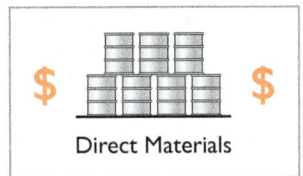
Direct Materials

Some raw materials cannot be easily associated with the finished product. These are called indirect materials. **Indirect materials** have one of two characteristics. (1) They do not physically become part of the finished product (such as polishing compounds used by Current Designs for the finishing touches on kayaks). Or, (2) they are impractical to trace to the finished product because their physical association with the finished product is too small in terms of cost (such as cotter pins and lock washers used in kayak rudder assembly). Companies account for indirect materials as part of **manufacturing overhead**.

Direct Labor

The work of factory employees that can be physically and directly associated with converting raw materials into finished goods is **direct labor**. Bottlers at **Coca-Cola**, bakers at **Sara Lee**, and equipment operators at **Current Designs** are employees whose activities are usually classified as direct labor. **Indirect labor** refers to the work of employees that has no physical association with the finished product or for which it is impractical to trace costs to the goods produced. Examples include wages of factory maintenance people, factory time-keepers, and factory supervisors. Like indirect materials, companies classify indirect labor as **manufacturing overhead**.

Direct Labor

Manufacturing Overhead

Manufacturing Overhead

Manufacturing overhead consists of costs that are indirectly associated with the manufacture of the finished product (see **Alternative Terminology**). Overhead costs also include manufacturing costs that cannot be classified as direct materials or direct labor. Manufacturing overhead includes indirect materials, indirect labor, depreciation on factory buildings and machines, and insurance, taxes, and maintenance on factory facilities.

One study of manufactured goods found the following magnitudes of the three different product costs as a percentage of the total product cost: direct materials 54%, direct labor 13%, and manufacturing overhead 33%. Note that the direct labor component is the smallest. This component of product cost is dropping substantially because of automation. Companies are working hard to increase productivity by decreasing labor. In some companies, direct labor has become as little as 5% of the total cost.

Tracing direct materials and direct labor costs to specific products is fairly straightforward. Good recordkeeping can tell a company how much plastic it used in making each type of gear, or how many hours of factory labor it took to assemble a part. But allocating overhead costs to specific products presents problems. How much of the purchasing agent's salary is attributable to the hundreds of different products made in the same plant? What about the grease that keeps the machines running smoothly, or the computers that make sure paychecks are generated on time? Boiled down to its simplest form, the question becomes: Which products cause the incurrence of which costs? In subsequent chapters, we show various methods of allocating overhead to products.

ALTERNATIVE TERMINOLOGY

Some companies use terms such as *factory overhead*, *indirect manufacturing costs*, and *burden* instead of manufacturing overhead.

Product versus Period Costs

Each of the manufacturing cost components—direct materials, direct labor, and manufacturing overhead—are product costs. As the term suggests, **product costs** are costs that are a necessary and integral part of producing the finished product (see **Alternative Terminology**). Companies record product costs, when incurred, as an asset called inventory. These costs do not become expenses until the company sells the finished goods inventory. At that point, the company records the expense as cost of goods sold.

Period costs are costs that are matched with the revenue of a specific time period rather than included as part of the cost of a salable product. These are nonmanufacturing costs. Period costs include selling and administrative expenses. In order to determine net income, companies deduct these costs from revenues in the period in which they are incurred.

Illustration 14.3 summarizes these relationships and cost terms. Our main concern in this chapter is with product costs.

ALTERNATIVE TERMINOLOGY

Product costs are also called *inventoriable* costs.

ILLUSTRATION 14.3

Product versus period costs

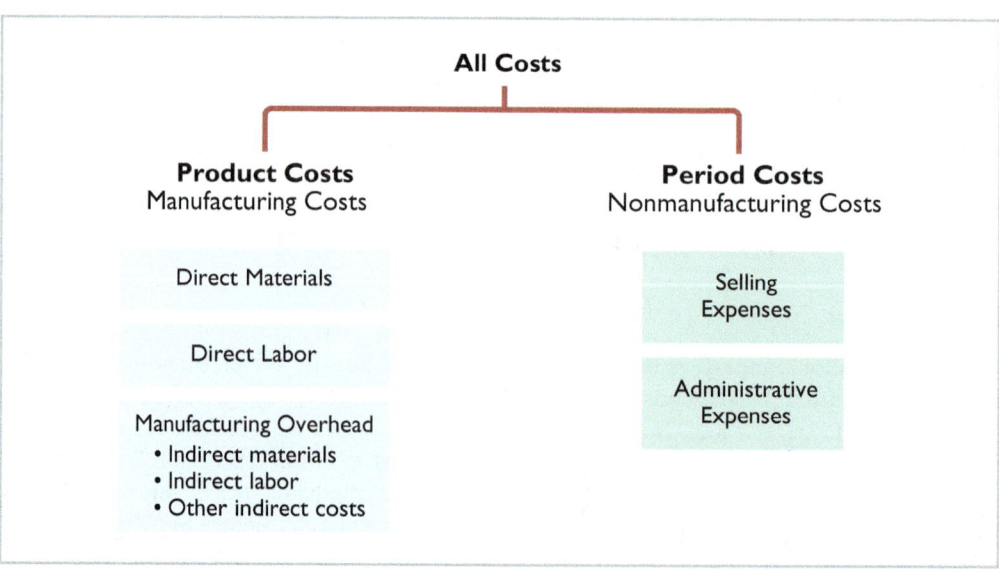

Illustration of Cost Concepts

To improve your understanding of cost concepts, we illustrate them here through an extended example. Suppose you started your own snowboard factory, Terrain Park Boards. Think that's impossible? **Burton Snowboards** was started by Jake Burton Carpenter, when he was only 23 years old. Jake initially experimented with 100 different prototype designs before settling on a final design. Then Jake, along with two relatives and a friend, started making 50 boards per day in Londonderry, Vermont. Unfortunately, while they made a lot of boards in their first year, they were only able to sell 300 of them. To get by during those early years, Jake taught tennis and tended bar to pay the bills.

Here are some of the costs that your snowboard factory, Terrain Park Boards, would incur.

1. The materials cost of each snowboard (wood cores, fiberglass, resins, metal screw holes, metal edges, and ink) is $30.
2. The labor costs (for example, to trim and shape each board using jig saws and band saws) are $40.
3. Depreciation on the factory building and equipment (for example, presses, grinding machines, and lacquer machines) used to make the snowboards is $25,000 per year.
4. Property taxes on the factory building (where the snowboards are made) are $6,000 per year.
5. Advertising costs (mostly online and catalogue) are $60,000 per year.
6. Sales commissions related to snowboard sales are $20 per snowboard.
7. Salaries for factory maintenance employees are $45,000 per year.
8. The salary of the plant manager is $70,000.
9. The cost of shipping is $8 per snowboard.

Illustration 14.4 shows how Terrain Park Boards would assign these manufacturing and selling costs to the various categories.

ILLUSTRATION 14.4

Assignment of costs to cost categories

Terrain Park Boards

Cost Item	Product Costs			Period Costs
	Direct Materials	Direct Labor	Manufacturing Overhead	
1. Material cost ($30 per board)	X			
2. Labor costs ($40 per board)		X		
3. Depreciation on factory equipment ($25,000 per year)			X	
4. Property taxes on factory building ($6,000 per year)			X	
5. Advertising costs ($60,000 per year)				X
6. Sales commissions ($20 per board)				X
7. Maintenance salaries (factory facilities, $45,000 per year)			X	
8. Salary of plant manager ($70,000 per year)			X	
9. Cost of shipping boards ($8 per board)				X

Total manufacturing costs are the sum of the **product costs**—direct materials, direct labor, and manufacturing overhead—incurred in the current period. If Terrain Park Boards produces 10,000 snowboards the first year, the total manufacturing costs would be $846,000, as shown in Illustration 14.5.

ILLUSTRATION 14.5

Computation of total manufacturing costs

Cost Number and Item	Manufacturing Cost
1. Material cost ($30 × 10,000)	$300,000
2. Labor cost ($40 × 10,000)	400,000
3. Depreciation on factory equipment	25,000
4. Property taxes on factory building	6,000
7. Maintenance salaries (factory facilities)	45,000
8. Salary of plant manager	70,000
Total manufacturing costs	**$846,000**

Once it knows the total manufacturing costs, Terrain Park Boards can compute the manufacturing cost per unit. Assuming 10,000 units, the cost to produce one snowboard is $84.60 ($846,000 ÷ 10,000 units).

The cost concepts discussed in this chapter are used extensively in subsequent chapters. So study Illustration 14.4 carefully. If you do not understand any of these classifications, go back and reread the appropriate section.

ACTION PLAN

- Direct materials: any raw materials physically and directly associated with the finished product.
- Direct labor: the work of factory employees directly associated with the finished product.
- Manufacturing overhead: any costs indirectly associated with the finished product.
- Costs that are not product costs are period costs.

DO IT! 2 | Managerial Cost Concepts

A bicycle company has these costs: tires, salaries of employees who put tires on the wheels, factory building depreciation, advertising expenditures, factory machine lubricants, spokes, salary of factory manager, salary of accountant, handlebars, and salaries of factory maintenance employees. Classify each cost as direct materials, direct labor, overhead, or a period cost.

Solution

Direct materials: Tires, spokes, and handlebars. **Direct labor:** Salaries of employees who put tires on the wheels. **Manufacturing overhead:** Factory building depreciation, factory machine lubricants, salary of factory manager, and salaries of factory maintenance employees. **Period costs:** Advertising expenditures and salary of accountant.

Related exercise material: BE14.3, BE14.4, BE14.5, BE14.6, DO IT! 14.2, E14.2, E14.3, E14.4, E14.5, E14.6, and E14.7.

Manufacturing Costs in Financial Statements

LEARNING OBJECTIVE 3
Demonstrate how to compute cost of goods manufactured and prepare financial statements for a manufacturer.

The financial statements of a manufacturer are very similar to those of a merchandiser. For example, you will find many of the same sections and same accounts in the financial statements of **Procter & Gamble** that you find in the financial statements of **Dick's Sporting Goods**. The principal differences between their financial statements occur in two places: the cost of goods sold section in the income statement and the current assets section in the balance sheet.

Income Statement

Under a periodic inventory system, the income statements of a merchandiser and a manufacturer differ in the cost of goods sold section. Merchandisers compute cost of goods sold by adding the beginning inventory to the **cost of goods purchased** and subtracting the ending inventory. Manufacturers compute cost of goods sold by adding the beginning finished goods inventory to the **cost of goods manufactured** and subtracting the ending finished goods inventory. **Illustration 14.6**, which assumes a periodic inventory system, shows these different methods.

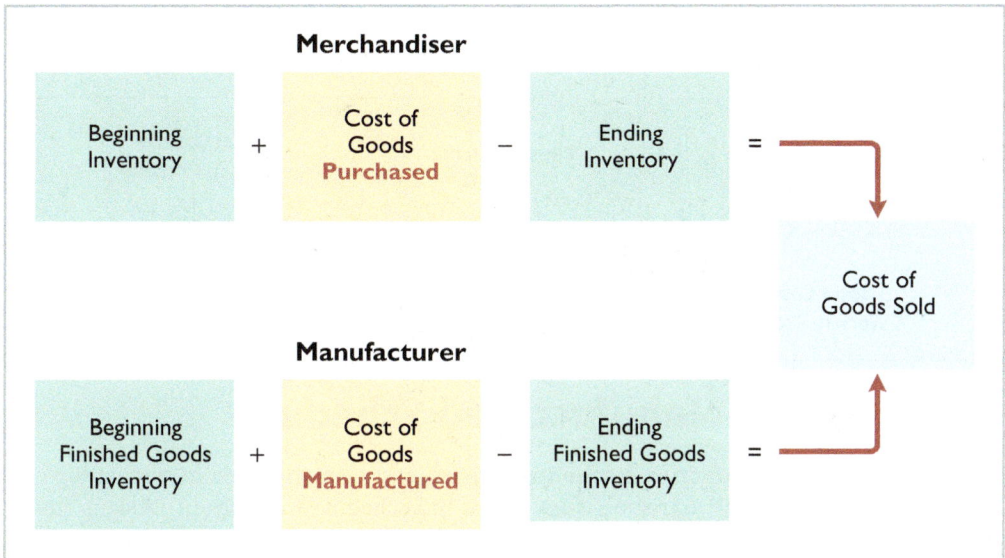

ILLUSTRATION 14.6

Cost of goods sold components

A number of accounts are involved in determining the cost of goods manufactured. To eliminate excessive detail, income statements typically show only the total cost of goods manufactured. A separate statement, called a Cost of Goods Manufactured Schedule, presents the details (see Illustration 14.9).

Illustration 14.7 shows the different presentations of the cost of goods sold sections for merchandising and manufacturing companies. The other sections of an income statement are similar for merchandisers and manufacturers.

ILLUSTRATION 14.7 Cost of goods sold sections of merchandising and manufacturing income statements

Merchandising Company Income Statement (partial) For the Year Ended December 31, 2022		Manufacturing Company Income Statement (partial) For the Year Ended December 31, 2022	
Cost of goods sold		Cost of goods sold	
Inventory, Jan. 1	$ 70,000	Finished goods inventory, Jan. 1	$ 90,000
Cost of goods purchased	650,000	Cost of goods manufactured	
		(see Illustration 14.9)	370,000
Cost of goods available for sale	720,000	Cost of goods available for sale	460,000
Less: Inventory,		Less: Finished goods inventory,	
Dec. 31	400,000	Dec. 31	80,000
Cost of goods sold	$320,000	Cost of goods sold	$380,000

Cost of Goods Manufactured

An example may help show how companies determine the cost of goods manufactured. Assume that on January 1, **Current Designs** has a number of kayaks in various stages of production. In total, these partially completed manufactured units are called **beginning work in process inventory**. These are kayaks that were worked on during the prior year but were not completed. As a result, these kayaks will be completed during the current year. The cost of beginning work in process inventory is based on the **manufacturing costs incurred in the prior period**.

Current Designs first incurs manufacturing costs in the current year to complete the kayaks that were in process on January 1. It then incurs manufacturing costs for production of new orders. The sum of the direct materials costs, direct labor costs, and manufacturing overhead incurred in the current year is the **total manufacturing costs** for the current period.

We now have two cost amounts: (1) the cost of the beginning work in process and (2) the total manufacturing costs for the current period. The sum of these costs is the **total cost of work in process** for the year.

At the end of the year, Current Designs may have some kayaks that are only partially completed. The costs of these units become the cost of the **ending work in process inventory**. To find the **cost of goods manufactured**, we subtract this cost from the total cost of work in process. **Illustration 14.8** shows the formula for determining the cost of goods manufactured.

ILLUSTRATION 14.8
Cost of goods manufactured formula

Beginning Work in Process Inventory + Total Manufacturing Costs = Total Cost of Work in Process

Total Cost of Work in Process − Ending Work in Process Inventory = Cost of Goods Manufactured

Cost of Goods Manufactured Schedule

The **cost of goods manufactured schedule** reports cost elements used in calculating cost of goods manufactured. **Illustration 14.9** shows the schedule for Current Designs (using assumed data). The schedule presents detailed data for direct materials and for manufacturing overhead (see **Decision Tools**).

Decision Tools

The cost of goods manufactured schedule helps managers determine if the company is maintaining control over the costs of production.

You should be able to distinguish between "Total manufacturing costs" and "Cost of goods manufactured." As Illustration 14.9 shows, total manufacturing costs is the sum of all manufacturing costs (direct materials, direct labor, and manufacturing overhead) **incurred during the period**. Cost of goods manufactured is the cost of those goods that were **completed during the period**. If we add beginning work in process inventory to the total manufacturing costs incurred during the period and then subtract the ending work in process inventory (the formula given in Illustration 14.8), we arrive at the cost of goods manufactured during the period.

ILLUSTRATION 14.9
Cost of goods manufactured schedule

Current Designs
Cost of Goods Manufactured Schedule
For the Year Ended December 31, 2022

Work in process, January 1			$ 18,400
Direct materials			
Raw materials inventory, January 1	$ 16,700		
Raw materials purchases	152,500		
Total raw materials available for use	169,200		
Less: Raw materials inventory, December 31	22,800		
Direct materials used		$146,400	
Direct labor		175,600	
Manufacturing overhead			
Indirect labor	14,300		
Factory repairs	12,600		
Factory utilities	10,100		
Factory depreciation	9,440		
Factory insurance	8,360		
Total manufacturing overhead		54,800	
Total manufacturing costs			376,800
Total cost of work in process			395,200
Less: Work in process, December 31			25,200
Cost of goods manufactured			$370,000

Balance Sheet

The balance sheet for a merchandising company shows just one category of inventory. In contrast, the balance sheet for a manufacturer may have three inventory accounts, as shown in **Illustration 14.10** for Current Designs' kayak inventory (see **Decision Tools**).

Decision Tools
The balance sheet helps managers determine whether sufficient inventory exists to meet forecasted demand.

ILLUSTRATION 14.10 Inventory accounts for a manufacturer

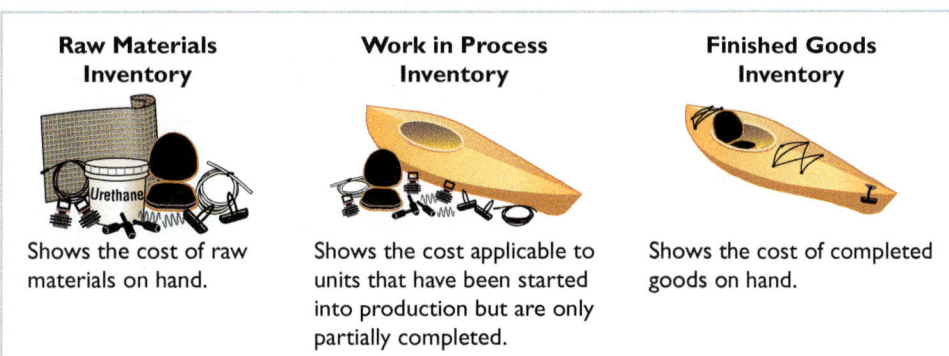

Raw Materials Inventory	Work in Process Inventory	Finished Goods Inventory
Shows the cost of raw materials on hand.	Shows the cost applicable to units that have been started into production but are only partially completed.	Shows the cost of completed goods on hand.

Finished Goods Inventory is to a manufacturer what Inventory is to a merchandiser. Each of these classifications represents the goods that the company has available for sale. The current assets sections presented in **Illustration 14.11** contrast the presentations of inventories for merchandising and manufacturing companies. The remainder of the balance sheet is similar for the two types of companies.

ILLUSTRATION 14.11 Current assets sections of merchandising and manufacturing balance sheets

Merchandising Company Balance Sheet December 31, 2022			Manufacturing Company Balance Sheet December 31, 2022		
Current assets			Current assets		
Cash		$100,000	Cash		$180,000
Accounts receivable (net)		210,000	Accounts receivable (net)		210,000
Inventory		400,000	Inventory		
Prepaid expenses		22,000	Finished goods	$80,000	
Total current assets		$732,000	Work in process	25,200	
			Raw materials	22,800	128,000
			Prepaid expenses		18,000
			Total current assets		$536,000

Each step in the accounting cycle for a merchandiser applies to a manufacturer. For example, prior to preparing financial statements, manufacturers make adjusting entries. The adjusting entries are essentially the same as those of a merchandiser. The closing entries are also similar for manufacturers and merchandisers.

DO IT! 3 | Cost of Goods Manufactured

The following information is available for Keystone Company.

		March 1	March 31
Raw materials inventory		$12,000	$10,000
Work in process inventory		2,500	4,000
Materials purchased in March	$ 90,000		
Direct labor in March	75,000		
Manufacturing overhead in March	220,000		

Prepare the cost of goods manufactured schedule for the month of March 2022.

ACTION PLAN

- Start with beginning work in process as the first item in the cost of goods manufactured schedule.
- Sum direct materials used, direct labor, and manufacturing overhead to determine total manufacturing costs.
- Sum beginning work in process and total manufacturing costs to determine total cost of work in process.
- Cost of goods manufactured is the total cost of work in process less ending work in process.

Solution

Keystone Company
Cost of Goods Manufactured Schedule
For the Month Ended March 31, 2022

Work in process, March 1			$ 2,500
Direct materials			
Raw materials, March 1	$ 12,000		
Raw materials purchases	90,000		
Total raw materials available for use	102,000		
Less: Raw materials, March 31	10,000		
Direct materials used		$ 92,000	
Direct labor		75,000	
Manufacturing overhead		220,000	
Total manufacturing costs			387,000
Total cost of work in process			389,500
Less: Work in process, March 31			4,000
Cost of goods manufactured			$385,500

Related exercise material: **BE14.7, BE14.8, BE14.9, BE14.10, DO IT! 14.3, E14.8, E14.9, E14.10, E14.11, E14.12, E14.13, E14.14, E14.15, E14.16, and E14.17.**

Managerial Accounting Today

LEARNING OBJECTIVE 4
Discuss trends in managerial accounting.

The business environment never stands still. Regulations are always changing, global competition continues to intensify, and technology is a source of constant upheaval. In this rapidly changing world, managerial accounting needs to continue to innovate in order to provide managers with the information they need.

Service Industries

Much of the U.S. economy has shifted toward an emphasis on services. Today, more than 50% of U.S. workers are employed by service companies. Airlines, marketing agencies, cable companies, and governmental agencies are just a few examples of service companies. How do service companies differ from manufacturing companies? One difference is that services are consumed immediately by customers. For example, when a restaurant produces a meal, that meal is not put in inventory but is instead consumed immediately. An airline uses special equipment to provide its product, but again, the output of that equipment is consumed immediately by the customer in the form of a flight. And a marketing agency performs services for its clients that are immediately consumed by the customer in the form of a marketing plan. For a manufacturing company, like **Boeing**, it often has a long lead time before its airplane is used or consumed by the customer.

This chapter's examples featured manufacturing companies because accounting for the manufacturing environment requires the use of the broadest range of accounts. That is, the accounts used by service companies represent a subset of those used by manufacturers because service companies are not producing inventory. Neither the restaurant, the airline, or the marketing agency discussed above produces an inventoriable product. However, just like a manufacturer, each needs to keep track of the costs of its services in order to know whether it is generating a profit (see **Ethics Note**). A successful restaurateur needs to know the cost of each offering on the menu, an airline needs to know the cost of flight service to each destination,

ETHICS NOTE

Do telecommunications companies have an obligation to provide service to remote or low-user areas for a fee that may be less than the cost of the service?

and a marketing agency needs to know the cost to develop a marketing plan. Thus, the techniques shown in this chapter, to accumulate manufacturing costs to determine manufacturing inventory, are equally useful for determining the costs of performing services.

For example, let's consider the costs that **Hewlett-Packard (HP)** might incur on a consulting engagement. A significant portion of its costs would be salaries of consulting personnel. It might also incur travel costs, materials, software costs, and depreciation charges on equipment. In the same way that it needs to keep track of the cost of manufacturing its computers and printers, HP needs to know what its costs are on each consulting job. It could prepare a cost of services performed schedule similar to the cost of goods manufactured schedule in Illustration 14.9. The structure would be essentially the same as the cost of goods manufactured schedule, but section headings would be reflective of the costs of the particular service organization.

Many of the examples we present in subsequent chapters will be based on service companies, as well as a number of end-of-chapter materials.

Service Company Insight   Allegiant Airlines

Low Fares but Decent Profits

© Stephen Strathdee/ iStockphoto

When other airlines were cutting flight service due to recession, **Allegiant Airlines** increased capacity by 21%. Sounds crazy, doesn't it? But it must know something because while the other airlines were losing money, it was generating profits. In fact, it often has the industry's highest profit margins. Consider also that its average one-way fare is only $83. So how does it make money? As a low-budget airline, it focuses on controlling costs.

Allegiant purchases used planes for $3 million each rather than new planes for $40 million. It flies out of small towns, so wages are low and competition is nonexistent. It minimizes hotel costs by having its flight crews finish their day in their home cities. The company also only flies a route if its 150-passenger planes are nearly full (it averages about 90% of capacity). The bottom line is that Allegiant knows its costs to the penny. Knowing what your costs are might not be glamorous, but it sure beats losing money.

Sources: Susan Carey, "For Allegiant, Getaways Mean Profits," *Wall Street Journal Online* (February 18, 2009); and Scott Mayerowitz, "Tiny Allegiant Air Thrives on Low Costs, High Fees," *http://bigstory.ap.org* (June 28, 2013).

What are some of the line items that would appear in the cost of services performed schedule of an airline? (Go to WileyPLUS for this answer and additional questions.)

Focus on the Value Chain

The **value chain** refers to all business processes associated with providing a product or performing a service. **Illustration 14.12** depicts the value chain for a manufacturer. Many of the most significant business innovations in recent years have resulted either directly, or indirectly, from a focus on the value chain. For example, so-called **lean manufacturing**, originally pioneered by Japanese automobile manufacturer **Toyota** but now widely practiced, reviews all business processes in an effort to increase productivity and eliminate waste, all while continually trying to improve quality.

ILLUSTRATION 14.12 A manufacturer's value chain

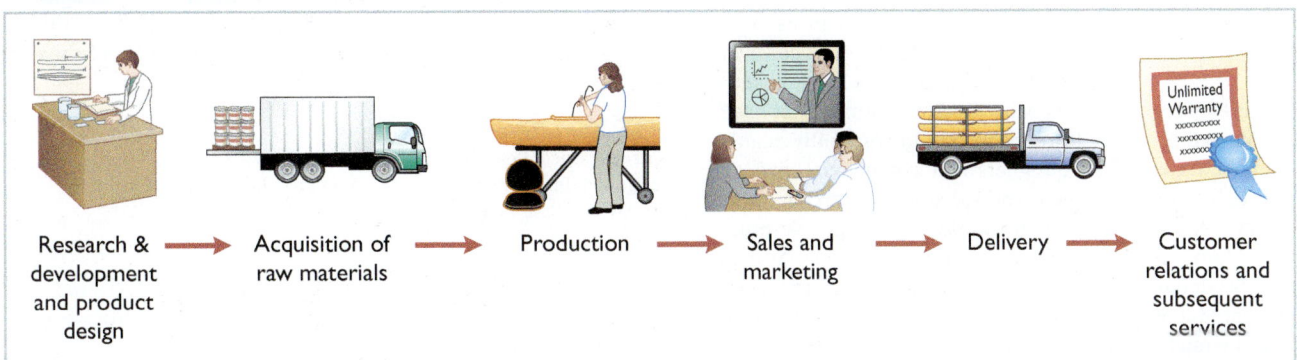

Research & development and product design → Acquisition of raw materials → Production → Sales and marketing → Delivery → Customer relations and subsequent services

Just-in-time (JIT) inventory methods, which have significantly lowered inventory levels and costs for many companies, are one innovation that resulted from the focus on the value chain. Under the JIT inventory method, goods are manufactured or purchased just in time for sale. For example, **Dell** can produce and deliver a custom computer within 48 hours of a customer's order. However, JIT also necessitates increased emphasis on product quality. Because JIT companies do not have excess inventory on hand, they cannot afford to stop production because of defects or machine breakdowns. If they stop production, deliveries will be delayed and customers will be unhappy. For example, a design flaw in an **Intel** computer chip was estimated to cost the company $1 billion in repairs and reduced revenue.

As a consequence, many companies now focus on **total quality management (TQM)** to reduce defects in finished products, with the goal of zero defects. **Toyota** was one of the pioneers of TQM processes as early as the 1940s. Some of the largest companies in the world, including **Ford** and **ExxonMobil**, have benefitted from these practices.

Another innovation, the **theory of constraints**, involves identification of "bottlenecks"—constraints within the value chain that limit a company's profitability. Once a major constraint has been identified and eliminated, the company moves on to fix the next most significant constraint. **General Motors** found that by applying the theory of constraints to its distribution system, it could more effectively meet the demands of its dealers and minimize the amount of excess inventory in its distribution system. This also reduced its need for overtime labor. An application of the theory of constraints is presented in Chapter 19.

Technology has played a big role in the focus on the value chain and the implementation of lean manufacturing. For example, **enterprise resource planning (ERP) systems**, such as those provided by **SAP**, provide a comprehensive, centralized, integrated source of information to manage all major business processes—from purchasing, to manufacturing, to sales, to human resources. ERP systems have, in some large companies, replaced as many as 200 individual software packages. In addition, the focus on improving efficiency in the value chain has also resulted in adoption of automated manufacturing processes. Many companies now use computer-integrated manufacturing. These systems often reduce the reliance on manual labor by using robotic equipment. This increases overhead costs as a percentage of total product costs.

As overhead costs have increased because of factory automation, the accuracy of overhead cost allocation to specific products has become more important. Managerial accounting devised an approach, called **activity-based costing (ABC)**, which allocates overhead based on each product's use of particular activities in making the product. In addition to providing more accurate product costing, ABC also can contribute to increased efficiency in the value chain. For example, suppose one of a company's overhead pools is allocated based on the number of setups that each product requires. If a particular product's cost is high because it is allocated a lot of overhead due to a high number of setups, management will be motivated to try to reduce the number of setups and thus reduce its overhead allocation. ABC is discussed further in Chapter 17.

Management Insight Inditex SA

Miguel Vidall/REUTERS/Alamy Stock Photo

Supplying Today's (Not Yesterday's) Fashions

In terms of total sales dollars, **Inditex SA** is the planet's largest fashion retailer. What does it do differently than its competitors? How did it double its sales over a recent seven-year period while competitors such as **Gap Inc.** stumbled badly? Inditex distinguishes itself in its value chain's ability to react quickly to constantly changing customer tastes. First, designers and commercial staff sit side by side in a massive, open workspace facility, taking direct input from sales staff around the world regarding new product ideas. Manufacturing facilities are located relatively near to company headquarters, allowing more direct input and oversight into production. Also, all goods (other than online sales) are shipped straight from the production facility to stores, rather than warehouses. As a result of its unique approach to how it designs, manufactures and distributes its goods, Inditex can actually sometimes get a new product from initial idea to the store shelf in two weeks rather than the industry norm of two to eight months. And because Inditex provides customers with designs that competitors don't have yet, it can charge higher prices while also continuing to look for ways to increase efficiency and thus cut costs.

Source: Patricia Kowsmann, "Fast Fashion: How a Zara Coat Went from Design to Fifth Avenue in 25 Days," *Wall Street Journal* (December 6, 2016).

What steps has Inditex taken that make its value chain unique? (Go to WileyPLUS for this answer and additional questions).

Balanced Scorecard

As companies implement various business practice innovations, managers sometimes focus too enthusiastically on the latest innovation, to the detriment of other areas of the business. For example, by focusing on total quality management, companies sometimes lose sight of cost/benefit considerations. Similarly, in focusing on reducing inventory levels through just-in-time inventory methods, companies sometimes lose sales due to inventory shortages. The **balanced scorecard** corrects for this limited perspective: This approach uses both financial and nonfinancial measures to evaluate all aspects of a company's operations in an integrated fashion. The performance measures are linked in a cause-and-effect fashion to ensure that they all tie to the company's overall objectives. For example, to increase return on assets, the company could try to increase sales. To increase sales, the company could try to increase customer satisfaction. To increase customer satisfaction, the company could try to reduce product defects. Finally, to reduce product defects, the company could increase employee training. The balanced scorecard, which is discussed further in Chapter 24, is now used by many companies, including **Hilton Hotels**, **Wal-Mart Stores, Inc.**, and **HP**.

Business Ethics

All employees within an organization are expected to act ethically in their business activities. Given the importance of ethical behavior to corporations and their owners (stockholders), an increasing number of organizations provide codes of business ethics for their employees.

Creating Proper Incentives

Companies like **Amazon.com**, **IBM**, and **Nike** use complex systems to monitor, control, and evaluate the actions of managers. Unfortunately, these systems and controls sometimes unwittingly create incentives for managers to take unethical actions. For example, because budgets are also used as an evaluation tool, some managers try to "game" the budgeting process by underestimating their division's predicted performance so that it will be easier to meet their performance targets. On the other hand, if budgets are set at unattainable levels, managers sometimes take unethical actions to meet the targets in order to receive higher compensation or, in some cases, to keep their jobs.

For example, at one time, airline manufacturer **Boeing** was plagued by a series of scandals including charges of over-billing, corporate espionage, and illegal conflicts of interest. Some long-time employees of Boeing blamed the decline in ethics on a change in the corporate culture that took place after Boeing merged with **McDonnell Douglas**. They suggested that evaluation systems implemented after the merger to evaluate employee performance gave employees the impression that they needed to succeed no matter what actions were required to do so.

In a recent example, the largest bank in the United States, **Wells Fargo**, admitted that it had fired 5,300 employees for opening more than 2 million accounts without customer approval or knowledge. According to the director of the Consumer Financial Protection Bureau, "Wells Fargo employees secretly opened unauthorized accounts to hit sales targets and receive bonuses."

Code of Ethical Standards

In response to corporate scandals, the U.S. Congress enacted the **Sarbanes-Oxley Act (SOX)** to help prevent lapses in internal control. One result of SOX was to clarify top management's responsibility for the company's financial statements. CEOs and CFOs are now required to certify that financial statements give a fair presentation of the company's operating results and its financial condition. In addition, top managers must certify that the company maintains an adequate system of internal controls to safeguard the company's assets and ensure accurate financial reports.

Another result of SOX is that companies now pay more attention to the composition of the board of directors. In particular, the audit committee of the board of directors must be comprised entirely of independent members (that is, non-employees) and must contain at least one financial expert. Finally, the law substantially increases the penalties for misconduct.

To provide guidance for managerial accountants, the Institute of Management Accountants (IMA) has developed a code of ethical standards, entitled *IMA Statement of Ethical Professional Practice*. Management accountants should not commit acts in violation of these standards. Nor should they condone such acts by others within their organizations. Throughout the text, we will address various ethical issues managers face.

Corporate Social Responsibility

The balanced scorecard attempts to take a broader, more inclusive view of corporate profitability measures. Many companies, however, have begun to evaluate not just corporate profitability but also **corporate social responsibility**. In addition to profitability, corporate social responsibility considers a company's efforts to employ sustainable business practices with regard to its employees, society, and the environment. This is sometimes referred to as the **triple bottom line** because it evaluates a company's performance with regard to **people, planet, and profit**. Recent reports indicate that over 50% of the 500 largest U.S. companies provide sustainability reports. Make no mistake, these companies are still striving to maximize profits—in a competitive world, they won't survive long if they don't. In fact, you might recognize a few of the names on a recent list (published by Corporate Knights) of the 100 most sustainable companies in the world. Are you surprised that **General Electric**, **adidas**, **BMW**, **Coca-Cola**, or **Apple** made the list? These companies have learned that with a long-term, sustainable approach, they can maximize profits while also acting in the best interest of their employees, their communities, and the environment. In fact, a monetary bonus was provided by 87% of the companies on the list to managers that met sustainability goals. At various points within this text, we will discuss situations where real companies use the very skills that you are learning to evaluate decisions from a sustainable perspective, such as in the following Insight box.

People, Planet, and Profit Insight   Phantom Tac

Geanina Bechea/Shutterstock

People Matter

Many clothing factories in developing countries are known for unsafe buildings, poor working conditions, and wage and labor violations. One of the owners of **Phantom Tac**, a clothing manufacturer in Bangladesh, did make efforts to develop sustainable business practices. This owner, David Mayor, provided funding for a training program for female workers. He also developed a website to educate customers about the workers' conditions. But Phantom Tac also had to make a profit. Things got tight when one of its customers canceled orders because Phantom Tac failed a social compliance audit. The company had to quit funding the training program and the website.

Recently, Bangladesh's textile industry has seen some significant improvements in working conditions and safety standards. As Brad Adams, Asia director of **Human Rights Watch**, notes, "The (Dhaka) government has belatedly begun to register unions, which is an important first step, but it now needs to ensure that factory owners stop persecuting their leaders and actually allow them to function."

Sources: Jim Yardley, "Clothing Brands Sidestep Blame for Safety Lapses," *The New York Times Online* (December 30, 2013); and Palash Ghosh, "Despite Low Pay, Poor Work Conditions, Garment Factories Empowering Millions of Bangladeshi Women," *International Business Times* (March 25, 2014).

What are some of the common problems for many clothing factories in developing countries? (Go to WileyPLUS for this answer and additional questions.)

Sustainable business practices present numerous issues for management and managerial accountants. First, companies need to decide what items need to be measured, generally those that are of utmost importance to its stakeholders. For example, a particular company might be most concerned with minimizing water pollution or maximizing employee safety. Then, for each item identified, the company determines measurable attributes that provide relevant information regarding the company's performance with regard to that item, such as the amount of waste released into public waterways or the number of accidents per 1,000 hours worked. Finally, the company needs to consider the materiality of the item, the cost of measuring these attributes, and the reliability of the measurements. If the company uses this information to make decisions, then accuracy is critical. Of particular concern is whether the measurements can be verified by an outside third party.

Unlike financial reporting, which is overseen by the Financial Accounting Standards Board (FASB), the reporting of sustainable business practices currently has no agreed-upon standard-setter. A number of organizations have, however, published guidelines. The guidelines published by the **Global Reporting Initiative** are among the most widely recognized and followed. **Illustration 14.13** provides a list of major categories provided by the Global Reporting Initiative for sustainability reporting and a sample of aspects that companies might consider within each category.

ILLUSTRATION 14.13 Sample categories in Global Reporting Initiative guidelines

		Social			
Economic	**Environmental**	**Labor Practices and Decent Work**	**Human Rights**	**Society**	**Product Responsibility**
Economic performance	Energy	Occupational health and safety	Non-discrimination	Anti-corruption	Customer health and safety
Market presence	Biodiversity	Training and education	Child labor	Anti-competitive behavior	Product and service labeling
Indirect economic impacts	Effluents and waste	Diversity and equal opportunity	Indigenous rights	Supplier assessment for impacts on society	Marketing communications
Procurement practices	Compliance	Labor practices grievance mechanisms	Supplier human rights assessment	Grievance mechanisms for impacts on society	Customer privacy

Source: Global Reporting Initiative, *G4 Sustainability Reporting Guidelines*, p. 9. The full report is available at *www.globalreporting.org*.

DO IT! 4 | Trends in Managerial Accounting

Match the descriptions that follow with the corresponding terms.

Descriptions:

1. _____ All activities associated with providing a product or performing a service.
2. _____ A method of allocating overhead based on each product's use of activities in making the product.
3. _____ Systems implemented to reduce defects in finished products with the goal of achieving zero defects.
4. _____ A performance-measurement approach that uses both financial and nonfinancial measures, tied to company objectives, to evaluate a company's operations in an integrated fashion.
5. _____ Inventory system in which goods are manufactured or purchased just as they are needed for use.
6. _____ A company's efforts to employ sustainable business practices with regards to its employees, society, and the environment.
7. _____ A code of ethical standards developed by the Institute of Management Accountants.

Terms:

a. Activity-based costing.
b. Balanced scorecard.
c. Corporate social responsibility.
d. Just-in-time (JIT) inventory.
e. Total quality management (TQM).
f. Statement of Ethical Professional Practice.
g. Value chain.

ACTION PLAN

- Develop a forward-looking view, in order to advise and provide information to various members of the organization.
- Understand current business trends and issues.

Solution

1. g 2. a 3. e 4. b 5. d 6. c 7. f

Related exercise material: **BE14.11, DO IT! 14.4, and E14.18.**

USING THE DECISION TOOLS | Current Designs

Current Designs faces many situations where it needs to apply the decision tools in this chapter, such as analyzing the balance sheet for optimal inventory levels. For example, assume that the market has responded enthusiastically to a new Current Designs' model, the Otter. As a result, the company has established a separate manufacturing facility to produce these kayaks. Now assume that the company produces 1,000 of these kayaks per month. Current Designs' monthly manufacturing costs and other data for the Otter are as follows.

1. Rent on manufacturing equipment (lease cost) — $2,000/month
2. Insurance on manufacturing building — $750/month
3. Raw materials (plastic, fiberglass, etc.) — $180/kayak
4. Utility costs for manufacturing facility — $1,000/month
5. Supplies for administrative office — $800/month
6. Wages for assembly line workers in manufacturing facility — $130/kayak
7. Depreciation on administrative office equipment — $650/month
8. Miscellaneous manufacturing materials (lubricants, solders, etc.) — $12/kayak
9. Property taxes on manufacturing building — $24,000/year
10. Manufacturing supervisor's salary — $5,000/month
11. Advertising for the Otter — $30,000/year
12. Sales commissions — $30/kayak
13. Depreciation on manufacturing building — $4,000/month

Instructions

a. Prepare an answer sheet with the following column headings.

Cost Item	Product Costs			Period Costs
	Direct Materials	Direct Labor	Manufacturing Overhead	

Enter each cost item on your answer sheet, placing an "X" mark under the appropriate headings.

b. Compute total manufacturing costs for the month.

Solution

a.

Cost Item	Product Costs			Period Costs
	Direct Materials	Direct Labor	Manufacturing Overhead	
1. Rent on manufacturing equipment ($2,000/month)			X	
2. Insurance on manufacturing building ($750/month)			X	
3. Raw materials ($180/kayak)	X			
4. Manufacturing utilities ($1,000/month)			X	
5. Office supplies ($800/month)				X
6. Wages for assembly workers ($130/kayak)		X		

		Product Costs			
Cost Item	Direct Materials	Direct Labor	Manufacturing Overhead	Period Costs
7. Depreciation on administrative office equipment ($650/month)				X
8. Miscellaneous manufacturing materials ($12/kayak)			X	
9. Property taxes on manufacturing building ($24,000/year)			X	
10. Manufacturing supervisor's salary ($5,000/month)			X	
11. Advertising cost ($30,000/year)				X
12. Sales commissions ($30/kayak)				X
13. Depreciation on manufacturing building ($4,000/month)			X	

b.

Cost Item	Manufacturing Cost
Rent on manufacturing equipment	$ 2,000
Insurance on manufacturing building	750
Raw materials ($180 × 1,000)	180,000
Manufacturing utilities	1,000
Labor ($130 × 1,000)	130,000
Miscellaneous materials ($12 × 1,000)	12,000
Property taxes on manufacturing building ($24,000 ÷ 12)	2,000
Manufacturing supervisor's salary	5,000
Depreciation on manufacturing building	4,000
Total manufacturing costs	$336,750

Current Designs' monthly manufacturing cost to produce 1,000 Otters is $336,750.

Review and Practice

Learning Objectives Review

1 Identify the features of managerial accounting and the functions of management.

The *primary users* of managerial accounting reports, issued as frequently as needed, are internal users, who are officers, department heads, managers, and supervisors in the company. The purpose of these reports is to provide special-purpose information for a particular user for a specific decision. The content of managerial accounting reports pertains to subunits of the business. It may be very detailed, and may extend beyond the double-entry accounting system. The reporting standard is relevance to the decision being made. No independent audits are required in managerial accounting.

The functions of management are planning, directing, and controlling. Planning requires management to look ahead and to establish objectives. Directing involves coordinating the diverse activities and human resources of a company to produce a smooth-running operation. Controlling is the process of keeping the activities on track.

2 Describe the classes of manufacturing costs and the differences between product and period costs.

Manufacturing costs are typically classified as either (1) direct materials, (2) direct labor, or (3) manufacturing overhead. Raw materials that can be physically and directly associated with the finished product during the manufacturing process are called direct materials. The work of factory employees that can be physically and directly associated with converting raw materials into finished goods is considered direct labor. Manufacturing overhead consists of costs that are indirectly associated with the manufacture of the finished product.

Product costs are costs that are a necessary and integral part of producing the finished product. Product costs are also called inventoriable costs. These costs do not become expenses until the company sells the finished goods inventory. Period costs are costs that are identified with a specific time period rather than with a salable product. These costs relate to nonmanufacturing costs and therefore are not inventoriable costs.

The difference between a merchandising and a manufacturing balance sheet is in the current assets section. The current assets section of a manufacturing company's balance sheet presents three inventory accounts: finished goods inventory, work in process inventory, and raw materials inventory.

3 Demonstrate how to compute cost of goods manufactured and prepare financial statements for a manufacturer.

Companies add the cost of the beginning work in process to the total manufacturing costs for the current year to arrive at the total cost of work in process for the year. They then subtract the ending work in process from the total cost of work in process to arrive at the cost of goods manufactured.

The difference between a merchandising and a manufacturing income statement is in the cost of goods sold section. A manufacturing cost of goods sold section shows beginning and ending finished goods inventories and the cost of goods manufactured.

4 Discuss trends in managerial accounting.

Managerial accounting has experienced many changes in recent years, including a shift toward service companies as well as an emphasis on ethical behavior. Improved practices include a focus on managing the value chain through techniques such as just-in-time inventory, total quality management, activity-based costing, and theory of constraints. The balanced scorecard is now used by many companies in order to attain a more comprehensive view of the company's operations. Finally, companies are now evaluating their performance with regard to their corporate social responsibility.

Decision Tools Review

Decision Checkpoints	Info Needed for Decision	Tool to Use for Decision	How to Evaluate Results
Is the company maintaining control over the costs of production?	Cost of material, labor, and overhead	Cost of goods manufactured schedule	Compare the cost of goods manufactured to revenue expected from product sales.
What is the composition of a manufacturing company's inventory?	Amount of raw materials, work in process, and finished goods inventories	Balance sheet	Determine whether there are sufficient finished goods, raw materials, and work in process inventories to meet forecasted demand.

Glossary Review

Activity-based costing (ABC) A method of allocating overhead based on each product's use of activities in making the product. (p. 14-16).

Balanced scorecard A performance-measurement approach that uses both financial and nonfinancial measures, tied to company objectives, to evaluate a company's operations in an integrated fashion. (p. 14-17).

Board of directors The group of officials elected by the stockholders of a corporation to formulate operating policies and select officers who will manage the company. (p. 14-5).

Chief executive officer (CEO) Corporate officer who has overall responsibility for managing the business and delegates responsibilities to other corporate officers. (p. 14-5).

Chief financial officer (CFO) Corporate officer who is responsible for all of the accounting and finance issues of the company. (p. 14-5).

Controller Financial officer responsible for a company's accounting records, system of internal control, and preparation of financial statements, tax returns, and internal reports. (p. 14-5).

Corporate social responsibility The efforts of a company to employ sustainable business practices with regard to its employees, society, and the environment. (p. 14-18).

Cost of goods manufactured Total cost of work in process less the cost of the ending work in process inventory. (p. 14-12).

Direct labor The work of factory employees that can be physically and directly associated with converting raw materials into finished goods. (p. 14-7).

Direct materials Raw materials that can be physically and directly associated with manufacturing the finished product. (p. 14-7).

Enterprise resource planning (ERP) system Software that provides a comprehensive, centralized, integrated source of information used to manage all major business processes. (p. 14-16).

Indirect labor Work of factory employees that has no physical association with the finished product or for which it is impractical to trace the costs to the goods produced. (p. 14-7).

Indirect materials Raw materials that do not physically become part of the finished product or for which it is impractical to trace to the finished product because their physical association with the finished product is too small. (p. 14-7).

Just-in-time (JIT) inventory Inventory system in which goods are manufactured or purchased just in time for sale. (p. 14-16).

Line positions Jobs that are directly involved in a company's primary revenue-generating operating activities. (p. 14-5).

Managerial accounting A field of accounting that provides economic and financial information for managers and other internal users. (p. 14-3).

Manufacturing overhead Manufacturing costs that are indirectly associated with the manufacture of the finished product. (p. 14-8).

Period costs Costs that are matched with the revenue of a specific time period and charged to expense as incurred. (p. 14-8).

Product costs Costs that are a necessary and integral part of producing the finished product. (p. 14-8).

Sarbanes-Oxley Act (SOX) Law passed by Congress intended to reduce unethical corporate behavior. (p. 14-17).

Staff positions Jobs that support the efforts of line employees. (p. 14-5).

Theory of constraints A specific approach used to identify and manage constraints in order to achieve the company's goals. (p. 14-16).

Total cost of work in process Cost of the beginning work in process plus total manufacturing costs for the current period. (p. 14-12).

Total manufacturing costs The sum of direct materials, direct labor, and manufacturing overhead incurred in the current period. (p. 14-10).

Total quality management (TQM) Systems implemented to reduce defects in finished products with the goal of achieving zero defects. (p. 14-16).

Treasurer Financial officer responsible for custody of a company's funds and for maintaining its cash position. (p. 14-5).

Triple bottom line The evaluation of a company's social responsibility performance with regard to people, planet, and profit. (p. 14-18).

Value chain All business processes associated with providing a product or performing a service. (p. 14-15).

Work in process inventory Partially completed manufactured units. (p. 14-11).

Practice Multiple-Choice Questions

1. **(LO 1)** Managerial accounting:
   a. is governed by generally accepted accounting principles.
   b. places emphasis on special-purpose information.
   c. pertains to the entity as a whole and is highly aggregated.
   d. is limited to cost data.

2. **(LO 1)** The management of an organization performs several broad functions. They are:
   a. planning, directing, and selling.
   b. planning, directing, and controlling.
   c. planning, manufacturing, and controlling.
   d. directing, manufacturing, and controlling.

3. **(LO 2)** Direct materials are a:

	Product Cost	Manufacturing Overhead Cost	Period Cost
a.	Yes	Yes	No
b.	Yes	No	No
c.	Yes	Yes	Yes
d.	No	No	No

4. **(LO 2)** Which of the following costs would a computer manufacturer include in manufacturing overhead?
   a. The cost of the disk drives.
   b. The wages earned by computer assemblers.
   c. The cost of the memory chips.
   d. Depreciation on testing equipment.

5. **(LO 2)** Which of the following is **not** an element of manufacturing overhead?
   a. Sales manager's salary.
   b. Plant manager's salary.
   c. Factory repairman's wages.
   d. Product inspector's salary.

6. **(LO 2)** Indirect labor is a:
   a. nonmanufacturing cost.
   b. raw material cost.
   c. product cost.
   d. period cost.

7. **(LO 2)** Which of the following costs are classified as a period cost?
   a. Wages paid to a factory custodian.
   b. Wages paid to a production department supervisor.
   c. Wages paid to a cost accounting department supervisor.
   d. Wages paid to an assembly worker.

8. **(LO 3)** For the year, Redder Company has cost of goods manufactured of $600,000, beginning finished goods inventory of $200,000, and ending finished goods inventory of $250,000. The cost of goods sold is:
   a. $450,000.
   b. $500,000.
   c. $550,000.
   d. $600,000.

9. **(LO 3)** Cost of goods available for sale is a step in the calculation of cost of goods sold of:
   a. a merchandising company but not a manufacturing company.
   b. a manufacturing company but not a merchandising company.
   c. a merchandising company and a manufacturing company.
   d. neither a manufacturing company nor a merchandising company.

10. **(LO 3)** A cost of goods manufactured schedule shows beginning and ending inventories for:
    a. raw materials and work in process only.
    b. work in process only.
    c. raw materials only.
    d. raw materials, work in process, and finished goods.

11. **(LO 3)** The formula to determine the cost of goods manufactured is:
    a. Beginning raw materials inventory + Total manufacturing costs − Ending work in process inventory.
    b. Beginning work in process inventory + Total manufacturing costs − Ending finished goods inventory.
    c. Beginning finished goods inventory + Total manufacturing costs − Ending finished goods inventory.
    d. Beginning work in process inventory + Total manufacturing costs − Ending work in process inventory.

12. **(LO 4)** After passage of the Sarbanes-Oxley Act:
    a. reports prepared by managerial accountants must by audited by CPAs.
    b. CEOs and CFOs must certify that financial statements give a fair presentation of the company's operating results.
    c. the audit committee, rather than top management, is responsible for the company's financial statements.
    d. reports prepared by managerial accountants must comply with generally accepted accounting principles (GAAP).

13. **(LO 4)** Which of the following managerial accounting techniques attempts to allocate manufacturing overhead in a more meaningful fashion?

    a. Just-in-time inventory.
    b. Total quality management.
    c. Balanced scorecard.
    d. Activity-based costing.

14. **(LO 4)** Corporate social responsibility refers to:

    a. the practice by management of reviewing all business processes in an effort to increase productivity and eliminate waste.
    b. an approach used to allocate overhead based on each product's use of activities.
    c. the attempt by management to identify and eliminate constraints within the value chain.
    d. efforts by companies to employ sustainable business practices with regard to employees and the environment.

Solutions

1. **b.** Managerial accounting emphasizes special-purpose information. The other choices are incorrect because (a) financial accounting is governed by generally accepted accounting principles, (c) financial accounting pertains to the entity as a whole and is highly aggregated, and (d) cost accounting and cost data are a subset of management accounting.

2. **b.** Planning, directing, and controlling are the broad functions performed by the management of an organization. The other choices are incorrect because (a) selling is performed by the sales group in the organization, not by management; (c) manufacturing is performed by the manufacturing group in the organization, not by management; and (d) manufacturing is performed by the manufacturing group in the organization, not by management.

3. **b.** Direct materials are a product cost only. Therefore, choices (a), (c), and (d) are incorrect as direct materials are not manufacturing overhead or a period cost.

4. **d.** Depreciation on testing equipment would be included in manufacturing overhead because it is indirectly associated with the finished product. The other choices are incorrect because (a) disk drives would be direct materials, (b) computer assembler wages would be direct labor, and (c) memory chips would be direct materials.

5. **a.** The sales manager's salary is not directly or indirectly associated with the manufacture of the finished product. The other choices are incorrect because (b) the plant manager's salary, (c) the factory repairman's wages, and (d) the product inspector's salary are all elements of manufacturing overhead.

6. **c.** Indirect labor is a product cost because it is part of the effort required to produce a product. The other choices are incorrect because (a) indirect labor is a manufacturing cost because it is part of the effort required to produce a product, (b) indirect labor is not a raw material cost because raw material costs only include direct materials and indirect materials, and (d) indirect labor is not a period cost because it is part of the effort required to produce a product.

7. **c.** Wages paid to a cost accounting department supervisor would be included in administrative expenses and classified as a period cost. The other choices are incorrect because (a) factory custodian wages are indirect labor which is manufacturing overhead and a product cost, (b) production department supervisor wages are indirect labor which is manufacturing overhead and a product cost, and (d) assembly worker wages is direct labor and is a product cost.

8. **c.** Cost of goods sold is computed as Beginning finished goods inventory ($200,000) + Cost of goods manufactured ($600,000) − Ending finished goods inventory ($250,000), or $200,000 + $600,000 − $250,000 = $550,000. Therefore, choices (a) $450,000, (b) $500,000, and (d) $600,000 are incorrect.

9. **c.** Both a merchandising company and a manufacturing company use cost of goods available for sale to calculate cost of goods sold. Therefore, choices (a) only a merchandising company, (b) only a manufacturing company, and (d) neither a manufacturing company or a merchandising company are incorrect.

10. **a.** A cost of goods manufactured schedule shows beginning and ending inventories for raw materials and work in process only. Therefore, choices (b) work in process only and (c) raw materials only are incorrect. Choice (d) is incorrect because the schedule does not include finished goods.

11. **d.** The formula to determine the cost of goods manufactured is Beginning work in process inventory + Total manufacturing costs − Ending work in process inventory. The other choices are incorrect because (a) raw materials inventory, (b) ending finished goods inventory, and (c) beginning finished goods inventory and ending finished goods inventory are not part of the computation.

12. **b.** CEOs and CFOs must certify that financial statements give a fair presentation of the company's operating results. The other choices are incorrect because (a) reports prepared by financial (not managerial) accountants must be audited by CPAs; (c) SOX clarifies that top management, not the audit committee, is responsible for the company's financial statements; and (d) reports by financial (not managerial) accountants must comply with GAAP.

13. **d.** Activity-based costing attempts to allocate manufacturing overhead in a more meaningful fashion. Therefore, choices (a) just-in-time inventory, (b) total quality management, and (c) balanced scorecard are incorrect.

14. **d.** Corporate social responsibility refers to efforts by companies to employ sustainable business practices with regard to employees and the environment. The other choices are incorrect because (a) defines lean manufacturing, (b) refers to activity-based costing, and (c) describes the theory of constraints.

Practice Brief Exercises

Classify manufacturing costs.

1. **(LO 1)** The following are selected data for Lopez Furniture.

Utilities for manufacturing equipment	$120,000
Wood	850,000
Depreciation on factory building	220,000
Wages for production workers	391,000
Fabric	313,000
Delivery expense	144,000
Property taxes on factory	70,000

Using the selected data above, determine total (a) direct materials, (b) direct labor, (c) manufacturing overhead, (d) product costs, and (e) period costs.

Solution

1. **a.** Wood ($850,000) + Fabric ($313,000) = $1,163,000
    b. Wages for production workers, $391,000
    c. Utilities ($120,000) + Depreciation ($220,000) + Property taxes ($70,000) = $410,000
    d. Direct materials ($1,163,000) + Direct labor ($391,000) + Manufacturing overhead ($410,000) = $1,964,000
    e. Delivery expense, $144,000

2. (LO 3) Cody Cellular has the following data: direct labor $100,000, direct materials used $90,000, total manufacturing overhead $110,000, beginning work in process $15,000, and ending work-in-process $24,000. Compute (a) total manufacturing costs, (b) total cost of work in process, and (c) cost of goods manufactured.

Compute total manufacturing costs and total cost of work in process.

Solution

2. **a.**

Direct materials use	$ 90,000
Direct labor	100,000
Total manufacturing overhead	110,000
Total manufacturing costs	$300,000

b.

Beginning work in process	$ 15,000
Total manufacturing costs	300,000
Total cost of work in process	$315,000

c.

Total cost of work in process	$315,000
Less ending work in process	(24,000)
Cost of goods manufactured	$291,000

3. (LO 3) The following are current asset items in alphabetical order for Asche Company's balance sheet at December 31, 2022. Prepare the current assets section (including a complete heading).

Prepare current assets section.

Accounts receivable	$100,000
Cash	29,000
Finished goods	47,000
Prepaid expenses	20,000
Raw materials	39,000
Short-term investments	51,000
Work in process	44,000

Solution

3.

Asche Company
Balance Sheet
December 31, 2022

Current assets		
Cash		$ 29,000
Short-term investments		51,000
Accounts receivable		100,000
Inventories		
Finished goods	$47,000	
Work in process	44,000	
Raw materials	39,000	130,000
Prepaid expenses		20,000
Total current assets		$330,000

Practice Exercises

Determine the total amount of various types of costs.

1. (LO 2) Fredricks Company reports the following costs and expenses in May.

Factory utilities	$ 15,600	Direct labor	$89,100
Depreciation on factory equipment	12,650	Sales salaries	46,400
Depreciation on delivery trucks	8,800	Property taxes on factory building	2,500
Indirect factory labor	48,900	Repairs to office equipment	2,300
Indirect materials	80,800	Factory repairs	2,000
Direct materials used	137,600	Advertising	18,000
Factory manager's salary	13,000	Office supplies used	5,640

Instructions

From the information, determine the total amount of:

a. Manufacturing overhead.

b. Product costs.

c. Period costs.

Solution

1. a.
Factory utilities	$ 15,600
Depreciation on factory equipment	12,650
Indirect factory labor	48,900
Indirect materials	80,800
Factory manager's salary	13,000
Property taxes on factory building	2,500
Factory repairs	2,000
Manufacturing overhead	$175,450

b.
Direct materials	$137,600
Direct labor	89,100
Manufacturing overhead	175,450
Product costs	$402,150

c.
Depreciation on delivery trucks	$ 8,800
Sales salaries	46,400
Repairs to office equipment	2,300
Advertising	18,000
Office supplies used	5,640
Period costs	$ 81,140

Compute cost of goods manufactured and sold.

2. (LO 3) Tommi Corporation incurred the following costs while manufacturing its product.

Materials used in production	$120,000	Advertising expense	$45,000
Depreciation on plant	60,000	Property taxes on plant	19,000
Property taxes on store	7,500	Delivery expense	21,000
Labor costs of assembly-line workers	110,000	Sales commissions	35,000
Factory supplies used	25,000	Salaries paid to sales clerks	50,000

Work-in-process inventory was $10,000 at January 1 and $14,000 at December 31. Finished goods inventory was $60,500 at January 1 and $50,600 at December 31. (Assume all materials were direct.)

Instructions

a. Compute cost of goods manufactured.

b. Compute cost of goods sold.

Solution

2. a.

Work-in-process, 1/1			$ 10,000
Direct materials used		$120,000	
Direct labor		110,000	
Manufacturing overhead			
Depreciation on plant	$60,000		
Factory supplies used	25,000		
Property taxes on plant	19,000		
Total manufacturing overhead		104,000	
Total manufacturing costs			334,000
Total cost of work-in-process			344,000
Less: Ending work-in-process			14,000
Cost of goods manufactured			$330,000

b.

Finished goods, 1/1	$ 60,500
Cost of goods manufactured	330,000
Cost of goods available for sale	390,500
Less: Finished goods, 12/31	50,600
Cost of goods sold	$339,900

Practice Problem

(LO 3) Superior Company has the following cost and expense data for the year ending December 31, 2022.

Prepare a cost of goods manufactured schedule, an income statement, and a partial balance sheet.

Raw materials, 1/1/22	$ 30,000	Property taxes, factory building	$ 6,000
Raw materials, 12/31/22	20,000	Sales revenue	1,500,000
Raw materials purchases	205,000	Delivery expenses	100,000
Work in process, 1/1/22	80,000	Sales commissions	150,000
Work in process, 12/31/22	50,000	Indirect labor	105,000
Finished goods, 1/1/22	110,000	Factory machinery rent	40,000
Finished goods, 12/31/22	120,000	Factory utilities	65,000
Direct labor	350,000	Depreciation, factory building	24,000
Factory manager's salary	35,000	Administrative expenses	300,000
Insurance, factory	14,000		

Instructions

a. Prepare a cost of goods manufactured schedule for Superior Company for 2022. (Assume that all raw materials used were direct materials.)

b. Prepare an income statement for Superior Company for 2022.

c. Assume that Superior Company's accounting records show the balances of the following current asset accounts: Cash $17,000, Accounts Receivable (net) $120,000, Prepaid Expenses $13,000, and Short-Term Investments $26,000. Prepare the current assets section of the balance sheet for Superior Company as of December 31, 2022.

Solution

a.

Superior Company
Cost of Goods Manufactured Schedule
For the Year Ended December 31, 2022

Work in process, 1/1			$ 80,000
Direct materials			
Raw materials inventory, 1/1	$ 30,000		
Raw materials purchases	205,000		
Total raw materials available for use	235,000		
Less: Raw materials inventory, 12/31	20,000		
Direct materials used		$215,000	
Direct labor		350,000	

(continued)

Manufacturing overhead			
Indirect labor	$105,000		
Factory utilities	65,000		
Factory machinery rent	40,000		
Factory manager's salary	35,000		
Depreciation, factory building	24,000		
Insurance, factory	14,000		
Property taxes, factory building	6,000		
Total manufacturing overhead		289,000	
Total manufacturing costs			854,000
Total cost of work in process			934,000
Less: Work in process, 12/31			50,000
Cost of goods manufactured			$884,000

b.

Superior Company
Income Statement
For the Year Ended December 31, 2022

Sales revenue		$1,500,000
Cost of goods sold		
Finished goods inventory, January 1	$110,000	
Cost of goods manufactured	884,000	
Cost of goods available for sale	994,000	
Less: Finished goods inventory, December 31	120,000	
Cost of goods sold		874,000
Gross profit		626,000
Operating expenses		
Administrative expenses	300,000	
Sales commissions	150,000	
Delivery expenses	100,000	
Total operating expenses		550,000
Net income		$ 76,000

c.

Superior Company
Balance Sheet (partial)
December 31, 2022

Current assets		
Cash		$ 17,000
Short-term investments		26,000
Accounts receivable (net)		120,000
Inventory		
Finished goods	$120,000	
Work in process	50,000	
Raw materials	20,000	190,000
Prepaid expenses		13,000
Total current assets		$366,000

WileyPLUS

Brief Exercises, DO IT! Exercises, Exercises, Problems, and many additional resources are available for practice in WileyPLUS.

Questions

1. a. "Managerial accounting is a field of accounting that provides economic information for all interested parties." Do you agree? Explain.

b. Joe Delong believes that managerial accounting serves only manufacturing firms. Is Joe correct? Explain.

2. Distinguish between managerial and financial accounting as to (a) primary users of reports, (b) types and frequency of reports, and (c) purpose of reports.

3. How do the content of reports and the verification of reports differ between managerial and financial accounting?

4. Linda Olsen is studying for the next accounting mid-term examination. Summarize for Linda what she should know about management functions.

5. "Decision-making is management's most important function." Do you agree? Why or why not?

6. Explain the primary difference between line positions and staff positions, and give examples of each.

7. Jerry Lang is unclear as to the difference between the balance sheets of a merchandising company and a manufacturing company. Explain the difference to Jerry.

8. How are manufacturing costs classified?

9. Mel Finney claims that the distinction between direct and indirect materials is based entirely on physical association with the product. Is Mel correct? Why?

10. Tina Burke is confused about the differences between a product cost and a period cost. Explain the differences to Tina.

11. Identify the differences in the cost of goods sold section of an income statement between a merchandising company and a manufacturing company.

12. The determination of the cost of goods manufactured involves the following factors: (A) beginning work in process inventory, (B) total manufacturing costs, and (C) ending work in process inventory. Identify the meaning of x in the following formulas:

   a. $A + B = x$
   b. $A + B - C = x$

13. Sealy Company has beginning raw materials inventory $12,000, ending raw materials inventory $15,000, and raw materials purchases $170,000. What is the cost of direct materials used?

14. Tate Inc. has beginning work in process $26,000, direct materials used $240,000, direct labor $220,000, total manufacturing overhead $180,000, and ending work in process $32,000. What are the total manufacturing costs?

15. Using the data in Question 14, what are (a) the total cost of work in process and (b) the cost of goods manufactured?

16. In what order should manufacturing inventories be listed in a balance sheet?

17. How does the output of manufacturing operations differ from that of service operations?

18. Discuss whether the product costing techniques discussed in this chapter apply equally well to manufacturers and service companies.

19. What is the value chain? Describe, in sequence, the main components of a manufacturer's value chain.

20. What is an enterprise resource planning (ERP) system? What are its primary benefits?

21. Why is product quality important for companies that implement a just-in-time inventory system?

22. Explain what is meant by "balanced" in the balanced scorecard approach.

23. In what ways can the budgeting process create incentives for unethical behavior?

24. What rules were enacted under the Sarbanes-Oxley Act to address unethical accounting practices?

25. What is activity-based costing, and what are its potential benefits?

Brief Exercises

BE14.1 (LO 1), C Complete the following comparison table between managerial and financial accounting.

Distinguish between managerial and financial accounting.

	Financial Accounting	Managerial Accounting
Primary users of reports		
Types of reports		
Frequency of reports		
Purpose of reports		
Content of reports		
Verification process		

BE14.2 (LO 1), C Listed below are the three functions of the management of an organization.

1. Planning.   2. Directing.   3. Controlling.

Identify which of the following statements best describes each of the above functions.

Identify the three management functions.

a. _____ requires management to look ahead and to establish objectives. A key objective of management is to add value to the business.

b. _____ involves coordinating the diverse activities and human resources of a company to produce a smooth-running operation. This function relates to the implementation of planned objectives.

c. _____ is the process of keeping the activities on track. Management determines whether goals are being met and what changes are necessary when there are deviations.

Classify manufacturing costs.

BE14.3 (LO 2), C Determine whether each of the following costs should be classified as direct materials (DM), direct labor (DL), or manufacturing overhead (MO).

a. _____ Frames and tires used in manufacturing bicycles.
b. _____ Wages paid to production workers.
c. _____ Insurance on factory equipment and machinery.
d. _____ Depreciation on factory equipment.

Classify manufacturing costs.

BE14.4 (LO 2), C Indicate whether each of the following costs of an automobile manufacturer would be classified as direct materials, direct labor, or manufacturing overhead.

a. _____ Windshield.
b. _____ Engine.
c. _____ Wages of assembly line worker.
d. _____ Depreciation of factory machinery.
e. _____ Factory machinery lubricants.
f. _____ Tires.
g. _____ Steering wheel.
h. _____ Salary of painting supervisor.

Identify product and period costs.

BE14.5 (LO 2), C Identify whether each of the following costs should be classified as product costs or period costs.

a. _____ Manufacturing overhead.
b. _____ Selling expenses.
c. _____ Administrative expenses.
d. _____ Advertising expenses.
e. _____ Direct labor.
f. _____ Direct materials.

Classify manufacturing costs.

BE14.6 (LO 2), C Presented below are Rook Company's monthly manufacturing cost data related to its tablet computer product.

a. Utilities for manufacturing equipment $116,000
b. Raw materials (CPU, chips, etc.) $ 85,000
c. Depreciation on manufacturing building $880,000
d. Wages for production workers $191,000

Enter each cost item in the following table, placing an "X" under the appropriate headings.

	Product Costs		
	Direct Materials	Direct Labor	Factory Overhead
a.			
b.			
c.			
d.			

Compute total manufacturing costs and total cost of work in process.

BE14.7 (LO 3), AP Francum Company has the following data: direct labor $209,000, direct materials used $180,000, total manufacturing overhead $208,000, and beginning work in process $25,000. Compute (a) total manufacturing costs and (b) total cost of work in process.

Prepare current assets section.

BE14.8 (LO 3), AP In alphabetical order below are current asset items for Roland Company's balance sheet at December 31, 2022. Prepare the current assets section (including a complete heading).

Accounts receivable	$200,000
Cash	62,000
Finished goods	91,000
Prepaid expenses	38,000
Raw materials	83,000
Work in process	87,000

Determine missing amounts in computing total manufacturing costs.

BE14.9 (LO 3), AP Presented below are incomplete manufacturing cost data. Determine the missing amounts for three different situations.

	Direct Materials Used	Direct Labor Used	Factory Overhead	Total Manufacturing Costs
1.	$40,000	$61,000	$ 50,000	?
2.	?	$75,000	$140,000	$296,000
3.	$55,000	?	$111,000	$310,000

BE14.10 (LO 3), AP Use the same data from BE14.9 above and the data below. Determine the missing amounts.

Determine missing amounts in computing cost of goods manufactured.

	Total Manufacturing Costs	Work in Process (1/1)	Work in Process (12/31)	Cost of Goods Manufactured
1.	?	$120,000	$82,000	?
2.	$296,000	?	$98,000	$331,000
3.	$310,000	$463,000	?	$715,000

BE14.11 (LO 4), C The Sarbanes-Oxley Act (SOX) has important implications for the financial community. Explain two implications of SOX.

Identify important regulatory changes.

DO IT! Exercises

DO IT! 14.1 (LO 1), C Indicate whether the following statements are true or false.

Identify managerial accounting concepts.

1. Managerial accounting reports focus on manufacturing and nonmanufacturing costs.
2. Financial accounting reports pertain to subunits of the business and are very detailed.
3. Managerial accounting reports must follow GAAP and are audited by CPAs.
4. Managers' activities and responsibilities can be classified into three broad functions: planning, directing, and controlling.

DO IT! 14.2 (LO 2), C A music company has these costs:

Identify managerial cost classifications.

Advertising	Paper inserts for CD cases
Blank CDs	CD plastic cases
Depreciation of CD image burner	Salaries of sales representatives
	Salaries of factory maintenance employees
Salary of factory manager	Salaries of employees who burn music onto CDs
Factory supplies used	

Classify each cost as a period or a product cost. Within the product cost category, indicate if the cost is part of direct materials (DM), direct labor (DL), or manufacturing overhead (MO).

DO IT! 14.3 (LO 3), AP The following information is available for Tomlin Company.

Prepare cost of goods manufactured schedule.

	April 1	April 30
Raw materials inventory	$10,000	$14,000
Work in process inventory	5,000	3,500

Materials purchased in April	$ 98,000
Direct labor in April	80,000
Manufacturing overhead in April	160,000

Prepare the cost of goods manufactured schedule for the month of April.

DO IT! 14.4 (LO 4), C Match the descriptions that follow with the corresponding terms.

Identify trends in managerial accounting.

Descriptions:

1. _____ Inventory system in which goods are manufactured or purchased just as they are needed for sale.
2. _____ A method of allocating overhead based on each product's use of activities in making the product.
3. _____ Systems that are especially important to firms adopting just-in-time inventory methods.
4. _____ Provides guidelines for companies to describe their sustainable business practices to external parties.
5. _____ Part of the value chain for a manufacturing company.
6. _____ The U.S. economy is trending toward this.
7. _____ A performance-measurement approach that uses both financial and nonfinancial measures, tied to company objectives, to evaluate a company's operations in an integrated fashion.
8. _____ Requires that top managers certify that the company maintains an adequate system of internal controls.

Terms:

a. Activity-based costing.
b. Balanced scorecard.
c. Total quality management (TQM).
d. Research and development, and product design.
e. Service industries.
f. Just-in-time (JIT) inventory.
g. Sarbanes-Oxley Act (SOX).
h. Global Reporting Initiative.

Exercises

Identify distinguishing features of managerial accounting.

E14.1 (LO 1), C Justin Bleeber has prepared the following list of statements about managerial accounting, financial accounting, and the functions of management.

1. Financial accounting focuses on providing information to internal users.
2. Staff positions are directly involved in the company's primary revenue-generating activities.
3. Preparation of budgets is part of financial accounting.
4. Managerial accounting applies only to merchandising and manufacturing companies.
5. Both managerial accounting and financial accounting deal with many of the same economic events.
6. Managerial accounting reports are prepared only quarterly and annually.
7. Financial accounting reports are general-purpose reports.
8. Managerial accounting reports pertain to subunits of the business.
9. Managerial accounting reports must comply with generally accepted accounting principles.
10. The company treasurer reports directly to the vice president of operations.

Instructions

Identify each statement as true or false. If false, indicate how to correct the statement.

Classify costs into three classes of manufacturing costs.

E14.2 (LO 2), C Presented below is a list of costs and expenses usually incurred by Barnum Corporation, a manufacturer of furniture, in its factory.

1. Salaries for assembly line inspectors.
2. Insurance on factory machines.
3. Property taxes on the factory building.
4. Factory repairs.
5. Upholstery used in manufacturing furniture.
6. Wages paid to assembly line workers.
7. Factory machinery depreciation.
8. Glue, nails, paint, and other small parts used in production.
9. Factory supervisors' salaries.
10. Wood used in manufacturing furniture.

Instructions

Classify the above items into the following categories: (a) direct materials, (b) direct labor, and (c) manufacturing overhead.

Identify types of cost and explain their accounting.

E14.3 (LO 2), C Trak Corporation incurred the following costs while manufacturing its bicycles.

Bicycle components	$100,000	Advertising expense	$45,000
Depreciation on plant	60,000	Property taxes on plant	14,000
Property taxes on store	7,500	Delivery expense	21,000
Labor costs of assembly-line workers	110,000	Sales commissions	35,000
Factory supplies used	13,000	Salaries paid to sales clerks	50,000

Instructions

a. Identify each of the above costs as direct materials, direct labor, manufacturing overhead, or period costs.
b. Explain the basic difference in accounting for product costs and period costs.

E14.4 (LO 2), AP Knight Company reports the following costs and expenses in May.

Factory utilities	$ 15,500	Direct labor	$69,100
Depreciation on factory equipment	12,650	Sales salaries	46,400
Depreciation on delivery trucks	3,800	Property taxes on factory building	2,500
Indirect factory labor	48,900	Repairs to office equipment	1,300
Indirect materials	80,800	Factory repairs	2,000
Direct materials used	137,600	Advertising	15,000
Factory manager's salary	8,000	Office supplies used	2,640

Determine the total amount of various types of costs.

Instructions

From the information, determine the total amount of:

a. Manufacturing overhead.

b. Product costs.

c. Period costs.

E14.5 (LO 2), C Gala Company is a manufacturer of laptop computers. Various costs and expenses associated with its operations are as follows.

1. Property taxes on the factory building.
2. Production superintendents' salaries.
3. Memory boards and chips used in assembling computers.
4. Depreciation on the factory equipment.
5. Salaries for assembly-line quality control inspectors.
6. Sales commissions paid to sell laptop computers.
7. Electrical components used in assembling computers.
8. Wages of workers assembling laptop computers.
9. Soldering materials used on factory assembly lines.
10. Salaries for the night security guards for the factory building.

Classify various costs into different cost categories.

The company intends to classify these costs and expenses into the following categories: (a) direct materials, (b) direct labor, (c) manufacturing overhead, and (d) period costs.

Instructions

List the items (1) through (10). For each item, indicate the cost category to which it belongs.

E14.6 (LO 2), C `Service` The administrators of Crawford County's Memorial Hospital are interested in identifying the various costs and expenses that are incurred in producing a patient's X-ray. A list of such costs and expenses is presented below.

1. Salaries for the X-ray machine technicians.
2. Wages for the hospital janitorial personnel.
3. Film costs for the X-ray machines.
4. Property taxes on the hospital building.
5. Salary of the X-ray technicians' supervisor.
6. Electricity costs for the X-ray department.
7. Maintenance and repairs on the X-ray machines.
8. X-ray department supplies.
9. Depreciation on the X-ray department equipment.
10. Depreciation on the hospital building.

Classify various costs into different cost categories.

The administrators want these costs and expenses classified as (a) direct materials, (b) direct labor, or (c) service overhead.

Instructions

List the items (1) through (10). For each item, indicate the cost category to which the item belongs.

E14.7 (LO 2), AP `Service` National Express reports the following costs and expenses in June 2022 for its delivery service.

Classify various costs into different cost categories.

Indirect materials	$ 6,400	Drivers' salaries	$16,000
Depreciation on delivery equipment	11,200	Advertising	4,600
Dispatcher's salary	5,000	Delivery equipment repairs	300
Property taxes on office building	870	Office supplies	650
CEO's salary	12,000	Office utilities	990
Gas and oil for delivery trucks	2,200	Repairs on office equipment	180

Instructions

Determine the total amount of (a) delivery service (product) costs and (b) period costs.

Compute cost of goods manufactured and sold.

E14.8 (LO 3), AP Lopez Corporation incurred the following costs while manufacturing its product.

Materials used in product	$120,000	Advertising expense	$45,000
Depreciation on plant	60,000	Property taxes on plant	14,000
Property taxes on store	7,500	Delivery expense	21,000
Labor costs of assembly-line workers	110,000	Sales commissions	35,000
Factory supplies used	23,000	Salaries paid to sales clerks	50,000

Work in process inventory was $12,000 at January 1 and $15,500 at December 31. Finished goods inventory was $60,000 at January 1 and $45,600 at December 31.

Instructions

a. Compute cost of goods manufactured.

b. Compute cost of goods sold.

Determine missing amounts in cost of goods manufactured schedule.

E14.9 (LO 3), AP An incomplete cost of goods manufactured schedule is presented below.

Hobbit Company
Cost of Goods Manufactured Schedule
For the Year Ended December 31, 2022

Work in process (1/1)			$210,000
Direct materials			
Raw materials inventory (1/1)	$?		
Add: Raw materials purchases	158,000		
Total raw materials available for use	?		
Less: Raw materials inventory (12/31)	22,500		
Direct materials used		$180,000	
Direct labor		?	
Manufacturing overhead			
Indirect labor	18,000		
Factory depreciation	36,000		
Factory utilities	68,000		
Total overhead		122,000	
Total manufacturing costs			?
Total cost of work in process			?
Less: Work in process (12/31)			81,000
Cost of goods manufactured			$540,000

Instructions

Complete the cost of goods manufactured schedule for Hobbit Company.

Determine the missing amount of different cost items.

E14.10 (LO 3), AN Manufacturing cost data for Copa Company are presented below.

	Case A	Case B	Case C
Direct materials used	$ (a)	$68,400	$130,000
Direct labor	57,000	86,000	(g)
Manufacturing overhead	46,500	81,600	102,000
Total manufacturing costs	195,650	(d)	253,700
Work in process 1/1/22	(b)	16,500	(h)
Total cost of work in process	221,500	(e)	337,000
Work in process 12/31/22	(c)	11,000	70,000
Cost of goods manufactured	185,275	(f)	(i)

Instructions

Indicate the missing amount for each letter (a) through (i).

E14.11 (LO 3), AN Incomplete manufacturing cost data for Horizon Company for 2022 are presented as follows for four different situations.

Determine the missing amount of different cost items, and prepare a condensed cost of goods manufactured schedule.

	Direct Materials Used	Direct Labor Used	Manufacturing Overhead	Total Manufacturing Costs	Work in Process 1/1	Work in Process 12/31	Cost of Goods Manufactured
(1)	$117,000	$140,000	$ 87,000	$ (a)	$33,000	$ (b)	$360,000
(2)	(c)	200,000	132,000	450,000	(d)	40,000	470,000
(3)	80,000	100,000	(e)	265,000	60,000	80,000	(f)
(4)	70,000	(g)	75,000	288,000	45,000	(h)	270,000

Instructions

a. Indicate the missing amount for each letter.

b. Prepare a condensed cost of goods manufactured schedule for situation (1) for the year ended December 31, 2022.

E14.12 (LO 3), AP Cepeda Corporation has the following cost records for June 2022.

Prepare a cost of goods manufactured schedule and a partial income statement.

Indirect factory labor	$ 4,500	Factory utilities	$ 400
Direct materials used	20,000	Depreciation, factory equipment	1,400
Work in process, 6/1/22	3,000	Direct labor	40,000
Work in process, 6/30/22	3,800	Maintenance, factory equipment	1,800
Finished goods, 6/1/22	5,000	Indirect materials	2,200
Finished goods, 6/30/22	7,500	Factory manager's salary	3,000

Instructions

a. Prepare a cost of goods manufactured schedule for June 2022.

b. Prepare an income statement through gross profit for June 2022 assuming sales revenue is $92,100.

E14.13 (LO 2, 3), AP `Service` Keisha Tombert, the bookkeeper for Washington Consulting, a political consulting firm, has recently completed a managerial accounting course at her local college. One of the topics covered in the course was the cost of goods manufactured schedule. Keisha wondered if such a schedule could be prepared for her firm. She realized that, as a service-oriented company, it would have no work in process inventory to consider.

Classify various costs into different categories and prepare cost of services performed schedule.

Listed below are the costs her firm incurred for the month ended August 31, 2022.

Supplies used on consulting contracts	$ 1,700
Supplies used in the administrative offices	1,500
Depreciation on equipment used for contract work	900
Depreciation used on administrative office equipment	1,050
Salaries of professionals working on contracts	15,600
Salaries of administrative office personnel	7,700
Janitorial services for professional offices	700
Janitorial services for administrative offices	500
Insurance on contract operations	800
Insurance on administrative operations	900
Utilities for contract operations	1,400
Utilities for administrative offices	1,300

Instructions

a. Prepare a schedule of cost of contract services performed (similar to a cost of goods manufactured schedule) for the month.

b. For those costs not included in (a), explain how they would be classified and reported in the financial statements.

Prepare a cost of goods manufactured schedule and a partial income statement.

E14.14 (LO 3), AP The following information is available for Aikman Company.

	January 1, 2022	2022	December 31, 2022
Raw materials inventory	$21,000		$30,000
Work in process inventory	13,500		17,200
Finished goods inventory	27,000		21,000
Materials purchased		$150,000	
Direct labor		220,000	
Manufacturing overhead		180,000	
Sales revenue		910,000	

Instructions

a. Compute cost of goods manufactured.

b. Prepare an income statement through gross profit.

c. Show the presentation of the ending inventories on the December 31, 2022, balance sheet.

d. How would the income statement and balance sheet of a merchandising company be different from Aikman's financial statements?

Indicate in which schedule or financial statement(s) different cost items will appear.

E14.15 (LO 3), C University Company produces collegiate apparel. From its accounting records, it prepares the following schedule and financial statements on a yearly basis.

a. Cost of goods manufactured schedule.

b. Income statement.

c. Balance sheet.

The following items are found in its ledger and accompanying data.

1. Direct labor.
2. Raw materials inventory, 1/1.
3. Work in process inventory, 12/31.
4. Finished goods inventory, 1/1.
5. Indirect labor.
6. Depreciation on factory machinery.
7. Work in process, 1/1.
8. Finished goods inventory, 12/31.
9. Factory maintenance salaries.
10. Cost of goods manufactured.
11. Depreciation on delivery equipment.
12. Cost of goods available for sale.
13. Direct materials used.
14. Heat and electricity for factory.
15. Repairs to roof of factory building.
16. Cost of raw materials purchases.

Instructions

List the items (1)–(16). For each item, indicate by using the appropriate letter or letters, the schedule and/or financial statement(s) in which the item will appear.

Prepare a cost of goods manufactured schedule, and present the ending inventories on the balance sheet.

E14.16 (LO 3), AP An analysis of the accounts of Roberts Company reveals the following manufacturing cost data for the month ended June 30, 2022.

Inventory	Beginning	Ending
Raw materials	$9,000	$13,100
Work in process	5,000	7,000
Finished goods	9,000	8,000

Costs incurred: raw materials purchases $54,000, direct labor $47,000, manufacturing overhead $19,900. The specific overhead costs were: indirect labor $5,500, factory insurance $4,000, machinery depreciation

$4,000, machinery repairs $1,800, factory utilities $3,100, and miscellaneous factory costs $1,500. Assume that all raw materials used were direct materials.

Instructions

a. Prepare the cost of goods manufactured schedule for the month ended June 30, 2022.

b. Show the presentation of the ending inventories on the June 30, 2022, balance sheet.

E14.17 (LO 3), AP Writing McQueen Motor Company manufactures automobiles. During September 2022, the company purchased 5,000 head lamps at a cost of $15 per lamp. Fifty of these lamps were used to replace the head lamps in autos used by traveling sales staff, and 4,600 lamps were put in autos manufactured during the month.

Of the autos put into production during September 2022, 90% were completed and transferred to the company's storage lot. Of the cars completed during the month, 70% were sold by September 30.

Determine the amount of cost to appear in various accounts, and indicate in which financial statements these accounts would appear.

Instructions

a. Determine the cost of head lamps that would appear in each of the following accounts at September 30, 2022: Raw Materials, Work in Process, Finished Goods, Cost of Goods Sold, and Selling Expenses.

b. Write a short memo to the chief accountant, indicating whether and where each of the accounts in (a) would appear on the income statement or on the balance sheet at September 30, 2022.

E14.18 (LO 4), C The following is a list of terms related to managerial accounting practices.

Identify various managerial accounting practices.

1. Activity-based costing.
2. Just-in-time inventory.
3. Balanced scorecard.
4. Value chain.

Instructions

Match each of the terms with the statement below that best describes the term.

a. _____ A performance-measurement technique that attempts to consider and evaluate all aspects of performance using financial and nonfinancial measures in an integrated fashion.

b. _____ The group of activities associated with providing a product or performing a service.

c. _____ An approach used to reduce the cost associated with handling and holding inventory by reducing the amount of inventory on hand.

d. _____ A method used to allocate overhead to products based on each product's use of the activities that cause the incurrence of the overhead cost.

Problems: Set A

P14.1A (LO 2), AP Ohno Company specializes in manufacturing a unique model of bicycle helmet. The model is well accepted by consumers, and the company has enough orders to keep the factory production at 10,000 helmets per month (80% of its full capacity). Ohno's monthly manufacturing cost and other expense data are as follows.

Classify manufacturing costs into different categories and compute the unit cost.

Rent on factory equipment	$11,000
Insurance on factory building	1,500
Raw materials (plastics, polystyrene, etc.)	75,000
Utility costs for factory	900
Supplies for general office	300
Wages for assembly line workers	58,000
Depreciation on office equipment	800
Miscellaneous materials (glue, thread, etc.)	1,100
Factory manager's salary	5,700
Property taxes on factory building	400
Advertising for helmets	14,000
Sales commissions	10,000
Depreciation on factory building	1,500

Instructions

a. DM $75,000
   DL $58,000
   MO $22,100
   PC $25,100

a. Prepare an answer sheet with the following column headings.

	Product Costs			
Cost Item	Direct Materials	Direct Labor	Manufacturing Overhead	Period Costs

Enter each cost item on your answer sheet, placing the dollar amount under the appropriate headings. Total the dollar amounts in each of the columns.

b. Compute the cost to produce one helmet.

Classify manufacturing costs into different categories and compute the unit cost.

P14.2A (LO 2), AP Bell Company, a manufacturer of audio systems, started its production in October 2022. For the preceding 3 years, Bell had been a retailer of audio systems. After a thorough survey of audio system markets, Bell decided to turn its retail store into an audio equipment factory.

Raw material costs for an audio system will total $74 per unit. Workers on the production lines are on average paid $12 per hour. An audio system usually takes 5 hours to complete. In addition, the rent on the equipment used to assemble audio systems amounts to $4,900 per month. Indirect materials cost $5 per system. A supervisor was hired to oversee production; her monthly salary is $3,000.

Factory janitorial costs are $1,300 monthly. Advertising costs for the audio system will be $9,500 per month. The factory building depreciation expense is $7,800 per year. Property taxes on the factory building will be $9,000 per year.

Instructions

a. DM $111,000
   DL $ 90,000
   MO $ 18,100
   PC $ 9,500

a. Prepare an answer sheet with the following column headings.

	Product Costs			
Cost Item	Direct Materials	Direct Labor	Manufacturing Overhead	Period Costs

Assuming that Bell manufactures, on average, 1,500 audio systems per month, enter each cost item on your answer sheet, placing the dollar amount per month under the appropriate headings. Total the dollar amounts in each of the columns.

b. Compute the cost to produce one audio system.

Indicate the missing amount of different cost items, and prepare a condensed cost of goods manufactured schedule, an income statement, and a partial balance sheet.

P14.3A (LO 3), AN Incomplete manufacturing costs, expenses, and selling data for two different cases are as follows.

	Case 1	Case 2
Direct materials used	$ 9,600	$ (g)
Direct labor	5,000	8,000
Manufacturing overhead	8,000	4,000
Total manufacturing costs	(a)	16,000
Beginning work in process inventory	1,000	(h)
Ending work in process inventory	(b)	3,000
Sales revenue	24,500	(i)
Sales discounts	2,500	1,400
Cost of goods manufactured	17,000	24,000
Beginning finished goods inventory	(c)	3,300
Cost of goods available for sale	22,000	(j)
Cost of goods sold	(d)	(k)
Ending finished goods inventory	3,400	2,500
Gross profit	(e)	7,000
Operating expenses	2,500	(l)
Net income	(f)	5,000

Instructions

b. Ending WIP $ 6,600
c. Current assets $29,000

a. Indicate the missing amount for each letter.

b. Prepare a condensed cost of goods manufactured schedule for Case 1.

c. Prepare an income statement and the current assets section of the balance sheet for Case 1. Assume that in Case 1 the other items in the current assets section are as follows: Cash $3,000, Receivables (net) $15,000, Raw Materials $600, and Prepaid Expenses $400.

P14.4A (LO 3), AP The following data were taken from the records of Clarkson Company for the fiscal year ended June 30, 2022.

Raw Materials Inventory 7/1/21	$ 48,000	Factory Insurance	$ 4,600
Raw Materials Inventory 6/30/22	39,600	Factory Machinery Depreciation	16,000
Finished Goods Inventory 7/1/21	96,000	Factory Utilities	27,600
Finished Goods Inventory 6/30/22	75,900	Office Utilities Expense	8,650
Work in Process Inventory 7/1/21	19,800	Sales Revenue	534,000
Work in Process Inventory 6/30/22	18,600	Sales Discounts	4,200
Direct Labor	139,250	Plant Manager's Salary	58,000
Indirect Labor	24,460	Factory Property Taxes	9,600
Accounts Receivable	27,000	Factory Repairs	1,400
		Raw Materials Purchases	96,400
		Cash	32,000

Prepare a cost of goods manufactured schedule, a partial income statement, and a partial balance sheet.

Instructions

a. Prepare a cost of goods manufactured schedule. (Assume all raw materials used were direct materials.)
b. Prepare an income statement through gross profit.
c. Prepare the current assets section of the balance sheet at June 30, 2022.

a. CGM $386,910
b. Gross profit $122,790
c. Current assets $193,100

P14.5A (LO 3), AN Empire Company is a manufacturer of smart phones. Its controller resigned in October 2022. An inexperienced assistant accountant has prepared the following income statement for the month of October 2022.

Prepare a cost of goods manufactured schedule and a correct income statement.

Empire Company
Income Statement
For the Month Ended October 31, 2022

Sales revenue		$780,000
Less: Operating expenses		
Raw materials purchases	$264,000	
Direct labor cost	190,000	
Advertising expense	90,000	
Selling and administrative salaries	75,000	
Rent on factory facilities	60,000	
Depreciation on sales equipment	45,000	
Depreciation on factory equipment	31,000	
Indirect labor cost	28,000	
Utilities expense	12,000	
Insurance expense	8,000	803,000
Net loss		$ (23,000)

Prior to October 2022, the company had been profitable every month. The company's president is concerned about the accuracy of the income statement. As her friend, you have been asked to review the income statement and make necessary corrections. After examining other manufacturing cost data, you have acquired additional information as follows.

1. Inventory balances at the beginning and end of October were:

	October 1	October 31
Raw materials	$18,000	$29,000
Work in process	20,000	14,000
Finished goods	30,000	50,000

2. Only 75% of the utilities expense and 60% of the insurance expense apply to factory operations. The remaining amounts should be charged to selling and administrative activities.

Instructions

a. Prepare a schedule of cost of goods manufactured for October 2022.
b. Prepare a correct income statement for October 2022.

a. CGM $581,800
b. NI $ 2,000

Continuing Cases

*Each of the remaining chapters includes a hypothetical case featuring **Current Designs**, the company described at the beginning of this chapter. Students can also work through this case following an **Excel tutorial** available in **WileyPLUS**. Each chapter's tutorial focuses on a different Excel function or feature.*

Current Designs

CD14 Mike Cichanowski founded **Wenonah Canoe** and later purchased **Current Designs**, a company that designs and manufactures kayaks. The kayak-manufacturing facility is located just a few minutes from the canoe company's headquarters in Winona, Minnesota.

Current Designs makes kayaks using two different processes. The rotational molding process uses high temperature to melt polyethylene powder in a closed rotating metal mold to produce a complete kayak hull and deck in a single piece. These kayaks are less labor-intensive and less expensive for the company to produce and sell.

Its other kayaks use the vacuum-bagged composite lamination process (which we will refer to as the composite process). Layers of fiberglass or Kevlar® are carefully placed by hand in a mold and are bonded with resin. Then, a high-pressure vacuum is used to eliminate any excess resin that would otherwise add weight and reduce strength of the finished kayak. These kayaks require a great deal of skilled labor as each boat is individually finished. The exquisite finish of the vacuum-bagged composite kayaks gave rise to Current Designs' tag line, "A work of art, made for life."

Current Designs has the following managers:

Mike Cichanowski, CEO
Diane Buswell, Controller
Deb Welch, Purchasing Manager
Bill Johnson, Sales Manager
Dave Thill, Kayak Plant Manager
Rick Thrune, Production Manager for Composite Kayaks

		Product Costs			Period Costs	Amount
Payee	Purpose	Direct Materials	Direct Labor	Manufacturing Overhead		
Winona Agency	Property insurance for the manufacturing plant					3,200
Bill Johnson (sales manager)	Payroll check—payment to sales manager					1,700
Xcel Energy	Electricity for manufacturing plant					450
Winona Printing	Price lists for salespeople					85
Jim Kaiser (sales representative)	Sales commissions					1,250
Dave Thill (plant manager)	Payroll check—payment to plant manager					1,450
Dana Schultz (kayak assembler)	Payroll check—payment to kayak assembler					760
Composite One	Bagging film used when kayaks are assembled; it is discarded after use					260
Fastenal	Shop supplies—brooms, paper towels, etc.					890
Ravago	Polyethylene powder which is the main ingredient for the rotational molded kayaks					3,170
Winona County	Property taxes on manufacturing plant					5,480
North American Composites	Kevlar® fabric for composite kayaks					4,930
Waste Management	Trash disposal for the company office building					660
None	Journal entry to record depreciation of manufacturing equipment					4,540

Instructions

a. What are the primary information needs of each manager?
b. Name one special-purpose management accounting report that could be designed for each manager. Include the name of the report, the information it would contain, and how frequently it should be issued.
c. When Diane Buswell, controller for Current Designs, reviewed the accounting records for a recent period, she noted the cost items and amounts shown above (amounts are assumed). Enter the amount for each item in the appropriate cost category. Then sum the amounts in each cost category column.

*The **Waterways case** starts in this chapter and continues in every remaining chapter. You will find the complete case for each chapter in **WileyPLUS**.*

Waterways

WP14 Waterways Corporation is a private corporation formed for the purpose of providing the products and the services needed to irrigate farms, parks, commercial projects, and private lawns. It has a centrally located factory in a U.S. city that manufactures the products it markets to retail outlets across the nation. It also maintains a division that performs installation and warranty servicing in six metropolitan areas.

The mission of Waterways is to manufacture quality parts that can be used for effective irrigation projects that also conserve water. By that effort, the company hopes to satisfy its customers, perform rapid and responsible service, and serve the community and the employees who represent them in each community.

The company has been growing rapidly, so management is considering new ideas to help the company continue its growth and maintain the high quality of its products.

Waterways was founded by Will Winkman, who is the company president and chief executive officer (CEO). Working with him from the company's inception is Will's brother, Ben, whose sprinkler designs and ideas about the installation of proper systems have been a major basis of the company's success. Ben is the vice president who oversees all aspects of design and production in the company.

The factory itself is managed by Todd Senter who hires his line managers to supervise the factory employees. The factory makes all of the parts for the irrigation systems. The purchasing department is managed by Helen Hines.

The installation and training division is overseen by vice president Henry Writer, who supervises the managers of the six local installation operations. Each of these local managers hires his or her own local service people. These service employees are trained by the home office under Henry Writer's direction because of the uniqueness of the company's products.

There is a small human resources department under the direction of Sally Fenton, a vice president who handles the employee paperwork, though hiring is actually performed by the separate departments. Teresa Totter is the vice president who heads the sales and marketing area; she oversees 10 well-trained salespeople.

The accounting and finance division of the company is run by Ann Headman, who is the chief financial officer (CFO) and a company vice president. She is a member of the Institute of Management Accountants and holds a certificate in management accounting. She has a small staff of accountants, including a controller and a treasurer, and a staff of accounting input operators who maintain the financial records.

A partial list of Waterways' accounts and their balances for the month of November follows.

Accounts Receivable	$ 275,000
Advertising Expenses	54,000
Cash	260,000
Depreciation—Factory Equipment	16,800
Depreciation—Office Equipment	2,400
Direct Labor	42,000
Factory Supplies Used	16,800
Factory Utilities	10,200
Finished Goods Inventory, November 30	68,800
Finished Goods Inventory, October 31	72,550
Indirect Labor	48,000
Office Supplies Expense	1,600
Other Administrative Expenses	72,000
Prepaid Expenses	41,250
Raw Materials Inventory, November 30	52,700
Raw Materials Inventory, October 31	38,000
Raw Materials Purchases	184,500
Rent—Factory Equipment	47,000

Repairs—Factory Equipment	$	4,500
Salaries		325,000
Sales Revenue		1,350,000
Sales Commissions		40,500
Work in Process Inventory, October 31		52,700
Work in Process Inventory, November 30		42,000

Instructions

a. Based on the information given, construct an organizational chart of Waterways Corporation.

b. A list of accounts and their values are given above. From this information, prepare a cost of goods manufactured schedule, an income statement, and a partial balance sheet for Waterways Corporation for the month of November.

Expand Your Critical Thinking

Decision-Making Across the Organization

CT14.1 Wendall Company specializes in producing fashion outfits. On July 31, 2022, a tornado touched down at its factory and general office. The inventories in the warehouse and the factory were completely destroyed as was the general office nearby. Next morning, through a careful search of the disaster site, however, Bill Francis, the company's controller, and Elizabeth Walton, the cost accountant, were able to recover a small part of manufacturing cost data for the current month.

"What a horrible experience," sighed Bill. "And the worst part is that we may not have enough records to use in filing an insurance claim."

"It was terrible," replied Elizabeth. "However, I managed to recover some of the manufacturing cost data that I was working on yesterday afternoon. The data indicate that our direct labor cost in July totaled $250,000 and that we had purchased $365,000 of raw materials. Also, I recall that the amount of raw materials used for July was $350,000. But I'm not sure this information will help. The rest of our records are blown away."

"Well, not exactly," said Bill. "I was working on the year-to-date income statement when the tornado warning was announced. My recollection is that our sales in July were $1,240,000 and our gross profit ratio has been 40% of sales. Also, I can remember that our cost of goods available for sale was $770,000 for July."

"Maybe we can work something out from this information!" exclaimed Elizabeth. "My experience tells me that our manufacturing overhead is usually 60% of direct labor."

"Hey, look what I just found," cried Elizabeth. "It's a copy of this June's balance sheet, and it shows that our inventories as of June 30 are Finished goods $38,000, Work in process $25,000, and Raw materials $19,000."

"Super," yelled Bill. "Let's go work something out."

In order to file an insurance claim, Wendall Company needs to determine the amount of its inventories as of July 31, 2022, the date of the tornado touchdown.

Instructions

With the class divided into groups, determine the amount of cost in the Raw Materials, Work in Process, and Finished Goods inventory accounts as of the date of the tornado touchdown.

Managerial Analysis

CT14.2 Tenrack is a fairly large manufacturing company located in the southern United States. The company manufactures tennis rackets, tennis balls, tennis clothing, and tennis shoes, all bearing the company's distinctive logo, a large green question mark on a white flocked tennis ball. The company's sales have been increasing over the past 10 years.

The tennis racket division has recently implemented several advanced manufacturing techniques. Robot arms hold the tennis rackets in place while glue dries, and machine vision systems check for defects. The engineering and design team uses computerized drafting and testing of new products. The following managers work in the tennis racket division:

Jason Dennis, Sales Manager (supervises all sales representatives)
Peggy Groneman, Technical Specialist (supervises computer programmers)
Dave Marley, Cost Accounting Manager (supervises cost accountants)
Kevin Carson, Production Supervisor (supervises all manufacturing employees)
Sally Renner, Engineer (supervises all new-product design teams)

Instructions

a. What are the primary information needs of each manager?

b. Which, if any, financial accounting report(s) is each likely to use?

c. Name one special-purpose management accounting report that could be designed for each manager. Include the name of the report, the information it would contain, and how frequently it should be issued.

Real-World Focus

CT14.3 **The Institute of Management Accountants** (IMA) is an organization dedicated to excellence in the practice of management accounting and financial management.

Instructions

Go to the IMA's website to locate the answers to the following questions.

a. How many members does the IMA have, and what are their job titles?

b. What are some of the benefits of joining the IMA as a student?

c. Use the chapter locator function to locate the IMA chapter nearest you, and find the name of the chapter president.

Communication Activity

CT14.4 Refer to P14.5A and add the following requirement.

Prepare a letter to the president of the company, Shelly Phillips, describing the changes you made. Explain clearly why net income is different after the changes. Keep the following points in mind as you compose your letter.

1. This is a letter to the president of a company, who is your friend. The style should be generally formal, but you may relax some requirements. For example, you may call the president by her first name.

2. Executives are very busy. Your letter should tell the president your main results first (for example, the amount of net income).

3. You should include brief explanations so that the president can understand the changes you made in the calculations.

Ethics Case

CT14.5 Steve Morgan, controller for Newton Industries, was reviewing production cost reports for the year. One amount in these reports continued to bother him—advertising. During the year, the company had instituted an expensive advertising campaign to sell some of its slower-moving products. It was still too early to tell whether the advertising campaign was successful.

There had been much internal debate as how to report advertising cost. The vice president of finance argued that advertising costs should be reported as a cost of production, just like direct materials and direct labor. He therefore recommended that this cost be identified as manufacturing overhead and reported as part of inventory costs until sold. Others disagreed. Morgan believed that this cost should be reported as an expense of the current period, so as not to overstate net income. Others argued that it should be reported as prepaid advertising and reported as a current asset.

The president finally had to decide the issue. He argued that these costs should be reported as inventory. His arguments were practical ones. He noted that the company was experiencing financial difficulty and expensing this amount in the current period might jeopardize a planned bond offering. Also, by reporting the advertising costs as inventory rather than as prepaid advertising, less attention would be directed to it by the financial community.

Instructions

a. Who are the stakeholders in this situation?

b. What are the ethical issues involved in this situation?

c. What would you do if you were Steve Morgan?

All About You

CT14.6 The primary purpose of managerial accounting is to provide information useful for management decisions. Many of the managerial accounting techniques that you learn in this course will be useful for decisions you make in your everyday life.

Instructions

For each of the following managerial accounting techniques, read the definition provided and then provide an example of a personal situation that would benefit from use of this technique.

a. Break-even point (Chapter 18).

b. Budget (Chapter 22).

c. Balanced scorecard (Chapter 24).

d. Capital budgeting (Chapter 25).

Considering Your Costs and Benefits

CT14.7 As noted in this chapter, because of global competition, companies have become increasingly focused on reducing costs. To reduce costs and remain competitive, many companies are turning to outsourcing. Outsourcing means hiring an outside supplier to provide elements of a product or service rather than producing them internally.

Suppose you are the managing partner in a CPA firm with 30 full-time staff. Larger firms in your community have begun to outsource basic tax-return preparation work to India. Should you outsource your basic tax-return work to India as well? You estimate that you would have to lay off six staff members if you outsource the work. The basic arguments for and against are as follows.

YES: The wages paid to Indian accountants are very low relative to U.S. wages. You will not be able to compete unless you outsource.

NO: Tax-return data is highly sensitive. Many customers will be upset to learn that their data is being emailed around the world.

Instructions

Write a response indicating your position regarding this situation. Provide support for your view.

CHAPTER 15

Job Order Costing

Chapter Preview

The following Feature Story about **Disney** describes how important accurate costing is to movie studios. In order to submit accurate bids on new film projects and to know whether it profited from past films, the company needs a good costing system. This chapter illustrates how costs are assigned to specific jobs, such as the production of *The Avengers 3*. We begin the discussion in this chapter with an overview of the flow of costs in a job order cost accounting system. We then use a case study to explain and illustrate the documents, entries, and accounts in this type of cost accounting system.

Feature Story

Profiting from the Silver Screen

Have you ever had the chance to tour a movie studio? There's a lot going on! Lots of equipment and lots of people with a variety of talents. Running a film studio, whether as an independent company or part of a major corporation, is a complex and risky business. Consider **Disney**, which has produced such classics as *Snow White and the Seven Dwarfs* and such colossal successes as *Frozen*. The movie studio has, however, also seen its share of losses. Disney's *Lone Ranger* movie brought in revenues of $260 million, but its production and marketing costs were a combined $375 million—a loss of $115 million.

Every time Disney or another movie studio makes a new movie, it is creating a unique product. Ideally, each new movie should be able to stand on its own, that is, the film should generate revenues that exceed its costs. In order to know whether a particular movie is profitable, the studio must keep track of all of the costs incurred to make and market the film. These costs include such items as salaries of the writers, actors, director, producer, and production team (e.g., film crew); licensing costs; depreciation on equipment; music; studio rental; and marketing and distribution costs. If you've ever watched the credits at the end of a movie, you know the list goes on and on.

The movie studio isn't the only one with an interest in knowing a particular project's profitability. Many of the people involved in making the movie, such as the screenwriters, actors, and producers, have at least part of their compensation tied to its profitability. As such, complaints about inaccurate accounting are common in the movie industry.

In particular, a few well-known and widely attended movies reported low profits, or even losses, once the accountants got done with them. How can this be? The issue is that a large portion of a movie's costs are overhead costs that can't be directly traced to a film, such as depreciation of film equipment and sets, facility maintenance costs, and executives' salaries. Actors and others often complain that these overhead costs are overallocated to their movie and therefore negatively affect their compensation.

To reduce the risk of financial flops, many of the big studios now focus on making sequels of previous hits. This might explain why, shortly after losing money on the *Lone Ranger*, Disney decided to make *The Avengers 2* and is now working on *The Avengers 3*—much safer bets.

 Watch the *Making a Hollywood Movie* video in WileyPLUS to learn more about job order costing in the real world.

Chapter Outline

LEARNING OBJECTIVES

LO 1 Describe cost systems and the flow of costs in a job order system.	• Process cost system • Job order cost system • Job order cost flow • Accumulating costs	**DO IT! 1** Accumulating Manufacturing Costs
LO 2 Use a job cost sheet to assign costs to work in process.	• Raw materials costs • Factory labor costs	**DO IT! 2** Work in Process
LO 3 Demonstrate how to determine and use the predetermined overhead rate.	• predetermined overhead rate • Applying manufacturing overhead	**DO IT! 3** Predetermined Overhead Rate
LO 4 Prepare entries for manufacturing and service jobs completed and sold.	• Finished goods • Cost of goods sold • Summary of job order cost flows • Job order for service companies • Pros and cons of job order costing	**DO IT! 4** Completion and Sale of Jobs
LO 5 Distinguish between under- and overapplied manufacturing overhead.	• Under- or overapplied manufacturing overhead	**DO IT! 5** Applied Manufacturing Overhead

Go to the Review and Practice section at the end of the chapter for a targeted summary and practice applications with solutions.
Visit WileyPLUS for additional tutorials and practice opportunities.

Cost Accounting Systems

LEARNING OBJECTIVE 1
Describe cost systems and the flow of costs in a job order system.

Cost accounting involves measuring, recording, and reporting product and service costs. Companies determine both the total cost and the unit cost of each product. The accuracy of the product cost information is critical to the success of the company. Companies use this information to determine which products to produce, what prices to charge, and how many units to produce. Accurate product cost information is also vital for effective evaluation of employee performance.

A **cost accounting system** consists of accounts for the various manufacturing and service costs. These accounts are fully integrated into the general ledger of a company. An important feature of a cost accounting system is the use of **a perpetual inventory system**. Such a system **provides immediate, up-to-date information on the cost of a product**.

There are two basic types of cost accounting systems: (1) a process cost system and (2) a job order cost system. Although cost accounting systems differ widely from company to company, most involve one of these two traditional product costing systems.

Process Cost System

A company uses a **process cost system** when it manufactures a large volume of similar products. Production is continuous. Examples of a process cost system are the manufacture of cereal by **Kellogg**, the refining of petroleum by **ExxonMobil**, and the production of ice cream by **Ben & Jerry's**. Process costing accumulates product-related costs **for a period of time** (such as a week or a month) instead of assigning costs to specific products or job orders. In process costing, companies assign the costs to departments or processes for the specified period of time. **Illustration 15.1** shows examples of the use of a process cost system. We will discuss the process cost system further in Chapter 16.

ILLUSTRATION 15.1 Process cost system

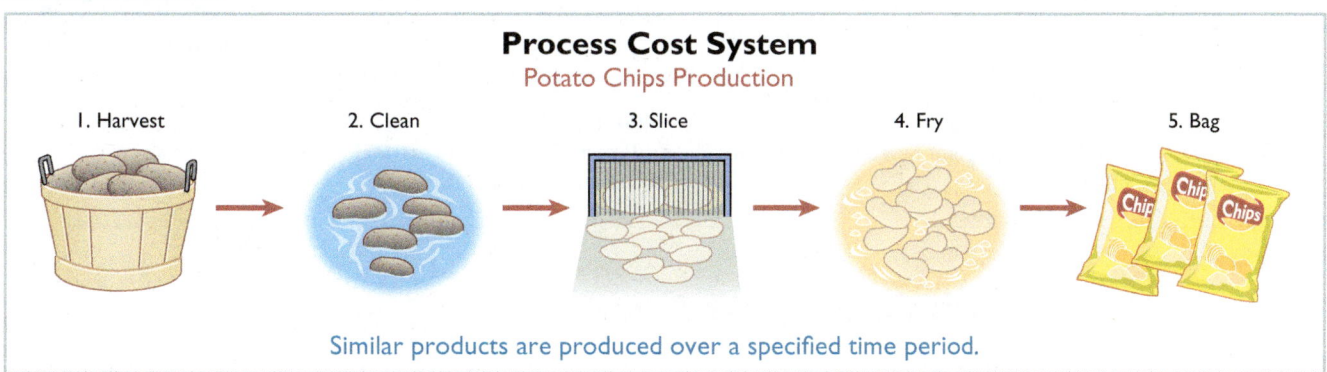

Job Order Cost System

Under a **job order cost system**, the company assigns costs to each **job** or to each **batch** of goods. An example of a job is the manufacture of a jet by **Boeing**, the production of a movie by **Disney**, or the making of a fire truck by **American LaFrance**. An example of a batch is the printing of 225 wedding invitations by a local print shop, or the printing of a weekly issue of *Fortune* magazine by a high-tech printer such as **Quad Graphics**.

An important feature of job order costing is that each job or batch has its own distinguishing characteristics. For example, each house is custom built, each consulting engagement by a CPA firm is unique, and each printing job is different. **The objective is to compute the cost**

per job. At each point in manufacturing a product or performing a service, the company can identify the job and its associated costs. A job order cost system measures costs for each job, rather than for set time periods. **Illustration 15.2** shows the recording of costs in a job order cost system for Disney as it produced two different films at the same time: an animated film and an action thriller.

ILLUSTRATION 15.2

Job order cost system for Disney

Can a company use both job order and process cost systems? Yes. For example, **General Motors** uses process cost accounting for its standard model cars, such as Malibu and Corvettes, and job order cost accounting for a custom-made limousine for the President of the United States.

The objective of both cost accounting systems is to provide unit cost information for product pricing, cost control, inventory valuation, and financial statement presentation.

Management Insight

© Tony Tremblay/iStockphoto

Jobs Won, Money Lost

Many companies suffer from poor cost accounting. As a result, they sometimes make products they should not be selling at all, or they buy product components that they could more profitably make themselves. Also, inaccurate cost data leads companies to misallocate capital and frustrates efforts by plant managers to improve efficiency.

For example, consider the case of a diversified company in the business of rebuilding diesel locomotives. The managers thought they were making money, but a consulting firm found that the company had seriously underestimated costs. The company bailed out of the business and not a moment too soon. Says the consultant who advised the company, "The more contracts it won, the more money it lost." Given that situation, a company cannot stay in business very long!

What type of costs do you think the company had been underestimating? (Go to WileyPLUS for this answer and additional questions).

Job Order Cost Flow

We first address the flow of costs for a manufacturer (service company costs are addressed in a later section). The flow of costs (direct materials, direct labor, and manufacturing overhead) in job order cost accounting parallels the physical flow of the materials as they are converted into finished goods and then sold. As shown in **Illustration 15.3**, companies first **accumulate** manufacturing costs in the form of raw materials, factory labor, or manufacturing overhead. They then **assign** manufacturing costs to the Work in Process Inventory account. When a job is completed, the company transfers the cost of the job to Finished Goods Inventory. Later when the goods are sold, the company transfers their cost to Cost of Goods Sold.

Illustration 15.3 provides a basic overview of the flow of costs in a manufacturing setting for production of a fire truck. A more detailed presentation of the flow of costs is summarized near the end of this chapter in Illustration 15.15. There are two major steps in the flow of costs: (1) *accumulating* the manufacturing costs incurred, and (2) *assigning* the accumulated costs to

ILLUSTRATION 15.3 Flow of costs in job order costing

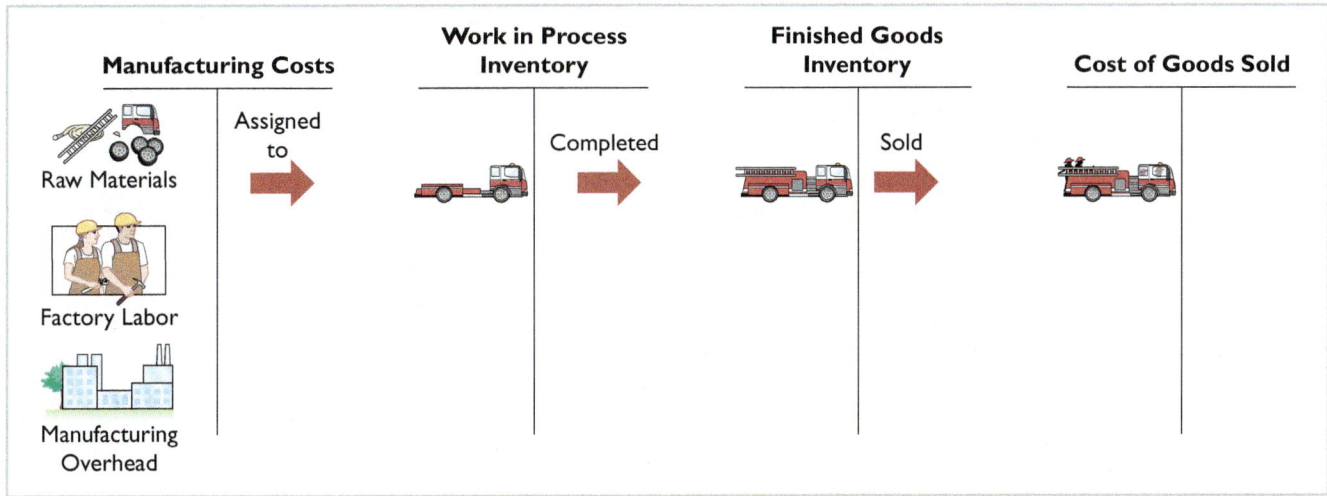

the work done. The following discussion shows that the company accumulates manufacturing costs incurred by debits to Raw Materials Inventory, Factory Labor, and Manufacturing Overhead. When the company incurs these costs, it does not attempt to associate the costs with specific jobs. The company makes additional entries to assign manufacturing costs incurred to specific jobs. In the remainder of this chapter, we will use a case study to explain how a job order cost system operates.

Accumulating Manufacturing Costs

To illustrate a job order cost system, we will use the January transactions of Wallace Company, which makes custom electronic sensors for corporate safety applications (such as fire and carbon monoxide) and security applications (such as theft and corporate espionage).

Raw Materials Costs

When Wallace receives the raw materials (both direct and indirect) it has purchased from a supplier, **it debits the cost of the materials to Raw Materials Inventory**. The company debits this account for the invoice cost of the raw materials and freight costs chargeable to the purchaser. It credits the account for purchase discounts taken and purchase returns and allowances. Wallace makes **no effort at this point to associate the cost of materials with specific jobs or orders**.

To illustrate, assume that Wallace purchases 2,000 lithium batteries (Stock No. AA2746) at $5 per unit ($10,000) and 800 electronic modules (Stock No. AA2850) at $40 per unit ($32,000) for a total cost of $42,000 ($10,000 + $32,000). The entry to record this purchase on January 4 is:

(1)[1]

Jan. 4	Raw Materials Inventory		42,000	
	Accounts Payable			42,000
	(Purchase of raw materials on account)			

Raw Materials Inventory	
42,000	

At this point, Raw Materials Inventory has a balance of $42,000, as shown in the T-account. As we will explain later in the chapter, the company subsequently assigns direct raw materials inventory to work in process and indirect raw materials inventory to manufacturing overhead.

---

[1] The numbers placed above the entries for Wallace Company are used for reference purposes in the summary provided in Illustration 15.15.

Factory Labor Costs

Some of a company's employees are involved in the manufacturing process, while others are not. As discussed in Chapter 14, wages and salaries of nonmanufacturing employees are expensed as period costs (e.g., Salaries and Wages Expense). Costs related to manufacturing employees are accumulated in Factory Labor to ensure their treatment as product costs. Factory labor consists of three costs: (1) wages payable related to factory workers, (2) employer payroll taxes on these wages, and (3) fringe benefits (such as sick pay, pensions, and vacation pay) incurred by the employer. **Companies debit labor costs to Factory Labor as they incur those costs.**

To illustrate, assume that Wallace incurs $32,000 of factory labor costs. Of that amount, $27,000 relates to wages payable and $5,000 relates to payroll taxes payable in February. The entry to record factory labor (both direct and indirect) for the month is:

Factory Labor
32,000	

(2)
Jan. 31	Factory Labor	32,000	
	Factory Wages Payable		27,000
	Employer Payroll Taxes Payable		5,000
	(To record factory labor costs)		

At this point, Factory Labor has a balance of $32,000, as shown in the T-account. The company subsequently assigns direct factory labor to work in process and indirect factory labor to manufacturing overhead.

Manufacturing Overhead Costs

A company has many types of overhead costs. If these overhead costs, such as property taxes, depreciation, insurance, and repairs, relate to overhead costs of a nonmanufacturing facility, such as an office building, then these costs are expensed as period costs (e.g., Property Tax Expense, Depreciation Expense, Insurance Expense, and Maintenance and Repairs Expense). If the costs relate to the manufacturing process, then they are accumulated in Manufacturing Overhead to ensure their treatment as product costs.

Using assumed data, the summary entry for manufacturing overhead (other than indirect materials and indirect labor) in Wallace Company is:

Manufacturing Overhead
13,800	

(3)
Jan. 31	Manufacturing Overhead	13,800	
	Utilities Payable		4,800
	Prepaid Insurance		2,000
	Accounts Payable (for repairs)		2,600
	Accumulated Depreciation		3,000
	Property Taxes Payable		1,400
	(To record overhead costs)		

At this point, Manufacturing Overhead has a balance of $13,800, as shown in the T-account. The company subsequently assigns manufacturing overhead to work in process.

ACTION PLAN

- In accumulating manufacturing costs, debit at least one of three accounts: Raw Materials Inventory, Factory Labor, and Manufacturing Overhead.

DO IT! 1 | Accumulating Manufacturing Costs

During the current month, Ringling Company incurs the following manufacturing costs:

a. Raw material purchases of $4,200 on account.

b. Factory labor of $18,000. Of that amount, $15,000 relates to wages payable and $3,000 relates to payroll taxes payable.

c. Factory utilities of $2,200 are payable, prepaid factory insurance of $1,800 has expired, and depreciation on the factory building is $3,500.

Prepare journal entries for each type of manufacturing cost.

Solution

a.	Raw Materials Inventory	4,200	
	Accounts Payable		4,200
	(Purchases of raw materials on account)		
b.	Factory Labor	18,000	
	Factory Wages Payable		15,000
	Employer Payroll Taxes Payable		3,000
	(To record factory labor costs)		
c.	Manufacturing Overhead	7,500	
	Utilities Payable		2,200
	Prepaid Insurance		1,800
	Accumulated Depreciation		3,500
	(To record overhead costs)		

Related exercise material: **BE15.1, BE15.2, DO IT! 15.1, E15.1, E15.7, E15.8, and E15.11.**

ACTION PLAN
- Manufacturing overhead costs may be recognized daily. Or, manufacturing overhead may be recorded periodically through a summary entry.

Assigning Manufacturing Costs

LEARNING OBJECTIVE 2
Use a job cost sheet to assign costs to work in process.

Assigning manufacturing costs to work in process results in the following entries.

1. **Debits** made to Work in Process Inventory.
2. **Credits** made to Raw Materials Inventory, Factory Labor, and Manufacturing Overhead.

An essential accounting record in assigning costs to jobs is a **job cost sheet**, as shown in **Illustration 15.4**. A **job cost sheet** is a form used to record the costs chargeable to a specific job and to determine the total and unit costs of the completed job (see **Decision Tools**).

Decision Tools
A completed job cost sheet helps managers to compare costs to those of previous periods to ensure that costs are in line.

ILLUSTRATION 15.4
Job cost sheet

Job Cost Sheet

Job No. _____ Quantity _____
Item _____ Date Requested _____
For _____ Date Completed _____

Date	Direct Materials	Direct Labor	Manufacturing Overhead

Cost of completed job
    Direct materials $ _____
    Direct labor   _____
    Manufacturing overhead   _____
Total cost $ _____
Unit cost (total dollars ÷ quantity) $ _____

Companies keep a separate job cost sheet for each job, typically as a computer file. The job cost sheets constitute the subsidiary ledger for the Work in Process Inventory control account in the general ledger. A **subsidiary ledger** consists of individual records for each individual item—in this case, each job. The Work in Process account is referred to as a **control account** because it summarizes the detailed data regarding specific jobs contained in the job cost sheets. **Each entry to Work in Process Inventory must be accompanied by a corresponding posting to one or more job cost sheets.**

Raw Materials Costs

> **ETHICS NOTE**
>
> Approvals are an important internal control feature of a requisition slip because they establish individual accountability over inventory.

Companies assign raw materials costs to jobs when their materials storeroom issues the materials in response to requests. Requests for issuing raw materials are made by production department personnel on a prenumbered **materials requisition slip**. The materials issued may be used directly on a job, or they may be considered indirect materials. As **Illustration 15.5** shows, the requisition should indicate the quantity and type of materials withdrawn and the account to be charged (see **Ethics Note**). Note in Illustration 15.5 the specific job to be charged (Job No. 101) as well as the internal control of prenumbering (R247) to enhance accountability. The company will charge direct materials to Work in Process Inventory, and indirect materials to Manufacturing Overhead.

ILLUSTRATION 15.5

Materials requisition slip

Wallace Company
Materials Requisition Slip

Deliver to: Assembly Department   Req. No. R247
Charge to: Work in Process–Job No. 101   Date: 1/6/22

Quantity	Description	Stock No.	Cost per Unit	Total
200	Lithium batteries	AA2746	$5.00	$1,000

Requested by _Bruce Howart_   Received by _Herb Crowley_
Approved by _Kap Shin_   Costed by _Heather Remmers_

The company may use any of the inventory costing methods (FIFO, LIFO, or average-cost) in costing the requisitions **to the individual job cost sheets**. In an automated system, the requisition is entered electronically. Once approved and delivered to production, the materials are charged automatically to an electronic job cost record.

Periodically, the company journalizes the requisitions. For example, if Wallace uses $24,000 of direct materials and $6,000 of indirect materials in January, the entry on January 31 is:

(4)

Jan. 31	Work in Process Inventory	24,000	
	Manufacturing Overhead	6,000	
	Raw Materials Inventory		30,000
	(To assign materials to jobs and overhead)		

This entry reduces Raw Materials Inventory by $30,000, increases Work in Process Inventory by $24,000 as the direct costs are assigned to jobs, and increases Manufacturing Overhead by $6,000, as the following shows.

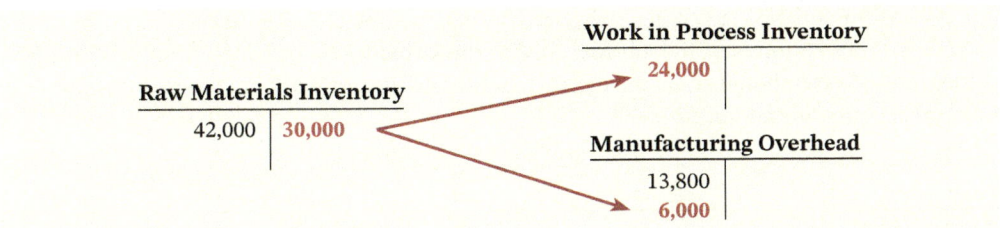

Illustration 15.6 shows the posting of requisition slip R247 to Job No. 101 for $1,000 and other assumed postings to the job cost sheets for materials. The requisition slips provide the basis for total direct materials costs of $12,000 for Job No. 101, $7,000 for Job No. 102,

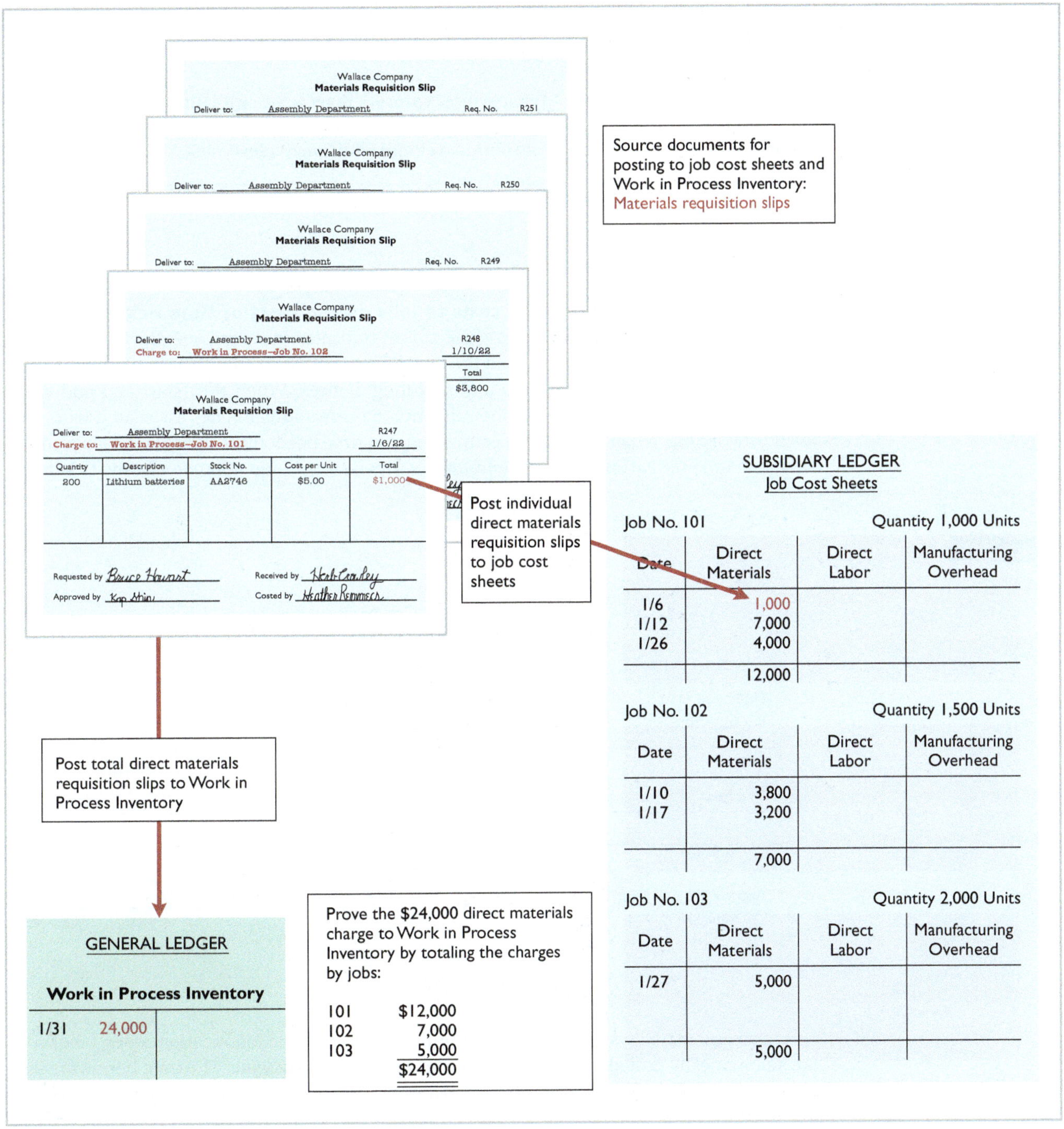

ILLUSTRATION 15.6 Job cost sheets–posting of direct materials

and $5,000 for Job No. 103. After the company has completed all postings, the sum of the direct materials columns of the job cost sheets (the **subsidiary** account amounts of $12,000, $7,000, and $5,000) should equal the direct materials debited to Work in Process Inventory (the **control** account amount of $24,000).

Management Insight IHS

The Cost of an iPhone? Just Tear One Apart

© TommL/iStockphoto

All companies need to know what it costs to make their own products—but a lot of companies would also like to know the cost of their competitors' products as well. That's where **IHS** steps in. IHS tears apart sophisticated electronic devices to tell you what it would cost to replicate.

In the case of smartphones, which often have more than 1,000 tiny components, that is no small feat. For example, consider that the components of a recent iPhone model cost about $221. Assembly adds only about another $5. However, the difference between what you pay (almost triple the total component cost) and the "cost" is not all profit. You also have to consider the additional nonproduction costs of research, design, marketing, patent fees, and selling costs.

Source: 2016 IHS Markit; https://9to5mac.com/2016/09/20/649-iphone-7-estimated-to-cost-apple-220-heres-the-component-breakdown.

What type of costs are marketing and selling costs, and how are they treated for accounting purposes? (Go to WileyPLUS for this answer and additional questions).

Factory Labor Costs

Companies assign factory labor costs to jobs on the basis of time tickets prepared when the work is performed. The **time ticket** indicates the employee, the hours worked, the account and job to be charged, and the total labor cost. Many companies accumulate these data through the use of bar coding and scanning devices. When they start and end work, employees scan bar codes on their identification badges and bar codes associated with each job they work on. When direct labor is involved, the time ticket must indicate the job number, as shown in **Illustration 15.7**. The employee's supervisor should approve all time tickets.

ILLUSTRATION 15.7

Time ticket

Wallace Company
Time Ticket

Employee: John Nash Date: 1/6/22
Charge to: Work in Process Employee No.: 124
  Job No.: 101

Time			Hourly Rate	Total Cost
Start	Stop	Total Hours		
0800	1200	4	10.00	40.00

Approved by Bob Kadler   Costed by M Cher

In an automated system, after factory employees scan their identification codes, labor costs are automatically posted to specific jobs at the appropriate pay scale. The time tickets are later sent to the payroll department, which applies the employee's hourly wage rate plus fringe benefits and computes the total labor cost. Finally, the company journalizes the time tickets. It debits the account Work in Process Inventory for direct labor and debits Manufacturing Overhead for indirect labor. For example, if the $32,000 total factory labor cost consists of $28,000 of direct labor and $4,000 of indirect labor, the entry is:

(5)

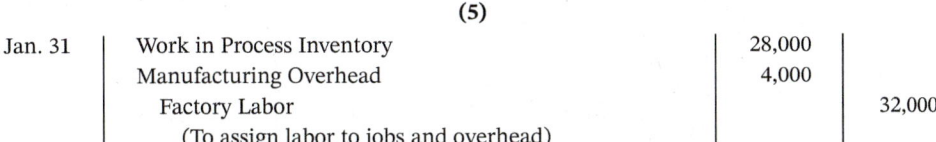
Jan. 31	Work in Process Inventory	28,000	
	Manufacturing Overhead	4,000	
	Factory Labor		32,000
	(To assign labor to jobs and overhead)		

As a result of this entry, Factory Labor is reduced by $32,000 so it has a zero balance, and labor costs are assigned to the appropriate manufacturing accounts. The entry increases Work in Process Inventory by $28,000 and increases Manufacturing Overhead by $4,000, as shown below.

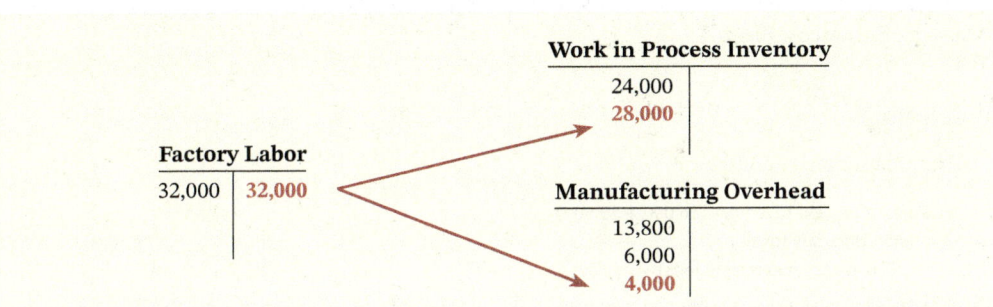

Let's assume that the labor costs chargeable to Wallace's three jobs are $15,000, $9,000, and $4,000. **Illustration 15.8** shows the Work in Process Inventory and job cost sheets

ILLUSTRATION 15.8 Job cost sheets–direct labor

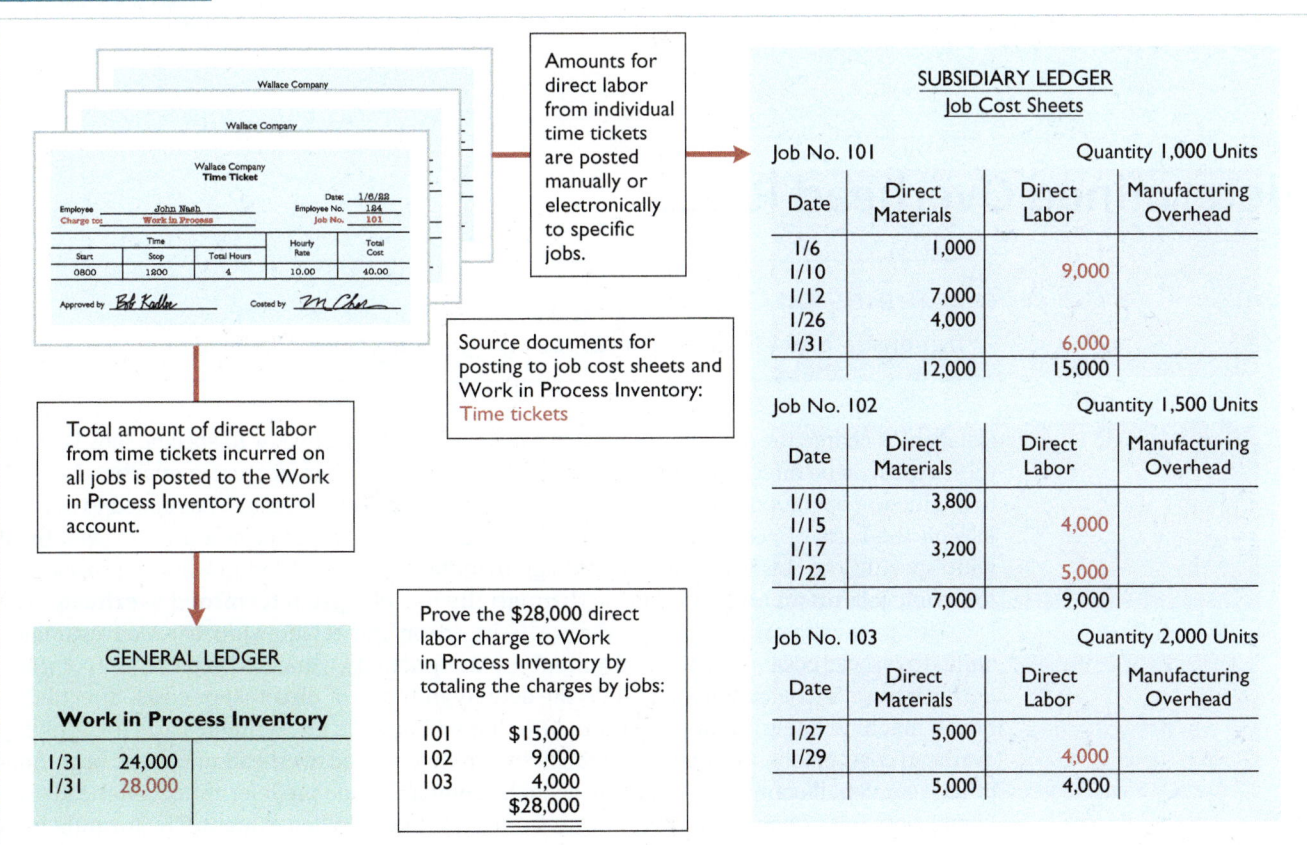

after posting. As in the case of direct materials, the sum of the postings to the direct labor columns of the job cost sheets (subsidiary accounts Job 101 $15,000, Job 102 $9,000, and Job 103 $4,000) should equal the posting of direct labor to the Work in Process Inventory control account ($28,000). Also, time card and job ticket hours should be periodically reconciled as an internal control.

ACTION PLAN

- Recognize that Work in Process Inventory is the control account for all unfinished job cost sheets.
- Debit Work in Process Inventory for the materials, labor, and overhead charged to the job cost sheets.
- Credit the accounts that were debited when the manufacturing costs were accumulated.

DO IT! 2 | Work in Process

Danielle Company is working on two job orders. The job cost sheets show the following:

    Direct materials—Job 120 $6,000; Job 121 $3,600
    Direct labor—Job 120 $4,000; Job 121 $2,000
    Manufacturing overhead—Job 120 $5,000; Job 121 $2,500

Prepare the three summary entries to record the assignment of costs to Work in Process from the data on the job cost sheets.

Solution

The three summary entries are:

Work in Process Inventory ($6,000 + $3,600)	9,600	
Raw Materials Inventory		9,600
(To assign materials to jobs)		
Work in Process Inventory ($4,000 + $2,000)	6,000	
Factory Labor		6,000
(To assign labor to jobs)		
Work in Process Inventory ($5,000 + $2,500)	7,500	
Manufacturing Overhead		7,500
(To assign overhead to jobs)		

Related exercise material: **BE15.3, BE15.4, BE15.5, DO IT! 15.2, E15.2, E15.7, and E15.8**.

Predetermined Overhead Rates

LEARNING OBJECTIVE 3
Demonstrate how to determine and use the predetermined overhead rate.

Companies charge the actual costs of direct materials and direct labor to specific jobs because these costs can be directly traced to specific jobs. In contrast, manufacturing **overhead** relates to production operations **as a whole**. As a result, overhead costs cannot be assigned to specific jobs on the basis of actual costs incurred because these costs cannot be traced to (identified with) specific jobs. Instead, companies assign manufacturing overhead to work in process and to specific jobs **on an estimated basis through the use of a predetermined overhead rate**.

The **predetermined overhead rate** is based on the relationship between estimated annual overhead costs and estimated annual operating activity, expressed in terms of a common **activity base**. The company may state the activity in terms of direct labor costs, direct labor hours, machine hours, or any other measure that will provide an equitable basis for applying overhead costs to jobs. Companies establish the predetermined overhead rate at the beginning of the year. Small companies often use a single, company-wide predetermined overhead rate. Large companies often use rates that vary from department to department. The formula for a predetermined overhead rate is shown in **Illustration 15.9**.

| Estimated Annual Overhead Costs | ÷ | Estimated Annual Operating Activity | = | **Predetermined Overhead Rate** |

ILLUSTRATION 15.9
Formula for predetermined overhead rate

Overhead consists only of indirect costs and relates to production operations as a whole. To know what "the whole" is, it might seem that the logical thing is to wait until the end of the year's operations. At that time, the company knows all of its actual costs for the period. As a practical matter, though, managers cannot wait until the end of the year. To price products effectively as they are completed, managers need information about product costs of specific jobs completed during the year. Using an estimated predetermined overhead rate enables a cost to be determined for the job immediately and identifies when actual costs may be different than planned. **Illustration 15.10** indicates how manufacturing overhead is assigned to work in process.

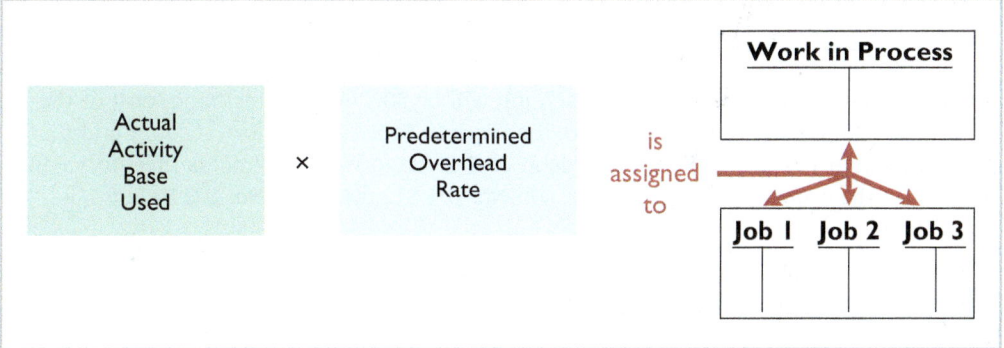

ILLUSTRATION 15.10
Using predetermined overhead rates

Wallace Company uses direct labor cost as the activity base. Assuming that the company estimates annual overhead costs to be $280,000 and direct labor costs for the year to be $350,000, the overhead rate is 80%, computed as shown in **Illustration 15.11**.

Estimated Annual Overhead Costs	÷	Estimated Direct Labor Cost	=	Predetermined Overhead Rate
$280,000	÷	$350,000	=	80%

ILLUSTRATION 15.11
Calculation of predetermined overhead rate

This means that for every dollar of direct labor, Wallace will assign 80 cents of manufacturing overhead to a job. The use of a predetermined overhead rate enables the company to determine the approximate total cost of each job **when it completes the job**.

Historically, companies used direct labor costs or direct labor hours as the activity base. The reason was the relatively high correlation between direct labor and manufacturing overhead. Today, more companies are using **machine hours as the activity base, due to increased reliance on automation in manufacturing operations**. Or, as mentioned in Chapter 14 (and discussed more fully in Chapter 17), many companies now use activity-based costing to more accurately assign overhead costs based on the activities that give rise to the costs.

A company may use more than one activity base. For example, if a job is manufactured in more than one factory department, each department may have its own overhead rate. In the Feature Story, **Disney** might use two bases in assigning overhead to film jobs: direct materials dollars for indirect materials, and direct labor hours for such costs as insurance and supervisor salaries.

Wallace Company applies manufacturing overhead to work in process after it assigns direct labor costs. It also applies manufacturing overhead to specific jobs at that time. For January, Wallace applied overhead of $22,400 in response to its assignment of $28,000 of direct labor costs (direct labor cost of $28,000 × 80%). The following entry records this application.

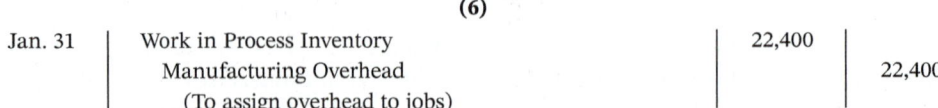

		(6)		
Jan. 31	Work in Process Inventory		22,400	
	Manufacturing Overhead			22,400
	(To assign overhead to jobs)			

This entry reduces the balance in Manufacturing Overhead and increases Work in Process Inventory by $22,400, as shown below.

Manufacturing Overhead		Work in Process Inventory	
13,800	22,400	24,000	
6,000		28,000	
4,000		22,400	
1,400			

The overhead that Wallace applies to each job will be 80% of the direct labor cost of the job for the month. **Illustration 15.12** shows the Work in Process Inventory account and the job cost sheets after posting. Note that the debit of $22,400 to Work in Process Inventory equals the sum of the overhead applied to jobs: Job No. 101 $12,000 1 Job No. 102 $7,200 1 Job No. 103 $3,200.

ILLUSTRATION 15.12 Job cost sheets–manufacturing overhead applied

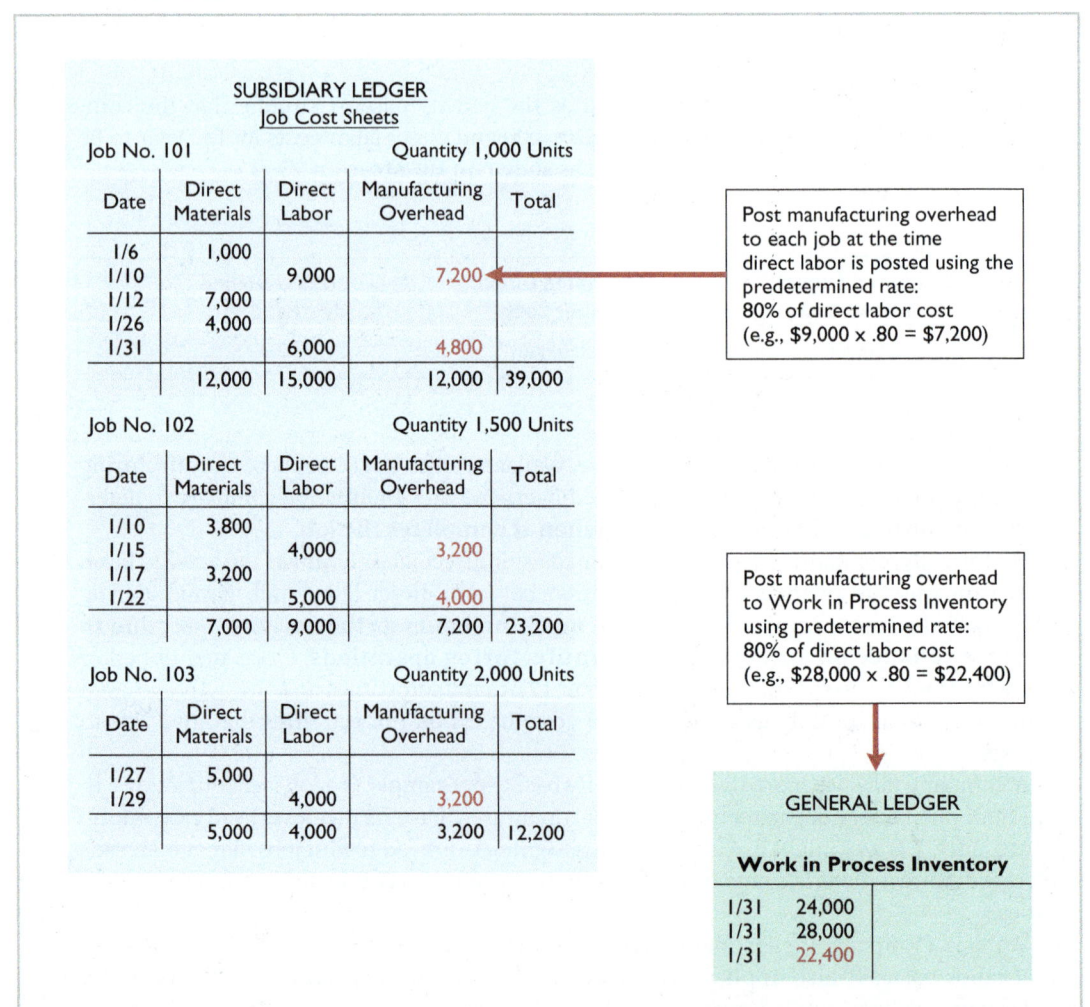

After posting the credit of $22,400 to manufacturing overhead, a debit balance remains. This means that the overhead applied to jobs using the predetermined rate was less than the actual amount of overhead incurred during the period. This situation is referred to as underapplied overhead. We address the treatment of under- and overapplied overhead in a later section.

At the end of each month, the **balance in Work in Process Inventory should equal the sum of the costs shown on the job cost sheets of unfinished jobs**. Illustration 15.13 presents proof of the agreement of the control and subsidiary accounts in Wallace. (It assumes that all jobs are still in process.)

Work in Process Inventory		Job Cost Sheets	
Jan. 31 24,000		No. 101	$ 39,000
31 28,000		102	23,200
31 22,400		103	12,200
74,400	←		$74,400

ILLUSTRATION 15.13
Proof of job cost sheets to work in process inventory

DO IT! 3 | Predetermined Overhead Rate

Stanley Company produces specialized safety devices. For the year, manufacturing overhead costs are estimated to be $160,000. Estimated machine usage is 40,000 hours. The company assigns overhead based on machine hours. Job No. 302 used 2,000 machine hours.

Compute the predetermined overhead rate, determine the amount of overhead to apply to Job No. 302, and prepare the entry to apply overhead to Job No. 302 on March 31.

Solution

Predetermined overhead rate = $160,000 ÷ 40,000 hours = $4.00 per machine hour
Amount of overhead applied to Job No. 302 = 2,000 hours × $4.00 = $8,000

The entry to record the application of overhead to Job No. 302 on March 31 is:

Work in Process Inventory	8,000	
Manufacturing Overhead		8,000
(To assign overhead to jobs)		

Related exercise material: **BE15.6, BE15.7, DO IT! 15.3, E15.5, and E15.6.**

ACTION PLAN
- The predetermined overhead rate is estimated annual overhead cost divided by estimated annual operating activity.
- Assignment of overhead to jobs is determined by multiplying the actual activity base used by the predetermined overhead rate.
- The entry to record the assignment of overhead transfers an amount out of Manufacturing Overhead into Work in Process Inventory.

Entries for Jobs Completed and Sold

LEARNING OBJECTIVE 4
Prepare entries for manufacturing and service jobs completed and sold.

Assigning Costs to Finished Goods

When a job is completed, Wallace Company summarizes the costs and completes the lower portion of the applicable job cost sheet. For example, if we assume that Wallace completes Job No. 101, a batch of electronic sensors, on January 31, the job cost sheet appears as shown in **Illustration 15.14**.

> **ILLUSTRATION 15.14**
> Completed job cost sheet

Job Cost Sheet

Job No.	101	Quantity	1,000
Item	Electronic Sensors	Date Requested	January 5
For	Tanner Company	Date Completed	January 31

Date	Direct Materials	Direct Labor	Manufacturing Overhead
1/6	$ 1,000		
1/10		$ 9,000	$ 7,200
1/12	7,000		
1/26	4,000		
1/31		6,000	4,800
	$12,000	$15,000	$12,000

Cost of completed job
 Direct materials $ 12,000
 Direct labor 15,000
 Manufacturing overhead 12,000
 Total cost $ 39,000
 Unit cost ($39,000 ÷ 1,000) $ 39.00

When a job is finished, Wallace makes an entry to transfer its total cost to finished goods inventory. The entry is as follows.

(7)

Jan. 31	Finished Goods Inventory	39,000	
	Work in Process Inventory		39,000
	(To record completion of Job No. 101)		

This entry increases Finished Goods Inventory and reduces Work in Process Inventory by $39,000, as shown in the T-accounts below.

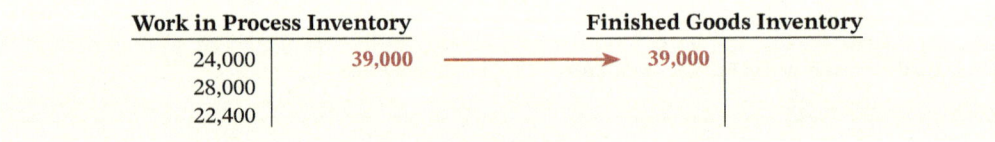

Finished Goods Inventory is a control account. It controls individual finished goods records in a finished goods subsidiary ledger.

Assigning Costs to Cost of Goods Sold

Companies recognize cost of goods sold when each sale occurs. To illustrate the entries a company makes when it sells a completed job, assume that on January 31 Wallace Company sells on account Job No. 101. The job cost $39,000, and it sold for $50,000. The entries to record the sale and recognize cost of goods sold are:

(8)

Jan. 31	Accounts Receivable	50,000	
	Sales Revenue		50,000
	(To record sale of Job No. 101)		
31	Cost of Goods Sold	39,000	
	Finished Goods Inventory		39,000
	(To record cost of Job No. 101)		

This entry increases Cost of Goods Sold and reduces Finished Goods Inventory by $39,000, as shown in the T-accounts below.

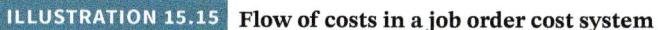

Finished Goods Inventory		Cost of Goods Sold
39,000	39,000	→ 39,000

Summary of Job Order Cost Flows

Illustration 15.15 shows a completed flowchart for a job order cost accounting system. All postings are keyed to entries 1–8 in the example presented in the previous pages for Wallace Company.

ILLUSTRATION 15.15 Flow of costs in a job order cost system

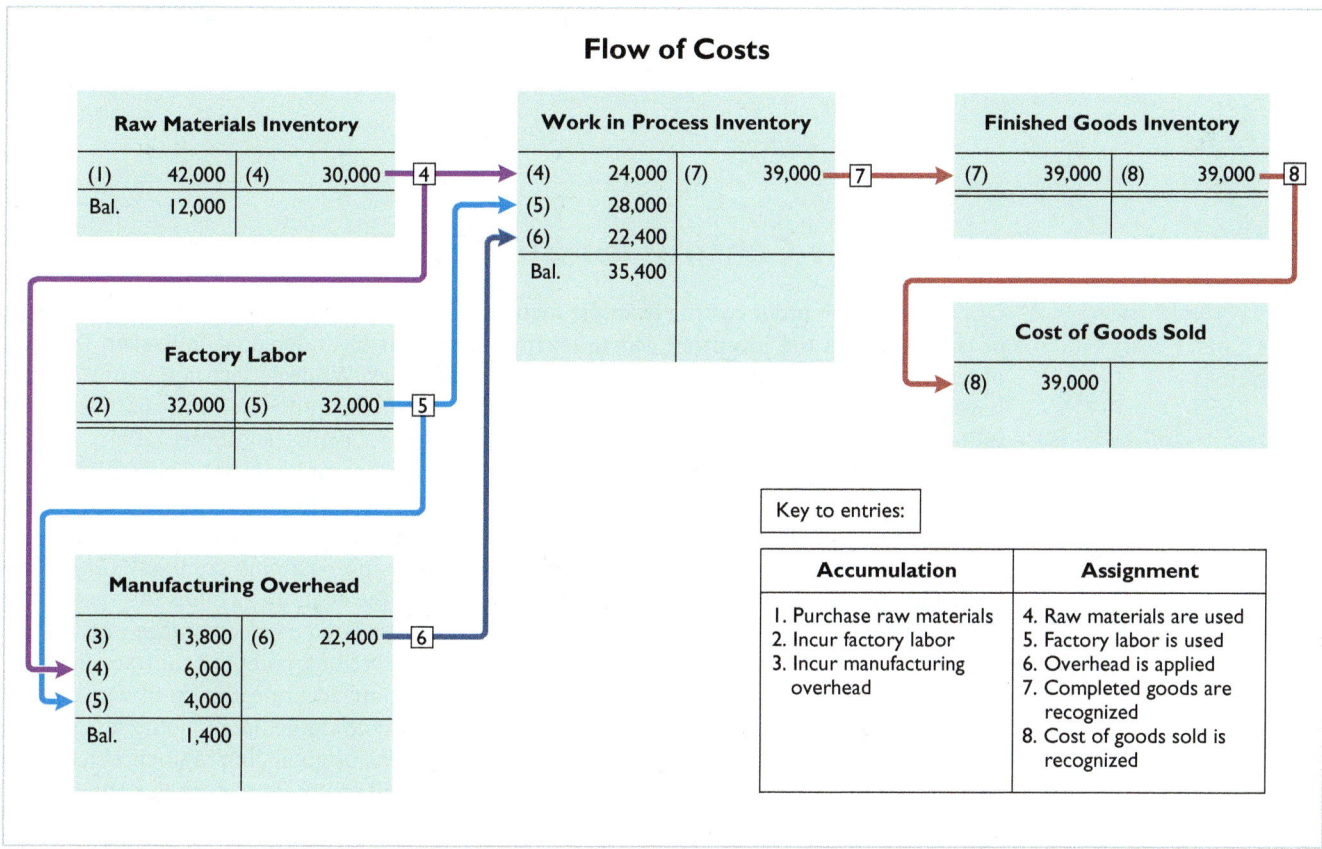

The cost flows in the diagram can be categorized as one of four types:

- **Accumulation.** The company first accumulates costs by (1) purchasing raw materials, (2) incurring labor costs, and (3) incurring manufacturing overhead costs.
- **Assignment to jobs.** Once the company has incurred manufacturing costs, it must assign them to specific jobs. For example, as it uses raw materials on specific jobs (4), the company assigns them to work in process or treats them as manufacturing overhead if the raw materials cannot be associated with a specific job. Similarly, the company either assigns factory labor (5) to work in process or treats it as manufacturing overhead if the factory labor cannot be associated with a specific job. Finally, the company assigns manufacturing overhead (6) to work in process using a *predetermined overhead rate*. This deserves emphasis: **Do not assign overhead using actual overhead costs but instead apply overhead using a predetermined rate.**
- **Completed jobs.** As jobs are completed (7), the company transfers the cost of the completed job out of work in process inventory into finished goods inventory.
- **When goods are sold.** As specific items are sold (8), the company transfers their cost out of finished goods inventory into cost of goods sold.

Illustration 15.16 summarizes the flow of documents in a job order cost system.

ILLUSTRATION 15.16 Flow of documents in a job order cost system

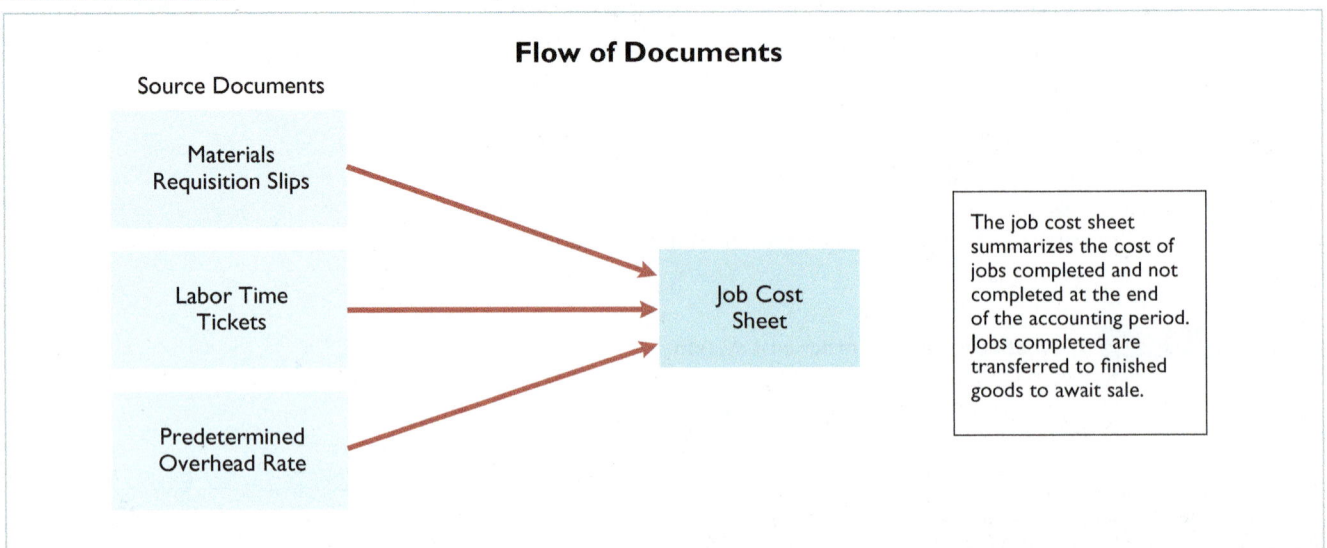

Job Order Costing for Service Companies

Our extended job order costing example focuses on a manufacturer so that you see the flow of costs through the inventory accounts. It is important to understand, however, that job order costing is also commonly used by service companies. While service companies do not have inventory, the techniques of job order costing are still quite useful in many service-industry environments. Consider, for example, the **Mayo Clinic** (healthcare), **PricewaterhouseCoopers** (accounting), and **Goldman Sachs** (investment banking). These companies need to keep track of the cost of jobs performed for specific customers to evaluate the profitability of medical treatments, audits, or investment banking engagements.

Many service organizations bill their customers using cost-plus contracts (discussed more fully in Chapter 23). Cost-plus contracts mean that the customer's bill is the sum of the costs incurred on the job, plus a profit amount that is calculated as a percentage of the costs incurred. In order to minimize conflict with customers and reduce potential contract disputes, service companies that use cost-plus contracts must maintain accurate and up-to-date costing records. Up-to-date cost records enable a service company to immediately notify a customer of cost overruns due to customer requests for changes to the original plan or unexpected complications. Timely recordkeeping allows the contractor and customer to consider alternatives before it is too late.

A service company that uses a job order cost system does not have inventory accounts. It does, however, use an account similar to Work in Process Inventory, referred to here as Service Contracts in Process, to record job costs prior to completion. To illustrate the journal entries for a service company under a job order cost system, consider the following transactions for Dorm Decor, an interior design company. The entry to record the assignment of $9,000 of supplies to projects ($7,000 direct and $2,000 indirect) is:

Service Contracts in Process	7,000	
Operating Overhead	2,000	
Supplies		9,000
(To assign supplies to projects)		

The entry to record the assignment of service salaries and wages of $100,000 ($84,000 direct and $16,000 indirect) is:

Service Contracts in Process	84,000	
Operating Overhead	16,000	
Service Salaries and Wages		100,000
(To assign personnel costs to projects)		

Dorm Decor applies operating overhead at a rate of 50% of direct labor costs. The entry to record the application of overhead ($84,000 × 50%) based on the $84,000 of direct labor costs is:

Service Contracts in Process	42,000	
Operating Overhead		42,000
(To assign operating overhead to projects)		

Upon completion of a design project (for State University) the job cost sheet shows a total cost of $34,000. The entry to record completion of this project is:

Cost of Completed Service Contracts	34,000	
Service Contracts in Process		34,000
(To record completion of State University project)		

Job cost sheets for a service company keep track of materials, labor, and overhead used on a particular job similar to a manufacturer. Several exercises at the end of this chapter apply job order costing to service companies.

Service Company Insight   General Electric

Sales Are Nice, but Service Revenue Pays the Bills

© Christian Lagereek/iStockphoto

Jet engines are one of the many products made by the industrial operations division of **General Electric (GE)**. At prices as high as $30 million per engine, you can bet that GE does its best to keep track of costs. It might surprise you that GE doesn't make much profit on the sale of each engine. So why does it bother making them? For the service revenue. During one recent year, about 75% of the division's revenues came from servicing its own products. One estimate is that the $13 billion in aircraft engines sold during a recent three-year period will generate about $90 billion in service revenue over the 30-year life of the engines. It hopes to have 44,000 engines in service by 2020.

Because of the high product costs, both the engines themselves and the subsequent service are most likely accounted for using job order costing. Accurate service cost records are important because GE needs to generate high profit margins (estimated to be 30%) on its service jobs to make up for the low margins on the original sale. It also needs good cost records for its service jobs in order to control its costs. Otherwise, a competitor, such as **Pratt and Whitney**, might submit lower bids for service contracts and take lucrative service jobs away from GE.

Sources: Paul Glader, "GE's Focus on Services Faces Test," *Wall Street Journal Online* (March 3, 2009); and Steve Heller, "General Electric's Untapped Opportunity in Aviation," *The Motley Fool* (August 27, 2016).

Explain why GE would use job order costing to keep track of the cost of repairing a malfunctioning engine for a major airline. (Go to WileyPLUS for this answer and additional questions.)

Advantages and Disadvantages of Job Order Costing

Job order costing is more precise in the assignment of costs to projects than process costing. For example, assume that a construction company, Juan Company, builds 10 custom homes a year at a total cost of $2,000,000. One way to determine the cost of the homes is to divide the total construction cost incurred during the year by the number of homes produced during the year. For Juan Company, an average cost of $200,000 ($2,000,000 ÷ 10) is computed. If the homes are nearly identical, then this approach is adequate for purposes of determining profit per home. But if the homes vary in terms of size, style, and material types, using the average cost of $200,000 to determine profit per home is inappropriate. Instead, Juan Company should use a job order cost system to determine the specific cost incurred to build each home and the amount of profit made on each. Thus, job order costing provides more useful information for determining the profitability of particular projects and for estimating costs when preparing bids on future jobs.

However, job order costing requires a significant amount of data entry. For Juan Company, it is much easier to simply keep track of total costs incurred during the year than it is to keep track of the costs incurred on each job (home built). Recording this information is time-consuming, and if the data is not entered accurately, then the product costs are incorrect. In recent years, technological advances, such as bar-coding devices for both labor costs and materials, have increased the accuracy and reduced the effort needed to record costs on specific jobs. These innovations expand the opportunities to apply job order costing in a wider variety of business settings, thus improving management's ability to control costs and make better informed decisions.

A common problem of all costing systems is how to assign overhead to the finished product. Overhead often represents more than 50% of a product's cost, and this cost is often difficult to assign meaningfully to the product. How, for example, is the salary of a project manager at Juan Company assigned to the various homes, which may differ in size, style, and cost of materials used? The accuracy of the job order cost system is largely dependent on the accuracy of the overhead allocation process. Even if the company does a good job of keeping track of the specific amounts of materials and labor used on each job, if the overhead costs are not assigned to individual jobs in a meaningful way, the product costing information is not useful. We address this issue in more detail in Chapter 17.

ACTION PLAN
- Debit Finished Goods Inventory for the cost of completed jobs.
- Debit Cost of Goods Sold for the cost of jobs sold.

DO IT! 4 | Completion and Sale of Jobs

During the current month, Onyx Corporation completed Job 109 and Job 112. Job 109 cost $19,000 and Job 112 cost $27,000. Job 112 was sold on account for $42,000. Journalize the entries for the completion of the two jobs and the sale of Job 112.

Solution

Finished Goods Inventory	46,000	
Work in Process Inventory		46,000
(To record completion of Job 109, costing $19,000 and Job 112, costing $27,000)		
Accounts Receivable	42,000	
Sales Revenue		42,000
(To record sale of Job 112)		
Cost of Goods Sold	27,000	
Finished Goods Inventory		27,000
(To record cost of goods sold for Job 112)		

Related exercise material: **BE15.8, BE15.9, DO IT! 15.4, E15.2, E15.3, E15.6, E15.7, and E15.10.**

Applied Manufacturing Overhead

LEARNING OBJECTIVE 5
Distinguish between under- and overapplied manufacturing overhead.

At the end of a period, companies prepare financial statements that present aggregate data on all jobs manufactured and sold. The cost of goods manufactured schedule in job order costing is the same as in Chapter 14 with one exception: **The schedule shows manufacturing overhead applied, rather than actual overhead costs. The company adds this amount to direct materials and direct labor to determine total manufacturing costs.**

Companies prepare the cost of goods manufactured schedule directly from the Work in Process Inventory account (see **Helpful Hint**). **Illustration 15.17** shows a condensed schedule for Wallace Company for January.

ILLUSTRATION 15.17
Cost of goods manufactured schedule

Wallace Company
Cost of Goods Manufactured Schedule
For the Month Ending January 31, 2022

Work in process, January 1		$ –0–
Direct materials used	$24,000	
Direct labor	28,000	
Manufacturing overhead applied	22,400	
Total manufacturing costs		74,400
Total cost of work in process		$74,400
Less: Work in process, January 31		35,400
Cost of goods manufactured		$39,000

HELPFUL HINT
Companies usually prepare monthly financial statements for management use only.

Note that the cost of goods manufactured ($39,000) agrees with the amount transferred from Work in Process Inventory to Finished Goods Inventory in journal entry No. 7 in Illustration 15.15.

Under- or Overapplied Manufacturing Overhead

Recall that overhead is applied based on an estimate of total annual overhead costs. This estimate will rarely be exactly equal to actual overhead incurred. Therefore, at the end of the year, after overhead has been applied to specific jobs, the Manufacturing Overhead account will likely have a remaining balance (see **Decision Tools**).

When Manufacturing Overhead has a **debit balance**, overhead is said to be underapplied. **Underapplied overhead** means that the overhead applied to work in process is less than the overhead incurred. Conversely, when manufacturing overhead has a **credit balance**, overhead is overapplied. **Overapplied overhead** means that the overhead applied to work in process is greater than the overhead incurred. **Illustration 15.18** shows these concepts.

Decision Tools
The Manufacturing Overhead account helps managers determine if overhead applied exceeded or was less than actual overhead costs.

ILLUSTRATION 15.18 Under- and overapplied overhead

Manufacturing Overhead	
Actual (Costs incurred)	Applied (Costs assigned)

If applied is **less** than actual, manufacturing overhead is underapplied.

If applied is **greater** than actual, manufacturing overhead is overapplied.

Year-End Balance

At the end of the year, all manufacturing overhead transactions are complete. There is no further opportunity for offsetting events to occur. At this point, Wallace Company eliminates any balance in Manufacturing Overhead by an adjusting entry. It considers under- or overapplied overhead to be an **adjustment to cost of goods sold**. Thus, Wallace **debits underapplied overhead to Cost of Goods Sold. It credits overapplied overhead to Cost of Goods Sold.**

To illustrate, as noted earlier in the chapter and shown below, after overhead of $22,400, Wallace has a $1,400 debit balance in Manufacturing Overhead at December 31. This occurred because the amount of overhead applied was less than the amount incurred during the period.

```
                Manufacturing Overhead
              ┌─ 13,800            22,400 ┐─ Applied
     Incurred─┤   6,000
              └─  4,000
                  1,400
```

The adjusting entry for the underapplied overhead is:

Dec. 31	Cost of Goods Sold	1,400	
	Manufacturing Overhead		1,400
	(To transfer underapplied overhead		
	to cost of goods sold)		

After Wallace posts this entry, Manufacturing Overhead has a zero balance. In preparing an income statement for the year, Wallace reports cost of goods sold **after adjusting it** for either under- or overapplied overhead.

Illustration 15.19 presents an income statement for Wallace after adjusting for the $1,400 of underapplied overhead.

ILLUSTRATION 15.19

Partial income statement

Wallace Company
Income Statement (partial)
For the Month Ending January 31, 2022

Sales revenue		$50,000
Cost of goods sold		
Finished goods inventory, January 1	$ -0-	
Cost of goods manufactured (see Illustration 15.17)	39,000	
Cost of goods available for sale	39,000	
Less: Finished goods inventory, January 31	-0-	
Cost of goods sold—unadjusted	39,000	
Add: Adjustment for underapplied overhead	1,400	
Cost of goods sold—adjusted		40,400
Gross profit		$ 9,600

For more accurate costing, significant under- or overapplied overhead at the end of the year should be allocated among ending work in process, finished goods, and cost of goods sold. The discussion of this allocation approach is left to more advanced courses.

ACTION PLAN

- Calculate the amount of overhead applied by multiplying the predetermined overhead rate by actual activity.
- If applied overhead is less than actual, overhead is underapplied.
- If applied overhead is greater than actual, overhead is overapplied.

DO IT! 5 | Applied Manufacturing Overhead

For Karr Company, the predetermined overhead rate is 140% of direct labor cost. During the month, Karr incurred $90,000 of factory labor costs, of which $80,000 is direct labor and $10,000 is indirect labor. Actual overhead incurred (including indirect labor) was $119,000.

Compute the amount of manufacturing overhead applied during the month. Determine the amount of under- or overapplied manufacturing overhead.

Solution

Manufacturing overhead applied = (140% × $80,000) = $112,000
Underapplied manufacturing overhead = ($119,000 − $112,000) = $7,000

Related exercise material: **BE15.10, DO IT! 15.5, E15.4, E15.5, E15.9, and E15.13.**

USING THE DECISION TOOLS | Disney

Disney faces many situations where it needs to apply the decision tools learned in this chapter, such as using a job cost sheet to determine a film's profitability. For example, assume Disney uses a job order cost system and applies overhead to production of its films on the basis of direct labor cost. In computing a predetermined overhead rate for the year 2022, the company estimated film production overhead to be $24 million and direct labor costs to be $20 million. In addition, it developed the following information.

Actual Costs Incurred During 2022

Direct materials used	$30,000,000
Direct labor cost incurred	21,000,000
Insurance, studio	500,000
Indirect labor	7,500,000
Studio maintenance	1,000,000
Rent on studio building	11,000,000
Depreciation on studio equipment	2,000,000

Instructions

Answer each of the following.

a. Why is Disney using a job order cost system?
b. On what basis does Disney apply its film production overhead? Compute the predetermined overhead rate for 2022.
c. Compute the amount of the under- or overapplied overhead for 2022.
d. Disney had balances in the beginning and ending films in process and finished films accounts as follows.

	1/1/22	12/31/22
Films in process	$ 5,000,000	$ 4,000,000
Finished films	13,000,000	11,000,000

Determine the (1) cost of films produced and (2) cost of films sold for Disney during 2022. Assume that any under- or overapplied overhead should be included in the cost of films sold.

e. During 2022, Film G408 (a short documentary film produced for a customer) was started and completed. Its cost sheet showed a total cost of $100,000, and Disney prices its film at 50% above its cost. What is the price to the customer if the company follows this pricing strategy?

Solution

a. Disney is using a job order cost system because it produces films. Each film is unique, with its own distinguishing characteristics.

b. Disney applies its overhead on the basis of direct labor cost. The predetermined overhead rate is 120%, computed as follows: $24,000,000 ÷ 20,000,000 = 120%.

c.
Actual film production overhead	$22,000,000*
Applied overhead cost ($21,000,000 × 120%)	25,200,000
Overapplied overhead	$ 3,200,000

*$500,000 + $7,500,000 + $1,000,000 + $11,000,000 + $2,000,000

d.

1.

Films in process, 1/1/22		$ 5,000,000
Direct materials used	$30,000,000	
Direct labor	21,000,000	
Film production overhead applied	25,200,000	
Total film production costs		76,200,000
Total cost of films in process		81,200,000
Less: Films in process, 12/31/22		4,000,000
Cost of films produced		$77,200,000

2.

Finished films, 1/1/22	$13,000,000
Cost of films produced (see above)	77,200,000
Cost of films available for sale	90,200,000
Finished films, 12/31/22	11,000,000
Cost of films sold (unadjusted)	79,200,000
Less: Overapplied overhead	3,200,000
Cost of films sold	$76,000,000

e.

Film G408 cost	$ 100,000
Markup percentage	× 50%
Markup	$ 50,000

Price to customer: $150,000 ($100,000 + $50,000)

Review and Practice

Learning Objectives Review

1 Describe cost systems and the flow of costs in a job order system.

Cost accounting involves the procedures for measuring, recording, and reporting product costs. From the data accumulated, companies determine the total cost and the unit cost of each product. The two basic types of cost accounting systems are process cost and job order cost.

In job order costing, companies first accumulate manufacturing costs in three accounts: Raw Materials Inventory, Factory Labor, and Manufacturing Overhead. They then assign the accumulated costs to Work in Process Inventory and eventually to Finished Goods Inventory and Cost of Goods Sold.

2 Use a job cost sheet to assign costs to work in process.

A job cost sheet is a form used to record the costs chargeable to a specific job and to determine the total and unit costs of the completed job. Job cost sheets constitute the subsidiary ledger for the Work in Process Inventory control account.

3 Demonstrate how to determine and use the predetermined overhead rate.

The predetermined overhead rate is based on the relationship between estimated annual overhead costs and estimated annual operating activity. This is expressed in terms of a common activity base, such as direct labor cost. Companies use this rate to assign overhead costs to work in process and to specific jobs.

4 Prepare entries for manufacturing and service jobs completed and sold.

When jobs are completed, companies debit the cost to Finished Goods Inventory and credit it to Work in Process Inventory. When a job is sold, the entries are (a) debit Cash or Accounts Receivable and credit Sales Revenue for the selling price, and (b) debit Cost of Goods Sold and credit Finished Goods Inventory for the cost of the goods.

5 Distinguish between under- and overapplied manufacturing overhead.

Underapplied manufacturing overhead indicates that the overhead assigned to work in process is less than the overhead incurred. Overapplied overhead indicates that the overhead assigned to work in process is greater than the overhead incurred.

Decision Tools Review

Decision checkpoints	Info Needed for Decision	Tool to Use for Decision	How to Evaluate Results
What is the cost of a job?	Cost of material, labor, and overhead assigned to a specific job	Job cost sheet	Compare costs to those of previous periods to ensure that costs are in line. Compare costs to estimated selling price or service fees charged to determine overall profitability.
Has the company over- or underapplied overhead for the period?	Actual overhead costs and overhead applied	Manufacturing Overhead account	If the account balance is a credit, overhead applied exceeded actual overhead costs. If the account balance is a debit, overhead applied was less than actual overhead costs.

Glossary Review

Cost accounting An area of accounting that involves measuring, recording, and reporting product and service costs. (p. 15-3).

Cost accounting system Manufacturing and service cost accounts that are fully integrated into the general ledger of a company. (p. 15-3).

Job cost sheet A form used to record the costs chargeable to a specific job and to determine the total and unit costs of the completed job. (p. 15-7).

Job order cost system A cost accounting system in which costs are assigned to each job or batch. (p. 15-3).

Materials requisition slip A document authorizing the issuance of raw materials from the storeroom to production. (p. 15-8).

Overapplied overhead A situation in which overhead applied to work in process is greater than the overhead incurred. (p. 15-21).

Predetermined overhead rate A rate based on the relationship between estimated annual overhead costs and estimated annual operating activity, expressed in terms of a common activity base. (p. 15-12).

Process cost system A cost accounting system used when a company manufactures a large volume of similar products. (p. 15-3).

Time ticket A document that indicates the employee, the hours worked, the account and job to be charged, and the total labor cost. (p. 15-10).

Underapplied overhead A situation in which overhead applied to work in process is less than the overhead incurred. (p. 15-21).

Practice Multiple-Choice Questions

1. **(LO 1)** Cost accounting involves the measuring, recording, and reporting of:
    a. product and service costs.
    b. future costs.
    c. manufacturing processes.
    d. managerial accounting decisions.

2. **(LO 1)** A company is more likely to use a job order cost system if:
    a. it manufactures a large volume of similar products.
    b. its production is continuous.
    c. it manufactures products with unique characteristics.
    d. it uses a periodic inventory system.

3. **(LO 1)** In accumulating raw materials costs, companies debit the cost of raw materials purchased in a perpetual system to:
    a. Raw Materials Purchases.
    b. Raw Materials Inventory.
    c. Purchases.
    d. Work in Process.

4. **(LO 1)** When incurred, factory labor costs are debited to:
    a. Work in Process.
    b. Factory Wages Expense.
    c. Factory Labor.
    d. Factory Wages Payable.

5. **(LO 1)** The flow of costs in job order costing:
    a. begins with work in process inventory and ends with finished goods inventory.
    b. begins as soon as a sale occurs.
    c. parallels the physical flow of materials as they are converted into finished goods and then sold.
    d. is necessary to prepare the cost of goods manufactured schedule.

6. **(LO 2)** Raw materials are assigned to a job when:
    a. the job is sold.
    b. the materials are purchased.
    c. the materials are received from the vendor.
    d. the materials are issued by the materials storeroom.

7. (LO 2) The source of information for assigning costs to job cost sheets are:

  a. invoices, time tickets, and the predetermined overhead rate.
  b. materials requisition slips, time tickets, and the actual overhead costs.
  c. materials requisition slips, payroll register, and the predetermined overhead rate.
  d. materials requisition slips, time tickets, and the predetermined overhead rate.

8. (LO 2) In recording the issuance of raw materials in a job order cost system, it would be **incorrect** to:

  a. debit Work in Process Inventory.
  b. debit Finished Goods Inventory.
  c. debit Manufacturing Overhead.
  d. credit Raw Materials Inventory.

9. (LO 2) The entry when direct factory labor is assigned to jobs is a debit to:

  a. Work in Process Inventory and a credit to Factory Labor.
  b. Manufacturing Overhead and a credit to Factory Labor.
  c. Factory Labor and a credit to Manufacturing Overhead.
  d. Factory Labor and a credit to Work in Process Inventory.

10. (LO 3) The formula for computing the predetermined manufacturing overhead rate is estimated annual overhead costs divided by estimated annual operating activity, expressed as:

  a. direct labor cost.
  b. direct labor hours.
  c. machine hours.
  d. Any of the above.

11. (LO 3) In Crawford Company, the predetermined overhead rate is 80% of direct labor cost. During the month, Crawford incurs $210,000 of factory labor costs, of which $180,000 is direct labor and $30,000 is indirect labor. Actual overhead incurred was $200,000. The amount of overhead debited to Work in Process Inventory should be:

  a. $200,000.
  b. $144,000.
  c. $168,000.
  d. $160,000.

12. (LO 4) Mynex Company completes Job No. 26 at a cost of $4,500 and later sells it for $7,000 cash. A **correct** entry is:

  a. debit Finished Goods Inventory $7,000 and credit Work in Process Inventory $7,000.
  b. debit Cost of Goods Sold $7,000 and credit Finished Goods Inventory $7,000.
  c. debit Finished Goods Inventory $4,500 and credit Work in Process Inventory $4,500.
  d. debit Accounts Receivable $7,000 and credit Sales Revenue $7,000.

13. (LO 5) At the end of an accounting period, a company using a job order cost system calculates the cost of goods manufactured:

  a. from the job cost sheet.
  b. from the Work in Process Inventory account.
  c. by adding direct materials used, direct labor incurred, and manufacturing overhead incurred.
  d. from the Cost of Goods Sold account.

14. (LO 4) Which of the following statements is **true**?

  a. Job order costing requires less data entry than process costing.
  b. Allocation of overhead is easier under job order costing than process costing.
  c. Job order costing provides more precise costing for custom jobs than process costing.
  d. The use of job order costing has declined because more companies have adopted automated accounting systems.

15. (LO 5) At end of the year, a company has a $1,200 debit balance in Manufacturing Overhead. The company:

  a. makes an adjusting entry by debiting Manufacturing Overhead Applied for $1,200 and crediting Manufacturing Overhead for $1,200.
  b. makes an adjusting entry by debiting Manufacturing Overhead Expense for $1,200 and crediting Manufacturing Overhead for $1,200.
  c. makes an adjusting entry by debiting Cost of Goods Sold for $1,200 and crediting Manufacturing Overhead for $1,200.
  d. makes no adjusting entry because differences between actual overhead and the amount applied are a normal part of job order costing and will average out over the next year.

16. (LO 5) Manufacturing overhead is underapplied if:

  a. actual overhead is less than applied.
  b. actual overhead is greater than applied.
  c. the predetermined rate equals the actual rate.
  d. actual overhead equals applied overhead.

Solutions

1. a. Cost accounting involves the measuring, recording, and reporting of product and service costs, not (b) future costs, (c) manufacturing processes, or (d) managerial accounting decisions.

2. c. A job costing system is more likely for products with unique characteristics. The other choices are incorrect because a process cost system is more likely for (a) large volumes of similar products or (b) if production is continuous. (d) is incorrect because the choice of a costing system is not dependent on whether a periodic or perpetual inventory system is used.

3. b. In a perpetual system, purchases of raw materials are debited to Raw Materials Inventory, not (a) Raw Materials Purchases, (c) Purchases, or (d) Work in Process.

4. c. When factory labor costs are incurred, they are debited to Factory Labor, not (a) Work in Process, (b) Factory Wages Expense, or (d) Factory Wages Payable (they are debited to Factory Labor and credited to Factory Wages Payable).

5. c. Job order costing parallels the physical flow of materials as they are converted into finished goods. The other choices are incorrect because job order costing begins (a) with raw materials, not work in process, and ends with cost of goods sold; and (b) as soon as raw materials are purchased, not when the sale occurs. (d) is incorrect because the cost of goods manufactured schedule is prepared from the Work in Process account and is only a portion of the costs in a job order system.

6. d. Raw materials are assigned to a job when the materials are issued by the materials storeroom, not when (a) the job is sold, (b) the materials are purchased, or (c) the materials are received from the vendor.

7. **d.** Materials requisition slips are used to assign direct materials, time tickets are used to assign direct labor, and the predetermined overhead rate is used to assign manufacturing overhead to job cost sheets. The other choices are incorrect because (a) materials requisition slips, not invoices, are used to assign direct materials; (b) the predetermined overhead rate, not the actual overhead costs, is used to assign manufacturing overhead; and (c) time tickets, not the payroll register, are used to assign direct labor.

8. **b.** Finished Goods Inventory is debited when goods are transferred from work in process to finished goods, not when raw materials are issued for a job. Choices (a), (c), and (d) are true statements.

9. **a.** When direct factory labor is assigned to jobs, the entry is a debit to Work in Process Inventory and a credit to Factory Labor. The other choices are incorrect because (b) Work in Process Inventory, not Manufacturing Overhead, is debited; (c) Work in Process Inventory, not Factory Labor, is debited and Factory Labor, not Manufacturing Overhead, is credited; and (d) Work in Process Inventory, not Factory Labor, is debited and Factory Labor, not Work in Process Inventory, is credited.

10. **d.** Any of the activity measures mentioned can be used in computing the predetermined manufacturing overhead rate. Choices (a) direct labor cost, (b) direct labor hours, and (c) machine hours can all be used in computing the predetermined manufacturing overhead rate, but (d) is the best answer.

11. **b.** Work in Process Inventory should be debited for $144,000 ($180,000 × 80%), the amount of manufacturing overhead applied, not (a) $200,000, (c) $168,000, or (d) $160,000.

12. **c.** When a job costing $4,500 is completed, Finished Goods Inventory is debited and Work in Process Inventory is credited for $4,500. Choices (a) and (b) are incorrect because the amounts should be for the cost of the job ($4,500), not the sale amount ($7,000). Choice (d) is incorrect because the debit should be to Cash, not Accounts Receivable.

13. **b.** At the end of an accounting period, a company using a job costing system prepares the cost of goods manufactured from the Work in Process Inventory account, not (a) the job cost sheet; (c) by adding direct materials used, direct labor incurred, and manufacturing overhead incurred; or (d) from the Cost of Goods Sold Account.

14. **c.** Job order costing provides more precise costing for custom jobs than process costing. The other choices are incorrect because (a) job order costing often requires significant data entry, (b) overhead allocation is a problem for all costing systems, and (d) the use of job order costing has increased due to automated accounting systems.

15. **c.** The company would make an adjusting entry for the underapplied overhead by debiting Cost of Goods Sold for $1,200 and crediting Manufacturing Overhead for $1,200, not by debiting (a) Manufacturing Overhead Applied for $1,200 or (b) Manufacturing Overhead Expense for $1,200. Choice (d) is incorrect because at the end of the year, a company makes an entry to eliminate any balance in Manufacturing Overhead.

16. **b.** Manufacturing overhead is underapplied if actual overhead is greater than applied overhead. The other choices are incorrect because (a) if actual overhead is less than applied, then manufacturing overhead is overapplied; (c) if the predetermined rate equals the actual rate, the actual overhead costs incurred equal the overhead costs applied, neither over- nor underapplied; and (d) if the actual overhead equals the applied overhead, neither over- nor underapplied occurs.

Practice Brief Exercises

1. **(LO 2)** During January, its first month of operations, Swarzak Company had factory labor of $9,000, of which $7,500 relates to factory wages payable and $1,500 relates to payroll taxes payable. Time tickets show that the factory labor of $9,000 was used as follows: Job 1 $3,200, Job 2 $2,600, Job 3 $2,200, and general factory use $1,000. Prepare summary journal entries to record factory labor.

Prepare entries to record factory labor.

Solution

1.	Jan. 31	Factory Labor	9,000	
		Factory Wages Payable		7,500
		Employer Payroll Taxes Payable		1,500
	Jan. 31	Work in Process Inventory	8,000	
		Manufacturing Overhead	1,000	
		Factory Labor		9,000

2. **(LO 3)** Brock Company estimates that annual manufacturing overhead costs will be $950,000. Annual direct labor cost is the base used to apply overhead, and it is estimated to be $500,000. During January, Brock incurred direct labor costs of $40,000. Prepare the entry to assign overhead to production.

Assign manufacturing overhead to production.

Solution

2. Overhead rate based on direct labor cost = ($950,000 ÷ $500,000) = 190%.

Jan. 31	Work in Process Inventory	76,000	
	Manufacturing Overhead ($40,000 × 190%)		76,000

Prepare entries for completion and sale of jobs.

3. (LO 4) In May, Huntzinger Company completes Jobs 14, 15, and 16. Job 14 cost $40,000, Job 15 $70,000, and Job 16 $35,000. On May 31, Job 14 is sold to a customer on account for $72,000. Journalize the entries for the completion of the three jobs and the sale of Job 14.

Solution

3.
May 31	Finished Goods Inventory		145,000	
	Work in Process Inventory			145,000
31	Accounts Receivable		72,000	
	Sales Revenue			72,000
31	Cost of Goods Sold		40,000	
	Finished Goods Inventory			40,000

Prepare adjusting entries for under- and overapplied overhead.

4. (LO 5) At December 31, balances in Manufacturing Overhead are Alex Company—debit $2,200, Katz Company—credit $1,900. Prepare the adjusting entry for each company at December 31, assuming the adjustment is made to cost of goods sold.

Solution

4.

Alex Company

Dec. 31	Cost of Goods Sold	2,200	
	Manufacturing Overhead		2,200

Katz Company

Dec. 31	Manufacturing Overhead	1,900	
	Cost of Goods Sold		1,900

Practice Exercises

Analyze a job cost sheet and prepare entries for manufacturing costs.

1. (LO 1, 2, 3, 4) A job order cost sheet for Michaels Company is shown below.

Job No. 92   **For 2,000 Units**

Date		Direct Materials	Direct Labor	Manufacturing Overhead
Beg. bal. Jan.	1	3,925	6,000	4,200
	8	6,000		
	12		8,500	6,375
	25	2,000		
	27		4,000	3,000
		11,925	18,500	13,575

Cost of completed job:
Direct materials	$11,925
Direct labor	18,500
Manufacturing overhead	13,575
Total cost	$44,000
Unit cost ($44,000 ÷ 2,000)	$ 22.00

Instructions

a. Answer the following questions.

1. What was the balance in Work in Process Inventory on January 1 if this was the only unfinished job?

2. If manufacturing overhead is applied on the basis of direct labor cost, what overhead rate was used in each year?

b. Prepare summary entries at January 31 to record the current year's transactions pertaining to Job No. 92.

Solution

1. a. 1. $14,125, or ($3,925 + $6,000 + $4,200).

   2. Last year 70%, or ($4,200 ÷ $6,000); this year 75% (either $6,375 ÷ $8,500 or $3,000 ÷ $4,000).

   b.

	Jan. 31	Work in Process Inventory	8,000	
		Raw Materials Inventory		8,000
		($6,000 + $2,000)		
	31	Work in Process Inventory	12,500	
		Factory Labor		12,500
		($8,500 + $4,000)		
	31	Work in Process Inventory	9,375	
		Manufacturing Overhead		9,375
		($6,375 + $3,000)		
	31	Finished Goods Inventory	44,000	
		Work in Process Inventory		44,000

2. (LO 3, 5) Kwik Kopy Company applies operating overhead to photocopying jobs on the basis of machine hours used. Overhead costs are estimated to total $290,000 for the year, and machine usage is estimated at 125,000 hours.

Compute the overhead rate and under- or overapplied overhead.

For the year, $295,000 of overhead costs are incurred and 130,000 hours are used.

Instructions

a. Compute the service overhead rate for the year.

b. What is the amount of under- or overapplied overhead at December 31?

c. Assuming the under- or overapplied overhead for the year is not allocated to inventory accounts, prepare the adjusting entry to assign the amount to cost of jobs finished.

Solution

2. a. $2.32 per machine hour ($290,000 ÷ 125,000).

   b. ($295,000) − ($2.32 × 130,000 machine hours)
      $295,000 − $301,600 = $6,600 overapplied

   c. | Operating Overhead | 6,600 | |
      |---|---|---|
      | Cost of Goods Sold | | 6,600 |

Practice Problem

(LO 3, 5) Cardella Company applies overhead on the basis of direct labor costs. The company estimates annual overhead costs will be $760,000 and annual direct labor costs will be $950,000. During February, Cardella works on two jobs: A16 and B17. Summary data concerning these jobs are as follows.

Compute predetermined overhead rate, apply overhead, and calculate under- or overapplied overhead.

Manufacturing Costs Incurred

Purchased $54,000 of raw materials on account.

Factory labor $76,000, plus $4,000 employer payroll taxes.

Manufacturing overhead incurred exclusive of indirect materials and indirect labor $59,800.

Assignment of Costs

Direct materials: Job A16 $27,000, Job B17 $21,000
Indirect materials: $3,000
Direct labor: Job A16 $52,000, Job B17 $26,000
Indirect labor: $2,000

By the end of February, the company completed Job A16 and sold it on account for $150,000. Job B17 was only partially completed.

Instructions

a. Compute the predetermined overhead rate.
b. Journalize the February transactions in the sequence followed in the chapter.
c. What was the amount of under- or overapplied manufacturing overhead?

Solution

a.

Estimated annual overhead costs	÷	Estimated annual operating activity	=	Predetermined overhead rate
$760,000	÷	$950,000	=	80%

b.

(1)

Feb. 28	Raw Materials Inventory	54,000	
	Accounts Payable		54,000
	(Purchase of raw materials on account)		

(2)

28	Factory Labor	80,000	
	Factory Wages Payable		76,000
	Employer Payroll Taxes Payable		4,000
	(To record factory labor costs)		

(3)

28	Manufacturing Overhead	59,800	
	Accounts Payable, Accumulated Depreciation, and Prepaid Insurance		59,800
	(To record overhead costs)		

(4)

28	Work in Process Inventory	48,000	
	Manufacturing Overhead	3,000	
	Raw Materials Inventory		51,000
	(To assign raw materials to production)		

(5)

28	Work in Process Inventory	78,000	
	Manufacturing Overhead	2,000	
	Factory Labor		80,000
	(To assign factory labor to production)		

(6)

28	Work in Process Inventory	62,400	
	Manufacturing Overhead		62,400
	(To assign overhead to jobs— 80% × $78,000)		

(7)

28	Finished Goods Inventory	120,600	
	Work in Process Inventory		120,600
	(To record completion of Job A16: direct materials $27,000, direct labor $52,000, and manufacturing overhead $41,600)		

(8)

28	Accounts Receivable	150,000	
	Sales Revenue		150,000
	(To record sale of Job A16)		

28	Cost of Goods Sold	120,600	
	Finished Goods Inventory		120,600
	(To record cost of sale for Job A16)		

c. Manufacturing Overhead has a debit balance of $2,400 as shown below.

Manufacturing Overhead

(3)	59,800	(6)	62,400
(4)	3,000		
(5)	2,000		
Bal.	2,400		

Thus, manufacturing overhead is underapplied for the month.

WileyPLUS

Brief Exercises, DO IT! Exercises, Exercises, Problems, and many additional resources are available for practice in WileyPLUS.

Questions

1. **a.** Mary Barett is not sure about the difference between cost accounting and a cost accounting system. Explain the difference to Mary.
   b. What is an important feature of a cost accounting system?
2. **a.** Distinguish between the two types of cost accounting systems.
   b. Can a company use both types of cost accounting systems?
3. What type of industry is likely to use a job order cost system? Give some examples.
4. What type of industry is likely to use a process cost system? Give some examples.
5. Your roommate asks your help in understanding the major steps in the flow of costs in a job order cost system. Identify the steps for your roommate.
6. There are three inventory control accounts in a job order system. Identify the control accounts and their subsidiary ledgers.
7. What source documents are used in accumulating direct labor costs?
8. "Entries to Manufacturing Overhead normally are only made daily." Do you agree? Explain.
9. Stan Kaiser is confused about the source documents used in assigning materials and labor costs. Identify the documents and give the entry for each document.
10. What is the purpose of a job cost sheet?
11. Indicate the source documents that are used in charging costs to specific jobs.
12. Explain the purpose and use of a "materials requisition slip" as used in a job order cost system.
13. Sam Bowden believes actual manufacturing overhead should be charged to jobs. Do you agree? Why or why not?
14. What elements are involved in computing a predetermined overhead rate?
15. How can the agreement of Work in Process Inventory and job cost sheets be verified?
16. Jane Neff believes that the cost of goods manufactured schedule in job order cost accounting is the same as shown in Chapter 14. Is Jane correct? Explain.
17. Matt Litkee is confused about under- and overapplied manufacturing overhead. Define the terms for Matt, and indicate the balance in the manufacturing overhead account applicable to each term.
18. "At the end of the year, under- or overapplied overhead is closed to Income Summary." Is this correct? If not, indicate the customary treatment of this amount.

Brief Exercises

BE15.1 (LO 1), C Dieker Company begins operations on January 1. Because all work is done to customer specifications, the company decides to use a job order cost system. Prepare a flowchart of a typical job order system with arrows showing the flow of costs. Identify the eight transactions.

Prepare a flowchart of a job order cost accounting system and identify transactions.

BE15.2 (LO 1), AP During January, its first month of operations, Dieker Company accumulated the following manufacturing costs: raw materials purchased $4,000 on account, factory labor incurred $6,000 of which $5,200 relates to factory wages payable and $800 relates to payroll taxes payable, and factory utilities payable $2,000. Prepare separate journal entries for each type of manufacturing cost.

Prepare entries in accumulating manufacturing costs.

Prepare entry for the assignment of raw materials costs.	**BE15.3 (LO 2), AP** In January, Dieker Company requisitions raw materials for production as follows: Job 1 $900, Job 2 $1,200, Job 3 $700, and general factory use $600. Prepare a summary journal entry to record raw materials used.
Prepare entry for the assignment of factory labor costs.	**BE15.4 (LO 2), AP** Factory labor data for Dieker Company is given in BE15.2. During January, time tickets show that the factory labor of $6,000 was used as follows: Job 1 $2,200, Job 2 $1,600, Job 3 $1,400, and general factory use $800. Prepare a summary journal entry to record factory labor used.
Prepare job cost sheets.	**BE15.5 (LO 2), AP** Data pertaining to job cost sheets for Dieker Company are given in BE15.3 and BE15.4. Prepare the job cost sheets for each of the three jobs using the format shown in Illustration 15.8. (*Note:* You may omit the column for Manufacturing Overhead.)
Compute predetermined overhead rates.	**BE15.6 (LO 3), AP** Marquis Company estimates that annual manufacturing overhead costs will be $900,000. Estimated annual operating activity bases are direct labor cost $500,000, direct labor hours 50,000, and machine hours 100,000. Compute the predetermined overhead rate for each activity base.
Assign manufacturing overhead to production.	**BE15.7 (LO 3), AP** During the first quarter, Francum Company incurs the following direct labor costs: January $40,000, February $30,000, and March $50,000. For each month, prepare the entry to assign overhead to production using a predetermined rate of 70% of direct labor cost.
Prepare entries for completion and sale of completed jobs.	**BE15.8 (LO 4), AP** In March, Stinson Company completes Jobs 10 and 11. Job 10 cost $20,000 and Job 11 $30,000. On March 31, Job 10 is sold to the customer for $35,000 in cash. Journalize the entries for the completion of the two jobs and the sale of Job 10.
Prepare entries for service salaries and wages and operating overhead.	**BE15.9 (LO 4), AP** Ruiz Engineering Contractors incurred service salaries and wages of $36,000 ($28,000 direct and $8,000 indirect) on an engineering project. The company applies overhead at a rate of 25% of direct labor. Record the entries to assign service salaries and wages and to apply overhead.
Prepare adjusting entries for under- and overapplied overhead.	**BE15.10 (LO 5), AP** At December 31, balances in Manufacturing Overhead are Shimeca Company—debit $1,200, Garcia Company—credit $900. Prepare the adjusting entry for each company at December 31, assuming the adjustment is made to cost of goods sold.

DO IT! Exercises

Prepare journal entries for manufacturing costs.	**DO IT! 15.1 (LO 1), AP** During the current month, Wacholz Company incurs the following manufacturing costs. a. Purchased raw materials of $18,000 on account. b. Incurred factory labor of $40,000. Of that amount, $31,000 relates to wages payable and $9,000 relates to payroll taxes payable. c. Factory utilities of $3,100 are payable, prepaid factory property taxes of $2,700 have expired, and depreciation on the factory building is $9,500. Prepare journal entries for each type of manufacturing cost. (Use a summary entry to record manufacturing overhead.)
Assign costs to work in process.	**DO IT! 15.2 (LO 2), AP** Milner Company is working on two job orders. The job cost sheets show the following.

	Job 201	Job 202
Direct materials	$7,200	$9,000
Direct labor	4,000	8,000
Manufacturing overhead	5,200	9,800

Prepare the three summary entries to record the assignment of costs to Work in Process from the data on the job cost sheets.

Compute and apply the predetermined overhead rate.	**DO IT! 15.3 (LO 3), AP** Washburn Company produces earbuds. During the year, manufacturing overhead costs are estimated to be $200,000. Estimated machine usage is 2,500 hours. The company assigns overhead based on machine hours. Job No. 551 used 90 machine hours. Compute the predetermined overhead rate, determine the amount of overhead to apply to Job No. 551, and prepare the entry to apply overhead to Job No. 551 on January 15.
Prepare entries for completion and sale of jobs.	**DO IT! 15.4 (LO 4), AP** During the current month, Standard Corporation completed Job 310 and Job 312. Job 310 cost $70,000 and Job 312 cost $50,000. Job 312 was sold on account for $90,000. Journalize the entries for the completion of the two jobs and the sale of Job 312.

DO IT! 15.5 (LO 5), AP For Eckstein Company, the predetermined overhead rate is 130% of direct labor cost. During the month, Eckstein incurred $100,000 of factory labor costs, of which $85,000 is direct labor and $15,000 is indirect labor. Actual overhead incurred was $115,000. Compute the amount of manufacturing overhead applied during the month. Determine the amount of under- or overapplied manufacturing overhead.

Apply manufacturing overhead and determine under- or overapplication.

Exercises

E15.1 (LO 1, 2), AP The wages payable related to factory workers for Larkin Company during the month of January are $76,000. The employer's payroll taxes for the factory payroll are $8,000. The fringe benefits to be paid by the employer on this payroll are $6,000. Of the total accumulated cost of factory labor, 85% is related to direct labor and 15% is attributable to indirect labor.

Prepare entries for factory labor.

Instructions

a. Prepare the entry to record the factory labor costs for the month of January.

b. Prepare the entry to assign factory labor to production.

E15.2 (LO 1, 2, 3, 4), AP Stine Company uses a job order cost system. On May 1, the company has a balance in Work in Process Inventory of $3,500 and two jobs in process: Job No. 429 $2,000, and Job No. 430 $1,500. During May, a summary of source documents reveals the following.

Prepare journal entries for manufacturing costs.

Job Number	Materials Requisition Slips		Labor Time Tickets	
429	$2,500		$1,900	
430	3,500		3,000	
431	4,400	$10,400	7,600	$12,500
General use		800		1,200
		$11,200		$13,700

Stine Company applies manufacturing overhead to jobs at an overhead rate of 60% of direct labor cost. Job No. 429 is completed during the month.

Instructions

a. Prepare summary journal entries to record (1) the requisition slips, (2) the time tickets, (3) the assignment of manufacturing overhead to jobs, and (4) the completion of Job No. 429.

b. Post the entries to Work in Process Inventory, and prove the agreement of the control account with the job cost sheets. (Use a T-account.)

E15.3 (LO 1, 2, 3, 4), AP A job order cost sheet for Ryan Company is shown below.

Analyze a job cost sheet and prepare entries for manufacturing costs.

Job No. 92				For 2,000 Units
Date		Direct Materials	Direct Labor	Manufacturing Overhead
Beg. bal. Jan.	1	5,000	6,000	4,200
	8	6,000		
	12		8,000	6,400
	25	2,000		
	27		4,000	3,200
		13,000	18,000	13,800

Cost of completed job:
   Direct materials $13,000
   Direct labor   18,000
   Manufacturing overhead   13,800
Total cost $44,800

Unit cost ($44,800 ÷ 2,000) $ 22.40

Instructions

a. On the basis of the foregoing data, answer the following questions.
   1. What was the balance in Work in Process Inventory on January 1 if this was the only unfinished job?
   2. If manufacturing overhead is applied on the basis of direct labor cost, what overhead rate was used in each year?

b. Prepare summary entries at January 31 to record the current year's transactions pertaining to Job No. 92.

Analyze costs of manufacturing and determine missing amounts.

E15.4 (LO 1, 5), AN Manufacturing cost data for Orlando Company, which uses a job order cost system, are presented below.

	Case A	Case B
Direct materials used	$ (a)	$ 83,000
Direct labor	50,000	140,000
Manufacturing overhead applied	42,500	(d)
Total manufacturing costs	145,650	(e)
Work in process 1/1/22	(b)	15,500
Total cost of work in process	201,500	(f)
Work in process 12/31/22	(c)	11,800
Cost of goods manufactured	192,300	(g)

Instructions

Indicate the missing amount for each letter. Assume that in all cases manufacturing overhead is applied on the basis of direct labor cost and the rate is the same.

Compute the manufacturing overhead rate and under- or overapplied overhead.

Excel

E15.5 (LO 3, 5), AN Ikerd Company applies manufacturing overhead to jobs on the basis of machine hours used. Overhead costs are estimated to total $300,000 for the year, and machine usage is estimated at 125,000 hours.

For the year, $322,000 of overhead costs are incurred and 130,000 hours are used.

Instructions

a. Compute the manufacturing overhead rate for the year.
b. What is the amount of under- or overapplied overhead at December 31?
c. Prepare the adjusting entry to assign the under- or overapplied overhead for the year to cost of goods sold.

Analyze job cost sheet and prepare entry for completed job.

E15.6 (LO 1, 2, 3, 4), AP A job cost sheet of Sandoval Company is given below.

Job Cost Sheet

JOB NO. 469   Quantity 2,500
ITEM White Lion Cages   Date Requested 7/2
FOR Todd Company   Date Completed 7/31

Date	Direct Materials	Direct Labor	Manufacturing Overhead
7/10	700		
12	900		
15		440	550
22		380	475
24	1,600		
27	1,500		
31		540	675

Cost of completed job:
    Direct materials   _____
    Direct labor   _____
    Manufacturing overhead   _____
Total cost   ══════
Unit cost   ══════

Instructions

a. Answer the following questions.

1. What are the source documents for direct materials, direct labor, and manufacturing overhead costs assigned to this job?
2. Overhead is applied on the basis of direct labor cost. What is the predetermined manufacturing overhead rate?
3. What are the total cost and the unit cost of the completed job? (Round unit cost to nearest cent.)

b. Prepare the entry to record the completion of the job.

E15.7 (LO 1, 2, 3, 4), AP Crawford Corporation incurred the following transactions.

Prepare entries for manufacturing and nonmanufacturing costs.

1. Purchased raw materials on account $46,300.
2. Raw materials of $36,000 were requisitioned to the factory. An analysis of the materials requisition slips indicated that $6,800 was classified as indirect materials.
3. Factory labor costs incurred were $59,900, of which $51,000 pertained to factory wages payable and $8,900 pertained to employer payroll taxes payable.
4. Time tickets indicated that $54,000 was direct labor and $5,900 was indirect labor.
5. Manufacturing overhead costs incurred on account were $80,500.
6. Depreciation on the company's office building was $8,100.
7. Manufacturing overhead was applied at the rate of 150% of direct labor cost.
8. Goods costing $88,000 were completed and transferred to finished goods.
9. Finished goods costing $75,000 to manufacture were sold on account for $103,000.

Instructions

Journalize the transactions. (Omit explanations.)

E15.8 (LO 1, 2, 3, 4), AP Enos Printing Corp. uses a job order cost system. The following data summarize the operations related to the first quarter's production.

Prepare entries for manufacturing and nonmanufacturing costs.

1. Materials purchased on account $192,000, and factory wages incurred $87,300.
2. Materials requisitioned and factory labor used by job:

Job Number	Materials	Factory Labor
A20	$ 35,240	$18,000
A21	42,920	22,000
A22	36,100	15,000
A23	39,270	25,000
General factory use	4,470	7,300
	$158,000	$87,300

3. Manufacturing overhead costs incurred on account $49,500.
4. Depreciation on factory equipment $14,550.
5. Depreciation on the company's office building was $14,300.
6. Manufacturing overhead rate is 90% of direct labor cost.
7. Jobs completed during the quarter: A20, A21, and A23.

Instructions

Prepare entries to record the operations summarized above. Prepare a schedule showing the individual cost elements and total cost for each job in item 7.

E15.9 (LO 1, 5), AP At May 31, 2022, the accounts of Lopez Company show the following.

Prepare a cost of goods manufactured schedule and partial financial statements.

1. May 1 inventories—finished goods $12,600, work in process $14,700, and raw materials $8,200.
2. May 31 inventories—finished goods $9,500, work in process $15,900, and raw materials $7,100.
3. Debit postings to work in process were direct materials $62,400, direct labor $50,000, and manufacturing overhead applied $40,000. (Assume that overhead applied was equal to overhead incurred.)
4. Sales revenue totaled $215,000.

Instructions

a. Prepare a condensed cost of goods manufactured schedule for May 2022.

b. Prepare an income statement for May 2022 through gross profit.

c. Indicate the balance sheet presentation of the manufacturing inventories at May 31, 2022.

Compute work in process and finished goods from job cost sheets.

E15.10 (LO 2, 4), AP Tierney Company begins operations on April 1. Information from job cost sheets shows the following.

Job Number	Manufacturing Costs Assigned			Month Completed
	April	May	June	
10	$5,200	$4,400		May
11	4,100	3,900	$2,000	June
12	1,200			April
13		4,700	4,500	June
14		5,900	3,600	Not complete

Job 12 was completed in April. Job 10 was completed in May. Jobs 11 and 13 were completed in June. Each job was sold for 25% above its cost in the month following completion.

Instructions

a. What is the balance in Work in Process Inventory at the end of each month?

b. What is the balance in Finished Goods Inventory at the end of each month?

c. What is the gross profit for May, June, and July?

Prepare entries for costs of services provided.

E15.11 (LO 1, 3, 4), AP **Service** The following are the job cost related accounts for the law firm of Colaw Associates and their manufacturing equivalents:

Law Firm Accounts	Manufacturing Firm Accounts
Supplies	Raw Materials
Salaries and Wages Payable	Factory Wages Payable
Operating Overhead	Manufacturing Overhead
Service Contracts in Process	Work in Process
Cost of Completed Service Contracts	Cost of Goods Sold

Cost data for the month of March follow.

1. Purchased supplies on account $1,800.
2. Issued supplies $1,200 (60% direct and 40% indirect).
3. Assigned labor costs based on time cards for the month which indicated labor costs of $70,000 (80% direct and 20% indirect).
4. Operating overhead costs incurred for cash totaled $40,000.
5. Operating overhead is applied at a rate of 90% of direct labor cost.
6. Work completed totaled $75,000.

Instructions

a. Journalize the transactions for March. (Omit explanations.)

b. Determine the balance of the Service Contracts in Process account. (Use a T-account.)

Determine cost of jobs and ending balance in work in process and overhead accounts.

E15.12 (LO 2, 3, 4), AP **Service** Don Lieberman and Associates, a CPA firm, uses job order costing to capture the costs of its audit jobs. There were no audit jobs in process at the beginning of November. Listed below are data concerning the three audit jobs conducted during November.

	Waters Inc.	Renolds Inc.	Bayfield Inc.
Direct materials	$600	$400	$200
Auditor labor costs	$5,400	$6,600	$3,375
Auditor hours	72	88	45

Overhead costs are applied to jobs on the basis of auditor hours, and the predetermined overhead rate is $50 per auditor hour. The Waters Inc. job is the only incomplete job at the end of November. Actual overhead for the month was $11,000.

Instructions

a. Determine the cost of each job.

b. Indicate the balance of the Service Contracts in Process account at the end of November.

c. Calculate the ending balance of the Operating Overhead account for November.

E15.13 (LO 3, 5), AP Service Tombert Decorating uses a job order cost system to collect the costs of its interior decorating business. Each client's consultation is treated as a separate job. Overhead is applied to each job based on the number of decorator hours incurred. Listed below are data for the current year.

Determine predetermined overhead rate, apply overhead, and determine whether balance under- or overapplied.

Estimated overhead	$960,000
Actual overhead	$982,800
Estimated decorator hours	40,000
Actual decorator hours	40,500

The company uses Operating Overhead in place of Manufacturing Overhead.

Instructions

a. Compute the predetermined overhead rate.

b. Prepare the entry to apply the overhead for the year.

c. Determine whether the overhead was under- or overapplied and by how much.

Problems: Set A

P15.1A (LO 1, 2, 3, 4, 5), AP Lott Company uses a job order cost system and applies overhead to production on the basis of direct labor costs. On January 1, 2022, Job 50 was the only job in process. The costs incurred prior to January 1 on this job were as follows: direct materials $20,000, direct labor $12,000, and manufacturing overhead $16,000. As of January 1, Job 49 had been completed at a cost of $90,000 and was part of finished goods inventory. There was a $15,000 balance in the Raw Materials Inventory account.

Prepare entries in a job order cost system and job cost sheets.

During the month of January, Lott Company began production on Jobs 51 and 52, and completed Jobs 50 and 51. Jobs 49 and 50 were also sold on account during the month for $122,000 and $158,000, respectively. The following additional events occurred during the month.

1. Purchased additional raw materials of $90,000 on account.

2. Incurred factory labor costs of $70,000. Of this amount $16,000 related to employer payroll taxes.

3. Incurred manufacturing overhead costs as follows: indirect materials $17,000, indirect labor $20,000, depreciation expense on equipment $12,000, and various other manufacturing overhead costs on account $16,000.

4. Assigned direct materials and direct labor to jobs as follows.

Job No.	Direct Materials	Direct Labor
50	$10,000	$ 5,000
51	39,000	25,000
52	30,000	20,000

Instructions

a. Calculate the predetermined overhead rate for 2022, assuming Lott Company estimates total manufacturing overhead costs of $840,000, direct labor costs of $700,000, and direct labor hours of 20,000 for the year.

b. Open job cost sheets for Jobs 50, 51, and 52. Enter the January 1 balances on the job cost sheet for Job 50.

c. Prepare the journal entries to record the purchase of raw materials, the factory labor costs incurred, and the manufacturing overhead costs incurred during the month of January.

d. Prepare the journal entries to record the assignment of direct materials, direct labor, and manufacturing overhead costs to production. In assigning manufacturing overhead costs, use the overhead rate calculated in (a). Post all costs to the job cost sheets as necessary.

e. Total the job cost sheets for any job(s) completed during the month. Prepare the journal entry (or entries) to record the completion of any job(s) during the month.

e. Job 50, $69,000
   Job 51, $94,000

f. Prepare the journal entry (or entries) to record the sale of any job(s) during the month.

g. What is the balance in the Finished Goods Inventory account at the end of the month? What does this balance consist of?

h. What is the amount of over- or underapplied overhead?

Prepare entries in a job order cost system and partial income statement.

P15.2A (LO 1, 2, 3, 4, 5), AP For the year ended December 31, 2022, the job cost sheets of Cinta Company contained the following data.

Job Number	Explanation	Direct Materials	Direct Labor	Manufacturing Overhead	Total Costs
7640	Balance 1/1	$25,000	$24,000	$28,800	$ 77,800
	Current year's costs	30,000	36,000	43,200	109,200
7641	Balance 1/1	11,000	18,000	21,600	50,600
	Current year's costs	43,000	48,000	57,600	148,600
7642	Current year's costs	58,000	55,000	66,000	179,000

Other data:

1. Raw materials inventory totaled $15,000 on January 1. During the year, $140,000 of raw materials were purchased on account.
2. Finished goods on January 1 consisted of Job No. 7638 for $87,000 and Job No. 7639 for $92,000.
3. Job No. 7640 and Job No. 7641 were completed during the year.
4. Job Nos. 7638, 7639, and 7641 were sold on account for $530,000.
5. Manufacturing overhead incurred on account totaled $120,000.
6. Other manufacturing overhead consisted of indirect materials $14,000, indirect labor $18,000, and depreciation on factory machinery $8,000.

Instructions

a. $179,000; Job 7642: $179,000

a. Prove the agreement of Work in Process Inventory with job cost sheets pertaining to unfinished work. (*Hint:* Use a single T-account for Work in Process Inventory.) Calculate each of the following, then post each to the T-account: (1) beginning balance, (2) direct materials, (3) direct labor, (4) manufacturing overhead, and (5) completed jobs.

b. Amount = $6,800

b. Prepare the adjusting entry for manufacturing overhead, assuming the balance is allocated entirely to Cost of Goods Sold.

c. $158,600

c. Determine the gross profit to be reported for 2022.

Prepare entries in a job order cost system and cost of goods manufactured schedule.

P15.3A (LO 1, 2, 3, 4, 5), AP Case Inc. is a construction company specializing in custom patios. The patios are constructed of concrete, brick, fiberglass, and lumber, depending upon customer preference. On June 1, 2022, the general ledger for Case Inc. contains the following data.

Raw Materials Inventory	$4,200	Manufacturing Overhead Applied	$32,640
Work in Process Inventory	$5,540	Manufacturing Overhead Incurred	$31,650

Subsidiary data for Work in Process Inventory on June 1 are as follows.

Job Cost Sheets

	Customer Job		
Cost Element	Rodgers	Stevens	Linton
Direct materials	$ 600	$ 800	$ 900
Direct labor	320	540	580
Manufacturing overhead	400	675	725
	$1,320	$2,015	$2,205

During June, raw materials purchased on account were $4,900, and all wages were paid. Additional overhead costs consisted of depreciation on equipment $900 and miscellaneous costs of $400 incurred on account.

A summary of materials requisition slips and time tickets for June shows the following.

Customer Job	Materials Requisition Slips	Time Tickets
Rodgers	$ 800	$ 850
Koss	2,000	800
Stevens	500	360
Linton	1,300	1,200
Rodgers	300	390
	4,900	3,600
General use	1,500	1,200
	$6,400	$4,800

Overhead was charged to jobs at the same rate of $1.25 per dollar of direct labor cost. The patios for customers Rodgers, Stevens, and Linton were completed during June and sold for a total of $18,900. Each customer paid in full.

Instructions

a. Journalize the June transactions: (1) for purchase of raw materials, factory labor costs incurred, and manufacturing overhead costs incurred; (2) assignment of direct materials, labor, and overhead to production; and (3) completion of jobs and sale of goods.
b. Post the entries to Work in Process Inventory.
c. Reconcile the balance in Work in Process Inventory with the costs of unfinished jobs.
d. Prepare a cost of goods manufactured schedule for June.

d. Cost of goods manufactured $14,740

P15.4A (LO 3, 5), AP Agassi Company uses a job order cost system in each of its three manufacturing departments. Manufacturing overhead is applied to jobs on the basis of direct labor cost in Department D, direct labor hours in Department E, and machine hours in Department K.

In establishing the predetermined overhead rates for 2022, the following estimates were made for the year.

Compute predetermined overhead rates, apply overhead, and calculate under- or overapplied overhead.

	Department		
	D	E	K
Manufacturing overhead	$1,200,000	$1,500,000	$900,000
Direct labor costs	$1,500,000	$1,250,000	$450,000
Direct labor hours	100,000	125,000	40,000
Machine hours	400,000	500,000	120,000

During January, the job cost sheets showed the following costs and production data.

	Department		
	D	E	K
Direct materials used	$140,000	$126,000	$78,000
Direct labor costs	$120,000	$110,000	$37,500
Manufacturing overhead incurred	$ 99,000	$124,000	$79,000
Direct labor hours	8,000	11,000	3,500
Machine hours	34,000	45,000	10,400

Instructions

a. Compute the predetermined overhead rate for each department.
b. Compute the total manufacturing costs assigned to jobs in January in each department.
c. Compute the under- or overapplied overhead for each department at January 31.

a. 80%, $12, $7.50
b. $356,000, $368,000, $193,500
c. $3,000, $(8,000), $1,000

P15.5A (LO 1, 2, 3, 4, 5), AN Phillips Corporation's fiscal year ends on November 30. The following accounts are found in its job order cost accounting system for the first month of the new fiscal year.

Analyze manufacturing accounts and determine missing amounts.

Raw Materials Inventory

Dec. 1	Beginning balance	(a)	Dec. 31	Requisitions	16,850
31	Purchases	17,225			
Dec. 31	Ending balance	7,975			

Work in Process Inventory

Dec.	1	Beginning balance	(b)	Dec. 31	Jobs completed		(f)
	31	Direct materials	(c)				
	31	Direct labor	8,400				
	31	Overhead	(d)				
Dec. 31		Ending balance	(e)				

Finished Goods Inventory

Dec.	1	Beginning balance	(g)	Dec. 31	Cost of goods sold		(i)
	31	Completed jobs	(h)				
Dec. 31		Ending balance	(j)				

Factory Labor

Dec. 31	Factory wages	12,025	Dec. 31	Wages assigned	(k)

Manufacturing Overhead

Dec. 31	Indirect materials	2,900	Dec. 31	Overhead applied	(m)
31	Indirect labor	(l)			
31	Other overhead	1,245			

Other data:

1. On December 1, two jobs were in process: Job No. 154 and Job No. 155. These jobs had combined direct materials costs of $9,750 and direct labor costs of $15,000. Overhead was applied at a rate that was 75% of direct labor cost.

2. During December, Job Nos. 156, 157, and 158 were started. On December 31, Job No. 158 was unfinished. This job had charges for direct materials $3,800 and direct labor $4,800, plus manufacturing overhead. All jobs, except for Job No. 158, were completed in December.

3. On December 1, Job No. 153 was in the finished goods warehouse. It had a total cost of $5,000. On December 31, Job No. 157 was the only job finished that was not sold. It had a cost of $4,000.

4. Manufacturing overhead was $1,470 underapplied in December.

c. $13,950
f. $52,450
i. $53,450

Instructions

List the letters (a) through (m) and indicate the amount pertaining to each letter.

Continuing Cases

Current Designs

CD15 Huegel Hollow Resort has ordered 20 rotomolded kayaks from **Current Designs**. Each kayak will be formed in the rotomolded oven, cooled, and then the excess plastic trimmed away. Then, the hatches, seat, ropes, and bungees will be attached to the kayak.

Dave Thill, the kayak plant manager, knows that manufacturing each kayak requires 54 pounds of polyethylene powder and a finishing kit (rope, seat, hardware, etc.). The polyethylene powder used in these kayaks costs $1.50 per pound, and the finishing kits cost $170 each. Each kayak will use two kinds of labor: 2 hours of more-skilled type I labor from people who run the oven and trim the plastic, and 3 hours of less-skilled type II labor from people who attach the hatches and seat and other hardware. The type I employees are paid $15 per hour, and the type II employees are paid $12 per hour. For purposes of this problem, assume that overhead is applied to all jobs at a rate of 150% of direct labor costs.

Instructions

Determine the total cost of the Huegel Hollow order and the cost of each individual kayak in the order. Identify costs as direct materials, direct labor, or manufacturing overhead.

Waterways

(*Note:* This is a continuation of the Waterways case from Chapter 14.)

WP15 Waterways has two major public-park projects to provide with comprehensive irrigation in one of its service locations this month. Job J57 and Job K52 involve 15 acres of landscaped terrain which will require special-order sprinkler heads to meet the specifications of the project. This problem asks you to help Waterways use a job order cost system to account for production of these parts.

Go to WileyPLUS for complete case details and instructions.

Comprehensive Case

CC15 Greetings Inc., a nationally recognized retailer of greeting cards and small gift items, decides to employ Internet technology to expand its sales opportunities. For this case, you will employ traditional job order costing techniques and then evaluate the resulting product costs.

Go to WileyPLUS for complete case details and instructions.

Comprehensive Cases *present realistic business situations that require students to apply topics learned in this and previous chapters.*

Expand Your Critical Thinking

Decision-Making Across the Organization

CT15.1 Khan Products Company uses a job order cost system. For a number of months, there has been an ongoing rift between the sales department and the production department concerning a special-order product, TC-1. TC-1 is a seasonal product that is manufactured in batches of 1,000 units. TC-1 is sold at cost plus a markup of 40% of cost.

The sales department is unhappy because fluctuating unit production costs significantly affect selling prices. Sales personnel complain that this has caused excessive customer complaints and the loss of considerable orders for TC-1.

The production department maintains that each job order must be fully costed on the basis of the costs incurred during the period in which the goods are produced. Production personnel maintain that the only real solution is for the sales department to increase sales in the slack periods.

Andrea Parley, president of the company, asks you as the company accountant to collect quarterly data for the past year on TC-1. From the cost accounting system, you accumulate the following production quantity and cost data.

	Quarter			
Costs	1	2	3	4
Direct materials	$100,000	$220,000	$ 80,000	$200,000
Direct labor	60,000	132,000	48,000	120,000
Manufacturing overhead	105,000	153,000	97,000	125,000
Total	$265,000	$505,000	$225,000	$445,000
Production in batches	5	11	4	10
Unit cost (per batch)	$ 53,000	$ 45,909	$ 56,250	$ 44,500

Instructions

With the class divided into groups, answer the following questions.

a. What manufacturing cost element is responsible for the fluctuating unit costs? Why?

b. What is your recommended solution to the problem of fluctuating unit cost?

c. Restate the quarterly data on the basis of your recommended solution.

Managerial Analysis

CT15.2 In the course of routine checking of all journal entries prior to preparing year-end reports, Betty Eller discovered several strange entries. She recalled that the president's son Joe had come in to help out during an especially busy time and that he had recorded some journal entries. She was relieved that there were only a few of his entries, and even more relieved that he had included rather lengthy explanations. The entries Joe made were:

(1)

Work in Process Inventory	25,000	
Cash		25,000

(This is for materials put into process. I don't find the record that we paid for these, so I'm crediting Cash because I know we'll have to pay for them sooner or later.)

(2)

Manufacturing Overhead	12,000	
Cash		12,000

(This is for bonuses paid to salespeople. I know they're part of overhead, and I can't find an account called "Non-Factory Overhead" or "Other Overhead" so I'm putting it in Manufacturing Overhead. I have the check stubs, so I know we paid these.)

(3)

Wages Expense	120,000	
Cash		120,000

(This is for the factory workers' wages. I have a note that employer payroll taxes are $18,000. I still think that's part of wages expense and that we'll have to pay it all in cash sooner or later, so I credited Cash for the wages and the taxes.)

(4)

Work in Process Inventory	3,000	
Raw Materials Inventory		3,000

(This is for the glue used in the factory. I know we used this to make the products, even though we didn't use very much on any one of the products. I got it out of inventory, so I credited an inventory account.)

Instructions

a. How should Joe have recorded each of the four events?

b. If the entry was not corrected, which financial statements (income statement or balance sheet) would be affected? What balances would be overstated or understated?

Real-World Focus

CT15.3 The **Institute of Management Accountants (IMA)** sponsors a certification for management accountants, allowing them to obtain the title of Certified Management Accountant.

Instructions

Go to the IMA website, choose **About IMA**, choose **CMA Certification**, and then **Getting Started**. Answer part (a) below. Next, choose **CMA Certification**, then **Current CMAs**, then **Maintain Your Certification**, and then click on **Download the CPE Requirements and Rules**. Answer part (b) below.

a. What is the experience qualification requirement?

b. How many hours of continuing education are required, and what types of courses qualify?

Communication Activity

CT15.4 You are the management accountant for Williams Company. Your company does custom carpentry work and uses a job order cost system. Williams sends detailed job cost sheets to its customers, along with an invoice. The job cost sheets show the date materials were used, the dollar cost of materials, and the hours and cost of labor. A predetermined overhead application rate is used, and the total overhead applied is also listed.

Nancy Kopay is a customer who recently had custom cabinets installed. Along with her check in payment for the work done, she included a letter. She thanked the company for including the detailed cost information but questioned why overhead was estimated. She stated that she would be interested in knowing exactly what costs were included in overhead, and she thought that other customers would, too.

Instructions

Prepare a letter to Ms. Kopay (address: 123 Cedar Lane, Altoona, KS 66651) and tell her why you did not send her information on exact costs of overhead included in her job. Respond to her suggestion that you provide this information.

Ethics Case

CT15.5 **Service** LRF Printing provides printing services to many different corporate clients. Although LRF bids most jobs, some jobs, particularly new ones, are negotiated on a "cost-plus" basis. Cost-plus means that the buyer is willing to pay the actual cost plus a return (profit) on these costs to LRF.

Alice Reiley, controller for LRF, has recently returned from a meeting where LRF's president stated that he wanted her to find a way to charge more costs to any project that was on a cost-plus basis. The president noted that the company needed more profits to meet its stated goals this period. By charging more costs to the cost-plus projects and therefore fewer costs to the jobs that were bid, the company should be able to increase its profit for the current year.

Alice knew why the president wanted to take this action. Rumors were that he was looking for a new position and if the company reported strong profits, the president's opportunities would be enhanced. Alice also recognized that she could probably increase the cost of certain jobs by changing the basis used to assign manufacturing overhead.

Instructions

a. Who are the stakeholders in this situation?
b. What are the ethical issues in this situation?
c. What would you do if you were Alice Reiley?

All About You

CT15.6 Many of you will work for a small business. Some of you will even own your own business. In order to operate a small business, you will need a good understanding of managerial accounting, as well as many other skills. Much information is available to assist people who are interested in starting a new business. A great place to start is the website provided by the **Small Business Administration**, which is an agency of the federal government whose purpose is to support small businesses.

Instructions

Go to the Small Business Administration website, search "Is entrepreneurship for you," and then answer part (a) below. Next, search "10 steps to starting a business" and then answer part (b) below.

a. What are some of the characteristics required of a small business owner?
b. What are the 10 steps for starting a business?

Considering Your Costs and Benefits

CT15.7 After graduating, you might decide to start a small business. As discussed in this chapter, owners of any business need to know how to calculate the cost of their products. In fact, many small businesses fail because they don't accurately calculate their product costs, so they don't know if they are making a profit or losing money—until it's too late.

Suppose that you decide to start a landscape business. You use an old pickup truck that you've fully paid for. You store the truck and other equipment in your parents' barn, and you store trees and shrubs on their land. Your parents will not charge you for the use of these facilities for the first two years, but beginning in the third year they will charge a reasonable rent. Your mother helps you by answering phone calls and providing customers with information. She doesn't charge you for this service, but she plans on doing it for only your first two years in business. In pricing your services, should you include charges for the truck, the barn, the land, and your mother's services when calculating your product cost? The basic arguments for and against are as follows.

YES: If you don't include charges for these costs, your costs are understated and your profitability is overstated.

NO: At this point, you are not actually incurring costs related to these activities; therefore, you shouldn't record charges.

Instructions

Write a response indicating your position regarding this situation. Provide support for your view.

CHAPTER 16

Process Costing

Chapter Preview

As the following Feature Story describes, the cost accounting system used by companies such as **Jones Soda** is **process cost accounting**. In contrast to job order cost accounting, which focuses on the individual job, process cost accounting focuses on the *processes* involved in mass-producing products that are identical or very similar in nature. The primary objective of this chapter is to explain and illustrate process costing.

Feature Story

The Little Guy Who Could

It isn't easy for a small company to get a foothold in the bottled beverage business. The giants, **The Coca-Cola Company** and **PepsiCo Inc.**, vigilantly defend their turf, constantly watching for new trends and opportunities. It is nearly impossible to get shelf space in stores, and consumer tastes can change faster than a bottle of soda can lose its fizz. But **Jones Soda Co.**, headquartered in Seattle, has overcome these and other obstacles to make a name for itself. Its corporate motto is, "Run with the little guy . . . create some change."

The company started as a Canadian distributor of other companies' beverages. Soon, it decided to make its own products under the corporate name Urban Juice and Soda Company. Eventually, its name changed to Jones Soda—the name of its most popular product. From the very start, Jones Soda was different. It sold soda from machines placed in tattoo parlors and piercing shops, and it sponsored a punk rock band as well as surfers and snowboarders. At one time, the company's product was the official drink at the **Seattle Seahawks'** stadium and was served on **Alaska Airlines**.

Today, Jones Soda makes a wide variety of products: soda-flavored candy, energy drinks, and product-promoting gear that includes t-shirts, sweatshirts, caps, shorts, and calendars. Its most profitable product is still its multi-flavored, pure cane soda with its creative labeling. If you've seen Jones Soda on a store shelf, then you know that it appears to have an infinite variety of labels. The bottle labels are actually created by customers and submitted on the company's website. (To see some of the best labels from the past, see the Gallery at the Jones Soda website.) If you would like some soda with a custom label of your own, you can design and submit a label and order a 12-pack.

Because Jones Soda has a dizzying array of product variations, keeping track of costs is of vital importance. Recently, management developed a reorganization plan that involved cost-cutting from top to bottom and eliminating unprofitable products. No matter how good your products are, if you don't keep your costs under control, you are likely to fail. Jones Soda's managers need accurate cost information regarding each primary product and each variation to ensure profitability. So while its marketing approach differs dramatically from the giants, Jones Soda needs the same kind of cost information as the big guys.

 Watch the *Jones Soda* video in WileyPLUS to learn more about process costing in the real world.

Chapter Outline

LEARNING OBJECTIVES

LO 1 Discuss the uses of a process cost system and how it compares to a job order system.	• Uses of process cost systems • Process costing for service companies • Comparing job order and process cost systems	**DO IT! 1** Compare Job Order and Process Cost Systems
LO 2 Explain the flow of costs in a process cost system and the journal entries to assign manufacturing costs.	• Process cost flow • Assigning manufacturing costs	**DO IT! 2** Manufacturing Costs in Process Costing
LO 3 Compute equivalent units.	• Weighted-average method • Refinements on the method	**DO IT! 3** Equivalent Units
LO 4 Complete the four steps to prepare a production cost report.	• Physical unit flow • Equivalent units of production • Unit production costs • Cost reconciliation schedule • Production cost report	**DO IT! 4** Cost Reconciliation Schedule

Go to the Review and Practice section at the end of the chapter for a targeted summary and practice applications with solutions.
Visit WileyPLUS for additional tutorials and practice opportunities.

Overview of Process Cost Systems

LEARNING OBJECTIVE 1
Discuss the uses of a process cost system and how it compares to a job order system.

Uses of Process Cost Systems

Companies use **process cost systems** to apply costs to similar products that are mass-produced in a continuous fashion. **Jones Soda Co.** uses a process cost system: Production of the soda, once it begins, continues until the completed bottles of soda emerge. The processing is the same for the entire production run—with precisely the same amount of materials, labor, and overhead. Each finished bottle of soda is indistinguishable from another.

A company such as **USX** uses process costing in the manufacturing of steel. **Kellogg** and **General Mills** use process costing for cereal production; **ExxonMobil** uses process costing for its oil refining. **Sherwin Williams** uses process costing for its paint products. At a bottling company like Jones Soda, the manufacturing process begins with the blending of ingredients. Next, automated machinery moves the bottles into position and fills them. The production process then caps, labels, packages, and forwards the bottles to the finished goods warehouse. **Illustration 16.1** shows this process.

ILLUSTRATION 16.1 Manufacturing processes

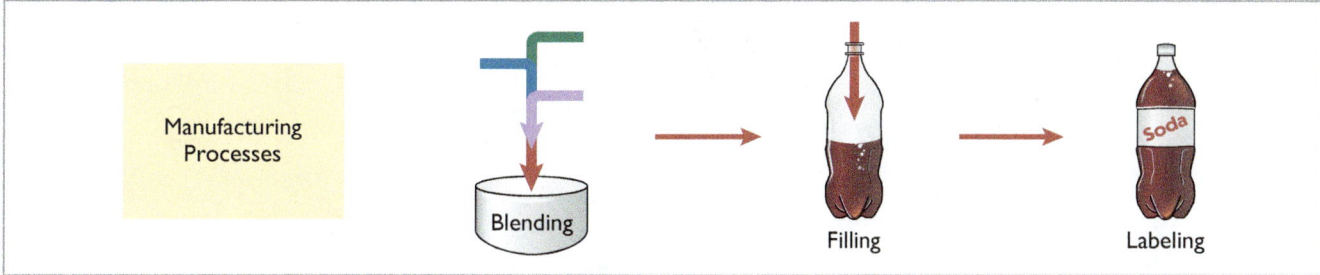

For Jones Soda, as well as the other companies just mentioned, once production begins, it continues until the finished product emerges. Each unit of finished product is like every other unit.

In comparison, a job order cost system assigns costs to a *specific job*. Examples are the construction of a customized home, the making of a movie, or the manufacturing of a specialized machine. **Illustration 16.2** provides examples of companies that primarily use either a process cost system or a job order cost system.

ILLUSTRATION 16.2 Process cost and job order cost companies and products

Process Cost System		Job Order Cost System	
Company	Product	Company	Product
Jones Soda, PepsiCo	Soft drinks	Young & Rubicam, J. Walter Thompson	Advertising
ExxonMobil, Royal Dutch Shell	Oil	Disney, Warner Brothers	Movies
Intel, Advanced Micro Devices	Computer chips	Center Ice Consultants, Ice Pro	Ice rinks
Dow Chemical, DuPont	Chemicals	Kaiser, Mayo Clinic	Patient health care

Process Costing for Service Companies

When considering service companies, you might initially think of specific, nonroutine tasks, such as rebuilding an automobile engine, consulting on a business acquisition, or defending a major lawsuit. However, many service companies perform repetitive, routine work. For example, **Jiffy Lube** regularly performs oil changes. **H&R Block** focuses on the routine aspects of basic tax practice. Service companies that perform individualized, nonroutine services will probably benefit from using a job order cost system. Those that perform routine, repetitive services will probably prefer a process cost system.

Similarities and Differences Between Job Order Cost and Process Cost Systems

In a job order cost system, companies assign costs to each job. In a process cost system, companies track costs through a series of connected manufacturing processes or departments, rather than by individual jobs. Thus, companies use process cost systems when they produce a large volume of uniform or relatively homogeneous products. **Illustration 16.3** shows the basic flow of costs in these two systems.

ILLUSTRATION 16.3 Job order cost and process cost flow

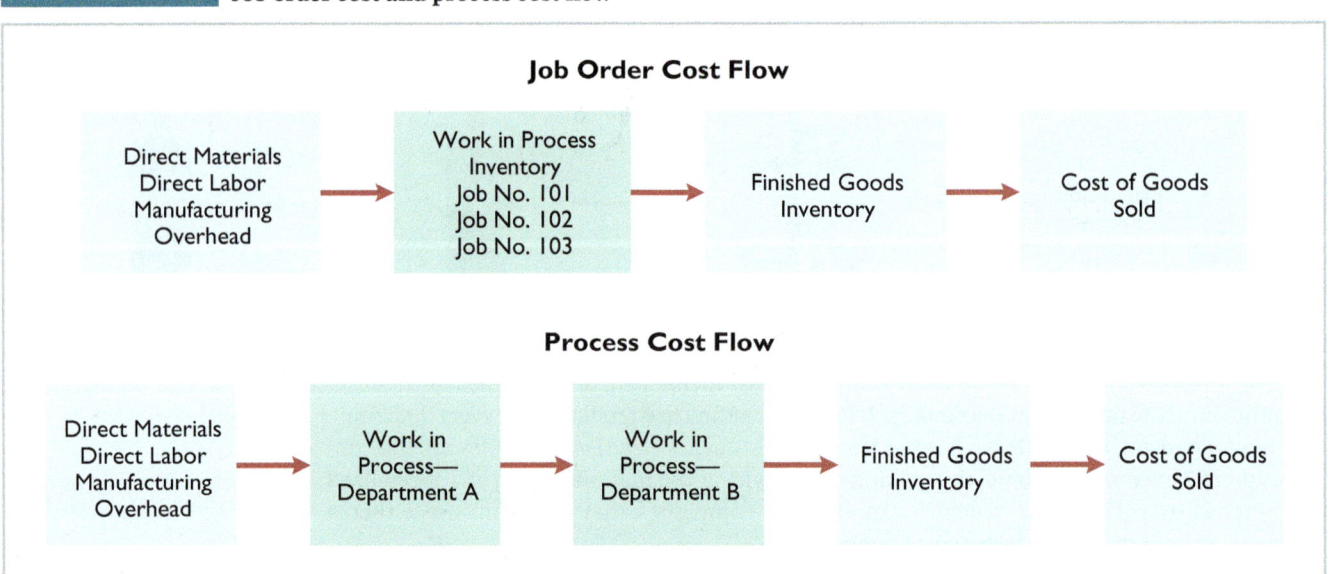

The following analysis highlights the basic similarities and differences between these two systems.

Similarities

Job order cost and process cost systems are similar in three ways:

1. **The manufacturing cost elements.** Both costing systems track three manufacturing cost elements—direct materials, direct labor, and manufacturing overhead.
2. **The accumulation of the costs of materials, labor, and overhead.** Both costing systems record the acquisition of raw materials as a debit to Raw Materials Inventory, incurred factory labor as a debit to Factory Labor, and manufacturing overhead costs as debits to Manufacturing Overhead.

3. **The flow of costs.** As noted above, both systems accumulate all manufacturing costs by debits to Raw Materials Inventory, Factory Labor, and Manufacturing Overhead. Both systems then assign these costs to the same accounts—Work in Process, Finished Goods Inventory, and Cost of Goods Sold. **The methods of assigning costs, however, differ significantly.** These differences are explained and illustrated later in the chapter.

Differences

The differences between a job order cost and a process cost system are as follows.

1. **The number of work in process accounts used.** A job order cost system uses only one work in process account. A process cost system uses multiple work in process accounts.
2. **Documents used to track costs.** A job order cost system charges costs to individual jobs and summarizes them in a job cost sheet. A process cost system summarizes costs in a production cost report for each department.
3. **The point at which costs are totaled.** A job order cost system totals costs when the job is completed. A process cost system totals costs at the end of a period of time.
4. **Unit cost computations.** In a job order cost system, the unit cost is the total cost per job divided by the units produced for that job. In a process cost system, the unit cost is total manufacturing costs for the period divided by the equivalent units produced during the period.

Illustration 16.4 summarizes the major differences between a job order cost and a process cost system.

Feature	Job Order Cost System	Process Cost System
Work in process accounts	One work in process account	Multiple work in process accounts
Documents used	Job cost sheets	Production cost reports
Determination of total manufacturing costs	Each job	Each period
Unit-cost computations	Cost of each job ÷ Units produced for the job	Total manufacturing costs ÷ Equivalent units produced during the period

ILLUSTRATION 16.4

Job order versus process cost systems

DO IT! 1 | Compare Job Order and Process Cost Systems

Indicate whether each of the following statements is true or false.

1. A law firm is likely to use process costing for major lawsuits.
2. A manufacturer of paintballs is likely to use process costing.
3. Both job order and process costing determine product costs at the end of a period of time, rather than when a product is completed.
4. Process costing does not keep track of manufacturing overhead.

ACTION PLAN
- Use job order costing in situations where unit costs are high, unit volume is low, and products are unique.
- Use process costing when there is a large volume of relatively homogeneous products.

Solution

1. False.   2. True.   3. False.   4. False.

Related exercise material: **DO IT! 16.1 and E16.1.**

Process Cost Flow and Assigning Costs

> **LEARNING OBJECTIVE 2**
> Explain the flow of costs in a process cost system and the journal entries to assign manufacturing costs.

Process Cost Flow

Illustration 16.5 shows the flow of costs in the process cost system for Tyler Company. Tyler manufactures roller blade and skateboard wheels that it sells to manufacturers and retail outlets. Manufacturing consists of two processes: machining and assembly. The Machining Department shapes, hones, and drills the raw materials. The Assembly Department assembles and packages the wheels.

ILLUSTRATION 16.5 Flow of costs in process cost system

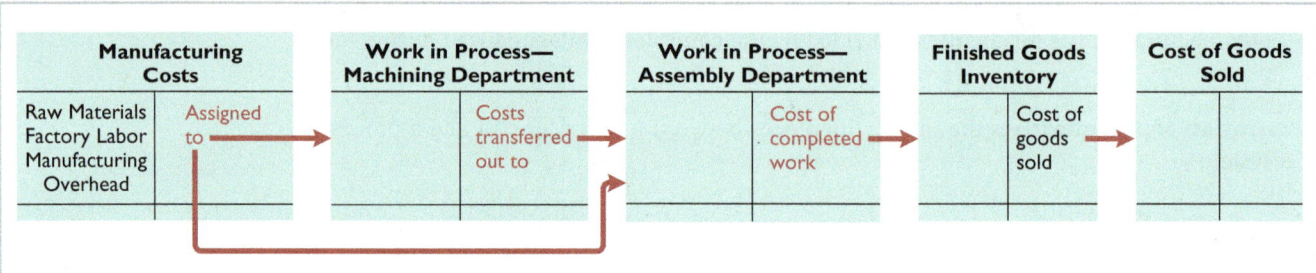

As the flow of costs indicates, the company can add materials, labor, and manufacturing overhead in both the Machining and Assembly Departments. When it finishes its work, the Machining Department transfers the partially completed units to the Assembly Department. The Assembly Department finishes the goods and then transfers them to the finished goods inventory. Upon sale, Tyler removes the goods from the finished goods inventory. Within each department, a similar set of activities is performed on each unit processed.

Assigning Manufacturing Costs—Journal Entries

As indicated, the accumulation of the costs of materials, labor, and manufacturing overhead is the same in a process cost system as in a job order cost system. That is, both systems follow these procedures:

- Debit all raw materials acquired to Raw Materials Inventory at the time of purchase.
- Debit all factory labor to Factory Labor as labor costs are incurred.
- Debit overhead costs to Manufacturing Overhead as these costs are incurred.

However, the assignment of the three manufacturing cost elements to Work in Process in a process cost system is different from a job order cost system. Here we'll look at how companies assign these manufacturing cost elements in a process cost system.

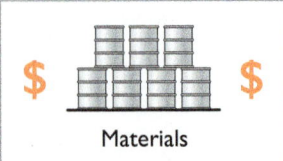

Materials Costs

All raw materials issued for production are a materials cost to the producing department. A process cost system may use materials requisition slips, but **it generally requires fewer requisitions than in a job order cost system. The materials are used for processes rather than for specific jobs** and therefore typically are for larger quantities.

At the beginning of the first process, a company usually adds most of the materials needed for production. However, other materials may be added at various points. For example, in the manufacture of **Hershey** candy bars, the chocolate and other ingredients are added at the beginning of the first process, and the wrappers and cartons are added at the end of the packaging process. Tyler Company adds materials at the beginning of each process. Suppose at the beginning of the current period that Tyler adds $50,000 of direct materials to the machining process and $20,000 of direct materials to the assembly process. Tyler makes the following entry to record the materials used.

Work in Process—Machining	50,000	
Work in Process—Assembly	20,000	
Raw Materials Inventory		70,000
(To record materials used)		

Factory Labor Costs

In a process cost system, as in a job order cost system, companies may use time tickets to determine the cost of labor assignable to production departments. Since they assign labor costs to a process rather than a job, they can obtain, from the payroll register or departmental payroll summaries, the labor cost chargeable to a process.

Suppose that Tyler Company incurs factory labor charges of $20,000 in the machining process and $13,000 in the assembly process. The entry to assign labor costs to machining and assembly for Tyler is:

Factory Labor

Work in Process—Machining	20,000	
Work in Process—Assembly	13,000	
Factory Labor		33,000
(To assign factory labor to production)		

Manufacturing Overhead Costs

The objective in assigning overhead in a process cost system is to allocate the overhead costs to the production departments on an objective and equitable basis. That basis is the activity that "drives" or causes the costs. A primary driver of overhead costs in continuous manufacturing operations is **machine time used**, not direct labor. Thus, companies **widely use machine hours** in allocating manufacturing overhead costs using predetermined overhead rates. Assume that based on machine hours that Tyler Company allocates overhead of $45,000 to the machining process and $17,000 to the assembly process. Tyler's entry to allocate overhead to the two processes is:

Manufacturing Overhead

Work in Process—Machining	45,000	
Work in Process—Assembly	17,000	
Manufacturing Overhead		62,000
(To assign overhead to production)		

Management Insight   Caterpillar

© SweetyMommy/iStockphoto

Choosing a Cost Driver

In one of its automated cost centers, **Caterpillar** inputs work into the cost center, where robotic machines process it and transfer the finished job to the next cost center without human intervention. One person tends all of the machines and spends more time maintaining machines than operating them. In such cases, overhead rates based on direct labor hours may be misleading. Surprisingly, some companies continue to assign manufacturing overhead on the basis of direct labor despite the fact that there is no cause-and-effect relationship between labor and overhead.

What is the result if a company uses the wrong "cost driver" to assign manufacturing overhead? (Go to WileyPLUS for this answer and additional questions.)

Transfer to Next Department

At the end of the month, Tyler Company needs an entry to record the cost of the goods transferred out of the Machining Department. In this case, the transfer is to the Assembly Department. Suppose Tyler transferred goods with a recorded cost of $87,000 from machining to assembly. Tyler makes the following entry.

Work in Process—Assembly	87,000	
Work in Process—Machining		87,000
(To record transfer of units to the Assembly Department)		

Transfer to Finished Goods

Suppose the Assembly Department completes units with a recorded cost of $114,000 and then transfers them to the finished goods warehouse. The entry for this transfer is as follows.

Finished Goods Inventory	114,000	
Work in Process—Assembly		114,000
(To record transfer of units to finished goods)		

Transfer to Cost of Goods Sold

Suppose Tyler Company sells finished good with a recorded cost of $27,000. It records the cost of goods sold as follows.

Cost of Goods Sold	27,000	
Finished Goods Inventory		27,000
(To record cost of units sold)		

ACTION PLAN

- In process cost accounting, keep separate work in process accounts for each process.
- When the costs are assigned to production, debit the separate work in process accounts.
- Transfer cost of completed units to the next process or to Finished Goods.

DO IT! 2 | Manufacturing Costs in Process Costing

Ruth Company manufactures ZEBO through two processes: blending and bottling. In June, raw materials used were Blending $18,000 and Bottling $4,000. Factory labor costs were Blending $12,000 and Bottling $5,000. Manufacturing overhead costs assigned were Blending $6,000 and Bottling $2,500. The company transfers units completed at a cost of $19,000 in the Blending Department to the Bottling Department. The Bottling Department transfers units completed at a cost of $11,000 to Finished Goods. Journalize the assignment of these costs to the two processes and the transfer of units as appropriate.

Solution

The entries are:

Work in Process—Blending	18,000	
Work in Process—Bottling	4,000	
Raw Materials Inventory		22,000
(To record materials used)		
Work in Process—Blending	12,000	
Work in Process—Bottling	5,000	
Factory Labor		17,000
(To assign factory labor to production)		
Work in Process—Blending	6,000	
Work in Process—Bottling	2,500	
Manufacturing Overhead		8,500
(To assign overhead to production)		
Work in Process—Bottling	19,000	
Work in Process—Blending		19,000
(To record transfer of units to the Bottling Department)		

Finished Goods Inventory	11,000	
Work in Process—Bottling		11,000
(To record transfer of units to finished goods)		

Related exercise material: **BE16.1, BE16.2, BE16.3, DO IT! 16.2, E16.2,** and **E16.4.**

Equivalent Units

LEARNING OBJECTIVE 3
Compute equivalent units.

Suppose you have a work-study job in the office of your college's president, and she asks you to compute the cost of instruction per full-time equivalent student at your college. The college's vice president for finance provides the information shown in **Illustration 16.6**.

Costs:	
Total cost of instruction	$9,000,000
Student population:	
Full-time students	900
Part-time students	1,000

ILLUSTRATION 16.6
Information for full-time student example

Part-time students take 60% of the classes of a full-time student during the year. **Illustration 16.7** shows how to compute the number of full-time equivalent students per year.

Full-Time Students	+	Equivalent Units of Part-Time Students	=	Full-Time Equivalent Students
900	+	(1,000 × 60%)	=	1,500

ILLUSTRATION 16.7
Full-time equivalent unit computation

The cost of instruction per full-time equivalent student is therefore the total cost of instruction ($9,000,000) divided by the number of full-time equivalent students (1,500), which is $6,000 ($9,000,000 ÷ 1,500).

A process cost system uses the same idea, called equivalent units of production. **Equivalent units of production** measure the work done during the period, expressed in fully completed units. Companies use this measure to determine the cost per unit of completed product.

Weighted-Average Method

The formula to compute equivalent units of production is shown in **Illustration 16.8**.

Units Completed and Transferred out	+	Equivalent Units of Ending Work in Process	=	Equivalent Units of Production

ILLUSTRATION 16.8
Equivalent units of production formula

To better understand this concept of equivalent units, consider the following two separate examples.

Example 1. In a specific period, the entire output of Sullivan Company's Blending Department consists of ending work in process of 4,000 units which are 60% complete as to materials, labor, and overhead. The equivalent units of production for the Blending Department are therefore 2,400 units (4,000 × 60%).

Example 2. The output of Kori Company's Packaging Department during the period consists of 10,000 units completed and transferred out, and 5,000 units in ending work in process which are 70% completed. The equivalent units of production are therefore 13,500 [10,000 + (5,000 × 70%)].

This method of computing equivalent units is referred to as the **weighted-average method**. It considers the degree of completion (weighting) of the units completed and transferred out and the ending work in process.

Refinements on the Weighted-Average Method

Kellogg Company has produced Eggo® Waffles since 1970. Three departments produce these waffles: Mixing, Baking, and Freezing/Packaging. The Mixing Department combines dry ingredients, including flour, salt, and baking powder, with liquid ingredients, including eggs and vegetable oil, to make waffle batter. **Illustration 16.9** provides information related to the Mixing Department at the end of June. Note that separate unit cost computations are needed for materials and conversion costs whenever the two types of costs do not occur in the process at the same time.

ILLUSTRATION 16.9
Information for Mixing Department

Mixing Department			
		Percentage Complete	
	Physical Units	Materials	Conversion Costs
Work in process, June 1	100,000	100%	70%
Started into production	800,000		
Total units to be accounted for	900,000		
Units transferred out	700,000		
Work in process, June 30	200,000	100%	60%
Total units accounted for	900,000		

ETHICS NOTE

An unethical manager might use incorrect completion percentages when determining equivalent units. This results in either raising or lowering costs. Since completion percentages are somewhat subjective, this form of income manipulation can be difficult to detect.

Illustration 16.9 indicates that the beginning work in process is 100% complete as to materials cost and 70% complete as to conversion costs (see **Ethics Note**). **Conversion costs are the sum of labor costs and overhead costs.** In other words, Kellogg adds both the dry and liquid ingredients (materials) at the beginning of the waffle-making process, and the conversion costs (labor and overhead) related to the mixing of these ingredients are incurred uniformly and are 70% complete. The ending work in process is 100% complete as to materials cost and 60% complete as to conversion costs.

We then use the Mixing Department information to determine equivalent units. **In computing equivalent units, the beginning work in process is not part of the equivalent-units-of-production formula.** The units transferred out to the Baking Department are fully complete as to both materials and conversion costs. The ending work in process is fully complete as to materials, but only 60% complete as to conversion costs. We therefore need to make **two equivalent unit computations**: one for materials, and the other for conversion costs. **Illustration 16.10** shows these computations.

ILLUSTRATION 16.10
Computation of equivalent units—Mixing Department

Mixing Department		
	Equivalent Units	
	Materials	Conversion Costs
Units transferred out	700,000	700,000
Work in process, June 30		
200,000 × 100%	200,000	
200,000 × 60%		120,000
Total equivalent units	900,000	820,000

We can refine the earlier formula used to compute equivalent units of production (Illustration 16.8) to show the computations for materials and for conversion costs, as shown in **Illustration 16.11**.

Units Completed and Transferred Out—Materials	+	Equivalent Units of Ending Work in Process—Materials	=	Equivalent Units of Production—Materials
Units Completed and Transferred Out—Conversion Costs	+	Equivalent Units of Ending Work in Process—Conversion Costs	=	Equivalent Units of Production—Conversion Costs

ILLUSTRATION 16.11

Refined equivalent units of production formula

People, Planet, and Profit Insight — General Electric

Haven't I Seen That Before?

© Nicole Hofmann/iStockphoto

For a variety of reasons, many companies, including **General Electric**, are making a big push to remanufacture goods that have been thrown away. Items getting a second chance include cell phones, computers, home appliances, car parts, vacuum cleaners, and medical equipment. Businesses have figured out that profit margins on remanufactured goods are significantly higher than on new goods. As commodity prices such as copper and steel increase, reusing parts makes more sense. Also, as more local governments initiate laws requiring that electronics and appliances be recycled rather than thrown away, the cost of remanufacturing declines because the gathering of used goods becomes far more efficient.

Besides benefitting the manufacturer, remanufacturing provides goods at a much lower price to consumers, reduces waste going to landfills, saves energy, reuses scarce resources, and reduces emissions. For example, it was estimated that a remanufactured car starter results in about 50% less carbon dioxide emissions than making a new one.

Source: James R. Hagerty and Paul Glader, "From Trash Heap to Store Shelf," *Wall Street Journal Online* (January 24, 2011).

In what ways might the relative composition (materials, labor, and overhead) of a remanufactured product's cost differ from that of a newly made product? (Go to WileyPLUS for this answer and additional questions.)

DO IT! 3 | Equivalent Units

The Fabricating Department for Outdoor Essentials has the following production and cost data for the current month.

Beginning Work in Process	Units Transferred Out	Ending Work in Process
–0–	15,000	10,000

Materials are entered at the beginning of the process. The ending work in process units are 30% complete as to conversion costs. Compute the equivalent units of production for (a) materials and (b) conversion costs.

Solution

a. Since materials are entered at the beginning of the process, the equivalent units of ending work in process are 10,000. Thus, 15,000 units + 10,000 units = 25,000 equivalent units of production for materials.

b. Since ending work in process is only 30% complete as to conversion costs, the equivalent units of ending work in process are 3,000 (10,000 units × 30%). Thus, 15,000 units + 3,000 units = 18,000 equivalent units of production for conversion costs.

ACTION PLAN

- To measure the work done during the period, expressed in fully completed units, compute equivalent units of production.
- Use the appropriate formula: Units completed and transferred out + Equivalent units of ending work in process = Equivalent units of production.

Related exercise material: **BE16.4, BE16.5, DO IT! 16.3, E16.5, E16.6, E16.8, E16.9, E16.10, E16.11, E16.13, E16.14, and E16.15.**

The Production Cost Report

> **LEARNING OBJECTIVE 4**
> Complete the four steps to prepare a production cost report.

As mentioned earlier, companies prepare a production cost report for each department. A **production cost report** is the key document that management uses to understand the activities in a department; it shows the production quantity and cost data related to that department. For example, in producing Eggo® Waffles, **Kellogg Company** uses three production cost reports: Mixing, Baking, and Freezing/Packaging. **Illustration 16.12** shows the flow of costs to make an Eggo® Waffle and the related production cost reports for each department.

ILLUSTRATION 16.12 Flow of costs in making Eggo® Waffles

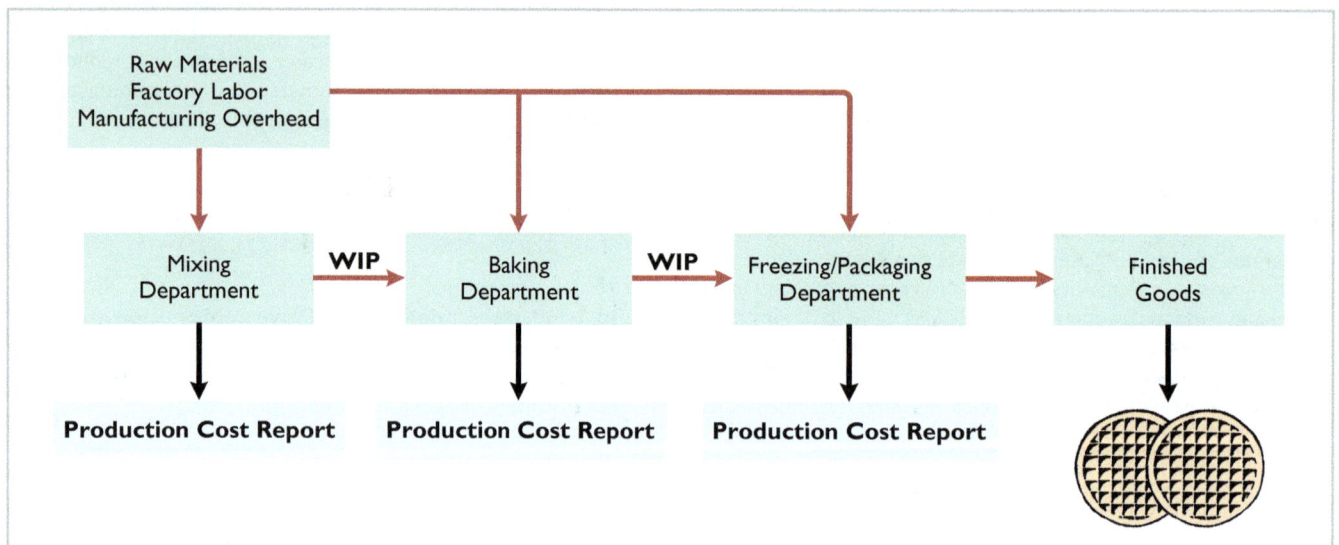

In order to complete a production cost report, the company must perform four steps, which as a whole make up the process cost system.

1. Compute the physical unit flow.
2. Compute the equivalent units of production.
3. Compute unit production costs.
4. Prepare a cost reconciliation schedule.

Illustration 16.13 shows assumed data for the Mixing Department at **Kellogg Company** for the month of June. We will use this information to complete a production cost report for the Mixing Department.

ILLUSTRATION 16.13 Unit and cost data—Mixing Department

Mixing Department

Units

Work in process, June 1	100,000
Direct materials: 100% complete	
Conversion costs: 70% complete	
Units started into production during June	800,000
Units completed and transferred out to Baking Department	700,000
Work in process, June 30	200,000
Direct materials: 100% complete	
Conversion costs: 60% complete	

ILLUSTRATION 16.13 (continued)

Costs

Work in process, June 1	
Direct materials: 100% complete	$ 50,000
Conversion costs: 70% complete	35,000
Cost of work in process, June 1	$ 85,000
Costs incurred during production in June	
Direct materials	$400,000
Conversion costs	170,000
Costs incurred in June	$570,000

Compute the Physical Unit Flow (Step 1)

Physical units are the actual units to be accounted for during a period, irrespective of any work performed. To keep track of these units, add the units started (or transferred) into production during the period to the units in process at the beginning of the period. This amount is referred to as the **total units to be accounted for**.

The total units then are accounted for by the output of the period. The output consists of units transferred out during the period and any units in process at the end of the period. This amount is referred to as the **total units accounted for**. **Illustration 16.14** shows the flow of physical units for Kellogg's Mixing Department for the month of June.

ILLUSTRATION 16.14
Physical unit flow—Mixing Department

Mixing Department

	Physical Units
Units to be accounted for	
Work in process, June 1	100,000
Started (transferred) into production	800,000
Total units	900,000
Units accounted for	
Completed and transferred out	700,000
Work in process, June 30	200,000
Total units	900,000

The records indicate that the Mixing Department must account for 900,000 units. Of this sum, 700,000 units were transferred to the Baking Department and 200,000 units were still in process.

Compute the Equivalent Units of Production (Step 2)

Once the physical flow of the units is established, Kellogg must measure the Mixing Department's productivity in terms of equivalent units of production. The Mixing Department adds materials at the beginning of the process, and it incurs conversion costs uniformly during the process (see **Helpful Hint**). Thus, we need two computations of equivalent units: one for materials and one for conversion costs. The equivalent unit computation is shown in **Illustration 16.15**. Recall that this computation ignores beginning work in process.

HELPFUL HINT
Materials are not always added at the beginning of the process. For example, materials are sometimes added uniformly during the process.

ILLUSTRATION 16.15

Computation of equivalent units—Mixing Department

	Equivalent Units	
	Materials	Conversion Costs
Units transferred out	700,000	700,000
Work in process, June 30		
200,000 × 100%	200,000	
200,000 × 60%		120,000
Total equivalent units	**900,000**	**820,000**

Compute Unit Production Costs (Step 3)

Armed with the knowledge of the equivalent units of production, we can now compute the unit production costs. **Unit production costs** are costs expressed in terms of equivalent units of production. When equivalent units of production are different for materials and conversion costs, we compute three unit costs: (1) materials, (2) conversion, and (3) total manufacturing.

The computation of total materials cost related to Eggo® Waffles is shown in **Illustration 16.16**.

ILLUSTRATION 16.16

Total materials cost computation

Work in process, June 1	
Direct materials cost	$ 50,000
Costs added to production during June	
Direct materials cost	400,000
Total materials cost	**$450,000**

Illustration 16.17 shows the computation of unit materials cost.

ILLUSTRATION 16.17

Unit materials cost computation

Total Materials Cost	÷	Equivalent Units of Materials	=	Unit Materials Cost
$450,000	÷	900,000	=	$0.50

Illustration 16.18 shows the computation of total conversion costs.

ILLUSTRATION 16.18

Total conversion costs computation

Work in process, June 1	
Conversion costs	$ 35,000
Costs added to production during June	
Conversion costs	170,000
Total conversion costs	**$205,000**

The computation of unit conversion cost is shown in **Illustration 16.19**.

ILLUSTRATION 16.19

Unit conversion cost computation

Total Conversion Costs	÷	Equivalent Units of Conversion Costs	=	Unit Conversion Cost
$205,000	÷	820,000	=	$0.25

Total manufacturing cost per unit is therefore computed as shown in **Illustration 16.20**.

Unit Materials Cost	+	Unit Conversion Cost	=	Total Manufacturing Cost per Unit
$0.50	+	$0.25	=	$0.75

ILLUSTRATION 16.20
Total manufacturing cost per unit

Prepare a Cost Reconciliation Schedule (Step 4)

We are now ready to determine the cost of goods transferred out of the Mixing Department to the Baking Department and the costs in ending work in process. Kellogg charged total costs of $655,000 to the Mixing Department in June, calculated as shown in **Illustration 16.21**.

Costs to be accounted for	
Work in process, June 1	$ 85,000
Started into production	570,000
Total costs	**$655,000**

ILLUSTRATION 16.21
Costs charged to Mixing Department

The company then prepares a cost reconciliation schedule (see **Illustration 16.22**) to assign these costs to (a) units transferred out to the Baking Department and (b) ending work in process.

Mixing Department
Cost Reconciliation Schedule

Costs accounted for		
Transferred out (700,000 × $0.75)		$525,000
Work in process, June 30		
Materials (200,000 × $0.50)	$100,000	
Conversion costs (120,000 × $0.25)	30,000	130,000
Total costs		**$655,000**

ILLUSTRATION 16.22
Cost reconciliation schedule—Mixing Department

Kellogg uses the total manufacturing cost per unit, $0.75, in costing the **units completed** and transferred to the Baking Department. In contrast, the unit cost of materials and the unit cost of conversion are needed in costing **units in process**. The **cost reconciliation schedule** shows that the **total costs accounted for** (Illustration 16.22) equal the **total costs to be accounted for** (Illustration 16.21).

Preparing the Production Cost Report

At this point, Kellogg is ready to prepare the production cost report for the Mixing Department. As indicated earlier, this report is an internal document for management that shows production quantity and cost data for a production department. **Illustration 16.23** shows the completed production cost report for the Mixing Department and identifies the four steps used in preparing it (see **Helpful Hint**).

Production cost reports provide a basis for evaluating the productivity of a department (see **Decision Tools**). In addition, managers can use the cost data to assess whether unit costs and total costs are reasonable. By comparing the quantity and cost data with predetermined goals, top management can also judge whether current performance is meeting planned objectives.

HELPFUL HINT
The four steps in preparing a production cost report:
1. Compute the physical unit flow.
2. Compute the equivalent units of production.
3. Compute unit production costs.
4. Prepare a cost reconciliation schedule.

Decision Tools
A production cost report helps managers evaluate overall profitability by comparing costs to previous periods, competitors, and expected selling price.

ILLUSTRATION 16.23 Production cost report

Mixing Department
Production Cost Report
For the Month Ended June 30, 2022

	Physical Units	Equivalent Units	
		Materials	Conversion Costs
Quantities			
Units to be accounted for	Step 1	Step 2	
Work in process, June 1	100,000		
Started into production	800,000		
Total units	900,000		
Units accounted for			
Transferred out	700,000	700,000	700,000
Work in process, June 30	200,000	200,000	120,000 (200,000 × 60%)
Total units	900,000	900,000	820,000

Costs		Materials	Conversion Costs	Total
Unit costs Step 3				
Total cost	(a)	$450,000	$205,000	$655,000
Equivalent units	(b)	900,000	820,000	
Unit costs [(a) ÷ (b)]		$0.50	$0.25	$0.75
Costs to be accounted for				
Work in process, June 1				$ 85,000
Started into production				570,000
Total costs				$655,000
Cost Reconciliation Schedule Step 4				
Costs accounted for				
Transferred out (700,000 × $0.75)				$525,000
Work in process, June 30				
Materials (200,000 × $0.50)			$100,000	
Conversion costs (120,000 × $0.25)			30,000	130,000
Total costs				$655,000

Costing Systems—Final Comments

Companies often use a combination of a process cost and a job order cost system. Called **operations costing**, this hybrid system is similar to process costing in its assumption that standardized methods are used to manufacture the product. At the same time, the product may have some customized, individual features that require the use of a job order cost system.

Consider, for example, **Ford Motor Company**. Each vehicle at a given plant goes through the same assembly line, but Ford uses different materials (such as seat coverings, paint, and tinted glass) for different vehicles. Similarly, **Kellogg**'s Pop-Tarts® toaster pastries go through numerous standardized processes—mixing, filling, baking, frosting, and packaging. The pastry dough, though, comes in different flavors—plain, chocolate, and graham—and fillings include Smucker's® real fruit, chocolate fudge, vanilla creme, brown sugar cinnamon, and s'mores.

A cost-benefit trade-off occurs as a company decides which costing system to use (see **Decision Tools**). A job order cost system, for example, provides detailed information related to the cost of the product. Because each job has its own distinguishing characteristics, the system can provide an accurate cost per job. This information is useful in controlling costs and pricing products. However, the cost of implementing a job order cost system is often expensive because of the accounting costs involved.

Decision Tools

A cost-benefit trade-off helps managers determine which costing system to use.

On the other hand, for a company like **Intel**, is there a benefit in knowing whether the cost of the one-hundredth computer chip produced is different from the one-thousandth chip produced? Probably not. An average cost of the product will suffice for control and pricing purposes.

In summary, when deciding to use one of these systems or a combination system, a company must weigh the costs of implementing the system against the benefits from the additional information provided.

DO IT! 4 | Cost Reconciliation Schedule

In March, Rodayo Manufacturing had the following unit production costs: materials $6 and conversion costs $9. On March 1, it had no work in process. During March, Rodayo transferred out 12,000 units. As of March 31, 800 units that were 25% complete as to conversion costs and 100% complete as to materials were in ending work in process. Assign the costs to the units transferred out and in process.

Solution

The assignment of costs is as follows.

Costs accounted for		
Transferred out (12,000 × $15)		$180,000
Work in process, March 31		
Materials (800 × $6)	$4,800	
Conversion costs (200* × $9)	1,800	6,600
Total costs		$186,600

*800 × 25%

Related exercise material: BE16.6, BE16.7, BE16.8, BE16.9, DO IT! 16.4, E16.3, E16.5, E16.6, E16.7, E16.8, E16.9, E16.10, E16.11, E16.13, E16.14, and E16.15.

ACTION PLAN
- Assign the total manufacturing cost of $15 per unit to the 12,000 units transferred out.
- Assign the materials cost and conversion costs based on equivalent units of production to units in ending work in process.

USING THE DECISION TOOLS | Jones Soda

Jones Soda Co. faces many situations where it needs to apply the decision tools learned in this chapter, such as using a production cost report to evaluate profitability. For example, suppose Jones Soda manufactures a high-end organic fruit soda, called Eternity, in 10-ounce plastic bottles. Because the market for beverages is highly competitive, the company is very concerned about keeping its costs under control. Eternity is manufactured through three processes: blending, filling, and labeling. Materials are added at the beginning of the process, and labor and overhead are incurred uniformly throughout each process. The company uses a weighted-average method to cost its product. A partially completed production cost report for the month of May for the Blending Department is shown below.

Jones Soda
Blending Department
Production Cost Report
For the Month Ended May 31, 2022

		Equivalent Units	
Quantities	Physical Units	Materials	Conversion Costs
Units to be accounted for	Step 1	Step 2	
Work in process, May 1	1,000		
Started into production	2,000		
Total units	3,000		
Units accounted for			
Transferred out	2,200	?	?
Work in process, May 31	800	?	?
Total units	3,000	?	?

Costs		Materials	Conversion Costs	Total
Unit costs [Step 3]				
Total cost	(a)	?	?	?
Equivalent units	(b)	?	?	
Unit costs [(a) ÷ (b)]		?	?	?
Costs to be accounted for				
Work in process, May 1				$ 56,300
Started into production				119,320
Total costs				$175,620

Cost Reconciliation Schedule [Step 4]

Costs accounted for				
Transferred out				?
Work in process, May 31				
Materials			?	
Conversion costs			?	?
Total costs				?

Additional information:
  Work in process, May 1, 1000 units
    Materials cost, 1,000 units (100% complete) $49,100
    Conversion costs, 1,000 units (70% complete)   7,200 $ 56,300
  Materials cost for May, 2,000 units $100,000
  Work in process, May 31, 800 units, 100% complete as
    to materials and 50% complete as to conversion costs

Instructions

a. Prepare a production cost report for the Blending Department for the month of May.
b. Prepare the journal entry to record the transfer of goods from the Blending Department to the Filling Department.
c. Explain why Jones Soda is using a process cost system to account for its costs.

Solution

a. A completed production cost report for the Blending Department is shown below. Computations to support the amounts reported follow the report.

Jones Soda
Blending Department
Production Cost Report
For the Month Ended May 31, 2022

Quantities	Physical Units	Equivalent Units	
		Materials	Conversion Costs
Units to be accounted for	[Step 1]	[Step 2]	
Work in process, May 1	1,000		
Started into production	2,000		
Total units	3,000		
Units accounted for			
Transferred out	2,200	2,200	2,200
Work in process, May 31	800	800	400 (800 × 50%)
Total units	3,000	3,000	2,600

		Materials	Conversion Costs	Total
Costs				
Unit costs Step 3				
Total cost	(a)	$149,100*	$26,520**	$175,620
Equivalent units	(b)	3,000	2,600	
Unit costs [(a) ÷ (b)]		$49.70	$10.20	$59.90
Costs to be accounted for				
Work in process, May 1				$ 56,300
Started into production				119,320
Total costs				$175,620

*Materials cost—$49,100 + $100,000
**Conversion costs—$7,200 + $19,320 ($119,320 − $100,000)

Cost Reconciliation Schedule Step 4

Costs accounted for			
Transferred out (2,200 × $59.90)			$131,780
Work in process, May 31			
Materials (800 × $49.70)		$39,760	
Conversion costs (400 × $10.20)		4,080	43,840
Total costs			$175,620

b. Work in Process—Filling   131,780
    Work in Process—Blending   131,780

c. Companies use process cost systems to apply costs to similar products that are mass-produced in a continuous fashion. Jones Soda uses a process cost system because production of the fruit soda, once it begins, continues until the soda emerges. The processing is the same for the entire run—with precisely the same amount of materials, labor, and overhead. Each bottle of Eternity soda is indistinguishable from another.

Appendix 16A   FIFO Method for Equivalent Units

LEARNING OBJECTIVE *5
Compute equivalent units using the FIFO method.

In this chapter, we demonstrated the weighted-average method of computing equivalent units. Some companies use a different method, referred to as the **first-in, first-out (FIFO) method**, to compute equivalent units. The purpose of this appendix is to illustrate how companies use the FIFO method to prepare a production cost report.

Equivalent Units Under FIFO

Under the FIFO method, companies compute equivalent units on a first-in, first-out basis. Some companies favor the FIFO method because the FIFO cost assumption usually corresponds to the actual physical flow of the goods. Under the FIFO method, companies therefore assume that the beginning work in process is completed before new work is started.

Using the FIFO method, equivalent units are the sum of the work performed to:

1. Finish the units of beginning work in process inventory.
2. Complete the units started into production during the period (referred to as the **units started and completed**).
3. Start, but only partially complete, the units in ending work in process inventory.

Normally, in a process cost system, some units will always be in process at both the beginning and end of the period.

Illustration

Illustration 16A.1 shows the physical flow of units for the Assembly Department of Shutters Inc. In addition, it indicates the degree of completion of the work in process accounts in regard to conversion costs.

ILLUSTRATION 16A.1

Physical unit flow—Assembly Department

Assembly Department	
	Physical Units
Units to be accounted for	
Work in process, June 1 (40% complete)	500
Started (transferred) into production	8,000
Total units	**8,500**
Units accounted for	
Completed and transferred out	8,100
Work in process, June 30 (75% complete)	400
Total units	**8,500**

In Illustration 16A.1, the units completed and transferred out (8,100) plus the units in ending work in process (400) equal the total units to be accounted for (8,500). Using FIFO, we then compute equivalent units for conversion costs as follows.

1. The 500 units of beginning work in process were 40% complete. Thus, 300 equivalent units (500 units × 60%) were required to complete the beginning inventory.
2. The units started and completed during the current month are **the units transferred out minus the units in beginning work in process**. For the Assembly Department, units started and completed are 7,600 (8,100 − 500).
3. The 400 units of ending work in process were 75% complete. Thus, equivalent units were 300 (400 × 75%).

Equivalent units for conversion costs for the Assembly Department are 8,200, computed as shown in **Illustration 16A.2**.

ILLUSTRATION 16A.2

Computation of equivalent units—FIFO method

Assembly Department			
Production Data	Work Added Physical Units	Equivalent This Period	Units
Work in process, June 1	500	60%	300
Started and completed	7,600	100%	7,600
Work in process, June 30	400	75%	300
Total	**8,500**		**8,200**

Comprehensive Example

To provide a complete illustration of the FIFO method, we will use the data for the Mixing Department at **Kellogg Company** for the month of June, as shown in **Illustration 16A.3**.

ILLUSTRATION 16A.3
Unit and cost data—Mixing Department

Mixing Department	
Units	
Work in process, June 1	100,000
Direct materials: 100% complete	
Conversion costs: 70% complete	
Units started into production during June	800,000
Units completed and transferred out to Baking Department	700,000
Work in process, June 30	200,000
Direct materials: 100% complete	
Conversion costs: 60% complete	
Costs	
Work in process, June 1	
Direct materials: 100% complete	$ 50,000
Conversion costs: 70% complete	35,000
Cost of work in process, June 1	$ 85,000
Costs incurred during production in June	
Direct materials	$400,000
Conversion costs	170,000
Costs incurred in June	$570,000

Compute the Physical Unit Flow (Step 1)

Illustration 16A.4 shows the physical flow of units for Kellogg's Mixing Department for the month of June.

ILLUSTRATION 16A.4
Physical unit flow—Mixing Department

Mixing Department	
	Physical Units
Units to be accounted for	
Work in process, June 1	100,000
Started (transferred) into production	800,000
Total units	**900,000**
Units accounted for	
Completed and transferred out	700,000
Work in process, June 30	200,000
Total units	**900,000**

Under the FIFO method, companies often expand the physical units schedule, as shown in **Illustration 16A.5**, to explain the transferred-out section. As a result, this section reports the beginning work in process and the units started and completed. These two items further explain the completed and transferred-out section.

ILLUSTRATION 16A.5
Physical unit flow (FIFO)—Mixing Department

Mixing Department	
	Physical Units
Units to be accounted for	
Work in process, June 1	100,000
Started (transferred) into production	800,000
Total units	**900,000**
Units accounted for	
Completed and transferred out	
Work in process, June 1	**100,000**
Started and completed	**600,000**
	700,000
Work in process, June 30	200,000
Total units	**900,000**

The records indicate that the Mixing Department must account for 900,000 units. Of this sum, 700,000 units were transferred to the Baking Department and 200,000 units were still in process.

Compute Equivalent Units of Production (Step 2)

As with the method presented in the chapter, once they determine the physical flow of the units, companies need to determine equivalent units of production. The Mixing Department adds materials at the beginning of the process, and it incurs conversion costs uniformly during the process (see **Helpful Hint**). Thus, Kellogg must make two computations of equivalent units: one for materials and one for conversion costs.

HELPFUL HINT

As noted earlier, materials are not always added at the beginning of the process. For example, companies sometimes add materials uniformly during the process.

Equivalent Units for Materials Since Kellogg adds materials at the beginning of the process, no additional materials costs are required to complete the beginning work in process. In addition, 100% of the materials costs has been incurred on the ending work in process. **Illustration 16A.6** shows the computation of equivalent units for materials.

ILLUSTRATION 16A.6
Computation of equivalent units—materials

Mixing Department—Materials			
Production Data	Physical Units	Materials Added This Period	Equivalent Units
Work in process, June 1	100,000	–0–	–0–
Started and finished	600,000	100%	600,000
Work in process, June 30	200,000	100%	200,000
Total	900,000		800,000

Equivalent Units for Conversion Costs The 100,000 units of beginning work in process were 70% complete in terms of conversion costs. Thus, the Mixing Department required 30,000 equivalent units (100,000 units × 30%) of conversion costs to complete the beginning inventory. In addition, the 200,000 units of ending work in process were 60% complete in terms of conversion costs. Thus, the equivalent units for conversion costs is 750,000, computed as shown in **Illustration 16A.7**.

ILLUSTRATION 16A.7
Computation of equivalent units—conversion costs

Mixing Department—Conversion Costs			
Production Data	Physical Units	Work Added This Period	Equivalent Units
Work in process, June 1	100,000	30%	30,000
Started and finished	600,000	100%	600,000
Work in process, June 30	200,000	60%	120,000
Total	900,000		750,000

Compute Unit Production Costs (Step 3)

Armed with the knowledge of the equivalent units of production, Kellogg can now compute the unit production costs. Unit production costs are costs expressed in terms of equivalent units of production. When equivalent units of production are different for materials and conversion costs, companies compute three unit costs: (1) materials, (2) conversion, and (3) total manufacturing.

Under the FIFO method, the unit costs of production are based entirely on the production costs incurred during the month. Thus, the costs in the beginning work in process are not relevant, because they were incurred on work done in the preceding month. As Illustration 16A.3 indicated, the costs incurred during production in June were as shown in **Illustration 16A.8.**

Direct materials	$400,000
Conversion costs	170,000
Total costs	$570,000

ILLUSTRATION 16A.8
Costs incurred during production in June

Illustration 16A.9 shows the computation of unit materials cost, unit conversion costs, and total unit cost related to Eggo® Waffles.

(1)	Total Materials Cost	÷	Equivalent Units of Materials	=	Unit Materials Cost
	$400,000	÷	800,000	=	$0.50
(2)	Total Conversion Costs	÷	Equivalent Units of Conversion Costs	=	Unit Conversion Cost
	$170,000	÷	750,000	=	$0.227 (rounded)*
(3)	Unit Materials Cost	+	Unit Conversion Cost	=	Total Manufacturing Cost per Unit
	$0.50	+	$0.227	=	$0.727

*For homework problems, round unit costs to three decimal places.

ILLUSTRATION 16A.9
Unit cost formulas and computations—Mixing Department

As shown, the unit costs are $0.50 for materials, $0.227 for conversion costs, and $0.727 for total manufacturing costs.

Prepare a Cost Reconciliation Schedule (Step 4)

Kellogg is now ready to determine the cost of goods transferred out of the Mixing Department to the Baking Department and the costs in ending work in process. The total costs charged to the Mixing Department in June are $655,000, calculated as shown in **Illustration 16A.10** (see Illustration 16A.3 for further detail).

Costs to be accounted for	
Work in process, June 1	$ 85,000
Started into production	570,000
Total costs	$655,000

ILLUSTRATION 16A.10
Costs charged to Mixing Department

Kellogg next prepares a cost reconciliation schedule to assign these costs to (1) units transferred out to the Baking Department and (2) ending work in process. Under the FIFO method, the first goods to be completed during the period are the units in beginning work in process. Thus, the cost of the beginning work in process is always assigned to the goods transferred to the next department (or finished goods, if processing is complete). Under the FIFO method, ending work in process also will be assigned only the production costs incurred in the current period. **Illustration 16A.11** shows a cost reconciliation schedule for the Mixing Department.

> **ILLUSTRATION 16A.11**
> Cost reconciliation report

Mixing Department Cost Reconciliation Schedule		
Costs accounted for		
Transferred out		
Work in process, June 1		$ 85,000
Costs to complete beginning work in process		
Conversion costs (30,000 × $0.227)		6,810
Total costs		91,810
Units started and completed (600,000 × $0.727)		435,950*
Total costs transferred out		527,760
Work in process, June 30		
Materials (200,000 × $0.50)	$100,000	
Conversion costs (120,000 × $0.227)	27,240	127,240
Total costs		**$655,000**

*Any rounding errors should be adjusted in the "Units started and completed" calculation.

As you can see, the total costs accounted for ($655,000 from Illustration 16A.11) equal the total costs to be accounted for ($655,000 from Illustration 16A.10).

Preparing the Production Cost Report

At this point, Kellogg is ready to prepare the production cost report for the Mixing Department. This report is an internal document for management that shows production quantity and cost data for a production department.

As discussed previously, there are four steps in preparing a production cost report:

1. Compute the physical unit flow.
2. Compute the equivalent units of production.
3. Compute unit production costs.
4. Prepare a cost reconciliation schedule.

Illustration 16A.12 shows the production cost report for the Mixing Department, with the four steps identified in the report.

As indicated in the chapter, production cost reports provide a basis for evaluating the productivity of a department (see **Helpful Hint**). In addition, managers can use the cost data to assess whether unit costs and total costs are reasonable. By comparing the quantity and cost data with predetermined goals, top management can also judge whether current performance is meeting planned objectives.

> **HELPFUL HINT**
> The two self-checks in the report are (1) total physical units accounted for must equal the total units to be accounted for, and (2) total costs accounted for must equal the total costs to be accounted for.

FIFO and Weighted-Average

The weighted-average method of computing equivalent units has **one major advantage**: It is simple to understand and apply. In cases where prices do not fluctuate significantly from period to period, the weighted-average method will be very similar to the FIFO method. In addition, companies that have been using just-in-time procedures effectively for inventory control purposes will have minimal inventory balances. Therefore, differences between the weighted-average and the FIFO methods will not be material.

Conceptually, the FIFO method is superior to the weighted-average method because it measures **current performance** using only costs incurred in the current period. Managers are, therefore, not held responsible for costs from prior periods over which they may not have had control. In addition, the FIFO method **provides current cost information**, which the company can use to establish **more accurate pricing strategies** for goods manufactured and sold in the current period.

ILLUSTRATION 16A.12 Production cost report—FIFO method

Mixing Department
Production Cost Report
For the Month Ended June 30, 2022

	Physical Units	Equivalent Units — Materials	Equivalent Units — Conversion Costs	
Quantities				
Units to be accounted for	Step 1	Step 2		
Work in process (WIP), June 1	100,000			
Started into production	800,000			
Total units	900,000			
Units accounted for				
Completed and transferred out				
Work in process, June 1	100,000	0	30,000	
Started and completed	600,000	600,000	600,000	
Work in process, June 30	200,000	200,000	120,000	
Total units	900,000	800,000	750,000	

Costs		Materials	Conversion Costs	Total
Unit costs Step 3				
Costs in June (excluding beginning WIP)	(a)	$400,000	$170,000	$570,000
Equivalent units	(b)	800,000	750,000	
Unit costs [(a) ÷ (b)]		$0.50	$0.227	$0.727
Costs to be accounted for				
Work in process, June 1				$ 85,000
Started into production				570,000
Total costs				$655,000

Cost Reconciliation Schedule Step 4			
Costs accounted for			
Transferred out			
Work in process, June 1		$ 85,000	
Costs to complete beginning work in process			
Conversion costs (30,000 × $0.227)		6,810	$ 91,810
Units started and completed (600,000 × $0.727)*			435,950
Total costs transferred out			527,760
Work in process, June 30			
Materials (200,000 × $0.50)		100,000	
Conversion costs (120,000 × $0.227)		27,240	127,240
Total costs			$655,000

*Any rounding errors should be adjusted in the "Units started and completed"

Review and Practice

Learning Objectives Review

1 Discuss the uses of a process cost system and how it compares to a job order system.

Companies that mass-produce similar products in a continuous fashion use process cost systems. Once production begins, it continues until the finished product emerges. Each unit of finished product is indistinguishable from every other unit.

Job order cost systems are similar to process cost systems in three ways. (1) Both systems track the same cost elements—direct materials, direct labor, and manufacturing overhead. (2) Both accumulate costs in the same accounts—Raw Materials Inventory, Factory Labor, and Manufacturing Overhead. (3) Both assign accumulated costs to the same accounts—Work in Process, Finished Goods Inventory, and Cost of Goods Sold. However, the methods used to assign costs differ significantly.

There are four main differences between the two cost systems. (1) A process cost system uses separate Work in Process accounts for each department or manufacturing process, rather than only one work in process account used in a job order cost system. (2) A process cost system summarizes costs in a production cost report for each department. A job order cost system charges costs to individual jobs and summarizes them in a job cost sheet. (3) Costs are totaled at the end of a time period in a process cost system but at the completion of a job in a job order cost system. (4) A process cost system calculates unit cost as Total manufacturing costs for the period ÷ Units produced during the period. A job order cost system calculates unit cost as Total cost per job ÷ Units produced.

2 Explain the flow of costs in a process cost system and the journal entries to assign manufacturing costs.

A process cost system assigns manufacturing costs for raw materials, labor, and overhead to work in process accounts for various departments or manufacturing processes. It transfers the costs of partially completed units from one department to another as those units move through the manufacturing process. The system transfers the costs of completed work to Finished Goods Inventory. Finally, when inventory is sold, the system transfers the costs to Cost of Goods Sold.

Entries to assign the costs of raw materials, labor, and overhead consist of a credit to Raw Materials Inventory, Factory Labor, and Manufacturing Overhead, and a debit to Work in Process for each department.

Entries to record the cost of goods transferred to another department are a credit to Work in Process for the department whose work is finished and a debit to Work in Process for the department to which the goods are transferred. The entry to record units completed and transferred to the warehouse is a credit to Work in Process for the department whose work is finished and a debit to Finished Goods Inventory. The entry to record the sale of goods is a credit to Finished Goods Inventory and a debit to Cost of Goods Sold.

3 Compute equivalent units.

Equivalent units of production measure work done during a period, expressed in fully completed units. Companies use this measure to determine the cost per unit of completed product. Equivalent units are the sum of units completed and transferred out plus equivalent units of ending work in process.

4 Complete the four steps to prepare a production cost report.

The four steps to complete a production cost report are as follows. (1) Compute the physical unit flow—that is, the total units to be accounted for. (2) Compute the equivalent units of production separately for direct materials and conversion costs. (3) Compute the unit production costs, expressed in terms of equivalent units of production. (4) Prepare a cost reconciliation schedule, which shows that the total costs accounted for equal the total costs to be accounted for.

The production cost report contains both quantity and cost data for a production department. There are four sections in the report: (1) number of physical units, (2) equivalent units determination, (3) unit costs, and (4) cost reconciliation schedule.

*5 Compute equivalent units using the FIFO method.

Equivalent units under the FIFO method are the sum of the work performed to (1) finish the units of beginning work in process inventory, if any; (2) complete the units started into production during the period; and (3) start, but only partially complete, the units in ending work in process inventory.

Decision Tools Review

Decision Checkpoints	Info Needed for Decision	Tool to Use for Decision	How to Evaluate Results
What is the cost of a product?	Cost of materials, labor, and overhead assigned to processes used to make the product	Production cost report	Compare costs to previous periods, to competitors, and to expected selling price to evaluate overall profitability.

(continues)

(continued)

Decision Checkpoints	Info Needed for Decision	Tool to Use for Decision	How to Evaluate Results
What costing method should be used?	Type of good produced or service performed	Cost of accounting system; benefits of additional information	The benefits of providing the additional information should exceed the costs of the accounting system needed to develop the information.

Glossary Review

Conversion costs The sum of labor costs and overhead costs. (p. 16-10).

Cost reconciliation schedule A schedule that shows that the total costs accounted for equal the total costs to be accounted for. (p. 16-15).

Equivalent units of production A measure of the work done during the period, expressed in fully completed units. (p. 16-9).

Operations costing A combination of a process cost and a job order cost system in which products are manufactured primarily by standardized methods, with some customization. (p. 16-16).

Physical units Actual units to be accounted for during a period, irrespective of any work performed. (p. 16-13).

Process cost system An accounting system used to apply costs to similar products that are mass-produced in a continuous fashion. (p. 16-3).

Production cost report An internal report for management that shows both production quantity and cost data for a production department. (p. 16-12).

Total units (costs) accounted for The sum of the units (costs) transferred out during the period plus the units (costs) in process at the end of the period. (p. 16-13).

Total units (costs) to be accounted for The sum of the units (costs) started (or transferred) into production during the period plus the units (costs) in process at the beginning of the period. (p. 16-13).

Unit production costs Costs expressed in terms of equivalent units of production. (p. 16-14).

Weighted-average method Method of computing equivalent units of production which considers the degree of completion (weighting) of the units completed and transferred out and the ending work in process. (p. 16-10).

Practice Multiple-Choice Questions

1. **(LO 1)** Which of the following items is not characteristic of a process cost system?
   a. Once production begins, it continues until the finished product emerges.
   b. The products produced are heterogeneous in nature.
   c. The focus is on continually producing homogeneous products.
   d. When the finished product emerges, all units have precisely the same amount of materials, labor, and overhead.

2. **(LO 1)** Indicate which of the following statements is **not** correct.
   a. Both a job order and a process cost system track the same three manufacturing cost elements—direct materials, direct labor, and manufacturing overhead.
   b. A job order cost system uses only one work in process account, whereas a process cost system uses multiple work in process accounts.
   c. Manufacturing costs are accumulated the same way in a job order and in a process cost system.
   d. Manufacturing costs are assigned the same way in a job order and in a process cost system.

3. **(LO 2)** In a process cost system, the flow of costs is:
   a. work in process, cost of goods sold, finished goods.
   b. finished goods, work in process, cost of goods sold.
   c. finished goods, cost of goods sold, work in process.
   d. work in process, finished goods, cost of goods sold.

4. **(LO 2)** In making journal entries to assign raw materials costs, a company using process costing:
   a. debits Finished Goods Inventory.
   b. often debits two or more work in process accounts.
   c. generally credits two or more work in process accounts.
   d. credits Finished Goods Inventory.

5. **(LO 2)** In a process cost system, manufacturing overhead:
   a. is assigned to finished goods at the end of each accounting period.
   b. is assigned to a work in process account for each job as the job is completed.
   c. is assigned to a work in process account for each production department on the basis of a predetermined overhead rate.
   d. is assigned to a work in process account for each production department as overhead costs are incurred.

6. **(LO 3)** Conversion costs are the sum of:
   a. fixed and variable overhead costs.
   b. direct labor costs and overhead costs.
   c. direct material costs and overhead costs.
   d. direct labor and indirect labor costs.

7. **(LO 3)** The Mixing Department's output during the period consists of 20,000 units completed and transferred out, and 5,000 units in ending work in process 60% complete as to materials and conversion

costs. Beginning inventory is 1,000 units, 40% complete as to materials and conversion costs. The equivalent units of production are:

  a. 22,600.
  b. 23,000.
  c. 24,000.
  d. 25,000.

8. **(LO 3)** In RYZ Company, there are zero units in beginning work in process, 7,000 units started into production, and 500 units in ending work in process 20% completed. The physical units to be accounted for are:

  a. 7,000.
  b. 7,360.
  c. 7,500.
  d. 7,340.

9. **(LO 3)** Mora Company has 2,000 units in beginning work in process, 20% complete as to conversion costs, 23,000 units transferred out to finished goods, and 3,000 units in ending work in process $33\frac{1}{3}\%$ complete as to conversion costs.

The beginning and ending inventory is fully complete as to materials costs. Equivalent units for materials and conversion costs are, respectively:

  a. 22,000, 24,000.
  b. 24,000, 26,000.
  c. 26,000, 24,000.
  d. 26,000, 26,000.

10. **(LO 4)** Fortner Company has no beginning work in process; 9,000 units are transferred out and 3,000 units in ending work in process are one-third finished as to conversion costs and fully complete as to materials cost. If total materials cost is $60,000, the unit materials cost is:

  a. $5.00.
  b. $5.45 rounded.
  c. $6.00.
  d. No correct answer is given.

11. **(LO 4)** Largo Company has unit costs of $10 for materials and $30 for conversion costs. If there are 2,500 units in ending work in process, 40% complete as to conversion costs, and fully complete as to materials cost, the total cost assignable to the ending work in process inventory is:

  a. $45,000.
  b. $55,000.
  c. $75,000.
  d. $100,000.

12. **(LO 4)** A production cost report:

  a. is an external report.
  b. shows both the production quantity and cost data related to a department.
  c. shows equivalent units of production but not physical units.
  d. contains six sections.

13. **(LO 4)** In a production cost report, units to be accounted for are calculated as:

  a. Units started into production + Units in ending work in process.
  b. Units started into production − Units in beginning work in process.
  c. Units transferred out + Units in beginning work in process.
  d. Units started into production + Units in beginning work in process.

*14. **(LO 5)** Hollins Company uses the FIFO method to compute equivalent units. It has 2,000 units in beginning work in process, 20% complete as to conversion costs, 25,000 units started and completed, and 3,000 units in ending work in process, 30% complete as to conversion costs. All units are 100% complete as to materials. Equivalent units for materials and conversion costs are, respectively:

  a. 28,000 and 26,600.
  b. 28,000 and 27,500.
  c. 27,000 and 26,200.
  d. 27,000 and 29,600.

*15. **(LO 5)** KLM Company uses the FIFO method to compute equivalent units. It has no beginning work in process; 9,000 units are started and completed and 3,000 units in ending work in process are one-third completed. All material is added at the beginning of the process. If total materials cost is $60,000, the unit materials cost is:

  a. $5.00.
  b. $6.00.
  c. $6.67 (rounded).
  d. No correct answer is given.

*16. **(LO 5)** Toney Company uses the FIFO method to compute equivalent units. It has unit costs of $10 for materials and $30 for conversion costs. If there are 2,500 units in ending work in process, 100% complete as to materials and 40% complete as to conversion costs, the total cost assignable to the ending work in process inventory is:

  a. $45,000.
  b. $55,000.
  c. $75,000.
  d. $100,000.

Solutions

1. **b.** The products produced are homogeneous, not heterogeneous, in nature. Choices (a), (c), and (d) are incorrect because they all represent characteristics of a process cost system.

2. **d.** Manufacturing costs are not assigned the same way in a job order and in a process cost system. Choices (a), (b), and (c) are true statements.

3. **d.** In a process cost system, the flow of costs is work in process, finished goods, cost of goods sold. Therefore, choices (a), (b), and (c) are incorrect.

4. **b.** The debit is often to two or more work in process accounts, not (a) a debit to Finished Goods Inventory, (c) credits to two or more work in process accounts, or (d) a credit to Finished Goods Inventory.

5. **c.** In a process cost system, manufacturing overhead is assigned to a work in process account for each production department on the basis of a predetermined overhead rate, not (a) to a finished goods account, (b) as the job is completed, or (d) as overhead costs are incurred.

6. **b.** Conversion costs are the sum of labor costs and overhead costs, not (a) the sum of fixed and variable overhead costs, (c) direct material costs and overhead costs, or (d) direct labor and indirect labor costs.

7. **b.** The equivalent units of production is the sum of units completed and transferred out (20,000) and the equivalent units of ending work in process inventory (5,000 units × 60%), or 20,000 + 3,000 = 23,000 units, not (a) 22,600 units, (c) 24,000 units, or (d) 25,000 units.

8. **a.** There are 7,000 physical units to be accounted for (0 units in beginning inventory + 7,000 units started), not (b) 7,360, (c) 7,500, or (d) 7,340.

9. **c.** The equivalent units for materials are 26,000 (23,000 units transferred out plus 3,000 in ending work in process inventory). The equivalent units for conversion costs are 24,000 (23,000 transferred out plus $33\frac{1}{3}\%$ of the ending work in process inventory or 1,000). Therefore, choices (a) 22,000, 24,000; (b) 24,000, 26,000; and (d) 26,000, 26,000 are incorrect.

10. **a.** $60,000 ÷ (9,000 + 3,000 units) = $5.00 per unit, not (b) $5.45 (rounded), (c) $6.00, or (d) no correct answer is given.

11. **b.** [(2,500 units × 100% complete) × $10] + [(2,500 units × 40% complete) × $30] or $25,000 + $30,000 = $55,000, not (a) $45,000, (c) $75,000, or (d) $100,000.

12. **b.** A production cost report shows costs charged to a department and costs accounted for as well as the production quantity. The other choices are incorrect because a production cost report

(a) is an internal, not external, report; (c) does show physical units; and (d) is prepared in four steps and does not contain six sections.

13. **d.** In a production cost report, units to be accounted for are calculated as Units started in production + Units in beginning work in process, not (a) Units in ending work in process, (b) minus Units in beginning work in process, or (c) Units transferred out.

*14. **b.** The equivalent units for materials are 28,000 [25,000 started and completed + (3,000 × 100%)]. The equivalent units for conversion costs are 27,500 [(2,000 × 80%) + 25,000 + (3,000 × 30%)]. Therefore, choices (a) 28,000, 26,600; (c) 27,000, 26,200; and (d) 27,000, 29,600 are incorrect.

*15. **a.** Unit materials cost is $5.00 [$60,000 ÷ (9,000 + 3,000)]. Therefore, choices (b) $6.00, (c) $6.67 (rounded), and (d) no correct answer are incorrect.

*16. **b.** The total cost assignable to the ending work in process is $55,000 [($10 × 2,500) + ($30 × 2,500 × 40%)]. Therefore, choices (a) $45,000, (c) $75,000, and (d) $100,000 are incorrect.

Practice Brief Exercises

1. (LO 2) Jeremiah Industries purchased $70,000 of raw materials on account. Supporting records show that the Assembly Department used $43,000 of the raw materials and the Finishing Department used the remainder. Prepare the journal entries relating to raw materials.

Journalize the assignment of materials.

Solution

1. Raw Materials Inventory　　　　　　　　　　　　　　　　　　70,000
    　　Accounts Payable　　　　　　　　　　　　　　　　　　　　　　　　70,000

    Work in Process—Assembly Department　　　　　　　　　　　43,000
    Work in Process—Finishing Department　　　　　　　　　　　27,000
    　　Raw Materials Inventory　　　　　　　　　　　　　　　　　　　　70,000

2. (LO 3) The Cooking Department of Caleb Foods has the following production data for October: beginning work in process 3,000 units that are 100% complete as to materials and 30% complete as to conversion costs; units transferred out 10,000 units; and ending work in process 6,000 units that are 100% complete as to materials and 60% complete as to conversion costs. Compute the equivalent units of production for (a) materials and (b) conversion costs for the month of October.

Compute equivalent units of production.

Solution

2.

	(a) Materials	(b) Conversion Costs
Units transferred out	10,000	10,000
Work in process, November 30		
Materials (6,000 × 100%)	6,000	
Conversion costs (6,000 × 60%)		3,600
Total equivalent units	16,000	13,600

3. (LO 4) Smith Company has the following production data for April: units transferred out 50,000, and ending work in process 8,000 units that are 100% complete for materials and 30% complete for conversion costs. If unit materials cost is $3 and unit conversion cost is $8, determine the costs to be assigned to the units transferred out and the units in ending work in process.

Compute costs to units transferred out and in process.

Solution

3.

Assignment of Costs	Equivalent Units	Unit Cost		
Transferred out				
Transferred out	50,000	$11		$550,000
Work in process, 4/30				
Materials	8,000	3	$24,000	
Conversion costs	2,400	8	19,200	43,200
Total costs				$593,200

4. (LO 4) Production costs chargeable to the Finishing Department in July in Lethbridge-Stewart Manufacturing are materials $60,000, labor $29,500, and overhead $11,000. Equivalent units of production are materials 30,000 and conversion costs 27,000. Production records indicate that 25,000 units were transferred out, and 5,000 units in ending work in process were 40% complete as to conversion costs and 100% complete as to materials.

Prepare unit costs and cost reconciliation schedule.

a. Compute the unit costs for materials and conversion costs.

b. Prepare a cost reconciliation schedule.

Solution

4. a.

Total materials costs	÷	Equivalent units of materials	=	Unit materials cost
$60,000	÷	30,000	=	$2.00

Total conversion costs*	÷	Equivalent units of conversion costs	=	Unit conversion cost
$40,500	÷	27,000	=	$1.50

*$29,500 + $11,000

b. Costs accounted for:

Transferred out	(25,000 × $3.50)			$ 87,500
Work in process				
Materials	(5,000 × $2.00)	$10,000		
Conversion costs	(2,000* × $1.50)	3,000		13,000
Total costs				$100,500

*5,000 × 40%

Practice Exercises

Journalize transactions.

1. (LO 2) Armando Company manufactures pizza sauce through two production departments: Cooking and Canning. In each process, materials and conversion costs are incurred evenly throughout the process. For the month of April, the work in process accounts show the following debits.

	Cooking	Canning
Beginning work in process	$ -0-	$ 4,000
Materials	25,000	8,000
Labor	8,500	7,500
Overhead	29,000	25,800
Costs transferred in		55,000

Instructions

Journalize the April transactions.

Solution

1. April 30	Work in Process—Cooking	25,000	
	Work in Process—Canning	8,000	
	Raw Materials Inventory		33,000
30	Work in Process—Cooking	8,500	
	Work in Process—Canning	7,500	
	Factory Labor		16,000
30	Work in Process—Cooking	29,000	
	Work in Process—Canning	25,800	
	Manufacturing Overhead		54,800
30	Work in Process—Canning	55,000	
	Work in Process—Cooking		55,000

Prepare a production cost report.

2. (LO 3, 4) The Sanding Department of Jo Furniture Company has the following production and manufacturing cost data for March 2022, the first month of operation.

Production: 11,000 units finished and transferred out; 4,000 units started that are 100% complete as to materials and 25% complete as to conversion costs.
Manufacturing costs: Materials $48,000; labor $42,000; and overhead $36,000.

Instructions

Prepare a production cost report.

Solution

2.

Jo Furniture Company
Sanding Department
Production Cost Report
For the Month Ended March 31, 2022

Quantities	Physical Units	Equivalent Units		
		Materials	Conversion Costs	
Units to be accounted for				
Work in process, March 1	0			
Started into production	15,000			
Total units	15,000			
Units accounted for				
Transferred out	11,000	11,000	11,000	
Work in process, March 31	4,000	4,000	1,000	(4,000 × 25%)
Total units	15,000	15,000	12,000	

Costs	Materials	Conversion Costs	Total
Unit costs			
Costs in March	$48,000	$78,000*	$126,000
Equivalent units	15,000	12,000	
Unit costs [(a) + (b)]	$3.20	$6.50	$9.70
Costs to be accounted for			
Work in process, March 1			$ 0
Started into production			126,000
Total costs			$126,000

Cost Reconciliation Schedule

Costs accounted for			
Transferred out (11,000 × $9.70)			$106,700
Work in process, March 31			
Materials (4,000 × $3.20)		$12,800	
Conversion costs (1,000 × $6.50)		6,500	19,300
Total costs			$126,000

*$42,000 + $36,000

Practice Problem

(LO 3, 4) Karlene Industries produces plastic ice cube trays in two processes: heating and stamping. All materials are added at the beginning of the Heating Department process. Karlene uses the weighted-average method to compute equivalent units.

Prepare a production cost report and journalize.

On November 1, the Heating Department had in process 1,000 trays that were 70% complete. During November, it started into production 12,000 trays. On November 30, 2022, 2,000 trays that were 60% complete were in process.

The following cost information for the Heating Department was also available.

Work in process, November 1:		Costs incurred in November:	
Materials	$ 640	Material	$3,000
Conversion costs	360	Labor	2,300
Cost of work in process, Nov. 1	$1,000	Overhead	4,050

Instructions

a. Prepare a production cost report for the Heating Department for the month of November 2022, using the weighted-average method.

b. Journalize the transfer of costs to the Stamping Department.

Solution

a.

Karlene Industries
Heating Department
Production Cost Report
For the Month Ended November 30, 2022

	Physical Units	Equivalent Units	
		Materials	Conversion Costs
Quantities	Step 1	Step 2	
Units to be accounted for			
Work in process, November 1	1,000		
Started into production	12,000		
Total units	13,000		
Units accounted for			
Transferred out	11,000	11,000	11,000
Work in process, November 30	2,000	2,000	1,200
Total units	13,000	13,000	12,200

Costs				
Unit costs Step 3		Materials	Conversion Costs	Total
Total cost	(a)	$ 3,640*	$ 6,710**	$10,350
Equivalent units	(b)	13,000	12,200	
Unit costs [(a) ÷ (b)]		$0.28	$0.55	$0.83
Costs to be accounted for				
Work in process, November 1				$ 1,000
Started into production				9,350
Total costs				$10,350

*$640 + $3,000
**$360 + $2,300 + $4,050

Cost Reconciliation Schedule Step 4

Costs accounted for			
Transferred out (11,000 × $0.83)			$ 9,130
Work in process, November 30			
Materials (2,000 × $0.28)		$560	
Conversion costs (1,200 × $0.55)		660	1,220
Total costs			$10,350

b.

Work in Process—Stamping	9,130	
Work in Process—Heating		9,130
(To record transfer of units to the Stamping Department)		

WileyPLUS

Brief Exercises, DO IT! Exercises, Exercises, Problems, and many additional resources are available for practice in WileyPLUS.

Note: All asterisked Questions, Exercises, and Problems relate to material in the appendix to this chapter.

Questions

1. Identify which costing system—job order or process cost—the following companies would primarily use: (a) **Quaker Oats**, (b) **Jif Peanut Butter**, (c) **Gulf Craft** (luxury yachts), and (d) **Warner Bros. Motion Pictures**.

2. Contrast the primary focus of job order cost accounting and of process cost accounting.

3. What are the similarities between a job order and a process cost system?

4. Your roommate is confused about the features of process cost accounting. Identify and explain the distinctive features for your roommate.

5. Sam Bowyer believes there are no significant differences in the flow of costs between job order cost accounting and process cost accounting. Is Bowyer correct? Explain.

6. **a.** What source documents are used in assigning (1) materials and (2) labor to production in a process cost system?

   b. What criterion and basis are commonly used in allocating overhead to processes?

7. At Ely Company, overhead is assigned to production departments at the rate of $5 per machine hour. In July, machine hours were 3,000 in the Machining Department and 2,400 in the Assembly Department. Prepare the entry to assign overhead to production.

8. Mark Haley is uncertain about the steps used to prepare a production cost report. State the procedures that are required in the sequence in which they are performed.

9. John Harbeck is confused about computing physical units. Explain to John how physical units to be accounted for and physical units accounted for are determined.

10. What is meant by the term "equivalent units of production"?

11. How are equivalent units of production computed?

12. Coats Company had zero units of beginning work in process. During the period, 9,000 units were completed, and there were 600 units of ending work in process. How many units were started into production?

13. Sanchez Co. has zero units of beginning work in process. During the period, 12,000 units were completed, and there were 500 units of ending work in process one-fifth complete as to conversion cost and 100% complete as to materials cost. What were the equivalent units of production for (a) materials and (b) conversion costs?

14. Hindi Co. started 3,000 units during the period. Its beginning inventory is 500 units one-fourth complete as to conversion costs and 100% complete as to materials costs. Its ending inventory is 300 units one-fifth complete as to conversion costs and 100% complete as to materials costs. How many units were transferred out this period?

15. Clauss Company transfers out 14,000 units and has 2,000 units of ending work in process that are 25% complete. Materials are entered at the beginning of the process and there is no beginning work in process. Assuming unit materials costs of $3 and unit conversion costs of $5, what are the costs to be assigned to units (a) transferred out and (b) in ending work in process?

16. **a.** Ann Quinn believes the production cost report is an external report for stockholders. Is Ann correct? Explain.

    b. Identify the sections in a production cost report.

17. What purposes are served by a production cost report?

18. At Trent Company, there are 800 units of ending work in process that are 100% complete as to materials and 40% complete as to conversion costs. If the unit cost of materials is $3 and the total costs assigned to the 800 units is $6,000, what is the per unit conversion cost?

19. What is the difference between operations costing and a process cost system?

20. How does a company decide whether to use a job order or a process cost system?

*21. Soria Co. started and completed 2,000 units for the period. Its beginning inventory is 800 units 25% complete and its ending inventory is 400 units 20% complete. Soria uses the FIFO method to compute equivalent units. How many units were transferred out this period?

*22. Reyes Company transfers out 12,000 units and has 2,000 units of ending work in process that are 25% complete. Materials are entered at the beginning of the process and there is no beginning work in process. Reyes uses the FIFO method to compute equivalent units. Assuming unit materials costs of $3 and unit conversion costs of $7, what are the costs to be assigned to units (a) transferred out and (b) in ending work in process?

Brief Exercises

BE16.1 (LO 2), AP Warner Company purchases $50,000 of raw materials on account, and it incurs $60,000 of factory labor costs. Journalize the two transactions on March 31, assuming the labor costs are not paid until April.

Journalize entries for accumulating costs.

BE16.2 (LO 2), AP Data for Warner Company are given in BE16.1. Supporting records show that (a) the Assembly Department used $24,000 of the raw materials and $35,000 of the factory labor, and (b) the Finishing Department used the remainder. Journalize the assignment of the costs to the processing departments on March 31.

Journalize the assignment of materials and labor costs.

BE16.3 (LO 2), AP Factory labor data for Warner Company are given in BE16.2. Manufacturing overhead is assigned to departments on the basis of 160% of labor costs. Journalize the assignment of overhead to the Assembly and Finishing Departments.

Journalize the assignment of overhead costs.

BE16.4 (LO 3), AP Goode Company has the following production data for selected months.

Compute equivalent units of production.

Month	Beginning Work in Process	Units Transferred Out	Ending Work in Process	
			Units	% Complete as to Conversion Cost
January	-0-	35,000	10,000	40%
March	-0-	40,000	8,000	75
July	-0-	45,000	16,000	25

Compute equivalent units of production.

Compute equivalent units of production for materials and conversion costs, assuming materials are entered at the beginning of the process.

BE16.5 (LO 3), AP The Smelting Department of Kiner Company has the following production data for November.

Beginning work in process 2,000 units that are 100% complete as to materials and 20% complete as to conversion costs; units transferred out 9,000 units; and ending work in process 7,000 units that are 100% complete as to materials and 40% complete as to conversion costs.

Compute the equivalent units of production for (a) materials and (b) conversion costs for the month of November.

Compute unit costs of production.

BE16.6 (LO 4), AP In Mordica Company, total materials costs are $33,000, and total conversion costs are $54,000. Equivalent units of production are materials 10,000 and conversion costs 12,000. Compute the unit costs for materials, conversion costs, and total manufacturing costs.

Assign costs to units transferred out and in process.

BE16.7 (LO 4), AP Trek Company has the following production data for April: units transferred out 40,000, and ending work in process 5,000 units that are 100% complete for materials and 40% complete for conversion costs. If unit materials cost is $4 and unit conversion cost is $7, determine the costs to be assigned to the units transferred out and the units in ending work in process.

Compute unit costs.

BE16.8 (LO 4), AP Production costs chargeable to the Finishing Department in June in Hollins Company are materials $12,000, labor $29,500, and overhead $18,000. Equivalent units of production are materials 20,000 and conversion costs 19,000. Compute the unit costs for materials and conversion costs.

Prepare cost reconciliation schedule.

BE16.9 (LO 4), AP Data for Hollins Company are given in BE16.8. Production records indicate that 18,000 units were transferred out, and 2,000 units in ending work in process were 50% complete as to conversion costs and 100% complete as to materials. Prepare a cost reconciliation schedule.

Assign costs to units transferred out and in process.

*BE16.10 (LO 5), AP Pix Company has the following production data for March: no beginning work in process, units started and completed 30,000, and ending work in process 5,000 units that are 100% complete for materials and 40% complete for conversion costs. Pix uses the FIFO method to compute equivalent units. If unit materials cost is $6 and unit conversion cost is $10, determine the costs to be assigned to the units transferred out and the units in ending work in process. The total costs to be assigned are $530,000.

Prepare a partial production cost report using the FIFO approach.

*BE16.11 (LO 5), AP Using the data in BE16.10, prepare the cost section of the production cost report for Pix Company using the FIFO approach.

Compute unit costs.

*BE16.12 (LO 5), AP Production costs chargeable to the Finishing Department in May at Kim Company are materials $8,000, labor $20,000, overhead $18,000, and transferred-in costs $67,000. Equivalent units of production are materials 20,000 and conversion costs 19,000. Kim uses the FIFO method to compute equivalent units. Compute the unit costs for materials and conversion costs. Transferred-in costs are considered materials costs.

DO IT! Exercises

Compare job order and process cost systems.

DO IT! 16.1 (LO 1), C Indicate whether each of the following statements is true or false.

1. Many hospitals use job order costing for small, routine medical procedures.
2. A manufacturer of computer flash drives would use a job order cost system.
3. A process cost system uses multiple work in process accounts.
4. A process cost system keeps track of costs on job cost sheets.

Assign and journalize manufacturing costs.

DO IT! 16.2 (LO 2), AP Kopa Company manufactures CH-21 through two processes: mixing and packaging. In July, the following costs were incurred.

	Mixing	Packaging
Raw materials used	$10,000	$28,000
Factory labor costs	8,000	36,000
Manufacturing overhead costs	12,000	54,000

Units completed at a cost of $21,000 in the Mixing Department are transferred to the Packaging Department. Units completed at a cost of $106,000 in the Packaging Department are transferred to Finished Goods. Journalize the assignment of these costs to the two processes and the transfer of units as appropriate.

DO IT! 16.3 (LO 3), AP The Assembly Department for Right pens has the following production data for the current month.

Compute equivalent units.

Beginning Work in Process	Units Transferred Out	Ending Work in Process
–0–	20,000	10,000

Materials are entered at the beginning of the process. The ending work in process units are 70% complete as to conversion costs. Compute the equivalent units of production for (a) materials and (b) conversion costs.

DO IT! 16.4 (LO 4), AP In March, Kelly Company had the following unit production costs: materials $10 and conversion costs $8. On March 1, it had no work in process. During March, Kelly transferred out 22,000 units. As of March 31, 4,000 units that were 40% complete as to conversion costs and 100% complete as to materials were in ending work in process.

Prepare cost reconciliation schedule.

a. Compute the total units to be accounted for.
b. Compute the equivalent units of production.
c. Prepare a cost reconciliation schedule, including the costs of materials transferred out and the costs of materials in process.

Exercises

E16.1 (LO 1), C Robert Wilkins has prepared the following list of statements about process cost accounting.

Understand process cost accounting.

1. Process cost systems are used to apply costs to similar products that are mass-produced in a continuous fashion.
2. A process cost system is used when each finished unit is indistinguishable from another.
3. Companies that produce soft drinks, movies, and computer chips would all use process cost accounting.
4. In a process cost system, costs are tracked by individual jobs.
5. Job order costing and process costing track different manufacturing cost elements.
6. Both job order costing and process costing account for direct materials, direct labor, and manufacturing overhead.
7. Costs flow through the accounts in the same basic way for both job order costing and process costing.
8. In a process cost system, only one work in process account is used.
9. In a process cost system, costs are summarized in a job cost sheet.
10. In a process cost system, the unit cost is total manufacturing costs for the period divided by the equivalent units produced during the period.

Instructions

Identify each statement as true or false. If false, indicate how to correct the statement.

E16.2 (LO 2), AP Harrelson Company manufactures pizza sauce through two production departments: Cooking and Canning. In each process, materials and conversion costs are incurred evenly throughout the process. For the month of April, the work in process accounts show the following debits.

Journalize transactions.

	Cooking	Canning
Beginning work in process	$ –0–	$ 4,000
Materials	21,000	9,000
Labor	8,500	7,000
Overhead	31,500	25,800
Costs transferred in		53,000

Instructions

Journalize the April transactions.

Answer questions on costs and production.

E16.3 (LO 2, 3, 4), AP The ledger of American Company has the following work in process account.

Work in Process—Painting						
5/1	Balance	3,590	5/31	Transferred out		?
5/31	Materials	5,160				
5/31	Labor	2,530				
5/31	Overhead	1,380				
5/31	Balance	?				

Production records show that there were 400 units in the beginning inventory, 30% complete, 1,600 units started, and 1,700 units transferred out. The beginning work in process had materials cost of $2,040 and conversion costs of $1,550. The units in ending inventory were 40% complete. Materials are entered at the beginning of the painting process.

Instructions

a. How many units are in process at May 31?

b. What is the unit materials cost for May?

c. What is the unit conversion cost for May?

d. What is the total cost of units transferred out in May?

e. What is the cost of the May 31 inventory?

Journalize transactions for two processes.

E16.4 (LO 2), AP Schrager Company has two production departments: Cutting and Assembly. July 1 inventories are Raw Materials $4,200, Work in Process—Cutting $2,900, Work in Process—Assembly $10,600, and Finished Goods $31,000. During July, the following transactions occurred.

1. Purchased $62,500 of raw materials on account.
2. Incurred $60,000 of factory labor. (Credit Wages Payable.)
3. Incurred $70,000 of manufacturing overhead; $40,000 was paid and the remainder is unpaid.
4. Requisitioned materials for Cutting $15,700 and Assembly $8,900.
5. Used factory labor for Cutting $33,000 and Assembly $27,000.
6. Applied overhead at the rate of $18 per machine hour. Machine hours were Cutting 1,680 and Assembly 1,720.
7. Transferred goods costing $67,600 from the Cutting Department to the Assembly Department.
8. Transferred goods costing $134,900 from Assembly to Finished Goods.
9. Sold goods costing $150,000 for $200,000 on account.

Instructions

Journalize the transactions. (Omit explanations.)

Compute physical units and equivalent units of production.

E16.5 (LO 3, 4), AP In Shady Company, materials are entered at the beginning of each process. Work in process inventories, with the percentage of work done on conversion costs, and production data for its Sterilizing Department in selected months during 2022 are as follows.

	Beginning Work in Process		Units Transferred Out	Ending Work in Process	
Month	Units	Conversion Cost%		Units	Conversion Cost%
January	-0-	—	11,000	2,000	60
March	-0-	—	12,000	3,000	30
May	-0-	—	14,000	7,000	80
July	-0-	—	10,000	1,500	40

Instructions

a. Compute the physical units for January and May.

b. Compute the equivalent units of production for (1) materials and (2) conversion costs for each month.

E16.6 (LO 3, 4), AP The Cutting Department of Cassel Company has the following production and cost data for July.

Determine equivalent units, unit costs, and assignment of costs.

Production	Costs	
1. Transferred out 12,000 units.	Beginning work in process	$ -0-
2. Started 3,000 units that are 60% complete as to conversion costs and 100% complete as to materials at July 31.	Materials	45,000
	Labor	16,200
	Manufacturing overhead	18,300

Materials are entered at the beginning of the process. Conversion costs are incurred uniformly during the process.

Instructions

a. Determine the equivalent units of production for (1) materials and (2) conversion costs.
b. Compute unit costs and prepare a cost reconciliation schedule.

E16.7 (LO 3, 4), AP The Sanding Department of Quik Furniture Company has the following production and manufacturing cost data for March 2022, the first month of operation.

Prepare a production cost report.

Production: 7,000 units finished and transferred out; 3,000 units started that are 100% complete as to materials and 20% complete as to conversion costs.

Manufacturing costs: Materials $33,000; labor $21,000; and overhead $36,000.

Instructions

Prepare a production cost report.

E16.8 (LO 3, 4), AP The Blending Department of Luongo Company has the following cost and production data for the month of April.

Determine equivalent units, unit costs, and assignment of costs.

Costs:
   Work in process, April 1
      Direct materials: 100% complete $100,000
      Conversion costs: 20% complete   70,000
      Cost of work in process, April 1 $170,000
   Costs incurred during production in April
      Direct materials $ 800,000
      Conversion costs   365,000
      Costs incurred in April $1,165,000

Units transferred out totaled 17,000. Ending work in process was 1,000 units that are 100% complete as to materials and 40% complete as to conversion costs.

Instructions

a. Compute the equivalent units of production for (1) materials and (2) conversion costs for the month of April.
b. Compute the unit costs for the month.
c. Determine the costs to be assigned to the units transferred out and in ending work in process.

E16.9 (LO 3, 4), AP Baden Company has gathered the following information.

Determine equivalent units, unit costs, and assignment of costs.

Units in beginning work in process	-0-
Units started into production	36,000
Units in ending work in process	6,000
Percent complete in ending work in process:	
Conversion costs	40%
Materials	100%
Costs incurred:	
Direct materials	$72,000
Direct labor	$61,000
Overhead	$101,000

Instructions

a. Compute equivalent units of production for materials and for conversion costs.

b. Determine the unit costs of production.

c. Show the assignment of costs to units transferred out and in process.

Determine equivalent units, unit costs, and assignment of costs.

E16.10 (LO 3, 4), AP Overton Company has gathered the following information.

Units in beginning work in process	20,000
Units started into production	164,000
Units in ending work in process	24,000
Percent complete in ending work in process:	
Conversion costs	60%
Materials	100%
Costs incurred:	
Direct materials	$101,200
Direct labor	$164,800
Overhead	$184,000

Instructions

a. Compute equivalent units of production for materials and for conversion costs.

b. Determine the unit costs of production.

c. Show the assignment of costs to units transferred out and in process.

Compute equivalent units, unit costs, and costs assigned.

→ Excel

E16.11 (LO 3, 4), AP The Polishing Department of Major Company has the following production and manufacturing cost data for September. Materials are entered at the beginning of the process.

Production: Beginning inventory 1,600 units that are 100% complete as to materials and 30% complete as to conversion costs; units started during the period are 42,900; ending inventory of 5,000 units 10% complete as to conversion costs.

Manufacturing costs: Beginning inventory costs, comprised of $20,000 of materials and $43,180 of conversion costs; materials costs added in Polishing during the month, $175,800; labor and overhead applied in Polishing during the month, $125,680 and $257,140, respectively.

Instructions

a. Compute the equivalent units of production for materials and conversion costs for the month of September.

b. Compute the unit costs for materials and conversion costs for the month.

c. Determine the costs to be assigned to the units transferred out and in process.

Explain the production cost report.

E16.12 (LO 4), S Writing David Skaros has recently been promoted to production manager. He has just started to receive various managerial reports, including the production cost report that you prepared. It showed that his department had 2,000 equivalent units in ending inventory. His department has had a history of not keeping enough inventory on hand to meet demand. He has come to you, very angry, and wants to know why you credited him with only 2,000 units when he knows he had at least twice that many on hand.

Instructions

Explain to him why his production cost report showed only 2,000 equivalent units in ending inventory. Write an informal memo. Be kind and explain very clearly why he is mistaken.

Prepare a production cost report.

E16.13 (LO 3, 4), AP The Welding Department of Healthy Company has the following production and manufacturing cost data for February 2022. All materials are added at the beginning of the process.

Manufacturing Costs			Production Data	
Beginning work in process			Beginning work in process	15,000 units
Materials	$18,000			1/10 complete
Conversion costs	14,175	$ 32,175	Units transferred out	55,000
Materials		180,000	Units started	51,000
Labor		67,380	Ending work in process	11,000 units
Overhead		61,445		1/5 complete

Instructions

Prepare a production cost report for the Welding Department for the month of February.

E16.14 (LO 3, 4), AP `Service` Remington Inc. is contemplating the use of process costing to track the costs of its operations. The operation consists of three segments (departments): Receiving, Shipping, and Delivery. Containers are received at Remington's docks and sorted according to the ship they will be carried on. The containers are loaded onto a ship, which carries them to the appropriate port of destination. The containers are then off-loaded and delivered to the Receiving Department.

Compute physical units and equivalent units of production.

Remington wants to begin using process costing in the Shipping Department. Direct materials represent the fuel costs to run the ship, and "Containers in transit" represents work in process. Listed below is information about the Shipping Department's first month's activity.

Containers in transit, April 1	0
Containers loaded	1,200
Containers in transit, April 30	350, 40% of direct materials and 20% of conversion costs

Instructions

a. Determine the physical flow of containers for the month.

b. Calculate the equivalent units for direct materials and conversion costs.

E16.15 (LO 3, 4), AP `Service` Santana Mortgage Company uses a process cost system to accumulate costs in its Application Department. When an application is completed, it is forwarded to the Loan Department for final processing. The following processing and cost data pertain to September.

Determine equivalent units, unit costs, and assignment of costs.

1. Applications in process on September 1: 100.
2. Applications started in September: 1,000.
3. Completed applications during September: 800.
4. Applications still in process at September 30: 100% complete as to materials (forms) and 60% complete as to conversion costs.

Beginning WIP:	
Direct materials	$ 1,000
Conversion costs	3,960
September costs:	
Direct materials	$ 4,500
Direct labor	12,000
Overhead	9,520

Materials are the forms used in the application process, and these costs are incurred at the beginning of the process. Conversion costs are incurred uniformly during the process.

Instructions

a. Determine the equivalent units of service (production) for materials and conversion costs.

b. Compute the unit costs and prepare a cost reconciliation schedule.

*E16.16 (LO 5), AP `Service` Using the data in E16.15, assume Santana Mortgage Company uses the FIFO method. Also, assume that the applications in process on September 1 were 100% complete as to materials (application forms) and 40% complete as to conversion costs. Assume overhead costs were $9,620 instead of $9,520.

Compute equivalent units, unit costs, and costs assigned.

Instructions

a. Determine the equivalent units of service (production) for materials and conversion costs.

b. Compute the unit costs and prepare a cost reconciliation schedule.

*E16.17 (LO 5), AP The Cutting Department of Lasso Company has the following production and cost data for August.

Determine equivalent units, unit costs, and assignment of costs.

Production	Costs	
1. Started and completed 10,000 units.	Beginning work in process	$ -0-
2. Started 2,000 units that are 40% completed at August 31.	Materials	45,000
	Labor	13,600
	Manufacturing overhead	16,100

Materials are entered at the beginning of the process. Conversion costs are incurred uniformly during the process. Lasso Company uses the FIFO method to compute equivalent units.

Instructions

a. Determine the equivalent units of production for (1) materials and (2) conversion costs.

b. Compute unit costs and show the assignment of manufacturing costs to units transferred out and in work in process.

Compute equivalent units, unit costs, and costs assigned.

*E16.18 (LO 5), AP The Smelting Department of Polzin Company has the following production and cost data for September.

Production: Beginning work in process 2,000 units that are 100% complete as to materials and 20% complete as to conversion costs; units started and finished 9,000 units; and ending work in process 1,000 units that are 100% complete as to materials and 40% complete as to conversion costs.

Manufacturing costs: Work in process, September 1, $15,200; materials added $60,000; labor and overhead $132,000.

Polzin uses the FIFO method to compute equivalent units.

Instructions

a. Compute the equivalent units of production for (1) materials and (2) conversion costs for the month of September.

b. Compute the unit costs for the month.

c. Determine the costs to be assigned to the units transferred out and in process.

Answer questions on costs and production.

*E16.19 (LO 5), AP The ledger of Hasgrove Company has the following work in process account.

		Work in Process—Painting			
3/1	Balance	3,680	3/31	Transferred out	?
3/31	Materials	6,600			
3/31	Labor	2,400			
3/31	Overhead	1,150			
3/31	Balance	?			

Production records show that there were 800 units in the beginning inventory, 30% complete, 1,100 units started, and 1,500 units transferred out. The units in ending inventory were 40% complete. Materials are entered at the beginning of the painting process. Hasgrove uses the FIFO method to compute equivalent units.

Instructions

Answer the following questions.

a. How many units are in process at March 31?

b. What is the unit materials cost for March?

c. What is the unit conversion cost for March?

d. What is the total cost of units started in February and completed in March?

e. What is the total cost of units started and finished in March?

f. What is the cost of the March 31 inventory?

Prepare a production cost report for a second process.

*E16.20 (LO 5), AP The Welding Department of Majestic Company has the following production and manufacturing cost data for February 2022. All materials are added at the beginning of the process. Majestic uses the FIFO method to compute equivalent units.

Manufacturing Costs		Production Data	
Beginning work in process	$ 32,175	Beginning work in process	15,000 units, 10% complete
Costs transferred in	135,000		
Materials	57,000	Units transferred out	54,000
Labor	35,100	Units transferred in	64,000
Overhead	68,400	Ending work in process	25,000 units 20% complete

Instructions

Prepare a production cost report for the Welding Department for the month of February. Transferred-in costs are considered materials costs.

Problems: Set A

P16.1A (LO 2), AP Fire Out Company manufactures its product, Vitadrink, through two manufacturing processes: Mixing and Packaging. All materials are entered at the beginning of each process. On October 1, 2022, inventories consisted of Raw Materials $26,000, Work in Process—Mixing $0, Work in Process—Packaging $250,000, and Finished Goods $289,000. The beginning inventory for Packaging consisted of 10,000 units that were 50% complete as to conversion costs and fully complete as to materials. During October, 50,000 units were started into production in the Mixing Department and the following transactions were completed.

Journalize transactions.

1. Purchased $300,000 of raw materials on account.
2. Issued raw materials for production: Mixing $210,000 and Packaging $45,000.
3. Incurred labor costs of $278,900.
4. Used factory labor: Mixing $182,500 and Packaging $96,400.
5. Incurred $810,000 of manufacturing overhead on account.
6. Applied manufacturing overhead on the basis of $23 per machine hour. Machine hours were 28,000 in Mixing and 6,000 in Packaging.
7. Transferred 45,000 units from Mixing to Packaging at a cost of $979,000.
8. Transferred 53,000 units from Packaging to Finished Goods at a cost of $1,315,000.
9. Sold goods costing $1,604,000 for $2,500,000 on account.

Instructions
Journalize the October transactions.

P16.2A (LO 3, 4), AP Rosenthal Company manufactures bowling balls through two processes: Molding and Packaging. In the Molding Department, the urethane, rubber, plastics, and other materials are molded into bowling balls. In the Packaging Department, the balls are placed in cartons and sent to the finished goods warehouse. All materials are entered at the beginning of each process. Labor and manufacturing overhead are incurred uniformly throughout each process. Production and cost data for the Molding Department during June 2022 are presented below.

Complete four steps necessary to prepare a production cost report.

Production Data	June
Beginning work in process units	–0–
Units started into production	22,000
Ending work in process units	2,000
Percent complete—ending inventory	40%

Cost Data	
Materials	$198,000
Labor	53,600
Overhead	112,800
Total	$364,400

Instructions
a. Prepare a schedule showing physical units of production.
b. Determine the equivalent units of production for materials and conversion costs.
c. Compute the unit costs of production.
d. Determine the costs to be assigned to the units transferred out and in process for June.
e. Prepare a production cost report for the Molding Department for the month of June.

c. Materials $9.00
CC $8.00
d. Transferred out $340,000
WIP $ 24,400

P16.3A (LO 3, 4), AP Thakin Industries Inc. manufactures dorm furniture in separate processes. In each process, materials are entered at the beginning, and conversion costs are incurred uniformly. Production and cost data for the first process in making a product are as follows.

Complete four steps necessary to prepare a production cost report.

Production Data—July	Cutting Department T12-Tables
Work in process units, July 1	–0–
Units started into production	20,000
Work in process units, July 31	3,000
Work in process percent complete	60%

Cost Data—July	
Work in process, July 1	$ –0–
Materials	380,000
Labor	234,400
Overhead	104,000
Total	$718,400

Instructions

a. 1. Compute the physical units of production.
2. Compute equivalent units of production for materials and for conversion costs.
3. Determine the unit costs of production.
4. Show the assignment of costs to units transferred out and in process.

b. Prepare the production cost report for July 2022.

a. 3. Materials $19
CC $18
4. Transferred
out $629,000
WIP $ 89,400

Assign costs and prepare production cost report.

P16.4A (LO 3, 4), AP Rivera Company has several processing departments. Costs charged to the Assembly Department for November 2022 totaled $2,280,000 as follows.

Work in process, November 1		
Materials	$79,000	
Conversion costs	48,150	$ 127,150
Materials added		1,589,000
Labor		225,920
Overhead		337,930

Production records show that 35,000 units were in beginning work in process 30% complete as to conversion costs, 660,000 units were started into production, and 25,000 units were in ending work in process 40% complete as to conversion costs. Materials are entered at the beginning of each process.

Instructions

a. Determine the equivalent units of production and the unit production costs for the Assembly Department.

b. Determine the assignment of costs to goods transferred out and in process.

c. Prepare a production cost report for the Assembly Department.

b. Transferred
out $2,211,000
WIP $ 69,000

Determine equivalent units and unit costs and assign costs.

P16.5A (LO 3, 4), AP Polk Company manufactures basketballs. Materials are added at the beginning of the production process and conversion costs are incurred uniformly. Production and cost data for the month of July 2022 are as follows.

Production Data—Basketballs	Units	Percentage Complete
Work in process units, July 1	500	60%
Units started into production	1,000	
Work in process units, July 31	600	40%

Cost Data—Basketballs		
Work in process, July 1		
Materials	$750	
Conversion costs	600	$1,350
Direct materials		2,400
Direct labor		1,580
Manufacturing overhead		1,240

Instructions

a. Calculate the following.
   1. The equivalent units of production for materials and conversion costs.
   2. The unit costs of production for materials and conversion costs.
   3. The assignment of costs to units transferred out and in process at the end of the accounting period.

b. Prepare a production cost report for the month of July for the basketballs.

a. 2. Materials $2.10
   3. Transferred
      out $4,590
      WIP $1,980

P16.6A (LO 3, 4), AP Hamilton Processing Company uses a weighted-average process cost system and manufactures a single product—an industrial carpet shampoo and cleaner used by many universities. The manufacturing activity for the month of October has just been completed. A partially completed production cost report for the month of October for the Mixing and Cooking Department is shown as follows.

Compute equivalent units and complete production cost report.

Hamilton Processing Company
Mixing and Cooking Department
Production Cost Report
For the Month Ended October 31

Quantities	Physical Units	Equivalent Units	
		Materials	Conversion Costs
Units to be accounted for			
Work in process, October 1 (all materials, 70% conversion costs)	20,000		
Started into production	150,000		
Total units	170,000		
Units accounted for			
Transferred out	120,000	?	?
Work in process, October 31 (60% materials, 40% conversion costs)	50,000	?	?
Total units accounted for	170,000	?	?

Costs

Unit costs	Materials	Conversion Costs	Total
Total cost	$240,000	$105,000	$345,000
Equivalent units	?	?	
Unit costs	$? +	$? =	$?

Costs to be accounted for	
Work in process, October 1	$ 30,000
Started into production	315,000
Total costs	$345,000

Cost Reconciliation Schedule

Costs accounted for			
Transferred out			$?
Work in process, October 31			
Materials		$?	
Conversion costs		?	?
Total costs			$?

Instructions

a. Prepare a schedule that shows how the equivalent units were computed so that you can complete the "Quantities: Units accounted for" equivalent units section shown in the production cost report, and compute October unit costs.

b. Complete the "Cost Reconciliation Schedule" part of the production cost report.

a. Materials $1.60
b. Transferred
   out $282,000
   WIP $ 63,000

Determine equivalent units and unit costs and assign costs for processes; prepare production cost report.

*P16.7A (LO 5), AP Owen Company manufactures bicycles and tricycles. For both products, materials are added at the beginning of the production process, and conversion costs are incurred uniformly. Owen Company uses the FIFO method to compute equivalent units. Production and cost data for the month of March are as follows.

Production Data—Bicycles	Units	Percentage Complete
Work in process units, March 1	200	80%
Units started into production	1,000	
Work in process units, March 31	300	40%

Cost Data—Bicycles	
Work in process, March 1	$19,280
Direct materials	50,000
Direct labor	25,900
Manufacturing overhead	30,000

Production Data—Tricycles	Units	Percentage Complete
Work in process units, March 1	100	75%
Units started into production	1,000	
Work in process units, March 31	60	25%

Cost Data—Tricycles	
Work in process, March 1	$ 6,125
Direct materials	30,000
Direct labor	14,300
Manufacturing overhead	20,000

Instructions

a. Calculate the following for both the bicycles and the tricycles.
  1. The equivalent units of production for materials and conversion costs.
  2. The unit costs of production for materials and conversion costs.
  3. The assignment of costs to units transferred out and in process at the end of the accounting period.

b. Prepare a production cost report for the month of March for the bicycles only.

a. Bicycles:
  1. Materials 1,000
  2. Materials $50
  3. Transferred
      out $102,380
      WIP $ 22,800

Continuing Cases

Current Designs

CD16 Building a kayak using the composite method is a very labor-intensive process. In the Fabrication Department, the kayaks go through several steps as employees carefully place layers of Kevlar® in a mold and then use resin to fuse together the layers. The excess resin is removed with a vacuum process, and the upper shell and lower shell are removed from the molds and assembled. The seat, hatch, and other components are added in the Finishing Department.

At the beginning of April, **Current Designs** had 30 kayaks in process in the Fabrication Department. Rick Thrune, the production manager, estimated that about 80% of the materials costs had been added to these boats, which were about 50% complete with respect to the conversion costs. The cost of this inventory had been calculated to be $8,400 in materials and $9,000 in conversion costs.

During April, 72 boats were started. At the end of the month, the 35 kayaks in the ending inventory had 20% of the materials and 40% of the conversion costs already added to them.

A review of the accounting records for April showed that materials with a cost of $17,500 had been requisitioned by the Fabrication Department and that the conversion costs for the month were $39,600.

Instructions

Complete a production cost report for April 2022 for the Fabrication Department using the weighted-average method.

Waterways

(*Note:* This is a continuation of the Waterways case from Chapters 14–15.)

WP16 Because most of the parts for its irrigation systems are standard, Waterways handles the majority of its manufacturing as a process cost system. There are multiple process departments. Three of these departments are the Molding, Cutting, and Welding Departments. All items eventually end up in the Packaging Department, which prepares items for sale in kits or individually. This problem asks you to help Waterways calculate equivalent units and prepare a production cost report.

Go to WileyPLUS for complete case details and instructions.

Expand Your Critical Thinking

Decision-Making Across the Organization

CT16.1 Florida Beach Company manufactures sunscreen, called NoTan, in 11-ounce plastic bottles. NoTan is sold in a competitive market. As a result, management is very cost-conscious. NoTan is manufactured through two processes: mixing and filling. Materials are entered at the beginning of each process, and labor and manufacturing overhead occur uniformly throughout each process. Unit costs are based on the cost per gallon of NoTan using the weighted-average costing approach.

On June 30, 2022, Mary Ritzman, the chief accountant for the past 20 years, opted to take early retirement. Her replacement, Joe Benili, had extensive accounting experience with motels in the area but only limited contact with manufacturing accounting. During July, Joe correctly accumulated the following production quantity and cost data for the Mixing Department.

Production quantities: Work in process, July 1, 8,000 gallons 75% complete; started into production 100,000 gallons; work in process, July 31, 5,000 gallons 20% complete. Materials are added at the beginning of the process.

Production costs: Beginning work in process $88,000, comprised of $21,000 of materials costs and $67,000 of conversion costs; incurred in July: materials $573,000, conversion costs $765,000.

Joe then prepared a production cost report on the basis of physical units started into production. His report showed a production cost of $14.26 per gallon of NoTan. The management of Florida Beach was surprised at the high unit cost. The president comes to you, as Mary's top assistant, to review Joe's report and prepare a correct report if necessary.

Instructions

With the class divided into groups, answer the following questions.

a. Show how Joe arrived at the unit cost of $14.26 per gallon of NoTan.

b. What error(s) did Joe make in preparing his production cost report?

c. Prepare a correct production cost report for July.

Managerial Analysis

CT16.2 Harris Furniture Company manufactures living room furniture through two departments: Framing and Upholstering. Materials are entered at the beginning of each process. For May, the following cost data are obtained from the two work in process accounts.

	Framing	Upholstering
Work in process, May 1	$ -0-	$?
Materials	450,000	?
Conversion costs	261,000	330,000
Costs transferred in	-0-	600,000
Costs transferred out	600,000	?
Work in process, May 31	111,000	?

Instructions

Answer the following questions.

a. If 3,000 sofas were started into production on May 1 and 2,500 sofas were transferred to Upholstering, what was the unit cost of materials for May in the Framing Department?

b. Using the data in (a) above, what was the per unit conversion cost of the sofas transferred to Upholstering?

c. Continuing the assumptions in (a) above, what is the percentage of completion of the units in process at May 31 in the Framing Department?

Real-World Focus

CT16.3 Paintball is now played around the world. The process of making paintballs is actually quite similar to the process used to make certain medical pills. In fact, paintballs were previously often made at the same factories that made pharmaceuticals.

Instructions

Do an Internet search on "video of paintball production," view that video, and then answer the following questions.

a. Describe in sequence the primary steps used to manufacture paintballs.

b. Explain the costs incurred by the company that would fall into each of the following categories: materials, labor, and overhead. Of these categories, which do you think would be the greatest cost in making paintballs?

c. Discuss whether a paintball manufacturer would use job order costing or process costing.

Communication Activity

CT16.4 Diane Barone was a good friend of yours in high school and is from your home town. While you chose to major in accounting when you both went away to college, she majored in marketing and management. You are now the accounting manager for the Snack Foods Division of Melton Enterprises. Your friend Diane was promoted to regional sales manager for the same division of Melton. Diane recently telephoned you. She explained that she was familiar with job cost sheets, which had been used by the Special Projects Division where she had formerly worked. She was, however, very uncomfortable with the production cost reports prepared by your division. She emailed you a list of her particular questions:

1. Since Melton occasionally prepares snack foods for special orders in the Snack Foods Division, why don't we track costs of the orders separately?
2. What is an equivalent unit?
3. Why am I getting four production cost reports? Isn't there one work in process account?

Instructions

Prepare a memo to Diane. Answer her questions and include any additional information you think would be helpful. You may write informally but do use proper grammar and punctuation.

Ethics Case

CT16.5 R. B. Dillman Company manufactures a high-tech component used in Bluetooth speakers that passes through two production processing departments, Molding and Assembly. Department managers are partially compensated on the basis of units of product completed and transferred out relative to units of product put into production. This was intended as encouragement to be efficient and to minimize waste.

Jan Wooten is the department head in the Molding Department, and Tony Ferneti is her quality control inspector. During the month of June, Jan hired three new employees who were not yet technically skilled. As a result, many of the units produced in June had minor molding defects. In order to maintain the department's normal high rate of completion, Jan told Tony to pass through inspection and on to the Assembly Department all units that had defects nondetectable to the human eye. "Company and industry tolerances on this product are too high anyway," says Jan. "Less than 2% of the units we produce are subjected in the market to the stress tolerance we've designed into them. The odds of those 2% being any of this month's units are even less. Anyway, we're saving the company money."

Instructions

a. Who are the potential stakeholders involved in this situation?

b. What alternatives does Tony have in this situation? What might the company do to prevent this situation from occurring?

Considering People, Planet, and Profit

CT16.6 In a recent year, an oil refinery in Texas City, Texas, on the Houston Ship Channel exploded. The explosion killed 14 people and sent a plume of smoke hundreds of feet into the air. The blast started as a fire in the section of the plant that increased the octane of the gasoline that was produced at the refinery. The Houston Ship Channel is the main waterway that allows commerce to flow from the Gulf of Mexico into Houston.

The Texas Commission on Environmental Quality expressed concern about the release of nitrogen oxides, benzene, and other known carcinogens as a result of the blast. Neighbors of the plant complained that the plant had been emitting carcinogens for years and that the regulators had ignored their complaints about emissions and unsafe working conditions.

Instructions

Answer the following questions.

a. Outline the costs that the company now faces as a result of the accident.
b. How could the company have reduced the costs associated with the accident?

CHAPTER 17

Activity-Based Costing

Chapter Preview

As indicated in the following Feature Story about **Precor**, the traditional costing systems described in earlier chapters are not the best answer for every company. Precor suspected that its traditional costing system was masking significant differences in its real cost structure, so it sought a new method of assigning costs. Similar searches by other companies for ways to improve operations and gather more accurate data for decision-making have resulted in the development of powerful management tools, including **activity-based costing (ABC)**. The primary objective of this chapter is to explain and illustrate activity-based costing.

Feature Story

Precor Is on Your Side

Do you feel like the whole world is conspiring against your efforts to get in shape? Is it humanly possible to resist the constant barrage of advertisements and fast-food servers who pleasantly encourage us to "supersize" it? Lest we think that we have no allies in our battle against the bulge, consider **Precor**.

Ever since it made the first ergonomically sound rowing machine in 1980, Precor's sole mission has been to provide exercise equipment. It makes elliptical trainers, exercise bikes, rowing machines, treadmills, multi-station strength systems, and many other forms of equipment designed to erase the cumulative effects of a fast-food nation. Its equipment is used in **Hilton** hotels, **Gold's Gym** franchises, and even in Madonna's **Hard Candy** fitness center in Moscow.

Building high-quality fitness equipment requires sizable investments by Precor in buildings and machinery. For example, Precor recently moved its facilities from Valencia, California, to Greensboro, North Carolina. In order to reduce costs and minimize environmental impact, the company installed low-flow water fixtures, high-efficiency heating and cooling systems, and state-of-the-art lighting in its $26 million, 230,000-square-foot facility. As a result of these efforts, Precor's new facility received a Leadership in Energy and Efficient Design (LEED) CI Gold Certification.

Because of its huge investments in property, plant, and equipment, overhead costs represent a large percentage of the cost of manufacturing Precor's exercise equipment. The combination of high overhead costs and a wide variety of products means that it is important that Precor assigns its overhead accurately to its various products. Without accurate cost information, Precor would not know whether its elliptical trainers and recumbent bicycles are making money, whether its AMT 100i adaptive motion trainer is priced high enough to cover its costs, or if its 240i Stretchtrainer is losing money.

To increase the accuracy of its costs, Precor uses a method of overhead allocation that focuses on identifying the types of activities that cause the company to incur costs. It then assigns overhead to products based on their relative usage of cost-incurring activities. By doing this, the allocation of overhead is less arbitrary than traditional overhead allocation methods. In short, before it can help us burn off the pounds, Precor needs to understand what drives its overhead costs.

Source: www.precor.com.

 Watch the *Precor* video in WileyPLUS to learn more about activity-based costing.

Chapter Outline

LEARNING OBJECTIVES

LO 1 Discuss the difference between traditional costing and activity-based costing.	• Traditional costing systems • Illustration of a traditional system • Need for a new approach • Activity-based costing	**DO IT! 1** Costing Systems
LO 2 Apply activity-based costing to a manufacturer.	• Identify and classify activities and allocate overhead to cost pools • Identify cost drivers • Compute activity-based overhead rates • Assign overhead costs • Comparing unit costs	**DO IT! 2** Apply ABC to Manufacturer
LO 3 Explain the benefits and limitations of activity-based costing.	• Advantage of multiple cost pools • Advantage of enhanced cost control • Advantage of better management decisions • Limitations of ABC	**DO IT! 3** Classify Activity Levels
LO 4 Apply activity-based costing to service industries.	• Traditional costing example • ABC example	**DO IT! 4** Apply ABC to Service Company

Go to the Review and Practice section at the end of the chapter for a targeted summary and practice applications with solutions.
Visit WileyPLUS for additional tutorials and practice opportunities.

Traditional vs. Activity-Based Costing

> **LEARNING OBJECTIVE 1**
> Discuss the difference between traditional costing and activity-based costing.

Traditional Costing Systems

It is probably impossible to determine the *exact* cost of a product or service. However, in order to achieve improved management decisions, companies strive to provide decision-makers with the most accurate cost estimates they can. The most accurate estimate of product cost occurs when the costs are traceable directly to the actual product or service. Direct materials and direct labor costs are the easiest to trace directly to the product through the use of material requisition forms and payroll time sheets. Overhead costs, on the other hand, are an indirect or common cost that generally cannot be easily or directly traced to individual products or services. Instead, companies use estimates to assign overhead costs to products and services.

Often, the most difficult part of computing accurate unit costs is determining the proper amount of **overhead cost** to assign to each product, service, or job. In our coverage of job order costing in Chapter 15 and of process costing in Chapter 16, we used a single or plantwide overhead rate throughout the year for the entire factory operation. That rate was called the **predetermined overhead rate**. For job order costing, we assumed that **direct labor (cost or hours)** was the relevant activity base for assigning all overhead costs to jobs. For process costing, we frequently assumed that **machine hours** was the relevant activity base for assigning all overhead to the process or department. **Illustration 17.1** displays a simplified (one-stage) traditional costing system relying on direct labor to assign overhead.

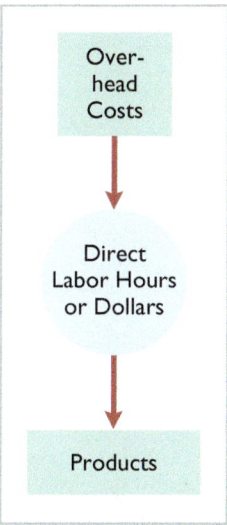

ILLUSTRATION 17.1

Traditional one-stage costing system

Illustration of a Traditional Costing System

To illustrate a traditional costing system, assume that Atlas Company produces two abdominal fitness products—the Ab Bench and the Ab Coaster. Each year, the company produces 25,000 Ab Benches but only 5,000 Ab Coasters. Each unit produced requires one hour of direct labor, for a total of 30,000 labor hours (25,000 + 5,000). The direct labor cost is $12 per unit for each product.

The direct materials cost per unit is $40 for the Ab Bench and $30 for the Ab Coaster. Therefore, the total manufacturing costs (excluding overhead) is $52 for the Ab Bench and $42 for the Ab Coaster, as shown in **Illustration 17.2**.

Atlas also expects to incur annual manufacturing overhead costs of $900,000. Atlas assigns overhead using a single predetermined overhead rate based on the 30,000 direct labor hours it expects to use this year. Thus, the predetermined overhead rate is $30 per direct labor hour ($900,000/30,000 direct labor hours).

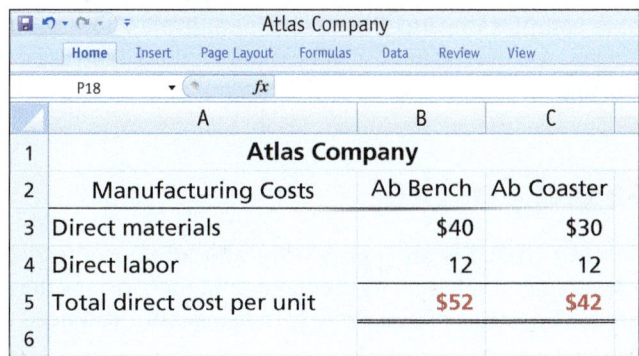

ILLUSTRATION 17.2

Direct costs per unit—traditional costing

Since both products require one direct labor hour per unit, both products are assigned overhead costs of $30 per unit under traditional costing. **Illustration 17.3** shows the total unit costs for the Ab Bench and the Ab Coaster.

ILLUSTRATION 17.3

Total unit costs—traditional costing

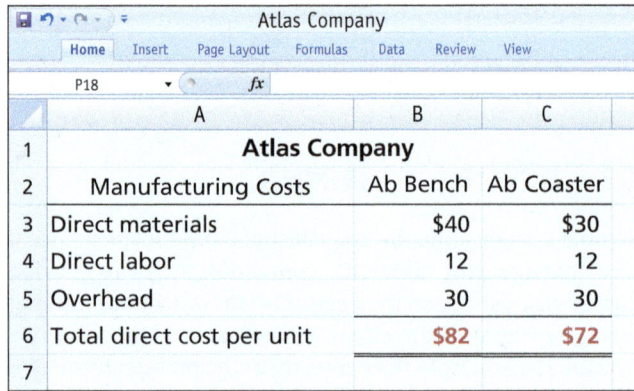

The Need for a New Approach

As shown in Illustration 17.3, Atlas assigns the same amount of overhead costs per unit to both the Ab Bench and the Ab Coaster because these two products use the same amount of direct labor hours per unit. However, using a single rate based on direct labor hours may not be the best approach for Atlas to assign its overhead.

Historically, the use of direct labor as the activity base seemed to make sense as direct labor made up a large portion of total manufacturing cost. Also, there often was a correlation between direct labor and the incurrence of overhead cost. Direct labor thus became the most popular basis for allocating overhead.

In recent years, however, manufacturers and service providers have experienced tremendous changes. Advances in computerized systems, technological innovations, global competition, and automation have altered the manufacturing environment drastically. As a result, the amount of direct labor used in many industries has greatly decreased, and total overhead costs resulting from depreciation on expensive equipment and machinery, utilities, repairs, and maintenance have significantly increased. When there is less (or no) correlation between direct labor and overhead costs incurred, plantwide predetermined overhead rates based on direct labor are misleading. Companies that use overhead rates based on direct labor when this correlation does not exist experience significant product cost distortions.

To minimize such distortions, many companies began to use machine hours instead of labor hours as the basis to assign overhead in an automated manufacturing environment. But, even machine hours may not serve as a good basis for plantwide allocation of overhead costs. For example, product design and engineering costs are not correlated with machine hours but instead with the number of different items a company produces. Companies that have complex processes need to use multiple allocation bases to compute accurate product costs. An overhead cost allocation method that uses multiple bases is **activity-based costing**.

Activity-Based Costing

Activity-based costing (ABC) is an approach for allocating overhead costs. Specifically, ABC allocates overhead to multiple activity cost pools and then assigns the activity cost pools to products and services by means of cost drivers. In using ABC, you need to understand the following concepts.

Key Concepts

Activity. Any event, action, transaction, or work sequence that incurs costs when producing a product or performing a service.

Activity cost pool. The overhead cost attributed to a distinct activity (e.g., ordering materials or setting up machines).

Cost driver. Any factor or activity that has a direct cause-effect relationship with the resources consumed.

Activity-based costing involves the following four steps, as shown in **Illustration 17.4**.

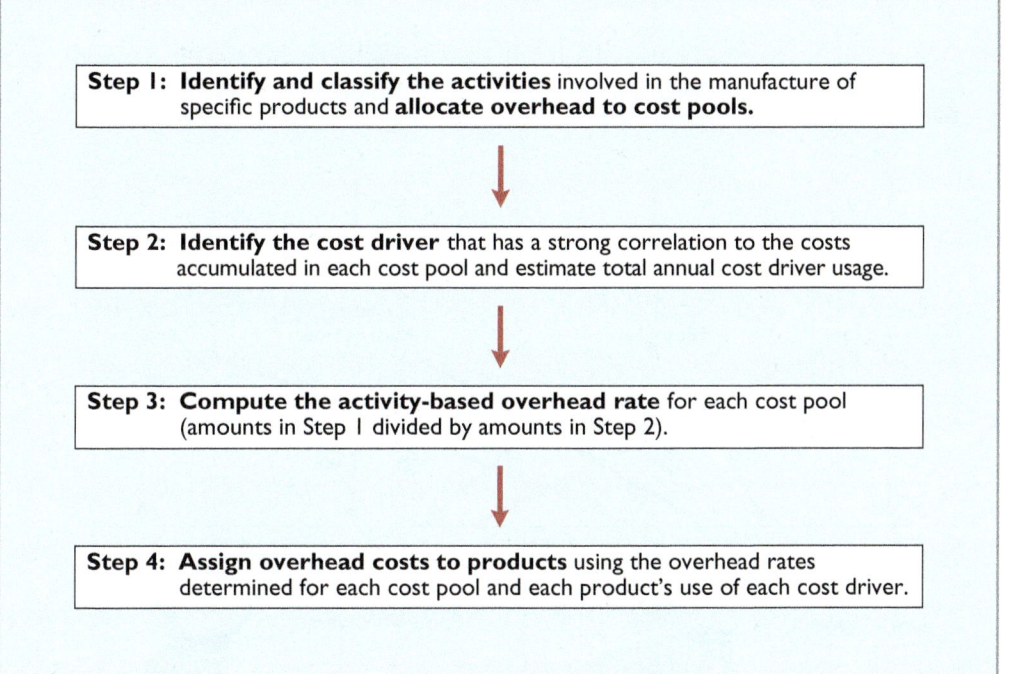

ILLUSTRATION 17.4

The four steps of activity-based costing

Step 1 allocates overhead costs to activity cost pools. (Traditional costing systems, in contrast, allocate these costs to departments or to jobs.) Examples of overhead cost pools are ordering materials, setting up machines, assembling products, and inspecting products. Steps 2–4 assign the overhead in the activity cost pools to products, using cost drivers. The cost drivers are activities undertaken to produce goods or perform services. Examples are number of purchase orders, number of setups, labor hours, and number of inspections.

Illustration 17.5 shows examples of activities, and possible cost drivers to measure them, for a company that manufactures two types of equipment—lawn mowers and snow throwers. In the first step, the company allocates overhead costs to activity cost pools. In this simplified example, the company has identified four activity cost pools: purchasing, storing, machining, and supervising. After the costs are allocated to the activity cost pools, the company uses cost drivers to determine the costs to assign to the individual products based on each product's use of each activity. For example, if lawn mowers require more activity by the purchasing department, as measured by the number of required purchase orders, then more of the overhead costs from the purchasing pool are assigned to the lawn mowers.

The more complex a product's manufacturing operation, the more activities and cost drivers it is likely to have. If there is little or no correlation between changes in the cost driver and consumption of the overhead cost, inaccurate product costs are inevitable.

ILLUSTRATION 17.5 Activities and related cost drivers

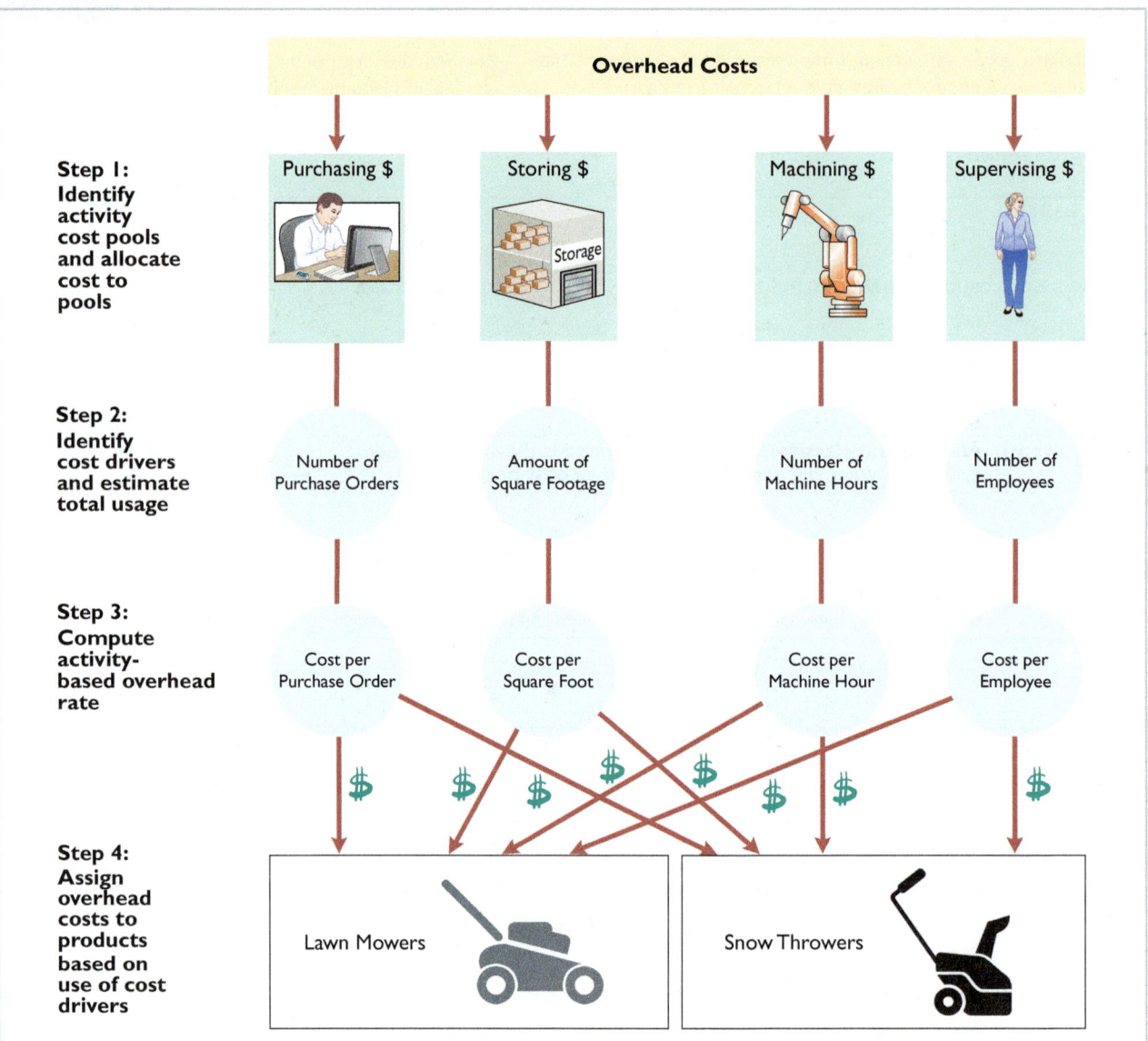

ACTION PLAN

- Understand that a traditional costing system assigns overhead on the basis of a single predetermined overhead rate.
- Understand that an ABC system allocates overhead to identified activity cost pools and then assigns costs to products using related cost drivers that measure the resources consumed.

DO IT! 1 | Costing Systems

Indicate whether the following statements are true or false.

1. A traditional costing system assigns overhead by means of multiple overhead rates.
2. Direct materials and direct labor costs are easier to trace to products than overhead.
3. As manufacturing processes have become more automated, more companies have chosen to assign overhead on the basis of direct labor costs.
4. In activity-based costing, an activity is any event, action, transaction, or work sequence that incurs cost when producing goods or performing services.

Solution

1. False.   2. True.   3. False.   4. True.

Related exercise material: **BE17.1, BE17.2, DO IT! 17.1, E17.1,** and **E17.2.**

ABC and Manufacturers

> **LEARNING OBJECTIVE 2**
> Apply activity-based costing to a manufacturer.

In this section, we present a simple case example that compares activity-based costing with traditional costing. It illustrates how ABC eliminates the cost distortions that can occur in traditional overhead cost allocation. As you study this example, you should understand that ABC does not *replace* an existing job order or process cost system. What ABC does is to segregate overhead into various cost pools in an effort to provide more accurate cost information. As a result, ABC supplements—rather than replaces—these cost systems.

Let's return to our Atlas Company example. Using the information from Illustration 17.3, we can calculate unit costs under ABC. As shown earlier in Illustration 17.4, activity-based costing involves the following four steps.

1. **Identify and classify the activities** involved in the manufacture of specific products and **allocate overhead to cost pools**.
2. **Identify the cost driver** that has a strong correlation to the costs accumulated in each cost pool and estimate total annual cost driver usage.
3. **Compute the activity-based overhead rate** for each cost pool.
4. **Assign overhead costs to products** using the overhead rates determined for each cost pool and each product's use of each cost driver.

Identify and Classify Activities and Allocate Overhead to Cost Pools (Step 1)

Activity-based costing starts with an analysis of the activities needed to manufacture a product or perform a service. This analysis should identify all resource-consuming activities. It requires documenting every activity undertaken to accomplish a task. Atlas Company identifies five activity cost pools: manufacturing, setups, purchase ordering, product development, and facility management.

Next, the company allocates overhead costs directly to the appropriate activity cost pool. For example, Atlas allocates all overhead costs directly associated with machine setups (such as salaries, supplies, and depreciation) to the setup cost pool. **Illustration 17.6** shows the five cost pools, along with the estimated overhead allocated to each cost pool. Note that the total estimated overhead is $900,000 under either traditional costing or ABC.

ILLUSTRATION 17.6
Activity cost pools and estimated overhead

Atlas Company	
Activity Cost Pools	Estimated Overhead
Manufacturing	$500,000
Setups	100,000
Purchase ordering	50,000
Product development	200,000
Facility management	50,000
Total	$900,000

Identify Cost Drivers (Step 2)

After costs are allocated to the activity cost pools, the company must identify the cost drivers for each cost pool. The cost driver must accurately measure the actual consumption of the activity by the various products. To achieve accurate costing, a **high degree of correlation** must exist between the cost driver and the actual consumption of the overhead costs in the cost pool.

Illustration 17.7 shows the cost drivers that Atlas Company identifies and their total expected use per activity cost pool. For example, the cost driver for the setup cost pool is the number of setups. A product that requires more setups will cause more setup costs to be incurred, and it therefore should be assigned more overhead costs from the setup cost pool. The total number of setups is estimated to be 2,000 for the year.

ILLUSTRATION 17.7
Cost drivers and their estimated use

Activity Cost Pools	Cost Drivers	Estimated Use of Cost Drivers per Activity
Manufacturing	Machine hours	50,000 machine hours
Setups	Number of setups	2,000 setups
Purchase ordering	Number of purchase orders	2,500 purchase orders
Product development	Products developed	2 products developed
Facility management	Square footage	25,000 square feet

Availability and ease of obtaining data relating to the cost driver is an important factor that must be considered in its selection.

Compute Activity-Based Overhead Rates (Step 3)

Next, the company computes an **activity-based overhead rate** per cost driver by dividing the estimated overhead per activity by the number of cost drivers estimated to be used per activity. This step is similar to calculating a predetermined overhead rate under the traditional costing approach except that instead of one rate for the company, there is one rate per cost pool. Illustration 17.8 shows the formula for this computation.

ILLUSTRATION 17.8
Formula for computing activity-based overhead rate

$$\frac{\text{Estimated Overhead per Activity}}{\text{Estimated Use of Cost Drivers per Activity}} = \text{Activity-Based Overhead Rate}$$

Atlas Company computes its activity-based overhead rates by using the estimated overhead per activity cost pool, shown in Illustration 17.6, and the estimated use of cost drivers per activity, shown in Illustration 17.7. These computations are presented in Illustration 17.9. For example, $100,000 was allocated to the setup pool and the estimated number of annual setups is 2,000. The activity-based rate for setups is therefore $50 per setup ($100,000 ÷ 2,000 setups).

ILLUSTRATION 17.9 Computation of activity-based overhead rates

Activity Cost Pools	Estimated Overhead	÷	Estimated Use of Cost Drivers per Activity	=	Activity-Based Overhead Rates
Manufacturing	$500,000		50,000 machine hours		$10 per machine hour
Setups	100,000		2,000 setups		$50 per setup
Purchase ordering	50,000		2,500 purchase orders		$20 per order
Product development	200,000		2 products developed		$100,000 per product
Facility management	50,000		25,000 square feet		$2 per square foot
Total	$900,000				

Assign Overhead Costs to Products (Step 4)

In allocating overhead costs, the company must know the estimated use of cost drivers **for each product**. Because of its low volume and higher number of components, the Ab Coaster requires more setups and purchase orders than the Ab Bench. **Illustration 17.10** shows the estimated use of cost drivers per product for each of Atlas Company's products. Note that of the 2,000 estimated total setups, 500 are expected to result from producing the Ab Bench and 1,500 are expected to result from the Ab Coaster.

ILLUSTRATION 17.10 Estimated use of cost drivers per product

Activity Cost Pools	Cost Drivers	Estimated Use of Cost Drivers per Activity	Estimated Use of Cost Drivers per Product	
			Ab Bench	Ab Coaster
Manufacturing	Machine hours	50,000 machine hours	30,000	20,000
Setups	Number of setups	2,000 setups	500	1,500
Purchase ordering	Number of purchase orders	2,500 purchase orders	750	1,750
Product development	Products developed	2 products developed	1	1
Facility management	Square feet	25,000 square feet	10,000	15,000

To assign overhead costs to each product, Atlas multiplies the activity-based overhead rates per cost driver (Illustration 17.9) by the number of cost drivers estimated to be used per product (Illustration 17.10). **Illustration 17.11** shows the overhead cost assigned to each product. For example, of the total of $100,000 allocated to the setup pool, $25,000 (500 setups × $50) is assigned to the Ab Bench and $75,000 (1,500 setups × $50) is assigned to the Ab Coaster.

ILLUSTRATION 17.11 Allocation of activity cost pools to products

Atlas Company

	Ab Bench			Ab Coaster		
Activity Cost Pools	Estimated Use of Cost Drivers per Product ×	Activity-Based Overhead Rates =	Cost Assigned	Estimated Use of Cost Drivers per Product ×	Activity-Based Overhead Rates =	Cost Assigned
Manufacturing	30,000	$10	$300,000	20,000	$10	$200,000
Setups	500	$50	25,000	1,500	$50	75,000
Purchase ordering	750	$20	15,000	1,750	$20	35,000
Product development	1	$100,000	100,000	1	$100,000	100,000
Facility management	10,000	$2.00	20,000	15,000	$2.00	30,000
Total costs assigned (a)			$460,000			$440,000
Units produced (b)			25,000			5,000
Overhead cost per unit [(a)÷(b)], rounded			$18.40			$88.00

Of the total overhead costs of $900,000 shown in Illustration 17.6, $460,000 was assigned to the Ab Bench and $440,000 to the Ab Coaster. Under ABC, the overhead cost per unit is $18.40 ($460,000 ÷ 25,000) for the Ab Bench and $88.00 ($440,000 ÷ 5,000) for the Ab Coaster. We see next how this per unit amount substantially differs from that computed under a traditional costing system.

Comparing Unit Costs

Illustration 17.12 compares the unit costs for Atlas Company's Ab Bench and Ab Coaster under traditional costing and ABC.

ILLUSTRATION 17.12

Comparison of unit product costs

	Ab Bench		Ab Coaster	
Manufacturing Costs	Traditional Costing	ABC	Traditional Costing	ABC
Direct materials	$40.00	$40.00	$30.00	$ 30.00
Direct labor	12.00	12.00	12.00	12.00
Overhead	30.00	18.40	30.00	88.00
Total direct cost per unit	$82.00	$70.40	$72.00	$130.00

Overstated $11.60

Understated $58.00

The comparison shows that unit costs under traditional costing are different and often misleading. Traditional costing overstates the cost of producing the Ab Bench by $11.60 per unit and understates the cost of producing the Ab Coaster by $58 per unit. These differences are attributable to how Atlas assigns manufacturing overhead across the two systems. Using a traditional costing system, each product was assigned the same amount of overhead ($30) because both products use the same amount of the cost driver (direct labor hours). In contrast, ABC assigns overhead to products based on multiple cost drivers. For example, under ABC, Atlas assigns 75% of the costs of equipment setups to Ab Coasters because Ab Coasters were responsible for 75% (1,500 ÷ 2,000) of the total number of setups.

Note that activity-based costing does not change the amount of total overhead costs. Under both traditional costing and ABC, Atlas spends the same amount of overhead—$900,000. However, ABC assigns overhead costs in a more accurate manner. Thus, ABC helps Atlas avoid some negative consequences of a traditional costing system, such as overpricing its Ab Benches and thereby possibly losing market share to competitors. Atlas has also been sacrificing profitability by underpricing the Ab Coaster.

Companies that move from traditional costing to ABC often have similar experiences as ABC shifts costs from high-volume products to low-volume products. This shift occurs because traditional overhead allocation uses volume-driven bases such as labor hours or machine hours. The traditional approach ignores the fact that many overhead costs are not correlated with volume. In addition, ABC recognizes products' use of resources, which also increases the accuracy of product costs.

Management Insight

© CGinspiration/iStockphoto

ABC Evaluated

Surveys of companies often show ABC usage of approximately 50%. Yet, in recent years, articles about ABC have expressed mixed opinions regarding its usefulness. To evaluate ABC practices and user satisfaction with ABC, a survey was conducted of 348 companies worldwide. Some of the interesting findings included the following: ABC methods are widely used across the entire value chain, rather than being primarily used to assign production-specific costs; only 25% of non-ABC companies think they are accurately tracing the costs of activities, while 70% of ABC companies think their company does this well; and respondents felt that ABC provides greater support for financial, operational, and strategic decisions. More than 87% of respondents said that their ideal costing system would include some form of ABC. Since this significantly exceeds the 50% of the respondents actually using it, ABC usage may well increase in the future.

Source: William Stratton, Denis Desroches, Raef Lawson, and Toby Hatch, "Activity-Based Costing: Is It Still Relevant?" *Management Accounting Quarterly* (Spring, 2009), pp. 31–39.

What might explain why so many companies say that ideally they would use ABC, but they haven't adopted it yet? (Go to WileyPLUS for this answer and additional questions.)

DO IT! 2 | Apply ABC to Manufacturer

Casey Company has five activity cost pools and two products. It estimates production of 200,000 units of its automobile scissors jack and 80,000 units of its truck hydraulic jack. Having identified its activity cost pools and the cost drivers for each cost pool, Casey Company accumulated the following data relative to those activity cost pools and cost drivers.

Annual Overhead Data

Activity Cost Pools	Cost Drivers	Estimated Overhead	Estimated Use of Cost Drivers per Activity	Estimated Use of Cost Drivers per Product	
				Scissors Jacks	Hydraulic Jacks
Ordering and receiving	Purchase orders	$ 200,000	2,500 orders	1,000	1,500
Machine setup	Setups	600,000	1,200 setups	500	700
Machining	Machine hours	2,000,000	800,000 hours	300,000	500,000
Assembling	Parts	1,800,000	3,000,000 parts	1,800,000	1,200,000
Inspecting and testing	Tests	700,000	35,000 tests	20,000	15,000
		$5,300,000			

Using the above data, do the following.

a. Prepare a schedule showing the computations of the activity-based overhead rates per cost driver.
b. Prepare a schedule assigning each activity's overhead cost to the two products.
c. Compute the overhead cost per unit for each product.
d. Comment on the comparative overhead cost per unit.

ACTION PLAN
- Determine the activity-based overhead rate by dividing the estimated overhead per activity by the estimated use of cost drivers per activity.

Solution

a. Computations of activity-based overhead rates per cost driver:

Activity Cost Pools	Estimated Overhead	÷	Estimated Use of Cost Drivers per Activity	=	Activity-Based Overhead Rates
Ordering and receiving	$ 200,000		2,500 purchase orders		$80 per order
Machine setup	600,000		1,200 setups		$500 per setup
Machining	2,000,000		800,000 machine hours		$2.50 per machine hour
Assembling	1,800,000		3,000,000 parts		$0.60 per part
Inspecting and testing	700,000		35,000 tests		$20 per test
	$5,300,000				

b. Assignment of each activity's overhead cost to products using ABC:

Activity Cost Pools	Scissors Jacks				Hydraulic Jacks			
	Estimated Use of Cost Drivers per Product	×	Activity-Based Overhead Rates	= Cost Assigned	Estimated Use of Cost Drivers per Product	×	Activity-Based Overhead Rates	= Cost Assigned
Ordering and receiving	1,000		$80	$ 80,000	1,500		$80	$ 120,000
Machine setup	500		$500	250,000	700		$500	350,000
Machining	300,000		$2.50	750,000	500,000		$2.50	1,250,000
Assembling	1,800,000		$0.60	1,080,000	1,200,000		$0.60	720,000
Inspecting and testing	20,000		$20	400,000	15,000		$20	300,000
Total assigned costs				$2,560,000				$2,740,000

> **ACTION PLAN**
> - Assign the overhead of each activity cost pool to the individual products by multiplying the estimated use of cost driver per product times the activity-based overhead rate.
> - Determine overhead cost per unit by dividing the overhead assigned to each product by the number of units of that product.

c. Computation of overhead cost per unit:

	Scissors Jack	Hydraulic Jack
Total costs assigned	$2,560,000	$2,740,000
Total units produced	200,000	80,000
Overhead cost per unit	$12.80	$34.25

d. These data show that the total overhead assigned to 80,000 hydraulic jacks exceeds the overhead assigned to 200,000 scissors jacks. The overhead cost per hydraulic jack is $34.25, but it is only $12.80 per scissors jack.

Related exercise material: **BE17.3, BE17.4, BE17.5, BE17.6, BE17.7, DO IT! 17.2, E17.3, E17.4, E17.5, E17.6, E17.7, and E17.8.**

ABC Benefits and Limitations

> **LEARNING OBJECTIVE 3**
> Explain the benefits and limitations of activity-based costing.

ABC has three primary benefits:

1. ABC employs more cost pools and therefore results in more accurate product costing.
2. ABC leads to enhanced control over overhead costs.
3. ABC supports better management decisions.

The Advantage of Multiple Cost Pools

The main mechanism by which ABC increases product cost accuracy is the use of multiple cost pools. Instead of one plantwide pool (or even several departmental pools) and a single cost driver, companies use numerous activity cost pools with more relevant cost drivers. Thus, costs are assigned more directly on the basis of the cost drivers used to produce each product.

Note that in the Atlas Company example, the *manufacturing* cost pool reflected multiple manufacturing activities, including machining, assembling, and painting. These activities were included in a single pool for simplicity. In many companies, the number of activities—and thus the number of pools—can be substantial. For example, **Clark-Hurth** (a division of **Clark Equipment Company**), a manufacturer of axles and transmissions, identified over 170 activities. **Compumotor** (a division of **Parker Hannifin**) identified over 80 activities in just the procurement function of its Material Control Department. **Illustration 17.13** shows a more likely "split" of the activities that were included in Atlas's manufacturing cost pool, reflecting separate pools and drivers for each of those activities.

Classification of Activity Levels

To gain the full advantage of having multiple cost pools, the costs within the pool must be correlated with the driver. To achieve this, a company's managers often characterize activities as belonging to one of the following four activity-level groups when designing an ABC system.

1. **Unit-level activities** are performed for each unit of production. For example, the assembly of cell phones is a unit-level activity because the amount of assembly the company performs increases with each additional cell phone assembled.

ILLUSTRATION 17.13 A more detailed view of Atlas's manufacturing activities

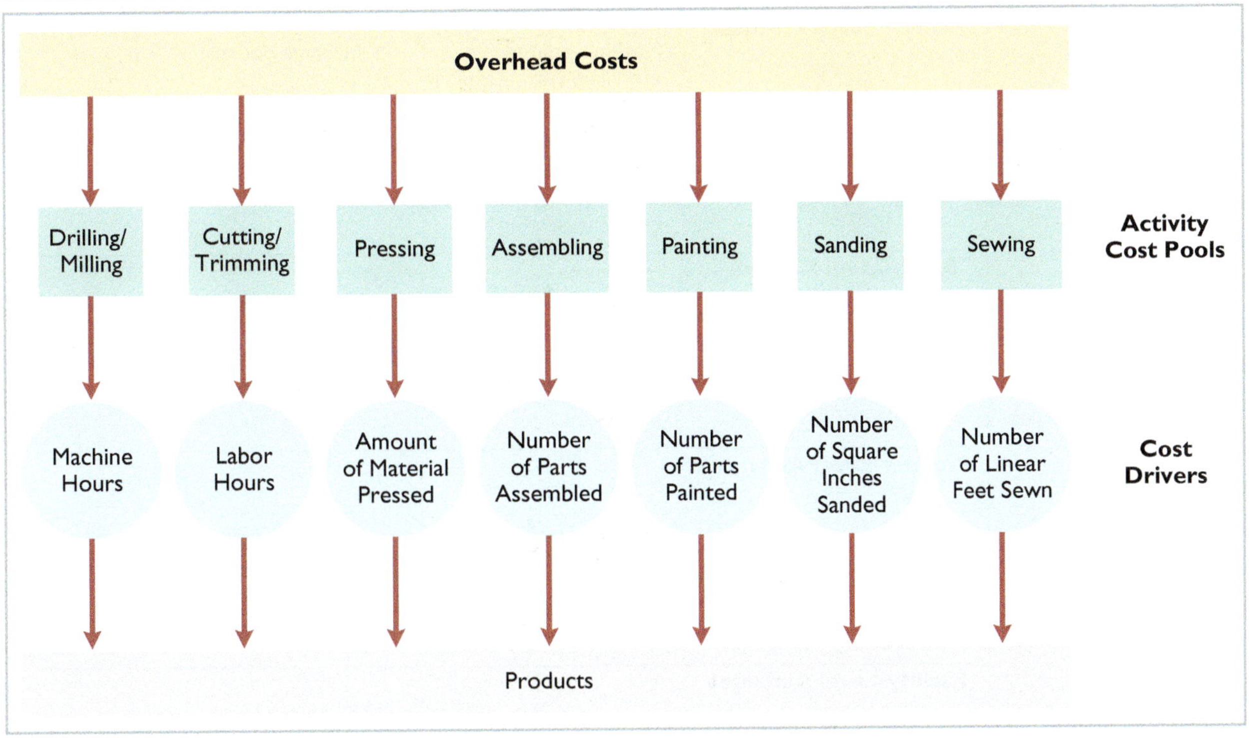

Overhead Costs

Activity Cost Pools	Cost Drivers
Drilling/Milling	Machine Hours
Cutting/Trimming	Labor Hours
Pressing	Amount of Material Pressed
Assembling	Number of Parts Assembled
Painting	Number of Parts Painted
Sanding	Number of Square Inches Sanded
Sewing	Number of Linear Feet Sewn

Products

2. **Batch-level activities** are performed every time a company produces another batch of a product. For example, suppose that to start processing a new batch of ice cream, an ice cream producer needs to set up its machines. The amount of time spent setting up and cleaning up machines increases with the number of batches produced, not with the number of units produced.
3. **Product-level activities** are performed every time a company produces a new type of product. For example, before a pharmaceutical company can produce and sell a new type of medicine, it must undergo very substantial product tests to ensure the product is effective and safe. The amount of time spent on testing activities increases with the number of products the company produces.
4. **Facility-level activities** are required to support or sustain an entire production process. Consider, for example, a hospital. The hospital building must be insured and heated, and the property taxes must be paid, no matter how many patients the hospital treats. These costs do not vary as a function of the number of units, batches, or products.

Companies may achieve greater accuracy in overhead cost allocation by recognizing these four different levels of activities and, from them, developing specific activity cost pools and their related cost drivers. **Illustration 17.14** depicts this four-level activity hierarchy, along with the types of activities and examples of cost drivers for those activities at each level.

Note that sometimes the classification of an activity will depend on the context. For example, in some circumstances, inspection is a batch-level activity that is driven by the number of batches or setups. This is because the company will have to ensure that the setup was done properly and did not cause a deviation from product specifications. However, inspection can also be a unit-level activity that is driven by the number of units produced.

The Advantage of Enhanced Cost Control

ABC leads to enhanced control over overhead costs. Under ABC, companies can trace many overhead costs directly to activities. In developing an ABC system, managers increase their awareness of the activities performed by the company in its production and supporting processes. This awareness helps managers classify activities as value-added or non-valued-added.

ILLUSTRATION 17.14

Hierarchy of activity levels

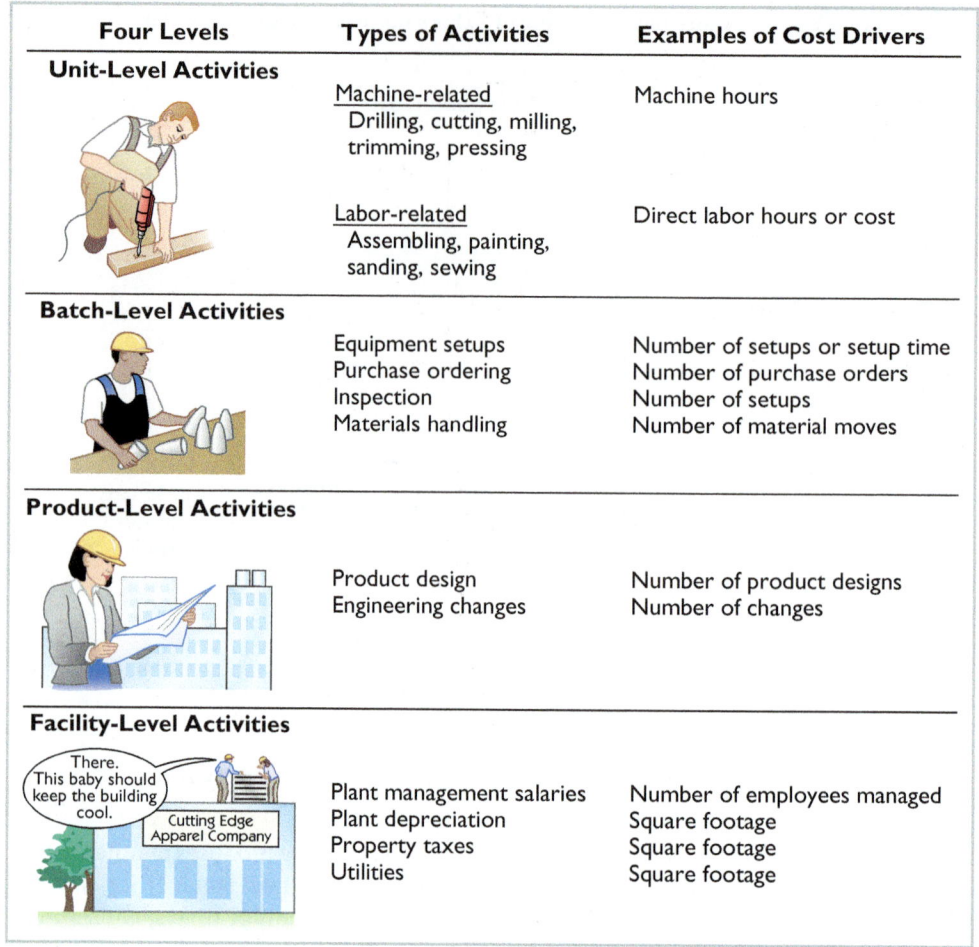

Value-added activities are those activities of **a company's operations** that increase the perceived value of a product or service to customers. Examples for the manufacture of **Precor** exercise equipment include engineering design, machining, assembly, and painting. Examples of value-added activities in a service company include performing surgery at a hospital, performing legal research at a law firm, or delivering packages by a freight company.

Non–value-added activities are those activities that, if eliminated, would not reduce the perceived value of a company's product or service. These activities simply **add cost to, or increase the time spent on, a product or service without increasing its perceived value**. One example is inventory storage. If a company **eliminated the need** to store inventory, it would not reduce the value of its product, but it would decrease its product costs. Other examples include moving materials, work in process, or finished goods from one location to another in the plant during the production process; waiting for manufacturing equipment to become available; inspecting goods; and fixing defective goods under warranty.

Companies often use **activity flowcharts** to help identify the ABC activities, such as the one shown in **Illustration 17.15** (see **Decision Tools**). The top part of this flowchart identifies activities as value-added (highlighted in red) or non–value-added. Two rows in the lower part of the flowchart show the number of days spent on each activity. The first row shows the number of days spent on each activity under the current manufacturing process. The second row shows the number of days estimated to be spent on each activity under management's proposed reengineered manufacturing process.

The proposed changes would reduce time spent on non–value-added activities by 17 days. This 17-day improvement is due entirely to moving inventory more quickly through the non–value-added processes—that is, by reducing inventory time in moving, storage, and waiting. Appendix 17A discusses a just-in-time inventory system, which some companies use to eliminate non–value-added activities related to inventory.

Not all activities labeled non–value-added are totally wasteful, nor can they be totally eliminated. For example, although inspection time is a non–value added activity from a

Decision Tools

The activity flowchart helps managers identify and reduce non–value-added activities.

ILLUSTRATION 17.15 Analyzing non–value-added activities to improve operations

Heartland Company
Activity Flowchart

					Activities							
NVA	NVA	NVA	NVA	VA		NVA	NVA	VA	NVA	NVA	NVA	VA
Receive and Inspect Materials	Move and Store Materials	Move Materials to Production and Wait	Set Up Machines	Machining		Inspect	Move and Wait	Assembly	Inspect and Test	Move to Storage	Store Finished Goods	Package and Ship
				Drill	Lathe							
Current Days 1	12	2.5	1.5	2	1	0.2	6	2	0.3	0.5	14	1

←——————————————— Total Current Average Time = 44 days ———————————————→

Proposed Days 1	4	1.5	1.5	2	1	0.2	2	2	0.3	0.5	10	1

←——————————————— Total Proposed Average Time = 27 days ———————————————→

Proposed reduction in non–value-added time = 17 days

VA = Value-added   NVA = Non–value-added

---

customer's perspective, few companies would eliminate their quality control functions. Similarly, moving and waiting time is non–value added, but it would be impossible to completely eliminate. Nevertheless, when managers recognize the non–value-added characteristic of these activities, they are motivated to minimize them as much as possible. Attention to such matters is part of the growing practice of activity-based management, which helps managers concentrate on **continuous improvement** of operations and activities.

Management Insight   General Mills

© Action Sports Photography/Shutterstock

What Does NASCAR Have to Do with Breakfast Cereal?

Often the best way to improve a process is to learn from observing a different process. Production-line technicians from food producer **General Mills** were flown to North Carolina to observe firsthand how race-car pit crews operate. In a NASCAR race, the value-added activity is driving toward the finish line; any time spent in the pit is non–value-added. Every split second saved in the pit increases the chances of winning. From what the General Mills technicians learned at the car race, as well as other efforts, they were able to reduce setup time from 5 hours to just 20 minutes.

What are the benefits of reducing setup time? (Go to WileyPLUS for this answer and additional questions.)

The Advantage of Better Management Decisions

Some companies experiencing the benefits of activity-based costing have applied it to a broader range of management activities. **Activity-based management (ABM)** extends the use of ABC from product costing to a comprehensive management tool that focuses on reducing costs and improving processes and decision-making.

Managers extend the use of ABC via ABM for both strategic and operational decisions or perspectives. For example, returning to Atlas Company, its managers might use ABC information about its Ab Benches and Ab Coasters to improve the efficiency of its operations. For example, after realizing that both products require a high volume of setup hours—as well as the costs of these hours—they might want to reduce the hours required to set up production runs. Such information may lead managers to increase the number of units produced with each setup or to optimize production schedules for the two products.

ABC also helps managers evaluate employees, departments, and business units. Atlas, for example, might use ABC information about salespeople's activities related to customer visits, number of orders, and post-sales customer service. Such information informs managers about how much effort salespeople are exerting, as well as how efficient they are in dealing with customers. Similarly, Atlas might use ABC information about each department's use of shared resources, like inventory space. Such information lets managers know which departments are the most efficient, which in turn leads to sharing best-practices information within the company. ABC information also helps Atlas to establish **performance standards** within the company, as well as **benchmark** its performance against other companies.

The implications of ABC are not limited to operational decisions. The differences in profitability between the Ab Benches and Ab Coasters may suggest a need to change the company's product mix. Such considerations, in turn, have implications for Atlas's marketing strategy. ABM may guide managers in considering different target customer markets for the two products. Or, managers might consider bundling the two products into a "home gym" set. As another, more extreme, example, managers might consider outsourcing production for one of the products or dropping one of the product lines altogether.

It is often the case that ABM for one perspective has implications for another perspective. For instance, the strategic decision to drop a product line is usually followed by operational decisions regarding what to do with employees' time or the machinery and equipment originally used to manufacture the dropped product. Similarly, increases in employees' efficiency following from operational decisions often lead to changes in employee hiring and compensation strategy. The interrelated nature of the strategic and operational perspectives often means that a decision is not made until the cascading implications of that decision are also identified and considered.

Some Limitations and Knowing When to Use ABC

ABC can be very beneficial, but it is not without its limitations.

1. **ABC can be expensive to use.** The increased cost of identifying multiple activities and applying numerous cost drivers discourages many companies from using ABC.
2. **ABC systems are more complex than traditional systems.**
3. **Some arbitrary allocations remain.** Even though more overhead costs can be assigned directly to products through ABC, some overhead costs might still be assigned by fairly arbitrary cost drivers. For example, Atlas Company allocated $50,000 of overhead pertaining to insurance and property taxes to the facility management cost pool. Atlas assigned this $50,000 using square footage used by each product (10,000 square feet for Ab Benches and 15,000 square feet for Ab Coasters). A more accurate driver of insurance costs might be replacement costs of production equipment for each product type. However, such information may not be readily available, and Atlas must make do with square footage.

So companies must ask, is the cost of implementation greater than the benefit of greater accuracy? For some companies, there may be no need to consider ABC at all because their existing system is sufficient.

In light of these limitations, how does a company know when to use ABC? The presence of one or more of the following factors would point to possible use:

1. Product lines differ greatly in volume and manufacturing complexity.
2. Product lines are numerous and diverse, requiring various degrees of support services.
3. Overhead costs constitute a significant portion of total costs.
4. The manufacturing process or the number of products has changed significantly, for example, from labor-intensive to capital-intensive due to automation.
5. Production or marketing managers are ignoring data provided by the existing system and are instead using "bootleg" costing data or other alternative data when pricing or making other product decisions.

Ultimately, it is important to realize that the redesign and installation of a product costing system is a significant decision that requires considerable costs and a major effort to accomplish (see **Decision Tools**). Therefore, financial managers need to be cautious and deliberate when initiating changes in costing systems, giving careful consideration to the relative costs and benefits. A key factor in implementing a successful ABC system is the support of top management, especially given that the benefits of ABC are not completely visible until *after* it has been implemented.

> **Decision Tools**
> Companies replace traditional costing with ABC when ABC provides more accurate information at a reasonable cost.

DO IT! 3 | Classify Activity Levels

Morgan Toy Company manufactures six primary product lines of toys in its Morganville plant. As a result of an activity analysis, the accounting department has identified eight activity cost pools. Each of the toy products is produced in large batches, with the whole plant devoted to one product at a time. Classify each of the following activities as either unit-level, batch-level, product-level, or facility-level: (a) engineering design, (b) machine setup, (c) toy design, (d) interviews of prospective employees, (e) inspections after each setup, (f) polishing parts, (g) assembling parts, and (h) health and safety.

ACTION PLAN
- You should use unit-level activities for each unit of product, batch-level activities for each batch of product, product-level activities for an entire product line, and facility-level activities for across the entire range of products.

Solution
a. Product-level. b. Batch-level. c. Product-level. d. Facility-level. e. Batch-level.
f. Unit-level. g. Unit-level. h. Facility-level.

Related exercise material: **BE17.10, BE17.11, BE17.12, DO IT! 17.3, E17.12,** and **E17.3**.

ABC and Service Industries

LEARNING OBJECTIVE 4
Apply activity-based costing to service industries.

Although initially developed and implemented by manufacturers, activity-based costing has been widely adopted in service industries as well. ABC is used by airlines, railroads, hotels, hospitals, banks, insurance companies, telephone companies, and financial services firms. The overall objective of ABC in service firms is no different than it is in a manufacturing company. That objective is to identify the key activities that generate costs and to keep track of how many of those activities are completed for each service performed (by job, service, contract, or customer).

The general approach to identifying activities, activity cost pools, and cost drivers is the same for service companies and for manufacturers. Also, the labeling of activities as value-added and non–value-added, and the attempt to reduce or eliminate non–value-added activities as much as possible, is just as valid in service industries as in manufacturing operations. What sometimes makes implementation of activity-based costing difficult in service industries is that, compared to manufacturers, **a larger proportion of overhead costs are company-wide costs** that cannot be easily traced to specific services performed by the company.

To illustrate the application of activity-based costing to a service company contrasted to traditional costing, we use a public accounting firm. This illustration is applicable to any service firm that performs numerous services for a client as part of a job, such as a law firm, consulting firm, or architect.

Traditional Costing Example

Assume that the public accounting firm of Check and Doublecheck prepares the condensed annual budget shown in **Illustration 17.16**. The firm engages in a number of services, including audit, tax, and computer consulting.

ILLUSTRATION 17.16
Condensed annual budget of a service firm under traditional costing

Check and Doublecheck, CPAs
Annual Budget

Revenue		$4,000,000
Direct labor	$1,200,000	
Overhead (estimated)	600,000	
Total costs		1,800,000
Operating income		$2,200,000

$$\frac{\text{Estimated overhead}}{\text{Direct labor cost}} = \text{Predetermined overhead rate}$$

$$\frac{\$600,000}{\$1,200,000} = 50\%$$

Direct labor is often the professional service performed. Under traditional costing, direct labor is the basis for overhead application to each job. As shown in Illustration 17.16, the predetermined overhead rate of 50% is calculated by dividing the total estimated overhead cost by the total direct labor cost. To determine the operating income earned on any job, Check and Doublecheck applies overhead at the rate of 50% of actual direct professional labor costs incurred. For example, assume that Check and Doublecheck records $140,000 of actual direct professional labor cost during its audit of Plano Molding Company, which was billed an audit fee of $260,000. Under traditional costing, using 50% as the rate for applying overhead to the job, Check and Doublecheck would compute applied overhead and operating income related to the Plano Molding Company audit as shown in **Illustration 17.17**.

ILLUSTRATION 17.17
Overhead applied under traditional costing system

Check and Doublecheck, CPAs
Plano Molding Company Audit

Revenue		$260,000
Less: Direct professional labor	$140,000	
Applied overhead (50% × $140,000)	70,000	210,000
Operating income		$ 50,000

This example, under traditional costing, uses only one cost driver (direct labor cost) to determine the overhead application rate.

Activity-Based Costing Example

Under *activity-based costing*, Check and Doublecheck distributes its estimated annual overhead costs of $600,000 to three activity cost pools. The firm computes activity-based overhead rates per cost driver by dividing the amount allocated to each activity overhead cost pool by the estimated number of cost drivers used per activity. **Illustration 17.18** shows an annual overhead budget using an ABC system.

ILLUSTRATION 17.18 Condensed annual budget of a service firm under activity-based costing

Check and Doublecheck, CPAs
Annual Overhead Budget

Activity Cost Pools	Cost Drivers	Estimated Overhead	÷	Estimated Use of Cost Drivers per Activity	=	Activity-Based Overhead Rates
Administration	Number of partner-hours	$335,000		3,350		$100 per partner-hour
Customer development	Revenue billed	160,000		$4,000,000		$0.04 per $1 of revenue
Recruiting and training	Direct professional hours	105,000		30,000		$3.50 per hour
		$600,000				

The assignment of the individual overhead activity rates to the actual number of activities used in the performance of the Plano Molding Company audit results in total overhead assigned of $57,200, as shown in **Illustration 17.19**.

ILLUSTRATION 17.19 Assigning overhead in a service company

Check and Doublecheck, CPAs
Plano Molding Company Audit

Activity Cost Pools	Cost Drivers	Actual Use of Drivers	Activity-Based Overhead Rates	Cost Assigned
Administration	Number of partner-hours	335	$100.00	$33,500
Customer development	Revenue billed	$260,000	$0.04	10,400
Recruiting and training	Direct professional hours	3,800	$3.50	13,300
				$57,200

Under activity-based costing, Check and Doublecheck assigns overhead costs of $57,200 to the Plano Molding Company audit, as compared to $70,000 under traditional costing. **Illustration 17.20** compares total costs and operating margins under the two costing systems.

ILLUSTRATION 17.20 Comparison of traditional costing with ABC in a service company

Check and Doublecheck, CPAs
Plano Molding Company Audit

	Traditional Costing		ABC	
Revenue		$260,000		$260,000
Expenses				
Direct professional labor	$140,000		$140,000	
Applied overhead	70,000		57,200	
Total expenses		210,000		197,200
Operating income		$ 50,000		$ 62,800
Profit margin		19.2%		24.2%

Illustration 17.20 shows that the assignment of overhead costs under traditional costing and ABC is different. The total cost assigned to performing the audit of Plano Molding Company is greater under traditional costing by $12,800 ($70,000 − $57,200), and the profit margin is significantly lower. Traditional costing understates the profitability of the audit.

Service Company Insight American Airlines

Traveling Light

Oleksiy Maksymenko-Photography/Alamy

Have you flown on **American Airlines** since baggage fees have been implemented? Did the fee make you so mad that you swore that the next time you flew, you would pack fewer clothes so you could use a carry-on bag instead? That is exactly how American Airlines (and the other airlines that charge baggage fees) hoped that you would react. Baggage handling is extremely labor-intensive. All that tagging, sorting, loading on carts, loading in planes, unloading, and sorting again add up to about $9 per bag. Baggage handling also involves equipment costs: sorters, carts, conveyors, tractors, and storage facilities. That's about another $4 of equipment-related overhead per bag. Finally, there is the additional fuel cost of a 40-pound item—about $2 in fuel for a 3-hour flight. These costs add up to $15 ($9 + $4 + $2).

Since airlines have implemented their baggage fees, fewer customers are checking bags. Not only does this save the airlines money, it also increases the amount of space available for hauling cargo. An airline can charge at least $80 for hauling a small parcel for same-day delivery service.

For those bags that do still get checked-in by customers, **Alaska Airlines** has reduced its costs by employing barcode scanning of every bag that goes on and off a plane to speed up its sorting process.

Source: Scott McCartney, "What It Costs an Airline to Fly Your Luggage," *Wall Street Journal* (November 25, 2008); and Scott McCartney, "The Best and Worst Airlines of 2016" *Wall Street Journal* (January 11, 2017).

Why do airlines charge even higher rates for heavier bags, bags that are odd shapes (e.g., ski bags), and bags with hazardous materials in them? (Go to WileyPLUS for this answer and additional questions.)

ACTION PLAN
- Divide the estimated overhead by the estimated use of cost driver per activity to determine activity-based overhead rate.
- Apply the activity-based overhead rate to jobs based on actual use of drivers.

DO IT! 4 | Apply ABC to Service Company

We Carry It, Inc. is a trucking company. It provides local, short-haul, and long-haul services. The company has developed the following three cost pools.

Activity Cost Pools	Cost Drivers	Estimated Overhead	Estimated Use of Cost Drivers per Activity
Loading and unloading	Number of pieces	$ 70,000	100,000 pieces
Travel	Miles driven	250,000	500,000 miles
Logistics	Hours	60,000	2,000 hours

a. Compute the activity-based overhead rate for each pool.
b. Determine the overhead assigned to Job A1027 which has 150 pieces, requires 200 miles of driving, and 0.75 hours of logistics.

Solution

a. The activity based overhead rates are as follows.

Activity Cost Pools	Estimated Overhead	÷	Estimated Use of Cost Drivers per Activity	=	Activity-Based Overhead Rate
Loading and unloading	$ 70,000		100,000 pieces		$0.70 per piece
Travel	250,000		500,000 miles		$0.50 per mile
Logistics	60,000		2,000 hours		$30 per hour

b. The overhead applied to job A1027 is (150 × $0.70) + (200 × $0.50) + (0.75 × $30) = $227.50

Related exercise material: **BE17.12, DO IT! 17.4, E17.14, E17.15, and E17.17.**

USING THE DECISION TOOLS | Precor

Precor faces many situations where it needs to apply the decision tools learned in this chapter. As mentioned in the Feature Story, Precor manufactures a line of high-end exercise equipment of commercial quality. Assume that the chief accountant has proposed changing from a traditional costing system to an activity-based costing system. The financial vice president is not convinced, so she requests that the next large order for equipment be costed under both systems for purposes of comparison and analysis. A new order from Slim-Way Salons, Inc. for 150 low-impact treadmills is identified as the test case. The following cost data relate to the Slim-Way order.

Data relevant to both costing systems

Direct materials	$55,500
Direct labor hours	820
Direct labor rate per hour	$ 18.00

Data relevant to the traditional costing system
Predetermined overhead rate is 300% of direct labor cost.

Data relevant to the activity-based costing system

Activity Cost Pools	Cost Drivers	Activity-Based Overhead Rate	Estimated Use of Cost Drivers for Treadmill Order
Engineering design	Engineering hours	$30 per hour	330
Machine setup	Setups	$200 per setup	22
Machining	Machine hours	$25 per hour	732
Assembly	Number of subassemblies	$8 per subassembly	1,500
Packaging and shipping	Packaging/shipping hours	$15 per hour	152
Building occupancy	Machine hours	$6 per hour	732

Instructions
Compute the total cost of the Slim-Way Salons, Inc. order under (a) the traditional costing system and (b) the activity-based costing system. (c) Evaluate the results.

Solution

a. Traditional costing system:

Direct materials		$ 55,500
Direct labor (820 × $18)		14,760
Overhead assigned ($14,760 × 300%)		44,280
Total costs assigned to Slim-Way order		$114,540
Number of low-impact treadmills		150
Cost per unit		$ 763.60

b. Activity-based costing system:

Direct materials		$ 55,500
Direct labor (820 × $18)		14,760
Overhead activities costs:		
Engineering design (330 hours @ $30)	$ 9,900	
Machine setup (22 setups @ $200)	4,400	
Machining (732 machine hours @ $25)	18,300	
Assembly (1,500 subassemblies @ $8)	12,000	
Packaging and shipping (152 hours @ $15)	2,280	
Building occupancy (732 hours @ $6)	4,392	51,272
Total costs assigned to Slim-Way order		$121,532
Number of low-impact treadmills		150
Cost per unit		$ 810.21

c. Precor will likely adopt ABC because of the difference in the cost per unit (which ABC found to be higher). More importantly, ABC provides greater insight into the sources and causes of the cost per unit. Managers are given greater insight into which activities to control in order to reduce costs. ABC will provide better product costing and greater profitability for the company.

Appendix 17A Just-in-Time Processing

> **LEARNING OBJECTIVE *5**
> Explain just-in-time (JIT) processing.

Traditionally, continuous process manufacturing has been based on a **just-in-case** philosophy: Inventories of raw materials are maintained *just in case* some items are of poor quality or a key supplier is shut down by a strike. Similarly, subassembly parts are manufactured and stored *just in case* they are needed later in the manufacturing process. Finished goods are completed and stored *just in case* unexpected and rush customer orders are received. This philosophy often results in a **"push approach,"** in which raw materials and subassembly parts are pushed through each process. Traditional processing often results in the buildup of extensive manufacturing inventories.

Primarily in response to foreign competition, many U.S. firms have switched to **just-in-time (JIT) processing**. JIT manufacturing is dedicated to having the right amount of materials, parts, or products just as they are needed. JIT first hit the United States in the early 1980s when automobile companies adopted it to compete with foreign automakers. Many companies, including **Dell**, **Caterpillar**, and **Harley-Davidson**, now successfully use JIT. Under JIT processing, companies receive raw materials **just in time** for use in production, they complete subassembly parts **just in time** for use in finished goods, and they complete finished goods **just in time** to be sold. Illustration 17A.1 shows the sequence of activities in just-in-time processing.

ILLUSTRATION 17A.1 Just-in-time processing

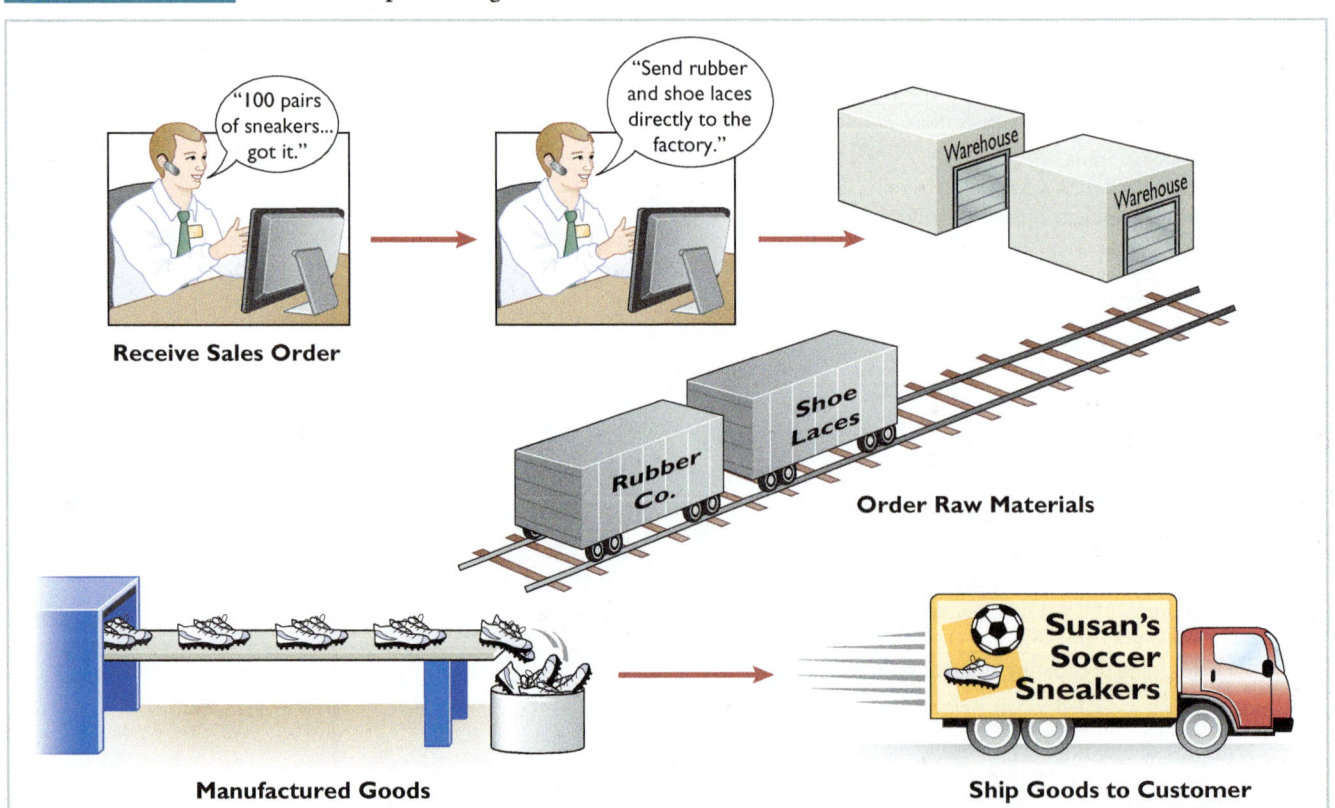

Objective of JIT Processing

An ultimate objective of JIT is to eliminate manufacturing inventories. Inventories have an adverse effect on net income because they tie up funds and storage space that could be put to more productive uses. JIT strives to eliminate inventories by using a "**pull approach**" in manufacturing. This approach begins with the customer placing an order with the company, which starts the process of pulling the product through the manufacturing process. A computer at the final workstation sends a signal to the preceding workstation. This signal indicates the exact materials (parts and subassemblies) needed to complete the production of a specified product for a specified time period, such as an eight-hour shift. The next-preceding process, in turn, sends its signal to other processes back up the line. The goal is a smooth continuous flow in the manufacturing process, with no buildup of inventories at any point.

Elements of JIT Processing

There are three important elements in JIT processing:

1. **Dependable suppliers.** Suppliers must be willing to deliver on short notice exact quantities of raw materials according to precise quality specifications (even including multiple deliveries within the same day) (see **Helpful Hint**). Suppliers must also be willing to deliver the raw materials at specified workstations rather than at a central receiving department. This type of purchasing requires constant and direct communication. Such communication is facilitated by an online computer linkage between the company and its suppliers.

2. **A multiskilled work force.** Under JIT, machines are often strategically grouped into work cells or workstations. Much of the work is automated. As a result, one worker may operate and maintain several different types of machines.

3. **A total quality control system.** The company must establish total quality control throughout the manufacturing operations (see **Helpful Hint**). Total quality control means **no defects**. Since the pull approach signals only required quantities, any defects at any workstation will shut down operations at subsequent workstations. Total quality control requires continuous monitoring by both line employees and supervisors at each workstation.

> **HELPFUL HINT**
> Buyer leverage is important in finding dependable suppliers. Companies like **GM** and **GE** have more success than smaller companies.

> **HELPFUL HINT**
> Without its emphasis on quality control, JIT would be impractical or even impossible. In JIT, quality is engineered into the production process.

Benefits of JIT Processing

The major benefits of implementing JIT processing are as follows.

1. Significant reduction or elimination of manufacturing inventories.
2. Enhanced product quality.
3. Reduction or elimination of rework costs and inventory storage costs.
4. Production cost savings from the improved flow of goods through the processes.

The effects in many cases have been dramatic. For example, after using JIT for two years, a major division of **Hewlett-Packard** found that work in process inventories (in dollars) were down 82%, scrap/rework costs were down 30%, space utilization improved by 40%, and labor efficiency improved 50%. As indicated, JIT not only reduces inventory but also enables a company to manufacture a better product faster and with less waste.

One of the major accounting benefits of JIT is the elimination of separate raw materials and work in process inventory accounts. These accounts are replaced by **one account**, Raw and In-Process Inventory. All materials and conversion costs are charged to this account. The reduction (or elimination) of in-process inventories results in a simpler computation of equivalent units of production.

A significant potential downside of JIT is the higher risk of not having materials when they are needed. As noted above, JIT requires dependable suppliers. But even dependable suppliers cannot overcome unexpected situations, such as natural disasters, that disrupt the supply chain.

Review and Practice

Learning Objectives Review

1 Discuss the difference between traditional costing and activity-based costing.

A traditional costing system assigns overhead to products on the basis of predetermined plantwide or departmentwide rates such as direct labor or machine hours. An ABC system allocates overhead to identified activity cost pools and then assigns costs to products using related cost drivers that measure the activities (resources) consumed.

The development of an activity-based costing system involves the following four steps. (1) Identify and classify the major activities involved in the manufacture of specific products and allocate overhead to cost pools. (2) Identify the cost driver that has a strong correlation to the costs accumulated in each cost pool and estimate total annual cost driver usage. (3) Compute the activity-based overhead rate for each cost pool. (4) Assign overhead costs to products using the overhead rates determined for each cost pool and each product's use of each cost driver.

2 Apply activity-based costing to a manufacturer.

To identify activity cost pools, a company must perform an analysis of each operation or process, documenting and timing every task, action, or transaction. Cost drivers identified for assigning activity cost pools must (a) accurately measure the actual consumption of the activity by the various products and (b) have related data easily available. The overhead allocated to each activity cost pool is divided by the estimated use of cost drivers to determine the activity-based overhead rate for each pool. Overhead is assigned to products by multiplying a particular product's estimated use of a cost driver by the activity-based overhead rate. This is done for each activity cost pool and then summed.

3 Explain the benefits and limitations of activity-based costing.

Features of ABC that make it a more accurate product costing system include (1) the increased number of cost pools used to assign overhead (including use of the activity-level hierarchy), (2) the enhanced control over overhead costs (including identification of non–value-added activities), and (3) the better management decisions it makes possible. The limitations of ABC are (1) the higher analysis and measurement costs that accompany multiple activity centers and cost drivers, and (2) the necessity still to assign some costs arbitrarily.

4 Apply activity-based costing to service industries.

The overall objective of using ABC in service industries is no different than for manufacturing industries—that is, improved costing of services performed (by job, service, contract, or customer). The general approach to costing is the same: analyze operations, identify activities, accumulate overhead costs by activity cost pools, and identify and use cost drivers to assign the cost pools to the services.

*5 Explain just-in-time (JIT) processing.

JIT is a processing system dedicated to having on hand the right materials and products just at the time they are needed, thereby reducing the amount of inventory and the time inventory is held. One of the principal accounting effects is that one account, Raw and In-Process Inventory, replaces both the raw materials and work in process inventory accounts.

Decision Tools Review

Decision Checkpoints	Info Needed for Decision	Tool to Use for Decision	How to Evaluate Results
How can activity-based management help managers?	Activities classified as value-added and non–value-added	Activity flowchart	The flowchart should motivate managers to minimize non–value-added activities. Managers should better understand the relationship between activities and the resources they consume.
When should we use ABC?	Knowledge of the products or product lines, the manufacturing process, and overhead costs	A detailed and accurate cost accounting system; cooperation between accountants and operating managers	Compare the results under both costing systems. If managers are better able to understand and control their operations using ABC and the costs are not prohibitive, the use of ABC would be beneficial.

Glossary Review

Activity Any event, action, transaction, or work sequence that incurs costs when producing a product or performing a service. (p. 17-5).

Activity-based costing (ABC) A costing system that allocates overhead to multiple activity cost pools and assigns the activity cost pools to products or services by means of cost drivers. (p. 17-4).

Activity-based management (ABM) Extends ABC from product costing to a comprehensive management tool that focuses on reducing costs and improving processes and decision-making. (p. 17-15).

Activity cost pool The overhead cost attributed to a distinct type of activity or related activities. (p. 17-5).

Batch-level activities Activities performed for each batch of products rather than for each unit. (p. 17-13).

Cost driver Any factor or activity that has a direct cause–effect relationship with the resources consumed. In ABC, cost drivers are used to assign activity cost pools to products or services. (p. 17-5).

Facility-level activities Activities required to support or sustain an entire production process. (p. 17-13).

*__Just-in-time (JIT) processing__ A processing system dedicated to having the right amount of materials, parts, or products arrive as they are needed, thereby reducing the amount of inventory. (p. 17-22).

Non–value-added activity An activity that, if eliminated, would not reduce the perceived value of a company's product or service. (p. 17-14).

Product-level activities Activities performed in support of an entire product line but not always performed every time a new unit or batch of products is produced. (p. 17-13).

Unit-level activities Activities performed for each unit of production. (p. 17-12).

Value-added activity An activity that increases the perceived value of a product or service to a customer. (p. 17-14).

Practice Multiple-Choice Questions

1. **(LO 1)** Activity-based costing (ABC):
   a. can be used only in a process cost system.
   b. focuses on units of production.
   c. focuses on activities needed to produce a good or perform a service.
   d. uses only a single basis of allocation.

2. **(LO 1)** Activity-based costing:
   a. is the initial phase of converting to a just-in-time operating environment.
   b. can be used only in a job order costing system.
   c. is a two-stage overhead cost allocation system that identifies activity cost pools and cost drivers.
   d. uses direct labor as its primary cost driver.

3. **(LO 1)** Any activity that causes resources to be consumed is called a:
   a. just-in-time activity.
   b. facility-level activity.
   c. cost driver.
   d. non–value-added activity.

4. **(LO 2)** Which of the following would be the **best** cost driver for the assembling cost pool?
   a. Number of product lines.
   b. Number of parts.
   c. Number of orders.
   d. Amount of square footage.

5. **(LO 2)** The overhead rate for machine setups is $100 per setup. Products A and B have 80 and 60 setups, respectively. The overhead assigned to each product is:
   a. Product A $8,000, Product B $8,000.
   b. Product A $8,000, Product B $6,000.
   c. Product A $6,000, Product B $6,000.
   d. Product A $6,000, Product B $8,000.

6. **(LO 2)** Donna Crawford Co. has identified an activity cost pool to which it has allocated estimated overhead of $1,920,000. It has estimated use of cost drivers for that activity to be 160,000 inspections. Widgets require 40,000 inspections, gadgets 30,000 inspections, and targets 90,000 inspections. The overhead assigned to each product is:
   a. Widgets $40,000, gadgets $30,000, targets $90,000.
   b. Widgets $640,000, gadgets $640,000, targets $640,000.
   c. Widgets $360,000, gadgets $480,000, targets $1,080,000.
   d. Widgets $480,000, gadgets $360,000, targets $1,080,000.

7. **(LO 3)** A frequently cited limitation of activity-based costing is:
   a. ABC results in more cost pools being used to assign overhead costs to products.
   b. certain overhead costs remain to be assigned by means of some arbitrary volume-based cost driver such as labor or machine hours.
   c. ABC leads to poorer management decisions.
   d. ABC results in less control over overhead costs.

8. **(LO 3)** A company should consider using ABC if:
   a. overhead costs constitute a small portion of total product costs.
   b. it has only a few product lines that require similar degrees of support services.
   c. direct labor constitutes a significant part of the total product cost and a high correlation exists between direct labor and changes in overhead costs.
   d. its product lines differ greatly in volume and manufacturing complexity.

9. (LO 3) An activity that adds costs to the product but does not increase its perceived value is a:

a. value-added activity.
b. cost driver.
c. cost/benefit activity.
d. non–value-added activity.

10. (LO 3) The following activity is value-added:

a. storage of raw materials.
b. moving parts from machine to machine.
c. producing a necessary product component on a machine.
d. All of the above.

11. (LO 3) A relevant facility-level cost driver for heating costs is:

a. machine hours.
b. direct materials.
c. floor space.
d. direct labor cost.

12. (LO 4) The first step in the development of an activity-based costing system for a service company is:

a. identify and classify activities and allocate overhead to cost pools.
b. assign overhead costs to products.
c. identify cost drivers.
d. compute overhead rates.

*13. (LO 5) Under just-in-time processing:

a. raw materials are received just in time for use in production.
b. subassembly parts are completed just in time for use in assembling finished goods.
c. finished goods are completed just in time to be sold.
d. All of the above.

*14. (LO 5) The primary objective of just-in-time processing is to:

a. accumulate overhead in activity cost pools.
b. eliminate or reduce all manufacturing inventories.
c. identify relevant activity cost drivers.
d. identify value-added activities.

Solutions

1. c. Focusing on activities needed to produce a good or perform a service is an accurate statement about activity-based costing. The other choices are incorrect because ABC (a) can be used in either a process cost or a job order cost system; (b) focuses on activities performed to produce a product, not on units of production; and (d) uses multiple bases of allocation, not just a single basis of allocation.

2. c. ABC is a two-stage overhead cost allocation system that identifies activity cost pools and cost drivers. The other choices are incorrect because ABC (a) is not necessarily part of the conversion to a just-in-time operating environment, (b) can be used in either a process cost or a job order cost system, and (d) uses other activities in addition to direct labor as cost drivers.

3. c. Activities that cause resources to be consumed are called cost drivers, not (a) just-in-time activities, (b) facility-level activities, or (d) non–value-added activities.

4. b. The number of parts would be the best cost driver for the assembling cost pool as it has a higher degree of correlation with the actual consumption of the overhead costs, that is, the assembling of parts, than (a) number of product lines, (c) number of orders, or (d) amount of square footage.

5. b. The overhead assigned to Product A is $8,000 ($100 × 80) and to Product B is $6,000 ($100 × 60), not (a) $8,000, $8,000; (c) $6,000, $6,000; or (d) $6,000, $8,000.

6. d. The overhead assigned to widgets is $480,000 [($1,920,000 ÷ 160,000) × 40,000], to gadgets is $360,000 [($1,920,000 ÷ 160,000) × 30,000], and to targets is $1,080,000 [($1,920,000 ÷ 160,000) × 90,000]. Therefore, choices (a) $40,000, $30,000, and $90,000; (b) $640,000, $640,000, and $640,000; and (c) $360,000, $480,000, and $1,080,000 are incorrect.

7. b. A limitation of ABC is that certain overhead costs remain to be assigned by means of some arbitrary volume-based cost driver. The other choices are incorrect because (a) more cost pools is an advantage of ABC, (c) ABC can lead to better management decisions, and (d) ABC results in more control over overhead costs.

8. d. A company should consider using ABC if its product lines differ greatly in volume and manufacturing complexity. For choices (a), (b), and (c), a traditional costing system should be sufficient and less expensive to implement.

9. d. Non–value-added activities add costs to a product but do not increase its perceived value, not (a) value-added activities, (b) cost drivers, or (c) cost/benefit activities.

10. c. Producing a necessary product component on a machine is a value-added activity as it is an integral part of manufacturing a product. Choices (a) and (b) are non–value-added activities, so therefore choice (d) is incorrect as well.

11. c. Floor space is a relevant facility-level cost driver for heating costs as a larger space will result in higher heating costs. The other choices are incorrect because (a) machine hours, (b) direct materials, and (d) direct labor cost are all unit-level cost drivers.

12. a. The first step in developing an ABC system is to identify and classify activities and allocate overhead to cost pools. The other choices are incorrect because (b) is Step 4, (c) is Step 2, and (d) is Step 3.

*13. d. All of the choices are accurate statements about just-in-time processing.

*14. b. Eliminating or reducing all manufacturing inventories is the primary objective of just-in-time processing. The other choices are incorrect because choices (a), (c), and (d) are part of the process of implementing an ABC system.

Practice Brief Exercises

1. (LO 2) Franco Company identifies three activities in its manufacturing process: machine setups, machining, and inspections. Estimated annual overhead cost for each activity is $280,000, $140,000, and $39,000, respectively. The cost driver for each activity and the estimated annual usage are number of setups 1,400, machine hours 7,000, and number of inspections 1,300. Compute the overhead rate for each activity.

Compute activity-based overhead rates.

Solution
1.

Machine setups	$280,000 ÷ 1,400 = $200 per setup
Machining	$140,000 ÷ 7,000 = $20 per machine hour
Inspections	$ 39,000 ÷ 1,300 = $30 per inspection

2. (LO 2) Dodge Inc. uses activity-based costing as the basis for information to set prices for its six lines of seasonal coats. Compute the activity-based overhead rates using the following budgeted data for each of the activity cost pools.

Compute activity-based overhead rates.

Activity Cost Pools	Estimated Overhead	Estimated Use of Cost Drivers per Activity
Designing	$ 300,000	6,000 designer hours
Sizing and cutting	3,000,000	150,000 machine hours
Stitching and trimming	1,200,000	40,000 labor hours
Wrapping and packing	420,000	28,000 finished units

Solution
2.

Activity Cost Pool	Estimated Overhead	÷	Expected Use of Cost Drivers per Activity	=	Activity-Based Overhead Rates
Designing	$ 300,000		6,000 designer hours		$50.00 per designer hour
Sizing and cutting	3,000,000		150,000 machine hours		$20.00 per machine hour
Stitching and trimming	1,200,000		40,000 labor hours		$30.00 per labor hour
Wrapping and packing	420,000		28,000 finished units		$15 per finished unit

3. (LO 2) Rankle, Inc. a manufacturer of tofu-based hot dogs, employs activity-based costing. The budgeted data for each of the activity cost pools is provided below for the year 2022.

Compute activity-based overhead rates.

Activity Cost Pools	Estimated Overhead	Estimated Use of Cost Drivers per Activity
Ordering and receiving	$ 280,000	5,600 orders
Food processing	1,400,000	40,000 machine hours
Packaging	560,000	22,400 labor hours

For 2022, the company had 5,400 orders and used 41,000 machine hours, and labor hours totaled 23,000. What is the total overhead applied?

Solution
3.

Activity Cost Pool	Estimated Overhead	÷	Estimated Use of Cost Drivers per Activity	=	Activity-Based Overhead Rates
Ordering and receiving	$ 280,000		5,600 orders		$50.00 per order
Food processing	1,400,000		40,000 machine hours		$35.00 per machine hour
Packaging	560,000		22,400 labor hours		$25.00 per labor hour

Cost Drivers	×	Overhead Rates	=	Total Overhead Applied
5,400 orders		$50.00		$ 270,000
41,000 machine hours		$35.00		1,435,000
23,000 labor hours		$25.00		575,000
				$2,280,000

Practice Exercises

Assign overhead using traditional costing and ABC.

1. (LO 1, 2) Domestic Fabrics has budgeted overhead costs of $955,000. It has assigned overhead on a plantwide basis to its two products (wool and cotton) using direct labor hours which are estimated to be 477,500 for the current year. The company has decided to experiment with activity-based costing and has created two activity cost pools and related activity cost drivers. These two cost pools are Cutting (cost driver is machine hours) and Design (cost driver is number of setups). Overhead allocated to the Cutting cost pool is $400,000, and $555,000 is allocated to the Design cost pool. Additional information related to these pools is as follows.

	Wool	Cotton	Total
Machine hours	100,000	100,000	200,000
Number of setups	1,000	500	1,500

Instructions

a. Determine the amount of overhead assigned to the wool product line and the cotton product line using activity-based costing.

b. What is the difference between the allocation of overhead to the wool and cotton product lines using activity-based costing versus the traditional approach, assuming direct labor hours were incurred evenly between the wool and cotton?

Solution

1. a.

Activity Cost Pools	Cost Drivers	Estimated Overhead
Cutting	Machine hours	$400,000
Design	Number of setups	555,000

Activity-based overhead rates:

Cutting	Design
$\dfrac{\$400{,}000}{200{,}000} = \$2$ per machine hour	$\dfrac{\$555{,}000}{1{,}500} = \$370$ per setup

	Wool	Cotton
Activity-based costing		
Cutting		
100,000 × $2	$200,000	
100,000 × $2		$200,000
Design		
1,000 × $370	370,000	
500 × $370		185,000
Total cost assigned	$570,000	$385,000

b. $\dfrac{\text{Estimated overhead}}{\text{Direct labors hours}} = \dfrac{\$955{,}000}{477{,}500} = \$2$ per direct labor hour

	Wool	Cotton
Traditional costing		
238,750* × $2	$477,500	
238,750 × $2		$477,500

*477,500 ÷ 2

The wool product line is assigned $92,500 ($570,000 − $477,500) more overhead cost when an activity-based costing system is used. As a result, the cotton product line is assigned $92,500 ($477,500 − $385,000) less.

Assign overhead using traditional costing and ABC; classify activities as value- or non–value-added.

2. (LO 1, 2, 3) Organic Products, Inc., uses a traditional product costing system to assign overhead costs uniformly to all products. To meet Food and Drug Administration (FDA) requirements and to assure its customers of safe, sanitary, and nutritious food, Organic engages in a high level of quality control. Organic assigns its quality-control overhead costs to all products at a rate of 20% of direct labor costs. Its direct labor cost for the month of June for its low-calorie dessert line is $55,000. In response to repeated requests from its financial vice president, Organic management agrees to adopt activity-based costing. Data relating to the low-calorie dessert line for the month of June are as follows.

Activity Cost Pools	Cost Drivers	Overhead Rate	Number of Cost Drivers Used per Activity
Inspections of material received	Number of pounds	$ 0.70 per pound	6,000 pounds
In-process inspections	Number of servings	$ 0.35 per serving	10,000 servings
FDA certification	Customer orders	$13.00 per order	450 orders

Instructions

a. Compute the quality-control overhead cost to be assigned to the low-calorie dessert product line for the month of June using (1) the traditional product costing system (direct labor cost is the cost driver), and (2) activity-based costing.

b. By what amount does the traditional product costing system undercost or overcost the low-calorie dessert line?

c. Classify each of the activities as value-added or non–value-added.

Solution

2. a. 1. Traditional product costing system:

   $55,000 × .20 = $11,000. Quality-control overhead costs assigned in June to the low-calorie dessert line are $11,000.

   2. Activity-based costing system:

Activity Cost Pools	Cost Drivers Used	×	Activity-Based Overhead Rate	=	Overhead Cost Assigned
Inspections of material received	6,000		$ 0.70		$ 4,200
In-process inspections	10,000		0.35		3,500
FDA certification	450		13.00		5,850
Total assigned cost for June					$13,550

b. As compared to ABC, the traditional costing system undercosts the quality-control overhead cost assigned to the low-calorie dessert product line by $2,550 ($13,550 − $11,000) in the month of June. That is a 23.2% ($2,550 ÷ $11,000) understatement.

c. All three activities, as quality-control related activities, are non–value-added activities.

Practice Problem

Assign overhead and compute unit costs.

(LO 2) Spreadwell Paint Company manufactures two high-quality base paints: an *oil-based* paint and a *latex* paint. Both are housepaints and are manufactured only in a neutral white color. Spreadwell sells the white base paints to franchised retail paint and decorating stores where pigments are added to tint (color) the paint as the customer desires. The oil-based paint is made with organic solvents (petroleum products) such as mineral spirits or turpentine. The latex paint is made with water; synthetic resin particles are suspended in the water, and dry and harden when exposed to air.

Spreadwell uses the same processing equipment to produce both paints in different production runs. Between batches, the vats and other processing equipment must be washed and cleaned.

After analyzing the company's entire operations, Spreadwell's accountants and production managers have identified activity cost pools and accumulated annual budgeted overhead costs by pool as follows.

Activity Cost Pools	Estimated Overhead
Purchasing	$ 240,000
Processing (weighing and mixing, grinding, thinning and drying, straining)	1,400,000
Packaging (quarts, gallons, and 5-gallons)	580,000
Testing	240,000
Storage and inventory control	180,000
Washing and cleaning equipment	560,000
Total annual budgeted overhead	$3,200,000

Following further analysis, activity cost drivers were identified and their estimated use by product and activity were scheduled as follows.

Activity Cost Pools	Cost Drivers	Estimated Cost Drivers per Activity	Estimated Use of Drivers per Product Oil-Based	Latex
Purchasing	Purchase orders	1,500 orders	800	700
Processing	Gallons processed	1,000,000 gallons	400,000	600,000
Packaging	Containers filled	400,000 containers	180,000	220,000
Testing	Number of tests	4,000 tests	2,100	1,900
Storing	Avg. gals. on hand	18,000 gallons	10,400	7,600
Washing	Number of batches	800 batches	350	450

Spreadwell has budgeted 400,000 gallons of oil-based paint and 600,000 gallons of latex paint for processing during the year.

Instructions

a. Prepare a schedule showing the computations of the activity-based overhead rates.
b. Prepare a schedule assigning each activity's overhead cost pool to each product.
c. Compute the overhead cost per unit for each product.

Solution

a. Computations of activity-based overhead rates:

Activity Cost Pools	Estimated Overhead	÷	Estimated Use of Cost Drivers	=	Activity-Based Overhead Rates
Purchasing	$ 240,000		1,500 orders		$160 per order
Processing	1,400,000		1,000,000 gallons		$1.40 per gallon
Packaging	580,000		400,000 containers		$1.45 per container
Testing	240,000		4,000 tests		$60 per test
Storing	180,000		18,000 gallons		$10 per gallon
Washing	560,000		800 batches		$700 per batch
	$3,200,000				

b. Assignment of activity cost pools to products:

Activity Cost Pools	Oil-Based Paint			Latex Paint		
	Estimated Use of Drivers	Overhead Rates	Cost Assigned	Estimated Use of Drivers	Overhead Rates	Cost Assigned
Purchasing	800	$160	$ 128,000	700	$160	$ 112,000
Processing	400,000	$1.40	560,000	600,000	$1.40	840,000
Packaging	180,000	$1.45	261,000	220,000	$1.45	319,000
Testing	2,100	$60	126,000	1,900	$60	114,000
Storing	10,400	$10	104,000	7,600	$10	76,000
Washing	350	$700	245,000	450	$700	315,000
Total overhead assigned			$1,424,000			$1,776,000

c. Computation of overhead cost assigned per unit:

	Oil-Based Paint	Latex Paint
Total overhead cost assigned	$1,424,000	$1,776,000
Total gallons produced	400,000	600,000
Overhead cost per gallon	$3.56	$2.96

WileyPLUS

Brief Exercises, DO IT! Exercises, Exercises, Problems, and many additional resources are available for practice in WileyPLUS.

Note: All asterisked Questions, Exercises, and Problems relate to material in the appendix to the chapter.

Questions

1. Under what conditions is direct labor a valid basis for allocating overhead?
2. What has happened in recent industrial history to reduce the usefulness of direct labor as the primary basis for allocating overhead to products?
3. In an automated manufacturing environment, what basis of overhead allocation is frequently more relevant than direct labor hours?
4. What is generally true about overhead allocation to high-volume products versus low-volume products under a traditional costing system?
5. What are the principal differences between activity-based costing (ABC) and traditional product costing?
6. What is the formula for computing activity-based overhead rates?
7. What steps are involved in developing an activity-based costing system?
8. Explain the preparation and use of a value-added/non–value-added activity flowchart in an ABC system.
9. What is an activity cost pool?
10. What is a cost driver?
11. What makes a cost driver accurate and appropriate?
12. What is the formula for assigning activity cost pools to products?
13. What is the primary benefit of activity-based costing?
14. What are the limitations of activity-based costing?
15. Under what conditions is ABC generally the superior overhead costing system?
16. What refinement has been made to enhance the efficiency and effectiveness of ABC for use in managing costs?
17. Of what benefit is classifying activities as value-added and non–value-added?
18. In what ways is the application of ABC to service industries the same as its application to manufacturing companies?
19. What is the relevance of the classification of levels of activity to ABC?
*20. a. Describe the philosophy and approach of just-in-time processing.
    b. Identify the major elements of JIT processing.

Brief Exercises

BE17.1 (LO 1), AP **Service** Digger Inc. sells a high-speed retrieval system for mining information. It provides the following information for the year.

Identify differences between costing systems.

	Budgeted	Actual
Overhead cost	$975,000	$950,000
Machine hours	50,000	45,000
Direct labor hours	100,000	92,000

Overhead is applied on the basis of direct labor hours. (a) Compute the predetermined overhead rate. (b) Determine the amount of overhead applied for the year. (c) Explain how an activity-based costing system might differ in terms of computing a predetermined overhead rate.

Identify differences between costing systems.

BE17.2 (LO 1), AP Finney Inc. has conducted an analysis of overhead costs related to one of its product lines using a traditional costing system (volume-based) and an activity-based costing system. Here are its results.

	Traditional Costing	ABC
Sales revenue	$600,000	$600,000
Overhead costs:		
Product RX3	$ 34,000	$ 50,000
Product Y12	36,000	20,000
	$ 70,000	$ 70,000

Explain how a difference in the overhead costs between the two systems may have occurred.

Identify cost drivers.

BE17.3 (LO 2), AP Splash Co. identifies the following activities that pertain to manufacturing overhead for its production of water polo balls: materials handling, machine setups, factory machine maintenance, factory supervision, and quality control. For each activity, identify an appropriate cost driver.

Identify cost drivers.

BE17.4 (LO 2), AP Mason Company manufactures four products in a single production facility. The company uses activity-based costing. The following activities have been identified through the company's activity analysis: (a) inventory control, (b) machine setups, (c) employee training, (d) quality inspections, (e) materials orderings, (f) drilling operations, and (g) building maintenance.

For each activity, name a cost driver that might be used to assign overhead costs to products.

Compute activity-based overhead rates.

BE17.5 (LO 2), AP Morgana Company identifies three activities in its manufacturing process: machine setups, machining, and inspections. Estimated annual overhead cost for each activity is $150,000, $375,000, and $87,500, respectively. The cost driver for each activity and the estimated annual usage are number of setups 2,500, machine hours 25,000, and number of inspections 1,750. Compute the overhead rate for each activity.

Compute activity-based overhead rates.

BE17.6 (LO 2), AP Weisman, Inc. uses activity-based costing as the basis for information to set prices for its six lines of seasonal coats. Compute the activity-based overhead rates using the following budgeted data for each of the activity cost pools.

Activity Cost Pools	Estimated Overhead	Estimated Use of Cost Drivers per Activity
Designing	$ 450,000	10,000 designer hours
Sizing and cutting	4,000,000	160,000 machine hours
Stitching and trimming	1,440,000	80,000 labor hours
Wrapping and packing	336,000	32,000 finished units

Compute activity-based overhead rates.

BE17.7 (LO 2), AP Spud, Inc. a manufacturer of gourmet potato chips, employs activity-based costing. The budgeted data for each of the activity cost pools is provided below for the year 2022.

Activity Cost Pools	Estimated Overhead	Estimated Use of Cost Drivers per Activity
Ordering and receiving	$ 84,000	12,000 orders
Food processing	480,000	60,000 machine hours
Packaging	1,760,000	440,000 labor hours

For 2022, the company had 11,000 orders and used 50,000 machine hours, and labor hours totaled 500,000. What is the total overhead applied?

Classify activities as value- or non–value-added.

BE17.8 (LO 3), AP Rich Novelty Company identified the following activities in its production and support operations. Classify each of these activities as either value-added or non–value-added.

a. Machine setup.
b. Design engineering.
c. Storing inventory.
d. Moving work in process.
e. Inspecting and testing.
f. Painting and packing.

Classify service company activities as value- or non–value-added.

BE17.9 (LO 3, 4), AN `Service` Pine and Danner is an architectural firm that is contemplating the implementation of activity-based costing. The following activities are performed daily by staff architects. Classify these activities as value-added or non–value-added: (a) designing and drafting, 3 hours; (b) staff meetings, 1 hour; (c) on-site supervision, 2 hours; (d) lunch, 1 hour; (e) consultation with client on specifications, 1.5 hours; and (f) entertaining a prospective client for dinner, 2 hours.

Classify activities according to level.

BE17.10 (LO 3, 4), AN `Service` Kwik Pix is a large digital processing center that serves 130 outlets in grocery stores, service stations, camera and photo shops, and drug stores in 16 nearby towns. Kwik Pix operates 24 hours a day, 6 days a week. Classify each of the following activity costs of Kwik Pix as either unit-level, batch-level, product-level, or facility-level.

a. Color printing materials.
b. Photocopy paper.
c. Depreciation of machinery (assume units-of-activity depreciation).
d. Setups for enlargements.
e. Supervisor's salary.
f. Ordering materials.
g. Pickup and delivery.
h. Commission to dealers.
i. Insurance on building.
j. Loading developing machines.

BE17.11 (LO 3), AP FixIt, Inc. operates 20 injection molding machines in the production of tool boxes of four different sizes, named the Apprentice, the Handyman, the Journeyman, and the Professional. Classify each of the following costs as unit-level, batch-level, product-level, or facility-level.

Classify activities according to level.

a. First-shift supervisor's salary.
b. Powdered raw plastic.
c. Dies for casting plastic components.
d. Depreciation on injection molding machines (assume units-of-activity depreciation).
e. Changing dies on machines.
f. Moving components to assembly department.
g. Engineering design.
h. Employee health and medical insurance coverage.

BE17.12 (LO 3, 4), AP Spin Cycle Architecture uses three activity pools to apply overhead to its projects. Each activity has a cost driver used to assign the overhead costs to the projects. The activities and related overhead costs are as follows: initial concept formation $40,000, design $300,000, and construction oversight $100,000. The cost drivers and estimated use are as follows.

Compute rates and activity levels.

Activities	Cost Drivers	Estimated Use of Cost Drivers per Activity
Initial concept formation	Number of project changes	20
Design	Square feet	150,000
Construction oversight	Number of months	100

a. Compute the predetermined overhead rate for each activity.
b. Classify each of these activities as unit-level, batch-level, product-level, or facility-level.

DO IT! Exercises

DO IT! 17.1 (LO 1), K Indicate whether the following statements are true or false.

Identify characteristics of traditional and ABC systems.

a. The reasoning behind ABC cost allocation is that products consume activities and activities consume resources.
b. Activity-based costing is an approach for allocating direct labor to products.
c. In today's increasingly automated environment, direct labor is never an appropriate basis for allocating costs to products.
d. A cost driver is any factor or activity that has a direct cause-effect relationship with resources consumed.
e. Activity-based costing segregates overhead into various cost pools in an effort to provide more accurate cost information.

DO IT! 17.2 (LO 2), AP Flynn Industries has three activity cost pools and two products. It estimates production 3,000 units of Product BC113 and 1,500 of Product AD908. Having identified its activity cost pools and the cost drivers for each pool, Flynn accumulated the following data relative to those activity cost pools and cost drivers.

Compute activity-based overhead rates and assign overhead using ABC.

	Annual Overhead Data			Estimated Use of Cost Drivers per Product	
Activity Cost Pools	Cost Drivers	Estimated Overhead	Estimated Use of Cost Drivers per Activity	Product BC113	Product AD908
Machine setup	Setups	$ 16,000	40	25	15
Machining	Machine hours	110,000	5,000	1,000	4,000
Packing	Orders	30,000	500	150	350

Using the above data, do the following:
a. Prepare a schedule showing the computations of the activity-based overhead rates per cost driver.
b. Prepare a schedule assigning each activity's overhead cost to the two products.
c. Compute the overhead cost per unit for each product. (Round to nearest cent.)
d. Comment on the comparative overhead cost per product.

Classify activities according to level.

DO IT! 17.3 (LO 3), C Adamson Company manufactures four lines of garden tools. As a result of an activity analysis, the accounting department has identified eight activity cost pools. Each of the product lines is produced in large batches, with the whole plant devoted to one product at a time. Classify each of the following activities or costs as either unit-level, batch level, product-level, or facility-level.

a. Machining parts.
b. Product design.
c. Plant maintenance.
d. Machine setup.
e. Assembling parts.
f. Purchasing raw materials.
g. Property taxes.
h. Painting garden tools.

Apply ABC to service company.

DO IT! 17.4 (LO 4), AP  Ready Ride is a trucking company. It provides local, short-haul, and long-haul services. It has developed the following three cost pools.

Activity Cost Pools	Cost Drivers	Estimated Overhead	Estimated Use of Cost Driver per Activity
Loading and unloading	Number of pieces	$ 90,000	90,000
Travel	Miles driven	450,000	600,000
Logistics	Hours	75,000	3,000

a. Compute the activity-based overhead rates for each pool.
b. Determine the overhead assigned to Job XZ3275 which has 150 pieces, requires 200 miles of driving, and 0.75 hours of logistics.

Exercises

Assign overhead using traditional costing and ABC.

Excel

E17.1 (LO 1, 2), AP Saddle Inc. has two types of handbags: standard and custom. The controller has decided to use a plantwide overhead rate based on direct labor costs. The president has heard of activity-based costing and wants to see how the results would differ if this system were used. Two activity cost pools were developed: machining and machine setup. Presented below is information related to the company's operations.

	Standard	Custom
Direct labor costs	$50,000	$100,000
Machine hours	1,000	1,000
Setup hours	100	400

Total estimated overhead costs are $240,000. Overhead cost allocated to the machining activity cost pool is $140,000, and $100,000 is allocated to the machine setup activity cost pool.

Instructions

a. Compute the overhead rate using the traditional (plantwide) approach.
b. Compute the overhead rates using the activity-based costing approach.
c. Determine the difference in allocation between the two approaches.

Explain difference between traditional and activity-based costing.

E17.2 (LO 1), AP Ayala Inc. has conducted the following analysis related to its product lines, using a traditional costing system (volume-based) and an activity-based costing system. The traditional and the activity-based costing systems assign the same amount of direct materials and direct labor costs.

		Total Costs	
Products	Sales Revenue	Traditional	ABC
Product 540X	$180,000	$55,000	$50,000
Product 137Y	160,000	50,000	35,000
Product 249S	70,000	15,000	35,000

Instructions

a. For each product line, compute operating income using the traditional costing system.

b. For each product line, compute operating income using the activity-based costing system.

c. Using the following formula, compute the percentage difference in operating income for each of the product lines of Ayala: [Operating Income (ABC) − Operating Income (traditional cost)] ÷ Operating Income (traditional cost). (Round to two decimals.)

d. Provide a rationale as to why the costs for Product 540X are approximately the same using either the traditional or activity-based costing system.

E17.3 (LO 1, 2), AN EcoFabrics has budgeted overhead costs of $945,000. It has assigned overhead on a plantwide basis to its two products (wool and cotton) using direct labor hours which are estimated to be 450,000 for the current year. The company has decided to experiment with activity-based costing and has created two activity cost pools and related activity cost drivers. These two cost pools are cutting (cost driver is machine hours) and design (cost driver is number of setups). Overhead allocated to the cutting cost pool is $360,000, and $585,000 is allocated to the design cost pool. Additional information related to these pools is as follows.

Assign overhead using traditional costing and ABC.

	Wool	Cotton	Total
Machine hours	100,000	100,000	200,000
Number of setups	1,000	500	1,500

Instructions

a. Determine the amount of overhead assigned to the wool product line and the cotton product line using activity-based costing.

b. What amount of overhead would be assigned to the wool and cotton product lines using the traditional approach, assuming direct labor hours were incurred evenly between the wool and cotton? How does this compare with the amount assigned using ABC in part (a)?

E17.4 (LO 1, 2), AN Altex Inc. manufactures two products: car wheels and truck wheels. To determine the amount of overhead to assign to each product line, the controller, Robert Hermann, has developed the following information.

Assign overhead using traditional costing and ABC.

	Car	Truck
Estimated wheels produced	40,000	10,000
Direct labor hours per wheel	1	3

Total estimated overhead costs for the two product lines are $770,000.

Instructions

a. Compute the overhead cost assigned to the car wheels and truck wheels, assuming that direct labor hours is used to assign overhead costs.

b. Hermann is not satisfied with the traditional method of allocating overhead because he believes that most of the overhead costs relate to the truck wheels product line because of its complexity. He therefore develops the following three activity cost pools and related cost drivers to better understand these costs.

Activity Cost Pools	Estimated Use of Cost Drivers	Estimated Overhead Costs
Setting up machines	1,000 setups	$220,000
Assembling	70,000 labor hours	280,000
Inspection	1,200 inspections	270,000

Compute the activity-based overhead rates for these three cost pools.

c. Compute the cost that is assigned to the car wheels and truck wheels product lines using an activity-based costing system, given the following information.

Estimated Use of Cost Drivers per Product

	Car	Truck
Number of setups	200	800
Direct labor hours	40,000	30,000
Number of inspections	100	1,100

d. What do you believe Hermann should do?

Assign overhead using traditional costing and ABC.

E17.5 (LO 1, 2), AN Perdon Corporation manufactures safes—large mobile safes, and large walk-in stationary bank safes. As part of its annual budgeting process, Perdon is analyzing the profitability of its two products. Part of this analysis involves estimating the amount of overhead to be assigned to each product line. The information shown below relates to overhead.

	Mobile Safes	Walk-In Safes
Units planned for production	200	50
Material moves per product line	300	200
Purchase orders per product line	450	350
Direct labor hours per product line	800	1,700

Instructions

a. The total estimated manufacturing overhead was $260,000. Under traditional costing (which assigns overhead on the basis of direct labor hours), what amount of manufacturing overhead costs are assigned to:

   1. One mobile safe?
   2. One walk-in safe?

b. The total estimated manufacturing overhead of $260,000 was comprised of $160,000 for materials handling costs and $100,000 for purchasing activity costs. Under activity-based costing (ABC):

   1. What amount of materials handling costs are assigned to:
      a. One mobile safe?
      b. One walk-in safe?
   2. What amount of purchasing activity costs are assigned to:
      a. One mobile safe?
      b. One walk-in safe?

c. Compare the amount of overhead assigned to one mobile safe and to one walk-in safe under the traditional costing approach versus under ABC.

Identify activity cost pools and cost drivers.

E17.6 (LO 2), AN Santana Corporation manufactures snowmobiles in its Blue Mountain, Wisconsin, plant. The following costs are budgeted for the first quarter's operations.

Machine setup, indirect materials	$ 4,000
Inspections	16,000
Tests	4,000
Insurance, plant	110,000
Engineering design	140,000
Depreciation, machinery	520,000
Machine setup, indirect labor	20,000
Property taxes	29,000
Oil, heating	19,000
Electricity, plant lighting	21,000
Engineering prototypes	60,000
Depreciation, plant	210,000
Electricity, machinery	36,000
Machine maintenance wages	19,000

Instructions

Classify the above costs of Santana Corporation into activity cost pools using the following: engineering, machinery, machine setup, quality control, factory costs. Next, identify a cost driver that may be used to assign each cost pool to each line of snowmobiles.

E17.7 (LO 2), AN Rojas Vineyards in Oakville, California, produces three varieties of non-alcoholic wine: merlot, viognier, and pinot noir. The winemaster, Russel Hansen, has identified the following activities as cost pools for accumulating overhead and assigning it to products.

Identify activity cost drivers.

1. Culling and replanting. Dead or overcrowded vines are culled, and new vines are planted or relocated. (Separate vineyards by variety.)
2. Tying. The posts and wires are reset, and vines are tied to the wires for the dormant season.
3. Trimming. At the end of the harvest, the vines are cut and trimmed back in preparation for the next season.
4. Spraying. The vines are sprayed with organic pesticides for protection against insects and fungi.
5. Harvesting. The grapes are hand-picked, placed in carts, and transported to the crushers.
6. Stemming and crushing. Cartfuls of bunches of grapes of each variety are separately loaded into machines that remove stems and gently crush the grapes.
7. Pressing and filtering. The crushed grapes are transferred to presses that mechanically remove the juices and filter out bulk and impurities.
8. Fermentation. The grape juice, by variety, is fermented in either stainless-steel tanks or oak barrels.
9. Aging. The wines are aged in either stainless-steel tanks or oak barrels for one to three years depending on variety.
10. Bottling and corking. Bottles are machine-filled and corked.
11. Labeling and boxing. Each bottle is labeled, as is each nine-bottle case, with the name of the vintner, vintage, and variety.
12. Storing. Packaged and boxed bottles are stored awaiting shipment.
13. Shipping. The wine is shipped to distributors and private retailers.
14. Heating and air-conditioning of plant and offices.
15. Maintenance of production equipment. Repairs, replacements, and general maintenance are performed in the off-season.

Instructions

For each of Rojas Vineyards' 15 activity cost pools, identify a probable cost driver that might be used to assign overhead costs to its three wine varieties.

E17.8 (LO 2), AN Wilmington, Inc. manufactures five models of kitchen appliances. The company is installing activity-based costing and has identified the following activities performed at its Mesa plant.

Identify activity cost drivers.

1. Designing new models.
2. Purchasing raw materials and parts.
3. Storing and managing inventory.
4. Receiving and inspecting raw materials and parts.
5. Interviewing and hiring new personnel.
6. Machine forming sheet steel into appliance parts.
7. Manually assembling parts into appliances.
8. Training all employees of the company.
9. Insuring all tangible fixed assets.
10. Supervising production.
11. Maintaining and repairing machinery and equipment.
12. Painting and packaging finished appliances.

Having analyzed its Mesa plant operations for purposes of installing activity-based costing, Wilmington, Inc. identified its activity cost centers. It now needs to identify relevant activity cost drivers in order to assign overhead costs to its products.

Instructions

Using the activities listed above, identify for each activity one or more cost drivers that might be used to assign overhead to Wilmington's five products.

E17.9 (LO 2, 3), AP Writing Air United, Inc. manufactures two products: missile range instruments and space pressure gauges. During April, 50 range instruments and 300 pressure gauges were produced, and overhead costs of $94,500 were estimated. An analysis of estimated overhead costs reveals the following activities.

Compute overhead rates and assign overhead using ABC.

Activities	Cost Drivers	Total Cost
1. Materials handling	Number of requisitions	$40,000
2. Machine setups	Number of setups	21,500
3. Quality inspections	Number of inspections	33,000
		$94,500

The cost driver volume for each product was as follows.

Cost Drivers	Instruments	Gauges	Total
Number of requisitions	400	600	1,000
Number of setups	200	300	500
Number of inspections	200	400	600

Instructions

a. Determine the overhead rate for each activity.

b. Assign the manufacturing overhead costs for April to the two products using activity-based costing.

c. Write a memorandum to the president of Air United explaining the benefits of activity-based costing.

Assign overhead using traditional costing and ABC.

E17.10 (LO 1, 2, 3), AP Kragan Clothing Company manufactures its own designed and labeled athletic wear and sells its products through catalog sales and retail outlets. While Kragan has for years used activity-based costing in its manufacturing activities, it has always used traditional costing in assigning its selling costs to its product lines. Selling costs have traditionally been assigned to Kragan's product lines at a rate of 70% of direct materials costs. Its direct materials costs for the month of March for Kragan's "high-intensity" line of athletic wear are $400,000. The company has decided to extend activity-based costing to its selling costs. Data relating to the "high-intensity" line of products for the month of March are as follows.

Activity Cost Pools	Cost Drivers	Overhead Rate	Number of Cost Drivers Used per Activity
Sales commissions	Dollar sales	$0.05 per dollar sales	$900,000
Advertising—TV	Minutes	$300 per minute	250
Advertising—Internet	Column inches	$10 per column inch	2,000
Catalogs	Catalogs mailed	$2.50 per catalog	60,000
Cost of catalog sales	Catalog orders	$1 per catalog order	9,000
Credit and collection	Dollar sales	$0.03 per dollar sales	900,000

Instructions

a. Compute the selling costs to be assigned to the "high-intensity" line of athletic wear for the month of March (1) using the traditional product costing system (direct materials cost is the cost driver), and (2) using activity-based costing.

b. By what amount does the traditional product costing system undercost or overcost the "high-intensity" product line relative to costing under ABC?

Assign overhead using traditional costing and ABC; classify activities as value- or non–value-added.

E17.11 (LO 1, 2, 3), AP Health 'R Us, Inc., uses a traditional product costing system to assign overhead costs uniformly to all its packaged multigrain products. To meet Food and Drug Administration requirements and to assure its customers of safe, sanitary, and nutritious food, Health 'R Us engages in a high level of quality control. Health 'R Us assigns its quality-control overhead costs to all products at a rate of 17% of direct labor costs. Its direct labor cost for the month of June for its low-calorie breakfast line is $70,000. In response to repeated requests from its financial vice president, Health 'R Us's management agrees to adopt activity-based costing. Data relating to the low-calorie breakfast line for the month of June are as follows.

Activity Cost Pools	Cost Drivers	Overhead Rate	Number of Cost Drivers Used per Activity
Inspections of material received	Number of pounds	$0.90 per pound	6,000 pounds
In-process inspections	Number of servings	$0.33 per serving	10,000 servings
FDA certification	Customer orders	$12.00 per order	420 orders

Instructions

a. Compute the quality-control overhead cost to be assigned to the low-calorie breakfast product line for the month of June (1) using the traditional product costing system (direct labor cost is the cost driver), and (2) using activity-based costing.

b. By what amount does the traditional product costing system undercost or overcost the low-calorie breakfast line relative to costing under ABC?

c. Classify each of the activities as value-added or non–value-added.

E17.12 (LO 3), AN Having itemized its costs for the first quarter of next year's budget, Santana Corporation desires to install an activity-based costing system. First, it identified the activity cost pools in which to accumulate factory overhead. Second, it identified the relevant cost drivers. (This was done in E17.6.)

Classify activities by level.

Instructions

Using the activity cost pools identified in E17.6, classify each of those cost pools as either unit-level, batch-level, product-level, or facility-level.

E17.13 (LO 3), AN William Mendel & Sons, Inc. is a small manufacturing company in La Jolla that uses activity-based costing. Mendel & Sons accumulates overhead in the following activity cost pools.

Classify activities by level.

1. Hiring personnel.
2. Managing parts inventory.
3. Purchasing.
4. Testing prototypes.
5. Designing products.
6. Setting up equipment.
7. Training employees.
8. Inspecting machined parts after each setup.
9. Machining.
10. Assembling.

Instructions

For each activity cost pool, indicate whether the activity cost pool would be unit-level, batch-level, product-level, or facility-level.

E17.14 (LO 4), AP **Service** Venus Creations sells window treatments (shades, blinds, and awnings) to both commercial and residential customers. The following information relates to its budgeted operations for the current year.

Assign overhead using traditional costing and ABC.

	Commercial		Residential	
Revenues		$300,000		$480,000
Direct materials costs	$ 30,000		$ 50,000	
Direct labor costs	100,000		300,000	
Overhead costs	85,000	215,000	150,000	500,000
Operating income (loss)		$ 85,000		($ 20,000)

The controller, Peggy Kingman, is concerned about the residential product line. She cannot understand why this line is not more profitable given that the installations of window coverings are less complex for residential customers. In addition, the residential client base resides in close proximity to the company office, so travel costs are not as expensive on a per client visit for residential customers. As a result, she has decided to take a closer look at the overhead costs assigned to the two product lines to determine whether a more accurate product costing model can be developed. Here are the three activity cost pools and related information she developed:

Activity Cost Pools	Estimated Overhead	Cost Drivers
Scheduling and travel	$85,000	Hours of travel
Setup time	90,000	Number of setups
Supervision	60,000	Direct labor cost

Estimated Use of Cost Drivers per Product

	Commercial	Residential
Scheduling and travel	750 hours	500 hours
Setup time	350 setups	250 setups

Instructions

a. Compute the activity-based overhead rates for each of the three cost pools, and determine the overhead cost assigned to each product line.

b. Compute the operating income for each product line, using the activity-based overhead rates.

c. What do you believe Peggy Kingman should do?

Identify activity cost pools.

E17.15 (LO 4), AP Service Snap Prints Company is a small printing and copying firm with three high-speed offset printing presses, five copiers (two color and three black-and-white), one collator, one cutting and folding machine, and one fax machine. To improve its pricing practices, owner-manager Terry Morton is installing activity-based costing. Additionally, Terry employs five employees: two printers/designers, one receptionist/bookkeeper, one salesperson/copy-machine operator, and one janitor/delivery clerk. Terry can operate any of the machines and, in addition to managing the entire operation, he performs the training, designing, selling, and marketing functions.

Instructions

As Snap Prints' independent accountant who prepares tax forms and quarterly financial statements, you have been asked to identify the activities that would be used to accumulate overhead costs for assignment to jobs and customers. Using your knowledge of a small printing and copying firm (and some imagination), identify at least 12 activity cost pools as the start of an activity-based costing system for Snap Prints Company.

Classify service company activities as value-added or non–value-added.

E17.16 (LO 3, 4), AN Service Lasso and Markowitz is a law firm that is initiating an activity-based costing system. Sam Lasso, the senior partner and strong supporter of ABC, has prepared the following list of activities performed by a typical attorney in a day at the firm.

Activities	Hours
Writing contracts and letters	1.5
Attending staff meetings	0.5
Taking depositions	1.0
Doing research	1.0
Traveling to/from court	1.0
Contemplating legal strategy	1.0
Eating lunch	1.0
Litigating a case in court	2.5
Entertaining a prospective client	1.5

Instructions

Classify each of the activities listed by Sam Lasso as value-added or non–value-added, and defend your classification. How much was value-added time and how much was non–value-added?

Apply ABC to service company.

E17.17 (LO 4), AP Service Manzeck Company operates a snow-removal service. The company owns five trucks, each of which has a snow plow in the front to plow driveways and a snowthrower in the back to clear sidewalks. Because plowing snow is very tough on trucks, the company incurs significant maintenance costs. Truck depreciation and maintenance represents a significant portion of the company's overhead. The company removes snow at residential locations, in which case the drivers spend the bulk of their time walking behind the snowthrower machine to clear sidewalks. On commercial jobs, the drivers spend most of their time plowing. Manzeck assigns overhead based on labor hours. Total estimated overhead costs for the year are $42,000. Total estimated labor hours are 1,500 hours. The average residential property requires 0.5 hours of labor, while the average commercial property requires 2.5 hours of labor. The following additional information is available.

Activity Cost Pools	Cost Drivers	Estimated Overhead	Estimated Use of Cost Drivers per Activity
Plowing	Square yards of surface plowed	$38,000	200,000
Snowthrowing	Linear feet of sidewalk cleared	$ 4,000	50,000

Instructions

a. Determine the predetermined overhead rate under traditional costing.

b. Determine the amount of overhead assigned to the average residential job using traditional costing based on labor hours.

c. Determine the activity-based overhead rates for each cost pool.

d. Determine the amount of overhead assigned to the average residential job using activity-based costing. Assume that the average residential job has 20 square yards of plowing and 60 linear feet of snowthrowing.

e. Discuss your findings from parts (b) and (d).

Problems: Set A

P17.1A (LO 1, 2, 3), AP Combat Fire, Inc. manufactures steel cylinders and nozzles for two models of fire extinguishers: (1) a home fire extinguisher and (2) a commercial fire extinguisher. The *home model* is a high-volume (54,000 units), half-gallon cylinder that holds 2 1/2 pounds of multi-purpose dry chemical at 480 PSI. The *commercial model* is a low-volume (10,200 units), two-gallon cylinder that holds 10 pounds of multi-purpose dry chemical at 390 PSI. Both products require 1.5 hours of direct labor for completion. Therefore, total annual direct labor hours are 96,300 or [1.5 hours × (54,000 + 10,200)]. Estimated annual manufacturing overhead is $1,584,280. Thus, the predetermined overhead rate is $16.45 or ($1,584,280 ÷ 96,300) per direct labor hour. The direct materials cost per unit is $18.50 for the home model and $26.50 for the commercial model. The direct labor cost is $19 per unit for both the home and the commercial models.

Assign overhead using traditional costing and ABC; compute unit costs; classify activities as value- or non–value-added.

The company's managers identified six activity cost pools and related cost drivers and accumulated overhead by cost pool as follows.

Activity Cost Pools	Cost Drivers	Estimated Overhead	Estimated Use of Cost Drivers	Estimated Use of Drivers by Product	
				Home	Commercial
Receiving	Pounds	$ 80,400	335,000	215,000	120,000
Forming	Machine hours	150,500	35,000	27,000	8,000
Assembling	Number of parts	412,300	217,000	165,000	52,000
Testing	Number of tests	51,000	25,500	15,500	10,000
Painting	Gallons	52,580	5,258	3,680	1,578
Packing and shipping	Pounds	837,500	335,000	215,000	120,000
		$1,584,280			

Instructions

a. Under traditional product costing, compute the total unit cost of each product. Prepare a simple comparative schedule of the individual costs by product (similar to Illustration 17.3).

b. Under ABC, prepare a schedule showing the computations of the activity-based overhead rates (per cost driver).

c. Prepare a schedule assigning each activity's overhead cost pool to each product based on the use of cost drivers. (Include a computation of overhead cost per unit, rounding to the nearest cent.)

d. Compute the total cost per unit for each product under ABC.

e. Classify each of the activities as a value-added activity or a non–value-added activity.

f. Comment on (1) the comparative overhead cost per unit for the two products under ABC, and (2) the comparative total costs per unit under traditional costing and ABC.

a. Unit cost—H.M. $62.18

c. Cost assigned—H.M. $1,086,500

d. Cost/unit—H.M. $57.62

P17.2A (LO 2), AP **Writing** Schultz Electronics manufactures two ultra high-definition television models: the Royale which sells for $1,600, and a new model, the Majestic, which sells for $1,300. The production cost computed per unit under traditional costing for each model in 2022 was as follows.

Assign overhead to products using ABC and evaluate decision.

Traditional Costing	Royale	Majestic
Direct materials	$ 700	$420
Direct labor ($20 per hour)	120	100
Manufacturing overhead ($38 per DLH)	228	190
Total per unit cost	$1,048	$710

In 2022, Schultz manufactured 25,000 units of the Royale and 10,000 units of the Majestic. The overhead rate of $38 per direct labor hour was determined by dividing total estimated manufacturing overhead of $7,600,000 by the total direct labor hours (200,000) for the two models.

Under traditional costing, the gross profit on the models was Royale $552 ($1,600 − $1,048) and Majestic $590 ($1,300 − $710). Because of this difference, management is considering phasing out the Royale model and increasing the production of the Majestic model.

Before finalizing its decision, management asks Schultz's controller to prepare an analysis using activity-based costing (ABC). The controller accumulates the following information about overhead for the year ended December 31, 2022.

Activity Cost Pools	Cost Drivers	Estimated Overhead	Estimated Use of Cost Drivers	Activity-Based Overhead Rate
Purchasing	Number of orders	$1,200,000	40,000	$30/order
Machine setups	Number of setups	900,000	18,000	$50/setup
Machining	Machine hours	4,800,000	120,000	$40/hour
Quality control	Number of inspections	700,000	28,000	$25/inspection

The cost drivers used for each product were:

Cost Drivers	Royale	Majestic	Total
Purchase orders	17,000	23,000	40,000
Machine setups	5,000	13,000	18,000
Machine hours	75,000	45,000	120,000
Inspections	11,000	17,000	28,000

Instructions

a. Assign the total 2022 manufacturing overhead costs to the two products using activity-based costing (ABC) and determine the overhead cost per unit.

b. What was the cost per unit and gross profit of each model using ABC?

c. Are management's future plans for the two models sound? Explain.

a. Royale $4,035,000

b. Cost/unit—Royale $981.40

Assign overhead costs using traditional costing and ABC; compare results.

P17.3A (LO 1, 2), AN Writing Shaker Stairs Co. designs and builds factory-made premium wooden stairways for homes. The manufactured stairway components (spindles, risers, hangers, hand rails) permit installation of stairways of varying lengths and widths. All are of white oak wood. Budgeted manufacturing overhead costs for the year 2022 are as follows.

Overhead Cost Pools	Amount
Purchasing	$ 75,000
Handling materials	82,000
Production (cutting, milling, finishing)	210,000
Setting up machines	105,000
Inspecting	90,000
Inventory control (raw materials and finished goods)	126,000
Utilities	180,000
Total budgeted overhead costs	$868,000

For the last 4 years, Shaker Stairs Co. has been charging overhead to products on the basis of machine hours. For the year 2022, 100,000 machine hours are budgeted.

Jeremy Nolan, owner-manager of Shaker Stairs Co., recently directed his accountant, Bill Seagren, to implement the activity-based costing system that he has repeatedly proposed. At Jeremy Nolan's request, Bill and the production foreman identify the following cost drivers and their usage for the previously budgeted overhead cost pools.

Activity Cost Pools	Cost Drivers	Estimated Use of Cost Drivers
Purchasing	Number of orders	600
Handling materials	Number of moves	8,000
Production (cutting, milling, finishing)	Direct labor hours	100,000
Setting up machines	Number of setups	1,250
Inspecting	Number of inspections	6,000
Inventory control (raw materials and finished goods)	Number of components	168,000
Utilities	Square feet occupied	90,000

Steve Hannon, sales manager, has received an order for 250 stairways from Community Builders, Inc., a large housing development contractor. At Steve's request, Bill prepares cost estimates for producing components for 250 stairways so Steve can submit a contract price per stairway to Community Builders. He accumulates the following data for the production of 250 stairways.

Direct materials	$103,600
Direct labor	$112,000
Machine hours	14,500
Direct labor hours	5,000
Number of purchase orders	60
Number of material moves	800
Number of machine setups	100
Number of inspections	450
Number of components	16,000
Number of square feet occupied	8,000

Instructions

a. Compute the predetermined overhead rate using traditional costing with machine hours as the basis.

b. What is the manufacturing cost per stairway under traditional costing? (Round to the nearest cent.)

c. What is the manufacturing cost per stairway under the proposed activity-based costing? (Round to the nearest cent. Prepare all of the necessary schedules.)

d. Which of the two costing systems is preferable in pricing decisions and why?

b. Cost/stairway $1,365.84

c. Cost/stairway $1,139.80

P17.4A (LO 1, 2), AN Benton Corporation produces two grades of non-alcoholic wine from grapes that it buys from California growers. It produces and sells roughly 3,000,000 liters per year of a low-cost, high-volume product called CoolDay. It sells this in 600,000 5-liter jugs. Benton also produces and sells roughly 300,000 liters per year of a low-volume, high-cost product called LiteMist. LiteMist is sold in 1-liter bottles. Based on recent data, the CoolDay product has not been as profitable as LiteMist. Management is considering dropping the inexpensive CoolDay line so it can focus more attention on the LiteMist product. The LiteMist product already demands considerably more attention than the CoolDay line.

Assign overhead costs using traditional costing and ABC; compare results.

Jack Eller, president and founder of Benton, is skeptical about this idea. He points out that for many decades the company produced only the CoolDay line and that it was always quite profitable. It wasn't until the company started producing the more complicated LiteMist wine that the profitability of CoolDay declined. Prior to the introduction of LiteMist, the company had basic equipment, simple growing and production procedures, and virtually no need for quality control. Because LiteMist is bottled in 1-liter bottles, it requires considerably more time and effort, both to bottle and to label and box than does CoolDay. The company must bottle and handle 5 times as many bottles of LiteMist to sell the same quantity as CoolDay. CoolDay requires 1 month of aging; LiteMist requires 1 year. CoolDay requires cleaning and inspection of equipment every 10,000 liters; LiteMist requires such maintenance every 600 liters.

Jack has asked the accounting department to prepare an analysis of the cost per liter using the traditional costing approach and using activity-based costing. The following information was collected.

	CoolDay	LiteMist
Direct materials per liter	$0.40	$1.20
Direct labor cost per liter	$0.50	$0.90
Direct labor hours per liter	0.05	0.09
Total direct labor hours	150,000	27,000

				Estimated Use of Cost Drivers per Product	
Activity Cost Pools	Cost Drivers	Estimated Overhead	Estimated Use of Cost Drivers	CoolDay	LiteMist
Grape processing	Cart of grapes	$ 145,860	6,600	6,000	600
Aging	Total months	396,000	6,600,000	3,000,000	3,600,000
Bottling and corking	Number of bottles	270,000	900,000	600,000	300,000
Labeling and boxing	Number of bottles	189,000	900,000	600,000	300,000
Maintain and inspect equipment	Number of inspections	240,800	800	350	450
		$1,241,660			

CHAPTER 17 Activity-Based Costing

Instructions

Answer each of the following questions. (Round all calculations to three decimal places.)

a. Cost/liter—C.D. $1.251

a. Under traditional product costing using direct labor hours, compute the total manufacturing cost per **liter** of both products.

b. Under ABC, prepare a schedule showing the computation of the activity-based overhead rates (per cost driver).

c. Cost/liter—C.D. $.241

c. Prepare a schedule assigning each activity's overhead cost pool to each product, based on the use of cost drivers. Include a computation of overhead cost per liter.

d. Compute the total manufacturing cost per liter for both products under ABC.

e. Write a memo to Jack Eller discussing the implications of your analysis for the company's plans. In this memo, provide a brief description of ABC as well as an explanation of how the traditional approach can result in distortions.

Assign overhead costs to services using traditional costing and ABC; compute overhead rates and unit costs; compare results.

P17.5A (LO 1, 2, 3, 4), AN Service Lewis and Stark is a public accounting firm that offers two primary services, auditing and tax-return preparation. A controversy has developed between the partners of the two service lines as to who is contributing the greater amount to the bottom line. The area of contention is the assignment of overhead. The tax partners argue for assigning overhead on the basis of 40% of direct labor dollars, while the audit partners argue for implementing activity-based costing. The partners agree to use next year's budgeted data for purposes of analysis and comparison. The following overhead data are collected to develop the comparison.

Activity Cost Pools	Cost Drivers	Estimated Overhead	Estimated Use of Cost Drivers	Estimated Use of Cost Drivers per Service	
				Audit	Tax
Employee training	Direct labor dollars	$216,000	$1,800,000	$1,100,000	$700,000
Typing and secretarial	Number of reports/forms	76,200	2,500	800	1,700
Computing	Number of minutes	204,000	60,000	27,000	33,000
Facility rental	Number of employees	142,500	40	22	18
Travel	Per expense reports	81,300	Direct	56,000	25,300
		$720,000			

Instructions

a. Using traditional product costing as proposed by the tax partners, compute the total overhead cost assigned to both services (audit and tax) of Lewis and Stark.

b. (2) Cost assigned—Tax $337,441

b. 1. Using activity-based costing, prepare a schedule showing the computations of the activity-based overhead rates (per cost driver).

2. Prepare a schedule assigning each activity's overhead cost pool to each service based on the use of the cost drivers.

c. Difference—Audit $57,441

c. Comment on the comparative overhead cost for the two services under both traditional costing and ABC.

Continuing Cases

Current Designs

CD17 As you learned in the previous chapters, Current Designs has two main product lines—composite kayaks, which are handmade and very labor-intensive, and rotomolded kayaks, which require less labor but employ more expensive equipment. Current Designs' controller, Diane Buswell, is now evaluating several different methods of assigning overhead to these products. It is important to ensure that costs are appropriately assigned to the company's products. At the same time, the system that is used must not be so complex that its costs are greater than its benefits.

Diane has decided to use the following activities and costs to evaluate the methods of assigning overhead.

Current Designs Activity Cost Pools

Activities	Cost
Designing new models	$121,100
Creating and testing prototypes	152,000
Creating molds for kayaks	188,500
Operating oven for the rotomolded kayaks	40,000
Operating the vacuum line for the composite kayaks	28,000
Supervising production employees	180,000
Curing time (the time that is needed for the chemical processes to finish before the next step in the production process; many of these costs are related to the space required in the building)	190,400
Total	**$900,000**

As Diane examines the data, she decides that the cost of operating the oven for the rotomolded kayaks and the cost of operating the vacuum line for the composite kayaks can be directly assigned to each of these product lines and do not need to be assigned with the other costs.

Instructions

For purposes of this analysis, assume that Current Designs uses $234,000 in direct labor costs to produce 1,000 composite kayaks and $286,000 in direct labor costs to produce 4,000 rotomolded kayaks each year.

a. One method of assigning overhead would assign the common costs to each product line by using an assignment basis such as the number of employees working on each type of kayak or the amount of factory space used for the production of each type of kayak. Diane knows that about 50% of the area of the plant and 50% of the employees work on the composite kayaks, and the remaining space and other employees work on the rotomolded kayaks. Using this information and remembering that the cost of operating the oven and vacuum line have been directly assigned, determine the total amount to be assigned to the composite kayak line and the rotomolded kayak line, and the amount to be assigned to each of the units in each line.

b. Another method of assigning overhead is to use direct labor dollars as an assignment basis. Remembering that the costs of the oven and the vacuum line have been assigned directly to the product lines, allocate the remaining costs using direct labor dollars as the allocation basis. Then, determine the amount of overhead that should be assigned to each unit of each product line using this method.

c. Activity-based costing requires a cost driver for each cost pool. Use the following information to assign the costs to the product lines using the activity-based costing approach.

Current Designs Cost Drivers

Activity Cost Pools	Cost Drivers	Driver Amount for Composite Kayaks	Driver Amount for Rotomolded Kayaks
Designing new models	Number of models	3	1
Creating and testing prototypes	Number of prototypes	6	2
Creating molds for kayaks	Number of molds	12	1
Supervising production employees	Number of employees	12	12
Curing time	Number of days of curing time	15,000	2,000

What amount of overhead should be assigned to each composite kayak using this method? What amount of overhead should be assigned to each rotomolded kayak using this method?

d. Which of the three methods do you think Current Designs should use? Why?

Waterways

(*Note:* This is a continuation of the Waterways case from Chapters 14–16.)

WP17 Waterways looked into ABC as a method of costing because of the variety of items it produces and the many different activities in which it is involved. This problem asks you to help Waterways use an activity-based costing system to account for its production activities.

Go to WileyPLUS for complete case details and instructions.

Comprehensive Case

CC17 In Chapter 15, you used job order costing techniques to help Greetings Inc., a retailer of greeting cards and small gift items, expand its operations. Your next task is to help the new unit, Wall Décor, become profitable through the use of activity-based costing. In this case, you will have the opportunity to discuss the cost/benefit trade-offs between simple ABC systems versus refined systems, and the potential benefit of using capacity rather than estimated sales when allocating fixed overhead costs.

Go to WileyPLUS for complete case details and instructions.

Expand Your Critical Thinking

Decision-Making Across the Organization

CT17.1 **Service** East Valley Hospital is a primary medical care facility and trauma center that serves 11 small, rural midwestern communities within a 40-mile radius. The hospital offers all the medical/surgical services of a typical small hospital. It has a staff of 18 full-time doctors and 20 part-time visiting specialists. East Valley has a payroll of 150 employees consisting of technicians, nurses, therapists, managers, directors, administrators, dieticians, secretaries, data processors, and janitors.

Instructions

With the class divided into groups, discuss and answer the following.

a. Using your (limited, moderate, or in-depth) knowledge of a hospital's operations, identify as many **activities** as you can that would serve as the basis for implementing an activity-based costing system.

b. For each of the activities listed in (a), identify a **cost driver** that would serve as a valid measure of the resources consumed by the activity.

Managerial Analysis

CT17.2 Ideal Manufacturing Company has supported a research and development (R&D) department that has for many years been the sole contributor to the company's new farm machinery products. The R&D activity is an overhead cost center that performs services only to in-house manufacturing departments (four different product lines), all of which produce agricultural/farm/ranch-related machinery products.

The department has never sold its services to outside companies. But, because of its long history of success, larger manufacturers of agricultural products have approached Ideal to hire its R&D department for special projects. Because the costs of operating the R&D department have been spiraling uncontrollably, Ideal's management is considering entertaining these outside approaches to absorb the increasing costs. However, (1) management doesn't have any cost basis for charging R&D services to outsiders, and (2) it needs to gain control of its R&D costs. Management decides to implement an activity-based costing system in order to determine the charges for both outsiders and the in-house users of the department's services.

R&D activities fall into four pools with the following annual costs.

Market analysis	$1,050,000
Product design	2,350,000
Product development	3,600,000
Prototype testing	1,400,000

Activity analysis determines that the appropriate cost drivers and their usage for the four activities are:

Activities	Cost Drivers	Total Estimated Drivers
Market analysis	Hours of analysis	15,000 hours
Product design	Number of designs	2,500 designs
Product development	Number of products	90 products
Prototype testing	Number of tests	500 tests

Instructions

a. Compute the activity-based overhead rate for each activity cost pool.

b. How much cost would be charged to an in-house manufacturing department that consumed 1,800 hours of market analysis time, was provided 280 designs relating to 10 products, and requested 92 engineering tests?

c. How much cost would serve as the basis for pricing an R&D bid with an outside company on a contract that would consume 800 hours of analysis time, require 178 designs relating to 3 products, and result in 70 engineering tests?

d. What is the benefit to Ideal Manufacturing of applying activity-based costing to its R&D activity for both in-house and outside charging purposes?

Real-World Focus

CT17.3 **Service** An article in *Cost Management*, by Kocakulah, Bartlett, and Albin entitled "ABC for Calculating Mortgage Loan Servicing Expenses" (July/August 2009, p. 36), discusses a use of ABC in the financial services industry.

Instructions

Read the article (obtain online or at your library) and then answer the following questions.

a. What are some of the benefits of ABC that relate to the financial services industry?

b. What are three things that the company's original costing method did not take into account?

c. What were some of the cost drivers used by the company in the ABC approach?

Ethics Case

CT17.4 Curtis Rich, the cost accountant for Hi-Power Mower Company, recently installed activity-based costing at Hi-Power's St. Louis lawn tractor (riding mower) plant where three models—the 8-horsepower Bladerunner, the 12-horsepower Quickcut, and the 18-horsepower Supercut—are manufactured. Curtis's new product costs for these three models show that the company's traditional costing system had been significantly undercosting the 18-horsepower Supercut. This was due primarily to the lower sales volume of the Supercut compared to the Bladerunner and the Quickcut.

Before completing his analysis and reporting these results to management, Curtis is approached by his friend Ed Gray, who is the production manager for the 18-horsepower Supercut model. Ed has heard from one of Curtis's staff about the new product costs and is upset and worried for his job because the new costs show the Supercut to be losing, rather than making, money.

At first, Ed condemns the new cost system, whereupon Curtis explains the practice of activity-based costing and why it is more accurate than the company's present system. Even more worried now, Ed begs Curtis, "Massage the figures just enough to save the line from being discontinued. You don't want me to lose my job, do you? Anyway, nobody will know."

Curtis holds firm but agrees to recompute all his calculations for accuracy before submitting his costs to management.

Instructions

a. Who are the stakeholders in this situation?
b. What, if any, are the ethical considerations in this situation?
c. What are Curtis's ethical obligations to the company? To his friend?

All About You

CT17.5 There are many resources available on the Internet to assist people in time management. Some of these resources are designed specifically for college students.

Instructions

Do an Internet search of Dartmouth College's time-management video. Watch the video and then answer the following questions.

a. What are the main tools of time management for students, and what is each used for?
b. At what time of day are students most inclined to waste time? What time of day is the best for studying complex topics?
c. How can employing time-management practices be a "liberating" experience?
d. Why is goal-setting important? What are the characteristics of good goals, and what steps should you take to help you develop your goals?

Considering Your Costs and Benefits

CT17.6 As discussed in the chapter, the principles underlying activity-based costing have evolved into the broader approach known as *activity-based management*. One of the common practices of activity-based management is to identify all business activities, classify each activity as either a value-added or a non–value-added activity, and then try to reduce or eliminate the time spent on non–value-added activities. Consider the implications of applying this same approach to your everyday life, at work and at school. How do you spend your time each day? How much of your day is spent on activities that help you accomplish your objectives, and how much of your day is spent on activities that do not add value?

Many self-help books and websites offer suggestions on how to improve your time management. Should you minimize the "non–value-added" hours in your life by adopting the methods suggested by these sources? The basic arguments for and against are as follows.

YES: There are a limited number of hours in a day. You should try to maximize your chances of achieving your goals by eliminating the time that you waste.

NO: Life is about more than working yourself to death. Being an efficiency expert doesn't guarantee that you will be happy. Schedules and daily planners are too constraining.

Instructions

Write a response indicating your position regarding this situation. Provide support for your view.

CHAPTER 18

Cost-Volume-Profit

Chapter Preview

As the following Feature Story indicates, to manage any size business you must understand how costs respond to changes in sales volume and the effect of costs and revenues on profits. A prerequisite to understanding cost-volume-profit (CVP) relationships is knowledge of how costs behave. In this chapter, we first explain the considerations involved in cost behavior analysis. Then, we discuss and illustrate CVP analysis.

Feature Story

Don't Worry—Just Get Big

It wasn't that Jeff didn't have a good job. He was a vice president at a Wall Street firm. But, despite his good position, he quit his job, moved to Seattle, and started an online retailer, which he named **Amazon.com**. Like any good entrepreneur, Jeff Bezos strove to keep his initial investment small. Operations were run out of his garage. And, to avoid the need for a warehouse, he took orders for books and had them shipped from other distributors' warehouses.

By its fourth month, Amazon was selling 100 books a day. In its first full year, it had $15.7 million in sales. The next year, sales increased eightfold. Two years later, sales were $1.6 billion.

Although its sales growth was impressive, Amazon's ability to lose money was equally amazing. One analyst nicknamed it *Amazon.bomb*, while another, predicting its demise, called it *Amazon.toast*. Why was it losing money? The company used every available dollar to reinvest in itself. It built massive warehouses and bought increasingly sophisticated (and expensive) computers and equipment to improve its distribution system. This desire to grow as fast as possible was captured in a T-shirt slogan at its company picnic, which read "Eat another hot dog, get big fast." This buying binge was increasing the company's fixed costs at a rate that exceeded its sales growth. Skeptics predicted that Amazon would soon run out of cash. It didn't.

At the end of one year, even as it announced record profits, Amazon's share price fell by 9%. Why? Because although the company was predicting that its sales revenue in the next quarter would increase by at least 28%, it predicted that its operating profit would fall by at least 2% and perhaps by as much as 34%. The company made no apologies. It explained that it was in the process of expanding from 39 distribution centers to 52. As Amazon's finance chief noted, "You're not as productive on those assets for some time. I'm very pleased with the investments we're making and we've shown over our history that we've been able to make great returns on the capital we invest in." In other words, eat another hot dog.

Sources: Christine Frey and John Cook, "How Amazon.com Survived, Thrived and Turned a Profit," *Seattle Post* (January 28, 2008); Stu Woo, "Sticker Shock Over Amazon Growth," *Wall Street Journal* (January 28, 2011); and Miriam Guttfried, "Amazon's Never-Ending Story," *Wall Street Journal* (April 25, 2014).

 Watch the *Southwest Airlines* video in WileyPLUS to learn more about cost-volume-profit analysis in the real world.

Chapter Outline
LEARNING OBJECTIVES

LO 1 Explain variable, fixed, and mixed costs and the relevant range.	• Variable costs • Fixed costs • Relevant range • Mixed costs	**DO IT! 1** Types of Costs
LO 2 Apply the high-low method to determine the components of mixed costs.	• High-low method • Identifying variable and fixed costs	**DO IT! 2** High-Low Method
LO 3 Prepare a CVP income statement to determine contribution margin.	• Basic components • CVP income statement	**DO IT! 3** CVP Income Statement
LO 4 Compute the break-even point using three approaches.	• Mathematical equation • Contribution margin technique • Graphic presentation	**DO IT! 4** Break-Even Analysis
LO 5 Determine the sales required to earn target net income and determine margin of safety.	• Target net income • Margin of safety	**DO IT! 5** Break-Even, Margin of Safety, and Target Net Income

Go to the Review and Practice section at the end of the chapter for a targeted summary and practice applications with solutions.
Visit WileyPLUS for additional tutorials and practice opportunities.

Cost Behavior Analysis

> **LEARNING OBJECTIVE 1**
> Explain variable, fixed, and mixed costs and the relevant range.

Cost behavior analysis is the study of how specific costs respond to changes in the level of business activity. As you might expect, some costs change when activity changes and others remain the same. For example, for an airline company such as **Southwest** or **United**, the longer the flight, the higher the fuel costs. On the other hand, **Massachusetts General Hospital**'s costs to staff the emergency room on any given night are relatively constant regardless of the number of patients treated. A knowledge of cost behavior helps management plan operations and decide between alternative courses of action. Cost behavior analysis applies to all types of entities.

The starting point in cost behavior analysis is measuring the key business activities. Activity levels may be expressed in terms of sales dollars (in a retail company), miles driven (in a trucking company), room occupancy (in a hotel), or dance classes taught (by a dance studio). Many companies use more than one measurement base. A manufacturer, for example, may use direct labor hours or units of output for manufacturing costs, and sales revenue or units sold for selling expenses.

For an activity level to be useful in cost behavior analysis, changes in the level or volume of activity should be correlated with changes in costs. The activity level selected is referred to as the activity index or driver. The **activity index** identifies the activity that causes changes in the behavior of costs. With an appropriate activity index, companies can classify the behavior of costs in response to changes in activity levels into three categories: variable, fixed, or mixed.

Variable Costs

Variable costs are costs that vary **in total** directly and proportionately with changes in the activity level. If the level increases 10%, total variable costs will increase 10%. If the level of activity decreases by 25%, variable costs will decrease 25%. Examples of variable costs include direct materials and direct labor for a manufacturer; cost of goods sold, sales commissions, and freight-out for a merchandiser; and gasoline in airline and trucking companies. A variable cost may also be defined as a cost that **remains the same *per unit* at every level of activity**.

To illustrate the behavior of a variable cost, assume that Damon Company manufactures tablet computers that contain cameras that cost $10. The activity index is the number of tablet computers produced. As Damon manufactures each tablet, the total cost of cameras installed in tablets increases by $10. As part (a) of **Illustration 18.1** shows, total cost of the cameras will be $20,000 (2,000 × $10) if Damon produces 2,000 tablets, and $100,000 when it produces 10,000 tablets. We also can see that a variable cost remains the same per unit as the level of activity changes. As part (b) of Illustration 18.1 shows, the unit cost of $10 for the cameras is the same whether Damon produces 2,000 or 10,000 tablets.

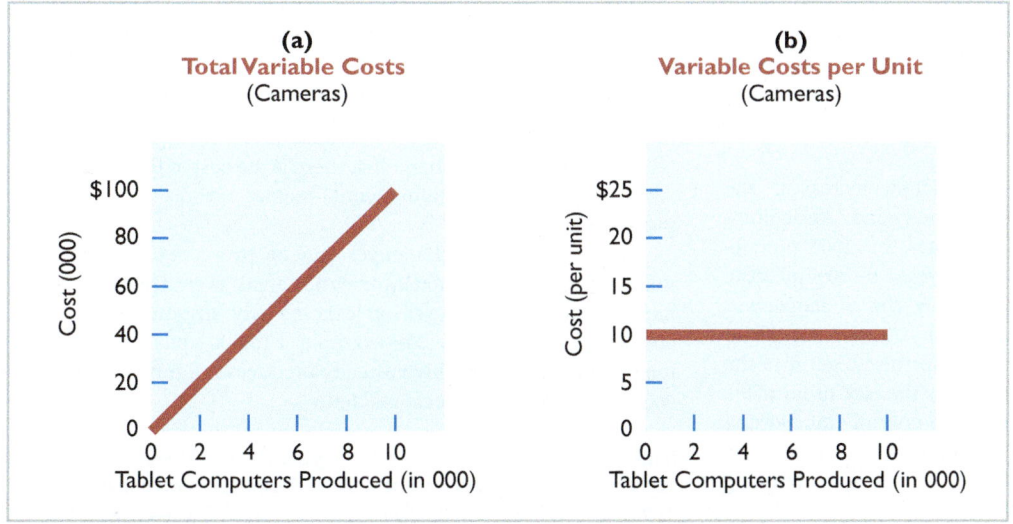

ILLUSTRATION 18.1
Behavior of total and unit variable costs; variable costs per unit remain constant

Companies that rely heavily on labor either to manufacture a product or perform a service, such as **Hilton** or **Marriott**, are likely to have a high percentage of variable costs. In contrast, companies that use a high proportion of machinery and equipment in producing revenue, such as **AT&T** or **Duke Energy Co.**, may have a lower percentage of variable costs.

Fixed Costs

Fixed costs are costs that **remain the same in total** regardless of changes in the activity level. Examples include property taxes, insurance, rent, supervisory salaries, and depreciation on buildings and equipment. Because total fixed costs remain constant as activity changes, it follows that **fixed costs *per unit* vary inversely with activity: As volume increases, unit cost declines, and vice versa**.

To illustrate the behavior of fixed costs, assume that Damon Company leases its productive facilities at a cost of $10,000 per month. Total fixed costs of the facilities remain a constant $10,000 at every level of activity, as part (a) of **Illustration 18.2** shows. But, **on a per unit basis, the cost of rent declines as activity increases**, as part (b) of Illustration 18.2 shows. At 2,000 units, the unit cost per tablet computer is $5 ($10,000 ÷ 2,000). When Damon produces 10,000 tablets, the unit cost of the rent is only $1 per tablet ($10,000 ÷ 10,000).

ILLUSTRATION 18.2

Behavior of total and unit fixed costs

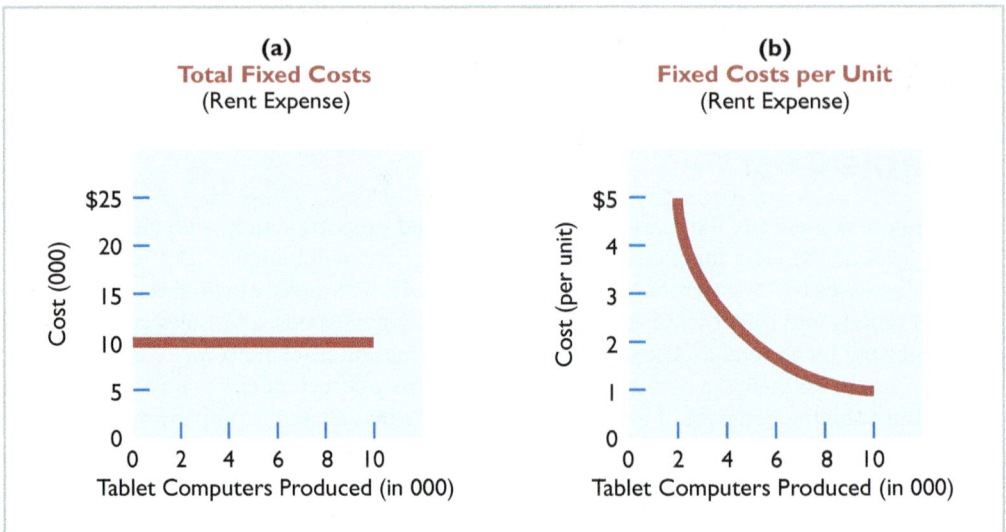

The trend for many manufacturers is to have more fixed costs and fewer variable costs. This trend is the result of increased use of automation and less use of employee labor. As a result, depreciation and lease charges (fixed costs) increase, whereas direct labor costs (variable costs) decrease.

People, Planet, and Profit Insight   BrightFarms

Gardens in the Sky

© Jani Bryson/iStockphoto

Because of population increases, the United Nations' Food and Agriculture Organization estimates that food production will need to increase by 70% by 2050. Also, by 2050, roughly 70% of people will live in cities, which means more food needs to be hauled further to get it to the consumer. To address the lack of farmable land and reduce the cost of transporting produce, some companies, such as New York-based **BrightFarms**, are building urban greenhouses.

This sounds great, but do the numbers work? Some variable costs would be reduced. For example, the use of pesticides, herbicides, fuel costs for shipping, and water would all drop. Soil erosion would be a non-issue since plants would be grown hydroponically (in a solution of water and minerals), and land requirements would be reduced because of vertical structures. But, other costs would be higher. First, there is the cost of the building. Also, any multistory building would require artificial lighting for plants on lower floors.

Until these cost challenges can be overcome, it appears that these urban greenhouses may not break even. On the other hand, rooftop greenhouses on existing city structures already appear financially viable. For example, a 15,000 square-foot rooftop greenhouse in Brooklyn already produces roughly 30 tons of vegetables per year for local residents.

Sources: "Vertical Farming: Does It Really Stack Up?" *The Economist* (December 9, 2010); and Jane Black, "BrightFarms Idea: Greenhouses That Cut Short the Path from Plant to Grocery Shelf," *The Washington Post* (May 7, 2013).

What are some of the variable and fixed costs that are impacted by hydroponic farming? (Go to WileyPLUS for this answer and additional questions.)

Relevant Range

In Illustration 18.1 part (a), a straight line is drawn throughout the entire range of the activity index for total variable costs. In essence, the assumption is that the costs are **linear**. If a relationship is linear (that is, straight-line), then changes in the activity index will result in a direct, proportional change in the total variable cost. For example, if the activity level doubles, the cost doubles.

It is now necessary to ask: Is the straight-line relationship realistic? In most business situations, a straight-line relationship **does not exist** for variable costs throughout the entire range of possible activity. At abnormally low levels of activity, it may be impossible to be cost-efficient. Small-scale operations may not allow the company to obtain quantity discounts for raw materials or to use specialized labor. In contrast, at abnormally high levels of activity, labor costs may increase sharply because of overtime pay. Also, at high activity levels, materials costs may jump significantly because of excess spoilage caused by worker fatigue.

As a result, in the real world, the relationship between the behavior of a variable cost and changes in the activity level is often **curvilinear**, as shown in part (a) of Illustration 18.3. In the curved sections of the line, a change in the activity index will not result in a direct, proportional change in the variable cost. That is, a doubling of the activity index will not result in an exact doubling of the variable cost. The variable cost may more than double, or it may be less than double.

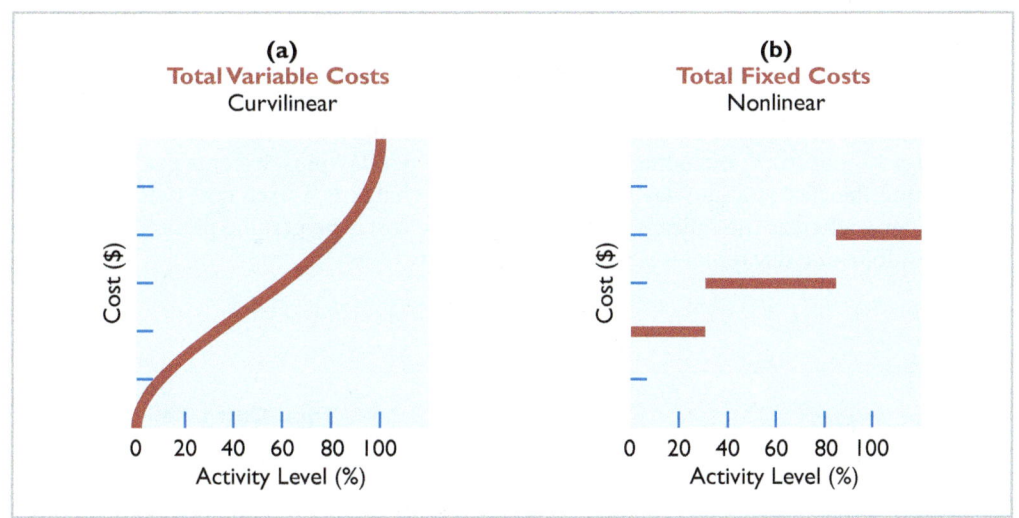

ILLUSTRATION 18.3

Nonlinear behavior of variable and fixed costs

Total fixed costs also do not have a straight-line relationship over the entire range of activity. Some fixed costs will not change. But it is possible for management to change other fixed costs (see **Helpful Hint**). For example, in some instances, salaried employees (fixed) are replaced with freelance workers (variable). Some costs are step costs. For example, once a company exceeds certain levels of activity, it may have to add an additional warehouse. Illustration 18.3, part (b), shows an example of step-cost behavior of total fixed costs through all potential levels of activity.

For most companies, operating at almost zero or at 100% capacity is the exception rather than the rule. Instead, companies often operate over a somewhat narrower range, such as 40–80% of capacity. The range over which a company expects to operate during a year is called the **relevant range** of the activity index (see **Alternative Terminology**). Within the relevant range, as both diagrams in Illustration 18.4 show, a straight-line relationship generally exists for both variable and fixed costs between 40 and 80% of capacity.

HELPFUL HINT

Fixed costs that may be changed by managers include research, such as new product development, and management training programs.

ALTERNATIVE TERMINOLOGY

The relevant range is also called the *normal* or *practical range*.

> **ILLUSTRATION 18.4**
> Linear behavior within relevant range

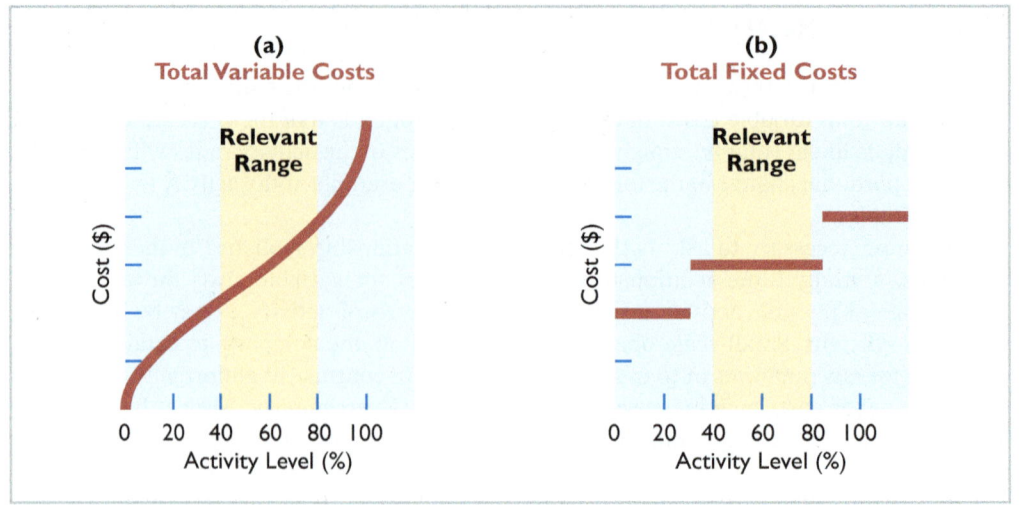

As you can see, although the linear (straight-line) relationship may not be completely realistic, **the linear assumption produces useful data for CVP analysis as long as the level of activity remains within the relevant range**.

Mixed Costs

Mixed costs are costs that contain both a variable- and a fixed-cost element. **Mixed costs, therefore, change in total but not proportionately with changes in the activity level.**

The rental of a **U-Haul** truck is a good example of a mixed cost. Assume that local rental terms for a 17-foot truck, including insurance, are $50 per day plus 50 cents per mile. When determining the cost of a one-day rental, the per day charge is a fixed cost (with respect to miles driven), whereas the mileage charge is a variable cost. The graphic presentation of the rental cost for a one-day rental is shown in **Illustration 18.5**.

> **ILLUSTRATION 18.5**
> Behavior of a mixed cost

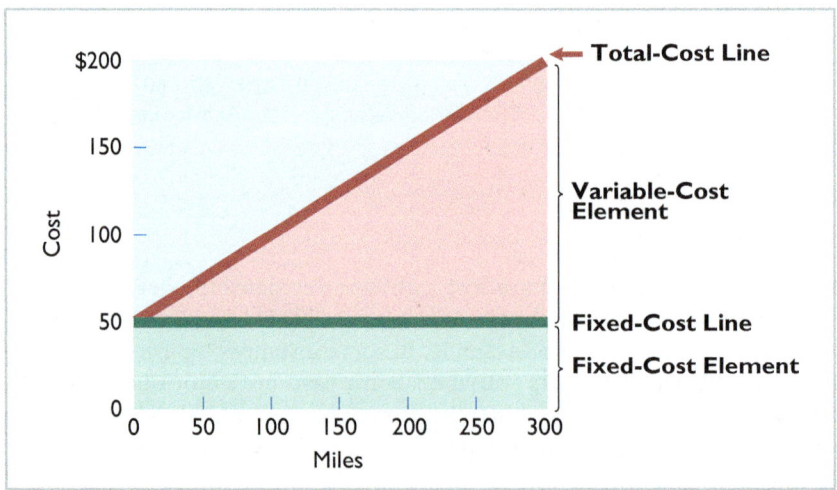

In this case, the fixed-cost element is the cost of having the service available. The variable-cost element is the cost of actually using the service (miles driven). Utility costs such as electricity are another example of a mixed cost. Each month the electric bill includes a flat service fee plus a usage charge.

DO IT! 1 | Types of Costs

Helena Company reports the following total costs at two levels of production.

	10,000 Units	20,000 Units
Direct materials	$20,000	$40,000
Maintenance	8,000	10,000
Direct labor	17,000	34,000
Indirect materials	1,000	2,000
Depreciation	4,000	4,000
Utilities	3,000	5,000
Rent	6,000	6,000

Classify each cost as variable, fixed, or mixed.

ACTION PLAN

- Recall that a variable cost varies in total directly and proportionately with each change in activity level.
- Recall that a fixed cost remains the same in total with each change in activity level.
- Recall that a mixed cost changes in total but not proportionately with each change in activity level.

Solution

Direct materials, direct labor, and indirect materials are variable costs because the total cost doubles with the doubling in activity.
Depreciation and rent are fixed costs because the total cost does not vary with the change in activity.
Maintenance and utilities are mixed costs because the total cost changes, but the change is not proportional to the change in activity.

Related exercise material: **BE18.1, BE18.2, BE18.3, DO IT! 18.1, E18.1, E18.2, E18.4, and E18.6.**

Mixed Costs Analysis

LEARNING OBJECTIVE 2
Apply the high-low method to determine the components of mixed costs.

For purposes of cost-volume-profit analysis, **mixed costs must be classified into their fixed and variable elements**. How does management make the classification? One possibility is to determine the variable and fixed components each time a mixed cost is incurred. But because of time and cost constraints, this approach is rarely followed. Instead, the usual approach is to collect data on the behavior of the mixed costs at various levels of activity. Analysts then identify the fixed- and variable-cost components. Companies use various types of analysis. One type of analysis, called the **high-low method**, is discussed next.

High-Low Method

The **high-low method** uses the total costs incurred at the high and low levels of activity to classify mixed costs into fixed and variable components. The difference in costs between the high and low levels represents variable costs, since only the variable-cost element can change as activity levels change.

The steps in computing fixed and variable costs under this method are as follows.

1. Determine variable cost per unit from the formula shown in Illustration 18.6. This is the slope of the cost function.

| Change in Total Costs at High versus Low Activity Level | ÷ | High minus Low Activity Level | = | Variable Cost per Unit |

ILLUSTRATION 18.6
Formula for variable cost per unit using high-low method

To illustrate, assume that Metro Transit Company has the maintenance costs and mileage data for its fleet of buses over a 6-month period shown in **Illustration 18.7**.

ILLUSTRATION 18.7
Assumed maintenance costs and mileage data

Month	Miles Driven	Total Cost	Month	Miles Driven	Total Cost
January	20,000	$30,000	April	50,000	$63,000
February	40,000	48,000	May	30,000	42,000
March	35,000	49,000	June	43,000	61,000

The high and low levels of activity are 50,000 miles in April and 20,000 miles in January. The maintenance costs at these two levels are $63,000 and $30,000, respectively. The difference in maintenance costs is $33,000 ($63,000 − $30,000), and the difference in miles is 30,000 (50,000 − 20,000). Therefore, for Metro Transit, variable cost per unit is $1.10, computed as follows.

$$\$33,000 \div 30,000 = \$1.10$$

2. **Determine the total fixed costs by subtracting the total variable costs at either the high or the low activity level from the total cost at that activity level.**

Illustration 18.8 shows the computations for Metro Transit.

ILLUSTRATION 18.8
High-low method computation of fixed costs

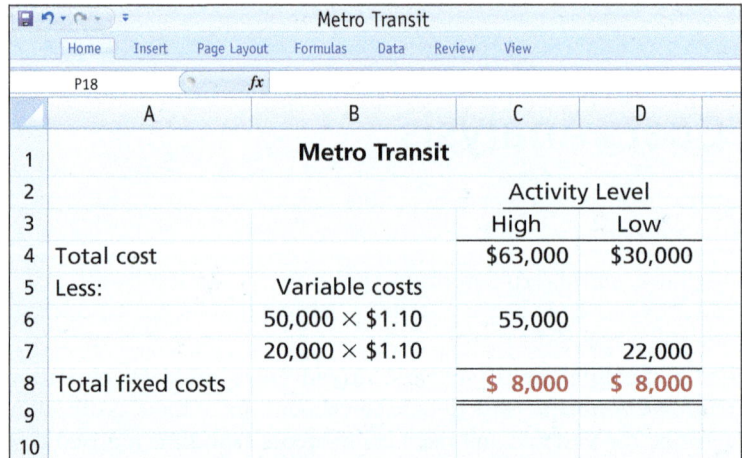

Maintenance costs are therefore **$8,000 per month of fixed costs plus $1.10 per mile of variable costs.** This is represented by the following formula, referred to as the total cost equation.

$$\text{Maintenance costs} = \$8,000 + (\$1.10 \times \text{Miles driven})$$

For example, at 45,000 miles, estimated maintenance costs would be $8,000 fixed and $49,500 variable ($1.10 × 45,000) for a total of $57,500.

The graph in **Illustration 18.9** plots the 6-month data for Metro Transit Company. The red line drawn in the graph connects the high and low data points (in squares) and therefore represents the equation that we just solved using the high-low method. The red, "high-low" line intersects the y-axis at $8,000 (the fixed-cost level), and it rises by its slope of $1.10 per unit (the variable cost per unit). Note that a completely different line would result if we chose any two of the other data points. That is, by choosing any two other data points, we would end up with a different estimate of fixed costs and a different variable cost per unit. Thus, from this scatter plot, we can see that while the high-low method is simple, the result is rather arbitrary. A better approach, which uses information from all the data points to estimate fixed and variable costs, is called *regression analysis*. A discussion of regression analysis is provided in Appendix 18A as well as in the Excel video available in WileyPLUS.

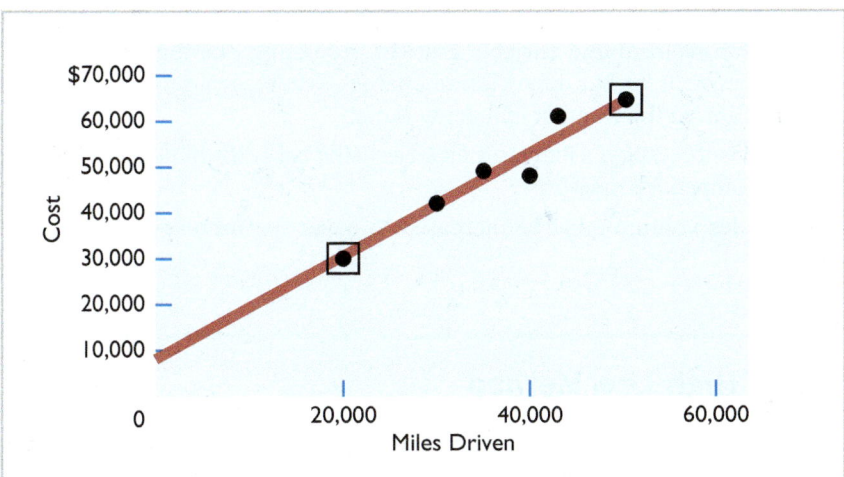

ILLUSTRATION 18.9

Scatter plot for Metro Transit Company

Management Insight   Kroger Co.

tiero/iStock/ Getty Images

Are Robotic Workers More Humane?

Warehouse distribution centers for large retailers and grocers employ more than 800,000 people in the United States. But many companies, such as grocer **Kroger Co.**, have a hard time finding and retaining warehouse workers. One reason? Studies have shown that some warehouse workers walk up to 20 miles and lift 50,000 pounds during a single day. As a result, as the needs for storage increases and companies are faced with the proposition of building massive new warehouses, some are choosing instead to invest in robotic warehousing systems.

Robots can provide many advantages over their human counterparts. Robots need aisles that are less than 30 inches wide, as opposed to traditional warehouse aisles that are 10 to 12 feet wide. Moving at speeds of up to 25 miles per hour, robots can drop off and retrieve warehouse cases about five times as fast as a human. Robotic systems cut labor costs by about 80%, and they cut warehouse size anywhere from 25% to 40%. However, a fully automated system costs between $40 to $80 million, so the switch to robotic systems is not a trivial decision.

Source: Robbie Whelan, "Fully Autonomous Robots: The Warehouse Workers of the Near Future," *Wall Street Journal* (September 20, 2016).

How would a company's variable and fixed costs change if it adopts a robotic system? (Go to WileyPLUS for this answer and additional questions).

Importance of Identifying Variable and Fixed Costs

Why is it important to segregate mixed costs into variable and fixed elements? The answer may become apparent if we look at the following four business decisions.

1. If **American Airlines** is to make a profit when it reduces all domestic fares by 30%, what reduction in costs or increase in passengers will be required?

   Answer: To make a profit when it cuts domestic fares by 30%, American Airlines will have to increase the number of passengers or cut its variable costs for those flights. Its fixed costs will not change.

2. If **Ford Motor Company** meets workers' demands for higher wages, what increase in sales revenue will be needed to maintain current profit levels?

   Answer: Higher wages at Ford Motor Company will increase the variable costs of manufacturing automobiles. To maintain present profit levels, Ford will have to cut other variable or fixed costs, sell more automobiles, or increase the price of its automobiles.

3. If **United States Steel Corp.**'s program to modernize plant facilities through significant equipment purchases reduces the work force by 50%, what will be the effect on the cost of producing one ton of steel?

Answer: The modernizing of plant facilities at United States Steel Corp. changes the proportion of fixed and variable costs of producing one ton of steel. Fixed costs increase because of higher depreciation charges, whereas variable costs decrease due to the reduction in the number of steelworkers.

4. What happens if **Kellogg's** increases its advertising expenses but cannot increase prices because of competitive pressure?

Answer: Sales volume must be increased to cover the increase in fixed advertising costs.

ACTION PLAN
- Determine the highest and lowest levels of activity.
- Compute variable cost per unit as Change in total costs ÷ (High − low activity level) = Variable cost per unit.
- Compute fixed cost as Total cost − (Variable cost per unit × Units produced) = Total fixed cost.

DO IT! 2 | High-Low Method

Byrnes Company accumulates the following data concerning a mixed cost, using units produced as the activity level.

	Units Produced	Total Cost
March	9,800	$14,740
April	8,500	13,250
May	7,000	11,100
June	7,600	12,000
July	8,100	12,460

a. Compute the variable-cost and fixed-cost elements using the high-low method.
b. Using the information from your answer to part (a), write the cost formula.
c. Estimate the total cost if the company produces 8,000 units.

Solution

a. Variable cost: ($14,740 − $11,100) ÷ (9,800 − 7,000) = $1.30 per unit
 Fixed cost: $14,740 − ($1.30 × 9,800 units) = $2,000
 or $11,100 − ($1.30 × 7,000 units) = $2,000
b. Cost = $2,000 + ($1.30 × units produced)
c. Total cost to produce 8,000 units: $2,000 + $10,400 ($1.30 × 8,000 units) = $12,400

Related exercise material: **BE18.4, BE18.5, DO IT! 18.2, E18.3, and E18.5.**

Cost-Volume-Profit Analysis

> **LEARNING OBJECTIVE 3**
> Prepare a CVP income statement to determine contribution margin.

Cost-volume-profit (CVP) analysis is the study of the effects of changes in costs and volume on a company's profits. CVP analysis is important in profit planning. It also is a critical factor in such management decisions as setting selling prices, determining product mix, and maximizing use of production facilities.

Basic Components

CVP analysis considers the interrelationships among the components shown in **Illustration 18.10**.

ILLUSTRATION 18.10 Components of CVP analysis

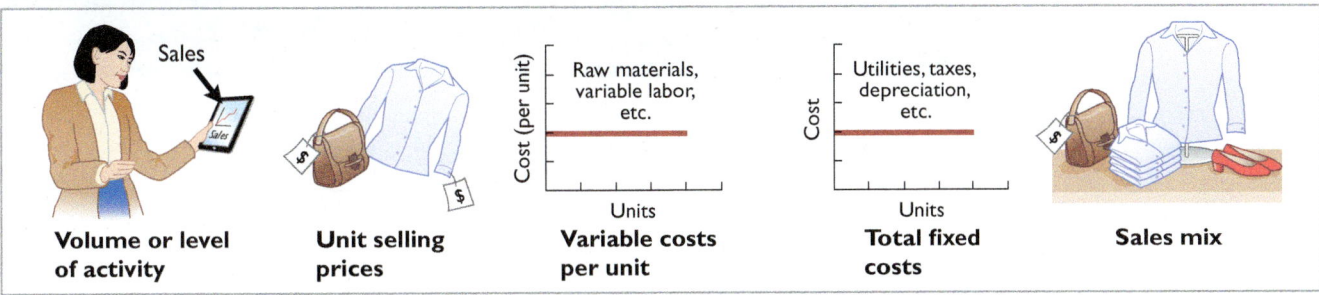

The following assumptions underlie each CVP analysis.

1. The behavior of both costs and revenues is linear throughout the relevant range of the activity index.
2. Costs can be classified accurately as either variable or fixed.
3. Changes in activity are the only factors that affect costs.
4. All units produced are sold.
5. When more than one type of product is sold, the sales mix will remain constant. That is, the percentage that each product represents of total sales will stay the same. Sales mix complicates CVP analysis because different products will have different cost relationships. In this chapter, we assume a single product. In Chapter 19, however, we examine the sales mix more closely.

When these assumptions are not valid, the CVP analysis may be inaccurate.

CVP Income Statement

Because CVP is so important for decision-making, management often wants this information reported in a **cost-volume-profit (CVP) income statement** format for internal use. The CVP income statement classifies costs as variable or fixed and computes a contribution margin. **Contribution margin (CM)** is the amount of revenue remaining after deducting variable costs. It is often stated both as a total amount and on a per unit basis.

We use Vargo Electronics Company to illustrate a CVP income statement. Vargo Electronics produces cell phones. **Illustration 18.11** presents relevant data for the cell phones sold by this company in June 2022.

Unit selling price of cell phone	$500
Unit variable costs*	$300
Total monthly fixed costs**	$200,000
Units sold	1,600

*Includes variable manufacturing costs and variable selling and administrative expenses.
**Includes fixed manufacturing costs and fixed selling and administrative expenses.

ILLUSTRATION 18.11
Assumed selling and cost data for Vargo Electronics

Note that in Illustration 18.11, as well as in the applications and assignment material of CVP analysis that follow, **we assume that the term "cost" includes all costs and expenses related to production and sale of the product. That is, cost includes manufacturing costs plus selling and administrative expenses.**

The CVP income statement for Vargo would therefore be reported as shown in **Illustration 18.12**.

A traditional income statement and a CVP income statement both report the same net income of $120,000. However, a traditional income statement does not classify costs as variable or fixed, and therefore it does not report a contribution margin. In addition, sometimes per unit amounts and percentage of sales amounts are shown in separate columns on a CVP income statement to facilitate CVP analysis. *Homework assignments specify which columns to present.*

ILLUSTRATION 18.12
CVP income statement, with net income

Vargo Electronics Company
CVP Income Statement
For the Month Ended June 30, 2022

	Total
Sales (1,600 × $500)	$800,000
Variable costs (1,600 × $300)	480,000
Contribution margin	320,000
Fixed costs	200,000
Net income	**$120,000**

Unit Contribution Margin

Illustration 18.13 shows the formula for **unit contribution margin** and the computation for Vargo Electronics.

ILLUSTRATION 18.13
Formula for unit contribution margin

Unit Selling Price	−	Unit Variable Costs	=	Unit Contribution Margin
$500	−	$300	=	$200

Decision Tools

The unit contribution margin indicates the increase in income that results from every additional unit sold after the break-even point.

Unit contribution margin indicates that for every cell phone sold, the selling price exceeds the variable costs by $200 (see **Decision Tools**). Vargo generates $200 per unit sold to cover fixed costs and contribute to net income. Because Vargo has fixed costs of $200,000, it must sell 1,000 cell phones ($200,000 ÷ $200) to cover its fixed costs.

At the point where total contribution margin exactly equals fixed costs, Vargo will report net income of zero. At this point, referred to as the **break-even point**, total costs (variable plus fixed) exactly equal total revenue. Illustration 18.14 shows Vargo's CVP income statement at the point where net income equals zero. It shows a contribution margin of $200,000, and a unit contribution margin of $200 ($500 − $300).

ILLUSTRATION 18.14
CVP income statement, with zero net income

Vargo Electronics Company
CVP Income Statement
For the Month Ended June 30, 2022

	Total	Per Unit
Sales (1,000 × $500)	$500,000	$500
Variable costs (1,000 × $300)	300,000	300
Contribution margin	200,000	$200
Fixed costs	200,000	
Net income	$ –0–	

It follows that for every cell phone sold above the break-even point of 1,000 units, **net income increases by the amount of the unit contribution margin, $200**. For example, assume that Vargo sold one more cell phone, for a total of 1,001 cell phones sold. In this case, Vargo reports net income of $200, as shown in Illustration 18.15.

ILLUSTRATION 18.15
CVP income statement, with net income and per unit data

Vargo Electronics Company
CVP Income Statement
For the Month Ended June 30, 2022

	Total	Per Unit
Sales (1,001 × $500)	$500,500	$500
Variable costs (1,001 × $300)	300,300	300
Contribution margin	200,200	$200
Fixed costs	200,000	
Net income	$ 200	

Contribution Margin Ratio

Some managers prefer to use a contribution margin ratio in CVP analysis. The contribution margin ratio is the contribution margin expressed as a percentage of sales. Vargo Electronics has a contribution margin ratio of 40% (contribution margin of $200,200 divided by sales of $500,500), as shown in the percent of sales column in **Illustration 18.16**.

ILLUSTRATION 18.16
CVP income statement, with net income and percent of sales data

Vargo Electronics Company
CVP Income Statement
For the Month Ended June 30, 2022

	Total	Percent of Sales
Sales (1,000 × $500)	$500,500	100%
Variable costs (1,000 × $300)	300,300	60
Contribution margin	**200,200**	**40%**
Fixed costs	200,000	
Net income	**$ 200**	

Alternatively, the **contribution margin ratio** can be determined by dividing the unit contribution margin by the unit selling price. **Illustration 18.17** shows the ratio for Vargo Electronics.

ILLUSTRATION 18.17
Formula for contribution margin ratio

Unit Contribution Margin	÷	Unit Selling Price	=	Contribution Margin Ratio
$200	÷	$500	=	40%

The contribution margin ratio of 40% means that Vargo generates 40 cents of contribution margin with each dollar of sales. That is, $0.40 of each sales dollar (40% × $1) is available to apply to fixed costs and to contribute to net income (see **Decision Tools**).

This expression of contribution margin is very helpful in determining the effect of changes in sales on net income. For example, if Vargo's sales increase $100,000, net income will increase $40,000 (40% × $100,000). Thus, by using the contribution margin ratio, managers can quickly determine increases in net income from any change in sales.

We can also see this effect through a CVP income statement. Assume that Vargo's current sales are $500,000 and it wants to know the effect of a $100,000 (200-unit) increase in sales. Vargo prepares the comparative CVP income statement analysis shown in **Illustration 18.18**.

Decision Tools
The contribution margin ratio indicates by how much every dollar of sales will increase income after the break-even point.

ILLUSTRATION 18.18 Comparative CVP income statements

Vargo Electronics Company
CVP Income Statement
For the Month Ended June 30, 2022

	No Change			With $100,000 Increase in Sales		
	Total	Per Unit	Percent of Sales	Total	Per Unit	Percent of Sales
Sales	$500,000	$500	100%	$600,000	$500	100%
Variable costs	300,000	300	60	360,000	300	60%
Contribution margin	**200,000**	**$200**	**40%**	**240,000**	**$200**	**40%**
Fixed costs	200,000			200,000		
Net income	**$ -0-**			**$ 40,000**		

The $40,000 increase in net income can be calculated on either a unit contribution margin basis (200 units × $200 per unit) or using the contribution margin ratio times the increase in sales dollars (40% × $100,000). Note that the unit contribution margin and contribution margin as a percentage of sales (that is, the contribution margin ratio) remain unchanged by the increase in sales.

Study these CVP income statements carefully. The concepts presented in these statements are used extensively in this and later chapters.

ACTION PLAN

- Provide a heading with the name of the company, name of statement, and period covered.
- Subtract variable costs from sales to determine contribution margin. Subtract fixed costs from contribution margin to determine net income.
- Express sales, variable costs and contribution margin on a per unit basis.

DO IT! 3 | CVP Income Statement

Ampco Industries produces and sells a cell phone-operated thermostat. Information regarding the costs and sales of thermostats during September 2022 are provided below.

Unit selling price of thermostat	$85
Unit variable costs	$32
Total monthly fixed costs	$190,000
Units sold	4,000

Prepare a CVP income statement for Ampco Industries for the month of September. Provide per unit values and total values.

Solution

Ampco Industries
CVP Income Statement
For the Month Ended September 30, 2022

	Total	Per Unit
Sales	$340,000	$85
Variable costs	128,000	32
Contribution margin	212,000	$53
Fixed costs	190,000	
Net income	$ 22,000	

Related exercise material: **BE18.6, BE18.7, DO IT! 18.3, and E18.7.**

Break-Even Analysis

LEARNING OBJECTIVE 4
Compute the break-even point using three approaches.

Decision Tools

Break-even analysis indicates the amount of sales units or sales dollars that a company needs to cover its costs.

A key relationship in CVP analysis is the level of activity at which total revenues equal total costs (both fixed and variable)—the **break-even point**. At this volume of sales, the company will realize no income but will suffer no loss. The process of finding the break-even point is called **break-even analysis**. Knowledge of the break-even point is useful to management when it considers decisions such as whether to introduce new product lines, change sales prices on established products, or enter new market areas (see **Decision Tools**).

The break-even point can be:

1. Computed from a mathematical equation.
2. Computed by using contribution margin.
3. Derived from a cost-volume-profit (CVP) graph.

The break-even point can be expressed either in **sales units** or **sales dollars**.

Mathematical Equation

Illustration 18.19 shows a common profit equation used as the basis for CVP analysis. This equation expresses net income as sales minus variable and fixed costs. Sales is expressed as the unit selling price ($500) times the number of units sold (Q). Variable costs are determined by multiplying the unit variable cost ($300) by the number of units sold (Q). When net income is set to zero, as it is in this illustration, this equation can be used to calculate the break-even point.

Sales	−	Variable Costs	−	Fixed Costs	=	Net Income
$500Q	−	$300Q	−	$200,000	=	$0

ILLUSTRATION 18.19
Profit equation

As shown in Illustration 18.14, net income equals zero when the contribution margin (sales minus variable costs) is equal to fixed costs. To reflect this, **Illustration 18.20** rewrites the equation with contribution margin (sales minus variable costs) on the left side, and fixed costs and net income of zero on the right. We can then compute the break-even point **in units** by **using unit selling prices** and **unit variable costs** and solving for the quantity (Q).

Sales	−	Variable Costs	−	Fixed Costs	=	Net Income
$500Q	−	$300Q	−	$200,000	=	$0
$500Q	−	$300Q	=	$200,000	+	$0
$200Q	=	$200,000				

$$Q = \frac{\$200,000}{\$200} = \frac{\text{Fixed Costs}}{\text{Unit Contribution Margin}}$$

$$Q = 1,000 \text{ units}$$

where

Q = number of units sold
$500 = unit selling price
$300 = unit variable costs
$200,000 = total fixed costs

ILLUSTRATION 18.20
Computation of break-even point in units

Thus, Vargo Electronics must sell 1,000 units to break even.

To find the amount of **sales dollars** required to break even, we multiply the units sold at the break-even point times the selling price per unit, as shown below.

$$1,000 \times \$500 = \$500,000 \text{ (break-even sales dollars)}$$

Contribution Margin Technique

Many managers employ the contribution margin to compute the break-even point.

Contribution Margin in Units

The final step in Illustration 18.20 divides fixed costs by the unit contribution margin (highlighted in red). Thus, rather than walk through all of the steps of the equation approach, we can simply employ this formula shown in **Illustration 18.21**.

Fixed Costs	÷	Unit Contribution Margin	=	Break-Even Point in Units
$200,000	÷	$200	=	1,000 units

ILLUSTRATION 18.21
Formula for break-even point in units using unit contribution margin

Why does this formula work? The unit contribution margin is the net amount by which each sale exceeds the variable costs per unit. Every sale generates this much to cover fixed costs. Consequently, if we divide fixed costs by the unit contribution margin, we know how many units we need to sell to break even.

Contribution Margin Ratio

As we will see in the next chapter, when a company has numerous products, it is not practical to determine the unit contribution margin for each product. In this case, using the contribution margin ratio is very useful for determining the break-even point in total dollars (rather than units). Recall that the contribution margin ratio is the percentage of each dollar of sales that is available to cover fixed costs and generate net income. Therefore, **to determine the sales dollars needed to cover fixed costs**, we divide fixed costs by the contribution margin ratio, as shown in **Illustration 18.22**.

ILLUSTRATION 18.22

Formula for break-even point in dollars using contribution margin ratio

Fixed Costs	÷	Contribution Margin Ratio	=	Break-Even Point in Dollars
$200,000	÷	40%	=	$500,000

To apply this formula to Vargo Electronics, consider that its 40% contribution margin ratio means that for every dollar sold, it generates 40 cents of contribution margin. The question is, how many dollars of sales does Vargo need in order to generate total contribution margin of $200,000 to pay off fixed costs? We divide the fixed costs of $200,000 by the 40 cents of contribution margin generated by each dollar of sales to arrive at $500,000 ($200,000 ÷ 40%). To prove this result, if we generate 40 cents of contribution margin for each dollar of sales, then the total contribution margin generated by $500,000 in sales is $200,000 ($500,000 × 40%).

Service Company Insight Flightserve

Digital Vision/
Getty Images

Charter Flights Offer a Good Deal

The Internet is wringing inefficiencies out of nearly every industry. While commercial aircraft spend roughly 4,000 hours a year in the air, chartered aircraft are flown only 500 hours annually. That means that they are sitting on the ground—not making any money—about 90% of the time.

One company, **Flightserve**, saw a business opportunity in that fact. For about the same cost as a first-class ticket, Flightserve matches up executives with charter flights in small "private jets."

The executive gets a more comfortable ride and avoids the hassle of big airports. Flightserve noted that the average charter jet has eight seats. When all eight seats are full, the company has an 80% profit margin. It breaks even at an average of 3.3 full seats per flight. Another company, **NetJets**, uses an alternative approach to increase utilization of jets and thus reduce fixed costs. It offers shared ownership in private jets.

Sources: "Jet Set Go," *The Economist* (March 18, 2000), p. 68; and Doug Gollan, "How NetJets' Private Jet Service Is Making Itself Whole Again," *Forbes* (June 3, 2015).

How did Flightserve determine that it would break even with 3.3 seats full per flight? (Go to WileyPLUS for this answer and additional questions.)

Graphic Presentation

An effective way to find the break-even point is to prepare a break-even graph. Because this graph also shows costs, volume, and profits, it is referred to as a **cost-volume-profit (CVP) graph**.

As the CVP graph in **Illustration 18.23** shows, sales volume is recorded along the horizontal axis. This axis should extend to the maximum level of expected sales. Both total revenues (sales) and total costs (fixed plus variable) are recorded on the vertical axis.

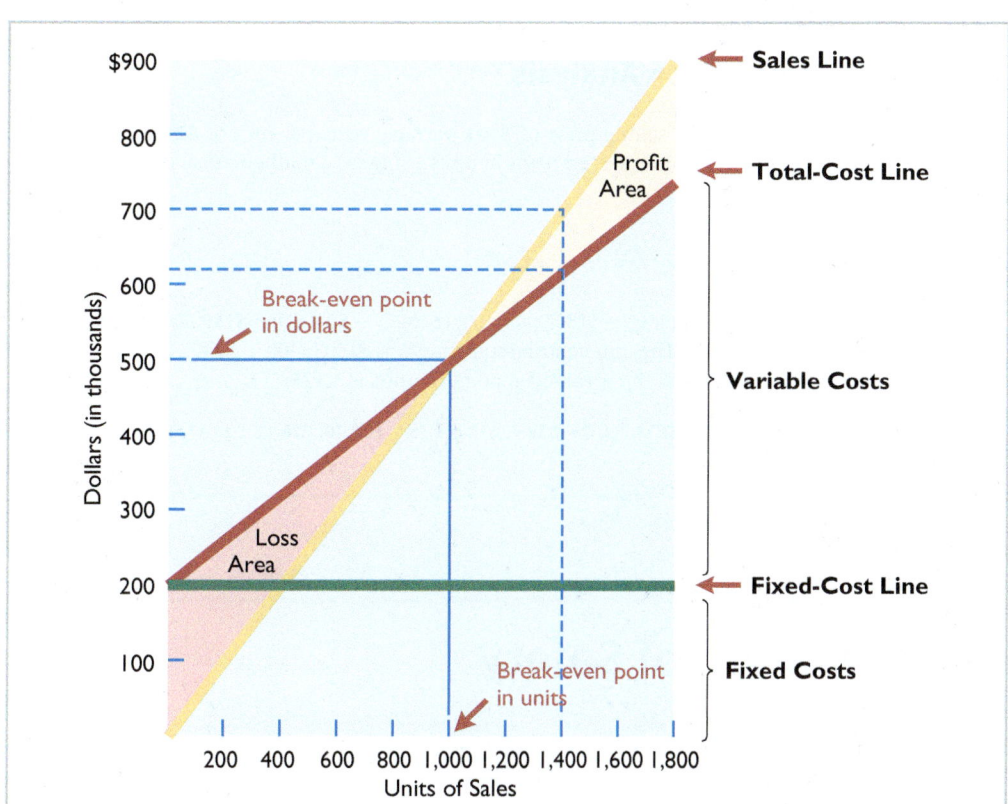

ILLUSTRATION 18.23

CVP graph

The construction of the graph, using the data for Vargo Electronics, is as follows.

1. Plot the sales line, starting at the zero activity level. For every cell phone sold, total revenue increases by $500. For example, at 200 units, sales are $100,000. At the upper level of activity (1,800 units), sales are $900,000. The revenue line is assumed to be linear through the full range of activity.

2. Plot the total fixed costs using a horizontal line. For the cell phones, this line is plotted at $200,000. The fixed costs are the same at every level of activity.

3. Plot the total-cost line. This starts at the fixed-cost line at zero activity. It increases by the variable costs at each level of activity. For each cell phone, variable costs are $300. Thus, at 200 units, total variable costs are $60,000 ($300 × 200) and the total cost is $260,000 ($60,000 + $200,000). At 1,800 units, total variable costs are $540,000 ($300 × 1,800) and total cost is $740,000 ($540,000 + $200,000). On the graph, the amount of the variable costs can be derived from the difference between the total-cost and fixed-cost lines at each level of activity.

4. Determine the break-even point from the intersection of the total-cost line and the sales line. The break-even point in dollars is found by drawing a horizontal line from the break-even point to the vertical axis. The break-even point in units is found by drawing a vertical line from the break-even point to the horizontal axis. For the cell phones, the break-even point is $500,000 of sales, or 1,000 units. At this sales level, Vargo will cover costs but make no profit.

The CVP graph also shows both the net income and net loss areas. Thus, the amount of income or loss at each level of sales can be derived from the sales and total-cost lines.

A CVP graph is useful because the effects of a change in any element in the CVP analysis can be quickly seen. For example, a 10% increase in selling price will change the location of the sales line. Likewise, the effects on total costs of wage increases can be quickly observed.

ACTION PLAN

- Apply the profit equation: Sales − Variable costs − Fixed costs = Net income.
- Apply the break-even formula: Fixed costs ÷ Unit contribution margin = Break-even point in units.

DO IT! 4 | Break-Even Analysis

Lombardi Company has a unit selling price of $400, variable costs per unit of $240, and fixed costs of $180,000. Compute the break-even point in units using (a) a mathematical equation and (b) unit contribution margin.

Solution

(a) The equation is $400Q − $240Q − $180,000 = $0; ($400Q − $240Q) = $180,000. The break-even point in units is 1,125. (b) The unit contribution margin is $160 ($400 − $240). The formula therefore is $180,000 ÷ $160, and the break-even point in units is 1,125.

Related exercise material: **BE18.8, BE18.9, DO IT! 18.4, E18.8, E18.9, E18.10, E18.11, E18.12,** and **E18.13**.

Target Net Income and Margin of Safety

> **LEARNING OBJECTIVE 5**
> Determine the sales required to earn target net income and determine margin of safety.

Target Net Income

Rather than simply "breaking even," management usually sets an income objective often called **target net income**. It then determines the sales necessary to achieve this specified level of income. Companies determine the sales necessary to achieve target net income by using one of the three approaches discussed earlier.

Mathematical Equation

We know that at the break-even point no profit or loss results for the company. By adding an amount for target net income to the same basic equation, we obtain the formula shown in **Illustration 18.24** for determining required sales.

ILLUSTRATION 18.24
Formula for sales to meet target net income

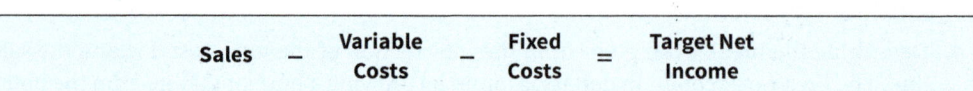

Recall that once the break-even point has been reached so that fixed costs are covered, each additional unit sold increases net income by the amount of the unit contribution margin. We can rewrite the equation with contribution margin (sales minus variable costs) on the left-hand side, and fixed costs and target net income on the right. Assuming that target net income is $120,000 for Vargo Electronics, the computation of required sales in units is as shown in **Illustration 18.25**.

ILLUSTRATION 18.25
Computation of required sales

	Sales	−	Variable Costs	−	Fixed Costs	=	Target Net Income
	$500Q	−	$300Q	−	$200,000	=	$120,000
	$500Q	−	$300Q	=	$200,000	+	$120,000

$$200Q = \$200,000 + \$120,000$$

$$Q = \frac{\$200,000 + \$120,000}{\$200} = \frac{\text{Fixed Costs} + \text{Target Net Income}}{\text{Unit Contribution Margin}}$$

$$Q = 1,600$$

where

Q = number of units sold
$500 = unit selling price
$300 = unit variable costs
$200,000 = total fixed costs
$120,000 = target net income

Vargo must sell 1,600 units to achieve target net income of $120,000. The sales dollars required to achieve the target net income is found by multiplying the units sold by the unit selling price [(1,600 × $500) = $800,000].

Contribution Margin Technique

As in the case of break-even sales, we can compute in either units or dollars the sales required to meet target net income. The formula to compute required sales in units for Vargo Electronics using the unit contribution margin can be seen in the final step of the equation approach in Illustration 18.25 (shown in red). We simply divide the sum of fixed costs and target net income by the unit contribution margin. **Illustration 18.26** shows this for Vargo.

ILLUSTRATION 18.26
Formula for sales in units using unit contribution margin

(Fixed Costs + Target Net Income)	÷	Unit Contribution Margin	=	Sales in Units
($200,000 + $120,000)	÷	$200	=	1,600 units

To achieve its desired target net income of $120,000, Vargo must sell 1,600 cell phones.

Illustration 18.27 presents the formula to compute the required sales in dollars for Vargo using the contribution margin ratio.

ILLUSTRATION 18.27
Formula for sales in dollars using contribution margin ratio

(Fixed Costs + Target Net Income)	÷	Contribution Margin Ratio	=	Sales in Dollars
($200,000 + $120,000)	÷	40%	=	$800,000

To achieve its desired target net income of $120,000, Vargo must generate sales of $800,000.

Graphic Presentation

We also can use the CVP graph in Illustration 18.23 to find the sales required to meet target net income. In the profit area of the graph, the distance between the sales line and the total-cost line at any point equals net income. We can find required sales by analyzing the differences between the two lines until the desired net income is found.

For example, suppose Vargo Electronics sells 1,400 cell phones. Illustration 18.23 shows that a vertical line drawn at 1,400 units intersects the sales line at $700,000 and the total-cost line at $620,000. The difference between the two amounts represents the net income (profit) of $80,000.

Margin of Safety

Margin of safety is the difference between actual or expected sales and sales at the break-even point. It measures the "cushion" that a particular level of sales provides. It tells us how far sales could fall before the company begins operating at a loss. The margin of safety is expressed in dollars or as a ratio.

The formula for stating the **margin of safety in dollars** is actual (or expected) sales minus break-even sales. **Illustration 18.28** shows the computation for Vargo Electronics, assuming that actual (expected) sales are $750,000.

ILLUSTRATION 18.28
Formula for margin of safety in dollars

Actual (Expected) Sales	−	Break-Even Sales	=	Margin of Safety in Dollars
$750,000	−	$500,000	=	$250,000

Vargo's margin of safety is $250,000. Its sales could fall $250,000 before it operates at a loss.

The **margin of safety ratio** is the margin of safety in dollars divided by actual (or expected) sales. **Illustration 18.29** shows the formula and computation for determining the margin of safety ratio.

ILLUSTRATION 18.29
Formula for margin of safety ratio

Margin of Safety in Dollars	÷	Actual (Expected) Sales	=	Margin of Safety Ratio
$250,000	÷	$750,000	=	33%

This means that the company's sales could fall by 33% before it operates at a loss.

The higher the margin of safety in dollars or the percentage, the lower the risk that the company will operate at a loss. Management evaluates the adequacy of the margin of safety in terms of such factors as the vulnerability of the product to competitive pressures and to downturns in the economy.

Service Company Insight   Rolling Stones

YAMIL LAGE/AFP/Getty Images

How a Rolling Stones' Tour Makes Money

Computations of break-even and margin of safety are important for service companies. Consider how the promoter for the **Rolling Stones**' tour used the break-even point and margin of safety. For example, say one outdoor show should bring 70,000 individuals for ticket sales of $2.45 million. The promoter guarantees $1.2 million to the Rolling Stones. In addition, 20% of ticket sales goes to the stadium in which the performance is staged. Add another $400,000 for other expenses such as ticket takers, parking attendants, advertising, and so on. The promoter also shares in sales of T-shirts and memorabilia for which the promoter will net over $7 million during the tour. From a successful Rolling Stones' tour, the promoter could make $35 million!

What amount of sales dollars are required for the promoter to break even? (Go to WileyPLUS for this answer and additional questions.)

ACTION PLAN
- Apply the formula for the break-even point in dollars.
- Apply the formulas for the margin of safety in dollars and the margin of safety ratio.
- Apply the formula for the sales in dollars.

DO IT! 5 | Break-Even, Margin of Safety, and Target Net Income

Zootsuit Inc. makes travel bags that sell for $56 each. For the coming year, management expects fixed costs to total $320,000 and variable costs to be $42 per unit. Compute the following: (a) break-even point in dollars using the contribution margin (CM) ratio; (b) the margin of safety and margin of safety ratio assuming actual sales are $1,382,400; and (c) the sales dollars required to earn net income of $410,000.

Solution

a. Contribution margin ratio = [($56 − $42) ÷ $56] = 25%
   Break-even sales in dollars = $320,000 ÷ 25% = $1,280,000

b. Margin of safety = $1,382,400 − $1,280,000 = $102,400
   Margin of safety ratio = $102,400 ÷ $1,382,400 = 7.4%

c. Sales in dollars = ($320,000 + $410,000) ÷ 25% = $2,920,000

Related exercise material: **BE18.10, BE18.11, BE18.12, DO IT! 18.5, E18.14, E18.15, E18.16, and E18.17.**

USING THE DECISION TOOLS | Amazon.com

Amazon.com faces many situations where it needs to apply the decision tools presented in this chapter, such as calculating the break-even point to determine a product's profitability. Amazon's dominance of the online retail space, selling other company's products, is well known. But not everyone may realize that Amazon also sells its own private-label electronics, including USB cables, mice, keyboards, and audio cables, under the brand name AmazonBasics. Assume that Amazon's management was provided with the following information regarding the production and sales of Bluetooth keyboards for tablet computers for 2022.

Cost Schedules

Variable costs	
Direct labor per keyboard	$ 8.00
Direct materials	4.00
Variable overhead	3.00
Variable cost per keyboard	$ 15.00
Fixed costs	
Manufacturing	$ 25,000
Selling	40,000
Administrative	70,000
Total fixed costs	$135,000
Selling price per keyboard	$25.00
Sales, 2022 (20,000 keyboards)	$500,000

Instructions

(Ignore any income tax considerations.)

a. What is the operating income for 2022?
b. What is the unit contribution margin for 2022?
c. What is the break-even point in units for 2022?
d. Assume that management set the sales target for the year 2023 at a level of $550,000 (22,000 keyboards). Amazon's management believes that to attain the sales target in 2023, the company must incur an additional selling expense of $10,000 for advertising in 2023, with all other costs remaining constant. What will be the break-even point in sales dollars for 2023 if the company spends the additional $10,000?
e. If the company spends the additional $10,000 for advertising in 2023, what is the sales level in dollars required to equal 2022 operating income?

Solution

a.

Sales	$500,000
Less:	
Variable costs (20,000 keyboards × $15)	300,000
Fixed costs	135,000
Operating income	$ 65,000

b. Selling price per keyboard $25
    Variable cost per keyboard   15
    Unit contribution margin $10

c. Fixed costs ÷ Unit contribution margin = Break-even point in units: $135,000 ÷ $10 = 13,500 units

d. Fixed costs ÷ Contribution margin ratio = Break-even point in dollars: $145,000* ÷ 40%** = $362,500

    *Fixed costs $135,000
      Additional advertising expense   10,000
    Revised fixed costs $145,000

    **Contribution margin ratio = Unit contribution margin ÷ Unit selling price: 40% = $10 ÷ $25

e. Sales = (Fixed costs + Target net income) ÷ Contribution margin ratio
    $525,000 = ($145,000 + $65,000) ÷ 40%

Appendix 18A   Regression Analysis

LEARNING OBJECTIVE *6
Describe how regression analysis is used to classify mixed costs.

The high-low method is often used to estimate fixed and variable costs for a mixed-cost situation. An advantage of the high-low method is that it is easy to apply. But, how accurate and reliable is the estimated cost equation that it produces? For example, consider the example shown in **Illustration 18A.1**, which indicates the cost equation line produced by the high-low method for Metro Transit Company's maintenance costs. How well does the high-low method represent the relationship between miles driven and total cost? This line is close to, and in some cases bisects, nearly all of the data points. Therefore, in this case, the high-low method provides a cost equation that is a very good fit for this data set. It identifies fixed and variable costs in an accurate and reliable way.

ILLUSTRATION 18A.1

Scatter plot for Metro Transit Company

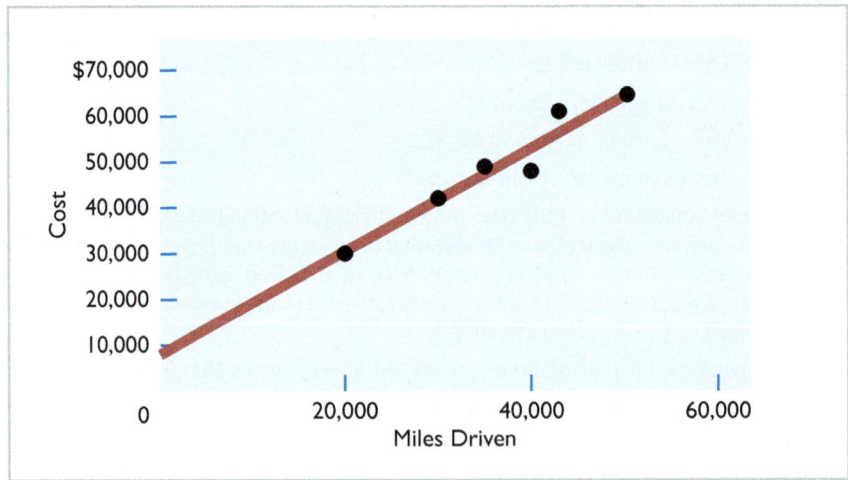

While the high-low method works well for the Metro Transit data set, a weakness of this method is that it employs only two data points and ignores the rest. If those two data points are representative of the entire data set, then the high-low method provides reasonable results (as seen in Illustration 18A.1). But, if the high and low data points are not representative of the rest of the data set, then the results are misleading. To illustrate, assume that Hanson Trucking Company has 12 months of maintenance cost data, as shown in **Illustration 18A.2**.

Month	Miles Driven	Total Cost	Month	Miles Driven	Total Cost
January	20,000	$30,000	July	15,000	$39,000
February	40,000	49,000	August	28,000	41,000
March	35,000	46,000	September	60,000	72,000
April	50,000	63,000	October	55,000	67,000
May	30,000	42,000	November	19,000	29,000
June	43,000	52,000	December	65,000	63,000

ILLUSTRATION 18A.2

Maintenance costs and mileage data for Hanson Trucking Company

The high and low activities are 65,000 miles in December and 15,000 miles in July. The maintenance costs at these two levels are $63,000 and $39,000, respectively. The difference in maintenance costs is $24,000 ($63,000 − $39,000), and the difference in miles is 50,000 (65,000 − 15,000). Therefore, for Hanson Trucking, variable cost per unit under the high-low method is $0.48 ($24,000 ÷ 50,000). To determine total variable cost, we multiply the number of miles by cost per mile. For example, at the low activity level of 15,000 miles, total variable cost is $7,200 (15,000 × $0.48). To determine fixed costs, we subtract total variable costs at the low activity level from the total cost at the low activity level ($39,000) as follows.

Fixed costs = $39,000 − ($0.48 × 15,000) = $31,800

Therefore, the cost equation based on the high-low method for this data produces the following formula:

Maintenance costs	=	Intercept	+	Slope
	=	$31,800	+	($0.48 × Miles driven)

Illustration 18A.3 shows a scatter plot of the data with a line representing the high-low method cost equation. Note that most of the data points for Hanson Trucking are a significant distance from the line. For example, at 19,000 miles, the observed maintenance cost is $29,000, but the equation predicts $40,920 [$31,800 + ($0.48 × 19,000)]. That is a difference of $11,920 ($40,920 − $29,000). In this case, the high-low method cost equation does not provide a good representation of the relationship between miles driven and maintenance costs. To derive a more representative cost equation, the company should employ regression analysis.

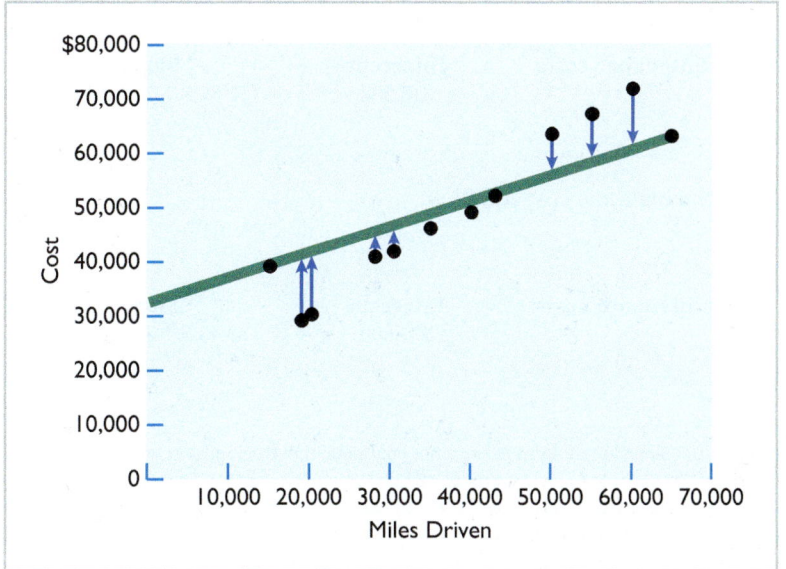

ILLUSTRATION 18A.3

Scatter plot for Hanson Trucking Company

Regression analysis is a statistical approach that estimates the cost equation by employing information from all data points, not just the highest and lowest ones. While it involves mathematical analysis taught in statistics courses (which we will not address here), we can provide you with a basic understanding of how regression analysis works. Consider Illustration 18A.3, which highlights the distance that each data point is from the high-low cost equation line. What regression analysis does is to find a cost equation that results in a cost equation line that minimizes the sum of the (squared) distances from the line to the data points.

Many software packages perform regression analysis. In **Illustration 18A.4**, we use the **Intercept** and **Slope** functions in Excel to estimate the regression equation for the Hanson Trucking Company data.[1] The Excel video provided in WileyPLUS demonstrates the use of the Intercept and Slope functions.

ILLUSTRATION 18A.4
Excel spreadsheet for Hanson Trucking Company

Month	Miles Driven	Total Cost	
January	20,000	30,000	
February	40,000	49,000	
March	35,000	46,000	
April	50,000	63,000	
May	30,000	42,000	
June	43,000	52,000	
July	15,000	39,000	
August	28,000	41,000	
September	60,000	72,000	
October	55,000	67,000	
November	19,000	29,000	
December	65,000	63,000	
	Formula		
Intercept	=INTERCEPT(C2:C13,B2:B13)	18,502	
Slope	=SLOPE(C2:C13,B2:B13)	0.81	

The resulting cost equation is:

Maintenance costs = Intercept + Slope
= $18,502 + ($0.81 × Miles driven)

Compare this to the high-low cost equation:

Maintenance costs = Intercept + Slope
= $31,800 + ($0.48 × Miles driven)

---

[1] To use the Intercept and Slope functions in Excel, enter your data in two columns in an Excel spreadsheet. The first column should be your "X" variable (miles driven, cells B2 to B13 in our example). The second column should be your "Y" variable (maintenance costs, cells C2 to C13 in our example). Next, in a separate cell, choosing from Excel's statistical functions, enter =Intercept(C2:C13,B2:B13) and in a different cell enter =Slope(C2:C13,B2:B13).

As **Illustration 18A.5** shows, the intercept and slope differ significantly between the regression equation (green) and the high-low equation (red).[2] The regression cost equation line does not bisect the high and low data points but instead follows a path that minimizes the cumulative distance from all of the data points. By doing so, it provides a cost equation that is more representative of the relationship between miles driven and total maintenance costs than the high-low method.

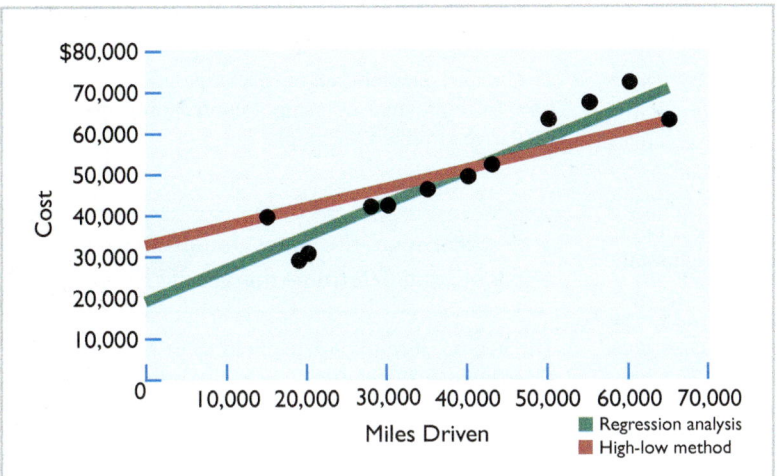

ILLUSTRATION 18A.5

Scatter plot and cost equation lines

Why should managers care about the accuracy of the cost equation? Managers make many decisions that require that mixed costs be separated into fixed and variable components. Inaccurate classifications of these costs might cause a manager to make an inappropriate decision. For example, Hanson Trucking Company's break-even point differs significantly depending on which of these two cost equations was used. If Hanson Trucking relies on the high-low method, it would have a distorted view of the level of sales it would need in order to break even. In addition, misrepresentation for fixed and variable costs could result in inappropriate decisions, such as whether to discontinue a product line. It would also result in inaccurate product costing under activity-based costing.

While regression analysis usually provides more reliable estimates of the cost equation, it does have its limitations.

1. The regression approach that we applied above assumes a linear relationship between the variables (that is, an increase or decrease in one variable results in a proportional increase or decrease in the other). If the actual relationship differs significantly from linearity, then linear regression can provide misleading results. (Nonlinear regression is addressed in advanced statistics courses.)

2. Regression estimates can be severely influenced by "outliers"—data points that differ significantly from the rest of the observations. It is therefore good practice to plot data points in a scatter graph to identify outliers and then investigate the reasons why they differ. In some cases, outliers must be adjusted for or eliminated.

3. Regression estimation is most accurate when it is based on a large number of data points. However, collecting data can be time-consuming and costly. In some cases, there simply are not enough observable data points to arrive at a reliable estimate.

---

[2] To plot a scatter graph in Excel, highlight the data and then click on Scatter under the Insert tab. To draw the cost equation line, click on the scatter plot, then select Layout and Trendline. In order to get the cost equation line to intercept the Y axis, under Trendline Options in the Backward field, enter the lowest value of your X variable. For example, for Hanson Trucking, we entered 15,000.

Review and Practice

Learning Objectives Review

1 Explain variable, fixed, and mixed costs and the relevant range.

Variable costs are costs that vary in total directly and proportionately with changes in the activity index. Fixed costs are costs that remain the same in total regardless of changes in the activity index.

The relevant range is the range of activity in which a company expects to operate during a year. It is important in CVP analysis because the behavior of costs is assumed to be linear throughout the relevant range.

Mixed costs change in total but not proportionately with changes in the activity level. For purposes of CVP analysis, mixed costs must be classified into their fixed and variable elements.

2 Apply the high-low method to determine the components of mixed costs.

Determine the variable costs per unit by dividing the change in total costs at the highest and lowest levels of activity by the difference in activity at those levels. Then, determine fixed costs by subtracting total variable costs from the amount of total costs at either the highest or lowest level of activity.

3 Prepare a CVP income statement to determine contribution margin.

The five components of CVP analysis are (1) volume or level of activity, (2) unit selling prices, (3) variable costs per unit, (4) total fixed costs, and (5) sales mix. Contribution margin is the amount of revenue remaining after deducting variable costs. It is identified in a CVP income statement, which classifies costs as variable or fixed. It can be expressed as a total amount, as a per unit amount, or as a ratio.

4 Compute the break-even point using three approaches.

The break-even point can be (a) computed from a mathematical equation, (b) computed by using a contribution margin technique, and (c) derived from a CVP graph.

5 Determine the sales required to earn target net income and determine margin of safety.

The general formula for required sales is Sales − Variable costs − Fixed costs = Target net income. Two other formulas are (1) Sales in units = (Fixed costs + Target net income) ÷ Unit contribution margin, and (2) Sales in dollars = (Fixed costs + Target net income) ÷ Contribution margin ratio.

Margin of safety is the difference between actual or expected sales and sales at the break-even point. The formulas for margin of safety are (1) Actual (expected) sales − Break-even sales = Margin of safety in dollars, and (2) Margin of safety in dollars ÷ Actual (expected) sales = Margin of safety ratio.

*6 Describe how regression analysis is used to classify mixed costs.

The high-low method provides a quick estimate of the cost equation for a mixed cost. However, the high-low method is based on only the highest and lowest data points. Regression analysis provides an estimate of the cost equation based on all data points. The cost equation line that results from regression analysis minimizes the sum of the (squared) distances of all of the data points from the cost equation line. Computer programs such as Excel enable easy estimation of the cost equation with regression.

Decision Tools Review

Decision Checkpoints	Info Needed for Decision	Tool to Use for Decision	How to Evaluate Results
What was the contribution toward fixed costs and income from each unit sold?	Selling price per unit and variable cost per unit	Unit contribution margin = Unit selling price − Unit variable cost	Every unit sold will increase income by the contribution margin.
What would be the increase in income as a result of an increase in sales?	Unit contribution margin and unit selling price	Contribution margin ratio = Unit contribution margin ÷ Unit selling price	Every dollar of sales will increase income by the contribution margin ratio.

(continues)

(continued)

Decision Checkpoints	Info Needed for Decision	Tool to Use for Decision	How to Evaluate Results
At what amount of sales does a company cover its costs?	Unit selling price, unit variable cost, and total fixed costs	Break-even point analysis *In units:* $$\text{Break-even point} = \frac{\text{Fixed costs}}{\text{Unit contribution margin}}$$ *In dollars:* $$\text{Break-even point} = \frac{\text{Fixed costs}}{\text{Contribution margin ratio}}$$	Below the break-even point, the company is unprofitable.

Glossary Review

Activity index The activity that causes changes in the behavior of costs. (p. 18-3).

Break-even point The level of activity at which total revenue equals total costs. (p. 18-12).

Contribution margin (CM) The amount of revenue remaining after deducting variable costs. (p. 18-11).

Contribution margin ratio The percentage of each dollar of sales that is available to apply to fixed costs and contribute to net income; calculated as unit contribution margin divided by unit selling price. (p. 18-13).

Cost behavior analysis The study of how specific costs respond to changes in the level of business activity. (p. 18-2).

Cost-volume-profit (CVP) analysis The study of the effects of changes in costs and volume on a company's profits. (p. 18-10).

Cost-volume-profit (CVP) graph A graph showing the relationship between costs, volume, and profits. (p. 18-16).

Cost-volume-profit (CVP) income statement A statement for internal use that classifies costs as fixed or variable and reports contribution margin in the body of the statement. (p. 18-11).

Fixed costs Costs that remain the same in total regardless of changes in the activity level. (p. 18-4).

High-low method A mathematical method that uses the total costs incurred at the high and low levels of activity to classify mixed costs into fixed and variable components. (p. 18-7).

Margin of safety The difference between actual or expected sales and sales at the break-even point. (p. 18-20).

Mixed costs Costs that contain both a variable- and a fixed-cost element and change in total but not proportionately with changes in the activity level. (p. 18-6).

*****Regression analysis** A statistical approach that estimates the cost equation by employing information from all data points to find the cost equation line that minimizes the sum of the squared distances from the line to the data points. (p. 18-24).

Relevant range The range of the activity index over which the company expects to operate during the year. (p. 18-5).

Target net income The income objective set by management. (p. 18-18).

Unit contribution margin The amount of revenue remaining per unit after deducting variable costs; calculated as unit selling price minus unit variable costs. (p. 18-12).

Variable costs Costs that vary in total directly and proportionately with changes in the activity level. (p. 18-3).

Practice Multiple-Choice Questions

1. **(LO 1)** Variable costs are costs that:
   a. vary in total directly and proportionately with changes in the activity level.
   b. remain the same per unit at every activity level.
   c. Neither of the above.
   d. Both (a) and (b) above.

2. **(LO 2)** The relevant range is:
   a. the range of activity in which variable costs will be curvilinear.
   b. the range of activity in which fixed costs will be curvilinear.
   c. the range over which the company expects to operate during a year.
   d. usually from zero to 100% of operating capacity.

3. **(LO 1, 2)** Mixed costs consist of a:
   a. variable-cost element and a fixed-cost element.
   b. fixed-cost element and a product-cost element.
   c. period-cost element and a product-cost element.
   d. variable-cost element and a period-cost element.

4. **(LO 1, 2)** Your cell phone service provider offers a plan that is classified as a mixed cost. The cost per month for 1,000 minutes is $50. If you use 2,000 minutes this month, your cost will be:
   a. $50.
   b. $100.
   c. more than $100.
   d. between $50 and $100.

5. **(LO 2)** Kendra Corporation's total utility costs during the past year were $1,200 during its highest month and $600 during its lowest month. These costs corresponded with 10,000 units of production during the high month and 2,000 units during the low month. What are the fixed and variable components of its utility costs using the high-low method?
   a. $0.075 variable and $450 fixed.
   b. $0.120 variable and $0 fixed.
   c. $0.300 variable and $0 fixed.
   d. $0.060 variable and $600 fixed.

6. (LO 3) Which of the following is **not** involved in CVP analysis?

a. Sales mix.
b. Unit selling prices.
c. Fixed costs per unit.
d. Volume or level of activity.

7. (LO 3) When comparing a traditional income statement to a CVP income statement:

a. net income will always be greater on the traditional statement.
b. net income will always be less on the traditional statement.
c. net income will always be identical on both.
d. net income will be greater or less depending on the sales volume.

8. (LO 3) Contribution margin:

a. is revenue remaining after deducting variable costs.
b. may be expressed as unit contribution margin.
c. is selling price less cost of goods sold.
d. Both (a) and (b) above.

9. (LO 3) Cournot Company sells 100,000 wrenches for $12 a unit. Fixed costs are $300,000, and net income is $200,000. What should be reported as variable expenses in the CVP income statement?

a. $700,000.
b. $900,000.
c. $500,000.
d. $1,000,000.

10. (LO 4) Gossen Company is planning to sell 200,000 pliers for $4 per unit. The contribution margin ratio is 25%. If Gossen will break even at this level of sales, what are the fixed costs?

a. $100,000.
b. $160,000.
c. $200,000.
d. $300,000.

11. (LO 4) Brownstone Company's contribution margin ratio is 30%. If Brownstone's sales revenue is $100 greater than its break-even sales in dollars, its net income:

a. will be $100.
b. will be $70.
c. will be $30.
d. cannot be determined without knowing fixed costs.

12. (LO 5) The mathematical equation for computing required sales to obtain target net income is Sales =

a. Variable costs + Target net income.
b. Variable costs + Fixed costs + Target net income.
c. Fixed costs + Target net income.
d. No correct answer is given.

13. (LO 5) Margin of safety is computed as:

a. Actual sales − Break-even sales.
b. Contribution margin − Fixed costs.
c. Break-even sales − Variable costs.
d. Actual sales − Contribution margin.

14. (LO 5) Marshall Company had actual sales of $600,000 when break-even sales were $420,000. What is the margin of safety ratio?

a. 25%.
b. 30%.
c. 33⅓%.
d. 45%.

Solutions

1. d. Variable costs vary in total directly and proportionately with changes in the activity level and remain the same per unit at every activity level. Choices (a) and (b) are correct, but (d) is the better and more complete answer. Since (a) and (b) are both true statements, choice (c) is incorrect.

2. c. The relevant range is the range over which the company expects to operate during a year. The other choices are incorrect because the relevant range is the range over which (a) variable costs are expected to be linear, not curvilinear, and (b) the company expects fixed costs to remain the same. Choice (d) is incorrect because this answer does not specifically define relevant range.

3. a. Mixed costs consist of a variable-cost element and a fixed-cost element, not (b) a product-cost element, (c) a period-cost element or a product-cost element, or (d) a period-cost element.

4. d. Your cost will include the fixed-cost component (flat service fee) which does not increase plus the variable cost (usage charge) for the additional 1,000 minutes which will increase your cost to between $50 and $100. Therefore, choices (a) $50, (b) $100, and (c) more than $100 are incorrect.

5. a. Variable is $0.075 [($1,200 − $600) ÷ (10,000 − 2,000)] and fixed is $450 [($1,200 − ($0.075 × 10,000)]. Therefore, choices (b) $0.120 variable and $0 fixed, (c) $0.300 variable and $0 fixed, and (d) $0.060 variable and $600 fixed are incorrect.

6. c. Total fixed costs, not fixed costs per unit, are involved in CVP analysis. Choices (a) sales mix, (b) unit selling prices, and (d) volume or level of activity are all involved in CVP analysis.

7. c. Net income will always be identical on both a traditional income statement and a CVP income statement. Therefore, choices (a), (b), and (d) are incorrect statements.

8. d. Contribution margin is revenue remaining after deducting variable costs and it may be expressed on a per unit basis. Choices (a) and (b) are accurate, but (d) is a better answer. Choice (c) is incorrect because it defines gross margin, not contribution margin.

9. a. Contribution margin is equal to fixed costs plus net income ($300,000 + $200,000 = $500,000). Since variable expenses are the difference between total sales ($1,200,000) and contribution margin ($500,000), $700,000 must be the amount of variable expenses in the CVP income statement. Therefore, choices (b) $900,000, (c) $500,000, and (d) $1,000,000 are incorrect.

10. c. Unit contribution margin is $1 ($4 × 25%). Fixed costs ÷ Unit contribution margin = Break-even point in units. Solving for fixed costs, 200,000 units × $1 per unit = $200,000, not (a) $100,000, (b) $160,000, or (d) $300,000.

11. c. If Brownstone's sales revenue is $100 greater than its break-even sales in dollars, its net income will be $30 or ($100 × 30%), not (a) $100 or (b) $70. Choice (d) is incorrect because net income can be determined without knowing fixed costs.

12. b. The correct equation is Sales = Variable costs + Fixed costs + Target net income. The other choices are incorrect because (a) needs fixed costs added, (b) needs variable costs added, and (d) there is a correct answer given (b).

13. a. Margin of safety is computed as Actual sales − Break-even sales. Therefore, choices (b) Contribution margin − Fixed costs, (c) Break-even sales − Variable costs, and (d) Actual sales − Contribution margin are incorrect.

14. b. The margin of safety ratio is computed by dividing the margin of safety in dollars of $180,000 ($600,000 − $420,000) by actual sales of $600,000. The result is 30% ($180,000 ÷ $600,000), not (a) 25%, (c) 33⅓%, or (d) 45%.

Practice Brief Exercises

1. (LO 2) Benji Company accumulates the following data concerning a mixed cost, using miles as the activity level.

Determine variable- and fixed-cost elements using the high-low method.

	Miles Driven	Total Cost		Miles Driven	Total Cost
January	7,500	$20,000	March	8,500	$22,000
February	8,200	21,100	April	8,300	21,750

Compute the variable- and fixed-cost elements using the high-low method.

Solution

1.

High		Low		Difference
$22,000	−	$20,000	=	$2,000
8,500	−	7,500	=	1,000

Variable cost per mile = $2,000 ÷ 1,000 = $2.00.

	High	Low
Total cost	$22,000	$20,000
Less: Variable costs		
8,500 × $2.00	17,000	
7,500 × $2.00		15,000
Total fixed costs	$ 5,000	$ 5,000

Mixed cost is $5,000 plus $2.00 per mile.

2. (LO 3) Determine the missing amounts.

Determine missing amounts for contribution margin.

Unit Selling Price	Unit Variable Costs	Unit Contribution Margin	Contribution Margin Ratio
$800	$520	(a)	(b)
500	(c)	$200	(d)
(e)	(f)	450	45%

Solution

2. a. ($800 − $520) = $280
   b. ($280 ÷ $800) = 35%
   c. ($500 − $200) = $300
   d. ($200 ÷ $500) = 40%
   e. ($450 ÷ 45%) = $1,000
   f. ($1,000 − $450) = $550

3. (LO 4) Jacob Company has a unit selling price of $600, variable costs per unit of $216, and fixed costs of $2,438,400. Compute the break-even point in units using (a) the mathematical equation and (b) unit contribution margin.

Compute the break-even point.

Solution

3. a. $600Q − $216Q − $2,438,400 = $0
   $384Q = $2,438,400
   Q = 6,350 units

   b. Contribution margin per unit = ($600 − $216) = $384
   Unit contribution margin = $2,438,400 ÷ $384 = 6,350 units

4. (LO 5) For Posh Company, actual sales are $1,500,000, and break-even sales are $1,300,000. Compute (a) the margin of safety in dollars and (b) the margin of safety ratio.

Compute the margin of safety and margin of safety ratio.

Solution

4. a. Margin of safety = $1,500,000 − $1,300,000 = $200,000
   b. Margin of safety ratio = $200,000 ÷ $1,500,000 = 13.3%

Practice Exercises

Determine fixed and variable costs using the high-low method and prepare graph.

1. (LO 1, 2) The controller of Teton Industries has collected the following monthly expense data for use in analyzing the cost behavior of maintenance costs.

Month	Total Maintenance Costs	Total Machine Hours
January	$2,900	300
February	3,000	400
March	3,600	600
April	4,300	790
May	3,200	500
June	4,500	800

Instructions

a. Determine the fixed-cost and variable-cost components using the high-low method.

b. Prepare a graph showing the behavior of maintenance costs, and identify the fixed-cost and variable-cost elements. Use 200 unit increments and $1,000 cost increments.

Solution

1. a. Maintenance Costs:

$$\frac{\$4,500 - \$2,900}{800 - 300} = \frac{\$1,600}{500} = \$3.20 \text{ variable cost per machine hour}$$

	800 Machine Hours	300 Machine Hours
Total costs	$4,500	$2,900
Less: Variable costs		
800 × $3.20	2,560	
300 × $3.20		960
Total fixed costs	$1,940	$1,940

Thus, maintenance costs are $1,940 per month plus $3.20 per machine hour.

b.

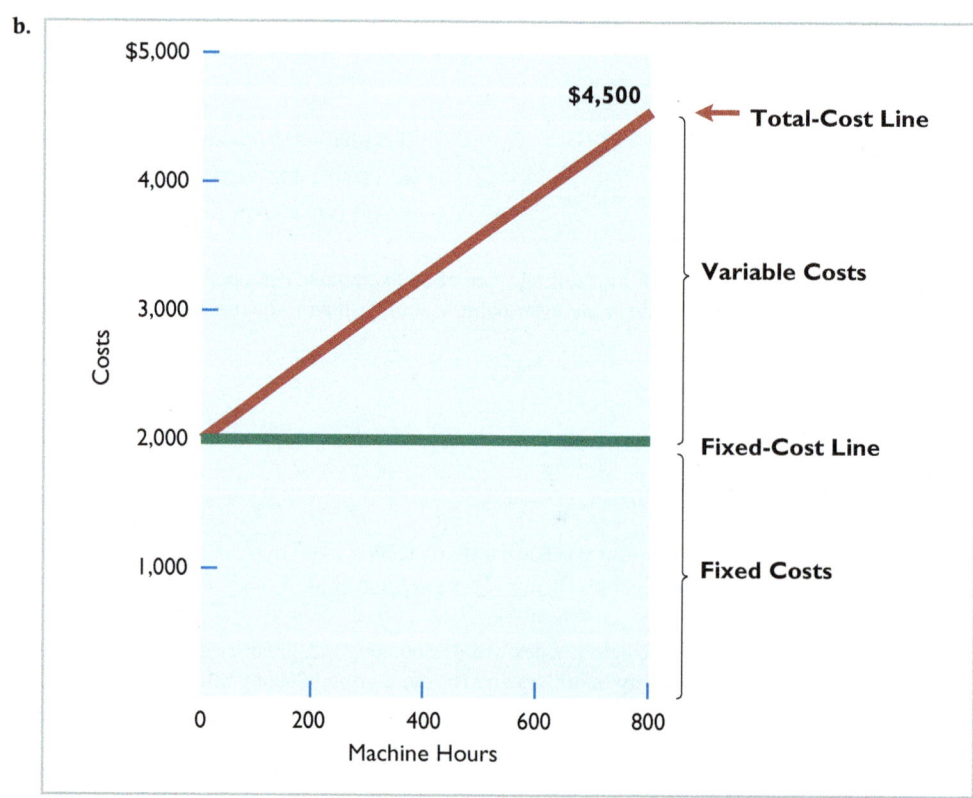

2. (LO 3, 4, 5) Zion Seating Co., a manufacturer of chairs, had the following data for 2022:

Sales	2,400 units
Sales price	$40 per unit
Variable costs	$15 per unit
Fixed costs	$19,500

Determine contribution margin ratio, break-even point in dollars, and margin of safety.

Instructions

a. What is the contribution margin ratio?
b. What is the break-even point in dollars?
c. What is the margin of safety in dollars and the margin of safety ratio?
d. If the company wishes to increase its total dollar contribution margin by 40% in 2023, by how much will it need to increase its sales if all other factors remain constant?

(CGA adapted)

Solution

2. a. Contribution margin ratio = Unit contribution margin ÷ Unit selling price
   ($40 − $15) ÷ $40 = 62.5%

   b. Break-even in dollars: $19,500 ÷ 62.5% = $31,200

   c. Margin of safety in dollars = (2,400 × $40) − $31,200 = $64,800
   Margin of safety ratio = $64,800 ÷ (2,400 × $40) = 67.5%

   d. Current contribution margin is $40 − $15 = $25
   Total contribution margin is $25 × 2,400 = $60,000
   40% increase in contribution margin is $60,000 × 40% = $24,000
   Total increase in sales required is $24,000 ÷ 62.5% = $38,400

Practice Problem

(LO 4, 5) Mabo Company makes calculators that sell for $20 each. For the coming year, management expects fixed costs to total $220,000 and variable costs to be $9 per unit.

Compute break-even point, contribution margin ratio, margin of safety, and sales for target net income.

Instructions

a. Compute break-even point in units using the mathematical equation.
b. Compute break-even point in dollars using the contribution margin (CM) ratio.
c. Compute the margin of safety percentage assuming actual sales are $500,000.
d. Compute the sales required in dollars to earn net income of $165,000.

Solution

a. Sales − Variable costs − Fixed costs = Net income
$20Q − $9Q − $220,000 = $0
$11Q = $220,000
Q = 20,000 units

b. Unit contribution margin = Unit selling price − Unit variable costs
$11 = $20 − $9
Contribution margin ratio = Unit contribution margin ÷ Unit selling price
55% = $11 ÷ $20
Break-even point in dollars = Fixed costs ÷ Contribution margin ratio
= $220,000 ÷ 55%
= $400,000

c. Margin of safety = $\dfrac{\text{Actual sales} - \text{Break-even sales}}{\text{Actual sales}}$

= $\dfrac{\$500{,}000 - \$400{,}000}{\$500{,}000}$

= 20%

d. Sales − Variable costs − Fixed costs = Net income
$20Q − $9Q − $220,000 = $165,000
$11Q = $385,000
Q = 35,000 units

35,000 units × $20 = $700,000 required sales

OR

(Fixed costs + Target net income) ÷ Contribution margin ratio = Sales in dollars
($220,000 + $165,000) ÷ .55 = $700,000

WileyPLUS

Brief Exercises, DO IT! Exercises, Exercises, Problems, and many additional resources are available for practice in WileyPLUS.

Note: All asterisked Questions, Exercises, and Problems relate to material in the appendix to this chapter.

Questions

1. **a.** What is cost behavior analysis?
   b. Why is cost behavior analysis important to management?

2. **a.** Scott Winter asks your help in understanding the term "activity index." Explain the meaning and importance of this term for Scott.
   b. State the two ways that variable costs may be defined.

3. Contrast the effects of changes in the activity level on total fixed costs and on unit fixed costs.

4. J. P. Alexander claims that the relevant range concept is important only for variable costs.
   a. Explain the relevant range concept.
   b. Do you agree with J. P.'s claim? Explain.

5. "The relevant range is indispensable in cost behavior analysis." Is this true? Why or why not?

6. Adam Antal is confused. He does not understand why rent on his apartment is a fixed cost and rent on a Hertz rental truck is a mixed cost. Explain the difference to Adam.

7. How should mixed costs be classified in CVP analysis? What approach is used to effect the appropriate classification?

8. At the high and low levels of activity during the month, direct labor hours are 90,000 and 40,000, respectively. The related costs are $165,000 and $100,000. What are the fixed and variable costs at each level of activity?

9. "Cost-volume-profit (CVP) analysis is based entirely on unit costs." Do you agree? Explain.

10. Faye Dunn defines contribution margin as the amount of profit available to cover operating expenses. Is there any truth in this definition? Discuss.

11. Marshall Company's GWhiz calculator sells for $40. Variable costs per unit are estimated to be $26. What are the unit contribution margin and the contribution margin ratio?

12. "Break-even analysis is of limited use to management because a company cannot survive by just breaking even." Do you agree? Explain.

13. Total fixed costs are $26,000 for Daz Inc. It has a unit contribution margin of $15, and a contribution margin ratio of 25%. Compute the break-even sales in dollars.

14. Peggy Turnbull asks your help in constructing a CVP graph. Explain to Peggy (a) how the break-even point is plotted, and (b) how the level of activity and dollar sales at the break-even point are determined.

15. Define the term "margin of safety." If Revere Company expects to sell 1,250 units of its product at $12 per unit, and break-even sales for the product are $13,200, what is the margin of safety ratio?

16. Huang Company's break-even sales are $500,000. Assuming fixed costs are $180,000, what sales volume is needed to achieve a target net income of $90,000?

17. The traditional income statement for Pace Company shows sales $900,000, cost of goods sold $600,000, and operating expenses $200,000. Assuming all costs and expenses are 70% variable and 30% fixed, prepare a CVP income statement through contribution margin.

*18. James Brooks estimated the variable and fixed components of his company's utility costs using the high-low method. He is concerned that the cost equation that resulted from the high-low method might not provide an accurate representation of his company's utility costs. What is the inherent weakness of the high-low method? What alternative approach might Brooks use, and what are its advantages?

*19. Mary Webster owns and manages a company that provides trenching services. Her clients are companies that need to lay power lines, gas lines, and fiber optic cable. Because trenching machines require considerable maintenance due to the demanding nature of the work, Mary has created a scatter plot that displays her monthly maintenance costs. If Mary were to estimate a cost equation line using regression analysis for the data in her scatter plot, what primary characteristic would that line display?

*20. What are some of the limitations of regression analysis?

Brief Exercises

BE18.1 (LO 1), C Monthly production costs in Dilts Company for two levels of production are as follows.

Cost	2,000 Units	4,000 Units
Indirect labor	$10,000	$20,000
Supervisory salaries	5,000	5,000
Maintenance	4,000	6,000

Indicate which costs are variable, fixed, and mixed, and give the reason for each answer.

Classify costs as variable, fixed, or mixed.

BE18.2 (LO 1), AN For Lodes Company, the relevant range of production is 40–80% of capacity. At 40% of capacity, a variable cost is $4,000 and a fixed cost is $6,000. Diagram the behavior of each cost within the relevant range assuming the behavior is linear.

Diagram the behavior of costs within the relevant range.

BE18.3 (LO 1), AN For Wesland Company, a mixed cost is $15,000 plus $18 per direct labor hour. Diagram the behavior of the cost using increments of 500 hours up to 2,500 hours on the horizontal axis and increments of $15,000 up to $60,000 on the vertical axis.

Diagram the behavior of a mixed cost.

BE18.4 (LO 2), AP Bruno Company accumulates the following data concerning a mixed cost, using miles as the activity level.

	Miles Driven	Total Cost		Miles Driven	Total Cost
January	8,000	$14,150	March	8,500	$15,000
February	7,500	13,500	April	8,200	14,490

Compute the variable- and fixed-cost elements using the high-low method.

Determine variable- and fixed-cost elements using the high-low method.

BE18.5 (LO 2), AP Markowis Corp. has collected the following data concerning its maintenance costs for the past 6 months.

	Units Produced	Total Cost
July	18,000	$36,000
August	32,000	48,000
September	36,000	55,000
October	22,000	38,000
November	40,000	74,500
December	38,000	62,000

Compute the variable- and fixed-cost elements using the high-low method.

Determine variable- and fixed-cost elements using the high-low method.

BE18.6 (LO 3), AN Determine the missing amounts.

	Unit Selling Price	Unit Variable Costs	Unit Contribution Margin	Contribution Margin Ratio
1.	$640	$352	(a)	(b)
2.	$300	(c)	$93	(d)
3.	(e)	(f)	$325	25%

Determine missing amounts for contribution margin.

BE18.7 (LO 3), AP Russell Inc. had sales of $2,200,000 for the first quarter of 2022. In making the sales, the company incurred the following costs and expenses.

	Variable	Fixed
Cost of goods sold	$920,000	$440,000
Selling expenses	70,000	45,000
Administrative expenses	86,000	98,000

Prepare a CVP income statement for the quarter ended March 31, 2022.

Prepare CVP income statement.

BE18.8 (LO 4), AP Rice Company has a unit selling price of $520, variable costs per unit of $286, and fixed costs of $163,800. Compute the break-even point in units using (a) the mathematical equation and (b) unit contribution margin.

Compute the break-even point.

BE18.9 (LO 4), AP Presto Corp. had total variable costs of $180,000, total fixed costs of $110,000, and total revenues of $300,000. Compute the required sales in dollars to break even.

Compute the break-even point.

BE18.10 (LO 5), AP For Flynn Company, variable costs are 70% of sales, and fixed costs are $195,000. Management's net income goal is $75,000. Compute the required sales in dollars needed to achieve management's target net income of $75,000. (Use the contribution margin approach.)

Compute sales for target net income.

18-34 CHAPTER 18 Cost-Volume-Profit

Compute the margin of safety and the margin of safety ratio.

BE18.11 (LO 5), AP For Astoria Company, actual sales are $1,000,000, and break-even sales are $800,000. Compute (a) the margin of safety in dollars and (b) the margin of safety ratio.

Compute the required sales in units for target net income.

BE18.12 (LO 5), AP Deines Corporation has fixed costs of $480,000. It has a unit selling price of $6, unit variable costs of $4.40, and a target net income of $1,500,000. Compute the required sales in units to achieve its target net income.

Compute variable and fixed cost elements using regression.

*BE18.13 (LO 6), AP** Data for Stiever Corporation's maintenance costs is shown below.

	Units Produced	Total Cost
July	18,000	$32,000
August	32,000	48,000
September	36,000	55,000
October	22,000	38,000
November	40,000	66,100
December	38,000	62,000

Compute the variable- and fixed-cost elements using regression analysis. Present your solution in the form of a cost equation. (We recommend that you use the Intercept and Slope functions in Excel.)

DO IT! Exercises

Classify types of costs.

DO IT! 18.1 (LO 1), C Amanda Company reports the following total costs at two levels of production.

	5,000 Units	10,000 Units
Indirect labor	$ 3,000	$ 6,000
Property taxes	7,000	7,000
Direct labor	28,000	56,000
Direct materials	22,000	44,000
Depreciation	4,000	4,000
Utilities	5,000	8,000
Maintenance	9,000	11,000

Classify each cost as variable, fixed, or mixed.

Compute costs using high-low method and estimate total cost.

DO IT! 18.2 (LO 2), AP Westerville Company accumulates the following data concerning a mixed cost, using units produced as the activity level.

	Units Produced	Total Cost
March	10,000	$18,000
April	9,000	16,650
May	10,500	18,580
June	8,800	16,200
July	9,500	17,100

a. Compute the variable- and fixed-cost elements using the high-low method.
b. Using the information from your answer to part (a), write the cost formula.
c. Estimate the total cost if the company produces 9,200 units.

Prepare CVP income statement.

DO IT! 18.3 (LO 3), AP Cedar Grove Industries produces and sells a cell phone-operated home security control. Information regarding the costs and sales of security controls during May 2022 are provided below.

Unit selling price of security control	$45
Unit variable costs	$22
Total monthly fixed costs	$120,000
Units sold	8,000

Prepare a CVP income statement for Cedar Grove Industries for the month of May. Provide per unit values and total values.

Compute break-even point in units.

DO IT! 18.4 (LO 4), AP Snow Cap Company has a unit selling price of $250, variable costs per unit of $170, and fixed costs of $160,000. Compute the break-even point in units using (a) the mathematical equation and (b) unit contribution margin.

DO IT! 18.5 (LO 5), AP Presto Company makes radios that sell for $30 each. For the coming year, management expects fixed costs to total $220,000 and variable costs to be $18 per unit.

a. Compute the break-even point in dollars using the contribution margin (CM) ratio.
b. Compute the margin of safety ratio assuming actual sales are $800,000.
c. Compute the sales dollars required to earn net income of $140,000.

Compute break-even point, margin of safety ratio, and sales for target net income.

Exercises

E18.1 (LO 1), C Bonita Company manufactures a single product. Annual production costs incurred in the manufacturing process are shown below for two levels of production.

Define and classify variable, fixed, and mixed costs.

	Costs Incurred			
Production in Units	5,000		10,000	
Production Costs	Total Cost	Cost/ Unit	Total Cost	Cost/ Unit
Direct materials	$8,000	$1.60	$16,000	$1.60
Direct labor	9,500	1.90	19,000	1.90
Utilities	2,000	0.40	3,300	0.33
Rent	4,000	0.80	4,000	0.40
Maintenance	800	0.16	1,400	0.14
Supervisory salaries	1,000	0.20	1,000	0.10

Instructions

a. Define the terms variable costs, fixed costs, and mixed costs.
b. Classify each cost above as either variable, fixed, or mixed.

E18.2 (LO 1), C Shingle Enterprises is considering manufacturing a new product. It projects the cost of direct materials and rent for a range of output as shown below.

Diagram cost behavior, determine relevant range, and classify costs.

Output in Units	Rent Expense	Direct Materials
1,000	$ 5,000	$ 4,000
2,000	5,000	7,200
3,000	8,000	9,000
4,000	8,000	12,000
5,000	8,000	15,000
6,000	8,000	18,000
7,000	8,000	21,000
8,000	8,000	24,000
9,000	10,000	29,300
10,000	10,000	35,000
11,000	10,000	44,000

Instructions

a. Diagram the behavior of each cost for output ranging from 1,000 to 11,000 units.
b. Determine the relevant range of activity for this product.
c. Calculate the variable costs per unit within the relevant range.
d. Indicate the fixed cost within the relevant range.

E18.3 (LO 1, 2), AN The controller of Norton Industries has collected the following monthly expense data for use in analyzing the cost behavior of maintenance costs.

Determine fixed and variable costs using the high-low method and prepare graph.

Month	Total Maintenance Costs	Total Machine Hours
January	$2,700	300
February	3,000	350
March	3,600	500
April	4,500	690
May	3,200	400
June	5,500	700

Instructions

a. Determine the fixed- and variable-cost components using the high-low method.

b. Prepare a graph showing the behavior of maintenance costs, and identify the fixed- and variable-cost elements. Use 100-hour increments and $1,000 cost increments.

Classify variable, fixed, and mixed costs.

E18.4 (LO 1), C Family Furniture Corporation incurred the following costs.

1. Wood used in the production of furniture.
2. Fuel used in delivery trucks.
3. Straight-line depreciation on factory building.
4. Screws used in the production of furniture.
5. Sales staff salaries.
6. Sales commissions.
7. Property taxes.
8. Insurance on buildings.
9. Hourly wages of furniture craftsmen.
10. Salaries of factory supervisors.
11. Utilities expense.
12. Telephone bill.

Instructions

Identify the costs above as variable, fixed, or mixed.

Determine fixed and variable costs using the high-low method and prepare graph.

E18.5 (LO 1, 2), AP The controller of Hall Industries has collected the following monthly expense data for use in analyzing the cost behavior of maintenance costs.

Month	Total Maintenance Costs	Total Machine Hours
January	$2,640	3,500
February	3,000	4,000
March	3,600	6,000
April	4,500	7,900
May	3,200	5,000
June	4,620	8,000

Instructions

a. Determine the fixed- and variable-cost components using the high-low method.

b. Prepare a graph showing the behavior of maintenance costs and identify the fixed- and variable-cost elements. Use 2,000-hour increments and $1,000 cost increments.

Determine fixed, variable, and mixed costs.

E18.6 (LO 1), AP PCB Corporation manufactures a single product. Monthly production costs incurred in the manufacturing process are shown below for the production of 3,000 units. The utilities and maintenance costs are mixed costs. The fixed portions of these costs are $300 and $200, respectively.

Production in Units	3,000
Production Costs	
Direct materials	$ 7,500
Direct labor	18,000
Utilities	2,100
Property taxes	1,000
Indirect labor	4,500
Supervisory salaries	1,900
Maintenance	1,100
Depreciation	2,400

Instructions

a. Identify the above costs as variable, fixed, or mixed.

b. Calculate the expected costs when production is 5,000 units.

Explain assumptions underlying CVP analysis.

E18.7 (LO 3), K Writing Marty Moser wants Moser Company to use CVP analysis to study the effects of changes in costs and volume on the company. Marty has heard that certain assumptions must be valid in order for CVP analysis to be useful.

Instructions

Prepare a memo to Marty Moser concerning the assumptions that underlie CVP analysis.

E18.8 (LO 3, 4), AP `Service` All That Blooms provides environmentally friendly lawn services for homeowners. Its operating costs are as follows.

Compute break-even point in units and dollars.

Depreciation	$1,400 per month
Advertising	$200 per month
Insurance	$2,000 per month
Weed and feed materials	$12 per lawn
Direct labor	$10 per lawn
Fuel	$2 per lawn

All That Blooms charges $60 per treatment for the average single-family lawn.

Instructions

Determine the company's break-even point in (a) number of lawns serviced per month and (b) dollars.

E18.9 (LO 3, 4), AP `Service` The Palmer Acres Inn is trying to determine its break-even point during its off-peak season. The inn has 50 rooms that it rents at $60 a night. Operating costs are as follows.

Compute break-even point.

Salaries	$5,900 per month
Utilities	$1,100 per month
Depreciation	$1,000 per month
Maintenance	$100 per month
Maid service	$14 per room
Other costs	$28 per room

Instructions

Determine the inn's break-even point in (a) number of rented rooms per month and (b) dollars.

E18.10 (LO 3, 4), AP `Service` In the month of March, Style Salon services 560 clients at an average price of $120. During the month, fixed costs were $21,024 and variable costs were 60% of sales.

Compute contribution margin and break-even point.

Instructions

a. Determine the total contribution margin in dollars, the per unit contribution margin, and the contribution margin ratio.

b. Using the contribution margin technique, compute the break-even point in dollars and in units.

E18.11 (LO 3, 4), AP `Service` Spencer Kars provides shuttle service between four hotels near a medical center and an international airport. Spencer Kars uses two 10-passenger vans to offer 12 round trips per day. A recent month's activity in the form of a cost-volume-profit income statement is shown below.

Compute break-even point.

Sales (1,500 passengers)		$36,000
Variable costs		
Fuel	$ 5,040	
Tolls and parking	3,100	
Maintenance	860	9,000
Contribution margin		27,000
Fixed costs		
Salaries	15,700	
Depreciation	1,300	
Insurance	1,000	18,000
Net income		$ 9,000

Instructions

a. Calculate the break-even point in (1) dollars and (2) number of passengers.

b. Without calculations, determine the contribution margin at the break-even point.

E18.12 (LO 3, 4), AP In 2021, Manhoff Company had a break-even point of $350,000 based on a selling price of $5 per unit and fixed costs of $112,000. In 2022, the selling price and the variable costs per unit did not change, but the break-even point increased to $420,000.

Compute variable costs per unit, contribution margin ratio, and increase in fixed costs.

Instructions

a. Compute the variable costs per unit and the contribution margin ratio for 2021.

b. Compute the increase in fixed costs for 2022.

Prepare CVP income statements.

E18.13 (LO 3, 4), AP Billings Company has the following information available for September 2022.

Unit selling price of video game consoles	$ 400
Unit variable costs	$ 280
Total fixed costs	$54,000
Units sold	600

Instructions

a. Compute the unit contribution margin.

b. Prepare a CVP income statement that shows both total and per unit amounts.

c. Compute Billings' break-even point in units.

d. Prepare a CVP income statement for the break-even point that shows both total and per unit amounts.

Compute various components to derive target net income under different assumptions.

E18.14 (LO 4, 5), AP Naylor Company had $210,000 of net income in 2021 when the selling price per unit was $150, the variable costs per unit were $90, and the fixed costs were $570,000. Management expects per unit data and total fixed costs to remain the same in 2022. The president of Naylor Company is under pressure from stockholders to increase net income by $52,000 in 2022.

Instructions

a. Compute the number of units sold in 2021.

b. Compute the number of units that would have to be sold in 2022 to reach the stockholders' desired profit level.

c. Assume that Naylor Company sells the same number of units in 2022 as it did in 2021. What would the selling price have to be in order to reach the stockholders' desired profit level?

Compute net income under different alternatives.

E18.15 (LO 5), AP Yams Company reports the following operating results for the month of August: sales $400,000 (units 5,000), variable costs $240,000, and fixed costs $90,000. Management is considering the following independent courses of action to increase net income.

1. Increase selling price by 10% with no change in total variable costs or units sold.
2. Reduce variable costs to 55% of sales.

Instructions

Compute the net income to be earned under each alternative. Which course of action will produce the higher net income?

Prepare a CVP graph and compute break-even point and margin of safety.

E18.16 (LO 4, 5), AP Glacial Company estimates that variable costs will be 62.5% of sales, and fixed costs will total $600,000. The selling price of the product is $4.

Instructions

a. Compute the break-even point in (1) units and (2) dollars.

b. Prepare a CVP graph, assuming maximum sales of $3,200,000. (*Note:* Use $400,000 increments for sales and costs and 100,000 increments for units.)

c. Assuming actual sales are $2 million, compute the margin of safety in (1) dollars and (2) as a ratio.

Determine contribution margin ratio, break-even point in dollars, and margin of safety.

E18.17 (LO 3, 4, 5), AP Felde Bucket Co., a manufacturer of rain barrels, had the following data for 2021:

Sales	2,500 units
Sales price	$40 per unit
Variable costs	$24 per unit
Fixed costs	$19,500

Instructions

a. What is the contribution margin ratio?

b. What is the break-even point in dollars?

c. What is the margin of safety in dollars and as a ratio?

d. If the company wishes to increase its total dollar contribution margin by 30% in 2022, by how much will it need to increase its sales if all other factors remain constant?

(CGA adapted)

Determine cost components using regression, prepare scatter plot, and estimate cost at particular level of activity.

*E18.18 (LO 6), AP The controller of Standard Industries has collected the following monthly expense data for analyzing the cost behavior of electricity costs.

	Total Electricity Costs	Total Machine Hours
January	$2,500	300
February	3,000	350
March	3,600	500
April	4,500	690
May	3,200	400
June	4,900	700
July	4,100	650
August	3,800	520
September	5,100	680
October	4,200	630
November	3,300	350
December	6,100	720

Instructions

a. Determine the fixed- and variable-cost components using regression analysis (We recommend the use of Excel.)

b. Prepare a scatter plot using Excel. Present the cost equation line estimated in part (a).

c. What electricity cost does the cost equation estimate for a level of activity of 500 machine hours? By what amount does this differ from March's observed cost for 500 machine hours?

Problems: Set A

P18.1A (LO 1, 2), AP The controller of Rather Production has collected the following monthly expense data for analyzing the cost behavior of electricity costs.

Determine cost components using high-low method, and estimate cost at particular level of activity.

	Total Electricity Costs	Total Machine Hours
January	$2,500	300
February	3,000	350
March	3,600	500
April	4,500	690
May	3,200	400
June	4,900	700
July	4,100	650
August	3,800	520
September	5,100	680
October	4,200	630
November	3,300	350
December	5,860	720

Instructions

a. Determine the fixed- and variable-cost components using the high-low method.

b. What electricity cost does the cost equation estimate for a level of activity of 500 machine hours? By what amount does this differ from March's observed cost for 500 machine hours?

c. What electricity cost does the cost equation estimate for a level of activity of 700 machine hours? By what amount does this differ from June's observed cost for 700 machine hours?

P18.2A (LO 1, 2, 3, 4), AN Service Vin Diesel owns the Fredonia Barber Shop. He employs four barbers and pays each a base rate of $1,250 per month. One of the barbers serves as the manager and receives an extra $500 per month. In addition to the base rate, each barber also receives a commission of $4.50 per haircut. Other costs are as follows.

Determine variable and fixed costs, compute break-even point, prepare a CVP graph, and determine net income.

Advertising	$200 per month
Rent	$1,100 per month
Barber supplies	$0.30 per haircut
Utilities	$175 per month plus $0.20 per haircut
Magazines	$25 per month

Vin currently charges $10 per haircut.

Instructions

a. VC $5

a. Determine the variable costs per haircut and the total monthly fixed costs.

b. Compute the break-even point in units and dollars.

c. Prepare a CVP graph, assuming a maximum of 1,800 haircuts in a month. Use increments of 300 haircuts on the horizontal axis and $3,000 on the vertical axis.

d. Determine net income, assuming 1,600 haircuts are given in a month.

Prepare a CVP income statement, compute break-even point, contribution margin ratio, margin of safety ratio, and sales for target net income.

P18.3A (LO 3, 4, 5), AN Jorge Company bottles and distributes B-Lite, a diet soft drink. The beverage is sold for 50 cents per 16-ounce bottle to retailers. For the year 2022, management estimates the following revenues and costs.

Sales	$1,800,000	Selling expenses—variable	$70,000
Direct materials	430,000	Selling expenses—fixed	65,000
Direct labor	360,000	Administrative expenses— variable	20,000
Manufacturing overhead— variable	380,000	Administrative expenses— fixed	60,000
Manufacturing overhead— fixed	280,000		

Instructions

a. Prepare a CVP income statement for 2022 based on management's estimates. (Show column for total amounts only.)

b. (1) 2,700,000 units

c. CM ratio 30%

b. Compute the break-even point in (1) units and (2) dollars.

c. Compute the contribution margin ratio and the margin of safety ratio. (Round to nearest full percent.)

d. Determine the sales dollars required to earn net income of $180,000.

Compute break-even point under alternative courses of action.

P18.4A (LO 4), E Tanek Corp.'s sales slumped badly in 2022. For the first time in its history, it operated at a loss. The company's income statement showed the following results from selling 500,000 units of product: sales $2,500,000, total costs and expenses $2,600,000, and net loss $100,000. Costs and expenses consisted of the amounts shown below.

	Total	Variable	Fixed
Cost of goods sold	$2,140,000	$1,590,000	$550,000
Selling expenses	250,000	92,000	158,000
Administrative expenses	210,000	68,000	142,000
	$2,600,000	$1,750,000	$850,000

Management is considering the following independent alternatives for 2023.

1. Increase unit selling price 20% with no change in costs, expenses, and sales volume.
2. Change the compensation of salespersons from fixed annual salaries totaling $150,000 to total salaries of $60,000 plus a 5% commission on sales.

Instructions

a. Compute the break-even point in dollars for 2023.

b. Alternative 1 $2,023,810

b. Compute the break-even point in dollars under each of the alternative courses of action. (Round all ratios to nearest full percent.) Which course of action do you recommend?

Compute break-even point and margin of safety ratio, and prepare a CVP income statement before and after changes in business environment.

P18.5A (LO 3, 4, 5), E Mary Willis is the advertising manager for Bargain Shoe Store. She is currently working on a major promotional campaign. Her ideas include the installation of a new lighting system and increased display space that will add $24,000 in fixed costs to the $270,000 currently spent. In addition, Mary is proposing that a 5% price decrease ($40 to $38) will produce a 20% increase in sales volume (20,000 to 24,000). Variable costs will remain at $24 per pair of shoes. Management is impressed with Mary's ideas but concerned about the effects that these changes will have on the break-even point and the margin of safety.

Instructions

a. Compute the current break-even point in units, and compare it to the break-even point in units if Mary's ideas are used.

b. Current margin of safety ratio 16%

b. Compute the margin of safety ratio for current operations and after Mary's changes are introduced. (Round to nearest full percent.)

c. Prepare a CVP income statement for current operations and after Mary's changes are introduced. (Show column for total amounts only.) Would you make the changes suggested?

P18.6A (LO 3, 4, 5), AN Viejol Corporation has collected the following information after its first year of sales. Sales were $1,600,000 on 100,000 units, selling expenses $250,000 (40% variable and 60% fixed), direct materials $490,000, direct labor $290,000, administrative expenses $270,000 (20% variable and 80% fixed), and manufacturing overhead $380,000 (70% variable and 30% fixed). Top management has asked you to do a CVP analysis so that it can make plans for the coming year. It has projected that unit sales will increase by 10% next year.

Compute contribution margin, fixed costs, break-even point, sales for target net income, and margin of safety ratio.

Instructions

a. Compute (1) the contribution margin for the current year and the projected year, and (2) the fixed costs for the current year. (Assume that fixed costs will remain the same in the projected year.)

b. Compute the break-even point in units and sales dollars for the current year.

c. The company has a target net income of $200,000. What is the required sales in dollars for the company to meet its target?

d. If the company meets its target net income number, by what percentage could its sales fall before it is operating at a loss? That is, what is its margin of safety ratio?

b. 120,000 units

P18.7A (LO 1, 3, 5), E Kaiser Industries carries no inventories. Its product is manufactured only when a customer's order is received. It is then shipped immediately after it is made. For its fiscal year ended October 31, 2022, Kaiser's break-even point was $1.3 million. On sales of $1.2 million, its income statement showed a gross profit of $180,000, direct materials cost of $400,000, and direct labor costs of $500,000. The contribution margin was $144,000, and variable manufacturing overhead was $50,000.

Determine variable and fixed costs.

Instructions

a. Calculate the following:
   1. Variable selling and administrative expenses.
   2. Fixed manufacturing overhead.
   3. Fixed selling and administrative expenses.

a. 2. $70,000

b. Ignoring your answer to part (a), assume that fixed manufacturing overhead was $100,000 and the fixed selling and administrative expenses were $80,000. The marketing vice president feels that if the company increased its advertising, sales could be increased by 25%. What is the maximum increased advertising cost the company can incur and still report the same income as before the advertising expenditure?

(CGA adapted)

Continuing Cases

Current Designs

CD18 Bill Johnson, sales manager, and Diane Buswell, controller, at Current Designs are beginning to analyze the cost considerations for one of the composite models of the kayak division. They have provided the following production and operational costs necessary to produce one composite kayak.

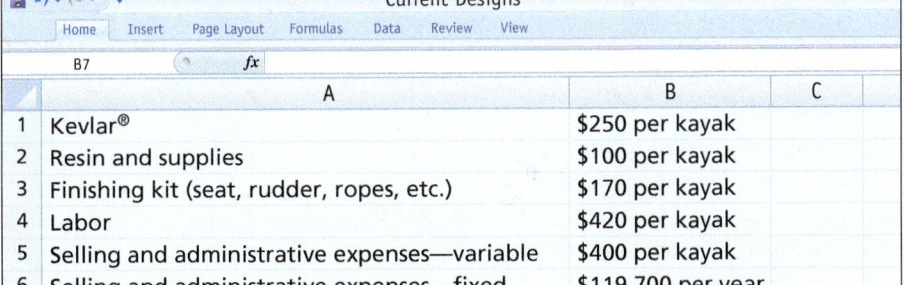

Bill and Diane have asked you to provide a cost-volume-profit analysis, to help them finalize the budget projections for the upcoming year. Bill has informed you that the selling price of the composite kayak will be $2,000.

Instructions

a. Calculate variable costs per unit.

b. Determine the unit contribution margin.

c. Using the unit contribution margin, determine the break-even point in units for this product line.

d. Assume that Current Designs plans to earn net income of $270,600 on this product line. Using the unit contribution margin, calculate the number of units that need to be sold to achieve this goal.

e. Based on the most recent sales forecast, Current Designs plans to sell 1,000 units of this model. Using your results from part (c), calculate the margin of safety and the margin of safety ratio.

Waterways

(*Note:* This is a continuation of the Waterways case from Chapters 14–17.)

WP18 The Vice President for Sales and Marketing at Waterways Corporation is planning for production needs to meet sales demand in the coming year. He is also trying to determine how the company's profits might be increased in the coming year. This problem asks you to use cost-volume-profit concepts to help Waterways understand contribution margins of some of its products and decide whether to mass-produce any of them.

Go to WileyPLUS for complete case details and instructions.

Expand Your Critical Thinking

Decision-Making Across the Organization

CT18.1 Creative Ideas Company has decided to introduce a new product. The new product can be manufactured by either a capital-intensive method or a labor-intensive method. The manufacturing method will not affect the quality of the product. The estimated manufacturing costs by the two methods are as follows.

	Capital-Intensive	Labor-Intensive
Direct materials	$5 per unit	$5.50 per unit
Direct labor	$6 per unit	$8.00 per unit
Variable overhead	$3 per unit	$4.50 per unit
Fixed manufacturing costs	$2,524,000	$1,550,000

Creative Ideas' market research department has recommended an introductory unit sales price of $32. The incremental selling expenses are estimated to be $502,000 annually plus $2 for each unit sold, regardless of manufacturing method.

Instructions

With the class divided into groups, answer the following.

a. Calculate the estimated break-even point in annual unit sales of the new product if Creative Ideas Company uses the:

   1. Capital-intensive manufacturing method.
   2. Labor-intensive manufacturing method.

b. Determine the annual unit sales volume at which Creative Ideas Company would be indifferent between the two manufacturing methods.

c. Explain the circumstance under which Creative Ideas should employ each of the two manufacturing methods.

(CMA adapted)

Managerial Analysis

CT18.2 The condensed income statement for the Peri and Paul partnership for 2022 is as follows.

Peri and Paul Company
Income Statement
For the Year Ended December 31, 2022

Sales (240,000 units)		$1,200,000
Cost of goods sold		800,000
Gross profit		400,000
Operating expenses		
Selling	$300,000	
Administrative	150,000	450,000
Net loss		$ (50,000)

A cost behavior analysis indicates that 75% of the cost of goods sold are variable, 40% of the selling expenses are variable, and 40% of the administrative expenses are variable.

Instructions

(Round to nearest unit, dollar, and percentage, where necessary. Use the CVP income statement format in computing profits.)

a. Compute the break-even point in total sales dollars and in units for 2022.

b. Peri has proposed a plan to get the partnership "out of the red" and improve its profitability. She feels that the quality of the product could be substantially improved by spending $0.25 more per unit on better raw materials. The selling price per unit could be increased to only $5.25 because of competitive pressures. Peri estimates that sales volume will increase by 25%. Compute net income under Peri's proposal and the break-even point in dollars. (Round the contribution margin ratio to three decimal places.)

c. Paul was a marketing major in college. He believes that sales volume can be increased only by intensive advertising and promotional campaigns. He therefore proposed the following plan as an alternative to Peri's: (1) increase variable selling expenses to $0.59 per unit, (2) lower the selling price per unit by $0.25, and (3) increase fixed selling expenses by $40,000. Paul quoted an old marketing research report that said that sales volume would increase by 60% if these changes were made. Compute net income under Paul's proposal and the break-even point in dollars. (Round the contribution margin ratio to three decimal places.)

d. Which plan should be accepted? Explain your answer.

Real-World Focus

CT18.3 The Coca-Cola Company hardly needs an introduction. A line taken from the cover of a recent annual report says it all: If you measured time in servings of Coca-Cola, "a billion Coca-Cola's ago was yesterday morning." On average, every U.S. citizen drinks 363 8-ounce servings of Coca-Cola products each year. Coca-Cola's primary line of business is the making and selling of syrup to bottlers. These bottlers then sell the finished bottles and cans of Coca-Cola to the consumer.

In the annual report of Coca-Cola, the information shown below was provided.

The Coca-Cola Company
Management Discussion

Our gross margin declined to 61 percent this year from 62 percent in the prior year, primarily due to costs for materials such as sweeteners and packaging.

The increases [in selling expenses] in the last two years were primarily due to higher marketing expenditures in support of our Company's volume growth.

We measure our sales volume in two ways: (1) gallon shipments of concentrates and syrups and (2) unit cases of finished product (bottles and cans of Coke sold by bottlers).

Instructions

Answer the following questions.

a. Are sweeteners and packaging a variable cost or a fixed cost? What is the impact on the contribution margin of an increase in the per unit cost of sweeteners or packaging? What are the implications for profitability?

b. In your opinion, are Coca-Cola's marketing expenditures a fixed cost, variable cost, or mixed cost? Give justification for your answer.

c. Which of the two measures cited for measuring volume represents the activity index as defined in this chapter? Why might Coca-Cola use two different measures?

Communication Activity

CT18.4 Your roommate asks for your help on the following questions about CVP analysis formulas.

a. How can the mathematical equation for break-even sales show both sales units and sales dollars?

b. How do the formulas differ for unit contribution margin and contribution margin ratio?

c. How can contribution margin be used to determine break-even sales in units and in dollars?

Instructions

Write a memo to your roommate stating the relevant formulas and answering each question.

Ethics Case

CT18.5 Scott Bestor is an accountant for Westfield Company. Early this year, Scott made a highly favorable projection of sales and profits over the next 3 years for Westfield's hot-selling computer PLEX. As a result of the projections Scott presented to senior management, the company decided to expand production in this area. This decision led to dislocations of some plant personnel who were reassigned to one of the company's newer plants in another state. However, no one was fired, and in fact the company expanded its workforce slightly.

Unfortunately, Scott rechecked his projection computations a few months later and found that he had made an error that would have reduced his projections substantially. Luckily, sales of PLEX have exceeded projections so far, and management is satisfied with its decision. Scott, however, is not sure what to do. Should he confess his honest mistake and jeopardize his possible promotion? He suspects that no one will catch the error because PLEX sales have exceeded his projections, and it appears that profits will materialize close to his projections.

Instructions

a. Who are the stakeholders in this situation?

b. Identify the ethical issues involved in this situation.

c. What are the possible alternative actions for Scott? What would you do in Scott's position?

All About You

CT18.6 Cost-volume-profit analysis can also be used in making personal financial decisions. For example, the purchase of a new car is one of your biggest personal expenditures. It is important that you carefully analyze your options.

Suppose that you are considering the purchase of a hybrid vehicle. Let's assume the following facts. The hybrid will initially cost an additional $4,500 above the cost of a traditional vehicle. The hybrid will get 40 miles per gallon of gas, and the traditional car will get 30 miles per gallon. Also, assume that the cost of gas is $3.60 per gallon.

Instructions

Using the facts above, answer the following questions.

a. What is the variable gasoline cost of going one mile in the hybrid car? What is the variable cost of going one mile in the traditional car?

b. Using the information in part (a), if "miles" is your unit of measure, what is the "contribution margin" of the hybrid vehicle relative to the traditional vehicle? That is, express the variable cost savings on a per-mile basis.

c. How many miles would you have to drive in order to break even on your investment in the hybrid car?

d. What other factors might you want to consider?

CHAPTER 19

Cost-Volume-Profit Analysis: Additional Issues

Chapter Preview

As the following Feature Story about **Whole Foods Market** suggests, the relationship between a company's fixed and variable costs can have a huge impact on its profitability. In particular, the trend toward cost structures dominated by fixed costs has significantly increased the volatility of many companies' net income. The purpose of this chapter is to demonstrate additional uses of cost-volume-profit analysis in making sound business decisions.

Feature Story

Not Even a Flood Could Stop It

America has a reputation as a country populated with people who won't buy a restaurant meal unless it can be ordered from the driver's seat of a car. Customers want to receive said "meal" 30 seconds later from a drive-up window and then consume the bagged product while driving one-handed down an 8-lane freeway. This is actually a fairly accurate depiction of the restaurant preferences (and eating habits) of one of the authors of this text. However, given the success of **Whole Foods Market**, this certainly cannot be true of all Americans.

Whole Foods Market began humbly in 1978 as a natural-foods store called SaferWay. (Get it? A play on **SafeWay** grocery stores.) It was founded in Austin, Texas, by 25 year-old John Mackey (a self-described college dropout) and 21 year-old Renee Lawson Hardy. They financed the first store by borrowing $45,000 from family and friends. The early days were "interesting." First, John and Renee got kicked out of their apartment for storing grocery products there. No problem—they just moved into the store. They bathed in the store's dishwasher with an attached hose. They did whatever it took to keep their costs down and the store going.

Two years later, John and Renee merged SaferWay with another store to form the first Whole Foods Market. The store's first year was very successful. Well, that is until everything in the store was completely destroyed by Austin's biggest flood in more than 70 years. They lost $400,000 in goods—and they had no insurance. But within 28 days, with tons of volunteer work and supportive creditors and vendors, the store reopened.

Today, Whole Foods operates approximately 270 stores. The size of the average store has actually declined in recent years. While huge stores (up to 80,000 square feet) were successful in a few cities, in most locations the fixed costs of such a large facility made it hard to achieve profit targets. Then, when sales became sluggish during the financial crisis of 2008, the company determined that it could reduce its fixed costs, such as rent and utility costs, by reducing its average store size by about 20%. However, with fewer square feet, managers must keep a close eye on the sales mix. They need to be aware of the relative contribution margins of each product line to maximize the profit per square foot while still providing the products its customers want.

Why is a company as successful as Whole Foods so concerned about controlling costs? The answer is that the grocery business runs on very thin margins. So while we doubt that anybody is bathing in the store's dishwashers anymore, Whole Foods is as vigilant about its costs today as it was during its first year of operations.

 Watch the *Whole Foods Market* video in WileyPLUS to learn more about the use of cost-volume-profit analysis in a changing business environment.

Chapter Outline

LEARNING OBJECTIVES

LO 1 Apply basic CVP concepts.	• Basic concepts • Basic computations • Business environment	**DO IT! 1** CVP Analysis
LO 2 Explain the term sales mix and its effects on break-even sales.	• Break-even in units • Break-even in dollars	**DO IT! 2** Sales Mix Break-Even
LO 3 Determine sales mix when a company has limited resources.	• Contribution margin per unit • Theory of constraints	**DO IT! 3** Sales Mix with Limited Resources
LO 4 Indicate how operating leverage affects profitability.	• Contribution margin ratio • Break-even point • Margin of safety ratio • Operating leverage	**DO IT! 4** Operating Leverage

Go to the Review and Practice section at the end of the chapter for a targeted summary and practice applications with solutions.
Visit WileyPLUS for additional tutorials and practice opportunities.

Basic CVP Concepts

> **LEARNING OBJECTIVE 1**
> Apply basic CVP concepts.

As indicated in Chapter 18, cost-volume-profit (CVP) analysis is the study of the effects of changes in costs and volume on a company's profit. CVP analysis is important to profit planning. It is also a critical factor in determining product mix, maximizing use of production facilities, and setting selling prices.

Basic Concepts

Because CVP is so important for decision-making, management often wants this information reported in a CVP income statement format for internal use. The CVP income statement classifies costs as variable or fixed, and computes a contribution margin. **Contribution margin** is the amount of revenue remaining after deducting variable costs. It is often stated both as a total amount and on a per unit basis.

Illustration 19.1 presents the CVP income statement for Vargo Electronics (which was shown in Illustration 18.12). Note that Vargo sold 1,600 cell phones at $500 per unit.

Vargo Electronics Company
CVP Income Statement
For the Month Ended June 30, 2022

	Total	Per Unit
Sales (1,600 cell phones)	$800,000	$500
Variable costs	480,000	300
Contribution margin	320,000	$200
Fixed costs	200,000	
Net income	$120,000	

ILLUSTRATION 19.1
Basic CVP income statement

Companies often prepare detailed CVP income statements. The CVP income statement in Illustration 19.2 uses the same base information as that presented in Illustration 19.1 but provides more detailed information (using assumed data) about the composition of expenses. The appendix to this chapter provides additional discussion of income statements used for decision-making.

In the applications of CVP analysis that follow, we assume that the term "cost" includes all costs and expenses related to production and sale of the product. That is, **cost includes manufacturing costs plus selling and administrative expenses**.

Basic Computations

Before we introduce additional issues of CVP analysis, let's review some of the basic concepts that you learned in Chapter 18, specifically break-even analysis, target net income, and margin of safety.

Break-Even Analysis

Vargo Electronics' CVP income statement (Illustration 19.2) shows that total contribution margin (sales minus variable expenses) is $320,000, and the company's unit contribution

ILLUSTRATION 19.2
Detailed CVP income statement

Vargo Electronics Company
CVP Income Statement
For the Month Ended June 30, 2022

		Total	Per Unit
Sales		$800,000	$500
Variable expenses			
Cost of goods sold	$400,000		
Selling expenses	60,000		
Administrative expenses	20,000		
Total variable expenses		480,000	300
Contribution margin		**320,000**	**$200**
Fixed expenses			
Cost of goods sold	120,000		
Selling expenses	40,000		
Administrative expenses	40,000		
Total fixed expenses		200,000	
Net income		**$120,000**	

margin is $200. Recall that contribution margin can also be expressed in the form of the **contribution margin ratio** (contribution margin divided by sales), which in the case of Vargo is 40% ($200 ÷ $500).

Illustration 19.3 demonstrates how to compute Vargo's break-even point in units (using unit contribution margin).

ILLUSTRATION 19.3
Break-even point in units

Fixed Costs	÷	Unit Contribution Margin	=	Break-Even Point in Units
$200,000	÷	$200	=	1,000 units

Illustration 19.4 shows the computation for the break-even point in dollars (using contribution margin ratio).

ILLUSTRATION 19.4
Break-even point in dollars

Fixed Costs	÷	Contribution Margin Ratio	=	Break-Even Point in Dollars
$200,000	÷	.40	=	$500,000

When a company is in its early stages of operation, its primary goal is to break even. Failure to break even will lead eventually to financial failure.

Target Net Income

Once a company achieves break-even, it then sets a sales goal that will generate a target net income. For example, assume that Vargo's management has a target net income of $250,000. Illustration 19.5 shows the required sales in units to achieve its target net income.

ILLUSTRATION 19.5 Target net income in units

(Fixed Costs + Target Net Income)	÷	Unit Contribution Margin	=	Sales in Units
($200,000 + $250,000)	÷	$200	=	2,250 units

Illustration 19.6 uses the contribution margin ratio to compute the required sales in dollars.

ILLUSTRATION 19.6 Target net income in dollars

(Fixed Costs + Target Net Income)	÷	Contribution Margin Ratio	=	Sales in Dollars
($200,000 + $250,000)	÷	.40	=	$1,125,000

In order to achieve net income of $250,000, Vargo has to sell 2,250 cell phones, for a total price of $1,125,000.

Margin of Safety

Another measure managers use to assess profitability is the margin of safety. The **margin of safety** tells us **how far sales can drop** before the company will be operating at a loss. Managers like to have a sense of how much cushion they have between their current situation and operating at a loss. This can be expressed in dollars or as a ratio. In Illustration 19.2, for example, Vargo reported sales of $800,000. At that sales level, its margin of safety in dollars and as a ratio are as shown in Illustrations 19.7 and 19.8.

ILLUSTRATION 19.7 Margin of safety in dollars

Actual (Expected) Sales	−	Break-Even Sales	=	Margin of Safety in Dollars
$800,000	−	$500,000	=	$300,000

As Illustration 19.8 indicates, Vargo's sales could drop by $300,000, or 37.5%, before the company would operate at a loss.

ILLUSTRATION 19.8 Margin of safety ratio

Margin of Safety in Dollars	÷	Actual (Expected) Sales	=	Margin of Safety in Ratio
$300,000	÷	$800,000	=	37.5%

CVP and Changes in the Business Environment

To better understand how CVP analysis works, let's look at three independent cases that might occur at Vargo Electronics. Each case uses the original cell phone sales and cost data, shown in Illustration 19.9.

Unit selling price	$500
Unit variable cost	$300
Total fixed costs	$200,000
Break-even sales	$500,000 or 1,000 units

ILLUSTRATION 19.9 Original cell phone sales and cost data

Case I

A competitor is offering a 10% discount on the selling price of its cell phones. Management must decide whether to offer a similar discount.

Question: What effect will a 10% discount on selling price have on the break-even point for cell phones?

Answer: A 10% discount on selling price reduces the selling price per unit to $450 [$500 − ($500 × 10%)]. Variable costs per unit remain unchanged at $300. Thus, the unit contribution margin is $150. Assuming no change in fixed costs, break-even sales are 1,333 units, computed as shown in Illustration 19.10.

Fixed Costs	÷	Unit Contribution Margin	=	Break-Even Sales
$200,000	÷	$150	=	1,333 units (rounded)

ILLUSTRATION 19.10 Computation of break-even sales in units

For Vargo, this change requires monthly sales to increase by 333 units, or 33⅓%, in order to break even. In reaching a conclusion about offering a 10% discount to customers, management must determine how likely it is to achieve the increased sales. Also, management should estimate the possible loss of sales if the competitor's discount price is not matched.

Case II

To meet the threat of foreign competition, management invests in new robotic equipment that will lower the amount of direct labor required to make cell phones. The company estimates that total fixed costs will increase 30% and that variable cost per unit will decrease 30%.

Question: What effect will the new equipment have on the sales volume required to break even?

Answer: Total fixed costs become $260,000 [$200,000 + (30% × $200,000)]. The variable cost per unit becomes $210 [$300 − (30% × $300)]. The new break-even point is approximately 897 units, computed as shown in **Illustration 19.11**.

ILLUSTRATION 19.11
Computation of break-even sales in units

Fixed Costs	÷	Unit Contribution Margin	=	Break-Even Sales
$260,000	÷	($500 − $210)	=	897 units (rounded)

These changes appear to be advantageous for Vargo. The break-even point is reduced by 103 units (1,000 − 897).

Case III

Vargo's principal supplier of raw materials has just announced a price increase. The higher cost is expected to increase the variable cost of cell phones by $25 per unit. Management decides that it does not want to increase the selling price of the cell phones. It plans a cost-cutting program that will save $17,500 in fixed costs per month. Vargo is currently realizing monthly net income of $80,000 on sales of 1,400 cell phones.

Question: What increase in units sold will be needed to maintain the same level of net income?

Answer: The variable cost per unit increases to $325 ($300 + $25). Fixed costs are reduced to $182,500 ($200,000 − $17,500). Because of the change in variable cost, the unit contribution margin becomes $175 ($500 − $325). **Illustration 19.12** shows the computation of the required number of units sold to achieve the target net income.

ILLUSTRATION 19.12
Computation of required sales

Fixed Costs + Target Net Income	÷	Unit Contribution Margin	=	Sales in Units
($182,500 + $80,000)	÷	$175	=	1,500

To achieve the required sales, Vargo Electronics will have to sell 1,500 cell phones, an increase of 100 units. If this does not seem to be a reasonable expectation, management will either have to make further cost reductions or accept less net income if the selling price remains unchanged.

We hope that the concepts reviewed in this section are now familiar to you. We are now ready to examine additional ways that companies use CVP analysis to assess profitability and to help in making effective business decisions.

Management Insight Amazon.com

Warchi/iStockphoto

Don't Just Look—Buy Something

When analyzing an Internet business such as **Amazon.com**, analysts closely watch the so-called "conversion rate." This rate is calculated by dividing the number of people who actually take action at an Internet site (buy something) by the total number of people who visit the site. Average conversion rates are from 3% to 5%. A rate below 2% is poor, while a rate above 10% is great.

Conversion rates have an obvious effect on the break-even point. Suppose you spend $10,000 on your site, which then attracts 5,000 visitors. If you get a 2% conversion rate (100 purchases), your site costs $100 per purchase ($10,000 ÷ 100). A 4% conversion rate lowers your cost to $50 per transaction, and an 8% conversion rate gets you down to $25. Studies show that conversion rates increase if the site has an easy-to-use interface, fast-performing screens, a convenient ordering process, and advertising that is both clever and clear.

Sources: J. William Gurley, "The One Internet Metric That Really Counts," *Fortune* (March 6, 2000), p. 392; and Milind Mody, "Chief Mentor: How Startups Can Win Customers Online," *Wall Street Journal* (May 11, 2011).

Besides increasing their conversion rates, what steps can online merchants use to lower their break-even points? (Go to WileyPLUS for this answer and additional questions).

DO IT! 1 | CVP Analysis

Krisanne Company reports the following operating results for the month of June.

Krisanne Company
CVP Income Statement
For the Month Ended June 30, 2022

	Total	Per Unit
Sales (5,000 units)	$300,000	$60
Variable costs	180,000	36
Contribution margin	120,000	$24
Fixed expenses	100,000	
Net income	$ 20,000	

To increase net income, management is considering reducing the selling price by 10%, with no changes to unit variable costs or fixed costs. Management is confident that this change will increase unit sales by 25%.

Using the contribution margin technique, compute the break-even point in units and dollars and margin of safety in dollars (a) assuming no changes to sales price or costs, and (b) assuming changes to sales price and volume as described above. (c) Comment on your findings.

ACTION PLAN
- Apply the formula for the break-even point in units.
- Apply the formula for the break-even point in dollars.
- Apply the formula for the margin of safety in dollars.

Solution

a. Assuming no changes to sales price or costs:
   Break-even point in units = 4,167 units (rounded) ($100,000 ÷ $24)
   Break-even point in sales dollars = $250,000 ($100,000 ÷ .40^a)
   Margin of safety in dollars = $50,000 ($300,000 − $250,000)
   ^{a}$24 ÷ $60

b. Assuming changes to sales price and volume:
   Break-even point in units = 5,556 units (rounded) ($100,000 ÷ $18^b)
   Break-even point in sales dollars = $300,000 ($100,000 ÷ ($18 ÷ $54^c))
   Margin of safety in dollars = $37,500 ($337,500^d − $300,000)
   ^{b}$60 − (.10 × $60) − 36 = $18
   ^{c}$60 − (.10 × $60)
   ^{d}5,000 + (.25 × 5,000) = 6,250 units, 6,250 units × $54 = $337,500

c. The increase in the break-even point and the decrease in the margin of safety indicate that management should not implement the proposed change. The increase in sales volume will result in contribution margin of $112,500 (6,250 × $18), which is $7,500 ($120,000 − $112,500) less than the current amount.

Related exercise material: **BE19.3, BE19.4, BE19.5, BE19.6, DO IT! 19.1, E19.1, E19.2, E19.3, E19.4, and E19.5**.

Sales Mix and Break-Even Sales

> **LEARNING OBJECTIVE 2**
> Explain the term sales mix and its effects on break-even sales.

To this point, our discussion of CVP analysis has assumed that a company sells only one product. However, most companies sell multiple products. When a company sells many products, it is important that management understand the financial implications of its sales mix. **Sales mix** is the relative percentage in which a company sells its multiple products. For example, if 80% of **Hewlett Packard**'s unit sales are printers and the other 20% are PCs, its sales mix is 80% printers to 20% PCs.

Sales mix is important to managers because different products often have substantially different contribution margins. For example, **Ford**'s SUVs and F150 pickup trucks have higher contribution margins compared to its economy cars. Similarly, first-class tickets sold by **United Airlines** provide substantially higher contribution margins than coach-class tickets. **Intel**'s sales of computer chips for netbook computers have increased, but the contribution margin on these chips is lower than for notebook and desktop PCs.

Break-Even Sales in Units

Companies can compute break-even sales for a mix of two or more products by determining the **weighted-average unit contribution margin of all the products**. To illustrate, assume that Vargo Electronics sells not only cell phones but high-definition TVs as well. Vargo sells its two products in the following amounts: 1,500 cell phones and 500 TVs. **Illustration 19.13** shows the sales mix, expressed as a percentage of the 2,000 total units sold.

ILLUSTRATION 19.13
Sales mix as a percentage of units sold

Cell Phones	TVs
1,500 units ÷ 2,000 units = 75%	500 units ÷ 2,000 units = 25%

That is, 75% of the 2,000 units sold are cell phones, and 25% of the 2,000 units sold are TVs. **Illustration 19.14** shows additional information related to Vargo. The unit contribution margin for cell phones is $200, and for TVs it is $500. Vargo's fixed costs total $275,000.

ILLUSTRATION 19.14
Per unit data—sales mix

Unit Data	Cell Phones	TVs
Selling price	$500	$1,000
Variable costs	300	500
Contribution margin	$200	$500
Sales mix—units	75%	25%
Fixed costs = $275,000		

To compute break-even for Vargo, we must determine the weighted-average unit contribution margin for the two products. We use the **weighted-average** contribution margin because Vargo sells three times as many cell phones as TVs. As a result, in determining an average unit contribution margin, three times as much weight should be placed on the contribution margin of the cell phones as on the TVs. The weighted-average contribution margin for a sales mix of 75% cell phones and 25% TVs is $275, which is computed as shown in **Illustration 19.15**.

ILLUSTRATION 19.15 Weighted-average unit contribution margin

Cell Phones				TVs				
(Unit Contribution Margin	×	Sales Mix Percentage)	+	(Unit Contribution Margin	×	Sales Mix Percentage)	=	Weighted-Average Unit Contribution Margin
($200	×	.75)	+	($500	×	.25)	=	$275

Similar to our calculation in the single-product setting, we can compute the break-even point in units by dividing the fixed costs by the weighted-average unit contribution margin of $275. **Illustration 19.16** shows the computation of break-even sales in units for Vargo, assuming $275,000 of fixed costs.

Fixed Costs	÷	Weighted-Average Unit Contribution Margin	=	Break-Even Point in Units
$275,000	÷	$275	=	1,000 units

ILLUSTRATION 19.16 Break-even point in units

Illustration 19.16 shows the break-even point for Vargo is 1,000 units—cell phones and TVs combined (see **Decision Tools**). Management needs to know how many of the 1,000 units sold are cell phones and how many are TVs. Applying the sales mix percentages that we computed previously of 75% for cell phones and 25% for TVs, these 1,000 units would be comprised of 750 cell phones (.75 × 1,000 units) and 250 TVs (.25 × 1,000). This is verified by the computations in **Illustration 19.17**, which shows that the total contribution margin is $275,000 when 1,000 units are sold. As required at the break-even point, this contribution margin equals the fixed costs of $275,000.

> **Decision Tools**
> The break-even point in units helps managers determine how many units of each product need to be sold to avoid a loss.

Product	Unit Sales	×	Unit Contribution Margin	=	Total Contribution Margin
Cell phones	750	×	$200	=	$150,000
TVs	250	×	500	=	125,000
	1,000				$275,000

ILLUSTRATION 19.17 Break-even proof—sales units

Management should continually review and update the company's sales mix. At any level of units sold, **net income will be greater if higher contribution margin units are sold rather than lower contribution margin units**. For Vargo, the TVs produce the higher contribution margin. Consequently, if Vargo instead sells 700 cell phones and 300 TVs (a sales mix of 70% cell phones and 30% TVs), net income would be higher than in the current sales mix even though total units sold (1,000 units) are the same.

An analysis of these relationships shows that a shift from low-margin sales to high-margin sales may increase net income even though there is a decline in total units sold. Likewise, a shift from high- to low-margin sales may result in a decrease in net income even though there is an increase in total units sold.

Break-Even Sales in Dollars

The calculation of the break-even point presented for Vargo Electronics in the previous section works well if a company has only a *small number* of products. In contrast, consider **3M**, the maker of Post-it Notes, which has more than 30,000 products. In order to calculate the break-even point for 3M using a weighted-average unit contribution margin, we would need to calculate 30,000 different unit contribution margins. That is not realistic.

Therefore, for a company with many products, we calculate the break-even point in terms of sales dollars (rather than units sold), using sales information for divisions or product lines

> **Decision Tools**
>
> The break-even point in dollars helps managers determine the sales dollars required from each division to avoid a loss.

(rather than individual products) (see **Decision Tools**). This requires that we compute both sales mix as a percentage of total dollar sales (rather than units sold) and the contribution margin ratio (rather than unit contribution margin).

To illustrate, suppose that Kale Garden Supply Company has two divisions—Indoor Plants and Outdoor Plants. Each division has hundreds of different types of plants and plant-care products. **Illustration 19.18** provides information necessary for determining the sales mix percentages for the two divisions of Kale Garden Supply.

ILLUSTRATION 19.18
Cost-volume-profit data for Kale Garden Supply

	Indoor Plant Division	Outdoor Plant Division	Company Total
Sales	$ 200,000	$ 800,000	$1,000,000
Variable costs	120,000	560,000	680,000
Contribution margin	$ 80,000	$ 240,000	$ 320,000
Sales mix percentage (in sales dollars) (Division sales ÷ Total sales)	$\frac{\$200,000}{\$1,000,000} = .20$	$\frac{\$800,000}{\$1,000,000} = .80$	

Illustration 19.19 shows the contribution margin ratio for each division (40% and 30%) and for the combined company (32%), which is computed by dividing the total contribution margin by total sales.

ILLUSTRATION 19.19
Contribution margin ratio for each division

	Indoor Plant Division	Outdoor Plant Division	Company Total
Contribution margin ratio (Contribution margin ÷ Sales)	$\frac{\$80,000}{\$200,000} = .40$	$\frac{\$240,000}{\$800,000} = .30$	$\frac{\$320,000}{\$1,000,000} = .32$

It is useful to note that the contribution margin ratio of 32% for the total company is a weighted average of the individual contribution margin ratios of the two divisions (40% and 30%). To illustrate, in **Illustration 19.20** we multiply each division's contribution margin ratio by its sales mix percentage, based on dollar sales, and then total these amounts. The calculation in Illustration 19.20 is useful because it enables us to determine how the break-even point changes when the sales mix changes.

ILLUSTRATION 19.20 Calculation of weighted-average contribution margin

Indoor Plant Division				Outdoor Plant Division				Weighted-Average Contribution Margin Ratio
(Contribution Margin Ratio	×	Sales Mix Percentage)	+	(Contribution Margin Ratio	×	Sales Mix Percentage)	=	
(.40	×	.20)	+	(.30	×	.80)	=	.32

Kale Garden Supply's break-even point in dollars is computed by dividing its fixed costs of $300,000 by the weighted-average contribution margin ratio of 32%, as shown in **Illustration 19.21**.

ILLUSTRATION 19.21
Calculation of break-even point in dollars

Fixed Costs	÷	Weighted-Average Contribution Margin Ratio	=	Break-Even Point in Dollars
$300,000	÷	.32	=	$937,500

This break-even point is based on the sales mix of 20% to 80%. We can determine the amount of sales contributed by each division by multiplying the sales mix percentage of each division by the total sales figure. Of the company's total break-even sales of $937,500, a total of $187,500 (.20 × $937,500) will come from the Indoor Plant Division, and $750,000 (.80 × $937,500) will come from the Outdoor Plant Division.

What would be the impact on the break-even point if a higher percentage of Kale Garden Supply's sales were to come from the Indoor Plant Division? Because the Indoor Plant Division enjoys a higher contribution margin ratio, this change in the sales mix would result in a higher weighted-average contribution margin ratio and consequently a lower break-even point in dollars. For example, if the sales mix changes to 50% for the Indoor Plant Division and 50% for the Outdoor Plant Division, the weighted-average contribution margin ratio would be 35% [(.40 × .50) + (.30 × .50)]. The new, lower, break-even point is $857,143 ($300,000 ÷ .35). The opposite would occur if a higher percentage of sales were expected from the Outdoor Plant Division. As you can see, the information provided using CVP analysis can help managers better understand the impact of sales mix on profitability.

Management Insight   Chipotle

Wouldn't You Rather Have a Chicken Burrito?

Stockbroker/MBI/Alamy Stock Photo

Restaurants serve a variety of products, and they certainly don't all have the same contribution margin. Obviously, restaurants would prefer that you buy products that provide them with a higher margin. For example, beef burritos cost more at **Chipotle**—so they provide a higher margin right? Wrong. Even though Chipotle charges more for beef burritos, the price difference still doesn't cover the higher raw materials cost of beef relative to chicken. So Chipotle's chicken products have a higher contribution margin than their beef entrees. Recently, Chipotle increased its price on its beef entrees relative to chicken by 40 cents, resulting in about an 80-cent price difference. The price increase still doesn't cover the difference in raw materials costs, but management is hoping that the higher price will cause some people to switch to chicken.

Source: Adam Levine-Weinberg, "Why Investors Will Love Chipotle Mexican Grill, Inc.'s Price Increase," *The Motley Fool* (May 31, 2014).

If Chipotle's customers switch from beef to chicken, what will happen to its revenues and its net income? (Go to WileyPLUS for this answer and additional questions.)

DO IT! 2 | Sales Mix Break-Even

Manzeck Bicycles International produces and sells three different types of mountain bikes. Information regarding the three models is shown below.

	Pro	Intermediate	Standard	Total
Units sold	5,000	10,000	25,000	40,000
Selling price	$800	$500	$350	
Variable costs	$500	$300	$250	

The company's total fixed costs to produce the bicycles are $7,500,000.

a. Determine the sales mix as a function of units sold for the three products.
b. Determine the weighted-average unit contribution margin.
c. Determine the total number of units that the company must sell to break even.
d. Determine the number of units of each model that the company must sell to break even.

ACTION PLAN
- The sales mix is the relative percentage of each product sold in units.
- The weighted-average unit contribution margin is the sum of the unit contribution margins multiplied by the respective sales mix percentage.
- Determine the break-even point in units by dividing the fixed costs by the weighted-average unit contribution margin.

Solution

a. The sales mix percentages as a function of units sold are:

Pro	Intermediate	Standard
5,000/40,000 = 12.5%	10,000/40,000 = 25%	25,000/40,000 = 62.5%

ACTION PLAN

- Determine the number of units of each model to sell by multiplying the total break-even units by the respective sales mix percentage for each product.

b. The weighted-average unit contribution margin is:

[.125 × ($800 − $500)] + [.25 × ($500 − $300)] + [.625 × ($350 − $250)] = $150

c. The break-even point in units is:

$7,500,000 ÷ $150 = 50,000 units

d. The break-even units to sell for each product are:

Pro:	50,000 units × 12.5%	=	6,250 units
Intermediate:	50,000 units × 25%	=	12,500 units
Standard:	50,000 units × 62.5%	=	31,250 units
			50,000 units

Related exercise material: **BE19.7, BE19.8, BE19.9, BE19.10, DO IT! 19.2, E19.6, E19.7, E19.8, E19.9, and E19.10.**

Sales Mix with Limited Resources

LEARNING OBJECTIVE 3

Determine sales mix when a company has limited resources.

In the previous discussion, we assumed a certain sales mix and then determined the break-even point given that sales mix. We now discuss how limited resources influence the sales-mix decision.

All companies have resource limitations. The limited resource may be floor space in a retail department store, or raw materials, direct labor hours, or machine capacity in a manufacturing company. When a company has limited resources, management must decide which products to make and sell in order to maximize net income (see **Decision Tools**).

To illustrate, recall that Vargo Electronics manufactures cell phones and TVs. The limiting resource is machine capacity, which is 3,600 hours per month. **Illustration 19.22** shows the relevant data.

Decision Tools

Determining the contribution margin per unit of limited resource helps managers decide which product should receive any additional capacity of the limited resource.

ILLUSTRATION 19.22
Contribution margin and machine hours

	Cell Phones	TVs
Unit contribution margin	$200	$500
Machine hours required per unit	.2	.625

HELPFUL HINT

CM alone is not enough to make this decision. The key factor is CM per unit of limited resource.

The TVs may appear to be more profitable since they have a higher unit contribution margin ($500) than the cell phones ($200). However, the cell phones take fewer machine hours to produce than the TVs. Therefore, it is necessary to find the **contribution margin per unit of limited resource**—in this case, contribution margin per machine hour (see **Helpful Hint**). This is obtained by dividing the unit contribution margin of each product by the number of units of the limited resource required for each product, as shown in **Illustration 19.23**.

ILLUSTRATION 19.23
Contribution margin per unit of limited resource

	Cell Phones	TVs
Unit contribution margin (a)	$200	$500
Machine hours required (b)	0.2	0.625
Contribution margin per unit of limited resource [(a) ÷ (b)]	$1,000	$800

The computation shows that the cell phones have a higher contribution margin per unit of limited resource. This would suggest that, given sufficient demand for cell phones, Vargo should shift the sales mix to produce more cell phones or increase machine capacity.

As indicated in Illustration 19.23, the constraint for the production of the TVs is the number of machine hours available to produce them. In addressing this problem, we have taken the limited number of machine hours as a given and have attempted to maximize the contribution margin given the constraint. One question that Vargo should ask, however, is whether this constraint can be reduced or eliminated. If Vargo is able to increase machine capacity from 3,600 hours to 4,200 hours, the additional 600 hours could be used to produce either the cell phones or TVs. The total contribution margin under each alternative is found by multiplying the machine hours by the contribution margin per unit of limited resource, as shown in **Illustration 19.24**.

	Cell Phones	TVs
Machine hours (a)	600	600
Contribution margin per unit of limited resource (b)	$ 1,000	$ 800
Contribution margin [(a) × (b)]	**$600,000**	**$480,000**

ILLUSTRATION 19.24

Incremental analysis—computation of total contribution margin

From this analysis, we can see that to maximize net income, all of the increased capacity should be used to make and sell the cell phones.

Vargo's manufacturing constraint might be due to a bottleneck in production or to poorly trained machine operators. In addition to finding ways to solve those problems, the company should consider other possible solutions, such as outsourcing part of the production, acquiring additional new equipment (discussed in Chapter 25), or striving to eliminate any non–value-added activities (see Chapter 17). As discussed in Chapter 14, this approach to evaluating constraints is referred to as the theory of constraints. The **theory of constraints** is a specific approach used to identify and manage constraints in order to achieve the company's goals. According to this theory, a company must continually identify its constraints and find ways to reduce or eliminate them, where appropriate.

Management Insight   Macy's

Something Smells

Liv Friis-Larsen/ iStockphoto

When fragrance sales went flat, retailers such as **Macy's** turned up the heat on fragrance manufacturers. They reduced the amount of floor space devoted to fragrances, leaving fragrance manufacturers fighting each other for the smaller space. The retailer doesn't just choose the fragrance with the highest contribution margin. Instead, it chooses the fragrance with the highest contribution margin per square foot for a given period of time. In this game, a product with a lower contribution margin, but a higher turnover, could well be the winner.

What is the limited resource for a retailer, and what implications does this have for sales mix? (Go to WileyPLUS for this answer and additional questions).

DO IT! 3 | Sales Mix with Limited Resources

Carolina Corporation manufactures and sells three different types of high-quality sealed ball bearings for mountain bike wheels. The bearings vary in terms of their quality specifications—primarily with respect to their smoothness and roundness. They are referred to as Fine, Extra-Fine, and Super-Fine bearings. Machine time is limited. More machine time is required to manufacture the Extra-Fine and Super-Fine bearings. Additional information is provided below.

ACTION PLAN
- Calculate the contribution margin per unit of limited resource for each product.

ACTION PLAN

- Apply the formula for the contribution margin per unit of limited resource.
- To maximize net income, shift sales mix to the product with the highest contribution margin per unit of limited resource.

	Product		
	Fine	Extra-Fine	Super-Fine
Selling price	$6.00	$10.00	$16.00
Variable costs and expenses	4.00	6.50	11.00
Contribution margin	$2.00	$ 3.50	$ 5.00
Machine hours required	0.02	0.04	0.08

a. Ignoring the machine time constraint, what strategy would appear optimal?
b. What is the contribution margin per unit of limited resource for each type of bearing?
c. If additional machine time could be obtained, how should the additional capacity be used?

Solution

a. The Super-Fine bearings have the highest unit contribution margin. Thus, ignoring any manufacturing constraints, it would appear that the company should shift toward production of more Super-Fine units.

b. The contribution margin per unit of limited resource (machine hours) is calculated as:

	Fine	Extra-Fine	Super-Fine
$\dfrac{\text{Unit contribution margin}}{\text{Limited resource consumed per unit}}$	$\dfrac{\$2}{.02} = \$100$	$\dfrac{\$3.5}{.04} = \$87.50$	$\dfrac{\$5}{.08} = \$62.50$

c. The Fine bearings have the highest contribution margin per unit of limited resource (machine time) even though they have the lowest unit contribution margin. Given the resource constraint, any additional capacity should be used to make Fine bearings, assuming that the market can absorb additional units.

Related exercise material: **BE19.11, BE19.12, DO IT! 19.3, E19.11, E19.12, and E19.13.**

Operating Leverage and Profitability

LEARNING OBJECTIVE 4
Indicate how operating leverage affects profitability.

Cost structure refers to the relative proportion of fixed versus variable costs that a company incurs. Cost structure can have a significant effect on profitability. For example, computer equipment manufacturer **Cisco Systems** has substantially reduced its fixed costs by choosing to outsource much of its production. By minimizing its fixed costs, Cisco is now less susceptible to economic swings. However, as the following discussion shows, its reduced reliance on fixed costs has also reduced its ability to experience the incredible profitability that it used to have during economic booms.

The choice of cost structure should be carefully considered. There are many ways that companies can influence their cost structure. For example, by acquiring sophisticated robotic equipment, many companies have reduced their use of manual labor. Similarly, some brokerage firms, such as **E*Trade**, have reduced their reliance on human brokers and have instead invested heavily in computers and online technology. In so doing, they have increased their reliance on fixed costs (through depreciation on the robotic equipment or computer equipment) and reduced their reliance on variable costs (the variable employee labor cost). Alternatively, some companies have reduced their fixed costs and increased their variable costs by outsourcing their production. **Nike**, for example, does very little manufacturing but instead outsources the manufacture of nearly all of its shoes. It has consequently converted many of its fixed costs into variable costs and therefore changed its cost structure.

Consider the following example of Vargo Electronics and one of its competitors, New Wave Company. Both make cell phones. Vargo uses a traditional, labor-intensive manufacturing process. New Wave has invested in a completely automated system. The factory employees are involved only in setting up, adjusting, and maintaining the machinery. **Illustration 19.25** shows CVP income statements for each company.

	Vargo Electronics	New Wave Company
Sales	$800,000	$800,000
Variable costs	480,000	160,000
Contribution margin	320,000	640,000
Fixed costs	200,000	520,000
Net income	$120,000	$120,000

ILLUSTRATION 19.25

CVP income statements for two companies

Both companies have the same sales and the same net income. However, because of the differences in their cost structures, they differ greatly in the risks and rewards related to increasing or decreasing sales. Let's evaluate the impact of cost structure on the profitability of the two companies.

Effect on Contribution Margin Ratio

First let's look at the contribution margin ratio. **Illustration 19.26** shows the computation of the contribution margin ratio for each company.

	Contribution Margin	÷	Sales	=	Contribution Margin Ratio
Vargo Electronics	$320,000	÷	$800,000	=	40%
New Wave	$640,000	÷	$800,000	=	80%

ILLUSTRATION 19.26

Contribution margin ratio for two companies

Because of its lower variable costs, New Wave has a contribution margin ratio of 80% versus only 40% for Vargo Electronics. That means that with every dollar of sales, New Wave generates 80 cents of contribution margin (and thus an 80-cent increase in net income), versus only 40 cents for Vargo. However, it also means that for every dollar that sales decline, New Wave loses 80 cents in net income, whereas Vargo will lose only 40 cents. New Wave's cost structure, which relies more heavily on fixed costs, makes it more sensitive to changes in sales revenue.

Effect on Break-Even Point

The difference in cost structure also affects the break-even point. The break-even point for each company is calculated in **Illustration 19.27**.

	Fixed Costs	÷	Contribution Margin Ratio	=	Break-Even Point in Dollars
Vargo Electronics	$200,000	÷	.40	=	$500,000
New Wave	$520,000	÷	.80	=	$650,000

ILLUSTRATION 19.27

Computation of break-even point for two companies

New Wave needs to generate $150,000 ($650,000 − $500,000) more in sales than Vargo Electronics before it breaks even. This makes New Wave riskier than Vargo because a company cannot survive for very long unless it at least breaks even.

Effect on Margin of Safety Ratio

We can also evaluate the relative impact that changes in sales would have on the two companies by computing the margin of safety ratio. **Illustration 19.28** shows the computation of the **margin of safety ratio** for the two companies.

ILLUSTRATION 19.28
Computation of margin of safety ratio for two companies

	(Actual Sales	−	Break-Even Sales)	÷	Actual Sales	=	Margin of Safety Ratio
Vargo Electronics	($800,000	−	$500,000)	÷	$800,000	=	38%
New Wave	($800,000	−	$650,000)	÷	$800,000	=	19%

The difference in the margin of safety ratio also reflects the difference in risk between the two companies. Vargo Electronics could sustain a 38% decline in sales before it would be operating at a loss. New Wave could sustain only a 19% decline in sales before it would be "in the red."

Operating Leverage

> **Decision Tools**
>
> Calculating the degree of operating leverage helps managers determine how sensitive the company's net income is to changes in sales.

Operating leverage refers to the extent to which a company's net income reacts to a given change in sales (see **Decision Tools**). Companies that have higher fixed costs relative to variable costs have higher operating leverage. When a company's sales revenue is increasing, high operating leverage is a good thing because it means that profits will increase rapidly. But when sales are declining, too much operating leverage can have devastating consequences.

Degree of Operating Leverage

How can we compare operating leverage between two companies? The **degree of operating leverage** provides a measure of a company's earnings volatility and can be used to compare companies. Degree of operating leverage is computed by dividing contribution margin by net income. This formula is presented in **Illustration 19.29** and applied to our two manufacturers of cell phones.

ILLUSTRATION 19.29
Computation of degree of operating leverage

	Contribution Margin	÷	Net Income	=	Degree of Operating Leverage
Vargo Electronics	$320,000	÷	$120,000	=	2.67
New Wave	$640,000	÷	$120,000	=	5.33

Due to its higher degree of operating leverage, New Wave's net income will react more to changes in sales. In fact, New Wave's earnings would go up (or down) by two times (5.33 ÷ 2.67 = 2.00) as much as Vargo Electronics' with an equal increase (or decrease) in sales. For example, suppose both companies experience a 10% decrease in sales. Vargo's net income will decrease by 26.7% (2.67 × 10%), while New Wave's will decrease by 53.3% (5.33 × 10%). Thus, New Wave's higher operating leverage exposes it to greater earnings volatility risk.

You should be careful not to conclude from this analysis that a cost structure that relies on higher fixed costs, and consequently has higher operating leverage, is necessarily bad. Some have suggested that Internet radio company **Pandora** has limited potential for growth in its profitability because it has very little operating leverage. When its revenues grow, its variable costs (fees it pays for the right to use music) grow proportionally. When used carefully, operating leverage can add considerably to a company's profitability. For example, computer equipment manufacturer **Komag** enjoyed a 66% increase in net income when its sales increased by only 8%. As one commentator noted, "Komag's fourth quarter illustrates the company's significant operating leverage; a small increase in sales leads to a big profit rise." However, as our illustration demonstrates, increased reliance on fixed costs increases a company's risk.

People, Planet, and Profit Insight

Alessandro2802/ Getty Images

Solar Power Generates More Than Electricity

When homeowners first began to put solar panels on their homes, electric utility companies encouraged them to do so. The power companies saw this as an opportunity to reduce their fixed investment in power-generating equipment. When homeowners generated more electricity than they needed, the extra electricity went into the grid, and the homeowner was compensated by the power company. It seemed to be a win-win situation. But now that solar power has become so widespread, power companies are concerned that they might have excess capacity and that they won't be able to charge customers enough to cover their fixed costs. So the power companies have been reducing the amount that they pay homeowners for excess electricity generated by solar power, and they are arguing that a larger portion of customers' bills should be fixed charges, as opposed to charges that vary with use. The power companies say that since so much of their costs are fixed costs, they need a dependable income stream to cover their fixed costs. Environmentalists worry that if a large percentage of a customer's bill is fixed (that is, doesn't vary with usage), then the customer won't have an incentive to conserve energy.

How do the homeowner solar panels represent a form of outsourcing? At what point did this create a dilemma for power companies? (Go to WileyPLUS for this answer and additional questions.)

DO IT! 4 | Operating Leverage

Rexfield Corp., a company specializing in crime scene investigations, is contemplating an investment in automated mass-spectrometers. Its current process relies on a high number of lab technicians. The new equipment would employ a computerized expert system. The company's CEO has requested a comparison of the old technology versus the new technology. The accounting department has prepared the following CVP income statements for use in your analysis.

	CSI Equipment	
	Old	New
Sales	$2,000,000	$2,000,000
Variable costs	1,400,000	600,000
Contribution margin	600,000	1,400,000
Fixed costs	400,000	1,200,000
Net income	$ 200,000	$ 200,000

Use the information provided above to do the following.

a. Compute the degree of operating leverage for the company under each scenario.
b. Discuss your results.

ACTION PLAN
- Divide contribution margin by net income to determine degree of operating leverage.
- A higher degree of operating leverage will result in a higher change in net income with a given change in sales.

Solution

a.

	Contribution Margin	÷	Net Income	=	Degree of Operating Leverage
Old	$600,000	÷	$200,000	=	3.00
New	$1,400,000	÷	$200,000	=	7.00

b. The degree of operating leverage measures the company's sensitivity to changes in sales. By switching to a cost structure dominated by fixed costs, the company would significantly increase its operating leverage. As a result, with a percentage change in sales, its percentage change in net income would be 2.33 (7.00 ÷ 3.00) times as much with the new technology as it would under the old.

Related exercise material: **BE19.13, BE19.14, BE19.15, DO IT! 19.4, E19.14, E19.15, and E19.16.**

USING THE DECISION TOOLS | Whole Foods Market

Whole Foods Market faces many decisions where it needs to apply the decision tools learned in this chapter, such as determining its cost structure. For example, suppose that Whole Foods Market has been approached by a robotics company with a proposal to significantly automate one of its stores. All stocking of shelves and bagging of groceries would be done by robots. Customers would check out through self-service scanners and point-of-sale terminals. Any assistance would be provided by robots. Management has compiled the following comparative data for one average-sized store.

	Old	New
Sales	$3,600,000	$3,600,000
Variable costs	2,800,000	2,000,000
Contribution margin	800,000	1,600,000
Fixed costs	480,000	1,280,000
Net income	$ 320,000	$ 320,000

Instructions

Use the information provided above to do the following.

a. Compute the degree of operating leverage for the company under each scenario, and discuss your results.

b. Compute the break-even point in dollars and margin of safety ratio for the company under each scenario, and discuss your results.

Solution

a.

	Contribution Margin	÷	Net Income	=	Degree of Operating Leverage
Old	$800,000	÷	$320,000	=	2.5
New	$1,600,000	÷	$320,000	=	5.0

The degree of operating leverage measures the company's sensitivity to changes in sales. By switching to a cost structure with higher fixed costs, Whole Foods would significantly increase its operating leverage. As a result, with a percentage change in sales, its percentage change in net income would be 2 times as much (5 ÷ 2.5) under the new structure as it would under the old.

b. To compute the break-even point in sales dollars, we first need to compute the contribution margin ratio under each scenario. Under the old structure, the contribution margin ratio would be .22 ($800,000 ÷ $3,600,000), and under the new it would be .44 ($1,600,000 ÷ $3,600,000).

	Fixed Costs	÷	Contribution Margin Ratio	=	Break-Even Point in Dollars
Old	$480,000	÷	.22	=	$2,181,818
New	$1,280,000	÷	.44	=	$2,909,090

Because Whole Foods' fixed costs would be substantially higher under the new cost structure, its break-even point would increase significantly, from $2,181,818 to $2,909,090. A higher break-even point is riskier because it means that the company must generate higher sales to be profitable.

The margin of safety ratio tells how far sales can fall before Whole Foods is operating at a loss.

	(Actual Sales − Break-Even Sales)	÷	Actual Sales	=	Margin of Safety Ratio
Old	($3,600,000 − $2,181,818)	÷	$3,600,000	=	.39
New	($3,600,000 − $2,909,090)	÷	$3,600,000	=	.19

Under the old structure, sales could fall by 39% before the company would be operating at a loss. Under the new structure, sales could fall by only 19%.

> On the one hand, grocery store sales are more stable than most products. Sales are less inclined to fluctuate with changes in the economy. However, Whole Foods sells many organic and unique products that have higher selling prices. It may be that during a recession, its customers might choose to switch to lower cost (e.g., non-organic) substitutes at traditional, high-volume grocery stores. If Whole Foods' sales are subject to significant swings, then changes in its cost structure could significantly affect its risk profile.

Appendix 19A | Absorption Costing vs. Variable Costing

LEARNING OBJECTIVE *5
Explain the differences between absorption costing and variable costing.

In this appendix, we present an approach called **variable costing**, which is consistent with the cost-volume-profit material presented in Chapters 18 and 19 and therefore readily supports CVP analysis. In the earlier chapters, we classified both variable and fixed manufacturing costs as product costs. In job order costing, for example, a job is assigned the costs of direct materials, direct labor, and **both** variable and fixed manufacturing overhead. This costing approach is referred to as **full** or **absorption costing**. It is so named because all manufacturing costs are charged to, or absorbed by, the product. Absorption costing is the approach used for external reporting under generally accepted accounting principles.

An alternative approach is to use **variable costing**. Under variable costing, only direct materials, direct labor, and variable manufacturing overhead costs are considered product costs. Companies using variable costing recognize fixed manufacturing overhead costs as period costs (expenses) when incurred. **Illustration 19A.1** shows the difference between absorption costing and variable costing.

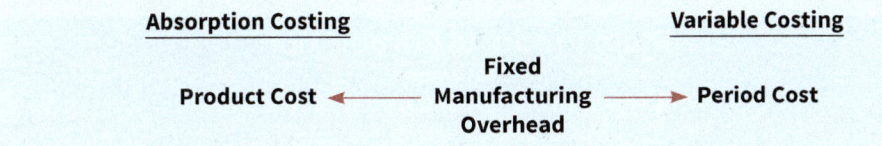

ILLUSTRATION 19A.1
Difference between absorption costing and variable costing

Under both absorption and variable costing, selling and administrative expenses are period costs.

Companies may not use variable costing for external financial reports because generally accepted accounting principles require that fixed manufacturing overhead be accounted for as a product cost.

Example Comparing Absorption Costing with Variable Costing

To illustrate absorption and variable costing, assume that Premium Products Corporation manufactures a polyurethane sealant, called Fix-It, for car windshields. Relevant data for Fix-It in January 2022, the first month of production, are shown in **Illustration 19A.2**.

Selling price	$20 per unit.
Units	Produced 30,000; sold 20,000; beginning inventory zero.
Variable unit costs	Manufacturing $9 (direct materials $5, direct labor $3, and variable overhead $1).
	Selling and administrative expenses $2.
Fixed costs	Manufacturing overhead $120,000.
	Selling and administrative expenses $15,000.

ILLUSTRATION 19A.2
Sealant sales and cost data for Premium Products Corporation

The per unit manufacturing cost under each costing approach is computed in **Illustration 19A.3**.

ILLUSTRATION 19A.3
Computation of per unit manufacturing cost

Type of Cost	Absorption Costing	Variable Costing
Direct materials	$5	$5
Direct labor	3	3
Variable manufacturing overhead	1	1
Fixed manufacturing overhead ($120,000 ÷ 30,000 units produced)	4	0
Manufacturing cost per unit	**$13**	**$9**

The manufacturing cost per unit is $4 higher ($13 − $9) for absorption costing. This occurs because fixed manufacturing overhead costs are a product cost under absorption costing. Under variable costing, they are, instead, a period cost, and so they are expensed. Based on these data, each unit sold and each unit remaining in inventory on the balance sheet is costed under absorption costing at $13 and under variable costing at $9.

Absorption Costing Example

Illustration 19A.4 shows the income statement for Premium Products using absorption costing. It shows that cost of goods manufactured is $390,000, computed by multiplying the 30,000 units produced times the manufacturing cost per unit of $13 (see Illustration 19A.3). Cost of goods sold is $260,000, after subtracting ending inventory of $130,000. Notice that the ending inventory of $130,000 includes fixed manufacturing overhead costs of $40,000 (10,000 × $4). Under absorption costing, $40,000 of the fixed manufacturing overhead is deferred to a future period as part of the cost of ending inventory. We will see that this is the primary difference between absorption costing and variable costing.

ILLUSTRATION 19A.4
Absorption costing income statement

Premium Products Corporation
Income Statement
For the Month Ended January 31, 2022
Absorption Costing

Sales (20,000 units × $20)		$400,000
Cost of goods sold		
Inventory, January 1	$ –0–	
Cost of goods manufactured (30,000 units × $13)	390,000	
Cost of goods available for sale	390,000	
Less: Inventory, January 31 (10,000 units × $13)	130,000	
Cost of goods sold (20,000 units × $13)		260,000
Gross profit		140,000
Variable selling and administrative expenses (20,000 × $2)	40,000	
Fixed selling and administrative expenses	15,000	55,000
Net income		**$ 85,000**

Variable Costing Example

As **Illustration 19A.5** shows, companies use the cost-volume-profit format in preparing a variable costing income statement. The variable manufacturing cost of $270,000 is computed by multiplying the 30,000 units produced times variable manufacturing cost of $9 per unit (see Illustration 19A.3). As in absorption costing, both variable and fixed selling and administrative expenses are treated as period costs.

ILLUSTRATION 19A.5
Variable costing income statement

Premium Products Corporation Income Statement For the Month Ended January 31, 2022 Variable Costing		
Sales (20,000 units × $20)		$400,000
Variable cost of goods sold		
Inventory, January 1	$ -0-	
Variable cost of goods manufactured		
(30,000 units × $9)	270,000	
Variable cost of goods available for sale	270,000	
Less: Inventory, January 31 (10,000 units × $9)	90,000	
Variable cost of goods sold	180,000	
Variable selling and administrative expenses		
(20,000 units × $2)	40,000	220,000
Contribution margin		180,000
Fixed manufacturing overhead	120,000	
Fixed selling and administrative expenses	15,000	135,000
Net income		**$ 45,000**

There is one primary difference between variable and absorption costing: **Under variable costing, companies charge the fixed manufacturing overhead as an expense in the current period.** Fixed manufacturing overhead costs of the current period, therefore, are not deferred to future periods through the ending inventory. As a result, absorption costing will show a **higher net income number** than variable costing **whenever units produced exceed units sold**.

This difference can be seen in the income statements in Illustrations 19A.4 and 19A.5. Note the difference in the computation of the ending inventory: $9 per unit in Illustration 19A.5, $13 per unit in Illustration 19A.4. This translates into a $40,000 difference in the ending inventories ($130,000 under absorption costing versus $90,000 under variable costing), which results in the $40,000 difference in net income. Under absorption costing, expensing $40,000 of the fixed overhead costs (10,000 units × $4) has been deferred (delayed) to a future period as part of inventory on the balance sheet. In contrast, under variable costing, all fixed manufacturing costs are expensed in the current period.

As shown, when units produced exceed units sold, income under absorption costing is *higher*. When units produced are less than units sold, income under absorption costing is *lower*. When units produced and sold are the same, net income will be *equal* under the two costing approaches. In this case, there is no increase in ending inventory. So fixed overhead costs of the current period are not deferred to future periods through the ending inventory.

Net Income Effects

To further illustrate the concepts underlying absorption and variable costing, we will look at an extended example using Overbay Inc., a manufacturer of special-purpose airplane drones. We assume that production volume stays the same each year over the 3-year period, but the number of units sold varies each year.

2021 Results

As indicated in **Illustration 19A.6**, the variable manufacturing cost per drone is $240,000, and the fixed manufacturing overhead cost per drone is $60,000 (assuming 10 drones). Total manufacturing cost per drone under absorption costing is therefore $300,000 ($240,000 + $60,000). Overbay also has variable selling and administrative expenses of $5,000 per drone. The fixed selling and administrative expenses are $80,000.

ILLUSTRATION 19A.6
Information for Overbay Inc.

	2021	2022	2023
Volume information			
Drones in beginning inventory	0	0	2
Drones produced	10	10	10
Drones sold	10	8	12
Drones in ending inventory	0	2	0
Financial information			
Selling price per drone	$400,000		
Variable manufacturing cost per drone	$240,000		
Fixed manufacturing overhead for the year	$600,000		
Fixed manufacturing overhead per drone	$ 60,000 ($600,000 ÷ 10)		
Variable selling and administrative expenses per drone	$ 5,000		
Fixed selling and administrative expenses	$ 80,000		

An absorption costing income statement for 2021 for Overbay Inc. is shown in **Illustration 19A.7**.

ILLUSTRATION 19A.7
Absorption costing income statement—2021

Overbay Inc.
Income Statement
For the Year Ended December 31, 2021
Absorption Costing

Sales (10 drones × $400,000)		$4,000,000
Cost of goods sold (10 drones × $300,000)		3,000,000
Gross profit		1,000,000
Variable selling and administrative expenses (10 drones × $5,000)	$50,000	
Fixed selling and administrative expenses	80,000	130,000
Net income		$ 870,000

Overbay reports net income of $870,000 under absorption costing.

Under a variable costing system, the income statement follows a cost-volume-profit (CVP) format. In this case, the manufacturing cost is comprised solely of the variable manufacturing costs of $240,000 per drone. The entire amount of fixed manufacturing overhead costs of $600,000 for the year are expensed in 2021. As in absorption costing, the fixed and variable selling and administrative expenses are period costs expensed in 2021. A variable costing income statement for Overbay Inc. for 2021 is shown in **Illustration 19A.8**.

ILLUSTRATION 19A.8
Variable costing income statement—2021

Overbay Inc.
Income Statement
For the Year Ended December 31, 2021
Variable Costing

Sales (10 drones × $400,000)		$4,000,000
Variable cost of goods sold (10 drones × $240,000)	$2,400,000	
Variable selling and administrative expenses (10 drones × $5,000)	50,000	2,450,000
Contribution margin		1,550,000
Fixed manufacturing overhead	600,000	
Fixed selling and administrative expenses	80,000	680,000
Net income		$ 870,000

As shown in Illustration 19A.8, the variable costing net income of $870,000 is the same as the absorption costing net income computed in Illustration 19A.7. **When the numbers of units** produced and sold are the same, net income is equal under the two costing approaches. Because no increase in ending inventory occurs, no fixed manufacturing overhead costs incurred in 2021 are deferred to future periods as part of ending inventory using absorption costing.

2022 Results

In 2022, Overbay produced 10 drones but sold only eight drones. As a result, there are two drones in ending inventory. The absorption costing income statement for 2022 is shown in **Illustration 19A.9**.

ILLUSTRATION 19A.9

Absorption costing income statement—2022

Overbay Inc.
Income Statement
For the Year Ended December 31, 2022
Absorption Costing

Sales (8 drones × $400,000)		$3,200,000
Cost of goods sold (8 drones × $300,000)		2,400,000
Gross profit		800,000
Variable selling and administrative expenses		
(8 drones × $5,000)	$40,000	
Fixed selling and administrative expenses	80,000	120,000
Net income		$ 680,000

Under absorption costing, the ending inventory of two drones is $600,000 ($300,000 × 2). As shown in Illustration 19A.6, each unit of ending inventory includes $60,000 ($600,000 ÷ 10) of fixed manufacturing overhead. Therefore, fixed manufacturing overhead costs of $120,000 ($60,000 × 2 drones) are deferred until a future period.

The variable costing income statement for 2022 is shown in **Illustration 19A.10**.

ILLUSTRATION 19A.10

Variable costing income statement—2022

Overbay Inc.
Income Statement
For the Year Ended December 31, 2022
Variable Costing

Sales (8 drones × $400,000)		$3,200,000
Variable cost of goods sold		
(8 drones × $240,000)	$1,920,000	
Variable selling and administrative expenses		
(8 drones × $5,000)	40,000	1,960,000
Contribution margin		1,240,000
Fixed manufacturing overhead	600,000	
Fixed selling and administrative expenses	80,000	680,000
Net income		$ 560,000

As shown in Illustrations 19A.9 and 19A.10, because the number of units produced (10) exceeds units sold (8), net income under absorption costing ($680,000) is higher than net income under variable costing ($560,000). The reason: The cost of the ending inventory is higher under absorption costing than under variable costing because fixed manufacturing overhead cost is retained in ending inventory. In 2022, under absorption costing, fixed manufacturing overhead of $120,000 is deferred and carried to future periods as part of inventory. Under variable costing, the $120,000 is expensed in the current period and, therefore the difference in the two net income numbers is $120,000 ($680,000 − $560,000).

2023 Results

In 2023, Overbay produced 10 drones and sold 12 (10 drones from the current year's production and 2 drones from the beginning inventory). As a result, there are no drones in ending inventory. The absorption costing income statement for 2023 is shown in **Illustration 19A.11**.

ILLUSTRATION 19A.11
Absorption costing income statement—2023

Overbay Inc.
Income Statement
For the Year Ended December 31, 2023
Absorption Costing

Sales (12 drones × $400,000)		$4,800,000
Cost of goods sold (12 drones × $300,000)		3,600,000
Gross profit		1,200,000
Variable selling and administrative expenses		
(12 drones × $5,000)	$60,000	
Fixed selling and administrative expenses	80,000	140,000
Net income		$1,060,000

Fixed manufacturing costs of $720,000 ($60,000 × 12 drones) are expensed as part of cost of goods sold in 2023. This $720,000 includes $120,000 of fixed manufacturing costs incurred during 2022 and included in beginning inventory, plus $600,000 of fixed manufacturing costs incurred during 2023. Given this result for the absorption costing statement, what would you now expect the result to be under variable costing? Let's take a look.

The variable costing income statement for 2023 is shown in **Illustration 19A.12**.

ILLUSTRATION 19A.12
Variable costing income statement—2023

Overbay Inc.
Income Statement
For the Year Ended December 31, 2023
Variable Costing

Sales (12 drones × $400,000)		$4,800,000
Variable cost of goods sold		
(12 drones × $240,000)	$2,880,000	
Variable selling and administrative expenses		
(12 drones × $5,000)	60,000	2,940,000
Contribution margin		1,860,000
Fixed manufacturing overhead	600,000	
Fixed selling and administrative expenses	80,000	680,000
Net income		$1,180,000

When drones produced (10) are less than drones sold (12), net income under absorption costing ($1,060,000) is less than net income under variable costing ($1,180,000). This difference of $120,000 ($1,180,000 − $1,060,000) results because $120,000 of fixed manufacturing overhead costs in beginning inventory are charged to 2023 under absorption costing, in addition to the $600,000 of fixed manufacturing overhead incurred during the current period. Under variable costing, there is no fixed manufacturing overhead cost in beginning or ending inventory.

Illustration 19A.13 summarizes the results of the three years.

ILLUSTRATION 19A.13
Comparison of net income under two costing approaches

	Net Income under Two Costing Approaches		
	2021	2022	2023
	Units Produced = Units Sold	Units Produced > Units Sold	Units Produced < Units Sold
Absorption costing	$870,000	$680,000	$1,060,000
Variable costing	870,000	560,000	1,180,000
Difference	$ –0–	$120,000	$ (120,000)

This relationship between production and sales and its effect on net income under the two costing approaches is shown in **Illustration 19A.14**.

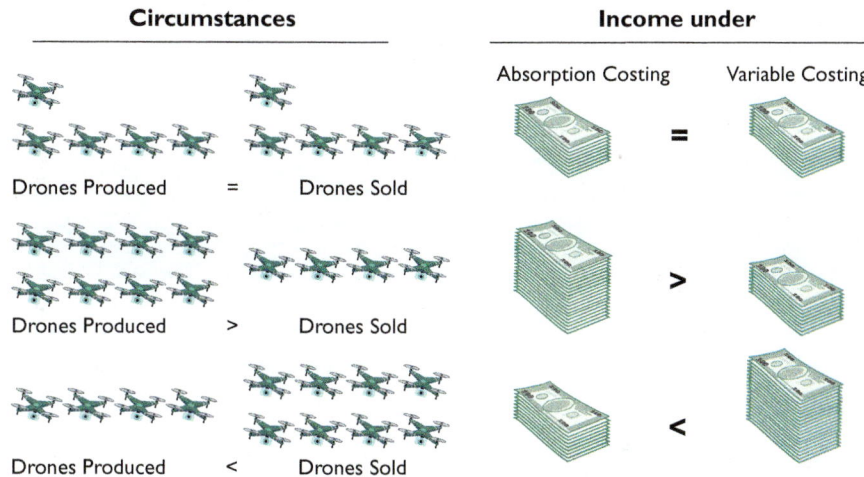

ILLUSTRATION 19A.14

Summary of income effects under absorption costing and variable costing

Decision-Making Concerns

Generally accepted accounting principles require that absorption costing be used for the costing of inventory for external reporting purposes. Net income measured under GAAP (absorption costing) is often used internally to evaluate performance, justify cost reductions, or evaluate new projects. Some companies, however, have recognized that net income calculated using GAAP does not highlight differences between variable and fixed costs and may lead to poor business decisions. Consequently, these companies use variable costing for internal reporting purposes. The following discussion and example highlight a significant problem related to the use of absorption costing for decision-making purposes.

When production exceeds sales, absorption costing reports a higher net income than variable costing. The reason is that some fixed manufacturing costs are not expensed in the current period but are deferred to future periods as part of inventory. As a result, **management may be tempted to overproduce in a given period in order to increase net income**. Although net income will increase, this decision to overproduce may not be in the company's best interest.

Suppose, for example, a division manager's compensation is based upon the division's net income. In such a case, the manager may decide to meet the net income targets by producing more units than will be sold. While this overproduction may increase the manager's compensation, the buildup of inventories in the long run will lead to additional costs to the company. Variable costing avoids this situation because net income under variable costing is unaffected by changes in production levels, as the following illustration shows.

Warren Lund, a division manager of Walker Enterprises, is under pressure to boost the performance of the Lighting Division in 2022. Unfortunately, recent profits have not met expectations. The expected sales for this year are 20,000 units. As he plans for the year, Warren has to decide whether to produce 20,000 or 30,000 units. **Illustration 19A.15** presents the facts available for the division.

Beginning inventory	0
Expected sales in units	20,000
Selling price per unit	$15
Variable manufacturing cost per unit	$6
Fixed manufacturing overhead cost (total)	$60,000
Fixed manufacturing overhead costs per unit	
Based on 20,000 units produced	$3 per unit ($60,000 ÷ 20,000 units)
Based on 30,000 units produced	$2 per unit ($60,000 ÷ 30,000 units)
Total manufacturing cost per unit	
Based on 20,000 units produced	$9 per unit ($6 variable + $3 fixed)
Based on 30,000 units produced	$8 per unit ($6 variable + $2 fixed)
Variable selling and administrative expenses per unit	$1
Fixed selling and administrative expenses	$15,000

ILLUSTRATION 19A.15

Variable costing income statement—2022

Illustration 19A.16 shows the division's results based upon the two possible levels of output under absorption costing.

ILLUSTRATION 19A.16

Absorption costing income statement—2022

Lighting Division
Income Statement
For the Year Ended December 31, 2022
Absorption Costing

	20,000 Produced	30,000 Produced
Sales (20,000 units × $15)	$300,000	$300,000
Cost of goods sold	180,000*	160,000**
Gross profit	120,000	140,000
Variable selling and administrative expenses (20,000 units × $1)	20,000	20,000
Fixed selling and administrative expenses	15,000	15,000
Net income	$ 85,000	$105,000

*20,000 units × $9; see red content in Illustration 19A.15.
**20,000 units × $8; see red content in Illustration 19A.15.

If the Lighting Division produces and sells 20,000 units, its net income under absorption costing is $85,000. If it produces 30,000 units but sells only 20,000 units, its net income is $105,000. By producing 30,000 units, the division has inventory of 10,000 units. This excess inventory causes net income to increase $20,000 because $20,000 of fixed costs (10,000 units × $2) are not charged to the current year, but are deferred to future periods.

What do you think Warren Lund might do in this situation? Given his concern about the profit numbers of the Lighting Division, he may be tempted to produce more units than are needed. Although this increased production will increase 2022 net income, it may be costly to the company in the long run because holding excess inventory is costly.

Now let's evaluate the same situation under variable costing. **Illustration 19A.17** shows a variable costing income statement for production at both 20,000 and 30,000 units, using the information from Illustration 19A.15.

ILLUSTRATION 19A.17

Variable costing income statement—2022

Lighting Division
Income Statement
For the Year Ended December 31, 2022
Variable Costing

	20,000 Produced	30,000 Produced
Sales (20,000 units × $15)	$300,000	$300,000
Variable cost of goods sold (20,000 units × $6)	120,000	120,000
Variable selling and administrative expenses (20,000 units × $1)	20,000	20,000
Contribution margin	160,000	160,000
Fixed manufacturing overhead	60,000	60,000
Fixed selling and administrative expenses	15,000	15,000
Net income	$ 85,000	$ 85,000

From this example, we see that under variable costing, net income is not affected by the number of units produced. Net income is $85,000 whether the division produces 20,000 or

30,000 units. Why? Because fixed manufacturing overhead is treated as a period expense. Unlike absorption costing, no fixed manufacturing overhead is deferred through inventory buildup. Therefore, under variable costing, production does not increase income; sales do. As a result, if the company uses variable costing, managers like Warren Lund cannot affect profitability by increasing production.

Potential Advantages of Variable Costing

Variable costing has a number of potential advantages relative to absorption costing:

1. Net income computed under variable costing is unaffected by changes in production levels. As a result, it is much easier to understand the impact of fixed and variable costs on the computation of net income when variable costing is used.
2. The use of variable costing is consistent with the cost-volume-profit material presented in Chapters 18 and 19 and therefore readily supports CVP analysis.
3. Net income computed under variable costing is closely tied to changes in sales levels (not production levels) and therefore provides a more realistic assessment of the company's success or failure during a period.
4. The presentation of fixed and variable cost components on the face of the variable costing income statement makes it easier to identify these costs and understand their effect on the business. Under absorption costing, the allocation of fixed costs to inventory makes it difficult to evaluate the impact of fixed costs on the company's results.

Companies that use just-in-time processing techniques to minimize their inventories will not have significant differences between absorption and variable costing net income.

DO IT! 5 | Variable Costing

Franklin Company produces and sells tennis balls. The following costs are available for the year ended December 31, 2022. The company has no beginning inventory. In 2022, 8,000,000 units were produced, but only 7,500,000 units were sold. The unit selling price was $0.50 per ball. Costs and expenses were as follows.

Variable costs per unit	
Direct materials	$0.10
Direct labor	0.05
Variable manufacturing overhead	0.08
Variable selling and administrative expenses	0.02
Annual fixed costs and expenses	
Manufacturing overhead	$500,000
Selling and administrative expenses	100,000

a. Compute the manufacturing cost of one unit of product using variable costing.
b. Prepare a 2022 income statement for Franklin Company using variable costing.

ACTION PLAN
- Recall that under variable costing, only variable manufacturing costs are treated as manufacturing (product) costs.
- Subtract all fixed costs, both manufacturing overhead and selling and administrative expenses, as period costs.

Solution

a. The cost of one unit of product under variable costing would be:

Direct materials	$0.10
Direct labor	0.05
Variable manufacturing overhead	0.08
	$0.23

b. The variable costing income statement would be as follows.

Franklin Company
Income Statement
For the Year Ended December 31, 2022
Variable Costing

Sales (7,500,000 × $0.50)		$3,750,000
Variable cost of goods sold (7,500,000 × $0.23)	$1,725,000	
Variable selling and administrative expenses (7,500,000 × .02)	150,000	1,875,000
Contribution margin		1,875,000
Fixed manufacturing overhead	500,000	
Fixed selling and administrative expenses	100,000	600,000
Net income		$1,275,000

Related exercise material: **BE19.16, BE19.17, BE19.18, BE19.19, E19.17, E19.18, and E19.19.**

Review and Practice

Learning Objectives Review

1 Apply basic CVP concepts.

The CVP income statement classifies costs and expenses as variable or fixed and reports contribution margin in the body of the statement. Contribution margin is the amount of revenue remaining after deducting variable costs. It can be expressed as a per unit amount or as a ratio. The break-even point in units is fixed costs divided by unit contribution margin. The break-even point in dollars is fixed costs divided by the contribution margin ratio. These formulas can also be used to determine units or sales dollars needed to achieve target net income, simply by adding target net income to fixed costs before dividing by the contribution margin. Margin of safety indicates how much sales can decline before the company is operating at a loss. It can be expressed in dollar terms or as a percentage.

2 Explain the term sales mix and its effects on break-even sales.

Sales mix is the relative proportion in which each product is sold when a company sells more than one product. For a company with a small number of different products, break-even sales in units is determined by using the weighted-average unit contribution margin of all the products. If the company sells many different products, then calculating the break-even point using unit information is not practical. Instead, in a company with many products, break-even sales in dollars is calculated using the weighted-average contribution margin ratio.

3 Determine sales mix when a company has limited resources.

When a company has limited resources, it is necessary to find the contribution margin per unit of limited resource. This amount is then multiplied by the units of limited resource to determine which product maximizes net income.

4 Indicate how operating leverage affects profitability.

Operating leverage refers to the degree to which a company's net income reacts to a change in sales. Operating leverage is determined by a company's relative use of fixed versus variable costs. Companies with high fixed costs relative to variable costs have high operating leverage. A company with high operating leverage experiences a sharp increase (decrease) in net income with a given increase (decrease) in sales. The degree of operating leverage is measured by dividing contribution margin by net income.

*5 Explain the differences between absorption costing and variable costing.

Under absorption costing, fixed manufacturing costs are product costs. Under variable costing, fixed manufacturing costs are period costs.

If production volume exceeds sales volume, net income under absorption costing will exceed net income under variable costing by the amount of fixed manufacturing costs included in ending inventory that results from units produced but not sold during the period. If production volume is less than sales volume, net income under absorption costing will be less than under variable costing by the amount of fixed manufacturing costs included in the units sold during the period that were not produced during the period.

The use of variable costing is consistent with cost-volume-profit analysis. Net income under variable costing is unaffected by changes in production levels. Instead, it is closely tied to changes in sales. The presentation of fixed costs in the variable costing approach makes it easier to identify fixed costs and to evaluate their impact on the company's profitability.

Decision Tools Review

Decision Checkpoints	Info Needed for Decision	Tool to Use for Decision		How to Evaluate Results
How many units of product A and product B do we need to sell to break even?	Fixed costs, weighted-average unit contribution margin, sales mix	Break-even point in units	$= \dfrac{\text{Fixed costs}}{\text{Weighted-average unit contribution margin}}$	To determine number of units of products A and B, allocate total break-even units based on unit sales mix.
How many dollars of sales are required from each division in order to break even?	Fixed costs, weighted-average contribution margin ratio, sales mix	Break-even point in sales	$= \dfrac{\text{Fixed costs}}{\text{Weighted-average contribution margin ratio}}$	To determine the sales dollars required from each division, allocate the total break-even sales using the sales revenue mix.
How many units of products A and B should we produce in light of a limited resource?	Unit contribution margin, limited resource required per unit	Contribution margin per unit of limited resource	$= \dfrac{\text{Unit contribution margin}}{\text{Limited resource per unit}}$	Any additional capacity of limited resource should be applied toward the product with higher contribution margin per unit of limited resource.
How sensitive is the company's net income to changes in sales?	Contribution margin and net income	Degree of operating leverage	$= \dfrac{\text{Contribution margin}}{\text{Net income}}$	Reports the change in net income that occurs with a given change in sales. A high degree of operating leverage means that the company's net income is very sensitive to changes in sales.

Glossary Review

*__Absorption costing__ A costing approach in which all manufacturing costs are charged to the product. (p. 19-19).

__Cost structure__ The relative proportion of fixed versus variable costs that a company incurs. (p. 19-14).

__Degree of operating leverage__ A measure of the extent to which a company's net income reacts to a change in sales. It is calculated by dividing contribution margin by net income. (p. 19-16).

__Operating leverage__ The extent to which a company's net income reacts to a change in sales. Operating leverage is determined by a company's relative use of fixed versus variable costs. (p. 19-16).

__Sales mix__ The relative percentage in which a company sells its multiple products. It can be calculated based on unit sales or sales revenue. (p. 19-8).

__Theory of constraints__ A specific approach used to identify and manage constraints in order to achieve the company's goals. (p. 19-13).

*__Variable costing__ A costing approach in which only variable manufacturing costs are product costs, and fixed manufacturing costs are period costs (expenses). (p. 19-19).

Practice Multiple-Choice Questions

1. **(LO 1)** Which one of the following is the format of a CVP income statement?
   a. Sales − Variable costs = Fixed costs + Net income.
   b. Sales − Fixed costs − Variable costs − Operating expenses = Net income.
   c. Sales − Cost of goods sold − Operating expenses = Net income.
   d. Sales − Variable costs − Fixed costs = Net income.

2. **(LO 1)** Croc Catchers calculates its contribution margin to be less than zero. Which statement is **true**?
   a. Its fixed costs are less than the variable costs per unit.
   b. Its profits are greater than its total costs.
   c. The company should sell more units.
   d. Its selling price is less than its variable costs.

3. **(LO 1)** Which one of the following describes the break-even point?
   a. It is the point where total sales equal total variable plus total fixed costs.
   b. It is the point where the contribution margin equals zero.
   c. It is the point where total variable costs equal total fixed costs.
   d. It is the point where total sales equal total fixed costs.

4. (LO 1) The following information is available for Chap Company.

Sales	$350,000
Cost of goods sold	$120,000
Total fixed expenses	$60,000
Total variable expenses	$100,000

Which amount would you find on Chap's CVP income statement?

a. Contribution margin of $250,000.
b. Contribution margin of $190,000.
c. Gross profit of $230,000.
d. Gross profit of $190,000.

5. (LO 1) Gabriel Corporation has fixed costs of $180,000 and variable costs of $8.50 per unit. It has a target income of $268,000. How many units must it sell at $12 per unit to achieve its target net income?

a. 51,429 units.   c. 76,571 units.
b. 128,000 units. d. 21,176 units.

6. (LO 1) Mackey Corporation has fixed costs of $150,000 and variable costs of $9 per unit. If sales price per unit is $12, what is break-even sales in dollars?

a. $200,000.   c. $480,000.
b. $450,000.   d. $600,000.

7. (LO 2) Sales mix is:

a. important to sales managers but not to accountants.
b. easier to analyze on absorption costing income statements.
c. a measure of the relative percentage of a company's variable costs to its fixed costs.
d. a measure of the relative percentage in which a company's products are sold.

8. (LO 2) Net income will be:

a. greater if more higher-contribution margin units are sold than lower-contribution margin units.
b. greater if more lower-contribution margin units are sold than higher-contribution margin units.
c. equal as long as total sales remain equal, regardless of which products are sold.
d. unaffected by changes in the mix of products sold.

9. (LO 3) If the unit contribution margin is $15 and it takes 3.0 machine hours to produce the unit, the contribution margin per unit of limited resource is:

a. $25.   c. $4.
b. $5.   d. None of the answer choices are correct.

10. (LO 3) MEM manufactures two products. Product X has a contribution margin of $26 and requires 4 hours of machine time. Product Y has a contribution margin of $14 and requires 2 hours of machine time. Assuming that machine time is limited to 3,000 hours, how should it allocate the machine time to maximize its income?

a. Use 1,500 hours to produce X and 1,500 hours to produce Y.
b. Use 2,250 hours to produce X and 750 hours to produce Y.
c. Use 3,000 hours to produce only X.
d. Use 3,000 hours to produce only Y.

11. (LO 3) When a company has a limited resource, it should apply additional capacity of that resource to providing more units of the product or service that has:

a. the highest contribution margin.
b. the highest selling price.
c. the highest gross profit.
d. the highest unit contribution margin of that limited resource.

12. (LO 4) The degree of operating leverage:

a. can be computed by dividing total contribution margin by net income.
b. provides a measure of the company's earnings volatility.
c. affects a company's break-even point.
d. All of the answer choices are correct.

13. (LO 4) A high degree of operating leverage:

a. indicates that a company has a larger percentage of variable costs relative to its fixed costs.
b. is computed by dividing fixed costs by contribution margin.
c. exposes a company to greater earnings volatility risk.
d. exposes a company to less earnings volatility risk.

14. (LO 4) Stevens Company has a degree of operating leverage of 3.5 at a sales level of $1,200,000 and net income of $200,000. If Stevens' sales fall by 10%, Stevens can be expected to experience a:

a. decrease in net income of $70,000.
b. decrease in contribution margin of $7,000.
c. decrease in operating leverage of 35%.
d. decrease in net income of $175,000.

*15. (LO 5) Fixed manufacturing overhead costs are recognized as:

a. period costs under absorption costing.
b. product costs under absorption costs.
c. product costs under variable costing.
d. part of ending inventory costs under both absorption and variable costing.

*16. (LO 5) Net income computed under absorption costing will be:

a. higher than net income computed under variable costing in all cases.
b. equal to net income computed under variable costing in all cases.
c. higher than net income computed under variable costing when units produced are greater than units sold.
d. higher than net income computed under variable costing when units produced are less than units sold.

Solutions

1. d. The format of a CVP income statement is Sales − Variable costs − Fixed costs = Net income. Therefore, choices (a), (b), and (c) are incorrect.

2. d. If contribution margin is less than zero, selling price is less than variable costs. The other choices are incorrect because if contribution margin is less than zero (a) selling price, not fixed costs, is less than variable costs; (b) neither profits or total costs can be determined from the contribution margin amount; and (c) selling more units will only increase the negativity of the contribution margin.

3. a. The break-even point is the point where total sales equal total variable costs plus total fixed costs. Choices (b), (c), and (d) are therefore incorrect.

4. a. The CVP income statement would show Sales ($350,000) − Total variable expenses ($100,000) = Contribution margin ($250,000), not (b) contribution margin of $190,000. Choices (c) and (d) are incorrect because gross profit does not appear on a CVP income statement.

5. b. Required sales in units to achieve net income = ($180,000 + $268,000)/($12 − $8.50) = 128,000 units, not (a) 51,429 units, (c) 76,571 units, or (d) 21,176 units.

6. d. Fixed costs ($150,000) ÷ Contribution margin ratio ($3 ÷ $12) = $600,000, not (a) $200,000, (b) $450,000, or (c) $480,000.

7. d. Sales mix is the relative percentage in which a company sells its multiple products. The other choices are incorrect because (a) sales mix is also important to accountants, and (b) absorption costing income statements are not needed. Choice (c) is an incorrect definition of sales mix.

8. a. Net income will be greater if more higher contribution margin units are sold than lower contribution units. Choices (b), (c), and (d) are therefore incorrect statements.

9. b. The contribution margin per unit of limited resource is Unit contribution margin ($15) ÷ Units of limited resource (3.0 machine hours) = $5, not (a) $25, (c) $4, or (d) none of the above.

10. d. Unit contribution margin of Product X ($26 ÷ 4) < unit contribution margin of Product Y ($14 ÷ 2), so the machine time should be applied toward the product with the higher unit contribution margin. Choices (a), (b), and (c) are incorrect because these options will not maximize MEM's income.

11. d. The company should apply additional capacity of the limited resource to providing more units of the product or service that has the highest unit contribution margin of that limited resource, not (a) the highest contribution margin, (b) the highest selling price, or (c) the highest gross profit.

12. d. All of the above statements about operating leverage are true. So while choices (a), (b), and (c) are true statements, choice (d) is the better answer.

13. c. A high degree of operating leverage exposes a company to greater earnings volatility risk. The other choices are incorrect because a high degree of operating leverage (a) means a company has higher fixed costs relative to variable costs, not vice versa; (b) is computed by dividing contribution margin by net income, not fixed costs by contribution margin; and (d) exposes a company to greater, not less, earnings volatility risk.

14. a. Net income ($200,000) × Operating leverage (3.5) × Decrease in sales (10%) = decrease in net income of $70,000, not (b) decrease in contribution margin of $7,000, (c) decrease in operating leverage of 35%, or (d) decrease in net income of $175,000.

*__15. b.__ Under absorption costing, fixed manufacturing overhead costs and variable manufacturing overhead costs are both product costs. The other choices are incorrect because (a) fixed manufacturing overhead costs are recognized as product costs under absorption costing, not period costs; (c) under variable costing, fixed manufacturing costs are recognized as period costs; and (d) fixed manufacturing costs are part of ending inventory under absorption costing only.

*__16. c.__ Net income is higher under absorption costing than under variable costing when units produced exceed units sold, not (a) higher in all cases, (b) equal to net income under variable costing in all cases, or (d) higher when units produced are less than units sold.

Practice Brief Exercises

1. (LO 2) Wifi Corporation sells three different models of a wifi extender. Model W5 sells for $60 and has variable costs of $45. Model W10 sells for $90 and has variable costs of $70. Model W15 sells for $300 and has variable costs of $260. The sales mix of the three models is W5, 50%; W10, 20%; and W15, 30%. What is the weighted-average unit contribution margin?

Compute weighted-average unit contribution margin based on sales mix.

Solution

1.

Model	Sales Mix Percentage	Unit Contribution Margin	Weighted-Average Unit Contribution Margin
W5	50%	$15 ($60 − $45)	$ 7.50
W10	20%	$20 ($90 − $70)	4.00
W15	30%	$40 ($300 − $260)	12.00
			$23.50

2. (LO 2) Information for Wifi Corporation is given in **Practice Brief Exercise 1**. If the company has fixed costs of $246,750, how many units of each model must the company sell in order to break even?

Compute break-even point in units for company with multiple products.

Solution

2. Total break-even = ($246,750 ÷ $23.50*) = 10,500 units

*Computed in **Practice Brief Exercise 1**

Sales Units

Units of W5 = .50 × 10,500 = 5,250
Units of W10 = .20 × 10,500 = 2,100
Units of W15 = .30 × 10,500 = 3,150
                                10,500

Show allocation of limited resources.

3. (LO 3) In Familia Company, data concerning two products are unit contribution margin—Product A $15, Product B $20; machine hours required for one unit—Product A 3, Product B 4. Compute the contribution margin per unit of limited resource for each product.

Solution

3.
	Product A	Product B
Unit contribution margin (a)	$15	$20
Machine hours required (b)	3	4
Contribution margin per unit of limited resource [(a) ÷ (b)]	$ 5	$ 5

Compute degree of operating leverage.

4. (LO 4) Rachel Potato Chips is considering the purchase of a new automated potato-cutting machine. The new machine will reduce variable labor costs but will increase depreciation expense. Contribution margin is expected to increase from $150,000 to $225,000. Net income is expected to be the same at $50,000. Compute the degree of operating leverage before and after the purchase of the new equipment. Interpret your results.

Solution

4. Degree of operating leverage (old) = $150,000 ÷ $50,000 = 3

   Degree of operating leverage (new) = $225,000 ÷ $50,000 = 4.5

   If Rachel's sales change, the resulting change in net income will be 1.5 times (4.5 ÷ 3) higher with the new machine than under the old system.

Practice Exercises

Compute break-even point in units for a company with more than one product.

1. (LO 2) Yard-King manufactures lawnmowers, weed-trimmers, and chainsaws. Its sales mix and unit contribution margins are as follows.

	Sales Mix	Unit Contribution Margin
Lawnmowers	30%	$35
Weed-trimmers	50%	$25
Chainsaws	20%	$50

Yard-King has fixed costs of $4,620,000.

Instructions

Compute the number of units of each product that Yard-King must sell in order to break even under this product mix.

Solution

1.
	Sales Mix Percentage	Unit Contribution Margin	Weighted-Average Contribution Margin
Lawnmowers	30%	$35	$10.50
Weed-trimmers	50	25	12.50
Chainsaws	20	50	10.00
			$33.00

Total break-even sales in units = $4,620,000 ÷ $33.00 = 140,000 units

	Sales Mix Percentage		Total Break-Even Sales		Sales Needed per Product
Lawnmowers	30%	×	140,000 units	=	42,000 units
Weed-trimmers	50	×	140,000	=	70,000
Chainsaws	20	×	140,000	=	28,000
Total units					140,000 units

2. (LO 3) Rene Company manufactures and sells three products. Relevant per unit data concerning each product are given below.

Compute contribution margin and determine the product to be manufactured.

	Product		
	A	B	C
Selling price	$12	$13	$15
Variable costs and expenses	$ 4	$ 8	$ 9
Machine hours to produce	2	1	2

Instructions

a. Compute the contribution margin per unit of limited resource (machine hours) for each product.

b. Assuming 4,500 additional machine hours are available, which product should be manufactured and why?

c. Prepare an analysis showing the total contribution margin if the additional hours are (1) divided equally among the products, and (2) allocated entirely to the product identified in (b) above.

Solution

2. a.

	Product		
	A	B	C
Unit contribution margin (a)	$8	$5	$6
Machine hours required (b)	2	1	2
Contribution margin per unit of limited resource (a) ÷ (b)	$4	$5	$3

b. Product B should be manufactured because it results in the highest contribution margin per machine hour.

c. 1.

	Product		
	A	B	C
Machine hours (a) (4,500 ÷ 3)	1,500	1,500	1,500
Contribution margin per unit of limited resource (b)	$ 4	$ 5	$ 3
Total contribution margin [(a)] × [(b)]	$6,000	$7,500	$4,500

The total contribution margin is $18,000 ($6,000 + $7,500 + $4,500)

2.

	Product B
Machine hours (a)	4,500
Contribution margin per unit of limited resource (b)	$ 5
Total contribution margin [(a) × (b)]	$22,500

3. (LO 4) The CVP income statements shown below are available for Vericelli Company and Boone Company.

Compute degree of operating leverage and evaluate impact of alternative cost structures on net income.

	Vericelli Co.	Boone Co.
Sales revenue	$600,000	$600,000
Variable costs	320,000	120,000
Contribution margin	280,000	480,000
Fixed costs	180,000	380,000
Net income	$100,000	$100,000

Instructions

a. Compute the degree of operating leverage for each company and interpret your results.

b. Assuming that sales revenue increases by 10%, prepare a variable costing income statement for each company.

c. Discuss how the cost structure of these two companies affects their operating leverage and profitability.

Solution

3. a.

	Contribution Margin	÷	Net Income	=	Degree of Operating Leverage
Vericelli	$280,000	÷	$100,000	=	2.8
Boone	480,000	÷	100,000	=	4.8

Boone has a higher degree of operating leverage. Its earnings would increase (decrease) by a greater amount than Vericelli if each experienced an equal increase (decrease) in sales.

b.

	Vericelli Co.	Boone Co.
Sales revenue	$660,000*	$660,000
Variable costs	352,000**	132,000***
Contribution margin	308,000	528,000
Fixed costs	180,000	380,000
Net income	$128,000	$148,000

*$600,000 × 1.1   **$320,000 × 1.1   ***$120,000 × 1.1

c. Each company experienced a $60,000 increase in sales. However, because of Boone's higher operating leverage, it experienced a $48,000 ($148,000 − $100,000) increase in net income while Vericelli experienced only a $28,000 ($128,000 − $100,000) increase. This is what we would have expected since Boone's degree of operating leverage exceeds that of Vericelli.

Practice Problem

Determine sales mix with limited resources.

(LO 3) Francis Corporation manufactures and sells three different types of water-sport wakeboards. The boards vary in terms of their quality specifications—primarily with respect to their smoothness and finish. They are referred to as Smooth, Extra-Smooth, and Super-Smooth boards. Machine time is limited. More machine time is required to manufacture the Extra-Smooth and Super-Smooth boards. Additional information on a per unit basis is provided below.

	Product		
	Smooth	Extra-Smooth	Super-Smooth
Selling price	$60	$100	$160
Variable costs and expenses	50	75	130
Contribution margin	$10	$ 25	$ 30
Machine hours required	0.25	0.40	0.60

Total fixed costs: $234,000

Instructions

Answer each of the following questions.

a. Ignoring the machine time constraint, what strategy would appear optimal?

b. What is the contribution margin per unit of limited resource for each type of board?

c. If additional machine time could be obtained, how should the additional capacity be used?

Solution

a. The Super-Smooth boards have the highest unit contribution margin. Thus, ignoring any manufacturing constraints, it would appear that the company should shift toward production of more Super-Smooth units.

b. The contribution margin per unit of limited resource is calculated as follows.

	Smooth	Extra-Smooth	Super-Smooth
Unit contribution margin	$10 = $40	$25 = $62.50	$30 = $50
Limited resource consumed per unit	.25	.40	.60

c. The Extra-Smooth boards have the highest contribution margin per unit of limited resource. Given the resource constraint, any additional capacity should be used to make Extra-Smooth boards.

WileyPLUS

Brief Exercises, DO IT! Exercises, Exercises, Problems, and many additional resources are available for practice in WileyPLUS.

Note: All asterisked Questions, Exercises, and Problems relate to material in the appendix to this chapter.

Questions

1. What is meant by CVP analysis?
2. Provide three examples of management decisions that benefit from CVP analysis.
3. Distinguish between a traditional income statement and a CVP income statement.
4. Describe the features of a CVP income statement that make it more useful for management decision-making than the traditional income statement that is prepared for external users.
5. The traditional income statement for Wheat Company shows sales $900,000, cost of goods sold $500,000, and operating expenses $200,000. Assuming all costs and expenses are 75% variable and 25% fixed, prepare a CVP income statement through contribution margin.
6. If management chooses to reduce its selling price to match that of a competitor, how will the break-even point be affected?
7. What is meant by the term sales mix? How does sales mix affect the calculation of the break-even point?
8. Performance Company sells two types of performance tires. The lower-priced model is guaranteed for only 50,000 miles; the higher-priced model is guaranteed for 150,000 miles. The unit contribution margin on the higher-priced tire is twice as high as that of the lower-priced tire. If the sales mix shifts so that the company begins to sell more units of the lower-priced tire, explain how the company's break-even point in units will change.
9. What approach should be used to calculate the break-even point of a company that has many products?
10. How is the contribution margin per unit of limited resource computed?
11. What is the theory of constraints? Provide some examples of possible constraints for a manufacturer.
12. What is meant by "cost structure?" Explain how a company's cost structure affects its break-even point.
13. What is operating leverage? How does a company increase its operating leverage?
14. How does the replacement of manual labor with automated equipment affect a company's cost structure? What implications does this have for its operating leverage and break-even point?
15. What is a measure of operating leverage, and how is it calculated?
16. Pine Company has a degree of operating leverage of 8. Fir Company has a degree of operating leverage of 4. Interpret these measures.
*17. Distinguish between absorption costing and variable costing.
*18. **a.** What is the major rationale for the use of variable costing?
  b. Discuss why variable costing cannot be used for financial reporting purposes.
*19. Doc Rowan Corporation sells one product, its waterproof hiking boot. It began operations in the current year and had an ending inventory of 8,500 units. The company sold 20,000 units throughout the year. Fixed manufacturing overhead is $5 per unit, and total manufacturing cost per unit is $20 (including fixed manufacturing overhead costs). What is the difference in net income between absorption and variable costing?
*20. If production equals sales, what, if any, is the difference between net income under absorption costing versus under variable costing?
*21. If production is greater than sales, how does absorption costing net income differ from variable costing net income?
*22. In the long run, will net income be higher or lower under variable costing compared to absorption costing?

Brief Exercises

Determine missing amounts for contribution margin.

BE19.1 (LO 1), AN Determine the missing amounts.

	Unit Selling Price	Unit Variable Costs	Unit Contribution Margin	Contribution Margin Ratio
1.	$250	$180	(a)	(b)
2.	$500	(c)	$200	(d)
3.	(e)	(f)	$330	30%

Prepare CVP income statement.

BE19.2 (LO 1), AP Hamby Inc. has sales of $2,000,000 for the first quarter of 2022. In making the sales, the company incurred the following costs and expenses.

	Variable	Fixed
Cost of goods sold	$760,000	$600,000
Selling expenses	95,000	60,000
Administrative expenses	79,000	66,000

Prepare a CVP income statement for the quarter ended March 31, 2022.

Compute the break-even point.

BE19.3 (LO 1), AP Eastland Corp. had total variable costs of $150,000, total fixed costs of $120,000, and total revenues of $250,000. Compute the required sales in dollars to break even.

Compute the break-even point.

BE19.4 (LO 1), AP Dilts Company has a unit selling price of $400, variable costs per unit of $250, and fixed costs of $210,000. Compute the break-even point in units using (a) the mathematical equation and (b) unit contribution margin.

Compute sales for target net income.

BE19.5 (LO 1), AP For Rivera Company, variable costs are 70% of sales, and fixed costs are $210,000. Management's net income goal is $60,000. Compute the required sales needed to achieve management's target net income of $60,000. (Use the mathematical equation approach.)

Compute the margin of safety and the margin of safety ratio.

BE19.6 (LO 1), AP For Kosko Company, actual sales are $1,200,000 and break-even sales are $960,000. Compute (a) the margin of safety in dollars and (b) the margin of safety ratio.

Compute weighted-average unit contribution margin based on sales mix.

BE19.7 (LO 2), AP NoFly Corporation sells three different models of a mosquito "zapper." Model A12 sells for $50 and has variable costs of $35. Model B22 sells for $100 and has variable costs of $70. Model C124 sells for $400 and has variable costs of $300. The sales mix of the three models is A12, 60%; B22, 15%; and C124, 25%. What is the weighted-average unit contribution margin?

Compute break-even point in units for company with multiple products.

BE19.8 (LO 2), AP Information for NoFly Corporation is given in BE19.7. If the company has fixed costs of $269,500, how many units of each model must the company sell in order to break even?

Compute break-even point in dollars for company with multiple product lines.

BE19.9 (LO 2), AP Dixie Candle Supply makes candles. The sales mix (as a percentage of total dollar sales) of its three product lines is birthday candles 30%, standard tapered candles 50%, and large scented candles 20%. The contribution margin ratio of each candle type is shown below.

Candle Type	Contribution Margin Ratio
Birthday	20%
Standard tapered	30%
Large scented	45%

a. What is the weighted-average contribution margin ratio?

b. If the company's fixed costs are $450,000 per year, what is the sales dollar amount of each type of candle that must be sold to break even?

Determine weighted-average contribution margin.

BE19.10 (LO 2), AP Faune Furniture Co. consists of two divisions, Bedroom Division and Dining Room Division. The results of operations for the most recent quarter are:

	Bedroom Division	Dining Room Division	Total
Sales	$500,000	$750,000	$1,250,000
Variable costs	225,000	450,000	675,000
Contribution margin	$275,000	$300,000	$ 575,000

a. Determine the company's sales mix based on sales revenue.

b. Determine the company's weighted-average contribution margin ratio.

BE19.11 (LO 3), AP In Marshall Company, data concerning two products are unit contribution margin—Product A $10, Product B $12; machine hours required for one unit—Product A 2, Product B 3. Compute the contribution margin per unit of limited resource for each product.

Show allocation of limited resources.

BE19.12 (LO 3), AP Sage Corporation manufactures two products with the following characteristics.

Show allocation of limited resources.

	Unit Contribution Margin	Machine Hours Required for Production
Product 1	$42	.15 hours
Product 2	$32	.10 hours

If Sage's machine hours are limited to 2,000 per month, determine which product it should produce.

BE19.13 (LO 4), AP Sam's Shingle Corporation is considering the purchase of a new automated shingle-cutting machine. The new machine will reduce variable labor costs but will increase depreciation expense. Contribution margin is expected to increase from $200,000 to $240,000. Net income is expected to be the same at $40,000. Compute the degree of operating leverage before and after the purchase of the new equipment. Interpret your results.

Compute degree of operating leverage.

BE19.14 (LO 4), AP Presented below are variable costing income statements for Diggs Company and Doggs Company. They are in the same industry, with the same net incomes, but different cost structures.

Compute break-even point with change in operating leverage.

	Diggs Co.	Doggs Co.
Sales	$200,000	$200,000
Variable costs	80,000	50,000
Contribution margin	120,000	150,000
Fixed costs	75,000	105,000
Net income	$ 45,000	$ 45,000

Compute the break-even point in dollars for each company and comment on your findings.

BE19.15 (LO 4), AP The degree of operating leverage for Montana Corp. and APK Co. are 1.6 and 5.4, respectively. Both have net incomes of $50,000. Determine their respective contribution margins.

Determine contribution margin from degree of operating leverage.

*BE19.16 (LO 5), AP The Rock Company produces basketballs. It incurred the following costs during the year.

Compute product costs under variable costing.

Direct materials	$14,400
Direct labor	$25,600
Fixed manufacturing overhead	$12,000
Variable manufacturing overhead	$29,400
Selling costs	$21,000

What are the total product costs for the company under variable costing?

*BE19.17 (LO 5), AP Information concerning The Rock Company is provided in BE19.16. What are the total product costs for the company under absorption costing?

Compute product costs under absorption costing.

*BE19.18 (LO 5), AP Burns Company incurred the following costs during the year: direct materials $20 per unit; direct labor $14 per unit; variable manufacturing overhead $15 per unit; variable selling and administrative costs $8 per unit; fixed manufacturing overhead $128,000; and fixed selling and administrative costs $10,000. Burns produced 8,000 units and sold 6,000 units. Determine the manufacturing cost per unit under (a) absorption costing and (b) variable costing.

Determine manufacturing cost per unit under absorption and variable costing.

*BE19.19 (LO 5), AP **Writing** Harris Company's fixed overhead costs are $4 per unit, and its variable overhead costs are $8 per unit. In the first month of operations, 50,000 units are produced, and 46,000 units are sold. Write a short memo to the chief financial officer explaining which costing approach will produce the higher income and what the difference will be.

Compute net income under absorption and variable costing.

DO IT! Exercises

Compute the break-even point and margin of safety under different alternatives.

DO IT! 19.1 (LO 1), AP Victoria Company reports the following operating results for the month of April.

Victoria Company
CVP Income Statement
For the Month Ended April 30, 2022

	Total	Per Unit
Sales (9,000 units)	$450,000	$50
Variable costs	270,000	30
Contribution margin	180,000	$20
Fixed expenses	150,000	
Net income	$ 30,000	

Management is considering the following course of action to increase net income: Reduce the selling price by 4%, with no changes to unit variable costs or fixed costs. Management is confident that this change will increase unit sales by 20%.

Using the contribution margin technique, compute the break-even point in units and dollars and margin of safety in dollars:

a. Assuming no changes to selling price or costs, and

b. Assuming changes to sales price and volume as described above.

Comment on your findings.

Compute sales mix, weighted-average contribution margin, and break-even point.

DO IT! 19.2 (LO 2), AP Snow Cap Springs produces and sells water filtration systems for homeowners. Information regarding its three models is shown below.

	Basic	Basic Plus	Premium	Total
Units sold	750	450	300	1,500
Selling price	$250	$400	$800	
Variable costs	$195	$285	$415	

The company's total fixed costs to produce the filtration systems are $180,700.

a. Determine the sales mix as a function of units sold for the three products.

b. Determine the weighted-average unit contribution margin.

c. Determine the total number of units that the company must produce to break even.

d. Determine the number of units of each model that the company must produce to break even.

Determine sales mix with limited resources.

DO IT! 19.3 (LO 3), AP Zoom Corporation manufactures and sells three different types of binoculars. They are referred to as Good, Better, and Best binoculars. Grinding and polishing time is limited. More time is required to grind and polish the lenses used in the Better and Best binoculars. Additional information is provided below.

	Product		
	Good	Better	Best
Selling price	$90.00	$330.00	$900.00
Variable costs and expenses	50.00	180.00	480.00
Contribution margin	$40.00	$150.00	$420.00
Grinding and polishing time required	0.5 hrs	1.5 hrs	6 hrs

a. Ignoring the time constraint, what strategy would appear to be optimal?

b. What is the contribution margin per unit of limited resource for each type of binocular?

c. If additional grinding and polishing time could be obtained, how should the additional capacity be used?

Determine operating leverage.

DO IT! 19.4 (LO 4), AP Bergen Hospital is contemplating an investment in an automated surgical system. Its current process relies on the a number of skilled physicians. The new equipment would employ a computer robotic system operated by a technician. The company requested an analysis of the old technology versus the new technology. The accounting department has prepared the following CVP income statements for use in your analysis.

	Old	New
Sales	$3,000,000	$3,000,000
Variable costs	1,600,000	700,000
Contribution margin	1,400,000	2,300,000
Fixed costs	1,000,000	1,900,000
Net income	$ 400,000	$ 400,000

a. Compute the degree of operating leverage for the company under each scenario.

b. Discuss your results.

Exercises

E19.1 (LO 1), AP **Service** The Soma Inn is trying to determine its break-even point. The inn has 75 rooms that are rented at $60 a night. Operating costs are as follows.

Salaries	$10,600 per month
Utilities	2,400 per month
Depreciation	1,500 per month
Maintenance	800 per month
Maid service	8 per room
Other costs	34 per room

Compute break-even point and margin of safety.

Instructions

a. Determine the inn's break-even point in (1) number of rented rooms per month and (2) dollars.

b. If the inn plans on renting an average of 50 rooms per day (assuming a 30-day month), what is (1) the monthly margin of safety in dollars and (2) the margin of safety ratio?

E19.2 (LO 1), AP **Service** In the month of June, Jose Hebert's Beauty Salon gave 4,000 haircuts, shampoos, and hair colorings at an average price of $30 each. During the month, fixed costs were $16,800 and variable costs were 75% of sales.

Compute contribution margin, break-even point, and margin of safety.

Instructions

a. Determine the contribution margin in dollars, per unit and as a ratio.

b. Using the contribution margin technique, compute the break-even point in dollars and in units.

c. Compute the margin of safety in dollars and as a ratio.

E19.3 (LO 1), AP Barnes Company reports the following operating results for the month of August: sales $325,000 (units 5,000); variable costs $210,000; and fixed costs $75,000. Management is considering the following independent courses of action to increase net income.

Compute net income under different alternatives.

1. Increase selling price by 10% with no change in total variable costs or sales volume.
2. Reduce variable costs to 58% of sales.
3. Reduce fixed costs by $15,000.

Instructions

Compute the net income to be earned under each alternative. Which course of action will produce the highest net income?

E19.4 (LO 1), AP **Service** Comfi Airways, Inc., a small two-plane passenger airline, has asked for your assistance in some basic analysis of its operations. Both planes seat 10 passengers each, and they fly commuters from Comfi's base airport to the major city in the state, Metropolis. Each month, 40 round-trip flights are made. The following is a recent month's activity in the form of a cost-volume-profit income statement.

Compute break-even point and prepare CVP income statement.

Fare revenues (400 passenger flights)		$48,000
Variable costs		
Fuel	$14,000	
Snacks and drinks	800	
Landing fees	2,000	
Supplies and forms	1,200	18,000
Contribution margin		30,000
Fixed costs		
Depreciation	3,000	
Salaries	15,000	
Advertising	500	
Airport hangar fees	1,750	20,250
Net income		$ 9,750

Instructions

a. Calculate the break-even point in (1) dollars and (2) number of passenger flights.

b. Without calculations, determine the contribution margin at the break-even point.

c. If ticket prices were decreased by 10%, passenger flights would increase by 25%. However, total variable costs would increase by the same percentage as passenger flights. Should the ticket price decrease be adopted?

Prepare a CVP income statement before and after changes in business environment.

E19.5 (LO 1), AP Carey Company had sales in 2021 of $1,560,000 on 60,000 units. Variable costs totaled $900,000, and fixed costs totaled $500,000.

A new raw material is available that will decrease the variable costs per unit by 20% (or $3). However, to process the new raw material, fixed operating costs will increase by $100,000. Management feels that one-half of the decline in the variable costs per unit should be passed on to customers in the form of a sales price reduction. The marketing department expects that this sales price reduction will result in a 5% increase in the number of units sold.

Instructions

Prepare a projected CVP income statement for 2022 (a) assuming the changes have not been made, and (b) assuming that changes are made as described.

Compute break-even point in units for a company with more than one product.

E19.6 (LO 2), AP Yard Tools manufactures lawnmowers, weed-trimmers, and chainsaws. Its sales mix and unit contribution margin are as follows.

	Sales Mix	Unit Contribution Margin
Lawnmowers	20%	$30
Weed-trimmers	50%	$20
Chainsaws	30%	$40

Yard Tools has fixed costs of $4,200,000.

Instructions

Compute the number of units of each product that Yard Tools must sell in order to break even under this product mix.

Compute service line break-even point and target net income in dollars for a company with more than one service.

E19.7 (LO 2), AN `Service` PDQ Repairs has 200 auto-maintenance service outlets nationwide. It performs primarily two lines of service: oil changes and brake repair. Oil change–related services represent 70% of its sales and provide a contribution margin ratio of 20%. Brake repair represents 30% of its sales and provides a 40% contribution margin ratio. The company's fixed costs are $15,600,000 (that is, $78,000 per service outlet).

Instructions

a. Calculate the dollar amount of each type of service that the company must provide in order to break even.

b. The company has a desired net income of $52,000 per service outlet. What is the dollar amount of each type of service that must be performed by each service outlet to meet its target net income per outlet?

Compute break-even point in dollars for a company with more than one service.

E19.8 (LO 2), AN `Service` Express Delivery is a rapidly growing delivery service. Last year, 80% of its revenue came from the delivery of mailing "pouches" and small, standardized delivery boxes (which provides a 20% contribution margin). The other 20% of its revenue came from delivering non-standardized boxes (which provides a 70% contribution margin). With the rapid growth of Internet retail sales, Express believes that there are great opportunities for growth in the delivery of non-standardized boxes. The company has fixed costs of $12,000,000.

Instructions

a. What is the company's break-even point in total sales dollars? At the break-even point, how much of the company's sales are provided by each type of service?

b. The company's management would like to hold its fixed costs constant but shift its sales mix so that 60% of its revenue comes from the delivery of non-standardized boxes and the remainder from pouches and small boxes. If this were to occur, what would be the company's break-even sales, and what amount of sales would be provided by each service type?

E19.9 (LO 2), AP Tiger Golf Accessories sells golf shoes, gloves, and a laser-guided range-finder that measures distance. Shown below are unit cost and sales data.

Compute break-even point in units for a company with multiple products.

	Pairs of Shoes	Pairs of Gloves	Range-Finder
Unit sales price	$100	$30	$260
Unit variable costs	60	10	200
Unit contribution margin	$ 40	$20	$ 60
Sales mix	35%	55%	10%

Fixed costs are $620,000.

Instructions

a. Compute the break-even point in units for the company.

b. Determine the number of units to be sold at the break-even point for each product line.

c. Verify that the mix of sales units determined in (b) will generate a zero net income.

E19.10 (LO 2), AP Personal Electronix sells computer tablets and MP3 players. The business is divided into two divisions along product lines. CVP income statements for a recent quarter's activity are presented below.

Determine break-even point in dollars for two divisions.

	Tablet Division	MP3 Player Division	Total
Sales	$600,000	$400,000	$1,000,000
Variable costs	420,000	260,000	680,000
Contribution margin	$180,000	$140,000	320,000
Fixed costs			120,000
Net income			$ 200,000

Instructions

a. Determine the sales mix percentage based on sales revenue and contribution margin ratio for each division.

b. Calculate the company's weighted-average contribution margin ratio.

c. Calculate the company's break-even point in dollars.

d. Determine the sales level in dollars for each division at the break-even point.

E19.11 (LO 3), AN Mars Company manufactures and sells three products. Relevant per unit data concerning each product are given below.

Compute contribution margin and determine the product to be manufactured.

	Product		
	A	B	C
Selling price	$9	$12	$15
Variable costs and expenses	$3	$10	$12
Machine hours to produce	2	1	2

Instructions

a. Compute the contribution margin per unit of limited resource (machine hours) for each product.

b. Assuming 3,000 additional machine hours are available, which product should be manufactured?

c. Prepare an analysis showing the total contribution margin if the additional hours are (1) divided equally among the products, and (2) allocated entirely to the product identified in (b) above.

Compute contribution margin and determine the products to be manufactured.

E19.12 (LO 3), AN Dalton Inc. produces and sells three products. Unit data concerning each product is shown below.

	Product		
	D	E	F
Selling price	$200	$300	$250
Direct labor costs	30	80	35
Other variable costs	95	80	145

The company has 2,000 hours of labor available to build inventory in anticipation of the company's peak season. Management is trying to decide which product should be produced. The direct labor hourly rate is $10.

Instructions

a. Determine the number of direct labor hours per unit.

b. Determine the contribution margin per direct labor hour.

c. Determine which product should be produced and the total contribution margin for that product.

Compute contribution margin and determine the products to be manufactured.

E19.13 (LO 3), AN Helena Company manufactures and sells two products. Relevant per unit data concerning each product follow.

	Product	
	Basic	Deluxe
Selling price	$40	$52
Variable costs	$22	$24
Machine hours	0.5	0.8

Instructions

a. Compute the contribution margin per machine hour for each product.

b. If 1,000 additional machine hours are available, which product should Helena manufacture?

c. Prepare an analysis showing the total contribution margin if the additional hours are:

1. Divided equally between the products.
2. Allocated entirely to the product identified in part (b).

Compute degree of operating leverage and evaluate impact of alternative cost structures on net income.

E19.14 (LO 4), AN The CVP income statements shown below are available for Armstrong Company and Contador Company.

	Armstrong Co.	Contador Co.
Sales	$500,000	$500,000
Variable costs	240,000	50,000
Contribution margin	260,000	450,000
Fixed costs	160,000	350,000
Net income	$100,000	$100,000

Instructions

a. Compute the degree of operating leverage for each company and interpret your results.

b. Assuming that sales revenue increases by 10%, prepare a variable costing income statement for each company.

c. Discuss how the cost structure of these two companies affects their operating leverage and profitability.

Compute degree of operating leverage and evaluate impact of alternative cost structures on net income and margin of safety.

E19.15 (LO 4), AN Service Casas Modernas of Juarez, Mexico, is contemplating a major change in its cost structure. Currently, all of its drafting work is performed by skilled draftsmen. Rafael Jiminez, Casas' owner, is considering replacing the draftsmen with a computerized drafting system. However, before making the change, Rafael would like to know the consequences of the change, since the volume of business varies significantly from year to year. Shown below are CVP income statements for each alternative.

	Manual System	Computerized System
Sales	$1,500,000	$1,500,000
Variable costs	1,200,000	600,000
Contribution margin	300,000	900,000
Fixed costs	100,000	700,000
Net income	$ 200,000	$ 200,000

Instructions

a. Determine the degree of operating leverage for each alternative.

b. Which alternative would produce the higher net income if sales increased by $150,000?

c. Using the margin of safety ratio, determine which alternative could sustain the greater decline in sales before operating at a loss.

E19.16 (LO 4), AN An investment banker is analyzing two companies that specialize in the production and sale of candied yams. Traditional Yams uses a labor-intensive approach, and Auto-Yams uses a mechanized system. CVP income statements for the two companies are shown below.

Compute degree of operating leverage and impact on net income of alternative cost structures.

	Traditional Yams	Auto-Yams
Sales	$400,000	$400,000
Variable costs	320,000	160,000
Contribution margin	80,000	240,000
Fixed costs	30,000	190,000
Net income	$ 50,000	$ 50,000

The investment banker is interested in acquiring one of these companies. However, she is concerned about the impact that each company's cost structure might have on its profitability.

Instructions

a. Calculate each company's degree of operating leverage. Determine which company's cost structure makes it more sensitive to changes in sales volume.

b. Determine the effect on each company's net income if sales decrease by 15% and if sales increase by 10%. Do not prepare income statements.

c. Which company should the investment banker acquire? Discuss.

*E19.17 (LO 5), AP Siren Company builds custom fishing lures for sporting goods stores. In its first year of operations, 2022, the company incurred the following costs.

Compute product cost and prepare an income statement under variable and absorption costing.

Variable Costs per Unit

Direct materials	$7.50
Direct labor	$3.45
Variable manufacturing overhead	$5.80
Variable selling and administrative expenses	$3.90

Fixed Costs per Year

Fixed manufacturing overhead	$225,000
Fixed selling and administrative expenses	$210,100

Siren Company sells the fishing lures for $25. During 2022, the company sold 80,000 lures and produced 90,000 lures.

Instructions

a. Assuming the company uses variable costing, calculate Siren's manufacturing cost per unit for 2022.

b. Prepare a variable costing income statement for 2022.

c. Assuming the company uses absorption costing, calculate Siren's manufacturing cost per unit for 2022.

d. Prepare an absorption costing income statement for 2022.

*E19.18 (LO 5), AN Langdon Company produced 9,000 units during the past year, but only 8,200 of the units were sold. The following additional information is also available.

Determine ending inventory under variable costing and determine whether absorption or variable costing would result in higher net income.

Direct materials used	$79,000
Direct labor incurred	$30,000
Variable manufacturing overhead	$21,500
Fixed manufacturing overhead	$45,000
Fixed selling and administrative expenses	$70,000
Variable selling and administrative expenses	$10,000

There was no work in process inventory at the beginning and end of the year, nor did Langdon have any beginning finished goods inventory.

Instructions

a. What would be Langdon Company's finished goods inventory cost on December 31 under variable costing?

b. Which costing method, absorption or variable costing, would show a higher net income for the year? By what amount?

Compute manufacturing cost under absorption and variable costing and explain difference.

*E19.19 (LO 5), AN Crate Express Co. produces wooden crates used for shipping products by ocean liner. In 2022, Crate Express incurred the following costs.

Wood used in crate production	$54,000
Nails (considered insignificant and a variable expense)	$ 350
Direct labor	$43,000
Utilities for the plant: $1,500 each month, plus $0.50 for each kilowatt-hour used each month	
Rent expense for the plant for the year	$21,400

Assume Crate Express used an average 500 kilowatt-hours each month over the past year.

Instructions

a. What is Crate Express's total manufacturing cost if it uses a variable costing approach?

b. What is Crate Express's total manufacturing cost if it uses an absorption costing approach?

c. What accounts for the difference in manufacturing costs between these two costing approaches?

Problems: Set A

Compute break-even point under alternative courses of action.

P19.1A (LO 1), AN Midlands Inc. had a bad year in 2021. For the first time in its history, it operated at a loss. The company's income statement showed the following results from selling 80,000 units of product: net sales $2,000,000; total costs and expenses $2,235,000; and net loss $235,000. Costs and expenses consisted of the following.

	Total	Variable	Fixed
Cost of goods sold	$1,568,000	$1,050,000	$ 518,000
Selling expenses	517,000	92,000	425,000
Administrative expenses	150,000	58,000	92,000
	$2,235,000	$1,200,000	$1,035,000

Management is considering the following independent alternatives for 2022.

1. Increase unit selling price 25% with no change in costs and expenses.
2. Change the compensation of salespersons from fixed annual salaries totaling $200,000 to total salaries of $40,000 plus a 5% commission on net sales.
3. Purchase new high-tech factory machinery that will change the proportion between variable and fixed cost of goods sold to 50:50.

Instructions

a. Compute the break-even point in dollars for 2021.

b. (2) $2,500,000

b. Compute the break-even point in dollars under each of the alternative courses of action for 2022. (Round to the nearest dollar.) Which course of action do you recommend?

Compute break-even point and margin of safety ratio, and prepare a CVP income statement before and after changes in business environment.

P19.2A (LO 1), AN Lorge Corporation has collected the following information after its first year of sales. Sales were $1,500,000 on 100,000 units; selling expenses $250,000 (40% variable and 60% fixed); direct materials $511,000; direct labor $290,000; administrative expenses $270,000 (20% variable and 80% fixed); and manufacturing overhead $350,000 (70% variable and 30% fixed). Top management has asked you to do a CVP analysis so that it can make plans for the coming year. It has projected that unit sales will increase by 10% next year.

Instructions

a. Compute (1) the contribution margin for the current year and the projected year, and (2) the fixed costs for the current year. (Assume that fixed costs will remain the same in the projected year.)

b. Compute the break-even point in units and sales dollars for the first year.

b. 157,000 units

c. The company has a target net income of $200,000. What is the required sales in dollars for the company to meet its target?

d. If the company meets its target net income number, by what percentage could its sales fall before it is operating at a loss? That is, what is its margin of safety ratio?

e. The company is considering a purchase of equipment that would reduce its direct labor costs by $104,000 and would change its manufacturing overhead costs to 30% variable and 70% fixed (assume total manufacturing overhead cost is $350,000, as above). It is also considering switching to a pure commission basis for its sales staff. This would change selling expenses to 90% variable and 10% fixed (assume total selling expense is $250,000, as above). Compute (1) the contribution margin and (2) the contribution margin ratio, and recompute (3) the break-even point in sales dollars. Comment on the effect each of management's proposed changes has on the break-even point.

e. (3) $1,735,714

P19.3A (LO 2), AN Service The Grand Inn is a restaurant in Flagstaff, Arizona. It specializes in southwestern style meals in a moderate price range. Paul Weld, the manager of Grand, has determined that during the last 2 years the sales mix and contribution margin ratio of its offerings are as follows.

Determine break-even sales under alternative sales strategies and evaluate results.

	Percent of Total Sales	Contribution Margin Ratio
Appetizers	15%	50%
Main entrees	50%	25%
Desserts	10%	50%
Beverages	25%	80%

Paul is considering a variety of options to try to improve the profitability of the restaurant. His goal is to generate a target net income of $117,000. The company has fixed costs of $1,053,000 per year.

Instructions

a. Calculate the total restaurant sales and the sales of each product line that would be necessary to achieve the desired target net income.

a. Total sales $2,600,000

b. Paul believes the restaurant could greatly improve its profitability by reducing the complexity and selling price of its entrees to increase the number of clients that it serves. It would then more heavily market its appetizers and beverages. He is proposing to reduce the contribution margin ratio on the main entrees to 10% by dropping the average selling price. He envisions an expansion of the restaurant that would increase fixed costs by $585,000. At the same time, he is proposing to change the sales mix to the following.

b. Total sales $3,375,000

	Percent of Total Sales	Contribution Margin Ratio
Appetizers	25%	50%
Main entrees	25%	10%
Desserts	10%	50%
Beverages	40%	80%

Compute the total restaurant sales, and the sales of each product line that would be necessary to achieve the desired target net income.

c. Suppose that Paul reduces the selling price on entrees and increases fixed costs as proposed in part (b), but customers are not swayed by the marketing efforts and the sales mix remains what it was in part (a). Compute the total restaurant sales and the sales of each product line that would be necessary to achieve the desired target net income. Comment on the potential risks and benefits of this strategy.

P19.4A (LO 3), AN Tanek Industries manufactures and sells three different models of wet-dry shop vacuum cleaners. Although the shop vacs vary in terms of quality and features, all are good sellers. Tanek is currently operating at full capacity with limited machine time.
Sales and production information relevant to each model follows.

Determine sales mix with limited resources.

	Product		
	Economy	Standard	Deluxe
Selling price	$30	$50	$100
Variable costs and expenses	$16	$20	$46
Machine hours required	0.5	0.8	1.6

b. Economy $28

Compute degree of operating leverage and evaluate impact of operating leverage on financial results.

P19.5A (LO 4), AN Writing The following CVP income statements are available for Blanc Company and Noir Company.

	Blanc Company	Noir Company
Sales	$500,000	$500,000
Variable costs	280,000	180,000
Contribution margin	220,000	320,000
Fixed costs	170,000	270,000
Net income	$ 50,000	$ 50,000

Instructions

a. BE, Blanc $386,364 BE, Noir $421,875

b. DOL, Blanc 4.4 DOL, Noir 6.4

a. Compute the break-even point in dollars and the margin of safety ratio (round to 3 places) for each company.

b. Compute the degree of operating leverage for each company and interpret your results.

c. Assuming that sales revenue increases by 20%, prepare a CVP income statement for each company.

d. Assuming that sales revenue decreases by 20%, prepare a CVP income statement for each company.

e. Discuss how the cost structure of these two companies affects their operating leverage and profitability.

Determine contribution margin, break-even point, target sales, and degree of operating leverage.

P19.6A (LO 1, 4), AN Bonita Beauty Corporation manufactures cosmetic products that are sold through a network of sales agents. The agents are paid a commission of 18% of sales. The income statement for the year ending December 31, 2022, is as follows.

Bonita Beauty Corporation
Income Statement
For the Year Ended December 31, 2022

Sales			$75,000,000
Cost of goods sold			
Variable		$31,500,000	
Fixed		8,610,000	40,110,000
Gross margin			34,890,000
Selling and marketing expenses			
Commissions		13,500,000	
Fixed costs		10,260,000	23,760,000
Operating income			$11,130,000

The company is considering hiring its own sales staff to replace the network of agents. It will pay its salespeople a commission of 8% and incur additional fixed costs of $7.5 million.

Instructions

a. $47,175,000

a. Under the current policy of using a network of sales agents, calculate the Bonita Beauty Corporation's break-even point in sales dollars for the year 2022.

b. Calculate the company's break-even point in sales dollars for the year 2022 if it hires its own sales force to replace the network of agents.

c. (2) 3.37

c. Calculate the degree of operating leverage at sales of $75 million if (1) Bonita Beauty uses sales agents, and (2) Bonita Beauty employs its own sales staff. Describe the advantages and disadvantages of each alternative.

d. Calculate the estimated sales volume in sales dollars that would generate an identical net income for the year ending December 31, 2022, regardless of whether Bonita Beauty Corporation employs its own sales staff and pays them an 8% commission or continues to use the independent network of agents.

(CMA-Canada adapted)

Prepare income statements under absorption costing and variable costing for a company with beginning inventory, and reconcile differences.

***P19.7A (LO 5), AN** Writing Jackson Company produces plastic that is used for injection-molding applications such as gears for small motors. In 2021, the first year of operations, Jackson produced 4,000 tons of plastic and sold 3,500 tons. In 2022, the production and sales results were exactly reversed. In each year, the selling price per ton was $2,000, variable manufacturing costs were 15% of the sales price of units produced, variable selling expenses were 10% of the selling price of units sold, fixed manufacturing costs were $2,800,000, and fixed administrative expenses were $500,000.

Instructions

a. Prepare income statements for each year using variable costing. (Use the format from Illustration 19A.5.)

b. Prepare income statements for each year using absorption costing. (Use the format from Illustration 19A.4.)

c. Reconcile the differences each year in net income under the two costing approaches.

d. Comment on the effects of production and sales on net income under the two costing approaches.

a. 2022 $2,700,000

b. 2022 $2,350,000

*P19.8A (LO 5), AN Writing Dilithium Batteries is a division of Enterprise Corporation. The division manufactures and sells a long-life battery used in a wide variety of applications. During the coming year, it expects to sell 60,000 units for $30 per unit. Nyota Uthura is the division manager. She is considering producing either 60,000 or 90,000 units during the period. Other information is presented in the schedule.

Prepare absorption and variable costing income statements and reconcile differences between absorption and variable costing income statements when sales level and production level change. Discuss relative usefulness of absorption costing versus variable costing.

Division Information for 2022

Beginning inventory	0
Expected sales in units	60,000
Selling price per unit	$30
Variable manufacturing costs per unit	$12
Fixed manufacturing overhead costs (total)	$540,000
Fixed manufacturing overhead costs per unit:	
Based on 60,000 units	$9 per unit ($540,000 ÷ 60,000)
Based on 90,000 units	$6 per unit ($540,000 ÷ 90,000)
Manufacturing costs per unit:	
Based on 60,000 units	$21 per unit ($12 variable + $9 fixed)
Based on 90,000 units	$18 per unit ($12 variable + $6 fixed)
Variable selling and administrative expenses	$2
Fixed selling and administrative expenses (total)	$50,000

Instructions

a. Prepare an absorption costing income statement, with one column showing the results if 60,000 units are produced and one column showing the results if 90,000 units are produced.

b. Prepare a variable costing income statement, with one column showing the results if 60,000 units are produced and one column showing the results if 90,000 units are produced.

c. Reconcile the difference in net incomes under the two approaches and explain what accounts for this difference.

d. Discuss the relative usefulness of the variable costing income statements versus the absorption costing income statements for decision making and for evaluating the manager's performance.

a. 90,000 units: NI $550,000

b. 90,000 units: NI $370,000

Continuing Cases

Current Designs

CD19 Current Designs manufactures two different types of kayaks, rotomolded kayaks and composite kayaks. The following information is available for each product line.

	Rotomolded	Composite
Sales price/unit	$950	$2,000
Variable costs/unit	$570	$1,340

The company's fixed costs are $820,000. An analysis of the sales mix identifies that rotomolded kayaks make up 80% of the total units sold.

Instructions

a. Determine the weighted-average unit contribution margin for Current Designs.

b. Determine the break-even point in units for Current Designs and identify how many units of each type of kayak will be sold at the break-even point. (Round to the nearest whole number.)

c. Assume that the sales mix changes, and rotomolded kayaks now make up 70% of total units sold. Calculate the total number of units that would need to be sold to earn a net income of $2,000,000 and identify how many units of each type of kayak will be sold at this level of income. (Round to the nearest whole number.)

d. Assume that Current Designs will have sales of $3,000,000 with two-thirds of the sales dollars in rotomolded kayaks and one-third of the sales dollars in composite kayaks. Assuming $660,000 of fixed costs are allocated to the rotomolded kayaks and $160,000 to the composite kayaks, prepare a CVP income statement for each product line.

e. Using the information in part (d), calculate the degree of operating leverage for each product line and interpret your findings. (Round to two decimal places.)

Waterways

(*Note:* This is a continuation of the Waterways case from Chapters 14–18.)

WP19 This problem asks you to perform break-even analysis based on Waterways' sales mix and to make sales mix decisions related to Waterways' use of its productive facilities. An optional extension of the problem (related to the chapter appendix) also asks you to prepare a variable costing income statement and an absorption costing income statement.

Go to WileyPLUS for complete case details and instructions.

Expand Your Critical Thinking

Decision-Making Across the Organization

CT19.1 E-Z Seats manufactures swivel seats for customized vans. It currently manufactures 10,000 seats per year, which it sells for $500 per seat. It incurs variable costs of $200 per seat and fixed costs of $2,000,000. It is considering automating the upholstery process, which is now largely manual. It estimates that if it does so, its fixed costs will be $3,000,000, and its variable costs will decline to $100 per seat.

Instructions

With the class divided into groups, answer the following questions.

a. Prepare a CVP income statement based on current activity.

b. Compute the contribution margin ratio, break-even point in dollars, margin of safety ratio, and degree of operating leverage based on current activity.

c. Prepare a CVP income statement assuming that the company invests in the automated upholstery system.

d. Compute the contribution margin ratio, break-even point in dollars, margin of safety ratio, and degree of operating leverage assuming the new upholstery system is implemented.

e. Discuss the implications of adopting the new system.

Managerial Analysis

CT19.2 For nearly 20 years, Specialized Coatings has provided painting and galvanizing services for manufacturers in its region. Manufacturers of various metal products have relied on the quality and quick turnaround time provided by Specialized Coatings and its 20 skilled employees. During the last year, as a result of a sharp upturn in the economy, the company's sales have increased by 30% relative to the previous year. The company has not been able to increase its capacity fast enough, so Specialized Coatings has had to turn work away because it cannot keep up with customer requests.

Top management is considering the purchase of a sophisticated robotic painting booth. The booth would represent a considerable move in the direction of automation versus manual labor. If Specialized Coatings purchases the booth, it would most likely lay off 15 of its skilled painters. To analyze the decision, the company compiled production information from the most recent year and then prepared a parallel compilation assuming that the company would purchase the new equipment and lay off the workers. Those data are shown below. As you can see, the company projects that during the last year it would have been far more profitable if it had used the automated approach.

	Current Approach	Automated Approach
Sales	$2,000,000	$2,000,000
Variable costs	1,500,000	1,000,000
Contribution margin	500,000	1,000,000
Fixed costs	380,000	800,000
Net income	$ 120,000	$ 200,000

Instructions

a. Compute and interpret the contribution margin ratio under each approach.

b. Compute the break-even point in sales dollars under each approach. Discuss the implications of your findings.

c. Using the current level of sales, compute the margin of safety ratio under each approach and interpret your findings.

d. Determine the degree of operating leverage for each approach at current sales levels. How much would the company's net income decline under each approach with a 10% decline in sales?

e. At what level of sales would the company's net income be the same under either approach?

f. Discuss the issues that the company must consider in making this decision.

Real-World Focus

CT19.3 In a recent report, the **Del Monte Foods Company** reported three separate operating segments: consumer products (which includes a variety of canned foods including tuna, fruit, and vegetables); pet products (which includes pet food and snacks and veterinary products); and soup and infant-feeding products (which includes soup, broth, and infant feeding and pureed products).

In its annual report, Del Monte uses absorption costing. As a result, information regarding the relative composition of its fixed and variable costs is not available. We have assumed that $860.3 million of its total operating expenses of $1,920.3 million are fixed and have allocated the remaining variable costs across the three divisions. Sales data, along with assumed expense data, are provided below.

	(in millions)	
	Sales	Variable Costs
Consumer products	$1,031.8	$ 610
Pet products	837.3	350
Soup and infant-feeding products	302.0	100
	$2,171.1	$1,060

Instructions

a. Compute each segment's contribution margin ratio and the sales mix.

b. Using the information computed in part (a), compute the company's break-even point in dollars, and then determine the amount of sales that would be generated by each division at the break-even point.

CT19.4 Service The external financial statements published by publicly traded companies are based on absorption cost accounting. As a consequence, it is very difficult to gain an understanding of the relative composition of the companies' fixed and variable costs. It is possible, however, to learn about a company's sales mix and the relative profitability of its various divisions. This exercise looks at the financial statements of **FedEx Corporation**.

Instructions

Go to the FedEx website and select Investor Relations near the bottom of the page. Under "Financial Information," choose "Annual Reports" and then choose "2013 Annual Report" to answer the following questions.

a. Read page 9 of the report under the heading "Description of Business." What are the four primary product lines of the company? What does the company identify as the key factors affecting operating results?

b. Page 21 of the report lists the operating expenses of FedEx Ground. Assuming that rentals, depreciation, and "other" are all fixed costs, prepare a variable costing income statement for 2013, and compute the division's contribution margin ratio and the break-even point in dollars.

c. Page 61, Note 14 ("Business segment information") provides additional information regarding the relative profitability of the business segments.

   (i) Calculate the sales mix for 2011 and 2013. (*Note:* Exclude "other" when you calculate total revenue.)

   (ii) The company does not provide the contribution margin for each division, but it does provide "operating margin" (operating income divided by revenues) on pages 18, 21, and 22 for three divisions. List these for each division for 2011 and 2013.

   (iii) Assuming that the "operating margin" (operating income divided by revenues) moves in parallel with each division's contribution margin, how has the shift in sales mix affected the company's profitability from 2011 to 2013?

Communication Activity

CT19.5 Easton Corporation makes two different boat anchors—a traditional fishing anchor and a high-end yacht anchor—using the same production machinery. The contribution margin of the yacht anchor is three times as high as that of the other product. The company is currently operating at full capacity and has been doing so for nearly two years. Bjorn Borg, the company's CEO, wants to cut back on production of the fishing anchor so that the company can make more yacht anchors. He says that this is a "no-brainer" because the contribution margin of the yacht anchor is so much higher.

Instructions

Write a short memo to Bjorn Borg describing the analysis that the company should do before it makes this decision and any other considerations that would affect the decision.

Ethics Case

*****CT19.6** Brett Stern was hired during January 2022 to manage the home products division of Hi-Tech Products. As part of his employment contract, he was told that he would get $5,000 of additional bonus for every 1% increase that the division's profits exceeded those of the previous year.

Soon after coming on board, Brett met with his plant managers and explained that he wanted the plants to be run at full capacity. Previously, the plant had employed just-in-time inventory practices and had consequently produced units only as they were needed. Brett stated that under previous management the company had missed out on too many sales opportunities because it didn't have enough inventory on hand. Because previous management had employed just-in-time inventory practices, when Brett came on board there was virtually no beginning inventory. The selling price and variable costs per unit remained the same from 2021 to 2022. Additional information is provided below.

	2021	2022
Net income	$ 300,000	$ 525,000
Units produced	25,000	30,000
Units sold	25,000	25,000
Fixed manufacturing overhead costs	$1,350,000	$1,350,000
Fixed manufacturing overhead costs per unit	$ 54	$ 45

Instructions

a. Calculate Brett's bonus based upon the net income shown above.

b. Recompute the 2021 and 2022 results using variable costing.

c. Recompute Brett's 2022 bonus under variable costing.

d. Were Brett's actions unethical? Do you think any actions need to be taken by the company?

All About You

CT19.7 Service Many of you will some day own your own business. One rapidly growing opportunity is no-frills workout centers. Such centers attract customers who want to take advantage of state-of-the-art fitness equipment but do not need the other amenities of full-service health clubs. One way to own your own fitness business is to buy a franchise. **Snap Fitness** is a Minnesota-based business that offers franchise opportunities. For a very low monthly fee ($26, without an annual contract), customers can access a Snap Fitness center 24 hours a day.

The Snap Fitness website indicates that start-up costs range from $60,000 to $184,000. This initial investment covers the following pre-opening costs: franchise fee, grand opening marketing, leasehold improvements, utility/rent deposits, and training.

Instructions

a. Suppose that Snap Fitness estimates that each location incurs $4,000 per month in fixed operating expenses plus $1,460 to lease equipment. A recent newspaper article describing no-frills fitness centers indicated that a Snap Fitness site might require only 300 members to break even. Using the information provided above and your knowledge of CVP analysis, estimate the amount of variable costs. (When performing your analysis, assume that the only fixed costs are the estimated monthly operating expenses and the equipment lease.)

b. Using the information from part (a), what would monthly sales in members and dollars have to be to achieve a target net income of $3,640 for the month?

c. Provide five examples of variable costs for a fitness center.

d. Go to a fitness-business website, such as **Curves**, **Snap Fitness**, or **Anytime Fitness**, and find information about purchasing a franchise. Summarize the franchise information needed to decide whether entering into a franchise agreement would be a good idea.

Considering People, Planet, and Profit

CT19.8 Many politicians, scientists, economists, and businesspeople have become concerned about the potential implications of global warming. The largest source of the emissions thought to contribute to global warming is from coal-fired power plants. The cost of alternative energy has declined, but it is still higher than coal. In 1980, wind-power electricity cost 80 cents per kilowatt hour. Using today's highly efficient turbines with rotor diameters of up to 125 meters, the cost can be as low as 4 cents (about the same as coal), or as much as 20 cents in places with less wind.

Some people have recently suggested that conventional cost comparisons are not adequate because they do not take environmental costs into account. For example, while coal is a very cheap energy source, it is also a significant contributor of greenhouse gases. Should environmental costs be incorporated into decision formulas when planners evaluate new power plants? The basic arguments for and against are as follows.

YES: As long as environmental costs are ignored, renewable energy will appear to be too expensive relative to coal.

NO: If one country decides to incorporate environmental costs into its decision-making process but other countries do not, the country that does so will be at a competitive disadvantage because its products will cost more to produce.

Instructions

Write a response indicating your position regarding this situation. Provide support for your view.

CHAPTER 20

Incremental Analysis

Chapter Preview

An important purpose of management accounting is to provide managers with relevant information for decision-making. Companies of all sorts must make product decisions. **Oral-B Laboratories** opted to produce a new, higher-priced toothbrush. **General Motors** announced the closure of its Oldsmobile Division. **Quaker Oats** decided to sell off a line of beverages, at a price more than $1 billion less than it paid for that product line only a few years before.

This chapter explains management's decision-making process and a decision-making approach called incremental analysis. The use of incremental analysis is demonstrated in a variety of situations.

Feature Story

Keeping It Clean

When you think of new, fast-growing, San Francisco companies, you probably think of fun products like smartphones, social networks, and game apps. You don't tend to think of soap. In fact, given that some of the biggest, most powerful companies in the world dominate the soap market (e.g., **Proctor & Gamble**, **Clorox**, and **Unilever**), starting a new soap company seems like an outrageously bad idea. But that didn't dissuade Adam Lowry and Eric Ryan from giving it a try. The long-time friends and former roommates combined their skills (Adam's chemical engineering and Eric's design and marketing) to start **Method Products**. Their goal: selling environmentally friendly soaps that actually remove dirt.

Within a year of its formation, the company had products on the shelves at **Target** stores. Within 5 years, Method was cited by numerous business publications as one of the fastest-growing companies in the country. It was easy—right? Wrong. Running a company is never easy, and given Method's commitment to sustainability, all of its business decisions are just a little more complex than usual. For example, the company wanted to use solar power to charge the batteries for the forklifts used in its factories. No problem, just put solar panels on the buildings. But because Method outsources its manufacturing, it doesn't actually own factory buildings. In fact, the company that does Method's manufacturing doesn't own the buildings either. Solution—Method parked old semi-trailers next to the factories and installed solar panels on those.

Since Method insists on using natural products and sustainable production practices, its production costs are higher than companies that don't adhere to these standards. Adam and Eric insist, however, that this actually benefits them because they have to be far more careful about controlling costs and far more innovative in solving problems. Consider Method's most recently developed laundry detergent. It is 8 times stronger than normal detergent, so it can be sold in a substantially smaller package. This reduces both its packaging and shipping costs. In fact, when the cost of the raw materials used for soap production recently jumped by as much as 40%, Method actually viewed it as an opportunity to grab market share. It determined that it could offset the cost increases in other places in its supply chain, thus absorbing the cost much easier than its big competitors.

In these and other instances, Adam and Eric identified their alternative courses of action, determined what was relevant to each choice and what wasn't, and then carefully evaluated the incremental costs of each alternative. When you are small and your competitors have some of the biggest marketing budgets in the world, you can't afford to make very many mistakes.

 Watch the *Method Products* video in WileyPLUS to learn more about incremental analysis in the real world.

Chapter Outline

LEARNING OBJECTIVES

LO 1 Describe management's decision-making process and incremental analysis.	• Incremental analysis approach • How incremental analysis works • Qualitative factors • Incremental analysis and ABC • Types of incremental analysis	**DO IT! 1** Incremental Analysis
LO 2 Analyze the relevant costs in accepting an order at a special price.	• Special price • Available capacity	**DO IT! 2** Special Orders
LO 3 Analyze the relevant costs in a make-or-buy decision.	• Make-or-buy • Opportunity cost	**DO IT! 3** Make or Buy
LO 4 Analyze the relevant costs and revenues in determining whether to sell or process materials further.	• Single-product case • Multiple-product case	**DO IT! 4** Sell or Process Further
LO 5 Analyze the relevant costs to be considered in repairing, retaining, or replacing equipment.	• Repair, retain, or replace equipment • Sunk costs	**DO IT! 5** Repair or Replace Equipment
LO 6 Analyze the relevant costs in deciding whether to eliminate an unprofitable segment or product.	• Unprofitable segments • Avoidable fixed costs • Effect of contribution margin	**DO IT! 6** Unprofitable Segments

Go to the Review and Practice section at the end of the chapter for a targeted summary and practice applications with solutions.
Visit WileyPLUS for additional tutorials and practice opportunities.

Decision-Making and Incremental Analysis

LEARNING OBJECTIVE 1
Describe management's decision-making process and incremental analysis.

Making decisions is an important management function. Management's decision-making process does not always follow a set pattern because decisions vary significantly in their scope, urgency, and importance. It is possible, though, to identify some steps that are frequently involved in the process. These steps are shown in **Illustration 20.1**.

ILLUSTRATION 20.1 Management's decision-making process

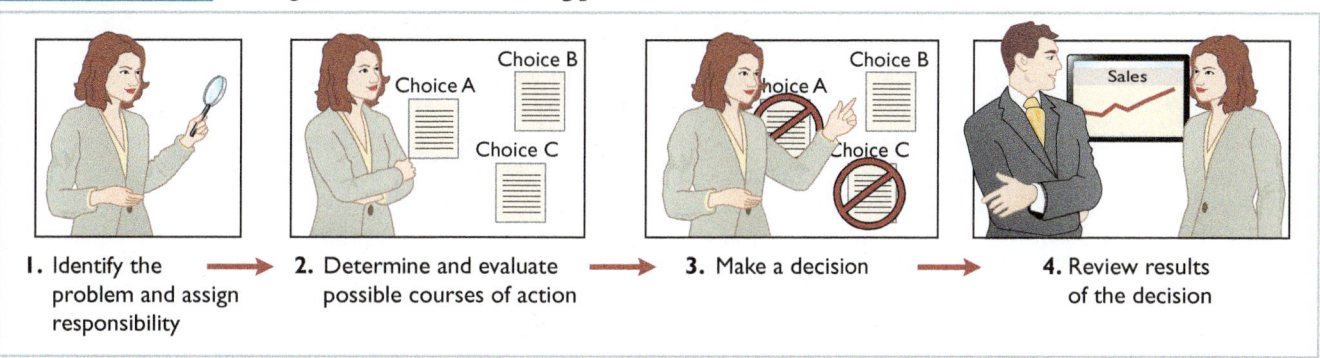

1. Identify the problem and assign responsibility
2. Determine and evaluate possible courses of action
3. Make a decision
4. Review results of the decision

Accounting's contribution to the decision-making process occurs primarily in Steps 2 and 4—evaluating possible courses of action and reviewing results. In Step 2, for each possible course of action, relevant revenue and cost data are provided. These show the expected overall effect on net income. In Step 4, internal reports are prepared that review the actual impact of the decision.

In making business decisions, management ordinarily considers both financial and nonfinancial information. **Financial** information is related to revenues and costs and their effect on the company's overall profitability. **Nonfinancial** information relates to such factors as the effect of the decision on employee turnover, the environment, or the overall image of the company in the community. (These are considerations that we touched on in our Chapter 14 discussion of corporate social responsibility.) Although nonfinancial information can be as important as financial information, we will focus primarily on financial information that is relevant to the decision.

Incremental Analysis Approach

Decisions involve a choice among alternative courses of action. Suppose you face the personal financial decision of whether to purchase or lease a car. The financial data relate to the cost of leasing versus the cost of purchasing. For example, leasing involves periodic lease payments; purchasing requires "up-front" payment of the purchase price. In other words, the financial information relevant to the decision is the data that vary in the future among the possible alternatives. The process used to identify the financial data that change under alternative courses of action is called incremental analysis (see **Alternative Terminology**). In some cases, you will find that when you use incremental analysis, both costs **and** revenues vary. In other cases, only costs **or** revenues vary.

Just as your decision to buy or lease a car affects your future financial situation, similar decisions, on a larger scale, affect a company's future. Incremental analysis identifies the probable effects of those decisions on future earnings. Such analysis inevitably involves estimates and uncertainty. Gathering data for incremental analyses may involve market analysts, engineers, and accountants. In quantifying the data, the accountant must produce the most reliable information available.

ALTERNATIVE TERMINOLOGY

Incremental analysis is also called *differential analysis* because the analysis focuses on differences.

How Incremental Analysis Works

The basic approach in incremental analysis is shown in **Illustration 20.2**.

ILLUSTRATION 20.2 Basic approach in incremental analysis

	Alternative A	Alternative B	Net Income Increase (Decrease)
Revenues	$125,000	$110,000	$ (15,000)
Costs	100,000	80,000	20,000
Net income	$ 25,000	$ 30,000	$ 5,000

> **Decision Tools**
> Incremental analysis helps managers choose the alternative that maximizes net income.

This example compares Alternative B with Alternative A. The net income column shows the differences between the alternatives. In this case, incremental revenue will be $15,000 less under Alternative B than under Alternative A. But a $20,000 incremental cost savings will be realized.[1] Thus, Alternative B will produce $5,000 more net income than Alternative A (see **Decision Tools**).

In the following pages, you will encounter three important cost concepts used in incremental analysis, as defined and discussed in **Illustration 20.3**.

ILLUSTRATION 20.3 Key cost concepts in incremental analysis

- **Relevant cost and revenues**   In incremental analysis, the only factors to be considered are those costs and revenues that differ across alternatives. Those factors are called **relevant costs and revenues**. Costs and revenues that do not differ across alternatives can be ignored when trying to choose between alternatives.

- **Opportunity cost**   Often in choosing one course of action, the company must give up the opportunity to benefit from some other course of action. For example, if a machine is used to make one type of product, the benefit of making another type of product with that machine is lost. This lost potential benefit is referred to as **opportunity cost**.

- **Sunk cost**   Costs that have already been incurred and will not be changed or avoided by any present or future decisions are referred to as **sunk costs**. For example, the amount you spent in the past to purchase or repair a laptop should have no bearing on your decision whether to buy a new laptop. **Sunk costs are not relevant costs.**

---

[1] Although income taxes are sometimes important in incremental analysis, they are ignored in the chapter for simplicity's sake.

Incremental analysis sometimes involves changes that at first glance might seem contrary to your intuition. For example, sometimes variable costs **do not change** under the alternative courses of action. Also, sometimes fixed costs **do change**. For example, direct labor, normally a variable cost, is not a relevant cost in deciding between the acquisition of two new factory machines if each asset requires the same amount of direct labor. In contrast, rent expense, normally a fixed cost, is a relevant cost in a decision whether to continue occupancy of a building or to purchase or lease a new building.

It is also important to understand that **the approaches to incremental analysis discussed in this chapter do not take into consideration the time value of money**. That is, amounts to be paid or received in future years are not discounted for the cost of interest in this chapter. Time value of money is addressed in Chapter 25 and Appendix G.

Service Company Insight — American Express

That Letter from AmEx Might Not Be a Bill

Tina Spruce/iStockphoto

No doubt every one of you has received an invitation from a credit card company to open a new account—some of you have probably received three in one day. But how many of you have received an offer of $300 to close out your credit card account? **American Express** decided to offer some of its customers $300 if they would give back their credit card. You could receive the $300 even if you hadn't paid off your balance yet, as long as you agreed to give up your credit card. Apparently, these customers cost more than they are worth.

Source: Aparajita Saha-Bubna and Lauren Pollock, "AmEx Offers Some Holders $300 to Pay and Leave," *Wall Street Journal Online* (February 23, 2009).

What are the relevant costs that American Express would need to know in order to determine to whom to make this offer? (Go to WileyPLUS for this answer and additional questions.)

Qualitative Factors

In this chapter, we focus primarily on the quantitative factors that affect a decision—those attributes that can be easily expressed in terms of numbers or dollars. However, many of the decisions involving incremental analysis have important qualitative features. Though not easily measured, they should not be ignored.

Consider, for example, the potential effects of the make-or-buy decision or of the decision to eliminate a line of business on existing employees and the community in which the plant is located. The cost savings that may be obtained from outsourcing or from eliminating a plant should be weighed against these qualitative attributes. One example would be the cost of lost morale that might result. Al "Chainsaw" Dunlap was a so-called "turnaround" artist who went into many companies, identified inefficiencies (using incremental analysis techniques), and tried to correct these problems to improve corporate profitability. Along the way, he laid off thousands of employees at numerous companies. As head of **Sunbeam**, it was Al Dunlap who lost his job because his Draconian approach failed to improve Sunbeam's profitability. It was reported that Sunbeam's employees openly rejoiced for days after his departure. Clearly, qualitative factors can matter.

Relationship of Incremental Analysis and Activity-Based Costing

In Chapter 17, we noted that many companies have shifted to activity-based costing to allocate overhead costs to products. The primary reason for using activity-based costing is that it results in a more accurate allocation of overhead. The concepts presented in this chapter are completely consistent with the use of activity-based costing. In fact, activity-based costing results in better identification of relevant costs and, therefore, better incremental analysis.

Types of Incremental Analysis

A number of different types of decisions involve incremental analysis. The more common types of decisions are whether to:

1. Accept an order at a special price.
2. Make or buy component parts or finished products.
3. Sell products or process them further.
4. Repair, retain, or replace equipment.
5. Eliminate an unprofitable business segment or product.

We consider each of these types of decisions in the following pages.

ACTION PLAN
- Past costs that cannot be changed as a result of any present or future action are sunk costs.
- Benefits lost by choosing one option over another are opportunity costs.

DO IT! 1 | Incremental Analysis

Owen T Corporation is comparing two different options. The company currently operates under Option 1, with revenues of $80,000 per year, maintenance expenses of $5,000 per year, and operating expenses of $38,000 per year. Option 2 provides revenues of $80,000 per year, maintenance expenses of $12,000 per year, and operating expenses of $32,000 per year. Option 1 employs a piece of equipment that was upgraded 2 years ago at a cost of $22,000. If Option 2 is chosen, it will free up resources that will increase revenues by $3,000.

Complete the following table to show the change in income from choosing Option 2 versus Option 1. Designate any sunk costs with an "S."

	Option 1	Option 2	Net Income Increase (Decrease)	Sunk (S)
Revenues				
Maintenance expenses				
Operating expenses				
Equipment upgrade				
Opportunity cost				

Solution

	Option 1	Option 2	Net Income Increase (Decrease)	Sunk (S)
Revenues	$80,000	$80,000	$ 0	
Maintenance expenses	5,000	12,000	(7,000)	
Operating expenses	38,000	32,000	6,000	
Equipment upgrade	22,000	0	0	S
Opportunity cost	3,000	0	3,000	
			$ 2,000	

Related exercise material: **BE20.1, BE20.2, DO IT! 20.1, E20.1,** and **E20.18.**

Special Orders

LEARNING OBJECTIVE 2
Analyze the relevant costs in accepting an order at a special price.

Sometimes a company has an opportunity to obtain additional business if it is willing to make a price concession to a specific customer. To illustrate, assume that Sunbelt Company produces 100,000 Smoothie blenders per month, which is 80% of plant capacity. Variable manufacturing costs are $8 per unit. Fixed manufacturing costs are $400,000, or $4 per unit. The Smoothie blenders are normally sold directly to retailers at $20 each. Sunbelt has an offer from Kensington Co. (a foreign wholesaler) to purchase an additional 2,000 blenders at $11 per unit. Acceptance of the offer would not affect normal sales of the product, and the additional units can be manufactured without increasing plant capacity. What should management do?

If management makes its decision on the basis of the total cost per unit of $12 ($8 variable + $4 fixed), the order would be rejected because costs per unit ($12) exceed revenues per unit ($11) by $1 per unit. However, since the units can be produced within existing plant capacity, the special order **will not increase fixed costs**. Let's identify the relevant data for the decision. First, the variable manufacturing costs increase $16,000 ($8 × 2,000). Second, the expected revenue increases $22,000 ($11 × 2,000). Thus, as shown in **Illustration 20.4**, Sunbelt increases its net income by $6,000 by accepting this special order (see **Helpful Hint**).

> **HELPFUL HINT**
> This is a good example of different costs for different purposes. In the long run all costs are relevant, but for this decision only costs that change are relevant.

ILLUSTRATION 20.4 Incremental analysis—accepting an order at a special price

	Reject Order	Accept Order	Net Income Increase (Decrease)
Revenues	$0	$22,000	$ 22,000
Costs	0	16,000	(16,000)
Net income	$0	$ 6,000	$ 6,000

Two points should be emphasized. First, we assume that sales of the product in other markets **would not be affected by this special order**. If other sales were affected, then Sunbelt would have to consider the change in profit due to lost sales in making the decision. Second, if Sunbelt is operating **at full capacity**, it is likely that the special order would be rejected. Under such circumstances, the company would have to expand plant capacity. In that case, the special order would have to absorb these additional fixed manufacturing costs, as well as the variable manufacturing costs.

DO IT! 2 | Special Orders

Cobb Company incurs costs of $28 per unit ($18 variable and $10 fixed) to make a product that normally sells for $42. A foreign wholesaler offers to buy 5,000 units at $25 each. The special order results in additional shipping costs of $1 per unit. Compute the increase or decrease in net income Cobb realizes by accepting the special order, assuming Cobb has excess operating capacity. Should Cobb Company accept the special order?

ACTION PLAN
- Identify all revenues that would change as a result of accepting the order.
- Identify all costs that would change as a result of accepting the order, and net this amount against the change in revenues.

Solution

	Reject	Accept	Net Income Increase (Decrease)
Revenues	$–0–	$125,000*	$125,000
Costs	–0–	95,000**	(95,000)
Net income	$–0–	$ 30,000	$ 30,000

*5,000 × $25
**(5,000 × $18) + (5,000 × $1)

The analysis indicates net income increases by $30,000; therefore, Cobb Company should accept the special order.

Related exercise material: **BE20.3, DO IT! 20.2, E20.2, E20.3, and E20.4**.

Make or Buy

> **LEARNING OBJECTIVE 3**
> Analyze the relevant costs in a make-or-buy decision.

When a manufacturer assembles component parts in producing a finished product, management must decide whether to make or buy the components. The decision to buy parts or services is often referred to as outsourcing. For example, as discussed in the Feature Story, a company such as **Method Products** may either make or buy the soaps used in its products. Similarly, **Hewlett-Packard Corporation** may make or buy the electronic circuitry, cases, and printer heads for its printers. **Boeing** recently sold some of its commercial aircraft factories in an effort to cut production costs and focus on engineering and final assembly rather than manufacturing. The decision to make or buy components should be made on the basis of incremental analysis.

Baron Company makes motorcycles and scooters. **Illustration 20.5** shows the annual costs it incurs in producing 25,000 ignition switches for scooters.

ILLUSTRATION 20.5
Annual product cost data

Direct materials	$ 50,000
Direct labor	75,000
Variable manufacturing overhead	40,000
Fixed manufacturing overhead	60,000
Total manufacturing costs	$225,000
Total cost per unit ($225,000 ÷ 25,000)	$9.00

Instead of making its own switches, Baron Company might purchase the ignition switches from Ignition, Inc. at a price of $8 per unit. What should management do?

At first glance, it appears that management should purchase the ignition switches for $8 rather than make them at a cost of $9. However, a review of operations indicates that if the ignition switches are purchased from Ignition, Inc., *all* of Baron's variable costs but only $10,000 of its fixed manufacturing costs will be eliminated (avoided). Thus, $50,000 of the fixed manufacturing costs remain if the ignition switches are purchased. The relevant costs for incremental analysis, therefore, are as shown in **Illustration 20.6**.

ILLUSTRATION 20.6 Incremental analysis—make or buy

	Make	Buy	Net Income Increase (Decrease)
Direct materials	$ 50,000	$ 0	$ 50,000
Direct labor	75,000	0	75,000
Variable manufacturing costs	40,000	0	40,000
Fixed manufacturing costs	60,000	50,000	10,000
Purchase price (25,000 × $8)	0	200,000	(200,000)
Total annual cost	$225,000	$250,000	$ (25,000)

This analysis indicates that Baron Company incurs $25,000 of additional costs by buying the ignition switches rather than making them. Therefore, Baron should continue to make the ignition switches even though the total manufacturing cost is $1 higher per unit than the purchase price. The primary cause of this result is that, even if the company purchases the ignition switches, it will still have fixed costs of $50,000 to absorb.

Opportunity Cost

The foregoing make-or-buy analysis is complete only if it is assumed that the productive capacity used to make the ignition switches cannot be converted to another purpose. If there is an opportunity to use this productive capacity in some other manner, then this opportunity cost must be considered. As indicated earlier, **opportunity cost** is the lost potential benefit that could have been obtained by following an alternative course of action (see **Ethics Note**).

To illustrate, assume that through buying the switches, Baron Company can use the released productive capacity to generate additional income of $38,000 from producing a different product. This lost income is an additional cost of continuing to make the switches in the make-or-buy decision. This opportunity cost is therefore added to the "Make" column for comparison. As shown in **Illustration 20.7**, it is now advantageous to buy the ignition switches because the company's income would increase by $13,000.

> **ETHICS NOTE**
>
> In the make-or-buy decision, it is important for management to take into account the social impact of its choice. For instance, buying may be the most economically feasible solution, but such action could result in the closure of a manufacturing plant and laying off many good workers.

ILLUSTRATION 20.7 Incremental analysis—make or buy, with opportunity cost

	Make	Buy	Net Income Increase (Decrease)
Total annual cost	$225,000	$250,000	$(25,000)
Opportunity cost	38,000	0	38,000
Total cost	$263,000	$250,000	$ 13,000

The qualitative factors in this decision include the possible loss of jobs for employees who produce the ignition switches. In addition, management must assess the supplier's ability to satisfy the company's quality control standards at the quoted price per unit on a timely basis.

Service Company Insight   Amazon.com

iStockphoto

Giving Away the Store?

In an earlier chapter, we discussed **Amazon.com**'s incredible growth. However, some analysts have questioned whether some of the methods that Amazon uses to increase its sales make good business sense. For example, a few years ago, Amazon initiated a "Prime" free-shipping subscription program. For a $99 fee per year, Amazon's customers get free shipping on as many goods as they want to buy. At the time, CEO Jeff Bezos promised that the program would be costly in the short-term but benefit the company in the long-term. Six years later, it was true that Amazon's sales had grown considerably. It was also estimated that its Prime customers buy two to three times as much as non-Prime customers. But, its shipping costs rose from 2.8% of sales to 4% of sales, which is remarkably similar to the drop in its gross margin from 24% to 22.3%. Amazon's order fulfillment center uses 30,000 robots and more than 100 million square feet of space. It generates significant fees from merchants that sell on its site and rely on its fulfillment services.

Sources: Martin Peers, "Amazon's Prime Numbers," *Wall Street Journal Online* (February 3, 2011); and Evan Niu, "Ever Wonder How Amazon.com Pays for All of That Free Shipping?" *The Motley Fool* (October 26, 2015).

What are the relevant revenues and costs that Amazon should consider relative to the decision whether to offer the Prime free-shipping subscription? (Go to WileyPLUS for this answer and additional questions.)

ACTION PLAN

- Look for the costs that change.
- Ignore the costs that do not change.
- Use the format in the chapter for your answer.
- Recognize that opportunity cost can make a difference.

DO IT! 3 | Make or Buy

Juanita Company must decide whether to make or buy some of its components for the appliances it produces. The costs of producing 166,000 electrical cords for its appliances are as follows.

Direct materials	$90,000	Variable overhead	$32,000
Direct labor	$20,000	Fixed overhead	$24,000

Instead of making the electrical cords at an average cost per unit of $1.00 ($166,000 ÷ 166,000), the company has an opportunity to buy the cords at $0.90 per unit. If the company purchases the cords, all variable costs and one-fourth of the fixed costs are eliminated.

a. Prepare an incremental analysis showing whether the company should make or buy the electrical cords.

b. Will your answer be different if the released productive capacity of the production facility will generate additional income of $5,000?

Solution

a.

	Make	Buy	Net Income Increase (Decrease)
Direct materials	$ 90,000	$ -0-	$ 90,000
Direct labor	20,000	-0-	20,000
Variable manufacturing costs	32,000	-0-	32,000
Fixed manufacturing costs	24,000	18,000*	6,000
Purchase price	-0-	149,400**	(149,400)
Total cost	$166,000	$167,400	$ (1,400)

*$24,000 × .75
**166,000 × $0.90

This analysis indicates that Juanita Company will incur $1,400 of additional costs if it buys the electrical cords rather than making them.

b.

	Make	Buy	Net Income Increase (Decrease)
Total cost	$166,000	$167,400	$(1,400)
Opportunity cost	5,000	-0-	5,000
Total cost	$171,000	$167,400	$ 3,600

Yes, the answer is different. The analysis shows that net income increases by $3,600 if Juanita Company purchases the electrical cords rather than making them.

Related exercise material: **BE20.4, DO IT! 20.3, E20.5, E20.6, E20.7, and E20.8.**

Sell or Process Further

LEARNING OBJECTIVE 4
Analyze the relevant costs and revenues in determining whether to sell or process materials further.

Many manufacturers have the option of selling products at a given point in the production cycle or continuing to process with the expectation of selling them at a later point at a higher price. For example, a bicycle manufacturer such as **Trek** could sell its bicycles to retailers either unassembled or assembled. A furniture manufacturer such as **IKEA** could sell its furniture to stores either unfinished or finished. The sell-or-process-further decision should be made on the basis of incremental analysis. The basic decision rule is: **Process further as long as the incremental revenue from such processing exceeds the incremental processing costs.**

Single-Product Case

Assume, for example, that Woodmasters Inc. makes tables. It sells unfinished tables for $50. The cost to manufacture an unfinished table is $35, computed as shown in **Illustration 20.8**.

Direct materials	$15
Direct labor	10
Variable manufacturing overhead	6
Fixed manufacturing overhead	4
Manufacturing cost per unit	**$35**

ILLUSTRATION 20.8
Per unit cost of unfinished table

Woodmasters currently has unused productive capacity that is expected to continue indefinitely. Some of this capacity could be used to finish the tables and sell them at $60 per unit. For a finished table, direct materials will increase $2 and direct labor costs will increase $4. Variable manufacturing overhead costs will increase by $2.40 (60% of direct labor). No increase is anticipated in fixed manufacturing overhead.

Should the company sell the unfinished tables, or should it process them further (see **Helpful Hint**)? **Illustration 20.9** shows the incremental analysis on a per unit basis.

HELPFUL HINT
Current net income is known. Net income from processing further is an estimate. In making its decision, management could add a "risk" factor for the estimate.

ILLUSTRATION 20.9 Incremental analysis—sell or process further

	Sell Unfinished	Process Further	Net Income Increase (Decrease)
Sales price per unit	$50.00	$60.00	$10.00
Cost per unit			
Direct materials	15.00	17.00	(2.00)
Direct labor	10.00	14.00	(4.00)
Variable manufacturing overhead	6.00	8.40	(2.40)
Fixed manufacturing overhead	4.00	4.00	0.00
Total	35.00	43.40	(8.40)
Net income per unit	$15.00	$16.60	$ 1.60

It would be advantageous for Woodmasters to process the tables further. The incremental revenue of $10.00 from the additional processing is $1.60 higher than the incremental processing costs of $8.40.

Multiple-Product Case

Sell-or-process-further decisions are particularly applicable to processes that produce multiple products simultaneously. In many industries, a number of end-products are produced from a single raw material and a common production process. These multiple end-products are commonly referred to as **joint products**. For example, in the meat-packing industry, **Armour** processes a cow or pig into meat, internal organs, hides, bones, and fat products. In the petroleum industry, **ExxonMobil** refines crude oil to produce gasoline, lubricating oil, kerosene, paraffin, and ethylene.

Illustration 20.10 presents a joint product situation for Marais Creamery involving a decision **to sell or process further** cream and skim milk. Cream and skim milk are joint products that result from the processing of raw milk.

ILLUSTRATION 20.10 Joint production process—Creamery

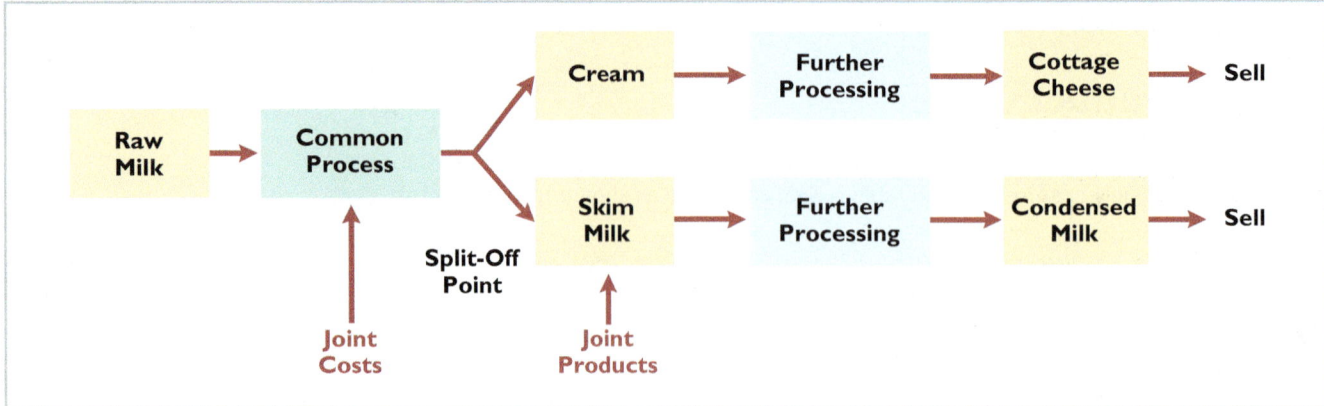

Marais incurs many costs prior to the manufacture of the cream and skim milk. All costs incurred prior to the point at which the two products are separately identifiable (the **split-off point**) are called **joint costs**. For purposes of determining the cost of each product, joint product costs must be allocated to the individual products. This is frequently done based on the relative sales value of the joint products. While this allocation is important for determination of product cost, **it is irrelevant for any sell-or-process-further decisions**. The reason is that these **joint product costs are sunk costs**. That is, they have already been incurred, and they cannot be changed or avoided by any subsequent decision.

Illustration 20.11 provides the daily cost and revenue data for Marais Creamery related to cream and cottage cheese.

ILLUSTRATION 20.11

Cost and revenue data per day for cream

Costs (per day)	
Joint cost allocated to cream	$ 9,000
Cost to process cream into cottage cheese	10,000

Revenues from Products (per day)	
Cream	$19,000
Cottage cheese	27,000

From this information, we can determine whether the company should simply sell the cream or process it further into cottage cheese. **Illustration 20.12** shows the necessary analysis. Note that the joint cost that is allocated to the cream is not included in this decision. It is not relevant to the decision because it is a sunk cost. It has been incurred in the past and will remain the same no matter whether the cream is subsequently processed into cottage cheese or not.

ILLUSTRATION 20.12 Analysis of whether to sell cream or process into cottage cheese

Incremental Analysis - Sell or process further - Cream or cottage cheese

A	B	C	D
	Sell	Process Further	Net Income Increase (Decrease)
Sales per day	$19,000	$27,000	$ 8,000
Cost per day to process cream into cottage cheese	0	10,000	(10,000)
Net income per day	$19,000	$17,000	$ (2,000)

From this analysis, we can see that Marais should not process the cream further because it will sustain an incremental loss of $2,000.

Illustration 20.13 provides the daily cost and revenue data for the company related to skim milk and condensed milk.

Costs (per day)	
Joint cost allocated to skim milk	$ 5,000
Cost to process skim milk into condensed milk	8,000
Revenues from Products (per day)	
Skim milk	$11,000
Condensed milk	26,000

ILLUSTRATION 20.13
Cost and revenue data per day for skim milk

Illustration 20.14 shows that Marais Company should process the skim milk into condensed milk, as it will increase net income by $7,000.

ILLUSTRATION 20.14 Analysis of whether to sell skim milk or process into condensed milk

Incremental Analysis - Sell or process further - Skim milk or condensed milk

	A	B	C	D
1		Sell	Process Further	Net Income Increase (Decrease)
2	Sales per day	$11,000	$26,000	$15,000
3	Cost per day to process skim milk into condensed milk	0	8,000	(8,000)
4	Net income per day	$11,000	$18,000	$ 7,000
5				

Again, note that the $5,000 of joint cost allocated to the skim milk is irrelevant in deciding whether to sell or process further. Why? The joint cost remains the same, whether or not further processing is performed.

These decisions need to be reevaluated as market conditions change. For example, if the price of skim milk increases relative to the price of condensed milk, it may become more profitable to sell the skim milk rather than process it into condensed milk. Consider also oil refineries. As market conditions change, the companies must constantly re-assess which products to produce from the oil they receive at their plants.

DO IT! 4 | Sell or Process Further

Easy Does It manufactures unpainted furniture for the do-it-yourself (DIY) market. It currently sells a child's rocking chair for $25. Production costs per unit are $12 variable and $8 fixed. Easy Does It is considering painting the rocking chair and selling it for $35. Variable costs to paint each chair are expected to be $9, and fixed costs are expected to be $2.

Prepare an analysis showing whether Easy Does It should sell unpainted or painted chairs.

Solution

	Sell	Process Further	Net Income Increase (Decrease)
Revenues	$25	$35	$10
Variable costs	12	21[a]	(9)
Fixed costs	8	10[b]	(2)
Net income	$ 5	$ 4	$(1)

[a]$12 + $9 [b]$8 + $2

The analysis indicates that the rocking chair should be sold unpainted because net income per chair will be $1 greater.

Related exercise material: **BE20.5, BE20.6, DO IT! 20.4, E20.9, E20.10, E20.11,** and **E20.12.**

ACTION PLAN
- Identify the revenues that change as a result of painting the rocking chair.
- Identify all costs that change as a result of painting the rocking chair, and net the amount against the revenues.

Repair, Retain, or Replace Equipment

LEARNING OBJECTIVE 5
Analyze the relevant costs to be considered in repairing, retaining, or replacing equipment.

Management often has to decide whether to continue using an asset, repair, or replace it. For example, **Delta Airlines** must decide whether to replace old jets with new, more fuel-efficient ones. To illustrate, assume that Jeffcoat Company has a factory machine that originally cost $110,000. It has a balance in Accumulated Depreciation of $70,000, so the machine's book value is $40,000. It has a remaining useful life of four years. The company is considering replacing this machine with a new machine. A new machine is available that costs $120,000. It is expected to have zero salvage value at the end of its four-year useful life. If the new machine is acquired, variable manufacturing costs are expected to decrease from $160,000 to $125,000 annually, and the old unit could be sold for $5,000. **Illustration 20.15** shows the incremental analysis for the **four-year period**.

ILLUSTRATION 20.15 Incremental analysis—retain or replace equipment

	Retain Equipment		Replace Equipment		Net Income Increase (Decrease)
Variable manufacturing costs	$640,000	a	$500,000	b	$140,000
New machine cost			120,000		(120,000)
Sale of old machine			(5,000)		5,000
Total	$640,000		$615,000		$ 25,000

a(4 years × $160,000)
b(4 years × $125,000)

In this case, it would be to the company's advantage to replace the equipment. The lower variable manufacturing costs due to replacement more than offset the cost of the new equipment. Note that the $5,000 received from the sale of the old machine is relevant to the decision because it will only be received if the company chooses to replace its equipment. In general, any trade-in allowance or cash disposal value of existing assets is relevant to the decision to retain or replace equipment.

One other point should be mentioned regarding Jeffcoat's decision: **The book value of the old machine does not affect the decision.** Book value is a **sunk cost**, which is a cost that cannot be changed by any present or future decision. **Sunk costs are not relevant in incremental analysis.** In this example, if the asset is retained, book value will be depreciated over its remaining useful life. Or, if the new unit is acquired, book value will be recognized as a loss of the current period. Thus, the effect of book value on cumulative future earnings is the same regardless of the replacement decision.

Sometimes, decisions regarding whether to replace equipment are clouded by behavioral decision-making errors. For example, suppose a manager spent $90,000 repairing a machine two months ago. Suppose that the machine now breaks down again. The manager might be inclined to think that because the company recently spent a large amount of money to repair the machine, the machine should be repaired again rather than replaced. However, the amount spent in the past to repair the machine is irrelevant to the current decision. It is a sunk cost.

Similarly, suppose a manager spent $5,000,000 to purchase a machine. Six months later, a new machine comes on the market that is significantly more efficient than the one recently purchased. The manager might be inclined to think that he or she should not buy the new machine because of the recent purchase. In fact, the manager might fear that buying a different machine so quickly might call into question the merit of the previous decision. Again, the fact that the company recently bought a machine is not relevant. Instead, the manager should use incremental analysis to determine whether the savings generated by the efficiencies of the new machine would justify its purchase.

DO IT! 5 | Repair or Replace Equipment

Rochester Roofing is faced with a decision. The company relies very heavily on the use of its 60-foot extension lift for work on large homes and commercial properties. Last year, the company spent $60,000 refurbishing the lift. It has just determined that another $40,000 of repair work is required. Alternatively, Rochester Roofing has found a newer used lift that is for sale for $170,000. The company estimates that both the old and new lifts would have useful lives of 6 years. However, the new lift is more efficient and thus would reduce operating expenses by about $20,000 per year. The company could also rent out the new lift for about $2,000 per year. The old lift is not suitable for rental. The old lift could currently be sold for $25,000 if the new lift is purchased. Prepare an incremental analysis that shows whether the company should repair or replace the equipment.

ACTION PLAN
- Those costs and revenues that differ across the alternatives are relevant to the decision.
- Past costs that cannot be changed are sunk costs.

Solution

	Retain Equipment	Replace Equipment	Net Income Increase (Decrease)
Operating expenses	$120,000*		$120,000
Repair costs	40,000		40,000
Rental revenue		$(12,000)**	12,000
New machine cost		170,000	(170,000)
Sale of old machine		(25,000)	25,000
Total cost	$160,000	$133,000	$ 27,000

*(6 years × $20,000)
**(6 years × $2,000)

The analysis indicates that purchasing the new machine would increase net income for the 6-year period by $27,000.

Related exercise material: **BE20.7, DO IT! 20.5, E20.13, and E20.14**.

Eliminate Unprofitable Segment or Product

LEARNING OBJECTIVE 6

Analyze the relevant costs in deciding whether to eliminate an unprofitable segment or product.

Management sometimes must decide whether to eliminate an unprofitable business segment or product. For example, in recent years, many airlines quit servicing certain cities or cut back on the number of flights. **Goodyear** quit producing several brands in the low-end tire market. Again, the key is to **focus on the relevant costs—the data that change under the alternative courses of action** (see **Helpful Hint**). To illustrate, assume that Venus Company manufactures tennis racquets in three models: Pro, Master, and Champ. Pro and Master are profitable lines. Champ (highlighted in red in the table below) operates at a loss. Condensed income statement data are as shown in **Illustration 20.16**.

You might think that total net income will increase by $20,000 to $240,000 if the unprofitable Champ line of racquets is eliminated. However, **net income may actually decrease if the Champ line is discontinued**. The reason is that the company's total fixed costs will be the same whether or not the Champ line is discontinued. That is, the fixed costs allocated to the Champ racquets cannot be eliminated, so they will have to be absorbed by the other products.

HELPFUL HINT
A decision to discontinue a segment based solely on the bottom line—net loss—is inappropriate.

ILLUSTRATION 20.16

Segment income data

	Pro	Master	Champ	Total
Sales	$800,000	$300,000	$100,000	$1,200,000
Variable costs	520,000	210,000	90,000	820,000
Contribution margin	280,000	90,000	10,000	380,000
Fixed costs	80,000	50,000	30,000	160,000
Net income	$200,000	$ 40,000	$(20,000)	$ 220,000

To illustrate, assume that the $30,000 of fixed costs applicable to the unprofitable segment are instead allocated ⅔ to the Pro model and ⅓ to the Master model if the Champ model is eliminated. Fixed costs will increase to $100,000 ($80,000 + $20,000) in the Pro line and to $60,000 ($50,000 + $10,000) in the Master line. **Illustration 20.17** shows the revised income statement.

ILLUSTRATION 20.17

Income data after eliminating unprofitable product line

	Pro	Master	Total
Sales	$800,000	$300,000	$1,100,000
Variable costs	520,000	210,000	730,000
Contribution margin	280,000	90,000	370,000
Fixed costs	100,000	60,000	160,000
Net income	$180,000	$ 30,000	$ 210,000

Total net income would decrease $10,000 ($220,000 − $210,000). This result is also obtained in the incremental analysis of the Champ racquets shown in **Illustration 20.18**.

ILLUSTRATION 20.18 Incremental analysis—eliminating unprofitable segment with no reduction in fixed costs

Incremental Analysis - Eliminating an unprofitable segment

	A	B	C	D
1		Continue	Eliminate	Net Income Increase (Decrease)
2	Sales	$100,000	$ 0	$(100,000)
3	Variable costs	90,000	0	90,000
4	Contribution margin	10,000	0	(10,000)
5	Fixed costs	30,000	30,000	0
6	Net income	$ (20,000)	$(30,000)	$ (10,000)

The loss in net income is attributable to the Champ line's $10,000 contribution margin ($220,000 − $210,000) that will not be realized if the segment is discontinued.

Assume the same facts as above, except now assume that $22,000 of the fixed costs attributed to the Champ line can be eliminated if the line is discontinued. **Illustration 20.19** presents the incremental analysis based on this revised assumption.

ILLUSTRATION 20.19 Incremental analysis—eliminating unprofitable segment with reduction in fixed costs

Incremental Analysis - Eliminating an unprofitable segment

	A	B	C	D
1		Continue	Eliminate	Net Income Increase (Decrease)
2	Sales	$100,000	$ 0	$(100,000)
3	Variable costs	90,000	0	90,000
4	Contribution margin	10,000	0	(10,000)
5	Fixed costs	30,000	8,000	22,000
6	Net income	$ (20,000)	$(8,000)	$ 12,000

In this case, because the company is able to eliminate some of its fixed costs by eliminating the division, it can increase its net income by $12,000. **This occurs because the $22,000 savings that results from the eliminated fixed costs exceeds the $10,000 in lost contribution margin by $12,000 ($22,000 − $10,000).**

In deciding on the future status of an unprofitable segment, management should consider the effect of elimination on related product lines. It may be possible for continuing product lines to obtain some or all of the sales lost by the discontinued product line. In some businesses, services or products may be linked—for example, free checking accounts at a bank, or coffee at a donut shop. In addition, management should consider the effect of eliminating the product line on employees who may have to be discharged or retrained.

Management Insight

Nerthuz / Getty Images

Batteries Are Included!

Top managers at every major car manufacturer face a massive "make or buy" decision. For example, consider the production of electric cars. By far, the most expensive component in an electric car is the battery, which costs about $7,500. The battery is critical to vehicle performance since it determines both the power and range of the vehicle. **Mercedes** and **Volkswagen** plan to make their own batteries, but **General Motors**, **BMW**, and **Renault** have decided to buy their batteries from suppliers such as Panasonic and Samsung.

It is not an easy decision. Battery production requires huge investments in plant assets and research and development. **Nissan** learned the hard way that making your own batteries can be a risky venture. It made a big investment in battery production for its electric car, the Leaf, but then suffered huge losses when sales of the Leaf were far below projections. Alternatively, **Tesla**, which only makes electric cars, has fully committed to making its own batteries. In fact, it often describes itself as a battery company.

Source: Stephen Milmot, "Auto Companies: Better with Batteries Not Included," *Wall Street Journal* (December 19, 2016).

What are the factors that companies must consider in deciding whether to make or to buy the batteries for their vehicles? (Go to WileyPLUS for this answer and additional questions.)

DO IT! 6 | Unprofitable Segments

Lambert, Inc. manufactures several types of accessories. For the year, the knit hats and scarves line had sales of $400,000, variable expenses of $310,000, and fixed expenses of $120,000. Therefore, the knit hats and scarves line had a net loss of $30,000. If Lambert eliminates the knit hats and scarves line, $20,000 of fixed costs will remain. Prepare an analysis showing whether the company should eliminate the knit hats and scarves line.

Solution

	Continue	Eliminate	Net Income Increase (Decrease)
Sales	$400,000	$ 0	$(400,000)
Variable costs	310,000	0	310,000
Contribution margin	90,000	0	(90,000)
Fixed costs	120,000	20,000	100,000
Net income	$(30,000)	$(20,000)	$ 10,000

The analysis indicates that Lambert should eliminate the knit hats and scarves line because net income will increase $10,000.

Related exercise material: **BE20.8, DO IT! 20.6, E20.15, E20.16, and E20.17.**

ACTION PLAN
- Identify the revenues that change as a result of eliminating a product line.
- Identify all costs that change as a result of eliminating a product line, and net the amount against the revenues.

USING THE DECISION TOOLS | Method Products

Method Products faces many situations where it needs to apply the decision tool learned in this chapter. For example, assume that in order to have control over the creative nature of its packaging, Method decides to manufacture (instead of outsourcing) some of its more creative soap dispensers. Suppose that the company has been approached by a plastic container manufacturer with a proposal to provide 500,000 Mickey and Minnie Mouse hand wash dispensers. Assume Method's cost of producing 500,000 of the dispensers is $110,000, broken down as follows.

Direct materials	$60,000	Variable manufacturing overhead	$12,000
Direct labor	$30,000	Fixed manufacturing overhead	$ 8,000

Instead of making the dispensers at an average cost per unit of $0.22 ($110,000 ÷ 500,000), Method has an opportunity to buy the dispensers at $0.215 per unit. If the dispensers are purchased, all variable costs and one-half of the fixed costs will be eliminated.

Instructions

a. Prepare an incremental analysis showing whether Method should make or buy the dispensers.

b. Will your answer be different if the released productive capacity resulting from the purchase of the dispensers will generate additional income of $25,000?

c. What additional qualitative factors might Method need to consider?

Solution

a.

	Make	Buy	Net Income Increase (Decrease)
Direct materials	$ 60,000	$ -0-	$ 60,000
Direct labor	30,000	-0-	30,000
Variable manufacturing costs	12,000	-0-	12,000
Fixed manufacturing costs	8,000	4,000*	4,000
Purchase price	-0-	107,500**	(107,500)
Total cost	$110,000	$111,500	$ (1,500)

*$8,000 × .50 **$0.215 × 500,000

This analysis indicates that Method will incur $1,500 of additional costs if it buys the dispensers. Method therefore would choose to make the dispensers.

b.

	Make	Buy	Net Income Increase (Decrease)
Total cost	$110,000	$111,500	$ (1,500)
Opportunity cost	25,000	-0-	25,000
Total cost	$135,000	$111,500	$23,500

Yes, the answer is different. The analysis shows that if additional capacity is released, net income will be increased by $23,500 if the dispensers are purchased. In this case, Method would choose to purchase the dispensers.

c. Method is very concerned about the image of its products. It charges a higher price for many of its products than those of its larger competitors. It therefore wants to ensure that the functionality of the dispenser, as well as the appearance, were up to its standards. Also, because of Method's commitment to sustainability, it would consider numerous qualitative issues. For example, is this supplier going to use sustainable manufacturing practices? Method currently requires that its suppliers meet its expectations regarding sustainability.

Review and Practice

Learning Objectives Review

1 Describe management's decision-making process and incremental analysis.

Management's decision-making process consists of (a) identifying the problem and assigning responsibility for the decision, (b) determining and evaluating possible courses of action, (c) making the decision, and (d) reviewing the results of the decision. Incremental analysis identifies financial data that change under alternative courses of action. These data are relevant to the decision because they vary across the possible alternatives.

2 Analyze the relevant costs in accepting an order at a special price.

The relevant costs are those that change if the order is accepted. The relevant information in accepting an order at a special price is the difference between the variable manufacturing costs to produce the special order and expected revenues. Any changes in fixed costs, opportunity cost, or other incremental costs or savings (such as additional shipping) should be considered.

3 Analyze the relevant costs in a make-or-buy decision.

In a make-or-buy decision, the relevant costs are (a) the variable manufacturing costs that will be saved as well as changes to fixed manufacturing costs, (b) the purchase price, and (c) opportunity cost.

4 Analyze the relevant costs and revenues in determining whether to sell or process materials further.

The decision rule for whether to sell or process materials further is: Process further as long as the incremental revenue from processing exceeds the incremental processing costs.

5 Analyze the relevant costs to be considered in repairing, retaining, or replacing equipment.

The relevant costs to be considered in determining whether equipment should be repaired, retained, or replaced are the effects on variable costs and the cost of the new equipment. Also, any disposal value of the existing asset must be considered.

6 Analyze the relevant costs in deciding whether to eliminate an unprofitable segment or product.

In deciding whether to eliminate an unprofitable segment or product, the relevant costs are the variable costs that drive the contribution margin, if any, produced by the segment or product. Opportunity cost and reduction of fixed expenses must also be considered.

Decision Tools Review

Decision Checkpoints	Info Needed for Decision	Tool to Use for Decision	How to Evaluate Results
Which alternative should the company choose?	All relevant costs including opportunity cost	Compare the relevant cost of each alternative	Choose the alternative that maximizes net income.

Glossary Review

Incremental analysis The process of identifying the financial data that change under alternative courses of action. (p. 20-3).

Joint costs For joint products, all costs incurred prior to the point at which the two products are separately identifiable (known as the split-off point). (p. 20-12).

Joint products Multiple end-products produced from a single raw material and a common production process. (p. 20-11).

Opportunity cost The potential benefit that is lost when one course of action is chosen rather than an alternative course of action. (p. 20-4).

Relevant costs and revenues Those costs and revenues that differ across alternatives. (p. 20-4).

Sunk cost A cost incurred in the past that cannot be changed or avoided by any present or future decision. (p. 20-4).

Practice Multiple-Choice Questions

1. **(LO 1)** Three of the steps in management's decision-making process are (1) review results of decision, (2) determine and evaluate possible courses of action, and (3) make the decision. The steps are prepared in the following order:
   a. (1), (2), (3).
   b. (3), (2), (1).
   c. (2), (1), (3).
   d. (2), (3), (1).

2. **(LO 1)** Incremental analysis is the process of identifying the financial data that:
   a. do not change under alternative courses of action.
   b. change under alternative courses of action.
   c. are mixed under alternative courses of action.
   d. No correct answer is given.

3. **(LO 1)** In making business decisions, management ordinarily considers:
   a. quantitative factors but not qualitative factors.
   b. financial information only.
   c. both financial and nonfinancial information.
   d. relevant costs, opportunity cost, and sunk costs.

4. **(LO 1)** A company is considering the following alternatives:

	Alternative A	Alternative B
Revenues	$50,000	$50,000
Variable costs	24,000	24,000
Fixed costs	12,000	15,000

   Which of the following are relevant in choosing between these alternatives?
   a. Revenues, variable costs, and fixed costs.
   b. Variable costs and fixed costs.
   c. Variable costs only.
   d. Fixed costs only.

5. **(LO 2)** It costs a company $14 of variable costs and $6 of fixed costs to produce product Z200 that sells for $30. A foreign buyer offers to purchase 3,000 units at $18 each. If the special offer is accepted and produced with unused capacity, net income will:
   a. decrease $6,000.
   b. increase $6,000.
   c. increase $12,000.
   d. increase $9,000.

6. **(LO 2)** It costs a company $14 of variable costs and $6 of fixed costs to produce product Z200. Product Z200 sells for $30. A buyer offers to purchase 3,000 units at $18 each. The seller will incur special shipping costs of $5 per unit. If the special offer is accepted and produced with unused capacity, net income will:
   a. increase $3,000.
   b. increase $12,000.
   c. decrease $12,000.
   d. decrease $3,000.

7. **(LO 3)** Jobart Company is currently operating at full capacity. It is considering buying a part from an outside supplier rather than making it in-house. If Jobart purchases the part, it can use the released productive capacity to generate additional income of $30,000 from producing a different product. When conducting incremental analysis in this make-or-buy decision, the company should:
   a. ignore the $30,000.
   b. add $30,000 to other costs in the "Make" column.
   c. add $30,000 to other costs in the "Buy" column.
   d. subtract $30,000 from the other costs in the "Make" column.

8. **(LO 3)** In a make-or-buy decision, relevant costs are:
   a. manufacturing costs that will be saved.
   b. the purchase price of the units.
   c. the opportunity cost.
   d. All of the above.

9. **(LO 3)** Derek is performing incremental analysis in a make-or-buy decision for Item X. If Derek buys Item X, he can use its released productive capacity to produce Item Z. Derek will sell Item Z for $12,000 and incur production costs of $8,000. Derek's incremental analysis should include an opportunity cost of:
   a. $12,000.
   b. $8,000.
   c. $4,000.
   d. $0.

10. **(LO 4)** The decision rule in a sell-or-process-further decision is: process further as long as the incremental revenue from processing exceeds:
    a. incremental processing costs.
    b. variable processing costs.
    c. fixed processing costs.
    d. No correct answer is given.

11. **(LO 4)** Walton, Inc. makes an unassembled product that it currently sells for $55. Production costs are $20. Walton is considering assembling the product and selling it for $68. The cost to assemble the product is estimated at $12. What decision should Walton make?
    a. Sell before assembly; net income per unit will be $12 greater.
    b. Sell before assembly; net income per unit will be $1 greater.
    c. Process further; net income per unit will be $13 greater.
    d. Process further; net income per unit will be $1 greater.

12. **(LO 5)** In a decision to retain or replace equipment, the book value of the old equipment is a (an):
    a. opportunity cost.
    b. sunk cost.
    c. incremental cost.
    d. marginal cost.

13. **(LO 6)** If an unprofitable segment is eliminated:
    a. net income will always increase.
    b. variable costs of the eliminated segment will have to be absorbed by other segments.
    c. fixed costs allocated to the eliminated segment will have to be absorbed by other segments.
    d. net income will always decrease.

14. **(LO 6)** A segment of Hazard Inc. has the following data.

Sales	$200,000
Variable expenses	140,000
Fixed expenses	100,000

    If this segment is eliminated, what will be the effect on the remaining company? Assume that 50% of the fixed expenses will be eliminated and the rest will be allocated to the segments of the remaining company.
    a. $120,000 increase.
    b. $10,000 decrease.
    c. $50,000 increase.
    d. $10,000 increase.

Solutions

1. d. The order of the steps in the decision process is (2) determine and evaluate possible courses of action, (3) make the decision, and (1) review the results of decision. Choices (a), (b), and (c) list the steps in the incorrect order.

2. b. Incremental analysis is the process of identifying the financial data that change under alternative courses of action, not the financial data that (a) do not change or (c) are mixed. Choice (d) is wrong as there is a correct answer given.

3. c. Management ordinarily considers both financial and nonfinancial information in making business decisions. The other choices are incorrect because they are all limited to financial data and do not consider nonfinancial information.

4. d. Fixed costs is the only relevant factor, that is, the only factor that differs across Alternatives A and B. The other choices are incorrect because they list either revenues, variable costs, or both, which are the same amounts for both alternatives.

5. c. If the special offer is accepted and produced with unused capacity, variable cost per unit = $14, income per unit = ($18 − $14), so net income will increase by $12,000 (3,000 × $4), not (a) decrease $6,000, (b) increase $6,000, or (d) increase $9,000.

6. d. If the special offer is accepted and produced with unused capacity, variable cost per unit = $19 ($14 variable + $5 shipping costs), income per unit = −$1 ($18 − $19), so net income will decrease by $3,000 (3,000 × −$1), not (a) increase $3,000, (b) increase $12,000, or (c) decrease $12,000.

7. b. Jobart Company should add $30,000 to other costs in the "Make" column as it represents lost income of continuing to make the part in-house. The other choices are incorrect because the $30,000 (a) should not be ignored as it is an opportunity cost, (c) represents potential lost income if the company continues to make the part instead of buying it so therefore should not be placed in the "Buy" column, and (d) should be added to, not subtracted from, the other costs in the "Make" column.

8. d. All the costs in choices (a), (b), and (c) are relevant in a make-or-buy decision. So although choices (a), (b), and (c) are true statements, choice (d) is a better answer.

9. c. Derek's opportunity cost in its make-or-buy decision is $12,000 (revenue for Item Z) − $8,000 (production costs for Item Z) = $4,000, not (a) $12,000, (b) $8,000, or (d) $0.

10. a. The decision rule in a sell-or-process-further decision is to process further as long as the incremental revenue from such processing exceeds incremental processing costs, not (b) variable processing costs or (c) fixed processing costs. Choice (d) is wrong as there is a correct answer given.

11. d. If Walton processes further, net income per unit will increase $13 ($68 − $55), which is $1 more than its additional production costs ($12). The other choices are therefore incorrect.

12. b. In the decision to retain or replace equipment, the book value of the old equipment is a sunk cost (it reflects the original cost less accumulated depreciation, neither of which is relevant to the decision), not (a) an opportunity cost, (c) an incremental cost, or (d) a marginal cost.

13. c. Even though the segment is eliminated, the fixed costs allocated to that segment will still have to be covered. This is done by having other segments absorb the fixed costs of that segment. Choices (a) and (d) are incorrect because net income can either increase or decrease if a segment is eliminated. Choice (b) is incorrect because when a segment is eliminated, the variable costs of that segment will also be eliminated and will not need to be absorbed by other segments.

14. b. If the segment continues, net income = −$40,000 ($200,000 − $140,000 − $100,000). If the segment is eliminated, the contribution margin will also be eliminated but $50,000 ($100,000 × .50) of the fixed costs will remain. Therefore, the effect of eliminating the segment will be a $10,000 decrease not (a) a $120,000 increase, (c) a $50,000 increase, or (d) a $10,000 increase.

Practice Brief Exercises

1. (LO 3) Flavia Industries incurs unit costs of $24 ($18 variable and $6 fixed) in making an assembly part for its finished product. A supplier offers to make 20,000 units of the assembly part at $17 per unit. If the offer is accepted, Flavia will save all variable costs but no fixed costs. Prepare an analysis showing the total cost saving, if any, Flavia will realize by buying the part.

Determine whether to make or buy a part.

Solution

1.

	Make	Buy	Net Income Increase (Decrease)
Variable manufacturing costs	$360,000	$ -0-	$360,000
Fixed manufacturing costs	120,000	120,000	-0-
Purchase price	-0-	340,000	(340,000)
Total annual cost	$480,000	$460,000	$ 20,000

The decision should be to buy the part.

2. (LO 4) Fast Speed Bicycle Inc. makes parts for unfinished bicycles that it sells for $125. Production costs are $40 variable and $20 fixed. Because of unused capacity, Fast Speed is considering finishing the bicycles and selling them for $200. Additional variable finishing costs are expected to be $65 with no increase in fixed costs. Prepare an analysis on a per unit basis showing whether Fast Speed should sell unfinished or unfinished bicycles.

Determine whether to sell or process further.

Solution

2.

	Sell	Process Further	Net Income Increase (Decrease)
Sales price per unit	$125	$200	$75
Cost per unit			
Variable	40	105	(65)
Fixed	20	20	0
Total	60	125	(65)
Net income per unit	$ 65	$ 75	$10

The bicycles should be processed further because the incremental revenues exceed incremental costs by $10 per unit.

Determine whether to eliminate an unprofitable segment.

3. (LO 6) Hava Racquets Company manufactures pickleball racquets in four different models. For the year, the SoftNet line had a net loss of $40,000 from sales of $250,000, variable costs of $180,000 and fixed costs of $110,000. If the SoftNet line is eliminated, $30,000 of fixed costs will remain. Prepare an analysis showing whether the SoftNet Line should be eliminated.

Solution

3.

	Continue	Eliminate	Net Income Increase (Decrease)
Sales	$250,000	$ -0-	$(250,000)
Variable costs	180,000	-0-	180,000
Contribution margin	70,000	-0-	(70,000)
Fixed costs	110,000	30,000	80,000
Net income	$ (40,000)	$(30,000)	$ 10,000

The SoftNet product line should be eliminated because $80,000 of fixed cost is eliminated whereas only $70,000 of contribution margin is realized if the line is continued. The $70,000 related to the contribution margin is lower than the $80,000 savings related to fixed costs and therefore a savings of $10,000 results by eliminating SoftNet.

Practice Exercises

Use incremental analysis for make-or-buy decision.

1. (LO 3) Maningly Inc. has been manufacturing its own lampshades for its table lamps. The company is currently operating at 100% of capacity. Variable manufacturing overhead is charged to production at the rate of 50% of direct labor cost. The direct materials and direct labor cost per unit to make the lampshades are $4 and $6, respectively. Normal production is 50,000 table lamps per year.

A supplier offers to make the lampshades at a price of $13.50 per unit. If Maningly accepts the supplier's offer; all variable manufacturing costs will be eliminated, but the $50,000 of fixed manufacturing overhead currently being charged to the lampshades will have to be absorbed by other products.

Instructions

a. Prepare the incremental analysis for the decision to make or buy the lampshades.

b. Should Maningly buy the lampshades?

c. Would your answer be different in (b) if the productive capacity released by not making the lampshades could be used to produce income of $40,000?

Solution

1. a.

	Make	Buy	Net Income Increase (Decrease)
Direct materials (50,000 × $4.00)	$200,000	$ 0	$ 200,000
Direct labor (50,000 × $6.00)	300,000	0	300,000
Variable manufacturing costs ($300,000 × 50%)	150,000	0	150,000
Fixed manufacturing costs	50,000	50,000	0
Purchase price (50,000 × $13.50)	0	675,000	(675,000)
Total annual cost	$700,000	$725,000	$ (25,000)

b. No, Maningly should not purchase the lampshades. As indicated by the incremental analysis, it would cost the company $25,000 more to purchase the lampshades.

c. Yes, by purchasing the lampshades, a total cost saving of $15,000 will result as shown below.

	Make	Buy	Net Income Increase (Decrease)
Total annual cost (from (a))	$700,000	$725,000	$(25,000)
Opportunity cost	40,000	0	40,000
Total cost	$740,000	$725,000	$ 15,000

---

2. (LO 4) A company manufactures three products using same production process. The costs incurred up to the split-off point are $200,000. These costs are allocated to the products on the basis of their sales value at the split-off point. The number of units produced, the selling prices per unit of the three products at the split-off point and after further processing, and the additional processing costs are as follows.

Use incremental analysis for whether to sell or process materials further.

Product	Number of Units Produced	Selling Price at Split-Off	Selling Price after Processing	Additional Processing Costs
D	3,000	$11.00	$15.00	$14,000
E	6,000	12.00	16.20	16,000
F	2,000	19.40	24.00	9,000

Instructions

a. Which information is relevant to the decision on whether or not to process the products further? Explain why this information is relevant.

b. Which product(s) should be processed further and which should be sold at the split-off point?

c. Would your decision be different if the company was using the quantity of output to allocate joint costs? Explain.

(CGA adapted)

Solution

2. a. The costs that are relevant in this decision are the incremental revenues and the incremental costs associated with processing the material past the split-off point. Any costs incurred up to the split-off point are sunk costs and therefore irrelevant to this decision.

b. Revenue after further processing:

Product D: $45,000 (3,000 units × $15.00 per unit)
Product E: $97,200 (6,000 units × $16.20 per unit)
Product F: $48,000 (2,000 units × $24.00 per unit)

Revenue at split-off:

Product D: $33,000 (3,000 units × $11.00 per unit)
Product E: $72,000 (6,000 units × $12.00 per unit)
Product F: $38,800 (2,000 units × $19.40 per unit)

	D	E	F
Incremental revenue	$ 12,000[a]	$ 25,200[b]	$ 9,200[c]
Incremental cost	(14,000)	(16,000)	(9,000)
Increase (decrease) in profit	$ (2,000)	$ 9,200	$ 200

[a]$45,000 − $33,000; [b]$97,200 − $72,000; [c]$48,000 − $38,800

Products E and F should be processed further, but Product D should not be processed further.

c. The decision would remain the same. It does not matter how the joint costs are allocated because joint costs are irrelevant to this decision.

Use incremental analysis for retaining or replacing equipment.

3. (LO 5) Tek Enterprises uses a computer to process its sales invoices. Lately, business has been so good that it takes an extra 3 hours per night, plus every third Saturday, to keep up with the volume of sales invoices. Management is considering updating its computer with a faster model that would eliminate all of the overtime processing.

	Current Machine	New Machine
Original purchase cost	$15,000	$25,000
Accumulated depreciation	6,000	—
Estimated annual operating costs	25,000	20,000
Useful life	6 years	6 years

If sold now, the current machine would have a salvage value of $5,000. If operated for the remainder of its useful life, the current machine would have zero salvage value. The new machine is expected to have zero salvage value after 6 years.

Instructions

Should the current machine be replaced? (Ignore the time value of money.)

Solution

3.

	Retain Machine	Replace Machine	Net Income Increase (Decrease)
Operating costs	$150,000*	$120,000**	$30,000
New machine cost	0	25,000	(25,000)
Salvage value (old)	0	(5,000)	5,000
Total	$150,000	$140,000	$10,000

*$25,000 × 6
**$20,000 × 6

The current machine should be replaced. The incremental analysis shows that net income for the 6-year period will be $10,000 higher by replacing the current machine.

Use incremental analysis for elimination of division.

4. (LO 6) Benai Lorenzo, a recent graduate of Bonita's accounting program, evaluated the operating performance of Wasson Company's six divisions. Benai made the following presentation to the Wasson board of directors and suggested the Ortiz Division be eliminated. "If the Ortiz Division is eliminated," she said, "our total profits would increase by $23,870."

	The Other Five Divisions	Ortiz Division	Total
Sales	$1,664,200	$ 96,200	$1,760,400
Cost of goods sold	978,520	76,470	1,054,990
Gross profit	685,680	19,730	705,410
Operating expenses	527,940	43,600	571,540
Net income	$ 157,740	$(23,870)	$ 133,870

In the Ortiz Division, cost of goods sold is $70,000 variable and $6,470 fixed, and operating expenses are $15,000 variable and $28,600 fixed. None of the Ortiz Division's fixed costs will be eliminated if the division is discontinued.

Instructions

Is Benai right about eliminating the Ortiz Division? Prepare an incremental analysis schedule to support your answer.

Solution

4.

	Continue	Eliminate	Net Income Increase (Decrease)
Sales	$ 96,200	$ 0	$(96,200)
Variable expenses			
Cost of goods sold	70,000	0	70,000
Operating expenses	15,000	0	15,000
Total variable	85,000	0	85,000
Contribution margin	11,200	0	(11,200)
Fixed expenses			
Cost of goods sold	6,470	6,470	0
Operating expenses	28,600	28,600	0
Total fixed	35,070	35,070	0
Net income (loss)	$(23,870)	$(35,070)	$(11,200)

Benai is incorrect. The incremental analysis shows that net income will be $11,200 less if the Ortiz Division is eliminated. This amount equals the contribution margin that would be lost by discontinuing the division.

Practice Problem

(LO 2) Walston Company produces kitchen cabinets for homebuilders across the western United States. The cost of producing 5,000 cabinets is as follows:

Materials	$ 500,000
Labor	250,000
Variable overhead	100,000
Fixed overhead	400,000
Total	$1,250,000

Use incremental analysis for a special order.

Walston also incurs selling expenses of $20 per cabinet. Wellington Corp. has offered Walston $165 per cabinet for a special order of 1,000 cabinets. The cabinets would be sold to homebuilders in the eastern United States and thus would not conflict with Walston's current sales. Selling expenses per cabinet would be only $5 per cabinet. Walston has available capacity to do the work.

Instructions

a. Prepare an incremental analysis for the special order.
b. Should Walston accept the special order? Why or why not?

Solution

a. Relevant costs per unit would be:

Materials	$500,000/5,000 = $100
Labor	250,000/5,000 = 50
Variable overhead	100,000/5,000 = 20
Selling expenses	5
Total relevant cost per unit	$175

	Reject Order	Accept Order	Net Income Increase (Decrease)
Revenues	$0	$165,000*	$ 165,000
Costs	0	175,000**	(175,000)
Net income	$0	$(10,000)	$ (10,000)

*$165 × 1,000; **$175 × 1,000

b. Walston should reject the offer. The incremental benefit of $165 per cabinet is less than the incremental cost of $175. By accepting the order, Walston's net income would actually decline by $10,000.

WileyPLUS

Brief Exercises, DO IT! Exercises, Exercises, Problems, and many additional resources are available for practice in WileyPLUS.

Questions

1. What steps are frequently involved in management's decision-making process?

2. Your roommate, Anna Polis, contends that accounting contributes to most of the steps in management's decision-making process. Is your roommate correct? Explain.

3. "Incremental analysis involves the accumulation of information concerning a single course of action." Do you agree? Why?

4. Sydney Greene asks for your help concerning the relevance of variable and fixed costs in incremental analysis. Help Sydney with her problem.

5. What data are relevant in deciding whether to accept an order at a special price?

6. Emil Corporation has an opportunity to buy parts at $9 each that currently cost $12 to make. What manufacturing costs are relevant to this make-or-buy decision?

7. Define the term "opportunity cost." How may this cost be relevant in a make-or-buy decision?

8. What is the decision rule in deciding whether to sell a product or process it further?

9. What are joint products? What accounting issue results from the production process that creates joint products?

10. How are allocated joint costs treated when making a sell-or-process-further decision?

11. Your roommate, Gale Dunham, is confused about sunk costs. Explain to your roommate the meaning of sunk costs and their relevance to a decision to retain or replace equipment.

12. Huang Inc. has one product line that is unprofitable. What circumstances may cause overall company net income to be lower if the unprofitable product line is eliminated?

Brief Exercises

Identify the steps in management's decision-making process.

BE20.1 (LO 1), AP The steps in management's decision-making process are listed in random order below. Indicate the order in which the steps should be executed.

_____ Make a decision.
_____ Identify the problem and assign responsibility.
_____ Review results of the decision.
_____ Determine and evaluate possible courses of action.

Determine incremental changes.

BE20.2 (LO 1), AP Bogart Company is considering two alternatives. Alternative A will have revenues of $160,000 and costs of $100,000. Alternative B will have revenues of $180,000 and costs of $125,000. Compare Alternative A to Alternative B showing incremental revenues, costs, and net income.

Determine whether to accept a special order.

BE20.3 (LO 2), AP At Bargain Electronics, it costs $30 per unit ($20 variable and $10 fixed) to make an MP3 player that normally sells for $45. A foreign wholesaler offers to buy 3,000 units at $25 each. Bargain Electronics will incur special shipping costs of $3 per unit. Assuming that Bargain Electronics has excess operating capacity, indicate the net income (loss) Bargain Electronics would realize by accepting the special order.

Determine whether to make or buy a part.

BE20.4 (LO 3), AP Manson Industries incurs unit costs of $8 ($5 variable and $3 fixed) in making an assembly part for its finished product. A supplier offers to make 10,000 of the assembly part at $6 per unit. If the offer is accepted, Manson will save all variable costs but no fixed costs. Prepare an analysis showing the total cost saving, if any, Manson will realize by buying the part.

Determine whether to sell or process further.

BE20.5 (LO 4), AP Pine Street Inc. makes unfinished bookcases that it sells for $62. Production costs are $36 variable and $10 fixed. Because it has unused capacity, Pine Street is considering finishing the bookcases and selling them for $70. Variable finishing costs are expected to be $6 per unit with no increase in fixed costs. Prepare an analysis on a per unit basis showing whether Pine Street should sell unfinished or finished bookcases.

Determine whether to sell or process further, joint products.

BE20.6 (LO 4), AP Each day, Adama Corporation processes 1 ton of a secret raw material into two resulting products, AB1 and XY1. When it processes 1 ton of the raw material, the company incurs joint processing costs of $60,000. It allocates $25,000 of these costs to AB1 and $35,000 of these costs to XY1. The resulting AB1 can be sold for $100,000. Alternatively, it can be processed further to make AB2 at an additional processing cost of $45,000, and sold for $150,000. Each day's batch of XY1 can be sold for $95,000. Or, it can be processed further to create XY2, at an additional processing cost of $50,000, and sold for $130,000. Discuss what products Adama Corporation should make.

BE20.7 (LO 5), AP Bryant Company has a factory machine with a book value of $90,000 and a remaining useful life of 5 years. It can be sold for $30,000. A new machine is available at a cost of $400,000. This machine will have a 5-year useful life with no salvage value. The new machine will lower annual variable manufacturing costs from $600,000 to $500,000. Prepare an analysis showing whether the old machine should be retained or replaced.

Determine whether to retain or replace equipment.

BE20.8 (LO 6), AP Lisah, Inc., manufactures golf clubs in three models. For the year, the Big Bart line has a net loss of $10,000 from sales $200,000, variable costs $180,000, and fixed costs $30,000. If the Big Bart line is eliminated, $20,000 of fixed costs will remain. Prepare an analysis showing whether the Big Bart line should be eliminated.

Determine whether to eliminate an unprofitable segment.

DO IT! Exercises

DO IT! 20.1 (LO 1), AN Nathan T Corporation is comparing two different options. Nathan T currently uses Option 1, with revenues of $65,000 per year, maintenance expenses of $5,000 per year, and operating expenses of $26,000 per year. Option 2 provides revenues of $60,000 per year, maintenance expenses of $5,000 per year, and operating expenses of $22,000 per year. Option 1 employs a piece of equipment which was upgraded 2 years ago at a cost of $17,000. If Option 2 is chosen, it will free up resources that will bring in an additional $4,000 of revenue. Complete the following table to show the change in income from choosing Option 2 versus Option 1. Designate Sunk costs with an "S."

Determine incremental costs.

	Option 1	Option 2	Net Income Increase (Decrease)	Sunk (S)
Revenues				
Maintenance expenses				
Operating expenses				
Equipment upgrade				
Opportunity cost				

DO IT! 20.2 (LO 2), AN Maize Company incurs a cost of $35 per unit, of which $20 is variable, to make a product that normally sells for $58. A foreign wholesaler offers to buy 6,000 units at $30 each. Maize will incur additional costs of $4 per unit to imprint a logo and to pay for shipping. Compute the increase or decrease in net income Maize will realize by accepting the special order, assuming Maize has sufficient excess operating capacity. Should Maize Company accept the special order?

Evaluate special order.

DO IT! 20.3 (LO 3), AN Wilma Company must decide whether to make or buy some of its components. The costs of producing 60,000 switches for its generators are as follows.

Evaluate make-or-buy opportunity.

Direct materials	$30,000	Variable overhead	$45,000
Direct labor	$42,000	Fixed overhead	$60,000

Instead of making the switches at an average cost of $2.95 ($177,000 ÷ 60,000), the company has an opportunity to buy the switches at $2.70 per unit. If the company purchases the switches, all the variable costs and one-fourth of the fixed costs will be eliminated. (a) Prepare an incremental analysis showing whether the company should make or buy the switches. (b) Would your answer be different if the released productive capacity will generate additional income of $34,000?

DO IT! 20.4 (LO 4), AP Mesa Verde manufactures unpainted furniture for the do-it-yourself (DIY) market. It currently sells a table for $75. Production costs per unit are $40 variable and $10 fixed. Mesa Verde is considering staining and sealing the table to sell it for $100. Variable costs per unit to finish each table are expected to be an additional $19 per unit, and fixed costs are expected to be an additional $3 per unit. Prepare an analysis showing whether Mesa Verde should sell unpainted or finished tables.

Sell or process further.

DO IT! 20.5 (LO 5), AP Darcy Roofing is faced with a decision. The company relies very heavily on the use of its 60-foot extension lift for work on large homes and commercial properties. Last year,

Repair or replace equipment.

Darcy Roofing spent $60,000 refurbishing the lift. It has just determined that another $40,000 of repair work is required. Alternatively, it has found a newer used lift that is for sale for $170,000. The company estimates that both lifts would have useful lives of 6 years. The new lift is more efficient and thus would reduce operating expenses by about $20,000 per year. Darcy Roofing could also rent out the new lift for about $10,000 per year. The old lift is not suitable for rental. The old lift could currently be sold for $25,000 if the new lift is purchased. Prepare an incremental analysis showing whether the company should repair or replace the equipment.

Analyze whether to eliminate unprofitable segment.

DO IT! 20.6 (LO 6), AP Gator Corporation manufactures several types of accessories. For the year, the gloves and mittens line had sales of $500,000, variable expenses of $370,000, and fixed expenses of $150,000. Therefore, the gloves and mittens line had a net loss of $20,000. If Gator eliminates the line, $38,000 of fixed costs will remain. Prepare an analysis showing whether the company should eliminate the gloves and mittens line.

Exercises

Analyze statements about decision-making and incremental analysis.

E20.1 (LO 1), C As a study aid, your classmate Pascal Adams has prepared the following list of statements about decision-making and incremental analysis.

1. The first step in management's decision-making process is, "Determine and evaluate possible courses of action."
2. The final step in management's decision-making process is to actually make the decision.
3. Accounting's contribution to management's decision-making process occurs primarily in evaluating possible courses of action and in reviewing the results.
4. In making business decisions, management ordinarily considers only financial information because it is objectively determined.
5. Decisions involve a choice among alternative courses of action.
6. The process used to identify the financial data that change under alternative courses of action is called incremental analysis.
7. Costs that are the same under all alternative courses of action sometimes affect the decision.
8. When using incremental analysis, some costs will always change under alternative courses of action, but revenues will not.
9. Variable costs will change under alternative courses of action, but fixed costs will not.

Instructions

Identify each statement as true or false. If false, indicate how to correct the statement.

Use incremental analysis for special-order decision.

E20.2 (LO 2), AN Gruden Company produces golf discs which it normally sells to retailers for $7 each. The cost of manufacturing 20,000 golf discs is:

Materials	$ 10,000
Labor	30,000
Variable overhead	20,000
Fixed overhead	40,000
Total	$100,000

Gruden also incurs 5% sales commission ($0.35) on each disc sold.

McGee Corporation offers Gruden $4.80 per disc for 5,000 discs. McGee would sell the discs under its own brand name in foreign markets not yet served by Gruden. If Gruden accepts the offer, its fixed overhead will increase from $40,000 to $46,000 due to the purchase of a new imprinting machine. No sales commission will result from the special order.

Instructions

a. Prepare an incremental analysis for the special order.
b. Should Gruden accept the special order? Why or why not?
c. What assumptions underlie the decision made in part (b)?

E20.3 (LO 2), AN Moonbeam Company manufactures toasters. For the first 8 months of 2022, the company reported the following operating results while operating at 75% of plant capacity:

Use incremental analysis for special order.

Sales (350,000 units)	$4,375,000
Cost of goods sold	2,600,000
Gross profit	1,775,000
Operating expenses	840,000
Net income	$ 935,000

Cost of goods sold was 70% variable and 30% fixed; operating expenses were 80% variable and 20% fixed.

In September, Moonbeam receives a special order for 15,000 toasters at $7.60 each from Luna Company of Ciudad Juarez. Acceptance of the order would result in an additional $3,000 of shipping costs but no increase in fixed costs.

Instructions

a. Prepare an incremental analysis for the special order.

b. Should Moonbeam accept the special order? Why or why not?

E20.4 (LO 2), AN Klean Fiber Company is the creator of Y-Go, a technology that weaves silver into its fabrics to kill bacteria and odor on clothing while managing heat. Y-Go has become very popular in undergarments for sports activities. Operating at capacity, the company can produce 1,000,000 Y-Go undergarments a year. The per unit and the total costs for an individual garment when the company operates at full capacity are as follows.

Use incremental analysis for special order.

	Per Undergarment	Total
Direct materials	$2.00	$2,000,000
Direct labor	0.75	750,000
Variable manufacturing overhead	1.00	1,000,000
Fixed manufacturing overhead	1.50	1,500,000
Variable selling expenses	0.25	250,000
Totals	$5.50	$5,500,000

The U.S. Army has approached Klean Fiber and expressed an interest in purchasing 250,000 Y-Go undergarments for soldiers in extremely warm climates. The Army would pay the unit cost for direct materials, direct labor, and variable manufacturing overhead costs. In addition, the Army has agreed to pay an additional $1 per undergarment to cover all other costs and provide a profit. Presently, Klean Fiber is operating at 70% capacity and does not have any other potential buyers for Y-Go. If Klean Fiber accepts the Army's offer, it will not incur any variable selling expenses related to this order.

Instructions

Using incremental analysis, determine whether Klean Fiber should accept the Army's offer.

E20.5 (LO 3), AN Pottery Ranch Inc. has been manufacturing its own finials for its curtain rods. The company is currently operating at 100% of capacity, and variable manufacturing overhead is charged to production at the rate of 70% of direct labor cost. The direct materials and direct labor cost per unit to make a pair of finials are $4 and $5, respectively. Normal production is 30,000 curtain rods per year.

A supplier offers to make a pair of finials at a price of $12.95 per unit. If Pottery Ranch accepts the supplier's offer, all variable manufacturing costs will be eliminated, but the $45,000 of fixed manufacturing overhead currently being charged to the finials will have to be absorbed by other products.

Use incremental analysis for make-or-buy decision.

Instructions

a. Prepare the incremental analysis for the decision to make or buy the finials.

b. Should Pottery Ranch buy the finials?

c. Would your answer be different in (b) if the productive capacity released by not making the finials could be used to produce income of $20,000?

E20.6 (LO 3), E Jobs, Inc. has recently started the manufacture of Tri-Robo, a three-wheeled robot that can scan a home for fires and gas leaks and then transmit this information to a smartphone. The cost structure to manufacture 20,000 Tri-Robos is as follows.

Use incremental analysis for make-or-buy decision.

	Cost
Direct materials ($50 per robot)	$1,000,000
Direct labor ($40 per robot)	800,000
Variable overhead ($6 per robot)	120,000
Allocated fixed overhead ($30 per robot)	600,000
Total	$2,520,000

Jobs is approached by Tienh Inc., which offers to make Tri-Robo for $115 per unit or $2,300,000.

Instructions

a. Using incremental analysis, determine whether Jobs should accept this offer under each of the following independent assumptions.

   1. Assume that $405,000 of the fixed overhead cost can be avoided.

   2. Assume that none of the fixed overhead can be avoided. However, if the robots are purchased from Tienh Inc., Jobs can use the released productive resources to generate additional income of $375,000.

b. Describe the qualitative factors that might affect the decision to purchase the robots from an outside supplier.

Prepare incremental analysis for make-or-buy decision.

E20.7 (LO 3), E Riggs Company purchases sails and produces sailboats. It currently produces 1,200 sailboats per year, operating at normal capacity, which is about 80% of full capacity. Riggs purchases sails at $250 each, but the company is considering using the excess capacity to manufacture the sails instead. The manufacturing cost per sail would be $100 for direct materials, $80 for direct labor, and $90 for overhead. The $90 overhead is based on $78,000 of annual fixed overhead that is allocated using normal capacity.

The president of Riggs has come to you for advice. "It would cost me $270 to make the sails," she says, "but only $250 to buy them. Should I continue buying them, or have I missed something?"

Instructions

a. Prepare a per unit analysis of the differential costs. Briefly explain whether Riggs should make or buy the sails.

b. If Riggs suddenly finds an opportunity to rent out the unused capacity of its factory for $77,000 per year, would your answer to part (a) change? Briefly explain.

c. Identify three qualitative factors that should be considered by Riggs in this make-or-buy decision.

(CGA adapted)

Prepare incremental analysis concerning make-or-buy decision.

E20.8 (LO 3), E Innova uses 1,000 units of the component IMC2 every month to manufacture one of its products. The unit costs incurred to manufacture the component are as follows.

Direct materials	$ 65.00
Direct labor	45.00
Overhead	126.50
Total	$236.50

Overhead costs include variable material handling costs of $6.50, which are applied to products on the basis of direct material costs. The remainder of the overhead costs are applied on the basis of direct labor dollars and consist of 60% variable costs and 40% fixed costs.

A vendor has offered to supply the IMC2 component at a price of $200 per unit.

Instructions

a. Should Innova purchase the component from the outside vendor if Innova's capacity remains idle?

b. Should Innova purchase the component from the outside vendor if it can use its facilities to manufacture another product? What information will Innova need to make an accurate decision? Show your calculations.

c. What are the qualitative factors that Innova will have to consider when making this decision?

(CGA adapted)

Use incremental analysis for further processing of materials decision.

E20.9 (LO 4), AN Anna Garden recently opened her own basketweaving studio. She sells finished baskets in addition to selling the raw materials needed by customers to weave baskets of their own. Unfortunately, owing to space limitations, Anna is unable to carry all varieties of kits originally assembled and must choose between two basic packages.

The Basic Kit includes undyed, uncut reeds (with dye included) for weaving one basket. This basic package costs Anna $16 and sells for $30. The second kit, called Stage 2, includes cut reeds that have already been dyed. With this kit the customer need only soak the reeds and weave the basket. Anna produces the Stage 2 kit by using the materials included in the Basic Kit. Because she is more efficient at cutting and dying reeds than her average customer, Anna is able to produce two Stage 2 kits in one hour from one Basic Kit. (She values her time at $18 per hour.) The Stage 2 kit sells for $36.

Instructions

Determine whether Anna's basketweaving studio should carry the Basic Kit with undyed and uncut reeds or the Stage 2 kit with reeds already dyed and cut. Prepare an incremental analysis to support your answer.

E20.10 (LO 4), AN Stahl Inc. produces three separate products from a common process costing $100,000. Each of the products can be sold at the split-off point or can be processed further and then sold for a higher price. Shown below are cost and selling price data for a recent period.

Determine whether to sell or process further, joint products.

	Sales Value at Split-Off Point	Cost to Process Further	Sales Value after Further Processing
Product 10	$60,000	$100,000	$190,000
Product 12	15,000	30,000	35,000
Product 14	55,000	150,000	215,000

Instructions

a. Determine total net income if all products are sold at the split-off point.

b. Determine total net income if all products are sold after further processing.

c. Using incremental analysis, determine which products should be sold at the split-off point and which should be processed further.

d. Determine total net income using the results from (c) and explain why the net income is different from that determined in (b).

E20.11 (LO 4), AN Kirk Minerals processes materials extracted from mines. The most common raw material that it processes results in three joint products: Spock, Uhura, and Sulu. Each of these products can be sold as is, or each can be processed further and sold for a higher price. The company incurs joint costs of $180,000 to process one batch of the raw material that produces the three joint products. The following cost and sales information is available for one batch of each product.

Determine whether to sell or process further, joint products.

	Sales Value at Split-Off Point	Allocated Joint Costs	Cost to Process Further	Sales Value of Processed Product
Spock	$210,000	$40,000	$110,000	$300,000
Uhura	300,000	60,000	85,000	400,000
Sulu	455,000	80,000	250,000	800,000

Instructions

Determine whether each of the three joint products should be sold as is, or processed further.

E20.12 (LO 4), E A company manufactures three products using the same production process. The costs incurred up to the split-off point are $200,000. These costs are allocated to the products on the basis of their sales value at the split-off point. The number of units produced, the selling prices per unit of the three products at the split-off point and after further processing, and the additional processing costs are as follows.

Prepare incremental analysis for whether to sell or process materials further.

Product	Number of Units Produced	Selling Price at Split-Off	Selling Price after Processing	Additional Processing Costs
D	4,000	$10.00	$15.00	$14,000
E	6,000	11.60	16.20	20,000
F	2,000	19.40	22.60	9,000

Instructions

a. Which information is relevant to the decision on whether or not to process the products further? Explain why this information is relevant.

b. Which product(s) should be processed further and which should be sold at the split-off point?

c. Would your decision be different if the company was using the quantity of output to allocate joint costs? Explain.

(CGA adapted)

Use incremental analysis for retaining or replacing equipment decision.

E20.13 (LO 5), E Service On January 2, 2021, Twilight Hospital purchased a $100,000 special radiology scanner from Bella Inc. The scanner had a useful life of 4 years and was estimated to have no disposal value at the end of its useful life. The straight-line method of depreciation is used on this scanner. Annual operating costs with this scanner are $105,000.

Approximately one year later, the hospital is approached by Dyno Technology salesperson, Jacob Cullen, who indicated that purchasing the scanner in 2021 from Bella Inc. was a mistake. He points out that Dyno has a scanner that will save Twilight Hospital $25,000 a year in operating expenses over its 3-year useful life. Jacob notes that the new scanner will cost $110,000 and has the same capabilities as the scanner purchased last year. The hospital agrees that both scanners are of equal quality. The new scanner will have no disposal value. Jacob agrees to buy the old scanner from Twilight Hospital for $50,000.

Instructions

a. If Twilight Hospital sells its old scanner on January 2, 2022, compute the gain or loss on the sale.

b. Using incremental analysis, determine if Twilight Hospital should purchase the new scanner on January 2, 2022.

c. Explain why Twilight Hospital might be reluctant to purchase the new scanner, regardless of the results indicated by the incremental analysis in (b).

Use incremental analysis for retaining or replacing equipment decision.

E20.14 (LO 5), AN Johnson Enterprises uses a computer to handle its sales invoices. Lately, business has been so good that it takes an extra 3 hours per night, plus every third Saturday, to keep up with the volume of sales invoices. Management is considering updating its computer with a faster model that would eliminate all of the overtime processing.

	Current Machine	New Machine
Original purchase cost	$15,000	$25,000
Accumulated depreciation	$ 6,000	—
Estimated annual operating costs	$25,000	$20,000
Remaining useful life	5 years	5 years

If sold now, the current machine would have a salvage value of $6,000. If operated for the remainder of its useful life, the current machine would have zero salvage value. The new machine is expected to have zero salvage value after 5 years.

Instructions

Prepare an incremental analysis to determine whether the current machine should be replaced.

Use incremental analysis concerning elimination of division.

E20.15 (LO 6), AN Veronica Mars, a recent graduate of Bell's accounting program, evaluated the operating performance of Dunn Company's six divisions. Veronica made the following presentation to Dunn's board of directors and suggested the Percy Division be eliminated. "If the Percy Division is eliminated," she said, "our total profits would increase by $26,000."

	The Other Five Divisions	Percy Division	Total
Sales	$1,664,200	$100,000	$1,764,200
Cost of goods sold	978,520	76,000	1,054,520
Gross profit	685,680	24,000	709,680
Operating expenses	527,940	50,000	577,940
Net income	$ 157,740	$ (26,000)	$ 131,740

In the Percy Division, cost of goods sold is $61,000 variable and $15,000 fixed, and operating expenses are $30,000 variable and $20,000 fixed. None of the Percy Division's fixed costs will be eliminated if the division is discontinued.

Instructions

Is Veronica right about eliminating the Percy Division? Prepare a schedule to support your answer.

E20.16 (LO 6), AN Cawley Company makes three models of tasers. Information on the three products is given below.

Use incremental analysis for elimination of a product line.

	Tingler	Shocker	Stunner
Sales	$300,000	$500,000	$200,000
Variable expenses	150,000	200,000	145,000
Contribution margin	150,000	300,000	55,000
Fixed expenses	120,000	230,000	95,000
Net income	$ 30,000	$ 70,000	$(40,000)

Fixed expenses consist of $300,000 of common costs allocated to the three products based on relative sales, as well as direct fixed expenses unique to each model of $30,000 (Tingler), $80,000 (Shocker), and $35,000 (Stunner). The common costs will be incurred regardless of how many models are produced. The direct fixed expenses would be eliminated if that model is phased out.

James Watt, an executive with the company, feels the Stunner line should be discontinued to increase the company's net income.

Instructions

a. Compute current net income for Cawley Company.

b. Compute net income by product line and in total for Cawley Company if the company discontinues the Stunner product line. (*Hint:* Allocate the $300,000 common costs to the two remaining product lines based on their relative sales.)

c. Should Cawley eliminate the Stunner product line? Why or why not?

E20.17 (LO 6), AN Tharp Company operates a small factory in which it manufactures two products: C and D. Production and sales results for last year were as follows.

Prepare incremental analysis concerning keeping or dropping a product to maximize operating income.

	C	D
Units sold	9,000	20,000
Selling price per unit	$95	$75
Variable cost per unit	50	40
Fixed cost per unit	24	24

For purposes of simplicity, the firm averages total fixed costs over the total number of units of C and D produced and sold.

The research department has developed a new product (E) as a replacement for product D. Market studies show that Tharp Company could sell 10,000 units of E next year at a price of $115; the variable cost per unit of E is $45. The introduction of product E will lead to a 10% increase in demand for product C and discontinuation of product D. If the company does not introduce the new product, it expects next year's results to be the same as last year's.

Instructions

Should Tharp Company introduce product E next year? Explain why or why not. Show calculations to support your decision.

(CMA-Canada adapted)

E20.18 (LO 1, 2, 3, 4, 5, 6), C The costs listed below relate to a variety of different decision situations.

Identify relevant costs for different decisions.

Cost	Decision
1. Unavoidable fixed overhead	Eliminate an unprofitable segment
2. Direct labor	Make or buy
3. Original cost of old equipment	Equipment replacement
4. Joint production costs	Sell or process further
5. Opportunity cost	Accepting a special order
6. Segment manager's salary	Eliminate an unprofitable segment (manager will be terminated)
7. Cost of new equipment	Equipment replacement
8. Incremental production costs	Sell or process further
9. Direct materials	Equipment replacement (the amount of materials required does not change)
10. Rent expense	Purchase or lease a building

Instructions

For each cost listed above, indicate if it is relevant or not to the related decision. For those costs determined to be irrelevant, briefly explain why.

Problems: Set A

Use incremental analysis for special order and identify nonfinancial factors in the decision.

P20.1A (LO 2), E Writing ThreePoint Sports Inc. manufactures basketballs for the Women's National Basketball Association (WNBA). For the first 6 months of 2022, the company reported the following operating results while operating at 80% of plant capacity and producing 120,000 units.

	Amount
Sales	$4,800,000
Cost of goods sold	3,600,000
Selling and administrative expenses	405,000
Net income	$ 795,000

Fixed costs for the period were cost of goods sold $960,000, and selling and administrative expenses $225,000.

In July, normally a slack manufacturing month, ThreePoint Sports receives a special order for 10,000 basketballs at $28 each from the Greek Basketball Association (GBA). Acceptance of the order would increase variable selling and administrative expenses $0.75 per unit because of shipping costs but would not increase fixed costs and expenses.

Instructions

a. NI increase $37,500

a. Prepare an incremental analysis for the special order.

b. Should ThreePoint Sports Inc. accept the special order? Explain your answer.

c. What is the minimum selling price on the special order to produce net income of $5.00 per ball?

d. What nonfinancial factors should management consider in making its decision?

Use incremental analysis related to make or buy, consider opportunity cost, and identify nonfinancial factors.

P20.2A (LO 3), E Writing The management of Shatner Manufacturing Company is trying to decide whether to continue manufacturing a part or to buy it from an outside supplier. The part, called CISCO, is a component of the company's finished product.

The following information was collected from the accounting records and production data for the year ending December 31, 2022.

1. 8,000 units of CISCO were produced in the Machining Department.

2. Variable manufacturing costs applicable to the production of each CISCO unit were: direct materials $4.80, direct labor $4.30, indirect labor $0.43, utilities $0.40.

3. Fixed manufacturing costs applicable to the production of CISCO were:

Cost Item	Direct	Allocated
Depreciation	$2,100	$ 900
Property taxes	500	200
Insurance	900	600
	$3,500	$1,700

All variable manufacturing and direct fixed costs will be eliminated if CISCO is purchased. Allocated costs will not be eliminated if CISCO is purchased. So if CISCO is purchased, the fixed manufacturing costs allocated to CISCO will have to be absorbed by other production departments.

4. The lowest quotation for 8,000 CISCO units from a supplier is $80,000.

5. If CISCO units are purchased, freight and inspection costs would be $0.35 per unit, and receiving costs totaling $1,300 per year would be incurred by the Machining Department.

Instructions

a. Prepare an incremental analysis for CISCO. Your analysis should have columns for (1) Make CISCO, (2) Buy CISCO, and (3) Net Income Increase/(Decrease).

b. Based on your analysis, what decision should management make?

c. Would the decision be different if Shatner Company has the opportunity to produce $3,000 of net income with the facilities currently being used to manufacture CISCO? Show computations.

d. What nonfinancial factors should management consider in making its decision?

a. NI (decrease) $(1,160)

c. NI increase $1,840

P20.3A (LO 4), AN Thompson Industrial Products Inc. (TIPI) is a diversified industrial-cleaner processing company. The company's Dargan plant produces two products: a table cleaner and a floor cleaner from a common set of chemical inputs (CDG). Each week, 900,000 ounces of chemical input are processed at a cost of $210,000 into 600,000 ounces of floor cleaner and 300,000 ounces of table cleaner. The floor cleaner has no market value until it is converted into a polish with the trade name FloorShine. The additional processing costs for this conversion amount to $240,000.

FloorShine sells at $20 per 30-ounce bottle. The table cleaner can be sold for $17 per 25-ounce bottle. However, the table cleaner can be converted into two other products by adding 300,000 ounces of another compound (TCP) to the 300,000 ounces of table cleaner. This joint process will yield 300,000 ounces each of table stain remover (TSR) and table polish (TP). The additional processing costs for this process amount to $100,000. Both table products can be sold for $14 per 25-ounce bottle.

The company decided not to process the table cleaner into TSR and TP based on the following analysis.

Determine if product should be sold or processed further.

	Table Cleaner	Process Further		Total
		Table Stain Remover (TSR)	Table Polish (TP)	
Production in ounces	300,000	300,000	300,000	
Revenues	$204,000	$168,000	$168,000	$336,000
Costs:				
CDG costs	70,000*	52,500	52,500	105,000**
TCP costs	0	50,000	50,000	100,000
Total costs	70,000	102,500	102,500	205,000
Weekly gross profit	$134,000	$ 65,500	$ 65,500	$131,000

*If table cleaner is not processed further, it is allocated 1/3 of the $210,000 of CDG cost, which is equal to 1/3 of the total physical output.
**If table cleaner is processed further, total physical output is 1,200,000 ounces. TSR and TP combined account for 50% of the total physical output and are each allocated 25% of the CDG cost.

Instructions

a. Determine if management made the correct decision to not process the table cleaner further by doing the following.

1. Calculate the company's total weekly gross profit assuming the table cleaner is not processed further.

2. Calculate the company's total weekly gross profit assuming the table cleaner is processed further.

3. Compare the resulting net incomes and comment on management's decision.

b. Using incremental analysis, determine if the table cleaner should be processed further.

2. Gross profit $186,000

(CMA adapted)

P20.4A (LO 5), S Service Writing At the beginning of last year (2021), Richter Condos installed a mechanized elevator for its tenants. The owner of the company, Ron Richter, recently returned from an industry equipment exhibition where he watched a computerized elevator demonstrated. He was impressed with the elevator's speed, comfort of ride, and cost efficiency. Upon returning from the exhibition, he asked his purchasing agent to collect price and operating cost data on the new elevator. In addition, he asked

Compute gain or loss, and determine if equipment should be replaced.

the company's accountant to provide him with cost data on the company's elevator. This information is presented below.

	Old Elevator	New Elevator
Purchase price	$120,000	$160,000
Estimated salvage value	0	0
Estimated useful life	5 years	4 years
Depreciation method	Straight-line	Straight-line
Annual operating costs other than depreciation:		
Variable	$ 35,000	$ 10,000
Fixed	23,000	8,500

Annual revenues are $240,000, and selling and administrative expenses are $29,000, regardless of which elevator is used. If the old elevator is replaced now, at the beginning of 2022, Richter Condos will be able to sell it for $25,000.

Instructions

a. Determine any gain or loss if the old elevator is replaced.

b. Prepare a 4-year summarized income statement for each of the following assumptions:

   1. The old elevator is retained.
   2. The old elevator is replaced.

b. 2. NI $539,000

c. NI increase $23,000

c. Using incremental analysis, determine if the old elevator should be replaced.

d. Write a memo to Ron Richter explaining why any gain or loss should be ignored in the decision to replace the old elevator.

Prepare incremental analysis concerning elimination of divisions.

P20.5A (LO 6), AN Brislin Company has four operating divisions. During the first quarter of 2022, the company reported aggregate income from operations of $213,000 and the following divisional results.

	Division			
	I	II	III	IV
Sales	$250,000	$200,000	$500,000	$450,000
Cost of goods sold	200,000	192,000	300,000	250,000
Selling and administrative expenses	75,000	60,000	60,000	50,000
Income (loss) from operations	$ (25,000)	$ (52,000)	$140,000	$150,000

Analysis reveals the following percentages of variable costs in each division.

	I	II	III	IV
Cost of goods sold	70%	90%	80%	75%
Selling and administrative expenses	40	60	50	60

Discontinuance of any division would save 50% of the fixed costs and expenses for that division.

Top management is very concerned about the unprofitable divisions (I and II). Consensus is that one or both of the divisions should be discontinued.

Instructions

a. Contribution margin I $80,000

a. Compute the contribution margin for Divisions I and II.

b. Prepare an incremental analysis concerning the possible discontinuance of (1) Division I and (2) Division II. What course of action do you recommend for each division?

c. Income III $132,800

c. Prepare a columnar condensed income statement for Brislin Company, assuming Division II is eliminated. (Use the CVP format.) Division II's unavoidable fixed costs are allocated equally to the continuing divisions.

d. Reconcile the total income from operations ($213,000) with the total income from operations without Division II.

Continuing Cases

Current Designs

CD20 Current Designs faces a number of important decisions that require incremental analysis. Consider each of the following situations independently.

Situation 1

Recently, Mike Cichanowski, owner and CEO of Current Designs, received a phone call from the president of a brewing company. He was calling to inquire about the possibility of Current Designs producing "floating coolers" for a promotion his company was planning. These coolers resemble a kayak but are about one-third the size. They are used to float food and beverages while paddling down the river on a weekend leisure trip. The company would be interested in purchasing 100 coolers for the upcoming summer. It is willing to pay $250 per cooler. The brewing company would pick up the coolers upon completion of the order.

Mike met with Diane Buswell, controller, to identify how much it would cost Current Designs to produce the coolers. After careful analysis, the following costs were identified.

Direct materials	$80/unit	Variable overhead	$20/unit
Direct labor	$60/unit	Fixed overhead	$1,000

Current Designs would be able to modify an existing mold to produce the coolers. The cost of these modifications would be approximately $2,000.

Instructions

a. Prepare an incremental analysis to determine whether Current Designs should accept this special order to produce the coolers.

b. Discuss additional factors that Mike and Diane should consider if Current Designs is currently operating at full capacity.

Situation 2

Current Designs is always working to identify ways to increase efficiency while becoming more environmentally conscious. During a recent brainstorming session, one employee suggested to Diane Buswell, controller, that the company should consider replacing the current rotomold oven as a way to realize savings from reduced energy consumption. The oven operates on natural gas, using 17,000 therms of natural gas for an entire year. A new, energy-efficient rotomold oven would operate on 15,000 therms of natural gas for an entire year. After seeking out price quotes from a few suppliers, Diane determined that it would cost approximately $250,000 to purchase a new, energy-efficient rotomold oven. She determines that the expected useful life of the new oven would be 10 years, and it would have no salvage value at the end of its useful life. Current Designs would be able to sell the current oven for $10,000.

Instructions

a. Prepare an incremental analysis to determine if Current Designs should purchase the new rotomold oven, assuming that the average price for natural gas over the next 10 years will be $0.65 per therm.

b. Diane is concerned that natural gas prices might increase at a faster rate over the next 10 years. If the company projects that the average natural gas price of the next 10 years could be as high as $0.85 per therm, discuss how that might change your conclusion in (a).

Situation 3

One of Current Designs' competitive advantages is found in the ingenuity of its owner and CEO, Mike Cichanowski. His involvement in the design of kayak molds and production techniques has led to Current Designs being recognized as an industry leader in the design and production of kayaks. This ingenuity was evident in an improved design of one of the most important components of a kayak, the seat. The "Revolution Seating System" is a one-of-a-kind, rotating axis seat that gives unmatched, full-contact, under-leg support. It is quickly adjustable with a lever-lock system that allows for a customizable seat position that maximizes comfort for the rider.

Having just designed the "Revolution Seating System," Current Designs must now decide whether to produce the seats internally or buy them from an outside supplier. The costs for Current Designs to produce the seats are as follows.

Direct materials	$20/unit	Direct labor	$15/unit
Variable overhead	$12/unit	Fixed overhead	$20,000

Current Designs will need to produce 3,000 seats this year; 25% of the fixed overhead will be avoided if the seats are purchased from an outside vendor. After soliciting prices from outside suppliers, the company determined that it will cost $50 to purchase a seat from an outside vendor.

Instructions

a. Prepare an incremental analysis showing whether Current Designs should make or buy the "Revolution Seating System."

b. Would your answer in (a) change if the productive capacity released by not making the seats could be used to produce income of $20,000?

Waterways

(*Note:* This is a continuation of the Waterways case from Chapters 14–19.)

WP20 Waterways Corporation is considering various business opportunities. It wants to make the best use of its production facilities to maximize income. This problem asks you to help Waterways do incremental analysis on these various opportunities.

Go to WileyPLUS for complete case details and instructions.

Expand Your Critical Thinking

Decision-Making Across the Organization

CT20.1 Aurora Company is considering the purchase of a new machine. The invoice price of the machine is $140,000, freight charges are estimated to be $4,000, and installation costs are expected to be $6,000. Salvage value of the new equipment is expected to be zero after a useful life of 5 years. Existing equipment could be retained and used for an additional 5 years if the new machine is not purchased. At that time, the salvage value of the equipment would be zero. If the new machine is purchased now, the existing machine would have to be scrapped. Aurora's accountant, Lisah Huang, has accumulated the following data regarding annual sales and expenses with and without the new machine.

1. Without the new machine, Aurora can sell 12,000 units of product annually at a per unit selling price of $100. If the new machine is purchased, the number of units produced and sold would increase by 10%, and the selling price would remain the same.

2. The new machine is faster than the old machine, and it is more efficient in its usage of materials. With the old machine the gross profit rate will be 25% of sales, whereas the rate will be 30% of sales with the new machine.

3. Annual selling expenses are $180,000 with the current equipment. Because the new equipment would produce a greater number of units to be sold, annual selling expenses are expected to increase by 10% if it is purchased.

4. Annual administrative expenses are expected to be $100,000 with the old machine, and $113,000 with the new machine.

5. The current book value of the existing machine is $36,000. Aurora uses straight-line depreciation.

Instructions

With the class divided into groups, prepare an incremental analysis for the 5 years showing whether Aurora should keep the existing machine or buy the new machine. (Ignore income tax effects.)

Managerial Analysis

CT20.2 MiniTek manufactures private-label small electronic products, such as alarm clocks, calculators, kitchen timers, stopwatches, and automatic pencil sharpeners. Some of the products are sold as sets, and others are sold individually. Products are studied as to their sales potential, and then cost estimates are made. The Engineering Department develops production plans, and then production begins. The company has generally had very successful product introductions. Only two products introduced by the company have been discontinued.

One of the products currently sold is a multi-alarm clock. The clock has four alarms that can be programmed to sound at various times and for varying lengths of time. The company has experienced a great deal of difficulty in making the circuit boards for the clocks. The production process has never operated smoothly. The product is unprofitable at the present time, primarily because of warranty repairs and product recalls. Two models of the clocks were recalled, for example, because they sometimes caused an electric shock when the alarms were being shut off. The Engineering Department is attempting to revise the manufacturing process, but the revision will take another 6 months at least.

The clocks were very popular when they were introduced, and since they are private-label, the company has not suffered much from the recalls. Presently, the company has a very large order for several items from **Kmart Stores**. The order includes 5,000 of the multi-alarm clocks. When the company suggested that Kmart purchase the clocks from another manufacturer, Kmart threatened to rescind the entire order unless the clocks were included.

The company has therefore investigated the possibility of having another company make the clocks for them. The clocks were bid for the Kmart order based on an estimated $6.90 cost to manufacture:

Circuit board, 1 each @ $2.00	$2.00
Plastic case, 1 each @ $0.80	0.80
Alarms, 4 @ $0.15 each	0.60
Labor, 15 minutes @ $12/hour	3.00
Overhead, $2.00 per labor hour	0.50

MiniTek could purchase clocks to fill the Kmart order for $10 from Trans-Tech Asia, a Korean manufacturer with a very good quality record. Trans-Tech has offered to reduce the price to $7.50 after MiniTek has been a customer for 6 months, placing an order of at least 1,000 units per month. If MiniTek becomes a "preferred customer" by purchasing 15,000 units per year, the price would be reduced still further to $4.50.

Omega Products, a local manufacturer, has also offered to make clocks for MiniTek. They have offered to sell 5,000 clocks for $5 each. However, Omega Products has been in business for only 6 months. They have experienced significant turnover in their labor force, and the local press has reported that the owners may face tax evasion charges soon. The owner of Omega Products is an electronic engineer, however, and the quality of the clocks is likely to be good.

If MiniTek decides to purchase the clocks from either Trans-Tech or Omega, all the costs to manufacture could be avoided, except a total of $1,000 in overhead costs for machine depreciation. The machinery is fairly new, and has no alternate use.

Instructions

a. What is the difference in profit under each of the alternatives if the clocks are to be sold for $14.50 each to Kmart?

b. What are the most important nonfinancial factors that MiniTek should consider when making this decision?

c. What do you think MiniTek should do in regard to the Kmart order? What should it do in regard to continuing to manufacture the multi-alarm clocks? Be prepared to defend your answer.

Real-World Focus

CT20.3 Founded in 1983 and foreclosed in 1996 **Beverly Hills Fan Company** was located in Woodland Hills, California. With 23 employees and sales of less than $10 million, the company was relatively small. Management felt that there was potential for growth in the upscale market for ceiling fans and lighting. They were particularly optimistic about growth in Mexican and Canadian markets.

Presented below is information from the president's letter in one of the company's last annual reports.

Beverly Hills Fan Company
President's Letter

An aggressive product development program was initiated during the past year resulting in new ceiling fan models planned for introduction this year. Award winning industrial designer Ron Rezek created several new fan models for the Beverly Hills Fan and L.A. Fan lines, including a new Showroom Collection, designed specifically for the architectural and designer markets. Each of these models has received critical acclaim, and order commitments for this year have been outstanding. Additionally, our Custom Color and special order fans continued to enjoy increasing popularity and sales gains as more and more customers desire fans that match their specific interior decors. Currently, Beverly Hills Fan Company offers a product line of over 100 models of contemporary, traditional, and transitional ceiling fans.

Instructions

a. What points did the company management need to consider before deciding to offer the special-order fans to customers?

b. How would have incremental analysis been employed to assist in this decision?

Communication Activity

CT20.4 Hank Jewell is a production manager at a metal fabricating plant. Last night, he read an article about a new piece of equipment that would dramatically reduce his division's costs. Hank was very excited about the prospect, and the first thing he did this morning was to bring the article to his supervisor, Preston Thiese, the plant manager. The following conversation occurred:

Hank: Preston, I thought you would like to see this article on the new PDD1130; they've made some fantastic changes that could save us millions of dollars.

Preston: I appreciate your interest, Hank, but I actually have been aware of the new machine for two months. The problem is that we just bought a new machine last year. We spent $2 million on that machine, and it was supposed to last us 12 years. If we replace it now, we would have to write its book value off of the books for a huge loss. If I go to top management now and say that I want a new machine, they will fire me. I think we should use our existing machine for a couple of years, and then when it becomes obvious that we have to have a new machine, I will make the proposal.

Instructions

Hank just completed a course in managerial accounting, and he believes that Preston is making a big mistake. Write a memo from Hank to Preston explaining Preston's decision-making error.

Ethics Case

CT20.5 Blake Romney became Chief Executive Officer of Peters Inc. two years ago. At the time, the company was reporting lagging profits, and Blake was brought in to "stir things up." The company has three divisions, electronics, fiber optics, and plumbing supplies. Blake has no interest in plumbing supplies, and one of the first things he did was to put pressure on his accountants to reallocate some of the company's fixed costs away from the other two divisions to the plumbing division. This had the effect of causing the plumbing division to report losses during the last two years; in the past it had always reported low, but acceptable, net income. Blake felt that this reallocation would shine a favorable light on him in front of the board of directors because it meant that the electronics and fiber optics divisions would look like they were improving. Given that these are "businesses of the future," he believed that the stock market would react favorably to these increases, while not penalizing the poor results of the plumbing division. Without this shift in the allocation of fixed costs, the profits of the electronics and fiber optics divisions would not have improved. But now the board of directors has suggested that the plumbing division be closed because it is reporting losses. This would mean that nearly 500 employees, many of whom have worked for Peters their whole lives, would lose their jobs.

Instructions

a. If a division is reporting losses, does that necessarily mean that it should be closed?

b. Was the reallocation of fixed costs across divisions unethical?

c. What should Blake do?

All About You

CT20.6 Managerial accounting techniques can be used in a wide variety of settings. As we have frequently pointed out, you can use them in many personal situations. They also can be useful in trying to find solutions for societal issues that appear to be hard to solve.

Instructions

Read the *Fortune* article, "The Toughest Customers: How Hardheaded Business Metrics Can Help the Hard-Core Homeless," by Cait Murphy (do an Internet search on the title), and then answer the following questions.

a. How does the article define "chronic" homelessness?

b. In what ways does homelessness cost a city money? What are the estimated costs of a chronic homeless person to various cities?

c. What are the steps suggested to address the problem?
   d. What is the estimated cost of implementing this program in New York? What results have been seen?
   e. In terms of incremental analysis, frame the relevant costs in this situation.

Considering Your Costs and Benefits

CT20.7 School costs money. Is this an expenditure that you should have avoided? A year of tuition at a public four-year college costs about $8,655, and a year of tuition at a public two-year college costs about $1,359. If you did not go to college, you might avoid mountains of school-related debt. In fact, each year, about 600,000 students decide to drop out of school. Many of them never return. Suppose that you are working two jobs and going to college, and that you are not making ends meet. Your grades are suffering due to your lack of available study time. You feel depressed. Should you drop out of school?

YES: You can always go back to school. If your grades are bad and you are depressed, what good is school doing you anyway?

NO: Once you drop out, it is very hard to get enough momentum to go back. Dropping out will dramatically reduce your long-term opportunities. It is better to stay in school, even if you take only one class per semester. While you cannot go back and redo your initial decision, you can look at some facts to evaluate the wisdom of your decision.

Instructions

Write a response indicating your position regarding this situation. Provide support for your view.

CHAPTER 21

Pricing

Chapter Preview

As the following Feature Story about **Zappos.com** indicates, few management decisions are more important than setting prices. **Intel**, for example, must sell computer chips at a price that is high enough to cover its costs and ensure a reasonable profit. But if the price is too high, the chips will not sell. In this chapter, we examine two types of pricing situations. The first part of the chapter addresses pricing for goods sold or services provided to external parties. The second part of the chapter addresses pricing decisions managers face when they sell goods to other divisions within the company.

Feature Story

They've Got Your Size—and Color

Nick Swinmurn was shopping for a pair of shoes. He found a store with the right style, but not the right color. The next store had the right color, but not the right size. After visiting numerous stores, he went home, figuring he would buy them online. After all, it was 1999, so you could buy everything online, right? Well, apparently not shoes. After an exhaustive search, Nick still came up shoeless.

Nick lived in San Francisco, where in 1999 everybody with even half an idea started an Internet company and became a millionaire. Or so it seemed. So Nick started **Zappos.com.** The company is dedicated to providing the best selection in shoes in terms of brands, styles, colors, size, and, most importantly, service.

To make sure that Zappos had a fighting chance of evolving from a half-baked idea to a thriving business, Nick brought in Tony Hsieh. At the age of 24, Tony had developed and recently sold a business to Microsoft for $265 million. Tony then brought in Alfred Lin to manage the company's finances. Tony and Alfred first met when Tony was running a pizza business and Alfred was Tony's best pizza customer. Together, Tony and Alfred have run Zappos based on 10 basic principles:

1. Deliver WOW through service.
2. Embrace and drive change.
3. Create fun and a little weirdness.
4. Be adventurous, creative, and open-minded.
5. Pursue growth and learning.
6. Build open and honest relationships with communication.
7. Build a positive team and family spirit.
8. Do more with less.
9. Be passionate and determined.
10. Be humble.

Are you looking for a pair of size 6 Giuseppe Zanotti heels for $1,295 or a pair of Keen size 17 sandals for $95? Zappos is committed to having what you want and getting it to you as fast as possible. Providing this kind of service is not cheap, however. It means having vast warehouses and sophisticated order processing systems. The company's price has to cover its costs and provide a reasonable profit yet still be competitive. If the price is too high, Zappos loses business. Too low and the company could lose its shirt (or in this case, shoes).

Source: www.zappos.com.

 Watch the *Zappos.com* video in WileyPLUS to learn more about how the company sets prices.

Chapter Outline

LEARNING OBJECTIVES

LO 1 Compute a target cost when the market determines a product price.	• Establishing a target cost	**DO IT! 1** Target Costing
LO 2 Compute a target selling price using cost-plus pricing.	• Cost-plus pricing • Limitations of cost-plus pricing • Variable-cost pricing	**DO IT! 2** Target Selling Price
LO 3 Use time-and-material pricing to determine the cost of services provided.	• Calculate labor rate • Calculate material loading charge	**DO IT! 3** Time-and-Material Pricing
LO 4 Determine a transfer price using the negotiated, cost-based, and market-based approaches.	• Negotiated transfer prices • Cost-based transfer prices • Market-based transfer prices • Effect of outsourcing on transfer pricing • Transfers between divisions in different countries	**DO IT! 4** Transfer Pricing

Go to the Review and Practice section at the end of the chapter for a targeted summary and practice applications with solutions.
Visit WileyPLUS for additional tutorials and practice opportunities.

Target Costing

> **LEARNING OBJECTIVE 1**
> Compute a target cost when the market determines a product price.

Establishing the price for any good or service is affected by many factors. Take the pharmaceutical industry as an example. Its approach to profitability has been to spend heavily on research and development in an effort to find and patent a few new drugs, price them high, and market them aggressively. Individuals in the United States sometimes question whether these prices are too high. For example, the price of EpiPens® received considerable criticism. The drug companies counter that they need to set these prices high to cover their substantial financial risks to develop these products. Illustration 21.1 indicates the many factors that can affect pricing decisions.

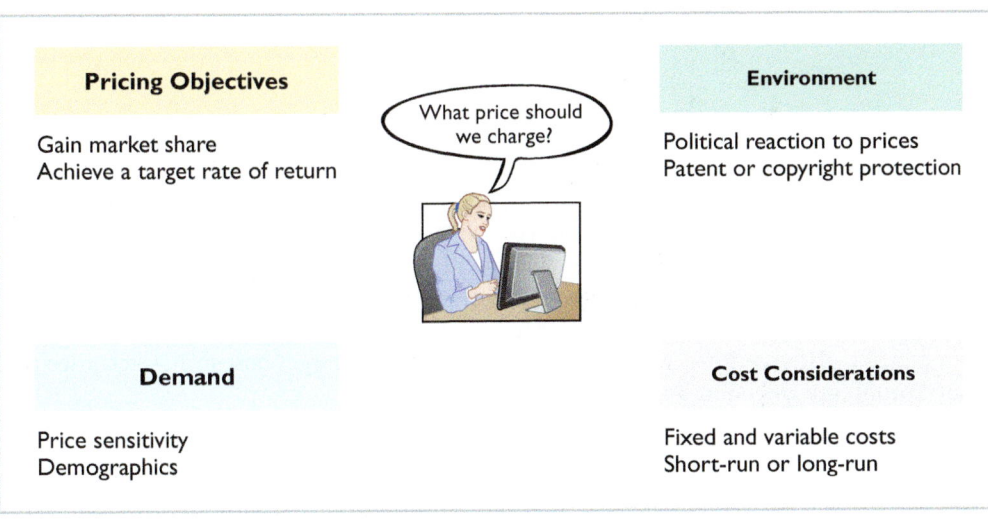

ILLUSTRATION 21.1
Pricing factors

In the long run, a company must price its product to cover its costs and earn a reasonable profit. But to price its product appropriately, it must have a good understanding of market forces at work. In most cases, a company does not set the prices. Instead, the price is set by the competitive market (the laws of supply and demand). For example, a company such as **ChevronTexaco** or **ExxonMobil** cannot set the price of gasoline by itself. These companies are called **price takers** because the price of gasoline is set by market forces (the supply of oil and the demand by customers). This is the case for any product that is not easily differentiated from competing products, such as farm products (corn or wheat) or minerals (coal or sand).

In other situations, the company sets the prices. This would be the case where the product is specially made for a customer, as in a one-of-a-kind product such as a designer dress by **Versace** or **Armani**. A company also sets the price when there are few or no other producers capable of manufacturing a similar item. An example would be a company that has a patent or copyright on a unique process, such as computer chips by **Intel**. Finally, a company can set prices when it effectively differentiates its product or service from others. Even in a competitive market like coffee, **Starbucks** has been able to differentiate its product and charge a premium for a cup of java.

Management Insight Amazon.com

Cyberstock/Alamy Stock Photo

Pricing to Sell

Managers at Amazon.com make many different pricing decisions for products with vastly different characteristics. For example, Amazon provides "cloud services" to both corporate and retail clients, as well as video rental, book sales, and order fulfillment services for thousands of different vendors. It also has produced and sold some of its own electronic devices, with varying degrees of success. For example, Amazon produced the Fire smartphone, which it tried unsuccessfully to sell for the same premium price as the iPhone (eventually, it had to offer steep discounts). On the other end of the price spectrum, it has offered tablets and e-reader devices (such as the Kindle) for extremely low prices. In fact, some have suggested that these products are sold below cost. Why would Amazon's management do that? Because the company makes money on the services delivered by tablets and e-readers, such as e-books and movies. (This is similar to Google, which provides many of its services for free but then makes advertising revenue as people use its free services.) In fact, even on its cheapest electronic devices, Amazon is cognizant of its costs. Although it desired to set the target price of its cheapest Kindle at $50, "the e-reader screen technology from its vendors ultimately proved too expensive to drop the retail price." Ultimately, Amazon decided it could not price the Kindle below $79.

Source: Greg Bensinger, "Amazon to Release $50 Tablet as It Struggles to Sell Pricier Devices," *Wall Street Journal* (September 7, 2015).

Why did Amazon choose to charge a premium price for its Fire smartphone, but it chooses to offer some of its tablet and Kindle models at prices that barely cover its costs? (Go to WileyPLUS for this answer and additional questions.)

Establishing a Target Cost

> **Decision Tools**
>
> Managers use the target cost formula in Illustration 21.2 to make decisions about manufacturing products or performing services.

Automobile manufacturers like Ford and Toyota face a competitive market. The price of an automobile is affected greatly by the laws of supply and demand, so no company in this industry can affect the price to a significant degree. Therefore, to earn a profit, companies in the auto industry must focus on controlling costs. This requires setting a **target cost** that provides a desired profit. Illustration 21.2 shows the relationship of target cost to market price and desired profit (see Decision Tools).

ILLUSTRATION 21.2

Target cost as related to price and profit

Market Price − Desired Profit = Target Cost

Assuming it reaches sales targets, if General Motors can produce its automobiles for its target cost (or less), it will meet its profit goal. If it cannot achieve its target cost, it will fail to achieve the desired profit, which will disappoint its stockholders.

In a competitive market, a company chooses the segment of the market it wants to compete in—that is, its market niche. For example, it may choose between selling luxury goods or economy goods in order to focus its efforts on one segment or the other. Once the company has identified the segment of the market in which it wants to compete, it conducts market research. This determines the features its product should have, and what the market price is for a product with those features. Once the company has determined this price, it can determine its target cost by setting a desired profit. The difference between the market price and the desired profit is the target cost of the product (shown in Illustration 21.2). After the company determines the target cost, it assembles a team of employees with expertise in a variety of areas (production and operations, marketing, and finance). The team's task is to design and develop a product that can meet quality specifications while not exceeding the target cost. The target cost includes all product and period costs necessary to make and market the product or service.

Service Company Insight Disney

How Much Did You Pay for That Seat?

Tomas Abad/Alamy Stock Photo

Pricing decisions are now frequently made by sophisticated computer algorithms. This is true for airlines, hotels, and even Broadway shows. Pricing for these service businesses is particularly important because no revenue is earned on an unused airplane seat, hotel room, or theater seat. These algorithms, which are based on models derived from vast amounts of data from previous customer experiences, strive to determine the best price to charge to fill the seats and maximize revenue. Prices are very dynamic, changing daily or hourly. As a result, it is not unusual to sit directly next to somebody that paid significantly more (or less) than you did on an airplane.

Experts says that the algorithm that **Disney** employs to determine ticket prices for its Broadway show "The Lion King" is among the best in the business. Disney's pricing model enabled "The Lion King" to nearly double its revenues compared to what they were six years earlier. As a consequence, the company is very reluctant to reveal specific information about its formulas.

Source: Patrick Healy, "Ticket Pricing Puts 'Lion King' Atop Broadway's Circle of Life," *The New York Times* (March 17, 2014).

What factors must the managers of a Broadway show consider setting prices? (Go to WileyPLUS for this answer and additional questions.)

DO IT! 1 | Target Costing

Fine Line Phones is considering introducing a fashion cover for its phones. Market research indicates that 200,000 units can be sold if the price is no more than $20. If Fine Line decides to produce the covers, it will need to invest $1,000,000 in new production equipment. Fine Line requires a minimum rate of return of 25% on all investments.

Determine the target cost per unit for the cover.

ACTION PLAN
- Recall that Market price − Desired profit = Target cost.
- The minimum rate of return is a company's desired profit.

Solution

The desired profit for this new product line is as follows.

Invested assets	×	Minimum rate of return	=	Desired profit
$1,000,000	×	25%	=	$250,000

Each cover must therefore result in $1.25 of profit ($250,000/200,000 units). The target cost per unit for the cover can then be calculated as follows.

Market price	−	Desired profit	=	Target cost per unit
$20	−	$1.25	=	$18.75 per unit

Related exercise material: **BE21.1, DO IT! 21.1, E21.1, and E21.2.**

Cost-Plus and Variable-Cost Pricing

LEARNING OBJECTIVE 2
Compute a target selling price using cost-plus pricing.

Cost-Plus Pricing

As discussed, in a competitive product environment, the price of a product is set by the market. In order to achieve its desired profit, the company focuses on achieving a target cost. In a less competitive environment, companies have a greater ability to set the product price. Commonly, when a company sets a product price, it does so as a function of, or relative to, the cost of the product or service. This is referred to as **cost-plus pricing**. Under cost-plus pricing, a company first determines a cost base and then adds a **markup** to the cost base to determine the **target selling price**.

If the cost base includes all of the costs required to produce and sell the product, then the markup represents the desired profit. This can be seen in **Illustration 21.3**, where the markup represents the difference between the selling price and cost—the profit on the product.

ILLUSTRATION 21.3
Relation of markup to cost and selling price

$$\text{Selling Price} - \text{Cost} = \text{Markup (Profit)}$$

Decision Tools

The formula in Illustration 21.4 represents how managers use cost-plus pricing to achieve the desired profit.

The size of the markup (profit) depends on the return the company hopes to generate on the amount it has invested. In determining the optimal markup, the company must consider competitive and market conditions, political and legal issues, and other relevant factors. Once the company has determined its cost base and its desired markup, it can add the two together to determine the target selling price. **Illustration 21.4** presents the basic cost-plus pricing formula (see **Decision Tools**).

ILLUSTRATION 21.4
Cost-plus pricing formula

$$\text{Cost} + \text{Markup} = \text{Target Selling Price}$$

To illustrate, assume that Thinkmore Products, Inc. is in the process of setting a selling price on its new video camera pen. It is a functioning pen that records up to 2 hours of audio and video. The per unit variable cost estimates for the video camera pen are as shown in **Illustration 21.5**.

ILLUSTRATION 21.5
Variable cost per unit

	Per Unit
Direct materials	$23
Direct labor	17
Variable manufacturing overhead	12
Variable selling and administrative expenses	8
Variable cost per unit	$60

To produce and sell its product, Thinkmore incurs fixed manufacturing overhead of $350,000 and fixed selling and administrative expenses of $300,000. To determine the cost per unit, we divide total fixed costs by the number of units the company expects to produce. **Illustration 21.6** shows the computation of fixed cost per unit for Thinkmore, assuming the production of 10,000 units.

ILLUSTRATION 21.6
Fixed cost per unit, 10,000 units

	Total Costs	÷	Budgeted Volume	=	Cost per Unit
Fixed manufacturing overhead	$350,000	÷	10,000	=	$35
Fixed selling and administrative expenses	300,000	÷	10,000	=	30
Fixed cost per unit (at 10,000 units)					$65

Management is ultimately evaluated based on its ability to generate a high return on the company's investment. This is frequently expressed as a return on investment (ROI) percentage, calculated as income divided by the average amount invested in a product or service. A higher percentage reflects a greater success in generating profits from the investment in a product or service. Chapter 23 provides a more in-depth discussion of the use of ROI to evaluate the performance of investment center managers.

To achieve a desired return on investment percentage, a product's markup should be determined by calculating the desired return on investment (ROI) per unit. This is calculated by multiplying the desired ROI percentage times the amount invested to produce the product, and then dividing this by the number of units produced. **Illustration 21.7** shows the computation used to determine a markup amount based on a desired ROI per unit for Thinkmore, assuming that the company expects to produce 10,000 units, desires a 20% ROI, and invests $2,000,000.

$$\frac{\text{Desired ROI Percentage} \times \text{Amount Invested}}{\text{Units Produced}} = \text{Markup (Desired ROI per Unit)}$$

$$\frac{20\% \times \$2{,}000{,}000}{10{,}000 \text{ units}} = \$40$$

ILLUSTRATION 21.7
Calculation of markup based on desired ROI per unit

Thinkmore expects to receive income of $400,000 (20% × $2,000,000) on its $2,000,000 investment. On a per unit basis, the markup based on the desired ROI per unit is $40 ($400,000 ÷ 10,000 units). Given the per unit costs shown above, **Illustration 21.8** computes the sales price to be $165.

	Per Unit
Variable cost	$ 60
Fixed cost	65
Total cost	125
Markup (desired ROI per unit)	40
Selling price per unit (at 10,000 units)	**$165**

ILLUSTRATION 21.8
Computation of selling price, 10,000 units

In most cases, companies like Thinkmore use a markup percentage on cost to determine the selling price. **Illustration 21.9** presents the formula to compute the markup percentage to achieve a desired ROI of $40 per unit.

$$\text{Markup (Desired ROI per Unit)} \div \text{Total Unit Cost} = \text{Markup Percentage}$$

$$\$40 \div \$125 = 32\%$$

ILLUSTRATION 21.9
Computation of markup percentage

Using a 32% markup on cost, Thinkmore would compute the target selling price as shown in **Illustration 21.10**.

$$\text{Total Unit Cost} + (\text{Total Unit Cost} \times \text{Markup Percentage}) = \text{Target Selling Price per Unit}$$

$$\$125 + (\$125 \times 32\%) = \$165$$

ILLUSTRATION 21.10
Computation of selling price—markup approach

Thinkmore should set the price for its video camera pen at $165 per unit.

Limitations of Cost-Plus Pricing

The cost-plus pricing approach has a major advantage: It is simple to compute. However, the cost model does not give consideration to the demand side. That is, will customers pay the price Thinkmore Products computed for its video camera pen? In addition, sales volume plays a large role in determining per unit costs. The lower the sales volume, for example, the higher the price Thinkmore must charge to meet its desired ROI. To illustrate, if the budgeted sales volume was 5,000 instead of 10,000, Thinkmore's variable cost per unit would remain the same. However, the fixed cost per unit would change as shown in **Illustration 21.11**.

ILLUSTRATION 21.11
Fixed cost per unit, 5,000 units

	Total Costs	÷	Budgeted Volume	=	Cost per Unit
Fixed manufacturing overhead	$350,000	÷	5,000	=	$ 70
Fixed selling and administrative expenses	300,000	÷	5,000	=	60
Fixed cost per unit (at 5,000 units)					$130

As indicated in Illustration 21.6, the fixed cost per unit for 10,000 units was $65. However, at a lower sales volume of 5,000 units, the fixed cost per unit increases to $130. Thinkmore's desired 20% ROI now results in a $80 ROI per unit [(20% × $2,000,000) ÷ 5,000]. Thinkmore computes the selling price at 5,000 units as shown in **Illustration 21.12**.

ILLUSTRATION 21.12
Computation of selling price, 5,000 units

	Per Unit
Variable cost	$ 60
Fixed cost	130
Total cost	190
Markup (desired ROI per unit)	80
Selling price per unit (at 5,000 units)	$270

As shown, the lower the budgeted volume, the higher the per unit price. The reason: Fixed costs and ROI are spread over fewer units, and therefore the fixed cost and ROI per unit increase. In this case, at 5,000 units, Thinkmore would have to mark up its total unit costs 42.11% to earn a desired ROI of $80 per unit, as shown below.

$$42.11\% = \frac{\$80 \text{ (desired ROI per unit)}}{\$190 \text{ (total unit cost)}}$$

The target selling price would then be $270, as indicated earlier:

$$\$190 + (\$190 \times 42.11\%) = \$270$$

The opposite effect will occur if budgeted volume is higher (say, at 12,000 units) because fixed costs and ROI can be spread over more units. As a result, the cost-plus model of pricing will achieve its desired ROI only when Thinkmore sells the quantity it budgeted. If actual volume is much less than budgeted volume, Thinkmore may sustain losses unless it can raise its prices.

Variable-Cost Pricing

In determining the target price for Thinkmore Products' video camera pen, we calculated the cost base by including all costs incurred. This approach is referred to as **full-cost pricing**. Instead of using full costs to set prices, some companies simply add a markup to their variable costs (thus excluding fixed manufacturing and fixed selling and administrative costs). Using **variable-cost pricing** as the basis for setting prices avoids the problem of using uncertain cost information (as discussed above for Thinkmore) related to fixed-cost-per-unit computations. Variable-cost pricing also is helpful in pricing special orders or when excess capacity exists.

The major disadvantage of variable-cost pricing is that managers may set the price too low and consequently fail to cover their fixed costs. In the long run, failure to cover fixed costs will lead to losses. As a result, companies that use variable-cost pricing must adjust their markups to make sure that the price set will provide a fair return. The use of variable costs as the basis for setting prices is discussed in Appendix 21A.

Management Insight Parker Hannifin

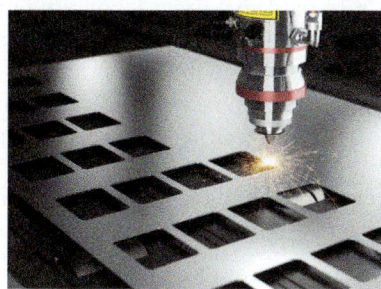
629603990/iStockphoto

At Least It Was Simple

For nearly 90 years, Parker Hannifin used the same simple approach to price its industrial parts. It calculated the production cost, then added on a percentage of the cost (about 35%) to arrive at the price. It didn't matter if a product was a premium product or a standard product. And if Parker reduced its production costs, it then also cut the price for the product. The problem with this approach was that it made it difficult for the company to ever substantially increase its profit margins. So the company's CEO decided to break with tradition and implement strategic pricing schemes similar to those used by retailers. It determined that for about a third of its products, it had a competitive advantage that would allow it to charge a higher markup. For example, there might be limited competition for the product, or its product might be of higher quality, or it might have the ability to produce a product faster. The company determined that the price increases raised net income by $200 million—not bad considering that net income was $130 million before the price increases.

Source: Timothy Aeppel, "Changing the Formula: Seeking Perfect Prices, CEO Tears Up the Rules," *Wall Street Journal Online* (March 27, 2007).

What kind of help might the sales staff need in implementing this new approach? (Go to WileyPLUS for this answer and additional questions.)

DO IT! 2 | Target Selling Price

Air Corporation produces air purifiers. The following per unit cost information is available: direct materials $16, direct labor $18, variable manufacturing overhead $11, variable selling and administrative expenses $6. Fixed selling and administrative expenses are $50,000, and fixed manufacturing overhead is $150,000. Using a 45% markup percentage on total per unit cost and assuming 10,000 units, compute the target selling price.

ACTION PLAN
- Calculate the total cost per unit.
- Multiply the total cost per unit by the markup percentage, then add this amount to the total cost per unit to determine the target selling price.

Solution

Direct materials	$16
Direct labor	18
Variable manufacturing overhead	11
Variable selling and administrative expenses	6
Fixed selling and administrative expenses	5*
Fixed manufacturing overhead	15**
Total unit cost	$71

$$\begin{pmatrix}\text{Total}\\\text{unit cost}\end{pmatrix} + \begin{pmatrix}\text{Total}\\\text{unit cost}\end{pmatrix} \times \begin{pmatrix}\text{Markup}\\\text{percentage}\end{pmatrix} = \begin{pmatrix}\text{Target selling}\\\text{price per unit}\end{pmatrix}$$

$$\$71 + (\$71 \times 45\%) = \$102.95$$

*$50,000 ÷ 10,000; **$150,000 ÷ 10,000

Related exercise material: **BE21.2, BE21.3, BE21.4, BE21.5, DO IT! 21.2, E21.3, E21.4, E21.5, E21.6, and E21.7.**

Time-and-Material Pricing

> **LEARNING OBJECTIVE 3**
> Use time-and-material pricing to determine the cost of services provided.

Another variation on cost-plus pricing is **time-and-material pricing**. Under this approach, the company sets two pricing rates—one for the **labor** used on a job and another for the **material**. The labor rate includes the hourly rate paid for direct labor time and other employee costs. The material charge is based on the cost of direct parts and materials used and a **material loading charge** for related overhead costs. Time-and-material pricing is widely used in service industries, especially professional firms such as public accounting, law, engineering, and consulting firms, as well as construction companies, repair shops, and printers.

To illustrate a time-and-material pricing situation, assume the data shown in **Illustration 21.13** for Lake Holiday Marina, a boat and motor repair shop.

ILLUSTRATION 21.13

Total annual budgeted time and material costs

Lake Holiday Marina
Budgeted Costs for the Year 2022

	Time Charges	Material Loading Charges*
Mechanics' wages and benefits	$103,500	—
Parts manager's salary and benefits	—	$11,500
Office employee's salary and benefits	20,700	2,300
Other overhead (supplies, depreciation, property taxes, advertising, utilities)	26,800	14,400
Total budgeted costs	$151,000	$28,200

*The material loading charges exclude the invoice cost of the materials.

Using time-and-material pricing involves three steps: (1) calculate the per hour labor charge, (2) calculate the charge for obtaining and holding materials, and (3) calculate the charges for a particular job.

Step 1: Calculate the Labor Rate The first step for time-and-material pricing is to determine a charge for labor time. The charge for labor time is expressed as a rate per hour of labor. This rate includes (1) the direct labor cost of the employees, including hourly pay rate plus fringe benefits; (2) selling, administrative, and similar overhead costs; and (3) an allowance for a desired profit or ROI per hour of employee time. In some industries, such as repair shops for autos and boats, the same hourly labor rate is charged regardless of which employee performs the work. In other industries, the rate that is charged is adjusted according to classification or level of the employee. A public accounting firm, for example, would charge different rates for the services of an assistant, senior, manager, or partner; a law firm would charge different rates for the work of a paralegal, associate, or partner.

Illustration 21.14 shows computation of the hourly charges for Lake Holiday Marina during 2022. The marina budgets 5,000 annual labor hours in 2022, and it desires a profit margin of $8 per hour of labor.

ILLUSTRATION 21.14 Computation of hourly time-charge rate

Lake Holiday Marina

	A	B	C	D	E	F
1	Per Hour	Total Cost	÷	Total Hours	=	Per Hour Charge
2	Hourly labor rate for repairs					
3	Mechanics' wages and benefits	$103,500	÷	5,000	=	$20.70
4	Overhead costs					
5	Office employee's salary and benefits	20,700	÷	5,000	=	4.14
6	Other overhead	26,800	÷	5,000	=	5.36
7	Total hourly cost	$151,000	÷	5,000	=	30.20
8	Profit margin					8.00
9	Rate charged per hour of labor					$38.20
10						

To determine the labor charge for a job, the marina multiplies this rate of $38.20 by the number of hours of labor used.

Step 2: Calculate the Material Loading Charge The charge for materials typically includes the invoice price of any materials used on the job plus a material loading charge. The **material loading charge** covers the costs of purchasing, receiving, handling, and storing materials, plus any desired profit margin on the materials themselves. The material loading charge is expressed as a **percentage** of the total estimated costs of parts and materials for the year. To determine this percentage, the company does the following. (1) It estimates its total annual costs for purchasing, receiving, handling, and storing materials. (2) It divides this amount by the total estimated cost of parts and materials. (3) It adds a desired profit margin on the materials themselves.

Illustration 21.15 shows computation of the material loading charge used by Lake Holiday Marina during 2022. The marina estimates that the total invoice cost of parts and materials used in 2022 will be $120,000. The marina desires a 20% profit margin on the invoice cost of parts and materials.

ILLUSTRATION 21.15 Computation of material loading charge

Lake Holiday Marina

	A	B	C	D	E	F
1		Material Loading Charges	÷	Total Invoice Cost, Parts and Materials	=	Material Loading Percentage
2	Overhead costs					
3	Parts manager's salary and benefits	$11,500				
4	Office employee's salary	2,300				
5		13,800	÷	$120,000	=	11.50%
6						
7	Other overhead	14,400	÷	120,000	=	12.00%
8		$28,200	÷	120,000	=	23.50%
9	Profit margin					20.00%
10	Material loading percentage					43.50%
11						

The marina's material loading charge on any particular job is 43.50% multiplied by the cost of materials used on the job. For example, if the marina used $100 of parts, the additional material loading charge would be $43.50.

Step 3: Calculate Charges for a Particular Job The charges for any particular job are the sum of (1) the labor charge, (2) the charge for the materials, and (3) the material loading charge. For example, suppose that Lake Holiday Marina prepares a price quotation to estimate the cost to refurbish a used 28-foot pontoon boat. Lake Holiday Marina estimates the job will require 50 hours of labor and $3,600 in parts and materials. **Illustration 21.16** shows the marina's price quotation.

ILLUSTRATION 21.16

Price quotation for time and material

Lake Holiday Marina
Time-and-Material Price Quotation

Job: Marianne Perino, repair of 28-foot pontoon boat		
Labor charges: 50 hours @ $38.20		$1,910
Material charges		
Cost of parts and materials	$3,600	
Material loading charge (43.5% × $3,600)	1,566	5,166
Total price of labor and material		$7,076

Decision Tools

The time-and-material price quotation covers costs for parts and labor as well as the desired profit margins on parts and labor.

Included in the $7,076 price quotation for the boat repair are charges for labor costs, overhead costs, materials costs, materials handling and storage costs, and a profit margin on both labor and parts (see **Decision Tools**). Lake Holiday Marina used labor hours as a basis for computing the time rate. Other companies, such as machine shops, plastic molding shops, and printers, might use machine hours.

Service Company Insight   Button Worldwide

Don Bayley/iStockphoto

It Ain't Like It Used to Be

For many decades, professionals in most service industries used some form of hourly based price, regardless of the outcome. But the most recent recession appears to have brought an end to that practice. Many customers are now demanding that bills be tied to actual performance, rather than to the amount of hours worked. For example, communications company **Button Worldwide**, which used to charge about $15,000 or more per month as its "retainer fee," now instead charges based on achieving particular outcomes. For example, the company might charge $10,000 if it obtains a desirable public speaking engagement for a company executive. Similarly, a digital marketing agency reduced its hourly fee from $135 to $80, but it gets a bonus if it achieves specified increases in the sales volume on a customer's website.

Source: Simona Covel, "Firms Try Alternative to Hourly Fees," *Wall Street Journal Online* (April 2, 2009).

What implications does this have for a service company's need for managerial accounting? (Go to WileyPLUS for this answer and additional questions.)

ACTION PLAN
- Calculate the labor charge.
- Calculate the material loading charge.
- Compute the bill for specific repair.

DO IT! 3 | Time-and-Material Pricing

Presented below are data for Harmon Electrical Repair Shop for next year.

Repair-technicians' wages	$130,000
Fringe benefits	30,000
Overhead	20,000

The desired profit margin per labor hour is $10. The material loading charge is 40% of invoice cost. Harmon estimates that 8,000 labor hours will be worked next year. If Harmon repairs a TV that takes 4 hours to repair and uses parts costing $50, compute the bill for this job.

Solution

	Total Cost	÷	Total Hours	=	Per Hour Charge
Repair-technicians' wages	$130,000	÷	8,000	=	$16.25
Fringe benefits	30,000	÷	8,000	=	3.75
Overhead	20,000	÷	8,000	=	2.50
	$180,000	÷	8,000	=	22.50
Profit margin					10.00
Rate charged per hour of labor					$32.50

Job: Repair TV

Labor charges: 4 hours @ $32.50		$130
Material charges		
Cost of parts and materials	$50	
Material loading charge (40% × $50)	20	70
Total price of labor and material		$200

Related exercise material: **BE21.6, DO IT! 21.3, E21.8, E21.9, and E21.10.**

Transfer Prices

LEARNING OBJECTIVE 4
Determine a transfer price using the negotiated, cost-based, and market-based approaches.

In today's global economy, growth is often vital to survival. Some companies grow "vertically," meaning they expand in the direction of either their suppliers or customers. For example, a manufacturer of bicycles like **Trek** may acquire a bicycle component manufacturer or a chain of bicycle shops. A movie production company like **Walt Disney** or **Time Warner** may acquire a movie theater chain or a cable television company.

In addition to customer sales, divisions within vertically integrated companies often transfer goods or services to other divisions in the company. When goods are transferred between divisions of the same company, the price used to record the transaction is the **transfer price**. Illustration 21.17 shows transfers between divisions for Aerobic Bicycle Company. As shown, the Component Division sells goods to the Company's Assembly Division, as well as to outside parties. Units sold to the Assembly Division are recorded at the transfer price.

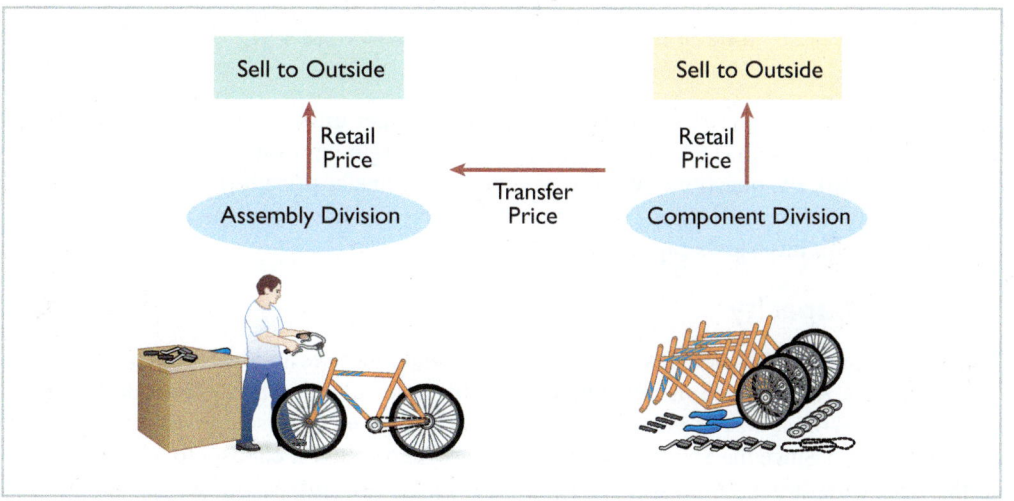

ILLUSTRATION 21.17

Transfer pricing example

The primary objective of transfer pricing is the same as that of pricing a product to an outside party. The objective is to maximize the return to the company. An additional objective of transfer pricing is to measure divisional performance accurately. Setting a transfer price is complicated because of competing interests among divisions within the company. For example, in the case of the bicycle company shown in Illustration 21.17, setting the transfer price high will benefit the Component Division (the selling division) but will hurt the Assembly Division (the purchasing division).

There are three possible approaches for determining a transfer price:

1. Negotiated transfer prices.
2. Cost-based transfer prices.
3. Market-based transfer prices.

Conceptually, a negotiated transfer price should work best, but due to practical considerations, companies often use the other two methods.

Negotiated Transfer Prices

A **negotiated transfer price** is determined through agreement of division managers. To illustrate negotiated transfer pricing, we examine Alberta Company. Until recently, Alberta focused exclusively on making rubber soles for work boots and hiking boots. It sold these rubber soles to boot manufacturers for $18 per sole and had a variable cost of $11 per sole. Last year, the company decided to take advantage of its strong reputation by expanding into the business of making hiking boots. As a consequence of this expansion, the company is now structured as two independent divisions, the Boot Division and the Sole Division. The company compensates the manager of each division based on achievement of profitability targets for that division.

The Boot Division manufactures leather uppers for hiking boots and attaches these uppers to rubber soles. Its variable costs, not including the sole, are $35 per boot. During its first year, the Boot Division purchased its rubber soles from an outside supplier for $17 per sole so as not to disrupt the operations of the Sole Division. However, top management now wants the Sole Division to provide at least some of the soles used by the Boot Division. **Illustration 21.18** shows the computation of the contribution margin per unit for each division when the Boot Division purchases soles from an outside supplier for $17 and the Sole Division sells to outside customers for $18 per sole.

ILLUSTRATION 21.18

Computation of contribution margin for two divisions, when Boot Division purchases soles from an outside supplier

Boot Division		Sole Division	
Selling price of boots	$90	Selling price of sole	$18
Variable cost of boot (not including sole)	35	Variable cost per sole	11
Cost of sole purchased from outside supplier	17	Contribution margin per unit	$ 7
Contribution margin per unit	**$38**		

Total contribution margin per unit $45 ($38 + $7)

This information indicates that the contribution margin per unit for the Boot Division is $38 and for the Sole Division is $7. The total contribution margin per unit is $45 ($38 + $7).

Now let's ask the question, "What would be a fair transfer price if the Sole Division sold 10,000 soles to the Boot Division?" The answer depends on how busy the Sole Division is—that is, whether it has excess capacity.

No Excess Capacity

Assume that the Sole Division has no excess capacity and produces and sells 80,000 soles to outside customers. As indicated in Illustration 21.18, the Sole Division charges outside customers $18 and has a variable cost of $11, so its contribution margin on units sold to outside customers is $7 ($18 − $11). Since the Sole Division has no excess capacity, if it chooses to sell 10,000 units to the Boot Division, it would have to forgo sales of 10,000 units to outside customers. The contribution margin on sales to outside customers that would be forgone as a result of an internal transfer is referred to as the **opportunity cost**.

Therefore, the Sole Division must receive from the Boot Division a payment that will at least cover its variable cost of $11 per sole **plus** its contribution margin—opportunity cost—of $7 per sole. The sum of the variable cost and the opportunity cost is referred to as the **minimum transfer price**. If the Sole Division cannot recover the minimum transfer price, it should not sell its soles to the Boot Division. The minimum transfer price that would be acceptable to the Sole Division is $18, as shown in Illustration 21.19 (see **Decision Tools**).

> **Decision Tools**
>
> The formula in Illustration 21.19 helps managers set prices for the transfer of goods between a company's divisions.

ILLUSTRATION 21.19

Minimum transfer price formula—no excess capacity

Variable Cost	+	Opportunity Cost	=	Minimum Transfer Price
$11	+	$7	=	$18

From the perspective of the Boot Division (the buyer), the most it will pay is what the sole would cost from an outside supplier. In this case, therefore, the Boot Division would pay no more than $17. As shown in Illustration 21.20, an acceptable transfer price is not available in this situation.

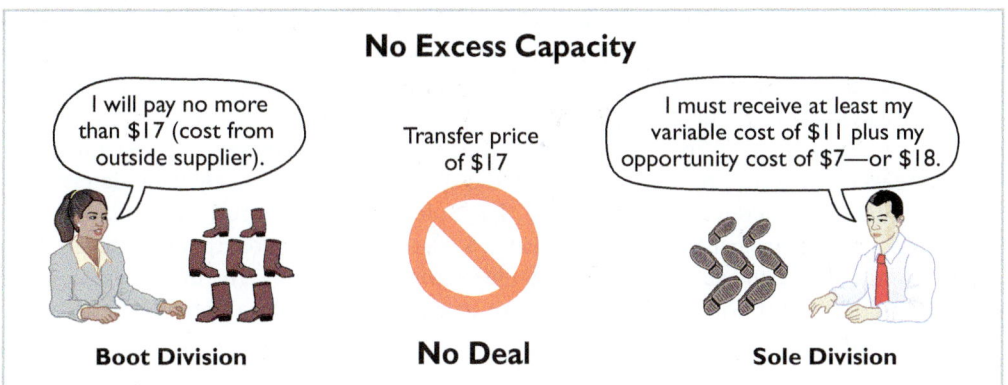

ILLUSTRATION 21.20

Transfer price negotiations—no excess capacity

Excess Capacity

What happens if the Sole Division **has excess capacity**? For example, assume the Sole Division can produce 80,000 soles but can sell only 70,000 soles in the open market. As a result, it has available capacity of 10,000 units. Because it has excess capacity, the Sole Division could provide 10,000 units to the Boot Division without losing its $7 contribution margin on these units. Therefore, as Illustration 21.21 shows, the minimum price it would now accept is $11.

ILLUSTRATION 21.21

Minimum transfer price formula—excess capacity

Variable Cost	+	Opportunity Cost	=	Minimum Transfer Price
$11	+	$0	=	$11

In this case, the Boot Division and the Sole Division should negotiate a transfer price within the range of $11 to $17, as shown in Illustration 21.22.

ILLUSTRATION 21.22

Transfer pricing negotiations—excess capacity

Given excess capacity, Alberta Company will increase its overall net income if the Boot Division purchases the 10,000 soles internally. This is true as long as the Sole Division's variable cost is less than the outside price of $17. The Sole Division will receive a positive contribution margin from any transfer price above its variable cost of $11. The Boot Division will benefit from any price below $17. At any transfer price above $17 the Boot Division will go to an outside supplier, a solution that would be undesirable to both divisions as well as to the company as a whole.

Variable Costs

In the minimum transfer price formula, **variable cost is defined as the variable cost of units sold *internally*.** In some instances, the variable cost of units sold internally will differ from the variable cost of units sold externally. For example, companies often can avoid some variable selling expenses when units are sold internally. In this case, the variable cost of units sold internally will be lower than that of units sold externally.

Alternatively, the variable cost of units sold internally could be higher than normal if the internal division requests a special order that requires more expensive materials or additional labor. For example, assume that the Boot Division designs a new high-margin, heavy-duty boot. The sole for this boot will use denser rubber with an intricate lug design. Alberta Company is not aware of any supplier that currently makes such a sole, nor does it feel that any other supplier can meet its quality expectations. As a consequence, there is no available market price to use as the transfer price.

We can, however, employ the formula for the minimum transfer price to assist in arriving at a reasonable solution. After evaluating the special sole, the Sole Division determines that its variable cost would be $19 per sole. The Sole Division is at full capacity. The Sole Division's opportunity cost at full capacity is the $7 ($18 − $11) per sole that it earns producing the standard sole and selling it to an outside customer. Therefore, the minimum transfer price that the Sole Division would be willing to accept for the special-order sole is as shown in **Illustration 21.23**.

ILLUSTRATION 21.23
Minimum transfer price formula—special order

Variable Cost	+	Opportunity Cost	=	Minimum Transfer Price
$19	+	$7	=	$26

The transfer price of $26 provides the Sole Division with enough revenue to cover its increased variable cost and its opportunity cost (contribution margin on its standard sole).

Units Transferred Are Unequal to Units Forgone

In some situations, when the division has no excess capacity, the number of units transferred internally differs from the number units forgone on sales to outside parties. This occurs if characteristics of the units transferred internally differ from standard units, and thus differ in terms of the amount of manufacturing resources required for production. For example, suppose that the Boot Division requests 7,000 units of a special, high-endurance sole that requires more manufacturing resources than a standard sole. To produce 7,000 units of the special sole for the Boot Division, the Sole Division will have to forgo sales of 10,000 units of its standard sole to outside customers. When the number of units transferred internally differs from the number of units of external sales forgone, a company must compute the opportunity cost per unit transferred internally. This is accomplished by first computing the total contribution margin on all units forgone and then dividing by the number of units transferred internally. The formula for the opportunity cost, applied to the special order from the Boot Division, is shown in **Illustration 21.24**.

ILLUSTRATION 21.24
Opportunity cost if units sold are unequal to units forgone

[(Selling Price	−	Variable Cost)	×	Units Forgone]	÷	Units Transferred Internally	=	Opportunity Cost
[($18	−	$11)	×	10,000]	÷	7,000	=	$10

Notice that, because the number of units forgone exceeds the number of units that will be transferred internally, the opportunity cost per unit of $10 exceeds the opportunity cost per unit of $7 that we computed previously on a standard unit.

Summary of Negotiated Transfer Pricing

Under negotiated transfer pricing, the selling division establishes a minimum transfer price, and the purchasing division establishes a maximum transfer price. This system provides a sound basis for establishing a transfer price because both divisions are better off if the proper decision-making rules are used. However, companies often do not use negotiated transfer pricing because:

- Market price information is sometimes not easily obtainable.
- A lack of trust between the two negotiating divisions may lead to a breakdown in the negotiations.
- Negotiations often lead to different pricing strategies from division to division, which is cumbersome and sometimes costly to implement.

Many companies, therefore, often use simple systems based on cost or market information to develop transfer prices.

Cost-Based Transfer Prices

An alternative to negotiated transfer pricing is cost-based pricing. A **cost-based transfer price** is based on the costs incurred by the division producing the goods or services. A cost-based transfer price can be based on variable costs alone, or on variable costs plus fixed costs. Also, in some cases the selling division may add a markup.

The cost-based approach sometimes results in improper transfer prices. Improper transfer prices can reduce company profits and provide unfair evaluations of division performance. To illustrate, assume that Alberta Company requires the division to use a transfer price based on the variable cost of the sole. With no excess capacity, the contribution margins per unit for the two divisions are as shown in **Illustration 21.25**.

ILLUSTRATION 21.25
Cost-based transfer price—10,000 units

Boot Division		Sole Division	
Selling price of boots	$90	Selling price of sole	$11
Variable cost of boot (not including sole)	35	Variable cost per sole	11
Cost of sole purchased from sole division	11	Contribution margin per unit	$ 0
Contribution margin per unit	$44		

Total contribution margin per unit $44 ($44 + $0)

This cost-based transfer system is a bad deal for the Sole Division as it reports no profit on the transfer of 10,000 soles to the Boot Division. If the Sole Division could sell these soles to an outside customer, it would make $70,000 [10,000 × ($18 − $11)]. The Boot Division, on the other hand, is delighted: its contribution margin per unit increases from $38 to $44, or $6 per boot. Thus, this transfer price results in an unfair evaluation of these two divisions.

Further examination of this example reveals that this transfer price reduces the company's overall profits. The Sole Division lost a contribution margin per unit of $7 (Illustration 21.18), and the Boot Division experiences only a $6 increase in its contribution margin per unit. Overall, Alberta Company loses $10,000 [10,000 boots × ($7 − $6)]. **Illustration 21.26** illustrates this deficiency.

> **ILLUSTRATION 21.26**
>
> Cost-based transfer price results—no excess capacity

The overall results change if the Sole Division **has excess capacity**. In this case, the Sole Division continues to report a zero profit on these 10,000 units but does not lose the $7 per unit of contribution margin (because it had excess capacity). The Boot Division gains $6. So overall, the company is better off by $60,000 (10,000 × $6). However, with a cost-based system, the Sole Division continues to report a zero profit on these 10,000 units.

The cost-based approach has disadvantages. First, a cost-based system does not reflect the division's true profitability. Second, **it does not provide adequate incentive for the Sole Division to control costs**. The division's costs are simply passed on to the next division.

Notwithstanding these disadvantages, the cost system is simple to understand and easy to use because the information is already available in the accounting system. In addition, market information is sometimes not available, so the only alternative is some type of cost-based system. As a result, cost-based transfer prices are the most common method used by companies to establish transfer prices.

Market-Based Transfer Prices

The **market-based transfer price** is based on existing market prices of competing goods or services. A market-based system is often considered the best approach because it is objective and generally provides the proper economic incentives. For example, if the Sole Division can charge the market price, it is indifferent as to whether soles are sold to outside customers or internally to the Boot Division—it does not lose any contribution margin. Similarly, the Boot Division pays a price for the soles that is at or reasonably close to market.

When the Sole Division has no excess capacity, the market-based system works reasonably well. The Sole Division receives market price, and the Boot Division pays market price.

If the Sole Division has excess capacity, however, the market-based system can lead to actions that are not in the best interest of the company. The minimum transfer price that the Sole Division should receive is its variable cost plus opportunity cost. If the Sole Division has excess capacity, its opportunity cost is zero. However, under the market-based system, the Sole Division transfers the goods at the market price of $18, for a contribution margin per unit of $7 ($18 − $11). The Boot Division manager has to accept the $18 sole price. This price may not accurately reflect a fair cost of the sole, given that the Sole Division had excess capacity. As a result, the Boot Division may overprice its boots in the market if it uses the market price of the sole plus a markup in setting the price of the boot. This action can lead to losses for Alberta overall.

As indicated earlier, in many cases, there simply is not a well-defined market for the good or service being transferred. When this is the case, a reasonable market value cannot be developed, so companies often resort to a cost-based system.

Effect of Outsourcing on Transfer Pricing

An increasing number of companies rely on **outsourcing**. Outsourcing involves contracting with an external party to provide a good or service, rather than performing the work internally. Some companies have taken outsourcing to the extreme by outsourcing all of their production. Many of these so-called **virtual companies** have well-established brand names though they do not manufacture any of their own products. Companies use incremental analysis (Chapter 20) to determine whether outsourcing is profitable. When companies outsource, fewer components are transferred internally between divisions. This reduces the need for transfer prices.

Transfers Between Divisions in Different Countries

As more companies "globalize" their operations, an increasing number of intercompany transfers are between divisions that are located in different countries. One estimate suggests that 60% of trade between countries is simply transfers between company divisions. Differences in tax rates across countries can complicate the determination of the appropriate transfer price. Appendix 21B discusses in more detail transfer pricing issues that occur when goods are exchanged between divisions in different countries.

DO IT! 4 | Transfer Pricing

The clock division of Control Central Corporation manufactures clocks and then sells them to customers for $10 per unit. Its variable cost is $4 per unit, and its fixed cost per unit is $2.50. Management would like the clock division to transfer 8,000 of these clocks to another division within the company at a price of $5. The clock division could avoid $0.50 per clock of variable packaging costs by selling internally.

a. Determine the minimum transfer price, assuming the clock division is not operating at full capacity.

b. Determine the minimum transfer price, assuming the clock division is operating at full capacity.

ACTION PLAN
- Determine whether the company is at full capacity or not.
- Determine variable cost and opportunity cost.
- Apply minimum transfer price formula.

Solution

a. If the clock division is not operating at full capacity, the opportunity cost for the clocks is $0. Since internal sales will eliminate $0.50 of packaging costs, the variable cost per clock is $3.50 ($4 − $0.50).

$$\text{Minimum transfer price} = \text{Variable cost} + \text{Opportunity cost}$$
$$\$3.50 = \$3.50 + \$0$$

b. If the clock division is already operating at full capacity, the opportunity cost for the clocks is $6 ($10 − $4). Since internal sales will eliminate $0.50 of packaging costs, the variable cost per clock is $3.50 ($4 − $0.50).

$$\text{Minimum transfer price} = \text{Variable cost} + \text{Opportunity cost}$$
$$\$9.50 = \$3.50 + \$6$$

Related exercise material: **BE21.7, BE21.8, BE21.9, DO IT! 21.4, E21.11, E21.12, E21.13, E21.14, and E21.15.**

USING THE DECISION TOOLS | Zappos.com

As mentioned in the Feature Story, **Zappos.com** faces many situations where it needs to apply the decision tools learned in this chapter. For example, suppose that Zappos is considering the idea of manufacturing a fun, low-cost, "energy" shoe and selling it under its own name. It has estimated the following information based upon a budgeted volume of 100,000 units.

	Per Unit	Total
Direct materials	$8.40	
Direct labor	$1.90	
Variable manufacturing overhead	$0.80	
Fixed manufacturing overhead		$940,000
Variable selling and administrative expenses	$0.90	
Fixed selling and administrative expenses		$320,000

Assume Zappos uses cost-plus pricing to set its selling price. Management also directs that the target price be set to provide a 25% return on investment (ROI) on invested assets of $4,200,000.

Instructions

a. Compute the markup percentage and target selling price on this new shoe.

b. Assuming that the volume is 50,000 units instead of 100,000 units, compute the markup percentage and target selling price that will allow Zappos to earn its desired ROI of 25%.

Solution

a.

Variable cost per unit

	Per Unit
Direct materials	$ 8.40
Direct labor	1.90
Variable manufacturing overhead	0.80
Variable selling and administrative expenses	0.90
Variable cost per unit	$12.00

Fixed cost per unit

	Total Costs	÷	Budgeted Volume	=	Cost per Unit
Fixed manufacturing overhead	$ 940,000	÷	100,000	=	$ 9.40
Fixed selling and administrative expenses	320,000	÷	100,000	=	3.20
Fixed cost per unit	$1,260,000				$12.60

Computation of selling price (100,000 units)

Variable cost per unit	$12.00
Fixed cost per unit	12.60
Total unit cost	24.60
Desired ROI per unit*	10.50
Selling price	$35.10

*($4,200,000 × .25) ÷ 100,000

The markup percentage is:

$$\frac{\text{Desired ROI per unit}}{\text{Total unit cost}} = \frac{\$10.50}{\$24.60} = 42.68\%$$

b. If the company produces 50,000 units, its selling price and markup percentage would be:

Computation of selling price (50,000 units)

Variable cost per unit	$12.00
Fixed cost per unit ($1,260,000 ÷ 50,000)	25.20
Total unit cost	37.20
Desired ROI per unit*	21.00
Selling price	$58.20

*($4,200,000 × .25) ÷ 50,000

The markup percentage would be:

$$\frac{\text{Desired ROI per unit}}{\text{Total unit cost}} = \frac{\$21.00}{\$37.20} = 56.45\%$$

Appendix 21A Absorption-Cost and Variable-Cost Pricing

LEARNING OBJECTIVE *5
Determine prices using absorption-cost pricing and variable-cost pricing.

In determining the target price for Thinkmore Products' video camera pen in the chapter, we calculated the cost base **by including all costs incurred**. This approach is referred to as **full-cost pricing**. Using total cost as the basis of the markup makes sense conceptually because, in the long run, the price must cover all costs and provide a reasonable profit. However, total cost is difficult to determine in practice. This is because period costs (selling and administrative expenses) are difficult to trace to a specific product. Activity-based costing can be used to overcome this difficulty to some extent.

In practice, companies sometimes use two other cost approaches: (1) absorption-cost pricing or (2) variable-cost pricing. Absorption-cost pricing is more popular than variable-cost pricing.[1] We illustrate both approaches because both have merit.

Absorption-Cost Pricing

Absorption-cost pricing is consistent with generally accepted accounting principles (GAAP). The reason: It includes both variable and fixed manufacturing costs as product costs. **It excludes from this cost base both variable and fixed selling and administrative costs.** Thus, companies must somehow provide for selling and administrative costs plus the target ROI. They do this through the markup.

The **first step** in absorption-cost pricing is to compute the unit **manufacturing cost**. For Thinkmore Products, this amounts to $87 per unit at a volume of 10,000 units, as shown in **Illustration 21A.1**.

	Per Unit
Direct materials	$23
Direct labor	17
Variable manufacturing overhead	12
Fixed manufacturing overhead ($350,000 ÷ 10,000)	35
Total unit manufacturing cost (absorption cost)	$87

ILLUSTRATION 21A.1
Computation of unit manufacturing cost

In addition, Thinkmore provides the information given in **Illustration 21A.2** regarding selling and administrative expenses per unit and desired ROI per unit.

Variable selling and administrative expenses	$ 8
Fixed selling and administrative expenses ($300,000 ÷ 10,000)	30
Total selling and administrative expenses per unit	$38
Desired ROI per unit (see Illustration 21.7)	$40

ILLUSTRATION 21A.2
Other information

The **second step** in absorption-cost pricing is to compute the markup percentage using the formula in **Illustration 21A.3**. Note that when companies use manufacturing cost per unit as the cost base to compute the markup percentage, the **percentage must cover the desired ROI and also the selling and administrative expenses**.

---

[1] For a discussion of cost-plus pricing, see Eunsup Skim and Ephraim F. Sudit, "How Manufacturers Price Products," *Management Accounting* (February 1995), pp. 37–39; and V. Govindarajan and R.N. Anthony, "How Firms Use Cost Data in Pricing Decisions," *Management Accounting* (65, no. 1), pp. 30–36.

ILLUSTRATION 21A.3
Markup percentage—absorption-cost pricing

Desired ROI per Unit	+	Selling and Administrative Expenses per Unit	=	Markup Percentage	×	Manufacturing Cost per Unit
$40	+	$38	=	MP	×	$87

Solving, we find:

$$MP = (\$40 + \$38) \div \$87 = 89.66\%$$

The **third** and final **step** is to set the target selling price. Using a markup percentage of 89.66% and absorption-cost pricing, Thinkmore computes the target selling price as shown in **Illustration 21A.4**.

ILLUSTRATION 21A.4
Computation of target price—absorption-cost pricing

Manufacturing Cost per Unit	+	(Markup Percentage	×	Manufacturing Cost per Unit)	=	Target Selling Price
$87	+	(89.66%	×	$87)	=	$165

Using a target price of $165 will produce the desired 20% return on investment for Thinkmore on its video camera pen at a volume level of 10,000 units, as shown in **Illustration 21A.5**.

ILLUSTRATION 21A.5
Proof of 20% ROI—absorption-cost pricing

Thinkmore Products, Inc.
Budgeted Absorption-Cost Income Statement

Revenue (10,000 camera pens × $165)	$1,650,000
Cost of goods sold (10,000 camera pens × $87)	870,000
Gross profit	780,000
Selling and administrative expenses	
[10,000 camera pens × ($8 + $30)]	380,000
Net income	$ 400,000

Budgeted ROI

$$\frac{\text{Net income}}{\text{Invested assets}} = \frac{\$400{,}000}{\$2{,}000{,}000} = 20\%$$

Markup Percentage

$$\frac{\text{Net income} + \text{Selling and administrative expenses}}{\text{Cost of goods sold}} = \frac{\$400{,}000 + \$380{,}000}{\$870{,}000} = 89.66\%$$

Because of the fixed-cost element, if Thinkmore sells more than 10,000 units, the ROI will be greater than 20%. If it sells fewer than 10,000 units, the ROI will be less than 20%. The markup percentage is also verified by adding $400,000 (the net income) and $380,000 (selling and administrative expenses) and then dividing by $870,000 (the cost of goods sold or the cost base).

Most companies that use cost-plus pricing use either absorption cost or full cost as the basis. The reasons for this tendency are as follows.

1. Absorption-cost information is most readily provided by a company's cost accounting system. Because absorption-cost data already exist in general ledger accounts, it is cost-effective to use the data for pricing.

2. Basing the cost-plus formula on only variable costs could encourage managers to set too low a price to boost sales. There is the fear that if managers use only variable costs, they will substitute variable costs for full costs, which can lead to repeated price cutting.

3. Absorption-cost or full-cost pricing provides the most defensible base for justifying prices to all interested parties—managers, customers, and government.

Variable-Cost Pricing

Under **variable-cost pricing**, the cost base consists of all of the **variable costs** associated with a product, including variable selling and administrative costs. **Because fixed costs are not included in the base, the markup must provide for all fixed costs (manufacturing, and selling and administrative) and the target ROI.** Variable-cost pricing is more useful for making short-run decisions because it considers variable-cost and fixed-cost behavior patterns separately.

The **first step** in variable-cost pricing is to compute the unit variable cost. For Thinkmore Products, this amounts to $60 per unit, as shown in **Illustration 21A.6**.

	Per Unit
Direct materials	$23
Direct labor	17
Variable manufacturing overhead	12
Variable selling and administrative expense	8
Total unit variable cost	$60

ILLUSTRATION 21A.6
Computation of unit variable cost

The **second step** in variable-cost pricing is to compute the markup percentage. **Illustration 21A.7** shows the formula for the markup percentage. For Thinkmore, fixed costs include fixed manufacturing overhead of $35 per unit ($350,000 ÷ 10,000) and fixed selling and administrative expenses of $30 per unit ($300,000 ÷ 10,000).

Desired ROI per Unit	+	Fixed Cost per Unit	=	Markup Percentage	×	Variable Cost per Unit
$40	+	($35 + $30)	=	MP	×	$60

ILLUSTRATION 21A.7
Computation of markup percentage—variable-cost pricing

Solving, we find:

$$MP = \frac{\$40 + (\$35 + \$30)}{\$60} = 175\%$$

The **third step** is to set the target selling price. Using a markup percentage of 175% and the variable-cost approach, Thinkmore computes the selling price as shown in **Illustration 21A.8**.

Variable Cost per Unit	+	(Markup Percentage	×	Variable Cost per Unit)	=	Target Selling Price
$60	+	(175%	×	$60)	=	$165

ILLUSTRATION 21A.8
Computation of target price—variable-cost pricing

Using a target price of $165 will produce the desired 20% return on investment for Thinkmore on its video camera pen at a volume level of 10,000 units, as shown in **Illustration 21A.9**.

Under any of the three pricing approaches we have looked at (full-cost, absorption-cost, and variable-cost), the desired ROI will be attained only if the budgeted sales volume for the period is attained. None of these approaches guarantees a profit or a desired ROI. Achieving a desired ROI is the result of many factors, some of which are beyond the company's control, such as market conditions, political and legal issues, customers' tastes, and competitive actions.

Because absorption-cost pricing includes allocated fixed costs, it does not make clear how the company's costs will change as volume changes. To avoid blurring the effects of cost behavior on net income, some managers therefore prefer variable-cost pricing. The specific reasons

ILLUSTRATION 21A.9
Proof of 20% ROI—variable-cost approach

Thinkmore Products, Inc.
Budgeted Variable-Cost Income Statement

Revenue (10,000 camera pens × $165)		$1,650,000
Variable costs (10,000 camera pens × $60)		600,000
Contribution margin		1,050,000
Fixed manufacturing overhead	$350,000	
Fixed selling and administrative expenses	300,000	650,000
Net income		$ 400,000

Budgeted ROI

$$\frac{\text{Net income}}{\text{Invested assets}} = \frac{\$400,000}{\$2,000,000} = \underline{\underline{20\%}}$$

Markup Percentage

$$\frac{\text{Net income} + \text{Fixed costs}}{\text{Variable costs}} = \frac{\$400,000 + \$650,000}{\$600,000} = \underline{\underline{175\%}}$$

for using variable-cost pricing, even though the basic accounting data are less accessible, are as follows.

1. Variable-cost pricing, being based on variable cost, is more consistent with cost-volume-profit analysis used by managers to measure the profit implications of changes in price and volume.

2. Variable-cost pricing provides the type of data managers need for pricing special orders. It reveals the incremental effect of accepting one more order.

3. Variable-cost pricing avoids arbitrary allocation of common fixed costs (such as executive salaries) to individual product lines.

Appendix 21B Transfers Between Divisions in Different Countries

LEARNING OBJECTIVE *6
Explain issues involved in transferring goods between divisions in different countries.

Companies must pay income tax in the country where they generate the income. In order to maximize income and minimize income tax, some companies attempt to report more income in countries with low tax rates, and less income in countries with high tax rates. They accomplish this by adjusting the transfer prices they use on internal transfers between divisions located in different countries. They allocate more contribution margin to the division in the low-tax-rate country, and allocate less to the division in the high-tax-rate country.

To illustrate, suppose that Alberta's Boot Division is located in a country with a corporate tax rate of 10%, and the Sole Division is located in a country with a tax rate of 30%. To maximize the company's combined after-tax profit, it would want to shift income from the Sole Division to the Boot Division because the Boot Division is taxed at a lower rate. **Illustration 21B.1** compares the after-tax contribution margin to the company using a transfer price of $18 versus a transfer price of $11.

Note that the **before-tax** total contribution margin to Alberta Company is $44 regardless of whether the transfer price is $18 or $11. However, the **after-tax** total contribution margin to Alberta Company is $38.20 using the $18 transfer price and $39.60 using the $11 transfer price.

ILLUSTRATION 21B.1
After-tax contribution margin per unit under alternative transfer prices

At $18 Transfer Price

Boot Division		Sole Division	
Selling price of boots	$90.00	Selling price of sole	$18.00
Variable cost of boot (not including sole)	35.00	Variable cost per sole	11.00
Cost of sole purchased internally	18.00		
Before-tax contribution margin	37.00	Before-tax contribution margin	7.00
Tax at 10%	3.70	Tax at 30%	2.10
After-tax contribution margin	$33.30	After-tax contribution margin	$ 4.90

Before-tax total contribution margin per unit to company = $37 + $7 = **$44**
After-tax total contribution margin per unit to company = $33.30 + $4.90 = **$38.20**

At $11 Transfer Price

Boot Division		Sole Division	
Selling price of boots	$90.00	Selling price of sole	$11.00
Variable cost of boot (not including sole)	35.00	Variable cost per sole	11.00
Cost of sole purchased internally	11.00		
Before-tax contribution margin	44.00	Before-tax contribution margin	0.00
Tax at 10%	4.40	Tax at 30%	0.00
After-tax contribution margin	$39.60	After-tax contribution margin	$ 0.00

Before-tax total contribution margin per unit to company = $44 + $0 = **$44**
After-tax total contribution margin per unit to company = $39.60 + $0 = **$39.60**

The reason: When Alberta uses the $11 transfer price, more of the contribution margin is attributed to the division that is in the country with the lower tax rate, so the company pays $1.40 less per unit in taxes [($3.70 + $2.10) − $4.40].

As this analysis shows, Alberta Company would be better off using the $11 transfer price. However, this presents some concerns. First, the Sole Division manager will not be happy with an $11 transfer price. This price may lead to unfair evaluations of the Sole Division's manager. Second, the company must ask whether it is legal and ethical to use an $11 transfer price when the market price clearly is higher than that.

Additional consideration of international transfer pricing is discussed in advanced accounting courses.

Review and Practice

Learning Objectives Review

1 Compute a target cost when the market determines a product price.

To compute a target cost, the company determines its target selling price. Once the target selling price is set, it determines its target cost by setting a desired profit. The difference between the target price and desired profit is the target cost of the product.

2 Compute a target selling price using cost-plus pricing.

Cost-plus pricing involves establishing a cost base and adding to this cost base a markup to determine a target selling price. The cost-plus pricing formula is expressed as follows: Target selling price = Cost + (Markup percentage × Cost).

3 Use time-and-material pricing to determine the cost of services provided.

Under time-and-material pricing, two pricing rates are set—one for the labor used on a job and another for the material. The labor rate includes direct labor time and other employee costs. The material charge is based on the cost of direct parts and materials used and a material loading charge for related overhead costs.

4 Determine a transfer price using the negotiated, cost-based, and market-based approaches.

The negotiated price is determined through agreement of division managers. Under a cost-based approach, the transfer price may be based on variable cost alone or on variable costs plus fixed costs. Companies may add a markup to these numbers. The cost-based approach often leads to poor performance evaluations and purchasing decisions. The advantage of the cost-based system is its simplicity. A market-based transfer price is based on existing competing market prices and services. A market-based system is often considered the best approach because it is objective and generally provides the proper economic incentives.

*5 Determine prices using absorption-cost pricing and variable-cost pricing.

Absorption-cost pricing uses total manufacturing cost as the cost base and provides for selling and administrative costs plus the target ROI through the markup. The target selling price is computed as: Manufacturing cost per unit + (Markup percentage × Manufacturing cost per unit).

Variable-cost pricing uses all of the variable costs, including selling and administrative costs, as the cost base and provides for fixed costs and target ROI through the markup. The target selling price is computed as: Variable cost per unit + (Markup percentage × Variable cost per unit).

*6 Explain issues involved in transferring goods between divisions in different countries.

Companies must pay income tax in the country where they generate the income. In order to maximize income and minimize income tax, many companies prefer to report more income in countries with low tax rates, and less income in countries with high tax rates. This is accomplished by adjusting the transfer prices they use on internal transfers between divisions located in different countries.

Decision Tools Review

Decision Checkpoints	Info Needed for Decision	Tool to Use for Decision	How to Evaluate Results
How does management use target costs to make decisions about manufacturing products or performing services?	Target selling price, desired profit, target cost	Target selling price less desired profit equals target cost	If actual cost exceeds target cost, the company will not earn desired profit. If desired profit is not achieved, company must evaluate whether to manufacture the product or perform the service.
What factors should be considered in determining selling price in a less competitive environment?	Total cost per unit and desired profit (cost-plus pricing)	Total cost per unit plus desired profit equals target selling price	Does company make its desired profit? If not, does the profit shortfall result from less volume?
How do we set prices for service jobs that require separate cost estimates for service labor and parts used?	Two pricing rates needed: one for labor use and another for materials	Compute labor rate charge and materials rate charge; in each of these calculations, add a profit margin	Is the company profitable under this pricing approach? Are employees earning reasonable wages?
What price should be charged for transfer of goods between divisions of a company?	Variable cost, opportunity cost, market prices	Variable cost plus opportunity cost provides minimum transfer price for seller	If income of division provides fair evaluation of managers, then transfer price is useful. Also, income of the company overall should not be reduced due to the transfer pricing approach.

Glossary Review

*****Absorption-cost pricing** An approach to pricing that defines the cost base as the manufacturing cost; it excludes both variable and fixed selling and administrative costs. (p. 21-21).

Cost-based transfer price A transfer price that uses as its foundation the costs incurred by the division producing the goods. (p. 21-17).

Cost-plus pricing A process whereby a product's selling price is determined by adding a markup to a cost base. (p. 21-5).

Full-cost pricing An approach to pricing that defines the cost base as all costs incurred. (p. 21-8).

Market-based transfer price A transfer price that is based on existing market prices of competing products. (p. 21-18).

Markup The amount added to a product's cost base to determine the product's selling price. (p. 21-6).

Material loading charge A charge added to cover the cost of purchasing, receiving, handling, and storing materials, plus any desired profit margin on the materials themselves. (p. 21-11).

Negotiated transfer price A transfer price that is determined by the agreement of the division managers. (p. 21-14).

Opportunity cost The contribution margin on sales to outside customers that would be forgone as a result of an internal transfer. (p. 21-15).

Outsourcing Contracting with an external party to provide a good or service, rather than performing the work internally. (p. 21-18).

Target cost The cost that will provide the desired profit on a product when the seller does not have control over the product's price. (p. 21-4).

Target selling price The selling price that will provide the desired profit on a product when the seller has the ability to determine the product's price. (p. 21-6).

Time-and-material pricing An approach to cost-plus pricing in which the company uses two pricing rates, one for the labor used on a job and another for the material. (p. 21-10).

Transfer price The price used to record the transfer of goods between two divisions of a company. (p. 21-13).

Variable-cost pricing An approach to pricing that defines the cost base as all variable costs; it excludes both fixed manufacturing and fixed selling and administrative costs. (pp. 21-8, 21-23).

Practice Multiple-Choice Questions

1. **(LO 1)** Target cost related to price and profit means that:
   a. cost and desired profit must be determined before selling price.
   b. cost and selling price must be determined before desired profit.
   c. price and desired profit must be determined before costs.
   d. costs can be achieved only if the company is at full capacity.

2. **(LO 1)** Classic Toys has examined the market for toy train locomotives. It believes there is a market niche in which it can sell locomotives at $80 each. It estimates that it could sell 10,000 of these locomotives annually. Variable costs to make a locomotive are expected to be $25. Classic anticipates a profit of $15 per locomotive. The target cost for the locomotive is:
   a. $80.
   b. $65.
   c. $40.
   d. $25.

3. **(LO 1, 2)** In a competitive, common-product environment, a seller would most likely use:
   a. time-and-material pricing.
   b. variable costing.
   c. target costing.
   d. cost-plus pricing.

4. **(LO 2)** Cost-plus pricing means that:
   a. Selling price = Variable cost + (Markup percentage + Variable cost).
   b. Selling price = Cost + (Markup percentage × Cost).
   c. Selling price = Manufacturing cost + (Markup percentage + Manufacturing cost).
   d. Selling price = Fixed cost + (Markup percentage × Fixed cost).

5. **(LO 2)** Adler Company is considering developing a new product. The company has gathered the following information on this product.

Expected total unit cost	$25
Estimated investment for new product	$500,000
Desired ROI	10%
Expected number of units to be produced and sold	1,000

   Given this information, the desired markup percentage and selling price are:
   a. markup percentage 10%; selling price $55.
   b. markup percentage 200%; selling price $75.
   c. markup percentage 10%; selling price $50.
   d. markup percentage 100%; selling price $55.

6. **(LO 2)** Mystique Co. provides the following information for the new product it recently introduced.

Total unit cost	$30
Desired ROI per unit	$10
Target selling price	$40

   What would be Mystique Co.'s percentage markup on cost?
   a. 125%.
   b. 75%.
   c. 33⅓%.
   d. 25%.

7. **(LO 3)** Crescent Electrical Repair has decided to price its work on a time-and-material basis. It estimates the following costs for the year related to labor.

Technician wages and benefits	$100,000
Office employee's salary and benefits	$ 40,000
Other overhead	$ 80,000

Crescent desires a profit margin of $10 per labor hour and budgets 5,000 hours of repair time for the year. The office employee's salary, benefits, and other overhead costs should be divided evenly between time charges and material loading charges. Crescent labor charge per hour would be:

a. $42.
b. $34.
c. $32.
d. $30.

8. **(LO 3)** Time-and-material pricing would most likely be used by a:

a. garden-fertilizer producer.
b. lawn-mower manufacturer.
c. tree farm.
d. lawn-care provider.

9. **(LO 3)** When a company uses time-and-material pricing, the material loading charge is expressed as a percentage of:

a. the total estimated labor costs for the year.
b. the total estimated costs of parts and materials for the year.
c. the total estimated overhead costs for the year.
d. the total estimated costs of parts, materials, and labor for the year.

10. **(LO 4)** The Plastics Division of Weston Company manufactures plastic molds and then sells them to customers for $70 per unit. Its variable cost is $30 per unit, and its fixed cost per unit is $10. Management would like the Plastics Division to transfer 10,000 of these molds to another division within the company at a price of $40. The Plastics Division is operating at full capacity. What is the minimum transfer price that the Plastics Division should accept?

a. $10.
b. $30.
c. $40.
d. $70.

11. **(LO 4)** Assume the same information as Question 10, except that the Plastics Division has available capacity of 10,000 units for plastic moldings. What is the minimum transfer price that the Plastics Division should accept?

a. $10.
b. $30.
c. $40.
d. $70.

12. **(LO 4)** The most common method used to establish transfer prices is the:

a. negotiated transfer pricing approach.
b. opportunity costing transfer pricing approach.
c. cost-based transfer pricing approach.
d. market-based transfer pricing approach.

*13. **(LO 5)** AST Electrical provides the following cost information related to its production of electronic circuit boards.

	Per Unit
Variable manufacturing cost	$40
Fixed manufacturing cost	$30
Variable selling and administrative expenses	$ 8
Fixed selling and administrative expenses	$12
Desired ROI per unit	$15

What is its markup percentage assuming that AST Electrical uses absorption-cost pricing?

a. 16.67%.
b. 50%.
c. 54.28%.
d. 118.75%.

*14. **(LO 5)** Assume the same information as Question 13 and determine AST Electrical's markup percentage using variable-cost pricing.

a. 16.67%.
b. 50%.
c. 54.28%.
d. 118.75%.

*15. **(LO 6)** Global Industries transfers parts between divisions in two countries, Eastland and Westland. Eastland's tax rate is 8%, and Westland's tax rate is 16%. If Global desired to minimize tax payments and maximize net income, it might consider establishing transfer prices that:

a. allocate contribution margin equally between Eastland and Westland.
b. allocate more contribution margin to Eastland.
c. allocate more contribution margin to Westland.
d. allocate half as much contribution margin to Eastland as it does to Westland.

Solutions

1. c. The selling price and the desired profit must be decided before costs are determined. Therefore, the other choices are incorrect.

2. b. The target cost for the locomotive is selling price less desired profit or $80 − $15 = $65, not (a) $80, (c) $40, or (d) $25.

3. c. A seller would most likely use target costing in a competitive common-product environment as the price is set by the market. In a less competitive environment, companies have a greater ability to set the product price and therefore could use (a) time-and-material pricing, (b) variable costing, or (d) cost-plus pricing.

4. b. In cost-plus pricing, Selling price = Cost + (Markup percentage × Cost). The other choices are therefore incorrect.

5. b. The desired markup percentage = [(.10 × $500,000) ÷ 1,000]/$25 = 200%. The selling price = $25 + $50 = $75. The other choices are therefore incorrect.

6. c. The percentage markup on cost = ($10 ÷ $30) = 33⅓%, not (a) 125%, (b) 75%, or (d) 25%.

7. a. The labor charge per hour = $10 + {[$100,000 + .5($40,000) + .5($80,000)] ÷ 5,000} = $42, not (b) $34, (c) $32, or (d) $30.

8. d. A lawn-care provider would be most likely to use time-and-material pricing as it is a service company. The other choices provide products rather than services.

9. b. In time-and-material pricing, the material loading charge is expressed as a percentage of the total estimated costs of parts and materials for the year. Therefore, the other choices are incorrect.

10. d. The minimum transfer price the Plastics Division should accept = Variable cost per unit + Opportunity cost per unit. Since the Plastics Division is operating at full capacity, the opportunity cost per unit is equal to the contribution margin per unit of $40 (selling price of $70 − variable cost per unit of $30). The minimum transfer price is therefore $30 + $40 = $70, not (a) $10, (b) $30, or (c) $40.

11. b. Since we assume the Plastics Division has excess capacity of 10,000 units, the minimum transfer price is equal to the variable cost per unit of $30, not (a) $10, (c) $40, or (d) $70.

12. **c.** The most common method to establish transfer prices is the cost-based transfer pricing approach as it is simple to use, easy to understand, and has available cost data. Negotiated transfer pricing and market-based transfer pricing are considered better approaches but often are not used because of lack of market price information or other considerations.

*13. **b.** Using the absorption-cost approach, add the desired ROI per unit ($15) and selling and administrative expenses per unit ($20) = $35 per unit, then divide that by the manufacturing cost per unit ($70), which equals the markup percentage of 50%, not (a) 16.67%, (c) 54.28%, or (d) 118.75%.

*14. **d.** Using variable-cost pricing, add the desired ROI per unit ($15), fixed manufacturing costs per unit ($30) and fixed selling and administrative expenses per unit ($12) = $57, then divide that by the total variable costs per unit ($40 + $8) = $57/$48 = 118.75%, not (a) 16.67%, (b) 50%, or (c) 54.28%.

*15. **b.** To minimize tax payments and maximize net income, Global's transfer prices might allocate more contribution margin to Eastland as it has a lower tax rate. (Note that the legal and ethical ramifications of this action would need to be considered.) The other choices are therefore incorrect.

Practice Brief Exercises

1. (LO 2) During the current year, Winston Corporation expects to produce 15,000 units and has budgeted the following: net income $500,000, variable costs $800,000, and fixed costs $700,000. It has invested assets of $2,000,000. The company's budgeted ROI was 20%. What was its budgeted markup percentage using a full-cost approach?

Compute ROI and markup percentage.

Solution

1. The markup percentage is equal to desired ROI per unit divided by total unit cost. The desired ROI per unit is computed as follows.

$$\text{Desired ROI per unit} = \frac{\$2,000,000 \times 30\%}{15,000 \text{ units}} = \$40$$

The total unit cost is computed as follows.

$$\text{Total unit cost} = \frac{\$800,000 + 700,000}{15,000 \text{ units}} = \$100$$

The budgeted markup percentage is computed as follows.

$$\frac{\text{Desired ROI per unit}}{\text{Total unit cost}} = \frac{\$40}{\$100} = \$40$$

2. (LO 3) Tanner Bicycle Repair charges $28 per hour of labor. It has a material loading percentage of 30%. On a recent job replacing the rear wheel and sprocket of a racing bike, Tanner worked 8 hours and used parts with a cost of $450. Calculate Tanner's total bill.

Use time-and-material pricing to determine bill.

Solution

2. Tanner's total bill would equal:

$$(8 \text{ hours} \times \$28) + \$450 + (\$450 \times 30\%) = \$809$$

3. (LO 4) The Memory Division of Ellie International produces a computer memory element that it sells to its customers for $30 per unit. Its variable cost per unit is $18, and its fixed cost per unit is $7. Top management of Ellie International would like the Memory Division to transfer 7,000 units to another division within the company at a price of $21. The Memory Division has sufficient excess capacity to provide the units. What is the minimum transfer price that the Memory Division should accept?

Determine minimum transfer price.

Solution

3. If the division has excess capacity, then its opportunity cost is zero. In this case, the minimum transfer price is:

$$\text{Minimum transfer price} = \$18 + \$0 = \$18$$

CHAPTER 21 Pricing

Determine minimum transfer price for special order.

4. (LO 4) Use the data from **Practice Brief Exercise 3** but assume that the units being requested are special high-performance units and that the division's variable cost would be $21 per unit (rather than $18). Assume the division is operating at full capacity. What is the minimum transfer price that the Memory Division should accept?

Solution

4. The minimum transfer price is equal to the division's variable cost plus its opportunity cost. In this case the minimum transfer price is:

$$\text{Minimum transfer price} = \$21 + (\$30 - \$18) = \$33$$

Practice Exercises

Use cost-plus pricing to determine various amounts.

1. (LO 2) Notown Recording Studio rents studio time to musicians in 2-hour blocks. Each session includes the use of the studio facilities, a digital recorded CD of the performance, and a professional music producer/mixer. Anticipated annual volume is 1,000 sessions. The company has invested $2,300,000 in the studio and expects a return on investment (ROI) of 15%. Budgeted costs for the coming year are as follows.

	Per Session	Total
Direct materials (CDs, etc.)	$ 20	
Direct labor	$400	
Variable overhead	$ 50	
Fixed overhead		$950,000
Variable selling and administrative expenses	$ 40	
Fixed selling and administrative expenses		$540,000

Instructions

a. Determine the total cost per session.
b. Determine the desired ROI per session.
c. Calculate the markup percentage on the total cost per session.
d. Calculate the target price per session.

Solution

1. a. Total cost per session:

	Per Session
Direct materials	$ 20
Direct labor	400
Variable overhead	50
Fixed overhead ($950,000 ÷ 1,000)	950
Variable selling & administrative expenses	40
Fixed selling & administrative expenses ($540,000 ÷ 1,000)	540
Total cost per session	$2,000

b. Desired ROI per session = (15% × $2,300,000) ÷ 1,000 = $345
c. Markup percentage on total cost per session = $345 ÷ $2,000 = 17.25%
d. Target price per session = $2,000 + ($2,000 × 17.25%) = $2,345

Determine minimum transfer price.

2. (LO 4) Mercury Corporation manufactures car audio systems. It is a division of Country-Wide Motors, which manufactures vehicles. Mercury sells car audio systems to other divisions of Country-Wide, as well as to other vehicle manufacturers and retail stores. The following information is available for Mercury's standard unit: variable cost per unit $31, fixed cost per unit $23, and selling price to outside customer $85. Country-Wide currently purchases a standard unit from an outside supplier for $80. Because of quality concerns and to ensure a reliable supply, the top management of Country-Wide has ordered Mercury to provide 200,000 units per year at a transfer price of $30 per unit. Mercury is already operating at full capacity. Mercury can avoid $2 per unit of variable selling costs by selling the unit internally.

Instructions

a. What is the minimum transfer price that Mercury should accept?
b. What is the potential loss to the corporation as a whole resulting from this forced transfer?
c. How should the company resolve this situation?

Solution

2. a. The minimum transfer price that Mercury should accept is:

   Minimum transfer price = ($31 − $2) + ($85 − $31) = $83

   b. The lost contribution margin per unit to the company is:

Contribution margin lost by Mercury	
{($85 − $31) − [$30 − ($31 − $2)]}	$53
Increased contribution margin to vehicle division ($80 − $30)	50
Net loss in contribution margin	$ 3

   Total lost contribution margin is $3 × 200,000 units = $600,000

   c. If management insists that it wants Mercury to provide the car audio systems and Mercury is operating at full capacity, then it must be willing to pay the minimum transfer price for those units. Otherwise, it will penalize the managers of Mercury by not giving them adequate credit for their contribution to the corporation's contribution margin.

Practice Problem

(LO 4) Revco Electronics is a division of International Motors, an automobile manufacturer. Revco produces car radio/CD players. Revco sells its products to other divisions of International Motors, as well as to other car manufacturers and electronics distributors. The following information is available regarding Revco's car radio/CD player.

Determine minimum transfer price under different situations.

Selling price of car radio/CD player to external customers	$49
Variable cost per unit	$28
Capacity	200,000 units

Instructions

Determine whether the goods should be transferred internally or purchased externally and what the appropriate transfer price should be under each of the following **independent** situations.

a. Revco Electronics is operating at full capacity. There is a saving of $4 per unit for variable cost if the car radio is made for internal sale. International Motors can purchase a comparable car radio from an outside supplier for $47.

b. Revco Electronics has sufficient existing capacity to meet the needs of International Motors. International Motors can purchase a comparable car radio from an outside supplier for $47.

c. International Motors wants to purchase a special-order car radio/CD player with additional features. It needs 15,000 units. Revco Electronics has determined that the additional variable cost would be $12 per unit. Revco Electronics has no spare capacity. It will have to forgo sales of 15,000 units to external parties in order to provide this special order.

Solution

a. Revco Electronics' opportunity cost (its lost contribution margin) would be $21 ($49 − $28). Using the formula for minimum transfer price, we determine:

Minimum transfer price	=	Variable cost	+	Opportunity cost
$45	=	($28 − $4)	+	$21

Since this minimum transfer price is less than the $47 it would cost if International Motors purchases from an external party, internal transfer should take place. Revco Electronics and International Motors should negotiate a transfer price between $45 and $47.

b. Since Revco Electronics has available capacity, its opportunity cost (its lost contribution margin) would be $0. Using the formula for minimum transfer price, we determine the following.

$$\begin{array}{rcccc} \text{Minimum transfer price} & = & \text{Variable cost} & + & \text{Opportunity cost} \\ \$28 & = & \$28 & + & \$0 \end{array}$$

Since International Motors can purchase the unit for $47 from an external party, the most it would be willing to pay would be $47. It is in the best interest of the company as a whole, as well as the two divisions, for a transfer to take place. The two divisions must reach a negotiated transfer price between $28 and $47 that recognizes the costs and benefits to each party and is acceptable to both.

c. Revco Electronics' opportunity cost (its lost contribution margin per unit) would be $21 ($49 − $28). Its variable cost would be $40 ($28 + $12). Using the formula for minimum transfer price, we determine the following.

$$\begin{array}{rcccc} \text{Minimum transfer price} & = & \text{Variable cost} & + & \text{Opportunity cost} \\ \$61 & = & \$40 & + & \$21 \end{array}$$

Note that in this case Revco Electronics has no available capacity. Its management may decide that it does not want to provide this special order because to do so will require that it cut off the supply of the standard unit to some of its existing customers. This may anger those customers and result in the loss of customers.

WileyPLUS

Brief Exercises, DO IT! Exercises, Exercises, Problems, and many additional resources are available for practice in WileyPLUS.

Note: All asterisked Questions, Exercises, and Problems relate to material in the appendices to this chapter.

Questions

1. What are the two types of pricing environments for sales to external parties?

2. In what situation does a company place the greatest focus on its target cost? How is the target cost determined?

3. What is the basic formula to determine the target selling price in cost-plus pricing?

4. Benz Corporation produces a filter that has a per unit cost of $18. The company would like a 30% markup. Using cost-plus pricing, determine the per unit selling price.

5. What is the basic formula for the markup percentage?

6. Stanley Corporation manufactures an electronic switch for dishwashers. The cost base per unit, excluding selling and administrative expenses, is $60. The per unit cost of selling and administrative expenses is $15. The company's desired ROI per unit is $6. Calculate its markup percentage on total unit cost.

7. Sheen Co. manufactures a standard cabinet for a Blu-ray player. The variable cost per unit is $16. The fixed cost per unit is $9. The desired ROI per unit is $6. Compute the markup percentage on total unit cost and the target selling price for the cabinet.

8. In what circumstances is time-and-material pricing most often used?

9. What is the material loading charge? How is it expressed?

10. What is a transfer price? Why is determining a fair transfer price important to division managers?

11. When setting a transfer price, what objective(s) should the company have in mind?

12. What are the three approaches for determining transfer prices?

13. Describe the cost-based approach to transfer pricing. What is the strength of this approach? What are the weaknesses of this approach?

14. What is the general formula for determining the minimum transfer price that the selling division should be willing to accept?

15. When determining the minimum transfer price, what is meant by the "opportunity cost"?

16. In what circumstances will a negotiated transfer price be used instead of a market-based price?

*17. What costs are excluded from the cost base when absorption-cost pricing is used to determine the markup percentage?

*18. Marie Corporation manufactures a fiber optic connector. The variable cost per unit is $16. The fixed cost per unit is $9. The company's desired ROI per unit is $3. Compute the markup percentage using variable-cost pricing.

*19. Explain how companies use transfer pricing between divisions located in different countries to reduce tax payments, and discuss the propriety of this approach.

Brief Exercises

BE21.1 (LO 1), AP Ortega Company manufactures computer hard drives. The market for hard drives is very competitive. The current market price for a computer hard drive is $45. Ortega would like a profit of $10 per drive. How can Ortega accomplish this objective?

Compute target cost.

BE21.2 (LO 2), AP Mussatto Corporation produces snowboards. The following per unit cost information is available: direct materials $12, direct labor $8, variable manufacturing overhead $6, fixed manufacturing overhead $14, variable selling and administrative expenses $4, and fixed selling and administrative expenses $12. Using a 30% markup percentage on total per unit cost, compute the target selling price.

Use cost-plus pricing to determine selling price.

BE21.3 (LO 2), AP Jaymes Corporation produces high-performance rotors. It expects to produce 50,000 rotors in the coming year. It has invested $10,000,000 to produce rotors. The company has a required return on investment of 12%. What is its ROI per unit?

Compute ROI per unit.

BE21.4 (LO 2), AP Morales Corporation produces microwave ovens. The following per unit cost information is available: direct materials $36, direct labor $24, variable manufacturing overhead $18, fixed manufacturing overhead $40, variable selling and administrative expenses $14, and fixed selling and administrative expenses $28. Its desired ROI per unit is $30. Compute its markup percentage using a total-cost approach.

Compute markup percentage.

BE21.5 (LO 2), AP During the current year, Chudrick Corporation expects to produce 10,000 units and has budgeted the following: net income $300,000, variable costs $1,100,000, and fixed costs $100,000. It has invested assets of $1,500,000. The company's budgeted ROI was 20%. What was its budgeted markup percentage using a full-cost approach?

Compute ROI and markup percentage.

BE21.6 (LO 3), AP Service Rooney Small Engine Repair charges $42 per hour of labor. It has a material loading percentage of 40%. On a recent job replacing the engine of a riding lawnmower, Rooney worked 10.5 hours and used parts with a cost of $700. Calculate Rooney's total bill.

Use time-and-material pricing to determine bill.

BE21.7 (LO 4), AP The Heating Division of Kobe International produces a heating element that it sells to its customers for $45 per unit. Its variable cost per unit is $25, and its fixed cost per unit is $10. Top management of Kobe International would like the Heating Division to transfer 15,000 heating units to another division within the company at a price of $29. The Heating Division is operating at full capacity. What is the minimum transfer price that the Heating Division should accept?

Determine minimum transfer price.

BE21.8 (LO 4), AP Use the data from BE21.7 but assume that the Heating Division has sufficient excess capacity to provide the 15,000 heating units to the other division. What is the minimum transfer price that the Heating Division should accept?

Determine minimum transfer price with excess capacity.

BE21.9 (LO 4), AP Use the data from BE21.7 but assume that the units being requested are special high-performance units and that the division's variable cost would be $27 per unit (rather than $25). What is the minimum transfer price that the Heating Division should accept?

Determine minimum transfer price for special order.

*derniBE21.10 (LO 5), AP** Using the data in BE21.4, compute the markup percentage using absorption-cost pricing.

Compute markup percentage using absorption-cost pricing.

BE21.11 (LO 5), AP Using the data in BE21.4, compute the markup percentage using variable-cost pricing.

Compute markup percentage using variable-cost pricing.

DO IT! Exercises

Determine target cost.

DO IT! 21.1 (LO 1), AP Maize Water is considering introducing a water filtration device for its 20-ounce water bottles. Market research indicates that 1,000,000 units can be sold if the price is no more than $3. If Maize Water decides to produce the filters, it will need to invest $2,000,000 in new production equipment. Maize Water requires a minimum rate of return of 16% on all investments.

Determine the target cost per unit for the filter.

Use cost-plus pricing to determine various amounts.

DO IT! 21.2 (LO 2), AP Gundy Corporation produces area rugs. The following per unit cost information is available: direct materials $18, direct labor $9, variable manufacturing overhead $5, fixed manufacturing overhead $6, variable selling and administrative expenses $3, and fixed selling and administrative expenses $7.

Using a 30% markup on total per unit cost, compute the target selling price.

Use time-and-material pricing to determine bill.

DO IT! 21.3 (LO 3), AP Service Presented below are data relating to labor for Verde Appliance Repair Shop.

Repair-technicians' wages	$110,000
Fringe benefits	40,000
Overhead	50,000

The desired profit margin per hour is $20. The material loading charge is 60% of invoice cost. Verde estimates that 5,000 labor hours will be worked next year. If Verde repairs a dishwasher that takes 1.5 hours to repair and uses parts of $70, compute the bill for the job.

Determine transfer prices.

DO IT! 21.4 (LO 4), AP The fastener division of Southern Fasteners manufactures zippers and then sells them to customers for $8 per unit. Its variable cost is $3 per unit, and its fixed cost per unit is $1.50. Management would like the fastener division to transfer 12,000 of these zippers to another division within the company at a price of $3. The fastener division could avoid $0.20 per zipper of variable packaging costs by selling internally.

Determine the minimum transfer price (a) assuming the fastener division is not operating at full capacity, and (b) assuming the fastener division is operating at full capacity.

Exercises

Compute target cost.

E21.1 (LO 1), AP Mesa Cheese Company has developed a new cheese slicer called Slim Slicer. The company plans to sell this slicer through its catalog, which it issues monthly. Given market research, Mesa believes that it can charge $20 for the Slim Slicer. Prototypes of the Slim Slicer, however, are costing $22. By using cheaper materials and gaining efficiencies in mass production, Mesa believes it can reduce Slim Slicer's cost substantially. Mesa wishes to earn a return of 40% of the selling price.

Instructions

a. Compute the target cost for the Slim Slicer.

b. When is target costing particularly helpful in deciding whether to produce a given product?

Compute target cost.

E21.2 (LO 1), AP Eckert Company is involved in producing and selling high-end golf equipment. The company has recently been involved in developing various types of laser guns to measure yardages on the golf course. One small laser gun, called LittleLaser, appears to have a very large potential market. Because of competition, Eckert does not believe that it can charge more than $90 for LittleLaser. At this price, Eckert believes it can sell 100,000 of these laser guns. Eckert will require an investment of $8,000,000 to manufacture, and the company wants an ROI of 20%.

Instructions

Determine the target cost for one LittleLaser.

Compute target cost and cost-plus pricing.

E21.3 (LO 1, 2), AP Leno Company makes swimsuits and sells these suits directly to retailers. Although Leno has a variety of suits, it does not make the All-Body suit used by highly skilled swimmers. The market research department believes that a strong market exists for this type of suit. The department indicates that the All-Body suit would sell for approximately $100. Given its experience, Leno believes the All-Body suit would have the following manufacturing costs.

Direct materials	$ 25
Direct labor	30
Manufacturing overhead	45
Total costs	$100

Instructions

a. Assume that Leno uses cost-plus pricing, setting the selling price 25% above its costs. (1) What would be the price charged for the All-Body swimsuit? (2) Under what circumstances might Leno consider manufacturing the All-Body swimsuit given this approach?

b. Assume that Leno uses target costing. What is the price that Leno would charge the retailer for the All-Body swimsuit?

c. What is the highest acceptable manufacturing cost Leno would be willing to incur to produce the All-Body swimsuit, if it desired a profit of $25 per unit? (Assume target costing.)

E21.4 (LO 2), AP Kaspar Corporation makes a commercial-grade cooking griddle. The following information is available for Kaspar Corporation's anticipated annual volume of 30,000 units.

Use cost-plus pricing to determine selling price.

	Per Unit	Total
Direct materials	$17	
Direct labor	$ 8	
Variable manufacturing overhead	$11	
Fixed manufacturing overhead		$300,000
Variable selling and administrative expenses	$ 4	
Fixed selling and administrative expenses		$150,000

The company uses a 40% markup percentage on total cost.

Instructions

a. Compute the total cost per unit.

b. Compute the target selling price.

E21.5 (LO 2), AP Schopp Corporation makes a mechanical stuffed alligator that sings the Martian national anthem. The following information is available for Schopp Corporation's anticipated annual volume of 500,000 units.

Use cost-plus pricing to determine various amounts.

	Per Unit	Total
Direct materials	$ 7	
Direct labor	$11	
Variable manufacturing overhead	$15	
Fixed manufacturing overhead		$3,000,000
Variable selling and administrative expenses	$14	
Fixed selling and administrative expenses		$1,500,000

The company has a desired ROI of 25%. It has invested assets of $28,000,000.

Instructions

a. Compute the total cost per unit.

b. Compute the desired ROI per unit.

c. Compute the markup percentage using total cost per unit.

d. Compute the target selling price.

E21.6 (LO 2), AP Service Alma's Recording Studio rents studio time to musicians in 2-hour blocks. Each session includes the use of the studio facilities, a digital recording of the performance, and a professional music producer/mixer. Anticipated annual volume is 1,000 sessions. The company has invested $2,352,000 in the studio and expects a return on investment (ROI) of 20%. Budgeted costs for the coming year are as follows.

Use cost-plus pricing to determine various amounts.

	Per Session	Total
Direct materials (CDs, etc.)	$ 20	
Direct labor	$400	
Variable overhead	$ 50	
Fixed overhead		$950,000
Variable selling and administrative expenses	$ 40	
Fixed selling and administrative expenses		$500,000

Instructions

a. Determine the total cost per session.

b. Determine the desired ROI per session.

c. Calculate the markup percentage on the total cost per session.

d. Calculate the target price per session.

Use cost-plus pricing to determine various amounts.

E21.7 (LO 2), AP Gibbs Corporation produces industrial robots for high-precision manufacturing. The following information is given for Gibbs Corporation.

	Per Unit	Total
Direct materials	$380	
Direct labor	$290	
Variable manufacturing overhead	$ 72	
Fixed manufacturing overhead		$1,500,000
Variable selling and administrative expenses	$ 55	
Fixed selling and administrative expenses		$ 324,000

The company has a desired ROI of 20%. It has invested assets of $54,000,000. It anticipates production of 3,000 units per year.

Instructions

a. Compute the cost per unit of the fixed manufacturing overhead and the fixed selling and administrative expenses.

b. Compute the desired ROI per unit. (Round to the nearest dollar.)

c. Compute the target selling price.

Use time-and-material pricing to determine bill.

E21.8 (LO 3), AP Service Second Chance Welding rebuilds spot welders for manufacturers. The following budgeted cost data for 2022 is available for Second Chance.

	Time Charges	Material Loading Charges
Technicians' wages and benefits	$228,000	—
Parts manager's salary and benefits	—	$42,500
Office employee's salary and benefits	38,000	9,000
Other overhead	15,200	24,000
Total budgeted costs	$281,200	$75,500

The company desires a $30 profit margin per hour of labor and a 20% profit margin on parts. It has budgeted for 7,600 hours of repair time in the coming year, and estimates that the total invoice cost of parts and materials in 2022 will be $400,000.

Instructions

a. Compute the rate charged per hour of labor.

b. Compute the material loading percentage. (Round to three decimal places.)

c. Pace Corporation has requested an estimate to rebuild its spot welder. Second Chance estimates that it would require 40 hours of labor and $2,000 of parts. Compute the total estimated bill.

Use time-and-material pricing to determine bill.

E21.9 (LO 3), AP Service Rey Custom Electronics (RCE) sells and installs complete security, computer, audio, and video systems for homes. On newly constructed homes it provides bids using time-and-material pricing. The following budgeted cost data are available.

	Time Charges	Material Loading Charges
Technicians' wages and benefits	$150,000	—
Parts manager's salary and benefits	—	$34,000
Office employee's salary and benefits	30,000	15,000
Other overhead	15,000	42,000
Total budgeted costs	$195,000	$91,000

The company has budgeted for 6,250 hours of technician time during the coming year. It desires a $38 profit margin per hour of labor and an 80% profit on parts. It estimates the total invoice cost of parts and materials in 2022 will be $700,000.

Instructions

a. Compute the rate charged per hour of labor.

b. Compute the material loading percentage.

c. RCE has just received a request for a bid from Buil Builders on a $1,200,000 new home. The company estimates that it would require 80 hours of labor and $40,000 of parts. Compute the total estimated bill.

E21.10 (LO 3), AP Service Wasson's Classic Cars restores classic automobiles to showroom status. Budgeted data for the current year are as follows.

Use time-and-material pricing to determine bill.

	Time Charges	Material Loading Charges
Restorers' wages and fringe benefits	$270,000	—
Purchasing agent's salary and fringe benefits	—	$ 67,500
Administrative salaries and fringe benefits	54,000	21,960
Other overhead costs	24,000	77,490
Total budgeted costs	$348,000	$166,950

The company anticipated that the restorers would work a total of 12,000 hours this year. Expected parts and materials were $1,260,000.

In late January, the company experienced a fire in its facilities that destroyed most of the accounting records. The accountant remembers that the hourly labor rate was $70.00 and that the material loading charge was 83.25%.

Instructions

a. Determine the profit margin per hour on labor.

b. Determine the profit margin on materials.

c. Determine the total price of labor and materials on a job that was completed after the fire that required 150 hours of labor and $60,000 in parts and materials.

E21.11 (LO 4), AP Writing Chen Company's Small Motor Division manufactures a number of small motors used in household and office appliances. The Household Division of Chen then assembles and packages such items as blenders and juicers. Both divisions are free to buy and sell any of their components internally or externally. The following costs relate to small motor LN233 on a per unit basis.

Determine minimum transfer price.

Fixed cost per unit	$ 5
Variable cost per unit	$11
Selling price per unit	$35

Instructions

a. Assuming that the Small Motor Division has excess capacity, compute the minimum acceptable price for the transfer of small motor LN233 to the Household Division.

b. Assuming that the Small Motor Division does not have excess capacity, compute the minimum acceptable price for the transfer of the small motor to the Household Division.

c. Explain why the level of capacity in the Small Motor Division has an effect on the transfer price.

E21.12 (LO 4), AN The Cycle Division of Ayala Company has the following per unit data related to its most recent cycle called Roadbuster.

Determine effect on income from transfer price.

Selling price		$2,200
Variable cost of goods sold		
Body frame	$300	
Other variable costs	900	1,200
Contribution margin		$1,000

Presently, the Cycle Division buys its body frames from an outside supplier. However Ayala has another division, FrameBody, that makes body frames for other cycle companies. The Cycle Division believes that FrameBody's product is suitable for its new Roadbuster cycle. Presently, FrameBody sells its frames for $350 per frame. The variable cost for FrameBody is $270. The Cycle Division is willing to pay $280 to purchase the frames from FrameBody.

Instructions

a. Assume that FrameBody has excess capacity and is able to meet all of the Cycle Division's needs. If the Cycle Division buys 1,000 frames from FrameBody, determine the following: (1) effect on the income of the Cycle Division; (2) effect on the income of FrameBody; and (3) effect on the income of Ayala.

b. Assume that FrameBody does not have excess capacity and therefore would lose sales if the frames were sold to the Cycle Division. If the Cycle Division buys 1,000 frames from FrameBody, determine the following: (1) effect on the income of the Cycle Division; (2) effect on the income of FrameBody; and (3) effect on the income of Ayala.

Determine minimum transfer price.

E21.13 (LO 4), AP Benson Corporation manufactures car stereos. It is a division of Berna Motors, which manufactures vehicles. Benson sells car stereos to Berna, as well as to other vehicle manufacturers and retail stores. The following information is available for Benson's standard unit: variable cost per unit $37, fixed cost per unit $23, and selling price to outside customer $86. Berna currently purchases a standard unit from an outside supplier for $80. Because of quality concerns and to ensure a reliable supply, the top management of Berna has ordered Benson to provide 200,000 units per year at a transfer price of $35 per unit. Benson is already operating at full capacity. Benson can avoid $3 per unit of variable selling costs by selling the unit internally.

Instructions

Answer each of the following questions.

a. What is the minimum transfer price that Benson should accept?

b. What is the potential loss to the corporation as a whole resulting from this forced transfer?

c. How should the company resolve this situation?

Compute minimum transfer price.

E21.14 (LO 4), AP The Bathtub Division of Kirk Plumbing Corporation has recently approached the Faucet Division with a proposal. The Bathtub Division would like to make a special "ivory" tub with gold-plated fixtures for the company's 50-year anniversary. It would make only 5,000 of these units. It would like the Faucet Division to make the fixtures and provide them to the Bathtub Division at a transfer price of $160. If sold externally, the estimated variable cost per unit would be $140. However, by selling internally, the Faucet Division would save $6 per unit on variable selling expenses. The Faucet Division is currently operating at full capacity. Its standard unit sells for $50 per unit and has variable costs of $29.

Instructions

Compute the minimum transfer price that the Faucet Division should be willing to accept, and discuss whether it should accept this offer.

Determine minimum transfer price.

E21.15 (LO 4), AP **Service** The Appraisal Department of Jean Bank performs appraisals of business properties for loans being considered by the bank and appraisals for home buyers that are financing their purchase through some other financial institution. The department charges $160 per home appraisal, and its variable costs are $130 per appraisal.

Recently, Jean Bank has opened its own Home-Loan Department and wants the Appraisal Department to perform 1,200 appraisals on all Jean Bank–financed home loans. Bank management feels that the cost of these appraisals to the Home-Loan Department should be $150. The variable cost per appraisal to the Home-Loan Department would be $8 less than those performed for outside customers due to savings in administrative costs.

Instructions

a. Determine the minimum transfer price, assuming the Appraisal Department has excess capacity.

b. Determine the minimum transfer price, assuming the Appraisal Department has no excess capacity.

c. Assuming the Appraisal Department has no excess capacity, should management force the department to charge the Home-Loan Department only $150? Discuss.

Determine minimum transfer price under different situations.

E21.16 (LO 4), AP Crede Inc. has two divisions. Division A makes and sells student desks. Division B manufactures and sells reading lamps.

Each desk has a reading lamp as one of its components. Division A can purchase reading lamps at a cost of $10 from an outside vendor. Division A needs 10,000 lamps for the coming year.

Division B has the capacity to manufacture 50,000 lamps annually. Sales to outside customers are estimated at 40,000 lamps for the next year. Reading lamps are sold at $12 each. Variable costs are $7 per lamp and include $1 of variable sales costs that are not incurred if lamps are sold internally to Division A. The total amount of fixed costs for Division B is $80,000.

Instructions

Consider the following independent situations.

a. What should be the minimum transfer price accepted by Division B for the 10,000 lamps and the maximum transfer price paid by Division A? Justify your answer.

b. Suppose Division B could use the excess capacity to produce and sell externally 15,000 units of a new product at a price of $7 per unit. The variable cost for this new product is $5 per unit. What should be the minimum transfer price accepted by Division B for the 10,000 lamps and the maximum transfer price paid by Division A? Justify your answer.

c. If Division A needs 15,000 lamps instead of 10,000 during the next year, what should be the minimum transfer price accepted by Division B and the maximum transfer price paid by Division A? Justify your answer.

(CGA adapted)

E21.17 (LO 4), AP Twyla Company is a multidivisional company. Its managers have full responsibility for profits and complete autonomy to accept or reject transfers from other divisions. Division A produces a subassembly part for which there is a competitive market. Division B currently uses this subassembly for a final product that is sold outside at $2,400. Division A charges Division B market price for the part, which is $1,500 per unit. Variable costs are $1,100 and $1,200 for Divisions A and B, respectively.

The manager of Division B feels that Division A should transfer the part at a lower price than market because at market, Division B is unable to make a profit.

Determine minimum transfer price under different situations.

Instructions

a. Calculate Division B's contribution margin if transfers are made at the market price, and calculate the company's total contribution margin.

b. Assume that Division A can sell all its production in the open market. Should Division A transfer the goods to Division B? If so, at what price?

c. Assume that Division A can sell in the open market only 500 units at $1,500 per unit out of the 1,000 units that it can produce every month. Assume also that a 20% reduction in price is necessary to sell all 1,000 units each month. Should transfers be made? If so, how many units should the division transfer and at what price? To support your decision, submit a schedule that compares the contribution margins under the following three different alternatives. Alternative 1: maintain price, no transfers; Alternative 2: cut price, no transfers; and Alternative 3: maintain price and transfers.

(CMA-Canada adapted)

*E21.18 (LO 5), AP Information for Schopp Corporation is given in E21.5.

Compute total cost per unit, ROI, and markup percentages using absorption-cost pricing and variable-cost pricing.

Instructions

Using the information given in E21.5, answer the following.

a. Compute the total cost per unit.
b. Compute the desired ROI per unit.
c. Using absorption-cost pricing, compute the markup percentage.
d. Using variable-cost pricing, compute the markup percentage.

*E21.19 (LO 5), AP Rap Corporation produces outdoor portable fireplace units. The following per unit cost information is available: direct materials $20, direct labor $25, variable manufacturing overhead $14, fixed manufacturing overhead $21, variable selling and administrative expenses $9, and fixed selling and administrative expenses $11. The company's ROI per unit is $24.

Compute markup percentage using absorption-cost pricing and variable-cost pricing.

Instructions

Compute Rap Corporation's markup percentage using (a) absorption-cost pricing and (b) variable-cost pricing.

*E21.20 (LO 5), AP Information for Gibbs Corporation is given in E21.7.

Compute various amounts using absorption-cost pricing and variable-cost pricing.

Instructions

Using the information given in E21.7, answer the following.

a. Compute the cost per unit of the fixed manufacturing overhead and the fixed selling and administrative expenses.

b. Compute the desired ROI per unit. (Round to the nearest dollar.)

c. Compute the markup percentage and target selling price using absorption-cost pricing. (Round the markup percentage to three decimal places.)

d. Compute the markup percentage and target selling price using variable-cost pricing. (Round the markup percentage to three decimal places.)

Problems: Set A

Use cost-plus pricing to determine various amounts.

P21.1A (LO 2), AP National Corporation needs to set a target price for its newly designed product M14–M16. The following data relate to this new product.

	Per Unit	Total
Direct materials	$25	
Direct labor	$40	
Variable manufacturing overhead	$10	
Fixed manufacturing overhead		$1,440,000
Variable selling and administrative expenses	$ 5	
Fixed selling and administrative expenses		$ 960,000

These costs are based on a budgeted volume of 80,000 units produced and sold each year. National uses cost-plus pricing methods to set its target selling price. The markup percentage on total unit cost is 40%.

Instructions

a. Variable cost per unit $80

a. Compute the total variable cost per unit, total fixed cost per unit, and total cost per unit for M14–M16.

b. Compute the desired ROI per unit for M14–M16.

c. Compute the target selling price for M14–M16.

d. Compute variable cost per unit, fixed cost per unit, and total cost per unit assuming that 60,000 M14–M16s are produced and sold during the year.

Use cost-plus pricing to determine various amounts.

P21.2A (LO 2), AP Lovell Computer Parts Inc. is in the process of setting a selling price on a new component it has just designed and developed. The following cost estimates for this new component have been provided by the accounting department for a budgeted volume of 50,000 units.

	Per Unit	Total
Direct materials	$50	
Direct labor	$26	
Variable manufacturing overhead	$20	
Fixed manufacturing overhead		$600,000
Variable selling and administrative expenses	$19	
Fixed selling and administrative expenses		$400,000

Lovell Computer Parts management requests that the total cost per unit be used in cost-plus pricing its products. On this particular product, management also directs that the target price be set to provide a 25% return on investment (ROI) on invested assets of $1,000,000.

Instructions

(Round all calculations to two decimal places.)

a. Compute the markup percentage and target selling price that will allow Lovell Computer Parts to earn its desired ROI of 25% on this new component.

b. Target selling price $146.25

b. Assuming that the volume is 40,000 units, compute the markup percentage and target selling price that will allow Lovell Computer Parts to earn its desired ROI of 25% on this new component.

Use time-and-material pricing to determine bill.

P21.3A (LO 3), AP **Service** Sutton's Electronic Repair Shop has budgeted the following time and material for 2022.

Sutton's Electronic Repair Shop
Budgeted Costs for the Year 2022

	Time Charges	Material Loading Charges
Shop employees' wages and benefits	$108,000	—
Parts manager's salary and benefits	—	$25,400
Office employee's salary and benefits	23,500	13,600
Overhead (supplies, depreciation, advertising, utilities)	26,000	16,000
Total budgeted costs	$157,500	$55,000

Sutton's budgets 5,000 hours of repair time in 2022 and will bill a profit of $10 per labor hour along with a 25% profit markup on the invoice cost of parts. The estimated invoice cost for parts to be used is $100,000.

On January 5, 2022, Sutton's is asked to submit a price estimate to fix a 72-inch flat-screen TV. Sutton's estimates that this job will consume 4 hours of labor and $200 in parts.

Instructions

a. Compute the labor rate for Sutton's Electronic Repair Shop for the year 2022.
b. Compute the material loading charge percentage for Sutton's Electronic Repair Shop for the year 2022.
c. Prepare a time-and-material price quotation for fixing the flat-screen TV.

c. $526

P21.4A (LO 4), AP Service Writing Word Wizard is a publishing company with a number of different book lines. Each line has contracts with a number of different authors. The company also owns a printing operation called Quick Press. The book lines and the printing operation each operate as a separate profit center. The printing operation earns revenue by printing books by authors under contract with the book lines owned by Word Wizard, as well as authors under contract with other companies. The printing operation bills out at $0.01 per page, and a typical book requires 500 pages of print. A manager from Business Books, one of Word Wizard's book lines, has approached the manager of the printing operation offering to pay $0.007 per page for 1,500 copies of a 500-page book. The book line pays outside printers $0.009 per page. The printing operation's variable cost per page is $0.004.

Determine minimum transfer price with no excess capacity and with excess capacity.

Instructions
Determine whether the printing should be done internally or externally, and the appropriate transfer price, under each of the following situations.

a. Assume that the printing operation is booked solid for the next 2 years, and it would have to cancel an obligation with an outside customer in order to meet the needs of the internal division.
b. Assume that the printing operation has available capacity.
c. The top management of Word Wizard believes that the printing operation should always do the printing for the company's authors. On a number of occasions, it has forced the printing operation to cancel jobs with outside customers in order to meet the needs of its own lines. Discuss the pros and cons of this approach.
d. Calculate the change in contribution margin to each division, and to the company as a whole, if top management forces the printing operation to accept the $0.007 per page transfer price when it has no available capacity.

d. Loss to company $(750)

P21.5A (LO 4), AP Gutierrez Company makes various electronic products. The company is divided into a number of autonomous divisions that can either sell to internal units or sell externally. All divisions are located in buildings on the same piece of property. The Board Division has offered the Chip Division $21 per unit to supply it with chips for 40,000 boards. It has been purchasing these chips for $22 per unit from outside suppliers. The Chip Division receives $22.50 per unit for sales made to outside customers on this type of chip. The variable cost of chips sold externally by the Chip Division is $14.50. It estimates that it will save $4.50 per chip of selling expenses on units sold internally to the Board Division. The Chip Division has no excess capacity.

Determine minimum transfer price with no excess capacity.

Instructions

a. Calculate the minimum transfer price that the Chip Division should accept. Discuss whether it is in the Chip Division's best interest to accept the offer.
b. Suppose that the Chip Division decides to reject the offer. What are the financial implications for each division, and for the company as a whole, of this decision?

b. Total loss to company $160,000

Determine minimum transfer price under different situations.

P21.6A (LO 4), AP Comm Devices (CD) is a division of Worldwide Communications, Inc. CD produces restaurant pagers and other personal communication devices. These devices are sold to other Worldwide divisions, as well as to other communication companies. CD was recently approached by the manager of the Personal Communications Division regarding a request to make a special emergency-response pager designed to receive signals from anywhere in the world. The Personal Communications Division has requested that CD produce 12,000 units of this special pager. The following facts are available regarding the Comm Devices Division.

Selling price of standard pager	$95
Variable cost of standard pager	$50
Additional variable cost of special pager	$30

Instructions

For each of the following independent situations, calculate the minimum transfer price, and discuss whether the internal transfer should take place or whether the Personal Communications Division should purchase the pager externally.

a. The Personal Communications Division has offered to pay the CD Division $105 per pager. The CD Division has no available capacity. The CD Division would have to forgo sales of 10,000 pagers to existing customers in order to meet the request of the Personal Communications Division. (*Note:* The number of special pagers to be produced does not equal the number of existing pagers that would be forgone.)

b. Minimum transfer price $140

b. The Personal Communications Division has offered to pay the CD Division $150 per pager. The CD Division has no available capacity. The CD Division would have to forgo sales of 16,000 pagers to existing customers in order to meet the request of the Personal Communications Division. (*Note:* The number of special pagers to be produced does not equal the number of existing pagers that would be forgone.

c. The Personal Communications Division has offered to pay the CD Division $100 per pager. The CD Division has available capacity.

Compute the target price using absorption-cost pricing and variable-cost pricing.

*P21.7A (LO 5), AP Stent Corporation needs to set a target price for its newly designed product EverReady. The following data relate to this new product.

	Per Unit	Total
Direct materials	$20	
Direct labor	$40	
Variable manufacturing overhead	$10	
Fixed manufacturing overhead		$1,600,000
Variable selling and administrative expenses	$ 5	
Fixed selling and administrative expenses		$1,120,000

The costs shown above are based on a budgeted volume of 80,000 units produced and sold each year. Stent uses cost-plus pricing methods to set its target selling price. Because some managers prefer absorption-cost pricing and others prefer variable-cost pricing, the accounting department provides information under both approaches using a markup of 50% on absorption cost and a markup of 80% on variable cost.

Instructions

a. Markup $45
b. Markup $60

a. Compute the target price for one unit of EverReady using absorption-cost pricing.

b. Compute the target price for one unit of EverReady using variable-cost pricing.

Compute various amounts using absorption-cost pricing and variable-cost pricing.

*P21.8A (LO 5), AP Writing Anderson Windows Inc. is in the process of setting a target price on its newly designed tinted window. Cost data relating to the window at a budgeted volume of 4,000 units are as follows.

	Per Unit	Total
Direct materials	$100	
Direct labor	$ 70	
Variable manufacturing overhead	$ 20	
Fixed manufacturing overhead		$120,000
Variable selling and administrative expenses	$ 10	
Fixed selling and administrative expenses		$102,000

Anderson Windows uses cost-plus pricing methods that are designed to provide the company with a 25% ROI on its tinted window line. A total of $1,016,000 in assets is committed to production of the new tinted window.

Instructions

a. Compute the markup percentage under absorption-cost pricing that will allow Anderson Windows to realize its desired ROI.

b. Compute the target price of the window under absorption-cost pricing, and show proof that the desired ROI is realized.

c. Compute the markup percentage under variable-cost pricing that will allow Anderson Windows to realize its desired ROI. (Round to three decimal places.)

d. Compute the target price of the window under variable-cost pricing, and show proof that the desired ROI is realized.

e. Since both absorption-cost pricing and variable-cost pricing produce the same target price and provide the same desired ROI, why do both methods exist? Isn't one method clearly superior to the other?

a. 45%

Continuing Cases

Current Designs

CD21 As a service to its customers, **Current Designs** repairs damaged kayaks. This is especially valuable to customers that have made a significant investment in the composite kayaks. To price the repair jobs, Current Designs uses time-and-material pricing with a desired profit margin of $20 per labor hour and a 50% materials loading charge.

Recently, Bill Johnson, Vice President of Sales and Marketing, received a phone call from a dealer in Brainerd, Minnesota. The dealer has a customer who recently damaged his composite kayak and would like an estimate of the cost to repair it. After the dealer emailed pictures of the damage, Bill reviewed the pictures with the repair technician and determined that the total materials charges for the repair would be $100. Bill estimates that the job will take 3 labor hours to complete. Following is the budgeted cost data for Current Designs:

Repair technician wages	$30,000
Fringe benefits	$10,000
Overhead	$10,000

Current Designs has allocated 2,000 hours of repair time for the upcoming year. The customer has agreed to transport the kayak to the Winona production facility for the repairs.

Instructions

Determine the price that Current Designs would charge to complete the repairs for the customer.

Waterways

(*Note:* This is a continuation of the Waterways case from Chapters 4–20.)

WP21 Waterways Corporation competes in a market economy in which its products must be sold at market prices. Its emphasis is therefore on manufacturing its products at a cost that allows the company to earn its desired profit. This problem asks you to consider various pricing situations for Waterways' projects.

Go to WileyPLUS for complete case details and instructions.

Comprehensive Case

CC21 Greetings, Inc., a retailer of greeting cards and small gift items, needs to change its transfer pricing strategy for its Wall Décor division. In this case, you will have the opportunity to evaluate profitability using two different transfer pricing approaches and comment on the terms of the proposed transfer pricing agreement.

Go to WileyPLUS for complete case details and instructions.

Expand Your Critical Thinking

Decision-Making Across the Organization

CT21.1 Lanier Manufacturing has multiple divisions that make a wide variety of products. Recently, the Bearing Division and the Wheel Division got into an argument over a transfer price. The Wheel Division needed bearings for garden tractor wheels. It normally buys its bearings from an outside supplier for $25 per set. The company's top management recently initiated a campaign to persuade the different divisions to buy their materials from within the company whenever possible. As a result, Hank Sherril, the purchasing manager for the Wheel Division, received a letter from the vice president of Purchasing, ordering him to contact the Bearing Division to discuss buying bearings from this division.

To comply with this request, Hank from the Wheel Division called Mary Plimpton of the Bearing Division, and asked the price for 15,000 bearings. Mary responded that the bearings normally sell for $36 per set. However, Mary noted that the Bearing Division would save $3 on marketing costs by selling internally, and would pass this cost savings on to the Wheel Division. She further commented that they were at full capacity, and therefore would not be able to provide any bearings presently. In the future, if they had available capacity, they would be happy to provide bearings.

Hank responded indignantly, "Thanks but no thanks." He said, "We can get all the bearings we need from Falk Manufacturing for $25 per set, and their quality is acceptable for our product." Mary snorted back, "Falk makes low-quality bearings. We incur a total cost of $22 per unit for units we sell externally. Our bearings can withstand heat of 2,000 degrees centigrade and are good to within .00001 centimeters. If you guys are happy buying low-quality bearings, then go ahead and buy from Falk."

Two weeks later, Hank's boss from the central office stopped in to find out whether he had placed an order with the Bearing Division. Hank responded that he would sooner buy his bearings from his worst enemy than from the Bearing Division.

Instructions

With the class divided into groups, prepare answers to the following questions.

a. Why might the company's top management want the divisions to start doing more business with one another?

b. Under what conditions should a buying division be forced to buy from an internal supplier? Under what conditions should a selling division be forced to sell to an internal division rather than to an outside customer?

c. The vice president of Purchasing thinks that this problem should be resolved by forcing the Bearing Division to sell to the Wheel Division at its cost of $22. Is this a good solution for the Wheel Division? Is this a good solution for the Bearing Division? Is this a good solution for the company?

d. Provide at least two other possible solutions to this problem. Discuss the merits and drawbacks of each.

Managerial Analysis

CT21.2 *Service* Construction on the Bonita Full-Service Car Wash is nearing completion. The owner is Dave Kear, a retired accounting professor. The car wash is strategically located on a busy street that separates an affluent suburban community from a middle-class community. It has two state-of-the-art stalls. Each stall can provide anything from a basic two-stage wash and rinse to a five-stage luxurious bath. It is all "touchless," that is, there are no brushes to potentially damage the car. Outside each stall, there is also a 400 horse-power vacuum. Dave likes to joke that these vacuums are so strong that they will pull the carpet right out of your car if you aren't careful.

Dave has some important decisions to make before he can open the car wash. First, he knows that there is one drive-through car wash only a 10-minute drive away. It is attached to a gas station; it charges $5 for a basic wash, and $4 if you also buy at least 8 gallons of gas. It is a "brush"-type wash with rotating brush heads. There is also a self-serve "stand outside your car and spray until you are soaked" car wash a 15-minute drive away from Dave's location. He went over and tried this out. He went through $3 in quarters to get the equivalent of a basic wash. He knows that both of these locations always have long lines, which is one reason why he decided to build a new car wash.

Dave is planning to offer three levels of wash service—Basic, Deluxe, and Premium. The Basic is all automated; it requires no direct intervention by employees. The Deluxe is all automated except that at the end an employee will wipe down the car and will put a window treatment on the windshield that reduces glare and allows rainwater to run off more quickly. The Premium level is a "pampered" service. This will include all the services of the Deluxe, plus a special wax after the machine wax, and an employee will vacuum the car, wipe down the entire interior, and wash the inside of the windows. To provide the Premium service, Dave will have to hire a couple of "car wash specialists" to do the additional pampering.

Dave has pulled together the following estimates, based on data he received from the local Chamber of Commerce and information from a trade association.

	Per Unit	Total
Direct materials per Basic wash	$0.30	
Direct materials per Deluxe wash	$0.80	
Direct materials per Premium wash	$1.10	
Direct labor per Basic wash	na	
Direct labor per Deluxe wash	$0.40	
Direct labor per Premium wash	$2.40	
Variable overhead per Basic wash	$0.10	
Variable overhead per Deluxe and Premium washes	$0.20	
Fixed overhead		$117,000
Variable selling and administrative expenses all washes	$0.10	
Fixed selling and administrative expenses		$130,500

The total estimated number of washes of any type is 45,000. Dave has invested assets of $393,750. He would like a return on investment (ROI) of 20%.

Instructions

Answer each of the following questions.

a. Identify the issues that Dave must consider in deciding on the price of each level of service of his car wash. Also discuss what issues he should consider in deciding on what levels of service to provide.

b. Dave estimates that of the total 45,000 washes, 20,000 will be Basic, 20,000 will be Deluxe, and 5,000 will be Premium. Calculate the selling price, using cost-plus pricing, that Dave should use for each type of wash to achieve his desired ROI of 20%.

c. During the first year, instead of selling 45,000 washes, Dave sold 43,000 washes. He was quite accurate in his estimate of first-year sales, but he was way off on the types of washes that he sold. He sold 3,000 Basic, 31,000 Deluxe, and 9,000 Premium. His actual total fixed expenses were as he expected, and his variable cost per unit was as estimated. Calculate Dave's actual net income and his actual ROI. (Round to two decimal places.)

d. Dave is using a traditional approach to allocate overhead. As a consequence, he is allocating overhead equally to all three types of washes, even though the Basic wash is considerably less complicated and uses very little of the technical capabilities of the machinery. What should Dave do to determine more accurate costs per unit? How will this affect his pricing and, consequently, his sales?

Real-World Focus

CT21.3 Merck & Co., Inc. is a global, research-driven pharmaceutical company that discovers, develops, manufactures, and markets a broad range of human and animal health products. The following are excerpts from the financial review section of the company's annual report.

Merck & Co., Inc.
Financial Review Section (partial)

In the United States, the Company has been working with private and governmental employers to slow the increase of health care costs.

Outside of the United States, in difficult environments encumbered by government cost containment actions, the Company has worked with payers to help them allocate scarce resources to optimize health care outcomes, limiting potentially detrimental effects of government actions on sales growth.

Several products face expiration of product patents in the near term.

The Company, along with other pharmaceutical manufacturers, received a notice from the Federal Trade Commission (FTC) that it was conducting an investigation into pricing practices.

Instructions

Answer each of the following questions.

a. In light of the above excerpts from Merck's annual report, discuss some unique pricing issues faced by companies that operate in the pharmaceutical industry.

b. What are some reasons why the same company often sells identical drugs for dramatically different prices in different countries? How can the same drug used for both humans and animals cost significantly different prices?

c. Suppose that Merck has just developed a revolutionary new drug. Discuss the steps it would go through in setting a price. Include a discussion of the information it would need to gather, and the issues it would need to consider.

CT21.4 Shopping "robots" have become very popular online. These are sites that will find the price of a specified product that is listed by retailers on the Internet ("e-tailers"). This allows the customer to search for the lowest possible price.

Instructions

Go to **DealTime**'s website. Under the heading "**Electronics**," click on **Blu-ray and DVD Players**, choose one of the models, and then answer the following questions.

a. Write down the name of the retailer and the price of the two lowest-priced units and the two highest-priced units.

b. As a consumer, what concerns might you have in clicking on the "buy" button?

c. Why might a consumer want to purchase a unit from a retailer that isn't offering the lowest price?

d. What implications does the existence of these sites have for retailers?

Communication Activity

CT21.5 *Service* Jane Fleming recently graduated from college with a degree in landscape architecture. Her father runs a tree, shrub, and perennial-flower nursery, and her brother has a business delivering topsoil, mulch, and compost. Jane has decided that she would like to start a landscape business. She believes that she can generate a nice profit for herself, while providing an opportunity for both her brother's and father's businesses to grow.

One potential problem that Jane is concerned about is that her father and brother tend to charge the highest prices of any local suppliers for their products. She is hoping that she can demonstrate that it would be in her interest, as well as theirs, for them to sell to her at a discounted price.

Instructions

Write a memo to Jane explaining what information she must gather, and what issues she must consider in working out an arrangement with her father and brother. In your memo, discuss how this situation differs from a "standard" transfer pricing problem, but also how it has many of the characteristics of a transfer pricing problem.

Ethics Case

CT21.6 *Service* Jumbo Airlines operates out of three main "hub" airports in the United States. Recently, Econo Airlines began operating a flight from Reno, Nevada, into Jumbo's Metropolis hub for $190. Jumbo Airlines offers a price of $425 for the same route. The management of Jumbo is not happy about Econo invading its turf. In fact, Jumbo has driven off nearly every other competing airline from its hub, so that today 90% of flights into and out of Metropolis are Jumbo Airline flights. Econo is able to offer a lower fare because its pilots are paid less, it uses older planes, and it has lower overhead costs. Econo has been in business for only 6 months, and it services only two other cities. It expects the Metropolis route to be its most profitable.

Jumbo estimates that it would have to charge $210 just to break even on this flight. It estimates that Econo can break even at a price of $160. Within one day of Econo's entry into the market, Jumbo dropped its price to $140, whereupon Econo matched its price. They both maintained this fare for a period of 9 months, until Econo went out of business. As soon as Econo went out of business, Jumbo raised its fare back to $425.

Instructions

Answer each of the following questions.

a. Who are the stakeholders in this case?

b. What are some of the reasons why Econo's break-even point is lower than that of Jumbo?

c. What are the likely reasons why Jumbo was able to offer this price for this period of time, while Econo couldn't?
d. What are some of the possible courses of action available to Econo in this situation?
e. Do you think that this kind of pricing activity is ethical? What are the implications for the stakeholders in this situation?

Considering Your Costs and Benefits

CT21.7 The January 2011 issue of *Strategic Finance* includes an article by J. Lockhart, A. Taylor, K. Thomas, B. Levetsovitis, and J. Wise entitled "When a Higher Price Pays Off."

Instructions

Read the article and answer the following questions.
a. Explain what is meant by a "low-cost" supplier versus a "low-priced" supplier.
b. **Clarus Technologies'** products are typically priced significantly higher than its competitors' products. How is it able to overcome the initial "sticker shock"?
c. List the five categories of costs that the authors used to compare the Tornado to competing products. Give examples of specific types of costs in each category.
d. The article discusses full-cost accounting as developed by the **Environmental Protection Agency (EPA)**. What are the characteristics of this approach, and what implications does the approach used in this article have for corporate social responsibility?

CHAPTER 22

Budgetary Planning

Chapter Preview

As the following Feature Story about **BabyCakes NYC** indicates, budgeting is critical to financial well-being. As a student, you budget your study time and your money. Families budget income and expenses. Governmental agencies budget revenues and expenditures. Businesses use budgets in planning and controlling their operations.

Our primary focus in this chapter is budgeting—specifically, how budgeting is used as a planning tool by management. Through budgeting, it should be possible for management to maintain enough cash to pay creditors as well as have sufficient raw materials to meet production requirements and adequate finished goods to meet expected sales.

Feature Story

What's in Your Cupcake?

The best business plans often result from meeting a basic human need. Many people would argue that cupcakes aren't necessarily essential to support life. But if you found out that allergies were going to deprive you forever of cupcakes, you might view baked goods in a whole new light. Such was the dilemma faced by Erin McKenna. When she found that her wheat allergies prevented her from consuming most baked sweets, she decided to open a bakery that met her needs. Her vegan and kosher bakery, **BabyCakes NYC**, advertises that it is refined-sugar-free, gluten-free, wheat-free, soy-free, dairy-free, and egg-free. So if you're one of the more than 10 million Americans with a food allergy or some other dietary constraint, this is probably the bakery for you.

Those of you that have spent a little time in the kitchen might wonder what kind of ingredients BabyCakes uses. To avoid the gluten in wheat, the company uses **Bob's Red Mill** rice flour, a garbanzo/fava bean mix, or oat flours. How does BabyCakes get all those great frosting colors without artificial dyes? The company achieves pink with beets, green with chlorophyll, yellow with turmeric, and blue/purple with red cabbage. To eliminate dairy and soy, the bakers use rice and coconut milk. And finally, to accomplish over-the-top deliciousness without refined sugar, BabyCakes uses agave nectar (a sweetener derived from cactus) and evaporated cane juice (often referred to as organic or unrefined sugar).

With cupcakes priced at over $3 per item and a brisk business, you might think that making money is easy for BabyCakes. But all of these specialty ingredients don't come cheap. In addition, BabyCakes' shops are located in Manhattan, Los Angeles, and Orlando, so rent isn't exactly inexpensive either. Despite these costs, Erin's first store made a profit its first year and did even better in later years. To achieve this profitability, Erin relies on careful budgeting. First, she needs to estimate how many items she will sell. Then, she determines her needs for materials, labor, and overhead. Prices for raw materials can fluctuate significantly, so Erin needs to update her budget accordingly. Finally, she has to budget for other products such as her cookbooks, baking kits, and T-shirts. Without a budget, Erin's business might not be so sweet.

 Watch the *BabyCakes NYC* video in WileyPLUS to learn more about real-world budgetary planning.

Chapter Outline

LEARNING OBJECTIVES

LO 1 State the essentials of effective budgeting and the components of the master budget.	• Budgeting and accounting • Benefits of budgeting • Effective budgeting essentials • Master budget	**DO IT! 1** Budget Terminology
LO 2 Prepare budgets for sales, production, and direct materials.	• Sales budget • Production budget • Direct materials budget	**DO IT! 2** Sales, Production, and Direct Materials Budgets
LO 3 Prepare budgets for direct labor, manufacturing overhead, and selling and administrative expenses, and a budgeted income statement.	• Direct labor budget • Manufacturing overhead budget • Selling and administrative expense budget • Budgeted income statement	**DO IT! 3** Budgeted Income Statement
LO 4 Prepare a cash budget and a budgeted balance sheet.	• Cash budget • Budgeted balance sheet	**DO IT! 4** Cash Budget
LO 5 Apply budgeting principles to nonmanufacturing companies.	• Merchandisers • Service companies • Not-for-profit organizations	**DO IT! 5** Merchandise Purchases Budget

Go to the Review and Practice section at the end of the chapter for a targeted summary and practice applications with solutions.
Visit WileyPLUS for additional tutorials and practice opportunities.

Effective Budgeting and the Master Budget

> **LEARNING OBJECTIVE 1**
> State the essentials of effective budgeting and the components of the master budget.

Planning is one of management's major responsibilities. As explained in Chapter 14, **planning** is the process of establishing company-wide objectives. A successful organization makes both long-term and short-term plans. These plans establish the objectives of the company and the proposed approach to accomplish them.

A **budget** is a formal written statement of management's plans for a specified future time period, expressed in financial terms. It represents the primary method of communicating agreed-upon objectives throughout the organization. Once adopted, a budget becomes an important basis for evaluating performance. It promotes efficiency and serves as a deterrent to waste and inefficiency. We consider the role of budgeting as a **control device** in Chapter 23.

Budgeting and Accounting

Accounting information makes major contributions to the budgeting process. From the accounting records, companies obtain historical data on revenues, costs, and expenses. These data are helpful in formulating future budget goals.

Accountants are responsible for presenting management's budgeting goals in financial terms. In this role, they translate management's plans and communicate the budget to employees throughout the company. They prepare periodic budget reports that provide the basis for measuring performance and comparing actual results with planned objectives. The budget itself and the administration of the budget, however, are entirely management responsibilities.

The Benefits of Budgeting

The primary benefits of budgeting are as follows.

1. It requires all levels of management to **plan ahead** and to formalize goals on a recurring basis.
2. It provides **definite objectives** for evaluating performance at each level of responsibility.
3. It creates an **early warning system** for potential problems so that management can make changes before things get out of hand.
4. It facilitates the **coordination of activities** within the business. It does this by correlating the goals of each segment with overall company objectives. Thus, the company can integrate production and sales promotion with expected sales.
5. It results in greater **management awareness** of the entity's overall operations and the impact on operations of external factors, such as economic trends.
6. It **motivates personnel** throughout the organization to meet planned objectives.

A budget is an aid to management; it is not a *substitute* for management. A budget cannot operate or enforce itself. Companies can realize the benefits of budgeting only when managers carefully administer budgets.

Essentials of Effective Budgeting

Effective budgeting depends on a **sound organizational structure**. In such a structure, authority and responsibility for all phases of operations are clearly defined. Budgets based on

research and analysis are more likely to result in realistic goals that will contribute to the growth and profitability of a company. And, the effectiveness of a budget program is directly related to its **acceptance by all levels of management**.

Once adopted, the budget is an important tool for evaluating performance. Managers should systematically and periodically review variations between actual and expected results to determine their cause(s). However, individuals should not be held responsible for variations that are beyond their control.

Length of the Budget Period

The budget period is not necessarily one year in length. **A budget may be prepared for any period of time.** Various factors influence the length of the budget period. These factors include the type of budget, the nature of the organization, the need for periodic appraisal, and prevailing business conditions.

The budget period should be long enough to provide an attainable goal under normal business conditions. Ideally, the time period should minimize the impact of seasonal or cyclical fluctuations. On the other hand, the budget period should not be so long that reliable estimates are impossible.

The **most common budget period is one year**. The annual budget, in turn, is often supplemented by monthly and quarterly budgets. Many companies use **continuous 12-month budgets**. These budgets drop the month just ended and add a future month. One benefit of continuous budgeting is that it keeps management planning a full year ahead.

Accounting Across the Organization

Businesses Often Feel Too Busy to Plan for the Future

Thinkstock/Comstock/ Getty Images, Inc.

A study by Willard & Shullman Group Ltd. found that fewer than 14% of businesses with less than 500 employees do an annual budget or have a written business plan. For many small businesses, the basic assumption is that, "As long as I sell as much as I can, and keep my employees paid, I'm doing OK." A few small business owners even say that they see no need for budgeting and planning. Most small business owners, though, say that they understand that budgeting and planning are critical for survival and growth. But given the long hours that they already work addressing day-to-day challenges, they also say that they are "just too busy to plan for the future."

Describe a situation in which a business "sells as much as it can" but cannot "keep its employees paid." (Go to WileyPLUS for this answer and additional questions.)

The Budgeting Process

The development of the budget for the coming year generally starts several months before the end of the current year. The budgeting process usually begins with the collection of data from each organizational unit of the company. Past performance is often the starting point from which future budget goals are formulated.

The budget is developed within the framework of a **sales forecast**. This forecast shows potential sales for the industry and the company's expected share of such sales. Sales forecasting involves a consideration of various factors: (1) general economic conditions, (2) industry trends, (3) market research studies, (4) anticipated advertising and promotion, (5) previous market share, (6) changes in prices, and (7) technological developments. The input of sales personnel and top management is essential to the sales forecast.

In small companies like **BabyCakes NYC**, the budgeting process is often informal. In larger companies, a **budget committee** has responsibility for coordinating the preparation of the budget. The committee ordinarily includes the president, treasurer, chief accountant (controller), and management personnel from each of the major areas of the company, such as sales, production, and research. The budget committee serves as a review board where managers can defend their budget goals and requests. Differences are reviewed, modified if necessary, and reconciled. The budget is then put in its final form by the budget committee, approved, and distributed.

Budgeting and Human Behavior

A budget can have a significant impact on human behavior. If done well, it can inspire managers to higher levels of performance. However, if done poorly, budgets can discourage additional effort and pull down the morale of managers. Why do these diverse effects occur? The answer is found in how the budget is developed and administered.

In developing the budget, each level of management should be invited to participate. This "bottom-to-top" approach is referred to as **participative budgeting**. One benefit of participative budgeting is that lower-level managers have more detailed knowledge of their specific area and thus are able to provide more accurate budgetary estimates. Also, when lower-level managers participate in the budgeting process, they are more likely to perceive the resulting budget as fair. The overall goal is to reach agreement on a budget that the managers consider fair and achievable, but which also meets the corporate goals set by top management. When this goal is met, the budget will provide positive motivation for the managers. In contrast, if managers view the budget as unfair and unrealistic, they may feel discouraged and uncommitted to budget goals. The risk of having unrealistic budgets is generally greater when the budget is developed from top management down to lower management than vice versa. **Illustration 22.1** graphically displays the flow of budget data from bottom to top under participative budgeting.

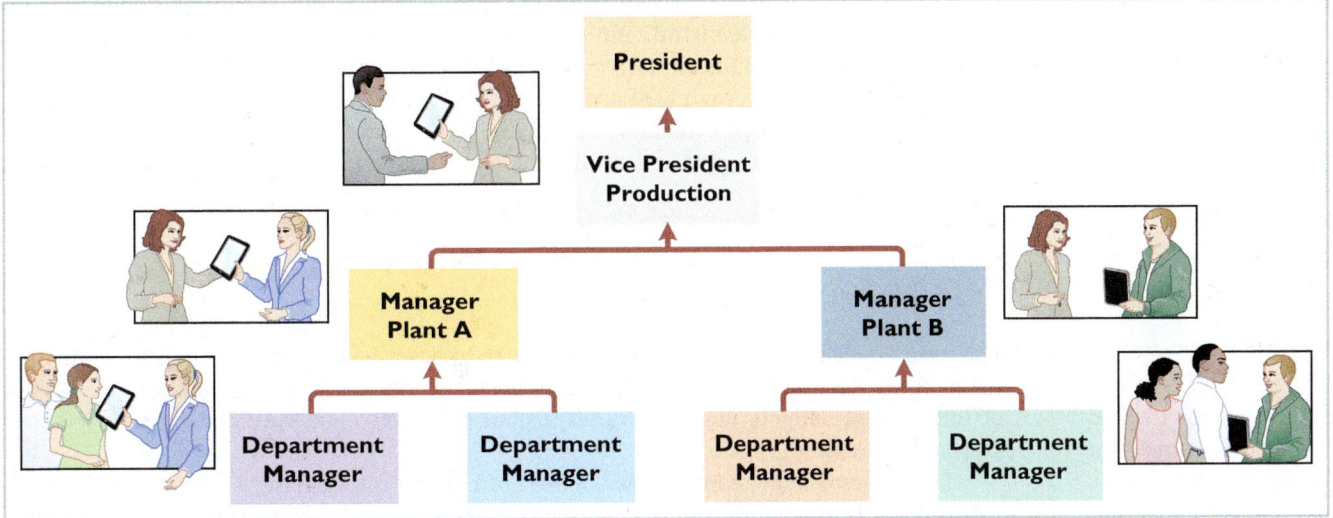

ILLUSTRATION 22.1 Flow of budget data under participative budgeting

For example, at one time, in an effort to revive its plummeting stock price, **Time Warner**'s top management determined and publicly announced bold new financial goals for the coming year. Unfortunately, these goals were not reached. The next year, the company got a new CEO who said the company would now actually set reasonable goals that it could meet. The new budgets were developed with each operating unit setting what it felt were optimistic but attainable goals. In the words of one manager, using this approach created a sense of teamwork.

Participative budgeting does, however, have potential disadvantages. First, the "give and take" of participative budgeting is time-consuming (and thus more costly). Under a "top-down" approach, the budget is simply developed by top management and then dictated to lower-level managers. A second disadvantage is that participative budgeting can foster budgetary "gaming" through budgetary slack. **Budgetary slack** occurs when managers intentionally underestimate budgeted revenues or overestimate budgeted expenses in order to make it easier to achieve budgetary goals for their division. To minimize budgetary slack, higher-level managers must carefully review and thoroughly question the budget projections provided to them by employees whom they supervise.

For the budget to be effective, top management must completely support the budget. The budget is an important tool for evaluating performance. It also can be used as a positive aid in achieving projected goals. The effect of an evaluation is positive when top management tempers criticism with advice and assistance. In contrast, a manager is likely to respond negatively if top management uses the budget exclusively to assess blame. A budget should not be used as a pressure device to force improved performance (see **Ethics Note**). In sum, a budget can be a manager's friend or foe.

> **ETHICS NOTE**
> Unrealistic budgets can lead to unethical employee behavior such as cutting corners on the job or distorting internal financial reports.

Budgeting and Long-Range Planning

Budgeting and long-range planning are not the same. One important difference is the **time period involved**. The maximum length of a budget is usually one year, and budgets are often prepared for shorter periods of time, such as a month or a quarter. In contrast, long-range planning usually encompasses a period of at least five years (see **Helpful Hint**).

A second significant difference is in **emphasis**. Budgeting focuses on achieving specific short-term goals, such as meeting annual profit objectives. **Long-range planning**, on the other hand, identifies long-term goals, selects strategies to achieve those goals, and develops policies and plans to implement the strategies. In long-range planning, management also considers anticipated trends in the economic and political environment and how the company should cope with them.

The final difference between budgeting and long-range planning relates to the **amount of detail presented**. Budgets, as you will see in this chapter, can be very detailed. Long-range plans contain considerably less detail. The data in long-range plans are intended more for a review of progress toward long-term goals than as a basis of control for achieving specific results. The primary objective of long-range planning is to develop the best strategy to maximize the company's performance over an extended future period.

> **HELPFUL HINT**
> A budget has more detail and is more concerned with short-term goals than a long-range plan.

The Master Budget

The term "budget" is actually a shorthand term to describe a variety of budget documents. All of these documents are combined into a master budget. The **master budget** is a set of interrelated budgets that constitutes a plan of action for a specified time period (see **Decision Tools**).

The master budget contains two classes of budgets. **Operating budgets** are the individual budgets that result in the preparation of the budgeted income statement. These budgets establish goals for the company's sales and production personnel. In contrast, **financial budgets** focus primarily on the cash resources needed to fund expected operations and planned capital expenditures. Financial budgets include the capital expenditure budget, the cash budget, and the budgeted balance sheet.

Illustration 22.2 shows the individual budgets included in a master budget, and the sequence in which they are prepared. The company first develops the operating budgets, beginning with the sales budget. Then, it prepares the financial budgets. We will explain and illustrate each budget shown in Illustration 22.2 except the capital expenditure budget. That budget is discussed under the topic of capital budgeting in Chapter 25.

> **Decision Tools**
> Managers use the master budget to determine if the company met its targets for such things as sales, production expenses, selling and administrative expenses, and net income.

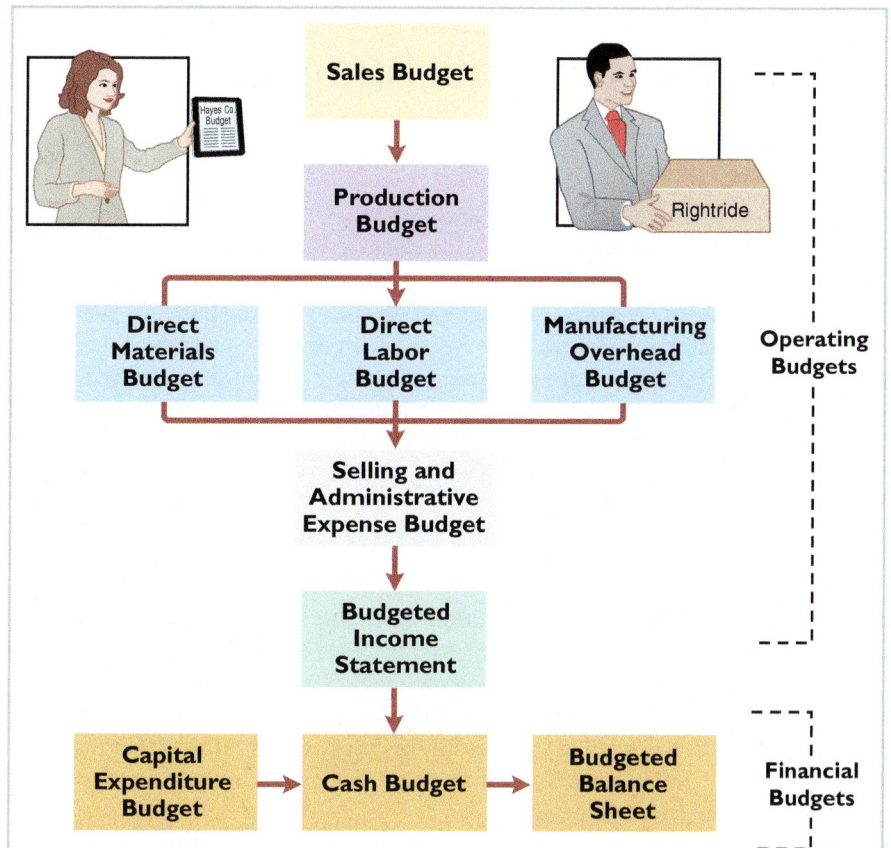

ILLUSTRATION 22.2

Components of the master budget

DO IT! 1 | Budget Terminology

Use this list of terms to complete the sentences that follow.

    Long-range planning   Participative budgeting
    Sales forecast   Operating budgets
    Master budget   Financial budgets

1. A _____ shows potential sales for the industry and a company's expected share of such sales.
2. _____ are used as the basis for the preparation of the budgeted income statement.
3. The _____ is a set of interrelated budgets that constitutes a plan of action for a specified time period.
4. _____ identifies long-term goals, selects strategies to achieve these goals, and develops policies and plans to implement the strategies.
5. Lower-level managers are more likely to perceive results as fair and achievable under a _____ approach.
6. _____ focus primarily on the cash resources needed to fund expected operations and planned capital expenditures.

ACTION PLAN

- Understand the budgeting process, including the importance of the sales forecast.
- Understand the difference between an operating budget and a financial budget.
- Differentiate budgeting from long-range planning.
- Realize that the master budget is a set of interrelated budgets.

Solution

1. Sales forecast.
2. Operating budgets.
3. Master budget.
4. Long-range planning.
5. Participative budgeting.
6. Financial budgets.

Related exercise material: **BE22.1, DO IT! 22.1, and E22.1.**

Sales, Production, and Direct Materials Budgets

LEARNING OBJECTIVE 2
Prepare budgets for sales, production, and direct materials.

We use a case study of Hayes Company in preparing the operating budgets. Hayes manufactures and sells an ergonomically designed bike seat with multiple customizable adjustments, called the Rightride. The budgets are prepared by quarters for the year ending December 31, 2022. Hayes Company begins its annual budgeting process on September 1, 2021, and it completes the budget for 2022 by December 1, 2021. The company begins by preparing the budgets for sales, production, and direct materials.

Sales Budget

HELPFUL HINT

For a retail or manufacturing company, the sales budget is the starting point for the master budget. It sets the level of activity for other functions such as production and purchasing.

As shown in the master budget in Illustration 22.2, **the sales budget is prepared first**. Each of the other budgets depends on the sales budget (see **Helpful Hint**). The **sales budget** is derived from the sales forecast. It represents management's best estimate of sales revenue for the budget period. An inaccurate sales budget may adversely affect net income. For example, an overly optimistic sales budget may result in excessive inventories that may have to be sold at reduced prices. In contrast, an unduly pessimistic sales budget may result in loss of sales revenue due to inventory shortages.

For example, at one time **Amazon.com** significantly underestimated demand for its e-book reader, the Kindle. As a consequence, it did not produce enough Kindles and was completely sold out well before the holiday shopping season. Not only did this represent a huge lost opportunity for Amazon, but it exposed the company to potential competitors, who were eager to provide customers with alternatives to the Kindle.

Forecasting sales is challenging. For example, consider the forecasting challenges faced by major sports arenas, whose revenues depend on the success of the home team. **Madison Square Garden**'s revenues from April to June were $193 million during a year when the Knicks made the NBA playoffs. But revenues were only $133.2 million a couple of years later when the team did not make the playoffs. Or, consider the challenges faced by Hollywood movie producers in predicting the complicated revenue stream produced by a new movie. Movie theater ticket sales represent only 20% of total revenue. The bulk of revenue comes from global sales, DVDs, video-on-demand, merchandising products, and videogames, all of which are difficult to forecast.

The sales budget is prepared by multiplying the expected unit sales volume for each product by its anticipated unit selling price. Hayes Company expects sales volume to be 3,000 units in the first quarter, with 500-unit increases in each succeeding quarter. **Illustration 22.3** shows the sales budget for the year, by quarter, based on a sales price of $60 per unit.

ILLUSTRATION 22.3

Sales budget

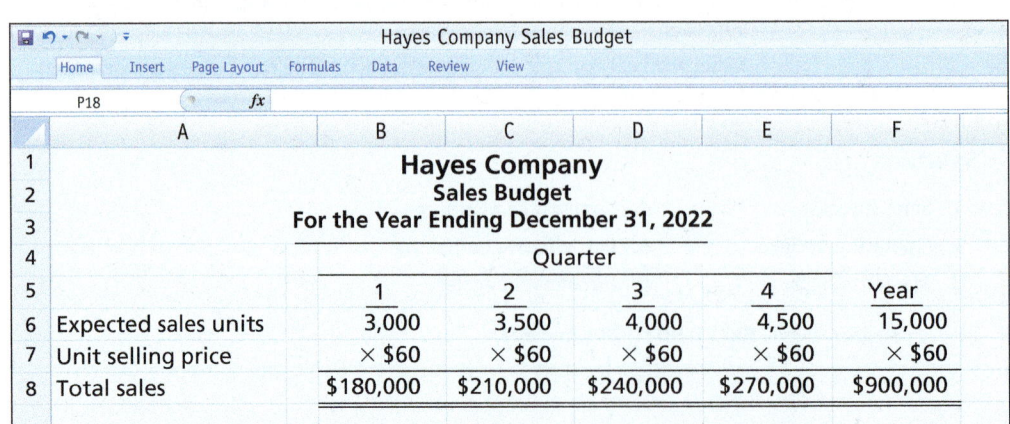

	Quarter				
	1	2	3	4	Year
Expected sales units	3,000	3,500	4,000	4,500	15,000
Unit selling price	× $60	× $60	× $60	× $60	× $60
Total sales	$180,000	$210,000	$240,000	$270,000	$900,000

Some companies classify the anticipated sales revenue as cash or credit sales and by geographic regions, territories, or salespersons.

Service Company Insight

Marcela Barsse/iStockphoto

The Implications of Budgetary Optimism

Companies aren't the only ones that have to estimate revenues. Governments at all levels (e.g., local, state or federal) prepare annual budgets. Most are required to submit balanced budgets, that is, estimated revenues are supposed to cover anticipated expenditures. Unfortunately, estimating government revenues can be as difficult as, or even more difficult than, estimating company revenues. For example, during a recent year, the median state government overestimated revenues by 10.2%, with four state governments missing by more than 25%.

What makes estimation so difficult for these governments? Most states rely on income taxes, which fluctuate widely with economic gyrations. Some states rely on sales taxes, which are problematic because the laws regarding sales taxes haven't adjusted for the shift from manufacturing to service companies and from brick-and-mortar stores to online sales.

Source: Conor Dougherty, "States Fumble Revenue Forecasts," *Wall Street Journal Online* (March 2, 2011).

Why is it important that government budgets accurately estimate future revenues during economic downturns? (Go to WileyPLUS for this answer and additional questions.)

Production Budget

The **production budget** shows the number of units of a product to produce to meet anticipated sales demand. Production requirements are determined from the formula shown in **Illustration 22.4**.[1]

| Expected Sales Units | + | Desired Ending Finished Goods Units | − | Beginning Finished Goods Units | = | Required Production Units |

ILLUSTRATION 22.4

Production requirements formula

Illustration 22.5 shows the production budget for Hayes Company, which is based on the formula shown in Illustration 22.4. For example, in the first quarter, expected sales are 3,000 units. Hayes Company believes it can meet future sales requirements by maintaining an ending inventory equal to 20% of the next quarter's budgeted sales volume. The ending finished goods inventory for the first quarter is 700 units (.20 × anticipated second-quarter sales of 3,500 units). If we then subtract the beginning finished goods units of 600 units (20% of first-quarter sales), we arrive at required production of 3,100 units. Illustration 22.5 shows the production budget.

A realistic estimate of ending inventory is essential in scheduling production requirements. Excessive inventories in one quarter may lead to cutbacks in production and employee layoffs in a subsequent quarter. On the other hand, inadequate inventories may result either in added costs for overtime work or in lost sales.

The production budget, in turn, provides the basis for the budgeted costs for each manufacturing cost element, as explained in the following discussion.

---

[1] This formula ignores any work in process inventories, which are assumed to be nonexistent in Hayes Company.

ILLUSTRATION 22.5 Production budget

Hayes Company
Production Budget
For the Year Ending December 31, 2022

	Quarter				
	1	2	3	4	Year
Expected sales units (Illustration 22.3)	3,000	3,500	4,000	4,500	
Add: Desired ending finished goods units[a]	700	800	900	1,000[b]	
Total required units	3,700	4,300	4,900	5,500	
Less: Beginning finished goods units[c]	600	700	800	900	
Required production units	3,100	3,600	4,100	4,600	15,400

[a] 20% of next quarter's sales
[b] Expected 2023 first-quarter sales, 5,000 units × .20
[c] 20% of estimated first-quarter 2022 sales units

Direct Materials Budget

The **direct materials budget** shows both the quantity and cost of direct materials to be purchased. The first step toward computing the cost of direct materials purchases is to compute the direct materials units required for production. **Illustration 22.6** shows the formula for this amount.

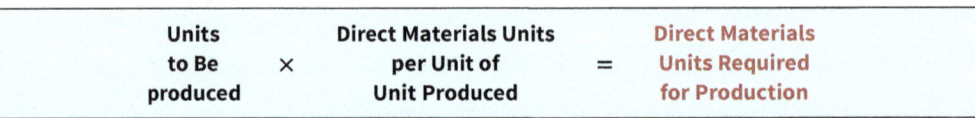

ILLUSTRATION 22.6 Formula for direct materials units required for production

Employing this formula, Illustration 22.9 shows that for Hayes Company's first quarter of production, there are 3,100 units to be produced, and each unit produced requires two pounds of raw materials. Therefore, the units of direct materials required for production is 6,200 pounds (3,100 × 2).

Next we can compute the direct materials units to be purchased using the formula shown in **Illustration 22.7**.

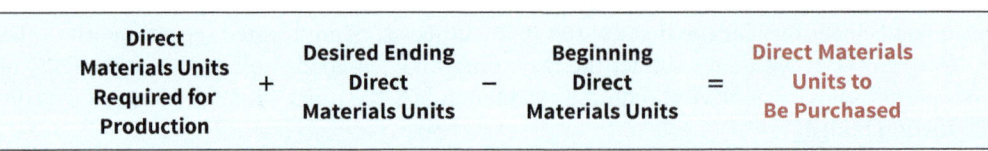

ILLUSTRATION 22.7 Formula for direct materials units to be purchased

Employing this formula, Illustration 22.9 shows that for Hayes Company's first quarter of production, the direct materials units required for production is 6,200 pounds (computed above). To that we add the desired ending direct materials units. For Hayes, this is assumed to be 10% of the next quarter's production requirements, or 720 pounds (.10 × 7,200). Then, we subtract the beginning direct materials units of 620 pounds (10% of this quarter's production requirements of 6,200) to arrive at the direct materials units to be purchased of 6,300 pounds.

Finally, to arrive at the cost of direct materials purchases, we employ the formula shown in **Illustration 22.8**.

ILLUSTRATION 22.8
Formula for cost of direct materials purchases

| Direct Materials Units to Be Purchased | × | Cost per Direct Materials Unit | = | Cost of Direct Materials Purchases |

Employing this formula, **Illustration 22.9** shows that for Hayes Company's first quarter of production, the cost of direct materials purchases is computed by multiplying the units to be purchased of 6,300 pounds by the cost per direct materials unit of $4 per pound, to arrive at $25,200 (6,300 × $4).

ILLUSTRATION 22.9 Direct materials budget

Hayes Company
Direct Materials Budget
For the Year Ending December 31, 2022

	Quarter				
	1	2	3	4	Year
Units to be produced (Illustration 22.5)	3,100	3,600	4,100	4,600	
Direct materials units per unit produced	× 2	× 2	× 2	× 2	
Direct materials units required for production	6,200	7,200	8,200	9,200	
Add: Desired ending direct materials (pounds)[a]	720	820	920	1,020[c]	
Total materials required	6,920	8,020	9,120	10,220	
Less: Beginning direct materials (pounds)	620[b]	720	820	920	
Direct materials units to be purchased (pounds)	6,300	7,300	8,300	9,300	
Cost per pound	× $4	× $4	× $4	× $4	
Cost of direct materials purchases	$25,200	$29,200	$33,200	$37,200	$124,800

[a]10% of next quarter's production requirements
[b]10% of estimated first-quarter pounds needed for production
[c]Total pounds needed for production is assumed to be 10,200 for the first quarter of 2023

The desired ending inventory is again a key component in the budgeting process. For example, inadequate inventories could result in temporary shutdowns of production. Because of its close proximity to suppliers, Hayes Company maintains an ending inventory of raw materials equal to 10% of the next quarter's production requirements.

Management Insight

Betting That Prices Won't Fall

© William Wang/iStockphoto

Sometimes things happen that cause managers to reevaluate their normal purchasing patterns. Consider, for example, the predicament that businesses faced when the price of many raw materials skyrocketed. Rubber, cotton, oil, corn, wheat, steel, copper, and spices—prices for seemingly everything were going straight up. Anticipating that prices might continue to go up, many managers decided to stockpile much larger quantities of raw materials to avoid paying even higher prices in the future.

For example, after cotton prices rose 92%, one manager of a printed T-shirt manufacturer decided to stockpile a huge supply of plain T-shirts in anticipation of additional price increases. While he normally has about 30 boxes of T-shirts in inventory, he purchased 2,500 boxes.

Source: Liam Pleven and Matt Wirz, "Companies Stock Up as Commodities Prices Rise," *Wall Street Journal Online* (February 3, 2011).

What are the potential downsides of stockpiling a huge amount of raw materials? (Go to WileyPLUS for this answer and additional questions.)

ACTION PLAN

- Know the form and content of the sales budget.
- Prepare the sales budget first, as the basis for the other budgets.
- Determine the units that must be produced to meet anticipated sales.
- Know how to compute the beginning and ending finished goods units.
- Determine the materials required to meet production needs.
- Know how to compute the beginning and ending direct materials units.

DO IT! 2 | Sales, Production, and Direct Materials Budgets

Soriano Company is preparing its master budget for 2022. Relevant data pertaining to its sales, production, and direct materials budgets are as follows.

Sales. Sales for the year are expected to total 1,200,000 units. Quarterly sales, as a percentage of total sales, are 20%, 25%, 30%, and 25%, respectively. The sales price is expected to be $50 per unit for the first three quarters and $55 per unit beginning in the fourth quarter. Sales in the first quarter of 2023 are expected to be 10% higher than the budgeted sales for the first quarter of 2022.

Production. Management desires to maintain the ending finished goods inventories at 25% of the next quarter's budgeted sales volume.

Direct materials. Each unit requires 3 pounds of raw materials at a cost of $5 per pound. Management desires to maintain raw materials inventories at 5% of the next quarter's production requirements. Assume the production requirements for the first quarter of 2023 are 810,000 pounds.

Prepare the sales, production, and direct materials budgets by quarters for 2022.

Solution

Soriano Company
Sales Budget
For the Year Ending December 31, 2022

	Quarter				
	1	2	3	4	Year
Expected unit sales[a]	240,000	300,000	360,000	300,000	1,200,000
Unit selling price	× $50	× $50	× $50	× $55	
Total sales	$12,000,000	$15,000,000	$18,000,000	$16,500,000	$61,500,000

[a]Specified quarterly percentage times annual units, e.g., first quarter of .20 × 1,200,000

Soriano Company
Production Budget
For the Year Ending December 31, 2022

	Quarter				
	1	2	3	4	Year
Expected unit sales	240,000	300,000	360,000	300,000	
Add: Desired ending finished goods units[a]	75,000	90,000	75,000	66,000[b]	
Total required units	315,000	390,000	435,000	366,000	
Less: Beginning finished goods units	60,000[c]	75,000	90,000	75,000	
Required production units	255,000	315,000	345,000	291,000	1,206,000

[a]25% of next quarter's unit sales
[b]Estimated first-quarter 2023 sales units: 240,000 + (240,000 × .10) = 264,000: 264,000 × .25
[c]25% of estimated first-quarter 2022 sales units (240,000 × .25)

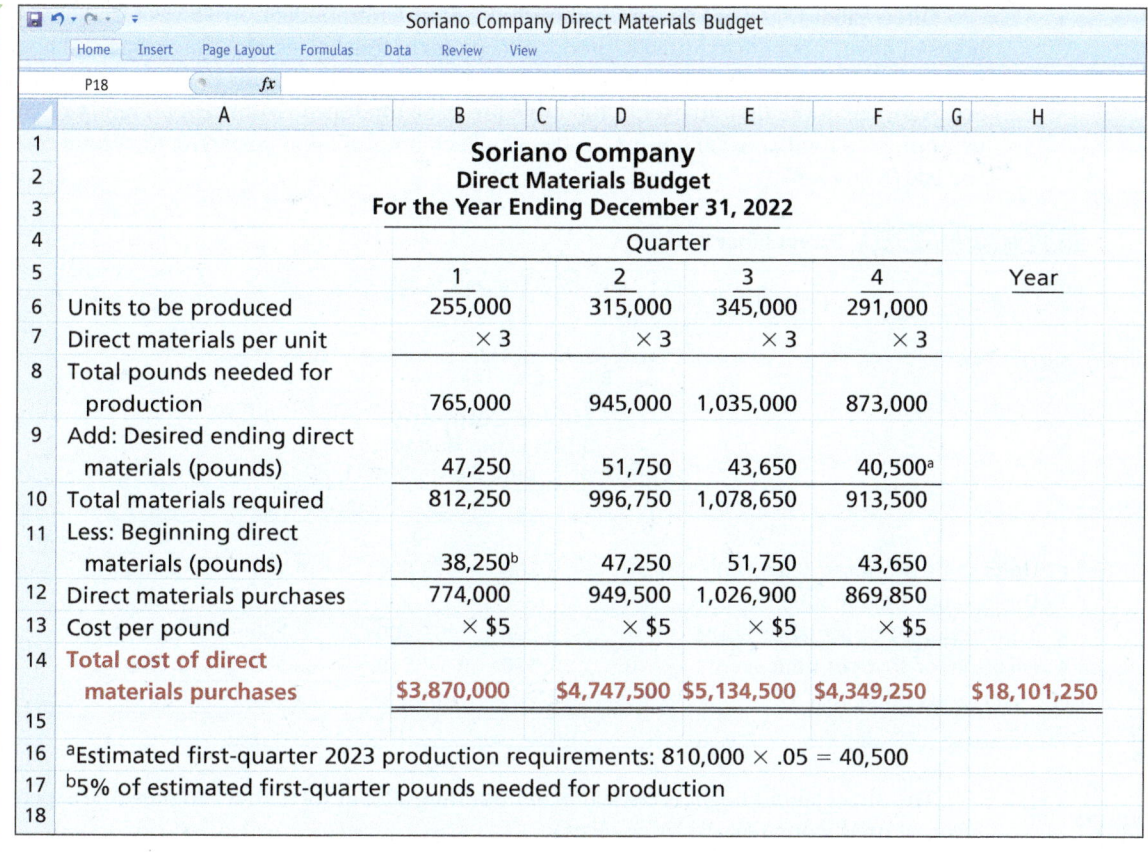

Direct Labor, Manufacturing Overhead, and S&A Expense Budgets

LEARNING OBJECTIVE 3
Prepare budgets for direct labor, manufacturing overhead, and selling and administrative expenses, and a budgeted income statement.

As shown in Illustration 22.2, the operating budgets culminate with preparation of the budgeted income statement. Before we can do that, we need to prepare budgets for direct labor, manufacturing overhead, and selling and administrative expenses.

Direct Labor Budget

Like the direct materials budget, the **direct labor budget** contains the quantity (hours) and cost of direct labor necessary to meet production requirements. The total direct labor cost is derived from the formula shown in **Illustration 22.10**.

ILLUSTRATION 22.10

Formula for direct labor cost

Units to Be Produced × Direct Labor Hours per Unit × Direct Labor Cost per Hour = Total Direct Labor Cost

Direct labor hours are determined from the production budget. At Hayes Company, two hours of direct labor are required to produce each unit of finished goods. The anticipated hourly wage rate is $10. **Illustration 22.11** employs the formula in Illustration 22.10 using these data. For example, in the first quarter, 3,100 units are to be produced requiring two hours of labor per unit, for a total of 6,200 hours (3,100 × $2). Each hour of labor costs $10, for a total cost of $62,000 (6,200 × $10).

ILLUSTRATION 22.11 Direct labor budget

Hayes Company
Direct Labor Budget
For the Year Ending December 31, 2022

	Quarter				
	1	2	3	4	Year
Units to be produced (Illustration 22.5)	3,100	3,600	4,100	4,600	
Direct labor time (hours) per unit	× 2	× 2	× 2	× 2	
Total required direct labor hours	6,200	7,200	8,200	9,200	
Direct labor cost per hour	× $10	× $10	× $10	× $10	
Total direct labor cost	$62,000	$72,000	$82,000	$92,000	$308,000

The direct labor budget is critical in maintaining a labor force that can meet the expected levels of production (see **Helpful Hint**).

HELPFUL HINT

An important assumption in Illustration 22.11 is that the company can add to and subtract from its work force as needed so that the $10 per hour labor cost applies to a wide range of possible production activity.

Manufacturing Overhead Budget

The **manufacturing overhead budget** shows the expected manufacturing overhead costs for the budget period. As **Illustration 22.12** shows, **this budget distinguishes between**

ILLUSTRATION 22.12 Manufacturing overhead budget

Hayes Company
Manufacturing Overhead Budget
For the Year Ending December 31, 2022

	Quarter				
	1	2	3	4	Year
Direct labor hours (Illustration 22.11)	6,200	7,200	8,200	9,200	30,800
Variable costs					
Indirect materials ($1.00/hour)	$ 6,200	$ 7,200	$ 8,200	$ 9,200	$ 30,800
Indirect labor ($1.40/hour)	8,680	10,080	11,480	12,880	43,120
Utilities ($0.40/hour)	2,480	2,880	3,280	3,680	12,320
Maintenance ($0.20/hour)	1,240	1,440	1,640	1,840	6,160
Total variable costs	18,600	21,600	24,600	27,600	92,400
Fixed costs					
Supervisory salaries	20,000	20,000	20,000	20,000	80,000
Depreciation	3,800	3,800	3,800	3,800	15,200
Property taxes and insurance	9,000	9,000	9,000	9,000	36,000
Maintenance	5,700	5,700	5,700	5,700	22,800
Total fixed costs	38,500	38,500	38,500	38,500	154,000
Total manufacturing overhead	$57,100	$60,100	$63,100	$66,100	$246,400
Manufacturing overhead rate per direct labor hour ($246,400 ÷ 30,800)					$8

variable and fixed overhead costs. Hayes Company expects variable costs to fluctuate with production volume on the basis of the following rates per direct labor hour: indirect materials $1.00, indirect labor $1.40, utilities $0.40, and maintenance $0.20. Thus, for the 6,200 direct labor hours to produce 3,100 units, budgeted indirect materials are $6,200 (6,200 × $1), and budgeted indirect labor is $8,680 (6,200 × $1.40). Hayes also recognizes that some maintenance is fixed. The amounts reported for fixed costs are assumed for our example. The accuracy of budgeted overhead cost estimates can be greatly improved by employing activity-based costing.

At Hayes Company, overhead is applied to production on the basis of direct labor hours. Thus, as Illustration 22.12 shows, the budgeted annual rate is $8 per hour ($246,400 ÷ 30,800).

Selling and Administrative Expense Budget

Hayes Company combines its operating expenses into one budget, the **selling and administrative expense budget**. This budget projects anticipated selling and administrative expenses for the budget period. This budget (**Illustration 22.13**) also classifies expenses as either variable or fixed. In this case, the variable expense rates per unit of sales are sales commissions $3 and freight-out $1. Variable expenses per quarter are based on the unit sales from the sales budget (see Illustration 22.3). For example, Hayes expects sales in the first quarter to be 3,000 units. Thus, sales commissions expense is $9,000 (3,000 × $3), and freight-out is $3,000 (3,000 × $1). Fixed expenses are based on assumed data.

ILLUSTRATION 22.13 Selling and administrative expense budget

Hayes Company Manufacturing Selling and Administrative Expense Budget

Hayes Company
Selling and Administrative Expense Budget
For the Year Ending December 31, 2022

	Quarter				
	1	2	3	4	Year
Budgeted sales in units (Illustration 22.3)	3,000	3,500	4,000	4,500	15,000
Variable expenses					
Sales commissions ($3 per unit)	$ 9,000	$10,500	$12,000	$13,500	$ 45,000
Freight-out ($1 per unit)	3,000	3,500	4,000	4,500	15,000
Total variable expenses	12,000	14,000	16,000	18,000	60,000
Fixed expenses					
Advertising	5,000	5,000	5,000	5,000	20,000
Sales salaries	15,000	15,000	15,000	15,000	60,000
Office salaries	7,500	7,500	7,500	7,500	30,000
Depreciation	1,000	1,000	1,000	1,000	4,000
Property taxes and insurance	1,500	1,500	1,500	1,500	6,000
Total fixed expenses	30,000	30,000	30,000	30,000	120,000
Total selling and administrative expenses	$42,000	$44,000	$46,000	$48,000	$180,000

Budgeted Income Statement

The **budgeted income statement** is the important end-product of the operating budgets. This budget indicates the expected profitability of operations for the budget period. The budgeted income statement provides the basis for evaluating company performance. Budgeted income statements often act as a call to action. For example, a board member at **XM Satellite Radio Holdings** felt that budgeted costs were too high relative to budgeted revenues. When management refused to cut its marketing and programming costs, the board member resigned. He felt that without the cuts, the company risked financial crisis.

As you would expect, the budgeted income statement is prepared from the various operating budgets. For example, to find the cost of goods sold, Hayes Company must first determine the total unit cost of producing one Rightride bicycle seat, as shown in **Illustration 22.14**.

ILLUSTRATION 22.14
Computation of total unit cost

Cost of One Rightride

Cost Element	Illustration	Quantity	Unit Cost	Total
Direct materials	22.9	2 pounds	$ 4.00	$ 8.00
Direct labor	22.11	2 hours	$10.00	20.00
Manufacturing overhead	22.12	2 hours	$ 8.00	16.00
Total unit cost				**$44.00**

Hayes then determines cost of goods sold by multiplying the units sold by the unit cost. Its budgeted cost of goods sold is $660,000 (15,000 × $44). All data for the income statement come from the individual operating budgets except the following: (1) interest expense is expected to be $100, and (2) income taxes are estimated to be $12,000. **Illustration 22.15** shows the budgeted multiple-step income statement.

ILLUSTRATION 22.15
Budgeted multiple-step income statement

Hayes Company
Budgeted Income Statement
For the Year Ending December 31, 2022

Sales (Illustration 22.3)	$900,000
Cost of goods sold (15,000 × $44)	660,000
Gross profit	240,000
Selling and administrative expenses (Illustration 22.13)	180,000
Income from operations	60,000
Interest expense	100
Income before income taxes	59,900
Income tax expense	12,000
Net income	$ 47,900

ACTION PLAN
- Recall that total unit cost consists of direct materials, direct labor, and manufacturing overhead.
- Recall that direct materials costs are included in the direct materials budget.
- Know the form and content of the income statement.
- Use the total unit sales information from the sales budget to compute annual sales and cost of goods sold.

DO IT! 3 | Budgeted Income Statement

Soriano Company is preparing its budgeted income statement for 2022. Relevant data pertaining to its sales, production, and direct materials budgets can be found in **DO IT! 2**.

In addition, Soriano budgets 0.5 hours of direct labor per unit, labor costs at $15 per hour, and manufacturing overhead at $25 per direct labor hour. Its budgeted selling and administrative expenses for 2022 are $12,000,000.

(a) Calculate the budgeted total unit cost. (b) Prepare the budgeted multiple-step income statement for 2022. (Ignore income taxes.)

Solution

a.

Cost Element	Quantity	Unit Cost	Total
Direct materials	3.0 pounds	$ 5	$15.00
Direct labor	0.5 hours	$15	7.50
Manufacturing overhead	0.5 hours	$25	12.50
Total unit cost			**$35.00**

b.

Soriano Company
Budgeted Income Statement
For the Year Ending December 31, 2022

Sales (1,200,000 units from sales budget)	$61,500,000
Cost of goods sold (1,200,000 × $35.00/unit)	42,000,000
Gross profit	19,500,000
Selling and administrative expenses	12,000,000
Net income	$ 7,500,000

Related exercise material: **BE22.8, DO IT! 22.3, E22.11,** and **E22.13.**

Cash Budget and Budgeted Balance Sheet

LEARNING OBJECTIVE 4
Prepare a cash budget and a budgeted balance sheet.

As shown in Illustration 22.2, the financial budgets consist of the capital expenditure budget, the cash budget, and the budgeted balance sheet. We will discuss the capital expenditure budget in Chapter 25.

Cash Budget

The **cash budget** shows anticipated cash flows. Because cash is so vital, this budget is often considered to be the most important financial budget (see **Decision Tools**). The cash budget contains three sections (cash receipts, cash disbursements, and financing) and the beginning and ending cash balances, as shown in **Illustration 22.16** (see **Helpful Hint**).

Decision Tools

Managers use the cash budget to determine if the company needs to borrow funds in the coming period.

ILLUSTRATION 22.16
Basic form of a cash budget

	A	B
1	Any Company	
2	Cash Budget	
3	Beginning cash balance	$X,XXX
4	Add: Cash receipts (itemized)	X,XXX
5	Total available cash	X,XXX
6	Less: Cash disbursements (itemized)	X,XXX
7	Excess (deficiency) of available cash over cash disbursements	X,XXX
8	Financing	X,XXX
9	Ending cash balance	$X,XXX

HELPFUL HINT

The cash budget is prepared after the other budgets because the information generated by the other budgets dictates the expected inflows and outflows of cash.

The **cash receipts section** includes expected receipts from the company's principal source(s) of revenue. These are usually cash sales and collections from customers on credit sales. This section also shows anticipated receipts of interest and dividends, and proceeds from planned sales of investments, plant assets, and the company's capital stock.

The **cash disbursements section** shows expected cash payments. Such payments include direct materials, direct labor, manufacturing overhead, and selling and administrative expenses. This section also includes projected payments for income taxes, dividends, investments, and plant assets.

The **financing section** shows expected borrowings and the repayment of the borrowed funds plus interest. Companies need this section when there is a cash deficiency or when the cash balance is below management's minimum required balance.

Data in the cash budget are prepared in sequence. The ending cash balance of one period becomes the beginning cash balance for the next period. Companies obtain data for preparing the cash budget from other budgets and from information provided by management. In practice, cash budgets are often prepared for the year on a monthly basis.

To minimize detail, we assume that Hayes Company prepares an annual cash budget by quarters. To prepare the cash budget, it is useful to prepare a schedule for collections from customers. This schedule is based on the following assumption.

1. **Sales (Illustration 22.3):** 60% are collected in the quarter sold and 40% are collected in the following quarter. Accounts receivable of $60,000 at December 31, 2021, are expected to be collected in full in the first quarter of 2022.

The schedule of cash collections from customers in **Illustration 22.17** applies this assumption. For example, in the first quarter, Hayes collects the $60,000 that was outstanding at the beginning of the quarter, as well as an additional $108,000 (.60 × $180,000), which is 60% of the first-quarter sales of $180,000. Total receipts in the first quarter are $168,000 ($60,000 + $108,000). In the second quarter, the company collects the remaining 40% of first-quarter sales of $72,000 (.40 × $180,000) as well as $126,000 (.60 × $210,000), which is 60% of second-quarter sales of $210,000. Second-quarter receipts are $198,000 ($72,000 + $126,000).

ILLUSTRATION 22.17
Collections from customers

Hayes Company
Schedule of Expected Collections from Customers

	Sales[a]	Collections by Quarter			
		1	2	3	4
Accounts receivable, 12/31/21		$ 60,000			
First quarter	$180,000	108,000[b]	$ 72,000[c]		
Second quarter	210,000		126,000	$ 84,000	
Third quarter	240,000			144,000	$ 96,000
Fourth quarter	270,000				162,000
Total collections		$168,000	$198,000	$228,000	$258,000

[a]Per Illustration 22.3; [b]$180,000 × .60; [c]$180,000 × .40

Next, it is useful to prepare a schedule of expected cash payments for direct materials, based on this second assumption:

2. **Direct materials (Illustration 22.9):** 50% are paid in the quarter purchased and 50% are paid in the following quarter. Accounts payable of $10,600 at December 31, 2021, are expected to be paid in full in the first quarter of 2022.

The schedule of cash payments for direct materials in **Illustration 22.18** applies this second assumption. For example, in the first quarter, Hayes pays the balance of its beginning accounts payable balance of $10,600 as well as pays $12,600, which is 50% of its first-quarter purchases of $25,200. The total payments in the first quarter are $23,200 ($10,600 + $12,600). In the second quarter, it pays $12,600 (.50 × $25,200) for the remaining 50% of its first-quarter purchases as well as $14,600 (.50 × $29,200) for 50% of the second-quarter purchases. Total payments in the second quarter are $27,200 ($12,600 + $14,600).

The preparation of Hayes Company's cash budget is based on the following additional assumptions.

3. The January 1, 2022, cash balance is expected to be $38,000. Hayes wishes to maintain a balance of at least $15,000.
4. Short-term investment securities are expected to be sold for $2,000 cash in the first quarter.
5. **Direct labor (Illustration 22.11):** 100% is paid in the quarter incurred.
6. **Manufacturing overhead (Illustration 22.12)** and selling and administrative expenses (Illustration 22.13): All items except depreciation are paid in the quarter incurred.
7. Management plans to purchase a truck in the second quarter for $10,000 cash.

ILLUSTRATION 22.18
Payments for direct materials

Hayes Company
Schedule of Expected Payments for Direct Materials

	Purchases[a]	Payments by Quarter			
		1	2	3	4
Accounts payable, 12/31/21		$10,600			
First quarter	$25,200	12,600[b]	$12,600[c]		
Second quarter	29,200		14,600	$14,600	
Third quarter	33,200			16,600	$16,600
Fourth quarter	37,200				18,600
Total payments		$23,200	$27,200	$31,200	$35,200

[a]Per Illustration 22.9; [b]$25,200 × .50; [c]$25,200 × .50

8. Hayes makes equal quarterly payments of its estimated $12,000 annual income taxes.
9. Loans are repaid in the earliest quarter in which there is sufficient cash (that is, when the cash on hand exceeds the $15,000 minimum required balance).

Illustration 22.19 shows the cash budget for Hayes Company. The budget indicates that Hayes will need $3,000 of financing in the second quarter to maintain a minimum cash

ILLUSTRATION 22.19 Cash budget

Hayes Company
Cash Budget
For the Year Ending December 31, 2022

	Assumption	Quarter			
		1	2	3	4
Beginning cash balance	3	$ 38,000	$ 25,500	$ 15,000	$ 19,400
Add: Receipts					
Collections from customers	1	168,000	198,000	228,000	258,000
Sale of investment securities	4	2,000	0	0	0
Total receipts		170,000	198,000	228,000	258,000
Total available cash		208,000	223,500	243,000	277,400
Less: Disbursements					
Direct materials	2	23,200	27,200	31,200	35,200
Direct labor	5	62,000	72,000	82,000	92,000
Manufacturing overhead	6	53,300[a]	56,300	59,300	62,300
Selling and administrative expenses	6	41,000[b]	43,000	45,000	47,000
Purchase of truck	7	0	10,000	0	0
Income tax expense	8	3,000	3,000	3,000	3,000
Total disbursements		182,500	211,500	220,500	239,500
Excess (deficiency) of available cash over cash disbursements		25,500	12,000	22,500	37,900
Financing					
Add: Borrowings		0	3,000	0	0
Less: Repayments including interest	9	0	0	3,100	0
Ending cash balance	3	$ 25,500	$ 15,000	$ 19,400	$ 37,900

[a]$57,100 − $3,800 depreciation
[b]$42,000 − $1,000 depreciation

balance of $15,000. Since there is an excess of available cash over disbursements of $22,500 at the end of the third quarter, the borrowing, plus $100 interest, is repaid in this quarter.

A cash budget contributes to more effective cash management. It shows managers when additional financing is necessary well before the actual need arises. And, it indicates when excess cash is available for investments or other purposes.

Management Insight   Kraft Heinz

Violka08/iStock/Getty Images

Starting from Scratch

Recently an increasing number of companies, including the giant food company **Kraft Heinz**, have adopted "zero-based budgeting." This budgeting approach requires that the budgeting process starts from scratch, rather than using the previous year's budget as a starting point. Every proposed cost must be justified and not just the large expenses. For example, **Pilgrim Pride Corp.**, "scrutinized how much paper it used to print documents, how much soap employees used to wash their hands, and how much Gatorade hourly employees at one processing facility drank during breaks." The move toward zero-based budgeting is due in part to pressure by shareholders to increase company performance, as well as management fear that if a company's operations aren't lean, it will be taken over by outside investors. Proponents point toward zero-based budgeting's ability to reduce wasteful spending practices such as first-class plane flights. But critics suggest that it often results in significant layoffs, destroys employee morale, and potentially reduces a company's ability to pursue growth opportunities. **Coca-Cola** recently implemented zero-based budgeting but calls it "zero-based work" to try to disassociate its efforts from some of the negative connotations associated with zero-based budgeting.

Source: David Kesmodel and Annie Gasparro, "Kraft-Heinz Deal Shows Brazilian Buyout Firm's Cost-Cutting Recipe," *Wall Street Journal* (March 2015).

What are some of the pros and cons of zero-based budgeting? (Go to WileyPLUS for this answer and additional questions.)

Budgeted Balance Sheet

The **budgeted balance sheet** is a projection of financial position at the end of the budget period. This budget is developed from the budgeted balance sheet for the preceding year and the budgets for the current year. Pertinent data from the budgeted balance sheet at December 31, 2021, are as follows.

Buildings and equipment	$182,000	Common stock	$225,000
Accumulated depreciation	$ 28,800	Retained earnings	$ 46,480

Illustration 22.20 shows Hayes Company's budgeted classified balance sheet at December 31, 2022.

ILLUSTRATION 22.20

Budgeted classified balance sheet

Hayes Company
Budgeted Balance Sheet
December 31, 2022

Assets

Current assets		
Cash		$ 37,900
Accounts receivable		108,000
Finished goods inventory		44,000
Raw materials inventory		4,080
Total current assets		193,980
Property, plant, and equipment		
Buildings and equipment	$192,000	
Less: Accumulated depreciation	48,000	144,000
Total assets		$337,980

	Liabilities and Stockholders' Equity	
Liabilities		
Accounts payable		$ 18,600
Stockholders' equity		
Common stock	$225,000	
Retained earnings	94,380	
Total stockholders' equity		319,380
Total liabilities and stockholders' equity		$337,980

The computations and sources of the amounts are explained below.

Cash: Ending cash balance $37,900, shown in the cash budget (Illustration 22.19).

Accounts receivable: 40% of fourth-quarter sales $270,000, shown in the schedule of expected collections from customers (Illustration 22.17).

Finished goods inventory: Desired ending inventory 1,000 units, shown in the production budget (Illustration 22.5) times the total unit cost $44 (shown in Illustration 22.14).

Raw materials inventory: Desired ending inventory 1,020 pounds, times the cost per pound $4, shown in the direct materials budget (Illustration 22.9).

Buildings and equipment: December 31, 2021, balance $182,000, plus purchase of truck for $10,000 (Illustration 22.19).

Accumulated depreciation: December 31, 2021, balance $28,800, plus $15,200 depreciation shown in manufacturing overhead budget (Illustration 22.12) and $4,000 depreciation shown in selling and administrative expense budget (Illustration 22.13).

Accounts payable: 50% of fourth-quarter purchases $37,200, shown in schedule of expected payments for direct materials (Illustration 22.18).

Common stock: Unchanged from the beginning of the year.

Retained earnings: December 31, 2021, balance $46,480, plus net income $47,900, shown in budgeted income statement (Illustration 22.15).

After budget data are entered into the computer, Hayes prepares the various budgets (sales, cash, etc.), as well as the budgeted financial statements. Using spreadsheets, management can also perform "what if" (sensitivity) analyses based on different hypothetical assumptions. For example, suppose that sales managers project that sales will be 10% higher in the coming quarter. What impact does this change have on the rest of the budgeting process and the financing needs of the business? The impact of the various assumptions on the budget is quickly determined by the spreadsheet. Armed with these analyses, managers make more informed decisions about the impact of various projects. They also anticipate future problems and business opportunities. As seen in this chapter, budgeting is an excellent use of computer spreadsheets.

DO IT! 4 | Cash Budget

Martian Company management wants to maintain a minimum monthly cash balance of $15,000. At the beginning of March, the cash balance is $16,500, expected cash receipts for March are $210,000, and cash disbursements are expected to be $220,000. How much cash, if any, must be borrowed to maintain the desired minimum monthly balance?

ACTION PLAN

- Write down the basic form of the cash budget, starting with the beginning cash balance, adding cash receipts for the period, deducting cash disbursements, and identifying the needed financing to achieve the desired minimum ending cash balance.
- Insert the data given into the outlined form of the cash budget.

Solution

Martian Company Cash Budget

Martian Company
Cash Budget
For the Month Ending March 31, 2022

Beginning cash balance	$ 16,500
Add: Cash receipts for March	210,000
Total available cash	226,500
Less: Cash disbursements for March	220,000
Excess (deficiency) of available cash over cash disbursements	6,500
Financing	8,500
Ending cash balance	$ 15,000

To maintain the desired minimum cash balance of $15,000, Martian Company must borrow $8,500 of cash.

Related exercise material: **BE22.9, DO IT! 22.4, E22.14, E22.15, and E22.16**.

Budgeting in Nonmanufacturing Companies

LEARNING OBJECTIVE 5
Apply budgeting principles to nonmanufacturing companies.

Budgeting is not limited to manufacturers. Budgets are also used by merchandisers, service companies, and not-for-profit organizations.

Merchandisers

As in manufacturing operations, the sales budget for a merchandiser is both the starting point and the key factor in the development of the master budget. The major differences between the master budgets of a merchandiser and a manufacturer are as follows.

1. A merchandiser **uses a merchandise purchases budget instead of a production budget**.
2. A merchandiser **does not use the manufacturing budgets (direct materials, direct labor, and manufacturing overhead)**.

The **merchandise purchases budget** shows the estimated cost of goods to be purchased to meet expected sales. The formula for determining budgeted merchandise purchases is as shown in **Illustration 22.21**.

ILLUSTRATION 22.21
Merchandise purchases formula

Budgeted Cost of Goods Sold + Desired Ending Merchandise Inventory − Beginning Merchandise Inventory = Required Merchandise Purchases

To illustrate, assume that the budget committee of Lima Company is preparing the merchandise purchases budget for July 2022. It estimates that budgeted sales will be $300,000 in July and $320,000 in August. Cost of goods sold is expected to be 70% of sales—that is, $210,000 in July (.70 × $300,000) and $224,000 in August (.70 × $320,000). The company's desired ending inventory is 30% of the following month's cost of goods sold. Required merchandise purchases for July are $214,200, computed as shown in **Illustration 22.22**.

ILLUSTRATION 22.22

Merchandise purchases budget

Lima Company
Merchandise Purchases Budget
For the Month Ending July 31, 2022

Budgeted cost of goods sold ($300,000 × .70)	$210,000
Add: Desired ending merchandise inventory ($224,000 × .30)	67,200
Total	277,200
Less: Beginning merchandise inventory ($210,000 × .30)	63,000
Required merchandise purchases for July	**$214,200**

When a merchandiser is departmentalized, it prepares separate budgets for each department (see infographic). For example, a grocery store prepares sales budgets and purchases budgets for each of its major departments, such as meats, dairy, and produce. The store then combines these budgets into a master budget for the store. When a retailer has branch stores, it prepares separate master budgets for each store. Then, it incorporates these budgets into master budgets for the company as a whole.

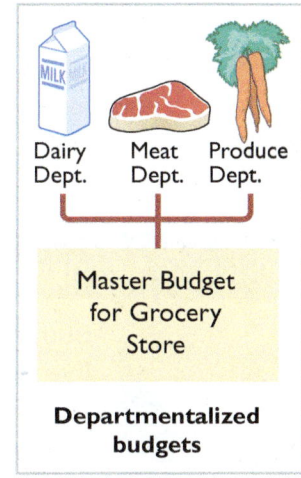

Departmentalized budgets

Service Companies

In a service company, such as a public accounting firm, a law office, or a medical practice, the critical factor in budgeting is **coordinating professional staff needs with anticipated services**. If a firm is overstaffed, several problems may result: Labor costs are disproportionately high. Profits are lower because of the additional salaries. Staff turnover sometimes increases because of lack of challenging work. In contrast, if a service company is understaffed, it may lose revenue because existing and prospective client needs for service cannot be met. Also, professional staff may seek other jobs because of excessive work loads.

Suppose that Stephan Lawn and Plowing Service estimates that it will service 300 small lawns, 200 medium lawns, and 100 large lawns during the month of July. It estimates its direct labor needs as 1 hour per small lawn, 1.75 hours for a medium lawn, and 2.75 hours for a large lawn. Its average cost for direct labor is $15 per hour. Stephan prepares a direct labor budget as shown in **Illustration 22.23**.

ILLUSTRATION 22.23

Direct labor budget for service company

Stephan Lawn and Plowing Service
Direct Labor Budget
For the Month Ending July 31, 2022

	Small	Medium	Large	Total
Lawns to be serviced	300	200	100	
Direct labor time (hours) per lawn	× 1	× 1.75	× 2.75	
Total required direct labor hours	300	350	275	
Direct labor cost per hour	× $15	× $15	× $15	
Total direct labor cost	**$4,500**	**$5,250**	**$4,125**	**$13,875**

Service companies can obtain budget data for service revenue from **expected output** or **expected input**. When output is used, it is necessary to determine the expected billings of clients for services performed. In a public accounting firm, for example, output is the sum of its billings in auditing, tax, and consulting services. When input data are used, each professional staff member projects his or her billable time. The firm then applies billing rates to billable time to produce expected service revenue.

Not-for-Profit Organizations

Budgeting is just as important for not-for-profit organizations as for profit-oriented businesses. The budget process, however, is different. In most cases, not-for-profit entities budget **on the basis of cash flows (expenditures and receipts), rather than on a revenue and expense basis**. Further, the starting point in the process is usually expenditures, not receipts. For the not-for-profit entity, management's task generally is to find the receipts needed to support the planned expenditures. The activity index is also likely to be significantly different. For example, in a not-for-profit entity, such as a university, budgeted faculty positions may be based on full-time equivalent students or credit hours expected to be taught in a department.

For some governmental units, voters approve the budget. In other cases, such as state governments and the federal government, legislative approval is required. After the budget is adopted, it must be followed. Overspending is often illegal. In governmental budgets, authorizations tend to be on a line-by-line basis. That is, the budget for a municipality may have a specified authorization for police and fire protection, garbage collection, street paving, and so on. The line-item authorization of governmental budgets significantly limits the amount of discretion management can exercise. The city manager often cannot use savings from one line item, such as street paving, to cover increased spending in another line item, such as snow removal.

Service Company Insight   Museum of Contemporary Art

Budget Shortfalls as Far as the Eye Can See

©ZUMA Press/Newscom/NewsCom

All organizations need to stick to budgets. The Museum of Contemporary Art in Los Angeles learned this the hard way. Over a 10-year period, its endowment shrunk from $50 million to $6 million as its newly hired director strove to build the museum's reputation through spending. The director consistently ran budget deficits, which eventually threatened the museum's survival.

The most recent recession created budgeting challenges for nearly all governmental agencies. Tax revenues dropped rapidly as earnings declined and unemployment skyrocketed. At the same time, sources of debt financing dried up. Even Princeton University, with the largest endowment per student of any U.S. university ($2 million per student), experienced a 25% drop in the value of its endowment when the financial markets plunged. Because the endowment supports 45% of the university's $1.25 billion budget, when the endowment fell the university had to make cuts. Many raises were capped at $2,000, administrative budgets were cut by 5%, and major construction projects were put on hold.

Sources: Edward Wyatt and Jori Finkel, "Soaring in Art, Museum Trips Over Finances," *Wall Street Journal Online* (December 4, 2008); Stu Woo, "California's Plans to Close Gap Become More Drastic," *Wall Street Journal Online* (January 8, 2009); and John Hechinger, "Princeton Cuts Budget as Endowment Slides," *Wall Street Journal Online* (January 9, 2009).

Why would a university's budgeted scholarships probably fall when the stock market suffers a serious drop? (Go to WileyPLUS for this answer and additional questions.)

DO IT! 5 | Merchandise Purchases Budget

Becker Company estimates that 2022 sales will be $15,000 in quarter 1, $20,000 in quarter 2, and $25,000 in quarter 3. Cost of goods sold is 80% of sales. Management desires to have ending finished goods inventory equal to 15% of the next quarter's expected cost of goods sold. Prepare a merchandise purchases budget by quarter for the first six months of 2022.

Solution

Becker Company Merchandise Purchases Budget
For the Six Months Ending June 30, 2022

	Quarter 1	Quarter 2	Six Months
Budgeted cost of goods sold (sales × .80)	$12,000	$16,000	
Add: Desired ending merchandise inventory (15% of next quarter's cost of goods sold)	2,400	3,000	
Total	14,400	19,000	
Less: Beginning merchandise inventory (15% this quarter's cost of goods sold)	1,800	2,400	
Required merchandise purchases	**$12,600**	**$16,600**	**$29,200**

ACTION PLAN
- Begin with budgeted cost of goods sold.
- Add desired ending merchandise inventory.
- Subtract beginning merchandise inventory.

Related exercise material: **BE22.10, DO IT! 22.5, E22.19, E22.20,** and **E22.21.**

USING THE DECISION TOOLS | BabyCakes NYC

As discussed in the Feature Story, **BabyCakes NYC** relies on budgeting to aid in the management of its cupcake operations. Assume that BabyCakes prepares monthly cash budgets. Relevant data from assumed operating budgets for 2022 are as follows:

	January	February
Sales	$460,000	$412,000
Direct materials purchases	185,000	210,000
Direct labor	70,000	85,000
Manufacturing overhead	50,000	65,000
Selling and administrative expenses	85,000	95,000

Assume that BabyCakes sells its cupcakes in its own shops as well as to other stores. Collections are expected to be 75% in the month of sale, and 25% in the month following sale. BabyCakes pays 60% of direct materials purchases in cash in the month of purchase, and the balance due in the month following the purchase. All other items above are paid in the month incurred. (Depreciation has been excluded from manufacturing overhead and selling and administrative expenses.)

Other data:
(1) Sales: December 2021, $320,000
(2) Purchases of direct materials: December 2021, $175,000
(3) Other receipts: January—Donation received, $2,000
    February—Sale of used equipment, $4,000
(4) Other disbursements: February—Purchased equipment, $10,000
(5) Repaid debt: January, $30,000

The company's cash balance on January 1, 2022, is expected to be $50,000. The company wants to maintain a minimum cash balance of $45,000.

Instructions

a. Prepare schedules for (1) expected collections from customers and (2) expected payments for direct materials purchases for January and February.

b. Prepare a cash budget for January and February in columnar form.

Solution

a. 1.

Expected Collections from Customers

	Sales	January	February
December	$320,000	$ 80,000	$ 0
January	460,000	345,000	115,000
February	412,000	0	309,000
Totals		$425,000	$424,000

2.

Expected Payments for Direct Materials

	Purchases	January	February
December	$175,000	$ 70,000	$ 0
January	185,000	111,000	74,000
February	210,000	0	126,000
Totals		$181,000	$200,000

b.

BabyCakes NYC
Cash Budget
For the Two Months Ending February 28, 2022

	January	February
Beginning cash balance	$ 50,000	$ 61,000
Add: Receipts		
Collections from customers	425,000	424,000
Donations received	2,000	0
Sale of used equipment	0	4,000
Total receipts	427,000	428,000
Total available cash	477,000	489,000
Less: Disbursements		
Direct materials	181,000	200,000
Direct labor	70,000	85,000
Manufacturing overhead	50,000	65,000
Selling and administrative expenses	85,000	95,000
Purchase of equipment	0	10,000
Total disbursements	386,000	455,000
Excess (deficiency) of available cash over cash disbursements	91,000	34,000
Financing		
Add: Borrowings	0	11,000
Less: Repayments	30,000	0
Ending cash balance	$ 61,000	$ 45,000

Review and Practice

Learning Objectives Review

1 State the essentials of effective budgeting and the components of the master budget.

The primary benefits of budgeting are that it (a) requires management to plan ahead, (b) provides definite objectives for evaluating performance, (c) creates an early warning system for potential problems, (d) facilitates coordination of activities, (e) results in greater management awareness, and (f) motivates personnel to meet planned objectives. The essentials of effective budgeting are (a) sound organizational structure, (b) research and analysis, and (c) acceptance by all levels of management.

The master budget consists of the following budgets: (a) sales, (b) production, (c) direct materials, (d) direct labor, (e) manufacturing overhead, (f) selling and administrative expense, (g) budgeted income statement, (h) capital expenditure budget, (i) cash budget, and (j) budgeted balance sheet.

2 Prepare budgets for sales, production, and direct materials.

The sales budget is derived from sales forecasts. The production budget starts with budgeted sales units, adds desired ending finished goods inventory, and subtracts beginning finished goods inventory to arrive at the required number of units to be produced. The direct materials budget starts with the direct materials units (e.g., pounds) required for budgeted production, adds desired ending direct materials units, and subtracts beginning direct materials units to arrive at required direct materials units to be purchased. This amount is multiplied by the direct materials cost (e.g., cost per pound) to arrive at the total cost of direct materials purchases.

3 Prepare budgets for direct labor, manufacturing overhead, and selling and administrative expenses, and a budgeted income statement.

The direct labor budget starts with the units to be produced as determined in the production budget. This amount is multiplied by the direct labor hours per unit and the direct labor cost per hour to arrive at the total direct labor cost. The manufacturing overhead budget lists all of the individual types of overhead costs, distinguishing between fixed and variable costs. The selling and administrative expense budget lists all of the individual types of selling and administrative expense items, distinguishing between fixed and variable costs. The budgeted income statement is prepared from the various operating budgets. Cost of goods sold is determined by calculating the budgeted cost to produce one unit, then multiplying this amount by the number of units sold.

4 Prepare a cash budget and a budgeted balance sheet.

The cash budget has three sections (receipts, disbursements, and financing) and the beginning and ending cash balances. Receipts and payments sections are determined after preparing separate schedules for collections from customers and payments to suppliers. The budgeted balance sheet is developed from the budgeted balance sheet from the preceding year and the various budgets for the current year.

5 Apply budgeting principles to nonmanufacturing companies.

Budgeting may be used by merchandisers for development of a merchandise purchases budget. In service companies, budgeting is a critical factor in coordinating staff needs with anticipated services. In not-for-profit organizations, the starting point in budgeting is usually expenditures, not receipts.

Decision Tools Review

Decision Checkpoints	Info Needed for Decision	Tool to Use for Decision	How to Evaluate Results
Has the company met its targets for sales, production expenses, selling and administrative expenses, and net income?	Sales forecasts, inventory levels, projected materials, labor, overhead, and selling and administrative requirements	Master budget—a set of interrelated budgets including sales, production, materials, labor, overhead, and selling and administrative expense budgets	Results are favorable if revenues exceed budgeted amounts, or if expenses are less than budgeted amounts.
Is the company going to need to borrow funds in the coming period?	Beginning cash balance, cash receipts, cash disbursements, and desired ending cash balance	Cash budget	The company will need to borrow money if the cash budget indicates a projected cash deficiency.

Glossary Review

Budget A formal written statement of management's plans for a specified future time period, expressed in financial terms. (p. 22-3).

Budgetary slack The amount by which a manager intentionally underestimates budgeted revenues or overestimates budgeted expenses in order to make it easier to achieve budgetary goals. (p. 22-6).

Budget committee A group responsible for coordinating the preparation of the budget. (p. 22-4).

Budgeted balance sheet A projection of financial position at the end of the budget period. (p. 22-20).

Budgeted income statement An estimate of the expected profitability of operations for the budget period. (p. 22-15).

Cash budget A projection of anticipated cash flows. (p. 22-17).

Direct labor budget A projection of the quantity and cost of direct labor necessary to meet production requirements. (p. 22-13).

Direct materials budget An estimate of the quantity and cost of direct materials to be purchased. (p. 22-10).

Financial budgets Individual budgets that focus primarily on the cash resources needed to fund expected operations and planned capital expenditures. (p. 22-6).

Long-range planning A formalized process of identifying long-term goals, selecting strategies to achieve those goals, and developing policies and plans to implement the strategies. (p. 22-6).

Manufacturing overhead budget An estimate of expected manufacturing overhead costs for the budget period. (p. 22-14).

Master budget A set of interrelated budgets that constitutes a plan of action for a specific time period. (p. 22-6).

Merchandise purchases budget The estimated cost of goods to be purchased by a merchandiser to meet expected sales. (p. 22-22).

Operating budgets Individual budgets that result in a budgeted income statement. (p. 22-6).

Participative budgeting A budgetary approach that starts with input from lower-level managers and works upward so that managers at all levels participate. (p. 22-5).

Production budget A projection of the units that must be produced to meet anticipated sales. (p. 22-9).

Sales budget An estimate of expected sales revenue for the budget period. (p. 22-8).

Sales forecast The projection of potential sales for the industry and the company's expected share of such sales. (p. 22-4).

Selling and administrative expense budget A projection of anticipated selling and administrative expenses for the budget period. (p. 22-15).

Practice Multiple-Choice Questions

1. **(LO 1)** Which of the following is **not** a benefit of budgeting?
   a. Management can plan ahead.
   b. An early warning system is provided for potential problems.
   c. It enables disciplinary action to be taken at every level of responsibility.
   d. The coordination of activities is facilitated.

2. **(LO 1)** A budget:
   a. is the responsibility of management accountants.
   b. is the primary method of communicating agreed-upon objectives throughout an organization.
   c. ignores past performance because it represents management's plans for a future time period.
   d. may promote efficiency but has no role in evaluating performance.

3. **(LO 1)** The essentials of effective budgeting do **not** include:
   a. top-down budgeting.
   b. management acceptance.
   c. research and analysis.
   d. sound organizational structure.

4. **(LO 1)** Compared to budgeting, long-range planning generally has the:
   a. same amount of detail.
   b. longer time period.
   c. same emphasis.
   d. same time period.

5. **(LO 2)** A sales budget is:
   a. derived from the production budget.
   b. management's best estimate of sales revenue for the year.
   c. not the starting point for the master budget.
   d. prepared only for credit sales.

6. **(LO 2)** The formula for the production budget is budgeted sales in units plus:
   a. desired ending merchandise inventory less beginning merchandise inventory.
   b. beginning finished goods units less desired ending finished goods units.
   c. desired ending direct materials units less beginning direct materials units.
   d. desired ending finished goods units less beginning finished goods units.

7. **(LO 2)** Direct materials inventories are kept in pounds in Byrd Company, and the total pounds of direct materials needed for production is 9,500. If the beginning inventory is 1,000 pounds and the desired ending inventory is 2,200 pounds, the total pounds to be purchased is:
   a. 9,400.
   b. 9,500.
   c. 9,700.
   d. 10,700.

8. **(LO 3)** The formula for computing the direct labor budget is to multiply the direct labor cost per hour by the:
   a. total required direct labor hours.
   b. physical units to be produced.
   c. equivalent units to be produced.
   d. No correct answer is given.

9. **(LO 3)** Each of the following budgets is used in preparing the budgeted income statement **except** the:

a. sales budget.
b. selling and administrative expense budget.
c. capital expenditure budget.
d. direct labor budget.

10. **(LO 3)** The budgeted income statement is:
    a. the end-product of the operating budgets.
    b. the end-product of the financial budgets.
    c. the starting point of the master budget.
    d. dependent on cash receipts and cash disbursements.

11. **(LO 4)** The budgeted balance sheet is:
    a. developed from the budgeted balance sheet for the preceding year and the budgets for the current year.
    b. the last operating budget prepared.
    c. used to prepare the cash budget.
    d. All of the above.

12. **(LO 4)** The format of a cash budget is:
    a. Beginning cash balance + Cash receipts + Cash from financing − Cash disbursements = Ending cash balance.
    b. Beginning cash balance + Cash receipts − Cash disbursements +/− Financing = Ending cash balance.
    c. Beginning cash balance + Net income − Cash dividends = Ending cash balance.
    d. Beginning cash balance + Cash revenues − Cash expenses = Ending cash balance.

13. **(LO 4)** Expected direct materials purchases in Read Company are $70,000 in the first quarter and $90,000 in the second quarter. Forty percent of the purchases are paid in cash as incurred, and the balance is paid in the following quarter. The budgeted cash payments for purchases in the second quarter are:
    a. $96,000.
    b. $90,000.
    c. $78,000.
    d. $72,000.

14. **(LO 5)** The budget for a merchandiser differs from a budget for a manufacturer because:
    a. a merchandise purchases budget replaces the production budget.
    b. the manufacturing budgets are not applicable.
    c. None of the above.
    d. Both (a) and (b) above.

15. **(LO 5)** In most cases, not-for-profit entities:
    a. prepare budgets using the same steps as those used by profit-oriented businesses.
    b. know budgeted cash receipts at the beginning of a time period, so they budget only for expenditures.
    c. begin the budgeting process by budgeting expenditures rather than receipts.
    d. can ignore budgets because they are not expected to generate net income.

Solutions

1. **c.** Budgeting does not necessarily enable disciplinary action to be taken at every level of responsibility. The other choices are all benefits of budgeting.

2. **b.** A budget is the primary method of communicating agreed-upon objectives throughout an organization. The other choices are incorrect because (a) a budget is the responsibility of all levels of management, not management accountants; (c) past performance is not ignored in the budgeting process but instead is the starting point from which future budget goals are formulated; and (d) the budget not only may promote efficiency but is an important tool for evaluating performance.

3. **a.** Top-down budgeting is not one of the essentials of effective budgeting. The other choices are true statements.

4. **b.** Long-range planning generally encompasses a period of at least 5 years whereas budgeting usually covers a period of 1 year. The other choices are incorrect because budgeting and long-range planning (a) do not have the same amount of detail, (c) do not have the same emphasis, and (d) do not cover the same time period.

5. **b.** A sales budget is management's best estimate of sales revenue for the year. The other choices are incorrect because a sales budget (a) is the first budget prepared and is the one budget that is not derived from any other budget, (c) is the starting point for the master budget, and (d) is prepared for both cash and credit sales.

6. **d.** The formula for the production budget is budgeted sales in units plus desired ending finished goods units less beginning finished goods units. The other choices are therefore incorrect.

7. **d.** Pounds to be purchased = Amount needed for production (9,500) + Desired ending inventory (2,200) − Beginning inventory (1,000) = 10,700, not (a) 9,400, (b) 9,500, or (c) 9,700.

8. **a.** Direct labor cost = Direct labor cost per hour × Total required direct labor hours. The other choices are therefore incorrect.

9. **c.** The capital expenditure budget is not used in preparing the budgeted income statement. The other choices are true statements.

10. **a.** The budgeted income statement is the end-product of the operating budgets, not (b) the financial budgets, (c) the starting point of the master budget, or (d) dependent on cash receipts and cash disbursements.

11. **a.** The budgeted balance sheet is developed from the budgeted balance sheet for the preceding year and the budgets for the current year. The other choices are therefore incorrect.

12. **b.** The format of a cash budget is Beginning cash balance + Cash receipts − Cash disbursements +/− Financing = Ending cash balance. The other choices are therefore incorrect.

13. **c.** Budgeted cash payments for the second quarter = Purchases for the first quarter ($42,000; $70,000 × .60) + 40% of the purchases for the second quarter ($36,000; $90,000 × .40) = $78,000, not (a) $96,000, (b) $90,000, or (d) $72,000.

14. **d.** The budget for a merchandiser uses a merchandise purchases budget in place of a production budget, and the manufacturing budgets are not applicable for a merchandiser. Therefore, as both choices (a) and (b) are correct, choice (d) is the best answer.

15. **c.** In most cases, not-for-profit entities begin the budgeting process by budgeting expenditures rather than receipts. The other choices are incorrect because in most cases not-for-profit entities (a) prepare budgets using different, not the same, steps as those used by profit-oriented enterprises; (b) budget for both expenditures and receipts; and (d) cannot ignore budgets.

Practice Brief Exercises

Prepare a production budget for two quarters.

1. (LO 2) Romana Company estimates that unit sales will be 20,000 in quarter 1, 24,000 in quarter 2, 27,000 in quarter 3, and 33,000 in quarter 4. Management desires to have an ending finished goods inventory equal to 20% of the next quarter's expected unit sales. Prepare a production budget by quarters for the first 6 months of 2022.

Solution

1.

Romana Company
Production Budget
For the Six Months Ending June 30, 2022

	Quarter 1	Quarter 2	Six Months
Expected unit sales	20,000	24,000	
Add: Desired ending finished goods	4,800[a]	5,400[c]	
Total required units	24,800	29,400	
Less: Beginning finished goods inventory	4,000[b]	3,500	
Required production units	20,800	25,900	46,700

[a] 24,000 × .2   [b] 20,000 × .2   [c] 27,000 × .2

Prepare a direct labor budget for 2 quarters.

2. (LO 3) For Jovanka Company, units to be produced are 7,000 in quarter 1 and 9,800 in quarter 2. It takes 2.2 hours to make a finished unit, and the expected hourly wage rate is $20 per hour. Prepare a direct labor budget by quarters for the 6 months ending June 30, 2022.

Solution

2.

Jovanka Company
Direct Labor Budget
For the Six Months Ending June 30, 2022

	Quarter 1	Quarter 2	Six Months
Units to be produced	7,000	9,800	
Direct labor time (hours) per unit	× 2.2	× 2.2	
Total required direct labor hours	15,400	21,560	
Direct labor cost per hour	× $20	× $20	
Total direct labor cost	$308,000	$431,200	$739,200

Prepare data for a cash budget.

3. (LO 4) Vislor Industries expects credit sales for January, February, and March to be $165,000, $200,000, and $220,000, respectively. It is expected that 70% of the sales will be collected in the month of sale, and 30% will be collected in the following month. Compute cash collections from customers for each month.

Solution

3.

	Collections from Customers		
Credit Sales	January	February	March
January, $165,000	$115,500	$ 49,500	
February, $200,000		140,000	$ 60,000
March, $220,000			154,000
	$115,500	$189,500	$214,000

Determine required merchandise purchases for 1 month.

4. (LO 5) Turlough Wholesalers is preparing its merchandise purchases budget. Budgeted sales are $300,000 for June and $380,000 for July. Cost of goods sold is expected to be 60% of sales. The company's desired ending inventory is 25% of the following month's cost of goods sold. Compute the required purchases for June.

Solution

4.
Budgeted cost of goods sold ($300,000 × 60%)	$180,000
Add: Desired ending inventory ($380,000 × 60% × 25%)	57,000
Total inventory required	237,000
Less: Beginning inventory ($300,000 × 60% × 25%)	45,000
Required merchandise purchases for April	$192,000

Practice Exercises

1. (LO 2) On January 1, 2022, the Heche Company budget committee has reached agreement on the following data for the 6 months ending June 30, 2022.

Sales units:	First quarter 5,000; second quarter 6,000; third quarter 7,000
Ending raw materials inventory:	40% of the next quarter's production requirements
Ending finished goods inventory:	30% of the next quarter's expected sales units
Third-quarter 2022 production:	7,500 units

The ending raw materials and finished goods inventories at December 31, 2021, follow the same percentage relationships to production and sales that occur in 2022. Two pounds of raw materials are required to make each unit of finished goods. Raw materials purchased are expected to cost $5 per pound.

Prepare production and direct materials budgets by quarter for 6 months.

Instructions

a. Prepare a production budget by quarters for the 6-month period ended June 30, 2022.

b. Prepare a direct materials budget by quarters for the 6-month period ended June 30, 2022.

Solution

1. a.

Heche Company
Production Budget
For the Six Months Ending June 30, 2022

	Quarter 1	Quarter 2	Six Months
Expected unit sales	5,000	6,000	
Add: Desired ending finished goods units	1,800[(1)]	2,100[(2)]	
Total required units	6,800	8,100	
Less: Beginning finished goods units	1,500[(3)]	1,800	
Required production units	**5,300**	**6,300**	**11,600**

[(1)].30 × 6,000; [(2)].30 × 7,000; [(3)].30 × 5,000

b.

Heche Company
Direct Materials Budget
For the Six Months Ending June 30, 2022

	Quarter 1	Quarter 2	Six Months
Units to be produced	5,300	6,300	
Direct materials per unit	× 2	× 2	
Total pounds needed for production	10,600	12,600	
Add: Desired ending direct materials (pounds)	5,040[(1)]	6,000[(2)]	
Total materials required	15,640	18,600	
Less: Beginning direct materials (pounds)	4,240[(3)]	5,040	
Direct materials purchase	11,400	13,560	
Cost per pound	× $5	× $5	
Total cost of direct materials purchase	**$57,000**	**$67,800**	**$124,800**

[(1)].40 × 12,600; [(2)]7,500 × (2 × .40); [(3)].40 × 10,600

Prepare a cash budget for 2 months.

2. (LO 4) Jake Company expects to have a cash balance of $45,000 on January 1, 2022. Relevant monthly budget data for the first 2 months of 2022 are as follows.

Collections from customers: January $100,000, February $160,000.

Payments for direct materials: January $60,000, February $80,000.

Direct labor: January $30,000, February $45,000. Wages are paid in the month they are incurred.

Manufacturing overhead: January $26,000, February $31,000. These costs include depreciation of $1,000 per month. All other overhead costs are paid as incurred.

Selling and administrative expenses: January $15,000, February $20,000. These costs are exclusive of depreciation. They are paid as incurred.

Sales of marketable securities in January are expected to realize $10,000 in cash. Jake Company has a line of credit at a local bank that enables it to borrow up to $25,000. The company wants to maintain a minimum monthly cash balance of $25,000.

Instructions

Prepare a cash budget for January and February.

Solution

2.

Jake Company
Cash Budget
For the Two Months Ending February 28, 2022

	January	February
Beginning cash balance	$ 45,000	$ 25,000
Add: Receipts		
Collections from customers	100,000	160,000
Sale of marketable securities	10,000	0
Total receipts	110,000	160,000
Total available cash	155,000	185,000
Less: Disbursements		
Direct materials	60,000	80,000
Direct labor	30,000	45,000
Manufacturing overhead	25,000*	30,000
Selling and administrative expenses	15,000	20,000
Total disbursements	130,000	175,000
Excess (deficiency) of available cash over cash		
Disbursements	25,000	10,000
Financing		
Borrowings	0	15,000
Repayments	0	0
Ending cash balance	$ 25,000	$ 25,000

*$26,000 − $1,000

Practice Problems

Prepare sales and production budgets.

1. (LO 2) Asheville Company is preparing its master budget for 2022. Relevant data pertaining to its sales and production budgets are as follows.

Sales. Sales for the year are expected to total 2,100,000 units. Quarterly sales, as a percentage of total sales, are 15%, 25%, 35%, and 25%, respectively. The sales price is expected to be $70 per unit for the first three quarters and $75 per unit beginning in the fourth quarter. Sales in the first quarter of 2023 are expected to be 10% higher than the budgeted sales volume for the first quarter of 2022.

Production. Management desires to maintain ending finished goods inventories at 20% of the next quarter's budgeted sales volume.

Instructions

Prepare the sales budget and production budget by quarters for 2022.

Solution

1.

Asheville Company Sales Budget and Production Budget

Asheville Company
For the Year Ending December 31, 2022
Sales Budget

	Quarter				
	1	2	3	4	Year
Expected unit sales[a]	315,000	525,000	735,000	525,000	2,100,000
Unit selling price	× $70	× $70	× $70	× $75	
Total sales	$22,050,000	$36,750,000	$51,450,000	$39,375,000	$149,625,000

Production Budget

	1	2	3	4	
Expected unit sales	315,000	525,000	735,000	525,000	
Add: Desired ending finished goods units	105,000	147,000	105,000	69,300[b]	
Total required units	420,000	672,000	840,000	594,300	
Less: Beginning finished goods units	63,000[c]	105,000	147,000	105,000	
Required production units	357,000	567,000	693,000	489,300	2,106,300

[a]Expected first-quarter unit sales 2,100,000 × .15; second and fourth quarters 2,100,000 × .25; third quarter 2,100,000 × .35
[b]Estimated first-quarter 2023 sales volume 315,000 + (315,000 × .10) = 346,500; 346,500 × .20
[c]20% of estimated first-quarter 2022 sales units (315,000 × .20)

2. **(LO 3, 4)** Barrett Company has completed all operating budgets other than the income statement for 2022. Selected data from these budgets follow.

Prepare budgeted cost of goods sold, income statement, and balance sheet.

Sales: $300,000
Purchases of raw materials: $145,000
Ending inventory of raw materials: $15,000
Direct labor: $40,000
Manufacturing overhead: $73,000, including $3,000 of depreciation expense
Selling and administrative expenses: $36,000 including depreciation expense of $1,000
Interest expense: $1,000
Principal payment on note: $2,000
Dividends declared: $2,000
Income tax rate: 30%

Other information:

Assume that the number of units produced equals the number sold.
Year-end accounts receivable: 4% of 2022 sales.
Year-end accounts payable: 50% of ending inventory of raw materials.
Interest, direct labor, manufacturing overhead, and selling and administrative expenses other than depreciation are paid as incurred.
Dividends declared and income taxes for 2022 will not be paid until 2023.

Barrett Company
Balance Sheet
December 31, 2021

Assets

Current assets		
Cash		$20,000
Raw materials inventory		10,000
Total current assets		30,000
Property, plant, and equipment		
Equipment	$40,000	
Less: Accumulated depreciation	4,000	36,000
Total assets		$66,000

Liabilities and Stockholders' Equity

Liabilities		
Accounts payable	$ 5,000	
Notes payable	22,000	
Total liabilities		$27,000
Stockholders' equity		
Common stock	25,000	
Retained earnings	14,000	
Total stockholders' equity		39,000
Total liabilities and stockholders' equity		$66,000

Instructions

a. Calculate budgeted cost of goods sold.

b. Prepare a budgeted multiple-step income statement for the year ending December 31, 2022.

c. Prepare a budgeted classified balance sheet as of December 31, 2022.

Solution

2. a. Beginning raw materials + Purchases − Ending raw materials = Cost of direct materials used ($10,000 + $145,000 − $15,000 = $140,000)

Direct materials used + Direct labor + Manufacturing overhead = Cost of goods sold ($140,000 + $40,000 + $73,000 = $253,000)

b.

Barrett Company
Budgeted Income Statement
For the Year Ending December 31, 2022

Sales	$300,000
Cost of goods sold	253,000
Gross profit	47,000
Selling and administrative expenses	36,000
Income from operations	11,000
Interest expense	1,000
Income before income tax expense	10,000
Income tax expense (30%)	3,000*
Net income	$ 7,000

*$10,000 * .30

c.

Barrett Company
Budgeted Balance Sheet
December 31, 2022

Assets

Current assets		
Cash[(1)]		$17,500
Accounts receivable (.04 × $300,000)		12,000
Raw materials inventory		15,000
Total current assets		44,500
Property, plant and equipment		
Equipment	$40,000	
Less: Accumulated depreciation[(2)]	8,000	32,000
Total assets		$76,500

Liabilities and Stockholders' Equity

Liabilities		
Accounts payable (.50 × $15,000)	$ 7,500	
Income taxes payable (see income statement)	3,000	
Dividends payable	2,000	
Note payable ($22,000 − $2,000)	20,000	
Total liabilities		$32,500
Stockholders' equity		
Common stock	25,000	
Retained earnings[(3)]	19,000	
Total stockholders' equity		44,000
Total liabilities and stockholders' equity		$76,500

[(1)]Beginning cash balance		$ 20,000
Add: Receipts		
Collections from customers [(1 − .04) × $300,000 sales)]		288,000
Total available cash		308,000
Less: Disbursements		
Direct materials ($5,000 + $145,000 − $7,500)	$142,500	
Direct labor	40,000	
Manufacturing overhead ($73,000 − $3,000)	70,000	
Selling and administrative expenses ($36,000 − $1,000)	35,000	
Total disbursements		287,500
Excess of available cash over cash disbursements		20,500
Financing		
Less: Repayment of principal and interest		3,000
Ending cash balance		$ 17,500

[(2)]$4,000 + $3,000 + $1,000

[(3)]Beginning retained earnings + Net income − Dividends declared = Ending retained earnings
($14,000 + $7,000 − $2,000 = $19,000)

WileyPLUS

Brief Exercises, DO IT! Exercises, Exercises, Problems, and many additional resources are available for practice in WileyPLUS.

Questions

1. **a.** What is a budget?
   b. How does a budget contribute to good management?

2. Kate Cey and Joe Coulter are discussing the benefits of budgeting. They ask you to identify the primary benefits of budgeting. Comply with their request.

3. Jane Gilligan asks your help in understanding the essentials of effective budgeting. Identify the essentials for Jane.

4. a. "Accounting plays a relatively unimportant role in budgeting." Do you agree? Explain.

   b. What responsibilities does management have in budgeting?

5. What criteria are helpful in determining the length of the budget period? What is the most common budget period?

6. Lori Wilkins maintains that the only difference between budgeting and long-range planning is time. Do you agree? Why or why not?

7. What is participative budgeting? What are its potential benefits? What are its potential disadvantages?

8. What is budgetary slack? What incentive do managers have to create budgetary slack?

9. Distinguish between a master budget and a sales forecast.

10. What budget is the starting point in preparing the master budget? What may result if this budget is inaccurate?

11. "The production budget shows both unit production data and unit cost data." Is this true? Explain.

12. Alou Company has 20,000 beginning finished goods units. Budgeted sales units are 160,000. If management desires 15,000 ending finished goods units, what are the required units of production?

13. In preparing the direct materials budget for Quan Company, management concludes that required purchases are 64,000 units. If 52,000 direct materials units are required in production and there are 9,000 units of beginning direct materials, what are the desired units of ending direct materials?

14. The production budget of Justus Company calls for 80,000 units to be produced. If it takes 45 minutes to make one unit and the direct labor rate is $16 per hour, what is the total budgeted direct labor cost?

15. Ortiz Company's manufacturing overhead budget shows total variable costs of $198,000 and total fixed costs of $162,000. Total production in units is expected to be 150,000. It takes 20 minutes to make one unit, and the direct labor rate is $15 per hour. Express the manufacturing overhead rate as (a) a percentage of direct labor cost, and (b) an amount per direct labor hour.

16. Everly Company's variable selling and administrative expenses are 12% of net sales. Fixed expenses are $50,000 per quarter. The sales budget shows expected sales of $200,000 and $240,000 in the first and second quarters, respectively. What are the total budgeted selling and administrative expenses for each quarter?

17. For Goody Company, the budgeted cost for one unit of product is direct materials $10, direct labor $20, and manufacturing overhead 80% of direct labor cost. If 25,000 units are expected to be sold at $65 each, what is the budgeted gross profit?

18. Indicate the supporting schedules used in preparing a budgeted income statement through gross profit for a manufacturer.

19. Identify the three sections of a cash budget. What balances are also shown in this budget?

20. Noterman Company has credit sales of $600,000 in January. Past experience suggests that 40% is collected in the month of sale, 50% in the month following the sale, and 10% in the second month following the sale. Compute the cash collections from January sales in January, February, and March.

21. What is the formula for determining required merchandise purchases for a merchandiser?

22. How might expected revenues in a service company be computed?

Brief Exercises

Prepare a diagram of a master budget.

BE22.1 (LO 1), AN Maris Company uses the following budgets: balance sheet, capital expenditure, cash, direct labor, direct materials, income statement, manufacturing overhead, production, sales, and selling and administrative expense. Prepare a diagram of the interrelationships of the budgets in the master budget. Indicate whether each budget is an operating or a financial budget.

Prepare a sales budget.

BE22.2 (LO 2), AP Paige Company estimates that unit sales will be 10,000 in quarter 1, 14,000 in quarter 2, 15,000 in quarter 3, and 18,000 in quarter 4. Using a sales price of $70 per unit, prepare the sales budget by quarters for the year ending December 31, 2022.

Prepare a production budget for 2 quarters.

BE22.3 (LO 2), AP Sales budget data for Paige Company are given in BE22.2. Management desires to have an ending finished goods inventory equal to 25% of the next quarter's expected unit sales. Prepare a production budget by quarters for the first 6 months of 2022.

Prepare a direct materials budget for 1 month.

BE22.4 (LO 2), AP Perine Company has 2,000 pounds of raw materials in its December 31, 2021, ending inventory. Required production for January and February of 2022 are 4,000 and 5,000 units, respectively. Two pounds of raw materials are needed for each unit, and the estimated cost per pound is $6. Management desires an ending inventory equal to 25% of next month's materials requirements. Prepare the direct materials budget for January.

Prepare a direct labor budget for 2 quarters.

BE22.5 (LO 3), AP For Gundy Company, units to be produced are 5,000 in quarter 1 and 7,000 in quarter 2. It takes 1.6 hours to make a finished unit, and the expected hourly wage rate is $15 per hour. Prepare a direct labor budget by quarters for the 6 months ending June 30, 2022.

Prepare a manufacturing overhead budget.

BE22.6 (LO 3), AP For Roche Inc., variable manufacturing overhead costs are expected to be $20,000 in the first quarter of 2022, with $5,000 increments in each of the remaining three quarters. Fixed overhead costs are estimated to be $40,000 in each quarter. Prepare the manufacturing overhead budget by quarters and in total for the year.

BE22.7 (LO 3), AP Elbert Company classifies its selling and administrative expense budget into variable and fixed components. Variable expenses are expected to be $24,000 in the first quarter, and $4,000 increments are expected in the remaining quarters of 2022. Fixed expenses are expected to be $40,000 in each quarter. Prepare the selling and administrative expense budget by quarters and in total for 2022.

Prepare a selling and administrative expense budget.

BE22.8 (LO 3), AP North Company has completed all of its operating budgets. The sales budget for the year shows 50,000 units and total sales of $2,250,000. The total unit cost of making one unit of sales is $25. Selling and administrative expenses are expected to be $300,000. Interest is estimated to be $10,000. Income taxes are estimated to be $200,000. Prepare a budgeted multiple-step income statement for the year ending December 31, 2022.

Prepare a budgeted income statement for the year.

BE22.9 (LO 4), AP Kaspar Industries expects credit sales for January, February, and March to be $220,000, $260,000, and $300,000, respectively. It is expected that 75% of the sales will be collected in the month of sale, and 25% will be collected in the following month. Compute cash collections from customers for each month.

Prepare data for a cash budget.

BE22.10 (LO 5), AP Moore Wholesalers is preparing its merchandise purchases budget. Budgeted sales are $400,000 for April and $480,000 for May. Cost of goods sold is expected to be 65% of sales. The company's desired ending inventory is 20% of the following month's cost of goods sold. Compute the required purchases for April.

Determine required merchandise purchases for 1 month.

DO IT! Exercises

DO IT! 22.1 (LO 1), K Use this list of terms to complete the sentences that follow.

Identify budget terminology.

    Long-range plans   Participative budgeting
    Sales forecast   Operating budgets
    Master budget   Financial budgets

1. _____ establish goals for the company's sales and production personnel.
2. The _____ is a set of interrelated budgets that constitutes a plan of action for a specified time period.
3. _____ reduces the risk of having unrealistic budgets.
4. _____ include the cash budget and the budgeted balance sheet.
5. The budget is formed within the framework of a _____.
6. _____ contain considerably less detail than budgets.

DO IT! 22.2 (LO 2), AP Pargo Company is preparing its master budget for 2022. Relevant data pertaining to its sales, production, and direct materials budgets are as follows.

Prepare sales, production, and direct materials budgets.

Sales. Sales for the year are expected to total 1,000,000 units. Quarterly sales are 20%, 25%, 25%, and 30%, respectively. The sales price is expected to be $40 per unit for the first three quarters and $45 per unit beginning in the fourth quarter. Sales in the first quarter of 2023 are expected to be 20% higher than the budgeted sales for the first quarter of 2022.

Production. Management desires to maintain the ending finished goods inventories at 25% of the next quarter's budgeted sales volume.

Direct materials. Each unit requires 2 pounds of raw materials at a cost of $12 per pound. Management desires to maintain raw materials inventories at 10% of the next quarter's production requirements. Assume the production requirements for first quarter of 2023 are 450,000 pounds.

Prepare the sales, production, and direct materials budgets by quarters for 2022.

DO IT! 22.3 (LO 3), AP Pargo Company is preparing its budgeted income statement for 2022. Relevant data pertaining to its sales, production, and direct materials budgets can be found in **DO IT! 22.2**.

Calculate budgeted total unit cost and prepare budgeted income statement.

    In addition, Pargo budgets 0.3 hours of direct labor per unit, labor costs at $15 per hour, and manufacturing overhead at $20 per direct labor hour. Its budgeted selling and administrative expenses for 2022 are $6,000,000.

    a. Calculate the budgeted total unit cost.
    b. Prepare the budgeted multiple-step income statement for 2022. (Ignore income taxes.)

DO IT! 22.4 (LO 4), AP Batista Company management wants to maintain a minimum monthly cash balance of $25,000. At the beginning of April, the cash balance is $25,000, expected cash receipts for

Determine amount of financing needed.

Prepare merchandise purchases budget.

DO IT! 22.5 (LO 5), AP Zeller Company estimates that 2022 sales will be $40,000 in quarter 1, $48,000 in quarter 2, and $58,000 in quarter 3. Cost of goods sold is 50% of sales. Management desires to have ending finished goods inventory equal to 10% of the next quarter's expected cost of goods sold. Prepare a merchandise purchases budget by quarter for the first 6 months of 2022.

Exercises

Explain the concept of budgeting.

E22.1 (LO 1), C Writing Trusler Company has always done some planning for the future, but the company has never prepared a formal budget. Now that the company is growing larger, it is considering preparing a budget.

Instructions

Write a memo to Jim Dixon, the president of Trusler Company, in which you define budgeting, identify the budgets that comprise the master budget, identify the primary benefits of budgeting, and discuss the essentials of effective budgeting.

Prepare a sales budget for 2 quarters.

E22.2 (LO 2), AP Edington Electronics Inc. produces and sells two models of calculators, XQ-103 and XQ-104. The calculators sell for $15 and $25, respectively. Because of the intense competition Edington faces, management budgets sales semiannually. Its projections for the first 2 quarters of 2022 are as follows.

	Unit Sales	
Product	Quarter 1	Quarter 2
XQ-103	20,000	22,000
XQ-104	12,000	15,000

No changes in selling prices are anticipated.

Instructions

Prepare a sales budget for the 2 quarters ending June 30, 2022. List the products and show for each quarter and for the 6 months, units, selling price, and total sales by product and in total.

Prepare a sales budget for 4 quarters.

E22.3 (LO 2), AP Service Thome and Crede, CPAs, are preparing their service revenue (sales) budget for the coming year (2022). The practice is divided into three departments: auditing, tax, and consulting. Billable hours for each department, by quarter, are provided below.

Department	Quarter 1	Quarter 2	Quarter 3	Quarter 4
Auditing	2,300	1,600	2,000	2,400
Tax	3,000	2,200	2,000	2,500
Consulting	1,500	1,500	1,500	1,500

Average hourly billing rates are auditing $80, tax $90, and consulting $110.

Instructions

Prepare the service revenue (sales) budget for 2022 by listing the departments and showing for each quarter and the year in total, billable hours, billable rate, and total revenue.

Prepare quarterly production budgets.

E22.4 (LO 2), AP Turney Company produces and sells automobile batteries, the heavy-duty HD-240. The 2022 sales forecast is as follows.

Quarter	HD-240
1	5,000
2	7,000
3	8,000
4	10,000

The January 1, 2022, inventory of HD-240 is 2,000 units. Management desires an ending inventory each quarter equal to 40% of the next quarter's sales. Sales in the first quarter of 2023 are expected to be 25% higher than sales in the same quarter in 2022.

Instructions

Prepare quarterly production budgets for each quarter and in total for 2022.

E22.5 (LO 2), AP DeWitt Industries has adopted the following production budget for the first 4 months of 2022.

Prepare a direct materials purchases budget.

Month	Units	Month	Units
January	10,000	March	5,000
February	8,000	April	4,000

Each unit requires 2 pounds of raw materials costing $3 per pound. On December 31, 2021, the ending raw materials inventory was 4,000 pounds. Management wants to have a raw materials inventory at the end of the month equal to 20% of next month's production requirements.

Instructions

Prepare a direct materials purchases budget by month for the first quarter.

E22.6 (LO 2), AP On January 1, 2022, the Hardin Company budget committee has reached agreement on the following data for the 6 months ending June 30, 2022.

Prepare production and direct materials budgets by quarters for 6 months.

Sales units: First quarter 5,000; second quarter 6,000; third quarter 7,000.

Ending raw materials inventory: 40% of the next quarter's production requirements.

Ending finished goods inventory: 25% of the next quarter's expected sales units.

Third-quarter production: 7,200 units.

The ending raw materials and finished goods inventories at December 31, 2021, follow the same percentage relationships to production and sales that occur in 2022. Three pounds of raw materials are required to make each unit of finished goods. Raw materials purchased are expected to cost $4 per pound.

Instructions

a. Prepare a production budget by quarters for the 6-month period ended June 30, 2022.

b. Prepare a direct materials budget by quarters for the 6-month period ended June 30, 2022.

E22.7 (LO 2), AP Rensing Ltd. estimates sales for the second quarter of 2022 will be as follows.

Calculate raw materials purchases in dollars.

Month	Units
April	2,550
May	2,675
June	2,390

The target ending inventory of finished products is as follows.

March 31	2,000
April 30	2,230
May 31	2,200
June 30	2,310

Two units of materials are required for each unit of finished product. Production for July is estimated at 2,700 units to start building inventory for the fall sales period. Rensing's policy is to have an inventory of raw materials at the end of each month equal to 50% of the following month's production requirements.

Raw materials are expected to cost $4 per unit throughout the period.

Instructions

Calculate the May raw materials purchases in dollars.

(CGA adapted)

E22.8 (LO 2), AP Fuqua Company's sales budget projects unit sales of part 198Z of 10,000 units in January, 12,000 units in February, and 13,000 units in March. Each unit of part 198Z requires 4 pounds of materials, which cost $2 per pound. Fuqua Company desires its ending raw materials inventory to equal 40% of the next month's production requirements, and its ending finished goods inventory to equal 20% of the next month's expected unit sales. These goals were met at December 31, 2021.

Prepare a production and a direct materials budget.

Instructions

a. Prepare a production budget for January and February 2022.

b. Prepare a direct materials budget for January 2022.

Prepare a direct labor budget.

E22.9 (LO 3), AP Rodriguez, Inc., is preparing its direct labor budget for 2022 from the following production budget based on a calendar year.

Quarter	Units	Quarter	Units
1	20,000	3	35,000
2	25,000	4	30,000

Each unit requires 1.5 hours of direct labor.

Instructions

Prepare a direct labor budget for 2022. Wage rates are expected to be $16 for the first 2 quarters and $18 for quarters 3 and 4.

Prepare production and direct labor budgets.

E22.10 (LO 2, 3), AP Lowell Company makes and sells artistic frames for pictures. The controller is responsible for preparing the master budget and has accumulated the following information for 2022.

	January	February	March	April	May
Estimated unit sales	12,000	14,000	13,000	11,000	11,000
Sales price per unit	$50.00	$47.50	$47.50	$47.50	$47.50
Direct labor hours per unit	2.0	2.0	1.5	1.5	1.5
Wage per direct labor hour	$8.00	$8.00	$8.00	$9.00	$9.00

Lowell has a labor contract that calls for a wage increase to $9.00 per hour on April 1. New labor-saving machinery has been installed and will be fully operational by March 1.

Lowell expects to begin the year with 17,600 frames on hand and has a policy of carrying an end-of-month inventory of 100% of the following month's sales, plus 40% of the second following month's sales.

Instructions

Prepare a production budget and a direct labor budget for Lowell Company by month and for the first quarter of the year. The direct labor budget should include direct labor hours.

(CMA-Canada adapted)

Prepare a manufacturing overhead budget for the year.

E22.11 (LO 3), AP Atlanta Company is preparing its manufacturing overhead budget for 2022. Relevant data consist of the following.

Units to be produced (by quarters): 10,000, 12,000, 14,000, 16,000.

Direct labor: time is 1.5 hours per unit.

Variable overhead costs per direct labor hour: indirect materials $0.80; indirect labor $1.20; and maintenance $0.50.

Fixed overhead costs per quarter: supervisory salaries $35,000; depreciation $15,000; and maintenance $12,000.

Instructions

Prepare the manufacturing overhead budget for the year, showing quarterly data.

Prepare a selling and administrative expense budget for 2 quarters.

E22.12 (LO 3), AP Kirkland Company combines its operating expenses for budget purposes in a selling and administrative expense budget. For the first 6 months of 2022, the following data are available.

1. Sales: 20,000 units quarter 1; 22,000 units quarter 2.
2. Variable costs per dollar of sales: sales commissions 5%, delivery expense 2%, and advertising 3%.
3. Fixed costs per quarter: sales salaries $12,000, office salaries $8,000, depreciation $4,200, insurance $1,500, utilities $800, and repairs expense $500.
4. Unit selling price: $20.

Instructions

Prepare a selling and administrative expense budget by quarters for the first 6 months of 2022.

E22.13 (LO 3), AP Fultz Company has accumulated the following budget data for the year 2022.

1. Sales: 30,000 units, unit selling price $85.
2. Cost of one unit of finished goods: direct materials 1 pound at $5 per pound, direct labor 3 hours at $15 per hour, and manufacturing overhead $5 per direct labor hour.
3. Inventories (raw materials only): beginning, 10,000 pounds; ending, 15,000 pounds.
4. Selling and administrative expenses: $170,000; interest expense: $30,000.
5. Income taxes: 30% of income before income taxes.

Prepare a budgeted income statement for the year.

Instructions

a. Prepare a schedule showing the computation of cost of goods sold for 2022.
b. Prepare a budgeted multiple-step income statement for 2022.

E22.14 (LO 4), AP Danner Company expects to have a cash balance of $45,000 on January 1, 2022. Relevant monthly budget data for the first 2 months of 2022 are as follows.

Prepare a cash budget for 2 months.

Collections from customers: January $85,000, February $150,000.

Payments for direct materials: January $50,000, February $75,000.

Direct labor: January $30,000, February $45,000. Wages are paid in the month they are incurred.

Manufacturing overhead: January $21,000, February $25,000. These costs include depreciation of $1,500 per month. All other overhead costs are paid as incurred.

Selling and administrative expenses: January $15,000, February $20,000. These costs are exclusive of depreciation. They are paid as incurred.

Sales of marketable securities in January are expected to realize $12,000 in cash. Danner Company has a line of credit at a local bank that enables it to borrow up to $25,000. The company wants to maintain a minimum monthly cash balance of $20,000.

Instructions

Prepare a cash budget for January and February.

E22.15 (LO 4), AP Deitz Corporation is projecting a cash balance of $30,000 in its December 31, 2021, balance sheet. Deitz's schedule of expected collections from customers for the first quarter of 2022 shows total collections of $185,000. The schedule of expected payments for direct materials for the first quarter of 2022 shows total payments of $43,000. Other information gathered for the first quarter of 2022 is sale of equipment $3,000, direct labor $70,000, manufacturing overhead $35,000, selling and administrative expenses $45,000, and purchase of securities $14,000. Deitz wants to maintain a balance of at least $25,000 cash at the end of each quarter.

Prepare a cash budget.

Instructions

Prepare a cash budget for the first quarter.

E22.16 (LO 4), AN The controller of Trenshaw Company wants to improve the company's control system by preparing a month-by-month cash budget. The following information is for the month ending July 31, 2022.

Prepare cash budget for a month.

June 30, 2022, cash balance	$45,000
Dividends to be declared on July 15*	12,000
Cash expenditures to be paid in July for operating expenses	40,800
Amortization expense in July	4,500
Cash collections to be received in July	90,000
Merchandise purchases to be paid in cash in July	56,200
Equipment to be purchased for cash in July	20,000

*Dividends are payable 30 days after declaration to shareholders of record on the declaration date.

Trenshaw Company wants to keep a minimum cash balance of $25,000.

Instructions

a. Prepare a cash budget for the month ended July 31, 2022, and indicate how much money, if any, Trenshaw Company will need to borrow to meet its minimum cash requirement.
b. Explain how cash budgeting can reduce the cost of short-term borrowing.

(CGA adapted)

Prepare schedules of expected collections and payments.

E22.17 (LO 4), AP Nieto Company's budgeted sales and direct materials purchases are as follows.

	Budgeted Sales	Budgeted D.M. Purchases
January	$200,000	$30,000
February	220,000	36,000
March	250,000	38,000

Nieto's sales are 30% cash and 70% credit. Credit sales are collected 10% in the month of sale, 50% in the month following sale, and 36% in the second month following sale; 4% are uncollectible. Nieto's purchases are 50% cash and 50% on account. Purchases on account are paid 40% in the month of purchase, and 60% in the month following purchase.

Instructions

a. Prepare a schedule of expected collections from customers for March.

b. Prepare a schedule of expected payments for direct materials for March.

Prepare schedules for cash receipts and cash payments, and determine ending balances for balance sheet.

E22.18 (LO 4), AP **Service** Green Landscaping Inc. is preparing its budget for the first quarter of 2022. The next step in the budgeting process is to prepare a cash receipts schedule and a cash payments schedule. To that end the following information has been collected.

Clients usually pay 60% of their fee in the month that service is performed, 30% the month after, and 10% the second month after receiving service.

Actual service revenue for 2021 and expected service revenues for 2022 are November 2021, $80,000; December 2021, $90,000; January 2022, $100,000; February 2022, $120,000; and March 2022, $140,000.

Purchases of landscaping supplies (direct materials) are paid 60% in the month of purchase and 40% the following month. Actual purchases for 2021 and expected purchases for 2022 are December 2021, $14,000; January 2022, $12,000; February 2022, $15,000; and March 2022, $18,000.

Instructions

a. Prepare the following schedules for each month in the first quarter of 2022 and for the quarter in total:

  1. Expected collections from clients.
  2. Expected payments for landscaping supplies.

b. Determine the following balances at March 31, 2022:

  1. Accounts receivable.
  2. Accounts payable.

Prepare a cash budget for 2 quarters.

E22.19 (LO 4, 5), AP **Service** Pletcher Dental Clinic is a medium-sized dental service specializing in family dental care. The clinic is currently preparing the master budget for the first 2 quarters of 2022. All that remains in this process is the cash budget. The following information has been collected from other portions of the master budget and elsewhere.

Beginning cash balance	$ 30,000
Required minimum cash balance	25,000
Payment of income taxes (2nd quarter)	4,000
Professional salaries:	
1st quarter	140,000
2nd quarter	140,000
Interest from investments (2nd quarter)	7,000
Overhead costs:	
1st quarter	77,000
2nd quarter	100,000
Selling and administrative costs, including $2,000 depreciation:	
1st quarter	50,000
2nd quarter	70,000
Purchase of equipment (2nd quarter)	50,000
Sale of equipment (1st quarter)	12,000
Collections from patients:	
1st quarter	235,000
2nd quarter	380,000
Interest payments (2nd quarter)	200

Instructions

Prepare a cash budget for each of the first two quarters of 2022.

E22.20 (LO 5), AP Service In May 2022, the budget committee of Grand Stores assembles the following data in preparation of budgeted merchandise purchases for the month of June.

Prepare a purchases budget and budgeted income statement for a merchandiser.

1. Expected sales: June $500,000, July $600,000.
2. Cost of goods sold is expected to be 75% of sales.
3. Desired ending merchandise inventory is 30% of the following (next) month's cost of goods sold.
4. The beginning inventory at June 1 will be the desired amount.

Instructions

a. Compute the budgeted merchandise purchases for June.
b. Prepare the budgeted multiple-step income statement for June through gross profit.

E22.21 (LO 5), AP Emeric and Ellie's Painting Service estimates that it will paint 10 small homes, 5 medium homes, and 2 large homes during the month of June 2022. The company estimates its direct labor needs as 40 hours per small home, 70 hours for a medium home, and 120 hours for a large home. Its average cost for direct labor is $18 per hour.

Prepare a direct labor budget for a service company.

Instructions

Prepare a direct labor budget for Emeric and Ellie's Painting Service for June 2022.

Problems: Set A

P22.1A (LO 2, 3), AP Cook Farm Supply Company manufactures and sells a pesticide called Snare. The following data are available for preparing budgets for Snare for the first 2 quarters of 2022.

Prepare budgeted income statement and supporting budgets.

1. Sales: quarter 1, 40,000 bags; quarter 2, 56,000 bags. Selling price is $60 per bag.
2. Direct materials: each bag of Snare requires 4 pounds of Gumm at a cost of $3.80 per pound and 6 pounds of Tarr at $1.50 per pound.
3. Desired inventory levels:

Type of Inventory	January 1	April 1	July 1
Snare (bags)	8,000	15,000	18,000
Gumm (pounds)	9,000	10,000	13,000
Tarr (pounds)	14,000	20,000	25,000

4. Direct labor: direct labor time is 15 minutes per bag at an hourly rate of $16 per hour.
5. Selling and administrative expenses are expected to be 15% of sales plus $175,000 per quarter.
6. Interest expense is $100,000 for the 2 quarters.
7. Income taxes are expected to be 30% of income before income taxes.

Your assistant has prepared two budgets: (1) the manufacturing overhead budget shows expected costs to be 125% of direct labor cost, and (2) the direct materials budget for Tarr shows the cost of Tarr purchases to be $297,000 in quarter 1 and $439,500 in quarter 2.

Instructions

Prepare the budgeted multiple-step income statement for the first 6 months and all required operating budgets by quarters. (*Note:* Use variable and fixed in the selling and administrative expense budget.) Do not prepare the manufacturing overhead budget or the direct materials budget for Tarr.

Net income $881,160
Cost per bag $33.20

P22.2A (LO 2, 3), AP Deleon Inc. is preparing its annual budgets for the year ending December 31, 2022. Accounting assistants furnish the data shown below.

Prepare sales, production, direct materials, direct labor, and income statement budgets.

	Product JB 50	Product JB 60
Sales budget:		
Anticipated volume in units	400,000	200,000
Unit selling price	$20	$25

	Product JB 50	Product JB 60
Production budget:		
Desired ending finished goods units	30,000	15,000
Beginning finished goods units	25,000	10,000
Direct materials budget:		
Direct materials per unit (pounds)	2	3
Desired ending direct materials pounds	30,000	10,000
Beginning direct materials pounds	40,000	15,000
Cost per pound	$3	$4
Direct labor budget:		
Direct labor time per unit	0.4	0.6
Direct labor rate per hour	$12	$12
Budgeted income statement:		
Total unit cost	$13	$20

An accounting assistant has prepared the detailed manufacturing overhead budget and the selling and administrative expense budget. The latter shows selling expenses of $560,000 for product JB 50 and $360,000 for product JB 60, and administrative expenses of $540,000 for product JB 50 and $340,000 for product JB 60. Interest expense is $150,000 (not allocated to products). Income taxes are expected to be 30%.

Instructions

Prepare the following budgets for the year. Show data for each product. Quarterly budgets should not be prepared.

a. Sales.
b. Production.
c. Direct materials.
d. Direct labor.
e. Multiple-step income statement (*Note:* income taxes are not allocated to the products).

a. Total sales $13,000,000
b. Required production units:
* JB 50, 405,000*
* JB 60, 205,000*
c. Total cost of direct materials purchases $4,840,000
d. Total direct labor cost $3,420,000
e. Net income $1,295,000

Prepare sales and production budgets and compute cost per unit under two plans.

P22.3A (LO 2), E Hill Industries had sales in 2021 of $6,800,000 and gross profit of $1,100,000. Management is considering two alternative budget plans to increase its gross profit in 2022.

Plan A would increase the selling price per unit from $8.00 to $8.40. Sales volume would decrease by 10% from its 2021 level. Plan B would decrease the selling price per unit by $0.50. The marketing department expects that the sales volume would increase by 100,000 units.

At the end of 2021, Hill has 40,000 units of inventory on hand. If Plan A is accepted, the 2022 ending inventory should be equal to 5% of the 2022 sales. If Plan B is accepted, the ending inventory should be equal to 60,000 units. Each unit produced will cost $1.80 in direct labor, $1.40 in direct materials, and $1.20 in variable overhead. The fixed overhead for 2022 should be $1,895,000.

Instructions

a. Prepare a sales budget for 2022 under each plan.
b. Prepare a production budget for 2022 under each plan.
c. Compute the production cost per unit under each plan. Why is the cost per unit different for each of the two plans? (Round to two decimals.)
d. Which plan should be accepted? (*Hint:* Compute the gross profit under each plan.)

c. Unit cost: Plan A $6.88
* Plan B $6.35*
d. Gross profit:
* Plan A $1,162,800*
* Plan B $1,092,500*

Prepare cash budget for 2 months.

P22.4A (LO 4), AP Colter Company prepares monthly cash budgets. Relevant data from operating budgets for 2022 are as follows:

	January	February
Sales	$360,000	$400,000
Direct materials purchases	120,000	125,000
Direct labor	90,000	100,000
Manufacturing overhead	70,000	75,000
Selling and administrative expenses	79,000	85,000

All sales are on account. Collections are expected to be 50% in the month of sale, 30% in the first month following the sale, and 20% in the second month following the sale. Sixty percent (60%) of direct materials purchases are paid in cash in the month of purchase, and the balance due is paid in the month following the purchase. All other items above are paid in the month incurred except for selling and administrative expenses that include $1,000 of depreciation per month.

Other data:

1. Credit sales: November 2021, $250,000; December 2021, $320,000.
2. Purchases of direct materials: December 2021, $100,000.
3. Other receipts: January—collection of December 31, 2021, notes receivable $15,000; February—proceeds from sale of securities $6,000.
4. Other disbursements: February—payment of $6,000 cash dividend.

The company's cash balance on January 1, 2022, is expected to be $60,000. The company wants to maintain a minimum cash balance of $50,000.

Instructions

a. Prepare schedules for (1) expected collections from customers and (2) expected payments for direct materials purchases for January and February.

b. Prepare a cash budget for January and February in columnar form.

a. January: collections $326,000; payments $112,000
b. Ending cash balance: January $51,000 February $50,000

P22.5A (LO 5), AP The budget committee of Suppar Company collects the following data for its San Miguel Store in preparing budgeted income statements for May and June 2022.

Prepare purchases and income statement budgets for a merchandiser.

1. Sales for May are expected to be $800,000. Sales in June and July are expected to be 5% higher than the preceding month.

2. Cost of goods sold is expected to be 75% of sales.

3. Company policy is to maintain ending merchandise inventory at 10% of the following month's cost of goods sold.

4. Operating expenses are estimated to be as follows:

Sales salaries	$35,000 per month
Advertising	6% of monthly sales
Delivery expense	2% of monthly sales
Sales commissions	5% of monthly sales
Rent expense	$5,000 per month
Depreciation	$800 per month
Utilities	$600 per month
Insurance	$500 per month

5. Interest expense is $2,000 per month. Income taxes are estimated to be 30% of income before income taxes.

Instructions

a. Prepare the merchandise purchases budget for each month in columnar form.

b. Prepare budgeted multiple-step income statements for each month in columnar form. Show in the statements the details of cost of goods sold.

a. Purchases:
May $603,000
June $633,150
b. Net income:
May $36,470
June $39,830

P22.6A (LO 3, 4), AP Krause Industries' balance sheet at December 31, 2021, is presented below.

Prepare budgeted cost of goods sold, income statement, retained earnings, and balance sheet.

Krause Industries
Balance Sheet
December 31, 2021

Assets

Current assets		
Cash		$ 7,500
Accounts receivable		73,500
Finished goods inventory (1,500 units)		24,000
Total current assets		105,000
Property, plant, and equipment		
Equipment	$40,000	
Less: Accumulated depreciation	10,000	30,000
Total assets		$135,000

Liabilities and Stockholders' Equity

Liabilities		
Notes payable		$ 25,000
Accounts payable		45,000
Total liabilities		70,000
Stockholders' equity		
Common stock	$40,000	
Retained earnings	25,000	
Total stockholders' equity		65,000
Total liabilities and stockholders' equity		$135,000

Budgeted data for the year 2022 include the following.

	2022 Quarter 4	2022 Total
Sales budget (8,000 units at $32)	$76,800	$256,000
Direct materials used	17,000	62,500
Direct labor	12,500	50,900
Manufacturing overhead applied	10,000	48,600
Selling and administrative expenses	18,000	75,000

To meet sales requirements and to have 2,500 units of finished goods on hand at December 31, 2022, the production budget shows 9,000 required units of output. The total unit cost of production is expected to be $18. Krause uses the first-in, first-out (FIFO) inventory costing method. Interest expense is expected to be $3,500 for the year. Income taxes are expected to be 40% of income before income taxes. In 2022, the company expects to declare and pay an $8,000 cash dividend.

The company's cash budget shows an expected cash balance of $5,880 at December 31, 2022. All sales and purchases are on account. It is expected that 60% of quarterly sales are collected in cash within the quarter and the remainder is collected in the following quarter. Direct materials purchased from suppliers are paid 50% in the quarter incurred and the remainder in the following quarter. Purchases in the fourth quarter were the same as the materials used. In 2022, the company expects to purchase additional equipment costing $9,000. $4,000 of depreciation expense on equipment is included in the budget data and split equally between manufacturing overhead and selling and administrative expenses. Krause expects to pay $8,000 on the outstanding notes payable balance plus all interest due and payable to December 31 (included in interest expense $3,500, above). Accounts payable at December 31, 2022, includes amounts due suppliers (see above) plus other accounts payable relating to manufacturing overhead of $7,200. Unpaid income taxes at December 31 will be $5,000.

Instructions

Net income $21,900
Total assets $116,600

Prepare a budgeted statement of cost of goods sold, budgeted multiple-step income statement and retained earnings statement for 2022, and a budgeted classified balance sheet at December 31, 2022.

Continuing Cases

Current Designs

CD22 Diane Buswell is preparing the 2022 budget for one of **Current Designs**' rotomolded kayaks. Extensive meetings with members of the sales department and executive team have resulted in the following unit sales projections for 2022.

Quarter 1	1,000 kayaks
Quarter 2	1,500 kayaks
Quarter 3	750 kayaks
Quarter 4	750 kayaks

Current Designs' policy is to have finished goods ending inventory in a quarter equal to 20% of the next quarter's anticipated sales. Preliminary sales projections for 2023 are 1,100 units for the first quarter and 1,500 units for the second quarter. Ending inventory of finished goods at December 31, 2021, will be 200 rotomolded kayaks.

Production of each kayak requires 54 pounds of polyethylene powder and a finishing kit (rope, seat, hardware, etc.). Company policy is that the ending inventory of polyethylene powder should be 25% of the amount needed for production in the next quarter. Assume that the ending inventory of polyethylene powder on December 31, 2021, is 19,400 pounds. The finishing kits can be assembled as they are needed. As a result, Current Designs does not maintain a significant inventory of the finishing kits.

The polyethylene powder used in these kayaks costs $1.50 per pound, and the finishing kits cost $170 each. Production of a single kayak requires 2 hours of time by more experienced, type I employees and 3 hours of finishing time by type II employees. The type I employees are paid $15 per hour, and the type II employees are paid $12 per hour.

Selling and administrative expenses for this line are expected to be $45 per unit sold plus $7,500 per quarter. Manufacturing overhead is assigned at 150% of labor costs.

Instructions

Prepare the production budget, direct materials budget, direct labor budget, manufacturing overhead budget, and selling and administrative budget for this product line by quarter and in total for 2022.

Waterways

(*Note:* This is a continuation of the Waterways case from Chapters 14–21.)

WP22 Waterways Corporation is preparing its budget for the coming year, 2022. The first step is to plan for the first quarter of that coming year. The company has gathered information from its managers in preparation of the budgeting process. This problem asks you to prepare the various budgets that comprise the master budget for 2022.

Go to WileyPLUS for complete case details and instructions.

Comprehensive Case

CC22.1 Service Auburn Circular Club is planning a major fundraiser that it hopes will become a successful annual event: sponsoring a professional rodeo. For this case, you will encounter many managerial accounting issues that would be common for a start-up business, such as CVP analysis (Chapter 18), incremental analysis (Chapter 20), and budgetary planning (Chapter 22).

CC22.2 Sweats Galore is a new business venture that will make custom sweatshirts using a silk-screen process. In helping the company's owner, Michael Woods, set up his business, you will have the opportunity to apply your understanding of CVP relationships (Chapter 18) and budgetary planning (Chapter 22).

Go to WileyPLUS for complete details and instructions for both cases.

Expand Your Critical Thinking

Decision-Making Across the Organization

CT22.1 Palmer Corporation operates on a calendar-year basis. It begins the annual budgeting process in late August when the president establishes targets for the total dollar sales and net income before taxes for the next year.

The sales target is given first to the marketing department. The marketing manager formulates a sales budget by product line in both units and dollars. From this budget, sales quotas by product line in units and dollars are established for each of the corporation's sales districts. The marketing manager also estimates the cost of the marketing activities required to support the target sales volume and prepares a tentative marketing expense budget.

The executive vice president uses the sales and profit targets, the sales budget by product line, and the tentative marketing expense budget to determine the dollar amounts that can be devoted to manufacturing and corporate office expense. The executive vice president prepares the budget for corporate expenses. She then forwards to the production department the product-line sales budget in units and the total dollar amount that can be devoted to manufacturing.

The production manager meets with the factory managers to develop a manufacturing plan that will produce the required units when needed within the cost constraints set by the executive vice president. The budgeting process usually comes to a halt at this point because the production department does not consider the financial resources allocated to be adequate.

When this standstill occurs, the vice president of finance, the executive vice president, the marketing manager, and the production manager meet together to determine the final budgets for each of the areas. This normally results in a modest increase in the total amount available for manufacturing costs and cuts in the marketing expense and corporate office expense budgets. The total sales and net income figures proposed by the president are seldom changed. Although the participants are seldom pleased with the compromise, these budgets are final. Each executive then develops a new detailed budget for the operations in his or her area.

None of the areas has achieved its budget in recent years. Sales often run below the target. When budgeted sales are not achieved, each area is expected to cut costs so that the president's profit target can be met. However, the profit target is seldom met because costs are not cut enough. In fact, costs often run above the original budget in all functional areas (marketing, production, and corporate office).

The president is disturbed that Palmer has not been able to meet the sales and profit targets. He hired a consultant with considerable experience with companies in Palmer's industry. The consultant reviewed the budgets for the past 4 years. He concluded that the product line sales budgets were reasonable and that the cost and expense budgets were adequate for the budgeted sales and production levels.

Instructions

With the class divided into groups, answer the following.

a. Discuss how the budgeting process employed by Palmer Corporation contributes to the failure to achieve the president's sales and profit targets.

b. Suggest how Palmer Corporation's budgeting process could be revised to correct the problems.

c. Should the functional areas be expected to cut their costs when sales volume falls below budget? Explain your answer.

(CMA adapted)

Managerial Analysis

CT22.2 Elliot & Hesse Inc. manufactures ergonomic devices for computer users. Some of its more popular products include anti-glare filters and privacy filters (for computer monitors) and keyboard stands with wrist rests. Over the past 5 years, it experienced rapid growth, with sales of all products increasing 20% to 50% each year.

Last year, some of the primary manufacturers of computers began introducing new products with some of the ergonomic designs, such as anti-glare filters and wrist rests, already built in. As a result, sales of Elliot & Hesse's accessory devices have declined somewhat. The company believes that the privacy filters will probably continue to show growth, but that the other products will probably continue to decline. When the next year's budget was prepared, increases were built into research and development so that replacement products could be developed or the company could expand into some other product line. Some product lines being considered are general-purpose ergonomic devices including back supports, foot rests, and sloped writing pads.

The most recent results have shown that sales decreased more than was expected for the anti-glare filters. As a result, the company may have a shortage of funds. Top management has therefore asked that all expenses be reduced 10% to compensate for these reduced sales. Summary budget information is as follows.

Direct materials	$240,000
Direct labor	110,000
Insurance	50,000
Depreciation	90,000
Machine repairs	30,000
Sales salaries	50,000
Office salaries	80,000
Factory salaries (indirect labor)	50,000
Total	$700,000

Instructions

Using the information above, answer the following questions.

a. What are the implications of reducing each of the costs? For example, if the company reduces direct materials costs, it may have to do so by purchasing lower-quality materials. This may affect sales in the long run.

b. Based on your analysis in (a), what do you think is the best way to obtain the $70,000 in cost savings requested? Be specific. Are there any costs that cannot or should not be reduced? Why?

Real-World Focus

CT22.3 Information regarding many approaches to budgeting can be found online. The following activity investigates the merits of "zero-based" budgeting, as discussed by Michael LaFaive, Director of Fiscal Policy of the **Mackinac Center for Public Policy**.

Instructions

Read the article at the Mackinac website and answer the following questions.

a. How does zero-based budgeting differ from standard budgeting procedures?

b. What are some potential advantages of zero-based budgeting?

c. What are some potential disadvantages of zero-based budgeting?

d. How often do departments in Oklahoma undergo zero-based budgeting?

Communication Activity

CT22.4 **Service** In order to better serve their rural patients, Drs. Joe and Rick Parcells (brothers) began giving safety seminars. Especially popular were their "emergency-preparedness" talks given to farmers. Many people asked whether the "kit" of materials the doctors recommended for common farm emergencies was commercially available.

After checking with several suppliers, the doctors realized that no other company offered the supplies they recommended in their seminars, packaged in the way they described. Their wives, Megan and Sue, agreed to make a test package by ordering supplies from various medical supply companies and assembling them into a "kit" that could be sold at the seminars. When these kits proved a runaway success, the sisters-in-law decided to market them. At the advice of their accountant, they organized this venture as a separate company, called Life Protection Products (LPP), with Megan Parcells as CEO and Sue Parcells as Secretary-Treasurer.

LPP soon started receiving requests for the kits from all over the country, as word spread about their availability. Even without advertising, LPP was able to sell its full inventory every month. However, the company was becoming financially strained. Megan and Sue had about $100,000 in savings, and they invested about half that amount initially. They believed that this venture would allow them to make money. However, at the present time, only about $30,000 of the cash remains, and the company is constantly short of cash.

Megan has come to you for advice. She does not understand why the company is having cash flow problems. She and Sue have not even been withdrawing salaries. However, they have rented a local building and have hired two more full-time workers to help them cope with the increasing demand. They do not think they could handle the demand without this additional help.

Megan is also worried that the cash problems mean that the company may not be able to support itself. She has prepared the cash budget shown below. All seminar customers pay for their products in full at the time of purchase. In addition, several large companies have ordered the kits for use by employees who work in remote sites. They have requested credit terms and have been allowed to pay in the month following the sale. These large purchasers amount to about 25% of the sales at the present time. LPP purchases the materials for the kits about 2 months ahead of time. Megan and Sue are considering slowing the growth of the company by simply purchasing less materials, which will mean selling fewer kits.

The workers are paid weekly. Megan and Sue need about $15,000 cash on hand at the beginning of the month to pay for purchases of raw materials. Right now they have been using cash from their savings, but as noted, only $30,000 is left.

Life Protection Products
Cash Budget
For the Quarter Ending June 30, 2022

	April	May	June
Cash balance, beginning	$15,000	$15,000	$15,000
Cash received			
From prior month sales	5,000	7,500	12,500
From current sales	15,000	22,500	37,500
Total cash on hand	35,000	45,000	65,000
Cash payments			
To employees	3,000	3,000	3,000
For products	25,000	35,000	45,000
Miscellaneous expenses	5,000	6,000	7,000
Postage	1,000	1,000	1,000
Total cash payments	34,000	45,000	56,000
Cash balance	$ 1,000	$ 0	$ 9,000
Borrow from savings	$14,000	$15,000	$ 1,000
Borrow from bank?	$ 0	$ 0	$ 5,000

Instructions

Write a response to Megan Parcells. Explain why LPP is short of cash. Will this company be able to support itself? Explain your answer. Make any recommendations you deem appropriate.

Ethics Case

CT22.5 You are an accountant in the budgetary, projections, and special projects department of Fernetti Conductor, Inc., a large manufacturing company. The president, Richard Brown, asks you on very short notice to prepare some sales and income projections covering the next 2 years of the company's much heralded new product lines. He wants these projections for a series of speeches he is making while on a 2-week trip to eight East Coast brokerage firms. The president hopes to bolster Fernetti's stock sales and price.

You work 23 hours in 2 days to compile the projections, hand-deliver them to the president, and are swiftly but graciously thanked as he departs. A week later, you find time to go over some of your computations and discover a miscalculation that makes the projections grossly overstated. You quickly inquire about the president's itinerary and learn that he has made half of his speeches and has half yet to make. You are in a quandary as to what to do.

Instructions

a. What are the consequences of telling the president of your gross miscalculations?

b. What are the consequences of not telling the president of your gross miscalculations?

c. What are the ethical considerations to you and the president in this situation?

All About You

CT22.6 In order to get your personal finances under control, you need to prepare a personal budget. Assume that you have compiled the following information regarding your expected cash flows for a typical month.

Rent payment	$ 500	Miscellaneous costs	$210
Interest income	50	Savings	50
Income tax withheld	300	Eating out	150
Electricity bill	85	Telephone and Internet costs	125
Groceries	100	Student loan payments	375
Wages earned	2,500	Entertainment costs	250
Insurance	100	Transportation costs	150

Instructions

Using the information above, prepare a personal budget. In preparing this budget, use the format included in the "Steps to Creating a Household Budget" article available at **the balance**'s website (go to the site and do a search for the article). Just skip any unused line items.

Considering Your Costs and Benefits

CT22.7 You might hear people say that they "need to learn to live within a budget." The funny thing is that most people who say this haven't actually prepared a personal budget, nor do they intend to. Instead, what they are referring to is a vaguely defined, poorly specified collection of rough ideas of how much they should spend on various aspects of their lives. However, you can't live within or even outside of something that doesn't exist. With that in mind, let's take a look at one aspect of personal-budget templates.

Many personal-budget worksheet templates that are provided for college students treat student loans as an income source. See, for example, the template included in the "Steps to Creating a Household Budget" article available at **the balance**'s website. Based on your knowledge of accounting, is this correct?

YES: Student loans provide a source of cash, which can be used to pay costs. As the saying goes, "It all spends the same." Therefore, student loans are income.

NO: Student loans must eventually be repaid; therefore, they are not income. As the name indicates, they are loans.

Instructions

Write a response indicating your position regarding this situation. Provide support for your view.

CHAPTER 23

Budgetary Control and Responsibility Accounting

Chapter Preview

In Chapter 22, we discussed the use of budgets for planning. We now consider how budgets are used by management to control operations. In the following Feature Story on the **Tribeca Grand Hotel**, we see that management uses the budget to adapt to the business environment. This chapter focuses on two aspects of management control: (1) budgetary control and (2) responsibility accounting.

Feature Story

Pumpkin Madeleines and a Movie

Perhaps no place in the world has a wider variety of distinctive, high-end accommodations than New York City. It's tough to set yourself apart in the Big Apple, but unique is what the **Tribeca Grand Hotel** is all about.

When you walk through the doors of this triangular-shaped building, nestled in one of Manhattan's most affluent neighborhoods, you immediately encounter a striking eight-story atrium. Although the hotel was completely renovated, it still maintains its funky mid-century charm. Just consider the always hip Church Bar. Besides serving up cocktails until 2 a.m., Church's also provides food. These are not the run-of-the-mill, chain hotel, borderline edibles. Church's chef is famous for tantalizing delectables such as duck rillettes, sea salt baked branzino, housemade pappardelle, and pumpkin madeleines.

Another thing that really sets the Tribeca Grand apart is its private screening room. As a guest, you can enjoy plush leather seating, state-of-the-art projection, and digital surround sound, all while viewing a cult classic from the hotel's film series. In fact, on Sundays, free screenings are available to guests and non-guests alike on a first-come-first-served basis.

To attract and satisfy a discerning clientele, the Tribeca Grand's management incurs higher and more unpredictable costs than those of a standard hotel. As fun as it might be to run a high-end hotel, management can't be cavalier about spending money. To maintain profitability, management closely monitors costs and revenues to make sure that they track with budgeted amounts. Further, because of unexpected fluctuations in demand for rooms (think hurricanes or bitterly cold winter weather), management must sometimes revise forecasts and budgets and adapt quickly. To evaluate performance and identify when changes need to be made, the budget needs to be flexible.

 Watch the *Tribeca Grand* video in WileyPLUS to learn more about real-world budgeting.

Chapter Outline

LEARNING OBJECTIVES

LO 1 Describe budgetary control and static budget reports.	• Budgetary control • Static budget reports	**DO IT! 1** Static Budget Reports
LO 2 Prepare flexible budget reports.	• Why flexible budgets? • Developing the flexible budget • Flexible budget—a case study • Flexible budget reports	**DO IT! 2** Flexible Budgets
LO 3 Apply responsibility accounting to cost and profit centers.	• Controllable vs. noncontrollable revenues and costs • Principles of performance evaluation • Responsibility reporting system • Types of responsibility centers	**DO IT! 3** Profit Center Responsibility Report
LO 4 Evaluate performance in investment centers.	• Return on investment (ROI) • Responsibility report • Judgmental factors in ROI • Improving ROI	**DO IT! 4** Performance Evaluation

Go to the Review and Practice section at the end of the chapter for a targeted summary and practice applications with solutions.
Visit WileyPLUS for additional tutorials and practice opportunities.

Budgetary Control and Static Budget Reports

LEARNING OBJECTIVE 1
Describe budgetary control and static budget reports.

Budgetary Control

One of management's responsibilities is to control company operations. Control consists of the steps taken by management to see that planned objectives are met. We now ask: How do budgets contribute to control of operations?

The use of budgets in controlling operations is known as **budgetary control**. Such control takes place by means of **budget reports** that compare actual results with planned objectives. The use of budget reports is based on the belief that planned objectives lose much of their potential value without some monitoring of progress along the way. Just as your professors give midterm exams to evaluate your progress, top management requires periodic reports on the progress of department managers toward their planned objectives.

Budget reports provide management with feedback on operations. The feedback for a crucial objective, such as having enough cash on hand to pay bills, may be made daily. For other objectives, such as meeting budgeted annual sales and operating expenses, monthly budget reports may suffice. Budget reports are prepared as frequently as needed. From these reports, management analyzes any differences between actual and planned results and determines their causes. Management then takes corrective action, or it decides to modify future plans. Budgetary control involves the activities shown in **Illustration 23.1**.

ILLUSTRATION 23.1

Budgetary control activities

Budgetary control works best when a company has a formalized reporting system. The reporting system does the following:

1. Identifies the name of the budget report, such as the sales budget or the manufacturing overhead budget.
2. States the frequency of the report, such as weekly or monthly.
3. Specifies the purpose of the report.
4. Indicates the primary recipient(s) of the report.

Illustration 23.2 provides a partial budgetary control system for a manufacturing company. Note the frequency of the reports and their emphasis on control. For example, there is a daily report on scrap and a weekly report on labor.

ILLUSTRATION 23.2 Budgetary control reporting system

Name of Report	Frequency	Purpose	Primary Recipient(s)
Sales	Weekly	Determine whether sales goals are met	Top management and sales manager
Labor	Weekly	Control direct and indirect labor costs	Vice president of production and production department managers
Scrap	Daily	Determine efficient use of materials	Production manager
Departmental overhead costs	Monthly	Control overhead costs	Department manager
Selling expenses	Monthly	Control selling expenses	Sales manager
Income statement	Monthly and quarterly	Determine whether income goals are met	Top management

Static Budget Reports

You learned in Chapter 22 that the master budget formalizes management's planned objectives for the coming year. When used in budgetary control, each budget included in the master budget is considered to be static. A **static budget** is a projection of budget data **at a single level of activity before actual activity occurs**. These budgets do not consider data for different levels of activity. As a result, companies always compare actual results with budget data at the activity level that was used in developing the master budget.

Examples

To illustrate the role of a static budget in budgetary control, we will use selected data prepared for Hayes Company in Chapter 22. **Illustration 23.3** provides budget and actual sales data for the Rightride product in the first and second quarters of 2022.

ILLUSTRATION 23.3
Budget and actual sales data

Sales	First Quarter	Second Quarter	Total
Budgeted	$180,000	$210,000	$390,000
Actual	179,000	199,500	378,500
Difference	$ 1,000	$ 10,500	$ 11,500

ALTERNATIVE TERMINOLOGY

The difference between budget and actual is sometimes called a *budget variance*.

The sales budget report for Hayes' first quarter is shown in **Illustration 23.4**. The rightmost column reports the difference between the budgeted and actual amounts (see **Alternative Terminology**).

ILLUSTRATION 23.4
Sales budget report—first quarter

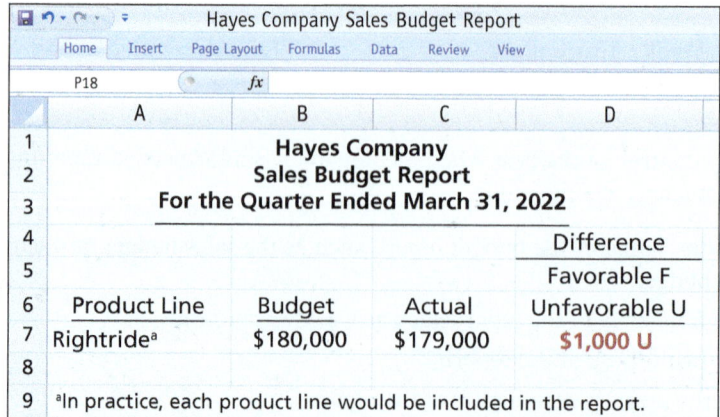

The report shows that sales are $1,000 under budget—an unfavorable result. This difference is less than 1% of budgeted sales ($1,000 ÷ $180,000 = .0056). Top management's reaction to differences is often influenced by the materiality (significance) of the difference. Since the difference of $1,000 is immaterial in this case, we assume that Hayes management takes no specific corrective action.

Illustration 23.5 shows the sales budget report for the second quarter. It contains one new feature: cumulative year-to-date information. This report indicates that sales for the second quarter are $10,500 below budget. This is 5% of budgeted sales ($10,500 ÷ $210,000). Top management may now conclude that the difference between budgeted and actual sales requires investigation.

ILLUSTRATION 23.5 Sales budget report—second quarter

Hayes Company Sales Budget Report
For the Quarter Ended June 30, 2022

Product Line	Second Quarter			Year-to-Date		
	Budget	Actual	Difference Favorable F Unfavorable U	Budget	Actual	Difference Favorable F Unfavorable U
Rightride	$210,000	$199,500	$10,500 U	$390,000	$378,500	$11,500 U

Management's analysis should start by asking the sales manager the cause(s) of the shortfall. Managers should consider the need for corrective action. For example, management may attempt to increase sales by offering sales incentives to customers or by increasing the advertising of Rightrides. Or, if management concludes that a downturn in the economy is responsible for the lower sales, it may modify planned sales and profit goals for the remainder of the year.

Uses and Limitations

From these examples, you can see that a master sales budget is useful in evaluating the performance of a sales manager. It is now necessary to ask: Is the master budget appropriate for evaluating a manager's performance in controlling costs? Recall that in a static budget, data are not modified or adjusted, regardless of changes in activity. It follows, then, that a static budget is appropriate in evaluating a manager's effectiveness in controlling costs when:

1. The actual level of activity closely approximates the master budget activity level, and/or
2. The behavior of the costs in response to changes in activity is fixed.

A static budget report is, therefore, appropriate for **fixed manufacturing costs** and for **fixed selling and administrative expenses**. But, as you will see shortly, static budget reports may not be a proper basis for evaluating a manager's performance in controlling variable costs.

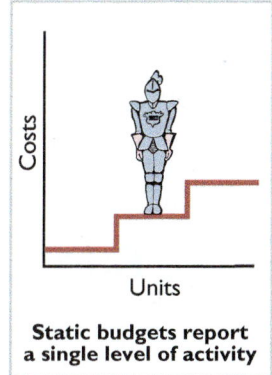

Static budgets report a single level of activity

DO IT! 1 | Static Budget Reports

Lawler Company expects to produce 5,000 units of product CV93 during the current month. Budgeted variable manufacturing costs per unit are direct materials $6, direct labor $15, and overhead $24. Monthly budgeted fixed manufacturing overhead costs are $10,000 for depreciation and $5,000 for supervision.

In the current month, Lawler actually produced 5,500 units and incurred the following costs: direct materials $33,900, direct labor $74,200, variable overhead $120,500, depreciation $10,000, and supervision $5,000.

Prepare a static budget report. (*Hint:* The Budget column is based on estimated production of 5,000 units while the Actual column is the actual costs incurred during the period.) Were costs controlled? Discuss limitations of this budget.

ACTION PLAN
- Classify each cost as variable or fixed.
- Determine the difference as favorable or unfavorable.
- Determine the difference in total variable costs, total fixed costs, and total costs.

Solution

Lawler Company

	Budget	Actual	Difference Favorable - F Unfavorable - U	
Production in units	5,000	5,500		
Variable costs				
Direct materials ($6)	$ 30,000	$ 33,900	$3,900	U
Direct labor ($15)	75,000	74,200	800	F
Overhead ($24)	120,000	120,500	500	U
Total variable costs	225,000	228,600	3,600	U
Fixed costs				
Depreciation	10,000	10,000	0	
Supervision	5,000	5,000	0	
Total fixed costs	15,000	15,000	0	
Total costs	$240,000	$243,600	$3,600	U

The static budget indicates that actual variable costs exceeded budgeted amounts by $3,600. Fixed costs were exactly as budgeted. The static budget gives the impression that the company did not control its variable costs. However, the static budget does not give consideration to the fact that the company produced 500 more units than planned. As a result, the static budget is not a good tool to evaluate variable costs. It is, however, a good tool to evaluate fixed costs as those should not vary with changes in production volume.

Related exercise material: **BE23.1, BE23.2, DO IT! 23.1, E23.1, and E23.2.**

Flexible Budget Reports

LEARNING OBJECTIVE 2
Prepare flexible budget reports.

Flexible budgets are static budgets at different activity levels

In contrast to a static budget, which is based on one level of activity, a **flexible budget** projects budget data for various levels of activity. In essence, **the flexible budget is a series of static budgets at different levels of activity**. The flexible budget recognizes that the budgetary process is more useful if it is adaptable to changed operating conditions.

Flexible budgets can be prepared for each of the types of budgets included in the master budget. For example, **Marriott Hotels** can budget revenues and net income on the basis of 60%, 80%, and 100% of room occupancy. Similarly, **American Van Lines** can budget its operating expenses on the basis of various levels of truck-miles driven. **Duke Energy** can budget revenue and net income on the basis of estimated billions of kwh (kilowatt hours) of residential, commercial, and industrial electricity generated. In the following pages, we will illustrate a flexible budget for manufacturing overhead.

Why Flexible Budgets?

Assume that you are the manager in charge of manufacturing overhead in the Assembly Department of Barton Robotics. In preparing the manufacturing overhead budget for 2022, you prepare the static budget shown in **Illustration 23.6** based on a production volume of 10,000 units of robotic controls (see **Helpful Hint**).

HELPFUL HINT
The master budget described in Chapter 22 is based on a static budget.

ILLUSTRATION 23.6
Static overhead budget

Barton Robotics
Manufacturing Overhead Budget (Static)
Assembly Department
For the Year Ended December 31, 2022

Budgeted production in units (robotic controls)	10,000
Budgeted costs	
Indirect materials	$ 250,000
Indirect labor	260,000
Utilities	190,000
Depreciation	280,000
Property taxes	70,000
Supervision	50,000
	$1,100,000

Fortunately for the company, the demand for robotic controls has increased, and Barton produces and sells 12,000 units during the year rather than 10,000. You are elated! Increased sales means increased profitability, which should mean a bonus or a raise for you and the employees in your department. Unfortunately, a comparison of Assembly Department actual and budgeted costs has put you on the spot. **Illustration 23.7** shows the budget report.

ILLUSTRATION 23.7
Overhead static budget report

Barton Robotics
Manufacturing Overhead Static Budget Report
For the Year Ended December 31, 2022

	Budget	Actual	Difference Favorable - F Unfavorable - U	
Production in units	10,000	12,000		
Costs				
Indirect materials	$ 250,000	$ 295,000	$ 45,000	U
Indirect labor	260,000	312,000	52,000	U
Utilities	190,000	225,000	35,000	U
Depreciation	280,000	280,000	0	
Property taxes	70,000	70,000	0	
Supervision	50,000	50,000	0	
	$1,100,000	$1,232,000	$132,000	U

This comparison uses budgeted cost data based on the original activity level (10,000 robotic controls). It indicates that the costs incurred by the Assembly Department are significantly **over budget** for three of the six overhead costs. There is a total unfavorable difference of $132,000, which is 12% over budget ($132,000 ÷ $1,100,000). Your supervisor is very unhappy. Instead of sharing in the company's success, you may find yourself looking for another job. What went wrong?

HELPFUL HINT

A static budget is not useful for performance evaluation if a company has substantial variable costs.

When you calm down and carefully examine the manufacturing overhead budget, you identify the problem: The budget data are not relevant! At the time the budget was developed, the company anticipated that only 10,000 units would be produced. Instead, 12,000 units were actually produced. Comparing actual costs incurred at a production level of 12,000 units with budgeted variable costs at an expected production level of 10,000 units is meaningless (see **Helpful Hint**). As production increases, the budget allowances for variable costs should increase proportionately. The variable costs in this example are indirect materials, indirect labor, and utilities.

Analyzing the budget data for these costs at 10,000 units, you arrive at the per unit results shown in **Illustration 23.8**.

ILLUSTRATION 23.8

Variable costs per unit

Item	Total Cost	Per Unit
Indirect materials	$250,000	$25
Indirect labor	260,000	26
Utilities	190,000	19
	$700,000	$70

Using these per unit costs, **Illustration 23.9** calculates the budgeted variable costs at 12,000 units.

ILLUSTRATION 23.9

Budgeted variable costs, 12,000 units

Item	Computation	Total
Indirect materials	$25 × 12,000	$300,000
Indirect labor	26 × 12,000	312,000
Utilities	19 × 12,000	228,000
		$840,000

Because fixed costs do not change in total as activity changes, the budgeted amounts for these costs remain the same. **Illustration 23.10** shows the budget report based on the flexible budget for **12,000 units** of production. (Compare this with Illustration 23.7.)

ILLUSTRATION 23.10

Overhead flexible budget report

Barton Robotics
Manufacturing Overhead Flexible Budget Report
For the Year Ended December 31, 2022

	Budget	Actual	Difference Favorable - F Unfavorable - U	
Production in units	12,000	12,000		
Variable costs				
Indirect materials ($25)	$ 300,000	$ 295,000	$5,000	F
Indirect labor ($26)	312,000	312,000	0	
Utilities ($19)	228,000	225,000	3,000	F
Total variable costs	840,000	832,000	8,000	F
Fixed costs				
Depreciation	280,000	280,000	0	
Property taxes	70,000	70,000	0	
Supervision	50,000	50,000	0	
Total fixed costs	400,000	400,000	0	
Total costs	$1,240,000	$1,232,000	$8,000	F

This flexible budget report indicates that the Assembly Department's costs are **under budget**—a favorable difference. Instead of worrying about being fired, you may be in line for a bonus or a raise after all! As this analysis shows, the only appropriate comparison is between actual costs at 12,000 units of production and budgeted costs at 12,000 units. Flexible budget reports provide this comparison (see **Decision Tools**).

> **Decision Tools**
> The flexible budget helps management evaluate whether cost changes resulting from different production volumes are reasonable.

Developing the Flexible Budget

The flexible budget uses the master budget as its basis. To develop the flexible budget, management uses the following steps.

1. Identify the activity index and the relevant range of activity.
2. Identify the variable costs, and determine the budgeted variable cost per unit of activity for each cost.
3. Identify the fixed costs, and determine the budgeted amount for each cost.
4. Prepare the budget for selected increments of activity within the relevant range.

The activity index chosen should significantly influence the costs being budgeted. For manufacturing overhead costs, for example, the activity index is usually the same as the index used in developing the predetermined overhead rate—that is, direct labor hours or machine hours. For selling and administrative expenses, the activity index usually is sales or net sales.

The choice of the increment of activity is largely a matter of judgment. For example, if the relevant range is 8,000 to 12,000 direct labor hours, increments of 1,000 hours may be selected. The flexible budget is then prepared for each increment within the relevant range.

Service Company Insight   NBCUniversal

Just What the Doctor Ordered?

Fox Broadcasting Company/Album/Newscom

Nobody is immune from the effects of declining revenues—not even movie stars. When the number of viewers of the television show "House," a medical drama, declined by almost 20%, **Fox Broadcasting** said it wanted to cut the license fee that it paid to **NBCUniversal** by 20%. What would NBCUniversal do in response? It might cut the size of the show's cast, which would reduce the payroll costs associated with the show. Or, it could reduce the number of episodes that take advantage of the full cast. Alternatively, it might threaten to quit providing the show to Fox altogether and instead present the show on its own NBC-affiliated channels.

Source: Sam Schechner, "Media Business Shorts: NBCU, Fox Taking Scalpel to 'House,'" *Wall Street Journal Online* (April 17, 2011).

Explain how the use of flexible budgets might help to identify the best solution to this problem. (Go to WileyPLUS for this answer and additional questions.)

Flexible Budget—A Case Study

To illustrate the flexible budget, we use Fox Company. Fox's management uses a **flexible budget for monthly comparisons** of actual and budgeted manufacturing overhead costs of the Finishing Department. The master budget for the year ending December 31, 2022, shows expected **annual** operating capacity of 120,000 direct labor hours and the overhead costs shown in **Illustration 23.11**.

ILLUSTRATION 23.11

Master budget data

Variable Costs		Fixed Costs	
Indirect materials	$180,000	Depreciation	$180,000
Indirect labor	240,000	Supervision	120,000
Utilities	60,000	Property taxes	60,000
Total	$480,000	Total	$360,000

The four steps for developing the flexible budget are applied as follows.

Step 1 **Identify the activity index and the relevant range of activity.** The activity index is direct labor hours. The relevant range is 8,000–12,000 direct labor hours per **month**.

Step 2 **Identify the variable costs, and determine the budgeted variable cost per unit of activity for each cost.** A cost is variable if total costs vary directly as a result of a change in the activity index, which is direct labor in this case. In this example, indirect materials, indirect labor, and utilities are variable costs. The variable cost per unit is found by dividing each total budgeted cost by the direct labor hours used in preparing the annual master budget (120,000 hours). **Illustration 23.12** shows the computations for Fox Company.

ILLUSTRATION 23.12
Computation of variable cost per direct labor hour

Variable Costs	Computation	Variable Cost per Direct Labor Hour
Indirect materials	$180,000 ÷ 120,000	$1.50
Indirect labor	$240,000 ÷ 120,000	2.00
Utilities	$ 60,000 ÷ 120,000	0.50
Total		$4.00

Step 3 **Identify the fixed costs, and determine the budgeted amount for each cost.** A cost is fixed if the total cost does not vary as a result of changes in the activity index. In this example, depreciation, supervision, and property taxes are fixed costs. Since Fox desires **monthly budget data**, it divides each annual budgeted cost by 12 to find the monthly amounts. Therefore, the monthly budgeted fixed costs are depreciation $15,000, supervision $10,000, and property taxes $5,000.

Step 4 **Prepare the budget for selected increments of activity within the relevant range.** Management prepares the budget in increments of 1,000 direct labor hours. Illustration 23.13 shows Fox's flexible budget.

ILLUSTRATION 23.13
Monthly overhead flexible budget

Fox Company
Monthly Manufacturing Overhead Flexible Budget
Finishing Department
For Months During the Year 2022

Activity level					
Direct labor hours	8,000	9,000	10,000	11,000	12,000
Variable costs					
Indirect materials ($1.50)[a]	$12,000[b]	$13,500	$15,000	$16,500	$18,000
Indirect labor ($2.00)[a]	16,000[c]	18,000	20,000	22,000	24,000
Utilities ($0.50)[a]	4,000[d]	4,500	5,000	5,500	6,000
Total variable costs	32,000	36,000	40,000	44,000	48,000
Fixed costs					
Depreciation	15,000	15,000	15,000	15,000	15,000
Supervision	10,000	10,000	10,000	10,000	10,000
Property taxes	5,000	5,000	5,000	5,000	5,000
Total fixed costs	30,000	30,000	30,000	30,000	30,000
Total costs	$62,000	$66,000	$70,000	$74,000	$78,000

[a]Cost per direct labor hour; [b]8,000 x $1.50; [c]8,000 x $2.00; [d]8,000 x $0.50

Fox uses the cost equation shown in **Illustration 23.14** to determine total budgeted costs at any level of activity.

$$\text{Fixed Costs} + \text{Variable Costs*} = \text{Total Budgeted Costs}$$

*Total variable cost per unit of activity × Activity level.

ILLUSTRATION 23.14

Cost equation for total budgeted costs

For Fox, fixed costs are $30,000 per month, and total variable cost per direct labor hour is $4 ($1.50 + $2.00 + $0.50). At 9,000 direct labor hours, total budgeted costs are $66,000 [$30,000 + ($4 × 9,000)]. At 8,622 direct labor hours, total budgeted costs are $64,488 [$30,000 + ($4 × 8,622)] (see **Helpful Hint**).

Total budgeted costs can also be shown graphically, as in **Illustration 23.15**. In the graph, the horizontal axis represents the activity index, and costs are indicated on the vertical axis. The graph highlights two activity levels (10,000 and 12,000). As shown, total budgeted costs at these activity levels are $70,000 [$30,000 + ($4 × 10,000)] and $78,000 [$30,000 + ($4 × 12,000)], respectively.

HELPFUL HINT

Using the data given for Fox, the amount of total costs to be budgeted for 10,600 direct labor hours would be $30,000 fixed + $42,400 variable (10,600 × $4) = $72,400 total.

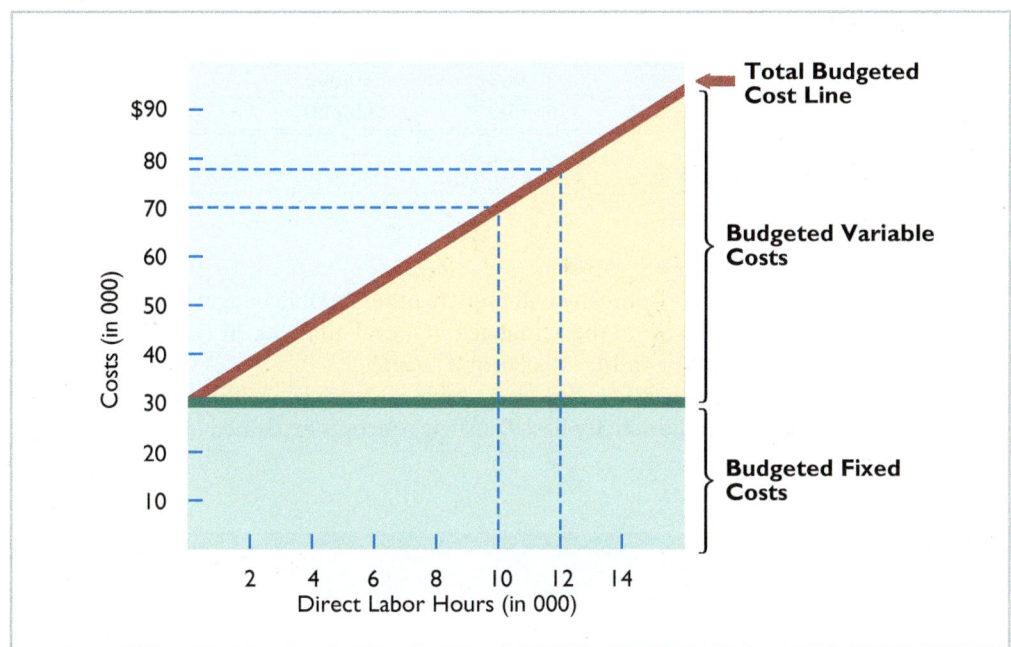

ILLUSTRATION 23.15

Graphic flexible budget data highlighting 10,000 and 12,000 activity levels

Flexible Budget Reports

Flexible budget reports are another type of internal report. The flexible budget report consists of two sections: (1) production data for a selected activity index, such as direct labor hours, and (2) cost data for variable and fixed costs. The report provides a basis for evaluating a manager's performance in two areas: production control and cost control. Flexible budget reports are widely used in production and service departments.

Illustration 23.16 shows a flexible budget report for the Finishing Department of Fox Company for the month of January. In this month, 9,000 hours are worked. The budget data are therefore based on the flexible budget for 9,000 hours in Illustration 23.13. The actual cost data are assumed.

How appropriate is this report in evaluating the Finishing Department manager's performance in controlling overhead costs? The report clearly provides a reliable basis. Both actual and budget costs are based on the activity level worked during January. Since variable costs generally are incurred directly by the department, the difference between the budget allowance for those hours and the actual costs is the responsibility of the department manager.

ILLUSTRATION 23.16
Overhead flexible budget report

Fox Company
Manufacturing Overhead Flexible Budget Report
Finishing Department
For the Month Ended January 31, 2022

	Budget at 9,000 DLH	Actual costs at 9,000 DLH	Difference Favorable - F Unfavorable - U	
Direct labor hours (DLH)				
Variable costs				
Indirect materials ($1.50)ᵃ	$13,500	$14,000	$ 500	U
Indirect labor ($2.00)ᵃ	18,000	17,000	1,000	F
Utilities ($0.50)ᵃ	4,500	4,600	100	U
Total variable costs	36,000	35,600	400	F
Fixed costs				
Depreciation	15,000	15,000	0	
Supervision	10,000	10,000	0	
Property taxes	5,000	5,000	0	
Total fixed costs	30,000	30,000	0	
Total costs	$66,000	$65,600	$ 400	F

ᵃCost per direct labor hour

In subsequent months, Fox Company will prepare other flexible budget reports. For each month, the budget data are based on the actual activity level attained. In February that level may be 11,000 direct labor hours, in July 10,000, and so on.

Note that this flexible budget is based on a single cost driver. A more accurate budget often can be developed using the activity-based costing concepts explained in Chapter 17.

Service Company Insight — San Diego Zoo

Budgets and the Exotic Newcastle Disease

Eric Isselée/iStockphoto

Exotic Newcastle Disease, one of the most infectious bird diseases in the world, kills so swiftly that many victims die before any symptoms appear. When it broke out in Southern California, it could have spelled disaster for the **San Diego Zoo**. "We have one of the most valuable collections of birds in the world, if not *the* most valuable," says Paula Brock, CFO of the Zoological Society of San Diego, which operates the zoo.

Bird exhibits were closed to the public for several months (the disease, which is harmless to humans, can be carried on clothes and shoes). The tires of arriving delivery trucks were sanitized, as were the shoes of anyone visiting the zoo's nonpublic areas. Zookeeper uniforms had to be changed and cleaned daily. And ultimately, the zoo, with $150 million in revenues, spent almost half a million dollars on quarantine measures.

It worked: No birds got sick. Better yet, the damage to the rest of the zoo's budget was minimized by another protective measure: the monthly budget reforecast. "When we get a hit like this, we still have to find a way to make our bottom line," says Brock. Thanks to a new planning process Brock had introduced a year earlier, the zoo's scientists were able to raise the financial alarm as they redirected resources to ward off the disease. "Because we had timely awareness," she says, "we were able to make adjustments to weather the storm."

Source: Tim Reason, "Budgeting in the Real World," *CFO Magazine* (July 12, 2005), www.cfodirect.com/cfopublic.nsf/vContentPrint/649A82C8FF8AB06B85257037004 (accessed July 2005).

What is the major benefit of tying a budget to the overall goals of the company? (Go to WileyPLUS for this answer and additional questions.)

DO IT! 2 | Flexible Budgets

In Strassel Company's flexible budget graph, the fixed cost line and the total budgeted cost line intersect the vertical axis at $36,000. The total budgeted cost line is $186,000 at an activity level of 50,000 direct labor hours. Compute total budgeted costs at 30,000 direct labor hours.

ACTION PLAN
- Apply the formula: Fixed costs + Variable costs (Total variable cost per unit × Activity level) = Total budgeted costs.

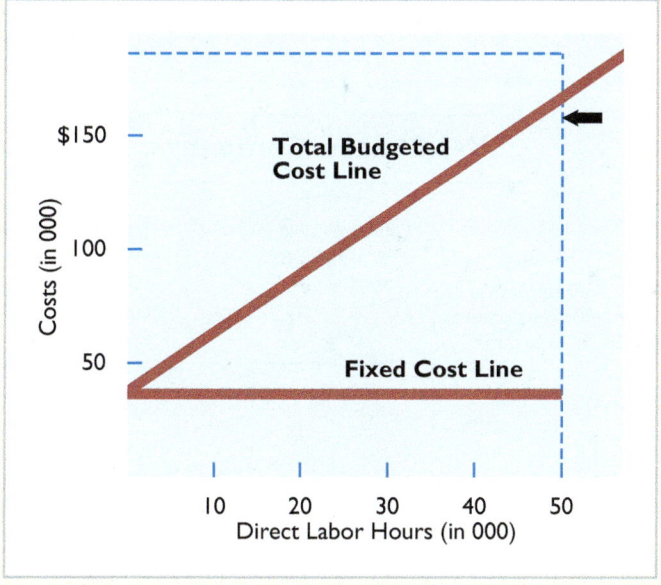

Solution

Using the graph, fixed costs are $36,000, and variable costs are $3 per direct labor hour [($186,000 − $36,000) ÷ 50,000]. Thus, at 30,000 direct labor hours, total budgeted costs are $126,000 [$36,000 + ($3 × 30,000)].

Related exercise material: **BE23.4, DO IT! 23.2, E23.3, and E23.5.**

Responsibility Accounting and Responsibility Centers

LEARNING OBJECTIVE 3
Apply responsibility accounting to cost and profit centers.

Like budgeting, responsibility accounting is an important part of management accounting. **Responsibility accounting** involves identifying and reporting costs (and revenues, where relevant) on the basis of the manager who has the authority to make the day-to-day decisions about the items. Under responsibility accounting, a manager's performance is evaluated on matters directly under that manager's control. Responsibility accounting can be used at every level of management in which the following conditions exist.

1. Costs and revenues can be directly associated with the specific level of management responsibility.

2. The costs and revenues can be controlled by employees at the level of responsibility with which they are associated.
3. Budget data can be developed for evaluating the manager's effectiveness in controlling the costs and revenues.

Illustration 23.17 depicts levels of responsibility for controlling costs.

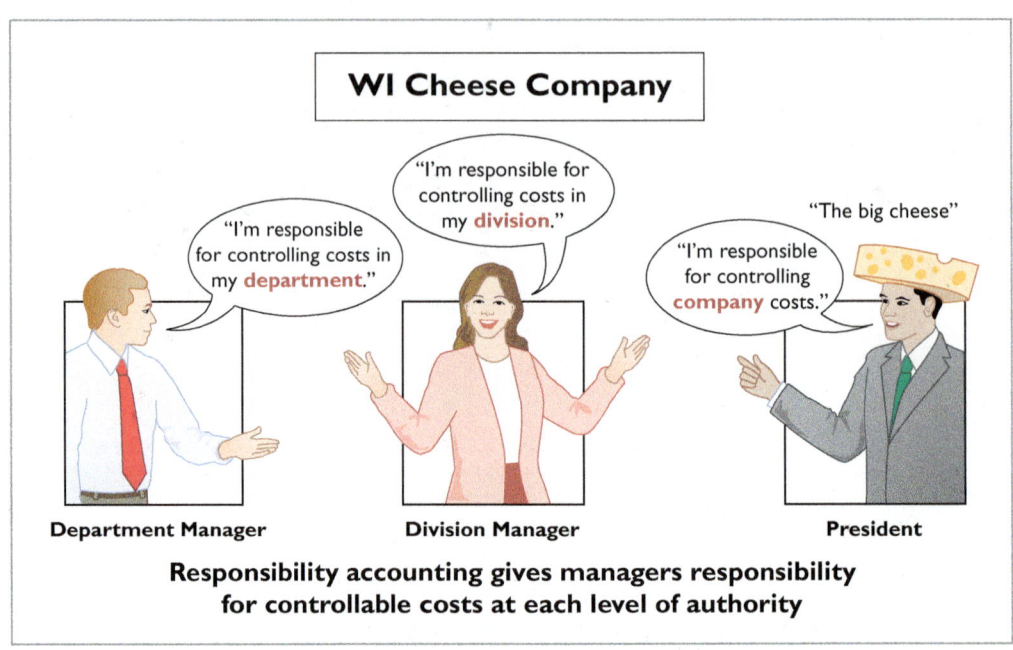

ILLUSTRATION 23.17

Responsibility for controllable costs at varying levels of management

> **HELPFUL HINT**
>
> All companies use responsibility accounting. Without some form of responsibility accounting, there would be chaos in discharging management's control function.

Under responsibility accounting, any individual who controls a specified set of activities can be a responsibility center. Thus, responsibility accounting may extend from the lowest level of control to the top strata of management. Once responsibility is established, the company first measures and reports the effectiveness of the individual's performance for the specified activity. It then reports that measure upward throughout the organization (see **Helpful Hint**).

Responsibility accounting is especially valuable in a decentralized company. **Decentralization** means that the control of operations is delegated to many managers throughout the organization. The term **segment** (or **division**) is sometimes used to identify an area of responsibility in decentralized operations. Under responsibility accounting, companies prepare segment reports periodically, such as monthly, quarterly, and annually, to evaluate managers' performance.

Responsibility accounting is an essential part of any effective system of budgetary control. The reporting of costs and revenues under responsibility accounting differs from budgeting in two respects:

1. A distinction is made between controllable and noncontrollable items.
2. Performance reports either emphasize or include only items controllable by the individual manager.

Responsibility accounting applies to both profit and not-for-profit entities. For-profit entities seek to maximize net income. Not-for-profit entities wish to provide services as efficiently as possible.

Management Insight   Procter & Gamble

Khuong Hoang/iStockphoto

Competition versus Collaboration

Many compensation and promotion programs encourage competition among employees for pay raises. To get ahead, you have to perform better than your fellow employees. While this may encourage hard work, it does not foster collaboration, and it can lead to distrust and disloyalty. Such negative effects have led some companies to believe that cooperation and collaboration, not competition, are essential in order to succeed in today's work environment.

As a consequence, many companies explicitly include measures of collaboration in their performance measures. For example, **Procter & Gamble** measures collaboration in employees' annual performance reviews. At **Cisco Systems**, the assessment of an employee's teamwork can affect the annual bonus by as much as 20%. A recent concern is that employees have become swamped in a confusing array of collaboration tools from Box Inc., Slack Technologies, Microsoft, Alphabet, and Facebook. In response, companies are trying to simplify the collaboration process.

Sources: Carol Hymowitz, "Rewarding Competitors Over Collaboration No Longer Makes Sense," *Wall Street Journal* (February 13, 2006); and Jay Greene, "Beware Collaboration—Tool Overload," *Wall Street Journal* (March 12, 2017).

How might managers of separate divisions be able to reduce division costs through collaboration? (Go to WileyPLUS for this answer and additional questions.)

Controllable versus Noncontrollable Revenues and Costs

All costs and revenues are controllable at some level of responsibility within a company. This truth underscores the adage by the CEO of any organization that "the buck stops here" (see **Helpful Hint**). Under responsibility accounting, the critical issue is **whether the cost or revenue is controllable at the level of responsibility with which it is associated**. A cost over which a manager has control is called a **controllable cost**. From this definition, it follows that:

1. All costs are controllable by top management because of the broad range of its authority.
2. Fewer costs are controllable as one moves down to each lower level of managerial responsibility because of the manager's decreasing authority.

In general, **costs incurred directly by a level of responsibility are controllable at that level** (see **Helpful Hint**). In contrast, costs incurred indirectly and allocated to a responsibility level are **noncontrollable costs** at that level.

> **HELPFUL HINT**
> There are more, not fewer, controllable costs as you move to higher levels of management.

> **HELPFUL HINT**
> The longer the time span, the more likely that the cost becomes controllable.

Principles of Performance Evaluation

Performance evaluation is at the center of responsibility accounting. It is a management function that compares actual results with budget goals. It involves both behavioral and reporting principles.

Management by Exception

Management by exception means that top management's review of a budget report is focused either entirely or primarily on significant differences between actual results and planned objectives. This approach enables top management to focus on problem areas. For example, many companies now use online reporting systems for employees to file their travel and entertainment expense reports. In addition to cutting reporting time in half, the online system enables managers to quickly analyze variances from travel budgets. This cuts down on expense account "padding" such as spending too much on meals or falsifying documents for costs that were never actually incurred.

As noted above, under management by exception, top management does not investigate every difference. For this approach to be effective, there must be guidelines for identifying which differences to investigate. The usual criteria are materiality and controllability.

Materiality Without quantitative guidelines, management would have to investigate every budget difference regardless of the amount. Materiality is usually expressed as a percentage difference from budget. For example, management may set the percentage difference at 5% for important items and 10% for other items. Managers will investigate all differences either over or under budget by the specified percentage. Costs over budget warrant investigation to determine why they were not controlled. Likewise, costs under budget merit investigation to determine whether costs critical to profitability are being curtailed. For example, if maintenance costs are budgeted at $80,000 but only $40,000 is spent, major unexpected breakdowns in productive facilities may occur in the future. Alternatively, as discussed in Chapter 22, cost might be under budget due to budgetary slack.

Alternatively, a company may specify a single percentage difference from budget for all items and supplement this guideline with a minimum dollar limit. For example, the exception criteria may be stated at 5% of budget or more than $10,000.

Controllability of the Item Exception guidelines are more restrictive for controllable items than for items the manager cannot control. In fact, there may be no guidelines for non-controllable items. For example, a large unfavorable difference between actual and budgeted property tax expense may not be flagged for investigation because the only possible causes are an unexpected increase in the tax rate or in the assessed value of the property. An investigation into the difference would be useless: The manager cannot control either cause.

Behavioral Principles

The human factor is critical in evaluating performance. Behavioral principles include the following.

1. **Managers of responsibility centers should have direct input into the process of establishing budget goals of their area of responsibility.** Without such input, managers may view the goals as unrealistic or arbitrarily set by top management. Such views adversely affect the managers' motivation to meet the targeted objectives.
2. **The evaluation of performance should be based entirely on matters that are controllable by the manager being evaluated.** Criticism of a manager on matters outside his or her control reduces the effectiveness of the evaluation process. It leads to negative reactions by a manager and to doubts about the fairness of the company's evaluation policies.
3. **Top management should support the evaluation process.** As explained earlier, the evaluation process begins at the lowest level of responsibility and extends upward to the highest level of management. Managers quickly lose faith in the process when top management ignores, overrules, or bypasses established procedures for evaluating a manager's performance.
4. **The evaluation process must allow managers to respond to their evaluations.** Evaluation is not a one-way street. Managers should have the opportunity to defend their performance. Evaluation without feedback is both impersonal and ineffective.
5. **The evaluation should identify both good and poor performance.** Praise for good performance is a powerful motivating factor for a manager. This is especially true when a manager's compensation includes rewards for meeting budget goals.

Reporting Principles

Performance evaluation under responsibility accounting should be based on certain reporting principles. These principles pertain primarily to the internal reports that provide the basis for evaluating performance. Performance reports should:

1. Contain only data that are controllable by the manager of the responsibility center.
2. Provide accurate and reliable budget data to measure performance.
3. Highlight significant differences between actual results and budget goals.
4. Be tailor-made for the intended evaluation by ensuring only controllable costs are included.
5. Be prepared at reasonable time intervals.

In recent years, companies have come under increasing pressure from influential shareholder groups to do a better job of linking executive pay to corporate performance. For example, software maker **Siebel Systems** unveiled an incentive plan after lengthy discussions with the California Public Employees' Retirement System. One unique feature of the plan is that managers' targets will be publicly disclosed at the beginning of each year for investors to evaluate.

Management Insight Honda

Kyodo/©AP/Wide World Photos

Flexible Manufacturing Requires Flexible Accounting

Flexible budgeting is useful because it enables managers to evaluate performance in light of changing conditions. But the ability to react quickly to changing conditions is even more important. Among automobile manufacturing facilities in the U.S., few plants are more flexible than **Honda**.

The manufacturing facilities of some auto companies can make slight alterations to the features of a vehicle in response to changes in demand for particular features. But for most plants, to switch from production of one type of vehicle to a completely different one typically takes months and costs hundreds of millions of dollars. At the Honda plant, however, the switch takes minutes. For example, it takes about five minutes to install different hand-like parts on the robots so they can switch from making Civic compacts to the longer, taller CR-V crossover. This ability to adjust quickly to changing demand gave Honda a huge advantage when gas prices surged and demand for more fuel-efficient cars increased quickly.

Source: Kate Linebaugh, "Honda's Flexible Plants Provide Edge," *Wall Street Journal Online* (September 23, 2008).

What implications do these improvements in production capabilities have for management accounting information and performance evaluation within the organization? (Go to WileyPLUS for this answer and additional questions.)

Responsibility Reporting System

A **responsibility reporting system** involves the preparation of a report for each level of responsibility in the company's organization chart (see **Decision Tools**). To illustrate such a system, we use the partial organization chart and production departments of Francis Chair Company in **Illustration 23.18**.

The responsibility reporting system begins with the lowest level of responsibility for controlling costs and moves upward to each higher level. **Illustration 23.19** details the connections between levels.

A brief description of the four reports for Francis Chair is as follows.

> **Decision Tools**
> Responsibility reports help to hold individual managers accountable for the costs and revenues under their control.

1. **Report D** is typical of reports that go to department managers. Similar reports are prepared for the managers of the Assembly and Enameling Departments.
2. **Report C** is an example of reports that are sent to plant managers. It shows the costs of the Chicago plant that are controllable at the second level of responsibility. In addition, Report C shows summary data for each department that is controlled by the plant manager. Similar reports are prepared for the Detroit and St. Louis plant managers.
3. **Report B** illustrates the reports at the third level of responsibility. It shows the controllable costs of the vice president of production and summary data on the three assembly plants for which this officer is responsible. Similar reports are prepared for the vice presidents of sales and finance.
4. **Report A** is typical of reports that go to the top level of responsibility—the president. It shows the controllable costs and expenses of this office and summary data on the vice presidents that are accountable to the president.

A responsibility reporting system permits management by exception at each level of responsibility. And, each higher level of responsibility can obtain the detailed report for each lower level of responsibility. For example, the vice president of production in Francis Chair may request the Chicago plant manager's report because this plant is $5,300 over budget.

ILLUSTRATION 23.18 Partial organization chart

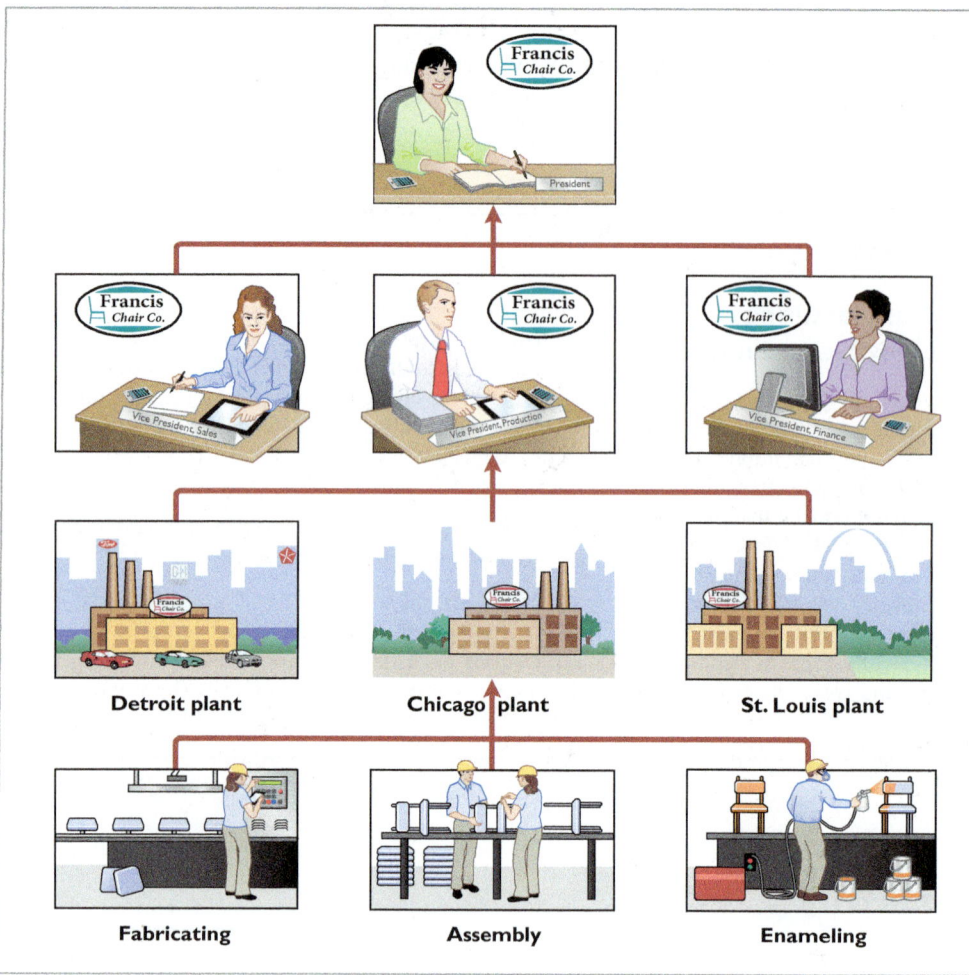

Report A
President sees summary data of vice presidents.

Report B
Vice president sees summary of controllable costs in his/her functional area.

Report C
Plant manager sees summary of controllable costs for each department in the plant.

Report D
Department manager sees controllable costs of his/her department.

This type of reporting system also permits comparative evaluations. In Illustration 23.19, the Chicago plant manager can easily rank the department managers' effectiveness in controlling manufacturing costs. Comparative rankings provide further incentive for a manager to control costs.

Types of Responsibility Centers

There are three basic types of responsibility centers: cost centers, profit centers, and investment centers. These classifications indicate the degree of responsibility the manager has for the performance of the center.

A **cost center** incurs costs (and expenses) but does not directly generate revenues. Managers of cost centers have the authority to incur costs. They are evaluated on their ability to control costs. **Cost centers are usually either production departments or service departments.** Production departments participate directly in making the product. Service departments provide only support services. In a **Ford Motor Company** automobile plant, the welding, painting, and assembling departments are production departments. Ford's maintenance, cafeteria, and human resources departments are service departments. All of them are cost centers.

A **profit center** incurs costs (and expenses) and also generates revenues. Managers of profit centers are judged on the profitability of their centers. Examples of profit centers include the individual departments of a retail store, such as clothing, furniture, and automotive products, and branch offices of banks (see **Helpful Hint**).

Like a profit center, an **investment center** incurs costs (and expenses) and generates revenues. In addition, an investment center has control over decisions regarding the assets

HELPFUL HINT
The jewelry department of **Macy's** department store is a profit center, while the makeup department of a movie studio is a cost center.

ILLUSTRATION 23.19 Responsibility reporting system

Report A
President sees summary data of vice presidents.

Report A

To President — Month: January

Controllable Costs:	Budget	Actual	Fav/Unfav	
President	$150,000	$151,500	$1,500	U
Vice Presidents:				
Sales	185,000	187,000	2,000	U
Production	1,179,000	1,186,300	7,300	U
Finance	100,000	101,000	1,000	U
Total	$1,614,000	$1,625,800	$11,800	U

Report B
Vice president sees summary of controllable costs in his/her functional area.

Report B

To Vice President Production — Month: January

Controllable Costs:	Budget	Actual	Fav/Unfav	
VP Production	$125,000	$126,000	$1,000	U
Assembly Plants:				
Detroit	420,000	418,000	2,000	F
Chicago	304,000	309,300	5,300	U
St. Louis	330,000	333,000	3,000	U
Total	$1,179,000	$1,186,300	$7,300	U

Report C
Plant manager sees summary of controllable costs for each department in the plant.

Report C

To Plant Manager-Chicago — Month: January

Controllable Costs:	Budget	Actual	Fav/Unfav	
Chicago Plant	$110,000	$113,000	$3,000	U
Departments:				
Fabricating	84,000	85,300	1,300	U
Enameling	62,000	64,000	2,000	U
Assembly	48,000	47,000	1,000	F
Total	$304,000	$309,300	$5,300	U

Report D
Department manager sees controllable costs of his/her department.

Report D

To Fabricating Dept. Manager — Month: January

Controllable Costs:	Budget	Actual	Fav/Unfav	
Direct Materials	$20,000	$20,500	$500	U
Direct Labor	40,000	41,000	1,000	U
Overhead	24,000	23,800	200	F
Total	$84,000	$85,300	$1,300	U

available for use. Investment center managers are evaluated on both the profitability of the center and the rate of return earned on the assets used. Investment centers are often associated with subsidiary companies. Utility **Duke Energy** has operating divisions such as electric utility, energy trading, and natural gas. Investment center managers control or significantly influence investment decisions related to such matters as plant expansion and entry into new market areas. **Illustration 23.20** depicts the three types of responsibility centers.

ILLUSTRATION 23.20 Types of responsibility centers

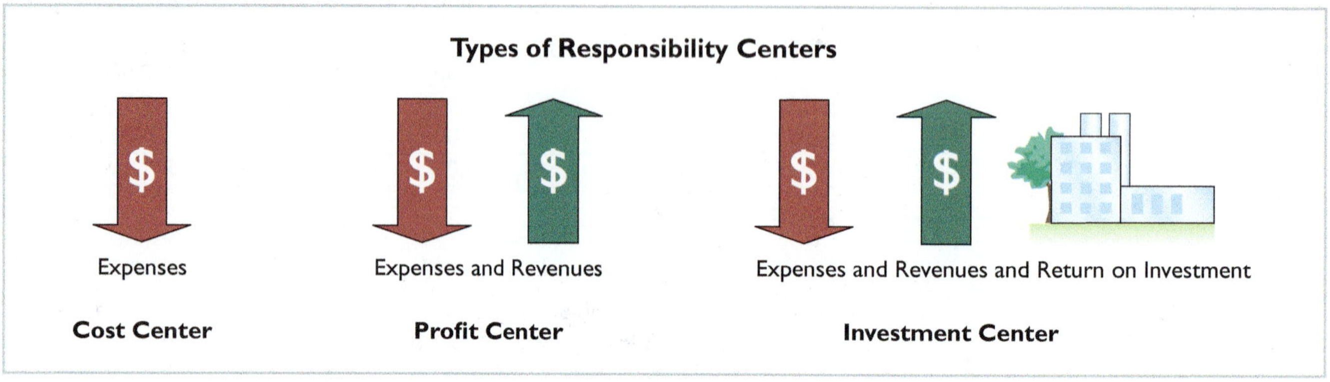

Responsibility Accounting for Cost Centers

The evaluation of a manager's performance for cost centers is based on his or her ability to meet budgeted goals for controllable costs. **Responsibility reports for cost centers compare actual controllable costs with flexible budget data.**

Illustration 23.21 shows a responsibility report. The report is adapted from the flexible budget report for Fox Company in Illustration 23.16. It assumes that the Finishing Department manager is able to control all manufacturing overhead costs except depreciation, property taxes, and his own monthly salary of $6,000. The remaining $4,000 ($10,000 − $6,000) of supervision costs are assumed to apply to other supervisory personnel within the Finishing Department, whose salaries are controllable by the manager.

ILLUSTRATION 23.21

Responsibility report for a cost center

Fox Company
Finishing Department
Responsibility Report
For the Month Ended January 31, 2022

Controllable Costs	Budget	Actual	Difference Favorable - F Unfavorable - U	
Indirect materials	$13,500	$14,000	$ 500	U
Indirect labor	18,000	17,000	1,000	F
Utilities	4,500	4,600	100	U
Supervision	4,000	4,000	0	
Total	$40,000	$39,600	$ 400	F

The report in Illustration 23.21 includes **only controllable costs**, and no distinction is made between variable and fixed costs. The responsibility report continues the concept of management by exception. In this case, top management may request an explanation of the $1,000 favorable difference in indirect labor and/or the $500 unfavorable difference in indirect materials if considered significant.

Responsibility Accounting for Profit Centers

To evaluate the performance of a profit center manager, upper management needs detailed information about both controllable revenues and controllable costs. The operating revenues earned by a profit center, such as sales, are controllable by the manager. All variable costs (and expenses) incurred by the center are also controllable by the manager because they vary with sales. However, to determine the controllability of fixed costs, it is necessary to distinguish between direct and indirect fixed costs.

Direct and Indirect Fixed Costs A profit center may have both direct and indirect fixed costs. **Direct fixed costs** relate specifically to one center and are incurred for the sole benefit of that center. Examples of such costs include the salaries established by the profit center manager for supervisory personnel and the cost of a timekeeping department for the center's employees. Since these fixed costs can be traced directly to a center, they are also called **traceable costs**. **Most direct fixed costs are controllable by the profit center manager.**

In contrast, **indirect fixed costs** pertain to a company's overall operating activities and are incurred for the benefit of more than one profit center. Management allocates indirect fixed costs to profit centers on some type of equitable basis. For example, property taxes on a building occupied by more than one center may be allocated on the basis of square feet of floor space used by each center. Or, the costs of a company's human resources department may be allocated to profit centers on the basis of the number of employees in each center. Because these fixed costs apply to more than one center, they are also called **common costs**. **Most indirect fixed costs are not controllable by the profit center manager.**

Responsibility Report The responsibility report for a profit center shows budgeted and actual **controllable revenues and costs**. The report is prepared using the cost-volume-profit income statement explained in Chapter 18 (see **Helpful Hint**). In the report:

1. Controllable fixed costs are deducted from contribution margin.
2. The excess of contribution margin over controllable fixed costs is identified as **controllable margin**.
3. Noncontrollable fixed costs are not reported.

Illustration 23.22 shows the responsibility report for the manager of the Marine Division, a profit center of Mantle Company. For the year, the Marine Division also had $60,000 of indirect fixed costs that were not controllable by the profit center manager and therefore were omitted from the report.

> **HELPFUL HINT**
> Recognize that we are emphasizing *financial* measures of performance. Companies are now making an effort to also stress *nonfinancial* performance measures such as product quality, labor productivity, market growth, materials' yield, manufacturing flexibility, and technological capability.

ILLUSTRATION 23.22
Responsibility report for profit center

Mantle Company
Marine Division
Responsibility Report
For the Year Ended December 31, 2022

	Budget	Actual	Difference Favorable - F Unfavorable - U	
Sales	$1,200,000	$1,150,000	$50,000	U
Variable costs				
Cost of goods sold	500,000	490,000	10,000	F
Selling and administrative	160,000	156,000	4,000	F
Total	660,000	646,000	14,000	F
Contribution margin	540,000	504,000	36,000	U
Controllable fixed costs				
Cost of goods sold	100,000	100,000	0	
Selling and administrative	80,000	80,000	0	
Total	180,000	180,000	0	
Controllable margin	$ 360,000	$ 324,000	$36,000	U

Controllable margin is considered to be the best measure of the manager's performance **in controlling revenues and costs**. The report in Illustration 23.22 shows that the manager's performance was below budgeted expectations by 10% ($36,000 ÷ $360,000) of the budgeted controllable margin. Top management would likely investigate the causes of this unfavorable result. Note that the report does not show the Marine Division's noncontrollable indirect fixed costs of $60,000. These costs would be included in a report on the profitability of the profit center.

Management also may choose to see **monthly** responsibility reports for profit centers. In addition, responsibility reports may include cumulative year-to-date results.

DO IT! 3 | Profit Center Responsibility Report

ACTION PLAN

- Deduct variable costs from sales to show contribution margin.
- Deduct controllable fixed costs from the contribution margin to show controllable margin.
- Do not report noncontrollable fixed costs.

Midwest Division operates as a profit center. It reports the following for the year:

	Budget	Actual
Sales	$1,500,000	$1,700,000
Variable costs	700,000	800,000
Controllable fixed costs	400,000	400,000
Noncontrollable fixed costs	200,000	200,000

Prepare a responsibility report for the Midwest Division for December 31, 2022.

Solution

Midwest Division
Responsibility Report
For the Year Ended December 31, 2022

	Budget	Actual	Difference Favorable F Unfavorable U	
Sales	$1,500,000	$1,700,000	$200,000	F
Variable costs	700,000	800,000	100,000	U
Contribution margin	800,000	900,000	100,000	F
Controllable fixed costs	400,000	400,000	0	
Controllable margin	$ 400,000	$ 500,000	$100,000	F

Related exercise material: **BE23.7, DO IT! 23.3,** and **E23.15.**

Investment Centers

LEARNING OBJECTIVE 4
Evaluate performance in investment centers.

As explained earlier, an investment center manager can control or significantly influence the investment funds available for use. Thus, the primary basis for evaluating the performance of a manager of an investment center is **return on investment (ROI)**. The return on investment is considered to be a useful performance measurement because it shows the **effectiveness of the manager in utilizing the assets at his or her disposal**.

Return on Investment (ROI)

The formula for computing ROI for an investment center, together with assumed illustrative data, is shown in **Illustration 23.23**.

Controllable Margin	÷	Average Operating Assets	=	Return on Investment (ROI)
$1,000,000	÷	$5,000,000	=	20%

ILLUSTRATION 23.23
ROI formula

Both factors in the formula are controllable by the investment center manager (see **Decision Tools**). Operating assets consist of current assets and plant assets used in operations by the center and controlled by the manager. Nonoperating assets such as idle plant assets and land held for future use are excluded. Average operating assets are usually based on the cost or book value of the assets at the beginning and end of the year. Based on these assigned values, the ROI of 20% indicates that, on average, the segment generates 20 cents of profit for every dollar invested in assets.

Decision Tools
The ROI formula helps managers determine if the investment center has used its assets effectively.

Responsibility Report

The scope of the investment center manager's responsibility significantly affects the content of the performance report. Since an investment center is an independent entity for operating purposes, **all fixed costs are controllable by its manager**. For example, the manager is responsible for depreciation on investment center assets. Therefore, more fixed costs are identified as controllable in the performance report for an investment center manager than in a performance report for a profit center manager. The report also shows budgeted and actual ROI below controllable margin.

To illustrate this responsibility report, we will now assume that the Marine Division of Mantle Company is an investment center. It has budgeted and actual average operating assets of $2,000,000. The manager can control $60,000 of additional fixed costs that were not controllable when the division was a profit center. **Illustration 23.24** shows the division's responsibility report.

ILLUSTRATION 23.24
Responsibility report for investment center

Mantle Company
Marine Division
Responsibility Report
For the Year Ended December 31, 2022

	Budget	Actual	Difference Favorable - F Unfavorable - U	
Sales	$ 1,200,000	$ 1,150,000	$ 50,000	U
Variable costs				
Cost of goods sold	500,000	490,000	10,000	F
Selling and administrative	160,000	156,000	4,000	F
Total	660,000	646,000	14,000	F
Contribution margin	540,000	504,000	36,000	U
Controllable fixed costs				
Cost of goods sold	100,000	100,000	0	
Selling and administrative	80,000	80,000	0	
Other fixed costs	60,000	60,000	0	
Total	240,000	240,000	0	
Controllable margin	$ 300,000	$ 264,000	$ 36,000	U
Return on investment	15.0%	13.2%	1.8%	U
	(a)	(b)	(c)	
	(a) $ 300,000 / $ 2,000,000	(b) $ 264,000 / $ 2,000,000	(c) $ 36,000 / $ 2,000,000	

The report shows that the manager's performance based on ROI was below budget expectations by 1.8% (15.0% versus 13.2%). Top management would likely want explanations for this unfavorable result.

Judgmental Factors in ROI

The return on investment approach includes two judgmental factors:

1. **Valuation of operating assets.** Operating assets may be valued at acquisition cost, book value, appraised value, or fair value. The first two bases are readily available from the accounting records.
2. **Margin (income) measure.** This measure may be controllable margin, income from operations, or net income.

Each of the alternative values for operating assets can provide a reliable basis for evaluating a manager's performance as long as it is consistently applied between reporting periods. However, the use of income measures other than controllable margin will not result in a valid basis for evaluating the performance of an investment center manager.

Improving ROI

The manager of an investment center can improve ROI by increasing controllable margin, and/or reducing average operating assets. To illustrate, we use the assumed data for the Laser Division of Berra Company shown in **Illustration 23.25**.

ILLUSTRATION 23.25
Assumed data for Laser Division

Sales	$2,000,000
Variable costs	1,100,000
Contribution margin (45%)	900,000
Controllable fixed costs	300,000
Controllable margin (a)	$ 600,000
Average operating assets (b)	$5,000,000
Return on investment (a) ÷ (b)	12%

Increasing Controllable Margin

Controllable margin can be increased by increasing sales or by reducing variable and controllable fixed costs as follows.

1. **Increase sales 10%.** Sales will increase $200,000 ($2,000,000 × .10). Assuming no change in the contribution margin percentage of 45% ($900,000 ÷ $2,000,000), contribution margin will increase $90,000 ($200,000 × .45). Controllable margin will increase by the same amount because controllable fixed costs will not change. Thus, controllable margin becomes $690,000 ($600,000 + $90,000). The new ROI is 13.8%, computed as shown in **Illustration 23.26**.

ILLUSTRATION 23.26
ROI computation—increase in sales

$$\text{ROI} = \frac{\text{Controllable margin}}{\text{Average operating assets}} = \frac{\$690,000}{\$5,000,000} = 13.8\%$$

An increase in sales benefits both the investment center and the company if it results in new business. It would not benefit the company if the increase was achieved at the expense of other investment centers.

2. **Decrease variable and fixed costs 10%.** Total costs decrease $140,000 [($1,100,000 + $300,000) × .10]. This reduction results in a corresponding increase in controllable margin. Thus, controllable margin becomes $740,000 ($600,000 + $140,000). The new ROI is 14.8%, computed as shown in **Illustration 23.27**.

$$\text{ROI} = \frac{\text{Controllable margin}}{\text{Average operating assets}} = \frac{\$740{,}000}{\$5{,}000{,}000} = 14.8\%$$

ILLUSTRATION 23.27
ROI computation—decrease in costs

This course of action is clearly beneficial when the reduction in costs is the result of eliminating waste and inefficiency. But, a reduction in costs that results from cutting expenditures on vital activities, such as required maintenance and inspections, is not likely to be acceptable to top management.

Reducing Average Operating Assets

Assume that average operating assets are reduced 10% or $500,000 ($5,000,000 × .10). Average operating assets become $4,500,000 ($5,000,000 − $500,000). Since controllable margin remains unchanged at $600,000, the new ROI is 13.3%, computed as shown in **Illustration 23.28**.

$$\text{ROI} = \frac{\text{Controllable margin}}{\text{Average operating assets}} = \frac{\$600{,}000}{\$4{,}500{,}000} = 13.3\%$$

ILLUSTRATION 23.28
ROI computation—decrease in operating assets

Reductions in operating assets may or may not be prudent. It is beneficial to eliminate overinvestment in inventories and to dispose of excessive plant assets. However, it is unwise to reduce inventories below expected needs or to dispose of essential plant assets.

Management Insight

PeopleImages/Getty Images

Is Your Job a Game?

As discussed in this chapter, the things you are held accountable for depend on your job responsibilities. Similarly, the form of a company's incentive and compensation structure varies depending on your level within the organization. If you are the chief executive officer (CEO), it is likely that a significant portion of your pay (about 30%) will be in the form of a stock-based bonus. This bonus is usually tied to overall company performance, typically measured by earnings per share and shareholder returns. But if you are a lower-level employee, your raises and bonuses might be structured similar to the incentives in video games. This so-called "gamification" has the ability to incentivize not just the most obvious aspect of your job but also many of the other functions that your manager deems important. For example, rather than just reward you for total sales made, your bonus under gamification might change if you "accurately enter their client's information into a sales tracker, assess the quality of sales leads or track how often they are going to sales meetings." It can also provide "points" for things like whether you lead a healthy lifestyle, collaborate with co-workers, and improve interpersonal skills.

Sources: Scott Thurm, "CEO Pay More Closely Matches Firms' Results," *Wall Street Journal* (September 11, 2013); and Farhad Manjoo, "The Gamification of the Office Approaches," *Wall Street Journal* (January 12, 2014).

Why is the reward system of top managers tied to different types of measures than those of lower-level managers? (Go to WileyPLUS for this answer and additional questions.)

DO IT! 4 | Performance Evaluation

The service division of Metro Industries reported the following results for 2022.

Sales	$400,000
Variable costs	320,000
Controllable fixed costs	40,800
Average operating assets	280,000

Management is considering the following independent courses of action in 2023 in order to maximize the return on investment for this division.

1. Reduce average operating assets by $80,000, with no change in controllable margin.
2. Increase sales $80,000, with no change in the contribution margin percentage.

a. Compute the controllable margin and the return on investment for 2022.
b. Compute the controllable margin and the expected return on investment for 2023 for each proposed alternative.

ACTION PLAN
- Recall key formulas: Sales − Variable costs = Contribution margin.
- Contribution margin − Controllable fixed costs = Controllable margin.
- Return on investment = Controllable margin ÷ Average operating assets.

Solution

a. Return on investment for 2022:

Sales	$400,000
Variable costs	320,000
Contribution margin	80,000
Controllable fixed costs	40,800
Controllable margin	$ 39,200

$$\text{Return on investment} \quad \frac{\$39,200}{\$280,000} = 14\%$$

b. Expected return on investment for alternative 1:

$$\frac{\$39,200}{\$280,000 - \$80,000} = 19.6\%$$

Expected return on investment for alternative 2:

Sales ($400,000 + $80,000)	$480,000
Variable costs ($320,000/$400,000 × $480,000)	384,000
Contribution margin	96,000
Controllable fixed costs	40,800
Controllable margin	$ 55,200

$$\text{Return on investment} \quad \frac{\$55,200}{\$280,000} = 19.7\%$$

Related exercise material: **BE23.8, BE23.9, BE23.10, DO IT! 23.4, E23.16,** and **E23.17.**

USING THE DECISION TOOLS | Tribeca Grand Hotel

The **Tribeca Grand Hotel**, which was discussed in the Feature Story, faces many situations where it needs to apply the decision tools learned in this chapter. For example, assume that the hotel's housekeeping budget contains the following items.

Variable costs	
Direct labor	$37,000
Laundry service	10,000
Supplies	6,000
Total variable	$53,000
Fixed costs	
Supervision	$17,000
Inspection costs	1,000
Insurance expenses	2,000
Depreciation	15,000
Total fixed	$35,000

The budget was based on an estimated 4,000-room rental for the month. During November, 3,000 rooms were actually rented, with the following costs incurred.

Variable costs	
Direct labor	$38,700
Laundry service	8,200
Supplies	5,100
Total variable	$52,000
Fixed costs	
Supervision	$19,300
Inspection costs	1,200
Insurance expenses	2,200
Depreciation	14,700
Total fixed	$37,400

Instructions

a. Determine which items would be controllable by the housekeeping manager. (Assume "supervision" excludes the housekeeping manager's own salary.)
b. How much should have been spent during the month for providing rental of 3,000 rooms?
c. Prepare a flexible housekeeping budget report for the housekeeping manager.
d. Prepare a responsibility report. Include only the costs that would have been controllable by the housekeeping manager.

Solution

a. The housekeeping manager should be able to control all the variable costs and the fixed costs of supervision and inspection. Insurance and depreciation ordinarily are not the responsibility of the housekeeping manager.

b. The total variable cost per unit is $13.25 ($53,000 ÷ 4,000). The total budgeted cost during the month to provide 3,000 room rentals is variable costs $39,750 (3,000 × $13.25) plus fixed costs ($35,000), for a total of $74,750 ($39,750 + $35,000).

c.

Tribeca Grand Hotel
Housekeeping Department
Housekeeping Budget Report (Flexible)
For the Month Ended November 30, 2022

	Budget at 3,000 Rooms	Actual at 3,000 Rooms	Difference Favorable F Unfavorable U
Variable costs			
Direct labor ($9.25)*	$27,750	$38,700	$10,950 U
Laundry service ($2.50)	7,500	8,200	700 U
Supplies ($1.50)	4,500	5,100	600 U
Total variable ($13.25)	39,750	52,000	12,250 U
Fixed costs			
Supervision	17,000	19,300	2,300 U
Inspection	1,000	1,200	200 U
Insurance	2,000	2,200	200 U
Depreciation	15,000	14,700	300 F
Total fixed	35,000	37,400	2,400 U
Total costs	$74,750	$89,400	$14,650 U

*Original budgeted amount divided by original budgeted units, e.g., $37,000 ÷ 4,000

d. Because a housekeeping department is a cost center, the responsibility report should include only the costs that are controllable by the housekeeping manager. In this type of report, no distinction is made between variable and fixed costs. Budget data in the report should be based on the rooms actually rented.

Tribeca Grand Hotel
Housekeeping Department
Housekeeping Responsibility Report
For the Month Ended November 30, 2022

Controllable Costs	Budget	Actual	Difference Favorable F Unfavorable U
Direct labor	$27,750	$38,700	$10,950 U
Laundry service	7,500	8,200	700 U
Supplies	4,500	5,100	600 U
Supervision	17,000	19,300	2,300 U
Inspection	1,000	1,200	200 U
Total	$57,750	$72,500	$14,750 U

Appendix 23A ROI vs. Residual Income

LEARNING OBJECTIVE *5
Explain the difference between ROI and residual income.

Although most companies use ROI to evaluate investment performance, ROI has a significant disadvantage. To illustrate, let's look at the Electronics Division of Pujols Company. It has an ROI of 20%, computed as shown in Illustration 23A.1.

ILLUSTRATION 23A.1
ROI formula

Controllable Margin ÷ Average Operating Assets = Return on Investment (ROI)

$1,000,000 ÷ $5,000,000 = 20%

The Electronics Division is considering producing a new product, a GPS device (hereafter referred to as Tracker) for its boats. To produce Tracker, operating assets will have to increase $2,000,000. Tracker is expected to generate an additional $260,000 of controllable margin. Illustration 23A.2 shows how Tracker will effect ROI.

ILLUSTRATION 23A.2
ROI comparison

	Without Tracker	Tracker	With Tracker
Controllable margin (a)	$1,000,000	$260,000	$1,260,000
Average operating assets (b)	$5,000,000	$2,000,000	$7,000,000
Return on investment [(a) ÷ (b)]	20%	13%	18%

The investment in Tracker reduces ROI from 20% to 18%.

Let's suppose that you are the manager of the Electronics Division and must make the decision to produce or not produce Tracker. If you were evaluated using ROI, you probably would not produce Tracker because your ROI would drop from 20% to 18%. The problem with this ROI analysis is that it ignores an important variable: the minimum rate of return on a company's operating assets. The **minimum rate of return** is the rate at which the Electronics Division can cover its costs and earn a profit. Assuming that the Electronics Division has a minimum rate of return of 10%, it should invest in Tracker because its ROI of 13% is greater than 10%.

Residual Income Compared to ROI

To evaluate performance using the minimum rate of return, companies use the residual income approach. **Residual income** is the income that remains after subtracting from the controllable margin the minimum rate of return on a company's average operating assets. The residual income for Tracker would be computed as shown in Illustration 23A.3.

ILLUSTRATION 23A.3
Residual income formula

Controllable Margin − Minimum Rate of Return × Average Operating Assets = Residual Income

$260,000 − 10% × $2,000,000 = $60,000

As shown, the residual income related to the Tracker investment is $60,000. **Illustration 23A.4** indicates how residual income changes as the additional investment is made.

ILLUSTRATION 23A.4
Residual income comparison

	Without Tracker	Tracker	With Tracker
Controllable margin (a)	$1,000,000	$260,000	$1,260,000
Average operating assets × 10% (b)	500,000	200,000	700,000
Residual income [(a) − (b)]	$ 500,000	$ 60,000	$ 560,000

This example illustrates how performance evaluation based on ROI can be misleading and can even cause managers to reject projects that would actually increase income for the company. As a result, many companies such as **Coca-Cola**, **Briggs & Stratton**, **Eli Lilly**, and **Siemens AG** use residual income (or a variant often referred to as economic value added) to evaluate investment alternatives and measure company performance.

Residual Income Weakness

It might appear from the above discussion that the goal of any company should be to maximize the total amount of residual income in each division. This goal, however, ignores the fact that one division might use substantially fewer assets to attain the same level of residual income as another division. For example, we know that to produce Tracker, the Electronics Division of Pujols Company used $2,000,000 of average operating assets to generate $260,000 of controllable margin. Now let's say a different division produced a product called SeaDog, which used $4,000,000 to generate $460,000 of controllable margin, as shown in **Illustration 23A.5**.

ILLUSTRATION 23A.5
Comparison of two products

	Tracker	SeaDog
Controllable margin (a)	$260,000	$460,000
Average operating assets × 10% (b)	200,000	400,000
Residual income [(a) − (b)]	$ 60,000	$ 60,000

If the performance of these two investments were evaluated using residual income, they would be considered equal: Both products have the same total residual income. This ignores, however, the fact that SeaDog required **twice** as many operating assets to achieve the same level of residual income.

Review and Practice

Learning Objectives Review

1 Describe budgetary control and static budget reports.

Budgetary control consists of (a) preparing periodic budget reports that compare actual results with planned objectives, (b) analyzing the differences to determine their causes, (c) taking appropriate corrective action, and (d) modifying future plans, if necessary.

Static budget reports are useful in evaluating the progress toward planned sales and profit goals. They are also appropriate in assessing a manager's effectiveness in controlling costs when (a) actual activity closely approximates the master budget activity level, and/or (b) the behavior of the costs in response to changes in activity is fixed.

2 Prepare flexible budget reports.

To develop the flexible budget it is necessary to: (a) Identify the activity index and the relevant range of activity. (b) Identify the variable costs, and determine the budgeted variable cost per unit of activity

3 Apply responsibility accounting to cost and profit centers.

Responsibility accounting involves accumulating and reporting revenues and costs on the basis of the individual manager who has the authority to make the day-to-day decisions about the items. The evaluation of a manager's performance is based on the matters directly under the manager's control. In responsibility accounting, it is necessary to distinguish between controllable and noncontrollable fixed costs and to identify three types of responsibility centers: cost, profit, and investment.

Responsibility reports for cost centers compare actual costs with flexible budget data. The reports show only controllable costs, and no distinction is made between variable and fixed costs. Responsibility reports show contribution margin, controllable fixed costs, and controllable margin for each profit center.

4 Evaluate performance in investment centers.

The primary basis for evaluating performance in investment centers is return on investment (ROI). The formula for computing ROI for investment centers is Controllable margin ÷ Average operating assets.

*5 Explain the difference between ROI and residual income.

ROI is controllable margin divided by average operating assets. Residual income is the income that remains after subtracting the minimum rate of return on a company's average operating assets. ROI sometimes provides misleading results because profitable investments are often rejected when the investment reduces ROI but increases overall profitability.

Text continues from previous page: for each cost. (c) Identify the fixed costs, and determine the budgeted amount for each cost. (d) Prepare the budget for selected increments of activity within the relevant range. Flexible budget reports permit an evaluation of a manager's performance in controlling production and costs.

Decision Tools Review

Decision Checkpoints	Info Needed for Decision	Tool to Use for Decision	How to Evaluate Results
Are the cost changes resulting from changed production levels reasonable?	Variable costs projected at different levels of production	Flexible budget	After taking into account different production levels, results are favorable if actual expenses are less than budgeted amounts at the actual activity level.
Have the individual managers been held accountable for the costs and revenues under their control?	Relevant costs and revenues, where the individual manager has authority to make day-to-day decisions about the items	Responsibility reports focused on cost centers, profit centers, and investment centers as appropriate	Compare budget to actual costs and revenues for controllable items.
Has the investment center performed up to expectations?	Controllable margin (contribution margin minus controllable fixed costs), and average investment center operating assets	Return on investment	Compare actual ROI to expected ROI based on the company's minimum required rate of return.

Glossary Review

Budgetary control The use of budgets to control operations. (p. 23-3).

Controllable cost A cost over which a manager has control. (p. 23-15).

Controllable margin Contribution margin less controllable fixed costs. (p. 23-21).

Cost center A responsibility center that incurs costs but does not directly generate revenues. (p. 23-18).

Decentralization Control of operations is delegated to many managers throughout the organization. (p. 23-14).

Direct fixed costs Costs that relate specifically to a responsibility center and are incurred for the sole benefit of the center. (p. 23-21).

Flexible budget A projection of budget data for various levels of activity. (p. 23-6).

Indirect fixed costs Costs that are incurred for the benefit of more than one profit center. (p. 23-21).

Investment center A responsibility center that incurs costs, generates revenues, and has control over decisions regarding the assets available for use. (p. 23-18).

Management by exception The review of budget reports by top management focused entirely or primarily on significant differences between actual results and planned objectives. (p. 23-15).

Noncontrollable costs Costs incurred indirectly and allocated to a responsibility center that are not controllable at that level. (p. 23-15).

Profit center A responsibility center that incurs costs and also generates revenues. (p. 23-18).

***Residual income** The income that remains after subtracting from the controllable margin the minimum rate of return on a company's average operating assets. (p. 23-28).

Responsibility accounting A part of management accounting that involves identifying and reporting revenues and costs on the basis of the manager who has the authority to make the day-to-day decisions about the items. (p. 23-13).

Responsibility reporting system The preparation of reports for each level of responsibility in the company's organization chart. (p. 23-17).

Return on investment (ROI) A measure of management's effectiveness in utilizing assets at its disposal in an investment center. (p. 23-22).

Segment (or division) An area of responsibility in decentralized operations. (p. 23-14).

Static budget A projection of budget data at one level of activity. (p. 23-4).

Practice Multiple-Choice Questions

1. **(LO 1)** Budgetary control involves all but one of the following:
   a. modifying future plans.
   b. analyzing differences.
   c. using static budgets but **not** flexible budgets.
   d. determining differences between actual and planned results.

2. **(LO 1)** Depending on the nature of the report, budget reports are prepared:
   a. daily.
   b. weekly.
   c. monthly.
   d. All of the above.

3. **(LO 1)** A production manager in a manufacturing company would most likely receive a:
   a. sales report.
   b. income statement.
   c. scrap report.
   d. shipping department overhead report.

4. **(LO 1)** A static budget is:
   a. a projection of budget data at several levels of activity within the relevant range of activity.
   b. a projection of budget data at a single level of activity.
   c. compared to a flexible budget in a budget report.
   d. never appropriate in evaluating a manager's effectiveness in controlling costs.

5. **(LO 1)** A static budget is useful in controlling costs when cost behavior is:
   a. mixed.
   b. fixed.
   c. variable.
   d. linear.

6. **(LO 2)** At zero direct labor hours in a flexible budget graph, the total budgeted cost line intersects the vertical axis at $30,000. At 10,000 direct labor hours, a horizontal line drawn from the total budgeted cost line intersects the vertical axis at $90,000. Fixed and variable costs may be expressed as:
   a. $30,000 fixed plus $6 per direct labor hour variable.
   b. $30,000 fixed plus $9 per direct labor hour variable.
   c. $60,000 fixed plus $3 per direct labor hour variable.
   d. $60,000 fixed plus $6 per direct labor hour variable.

7. **(LO 2)** At 9,000 direct labor hours, the flexible budget for indirect materials (a variable cost) is $27,000. If $28,000 of indirect materials costs are incurred at 9,200 direct labor hours, the flexible budget report should show the following difference for indirect materials:
   a. $1,000 unfavorable.
   b. $1,000 favorable.
   c. $400 favorable.
   d. $400 unfavorable.

8. **(LO 3)** Under responsibility accounting, the evaluation of a manager's performance is based on matters that the manager:
   a. directly controls.
   b. directly and indirectly controls.
   c. indirectly controls.
   d. has shared responsibility for with another manager.

9. **(LO 3)** Responsibility centers include:
   a. cost centers.
   b. profit centers.
   c. investment centers.
   d. All of the above.

10. **(LO 3)** Responsibility reports for cost centers:
    a. distinguish between fixed and variable costs.
    b. use static budget data.
    c. include both controllable and noncontrollable costs.
    d. include only controllable costs.

11. **(LO 3)** The accounting department of a manufacturing company is an example of:
    a. a cost center.
    b. a profit center.
    c. an investment center.
    d. a contribution center.

12. **(LO 3)** To evaluate the performance of a profit center manager, upper management needs detailed information about:
    a. controllable costs.
    b. controllable revenues.
    c. controllable costs and revenues.
    d. controllable costs and revenues and average operating assets.

13. **(LO 3)** In a responsibility report for a profit center, controllable fixed costs are deducted from contribution margin to show:
    a. profit center margin.
    b. controllable margin.
    c. net income.
    d. income from operations.

14. **(LO 4)** In the formula for return on investment (ROI), the factors for controllable margin and operating assets are, respectively:
    a. controllable margin percentage and total operating assets.
    b. controllable margin dollars and average operating assets.
    c. controllable margin dollars and total assets.
    d. controllable margin percentage and average operating assets.

15. **(LO 4)** A manager of an investment center can improve ROI by:
    a. increasing average operating assets.
    b. reducing sales.
    c. increasing variable costs.
    d. reducing variable and/or controllable fixed costs.

Solutions

1. **c.** Budgetary control involves using flexible budgets and sometimes static budgets. The other choices are all part of budgetary control.

2. **d.** Budget reports are prepared daily, weekly, or monthly. The other choices are correct, but choice (d) is the better answer.

3. **c.** A production manager in a manufacturing company would most likely receive a scrap report. The other choices are incorrect because (a) top management or a sales manager would most likely receive a sales report, (b) top management would most likely receive an income statement, and (d) a department manager would most likely receive a shipping department overhead report.

4. **b.** A static budget is a projection of budget data at a single level of activity. The other choices are incorrect because a static budget (a) is a projection of budget data at a single level of activity, not at several levels of activity within the relevant range of activity; (c) is not compared to a flexible budget in a budget report; and (d) is appropriate in evaluating a manager's effectiveness in controlling fixed costs.

5. **b.** A static budget is useful for controlling fixed costs. The other choices are incorrect because a static budget is not useful for controlling (a) mixed costs, (c) variable costs, or (d) linear costs.

6. **a.** The intersection point of $90,000 is total budgeted costs, or budgeted fixed costs plus budgeted variable costs. Fixed costs are $30,000 (amount at zero direct labor hours), so budgeted variable costs are $60,000 [$90,000 (Total costs) − $30,000 (Fixed costs)]. Budgeted variable costs ($60,000) divided by total activity level (10,000 direct labor hours) gives the variable cost per unit of $6 per direct labor hour. The other choices are therefore incorrect.

7. **d.** Budgeted indirect materials per direct labor hour (DLH) is $3 ($27,000/9,000). At an activity level of 9,200 direct labor hours, budgeted indirect materials are $27,600 (9,200 × $3 per DLH) but actual indirect materials costs are $28,000, resulting in a $400 unfavorable difference. The other choices are therefore incorrect.

8. **a.** The evaluation of a manager's performance is based only on matters that the manager directly controls. The other choices are therefore incorrect as they include indirect controls and shared responsibility.

9. **d.** Cost centers, profit centers, and investment centers are all responsibility centers. The other choices are correct, but choice (d) is the better answer.

10. **d.** Responsibility reports for cost centers report only controllable costs; they (a) do not distinguish between fixed and variable costs; (b) use flexible budget data, not static budget data; and (c) do not include noncontrollable costs.

11. **a.** The accounting department of a manufacturing company is an example of a cost center, not (b) a profit center, (c) an investment center, or (d) contribution center.

12. **c.** To evaluate the performance of a profit center manager, upper management needs detailed information about controllable costs and revenues, not just (a) controllable costs or (b) controllable revenues. Choice (d) is incorrect because upper management does not need information about average operating assets.

13. **b.** Contribution margin less controllable fixed costs is the controllable margin, not (a) the profit center margin, (c) net income, or (d) income from operations.

14. **b.** The factors in the formula for ROI are controllable margin dollars and average operating assets. The other choices are therefore incorrect.

15. **d.** Reducing variable or controllable fixed costs will cause the controllable margin to increase, which is one way a manager of an investment center can improve ROI. The other choices are incorrect because (a) increasing average operating assets will lower ROI; (b) reducing sales will cause contribution margin to go down, thereby decreasing controllable margin since there will be less contribution margin to cover controllable fixed costs and resulting in lower ROI; and (c) increasing variable costs will cause the contribution margin to be lower, thereby decreasing controllable margin and resulting in lower ROI.

Practice Brief Exercises

Prepare a flexible budget for variable costs.

1. (LO 2) Borusa Company expects to produce 600,000 units of its product Eldrad in 2022. Monthly production is expected to range from 40,000 to 60,000 units. Budgeted variable manufacturing costs per unit are direct materials $4, direct labor $5, and overhead $8. Budgeted fixed manufacturing costs per unit are $2 for depreciation and $1.50 for supervision. Prepare a flexible manufacturing budget for the relevant range value using 10,000-unit increments.

Solution

1.

Borusa Company
Monthly Flexible Manufacturing Budget
For the Year 2022

Activity level			
Finished units	40,000	50,000	60,000
Variable costs			
Direct materials ($4)	$160,000	$ 200,000	$ 240,000
Direct labor ($5)	200,000	250,000	300,000
Overhead ($8)	320,000	400,000	480,000
Total variable costs ($17)	$680,000	$ 850,000	$1,020,000
Fixed costs			
Depreciation*	100,000	100,000	100,000
Supervision**	75,000	75,000	75,000
Total fixed costs	175,000	175,000	175,000
Total costs	$855,000	$1,025,000	$1,195,000

*($2 × 600,000) ÷ 12; **($1.50 × 600,000) ÷ 12

2. (LO 3) Goth Company accumulates the following summary data for the year ending December 31, 2022, for its Chancellor Division, which it operates as a profit center: sales—$2,000,000 budget, $1,940,000 actual; variable costs—$1,000,000 budget, $980,000 actual; and controllable fixed costs—$300,000 budget, $317,000 actual. Prepare a responsibility report for the Chancellor Division.

Prepare a responsibility report for a profit center.

Solution

2.

Goth Company
Chancellor Division
Responsibility Report
For the Year Ended December 31, 2022

	Budget	Actual	Difference Favorable F Unfavorable U
Sales	$2,000,000	$1,940,000	$60,000 U
Variable costs	1,000,000	980,000	20,000 F
Contribution margin	1,000,000	960,000	40,000 U
Controllable fixed costs	300,000	317,000	17,000 U
Controllable margin	$ 700,000	$ 643,000	$57,000 F

3. (LO 4) For its three investment centers, Usher Company accumulates the following data:

Compute return on investment using the ROI formula.

	I	II	III
Sales	$2,000,000	$4,000,000	$4,000,000
Controllable margin	1,200,000	2,100,000	2,400,000
Average operating assets	4,000,000	7,000,000	9,600,000

Compute the return on investment (ROI) for each center.

Solution

3.

I   ($1,200,000 ÷ $4,000,000) = 30%
II ($2,100,000 ÷ $7,000,000) = 30%
III ($2,400,000 ÷ $9,600,000) = 25%

Practice Exercises

1. (LO 2) Felix Company uses a flexible budget for manufacturing overhead based on direct labor hours. Variable manufacturing overhead costs per direct labor hour are as follows.

Prepare flexible manufacturing overhead budget.

Indirect labor	$0.70
Indirect materials	0.50
Utilities	0.40

Budgeted fixed overhead costs per month are supervision $4,000, depreciation $3,000, and property taxes $800. The company believes it will normally operate in a range of 7,000–10,000 direct labor hours per month.

Instructions

Prepare a monthly flexible manufacturing overhead budget for 2022 for the expected range of activity, using increments of 1,000 direct labor hours.

Solution

1.

Felix Company
Monthly Flexible Manufacturing Overhead Budget
For the Year 2022

Activity level				
Direct labor hours	7,000	8,000	9,000	10,000
Variable costs				
Indirect labor ($.70)	$ 4,900	$ 5,600	$ 6,300	$ 7,000
Indirect materials ($.50)	3,500	4,000	4,500	5,000
Utilities ($.40)	2,800	3,200	3,600	4,000
Total variable costs ($1.60)	11,200	12,800	14,400	16,000
Fixed costs				
Supervision	4,000	4,000	4,000	4,000
Depreciation	3,000	3,000	3,000	3,000
Property taxes	800	800	800	800
Total fixed costs	7,800	7,800	7,800	7,800
Total costs	$19,000	$20,600	$22,200	$23,800

Compute ROI for current year and for possible future changes.

2. (LO 4) The White Division of Mesin Company reported the following data for the current year.

Sales	$3,000,000
Variable costs	2,400,000
Controllable fixed costs	400,000
Average operating assets	5,000,000

Top management is unhappy with the investment center's return on investment (ROI). It asks the manager of the White Division to submit plans to improve ROI in the next year. The manager believes it is feasible to consider the following independent courses of action.

1. Increase sales by $300,000 with no change in the contribution margin percentage.
2. Reduce variable costs by $100,000.
3. Reduce average operating assets by 4%.

Instructions

a. Compute the return on investment (ROI) for the current year.
b. Using the ROI formula, compute the ROI under each of the proposed courses of action. (Round to one decimal.)

Solution

2. a. Controllable margin = ($3,000,000 − $2,400,000 − $400,000) = $200,000
   ROI = $200,000 ÷ $5,000,000 = 4%

   b. 1. Contribution margin percentage is 20%, or [($3,000,000 − $2,400,000) ÷ $3,000,000]
      Increase in controllable margin = $300,000 × 20% = $60,000
      ROI = ($200,000 + $60,000) ÷ $5,000,000 = 5.2%
   2. ($200,000 + $100,000) ÷ $5,000,000 = 6%
   3. $200,000 ÷ [$5,000,000 − ($5,000,000 × .04)] = 4.2%

Practice Problem

Prepare flexible budget report.

(LO 2) Glenda Company uses a flexible budget for manufacturing overhead based on direct labor hours. For 2022, the master overhead budget for the Packaging Department based on 300,000 direct labor hours was as follows.

	Variable Costs			Fixed Costs	
Indirect labor		$360,000	Supervision		$ 60,000
Supplies and lubricants		150,000	Depreciation		24,000
Maintenance		210,000	Property taxes		18,000
Utilities		120,000	Insurance		12,000
		$840,000			$114,000

During July, 24,000 direct labor hours were worked. The company incurred the following variable costs in July: indirect labor $30,200, supplies and lubricants $11,600, maintenance $17,500, and utilities $9,200. Actual fixed overhead costs were the same as monthly budgeted fixed costs.

Instructions

Prepare a flexible budget report for the Packaging Department for July.

Solution

Glenda Company
Manufacturing Overhead Budget Report (Flexible)
Packaging Department
For the Month Ended July 31, 2022

Direct labor hours (DLH)	Budget 24,000 DLH	Actual Costs 24,000 DLH	Difference Favorable F Unfavorable U
Variable costs			
Indirect labor ($1.20[a])	$28,800	$30,200	$1,400 U
Supplies and lubricants ($0.50[a])	12,000	11,600	400 F
Maintenance ($0.70[a])	16,800	17,500	700 U
Utilities ($0.40[a])	9,600	9,200	400 F
Total variable	67,200	68,500	1,300 U
Fixed costs			
Supervision	$ 5,000[b]	$ 5,000	–0–
Depreciation	2,000[b]	2,000	–0–
Property taxes	1,500[b]	1,500	–0–
Insurance	1,000[b]	1,000	–0–
Total fixed	9,500	9,500	–0–
Total costs	$76,700	$78,000	$1,300 U

[a]($360,000 ÷ 300,000; $150,000 ÷ 300,000; $210,000 ÷ 300,000; $120,000 ÷ 300,000).
[b]Annual cost divided by 12.

WileyPLUS

Brief Exercises, DO IT! Exercises, Exercises, Problems, and many additional resources are available for practice in WileyPLUS.

Note: All asterisked Questions, Exercises, and Problems relate to material in the appendix to the chapter.

Questions

1. **a.** What is budgetary control?
   b. Fred Barone is describing budgetary control. What steps should be included in Fred's description?

2. The following purposes are part of a budgetary reporting system: (a) Determine efficient use of materials. (b) Control overhead costs. (c) Determine whether income objectives are being met. For each

purpose, indicate the name of the report, the frequency of the report, and the primary recipient(s) of the report.

3. How may a budget report for the second quarter differ from a budget report for the first quarter?

4. Ken Bay questions the usefulness of a master sales budget in evaluating sales performance. Is there justification for Ken's concern? Explain.

5. Under what circumstances may a static budget be an appropriate basis for evaluating a manager's effectiveness in controlling costs?

6. "A flexible budget is really a series of static budgets." Is this true? Why?

7. The static manufacturing overhead budget based on 40,000 direct labor hours shows budgeted indirect labor costs of $54,000. During March, the department incurs $64,000 of indirect labor while working 45,000 direct labor hours. Is this a favorable or unfavorable performance? Why?

8. A static overhead budget based on 40,000 direct labor hours shows Factory Insurance $6,500 as a fixed cost. At the 50,000 direct labor hours worked in March, factory insurance costs were $6,300. Is this a favorable or unfavorable performance? Why?

9. Megan Pedigo is confused about how a flexible budget is prepared. Identify the steps for Megan.

10. Cali Company has prepared a graph of flexible budget data. At zero direct labor hours, the total budgeted cost line intersects the vertical axis at $20,000. At 10,000 direct labor hours, the line drawn from the total budgeted cost line intersects the vertical axis at $85,000. How may the fixed and variable costs be expressed?

11. The flexible budget formula is fixed costs $50,000 plus variable costs of $4 per direct labor hour. What is the total budgeted cost at (a) 9,000 hours and (b) 12,345 hours?

12. What is management by exception? What criteria may be used in identifying exceptions?

13. What is responsibility accounting? Explain the purpose of responsibility accounting.

14. Eve Rooney is studying for an accounting examination. Describe for Eve what conditions are necessary for responsibility accounting to be used effectively.

15. Distinguish between controllable and noncontrollable costs.

16. How do responsibility reports differ from budget reports?

17. What is the relationship, if any, between a responsibility reporting system and a company's organization chart?

18. Distinguish among the three types of responsibility centers.

19. (a) What costs are included in a performance report for a cost center? (b) In the report, are variable and fixed costs identified?

20. How do direct fixed costs differ from indirect fixed costs? Are both types of fixed costs controllable?

21. Jane Nott is confused about controllable margin reported in an income statement for a profit center. How is this margin computed, and what is its primary purpose?

22. What is the primary basis for evaluating the performance of the manager of an investment center? Indicate the formula for this basis.

23. Explain the ways that ROI can be improved.

24. Indicate two behavioral principles that pertain to (a) the manager being evaluated and (b) top management.

*25. What is a major disadvantage of using ROI to evaluate investment and company performance?

*26. What is residual income, and what is one of its major weaknesses?

Brief Exercises

Prepare static budget report.

BE23.1 (LO 1), AP For the quarter ended March 31, 2022, Croix Company accumulates the following sales data for its newest guitar, The Edge: $315,000 budget; $305,000 actual. Prepare a static budget report for the quarter.

Prepare static budget report for 2 quarters.

BE23.2 (LO 1), AP Data for Croix Company are given in BE23.1. In the second quarter, budgeted sales were $380,000, and actual sales were $384,000. Prepare a static budget report for the second quarter and for the year to date.

Show usefulness of flexible budgets in evaluating performance.

BE23.3 (LO 2), E In Rooney Company, direct labor is $20 per hour. The company expects to operate at 10,000 direct labor hours each month. In January 2022, direct labor totaling $206,000 is incurred in working 10,400 hours. Prepare (a) a static budget report and (b) a flexible budget report. Evaluate the usefulness of each report.

Prepare a flexible budget for variable costs.

BE23.4 (LO 2), AP Gundy Company expects to produce 1,200,000 units of Product XX in 2022. Monthly production is expected to range from 80,000 to 120,000 units. Budgeted variable manufacturing costs per unit are direct materials $5, direct labor $6, and overhead $8. Budgeted fixed manufacturing costs per unit for depreciation are $2 and for supervision are $1. Prepare a flexible manufacturing budget for the relevant range value using 20,000 unit increments.

Prepare flexible budget report.

BE23.5 (LO 2), AN Data for Gundy Company are given in BE23.4. In March 2022, the company incurs the following costs in producing 100,000 units: direct materials $520,000, direct labor $596,000, and variable overhead $805,000. Actual fixed costs were equal to budgeted fixed costs. Prepare a flexible budget report for March. Were costs controlled?

BE23.6 (LO 3), AP In the Assembly Department of Hannon Company, budgeted and actual manufacturing overhead costs for the month of April 2022 were as follows.

	Budget	Actual
Indirect materials	$16,000	$14,300
Indirect labor	20,000	20,600
Utilities	10,000	10,850
Supervision	5,000	5,000

All costs are controllable by the department manager. Prepare a responsibility report for April for the cost center.

Prepare a responsibility report for a cost center.

BE23.7 (LO 3), AP Torres Company accumulates the following summary data for the year ending December 31, 2022, for its Water Division, which it operates as a profit center: sales—$2,000,000 budget, $2,080,000 actual; variable costs—$1,000,000 budget, $1,050,000 actual; and controllable fixed costs—$300,000 budget, $305,000 actual. Prepare a responsibility report for the Water Division for the year ending December 31, 2022.

Prepare a responsibility report for a profit center.

BE23.8 (LO 4), AP For the year ending December 31, 2022, Cobb Company accumulates the following data for the Plastics Division which it operates as an investment center: contribution margin—$700,000 budget, $710,000 actual; controllable fixed costs—$300,000 budget, $302,000 actual. Average operating assets for the year were $2,000,000. Prepare a responsibility report for the Plastics Division beginning with contribution margin for the year ending December 31, 2022.

Prepare a responsibility report for an investment center.

BE23.9 (LO 4), AP For its three investment centers, Gerrard Company accumulates the following data:

	I	II	III
Sales	$2,000,000	$4,000,000	$4,000,000
Controllable margin	1,400,000	2,000,000	3,600,000
Average operating assets	5,000,000	8,000,000	10,000,000

Compute the return on investment (ROI) for each center.

Compute return on investment using the ROI formula.

BE23.10 (LO 4), AP Data for the investment centers for Gerrard Company are given in BE23.9. The centers expect the following changes in the next year: (I) increase sales 15%, (II) decrease controllable fixed costs $400,000, and (III) decrease average operating assets $500,000. Compute the expected return on investment (ROI) for each center. Assume center I has a contribution margin percentage of 70%.

Compute return on investment under changed conditions.

*BE23.11 (LO 5), AP Sterling, Inc. reports the following financial information for its sports clothing segment.

Average operating assets	$3,000,000
Controllable margin	$ 630,000
Minimum rate of return	10%

Compute the return on investment and the residual income for the segment.

Compute ROI and residual income.

*BE23.12 (LO 5), AP Presented below is information related to the Southern Division of Lumber, Inc.

Contribution margin	$1,200,000
Controllable margin	$ 800,000
Average operating assets	$4,000,000
Minimum rate of return	15%

Compute the Southern Division's return on investment and residual income.

Compute ROI and residual income.

DO IT! Exercises

DO IT! 23.1 (LO 1), AP Wade Company estimates that it will produce 6,000 units of product IOA during the current month. Budgeted variable manufacturing costs per unit are direct materials $7, direct labor $13, and overhead $18. Monthly budgeted fixed manufacturing overhead costs are $8,000 for depreciation and $3,800 for supervision.

In the current month, Wade actually produced 6,500 units and incurred the following costs: direct materials $38,850, direct labor $76,440, variable overhead $116,640, depreciation $8,000, and supervision $4,000.

Prepare and evaluate a static budget report.

Prepare a static budget report. *Hint:* The Budget column is based on estimated production while the Actual column is the actual cost incurred during the period. (*Note:* You do not need to prepare the heading.) Were costs controlled? Discuss limitations of the budget.

Compute total budgeted costs in flexible budget.

DO IT! 23.2 (LO 2), AP In Pargo Company's flexible budget graph, the fixed cost line and the total budgeted cost line intersect the vertical axis at $90,000. The total budgeted cost line is $350,000 at an activity level of 50,000 direct labor hours. Compute total budgeted costs at 65,000 direct labor hours.

Prepare a responsibility report.

DO IT! 23.3 (LO 3), AP The Rockies Division operates as a profit center. It reports the following for the year ending December 31, 2022.

	Budget	Actual
Sales	$2,000,000	$1,890,000
Variable costs	800,000	760,000
Controllable fixed costs	550,000	550,000
Noncontrollable fixed costs	250,000	250,000

Prepare a responsibility report for the Rockies Division at December 31, 2022.

Compute ROI and expected return on investments.

DO IT! 23.4 (LO 4), AP The service division of Raney Industries reported the following results for 2022.

Sales	$500,000
Variable costs	300,000
Controllable fixed costs	75,000
Average operating assets	625,000

Management is considering the following independent courses of action in 2023 in order to maximize the return on investment for this division.

1. Reduce average operating assets by $125,000, with no change in controllable margin.
2. Increase sales $100,000, with no change in the contribution margin percentage.

a. Compute the controllable margin and the return on investment for 2022.
b. Compute the controllable margin and the expected return on investment for 2023 for each proposed alternative.

Exercises

Understand the concept of budgetary control.

E23.1 (LO 1, 2), K Connie Rice has prepared the following list of statements about budgetary control.

1. Budget reports compare actual results with planned objectives.
2. All budget reports are prepared on a weekly basis.
3. Management uses budget reports to analyze differences between actual and planned results and to determine their causes.
4. As a result of analyzing budget reports, management may either take corrective action or modify future plans.
5. Budgetary control works best when a company has an informal reporting system.
6. The primary recipients of the sales report are the sales manager and the production supervisor.
7. The primary recipient of the scrap report is the production manager.
8. A static budget is a projection of budget data at a single level of activity.
9. Top management's reaction to unfavorable differences is not influenced by the materiality of the difference.
10. A static budget is not appropriate in evaluating a manager's effectiveness in controlling costs unless the actual activity level approximates the static budget activity level or the behavior of the costs is fixed.

Instructions

Identify each statement as true or false. If false, indicate how to correct the statement.

Prepare and evaluate static budget report.

E23.2 (LO 1), AN Crede Company budgeted selling expenses of $30,000 in January, $35,000 in February, and $40,000 in March. Actual selling expenses were $31,200 in January, $34,525 in February, and $46,000 in March. The company considers any difference that is less than 5% of the budgeted amount to be immaterial.

Instructions

a. Prepare a selling expense report that compares budgeted and actual amounts by month and for the year to date.

b. What is the purpose of the report prepared in (a), and who would be the primary recipient?

c. What would be the likely result of management's analysis of the report?

E23.3 (LO 2), AP Myers Company uses a flexible budget for manufacturing overhead based on direct labor hours. Variable manufacturing overhead costs per direct labor hour are as follows.

Prepare flexible manufacturing overhead budget.

Indirect labor	$1.00
Indirect materials	0.70
Utilities	0.40

Fixed overhead costs per month are supervision $4,000, depreciation $1,200, and property taxes $800. The company believes it will normally operate in a range of 7,000–10,000 direct labor hours per month.

Instructions

Prepare a monthly manufacturing overhead flexible budget for 2022 for the expected range of activity, using increments of 1,000 direct labor hours.

E23.4 (LO 2), AN Writing Using the information in E23.3, assume that in July 2022, Myers Company incurs the following manufacturing overhead costs.

Prepare flexible budget reports for manufacturing overhead costs, and comment on findings.

Variable Costs		Fixed Costs	
Indirect labor	$8,800	Supervision	$4,000
Indirect materials	5,800	Depreciation	1,200
Utilities	3,200	Property taxes	800

Instructions

a. Prepare a flexible budget performance report, assuming that the company worked 9,000 direct labor hours during the month.

b. Prepare a flexible budget performance report, assuming that the company worked 8,500 direct labor hours during the month.

c. Comment on your findings.

E23.5 (LO 2), AP Fallon Company uses flexible budgets to control its selling expenses. Monthly sales are expected to range from $170,000 to $200,000. Variable costs and their percentage relationship to sales are sales commissions 6%, advertising 4%, travel 3%, and delivery 2%. Fixed selling expenses will consist of sales salaries $35,000, depreciation on delivery equipment $7,000, and insurance on delivery equipment $1,000.

Prepare flexible selling expense budget.

Instructions

Prepare a monthly selling expense flexible budget for each $10,000 increment of sales within the relevant range for the year ending December 31, 2022.

E23.6 (LO 2), AN Writing The actual selling expenses incurred in March 2022 by Fallon Company are as follows.

Prepare flexible budget reports for selling expenses.

Variable Expenses		Fixed Expenses	
Sales commissions	$11,000	Sales salaries	$35,000
Advertising	6,900	Depreciation	7,000
Travel	5,100	Insurance	1,000
Delivery	3,450		

Instructions

a. Prepare a flexible budget performance report for March using the budget data in E23.5, assuming that March sales were $170,000.

b. Prepare a flexible budget performance report, assuming that March sales were $180,000.

c. Comment on the importance of using flexible budgets in evaluating the performance of the sales manager.

E23.7 (LO 2), AP Appliance Possible Inc. (AP) is a manufacturer of toaster ovens. To improve control over operations, the president of AP wants to begin using a flexible budgeting system, rather than use only the current master budget. The following data are available for AP's expected costs at production levels of 90,000, 100,000, and 110,000 units.

Prepare flexible budget report.

Variable costs	
Manufacturing	$6 per unit
Administrative	$4 per unit
Selling	$3 per unit
Fixed costs	
Manufacturing	$160,000
Administrative	$ 80,000

Instructions

a. Prepare a flexible budget for each of the possible production levels: 90,000, 100,000, and 110,000 units.

b. If AP sells the toaster ovens for $16 each, how many units will it have to sell to make a profit of $60,000 before taxes?

(CGA adapted)

Prepare flexible budget report; compare flexible and static budgets.

E23.8 (LO 1, 2), E Service Writing Rensing Groomers is in the dog-grooming business. Its operating costs are described by the following formulas:

Grooming supplies (variable)	$y = \$0 + \$5x$
Direct labor (variable)	$y = \$0 + \$14x$
Overhead (mixed)	$y = \$10,000 + \$1x$

Milo, the owner, has determined that direct labor is the cost driver for all three categories of costs.

Instructions

a. Prepare a flexible budget for activity levels of 550, 600, and 700 direct labor hours.

b. Explain why the flexible budget is more informative than the static budget.

c. Calculate the total cost per direct labor hour at each of the activity levels specified in part (a).

d. The groomers at Rensing normally work a total of 650 direct labor hours during each month. Each grooming job normally takes a groomer 1.3 hours. Milo wants to earn a profit equal to 40% of the costs incurred. Determine what he should charge each pet owner for grooming.

(CGA adapted)

Prepare flexible budget report, and answer question.

E23.9 (LO 1, 2), E As sales manager, Joe Batista was given the following static budget report for selling expenses in the Clothing Department of Soria Company for the month of October.

Soria Company
Clothing Department
Budget Report
For the Month Ended October 31, 2022

	Budget	Actual	Difference Favorable F Unfavorable U
Sales in units	8,000	10,000	2,000 F
Variable expenses			
Sales commissions	$ 2,400	$ 2,600	$ 200 U
Advertising expense	720	850	130 U
Travel expense	3,600	4,100	500 U
Free samples given out	1,600	1,400	200 F
Total variable	8,320	8,950	630 U
Fixed expenses			
Rent	1,500	1,500	–0–
Sales salaries	1,200	1,200	–0–
Office salaries	800	800	–0–
Depreciation—autos (sales staff)	500	500	–0–
Total fixed	4,000	4,000	–0–
Total expenses	$12,320	$12,950	$ 630 U

As a result of this budget report, Joe was called into the president's office and congratulated on his fine sales performance. He was reprimanded, however, for allowing his costs to get out of control. Joe knew something was wrong with the performance report that he had been given. However, he was not sure what to do, and comes to you for advice.

Instructions

a. Prepare a budget report based on flexible budget data to help Joe.

b. Should Joe have been reprimanded? Explain.

E23.10 (LO 2, 3), AP Chubbs Inc.'s manufacturing overhead budget for the first quarter of 2022 contained the following data.

Prepare flexible budget and responsibility report for manufacturing overhead.

Variable Costs		Fixed Costs	
Indirect materials	$12,000	Supervisory salaries	$36,000
Indirect labor	10,000	Depreciation	7,000
Utilities	8,000	Property taxes and insurance	8,000
Maintenance	6,000	Maintenance	5,000

Actual variable costs were indirect materials $13,500, indirect labor $9,500, utilities $8,700, and maintenance $5,000. Actual fixed costs equaled budgeted costs except for property taxes and insurance, which were $8,300. The actual activity level equaled the budgeted level.

All costs are considered controllable by the production department manager except for depreciation, and property taxes and insurance.

Instructions

a. Prepare a manufacturing overhead flexible budget report for the first quarter.

b. Prepare a responsibility report for the first quarter.

E23.11 (LO 2, 3), AP **Service** **Writing** UrLink Company is a newly formed company specializing in high-speed Internet service for home and business. The owner, Lenny Kirkland, had divided the company into two segments: Home Internet Service and Business Internet Service. Each segment is run by its own supervisor, while basic selling and administrative services are shared by both segments.

Prepare and discuss a responsibility report.

Lenny has asked you to help him create a performance reporting system that will allow him to measure each segment's performance in terms of its profitability. To that end, the following information has been collected on the Home Internet Service segment for the first quarter of 2022.

	Budget	Actual
Service revenue	$25,000	$26,200
Allocated portion of:		
Building depreciation	11,000	11,000
Advertising	5,000	4,200
Billing	3,500	3,000
Property taxes	1,200	1,000
Material and supplies	1,600	1,200
Supervisory salaries	9,000	9,500
Insurance	4,000	3,900
Wages	3,000	3,250
Gas and oil	2,800	3,400
Equipment depreciation	1,500	1,300

Instructions

a. Prepare a responsibility report for the first quarter of 2022 for the Home Internet Service segment.

b. Write a memo to Lenny Kirkland discussing the principles that should be used when preparing performance reports.

E23.12 (LO 2), AP Venetian Company has two production departments, Fabricating and Assembling. At a department managers' meeting, the controller uses flexible budget graphs to explain total budgeted costs. Separate graphs based on direct labor hours are used for each department. The graphs show the following.

State total budgeted cost formulas, and prepare flexible budget graph.

1. At zero direct labor hours, the total budgeted cost line and the fixed cost line intersect the vertical axis at $50,000 in the Fabricating Department and $40,000 in the Assembling Department.

2. At normal capacity of 50,000 direct labor hours, the line drawn from the total budgeted cost line intersects the vertical axis at $150,000 in the Fabricating Department, and $120,000 in the Assembling Department.

Instructions

a. State the total budgeted cost formula for each department.

b. Compute the total budgeted cost for each department, assuming actual direct labor hours worked were 53,000 and 47,000, in the Fabricating and Assembling Departments, respectively.

c. Prepare the flexible budget graph for the Fabricating Department, assuming the maximum direct labor hours in the relevant range is 100,000. Use increments of 10,000 direct labor hours on the horizontal axis and increments of $50,000 on the vertical axis.

Prepare reports in a responsibility reporting system.

E23.13 (LO 3), AP Fey Company's organization chart includes the president; the vice president of production; three assembly plants—Dallas, Atlanta, and Tucson; and two departments within each plant—Machining and Finishing. Budget and actual manufacturing cost data for July 2022 are as follows.

Finishing Department—Dallas: direct materials $42,500 actual, $44,000 budget; direct labor $83,400 actual, $82,000 budget; manufacturing overhead $51,000 actual, $49,200 budget.

Machining Department—Dallas: total manufacturing costs $220,000 actual, $219,000 budget.

Atlanta Plant: total manufacturing costs $424,000 actual, $420,000 budget.

Tucson Plant: total manufacturing costs $494,200 actual, $496,500 budget.

The Dallas plant manager's office costs were $95,000 actual and $92,000 budget. The vice president of production's office costs were $132,000 actual and $130,000 budget. Office costs are not allocated to departments and plants.

Instructions

Using the format shown in Illustration 23.19, prepare the reports in a responsibility system for:

a. The Finishing Department—Dallas.

b. The plant manager—Dallas.

c. The vice president of production.

Prepare a responsibility report for a cost center.

E23.14 (LO 3), AN The Mixing Department manager of Malone Company is able to control all overhead costs except rent, property taxes, and salaries. Budgeted monthly overhead costs for the Mixing Department, in alphabetical order, are:

Indirect labor	$12,000	Property taxes	$ 1,000
Indirect materials	7,700	Rent	1,800
Lubricants	1,675	Salaries	10,000
Maintenance	3,500	Utilities	5,000

Actual costs incurred for January 2022 are indirect labor $12,250, indirect materials $10,200, lubricants $1,650, maintenance $3,500, property taxes $1,100, rent $1,800, salaries $10,000, and utilities $6,400.

Instructions

a. Prepare a responsibility report for January 2022.

b. What would be the likely result of management's analysis of the report?

Compute missing amounts in responsibility reports for three profit centers, and prepare a report.

E23.15 (LO 3), AN Horatio Inc. has three divisions which are operated as profit centers. Actual operating data for the divisions listed alphabetically are as follows.

Operating Data	Women's Shoes	Men's Shoes	Children's Shoes
Contribution margin	$270,000	(3)	$180,000
Controllable fixed costs	100,000	(4)	(5)
Controllable margin	(1)	$ 90,000	95,000
Sales	600,000	450,000	(6)
Variable costs	(2)	320,000	250,000

Instructions

a. Compute the missing amounts. Show computations.

b. Prepare a responsibility report for the Women's Shoes Division assuming (1) the data are for the month ended June 30, 2022, and (2) all data equal budget except variable costs which are $5,000 over budget.

Prepare a responsibility report for a profit center, and compute ROI.

E23.16 (LO 3, 4), AP The Sports Equipment Division of Harrington Company is operated as a profit center. Sales for the division were budgeted for 2022 at $900,000. The only variable costs budgeted for the division were cost of goods sold ($440,000) and selling and administrative ($60,000). Fixed costs were budgeted at $100,000 for cost of goods sold, $90,000 for selling and administrative, and $70,000 for noncontrollable fixed costs. Actual results for these items were:

Sales	$880,000
Cost of goods sold	
Variable	408,000
Fixed	105,000
Selling and administrative	
Variable	61,000
Fixed	66,000
Noncontrollable fixed	90,000

Instructions

a. Prepare a responsibility report for the Sports Equipment Division for 2022.

b. Assume the division is an investment center, and average operating assets were $1,000,000. The noncontrollable fixed costs are controllable at the investment center level. Compute ROI using the actual amounts.

E23.17 (LO 4), AP The South Division of Wiig Company reported the following data for the current year.

Compute ROI for current year and for possible future changes.

Sales	$3,000,000
Variable costs	1,950,000
Controllable fixed costs	600,000
Average operating assets	5,000,000

Top management is unhappy with the investment center's return on investment (ROI). It asks the manager of the South Division to submit plans to improve ROI in the next year. The manager believes it is feasible to consider the following independent courses of action.

1. Increase sales by $300,000 with no change in the contribution margin percentage.
2. Reduce variable costs by $150,000.
3. Reduce average operating assets by 4%.

Instructions

a. Compute the return on investment (ROI) for the current year.

b. Using the ROI formula, compute the ROI under each of the proposed courses of action. (Round to one decimal.)

E23.18 (LO 4), AP **Service** **Writing** The Dinkle and Frizell Dental Clinic provides both preventive and orthodontic dental services. The two owners, Reese Dinkle and Anita Frizell, operate the clinic as two separate investment centers: Preventive Services and Orthodontic Services. Each of them is in charge of one of the centers: Reese for Preventive Services and Anita for Orthodontic Services. Each month, they prepare an income statement for the two centers to evaluate performance and make decisions about how to improve the operational efficiency and profitability of the clinic.

Prepare a responsibility report for an investment center.

Recently, they have been concerned about the profitability of the Preventive Services operations. For several months, it has been reporting a loss. The responsibility report for the month of May 2022 is shown below.

	Actual	Difference from Budget
Service revenue	$40,000	$1,000 F
Variable costs		
Filling materials	5,000	100 U
Novocain	3,900	100 U
Supplies	1,900	350 F
Dental assistant wages	2,500	–0–
Utilities	500	110 U
Total variable costs	13,800	40 F
Fixed costs		
Allocated portion of receptionist's salary	3,000	200 U
Dentist salary	9,800	400 U
Equipment depreciation	6,000	–0–
Allocated portion of building depreciation	15,000	1,000 U
Total fixed costs	33,800	1,600 U
Operating income (loss)	$(7,600)	$ 560 U

In addition, the owners know that the investment in operating assets at the beginning of the month was $82,400, and it was $77,600 at the end of the month. They have asked for your assistance in evaluating their current performance reporting system.

Instructions

a. Prepare an investment center responsibility report for the Preventative Services segment for May 2022.

b. Write a memo to the owners discussing the deficiencies of their current reporting system.

Prepare missing amounts in responsibility reports for three investment centers.

E23.19 (LO 4), AN Service The Ferrell Transportation Company uses a responsibility reporting system to measure the performance of its three investment centers: Planes, Taxis, and Limos. Segment performance is measured using a system of responsibility reports and return on investment calculations. The allocation of resources within the company and the segment managers' bonuses are based in part on the results shown in these reports.

Recently, the company was the victim of a computer virus that deleted portions of the company's accounting records. This was discovered when the current period's responsibility reports were being prepared. The printout of the actual operating results appeared as follows.

	Planes	Taxis	Limos
Service revenue	$?	$500,000	$?
Variable costs	5,500,000	?	300,000
Contribution margin	?	250,000	480,000
Controllable fixed costs	1,500,000	?	?
Controllable margin	?	80,000	210,000
Average operating assets	25,000,000	?	1,500,000
Return on investment	12%	10%	?

Instructions

Determine the missing pieces of information above.

Compare ROI and residual income.

*E23.20 (LO 5), AN Presented below is selected information for three regional divisions of Medina Company.

	Divisions		
	North	West	South
Contribution margin	$ 300,000	$ 500,000	$ 400,000
Controllable margin	$ 140,000	$ 360,000	$ 210,000
Average operating assets	$1,000,000	$2,000,000	$1,500,000
Minimum rate of return	13%	16%	10%

Instructions

a. Compute the return on investment for each division.

b. Compute the residual income for each division.

c. Assume that each division has an investment opportunity that would provide a rate of return of 16%.

   1. If ROI is used to measure performance, which division or divisions will probably make the additional investment?

   2. If residual income is used to measure performance, which division or divisions will probably make the additional investment?

Fill in information related to ROI and residual income.

*E23.21 (LO 5), AN Presented below is selected financial information for two divisions of Samberg Brewing.

	Lager	Lite Lager
Contribution margin	$500,000	$ 300,000
Controllable margin	200,000	(c)
Average operating assets	(a)	$1,200,000
Minimum rate of return	(b)	11%
Return on investment	16%	(d)
Residual income	$100,000	$ 204,000

Instructions

Supply the missing information for the lettered items.

Problems: Set A

P23.1A (LO 2), AN **Writing** Bumblebee Company estimates that 300,000 direct labor hours will be worked during the coming year, 2022, in the Packaging Department. On this basis, the following budgeted manufacturing overhead cost data are computed for the year.

Prepare flexible budget and budget report for manufacturing overhead.

Fixed Overhead Costs		Variable Overhead Costs	
Supervision	$ 96,000	Indirect labor	$126,000
Depreciation	72,000	Indirect materials	90,000
Insurance	30,000	Repairs	69,000
Rent	24,000	Utilities	72,000
Property taxes	18,000	Lubricants	18,000
	$240,000		$375,000

It is estimated that direct labor hours worked each month will range from 27,000 to 36,000 hours.

During October, 27,000 direct labor hours were worked and the following overhead costs were incurred.

Fixed overhead costs: supervision $8,000, depreciation $6,000, insurance $2,460, rent $2,000, and property taxes $1,500.

Variable overhead costs: indirect labor $12,432, indirect materials $7,680, repairs $6,100, utilities $6,840, and lubricants $1,920.

Instructions

a. Prepare a monthly manufacturing overhead flexible budget for each increment of 3,000 direct labor hours over the relevant range for the year ending December 31, 2022.

b. Prepare a flexible budget report for October.

c. Comment on management's efficiency in controlling manufacturing overhead costs in October.

a. Total costs: DLH 27,000, $53,750; DLH 36,000, $65,000

b. Total $1,182 U

P23.2A (LO 2), E Zelmer Company manufactures tablecloths. Sales have grown rapidly over the past 2 years. As a result, the president has installed a budgetary control system for 2022. The following data were used in developing the master manufacturing overhead budget for the Ironing Department, which is based on an activity index of direct labor hours.

Prepare flexible budget, budget report, and graph for manufacturing overhead.

Variable Costs	Rate per Direct Labor Hour	Annual Fixed Costs	
Indirect labor	$0.40	Supervision	$48,000
Indirect materials	0.50	Depreciation	18,000
Factory utilities	0.30	Insurance	12,000
Factory repairs	0.20	Rent	30,000

The master overhead budget was prepared on the expectation that 480,000 direct labor hours will be worked during the year. In June, 41,000 direct labor hours were worked. At that level of activity, actual costs were as shown below.

Variable—per direct labor hour: indirect labor $0.44, indirect materials $0.48, factory utilities $0.32, and factory repairs $0.25.

Fixed: same as budgeted.

Instructions

a. Prepare a monthly manufacturing overhead flexible budget for the year ending December 31, 2022, assuming production levels range from 35,000 to 50,000 direct labor hours. Use increments of 5,000 direct labor hours.

b. Prepare a budget report for June comparing actual results with budget data based on the flexible budget.

c. Were costs effectively controlled? Explain.

d. State the formula for computing the total budgeted costs for the Ironing Department.

e. Prepare the flexible budget graph, showing total budgeted costs at 35,000 and 45,000 direct labor hours. Use increments of 5,000 direct labor hours on the horizontal axis and increments of $10,000 on the vertical axis.

a. Total costs: 35,000 DLH, $58,000; 50,000 DLH, $79,000

b. Budget $66,400 Actual $70,090

State total budgeted cost formula, and prepare flexible budget reports for 2 time periods.

P23.3A (LO 1, 2), AN Ratchet Company uses budgets in controlling costs. The August 2022 budget report for the company's Assembling Department is as follows.

Ratchet Company
Budget Report
Assembling Department
For the Month Ended August 31, 2022

Manufacturing Costs	Budget	Actual	Difference Favorable F Unfavorable U
Variable costs			
Direct materials	$ 48,000	$ 47,000	$1,000 F
Direct labor	54,000	51,200	2,800 F
Indirect materials	24,000	24,200	200 U
Indirect labor	18,000	17,500	500 F
Utilities	15,000	14,900	100 F
Maintenance	12,000	12,400	400 U
Total variable	171,000	167,200	3,800 F
Fixed costs			
Rent	12,000	12,000	–0–
Supervision	17,000	17,000	–0–
Depreciation	6,000	6,000	–0–
Total fixed	35,000	35,000	–0–
Total costs	$206,000	$202,200	$3,800 F

The monthly budget amounts in the report were based on an expected production of 60,000 units per month or 720,000 units per year. The Assembling Department manager is pleased with the report and expects a raise, or at least praise for a job well done. The company president, however, is unhappy with the results for August because only 58,000 units were produced.

Instructions

a. State the total monthly budgeted cost formula.

b. Budget $200,300

b. Prepare a budget report for August using flexible budget data. Why does this report provide a better basis for evaluating performance than the report based on static budget data?

c. Budget $217,400
Actual $218,920

c. In September, 64,000 units were produced. Prepare the budget report using flexible budget data, assuming (1) each variable cost was 10% higher than its actual cost in August, and (2) fixed costs were the same in September as in August.

Prepare responsibility report for a profit center.

P23.4A (LO 3), AN Writing Clarke Inc. operates the Patio Furniture Division as a profit center. Operating data for this division for the year ended December 31, 2022, are as shown below.

	Budget	Difference from Budget
Sales	$2,500,000	$50,000 F
Cost of goods sold		
Variable	1,300,000	41,000 F
Controllable fixed	200,000	3,000 U
Selling and administrative		
Variable	220,000	6,000 U
Controllable fixed	50,000	2,000 U
Noncontrollable fixed costs	70,000	4,000 U

In addition, Clarke incurs $180,000 of indirect fixed costs that were budgeted at $175,000. Twenty percent (20%) of these costs are allocated to the Patio Furniture Division.

Instructions

a. Contribution margin $85,000 F
Controllable margin $80,000 F

a. Prepare a responsibility report for the Patio Furniture Division for the year.

b. Comment on the manager's performance in controlling revenues and costs.

c. Identify any costs excluded from the responsibility report and explain why they were excluded.

P23.5A (LO 4), E Optimus Company manufactures a variety of tools and industrial equipment. The company operates through three divisions. Each division is an investment center. Operating data for the Home Division for the year ended December 31, 2022, and relevant budget data are as follows.

Prepare responsibility report for an investment center, and compute ROI.

	Actual	Comparison with Budget
Sales	$1,400,000	$100,000 favorable
Variable cost of goods sold	665,000	45,000 unfavorable
Variable selling and administrative expenses	125,000	25,000 unfavorable
Controllable fixed cost of goods sold	170,000	On target
Controllable fixed selling and administrative expenses	80,000	On target

Average operating assets for the year for the Home Division were $2,000,000 which was also the budgeted amount.

Instructions

a. Prepare a responsibility report (in thousands of dollars) for the Home Division.

b. Evaluate the manager's performance. Which items will likely be investigated by top management?

c. Compute the expected ROI in 2022 for the Home Division, assuming the following independent changes to actual data.

1. Variable cost of goods sold is decreased by 5%.
2. Average operating assets are decreased by 10%.
3. Sales are increased by $200,000, and this increase is expected to increase contribution margin by $80,000.

a. Controllable margin: Budget $330; Actual $360

P23.6A (LO 3), AN Durham Company uses a responsibility reporting system. It has divisions in Denver, Seattle, and San Diego. Each division has three production departments: Cutting, Shaping, and Finishing. The responsibility for each department rests with a manager who reports to the division production manager. Each division manager reports to the vice president of production. There are also vice presidents for marketing and finance. All vice presidents report to the president.

In January 2022, controllable actual and budget manufacturing overhead cost data for the departments and divisions were as shown below.

Prepare reports for cost centers under responsibility accounting, and comment on performance of managers.

Manufacturing Overhead	Actual	Budget
Individual costs—Cutting Department—Seattle		
Indirect labor	$ 73,000	$ 70,000
Indirect materials	47,900	46,000
Maintenance	20,500	18,000
Utilities	20,100	17,000
Supervision	22,000	20,000
	$183,500	$171,000
Total costs		
Shaping Department—Seattle	$158,000	$148,000
Finishing Department—Seattle	210,000	205,000
Denver division	678,000	673,000
San Diego division	722,000	715,000

Additional overhead costs were incurred as follows: Seattle division production manager—actual costs $52,500, budget $51,000; vice president of production—actual costs $65,000, budget $64,000; president—actual costs $76,400, budget $74,200. These expenses are not allocated.

The vice presidents who report to the president, other than the vice president of production, had the following expenses.

Vice President	Actual	Budget
Marketing	$133,600	$130,000
Finance	109,000	104,000

a. $12,500 U
b. $29,000 U
c. $42,000 U
d. $52,800 U

Compare ROI and residual income.

Instructions

Using the format in Illustration 23.19, prepare the following responsibility reports.

a. Manufacturing overhead—Cutting Department manager—Seattle division.
b. Manufacturing overhead—Seattle division manager.
c. Manufacturing overhead—vice president of production.
d. Manufacturing overhead and expenses—president.

*P23.7A (LO 5), AN Writing Sentinel Industries has manufactured prefabricated houses for over 20 years. The houses are constructed in sections to be assembled on customers' lots. Sentinel expanded into the precut housing market when it acquired Jensen Company, one of its suppliers. In this market, various types of lumber are precut into the appropriate lengths, banded into packages, and shipped to customers' lots for assembly. Sentinel designated the Jensen Division as an investment center.

Sentinel uses return on investment (ROI) as a performance measure with investment defined as average operating assets. Management bonuses are based in part on ROI. All investments are expected to earn a minimum rate of return of 18%. Jensen's ROI has ranged from 20.1% to 23.5% since it was acquired. Jensen had an investment opportunity in 2022 that had an estimated ROI of 19%. Jensen management decided against the investment because it believed the investment would decrease the division's overall ROI.

Selected financial information for Jensen is presented below. The division's average operating assets were $12,300,000 for the year 2022.

Sentinel Industries
Jensen Division
Selected Financial Information
For the Year Ended December 31, 2022

Sales	$24,000,000
Contribution margin	9,100,000
Controllable margin	2,460,000

Instructions

a. Calculate the following performance measures for 2022 for the Jensen Division.
   1. Return on investment (ROI).
   2. Residual income.
b. Would the management of Jensen Division have been more likely to accept the investment opportunity it had in 2022 if residual income were used as a performance measure instead of ROI? Explain your answer.

(CMA adapted)

Continuing Cases

Current Designs

CD23 The **Current Designs** staff has prepared the annual manufacturing budget for the rotomolded line based on an estimated annual production of 4,000 kayaks during 2022. Each kayak will require 54 pounds of polyethylene powder and a finishing kit (rope, seat, hardware, etc.). The polyethylene powder used in these kayaks costs $1.50 per pound, and the finishing kits cost $170 each. Each kayak will use two kinds of labor—2 hours of type I labor from people who run the oven and trim the plastic, and 3 hours of work from type II workers who attach the hatches and seat and other hardware. The type I employees are paid $15 per hour, and the type II are paid $12 per hour.

Manufacturing overhead is budgeted at $396,000 for 2022, broken down as follows.

Variable costs	
Indirect materials	$ 40,000
Manufacturing supplies	53,800
Maintenance and utilities	88,000
	181,800

Fixed costs
Supervision	90,000
Insurance	14,400
Depreciation	109,800
	214,200
Total	$396,000

During the first quarter, ended March 31, 2022, 1,050 units were actually produced with the following costs.

Polyethylene powder	$ 87,000
Finishing kits	178,840
Type I labor	31,500
Type II labor	39,060
Indirect materials	10,500
Manufacturing supplies	14,150
Maintenance and utilities	26,000
Supervision	20,000
Insurance	3,600
Depreciation	27,450
Total	$438,100

Instructions

a. Prepare the annual manufacturing budget for 2022, assuming that 4,000 kayaks will be produced.

b. Prepare the flexible budget for manufacturing for the quarter ended March 31, 2022. Assume activity levels of 900, 1,000, and 1,050 units.

c. Assuming the rotomolded line is treated as a cost center, prepare a flexible budget report for manufacturing for the quarter ended March 31, 2022, when 1,050 units were produced.

Waterways

(*Note:* This is a continuation of the Waterways case from Chapters 14–22.)

WP23 Waterways Corporation is continuing its budget preparations. This problem gives you static budget information as well as actual overhead costs, and asks you to calculate amounts related to budgetary control and responsibility accounting.

Go to WileyPLUS for complete case details and instructions.

Expand Your Critical Thinking

Decision-Making Across the Organization

CT23.1 Service Green Pastures is a 400-acre farm on the outskirts of the Kentucky Bluegrass, specializing in the boarding of broodmares and their foals. A recent economic downturn in the thoroughbred industry has made the boarding business extremely competitive. To meet the competition, Green Pastures planned in 2022 to entertain clients, advertise more extensively, and absorb expenses formerly paid by clients such as veterinary and blacksmith fees.

The budget report for 2022 follows. As shown, the static income statement budget for the year is based on an expected 21,900 boarding days at $25 per mare. The variable expenses per mare per day were budgeted: feed $5, veterinary fees $3, blacksmith fees $0.25, and supplies $0.55. All other budgeted expenses were either semifixed or fixed.

During the year, management decided not to replace a worker who quit in March, but it did issue a new advertising brochure and did more entertaining of clients.[1]

Green Pastures
Static Budget Income Statement
For the Year Ended December 31, 2022

	Actual	Master Budget	Difference
Number of mares	52	60	8 U
Number of boarding days	19,000	21,900	2,900 U
Sales	$380,000	$547,500	$167,500 U
Less: Variable expenses			
Feed	104,390	109,500	5,110 F
Veterinary fees	58,838	65,700	6,862 F
Blacksmith fees	4,984	5,475	491 F
Supplies	10,178	12,045	1,867 F
Total variable expenses	178,390	192,720	14,330 F
Contribution margin	201,610	354,780	153,170 U
Less: Fixed expenses			
Depreciation	40,000	40,000	-0-
Insurance	11,000	11,000	-0-
Utilities	12,000	14,000	2,000 F
Repairs and maintenance	10,000	11,000	1,000 F
Labor	88,000	95,000	7,000 F
Advertisement	12,000	8,000	4,000 U
Entertainment	7,000	5,000	2,000 U
Total fixed expenses	180,000	184,000	4,000 F
Net income	$ 21,610	$170,780	$149,170 U

Instructions

With the class divided into groups, answer the following.

a. Based on the static budget report:
   1. What was the primary cause(s) of the decline in net income?
   2. Did management do a good, average, or poor job of controlling expenses?
   3. Were management's decisions to stay competitive sound?
b. Prepare a flexible budget report for the year.
c. Based on the flexible budget report, answer the three questions in part (a) above.
d. What course of action do you recommend for the management of Green Pastures?

Managerial Analysis

CT23.2 Lanier Company manufactures expensive watch cases sold as souvenirs. Three of its sales departments are Retail Sales, Wholesale Sales, and Outlet Sales. The Retail Sales Department is a profit center. The Wholesale Sales Department is a cost center. Its managers merely take orders from customers who purchase through the company's wholesale catalog. The Outlet Sales Department is an investment center because each manager is given full responsibility for an outlet store location. The manager can hire and discharge employees, purchase, maintain, and sell equipment, and in general is fairly independent of company control.

Mary Gammel is a manager in the Retail Sales Department. Stephen Flott manages the Wholesale Sales Department. Jose Gomez manages the Golden Gate Club outlet store in San Francisco. The following are the budget responsibility reports for each of the three departments.

---

[1] Data for this case are based on Hans Sprohge and John Talbott, "New Applications for Variance Analysis," *Journal of Accountancy* (AICPA, New York), April 1989, pp. 137–141.

Budget

	Retail Sales	Wholesale Sales	Outlet Sales
Sales	$ 750,000	$ 400,000	$200,000
Variable costs			
Cost of goods sold	150,000	100,000	25,000
Advertising	100,000	30,000	5,000
Sales salaries	75,000	15,000	3,000
Printing	10,000	20,000	5,000
Travel	20,000	30,000	2,000
Fixed costs			
Rent	50,000	30,000	10,000
Insurance	5,000	2,000	1,000
Depreciation	75,000	100,000	40,000
Investment in assets	1,000,000	1,200,000	800,000

Actual Results

	Retail Sales	Wholesale Sales	Outlet Sales
Sales	$ 750,000	$ 400,000	$200,000
Variable costs			
Cost of goods sold	192,000	122,000	26,500
Advertising	100,000	30,000	5,000
Sales salaries	75,000	15,000	3,000
Printing	10,000	20,000	5,000
Travel	14,000	21,000	1,500
Fixed costs			
Rent	40,000	50,000	12,300
Insurance	5,000	2,000	1,000
Depreciation	80,000	90,000	56,000
Investment in assets	1,000,000	1,200,000	800,000

Instructions

a. Determine which of the items should be included in the responsibility report for each of the three managers.

b. Compare the budgeted measures with the actual results. Decide which results should be called to the attention of each manager.

Real-World Focus

CT23.3 Computer Associates International, Inc., the world's leading business software company, delivers the end-to-end infrastructure to enable e-business through innovative technology, services, and education. Recently, Computer Associates had 19,000 employees worldwide and revenue of over $6 billion.

The following information is from the company's annual report.

Computer Associates International, Inc.
Management Discussion

The Company has experienced a pattern of business whereby revenue for its third and fourth fiscal quarters reflects an increase over first- and second-quarter revenue. The Company attributes this increase to clients' increased spending at the end of their calendar year budgetary periods and the culmination of its annual sales plan. Since the Company's costs do not increase proportionately with the third- and fourth-quarters' increase in revenue, the higher revenue in these quarters results in greater profit margins and income. Fourth-quarter profitability is traditionally affected by significant new hirings, training, and education expenditures for the succeeding year.

Instructions

a. Why don't the company's costs increase proportionately as the revenues increase in the third and fourth quarters?

b. What type of budgeting seems appropriate for the Computer Associates situation?

Communication Activity

CT23.4 The manufacturing overhead budget for Fleming Company contains the following items.

Variable costs		Fixed costs	
Indirect materials	$22,000	Supervision	$17,000
Indirect labor	12,000	Inspection costs	1,000
Maintenance expense	10,000	Insurance expense	2,000
Manufacturing supplies	6,000	Depreciation	15,000
Total variable	$50,000	Total fixed	$35,000

The budget was based on an estimated 2,000 units being produced. During the past month, 1,500 units were produced, and the following costs incurred.

Variable costs		Fixed costs	
Indirect materials	$22,500	Supervision	$18,400
Indirect labor	13,500	Inspection costs	1,200
Maintenance expense	8,200	Insurance expense	2,200
Manufacturing supplies	5,000	Depreciation	14,700
Total variable	$49,200	Total fixed	$36,500

Instructions

a. Determine which items would be controllable by Fred Bedner, the production manager.

b. How much should have been spent during the month for the manufacture of the 1,500 units?

c. Prepare a flexible manufacturing overhead budget report for Mr. Bedner.

d. Prepare a responsibility report. Include only the costs that would have been controllable by Mr. Bedner. Assume that the supervision cost above includes Mr. Bedner's salary of $10,000, both at budget and actual. In an attached memo, describe clearly for Mr. Bedner the areas in which his performance needs to be improved.

Ethics Case

CT23.5 American Products Corporation participates in a highly competitive industry. In order to meet this competition and achieve profit goals, the company has chosen the decentralized form of organization. Each manager of a decentralized investment center is measured on the basis of profit contribution, market penetration, and return on investment. Failure to meet the objectives established by corporate management for these measures has not been acceptable and usually has resulted in demotion or dismissal of an investment center manager.

An anonymous survey of managers in the company revealed that the managers feel the pressure to compromise their personal ethical standards to achieve the corporate objectives. For example, at certain plant locations there was pressure to reduce quality control to a level which could not assure that all unsafe products would be rejected. Also, sales personnel were encouraged to use questionable sales tactics to obtain orders, including gifts and other incentives to purchasing agents.

The chief executive officer is disturbed by the survey findings. In his opinion, such behavior cannot be condoned by the company. He concludes that the company should do something about this problem.

Instructions

a. Who are the stakeholders (the affected parties) in this situation?

b. Identify the ethical implications, conflicts, or dilemmas in the above described situation.

c. What might the company do to reduce the pressures on managers and to decrease the ethical conflicts?

(CMA adapted)

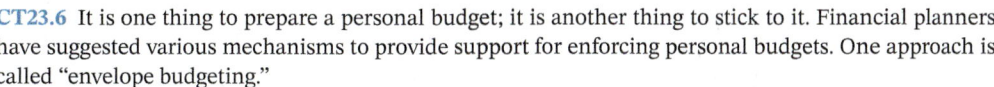

All About You

CT23.6 It is one thing to prepare a personal budget; it is another thing to stick to it. Financial planners have suggested various mechanisms to provide support for enforcing personal budgets. One approach is called "envelope budgeting."

Instructions

Do an Internet search on "envelope system money management" and then answer the following questions.

a. Summarize the process of envelope budgeting.

b. Evaluate whether you think you would benefit from envelope budgeting. What do you think are its strengths and weaknesses relative to your situation?

Considering Your Costs and Benefits

CT23.7 Preparing a personal budget is a great first step toward control over your personal finances. It is especially useful to prepare a budget when you face a big decision. For most people, the biggest decision they will ever make is whether to purchase a house. The percentage of people in the United States who own a home is high compared to many other countries. This is partially the result of U.S. government programs and incentives that encourage home ownership. For example, the interest on a home mortgage is tax-deductible.

Before purchasing a house, you should first consider whether buying it is the best choice for you. Suppose you just graduated from college and are moving to a new community. Should you immediately buy a new home?

YES: If I purchase a home, I am making my housing cost more like a "fixed cost," thus minimizing increases in my future housing costs. Also, I benefit from the appreciation in my home's value. Although recent turbulence in the economy has caused home prices in many communities to decline, I know that over the long term, home prices have increased across the country.

NO: I just moved to a new town, so I don't know the housing market. I am new to my job, so I don't know whether I will like it or my new community. Also, if my job does go well, it is likely that my income will increase in the next few years, so I will able to afford a better house if I wait. Therefore, the flexibility provided by renting is very valuable to me at this point in my life.

Instructions

Write a response indicating your position regarding this situation. Provide support for your view.

CHAPTER 24

Standard Costs and Balanced Scorecard

Chapter Preview

Standards are a fact of life. You met the admission standards for the school you are attending. The vehicle that you drive had to meet certain governmental emissions standards. The hamburgers and salads that you eat in a restaurant have to meet certain health and nutritional standards before they can be sold. As described in the following Feature Story, **Starbucks** has standards for the costs of its materials, labor, and overhead. The reason for standards in these cases is very simple: They help to ensure that overall product quality is high while keeping costs under control.

In this chapter, we continue the study of controlling costs. You will learn how to evaluate performance using standard costs and a balanced scorecard.

Feature Story

80,000 Different Caffeinated Combinations

When Howard Schultz purchased a small Seattle coffee-roasting business in 1987, he set out to create a new kind of company. He thought the company should sell coffee by the cup in its store, in addition to the bags of roasted beans it already sold. He also saw the store as a place where you could order a beverage, custom-made to your unique tastes, in an environment that would give you the sense that you had escaped, if only momentarily, from the chaos we call life. Finally, Schultz believed that the company would prosper if employees shared in its success.

In a little more than 20 years, Howard Schultz's company, **Starbucks**, grew from that one store to over 17,000 locations in 54 countries. That is an incredible rate of growth, and it didn't happen by accident. While Starbucks does everything it can to maximize the customer's experience, behind the scenes it needs to control costs. Consider the almost infinite options of beverage combinations and variations at Starbucks. The company must determine the most efficient way to make each beverage, it must communicate these methods in the form of standards to its employees, and it must then evaluate whether those standards are being met.

Schultz's book, *Onward: How Starbucks Fought for Its Life Without Losing Its Soul*, describes a painful period in which Starbucks had to close 600 stores and lay off thousands of employees. However, when a prominent shareholder suggested that the company eliminate its employee healthcare plan, as so many other companies had done, Schultz refused. The healthcare plan represented one of the company's most tangible commitments to employee well-being as well as to corporate social responsibility. Schultz feels strongly that providing health care to the company's employees is an essential part of the standard cost of a cup of Starbucks' coffee.

 In WileyPLUS, watch the *Starbucks* video to learn more about how the company sets standards, and watch the *Southwest Airlines* video to learn more about the real-world use of the balanced scorecard.

Chapter Outline

LEARNING OBJECTIVES

LO 1 Describe standard costs.	• Distinguishing between standards and budgets • Setting standard costs	**DO IT! 1** Standard Costs
LO 2 Determine direct materials variances.	• Analyzing and reporting variances • Calculating direct materials variances	**DO IT! 2** Direct Materials Variances
LO 3 Determine direct labor and total manufacturing overhead variances.	• Direct labor variances • Manufacturing overhead variances	**DO IT! 3** Labor and Manufacturing Overhead Variances
LO 4 Prepare variance reports and balanced scorecards.	• Reporting variances • Income statement presentation of variances • Balanced scorecard	**DO IT! 4** Reporting Variances

Go to the Review and Practice section at the end of the chapter for a targeted summary and practice applications with solutions.
Visit WileyPLUS for additional tutorials and practice opportunities.

Overview of Standard Costs

LEARNING OBJECTIVE 1
Describe standard costs.

Standards are common in business. Those imposed by government agencies are often called **regulations**. They include the Fair Labor Standards Act, the Equal Employment Opportunity Act, and a multitude of environmental standards. Standards established internally by a company may extend to personnel matters, such as employee absenteeism and ethical codes of conduct, quality control standards for products, and standard costs for goods and services. In managerial accounting, standard costs are predetermined unit costs, which companies use as measures of performance.

We focus on manufacturing operations in this chapter. But you should recognize that standard costs also apply to many types of service businesses as well. For example, a fast-food restaurant such as McDonald's knows the price it should pay for pickles, beef, buns, and other ingredients. It also knows how much time it should take an employee to flip hamburgers. If the company pays too much for pickles or if employees take too much time to prepare Big Macs, McDonald's notices the deviations from standards and takes corrective action. Not-for-profit entities, such as universities, charitable organizations, and governmental agencies, also may use standard costs as measures of performance.

Standard costs offer a number of advantages to an organization, as shown in Illustration 24.1. The organization will realize these advantages only when standard costs are carefully established and prudently used. Using standards solely as a way to place blame can have a negative effect on managers and employees. To minimize this effect, many companies offer wage incentives to those who meet the standards.

ILLUSTRATION 24.1 Advantages of standard costs

Advantages of Standard Costs

Facilitate management planning

Promote greater economy by making employees more "cost-conscious"

Useful in setting selling prices

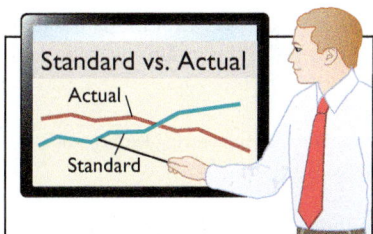

Contribute to management control by providing basis for evaluation of cost control

Useful in highlighting variances in management by exception

Simplify costing of inventories and reduce clerical costs

Distinguishing Between Standards and Budgets

Both **standards** and **budgets** are predetermined costs, and both contribute to management planning and control. There is a difference, however, in the way the terms are expressed. A standard is a **unit** amount. A budget is a **total** amount. Thus, it is customary to state that the **standard cost** of direct labor for a unit of product is, say, $10. If the company produces 5,000 units of the product, the $50,000 of direct labor is the **budgeted** labor cost. A standard is the budgeted **cost per unit** of product. A standard is therefore concerned with each individual cost component that makes up the entire budget.

There are important accounting differences between budgets and standards. Except in the application of manufacturing overhead to jobs and processes, budget data are not journalized in cost accounting systems. In contrast, as we illustrate in the appendix to this chapter, standard costs may be incorporated into cost accounting systems. Also, a company may report its inventories at standard cost in its financial statements, but it would not report inventories at budgeted costs.

Setting Standard Costs

The setting of standard costs to produce a unit of product is a difficult task. It requires input from all persons who have responsibility for costs and quantities. To determine the standard cost of direct materials, management consults purchasing agents, product managers, quality control engineers, and production supervisors. In setting the standard cost for direct labor, managers obtain pay rate data from the payroll department. Industrial engineers generally determine the labor time requirements. The managerial accountant provides important input for the standard-setting process by accumulating historical cost data and by knowing how costs respond to changes in activity levels.

To be effective in controlling costs, standard costs need to be current at all times. Thus, standards are under continuous review. They should change whenever managers determine that the existing standard is not a good measure of performance. Circumstances that warrant revision of a standard include changed wage rates resulting from a new union contract, a change in product specifications, or the implementation of a new manufacturing method.

Ideal versus Normal Standards

Companies set standards at one of two levels: ideal or normal. **Ideal standards** represent optimum levels of performance under perfect operating conditions. **Normal standards** represent efficient levels of performance that are attainable under expected operating conditions.

Some managers believe ideal standards will stimulate workers to ever-increasing improvement. However, most managers believe that ideal standards lower the morale of the workforce because they are difficult, if not impossible, to meet (see **Ethics Note**). Very few companies use ideal standards.

Most companies that use standards set them at a normal level. Properly set, normal standards should be **rigorous but attainable**. Normal standards allow for rest periods, machine breakdowns, and other "normal" contingencies in the production process. In the remainder of this chapter, we will assume that standard costs are set at a normal level.

> **ETHICS NOTE**
> When standards are set too high, employees sometimes feel pressure to consider unethical practices to meet these standards.

Accounting Across the Organization   U.S. Navy

SpotX/iStockphoto

How Do Standards Help a Business?

A number of organizations, including corporations, consultants, and governmental agencies, share information regarding performance standards in an effort to create a standard set of measures for thousands of business processes. The group, referred to as the Open Standards Benchmarking Collaborative, includes **IBM**, **Procter and Gamble**, the **U.S. Navy**, and the **World Bank**. Companies that are interested in participating can go to the group's website and enter their information.

Source: Becky Partida, "Benchmark Your Manufacturing Performance," Control Engineering (February 4, 2013).

How will the creation of such standards help a business or organization? (Go to WileyPLUS for this answer and additional questions.)

A Case Study

To establish the standard cost of producing a product, it is necessary to establish standards for each manufacturing cost element—direct materials, direct labor, and manufacturing overhead. The standard for each element is derived from the standard price to be paid and the standard quantity to be used.

To illustrate, we use an extended example. Xonic Beverage Company uses standard costs to measure performance at the production facility of its caffeinated energy drink, Xonic Tonic. Xonic produces one-gallon containers of concentrated syrup that it sells to coffee and smoothie shops, and other retail outlets. The syrup is mixed with ice water or ice "slush" before serving. The potency of the beverage varies depending on the amount of concentrated syrup used.

Direct Materials The **direct materials price standard** is the cost per finished unit of product of direct materials that should be incurred. This standard is based on the purchasing department's best estimate of the **cost of raw materials**. This cost is frequently based on current purchase prices. The price standard also includes an amount for related costs such as receiving, storing, and handling. **Illustration 24.2** shows the materials price standard per pound of material for Xonic Tonic.

Item	Price
Purchase price, net of discounts	$2.70
Freight	0.20
Receiving and handling	0.10
Standard direct materials price per pound	**$3.00**

ILLUSTRATION 24.2
Setting direct materials price standard

The **direct materials quantity standard** is the quantity of direct materials that management determines should be used per unit of finished goods. This standard is expressed as a physical measure, such as pounds, barrels, or board feet. In setting the standard, management considers both the quality and quantity of materials required to manufacture the product. The standard includes allowances for unavoidable waste and normal spoilage. The standard quantity per unit for Xonic Tonic is shown in **Illustration 24.3**.

Item	Quantity (Pounds)
Required materials	3.5
Allowance for waste	0.4
Allowance for spoilage	0.1
Standard direct materials quantity per unit	**4.0**

ILLUSTRATION 24.3
Setting direct materials quantity standard

The standard direct materials cost per unit is the standard direct materials price times the standard direct materials quantity. For Xonic, the standard direct materials cost per gallon of Xonic Tonic is $12.00 ($3 × 4 pounds).

Direct Labor The **direct labor price standard** is the rate per hour that should be incurred for direct labor (see **Alternative Terminology**). This standard is based on current wage rates, adjusted for anticipated changes such as cost of living adjustments (COLAs). The price standard also generally includes employer payroll taxes and fringe benefits, such as paid holidays and vacations. For Xonic, the direct labor price standard is as shown in **Illustration 24.4**.

ALTERNATIVE TERMINOLOGY
The direct labor price standard is also called the *direct labor rate standard*.

Item	Price
Hourly wage rate	$12.50
COLA	0.25
Payroll taxes	0.75
Fringe benefits	1.50
Standard direct labor rate per hour	**$15.00**

ILLUSTRATION 24.4
Setting direct labor price standard

ALTERNATIVE TERMINOLOGY

The direct labor quantity standard is also called the *direct labor efficiency standard*.

The **direct labor quantity standard** is the time that management determines should be required to make one unit of the product (see **Alternative Terminology**). This standard is especially critical in labor-intensive companies. Allowances should be made in this standard for rest periods, cleanup, machine setup, and machine downtime. **Illustration 24.5** shows the direct labor quantity standard for Xonic.

ILLUSTRATION 24.5

Setting direct labor quantity standard

Item	Quantity (Hours)
Actual production time	1.5
Rest periods and cleanup	0.2
Setup and downtime	0.3
Standard direct labor hours per unit	**2.0**

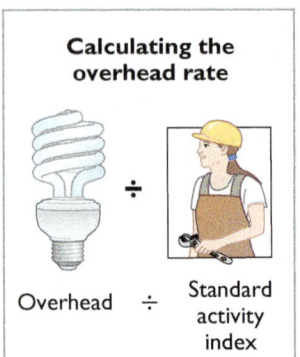

Calculating the overhead rate

Overhead ÷ Standard activity index

The standard direct labor cost per unit of finished product is the standard direct labor rate times the standard direct labor hours. For Xonic, the standard direct labor cost per gallon is $30 ($15 × 2 hours).

Manufacturing Overhead For manufacturing overhead, companies use a **standard predetermined overhead rate** in setting the standard. This overhead rate is determined by dividing budgeted overhead costs by an expected standard activity index. For example, the index may be standard direct labor hours or standard machine hours.

As discussed in Chapter 17, many companies employ activity-based costing (ABC) to allocate overhead costs. Because ABC uses multiple activity indices to allocate overhead costs, it results in a better correlation between activities and costs incurred than do other methods. As a result, the use of ABC can significantly improve the usefulness of standard costing for management decision-making.

Xonic uses standard direct labor hours as the activity index. The company expects to produce 13,200 gallons of Xonic Tonic during the year at normal capacity. **Normal capacity** is the average activity output that a company should experience over the long run. Since it takes two direct labor hours for each gallon, total standard direct labor hours are 26,400 (13,200 gallons × 2 hours).

At normal capacity of 26,400 direct labor hours, overhead costs are budgeted to be $132,000. Of that amount, $79,200 are variable and $52,800 are fixed. **Illustration 24.6** shows computation of the standard predetermined overhead rates for Xonic.

ILLUSTRATION 24.6

Computing predetermined overhead rates

	Budgeted Overhead Costs	Amount	÷	Standard Direct Labor Hours	=	Overhead Rate per Direct Labor Hour
Variable		$ 79,200		26,400		$3.00
Fixed		52,800		26,400		2.00
Total		$132,000		26,400		**$5.00**

The standard manufacturing overhead cost per unit is the predetermined overhead rate times the activity index quantity standard. For Xonic, which uses direct labor hours as its activity index, the standard manufacturing overhead cost per gallon of Xonic Tonic is $10 ($5 × 2 hours).

Total Standard Cost per Unit After a company has established the standard quantity and price per unit of finished product for each cost element, it can determine the total standard cost. The total standard cost per unit is the sum of the standard costs of direct materials, direct labor, and manufacturing overhead. The total standard cost per gallon of Xonic Tonic is $52, as the standard cost card in **Illustration 24.7** shows.

ILLUSTRATION 24.7
Standard cost per gallon of Xonic Tonic

Product: Xonic Tonic		Unit Measure: Gallon		
Manufacturing Cost Elements	Standard Quantity	× Standard Price	=	Standard Cost
Direct materials	4 pounds	$ 3.00		$12.00
Direct labor	2 hours	$15.00		30.00
Manufacturing overhead	2 hours	$ 5.00		10.00
				$52.00

The company prepares a standard cost card for each product. This card provides the basis for determining variances from standards.

DO IT! 1 | Standard Costs

Ridette Inc. accumulated the following standard cost data concerning product Cty31.

Direct materials per unit: 1.5 pounds at $4 per pound
Direct labor per unit: 0.25 hours at $13 per hour.
Manufacturing overhead: allocated based on direct labor hours at a predetermined rate of $15.60 per direct labor hour.

Compute the standard cost of one unit of product Cty31.

Solution

Manufacturing Cost Element	Standard Quantity	× Standard Price	=	Standard Cost
Direct materials	1.5 pounds	$ 4.00		$ 6.00
Direct labor	0.25 hours	$13.00		3.25
Manufacturing overhead	0.25 hours	$15.60		3.90
Total				$13.15

Related exercise material: **BE24.2, BE24.3, DO IT! 24.1, E24.1, E24.2, and E24.3.**

ACTION PLAN
- Know that standard costs are predetermined unit costs.
- To establish the standard cost of producing a product, establish the standard for each manufacturing cost element—direct materials, direct labor, and manufacturing overhead.
- Compute the standard cost for each element from the standard price to be paid and the standard quantity to be used.

Direct Materials Variances

LEARNING OBJECTIVE 2
Determine direct materials variances.

Analyzing and Reporting Variances

One of the major management uses of standard costs is to identify variances from standards. **Variances** are the differences between total actual costs and total standard costs (see **Alternative Terminology**).

To illustrate, assume that in producing 1,000 gallons of Xonic Tonic in the month of June, Xonic incurred the costs listed in **Illustration 24.8**.

ALTERNATIVE TERMINOLOGY
In business, the term *variance* is also used to indicate differences between total budgeted and total actual costs.

> **ILLUSTRATION 24.8**
> Actual production costs

Direct materials	$13,020
Direct labor	31,080
Variable overhead	6,500
Fixed overhead	4,400
Total actual costs	$55,000

Companies determine total standard costs by multiplying the units produced by the standard cost per unit. The total standard cost of Xonic Tonic is $52,000 (1,000 gallons × $52). Thus, the total variance is $3,000, as shown in **Illustration 24.9**.

> **ILLUSTRATION 24.9**
> Computation of total variance

Actual costs	$55,000
Less: Standard costs	52,000
Total variance	**$ 3,000**

Note that the variance is expressed in total dollars, not on a per unit basis.

When actual costs exceed standard costs, the variance is **unfavorable**. The $3,000 variance in June for Xonic Tonic is unfavorable. An unfavorable variance has a negative connotation as it reduces profit. It suggests that the company paid too much for one or more of the manufacturing cost elements or that it used the elements inefficiently.

If actual costs are less than standard costs, the variance is **favorable**. A favorable variance has a positive connotation. It suggests efficiencies in incurring manufacturing costs and in using direct materials, direct labor, and manufacturing overhead.

However, be careful: A favorable variance could be obtained by using inferior materials. In printing wedding invitations, for example, a favorable variance could result from using an inferior grade of paper. Or, a favorable variance might be achieved in installing tires on an automobile assembly line by tightening only half of the lug bolts. A variance is not favorable if the company has sacrificed quality control standards.

To interpret a variance, you must analyze its components. A variance can result from differences related to the cost of materials, labor, or overhead. **Illustration 24.10** shows that the total variance is the sum of the materials, labor, and overhead variances.

> **ILLUSTRATION 24.10**
> Components of total variance

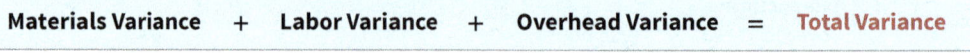

Materials Variance + Labor Variance + Overhead Variance = Total Variance

In the following discussion, you will see that the materials variance and the labor variance are the sum of variances resulting from price differences and quantity differences. **Illustration 24.11** shows a format for computing the price and quantity variances.

> **ILLUSTRATION 24.11**
> Breakdown of materials or labor variance into price and quantity variances

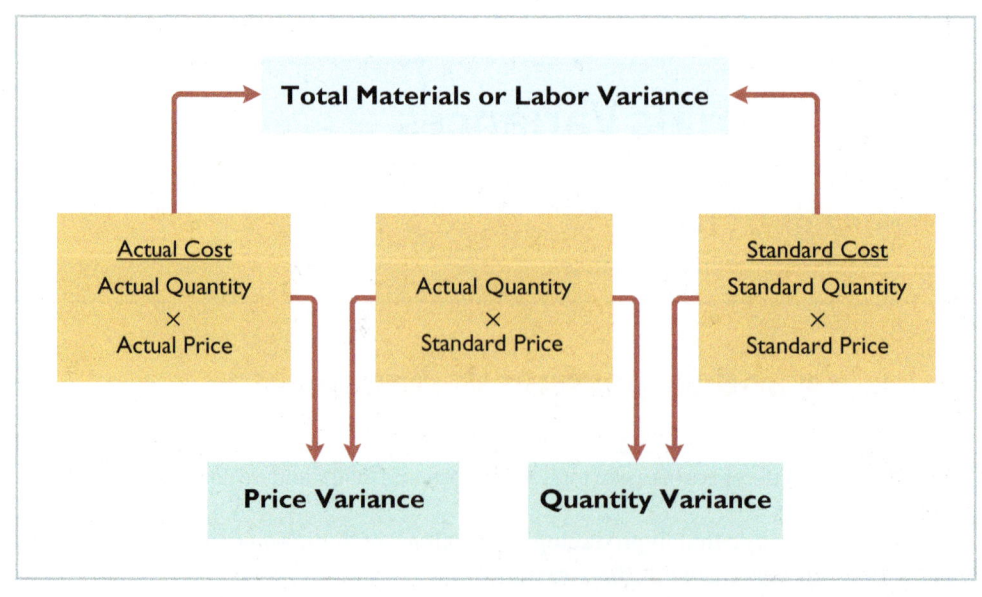

Note that the left side of the matrix is actual cost (actual quantity times actual price). The right hand is standard cost (standard quantity times standard price). The difference between these two amounts (shown in the blue box in Illustration 24.11) is the total materials or labor variance. The only additional element you need in order to compute the price and quantity variances is the middle element, the actual quantity at the standard price.

To compute the price variance, we hold the quantity constant (at the actual quantity) but vary the price (actual versus standard). Similarly, to compute the quantity variance, we hold the price constant (at the standard price) but vary the quantity (actual versus standard).

Calculating Direct Materials Variances

Part of Xonic's total variance of $3,000 is due to a materials variance (see **Decision Tools**). In completing the order for 1,000 gallons of Xonic Tonic, the company used 4,200 pounds of direct materials. From Illustration 24.3, we know that Xonic's standards require it to use 4 pounds of materials per gallon produced, so it should have only used 4,000 (4 × 1,000) pounds of direct materials to produce 1,000 gallons. The direct materials were purchased at a price of $3.10 per unit. Illustration 24.2 shows that the standard cost of each pound of direct materials is $3 instead of the $3.10 actually paid. **Illustration 24.12** shows that the **total materials variance** is computed as the difference between the amount paid (actual quantity times actual price) and the amount that should have been paid based on standards (standard quantity times standard price of materials).

> **Decision Tools**
> The materials price and materials quantity variances help managers determine if they have met their price and quantity objectives regarding materials.

Actual Quantity × Actual Price	−	Standard Quantity × Standard Price	=	Total Materials Variance
(AQ) × (AP)		(SQ) × (SP)		(TMV)
(4,200 × $3.10)	−	(4,000* × $3.00)		
$13,020	−	$12,000	=	$1,020 U

*1,000 units × 4 pounds

ILLUSTRATION 24.12
Formula for total materials variance

Thus, for Xonic, the total materials variance is $1,020 ($13,020 − $12,000) unfavorable (abbreviated as "U"). It is unfavorable because the actual cost exceeded the standard cost.

The total materials variance could be caused by differences in the price paid for the materials or by differences in the amount of materials used. **Illustration 24.13** shows that the total materials variance is the sum of the materials price variance and the materials quantity variance.

Materials Price Variance	+	Materials Quantity Variance	=	Total Materials Variance

ILLUSTRATION 24.13
Components of total materials variance

The materials price variance results from a difference between the actual price and the standard price. **Illustration 24.14** shows that the **materials price variance** is computed as the difference between the actual amount paid (actual quantity of materials times actual price) and the standard amount that should have been paid for the materials used (actual quantity of materials times standard price).[1]

Actual Quantity × Actual Price	−	Actual Quantity × Standard Price	=	Materials Price Variance
(AQ) × (AP)		(AQ) × (SP)		(MPV)
(4,200 × $3.10)	−	(4,200 × $3.00)		
$13,020	−	$12,600	=	$420 U

ILLUSTRATION 24.14
Formula for materials price variance

For Xonic, the materials price variance is $420 ($13,020 − $12,600) unfavorable.

---
[1]Assume that all materials purchased during the period are used in production and that no units remain in inventory at the end of the period.

The price variance can also be computed by multiplying the actual quantity purchased by the difference between the actual and standard price per unit (see **Helpful Hint**). The computation in this case is 4,200 × ($3.10 − $3.00) = $420 U.

As seen in Illustration 24.13, the other component of the materials variance is the quantity variance. The quantity variance results from differences between the amount of material actually used and the amount that should have been used. As shown in **Illustration 24.15**, the **materials quantity variance** is computed as the difference between the standard cost of the actual quantity (actual quantity times standard price) and the standard cost of the amount that should have been used (standard quantity times standard price for materials).

> **HELPFUL HINT**
> The alternative formula is:
> $\boxed{AQ} \times \boxed{AP - SP} = \boxed{MPV}$

ILLUSTRATION 24.15
Formula for materials quantity variance

Actual Quantity × Standard Price		Standard Quantity × Standard Price		Materials Quantity Variance
(AQ) × (SP)	−	(SQ) × (SP)	=	(MQV)
(4,200 × $3.00)	−	(4,000 × $3.00)		
$12,600	−	$12,000	=	$600 U

> **HELPFUL HINT**
> The alternative formula is:
> $\boxed{SP} \times \boxed{AQ - SQ} = \boxed{MQV}$

Thus, for Xonic, the materials quantity variance is $600 ($12,600 − $12,000) unfavorable.

The quantity variance can also be computed by applying the standard price to the difference between actual and standard quantities used (see **Helpful Hint**). The computation in this example is $3.00 × (4,200 − 4,000) = $600 U.

Illustration 24.16 summarizes the total materials variance of $1,020 U.

ILLUSTRATION 24.16
Summary of materials variances

Materials price variance	$ 420 U
Materials quantity variance	600 U
Total materials variance	**$1,020 U**

Companies sometimes use a matrix to analyze a variance. **When the matrix is used, a company computes the amounts using the formulas for each cost element first and then computes the variances. Illustration 24.17** shows the completed matrix for the direct materials variance for Xonic. The matrix provides a convenient structure for determining each variance.

ILLUSTRATION 24.17 Matrix for direct materials variances

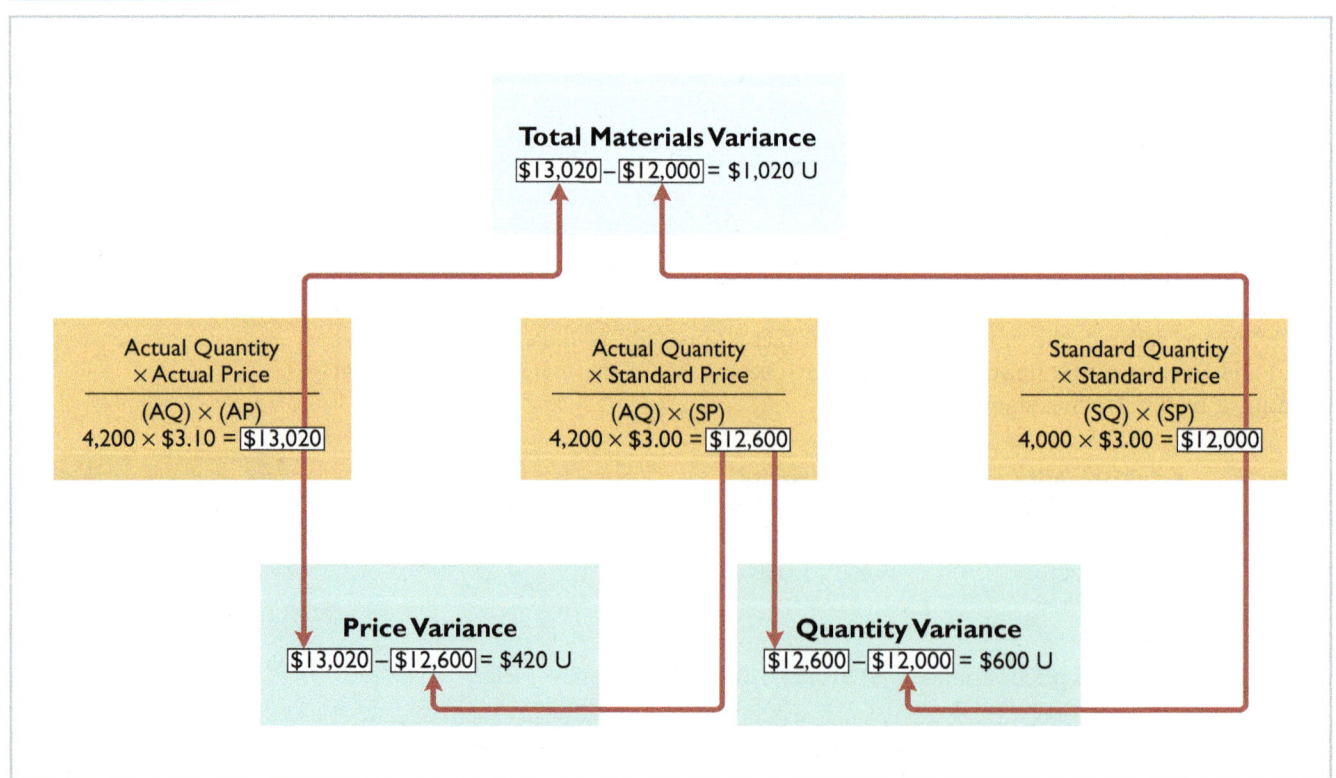

Causes of Materials Variances

What are the causes of a variance? The causes may relate to both internal and external factors. The investigation of a **materials price variance usually begins in the purchasing department**. Many factors affect the price paid for raw materials. These include availability of quantity and cash discounts, the quality of the materials requested, and the delivery method used. To the extent that these factors are considered in setting the price standard, the purchasing department is responsible for any variances.

However, a variance may be beyond the control of the purchasing department. Sometimes, for example, prices may rise faster than expected. Moreover, actions by groups over which the company has no control, such as the OPEC nations' oil price increases, may cause an unfavorable variance. For example, during a recent year, **Kraft Foods** and **Kellogg Company** both experienced unfavorable materials price variances when the cost of dairy and wheat products jumped unexpectedly. There are also times when a production department may be responsible for the price variance. This may occur when a rush order forces the company to pay a higher price for the materials.

The starting point for determining the cause(s) of a significant **materials quantity variance is in the production department**. If the variances are due to inexperienced workers, faulty machinery, or carelessness, the production department is responsible. However, if the materials obtained by the purchasing department were of inferior quality, then the purchasing department is responsible.

DO IT! 2 | Direct Materials Variances

The standard cost of Wonder Walkers includes two units of direct materials at $8.00 per unit. During July, the company buys 22,000 units of direct materials at $7.50 and uses those materials to produce 10,000 Wonder Walkers. Compute the total, price, and quantity variances for materials.

Solution
Standard quantity = 10,000 × 2 = 20,000
Substituting amounts into the formulas, the variances are:

Total materials variance = (22,000 × $7.50) − (20,000 × $8.00) = $5,000 unfavorable
Materials price variance = (22,000 × $7.50) − (22,000 × $8.00) = $11,000 favorable
Materials quantity variance = (22,000 × $8.00) − (20,000 × $8.00) = $16,000 unfavorable

Related exercise material: **BE24.4, DO IT! 24.2, and E24.5**.

ACTION PLAN
Use the formulas for computing each of the materials variances:
- Total materials variance = (AQ × AP) − (SQ × SP)
- Materials price variance = (AQ × AP) − (AQ × SP)
- Materials quantity variance = (AQ × SP) − (SQ × SP)

Direct Labor and Manufacturing Overhead Variances

LEARNING OBJECTIVE 3
Determine direct labor and total manufacturing overhead variances.

Direct Labor Variances

The process of determining direct labor variances is the same as for determining the direct materials variances (see **Decision Tools**). In completing the Xonic Tonic order, the company incurred 2,100 direct labor hours. The standard hours allowed for the units produced were

Decision Tools
Labor price and labor quantity variances help managers to determine if they have met their price and quantity objectives regarding labor.

2,000 hours (1,000 gallons × 2 hours). The standard labor rate was $15 per hour, and the actual labor rate was $14.80.

The total labor variance is the difference between the amount actually paid for labor versus the amount that should have been paid. **Illustration 24.18** shows that the **total labor variance** is computed as the difference between the amount actually paid for labor (actual hours times actual rate) and the amount that should have been paid (standard hours times standard rate for labor).

ILLUSTRATION 24.18
Formula for total labor variance

Actual Hours × Actual Rate	−	Standard Hours × Standard Rate	=	Total Labor Variance
(AH) × (AR)		(SH) × (SR)		(TLV)
(2,100 × $14.80)	−	(2,000 × $15.00)		
$31,080	−	$30,000	=	$1,080 U

The total labor variance is $1,080 ($31,080 − $30,000) unfavorable.

The total labor variance is caused by differences in the labor rate or difference in labor hours. **Illustration 24.19** shows that the total labor variance is the sum of the labor price variance and the labor quantity variance.

ILLUSTRATION 24.19
Components of total labor variance

Labor Price Variance	+	Labor Quantity Variance	=	Total Labor Variance

The labor price variance results from the difference between the rate paid to workers versus the rate that was supposed to be paid. **Illustration 24.20** shows that the **labor price variance** is computed as the difference between the actual amount paid (actual hours times actual rate) and the amount that should have been paid for the number of hours worked (actual hours times standard rate for labor).

ILLUSTRATION 24.20
Formula for labor price variance

Actual Hours × Actual Rate	−	Actual Hours × Standard Rate	=	Labor Price Variance
(AH) × (AR)		(AH) × (SR)		(LPV)
(2,100 × $14.80)	−	(2,100 × $15.00)		
$31,080	−	$31,500	=	$420 F

For Xonic, the labor price variance is $420 ($31,080 − $31,500) favorable.

HELPFUL HINT

The alternative formula is:
$$\boxed{AH} \times \boxed{AR - SR} = \boxed{LPV}$$

The labor price variance can also be computed by multiplying actual hours worked by the difference between the actual pay rate and the standard pay rate (see **Helpful Hint**). The computation in this example is 2,100 × ($15.00 − $14.80) = $420 F.

The other component of the total labor variance is the labor quantity variance. The labor quantity variance results from the difference between the actual number of labor hours and the number of hours that should have been worked for the quantity produced. **Illustration 24.21** shows that the **labor quantity variance** is computed as the difference between the amount that should have been paid for the hours worked (actual hours times standard rate) and the amount that should have been paid for the amount of hours that should have been worked (standard hours times standard rate for labor).

ILLUSTRATION 24.21
Formula for labor quantity variance

Actual Hours × Standard Rate	−	Standard Hours × Standard Rate	=	Labor Quantity Variance
(AH) × (SR)		(SH) × (SR)		(LQV)
(2,100 × $15.00)	−	(2,000 × $15.00)		
$31,500	−	$30,000	=	$1,500 U

Thus, for Xonic, the labor quantity variance is $1,500 ($31,500 − $30,000) unfavorable.

The same result can be obtained by multiplying the standard rate by the difference between actual hours worked and standard hours allowed (see **Helpful Hint**). In this case, the computation is $15.00 × (2,100 − 2,000) = $1,500 U.

Illustration 24.22 summarizes the total direct labor variance of $1,080 U.

> **HELPFUL HINT**
> The alternative formula is:
> $SR \times (AH - SH) = LQV$

Labor price variance	$ 420 F
Labor quantity variance	1,500 U
Total direct labor variance	**$1,080 U**

ILLUSTRATION 24.22

Summary of labor variances

These results can also be obtained from the matrix in **Illustration 24.23**.

ILLUSTRATION 24.23 Matrix for direct labor variances

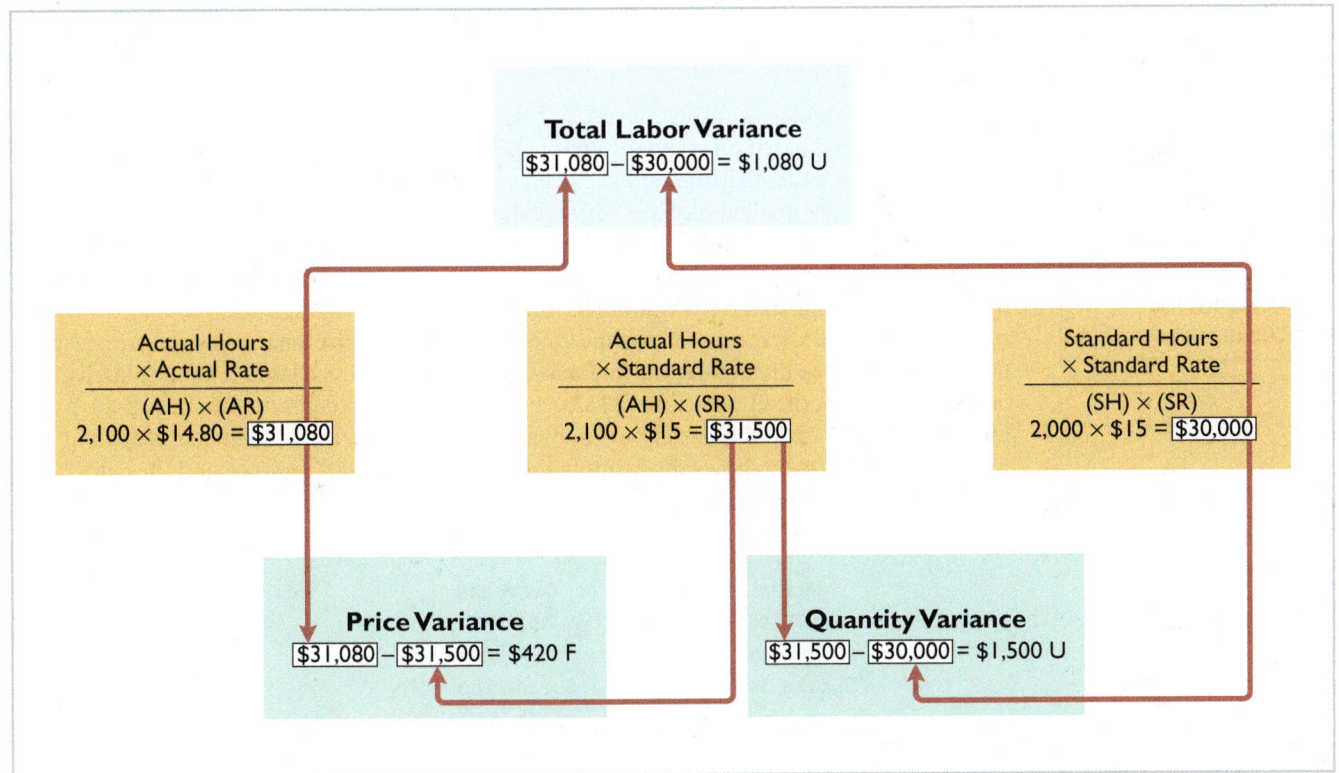

Causes of Labor Variances

Labor price variances usually result from two factors: (1) paying workers **different wages than expected**, and (2) **misallocation of workers**. In companies where pay rates are determined by union contracts, labor price variances should be infrequent. When workers are not unionized, there is a much higher likelihood of such variances. The responsibility for these variances rests with the manager who authorized the wage change.

Misallocation of the workforce refers to using skilled workers in place of unskilled workers and vice versa. The use of an inexperienced worker instead of an experienced one will result in a favorable price variance because of the lower pay rate of the unskilled worker. An unfavorable price variance would result if a skilled worker were substituted for an inexperienced one. The production department generally is responsible for labor price variances resulting from misallocation of the workforce.

Labor quantity variances relate to the **efficiency of workers**. The cause of a quantity variance generally can be traced to the production department. The causes of an unfavorable variance may be poor training, worker fatigue, faulty machinery, or carelessness. These causes are the responsibility of the **production department**. However, if the excess time is due to inferior materials, the responsibility falls outside the production department and resides instead with the purchasing department.

Manufacturing Overhead Variances

The **total overhead variance** is the difference between the actual overhead costs and overhead costs applied based on standard hours allowed for the amount of goods produced. As indicated in Illustration 24.8, Xonic incurred overhead costs of $10,900 to produce 1,000 gallons of Xonic Tonic in June. The computation of the actual overhead is comprised of a variable and a fixed component. **Illustration 24.24** shows this computation.

ILLUSTRATION 24.24
Actual overhead costs

Variable overhead	$ 6,500
Fixed overhead	4,400
Total actual overhead	**$10,900**

Decision Tools

The total manufacturing overhead variance helps managers to determine if they have met their objectives regarding manufacturing overhead.

To find the total overhead variance in a standard costing system, we determine the overhead costs applied based on standard hours allowed (see **Decision Tools**). **Standard hours allowed** are the hours that *should* have been worked for the units produced. Overhead costs for Xonic Tonic are applied based on direct labor hours. Because it takes two hours of direct labor to produce one gallon of Xonic Tonic, for the 1,000-gallon Xonic Tonic order, the standard hours allowed are 2,000 hours (1,000 gallons × 2 hours). We then apply the predetermined overhead rate to the 2,000 standard hours allowed.

Recall from Illustration 24.6 that the amount of budgeted overhead costs at normal capacity of $132,000 was divided by normal capacity of 26,400 direct labor hours, to arrive at a predetermined overhead rate of $5 ($132,000 ÷ 26,400). The predetermined rate of $5 is then multiplied by the 2,000 standard hours allowed, to determine the overhead costs applied.

Illustration 24.25 shows the formula for the total overhead variance and the calculation for Xonic for the month of June.

ILLUSTRATION 24.25
Formula for total overhead variance

Actual Overhead	−	Overhead Applied*	=	Total Overhead Variance
$10,900	−	$10,000	=	$900 U
($6,500 + $4,400)		($5 × 2,000 hours)		

*Based on standard hours allowed.

Thus, for Xonic, the total overhead variance is $900 unfavorable.

The overhead variance is generally analyzed through a price and a quantity variance. (These computations are discussed in more detail in advanced courses.) The name usually given to the price variance is the **overhead controllable variance**; the quantity variance is referred to as the **overhead volume variance**. Appendix 24B discusses how the total overhead variance can be broken down into these two variances.

Causes of Manufacturing Overhead Variances

One reason for an overhead variance relates to over- or underspending on overhead items. For example, overhead may include indirect labor for which a company paid wages higher than the standard labor price allowed. Or, the price of electricity to run the company's machines increased, and the company did not anticipate this additional cost. Companies should investigate any spending variances to determine whether they will continue in the future. Generally, the responsibility for these variances rests with the production department.

The overhead variance can also result from the inefficient use of overhead. For example, because of poor maintenance, a number of the manufacturing machines are experiencing breakdowns on a consistent basis, leading to reduced production. Or, the flow of materials through the production process is impeded because of a lack of skilled labor to perform the necessary production tasks, due to a lack of planning. In both of these cases, the production department is responsible for the cause of these variances. On the other hand, overhead can also be underutilized because of a lack of sales orders. When the cause is a lack of sales orders, the responsibility rests outside the production department and resides instead with the sales department. For example, at one point **Chrysler** experienced a very significant unfavorable overhead variance because plant capacity was maintained at excessively high levels, due to overly optimistic sales forecasts.

People, Planet, and Profit Insight Starbucks

What's Brewing at Starbucks?

Archer Colin/SIPA/NewsCom

It's easy for a company to say it's committed to corporate social responsibility. But **Starbucks** actually spells out measurable goals. Recently, the company published its annual *Global Responsibility Report* in which it describes its goals, achievements, and even its shortcomings related to corporate social responsibility. For example, Starbucks achieved its goal of getting more than 50% of its electricity from renewable sources. It also has numerous goals related to purchasing coffee from sources that are certified as responsibly grown and ethically traded; providing funds for loans to coffee farmers; and fostering partnerships with **Conservation International** to provide training to farmers on ecologically friendly growing.

The report also candidly explains that the company did not meet its goal to cut energy consumption by 25%. It also fell far short of its goal of getting customers to reuse their cups. In those instances where it didn't achieve its goals, Starbucks set new goals and described steps it would take to achieve them. You can view the company's *Global Responsibility Report* at the Starbucks website.

Source: "Starbucks Launches 10th Global Responsibility Report," *Business Wire* (April 18, 2011).

What implications does Starbucks' commitment to corporate social responsibility have for the standard cost of a cup of coffee? (Go to WileyPLUS for this answer and additional questions.)

DO IT! 3 | Labor and Manufacturing Overhead Variances

The standard cost of Product YY includes 3 hours of direct labor at $12.00 per hour. The predetermined overhead rate is $20.00 per direct labor hour. During July, the company incurred 3,500 hours of direct labor at an average rate of $12.40 per hour and $71,300 of manufacturing overhead costs. It produced 1,200 units.

a. Compute the total, price, and quantity variances for labor.
b. Compute the total overhead variance.

Solution

Substituting amounts into the formulas, the variances are:

Total labor variance = (3,500 × $12.40) − (3,600 × $12.00) = $200 unfavorable

Labor price variance = (3,500 × $12.40) − (3,500 × $12.00) = $1,400 unfavorable

Labor quantity variance = (3,500 × $12.00) − (3,600 × $12.00) = $1,200 favorable

Total overhead variance = $71,300 − $72,000* = $700 favorable

*(1,200 × 3 hours) × $20.00

Related exercise material: **BE24.5, BE24.6, DO IT! 24.3, E24.4, E24.6, E24.7, E24.8, and E24.11.**

ACTION PLAN
- Use the formulas for computing each of the variances:

  Total labor variance = (AH × AR) − (SH × SR)
  Labor price variance = (AH × AR) − (AH × SR)
  Labor quantity variance = (AH × SR) − (SH × SR)
  Total overhead variance = Actual overhead − Overhead applied*

*Based on standard hours allowed.

Variance Reports and Balanced Scorecards

LEARNING OBJECTIVE 4
Prepare variance reports and balanced scorecards.

Reporting Variances

All variances should be reported to appropriate levels of management as soon as possible. The sooner managers are informed, the sooner they can evaluate problems and take corrective action.

The form, content, and frequency of variance reports vary considerably among companies. One approach is to prepare a weekly report for each department that has primary responsibility for cost control. Under this approach, materials price variances are reported to the purchasing department, and all other variances are reported to the production department that did the work. The report for Xonic shown in Illustration 24.26, with the materials for the Xonic Tonic order listed first, illustrates this approach.

ILLUSTRATION 24.26

Materials price variance report

Xonic
Variance Report—Purchasing Department
For Week Ended June 8, 2022

Type of Materials	Quantity Purchased	Actual Price	Standard Price	Price Variance	Explanation
X100	4,200 lbs.	$3.10	$3.00	$420 U	Rush order
X142	1,200 units	2.75	2.80	60 F	Quantity discount
A85	600 doz.	5.20	5.10	60 U	Regular supplier on strike
Total price variance				**$420 U**	

The explanation column is completed after consultation with the purchasing department manager.

Variance reports facilitate the principle of "management by exception" explained in Chapter 23. For example, the vice president of purchasing can use the report shown above to evaluate the effectiveness of the purchasing department manager. Or, the vice president of production can use production department variance reports to determine how well each production manager is controlling costs. In using variance reports, top management normally looks for **significant variances**. These may be judged on the basis of some quantitative measure, such as more than 10% of the standard or more than $1,000.

Income Statement Presentation of Variances

In income statements **prepared for management** under a standard cost accounting system, **cost of goods sold is stated at standard cost and the variances are disclosed separately**. Unfavorable variances increase cost of goods sold, while favorable variances decrease cost of goods sold. Illustration 24.27 shows the presentation of variances in an income statement. This income statement is based on the production and sale of 1,000 units of Xonic Tonic at $70 per unit. It also assumes selling and administrative costs of $3,000. Observe that each variance is shown, as well as the total net variance. In this example, variations from standard costs reduced net income by $3,000.

Standard costs may be used in financial statements prepared for stockholders and other external users. The costing of inventories at standard costs is in accordance with generally accepted accounting principles when there are no significant differences between actual costs and standard costs. Hewlett-Packard and Jostens, Inc., for example, report their inventories at standard costs. However, if there are significant differences between actual and standard costs, the financial statements must report inventories and cost of goods sold at actual costs.

It is also possible to show the variances in an income statement prepared in the variable costing (CVP) format. To do so, it is necessary to analyze the overhead variances into variable and fixed components. This type of analysis is explained in cost accounting texts.

ILLUSTRATION 24.27
Variances in income statement for management

Xonic
Income Statement
For the Month Ended June 30, 2022

Sales revenue		$70,000
Cost of goods sold (at standard)		52,000
Gross profit (at standard)		18,000
Variances		
Materials price	$ 420 U	
Materials quantity	600 U	
Labor price	420 F	
Labor quantity	1,500 U	
Overhead	900 U	
Total variance unfavorable		3,000
Gross profit (actual)		15,000
Selling and administrative expenses		3,000
Net income		$12,000

Balanced Scorecard

Financial measures (measurement of dollars), such as variance analysis and return on investment (ROI), are useful tools for evaluating performance. However, many companies now supplement these financial measures with nonfinancial measures to better assess performance and anticipate future results. For example, airlines like **Delta** and **United** use capacity utilization as an important measure to understand and predict future performance. Companies that publish the *New York Times* and the *Chicago Tribune* newspapers use circulation figures as another measure by which to assess performance. **Penske Automotive Group**, the owner of 300 dealerships, rewards executives for meeting employee retention targets. Illustration 24.28 lists some key nonfinancial measures used in various industries.

ILLUSTRATION 24.28 Nonfinancial measures used in various industries

Industry	Measure
Automobiles	Capacity utilization of plants. Average age of key assets. Impact of strikes. Brand-loyalty statistics.
Computer Systems	Market profile of customer end-products. Number of new products. Employee stock ownership percentages. Number of scientists and technicians used in R&D.
Chemicals	Customer satisfaction data. Factors affecting customer product selection. Number of patents and trademarks held. Customer brand awareness.
Regional Banks	Number of ATMs by state. Number of products used by average customer. Percentage of customer service calls handled by interactive voice response units. Personnel cost per employee. Credit card retention rates.

Source: Financial Accounting Standards Board, *Business Reporting: Insights into Enhancing Voluntary Disclosures* (Norwalk, Conn.: FASB, 2001).

Most companies recognize that both financial and nonfinancial measures can provide useful insights into what is happening in the company. As a result, many companies now use a broad-based measurement approach, called the **balanced scorecard**, to evaluate performance. The balanced scorecard incorporates financial and nonfinancial measures in an integrated system that links performance measurement with a company's strategic goals. Nearly 50% of the largest companies in the United States, including **Unilever**, **Chase**, and **Wal-Mart Stores Inc.**, are using the balanced scorecard approach.

The balanced scorecard evaluates company performance from a series of "perspectives." The four most commonly employed perspectives are as follows.

1. The financial perspective is the most traditional view of the company. It employs financial measures of performance used by most firms.
2. The customer perspective evaluates the company from the viewpoint of those people who buy its products or services. This view compares the company to competitors in terms of price, quality, product innovation, customer service, and other dimensions.
3. The internal process perspective evaluates the internal operating processes critical to success. All critical aspects of the value chain—including product development, production, delivery, and after-sale service—are evaluated to ensure that the company is operating effectively and efficiently.
4. The learning and growth perspective evaluates how well the company develops and retains its employees. This would include evaluation of such things as employee skills, employee satisfaction, training programs, and information dissemination.

Within each perspective, the balanced scorecard identifies objectives that contribute to attainment of strategic goals. Illustration 24.29 shows examples of objectives within each perspective.

ILLUSTRATION 24.29 Examples of objectives within the four perspectives of balanced scorecard

Perspective	Objective
Financial	Return on assets. Net income. Credit rating. Share price. Profit per employee.
Customer	Percentage of customers who would recommend product. Customer retention. Response time per customer request. Brand recognition. Customer service expense per customer.
Internal Process	Percentage of defect-free products. Stockouts. Labor utilization rates. Waste reduction. Planning accuracy.
Learning and Growth	Percentage of employees leaving in less than one year. Number of cross-trained employees. Ethics violations. Training hours. Reportable accidents.

The objectives are linked across perspectives in order to tie performance measurement to company goals. The financial-perspective objectives are normally set first, and then objectives are set in the other perspectives in order to accomplish the financial goals.

For example, within the financial perspective, a common goal is to increase profit per dollars invested as measured by ROI. In order to increase ROI, a customer-perspective objective might be to increase customer satisfaction as measured by the percentage of customers who would recommend the product to a friend. In order to increase customer satisfaction, an internal-process-perspective objective might be to increase product quality as measured by the percentage of defect-free units. Finally, in order to increase the percentage of defect-free units, the learning-and-growth-perspective objective might be to reduce factory employee turnover as measured by the percentage of employees leaving in under one year.

Illustration 24.30 illustrates this linkage across perspectives.

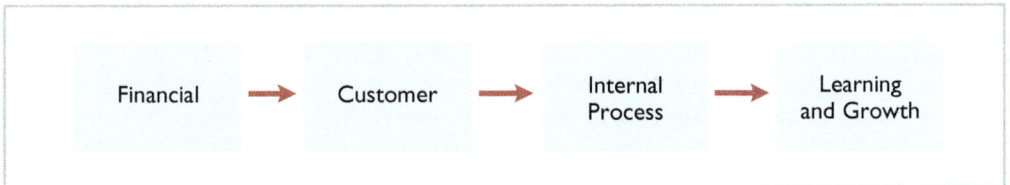

ILLUSTRATION 24.30

Linked process across balanced scorecard perspectives

Through this linked process, the company can better understand how to achieve its goals and what measures to use to evaluate performance.

In summary, the balanced scorecard does the following:

1. Employs both **financial and nonfinancial measures**. (For example, ROI is a financial measure; employee turnover is a nonfinancial measure.)
2. **Creates linkages** so that high-level corporate goals can be communicated all the way down to the shop floor.
3. **Provides measurable objectives for nonfinancial measures** such as product quality, rather than vague statements such as "We would like to improve quality."
4. Integrates all of the company's goals into a single performance measurement system, so that **an inappropriate amount of weight will not be placed on any single goal**.

Service Company Insight   United Airlines

PhotoDisc, Inc./ Getty Images

It May Be Time to Fly United Again

Many of the benefits of a balanced scorecard approach are evident in the improved operations at **United Airlines**. At the time it filed for bankruptcy, United had a reputation for some of the worst service in the airline business. But when Glenn Tilton took over as United's chief executive officer, he recognized that things had to change.

He implemented an incentive program that allows all of United's 63,000 employees to earn a bonus of 2.5% or more of their wages if the company "exceeds its goals for on-time flight departures and for customer intent to fly United again." After instituting this program, the company's on-time departures were among the best, its customer complaints were reduced considerably, and the number of customers who said that they would fly United again was at its highest level ever. However, after a highly publicized incident where a traveler was injured as he was dragged off an overbooked flight, United must once again overcome a negative public image.

Sources: Susan Carey, "Friendlier Skies: In Bankruptcy, United Airlines Forges a Path to Better Service," *Wall Street Journal* (June 15, 2004); and Emre Serpen, "More to Maintain," *Airline Business* (November 2012), pp. 38–40.

Which of the perspectives of a balanced scorecard were the focus of United's CEO? (Go to WileyPLUS for this answer and additional questions.)

DO IT! 4 | Reporting Variances

Polar Vortex Corporation experienced the following variances: materials price $250 F, materials quantity $1,100 F, labor price $700 U, labor quantity $300 F, and overhead $800 F. Sales revenue was $102,700, and cost of goods sold (at standard) was $61,900. Determine the actual gross profit.

ACTION PLAN

- Gross profit at standard is sales revenue less cost of goods sold at standard.
- Adjust standard gross profit by adding a net favorable variance or subtracting a net unfavorable variance.

Solution

Sales revenue		$102,700
Cost of goods sold (at standard)		61,900
Standard gross profit		40,800
Variances		
Materials price	$ 250 F	
Materials quantity	1,100 F	
Labor price	700 U	
Labor quantity	300 F	
Overhead	800 F	
Total variance favorable		1,750
Gross profit (actual)		$ 42,550

Related exercise material: **DO IT! 24.4, E24.10, E24.14, and E24.15.**

USING THE DECISION TOOLS | Starbucks

Starbucks faces many situations where it needs to apply the decision tools learned in this chapter. Assume that during the past month, Starbucks produced 10,000 50-pound sacks of dark roast Sumatra coffee beans, with the standard cost for one 50-pound sack of dark roast Sumatra as follows.

	Standard			
Manufacturing Cost Elements	Quantity	× Price	=	Cost
Direct materials (unroasted beans)	60 lbs.	× $ 2.00	=	$120.00
Direct labor	0.25 hours	× $16.00	=	4.00
Overhead	0.25 hours	× $48.00	=	12.00
				$136.00

During the month, the following transactions occurred in manufacturing the 10,000 50-pound sacks of Sumatra coffee.

1. Purchased 620,000 pounds of unroasted beans at a price of $1.90 per pound for a total cost of $1,178,000.
2. All materials purchased during the period were used to make coffee during the period.
3. 2,300 direct labor hours were worked at a total labor cost of $36,340 (an average hourly rate of $15.80).
4. Variable manufacturing overhead incurred was $34,600, and fixed overhead incurred was $84,000.

The manufacturing overhead rate of $48.00 is based on a normal capacity of 2,600 direct labor hours. The total overhead budget at this capacity is $83,980 fixed and $40,820 variable.

Instructions

Determine whether Starbucks met its price and quantity objectives relative to materials, labor, and overhead.

Solution

To determine whether Starbucks met its price and quantity objectives, compute the total variance and the variances for direct materials and direct labor, and calculate the total variance for manufacturing overhead.

Total Variance

Actual cost incurred:	
Direct materials	$1,178,000
Direct labor	36,340
Overhead	118,600
Total actual costs	1,332,940
Less: Standard cost (10,000 × $136.00)	1,360,000
Total variance	$ 27,060 F

Direct Materials Variances

Total	= $1,178,000	− $1,200,000 (600,000 × $2.00)	= $22,000 F
Price	= $1,178,000 (620,000 × $1.90)	− $1,240,000 (620,000 × $2.00)	= $62,000 F
Quantity	= $1,240,000 (620,000 × $2.00)	− $1,200,000 (600,000 × $2.00)	= $40,000 U

Direct Labor Variances

Total	= $36,340 (2,300 × $15.80)	− $40,000 (2,500* × $16.00)	= $ 3,660 F
Price	= $36,340 (2,300 × $15.80)	− $36,800 (2,300 × $16.00)	= $ 460 F
Quantity	= $36,800 (2,300 × $16.00)	− $40,000 (2,500* × $16.00)	= $ 3,200 F

*10,000 × .25

Overhead Variance

Total	= $118,600 ($84,000 + $34,600)	− $120,000 (2,500 × $48)	= $ 1,400 F

Starbucks' total variance was a favorable $27,060. The total materials, labor, and overhead variances were favorable. The company did have an unfavorable materials quantity variance, but this was outweighed by the favorable materials price variance.

Appendix 24A Standard Cost Accounting System

LEARNING OBJECTIVE *5
Identify the features of a standard cost accounting system.

A **standard cost accounting system** is a double-entry system of accounting. In this system, companies use standard costs in making entries, and they formally recognize variances in the accounts. Companies may use a standard cost system with either job order or process costing.

In this appendix, we will explain and illustrate a **standard cost, job order cost accounting system**. The system is based on two important assumptions:

1. Variances from standards are recognized at the earliest opportunity.
2. The Work in Process account is maintained exclusively on the basis of standard costs.

In practice, there are many variations among standard cost systems. The system described here should prepare you for systems you see in the "real world."

Journal Entries

We will use the transactions of Xonic to illustrate the journal entries. Note as you study the entries that the major difference between the entries here and those for the job order cost accounting system in Chapter 15 is the **variance accounts**.

1. Purchase raw materials on account for $13,020 when the standard cost is $12,600.

Raw Materials Inventory	12,600	
Materials Price Variance	420	
Accounts Payable		13,020
(To record purchase of materials)		

Xonic debits the inventory account for actual quantities at standard cost. This enables the perpetual materials records to show actual quantities. Xonic debits the price variance, which is unfavorable, to Materials Price Variance.

2. Incur direct labor costs of $31,080 when the standard labor cost is $31,500.

Factory Labor	31,500	
Labor Price Variance		420
Factory Wages Payable		31,080
(To record direct labor costs)		

Like the raw materials inventory account, Xonic debits Factory Labor for actual hours worked at the standard hourly rate of pay. In this case, the labor variance is favorable. Thus, Xonic credits Labor Price Variance.

3. Incur actual manufacturing overhead costs of $10,900.

Manufacturing Overhead	10,900	
Accounts Payable/Cash/Acc. Depreciation		10,900
(To record overhead incurred)		

The controllable overhead variance (see Appendix 24B) is not recorded at this time. It depends on standard hours applied to work in process. This amount is not known at the time overhead is incurred.

4. Issue raw materials for production at a cost of $12,600 when the standard cost is $12,000.

Work in Process Inventory	12,000	
Materials Quantity Variance	600	
Raw Materials Inventory		12,600
(To record issuance of raw materials)		

Xonic debits Work in Process Inventory for standard materials quantities used at standard prices. It debits the variance account because the variance is unfavorable. The company credits Raw Materials Inventory for actual quantities at standard prices.

5. Assign factory labor to production at a cost of $31,500 when standard cost is $30,000.

Work in Process Inventory	30,000	
Labor Quantity Variance	1,500	
Factory Labor		31,500
(To assign factory labor to jobs)		

Xonic debits Work in Process Inventory for standard labor hours at standard rates. It debits the unfavorable variance to Labor Quantity Variance. The credit to Factory Labor produces a zero balance in this account.

6. Apply manufacturing overhead to production $10,000.

Work in Process Inventory	10,000	
Manufacturing Overhead		10,000
(To assign overhead to jobs)		

Xonic debits Work in Process Inventory for standard hours allowed multiplied by the standard overhead rate.

7. Transfer completed work to finished goods $52,000.

Finished Goods Inventory	52,000	
Work in Process Inventory		52,000
(To record transfer of completed work to finished goods)		

In this example, both inventory accounts are at standard cost.

8. Sell the 1,000 gallons of Xonic Tonic for $70,000.

Accounts Receivable	70,000	
Cost of Goods Sold	52,000	
Sales		70,000
Finished Goods Inventory		52,000
(To record sale of finished goods and the cost of goods sold)		

The company debits Cost of Goods Sold at standard cost. Gross profit, in turn, is the difference between sales and the standard cost of goods sold.

9. Recognize unfavorable total overhead variance:

Overhead Variance	900	
Manufacturing Overhead		900
(To recognize overhead variances)		

Prior to this entry, a debit balance of $900 existed in Manufacturing Overhead because overhead of $10,900 was incurred but only $10,000 of overhead was applied. This entry therefore adjusts the account to a zero balance in the Manufacturing Overhead account. The information needed for this entry is often not available until the end of the accounting period.

Ledger Accounts

Illustration 24A.1 shows the cost accounts for Xonic after posting the entries. Note that five variance accounts, highlighted in red, are included in the ledger (see **Helpful Hint**). The six other accounts are the same as those illustrated for a job order cost system in Chapter 15, in which only actual costs were used.

HELPFUL HINT

Each debit balance in variance accounts indicates an unfavorable variance; each credit balance indicates a favorable variance.

ILLUSTRATION 24A.1
Cost accounts with variances

Raw Materials Inventory
(1)	12,600	(4)	12,600

Materials Price Variance
(1) 420	

Work in Process Inventory
(4)	12,000	(7)	52,000
(5)	30,000		
(6)	10,000		

Factory Labor
(2)	31,500	(5)	31,500

Materials Quantity Variance
(4) 600	

Finished Goods Inventory
(7)	52,000	(8)	52,000

Manufacturing Overhead
(3)	10,900	(6)	10,000
		(9)	900

Labor Price Variance
(2)	420

Cost of Goods Sold
(8) 52,000	

Labor Quantity Variance
(5) 1,500	

Overhead Variance
(9) 900	

Appendix 24B Overhead Controllable and Volume Variances

LEARNING OBJECTIVE *6
Compute overhead controllable and volume variances.

As indicated in the chapter, the total overhead variance is generally analyzed through a price variance and a quantity variance. The name usually given to the price variance is the **overhead controllable variance**; the quantity variance is referred to as the **overhead volume variance**.

Overhead Controllable Variance

The **overhead controllable variance** shows whether overhead costs are effectively controlled. To compute this variance, the company compares actual overhead costs incurred with budgeted costs for the **standard hours allowed**. The budgeted costs are determined from a flexible manufacturing overhead budget. The concepts related to a flexible budget were discussed in Chapter 23.

For Xonic, the budget formula for manufacturing overhead is variable manufacturing overhead cost of $3 per hour of labor plus fixed manufacturing overhead costs of $4,400 ($52,800 ÷ 12, per Illustration 24.6). **Illustration 24B.1** shows the monthly flexible budget for Xonic.

ILLUSTRATION 24B.1

Flexible budget using standard direct labor hours

	B	C	D	E
Xonic				
Flexible Manufacturing Overhead Monthly Budget				
Activity Index				
Standard direct labor hours	1,800	2,000	2,200	2,400
Costs				
Variable costs				
Indirect materials	$1,800	$ 2,000	$ 2,200	$ 2,400
Indirect labor	2,700	3,000	3,300	3,600
Utilities	900	1,000	1,100	1,200
Total variable costs	5,400	6,000	6,600	7,200
Fixed costs				
Supervision	3,000	3,000	3,000	3,000
Depreciation	1,400	1,400	1,400	1,400
Total fixed costs	4,400	4,400	4,400	4,400
Total costs	$9,800	$10,400	$11,000	$11,600

As shown, the budgeted costs for 2,000 standard hours are $10,400 ($6,000 variable and $4,400 fixed).

Illustration 24B.2 shows the formula for the overhead controllable variance and the calculation for Xonic at 1,000 units of output (2,000 standard labor hours).

ILLUSTRATION 24B.2
Formula for overhead controllable variance

Actual Overhead	−	Overhead Budgeted*	=	Overhead Controllable Variance
$10,900 ($6,500 + $4,400)	−	$10,400 ($6,000 + $4,400)	=	$500 U

*Based on standard hours allowed.

The overhead controllable variance for Xonic is $500 unfavorable.

Most controllable variances are associated with variable costs, which are controllable costs. Fixed costs are often known at the time the budget is prepared and are therefore not as likely to deviate from the budgeted amount. In Xonic's case, all of the overhead controllable variance is due to the difference between the actual variable overhead costs ($6,500) and the budgeted variable costs ($6,000).

Management can compare actual and budgeted overhead for each manufacturing overhead cost that contributes to the controllable variance. In addition, management can develop cost and quantity variances for each overhead cost, such as indirect materials and indirect labor.

Overhead Volume Variance

The **overhead volume variance** is the difference between normal capacity hours and standard hours allowed times the fixed overhead rate. The overhead volume variance relates to whether fixed costs were under- or overapplied during the year. For example, the overhead volume variance answers the question of whether Xonic effectively used its fixed costs. If Xonic produces less Xonic Tonic than normal capacity would allow, an unfavorable variance results. Conversely, if Xonic produces more Xonic Tonic than what is considered normal capacity, a favorable variance results.

Illustration 24B.3 provides the formula for computing the overhead volume variance.

ILLUSTRATION 24B.3
Formula for overhead volume variance

Fixed Overhead Rate	×	(Normal Capacity Hours − Standard Hours Allowed)	=	Overhead Volume Variance

To illustrate the fixed overhead rate computation, recall that Xonic budgeted fixed overhead cost for the year of $52,800 (Illustration 24.6). At normal capacity, 26,400 standard direct labor hours are required. The fixed overhead rate is therefore $2 per hour ($52,800 ÷ 26,400 hours).

Xonic produced 1,000 units of Xonic Tonic in June. The standard hours allowed for the 1,000 gallons produced in June is 2,000 (1,000 gallons × 2 hours). For Xonic, normal capacity for June is 1,100, so standard direct labor hours for June at normal capacity is 2,200 (26,400 annual hours ÷ 12 months). The computation of the overhead volume variance in this case is as shown in **Illustration 24B.4**.

ILLUSTRATION 24B.4
Computation of overhead volume variance for Xonic

Fixed Overhead Rate	×	(Normal Capacity Hours − Standard Hours Allowed)	=	Overhead Volume Variance
$2	×	(2,200 − 2,000)	=	$400 U

In Xonic's case, a $400 unfavorable volume variance results. The volume variance is unfavorable because Xonic produced only 1,000 gallons rather than the normal capacity of 1,100 gallons in the month of June. As a result, it underapplied fixed overhead for that period.

In computing the overhead variances, it is important to remember the following.

1. Standard hours allowed are used in each of the variances.
2. Budgeted costs for the controllable variance are derived from the flexible budget.
3. The controllable variance generally pertains to variable costs.
4. The volume variance pertains solely to fixed costs.

Review and Practice

Learning Objectives Review

1 Describe standard costs.

Both standards and budgets are predetermined costs. The primary difference is that a standard is a unit amount, whereas a budget is a total amount. A standard may be regarded as the budgeted cost per unit of product.

Standard costs offer a number of advantages. They (a) facilitate management planning, (b) promote greater economy, (c) are useful in setting selling prices, (d) contribute to management control, (e) permit "management by exception," and (f) simplify the costing of inventories and reduce clerical costs.

The direct materials price standard should be based on the delivered cost of raw materials plus an allowance for receiving and handling. The direct materials quantity standard should establish the required quantity plus an allowance for waste and spoilage.

The direct labor price standard should be based on current wage rates and anticipated adjustments such as COLAs. It also generally includes payroll taxes and fringe benefits. Direct labor quantity standards should be based on required production time plus an allowance for rest periods, cleanup, machine setup, and machine downtime.

For manufacturing overhead, a standard predetermined overhead rate is used. It is based on an expected standard activity index such as standard direct labor hours or standard machine hours.

2 Determine direct materials variances.

The formulas for the direct materials variances are as follows.

$$\begin{pmatrix}\text{Actual quantity}\\ \times \text{ Actual price}\end{pmatrix} - \begin{pmatrix}\text{Standard quantity}\\ \times \text{ Standard price}\end{pmatrix} = \begin{array}{l}\text{Total}\\ \text{materials}\\ \text{variance}\end{array}$$

$$\begin{pmatrix}\text{Actual quantity}\\ \times \text{ Actual price}\end{pmatrix} - \begin{pmatrix}\text{Actual quantity}\\ \times \text{ Standard price}\end{pmatrix} = \begin{array}{l}\text{Materials}\\ \text{price}\\ \text{variance}\end{array}$$

$$\begin{pmatrix}\text{Actual quantity}\\ \times \text{ Standard price}\end{pmatrix} - \begin{pmatrix}\text{Standard quantity}\\ \times \text{ Standard price}\end{pmatrix} = \begin{array}{l}\text{Materials}\\ \text{quantity}\\ \text{variance}\end{array}$$

3 Determine direct labor and total manufacturing overhead variances.

The formulas for the direct labor variances are as follows.

$$\begin{pmatrix}\text{Actual hours}\\ \times \text{ Actual rate}\end{pmatrix} - \begin{pmatrix}\text{Standard hours}\\ \times \text{ Standard rate}\end{pmatrix} = \begin{array}{l}\text{Total}\\ \text{labor}\\ \text{variance}\end{array}$$

$$\begin{pmatrix}\text{Actual hours}\\ \times \text{ Actual rate}\end{pmatrix} - \begin{pmatrix}\text{Actual hours}\\ \times \text{ Standard rate}\end{pmatrix} = \begin{array}{l}\text{Labor}\\ \text{price}\\ \text{variance}\end{array}$$

$$\begin{pmatrix}\text{Actual hours}\\ \times \text{ Standard rate}\end{pmatrix} - \begin{pmatrix}\text{Standard hours}\\ \times \text{ Standard rate}\end{pmatrix} = \begin{array}{l}\text{Labor}\\ \text{quantity}\\ \text{variance}\end{array}$$

The formula for the total manufacturing overhead variance is as follows.

$$\begin{pmatrix}\text{Actual}\\ \text{overhead}\end{pmatrix} - \begin{pmatrix}\text{Overhead}\\ \text{applied at}\\ \text{standard hours}\\ \text{allowed}\end{pmatrix} = \begin{array}{l}\text{Total overhead}\\ \text{variance}\end{array}$$

4 Prepare variance reports and balanced scorecards.

Variances are reported to management in variance reports. The reports facilitate management by exception by highlighting significant differences. Under a standard costing system, an income statement prepared for management will report cost of goods sold at standard cost and then disclose each variance separately.

The balanced scorecard incorporates financial and nonfinancial measures in an integrated system that links performance measurement and a company's strategic goals. It employs four perspectives: financial, customer, internal process, and learning and growth. Objectives are set within each of these perspectives that link to objectives within the other perspectives.

*5 Identify the features of a standard cost accounting system.

In a standard cost accounting system, companies journalize and post standard costs, and they maintain separate variance accounts in the ledger.

*6 Compute overhead controllable and volume variances.

The total overhead variance is generally analyzed through a price variance and a quantity variance. The name usually given to the price variance is the overhead controllable variance. The quantity variance is referred to as the overhead volume variance.

Decision Tools Review

Decision Checkpoints	Info Needed for Decision	Tool to Use for Decision	How to Evaluate Results
Has management accomplished its price and quantity objectives regarding materials?	Actual cost and standard cost of materials	Materials price and materials quantity variances	Positive (favorable) variances suggest that price and quantity objectives have been met.
Has management accomplished its price and quantity objectives regarding labor?	Actual cost and standard cost of labor	Labor price and labor quantity variances	Positive (favorable) variances suggest that price and quantity objectives have been met.
Has management accomplished its objectives regarding manufacturing overhead?	Actual cost and standard cost of manufacturing overhead	Total manufacturing overhead variance	Positive (favorable) variances suggest that manufacturing overhead objectives have been met.

Glossary Review

Balanced scorecard An approach that incorporates financial and nonfinancial measures in an integrated system that links performance measurement and a company's strategic goals. (p. 24-18).

Customer perspective A viewpoint employed in the balanced scorecard to evaluate the company from the perspective of those people who buy and use its products or services. (p. 24-18).

Direct labor price standard The rate per hour that management determines should be incurred for direct labor to produce one unit of product. (p. 24-5).

Direct labor quantity standard The time that management determines should be required to produce one unit of product. (p. 24-6).

Direct materials price standard The cost per unit of direct materials that management determines should be incurred to produce one unit of product. (p. 24-5).

Direct materials quantity standard The quantity of direct materials that management determines should be used per unit of finished goods. (p. 24-5).

Financial perspective A viewpoint employed in the balanced scorecard to evaluate a company's performance using financial measures. (p. 24-18).

Ideal standards Standards based on the optimum level of performance under perfect operating conditions. (p. 24-4).

Internal process perspective A viewpoint employed in the balanced scorecard to evaluate the effectiveness and efficiency of a company's value chain, including product development, production, delivery, and after-sale service. (p. 24-18).

Labor price variance The difference between the actual hours times the actual rate and the actual hours times the standard rate for labor. (p. 24-12).

Labor quantity variance The difference between actual hours times the standard rate and standard hours times the standard rate for labor. (p. 24-12).

Learning and growth perspective A viewpoint employed in the balanced scorecard to evaluate how well a company develops and retains its employees. (p. 24-18).

Materials price variance The difference between the actual quantity times the actual price and the actual quantity times the standard price for materials. (p. 24-9).

Materials quantity variance The difference between the actual quantity times the standard price and the standard quantity times the standard price for materials. (p. 24-10).

Normal capacity The average activity output that a company should experience over the long run. (p. 24-6).

Normal standards Standards based on an efficient level of performance that are attainable under expected operating conditions. (p. 24-4).

*****Overhead controllable variance** The difference between actual overhead incurred and overhead budgeted for the standard hours allowed. (p. 24-24).

*****Overhead volume variance** The difference between normal capacity hours and standard hours allowed times the fixed overhead rate. (p. 24-25).

*****Standard cost accounting system** A double-entry system of accounting in which standard costs are used in making entries, and variances are recognized in the accounts. (p. 24-21).

Standard costs Predetermined unit costs which companies use as measures of performance. (p. 24-3).

Standard hours allowed The hours that should have been worked for the units produced. (p. 24-14).

Standard predetermined overhead rate An overhead rate determined by dividing budgeted overhead costs by an expected standard activity index. (p. 24-6).

Total labor variance The difference between actual hours times the actual rate and standard hours times the standard rate for labor. (p. 24-12).

Total materials variance The difference between the actual quantity times the actual price and the standard quantity times the standard price of materials. (p. 24-9).

Total overhead variance The difference between actual overhead costs and overhead costs applied to work done, based on standard hours allowed. (p. 24-14).

Variance The difference between total actual costs and total standard costs. (p. 24-7).

Practice Multiple-Choice Questions

1. **(LO 1)** Standards differ from budgets in that:
   a. budgets but not standards may be used in valuing inventories.
   b. budgets but not standards may be journalized and posted.
   c. budgets are a total amount and standards are a unit amount.
   d. only budgets contribute to management planning and control.

2. **(LO 1)** Standard costs:
   a. are imposed by governmental agencies.
   b. are predetermined unit costs which companies use as measures of performance.
   c. can be used by manufacturing companies but not by service or not-for-profit companies.
   d. All of the above.

3. **(LO 1)** The advantages of standard costs include all of the following **except**:
   a. management by exception may be used.
   b. management planning is facilitated.
   c. they may simplify the costing of inventories.
   d. management must use a static budget.

4. **(LO 1)** Normal standards:
   a. allow for rest periods, machine breakdowns, and setup time.
   b. represent levels of performance under perfect operating conditions.
   c. are rarely used because managers believe they lower workforce morale.
   d. are more likely than ideal standards to result in unethical practices.

5. **(LO 1)** The setting of standards is:
   a. a managerial accounting decision.
   b. a management decision.
   c. a worker decision.
   d. preferably set at the ideal level of performance.

6. **(LO 2)** Each of the following formulas is correct **except**:
   a. Labor price variance = (Actual hours × Actual rate) − (Actual hours × Standard rate).
   b. Total overhead variance = Actual overhead − Overhead applied.
   c. Materials price variance = (Actual quantity × Actual price) − (Standard quantity × Standard price).
   d. Labor quantity variance = (Actual hours × Standard rate) − (Standard hours × Standard rate).

7. **(LO 2)** In producing product AA, 6,300 pounds of direct materials were used at a cost of $1.10 per pound. The standard was 6,000 pounds at $1.00 per pound. The direct materials quantity variance is:
   a. $330 unfavorable.
   b. $300 unfavorable.
   c. $600 unfavorable.
   d. $630 unfavorable.

8. **(LO 3)** In producing product ZZ, 14,800 direct labor hours were used at a rate of $8.20 per hour. The standard was 15,000 hours at $8.00 per hour. Based on these data, the direct labor:
   a. quantity variance is $1,600 favorable.
   b. quantity variance is $1,600 unfavorable.
   c. price variance is $3,000 favorable.
   d. price variance is $3,000 unfavorable.

9. **(LO 3)** Which of the following is **correct** about the total overhead variance?
   a. Budgeted overhead and overhead applied are the same.
   b. Total actual overhead is composed of variable overhead, fixed overhead, and period costs.
   c. Standard hours actually worked are used in computing the variance.
   d. Standard hours allowed for the work done is the measure used in computing the variance.

10. **(LO 3)** The formula for computing the total overhead variance is:
    a. actual overhead less overhead applied.
    b. overhead budgeted less overhead applied.
    c. actual overhead less overhead budgeted.
    d. No correct answer is given.

11. **(LO 4)** Which of the following is **incorrect** about variance reports?
    a. They facilitate "management by exception."
    b. They should only be sent to the top level of management.
    c. They should be prepared as soon as possible.
    d. They may vary in form, content, and frequency among companies.

12. **(LO 4)** In using variance reports to evaluate cost control, management normally looks into:
    a. all variances.
    b. favorable variances only.
    c. unfavorable variances only.
    d. both favorable and unfavorable variances that exceed a predetermined quantitative measure such as a percentage or dollar amount.

13. (LO 4) Generally accepted accounting principles allow a company to:

  a. report inventory at standard cost but cost of goods sold must be reported at actual cost.

  b. report cost of goods sold at standard cost but inventory must be reported at actual cost.

  c. report inventory and cost of goods sold at standard cost as long as there are no significant differences between actual and standard cost.

  d. report inventory and cost of goods sold only at actual costs; standard costing is never permitted.

14. (LO 4) Which of the following would **not** be an objective used in the customer perspective of the balanced scorecard approach?

  a. Percentage of customers who would recommend product to a friend.

  b. Customer retention.

  c. Brand recognition.

  d. Earnings per share.

*15. (LO 5) Which of the following is **incorrect** about a standard cost accounting system?

  a. It is applicable to job order costing.

  b. It is applicable to process costing.

  c. It reports only favorable variances.

  d. It keeps separate accounts for each variance.

*16. (LO 6) The formula to compute the overhead volume variance is:

  a. Fixed overhead rate × (Standard hours − Actual hours).

  b. Fixed overhead rate × (Normal capacity hours − Actual hours).

  c. Fixed overhead rate × (Normal capacity hours − Standard hours allowed).

  d. (Variable overhead rate + Fixed overhead rate) × (Normal capacity hours − Standard hours allowed).

Solutions

1. c. Budgets are expressed in total amounts, and standards are expressed in unit amounts. The other choices are incorrect because (a) standards, not budgets, may be used in valuing inventories; (b) standards, not budgets, may be journalized and posted; and (d) both budgets and standards contribute to management planning and control.

2. b. Standard costs are predetermined units costs which companies use as measures of performance. The other choices are incorrect because (a) only those that are called regulations are imposed by governmental agencies, (c) standard costs can be used by all types of companies, and (d) choices (a) and (c) are incorrect.

3. d. Standard costs are separate from a static budget. The other choices are all advantages of using standard costs.

4. a. Normal standards allow for rest periods, machine breakdowns, and setup time. The other choices are incorrect because they describe ideal standards, not normal standards.

5. b. Standards are set by management. The other choices are incorrect because setting standards requires input from (a) managerial accountants and (c) sometimes workers, but the final decision is made by management. Choice (d) is incorrect because setting standards at the ideal level of performance is uncommon because of the perceived negative effect on worker morale.

6. c. Materials price variance = (Actual quantity × Actual price) − (Actual quantity (not Standard quantity) × Standard price). The other choices are correct formulas.

7. b. The direct materials quantity variance is (6,300 × $1.00) − (6,000 × $1.00) = $300. This variance is unfavorable because more material was used than prescribed by the standard. The other choices are therefore incorrect.

8. a. The direct labor quantity variance is (14,800 × $8) − (15,000 × $8) = $1,600. This variance is favorable because fewer labor hours were used than prescribed by the standard. The other choices are therefore incorrect.

9. d. Standard hours allowed for work done is the measure used in computing the variance. The other choices are incorrect because (a) budgeted overhead is used to calculate the predetermined overhead rate while overhead applied is equal to standard hours allowed times the predetermined overhead rate, (b) overhead is a product cost and does not include period costs, and (c) standard hours allowed, not hours actually worked, are used in computing the overhead variance.

10. a. Total overhead variance equals actual overhead less overhead applied. The other choices are therefore incorrect.

11. b. Variance reports should be sent to the level of management responsible for the area in which the variance occurred so it can be remedied as quickly as possible. The other choices are correct statements.

12. d. In using variance reports to evaluate cost control, management normally looks into both favorable and unfavorable variances that exceed a predetermined quantitative measure such as percentage or dollar amount. The other choices are therefore incorrect.

13. c. GAAP allows a company to report both inventory and cost of goods sold at standard cost as long as there are no significant differences between actual and standard cost. The other choices are therefore incorrect.

14. d. Earnings per share is not an objective used in the customer perspective of the balanced scorecard approach. The other choices are all true statements.

*15. c. A standard cost accounting system reports both favorable and unfavorable variances. The other choices are all correct statements.

*16. c. The formula to compute the overhead volume variance is Fixed overhead rate × (Normal capacity hours − Standard hours allowed). The other choices are therefore incorrect.

Practice Brief Exercises

Set direct materials standard.

1. **(LO 1)** Castellen Company accumulates the following data concerning raw materials in making one quart of finished product. (1) Price—purchase price $3.00; terms 2/10, n/30; freight-in $0.25; and receiving and handling $0.10. (2) Quantity—required materials 2.7 pounds, allowance for waste and spoilage 0.3 pounds. Compute the following.

    a. Standard direct materials price per quart.
    b. Standard direct materials quantity per quart.
    c. Total standard materials cost per quart

Solution

1. a. Standard direct materials price per quart = ($3.00 − $0.06 + $0.25 + $0.10) = $3.29
   b. Standard direct materials quantity per quart = (2.7 + .3) = 3 pounds
   c. Standard materials cost per quart = ($3.29 × 3) = $9.71

Compute direct materials variances.

2. **(LO 2)** Spandrell Company's standard materials cost per unit of output is $12 (3 pounds × $4). During July, the company purchases and uses 5,800 pounds of materials costing $22,910 in making 2,000 units of finished product. Compute the total, price, and quantity materials variances.

Solution

2. Total materials variance = [(5,800 × $3.95*) − (6,000** × $4.00)] = $1,090 F

   Materials price variance = [(5,800 × $3.95) − (5,800 × $4.00)] = $290 F

   Materials quantity variance [(5,800 × $4.00) − (6,000 × $4.00)] = $800 F

   *$22,910 ÷ 5,800; **2,000 × 3

Compute direct labor variances.

3. **(LO 3)** Timemore Company's standard labor cost per unit of output is $34 (2 hours × $17 per hour). During August, the company incurs 1,960 hours of direct labor at an hourly cost of $17.20 per hour in making 1,000 units of finished product. Compute the total, price, and quantity labor variances.

Solution

3. Total labor variance = [(1,960 × $17.20) − (2,000 × $17.00)] = $288 F

   Labor price variance = [(1,960 × $17.20) − (1,960 × $17.00)] = $392 U

   Labor quantity variance = [(1,960 × $17.00) − (2,000 × $17.00)] = $680 F

Practice Exercises

Compute materials and labor variances.

1. **(LO 2, 3)** Hector Inc., which produces a single product, has prepared the following standard cost sheet for one unit of the product.

Direct materials (6 pounds at $2.50 per pound)	$15.00
Direct labor (3.1 hours at $12.00 per hour)	$37.20

    During the month of April, the company manufactures 250 units and incurs the following actual costs.

Direct materials purchased and used (1,600 pounds)	$4,192
Direct labor (760 hours)	$8,740

Instructions

Compute the total, price, and quantity variances for materials and labor.

Solution

1. Total materials variance:

$$
\begin{array}{ccc}
(AQ \times AP) & - & (SQ \times SP) \\
(1{,}600 \times \$2.62^{*}) & & (1{,}500^{**} \times \$2.50) \\
\$4{,}192 & - & \$3{,}750 = \$442 \text{ U}
\end{array}
$$

*$4,192 ÷ 1,600   **250 × 6

Materials price variance:

$$
\begin{array}{ccc}
(AQ \times AP) & - & (AQ \times SP) \\
(1{,}600 \times \$2.62) & & (1{,}600 \times \$2.50) \\
\$4{,}192 & - & \$4{,}000 = \$192 \text{ U}
\end{array}
$$

Materials quantity variance:

$$
\begin{array}{ccc}
(AQ \times SP) & - & (SQ \times SP) \\
(1{,}600 \times \$2.50) & & (1{,}500 \times \$2.50) \\
\$4{,}000 & - & \$3{,}750 = \$250 \text{ U}
\end{array}
$$

Total labor variance:

$$
\begin{array}{ccc}
(AH \times AR) & - & (SH \times SR) \\
(760 \times \$11.50^{*}) & & (775^{**} \times \$12.00) \\
\$8{,}740 & - & \$9{,}300 = \$560 \text{ F}
\end{array}
$$

*$8,740 ÷ 760   **250 × 3.1

Labor price variance:

$$
\begin{array}{ccc}
(AH \times AR) & - & (AH \times SR) \\
(760 \times \$11.50) & & (760 \times \$12.00) \\
\$8{,}740 & - & \$9{,}120 = \$380 \text{ F}
\end{array}
$$

Labor quantity variance:

$$
\begin{array}{ccc}
(AH \times SR) & - & (SH \times SR) \\
(760 \times \$12.00) & & (775 \times \$12.00) \\
\$9{,}120 & - & \$9{,}300 = \$180 \text{ F}
\end{array}
$$

2. (LO 3) Manufacturing overhead data for the production of Product H by Yamato Company are as follows.

Compute overhead variances.

Overhead incurred for 35,000 actual direct labor hours worked	$140,000
Overhead rate (variable $3; fixed $1) at normal capacity of 36,000 direct labor hours	$4
Standard hours allowed for work done	34,000

Instructions
Compute the total overhead variance.

Solution

2. Total overhead variance:

$$
\begin{array}{ccc}
\text{Actual Overhead} & - & \text{Overhead Applied} \\
\$140{,}000 & - & \$136{,}000 = \$4{,}000 \text{ U} \\
 & & (34{,}000 \times \$4)
\end{array}
$$

Practice Problem

(LO 2, 3) Manlow Company makes a cologne called Allure. The standard cost for one bottle of Allure is as follows.

Compute variances.

Manufacturing Cost Elements	Standard Quantity	×	Price	=	Cost
Direct materials	6 oz.	×	$ 0.90	=	$ 5.40
Direct labor	0.5 hrs.	×	$12.00	=	6.00
Manufacturing overhead	0.5 hrs.	×	$ 4.80	=	2.40
					$13.80

During the month, the following transactions occurred in manufacturing 10,000 bottles of Allure.

1. 58,000 ounces of materials were purchased at $1.00 per ounce.
2. All the materials purchased were used to produce the 10,000 bottles of Allure.
3. 4,900 direct labor hours were worked at a total labor cost of $56,350.
4. Variable manufacturing overhead incurred was $15,000 and fixed overhead incurred was $10,400.

The manufacturing overhead rate of $4.80 is based on a normal capacity of 5,200 direct labor hours. The total budget at this capacity is $10,400 fixed and $14,560 variable.

Instructions

a. Compute the total variance and the variances for direct materials and direct labor elements.
b. Compute the total variance for manufacturing overhead.

Solution

a.

Total Variance

Actual costs incurred	
Direct materials	$ 58,000
Direct labor	56,350
Manufacturing overhead	25,400
	139,750
Standard cost (10,000 × $13.80)	138,000
Total variance	$ 1,750 U

Direct Materials Variances

Total	= $58,000 (58,000 × $1.00)	−	$54,000 (60,000* × $0.90)	=	$4,000 U
Price	= $58,000 (58,000 × $1.00)	−	$52,200 (58,000 × $0.90)	=	$5,800 U
Quantity	= $52,200 (58,000 × $0.90)	−	$54,000 (60,000 × $0.90)	=	$1,800 F

*10,000 × 6

Direct Labor Variances

Total	= $56,350 (4,900 × $11.50*)	−	$60,000 (5,000** × $12.00)	=	$3,650 F
Price	= $56,350 (4,900 × $11.50)	−	$58,800 (4,900 × $12.00)	=	$2,450 F
Quantity	= $58,800 (4,900 × $12.00)	−	$60,000 (5,000 × $12.00)	=	$1,200 F

*56,350 ÷ 4,900; **10,000 × 0.5

b.

Overhead Variance

Total	= $25,400 ($15,000 + $10,400)	−	$24,000 (5,000 × $4.80)	=	$1,400 U

WileyPLUS

Brief Exercises, DO IT! Exercises, Exercises, Problems, and many additional resources are available for practice in WileyPLUS.

Note: All asterisked Questions, Exercises, and Problems relate to material in the appendices to the chapter.

Questions

1. a. "Standard costs are the expected total cost of completing a job." Is this correct? Explain.

b. "A standard imposed by a governmental agency is known as a regulation." Do you agree? Explain.

2. a. Explain the similarities and differences between standards and budgets.

b. Contrast the accounting for standards and budgets.

3. Standard costs facilitate management planning. What are the other advantages of standard costs?

4. Contrast the roles of the management accountant and management in setting standard costs.

5. Distinguish between an ideal standard and a normal standard.

6. What factors should be considered in setting (a) the direct materials price standard and (b) the direct materials quantity standard?

7. "The objective in setting the direct labor quantity standard is to determine the aggregate time required to make one unit of product." Do you agree? What allowances should be made in setting this standard?

8. How is the predetermined overhead rate determined when standard costs are used?

9. What is the difference between a favorable cost variance and an unfavorable cost variance?

10. In each of the following formulas, supply the words that should be inserted for each number in parentheses.
    a. (Actual quantity × (1)) − (Standard quantity × (2)) = Total materials variance
    b. ((3) × Actual price) − (Actual quantity × (4)) = Materials price variance
    c. (Actual quantity × (5)) − ((6) × Standard price) = Materials quantity variance

11. In the direct labor variance matrix, there are three factors: (1) Actual hours × Actual rate, (2) Actual hours × Standard rate, and (3) Standard hours × Standard rate. Using the numbers, indicate the formulas for each of the direct labor variances.

12. Mikan Company's standard predetermined overhead rate is $9 per direct labor hour. For the month of June, 26,000 actual hours were worked, and 27,000 standard hours were allowed. How much overhead was applied?

13. How often should variances be reported to management? What principle may be used with variance reports?

14. What circumstances may cause the purchasing department to be responsible for both an unfavorable materials price variance and an unfavorable materials quantity variance?

15. What are the four perspectives used in the balanced scorecard? Discuss the nature of each, and how the perspectives are linked.

16. Kerry James says that the balanced scorecard was created to replace financial measures as the primary mechanism for performance evaluation. He says that it uses only nonfinancial measures. Is this true?

17. What are some examples of nonfinancial measures used by companies to evaluate performance?

18. (a) How are variances reported in income statements prepared for management? (b) May standard costs be used in preparing financial statements for stockholders? Explain.

*19. (a) Explain the basic features of a standard cost accounting system. (b) What type of balance will exist in the variance account when (1) the materials price variance is unfavorable and (2) the labor quantity variance is favorable?

*20. If the $9 per hour overhead rate in Question 12 includes $5 variable, and actual overhead costs were $248,000, what is the overhead controllable variance for June? The normal capacity hours were 28,000. Is the variance favorable or unfavorable?

*21. What is the purpose of computing the overhead volume variance? What is the basic formula for this variance?

*22. Alma Ortiz does not understand why the overhead volume variance indicates that fixed overhead costs are under or overapplied. Clarify this matter for Alma.

*23. John Hsu is attempting to outline the important points about overhead variances on a class examination. List four points that John should include in his outline.

Brief Exercises

BE24.1 (LO 1), AP Lopez Company uses both standards and budgets. For the year, estimated production of Product X is 500,000 units. Total estimated cost for materials and labor are $1,400,000 and $1,700,000. Compute the estimates for (a) a standard cost and (b) a budgeted cost.

Distinguish between a standard and a budget.

BE24.2 (LO 1), AP Tang Company accumulates the following data concerning raw materials in making its finished product. (1) Price per pound of raw materials is net purchase price $2.30, freight-in $0.20, and receiving and handling $0.10. (2) Quantity per gallon of finished product is required materials 3.6 pounds and allowance for waste and spoilage 0.4 pounds. Compute the following.
  a. Standard direct materials price per pound of raw materials.
  b. Standard direct materials quantity per gallon.
  c. Total standard materials cost per gallon.

Set direct materials standard.

BE24.3 (LO 1), AP Labor data for making one gallon of finished product in Bing Company are as follows. (1) Price—hourly wage rate $14.00, payroll taxes $0.80, and fringe benefits $1.20. (2) Quantity—actual production time 1.1 hours, rest periods and cleanup 0.25 hours, and setup and downtime 0.15 hours. Compute the following.
  a. Standard direct labor rate per hour.
  b. Standard direct labor hours per gallon.
  c. Standard labor cost per gallon.

Set direct labor standard.

BE24.4 (LO 2), AP Simba Company's standard materials cost per unit of output is $10 (2 pounds × $5). During July, the company purchases and uses 3,200 pounds of materials costing $16,192 in making 1,500 units of finished product. Compute the total, price, and quantity materials variances.

Compute direct materials variances.

Compute direct labor variances.	**BE24.5 (LO 3), AP** Mordica Company's standard labor cost per unit of output is $22 (2 hours × $11 per hour). During August, the company incurs 2,150 hours of direct labor at an hourly cost of $10.80 per hour in making 1,000 units of finished product. Compute the total, price, and quantity labor variances.
Compute total overhead variance.	**BE24.6 (LO 3), AP** In October, Pine Company reports 21,000 actual direct labor hours, and it incurs $118,000 of manufacturing overhead costs. Standard hours allowed for the work done is 20,600 hours. The predetermined overhead rate is $6 per direct labor hour. Compute the total overhead variance.
Match balanced scorecard perspectives.	**BE24.7 (LO 4), AP** The four perspectives in the balanced scorecard are (1) financial, (2) customer, (3) internal process, and (4) learning and growth. Match each of the following objectives with the perspective it is most likely associated with: (a) plant capacity utilization, (b) employee work days missed due to injury, (c) return on assets, and (d) brand recognition.
Journalize materials variances.	*BE24.8 (LO 5), AP** Journalize the following transactions for Combs Company. a. Purchased 6,000 units of raw materials on account for $11,500. The standard cost was $12,000. b. Issued 5,600 units of raw materials for production. The standard units were 5,800.
Journalize labor variances.	*BE24.9 (LO 5), AP** Journalize the following transactions for Shelton, Inc. a. Incurred direct labor costs of $24,000 for 3,000 hours. The standard labor cost was $24,900. b. Assigned 3,000 direct labor hours costing $24,000 to production. Standard hours were 3,150.
Compute the overhead controllable variance.	*BE24.10 (LO 6), AP** Some overhead data for Pine Company are given in BE24.6. In addition, the flexible manufacturing overhead budget shows that budgeted costs are $4 variable per direct labor hour and $50,000 fixed. Compute the overhead controllable variance.
Compute overhead volume variance.	*BE24.11 (LO 6), AP** Using the data in BE24.6 and BE24.10, compute the overhead volume variance. Normal capacity was 25,000 direct labor hours.

DO IT! Exercises

Compute standard cost.	**DO IT! 24.1 (LO 1), AP** Larkin Company accumulated the following standard cost data concerning product I-Tal. Direct materials per unit: 2 pounds at $5 per pound Direct labor per unit: 0.2 hours at $16 per hour Manufacturing overhead: Allocated based on direct labor hours at a predetermined rate of $20 per direct labor hour Compute the standard cost of one unit of product I-Tal.
Compute materials variance.	**DO IT! 24.2 (LO 2), AP** The standard cost of product 777 includes 2 units of direct materials at $6.00 per unit. During August, the company bought 29,000 units of materials at $6.30 and used those materials to produce 16,000 units. Compute the total, price, and quantity variances for materials.
Compute labor and manufacturing overhead variances.	**DO IT! 24.3 (LO 3), AP** The standard cost of product 5252 includes 1.9 hours of direct labor at $14.00 per hour. The predetermined overhead rate is $22.00 per direct labor hour. During July, the company incurred 4,000 hours of direct labor at an average rate of $14.30 per hour and $81,300 of manufacturing overhead costs. It produced 2,000 units. a. Compute the total, price, and quantity variances for labor. b. Compute the total overhead variance.
Prepare variance report.	**DO IT! 24.4 (LO 4), AP** Tropic Zone Corporation experienced the following variances: materials price $350 U, materials quantity $1,700 F, labor price $800 F, labor quantity $500 F, and total overhead $1,200 U. Sales revenue was $92,100, and cost of goods sold (at standard) was $51,600. Determine the actual gross profit.

Exercises

Compute budget and standard.	**E24.1 (LO 1), AP** Writing Parsons Company is planning to produce 2,000 units of product in 2022. Each unit requires 3 pounds of materials at $5 per pound and a half-hour of labor at $16 per hour. The overhead rate is 70% of direct labor.

Instructions

a. Compute the budgeted amounts for 2022 for direct materials to be used, direct labor, and applied overhead.

b. Compute the standard cost of one unit of product.

c. What are the potential advantages to a corporation of using standard costs?

E24.2 (LO 1), AP Hank Itzek manufactures and sells homemade wine, and he wants to develop a standard cost per gallon. The following are required for production of a 50-gallon batch.

Compute standard materials costs.

3,000 ounces of grape concentrate at $0.06 per ounce
54 pounds of granulated sugar at $0.30 per pound
60 lemons at $0.60 each
50 yeast tablets at $0.25 each
50 nutrient tablets at $0.20 each
2,600 ounces of water at $0.005 per ounce

Hank estimates that 4% of the grape concentrate is wasted, 10% of the sugar is lost, and 25% of the lemons cannot be used.

Instructions

Compute the standard cost of the ingredients for one gallon of wine. (Carry computations to two decimal places.)

E24.3 (LO 1), AP Stefani Company has gathered the following information about its product.

Compute standard cost per unit.

Direct materials. Each unit of product contains 4.5 pounds of materials. The average waste and spoilage per unit produced under normal conditions is 0.5 pounds. Materials cost $5 per pound, but Stefani always takes the 2% cash discount all of its suppliers offer. Freight costs average $0.25 per pound.

Direct labor. Each unit requires 2 hours of labor. Setup, cleanup, and downtime average 0.4 hours per unit. The average hourly pay rate of Stefani's employees is $12. Payroll taxes and fringe benefits are an additional $3 per hour.

Manufacturing overhead. Overhead is applied at a rate of $7 per direct labor hour.

Instructions

Compute Stefani's total standard cost per unit.

E24.4 (LO 1, 3), AP **Service** Monte Services, Inc. is trying to establish the standard labor cost of a typical brake repair. The following data have been collected from time and motion studies conducted over the past month.

Compute labor cost and labor quantity variance.

Actual time spent on the brake repair	1.0 hour
Hourly wage rate	$12
Payroll taxes	10% of wage rate
Setup and downtime	20% of actual labor time
Cleanup and rest periods	30% of actual labor time
Fringe benefits	25% of wage rate

Instructions

a. Determine the standard direct labor hours per brake repair.

b. Determine the standard direct labor hourly rate.

c. Determine the standard direct labor cost per brake repair.

d. If a brake repair took 1.6 hours at the standard hourly rate, what was the direct labor quantity variance?

E24.5 (LO 2), AP The standard cost of Product B manufactured by Pharrell Company includes three units of direct materials at $5.00 per unit. During June, 29,000 units of direct materials are purchased at a cost of $4.70 per unit, and 29,000 units of direct materials are used to produce 9,400 units of Product B.

Compute materials price and quantity variances.

Instructions

a. Compute the total materials variance and the price and quantity variances.

b. Repeat (a), assuming the purchase price is $5.15 and the quantity purchased and used is 28,000 units.

E24.6 (LO 3), AP Lewis Company's standard labor cost of producing one unit of Product DD is 4 hours at the rate of $12.00 per hour. During August, 40,600 hours of labor are incurred at a cost of $12.15 per hour to produce 10,000 units of Product DD.

Compute labor price and quantity variances.

Compute materials and labor variances.

Instructions

a. Compute the total labor variance.

b. Compute the labor price and quantity variances.

c. Repeat (b), assuming the standard is 4.1 hours of direct labor at $12.25 per hour.

E24.7 (LO 2, 3), AP Levine Inc., which produces a single product, has prepared the following standard cost sheet for one unit of the product.

Direct materials (8 pounds at $2.50 per pound)	$20
Direct labor (3 hours at $12.00 per hour)	$36

During the month of April, the company manufactures 230 units and incurs the following actual costs.

Direct materials purchased and used (1,900 pounds)	$5,035
Direct labor (700 hours)	$8,120

Instructions

Compute the total, price, and quantity variances for materials and labor.

Compute the materials and labor variances and list reasons for unfavorable variances.

E24.8 (LO 2, 3), AN Writing The following direct materials and direct labor data pertain to the operations of Laurel Company for the month of August.

Costs		Quantities	
Actual labor rate	$13 per hour	Actual hours incurred and used	4,150 hours
Actual materials price	$128 per ton	Actual quantity of materials purchased and used	1,220 tons
Standard labor rate	$12.50 per hour	Standard hours used	4,300 hours
Standard materials price	$130 per ton	Standard quantity of materials used	1,200 tons

Instructions

a. Compute the total, price, and quantity variances for materials and labor.

b. Provide two possible explanations for each of the unfavorable variances calculated above, and suggest where responsibility for the unfavorable result might be placed.

Determine amounts from variance report.

E24.9 (LO 2, 3), AN You have been given the following information about the production of Usher Co., and are asked to provide the plant manager with information for a meeting with the vice president of operations.

	Standard Cost Card
Direct materials (5 pounds at $4 per pound)	$20.00
Direct labor (0.8 hours at $10)	8.00
Variable overhead (0.8 hours at $3 per hour)	2.40
Fixed overhead (0.8 hours at $7 per hour)	5.60
	$36.00

The following is a variance report for the most recent period of operations.

		Variances	
Costs	Total Standard Cost	Price	Quantity
Direct materials	$410,000	$2,095 F	$ 9,000 U
Direct labor	164,000	3,906 U	22,000 U

Instructions

a. How many units were produced during the period?

b. How many pounds of raw materials were purchased and used during the period?

c. What was the actual cost per pound of raw materials?

d. How many actual direct labor hours were worked during the period?

e. What was the actual rate paid per direct labor hour?

(CGA adapted)

E24.10 (LO 3, 4), AP During March 2022, Toby Tool & Die Company worked on four jobs. A review of direct labor costs reveals the following summary data.

Prepare a variance report for direct labor.

Job Number	Actual Hours	Actual Costs	Standard Hours	Standard Costs	Total Variance
A257	221	$4,420	225	$4,500	$ 80 F
A258	450	9,450	430	8,600	850 U
A259	300	6,180	300	6,000	180 U
A260	116	2,088	110	2,200	112 F
Total variance					$838 U

Analysis reveals that Job A257 was a repeat job. Job A258 was a rush order that required overtime work at premium rates of pay. Job A259 required a more experienced replacement worker on one shift. Work on Job A260 was done for one day by a new trainee when a regular worker was absent.

Instructions

Prepare a report for the plant supervisor on direct labor cost variances for March. The report should have columns for (1) Job No., (2) Actual Hours, (3) Standard Hours, (4) Quantity Variance, (5) Actual Rate, (6) Standard Rate, (7) Price Variance, and (8) Explanation.

E24.11 (LO 3), AN Manufacturing overhead data for the production of Product H by Shakira Company, assuming the company uses a standard cost system, are as follows.

Compute overhead variance.

Overhead incurred for 52,000 actual direct labor hours worked	$263,000
Overhead rate (variable $3; fixed $2) at normal capacity of 54,000 direct labor hours	$5
Standard hours allowed for work done	52,000

Instructions

Compute the total overhead variance.

E24.12 (LO 3), AP Byrd Company produces one product, a putter called GO-Putter. Byrd uses a standard cost system and determines that it should take one hour of direct labor to produce one GO-Putter. The normal production capacity for this putter is 100,000 units per year. The total budgeted overhead at normal capacity is $850,000 comprised of $250,000 of variable costs and $600,000 of fixed costs. Byrd applies overhead on the basis of direct labor hours.

Compute overhead variances.

During the current year, Byrd produced 95,000 putters, worked 94,000 direct labor hours, and incurred variable overhead costs of $256,000 and fixed overhead costs of $600,000.

Instructions

a. Compute the predetermined variable overhead rate and the predetermined fixed overhead rate.

b. Compute the applied overhead for Byrd for the year.

c. Compute the total overhead variance.

E24.13 (LO 2, 3), AP **Writing** Ceelo Company purchased (at a cost of $10,200) and used 2,400 pounds of materials during May. Ceelo's standard cost of materials per unit produced is based on 2 pounds per unit at a cost $5 per pound. Production in May was 1,050 units.

Compute variances for materials.

Instructions

a. Compute the total, price, and quantity variances for materials.

b. Assume Ceelo also had an unfavorable labor quantity variance. What is a possible scenario that would provide one cause for the variances computed in (a) and the unfavorable labor quantity variance?

E24.14 (LO 2, 4), AP **Service** Picard Landscaping plants grass seed as the basic landscaping for business campuses. During a recent month, the company worked on three projects (Remington, Chang, and Wyco). The company is interested in controlling the materials costs, namely the grass seed, for these plantings projects.

Prepare a variance report.

In order to provide management with useful cost control information, the company uses standard costs and prepares monthly variance reports. Analysis reveals that the purchasing agent mistakenly purchased poor-quality seed for the Remington project. The Chang project, however, received higher-than-standard-quality seed that was on sale. The Wyco project received standard-quality seed. However, the price had increased and a new employee was used to spread the seed.

Shown below are quantity and cost data for each project.

Project	Actual Quantity	Actual Costs	Standard Quantity	Standard Costs	Total Variance
Remington	500 lbs.	$1,200	460 lbs.	$1,150	$ 50 U
Chang	400	920	410	1,025	105 F
Wyco	550	1,430	480	1,200	230 U
Total variance					$175 U

Instructions

a. Prepare a variance report for the purchasing department with the following columns: (1) Project, (2) Actual Pounds Purchased, (3) Actual Price per Pound, (4) Standard Price per Pound, (5) Price Variance, and (6) Explanation.

b. Prepare a variance report for the production department with the following columns: (1) Project, (2) Actual Pounds, (3) Standard Pounds, (4) Standard Price per Pound, (5) Quantity Variance, and (6) Explanation.

Complete variance report.

E24.15 (LO 4), AP Urban Corporation prepared the following variance report.

Urban Corporation
Variance Report—Purchasing Department
For the Week Ended January 9, 2022

Type of Materials	Quantity Purchased	Actual Price	Standard Price	Price Variance	Explanation
Rogue11	? lbs.	$5.20	$5.00	$5,500 ?	Price increase
Storm17	7,000 oz.	?	3.30	1,050 U	Rush order
Beast29	22,000 units	0.40	?	660 F	Bought larger quantity

Instructions

Fill in the appropriate amounts or letters for the question marks in the report.

Prepare income statement for management.

E24.16 (LO 4), AP Fisk Company uses a standard cost accounting system. During January, the company reported the following manufacturing variances.

Materials price variance	$1,200 U	Labor quantity variance	$750 U
Materials quantity variance	800 F	Overhead variance	800 U
Labor price variance	550 U		

In addition, 8,000 units of product were sold at $8 per unit. Each unit sold had a standard cost of $5. Selling and administrative expenses were $8,000 for the month.

Instructions

Prepare an income statement for management for the month ended January 31, 2022.

Identify performance evaluation terminology.

E24.17 (LO 1, 4), C The following is a list of terms related to performance evaluation.

1. Balanced scorecard
2. Variance
3. Learning and growth perspective
4. Nonfinancial measures
5. Customer perspective
6. Internal process perspective
7. Ideal standards
8. Normal standards

Instructions

Match each of the following descriptions with one of the terms above.

a. The difference between total actual costs and total standard costs.

b. An efficient level of performance that is attainable under expected operating conditions.

c. An approach that incorporates financial and nonfinancial measures in an integrated system that links performance measurement and a company's strategic goals.

d. A viewpoint employed in the balanced scorecard to evaluate how well a company develops and retains its employees.

e. An evaluation tool that is not based on dollars.

f. A viewpoint employed in the balanced scorecard to evaluate the company from the perspective of those people who buy its products or services.

g. An optimum level of performance under perfect operating conditions.

h. A viewpoint employed in the balanced scorecard to evaluate the efficiency and effectiveness of the company's value chain.

E24.18 (LO 4), C Indicate which of the four perspectives in the balanced scorecard is most likely associated with the objectives that follow.

Identity balanced scorecard perspectives.

1. Percentage of repeat customers.
2. Number of suggestions for improvement from employees.
3. Contribution margin.
4. Brand recognition.
5. Number of cross-trained employees.
6. Amount of setup time.

E24.19 (LO 4), C Indicate which of the four perspectives in the balanced scorecard is most likely associated with the objectives that follow.

Identify balance scorecard perspectives.

1. Ethics violations.
2. Credit rating.
3. Customer retention.
4. Stockouts.
5. Reportable accidents.
6. Brand recognition.

*E24.20 (LO 5), AP Vista Company installed a standard cost system on January 1. Selected transactions for the month of January are as follows.

Journalize entries in a standard cost accounting system.

1. Purchased 18,000 units of raw materials on account at a cost of $4.50 per unit. Standard cost was $4.40 per unit.
2. Issued 18,000 units of raw materials for jobs that required 17,500 standard units of raw materials.
3. Incurred 15,300 actual hours of direct labor at an actual rate of $5.00 per hour. The standard rate is $5.50 per hour. (Credit Factory Wages Payable.)
4. Performed 15,300 hours of direct labor on jobs when standard hours were 15,400.
5. Applied overhead to jobs at the rate of 100% of direct labor cost for standard hours allowed.

Instructions

Journalize the January transactions.

*E24.21 (LO 2, 3, 5), AN Lopez Company uses a standard cost accounting system. Some of the ledger accounts have been destroyed in a fire. The controller asks your help in reconstructing some missing entries and balances.

Answer questions concerning missing entries and balances.

Instructions

Answer the following questions.

a. Materials Price Variance shows a $2,000 unfavorable balance. Accounts Payable shows $138,000 of raw materials purchases. What was the amount debited to Raw Materials Inventory for raw materials purchased?

b. Materials Quantity Variance shows a $3,000 favorable balance. Raw Materials Inventory shows a zero balance. What was the amount debited to Work in Process Inventory for direct materials used?

c. Labor Price Variance shows a $1,500 favorable balance. Factory Labor shows a debit of $145,000 for wages incurred. What was the amount credited to Factory Wages Payable?

d. Factory Labor shows a credit of $145,000 for direct labor used. Labor Quantity Variance shows a $900 favorable balance. What was the amount debited to Work in Process for direct labor used?

e. Overhead applied to Work in Process totaled $165,000. If the total overhead variance was $1,200 favorable, what was the amount of overhead costs debited to Manufacturing Overhead?

*E24.22 (LO 5), AP Data for Levine Inc. are given in E24.7.

Journalize entries for materials and labor variances.

Instructions

Journalize the entries to record the materials and labor variances.

Compute manufacturing overhead variances and interpret findings.

*E24.23 (LO 6), AN **Writing** The information shown below was taken from the annual manufacturing overhead cost budget of Connick Company.

Variable manufacturing overhead costs	$34,650
Fixed manufacturing overhead costs	$19,800
Normal production level in labor hours	16,500
Normal production level in units	4,125
Standard labor hours per unit	4

During the year, 4,050 units were produced, 16,100 hours were worked, and the actual manufacturing overhead was $55,500. Actual fixed manufacturing overhead costs equaled budgeted fixed manufacturing overhead costs. Overhead is applied on the basis of direct labor hours.

Instructions

a. Compute the total, fixed, and variable predetermined manufacturing overhead rates.

b. Compute the total, controllable, and volume overhead variances.

c. Briefly interpret the overhead controllable and volume variances computed in (b).

Compute overhead variances.

*E24.24 (LO 6), AN **Service** The loan department of Calgary Bank uses standard costs to determine the overhead cost of processing loan applications. During the current month, a fire occurred, and the accounting records for the department were mostly destroyed. The following data were salvaged from the ashes.

Standard variable overhead rate per hour	$9
Standard hours per application	2
Standard hours allowed	2,000
Standard fixed overhead rate per hour	$6
Actual fixed overhead cost	$12,600
Variable overhead budget based on standard hours allowed	$18,000
Fixed overhead budget	$12,600
Overhead controllable variance	$ 1,200 U

Instructions

a. Determine the following.
   1. Total actual overhead cost.
   2. Actual variable overhead cost.
   3. Variable overhead costs applied.
   4. Fixed overhead costs applied.
   5. Overhead volume variance.

b. Determine how many loans were processed.

Compute variances.

*E24.25 (LO 6), AP Seacrest Company's overhead rate was based on estimates of $200,000 for overhead costs and 20,000 direct labor hours. Seacrest's standards allow 2 hours of direct labor per unit produced. Production in May was 900 units, and actual overhead incurred in May was $19,500. The overhead budgeted for 1,800 standard direct labor hours is $17,600 ($5,000 fixed and $12,600 variable).

Instructions

a. Compute the total, controllable, and volume variances for overhead.

b. What are possible causes of the variances computed in part (a)?

Problems: Set A

Compute variances.

P24.1A (LO 2, 3), AP Rogen Corporation manufactures a single product. The standard cost per unit of product is shown below.

Direct materials—1 pound plastic at $7.00 per pound	$ 7.00
Direct labor—1.6 hours at $12.00 per hour	19.20
Variable manufacturing overhead	12.00
Fixed manufacturing overhead	4.00
Total standard cost per unit	$42.20

The predetermined manufacturing overhead rate is $10 per direct labor hour ($16.00 ÷ 1.6). It was computed from a master manufacturing overhead budget based on normal production of 8,000 direct labor hours (5,000 units) for the month. The master budget showed total variable costs of $60,000 ($7.50 per hour) and total fixed overhead costs of $20,000 ($2.50 per hour). Actual costs for October in producing 4,800 units were as follows.

Direct materials (5,100 pounds)	$ 36,720
Direct labor (7,400 hours)	92,500
Variable overhead	59,700
Fixed overhead	21,000
Total manufacturing costs	$209,920

The purchasing department buys the quantities of raw materials that are expected to be used in production each month. Raw materials inventories, therefore, can be ignored.

Instructions

a. Compute all of the materials and labor variances.

b. Compute the total overhead variance.

a. MPV $1,020 U

P24.2A (LO 2, 3, 4), AP Ayala Corporation accumulates the following data relative to jobs started and finished during the month of June 2022.

Compute variances, and prepare income statement.

Costs and Production Data	Actual	Standard
Raw materials unit cost	$2.25	$2.10
Raw materials units	10,600	10,000
Direct labor payroll	$120,960	$120,000
Direct labor hours	14,400	15,000
Manufacturing overhead incurred	$189,500	
Manufacturing overhead applied		$193,500
Machine hours expected to be used at normal capacity		42,500
Budgeted fixed overhead for June		$55,250
Variable overhead rate per machine hour		$3.00
Fixed overhead rate per machine hour		$1.30

Overhead is applied on the basis of standard machine hours. Three hours of machine time are required for each direct labor hour. The jobs were sold for $400,000. Selling and administrative expenses were $40,000. Assume that the amount of raw materials purchased equaled the amount used.

Instructions

a. Compute all of the variances for (1) direct materials and (2) direct labor.

b. Compute the total overhead variance.

c. Prepare an income statement for management. (Ignore income taxes.)

a. LQV $4,800 F

P24.3A (LO 2, 3, 4), AN Writing Rudd Clothiers is a small company that manufactures tall-men's suits. The company has used a standard cost accounting system. In May 2022, 11,250 suits were produced. The following standard and actual cost data applied to the month of May when normal capacity was 14,000 direct labor hours. All materials purchased were used.

Compute and identify significant variances.

Cost Element	Standard (per unit)	Actual
Direct materials	8 yards at $4.40 per yard	$375,575 for 90,500 yards ($4.15 per yard)
Direct labor	1.2 hours at $13.40 per hour	$200,925 for 14,250 hours ($14.10 per hour)
Overhead	1.2 hours at $6.10 per hour (fixed $3.50; variable $2.60)	$49,000 fixed overhead $37,000 variable overhead

Overhead is applied on the basis of direct labor hours. At normal capacity, budgeted fixed overhead costs were $49,000, and budgeted variable overhead was $36,400.

Instructions

a. Compute the total, price, and quantity variances for (1) materials and (2) labor.

b. Compute the total overhead variance.

c. Which of the materials and labor variances should be investigated if management considers a variance of more than 4% from standard to be significant?

a. MPV $22,625 F

Answer questions about variances.

P24.4A (LO 2, 3), AN Kansas Company uses a standard cost accounting system. In 2022, the company produced 28,000 units. Each unit took several pounds of direct materials and 1.6 standard hours of direct labor at a standard hourly rate of $12.00. Normal capacity was 50,000 direct labor hours. During the year, 117,000 pounds of raw materials were purchased at $0.92 per pound. All materials purchased were used during the year.

Instructions

a. If the materials price variance was $3,510 favorable, what was the standard materials price per pound?

b. 4.0 pounds

b. If the materials quantity variance was $4,750 unfavorable, what was the standard materials quantity per unit?

c. What were the standard hours allowed for the units produced?

d. If the labor quantity variance was $7,200 unfavorable, what were the actual direct labor hours worked?

e. If the labor price variance was $9,080 favorable, what was the actual rate per hour?

f. $7.20 per DLH

f. If total budgeted manufacturing overhead was $360,000 at normal capacity, what was the predetermined overhead rate?

g. What was the standard cost per unit of product?

h. How much overhead was applied to production during the year?

i. Using one or more answers above, what were the total costs assigned to work in process?

Compute variances, prepare an income statement, and explain unfavorable variances.

P24.5A (LO 2, 3, 4), AP `Service` `Writing` Hart Labs, Inc. provides mad cow disease testing for both state and federal governmental agricultural agencies. Because the company's customers are governmental agencies, prices are strictly regulated. Therefore, Hart Labs must constantly monitor and control its testing costs. Shown below are the standard costs for a typical test.

Direct materials (2 test tubes @ $1.46 per tube)	$ 2.92
Direct labor (1 hour @ $24 per hour)	24.00
Variable overhead (1 hour @ $6 per hour)	6.00
Fixed overhead (1 hour @ $10 per hour)	10.00
Total standard cost per test	$42.92

The lab does not maintain an inventory of test tubes. As a result, the tubes purchased each month are used that month. Actual activity for the month of November 2022, when 1,475 tests were conducted, resulted in the following.

Direct materials (3,050 test tubes)	$ 4,270
Direct labor (1,550 hours)	35,650
Variable overhead	7,400
Fixed overhead	15,000

Monthly budgeted fixed overhead is $14,000. Revenues for the month were $75,000, and selling and administrative expenses were $5,000.

Instructions

a. LQV $1,800 U

a. Compute the price and quantity variances for direct materials and direct labor.

b. Compute the total overhead variance.

c. Prepare an income statement for management.

d. Provide possible explanations for each unfavorable variance.

Journalize and post standard cost entries, and prepare income statement.

*P24.6A (LO 2, 3, 4, 5), AP Jorgensen Corporation uses standard costs with its job order cost accounting system. In January, an order (Job No. 12) for 1,900 units of Product B was received. The standard cost of one unit of Product B is as follows.

Direct materials	3 pounds at $1.00 per pound	$ 3.00
Direct labor	1 hour at $8.00 per hour	8.00
Overhead	2 hours (variable $4.00 per machine hour; fixed $2.25 per machine hour)	12.50
Standard cost per unit		$23.50

Normal capacity for the month was 4,200 machine hours. During January, the following transactions applicable to Job No. 12 occurred.

1. Purchased 6,200 pounds of raw materials on account at $1.05 per pound.
2. Requisitioned 6,200 pounds of raw materials for Job No. 12.
3. Incurred 2,000 hours of direct labor at a rate of $7.80 per hour.
4. Worked 2,000 hours of direct labor on Job No. 12.
5. Incurred manufacturing overhead on account $25,000.
6. Applied overhead to Job No. 12 on basis of standard machine hours allowed.
7. Completed Job No. 12.
8. Billed customer for Job No. 12 at a selling price of $65,000.

Instructions

a. Journalize the transactions.
b. Post to the job order cost accounts.
c. Prepare the entry to recognize the total overhead variance.
d. Prepare the January 2022 income statement for management. Assume selling and administrative expenses were $2,000.

d. NI $15,890

*P24.7A (LO 6), AP Using the information in P24.1A, compute the overhead controllable variance and the overhead volume variance.

Compute overhead controllable and volume variances.

*P24.8A (LO 6), AP Using the information in P24.2A, compute the overhead controllable variance and the overhead volume variance.

Compute overhead controllable and volume variances.

*P24.9A (LO 6), AP Using the information in P24.3A, compute the overhead controllable variance and the overhead volume variance.

Compute overhead controllable and volume variances.

*P24.10A (LO 6), AP Using the information in P24.5A, compute the overhead controllable variance and the overhead volume variance.

Compute overhead controllable and volume variances.

Continuing Cases

Current Designs

CD24 The executive team at **Current Designs** has gathered to evaluate the company's operations for the last month. One of the topics on the agenda is the special order from Huegel Hollow, which was presented in CD2. Recall that Current Designs had a special order to produce a batch of 20 kayaks for a client, and you were asked to determine the cost of the order and the cost per kayak.

Mike Cichanowski asked the others if the special order caused any particular problems in the production process. Dave Thill, the production manager, made the following comments: "Since we wanted to complete this order quickly and make a good first impression on this new customer, we had some of our most experienced type I workers run the rotomold oven and do the trimming. They were very efficient and were able to complete that part of the manufacturing process even more quickly than the regular crew. However, the finishing on these kayaks required a different technique than what we usually use, so our type II workers took a little longer than usual for that part of the process."

Deb Welch, who is in charge of the purchasing function, said, "We had to pay a little more for the polyethylene powder for this order because the customer wanted a color that we don't usually stock. We also ordered a little extra since we wanted to make sure that we had enough to allow us to calibrate the equipment. The calibration was a little tricky, and we used all of the powder that we had purchased. Since the number of kayaks in the order was fairly small, we were able to use some rope and other parts that were left over from last year's production in the finishing kits. We've seen a price increase for these components in the last year, so using the parts that we already had in inventory cut our costs for the finishing kits."

Instructions

a. Based on the comments above, predict whether each of the following variances will be favorable or unfavorable. If you don't have enough information to make a prediction, use "NEI" to indicate "Not Enough Information."

1. Quantity variance for polyethylene powder.
2. Price variance for polyethylene powder.
3. Quantity variance for finishing kits.
4. Price variance for finishing kits.
5. Quantity variance for type I workers.
6. Price variance for type I workers.
7. Quantity variance for type II workers.
8. Price variance for type II workers.

b. Diane Buswell examined some of the accounting records and reported that Current Designs purchased 1,200 pounds of pellets for this order at a total cost of $2,040. Twenty (20) finishing kits were assembled at a total cost of $3,240. The payroll records showed that the type I employees worked 38 hours on this project at a total cost of $570. The type II finishing employees worked 65 hours at a total cost of $796.25. A total of 20 kayaks were produced for this order.

The standards that had been developed for this model of kayak were used in CD2 and are reproduced here. For each kayak:

54 pounds of polyethylene powder at $1.50 per pound

1 finishing kit (rope, seat, hardware, etc.) at $170

2 hours of type I labor from people who run the oven and trim the plastic at a standard wage rate of $15 per hour

3 hours of type II labor from people who attach the hatches and seat and other hardware at a standard wage rate of $12 per hour.

Calculate the eight variances that are listed in part (a) of this problem.

Waterways

(This is a continuation of the Waterways case from Chapters 14–23.)

WP24 Waterways Corporation uses very stringent standard costs in evaluating its manufacturing efficiency. These standards are not "ideal" at this point, but management is working toward that as a goal. This problem asks you to calculate and evaluate the company's variances.

Go to WileyPLUS for complete case details and instructions.

Expand Your Critical Thinking

Decision-Making Across the Organization

CT24.1 Service Milton Professionals, a management consulting firm, specializes in strategic planning for financial institutions. James Hahn and Sara Norton, partners in the firm, are assembling a new strategic planning model for use by clients. The model is designed for use on most personal computers and replaces a rather lengthy manual model currently marketed by the firm. To market the new model, James and Sara will need to provide clients with an estimate of the number of labor hours and computer time needed to operate the model. The model is currently being test-marketed at five small financial institutions. These financial institutions are listed below, along with the number of combined computer/labor hours used by each institution to run the model one time.

Financial Institutions	Computer/Labor Hours Required
Midland National	25
First State	45
Financial Federal	40
Pacific America	30
Lakeview National	30
Total	170
Average	34

Any company that purchases the new model will need to purchase user manuals for the system. User manuals will be sold to clients in cases of 20, at a cost of $320 per case. One manual must be used each time the model is run because each manual includes a nonreusable computer-accessed password for operating the system. Also required are specialized computer forms that are sold only by Milton. The specialized forms are sold in packages of 250, at a cost of $60 per package. One application of the model requires the use of 50 forms. This amount includes two forms that are generally wasted in each application due to printer alignment errors. The overall cost of the strategic planning model to clients is $12,000. Most clients will use the model four times annually.

Milton must provide its clients with estimates of ongoing costs incurred in operating the new planning model, and would like to do so in the form of standard costs.

Instructions

With the class divided into groups, answer the following.

a. What factors should be considered in setting a standard for computer/labor hours?

b. What alternatives for setting a standard for computer/labor hours might be used?

c. What standard for computer/labor hours would you select? Justify your answer.

d. Determine the standard materials cost associated with the user manuals and computer forms for each application of the strategic planning model.

Managerial Analysis

*CT24.2 Ana Carillo and Associates is a medium-sized company located near a large metropolitan area in the Midwest. The company manufactures cabinets of mahogany, oak, and other fine woods for use in expensive homes, restaurants, and hotels. Although some of the work is custom, many of the cabinets are a standard size.

One such non-custom model is called Luxury Base Frame. Normal production is 1,000 units. Each unit has a direct labor hour standard of 5 hours. Overhead is applied to production based on standard direct labor hours. During the most recent month, only 900 units were produced; 4,500 direct labor hours were allowed for standard production, but only 4,000 hours were used. Standard and actual overhead costs were as follows.

	Standard (1,000 units)	Actual (900 units)
Indirect materials	$ 12,000	$ 12,300
Indirect labor	43,000	51,000
(Fixed) Manufacturing supervisors salaries	22,500	22,000
(Fixed) Manufacturing office employees salaries	13,000	12,500
(Fixed) Engineering costs	27,000	25,000
Computer costs	10,000	10,000
Electricity	2,500	2,500
(Fixed) Manufacturing building depreciation	8,000	8,000
(Fixed) Machinery depreciation	3,000	3,000
(Fixed) Trucks and forklift depreciation	1,500	1,500
Small tools	700	1,400
(Fixed) Insurance	500	500
(Fixed) Property taxes	300	300
Total	$144,000	$150,000

Instructions

a. Determine the overhead application rate.

b. Determine how much overhead was applied to production.

c. Calculate the total overhead variance, controllable variance, and volume variance.

d. Decide which overhead variances should be investigated.

e. Discuss causes of the overhead variances. What can management do to improve its performance next month?

Real-World Focus

CT24.3 Glassmaster Company is organized as two divisions and one subsidiary. One division focuses on the manufacture of filaments such as fishing line and sewing thread; the other division manufactures antennas and specialty fiberglass products. Its subsidiary manufactures flexible steel wire controls and molded control panels.

The annual report of Glassmaster provides the following information.

> **Glassmaster Company**
> **Management Discussion**
>
> Gross profit margins for the year improved to 20.9% of sales compared to last year's 18.5%. All operations reported improved margins due in large part to improved operating efficiencies as a result of cost reduction measures implemented during the second and third quarters of the fiscal year and increased manufacturing throughout due to higher unit volume sales. Contributing to the improved margins was a favorable materials price variance due to competitive pricing by suppliers as a result of soft demand for petrochemical-based products. This favorable variance is temporary and will begin to reverse itself as stronger worldwide demand for commodity products improves in tandem with the economy. Partially offsetting these positive effects on profit margins were competitive pressures on sales prices of certain product lines. The company responded with pricing strategies designed to maintain and/or increase market share.

Instructions

a. Is it apparent from the information whether Glassmaster utilizes standard costs?

b. Do you think the price variance experienced should lead to changes in standard costs for the next fiscal year?

CT24.4 **Service** The **Balanced Scorecard Institute** is a great resource for information about implementing the balanced scorecard. One item of interest provided at its website is an example of a balanced scorecard for a regional airline.

Instructions

Go to the Balanced Scorecard Institute website, do a search on "Examples and Success Stories," scroll down to select the Regional Airline example under Commercial Organizations, and then answer the following questions.

a. What are the objectives identified for the airline for each perspective?

b. What measures are used for the objectives in the customer perspective?

c. What initiatives are planned to achieve the objective in the learning perspective?

Communication Activity

CT24.5 The setting of standards is critical to the effective use of standards in evaluating performance.

Instructions

Explain the following in a memo to your instructor.

a. The comparative advantages and disadvantages of ideal versus normal standards.

b. The factors that should be included in setting the price and quantity standards for direct materials, direct labor, and manufacturing overhead.

Ethics Case

CT24.6 At Symond Company, production workers in the Painting Department are paid on the basis of productivity. The labor time standard for a unit of production is established through periodic time studies conducted by Douglas Management Consultants. In a time study, the actual time required to complete a specific task by a worker is observed. Allowances are then made for preparation time, rest periods, and cleanup time. Bill Carson is one of several veterans in the Painting Department.

Bill is informed by Douglas that he will be used in the time study for the painting of a new product. The findings will be the basis for establishing the labor time standard for the next 6 months. During the test, Bill deliberately slows his normal work pace in an effort to obtain a labor time standard that will be easy to meet. Because it is a new product, the Douglas representative who conducted the test is unaware that Bill did not give the test his best effort.

Instructions

a. Who was benefited and who was harmed by Bill's actions?

b. Was Bill ethical in the way he performed the time study test?

c. What measure(s) might the company take to obtain valid data for setting the labor time standard?

All About You

CT24.7 From the time you first entered school many years ago, instructors have been measuring and evaluating you by imposing standards. In addition, many of you will pursue professions that administer professional examinations to attain recognized certification. A federal commission presented proposals suggesting all public colleges and universities should require standardized tests to measure their students' learning.

Instructions

Do an Internet search on "Union Tribune U.S. panel endorses standards for college," read the **San Diego Union-Tribune** article, and then answer the following questions.

a. What areas of concern did the panel's recommendations address?

b. What are possible advantages of standard testing?

c. What are possible disadvantages of standard testing?

d. Would you be in favor of standardized tests?

Considering Your Costs and Benefits

CT24.8 **Writing** Do you think that standard costs are used only in making products like wheel bearings and hamburgers? Think again. Standards influence virtually every aspect of our lives. For example, the next time you call to schedule an appointment with your doctor, ask the receptionist how many minutes the appointment is scheduled for. Doctors are under increasing pressure to see more patients each day, which means the time spent with each patient is shorter. As insurance companies and employers push for reduced medical costs, every facet of medicine has been standardized and analyzed. Doctors, nurses, and other medical staff are evaluated in every part of their operations to ensure maximum efficiency. While keeping medical treatment affordable seems like a worthy goal, what are the potential implications for the quality of health care? Does a focus on the bottom line result in a reduction in the quality of health care?

A simmering debate has centered on a very basic question: To what extent should accountants, through financial measures, influence the type of medical care that you receive? Suppose that your local medical facility is in danger of closing because it has been losing money. Should the facility put in place incentives that provide bonuses to doctors if they meet certain standard-cost targets for the cost of treating specific ailments?

YES: If the facility is in danger of closing, then someone should take steps to change the medical practices to reduce costs. A closed medical facility is of no use to me, my family, or the community.

NO: I don't want an accountant deciding the right medical treatment for me. My family and I deserve the best medical care.

Instructions

Write a response indicating your position regarding this situation. Provide support for your view.

CHAPTER 25

Planning for Capital Investments

Chapter Preview

Companies like **Holland America Line** (as discussed in the following Feature Story) must constantly determine how to invest their resources. Other examples: **Dell** announced plans to spend $1 billion on data centers for cloud computing. **ExxonMobil** announced that two wells off the Brazilian coast, which it had spent hundreds of millions of dollars to drill, would produce no oil. **Renault** and **Nissan** spent over $5 billion during a nearly 20-year period to develop electric cars, such as the Leaf.

The process of making such capital expenditure decisions is referred to as **capital budgeting**. Capital budgeting involves choosing among various capital projects to find those that will maximize a company's return on its financial investment. The purpose of this chapter is to discuss the various techniques used to make effective capital budgeting decisions.

Feature Story

Floating Hotels

Do you own a boat? Maybe you think it's a nice boat, but how many swimming pools, movie theaters, shopping malls, or restaurants does it have on board? If you are in the cruise-line business, like **Holland America Line**, you need all of these amenities and more just to stay afloat. Holland America Line is considered by many to be the leader of the premium luxury-liner segment.

Carnival Corporation, which owns Holland America Line and other cruise lines, is one of the largest vacation companies in the world. During one recent three-year period, Carnival spent more than $3 billion per year on capital expenditures. That's a big number, but keep in mind that Carnival estimates that at any given time there are 270,000 people (200,000 customers and 70,000 crew) on its 100 ships somewhere in the world.

The cruise industry is a tricky business. When times are good, customers are looking for ways to splurge. But when times get tough, people are more inclined to take a trip in a minivan than a luxury yacht. So, if you are a cruise line executive, it's important to time your investment properly. For example, during one stretch of solid global economic growth, many cruise lines decided to add capacity. The industry built 14 new ships at a total price of $4.7 billion. (That's an average price of about $330 million.) But, it takes up to three years to build one of these giant vessels. Unfortunately, by the time the ships were completed, the economy was in a nose-dive.

To maintain passenger numbers during the recession, cruise prices had to be cut by up to 40%. While the lower prices attracted lots of customers, that wasn't enough to offset an overall decline in revenue of 10%. The industry had added capacity at just the wrong time.

 Watch the *Holland America Line* video in WileyPLUS to learn more about real-world capital budgeting.

Chapter Outline

LEARNING OBJECTIVES

LO 1 Describe capital budgeting inputs and apply the cash payback technique.	• Cash flow information • Cash payback	**DO IT! 1** Cash Payback Period
LO 2 Use the net present value method.	• Equal annual cash flows • Unequal annual cash flows • Choosing a discount rate • Simplifying assumptions • Comprehensive example	**DO IT! 2** Net Present Value
LO 3 Identify capital budgeting challenges and refinements.	• Intangible benefits • Profitability index for mutually exclusive projects • Risk analysis • Post-audit of investment projects	**DO IT! 3** Profitability Index
LO 4 Use the internal rate of return method.	• Comparing discounted cash flow methods	**DO IT! 4** Internal Rate of Return
LO 5 Use the annual rate of return method.	• Based on accrual-accounting data	**DO IT! 5** Annual Rate of Return

Go to the Review and Practice section at the end of the chapter for a targeted summary and practice applications with solutions.
Visit WileyPLUS for additional tutorials and practice opportunities.

Capital Budgeting and Cash Payback

LEARNING OBJECTIVE 1
Describe capital budgeting inputs and apply the cash payback technique.

Many companies follow a carefully prescribed capital budgeting process similar to the following. At least once a year, top management requests proposals for projects from departments, plants, and authorized personnel. A capital budgeting committee screens the proposals and submits its findings to the officers of the company. The officers select the projects they believe to be most worthy of funding. They submit this list of projects to the board of directors. Ultimately, the directors approve the capital expenditure budget for the year. **Illustration 25.1** shows this process.

ILLUSTRATION 25.1 Corporate capital budget authorization process

1. Project proposals are requested from departments, plants, and authorized personnel.
2. Proposals are screened by a capital budget committee.
3. Officers determine which projects are worthy of funding.
4. Board of directors approves capital budget.

The involvement of top management and the board of directors in the process demonstrates the importance of capital budgeting decisions. These decisions often have a significant impact on a company's future profitability. In fact, poor capital budgeting decisions can cost a lot of money. Such decisions have even led to the bankruptcy of some companies.

Cash Flow Information

In this chapter, we look at several methods that help companies make effective capital budgeting decisions. Most of these methods employ **cash flow numbers**, rather than accrual accounting revenues and expenses. Remember from your financial accounting course that accrual accounting records **revenues** and **expenses**, rather than cash inflows and cash outflows. In fact, revenues and expenses measured during a period often differ significantly from their cash flow counterparts. Accrual accounting has advantages over cash accounting in many contexts. **For purposes of capital budgeting, though, estimated cash inflows and outflows are the preferred inputs.** Why? Because ultimately the value of all financial investments is determined by the value of cash flows received and paid.

Sometimes cash flow information is not available. In this case, companies can make adjustments to accrual accounting numbers to estimate cash flow. Often, they estimate net annual cash flow by adding back depreciation expense to net income. Depreciation expense is added back because it is an expense that does not require an outflow of cash. By adding depreciation expense back to net income, companies approximate net annual cash flow. Suppose, for example, that Reno Company's net income of $13,000 includes a charge for depreciation expense of $26,000. Its estimated net annual cash flow would be $39,000 ($13,000 + $26,000).

Illustration 25.2 lists some typical cash outflows and inflows related to equipment purchase and replacement.

ILLUSTRATION 25.2
Typical cash flows relating to capital budgeting decisions

Cash Outflows
Initial investment
Repairs and maintenance
Increased operating costs
Overhaul of equipment

Cash Inflows
Proceeds from sale of old equipment
Increased cash received from customers
Reduced cash outflows related to operating costs
Salvage value of equipment

These cash flows are the inputs that are considered relevant in capital budgeting decisions.

The capital budgeting decision, under any technique, depends in part on a variety of considerations:

- **The availability of funds:** Does the company have unlimited funds, or will it have to ration capital investments?
- **Relationships among proposed projects:** Are proposed projects independent of each other, or does the acceptance or rejection of one depend on the acceptance or rejection of another?
- **The company's basic decision-making approach:** Does the company want to produce an accept-reject decision or a ranking of desirability among possible projects?
- **The risk associated with a particular project:** How certain are the projected returns? The certainty of estimates varies with such issues as market considerations or the length of time before returns are expected.

Illustrative Data

To compare the results of the various capital budgeting techniques, we use a continuing example. Assume that Stewart Shipping Company is considering an investment of $130,000 in new equipment. The new equipment is expected to last 10 years. It is estimated to have a zero salvage value at the end of its useful life. The expected annual cash inflows are $200,000, and the annual cash outflows are $176,000. Illustration 25.3 summarizes these data.

ILLUSTRATION 25.3
Investment information for Stewart Shipping example

Initial investment	$130,000
Estimated useful life	10 years
Estimated salvage value	–0–
Estimated annual cash flows	
Cash inflows from customers	$200,000
Cash outflows for operating costs	176,000
Net annual cash flow	$ 24,000

In the following two sections, we examine two popular techniques for evaluating capital investments: cash payback and the net present value method.

Cash Payback

The **cash payback technique** identifies the time period required to recover the cost of the capital investment from the net annual cash flow produced by the investment. Illustration 25.4 presents the formula for computing the cash payback period assuming equal annual cash flows.

| Cost of Capital Investment | ÷ | Net Annual Cash Flow | = | Cash Payback Period |

ILLUSTRATION 25.4
Cash payback formula

The cash payback period in the Stewart Shipping example is 5.42 years, computed as follows (see **Helpful Hint**).

$$\$130,000 \div \$24,000 = 5.42 \text{ years}$$

HELPFUL HINT
Net annual cash flow can also be approximated by "Net cash provided by operating activities" from the statement of cash flows.

The evaluation of the payback period is often related to the expected useful life of the asset. For example, assume that at Stewart Shipping a project is unacceptable if the payback period is longer than 60% of the asset's expected useful life. The 5.42-year payback period is 54.2% (5.42 ÷ 10) of the project's expected useful life. Thus, the project is acceptable.

It follows that when the payback technique is used to decide among acceptable alternative projects, **the shorter the payback period, the more attractive the investment**. This is true for two reasons: First, the earlier the investment is recovered, the sooner the company can use the cash funds for other purposes. Second, the risk of loss from obsolescence and changed economic conditions is less in a shorter payback period.

The preceding computation of the cash payback period assumes **equal** net annual cash flows in each year of the investment's life. In many cases, this assumption is not valid. In the case of **uneven** net annual cash flows, the company determines the cash payback period **when the cumulative net cash flows from the investment equal the cost of the investment**.

To illustrate, assume that Chen Company proposes an investment in a new website that is estimated to cost $300,000. **Illustration 25.5** shows the proposed investment cost, net annual cash flows, cumulative net cash flows, and the cash payback period.

Year	Investment	Net Annual Cash Flow	Cumulative Net Cash Flow
0	$300,000		
1		$ 60,000	$ 60,000
2		90,000	150,000
3		90,000	240,000
4		120,000	360,000
5		100,000	460,000

Cash payback period = 3.5 years

ILLUSTRATION 25.5
Computation of cash payback period—unequal cash flows

As Illustration 25.5 shows, at the end of year 3, cumulative net cash flow of $240,000 is less than the investment cost of $300,000, but at the end of year 4 the cumulative cash inflow of $360,000 exceeds the investment cost. The cash flow needed in year 4 to equal the investment cost is $60,000 ($300,000 − $240,000). Assuming the cash inflow occurred evenly during year 4, we divide $60,000 by the net annual cash flow in year 4 ($120,000) to determine the point during the year when the cash payback occurs. Thus, we get 0.50 ($60,000/$120,000), or half of the year, and the cash payback period is 3.5 years.

The cash payback technique may be useful as an initial screening tool. It may be the most critical factor in the capital budgeting decision for a company that desires a fast turnaround of its investment because of a weak cash position. It also is relatively easy to compute and understand.

However, cash payback should not ordinarily be the only basis for the capital budgeting decision because it **ignores the expected profitability of the project**. To illustrate, assume that Projects A and B have the same payback period, but Project A's useful life is double the useful life of Project B. Project A's earning power, therefore, is twice as long as Project B's. A further—and major—disadvantage of this technique is that it **ignores the time value of money**. We address time value of money with the approach described in the next section.

ACTION PLAN

- Annual cash inflows − Annual cash outflows = Net annual cash flow.
- Cash payback period = Cost of capital investment/Net annual cash flow.

DO IT! 1 | Cash Payback Period

Watertown Paper Corporation is considering adding another machine for the manufacture of corrugated cardboard. The machine would cost $900,000. It would have an estimated life of 6 years and no salvage value. The company estimates that annual cash inflows would increase by $400,000 and that annual cash outflows would increase by $190,000. Compute the cash payback period.

Solution

Estimated annual cash inflows	$400,000
Estimated annual cash outflows	190,000
Net annual cash flow	$210,000

Cash payback period = $900,000/$210,000 = 4.3 years

Related exercise material: **BE25.1** and **DO IT! 25.1**.

Net Present Value Method

LEARNING OBJECTIVE 2
Use the net present value method.

The time value of money can have a significant impact on a capital budgeting decision. Cash flows that occur early in the life of an investment are worth more than those that occur later—because of the time value of money. Therefore, it is useful to recognize the timing of cash flows when evaluating projects.

Capital budgeting techniques that take into account both the time value of money and the estimated net cash flows from an investment are called **discounted cash flow techniques**. They are generally recognized as the most informative and best conceptual approaches to making capital budgeting decisions. The expected net cash flow used in discounting cash flows consists of the annual net cash flows plus the estimated liquidation proceeds (salvage value) when the asset is sold for salvage at the end of its useful life.

The primary discounted cash flow technique is the **net present value method**. A second method, discussed later in the chapter, is the **internal rate of return**. At this point, **we recommend that you examine Appendix G** to review the time value of money concepts upon which these methods are based. Also, the Excel tutorial provided in WileyPLUS for this chapter demonstrates the use of the NPV (net present value) and IRR (internal rate of return) functions in Excel.

The **net present value (NPV) method** involves discounting net cash flows to their present value and then comparing that present value with the capital outlay required by the investment (see **Decision Tools**). The difference between these two amounts is referred to as **net present value (NPV)**. Company management determines what interest rate to use in discounting the future net cash flows. This rate, often referred to as the **discount rate** or **required rate of return**, is discussed in a later section.

The NPV decision rule is this: **A proposal is acceptable when net present value is zero or positive**. A zero or positive NPV indicates that the rate of return on the investment equals or exceeds (respectively) the required rate of return. The **required rate of return** is management's minimum acceptable rate of return on investments, sometimes called the discount rate or cost of capital. When net present value is negative, the project is unacceptable. **Illustration 25.6** shows the net present value decision criteria.

Decision Tools

Using the net present value method helps companies to determine whether or not to invest in proposed projects.

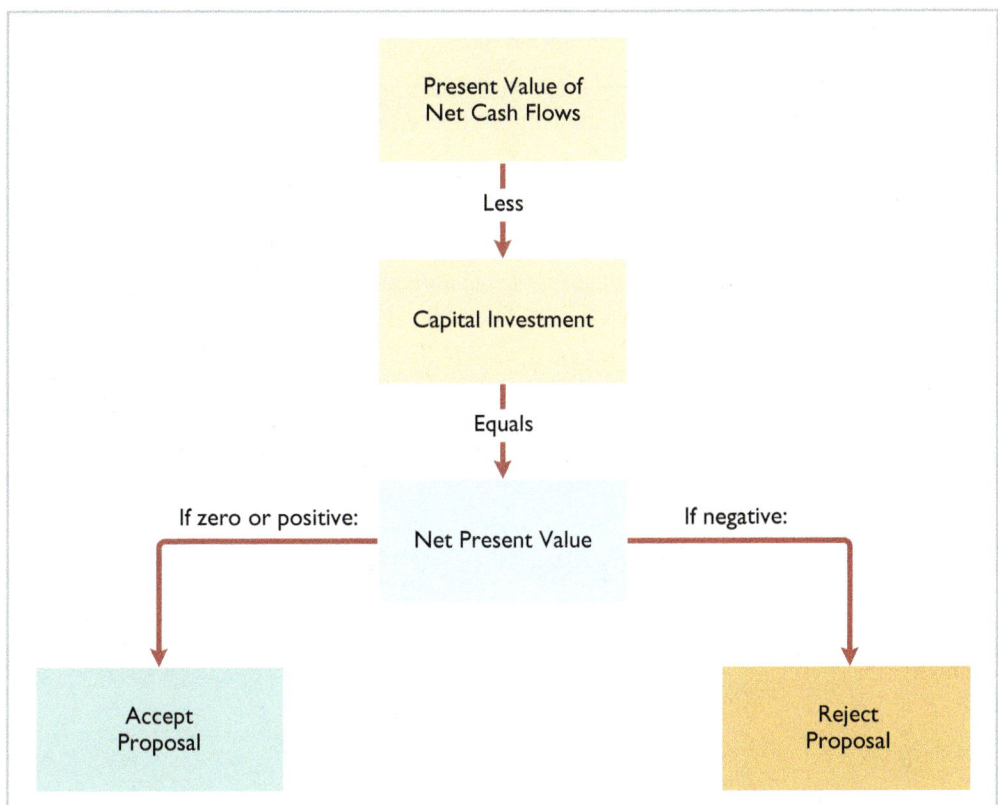

ILLUSTRATION 25.6

Net present value decision criteria

When making a selection among acceptable proposals, **the higher the positive net present value, the more attractive the investment**. The application of this method to two cases is described in the next two sections. In each case, we assume that the investment has no salvage value at the end of its useful life.

Equal Annual Cash Flows

In our Stewart Shipping Company example, the company's net annual cash flows are $24,000. If we assume this amount **is uniform over the asset's useful life**, we can compute the present value of the net annual cash flows by using the present value of an annuity of 1 for 10 payments (from Table 4, Appendix G). Assuming a discount rate of 12%, the present value of net cash flows are as shown in Illustration 25.7 (rounded to the nearest dollar) (see **Helpful Hint**).

> **HELPFUL HINT**
> The ABC Co. expects equal cash flows over an asset's 5-year useful life. The discount factor it should use in determining present values if management wants a 12% return is 3.60478 (using Table 4).

	Present Value at 12%
Discount factor for 10 periods	5.65022
Present value of net cash flows: $24,000 × 5.65022	$135,605

ILLUSTRATION 25.7

Computation of present value of equal net annual cash flows

Illustration 25.8 shows the analysis of the proposal by the net present value method.

	12%
Present value of net cash flows	$135,605
Less: Capital investment	130,000
Net present value	**$ 5,605**

ILLUSTRATION 25.8

Computation of net present value—equal net annual cash flows

The proposed capital expenditure is acceptable at a required rate of return of 12% because the net present value is positive. The positive NPV indicates the expected return on the investment exceeds 12%.

Unequal Annual Cash Flows

When net annual cash flows are unequal, we cannot use annuity tables to calculate their present value. Instead, we use tables showing the **present value of a single future amount for each annual cash flow**.

To illustrate, assume that Stewart Shipping Company expects the same total net cash flows of $240,000 over the life of the investment. But because of a declining market demand for the product over the life of the equipment, the net annual cash flows are higher in the early years and lower in the later years. The present value of the net annual cash flows is calculated as shown in **Illustration 25.9**, using discount factors from Table 3 in Appendix G (see **Helpful Hint**).

HELPFUL HINT
Appendix G demonstrates the use of a financial calculator to solve time value of money problems.

ILLUSTRATION 25.9
Computation of present value of unequal annual cash flows

Year	Assumed Net Annual Cash Flows (1)	Discount Factor 12% (2)	Present Value 12% (1) × (2)
1	$ 34,000	.89286	$ 30,357
2	30,000	.79719	23,916
3	27,000	.71178	19,218
4	25,000	.63552	15,888
5	24,000	.56743	13,618
6	22,000	.50663	11,146
7	21,000	.45235	9,499
8	20,000	.40388	8,078
9	19,000	.36061	6,852
10	18,000	.32197	5,795
	$240,000		$144,367

Therefore, the analysis of the proposal by the net present value method is as shown in **Illustration 25.10**.

ILLUSTRATION 25.10
Computation of net present value—unequal annual cash flows

	12%
Present value of net cash flows	$144,367
Less: Capital investment	130,000
Net present value	**$ 14,367**

In this example, the present value of the net cash flows is greater than the $130,000 capital investment. Thus, the project is acceptable at a 12% required rate of return. The difference between the present values using the 12% rate under equal cash flows ($135,605) and unequal cash flows ($144,367) is due to the pattern of the flows. Since more money is received sooner under this particular uneven cash flow scenario, its present value is greater.

Management Insight   Verizon

SchulteProductions/Getty Images.

Can You Hear Me—Better?

What's better than 3G wireless service? 4G. But the question for wireless service providers is whether customers will be willing to pay extra for that improvement. Verizon has spent billions on upgrading its networks in the past few years, so it now offers 4G LTE service to 97% of the nation. Verizon is hoping that its investment in 4G works out better than its $23 billion investment in its FIOS fiber-wired network for TV and ultrahigh-speed Internet. One analyst estimates that the present value of each FIOS customer is $800 less than the cost of the connection.

Sources: Martin Peers, "Investors: Beware Verizon's Generation GAP," *Wall Street Journal Online* (January 26, 2010); and Chad Fraser, "What Warren Buffett Sees in Verizon," *Investing Daily* (May 30, 2014).

If customers are slow to initially adopt 4G, how might the conclusions of a cash payback analysis of Verizon's 4G investment differ from a present value analysis? (Go to WileyPlus for this answer and additional questions.)

Choosing a Discount Rate

Now that you understand how companies apply the net present value method, it is logical to ask a related question: How is a discount rate (required rate of return) determined in real capital budgeting decisions? In most instances, a company uses a required rate of return equal to its **cost of capital**—that is, the rate that it must pay to obtain funds from creditors and stockholders.

The cost of capital is a weighted average of the rates paid on borrowed funds as well as on funds provided by investors in the company's common stock and preferred stock (see **Helpful Hint**). If management believes a project is riskier than the company's usual line of business, the discount rate should be increased. That is, the discount rate has two elements, a cost of capital element and a risk element. Often, companies assume the risk element is equal to zero.

Using an incorrect discount rate can lead to incorrect capital budgeting decisions. Consider again the Stewart Shipping example in Illustration 25.8, where we used a discount rate of 12%. Suppose that this rate does not take into account the fact that this project is riskier than most of the company's investments. A more appropriate discount rate, given the risk, might be 15%. **Illustration 25.11** compares the net present values at the two rates. At the higher, more appropriate discount rate of 15%, the net present value is negative. The negative NPV indicates that the expected rate of return on the investment is less than the required rate of return of 15%. The company should reject the project (discount factors from Appendix G, Table 4).

> **HELPFUL HINT**
> Cost of capital is the rate that management expects to pay on all borrowed and equity funds. It does not relate to the cost of funding a *specific* project.

	Present Values at Different Discount Rates	
	12%	15%
Discount factor for 10 payments	5.65022	5.01877
Present value of net cash flows:		
$24,000 × 5.65022	$135,605	
$24,000 × 5.01877		$120,450
Less: Capital investment	130,000	130,000
Positive (negative) net present value	$ 5,605	$ (9,550)

ILLUSTRATION 25.11
Comparison of net present values at different discount rates

The discount rate is often referred to by alternative names, including the **required rate of return**, the **hurdle rate**, and the **cutoff rate**. Determination of the cost of capital varies somewhat depending on whether the entity is a for-profit or not-for-profit business. Calculation of the cost of capital is discussed more fully in advanced accounting and finance courses.

Simplifying Assumptions

In our examples of the net present value method, we made a number of simplifying assumptions:

- **All cash flows occur at the end of each year.** In reality, cash flows will occur at uneven intervals throughout the year. However, it is far simpler to assume that all cash flows come at the end (or in some cases the beginning) of the year. In fact, this assumption is frequently made in practice.
- **All cash flows are immediately reinvested in another project that has a similar return.** In most capital budgeting situations, companies receive cash flows during each year of a project's life. In order to determine the return on the investment, some assumption must be made about how the cash flows are reinvested in the year that they are received. It is customary to assume that cash flows received are reinvested in some other project of similar return until the end of the project's life.
- **All cash flows can be predicted with certainty.** The outcomes of business investments are full of uncertainty, as the **Holland America Line** Feature Story shows. There is no way of knowing how popular a new product will be, how long a new machine will last, or what competitors' reactions might be to changes in a product. But, in order to

make investment decisions, analysts must estimate future outcomes. In this chapter, we have assumed that future amounts are known with certainty.[1] In reality, little is known with certainty. More advanced capital budgeting techniques deal with uncertainty by considering the probability that various outcomes will occur.

Comprehensive Example

Best Taste Foods is considering investing in new equipment to produce fat-free snack foods. Management believes that although demand for fat-free foods has leveled off, fat-free foods are here to stay. The estimated costs, cost of capital, and cash flows shown in **Illustration 25.12** were determined in consultation with the marketing, production, and finance departments.

ILLUSTRATION 25.12
Investment information for Best Taste Foods example

Initial investment	$1,000,000
Cost of equipment overhaul in 5 years	$200,000
Salvage value of equipment in 10 years	$20,000
Cost of capital (discount rate)	15%
Estimated annual cash flows	
Cash inflows received from sales	$500,000
Cash outflows for cost of goods sold	$200,000
Maintenance costs	$30,000
Other direct operating costs	$40,000

Remember that we are using cash flows in our analysis, not accrual revenues and expenses. Thus, for example, the direct operating costs would not include depreciation expense, since depreciation expense does not use cash. **Illustration 25.13** presents the computation of the net annual cash flows of this project.

ILLUSTRATION 25.13
Computation of net annual cash flow

Cash inflows received from sales	$ 500,000
Cash outflows for cost of goods sold	(200,000)
Maintenance costs	(30,000)
Other direct operating costs	(40,000)
Net annual cash flow	**$ 230,000**

Illustration 25.14 shows computation of the net present value for this proposed investment (discount factors from Appendix G, Tables 3 and 4).

ILLUSTRATION 25.14
Computation of net present value for Best Taste Foods investment

Event	Time Period	Cash Flow	×	15% Discount Factor	=	Present Value
Net annual cash flow	1–10	$ 230,000	×	5.01877	=	$1,154,317
Salvage value	10	20,000		.24719		4,944
Less: Equipment purchase	0	1,000,000		1.00000		1,000,000
Less: Equipment overhaul	5	200,000		.49718		99,436
Net present value						**$ 59,825**

Because the net present value of the project is positive, Best Taste should accept the project.

---

[1]One exception is a brief discussion of sensitivity analysis later in the chapter.

DO IT! 2 | Net Present Value

Watertown Paper Corporation is considering adding another machine for the manufacture of corrugated cardboard. The machine would cost $900,000. It would have an estimated life of 6 years and no salvage value. The company estimates that annual cash inflows would increase by $400,000 and that annual cash outflows would increase by $190,000. Management has a required rate of return of 9%. Calculate the net present value on this project and discuss whether it should be accepted.

ACTION PLAN
- Recall that estimated annual cash inflows − Estimated annual cash outflows = Net annual cash flow.
- Use the NPV technique to calculate the difference between net cash flows and the initial investment.
- Accept the project if the net present value is positive.

Solution

Estimated annual cash inflows	$400,000
Estimated annual cash outflows	190,000
Net annual cash flow	$210,000

	Cash Flow	9% Discount Factor	Present Value
Present value of net annual cash flows	$210,000	4.48592[a]	$942,043
Less: Capital investment			900,000
Net present value			$ 42,043

[a]Table 4, Appendix G, 9%, 6 years

Since the net present value is greater than zero, Watertown should accept the project.

Related exercise material: **BE25.2, BE25.3, DO IT! 25.2, E25.1, E25.2, and E25.3**.

Capital Budgeting Challenges and Refinements

LEARNING OBJECTIVE 3
Identify capital budgeting challenges and refinements.

Now that you understand how the net present value method works, we can add some "additional wrinkles." Specifically, these are the impact of intangible benefits, a way to compare mutually exclusive projects, refinements that take risk into account, and the need to conduct post-audits of investment projects.

Intangible Benefits

The NPV evaluation techniques employed thus far rely on tangible costs and benefits that can be relatively easily quantified. Some investment projects, especially high-tech projects, fail to make it through initial capital budget screens because only the project's tangible benefits are considered. **Intangible benefits** might include increased quality, improved safety, or enhanced employee loyalty. By ignoring intangible benefits, capital budgeting techniques might incorrectly eliminate projects that could be financially beneficial to the company.

To avoid rejecting projects that actually should be accepted, analysts suggest two possible approaches:

1. Calculate net present value ignoring intangible benefits. Then, if the NPV is negative, ask whether the project offers any intangible benefits that are worth at least the amount of the negative NPV.
2. Project conservative estimates of the value of the intangible benefits, and incorporate these values into the NPV calculation.

Example

Assume that Berg Company is considering the purchase of a new mechanical robot to be used for soldering electrical connections. **Illustration 25.15** shows the estimates related to this proposed purchase (discount factor from Appendix G, Table 4).

ILLUSTRATION 25.15
Investment information for Berg Company example

Initial investment	$200,000	
Annual cash inflows	$ 50,000	
Annual cash outflows	20,000	
Net annual cash flow	**$ 30,000**	
Estimated life of equipment	10 years	
Discount rate	12%	

	Cash Flows	×	12% Discount Factor	=	Present Value
Present value of net annual cash flows	$30,000	×	5.65022	=	$169,507
Less: Initial investment					200,000
Net present value					**$ (30,493)**

Based on the negative net present value of $30,493, the proposed project is not acceptable. This calculation, however, ignores important information. First, the company's engineers believe that purchasing this machine will improve the quality of electrical connections in the company's products. As a result, future warranty costs may be reduced. Also, this higher quality may translate into higher future sales. Finally, the new machine will be safer than the current machine.

The managers at Berg Company do not have confidence in their ability to accurately estimate these potentially higher revenues and lower costs. But Berg can incorporate this new information into the capital budgeting decision in the two ways discussed earlier. First, management might simply ask whether the reduced warranty costs, increased sales, and improved safety benefits have an estimated total present value to the company of at least $30,493. If yes, then the project is acceptable.

Alternatively, analysts can estimate the annual cash flows of these benefits. In our initial calculation, we assumed each of these benefits to have a value of zero. It seems likely that their actual values are much higher than zero. Given the difficulty of estimating these benefits, however, conservative values should be assigned to them. If, after using conservative estimates, the net present value is positive, Berg should accept the project.

To illustrate, assume that Berg estimates that improved sales will increase cash inflows by $10,000 annually as a result of an increase in perceived quality. Berg also estimates that annual cost outflows would be reduced by $5,000 as a result of lower warranty claims, reduced injury claims, and fewer missed work days. Consideration of the intangible benefits results in the revised NPV calculation shown in **Illustration 25.16** (discount factor from Appendix G, Table 4).

ILLUSTRATION 25.16
Revised investment information for Berg Company example, including intangible benefits

Initial investment	$200,000	
Annual cash inflows (revised)	$ 60,000 ($50,000 + $10,000)	
Annual cash outflows (revised)	15,000 ($20,000 − $5,000)	
Net annual cash flow	**$ 45,000**	
Estimated life of equipment	10 years	
Discount rate	12%	

	Cash Flows	×	12% Discount Factor	=	Present Value
Present value of net annual cash flows	$45,000	×	5.65022	=	$254,260
Less: Initial investment					200,000
Net present value					**$ 54,260**

Using these conservative estimates of the value of the additional benefits, Berg should accept the project.

Ethics Insight

It Need Not Cost an Arm and a Leg

Carol Gering/iStockphoto

Most manufacturers say that employee safety matters above everything else. But how many back up this statement with investments that improve employee safety? Recently, a woodworking hobbyist, who also happens to be a patent attorney with a Ph.D. in physics, invented a mechanism that automatically shuts down a power saw when the saw blade comes in contact with human flesh. The blade stops so quickly that only minor injuries result.

Power saws injure 40,000 Americans each year, and 4,000 of those injuries are bad enough to require amputation. Therefore, one might think that power-saw companies would be lined up to incorporate this mechanism into their saws. But, in the words of one power-tool company, "Safety doesn't sell." Since existing saw manufacturers were unwilling to incorporate the device into their saws, eventually the inventor started his own company to build the devices and sell them directly to businesses that use power saws.

Source: Melba Newsome, "An Edgy New Idea," *Time: Inside Business* (May 2006), p. A16.

In addition to the obvious humanitarian benefit of reducing serious injuries, how else might the manufacturer of this product convince potential customers of its worth? (Go to WileyPLUS for this answer and additional questions.)

Profitability Index for Mutually Exclusive Projects

In theory, companies should accept all projects with positive NPVs. However, companies rarely are able to adopt all positive-NPV proposals. First, proposals often are **mutually exclusive**. This means that if the company adopts one proposal, it would be impossible or impractical also to adopt the other proposal. For example, a company may be considering the purchase of a new packaging machine and is looking at various brands and models. It needs only one packaging machine. Once the company has determined which brand and model to purchase, the others will not be purchased—even though they also may have positive net present values.

Even in instances where projects are not mutually exclusive, managers often must choose between various positive-NPV projects because of **limited resources**. For example, the company might have ideas for two new lines of business, each of which has a projected positive NPV. However, both of these proposals require skilled personnel, and the company determines that it will not be able to find enough skilled personnel to staff both projects. Management will have to choose the project it thinks is a better option.

When choosing between alternative proposals, it is tempting simply to choose the project with the higher NPV. Consider the following example of two mutually exclusive projects. Each is assumed to have a 10-year life and a 12% discount rate (discount factors from Appendix G, Tables 3 and 4). **Illustration 25.17** shows the estimates for each project and the computation of the present value of the net cash flows.

	Project A	Project B
Initial investment	$40,000	$ 90,000
Net annual cash inflow	10,000	19,000
Salvage value	5,000	10,000
Present value of net cash flows		
($10,000 × 5.65022) + ($5,000 × .32197)	58,112	
($19,000 × 5.65022) + ($10,000 × .32197)		110,574

ILLUSTRATION 25.17

Investment information for mutually exclusive projects

Illustration 25.18 computes the net present values of Project A and Project B by subtracting the initial investment from the present value of the net cash flows.

ILLUSTRATION 25.18
Net present value computation

	Project A	Project B
Present value of net cash flows	$58,112	$110,574
Less: Initial investment	40,000	90,000
Net present value	**$18,112**	**$ 20,574**

As Project B has the higher NPV, it would seem that the company should adopt it. However, Project B also requires more than twice the original investment of Project A. In choosing between the two projects, the company should also include in its calculations the amount of the original investment.

One relatively simple method of comparing alternative projects is the **profitability index**. This method takes into account both the size of the original investment and the discounted cash flows. The profitability index is calculated by dividing the present value of net cash flows that occur after the initial investment by the amount of the initial investment, as **Illustration 25.19** shows.

ILLUSTRATION 25.19
Formula for profitability index

$$\text{Present Value of Net Cash Flows} \div \text{Initial Investment} = \text{Profitability Index}$$

> **Decision Tools**
> The profitability index helps a company determine which investment proposal to accept.

The profitability index allows comparison of the relative desirability of projects that require differing initial investments (see **Decision Tools**). Note that any project with a positive NPV will have a profitability index above 1. The profitability index for each of the mutually exclusive projects is calculated in **Illustration 25.20**.

ILLUSTRATION 25.20
Calculation of profitability index

$$\text{Profitability Index} = \frac{\text{Present Value of Net Cash Flows}}{\text{Initial Investment}}$$

Project A: $\dfrac{\$58,112}{\$40,000} = 1.45$

Project B: $\dfrac{\$110,574}{\$90,000} = 1.23$

In this case, the profitability index of Project A exceeds that of Project B. Thus, Project A is more desirable. Again, if these were not mutually exclusive projects and if resources were not limited, then the company should invest in both projects since both have positive NPVs. Additional considerations related to preference decisions are discussed in more advanced courses.

Risk Analysis

A simplifying assumption made by many financial analysts is that projected results are known with certainty. In reality, projected results are only estimates based upon the forecaster's belief as to the most probable outcome. One approach for dealing with such uncertainty is **sensitivity analysis**. Sensitivity analysis uses a number of outcome estimates to get a sense of the variability among potential returns. An example of sensitivity analysis was presented in Illustration 25.11, where we illustrated the impact on NPV of different discount rate assumptions. A higher-risk project would be evaluated using a higher discount rate.

Similarly, to take into account that more distant cash flows are often more uncertain, a higher discount rate can be used to discount more distant cash flows. Other techniques to address uncertainty are discussed in advanced courses.

People, Planet, and Profit Insight

Elnur/Shutterstock

Big Spenders

Investments in electricity production and transmission represent some of society's biggest capital budgeting decisions. For example, billionaire Philip Anschutz is backing a project to build a 3,000-megawatt Wyoming wind farm as well as a 730-mile transmission line that would efficiently transfer the electricity to Las Vegas, where it could then travel on existing lines to locations in California. Total cost: $9 billion. This would be the biggest wind farm in the United States except that an even bigger, 4,000-megawatt wind farm is being planned by a different group of investors. In the past, these investments were made by regulated utility companies which were allowed to pass on their costs to customers and thus essentially guaranteed a steady revenue stream. Today, many of the biggest projects are instead being financed by private investors. These investors will be selling their electricity in energy markets driven by market demand. This provides for more potential upside on their investment but also more uncertainty regarding revenue flows.

Source: Russell Gold, "Investors Are Building Their Own Green-Power Lines," *Wall Street Journal* (April 6, 2017).

How does the financing of today's big energy investments differ from big energy capital investments of the past, and what are the implications? (Go to WileyPLUS for this answer and additional questions.)

Post-Audit of Investment Projects

Any well-run organization should perform an evaluation, called a **post-audit**, of its investment projects after their completion. A post-audit is a thorough evaluation of how well a project's actual performance matches the original projections. An example of a post-audit is seen in a situation that occurred at **Campbell Soup**. The company made the original decision to invest in the Intelligent Quisine line based on management's best estimates of future cash flows. During the development phase of the project, Campbell hired an outside consulting firm to evaluate the project's potential for success. Because actual results during the initial years were far below the estimated results and because the future also did not look promising, the project was terminated.

Performing a post-audit is important for a variety of reasons. First, if managers know that the company will compare their estimates to actual results, they will be more likely to submit reasonable and accurate data when they make investment proposals. This clearly is better for the company than for managers to submit overly optimistic estimates in an effort to get pet projects approved. Second, as seen with Campbell Soup, a post-audit provides a formal mechanism by which the company can determine whether existing projects should be supported or terminated. Third, post-audits improve future investment proposals because, by evaluating past successes and failures, managers improve their estimation techniques.

A post-audit involves the same evaluation techniques used in making the original capital budgeting decision—for example, use of the NPV method. The difference is that, in the post-audit, analysts insert actual figures, where known, and they revise estimates of future amounts based on new information. The managers responsible for the estimates used in the original proposal must explain the reasons for any significant differences between their estimates and actual results.

Post-audits are not foolproof. In the case of Campbell Soup, some observers suggested that the company was too quick to abandon the project. Industry analysts suggested that with more time and more advertising expenditures, the company might have enjoyed success.

DO IT! 3 | Profitability Index

Taz Corporation has decided to invest in renewable energy sources to meet part of its energy needs for production. It is considering solar power versus wind power. After considering cost savings as well as incremental revenues from selling excess electricity into the power grid, it has determined the following.

	Solar	Wind
Present value of annual cash flows	$78,580	$168,450
Initial investment	$45,500	$125,300

Determine the net present value and profitability index of each project. Which energy source should it choose?

ACTION PLAN
- Determine the present value of annual cash flows of each mutually exclusive project.
- Determine profitability index by dividing the present value of annual cash flows by the amount of the initial investment.
- Choose project with highest profitability index.

Solution

	Solar	Wind
Present value of annual cash flows	$78,580	$168,450
Less: Initial investment	45,500	125,300
Net present value	$33,080	$ 43,150
Profitability index	1.73*	1.34**

*$78,580 ÷ $45,500
**$168,450 ÷ $125,300

While the investment in wind power generates the higher net present value, it also requires a substantially higher initial investment. The profitability index favors solar power, which suggests that the additional net present value of wind is outweighed by the cost of the initial investment. The company should choose solar power.

Related exercise material: **BE25.5, DO IT! 25.3, and E25.4**.

Internal Rate of Return

LEARNING OBJECTIVE 4
Use the internal rate of return method.

Decision Tools

The IRR helps a company determine if it should invest in a proposed project.

The **internal rate of return method** differs from the net present value method in that it finds the **interest yield of the potential investment**. The **internal rate of return (IRR)** is the interest rate that causes the present value of the proposed capital expenditure to equal the present value of the expected net annual cash flows (that is, NPV equal to zero). Because it recognizes the time value of money, the internal rate of return method is (like the NPV method) a discounted cash flow technique (see **Decision Tools**).

How do we determine the internal rate of return? One way is to use a financial calculator (see Appendix G) or electronic spreadsheet (see the Excel tutorial provided in WileyPLUS) to solve for this rate. Or, we can use a trial-and-error procedure.

To illustrate, assume that Stewart Shipping Company is considering the purchase of a new front-end loader at a cost of $244,371. Net annual cash flows from this loader are estimated to be $100,000 a year for three years. To determine the internal rate of return on this front-end loader, the company finds the discount rate that results in a net present value of zero. As **Illustration 25.21** shows, at a rate of return of 10%, Stewart Shipping has a positive net present value of $4,315. At a rate of return of 12%, it has a negative net present value of $4,188. At an 11% rate, the net present value is zero. Therefore, 11% is the internal rate of return for this investment (discount factors from Appendix G, Table 3).

ILLUSTRATION 25.21 Estimation of internal rate of return

Year	Net Annual Cash Flows	Discount Factor 10%	Present Value 10%	Discount Factor 11%	Present Value 11%	Discount Factor 12%	Present Value 12%
1	$100,000	.90909	$ 90,909	.90090	$ 90,090	.89286	$ 89,286
2	$100,000	.82645	82,645	.81162	81,162	.79719	79,719
3	$100,000	.75132	75,132	.73119	73,119	.71178	71,178
			248,686		244,371		240,183
Less: Initial investment			244,371		244,371		244,371
Net present value			$ 4,315		$ -0-		$ (4,188)

An easier approach to solving for the internal rate of return can be used if the net annual cash flows are **equal**, as in the Stewart Shipping example. In this special case, we can find the internal rate of return using the formula provided in **Illustration 25.22**.

| Capital Investment | ÷ | Net Annual Cash Flows | = | Internal Rate of Return Factor |

ILLUSTRATION 25.22

Formula for internal rate of return—even cash flows

Applying this formula to the Stewart Shipping example, we find:

$$\$244{,}371 \div 100{,}000 = 2.44371$$

We then look up the factor 2.44371 in Table 4 of Appendix G in the three-payment row and find it under 11%. Row 3 is reproduced for your convenience.

Table 4 Present Value of an Annuity of 1									
(n) Payments	4%	5%	6%	7%	8%	9%	10%	11%	12%	15%
3	2.77509	2.72325	2.67301	2.62432	2.57710	2.53130	2.48685	**2.44371**	2.40183	2.28323

Recognize that if the cash flows are **uneven**, then a trial-and-error approach or a financial calculator or computerized spreadsheet must be used.

Once managers know the internal rate of return, they compare it to the company's required rate of return (the discount rate). The IRR decision rule is as follows: **Accept the project when the internal rate of return is equal to or greater than the required rate of return. Reject the project when the internal rate of return is less than the required rate of return.** **Illustration 25.23** shows these relationships. The internal rate of return method is widely used in practice, largely because most managers find the internal rate of return easy to interpret.

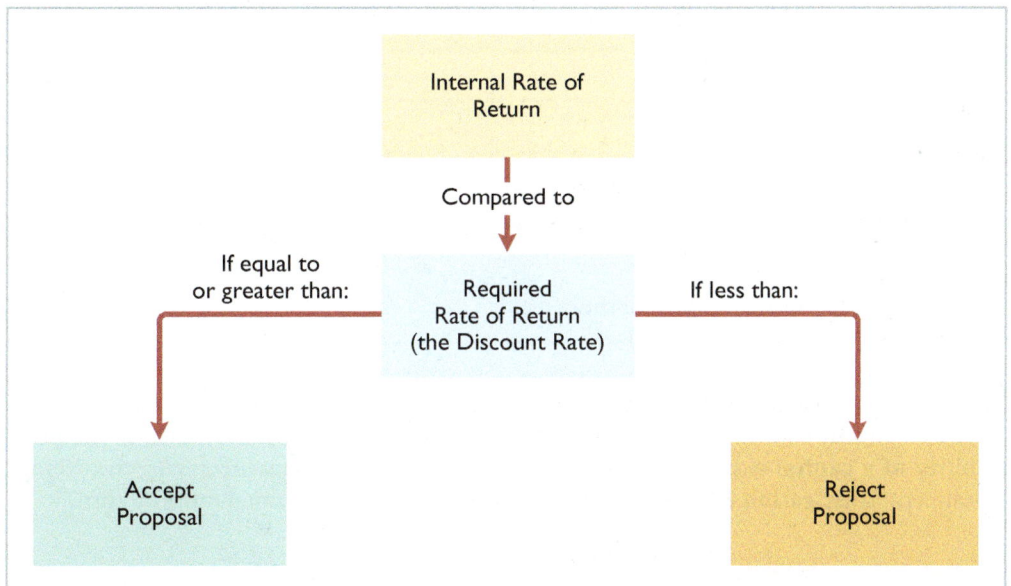

ILLUSTRATION 25.23

Internal rate of return decision criteria

Comparing Discounted Cash Flow Methods

Illustration 25.24 compares the two discounted cash flow methods—net present value and internal rate of return. When properly used, either method will provide management with relevant quantitative data for making capital budgeting decisions.

ILLUSTRATION 25.24

Comparison of discounted cash flow methods

	Net Present Value	Internal Rate of Return
1. Objective	Compute net present value (a dollar amount).	Compute internal rate of return (a percentage).
2. Decision Rule	If net present value is zero or positive, accept the proposal. If net present value is negative, reject the proposal.	If internal rate of return is equal to or greater than the required rate of return, accept the proposal. If internal rate of return is less than the required rate of return, reject the proposal.

ACTION PLAN

- Estimated annual cash inflows − Estimated annual cash outflows = Net annual cash flow.
- Capital investment/Net annual cash flows = Internal rate of return factor.
- Look up the factor in the present value of an annuity table to find the internal rate of return.
- Accept the project if the internal rate of return is equal to or greater than the required rate of return.

DO IT! 4 | Internal Rate of Return

Watertown Paper Corporation is considering adding another machine for the manufacture of corrugated cardboard. The machine would cost $900,000. It would have an estimated life of 6 years and no salvage value. The company estimates that annual cash inflows would increase by $400,000 and that annual cash outflows would increase by $190,000. Management has a required rate of return of 9%. Calculate the internal rate of return on this project and discuss whether it should be accepted.

Solution

Estimated annual cash inflows	$400,000
Estimated annual cash outflows	190,000
Net annual cash flow	$210,000

$900,000/$210,000 = 4.285714. Using Table 4 of Appendix G and the factors that correspond with the six-payment row, 4.285714 is between the factors for 10% and 11%. Since the project has an internal rate that is greater than 10% and the required rate of return is only 9%, the project should be accepted.

Related exercise material: **BE25.7, BE25.8, DO IT! 25.4, E25.5, E25.6, and E25.7.**

Annual Rate of Return

LEARNING OBJECTIVE 5
Use the annual rate of return method.

The final capital budgeting technique we will look at is the **annual rate of return method**. It is based directly on accrual accounting data rather than on cash flows. It indicates **the profitability of a capital expenditure** by dividing expected annual net income by the average investment. **Illustration 25.25** shows the formula for computing annual rate of return.

ILLUSTRATION 25.25

Annual rate of return formula

Expected Annual Net Income	÷	Average Investment	=	Annual Rate of Return

Assume that Reno Company is considering an investment of $130,000 in new equipment. The new equipment is expected to last five years and have zero salvage value at the end of its useful life. Reno uses the straight-line method of depreciation for accounting purposes. **Illustration 25.26** shows the expected annual revenues and costs of the new product that will be produced from the investment.

Sales		$200,000
Less: Costs and expenses		
Manufacturing costs (exclusive of depreciation)	$132,000	
Depreciation expense ($130,000 ÷ 5)	26,000	
Selling and administrative expenses	22,000	180,000
Income before income taxes		20,000
Income tax expense		7,000
Net income		$ 13,000

ILLUSTRATION 25.26
Estimated annual net income from Reno Company's capital expenditure

Reno's expected annual net income is $13,000. Average investment is derived from the formula shown in **Illustration 25.27**.

$$\frac{\text{Original Investment} + \text{Value at End of Useful Life}}{2} = \text{Average Investment}$$

ILLUSTRATION 25.27
Formula for computing average investment

The value at the end of useful life is equal to the asset's salvage value, if any. For Reno, average investment is $65,000 [($130,000 + $0) ÷ 2]. The expected annual rate of return for Reno's investment in new equipment is therefore 20%, computed as follows.

$$\$13,000 \div \$65,000 = 20\%$$

Management then compares the annual rate of return with its **required rate of return** for investments of similar risk. The required rate of return is generally based on the company's cost of capital. The decision rule is: **A project is acceptable if its rate of return is greater than management's required rate of return. It is unacceptable when the reverse is true.** When companies use the rate of return technique in deciding among several acceptable projects, **the higher the rate of return for a given risk, the more attractive the investment**.

The principal advantages of this method are the simplicity of its calculation and management's familiarity with the accounting terms used in the computation. A major limitation of the annual rate of return method is that it does not consider the time value of money. For example, no consideration is given as to whether cash inflows will occur early or late in the life of the investment. As explained in Appendix G, recognition of the time value of money can make a significant difference between the future value and the discounted present value of an investment. A second disadvantage is that this method relies on accrual accounting numbers rather than expected cash flows (see **Helpful Hint**).

HELPFUL HINT
A capital budgeting decision based on only one technique may be misleading. It is often wise to analyze an investment from a number of different perspectives.

DO IT! 5 | Annual Rate of Return

Watertown Paper Corporation is considering adding another machine for the manufacture of corrugated cardboard. The machine would cost $900,000. It would have an estimated life of 6 years and no salvage value. The company estimates that annual revenues would increase by $400,000 and that annual expenses excluding depreciation would increase by $190,000. It uses the straight-line method to compute depreciation expense. Management has a required rate of return of 9%. Compute the annual rate of return.

ACTION PLAN
- Expected annual net income = Annual revenues − Annual expenses (including depreciation expense).
- Average investment = (Original investment + Value at end of useful life)/2.

ACTION PLAN

- Annual rate of return = Expected annual net income/Average investment.

Solution

Revenues		$400,000
Less:		
Expenses (excluding depreciation)	$190,000	
Depreciation ($900,000/6 years)	150,000	340,000
Annual net income		$ 60,000

Average investment = ($900,000 + $0)/2 = $450,000.
Annual rate of return = $60,000/$450,000 = 13.3%.

Since the annual rate of return (13.3%) is greater than Watertown's required rate of return (9%), the proposed project is acceptable.

Related exercise material: **BE25.9, DO IT! 25.5, E25.8, E25.9, E25.10, and E25.11.**

USING THE DECISION TOOLS | Holland America Line

As noted in the Feature Story, **Holland America Line** must continually make significant capital investments in ships. Some of these decisions require comparisons of strategic alternatives. For example, not all of the company's ships are the same size. Different-sized ships offer alternative advantages and disadvantages. Suppose the company engages in ferrying activities and is trying to decide between two investment options. It is weighing the purchase of three larger ships for a total of $2,500,000 versus five smaller ships for a total of $1,400,000. Information regarding these two alternatives is provided below.

	Three Larger Ships	Five Smaller Ships
Initial investment	$2,500,000	$1,400,000
Estimated useful life	20 years	20 years
Annual revenues (accrual)	$500,000	$380,000
Annual expenses (accrual)	$200,000	$180,000
Annual cash inflows	$550,000	$430,000
Annual cash outflows	$222,250	$206,350
Estimated salvage value	$500,000	$0
Discount rate	9%	9%

Instructions

Evaluate each of these mutually exclusive proposals employing (a) cash payback, (b) net present value, (c) profitability index, (d) internal rate of return, and (e) annual rate of return. Discuss the implications of your findings.

Solution

	Three Larger Ships	Five Smaller Ships
a. Cash payback	$\dfrac{\$2,500,000}{\$327,750^*} = 7.63$ years	$\dfrac{\$1,400,000}{\$223,650^{**}} = 6.26$ years

*$550,000 − $222,250; **$430,000 − $206,350

b. Net present value
  Present value of net cash flows

$327,750 × 9.12855 =	$2,991,882	$223,650 × 9.12855 =	$2,041,600
$500,000 × 0.17843 =	89,215		
	3,081,097		
Less: Initial investment	2,500,000		1,400,000
Net present value	$ 581,097		$ 641,600

c. Profitability index $\dfrac{\$3,081,097}{\$2,500,000} = 1.23$ $\dfrac{\$2,041,600}{\$1,400,000} = 1.46$

d. The internal rate of return can be approximated by experimenting with different discount rates to see which one comes the closest to resulting in a net present value of zero. Doing this, we find that the larger ships have an internal rate of return of approximately 12%, while the internal rate of return of the smaller ships is approximately 15% as shown below.

Internal rate of return

Cash Flows	×	12% Discount Factor	=	Present Value	Cash Flows	×	15% Discount Factor	=	Present Value
$327,750	×	7.46944	=	$2,448,109	$223,650	×	6.25933	=	$1,399,899
$500,000	×	0.10367	=	51,835					
				$2,499,944					
Less: Capital investment				2,500,000					1,400,000
Net present value				$ (56)					$ (101)

e. Annual rate of return

Three Larger Ships

Average investment

$$\frac{(\$2,500,000 + \$500,000)}{2} = \$1,500,000$$

$$\text{Annual rate of return} \quad \frac{\$300,000^*}{\$1,500,000} = .20 = 20\%$$

Five Smaller Ships

$$\frac{(\$1,400,000 + \$0)}{2} = \$700,000$$

$$\frac{\$200,000^{**}}{\$700,000} = .286 = 28.6\%$$

*$500,000 − $200,000; **$380,000 − $180,000

Although the annual rate of return is higher for the smaller ships, annual rate of return has the disadvantage of ignoring time value of money, as well as using accrual numbers rather than cash flows. The cash payback of the smaller ships is also shorter, but this method also ignores the time value of money. Thus, while these two methods can be used for a quick assessment, neither should be relied upon as the sole evaluation tool.

From the net present value calculation, it would appear that the two alternatives are nearly identical in their acceptability. However, the profitability index indicates that the small-ship investment is far more desirable because it generates its cash flows with a much smaller initial investment. A similar result is found by using the internal rate of return. Overall, assuming that the company will select only one alternative, it would appear that the small-ship option should be chosen.

Review and Practice

Learning Objectives Review

1 Describe capital budgeting inputs and apply the cash payback technique.

Management gathers project proposals from each department; a capital budget committee screens the proposals and recommends worthy projects. Company officers decide which projects to fund, and the board of directors approves the capital budget. In capital budgeting, estimated cash inflows and outflows, rather than accrual-accounting numbers, are the preferred inputs.

The cash payback technique identifies the time period required to recover the cost of the investment. The formula when net annual cash flows are equal is: Cost of capital investment ÷ Estimated net annual cash flow = Cash payback period. The shorter the payback period, the more attractive the investment.

2 Use the net present value method.

The net present value method compares the present value of future cash inflows with the capital investment to determine net present value. The NPV decision rule is: Accept the project if net present value is zero or positive. Reject the project if net present value is negative.

3 Identify capital budgeting challenges and refinements.

Intangible benefits are difficult to quantify and thus are often ignored in capital budgeting decisions. This can result in incorrectly rejecting some projects. One method for considering intangible benefits is to calculate the NPV, ignoring intangible benefits. If the resulting NPV is below zero, evaluate whether the benefits are worth at least the amount of the negative net present value. Alternatively, intangible benefits can be incorporated into the NPV calculation, using conservative estimates of their value.

The profitability index is a tool for comparing the relative merits of alternative capital investment opportunities. It is computed as Present value of net cash flows ÷ Initial investment. The higher the index, the more desirable the project.

A post-audit is an evaluation of a capital investment's actual performance. Post-audits create an incentive for managers to make accurate estimates. Post-audits also are useful for determining whether a company should continue, expand, or terminate a project. Finally, post-audits provide feedback that is useful for improving estimation techniques.

4 Use the internal rate of return method.

The objective of the internal rate of return method is to find the interest yield of the potential investment, which is expressed as a percentage rate. The IRR decision rule is: Accept the project when the internal rate of return is equal to or greater than the required rate of return. Reject the project when the internal rate of return is less than the required rate of return.

5 Use the annual rate of return method.

The annual rate of return uses accrual accounting data to indicate the profitability of a capital investment. It is calculated as Expected annual net income ÷ Amount of the average investment. The higher the rate of return, the more attractive the investment.

Decision Tools Review

Decision Checkpoints	Info Needed for Decision	Tool to Use for Decision	How to Evaluate Results
Should the company invest in a proposed project?	Cash flow estimates, discount rate	Net present value = Present value of net cash flows less capital investment	The investment is financially acceptable if net present value is zero or positive.
Which investment proposal should a company accept?	Estimated cash flows and discount rate for each proposal	Profitability index = Present value of net cash flows / Initial investment	The investment proposal with the highest profitability index should be accepted.
Should the company invest in a proposed project?	Estimated cash flows and the required rate of return (hurdle rate)	Internal rate of return = Interest rate that results in a net present value of zero	If the internal rate of return exceeds the required rate of return for the project, then the project is financially acceptable.

Glossary Review

Annual rate of return method The determination of the profitability of a capital expenditure, computed by dividing expected annual net income by the average investment. (p. 25-18).

Capital budgeting The process of making capital expenditure decisions in business. (p. 25-1).

Cash payback technique A capital budgeting technique that identifies the time period required to recover the cost of a capital investment from the net annual cash flow produced by the investment. (p. 25-4).

Cost of capital The weighted-average rate of return that the firm must pay to obtain funds from creditors and stockholders. (p. 25-9).

Discounted cash flow technique A capital budgeting technique that considers both the estimated net cash flows from the investment and the time value of money. (p. 25-6).

Discount rate The interest rate used in discounting the future net cash flows to determine present value. (p. 25-6).

Internal rate of return (IRR) The interest rate that will cause the present value of the proposed capital expenditure to equal the present value of the expected net annual cash flows. (p. 25-16).

Internal rate of return (IRR) method A method used in capital budgeting that results in finding the interest yield of the potential investment. (p. 25-16).

Net present value (NPV) The difference that results when the original capital outlay is subtracted from the discounted net cash flows. (p. 25-6).

Net present value (NPV) method A method used in capital budgeting in which net cash flows are discounted to their present value and then compared to the capital outlay required by the investment. (p. 25-6).

Post-audit A thorough evaluation of how well a project's actual performance matches the original projections. (p. 25-15).

Profitability index A method of comparing alternative projects that takes into account both the size of the investment and its discounted net cash flows. It is computed by dividing the present value of net cash flows by the initial investment. (p. 25-14).

Required rate of return Management's minimum acceptable rate of return on investments, sometimes called the discount rate or cost of capital. (p. 25-6).

Sensitivity analysis An approach that uses a number of outcome estimates to get a sense of the variability among potential returns. (p. 25-14).

Practice Multiple-Choice Questions

1. **(LO 1)** Which of the following is **not** an example of a capital budgeting decision?
   a. Decision to build a new plant.
   b. Decision to renovate an existing facility.
   c. Decision to buy a piece of machinery.
   d. All of these are capital budgeting decisions.

2. **(LO 1)** What is the order of involvement of the following parties in the capital budgeting authorization process?
   a. Plant managers, officers, capital budget committee, board of directors.
   b. Board of directors, plant managers, officers, capital budget committee.
   c. Plant managers, capital budget committee, officers, board of directors.
   d. Officers, plant managers, capital budget committee, board of directors.

3. **(LO 1)** What is a weakness of the cash payback approach?
   a. It uses accrual-based accounting numbers.
   b. It ignores the time value of money.
   c. It ignores the useful life of alternative projects.
   d. Both (b) and (c) are true.

4. **(LO 1)** Siegel Industries is considering two capital budgeting projects. Project A requires an initial investment of $48,000. It is expected to produce net annual cash flows of $7,000. Project B requires an initial investment of $75,000 and is expected to produce net annual cash flows of $12,000. Using the cash payback technique to evaluate the two projects, Siegel should accept:
   a. Project A because it has a shorter cash payback period.
   b. Project B because it has a shorter cash payback period.
   c. Project A because it requires a smaller initial investment.
   d. Project B because it produces a larger net annual cash flow.

5. **(LO 2)** Which is a **true** statement regarding using a higher discount rate to calculate the net present value of a project?
   a. It will make it less likely that the project will be accepted.
   b. It will make it more likely that the project will be accepted.
   c. It is appropriate to use a higher rate if the project is perceived as being less risky than other projects being considered.
   d. It is appropriate to use a higher rate if the project will have a short useful life relative to other projects being considered.

6. **(LO 2)** A positive net present value means that the:
   a. project's rate of return is less than the cutoff rate.
   b. project's rate of return exceeds the required rate of return.
   c. project's rate of return equals the required rate of return.
   d. project is unacceptable.

7. **(LO 2)** Which of the following is **not** an alternative name for the discount rate?
   a. Hurdle rate.
   b. Required rate of return.
   c. Cutoff rate.
   d. All of these are alternative names for the discount rate.

8. **(LO 3)** If a project has intangible benefits whose value is hard to estimate, the best thing to do is:
   a. ignore these benefits, since any estimate of their value will most likely be wrong.
   b. include a conservative estimate of their value.
   c. ignore their value in your initial net present value calculation, but then estimate whether their potential value is worth at least the amount of the net present value deficiency.
   d. Either (b) or (c) is correct.

9. **(LO 3)** An example of an intangible benefit provided by a capital budgeting project is:
   a. the salvage value of the capital investment.
   b. a positive net present value.
   c. a decrease in customer complaints regarding poor quality.
   d. an internal rate of return greater than zero.

10. **(LO 3)** The following information is available for a potential capital investment.

Initial investment	$80,000
Salvage value	10,000
Net annual cash flow	14,820
Present value of net annual cash flows	98,112
Net present value	18,112
Useful life	10 years

    The potential investment's profitability index (rounded to two decimals) is:
    a. 5.40.   c. 1.23.
    b. 1.19.   d. 1.40.

11. **(LO 3)** A post-audit of an investment project should be performed:
    a. on all significant capital expenditure projects.
    b. on all projects that management feels might be financial failures.
    c. on randomly selected projects.
    d. only on projects that enjoy tremendous success.

12. **(LO 4)** A project should be accepted if its internal rate of return exceeds:
    a. zero.
    b. the rate of return on a government bond.
    c. the company's required rate of return.
    d. the rate the company pays on borrowed funds.

13. **(LO 4)** The following information is available for a potential capital investment.

Initial investment	$60,000
Net annual cash flow	15,400
Net present value	3,143
Useful life	5 years

    The potential investment's internal rate of return is approximately:
    a. 5%.   c. 4%.
    b. 10%. d. 9%.

14. (LO 5) Which of the following is **incorrect** about the annual rate of return technique?

a. The calculation is simple.

b. The accounting terms used are familiar to management.

c. The timing of the cash inflows is not considered.

d. The time value of money is considered.

15. (LO 5) The following information is available for a potential capital investment.

Initial investment	$120,000
Annual net income	15,000
Net annual cash flow	27,500
Salvage value	20,000
Useful life	8 years

The potential investment's annual rate of return is approximately:

a. 21%.

b. 15%.

c. 30%.

d. 39%.

Solutions

1. d. Choices (a), (b), and (c) are all examples of capital budgeting decisions, so choice (d) is the best answer.

2. c. The process of authorizing capital budget expenditures starts with plant managers, moves on to the capital budgeting committee, goes next to the officers of the firm and finally is acted upon by the board of directors. The other choices are therefore incorrect.

3. d. Choices (b) and (c) are both correct; therefore, choice (d) is the best answer. Choice (a) is incorrect as the use of accrual-based accounting numbers is not a weakness of the cash payback approach.

4. b. Project B ($75,000 ÷ $12,000) has a shorter cash payback period than Project A ($48,000 ÷ $7,000). The other choices are therefore incorrect.

5. a. If a higher discount rate is used in calculating the net present value of a project, the resulting net present value will be lower and the project will be less likely to be accepted. The other choices are therefore incorrect.

6. b. A positive net present value means that the project's rate of return exceeds the required rate of return. The other choices are therefore incorrect.

7. d. Choices (a), (b), and (c) are all alternative names for the discount rate; therefore, choice (d) is the best answer.

8. d. Choices (b) and (c) are both reasonable approaches to including intangible benefits in the capital budgeting process; therefore, choice (d) is the best answer. Choice (a) is incorrect because even though these intangible benefits may be hard to quantify, they should not be ignored in the capital budgeting process.

9. c. A decrease in customer complaints regarding poor quality is one example of an intangible benefit provided by a capital budgeting project. The other choices are incorrect because (a) salvage value, (b) net present value, and (d) internal rate of return are all quantitative measures, i.e., tangible.

10. c. ($18,112 + $80,000) ÷ $80,000 = 1.23, not (a) 5.40, (b) 1.19, or (d) 1.40.

11. a. A post-audit should be performed on all significant capital expenditure projects, not just on (b) financial failures, (c) randomly selected projects, or (d) tremendous successes, because the feedback gained will help to improve the process in the future and also will give managers an incentive to be more realistic in preparing capital expenditure proposals.

12. c. A project should be accepted if its internal rate of return exceeds the company's required rate of return, not (a) zero, (b) the rate of return on a government bond, or (d) the rate the company pays on borrowed funds.

13. d. ($60,000 ÷ $15,400) equals 3.8961, which corresponds with approximately 9% in Table 4 of Appendix G, not (a) 5%, (b) 10%, or (c) 4%.

14. d. The time value of money is not considered when applying the annual rate of return method. The other choices are correct statements.

15. a. $15,000 ÷ [($120,000 + $20,000) ÷ 2] = 21%, not (b) 15%, (c) 30%, or (d) 39%.

Practice Brief Exercises

Compute the cash payback period for a capital investment.

1. (LO 1) Carson Company is considering purchasing new equipment for $600,000. Annual depreciation over the 8-year useful life of the equipment is $75,000. It is expected that the equipment will produce net annual cash inflows of $100,000 over its 8-year useful life. Compute the cash payback period.

Solution

1. Cash payback period = $600,000/$100,000 = 6 years

Compute net present values.

2. (LO 2) Hilred Company is considering two different, mutually exclusive capital expenditure proposals. Project A will cost $400,000, has an expected useful life of 8 years, a salvage value of zero, and is expected to increase net annual cash flows by $80,000. Project B will also cost $400,000, has an expected useful life of 8 years, a salvage value of $100,000, and is expected to increase net annual cash flows by $70,000. A discount rate of 10% is appropriate for both projects. Compute the net present value of each project. Which project should be accepted?

Solution

2.

Project A

	Cash Flows	×	10% Discount Factor	=	Present Value
Present value of net annual cash flows	$ 80,000	×	5.33493	=	$426,794
Present value of salvage value	0	×	.46651	=	0
					426,794
Less: Capital investment					400,000
Net present value					$ 26,794

Project B

	Cash Flows	×	10% Discount Factor	=	Present Value
Present value of net annual cash flows	$ 70,000	×	5.33493	=	$373,445
Present value of salvage value	100,000	×	.46651	=	46,651
					420,096
Less: Capital investment					400,000
Net present value					$ 20,096

Project A has a higher net present value than Project B, and it should therefore be accepted.

---

3. (LO 5) King-Roken Company is considering investing in new automated equipment. It is expected that the equipment will increase annual revenues by $200,000 and annual expenses by $120,000 (including depreciation). The equipment will cost $540,000 and have a $20,000 salvage value at the end of its 10-year useful life. Calculate the annual rate of return.

Calculate annual rate of return.

Solution

3. The annual rate of return is calculated by dividing expected annual income by the average investment. The company's expected annual income is:

$$\$200{,}000 - \$120{,}000 = \$80{,}000$$

Its average investment is:

$$\frac{\$540{,}000 + \$20{,}000}{2} = \$280{,}000$$

Therefore, its annual rate of return is:

$$\$80{,}000 / \$280{,}000 = 28.6\%$$

Practice Exercises

1. (LO 1, 4) BTMS Inc. wants to purchase a new machine for $30,000. Installation costs are $1,500. The old machine was bought five years ago and had an expected economic life of 10 years without salvage value. This old machine now has a book value of $2,000, and BTMS Inc. expects to sell it for that amount. The new machine would decrease operating costs by $8,000 each year of its economic life. The straight-line depreciation method would be used for the new machine, for a five-year period with no salvage value.

Calculate payback period, internal rate of return, and apply decision rules.

Instructions

a. Determine the cash payback period.

b. Determine the approximate internal rate of return.

c. Assuming the company has a required rate of return of 10%, state your conclusion on whether the new machine should be purchased.

(CGA adapted)

Solution

1. a. Total net investment = $30,000 + $1,500 − $2,000 = $29,500
Annual net cash flow = $8,000
Payback period = $29,500 ÷ $8,000 = 3.7 years

b. Net present value approximates zero when discount rate is 11%.

Item	Amount	Years	PV Factor	Present Value
Net annual cash flows	$8,000	1–5	3.69590	$29,567
Less: Capital investment				29,500
Net present value				$ 67

c. Because the approximate internal rate of return of 11% exceeds the required rate of return of 10%, the investment should be accepted.

Calculate payback, annual rate of return, and net present value

2. (LO 1, 2, 5) MCA Corporation is reviewing an investment proposal. The initial cost is $105,000. Estimates of the book value of the investment at the end of each year, the net cash flows for each year, and the net income for each year are presented in the schedule below. All cash flows are assumed to take place at the end of the year. The salvage value of the investment at the end of each year is equal to its book value. There would be no salvage value at the end of the investment's life.

Investment Proposal

Year	Book Value	Annual Cash Flows	Annual Net Income
1	$70,000	$45,000	$16,000
2	42,000	40,000	18,000
3	21,000	35,000	20,000
4	7,000	30,000	22,000
5	0	25,000	24,000

MCA Corporation uses a 15% target rate of return for new investment proposals.

Instructions

a. What is the cash payback period for this proposal?
b. What is the annual rate of return for the investment?
c. What is the net present value of the investment?

(CMA-Canada adapted)

Solution

2. a.

	Year	Amount	Balance
Initial investment	0	$(105,000)	$(105,000)
Less: Cash flow	1	45,000	(60,000)
	2	40,000	(20,000)
	3	35,000	15,000

Payback period = 2 + ($20,000 ÷ $35,000) = 2.57 years

b. Average annual net income = ($16,000 + $18,000 + $20,000 + $22,000 + $24,000) ÷ 5 = $20,000
Average investment = ($105,000 + $0) ÷ 2 = $52,500
Annual rate of return = $20,000 ÷ $52,500 = 38.10%

c.

	Year	Discount Factor, 15%	Amount	Present Value
Net cash flows	1	0.86957	$45,000	$ 39,131
	2	0.75614	40,000	30,246
	3	0.65752	35,000	23,013
	4	0.57175	30,000	17,153
	5	0.49718	25,000	12,430
Present value of cash inflows				121,973
Less: Initial investment				105,000
Net present value				$ 16,973

Practice Problem

(LO 1, 2, 5) Cornfield Company is considering a long-term capital investment project in laser equipment. This will require an investment of $280,000, and it will have a useful life of 5 years. Annual net income is expected to be $16,000 a year. Depreciation is computed by the straight-line method with no salvage value. The company's cost of capital is 10%, and it desires a cash payback of 60% of a project's useful life or less. (*Hint:* Assume cash flows can be computed by adding back depreciation expense.)

Compute annual rate of return, cash payback, and net present value.

Instructions

(Round all computations to two decimal places unless directed otherwise.)

a. Compute the cash payback period for the project.
b. Compute the net present value for the project. (Round to nearest dollar.)
c. Compute the annual rate of return for the project.
d. Should the project be accepted? Why?

Solution

a. $280,000 ÷ $72,000 ($16,000 + $56,000) = 3.89 years

b.

	Present Value at 10%
Discount factor for 5 payments	3.79079
Present value of net cash flows:	
$72,000 × 3.79079	$272,937
Less: Capital investment	280,000
Negative net present value	$ (7,063)

c. $16,000 ÷ $140,000 ($280,000 ÷ 2) = 11.4%

d. The annual rate of return of 11.4% is reasonable. However, the cash payback period is 78% of the project's useful life, and net present value is negative. The recommendation is to reject the project.

WileyPLUS

Brief Exercises, DO IT! Exercises, Exercises, Problems, and many additional resources are available for practice in WileyPLUS.

Questions

1. Describe the process a company may use in screening and approving the capital expenditure budget.

2. What are the advantages and disadvantages of the cash payback technique?

3. Tom Wells claims the formula for the cash payback technique is the same as the formula for the annual rate of return technique. Is Tom correct? What is the formula for the cash payback technique?

4. Two types of present value tables may be used with the discounted cash flow techniques. Identify the tables and the circumstance(s) when each table should be used.

5. What is the decision rule under the net present value method?

6. Discuss the factors that determine the appropriate discount rate to use when calculating the net present value.

7. What simplifying assumptions were made in the chapter regarding the calculation of net present value?

8. What are some examples of potential intangible benefits of investment proposals? Why do these intangible benefits complicate the capital budgeting evaluation process? What might happen if intangible benefits are ignored in a capital budgeting decision?

9. What steps can be taken to incorporate intangible benefits into the capital budget evaluation process?

10. What advantages does the profitability index provide over direct comparison of net present value when comparing two projects?

11. What is a post-audit? What are the potential benefits of a post-audit?

12. Identify the steps required in using the internal rate of return method when the net annual cash flows are equal.

13. El Cajon Company uses the internal rate of return method. What is the decision rule for this method?

14. What are the strengths of the annual rate of return approach? What are its weaknesses?

15. Your classmate, Mike Dawson, is confused about the factors that are included in the annual rate of return technique. What is the formula for this technique?

16. Sveta Pace is trying to understand the term "cost of capital." Define the term and indicate its relevance to the decision rule under the internal rate of return technique.

Brief Exercises

Compute the cash payback period for a capital investment.

BE25.1 (LO 1), AP Rihanna Company is considering purchasing new equipment for $450,000. It is expected that the equipment will produce net annual cash flows of $60,000 over its 10-year useful life. Annual depreciation will be $45,000. Compute the cash payback period.

Compute net present value of an investment.

BE25.2 (LO 2), AN Hsung Company accumulates the following data concerning a proposed capital investment: cash cost $215,000, net annual cash flows $40,000, and present value factor of cash inflows for 10 years is 5.65 (rounded). Determine the net present value, and indicate whether the investment should be made.

Compute net present value of an investment.

BE25.3 (LO 2), AP Thunder Corporation, an amusement park, is considering a capital investment in a new exhibit. The exhibit would cost $136,000 and have an estimated useful life of 5 years. It can be sold for $60,000 at the end of that time. (Amusement parks need to rotate exhibits to keep people interested.) It is expected to increase net annual cash flows by $25,000. The company's borrowing rate is 8%. Its cost of capital is 10%. Calculate the net present value of this project to the company.

Compute net present value of an investment and consider intangible benefits.

BE25.4 (LO 2, 3), AN Caine Bottling Corporation is considering the purchase of a new bottling machine. The machine would cost $200,000 and has an estimated useful life of 8 years with zero salvage value. Management estimates that the new bottling machine will provide net annual cash flows of $34,000. Management also believes that the new bottling machine will save the company money because it is expected to be more reliable than other machines, and thus will reduce downtime. How much would the reduction in downtime have to be worth in order for the project to be acceptable? Assume a discount rate of 9%. (*Hint:* Calculate the net present value.)

Compute net present value and profitability index.

BE25.5 (LO 2, 3), AN McKnight Company is considering two different, mutually exclusive capital expenditure proposals. Project A will cost $400,000, has an expected useful life of 10 years, a salvage value of zero, and is expected to increase net annual cash flows by $70,000. Project B will cost $310,000, has an expected useful life of 10 years, a salvage value of zero, and is expected to increase net annual cash flows by $55,000. A discount rate of 9% is appropriate for both projects. Compute the net present value and profitability index of each project. Which project should be accepted?

Perform a post-audit.

BE25.6 (LO 3), AN Quillen Company is performing a post-audit of a project completed one year ago. The initial estimates were that the project would cost $250,000, would have a useful life of 9 years, zero salvage value, and would result in net annual cash flows of $46,000 per year. Now that the investment has been in operation for 1 year, revised figures indicate that it actually cost $260,000, will have a total useful life of 11 years (including the year just completed), and will produce net annual cash flows of $39,000 per year. Evaluate the success of the project. Assume a discount rate of 10%.

Calculate internal rate of return.

BE25.7 (LO 4), AP Kanye Company is evaluating the purchase of a rebuilt spot-welding machine to be used in the manufacture of a new product. The machine will cost $176,000, has an estimated useful life of 7 years, a salvage value of zero, and will increase net annual cash flows by $35,000. What is its approximate internal rate of return?

Calculate internal rate of return.

BE25.8 (LO 4), AN Viera Corporation is considering investing in a new facility. The estimated cost of the facility is $2,045,000. It will be used for 12 years, then sold for $716,000. The facility will generate annual cash inflows of $400,000 and will need new annual cash outflows of $150,000. The company has a required rate of return of 7%. Calculate the internal rate of return on this project, and discuss whether the project should be accepted.

BE25.9 (LO 5), AP Swift Oil Company is considering investing in a new oil well. It is expected that the oil well will increase annual revenues by $130,000 and will increase annual expenses by $70,000 including depreciation. The oil well will cost $490,000 and will have a $10,000 salvage value at the end of its 10-year useful life. Calculate the annual rate of return.

Compute annual rate of return.

DO IT! Exercises

DO IT! 25.1 (LO 1), AP Wayne Company is considering a long-term investment project called ZIP. ZIP will require an investment of $140,000. It will have a useful life of 4 years and no salvage value. Annual cash inflows would increase by $80,000, and annual cash outflows would increase by $40,000. Compute the cash payback period.

Compute the cash payback period for an investment.

DO IT! 25.2 (LO 2), AN Wayne Company is considering a long-term investment project called ZIP. ZIP will require an investment of $120,000. It will have a useful life of 4 years and no salvage value. Annual cash inflows would increase by $80,000, and annual cash outflows would increase by $40,000. The company's required rate of return is 12%. Calculate the net present value on this project and discuss whether it should be accepted.

Calculate net present value of an investment.

DO IT! 25.3 (LO 3), AP Ranger Corporation has decided to invest in renewable energy sources to meet part of its energy needs for production. It is considering solar power versus wind power. After considering cost savings as well as incremental revenues from selling excess electricity into the power grid, it has determined the following.

Compute profitability index.

	Solar	Wind
Present value of annual cash flows	$52,580	$128,450
Initial investment	$39,500	$105,300

Determine the net present value and profitability index of each project. Which energy source should it choose?

DO IT! 25.4 (LO 4), AN Wayne Company is considering a long-term investment project called ZIP. ZIP will require an investment of $120,000. It will have a useful life of 4 years and no salvage value. Annual cash inflows would increase by $80,000, and annual cash outflows would increase by $40,000. The company's required rate of return is 12%. Calculate the internal rate of return on this project and discuss whether it should be accepted.

Calculate internal rate of return.

DO IT! 25.5 (LO 5), AP Wayne Company is considering a long-term investment project called ZIP. ZIP will require an investment of $120,000. It will have a useful life of 4 years and no salvage value. Annual revenues would increase by $80,000, and annual expenses (excluding depreciation) would increase by $41,000. Wayne uses the straight-line method to compute depreciation expense. The company's required rate of return is 12%. Compute the annual rate of return.

Calculate annual rate of return.

Exercises

E25.1 (LO 1, 2), AN Linkin Corporation is considering purchasing a new delivery truck. The truck has many advantages over the company's current truck (not the least of which is that it runs). The new truck would cost $56,000. Because of the increased capacity, reduced maintenance costs, and increased fuel economy, the new truck is expected to generate cost savings of $8,000. At the end of 8 years, the company will sell the truck for an estimated $27,000. Traditionally the company has used a rule of thumb that a proposal should not be accepted unless it has a payback period that is less than 50% of the asset's estimated useful life. Larry Newton, a new manager, has suggested that the company should not rely solely on the payback approach, but should also employ the net present value method when evaluating new projects. The company's cost of capital is 8%.

Compute cash payback and net present value.

Instructions

a. Compute the cash payback period and net present value of the proposed investment.

b. Does the project meet the company's cash payback criteria? Does it meet the net present value criteria for acceptance? Discuss your results.

Compute cash payback period and net present value.

E25.2 (LO 1, 2), AN Doug's Custom Construction Company is considering three new projects, each requiring an equipment investment of $22,000. Each project will last for 3 years and produce the following net annual cash flows.

Year	AA	BB	CC
1	$ 7,000	$10,000	$13,000
2	9,000	10,000	12,000
3	12,000	10,000	11,000
Total	$28,000	$30,000	$36,000

The equipment's salvage value is zero, and Doug uses straight-line depreciation. Doug will not accept any project with a cash payback period over 2 years. Doug's required rate of return is 12%.

Instructions

a. Compute each project's payback period, indicating the most desirable project and the least desirable project using this method. (Round to two decimals and assume in your computations that cash flows occur evenly throughout the year.)

b. Compute the net present value of each project. Does your evaluation change? (Round to nearest dollar.)

Calculate net present value and apply decision rule.

E25.3 (LO 2), AN Hillsong Inc. manufactures snowsuits. Hillsong is considering purchasing a new sewing machine at a cost of $2.45 million. Its existing machine was purchased five years ago at a price of $1.8 million; six months ago, Hillsong spent $55,000 to keep it operational. The existing sewing machine can be sold today for $250,000. The new sewing machine would require a one-time, $85,000 training cost. Operating costs would decrease by the following amounts for years 1 to 7:

Year	
1	$390,000
2	400,000
3	411,000
4	426,000
5	434,000
6	435,000
7	436,000

The new sewing machine would be depreciated according to the declining-balance method at a rate of 20%. The salvage value is expected to be $400,000. This new equipment would require maintenance costs of $100,000 at the end of the fifth year. The cost of capital is 9%.

Instructions

Use the net present value method to determine whether Hillsong should purchase the new machine to replace the existing machine, and state the reason for your conclusion.

(CGA adapted)

Compute net present value and profitability index.

E25.4 (LO 2, 3), AN BAK Corp. is considering purchasing one of two new diagnostic machines. Either machine would make it possible for the company to bid on jobs that it currently isn't equipped to do. Estimates regarding each machine are provided below.

	Machine A	Machine B
Original cost	$75,500	$180,000
Estimated life	8 years	8 years
Salvage value	–0–	–0–
Estimated annual cash inflows	$20,000	$40,000
Estimated annual cash outflows	$5,000	$10,000

Instructions

Calculate the net present value and profitability index of each machine. Assume a 9% discount rate. Which machine should be purchased?

Determine internal rate of return.

E25.5 (LO 4), AN Bruno Corporation is involved in the business of injection molding of plastics. It is considering the purchase of a new computer-aided design and manufacturing machine for $430,000. The company believes that with this new machine it will improve productivity and increase quality, resulting in an increase in net annual cash flows of $101,000 for the next 6 years. Management requires a 10% rate of return on all new investments.

Instructions

Calculate the internal rate of return on this new machine. Should the investment be accepted?

E25.6 (LO 1, 4), AN BSU Inc. wants to purchase a new machine for $29,300, excluding $1,500 of installation costs. The old machine was purchased five years ago and had an expected economic life of 10 years with no salvage value. The old machine has a book value of $2,000, and BSU Inc. expects to sell it for that amount. The new machine will decrease operating costs by $7,000 each year of its economic life. The straight-line depreciation method will be used for the new machine for a six-year period with no salvage value.

Calculate cash payback period, internal rate of return, and apply decision rules.

Instructions

a. Determine the cash payback period.

b. Determine the approximate internal rate of return.

c. Assuming the company has a required rate of return of 10%, state your conclusion on whether the new machine should be purchased.

(CGA adapted)

E25.7 (LO 4), AN Iggy Company is considering three capital expenditure projects. Relevant data for the projects are as follows.

Determine internal rate of return.

Project	Investment	Annual Income	Life of Project
22A	$240,000	$15,500	6 years
23A	270,000	20,600	9 years
24A	280,000	15,700	7 years

Annual income is constant over the life of the project. Each project is expected to have zero salvage value at the end of the project. Iggy Company uses the straight-line method of depreciation.

Instructions

a. Determine the internal rate of return for each project. Round the internal rate of return factor to three decimals.

b. If Iggy Company's required rate of return is 10%, which projects are acceptable?

E25.8 (LO 5), AP **Service** Pierre's Hair Salon is considering opening a new location in French Lick, California. The cost of building a new salon is $300,000. A new salon will normally generate annual revenues of $70,000, with annual expenses (including depreciation) of $41,500. At the end of 15 years the salon will have a salvage value of $80,000.

Calculate annual rate of return.

Instructions

Calculate the annual rate of return on the project.

E25.9 (LO 1, 5), AP **Service** Legend Service Center just purchased an automobile hoist for $32,400. The hoist has an 8-year life and an estimated salvage value of $3,000. Installation costs and freight charges were $3,300 and $700, respectively. Legend uses straight-line depreciation.

Compute cash payback period and annual rate of return.

The new hoist will be used to replace mufflers and tires on automobiles. Legend estimates that the new hoist will enable his mechanics to replace five extra mufflers per week. Each muffler sells for $72 installed. The cost of a muffler is $36, and the labor cost to install a muffler is $16.

Instructions

a. Compute the cash payback period for the new hoist.

b. Compute the annual rate of return for the new hoist. (Round to one decimal.)

E25.10 (LO 1, 2, 5), AP Vilas Company is considering a capital investment of $190,000 in additional productive facilities. The new machinery is expected to have a useful life of 5 years with no salvage value. Depreciation is by the straight-line method. During the life of the investment, annual net income and net annual cash flows are expected to be $12,000 and $50,000, respectively. Vilas has a 12% cost of capital rate, which is the required rate of return on the investment.

Compute annual rate of return, cash payback period, and net present value.

Instructions

(Round to two decimals.)

a. Compute (1) the cash payback period and (2) the annual rate of return on the proposed capital expenditure.

b. Using the discounted cash flow technique, compute the net present value.

E25.11 (LO 1, 2, 5), AP Drake Corporation is reviewing an investment proposal. The initial cost is $105,000. Estimates of the book value of the investment at the end of each year, the net cash flows for each year, and

Calculate payback, annual rate of return, and net present value.

the net income for each year are presented in the schedule below. All cash flows are assumed to take place at the end of the year. The salvage value of the investment at the end of each year is assumed to equal its book value. There would be no salvage value at the end of the investment's life.

Investment Proposal

Year	Book Value	Annual Cash Flows	Annual Net Income
1	$70,000	$45,000	$10,000
2	42,000	40,000	12,000
3	21,000	35,000	14,000
4	7,000	30,000	16,000
5	0	25,000	18,000

Drake Corporation uses an 11% target rate of return for new investment proposals.

Instructions

a. What is the cash payback period for this proposal?

b. What is the annual rate of return for the investment?

c. What is the net present value of the investment?

(CMA-Canada adapted)

Problems: Set A

Compute annual rate of return, cash payback, and net present value.

P25.1A (LO 1, 2, 5), AN U3 Company is considering three long-term capital investment proposals. Each investment has a useful life of 5 years. Relevant data on each project are as follows.

	Project Bono	Project Edge	Project Clayton
Capital investment	$160,000	$175,000	$200,000
Annual net income:			
Year 1	14,000	18,000	27,000
2	14,000	17,000	23,000
3	14,000	16,000	21,000
4	14,000	12,000	13,000
5	14,000	9,000	12,000
Total	$ 70,000	$ 72,000	$ 96,000

Depreciation is computed by the straight-line method with no salvage value. The company's cost of capital is 15%. (Assume that cash flows occur evenly throughout the year.)

Instructions

a. Compute the cash payback period for each project. (Round to two decimals.)

b. Compute the net present value for each project. (Round to nearest dollar.)

c. Compute the annual rate of return for each project. (Round to two decimals.) (*Hint:* Use average annual net income in your computation.)

d. Rank the projects on each of the foregoing bases. Which project do you recommend?

b. E $(7,312); C $2,163

Compute annual rate of return, cash payback, and net present value.

P25.2A (LO 1, 2, 5), AN **Service** **Writing** Lon Timur is an accounting major at a midwestern state university located approximately 60 miles from a major city. Many of the students attending the university are from the metropolitan area and visit their homes regularly on the weekends. Lon, an entrepreneur at heart, realizes that few good commuting alternatives are available for students doing weekend travel. He believes that a weekend commuting service could be organized and run profitably from several suburban and downtown shopping mall locations. Lon has gathered the following investment information.

1. Five used vans would cost a total of $75,000 to purchase and would have a 3-year useful life with negligible salvage value. Lon plans to use straight-line depreciation.

2. Ten drivers would have to be employed at a total payroll expense of $48,000.

3. Other annual out-of-pocket expenses associated with running the commuter service would include Gasoline $16,000, Maintenance $3,300, Repairs $4,000, Insurance $4,200, and Advertising $2,500.

4. Lon has visited several financial institutions to discuss funding. The best interest rate he has been able to negotiate is 15%. Use this rate for cost of capital.

5. Lon expects each van to make ten round trips weekly and carry an average of six students each trip. The service is expected to operate 30 weeks each year, and each student will be charged $12.00 for a round-trip ticket.

Instructions

a. Determine the annual (1) net income and (2) net annual cash flows for the commuter service.

b. Compute (1) the cash payback period and (2) the annual rate of return. (Round to two decimals.)

c. Compute the net present value of the commuter service. (Round to the nearest dollar.)

d. What should Lon conclude from these computations?

a. (1) $5,000

b. (1) 2.5 years

P25.3A (LO 2, 3, 4), AN Service Brooks Clinic is considering investing in new heart-monitoring equipment. It has two options. Option A would have an initial lower cost but would require a significant expenditure for rebuilding after 4 years. Option B would require no rebuilding expenditure, but its maintenance costs would be higher. Since the Option B machine is of initial higher quality, it is expected to have a salvage value at the end of its useful life. The following estimates were made of the cash flows. The company's cost of capital is 8%.

Compute net present value, profitability index, and internal rate of return.

	Option A	Option B
Initial cost	$160,000	$227,000
Annual cash inflows	$71,000	$80,000
Annual cash outflows	$30,000	$31,000
Cost to rebuild (end of year 4)	$50,000	$0
Salvage value	$0	$8,000
Estimated useful life	7 years	7 years

Instructions

a. Compute the (1) net present value, (2) profitability index, and (3) internal rate of return for each option. (*Hint:* To solve for internal rate of return, experiment with alternative discount rates to arrive at a net present value of zero.)

b. Which option should be accepted?

a. (1) NPV A $16,709
(3) IRR B 12%

P25.4A (LO 2, 3), E Service Jane's Auto Care is considering the purchase of a new tow truck. The garage doesn't currently have a tow truck, and the $60,000 price tag for a new truck would represent a major expenditure. Jane Austen, owner of the garage, has compiled the estimates shown below in trying to determine whether the tow truck should be purchased.

Compute net present value considering intangible benefits.

Initial cost	$60,000
Estimated useful life	8 years
Net annual cash flows from towing	$8,000
Overhaul costs (end of year 4)	$6,000
Salvage value	$12,000

Jane's good friend, Rick Ryan, stopped by. He is trying to convince Jane that the tow truck will have other benefits that Jane hasn't even considered. First, he says, cars that need towing need to be fixed. Thus, when Jane tows them to her facility, her repair revenues will increase. Second, he notes that the tow truck could have a plow mounted on it, thus saving Jane the cost of plowing her parking lot. (Rick will give her a used plow blade for free if Jane will plow Rick's driveway.) Third, he notes that the truck will generate goodwill; people who are rescued by Jane's tow truck will feel grateful and might be more inclined to use her service station in the future or buy gas there. Fourth, the tow truck will have "Jane's Auto Care" on its doors, hood, and back tailgate—a form of free advertising wherever the tow truck goes. Rick estimates that, at a minimum, these benefits would be worth the following.

Additional annual net cash flows from repair work	$3,000
Annual savings from plowing	750
Additional annual net cash flows from customer "goodwill"	1,000
Additional annual net cash flows resulting from free advertising	750

The company's cost of capital is 9%.

Instructions

a. Calculate the net present value, ignoring the additional benefits described by Rick. Should the tow truck be purchased?

a. NPV $(13,950)

b. NPV $16,491

Compute net present value and internal rate of return with sensitivity analysis.

a. NPV $207,277

d. IRR 12%

b. Calculate the net present value, incorporating the additional benefits suggested by Rick. Should the tow truck be purchased?

c. Suppose Rick has been overly optimistic in his assessment of the value of the additional benefits. At a minimum, how much would the additional benefits have to be worth in order for the project to be accepted?

P25.5A (LO 2, 3, 4), E Service Coolplay Corp. is thinking about opening a soccer camp in southern California. To start the camp, Coolplay would need to purchase land and build four soccer fields and a sleeping and dining facility to house 150 soccer players. Each year, the camp would be run for 8 sessions of 1 week each. The company would hire college soccer players as coaches. The camp attendees would be male and female soccer players ages 12–18. Property values in southern California have enjoyed a steady increase in value. It is expected that after using the facility for 20 years, Coolplay can sell the property for more than it was originally purchased for. The following amounts have been estimated.

Cost of land	$300,000
Cost to build soccer fields, dorm and dining facility	$600,000
Annual cash inflows assuming 150 players and 8 weeks	$920,000
Annual cash outflows	$840,000
Estimated useful life	20 years
Salvage value	$1,500,000
Discount rate	8%

Instructions

a. Calculate the net present value of the project.

b. To gauge the sensitivity of the project to these estimates, assume that if only 125 players attend each week, annual cash inflows will be $805,000 and annual cash outflows will be $750,000. What is the net present value using these alternative estimates? Discuss your findings.

c. Assuming the original facts, what is the net present value if the project is actually riskier than first assumed and an 10% discount rate is more appropriate?

d. Assume that during the first 5 years, the annual net cash flows each year were only $40,000. At the end of the fifth year, the company is running low on cash, so management decides to sell the property for $1,332,000. What was the actual internal rate of return on the project? Explain how this return was possible given that the camp did not appear to be successful.

Continuing Cases

Current Designs

CD25 A company that manufactures recreational pedal boats has approached Mike Cichanowski to ask if he would be interested in using **Current Designs'** rotomold expertise and equipment to produce some of the pedal boat components. Mike is intrigued by the idea and thinks it would be an interesting way of complementing the present product line.

One of Mike's hesitations about the proposal is that the pedal boats are a different shape than the kayaks that Current Designs produces. As a result, the company would need to buy an additional rotomold oven in order to produce the pedal boat components. This project clearly involves risks, and Mike wants to make sure that the returns justify the risks. In this case, since this is a new venture, Mike thinks that a 15% discount rate is appropriate to use to evaluate the project.

As an intern at Current Designs, Mike has asked you to prepare an initial evaluation of this proposal. To aid in your analysis, he has provided the following information and assumptions.

1. The new rotomold oven will have a cost of $256,000, a salvage value of $0, and an 8-year useful life. Straight-line depreciation will be used.

2. The projected revenues, costs, and results for each of the 8 years of this project are as follows.

Sales		$220,000
Less:		
Manufacturing costs	$140,000	
Depreciation	32,000	
Shipping and administrative costs	22,000	194,000
Income before income taxes		26,000
Income tax expense		10,800
Net income		$ 15,200

Instructions

a. Compute the annual rate of return. (Round to two decimal places.)
b. Compute the payback period. (Round to two decimal places.)
c. Compute the net present value using a discount rate of 9%. (Round to nearest dollar.) Should the proposal be accepted using this discount rate?
d. Compute the net present value using a discount rate of 15%. (Round to nearest dollar.) Should the proposal be accepted using this discount rate?

Waterways

(*Note:* This is a continuation of the Waterways case from Chapters 14–24.)

WP25 Waterways Corporation puts much emphasis on cash flow when it plans for capital investments. The company chose its discount rate of 8% based on the rate of return it must pay its owners and creditors. Using that rate, Waterways then uses different methods to determine the best decisions for making capital outlays. Waterways is considering buying five new backhoes to replace the backhoes it now has. This problem asks you to evaluate that decision, using various capital budgeting techniques.

Go to WileyPLUS for complete case details and instructions.

Comprehensive Cases

CC25.1 For this case, revisit the Greetings Inc. company presented in earlier chapters. The company is now searching for new opportunities for growth. This case will provide you with the opportunity to evaluate a proposal based on initial estimates as well as conduct sensitivity analysis. It also requires evaluation of the underlying assumptions used in the analysis.

CC25.2 Armstrong Helmet Company needs to determine the cost for a given product. For this case, you will have the opportunity to explore cost-volume-profit relationships and prepare a set of budgets.

Go to WileyPLUS for details and instructions for both cases.

Expand Your Critical Thinking

Decision-Making Across the Organization

CT25.1 Luang Company is considering the purchase of a new machine. Its invoice price is $122,000, freight charges are estimated to be $3,000, and installation costs are expected to be $5,000. Salvage value of the new machine is expected to be zero after a useful life of 4 years. Existing equipment could be retained and used for an additional 4 years if the new machine is not purchased. At that time, the salvage value of the equipment would be zero. If the new machine is purchased now, the existing machine would be scrapped. Luang's accountant, Lisa Hsung, has accumulated the following data regarding annual sales and expenses with and without the new machine.

1. Without the new machine, Luang can sell 10,000 units of product annually at a per unit selling price of $100. If the new unit is purchased, the number of units produced and sold would increase by 25%, and the selling price would remain the same.

2. The new machine is faster than the old machine, and it is more efficient in its usage of materials. With the old machine the gross profit rate will be 28.5% of sales, whereas the rate will be 30% of sales with the new machine. (*Note:* These gross profit rates do not include depreciation on the machines. For purposes of determining net income, treat depreciation expense as a separate line item.)

3. Annual selling expenses are $160,000 with the current equipment. Because the new equipment would produce a greater number of units to be sold, annual selling expenses are expected to increase by 10% if it is purchased.

4. Annual administrative expenses are expected to be $100,000 with the old machine, and $112,000 with the new machine.

5. The current book value of the existing machine is $40,000. Luang uses straight-line depreciation.

6. Luang's management has a required rate of return of 15% on its investment and a cash payback period of no more than 3 years.

Instructions

With the class divided into groups, answer the following. (Ignore income tax effects.)

a. Calculate the annual rate of return for the new machine. (Round to two decimals.)
b. Compute the cash payback period for the new machine. (Round to two decimals.)
c. Compute the net present value of the new machine. (Round to the nearest dollar.)
d. On the basis of the foregoing data, would you recommend that Luang buy the machine? Why?

Managerial Analysis

CT25.2 Hawke Skateboards is considering building a new plant. Bob Skerritt, the company's marketing manager, is an enthusiastic supporter of the new plant. Lucy Liu, the company's chief financial officer, is not so sure that the plant is a good idea. Currently, the company purchases its skateboards from foreign manufacturers. The following figures were estimated regarding the construction of a new plant.

Cost of plant	$4,000,000	Estimated useful life	15 years
Annual cash inflows	4,000,000	Salvage value	$2,000,000
Annual cash outflows	3,540,000	Discount rate	11%

Bob Skerritt believes that these figures understate the true potential value of the plant. He suggests that by manufacturing its own skateboards the company will benefit from a "buy American" patriotism that he believes is common among skateboarders. He also notes that the firm has had numerous quality problems with the skateboards manufactured by its suppliers. He suggests that the inconsistent quality has resulted in lost sales, increased warranty claims, and some costly lawsuits. Overall, he believes sales will be $200,000 higher than projected above, and that the savings from lower warranty costs and legal costs will be $60,000 per year. He also believes that the project is not as risky as assumed above, and that a 9% discount rate is more reasonable.

Instructions

Answer each of the following.

a. Compute the net present value of the project based on the original projections.
b. Compute the net present value incorporating Bob's estimates of the value of the intangible benefits, but still using the 11% discount rate.
c. Compute the net present value using the original estimates, but employing the 9% discount rate that Bob suggests is more appropriate.
d. Comment on your findings.

Real-World Focus

CT25.3 Tecumseh Products Company has its headquarters in Tecumseh, Michigan. It describes itself as "a global multinational corporation producing mechanical and electrical components essential to industries creating end-products for health, comfort, and convenience." The following was excerpted from the management discussion and analysis section of a recent annual report.

Tecumseh Products Company
Management Discussion and Analysis

The company has invested approximately $50 million in a scroll compressor manufacturing facility in Tecumseh, Michigan. After experiencing setbacks in developing a commercially acceptable scroll compressor, the Company is currently testing a new generation of scroll product. The Company is unable to predict when, or if, it will offer a scroll compressor for commercial sale, but it does anticipate that reaching volume production will require a significant additional investment. Given such additional investment and current market conditions, management is currently reviewing its options with respect to scroll product improvement, cost reductions, joint ventures and alternative new products.

Instructions

Discuss issues the company should consider and techniques the company should employ to determine whether to continue pursuing this project.

CT25.4 Campbell Soup Company is an international provider of soup products. Management is very interested in continuing to grow the company in its core business, while "spinning off" those businesses that are not part of its core operation.

Instructions

Go to the home page of Campbell Soup Company and access its current annual report. Review the financial statements and management's discussion and analysis, and answer the following questions.

   a. What was the total amount of capital expenditures in the current year, and how does this amount compare with the previous year? In your response, note what year you are using.

   b. What interest rate did the company pay on new borrowings in the current year?

   c. Assume that this year's capital expenditures are expected to increase cash flows by $50 million. What is the expected internal rate of return (IRR) for these capital expenditures? (Assume a 10-year period for the cash flows.)

Communication Activity

CT25.5 Refer back to E25.9 to address the following.

Instructions

Prepare a memo to Maria Fierro, your supervisor. Show your calculations from E25.9 (a) and (b). In one or two paragraphs, discuss important nonfinancial considerations. Make any assumptions you believe to be necessary. Make a recommendation based on your analysis.

Ethics Case

CT25.6 NuComp Company operates in a state where corporate taxes and workers' compensation insurance rates have recently doubled. NuComp's president has just assigned you the task of preparing an economic analysis and making a recommendation relative to moving the entire operation to Missouri. The president is slightly in favor of such a move because Missouri is his boyhood home and he also owns a fishing lodge there.

You have just completed building your dream house, moved in, and sodded the lawn. Your children are all doing well in school and sports and, along with your spouse, want no part of a move to Missouri. If the company does move, so will you because the town is a one-industry community and you and your spouse will have to move to have employment. Moving when everyone else does will cause you to take a big loss on the sale of your house. The same hardships will be suffered by your coworkers, and the town will be devastated.

In compiling the costs of moving versus not moving, you have latitude in the assumptions you make, the estimates you compute, and the discount rates and time periods you project. You are in a position to influence the decision singlehandedly.

Instructions

   a. Who are the stakeholders in this situation?
   b. What are the ethical issues in this situation?
   c. What would you do in this situation?

All About You

CT25.7 Numerous articles have been written that identify early warning signs that you might be getting into trouble with your personal debt load. You can find many good articles on this topic on the Web.

Instructions

Find an article that identifies early warning signs of personal debt trouble. Write a summary of the article and bring your summary and the article to class to share.

Considering Your Costs and Benefits

CT25.8 The March 31, 2011, edition of the *Wall Street Journal* includes an article by Russell Gold entitled "Solar Gains Traction—Thanks to Subsidies."

Instructions

Read the article and then answer the following questions.

   a. What was the total cost of the solar panels installed? What was the "out-of-pocket" cost to the couple?

   b. Using the total annual electricity bill of $5,000 mentioned in the story, what is the cash payback of the project using the total cost? What is the cash payback based on the "out-of-pocket" cost?

   c. Solar panel manufacturers estimate that solar panels can last up to 40 years with only minor maintenance costs. Assuming no maintenance costs, a 6% rate of interest, a more conservative 20-year life, and zero salvage value, what is the net present value of the project based on the total cost? What is the net present value of the project based on the "out-of-pocket" cost?

   d. What was the wholesale price of panels per watt at the time the article was written? At what price per watt does the article say that subsidies will no longer be needed? Does this price appear to be achievable?

Appendix A

Specimen Financial Statements: Apple Inc.

Once each year, a corporation communicates to its stockholders and other interested parties by issuing a complete set of audited financial statements. The **annual report**, as this communication is called, summarizes the financial results of the company's operations for the year and its plans for the future. Many annual reports are attractive, multicolored, glossy public relations pieces, containing pictures of corporate officers and directors as well as photos and descriptions of new products and new buildings. Yet the basic function of every annual report is to report financial information, almost all of which is a product of the corporation's accounting system.

The content and organization of corporate annual reports have become fairly standardized. Excluding the public relations part of the report (pictures, products, etc.), the following are the traditional financial portions of the annual report:

- Financial Highlights
- Letter to the Stockholders
- Management's Discussion and Analysis
- Financial Statements
- Notes to the Financial Statements
- Management's Responsibility for Financial Reporting
- Management's Report on Internal Control over Financial Reporting
- Report of Independent Registered Public Accounting Firm
- Selected Financial Data

The official SEC filing of the annual report is called a **Form 10-K**, which often omits the public relations pieces found in most standard annual reports. On the following pages, we present **Apple Inc.**'s financial statements taken from the company's 2017 Form 10-K. The complete Form 10-K, including notes to the financial statements, is available at the company's website.

Apple Inc.
CONSOLIDATED STATEMENTS OF OPERATIONS
(In millions, except number of shares which are reflected in thousands and per share amounts)

	Years ended		
	September 30, 2017	September 24, 2016	September 26, 2015
Net sales	$ 229,234	$ 215,639	$ 233,715
Cost of sales	141,048	131,376	140,089
Gross margin	88,186	84,263	93,626
Operating expenses:			
Research and development	11,581	10,045	8,067
Selling, general and administrative	15,261	14,194	14,329
Total operating expenses	26,842	24,239	22,396
Operating income	61,344	60,024	71,230
Other income/(expense), net	2,745	1,348	1,285
Income before provision for income taxes	64,089	61,372	72,515
Provision for income taxes	15,738	15,685	19,121
Net income	$ 48,351	$ 45,687	$ 53,394
Earnings per share:			
Basic	$ 9.27	$ 8.35	$ 9.28
Diluted	$ 9.21	$ 8.31	$ 9.22
Shares used in computing earnings per share:			
Basic	5,217,242	5,470,820	5,753,421
Diluted	5,251,692	5,500,281	5,793,069
Cash dividends declared per share	$ 2.40	$ 2.18	$ 1.98

See accompanying Notes to Consolidated Financial Statements.

Apple Inc.
CONSOLIDATED STATEMENTS OF COMPREHENSIVE INCOME
(In millions)

	Years ended		
	September 30, 2017	September 24, 2016	September 26, 2015
Net income	$ 48,351	$ 45,687	$ 53,394
Other comprehensive income/(loss):			
Change in foreign currency translation, net of tax effects of $(77), $8 and $201, respectively	224	75	(411)
Change in unrealized gains/losses on derivative instruments:			
Change in fair value of derivatives, net of tax benefit/(expense) of $(478), $(7) and $(441), respectively	1,315	7	2,905
Adjustment for net (gains)/losses realized and included in net income, net of tax expense/(benefit) of $475, $131 and $630, respectively	(1,477)	(741)	(3,497)
Total change in unrealized gains/losses on derivative instruments, net of tax	(162)	(734)	(592)
Change in unrealized gains/losses on marketable securities:			
Change in fair value of marketable securities, net of tax benefit/(expense) of $425, $(863) and $264, respectively	(782)	1,582	(483)
Adjustment for net (gains)/losses realized and included in net income, net of tax expense/(benefit) of $35, $(31) and $(32), respectively	(64)	56	59
Total change in unrealized gains/losses on marketable securities, net of tax	(846)	1,638	(424)
Total other comprehensive income/(loss)	(784)	979	(1,427)
Total comprehensive income	$ 47,567	$ 46,666	$ 51,967

See accompanying Notes to Consolidated Financial Statements.

Apple Inc.
CONSOLIDATED BALANCE SHEETS
(In millions, except number of shares which are reflected in thousands and par value)

	September 30, 2017	September 24, 2016
ASSETS:		
Current assets:		
Cash and cash equivalents	$ 20,289	$ 20,484
Short-term marketable securities	53,892	46,671
Accounts receivable, less allowances of $58 and $53, respectively	17,874	15,754
Inventories	4,855	2,132
Vendor non-trade receivables	17,799	13,545
Other current assets	13,936	8,283
Total current assets	128,645	106,869
Long-term marketable securities	194,714	170,430
Property, plant and equipment, net	33,783	27,010
Goodwill	5,717	5,414
Acquired intangible assets, net	2,298	3,206
Other non-current assets	10,162	8,757
Total assets	$ 375,319	$ 321,686
LIABILITIES AND SHAREHOLDERS' EQUITY:		
Current liabilities:		
Accounts payable	$ 49,049	$ 37,294
Accrued expenses	25,744	22,027
Deferred revenue	7,548	8,080
Commercial paper	11,977	8,105
Current portion of long-term debt	6,496	3,500
Total current liabilities	100,814	79,006
Deferred revenue, non-current	2,836	2,930
Long-term debt	97,207	75,427
Other non-current liabilities	40,415	36,074
Total liabilities	241,272	193,437
Commitments and contingencies		
Shareholders' equity:		
Common stock and additional paid-in capital, $0.00001 par value: 12,600,000 shares authorized; 5,126,201 and 5,336,166 shares issued and outstanding, respectively	35,867	31,251
Retained earnings	98,330	96,364
Accumulated other comprehensive income/(loss)	(150)	634
Total shareholders' equity	134,047	128,249
Total liabilities and shareholders' equity	$ 375,319	$ 321,686

See accompanying Notes to Consolidated Financial Statements.

Apple Inc.
CONSOLIDATED STATEMENTS OF SHAREHOLDERS' EQUITY
(In millions, except number of shares which are reflected in thousands)

	Common Stock and Additional Paid-In Capital		Retained Earnings	Accumulated Other Comprehensive Income/(Loss)	Total Shareholders' Equity
	Shares	Amount			
Balances as of September 27, 2014	5,866,161	$ 23,313	$ 87,152	$ 1,082	$ 111,547
Net income	—	—	53,394	—	53,394
Other comprehensive income/(loss)	—	—	—	(1,427)	(1,427)
Dividends and dividend equivalents declared	—	—	(11,627)	—	(11,627)
Repurchase of common stock	(325,032)	—	(36,026)	—	(36,026)
Share-based compensation	—	3,586	—	—	3,586
Common stock issued, net of shares withheld for employee taxes	37,624	(231)	(609)	—	(840)
Tax benefit from equity awards, including transfer pricing adjustments	—	748	—	—	748
Balances as of September 26, 2015	5,578,753	27,416	92,284	(345)	119,355
Net income	—	—	45,687	—	45,687
Other comprehensive income/(loss)	—	—	—	979	979
Dividends and dividend equivalents declared	—	—	(12,188)	—	(12,188)
Repurchase of common stock	(279,609)	—	(29,000)	—	(29,000)
Share-based compensation	—	4,262	—	—	4,262
Common stock issued, net of shares withheld for employee taxes	37,022	(806)	(419)	—	(1,225)
Tax benefit from equity awards, including transfer pricing adjustments	—	379	—	—	379
Balances as of September 24, 2016	5,336,166	31,251	96,364	634	128,249
Net income	—	—	48,351	—	48,351
Other comprehensive income/(loss)	—	—	—	(784)	(784)
Dividends and dividend equivalents declared	—	—	(12,803)	—	(12,803)
Repurchase of common stock	(246,496)	—	(33,001)	—	(33,001)
Share-based compensation	—	4,909	—	—	4,909
Common stock issued, net of shares withheld for employee taxes	36,531	(913)	(581)	—	(1,494)
Tax benefit from equity awards, including transfer pricing adjustments	—	620	—	—	620
Balances as of September 30, 2017	5,126,201	$ 35,867	$ 98,330	$ (150)	$ 134,047

See accompanying Notes to Consolidated Financial Statements.

Apple Inc.
CONSOLIDATED STATEMENTS OF CASH FLOWS
(In millions)

	Years ended		
	September 30, 2017	September 24, 2016	September 26, 2015
Cash and cash equivalents, beginning of the year	$ 20,484	$ 21,120	$ 13,844
Operating activities:			
Net income	48,351	45,687	53,394
Adjustments to reconcile net income to cash generated by operating activities:			
Depreciation and amortization	10,157	10,505	11,257
Share-based compensation expense	4,840	4,210	3,586
Deferred income tax expense	5,966	4,938	1,382
Other	(166)	486	385
Changes in operating assets and liabilities:			
Accounts receivable, net	(2,093)	527	417
Inventories	(2,723)	217	(238)
Vendor non-trade receivables	(4,254)	(51)	(3,735)
Other current and non-current assets	(5,318)	1,055	(283)
Accounts payable	9,618	1,837	5,001
Deferred revenue	(626)	(1,554)	1,042
Other current and non-current liabilities	(154)	(2,033)	9,058
Cash generated by operating activities	63,598	65,824	81,266
Investing activities:			
Purchases of marketable securities	(159,486)	(142,428)	(166,402)
Proceeds from maturities of marketable securities	31,775	21,258	14,538
Proceeds from sales of marketable securities	94,564	90,536	107,447
Payments made in connection with business acquisitions, net	(329)	(297)	(343)
Payments for acquisition of property, plant and equipment	(12,451)	(12,734)	(11,247)
Payments for acquisition of intangible assets	(344)	(814)	(241)
Payments for strategic investments, net	(395)	(1,388)	—
Other	220	(110)	(26)
Cash used in investing activities	(46,446)	(45,977)	(56,274)
Financing activities:			
Proceeds from issuance of common stock	555	495	543
Excess tax benefits from equity awards	627	407	749
Payments for taxes related to net share settlement of equity awards	(1,874)	(1,570)	(1,499)
Payments for dividends and dividend equivalents	(12,769)	(12,150)	(11,561)
Repurchases of common stock	(32,900)	(29,722)	(35,253)
Proceeds from issuance of term debt, net	28,662	24,954	27,114
Repayments of term debt	(3,500)	(2,500)	—
Change in commercial paper, net	3,852	(397)	2,191
Cash used in financing activities	(17,347)	(20,483)	(17,716)
Increase/(Decrease) in cash and cash equivalents	(195)	(636)	7,276
Cash and cash equivalents, end of the year	$ 20,289	$ 20,484	$ 21,120
Supplemental cash flow disclosure:			
Cash paid for income taxes, net	$ 11,591	$ 10,444	$ 13,252
Cash paid for interest	$ 2,092	$ 1,316	$ 514

See accompanying Notes to Consolidated Financial Statements.

Specimen Financial Statements: Columbia Sportswear Company

Columbia Sportswear Company is a leader in outdoor sportswear. The following are Columbia's financial statements as presented in its 2016 annual report. The complete annual report, including notes to the financial statements, is available at the company's website.

COLUMBIA SPORTSWEAR COMPANY

CONSOLIDATED STATEMENTS OF OPERATIONS

(In thousands, except per share amounts)

	Year Ended December 31,		
	2016	2015	2014
Net sales	$ 2,377,045	$ 2,326,180	$ 2,100,590
Cost of sales	1,266,697	1,252,680	1,145,639
Gross profit	1,110,348	1,073,500	954,951
Selling, general and administrative expenses	864,084	831,971	763,063
Net licensing income	10,244	8,192	6,956
Income from operations	256,508	249,721	198,844
Interest income, net	2,003	1,531	1,004
Interest expense on note payable to related party (Note 22)	(1,041)	(1,099)	(1,053)
Other non-operating expense	(572)	(2,834)	(274)
Income before income tax	256,898	247,319	198,521
Income tax expense (Note 10)	(58,459)	(67,468)	(56,662)
Net income	198,439	179,851	141,859
Net income attributable to non-controlling interest	6,541	5,514	4,686
Net income attributable to Columbia Sportswear Company	$ 191,898	$ 174,337	$ 137,173
Earnings per share attributable to Columbia Sportswear Company (Note 16):			
Basic	$ 2.75	$ 2.48	$ 1.97
Diluted	2.72	2.45	1.94
Weighted average shares outstanding (Note 16):			
Basic	69,683	70,162	69,807
Diluted	70,632	71,064	70,681

See accompanying notes to consolidated financial statements

COLUMBIA SPORTSWEAR COMPANY
CONSOLIDATED STATEMENTS OF COMPREHENSIVE INCOME
(In thousands)

	Year Ended December 31,		
	2016	2015	2014
Net income	$ 198,439	$ 179,851	$ 141,859
Other comprehensive loss:			
Unrealized holding gains (losses) on available-for-sale securities (net of tax effects of $0, ($3), and ($5), respectively)	(2)	(6)	10
Unrealized gains (losses) on derivative transactions (net of tax effects of ($1,922), ($849) and ($1,507), respectively)	843	(2,908)	7,751
Foreign currency translation adjustments (net of tax effects of ($347), ($760) and $1,023, respectively)	(4,485)	(34,887)	(27,789)
Other comprehensive loss	(3,644)	(37,801)	(20,028)
Comprehensive income	194,795	142,050	121,831
Comprehensive income attributable to non-controlling interest	4,678	4,382	4,185
Comprehensive income attributable to Columbia Sportswear Company	$ 190,117	$ 137,668	$ 117,646

See accompanying notes to consolidated financial statements

COLUMBIA SPORTSWEAR COMPANY
CONSOLIDATED BALANCE SHEETS
(In thousands)

	December 31,	
	2016	2015
ASSETS		
Current Assets:		
Cash and cash equivalents	$ 551,389	$ 369,770
Short-term investments	472	629
Accounts receivable, net (Note 5)	333,678	371,953
Inventories	487,997	473,637
Prepaid expenses and other current assets	38,487	33,400
Total current assets	1,412,023	1,249,389
Property, plant, and equipment, net (Note 6)	279,650	291,687
Intangible assets, net (Note 7)	133,438	138,584
Goodwill (Note 7)	68,594	68,594
Deferred income taxes (Note 10)	92,494	76,181
Other non-current assets	27,695	21,718
Total assets	$ 2,013,894	$ 1,846,153
LIABILITIES AND EQUITY		
Current Liabilities:		
Short-term borrowings (Note 8)	$ —	$ 1,940
Accounts payable	215,048	217,230
Accrued liabilities (Note 9)	142,158	141,862
Income taxes payable (Note 10)	5,645	5,038
Total current liabilities	362,851	366,070
Note payable to related party (Note 22)	14,053	15,030
Other long-term liabilities (Notes 11, 12)	42,622	40,172
Income taxes payable (Note 10)	12,710	8,839
Deferred income taxes (Note 10)	147	229
Total liabilities	432,383	430,340
Commitments and contingencies (Note 13)		
Shareholders' Equity:		
Preferred stock; 10,000 shares authorized; none issued and outstanding	—	—
Common stock (no par value); 250,000 shares authorized; 69,873 and 69,277 issued and outstanding (Note 14)	53,801	34,776
Retained earnings	1,529,636	1,385,860
Accumulated other comprehensive loss (Note 17)	(22,617)	(20,836)
Total Columbia Sportswear Company shareholders' equity	1,560,820	1,399,800
Non-controlling interest (Note 4)	20,691	16,013
Total equity	1,581,511	1,415,813
Total liabilities and equity	$ 2,013,894	$ 1,846,153

See accompanying notes to consolidated financial statements

COLUMBIA SPORTSWEAR COMPANY
CONSOLIDATED STATEMENTS OF CASH FLOWS
(In thousands)

	Year Ended December 31,		
	2016	2015	2014
Cash flows from operating activities:			
Net income	$ 198,439	$ 179,851	$ 141,859
Adjustments to reconcile net income to net cash provided by operating activities:			
Depreciation and amortization	60,016	56,521	54,017
Loss on disposal or impairment of property, plant, and equipment	4,805	5,098	481
Deferred income taxes	(19,178)	(11,709)	(6,978)
Stock-based compensation	10,986	11,672	11,120
Excess tax benefit from employee stock plans	—	(7,873)	(4,927)
Changes in operating assets and liabilities:			
Accounts receivable	36,710	(40,419)	(31,478)
Inventories	(18,777)	(103,296)	(62,086)
Prepaid expenses and other current assets	(5,452)	4,411	(4,869)
Other assets	(5,948)	(2,524)	4,291
Accounts payable	1,483	11,418	41,941
Accrued liabilities	4,847	(2,017)	35,051
Income taxes payable	4,768	(10,994)	1,166
Other liabilities	2,468	4,966	6,195
Net cash provided by operating activities	275,167	95,105	185,783
Cash flows from investing activities:			
Acquisition of business, net of cash acquired	—	—	(188,467)
Purchases of short-term investments	(21,263)	(38,208)	(48,243)
Sales of short-term investments	21,263	64,980	112,895
Capital expenditures	(49,987)	(69,917)	(60,283)
Proceeds from sale of property, plant, and equipment	97	144	71
Net cash used in investing activities	(49,890)	(43,001)	(184,027)
Cash flows from financing activities:			
Proceeds from credit facilities	62,885	53,429	52,356
Repayments on credit facilities	(64,825)	(51,479)	(52,205)
Proceeds from issuance of common stock under employee stock plans	13,167	17,442	22,277
Tax payments related to restricted stock unit issuances	(5,117)	(4,895)	(3,141)
Excess tax benefit from employee stock plans	—	7,873	4,927
Repurchase of common stock	(11)	(70,068)	(15,000)
Cash dividends paid	(48,122)	(43,547)	(39,836)
Proceeds from note payable to related party	—	—	16,072
Net cash used in financing activities	(42,023)	(91,245)	(14,550)
Net effect of exchange rate changes on cash	(1,635)	(4,647)	(11,137)
Net increase (decrease) in cash and cash equivalents	181,619	(43,788)	(23,931)
Cash and cash equivalents, beginning of year	369,770	413,558	437,489
Cash and cash equivalents, end of year	$ 551,389	$ 369,770	$ 413,558
Supplemental disclosures of cash flow information:			
Cash paid during the year for income taxes	$ 70,424	$ 87,350	$ 53,958
Cash paid during the year for interest on note payable to related party	1,049	1,115	838
Supplemental disclosures of non-cash investing activities:			
Capital expenditures incurred but not yet paid	2,710	4,698	7,196

See accompanying notes to consolidated financial statements

COLUMBIA SPORTSWEAR COMPANY
CONSOLIDATED STATEMENTS OF EQUITY
(In thousands)

	Columbia Sportswear Company Shareholders' Equity					
	Common Stock			Accumulated Other	Non-	
	Shares Outstanding	Amount	Retained Earnings	Comprehensive Income (Loss)	Controlling Interest	Total
BALANCE, JANUARY 1, 2014	69,190	$52,325	$1,157,733	$35,360	$7,446	$1,252,864
Net income	—	—	137,173	—	4,686	141,859
Other comprehensive income (loss):						
Unrealized holding gains on available-for-sale securities, net	—	—	—	10	—	10
Unrealized holding gains on derivative transactions, net	—	—	—	7,751	—	7,751
Foreign currency translation adjustment, net	—	—	—	(27,288)	(501)	(27,789)
Cash dividends ($0.57 per share)	—	—	(39,836)	—	—	(39,836)
Issuance of common stock under employee stock plans, net	1,059	19,136	—	—	—	19,136
Tax adjustment from stock plans	—	5,119	—	—	—	5,119
Stock-based compensation expense	—	11,120	—	—	—	11,120
Repurchase of common stock	(421)	(15,000)	—	—	—	(15,000)
BALANCE, DECEMBER 31, 2014	69,828	72,700	1,255,070	15,833	11,631	1,355,234
Net income	—	—	174,337	—	5,514	179,851
Other comprehensive loss:						
Unrealized holding losses on available-for-sale securities, net	—	—	—	(6)	—	(6)
Unrealized holding losses on derivative transactions, net	—	—	—	(2,908)	—	(2,908)
Foreign currency translation adjustment, net	—	—	—	(33,755)	(1,132)	(34,887)
Cash dividends ($0.62 per share)	—	—	(43,547)	—	—	(43,547)
Issuance of common stock under employee stock plans, net	835	12,547	—	—	—	12,547
Tax adjustment from stock plans	—	7,925	—	—	—	7,925
Stock-based compensation expense	—	11,672	—	—	—	11,672
Repurchase of common stock	(1,386)	(70,068)	—	—	—	(70,068)
BALANCE, DECEMBER 31, 2015	69,277	34,776	1,385,860	(20,836)	16,013	1,415,813
Net income	—	—	191,898	—	6,541	198,439
Other comprehensive income (loss):						
Unrealized holding losses on available-for-sale securities, net	—	—	—	(2)	—	(2)
Unrealized holding gains on derivative transactions, net	—	—	—	686	157	843
Foreign currency translation adjustment, net	—	—	—	(2,465)	(2,020)	(4,485)
Cash dividends ($0.69 per share)	—	—	(48,122)	—	—	(48,122)
Issuance of common stock under employee stock plans, net	596	8,050	—	—	—	8,050
Stock-based compensation expense	—	10,986	—	—	—	10,986
Repurchase of common stock	—	(11)	—	—	—	(11)
BALANCE, DECEMBER 31, 2016	69,873	$53,801	$1,529,636	$(22,617)	$20,691	$1,581,511

See accompanying notes to consolidated financial statements

Appendix C

Specimen Financial Statements: VF Corporation

VF Corporation is a leader in outdoor sportswear. The following are VF's financial statements as presented in its 2016 annual report. The complete annual report, including notes to the financial statements, is available at the company's website.

VF CORPORATION
Consolidated Balance Sheets

	December 2016	December 2015
	In thousands, except share amounts	
ASSETS		
Current assets		
Cash and equivalents	$ 1,227,862	$ 944,423
Accounts receivable, less allowance for doubtful accounts of $21,131 in 2016 and $23,275 in 2015	1,197,678	1,289,962
Inventories	1,569,325	1,555,360
Other current assets	298,233	284,215
Current assets of discontinued operations	—	89,176
Total current assets	4,293,098	4,163,136
Property, plant and equipment	939,650	945,491
Intangible assets	1,839,698	1,948,611
Goodwill	1,736,959	1,788,407
Other assets	929,882	583,866
Other assets of discontinued operations	—	210,031
Total assets	$ 9,739,287	$ 9,639,542
LIABILITIES AND STOCKHOLDERS' EQUITY		
Current liabilities		
Short-term borrowings	$ 26,029	$ 449,590
Current portion of long-term debt	253,689	3,351
Accounts payable	664,644	680,606
Accrued liabilities	841,038	782,148
Current liabilities of discontinued operations	—	26,018
Total current liabilities	1,785,400	1,941,713
Long-term debt	2,039,180	1,401,820
Other liabilities	973,786	900,256
Other liabilities of discontinued operations	—	10,915
Commitments and contingencies		
Total liabilities	4,798,366	4,254,704
Stockholders' equity		
Preferred Stock, par value $1; shares authorized, 25,000,000; no shares outstanding in 2016 and 2015	—	—
Common Stock, stated value $0.25; shares authorized, 1,200,000,000; 414,012,954 shares outstanding in 2016 and 426,614,274 shares outstanding in 2015	103,503	106,654
Additional paid-in capital	3,333,423	3,192,675
Accumulated other comprehensive loss	(1,041,463)	(1,043,222)
Retained earnings	2,545,458	3,128,731
Total stockholders' equity	4,940,921	5,384,838
Total liabilities and stockholders' equity	$ 9,739,287	$ 9,639,542

See notes to consolidated financial statements.

VF CORPORATION
Consolidated Statements of Income

	Year Ended December		
	2016	2015	2014
	In thousands, except per share amounts		
Net sales	$ 11,902,314	$ 11,909,635	$ 11,757,399
Royalty income	116,689	123,020	124,331
Total revenues	12,019,003	12,032,655	11,881,730
Costs and operating expenses			
Cost of goods sold	6,196,335	6,235,699	6,112,880
Selling, general and administrative expenses	4,243,798	4,009,029	3,970,536
Impairment of goodwill and intangible assets	79,644	—	—
Total costs and operating expenses	10,519,777	10,244,728	10,083,416
Operating income	1,499,226	1,787,927	1,798,314
Interest income	9,094	7,152	6,911
Interest expense	(94,730)	(88,772)	(86,104)
Other income (expense), net	2,001	1,028	(5,545)
Income from continuing operations before income taxes	1,415,591	1,707,335	1,713,576
Income taxes	243,064	392,204	385,827
Income from continuing operations	1,172,527	1,315,131	1,327,749
Loss from discontinued operations, net of tax	(98,421)	(83,538)	(280,244)
Net income	$ 1,074,106	$ 1,231,593	$ 1,047,505
Earnings per common share - basic			
Continuing operations	$ 2.82	$ 3.09	$ 3.07
Discontinued operations	(0.24)	(0.19)	(0.65)
Total earnings per common share - basic	$ 2.58	$ 2.90	$ 2.42
Earnings per common share - diluted			
Continuing operations	$ 2.78	$ 3.04	$ 3.02
Discontinued operations	(0.24)	(0.19)	(0.64)
Total earnings per common share - diluted	$ 2.54	$ 2.85	$ 2.38
Cash dividends per common share	$ 1.5300	$ 1.3300	$ 1.1075

See notes to consolidated financial statements.

VF CORPORATION
Consolidated Statements of Comprehensive Income

	Year Ended December		
	2016	2015	2014
	In thousands		
Net income	$ 1,074,106	$ 1,231,593	$ 1,047,505
Other comprehensive income (loss)			
Foreign currency translation and other			
Gains (losses) arising during year	(52,028)	(361,814)	(469,663)
Less income tax effect	(24,382)	586	6,075
Defined benefit pension plans			
Current year actuarial gains (losses) and plan amendments	(5,384)	(62,556)	(203,234)
Amortization of net deferred actuarial losses	65,212	61,966	37,518
Amortization of deferred prior service costs	2,584	3,038	5,445
Reclassification of net actuarial loss from settlement charge	50,922	4,062	—
Less income tax effect	(43,836)	(1,571)	60,588
Derivative financial instruments			
Gains (losses) arising during year	90,708	89,993	88,387
Less income tax effect	(9,672)	(34,668)	(34,736)
Reclassification to net income for (gains) losses realized	(107,457)	(64,976)	32,111
Less income tax effect	35,092	25,404	(12,619)
Marketable securities			
Gains (losses) arising during year	—	495	(698)
Less income tax effect	—	(195)	274
Reclassification to net income for (gains) losses realized	—	(1,177)	—
Less income tax effect	—	463	—
Other comprehensive income (loss)	1,759	(340,950)	(490,552)
Comprehensive income	$ 1,075,865	$ 890,643	$ 556,953

See notes to consolidated financial statements.

VF CORPORATION

Consolidated Statements of Cash Flows

	Year Ended December		
	2016	2015	2014
	In thousands		
Operating activities			
Net income	$ 1,074,106	$ 1,231,593	$ 1,047,505
Adjustments to reconcile net income to cash provided by operating activities:			
Impairment of goodwill and intangible assets	79,644	143,562	396,362
Depreciation and amortization	281,577	272,075	274,883
Stock-based compensation	67,762	73,420	104,313
Provision for doubtful accounts	17,283	12,006	(2,198)
Pension expense in excess of (less than) contributions	89,005	(208,709)	(9,864)
Deferred income taxes	(71,625)	7,088	(78,064)
Loss on sale of businesses	104,357	—	—
Other, net	(15,232)	(34,784)	4,112
Changes in operating assets and liabilities:			
Accounts receivable	47,102	(124,248)	854
Inventories	(37,210)	(175,098)	(130,540)
Accounts payable	(9,553)	14,225	69,807
Income taxes	(129,574)	4,206	20,293
Accrued liabilities	28,904	(14,505)	41,989
Other assets and liabilities	(48,627)	2,599	22,614
Cash provided by operating activities	1,477,919	1,203,430	1,762,066
Investing activities			
Capital expenditures	(175,840)	(254,501)	(234,077)
Proceeds from sale of businesses, net of cash sold	115,983	—	—
Software purchases	(44,226)	(63,283)	(67,943)
Other, net	(8,331)	(5,038)	(27,235)
Cash used by investing activities	(112,414)	(322,822)	(329,255)
Financing activities			
Net (decrease) increase in short-term borrowings	(421,069)	432,262	4,761
Payments on long-term debt	(13,276)	(3,975)	(4,760)
Payment of debt issuance costs	(6,807)	(1,475)	—
Proceeds from long-term debt	951,817	—	—
Purchases of treasury stock	(1,000,468)	(732,623)	(727,795)
Cash dividends paid	(635,994)	(565,275)	(478,933)
Proceeds from issuance of Common Stock, net of shares withheld for taxes	48,918	30,871	34,869
Cash used by financing activities	(1,076,879)	(840,215)	(1,171,858)
Effect of foreign currency rate changes on cash and equivalents	(6,369)	(66,683)	(65,461)
Net change in cash and equivalents	282,257	(26,290)	195,492
Cash and equivalents — beginning of year [a]	945,605	971,895	776,403
Cash and equivalents — end of year [a]	$ 1,227,862	$ 945,605	$ 971,895

[a] The cash flows related to discontinued operations have not been segregated and are included in the Consolidated Statements of Cash Flows. The cash and equivalents amount presented at December 2015 differs from cash and equivalents in the Consolidated Balance Sheet due to cash included in "Current assets of discontinued operations."

See notes to consolidated financial statements.

VF CORPORATION
Consolidated Statements of Stockholders' Equity

	Common Stock Shares	Common Stock Amounts	Additional Paid-in Capital	Accumulated Other Comprehensive Loss	Retained Earnings
			In thousands, except share amounts		
Balance, December 2013	440,310,370	$ 110,078	$ 2,746,590	$ (211,720)	$ 3,432,090
Net income	—	—	—	—	1,047,505
Dividends on Common Stock	—	—	—	—	(478,933)
Purchase of treasury stock	(12,037,000)	(3,009)	—	—	(724,786)
Stock-based compensation, net	4,586,521	1,146	246,596	—	(44,123)
Foreign currency translation and other	—	—	—	(463,588)	—
Defined benefit pension plans	—	—	—	(99,683)	—
Derivative financial instruments	—	—	—	73,143	—
Marketable securities	—	—	—	(424)	—
Balance, December 2014	432,859,891	108,215	2,993,186	(702,272)	3,231,753
Net income	—	—	—	—	1,231,593
Dividends on Common Stock	—	—	—	—	(565,275)
Purchase of treasury stock	(10,036,100)	(2,509)	—	—	(730,114)
Stock-based compensation, net	3,790,483	948	199,489	—	(39,226)
Foreign currency translation and other	—	—	—	(361,228)	—
Defined benefit pension plans	—	—	—	4,939	—
Derivative financial instruments	—	—	—	15,753	—
Marketable securities	—	—	—	(414)	—
Balance, December 2015	426,614,274	106,654	3,192,675	(1,043,222)	3,128,731
Net income	—	—	—	—	1,074,106
Dividends on Common Stock	—	—	—	—	(635,994)
Purchase of treasury stock	(15,932,075)	(3,983)	—	—	(996,485)
Stock-based compensation, net	3,330,755	832	140,748	—	(24,900)
Foreign currency translation and other	—	—	—	(76,410)	—
Defined benefit pension plans	—	—	—	69,498	—
Derivative financial instruments	—	—	—	8,671	—
Balance, December 2016	414,012,954	$ 103,503	$ 3,333,423	$ (1,041,463)	$ 2,545,458

See notes to consolidated financial statements.

Appendix D

Specimen Financial Statements: Amazon.com, Inc.

Amazon.com, Inc. is the world's largest online retailer. It also produces consumer electronics—notably the Kindle e-book reader and the Alexa digital assistant in its Echo speakers—and is a major provider of cloud computing services. The following are Amazon's financial statements as presented in the company's 2016 annual report. The complete annual report, including notes to the financial statements, is available at the company's website.

AMAZON.COM, INC.
CONSOLIDATED STATEMENTS OF CASH FLOWS
(in millions)

	Year Ended December 31,		
	2014	2015	2016
CASH AND CASH EQUIVALENTS, BEGINNING OF PERIOD	$ 8,658	$ 14,557	$ 15,890
OPERATING ACTIVITIES:			
Net income (loss)	(241)	596	2,371
Adjustments to reconcile net income (loss) to net cash from operating activities:			
Depreciation of property and equipment, including internal-use software and website development, and other amortization, including capitalized content costs	4,746	6,281	8,116
Stock-based compensation	1,497	2,119	2,975
Other operating expense, net	129	155	160
Other expense (income), net	59	250	(20)
Deferred income taxes	(316)	81	(246)
Excess tax benefits from stock-based compensation	(6)	(119)	(829)
Changes in operating assets and liabilities:			
Inventories	(1,193)	(2,187)	(1,426)
Accounts receivable, net and other	(1,039)	(1,755)	(3,367)
Accounts payable	1,759	4,294	5,030
Accrued expenses and other	706	913	1,724
Additions to unearned revenue	4,433	7,401	11,931
Amortization of previously unearned revenue	(3,692)	(6,109)	(9,976)
Net cash provided by (used in) operating activities	6,842	11,920	16,443
INVESTING ACTIVITIES:			
Purchases of property and equipment, including internal-use software and website development, net	(4,893)	(4,589)	(6,737)
Acquisitions, net of cash acquired, and other	(979)	(795)	(116)
Sales and maturities of marketable securities	3,349	3,025	4,733
Purchases of marketable securities	(2,542)	(4,091)	(7,756)
Net cash provided by (used in) investing activities	(5,065)	(6,450)	(9,876)
FINANCING ACTIVITIES:			
Excess tax benefits from stock-based compensation	6	119	829
Proceeds from long-term debt and other	6,359	353	621
Repayments of long-term debt and other	(513)	(1,652)	(354)
Principal repayments of capital lease obligations	(1,285)	(2,462)	(3,860)
Principal repayments of finance lease obligations	(135)	(121)	(147)
Net cash provided by (used in) financing activities	4,432	(3,763)	(2,911)
Foreign currency effect on cash and cash equivalents	(310)	(374)	(212)
Net increase (decrease) in cash and cash equivalents	5,899	1,333	3,444
CASH AND CASH EQUIVALENTS, END OF PERIOD	$ 14,557	$ 15,890	$ 19,334
SUPPLEMENTAL CASH FLOW INFORMATION:			
Cash paid for interest on long-term debt	$ 91	$ 325	$ 290
Cash paid for interest on capital and finance lease obligations	86	153	206
Cash paid for income taxes, net of refunds	177	273	412
Property and equipment acquired under capital leases	4,008	4,717	5,704
Property and equipment acquired under build-to-suit leases	920	544	1,209

See accompanying notes to consolidated financial statements.

AMAZON.COM, INC.
CONSOLIDATED STATEMENTS OF OPERATIONS
(in millions, except per share data)

	Year Ended December 31,		
	2014	2015	2016
Net product sales	$ 70,080	$ 79,268	$ 94,665
Net service sales	18,908	27,738	41,322
Total net sales	88,988	107,006	135,987
Operating expenses:			
Cost of sales	62,752	71,651	88,265
Fulfillment	10,766	13,410	17,619
Marketing	4,332	5,254	7,233
Technology and content	9,275	12,540	16,085
General and administrative	1,552	1,747	2,432
Other operating expense, net	133	171	167
Total operating expenses	88,810	104,773	131,801
Operating income	178	2,233	4,186
Interest income	39	50	100
Interest expense	(210)	(459)	(484)
Other income (expense), net	(118)	(256)	90
Total non-operating income (expense)	(289)	(665)	(294)
Income (loss) before income taxes	(111)	1,568	3,892
Provision for income taxes	(167)	(950)	(1,425)
Equity-method investment activity, net of tax	37	(22)	(96)
Net income (loss)	$ (241)	$ 596	$ 2,371
Basic earnings per share	$ (0.52)	$ 1.28	$ 5.01
Diluted earnings per share	$ (0.52)	$ 1.25	$ 4.90
Weighted-average shares used in computation of earnings per share:			
Basic	462	467	474
Diluted	462	477	484

See accompanying notes to consolidated financial statements.

AMAZON.COM, INC.
CONSOLIDATED STATEMENTS OF COMPREHENSIVE INCOME (LOSS)
(in millions)

	Year Ended December 31,		
	2014	2015	2016
Net income (loss)	$ (241)	$ 596	$ 2,371
Other comprehensive income (loss):			
Foreign currency translation adjustments, net of tax of $(3), $10, and $(49)	(325)	(210)	(279)
Net change in unrealized gains (losses) on available-for-sale securities:			
Unrealized gains (losses), net of tax of $1, $(5), and $(12)	2	(7)	9
Reclassification adjustment for losses (gains) included in "Other income (expense), net," net of tax of $(1), $0, and $0	(3)	5	8
Net unrealized gains (losses) on available-for-sale securities	(1)	(2)	17
Total other comprehensive income (loss)	(326)	(212)	(262)
Comprehensive income (loss)	$ (567)	$ 384	$ 2,109

See accompanying notes to consolidated financial statements.

AMAZON.COM, INC.
CONSOLIDATED BALANCE SHEETS
(in millions, except per share data)

	December 31, 2015	December 31, 2016
ASSETS		
Current assets:		
Cash and cash equivalents	$ 15,890	$ 19,334
Marketable securities	3,918	6,647
Inventories	10,243	11,461
Accounts receivable, net and other	5,654	8,339
Total current assets	35,705	45,781
Property and equipment, net	21,838	29,114
Goodwill	3,759	3,784
Other assets	3,445	4,723
Total assets	$ 64,747	$ 83,402
LIABILITIES AND STOCKHOLDERS' EQUITY		
Current liabilities:		
Accounts payable	$ 20,397	$ 25,309
Accrued expenses and other	10,372	13,739
Unearned revenue	3,118	4,768
Total current liabilities	33,887	43,816
Long-term debt	8,227	7,694
Other long-term liabilities	9,249	12,607
Commitments and contingencies (Note 7)		
Stockholders' equity:		
Preferred stock, $0.01 par value:		
Authorized shares — 500		
Issued and outstanding shares — none	—	—
Common stock, $0.01 par value:		
Authorized shares — 5,000		
Issued shares — 494 and 500		
Outstanding shares — 471 and 477	5	5
Treasury stock, at cost	(1,837)	(1,837)
Additional paid-in capital	13,394	17,186
Accumulated other comprehensive loss	(723)	(985)
Retained earnings	2,545	4,916
Total stockholders' equity	13,384	19,285
Total liabilities and stockholders' equity	$ 64,747	$ 83,402

See accompanying notes to consolidated financial statements.

AMAZON.COM, INC.
CONSOLIDATED STATEMENTS OF STOCKHOLDERS' EQUITY
(in millions)

	Common Stock		Treasury Stock	Additional Paid-In Capital	Accumulated Other Comprehensive Income (Loss)	Retained Earnings	Total Stockholders' Equity
	Shares	Amount					
Balance as of January 1, 2014	459	$ 5	$ (1,837)	$ 9,573	$ (185)	$ 2,190	$ 9,746
Net loss	—	—	—	—	—	(241)	(241)
Other comprehensive income (loss)	—	—	—	—	(326)	—	(326)
Exercise of common stock options	6	—	—	2	—	—	2
Excess tax benefits from stock-based compensation	—	—	—	6	—	—	6
Stock-based compensation and issuance of employee benefit plan stock	—	—	—	1,510	—	—	1,510
Issuance of common stock for acquisition activity	—	—	—	44	—	—	44
Balance as of December 31, 2014	465	5	(1,837)	11,135	(511)	1,949	10,741
Net income	—	—	—	—	—	596	596
Other comprehensive income (loss)	—	—	—	—	(212)	—	(212)
Exercise of common stock options	6	—	—	4	—	—	4
Excess tax benefits from stock-based compensation	—	—	—	119	—	—	119
Stock-based compensation and issuance of employee benefit plan stock	—	—	—	2,131	—	—	2,131
Issuance of common stock for acquisition activity	—	—	—	5	—	—	5
Balance as of December 31, 2015	471	5	(1,837)	13,394	(723)	2,545	13,384
Net income	—	—	—	—	—	2,371	2,371
Other comprehensive income (loss)	—	—	—	—	(262)	—	(262)
Exercise of common stock options	6	—	—	1	—	—	1
Excess tax benefits from stock-based compensation	—	—	—	829	—	—	829
Stock-based compensation and issuance of employee benefit plan stock	—	—	—	2,962	—	—	2,962
Balance as of December 31, 2016	477	$ 5	$ (1,837)	$ 17,186	$ (985)	$ 4,916	$ 19,285

See accompanying notes to consolidated financial statements.

Appendix E

Specimen Financial Statements: Wal-Mart Stores, Inc.

The following are **Wal-Mart Stores, Inc.**'s financial statements as presented in the company's annual report for the year ended January 31, 2017. The complete annual report, including notes to the financial statements, is available at the company's website.

Wal-Mart Stores, Inc.
Consolidated Statement of Income

	Fiscal Years Ended January 31,		
(Amounts in millions, except per share data)	2017	2016	2015
Revenues:			
Net sales	$481,317	$478,614	$482,229
Membership and other income	4,556	3,516	3,422
Total revenues	485,873	482,130	485,651
Costs and expenses:			
Cost of sales	361,256	360,984	365,086
Operating, selling, general and administrative expenses	101,853	97,041	93,418
Operating income	22,764	24,105	27,147
Interest:			
Debt	2,044	2,027	2,161
Capital lease and financing obligations	323	521	300
Interest income	(100)	(81)	(113)
Interest, net	2,267	2,467	2,348
Income from continuing operations before income taxes	20,497	21,638	24,799
Provision for income taxes	6,204	6,558	7,985
Income from continuing operations	14,293	15,080	16,814
Income from discontinued operations, net of income taxes	—	—	285
Consolidated net income	14,293	15,080	17,099
Consolidated net income attributable to noncontrolling interest	(650)	(386)	(736)
Consolidated net income attributable to Walmart	$ 13,643	$ 14,694	$ 16,363
Basic net income per common share:			
Basic income per common share from continuing operations attributable to Walmart	$ 4.40	$ 4.58	$ 5.01
Basic income per common share from discontinued operations attributable to Walmart	—	—	0.06
Basic net income per common share attributable to Walmart	$ 4.40	$ 4.58	$ 5.07
Diluted net income per common share:			
Diluted income per common share from continuing operations attributable to Walmart	$ 4.38	$ 4.57	$ 4.99
Diluted income per common share from discontinued operations attributable to Walmart	—	—	0.06
Diluted net income per common share attributable to Walmart	$ 4.38	$ 4.57	$ 5.05
Weighted-average common shares outstanding:			
Basic	3,101	3,207	3,230
Diluted	3,112	3,217	3,243
Dividends declared per common share	$ 2.00	$ 1.96	$ 1.92

See accompanying notes.

Wal-Mart Stores, Inc.
Consolidated Statement of Comprehensive Income

(Amounts in millions)	Fiscal Years Ended January 31,		
	2017	2016	2015
Consolidated net income	$14,293	$15,080	$17,099
Less consolidated net income attributable to nonredeemable noncontrolling interest	(650)	(386)	(736)
Consolidated net income attributable to Walmart	13,643	14,694	16,363
Other comprehensive income (loss), net of income taxes			
Currency translation and other	(2,882)	(5,220)	(4,558)
Net investment hedges	413	366	379
Cash flow hedges	21	(202)	(470)
Minimum pension liability	(397)	86	(69)
Other comprehensive income (loss), net of income taxes	(2,845)	(4,970)	(4,718)
Less other comprehensive income (loss) attributable to nonredeemable noncontrolling interest	210	541	546
Other comprehensive income (loss) attributable to Walmart	(2,635)	(4,429)	(4,172)
Comprehensive income, net of income taxes	11,448	10,110	12,381
Less comprehensive income (loss) attributable to nonredeemable noncontrolling interest	(440)	155	(190)
Comprehensive income attributable to Walmart	$11,008	$10,265	$12,191

See accompanying notes.

Wal-Mart Stores, Inc.
Consolidated Balance Sheets

	As of January 31,	
(Amounts in millions)	2017	2016
ASSETS		
Current assets:		
Cash and cash equivalents	$ 6,867	$ 8,705
Receivables, net	5,835	5,624
Inventories	43,046	44,469
Prepaid expenses and other	1,941	1,441
Total current assets	57,689	60,239
Property and equipment:		
Property and equipment	179,492	176,958
Less accumulated depreciation	(71,782)	(66,787)
Property and equipment, net	107,710	110,171
Property under capital lease and financing obligations:		
Property under capital lease and financing obligations	11,637	11,096
Less accumulated amortization	(5,169)	(4,751)
Property under capital lease and financing obligations, net	6,468	6,345
Goodwill	17,037	16,695
Other assets and deferred charges	9,921	6,131
Total assets	**$198,825**	**$199,581**
LIABILITIES AND EQUITY		
Current liabilities:		
Short-term borrowings	$ 1,099	$ 2,708
Accounts payable	41,433	38,487
Accrued liabilities	20,654	19,607
Accrued income taxes	921	521
Long-term debt due within one year	2,256	2,745
Capital lease and financing obligations due within one year	565	551
Total current liabilities	66,928	64,619
Long-term debt	36,015	38,214
Long-term capital lease and financing obligations	6,003	5,816
Deferred income taxes and other	9,344	7,321
Commitments and contingencies		
Equity:		
Common stock	305	317
Capital in excess of par value	2,371	1,805
Retained earnings	89,354	90,021
Accumulated other comprehensive loss	(14,232)	(11,597)
Total Walmart shareholders' equity	77,798	80,546
Nonredeemable noncontrolling interest	2,737	3,065
Total equity	80,535	83,611
Total liabilities and equity	**$198,825**	**$199,581**

See accompanying notes.

Wal-Mart Stores, Inc.
Consolidated Statements of Shareholders' Equity and Redeemaole Noncontrolling Interest

(Amounts in millions)	Common Stock Shares	Common Stock Amount	Capital in Excess of Par Value	Retained Earnings	Accumulated Other Comprehensive Loss	Total Walmart Shareholders' Equity	Nonredeemable Noncontrolling Interest	Total Equity	Redeemable Noncontrolling Interest
Balances as of February 1, 2014	3,233	$323	$2,362	$76,566	$ (2,996)	$76,255	$5,084	$81,339	$ 1,491
Consolidated net income	—	—	—	16,363	—	16,363	736	17,099	—
Other comprehensive loss, net of income taxes	—	—	—	—	(4,172)	(4,172)	(546)	(4,718)	—
Cash dividends declared ($1.92 per share)	—	—	—	(6,185)	—	(6,185)	—	(6,185)	—
Purchase of Company stock	(13)	(1)	(29)	(950)	—	(980)	—	(980)	—
Purchase of redeemable noncontrolling interest	—	—	—	—	—	—	—	—	(1,491)
Other	8	1	129	(17)	—	113	(731)	(618)	—
Balances as of January 31, 2015	3,228	323	2,462	85,777	(7,168)	81,394	4,543	85,937	—
Consolidated net income	—	—	—	14,694	—	14,694	386	15,080	—
Other comprehensive loss, net of income taxes	—	—	—	—	(4,429)	(4,429)	(541)	(4,970)	—
Cash dividends declared ($1.96 per share)	—	—	—	(6,294)	—	(6,294)	—	(6,294)	—
Purchase of Company stock	(65)	(6)	(102)	(4,148)	—	(4,256)	—	(4,256)	—
Cash dividend declared to noncontrolling interest	—	—	—	—	—	—	(691)	(691)	—
Other	(1)	—	(555)	(8)	—	(563)	(632)	(1,195)	—
Balances as of January 31, 2016	3,162	317	1,805	90,021	(11,597)	80,546	3,065	83,611	—
Consolidated net income	—	—	—	13,643	—	13,643	650	14,293	—
Other comprehensive loss, net of income taxes	—	—	—	—	(2,635)	(2,635)	(210)	(2,845)	—
Cash dividends declared ($2.00 per share)	—	—	—	(6,216)	—	(6,216)	—	(6,216)	—
Purchase of Company stock	(120)	(12)	(174)	(8,090)	—	(8,276)	—	(8,276)	—
Cash dividend declared to noncontrolling interest	—	—	—	—	—	—	(519)	(519)	—
Other	6	—	740	(4)	—	736	(249)	487	—
Balances as of January 31, 2017	3,048	$305	$2,371	$89,354	$(14,232)	$77,798	$2,737	$80,535	$ —

See accompanying notes.

Wal-Mart Stores, Inc.
Consolidated Statements of Cash Flow

	Fiscal Years Ended January 31,		
(Amounts in millions)	2017	2016	2015
Cash flows from operating activities:			
Consolidated net income	$ 14,293	$ 15,080	$ 17,099
Income from discontinued operations, net of income taxes	—	—	(285)
Income from continuing operations	14,293	15,080	16,814
Adjustments to reconcile income from continuing operations to net cash provided by operating activities:			
Depreciation and amortization	10,080	9,454	9,173
Deferred income taxes	761	(672)	(503)
Other operating activities	206	1,410	785
Changes in certain assets and liabilities, net of effects of acquisitions:			
Receivables, net	(402)	(19)	(569)
Inventories	1,021	(703)	(1,229)
Accounts payable	3,942	2,008	2,678
Accrued liabilities	1,137	1,303	1,249
Accrued income taxes	492	(472)	166
Net cash provided by operating activities	31,530	27,389	28,564
Cash flows from investing activities:			
Payments for property and equipment	(10,619)	(11,477)	(12,174)
Proceeds from the disposal of property and equipment	456	635	570
Proceeds from the disposal of certain operations	662	246	671
Purchase of available for sale securities	(1,901)	—	—
Investment and business acquisitions, net of cash acquired	(2,463)	—	—
Other investing activities	(122)	(79)	(192)
Net cash used in investing activities	(13,987)	(10,675)	(11,125)
Cash flows from financing activities:			
Net change in short-term borrowings	(1,673)	1,235	(6,288)
Proceeds from issuance of long-term debt	137	39	5,174
Payments of long-term debt	(2,055)	(4,432)	(3,904)
Dividends paid	(6,216)	(6,294)	(6,185)
Purchase of Company stock	(8,298)	(4,112)	(1,015)
Dividends paid to noncontrolling interest	(479)	(719)	(600)
Purchase of noncontrolling interest	(90)	(1,326)	(1,844)
Other financing activities	(255)	(513)	(409)
Net cash used in financing activities	(18,929)	(16,122)	(15,071)
Effect of exchange rates on cash and cash equivalents	(452)	(1,022)	(514)
Net increase (decrease) in cash and cash equivalents	(1,838)	(430)	1,854
Cash and cash equivalents at beginning of year	8,705	9,135	7,281
Cash and cash equivalents at end of year	$ 6,867	$ 8,705	$ 9,135
Supplemental disclosure of cash flow information:			
Income taxes paid	4,507	8,111	8,169
Interest paid	2,351	2,540	2,433

See accompanying notes.

Specimen Financial Statements: Louis Vuitton

Louis Vuitton is a French company and is one of the leading international fashion houses in the world. Louis Vuitton has been named the world's most valuable luxury brand. Note that its financial statements are IFRS-based and are presented in euros (€). The complete financial statements are available at the company's website.

CONSOLIDATED INCOME STATEMENT

(EUR millions, except for earnings per share)	Notes	2016	2015	2014
Revenue	23-24	**37,600**	**35,664**	**30,638**
Cost of sales		(13,039)	(12,553)	(10,801)
Gross margin		**24,561**	**23,111**	**19,837**
Marketing and selling expenses		(14,607)	(13,830)	(11,744)
General and administrative expenses		(2,931)	(2,663)	(2,373)
Income (loss) from joint ventures and associates	7	3	(13)	(5)
Profit from recurring operations	23-24	**7,026**	**6,605**	**5,715**
Other operating income and expenses	25	(122)	(221)	(284)
Operating profit		**6,904**	**6,384**	**5,431**
Cost of net financial debt		(83)	(78)	(115)
Other financial income and expenses		(349)	(336)	3,062
Net financial income (expense)	26	**(432)**	**(414)**	**2,947**
Income taxes	27	(2,109)	(1,969)	(2,273)
Net profit before minority interests		**4,363**	**4,001**	**6,105**
Minority interests	17	(382)	(428)	(457)
Net profit, Group share		**3,981**	**3,573**	**5,648**
Basic Group share of net earnings per share *(EUR)*	28	**7.92**	**7.11**	**11.27**
Number of shares on which the calculation is based		502,911,125	502,395,491	501,309,369
Diluted Group share of net earnings per share *(EUR)*	28	**7.89**	**7.08**	**11.21**
Number of shares on which the calculation is based		504,640,459	504,894,946	503,861,733

CONSOLIDATED STATEMENT OF COMPREHENSIVE GAINS AND LOSSES

(EUR millions)	Notes	2016	2015	2014
Net profit before minority interests		4,363	4,001	6,105
Translation adjustments	15.4	109	631	534
Amounts transferred to income statement		(32)	-	-
Tax impact		(9)	135	104
		68	766	638
Change in value of available for sale financial assets	8, 13	18	(32)	494
Amounts transferred to income statement		4	(91)	(3,326)
Tax impact		1	20	184
		23	(103)	(2,648)
Change in value of hedges of future foreign currency cash flows		48	(63)	(30)
Amounts transferred to income statement		(26)	33	(163)
Tax impact		(2)	3	57
		20	(27)	(136)
Gains and losses recognized in equity, transferable to income statement		111	636	(2,146)
Change in value of vineyard land	6	30	64	(17)
Amounts transferred to consolidated reserves		-	-	(10)
Tax impact		108	(21)	9
		138	43	(18)
Employee benefit commitments: change in value resulting from actuarial gains and losses	29	(86)	42	(161)
Tax impact		17	(16)	52
		(69)	26	(109)
Gains and losses recognized in equity, not transferable to income statement		69	69	(127)
Comprehensive income		4,543	4,706	3,832
Minority interests		(434)	(558)	(565)
Comprehensive income, Group share		4,109	4,148	3,267

CONSOLIDATED BALANCE SHEET

ASSETS (EUR millions)	Notes	2016	2015	2014
Brands and other intangible assets	3	13,335	13,572	13,031
Goodwill	4	10,401	10,122	8,810
Property, plant and equipment	6	12,139	11,157	10,387
Investments in joint ventures and associates	7	770	729	519
Non-current available for sale financial assets	8	744	574	580
Other non-current assets	9	777	552	489
Deferred tax	27	2,058	1,945	1,436
Non-current assets		**40,224**	**38,651**	**35,252**
Inventories and work in progress	10	10,546	10,096	9,475
Trade accounts receivable	11	2,685	2,521	2,274
Income taxes		280	384	354
Other current assets	12	2,343	2,355	1,916
Cash and cash equivalents	14	3,544	3,594	4,091
Current assets		**19,398**	**18,950**	**18,110**
Total assets		**59,622**	**57,601**	**53,362**

LIABILITIES AND EQUITY (EUR millions)	Notes	2016	2015	2014
Share capital	15.1	152	152	152
Share premium account	15.1	2,601	2,579	2,655
Treasury shares and LVMH share-settled derivatives	15.2	(520)	(240)	(374)
Cumulative translation adjustment	15.4	1,165	1,137	492
Revaluation reserves		1,049	949	1,019
Other reserves		17,965	16,189	12,171
Net profit, Group share		3,981	3,573	5,648
Equity, Group share		26,393	24,339	21,763
Minority interests	17	1,510	1,460	1,240
Equity		**27,903**	**25,799**	**23,003**
Long-term borrowings	18	3,932	4,511	5,054
Non-current provisions	19	2,342	1,950	2,291
Deferred tax	27	4,137	4,685	4,392
Other non-current liabilities	20	8,498	7,957	6,447
Non-current liabilities		**18,909**	**19,103**	**18,184**
Short-term borrowings	18	3,447	3,769	4,189
Trade accounts payable	21.1	4,184	3,960	3,606
Income taxes		428	640	549
Current provisions	19	352	421	332
Other current liabilities	21.2	4,399	3,909	3,499
Current liabilities		**12,810**	**12,699**	**12,175**
Total liabilities and equity		**59,622**	**57,601**	**53,362**

CONSOLIDATED STATEMENT OF CHANGES IN EQUITY

(EUR millions)	Number of shares	Share capital	Share premium account	Treasury shares and LVMH share-settled derivatives	Cumulative translation adjustment	Revaluation reserves				Net profit and other reserves	Total equity		
						Available for sale financial assets	Hedges of future foreign currency cash flows	Vineyard land	Employee benefit commitments		Group share	Minority interests	Total
Notes		15.1		15.2	15.4							17	
As of December 31, 2013	507,793,661	152	3,849	(451)	(8)	2,855	136	946	(37)	19,437	26,879	1,028	27,907
Gains and losses recognized in equity					500	(2,648)	(122)	(15)	(96)	-	(2,381)	108	(2,273)
Net profit										5,648	5,648	457	6,105
Comprehensive income		-	-	-	500	(2,648)	(122)	(15)	(96)	5,648	3,267	565	3,832
Stock option plan and similar expenses										37	37	2	39
(Acquisition)/disposal of treasury shares and LVMH share-settled derivatives				27						(17)	10	-	10
Exercise of LVMH share subscription options	980,323		59								59	-	59
Retirement of LVMH shares	(1,062,271)		(50)	50							-	-	-
Capital increase in subsidiaries											-	3	3
Interim and final dividends paid										(1,579)	(1,579)	(328)	(1,907)
Distribution in kind of Hermès shares (a)			(1,203)							(5,652)	(6,855)	-	(6,855)
Changes in control of consolidated entities										(5)	(5)	11	6
Acquisition and disposal of minority interests' shares										(2)	(2)	32	30
Purchase commitments for minority interests' shares										(48)	(48)	(73)	(121)
As of December 31, 2014	507,711,713	152	2,655	(374)	492	207	14	931	(133)	17,819	21,763	1,240	23,003
Gains and losses recognized in equity					645	(103)	(25)	33	25	-	575	130	705
Net profit										3,573	3,573	428	4,001
Comprehensive income		-	-	-	645	(103)	(25)	33	25	3,573	4,148	558	4,706
Stock option plan and similar expenses										35	35	2	37
(Acquisition)/disposal of treasury shares and LVMH share-settled derivatives				23						(13)	10	-	10
Exercise of LVMH share subscription options	552,137		35								35	-	35
Retirement of LVMH shares	(1,124,740)		(111)	111							-	-	-
Capital increase in subsidiaries											-	89	89
Interim and final dividends paid										(1,659)	(1,659)	(229)	(1,888)
Changes in control of consolidated entities										(9)	(9)	1	(8)
Acquisition and disposal of minority interests' shares										5	5	(3)	2
Purchase commitments for minority interests' shares										11	11	(198)	(187)
As of December 31, 2015	507,139,110	152	2,579	(240)	1,137	104	(11)	964	(108)	19,762	24,339	1,460	25,799
Gains and losses recognized in equity					28	23	19	113	(55)	-	128	52	180
Net profit										3,981	3,981	382	4,363
Comprehensive income		-	-	-	28	23	19	113	(55)	3,981	4,109	434	4,543
Stock option plan and similar expenses										39	39	2	41
(Acquisition)/disposal of treasury shares and LVMH share-settled derivatives				(322)						(21)	(343)	-	(343)
Exercise of LVMH share subscription options	907,929		64								64	-	64
Retirement of LVMH shares	(920,951)		(42)	42							-	-	-
Capital increase in subsidiaries											-	41	41
Interim and final dividends paid										(1,811)	(1,811)	(272)	(2,083)
Changes in control of consolidated entities										(5)	(5)	22	17
Acquisition and disposal of minority interests' shares										(56)	(56)	(35)	(91)
Purchase commitments for minority interests' shares										57	57	(142)	(85)
As of December 31, 2016	507,126,088	152	2,601	(520)	1,165	127	8	1,077	(163)	21,946	26,393	1,510	27,903

(a) See Note 8.

CONSOLIDATED CASH FLOW STATEMENT

(EUR millions)	Notes	2016	2015	2014
I. OPERATING ACTIVITIES AND OPERATING INVESTMENTS				
Operating profit		6,904	6,384	5,431
Income/(loss) and dividends from joint ventures and associates	7	18	27	26
Net increase in depreciation, amortization and provisions		2,143	2,081	1,895
Other computed expenses		(177)	(456)	(188)
Other adjustments		(155)	(91)	(84)
Cash from operations before changes in working capital		**8,733**	**7,945**	**7,080**
Cost of net financial debt: interest paid		(59)	(75)	(116)
Tax paid		(1,923)	(1,807)	(1,639)
Net cash from operating activities before changes in working capital		**6,751**	**6,063**	**5,325**
Change in working capital	14.2	(512)	(429)	(718)
Net cash from operating activities		**6,239**	**5,634**	**4,607**
Operating investments	14.3	(2,265)	(1,955)	(1,775)
Net cash from operating activities and operating investments (free cash flow)		**3,974**	**3,679**	**2,832**
II. FINANCIAL INVESTMENTS				
Purchase of non-current available for sale financial assets (a)	8, 13	(28)	(78)	(57)
Proceeds from sale of non-current available for sale financial assets	8	91	68	160
Dividends received	8	6	4	69
Tax paid related to non-current available for sale financial assets and consolidated investments		(461)	(265)	(237)
Impact of purchase and sale of consolidated investments	2.4	310	(240)	(167)
Net cash from (used in) financial investments		**(82)**	**(511)**	**(232)**
III. TRANSACTIONS RELATING TO EQUITY				
Capital increases of LVMH SE	15.1	64	35	59
Capital increases of subsidiaries subscribed by minority interests	17	41	81	3
Acquisition and disposals of treasury shares and LVMH share-settled derivatives	15.2	(352)	1	1
Interim and final dividends paid by LVMH SE (b)	15.3	(1,810)	(1,671)	(1,619)
Tax paid related to interim and final dividends paid		(145)	(304)	(79)
Interim and final dividends paid to minority interests in consolidated subsidiaries	17	(267)	(228)	(336)
Purchase and proceeds from sale of minority interests	2.4	(95)	(4)	10
Net cash from (used in) transactions relating to equity		**(2,564)**	**(2,090)**	**(1,961)**
Change in cash before financing activities		**1,328**	**1,078**	**639**
IV. FINANCING ACTIVITIES				
Proceeds from borrowings	18.1	913	1,008	2,407
Repayment of borrowings	18.1	(2,134)	(2,443)	(2,100)
Purchase and proceeds from sale of current available for sale financial assets (a)	8, 13	(113)	(3)	(106)
Net cash from (used in) financing activities		**(1,334)**	**(1,438)**	**201**
V. EFFECT OF EXCHANGE RATE CHANGES		(47)	(33)	27
NET INCREASE (DECREASE) IN CASH AND CASH EQUIVALENTS (I+II+III+IV+V)		**(53)**	**(393)**	**867**
CASH AND CASH EQUIVALENTS AT BEGINNING OF PERIOD	14.1	3,390	3,783	2,916
CASH AND CASH EQUIVALENTS AT END OF PERIOD	14.1	3,337	3,390	3,783
TOTAL TAX PAID		**(2,529)**	**(2,376)**	**(1,955)**

(a) The cash impact of non-current available for sale financial assets used to hedge net financial debt (see Note 18) is presented under "IV. Financing activities" as "Purchase and proceeds from sale of current available for sale financial assets".
(b) The distribution in kind of Hermès shares in 2014 had no impact on cash, apart from related tax effects. See Note 8.

Appendix G

Time Value of Money

Appendix Preview

Would you rather receive $1,000 today or a year from now? You should prefer to receive the $1,000 today because you can invest the $1,000 and then earn interest on it. As a result, you will have more than $1,000 a year from now. What this example illustrates is the concept of the **time value of money**. Everyone prefers to receive money today rather than in the future because of the interest factor.

Appendix Outline

LEARNING OBJECTIVES	
1. Compute interest and future values.	• Nature of interest • Future value of a single amount • Future value of an annuity
2. Compute present values.	• Present value variables • Present value of a single amount • Present value of an annuity • Time periods and discounting • Present value of a long-term note or bond
3. Compute the present value in capital budgeting situations.	• Using alternative discount rates
4. Use a financial calculator to solve time value of money problems.	• Present value of a single sum • Present value of an annuity • Future value of a single sum • Future value of an annuity • Internal rate of return • Useful financial calculator applications

Interest and Future Values

LEARNING OBJECTIVE 1
Compute interest and future values.

Nature of Interest

Interest is payment for the use of another person's money. It is the difference between the amount borrowed or invested (called the **principal**) and the amount repaid or collected. The amount of interest to be paid or collected is usually stated as a rate over a specific period of time. The rate of interest is generally stated as an annual rate.

The amount of interest involved in any financing transaction is based on three elements:

1. **Principal (p):** The original amount borrowed or invested.
2. **Interest Rate (i):** An annual percentage of the principal.
3. **Time (n):** The number of periods that the principal is borrowed or invested.

Simple Interest

Simple interest is computed on the principal amount only. It is the return on the principal for one period (we use an annual interest rate unless stated otherwise). Simple interest is usually expressed as shown in **Illustration G.1**.

ILLUSTRATION G.1
Interest computation

$$\text{Interest} = \underset{p}{\text{Principal}} \times \underset{i}{\text{Rate}} \times \underset{n}{\text{Time}}$$

For example, if you borrowed $5,000 for 2 years at a simple interest rate of 12% annually, you would pay $1,200 in total interest, computed as follows.

$$\begin{aligned}\text{Interest} &= p \times i \times n \\ &= \$5,000 \times .12 \times 2 \\ &= \$1,200\end{aligned}$$

Compound Interest

Compound interest is computed on principal **and** on any interest earned that has not been paid or withdrawn. It is the return on (or growth of) the principal for two or more time periods. Compounding computes interest not only on the principal but also on the interest earned to date on that principal, assuming the interest is left on deposit.

To illustrate the difference between simple and compound interest, assume that you deposit $1,000 in Bank Two, where it will earn simple interest of 9% per year, and you deposit another $1,000 in Citizens Bank, where it will earn compound interest of 9% per year compounded annually. Also assume that in both cases you will not withdraw any cash until three years from the date of deposit. **Illustration G.2** shows the computation of interest to be received and the accumulated year-end balances.

ILLUSTRATION G.2 Simple versus compound interest

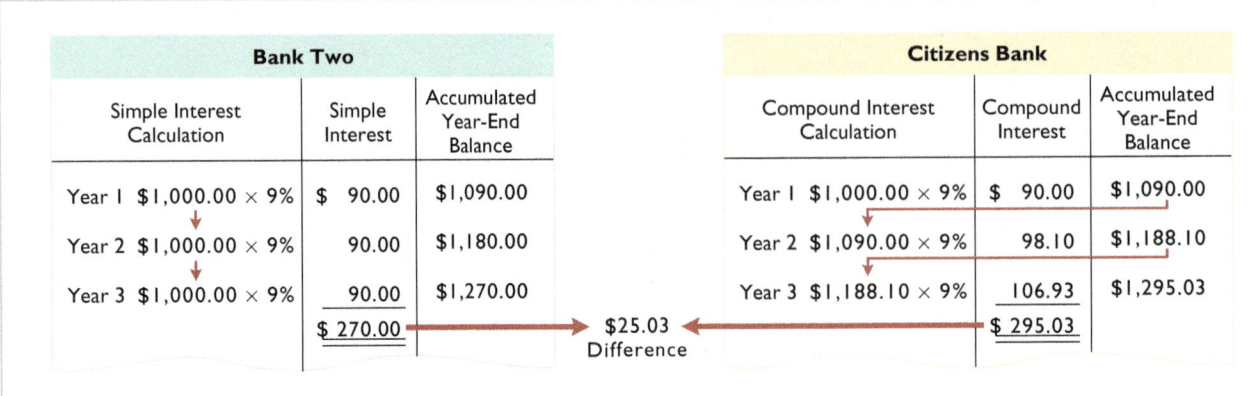

Note in Illustration G.2 that simple interest uses the initial principal of $1,000 to compute the interest in all three years. Compound interest uses the accumulated balance (principal plus interest to date) at each year-end to compute interest in the succeeding year—which explains why your compound interest account is larger.

Obviously, if you had a choice between investing your money at simple interest or at compound interest, you would choose compound interest, all other things—especially risk—being equal. In the example, compounding provides $25.03 of additional interest income. For practical purposes, compounding assumes that unpaid interest earned becomes a part of the principal, and the accumulated balance at the end of each year becomes the new principal on which interest is earned during the next year.

Most business situations use compound interest. Simple interest is generally applicable only to short-term situations of one year or less.

Future Value of a Single Amount

The **future value of a single amount** is the value at a future date of a given amount invested, assuming compound interest. For example, in Illustration G.2, $1,295.03 is the future value of the $1,000 investment earning 9% for three years. The $1,295.03 is determined more easily by using the formula shown in **Illustration G.3**.

$$FV = p \times (1 + i)^n$$

ILLUSTRATION G.3

Formula for future value

where:

FV = future value of a single amount
p = principal (or present value; the value today)
i = interest rate for one period
n = number of periods

The $1,295.03 is computed as follows.

$$\begin{aligned} FV &= p \times (1 + i)^n \\ &= \$1{,}000 \times (1 + .09)^3 \\ &= \$1{,}000 \times 1.29503 \\ &= \$1{,}295.03 \end{aligned}$$

The 1.29503 is computed by multiplying (1.09 × 1.09 × 1.09). The amounts in this example can be depicted in the time diagram shown in **Illustration G.4**.

ILLUSTRATION G.4 Time diagram

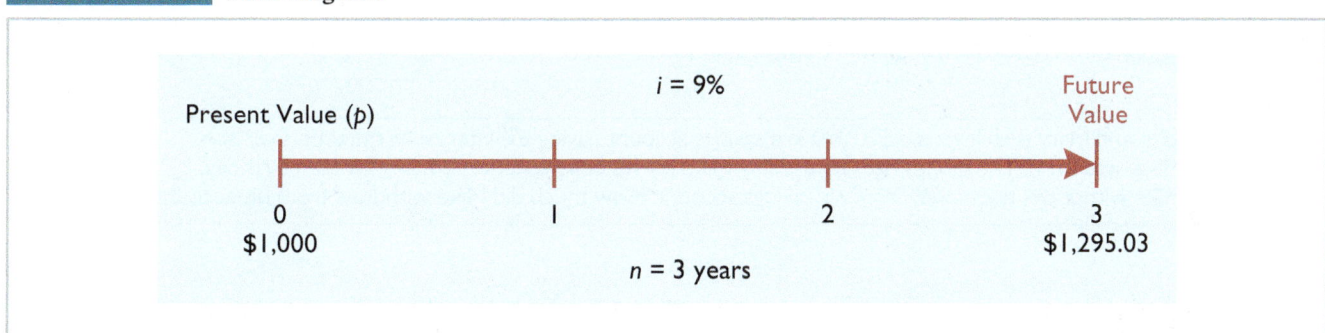

Another method used to compute the future value of a single amount involves a compound interest table. This table shows the future value of 1 for n periods. **Table 1** is such a table.

In Table 1, n is the number of compounding periods, the percentages are the periodic interest rates, and the 5-digit decimal numbers in the respective columns are the future value of 1 factors. To use Table 1, you multiply the principal amount by the future value factor for the specified number of periods and interest rate. For example, the future value factor for two periods at 9% is 1.18810. Multiplying this factor by $1,000 equals $1,188.10—which is the

TABLE 1 Future Value of 1

(n) Periods	4%	5%	6%	7%	8%	9%	10%	11%	12%	15%
0	1.00000	1.00000	1.00000	1.00000	1.00000	1.00000	1.00000	1.00000	1.00000	1.00000
1	1.04000	1.05000	1.06000	1.07000	1.08000	1.09000	1.10000	1.11000	1.12000	1.15000
2	1.08160	1.10250	1.12360	1.14490	1.16640	1.18810	1.21000	1.23210	1.25440	1.32250
3	1.12486	1.15763	1.19102	1.22504	1.25971	1.29503	1.33100	1.36763	1.40493	1.52088
4	1.16986	1.21551	1.26248	1.31080	1.36049	1.41158	1.46410	1.51807	1.57352	1.74901
5	1.21665	1.27628	1.33823	1.40255	1.46933	1.53862	1.61051	1.68506	1.76234	2.01136
6	1.26532	1.34010	1.41852	1.50073	1.58687	1.67710	1.77156	1.87041	1.97382	2.31306
7	1.31593	1.40710	1.50363	1.60578	1.71382	1.82804	1.94872	2.07616	2.21068	2.66002
8	1.36857	1.47746	1.59385	1.71819	1.85093	1.99256	2.14359	2.30454	2.47596	3.05902
9	1.42331	1.55133	1.68948	1.83846	1.99900	2.17189	2.35795	2.55803	2.77308	3.51788
10	1.48024	1.62889	1.79085	1.96715	2.15892	2.36736	2.59374	2.83942	3.10585	4.04556
11	1.53945	1.71034	1.89830	2.10485	2.33164	2.58043	2.85312	3.15176	3.47855	4.65239
12	1.60103	1.79586	2.01220	2.25219	2.51817	2.81267	3.13843	3.49845	3.89598	5.35025
13	1.66507	1.88565	2.13293	2.40985	2.71962	3.06581	3.45227	3.88328	4.36349	6.15279
14	1.73168	1.97993	2.26090	2.57853	2.93719	3.34173	3.79750	4.31044	4.88711	7.07571
15	1.80094	2.07893	2.39656	2.75903	3.17217	3.64248	4.17725	4.78459	5.47357	8.13706
16	1.87298	2.18287	2.54035	2.95216	3.42594	3.97031	4.59497	5.31089	6.13039	9.35762
17	1.94790	2.29202	2.69277	3.15882	3.70002	4.32763	5.05447	5.89509	6.86604	10.76126
18	2.02582	2.40662	2.85434	3.37993	3.99602	4.71712	5.55992	6.54355	7.68997	12.37545
19	2.10685	2.52695	3.02560	3.61653	4.31570	5.14166	6.11591	7.26334	8.61276	14.23177
20	2.19112	2.65330	3.20714	3.86968	4.66096	5.60441	6.72750	8.06231	9.64629	16.36654

accumulated balance at the end of year 2 in the Citizens Bank example in Illustration G.2. The $1,295.03 accumulated balance at the end of the third year is calculated from Table 1 by multiplying the future value factor for three periods (1.29503) by the $1,000.

The demonstration problem in **Illustration G.5** shows how to use Table 1.

ILLUSTRATION G.5 Demonstration problem—Using Table 1 for *FV* of 1

John and Mary Rich invested $20,000 in a savings account paying 6% interest at the time their son, Mike, was born. The money is to be used by Mike for his college education. On his 18th birthday, Mike withdraws the money from his savings account. How much did Mike withdraw from his account?

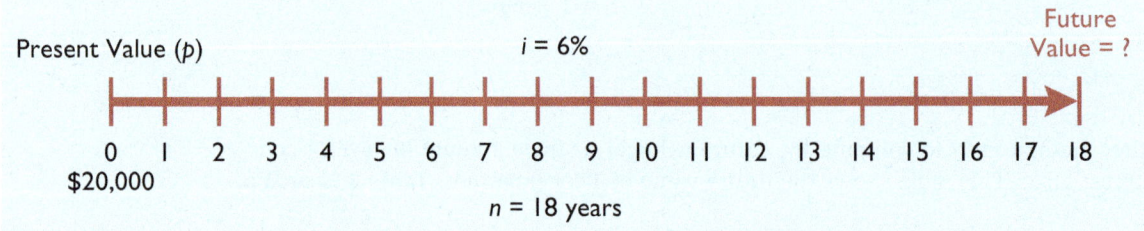

Answer: The future value factor from Table 1 is 2.85434 (18 periods at 6%). The future value of $20,000 earning 6% per year for 18 years is **$57,086.80** ($20,000 × 2.85434).

Future Value of an Annuity

The preceding discussion involved the accumulation of only a single principal sum. Individuals and businesses frequently encounter situations in which a **series** of equal dollar amounts are to be paid or received at evenly spaced time intervals (periodically), such as loans or lease (rental) contracts. A series of payments or receipts of equal dollar amounts is referred to as an **annuity**.

The **future value of an annuity** is the sum of all the payments (receipts) plus the accumulated compound interest on them. In computing the future value of an annuity, it is necessary to know (1) the interest rate, (2) the number of payments (receipts), and (3) the amount of the periodic payments (receipts).

To illustrate the computation of the future value of an annuity, assume that you invest $2,000 at the end of each year for three years at 5% interest compounded annually. This situation is depicted in the time diagram in **Illustration G.6**.

ILLUSTRATION G.6 Time diagram for a three-year annuity

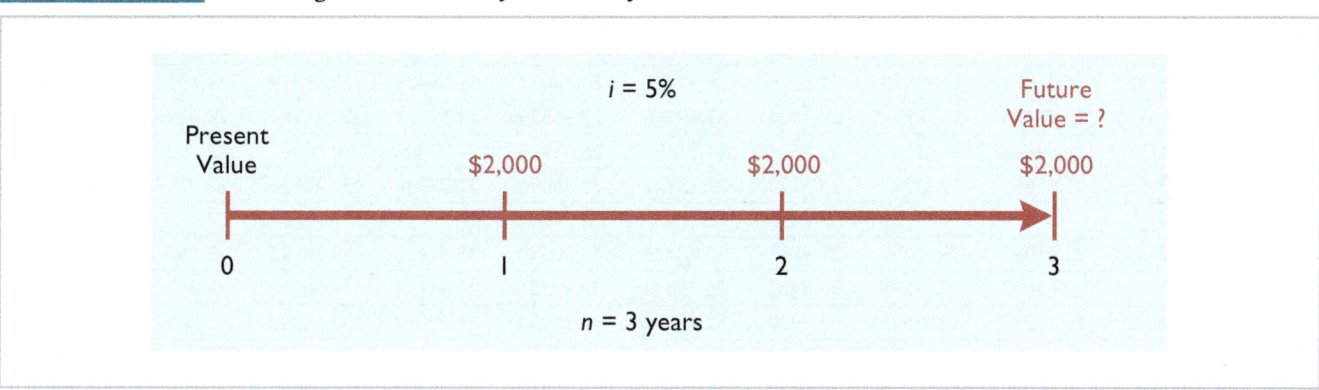

The $2,000 invested at the end of year 1 will earn interest for two years (years 2 and 3), and the $2,000 invested at the end of year 2 will earn interest for one year (year 3). However, the last $2,000 investment (made at the end of year 3) will not earn any interest. Using the future value factors from Table 1, the future value of these periodic payments is computed as shown in **Illustration G.7**.

Invested at End of Year	Number of Compounding Periods	Amount Invested	×	Future Value of 1 Factor at 5%	=	Future Value
1	2	$2,000		1.10250		$2,205
2	1	2,000		1.05000		2,100
3	0	2,000		1.00000		2,000
				3.15250		$6,305

ILLUSTRATION G.7
Future value of periodic payment computation

The first $2,000 investment is multiplied by the future value factor for two periods (1.1025) because two years' interest will accumulate on it (in years 2 and 3). The second $2,000 investment will earn only one year's interest (in year 3) and therefore is multiplied by the future value factor for one year (1.0500). The final $2,000 investment is made at the end of the third year and will not earn any interest. Thus, $n = 0$ and the future value factor is 1.00000. Consequently, the future value of the last $2,000 invested is only $2,000 since it does not accumulate any interest.

Calculating the future value of each individual cash flow is required when the periodic payments or receipts are not equal in each period. However, when the periodic payments (receipts) are **the same in each period**, the future value can be computed by using a future value of an annuity of 1 table. **Table 2** is such a table.

Table 2 shows the future value of 1 to be received periodically for a given number of payments. It assumes that each payment is made at the **end** of each period. We can see from Table 2

TABLE 2 Future Value of an Annuity of 1

(n) Payments	4%	5%	6%	7%	8%	9%	10%	11%	12%	15%
1	1.00000	1.00000	1.00000	1.0000	1.00000	1.00000	1.00000	1.00000	1.00000	1.00000
2	2.04000	2.05000	2.06000	2.0700	2.08000	2.09000	2.10000	2.11000	2.12000	2.15000
3	3.12160	3.15250	3.18360	3.2149	3.24640	3.27810	3.31000	3.34210	3.37440	3.47250
4	4.24646	4.31013	4.37462	4.4399	4.50611	4.57313	4.64100	4.70973	4.77933	4.99338
5	5.41632	5.52563	5.63709	5.7507	5.86660	5.98471	6.10510	6.22780	6.35285	6.74238
6	6.63298	6.80191	6.97532	7.1533	7.33592	7.52334	7.71561	7.91286	8.11519	8.75374
7	7.89829	8.14201	8.39384	8.6540	8.92280	9.20044	9.48717	9.78327	10.08901	11.06680
8	9.21423	9.54911	9.89747	10.2598	10.63663	11.02847	11.43589	11.85943	12.29969	13.72682
9	10.58280	11.02656	11.49132	11.9780	12.48756	13.02104	13.57948	14.16397	14.77566	16.78584
10	12.00611	12.57789	13.18079	13.8164	14.48656	15.19293	15.93743	16.72201	17.54874	20.30372
11	13.48635	14.20679	14.97164	15.7836	16.64549	17.56029	18.53117	19.56143	20.65458	24.34928
12	15.02581	15.91713	16.86994	17.8885	18.97713	20.14072	21.38428	22.71319	24.13313	29.00167
13	16.62684	17.71298	18.88214	20.1406	21.49530	22.95339	24.52271	26.21164	28.02911	34.35192
14	18.29191	19.59863	21.01507	22.5505	24.21492	26.01919	27.97498	30.09492	32.39260	40.50471
15	20.02359	21.57856	23.27597	25.1290	27.15211	29.36092	31.77248	34.40536	37.27972	47.58041
16	21.82453	23.65749	25.67253	27.8881	30.32428	33.00340	35.94973	39.18995	42.75328	55.71747
17	23.69751	25.84037	28.21288	30.8402	33.75023	36.97351	40.54470	44.50084	48.88367	65.07509
18	25.64541	28.13238	30.90565	33.9990	37.45024	41.30134	45.59917	50.39593	55.74972	75.83636
19	27.67123	30.53900	33.75999	37.3790	41.44626	46.01846	51.15909	56.93949	63.43968	88.21181
20	29.77808	33.06595	36.78559	40.9955	45.76196	51.16012	57.27500	64.20283	72.05244	102.44358

that the future value of an annuity of 1 factor for three payments at 5% is 3.15250. The future value factor is the total of the three individual future value factors was shown in Illustration G.7. Multiplying this amount by the annual investment of $2,000 produces a future value of $6,305. The demonstration problem in **Illustration G.8** shows how to use Table 2.

ILLUSTRATION G.8 Demonstration problem—Using Table 2 for *FV* of an annuity of 1

John and Char Lewis's daughter, Debra, has just started high school. They decide to start a college fund for her and will invest $2,500 in a savings account at the end of each year she is in high school (4 payments total). The account will earn 6% interest compounded annually. How much will be in the college fund at the time Debra graduates from high school?

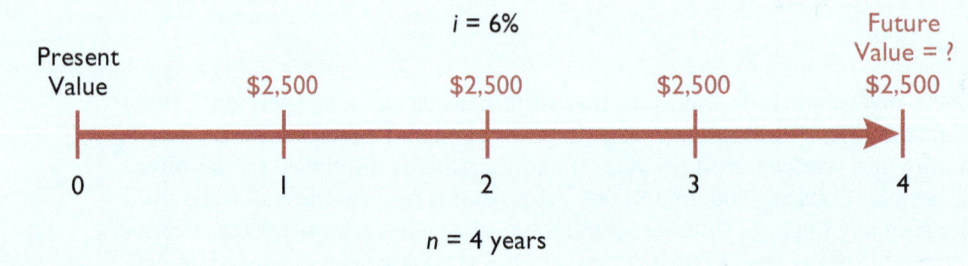

Answer: The future value factor from Table 2 is 4.37462 (4 payments at 6%). The future value of $2,500 invested each year for 4 years at 6% interest is **$10,936.55** ($2,500 × 4.37462).

Present Values

> **LEARNING OBJECTIVE 2**
> Compute present values.

Present Value Variables

The **present value** is the value now of a given amount to be paid or received in the future, assuming compound interest. The present value, like the future value, is based on three variables: (1) the dollar amount to be received (future amount), (2) the length of time until the amount is received (number of periods), and (3) the interest rate (the discount rate). The process of determining the present value is referred to as **discounting the future amount**.

Present value computations are used in measuring many items. For example, the present value of principal and interest payments is used to determine the market price of a bond. Determining the amount to be reported for notes payable and lease liabilities also involves present value computations. In addition, capital budgeting and other investment proposals are evaluated using present value computations. Finally, all rate of return and internal rate of return computations involve present value techniques.

Present Value of a Single Amount

To illustrate present value, assume that you want to invest a sum of money today that will provide $1,000 at the end of one year. What amount would you need to invest today to have $1,000 one year from now? If you want a 10% rate of return, the investment or present value is $909.09 ($1,000 ÷ 1.10). The formula for calculating present value is shown in **Illustration G.9**.

$$\text{Present Value } (PV) = \text{Future Value } (FV) \div (1 + i)^n$$

ILLUSTRATION G.9
Formula for present value

The computation of $1,000 discounted at 10% for one year is as follows.

$$\begin{aligned} PV &= FV \div (1 + i)^n \\ &= \$1,000 \div (1 + .10)^1 \\ &= \$1,000 \div 1.10 \\ &= \$909.09 \end{aligned}$$

The future amount ($1,000), the discount rate (10%), and the number of periods (1) are known. The variables in this situation are depicted in the time diagram in **Illustration G.10**.

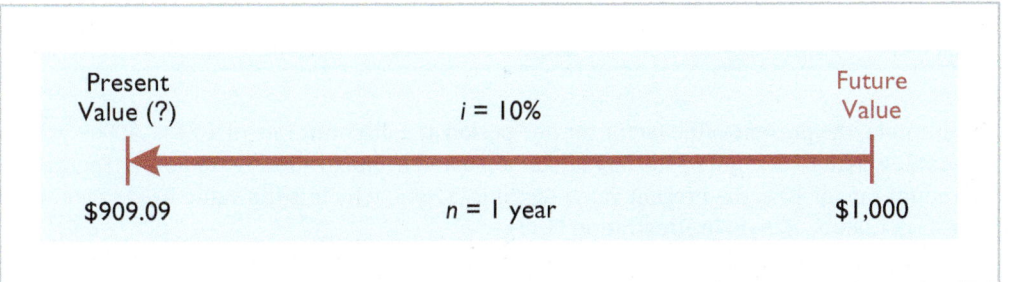

ILLUSTRATION G.10
Finding present value if discounted for one period

If the single amount of $1,000 is to be received **in two years** and discounted at 10%, the formula $PV = \$1,000 \div (1 + .10)^2$ is used, where $(1 + .10)^2$ is equal to 1.21 (1.10 × 1.10). Its present value is $826.45 ($1,000 ÷ 1.21), depicted in **Illustration G.11**.

ILLUSTRATION G.11
Finding present value if discounted for two periods

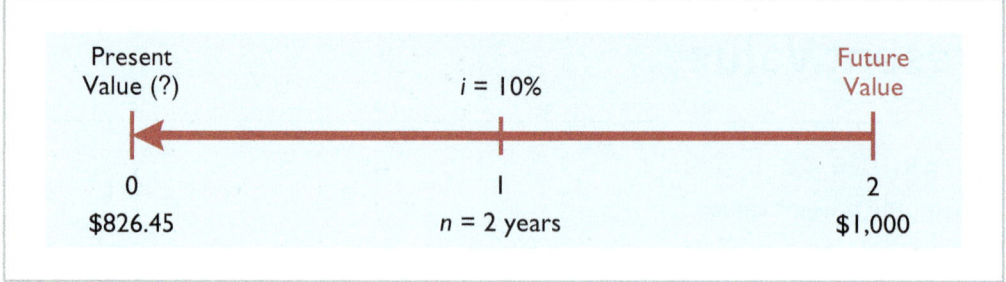

The present value of 1 may also be determined through tables that show the present value of 1 for n periods. In **Table 3**, n is the number of discounting periods involved. The percentages are the periodic interest rates or discount rates, and the 5-digit decimal numbers in the respective columns are the present value of 1 factors.

When using Table 3, the future value is multiplied by the present value factor specified at the intersection of the number of periods and the discount rate.

TABLE 3 Present Value of 1

(n) Periods	4%	5%	6%	7%	8%	9%	10%	11%	12%	15%
1	.96154	.95238	.94340	.93458	.92593	.91743	.90909	.90090	.89286	.86957
2	.92456	.90703	.89000	.87344	.85734	.84168	.82645	.81162	.79719	.75614
3	.88900	.86384	.83962	.81630	.79383	.77218	.75132	.73119	.71178	.65752
4	.85480	.82270	.79209	.76290	.73503	.70843	.68301	.65873	.63552	.57175
5	.82193	.78353	.74726	.71299	.68058	.64993	.62092	.59345	.56743	.49718
6	.79031	.74622	.70496	.66634	.63017	.59627	.56447	.53464	.50663	.43233
7	.75992	.71068	.66506	.62275	.58349	.54703	.51316	.48166	.45235	.37594
8	.73069	.67684	.62741	.58201	.54027	.50187	.46651	.43393	.40388	.32690
9	.70259	.64461	.59190	.54393	.50025	.46043	.42410	.39092	.36061	.28426
10	.67556	.61391	.55839	.50835	.46319	.42241	.38554	.35218	.32197	.24719
11	.64958	.58468	.52679	.47509	.42888	.38753	.35049	.31728	.28748	.21494
12	.62460	.55684	.49697	.44401	.39711	.35554	.31863	.28584	.25668	.18691
13	.60057	.53032	.46884	.41496	.36770	.32618	.28966	.25751	.22917	.16253
14	.57748	.50507	.44230	.38782	.34046	.29925	.26333	.23199	.20462	.14133
15	.55526	.48102	.41727	.36245	.31524	.27454	.23939	.20900	.18270	.12289
16	.53391	.45811	.39365	.33873	.29189	.25187	.21763	.18829	.16312	.10687
17	.51337	.43630	.37136	.31657	.27027	.23107	.19785	.16963	.14564	.09293
18	.49363	.41552	.35034	.29586	.25025	.21199	.17986	.15282	.13004	.08081
19	.47464	.39573	.33051	.27615	.23171	.19449	.16351	.13768	.11611	.07027
20	.45639	.37689	.31180	.25842	.21455	.17843	.14864	.12403	.10367	.06110

For example, the present value factor for one period at a discount rate of 10% is .90909, which is the value used to compute $909.09 ($1,000 × .90909) in Illustration G.10. For two periods at a discount rate of 10%, the present value factor is .82645, which is the value used to compute $826.45 ($1,000 × .82645) in Illustration G.11.

Note that a higher discount rate produces a smaller present value. For example, using a 15% discount rate, the present value of $1,000 due one year from now is $869.57 ($1,000 × .86957), versus $909.09 at 10%. Also note that the further in the future that the future value is, the smaller the present value. For example, using the same discount rate of 10%, the present value of $1,000 due in **five years** at 10% is $620.92 ($1,000 × .62092). The present value of $1,000 due in **one year** is $909.09, a difference of $288.17.

The following two demonstration problems (**Illustrations G.12** and **G.13**) illustrate how to use Table 3.

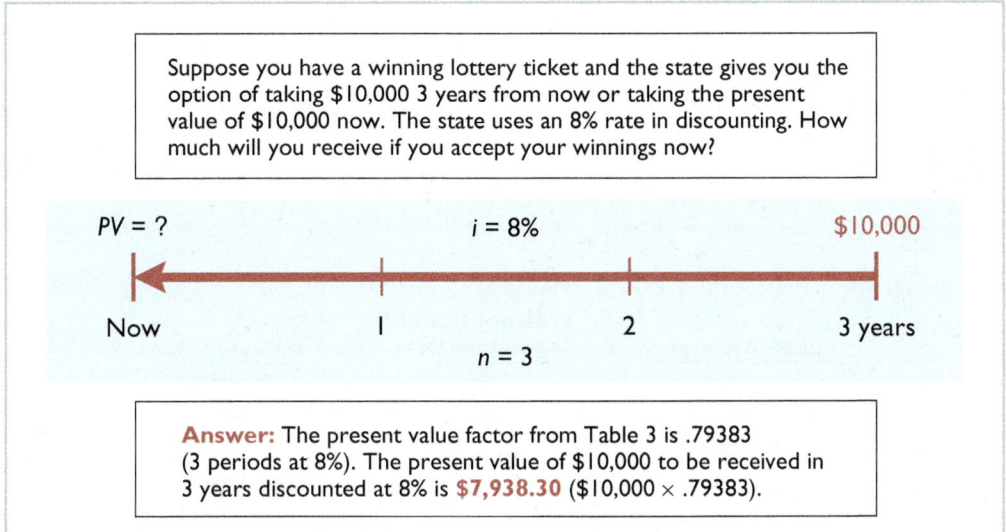

ILLUSTRATION G.12

Demonstration problem—Using Table 3 for *PV* of 1

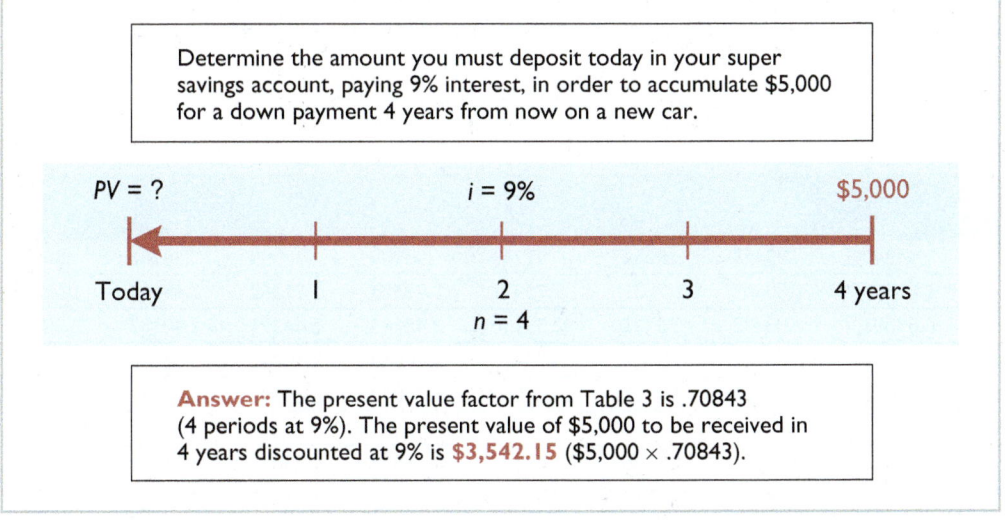

ILLUSTRATION G.13

Demonstration problem—Using Table 3 for *PV* of 1

Present Value of an Annuity

The preceding discussion involved the discounting of only a single future amount. Businesses and individuals frequently engage in transactions in which a series of equal dollar amounts are to be received or paid at evenly spaced time intervals (periodically). Examples of a series of periodic receipts or payments are loan agreements, installment sales, mortgage notes, lease (rental) contracts, and pension obligations. As discussed earlier, these periodic receipts or payments are **annuities**.

The **present value of an annuity** is the value now of a series of future receipts or payments, discounted assuming compound interest. In computing the present value of an annuity, it is necessary to know (1) the discount rate, (2) the number of payments (receipts), and (3) the amount of the periodic receipts or payments. To illustrate the computation of the present value of an annuity, assume that you will receive $1,000 cash annually for three years at a time when the discount rate is 10%. This situation is depicted in the time diagram in **Illustration G.14**. **Illustration G.15** shows the computation of its present value in this situation.

ILLUSTRATION G.14
Time diagram for a three-year annuity

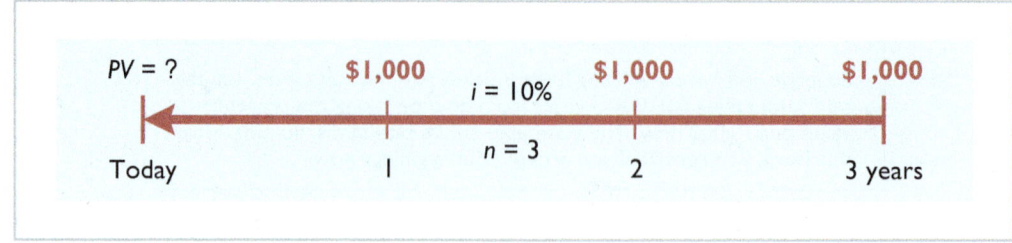

ILLUSTRATION G.15
Present value of a series of future amounts computation

Future Amount	×	Present Value of 1 Factor at 10%	=	Present Value
$1,000 (1 year away)		.90909		$ 909.09
1,000 (2 years away)		.82645		826.45
1,000 (3 years away)		.75132		751.32
		2.48686		$2,486.86

This method of calculation is required when the periodic cash flows are not uniform in each period. However, when the future receipts are the same in each period, an annuity table can be used. As illustrated in **Table 4**, an annuity table shows the present value of 1 to be received periodically for a given number of payments. It assumes that each payment is made at the end of each period.

TABLE 4 Present Value of an Annuity of 1

(n) Payments	4%	5%	6%	7%	8%	9%	10%	11%	12%	15%
1	.96154	.95238	.94340	.93458	.92593	.91743	.90909	.90090	.89286	.86957
2	1.88609	1.85941	1.83339	1.80802	1.78326	1.75911	1.73554	1.71252	1.69005	1.62571
3	2.77509	2.72325	2.67301	2.62432	2.57710	2.53130	2.48685	2.44371	2.40183	2.28323
4	3.62990	3.54595	3.46511	3.38721	3.31213	3.23972	3.16986	3.10245	3.03735	2.85498
5	4.45182	4.32948	4.21236	4.10020	3.99271	3.88965	3.79079	3.69590	3.60478	3.35216
6	5.24214	5.07569	4.91732	4.76654	4.62288	4.48592	4.35526	4.23054	4.11141	3.78448
7	6.00205	5.78637	5.58238	5.38929	5.20637	5.03295	4.86842	4.71220	4.56376	4.16042
8	6.73274	6.46321	6.20979	5.97130	5.74664	5.53482	5.33493	5.14612	4.96764	4.48732
9	7.43533	7.10782	6.80169	6.51523	6.24689	5.99525	5.75902	5.53705	5.32825	4.77158
10	8.11090	7.72173	7.36009	7.02358	6.71008	6.41766	6.14457	5.88923	5.65022	5.01877
11	8.76048	8.30641	7.88687	7.49867	7.13896	6.80519	6.49506	6.20652	5.93770	5.23371
12	9.38507	8.86325	8.38384	7.94269	7.53608	7.16073	6.81369	6.49236	6.19437	5.42062
13	9.98565	9.39357	8.85268	8.35765	7.90378	7.48690	7.10336	6.74987	6.42355	5.58315
14	10.56312	9.89864	9.29498	8.74547	8.24424	7.78615	7.36669	6.98187	6.62817	5.72448
15	11.11839	10.37966	9.71225	9.10791	8.55948	8.06069	7.60608	7.19087	6.81086	5.84737
16	11.65230	10.83777	10.10590	9.44665	8.85137	8.31256	7.82371	7.37916	6.97399	5.95424
17	12.16567	11.27407	10.47726	9.76322	9.12164	8.54363	8.02155	7.54879	7.11963	6.04716
18	12.65930	11.68959	10.82760	10.05909	9.37189	8.75563	8.20141	7.70162	7.24967	6.12797
19	13.13394	12.08532	11.15812	10.33560	9.60360	8.95012	8.36492	7.83929	7.36578	6.19823
20	13.59033	12.46221	11.46992	10.59401	9.81815	9.12855	8.51356	7.96333	7.46944	6.25933

Table 4 shows that the present value of an annuity of 1 factor for three payments at 10% is 2.48685.[1] This present value factor is the total of the three individual present value factors, as shown in Illustration G.15. Applying this amount to the annual cash flow of $1,000 produces a present value of $2,486.85.

The following demonstration problem (**Illustration G.16**) illustrates how to use Table 4.

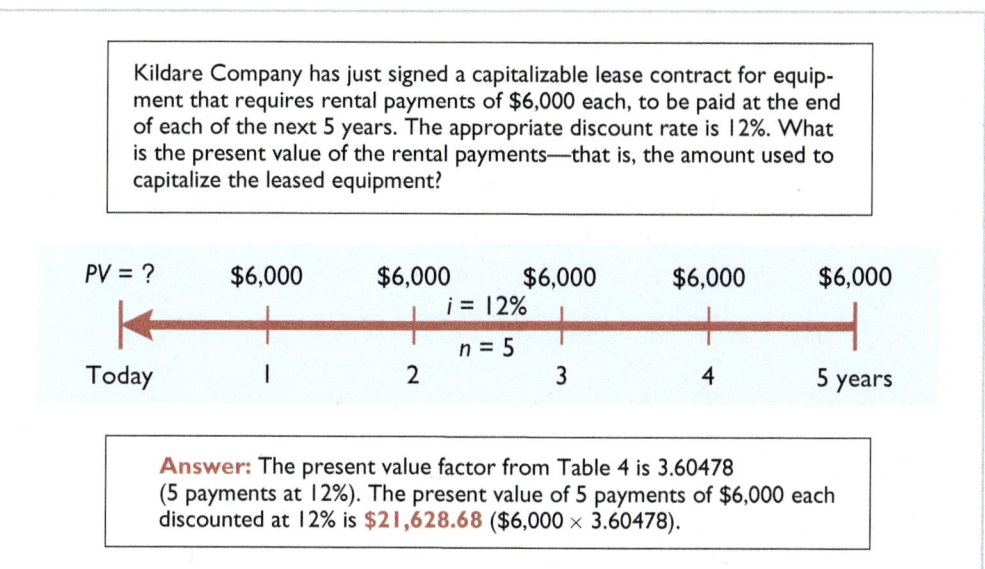

ILLUSTRATION G.16

Demonstration problem—Using Table 4 for *PV* of an annuity of 1

Time Periods and Discounting

In the preceding calculations, the discounting was done on an annual basis using an annual interest rate. Discounting may also be done over shorter periods of time such as monthly, quarterly, or semiannually.

When the time frame is less than one year, it is necessary to convert the annual interest rate to the applicable time frame. Assume, for example, that the investor in Illustration G.14 received $500 **semiannually** for three years instead of $1,000 annually. In this case, the number of periods becomes six (3 × 2), the discount rate is 5% (10% ÷ 2), the present value factor from Table 4 is 5.07569 (6 periods at 5%), and the present value of the future cash flows is $2,537.85 (5.07569 × $500). This amount is slightly higher than the $2,486.86 computed in Illustration G.15 because interest is computed twice during the same year. That is, during the second half of the year, interest is earned on the first half-year's interest. Each period's $1,000 is received and earns interest six months sooner.

Present Value of a Long-Term Note or Bond

The present value (or market price) of a long-term note or bond is a function of three variables: (1) the payment amounts, (2) the length of time until the amounts are paid, and (3) the discount rate. Our example uses a five-year bond issue.

The first variable (dollars to be paid) is made up of two elements: (1) a series of interest payments (an annuity) and (2) the principal amount (a single sum). To compute the present

---

[1]The difference of .00001 between 2.48686 and 2.48685 is due to rounding.

value of the bond, both the interest payments and the principal amount must be discounted—two different computations. The time diagrams for a bond due in five years are shown in **Illustration G.17**.

ILLUSTRATION G.17 Time diagrams for the present value of a bond

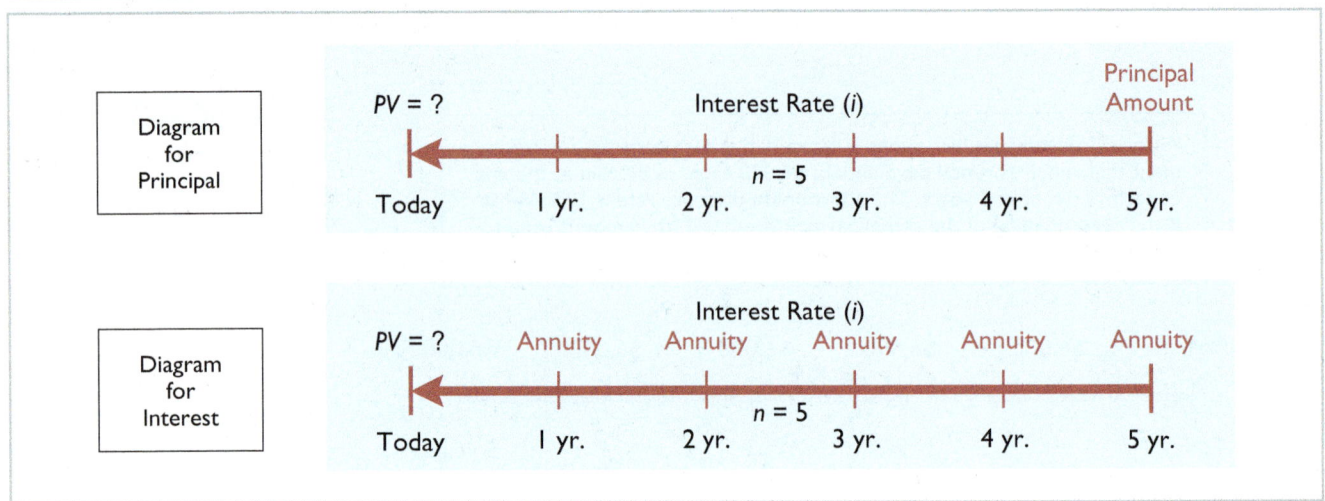

When the investor's market interest rate is equal to the bond's contractual interest rate, the present value of the bonds will equal the face value of the bonds. To illustrate, assume a bond issue of 5%, 10-year bonds with a face value of $100,000 with interest payable **annually** on January 1. If the discount rate is the same as the contractual rate, the bonds will sell at face value. In this case, the investor will receive (1) $100,000 at maturity and (2) a series of ten $5,000 interest payments ($100,000 × 5%) over the term of the bonds. The length of time is expressed in terms of interest periods—in this case—10, and the discount rate per interest period, 5%. The time diagram in **Illustration G.18** depicts the variables involved in this discounting situation.

ILLUSTRATION G.18 Time diagram for present value of a 5%, 10-year bond paying interest annually

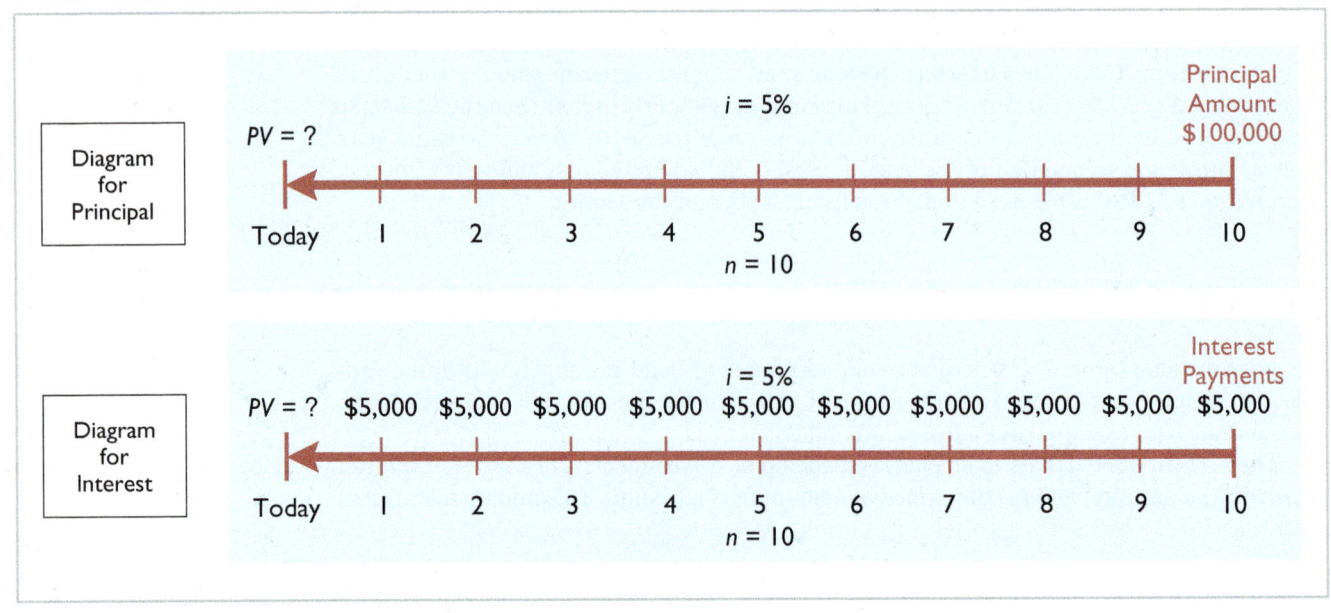

Illustration G.19 shows the computation of the present value of these bonds.

5% Contractual Rate—5% Discount Rate

Present value of principal to be received at maturity	
$100,000 × PV of 1 due in 10 periods at 5%	
$100,000 × .61391 (Table 3)	$ 61,391
Present value of interest to be received periodically over the term of the bonds	
$5,000 × PV of 1 due periodically for 10 periods at 5%	
$5,000 × 7.72173 (Table 4)	38,609*
Present value of bonds	**$100,000**

*Rounded

ILLUSTRATION G.19
Present value of principal and interest—face value

Now assume that the investor's required rate of return is 6%, not 5%. The future amounts are again $100,000 and $5,000, respectively, but now a discount rate of 6% must be used. The present value of the bonds is $92,639, as computed in Illustration G.20.

5% Contractual Rate—6% Discount Rate

Present value of principal to be received at maturity	
$100,000 × .55839 (Table 3)	$55,839
Present value of interest to be received periodically over the term of the bonds	
$5,000 × 7.36009 (Table 4)	36,800
Present value of bonds	**$92,639**

ILLUSTRATION G.20
Present value of principal and interest—discount

Conversely, if the discount rate is 4% and the contractual rate is 5%, the present value of the bonds is $108,111, computed as shown in Illustration G.21.

5% Contractual Rate—4% Discount Rate

Present value of principal to be received at maturity	
$100,000 × .67556 (Table 3)	$ 67,556
Present value of interest to be received periodically over the term of the bonds	
$5,000 × 8.11090 (Table 4)	40,555*
Present value of bonds	**$108,111**

*Rounded

ILLUSTRATION G.21
Present value of principal and interest—premium

The above discussion relied on present value tables in solving present value problems. Calculators may also be used to compute present values without the use of these tables. Many calculators, especially financial calculators, have present value (*PV*) functions that allow you to calculate present values by merely inputting the proper amount, discount rate, periods, and pressing the PV key. We discuss the use of financial calculators in a later section.

Capital Budgeting Situations

LEARNING OBJECTIVE 3
Compute the present value in capital budgeting situations.

The decision to make long-term capital investments is best evaluated using discounting techniques that recognize the time value of money. To do this, many companies calculate the present value of the cash flows involved in a capital investment.

To illustrate, Nagel-Siebert Trucking Company, a cross-country freight carrier in Montgomery, Illinois, is considering adding another truck to its fleet because of a purchasing opportunity. **Navistar Inc.**, Nagel-Siebert's primary supplier of overland rigs, is overstocked and offers to sell its biggest rig for $154,000 cash payable upon delivery. Nagel-Siebert knows that the rig will produce a net cash flow per year of $40,000 for five years (received at the end of each year), at which time it will be sold for an estimated salvage value of $35,000. Nagel-Siebert's discount rate in evaluating capital expenditures is 10%. Should Nagel-Siebert commit to the purchase of this rig?

The cash flows that must be discounted to present value by Nagel-Siebert are as follows.

Cash payable on delivery (today): $154,000.

Net cash flow from operating the rig: $40,000 for 5 years (at the end of each year).

Cash received from sale of rig at the end of 5 years: $35,000.

The time diagrams for the latter two cash flows are shown in **Illustration G.22**.

ILLUSTRATION G.22 Time diagrams for Nagel-Siebert Trucking Company

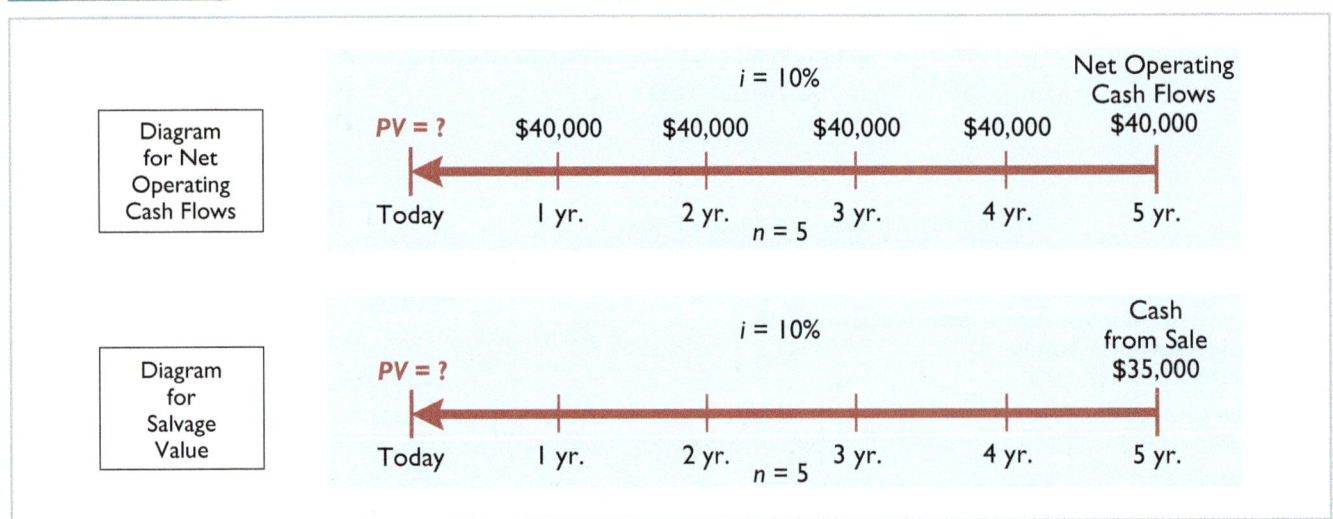

Notice from the diagrams that computing the present value of the net operating cash flows ($40,000 at the end of each year) is **discounting an annuity** (Table 4), while computing the present value of the $35,000 salvage value is **discounting a single sum** (Table 3). The computation of these present values is shown in **Illustration G.23**.

ILLUSTRATION G.23

Present value computations at 10%

Present Values Using a 10% Discount Rate

Present value of net operating cash flows received annually over 5 years
$40,000 × PV of 1 received annually for 5 years at 10%
$40,000 × 3.79079 $151,631.60

Present value of salvage value (cash) to be received in 5 years
$35,000 × PV of 1 received in 5 years at 10%
$35,000 × .62092   21,732.20

Present value of cash **inflows**   173,363.80

Present value of cash **outflows** (purchase price due today at 10%)
$154,000 × PV of 1 due today
$154,000 × 1.00000   (154,000.00)

Net present value   **$ 19,363.80**

Because the present value of the cash receipts (inflows) of $173,363.80 ($151,631.60 + $21,732.20) exceeds the present value of the cash payments (outflows) of $154,000.00, the net present value of $19,363.80 is positive, and **the decision to invest should be accepted**.

Now assume that Nagel-Siebert uses a discount rate of 15%, not 10%, because it wants a greater return on its investments in capital assets. The cash receipts and cash payments by Nagel-Siebert are the same. The present values of these receipts and cash payments discounted at 15% are shown in **Illustration G.24**.

ILLUSTRATION G.24

Present value computations at 15%

Present Values Using a 15% Discount Rate

Present value of net operating cash flows received annually
over 5 years at 15%
$40,000 × 3.35216 $134,086.40

Present value of salvage value (cash) to be received in 5 years at 15%
$35,000 × .49718   17,401.30

Present value of cash **inflows** $151,487.70

Present value of cash **outflows** (purchase price due today at 15%)
$154,000 × 1.00000   (154,000.00)

Net present value   **$ (2,512.30)**

Because the present value of the cash payments (outflows) of $154,000.00 exceeds the present value of the cash receipts (inflows) of $151,487.70 ($134,086.40 + $17,401.30), the net present value of $2,512.30 is negative, and **the investment should be rejected**.

The above discussion relied on present value tables in solving present value problems. As we show in the next section, calculators may also be used to compute present values without the use of these tables. Financial calculators have present value (PV) functions that allow you to calculate present values by merely identifying the proper amount, discount rate, periods, and pressing the PV key.

Using Financial Calculators

LEARNING OBJECTIVE 4
Use a financial calculator to solve time value of money problems.

Business professionals, once they have mastered the underlying time value of money concepts, often use a financial calculator to solve these types of problems. To use financial calculators, you enter the time value of money variables into the calculator. **Illustration G.25** shows the five most common keys used to solve time value of money problems.[2]

ILLUSTRATION G.25

Financial calculator keys

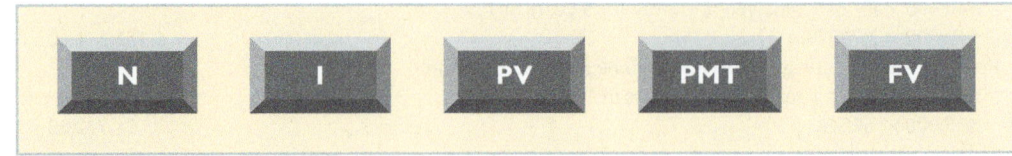

where:

- N = number of periods
- I = interest rate per period (some calculators use I/YR or i)
- PV = present value (occurs at the beginning of the first period)
- PMT = payment (all payments are equal, and none are skipped)
- FV = future value (occurs at the end of the last period)

In solving time value of money problems in this appendix, you will generally be given three of four variables and will have to solve for the remaining variable. The fifth key (the key not used) is given a value of zero to ensure that this variable is not used in the computation.

Present Value of a Single Sum

To illustrate how to solve a present value problem using a financial calculator, assume that you want to know the present value of $84,253 to be received in five years, discounted at 11% compounded annually. **Illustration G.26** depicts this problem.

ILLUSTRATION G.26

Calculator solution for present value of a single sum

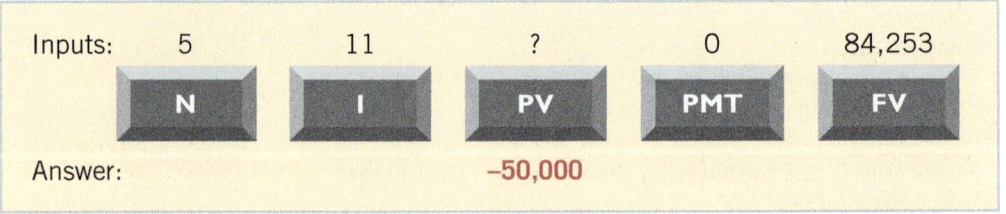

Illustration G.26 shows you the information (inputs) to enter into the calculator: N = 5, I = 11, PMT = 0, and FV = 84,253. You then press PV for the answer: −$50,000. As indicated, the PMT key was given a value of zero because a series of payments did not occur in this problem.

Plus and Minus

The use of plus and minus signs in time value of money problems with a financial calculator can be confusing. Most financial calculators are programmed so that the positive and negative cash flows in any problem offset each other. In the present value problem above, we identified the $84,253 future value initial investment as a positive (inflow); the answer −$50,000 was shown as a negative amount, reflecting a cash outflow. If the 84,253 were entered as a negative, then the final answer would have been reported as a positive 50,000.

Hopefully, the sign convention will not cause confusion. If you understand what is required in a problem, you should be able to interpret a positive or negative amount in determining the solution to a problem.

Compounding Periods

In the problem above, we assumed that compounding occurs once a year. Some financial calculators have a default setting, which assumes that compounding occurs 12 times a year. You must determine what default period has been programmed into your calculator and change it as necessary to arrive at the proper compounding period.

---

[2]On many calculators, these keys are actual buttons on the face of the calculator; on others, they appear on the display after the user accesses a present value menu.

Rounding

Most financial calculators store and calculate using 12 decimal places. As a result, because compound interest tables generally have factors only up to five decimal places, a slight difference in the final answer can result. In most time value of money problems, the final answer will not include more than two decimal places.

Present Value of an Annuity

To illustrate how to solve a present value of an annuity problem using a financial calculator, assume that you are asked to determine the present value of rental receipts of $6,000 each to be received at the end of each of the next five years, when discounted at 12%, as pictured in Illustration G.27.

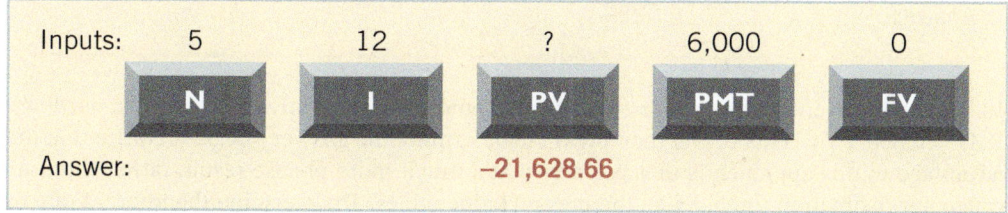

ILLUSTRATION G.27
Calculator solution for present value of an annuity

In this case, you enter N = 5, I = 12, PMT = 6,000, FV = 0, and then press PV to arrive at the answer of −$21,628.66.

Future Value of a Single Sum

Now let us look at an investment to illustrate how to solve a future value problem using a financial calculator. Assume that you will invest $20,000 today into a fund and you intend to leave it there for 15 years. The fund earns 7% interest. Illustration G.28 shows how to compute the future value of the fund at the end of year 15.

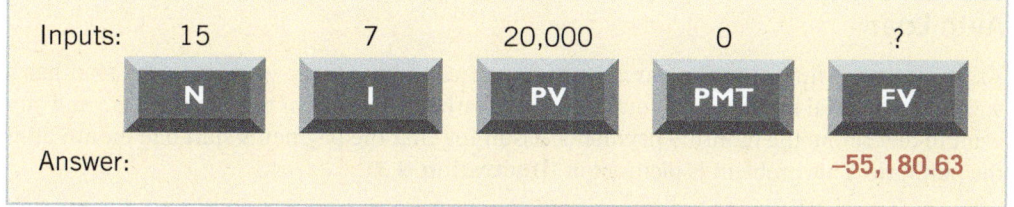

ILLUSTRATION G.28
Calculator solution for future value of single sum

In this case, you enter N = 15, I = 7, PV = 20,000, PMT = 0, and then press FV to calculate the future value of −$55,180.63.

Future Value of an Annuity

You can use a financial calculator to solve a future value of an annuity problem for an annuity investment. Assume that you will invest $8,000 into a fund at the end of each of the next eight years. The fund earns 9% interest. Illustration G.29 shows how to compute the future value of the fund at the end of the eighth year.

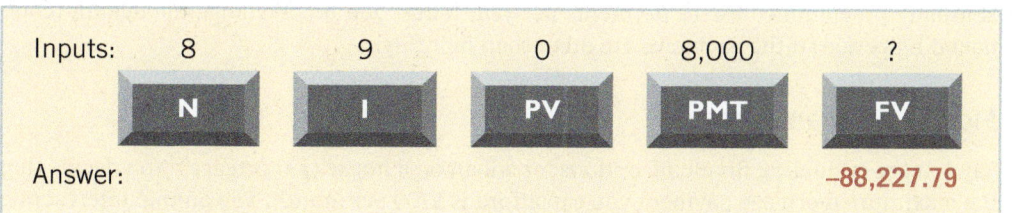

ILLUSTRATION G.29
Calculator solution for future value of an annuity

In this case, you enter N = 8, I = 9, PV = 0, PMT = 8,000, and then press FV to determine the future value of −$88,227.79.

Internal Rate of Return

You can also use these same calculator keys to compute the internal rate of return of an investment that has equal cash flows. Suppose that a purchase of a piece of equipment with a seven-year life requires an initial investment of $54,000, has positive cash flows of $7,800 per year, and has an estimated salvage value of $11,000. The computation is shown in **Illustration G.30**.

ILLUSTRATION G.30
Calculator solution for internal rate of return

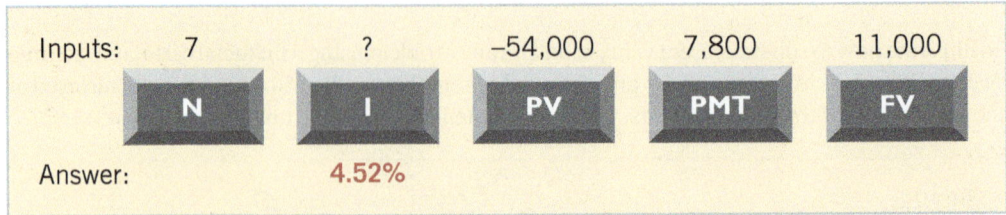

In this case, you enter N = 7, PV = −54,000 (we entered as a negative, since it is an outflow), PMT = 7,800, FV = 11,000, and then press I to determine the answer of 4.52%. Notice that the advantage to this approach is that you arrive at a much more precise result, rather than the rough approximation provided by the present value tables. To determine the internal rate of return using your calculator for an investment with unequal cash flows, you need to employ the cash flow key (CF) and the internal rate of return key (IRR). The use of these function keys varies across calculators, so you should consult the user manual for your calculator or the manufacturer's website for specific information.

Useful Applications of the Financial Calculator

With a financial calculator, you can solve for any interest rate or for any number of periods in a time value of money problem. Here are some examples of these applications.

Auto Loan

Assume you are financing the purchase of a used car with a three-year loan. The loan has a 9.5% stated annual interest rate, compounded monthly. The price of the car is $6,000, and you want to determine the monthly payments, assuming that the payments start one month after the purchase. This problem is pictured in **Illustration G.31**.

ILLUSTRATION G.31
Calculator solution for auto loan payments

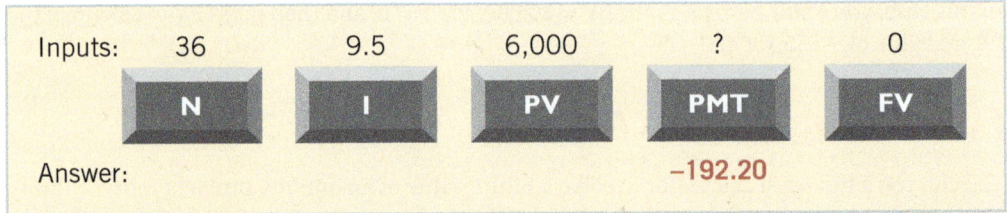

To solve this problem, you enter N = 36 (12 × 3), I = 9.5, PV = 6,000, FV = 0, and then press PMT. You will find that the monthly payments will be $192.20. Note that the payment key is usually programmed for 12 payments per year. Thus, you must change the default (compounding period) if the payments are other than monthly.

Mortgage Loan Amount

Say you are evaluating financing options for a loan on a house (a mortgage). You decide that the maximum mortgage payment you can afford is $700 per month. The annual interest rate is 8.4%. If you get a mortgage that requires you to make monthly payments over a 15-year period, what is the maximum home loan you can afford? **Illustration G.32** depicts this problem.

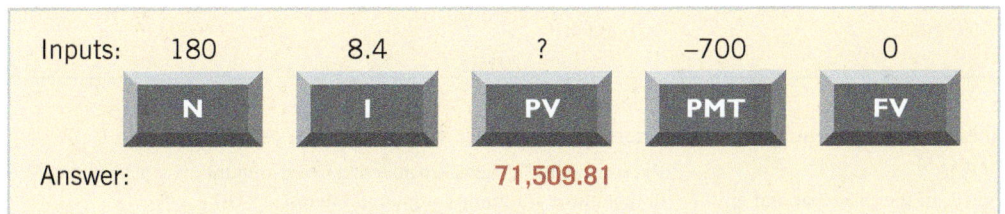

ILLUSTRATION G.32
Calculator solution for mortgage amount

You enter N = 180 (12 × 15 years), I = 8.4, PMT = −700, FV = 0, and then press PV. With the payments-per-year key set at 12, you find a present value of $71,509.81—the maximum home loan you can afford, given that you want to keep your mortgage payments at $700. Note that by changing any of the variables, you can quickly conduct "what-if" analyses for different situations.

Review

Learning Objectives Review

1 Compute interest and future values.

Simple interest is computed on the principal only, while compound interest is computed on the principal and any interest earned that has not been withdrawn.

To solve for future value of a single amount, prepare a time diagram of the problem. Identify the principal amount, the number of compounding periods, and the interest rate. Using the future value of 1 table, multiply the principal amount by the future value factor specified at the intersection of the number of periods and the interest rate.

To solve for future value of an annuity, prepare a time diagram of the problem. Identify the amount of the periodic payments (receipts), the number of payments (receipts), and the interest rate. Using the future value of an annuity of 1 table, multiply the amount of the payments by the future value factor specified at the intersection of the number of periods and the interest rate.

2 Compute present values.

The following three variables are fundamental to solving present value problems: (1) the future amount, (2) the number of periods, and (3) the interest rate (the discount rate).

To solve for present value of a single amount, prepare a time diagram of the problem. Identify the future amount, the number of discounting periods, and the discount (interest) rate. Using the present value of a single amount table, multiply the future amount by the present value factor specified at the intersection of the number of periods and the discount rate.

To solve for present value of an annuity, prepare a time diagram of the problem. Identify the amount of future periodic receipts or payments (annuities), the number of payments (receipts), and the discount (interest) rate. Using the present value of an annuity of 1 table, multiply the amount of the annuity by the present value factor specified at the intersection of the number of payments and the interest rate.

To compute the present value of notes and bonds, determine the present value of the principal amount and the present value of the interest payments. Multiply the principal amount (a single future amount) by the present value factor (from the present value of 1 table) intersecting at the number of periods (number of interest payments) and the discount rate. To determine the present value of the series of interest payments, multiply the amount of the interest payment by the present value factor (from the present value of an annuity of 1 table) intersecting at the number of periods (number of interest payments) and the discount rate. Add the present value of the principal amount to the present value of the interest payments to arrive at the present value of the note or bond.

3 Compute the present value in capital budgeting situations.

Compute the present values of all cash inflows and all cash outflows related to the capital budgeting proposal (an investment-type decision). If the **net** present value is positive, accept the proposal (make the investment). If the **net** present value is negative, reject the proposal (do not make the investment).

4 Use a financial calculator to solve time value of money problems.

Financial calculators can be used to solve the same and additional problems as those solved with time value of money tables. Enter into the financial calculator the amounts for all of the known elements of a time value of money problem (periods, interest rate, payments, future or present value), and it solves for the unknown element. Particularly useful situations involve interest rates and compounding periods not presented in the tables.

Glossary Review

Annuity A series of equal dollar amounts to be paid or received at evenly spaced time intervals (periodically). (p. G-5).

Compound interest The interest computed on the principal and any interest earned that has not been paid or withdrawn. (p. G-2).

Discounting the future amount(s) The process of determining present value. (p. G-7).

Future value of an annuity The sum of all the payments (receipts) plus the accumulated compound interest on them. (p. G-5).

Future value of a single amount The value at a future date of a given amount invested, assuming compound interest. (p. G-3).

Interest Payment for the use of another person's money. (p. G-2).

Present value The value now of a given amount to be paid or received in the future, assuming compound interest. (p. G-7).

Present value of an annuity The value now of a series of future receipts or payments, discounted assuming compound interest. (p. G-9).

Principal The amount borrowed or invested. (p. G-2).

Simple interest The interest computed on the principal only. (p. G-2).

WileyPLUS

Many additional resources are available for practice in WileyPLUS.

Brief Exercises

(Use tables to solve exercises BEG.1 to BEG.23.)

Compute the future value of a single amount.

BEG.1 (LO 1) Jozy Altidore invested $6,000 at 5% annual interest, and left the money invested without withdrawing any of the interest for 12 years. At the end of the 12 years, Jozy withdrew the accumulated amount of money. (a) What amount did Jozy withdraw, assuming the investment earns simple interest? (b) What amount did Jozy withdraw, assuming the investment earns interest compounded annually?

Use future value tables.

BEG.2 (LO 1) For each of the following cases, indicate (a) what interest rate columns and (b) what number of periods you would refer to in looking up the future value factor.

1. In Table 1 (future value of 1):

	Annual Rate	Number of Years Invested	Compounded
Case A	5%	3	Annually
Case B	12%	4	Semiannually

2. In Table 2 (future value of an annuity of 1):

	Annual Rate	Number of Years Invested	Compounded
Case A	3%	8	Annually
Case B	8%	6	Semiannually

Compute the future value of a single amount.

BEG.3 (LO 1) Liam Company signed a lease for an office building for a period of 12 years. Under the lease agreement, a security deposit of $9,600 is made. The deposit will be returned at the expiration of the lease with interest compounded at 4% per year. What amount will Liam receive at the time the lease expires?

Compute the future value of an annuity.

BEG.4 (LO 1) Bates Company issued $1,000,000, 10-year bonds. It agreed to make annual deposits of $78,000 to a fund (called a sinking fund), which will be used to pay off the principal amount of the bond at the end of 10 years. The deposits are made at the end of each year into an account paying 6% annual interest. What amount will be in the sinking fund at the end of 10 years?

Compute the future value of a single amount and of an annuity.

BEG.5 (LO 1) Andrew and Emma Garfield invested $8,000 in a savings account paying 5% annual interest when their daughter, Angela, was born. They also deposited $1,000 on each of her birthdays until she was 18 (including her 18th birthday). How much was in the savings account on her 18th birthday (after the last deposit)?

BEG.6 (LO 1) Hugh Curtin borrowed $35,000 on July 1, 2022. This amount plus accrued interest at 8% compounded annually is to be repaid on July 1, 2027. How much will Hugh have to repay on July 1, 2027?

Compute the future value of a single amount.

BEG.7 (LO 2) For each of the following cases, indicate (a) what interest rate columns and (b) what number of periods you would refer to in looking up the discount rate.

Use present value tables.

1. In Table 3 (future value of 1):

	Annual Rate	Number of Years Invested	Discounts Per Year
Case A	12%	7	Annually
Case B	8%	11	Semiannually
Case C	10%	8	Semiannually

2. In Table 2 (future value of an annuity of 1):

	Annual Rate	Number of Years Involved	Number of Payments Involved	Frequency of Payments
Case A	10%	20	20	Annually
Case B	10%	7	7	Annually
Case C	6%	5	10	Semiannually

BEG.8 (LO 2) **a.** What is the present value of $25,000 due 9 periods from now, discounted at 10%?

Determine present values.

b. What is the present value of $25,000 to be received at the end of each of 6 periods, discounted at 9%?

BEG.9 (LO 2) Messi Company is considering an investment that will return a lump sum of $900,000 6 years from now. What amount should Messi Company pay for this investment to earn an 8% return?

Compute the present value of a single amount investment.

BEG.10 (LO 2) Lloyd Company earns 6% on an investment that will return $450,000 8 years from now. What is the amount Lloyd should invest now to earn this rate of return?

Compute the present value of a single amount investment.

BEG.11 (LO 2) Robben Company is considering investing in an annuity contract that will return $40,000 annually at the end of each year for 15 years. What amount should Robben Company pay for this investment if it earns an 8% return?

Compute the present value of an annuity investment.

BEG.12 (LO 2) Kaehler Enterprises earns 5% on an investment that pays back $80,000 at the end of each of the next 6 years. What is the amount Kaehler Enterprises invested to earn the 5% rate of return?

Compute the present value of an annual investment.

BEG.13 (LO 2) Dempsey Railroad Co. is about to issue $400,000 of 10-year bonds paying an 11% interest rate, with interest payable annually. The discount rate for such securities is 10%. How much can Dempsey expect to receive for the sale of these bonds?

Compute the present value of bonds.

BEG.14 (LO 2) Assume the same information as BEG.13 except that the discount rate is 12% instead of 10%. In this case, how much can Dempsey expect to receive from the sale of these bonds?

Compute the present value of bonds.

BEG.15 (LO 2) Neymar Taco Company receives a $75,000, 6-year note bearing interest of 4% (paid annually) from a customer at a time when the discount rate is 6%. What is the present value of the note received by Neymar?

Compute the present value of a note.

BEG.16 (LO 2) Gleason Enterprises issued 6%, 8-year, $2,500,000 par value bonds that pay interest annually on April 1. The bonds are dated April 1, 2022, and are issued on that date. The discount rate of interest for such bonds on April 1, 2022, is 8%. What cash proceeds did Gleason receive from issuance of the bonds?

Compute the present value of bonds.

BEG.17 (LO 2) Frazier Company issues a 10%, 5-year mortgage note on January 1, 2022, to obtain financing for new equipment. Land is used as collateral for the note. The terms provide for semiannual installment payments of $48,850. What are the cash proceeds received from the issuance of the note?

Compute the present value of a note.

BEG.18 (LO 2) If Colleen Mooney invests $4,765.50 now and she will receive $12,000 at the end of 12 years, what annual rate of interest will Colleen earn on her investment? (*Hint:* Use Table 3.)

Compute the interest rate on a single amount.

BEG.19 (LO 2) Tim Howard has been offered the opportunity of investing $36,125 now. The investment will earn 11% per year and at the end of that time will return Tim $75,000. How many years must Tim wait to receive $75,000? (*Hint:* Use Table 3.)

Compute the number of periods of a single amount.

BEG.20 (LO 2) Joanne Quick made an investment of $10,271.38. From this investment, she will receive $1,200 annually for the next 15 years starting one year from now. What rate of interest will Joanne's investment be earning for her? (*Hint:* Use Table 4.)

Compute the interest rate on an annuity.

Compute the number of periods of an annuity.

BEG.21 (LO 2) Kevin Morales invests $7,793.83 now for a series of $1,300 annual returns beginning one year from now. Kevin will earn a return of 9% on the initial investment. How many annual payments of $1,300 will Kevin receive? (*Hint:* Use Table 4.)

Compute the present value of a machine for purposes of making a purchase decision.

BEG.22 (LO 3) Barney Googal owns a garage and is contemplating purchasing a tire retreading machine for $12,820. After estimating costs and revenues, Barney projects a net cash inflow from the retreading machine of $2,700 annually for 7 years. Barney hopes to earn a return of 9% on such investments. What is the present value of the retreading operation? Should Barney Googal purchase the retreading machine?

Compute the maximum price to pay for a machine.

BEG.23 (LO 3) Snyder Company is considering purchasing equipment. The equipment will produce the following cash inflows: Year 1, $25,000; Year 2, $30,000; and Year 3, $40,000. Snyder requires a minimum rate of return of 11%. What is the maximum price Snyder should pay for this equipment?

Determine interest rate.

BEG.24 (LO 4) Carly Simon wishes to invest $18,000 on July 1, 2022, and have it accumulate to $50,000 by July 1, 2032. Use a financial calculator to determine at what exact annual rate of interest Carly must invest the $18,000.

Determine interest rate.

BEG.25 (LO 4) On July 17, 2021, Keith Urban borrowed $42,000 from his grandfather to open a clothing store. Starting July 17, 2022, Keith has to make 10 equal annual payments of $6,500 each to repay the loan. Use a financial calculator to determine what interest rate Keith is paying.

Determine interest rate.

BEG.26 (LO 4) As the purchaser of a new house, Carrie Underwood has signed a mortgage note to pay the Nashville National Bank and Trust Co. $8,400 every 6 months for 20 years, at the end of which time she will own the house. At the date the mortgage is signed, the purchase price was $198,000 and Underwood made a down payment of $20,000. The first payment will be made 6 months after the date the mortgage is signed. Using a financial calculator, compute the exact rate of interest earned on the mortgage by the bank.

Various time value of money situations.

BEG.27 (LO 4) Using a financial calculator, solve for the unknowns in each of the following situations.

a. On June 1, 2021, Jennifer Lawrence purchases lakefront property from her neighbor, Josh Hutcherson, and agrees to pay the purchase price in seven payments of $16,000 each, the first payment to be payable June 1, 2022. (Assume that interest compounded at an annual rate of 7.35% is implicit in the payments.) What is the purchase price of the property?

b. On January 1, 2021, Gerrard Corporation purchased 200 of the $1,000 face value, 8% coupon, 10-year bonds of Sterling Inc. The bonds mature on January 1, 2031, and pay interest annually beginning January 1, 2022. Gerrard purchased the bonds to yield 10.65%. How much did Gerrard pay for the bonds?

Various time value of money situations.

BEG.28 (LO 4) Using a financial calculator, provide a solution to each of the following situations.

a. Lynn Anglin owes a debt of $42,000 from the purchase of her new sport utility vehicle. The debt bears annual interest of 7.8% compounded monthly. Lynn wishes to pay the debt and interest in equal monthly payments over 8 years, beginning one month hence. What equal monthly payments will pay off the debt and interest?

b. On January 1, 2022, Roger Molony offers to buy Dave Feeney's used snowmobile for $8,000, payable in five equal annual installments, which are to include 7.25% interest on the unpaid balance and a portion of the principal. If the first payment is to be made on December 31, 2022, how much will each payment be?

Determine internal rate of return.

BEG.29 (LO 4) Renolds Corporation is considering two alternative investments in excavating equipment. Investment A requires an initial investment of $184,000, has positive cash flows of $27,500 per year, and has an estimated salvage value of $21,000. Investment B requires an initial investment of $234,000, has positive cash flows of $32,800 per year, and has an estimated salvage value of $19,000. Each piece of equipment is expected to have a 12-year useful life. Use a financial calculator to determine the internal rate of return of each project to decide which is more desirable. (Round to two decimal places, e.g., 9.74%.)

Appendix H

Reporting and Analyzing Investments

Appendix Preview

Some companies believe in aggressive growth through investing in the stock of existing companies. Besides purchasing stock, companies also purchase other securities such as bonds issued by corporations or by governments. Companies can make investments for a short or long period of time, as a passive investment, or with the intent to control another company. As you will see in this appendix, the way in which a company accounts for its investments is determined by a number of factors.

Appendix Outline

LEARNING OBJECTIVES

1.	Explain how to account for debt investments.	• Why corporations invest • Accounting for debt investments
2.	Explain how to account for stock investments.	• Holdings of less than 20% • Holdings between 20% and 50% • Holdings of more than 50%
3.	Discuss how debt and stock investments are reported in the financial statements.	• Debt securities • Equity securities • Balance sheet presentation • Presentation of realized and unrealized gain or loss

Accounting for Debt Investments

LEARNING OBJECTIVE 1
Explain how to account for debt investments.

Why Corporations Invest

Corporations purchase investments in debt or equity securities generally for one of three reasons. First, a corporation may **have excess cash** that it does not need for the immediate purchase of operating assets. For example, many companies experience seasonal fluctuations in sales. A Cape Cod marina has more sales in the spring and summer than in the fall and winter. The reverse is true for an Aspen ski shop. Thus, at the end of an operating cycle, many companies may have cash on hand that is temporarily idle until the start of another operating cycle. These companies may invest the excess funds to earn—through interest and dividends—a greater return than they would get by just holding the funds in the bank. **Illustration H.1** shows the role that such temporary investments play in the operating cycle.

ILLUSTRATION H.1
Temporary investments and the operating cycle

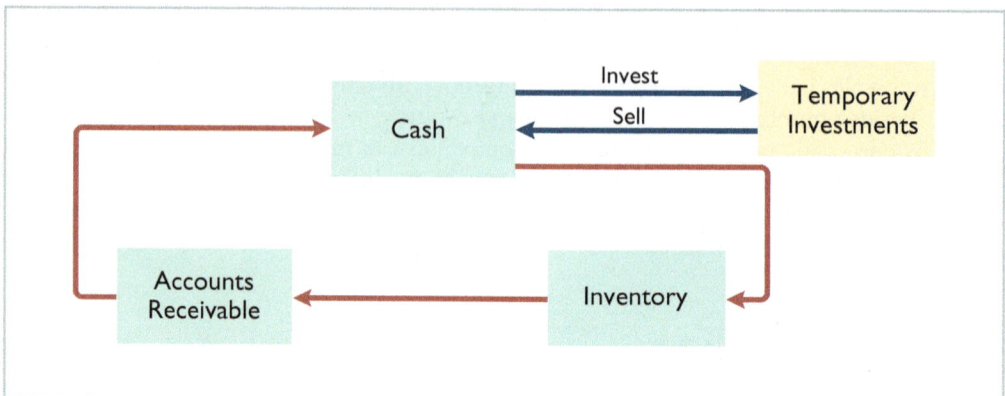

A second reason some companies such as banks purchase investments is to generate **earnings from investment income**. Although banks make most of their earnings by lending money, they also generate earnings by investing in primarily debt securities. Banks purchase investment securities because loan demand varies both seasonally and with changes in the economic climate. Thus, when loan demand is low, a bank must find other uses for its cash.

Some companies attempt to generate investment income through speculative investments. That is, they are speculating that the investment will increase in value and thus result in positive returns. Therefore, they invest mostly in the common stock of other corporations.

Third, companies also invest for **strategic reasons**. A company may purchase a non-controlling interest in another company in a related industry in which it wishes to establish a presence. Or, a company can exercise some influence over one of its customers or suppliers by purchasing a significant, but not controlling, interest in that company. Another option is for a corporation to purchase a controlling interest in another company in order to enter a new industry without incurring the costs and risks associated with starting from scratch.

In summary, businesses invest in other companies for the reasons shown in **Illustration H.2**.

ILLUSTRATION H.2
Why corporations invest

Reason	Typical Investment
To house excess cash until needed	Low-risk, highly liquid, short-term securities such as government-issued securities
To generate earnings	Banks and financial institutions often purchase debt securities, while mutual funds and index funds purchase both debt and stock securities
To meet strategic goals	Stocks of companies in a related industry or in an unrelated industry that the company wishes to enter

Accounting for Debt Investments

Debt investments are investments in government and corporation bonds. In accounting for debt investments, companies must make entries to record (1) the acquisition, (2) the interest revenue, and (3) the sale.

Recording Acquisition of Bonds

At acquisition, debt investments are recorded at cost. Cost includes all expenditures necessary to acquire these investments, such as the price paid plus brokerage fees (commissions), if any.

For example, assume that Kuhl Corporation acquires 50 Doan Inc. 8%, 10-year, $1,000 bonds on January 1, 2022, at a cost of $50,000. Kuhl records the investment as:

Jan. 1	Debt Investments		50,000	
	Cash			50,000
	(To record purchase of 50 Doan Inc. bonds)			

Recording Bond Interest

The Doan Inc. bonds pay interest of $4,000 annually on January 1 ($50,000 × 8%). If Kuhl Corporation's fiscal year ends on December 31, it accrues the interest of $4,000 earned since January 1. The adjusting entry is:

Dec. 31	Interest Receivable		4,000	
	Interest Revenue			4,000
	(To accrue interest on Doan Inc. bonds)			

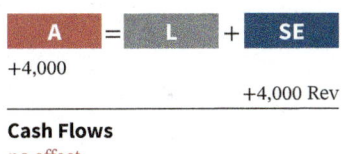

Kuhl reports Interest Receivable as a current asset in the balance sheet. It reports Interest Revenue under "Other revenues and gains" in the income statement.

Kuhl records receipt of the interest on January 1 as follows.

Jan. 1	Cash		4,000	
	Interest Receivable			4,000
	(To record receipt of accrued interest)			

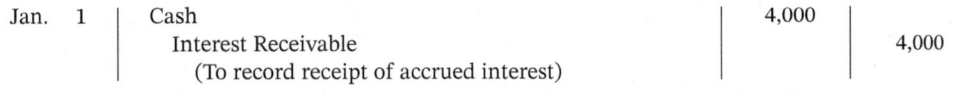

A credit to Interest Revenue at this time would be incorrect. Why? Because the company earned and accrued the interest revenue in the preceding accounting period.

Recording Sale of Bonds

When Kuhl Corporation sells the bond investments, it credits the investment account for the cost of the bonds. The company records as a gain or loss any difference between the net proceeds from the sale (sales price less brokerage fees) and the cost of the bonds (see **Helpful Hint**).

Assume, for example, that Kuhl receives net proceeds of $53,000 on the sale of the Doan Inc. bonds on January 1, 2023, after receiving the interest due. Since the securities cost $50,000, Kuhl has realized a gain of $3,000. It records the sale as follows.

Jan. 1	Cash		53,000	
	Debt Investments			50,000
	Gain on Sale of Debt Investments			3,000
	(To record sale of Doan Inc. bonds)			

HELPFUL HINT
The accounting for short-term debt investments and long-term debt investments is similar. Any exceptions are discussed in more advanced courses.

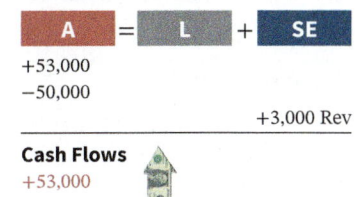

Kuhl reports the gain on the sale of debt investments under "Other revenues and gains" in the income statement and reports losses under "Other expenses and losses."

Accounting for Stock Investments

LEARNING OBJECTIVE 2
Explain how to account for stock investments.

Stock investments are investments in the capital stock of corporations. When a company holds stock (and/or debt) of several different corporations, the group of securities is an **investment portfolio**.

The accounting for investments in common stock depends on the extent of the investor's influence over the operating and financial affairs of the issuing corporation (the **investee**). Illustration H.3 shows the general guidelines.

ILLUSTRATION H.3
Accounting guidelines for stock investments

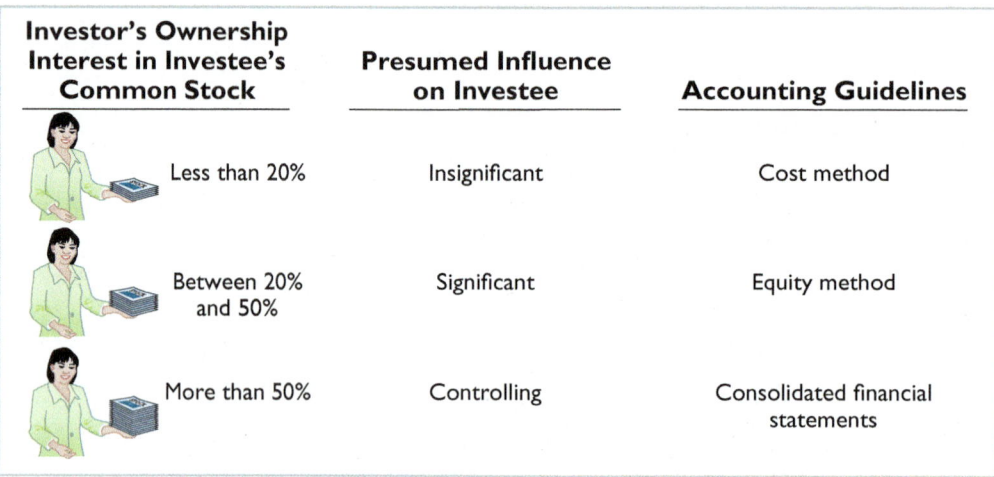

Companies are required to use judgment instead of blindly following the guidelines.[1] We explain and illustrate the application of each guideline next.

Holdings of Less Than 20%

In the accounting for stock investments of less than 20%, companies use the cost method. Under the **cost method**, companies record the investment at cost and recognize revenue only when cash dividends are received.

Recording Acquisition of Stock

At acquisition, stock investments are recorded at cost. Cost includes all expenditures necessary to acquire these investments, such as the price paid plus brokerage fees (commissions), if any.

Assume, for example, that on July 1, 2022, Sanchez Corporation acquires 1,000 shares (10% ownership) of Beal Corporation common stock at $40 per share. The entry for the purchase is:

A	=	L	+	SE
+40,000				
−40,000				

Cash Flows
−40,000

July 1	Stock Investments		40,000	
	Cash			40,000
	(To record purchase of 1,000 shares of			
	Beal common stock)			

---

[1]Among the factors that companies should consider in determining an investor's influence are whether (1) the investor has representation on the investee's board of directors, (2) the investor participates in the investee's policy-making process, (3) there are material transactions between the investor and the investee, and (4) the common stock held by other stockholders is concentrated or dispersed.

Recording Dividends

During the time the company holds the stock, it makes entries for any cash dividends received. Thus, if Sanchez Corporation receives a $2 per share dividend on December 31, the entry is:

Dec. 31	Cash (1,000 × $2)	2,000	
	Dividend Revenue		2,000
	(To record receipt of a cash dividend)		

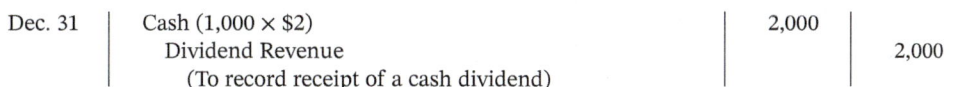

Sanchez reports Dividend Revenue under "Other revenues and gains" in the income statement.

Recording Sale of Stock

When a company sells a stock investment, it recognizes the difference between the net proceeds from the sale (sales price less brokerage fees) and the cost of the stock as a gain or a loss.

Assume, for instance, that Sanchez Corporation receives net proceeds of $39,500 on the sale of its Beal Corporation stock on February 10, 2023. Because the stock cost $40,000, Sanchez has incurred a loss of $500. It records the sale as:

Feb. 10	Cash	39,500	
	Loss on Sale of Stock Investments	500	
	Stock Investments		40,000
	(To record sale of Beal common stock)		

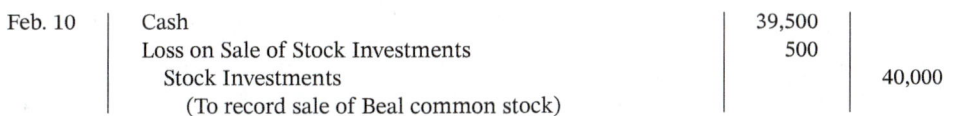
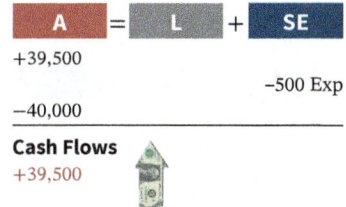

Sanchez reports the loss account under "Other expenses and losses" in the income statement and shows a gain on sale under "Other revenues and gains."

Holdings Between 20% and 50%

When an investor company owns only a small portion of the shares of stock of another company, the investor cannot exercise control over the investee. But when an investor owns between 20% and 50% of the common stock of a corporation, it is presumed that the investor has significant influence over the financial and operating activities of the investee. The investor probably has a representative on the investee's board of directors. Through that representative, the investor begins to exercise some control over the investee—and the investee company in some sense becomes part of the investor company.

For example, even prior to purchasing all of **Turner Broadcasting**, **Time Warner** owned 20% of Turner. Because it exercised significant control over major decisions made by Turner, Time Warner used an approach called the equity method. Under the **equity method, the investor records its share of the net income of the investee in the year when it is earned**. An alternative might be to delay recognizing the investor's share of net income until a cash dividend is declared. But that approach would ignore the fact that the investor and investee are, in some sense, one company, making the investor better off by the investee's net income.

Under the **equity method**, the company initially records the investment in common stock at cost. After that, it adjusts the investment account **annually** to show the investor's equity in the investee. Each year, the investor does the following. (1) It increases (debits) the investment account and increases (credits) revenue for its share of the investee's net income.[2] (2) The investor also decreases (credits) the investment account for the amount of dividends received. The investment account is reduced for dividends received because payment of a dividend decreases the net assets of the investee.

---

[2] Conversely, the investor increases (debits) a loss account and decreases (credits) the investment account for its share of the investee's net loss.

Recording Acquisition of Stock

Assume that Milar Corporation acquires 30% of the common stock of Beck Company for $120,000 on January 1, 2022. The entry to record this transaction is:

Jan. 1	Stock Investments	120,000	
	Cash		120,000
	(To record purchase of Beck common stock)		

Recording Revenue and Dividends

For 2022, Beck reports net income of $100,000. It declares and pays a $40,000 cash dividend. Milar must record (1) its share of Beck's income, $30,000 (30% × $100,000), and (2) the reduction in the investment account for the dividends received, $12,000 (30% × $40,000). The entries are:

(1)

Dec. 31	Stock Investments	30,000	
	Revenue from Stock Investments		30,000
	(To record 30% equity in Beck's 2022 net income)		

(2)

Dec. 31	Cash	12,000	
	Stock Investments		12,000
	(To record dividends received)		

After Milar posts the transactions for the year, the investment and revenue accounts are as shown in **Illustration H.4**.

ILLUSTRATION H.4
Investment and revenue accounts after posting

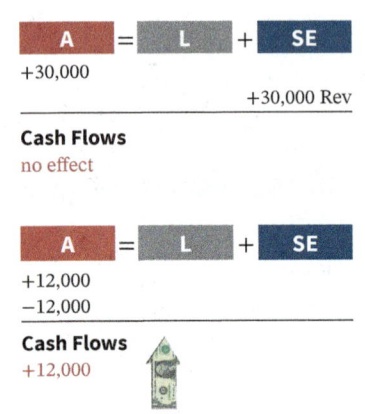

Stock Investments				Revenue from Stock Investments	
Jan. 1	120,000	Dec. 31	12,000	Dec. 31	30,000
Dec. 31	30,000				
Dec. 31 Bal.	138,000				

During the year, the investment account increased by $18,000. This $18,000 is explained as follows: (1) Milar records a $30,000 increase in revenue from its stock investment in Beck, and (2) Milar records a $12,000 decrease due to dividends received from its stock investment in Beck.

Note that the difference between reported revenue under the cost method and reported revenue under the equity method can be significant. For example, Milar would report only $12,000 of dividend revenue (30% × $40,000) if it used the cost method.

Holdings of More Than 50%

A company that owns more than 50% of the common stock of another entity is known as the **parent company**. The entity whose stock is owned by the parent company is called the **subsidiary (affiliated) company**. Because of its stock ownership, the parent company has a **controlling interest** in the subsidiary company.

When a company owns more than 50% of the common stock of another company, it usually prepares **consolidated financial statements**. Consolidated financial statements present the assets and liabilities of the parent and subsidiary companies. They also present the total revenues and expenses of the parent and subsidiary companies. Companies prepare consolidated statements **in addition to** the financial statements for the individual parent and subsidiary companies.

As noted earlier, prior to acquiring all of **Turner Broadcasting**, **Time Warner** accounted for its investment in Turner using the equity method. Time Warner's net investment in Turner was reported in a single line item—Other investments. After the merger, Time Warner instead consolidated Turner's results with its own. Under this approach, Time Warner included the individual assets and liabilities of Turner with its own assets. That is, Turner's plant and equipment were added to Time Warner's plant and equipment, its receivables were added to Time Warner's receivables, and so on. A similar sort of consolidation went on when **AOL** merged with Time Warner (see **Helpful Hint**).

Consolidated statements are useful to the stockholders, board of directors, and management of the parent company. Consolidated statements indicate to creditors, prospective investors, and regulatory agencies the magnitude and scope of operations of the companies under common control. For example, regulators and the courts undoubtedly used the consolidated statements of **AT&T** to determine whether a breakup of the company was in the public interest. **Illustration H.5** lists three companies that prepare consolidated statements and some of the companies they have owned.

> **HELPFUL HINT**
> If the parent (A) has three wholly owned subsidiaries (B, C, and D), there are four separate legal entities but only one economic entity from the viewpoint of the shareholders of the parent company.

PepsiCo	Cendant	The Walt Disney Company
Frito-Lay	Howard Johnson	Capital Cities/ABC, Inc.
Tropicana	Ramada Inn	Disneyland, Disney World
Quaker Oats	Century 21	Mighty Ducks
Pepsi-Cola	Coldwell Banker	Anaheim Angels
Gatorade	Avis	ESPN

ILLUSTRATION H.5
Examples of consolidated companies and their subsidiaries

Reporting Investments in Financial Statements

LEARNING OBJECTIVE 3
Discuss how debt and stock investments are reported in the financial statements.

The value of debt and stock investments may fluctuate greatly during the time they are held. For example, in a 12-month period, the stock of **Time Warner** hit a high of $58\frac{1}{2}$ and a low of 9. In light of such price fluctuations, how should companies value investments at the balance sheet date? Valuation could be at cost, at fair value, or at the lower-of-cost-or-market value.

Many people argue that fair value offers the best approach because it represents the expected cash realizable value of securities. **Fair value** is the amount for which a security could be sold in a normal market. Others counter that unless a security is going to be sold soon, the fair value is not relevant because the price of the security will likely change again.

Debt Securities

For purposes of valuation and reporting at a financial statement date, debt investments are classified into three categories:

1. **Trading securities** are bought and held primarily for sale in the near term to generate income on short-term price differences.
2. **Available-for-sale securities** are held with the intent of selling them sometime in the future.
3. **Held-to-maturity securities** are debt securities that the investor has the intent and ability to hold to maturity.[3]

---

[3]This category is provided for completeness. The accounting and valuation issues related to held-to-maturity securities are discussed in more advanced accounting courses.

Illustration H.6 shows the valuation guidelines for these debt securities.

ILLUSTRATION H.6 Valuation guidelines for debt securities

Trading Securities

Trading securities are held with the intention of selling them in a short period of time (generally less than three months and sometimes less than a full day). **Trading** means frequent buying and selling. As indicated in Illustration H.6, companies adjust trading securities to fair value at the end of each period (an approach referred to as **mark-to-market** accounting). They report changes from cost **as part of net income**. The changes are reported as **unrealized gains or losses** because the securities have not been sold. The unrealized gain or loss is the difference between the **total cost** of trading securities and their **total fair value**. Companies classify trading securities as a current asset.

As an example, **Illustration H.7** shows the costs and fair values for investments classified as trading securities for Pace Corporation on December 31, 2022. Pace has an unrealized gain of $7,000 because total fair value ($147,000) is $7,000 greater than total cost ($140,000).

ILLUSTRATION H.7 Valuation of trading securities

Trading Securities, December 31, 2022

Investments	Cost	Fair Value	Unrealized Gain (Loss)
Yorkville Company bonds	$ 50,000	$ 48,000	$(2,000)
Kodak Company bonds	90,000	99,000	9,000
Total	$140,000	$147,000	$ 7,000

HELPFUL HINT

Companies report an unrealized gain or loss in the income statement because of the likelihood that the securities will be sold at fair value since they are a short-term investment.

The fact that trading securities are a short-term investment increases the likelihood that Pace will sell them at fair value for a gain. Pace records fair value and the unrealized gain through an adjusting entry at the time it prepares financial statements (see **Helpful Hint**). In this entry, the company uses a valuation allowance account, Fair Value Adjustment—Trading, to record the difference between the total cost and the total fair value of the securities. The adjusting entry for Pace is:

Dec. 31	Fair Value Adjustment—Trading	7,000	
	Unrealized Gain or Loss—Income		7,000
	(To record unrealized gain on trading securities)		

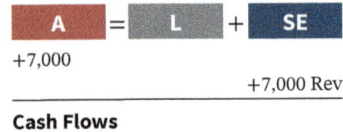

A = L + SE
+7,000
          +7,000 Rev

Cash Flows
no effect

The use of the Fair Value Adjustment—Trading account enables the company to maintain a record of the investment cost. Actual cost is needed to determine the gain or loss realized when the securities are sold. The company adds the debit balance (or subtracts a credit balance) of the Fair Value Adjustment—Trading account to the cost of the investments to arrive at a fair value for the trading securities.

The fair value of the securities is the amount companies report on the balance sheet. They report the unrealized gain on the income statement under "Other revenues and gains." The term **income** in the account title indicates that the gain affects net income.

If the total cost of the trading securities is greater than total fair value, an unrealized loss has occurred. In such a case, the adjusting entry is a debit to Unrealized Gain or Loss—Income and a credit to Fair Value Adjustment—Trading. Companies report the unrealized loss under "Other expenses and losses" in the income statement.

The Fair Value Adjustment—Trading account is carried forward into future accounting periods. No entries are made to this account during the period. At the end of each reporting period, a company adjusts the balance in the account to the difference between cost and fair value at that time. It closes the Unrealized Gain or Loss—Income account at the end of the reporting period.

Available-for-Sale Securities

As indicated earlier, available-for-sale securities are held with the intent of selling them sometime in the future. If the intent is to sell the securities within the next year or operating cycle, a company classifies the securities as current assets in the balance sheet. Otherwise, it classifies them as long-term assets in the investments section of the balance sheet.

Companies also report available-for-sale securities at fair value. The procedure for determining fair value and unrealized gain or loss for these securities is the same as that for trading securities. To illustrate, assume that Shelton Corporation has two securities that are classified as available-for-sale. **Illustration H.8** provides information on the cost, fair value, and amount of the unrealized gain or loss on December 31, 2022. There is an unrealized loss of $9,537 because total cost ($293,537) is $9,537 more than total fair value ($284,000).

ILLUSTRATION H.8
Valuation of available-for-sale securities

Available-for-Sale Securities, December 31, 2022

Investments	Cost	Fair Value	Unrealized Gain (Loss)
Campbell Soup Co. bonds	$ 93,537	$103,600	$10,063
Hershey Foods bonds	200,000	180,400	(19,600)
Total	$293,537	$284,000	$(9,537)

Both the adjusting entry and the reporting of the unrealized loss from Shelton's available-for-sale securities differ from those illustrated for trading securities. The differences result because these securities are not going to be sold in the near term. Thus, prior to actual sale it is much more likely that changes in fair value may reverse the unrealized loss. Therefore, Shelton does not report an unrealized loss in the income statement. Instead, the company reports it as an item of other comprehensive income in the comprehensive income statement, as discussed in Chapter 5. In the adjusting entry, Shelton identifies the fair value adjustment account with available-for-sale securities, and identifies the unrealized gain or loss account with stockholders' equity (see **Helpful Hint**). The adjusting entry for Shelton to record the unrealized loss of $9,537 is:

HELPFUL HINT
The entry is the same regardless of whether the securities are considered short-term or long-term.

Dec. 31	Unrealized Gain or Loss—Equity	9,537	
	Fair Value Adjustment—Available-for-Sale		9,537
	(To record unrealized loss on available-for-sale securities)		

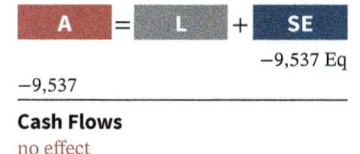

If total fair value exceeds total cost, Shelton would record the adjusting entry as an increase (debit) to Fair Value Adjustment—Available-for-Sale and a credit to Unrealized Gain or Loss—Equity.

Shelton's unrealized loss of $9,537 would appear in the comprehensive income statement as shown in Illustration H.9.

ILLUSTRATION H.9
Comprehensive income statement

Shelton Corporation
Comprehensive Income Statement
For the Year Ended December 31, 2022

Net income	$118,000
Other comprehensive income	
Unrealized loss on available-for-sale securities	(9,537)
Comprehensive income	$108,463

ETHICS NOTE

Recently, the SEC accused investment bank **Morgan Stanley** of overstating the value of certain bond investments by $75 million. The SEC stated that, in applying fair value accounting, Morgan Stanley used its own more optimistic assumptions rather than relying on external pricing sources.

For available-for-sale securities, the company carries forward the Unrealized Gain or Loss—Equity account to future periods. At each future balance sheet date, the account is adjusted with the Fair Value Adjustment—Available-for-Sale account to show the difference between cost and fair value at that time (see **Ethics Note**).

Equity Securities

The valuation and reporting of equity securities at a financial statement date depends on the levels of influence involved, as shown in **Illustration H.10**.

ILLUSTRATION H.10
Accounting and reporting for equity securities by category

Category	Valuation	Unrealized Gains or Losses	Other Income Effects
Holdings less than 20%	Fair value	Recognized in net income	Dividends declared; gains and losses from sale.
Holdings between 20% and 50%	Equity	Not recognized	Proportionate share of investee's net income.
Holdings more than 50%	Consolidation	Not recognized	Not applicable.

When an investor has an interest of less than 20%, it is presumed that the investor has little or no influence over the investee. In such cases, if market prices are available subsequent to acquisition, the company values and reports the stock investment using the fair value method.

Illustration of Stock Holdings Less Than 20%

At December 31, 2022, Shelton Corporation has two equity securities in which it has less than a 20% ownership interest and therefore has little or no influence over these companies. Shelton has the following cost and fair value for these two companies, as shown in **Illustration H.11**.

ILLUSTRATION H.11
Computation of fair value adjustment—equity security portfolio (2022)

Investments	Cost	Fair Value	Unrealized Gain (Loss)
Twitter Co.	$259,700	$275,000	$ 15,300
Campbell Soup Co.	317,500	304,000	(13,500)
Totals	$577,200	$579,000	$ 1,800

For Shelton's equity securities portfolio, the gross unrealized gain is $15,300 and the gross unrealized loss is $13,500, resulting in a net unrealized gain of $1,800. That is, the fair value of the equity securities portfolio is above cost by $1,800.

Shelton records the net unrealized gains and losses related to changes in the fair value equity securities in an Unrealized Gain or Loss—Income account. In this case, Shelton prepares an adjusting entry debiting the Fair Value Adjustment—Stock account and crediting the Unrealized Gain or Loss—Income account to record the increase in fair value and to record the gain as follows.

December 31, 2022

Fair Value Adjustment—Stock	1,800	
Unrealized Gain or Loss—Income		1,800
(To record unrealized gain on equity securities)		

Similar to trading securities, Shelton adjusts the balance in the Fair Value Adjustment—Stock account for the difference between cost and fair value. In addition, the unrealized gain related to Shelton's equity securities are reported in the "Other revenues and gains" section of the income statement.

Balance Sheet Presentation

In the balance sheet presentation, companies must classify investments as either short-term or long-term.

Short-Term Investments

Short-term investments (also called **marketable securities**) are securities held by a company that are (1) **readily marketable** and (2) **intended to be converted into cash** within the next year or operating cycle, whichever is longer (see **Helpful Hint**). Investments that do not meet **both criteria** are classified as **long-term investments**.

Readily Marketable An investment is readily marketable when it can be sold easily whenever the need for cash arises. Short-term paper[4] meets this criterion because a company can readily sell it to other investors. Stocks and bonds traded on organized securities markets, such as the New York Stock Exchange, are readily marketable because they can be bought and sold daily. In contrast, there may be only a limited market for the securities issued by small corporations and no market for the securities of a privately held company.

Intent to Convert Intent to convert means that management intends to sell the investment within the next year or operating cycle, whichever is longer. Generally, this criterion is satisfied when the investment is considered a resource that the company will use whenever the need for cash arises. For example, a ski resort may invest idle cash during the summer months with the intent to sell the securities to buy supplies and equipment shortly before the next winter season. This investment is considered short-term even if lack of snow cancels the next ski season and eliminates the need to convert the securities into cash as intended.

Because of their high liquidity, companies list short-term investments immediately below Cash in the current assets section of the balance sheet. Short-term investments are reported at fair value. For example, Weber Corporation would report its trading securities as shown in **Illustration H.12**.

HELPFUL HINT
Trading securities are always classified as short-term. Available-for-sale securities can be either short-term or long-term.

Weber Corporation	
Balance Sheet (partial)	
Current assets	
Cash	$21,000
Debt investments (at fair value)	**60,000**

ILLUSTRATION H.12
Balance sheet presentation of short-term investments

---

[4]Short-term paper includes (1) certificates of deposits (CDs) issued by banks, (2) money market certificates issued by banks and savings and loan associations, (3) Treasury bills issued by the U.S. government, and (4) commercial paper issued by corporations with good credit ratings.

Long-Term Investments

Companies generally report long-term investments in a separate section of the balance sheet immediately below "Current assets," as shown in **Illustration H.13**. Long-term investments in available-for-sale securities and stock holdings of less than 20% are reported at fair value. Investments in common stock accounted for under the equity method are reported at equity.

ILLUSTRATION H.13
Balance sheet presentation of long-term investments

Weber Corporation Balance Sheet (partial)	
Investments	
Debt investment (at fair value)	$100,000
Stock investments (at fair value)	**50,000**
Stock investments (at equity)	**150,000**
Total investments	$300,000

Presentation of Realized and Unrealized Gain or Loss

Companies must present in the financial statements gains and losses on investments, whether realized or unrealized. In the income statement, companies report gains and losses, as well as interest and dividend revenue, in the nonoperating activities section under the categories listed in **Illustration H.14**.

ILLUSTRATION H.14
Nonoperating items related to investments

Other Revenues and Gains	Other Expenses and Losses
Interest Revenue	Loss on Sale of Investments
Dividend Revenue	Unrealized Loss
Gain on Sale of Investments	
Unrealized Gain	

Recall that companies report the cumulative amount of other comprehensive income items from the current and previous years as a separate component of stockholders' equity. To illustrate, assume that Muzzillo Inc. has common stock of $3,000,000, retained earnings of $1,500,000, and an accumulated other comprehensive loss of $100,000. **Illustration H.15** shows the financial statement presentation of the accumulated other comprehensive loss.

ILLUSTRATION H.15
Unrealized loss in stockholders' equity section

Muzzillo Inc. Balance Sheet (partial)	
Stockholders' equity	
Common stock	$3,000,000
Retained earnings	1,500,000
Total paid-in capital and retained earnings	4,500,000
Accumulated other comprehensive loss	**(100,000)**
Total stockholders' equity	$4,400,000

A classified balance sheet is shown in **Illustration H.16**. This balance sheet includes (highlighted in red) short-term and long-term debt and stock investments as well as a presentation of accumulated other comprehensive income.

ILLUSTRATION H.16
Classified balance sheet

Pace Corporation
Balance Sheet
December 31, 2022

Assets

Current assets			
Cash			$ 21,000
Debt investments (at fair value)			**147,000**
Accounts receivable		$ 84,000	
Less: Allowance for doubtful accounts		4,000	80,000
Inventory, at FIFO cost			43,000
Prepaid insurance			23,000
Total current assets			314,000
Investments			
Debt investments (at fair value)		**20,000**	
Stock investments (at fair value)		**30,000**	
Stock investments (at equity)		**150,000**	
Total investments			200,000
Property, plant, and equipment			
Land			200,000
Buildings	$800,000		
Less: Accumulated depreciation—buildings	200,000	600,000	
Equipment	180,000		
Less: Accumulated depreciation—equipment	54,000	126,000	
Total property, plant, and equipment			926,000
Intangible assets			
Goodwill			270,000
Total assets			$1,710,000

Liabilities and Stockholders' Equity

Current liabilities			
Accounts payable			$ 185,000
Federal income taxes payable			60,000
Interest payable			10,000
Total current liabilities			255,000
Long-term liabilities			
Bonds payable, 10%, due 2027		$ 300,000	
Less: Discount on bonds		10,000	
Total long-term liabilities			290,000
Total liabilities			545,000
Stockholders' equity			
Paid-in capital			
Common stock, $10 par value, 200,000 shares authorized, 80,000 shares issued and outstanding		800,000	
In excess of par—common stock		100,000	
Total paid-in capital		900,000	
Retained earnings (Note 1)		255,000	
Total paid-in capital and retained earnings		1,155,000	
Add: Accumulated other comprehensive income		**10,000**	
Total stockholders' equity			1,165,000
Total liabilities and stockholders' equity			$1,710,000

Note 1. Retained earnings of $100,000 is restricted for plant expansion.

Review

Learning Objectives Review

1 Explain how to account for debt investments.

Corporations invest for three common reasons: (a) they have excess cash, (b) they view investment income as a significant revenue source, and (c) they have strategic goals such as gaining control of a competitor or supplier or moving into a new line of business.

Entries for investments in debt securities are required when companies purchase bonds, receive or accrue interest, and sell bonds.

2 Explain how to account for stock investments.

Entries for investments in common stock are required when companies purchase stock, receive dividends, and sell stock. When ownership is less than 20%, the cost method is used—the investment is recorded at cost. When ownership is between 20% and 50%, the equity method should be used—the investor records its share of the net income of the investee in the year it is earned.

When a company owns more than 50% of the common stock of another company, consolidated financial statements are usually prepared. These statements are especially useful to the stockholders, board of directors, and management of the parent company.

3 Discuss how debt and stock investments are reported in the financial statements.

Investments in debt securities are classified as trading, available-for-sale, or held-to-maturity for valuation and reporting purposes. Trading securities are reported as current assets at fair value, with changes from cost reported in net income. Available-for-sale securities are also reported at fair value, with the changes from cost reported as items of other comprehensive income. Available-for-sale securities are classified as short-term or long-term depending on their expected realization.

Investments in stock when ownership is less than 20% are reported at fair values, with changes from cost reported in net income.

Short-term investments are securities held by a company that are readily marketable and intended to be converted to cash within the next year or operating cycle, whichever is longer. Investments that do not meet both criteria are classified as long-term investments.

Glossary Review

Available-for-sale securities Securities that are held with the intent of selling them sometime in the future. (p. H-7).

Consolidated financial statements Financial statements that present the assets and liabilities controlled by the parent company and the total revenues and expenses of the parent and subsidiary companies. (p. H-6).

Controlling interest Ownership of more than 50% of the common stock of another entity. (p. H-6).

Cost method An accounting method in which the investment in common stock is recorded at cost and revenue is recognized only when cash dividends are received. (p. H-4).

Debt investments Investments in government and corporation bonds. (p. H-3).

Equity method An accounting method in which the investment in common stock is initially recorded at cost, and the investment account is then adjusted annually to show the investor's equity in the investee. (p. H-5).

Fair value Amount for which a security could be sold in a normal market. (p. H-7).

Held-to-maturity securities Debt securities that the investor has the intent and ability to hold to maturity. (p. H-7).

Long-term investments Investments that are not readily marketable or that management does not intend to convert into cash within the next year or operating cycle, whichever is longer. (p. H-11).

Mark-to-market A method of accounting for certain investments that requires that they be adjusted to their fair value at the end of each period. (p. H-8).

Parent company A company that owns more than 50% of the common stock of another entity. (p. H-6).

Short-term investments (marketable securities) Investments that are readily marketable and intended to be converted into cash within the next year or operating cycle, whichever is longer. (p. H-11).

Stock investments Investments in the capital stock of corporations. (p. H-4).

Subsidiary (affiliated) company A company in which more than 50% of its stock is owned by another company. (p. H-6).

Trading securities Securities bought and held primarily for sale in the near term to generate income on short-term price differences. (p. H-7).

Questions

1. What are the reasons that companies invest in securities?
2. **a.** What is the cost of an investment in bonds?
   b. When is interest on bonds recorded?
3. Geena Jaymes is confused about losses and gains on the sale of debt investments. Explain these issues to Geena:
   a. How the gain or loss is computed.
   b. The statement presentation of gains and losses.
4. Heliy Company sells bonds that it was holding as an investment that cost $40,000 for $45,000, including $1,000 of accrued interest revenue. In recording the sale, Heliy books a $5,000 gain. Is this correct? Explain.
5. What is the cost of an investment in stock?
6. To acquire Gaines Corporation stock, Palmer Co. pays $61,500 in cash. What entry should be made for this investment, assuming the stock is readily marketable?
7. **a.** When should a long-term investment in common stock be accounted for by the equity method?
   b. When is revenue recognized under the equity method?
8. Stetson Corporation uses the equity method to account for its ownership of 30% of the common stock of Pike Packing. During 2022, Pike reported a net income of $80,000 and declares and pays cash dividends of $10,000. What recognition should Stetson Corporation give to these events?
9. What constitutes "significant influence" when an investor's financial interest is less than 50%?
10. Distinguish between the cost and equity methods of accounting for investments in stocks.
11. What are consolidated financial statements?
12. What are the valuation guidelines for trading and available-for-sale debt investments at a balance sheet date?
13. Pat Ernst is the controller of J-Products, Inc. At December 31, the end of its first year of operations, the company's investments in trading debt securities cost $74,000 and have a fair value of $70,000. Indicate how Pat would report these data in the financial statements prepared on December 31.
14. Using the data in Question 13, how would Pat report the data if the investments were long-term and the debt securities were classified as available-for-sale?
15. Boise Company's investments in equity securities at December 31 show total cost of $202,000 and total fair value of $210,000. Boise has less than a 20% ownership interest in the equity securities. Prepare the adjusting entry.
16. Where is Accumulated Other Comprehensive Loss reported on the balance sheet?
17. Bargain Wholesale Supply owns stock in Cyrus Corporation, which it intends to hold indefinitely because of some negative tax consequences if sold. Should the investment in Cyrus be classified as a short-term investment? Why?

Brief Exercises

BEH.1 (**LO 1**) Craig Corporation purchased debt investments for $40,800 on January 1, 2022. On July 1, 2022, Craig received cash interest of $1,660. Journalize the purchase and the receipt of interest. Assume no interest has been accrued. *Journalize entries for debt investments.*

BEH.2 (**LO 2**) On August 1, Snow Company buys 1,000 shares of BCN common stock for $35,600 cash. On December 1, the stock investments are sold for $38,000 in cash. Journalize the purchase and sale of the common stock. *Journalize entries for stock investments.*

BEH.3 (**LO 2**) Tote Company owns 25% of Toppe Company. For the current year, Toppe reports net income of $150,000 and declares and pays a $60,000 cash dividend. Record Tote's equity in Toppe's net income and the receipt of dividends from Toppe. *Journalize transactions under the equity method.*

BEH.4 (**LO 3**) Cost and fair value data for the trading debt securities of Lecler Company at December 31, 2022, are $62,000 and $59,600, respectively. Prepare the adjusting entry to record the securities at fair value. *Prepare adjusting entry using fair value.*

BEH.5 (**LO 3**) For the data presented in BEH.4, show the financial statement presentation of the trading securities and related accounts. *Indicate statement presentation using fair value.*

BEH.6 (**LO 3**) In its first year of operations, Machin Corporation purchased available-for-sale debt securities costing $72,000 as a long-term investment. At December 31, 2022, the fair value of the securities is $69,000. Prepare the adjusting entry to record the securities at fair value. *Prepare adjusting entry using fair value.*

Indicate statement presentation using fair value.

BEH.7 (LO 3) For the data presented in BEH.6, show the financial statement presentation of the securities and related accounts. Assume the securities are noncurrent.

Prepare investments section of balance sheet.

BEH.8 (LO 3) Perth Corporation has these long-term investments: common stock of Vejas Co. (10% ownership), cost $108,000, fair value $112,000; common stock of Penn Inc. (30% ownership), cost $210,000, equity $230,000; and debt investment, cost $90,000, fair value, $150,000. Prepare the investments section of the balance sheet.

Exercises

Journalize debt investment transactions, and accrue interest.

EH.1 (LO 1) Chopin Corporation had these transactions pertaining to debt investments:

Jan. 1	Purchased 90 Martine Co. 10% bonds (each with a face value of $1,000) for $90,000 cash. Interest is payable annually on December 31.
Dec. 31	Received annual interest on Martine Co. bonds.
Dec. 31	Sold 30 Martine Co. bonds for $32,000.

Instructions

Journalize the transactions.

Journalize stock investment transactions, and explain income statement presentation.

EH.2 (LO 2, 3) Soylent Company had these transactions pertaining to stock investments:

Feb. 1	Purchased 1,200 shares of BJ common stock (2% of outstanding shares) for $8,400.
July 1	Received cash dividends of $2 per share on BJ common stock.
Sept. 1	Sold 500 shares of BJ common stock for $5,400.
Dec. 1	Received cash dividends of $1 per share on BJ common stock.

Instructions

a. Journalize the transactions.

b. Explain how dividend revenue and the gain (loss) on sale should be reported in the income statement.

Journalize transactions for investments in stock.

EH.3 (LO 2) Cooper Inc. had these transactions pertaining to investments in common stock:

Jan. 1	Purchased 1,200 shares of Gate Corporation common stock (5% of outstanding shares) for $59,200 cash.
July 1	Received a cash dividend of $7 per share.
Dec. 1	Sold 900 shares of Gate Corporation common stock for $47,200 cash.
31	Received a cash dividend of $7 per share.

Instructions

Journalize the transactions.

Journalize and post transactions under the equity method.

EH.4 (LO 2) On January 1, Lyon Corporation purchased a 25% equity investment in Shane Corporation for $150,000. At December 31, Shane declared and paid a $80,000 cash dividend and reported net income of $380,000.

Instructions

a. Journalize the transactions.

b. Determine the amount to be reported as an investment in Shane stock at December 31.

Journalize entries under cost and equity methods.

EH.5 (LO 2) These are two independent situations:

1. Sosey Cosmetics acquired 12% of the 300,000 shares of common stock of Elite Fashion at a total cost of $14 per share on March 18, 2022. On June 30, Elite declared and paid a $75,000 dividend. On December 31, Elite reported net income of $244,000 for the year. At December 31, the market price of Elite Fashion was $16 per share.

2. Williams Inc. obtained significant influence over Kasey Corporation by buying 25% of Kasey's 30,000 outstanding shares of common stock at a total cost of $11 per share on January 1, 2022. On June 15, Kasey declared and paid a cash dividend of $35,000. On December 31, Kasey reported a net income of $120,000 for the year.

Instructions

Prepare all the necessary journal entries for 2022 for (a) Sosey Cosmetics and (b) Williams Inc.

EH.6 (LO 3) At December 31, 2022, the trading debt securities for Gwynn, Inc. are as follows.

Prepare adjusting entry to record fair value, and indicate statement presentation.

Security	Cost	Fair Value
A	$18,100	$16,000
B	12,500	14,800
C	23,000	18,000
Total	$53,600	$48,800

Instructions

a. Prepare the adjusting entry at December 31, 2022, to report the securities at fair value.

b. Show the balance sheet and income statement presentation at December 31, 2022, after adjustment to fair value.

EH.7 (LO 3) **Writing** Data for debt investments are presented in EH.6. Assume instead that the investments are classified as available-for-sale debt securities with the same cost and fair value data as indicated in EH.6. The securities are considered to be a long-term investment.

Prepare adjusting entry to record fair value, and indicate statement presentation.

Instructions

a. Prepare the adjusting entry at December 31, 2022, to report the securities at fair value.

b. Show the statement presentation at December 31, 2022, after adjustment to fair value.

c. Pam Jenks, a member of the board of directors, does not understand the reporting of the unrealized gains or losses on trading debt securities and available-for-sale debt securities. Write a letter to Ms. Jenks explaining the reporting and the purposes it serves.

EH.8 (LO 3) Weston Company has these data at December 31, 2022, the end of its first year of operations.

Prepare adjusting entries for fair value, and indicate statement presentation for two classes of securities.

Debt Securities	Cost	Fair Value
Trading	$110,000	$122,000
Available-for-sale	100,000	96,000

The available-for-sale securities are held as a long-term investment.

Instructions

a. Prepare the adjusting entries to report each class of securities at fair value.

b. Indicate the statement presentation of each class of securities and the related unrealized gain (loss) accounts.

Problems

PH.1 (LO 1) Penn Farms is a grower of hybrid seed corn for Bend Genetics Corporation. It has had two exceptionally good years and has elected to invest its excess funds in bonds. The following selected transactions relate to bonds acquired as an investment by Penn Farms, whose fiscal year ends on December 31.

Journalize debt investment transactions.

2022

Jan. 1 Purchased at par $600,000 of Dover Corporation 10-year, 7% bonds dated January 1, 2022, directly from the issuing corporation. The bonds pay interest annually on January 1.

Dec. 31 Accrual of interest at year-end on the Dover bonds.

Assume that all intervening transactions and adjustments have been properly recorded and the number of bonds owned has not changed from December 31, 2022, to December 31, 2024.

2025

Jan. 1 Received the annual interest on the Dover bonds.
Jan. 1 Sold $300,000 of Dover bonds at 110% of face value (110).
Dec. 31 Accrual of interest at year-end on the Dover bonds.

Gain on sale of debt investments $30,000

Instructions

Journalize the listed transactions for the years 2022 and 2025.

Journalize investment transactions, prepare adjusting entry, and show financial statement presentation.

PH.2 (LO 1, 2, 3) In January 2022, the management of Northern Company concludes that it has sufficient cash to purchase some short-term investments in debt and stock securities. During the year, the following transactions occurred.

Jan. 1	Purchased 70 $1,000, 8% TRC bonds for $70,000. Interest is payable annually on December 31.	
Feb. 1	Purchased 1,200 shares of LAF common stock for $51,600.	
Mar. 1	Purchased 500 shares of NCL common stock for $18,500.	
July 1	Received a cash dividend of $0.80 per share on the LAF common stock.	
Aug. 1	Sold 200 shares of LAF common stock at $42 per share.	
Sept. 1	Received $2 per share cash dividend on the NCL common stock.	
Dec. 31	Received the annual interest on the TRC bonds.	
Dec. 31	Sold the TRC bonds for $75,700.	

At December 31, the fair values of the LAF and NCL common stocks were $39 and $30 per share, respectively. These stock investments by Northern Company provide less than a 20% ownership interest.

Instructions

a. Loss on sale of stock investment $200

a. Journalize the transactions and post to the accounts Debt Investments and Stock Investments. (Use the T-account form.)

b. Prepare the adjusting entry at December 31, 2022, to report the investments at fair value.

c. Show the balance sheet presentation of investment securities at December 31, 2022.

d. Identify the income statement accounts and give the statement classification of each account.

Journalize transactions, prepare adjusting entry for stock investments, and show balance sheet presentation.

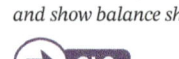

PH.3 (LO 2, 3) On December 31, 2021, the end of its first year of operations, Botani Associates owned the following securities that are held as long-term investments.

Common Stock	Shares	Cost
C Co.	1,000	$48,000
D Co.	5,000	36,000
E Co.	1,200	24,000

On this date, the total fair value of the securities was equal to its cost. The securities are not held for influence or control over the investees. In 2022, the following transactions occurred.

July 1	Received $2.00 per share semiannual cash dividend on D Co. common stock.
Aug. 1	Received $0.50 per share cash dividend on C Co. common stock.
Sept. 1	Sold 1,000 shares of D Co. common stock for cash at $9 per share.
Oct. 1	Sold 300 shares of C Co. common stock for cash at $53 per share.
Nov. 1	Received $1 per share cash dividend on E Co. common stock.
Dec. 15	Received $0.50 per share cash dividend on C Co. common stock.
31	Received $2.20 per share semiannual cash dividend on D Co. common stock.

At December 31, the fair values per share of the common stocks were C Co. $47, D Co. $7, and E Co. $24. These investments should be classified as long-term.

Instructions

a. Journalize the 2022 transactions and post to the account Stock Investments. (Use the T-account form.)

b. Unrealized loss $3,300

b. Prepare the adjusting entry at December 31, 2022, to show the securities at fair value. Botani has less than a 20% ownership interest in all these common stocks (C Co., D Co., and E Co.).

c. Show the balance sheet presentation of the investments at 2022. These investments should be classified as long-term.

Prepare entries under cost and equity methods, and prepare memorandum.

PH.4 (LO 2) Writing Wellman Company acquired 30% of the outstanding common stock of Grinwold Inc. on January 1, 2022, by paying $1,800,000 for 60,000 shares. Grinwold declared and paid a $0.50 per share cash dividend on June 30 and again on December 31, 2022. Grinwold reported net income of $800,000 for the year.

Instructions

a. Total dividend revenue for 2022 $60,000

a. Prepare the journal entries for Wellman Company for 2022, assuming Wellman cannot exercise significant influence over Grinwold. (Use the cost method.)

b. Revenue from stock investments $240,000

b. Prepare the journal entries for Wellman Company for 2022, assuming Wellman can exercise significant influence over Grinwold. (Use the equity method.)

c. The board of directors of Wellman Company is confused about the differences between the cost and equity methods. Prepare a memorandum for the board that explains each method and shows in tabular form the account balances under each method at December 31, 2022.

PH.5 (LO 2, 3) Here is Kalvin Company's portfolio of long-term stock investments at December 31, 2021, the end of its first year of operations.

Journalize stock transactions, and show balance sheet presentation.

	Cost
1,400 shares of Batone Inc. common stock	$73,500
1,200 shares of Mendez Corporation common stock	84,000
800 shares of P. Tillman Corporation preferred stock	33,600

On December 31, the total cost of the portfolio equaled the total fair value. Kalvin had the following transactions related to the securities during 2022.

Jan. 20	Sold all 1,400 shares of Batone Inc. common stock at $55 per share.
28	Purchased 400 shares of $10 par value common stock of P. Wahl Corporation at $78 per share.
30	Received a cash dividend of $1.25 per share on Mendez Corporation common stock.
Feb. 8	Received cash dividends of $0.40 per share on P. Tillman Corporation preferred stock.
18	Sold all 800 shares of P. Tillman preferred stock at $35 per share.
July 30	Received a cash dividend of $1.10 per share on Mendez Corporation common stock.
Sept. 6	Purchased an additional 600 shares of the $10 par value common stock of P. Wahl Corporation at $82 per share.
Dec. 1	Received a cash dividend of $1.50 per share on P. Wahl Corporation common stock.

At December 31, 2022, the fair values of the securities were:

Mendez Corporation common stock	$65 per share
P. Wahl Corporation common stock	$77 per share

Kalvin uses separate account titles for each investment, such as Investment in Mendez Corporation Common Stock.

Instructions

a. Prepare journal entries to record the transactions.
b. Prepare the adjusting entry at December 31, 2022, to report the portfolio at fair value.
c. Show the balance sheet presentation at December 31, 2022.

a. Loss on sale of Tillman stock
investments $5,600
b. Unrealized loss $9,400

PH.6 (LO 3) The following data, presented in alphabetical order, are taken from the records of Manfreid Corporation.

Prepare a balance sheet.

Accounts payable	$ 150,000
Accounts receivable	90,000
Accumulated depreciation—buildings	180,000
Accumulated depreciation—equipment	52,000
Allowance for doubtful accounts	6,000
Bonds payable (10%, due 2033)	350,000
Buildings	900,000
Cash	63,000
Common stock ($5 par value; 500,000 shares authorized, 240,000 shares issued)	1,200,000
Debt investments (long-term, at fair value)	400,000
Discount on bonds payable	20,000
Dividends payable	50,000
Equipment	275,000
Goodwill	190,000
Income taxes payable	70,000
Inventory	170,000
Land	410,000
Notes payable (due 2023)	70,000
Paid-in capital in excess of par value	464,000
Prepaid insurance	16,000
Retained earnings	310,000
Stock investments (Horton Inc. stock, 30% ownership, at equity)	240,000
Stock investments (short-term, at fair value)	128,000

Instructions

Prepare a balance sheet at December 31, 2022.

Total assets $2,644,000

Appendix I

Payroll Accounting

Appendix Preview

Payroll and related fringe benefits often make up a large percentage of current liabilities. Employee compensation is often the most significant expense that a company incurs. However, payroll accounting involves more than paying employees' wages. Companies are required by law to maintain payroll records for each employee, to file and pay payroll taxes, and to comply with state and federal tax laws related to employee compensation.

Appendix Outline

LEARNING OBJECTIVES

1. Record the payroll for a pay period.	• Determining the payroll • Recording the payroll
2. Record employer payroll taxes.	• FICA taxes • Federal unemployment taxes • State unemployment taxes • Recording employer payroll taxes • Filing and remitting payroll taxes
3. Discuss the objectives of internal control for payroll.	• Objectives of internal control for payroll • Internal control activities

Recording the Payroll

LEARNING OBJECTIVE 1
Record the payroll for a pay period.

The term "payroll" **pertains to both salaries and wages of employees**. Managerial, administrative, and sales personnel are generally paid **salaries**. Salaries are often expressed in terms of a specified amount per month or per year rather than an hourly rate. Store clerks, factory employees, and manual laborers are normally paid **wages**. Wages are based on a rate per hour or on a piecework basis (such as per unit of product). Frequently, people use the terms "salaries" and "wages" interchangeably.

The term "payroll" **does not apply to payments made for services of professionals** such as certified public accountants, attorneys, and architects. Such professionals are independent contractors rather than salaried employees. Payments to them are called **fees**. This distinction is important because government regulations relating to the payment and reporting of payroll taxes apply only to employees.

Determining the Payroll

Determining the payroll involves computing three amounts: (1) gross earnings, (2) payroll deductions, and (3) net pay.

Gross Earnings

Gross earnings is the total compensation earned by an employee. It consists of wages or salaries, plus any bonuses and commissions.

Companies determine total **wages** for an employee by multiplying the hours worked by the hourly rate of pay. In addition to the hourly pay rate, most companies are required by law to pay hourly workers a minimum of 1½ times the regular hourly rate for overtime work in excess of eight hours per day or 40 hours per week. In addition, many employers pay overtime rates for work done at night, on weekends, and on holidays.

For example, assume that Michael Jordan, an employee of Academy Company, worked 44 hours for the weekly pay period ending January 14. His regular wage is $12 per hour. For any hours in excess of 40, the company pays at 1½ times the regular rate. Academy computes Jordan's gross earnings (total wages) as shown in **Illustration I.1**.

ILLUSTRATION I.1
Computation of total wages

Type of Pay	Hours	×	Rate	=	Gross Earnings
Regular	40	×	$12	=	$480
Overtime	4	×	18	=	72
Total wages					**$552**

This computation assumes that Jordan receives 1½ times his regular hourly rate ($12 × 1.5) for his overtime hours. Union contracts often require that overtime rates be as much as twice the regular rates.

An employee's **salary** is generally based on a monthly or yearly rate. The company then prorates these rates to its payroll periods (e.g., biweekly or monthly). Most executive and administrative positions are salaried. Federal law does not require overtime pay for employees in such positions.

Many companies have **bonus** agreements for employees (see **Ethics Note**). One survey found that over 94% of the largest U.S. manufacturing companies offer annual bonuses to key executives. Bonus arrangements may be based on such factors as increased sales or net income. Companies may pay bonuses in cash and/or by granting employees the opportunity to acquire shares of company stock at favorable prices (called stock option plans).

ETHICS NOTE

Bonuses often reward outstanding individual performance, but successful corporations also need considerable teamwork. A challenge is to motivate individuals while preventing an unethical employee from taking another's idea for his or her own advantage.

Payroll Deductions

As anyone who has received a paycheck knows, gross earnings are usually very different from the amount actually received. The difference is due to **payroll deductions**.

Payroll deductions may be mandatory or voluntary. **Mandatory deductions are required by law and consist of FICA taxes and income taxes.** Voluntary deductions are at the option of the employee. **Illustration I.2** summarizes common types of payroll deductions. Such deductions do not result in payroll tax expense to the employer. The employer is merely a collection agent, and subsequently transfers the deducted amounts to the government and designated recipients.

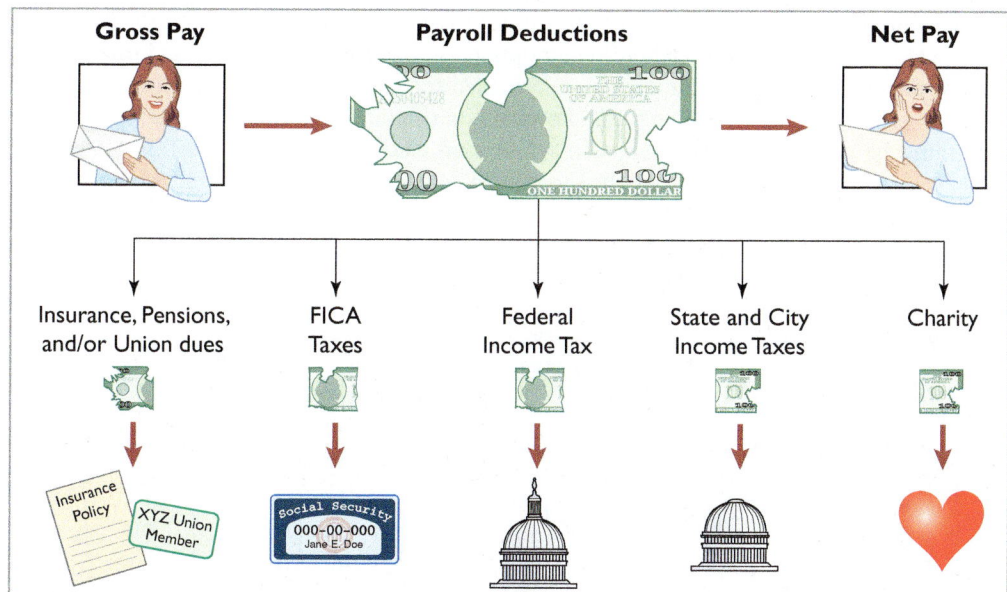

ILLUSTRATION I.2
Payroll deductions

FICA Taxes In 1937, Congress enacted the Federal Insurance Contribution Act (FICA). **FICA taxes are designed to provide workers with supplemental retirement, employment disability, and medical benefits.** In 1965, Congress extended benefits to include Medicare for individuals over 65 years of age. The benefits are financed by a tax levied on employees' earnings.

FICA taxes consist of a Social Security tax and a Medicare tax. They are paid by both employee and employer. The FICA tax rate is 7.65% (6.2% Social Security tax up to $127,200 plus 1.45% Medicare tax) of salary and wages for each employee.[1] In addition, the Medicare tax of 1.45% continues for an employee's salary and wages in excess of $127,200. These tax rate and tax base requirements are shown in **Illustration I.3**.

Social Security taxes	
Employee and employer	**6.2%** on salary and wages up to **$127,200**
Medicare taxes	
Employee and employer	**1.45%** on all salary and wages without limitation

ILLUSTRATION I.3
FICA tax rate and tax base

To illustrate the computation of FICA taxes, assume that Mario Ruiz has total wages for the year of $100,000. In this case, Mario pays FICA taxes of $7,650 ($100,000 × 7.65%). If Mario has total wages of $130,000, Mario pays FICA taxes of $9,771 (rounded to the nearest dollar), as shown in **Illustration I.4**.

Social Security tax	($127,200 × 6.2%)	$7,886
Medicare tax	($130,000 × 1.45%)	1,885
Total FICA taxes		**$9,771**

ILLUSTRATION I.4
FICA tax computation

Mario's employer is also required to pay $9,771.

Income Taxes Under the U.S. pay-as-you-go system of federal income taxes, employers are required to withhold income taxes from employees each pay period. Four variables determine the amount to be withheld: (1) the employee's gross earnings, (2) marital status, (3) the number of allowances claimed by the employee, and (4) the length of the pay period. The number of allowances claimed typically includes the employee, his or her spouse, and other dependents.

---

[1]The $127,200 limit is based upon recent guidelines set by the Social Security Administration.

Withholding tables furnished by the Internal Revenue Service indicate the amount of income tax to be withheld. Withholding amounts are based on gross wages and the number of allowances claimed. Separate tables are provided for weekly, biweekly, semimonthly, and monthly pay periods. **Illustration I.5** shows the withholding tax table for Michael Jordan (assuming he earns $552 per week, is married, and claims two allowances). For a weekly salary of $552 with two allowances, the income tax to be withheld is $24 (highlighted in red).

ILLUSTRATION I.5
Withholding tax table

MARRIED Persons — WEEKLY Payroll Period
(For Wages Paid through December 2022)

If the wages are —		And the number of withholding allowances claimed is —										
At least	But less than	0	1	2	3	4	5	6	7	8	9	10
		The amount of income tax to be withheld is —										
500	510	34	27	19	11	4	0	0	0	0	0	0
510	520	35	28	20	12	5	0	0	0	0	0	0
520	530	37	29	21	13	6	0	0	0	0	0	0
530	540	38	30	22	14	7	0	0	0	0	0	0
540	550	40	31	23	15	8	0	0	0	0	0	0
550	560	41	32	24	16	9	1	0	0	0	0	0
560	570	43	33	25	17	10	2	0	0	0	0	0
570	580	44	34	26	18	11	3	0	0	0	0	0
580	590	46	35	27	19	12	4	0	0	0	0	0
590	600	47	36	28	20	13	5	0	0	0	0	0
600	610	49	38	29	21	14	6	0	0	0	0	0
610	620	50	39	30	22	15	7	0	0	0	0	0
620	630	52	41	31	23	16	8	1	0	0	0	0
630	640	53	42	32	24	17	9	2	0	0	0	0
640	650	55	44	33	25	18	10	3	0	0	0	0
650	660	56	45	34	26	19	11	4	0	0	0	0
660	670	58	47	35	27	20	12	5	0	0	0	0
670	680	59	48	37	28	21	13	6	0	0	0	0
680	690	61	50	38	29	22	14	7	0	0	0	0
690	700	62	51	40	30	23	15	8	0	0	0	0

In addition, most states (and some cities) require **employers** to withhold income taxes from employees' earnings. As a rule, the amounts withheld are a percentage (specified in the state revenue code) of the amount withheld for the federal income tax. Or they may be a specified percentage of the employee's earnings. For the sake of simplicity, we have assumed that Jordan's wages are subject to state income taxes of 2%, or $11.04 (2% × $552) per week.

There is no limit on the amount of gross earnings subject to income tax withholdings. In fact, under our progressive system of taxation, the higher the earnings, the higher the percentage of income withheld for taxes.

Other Deductions Employees may voluntarily authorize withholdings for charitable organizations, retirement, and other purposes. All voluntary deductions from gross earnings should be authorized in writing by the employee. The authorization(s) may be made individually or as part of a group plan. Deductions for charitable organizations, such as the United Fund, or for financial arrangements, such as U.S. savings bonds and repayment of loans from company credit unions, are made individually. Deductions for union dues, health and life insurance, and pension plans are often made on a group basis. We assume that Jordan has weekly voluntary deductions of $10 for the United Fund and $5 for union dues.

Net Pay

ALTERNATIVE TERMINOLOGY
Net pay is also called *take-home pay.*

Academy Company determines **net pay** by subtracting payroll deductions from gross earnings (see **Alternative Terminology**). **Illustration I.6** shows the computation of Jordan's net pay for the pay period.

Gross earnings			$552.00
Payroll deductions:			
FICA taxes		$42.23	
Federal income taxes		24.00	
State income taxes		11.04	
United Fund		10.00	
Union dues		5.00	92.27
Net pay			**$459.73**

ILLUSTRATION I.6

Computation of net pay

Assuming that Michael Jordan's wages for each week during the year are $552, total wages for the year are $28,704 (52 × $552). Thus, all of Jordan's wages are subject to FICA tax during the year. In comparison, let's assume that Jordan's department head earns $3,000 per week, or $156,000 for the year. Since only the first $127,200 is subject to Social Security taxes, the maximum FICA withholdings on the department head's earnings would be $10,148 [($127,200 × 6.20%) + ($156,000 × 1.45%)].

Recording the Payroll

Recording the payroll involves maintaining payroll department records, recognizing payroll expenses and liabilities, and recording payment of the payroll.

Maintaining Payroll Department Records

To comply with state and federal laws, an employer must keep a cumulative record of each employee's gross earnings, deductions, and net pay during the year. The record that provides this information is the **employee earnings record**. **Illustration I.7** shows Michael Jordan's employee earnings record.

ILLUSTRATION I.7 Employee earnings record

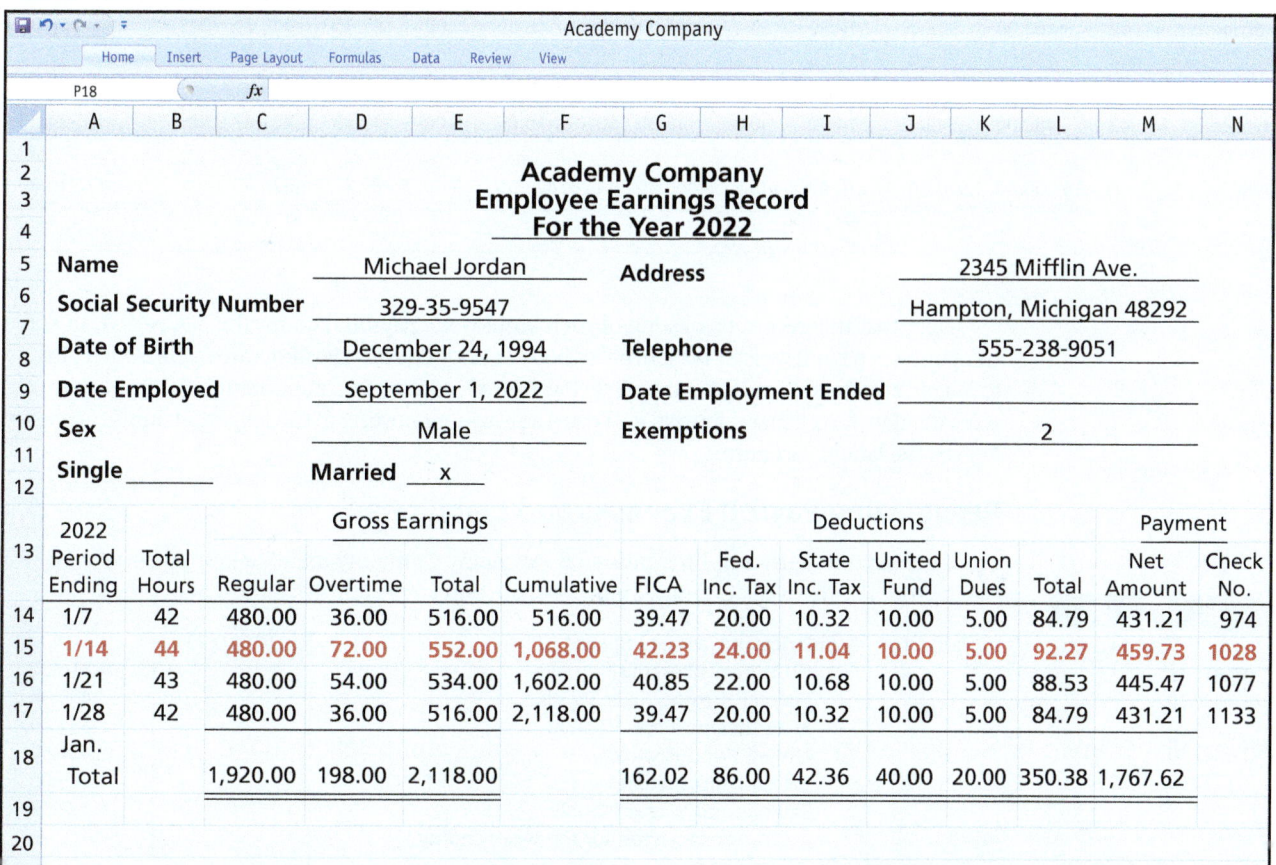

Companies keep a separate earnings record for each employee and update these records after each pay period. The employer uses the cumulative payroll data on the earnings record to (1) determine when an employee has earned the maximum earnings subject to FICA taxes, (2) file state and federal payroll tax returns (as explained later), and (3) provide each employee with a statement of gross earnings and tax withholdings for the year. Illustration I.11 shows this statement.

In addition to employee earnings records, many companies find it useful to prepare a **payroll register**. This record accumulates the gross earnings, deductions, and net pay by employee for each pay period. **Illustration I.8** presents Academy Company's payroll register. It provides the documentation for preparing a paycheck for each employee. For example, it shows the data for Michael Jordan in the wages section. In this example, Academy's total weekly payroll is $17,210, as shown in the salary and wages expense column (column N, row 31).

ILLUSTRATION I.8 Payroll register

Academy Company
Payroll Register
For the Week Ending January 14, 2022

Employee	Total Hours	Regular	Over-time	Gross	FICA	Federal Income Tax	State Income Tax	United Fund	Union Dues	Total	Net Pay	Check No.	Salaries and Wages Expense
Arnold, Patricia	40	580.00		580.00	44.37	61.00	11.60	15.00		131.97	448.03	998	580.00
Canton, Matthew	40	590.00		590.00	45.14	63.00	11.80	20.00		139.94	450.06	999	590.00
Mueller, William	40	530.00		530.00	40.55	54.00	10.60	11.00		116.15	413.85	1000	530.00
Bennett, Robin	42	480.00	36.00	516.00	39.47	35.00	10.32	18.00	5.00	107.79	408.21	1025	516.00
Jordan, Michael	44	480.00	72.00	552.00	42.23	24.00	11.04	10.00	5.00	92.27	459.73	1028	552.00
Milroy, Lee	43	480.00	54.00	534.00	40.85	46.00	10.68	10.00	5.00	112.53	421.47	1029	534.00
Total		16,200.00	1,010.00	17,210.00	1,316.57	3,490.00	344.20	421.50	115.00	5,687.27	11,522.73		17,210.00

Note that this record is a listing of each employee's payroll data for the pay period. In some companies, a payroll register is a journal or book of original entry. Postings are made from it directly to ledger accounts. In other companies, the payroll register is a memorandum record that provides the data for a general journal entry and subsequent posting to the ledger accounts. Academy follows the latter procedure.

Recognizing Payroll Expenses and Liabilities

From the payroll register in Illustration I.8, Academy Company makes a journal entry to record the payroll. For the week ending January 14, the entry is as follows.

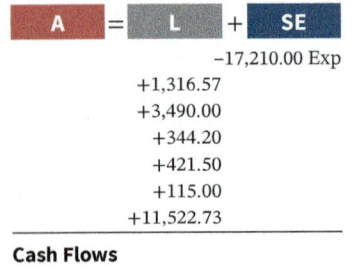

Jan. 14	Salaries and Wages Expense		17,210.00	
	FICA Taxes Payable			1,316.57
	Federal Income Taxes Payable			3,490.00
	State Income Taxes Payable			344.20
	United Fund Payable			421.50
	Union Dues Payable			115.00
	Salaries and Wages Payable			11,522.73
	(To record payroll for the week ending January 14)			

Cash Flows
no effect

The company credits specific liability accounts for the mandatory and voluntary deductions made during the pay period. In the example, Academy debits Salaries and Wages Expense for the gross earnings of its employees. The amount credited to Salaries and Wages Payable is the sum of the individual checks the employees will receive.

Recording Payment of the Payroll

A company makes payments by check (or electronic funds transfer) either from its regular bank account or a payroll bank account. Each paycheck is usually accompanied by a detachable **statement of earnings** document. This shows the employee's gross earnings, payroll deductions, and net pay, both for the period and for the year-to-date. Academy Company uses its regular bank account for payroll checks. **Illustration I.9** shows the paycheck and statement of earnings for Michael Jordan (see **Helpful Hint**).

ILLUSTRATION I.9
Paycheck and statement of earnings

HELPFUL HINT
None of the income tax liabilities result in payroll tax expense for the employer because the employer is acting only as a collection agent for the government.

Following payment of the payroll, the company enters the check numbers in the payroll register. Academy records payment of the payroll as follows.

Jan. 14	Salaries and Wages Payable	11,522.73	
	Cash		11,522.73
	(To record payment of payroll)		

A = L + SE
     −11,522.73
−11,522.73

Cash Flows
−11,522.73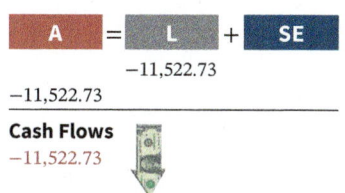

Many medium- and large-size companies use a payroll processing center that performs payroll recordkeeping services. Companies send the center payroll information about employee pay rates and hours worked. The center maintains the payroll records and prepares the payroll checks. In most cases, it costs less to process the payroll through the center (outsource) than if the company did so internally.

Employer Payroll Taxes

LEARNING OBJECTIVE 2
Record employer payroll taxes.

Payroll tax expense for businesses results from three taxes that governmental agencies levy **on employers**. These taxes are (1) FICA, (2) federal unemployment tax, and (3) state unemployment tax. These taxes plus such items as paid vacations and pensions are collectively referred to as **fringe benefits**. As indicated earlier, the cost of fringe benefits in many companies is substantial.

FICA Taxes

Each employee must pay FICA taxes. In addition, employers must match each employee's FICA contribution. This means the employer must remit to the federal government 12.4% of each employee's first $127,200 of taxable earnings, plus 2.9% of each employee's earnings, regardless of amount. The matching contribution results in **payroll tax expense** to the employer. The employer's tax is subject to the same rate and maximum earnings as the employee's. The company uses the same account, FICA Taxes Payable, to record both the employee's and the employer's FICA contributions. For the January 14 payroll, Academy Company's FICA tax contribution is $1,316.57 ($17,210.00 × 7.65%).

Federal Unemployment Taxes

The Federal Unemployment Tax Act (FUTA) is another feature of the federal Social Security program. **Federal unemployment taxes** provide benefits for a limited period of time to employees who lose their jobs through no fault of their own. The FUTA tax rate is currently 6.0% of taxable wages. The taxable wage base is the first $7,000 of wages paid to each employee in a calendar year. Employers who pay the state unemployment tax on a timely basis will receive an offset credit of up to 5.4%. Therefore, the net federal tax rate is generally 0.6% (6.0% − 5.4%). This rate would equate to a maximum of $42 of federal tax per employee per year (0.6% × $7,000). State tax rates are based on state law.

The **employer** bears the entire federal unemployment tax (see **Helpful Hint**). There is no deduction or withholding from employees. Companies use the account Federal Unemployment Taxes Payable to recognize this liability. The federal unemployment tax for Academy Company for the January 14 payroll is $103.26 ($17,210.00 × 0.6%).

> **HELPFUL HINT**
> Both the employer and employee pay FICA taxes. Federal unemployment taxes and (in most states) the state unemployment taxes are borne entirely by the employer.

State Unemployment Taxes

All states have unemployment compensation programs under state unemployment tax acts (SUTA). Like federal unemployment taxes, **state unemployment taxes** provide benefits to employees who lose their jobs. These taxes are levied on employers.[2] The basic rate is usually 5.4% on the first $7,000 of wages paid to an employee during the year. The state adjusts the basic rate according to the employer's experience rating. Companies with a history of stable employment may pay less than 5.4%. Companies with a history of unstable employment may pay more than the basic rate. Regardless of the rate paid, the company's credit on the federal unemployment tax is still 5.4%.

Companies use the account State Unemployment Taxes Payable for this liability. The state unemployment tax for Academy Company for the January 14 payroll is $929.34 ($17,210.00 × 5.4%). **Illustration I.10** summarizes the types of employer payroll taxes.

---

[2]In a few states, the employee is also required to make a contribution. *In this appendix, including the homework, we will assume that the tax is only on the employer.*

ILLUSTRATION I.10 Employer payroll taxes

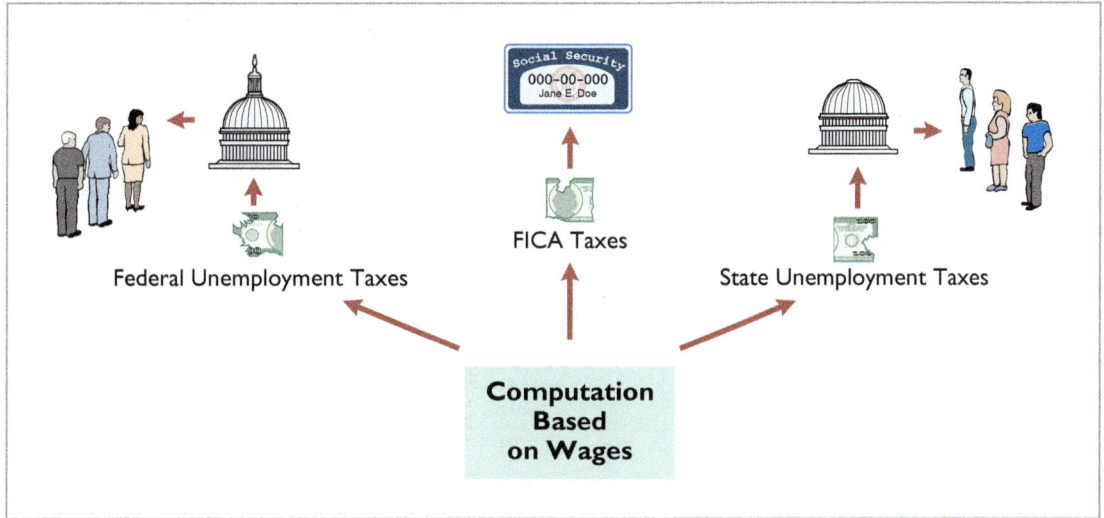

Recording Employer Payroll Taxes

Companies usually record employer payroll taxes at the same time they record the payroll. The entire amount of gross pay ($17,210.00) shown in the payroll register in Illustration I.8 is subject to each of the three taxes mentioned previously. Accordingly, Academy records the payroll tax expense associated with the January 14 payroll with the following entry.

Jan. 14	Payroll Tax Expense	2,349.17	
	FICA Taxes Payable		1,316.57
	Federal Unemployment Taxes Payable		103.26
	State Unemployment Taxes Payable		929.34
	(To record employer's payroll taxes on January 14 payroll)		

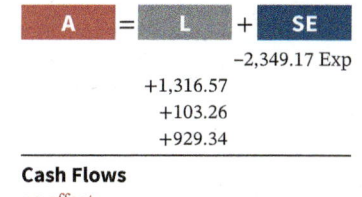

Note that Academy uses separate liability accounts instead of a single credit to Payroll Taxes Payable. Why? Because these liabilities are payable to different taxing authorities at different dates. Companies classify the liability accounts in the balance sheet as current liabilities since they will be paid within the next year. They classify Payroll Tax Expense on the income statement as an operating expense.

Filing and Remitting Payroll Taxes

Preparation of payroll tax returns is the responsibility of the payroll department. The treasurer's department makes the tax payment. Much of the information for the returns is obtained from employee earnings records.

For purposes of reporting and remitting to the IRS, the company combines the FICA taxes and federal income taxes that it withheld. **Companies must report the taxes quarterly**, no later than one month following the close of each quarter. The remitting requirements depend on the amount of taxes withheld and the length of the pay period. Companies remit funds through deposits in either a Federal Reserve bank or an authorized commercial bank.

Companies generally file and remit federal unemployment taxes **annually** on or before January 31 of the subsequent year. Earlier payments are required when the tax exceeds a specified amount. Companies usually must file and pay state unemployment taxes by the **end of the month following each quarter**. When payroll taxes are paid, companies debit payroll liability accounts and credit Cash.

Employers also must provide each employee with a **Wage and Tax Statement (Form W-2)** by January 31 following the end of a calendar year. This statement shows gross earnings, FICA taxes withheld, and income taxes withheld for the year. The required W-2 form for Michael Jordan, using assumed annual data, is shown in **Illustration I.11**. The employer must send a copy of each employee's Wage and Tax Statement (Form W-2) to the Social Security Administration. This agency subsequently furnishes the Internal Revenue Service with the income data required.

ILLUSTRATION I.11 W-2 form

a Employee's social security number: 329-35-9547		
b Employer identification number (EIN): 36-2167852	1 Wages, tips, other compensation: 26,300.00	2 Federal income tax withheld: 2,248.00
c Employer's name, address, and ZIP code: Academy Company, 19 Center St., Hampton, MI 48291	3 Social security wages: 26,300.00	4 Social security tax withheld: 1,630.60
	5 Medicare wages and tips: 26,300.00	6 Medicare tax withheld: 381.35
	7 Social security tips	8 Allocated tips
d Control number	9 Advance EIC payment	10 Dependent care benefits
e Employee's first name and initial: Michael Last name: Jordan	11 Nonqualified plans	12a See instructions for box 12
2345 Mifflin Ave., Hampton, MI 48292	13 Statutory employee / Retirement plan / Third-party sick pay	12b
	14 Other	12c
		12d
f Employee's address and ZIP code		
15 State: MI Employer's state ID number: 423-1466-3	16 State wages, tips, etc.: 26,300.00 17 State income tax: 526.00	18 Local wages, tips, etc. 19 Local income tax 20 Locality name

Form **W-2** Wage and Tax Statement **2022** Department of the Treasury—Internal Revenue Service

Copy A For Social Security Administration — Send this entire page with Form W-3 to the Social Security Administration; photocopies are **not** acceptable.

For Privacy Act and Paperwork Reduction Act Notice, see back of Copy D.

Cat. No. 10134D

Internal Control for Payroll

> **LEARNING OBJECTIVE 3**
> Discuss the objectives of internal control for payroll.

Chapter 7 introduced internal control. As applied to payrolls, the objectives of internal control are (1) to safeguard company assets against unauthorized payments of payrolls, and (2) to ensure the accuracy and reliability of the accounting records pertaining to payrolls.

Irregularities often result if internal control is lax. Frauds involving payroll include overstating hours, using unauthorized pay rates, adding fictitious employees to the payroll, continuing terminated employees on the payroll, and distributing duplicate payroll checks. Moreover, inaccurate records will result in incorrect paychecks, financial statements, and payroll tax returns.

Payroll activities involve four functions: hiring employees, timekeeping, preparing the payroll, and paying the payroll. For effective internal control, companies should assign these four functions to different departments or individuals. **Illustration I.12** highlights these functions and illustrates their internal control features.

> **ILLUSTRATION I.12** Internal control for payroll

Review

Learning Objectives Review

1 Record the payroll for a pay period.

The computation of the payroll involves gross earnings, payroll deductions, and net pay. In recording the payroll, Salaries and Wages Expense is debited for gross earnings, individual tax and other liability accounts are credited for payroll deductions, and Salaries and Wages Payable is credited for net pay. When the payroll is paid, Salaries and Wages Payable is debited, and Cash is credited.

2 Record employer payroll taxes.

Employer payroll taxes consist of FICA, federal unemployment taxes, and state unemployment taxes. The taxes are usually accrued at the time the payroll is recorded by debiting Payroll Tax Expense and crediting separate liability accounts for each type of tax.

3 Discuss the objectives of internal control for payroll.

The objectives of internal control for payroll are (1) to safeguard company assets against unauthorized payments of payrolls, and (2) to ensure the accuracy and reliability of the accounting records pertaining to payrolls.

Glossary Review

Bonus Compensation to management personnel and other employees, based on factors such as increased sales or the amount of net income. (p. I-2).

Employee earnings record A cumulative record of each employee's gross earnings, deductions, and net pay during the year. (p. I-5).

Federal unemployment taxes Taxes imposed on the employer that provide benefits for a limited time period to employees who lose their jobs through no fault of their own. (p. I-8).

Fees Payments made for the services of professionals. (p. I-2).

FICA taxes Taxes designed to provide workers with supplemental retirement, employment disability, and medical benefits. (p. I-3).

Gross earnings Total compensation earned by an employee. (p. I-2).

Net pay Gross earnings less payroll deductions. (p. I-4).

Payroll deductions Deductions from gross earnings to determine the amount of a paycheck. (p. I-2).

Payroll register A payroll record that accumulates the gross earnings, deductions, and net pay by employee for each pay period. (p. I-6).

APPENDIX I Payroll Accounting

Salaries Specified amount per month or per year paid to managerial, administrative, and sales personnel. (p. I-1).

Statement of earnings A document attached to a paycheck that indicates the employee's gross earnings, payroll deductions, and net pay. (p. I-7).

State unemployment taxes Taxes imposed on the employer that provide benefits to employees who lose their jobs. (p. I-8).

Wage and Tax Statement (Form W-2) A form showing gross earnings, FICA taxes withheld, and income taxes withheld which is prepared annually by an employer for each employee. (p. I-9).

Wages Amounts paid to employees based on a rate per hour or on a piecework basis. (p. I-1).

WileyPLUS

Many additional resources are available for practice in WileyPLUS.

Questions

1. What is the difference between gross pay and net pay? Which amount should a company record as wages or salaries expense?

2. Which payroll tax is levied on both employers and employees?

3. Are the federal and state income taxes withheld from employee paychecks a payroll tax expense for the employer? Explain your answer.

4. What do the following acronyms stand for: FICA, FUTA, and SUTA?

5. What information is shown on a W-2 statement?

6. Distinguish between the two types of payroll deductions and give examples of each.

7. What are the primary uses of the employee earnings record?

8. (a) Identify the three types of employer payroll taxes. (b) How are tax liability accounts and Payroll Tax Expense classified in the financial statements?

9. You are a newly hired accountant with Nolasco Company. On your first day, the controller asks you to identify the main internal control objectives related to payroll accounting. How would you respond?

10. What are the four functions associated with payroll activities?

Brief Exercises

Compute gross earnings and net pay.

BEI.1 (LO 1), AP Beth Corbin's regular hourly wage rate is $16, and she receives an hourly rate of $24 for work in excess of 40 hours. During a January pay period, Beth works 45 hours. Beth's federal income tax withholding is $95, she has no voluntary deductions, and the FICA tax rate is 7.65%. Compute Beth Corbin's gross earnings and net pay for the pay period.

Record a payroll and the payment of wages.

BEI.2 (LO 1), AP Data for Beth Corbin are presented in BEI.1. Prepare the journal entries to record (a) Beth's pay for the period and (b) the payment of Beth's wages. Use January 15 for the end of the pay period and the payment date.

Record employer payroll taxes.

BEI.3 (LO 2), AP In January, gross earnings in Lugo Company totaled $80,000. All earnings are subject to 7.65% FICA taxes, 5.4% state unemployment taxes, and 0.6% federal unemployment taxes. Prepare the entry to record January payroll tax expense.

Identify payroll functions.

BEI.4 (LO 3), AP Swenson Company has the following payroll procedures.

 a. Supervisor approves overtime work.
 b. The human resources department prepares hiring authorization forms for new hires.
 c. A second payroll department employee verifies payroll calculations.
 d. The treasurer's department pays employees.

Identify the payroll function to which each procedure pertains.

Exercises

Compute net pay and record pay for one employee.

EI.1 (LO 1), AP Maria Garza's regular hourly wage rate is $16, and she receives a wage of 1½ times the regular hourly rate for work in excess of 40 hours. During a March weekly pay period, Maria worked 42 hours. Her gross earnings prior to the current week were $6,000. Maria is married and claims three withholding allowances. Her only voluntary deduction is for group hospitalization insurance at $25 per week.

Instructions

a. Compute the following amounts for Maria's wages for the current week.

1. Gross earnings.
2. FICA taxes. (Assume a 7.65% rate on maximum of $127,200.)
3. Federal income taxes withheld. (Use the withholding table in Illustration I.5.)
4. State income taxes withheld. (Assume a 2.0% rate.)
5. Net pay.

b. Record Maria's pay.

EI.2 (LO 1), AP Employee earnings records for Slaymaker Company reveal the following gross earnings for four employees through the pay period of December 15.

Compute maximum FICA deductions.

J. Seligman	$93,500	L. Marshall	$115,100
R. Eby	$113,600	T. Olson	$140,000

For the pay period ending December 31, each employee's gross earnings is $4,500. The FICA tax rate is 7.65% on gross earnings of $127,200.

Instructions

Compute the FICA withholdings that should be made for each employee for the December 31 pay period. (Show computations.)

EI.3 (LO 1, 2), AP Ramirez Company has the following data for the weekly payroll ending January 31.

Prepare payroll register and record payroll and payroll tax expense.

Employee	M	T	W	T	F	S	Hourly Rate	Federal Income Tax Withholding	Health Insurance
L. Helton	8	8	9	8	10	3	$12	$34	$10
R. Kenseth	8	8	8	8	8	2	14	37	25
D. Tavaras	9	10	8	8	9	0	15	58	25

Employees are paid 1½ times the regular hourly rate for all hours worked in excess of 40 hours per week. FICA taxes are 7.65% on the first $127,200 of gross earnings. Ramirez Company is subject to 5.4% state unemployment taxes and 0.6% federal unemployment taxes on the first $7,000 of gross earnings.

Instructions

a. Prepare the payroll register for the weekly payroll.

b. Prepare the journal entries to record the payroll and Ramirez's payroll tax expense.

EI.4 (LO 1), AP Selected data from a February payroll register for Sutton Company are presented below. Some amounts are intentionally omitted.

Compute missing payroll amounts and record payroll.

Gross earnings:		State income taxes	$ (3)
Regular	$9,100	Union dues	100
Overtime	(1)	Total deductions	(4)
Total	(2)	Net pay	$7,595
Deductions:		Account debited:	
FICA taxes	$ 765	Salaries and wages expense	(5)
Federal income taxes	1,140		

FICA taxes are 7.65%. State income taxes are 4% of gross earnings.

Instructions

a. Fill in the missing amounts.

b. Journalize the February payroll and the payment of the payroll.

EI.5 (LO 2), AP According to a payroll register summary of Frederickson Company, the amount of employees' gross pay in December was $850,000, of which $80,000 was not subject to Social Security taxes of 6.2% and $750,000 was not subject to state and federal unemployment taxes.

Determine employer's payroll taxes; record payroll tax expense.

Instructions

a. Determine the employer's payroll tax expense for the month, using the following rates: FICA 7.65%, state unemployment 5.4%, and federal unemployment 0.6%.

b. Prepare the journal entry to record December payroll tax expense.

Problems

Prepare payroll register and payroll entries.

PI.1 (LO 1, 2), AP Mann Hardware has four employees who are paid on an hourly basis plus time-and-a-half for all hours worked in excess of 40 a week. Payroll data for the week ended March 15, 2022, are presented as follows.

Employee	Hours Worked	Hourly Rate	Federal Income Tax Withholdings	United Fund
Ben Abel	40	$15.00	$?	$5.00
Rita Hager	42	16.00	?	5.00
Jack Never	44	13.00	60.00	8.00
Sue Perez	46	13.00	61.00	5.00

Abel and Hager are married. They claim 0 and 4 withholding allowances, respectively. The following tax rates are applicable: FICA 7.65%, state income taxes 3%, state unemployment taxes 5.4%, and federal unemployment 0.6%.

Instructions

a. Net pay $2,039.30

b. Payroll tax expense $349.43

d. Cash paid $578.02

a. Prepare a payroll register for the weekly payroll. (Use the wage-bracket withholding table in the text for federal income tax withholdings.)

b. Journalize the payroll on March 15, 2022, and the accrual of employer payroll taxes.

c. Journalize the payment of the payroll on March 16, 2022.

d. Journalize the deposit in a Federal Reserve bank on March 31, 2022, of the FICA and federal income taxes payable to the government.

Journalize payroll transactions and adjusting entries.

PI.2 (LO 1, 2), AP The following payroll liability accounts are included in the ledger of Harmon Company on January 1, 2022.

FICA Taxes Payable	$ 760.00
Federal Income Taxes Payable	1,204.60
State Income Taxes Payable	108.95
Federal Unemployment Taxes Payable	288.95
State Unemployment Taxes Payable	1,954.40
Union Dues Payable	870.00
U.S. Savings Bonds Payable	360.00

In January, the following transactions occurred.

Jan. 10 Sent check for $870.00 to union treasurer for union dues.
12 Remitted check for $1,964.60 to the Federal Reserve bank for FICA taxes and federal income taxes withheld.
15 Purchased U.S. Savings Bonds for employees by writing check for $360.00.
17 Paid state income taxes withheld from employees.
20 Paid federal and state unemployment taxes.
31 Completed monthly payroll register, which shows salaries and wages $58,000, FICA taxes withheld $4,437, federal income taxes payable $2,158, state income taxes payable $454, union dues payable $400, United Fund contributions payable $1,888, and net pay $48,663.
31 Prepared payroll checks for the net pay and distributed checks to employees.

At January 31, the company also makes the following accrued adjustments pertaining to employee compensation.

1. Employer payroll taxes: FICA taxes 7.65%, federal unemployment taxes 0.6%, and state unemployment taxes 5.4%.
2. Vacation pay: 6% of gross earnings. (Use Vacation Benefit Expense to record the transaction.)

b. Payroll tax expense $8,033; Vacation benefit expense $3,480

Instructions

a. Journalize the January transactions.

b. Journalize the adjustments pertaining to employee compensation at January 31.

P1.3 (LO 1, 2), AP For the year ended December 31, 2022, Denkinger Electrical Repair Company reports the following summary payroll data.

Prepare entries for payroll and payroll taxes; prepare W-2 data.

Gross earnings:	
Administrative salaries	$200,000
Electricians' wages	370,000
Total	$570,000
Deductions:	
FICA taxes	$ 38,645
Federal income taxes withheld	174,400
State income taxes withheld (3%)	17,100
United Fund contributions payable	27,500
Health insurance premiums	17,200
Total	$274,845

Denkinger Company's payroll taxes are Social Security tax 6.2%, Medicare tax 1.45%, state unemployment 2.5% (due to a stable employment record), and 0.6% federal unemployment. Gross earnings subject to Social Security taxes of 6.2% total $490,000, and gross earnings subject to unemployment taxes total $135,000. No employee exceeds the $127,200 limit related to FICA taxes.

Instructions

a. Prepare a summary journal entry at December 31 for the full year's payroll.
b. Journalize the adjusting entry at December 31 to record the employer's payroll taxes.
c. The W-2 Wage and Tax Statement requires the following dollar data.

a. Salaries and wages payable $295,155
b. Payroll tax expense $43,100

Wages, Tips, Other Compensation	Federal Income Tax Withheld	State Income Tax Withheld	FICA Wages	FICA Tax Withheld

Complete the required data for the following employees.

Employee	Gross Earnings	Federal Income Tax Withheld
Maria Sandoval	$59,000	$28,500
Jennifer Mingenback	26,000	10,200

Appendix J

Subsidiary Ledgers and Special Journals

Appendix Preview

A reliable accounting information system is a necessity for any company. Whether companies use pen, pencil, or computers in maintaining accounting records, certain principles and procedures apply. The purpose of this appendix is to explain and illustrate two components of an accounting information system: subsidiary ledgers and special journals.

Appendix Outline

LEARNING OBJECTIVES

1. Describe the nature and purpose of a subsidiary ledger.	• Subsidiary ledger example • Advantages of subsidiary ledgers
2. Record transactions in special journals.	• Sales journal • Cash receipts journal • Purchases journal • Cash payments journal • Effects of special journals on the general journal • Cybersecurity

Subsidiary Ledgers

LEARNING OBJECTIVE 1
Describe the nature and purpose of a subsidiary ledger.

Imagine a business that has several thousand charge (credit) customers and shows the transactions with these customers in only one general ledger account—Accounts Receivable. It would be nearly impossible to determine the balance owed by an individual customer at any specific time. Similarly, the amount payable to one creditor would be difficult to locate quickly from a single Accounts Payable account in the general ledger.

Instead, companies use subsidiary ledgers to keep track of individual balances. A **subsidiary ledger** is a group of accounts with a common characteristic (for example, all accounts receivable). It is an addition to, and an expansion of, the general ledger. The subsidiary ledger frees the general ledger from the details of individual balances.

J-1

Two common subsidiary ledgers are as follows.

1. The **accounts receivable** (or **customers') subsidiary ledger**, which collects transaction data of individual customers.
2. The **accounts payable** (or **creditors') subsidiary ledger**, which collects transaction data of individual creditors.

In each of these subsidiary ledgers, companies usually arrange individual accounts in alphabetical order.

A general ledger account summarizes the detailed data from a subsidiary ledger. For example, the detailed data from the accounts receivable subsidiary ledger are summarized in Accounts Receivable in the general ledger. The general ledger account that summarizes subsidiary ledger data is called a **control account**. Illustration J.1 presents an overview of the relationship of subsidiary ledgers to the general ledger. In Illustration J.1, the general ledger control accounts and subsidiary ledger accounts are in green. Note that Cash and Common Stock in this illustration are not control accounts because there are no subsidiary ledger accounts related to these accounts.

ILLUSTRATION J.1 Relationship of general ledger and subsidiary ledgers

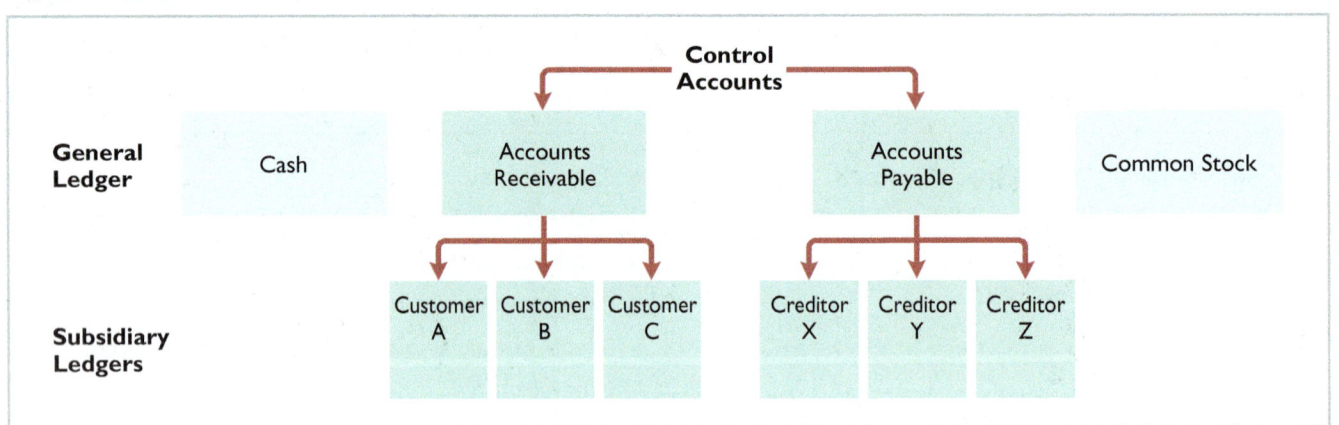

At the end of an accounting period, **each general ledger control account balance must equal the composite balance of the individual accounts in the related subsidiary ledger.** For example, the balance in Accounts Payable in Illustration J.1 must equal the total of the subsidiary balances of Creditors X + Y + Z.

Subsidiary Ledger Example

Illustration J.2 lists sales and collection transactions for Pujols Enterprises.

ILLUSTRATION J.2
Sales and collection transactions

	Credit Sales				Collections on Account	
Jan. 10	Aaron Co.	$ 6,000		Jan. 19	Aaron Co.	$4,000
12	Branden Inc.	3,000		21	Branden Inc.	3,000
20	Caron Co.	3,000		29	Caron Co.	1,000
		$12,000				$8,000

Illustration J.3 provides an example of a control account and subsidiary ledger based on these transactions. (Due to space considerations, the explanation column in these accounts is not shown in this and subsequent illustrations.)

ILLUSTRATION J.3 Relationship between general and subsidiary ledgers

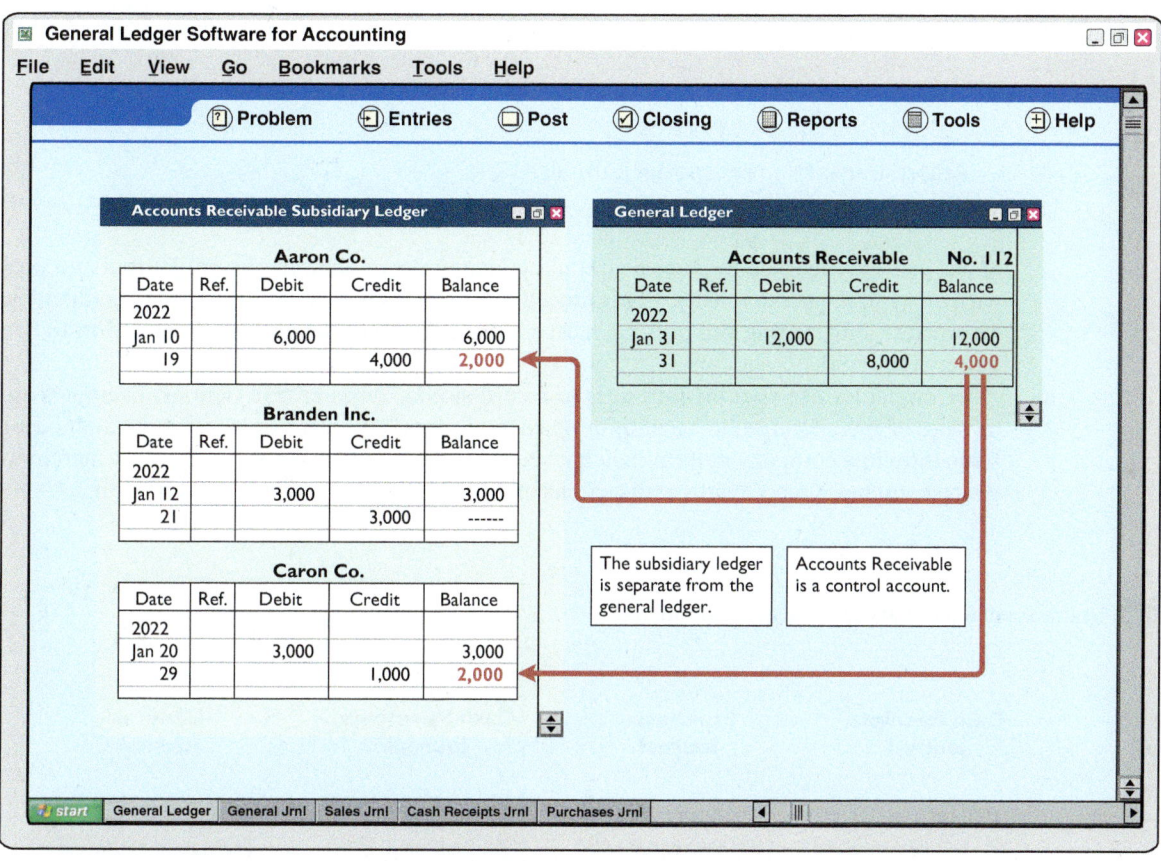

Pujols can reconcile the total debits ($12,000) and credits ($8,000) in Accounts Receivable in the general ledger to the detailed debits and credits in the subsidiary accounts. Also, the balance of $4,000 in the control account agrees with the total of the balances in the individual accounts (Aaron Co. $2,000 + Branden Inc. $0 + Caron Co. $2,000) in the subsidiary ledger.

As Illustration J.3 shows, companies make monthly postings to the control accounts in the general ledger. This practice allows them to prepare monthly financial statements. Companies post to the individual accounts in the subsidiary ledger daily. Daily posting ensures that account information is current. This enables the company to monitor credit limits, bill customers, and answer inquiries from customers about their account balances.

Advantages of Subsidiary Ledgers

Subsidiary ledgers have several advantages:

1. **They show in a single account transactions affecting one customer or one creditor**, thus providing up-to-date information on specific account balances.
2. **They free the general ledger of excessive details.** As a result, a trial balance of the general ledger does not contain vast numbers of individual account balances.
3. **They help locate errors in individual accounts** by reducing the number of accounts in one ledger and by using control accounts.
4. **They make possible a division of labor in posting.** One employee can post to the general ledger while someone else posts to the subsidiary ledgers.

Special Journals

LEARNING OBJECTIVE 2
Record transactions in special journals.

So far you have learned to journalize transactions in a two-column general journal and post each entry to the general ledger. This procedure is satisfactory in only very small companies. To expedite journalizing and posting, most companies use special journals **in addition to the general journal**.

Companies use **special journals** to record similar types of transactions. Examples are all sales of merchandise on account or all cash receipts. The types of transactions that occur frequently in a company determine what special journals the company uses. Most merchandising companies record daily transactions using the journals shown in Illustration J.4.

ILLUSTRATION J.4 Use of special journals and the general journal

Sales Journal	Cash Receipts Journal	Purchases Journal	Cash Payments Journal	General Journal
Used for: All sales of merchandise on account	Used for: All cash received (including cash sales)	Used for: All purchases of merchandise on account	Used for: All cash paid (including cash purchases)	Used for: Transactions that cannot be entered in a special journal, including correcting, adjusting, and closing entries

If a transaction cannot be recorded in a special journal, the company records it in the general journal. For example, if a company had special journals for only the four types of transactions listed above, it would record purchase returns and allowances that do not affect cash in the general journal. Similarly, **correcting, adjusting, and closing entries are recorded in the general journal**. In some situations, companies might use special journals other than those listed above. For example, when sales returns and allowances that do not affect cash are frequent, a company might use a special journal to record these transactions.

Special journals **permit greater division of labor** because several people can record entries in different journals at the same time. For example, one employee may journalize all cash receipts, and another may journalize all credit sales. Also, the use of special journals **reduces the time needed to complete the posting process**. With special journals, companies may post some accounts monthly, instead of daily, as we will illustrate later in this appendix (see **Helpful Hint**). On the following pages, we discuss the four special journals shown in Illustration J.4.

> **HELPFUL HINT**
> Postings are also made daily to individual ledger accounts in the inventory subsidiary ledger to maintain a perpetual inventory.

Sales Journal

In the **sales journal**, companies record **sales of merchandise on account**. Cash sales of merchandise go in the cash receipts journal. Credit sales of assets other than merchandise go in the general journal.

Journalizing Credit Sales

To demonstrate use of a sales journal, we will use data for Karns Wholesale Supply, which uses a **perpetual inventory system**. Under this system, each entry in the sales journal results in one entry **at selling price** and another entry **at cost**. The entry at selling price is a debit to Accounts Receivable (a control account) and a credit of equal amount to Sales Revenue. The entry at cost is a debit to Cost of Goods Sold and a credit of equal amount to Inventory (a control account). Using a sales journal with two amount columns, the company can show on only one line a sales transaction at both selling price and cost. **Illustration J.5** shows this two-column sales journal of Karns Wholesale Supply, using assumed credit sales transactions (for sales invoices 101–107).

ILLUSTRATION J.5 Journalizing the sales journal—perpetual inventory system

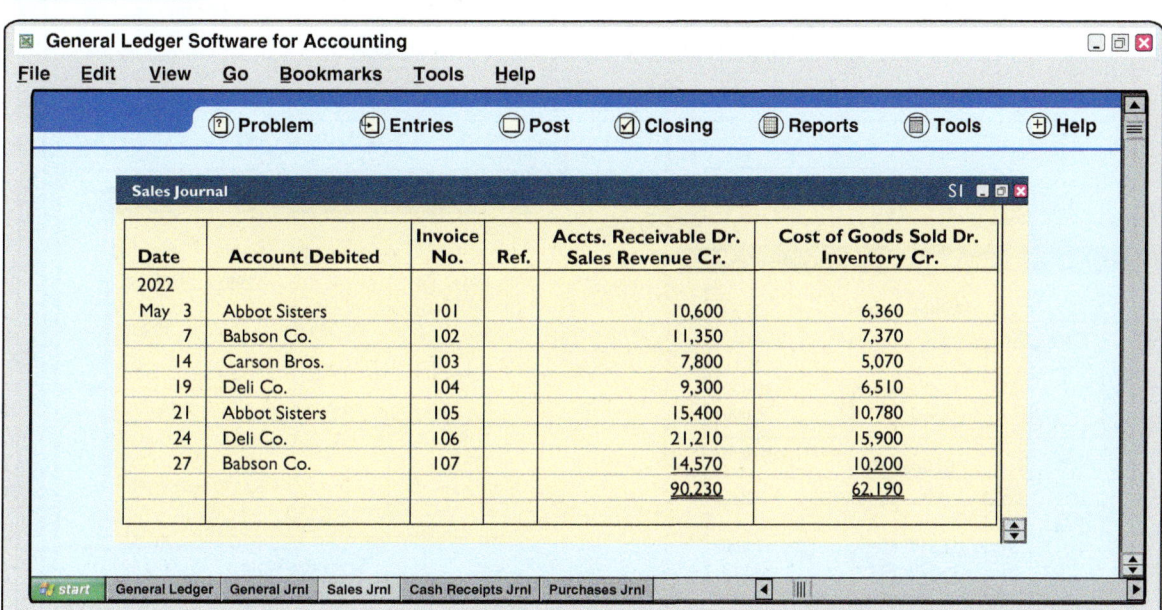

Note that, unlike the general journal, an explanation is not required for each entry in a special journal. Also, the use of prenumbered invoices ensures that all invoices are journalized. Finally, the reference (Ref.) column is not used in journalizing. It is used in posting the sales journal, as explained next.

Posting the Sales Journal

Companies make daily postings from the sales journal **to the individual accounts receivable** in the subsidiary ledger. Posting **to the general ledger** is done **monthly**. **Illustration J.6** shows both the daily and monthly postings.

A check mark (✓) is inserted in the reference posting column to indicate that the daily posting to the customer's account has been made. If the subsidiary ledger accounts were numbered, the account number would be entered in place of the check mark. At the end of the month, Karns posts the column totals of the sales journal to the general ledger. Here, the column totals are as follows. From the selling-price column, a debit of $90,230 to Accounts Receivable (account No. 112) and a credit of $90,230 to Sales Revenue (account No. 401); from the cost column, a debit of $62,190 to Cost of Goods Sold (account No. 505) and a credit of $62,190 to Inventory (account No. 120). Karns inserts the account numbers below the column totals to indicate that the postings have been made. In both the general ledger and subsidiary ledger accounts, the reference **S1** indicates that the posting came from page 1 of the sales journal.

ILLUSTRATION J.6 Posting the sales journal

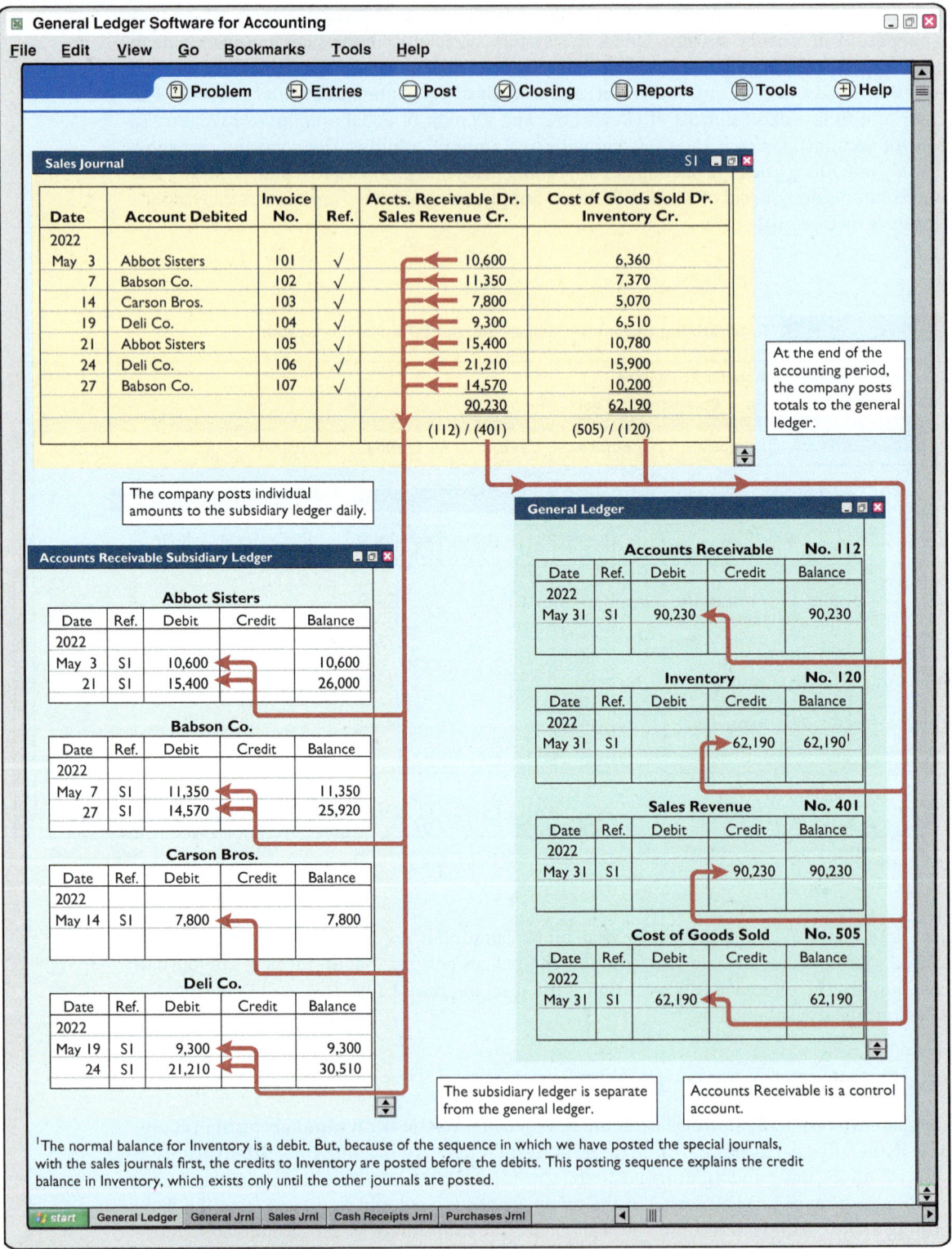

Proving the Ledgers

The next step is to "prove" the ledgers. To do so, Karns must determine two things: (1) The total of the general ledger debit balances must equal the total of the general ledger credit balances. (2) The sum of the subsidiary ledger balances must equal the balance in the control account. **Illustration J.7** shows the proof of the postings from the sales journal to the general and subsidiary ledger.

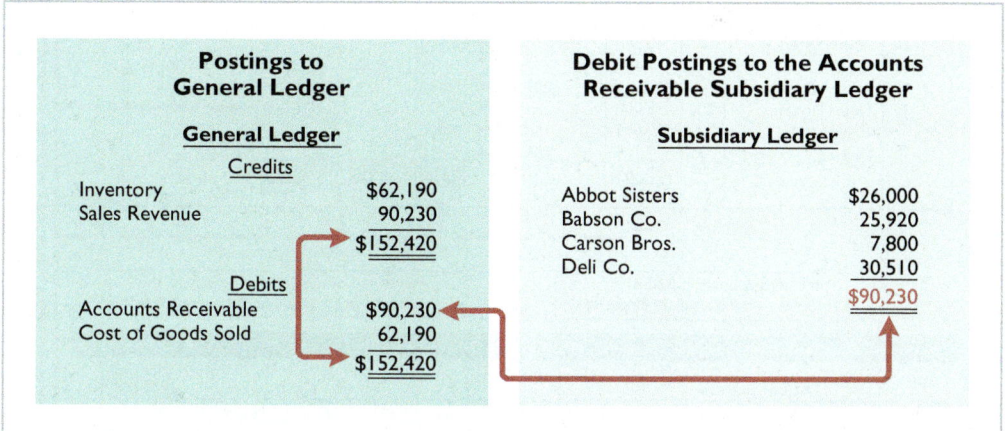

ILLUSTRATION J.7
Proving the equality of the postings from the sales journal

Advantages of the Sales Journal

Use of a special journal to record sales on account has several advantages. First, the one-line entry for each sales transaction saves time. In the sales journal, it is not necessary to write out the four account titles for each transaction. Second, only totals, rather than individual entries, are posted to the general ledger. This saves posting time and reduces the possibilities of posting errors. Finally, a division of labor results because one individual can take responsibility for the sales journal.

Cash Receipts Journal

In the **cash receipts journal**, companies record all receipts of cash. The most common types of cash receipts are cash sales of merchandise and collections of accounts receivable. Many other possibilities exist, such as receipt of money from bank loans and cash proceeds from disposal of equipment. A one- or two-column cash receipts journal would not have space enough for all possible cash receipt transactions. Therefore, companies use a multi-column cash receipts journal.

Generally, a cash receipts journal includes the following columns: debit columns for Cash and Sales Discounts, and credit columns for Accounts Receivable, Sales Revenue, and "Other Accounts." Companies use the Other Accounts category when the cash receipt does not involve a cash sale or a collection of accounts receivable. Under a perpetual inventory system, each sales entry also is accompanied by an entry that debits Cost of Goods Sold and credits Inventory for the cost of the merchandise sold. **Illustration J.8** shows a six-column cash receipts journal.

ILLUSTRATION J.8

Journalizing and posting the cash receipts journal

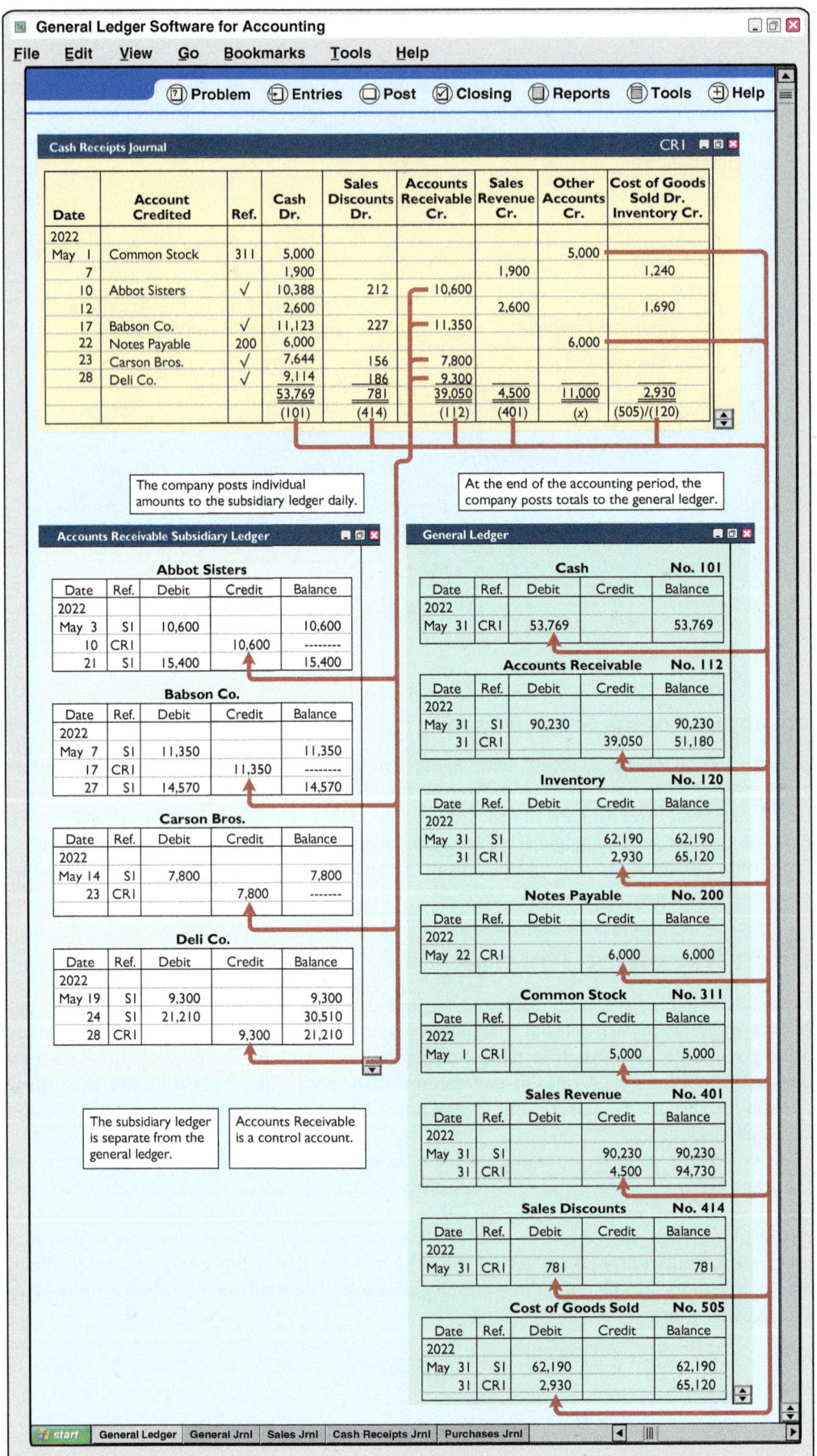

Companies may use additional credit columns if these columns significantly reduce postings to a specific account. For example, a loan company, such as **Household International**, receives thousands of cash collections from customers. Using separate credit columns for Loans Receivable and Interest Revenue, rather than the Other Accounts credit column, would reduce postings.

Journalizing Cash Receipts Transactions

To illustrate the journalizing of cash receipts transactions, we will continue with the May transactions of Karns Wholesale Supply. Collections from customers relate to the entries recorded in the sales journal in Illustration J.5. The entries in the cash receipts journal are based on the following cash receipts.

May	1	Stockholders invested $5,000 in the business.
	7	Cash sales of merchandise total $1,900 (cost, $1,240).
	10	Received a check for $10,388 from Abbot Sisters in payment of invoice No. 101 for $10,600 less a 2% discount.
	12	Cash sales of merchandise total $2,600 (cost, $1,690).
	17	Received a check for $11,123 from Babson Co. in payment of invoice No. 102 for $11,350 less a 2% discount.
	22	Received cash by signing a note for $6,000.
	23	Received a check for $7,644 from Carson Bros. in full for invoice No. 103 for $7,800 less a 2% discount.
	28	Received a check for $9,114 from Deli Co. in full for invoice No. 104 for $9,300 less a 2% discount.

Further information about the columns in the cash receipts journal is listed below.

Debit Columns:

1. **Cash.** Karns enters in this column the amount of cash actually received in each transaction. The column total indicates the total cash receipts for the month.
2. **Sales Discounts.** Karns includes a Sales Discounts column in its cash receipts journal. By doing so, it does not need to enter sales discount items in the general journal. As a result, the cash receipts journal shows on one line the collection of an account receivable within the discount period.

Credit Columns:

3. **Accounts Receivable.** Karns uses the Accounts Receivable column to record cash collections on account. The amount entered here is the amount to be credited to the individual customer's account (see **Helpful Hint**).
4. **Sales Revenue.** The Sales Revenue column records all cash sales of merchandise. Cash sales of other assets (plant assets, for example) are not reported in this column.
5. **Other Accounts.** Karns uses the Other Accounts column whenever the credit is other than to Accounts Receivable or Sales Revenue. For example, in the first entry, Karns enters $5,000 as a credit to Common Stock. This column is often referred to as the sundry accounts column.

Debit and Credit Column:

6. **Cost of Goods Sold and Inventory.** This column records debits to Cost of Goods Sold and credits to Inventory.

In a multi-column journal, generally only one line is needed for each entry. Debit and credit amounts for each line must be equal. When Karns journalizes the collection from Abbot Sisters on May 10, for example, three amounts are indicated. Note also that the Account Credited column identifies both general ledger and subsidiary ledger account titles. General ledger

> **HELPFUL HINT**
>
> A *subsidiary ledger* account is entered when the entry involves a collection of accounts receivable. A *general ledger* account is entered when the account is not shown in a special column (and an amount must be entered in the Other Accounts column). Otherwise, no account is shown in the Account Credited column.

accounts are illustrated in the May 1 and May 22 entries. A subsidiary account is illustrated in the May 10 entry for the collection from Abbot Sisters.

When Karns has finished journalizing a multi-column journal, it totals the amount columns and compares the totals to prove the equality of debits and credits. **Illustration J.9** shows the proof of the equality of Karns' cash receipts journal.

ILLUSTRATION J.9

Proving the equality of the cash receipts journal

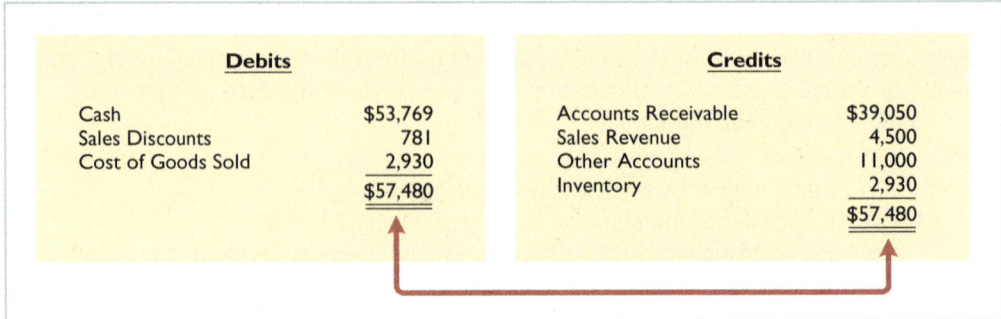

Totaling the columns of a journal and proving the equality of the totals is called **footing** and **crossfooting** a journal.

Posting the Cash Receipts Journal

Posting a multi-column journal (Illustration J.8) involves the following steps.

1. **At the end of the month**, the company posts all column totals, except for the Other Accounts total, to the account title(s) specified in the column heading (such as Cash or Accounts Receivable). The company then enters account numbers below the column totals to show that they have been posted. For example, Karns has posted cash to account No. 101, accounts receivable to account No. 112, inventory to account No. 120, sales revenue to account No. 401, sales discounts to account No. 414, and cost of goods sold to account No. 505.

2. The company **separately posts the individual amounts comprising the Other Accounts total** to the general ledger accounts specified in the Account Credited column. See, for example, the credit posting to Common Stock. The total amount of this column has not been posted. The symbol (X) is inserted below the total to this column to indicate that the amount has not been posted.

3. The individual amounts in a column, posted in total to a control account (Accounts Receivable, in this case), are posted **daily to the subsidiary ledger** account specified in the Account Credited column. See, for example, the credit posting of $10,600 to Abbot Sisters.

The symbol **CR**, used in both the subsidiary and general ledgers, identifies postings from the cash receipts journal.

Proving the Ledgers

After posting of the cash receipts journal is completed, Karns proves the ledgers. As shown in **Illustration J.10**, the general ledger totals agree. Also, the sum of the subsidiary ledger balances equals the control account balance.

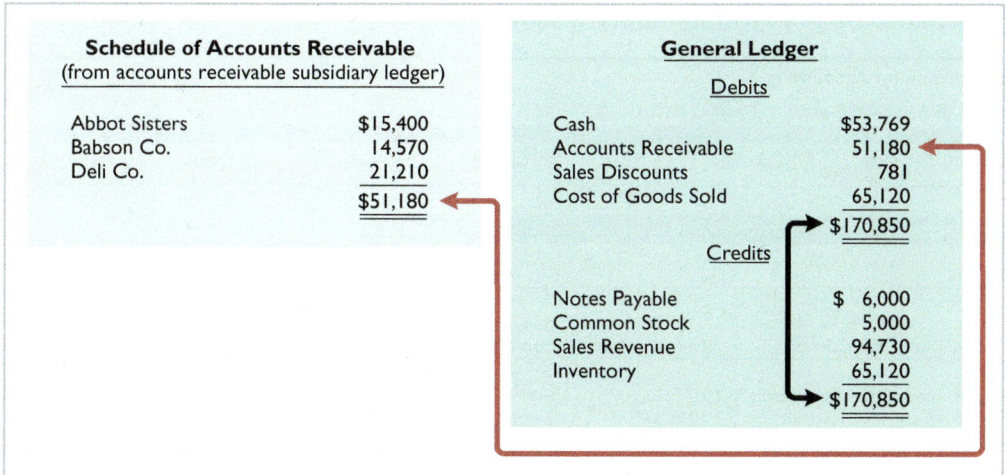

ILLUSTRATION J.10
Proving the ledgers after posting the sales and the cash receipts journals

Purchases Journal

In the **purchases journal**, companies record all purchases of merchandise on account. Each entry in this journal results in a debit to Inventory and a credit to Accounts Payable (see **Helpful Hint**). For example, consider the following credit purchase transactions for Karns Wholesale Supply in **Illustration J.11**.

> **HELPFUL HINT**
> A single-column purchases journal needs only to be footed to prove the equality of debits and credits.

Date	Supplier	Amount
5/6	Jasper Manufacturing Inc.	$11,000
5/10	Eaton and Howe Inc.	7,200
5/14	Fabor and Son	6,900
5/19	Jasper Manufacturing Inc.	17,500
5/26	Fabor and Son	8,700
5/29	Eaton and Howe Inc.	12,600

ILLUSTRATION J.11
Credit purchases transactions

Illustration J.12 shows the purchases journal for Karns based on these transactions. When using a one-column purchases journal (as in Illustration J.12), a company cannot journalize other types of purchases on account or cash purchases in it. For example, using the purchases journal shown in Illustration J.12, Karns would have to record credit purchases of equipment or supplies in the general journal. Likewise, all cash purchases would be entered in the cash payments journal. As illustrated later, companies that make numerous credit purchases for items other than merchandise often expand the purchases journal to a multi-column format. (See Illustration J.14.)

Journalizing Credit Purchases of Merchandise

The journalizing procedure is similar to that for a sales journal. Companies make entries in the purchases journal from purchase invoices. In contrast to the sales journal, the purchases journal may not have an invoice number column because invoices received from different suppliers will not be in numerical sequence. To ensure that they record all purchase invoices, some companies consecutively number each invoice upon receipt and then use an internal document number column in the purchases journal.

ILLUSTRATION J.12 Journalizing and posting the purchases journal

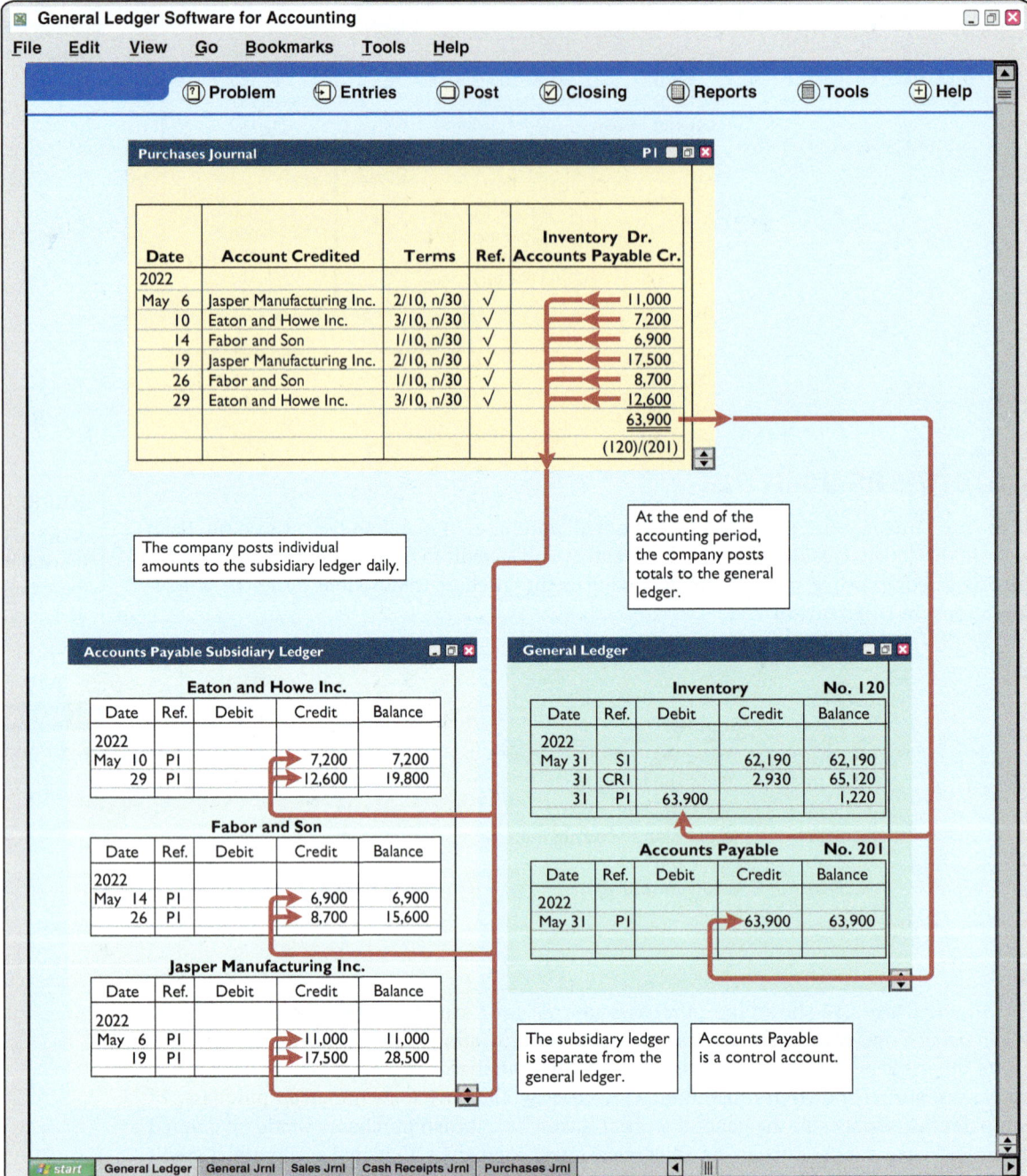

Posting the Purchases Journal

HELPFUL HINT

Postings to subsidiary ledger accounts are done daily because it is often necessary to know a current balance for the subsidiary accounts.

The procedures for posting the purchases journal are similar to those for the sales journal. In this case, Karns makes **daily** postings to the **accounts payable ledger**; it makes **monthly** postings to Inventory and Accounts Payable in the general ledger (see **Helpful Hint**). In both ledgers, Karns uses **P1** in the reference column to show that the postings are from page 1 of the purchases journal.

Proof of the equality of the postings from the purchases journal to both ledgers is shown in **Illustration J.13**.

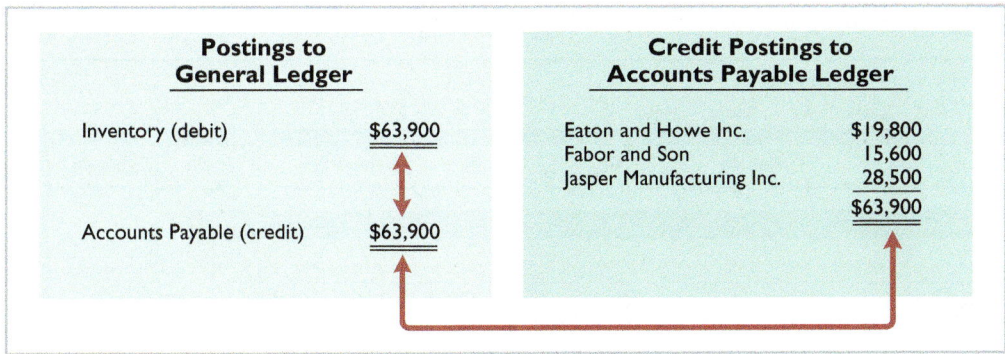

ILLUSTRATION J.13

Proving the equality of the purchases journal

Expanding the Purchases Journal

As noted earlier, some companies expand the purchases journal to include all types of purchases on account. Instead of one column for Inventory and Accounts Payable, they use a multi-column format. This format usually includes a credit column for Accounts Payable and debit columns for purchases of Inventory, Office Supplies, Store Supplies, and Other Accounts. **Illustration J.14** shows a multi-column purchases journal for Hanover Co. The posting procedures are similar to those shown earlier for posting the cash receipts journal.

ILLUSTRATION J.14 Multi-column purchases journal

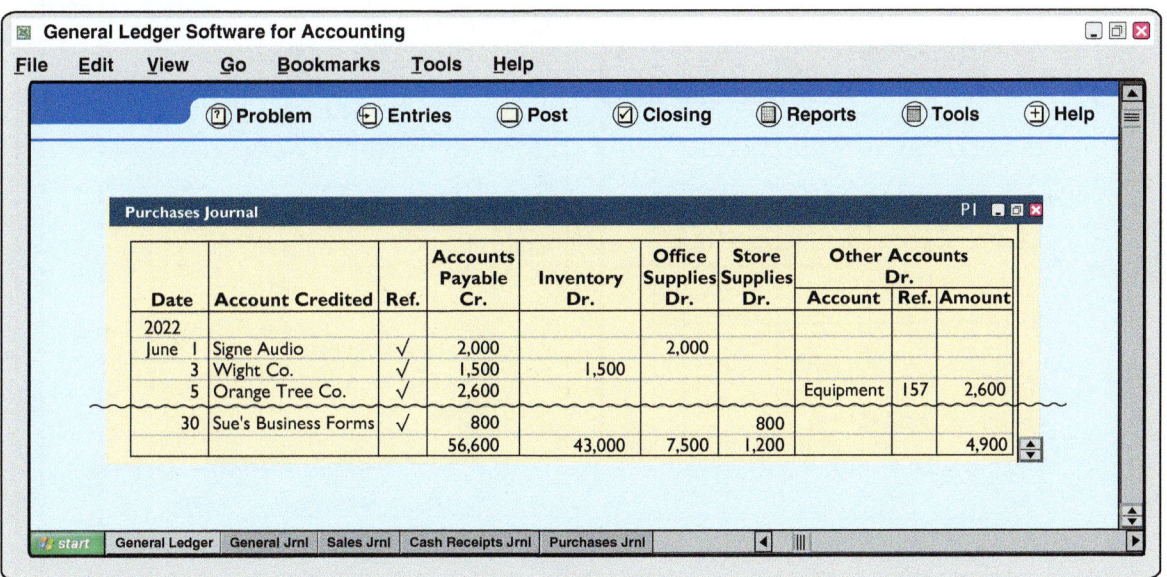

Cash Payments Journal

In a **cash payments (cash disbursements) journal**, companies record all disbursements of cash. Entries are made from prenumbered checks. Because companies make cash payments for various purposes, the cash payments journal has multiple columns. **Illustration J.15** shows a four-column journal.

Journalizing Cash Payments Transactions

The procedures for journalizing transactions in this journal are similar to those for the cash receipts journal. Karns records each transaction on one line, and for each line there must be equal debit and credit amounts. The entries in the cash payments

ILLUSTRATION J.15 Journalizing and posting the cash payments journal

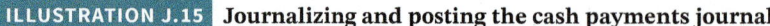

journal in Illustration J.15 are based on the following transactions for Karns Wholesale Supply.

May 1 Issued check No. 101 for $1,200 for the annual premium on a fire insurance policy.
    3 Issued check No. 102 for $100 in payment of freight when terms were FOB shipping point.
    8 Issued check No. 103 for $4,400 for the purchase of merchandise.
   10 Sent check No. 104 for $10,780 to Jasper Manufacturing Inc. in payment of May 6 invoice for $11,000 less a 2% discount.
   19 Mailed check No. 105 for $6,984 to Eaton and Howe Inc. in payment of May 10 invoice for $7,200 less a 3% discount.
   23 Sent check No. 106 for $6,831 to Fabor and Son in payment of May 14 invoice for $6,900 less a 1% discount.
   28 Sent check No. 107 for $17,150 to Jasper Manufacturing Inc. in payment of May 19 invoice for $17,500 less a 2% discount.
   30 Issued check No. 108 for $500 to stockholders as a dividend.

Note that whenever Karns enters an amount in the Other Accounts column, it must identify a specific general ledger account in the Account Debited column. The entries for checks No. 101, 102, 103, and 108 illustrate this situation. Similarly, Karns must identify a subsidiary account in the Account Debited column whenever it enters an amount in the Accounts Payable column. See, for example, the entry for check No. 104.

After Karns journalizes the cash payments journal, it totals the columns. The totals are then balanced to prove the equality of debits and credits.

Posting the Cash Payments Journal

The procedures for posting the cash payments journal are similar to those for the cash receipts journal. Karns posts the amounts recorded in the Accounts Payable column individually to the subsidiary ledger and in total to the control account. It posts Inventory and Cash only in total at the end of the month. Transactions in the Other Accounts column are posted individually to the appropriate account(s) affected. The company does not post totals for the Other Accounts column.

Illustration J.15 shows the posting of the cash payments journal. Note that Karns uses the symbol **CP** as the posting reference. After postings are completed, the company proves the equality of the debit and credit balances in the general ledger. In addition, the control account balances should agree with the subsidiary ledger total balance. **Illustration J.16** shows the agreement of these balances.

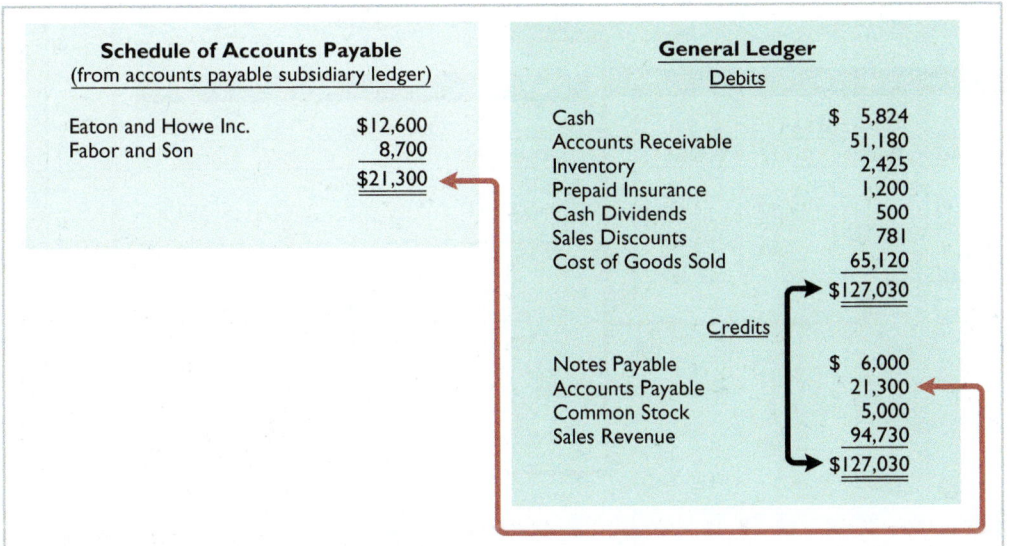

ILLUSTRATION J.16

Proving the ledgers after postings from the sales, cash receipts, purchases, and cash payments journals

Effects of Special Journals on the General Journal

Special journals for sales, purchases, and cash substantially reduce the number of entries that companies make in the general journal. **Only transactions that cannot be entered in a special journal are recorded in the general journal.** For example, a company may use the general journal to record such transactions as granting of credit to a customer for a sales return or allowance, granting of credit from a supplier for purchases returned, acceptance of a note receivable from a customer, and purchase of equipment by issuing a note payable. Also, **correcting, adjusting, and closing entries are made in the general journal**.

The general journal has columns for date, account title and explanation, reference, and debit and credit amounts. When control and subsidiary accounts are not involved, the procedures for journalizing and posting of transactions are the same as those described in earlier chapters. When control and subsidiary accounts *are* involved, companies make two changes from the earlier procedures:

1. In **journalizing**, they identify both the control and the subsidiary accounts.
2. In **posting**, there must be a **dual posting**: once to the control account and once to the subsidiary account.

To illustrate, assume that on May 31, Karns Wholesale Supply returns $500 of merchandise for credit to Fabor and Son. **Illustration J.17** shows the entry in the general journal and the posting of the entry. If Karns receives cash instead of credit on this return, then it would record the transaction in the cash receipts journal.

The general journal indicates two accounts (Accounts Payable, and Fabor and Son) for the debit, and two postings ("201/✓") in the reference column. One debit is posted to the control account and another debit to the creditor's account in the subsidiary ledger.

ILLUSTRATION J.17 Journalizing and posting the general journal

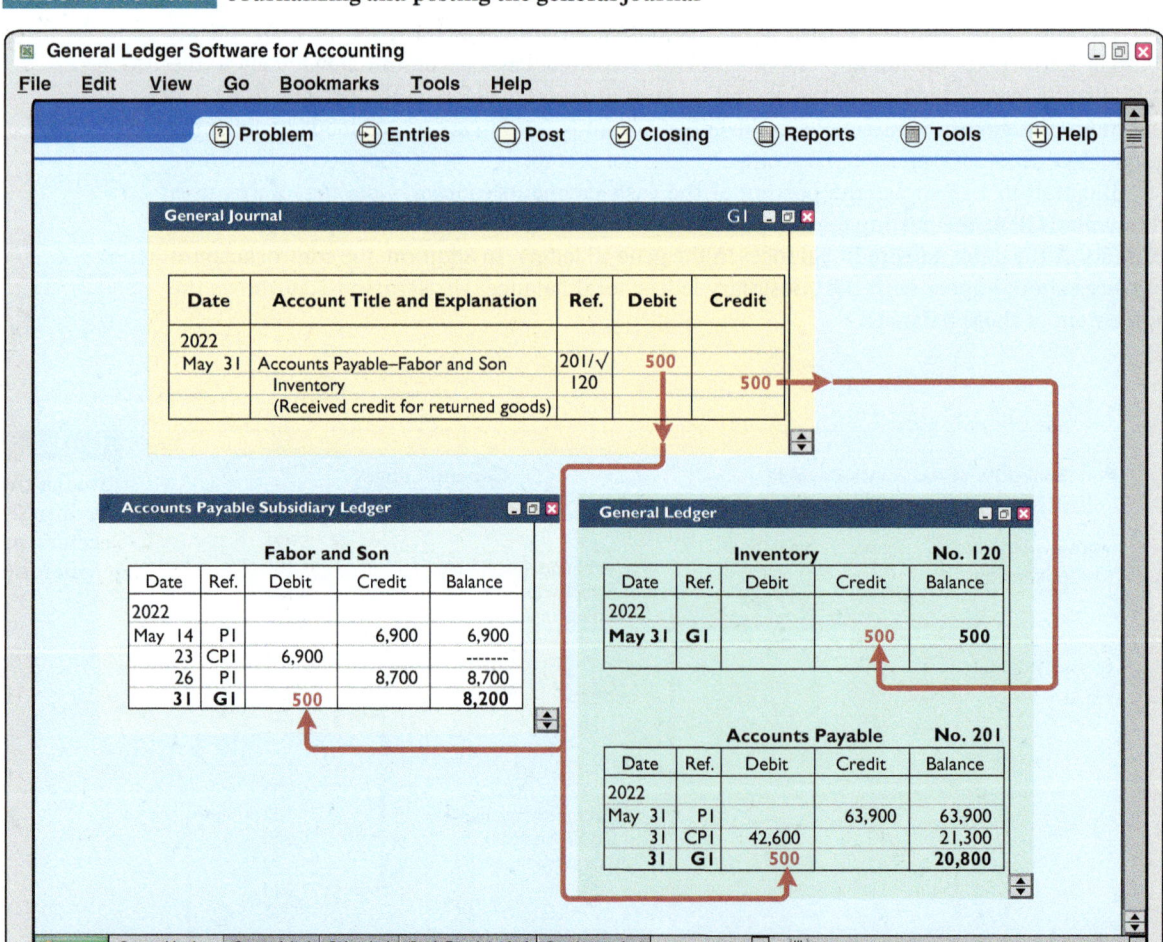

Cybersecurity: A Final Comment

Have you ever been hacked? With the increasing use of cell phones, tablets, and other social media outlets, a real risk exists that your confidential information may be stolen and used illegally. Companies, individuals, and even nations have all been victims of **cybercrime**—a crime that involves the Internet, a computer system, or computer technology.

For companies, cybercrime is clearly a major threat as the hacking of employees' or customers' records related to cybercrime can cost millions of dollars. Unfortunately, the numbers of security breaches are increasing. A security breach at **Target**, for example, cost the company a minimum of $20 million, the CEO lost his job, and sales plummeted.

Here are three reasons for the rise in the successful hacks of corporate computer records.

1. Companies and their employees continue to increase their activity on the Internet, primarily due to the use of mobile devices and cloud computing.
2. Companies today collect and store unprecedented amounts of personal data on customers and employees.
3. Companies often take measures to protect themselves from cybersecurity attacks but then fail to check if employees are carrying out the proper security guidelines.

Note that cybersecurity risks extend far beyond company operations and compliance. Many hackers target highly sensitive intellectual information or other strategic assets. **Illustration J.18** highlights the type of hackers and their motives, targets and impacts.

Companies now recognize that cybersecurity systems that protect confidential data must be implemented. It follows that companies (and nations and individuals) must continually verify that their cybersecurity defenses are sound and uncompromised.

ILLUSTRATION J.18 Profiles of hackers

Malicious Actors	Motives	Targets	Impacts
Nation-state	• Economic, political, and/or military advantage	• Trade secrets • Sensitive business information • Emerging technologies • Critical infrastructure	• Loss of competitive advantage • Disruption to critical infrastructure
Organized crime	• Immediate financial gain • Collect information for future financial gains	• Financial/payment systems • Personally identifiable information • Payment card information • Protected health information	• Costly regulatory inquiries and penalties • Consumer and shareholder lawsuits • Loss of consumer confidence
Hacktivists	• Influence political and/or social change • Pressure businesses to change their practices	• Corporate secrets • Sensitive business information • Information related to key executives, employees, customers, and business partners	• Disruption of business activities • Harm to brand and reputation • Loss of consumer confidence
Insiders	• Personal advantage, monetary gain • Professional revenge • Patriotism	• Sales, deals, market strategies • Corporate secrets, intellectual property • Business operations • Personnel information	• Trade secret disclosure • Operational disruption • Harm to brand and reputation • National security impact

Source: PriceWaterhouseCoopers, "Answering Your Cybersecurity Questions" (January 2014).

Review

Learning Objectives Review

1 Describe the nature and purpose of a subsidiary ledger.

A subsidiary ledger is a group of accounts with a common characteristic. It facilitates the recording process by freeing the general ledger from details of individual balances.

2 Record transactions in special journals.

Companies use special journals to group similar types of transactions. In a special journal, generally only one line is used to record a complete transaction.

In posting a multi-column journal:

a. Companies post all column totals except for the Other Accounts column once at the end of the month to the account title specified in the column heading.

b. Companies do not post the total of the Other Accounts column. Instead, the individual amounts comprising the total are posted separately to the general ledger accounts specified in the Account Credited (Debited) column.

c. The individual amounts in a column posted in total to a control account are posted daily to the subsidiary ledger accounts specified in the Account Credited (Debited) column.

Glossary Review

Accounts payable (creditors') subsidiary ledger A subsidiary ledger that collects transaction data of individual creditors. (p. J-2).

Accounts receivable (customers') subsidiary ledger A subsidiary ledger that collects transaction data of individual customers. (p. J-2).

Cash payments (cash disbursements) journal A special journal that records all cash paid. (p. J-13).

Cash receipts journal A special journal that records all cash received. (p. J-7).

Control account An account in the general ledger that summarizes subsidiary ledger data. (p. J-2).

Cybercrime A crime that involves the Internet, a computer system, or computer technology. (p. J-17).

Purchases journal A special journal that records all purchases of merchandise on account. (p. J-11).

Sales journal A special journal that records all sales of merchandise on account. (p. J-4).

Special journals Journals that record similar types of transactions, such as all credit sales. (p. J-4).

Subsidiary ledger A group of accounts with a common characteristic. (p. J-1).

WileyPLUS

Many additional resources are available for practice in WileyPLUS.

Questions

1. What are the advantages of using subsidiary ledgers?

2. (a) When do companies normally post to (1) the subsidiary accounts and (2) the general ledger control accounts? (b) Describe the relationship between a control account and a subsidiary ledger.

3. Identify and explain the four special journals discussed in this appendix. List an advantage of using each of these journals rather than using only a general journal.

4. Burguet Company uses special journals. It recorded in a sales journal a sale made on account to P. Starch for $435. A few days later, P. Starch returns $70 worth of merchandise for credit. Where should Burguet Company record the sales return? Why?

5. A $500 purchase of merchandise on account from Liu Company was properly recorded in the purchases journal. When posted, however, the amount recorded in the subsidiary ledger was $50. How might this error be discovered?

6. Why would special journals used in different businesses not be identical in format? What type of business would maintain a cash receipts journal but not include a column for accounts receivable?

7. The cash and the accounts receivable columns in the cash receipts journal were mistakenly over-added by $4,000 at the end of the month. (a) Will the customers' ledger agree with the Accounts Receivable control account? (b) Assuming no other errors, will the trial balance totals be equal?

8. One column total of a special journal is posted at month-end to only two general ledger accounts. One of these two accounts is Accounts Receivable. What is the name of this special journal? What is the other general ledger account to which that same month-end total is posted?

9. In what journal would the following transactions be recorded? (Assume that a two-column sales journal and a single-column purchases journal are used.)

   a. Recording of depreciation expense for the year.
   b. Credit given to a customer for merchandise purchased on credit and returned.
   c. Sales of merchandise for cash.
   d. Sales of merchandise on account.
   e. Collection of cash on account from a customer.
   f. Purchase of office supplies on account.

10. In what journal would the following transactions be recorded? (Assume that a two-column sales journal and a single-column purchases journal are used.)

    a. Cash received from signing a note payable.
    b. Investment of cash by stockholders.
    c. Closing of the expense accounts at the end of the year.
    d. Purchase of merchandise on account.
    e. Credit received for merchandise purchased and returned to supplier.
    f. Payment of cash on account due a supplier.

11. What transactions might be included in a multi-column purchases journal that would not be included in a single-column purchases journal?

12. Give an example of a transaction in the general journal that causes an entry to be posted twice (i.e., to two accounts), one in the general ledger, the other in the subsidiary ledger. Does this affect the debit/credit equality of the general ledger?

13. Give some examples of appropriate general journal transactions for an organization using special journals.

Brief Exercises

BEJ.1 (LO 1), C Presented below is information related to Cortes Company for its first month of operations. Identify the balances that appear in the accounts receivable subsidiary ledger and the accounts receivable balance that appears in the general ledger at the end of January.

Identify subsidiary ledger balances.

		Credit Sales				Cash Collections	
Jan.	7	Adcock Co.	$10,000	Jan.	17	Adcock Co.	$7,000
	15	Cruz Co.	7,000		24	Cruz Co.	6,000
	23	Morissy Co.	9,000		29	Morissy Co.	9,000

BEJ.2 (LO 1), C Identify in what ledger (general or subsidiary) each of the following accounts is shown.

Identify subsidiary ledger accounts.

a. Rent Expense.
b. Accounts Receivable—Molina.
c. Notes Payable.
d. Accounts Payable—Unruh.

BEJ.3 (LO 2), C Identify the journal in which each of the following transactions is recorded.

Identify special journals.

a. Cash sales.
b. Payment of cash dividends.
c. Cash purchase of land.
d. Credit sales.
e. Purchase of merchandise on account.
f. Receipt of cash for services performed.

BEJ.4 (LO 2), C Indicate whether each of the following debits and credits is included in the cash receipts journal. (Use "Yes" or "No" to answer this question.)

Identify entries to cash receipts journal.

a. Debit to Sales Revenue.
b. Credit to Inventory.
c. Credit to Accounts Receivable.
d. Debit to Accounts Payable.

BEJ.5 (LO 2), C Kiner Co. uses special journals and a general journal. Identify the journal in which each of the following transactions is recorded.

Identify transactions for special journals.

a. Purchased equipment on account.
b. Purchased merchandise on account.
c. Paid utility expense in cash.
d. Sold merchandise on account.

BEJ.6 (LO 2), C Identify the special journal(s). in which the following column headings appear.

Identify transactions for special journals.

a. Sales Discounts Dr.
b. Accounts Receivable Cr.
c. Cash Dr.
d. Sales Revenue Cr.
e. Inventory Dr.

Indicate postings to cash receipts journal.

BEJ.7 (LO 2), C Merando Computer Components Inc. uses a multi-column cash receipts journal. Indicate which column(s) is/are posted only in total, only daily, or both in total and daily.

a. Accounts Receivable.
b. Sales Discounts.
c. Cash.
d. Other Accounts.

Exercises

Determine control account balances, and explain posting of special journals.

EJ.1 (LO 1, 2), AP Lanley Company uses both special journals and a general journal as described in this appendix. On June 30, after all monthly postings had been completed, the Accounts Receivable control account in the general ledger had a debit balance of $314,000; the Accounts Payable control account had a credit balance of $77,000.

The July transactions recorded in the special journals are summarized below. No entries affecting accounts receivable and accounts payable were recorded in the general journal for July.

Sales journal	Total sales $161,400
Purchases journal	Total purchases $54,100
Cash receipts journal	Accounts receivable column total $131,000
Cash payments journal	Accounts payable column total $47,500

Instructions

a. What is the balance of the Accounts Receivable control account after the monthly postings on July 31?

b. What is the balance of the Accounts Payable control account after the monthly postings on July 31?

c. To what account(s) is the column total of $161,400 in the sales journal posted?

d. To what account(s) is the accounts receivable column total of $131,000 in the cash receipts journal posted?

Explain postings to subsidiary ledger.

EJ.2 (LO 1), AP Writing Presented below is the subsidiary Accounts Receivable account of Martha Nott.

Date	Ref.	Debit	Credit	Balance
2022				
Sept. 2	S31	61,000		61,000
9	G4		14,000	47,000
27	CR8		47,000	—

Instructions

Write a memo to Erica Grier, chief financial officer, that explains each transaction.

Post various journals to control and subsidiary accounts.

EJ.3 (LO 1, 2), AP On September 1, the balance of the Accounts Receivable control account in the general ledger of Stark Company was $10,960. The customers' subsidiary ledger contained account balances as follows: Zeyen $1,440, Milo $2,640, Baez $2,060, and Dey $4,820. At the end of September, the various journals contained the following information.

Sales journal: Sales to Dey $800; to Zeyen $1,260; to Guy $1,330; to Baez $1,260.

Cash receipts journal: Cash received from Baez $1,310; from Dey $2,300; from Guy $380; from Milo $1,800; from Zeyen $1,240.

General journal: An allowance is granted to Dey $185.

Instructions

a. Set up control and subsidiary accounts and enter the beginning balances. Do not construct the journals.

b. Post the various journals. Post the items as individual items or as totals, whichever would be the appropriate procedure. (No sales discounts given.)

c. Prepare a schedule of accounts receivable and prove the agreement of the controlling account with the subsidiary ledger at September 30, 2022.

EJ.4 (LO 1, 2), AP Bill Porter Company has a balance in its Accounts Receivable control account of $10,200 on January 1, 2022. The subsidiary ledger contains three accounts: Connor Company, balance $4,000; Uhlig Company, balance $2,500; and Matson Company. During January, the following receivable-related transactions occurred.

Determine control and subsidiary ledger balances for accounts receivable.

	Credit Sales	Collections	Returns
Connor Company	$9,000	$8,000	$ –0–
Uhlig Company	7,000	2,500	3,000
Matson Company	8,300	9,000	–0–

Instructions

a. What is the January 1 balance in the Matson Company subsidiary account?

b. What is the January 31 balance in the control account?

c. Compute the balances in the subsidiary accounts at the end of the month.

d. Which January transaction would not be recorded in a special journal?

EJ.5 (LO 1, 2), AP Gonzalez Company has a balance in its Accounts Payable control account of $8,250 on January 1, 2022. The subsidiary ledger contains three accounts: Rye Company, balance $3,000; Keyes Company, balance $1,875; and Colaw Company. During January, the following receivable-related transactions occurred.

Determine control and subsidiary ledger balances for accounts payable.

	Purchases	Payments	Returns
Rye Company	$6,750	$6,000	$ –0–
Keyes Company	5,250	1,900	2,300
Colaw Company	6,375	6,750	–0–

Instructions

a. What is the January 1 balance in the Colaw Company subsidiary account?

b. What is the January 31 balance in the control account?

c. Compute the balances in the subsidiary accounts at the end of the month.

d. Which January transaction would not be recorded in a special journal?

EJ.6 (LO 2), AP Norren Company uses special journals and a general journal. The following transactions occurred during September 2022.

Record transactions in sales and purchases journal.

Sept. 2 Sold merchandise on account to J. Yancey, invoice no. 101, $780, terms n/30. The cost of the merchandise sold was $420.

10 Purchased merchandise on account from H. Heerey $600, terms 2/10, n/30.

12 Purchased office equipment on account from Y. Kojima $6,500.

21 Sold merchandise on account to K. Pricer, invoice no. 102 for $800, terms 2/10, n/30. The cost of the merchandise sold was $480.

25 Purchased merchandise on account from G. Jeanik $835, terms n/30.

27 Sold merchandise to D. Schaff for $700 cash. The cost of the merchandise sold was $400.

Instructions

a. Prepare a sales journal (see Illustration J.6) and a single-column purchases journal (see Illustration J.12). (Use page 1 for each journal.)

b. Record the transaction(s) for September that should be journalized in the sales journal and the purchases journal.

EJ.7 (LO 2), AP Milner Co. uses special journals and a general journal. The following transactions occurred during May 2022.

Record transactions in cash receipts and cash payments journal.

May 1 M. Milner invested $48,000 cash in the business in exchange for common stock.

2 Sold merchandise to A. Belton for $6,340 cash. The cost of the merchandise sold was $4,200.

3 Purchased merchandise for $7,200 from E. Stein using check no. 101.

14 Paid salary to M. Hunt $700 by issuing check no. 102.

16 Sold merchandise on account to S. Spies for $900, terms n/30. The cost of the merchandise sold was $630.

22 A check of $9,000 is received from N. Feeney in full for invoice 101; no discount given.

J-22 APPENDIX J Subsidiary Ledgers and Special Journals

Instructions

a. Prepare a multi-column cash receipts journal (see Illustration J.8) and a multi-column cash payments journal (see Illustration J.15). (Use page 1 for each journal.)

b. Record the transaction(s) for May that should be journalized in the cash receipts journal and cash payments journal.

Explain journalizing in cash journals.

EJ.8 (LO 2), AP Eaton Company uses the columnar cash journals illustrated in the text. In April, the following selected cash transactions occurred.

1. Made a cash refund to a customer for the return of damaged goods.
2. Received collection from customer within the 3% discount period.
3. Purchased merchandise for cash.
4. Paid a creditor within the 3% discount period.
5. Received collection from customer after the 3% discount period had expired.
6. Paid freight on merchandise purchased.
7. Paid cash for office equipment.
8. Received cash refund from supplier for merchandise returned.
9. Paid cash dividend to stockholders.
10. Made cash sales.

Instructions

Indicate (a) the journal and (b) the columns in the journal that should be used in recording each transaction.

Journalize transactions in general journal and post.

EJ.9 (LO 1, 2), AP **Writing** Nolasco Company has the following selected transactions during March.

Mar. 2 Purchased equipment costing $9,400 from Brantly Company on account.
5 Received credit of $410 from Dumont Company for merchandise damaged in shipment to Nolasco.
7 Issued credit of $390 to Horst Company for merchandise the customer returned. The returned merchandise had a cost of $240.

Nolasco Company uses a one-column purchases journal, a sales journal, the columnar cash journals used in the text, and a general journal.

Instructions

a. Journalize the transactions in the general journal.

b. In a brief memo to the president of Nolasco Company, explain the postings to the control and subsidiary accounts from each type of journal.

Indicate journalizing in special journals.

EJ.10 (LO 2), AP Below are some typical transactions incurred by Barone Company.

1. Payment of creditors on account.
2. Return of merchandise sold for credit.
3. Collection on account from customers.
4. Sale of land for cash.
5. Sale of merchandise on account.
6. Sale of merchandise for cash.
7. Received credit for merchandise purchased on credit.
8. Sales discount taken on goods sold.
9. Payment of employee wages.
10. Payment of cash dividend to stockholders.
11. Depreciation on building.
12. Purchase of office supplies for cash.
13. Purchase of merchandise on account.

Instructions

For each transaction, indicate whether it would normally be recorded in a cash receipts journal, cash payments journal, sales journal, single-column purchases journal, or general journal.

EJ.11 (LO 1), AP The general ledger of Raysom Company contained the following Accounts Payable control account (in T-account form). Also shown is the related subsidiary ledger.

Explain posting to control account and subsidiary ledger.

General Ledger

Accounts Payable

Feb.	15	General journal	1,400	Feb.	1	Balance	26,025
	28	?	?		5	General journal	195
					11	General journal	550
					28	Purchases	13,400
				Feb.	28	Balance	9,800

Accounts Payable Ledger

Keyser

	Feb. 28	Bal. 4,600

Stine

	Feb. 28	Bal. 2,100

Robillard

	Feb. 28	Bal. ?

Instructions

a. Indicate the missing posting reference and amount in the control account, and the missing ending balance in the subsidiary ledger.

b. Indicate the amounts in the control account that were dual-posted (i.e., posted to the control account and the subsidiary accounts).

EJ.12 (LO 1, 2), AP Selected accounts from the ledgers of Ramos Company at July 31 showed the following.

Prepare purchases and general journals.

General Ledger

Equipment   No. 153

Date	Explanation	Ref.	Debit	Credit	Balance
July 1		G1	3,900		3,900

Accounts Payable   No. 201

Date	Explanation	Ref.	Debit	Credit	Balance
July 1		G1		3,900	3,900
15		G1		600	4,500
18		G1	380		4,120
25		G1	200		3,920
31		P1		8,500	12,420

Inventory   No. 120

Date	Explanation	Ref.	Debit	Credit	Balance
July 15		G1	600		600
18		G1		380	220
25		G1		200	20
31		P1	8,500		8,520

Accounts Payable Ledger

Alaska Equipment Co.

Date	Explanation	Ref.	Debit	Credit	Balance
July 1		G1		3,900	3,900

Carolina Co.

Date	Explanation	Ref.	Debit	Credit	Balance
July 3		P1		2,400	2,400
20		P1		700	3,100

Florida Corp

Date	Explanation	Ref.	Debit	Credit	Balance
July 17		P1		1,400	1,400
18		G1	380		1,020
29		P1		1,600	2,620

Kentucky Co.

Date	Explanation	Ref.	Debit	Credit	Balance
July 14		P1		1,300	1,300
25		G1	200		1,100

Nevada Co.

Date	Explanation	Ref.	Debit	Credit	Balance
July 12		P1		500	500
21		P1		600	1,100

Oklahoma Inc.

Date	Explanation	Ref.	Debit	Credit	Balance
July 15		G1		600	600

Instructions

From the data prepare:

a. The single-column purchases journal for July.

b. The general journal entries for July.

Determine correct posting amount to control account.

EJ.13 (LO 1, 2), AP Castro Products uses both special journals and a general journal as described in this appendix. Castro also posts customers' accounts in the accounts receivable subsidiary ledger. The postings for the most recent month are included in the subsidiary T-accounts below.

Dingel				Lopez		
Bal.	340		250	Bal.	150	150
	280				240	

Epping				Rivera		
Bal.	–0–		145	Bal.	120	120
	145				190	
					130	

Instructions

Determine the correct amount of the end-of-month posting from the sales journal to the Accounts Receivable control account.

Compute balances in various accounts.

EJ.14 (LO 2), AP Selected account balances for Ramano Company at January 1, 2022, are presented below.

Accounts Payable	$19,000
Accounts Receivable	22,000
Cash	17,000
Inventory	13,500

Ramano's sales journal for January shows a total of $100,000 in the selling-price column, and its one-column purchases journal for January shows a total of $72,000.

The column totals in Ramano's cash receipts journal are Cash Dr. $64,000; Sales Discounts Dr. $1,100; Accounts Receivable Cr. $48,000; Sales Revenue Cr. $6,000; and Other Accounts Cr. $11,100.

The column totals in Ramano's cash payments journal for January are Cash Cr. $55,000; Inventory Cr. $1,000; Accounts Payable Dr. $46,000; and Other Accounts Dr. $10,000. Ramano's total cost of goods sold for January is $63,600.

Accounts Payable, Accounts Receivable, Cash, Inventory, and Sales Revenue are not involved in the "Other Accounts" column in either the cash receipts or cash payments journal, and are not involved in any general journal entries.

Instructions

Compute the January 31 balance for Ramano in the following accounts.

a. Accounts Payable.
b. Accounts Receivable.
c. Cash.
d. Inventory.
e. Sales Revenue.

Problems

Journalize transactions in cash receipts journal; post to control account and subsidiary ledger.

PJ.1 (LO 1, 2), AP Parsons Company's chart of accounts includes the following selected accounts.

101	Cash	401	Sales Revenue
112	Accounts Receivable	414	Sales Discounts
120	Inventory	505	Cost of Goods Sold
311	Common Stock		

On April 1, the accounts receivable ledger of Parsons Company showed the following balances: Park $1,550, Kolten $1,200, Hurt Co. $2,900, and Afzal $1,800. The April transactions involving the receipt of cash were as follows.

Apr. 1 Stockholders invested $7,200 additional cash in the business, in exchange for common stock.
      4 Received check for payment of account from Afzal less 2% cash discount.
      5 Received check for $990 in payment of invoice no. 307 from Hurt Co.
      8 Made cash sales of merchandise totaling $7,845. The cost of the merchandise sold was $4,347.
     10 Received check for $600 in payment of invoice no. 309 from Park.
     11 Received cash refund from a supplier for damaged merchandise $680.
     23 Received check for $1,500 in payment of invoice no. 310 from Hurt Co.
     29 Received check for payment of account from Kolten.

Instructions

a. Journalize the preceding transactions in a six-column cash receipts journal with columns for Cash Dr., Sales Discounts Dr., Accounts Receivable Cr., Sales Revenue Cr., Other Accounts Cr., and Cost of Goods Sold Dr./Inventory Cr. Foot and crossfoot the journal.

b. Insert the beginning balances in the Accounts Receivable control and subsidiary accounts, and post the April transactions to these accounts.

c. Prove the agreement of the control account and subsidiary account balances.

a. Balancing totals $21,815

c. Accounts Receivable $1,360

PJ.2 (LO 1, 2), AP Venson Company's chart of accounts includes the following selected accounts.

Journalize transactions in cash payments journal; post to control account and subsidiary ledgers.

101 Cash
120 Inventory
130 Prepaid Insurance
157 Equipment
201 Accounts Payable
332 Cash Dividends
505 Cost of Goods Sold

On October 1, the accounts payable ledger of Venson Company showed the following balances: Coulsen Company $2,700, Flynn Co. $2,500, Noy Co. $2,100, and Trent Company $3,700. The October transactions involving the payment of cash were as follows.

Oct. 1 Purchased merchandise, check no. 63, $300.
      3 Purchased equipment, check no. 64, $1,200.
      5 Paid Coulsen Company balance due of $2,700, less 2% discount, check no. 65, $2,646.
     10 Purchased merchandise, check no. 66, $2,250.
     15 Paid Noy Co. balance due of $2,100, check no. 67.
     16 Paid cash dividend of $400, check no. 68.
     19 Paid Flynn Co. in full for invoice no. 610, $1,800 less 2% cash discount, check no. 69, $1,764.
     29 Paid Trent Company in full for invoice no. 264, $2,500, check no. 70.

Instructions

a. Journalize the transactions above in a four-column cash payments journal with columns for Other Accounts Dr., Accounts Payable Dr., Inventory Cr., and Cash Cr. Foot and crossfoot the journal.

b. Insert the beginning balances in the Accounts Payable control and subsidiary accounts, and post the October transactions to these accounts.

c. Prove the agreement of the control account and the subsidiary account balances.

a. Balancing totals $13,250

c. Accounts Payable $1,900

PJ.3 (LO 1, 2), AP The chart of accounts of Beldona Company includes the following selected accounts.

Journalize transactions in multi-column purchases journal; post to the general and subsidiary ledgers.

112 Accounts Receivable
120 Inventory
126 Supplies
157 Equipment
201 Accounts Payable
401 Sales Revenue
412 Sales Returns and Allowances
505 Cost of Goods Sold
610 Advertising Expense

In July, the following selected transactions were completed. All purchases and sales were on account. The cost of all merchandise sold was 70% of the sales price.

July 1 Purchased merchandise from Dent Company $7,600.
      2 Received freight bill from Rensing Shipping on Dent purchase $400.
      3 Made sales to Dayley Company $1,300 and to Orsen Bros. $2,000.
      5 Purchased merchandise from Langer Company $3,200.
      8 Received credit on merchandise returned to Langer Company $300.
     13 Purchased store supplies from Abel Supply $910.
     15 Purchased merchandise from Dent Company $3,600 and from Goran Company $3,300.
     16 Made sales to Gentry Company $3,450 and to Orsen Bros. $1,570.
     18 Received bill for advertising from Wei Advertisements $600.
     21 Made sales to Dayley Company $310 and to Musky Company $2,800.
     22 Granted allowance to Dayley Company for merchandise damaged in shipment $65.
     24 Purchased merchandise from Langer Company $3,000.
     26 Purchased equipment from Abel Supply $900.
     28 Received freight bill from Rensing Shipping on Langer purchase of July 24, $380.
     30 Made sales to Gentry Company $5,600.

Instructions

a. Purchases journal—
   Accounts Payable $23,890
   Sales journal—Sales revenue
   column total $17,030

c. Accounts Receivable $16,965
   Accounts Payable $23,590

Journalize transactions in special journals.

a. Journalize the preceding transactions in a purchases journal, a sales journal, and a general journal. The purchases journal should have the following column headings: Date, Account Credited (Debited), Ref., Accounts Payable Cr., Inventory Dr., and Other Accounts Dr.

b. Post to both the general and subsidiary ledger accounts. (Assume that all accounts have zero beginning balances.)

c. Prove the agreement of the control and subsidiary accounts.

PJ.4 (LO 1, 2), AP Selected accounts from the chart of accounts of Rivera Company are shown below.

101 Cash
112 Accounts Receivable
120 Inventory
126 Supplies
157 Equipment
201 Accounts Payable

401 Sales Revenue
412 Sales Returns and Allowances
414 Sales Discounts
505 Cost of Goods Sold
726 Salaries and Wages Expense

The cost of all merchandise sold was 60% of the sales price. During January, Rivera completed the following transactions.

Jan. 3 Purchased merchandise on account from Quayle Co. $10,000.
      4 Purchased supplies for cash $80.
      4 Sold merchandise on account to Gant $5,600, invoice no. 371, terms 1/10, n/30.
      5 Returned $300 worth of damaged goods purchased on account from Quayle Co. on January 3.
      6 Made cash sales for the week totaling $3,750.
      8 Purchased merchandise on account from Eubank Co. $4,500.
      9 Sold merchandise on account to Notson Corp. $6,400, invoice no. 372, terms 1/10, n/30.
     11 Purchased merchandise on account from Akers Co. $3,700.
     13 Paid in full Quayle Co. on account less a 2% discount.
     13 Made cash sales for the week totaling $6,260.
     15 Received payment from Notson Corp. for invoice no. 372.
     15 Paid semi-monthly salaries of $14,300 to employees.
     17 Received payment from Gant for invoice no. 371.
     17 Sold merchandise on account to Loeb Co. $1,200, invoice no. 373, terms 1/10, n/30.
     19 Purchased equipment on account from Barb Corp. $5,500.
     20 Cash sales for the week totaled $3,200.
     20 Paid in full Eubank Co. on account less a 2% discount.
     23 Purchased merchandise on account from Quayle Co. $7,800.
     24 Purchased merchandise on account from Fifer Corp. $5,100.
     27 Made cash sales for the week totaling $4,230.
     30 Received payment from Loeb Co. for invoice no. 373.
     31 Paid semi-monthly salaries of $14,300 to employees.
     31 Sold merchandise on account to Gant $9,330, invoice no. 374, terms 1/10, n/30.

Rivera Company uses the following journals.

1. Sales journal.
2. Single-column purchases journal.
3. Cash receipts journal with columns for Cash Dr., Sales Discounts Dr., Accounts Receivable Cr., Sales Revenue Cr., Other Accounts Cr., and Cost of Goods Sold Dr./Inventory Cr.
4. Cash payments journal with columns for Other Accounts Dr., Accounts Payable Dr., Inventory Cr., and Cash Cr.
5. General journal.

Instructions

Using the selected accounts provided:

a. Record the January transactions in the appropriate journal noted.
b. Foot and crossfoot all special journals.
c. Show how postings would be made by placing ledger account numbers and checkmarks as needed in the journals. (Actual posting to ledger accounts is not required.)

a. Sales journal $22,530
Purchases journal $31,100
Cash receipts journal balancing total $30,640
Cash payments journal balancing total $42,880

PJ.5 (LO 1, 2), AP Presented below are the purchases and cash payments journals for Ramirez Co. for its first month of operations.

Journalize in sales and cash receipts journals; post; prepare a trial balance; prove control to subsidiary; prepare adjusting entries; prepare an adjusted trial balance.

Purchases Journal   P1

Date		Account Credited	Ref.	Inventory Dr. Accounts Payable Cr.
July	4	T. Donley		6,500
	5	K. Farmer		8,100
	11	M. Huang		5,920
	13	D. Sampson		15,300
	20	G. Young		7,900
				43,720

Cash Payments Journal   CP1

Date		Account Debited	Ref.	Other Accounts Dr.	Accounts Payable Dr.	Inventory Cr.	Cash Cr.
July	4	Supplies		600			600
	10	K. Farmer			8,100	81	8,019
	11	Prepaid Rent		6,000			6,000
	15	T. Donley			6,500		6,500
	19	Cash Dividends		2,500			2,500
	21	D. Sampson			15,300	153	15,147
				9,100	29,900	234	38,766

In addition, the following transactions have not been journalized for July. The cost of all merchandise sold was 65% of the sales price.

July 1   A. Ramirez invested $80,000 in cash in exchange for common stock.
    6   Sold merchandise on account to Edwards Co. $6,600 terms 1/10, n/30.
    7   Made cash sales totaling $6,300.
    8   Sold merchandise on account to Carmoni $3,600, terms 1/10, n/30.
   10   Sold merchandise on account to L. Nunez $4,900, terms 1/10, n/30.
   13   Received payment in full from Carmoni.
   16   Received payment in full from L. Nunez.
   20   Received payment in full from Edwards Co.
   21   Sold merchandise on account to M. Putzi $5,000, terms 1/10, n/30.
   29   Returned damaged goods to T. Donley and received cash refund of $450.

Instructions

a. Open the following accounts in the general ledger.

    101 Cash   131 Prepaid Rent
    112 Accounts Receivable   201 Accounts Payable
    120 Inventory   311 Common Stock
    127 Supplies   332 Cash Dividends

401 Sales Revenue
414 Sales Discounts
505 Cost of Goods Sold

631 Supplies Expense
729 Rent Expense

b. Sales journal total $20,100
Cash receipts journal balancing total $101,850

e. Totals $120,220

f. Accounts Receivable $5,000
Accounts Payable $13,820

h. Totals $120,220

Journalize in special journals; post; prepare a trial balance.

GLS

b. Journalize the transactions that have not been journalized in the sales journal, the cash receipts journal (see Illustration J.8), and the general journal.

c. Post to the accounts receivable and accounts payable subsidiary ledgers. Follow the sequence of transactions as shown in the problem.

d. Post the individual entries and totals to the general ledger.

e. Prepare a trial balance at July 31, 2022.

f. Determine whether the subsidiary ledgers agree with the control accounts in the general ledger.

g. The following adjustments at the end of July are necessary.

   1. A count of supplies indicates that $170 is still on hand.
   2. Recognize rent expense for July, $500.

   Prepare the necessary entries in the general journal. Post the entries to the general ledger.

h. Prepare an adjusted trial balance at July 31, 2022.

PJ.6 (LO 1, 2), AP The post-closing trial balance for Bensen Co. is as follows.

Bensen Co.
Post-Closing Trial Balance
December 31, 2021

	Debit	Credit
Cash	$ 41,500	
Accounts Receivable	15,000	
Notes Receivable	45,000	
Inventory	20,000	
Equipment	7,500	
Accumulated Depreciation—Equipment		$ 1,500
Accounts Payable		43,000
Common Stock		84,500
	$129,000	$129,000

The subsidiary ledgers contain the following information: (1) accounts receivable—M. Cedeno $2,500, J. Deitz $7,500, and E. Divine $5,000; (2) accounts payable—B. Forrest $10,000, L. Gold $18,000, and A. Pele $15,000. The cost of all merchandise sold was 60% of the sales price.

The transactions for January 2022 are as follows.

Jan. 3 Sell merchandise to T. Raynor $4,600, terms 2/10, n/30.
   5 Purchase merchandise from P. Weng $2,800, terms 2/10, n/30.
   7 Receive a check from E. Divine $3,500.
   11 Pay freight on merchandise purchased $300.
   12 Pay rent of $1,000 for January.
   13 Receive payment in full from T. Raynor.
   14 Post all entries to the subsidiary ledgers. Issued credit of $300 to M. Cedeno for returned merchandise.
   15 Send A. Pele a check for $14,850 in full payment of account, discount $150.
   17 Purchase merchandise from E. Nanco $1,600, terms 2/10, n/30.
   18 Pay sales salaries of $2,500 and office salaries $2,000.
   20 Give L. Gold a 60-day note for $18,000 in full payment of account payable.
   23 Total cash sales amount to $9,100.
   24 Post all entries to the subsidiary ledgers. Sell merchandise on account to J. Deitz $7,400, terms 1/10, n/30.
   27 Send P. Weng a check for $950.
   29 Receive payment on a note of $37,000 from W. Lague.
   30 Post all entries to the subsidiary ledgers. Return merchandise of $300 to E. Nanco for credit.

Instructions

a. Open general and subsidiary ledger accounts for the following.

101	Cash	311	Common Stock
112	Accounts Receivable	401	Sales Revenue
115	Notes Receivable	412	Sales Returns and Allowances
120	Inventory	414	Sales Discounts
157	Equipment	505	Cost of Goods Sold
158	Accumulated Depreciation—Equipment	726	Salaries and Wages Expense
200	Notes Payable	729	Rent Expense
201	Accounts Payable		

b. Record the January transactions in a sales journal, a single-column purchases journal, a cash receipts journal (see Illustration J.8), a cash payments journal (see Illustration J.15), and a general journal.

c. Post the appropriate amounts to the general ledger.

d. Prepare a trial balance at January 31, 2022.

e. Determine whether the subsidiary ledgers agree with controlling accounts in the general ledger.

b. Sales journal $12,000
Purchases journal $4,400
Cash receipts journal (balancing) $54,200
Cash payments journal (balancing) $21,750

d. Totals $138,250

e. Accounts Receivable $18,600
Accounts Payable $13,150

Comprehensive Accounting Cycle Review

ACR Zweifel Company has the following opening account balances in its general and subsidiary ledgers on January 1 and uses the periodic inventory system. All accounts have normal debit and credit balances.

General Ledger

Account Number	Account Title	January 1 Opening Balance
101	Cash	$32,750
112	Accounts Receivable	13,000
115	Notes Receivable	42,000
120	Inventory	20,000
125	Supplies	1,000
130	Prepaid Insurance	2,000
157	Equipment	6,450
158	Accumulated Depreciation—Equip.	1,500
201	Accounts Payable	35,000
311	Common Stock	70,000
320	Retained Earnings	10,700

Schedule of Accounts Receivable
(from accounts receivable subsidiary ledger)

Customer	January 1 Opening Balance
G. Dukes	$1,800
M. Hall	7,200
L. Longhini	4,000

Schedule of Accounts Payable
(from accounts payable subsidiary ledger)

Creditor	January 1 Opening Balance
O. Kitson	$ 9,000
D. Markoff	15,000
L. Quinn	11,000

In addition, the following transactions have not been journalized for January 2022.

Jan. 3 Sell merchandise on account to W. Rayms $3,600, invoice no. 510, and M. Fischer $1,800, invoice no. 511.

5 Purchase merchandise on account from K. Zapfel $3,000 and J. Liotta $2,400.

7 Receive checks for $4,000 from L. Longhini and $2,000 from M. Hall.

8 Pay freight on merchandise purchased $180.

9 Send checks to O. Kitson for $9,000 and L. Quinn for $11,000.

9 Issue credit of $240 to M. Fischer for merchandise returned.

10 Cash sales total $15,500 from January 1 to January 10. Make one journal entry for these sales.

11 Sell merchandise on account to G. Dukes for $1,900, invoice no. 512, and to L. Longhini $900, invoice no. 513.

	12	Pay rent of $1,000 for January.
	13	Receive payment in full from W. Rayms and M. Fischer.
	15	Pay cash dividend of $650.
	16	Purchase merchandise on account from L. Quinn for $15,000, from O. Kitson for $13,900, and from K. Zapfel for $1,500.
	17	Pay $400 cash for office supplies.
	18	Return $200 of merchandise to O. Kitson and receive credit.
	20	Cash sales total $17,750 from January 11 to January 20. Make one journal entry for these sales.
	21	Issue $15,000 note to D. Markoff in payment of balance due.
	21	Receive payment in full from L. Longhini.
	22	Sell merchandise on account to W. Rayms for $3,700, invoice no. 514, and to G. Dukes for $800, invoice no. 515.
	23	Send checks to L. Quinn and O. Kitson in full payment.
	25	Sell merchandise on account to M. Hall for $3,500, invoice no. 516, and to M. Fischer for $6,100, invoice no. 517.
	27	Purchase merchandise on account from L. Quinn for $12,500, from J. Liotta $1,200, and from K. Zapfel for $2,800.
	28	Pay $200 cash for office supplies.
	31	Cash sales total $22,920 from January 21 to January 31. Make one journal entry for these sales.
	31	Pay sales salaries of $4,300 and office salaries of $3,100.

Instructions

a. Record the January transactions in the appropriate journal—sales, purchases, cash receipts, cash payments, and general.

b. Post the journals to the general and subsidiary ledgers. Add and number new accounts in an orderly fashion as needed.

c. *Trial balance totals $199,270*
   Adj. T/B totals $199,425

c. Prepare a trial balance at January 31, 2022, using a worksheet. Complete the worksheet using the following additional information.

   1. Office supplies at January 31 total $580.
   2. Insurance coverage expires on October 31, 2022.
   3. Annual depreciation on the equipment is $1,500.
   4. Interest of $30 has accrued on the note payable.
   5. Inventory at January 31 is $12,600.

d. *Net income $8,775*
   Total assets $127,255

d. Prepare a multiple-step income statement and a retained earnings statement for January and a classified balance sheet at the end of January.

e. Prepare and post the adjusting and closing entries.

f. *Post-closing T/B totals $128,880*

f. Prepare a post-closing trial balance, and determine whether the subsidiary ledgers agree with the control accounts in the general ledger.

Appendix K

Accounting for Partnerships

Appendix Preview

In this appendix, we discuss reasons why businesses select the partnership form of organization. We also explain the major issues in accounting for partnerships.

Appendix Outline

LEARNING OBJECTIVES

1. Discuss and account for the formation of a partnership.	• Characteristics of partnerships • Organizations with partnership characteristics • Advantages and disadvantages of partnerships • The partnership agreement • Accounting for a partnership formation
2. Explain how to account for net income or net loss of a partnership.	• Dividing net income or net loss • Partnership financial statements
3. Explain how to account for the liquidation of a partnership.	• No capital deficiency • Capital deficiency
4. Prepare journal entries when a partner is either admitted or withdraws.	• Admission of a partner • Withdrawal of a partner

Forming a Partnership

LEARNING OBJECTIVE 1
Discuss and account for the formation of a partnership.

A **partnership** is an association of two or more persons to carry on as co-owners of a business for profit. Partnerships are sometimes used in small retail, service, or manufacturing companies. Accountants, lawyers, and doctors also find it desirable to form partnerships with other professionals in the field.

Characteristics of Partnerships

Partnerships are fairly easy to form. People form partnerships simply by a verbal agreement or more formally by written agreement. We explain the principal characteristics of partnerships in the following sections.

K-1

Association of Individuals

Association of Individuals

A partnership is a legal entity. A partnership can own property (land, buildings, equipment) and can sue or be sued. **A partnership also is an accounting entity.** Thus, the personal assets, liabilities, and transactions of the partners are excluded from the accounting records of the partnership, just as they are in a proprietorship.

The net income of a partnership is not taxed as a separate entity. But, a partnership must file an information tax return showing partnership net income and each partner's share of that net income. Each partner's share is taxable at **personal tax rates**, regardless of the amount of net income each withdraws from the business during the year.

Mutual Agency

Mutual Agency

Mutual agency means that each partner acts on behalf of the partnership when engaging in partnership business. The act of any partner is binding on all other partners. This is true even when partners act beyond the scope of their authority, so long as the act appears to be appropriate for the partnership. For example, a partner of a grocery store who purchases a delivery truck creates a binding contract in the name of the partnership, even if the partnership agreement denies this authority. On the other hand, if a partner in a law firm purchased a snowmobile for the partnership, such an act would not be binding on the partnership. The purchase is clearly outside the scope of partnership business.

Limited Life

Limited Life

Corporations have unlimited life. Partnerships do not. A partnership may be ended voluntarily at any time through the acceptance of a new partner or the withdrawal of a partner. It may be ended involuntarily by the death or incapacity of a partner. **Partnership dissolution** occurs whenever a partner withdraws or a new partner is admitted. Dissolution does not necessarily mean that the business ends. If the continuing partners agree, operations can continue without interruption by forming a new partnership.

Unlimited Liability

Unlimited Liability

Each partner is **personally and individually liable** for all partnership liabilities. Creditors' claims attach first to partnership assets. If these are insufficient, the claims then attach to the personal resources of any partner, irrespective of that partner's equity in the partnership. Because each partner is responsible for all the debts of the partnership, each partner is said to have **unlimited liability**.

Co-Ownership of Property

Partners jointly own partnership assets. If the partnership is dissolved, each partner has a claim on total assets equal to the balance in his or her respective capital account. This claim does not attach to **specific assets** that an individual partner contributed to the firm. Similarly, if a partner invests a building in the partnership valued at $100,000 and the building is later sold at a gain of $20,000, the partners all share in the gain.

Partnership net income (or net loss) is also co-owned. **If the partnership contract does not specify to the contrary, all net income or net loss is shared equally by the partners.** As you will see later, though, partners may agree to unequal sharing of net income or net loss.

Organizations with Partnership Characteristics

If you are starting a business with a friend and each of you has little capital and your business is not risky, you probably want to use a partnership. As indicated above, the partnership is easy to establish and its cost is minimal. These types of partnerships are often called **regular**

partnerships. However if your business is risky—say, roof repair or performing some type of professional service—you will want to limit your liability and not use a regular partnership. As a result, special forms of business organizations with partnership characteristics are now often used to provide protection from unlimited liability for people who wish to work together in some activity.

The special partnership forms are limited partnerships, limited liability partnerships, and limited liability companies. These special forms use the same accounting procedures as those described for a regular partnership. In addition, for taxation purposes, all the profits and losses pass through these organizations (similar to the regular partnership) to the owners, who report their share of partnership net income or losses on their personal tax returns.

Limited Partnerships

In a **limited partnership**, one or more partners have **unlimited liability** and one or more partners have **limited liability** for the debts of the firm (see **International Note**). Those with unlimited liability are **general partners**. Those with limited liability are **limited partners**. Limited partners are responsible for the debts of the partnership up to the limit of their investment in the firm.

The words "Limited Partnership," "Ltd.," or "LP" identify this type of organization. For the privilege of limited liability, the limited partner usually accepts less compensation than a general partner and exercises less influence in the affairs of the firm. If the limited partners get involved in management, they risk their liability protection.

Limited Liability Partnership

Most states allow professionals such as lawyers, doctors, and accountants to form a **limited liability partnership** or "LLP." The LLP is designed to protect innocent partners from malpractice or negligence claims resulting from the acts of another partner (see **Helpful Hint**). LLPs generally carry large insurance policies as protection against malpractice suits. These professional partnerships vary in size from a medical partnership of three to five doctors, to 150 to 200 partners in a large law firm, to more than 2,000 partners in an international accounting firm.

Limited Liability Companies

A hybrid form of business organization with certain features like a corporation and others like a limited partnership is the **limited liability company** or "LLC." An LLC usually has a limited life. The owners, called **members**, have limited liability like owners of a corporation. Whereas limited partners do not actively participate in the management of a limited partnership (LP), the members of a limited liability company (LLC) can assume an active management role. For income tax purposes, the IRS usually classifies an LLC as a partnership.

Illustration K.1 summarizes different forms of organizations that have partnership characteristics.

Advantages and Disadvantages of Partnerships

Why do people choose partnerships? One major advantage of a partnership is to combine the skills and resources of two or more individuals. In addition, partnerships are easily formed and are relatively free from government regulations and restrictions. A partnership does not have to contend with the "red tape" that a corporation must face. Also, partners generally can make decisions quickly on substantive business matters without having to consult a board of directors.

On the other hand, partnerships also have some major disadvantages. **Unlimited liability** is particularly troublesome. Many individuals fear they may lose not only their initial investment but also their personal assets if those assets are needed to pay partnership creditors.

International Note

Much of the funding for successful new U.S. businesses comes from "venture capital" firms, which are organized as limited partnerships. To develop its own venture capital industry, China has taken steps to model its partnership laws to allow for limited partnerships like those in the United States.

HELPFUL HINT

In an LLP, *all* partners have limited liability. There are no general partners.

ILLUSTRATION K.1

Different forms of organizations with partnership characteristics

	Major Advantages	Major Disadvantages
Regular Partnership  General Partners	Simple and inexpensive to create and operate.	Owners (partners) personally liable for business debts.
Limited Partnership  General Partner / Limited Partners	Limited partners have limited personal liability for business debts as long as they do not participate in management. General partners can raise cash without involving outside investors in management of business.	General partners personally liable for business debts. More expensive to create than regular partnership. Suitable mainly for companies that invest in real estate.
Limited Liability Partnership 	Mostly of interest to partners in old-line professions such as law, medicine, and accounting. Owners (partners) are not personally liable for the malpractice of other partners.	Unlike a limited liability company, owners (partners) remain personally liable for many types of obligations owed to business creditors, lenders, and landlords. Often limited to a short list of professions.
Limited Liability Company 	Owners have limited personal liability for business debts even if they participate in management.	More expensive to create than regular partnership.

Source: www.nolo.com.

Illustration K.2 summarizes the advantages and disadvantages of the regular partnership form of business organization. As indicated previously, different types of partnership forms have evolved to reduce some of the disadvantages.

ILLUSTRATION K.2

Advantages and disadvantages of a partnership

Advantages	Disadvantages
Combining skills and resources of two or more individuals	Mutual agency
Ease of formation	Limited life
Freedom from governmental regulations and restrictions	Unlimited liability
Ease of decision-making	

The Partnership Agreement

Ideally, the agreement of two or more individuals to form a partnership should be expressed in a written contract, called the **partnership agreement** or **articles of co-partnership**. The partnership agreement contains such basic information as the name and principal location of the firm, the purpose of the business, and date of inception. In addition, it should specify relationships among the partners, such as:

1. Names and capital contributions of partners.
2. Rights and duties of partners.
3. Basis for sharing net income or net loss.
4. Provision for withdrawals of assets.
5. Procedures for submitting disputes to arbitration.
6. Procedures for the withdrawal or addition of a partner.
7. Rights and duties of surviving partners in the event of a partner's death.

We cannot overemphasize the importance of a written contract. The agreement should attempt to anticipate all possible situations, contingencies, and disagreements (see **Ethics Note**). The help of a lawyer is highly desirable in preparing the agreement.

> **ETHICS NOTE**
>
> A well-developed partnership agreement specifies in clear and concise language the process by which the partners will resolve ethical and legal problems. This issue is especially significant when the partnership experiences financial distress.

Accounting for a Partnership Formation

We now turn to the basic accounting for partnerships. The major accounting issues relate to forming the partnership, dividing income or loss, and preparing financial statements.

When forming a partnership, each partner's initial investment in a partnership is entered in the partnership records. The partnership should record these investments at the **fair value of the assets at the date of their transfer to the partnership**. All partners must agree to the values assigned.

To illustrate, assume that A. Rolfe and T. Shea combine their proprietorships to start a partnership named U.S. Software. The firm will specialize in developing financial modeling software. Rolfe and Shea have the assets shown in **Illustration K.3** prior to the formation of the partnership.

	Book Value		Fair Value	
	A. Rolfe	T. Shea	A. Rolfe	T. Shea
Cash	$ 8,000	$ 9,000	$ 8,000	$ 9,000
Equipment	5,000		4,000	
Accumulated depreciation—equipment	(2,000)			
Accounts receivable		4,000		4,000
Allowance for doubtful accounts		(700)		(1,000)
	$11,000	$12,300	$12,000	$12,000

ILLUSTRATION K.3
Book and fair values of assets invested

*Items under **owners' equity (OE)** in the accounting equation analyses are not labeled in this partnership appendix. Nearly all affect partners' **capital** accounts.*

The partnership records the investments as follows.

Investment of A. Rolfe

Cash	8,000	
Equipment	4,000	
A. Rolfe, Capital		12,000
(To record investment of Rolfe)		

Investment of T. Shea

Cash	9,000	
Accounts Receivable	4,000	
Allowance for Doubtful Accounts		1,000
T. Shea, Capital		12,000
(To record investment of Shea)		

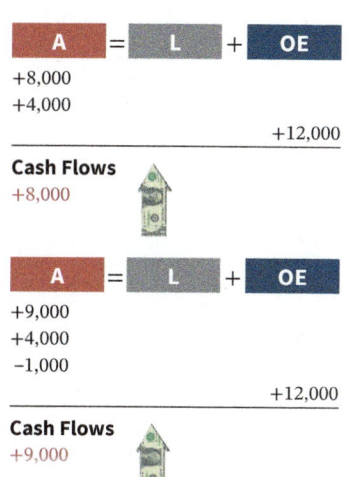

A = L + OE
+8,000
+4,000
                +12,000

Cash Flows
+8,000

A = L + OE
+9,000
+4,000
−1,000
                +12,000

Cash Flows
+9,000

Note that the partnership records neither the original cost of the equipment ($5,000) nor its book value ($5,000 − $2,000). It records the equipment at its fair value, $4,000. The partnership does not carry forward any accumulated depreciation from the books of previous entities (in this case, the two proprietorships).

In contrast, the gross claims on customers ($4,000) are carried forward to the partnership. The partnership adjusts the allowance for doubtful accounts to $1,000, to arrive at a cash (net) realizable value of $3,000. A partnership may start with an allowance for doubtful accounts because it will continue to collect existing accounts receivable, some of which are expected to be uncollectible. In addition, this procedure maintains the control and subsidiary relationship between Accounts Receivable and the accounts receivable subsidiary ledger.

After formation of the partnership, the accounting for transactions is similar to any other type of business organization. For example, the partners record all transactions with outside parties, such as the purchase or sale of inventory and the payment or receipt of cash, the same as would a sole proprietor.

The steps in the accounting cycle described in Chapter 4 also apply to a partnership. For example, the partnership prepares a trial balance and journalizes and posts adjusting entries. A worksheet may be used. There are minor differences in journalizing and posting closing entries and in preparing financial statements, as we explain in the following sections. The differences occur because there is more than one owner.

Accounting for Partnership Net Income or Net Loss

LEARNING OBJECTIVE 2
Explain how to account for net income or net loss of a partnership.

Dividing Net Income or Net Loss

Partners equally share partnership net income or net loss unless the partnership contract indicates otherwise. The same basis of division usually applies to both net income and net loss. It is customary to refer to this basis as the **income ratio**, the **income and loss ratio**, or the **profit and loss (P&L) ratio**. Because of its wide acceptance, we use the term income ratio to identify the basis for dividing net income and net loss. The partnership recognizes a partner's share of net income or net loss in the accounts through closing entries.

Closing Entries

As in the case of a proprietorship, a partnership must make four entries in preparing closing entries. The entries are:

1. Debit each revenue account for its balance, and credit Income Summary for total revenues.
2. Debit Income Summary for total expenses, and credit each expense account for its balance.
3. Debit Income Summary for its balance, and credit each partner's capital account for his or her share of net income. Or, credit Income Summary, and debit each partner's capital account for his or her share of net loss.
4. Debit each partner's capital account for the balance in that partner's drawings account, and credit each partner's drawings account for the same amount.

The first two entries are the same as in a corporation. The last two entries are different because (1) there are two or more owners' capital and drawings accounts, and (2) it is necessary to divide net income (or net loss) among the partners.

To illustrate the last two closing entries, assume that AB Company has net income of $32,000 for 2022. The partners, L. Arbor and D. Barnett, share net income and net loss equally.

Drawings for the year were Arbor $8,000 and Barnett $6,000. The last two closing entries are as follows.

Date	Account	Debit	Credit
Dec. 31	Income Summary	32,000	
	L. Arbor, Capital ($32,000 × 50%)		16,000
	D. Barnett, Capital ($32,000 × 50%)		16,000
	(To transfer net income to partners' capital accounts)		
Dec. 31	L. Arbor, Capital	8,000	
	D. Barnett, Capital	6,000	
	L. Arbor, Drawings		8,000
	D. Barnett, Drawings		6,000
	(To close drawings accounts to capital accounts)		

A = L + OE
−32,000
+16,000
+16,000

Cash Flows
no effect

A = L + OE
−8,000
−6,000
+8,000
+6,000

Cash Flows
no effect

Assume that the beginning capital balance is $47,000 for Arbor and $36,000 for Barnett. After posting the closing entries, the capital and drawings accounts will appear as shown in **Illustration K.4**.

L. Arbor, Capital					D. Barnett, Capital				
12/31 Clos.	8,000	1/1 Bal.	47,000		12/31 Clos.	6,000	1/1 Bal.	36,000	
		12/31 Clos.	16,000				12/31 Clos.	16,000	
		12/31 Bal.	55,000				12/31 Bal.	46,000	

L. Arbor, Drawings					D. Barnett, Drawings				
12/31 Bal.	8,000	12/31 Clos.	8,000		12/31 Bal.	6,000	12/31 Clos.	6,000

ILLUSTRATION K.4
Partners' capital and drawings accounts after closing

As in a proprietorship, the partners' capital accounts are permanent accounts. Their drawings accounts are temporary accounts. Normally, the capital accounts will have credit balances, and the drawings accounts will have debit balances. Drawings accounts are debited when partners withdraw cash or other assets from the partnership for personal use.

Income Ratios

As noted earlier, the partnership agreement should specify the basis for sharing net income or net loss. The following are typical income ratios.

1. A fixed ratio, expressed as a proportion (6:4), a percentage (70% and 30%), or a fraction (2/3 and 1/3) (see **Helpful Hint**).
2. A ratio based either on capital balances at the beginning of the year or on average capital balances during the year.
3. Salaries to partners and the remainder on a fixed ratio.
4. Interest on partners' capital balances and the remainder on a fixed ratio.
5. Salaries to partners, interest on partners' capital, and the remainder on a fixed ratio.

The objective is to settle on a basis that will equitably reflect the partners' capital investment and service to the partnership.

A **fixed ratio** is easy to apply, and it may be an equitable basis in some circumstances. Assume, for example, that Hughes and Lane are partners. Each contributes the same amount of capital, but Hughes expects to work full-time in the partnership and Lane expects to work only half-time. Accordingly, the partners agree to a fixed ratio of 2/3 to Hughes and 1/3 to Lane.

A **ratio based on capital balances** may be appropriate when the funds invested in the partnership are considered the critical factor. Capital ratios may also be equitable when the partners hire a manager to run the business and do not plan to take an active role in daily operations.

HELPFUL HINT

A proportion such as 4:4:2 has a denominator of 10 (4 + 4 + 2). Thus, the basis for sharing net income or loss is 4/10, 4/10, and 2/10.

The three remaining ratios (items 3, 4, and 5) give specific recognition to differences among partners. These ratios provide salary allowances for time worked and interest allowances for capital invested. Then, the partnership allocates any remaining net income or net loss on a fixed ratio.

Salaries to partners and interest on partners' capital are not expenses of the partnership. Therefore, these items do not enter into the matching of expenses with revenues and the determination of net income or net loss. For a partnership, as for other entities, salaries and wages expense pertains to the cost of services performed by employees. Likewise, interest expense relates to the cost of borrowing from creditors. But partners, as owners, are not considered either **employees** or **creditors**. When the partnership agreement permits the partners to make monthly withdrawals of cash based on their "salary," the partnership debits these withdrawals to the partner's drawings account.

Salaries, Interest, and Remainder on a Fixed Ratio

Under income ratio (5) in the list above, the partnership must apply salaries and interest **before** it allocates the remainder on the specified fixed ratio. **This is true even if the provisions exceed net income. It is also true even if the partnership has suffered a net loss for the year.** The partnership's income statement should show, below net income, detailed information concerning the division of net income or net loss.

To illustrate, assume that Sara King and Ray Lee are co-partners in the Kingslee Company. The partnership agreement provides for (1) salary allowances of $8,400 to King and $6,000 to Lee, (2) interest allowances of 10% on capital balances at the beginning of the year, and (3) the remaining income to be divided equally. Capital balances on January 1 were King $28,000, and Lee $24,000. In 2022, partnership net income is $22,000. The division of net income is as shown in **Illustration K.5**.

ILLUSTRATION K.5
Division of net income schedule

Kingslee Company
Division of Net Income
For the Year Ended December 31, 2022

Net income $ 22,000

Division of Net Income

	Sara King	Ray Lee	Total
Salary allowance	$ 8,400	$6,000	$14,400
Interest allowance on partners' capital			
Sara King ($28,000 × 10%)	2,800		
Ray Lee ($24,000 × 10%)		2,400	
Total interest allowance			5,200
Total salaries and interest	11,200	8,400	19,600
Remaining income, $2,400			
($22,000 − $19,600)			
Sara King ($2,400 × 50%)	1,200		
Ray Lee ($2,400 × 50%)		1,200	
Total remainder			2,400
Total division of net income	**$12,400**	**$9,600**	**$22,000**

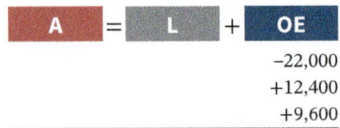

Cash Flows
no effect

Kingslee records the division of net income as follows.

Dec. 31	Income Summary	22,000	
	Sara King, Capital		12,400
	Ray Lee, Capital		9,600
	(To close net income to partners' capital)		

Now let's look at a situation in which the salary and interest allowances **exceed** net income. Assume that Kingslee Company's net income is only $18,000. In this case, the salary and interest allowances will create a deficiency of $1,600 ($18,000 − $19,600). The computations of the allowances are the same as those in the preceding example. Beginning with total salaries and interest, we complete the division of net income as shown in Illustration K.6.

ILLUSTRATION K.6
Division of net income—income deficiency

	Sara King	Ray Lee	Total
Total salaries and interest	$11,200	$8,400	$19,600
Remaining deficiency ($1,600)			
($18,000 − $19,600)			
Sara King ($1,600 × 50%)	(800)		
Ray Lee ($1,600 × 50%)		(800)	
Total remainder			(1,600)
Total division	**$10,400**	**$7,600**	**$18,000**

Partnership Financial Statements

The financial statements of a partnership are similar to those of a proprietorship. The differences are due to the number of owners involved. The income statement for a partnership is identical to the income statement for a proprietorship except for the division of net income, as shown earlier.

The owners' equity statement for a partnership is called the **partners' capital statement**. It explains the changes in each partner's capital account and in total partnership capital during the year. Illustration K.7 shows the partners' capital statement for Kingslee Company (see **Helpful Hint**). It is based on the division of $22,000 of net income in Illustration K.5. The statement includes assumed data for the additional investment and drawings. The partnership prepares the partners' capital statement from the income statement and the partners' capital and drawings accounts.

ILLUSTRATION K.7
Partners' capital statement

Kingslee Company
Partners' Capital Statement
For the Year Ended December 31, 2022

	Sara King	Ray Lee	Total
Capital, January 1	$28,000	$24,000	$52,000
Add: Additional investment	2,000		2,000
Net income	12,400	9,600	22,000
	42,400	33,600	76,000
Less: Drawings	7,000	5,000	12,000
Capital, December 31	**$35,400**	**$28,600**	**$64,000**

HELPFUL HINT
As in a proprietorship, partners' capital may change due to (1) additional investment, (2) drawings, and (3) net income or net loss.

The balance sheet for a partnership is the same as for a proprietorship except for the owners' equity section. For a partnership, the balance sheet shows the capital balances of each partner. Illustration K.8 shows the owners' equity section for Kingslee Company.

ILLUSTRATION K.8
Owners' equity section of a partnership balance sheet

Kingslee Company
Balance Sheet (partial)
December 31, 2022

Total liabilities (assumed amount)		$115,000
Owners' equity		
Sara King, capital	$35,400	
Ray Lee, capital	28,600	
Total owners' equity		64,000
Total liabilities and owners' equity		$179,000

Accounting for Partnership Liquidation

LEARNING OBJECTIVE 3
Explain how to account for the liquidation of a partnership.

Liquidation of a business involves selling the assets of the firm, paying liabilities, and distributing any remaining assets. Liquidation may result from the sale of the business by mutual agreement of the partners, from the death of a partner, or from bankruptcy. **Partnership liquidation** ends both the legal and economic life of the entity.

From an accounting standpoint, the partnership should complete the accounting cycle for the final operating period prior to liquidation. This includes preparing adjusting entries and financial statements. It also involves preparing closing entries and a post-closing trial balance. Thus, only balance sheet accounts should be open as the liquidation process begins.

In liquidation, the sale of noncash assets for cash is called **realization**. Any difference between book value and the cash proceeds is called the **gain or loss on realization**. To liquidate a partnership, it is necessary to:

ETHICS NOTE
The process of selling noncash assets and then distributing the cash reduces the likelihood of partner disputes. If instead the partnership distributes noncash assets to partners to liquidate the firm, the partners would need to agree on the value of the noncash assets, which can be very difficult to determine.

1. Sell noncash assets for cash and recognize a gain or loss on realization (see **Ethics Note**).
2. Allocate gain/loss on realization to the partners based on their income ratios.
3. Pay partnership liabilities in cash.
4. Distribute remaining cash to partners on the basis of their **capital balances**.

Each of the steps must be performed in sequence. The partnership must pay creditors **before** partners receive any cash distributions. Also, an accounting entry must record each step.

When a partnership is liquidated, all partners may have credit balances in their capital accounts. This situation is called **no capital deficiency**. Or, one or more partners may have a debit balance in the capital account. This situation is termed a **capital deficiency**. To illustrate each of these conditions, assume that Ace Company is liquidated when its ledger has the assets, liabilities, and owners' equity accounts shown in **Illustration K.9**.

ILLUSTRATION K.9
Account balances prior to liquidation

Assets		Liabilities and Owners' Equity	
Cash	$ 5,000	Notes Payable	$15,000
Accounts Receivable	15,000	Accounts Payable	16,000
Inventory	18,000	R. Arnet, Capital	15,000
Equipment	35,000	P. Carey, Capital	17,800
Accum. Depr.—Equipment	(8,000)	W. Eaton, Capital	1,200
	$65,000		$65,000

No Capital Deficiency

The partners of Ace Company agree to liquidate the partnership on the following terms. (1) The partnership will sell its noncash assets to Jackson Enterprises for $75,000 cash. (2) The partnership will pay its partnership liabilities. The income ratios of the partners are 3:2:1, respectively (see **Helpful Hint**). The steps in the liquidation process are as follows.

HELPFUL HINT
The income ratios' denominator for Ace Company is 6 (3 + 2 + 1).

1. Ace sells the noncash assets (accounts receivable, inventory, and equipment) for $75,000. The book value of these assets is $60,000 ($15,000 + $18,000 + $35,000 − $8,000). Thus, Ace realizes a gain of $15,000 on the sale. The entry is:

(1)		
Cash	75,000	
Accumulated Depreciation–Equipment	8,000	
Accounts Receivable		15,000
Inventory		18,000
Equipment		35,000
Gain on Realization		15,000
(To record realization of noncash assets)		

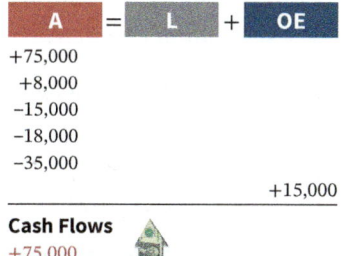

2. Ace allocates the $15,000 gain on realization to the partners based on their income ratios, which are 3:2:1. The entry is:

(2)		
Gain on Realization	15,000	
R. Arnet, Capital ($15,000 × 3/6)		7,500
P. Carey, Capital ($15,000 × 2/6)		5,000
W. Eaton, Capital ($15,000 × 1/6)		2,500
(To allocate gain to partners' capital accounts)		

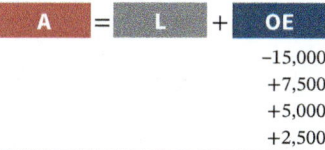

3. Partnership liabilities consist of Notes Payable $15,000 and Accounts Payable $16,000. Ace pays creditors in full by a cash payment of $31,000. The entry is:

(3)		
Notes Payable	15,000	
Accounts Payable	16,000	
Cash		31,000
(To record payment of partnership liabilities)		

4. Ace distributes the remaining cash to the partners on the basis of **their capital balances**. After posting the entries in the first three steps, all partnership accounts, including Gain on Realization, will have zero balances except for four accounts: Cash $49,000; R. Arnet, Capital $22,500; P. Carey, Capital $22,800; and W. Eaton, Capital $3,700, as shown in **Illustration K.10**.

ILLUSTRATION K.10 Ledger balances before distribution of cash

Cash				R. Arnet, Capital			P. Carey, Capital			W. Eaton, Capital		
Bal.	5,000	(3)	31,000		Bal.	15,000		Bal.	17,800		Bal.	1,200
(1)	75,000				(2)	7,500		(2)	5,000		(2)	2,500
Bal.	**49,000**				**Bal.**	**22,500**		**Bal.**	**22,800**		**Bal.**	**3,700**

Ace records the distribution of cash as follows.

(4)		
R. Arnet, Capital	22,500	
P. Carey, Capital	22,800	
W. Eaton, Capital	3,700	
Cash		49,000
(To record distribution of cash to partners)		

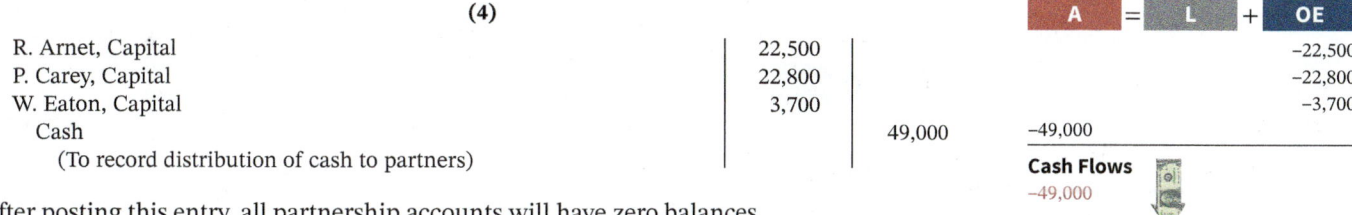

After posting this entry, all partnership accounts will have zero balances.

A word of caution: **Partnerships should not distribute remaining cash to partners on the basis of their income-sharing ratios.** On this basis, Arnet would receive three-sixths, or $24,500, which would produce an erroneous debit balance of $2,000. The income ratio is the proper basis for allocating net income or loss. **It is not a proper basis for making the final distribution of cash to the partners.**

Schedule of Cash Payments

ALTERNATIVE TERMINOLOGY

The schedule of cash payments is sometimes called a *safe cash payments schedule*.

The **schedule of cash payments** shows the distribution of cash to the partners in a partnership liquidation (see **Alternative Terminology**). The schedule of cash payments is organized around the basic accounting equation. **Illustration K.11** shows the schedule for Ace Company. The numbers in parentheses in column B refer to the four required steps in the liquidation of a partnership. They also identify the accounting entries that Ace must make. The cash payments schedule is especially useful when the liquidation process extends over a period of time.

ILLUSTRATION K.11 Schedule of cash payments, no capital deficiency

Ace Company — Schedule of Cash Payments

#	Item	B	Cash	+	Noncash Assets	=	Liabilities	+	R. Arnet, Capital	+	P. Carey, Capital	+	W. Eaton, Capital
3	Balances before liquidation		5,000	+	60,000	=	31,000	+	15,000	+	17,800	+	1,200
4	Sale of noncash assets and allocation of gain	(1)&(2)	75,000	+	(60,000)	=			7,500	+	5,000	+	2,500
5	New balances		80,000	+	–0–	=	31,000	+	22,500	+	22,800	+	3,700
6	Pay liabilities		(31,000)			=	(31,000)						
7	New balances	(3)	49,000	+	–0–	=	–0–	+	22,500	+	22,800	+	3,700
8	Cash distribution to partners	(4)	(49,000)			=			(22,500)	+	(22,800)	+	(3,700)
9	Final balances		–0–		–0–		–0–		–0–		–0–		–0–

Capital Deficiency

A capital deficiency may result from recurring net losses, excessive drawings, or losses from realization suffered during liquidation. To illustrate, assume that Ace Company is on the brink of bankruptcy. The partners decide to liquidate by having a "going-out-of-business" sale. They sell merchandise at substantial discounts, and sell the equipment at auction. Cash proceeds from these sales and collections from customers total only $42,000. Thus, the loss from liquidation is $18,000 ($60,000 − $42,000). The steps in the liquidation process are as follows.

1. The entry for the realization of noncash assets is:

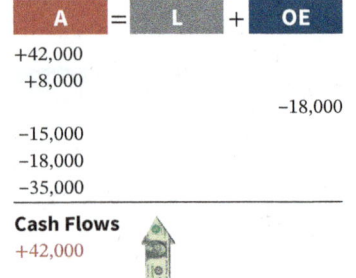

(1)		
Cash	42,000	
Accumulated Depreciation—Equipment	8,000	
Loss on Realization	18,000	
Accounts Receivable		15,000
Inventory		18,000
Equipment		35,000
(To record realization of noncash assets)		

2. Ace allocates the loss on realization to the partners on the basis of their income ratios. The entry is:

(2)

R. Arnet, Capital ($18,000 × 3/6)	9,000	
P. Carey, Capital ($18,000 × 2/6)	6,000	
W. Eaton, Capital ($18,000 × 1/6)	3,000	
Loss on Realization		18,000
(To allocate loss on realization to partners)		

3. Ace pays the partnership liabilities. This entry is the same as the previous one.

(3)

Notes Payable	15,000	
Accounts Payable	16,000	
Cash		31,000
(To record payment of partnership liabilities)		

4. After posting the three entries, two accounts will have debit balances—Cash $16,000 and W. Eaton, Capital $1,800. Two accounts will have credit balances—R. Arnet, Capital $6,000 and P. Carey, Capital $11,800. All four accounts are shown in **Illustration K.12**.

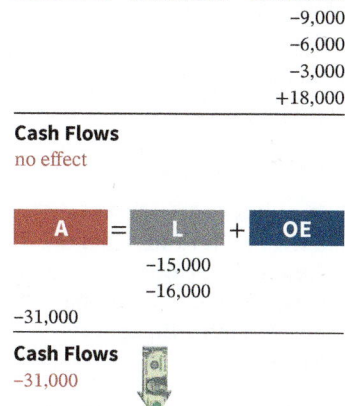

ILLUSTRATION K.12 Ledger balances before distribution of cash

Cash				R. Arnet, Capital			P. Carey, Capital			W. Eaton, Capital		
Bal.	5,000	(3)	31,000	(2)	9,000	Bal. 15,000	(2)	6,000	Bal. 17,800	(2)	3,000	Bal. 1,200
(1)	42,000					Bal. 6,000			Bal. 11,800	Bal.	1,800	
Bal.	16,000											

Eaton has a capital deficiency of $1,800 and so owes the partnership $1,800. Arnet and Carey have a legally enforceable claim for that amount against Eaton's personal assets. Note that the distribution of cash is still made on the basis of capital balances. But, the amount will vary depending on how Eaton settles the deficiency. Two alternatives are presented in the following sections.

Payment of Deficiency

If the partner with the capital deficiency pays the amount owed the partnership, the deficiency is eliminated. To illustrate, assume that Eaton pays $1,800 to the partnership. The entry is:

(a)

Cash	1,800	
W. Eaton, Capital		1,800
(To record payment of capital deficiency by Eaton)		

Illustration K.13 shows the account balances after posting this entry.

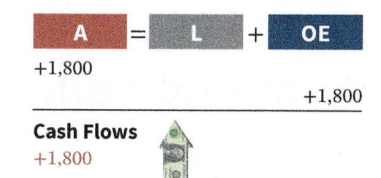

ILLUSTRATION K.13 Ledger balances after paying capital deficiency

Cash				R. Arnet, Capital			P. Carey, Capital			W. Eaton, Capital		
Bal.	5,000	(3)	31,000	(2)	9,000	Bal. 15,000	(2)	6,000	Bal. 17,800	(2)	3,000	Bal. 1,200
(1)	42,000					Bal. 6,000			Bal. 11,800			(a) 1,800
(a)	1,800											Bal. –0–
Bal.	17,800											

K-14 APPENDIX K Accounting for Partnerships

The cash balance of $17,800 is now equal to the credit balances in the capital accounts (Arnet $6,000 + Carey $11,800). Ace now distributes cash on the basis of these balances. The entry is:

R. Arnet, Capital	6,000	
P. Carey, Capital	11,800	
Cash		17,800
(To record distribution of cash to the partners)		

After posting this entry, all accounts will have zero balances.

Nonpayment of Deficiency

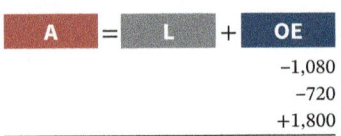

HELPFUL HINT

The ratios with all three partners were 3:2:1 and the denominator was therefore 6. Leaving out Eaton, the denominator changes to 5 (3 + 2).

If a partner with a capital deficiency is unable to pay the amount owed to the partnership, the partners with credit balances must absorb the loss. The partnership allocates the loss on the basis of the income ratios that exist between the partners with credit balances.

The income ratios of Arnet and Carey are 3:2, or 3/5 and 2/5, respectively (see **Helpful Hint**). Thus, Ace would make the following entry to remove Eaton's capital deficiency.

(a)

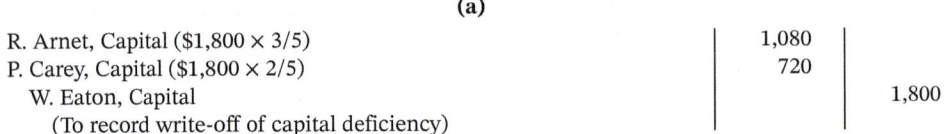

R. Arnet, Capital ($1,800 × 3/5)	1,080	
P. Carey, Capital ($1,800 × 2/5)	720	
W. Eaton, Capital		1,800
(To record write-off of capital deficiency)		

After posting this entry, the cash and capital accounts will have the balances shown in **Illustration K.14**.

ILLUSTRATION K.14 Ledger balances after nonpayment of capital deficiency

Cash				R. Arnet, Capital				P. Carey, Capital				W. Eaton, Capital			
Bal.	5,000	(3)	31,000	(2)	9,000	Bal.	15,000	(2)	6,000	Bal.	17,800	(2)	3,000	Bal.	1,200
(1)	42,000			(a)	1,080			(a)	720					(a)	1,800
Bal.	16,000					Bal.	4,920			Bal.	11,080			Bal.	-0-

The cash balance ($16,000) now equals the sum of the credit balances in the capital accounts (Arnet $4,920 + Carey $11,080). Ace records the distribution of cash as:

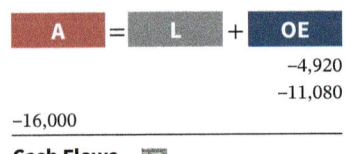

R. Arnet, Capital	4,920	
P. Carey, Capital	11,080	
Cash		16,000
(To record distribution of cash to the partners)		

After posting this entry, all accounts will have zero balances.

Admission and Withdrawal of Partners

LEARNING OBJECTIVE 4
Prepare journal entries when a partner is either admitted or withdraws.

We have now explained how the basic accounting for a partnership works. We next look at how to account for a common occurrence in partnerships—the addition or withdrawal of a partner.

Admission of a Partner

The admission of a new partner results in the **legal dissolution** of the existing partnership and the beginning of a new one. From an economic standpoint, however, the admission of a new partner (or partners) may be of minor significance in the continuity of the business. For example, in large public accounting or law firms, partners are admitted annually without any change in operating policies. **To recognize the economic effects, it is necessary only to open a capital account for each new partner.** In the entries illustrated below, we assume that the accounting records of the predecessor firm will continue to be used by the new partnership.

A new partner may be admitted either by (1) purchasing the interest of one or more existing partners or (2) investing assets in the partnership. The former affects only the capital accounts of the partners who are parties to the transaction. The latter increases both net assets and total capital of the partnership.

Purchase of a Partner's Interest

The **admission** of a partner **by purchase of an interest** is a personal transaction between one or more existing partners and the new partner (see **Helpful Hint**). Each party acts as an individual separate from the partnership entity. The individuals involved negotiate the price paid. It may be equal to or different from the capital equity acquired. The purchase price passes directly from the new partner to the partners who are giving up part or all of their ownership claims.

Any money or other consideration exchanged is the personal property of the participants and **not** the property of the partnership. Upon purchase of an interest, the new partner acquires each selling partner's capital interest and income ratio.

Accounting for the purchase of an interest is straightforward. The partnership records only the changes in partners' capital. **Partners' capital accounts are debited for any ownership claims sold.** At the same time, the new partner's capital account is credited for the capital equity purchased. Total assets, total liabilities, and total capital remain unchanged, as do all individual asset and liability accounts.

To illustrate, assume that L. Carson agrees to pay $10,000 each to C. Ames and D. Barker for $33^{1}/_{3}\%$ (one-third) of their interest in the Ames–Barker partnership. At the time of the admission of Carson, each partner has a $30,000 capital balance. Both partners, therefore, give up $10,000 of their capital equity. The entry to record the admission of Carson is:

> **HELPFUL HINT**
>
> In a purchase of an interest, the partnership is not a participant in the transaction. In this transaction, the new partner contributes *no* cash to the partnership.

C. Ames, Capital	10,000	
D. Barker, Capital	10,000	
L. Carson, Capital		20,000
(To record admission of Carson by purchase)		

Illustration K.15 shows the effect of this transaction on net assets and partners' capital.

ILLUSTRATION K.15 Ledger balances after purchase of a partner's interest

Net Assets	C. Ames, Capital		D. Barker, Capital		L. Carson, Capital
60,000	**10,000**	30,000	**10,000**	30,000	20,000
		Bal. 20,000		Bal. 20,000	

Note that net assets remain unchanged at $60,000, and each partner has a $20,000 capital balance. Ames and Barker continue as partners in the firm, but the capital interest of each has changed. The cash paid by Carson goes directly to the individual partners and not to the partnership.

Regardless of the amount paid by Carson for the one-third interest, the entry is exactly the same. If Carson pays $12,000 each to Ames and Barker for one-third of the partnership, the partnership still makes the entry shown above.

Investment of Assets in a Partnership

The admission of a partner by an investment of assets is a transaction between the new partner and the partnership. Often referred to simply as **admission by investment**, the transaction **increases both the net assets and total capital of the partnership.**

Assume, for example, that instead of purchasing an interest, Carson invests $30,000 in cash in the Ames-Barker partnership for a 33 1/3% capital interest. In such a case, the entry is:

Cash	30,000	
L. Carson, Capital		30,000
(To record admission of Carson by investment)		

Illustration K.16 shows the effects of this transaction on the partnership accounts.

ILLUSTRATION K.16 Ledger balances after investment of assets

Net Assets		C. Ames, Capital	D. Barker, Capital	L. Carson, Capital
60,000		30,000	30,000	30,000
30,000				
Bal. 90,000				

Note that both net assets and total capital have increased by $30,000.

Remember that Carson's one-third capital interest might not result in a one-third income ratio. The new partnership agreement should specify Carson's income ratio, and it may or may not be equal to the one-third capital interest.

The comparison of the net assets and capital balances in **Illustration K.17** shows the different effects of the purchase of an interest and admission by investment.

ILLUSTRATION K.17
Comparison of purchase of an interest and admission by investment

Purchase of an Interest		Admission by Investment	
Net assets	$60,000	Net assets	$90,000
Capital		Capital	
C. Ames	$20,000	C. Ames	$30,000
D. Barker	20,000	D. Barker	30,000
L. Carson	20,000	L. Carson	30,000
Total capital	$60,000	Total capital	$90,000

When a new partner purchases an interest, the total net assets and total capital of the partnership **do not change**. When a partner is admitted by investment, both the total net assets and the total capital **change** by the amount of the new investment.

In the case of admission by investment, further complications occur when the new partner's investment differs from the capital equity acquired. When those amounts are not the same, the difference is considered a **bonus** either to (1) the existing (old) partners or (2) the new partner.

Bonus to Old Partners For both personal and business reasons, the existing partners may be unwilling to admit a new partner without receiving a bonus. In an established firm, existing partners may insist on a bonus as compensation for the work they have put into the company over the years. Two accounting factors underlie the business reason. First, total partners' capital equals the **book value** of the recorded net assets of the partnership. When the new partner is admitted, the fair values of assets such as land and buildings may be higher than their book values. The bonus will help make up the difference between fair value and book value. Second, when the partnership has been profitable, goodwill may exist. But, the partnership balance sheet does not report goodwill. The new partner is usually willing to pay the bonus to become a partner.

A bonus to old partners results when the new partner's investment in the firm is greater than the capital credit on the date of admittance. The bonus results in **an increase in the capital balances of the old partners**. **The partnership allocates the bonus to them on the basis of their income ratios before the admission of the new partner.** To illustrate, assume that the Bart-Cohen partnership, owned by Sam Bart and Tom Cohen, has total capital of $120,000. Lea Eden acquires a 25% ownership (capital) interest in the partnership by making a cash investment of $80,000. The procedure for determining Eden's capital credit and the bonus to the old partners is as follows.

1. **Determine the total capital of the new partnership.** Add the new partner's investment to the total capital of the old partnership. In this case, the total capital of the new firm is $200,000, computed as follows.

Total capital of existing partnership	$120,000
Investment by new partner, Eden	80,000
Total capital of new partnership	$200,000

2. **Determine the new partner's capital credit.** Multiply the total capital of the new partnership by the new partner's ownership interest. Eden's capital credit is $50,000 ($200,000 × 25%).
3. **Determine the amount of bonus.** Subtract the new partner's capital credit from the new partner's investment. The bonus in this case is $30,000 ($80,000 − $50,000).
4. **Allocate the bonus to the old partners on the basis of their income ratios.** Assuming the ratios are Bart 60%, and Cohen 40%, the allocation is Bart $18,000 ($30,000 × 60%) and Cohen $12,000 ($30,000 × 40%).

The entry to record the admission of Eden is:

Cash	80,000	
Sam Bart, Capital		18,000
Tom Cohen, Capital		12,000
Lea Eden, Capital		50,000
(To record admission of Eden and bonus to old partners)		

A	=	L	+	OE
+80,000				+18,000
				+12,000
				+50,000

Cash Flows
+80,000

Bonus to New Partner A bonus to a new partner results when the new partner's investment in the firm is less than his or her capital credit. This may occur when the new partner possesses special attributes that the partnership wants. For example, the new partner may be able to supply cash that the firm needs for expansion or to meet maturing debts. Or the new partner may be a recognized expert in a relevant field. Thus, an engineering firm may be willing to give a renowned engineer a bonus to join the firm. The partners of a restaurant may offer a bonus to a sports celebrity in order to add the athlete's name to the partnership. A bonus to a new partner may also result when recorded book values on the partnership books are higher than their fair values.

A bonus to a new partner results in a **decrease in the capital balances of the old partners**. **The amount of the decrease for each partner is based on the income ratios before the admission of the new partner.** To illustrate, assume that Lea Eden invests $20,000 in cash for a 25% ownership interest in the Bart–Cohen partnership. **Illustration K.18** shows the computations for Eden's capital credit and the bonus, using the four procedures described in the preceding section.

1.	Total capital of Bart–Cohen partnership		$120,000
	Investment by new partner, Eden		20,000
	Total capital of new partnership		$140,000
2.	**Eden's capital credit** (25% × $140,000)		**$ 35,000**
3.	**Bonus to Eden** ($35,000 − $20,000)		**$ 15,000**
4.	Allocation of bonus to old partners:		
	Bart ($15,000 × 60%)	$9,000	
	Cohen ($15,000 × 40%)	6,000	$ 15,000

ILLUSTRATION K.18

Computation of capital credit and bonus to new partner

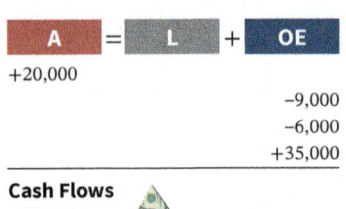

The partnership records the admission of Eden as follows.

Cash	20,000	
Sam Bart, Capital		9,000
Tom Cohen, Capital		6,000
Lea Eden, Capital		35,000
(To record Eden's admission and bonus)		

Withdrawal of a Partner

Now let's look at the opposite situation–the withdrawal of a partner. A partner may withdraw from a partnership **voluntarily**, by selling his or her equity in the firm. Or, he or she may withdraw **involuntarily**, by reaching mandatory retirement age or by dying. The withdrawal of a partner, like the admission of a partner, legally dissolves the partnership. The legal effects may be recognized by dissolving the firm. However, it is customary to record only the economic effects of the partner's withdrawal, while the firm continues to operate and reorganizes itself legally.

As indicated earlier, the partnership agreement should specify the terms of withdrawal. The withdrawal of a partner may be accomplished by (1) payment from partners' personal assets or (2) payment from partnership assets. The former affects only the partners' capital accounts. The latter decreases total net assets and total capital of the partnership.

Payment from Partners' Personal Assets

Withdrawal by payment from partners' personal assets is a personal transaction between the partners. **It is the direct opposite of admitting a new partner who purchases a partner's interest.** The remaining partners pay the retiring partner directly from their personal assets. **Partnership assets are not involved in any way, and total capital does not change.** The effect on the partnership is limited to changes in the partners' capital balances.

To illustrate, assume that partners Morz, Nead, and Odom have capital balances of $25,000, $15,000, and $10,000, respectively. Morz and Nead agree to buy out Odom's interest. Each of them agrees to pay Odom $8,000 in exchange for one-half of Odom's total interest of $10,000. The entry to record the withdrawal is:

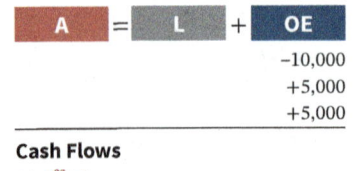

J. Odom, Capital	10,000	
A. Morz, Capital		5,000
M. Nead, Capital		5,000
(To record purchase of Odom's interest)		

The effect of this entry on the partnership accounts is shown in **Illustration K.19**.

ILLUSTRATION K.19 Ledger balances after payment from partners' personal assets

Net Assets	A. Morz, Capital	M. Nead, Capital	J. Odom, Capital
50,000	25,000	15,000	10,000 10,000
	5,000	5,000	Bal. –0–
	Bal. 30,000	Bal. 20,000	

Note that net assets and total capital remain the same at $50,000.

What about the $16,000 paid to Odom? You've probably noted that it is not recorded. The entry debited Odom's capital only for $10,000, not for the $16,000 that she received. Similarly, both Morz and Nead credit their capital accounts for only $5,000, not for the $8,000 they each paid.

After Odom's withdrawal, Morz and Nead will share net income or net loss equally unless they indicate another income ratio in the partnership agreement.

Payment from Partnership Assets

Withdrawal by payment from partnership assets is a transaction that involves the partnership. **Both partnership net assets and total capital decrease as a result.** Using partnership assets to pay for a withdrawing partner's interest is the **reverse** of admitting a partner through the investment of assets in the partnership.

Many partnership agreements provide that the amount paid should be based on the fair value of the assets at the time of the partner's withdrawal. When this basis is required, some maintain that any differences between recorded asset balances and their fair values should be (1) recorded by an adjusting entry, and (2) allocated to all partners on the basis of their income ratios. This position has serious flaws. Recording the revaluations violates the historical cost principle, which requires that assets be stated at original cost. It also violates the going-concern assumption, which assumes the entity will continue indefinitely. The terms of the partnership contract should not dictate the accounting for this event.

In accounting for a withdrawal by payment from partnership assets, the partnership should not record asset revaluations. Instead, it should consider any difference between the amount paid and the withdrawing partner's capital balance as **a bonus** to the retiring partner or to the remaining partners.

Bonus to Retiring Partner

A partnership may pay a bonus to a retiring partner when:

1. The fair value of partnership assets is more than their book value,
2. There is unrecorded goodwill resulting from the partnership's superior earnings record, or
3. The remaining partners are eager to remove the partner from the firm.

The partnership deducts the bonus from the remaining partners' capital balances on the basis of their income ratios at the time of the withdrawal.

To illustrate, assume that the following capital balances exist in the RST partnership: Roman $50,000, Sand $30,000, and Terk $20,000. The partners share income in the ratio of 3:2:1, respectively. Terk retires from the partnership and receives a cash payment of $25,000 from the firm. The procedure for determining the bonus to the retiring partner and the allocation of the bonus to the remaining partners is as follows.

1. **Determine the amount of the bonus.** Subtract the retiring partner's capital balance from the cash paid by the partnership. The bonus in this case is $5,000 ($25,000 − $20,000).

2. **Allocate the bonus to the remaining partners on the basis of their income ratios.** The ratios of Roman and Sand are 3:2. Thus, the allocation of the $5,000 bonus is: Roman $3,000 ($5,000 × 3/5) and Sand $2,000 ($5,000 × 2/5).

The partnership records the withdrawal of Terk as follows (see **Helpful Hint**).

B. Terk, Capital	20,000	
F. Roman, Capital		3,000
D. Sand, Capital		2,000
Cash		25,000
(To record withdrawal of and bonus to Terk)		

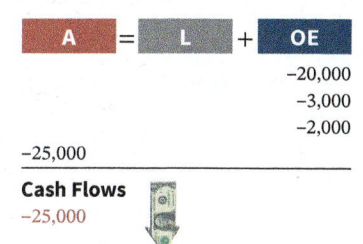

HELPFUL HINT
Compare this entry to the following one.

The remaining partners, Roman and Sand, will recover the bonus given to Terk as the partnership sells or uses the undervalued assets.

Bonus to Remaining Partners

The retiring partner may give a bonus to the remaining partners when:

1. Recorded assets are overvalued.
2. The partnership has a poor earnings record.
3. The partner is eager to leave the partnership.

In such cases, the cash paid to the retiring partner will be less than the retiring partner's capital balance. **The partnership allocates (credits) the bonus to the capital accounts of the remaining partners on the basis of their income ratios.**

To illustrate, assume instead that the partnership pays Terk only $16,000 for her $20,000 equity when she withdraws from the partnership. In that case:

1. The bonus to remaining partners is $4,000 ($20,000 − $16,000).
2. The allocation of the $4,000 bonus is Roman $2,400 ($4,000 × 3/5) and Sand $1,600 ($4,000 × 2/5).

Under these circumstances, the entry to record the withdrawal is as follows (see **Helpful Hint**).

HELPFUL HINT
Compare this entry to the previous one.

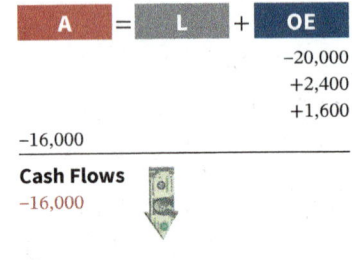

	Debit	Credit
B. Terk, Capital	20,000	
F. Roman, Capital		2,400
D. Sand, Capital		1,600
Cash		16,000
(To record withdrawal of Terk and bonus to remaining partners)		

Note that if Sand had withdrawn from the partnership, Roman and Terk would divide any bonus on the basis of their income ratio, which is 3:1 or 75% and 25%.

Death of a Partner

The death of a partner dissolves the partnership. However, partnership agreements usually contain a provision for the surviving partners to continue operations. When a partner dies, it usually is necessary to determine the partner's equity at the date of death. This is done by (1) determining the net income or loss for the year to date, (2) closing the books, and (3) preparing financial statements. The partnership agreement may also require an independent audit and a revaluation of assets.

The surviving partners may agree to purchase the deceased partner's equity from their personal assets. Or they may use partnership assets to settle with the deceased partner's estate. In both instances, the entries to record the withdrawal of the partner are similar to those presented earlier.

To facilitate payment from partnership assets, some partnerships obtain life insurance policies on each partner, with the partnership named as the beneficiary. The partnership then uses the proceeds from the insurance policy on the deceased partner to settle with the estate.

Review

Learning Objectives Review

1 Discuss and account for the formation of a partnership.

The principal characteristics of a partnership are (a) association of individuals, (b) mutual agency, (c) limited life, (d) unlimited liability, and (e) co-ownership of property. When formed, a partnership records each partner's initial investment at the fair value of the assets at the date of their transfer to the partnership.

2 Explain how to account for net income or net loss of a partnership.

Partnerships divide net income or net loss on the basis of the income ratio, which may be (a) a fixed ratio, (b) a ratio based on beginning or average capital balances, (c) salaries to partners and the remainder on a fixed ratio, (d) interest on partners' capital and the remainder on a fixed ratio, and (e) salaries to partners, interest on partners' capital, and the remainder on a fixed ratio.

The financial statements of a partnership are similar to those of a proprietorship. The principal differences are as follows. (a) The partnership shows the division of net income on the income statement. (b) The owners' equity statement is called a partners' capital statement. (c) The partnership reports each partner's capital on the balance sheet.

3 Explain how to account for the liquidation of a partnership.

When a partnership is liquidated, it is necessary to record the (a) sale of noncash assets, (b) allocation of the gain or loss on realization, (c) payment of partnership liabilities, and (d) distribution of cash to the partners on the basis of their capital balances.

4 Prepare journal entries when a partner is either admitted or withdraws.

The entry to record the admittance of a new partner by purchase of a partner's interest affects only partners' capital accounts. The entries to record the admittance by investment of assets in the partnership (a) increase both net assets and total capital and (b) may result in recognition of a bonus to either the old partners or the new partner.

The entry to record a withdrawal from the firm when the partners pay from their personal assets affects only partners' capital accounts. The entry to record a withdrawal when payment is made from partnership assets (a) decreases net assets and total capital and (b) may result in recognizing a bonus either to the retiring partner or the remaining partners.

Glossary Review

Admission by investment Admission of a partner by investing assets in the partnership, causing both partnership net assets and total capital to increase. (p. K-15).

Admission by purchase of an interest Admission of a partner in a personal transaction between one or more existing partners and the new partner; does not change total partnership assets or total capital. (p. K-15).

Capital deficiency A debit balance in a partner's capital account after allocation of gain or loss. (p. K-10).

General partners Partners who have unlimited liability for the debts of the firm. (p. K-3).

Income ratio The basis for dividing net income and net loss in a partnership. (p. K-6).

Limited liability company A form of business organization, usually classified as a partnership for tax purposes and usually with limited life, in which partners, who are called members, have limited liability. (p. K-3).

Limited liability partnership A partnership of professionals in which partners are given limited liability and the public is protected from malpractice by insurance carried by the partnership. (p. K-3).

Limited partners Partners whose liability for the debts of the firm is limited to their investment in the firm. (p. K-3).

Limited partnership A partnership in which one or more general partners have unlimited liability and one or more partners have limited liability for the obligations of the firm. (p. K-3).

No capital deficiency All partners have credit balances after allocation of gain or loss. (p. K-10).

Partners' capital statement The owners' equity statement for a partnership which shows the changes in each partner's capital account and in total partnership capital during the year. (p. K-9).

Partnership An association of two or more persons to carry on as co-owners of a business for profit. (p. K-1).

Partnership agreement A written contract expressing the voluntary agreement of two or more individuals in a partnership. (p. K-4).

Partnership dissolution A change in partners due to withdrawal or admission, which does not necessarily terminate the business. (p. K-2).

Partnership liquidation An event that ends both the legal and economic life of a partnership. (p. K-10).

Schedule of cash payments A schedule showing the distribution of cash to the partners in a partnership liquidation. (p. K-12).

Withdrawal by payment from partners' personal assets Withdrawal of a partner in a personal transaction between partners; does not change total partnership assets or total capital. (p. K-18).

Withdrawal by payment from partnership assets Withdrawal of a partner in a transaction involving the partnership, causing both partnership net assets and total capital to decrease. (p. K-18).

WileyPLUS

Many additional resources are available for practice in WileyPLUS.

Questions

1. The characteristics of a partnership include the following: (a) association of individuals, (b) limited life, and (c) co-ownership of property. Explain each of these terms.

2. Kevin Mathis is confused about the partnership characteristics of (a) mutual agency and (b) unlimited liability. Explain these two characteristics for Kevin.

3. Lance Kosinski and Matt Morrisen are considering a business venture. They ask you to explain the advantages and disadvantages of the partnership form of organization.

4. Why might a company choose to use a limited partnership?

5. Newland and Palermo form a partnership. Newland contributes land with a book value of $50,000 and a fair value of $60,000. Newland also contributes equipment with a book value of $52,000 and a fair value of $57,000. The partnership assumes a $20,000 mortgage on the land. What should be the balance in Newland's capital account upon formation of the partnership?

6. W. Jenson, N. Emch, and W. Gilligan have a partnership called Outlaws. A dispute has arisen among the partners. Jenson has invested twice as much in assets as the other two partners, and he believes net income and net losses should be shared in accordance with the capital ratios. The partnership agreement does not specify the division of profits and losses. How will net income and net loss be divided?

7. Mutt and Jeff are discussing how income and losses should be divided in a partnership they plan to form. What factors should be considered in determining the division of net income or net loss?

8. M. Elston and R. Ogle have partnership capital balances of $40,000 and $80,000, respectively. The partnership agreement indicates that net

income or net loss should be shared equally. If net income for the partnership is $42,000, how should the net income be divided?

9. S. Pletcher and F. Holt share net income and net loss equally. (a) Which account(s) is (are) debited and credited to record the division of net income between the partners? (b) If S. Pletcher withdraws $30,000 in cash for personal use instead of salary, which account is debited and which is credited?

10. Partners T. Greer and R. Parks are provided salary allowances of $30,000 and $25,000, respectively. They divide the remainder of the partnership income in a ratio of 3:2. If partnership net income is $40,000, how much is allocated to Greer and Parks?

11. Are the financial statements of a partnership similar to those of a proprietorship? Discuss.

12. How does the liquidation of a partnership differ from the dissolution of a partnership?

13. Roger Fuller and Mike Rangel are discussing the liquidation of a partnership. Roger maintains that all cash should be distributed to partners on the basis of their income ratios. Is he correct? Explain.

14. In continuing their discussion from Question 13, Mike says that even in the case of a capital deficiency, all cash should still be distributed on the basis of capital balances. Is Mike correct? Explain.

15. Norris, Madson, and Howell have income ratios of 5:3:2 and capital balances of $34,000, $31,000, and $28,000, respectively. Noncash assets are sold at a gain and allocated to the partners. After creditors are paid, $103,000 of cash is available for distribution to the partners. How much cash should be paid to Madson?

16. Before the final distribution of cash, account balances are Cash $27,000; S. Shea, Capital $19,000 (Cr.); L. Seastrom, Capital $12,000 (Cr.); and M. Luthi, Capital $4,000 (Dr.). Luthi is unable to pay any of the capital deficiency. If the income-sharing ratios are 5:3:2, respectively, how much cash should be paid to L. Seastrom?

17. Why is **Apple** not a partnership?

18. Susan Turnbull decides to purchase from an existing partner for $50,000 a one-third interest in a partnership. What effect does this transaction have on partnership net assets?

19. Jerry Park decides to invest $25,000 in a partnership for a one-sixth capital interest. How much do the partnership's net assets increase? Does Park also acquire a one-sixth income ratio through this investment?

20. Jill Parsons purchases for $72,000 Jamar's interest in the Tholen-Jamar partnership. Assuming that Jamar has a $68,000 capital balance in the partnership, what journal entry is made by the partnership to record this transaction?

21. Jaime Keller has a $41,000 capital balance in a partnership. She sells her interest to Sam Parmenter for $45,000 cash. What entry is made by the partnership for this transaction?

22. Andrea Riley retires from the partnership of Jaggard, Pester, and Riley. She receives $85,000 of partnership assets in settlement of her capital balance of $81,000. Assuming that the income-sharing ratios are 5:3:2, respectively, how much of Riley's bonus is debited to Pester's capital account?

23. Your roommate argues that partnership assets should be revalued in situations like those in Question 21. Why is this generally not done?

24. How is a deceased partner's equity determined?

Brief Exercises

Journalize entries in forming a partnership.

BEK.1 (LO 1), AP Barbara Ripley and Fred Nichols decide to organize the All-Star partnership. Ripley invests $15,000 cash, and Nichols contributes $10,000 cash and equipment having a book value of $3,500. Prepare the entry to record Nichols's investment in the partnership, assuming the equipment has a fair value of $4,000.

Prepare portion of opening balance sheet for partnership.

BEK.2 (LO 1), AP Penner and Torres decide to merge their proprietorships into a partnership called Pentor Company. The balance sheet of Torres Co. shows:

Accounts receivable	$16,000	
Less: Allowance for doubtful accounts	1,200	$14,800
Equipment	20,000	
Less: Accumulated depreciation—equip.	7,000	13,000

The partners agree that the net realizable value of the receivables is $14,500 and that the fair value of the equipment is $11,000. Indicate how the accounts should appear in the opening balance sheet of the partnership.

Journalize the division of net income using fixed income ratios.

BEK.3 (LO 2), AP Rod Dall Co. reports net income of $75,000. The income ratios are Rod 60% and Dall 40%. Indicate the division of net income to each partner, and prepare the entry to distribute the net income.

Compute division of net income with a salary allowance and fixed ratios.

BEK.4 (LO 2), AP PFW Co. reports net income of $45,000. Partner salary allowances are Pitts $15,000, Filbert $5,000, and Witten $5,000. Indicate the division of net income to each partner, assuming the income ratio is 50:30:20, respectively.

Show division of net income when allowances exceed net income.

BEK.5 (LO 2), AP Nabb & Fry Co. reports net income of $31,000. Interest allowances are Nabb $7,000 and Fry $5,000, salary allowances are Nabb $15,000 and Fry $10,000, and the remainder is shared equally. Show the distribution of income.

BEK.6 (LO 3), AP After liquidating noncash assets and paying creditors, account balances in the Mann Co. are Cash $21,000; A, Capital (Cr.) $8,000; B, Capital (Cr.) $9,000; and C, Capital (Cr.) $4,000. The partners share income equally. Journalize the final distribution of cash to the partners.

Journalize final cash distribution in liquidation.

BEK.7 (LO 4), AP Gamma Co. capital balances are Barr $30,000, Croy $25,000, and Eubank $22,000. The partners share income equally. Tovar is admitted to the firm by purchasing one-half of Eubank's interest for $13,000. Journalize the admission of Tovar to the partnership.

Journalize admission by purchase of an interest.

BEK.8 (LO 4), AP In Eastwood Co., capital balances are Irey $40,000 and Pedigo $50,000. The partners share income equally. Vernon is admitted to the firm with a 45% interest by an investment of cash of $58,000. Journalize the admission of Vernon.

Journalize admission by investment.

BEK.9 (LO 4), AP Capital balances in Pelmar Co. are Lango $40,000, Oslo $30,000, and Fernetti $20,000. Lango and Oslo each agree to pay Fernetti $12,000 from their personal assets. Lango and Oslo each receive 50% of Fernetti's equity. The partners share income equally. Journalize the withdrawal of Fernetti.

Journalize withdrawal paid by personal assets.

BEK.10 (LO 4), AP Data pertaining to Pelmar Co. are presented in BEK.9. Instead of payment from personal assets, assume that Fernetti receives $24,000 from partnership assets in withdrawing from the firm. Journalize the withdrawal of Fernetti.

Journalize withdrawal paid by partnership assets.

Exercises

EK.1 (LO 1), C Mark Rensing has prepared the following list of statements about partnerships.

Identify characteristics of partnership.

1. A partnership is an association of three or more persons to carry on as co-owners of a business for profit.
2. The legal requirements for forming a partnership can be quite burdensome.
3. A partnership is not an entity for financial reporting purposes.
4. The net income of a partnership is taxed as a separate entity.
5. The act of any partner is binding on all other partners, even when partners perform business acts beyond the scope of their authority.
6. Each partner is personally and individually liable for all partnership liabilities.
7. When a partnership is dissolved, the assets legally revert to the original contributor.
8. In a limited partnership, one or more partners have unlimited liability and one or more partners have limited liability for the debts of the firm.
9. Mutual agency is a major advantage of the partnership form of business.

Instructions
Identify each statement as true or false. If false, indicate how to correct the statement.

EK.2 (LO 1), AP K. Decker, S. Rosen, and E. Toso are forming a partnership. Decker is transferring $50,000 of personal cash to the partnership. Rosen owns land worth $15,000 and a small building worth $80,000, which she transfers to the partnership. Toso transfers to the partnership cash of $9,000, accounts receivable of $32,000, and equipment worth $39,000. The partnership expects to collect $29,000 of the accounts receivable.

Journalize entry for formation of a partnership.

Instructions
a. Prepare the journal entries to record each of the partners' investments.
b. What amount would be reported as total owners' equity immediately after the investments?

EK.3 (LO 1), AP Suzy Vopat has owned and operated a proprietorship for several years. On January 1, she decides to terminate this business and become a partner in the firm of Vopat and Sigma. Vopat's investment in the partnership consists of $12,000 in cash, and the following assets of the proprietorship: accounts receivable $14,000 less allowance for doubtful accounts of $2,000, and equipment $30,000 less accumulated depreciation of $4,000. It is agreed that the allowance for doubtful accounts should be $3,000 for the partnership. The fair value of the equipment is $23,500.

Journalize entry for formation of a partnership.

Instructions
Journalize Vopat's admission to the firm of Vopat and Sigma.

Prepare schedule showing distribution of net income and closing entry.

EK.4 (LO 2), AP McGill and Smyth have capital balances on January 1 of $50,000 and $40,000, respectively. The partnership income-sharing agreement provides for (1) annual salaries of $22,000 for McGill and $13,000 for Smyth, (2) interest at 10% on beginning capital balances, and (3) remaining income or loss to be shared 60% by McGill and 40% by Smyth.

Instructions

a. Prepare a schedule showing the distribution of net income, assuming net income is (1) $50,000 and (2) $36,000.

b. Journalize the allocation of net income in each of the situations above.

Prepare journal entries to record allocation of net income.

EK.5 (LO 2), AP Coburn (beginning capital, $60,000) and Webb (beginning capital $90,000) are partners. During 2022, the partnership earned net income of $80,000, and Coburn made drawings of $18,000 while Webb made drawings of $24,000.

Instructions

a. Assume the partnership income-sharing agreement calls for income to be divided 45% to Coburn and 55% to Webb. Prepare the journal entry to record the allocation of net income.

b. Assume the partnership income-sharing agreement calls for income to be divided with a salary of $30,000 to Coburn and $25,000 to Webb, with the remainder divided 45% to Coburn and 55% to Webb. Prepare the journal entry to record the allocation of net income.

c. Assume the partnership income-sharing agreement calls for income to be divided with a salary of $40,000 to Coburn and $35,000 to Webb, interest of 10% on beginning capital, and the remainder divided 50%–50%. Prepare the journal entry to record the allocation of net income.

d. Compute the partners' ending capital balances under the assumption in part (c).

Prepare partners' capital statement and partial balance sheet.

EK.6 (LO 2), AP For National Co., beginning capital balances on January 1, 2022, are Nancy Payne $20,000 and Ann Dody $18,000. During the year, drawings were Payne $8,000 and Dody $5,000. Net income was $40,000, and the partners share income equally.

Instructions

a. Prepare the partners' capital statement for the year.

b. Prepare the owners' equity section of the balance sheet at December 31, 2022.

Prepare a classified balance sheet of a partnership.

EK.7 (LO 2), AP Terry, Nick, and Frank are forming The Doctor Partnership. Terry is transferring $30,000 of personal cash and equipment worth $25,000 to the partnership. Nick owns land worth $28,000 and a small building worth $75,000, which he transfers to the partnership. There is a long-term mortgage of $20,000 on the land and building, which the partnership assumes. Frank transfers cash of $7,000, accounts receivable of $36,000, supplies worth $3,000, and equipment worth $27,000 to the partnership. The partnership expects to collect $32,000 of the accounts receivable.

Instructions

Prepare a classified balance sheet for the partnership after the partners' investments on December 31, 2022.

Prepare cash payments schedule.

EK.8 (LO 3), AP Sedgwick Company at December 31 has cash $20,000, noncash assets $100,000, liabilities $55,000, and the following capital balances: Floyd $45,000 and DeWitt $20,000. The firm is liquidated, and $105,000 in cash is received for the noncash assets. Floyd and DeWitt income ratios are 60% and 40%, respectively.

Instructions

Prepare a schedule of cash payments.

Journalize transactions in a liquidation.

EK.9 (LO 3), AP Data for Sedgwick Company are presented in EK.8. Sedgwick Company now decides to liquidate the partnership.

Instructions

Prepare the entries to record:

a. The sale of noncash assets.

b. The allocation of the gain or loss on realization to the partners.

c. Payment of creditors.

d. Distribution of cash to the partners.

EK.10 (LO 3), AP Prior to the distribution of cash to the partners, the accounts in the VUP Company are Cash $24,000; Vogel, Capital (Cr.) $17,000; Utech, Capital (Cr.) $15,000; and Pena, Capital (Dr.) $8,000. The income ratios are 5:3:2, respectively. VUP Company decides to liquidate the company.

Journalize transactions with a capital deficiency.

Instructions

a. Prepare the entry to record (1) Pena's payment of $8,000 in cash to the partnership and (2) the distribution of cash to the partners with credit balances.

b. Prepare the entry to record (1) the absorption of Pena's capital deficiency by the other partners and (2) the distribution of cash to the partners with credit balances.

EK.11 (LO 4), AP K. Kolmer, C. Eidman, and C. Ryno share income on a 5:3:2 basis. They have capital balances of $34,000, $26,000, and $21,000, respectively, when Don Jernigan is admitted to the partnership.

Journalize admission of a new partner by purchase of an interest.

Instructions

Prepare the journal entry to record the admission of Don Jernigan under each of the following assumptions.

a. Purchase of 50% of Kolmer's equity for $19,000.

b. Purchase of 50% of Eidman's equity for $12,000.

c. Purchase of $33^1/_3$% of Ryno's equity for $9,000.

EK.12 (LO 4), AP S. Pagan and T. Tabor share income on a 6:4 basis. They have capital balances of $100,000 and $60,000, respectively, when W. Wolford is admitted to the partnership.

Journalize admission of a new partner by investment.

Instructions

Prepare the journal entry to record the admission of W. Wolford under each of the following assumptions.

a. Investment of $90,000 cash for a 30% ownership interest with bonuses to the existing partners.

b. Investment of $50,000 cash for a 30% ownership interest with a bonus to the new partner.

EK.13 (LO 4), AP N. Essex, C. Gilmore, and C. Heganbart have capital balances of $50,000, $40,000, and $30,000, respectively. Their income ratios are 4:4:2. Heganbart withdraws from the partnership under each of the following independent conditions.

Journalize withdrawal of a partner with payment from partners' personal assets.

1. Essex and Gilmore agree to purchase Heganbart's equity by paying $17,000 each from their personal assets. Each purchaser receives 50% of Heganbart's equity.

2. Gilmore agrees to purchase all of Heganbart's equity by paying $22,000 cash from her personal assets.

3. Essex agrees to purchase all of Heganbart's equity by paying $26,000 cash from his personal assets.

Instructions

Journalize the withdrawal of Heganbart under each of the assumptions above.

EK.14 (LO 4), AP B. Higgins, J. Mayo, and N. Rice have capital balances of $95,000, $75,000, and $60,000, respectively. They share income or loss on a 5:3:2 basis. Rice withdraws from the partnership under each of the following conditions.

Journalize withdrawal of a partner with payment from partnership assets.

1. Rice is paid $64,000 in cash from partnership assets, and a bonus is granted to the retiring partner.

2. Rice is paid $52,000 in cash from partnership assets, and bonuses are granted to the remaining partners.

Instructions

Journalize the withdrawal of Rice under each of the assumptions above.

EK.15 (LO 4), AP Foss, Albertson, and Espinosa are partners who share profits and losses 50%, 30%, and 20%, respectively. Their capital balances are $100,000, $60,000, and $40,000, respectively.

Journalize entry for admission and withdrawal of partners.

Instructions

a. Assume Garrett joins the partnership by investing $88,000 for a 25% interest with bonuses to the existing partners. Prepare the journal entry to record his investment.

b. Assume instead that Foss leaves the partnership. Foss is paid $110,000 with a bonus to the retiring partner. Prepare the journal entry to record Foss's withdrawal.

Problems

Prepare entries for formation of a partnership and a balance sheet.

PK.1 (LO 1, 2), AP The post-closing trial balances of two proprietorships on January 1, 2022, are presented below.

	Sorensen Company		Lucas Company	
	Dr.	Cr.	Dr.	Cr.
Cash	$ 14,000		$12,000	
Accounts receivable	17,500		26,000	
Allowance for doubtful accounts		$ 3,000		$ 4,400
Inventory	26,500		18,400	
Equipment	45,000		29,000	
Accumulated depreciation—equipment		24,000		11,000
Notes payable		18,000		15,000
Accounts payable		22,000		31,000
Sorensen, capital		36,000		
Lucas, capital				24,000
	$103,000	$103,000	$85,400	$85,400

Sorensen and Lucas decide to form a partnership, Solu Company, with the following agreed upon valuations for noncash assets.

	Sorensen Company	Lucas Company
Accounts receivable	$17,500	$26,000
Allowance for doubtful accounts	4,500	4,000
Inventory	28,000	20,000
Equipment	25,000	15,000

All cash will be transferred to the partnership, and the partnership will assume all the liabilities of the two proprietorships. Further, it is agreed that Sorensen will invest an additional $5,000 in cash, and Lucas will invest an additional $19,000 in cash.

Instructions

a. Prepare separate journal entries to record the transfer of each proprietorship's assets and liabilities to the partnership.

b. Journalize the additional cash investment by each partner.

c. Prepare a classified balance sheet for the partnership on January 1, 2022.

a. Sorensen, Capital $40,000
Lucas, Capital $23,000

c. Total assets $173,000

Journalize divisions of net income and prepare a partners' capital statement.

PK.2 (LO 2), AP At the end of its first year of operations on December 31, 2022, NBS Company's accounts show the following.

Partner	Drawings	Capital
Art Niensted	$23,000	$48,000
Greg Bolen	14,000	30,000
Krista Sayler	10,000	25,000

The capital balance represents each partner's initial capital investment. Therefore, net income or net loss for 2022 has not been closed to the partners' capital accounts.

Instructions

a. Journalize the entry to record the division of net income for the year 2022 under each of the following independent assumptions.

a. 1. Niensted $18,000

1. Net income is $30,000. Income is shared 6:3:1.

2. Niensted $20,000

2. Net income is $40,000. Niensted and Bolen are given salary allowances of $15,000 and $10,000, respectively. The remainder is shared equally.

3. Niensted $17,700

3. Net income is $19,000. Each partner is allowed interest of 10% on beginning capital balances. Niensted is given a $15,000 salary allowance. The remainder is shared equally.

b. Prepare a schedule showing the division of net income under assumption (3) above.

c. Prepare a partners' capital statement for the year under assumption (3) above

c. Niensted $42,700

PK.3 (LO 3), AP The partners in Crawford Company decide to liquidate the firm when the balance sheet shows the following.

Prepare entries with a capital deficiency in liquidation of a partnership.

Crawford Company
Balance Sheet
May 31, 2022

Assets		Liabilities and Owners' Equity	
Cash	$ 27,500	Notes payable	$ 13,500
Accounts receivable	25,000	Accounts payable	27,000
Allowance for doubtful accounts	(1,000)	Salaries and wages payable	4,000
Inventory	34,500	A. Jamison, capital	33,000
Equipment	21,000	S. Moyer, capital	21,000
Accumulated depreciation—equipment	(5,500)	P. Roper, capital	3,000
	$101,500		$101,500

The partners share income and loss 5:3:2. During the process of liquidation, the following transactions were completed in the following sequence.

1. A total of $51,000 was received from converting noncash assets into cash.
2. Gain or loss on realization was allocated to partners.
3. Liabilities were paid in full.
4. P. Roper paid his capital deficiency.
5. Cash was paid to the partners with credit balances.

Instructions

a. Prepare the entries to record the transactions.

b. Post to the cash and capital accounts.

c. Assume that Roper is unable to pay the capital deficiency.

   1. Prepare the entry to allocate Roper's debit balance to Jamison and Moyer.

   2. Prepare the entry to record the final distribution of cash.

a. Loss on realization $23,000
Cash paid: to Jamison
$21,500; to Moyer $14,100

PK.4 (LO 4), AP At April 30, partners' capital balances in PDL Company are G. Donley $52,000, C. Lamar $48,000, and J. Pinkston $18,000. The income sharing ratios are 5:4:1, respectively. On May 1, the PDLT Company is formed by admitting J. Terrell to the firm as a partner.

Journalize admission of a partner under different assumptions.

Instructions

a. Journalize the admission of Terrell under each of the following independent assumptions.

   1. Terrell purchases 50% of Pinkston's ownership interest by paying Pinkston $16,000 in cash.
   2. Terrell purchases 33 1/3% of Lamar's ownership interest by paying Lamar $15,000 in cash.
   3. Terrell invests $62,000 for a 30% ownership interest, and bonuses are given to the old partners.
   4. Terrell invests $42,000 for a 30% ownership interest, which includes a bonus to the new partner.

b. Lamar's capital balance is $32,000 after admitting Terrell to the partnership by investment. If Lamar's ownership interest is 20% of total partnership capital, what were (1) Terrell's cash investment and (2) the bonus to the new partner?

a. 1. Terrell $9,000
2. Terrell $16,000
3. Terrell $54,000
4. Terrell $48,000

PK.5 (LO 4), AP On December 31, the capital balances and income ratios in TEP Company are as follows.

Journalize withdrawal of a partner under different assumptions.

Partner	Capital Balance	Income Ratio
Trayer	$60,000	50%
Emig	40,000	30%
Posada	30,000	20%

Instructions

a. Journalize the withdrawal of Posada under each of the following assumptions.

   1. Each of the continuing partners agrees to pay $18,000 in cash from personal funds to purchase Posada's ownership equity. Each receives 50% of Posada's equity.

a. 1. Emig, Capital $15,000

2. Emig, Capital $30,000
3. Bonus $4,000
4. Bonus $8,000

2. Emig agrees to purchase Posada's ownership interest for $25,000 cash.
3. Posada is paid $34,000 from partnership assets, which includes a bonus to the retiring partner.
4. Posada is paid $22,000 from partnership assets, and bonuses to the remaining partners are recognized.

b. If Emig's capital balance after Posada's withdrawal is $43,600, what were (1) the total bonus to the remaining partners and (2) the cash paid by the partnership to Posada?

Appendix L

Accounting for Sole Proprietorships

Appendix Preview

Chapter 1 identified three forms of business organization. Two forms, the sole proprietorship and the partnership, were discussed only briefly. Emphasis was placed on the corporate form in Chapter 1 as well as in subsequent chapters. The purpose of this appendix is to discuss and illustrate the accounting for the operations and financial condition of a sole proprietorship.

Appendix Outline

LEARNING OBJECTIVES

1. Identify the differences in equity accounts between a corporation and a sole proprietorship.	• Owner's capital account • Drawing account
2. Discuss the accounts that increase and decrease owner's equity.	• Owner's equity in a sole proprietorship • Recording transactions of a sole proprietorship
3. Describe the differences between a retained earnings statement and an owner's equity statement.	• Using the adjusted trial balance • Reporting equity
4. Explain the process of closing the books for a sole proprietorship.	• Preparing a post-closing trial balance for a sole proprietorship

Corporation versus Sole Proprietorship Equity Accounts

LEARNING OBJECTIVE 1
Identify the differences in equity accounts between a corporation and a sole proprietorship.

The primary difference between accounting and reporting for a sole proprietorship and a corporation involves accounting for equity transactions. Because a sole proprietorship has a single owner rather than numerous stockholders, a sole proprietorship uses a permanent **owner's capital account**, such as "Sally Jones, Capital," instead of Common Stock and Retained Earnings. In a sole proprietorship, there is no need to separate owner's investments from net income retained for dividends because the sole proprietor does not declare or receive dividends. Instead, withdrawals by the owner of cash or other assets from the business for personal use are recorded in a temporary **drawing** account. The different equity accounts are contrasted as shown in **Illustration L.1**.

ILLUSTRATION L.1
Equity section of the balance sheet—corporation vs. proprietorship

Corporation	Sole Proprietorship
Stockholders' equity	Owner's equity
Common stock	Owner's name, capital
Retained earnings	

For purposes of comparing the accounting for a corporation with a sole proprietorship, the illustrations in this appendix assume a sole proprietorship owned by R. Neal and named Sierra Company. **Except for equity transactions, we use the same accounts, amounts, and transactions as those of Sierra Corporation presented in Chapters 1 through 4.**

Accounts that Change Owner's Equity

LEARNING OBJECTIVE 2
Discuss the accounts that increase and decrease owner's equity.

Owner's Equity in a Sole Proprietorship

The ownership claim on total assets is known as **owner's equity**. It is equal to total assets minus total liabilities.

Increases in Owner's Equity

In a proprietorship, owner's equity is increased by owner's investments and revenues.

Investments by Owner **Investments by owner** are the assets the owner puts into the business. These investments increase owner's equity.

Revenues **Revenues** are the gross increase in owner's equity resulting from business activities entered into for the purpose of earning income.

Decreases in Owner's Equity

In a proprietorship, owner's equity is decreased by owner's drawings and expenses.

Drawings An owner may withdraw cash or other assets for personal use. These withdrawals could be recorded as a direct decrease of owner's equity. However, it is generally considered preferable to use a separate classification called **drawings** to determine the total withdrawals for each accounting period. **Drawings decrease owner's equity.**

Expenses **Expenses** are the cost of assets consumed or services used in the process of earning revenue. They are **decreases in owner's equity that result from operating the business.**

In summary, owner's equity is increased by an owner's investments and by revenues from business operations. In contrast, owner's equity is decreased by an owner's withdrawals of assets and by expenses. These relationships are shown in **Illustration L.2**. **Net income** results when revenues exceed expenses. A **net loss** occurs when expenses exceed revenues.

ILLUSTRATION L.2
Increases and decreases in owner's equity

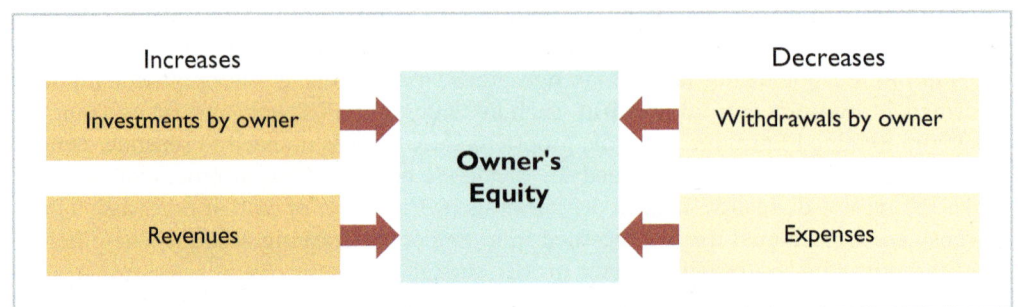

Recording Transactions of a Proprietorship

Chapter 3 described the basic steps employed in the accounting process as follows:

- Analyze transactions.
- Record transactions in the journal.
- Post journal entries to the general ledger.
- Prepare a trial balance.

These same steps apply to all forms of business. Illustration 3.4 presented the impact of Sierra's transactions on its accounting equation. **Illustration L.3** shows how the same transactions would have been recorded for a sole proprietor. The only differences are related to the accounts used to record equity transactions. Those differences are highlighted here in red.

ILLUSTRATION L.3 Summary of transactions

							BALANCE SHEET										INCOME STATEMENT
			Assets				=		Liabilities				+	Owner's Equity			
	Cash	+	Supplies	+	Prepd. Insur.	+	Equip-ment	=	Notes Pay.	+	Accts. Pay.	+	Unearned Serv. Rev.	+	R. Neal, Capital		
(1)	+$10,000														+$10,000		Investment by owner
(2)	+5,000								+$5,000								
(3)	−5,000						+$5,000										
(4)	+1,200												+$1,200				
(5)	+10,000														+10,000		Service Revenue
(6)	−900														−900		Rent Expense
(7)	−600				+$600												
(8)			+$2,500								+$2,500						
(9)																	
(10)	−500														−500		Drawings
(11)	−4,000														−4,000		Sal./Wages Expense
	$15,200	+	$2,500	+	$600	+	$5,000	=	$5,000	+	$2,500	+	$1,200	+	$14,600		

$23,300 = $23,300

Retained Earnings Statement versus Owner's Equity Statement

LEARNING OBJECTIVE 3
Describe the differences between a retained earnings statement and an owner's equity statement.

Chapter 4 described accounting for adjusting entries. A sole proprietor makes the same types of adjustments as a corporation. After recording and posting all of the adjustments, an adjusted trial balance is prepared. **Illustrations L.4** and **L.5** show how the adjusted trial balance is used to prepare a sole proprietor's financial statements.

The primary differences between these statements and those of a corporation (presented in Illustrations 4.27 and 4.28) relate to the way equity is reported. A sole proprietor prepares an **owner's equity statement** rather than a retained earnings statement and uses different titles for the equity items shown on the balance sheet.

APPENDIX L Accounting for Sole Proprietorships

ILLUSTRATION L.4 Preparation of the income statement and owner's equity statement from the adjusted trial balance

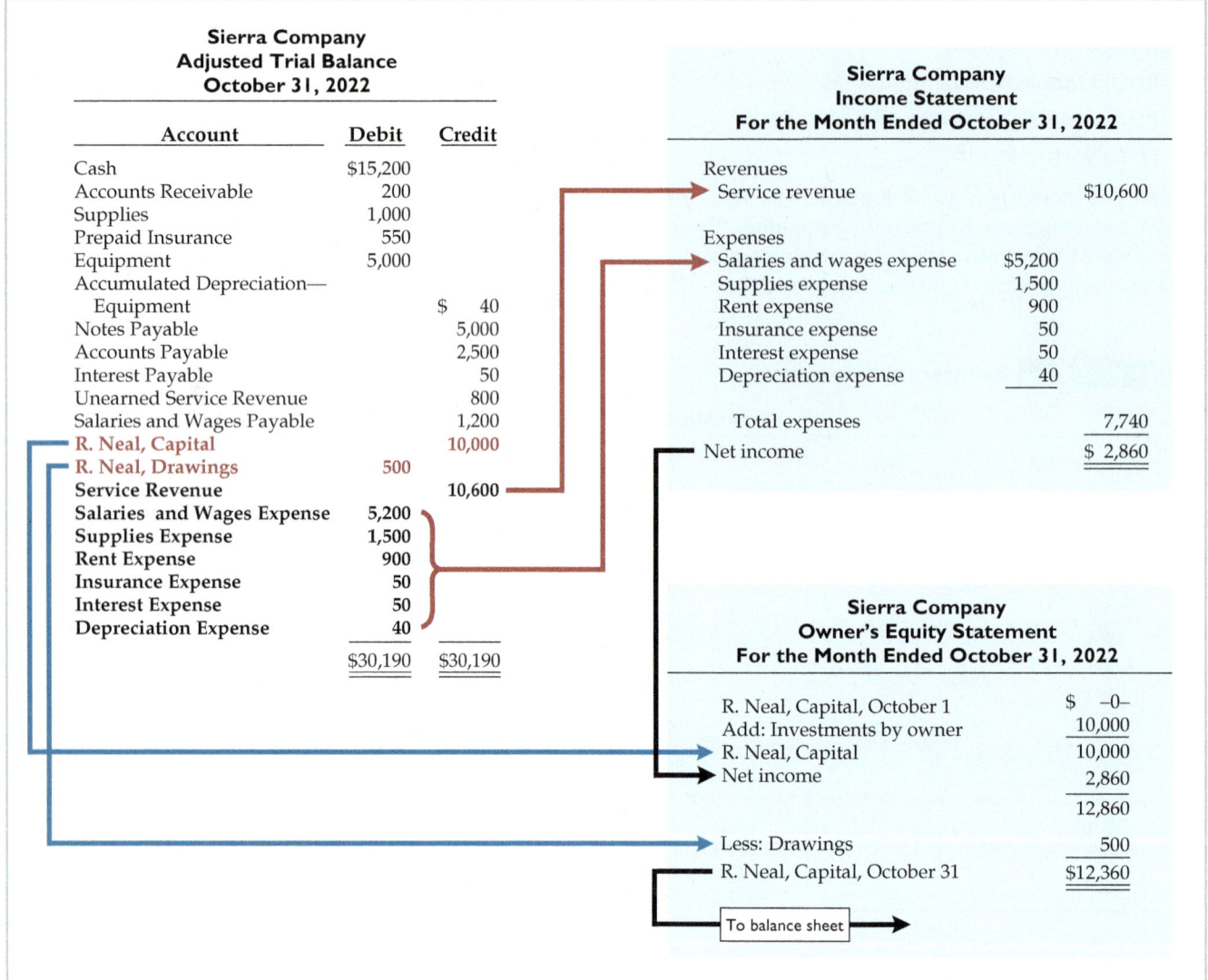

Closing the Books for a Sole Proprietorship

LEARNING OBJECTIVE 4
Explain the process of closing the books for a sole proprietorship.

At the end of the accounting period, the temporary account balances are transferred to the permanent owner's equity account, Owner's Capital, through the preparation of closing entries. **Closing entries** for a proprietorship formally recognize in the ledger the transfer of net income (or net loss) and owner's drawing to owner's capital. The results of these entries are shown in the owner's equity statement.

Journalizing and posting closing entries is a required step in the accounting cycle. (See Illustrations 4.32 and 4.33 for Sierra Corporation.)

In preparing closing entries for a proprietorship, each income statement account could be closed directly to owner's capital. However, to do so would result in excessive detail in

ILLUSTRATION L.5 Preparation of the balance sheet from the adjusted trial balance

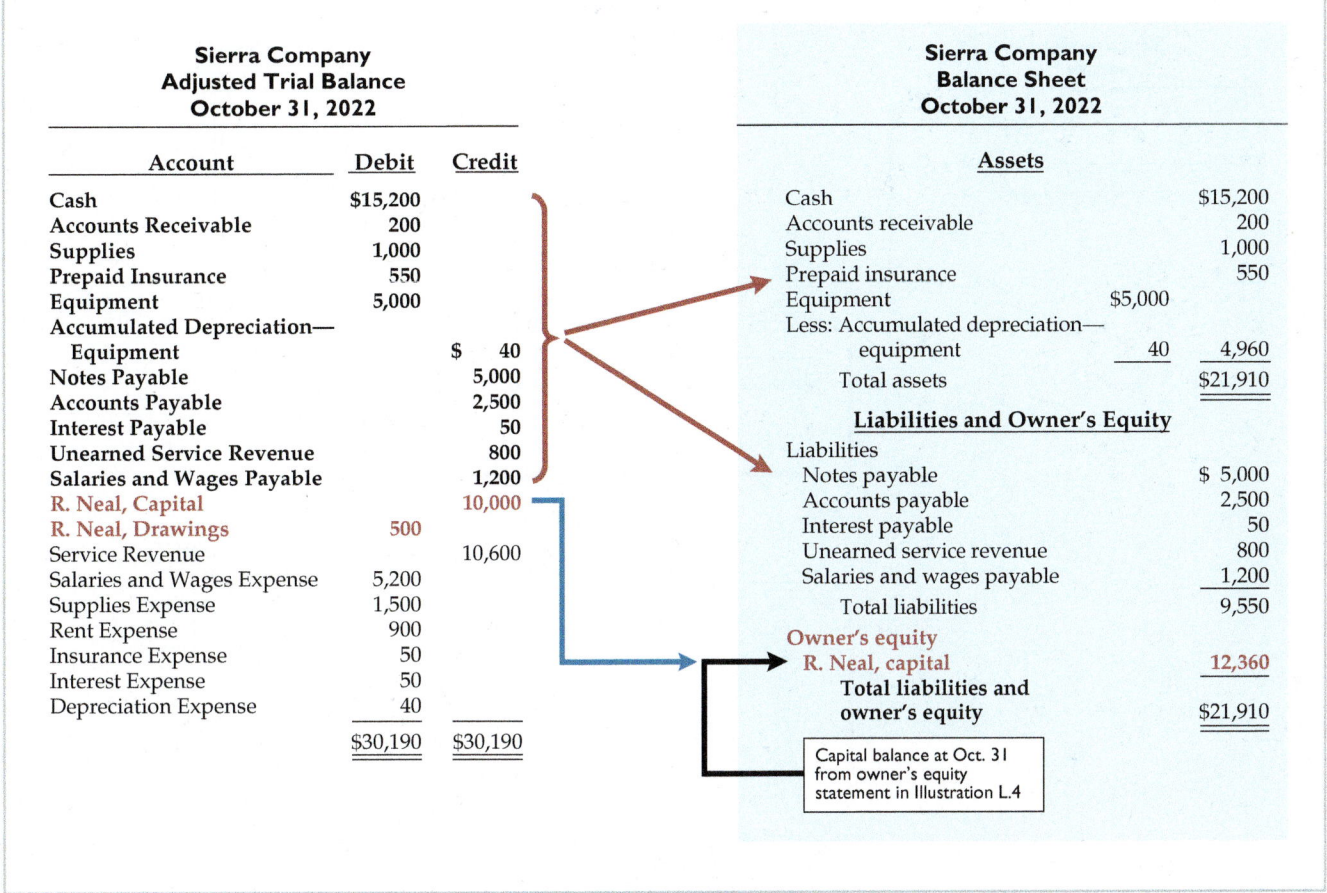

the permanent owner's capital account. Instead, the revenue and expense accounts are closed, in the same manner as for a corporation, to another temporary account, **Income Summary**. Only the net income or net loss is transferred from this account to Owner's Capital.

Closing entries for a proprietorship may be prepared directly from the adjusted balances in the ledger, from the income statement and balance sheet columns of the worksheet, or from the income and owner's equity statements. Separate closing entries could be prepared for each nominal account, but the following four entries accomplish the desired result more efficiently:

1. Debit each revenue account for its balance, and credit Income Summary for total revenues.
2. Debit Income Summary for total expenses, and credit each expense account for its balance.
3. Debit Income Summary and credit Owner's Capital for the amount of net income.
4. Debit Owner's Capital for the balance in the Owner's Drawings account, and credit Owner's Drawings for the same amount (see **Helpful Hint**).

HELPFUL HINT
Owner's Drawings is closed directly to Owner's Capital and not to Income Summary because Owner's Drawings is not an expense.

The four entries are referenced in the diagram of the closing process shown in **Illustration L.6** and in the journal entries in **Illustration L.7** (see **Helpful Hint**). The posting of closing entries is shown in **Illustration L.8**.

If there were a net loss because expenses exceeded revenues, entry 3 in Illustration L.6 would be reversed: credit Income Summary and debit Owner's Capital.

APPENDIX L Accounting for Sole Proprietorships

ILLUSTRATION L.6 Diagram of closing process

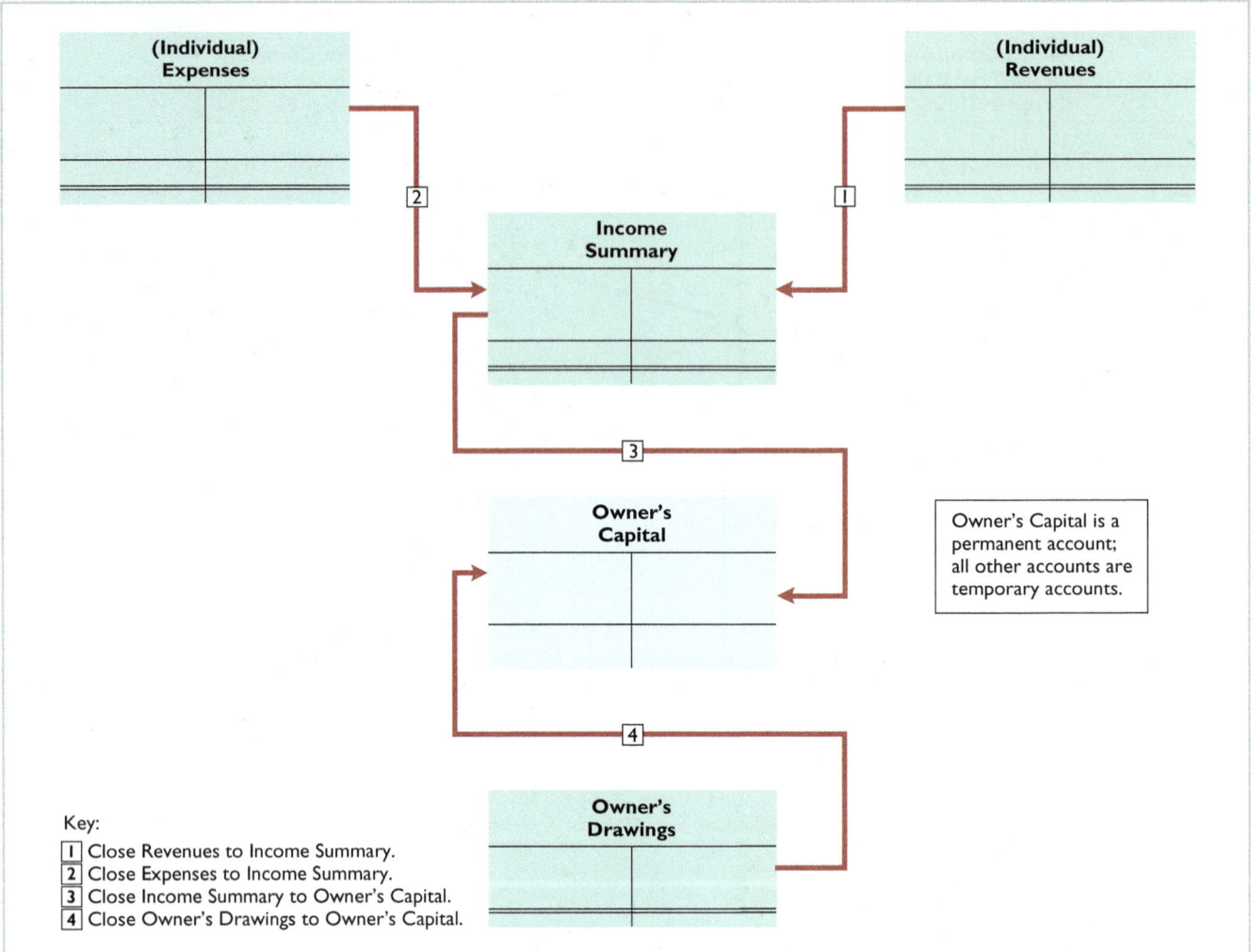

Key:
1. Close Revenues to Income Summary.
2. Close Expenses to Income Summary.
3. Close Income Summary to Owner's Capital.
4. Close Owner's Drawings to Owner's Capital.

Owner's Capital is a permanent account; all other accounts are temporary accounts.

ILLUSTRATION L.7 Closing entries journalized

	General Journal		
Date	Account Titles and Explanation	Debit	Credit
	Closing Entries		
	(1)		
2022 Oct. 31	Service Revenue	10,600	
	Income Summary		10,600
	(To close revenue account)		
	(2)		
31	Income Summary	7,740	
	Salaries and Wages Expense		5,200
	Supplies Expense		1,500
	Rent Expense		900
	Insurance Expense		50
	Interest Expense		50
	Depreciation Expense		40
	(To close expense accounts)		
	(3)		
31	Income Summary	2,860	
	R. Neal, Capital		2,860
	(To close net income to owner's capital)		
	(4)		
31	R. Neal, Capital	500	
	R. Neal, Drawings		500
	(To close drawings to owner's capital)		

HELPFUL HINT

Income Summary is a very descriptive title. Total revenues are closed to Income Summary, total expenses are closed to Income Summary, and the balance in Income Summary is a net income or net loss.

ILLUSTRATION L.8 Posting of closing entries

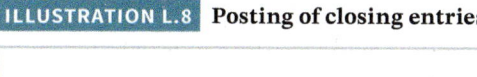

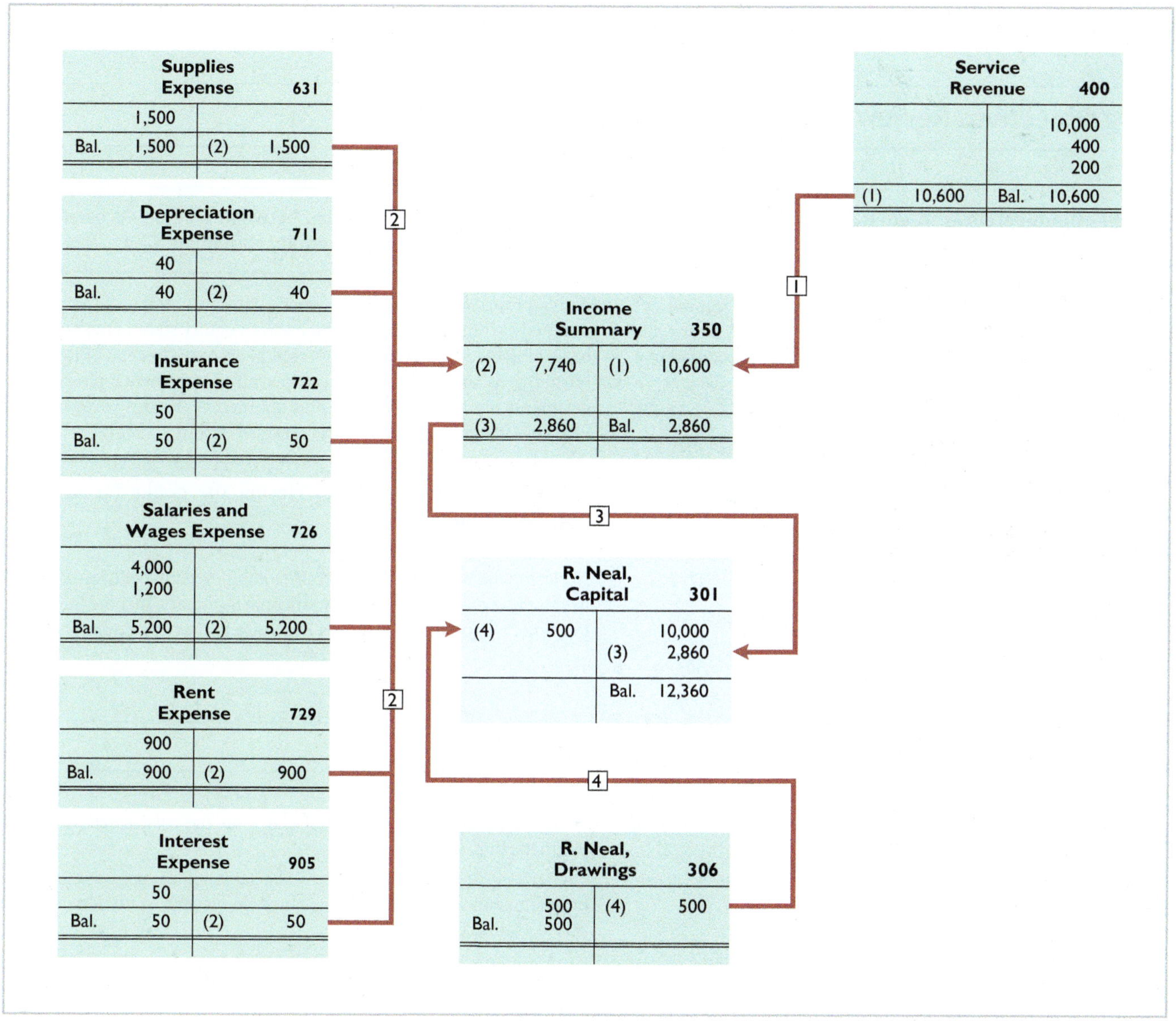

Preparing a Post-Closing Trial Balance for a Proprietorship

After all closing entries are journalized and posted, the **post-closing trial balance** is prepared from the ledger. A post-closing trial balance is a list of all permanent accounts and their balances after closing entries are journalized and posted. As with a corporation, **the purpose of a proprietorship post-closing trial balance is to prove the equality of the permanent account balances that are carried forward into the next accounting period**. Since all temporary accounts will have zero balances, **the post-closing trial balance will contain only permanent—balance sheet—accounts**.

Review

Learning Objectives Review

1 Identify the differences in equity accounts between a corporation and a sole proprietorship.

A sole proprietorship uses a permanent owner's equity capital account instead of Common Stock and Retained Earnings. Withdrawals of cash or other assets by the owner for personal use are recorded in a temporary drawing account.

2 Discuss the accounts that increase and decrease owner's equity.

Investments by the owner and revenue increase owner's equity. Owner's drawings and expenses decrease owner's equity.

3 Describe the differences between a retained earnings statement and an owner's equity statement.

A sole proprietor prepares an owner's equity statement rather than a retained earnings statement. The owner's equity statement shows the beginning balance in the owner's capital account (instead of Retained Earnings, as shown in the retained earnings statement), plus any investments made by the owner, plus net income, less any drawings (in place of Dividends, shown in the retained earnings statement).

4 Explain the process of closing the books for a sole proprietorship.

In closing the books for a sole proprietorship, separate entries are made to close revenues and expenses to Income Summary, Income Summary to Owner's Capital, and Owner's Drawings to Owner's Capital.

Glossary Review

Drawings Withdrawal of cash or other assets from a sole proprietorship for the personal use of the owner. (p. L.2)

Investments by owner The assets put into the business by a sole proprietor. (p. L.2)

Owner's equity The ownership claim on the total assets of a sole proprietorship. (p. L.2)

Owner's equity statement The financial statement prepared for a sole proprietorship to summarize the changes in owner's equity for a specific period of time. (p. L.4)

WileyPLUS

Many additional resources are available for practice in WileyPLUS.

Questions

1. What is the basic accounting equation for a sole proprietorship?
2. What are the differences in the equity accounts of a sole proprietorship versus those of a corporation?
3. What items affect owner's equity, and in what direction?
4. In February 2022, Ken Moran invested an additional $10,000 in his business, Moran's Pharmacy, which is organized as a proprietorship. Moran's accountant, Terry Baden, recorded this receipt as an increase in cash revenues. Is this treatment appropriate? Why or why not?
5. What are the steps in preparing an owner's equity statement?
6. Identify the account(s) debited and credited in each of the required closing entries for a sole proprietorship, assuming the company has net income for the year.

Brief Exercises

BEL.1 (LO 2), C Presented below are three business transactions. On a sheet of paper, list the letters (a), (b), (c) with columns for assets, liabilities, and owner's equity. For each column, indicate whether the transactions increased (+), decreased (−), or had no effect (NE) on assets, liabilities, and owner's equity.

Determine effect of transactions on basic accounting equation.

   a. Invested cash in the business.
   b. Withdrawal of cash by owner.
   c. Received cash from a customer who had previously been billed for services performed.

BEL.2 (LO 2), C Presented below are three transactions. Mark each transaction as affecting owner's investment (I), owner's drawings (D), revenue (R), expense (E), or not affecting owner's equity (NOE).

Determine effect of transactions on owner's equity.

   a. Received cash for services performed.
   b. Paid cash to purchase equipment.
   c. Paid employee salaries.

BEL.3 (LO 2), C For each of the following accounts, indicate the effects of (a) a debit and (b) a credit on the accounts and (c) the normal balance of the account.

Indicate debit and credit effects and normal balance.

   1. Accounts Payable.
   2. Advertising Expense.
   3. Service Revenue.
   4. Accounts Receivable.
   5. A. L. Brislin, Capital.
   6. A. L. Brislin, Drawings.

Exercises

EL.1 (LO 2), AP Writing An analysis of the transactions made by Rodriguez & Co., a certified public accounting firm, for the month of August is shown below. Each increase and decrease in owner's equity is explained.

Analyze transactions and compute net income.

	Cash	+ Accounts Receivable	+ Supplies	+ Equipment	= Accounts Payable	+ Owner's Equity Rodriguez, Capital	
1.	+$12,000					+$12,000	Investment
2.	−2,000			+$5,000	+$3,000		
3.	−750		+$750				
4.	+2,600	+$3,700				+6,300	Service Revenue
5.	−1,500				−1,500		
6.	−2,000					−2,000	Drawings
7.	−650					−650	Rent Expense
8.	+450	−450					
9.	−2,900					−2,900	Sal./Wag. Expense
10.					+500	−500	Utilities Expense

Instructions

   a. Describe each transaction that occurred for the month.
   b. Determine how much owner's equity increased for the month.
   c. Compute the amount of net income for the month.

Prepare an owner's equity statement.

EL.2 (LO 3), AP Presented below is information related to the sole proprietorship of Kurt Cooper, attorney.

Legal service revenue—2022	$360,000
Total expenses—2022	211,000
Assets, January 1, 2022	85,000
Liabilities, January 1, 2022	62,000
Assets, December 31, 2022	168,000
Liabilities, December 31, 2022	70,000
Drawings—2022	?

Instructions

Prepare the 2022 owner's equity statement for Kurt Cooper's legal practice.

Prepare income statement, owner's equity statement, and balance sheet.

EL.3 (LO 1, 2, 3, 4), AP The adjusted trial balance of Lorenz Company at the end of its fiscal year is:

Lorenz Company
Adjusted Trial Balance
July 31, 2022

No.	Account Titles	Debit	Credit
101	Cash	$ 14,940	
112	Accounts Receivable	8,780	
157	Equipment	15,900	
167	Accumulated Depreciation—Equipment		$ 5,400
201	Accounts Payable		4,220
208	Unearned Rent Revenue		1,800
301	J. D. Lorenz, Capital		45,200
306	J. D. Lorenz, Drawings	14,000	
404	Service Revenue		65,100
429	Rent Revenue		6,500
711	Depreciation Expense	4,000	
720	Salaries and Wages Expense	55,700	
732	Utilities Expense	14,900	
		$128,220	$128,220

Instructions

a. Prepare an income statement and an owner's equity statement for the year. Lorenz did not make any capital investments during the year.

b. Prepare a classified balance sheet at July 31.

Problems

Prepare income statement, owner's equity statement, and balance sheet.

a. Net income $ 3,600
Owner's equity $ 46,900
Total assets $ 77,700

PL.1 (LO 1, 2, 3, 4), AP On May 1, Steven Rumford started Skyline Flying School, a company that provides flying lessons, by investing $45,000 cash in the business. Following are the assets and liabilities of the company on May 31, 2022, and the revenues and expenses for the month of May.

Cash	$ 6,500	Notes Payable	$30,000
Accounts Receivable	7,200	Rent Expense	1,200
Equipment	64,000	Maintenance and Repairs Expense	400
Service Revenue	8,600	Gasoline Expense	2,500
Advertising Expense	500	Insurance Expense	400
		Accounts Payable	800

Steven Rumford made no additional investment in May, but he withdrew $1,700 in cash for personal use.

Instructions

a. Prepare an income statement and owner's equity statement for the month of May and a balance sheet at May 31.

b. Prepare an income statement and owner's equity statement for May assuming that the data above need to be adjusted for the following items: (1) $900 worth of services were performed and billed but not collected at May 31, and (2) $3,300 of gasoline expense was incurred but not paid.

b. Net income $ 1,200
Owner's equity $ 44,500

PL.2 (LO 1, 2, 3, 4), AP The adjusted trial balance columns of the worksheet for Whitmore Company are as follows.

Prepare financial statements, closing entries, and post-closing trial balance.

Whitmore Company
Adjusted Trial Balance
For the Year Ended December 31, 2022

Account No.	Account Titles	Adjusted Trial Balance Debit	Credit
101	Cash	$ 20,800	
112	Accounts Receivable	15,400	
126	Supplies	2,300	
130	Prepaid Insurance	4,800	
151	Equipment	44,000	
152	Accumulated Depreciation—Equipment		$ 18,000
200	Notes Payable		20,000
201	Accounts Payable		8,000
212	Salaries and Wages Payable		3,000
230	Interest Payable		1,000
301	B. Whitmore, Capital		36,000
306	B. Whitmore, Drawings	12,000	
400	Service Revenue		79,000
610	Advertising Expense	12,000	
631	Supplies Expense	3,700	
711	Depreciation Expense	6,000	
722	Insurance Expense	4,000	
726	Salaries and Wages Expense	39,000	
905	Interest Expense	1,000	
	Totals	$165,000	$165,000

Instructions

a. Prepare an income statement, owner's equity statement, and a classified balance sheet. $10,000 of the notes payable become due in 2023. B. Whitmore did not make any additional investments in the business during 2022.

b. Prepare the closing entries.

c. Post the closing entries. Use the three-column form of account. Income summary is No. 350.

d. Prepare a post-closing trial balance.

a. Net income $13,300
Current assets $43,300
Current liabilities $22,000

d. Post-closing trial balance $87,300

PL.3 (LO 1, 2, 3, 4), AP The adjusted trial balance columns of the worksheet for Rick Pool Company, owned by Rick Pool, are as follows.

Prepare financial statements, closing entries, and post-closing trial balance.

Rick Pool Company
Adjusted Trial Balance
For the Year Ended December 31, 2022

Account No.	Account Titles	Adjusted Trial Balance Debit	Adjusted Trial Balance Credit
101	Cash	$ 13,600	
112	Accounts Receivable	15,400	
126	Supplies	1,500	
130	Prepaid Insurance	2,800	
151	Equipment	34,000	
152	Accumulated Depreciation—Equipment		$ 8,000
200	Notes Payable		16,000
201	Accounts Payable		6,000
212	Salaries and Wages Payable		3,000
230	Interest Payable		500
301	Rick Pool, Capital		25,000
306	Rick Pool, Drawings	10,000	
400	Service Revenue		88,000
610	Advertising Expense	12,000	
631	Supplies Expense	5,700	
711	Depreciation Expense	4,000	
722	Insurance Expense	5,000	
726	Salaries and Wages Expense	42,000	
905	Interest Expense	500	
	Totals	$146,500	$146,500

Instructions

a. Net income $18,800
Current assets $33,300
Current liabilities $19,500

d. Post-closing trial balance $67,300

a. Prepare an income statement, owner's equity statement, and a classified balance sheet (*Note:* $10,000 of the notes payable become due in 2023.) Rick Pool did not make any additional investments in the business during the year.

b. Prepare the closing entries. Use J14 for the journal page.

c. Post the closing entries. Use the three-column form of account. Income Summary is No. 350.

d. Prepare a post-closing trial balance.

Company Index

A
Abercrombie and Fitch, 14-6
Abitibi Consolidated Inc., 1-30
Adelphia, 2-18
adidas, 8-25, 8-42, 10-41, 11-29, 14-18
Advanced Micro Devices, 11-8, 16-3
Ag. Chem, 7-24
Ahold NV, 4-66
AIG, 1-5
Airbus, 9-54
AirTran Airways, 9-14
Alaska Airlines, 16-2, 17-20
Allegiant Airlines, 14-15
Alliance Atlantis Communications Inc., 9-43
Alphabet, Inc., 2-1, 2-5, 2-7
Amazon.com, Inc., 1-11, 1-36, 1-38–1-39, 2-5, 2-42, 3-57, 4-62–4-63, 5-3, 5-5, 5-51, 6-45, 7-54, 8-43, 8-44, 9-19, 9-51–9-52, 10-54, 11-51, 12-19, 12-58–12-59, 13-51, 13-52–13-53, 14-17, 18-1–18-2, 18-21–18-22, 19-7, 20-9, 21-4, 22-8, D-1–D-4
American Accounting Association, 1-41
American Airlines, 4-11, 9-1, 14-4, 17-20, 18-9
American Cancer Society, 11-3
American Eagle Outfitters, 2-26–2-27, 2-36
American Express, 8-5, 8-12, 8-23, 20-5
American LaFrance, 15-3
American Van Lines, 23-6
Anytime Fitness, 19-51
Apple Inc., 1-4, 1-27, 1-38, 2-10, 2-29, 2-42, 2-47, 3-42, 3-56–3-57, 4-4, 4-43, 4-62, 5-38, 5-51, 6-45, 7-40, 7-53, 8-19, 8-32, 8-43, 9-25, 9-31, 9-51, 10-11, 10-39, 10-53, 11-2, 11-3, 11-38, 11-51, 12-2, 12-20, 12-45, 12-58, 12-59, 13-38, 13-51, 13-52, 14-18, A-1–A-5
Armani, 21-3
Armour, 20-11
Aviation Partners, 9-54

B
Baan NV, 4-66
BabyCakes NYC, 22-1–22-2, 22-4–22-5, 22-25–22-26
Balanced Scorecard Institute, 24-46
Bank of America, 7-55, 8-11
Bank One Corporation, 3-9
Barnes & Noble, 9-19, 10-55, 13-44
Barriques, 7-1–7-3, 7-8, 7-13
Ben & Jerry's, 11-54, 15-3
Berkshire Hathaway, 11-21
Best Buy Co., Inc., 2-1, 2-2, 2-9–2-13, 2-16, 2-17, 2-20–2-21, 2-35, 4-13, 5-14, 5-54, 9-22, 9-52, 11-21, 13-52
Beverly Hills Fan Company, 20-39
Blockbuster, Inc., 1-17
BMW, 14-18, 20-17
Bob Evans Farms, 2-30, 13-40
Bob's Red Mill, 22-2
Boeing Capital Corporation, 9-7
Boeing Company, 2-33, 2-44, 9-3, 9-16, 9-54, 10-45, 14-14, 14-17, 15-3, 20-8
Boise Cascade Corporation, 9-29
Borders Group, 10-55
BorderStylo LLC, 9-20
Box, 12-15
BP, 6-14
Briggs and Stratton, 23-29
BrightFarms, 18-4
Bristol Myers Squibb, 4-24, 6-12, 13-8
Burton Snowboards, 14-9
Button Worldwide, 21-12

C
Calico Corners, 8-33
Callaway Golf Company, 2-34
Campbell Soup Company, 1-36, 6-12, 9-10, 9-37, 14-4, 25-15, 25-36–25-37
Canwest Global Communications Corp., 12-46
Cargill Inc., 11-3
Carnival Corporation, 25-2
Carrefour SA, 5-51–5-52
Caterpillar Financial Services, 8-23
Caterpillar Inc., 6-1–6-3, 6-13, 6-18–6-19, 6-48, 8-23, 9-3, 11-3, 16-7, 17-22
CBS, 9-20
Cendant, H-7
Center Ice Consultants, 16-3
Cerberus, 10-2
Chase, 24-18
Chevron Texaco, 21-3
Chicago Bears, 3-15
Chicago Cubs, 3-15
Chieftain International, Inc., 3-58
Chipotle, 14-6, 19-11
Chrysler, 10-1–10-2, 24-15
Cisco Systems, 4-26, 13-8, 19-14, 23-15
Citibank Visa, 8-28
Citicorp, 1-5
Citigroup, 1-3, 2-10, 4-3, 10-56
Clark Equipment Company, 17-12
Clark Hurth, 17-12
Clarus Technologies, 21-47
Clif Bar & Company, 1-4, 1-41–1-42
The Clorox Company, 5-43, 20-1
CNH Global, 6-19
Coca-Cola Company, 1-3, 1-42, 5-52, 8-33, 9-25, 12-52, 13-51, 14-7, 14-18, 16-1, 18-43–18-44, 22-20, 23-29
Columbia Sportswear Company, 1-2, 1-7, 1-16, 1-18, 1-38, 2-1, 2-42, 3-57, 4-62, 5-51, 6-45, 7-53, 8-43, 9-51, 10-54, 11-51, 12-46, 12-58, 13-51, B-1–B-4
Commercial Capital LLC, 8-45
Commonwealth Edison, 11-18
Compumotor, 17-12
Computer Associates International, Inc., 23-51–23-52
Con Agra Foods, 4-23–4-24, 5-18, 11-15
ConocoPhillips, 9-22
Conservation International, 24-15
Continental Bank, 9-7
Cooper Tire & Rubber Company, 2-5, 9-7
Costco Wholesale Corp., 5-13–5-14, 12-5
Countrywide Financial Corporation, 8-20
Credit Suisse Group, 3-21
Current Designs, 14-1–14-2, 14-3, 14-4, 14-7, 14-11–14-12, 14-20–14-21, 14-40–14-41, 15-40–15-41, 16-44–16-45, 18-41–18-42, 19-47–19-48, 20-37–20-38, 21-43, 22-46–22-47, 23-48–23-49, 24-43–24-44, 25-34–25-35
Curves, 19-51
Cyan, 12-15
Cypress Semiconductor Corporation, 12-46

D
Daimler, 10-2
Dayton Hudson, 7-25
DealTime, 21-46
Deere & Company, 6-39–6-40, 8-19
Del Monte Foods Company, 19-49
Dell, 14-4, 14-16, 17-22, 25-1
Dell Financial Services, 9-7
Deloitte & Touche, 1-17
Delta Air Lines, 2-17, 4-3, 4-11, 7-25, 9-16, 9-26–9-27, 20-14, 24-17
Dewey & LeBoeuf LLP, 1-6
Dick's Sporting Goods, 5-23, 5-24, 14-10
Discover, 8-12, 8-23
Disney Company, 1-5, 2-6, 2-17, 9-14, 9-22, 15-1–15-2, 15-3, 15-4, 15-13, 15-23, 16-3, 21-5, 21-13, H-7
Dow Chemical, 1-11, 16-3
DPR Construction, 14-6
Duke Energy Co., 1-5, 13-7, 14-4, 18-3, 23-6, 23-20, H-7
Dunkin' Donuts, Inc., 2-17
Dunn & Bradstreet, 13-9
DuPont, 5-25, 10-9, 10-10, 16-3
Dynegy, 1-5

E
E*Trade Financial, 19-14
EarthLink, 11-18
Eastman Kodak, 12-1
eBay, 5-18
Eli Lilly, 7-4, 23-29
Enron Corporation, 1-5, 5-18, 10-19, 10-22, 10-56, 11-4, 13-8, 14-4
Environmental Protection Agency (EPA), 21-47
Ernst & Young, 7-54
Eskimo Pie Corporation, 1-28
ExxonMobil, 1-3, 2-13, 6-14, 7-17, 14-16, 15-3, 16-3, 20-11, 21-3, 25-1

F
Facebook, 1-11, 11-1–11-3, 11-6, 11-7, 11-9, 11-12, 11-15–11-16, 11-26, 14-5
Fannie Mae, 3-9, 4-16
FedEx Corporation, 8-38, 9-43, 14-4, 19-49–19-50
Fiat/Chrysler, 1-42
FinAid, 1-41
FireEye, 12-15
Fitch, 13-17
Flightserve, 18-16

I-1

COMPANY INDEX

Ford Motor Company, 1-5, 3-21, 5-4, 6-3, 6-16, 8-23, 9-22, 10-1–10-2, 10-20, 10-21, 10-23–10-24, 14-16, 16-16, 18-9, 19-8, 21-4, 23-18
Ford Motor Credit Corp. (FMCC), 8-23
Fox Broadcasting, 9-20, 23-9

G

Gap, Inc., 2-42–2-43, 14-16
GE Capital, 8-23
General Dynamics Corp., 13-4
General Electric (GE), 1-5, 5-11, 8-23, 10-45, 11-15, 14-5, 14-18, 15-19, 16-11, 17-23
General Mills, 9-10, 13-9, 16-3, 17-15
General Motors (GM), 1-3, 1-4, 1-5, 2-13, 3-3, 6-43, 8-33, 10-1–10-2, 10-5, 10-9, 10-19–10-21, 10-24, 13-7, 13-39, 14-4, 14-16, 15-4, 17-23, 20-1, 20-17, 21-4
Glassmaster Company, 24-45–24-46
Global Crossing, 10-19
Global Reporting Initiative, 14-19
Goldman Sachs, 1-5, 15-18
Gold's Gym, 17-1
Goodyear, 20-15
Google, Inc., 1-11, 2-13, 9-18, 9-19, 9-20, 11-1, 11-2, 11-8, 11-20, 13-3, 21-4. *See also* Alphabet, Inc.
Grant Thornton LLP, 1-30
Green Bay Packers, 3-1, 3-58
Groupon, Inc., 4-1–4-2, 4-31–4-32, 11-23
Gulf Craft, 16-32
Gulf Oil, 11-6

H

H. J. Heinz Company, 2-26, 2-33
H&R Block, 16-4
Hain Celestial Group, 3-19
Hard Candy, 17-1
Harley-Davidson, 17-22
HealthSouth, 1-5
Hechinger Co., 10-54
Heinz Company, 2-33, 22-20
Hershey, 16-7
Hewlett-Packard (HP), 14-4, 14-15, 14-17, 17-23, 19-8, 20-8, 24-16
hhgregg, 2-9, 2-12, 2-13
Hilton Hotels, 9-7, 14-17, 17-1, 18-3
Holland America Line, 25-1, 25-2, 25-9–25-21
Home Depot, 6-4, 10-54
Honda, 23-17
Honeywell International, 13-7
Host Marriott Corporation, 11-51–11-52
Hughes Aircraft Co., 13-4
Human Rights Watch, 14-18

I

IBM, 1-41, 5-18, 11-3, 11-6, 12-18–12-19, 13-5, 13-7, 14-17, 24-4
Ice Pro, 16-3
IHS, 15-10
IKEA, 20-10–20-11
Inditex SA, 14-16
The Institute of Management Accountants (IMA), 14-40, 15-42
Institutional Shareholder Services, 11-7
Intel Corporation, 1-42, 5-25, 7-25, 8-21, 9-19, 12-21–12-22, 14-16, 16-3, 16-17, 19-8, 21-1, 21-3
InterContinental, 9-7

International Outsourcing Services, LLC, 3-17
IT&T, 1-1

J

J. Walter Thompson, 16-3
JCPenney Company, Inc., 7-25, 8-4, 8-32, 12-5
JetBlue Airways, 9-2, 9-3, 9-5, 9-7, 9-23–9-25, 12-20
Jif Peanut Butter, 16-32
Jiffy Lube, 16-4
John Deere Capital Corporation, 9-7
Johnson & Johnson, 1-39–1-40
Jones Soda Co., 16-1–16-2, 16-3, 16-17–16-19
Jostens, Inc., 24-16
J.P. Morgan Leasing, 9-7
JPMorgan Chase, 1-36, 3-9, 8-11

K

Kaiser, 16-3
Kansas Farmers' Vertically Integrated Cooperative, Inc., 3-32–3-33
Kellogg Company, Inc., 1-33, 11-26, 12-19, 13-9, 13-29–13-30, 15-3, 16-3, 16-10, 16-12–16-16, 16-20–16-24, 18-10, 24-11
Kmart Stores, 8-20, 20-39
Kohl's Corporation, 7-39, 12-5
Komag, 19-16
Kraft Foods, 3-17, 22-20, 24-11
Krispy Kreme Doughnuts, Inc., 3-46
Kroger Co., 5-4, 5-23, 6-12, 18-9

L

Laser Recording Systems, 4-63
LDK Solar Co., 12-19
Lease Finance Corporation, 9-7
Leslie Fay, 6-4, 6-48
Limited Brands, 2-30
Linens' n Things, 8-20
Lockheed, 9-16
Louis Vuitton, 1-43, 2-47, 3-62, 4-66, 5-55, 6-49, 7-57, 8-48, 9-56, 10-59, 11-56, 12-62, 13-55, F-1–F-5
Lucent, 14-4

M

Macy's, 19-13, 23-18
Madison Square Garden, 22-8
Manitowoc Company, 6-20–6-21
MarketWatch, 13-52
Marriott Corporation, 9-7, 9-10, 9-20, 11-51–11-52, 18-3, 23-6
Massachusetts General Hospital, 1-5, 18-3
MasterCard, 8-12, 8-23
Mattel Corporation, 7-29–7-30
Maxwell Car Company, 10-1
Mayo Clinic, 15-18, 16-3
McDonald's Corporation, 1-5, 1-42, 9-18, 9-38, 10-30, 10-46, 11-3, 12-52, 24-3
McDonnell Douglas, 2-44, 14-17
McKesson Corporation, 5-3, 6-48, 7-25
Medtronic, Inc., 10-12
Mercedes, 20-17
Merck & Co., Inc., 1-31, 5-23, 21-45–21-46
Merrill Lynch, 1-5
Method Products, 20-1–20-2, 20-8, 20-18
MF Global Holdings Ltd, 3-2, 3-12, 3-30, 11-4
Microsoft, 1-3, 1-4, 2-13, 3-3, 5-11, 5-18, 5-25, 9-3, 9-18, 9-22, 11-2, 11-26, 12-1–12-2, 12-18–12-20, 13-39, 14-3, 21-2

MobileIron, 12-15
Moody's, 13-9, 13-17
Morgan Stanley, H-10
Morrow Snowboards, Inc., 5-6
The Motley Fool, 2-2
Motorola, 6-12, 13-4
Mountain Equipment Cooperative (MEC), 5-25–5-26
MSN.com, 13-19
Museum of Contemporary Art, 22-24

N

NationsBank, 7-55
Navistar Inc., G-14
NBC Universal, 9-20, 23-9
NEC, 4-66
Nestlé, 1-42
Netflix, 12-59, 13-52
NetJets, 18-16
New York Stock Exchange, 1-3
NFL, 9-20
Nike, Inc., 1-34, 2-7, 2-13, 5-25, 7-26, 8-1–8-2, 8-8–8-9, 8-22, 8-24, 8-25, 8-42, 9-18, 9-38–9-39, 11-3, 11-9, 11-13, 11-15, 11-20, 11-26, 11-27, 11-29, 12-20, 13-14, 13-42–13-43, 14-17, 19-14
Nissan, 20-17, 25-1
Nordstrom, Inc., 2-35, 8-13, 9-3, 13-43
The North Face, 1-36
Northwest Airlines, 9-6
Novartis AG, 10-22

O

Oakely, Inc., 6-35
Obsidian Energy, 3-19
Office Depot, Inc., 5-3, 5-41, 6-17, 8-38
Office Max, 4-24
Oracle Corporation, 1-30, 14-6
Oral-B Laboratories, 20-1

P

Packard Bell, 8-21
PairGain Technologies, 2-2
Pandora, 19-16
Parker Hannitin, 17-12, 21-9
Parmalat, 7-56, 12-13
Penske Automotive Group, 24-17
PepsiCo Inc., 1-4, 3-17, 5-14, 5-52, 6-14, 6-39, 11-3, 12-52, 13-51, 16-1, 16-3, H-7
Phantom Tac, 14-18
Phillip Morris International, 10-12
Pilgrim's Pride Corp., 4-24, 5-18, 22-20
Pratt and Whitney, 15-19
Precor, 17-1–17-2, 17-14, 17-21–17-22
PricewaterhouseCoopers, 1-40, 1-41, 15-18
Princeton University, 22-24
Procter & Gamble, 1-5, 11-9, 13-4, 14-10, 20-1, 23-15, 24-4
Promodes SA, 5-51–5-52
Prudential Real Estate, 1-5

Q

Quad Graphics, 15-3
Quaker Oats, 6-14, 16-32, 20-1
Qualcomm, 12-21, 12-22

R

Radio Shack, 5-23
RBC Financial Group, 4-47
Reebok International Ltd., 6-12, 11-14

REI (Recreational Equipment Incorporated), 5-1–5-3, 5-7, 5-11, 5-14–5-17, 5-23–5-25
REL Consultancy Group, 2-12
Renault, 20-17, 25-1
Rite Aid, 8-3
Rolling Stones, 18-20
Royal Ahold, 7-56
Royal Dutch Shell, 6-14, 9-20, 16-3

S
SafeNet, 11-8
SaferWay, 19-2
Safeway, 5-23, 7-5, 19-2
Saks Fifth Avenue, 5-23
Salvation Army, 11-3
Samsung, 14-6
San Diego Union Tribune, 24-47
San Diego Zoo, 23-12
SAP, 14-16
Sara Lee, 14-7
Satyam Computer Services, 7-56
The Scotts Company, 8-44–8-45
Sears Holdings, 5-18, 8-45
Seattle Seahawks, 16-2
Securities and Exchange Commission (SEC), 4-63
Shell, 6-14, 9-20
Sherwin Williams, 16-3
Siebel Systems, 23-17
Siemens AG, 23-29
Simon Properties, 10-12
Skechers USA, 8-1, 8-11, 8-20–8-22, 8-25
Skype, 5-18
SkyTrax, 9-2
Small Business Administration, 15-43
Snap Fitness, 19-50–19-51
Sony, 1-42, 6-18
Southwest Airlines, 1-30, 2-4, 4-47, 9-2, 9-3, 9-14, 9-23–9-25, 10-5, 10-50–10-51, 12-19, 18-2
Sports Authority Inc., 6-5
Sportsco Investments, 1-30
Sprint Corporation, 10-4
Standard & Poor's, 10-55, 11-13, 11-17, 13-9, 13-17
Standard Oil Company of California, 9-29

Stanley Black & Decker Manufacturing Company, 6-12
Staples, Inc., 13-40
Starbucks, 6-12, 6-47, 12-19, 21-3, 24-1–24-2, 24-15, 24-20–24-21
Subway, 9-20
Sunbeam, 20-5
SUPERVALU, 11-39

T
Target Corporation, 2-41, 4-47, 5-23, 6-4, 6-17, 7-17, 7-25, 12-5, 13-50, 20-2
Tecumseh Products Company, 25-36
Tektronix Inc., 11-23
Texas Instruments, Inc., 2-34
the balance, 22-50
3M Company, 8-34, 10-46
Tiffany and Co., 5-23
Time Warner, 1-5, 21-13, 22-5, H-5, H-7
Time Warner Cable, 10-10
Tootsie Roll Industries, Inc., 3-3, 11-25
Topps Company, Inc., 13-40
Toronto Blue Jays, 4-47
Toyota, 1-42, 9-20, 10-20, 14-15, 14-16, 21-4
Trek, 1-5, 20-10, 21-13
Tribeca Grand Hotel, 23-1–23-2, 23-26–23-27
True Value Hardware, 6-4
Turner Broadcasting, H-5, H-7
Tweeter Home Entertainment, 2-20–2-21

U
U-Haul, 18-6
Ultimate Electronics, 4-47
Unilever, 20-1, 24-18
United Airlines, 1-5, 4-11, 9-1, 10-5, 12-1, 18-2, 19-8, 24-17, 24-19
United Parcel Service (UPS), 13-7
United States Steel Corp., 10-9, 12-19, 18-9
US Bancorp Equipment Finance, 9-7
U.S. Navy, 24-4
USAir, 10-9
USX, 16-3

V
ValuJet, 9-2
Verizon Communications, Inc., 10-11, 13-7, 25-8

Versace, 21-3
VF Corporation, 1-18, 1-38, 2-42, 3-57, 4-62, 5-51, 6-45, 7-53, 8-43, 9-51, 10-54, 11-51, 12-58, 13-51
Visa, 8-12, 8-13, 8-23, C-1–C-4
Vodafone/Mannesmann, 1-42
Volkswagen, 20-17

W
Wachovia, 8-5
Walgreen Company, 5-3, 6-12, 11-44
Wal-Mart Stores, Inc., 1-38–1-39, 2-41, 2-42, 3-57, 4-62–4-63, 5-2, 5-3, 5-23, 5-25, 5-51, 5-52, 6-4, 6-15, 6-17–6-18, 6-45, 7-17, 7-54, 8-43–8-44, 9-3, 9-51–9-52, 10-54, 11-26, 11-51, 12-5, 12-20, 12-58–12-59, 13-50–13-52, 14-17, 24-18, E-1–E-5
The Walt Disney Company. *See* Disney Company
Warner Brothers Motion Pictures, 16-3, 16-32
Waste Management Company, 3-9
Wells Fargo & Company, 7-3, 8-5, 8-11, 11-44, 14-17
Wendy's International, 6-12, 9-3, 11-52
Wenonah Canoe, 14-1–14-2, 14-40
Whole Foods Market, 14-6, 19-1–19-2, 19-18–19-19
Windstream Holdings, 11-18
Winnebago Industries, Inc., 6-35
Workday, 8-24
World Bank, 24-4
WorldCom, 1-5, 4-24, 7-9, 9-6, 10-19, 11-4, 13-8, 13-14

X
Xerox, 1-39, 4-24, 14-4
XM Satellite Radio Holdings, 22-15

Y
Yahoo! Finance, 1-39, 2-43, 12-59
Yahoo! Inc., 2-37–2-38
Young & Rubicam, 16-3

Z
Zappos.com, 21-1–21-2, 21-19–21-20

Subject Index

A

ABC. *See* Activity-based costing
ABM. *See* Activity-based management
Absorption costing
  comparison example, 19-19–19-21
  comparison of, 19-24
  decision-making concerns, 19-25–19-27
  defined, 19-19, 19-29
  example, 19-20
  fixed manufacturing overhead and, 19-21
  GAAP and, 19-25
  income statements, 19-20, 19-22, 19-23, 19-24, 19-26
  net income effects, 19-21–19-25
  summary of income effects, 19-25
  variable costing versus, 19-19–19-27
Absorption-cost pricing. *See also* Pricing
  allocated fixed costs, 21-23
  as basis, 21-22, 21-23
  defined, 21-21, 21-27
  information, 21-22
  markup percentage computation, 21-21–21-22
  proof of 20% ROI, 21-22
  steps for, 21-21–21-22
  target price computation, 21-22
  unit manufacturing cost computation, 21-21
Accelerated-depreciation method, 9-11, 9-28, 9-30
Account titles, in journals, 3-19
Accounting. *See also* Accrual-basis accounting; Cash-basis accounting; Managerial accounting
  and authorization of capital stock, 11-8
  for bond transactions, 10-12–10-18
  budgeting and, 22-3
  business importance of, 1-1–1-2
  careers in, 1-5
  cost, 15-3–15-7
  defined, 1-3, 1-19
  financial versus managerial, 14-3, 14-4
  mark-to-market, H-8, H-14
  for partnerships, K-5–K-14
  payroll, I-1–I-16
  process cost, 16-1
  responsibility, 23-13–23-22
  for sole proprietorships, L-1–L-12
  uses of information in, 1-3–1-7
  worksheets vs. records in, 4-33
Accounting cycle
  defined, 3-3
  summary of, 4-28–4-30
Accounting equation
  for accounts receivable, 3-7
  analyzing transactions with, 3-3–3-11
  balancing of, 3-4
  basic, 1-11, 1-20, 3-4, 3-16
  defined, 2-4
  expanded, 3-5, 3-16
Accounting information system, 3-1–3-62
  debits, credits, and accounts in, 3-11–3-17

  defined, 1-7, 3-3, 3-34
  journal in, 3-17–3-20
  posting in, 3-20–3-29
  transaction analysis, 3-3–3-11
  trial balance and, 3-30–3-33
Accounting principle, change in, 13-6–13-7, 13-32
Accounting time periods, 4-2–4-3
Accounting transactions
  accuracy in recording of, 3-9, 3-19
  analyzing, 3-4–3-9
  defined, 3-3, 3-34
  identification process, 3-4
  summary of, 3-10
Account(s), 3-11–3-17. *See also specific types*
  basic form of, 3-11, 3-12
  chart of, 3-20–3-21, 3-34
  debit and credit procedures for, 3-12–3-15
  defined, 3-11, 3-34
  purchases on, 3-8, 3-26, 5-29
  in recording process, 3-22
  stockholders' equity relationships, 3-15–3-16
  summary of debit/credit rules, 3-16–3-17
Accounts payable, 1-9, 12-11, 12-32
Accounts payable (or creditors') subsidiary ledger, J-2, J-18
Accounts receivable, 8-3–8-14
  aging the, 8-9, 8-26
  and cash, 8-24
  defined, 1-8, 3-7, 8-3, 8-26
  disposing of, 8-12–8-14
  managing, 8-18–8-21
  recognizing, 8-3–8-5
  and statement of cash flows, 12-10–12-11, 12-25, 12-32
  valuing, 8-5–8-11
Accounts receivable (or customers') subsidiary ledger, J-2, J-18
Accounts receivable outstanding, average, 8-22
Accounts receivable turnover, 8-22, 8-26, 13-19–13-20, 13-32
Accrual-basis accounting, 4-1–4-66
  accounting cycle summary, 4-28–4-30
  accruals in, 4-14–4-21
  adjusted trial balance, 4-21–4-25
  adjusting entries, 4-5–4-21
  cash-basis accounting vs., 4-5
  closing the books, 4-26–4-28
  deferrals in, 4-7–4-14
  defined, 4-5, 4-36
  expense recognition principle, 4-4
  net income from, 12-9, 12-23–12-28
  revenue recognition principle, 4-3–4-4
  statements of cash flows and, 12-7
  worksheets for, 4-33–4-34
Accruals, 4-14–4-21
  for expenses, 4-16–4-18
  relationships between, 4-19–4-20
  for revenues, 4-14–4-16
  types of, 4-6
Accrued expenses

  adjusting entries for, 4-16–4-18
  defined, 4-6, 4-16, 4-36
Accrued interest, 4-16–4-17
Accrued revenues, 4-6, 4-14–4-16, 4-36
Accrued salaries, 4-17–4-18
Accumulated depreciation, 2-5, 12-33
Accumulated Other Comprehensive Income, 11-24, 11-32
Accumulated profit or loss, 11-55
Accumulating manufacturing costs
  defined, 15-4
  factory labor costs, 15-5
  manufacturing overhead costs, 15-6
  raw materials costs, 15-5
Accuracy, in recording transactions, 3-9, 3-19
Acquisition(s)
  of bonds, recording, H-3
  cost allocation in, 9-8
  IFRS for, 1-42
  of stock, recording, H-4, H-6
Activities
  batch-level, 17-13, 17-25
  coordination, budgeting and, 22-3
  defined, 17-5, 17-25
  examples of, 17-5, 17-6
  facility-level, 17-13, 17-25
  hierarchy of levels, 17-14
  identifying and classifying, 17-7
  levels, classification of, 17-12–17-13, 17-17
  non-value-added, 17-14, 17-15, 17-25
  product-level, 17-13, 17-25
  unit-level, 17-12, 17-25
  value-added, 17-14, 17-15, 17-25
Activity base, 15-12
Activity cost pools, 17-16–17-17
  allocating overhead to, 17-7
  allocating to products, 17-9
  defined, 17-5, 17-25
Activity flowcharts, 17-14
Activity index
  defined, 18-3, 18-27
  in flexible budget preparation, 23-10
Activity-based costing (ABC), 17-1–17-48
  activities identification and classification, 17-7
  activity-based overhead rates computation, 17-8
  applying, 17-11–17-12
  arbitrary allocations and, 17-16
  benefits of, 17-1, 17-12–17-16
  better management decisions advantage, 17-15–17-16
  complexity of, 17-16
  concepts, 17-5
  cost drivers identification, 17-8
  cost pools overhead allocation, 17-7
  defined, 14-16, 14-22, 17-4, 17-25
  enhanced cost control advantage, 17-13–17-15
  evaluation, 17-10
  expense of using, 17-16

incremental analysis relationship, 20-5
knowing when to use, 17-16–17-17
limitations, 17-16–17-17
manufacturers and, 17-7–17-12
moving from traditional costing to, 17-10
multiple bases, 17-4
multiple cost pools advantage, 17-12–17-13
overhead costs assignment, 17-9
service companies and, 17-17–17-20
service company example, 17-18–17-19
steps of, 17-5
total overhead costs and, 17-10
unit costs comparison, 17-10
Activity-based management (ABM)
benchmarks and, 17-16
defined, 17-15, 17-25
performance standards and, 17-16
Activity-based overhead rate
computation, 17-8
defined, 17-8
formula, 17-8
Adding value, 14-4
Additional paid-in capital, 11-24
Additions and improvements, to plant assets, 9-6, 9-30
Adjustable interest rates, 10-30
Adjusted cash balance, 7-22–7-23
Adjusted trial balance, 4-21–4-25
defined, 4-21, 4-36
financial statements from, 4-22–4-24
preparation of balance sheet (sole proprietorship) from, L-5
preparing, 4-21–4-22
and quality of earnings, 4-23–4-24
Adjusting entries, 4-5–4-21
for accruals, 4-6, 4-14–4-21
for accrued expenses, 4-16–4-18
for accrued revenues, 4-14–4-16
for bad debt expense, 8-10
from bank reconciliation, 7-22–7-23
for deferrals, 4-6–4-14
defined, 4-36
GAAP vs. IFRS, 4-65–4-66
improper, 4-24
for merchandising operations, 5-29–5-30
need for, 4-5–4-6, 4-10–4-11
for prepaid expenses, 4-7–4-11
relationships between, 4-19–4-21
trial balance and, 4-6–4-7, 4-21–4-25
for underapplied overhead, 15-22
for unearned revenues, 4-11–4-13
Administrative expenses, 1-9
Admission by investment
bonus to new partner, K-17–K-18
bonus to old partners, K-16–K-17
defined, K-15, K-21
purchase of and interest versus, K-16
Admission by purchase of an interest, K-15, K-16, K-21
Admission of partners
by investment, K-15–K-18, K-21
legal dissolution of partnership and, K-14–K-15
by purchase of and interest, K-15, K-21
Affiliated (subsidiary) company, H-6, H-7, H-14
After-tax contribution margin, 21-24–21-25
Agents, of corporations, 11-3

Aging schedule, 8-9, 8-20, 8-21
Aging the accounts receivable, 8-9, 8-26
Airline industry
baggage fees, 17-20
charter flights versus, 18-16
fares and profits in, 14-15
incentive program, 24-19
successful business models in, 9-1–9-2
Allocation, cost, 4-10, 4-11, 9-8
Allowance method, 8-6–8-11
defined, 8-6, 8-26
estimating the allowance, 8-8–8-11
recording estimated uncollectibles, 8-7
recording write-off, 8-7–8-8
recovery of uncollectible account, 8-8
Allowances
adjusting entries for credit sales with, 5-29–5-30
debit balance and, 8-10
for Doubtful Accounts, 8-7, 8-11
estimating, 8-8–8-11
in perpetual inventory system, 5-9
purchase, 5-9, 5-31
sales, 5-12–5-13, 5-28–5-31
Alternative accounting methods, quality of earnings, 13-7
Amortization
amount computation, 10-27
bond discount, 10-15, 10-24–10-25, 10-27–10-28
bond premium, 10-16, 10-26, 10-29–10-30
and cash flow, 9-25
defined, 9-18, 9-30
effective-interest, 10-27–10-30, 10-32
of intangible assets, 9-18–9-19
straight-line, 10-24–10-26, 10-32
Amortization schedule
bond discount, 10-25, 10-28
bond premium, 10-26, 10-29
Amount due at maturity, for note, 8-17
Annual interest payments, bond with, G-12–G-13
Annual interest rates, 8-16
Annual rate, depreciation and, 9-10
Annual rate of return method. *See also* Capital budgeting
advantages and limitations of, 25-19
defined, 25-18, 25-22
formula, 25-18
formula for computing average investment, 25-19
profitability indication, 25-18
required rate of return comparison, 25-19
Annual recurring expenditures, equipment, 9-5
Annual reports, 1-16–1-18
auditor's report, 1-17
defined, 1-16, 1-19, A-1
management discussion and analysis (MD&A), 1-16
notes to the financial statements, 1-16
Annuities
defined, G-5, G-9, G-20
discounting, G-14
future value of, G-5–G-6, G-17, G-20
present value of, G-9–G-11, G-17, G-20
Applied manufacturing overhead
defined, 15-20
job cost sheets, 15-14

overapplied overhead, 15-21–15-22, 15-25
underapplied overhead, 15-21–15-22, 15-25
Approvals, 15-8
Articles of incorporation (charters), 11-6, 11-32
Asset misappropriation, 7-16
Asset turnover
defined, 9-24, 9-30, 13-24, 13-32
as profitability ratio, 9-26, 13-24–13-25
Assets
and accrued revenues, 4-14, 4-15
and bonds issued at discount, 10-14
classified balance sheet, 2-5–2-7
current, 2-3–2-5, 2-12, 2-22, 12-10–12-11
debit/credit procedures for, 3-12–3-13
debt to assets ratio, 2-13, 2-22, 13-21–13-22, 13-32
defined, 1-8, 1-19
depreciable, 9-8
intangible. *See* Intangible assets
long-lived. *See* Long-lived assets
noncash, 11-11, 12-10–12-11
noncurrent, 12-13–12-14, 12-28
plant. *See* Plant assets
and prepaid expenses, 4-8, 4-10
receivables as percentage of, 8-3
return on. *See* Return on assets
total, 9-3, 11-17, 13-12
valuation of, 9-4
Assigning costs to finished goods, 15-15–15-16
Assigning costs to goods sold, 15-16–15-17
Assigning manufacturing costs
credit entries, 15-7
debit entries, 15-7
defined, 15-4
factory labor costs, 15-10–15-11, 16-7
job cost sheet and, 15-7–15-8
in job order cost system, 15-7–15-11
manufacturing overhead costs, 16-7
material costs, 16-6–16-7
in process cost system, 16-6–16-9
raw materials costs, 15-8–15-10
transfer to cost of goods sold, 16-8
transfer to finished goods, 16-8
transfer to next department, 16-8
Auditors, 1-17, 7-9, 7-34
Auditor's report, 1-17, 1-19
Authorized stock, 11-7–11-8, 11-32
Auto industry
debt in, 10-1–10-2
flexible manufacturing in, 23-17
make or buy decision, 20-17
Auto loan application, G-18
Available-for-sale securities
defined, 13-5, 13-32, H-7, H-14
financial statement reporting on, H-9–H-10
valuation of, H-8
Average accounts receivable outstanding, 8-22
Average collection period, 8-22, 8-27, 13-20, 13-32
Average-cost method
cost flow assumptions in, 6-11–6-12
defined, 6-11, 6-26
financial statement and tax effects of, 6-13–6-14
periodic, 6-8
in perpetual inventory system, 6-23

B

Background checks, 7-10
Bad debt expense, 8-5, 8-8, 8-10, 8-27
Bad debts, material, 8-6
Bad loans, 8-20
Balance sheets, 1-11–1-12
  accrued revenues on, 4-15
  from adjusted trial balance, 4-24
  and adjusting entries, 4-6, 4-14, 4-19
  Amazon.com, Inc., D-3
  Apple Inc., A-3
  budgeted, 2-28, 22-20–22-21
  classified, 2-3–2-8, 2-10–2-13, 2-22, 2-45–2-46, H-13
  Columbia Sportswear Company, B-2
  comparative, 12-6–12-8, 12-22–12-23, 12-31
  cost flow methods and, 6-13
  debits and credits for accounts on, 3-16–3-17
  defined, 1-9, 1-11, 1-19
  fair value on, H-9
  horizontal analysis of, 13-11
  interrelationships of other statements and, 1-13, 1-14
  inventory errors and, 6-25
  investments on, H-11–H-13
  liabilities on, 10-19, 10-20
  long-term notes payable on, 10-31
  Louis Vuitton, F-3
  manufacturing costs, 14-13
  and net change cash, 12-14–12-15, 12-29
  off-balance-sheet financing, 10-22, 10-32
  partnership, K-9–K-10
  prepaid expenses on, 4-8, 4-11
  receivables presentation on, 8-19
  stockholders' equity on, 11-24–11-25
  and stockholders' equity relationship, 3-16
  uncollectible debt and, 8-8
  unearned revenues on, 4-13
  use of, 1-11–1-12
  vertical analysis of, 13-12–13-13
  VF Corporation, C-1
  Wal-Mart Stores, Inc., E-3
Balanced scorecard, 24-17–24-20
  defined, 14-17, 14-22, 24-18, 24-27
  examples of objectives, 24-18
  linked processes across, 24-19
  perspectives, 24-18
  summary, 24-19
  United Airlines and, 24-19
Bank, reconciliation items per, 7-20
Bank accounts, 7-17–7-23
  electronic funds transfers (EFTs), 7-17–7-18
  reconciliation of, 7-19–7-23
  statements, 7-18–7-19
Bank charges expense, 7-22–7-23
Bank errors, 7-20
Bank lines of credit, 10-20
Bank reconciliation, 7-19–7-23
  defined, 7-17, 7-19, 7-34
  entries from, 7-22–7-23
  example, 7-21–7-22
  procedure, 7-19–7-21
Bank statements, 7-18–7-19, 7-34
Base amount, for vertical analysis, 13-12
Base period, changes since, 13-10
Base year, current year compared to, 13-10
Basic accounting equation, 1-11, 1-20, 3-4, 3-16
Batch-level activities, 17-13, 17-25
Before-tax contribution margin, 21-24

Beginning inventory, errors with, 6-24
Benchmarks, 17-16
Benford's Law, 13-14
Bezos, Jeff, 18-1–18-2
Billing, for receivables, 8-12, 8-23
Board of directors, 14-5, 14-22
Boards of directors, financial statements for, H-7
Bond certificates, 10-9, 10-10, 10-32
Bond indenture, 10-9, 10-32
Bond interest expense, 10-27
Bond interest paid, 10-27
Bond interest, recording, H-3
Bond prices
  and interest rates, 10-14
  quotes of, 10-9, 10-10, 10-12
Bonding, 7-9, 7-34
Bonds, 10-8–10-18
  accounting for transactions with, 10-12–10-18
  acquisition of, recording, H-3
  callable, 10-9, 10-32
  common stock financing vs., 11-27
  convertible, 10-9, 10-32
  debenture, 10-32
  defined, 10-8, 10-32
  effective-interest method of amortization, 10-27–10-30
  green, 10-18
  issuing of, 10-9, 10-11–10-12
  market price determination, 10-10–10-12
  mortgage, 10-9, 10-32
  present value of, G-11–G-13
  sale of, recording, H-3
  secured, 10-9, 10-32
  sinking fund, 10-9
  straight-line amortization, 10-24–10-26
  trading of, 10-9–10-10
  types of, 10-8–10-9
  unsecured (debenture), 10-9, 10-32
  zero-interest, 10-10
Bonds payable
  discount on, 10-14, 10-25
  as financing activity, 1-8
  premium on, 10-15, 10-26
  and statement of cash flows, 12-14, 12-28, 12-32
Bonuses
  admission of a partner, K-16–K-18
  payroll, I-2, I-11
  withdrawal of a partner, K-19–K-20
Book errors, 7-21, 7-22
Book value
  of bonds, 10-14, 10-17
  and declining-balance method, 9-27
  defined, 4-11, 4-36
  in depreciation, 9-8
  and effective-interest amortization, 10-27
Books, reconciling items per, 7-21
Borrowing, costs of, 10-14–10-16
Bowerman, Bill, 8-1, 8-2, 11-3
Break-even analysis
  contribution margin technique, 18-15–18-16
  defined, 18-14
  graphic representation, 18-16–18-17
  mathematical equation, 18-15
  overview of, 19-3–19-4
Break-even point
  in break-even analysis, 18-14
  computation for two companies, 19-15

  computing/deriving, 18-14
  cost structure effect on, 19-15
  defined, 18-12, 18-27
  in dollars, 18-16, 19-4
  expression of, 18-14
  formula using unit contribution margin, 18-15
  in units, 18-15, 19-4, 19-9
Break-even sales
  in dollars, 19-9–19-11
  sales mix and, 19-8–19-12
  in units, 19-5, 19-6
Budget committee, 22-4–22-5, 22-28
Budget periods, 22-4
Budget reports
  defined, 23-3
  flexible, 23-11–23-12
  function of, 23-3
  overhead static, 23-7
  static, 23-4–23-6
Budgetary control, 23-1–23-13
  activities, 23-3
  defined, 23-3, 23-30
  flexible budget reports and, 23-6–23-13
  reporting system, 23-3–23-4
  static budget reports and, 23-4–23-6
Budgetary optimism, 22-9
Budgeted balance sheet
  computation and sources of amounts, 22-21
  defined, 2-20, 2-28
  illustrated, 2-20–2-21
Budgeted income statement, 2-28, 22-15–22-16
Budgeting, 22-1–22-50
  accounting and, 22-3
  benefits of, 22-3
  budget period and, 22-4
  budgeted balance sheet and, 22-20–22-21, 22-28
  budgeted income statement and, 2-28, 22-15–22-16
  capital, 25-1–25-37, G-14–G-15
  cash, 7-27–7-29
  cash budget and, 22-17–22-20
  as control device, 22-3
  in coordination of activities, 22-3
  direct labor budget and, 22-13–22-14, 22-28
  direct materials budget and, 22-10–22-11, 22-28
  as early warning system, 22-3
  effective, 22-3–22-7
  essentials of, 22-3–22-6
  human behavior and, 22-5–22-6
  long-range planning and, 22-6
  in management awareness, 22-3
  manufacturing overhead budget and, 22-14–22-15, 22-28
  master budget and, 22-6–22-7, 22-28
  for merchandisers, 22-22–22-23, 22-28
  in nonmanufacturing companies, 22-22–22-25
  for not-for-profit organizations, 22-24
  objectives, 22-3
  organizational structure and, 22-3–22-4
  in personnel motivation, 22-3
  in planning, 22-3
  process, 22-4–22-5
  production budget and, 22-9–22-10, 22-28
  sales budget and, 22-6–22-7, 22-28

selling and administrative expense budget and, 22-15, 22-28
for service companies, 22-23–22-24
"zero-based," 22-20
Budgets
cash, 7-27–7-30
defined, 22-3, 22-28
details and goals, 22-6
direct labor, 22-13–22-14, 22-23, 22-28
direct materials, 22-10–22-11, 22-28
ethics and, 22-6
Exotic Newcastle Disease and, 23-12
financial, 22-6, 22-8
flexible, 23-6–23-13
manufacturing overhead, 22-14–22-15, 22-28
master, 22-6–22-7, 22-28
merchandise purchase, 22-22–22-23, 22-28
operating, 22-6, 22-28
over, 23-7
preparation framework, 22-4
production, 22-9–22-10
sales, 22-8–22-9, 22-28
selling and administrative expense, 22-15, 22-28
shortfalls, 22-24
standards versus, 24-4
static, 23-4–23-6, 23-7–23-8
under, 23-9
unrealistic, 22-6
Buffett, Warren, 11-21, 13-1, 13-2
Buildings
accumulated depreciation on, 12-33
cost of, 9-5
and statement of cash flows, 12-13, 12-28, 12-32
Bulletin boards, investment information on, 2-2
Business activities, 1-7–1-9. *See also specific types*
Business documents, for sales transactions, 5-11
Business organization, 1-2–1-3. *See also Corporations*
Business size, internal controls and, 7-11
Business transactions, organizing information related to, 3-1–3-2
Buyer leverage, 17-17
Buyers, freight costs incurred by, 5-8
Buy-or-lease decision, 9-7
By-laws, 11-6

C

Callable bonds, 10-9, 10-32
Canceled checks, 7-19
Capital
corporate, 11-9–11-10
corporations' acquisition of, 11-4
legal, 11-8
paid-in. *See* Paid-in capital
working, 2-11, 2-12, 2-23
Capital budgeting, 25-1–25-37
annual rate of return method, 25-18
authorization process, 25-3
cash flow information and, 25-3–25-4
cash payback and, 25-4–25-6
challenges and refinements, 25-11–25-16
decision considerations, 25-4
defined, 25-1, 25-22
discounted cash flow techniques, 25-6, 25-22

illustrative data, 25-4
intangible benefits, 25-11–25-13
internal rate of return (IRR) method, 25-16–25-18
mutually exclusive projects, 25-13–25-14
net present value (NPV) method, 25-6–25-11
post-audit, 25-15
profitability index and, 25-13–25-14
risk analysis, 25-14
sensitivity analysis, 25-14, 25-22
situations, G-14–G-15
time value of money and, 25-6
Capital deficiency. *See also* Partnership liquidation
causes of, K-12
defined, K-10, K-21
ledger balances after nonpayment, K-14
ledger balances before distribution, K-13
nonpayment of deficiency, K-14
steps in liquidation process, K-12–K-13
Capital expenditures, 9-3, 9-6, 9-30
Capital stock, 11-8, 11-24. *See also* Common stock; Preferred stock
Capitalization
Improper, 9-3–9-4
of research and development costs, 9-19
of retained earnings. *See* Stock dividends
Captive finance companies, 8-23
Carrying value. *See* Book value
Cash, 7-12–7-32
accumulation of, 12-1–12-2
and adjusting entries, 4-30
and amortization/depreciation, 9-25
as asset, 1-8
in bank accounts, 7-17–7-23
budgeting of, 7-27–7-30
burn rate, 12-15
for cash dividends, 11-15–11-16
change in (T-account method), 12-35
common par value stock for, 11-10–11-11
from customer in advance, 3-6–3-7, 3-24
defined, 7-34
and depreciation, 9-8
for employee salaries, 3-9, 3-27
equipment purchase for, 3-6, 3-23
excess, investing and, H-1–H-2
GAAP vs. IFRS and, 7-56–7-57
insurance policy purchased for, 3-8, 3-25
internal controls for, 7-12–7-17
and inventory cost flow method, 6-13–6-14
and liabilities, 10-19
management of, 7-25–7-27
negative, operating with, 12-19
net change in (direct method), 12-29
net change in (indirect method), 12-14–12-15, 12-33
note issued in exchange for, 3-6, 3-23
payment of rent with, 3-25
petty cash fund, 7-30–7-32
POS systems for tracking, 7-1–7-2
and quality of earnings ratio, 5-24–5-25
and receivables management, 8-24
reporting, 7-24–7-25
restricted, 7-24–7-25, 7-34
from sales of receivables, 8-12, 8-23
services performed for, 3-7, 3-24
stockholder investment of, 3-5–3-6, 3-22
and stockholders' equity, 11-25
and trial balance, 3-31

Cash (net) realizable value
after write-off of uncollectible debt, 8-8
defined, 8-6, 8-27
lower-of-cost-or-net realizable value, 6-16, 6-19–6-20, 6-27
of notes receivable, 8-16
Cash balance, retained earnings and, 11-23
Cash budgets. *See also* Budgeting; Budgets
basic form of, 7-28, 22-17
collections from customers and, 22-18
defined, 7-27, 7-34, 22-17, 22-28
in effective cash management, 7-29, 22-20
illustrated, 7-28, 22-19
payments for materials and, 22-19
sections, 7-27–7-28, 22-17
Cash controls, 7-12–7-17
for disbursements, 7-14–7-16
for petty cash fund, 7-16
for receipts, 7-12–7-14
Cash disbursements, 7-14–7-16, 7-27
Cash dividends, 11-15–11-17, 11-23, 11-32
Cash drawers, transfer of, 7-5
Cash equivalent price, 9-4, 9-31
Cash equivalents, 7-24, 7-34
Cash financing transactions, 12-3
Cash flow numbers, 25-3
"Cash Flow Statements" (*IAS 7*), 12-61
Cash flows. *See also* Statements of cash flows
adjusting entries and, 4-9
analyzing, for accounting transactions, 3-22–3-27
capital budgeting and, 25-3–25-4
classification of, 12-3–12-4
determination of, 12-6
equal annual, 25-7
from financing activities, 10-19
free, 2-14, 2-22, 12-19–12-21, 12-38, 13-22–13-23
future, 12-3
from investing activities, 9-25
monitoring of, 12-20
from operating activities, 9-25, 12-3, 12-4
product life cycle impact on, 12-18
unequal annual, 25-8
Cash investing transactions, 12-3
Cash management
cash budgets and, 7-29, 22-20
international sales and, 7-26
overview, 7-25–7-26
principles of, 7-26–7-27
Cash over and short, 7-32
Cash payback
defined, 25-4, 25-22
formula, 25-5
period, computation of, 25-5
technique drawbacks, 25-5
Cash payments
in direct method (statement of cash flows), 12-23–12-28
for income taxes, 12-27–12-28
for interest, 12-27
for operating expenses, 12-26
to suppliers, 12-25–12-26
Cash payments (cash disbursements) journal. *See also* Special journals
defined, J-13, J-18
journalizing, J-13–J-15
posting, J-14, J-15
proofing the ledgers, J-15

Cash receipts
  acceleration of, 8-23
  in cash budget, 7-27
  controls for, 7-12–7-14
  from customers, 12-24–12-25
  in direct method (statement of cash flows), 12-23–12-25
Cash receipts journal. *See also* Special journals
  columns, J-7–J-9
  credit columns, J-9
  debit and credit columns, J-9–J-10
  debit columns, J-9
  defined, J-7, J-18
  journalizing, J-8, J-9–J-10
  posting, J-8, J-10
  proving equality of, J-10
  proving the ledgers, J-10–J-11
Cash register documents, 5-11
Cash-and-carry sales, 8-1–8-2
Cash-basis accounting
  accrual- vs., 4-5
  converting net income to, 12-9, 12-23–12-28
  defined, 4-5, 4-36
  and statements of cash flows, 12-7
Casualty losses, 5-18
Certified public accountant (CPA), 1-17, 1-20
Change in accounting principle, 13-6–13-7, 13-32
Channel stuffing, 13-8
Chart of accounts, 3-20–3-21, 3-34
Charters, corporate, 11-6, 11-32
Check register, 7-15
Check(s) canceled
  defined, 7-19
  disbursements via, 7-14
  NSF, 7-19, 7-22, 7-34
  outstanding, 7-20, 7-21, 7-34
Chief executive officer (CEO), 14-5, 14-6, 14-22
Chief financial officer (CFO), 14-5, 14-22
Classified balance sheet, 2-3–2-8
  current assets on, 2-3–2-5
  current liabilities on, 2-7
  defined, 2-3, 2-22
  GAAP vs. IFRS, 2-45–2-46
  intangible assets on, 2-5–2-6
  investments on, H-13
  liquidity measures from, 2-10–2-12
  long-term investments on, 2-5
  long-term liabilities on, 2-7
  property, plant, and equipment on, 2-5
  ratio analysis with, 2-10–2-13
  solvency measures on, 2-12–2-13
  stockholders' equity, 2-7–2-8
Closely held corporations (privately held corporations), 11-3, 11-32
Closing entries
  defined, 4-26, 4-36
  journalized, 4-27
  net loss in, 11-23
  partnerships, K-6–K-7
  preparing, 4-26–4-27
  sole proprietorships, L-4–L-7
Closing the books, 4-26–4-28
Collection agents, 10-4
Collection period, average, 8-22, 8-27, 13-20, 13-32

Collections
  monitoring of, 8-20–8-21
  sale of receivables and, 8-12, 8-23
Combined statement of income and comprehensive income, 13-5
Common stock
  accounting for, 11-11–11-12
  bond financing vs., 11-27
  debit/credit procedures for, 3-13–3-14
  defined, 1-8, 1-20, 2-7
  dividends on, 11-17
  and paid-in capital, 11-9
  par value, 11-11–11-12
  return on common stockholders' equity, 11-26–11-27, 11-32
  and statement of cash flows, 12-14, 12-28, 12-32
  and stockholder rights, 11-6
Common stock dividends distributable, 11-30
Communication, in internal control system, 7-4
Company officers, 1-4
Comparability, financial information, 2-17, 2-22
Comparative balance sheets, 12-6–12-8, 12-22–12-23, 12-31
Comparative CVP income statements, 18-13
Compensation, for managers, 11-4
Competition versus collaboration, 23-15
Complete information, 2-17
Component depreciation, 9-55
Composition, of current assets, 2-12
Compound interest, G-2–G-3, G-20
Compounding periods, G-16
Comprehensive income, 13-5–13-6
  accumulated other, 11-24, 11-32
  complete statement of, 13-6
  defined, 5-19, 5-20, 5-31, 13-5, 13-32
  example, 13-5
  format, 13-5–13-6
  other, 5-55, 11-24, 11-32
Comprehensive income statements
  available-for-sale securities on, H-10
  defined, 5-19, 5-31
  financial analysis with, 13-5, 13-6
  for merchandising operations, 5-19–5-20
Concentration, of credit risk, 8-21, 8-27
Confirmatory value, of information, 2-17
Conservatism, 6-16
Consigned goods, 6-5–6-6, 6-26
Consistency concept
  for cost flow method use, 6-14
  defined, 6-26
  for financial information, 2-17, 2-22
  for financial statement preparation, 13-6
Consolidated financial statements
  Amazon.com, Inc., D-1–D-4
  Apple Inc., A-1–A-5
  Columbia Sportswear Company, B-1–B-4
  defined, H-6, H-14
  Louis Vuitton, F-1–F-5
  for stock investments over 50%, H-6–H-7
  VF Corporation, C-1–C-4
  Wal-Mart Stores, Inc., E-1–E-5
Constraints, theory of, 19-13
Constructed buildings, cost of, 9-5
Consumer cooperatives (co-ops), 5-1–5-2
Contingencies, 10-22, 10-32
Continuous improvement, 17-15

Continuous life, corporations and, 11-4
Contra accounts
  asset, 4-10, 4-36
  revenue, 5-13, 5-31
  treasury stock, 11-14
Contractual interest rate, 10-9, 10-13, 10-32
Contribution margin (CM)
  after-tax, 21-24–21-25
  break-even point and, 18-12, 18-27
  defined, 18-11, 18-27, 19-3
  machine hours and, 19-12
  per square foot, 19-13
  per unit of limited resource, 19-12
  for restaurants, 19-11
  in target net income, 18-19
  before-tax, 21-24
  technique, 18-15–18-16
  total, computation of, 19-13
  unit, 18-12, 18-15–18-16, 18-27
  weighted-average, 19-8–19-9
Contribution margin ratio
  in break-even point formula, 18-16
  in break-even sales in dollars, 19-10
  cost structure effect on, 19-15
  defined, 18-13, 18-27, 19-4
  formula for, 18-13
  formula for sales in dollars using, 18-19
  for two companies, 19-15
Control account, 15-8, J-2, J-18
Control activities, 7-4–7-12
  defined, 7-4
  documentation procedures, 7-7
  human resource controls, 7-9–7-10
  independent internal verification, 7-8–7-9
  physical controls, 7-7–7-8
  responsibility establishment, 7-5
  segregation of duties, 7-5–7-7
Control devices, budgeting, 22-3
Control environment, 7-4
Controllable costs, 23-15, 23-30
Controllable margin
  defined, 23-21, 23-30
  increasing, 23-24–23-25
  as manager performance measure, 23-22
Controller, 11-4, 14-5, 14-22
Controlling function, 14-3, 14-4
Controlling interest, H-6, H-14
Controls. *See* Internal controls
Conversion costs
  defined, 16-10, 16-27
  total, computation, 16-14
  unit, computation, 16-14
Conversion rate, 19-7
Convertible bonds, 10-9, 10-32
"Cookie jar," tapping the, 8-11
Co-ops (consumer cooperatives), 5-1–5-2
Copyrights, 9-19, 9-31
Corporate capital, 11-9–11-10. *See also* Stockholders' equity
Corporate life cycle, 12-17–12-19
Corporate social responsibility, 1-13, 11-7, 14-18–14-19, 14-22, 24-15
Corporations, 11-3–11-10
  capital for, 11-9–11-10
  characteristics of, 11-3–11-5
  defined, 1-3, 1-20, 11-3, 11-32
  forming, 11-6
  privately held, 11-3, 11-32

publicly held, 11-3, 11-32
reasons for investing by, H-1–H-2
S corporation, 11-5
stock issuance by, 11-7–11-9
stockholder rights at, 11-6–11-7
Correct cash balance, 7-22
Corruption, 7-16
Cost accounting, 15-3, 15-4, 15-25
Cost accounting systems
  accumulating manufacturing costs, 15-5–15-7
  defined, 15-3, 15-25
  job order cost flow, 15-4–15-5
  job order cost system, 15-3–15-4
  process cost system, 15-3, 15-25
Cost allocation, 4-10, 4-11, 9-8
Cost behavior analysis
  activity index and, 18-3
  defined, 18-2, 18-27
  fixed costs, 18-4
  mixed costs, 18-6
  relevant range, 18-5–18-6
  variable costs, 18-3
Cost centers. *See also* Responsibility centers
  defined, 23-18, 23-30
  responsibility accounting for, 23-20
  responsibility report for, 23-20
Cost constraint, 2-19, 2-22
Cost conversion, equivalent units for, 16-22
Cost drivers
  choosing, 16-7
  defined, 17-5, 17-25
  estimated use, 17-8
  estimated use per product, 17-9, 17-11
  examples of, 17-5, 17-6
  high degree of correlation, 17-8
  identifying, 17-8
Cost equation
  accuracy of, 18-25
  regression analysis and, 18-22–18-25
Cost factor, in depreciation, 9-9
Cost flow assumptions, 6-7–6-12
  average-cost method, 6-11–6-12
  FIFO method, 6-8–6-9
  LIFO method, 6-10–6-11
Cost flow methods, inventory. *See* Inventory cost flow methods
Cost flows
  job order, 15-17–15-18
  in merchandising operations, 5-4–5-6
Cost method
  for stock investments, H-4, H-14
  for treasury stock purchase, 11-13–11-14
Cost of capital, 25-9, 25-22
Cost of goods available for sale, 6-8
Cost of goods manufactured
  defined, 14-12, 14-22
  finding, 14-11–14-12
  formula, 14-12
Cost of goods manufactured schedule, 14-11, 14-12, 15-20
Cost of goods purchased, 5-27, 14-11
Cost of goods sold
  adjustment to, 15-21–15-22
  components, 14-11
  defined, 1-9, 5-3, 5-31
  in FIFO method, 6-9
  in gross profit calculation, 5-17
  in LIFO method, 6-11

  manufacturer calculation of, 14-11
  in periodic inventory system, 5-5, 5-21–5-22, 6-8
  in perpetual inventory system, 5-4, 5-11, 5-21
  transfer to, 16-8
Cost reconciliation schedule
  defined, 16-15, 16-27
  illustrated, 16-15, 16-24
  preparing (FIFO), 16-23–16-24
  preparing (weighted-average), 16-15
Cost structure
  choice of, 19-14
  defined, 19-14, 19-29
  effect on break-even point, 19-15
  effect on contribution margin ratio, 19-15
  effect on margin of safety ratio, 19-16
Cost-based transfer prices
  defined, 21-17, 21-27
  drawbacks, 21-17
  excess capacity, 21-18
  no excess capacity, 21-18
  results, no excess capacity, 21-18
Costing systems. *See also* Activity-based costing (ABC); Job order costing; Process cost systems
  direct costs per unit, 17-3
  elements of, 17-3
  illustrated, 17-3–17-4
  need for new approach, 17-4
  overhead applied under, 17-18
  service company example, 17-18
  service firms under, 17-18
  total unit costs, 17-4
  traditional, 17-3–17-4
  unit coss and, 17-10
Cost-plus pricing. *See also* Pricing
  advantage of, 21-7
  basis, 21-22
  defined, 21-5, 21-27
  limitations of, 21-7–21-8
  markup and, 21-6, 21-7
  selling price computation and, 21-7
  target selling price and, 21-6
Cost(s). *See also* Manufacturing costs
  assignment to cost categories, 14-9
  of borrowing, 10-14–10-16
  controllable, 23-15, 23-30
  conversion, 16-10, 16-14
  debt investments at, H-3
  depreciable, 9-9, 9-31
  fixed, 18-4, 18-5–18-6, 18-8, 18-9–18-10
  flow of, 5-4–5-6
  freight, 5-8–5-9, 5-27
  initial, for patents, 9-19
  interest and building, 9-5
  joint, 20-12, 20-19
  managerial concepts of, 14-7–14-10
  mixed, 18-6, 18-7–18-10
  noncontrollable, 23-15, 23-30
  opportunity, 20-4, 20-9, 20-19, 21-15, 21-27
  organization, 11-6, 11-32
  period, 14-8, 14-23
  of plant assets, 9-3–9-6
  product, 14-8, 14-10
  production, 14-23
  relevant, 20-4, 20-6–20-7, 20-19
  research and development, 9-19, 9-31
  standard, 24-3–24-7
  sunk, 20-4, 20-19

  target, 21-4
  total manufacturing, 14-10
  variable, 18-3, 18-5–18-6, 18-9–18-10, 18-27
  weighted-average unit, 6-11, 6-27
Cost-volume-profit (CVP), 18-1–18-44, 19-1–19-51
  basic components, 18-10–18-11
  basic computations, 19-3–19-5
  basic concepts, 19-3
  break-even analysis, 18-14–18-18, 19-3–19-4
  cost behavior analysis and, 18-2–18-7
  margin of safety and, 18-20, 18-27, 19-5
  mixed costs analysis, 18-7
  prerequisite to understanding, 18-1
  target net income and, 18-18–18-19, 19-4–19-5
Cost-volume-profit (CVP) analysis
  applications of, 19-3
  assumptions, 18-11
  changes in business environment and, 19-5–19-6
  CVP income statement, 18-11–18-14
  defined, 18-10, 18-27
  variable costing and, 19-19, 19-27
Cost-volume-profit (CVP) graph
  construction of, 18-17
  defined, 18-16
  illustrated, 18-17
  in target net income, 18-19
  use of, 18-17
Cost-volume-profit (CVP) income statement
  basic, 19-3
  comparative, 18-13
  contribution margin ratio and, 18-13–18-14
  defined, 18-11, 18-27
  detailed, 19-4
  with net income, 18-12
  with net income and per unit data, 18-12
  with net income and percent of sales data, 18-13
  traditional income statement versus, 18-11
  for two companies, 19-15
  unit contribution margin and, 18-12
  with zero net income, 18-12
Coupons, 3-17, 4-1–4-2
CPA (certified public accountant), 1-17, 1-20
Credit
  bank lines of, 10-20
  extending, 8-19–8-20
  purchase discounts and terms for, 5-9–5-10
Credit balances
  defined, 3-12
  for liability accounts, 3-13
  for revenue accounts, 3-15
  on worksheet for indirect method (statement of cash flows), 12-29
Credit cards, 8-12–8-13
Credit crisis, bad loans in, 8-20
Credit procedures, 3-12–3-15
  for assets and liabilities, 3-12–3-13
  for stockholders' equity, 3-13–3-15
Credit ratings, 13-17
Credit risk, 8-21, 8-27
Credit sales
  adjusting entries for, 5-29–5-30
  with credit cards, 8-12–8-13
  in perpetual inventory systems, 5-14
Crediting, 3-11
Creditors, 1-4, 1-5, 1-7

SUBJECT INDEX

Credits (Cr.), 3-11–3-12
  in assigning manufacturing costs, 15-7
  on bank statements, 7-18–7-19
  debits in transactions and, 3-12
  defined, 3-11, 3-34
  for notes receivable, 8-14
  in recording process, 3-22
  rules for, 3-16–3-17
  trial balance and, 3-30
  on worksheet for indirect method (statement of cash flows), 12-30
Cumulative dividends, 11-18, 11-32
Current assets, 2-3–2-5
  on classified balance sheet, 2-3–2-5
  composition of, 2-12
  defined, 2-3, 2-22
  noncash, 12-10–12-11
Current liabilities, 10-3–10-8
  changes to, 12-11–12-12
  on classified balance sheet, 2-7
  current maturities of long-term debt, 10-5
  defined, 2-7, 2-22, 10-3, 10-32
  interest payable as, 10-13
  notes payable, 10-3–10-4, 10-31
  payroll and payroll taxes payable, 10-6–10-8
  sales taxes payable, 10-4
  unearned revenues, 10-5
Current maturities of long-term debt, 10-5
Current ratio
  classified balance sheet and, 2-11–2-12
  defined, 2-11, 2-22, 13-19, 13-32
  for liabilities, 10-20
  as liquidity ratio, 13-19
  managing, 13-16
Customer perspective, 24-18, 24-19, 24-27
Customers
  cash in advance from, 3-6–3-7, 3-24
  cash receipts from, 12-24–12-25
  as external users, 1-5
Cutoff rate. *See* Discount rate
CVP. *See* Cost-volume-profit
Cybercrime, J-17, J-18

D

Data analytics
  and financial analysis, 13-17
  for perpetual inventory systems, 5-14
Days in inventory, 6-17–6-18, 6-26, 13-21, 13-32
Debenture (unsecured) bonds, 10-9, 10-32
Debit balance
  allowance account and, 8-10
  for asset accounts, 3-13
  defined, 3-12
  for expense accounts, 3-15
  on worksheet for indirect method, 12-29
Debit procedures, 3-12–3-15
  for assets and liabilities, 3-12–3-13
  for stockholders' equity, 3-13–3-15
Debiting, 3-11
Debits (Dr.), 3-11–3-12
  in assigning manufacturing costs, 15-7
  on bank statements, 7-19
  credits in transaction and, 3-12
  defined, 3-11, 3-34
  for notes receivable, 8-14
  for purchase of treasury stock, 11-13
  in recording process, 3-22
  rules for, 3-16–3-17
  trial balance and, 3-30
  on worksheet for indirect method, 12-30
Debt. *See also* Liabilities
  in auto industry, 10-1–10-2
  disclosure of, 10-19
  good, 2-13
  long-term. *See* Long-term liabilities
Debt covenants, 10-22–10-23
Debt investments, H-1–H-3, H-14
Debt masking, 10-22
Debt securities, H-7–H-10
Debt to assets ratio, 2-13, 2-22, 13-21–13-22, 13-32
Debt to equity ratio, 2-13, 13-22
Debt vs. equity decision, 11-27–11-28
Decentralization, 23-14, 23-30
Decision tools
  accounting equation, 3-4
  accounts receivable turnover, 8-22
  activity flowchart, 17-14
  activity-based costing (ABC), 17-17
  aging schedule for accounts receivable, 8-20
  asset turnover, 9-24
  average collection period, 8-22
  balance sheet, 1-11, 14-13
  break-even analysis, 18-14
  break-even point in dollars, 19-10
  break-even point in units, 19-9
  cash budget, 22-17, 22-28
  changes in accounting principle, 13-7
  contingencies, 10-22
  contribution margin per unit, 19-12
  contribution margin ratio, 18-13
  control activities, 7-5
  cost flow methods and, 6-12
  cost of goods manufactured schedule, 14-12
  cost–benefit analysis, 11-3
  cost-benefit trade-off, 16-16
  cost-plus pricing, 21-6
  credit risk concentration, 8-21
  current ratio, 2-11
  debt to assets ratio, 2-13
  degree of operating leverage, 19-16
  discontinued operations, 13-4
  earnings per share, 2-10
  flexible budget, 23-9
  free cash flow, 2-14, 12-19
  gross profit rate, 5-22
  horizontal analysis, 13-10
  income statement, 1-10
  incremental analysis, 20-4
  intangibles amortization, 9-19
  internal rate of return (IRR), 25-16
  inventory turnover and days in inventory, 6-17
  labor price variance, 24-11
  labor quantity variance, 24-11
  LIFO to FIFO inventory conversion, 6-18
  liquidity measures, 10-20
  Manufacturing Overhead account, 15-21
  master budget, 22-6
  materials price variance, 24-9
  materials quantity variance, 24-9
  negotiated transfer pricing, 21-15
  net present value (NPV) method, 25-6
  payout ratio, 11-26
  production cost report, 16-15
  profit margin, 5-23
  profitability index, 25-14
  ratio analysis, 13-14
  responsibility reports, 23-17
  restricted cash, 7-25
  retained earnings statement, 1-11
  return on assets, 9-23
  return on common stockholders' equity, 11-26
  revenue and expense recognition principles, 4-4
  ROI formula, 23-23
  statement of cash flows, 1-12
  target cost formula, 21-4
  time-and-material price quotation, 21-12
  times interest earned, 10-21
  total manufacturing overhead variance, 24-14
  trial balance, 3-30
  unit contribution margin, 18-12
  vertical analysis, 13-12
Decision-making
  alternative courses of action and, 20-3
  financial and nonfinancial information in, 20-3
  incremental analysis and, 20-3–20-6
  management functions and, 14-4
  management process of, 20-3
  qualitative factors and, 20-5
Decisions
  eliminate unprofitable segment, 20-15–20-17
  make or buy, 20-8–20-10
  repair, retain, or replace equipment, 20-14–20-15
  sell or process further, 20-10–20-13
  special orders, 20-6–20-7
  types of, 20-6
Declaration date, 11-16, 11-32
Declared dividends, 11-16
Decline phase, of life cycle, 12-17–12-19
Declining-balance method, 9-11–9-13, 9-27–9-28, 9-31
Deferrals, 4-6–4-14
  prepaid expenses, 4-7–4-11
  types of, 4-6
  unearned revenues, 4-11–4-13
Deficits, 11-23, 11-32
Degree of operating leverage, 19-16, 19-29
Delivery truck, cost of, 9-5
Deposits, in bank reconciliation, 7-21
Deposits in transit, 7-20, 7-34
Depreciable assets, 9-8
Depreciable cost, 9-9, 9-31
Depreciation, 9-8–9-15
  accelerated-depreciation method, 9-11, 9-28, 9-30
  accumulated, 2-5, 12-33
  adjusting entries for, 4-10–4-11
  and cash flow, 9-25
  comparison of methods, 9-12–9-13
  component, 9-55
  declining-balance method, 9-11–9-13, 9-27–9-28, 9-31
  defined, 2-5, 4-10, 4-36, 9-8, 9-31
  double-declining-balance method, 9-27
  as expense, 12-9
  factors in computing, 9-8–9-9
  impairments, 9-14–9-15
  methods, 9-9–9-13
  revising, 9-13–9-15
  straight-line, 9-9–9-13, 9-27, 9-31

units-of-activity method, 9-12–9-13, 9-28–9-29, 9-31
Depreciation expense
  in direct method, 12-26–12-27
  in indirect method, 12-9
  total, 9-12
Depreciation rate, declining-balance method, 9-27
Depreciation schedules
  declining-balance, 9-11
  defined, 9-10
  double-declining-balance, 9-28
  straight-line, 9-10
  units-of-activity, 9-12, 9-29
Differential analysis. *See also* Incremental analysis
  basic approach to, 20-4
  functioning of, 20-4–20-5
  key cost concepts in, 20-4
  opportunity cost and, 20-4
  relevant cost and revenues and, 20-4
  sunk cost and, 20-4
Direct fixed costs, 23-21, 23-30
Direct issuance of stock, 11-8
Direct labor
  defined, 14-7, 14-22
  job costs sheets, 15-11
  tracing costs to products, 14-8
  in traditional costing systems, 17-3
Direct labor budget. *See also* Budgeting; Budgets
  cost formula, 22-13
  defined, 22-13, 22-28
  illustrated, 22-14
  for service company, 22-23
Direct labor efficiency standard, 24-6
Direct labor price standard, 24-5, 24-27
Direct labor quantity standard, 24-6, 24-27
Direct labor rate standard, 24-5
Direct labor variances
  breakdown of, 24-8
  causes of, 24-13–24-14
  labor price variance and, 24-12
  labor quantity variance and, 24-12–24-13
  matrix for, 24-13
  overview of, 24-11–24-12
  summary of, 24-13
  total labor variance and, 24-12
Direct materials
  defined, 14-7, 14-22
  job cost sheets, posting of, 15-9
  payments for, 22-19
  tracing costs to products, 14-8
Direct materials budget. *See also* Budgeting; Budgets
  cost of purchases formula, 22-10
  defined, 22-10, 22-28
  ending inventory and, 22-11, 22-28
  illustrated, 22-11
  units purchased formula, 22-10
  units required formula, 22-10
Direct materials price standard, 24-5, 24-27
Direct materials quantity standard, 24-5, 24-27
Direct materials variances
  analyzing and reporting, 24-7–24-11
  breakdown of, 24-8
  calculating, 24-9–24-10
  causes of, 24-11
  materials price variance and, 24-9–24-10

materials quality variance and, 24-10
matrix for, 24-10
summary of, 24-10
total materials variance and, 24-9
Direct method (statement of cash flows), 12-22–12-29
  defined, 12-7, 12-38
  financial information for, 12-22–12-23
  financing activities, 12-14, 12-28–12-29
  indirect vs., 12-7
  investing activities, 12-14, 12-28–12-29
  net change in cash, 12-29
  operating activities, 12-23–12-28
Direct write-off method, 8-5–8-6, 8-27
Directing function, 14-3, 14-4
Disbursements, cash, 7-14–7-16, 7-27
Discontinued operations, 13-4, 13-32
Discount period, 5-9
Discount rate
  choosing, 25-9
  defined, 25-6, 25-22
  net present value comparison and, 25-9
Discounted cash flow techniques, 25-22
Discounting
  in capital budgeting situations, G-14–G-15
  the future amount, G-7, G-20
  inventory and, 6-18
  time periods and, G-11
Discounts
  amortizing, 10-15, 10-24–10-25, 10-27–10-28
  on bonds, 10-13–10-15
  on bonds payable, 10-14, 10-25
  defined, 10-13, 10-32
  effective-interest amortization of, 10-27–10-28
  issuing bonds at, 10-14–10-15
  "Korean," 2-16
  present value of principal and interest, G-13
  purchase, 5-9–5-10, 5-27, 5-31
  sales, 5-13–5-14, 5-28, 5-31
  straight-line amortization of, 10-24–10-25
Dishonored (defaulted) note, 8-17–8-18, 8-27
Disposal
  of accounts receivable, 8-12–8-14
  of component, 13-4
  of notes receivable, 8-16–8-18
  of plant assets, 9-15–9-17, 12-10, 12-26–12-27
Dividend preferences, 11-17–11-19
Dividend record, 11-26
Dividend revenue, 5-18
Dividends, 11-15–11-20
  ability to pay, 12-3
  cash, 11-15–11-17, 11-23, 11-32
  cumulative, 11-18, 11-32
  debit/credit procedures for, 3-14
  declared, 11-16
  defined, 1-8, 1-20, 3-9, 11-15, 11-32
  payment of, 3-9, 3-27, 12-28
  recording, H-5, H-6
  size of, 11-17
  on statement of cash flows, 2-14
  stock, 11-19–11-20, 11-22, 11-30, 11-32
Dividends in arrears, 11-18, 11-32
Documentation procedures, 7-7, 7-12, 7-15, 9-6
Dollar amount changes, in horizontal analysis, 13-10
Dollars
  break-even point in, 18-6, 19-4
  break-even sales in, 19-9–19-11

contribution margin ratio formula for sales in, 18-19
margin of safety in, 19-5
target net income in, 19-5
Double taxation, 11-5
Double-declining-balance method, 9-11, 9-27–9-28
Double-entry system, 3-12, 3-35
Doubtful Accounts, Allowance for, 8-7, 8-11
Down payments, 9-7
Dr. *See* Debits
Drawings, L-2, L-8
Due date, maturity date and, 8-15
The Dun & Bradstreet Reference Book of American Business, 8-20

E
Earnings
  from investment income, H-2
  quality of, 4-23–4-24, 4-36, 13-7–13-8, 13-32
  quality of earnings ratio, 5-24–5-25, 5-31
Earnings management, 4-23, 4-36, 9-14
Earnings per share (EPS)
  defined, 2-10, 2-22, 13-25, 13-32
  from income statement, 2-10
  as profitability ratio, 13-25–13-26
Earnings performance, stockholders' equity, 11-26–11-27
Economic entity assumption, 2-18, 2-22
Effective-interest method of amortization, 10-27–10-30
  bond discount, 10-27–10-28
  bond premium, 10-29–10-30
  defined, 10-27, 10-32
Effective-interest rate, 10-27, 10-32
EFTs. *See* Electronic funds transfers
Electronic funds transfers (EFTs), 7-14, 7-17–7-18, 7-22, 7-34
Electronics
  recycling, 4-18
  sales returns of, 5-13
Employee earnings record, I-5–I-6, I-11
Employee safety, 25-13
Employees. *See also* Payroll
  bonding of, 7-9
  hiring of, 3-8–3-9, 3-26
  as internal users of financial statements, 1-4
  rotating duties of, 7-9
  salaries, cash payment for, 3-9, 3-27
  theft by, 7-16
Employer payroll taxes
  defined, I-8
  federal unemployment taxes, I-8
  FICA taxes, 10-7, I-8
  filing and remitting, I-9–I-10
  as fringe benefits, I-8
  illustrated, I-8
  recording, I-9
  state unemployment taxes, I-8
  Wage and Tax Statement (Form W-2) and, I-9–I-10
Ending inventory, 6-9, 6-10, 6-24
Enterprise resource planning (ERP) system, 14-16, 14-22
EPS. *See* Earnings per share
Equal annual cash flows, 25-7
Equation analyses, 4-15

I-12 SUBJECT INDEX

Equipment. *See also* Property, plant, and equipment
  accumulated depreciation on, 12-33
  cost of, 9-5–9-6
  purchase of, for cash, 3-6, 3-23
  repair or replace decision, 20-14–20-15
  and statement of cash flows, 12-14, 12-28, 12-32
Equity
  debt to equity ratio, 2-13, 13-22
  in sole proprietorship, 11-10
  stockholders.' *See* Stockholders' equity
  trading on the, 13-24
Equity method, H-5, H-14
Equity securities, H-10–H-11
Equity vs. debt decision, 11-27–11-28
Equivalent units of production
  computation, 16-9, 16-10–16-11
  computation (FIFO), 16-22–16-23
  computation (weighted-average), 16-13–16-14
  conversion costs, 16-10, 16-14, 16-22, 16-27
  defined, 16-9, 16-27
  first-in, first-out (FIFO) method for, 16-19–16-25
  formula, 16-9
  incorrect completion percentages and, 16-10
  for materials, 16-22
  refinements, 16-10–16-11
  weighted-average method for, 16-9–16-10
ERP (Enterprise resource planning) system, 14-16, 14-22
Errors
  and bank reconciliation, 7-19–7-21
  and faithful representation, 2-17
  inventory, 6-23–6-25
  irregularities vs., 3-31
  and journalizing, 3-19, 3-30
  and posting, 3-30
Ethics
  allowance for doubtful accounts, 8-11
  approvals and, 15-8
  business, 14-17–14-18
  cases, steps in analyzing, 1-6
  cash equivalents and, 7-24
  of cash flow as performance measure, 12-3
  code of ethical standards and, 14-17–14-18
  compensation for managers, 11-4
  cost allocation in acquisition, 9-8
  credit card finance charges, 8-12
  current ratio and, 2-12
  earnings management, 5-18
  economic entity assumption, 2-18
  employee safety and, 25-13
  employee theft, 7-16
  equivalent units determination and, 16-10
  errors vs. irregularities, 3-31
  fair value accounting, H-10
  falsifying inventory, 6-4
  in financial reporting, 1-5–1-6
  financial reporting quality, 5-11
  fraudulent store coupons, 3-17
  improper adjusting entries, 4-16
  incentives and, 14-17
  income statement and, 1-10
  inventory fraud, 6-24
  liabilities reporting, 10-19
  make-or-buy decision, 20-9
  overstatement of value, 3-21

  petty cash fund, 7-16
  physical inventory, 6-4
  receivables reporting, 8-3
  reporting other gains and losses, 5-18
  specific identification method, 6-7
  standards and, 24-4
  treasury stock, 11-14
  unrealistic budgets and, 22-6
European Union, 2-16, 3-12
Excel functions, 18-24
Excess capacity
  cost-based transfer price, 21-18
  given, 21-16
  negotiated transfer price, 21-15–21-16
  no, cost-based transfer price, 21-18
  no, negotiated transfer price, 21-14–21-15
Exchange, of plant assets, 9-15
Exclusive right, 2-6
Exotic Newcastle Disease, 23-12
Expanded accounting equation, 3-5, 3-16
Expenditures
  annual recurring, 9-5
  capital, 9-3, 9-6, 9-30
  in cash management, 7-26–7-27
  improperly capitalized, 9-3–9-4
  for plant assets, 9-3–9-7
  revenue, 9-3, 9-31
  during useful life, 9-6
Expense accounts, 4-8, 4-16, 4-17
Expense recognition principle, 4-4, 4-6, 4-36
Expenses. *See also* Interest expense; Prepaid expenses (prepayments)
  accrued, 4-6, 4-16–4-18, 4-36
  administrative, 1-9
  bad debt, 8-5, 8-8, 8-10, 8-27
  bank charges, 7-22–7-23
  bond interest, 10-27
  debit/credit procedures for, 3-15
  decreases in owner's equity, L-2
  defined, 1-8, 1-20
  depreciation, 9-12, 12-9, 12-26–12-27
  forms of, 1-8–1-9
  income tax, 1-9, 5-18–5-19, 5-31
  marketing, 1-9
  noncash, 12-9
  operating, 5-8–5-9, 5-17, 9-20, 12-26
  other expenses and losses, 5-18, H-12
  and profit margin, 5-23
  research and development, 9-19
  selling, 1-9
  on single-step income statement, 5-15
  stockholders' equity and, 3-7, 3-8, 3-15
Expiration, of prepaid expenses, 4-8
External users, 1-4–1-5

F

Face value (par value)
  of bonds, 10-9, 10-12
  defined, 8-16, 10-32
  issuing bonds at, 10-13
  present value of principal and interest, G-13
  of stock, 11-8–11-9
Facility-level activities, 17-13, 17-25
Factoring, 8-12–8-14
Factors, 8-12, 8-27
Factory labor costs

  accumulating, 15-6
  assigning, 15-10–15-12, 16-7
  in job order cost system, 15-6, 15-10–15-12
  in process cost system, 16-7
Factory machinery, cost of, 9-6
Factory overhead. *See* Manufacturing overhead
Fair value
  and cash equivalent price, 9-4
  defined, H-7, H-14
  in depreciation, 9-8
  for equity securities, H-10
  ethical reporting of, H-10
  and impairment, 9-14
  of securities, H-9
  total, H-8
Fair value per share, 11-19–11-20
Fair value principle, 2-18, 2-22
Faithful representation, 2-16, 2-17, 2-22
FASB. *See* Financial Accounting Standards Board
Federal unemployment taxes, I-8, I-11
Fees, I-2, I-11
FICA taxes
  computation, I-3
  defined, I-3, I-11
  as payroll tax expense, 10-7, I-8
  withholding, 10-6
FIFO. *See* First-in, first-out (FIFO) method
Finance charges, credit card, 8-12
Finance directors, 1-4
Financial Accounting Standards Board (FASB)
  Accounting Standards Codification, 1-41
  defined, 2-16, 2-22
  fair value principle of, 2-18
  IASB joint project, 5-15
  on restricted cash, 7-25
  on statement of cash flows format, 12-5
  on statements of cash flows, 12-7
Financial accounting versus managerial accounting, 14-3, 14-4
Financial analysis, 13-1–13-55
  and data analytics, 13-17
  GAAP vs. IFRS, 13-54
  horizontal analysis, 13-10–13-12
  quality of earnings, 13-7–13-8
  ratio analysis, 13-14–13-30
  sustainable income, 13-3–13-7
  vertical analysis, 13-12–13-14
Financial budgets, 22-6, 22-8
Financial calculators, G-15–G-19
  auto loan, G-18
  future value of annuity, G-17
  future value of single sum, G-17
  internal rate of return, G-18
  mortgage loan amount, G-18–G-19
  present value of a single sum, G-16–G-17
  present value of annuity, G-17
Financial information
  defined, 20-3
  enhancing qualities of, 2-17
  for statement of cash flows, 12-7–12-9, 12-22–12-23
  useful, 2-16–2-17
  users of, 1-3–1-5
Financial markets, IFRS and, 1-42
Financial perspective, 24-18, 24-19, 24-27
Financial pressure, in fraud triangle, 7-3
Financial reporting, 2-15–2-21

assumptions in, 2-17–2-18
cost constraint and, 2-19
ethics in, 1-5–1-6
principles in, 2-18–2-19
quality of, 5-11
standard-setting environment and, 2-16
useful information, 2-16–2-17
Financial statement fraud, 7-16
Financial statements, 1-1–1-43, 2-1–2-47. *See also* Consolidated financial statements
from adjusted trial balance, 4-21–4-24
adjusting entries in preparation of, 4-6
balance sheet, 1-9, 1-11–1-12, 1-19
classified balance sheet, 2-3–2-8
defined, 1-9
depreciation and, 4-11
discount on bonds payable on, 10-14
financial reporting concepts, 2-15–2-21
income statement, 1-9, 1-10, 1-20
interrelationships of, 1-13–1-14
inventory on, 6-3, 6-15–6-16
investment reporting for, H-7–H-13
liabilities on, 10-18–10-19
long-lived assets on, 9-21–9-23
manufacturing costs in, 14-10–14-14
notes to, 1-16, 1-20, 9-13, 12-5
partnership, K-9–K-10
premium on bonds payable on, 10-15
ratio analysis, 2-8–2-15
receivables on, 8-19
retained earnings statement, 1-9, 1-11, 1-20
statement of cash flows, 1-10, 1-12–1-13, 1-20
stock dividends on, 11-30
stockholders' equity on, 11-22–11-25
trial balance in preparation of, 3-30
types of, 1-9–1-10
Financing
on cash budget, 7-28
cash transactions, 12-3
off-balance-sheet, 10-22, 10-32
Financing activities
and cash account, 3-31
cash flows from, 10-19, 12-3, 12-4
defined, 1-7–1-8, 12-38
in direct method (statement of cash flows), 12-14, 12-28–12-29
in indirect method (statement of cash flows), 12-13–12-14
inflows and outflows for, 12-15
noncash, 12-5
on statement of cash flows, 1-12
Finished goods
assigning costs to, 15-15–15-16
just in time, 17-22
transfer to, 16-8
Finished goods inventory, 6-3, 6-26
First-in, first-out (FIFO) method
comprehensive example, 16-20–16-24
computation of equivalent units, 16-20, 16-22
cost flow assumptions in, 6-8–6-9
cost reconciliation schedule preparation, 16-23–16-24
current cost information, 16-24–16-25
current performance measurement, 16-24
defined, 6-8, 6-26, 16-19
for equivalent units, 16-19–16-25
financial statement and tax effects of, 6-13–6-14
illustrated, 16-20

LIFO conversion to, 6-18–6-19
periodic, 6-8
in perpetual inventory system, 6-22
physical unit flow, 16-20
physical unit flow computation, 16-21–16-22
production cost report preparation, 16-24
unit production costs computation, 16-22–16-23
weighted-average method versus, 16-24–16-25
Fiscal year, 2-17, 4-3, 4-36
FISH assumption, 6-10
Fixed assets, free cash flow and, 12-19
Fixed costs
behavior of, 18-4
changed by managers, 18-5
defined, 18-4, 18-27
direct, 23-21, 23-30
in flexible budget preparation, 23-10
high-low method computation of, 18-8
importance of identifying, 18-9–18-10
indirect, 23-21, 23-30
nonlinear behavior of, 18-5
overhead, 22-15
per unit, cost-plus pricing, 21-6, 21-8
Fixed interest rates, 10-30
Fixed ratio, K-7
Flexible budget reports
defined, 23-11
illustrated, 23-12
overhead, 23-8, 23-12
use of, 23-12–23-13
Flexible budgets. *See also* Budgeting; Budgets
activity index and relevant range identification, 23-10
basis of, 23-9
case study, 23-9–23-11
cost equation, 23-11
defined, 23-6, 23-30
developing, 23-9, 23-10
fixed costs identification, 23-10
flexible manufacturing and, 23-17
graphic data, 23-11
master budget data for, 23-9
for monthly comparisons, 23-9
monthly overhead, 23-10
preparing, 23-10
reasons for using, 23-7–23-9
with standard direct labor hours, 24-24
steps for, 23-9, 23-10
types of, 23-6
variable costs identification, 23-10
Flexible manufacturing, 23-17
Flow of costs
illustrated, 5-4
job order cost system, 15-5, 15-16–15-17
for merchandising company, 5-4
periodic system, 5-5
perpetual system, 5-4, 5-5–5-6
as process and job cost systems similarity, 16-5
process cost system, 16-6
FOB (free on board), 5-8
FOB destination, 5-8, 5-31, 6-5, 6-26
FOB shipping point, 5-8, 5-31, 6-5, 6-26
Form 10-K, A-1
Franchises, 9-20, 9-31
Fraud
accounts receivable, 8-4

bank reconciliation and, 7-19
capital expenditures, 9-6
cash overstatements, 12-13
cash's susceptibility to, 7-12
defined, 7-3, 7-34
examples of, 7-5–7-10
financial analysis to detect, 13-14
financial statement, 7-16
GAAP vs. IFRS and, 7-56–7-57
and internal controls, 7-3–7-24
inventory, 6-6, 6-24
in merchandising operations, 5-12
payroll, 10-7
Sarbanes-Oxley Act and, 7-3–7-4
stockholders' equity, 11-8
Fraud triangle, 7-3, 7-34
Free cash flow, 12-19–12-21
calculation of, 2-14, 12-20
defined, 2-14, 2-22, 12-19, 12-38, 13-22–13-23, 13-32
as solvency ratio, 13-22–13-23
Free on board (FOB), 5-8
Freight costs, 5-8–5-9, 5-27
Freight-in, 5-27
Full costing. *See* Absorption costing
Full disclosure principle, 2-19, 2-22, 12-5
Full-cost pricing
as basis, 21-22, 21-23
defined, 21-8, 21-21, 21-27
Future amount, discounting, G-7, G-20
Future value, G-3–G-6. *See also* Time value of money
Future value of a single amount, G-3–G-4, G-17, G-20
Future value of an annuity, G-5–G-6, G-17, G-20

G

GAAP. *See* Generally accepted accounting principles
Gain(s)
on bonds redeemed before maturity, 10-17
on disposal of plant assets, 9-16, 12-10
and net income, 12-9
other revenues and gains, 5-18, H-12
realized, presentation of, H-12–H-13
unrealized, presentation of, H-8, H-12
"Gamification," 23-25
General journal, 3-18, 3-28, 3-35, 4-19
General ledger
adjusting entries on, 4-20
after write-off of uncollectible accounts, 8-8
control account, J-2
defined, 3-20, 3-35
example, 3-29
journalizing, J-16
posting, J-16
relationship with subsidiary ledgers, J-2, J-3
special journals effects on, J-16
use of, J-4
General partners, K-3, K-21
Generally accepted accounting principles (GAAP)
absorption costing and, 19-25
adjusting entries, 4-65–4-66
capital disclosure categories, 11-24
cash, 7-56–7-57
and cash-basis accounting, 4-5
classified balance sheet, 2-45–2-46

Generally accepted accounting principles (GAAP) *(Cont'd)*
  defined, 1-42, 2-16, 2-22
  effective-interest method of amortization, 10-27
  financial statement analysis, 13-54
  financial statements required, 1-9
  for fraud, 7-56–7-57
  income statement presentation, 13-54
  internal controls, 7-56–7-57
  inventory and, 6-48–6-49
  liabilities, 10-58
  long-lived assets, 9-54–9-55
  managerial accounting reports and, 14-6
  measurement principles, 2-18
  merchandising operations, 5-54–5-55
  pro forma income, 13-8
  receivables, 8-47
  recording process, 3-60–3-61
  revenue/expense recognition, 4-4
  statement of cash flows, 12-61–12-62
  stockholders' equity, 11-54–11-55
Gift cards, 4-13
Given excess capacity, 21-16
Going concern assumption, 2-18, 2-22
Goods. *See also* Cost of goods purchased; Cost of goods sold
  consigned, 6-5–6-6, 6-26
  determining ownership of, 6-4–6-6
  finished, 15-15–15-16, 16-8, 17-22
  remanufacturing, 16-11
Goods in transit, 6-4–6-5
Goodwill, 2-6, 9-20–9-21, 9-31
Government regulations, corporations and, 11-4
Grace period, credit card, 8-12
Green bonds, 10-18
Green marketing, 5-14
Gross earnings, I-2, I-11
Gross margin. *See* Gross profit
Gross pay, 10-6
Gross profit
  defined, 5-17, 5-31
  gross profit rate vs., 5-22
  on multiple-step income statement, 5-16, 5-17, 5-19
Gross profit rate
  computation of, 5-22–5-23
  defined, 5-22, 5-31, 13-25, 13-32
  for merchandising operations, 5-22–5-23
  as profitability ratio, 13-25
Growth phase, of life cycle, 12-17, 12-18
Guarantees, of dividends, 11-18

H

Hackers, profiles of, J-17
Hedges, 7-26
Held-to-maturity securities, H-7, H-8, H-14
High-low method. *See also* Mixed costs
  advantage of, 18-22
  computation of fixed costs, 18-8
  defined, 18-7, 18-27
  formula, 18-7
  regression analysis versus, 18-24
  steps for computation in, 18-7–18-8
  use of, 18-22–18-23
High-tech companies, 11-1–11-2, 12-15
Hiring of new employees, 3-8–3-9, 3-26

Historical cost principle, 2-18, 2-22, 9-3
Honor of notes receivable, 8-17
Horizontal analysis, 13-10–13-12, 13-32
Human element, internal controls and, 7-11
Human resource controls
  activities, 7-9–7-10
  for cash controls, 7-12, 7-15
  missing, 5-12, 7-10, 10-7
Hurdle rate. *See* Discount rate

I

IASB. *See* International Accounting Standards Board
Ideal standards, 24-4, 24-27
Idle cash, investing, 7-27
IFRS. *See* International Financial Reporting Standards
IMA Statement of Ethical Professional Practice, 14-18
Impairments, 9-14–9-15, 9-31
Imprest system. *See* Petty cash fund
Improper adjusting entries, 4-24
Improper recognition, quality of earnings, 13-8
Improperly capitalized expenditures, 9-3–9-4
Incentive and compensation structure, 23-25
Incentives, creating, 14-17
Income. *See also* Comprehensive income; Net income
  investment, H-2
  for merchandising operations, 5-3
  from operations, 5-16, 5-18, 5-19
  pro forma, 13-8, 13-32
  residual, 23-8–23-9, 23-31
  sustainable, 13-3–13-7, 13-32
  from trading securities, H-9
Income before income taxes, 5-18
Income ratios, K-6, K-7–K-8
Income statements
  absorption costing, 19-20, 19-22, 19-23, 19-24, 19-26
  accrued revenues on, 4-15
  and adjusting entries, 4-6, 4-14, 4-19
  budgeted, 2-28, 22-15–22-16
  cash flows and, 12-4
  comprehensive, 5-19–5-20, 5-31, 13-5, 13-6, H-10
  cost flow methods and, 6-12–6-13
  CVP, 18-11–18-14, 19-3
  defined, 1-9, 1-20
  depreciation on, 9-9
  ethics and, 1-10
  GAAP vs. IFRS, 13-54
  horizontal analysis of, 13-11
  interrelationships of other statements and, 1-13, 1-14
  inventory errors and, 6-24–6-25
  manufacturing costs, 14-11
  for merchandising operations, 5-15–5-20
  multiple-step, 5-16–5-19
  non-recurring charges on, 13-4
  ratio analysis with, 2-9–2-10
  single-step, 5-15–5-16
  and statements of cash flows, 12-7, 12-8, 12-23, 12-31
  and stockholders' equity relationship, 3-16

  use of, 1-10
  variable costing, 19-21, 19-22, 19-23, 19-24, 19-25, 19-26
  variances presentation, 24-16–24-17
  vertical analysis of, 13-13
  VF Corporation, C-2
  Wal-Mart Stores, Inc., E-1
Income Summary, 4-26, 4-27, 4-36, L-5
Income tax expense, 1-9, 5-18–5-19, 5-31
Income taxes
  cash payments for, 12-27–12-28
  depreciation and, 9-13
  as payroll deduction, I-3–I-4
Income taxes payable
  and cash payments for income taxes, 12-27
  as operating activity, 1-9
  and statement of cash flows, 12-12, 12-32
Incremental analysis, 20-1–20-41
  activity-based costing (ABC) relationship, 20-5
  approach, 20-3
  computation of total contribution margin, 19-13
  decision-making and, 20-3
  defined, 20-3, 20-19
  eliminate unprofitable segment, 20-15–20-17
  make or buy, 20-8–20-10
  opportunity cost, 20-4, 20-9
  qualitative factors and, 20-5
  relevant cost and revenues and, 20-4, 20-6–20-7
  repair, retain, or replace equipment, 20-14–20-15
  sell or process further, 20-10–20-13
  special order, 20-6–20-7
  sunk cost and, 20-4
  types of, 20-6
Indefinite life, intangible assets with, 9-18
Independent internal verification
  as cash control, 7-12, 7-15
  as control activity, 7-8–7-9
  missing, 6-6, 8-4, 9-6, 10-7, 11-8, 12-13, 13-14
Indirect fixed costs, 23-21, 23-30
Indirect issuance of stock, 11-8
Indirect labor, 14-7, 14-22
Indirect materials, 14-7, 14-22
Indirect method (statement of cash flows), 12-6–12-17
  defined, 12-7, 12-38
  direct vs., 12-7
  financial information for, 12-7–12-9
  financing activities, 12-13–12-14
  investing activities, 12-13–12-14
  net change in cash, 12-14–12-15
  operating activities, 12-9–12-13
  worksheet for, 12-29–12-34
Industry averages, 2-8, 13-9, 13-15, 13-19
Industry comparisons
  of gross profit rate, 5-22
  of profit margin, 5-24
Inflation, revenue, 4-24
Information, in internal control system, 7-4
Information technology, IFRS and, 1-42
Initial cost, patent, 9-19
Installment payment schedule, mortgage, 10-30
Insurance, adjusting entries for, 4-8–4-10
Insurance policies, 3-8, 3-25

Intangible assets, 9-18–9-23
　accounting for, 9-18–9-19
　on classified balance sheet, 2-5–2-6
　defined, 2-5, 2-22, 9-1, 9-18, 9-31
　presentation of, 9-21–9-23
　types of, 9-19–9-21
Intangible benefits, 25-11–25-13
Intended use, of land, 9-4
Intent to convert, investments, H-11
Intercompany comparisons, 2-8, 13-9, 13-13, 13-15, 13-19
Interest
　accrued, 4-16–4-17
　on bonds, 10-11, H-3
　cash payments for, 12-27
　compound, G-2–G-3, G-20
　defined, G-2, G-20
　on notes payable, 10-3
　on notes receivable, 8-15–8-16
　and purchase discounts, 5-10
　simple, G-2, G-20
Interest costs, in building costs, 9-5
Interest expense
　and accrued expenses, 4-17
　bond, 10-14, 10-27
　defined, 1-9
　as other expenses and losses, 5-18
Interest paid, bond, 10-27
Interest payable, 1-9, 10-13
Interest rates
　annual, 8-16
　bond prices and, 10-14
　contractual, 10-9, 10-13, 10-32
　defined, G-2
　effective, 10-27, 10-32
　for long-term notes payable, 10-30
　market, 10-11, 10-32
Interest receivable, 8-17
Interest revenue, 1-8, 5-18
Internal audit staff, 14-5
Internal auditors, 7-9, 7-34
Internal controls, 7-3–7-24
　with bank accounts, 7-17–7-23
　for cash, 7-12–7-17
　data analytics and, 7-10–7-11
　defined, 7-4, 7-34
　and fraud, 7-3
　GAAP vs. IFRS and, 7-56–7-57
　human resource, 5-12, 7-9–7-10, 7-12, 7-15, 10-7
　limitations of, 7-11–7-12
　missing, 5-12, 6-6, 7-5, 7-7–7-10, 8-4, 9-6, 10-7, 11-8, 12-13, 13-14
　for payroll, I-10–I-11
　with petty cash fund, 7-31, 7-32
　physical, 5-12, 7-7–7-8, 7-12, 7-15
　principles of activities, 7-4–7-10
　and Sarbanes-Oxley Act, 7-3–7-4
Internal process perspective, 24-18, 24-19, 24-27
Internal rate of return (IRR)
　defined, 25-16, 25-22
　estimation of, 25-16
　financial calculator computation of, G-18
　formula, 25-17
Internal rate of return (IRR) method. See also Capital budgeting
　decision criteria, 25-17
　defined, 25-16, 25-22

　even cash flows, 25-17
　interest yield of potential investment, 25-16
　net present value (NPV) method comparison, 25-17–25-18
Internal Revenue Service, 4-2
Internal users, 1-4
International Accounting Standards Board (IASB), 2-16, 2-22, 5-15
International Financial Reporting Standards (IFRS)
　adjusting entries, 4-65–4-66
　asset valuation, 9-4
　capital disclosure categories, 11-24
　cash, 7-56–7-57
　classified balance sheet, 2-45–2-46
　defined, 1-42, 2-16, 2-22
　financial statement analysis, 13-54
　financial statements required, 1-9
　for fraud, 7-56–7-57
　income statement presentation, 13-54
　internal controls, 7-56–7-57
　inventory and, 6-48–6-49
　liabilities, 10-58
　long-lived assets, 9-54–9-55
　merchandising operations, 5-54–5-55
　receivables, 8-47
　recording process, 3-60–3-61
　research and development costs, 9-19
　statement of cash flows, 12-61–12-62
　stockholders' equity, 11-54–11-55
International sales, cash management and, 7-26
Internet sales, 19-7
Intracompany comparisons, 2-8, 13-9, 13-15, 13-19
Introductory phase, of life cycle, 12-17, 12-18
Inventoriable costs. See Product costs
Inventory, 6-1–6-49. See also Periodic inventory system; Perpetual inventory system
　analyzing, 6-16–6-21
　beginning, 6-24
　in cash management, 7-26, 7-27
　and cash payments to suppliers, 12-25
　classifying, 6-2–6-3
　control of, 5-5–5-6
　days in, 6-17–6-18, 6-26, 13-21, 13-32
　defined, 1-8
　ending, 6-9, 6-10, 6-24
　errors in, 6-23–6-25
　finished goods, 6-3, 6-26
　GAAP vs. IFRS, 6-48–6-49
　just-in-time, 6-3, 6-17–6-18, 6-26, 14-16, 14-22
　merchandising, 6-3
　physical, 5-4, 6-4
　presentation of, 6-15–6-16
　quantities, determining, 6-4–6-6
　and statement of cash flows, 12-11, 12-32
　work in process, 14-11, 14-23
Inventory cost flow methods, 6-6–6-15
　assumptions, 6-7–6-12
　consistent use of, 6-14
　financial effects of, 6-6–6-15
　financial statement effects, 6-12–6-13
　in perpetual inventory systems, 6-21–6-23
　specific identification method, 6-7
　tax effects, 6-13–6-14
Inventory management, 6-1–6-2
Inventory turnover, 6-17–6-19, 6-26, 13-20–13-21, 13-32

Inverse proportionality, 11-20
Investees, H-4
Investing activities
　and cash account, 3-31
　cash flows from, 9-25, 12-3, 12-4
　defined, 1-7, 1-8, 12-38
　direct method (statement of cash flows), 12-14, 12-28–12-29
　indirect method (statement of cash flows), 12-13–12-14
　inflows and outflows for, 12-15
　noncash, 12-5
　on statement of cash flows, 1-12
Investment centers. See also Responsibility centers
　defined, 23-18, 23-30
　improving ROI and, 23-24–23-25
　judgmental factors in ROI and, 23-24
　responsibility accounting for, 23-22–23-25
　responsibility report, 23-23–23-24
　return on investment (ROI) and, 23-22–23-23
Investment income, H-2
Investment portfolios, H-4
Investments, H-1–H-19
　in bonds, 10-11–10-12
　bulletin board information on, 2-2
　capital, planning for, 25-1–25-37
　cash flows from, 12-4
　debt, H-1–H-3, H-14
　financial statement reporting for, H-7–H-13
　of idle cash, 7-27
　as investing activity, 1-8
　liquid, 7-27
　long-term, 2-5, 2-22, H-3, H-12, H-14
　nonoperating items related to, H-12
　by owner, L-2, L-8
　readily marketable, H-11
　risk-free, 7-27
　short-term, H-3, H-11, H-14
　stock, H-4–H-12, H-14
Investors, 1-4, 1-5
Invoices
　prenumbered, 7-7
　purchase, 5-7, 5-31
　sales, 5-7, 5-11, 5-31
iPhones
　cost, tearing apart and, 15-10
　sales, reporting revenues from, 4-4
Irregularities, errors vs., 3-31

J
JIT inventory. See Just-in-time inventory
Job cost sheets
　completed, 15-16
　defined, 15-7, 15-25
　direct labor, 15-11
　direct materials, 15-9
　illustrated, 15-7
　individual, 15-8
　manufacturing overhead applied, 15-14
　for service companies, 15-19
　subsidiary ledger, 15-8
Job order cost system
　combined with process cost system, 16-16
　companies and products, 16-3
　cost-benefit trade-off, 16-17
　defined, 15-3, 15-25
　differences with process cost system, 16-5
　documents used to track costs, 16-5

I-16 SUBJECT INDEX

Job order cost system (Cont'd)
  flow of costs in, 15-17–15-18, 16-4
  flow of documents in, 15-18
  illustrated, 15-3
  number of work process accounts used, 16-5
  objective, 15-3–15-4
  point at which costs are totaled, 16-5
  process cost system versus, 16-4–16-5
  service companies, 15-18–15-19
  similarities with process cost system, 16-4–16-5
  unit cost computations, 16-5
Job order costing, 15-1–15-43
  accumulating manufacturing costs, 15-5–15-7
  advantages and disadvantages of, 15-19–15-20
  applied manufacturing overhead and, 15-20–15-22
  assigning manufacturing costs, 15-7–15-12
  cost accounting systems and, 15-3–15-7
  data entry and, 15-20
  entries for jobs completed and sold and, 15-15–15-17
  flow of costs in, 15-5
  flow summary, 15-17–15-18
  overhead assignment and, 15-20
  precision and, 15-19
  predetermined overhead rates and, 15-12–15-15, 15-25
  for service companies, 15-18–15-19
Jobs
  assignment to, 15-17
  completed, 15-15–15-16, 15-17
  sold, 15-16–15-17, 15-17
Joint costs, 20-12, 20-19
Joint products, 20-11, 20-19
Journalizing
  account titles in, 3-19
  of bond transactions, 10-10, 10-12
  cash payments (cash disbursements) journal, J-13–J-15
  cash receipts journal, J-8, J-9–J-10
  of closing entries, 4-27, L-4, L-6
  defined, 3-18, 3-35
  and errors, 3-18, 3-30
  general ledger, J-16
  purchases journal, J-11, J-12
  sales journal, J-5
  and stock splits, 11-22
  summary illustration of, 3-28
  trial balance and, 3-30
  and worksheet for statement of cash flows, 12-30
Journals, 3-17–3-20
  defined, 3-17, 3-35
  general, 3-18, 3-28, 3-35, 4-19
  posting from, 3-21
  recording in, 3-18–3-20
  special, J-4–J-16
Just-in-time (JIT) inventory, 6-3, 6-17–6-18, 6-26, 14-16, 14-22
Just-in-time (JIT) processing
  benefits of, 17-23
  defined, 17-22, 17-25
  downside of, 17-23
  elements of, 17-23
  illustrated, 17-22
  multiskilled work force, 17-23
  objective, 17-23
  pull approach, 17-23
  suppliers, 17-23
  total quality control system, 17-23

K
Knight, Phil, 8-1, 8-2, 11-3
Korean discount, 2-16

L
Labor. See also Factory labor costs
  direct, 14-7, 14-8, 14-22, 15-11, 17-3
  indirect, 14-7, 14-22
  rate calculation, 21-10–21-11
  time ticket and, 15-10, 15-25
  in time-and-material pricing, 21-10
Labor price variance, 24-12, 24-13, 24-27
Labor quantity variance, 24-12, 24-14, 24-27
Labor unions, 1-5
Land
  cost of, 9-4
  and depreciation, 9-8
  improvements, cost of, 9-4
  and statement of cash flows, 12-13, 12-28, 12-32
Large stock dividend, 11-19
Last-in, first-out (LIFO)
  conversion to FIFO from, 6-18–6-19
  cost flow assumptions in, 6-10–6-11
  defined, 6-10, 6-26
  fairness of, 6-14
  financial statement and tax effects of, 6-13–6-14
  periodic, 6-8
  in perpetual inventory system, 6-22–6-23
LCNRV. See Lower-of-cost-or-net realizable value
Lean manufacturing, 14-15
Learning and growth perspective, 24-18, 24-19, 24-27
Leases, 9-7
Ledgers
  defined, 3-17, 3-20, 3-35
  general, 3-20, 3-29, 3-35, 4-20, 8-8, J-3–J-4, J-16
  subsidiary, 15-8, J-1–J-3, J-18
Legal capital, 11-8
Legal entities, corporations as, 11-3, 11-5
Legal liability, 1-3
Lessee, 9-7, 9-31
Lessor, 9-7, 9-31
Leveraging, 13-24, 13-32
Liabilities, 10-1–10-59. See also Current liabilities; Long-term liabilities
  and accrued expenses, 4-16, 4-17
  analyzing, 10-20–10-24
  bonds, 10-8–10-18
  in cash management, 7-26, 7-27
  debit/credit procedures for, 3-12–3-13
  defined, 1-7, 1-20
  and dividends in arrears, 11-18
  effective-interest amortization of, 10-27–10-30
  GAAP vs. IFRS, 10-58
  long-term notes payable, 10-30–10-31
  noncurrent, 12-14, 12-29
  presentation of, 10-18–10-19
  straight-line amortization of, 10-24–10-26
  total, 13-12
  and unearned revenues, 4-12, 4-13
Licenses, 9-20, 11-6
LIFO. See Last-in, first-out
LIFO conformity rule, 6-14
LIFO reserve, 6-18–6-19, 6-27
Limited liability company (LLC), K-3, K-4, K-21
Limited liability of stockholders, corporations and, 11-3
Limited liability partnership (LLP), K-3, K-4, K-21
Limited life, intangible assets with, 9-18
Limited partners, K-3, K-4, K-21
Line positions, 14-5, 14-22
Liquid investments, 7-27
Liquidation
  elements of, K-10
  partnership, K-10–K-14
Liquidity
  from classified balance sheet, 2-10–2-12
  defined, 2-10, 2-22
  and excess working capital, 2-12
  liabilities and, 10-20
  of receivables, 8-21–8-22
Liquidity ratios
  accounts receivable turnover and, 13-19–13-20
  average collection period, 13-20
  current ratio, 2-11–2-12, 13-19
  days in inventory, 13-21
  defined, 2-9, 2-11, 2-22, 10-20, 13-15, 13-19, 13-32
  inventory turnover, 13-20–13-21
  summary of, 13-16
LISH assumption, 6-9
Loans, bad, 8-20
Long-lived assets, 9-1–9-56
  analyzing, 9-23–9-27
  cash flows related to, 12-4
  depreciation of, 9-8–9-15, 9-27–9-29
  disposing of, 9-15–9-17
  expenditures for, 9-3–9-7
  GAAP vs. IFRS, 9-54–9-55
  intangible assets, 9-18–9-21
  plant assets, 9-3–9-17
  presentation of, 9-21–9-23
Long-range planning
  budgeting and, 22-6
  defined, 22-6, 22-8
Long-term debt. See Long-term liabilities
Long-term investments
  accounting for, H-3
  on balance sheets, H-12
  on classified balance sheet, 2-5
  defined, 2-5, 2-22, H-14
Long-term liabilities
  bonds, 10-8–10-18
  cash flows and, 12-4
  on classified balance sheet, 2-7
  current maturities of, 10-5
  defined, 2-7, 2-22, 10-3, 10-8, 10-32
  notes payable, 10-31
Long-term notes payable, 10-30–10-31
Long-term notes, present value of, G-11–G-13
Loss(es)
  accounts receivable, 8-6
  accumulated, 11-55
  casualty, 5-18

from discontinued operations, 13-4
on disposal of plant assets, 9-16–9-17, 12-10, 12-26–12-27
net, 1-9, 1-20, 11-23
and net income, 12-9
other expenses and losses, 5-18, H-12
realized, H-12–H-13
unrealized, 13-6, H-8, H-12
Lower-of-cost-or-net realizable value (LCNRV), 6-16, 6-19–6-20, 6-27

M

Machine hours, 16-7, 17-3
Machine time used, 16-7
Machinery, cost of, 9-6
MACRS (Modified Accelerated Cost Recovery System), 9-13
Madoff, Bernard, 7-23
Mail receipts, 7-14
Make or buy decisions, 20-8–20-10, 20-17
Makers, promissory note, 8-14, 8-27
Management (managers), 11-4, H-7
Management by exception
  controllability of the item, 23-16
  defined, 23-15, 23-30
  materiality, 23-16
Management discussion and analysis (MD&A), 1-16, 1-20
Management functions
  controlling, 14-3, 14-4
  directing, 14-3, 14-4
  planning, 14-3, 14-4
  types of, 14-3
Managerial accounting, 14-1–14-44
  balanced scorecard, 14-17, 14-22
  basics, 14-3–14-6
  business ethics and, 14-17–14-18
  corporate social responsibility and, 14-18–14-19, 14-22
  defined, 14-3, 14-22
  financial accounting versus, 14-3, 14-4
  GAAP and, 14-6
  management functions and, 14-3–14-4
  organizational structure and, 14-4–14-16
  overview, 14-6
  service industries, 14-14–14-15
  today, 14-14–14-19
  tools, 14-1
  trends in, 14-16
  unit cost determination, 14-3
  value chain and, 14-15–14-16
Managerial costs
  assignment to cost categories, 14-9
  concepts of, 14-7–14-10
  illustrated, 14-9
  manufacturing costs, 14-7–14-8
  product versus period costs, 14-8
Manufacturing
  ABC and, 17-7–17-12
  activities and processes, 14-7
  flexible, 23-17
  and inventory, 6-3
  lean, 14-15
  processes, 16-3
  remanufacturing goods and, 16-11
  value chain, 14-15

Manufacturing costs
  absorption-cost pricing, 21-21
  accumulating, 15-4, 15-5–15-6
  assigning, 15-4
  balance sheet, 14-13
  cost of goods manufactured schedule, 14-11, 14-12
  defined, 14-7
  direct labor, 14-7
  direct materials, 14-7
  factory labor, 15-6
  in financial statements, 14-10–14-14
  fixed, 23-5
  income statement, 14-11
  indirect labor, 14-7
  indirect materials, 14-7
  manufacturing overhead, 15-6
  overhead, 14-8, 15-6, 16-7
  per unit, calculation of, 19-20
  product versus period costs and, 14-8
  raw materials, 15-5
  total, 14-10, 14-23
  unit, 21-21
Manufacturing overhead
  applied, 15-20–15-22
  assigning to products, 17-9
  defined, 14-8, 14-23
  indirect materials and, 14-7
  overapplied, 15-21–15-22, 15-25
  predetermined overhead rates, 15-12–15-15, 15-25
  underapplied, 15-21–15-22, 15-25
  year-end balance, 15-21–15-22
Manufacturing overhead account, 15-21
Manufacturing overhead budget. *See also* Budgeting; Budgets
  defined, 22-14, 22-28
  illustrated, 22-14
  variable versus fixed overhead costs and, 22-15
Manufacturing overhead costs
  accumulating, 15-6
  in job order cost system, 15-6
  in process cost system, 16-7
Margin of safety
  defined, 18-20, 18-27, 19-5
  in dollars, 19-5
  formula for, 18-20
Margin of safety ratio
  computation for two companies, 19-16
  cost structure effect on, 19-16
  defined, 18-20
  formula, 19-5
Market interest rate, 10-11, 10-32
Market price, of bonds, 10-10–10-12
Marketable securities, H-11, H-14
Market-based transfer prices, 21-18, 21-27
Marketing expenses, 1-9
Marketing managers, 1-4
Marketing return on investment, 9-24
Mark-to-market accounting, H-8, H-14
Markup
  adding to variable costs, 21-8
  computation, based on ROI per unit, 21-7
  defined, 21-6, 21-27
Markup percentage
  absorption-cost pricing, 21-21–21-22
  cost-plus pricing, 21-7
  variable-cost pricing, 21-23

Master budgets. *See also* Budgeting; Budgets
  classes of budgets, 22-8
  components of, 22-7
  defined, 22-6, 22-8
  as flexible budget basis, 23-9
Matching principle (expense recognition principle), 4-4, 4-6, 4-36
Material bad debts, 8-6
Material disposal, 4-18
Material loading charge
  calculating, 21-11–21-12
  defined, 21-10
  job charges calculation, 21-12
  labor rate calculation, 21-10–21-11
  material loading charge calculation, 21-11–21-12
  as percentage, 21-11
Materiality, 2-17, 2-22
Materials
  direct, 14-7, 14-8, 14-22, 15-9, 22-19
  equivalent units for, 16-22
  indirect, 14-7, 14-22
  for processes, 16-6–16-7
  raw, 14-7, 15-5, 15-8–15-10
  time for adding, 16-13, 16-22
  in time-and-material pricing, 21-10
Materials cost
  in process cost system, 16-6–16-7
  raw, 15-5, 15-8–15-10
  total, 16-14
  unit, 16-14
Materials price variance, 24-9–24-10, 24-11, 24-27
Materials price variance report, 24-16
Materials quantity variance, 24-10, 24-11, 24-27
Materials requisition slip, 15-8, 15-25
Maturity date
  of bonds, 10-9
  defined, 10-9, 10-32
  of notes receivable, 8-15
  redeeming bonds at/before, 10-17
Maturity phase, of life cycle, 12-17, 12-18
Maturity value, 8-17
MD&A (management discussion and analysis), 1-16, 1-20
Measurement principles, 2-18
Medicare taxes, 10-6, 10-7. *See also* FICA taxes
Merchandise purchase budgets
  defined, 22-22, 22-28
  illustrated, 22-23
  purchases formula, 22-23
Merchandise transactions, under periodic inventory system, 5-26–5-27
Merchandisers, budgeting and, 22-22–22-23
Merchandising inventory, 6-3
Merchandising operations, 5-1–5-55
  adjusting entries for, 5-29–5-30
  flow of costs, 5-4–5-6
  GAAP vs. IFRS, 5-54–5-55
  gross profit rate and profit margin, 5-22–5-26
  income statements for, 5-15–5-20
  inventory for, 6-2–6-3
  operating cycles, 5-3–5-4, 7-25–7-26
  periodic inventory system for, 5-21–5-22, 5-26–5-28
  perpetual inventory system for, 5-6–5-15
  purchase transactions for, 5-6–5-10
  sales transactions for, 5-11–5-15

Merchandising profit, 5-17
Mergers and acquisitions, 1-42
Minimum rate of return, 23-28
Minimum transfer price, 21-15, 21-16
Minus sign, in time value of money problems, G-16
Mixed costs
  analysis, 18-7–18-10
  behavior of, 18-6
  classification, 18-7
  defined, 18-6, 18-27
  high-low method, 18-7–18-9
  identifying variable and fixed costs and, 18-9–18-10
Modified Accelerated Cost Recovery System (MACRS), 9-13
Monetary unit assumption, 2-18, 2-23
Monitoring
  of cash, 7-25–7-27
  of collections, 8-20–8-21
  of internal controls, 7-4
  of payment of liabilities, 7-26, 7-27
Mortgage bonds, 10-9, 10-32
Mortgage loan application, G-18–G-19
Mortgage notes payable, 10-30, 10-32
Mortgages, 10-30
Multinational corporations, 1-42
Multiple-step income statement, 5-16–5-19
Mutual agency, K-2
Mutually exclusive projects, 25-13–25-14

N

National credit card sales, 8-12–8-13
Natural disasters, just-in-time inventory and, 6-3
Negotiated transfer prices. *See also* Transfer prices
  defined, 21-14, 21-27
  excess capacity, 21-15
  minimum transfer price and, 21-15
  no excess capacity, 21-14–21-15
  summary, 21-17
  units transferred are unequal to units forgone, 21-16–21-17
  variable costs, 21-16
"Net 30," 5-9
Net cash, net income vs., 12-5
Net cash provided/used by operating activities
  and adjusting entries, 4-30
  in direct method (statement of cash flows), 12-23–12-28
  in indirect method (statement of cash flows), 12-9–12-13
  and net income, 12-3
  on statements of cash flows, 2-13–2-14
Net change in cash, 12-14–12-15, 12-29, 12-33
Net income
  absorption costing and, 19-21–19-25
  from accrual to cash basis, 12-9, 12-23–12-28
  accrued expenses and, 4-17
  accrued revenues and, 4-15
  adjusting entries and, 4-30
  comparison under two costing approaches, 19-24
  comprehensive income and, 5-20
  defined, 1-9, 1-20
  in equity method, H-5
  income statement and, 1-10
  inventory errors and, 6-24
  on multiple-step income statement, 5-16

net cash vs., 12-5
partnerships, K-6–K-10
payout ratio and, 11-23
as performance measure, 12-3
prepaid expenses and, 4-8, 4-11
processing further, 20-11
in specific identification method, 6-7
trading securities and, H-8
variable costing and, 19-21–19-25
Net loss
  in closing entries, 11-23
  defined, 1-9, 1-20
  partnerships, K-6–K-10
Net pay, 10-6, I-4–I-5, I-11
Net present value (NPV)
  comparison at discount rates, 25-9
  computation, comprehensive example, 25-10
  computation, equal net annual cash flows, 25-7
  computation, unequal annual cash flows, 25-8
  defined, 25-6, 25-22
Net present value (NPV) method. *See also* Capital budgeting
  comprehensive example, 25-10–25-11
  decision criteria, 25-7
  decision rule, 25-6
  defined, 25-6, 25-22
  discount rate and, 25-6, 25-9
  equal annual cash flows, 25-7
  internal rate of return (IRR) method comparison, 25-17–25-18
  simplifying assumptions, 25-9–25-10
  unequal annual cash flows, 25-7
Net realizable value. *See* Cash (net) realizable value
Net sales, 5-17, 5-31, 13-10
Neutrality, of information, 2-17
No capital deficiency. *See also* Partnership liquidation
  defined, K-10, K-21
  schedule of cash payments, K-12
  steps, K-11
Nominal (temporary) accounts, 4-26, 4-30
Noncash activities, 12-4–12-5, 12-32
Noncash assets, 11-11, 12-10–12-11
Noncash expenses, 12-9
Noncontrollable costs, 23-15, 23-30
Noncurrent assets, 12-13–12-14, 12-28
Noncurrent liabilities, 12-14, 12-29
Nonfinancial information, 20-3
Nonfinancial measures, 24-17
Nonoperating activities, 5-18, 5-19
Non-recurring charges, 13-4
Non-value added activities, 17-14, 17-15, 17-25
No-par value stock, 11-9, 11-32
Normal balance
  for assets and liabilities, 3-13
  for common stock, 3-14
  for contra asset accounts, 4-10
  defined, 3-13
  for dividends, 3-14
  for retained earnings, 3-14
  for revenues and expenses, 3-15
Normal capacity, 24-6, 24-27
Normal standards, 24-4, 24-27
Notes payable
  as current liabilities, 10-3–10-4
  defined, 10-3, 10-32

as financing activity, 1-7–1-8
issue of, 3-6, 3-23
as long-term liability, 10-30–10-31
mortgage, 10-30, 10-32
Notes receivable, 8-14–8-18
  defined, 8-3, 8-27
  disposing of, 8-16–8-18
  interest computation for, 8-15–8-16
  maturity date determination, 8-15
  recognizing, 8-16
  valuing, 8-16
Notes to financial statements, 1-16, 1-20, 9-13, 12-5
Not-for-profit organizations
  budgeting for, 22-24
  responsibility accounting in, 23-14
NPV. *See* Net present value
NSF checks, 7-19, 7-22, 7-34

O

Obsolescence, 9-7, 9-8
Off-balance-sheet financing, 10-22, 10-32
One-time items, 4-23, 4-24
Operating activities
  and cash account, 3-31
  cash flows from, 9-25, 12-3, 12-4
  defined, 1-7–1-9, 12-38
  in direct method (statement of cash flows), 12-23–12-28
  in indirect method (statement of cash flows), 12-9–12-13
  net cash provided/used by, 4-30, 12-3, 12-9–12-14, 12-23–12-28
  on statement of cash flows, 1-12
Operating assets, average, 23-25
Operating budgets, 22-6, 22-28
Operating cycles
  defined, 2-3, 2-23
  intent to convert during, H-11
  of merchandising operations, 5-3–5-4, 7-26–7-27
  temporary investments in, H-2
Operating expenses
  cash payments for, 12-26
  for franchises/licenses, 9-20
  freight costs as, 5-8–5-9
  on multiple-step income statement, 5-17
Operating leverage
  defined, 19-16, 19-29
  degree of, 19-16, 19-29
  profitability and, 19-14–19-16
Operations
  income from, 5-16
  loss from, 13-4
Operations costing, 16-16, 16-27
Opportunity, in fraud triangle, 7-3
Opportunity costs
  defined, 20-4, 20-19
  make or buy and, 20-9
  negotiated transfer prices and, 21-15
  units sold unequal to units forgone, 21-16
Ordinary repairs, 9-6, 9-31
Organization costs, 11-6, 11-32
Organizational charts
  corporate, 11-5, 14-5
  defined, 14-4
  illustrated, 11-5, 14-5
Organizational structure, 14-4–14-6, 22-3–22-4
Other assets. *See* Intangible assets

Other comprehensive income, 5-55, 11-24, 11-32
Other deposits, 7-21
Other expenses and losses, 5-18, H-12
Other payments, 7-21
Other receivables, 8-3, 8-27
Other revenues and gains, 5-18, H-12
Outsourcing
   defined, 21-18, 21-27
   effect on transfer pricing, 21-18–21-19
Outstanding checks, 7-20, 7-21, 7-34
Outstanding stock, 11-14, 11-32
Overapplied overhead, 15-21–15-22, 15-25
Overhead controllable variance, 24-14, 24-24–24-25
Overhead volume variance, 24-14, 24-25
Over-the-counter receipts, 7-13–7-14
Owners, of corporations, 11-3
Owner's equity
   accounts, 11-10
   decreases in, L-2
   defined, L-2, L-8
   increases in, L-2
Owner's equity statement, L-3–L-4
Ownership
   of goods, 6-4–6-6
   stock dividends and, 11-19
Ownership rights, transferable, 11-4

P

Paid-in capital
   additional, 11-24
   defined, 11-9, 11-32
   and net losses, 11-23
   stock dividends and, 11-19
   stock splits and, 11-21
"Paper or phantom profits," 6-13
Par value. *See* Face value
Par value stock, 11-8–11-11, 11-32
Parent company, H-6, H-7, H-14
Participative budgeting. *See also* Budgeting
   defined, 22-5, 22-28
   disadvantages of, 22-6
   flow of budget data under, 22-5
Partners
   admission of, K-14–K-18
   death of, K-20
   general, K-3, K-21
   limited, K-3, K-21
   withdrawal of, K-18–K-20
Partners' capital statement, K-9, K-21
Partnership agreement, K-4–K-5, K-21
Partnership dissolution, K-2, K-21
Partnership liquidation
   capital deficiency, K-10, K-13–K-14
   defined, K-10, K-21
   elements of, K-10
   no capital deficiency, K-10, K-11–K-12
Partnerships
   accounting for, K-5–K-14
   admission of partner, K-14–K-18, K-16
   advantages and disadvantages of, K-3–K-4
   association of individuals, K-2
   balance sheet, K-9–K-10
   characteristics of, K-1–K-2
   closing entries, K-6–K-7
   co-ownership of property, K-2
   defined, 1-3, 1-20, K-1, K-21
   fair value of assets, K-5
   financial statements, K-9–K-10
   fixed ratio and, K-7, K-8–K-9
   formation, accounting for, K-5–K-6
   income ratios and, K-6, K-7–K-8
   limited, K-3, K-21
   limited liability company (LLC), K-3, K-21
   limited liability (LLP), K-3, K-21
   limited life, K-2
   mutual agency, K-2
   net income or net loss, K-6–K-10
   organizations with characteristics of, K-2–K-3
   partners' capital statement, K-9
   salaries and interest, K-8–K-9
   unlimited liability, K-2, K-3
   withdrawal of partner, K-18–K-20
Patents, 9-18, 9-19, 9-31
Pay, gross vs. net, 10-6
Pay periods, 4-17
Payees, promissory note, 8-14, 8-27
Payment date, 11-16–11-17, 11-32
Payment period, receivables and, 8-20
Payments. *See also* Cash payments; Prepaid expenses (prepayments)
   annual interest, bonds with, G-12–G-13
   of dividends, 3-9, 3-27
   for employee salaries, 3-9, 3-27
   other, in bank reconciliation, 7-21
   from petty cash, 7-31
   of rent, 3-7–3-8, 3-25
Payout ratio
   defined, 11-26, 11-32, 13-26, 13-32
   as profitability ratio, 13-26–13-27
   and stockholders' equity, 11-26
Payroll
   accounting, I-1–I-16
   deductions and, I-2–I-4
   determining, I-2–I-5
   employer taxes, I-8–I-10
   gross earnings and, I-2
   internal control for, I-10–I-11
   net pay and, I-4–I-5
   overview, 10-6–10-7
   professional services and, I-2
   recording, I-1–I-2, I-5–I-7
Payroll deductions
   defined, I-2, I-11
   FICA taxes, I-3
   illustrated, I-3
   income taxes, I-3–I-4
   mandatory, I-2
   types of, 10-6
   voluntary, I-2
   withholding tables, I-4
Payroll register, I-6, I-11
Payroll taxes payable, 10-6–10-8
PCAOB. *See* Public Company Accounting Oversight Board
P-E (price-earnings) ratio, 13-26, 13-32
Pension plans, 13-7
Percentage, ratio as, 13-15
Percentage changes, in horizontal analysis, 13-10
Percentage-of-receivables basis, 8-9, 8-27
Performance evaluation
   behavioral principles, 23-16
   financial performance, 23-21
   human factor in, 23-16
   management by exception, 23-15–23-16, 23-30
   nonfinancial performance, 23-21
   principles of, 23-15–23-17
   reporting principles, 23-16–23-17
Performance standards, 17-16
Period costs, 14-8
Periodic depreciation, revising, 9-13–9-15
Periodic interest expense, 10-27
Periodic inventory system, 5-26–5-28
   cost flow assumptions, 6-8
   cost of goods sold under, 5-21–5-22
   defined, 5-5, 5-26, 5-31
   flow of costs in, 5-5
   freight costs, 5-27
   merchandise transactions in, 5-26–5-27
   perpetual system vs., 5-5–5-6, 5-28
   purchases of merchandise in, 5-27
   sales of merchandise, 5-27–5-28
Periodicity assumption
   defined, 2-18, 2-23, 4-3, 4-36
   and IFRS, 4-65
   and revenue/expense recognition, 4-3, 4-4
Permanent accounts, 4-26, 4-27, 4-36
Perpetual inventory system, 5-4–5-15
   cost flow assumptions, 6-8
   cost of goods sold in, 5-21
   defined, 5-4, 5-31
   flow of costs in, 5-4
   information on product cost, 15-3
   inventory cost flow methods in, 6-21–6-23
   periodic system vs., 5-5–5-6, 5-28
   purchases under, 5-6–5-10
   sales under, 5-11–5-15
Petty cash fund
   controls over, 7-16
   defined, 7-16, 7-34
   disbursement from, 7-14
   operation of, 7-30–7-32
Petty cash receipts, 7-31
Physical controls
   as cash controls, 7-12, 7-15
   defined, 7-7
   missing, 5-12, 7-8
   types of, 7-8
Physical custody, recordkeeping and, 7-6–7-7
Physical inventory, 5-4, 6-4
Physical units, 16-13, 16-27. *See also* Units
Planning
   budgeting and, 22-3, 22-6
   for capital investments, 25-1–25-37
   defined, 22-3
   enterprise resource (ERP), 14-16, 14-22
   long-range, 22-6
   as management function, 14-3, 14-4
Plant assets, 9-3–9-17. *See also* Long-lived assets; Property, plant, and equipment
   analyzing, 9-23–9-27
   defined, 9-1, 9-3, 9-31
   depreciation of, 9-8–9-15
   disposal of, 9-15–9-17, 12-10, 12-26–12-27
   expenditures for, 9-3–9-7
   presentation of, 9-21–9-23
Plus sign, in time value of money problems, G-16
Point-of-sale (POS) systems, 7-1–7-2, 10-4
Ponzi scheme, 7-23
Post-audit, 25-15, 25-22

Post-closing trial balance, 4-27–4-28, 4-36, L-7
Posting, 3-20–3-29
 Bad Debt accounts after, 8-10
 cash payments (cash disbursements) journal, J-14, J-15
 cash receipts journal, J-8, J-10
 chart of accounts and, 3-20–3-21
 of closing entries, 4-28
 defined, 3-21, 3-35
 general ledger, J-16
 of job cost sheets, 15-9
 in ledger, 3-20
 purchases journal, J-12
 sales journal, J-5–J-6
 steps in, 3-21
 summary illustration of, 3-28
 trial balance and, 3-30
 and worksheet for statement of cash flows, 12-30
Practical range. See Relevant range
Predetermined overhead rate
 calculation of, 15-13
 computing, 24-6
 defined, 15-12, 15-25
 formula, 15-13
 standard, 24-6, 24-27
 in traditional costing systems, 17-3
 using, 15-13–15-15
Predictive value, of information, 2-17
Preemptive right, 11-6
Preferred stock
 defined, 11-12, 11-32
 dividends on, 11-17–11-19
 issuing, 11-12–11-13
Premiums
 amortizing, 10-16, 10-26, 10-29–10-30
 on bonds, 10-13–10-16
 on bonds payable, 10-15, 10-26
 defined, 10-13, 10-32
 effective-interest amortization of, 10-29–10-30
 issuing bonds at, 10-15–10-16
 present value of principal and interest, G-13
 straight-line amortization of, 10-26
Prenumbered invoices, 7-7
Prepaid expenses (prepayments)
 adjusting entries for, 4-7–4-11
 defined, 4-6, 4-7
 depreciation, 4-10–4-11
 for insurance, 4-8–4-10
 and statement of cash flows, 12-11, 12-32
 for supplies, 4-8–4-9
Present value, G-7–G-13. See also Time value of money
 of bonds, 10-10
 in capital budgeting, G-14–G-15
 defined, 10-10, 10-32, G-7, G-20
 discounting future amount and, G-7
 of long-term notes or bonds, G-11–G-13
 positive net, 25-7
 of series of future amounts, G-10
 of single amount, G-7–G-9
 of single future amount for annual cash flow, 25-8
 of a single sum, G-16–G-17
 of unequal annual cash flows, 25-8
Present value of an annuity, G-9–G-11, G-17, G-20

"Presentation of Financial Statements" (IAS No. 1 [revised]), 7-56
Price takers, 21-3
Price-earnings (P-E) ratio, 13-26, 13-32
Pricing, 21-1–21-47
 absorption-cost, 21-21–21-23
 cost-plus, 21-5–21-8
 decisions by computer algorithms, 21-5
 factors, 21-3
 full-cost, 21-8, 21-21, 21-27
 profit margins and, 21-9
 to sell, 21-4
 service companies, 21-12
 target costing and, 21-3–21-5
 time-and-material, 21-10–21-12
 transfer, 21-13–21-19, 21-27
 variable-cost, 21-8–21-9, 21-23–21-24, 21-27
Principal, 10-11, G-2, G-20
Privately held corporations, 11-3, 11-32
Pro forma income, 13-8, 13-32
Pro rata basis, defined, 11-15
Process cost accounting, 16-1
Process cost systems, 16-1–16-47
 assigning manufacturing costs in, 16-6–16-9
 combined with job order cost system, 16-16
 companies and products, 16-3
 cost-benefit trade-off, 16-16–16-17
 defined, 15-3, 16-27
 differences with job order cost system, 16-5
 documents used to track costs, 16-5
 factory labor costs, 16-7
 flow of costs in, 16-4, 16-6
 job order cost system versus, 16-4–16-5
 manufacturing overhead costs, 16-7
 material costs, 16-6–16-7
 number of work process accounts used, 16-5
 overview of, 16-3–16-5
 point at which costs are totaled, 16-5
 production cost report, 16-12–16-17
 for service companies, 16-4
 similarities with job order cost system, 16-4–16-5
 transfer to cost of goods sold, 16-8
 transfer to finished goods, 16-8
 transfer to next department, 16-8
 unit cost computations, 16-5
 uses of, 16-3
Process further
 decision, 20-10–20-13
 multiple-product case, 20-11
 net income from, 20-11
 single-product case, 20-11
Process improvement, 17-15
Product costs
 defined, 14-8
 period costs versus, 14-8
 in total manufacturing costs, 14-10
Product life cycle, 12-17–12-19, 12-38
Production, inventory and, 6-3
Production budget. See also Budgeting; Budgets
 defined, 22-9, 22-28
 ending inventory estimate and, 22-9
 illustrated, 22-10
 requirements formula, 22-9
Production cost report
 cost reconciliation schedule preparation, 16-15, 16-23–16-24

 defined, 16-12, 16-27
 equivalent units of production computation, 16-13–16-14, 16-22
 illustrated, 16-16, 16-25
 physical unit flow computation, 16-13, 16-21–16-22
 preparing (FIFO), 16-24
 preparing (weighted-average), 16-15
 self-checks, 16-24
 steps for completion, 16-12, 16-15
 unit production costs computation, 16-14–16-15, 16-22–16-23
Production supervisors, 1-4
Product-level activities, 17-13, 17-25
Products
 assigning overhead costs to, 17-9
 comparison of unit costs, 17-10
 eliminate unprofitable decision, 20-15–20-17
 joint, 20-11, 20-19
Profit
 accumulated, 11-55
 gross, 5-16, 5-17, 5-19, 5-22, 5-31
 and marketing ROI, 9-24
 merchandising vs. overall, 5-17
 retained, 11-55
Profit centers. See also Responsibility centers
 controllable margin and, 23-21–23-22
 defined, 23-18, 23-30
 direct fixed costs and, 23-21
 indirect fixed costs and, 23-21
 responsibility accounting for, 23-21–23-22
 responsibility report for, 23-21
Profit margin
 computation of, 5-23–5-25
 defined, 5-23, 5-31, 13-24, 13-32
 long-lived assets and, 9-24, 9-25
 for merchandising operations, 5-23–5-25
 as profitability ratio, 13-24
Profitability index
 calculation of, 25-14
 defined, 25-14, 25-22
 for mutually exclusive projects, 25-13–25-14
Profitability ratios
 asset turnover, 13-24–13-25
 defined, 2-9, 2-23, 13-16, 13-19, 13-23, 13-32
 earnings per share, 13-25–13-26
 gross profit rate, 13-25
 payout ratio, 13-26–13-27
 price-earnings ratio, 13-26
 profit margin, 13-24
 return on assets, 13-24
 return on common stockholders' equity, 13-23
 summary of, 13-16
Promissory notes, 8-14–8-15, 8-27
Property, plant, and equipment. See also Equipment; Plant assets
 on classified balance sheet, 2-5
 defined, 1-8, 2-5, 2-23
Property taxes payable, 1-9
Proportion, ratio as, 13-15
Prorating of depreciation, 9-10
Public companies, high-tech, 11-1–11-2
Public Company Accounting Oversight Board (PCAOB), 2-16, 2-23, 7-3
Publicly held corporations, 11-3, 11-32
Pull approach, 17-23
Purchase allowances, 5-9, 5-31

Purchase discounts, 5-9–5-10, 5-27, 5-31
Purchase invoices, 5-7, 5-31
Purchase returns, 5-9, 5-27, 5-31
Purchased buildings, cost of, 9-5
Purchases
  and average-cost method, 6-23
  of businesses, 9-21
  and cash payments to suppliers, 12-25
  of equipment, 3-6, 3-23
  of insurance policies, 3-8, 3-25
  in periodic inventory system, 5-27, 5-28
  in perpetual inventory system, 5-6–5-10
  transaction summary, 5-10
  of treasury stock, 11-13–11-15
Purchases journal. *See also* Special journals
  defined, J-11, J-18
  expanding, J-13
  journalizing, J-11, J-12
  multi-column, illustrated, J-13
  posting, J-12
  proving equality of, J-13
Purchases on account, 3-8, 3-26, 5-29
Purchasing activities, 7-6
Purchasing patterns, 22-11
Push approach, 17-22

Q

Qualitative factors, 20-5
Quality control, JIT processing and, 17-23
Quality of earnings, 13-7–13-8
  and adjusted trial balance, 4-23–4-24
  alternative accounting methods, 13-7
  defined, 4-23, 4-36, 13-7, 13-32
  improper recognition, 13-8
  pro forma income, 13-8
Quality of earnings ratio, 5-24–5-25, 5-31
Quarterly dividend rate, 11-15

R

Rate, ratio expressed as, 13-15
Ratio analysis, 2-8–2-15, 13-14–13-30
  classifications, 2-9
  with classified balance sheet, 2-10–2-13
  and data analytics, 13-17
  defined, 2-8, 2-23, 13-32
  example of, 13-17–13-27
  with income statement, 2-9–2-10
  liquidity ratios, 13-15–13-16, 13-19–13-21
  profitability ratios, 13-16–13-17, 13-19, 13-23–13-27
  solvency ratios, 13-16, 13-19, 13-21–13-23
  with statement of cash flows, 2-13–2-14
Rationalization, in fraud triangle, 7-3
Ratios, 2-8, 2-23, 13-14, 13-32. *See also specific ratios*
Raw materials, 6-3, 6-27, 14-7, 17-22
Raw materials costs
  accumulating, 15-5
  assigning, 15-8–15-10
  job cost sheets and, 15-8–15-9
  materials requisition slip and, 15-8, 15-25
Readily marketable, investments, H-11
Real (permanent) accounts, 4-26, 4-27, 4-36
Realized gains and losses, H-12–H-13
Reasonable assurance, 7-11
Receipts. *See also* Cash receipts
  mail, 7-14
  over-the-counter, 7-13–7-14
  petty cash, 7-31

Receivables, 8-1–8-48
  accounts receivable, 8-3–8-14
  in cash management, 7-26, 7-27
  defined, 8-3, 8-27
  GAAP vs. IFRS, 8-47
  interest receivable, 8-17
  liquidity, evaluating, 8-21–8-22
  managing, 8-19–8-25
  notes receivable, 8-3, 8-14–8-18
  other, 8-3, 8-27
  presentation of, 8-18–8-19
  sales of, 8-12–8-14
  size and sale of, 8-23
  trade, 8-3, 8-27
Receivables management, 8-19–8-25
  accelerating cash receipts for, 8-23
  data analytics and, 8-24
  liquidity evaluation for, 8-21–8-22
  steps in, 8-19–8-21
Reconciling items, 7-20–7-21, 12-30, 12-32–12-33
Record date, 11-16, 11-32
Recording payroll
  employee earnings record and, I-5–I-6
  expenses and liabilities and, I-6–I-7
  payment, I-7
  payroll register and, I-6
  statement of earnings and, I-7
Recording process, 3-17–3-27
  chart of accounts and, 3-20–3-21
  described, 3-17
  example, 3-22–3-27
  GAAP vs. IFRS, 3-60–3-61
  journal in, 3-17–3-20, 3-28
  ledger in, 3-20
  posting in, 3-21, 3-28–3-29
Recording transactions of proprietorships, L-3
Recordkeeping, physical custody and, 7-6–7-7
Recovery of uncollectible accounts, 8-8
Redemption, bond, 10-17
Regression analysis
  defined, 18-24, 18-27
  high-low method versus, 18-24
  limitations, 18-25
  software packages, 18-24
Regulations, 24-3
Regulatory agencies, 1-5
Related activities, segregation of, 7-6
Relevance, financial information, 2-16, 2-17, 2-23
Relevant costs
  defined, 20-4, 20-19
  in special orders, 20-6–20-7
Relevant range
  defined, 18-5, 18-27
  in flexible budget preparation, 23-10
  linear behavior within, 18-6
Relevant revenues, 20-4, 20-19
Rent payment, 3-7–3-8, 3-25
Rent revenue, 5-18
Repair or replace equipment decision, 20-14–20-15
Repairs, ordinary, 9-6, 9-31
Replenishing petty cash fund, 7-31–7-32
Required rate of return, 25-6, 25-22. *See also* Discount rate
Required sales, 19-6

Research and development costs, 9-19, 9-31
Reserves, 11-55
Residual claims, 11-6
Residual income
  comparison, 23-29
  defined, 23-28, 23-31
  formula, 23-28
  ROI versus, 23-28–23-29
  weakness, 23-29
Residual value, 9-55
Responsibility, control activities and, 7-5, 7-12, 7-15
Responsibility accounting, 23-13–23-26
  characteristics of, 23-14
  controllable versus noncontrollable revenues and costs and, 23-15
  for cost center, 23-20
  decentralization and, 23-14
  defined, 23-13, 23-31
  illustrated, 23-14
  for investment center, 23-22–23-25
  need for, 23-14
  not-for-profit entities, 23-14
  performance evaluation, 23-15–23-17
  for profit center, 23-21–23-22
  for-profit entities, 23-14
  reporting of costs and revenues under, 23-14
  segments (divisions) and, 23-14
  uses of, 23-13–23-14
Responsibility centers
  cost center, 23-18, 23-20, 23-30
  investment center, 23-18, 23-22–23-25, 23-30
  profit center, 23-18, 23-21–23-22, 23-30
  types of, 23-18–23-20
Responsibility reporting system
  benefits of, 23-17–23-18
  defined, 23-17, 23-31
  illustrated, 23-19
  report types, 23-17, 23-18
Responsibility reports
  for cost center, 23-20
  for investment center, 23-23–23-24
  for profit center, 23-21
Restricted cash, 7-24–7-25, 7-34
Retailers, 5-3, 8-12, 8-13
Retained earnings
  cash dividends and, 11-15
  debit/credit procedures for, 3-14
  defined, 1-11, 1-20, 11-32
  presentation of, 11-22–11-23
  and statement of cash flows, 12-14, 12-28, 12-33
  stock dividends and, 11-19
  stock splits and, 11-21
  stockholders' equity and, 2-7, 11-9–11-10
Retained earnings restrictions, 11-23, 11-32
Retained earnings statement
  as decision tool, 1-11
  defined, 1-9, 1-20
  illustrated, 1-11
  interrelationships of other statements and, 1-13, 1-14
  owner's equity statement versus, L-3–L-4
  and stockholders' equity relationship, 3-16
  use of, 1-11
Retained profits, 11-55
Retirement, of plant assets, 9-15, 9-17

Return on assets, 9-23–9-25
  composition of, 13-25
  defined, 9-23, 9-31, 13-32
  as profitability ratio, 13-24
  and ROE, 11-27, 11-28
Return on common stockholders' equity (ROE)
  defined, 11-26, 11-32, 13-23, 13-32
  as profitability ratio, 11-26–11-28, 13-23
Return on investment (ROI)
  absorption-cost pricing, 21-22
  comparison, 23-28
  computation, decrease in costs, 23-25
  computation, decrease in operating assets, 23-25
  computation, increase in sales, 23-24
  defined, 23-22, 23-31
  formula, 23-23
  improving, 23-24–23-25
  judgmental factors in, 23-24
  margin (income) measure and, 23-24
  marketing, as profit indicator, 9-24
  residual income versus, 23-28–23-29
  valuation of operating assets and, 23-24
  variable-cost pricing, 21-24
Returns
  adjusting entries for credit sales with, 5-29–5-30
  in perpetual inventory system, 5-9
  purchase, 5-9, 5-27, 5-31
  sales, 5-12–5-13, 5-28–5-31
Revenue (change in asset–liability balance)
  from accrued revenues, 4-14
  and cash in advance from customer, 3-6
  defined, 1-8
  dividend, 5-18
  from gift cards, 4-13
  interest, 1-8, 5-18
  rent, 5-18
  sales. See Sales revenue (sales)
  service, 1-8, 3-24
  sources of, 1-8
  from stock investments, H-6
  stockholders' equity and, 3-7
  from unearned revenues, 3-24, 4-12, 4-13
Revenue expenditures, 9-3, 9-31
Revenue recognition principle
  and adjusting entries, 4-6
  defined, 4-3–4-4, 4-36
  and GAAP, 4-66
Revenues (earnings on sales)
  accrued, 4-6, 4-14–4-16, 4-36
  in allowance method for uncollectible accounts, 8-6
  debit/credit procedures for, 3-15
  defined, 1-8, 1-20
  inflating, 4-24
  other revenues and gains, 5-18, H-12
  reporting accurately, 4-4
  on single-step income statement, 5-15
  unearned, 4-6, 4-11–4-13, 4-36, 10-5
Reversing entries, 4-28, 4-36
Revised depreciation, 9-13–9-15
Rights
  ownership, 11-4
  of stockholders, 11-6–11-7
  voting, 5-1–5-2
Risk, internal control and, 7-11
Risk assessment, 7-4
Risk-free investments, 7-27

ROE. See Return on common stockholders' equity
ROI. See Return on investment (ROI)
Rounding, G-17

S
S corporation, 11-5
Safe cash payments schedule, K-12
Salaries
  accrued, 4-17–4-18
  defined, I-1, I-12
  partnerships, K-8–K-9
  payment of cash for, 3-9, 3-27
  rate basis, I-2
Sales
  break-even, 19-5–19-6
  break-even, in dollars, 19-9–19-11
  required, 19-6
Sales activities (sales)
  of bonds, H-3
  cash, 8-12
  credit, 5-29–5-30
  international, 7-26
  of plant assets, 9-15–9-17
  of receivables, 8-23
  segregation of duties and, 7-6
  of stock, H-5
Sales budget. See also Budgeting; Budgets
  defined, 22-8, 22-28
  illustrated, 22-8
  preparation of, 22-8–22-9
Sales discounts
  defined, 5-13, 5-31
  in periodic inventory system, 5-28
  in perpetual inventory system, 5-13–5-14
Sales forecast, 22-4, 22-28
Sales invoices, 5-7, 5-11, 5-31
Sales journal. See also Special journals
  advantages of, J-7
  credit sales, J-5
  defined, J-4, J-18
  journalizing, J-5
  posting, J-5–J-6
  proving the equality of, J-7
  proving the ledgers, J-7
Sales mix
  break-even sales in dollars and, 19-9–19-11
  break-even sales in units and, 19-8
  defined, 19-8, 19-29
  importance of, 19-8
  with limited resources, 19-12–19-14
  as percentage of units sold, 19-8
Sales returns and allowances, 5-28–5-31
  adjusting entries for, 5-29–5-30
  defined, 5-12, 5-31
  in periodic inventory systems, 5-28
  in perpetual inventory system, 5-12–5-13
Sales revenue (sales)
  defined, 1-8, 5-3, 5-31
  on multiple-step income statement, 5-17
  net, 5-17, 5-31, 13-10
  in periodic inventory system, 5-27–5-28
  in perpetual inventory system, 5-4, 5-11–5-15
Sales taxes payable, 1-9, 10-4
Salvage value, 9-9, 9-27, 9-29
Sarbanes-Oxley Act (SOX)
  defined, 1-6, 1-20, 7-3, 7-34, 14-23

  effects of, 1-6
  employee tracking under, 7-11
  fraud and, 7-3–7-4
  IFRS and, 7-56, 7-57
  results of, 14-17
  transaction-recording errors and, 3-9
Scatter plots, 18-22, 18-23, 18-25
Schedule of cash payments, K-12, K-21
SEC. See Securities and Exchange Commission
Secured bonds, 10-9, 10-32
Securities. See also Investments
  available-for-sale, 13-5, 13-32, H-7–H-10, H-14
  debt, H-7–H-10
  equity, H-10–H-11
  held-to-maturity, H-7, H-8, H-14
  marketable, H-11, H-14
  trading, 13-5, 13-32, H-7–H-9, H-14
Securities and Exchange Commission (SEC)
  on debt masking, 10-22
  defined, 2-16, 2-23, 4-1, 4-63
  on fair value accounting, H-10
  on financial analysis, 13-17
  and Madoff's Ponzi scheme, 7-23
  on pro forma income, 13-8
  regulations for corporations from, 11-4
Segments (divisions), 23-14, 23-31
Segregation of duties
  as cash control, 7-12, 7-15
  as control activity, 7-5–7-7
  independent internal verification vs., 7-9
  missing, 8-4
  and write-off of uncollectible account, 8-7
Sell or process further decision
  defined, 20-10–20-11
  illustrated, 20-11
  multiple-product case, 20-11–20-13
  single-product case, 20-11
Sellers, freight costs incurred by, 5-8–5-9
Selling and administrative expense budget, 22-15, 22-28
Selling expenses, 1-9
Selling price, profit margin, 5-23
Semiannual payments, discounting for, G-11
Sensitivity analysis, 25-14, 25-22
Service companies
  ABC costing example, 17-18–17-19
  activity-based costing and, 17-17–17-20
  assigning overhead in, 17-19
  break-even point in, 18-20
  budgetary optimism and, 22-9
  budgeting for, 22-23–22-24
  comparison of traditional costing with ABC in, 17-19
  job order costing for, 15-18–15-19
  managerial accounting in, 14-14–14-15
  margin of safety, 18-20
  operating cycles for, 5-3
  pricing, 21-12
  process cost systems for, 16-4
  sales versus service revenue, 15-19
  traditional costing example, 17-18
Service revenue, 1-8, 3-24
Services
  cash for performance of, 3-7, 3-24
  stock issuance in exchange for, 11-11
Shareholders. See Stockholders
Short-term investments, H-3, H-11, H-14

Shrinkage, inventory, 5-4
Simple interest, G-2
Single amount
  future value of, G-3–G-4, G-20
  present value of, G-7–G-9
Single sum
  discounting, G-14
  future value of, G-17
  present value of, G-16–G-17
Single-step income statement, 5-15–5-16
Sinking fund bonds, 10-9
Slush funds, 7-16
Small stock dividend, 11-19
Social Security taxes, 10-6, 10-7. *See also* FICA taxes
Sole proprietorships
  accounting for, L-1–L-12
  accounting for corporations versus, L-1
  balance sheet, L-2
  closing books for, L-4–L-7
  closing entries, journalizing, L-4, L-6
  closing entries, posting, L-4, L-7
  closing entries, preparing, L-4–L-5
  defined, 1-3, 1-20
  diagram of closing process, L-6
  drawings, L-2, L-8
  expenses, L-2, L-8
  Income Summary account, L-5
  investments by owner, L-2, L-8
  owners' equity account, 11-10
  owner's equity in, L-2
  owner's equity statement, L-3–L-4
  preparing post-closing trial balance for, L-7
  recording transactions of, L-3
Solvency
  classified balance sheet and, 2-12–2-13
  debt vs. equity decision and, 11-28
  defined, 2-12, 2-23
  liabilities and, 10-20–10-22
Solvency ratios
  debt to assets ratio, 2-13, 13-21–13-22
  defined, 2-9, 2-12, 2-23, 10-20, 13-16, 13-19, 13-21, 13-32
  free cash flow, 13-22–13-23
  liabilities and, 10-21–10-22
  summary of, 13-16
  times interest earned, 13-22
Source documents, 3-17
SOX. *See* Sarbanes-Oxley Act
Special journals
  cash payments journal, J-4, J-13–J-15, J-18
  cash receipts journal, J-4, J-7–J-11, J-18
  defined, J-4, J-18
  effects on general journal, J-16
  purchases journal, J-4, J-11–J-13, J-18
  sales journal, J-4–J-7, J-18
  use of, J-4
Special orders
  incremental analysis and, 20-6–20-7
  minimum transfer price formula, 21-16
  variable-cost pricing for, 21-8
Specific identification method, 6-7, 6-27
Staff positions, 14-5, 14-23
Stakeholders, consolidated financial statements for, H-7
Standard cost accounting system
  assumptions, 24-21

defined, 24-21, 24-27
journal entries, 24-21–24-23
ledger accounts, 24-23
Standard costs
  advantage of, 24-3
  case study, 24-5–24-7
  defined, 24-3, 24-27
  overview of, 24-3–24-7
  setting, 24-4–24-7
Standard hours allowed, 24-14, 24-27
Standard predetermined overhead rate, 24-6, 24-27
Standards
  budgets versus, 24-4
  defined, 24-4
  direct labor price, 24-5, 24-27
  direct labor quantity, 24-6, 24-27
  direct materials price, 24-5, 24-27
  direct materials quantity, 24-5, 24-27
  ethics and, 24-4
  in helping business, 24-4
  ideal, 24-4, 24-27
  normal, 24-4, 24-27
State unemployment taxes, I-8, I-12
Stated rate (contractual interest rate), 10-9, 10-13, 10-32
Stated value, 11-9, 11-32
Stated value per share, 11-20
Statement of changes in equity, Louis Vuitton, F-4
Statement of comprehensive gains and losses, Louis Vuitton, F-2
Statement of earnings, I-7, I-12
Statements of cash flows, 1-12–1-13, 12-1–12-62
  Amazon.com, Inc., D-1
  analyzing, 12-17–12-22
  Apple Inc., A-5
  classification of cash flows and, 12-3–12-4
  Columbia Sportswear Company, B-3
  defined, 1-10, 1-20, 12-38
  direct method of preparing, 12-7, 12-22–12-29
  format of, 12-5–12-6
  GAAP vs. IFRS, 12-61–12-62
  indirect method of preparing, 12-6–12-17, 12-29–12-34
  interrelationships of other statements and, 1-13, 1-14
  investing/financing activities and, 12-13–12-14, 12-28–12-29
  Louis Vuitton, F-5
  net cash provided/used by operating activities and, 12-9–12-14, 12-23–12-28
  net change in cash for, 12-14–12-15, 12-29
  preparation of, 12-6–12-17, 12-22–12-36
  ratio analysis with, 2-13–2-14
  significant noncash activities and, 12-4–12-5
  stockholders' equity and, 11-25
  T-account approach, 12-34–12-36
  use of, 1-12–1-13, 12-3
  VF Corporation, C-3
  Wal-Mart Stores, Inc., E-5
  worksheet for preparing, 12-29–12-34
Statements of comprehensive income
  Amazon.com, Inc., D-2
  Apple Inc., A-2
  Columbia Sportswear Company, B-2
  defined, 11-54

illustrated, 13-3
VF Corporation, C-2
Wal-Mart Stores, Inc., E-2
Statements of equity, Columbia Sportswear Company, B-4
Statements of operations
  Amazon.com, Inc., D-2
  Apple Inc., A-2
  Columbia Sportswear Company, B-1
Statements of shareholders' equity
  Amazon.com, Inc., D-4
  Apple Inc., A-4
  VF Corporation, C-4
  Wal-Mart Stores, Inc., E-4
Static budget reports, 23-4
Static budgets
  defined, 23-4, 23-31
  examples of, 23-4–23-5
  overhead, 23-7
  performance evaluation and, 23-8
  uses and limitations of, 23-5
Stock. *See also* Common stock; Stock investments
  acquisition of, recording, H-4, H-6
  authorized, 11-7–11-8, 11-32
  capital, 11-8, 11-24
  issuing, 11-7–11-9
  no-par value, 11-9, 11-32
  outstanding, 11-14, 11-32
  par value, 11-8–11-11, 11-32
  preferred, 11-12–11-13, 11-17–11-19, 11-32
  sale of, H-5
  treasury, 11-13–11-15, 11-32
Stock certificates, 11-7
Stock dividends
  defined, 11-19, 11-32
  effects of, 11-20, 11-22
  entries for, 11-30
  large, 11-19
  preparing entries for, 11-30
  reasons for issuing, 11-19
  size determination, 11-19
  small, 11-19, 11-20
Stock investments, H-4–H-12
  accounting for, H-4–H-12
  defined, H-4, H-14
  with holdings between 20% and 50%, H-5–H-6
  with holdings of less than 20%, H-4–H-5
  with holdings of more than 50%, H-6–H-7
Stock price, inventory system and, 5-6
Stock quotes, 11-12
Stock splits, 11-20–11-22, 11-32
Stockholders
  cash investment by, 3-5–3-6, 3-22
  control of, 11-27
  defined, 1-3
  rights of, 11-6–11-7
Stockholders' equity, 11-1–11-56
  accrued expenses and, 4-17
  analyzing, 11-26–11-29
  cash flows and, 12-4
  changes in, 12-14, 12-28
  on classified balance sheet, 2-7
  common stock, 11-11–11-12
  corporate form of organization and, 11-3–11-10
  debit/credit procedures for, 3-13–3-15
  defined, 1-11, 1-20, 2-7

Stockholders' equity *(Cont'd)*
  dividends, 3-9, 11-15–11-20, 11-30
  expenses and, 3-7, 3-8, 3-15
  GAAP vs. IFRS, 11-54–11-55
  preferred stock, 11-12–11-13
  prepaid expenses and, 4-8, 4-10, 4-11
  presentation of, 11-22–11-25
  relationships of items impacting, 3-15–3-16
  return on, 11-26–11-28, 11-32, 13-23, 13-32
  revenue and, 3-7
  stock splits, 11-20–11-22
  total, 11-20, 11-21, 13-12
  treasury stock, 11-13–11-15
  and unearned revenues, 4-13
  unrealized loss in, 13-6, H-12
Straight-line amortization, 10-24–10-26
  bond discount, 10-24–10-25
  bond premium, 10-26
  defined, 10-24–10-25, 10-32
Straight-line depreciation, 9-9–9-13, 9-27, 9-31
Strategic goals, investments related to, H-2
Subsidiary (affiliated) company, H-6, H-7, H-14
Subsidiary ledgers
  accounts payable (or creditors'), J-2, J-18
  accounts receivable (or customers'), J-2, J-18
  advantages of, J-3
  defined, 15-8, J-1, J-18
  example, J-2–J-3
  general ledger relationship, J-2, J-3
  types of, J-2
Sunk costs, 20-4, 20-19
Supplementary schedules, for noncash activities, 12-5
Suppliers
  cash payments to, 12-25–12-26
  in JIT processing, 17-23
Supplies
  adjusting entries for, 4-8, 4-9
  as asset, 1-8
  purchasing, on account, 3-8, 3-26
Sustainability reports and reporting, 7-4, 9-22–9-23
Sustainable business practices, 14-18
Sustainable income, 13-3–13-7
  changes in accounting principle and, 13-6–13-7
  comprehensive income and, 13-5–13-6
  defined, 13-3, 13-32
  discontinued operations and, 13-4
Swinmurn, Nick, 21-1–21-2

T
Tabular summary, of account, 3-12
T-account approach (statement of cash flows), 12-34–12-36
T-accounts
  for cash payments to suppliers, 12-26
  for cash receipts from customers, 12-25
  defined, 3-11, 3-35
Target cost, 21-4
Target costing, 21-3–21-5
Target net income
  contribution margin technique, 18-19
  defined, 18-18, 18-27
  in dollars, 19-5
  formula for sales to meet, 18-18
  graphic representation, 18-19

  mathematical equation, 18-18–18-19
  in units, 19-4
Target price
  absorption-cost pricing, 21-23
  defined, 21-6, 21-27
  variable-cost pricing, 21-23
Taxes. *See also* Income tax expense; Income taxes; Income taxes payable
  business organization and, 1-3
  and buy-or-lease decision, 9-7
  for corporations, 11-5
  and debt vs. equity decision, 11-27
  employer payroll, I-8–I-10
  FICA, 10-6, 10-7, I-3–I-4, I-9
  inventory cost flow methods and, 6-13–6-14
  payroll taxes payable, 10-6–10-8
  property taxes payable, 1-9
  sales taxes payable, 1-9, 10-4
Taxing authorities, 1-5
Tech companies, 11-1–11-2, 12-15
Temporary accounts, 4-26, 4-36
Temporary investments, H-2
Theory of constraints, 14-16, 14-23, 19-13, 19-29
30-year bonds, 10-12
Time, interest and, G-2
Time diagrams, 10-11, G-3, G-5, G-10, G-12, G-14
Time periods
  accounting, 4-2–4-3
  for computing interest, 4-16
  discounting and, G-11
Time ticket, 15-10, 15-25
Time value of money, G-1–G-22
  in capital budgeting, G-14–G-15
  on capital budgeting decision, 25-6
  concept, G-1
  defined, 10-10, 10-32
  financial calculator applications, G-15–G-19
  future value and, G-3–G-6
  interest and, G-2–G-3
  and market price of bonds, 10-10–10-11
  present value and, G-7–G-13
Time-and-material pricing
  defined, 21-10, 21-27
  labor in, 21-10
  material in, 21-10
  steps for, 21-10–21-12
Timeliness, financial information, 2-17, 2-23
Times interest earned
  defined, 10-21, 10-32, 13-22, 13-32
  liabilities and, 10-21
  as solvency ratio, 13-22
Total assets
  and capital dividends, 11-17
  plant assets as percentage of, 9-3
  vertical analysis of, 13-12
Total conversion costs, 16-15
Total cost of borrowing, 10-14–10-15, 10-16
Total cost of work in process, 14-12, 14-23
Total depreciation expense, 9-12
Total labor variance, 24-12, 24-27
Total liabilities, 13-12
Total manufacturing costs, 14-10, 14-23, 16-15
Total materials costs, 16-14
Total materials variance, 24-9, 24-27
Total overhead variance, 24-14, 24-27
Total quality control system, 17-23

Total quality management (TQM), 14-16, 14-23
Total stockholders' equity, 11-20, 11-21, 13-12
Total units accounted for, 16-13, 16-27
Total units to be accounted for, 16-13, 16-27
TQM (total quality management), 14-16, 14-23
Trade receivables, 8-3, 8-27
Trademarks (trade names), 9-20, 9-31
Trading, H-8
Trading on the equity, 13-24
Trading securities
  defined, 13-5, 13-32, H-7, H-14
  financial statement reporting on, H-7–H-9
  as short-term investments, H-11
Traditional costing. *See* Costing systems
Transaction analysis, 3-4–3-9, 3-22
Transfer prices. *See also* Pricing
  alternative, 21-24–21-25
  cost-based, 21-17–21-18, 21-27
  defined, 21-13, 21-27
  determination approaches, 21-14
  example, 21-3
  market-based, 21-18, 21-27
  minimum, 21-15
  negotiated, 21-14–21-17, 21-27
  outsourcing effect on, 21-18–21-19
  primary objective, 21-4
  transfers between divisions in different countries and, 21-19, 21-24–21-25
Transfer to cost of goods sold, 16-8
Transfer to finished goods, 16-8
Transfer to next department, 16-8
Transferable ownership rights, 11-4
Transfers between division in different countries, 21-19, 21-24–21-25
Treasurer, 7-26, 7-34, 11-4, 14-5, 14-23
Treasury stock, 11-13–11-15, 11-32
Trend (horizontal) analysis, 13-10–13-12, 13-32
Trial balance, 3-30–3-33
  adjusted, 4-21–4-25, 4-36
  adjusting entries and, 4-6–4-7
  defined, 3-30, 3-35
  limitations of, 3-31
  post-closing, 4-27–4-28, 4-36, L-7
Triple bottom line, 14-18, 14-23
True cash balance, 7-22
Trustees, bond, 10-9
Turnover
  accounts receivable, 8-22, 8-26, 13-19–13-20, 13-32
  asset, 9-24, 9-26, 9-30, 13-24–13-25, 13-32
  inventory, 6-17–6-19, 6-26, 13-20–13-21, 13-32

U
Unamortized discount on bonds payable, 10-14, 10-25
Uncollectible accounts, 8-5–8-11
  allowance method, 8-6–8-11
  direct write-off method for, 8-5–8-6
  estimates of, 8-7
  write-offs of, 8-7–8-8
Underapplied overhead, 15-21–15-22, 15-25
Understandability, financial information, 2-17, 2-23
Underwriting, stock issue, 11-8
Unearned revenues
  adjusting entries for, 4-11–4-13
  as current liability, 10-5
  defined, 4-6, 4-11, 4-36

Unearned service revenue, 3-24
Unequal annual cash flows, 25-8
Unit contribution margin. *See also* Contribution margin (CM)
   in break-even point computation, 18-15–18-16
   defined, 18-12, 18-27
   weighted-average, 19-8–19-9
Unit production costs
   computation (FIFO), 16-22–16-23
   computation (weighted-average), 16-14–16-15
   defined, 16-14, 16-27
United States
   accounting for specific events in Europe vs., 3-12
   cost flow methods used in, 6-12, 6-14
   depreciation methods used by companies in, 9-9
   leases by firms in, 9-7
Unit-level activities, 17-12, 17-25
Units
   break-even point in, 18-15, 19-4, 19-9
   break-even sales in, 19-5–19-6, 19-8–19-9
   conversion cost, 16-14
   flow, FIFO method, 16-20, 16-21–16-22
   flow, weighted-average method, 16-13
   materials cost, 16-14
   production costs, 16-14–16-15, 16-27
   target net income in, 19-4
   total accounted for, 16-13, 16-27
   total to be accounted for, 16-13, 16-27
   transferred are unequal to forgone, 21-16–21-17
Units completed, 16-15
Units in process, 16-15
Units-of-activity method, 9-12–9-13, 9-28–9-29, 9-31
Unprofitable segments
   elimination decision, 20-15–20-17
   income data, 20-16
   incremental analysis, 20-16
Unqualified opinion, 1-17
Unrealized gains, H-8, H-12
Unrealized losses, 13-6, H-8, H-12
Unsecured (debenture) bonds, 10-9, 10-32
U.S. Commerce Department, 12-2
U.S. Patent Office, 9-20
Useful information, qualities of, 2-16–2-17
Useful life
   amortization over, 9-18
   defined, 4-10, 4-36
   in depreciation, 9-9
   expenditures during, 9-6
Users
   defined, 1-4
   external, 1-4–1-5
   internal, 1-4

V

Vacations, employee, 7-9
Valuation
   accounts receivable, 8-5–8-11
   asset, 9-4
   of available-for-sale securities, H-9
   corporate social responsibility and, 11-7
   of debt securities, H-8
   notes receivable, 8-16
   of trading securities, H-8
Valuation accounts, 10-16
Value
   adding, 14-4
   overstatement of, 3-21
   residual, 9-55
Value chain
   defined, 14-15, 14-23
   illustrated, 14-15
   in managerial accounting, 14-15–14-16
Value investing, 13-2
Value-added activities, 17-14, 17-15, 17-25
Variable costing
   absorption costing versus, 19-19–19-27
   comparison example, 19-19–19-21
   comparison of, 19-24
   CVP analysis and, 19-19, 19-27
   decision-making concerns, 19-25–19-27
   defined, 19-19, 19-29
   example, 19-20–19-21
   fixed manufacturing overhead and, 19-21
   income statements, 19-21, 19-22, 19-23, 19-24, 19-25, 19-26
   net income effects, 19-21–19-25
   potential advantages of, 19-27
   summary of income effects, 19-25
Variable costs
   behavior of, 18-3
   budgeted, 23-8
   defined, 18-3, 18-27, 21-16
   in flexible budget preparation, 23-10
   importance of identifying, 18-9–18-10
   linear behavior within relevant range, 18-6
   negotiated transfer pricing, 21-16
   nonlinear behavior of, 18-5
   overhead, 22-15
   per unit, cost-plus pricing, 21-6
   in variable cost pricing, 21-23
Variable-cost pricing. *See also* Pricing
   cost base of, 21-23
   defined, 21-8, 21-23, 21-27
   disadvantage of, 21-9
   markup percentage computation, 21-23
   proof of 20% ROI, 21-24
   reasons for using, 21-24
   in short-run decisions, 21-23
   for special orders, 21-8
   steps for, 21-23
   target price computation, 21-23
   unit variable cost computation, 21-23
   use of, 21-8
Variance accounts, 24-21–24-23
Variance reports, 24-16–24-17
Variances
   in business, 24-7
   defined, 24-7, 24-27
   direct labor, 24-8, 24-11–24-14
   direct materials, 24-7–24-11
   favorable, 24-8
   income statement presentation of, 24-16–24-17
   labor price, 24-12, 24-13, 24-27
   labor quantity, 24-12–24-13, 24-14, 24-27
   manufacturing overhead, 24-14–24-15
   materials price, 24-9–24-10, 24-11, 24-27
   materials quality, 24-10, 24-27
   overhead controllable, 24-14, 24-24–24-25
   overhead volume, 24-14, 24-25
   reporting, 24-16–24-17
   significant, 24-16
   total, 24-8
   total labor, 24-12, 24-27
   total materials, 24-9, 24-27
   unfavorable, 24-8
Venture capital firms, K-3
Verifiability, financial information, 2-17, 2-23
Vertical analysis, 13-12–13-14, 13-32
Vice president of operations, 14-5–14-6
Virtual close, 4-26
Voting rights, 5-1–5-2
Voucher register, 7-15
Voucher system, 7-14–7-16, 7-34
Vouchers, 7-15, 7-34

W

Wage and Tax Statement (Form W-2), I-9–I-10, I-12
Wages. *See also* Payroll
   defined, I-1, I-12
   total, computation of, I-2
Wages payable, I-9
Weighted-average contribution margin
   calculation of, 19-10
   unit, 19-8–19-9
Weighted-average method
   defined, 16-9, 16-27
   examples, 16-9–16-10
   FIFO versus, 16-24–16-25
   formula, 16-9
   refinements on, 16-10–16-11
Weighted-average unit cost, 6-11, 6-27
Wholesalers, 5-3
Wireless service providers, 25-8
Withdrawal by payment from partners' personal assets, K-18, K-21
Withdrawal by payment from partnership assets
   bonus to remaining partners, K-19–K-20
   bonus to retiring partner, K-19
   defined, K-18, K-21
Withdrawal of a partner
   death of a partner, K-20
   overview, K-18
   by payment from partners' personal assets, K-18, K-21
   by payment from partnership assets, K-18–K-20, K-21
Withholding tax tables, I-4
Work force, in JIT processing, 17-23
Work in process, 6-3, 6-27
Work in process inventory
   balance in, 15-15
   defined, 14-11, 14-23
   entries in, 15-8
   proof of job cost sheets in, 15-15
Working capital, 2-11, 2-12, 2-23
Worksheets, 4-33–4-34, 4-36
Write-downs, 9-14–9-15
Write-offs, 8-7–8-8

Y

Year-ends, 2-17

Z

"Zero-based budgeting," 22-20
Zero-interest bonds, 10-10